4500+ Questions to Boost Your NEET Rank

NEET power house Physics

Chapterwise
Topicwise

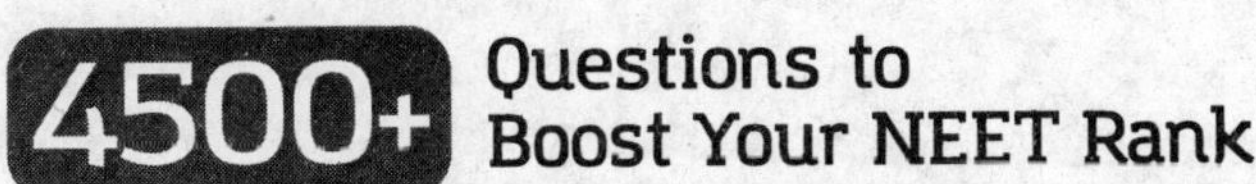

NEET power house Physics

Chapterwise
Topicwise

Questions of
Last 19 Years'

Authors
Digvijay Singh, Mansi Garg
Manish Dangwal

ARIHANT PRAKASHAN (SERIES), MEERUT

Administrative & Production Offices

Regd. Office

'Ramchhaya' 4577/15, Agarwal Road, Darya Ganj, New Delhi -110002
Tele: 011- 47630600, 43518550

Head Office

Kalindi, TP Nagar, Meerut (UP) - 250002 Tel: 0121-7156203, 7156204

Sales & Support Offices

Agra, Ahmedabad, Bengaluru, Bareilly, Chennai, Delhi, Guwahati, Hyderabad, Jaipur, Jhansi, Kolkata, Lucknow, Nagpur & Pune.

PRICE ₹795.00

Published by Arihant Publications (India) Ltd.

For further information about the books published by Arihant, log on to www.arihantbooks.com or e-mail at info@arihantbooks.com

Follow us on    

PREFACE

Once you have an idea of what you are going to be asked in a test, you are more comfortable to tackle it, and your performance in the test improves dramatically. Once you know the importance of different chapters and topics from the syllabi for a exam by going through chapterwise and topical segregation of previous years' questions, you can strategically plan out your preparation for the exam by allotting your time accordingly for the chapters or the topics of the chapters.

This book Chapterwise & Topicwise Medical Entrances Solved Papers Physics has Previous Years' Medical Entrance Questions with their Solutions to fulfill the above mentioned needs of understanding the nature & pattern of questions being asked in NEET and other Medical Entrances.

The Salient Features of the Book are

- It covers all the questions with explanations from year 2005 to 2023 for all Medical entrance exams in India (both National as well as Regional).
- Chapterwise division and topical categorisation has been done keeping in mind the syllabi of NEET & NCERT Textbooks and the learning facilitation to the students in the subject of Physics.
- Questions of all Medical entrances are grouped according to the year.
- Extreme care is taken, while solving the questions and compiling their answers for their accuracy.

We hope that the book will be of utmost help to you in your NEET Preparation and propel you to success. Suggestions for further improvement will be welcomed.

Publisher

CONTENTS

PART I *Based on Class XIth NCERT*

PART II *Based on Class XIIth NCERT*

01

Units and Measurements

Quick Review

Physical Quantities

All the quantities which are used to describe the laws of physics are called physical quantities, e.g. length, mass, volume, etc.

To express the measurement of a physical quantity, we need to know two things as given below

(*i*) The unit in which the quantity is measured.

(*ii*) The numerical value or the magnitude of the quantity.

i.e. The number of times that unit is contained in the given physical quantity = nu

$$\therefore \quad n \propto \frac{1}{u}$$

$$\Rightarrow \quad nu = \text{constant}$$

where, n = numerical value of the physical quantity and u = size of unit.

Physical Units

The standard amount of a physical quantity chosen to measure the physical quantity of same kind is called a physical unit.

Fundamental Quantities and Fundamental Units

Those physical quantities which are independent of other physical quantities and not defined in terms of other physical quantities, are called **fundamental** or **base quantities.**

The units of these quantities are called **fundamental** or **base units.**

Table below gives the seven fundamental quantities and their SI units

Base Quantity	SI Units		
	Name	Symbol	Definition
Length	Metre	m	The metre is the length of the path travelled by light in vacuum during a time interval of 1/299792458 of a second.
Mass	Kilogram	kg	The kilogram is equal to the mass of the international prototype of the kilogram (a platinum-iridium alloy cylinder) kept at international Bureau of Weights and Measures at Sevres, near Paris, France.
Time	Second	s	The second is the duration of 9192631770 periods of the radiation corresponding to the transition between the two hyperfine levels of the ground state of the cesium-133 atom.
Electric current	Ampere	A	The ampere is that constant current which if maintained in two straight parallel conductors of infinite length, of negligible circular cross-section and placed 1 m apart in vacuum, would produce a force between these conductors equal to 2×10^{-7} N/m of length.
Thermo-dynamic temperature	Kelvin	K	The kelvin is the fraction 1/273.16 of the thermo-dynamic temperature of the triple point of water.

Base Quantity	SI Units		
	Name	**Symbol**	**Definition**
Amount of substance	Mole	mol	The mole is the amount of substance of a system which contains as many elementary entities as there are atoms in 0.012 kg of carbon-12.
Luminous intensity	Candela	cd	The candela is the luminous intensity in a given direction of a source that emits monochromatic radiation of frequency 540×10^{12} Hz and that has a radiant intensity in that direction of 1/683 watt/steradian

Derived Quantities and Derived Units

The quantities which can be expressed in terms of the fundamental quantities are called **derived quantities**. The units of these quantities are called **derived units**.

e.g. Unit of speed = ms^{-1} can be derived from fundamental unit, i.e. unit of length and time as

$$\text{Speed} = \frac{\text{Distance}}{\text{Time}} = \frac{m}{s} = ms^{-1}$$

Supplementary Quantities and Supplementary Units

Other than fundamental and derived quantities, there are two more quantities called as **supplementary quantities.** The units of these quantities are known as **supplementary units.**

Table below gives the supplementary quantities and their SI units

Supplementary Quantity	SI Units		
	Name	**Symbol**	**Definition**
Plane angle	Radian	rad	One radian is the angle subtended at the centre by an arc equal in length to the radius of the circle. i.e. $d\theta = \frac{ds}{r}$
Solid angle	Steradian	sr	One steradian is the solid angle subtended at the centre of a sphere, by that surface of the sphere, which is equal in area to the square of radius of the sphere. i.e. $d\Omega = \frac{dA}{r^2}$

Systems of Unit

A complete set of units which is used to measure all kinds of fundamental and derived quantities is called a system of units.

Some of the commonly used systems of units are as follows

(*i*) CGS System

In this system, the units of length, mass and time are centimetre (cm), gram (g) and second (s), respectively. The unit of force is dyne and that of work or energy is erg.

(*ii*) FPS System

In this system, the units of length, mass and time are foot, pound and second, respectively. The unit of force in this system is poundal.

(*iii*) MKS System

In this system, the units of length, mass and time are metre (m), kilogram (kg) and second (s) respectively. The unit of force is newton (N) and that of work or energy is joule (J).

(*iv*) International System (SI) of Units

This system of units helps in revolutionary changes over the MKS system and is known as **rationalised MKS system.** It is helpful to obtain all the physical quantities in physics.

Some Other Units (Not Contained in SI Units)

Length

(*i*) 1 micron = $1 \mu m = 10^{-6}$ m

(*ii*) 1 nanometre = $1 nm = 10^{-9}$ m

(*iii*) 1 angstrom = $1 Å = 10^{-10} m = 10^{-8} cm = 10^{-4} \mu m$

(*iv*) 1 fermi = $1 fm = 10^{-15}$ m

(*v*) 1 astronomical unit = $1 AU = 1.496 \times 10^{11}$ m

(*vi*) 1 light year = $1 ly = 9.467 \times 10^{15}$ m

(*vii*) 1 parsec = $3.08 \times 10^{16} m = 3.26 ly = 206267$ AU

Mass

(*i*) 1 quintal = 100 kg

(*ii*) 1 tonne or 1 metric ton = 1000 kg = 10 quintal

(iii) 1 megagram = 10^3 kg

(*iv*) 1 gigagram = 10^6 kg

(*v*) 1 teragram = 10^9 kg

(*vi*) 1 slug = 14.57 kg

(*vii*) 1 pound = 1 lb = 0.4536 kg

Time

(*i*) 1 millisecond = 10^{-3} s (*ii*) 1 microsecond = 10^{-6} s

(*iii*) 1 shake = 10^{-8} s (*iv*) 1 nanosecond = 10^{-9} s

(*v*) 1 picosecond = 10^{-12} s

(*vii*) 1 hour = 60 min = 3600 s

(*viii*) 1 day = 24 h = 86400 s

(*ix*) 1 year = 365 days = 3.15×10^7 s

(*x*) 1 century = 100 years

Common SI prefixes and symbols for multiples and sub-multiples are given in tabular form below

Multiple			Sub-multiple		
Factor	Prefix	Symbol	Factor	Prefix	Symbol
10^{18}	Exa	E	10^{-18}	atto	a
10^{15}	Peta	P	10^{-15}	femto	f
10^{12}	Tera	T	10^{-12}	pico	p
10^{9}	Giga	G	10^{-9}	nano	n
10^{6}	Mega	M	10^{-6}	micro	μ
10^{3}	Kilo	k	10^{-3}	milli	m
10^{2}	Hecto	h	10^{-2}	centi	c
10^{1}	Deca	da	10^{-1}	deci	d

Errors

The difference between the true value and the measured value of a quantity is called error of measurement.

In general, the errors can be classified as given below

(*i*) **Systematic Error** The error which associates with system itself. e.g., (a) Instrumental error, (b) Imperfection in technique or procedure (c) Personal errors (d) Errors due to external cause.

(*ii*) **Random Error** The error which occurs irregularly and is random in magnitude and direction.

(*iii*) **Least Count Error** The error which associates with the resolution or the smallest limiting value that an instrument can measure.

Some mathematical terms used for error calculation are given below

(*i*) **Absolute Error** The difference between the true value and the measured value of a quantity is called absolute error,

$$\Delta a_n = a_{\text{mean}} - a_n$$

where, $a_{\text{mean}} = \sum_{i=1}^{n} \frac{a_i}{n}$

(*ii*) **Mean Absolute Error** The arithmetic mean of the magnitude of absolute errors in all the measurement is called mean absolute error.

$$\overline{\Delta a} = \frac{|\Delta a_1| + |\Delta a_2| + \ldots + |\Delta a_n|}{n}$$

(*iii*) **Relative Error or Fractional Error** The ratio of mean absolute error to the true value is called relative error.

$$\text{Relative error} = \frac{\text{Mean absolute error}}{\text{True value}} = \frac{\overline{\Delta a}}{a_m}$$

(*iv*) **Percentage Error** The relative error expressed in percentage is called percentage error.

$$\text{Percentage error} = \frac{\overline{\Delta a}}{a_m} \times 100\%$$

Combination of Errors

(*i*) **Error in Addition or Subtraction**

Let $x = a + b$ or $x = a - b$

If the measured values of two quantities a and b are $(a \pm \Delta a)$ and $(b \pm \Delta b)$, where Δa, Δb are the absolute errors in the measurement of a and b, then maximum absolute error in their addition or subtraction is

$$\Delta x = \pm (\Delta a + \Delta b)$$

(*ii*) **Error in Multiplication or Division**

Let $x = a \times b$ or $x = \frac{a}{b}$

If the measured values of a and b are $(a \pm \Delta a)$ and $(b \pm \Delta b)$, then maximum relative error,

$$\frac{\Delta x}{x} = \pm \left(\frac{\Delta a}{a} + \frac{\Delta b}{b} \right)$$

(*iii*) **Error in a quantity Raised to a Power**

Let $z = a^p b^q / c^r$

If the measured values of a, b and c are $(a \pm \Delta a)$, $(b \pm \Delta b)$ and $(c \pm \Delta c)$, then maximum error,

$$\frac{\Delta z}{z} = \pm \left[p\left(\frac{\Delta a}{a}\right) + q\left(\frac{\Delta b}{b}\right) + r\left(\frac{\Delta c}{c}\right) \right]$$

Note
- **Accuracy** is the closeness of measurements to the true value of physical quantity.
- **Precision** is the resolution or limit to which the physical quantity is measured.
- Least count of Vernier callipers = 1MSD (Main Scale Division) – 1VSD (Vernier Scale Division)

Significant Figures

The rules for determining the number of significant figures are as given below

***Rule* 1** All the non-zero digits are significant. e.g. $x = 1234$, has four significant figures.

***Rule* 2** All the zeroes between two non-zero digits are significant, no matter where the decimal point is, if at all. e.g. $x = 1007$, has four significant figures and $x = 10.07$ also contains four significant figures.

***Rule* 3** If the number is less than one, the zeroes on the right of decimal point and to the left of first non-zero digit are not significant.

e.g. In $0.\underline{0}\underline{0}55704$, the underlined zeroes are not significant. The zero between 7 and 4 is significant. The number of significant figure is 5.

***Rule* 4** In a number without a decimal point, the terminal or trailing zeroes are not significant. e.g. $x = 3210$, has three significant figures, the trailing zeroes are not significant.

***Rule* 5** Trailing zeroes in a number with a decimal point are significant.
e.g. 3.500, has four significant figures.

***Rule* 6** The multiplying or dividing factors, which are neither rounded numbers nor numbers representing measured values are exact and have infinite number of significant digits as per the condition.
e.g. In radius, $r = d/2$ and circumference, $S = 2\pi r$, the factor 2 is an exact number. It can be written as 2.0, 2.00 and 2.000 etc., as required.

Rounding Off

The process of omitting the non-significant digits and retaining only the desired number of significant digits, incorporating the required modifications to the last significant digit is called rounding off the number.

Rules for Rounding Off a Measurement

***Rule* 1** If the number lying to the right of cut-off digit is less than 5, then the cut-off digit is retained as such. However, if it is more than 5, then the cut-off digit is increased by 1.

e.g. $x = 6.24$ is rounded off to 6.2 to two significant digits and $x = 5.328$ is rounded off to 5.33 to three significant digits.

***Rule* 2** If the insignificant digit to be dropped is 5, then the rule is

(*i*) if the preceding digit is even, the insignificant digit is simply dropped.

(*ii*) if the preceding digit is odd, the preceding digit is raised by 1.

e.g. $x = 6.265$ is rounded off to $x = 6.26$ to three significant digits and $x = 6.275$ is rounded off to $x = 6.28$ to three significant digits.

***Rule* 3** The exact numbers like π, 2, 3 and 4 etc., that appear in formulae and are known to have infinite significant figures, can be rounded off to a limited number of significant figures as per the requirement.

Order of Magnitude

Any physical quantity can be expressed in the form of $a \times 10^b$ (in terms of magnitude), where a is a number lying between 1 and 10 and b is any negative or positive exponent of 10, then the exponent b is called the **order of magnitude** of the physical quantity, and the expression of a quantity as $a \times 10^b$ is called **scientific notation.**

e.g. The speed of light is given as 3.00×10^8 m/s, so the order of magnitude of the speed of light is 8.

Dimensions of Physical Quantities

The dimensions of a physical quantity are the powers (or exponents) to which the fundamental quantities must be raised to represent that quantity.

e.g. $$\text{Density} = \frac{\text{Mass}}{\text{Volume}} = \frac{\text{Mass}}{(\text{Length})^3}$$

or $$\text{Density} = (\text{Mass})\,(\text{Length})^{-3}$$

Thus, the dimensions of density are 1 in mass and – 3 in length. The dimensions of all other fundamental quantities are zero.

Dimensional Formula and Dimensional Equation

The expression of a physical quantity in terms of its dimensions is called its **dimensional formula**. e.g., Dimensional formula for density is $[ML^{-3}T^0]$, the dimensional formula of force is $[MLT^{-2}]$ and that for acceleration is $[M^0LT^{-2}]$.

An equation which contains a physical quantity on one side and its dimensional formula on the other side, is called the **dimensional equation** of that quantity.

Dimensional equations for a few physical quantities are given below

Speed $[v] = [M^0LT^{-1}]$

Area $[A] = [M^0L^2T^0]$

Force $[F] = [MLT^{-2}]$

Principle of Homogeneity

This principle states that, the dimensions of each term on both sides of an equation must be the same.

Dimensional Analysis and its Applications

The method of studying a physical phenomenon on the basis of dimensions is called **dimensional analysis**. The following are the three main used of dimensional analysis

(*i*) To convert a physical quantity from one system of units to another.

(*ii*) To check the correctness of a given physical relation.

(*iii*) To derive a relationship between different physical quantities.

Topical Practice Questions

All the exam questions of this chapter have been divided into 3 topics as listed below

Topic 1

Units

2019

1 The SI unit of thermal conductivity is **[NEET]**

(a) $J\,m^{-1}K^{-1}$ (b) $W\,m\,K^{-1}$
(c) $W\,m^{-1}K^{-1}$ (d) $J\,m\,K^{-1}$

2014

2 Unit of emf is **[WB JEE]**

(a) joule/ampere (b) volt/ampere
(c) $\dfrac{\text{henry-ampere}}{\text{second}}$ (d) joule/coulomb

3 If the unit of force is kN, the length is 1 km and time 100 s, then what will be the unit of mass? **[KCET]**

(a) 1000 kg (b) 1 kg
(c) 10000 kg (d) 100 kg

2012

4 The damping force on an oscillator is directly proportional to the velocity. The unit of the constant of proportionality is **[CBSE AIPMT]**

(a) $kg\,ms^{-1}$ (b) $kg\,ms^{-2}$
(c) kgs^{-1} (d) kgs

5 SI unit of permittivity is **[AIIMS, Manipal]**

(a) $C^2m^2N^2$ (b) $C^2m^{-2}N^{-1}$
(c) $C^2m^2N^{-1}$ (d) $C^{-1}m^2N^{-2}$

2011

6 The SI unit of activity of a radioactive sample is **[J&K CET]**

(a) curie (b) rutherford
(c) becquerel (d) millicurie

2010

7 Unit of electrical conductivity is **[UP CPMT]**

(a) ohm (b) siemen
(c) $m\,mho^{-1}$ (d) $mho\,m^{-1}$

8 The unit of magnetic moment is **[Guj CET]**

(a) TJ^{-1} (b) JT^{-1}
(c) Am^{-2} (d) Am^{-1}

9 The unit of specific conductivity is **[Manipal]**

(a) $\Omega\,cm^{-1}$ (b) $\Omega\,cm^{-2}$
(c) $\Omega^{-1}\,cm$ (d) $\Omega^{-1}cm^{-1}$

10 Which one of the following quantities has not been expressed in proper units? **[Kerala CEE]**

(a) Torque Nm
(b) Stress Nm^{-2}
(c) Modulus of elasticity Nm^{-2}
(d) Power Nms^{-1}
(e) Surface tension Nm^{-2}

2008

11 If 'muscle times speed equals power', then what is the ratio of the SI unit and the CGS unit of muscle? **[Manipal]**

(a) 10^5 (b) 10^3 (c) 10^7 (d) 10^{-5}

12 Match the following columns. **[Kerala CEE]**

Column I	Column II
A. Capacitance	P. volt $(\text{ampere})^{-1}$
B. Magnetic induction	Q. volt-sec $(\text{ampere})^{-1}$
C. Inductance	R. newton $(\text{ampere})^{-1}$ $(\text{metre})^{-1}$
D. Resistance	S. $\text{coulomb}^2(\text{joule})^{-1}$

	A	B	C	D
(a)	Q	R	S	P
(b)	S	R	Q	P
(c)	R	S	P	Q
(d)	S	P	Q	R
(e)	Q	S	P	R

2007

13 Parsec is the unit of **[BHU]**

(a) time (b) distance
(c) frequency (d) angular acceleration

2006

14 Given that, $y = A\sin\left[\left(\dfrac{2\pi}{\lambda}(ct - x)\right)\right]$, where y and x are measured in metre. Which of the following statements is true? **[AFMC]**

(a) The unit of λ is same as that of x and A.
(b) The unit of λ is same as that of x but not of A.
(c) The unit of c is same as that of $\dfrac{2\pi}{\lambda}$.
(d) The unit of $(ct - x)$ is same as that of $\dfrac{2\pi}{\lambda}$.

15 Which one of the following is not a derived unit? **[Kerala CEE]**

(a) Frequency (b) Planck's constant
(c) Gravitational constant (d) Charge
(e) Electric current

16 The magnitude of any physical quantity **[Punjab PMET]**

(a) depends on the method of measurement
(b) does not depend on the method of measurement
(c) is more in SI system than in CGS system
(d) directly proportional to fundamental unit of mass, length and time

17 The volume of a cube in m^3 is equal to the surface area of the cube in m^2. The volume of the cube is **[DUMET]**

(a) $64\,m^3$ (b) $216\,m^3$ (c) $512\,m^3$ (d) $195\,m^3$

18 The unit of Stefan's constant is **[KCET]**
(a) $Wm^{-2}K^{-1}$ (b) $Wm\,K^{-4}$
(c) $Wm^{-2}K^{-4}$ (d) $Nm^{-2}K^{-4}$

19 What is the SI unit of electric field intensity? **[Guj CET]**
(a) cm (b) Vm^{-1}
(c) Am^{-1} (d) None of these

20 If the magnetic flux is represented in weber, then the unit of magnetic induction will be **[Guj CET]**
(a) Wbm^{-2} (b) Wbm
(c) Wbm^2 (d) Wbm^{-1}

2005

21 If the unit of force and length are doubled, then the unit of energy will be **[Kerala CEE]**
(a) 1/4 times the original (b) 1/2 times the original
(c) 2 times the original (d) 4 times the original
(e) None of these

22 Density of liquid in CGS system is 0.625 g cm^{-3}. What is its magnitude in SI system? **[J&K CET]**
(a) 0.625 (b) 0.0625
(c) 0.00625 (d) 625

23 Some physical quantities are given in the Column I, the related units are given in the Column II. Match the correct pairs in the columns. **[DUMET]**

Column I	Column II
A. Magnetic field intensity	P. Wbm^{-1}
B. Magnetic flux	Q. Wbm^{-2}
C. Magnetic potential	R. Wb
D. Magnetic induction	S. Am^{-1}

	A	B	C	D		A	B	C	D
(a)	S	R	P	Q	(b)	S	R	Q	P
(c)	P	S	Q	R	(d)	R	P	S	Q

Answers

1 (c)	2 (c)	3 (c)	4 (c)	5 (b)	6 (c)	7 (d)	8 (b)	9 (d)	10 (e)
11 (a)	12 (b)	13 (b)	14 (a)	15 (e)	16 (b)	17 (b)	18 (c)	19 (b)	20 (a)
21 (d)	22 (d)	23 (a)							

Explanations

1 *(c)* The SI unit of thermal conductivity is $Wm^{-1}K^{-1}$.

2 *(c)* From the formula of emf, $\varepsilon = L\dfrac{dI}{dt}$

$\Rightarrow \quad \varepsilon = \dfrac{\text{henry-ampere}}{\text{second}}$

3 *(c)* We know that, $F = ma$ ...(i)

As, $a = \dfrac{v}{t} = \dfrac{s}{t\cdot t}$ $\left[\because v = \dfrac{s}{t}\right]$

So, $a = st^{-2}$ ...(ii)

From Eqs. (i) and (ii), we get

$\Rightarrow \quad F = mst^{-2}$

Given, $F = \text{kN} = 10^3\text{ N}$,

$s = 1\text{km} = 10^3\text{ m} = 1000\text{m}$ and $t = 100\text{s}$

Let x kg be unit of mass, then

Putting these values, we get

$f = (x\text{kg})(1000\text{ m})(100\text{s})^{-2}$

$\Rightarrow 1000 = x \times 1000 \times \dfrac{1}{10000}$

$\therefore \quad x = 10000\text{kg} = 10^4\text{ kg}$

4 *(c)* Given, damping force $\propto$ velocity

$F \propto v \Rightarrow F = kv$

$\Rightarrow \quad k = \dfrac{F}{v}$

unit of $k = \dfrac{\text{unit of } F}{\text{unit of } v} = \dfrac{\text{kgms}^{-2}}{\text{ms}^{-1}}$

$= \text{kgs}^{-1}$

5 *(b)* From Coulomb's law,

$F = \dfrac{1}{4\pi\varepsilon_0}\dfrac{q_1q_2}{r^2}$

or $\quad \varepsilon_0 = \dfrac{q_1q_2}{4\pi Fr^2}$

$\therefore$ Unit of ε_0 (permittivity)

$= \dfrac{C^2}{Nm^2} = C^2m^{-2}N^{-1}$

6 *(c)* The SI unit of activity of a radioactive sample is becquerel.

7 *(d)* Unit of electrical conductivity is mho m^{-1} or siemen m^{-1}.

8 *(b)* Magnetic moment is the strength of magnet. Its SI unit is Am^2 or NmT^{-1} or JT^{-1}.

9. *(d)* Specific conductivity

$= \dfrac{1}{\text{Specific resistance}}$

$= \dfrac{1}{\Omega\text{cm}} = (\Omega\text{ cm})^{-1}$

$= \Omega^{-1}\text{cm}^{-1}$

10 *(e)* The unit of surface tension is Nm^{-1}, so the given unit of surface tension Nm^{-2} is incorrect.

11 *(a)* Muscle $\times$ Speed = Power

or Muscle $= \dfrac{\text{Power}}{\text{Speed}} = \dfrac{\text{Work}}{\text{Time} \times \text{Speed}}$

$= \dfrac{\text{Force} \times \text{Displacement}}{\text{Displacement}}$

= Force

Now, ratio of SI unit and CGS unit of muscle

$= \dfrac{\text{SI unit of force}}{\text{CGS unit of force}}$

$= \dfrac{\text{kg} \times \text{m} \times \text{s}^{-2}}{\text{g} \times \text{cm} \times \text{s}^{-2}}$

$= 10^3 \times 10^2 = 10^5$

12 *(b)* Capacitance,

$C = \dfrac{Q}{V} = \dfrac{Q^2}{W} = (\text{coulomb})^2\text{joule}^{-1}$

Magnetic induction,

$B = \dfrac{F}{il} = \dfrac{\text{newton}}{\text{ampere} \times \text{metre}}$

$= (\text{newton})(\text{ampere})^{-1}(\text{metre})^{-1}$

Inductance,

$L=\frac{e}{dI/dt}=\frac{\text{volt}}{\text{ampere /second}}$

$=\text{volt-sec(ampere)}^{-1}$

Resistance, $R=\frac{V}{I}=\frac{\text{volt}}{\text{ampere}}$

$=\text{volt (ampere)}^{-1}$

$A\rightarrow S,\ B\rightarrow R,\ C\rightarrow Q,\ D\rightarrow P$

13 *(b)* The parsec is a unit of distance and one parsec is approximately equal to 3.08×10^{16}m.

14 *(a)* Here, $\frac{2\pi}{\lambda}(ct-x)$ is dimensionless.

Hence, $\frac{ct}{\lambda}$ is also dimensionless and unit of it is same as that of $\frac{x}{\lambda}$. Therefore, unit of λ is same as that of x.

Also, unit of y is same as that of A, which is also the unit of x.

Hence, statement (a) is correct.

15 *(e)* The units of all physical quantities other than length, mass, time, electric current, temperature, luminous intensity and amount of substance are obtained by raising one or more of the fundamental units to suitable power. Such units are called derived units. Hence, option (e) is correct.

16 *(b)* The magnitude of any physical quantity does not depend on the method of measurement because magnitude is a absolute value.

17 *(b)* Let length of side of the cube be a, then volume of the cube $=a^3$

Also, surface area of the cube $=6a^2$

Given, volume of cube = surface area of cube

$a^3=6a^2$

$\Rightarrow\quad a=6\text{m}$

Thus, volume of the cube

$=(6)^3=216\text{ m}^3$

18 *(c)* According to Stefan's law, the energy radiated per second or power radiated is given by

$P=\sigma AT^4$

$\Rightarrow\quad \sigma=\frac{P}{AT^4}$

Therefore, unit of σ is

$\frac{\text{W}}{\text{m}^2\text{K}^4}=\text{Wm}^{-2}\text{K}^{-4}$

19 *(b)* Electric field intensity, $E=-\frac{\partial V}{\partial r}$

$\therefore$ SI unit of $E=\text{V/m}$ or Vm^{-1}.

20 *(a)* Magnetic induction $=\frac{\text{Magnetic flux}}{\text{Area}}$

$\therefore$ Unit of magnetic induction

$=\frac{\text{weber}}{\text{metre}^2}=\frac{\text{Wb}}{\text{m}^2}=\text{Wbm}^{-2}$

21 *(d)* Energy = Work = Force × Length

So, on doubling unit of force and length, then the unit of energy will be 4 times the original.

22 *(d)* We know that, density $=\frac{\text{mass}}{\text{volume}}$

In CGS units, $d=0.625\text{ g cm}^{-3}$

In SI units, $d=\frac{0.625\times10^{-3}\text{ kg}}{10^{-6}\text{m}^3}$

$=625\text{ kg m}^{-3}$

23 *(a)* Unit of magnetic field intensity is Am^{-1}.

Unit of magnetic flux is Wb (weber).

Unit of magnetic potential is Wbm^{-1}.

Unit of magnetic induction is Wbm^{-2}.

$A\rightarrow S,\ B\rightarrow R,\ C\rightarrow P,\ D\rightarrow Q$

Topic 2

Errors and Significant Figures

2019

1 In an experiment, the percentage of error occurred in the measurement of physical quantities A, B, C and D are 1%, 2%, 3% and 4% respectively. Then the maximum percentage of error in the measurement X, where,

$X=\frac{A^2B^{1/2}}{C^{1/3}D^3}$ will be **[NEET]**

(a) 16% (b) −10% (c) 10% (d) $\left(\frac{3}{13}\right)$%

2 The main scale of a Vernier calliper has n divisions/cm. n divisions of the Vernier scale coincide with $(n-1)$ divisions of main scale. The least count of the vernier callipers is **[NEET]**

(a) $\frac{1}{(n+1)(n-1)}$ cm (b) $\frac{1}{n}$ cm

(c) $\frac{1}{n^2}$ cm (d) $\frac{1}{n(n+1)}$ cm

3 Calculate the mean percentage error in five observations, 80.0, 80.5, 81.0, 81.5 and 82. **[AIIMS]**

(a) 0.74% (b) 1.74%

(c) 0.38% (d) 1.38%

2018

4 $R=65\pm1\Omega$ L, $l=5\pm0.1$ mm and $d=10\pm0.5$ mm. Find error in calculation of resistivity. **[JIPMER]**

(a) 21% (b) 13%

(c) 16% (d) 41%

5 A student measured the diameter of a small steel ball using a screw gauge of least count 0.001 cm. The main scale reading is 5 mm and zero of circular scale division coincides with 25 divisions above the reference level. If screw gauge has a zero error of −0.004 cm, the correct diameter of the ball is **[NEET]**

(a) 0.053 cm (b) 0.525 cm

(c) 0.521 cm (d) 0.529 cm

6 In an experiment to measure, the height of a bridge by dropping stone into water underneath. If the error in measurement of time is 0.2s at the end of 4s, then the error in estimation of height of bridge will be (neglect the water resistance, i.e. thrust) **[AIIMS]**

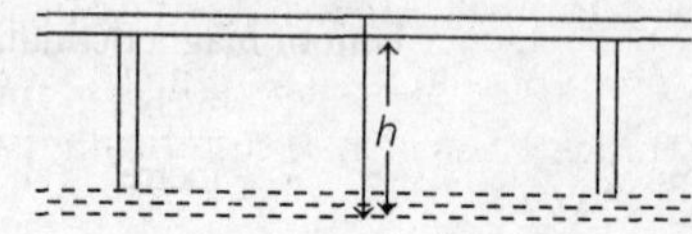

(a) ± 19.68 m (b) ± 17.22 m
(c) ± 7.84 m (d) ± 12.22 m

2014

7 If the absolute errors in two physical quantities A and B are a and b respectively, then the absolute error in the value of $A - B$ is **[EAMCET]**
(a) $b - a$ (b) $a \neq b$ (c) $a + b$ (d) $a - b$

2013

8 A physical quantity Q is found to depend on observables x, y and z obeying relation $Q = \frac{x^3 y^2}{z}$. The percentage error in the measurements of x, y and z are 1%, 2% and 4% respectively. What is the percentage error in the quantity Q? **[KCET]**
(a) 4% (b) 3% (c) 11% (d) 1%

2012

9 In an experiment, four quantities a, b, c and d are measured with percentage error 1%, 2%, 3% and 4% respectively. Quantity P is calculated as follows

$P = \frac{a^3 b^2}{cd}$, % error in P is **[NEET]**
(a) 14% (b) 10% (c) 7% (d) 4%

10 The error in the measurement of radius of sphere is 0.3%, what is the percentage error in the measurement of its volume? **[UP CPMT]**
(a) 0.3 % (b) 0.6% (c) 0.9% (d) $\frac{4}{3}\pi(0.3)^3$

11 In a slide calliper, $(m + 1)$ number of Vernier divisions is equal to m number of smallest main scale divisions. If d unit is the magnitude of the smallest main scale division, then the magnitude of the Vernier constant is **[WB JEE]**
(a) $d/(m+1)$ unit (b) d/m unit
(c) $md/(m+1)$ unit (d) $(m+1)\,d/m$ unit

12 A physical quantity x is given by $x = \frac{2k^3 l^2}{m\sqrt{n}}$.

The percentage error in the measurements of k, l, m and n are 1%, 2%, 3% and 4% respectively. The value of x is uncertain by **[AMU]**
(a) 8% (b) 10%
(c) 12% (d) None of these

2010

13 The length of a strip measured with a metre rod is 10.0 cm. Its width measured with a vernier calipers is 1.00 cm. The least count of the metre rod is 0.1 cm and that of vernier calipers 0.01 cm. What will be error in its area? **[BVP]**
(a) $\pm 13\%$ (b) $\pm 7\%$ (c) $\pm 4\%$ (d) $\pm 2\%$

14 Each side of a cube is measured to be 7.203 m. What are the total surface area and the volume of the cube to appropriate significant figures? **[Manipal]**
(a) 373.7 m^2, 311.3 m^3
(b) 311.3 m^2, 373.7 m^3
(c) 273.4 m^2, 342.4 m^3
(d) 423.4 m^2, 437.4 m^3

15 You measure two quantities as $A = 1.0 \text{ m} \pm 0.2$ m, $B = 2.0 \text{m} \pm 0.2$ m. We should report correct value for $\sqrt{AB}$ as **[AMU]**
(a) $1.4 \text{m} \pm 0.4 \text{m}$ (b) $1.41 \text{m} \pm 0.15$ m
(c) $1.4 \text{ m} \pm 0.3$ m (d) $1.4 \text{m} \pm 0.2 \text{m}$

16 The length and breadth of a rectangular sheet have been measured by a measuring scale to an accuracy of 0.1 cm. If the measured values are 35.2 cm and 21.7 cm, respectively, then find the relative error in the area of the sheet. **[Manipal]**
(a) $\pm 8 \times 10^{-2}$ (b) $\pm 4 \times 10^{-3}$
(c) $\pm 7.45 \times 10^{-3}$ (d) $\pm 9 \times 10^{-6}$

17 Choose the incorrect statement out of the following. **[AMU]**
(a) Every measurement by any measuring instrument has some errors.
(b) Every calculated physical quantity that is based on measured values has some errors.
(c) A measurement can have more accuracy but less precision and *vice-versa*.
(d) The percentage error is different from relative error.

2009

18 The number of significant figures in the numbers 4.8000×10^4 and 48000.50 are respectively, **[Kerala CEE]**
(a) 5 and 6 (b) 5 and 7
(c) 2 and 7 (d) 2 and 6

19 Percentage error in the measurement of mass and speed are 2% and 3% respectively. The error in the estimation of kinetic energy obtained by measuring mass and speed will be **[AIIMS]**
(a) 12% (b) 10%
(c) 2% (d) 8%

20 If the length of a pendulum is increased by 2%, then in a day, the pendulum **[Kerala CEE]**
(a) loses 764 s (b) loses 924 s
(c) gains 236 s (d) loses 864 s
(e) gains 346 s

2008

21 If the error in the measurement of radius of a sphere is 2%, then the error in the determination of volume of the sphere will be **[CBSE AIPMT]**
(a) 4% (b) 6% (c) 8% (d) 2%

22 **Assertion** The error in the measurement of radius of the sphere is 0.3%. The permissible error in its surface area is 0.6%.
Reason The permissible error is calculated by the formula $\frac{\Delta A}{A} = \frac{4\Delta r}{r}$. **[AIIMS]**
(a) Both Assertion and Reason are correct and Reason is the correct explanation of Assertion.
(b) Both Assertion and Reason are correct but Reason is not the correct explanation of Assertion.
(c) Assertion is correct but Reason is incorrect.
(d) Both Assertion and Reason are incorrect.

23 The period of oscillation of a simple pendulum in the experiment is recorded as 2.63 s, 2.56 s, 2.42 s, 2.71 s and 2.80 s respectively. The average absolute error is **[AMU]**
(a) 0.1 s (b) 0.11 s (c) 0.01 s (d) 1.0 s

2007

24 If voltage $V = (100 \pm 5)$ V and current $I = (10 \pm 0.2)$ A, the percentage error in resistance R is **[Kerala CEE]**
(a) 5.2% (b) 25% (c) 7% (d) 10%
(e) 2.5%

25 A wire has a mass (0.3 ± 0.003) g, radius (0.5 ± 0.005) mm and length (0.6 ± 0.006) cm. The maximum percentage error in the measurement of its density **[WB JEE]**
(a) 1 (b) 2 (c) 3 (d) 4

2006

26 The length, breadth and thickness of a block are given by $l = 12$ cm, $b = 6$ cm and $t = 2.45$ cm. The volume of the block according to the idea of significant figures should be **[MP PMT]**
(a) 1×10^2 cm^3 (b) 2×10^2 cm^3
(c) 1.764×10^2 cm^3 (d) None of these

2005

27 If the radius of a sphere is (5.3 ± 0.1) cm. Then, percentage error in its volume will be **[AFMC]**
(a) $3 + 6.01 \times \frac{100}{5.3}$ (b) $\frac{1}{3} \times 0.01 \times \frac{100}{5.3}$
(c) $\left(\frac{3 \times 0.1}{5.3}\right) \times 100$ (d) $\frac{0.1}{5.3} \times 100$

28 If the length of rod A is 3.25 ± 0.01 cm and that of B is 4.19 ± 0.01 cm, then the rod B is longer than rod A by **[J&K CET]**
(a) 0.94 ± 0.00 cm (b) 0.94 ± 0.01 cm
(c) 0.94 ± 0.02 cm (d) 0.94 ± 0.005 cm

29 The radius of a sphere is measured to be (2.1 ± 0.5) cm. Calculate its surface area with error limits **[JCECE]**
(a) (55.4 ± 26.4) cm^2 (b) (55.4 ± 0.02) cm^2
(c) (55.4 ± 2.64) cm^2 (d) (55.4 ± 0.26) cm^2

Answers

1 (a)	2 (c)	3 (a)	4 (b)	5 (d)	6 (c)	7 (c)	8 (c)	9 (a)	10 (c)
11 (c)	12 (c)	13 (d)	14 (b)	15 (d)	16 (c)	17 (d)	18 (b)	19 (d)	20 (d)
21 (b)	22 (c)	23 (b)	24 (c)	25 (d)	26 (b)	27 (c)	28 (c)	29 (a)	

Explanations

1 (a) Given, $X = \frac{A^2 B^{1/2}}{C^{1/3} D^3}$

The percentage error in X is given by

$$\frac{\Delta X}{X} \times 100 = 2\left(\frac{\Delta A}{A}\right) \times 100 + \frac{1}{2}\left(\frac{\Delta B}{B}\right) \times 100 + \frac{1}{3}\left(\frac{\Delta C}{C}\right) \times 100 + 3\left(\frac{\Delta D}{D}\right) \times 100 \quad \text{...(i)}$$

Given, $\frac{\Delta A}{A} \times 100 = 1\%$, $\frac{\Delta B}{B} \times 100 = 2\%$, $\frac{\Delta C}{C} \times 100 = 3\%$, $\frac{\Delta D}{D} \times 100 = 4\%$

Substituting these values in Eq. (i), we get

$$\frac{\Delta X}{X} \times 100 = 2(1\%) + \frac{1}{2}(2\%) + \frac{1}{3}(3\%) + 3(4\%)$$
$$= 2\% + 1\% + 1\% + 12\% = 16\%$$

Thus, maximum % error in X is 16%.

2 (c) As it is given that, n divisions of Vernier scale coincide with $(n-1)$ divisions of main scale, i.e.

$$n(\text{VSD}) = (n-1)\text{MSD}$$
$$\Rightarrow \quad 1\text{VSD} = \frac{(n-1)}{n}\text{MSD} \quad \text{...(i)}$$

The least count is the difference between one Main Scale Division (MSD) and one Vernier Scale Division (VSD).

$\therefore$ Least Count (LC) = 1MSD − 1VSD

$$= 1\text{MSD} - \frac{(n-1)}{n}\text{MSD} \quad \text{[From Eq. (i)]}$$
$$= \left(1 - \frac{(n-1)}{n}\right)\text{MSD} = \frac{1}{n}\text{MSD}$$

Given, $1\text{MSD} = \frac{1}{n}$ cm

$$\Rightarrow \text{LC} = \frac{1}{n} \times \frac{1}{n} \text{ cm} = \frac{1}{n^2} \text{ cm}$$

3 (a) Mean of the five observations,

$$\mu = \frac{80.0 + 80.5 + 81.0 + 81.5 + 82}{5} = \frac{405.0}{5} = 81$$

$\therefore$ Mean error

$$= \frac{\left[\begin{array}{l}|80-\mu| + |80.5-\mu| + |81.0-\mu| \\ \quad + |81.5-\mu| + |82-\mu|\end{array}\right]}{5}$$

$$= \frac{\left[\begin{array}{l}|80-81| + |80.5-81| + |81.0-81| \\ \quad + |81.5-81| + |82-81|\end{array}\right]}{5}$$

$$= \frac{1 + 0.5 + 0 + 0.5 + 1}{5} = \frac{3}{5} = 0.6$$

$\therefore$ Mean % error $= \frac{0.6}{81} \times 100\% = 0.74\%$

4 (b) Given, $R = 65\ \Omega$, $\Delta R = 1\Omega$, $l = 5\times10^{-3}$ m, $\Delta l = 0.1\times10^{-3}$ m, $d = 10\times10^{-3}$ m and $\Delta d = 0.5\times10^{-3}$ m.

$\because$ Resistivity, $\rho = \frac{RA}{l}$

or $\rho = \frac{R\pi\ (d/2)^2}{l} = \frac{\pi R d^2}{4l}$

$$\therefore \frac{\Delta\rho}{\rho} = \frac{\Delta R}{R} + 2\frac{\Delta d}{d} + \frac{\Delta l}{l}$$

$$\therefore \frac{\Delta\rho}{\rho} = \frac{1}{65} + 2\left(\frac{0.5\times10^{-3}}{10\times10^{-3}}\right) + \frac{0.1\times10^{-3}}{5\times10^{-3}}$$

or $\frac{\Delta\rho}{\rho} = 0.0153 + 0.1 + 0.02$

or $\frac{\Delta\rho}{\rho} \approx 0.1353$

So, error in calculation of resistivity is 13.5% ≈ 13%.

5 (d) Given, least count of screw gauge, LC = 0.001 cm

Main Scale Reading (MSR) = 5 mm = 0.5 cm

Number of coinciding divisions on the circular scale, i.e. Vernier Scale Reading, (VSR) = 25

Here, zero error = – 0.004 cm

Final reading obtained from the screw gauge is given as

MSR + VSR × LC – zero error

Final reading from the screw gauge

= 0.5 + 25 × 0.001 – (–0.004)

= 0.5 + 0.025 + 0.004

= 0.5 + 0.029

= 0.529 cm

Thus, the diameter of the ball is 0.529 cm.

6 (c) We know that, $s = ut + \frac{1}{2}at^2$

or $h = (0)t + \frac{1}{2}\times 9.8\times(4)^2 \quad \left(\begin{array}{l}\because a = g \\ \because u = 0\end{array}\right)$

$= 78.4$ m

Given, $\Delta t = 0.2$ s

$t = 4$ s

Now, for error,

$$\frac{\Delta h}{h} = \pm 2\left(\frac{\Delta t}{t}\right) = \pm 2\left(\frac{0.2}{4}\right) = \pm 0.1$$

or $\Delta h = \pm 0.1\times h$

$= \pm 0.1\times 78.4$

$= \pm 7.84$ m

7 (c) The absolute error in the value $A - B$ will be $\Delta x = \pm(a+b)$, where, a and b are absolute errors in quantity A and B, respectively.

8 (c) Given, $Q = \frac{x^3y^2}{z}$

According to percentage error formula,

$$\frac{\Delta Q}{Q}\times 100 = 3\left|\frac{\Delta x}{x}\right| + 2\left|\frac{\Delta y}{y}\right| + \left|\frac{\Delta z}{z}\right| \times 100$$

$$\left[\because \frac{\Delta x}{x} = 1\%, \frac{\Delta y}{y} = 2\% \text{ and } \frac{\Delta z}{z} = 40\%\right]$$

$= 3\times1\% + 2\times2\% + 1\times4\%$

$= 3\% + 4\% + 4\% = 11\%$

9 (a) Given, $P = \frac{a^3b^2}{cd}$

$$\therefore \left(\frac{\Delta P}{P}\times 100\right) = \left(\frac{3\Delta a}{a} + \frac{2\Delta b}{b} + \frac{\Delta c}{c} + \frac{\Delta d}{d}\right)\times 100$$

$$= 3\left(\frac{\Delta a}{a}\times100\right) + 2\left(\frac{\Delta b}{b}\times100\right) + \left(\frac{\Delta c}{c}\times100\right) + \left(\frac{\Delta d}{d}\times100\right)$$

$$\left[\begin{array}{l}\because \frac{\Delta a}{a}\times100\% = 1\%, \frac{\Delta b}{b}\times100 = 2\%, \\ \frac{\Delta c}{c}\times100 = 3\% \text{ and } \frac{\Delta d}{d}\times100 = 4\%\end{array}\right]$$

$= (3\times1) + (2\times2) + (1\times3) + (1\times4)$

$= 3 + 4 + 3 + 4 = 14\%$

10 (c) Error in radius, $\frac{\Delta r}{r} = 0.3\%$

Volume of sphere $= \frac{4}{3}\pi r^3$

$\therefore$ Error in volume $= 3\times\frac{\Delta r}{r}$

$= (3\times0.3)\% = 0.9\%$

11 (c) $(m+1)$ Vernier scale division $= m$ main scale division.

One division on Vernier scale

$= \left(\frac{m}{m+1}\right)$ main scale division.

Vernier constant

$= \left(\frac{m}{m+1}\right)d = \frac{md}{m+1}$ unit

12 (c) Given, $x = \frac{2k^3l^2}{m\sqrt{n}}$

Percentage error in x

$= 3\%k + 2\%l + \%m + \frac{1}{2}\%n$

$$= 3\left(\frac{\Delta k}{k}\times100\right) + 2\left(\frac{\Delta l}{l}\times100\right) + \left(\frac{\Delta m}{m}\times100\right) + \frac{1}{2}\left(\frac{\Delta n}{n}\times100\right)$$

$= 3\times1\% + 2\times2\% + 1\times3\% + \frac{1}{2}\times4\%$

$= 12\%$

13 (d) Area of strip $(A) = lb$

where, l = length and b = breadth.

The percentage error in area is given by

$$\left(\frac{\Delta A}{A}\right)\times100 = \left(\frac{\Delta l}{l}\right)\times100 + \left(\frac{\Delta b}{b}\right)\times100$$

$$= \frac{0.1}{10}\times100 + \frac{0.01}{1}\times100 = \pm 2\%$$

14 (b) The number of significant figures in the measured length is 4. The calculated area and the volume should therefore be rounded off to 4 significant figures.

Surface area of the cube

$= 6\ (7.203)^2 = 311.299254$

$= 311.3\ \text{m}^2$

Volume of the cube

$= (7.203)^3 = 373.714754$

$= 373.7\ \text{m}^3$

15. (d) Given, $A = 1.0\ \text{m} \pm 0.2$ m, $B = 2.0\ \text{m} \pm 0.2$ m

Let, $Y = \sqrt{AB} = \sqrt{(1.0)(2.0)} = 1.414$ m

Rounding off to two significant digit $Y = 1.4$ m

$$\frac{\Delta Y}{Y} = \frac{1}{2}\left[\frac{\Delta A}{A} + \frac{\Delta B}{B}\right]$$

$$= \frac{1}{2}\left[\frac{0.2}{1.0} + \frac{0.2}{2.0}\right] = \frac{0.6}{2\times2.0}$$

$$\Rightarrow \Delta Y = \frac{0.6Y}{2\times2.0} = \frac{0.6\times1.4}{2\times2.0} = 0.212$$

Rounding off to one significant digit $\Delta Y = 0.2\,\text{m}$

Thus, correct value for $\sqrt{AB}$

$$= r + \Delta r = 1.4 \pm 0.2\text{m}$$

16 (c) Here, length of sheet $l = (35.2 \pm 0.1)$ cm and breadth of sheet $b = (21.7 \pm 0.1)$ cm

$\therefore$ Relative error in surface area of the sheet,

$$\left(\frac{\Delta s}{s}\right)_{max} = \frac{\Delta l}{l} + \frac{\Delta b}{b} = \frac{0.1}{35.2} + \frac{0.1}{21.7}$$

$$= 2.841 \times 10^{-3} + 4.608 \times 10^{-3}$$

$$= 7.449 \times 10^{-3} = \pm 7.45 \times 10^{-3}$$

17 (d) When the relative error is expressed in percentage, we call it as percentage error.

Thus, statement (d) is incorrect while all other statements regarding measurement of a quantity are correct.

18 (b) 4.8000×10^4 has 4, 8, 0, 0, 0 (5 significant digits).

48000.50 has 4, 8, 0, 0, 0, 5, 0 (7 significant digits).

For number more than 1 digit, after decimal place are significant. Power of 10 does not affect number of significant figures or digits.

19 (d) Kinetic energy, $K = \frac{1}{2}mv^2$

Fractional error in kinetic energy,

$$\frac{\Delta K}{K} = \frac{\Delta m}{m} + \frac{2\Delta v}{v}$$

Percentage error in kinetic energy is

$$= \frac{\Delta m}{m} \times 100 + \frac{2\Delta v}{v} \times 100$$

Given,

$$\frac{\Delta m}{m} \times 100 = 2\% \text{ and } \frac{\Delta v}{v} \times 100 = 3\%$$

So, percentage error in kinetic energy

$$= 2 + (2 \times 3) = 2 + 6 = 8\%$$

20 (d) Time period, $T = 2\pi\sqrt{\frac{l}{g}}$

or $$\frac{\Delta T}{T} = \frac{1}{2}\frac{\Delta l}{l}$$

For 1 s ,

$$\Delta T = \frac{1}{2}\left(\frac{\Delta l}{l}\right)T = \frac{1}{2} \times 0.02 \times T$$

$= 0.01\,T$

For a day, the pendulum loses,

$$\Delta T = 24 \times 60 \times 60 \times 0.01 = 864\text{ s}$$

21 (b) Volume of a sphere $= \frac{4}{3}\pi\,(\text{radius})^3$

or $$V = \frac{4}{3}\pi R^3$$

The fractional error in V is $\frac{\Delta V}{V} = \frac{3\Delta R}{R}$

Given, $\frac{\Delta R}{R} \times 100 = 2\%$

$$\frac{\Delta V}{V} \times 100 = 3 \times 2\% = 6\%$$

22 (c) Surface area of sphere, $A = 4\pi r^2$ (error will not be involved in constant 4π)

Fractional error, $\frac{\Delta A}{A} = \frac{2\Delta r}{r}$

$$\frac{\Delta A}{A} \times 100 = 2 \times 0.3\% = 0.6\%$$

but $\frac{\Delta A}{A} = \frac{4\Delta r}{r}$ is false.

23 (b) Average value

$$= \frac{2.63 + 2.56 + 2.42 + 2.71 + 2.80}{5}$$

$= 2.62$ s

Now, $|\Delta T_1| = |2.62 - 2.63| = 0.01$

$|\Delta T_2| = |2.62 - 2.56| = 0.06$

$|\Delta T_3| = |2.62 - 2.42| = 0.20$

$|\Delta T_4| = |2.62 - 2.71| = 0.09$

$|\Delta T_5| = |2.62 - 2.80| = 0.18$

$$\Delta T = \frac{\left[\begin{array}{c}|\Delta T_1| + |\Delta T_2| + |\Delta T_3| \\ + |\Delta T_4| + |\Delta T_5|\end{array}\right]}{5}$$

$$= \frac{0.54}{5} = 0.108$$

$$\Delta T \simeq 0.11\text{ s}$$

24 (c) Given, voltage, $V = (100 \pm 5)$ V,

Current, $I = (10 \pm 0.2)$ A

From Ohm's law, $V = IR$

$\therefore$ Resistance, $R = \frac{V}{I}$

Maximum percentage error in resistance,

$$\left(\frac{\Delta R}{R} \times 100\right) = \left(\frac{\Delta V}{V} \times 100\right) + \left(\frac{\Delta I}{I} \times 100\right)$$

$$= \left(\frac{5}{100} \times 100\right) + \left(\frac{0.2}{10} \times 100\right)$$

$= 5 + 2 = 7\%$

25 (d) Density, $\rho = \frac{m}{\pi r^2 L}$

$$\therefore \frac{\Delta\rho}{\rho} \times 100 = \left[\frac{\Delta m}{m} + \frac{2\Delta r}{r} + \frac{\Delta L}{L}\right] \times 100$$

$$= \left(\frac{0.003}{0.3} \times 100\right) + \left(2 \times \frac{0.005}{0.5} \times 100\right) + \left(\frac{0.006}{0.6} \times 100\right) \text{(given)}$$

$= 1 + 2 + 1 = 4\%$

So, the maximum percentage error in density $= 4\%$.

26 (b) Using the relation for volume,

V = Length × Breadth × Thickness

$= 12 \times 6 \times 2.45 = 176.4\text{ cm}^3$

$V = 1.764 \times 10^2\text{cm}^3$

The minimum number of significant figure is 1 in breadth. Hence, the volume will contain only one significant figure. Therefore, volume,

$$V = 2 \times 10^2\text{ cm}^3.$$

27 (c) Volume of sphere, $V = \frac{4}{3}\pi r^3$

Percentage error in volume

$$= \frac{3 \times \Delta r}{r} \times 100$$

$$= \left(\frac{3 \times 0.1}{5.3}\right) \times 100$$

28 (c) Length of rod A,

$L_A = 3.25 \pm 0.01$ cm

and length B,

$L_B = 4.19 \pm 0.01$cm

Then, the rod B is longer than rod A by a length,

$\Delta l = L_B - L_A$

$\Delta l = (4.19 \pm 0.01) - (3.25 \pm 0.01)$

$\Delta l = (0.94 \pm 0.02)$ cm

29 (a) Surface area,

$$S = 4\pi r^2 = 4 \times \frac{22}{7} \times (2.1)^2$$

$= 55.44 = 55.4\text{ cm}^2$

Further, $\frac{\Delta S}{S} = 2 \cdot \frac{\Delta r}{r}$

or $$\Delta S = 2\left(\frac{\Delta r}{r}\right)(S)$$

$$= \frac{2 \times 0.5 \times 55.4}{2.1}$$

$= 26.38 = 26.4\text{ cm}^2$

$\therefore$ $S = (55.4 \pm 26.4)\text{ cm}^2$

Topic 3

Dimensions

2019

1 If mass [M], distance [L] and time [T] are fundamental quantities, then find the dimensions of torque. **[JIPMER]**
(a) $[ML^2T^{-2}]$ (b) $[MLT^{-2}]$ (c) $[MLT]$ (d) $[ML^2T]$

2 What is dimensions of energy in terms of linear momentum [p], area [A] and time [T]? **[JIPMER]**
(a) $[p^1A^1T^1]$
(b) $[p^2A^2T^{-1}]$
(c) $[p^1A^{1/2}T^{-1}]$
(d) $[p^{1/2}A^{1/2}T^{-1}]$

2018

3 Dimensions of force is **[JIPMER]**
(a) $[M^2L^1T^{-1}]$
(b) $[M^1L^1T^{-2}]$
(c) $[M^2L^{-1}T^{-2}]$
(d) $[M^1L^1T^{-1}]$

4 If the formula, $X = 3YZ^2$, X and Z have dimensions of capacitance and magnetic induction. The dimensions of Y in MKSQ system are **[AIIMS]**
(a) $[M^{-3}L^{-2}T^4Q^4]$
(b) $[ML^2T^8Q^4]$
(c) $[M^{-2}L^{-3}T^2Q^4]$
(d) $[M^{-2}L^{-2}TQ^2]$

2017

5 A physical quantity of the dimensions of length that can be formed out of c, G and $\frac{e^2}{4\pi\varepsilon_0}$ is [c is velocity of light, G is universal constant of gravitation and e is charge] **[NEET]**
(a) $\frac{1}{c^2}\left[G\frac{e^2}{4\pi\varepsilon_0}\right]^{1/2}$
(b) $c^2\left[G\frac{e^2}{4\pi\varepsilon_0}\right]^{1/2}$
(c) $\frac{1}{c^2}\left[\frac{e^2}{G\,4\pi\varepsilon_0}\right]^{1/2}$
(d) $\frac{1}{c}G\frac{e^2}{4\pi\varepsilon_0}$

2016

6 Planck's constant (h), speed of light in vacuum (c) and Newton's gravitational constant (G) are three fundamental constants. Which of the following combinations of these has the dimensions of length? **[NEET]**
(a) $\frac{\sqrt{hG}}{c^{3/2}}$ (b) $\frac{\sqrt{hG}}{c^{5/2}}$ (c) $\sqrt{\frac{hc}{G}}$ (d) $\sqrt{\frac{Gc}{h^{3/2}}}$

2015

7 If energy (E), velocity (v) and time (T) are chosen as the fundamental quantities, the dimensional formula of surface tension will be **[AIPMT]**
(a) $[E\,v^{-2}T^{-1}]$
(b) $[E\,v^{-1}T^{-2}]$
(c) $[E\,v^{-2}T^{-2}]$
(d) $[E^{-2}\,v^{-1}T^{-3}]$

2014

8 If force (F), velocity (v) and time (T) are taken as fundamental units, then the dimensions of mass is **[CBSE AIPMT]**
(a) $[FvT^{-1}]$
(b) $[FvT^{-2}]$
(c) $[Fv^{-1}T^{-1}]$
(d) $[Fv^{-1}T]$

9 The dimensional formula for Reynold's number is **[MHT CET]**
(a) $[M^0L^0T^0]$
(b) $[MLT]$
(c) $[ML^{-1}T]$
(d) $[MLT^{-1}]$

10 The relation between force F and density d is $F = \frac{x}{\sqrt{d}}$. The dimensions of x is **[MHT CET]**
(a) $[M^{3/2}L^{-1/2}T^{-2}]$
(b) $[M^{1/2}L^{-1/2}T^{-2}]$
(c) $[M^{3/2}L^{-1}T^{-2}]$
(d) $[M^{1/2}L^{-1}T^{-2}]$

11 If n denotes a positive integer, h the Planck's constant, q the charge and B the magnetic field, then the quantity $\left[\frac{nh}{2\pi qB}\right]$ has the dimensions of **[WB JEE]**
(a) area
(b) length
(c) speed
(d) acceleration

12 In which of the following pairs, the two physical quantities have different dimensions? **[WB JEE]**
(a) Planck's constant and angular momentum
(b) Impulse and linear momentum
(c) Moment of inertia and moment of a force
(d) Energy and torque

13 What is the dimensional formula of gravitational constant G? **[UK PMT]**
(a) $[M^{-1}L^3T^{-2}]$
(b) $[M^2L^{-3}T^{-2}]$
(c) $[M^{-1}L^2T^{-2}]$
(d) $[M^{-1}L^3T^{-1}]$

14 The dimensional formula of magnetic flux is **[Guj CET]**
(a) $[ML^2T^{-2}A^{-1}]$
(b) $[ML^2T^{-3}A^{-1}]$
(c) $[M^{-1}L^{-2}T^2A]$
(d) $[ML^3T^{-2}A^{-1}]$

15 The dimensional formula for electric field is **[Guj CET]**
(a) $[ML^2T^{-3}A^{-1}]$
(b) $[ML^2T^{-3}A^{-2}]$
(c) $[MLT^{-3}A^{-1}]$
(d) $[M^0L^0T^0A^0]$

2013

16 The dimensions of $\frac{1}{2}\varepsilon_0E^2$ (ε_0 is permittivity of free space, E is electric field) are **[AIIMS]**
(a) $[MLT^{-1}]$
(b) $[ML^2T^{-3}]$
(c) $[ML^{-1}T^{-2}]$
(d) $[ML^2T^{-1}]$

17 The displacement of an oscillating particle is given by $y = A\sin(Bx + Ct + D)$. The dimensional formula for $(ABCD)$ is **[UP CPMT]**
(a) $[M^0L^{-1}T^0]$ (b) $[M^0L^0T^{-1}]$
(c) $[M^0L^{-1}T^{-1}]$ (d) $[M^0\ L^0T^0]$

18 If C and R stands for capacitance and resistance, then the dimensions of CR is **[Manipal]**
(a) $[M^0L^0T]$
(b) $[ML^0T]$
(c) $[M^0L^0T^2]$
(d) not expressible in terms of M, L and T

2012

19 The dimensions of angular momentum are **[WB JEE]**
(a) $[M^0LT^{-1}]$ (b) $[ML^2T^{-1}]$ (c) $[MLT^{-1}]$ (d) $[M^2LT^{-2}]$

2011

20 The dimensions of $(\mu_0\varepsilon_0)^{-1/2}$ are **[CBSE AIPMT]**
(a) $[L^{-1}T]$ (b) $[LT^{-1}]$
(c) $[L^{-1/2}T^{1/2}]$ (d) $[L^{1/2}T^{-1/2}]$

21 Surface tension has the same dimensions as that of **[Kerala CEE]**
(a) coefficient of viscosity (b) impulse
(c) momentum (d) spring constant
(e) frequency

22 What is the dimensions of surface tension? **[WB JEE]**
(a) $[MLT^0]$ (b) $[MLT^{-1}]$ (c) $[ML^0T^{-2}]$ (d) $[ML^0T^{-1}]$

23 The dimensions of impulse are **[J&K CET]**
(a) $[MLT^{-1}]$ (b) $[ML^2T^{-1}]$
(c) $[ML^{-1}T^{-1}]$ (d) $[MT^{-1}]$

24 If C be the capacitance and V be the electric potential, then the dimensional formula of CV^2 is **[KCET]**
(a) $[ML^2T^{-2}A^0]$ (b) $[MLT^{-2}A^{-1}]$
(c) $[M^0LT^{-2}A^0]$ (d) $[ML^{-3}TA]$

25 The relation $p = \frac{\alpha}{\beta}e^{\frac{-\alpha Z}{k\theta}}$, where p is pressure, Z is distance, k is Boltzmann constant and θ is temperature. The dimensional formula of β will be **[AFMC]**
(a) $[M^0L^2T^0]$ (b) $[ML^2T]$
(c) $[ML^0T^{-1}]$ (d) $[M^0L^2T^{-1}]$

26 If $p = \frac{RT}{V-b}e^{-\alpha V/RT}$, then dimensional formula of α is **[UP CPMT]**
(a) p (b) R (c) T (d) V

27 Velocity v is given by $v = at^2 + bt + c$, where t is time. What are the dimensions of a, b and c respectively? **[UP CPMT]**
(a) $[LT^{-3}]$, $[LT^{-2}]$ and $[LT^{-1}]$
(b) $[LT^{-1}]$, $[LT^{-2}]$ and $[LT^{-3}]$
(c) $[LT^{-2}]$, $[LT^{-3}]$ and $[LT^{-1}]$
(d) $[LT^{-1}]$, $[LT^{-3}]$ and $[LT^{-2}]$

28 The dimensions of electromotive force in terms of current [A] are **[BVP]**
(a) $[ML^{-2}A^{-2}]$ (b) $[ML^2T^{-2}A^{-2}]$
(c) $[ML^2T^{-2}A^{-2}]$ (d) $[ML^2T^{-3}A^{-1}]$

29 Dimensions of capacitance are **[Manipal]**
(a) $[M^{-1}L^{-2}T^4A^2]$ (b) $[MLT^{-3}A^{-1}]$
(c) $[ML^2T^{-3}A^{-1}]$ (d) $[M^{-1}L^{-2}T^3A^{-1}]$

30 From the dimensional consideration, which of the following equations is correct? **[Haryana PMT]**
(a) $T = 2\pi\sqrt{\frac{R^3}{GM}}$ (b) $T = 2\pi\sqrt{\frac{GM}{R^3}}$
(c) $T = 2\pi\sqrt{\frac{GM}{R^2}}$ (d) $T = 2\pi\sqrt{\frac{R^2}{GM}}$

31 If E, M, L and G denote energy, mass, angular momentum and gravitational constant respectively, then the quantity (E^2L^2/M^5G^2) has the dimensions of **[AMU]**
(a) angle (b) length
(c) mass (d) None of these

32. A uniform wire of length L, diameter D and density ρ is stretched under a tension T. The correct relation between its fundamental frequency f, the length L and the diameter D is **[KCET]**
(a) $f \propto \frac{1}{LD}$ (b) $f \propto \frac{1}{L\sqrt{D}}$
(c) $f \propto \frac{1}{D^2}$ (d) $f \propto \frac{1}{LD^2}$

33 The dimensions of resistance are same as those of ..., where, h is the Planck's constant and e is the charge. **[KCET]**
(a) $\frac{h^2}{e^2}$ (b) $\frac{h^2}{e}$
(c) $\frac{h}{e^2}$ (d) $\frac{h}{e}$

34 The dimensional formula of resistivity(s) **[Guj CET]**
(a) $[M^0L^1T^{-1}A^{-1}]$ (b) $[M^0L^0T^{-1}A^{-1}]$
(c) $[M^1L^1T^{-1}A^{-3}]$ (d) $[M^1L^3T^{-3}A^{-2}]$

35 The equation of state of some gases can be expressed as $\left(p + \frac{a}{V^2}\right)(V - b) = RT$, where p is absolute the pressure, V is the volume, T is absolute temperature and a and b are constants. The dimensional formula of a is **[JCECE]**
(a) $[ML^5T^{-2}]$ (b) $[M^{-1}L^5T^{-2}]$
(c) $[ML^{-1}T^{-2}]$ (d) $[ML^{-5}T^{-2}]$

36 If force F, length L and time T be considered fundamental units, then units of mass will be **[VMMC]**
(a) $[FLT^{-2}]$ (b) $[FL^{-2}T^{-1}]$
(c) $[FL^{-1}T^2]$ (d) $[F^2LT^{-2}]$

2009

37 An object is moving through the liquid. The viscous damping force acting on it is proportional to the velocity. Then, dimensional formula of constant of proportionality is **[UP CPMT, Punjab PMET]**

(a) $[ML^{-1}T^{-1}]$ (b) $[MLT^{-1}]$
(c) $[M^0LT^{-1}]$ (d) $[ML^0T^{-1}]$

2008

38 Which two of the following five physical parameters have the same dimensions? **[CBSE AIPMT]**

I. Energy density II. Refractive index
III. Dielectric constant IV. Young's modulus
V. Magnetic field

(a) I and IV (b) III and V
(c) I and II (d) I and V

39 The speed of light c, gravitational constant G and Planck's constant h are taken as fundamental units in a system. The dimensions of time in this new system should be **[AIIMS]**

(a) $[G^{1/2}h^{1/2}c^{-5/2}]$ (b) $[G^{-1/2}h^{1/2}c^{1/2}]$
(c) $[G^{1/2}h^{1/2}c^{-3/2}]$ (d) $[G^{1/2}h^{1/2}c^{1/2}]$

40 The physical quantity having the dimensions $[M^{-1}L^{-3}T^3A^2]$ is **[AFMC]**

(a) resistance
(b) resistivity
(c) electrical conductivity
(d) electromotive force

41 If p represents radiation pressure, c represents speed of light and Q represents radiation energy striking a unit area per second, then non-zero integers x, y and z such that $p^xQ^yc^z$ is dimensionless, are **[BHU]**

(a) $x=1, y=1, z=-1$ (b) $x=1, y=-1, z=1$
(c) $x=-1, y=1, z=1$ (d) $x=1, y=1, z=1$

42 Dimensions of resistance in an electrical circuit, in terms of dimension of mass M, length L, time T and current A, would be **[UP CPMT]**

(a) $[ML^2T^{-3}A^{-1}]$ (b) $[ML^2T^{-2}]$
(c) $[ML^2T^{-1}A^{-1}]$ (d) $[ML^2T^{-3}A^{-2}]$

43 The velocity v (in cms^{-1}) of a particle is given in terms of time t (in second) by the equation

$$v = at + \frac{b}{t+c}$$

The dimensions of a, b and c are **[Manipal]**

	a	b	c
(a)	$[L^2]$	$[T]$	$[LT^2]$
(b)	$[LT^2]$	$[LT]$	$[L]$
(c)	$[LT^{-2}]$	$[L]$	$[T]$
(d)	$[L]$	$[LT]$	$[T^2]$

44 The physical quantities not having same dimensions are **[RPMT]**

(a) torque and work
(b) momentum and Planck's constant
(c) stress and Young's modulus
(d) speed and $(\mu_0\varepsilon_0)^{-1/2}$

45 Given that T stands for time period and l stands for the length of simple pendulum. If g is the acceleration due to gravity, then which of the following statements about the relation $T^2 = l/g$ is correct? **[MP PMT]**

(a) It is correct both dimensionally as well as numerically.
(b) It is neither dimensionally correct nor numerically.
(c) It is dimensionally correct but not numerically.
(d) It is numerically correct but not dimensionally.

46 If force F, work W and velocity v are taken as fundamental quantities, then the dimensional formula of time T is **[Punjab PMET]**

(a) [WFv] (b) $[WFv^{-1}]$
(c) $[W^{-1}F^{-1}v]$ (d) $[WF^{-1}v^{-1}]$

47 If power P, surface tension T and Planck's constant h are arranged, so that the dimensions of time in their dimensional formulae are in ascending order, then which of the following is correct? **[EAMCET]**

(a) P, T, h (b) P, h, T
(c) T, P, h (d) T, h, P

48 Consider the following equation of Bernoulli's theorem

$$p + \frac{1}{2}\rho v^2 + \rho gh = k \text{ (constant)}.$$

The dimensions of k/p are same as that of which of the following? **[DUMET]**

(a) Thrust (b) Pressure
(c) Angle (d) Viscosity

49 If E = energy, G = gravitational constant, I = impulse and M = mass, then dimensions of $\frac{GIM^2}{E^2}$ are same as that of **[BCECE]**

(a) time (b) mass
(c) length (d) force

2007

50 The speed v of ripples on the surface of water depends on surface tension σ, density ρ and wavelength λ. The square of speed v is proportional to **[AIIMS]**

(a) $\frac{\sigma}{\rho\lambda}$ (b) $\frac{\rho}{\sigma\lambda}$ (c) $\frac{\lambda}{\sigma\rho}$ (d) $\rho\lambda\sigma$

51 The ratio of the dimensions of Planck's constant and that of the moment of inertia is the dimension of **[AFMC]**

(a) frequency (b) velocity
(c) angular momentum (d) time

52 Which of the following units denotes the dimensions $[ML^2/Q^2]$, where Q denotes the electric charge? **[BHU]**

(a) Wbm^{-2} (b) Henry (H)
(c) Hm^{-2} (d) Weber (Wb)

53 Using mass M, length L, time T and current A as fundamental quantities, the dimensions of permeability are **[UP CPMT]**

(a) $[M^{-1}LT^{-2}A]$ (b) $[ML^{-2}T^{-2}A^{-1}]$
(c) $[MLT^{-2}A^{-2}]$ (d) $[MLT^{-1}A^{-1}]$

54 The only mechanical quantity which has negative dimension of mass is **[J&K CET]**

(a) angular momentum
(b) torque
(c) coefficient of thermal conductivity
(d) gravitational constant

55 The dimension of $\frac{e^2}{4\pi\varepsilon_0 hc}$, where e, ε_0, h and c are electric charge, electric permittivity, Planck's constant and velocity of light in vacuum respectively **[Punjab PMET]**

(a) $[M^0L^0T^0]$ (b) $[ML^0T^0]$
(c) $[M^0LT^0]$ (d) $[M^0L^0T]$

56 The position of the particle moving along Y-axis is given as $y = At^2 - Bt^3$, where y is measured in metre and t in second. Then, the dimensions of B are **[AMU]**

(a) $[LT^{-2}]$ (b) $[LT^{-1}]$
(c) $[LT^{-3}]$ (d) $[MLT^{-2}]$

57 Write dimensional formula for the intensity of radiation. **[Guj CET]**

(a) $[ML^0T^3]$ (b) $[ML^0T^{-3}]$
(c) $[ML^2T^{-2}]$ (d) $[ML^2T^{-3}]$

58 A gas bubble formed from an explosion under water oscillates with a period T proportional to $p^a d^b E^c$, where p is pressure, d is the density of water and E is the total energy of explosion. The values of a, b and c are **[BCECE]**

(a) $a = 1, b = 1, c = 2$
(b) $a = 1, b = 2, c = 1$
(c) $a = \frac{5}{6}, b = \frac{1}{2}, c = \frac{1}{3}$
(d) $a = -\frac{5}{6}, b = \frac{1}{2}, c = \frac{1}{3}$

2006

59 If σ = surface charge density, ε = electric permittivity, then the dimensions of σ/ε is same as **[Punjab PMET]**

(a) electric force
(b) electric field intensity
(c) pressure
(d) electric charge

60 The magnetic force on a point charge is $\mathbf{F} = q(\mathbf{v} \times \mathbf{B})$. Here, q = electric charge, $\mathbf{v}$ = velocity of point charge $\mathbf{B}$ = magnetic field. The dimensions of $\mathbf{B}$ are **[AMU]**

(a) $[MLT^{-1}A]$ (b) $[M^2LT^{-2}A^{-1}]$
(c) $[MT^{-2}A^{-1}]$ (d) None of these

61 Some physical constants are given in Column I and their dimensional formulae are given in Column II. Match the correct pairs in the columns. **[EAMCET]**

Column I	Column II
A. Planck's constant	P. $[ML^{-1}T^{-2}]$
B. Gravitational constant	Q. $[ML^{-1}T^{-1}]$
C. Bulk modulus	R. $[ML^2T^{-1}]$
D. Coefficient of viscosity	S. $[M^{-1}L^3T^{-2}]$

	A	B	C	D
(a)	S	R	Q	P
(b)	Q	P	R	S
(c)	R	Q	P	S
(d)	R	S	P	Q

62 What is dimensional formula of thermal conductivity? **[DUMET]**

(a) $[MLT^{-1}Q^{-1}]$ (b) $[MLT^{-3}Q^{-1}]$
(c) $[M^2LT^{-3}Q^{-2}]$ (d) $[ML^2T^{-2}Q]$

2005

63 **Assertion** Specific gravity of a fluid is a dimensionless quantity. **[AIIMS]**

Reason It is the ratio of density of fluid to the density of water.

(a) Both Assertion and Reason are correct and Reason is the correct explanation of Assertion.
(b) Both Assertion and Reason are correct but Reason is not the correct explanation of Assertion.
(c) Assertion is correct but Reason is incorrect.
(d) Both Assertion and Reason are incorrect.

64 In a system of units, if force F, acceleration A and time T are taken as fundamental units, then the dimensional formula of energy is **[BHU]**

(a) $[FA^2T]$ (b) $[FAT^2]$ (c) $[F^2AT]$ (d) $[FAT]$

65 If a, b, c and d are mass, length, time and current respectively, then b^2a/c^3d has the dimension of **[Haryana PMT]**

(a) capacitance (b) electric field
(c) permittivity (d) electric potential

66 The dimensions of self-inductance L are **[J&K CET]**

(a) $[ML^2T^{-2}A^{-2}]$ (b) $[ML^2T^{-1}A^{-2}]$
(c) $[ML^2T^{-1}A^{-1}]$ (d) $[ML^{-2}T^{-2}A^{-2}]$

67 Suppose refractive index μ is given as $\mu = A + B/\lambda^2$, where A and B are constants and λ is wavelength, then the dimension of B is same as that of **[AMU]**

(a) wavelength (b) pressure
(c) area (d) volume

68 A force F is given by $F = at + bt^2$, where t is time. What are the dimensions of a and b? **[DUMET]**

(a) $[MLT^{-1}]$ and $[MLT^0]$ (b) $[MLT^{-3}]$ and $[ML^2T^{-4}]$
(c) $[MLT^{-4}]$ and $[MLT]$ (d) $[MLT^{-3}]$ and $[MLT^{-4}]$

Answers

1 (a)	2 (c)	3 (b)	4 (a)	5 (a)	6 (a)	7 (c)	8 (d)	9 (a)	10 (a)
11 (a)	12 (c)	13 (a)	14 (a)	15 (c)	16 (c)	17 (b)	18 (a)	19 (b)	20 (b)
21 (d)	22 (c)	23 (a)	24 (a)	25 (a)	26 (a)	27 (a)	28 (d)	29 (a)	30 (a)
31 (d)	32 (a)	33 (c)	34 (d)	35 (a)	36 (c)	37 (d)	38 (a)	39 (a)	40 (c)
41 (b)	42 (d)	43 (c)	44 (b)	45 (c)	46 (d)	47 (a)	48 (c)	49 (a)	50 (a)
51 (a)	52 (b)	53 (c)	54 (d)	55 (a)	56 (c)	57 (b)	58 (d)	59 (b)	60 (c)
61 (d)	62 (b)	63 (a)	64 (b)	65 (d)	66 (a)	67 (c)	68 (d)		

Explanations

1 (a) Dimensions of torque,

$$\tau = \mathbf{F} \times \mathbf{r}$$
$$= [\text{MLT}^{-2}][\text{L}]$$
$$= [\text{ML}^2\text{T}^{-2}]$$

2 (c) Dimensions of energy in terms of linear momentum (p) area (A) and time (T), is related of

$$E = p^a A^b T^c \quad \dots \text{(i)}$$

Writing dimensional formula of both side, we get

$$[\text{ML}^2\text{T}^{-2}] = [\text{MLT}^{-1}]^a [\text{L}^2]^b [\text{T}]^c$$
$$[\text{ML}^2\text{T}^{-2}] = [\text{M}^a \text{L}^{a+2b} \text{T}^{-a+c}]$$

Comparing the exponents,

$$a = 1, a + 2b = 2$$
$$2b = 1$$
$$b = \frac{1}{2}$$
$$-a + c = -2 \quad -1 + c = -2$$
$$\Rightarrow \quad c = -1$$

$\therefore$ From Eq. (i), we have

$$\Rightarrow \quad E = [\text{pA}^{1/2}\text{T}^{-1}]$$

3 (b) We know that,

$$F = ma = \frac{m(d)}{t^2} = \frac{[\text{M}][\text{L}]}{\text{T}^2}$$
$$= [\text{M}^1\text{L}^1\text{T}^{-2}]$$

4 (a) According to question,

$$[X] = [C]$$
$$= [\text{M}^{-1}\text{L}^{-2}\text{T}^2\text{Q}^2]$$

and $[Z] = [B] = [\text{MT}^{-1}\text{Q}^{-1}]$

$$\because \quad Y = \frac{[X]}{[Z^2]}$$
$$Y = \frac{[\text{M}^{-1}\text{L}^{-2}\text{T}^2\text{Q}^2]}{[\text{M}^2\text{T}^{-2}\text{Q}^{-2}]}$$
$$Y = [\text{M}^{-3}\text{L}^{-2}\text{T}^4\text{Q}^4]$$

5 (a) As, force, $F = \dfrac{e^2}{4\pi\varepsilon_0 r^2}$

$$\Rightarrow \quad \frac{e^2}{4\pi\varepsilon_0} = r^2 \cdot F$$

Putting dimensions of r and F, we get

$$\Rightarrow \left[\frac{e^2}{4\pi\varepsilon_0}\right] = [\text{ML}^3\text{T}^{-2}] \quad \dots \text{(i)}$$

Also, force, $F = \dfrac{Gm^2}{r^2}$

$$\Rightarrow [G] = [\text{M}^{-1}\text{L}^3\text{T}^{-2}] \quad \dots \text{(ii)}$$

and $\left[\dfrac{1}{c^2}\right] = \dfrac{1}{[\text{L}^2\text{T}^{-2}]} = [\text{L}^{-2}\text{T}^2] \quad \dots \text{(iii)}$

Now, checking optionwise

$$\frac{1}{c^2}\left(\frac{Ge^2}{4\pi\varepsilon_0}\right)^{1/2}$$
$$= [\text{L}^{-2}\text{T}^2][\text{L}^6\text{T}^{-4}]^{1/2} = [\text{L}]$$

6 (a) In forms of h, c and G length can be expressed as $L = (h)^a (c)^b (G)^c$.

Writing dimensions on both sides, we get

$$[\text{M}^0\text{LT}^0] = [\text{ML}^2\text{T}^{-1}]^a [\text{LT}^{-1}]^b [\text{M}^{-1}\text{L}^3\text{T}^{-2}]^c$$
$$= \text{M}^{a-c}\text{L}^{2a+b+3c}\text{T}^{-a-b-2c}$$

On comparing powers of M, L and T on both sides, we get

$$a - c = 0, 2a + b + 3c = 1$$

and $\quad -a - b - 2c = 0$

On solving, we get

$$a = c = \frac{1}{2} \text{ and } b = -\frac{3}{2}$$

$\therefore$ Dimensions of length,

$$L = (h)^{1/2}(c)^{-3/2}(G)^{1/2}$$
$$= \frac{\sqrt{hG}}{c^{3/2}}$$

7 (c) We know that,

$$\text{Surface tension, } (S) = \frac{\text{Force}[F]}{\text{Length}[L]}$$

So, $[\text{S}] = \dfrac{[\text{MLT}^{-2}]}{[\text{L}]} = [\text{ML}^0\text{T}^{-2}]$

$$\text{Energy } (E) = \text{Force} \times \text{Displacement}$$
$$\Rightarrow \quad [\text{E}] = [\text{ML}^2\text{T}^{-2}]$$
$$\text{Velocity } (v) = \frac{\text{Displacement}}{\text{Time}}$$
$$\Rightarrow \quad [\text{v}] = [\text{LT}^{-1}]$$

As, $\quad S \propto E^a v^b T^c$

where, a, b, c are constants.

From the principle of homogeneity,

$$[\text{LHS}] = [\text{RHS}]$$
$$\Rightarrow [\text{ML}^0\text{T}^{-2}] = [\text{ML}^2\text{T}^{-2}]^a [\text{LT}^{-1}]^b [\text{T}]^c$$
$$\Rightarrow [\text{ML}^0\text{T}^{-2}] = [\text{M}^a\text{L}^{2a+b}\text{T}^{-2a-b+c}]$$

Equating the power on both sides, we get

$$a = 1, 2a + b = 0 \Rightarrow b = -2$$
$$-2a - b + c = -2$$
$$\Rightarrow \quad c = (2a + b) - 2$$
$$= 0 - 2 = -2$$

So, $\quad [\text{S}] = [\text{Ev}^{-2}\text{T}^{-2}]$

8 (d) We know that, $F = ma \quad \left(\because \; a = \dfrac{v}{t}\right)$

$$\Rightarrow \quad F = \frac{mv}{t} \quad \Rightarrow \quad m = \frac{Ft}{v}$$

$\therefore$ Dimensions of

$$[\text{M}] = \frac{[\text{F}][\text{T}]}{[\text{v}]} = [\text{Fv}^{-1}\text{T}]$$

9 (a) Reynold's number describes the ratio of inertial force per unit area to viscous force per unit area for a flowing fluid. Thus, Reynold's number is the ratio of two physical quantity of same dimension which cancel out each other. Hence, Reynold's number is dimensionless $[\text{M}^0\text{L}^0\text{T}^0]$ quantity.

10 *(a)* Given, $F = \frac{x}{\sqrt{d}}$

Substituting dimensions,

$$[MLT^{-2}] = \frac{x}{\sqrt{[ML^{-3}]}}$$

$$\Rightarrow \quad x = [M^{3/2}L^{-1/2}T^{-2}]$$

11 *(a)* $\left[\frac{nh}{2\pi qB}\right]$ where, n and 2π are dimensionless quantities.

So, $[h] = [mvr]$

$$[qB] = \left[\frac{qvB}{v}\right] = \left[\frac{F}{v}\right]$$

$$\therefore \left[\frac{mvr}{F/v}\right] = \frac{[mvr][v]}{[F]}$$

$$= \frac{[mv^2r]}{\left[\frac{mv^2}{r}\right]} = [r^2] = \text{Area}$$

12 *(c)*

(a) Planck's constant $= \frac{\text{Energy}}{\text{Frequency}}$

$$= \frac{[ML^2T^{-2}]}{[T^{-1}]} = [ML^2T^{-1}]$$

and angular momentum = moment of inertia × angular velocity

$$= [ML^2] \times [T^{-1}] = [ML^2T^{-1}]$$

(b) Impulse = Force × Time

$$= [MLT^{-2}][T] = [MLT^{-1}]$$

and linear momentum

$$= \text{Mass} \times \text{Velocity}$$
$$= [M][LT^{-1}] = [MLT^{-1}]$$

(c) Moment of inertia

$$= \text{Mass} \times (\text{Distance})^2$$
$$= [M][L^2] = [ML^2]$$

and moment of force

$$= \text{force} \times \text{distance}$$
$$= [MLT^{-2}][L] = [ML^2T^{-2}]$$

(d) Energy $= [ML^2T^{-2}]$ and

torque $= [ML^2T^{-2}]$

13 *(a)* From Newton's law of gravitation,

$$F = \frac{Gm_1m_2}{r^2}$$

where, F = force between two bodies

m_1, m_2 = masses of two bodies,

r = distance between the masses

and G = universal gravitational constant.

$$\Rightarrow \quad G = \frac{F \cdot r^2}{m_1m_2} \quad \text{...(i)}$$

Putting the dimensions of all the known physical quantities given in Eq. (i), we get

i.e. $[F] = [M \times a] = [MLT^{-2}]$, $[r] = [L]$, $[m] = [M]$

$$[G] = \frac{[MLT^{-2}][L^2]}{[M^2]} = \left[\frac{L^3T^{-2}}{M}\right]$$

$$\Rightarrow \quad [G] = [M^{-1}L^3T^{-2}]$$

14 *(a)* Dimensions of ϕ_B = Unit of $B \times$ Unit of A

$$= \frac{\text{newton}}{\text{ampere - metre}} \times \text{metre}^2$$

$$= \frac{\text{newton} \times \text{metre}}{\text{ampere}}$$

$$= \frac{\text{kg ms}^{-2} \times \text{m}}{\text{A}} = \text{kgm}^2\text{s}^{-2}\text{A}^{-1}$$

$$= [ML^2T^{-2}A^{-1}]$$

15 *(c)* The unit of electric field E is

$$= \frac{\text{newton}}{\text{coulomb}} = \frac{\text{kg-ms}^{-2}}{\text{amp-s}}$$

$$= \text{kg-m s}^{-3}\text{ amp}^{-1}$$

$\therefore$ Dimensions of electric field are $[MLT^{-3}A^{-1}]$.

16 *(c)* Quantity $\frac{1}{2}\varepsilon_0E^2$ is the electrostatic energy per unit volume.

$$\therefore \text{Its dimensions} = \frac{[ML^2T^{-2}]}{[L^3]}$$
$$= [ML^{-1}T^{-2}]$$

17 *(b)* Displacment,

$$y = A\sin(Bx + Ct + D)$$
$$A = y = [L]$$

As each term inside the brackets is dimensionless, so

$$B = \frac{1}{x} = [L^{-1}]$$

$$C = \frac{1}{t} = [T^{-1}]$$

and D is dimensionless.

$$\therefore \quad [ABCD] = [L][L^{-1}][T^{-1}]$$
$$= [M^0L^0T^{-1}]$$

18 *(a)* The capacitance of a conductor is defined as the ratio of the charge given to the rise in the potential of the conductor.

i.e. $C = \frac{q}{V} = \frac{q^2}{W} \quad \left(V = \frac{W}{q}\right)$

$$C = \frac{\text{ampere}^2\text{-s}^2}{\text{kg-m}^2/\text{s}^2}$$

Hence, dimensions of C are $[M^{-1}L^{-2}T^4A^2]$.

From Ohm's law, $V = iR$, therefore unit of resistance,

$$R = \frac{V}{i} = \frac{\text{volt}}{\text{ampere}}$$

$$= \text{kg-m}^2\text{s}^{-3}\text{ampere}^{-2}$$

$\therefore$ Dimensions of $R = [ML^2T^{-3}A^{-2}]$

$\therefore$ Dimensions of RC

$$= [M^{-1}L^{-2}T^4A^2][ML^2T^{-3}A^{-2}]$$
$$= [M^0L^0T]$$

Alternative

In a CR circuit, the product of CR is the capacitive time constant of the circuit. If C is in farad, R is in ohm, then time constant is in second.

Hence, dimensions of $CR = [M^0L^0T]$.

19 *(b)* Dimensions of angular momentum, $L = p \times r = [MLT^{-1}][L] = [ML^2T^{-1}]$

20 *(b)* This expression is for the speed of light and the dimensions of speed of light is $[LT^{-1}]$.

21 *(d)* Surface tension, S

$$= \frac{\text{Force}}{\text{Length}} = \frac{[MLT^{-2}]}{[L]} = [MT^{-2}]$$

Spring constant, R

$$= \frac{\text{Force}}{\text{Elongation}} = \frac{[MLT^{-2}]}{[L]}$$
$$= [MT^{-2}]$$

22 *(c)* We know that, $T = \frac{F}{l}$

$$\text{Dimensions of } T = \frac{\text{Dimensions of } F}{\text{Dimensions of } L}$$

$$= \frac{[MLT^{-2}]}{[L]} = [ML^0T^{-2}]$$

23 *(a)* The dimensions of impulse are

$$= Ft = [MLT^{-2}][T] = [MLT^{-1}]$$

24 *(a)* We know that, energy, $E = \frac{1}{2}CV^2$

Dimensions of CV^2 = Dimensions of energy, E

$$= [ML^2T^{-2}A^0]$$

25 *(a)* In the given equation, $\frac{\alpha Z}{k\theta}$ should be dimensionless.

$$\therefore \quad \alpha = \frac{k\theta}{Z}$$

$$\Rightarrow [\alpha] = \frac{[ML^2T^{-2}K^{-1}][K]}{[L]} = [MLT^{-2}]$$

and $p = \frac{\alpha}{\beta} \Rightarrow [\beta] = \left[\frac{\alpha}{p}\right] = \frac{[MLT^{-2}]}{[ML^{-1}T^{-2}]}$

$$= [M^0 L^2 T^0]$$

26 (a) Given, $p = \frac{RT}{V-b} e^{-\alpha V/RT}$

So, $\frac{\alpha V}{RT}$ is dimensionless.

Hence, $[\alpha] = \left[\frac{RT}{V}\right] = \frac{[ML^2T^{-2}\theta^{-1}][\theta]}{[L^3]}$

$$= [ML^{-1}T^{-2}]$$

This is dimensional formula of pressure (p).

27 (a) Dimensions of velocity are

$$[v] = [L][T^{-1}]$$

So, dimensions of $[at^2] = [LT^{-1}]$

$$\Rightarrow [a][T^2] = [LT^{-1}]$$

$$\Rightarrow [a] = [LT^{-3}]$$

Dimensions of $[bt] = [LT^{-1}]$

$$\Rightarrow [b][T] = [LT^{-1}]$$

$$\Rightarrow [b] = [LT^{-2}]$$

Dimensions of $[c] = [LT^{-1}]$

28 (d) Electromotive force = Potential difference

$$\Rightarrow V = \frac{W}{q} = \frac{[ML^2T^{-2}]}{[AT]}$$

$$= [ML^2T^{-3}A^{-1}]$$

29 (a) The capacitance C of a conductor is defined as the ratio of charge q given to raise the potential V of the conductor, i.e.

$$C = \frac{q}{V}$$

$$\therefore \text{Farad} = \frac{\text{Coulomb}}{\text{Volt}} = \frac{\text{Coulomb}}{\text{Joule / Coulomb}}$$

$$= \frac{(\text{Coulomb})^2}{\text{Joule}}$$

$$= \frac{(\text{amp - s})^2}{\text{newton - m}}$$

$$= \frac{\text{amp}^2\text{-s}^2}{(\text{kg - m s}^{-2}) \times \text{m}}$$

$$= \frac{\text{amp}^2\text{-s}^4}{\text{kg-m}^2}$$

$$= \text{kg}^{-1}\,\text{m}^{-2}\,\text{s}^4\,\text{amp}^2$$

So, the dimensions of capacitance are $[M^{-1}L^{-2}T^4A^2]$.

30 (a) Taking, $T = 2\pi\sqrt{\frac{R^3}{GM}}$

Substituting the dimensions,

$$\text{LHS} = T = [T]$$

$$\text{RHS} = 2\pi\sqrt{\frac{R^3}{GM}}$$

$$= \sqrt{\frac{[L]^3}{[M^{-1}L^3T^{-2}][M]}}$$

$$= \sqrt{[T]^2} = [T]$$

Thus, LHS = RHS for $T = 2\pi\sqrt{\frac{R^3}{GM}}$.

31 (d) Dimensions of $E = [ML^2T^{-2}]$

Dimensions of $M = [M]$

Dimensions of $L = [ML^2T^{-1}]$

Dimensions of $G = [M^{-1}L^3T^{-2}]$

$\therefore$ Dimensions of

$$\left[\frac{E^2L^2}{M^5G^2}\right] = \frac{[ML^2T^{-2}]^2\,[ML^2T^{-1}]^2}{[M]^5\,[M^{-1}L^3T^{-2}]^2}$$

$$= [ML^2T^{-2}]$$

32 (a) Fundamental frequency,

$$f = \frac{1}{2L}\sqrt{\frac{T}{\mu}}$$

$$\Rightarrow f = \frac{1}{2L}\sqrt{\frac{T}{\rho\pi\frac{D^2}{4}}} = \frac{1}{LD}\sqrt{\frac{T}{\pi\rho}}$$

$$\therefore f \propto \frac{1}{LD}$$

(as T, π and ρ are constants)

33 (c) Now, for $\left[\frac{h}{e^2}\right] = \frac{[ML^2T^{-1}]}{[AT]^2}$

$$= [ML^2T^{-3}A^{-2}]$$

As, we know that dimensional formula of resistance is $[ML^2T^3A^{-2}]$.

34 (d) The resistivity(s) is $\rho = \frac{RA}{L}$

Resistance, $R = \frac{V}{i} = \frac{W}{qi} = \frac{W}{i^2t}$ $(\because q = it)$

$$= \frac{[ML^2T^{-2}]}{[A^2T]}$$

$$\Rightarrow R = [ML^2T^{-3}A^{-2}]$$

Thus, dimensional formula of ρ is

$$= [M^1L^3T^{-3}A^{-2}]$$

35 (a) In equation p, V and T are pressure, volume and temperature, respectively.

$$\left(p + \frac{a}{V^2}\right)(V - b) = RT$$

$\therefore$ Dimensions of $\frac{a}{V^2}$

= Dimensions of p.

Dimensions of a = Dimensions of $p \times$ Dimensions of V^2

$$= [ML^{-1}T^{-2}][L^6]$$

$$= [ML^5T^{-2}]$$

36 (c) Let $[M] \propto [F^aL^bT^c]$

So, using dimensions, we have

$$[ML^0T^0] = [MLT^{-2}]^a[L]^b[T]^c$$

$$= [M^aL^{a+b}T^{-2a+c}]$$

$$\Rightarrow a = 1, a + b = 0$$

$$\Rightarrow b = -1$$

and $-2a + c = 0$

$$\Rightarrow c = 2$$

So, unit of mass is $[FL^{-1}T^2]$.

37 (d) We have, $F \propto v \Rightarrow F = kv$

$$\Rightarrow [k] = \left[\frac{F}{v}\right] = \left[\frac{MLT^{-2}}{LT^{-1}}\right]$$

$$= [ML^0T^{-1}]$$

38. (a) I. Energy density $= \frac{\text{Energy}}{\text{Volume}}$

$$= \frac{[ML^2T^{-2}]}{[L^3]}$$

$$= [ML^{-1}T^{-2}]$$

II. Refractive index has no dimensions.

III. Dielectric constant has no dimensions.

IV. Young's modulus,

$$Y = \frac{Fl}{A\Delta l} = \frac{[MLT^{-2}][L]}{[L]^2[L]}$$

$$= [ML^{-1}T^{-2}]$$

V. Magnetic field,

$$B = \frac{F}{Il} = \frac{[MLT^{-2}]}{[A][L]}$$

$$= [MT^{-2}A^{-1}]$$

39 (a) Time $\propto c^xG^yh^z$

$$\Rightarrow T = k\,c^xG^yh^z$$

$$\Rightarrow [M^0L^0T] = [LT^{-1}]^x\,[M^{-1}L^3T^{-2}]^y\,[ML^2T^{-1}]^z$$

$$\Rightarrow [M^0L^0T] = [M^{-y+z}L^{x+3y+2z}T^{-x-2y-z}]$$

Comparing the powers of M, L and T, we get

$$-y + z = 0 \quad \ldots(i)$$

$$x + 3y + 2z = 0 \quad \ldots(ii)$$

$$-x - 2y - z = 1 \quad \ldots(iii)$$

On solving Eqs. (i), (ii) and (iii), we get

$$x=-\frac{5}{2},\ y=z=\frac{1}{2}$$

Hence, dimensions of time are $[G^{1/2}h^{1/2}c^{-5/2}]$.

40 *(c)* Electrical conductivity,

$$\sigma=\frac{1}{\rho}=\frac{ne^2\tau}{m}=\frac{[L^{-3}][AT]^2[T]}{[M]}$$

or $[\sigma]=\frac{1}{[\rho]}=[M^{-1}L^{-3}A^2T^3]$

41 *(b)* Pressure $=\frac{\text{Force}}{\text{Area}}$

$$[p]=\frac{[F]}{[A]}=[ML^{-1}T^{-2}],$$

$$[c]=[LT^{-1}]$$

$$[Q]=\frac{[E]}{[A][T]}=[MT^{-3}]$$

As given, $p^xQ^yc^z=[M^0L^0T^0]$

$$[ML^{-1}T^{-2}]^x[LT^{-1}]^z[MT^{-3}]^y=[M^0L^0T^0]$$

$$\Rightarrow\ M^{x+y}L^{-x+z}T^{-2x-z-3y}=[M^0L^0T^0]$$

$\therefore$ $x+y=0$ ...(i)

$-x+z=0$ ...(ii)

$-2x-z-3y=0$ ...(iii)

On solving Eqs. (i), (ii) and (iii), we get $x=1,\ y=-1,z=1$.

42 *(d)* Resistance,

$$R=\frac{\text{Potential difference}}{\text{Current}}$$

$$=\frac{V}{I}=\frac{W}{qI}\quad\left[\because V=\frac{W}{Q}\right]$$

So, dimensions of R

$$=\frac{[\text{Dimensions of work}]}{[\text{Dimensions of charge}][\text{Dimensions of current}]}$$

$$=\frac{[ML^2T^{-2}]}{[AT][A]}=[ML^2T^{-3}A^{-2}]$$

43 *(c)* Given, $v=at+\frac{b}{t+c}$

or $[at]=[v]=[LT^{-1}]$

$$\therefore\ [a]=\frac{[LT^{-1}]}{[T]}=[LT^{-2}]$$

Dimension of $c=[t]=[T]$ (we can add quantities of same dimensions only).

$$\left[\frac{b}{t+c}\right]=[v]=[LT^{-1}]$$

or $[b]=[LT^{-1}][T]=[L]$

44 *(b)* Planck's constant,

$$h=\text{Js}=[ML^2T^{-2}][T]$$
$$=[ML^2T^{-1}]$$

Momentum, $p=\text{kg-ms}^{-1}$

$$=[M][L][T]^{-1}=[MLT^{-1}]$$

45 *(c)* The correct relation for time period of simple pendulum is $T=2\pi(l/g)^{1/2}$. So, the given relation is numerically incorrect as the factor of 2π is missing. But, it is dimensionally correct.

46 *(d)* Let $T\propto F^aW^bv^c$ ...(i)

$$[T]=[MLT^{-2}]^a[ML^2T^{-2}]^b[LT^{-1}]^c$$

$$[T]=[M^{a+b}][L^{a+2b+c}][T^{-2a-2b-c}]$$

On comparing the powers, we get

$a+b=0$ ...(ii)

$a+2b+c=0$ ...(iii)

$-2a-2b-c=1$ ...(iv)

On solving Eqs. (ii), (iii) and (iv), we get

$$a=-1,\ b=1,\ c=-1$$

Therefore, from Eq. (i),

$$[T]=k[F^{-1}Wv^{-1}]$$

Taking $k=1$ in SI system, we have

$$[T]=[WF^{-1}v^{-1}]$$

47 *(a)* Dimensions of power,

$$P=\frac{\text{Work}}{\text{Time}}=\frac{[ML^2T^{-2}]}{[T]}=[ML^2T^{-3}]$$

Dimensions of surface tension,

$$T=\frac{\text{Force}}{\text{Length}}=\frac{[MLT^{-2}]}{[L]}=[ML^0T^{-2}]$$

Dimensions of Planck's constant,

$$h=\frac{\text{Energy}}{\text{Frequency}}$$

$$=\frac{[ML^2T^{-2}]}{[T^{-1}]}=[ML^2T^{-1}]$$

From the dimensional formulae, the ascending order of time is power(P), surface tension (T) and Planck's constant (h).

48 *(c)* The given equation of Bernoulli's theorem is

$$p+\frac{1}{2}\rho v^2+\rho gh=k$$

where, p is pressure, ρ is density, g is acceleration due to gravity and h is height. We know that, every equation relating physical quantities should be in dimensional balance. It means dimensions of terms on both sides must be same.

Hence, k has same dimensions as p and so $\frac{k}{p}$ is dimensionless. Out of the given four options, angle is a dimensionless quantity.

49 *(a)* Dimensions of $\frac{GIM^2}{E^2}$

$$=\frac{[M^{-1}L^3T^{-2}][MLT^{-1}][M^2]}{[ML^2T^{-2}]^2}$$

$$=[T]=\text{dimension of time}$$

50 *(a)* Let $v\propto\sigma^a\rho^b\lambda^c$

Equating dimensions on both sides, we get

$$[M^0LT^{-1}]\propto[MT^{-2}]^a[ML^{-3}]^b[L]^c$$
$$\propto[M]^{a+b}[L]^{-3b+c}[T]^{-2a}$$

Equating the powers of M, L, T on both sides, we get

$a+b=0$ ...(i)

$-3b+c=1$ ...(ii)

$-2a=-1$ ...(iii)

On solving Eqs. (i), (ii) and (iii) we get

$$a=\frac{1}{2},\ b=\frac{-1}{2},\ c=-\frac{1}{2}$$

$$\Rightarrow\ v\propto\sigma^{1/2}\rho^{-1/2}\lambda^{-1/2}$$

$$\therefore\ v^2\propto\frac{\sigma}{\rho\lambda}$$

51 *(a)* The ratio

$$=\frac{\text{Planck's constant }(h)}{\text{Moment of inertia }(I)}=\frac{E/v}{I}$$

$$=\frac{E\times T}{I}=\frac{(\text{kg-m}^2/\text{s}^2)\times\text{s}}{(\text{kg-m}^2)}$$

$$=\frac{1}{\text{s}}=\frac{1}{\text{Time}}=\text{Frequency}$$

Thus, dimension of $\frac{h}{I}$ is same as that of frequency.

52 *(b)* Magnetic energy $=\frac{1}{2}LI^2=\frac{LQ^2}{2t^2}$

where, $L=$ inductance, $I=$ current, $Q=$ charge and $t=$ time.

Energy has the dimensions $=[ML^2T^{-2}]$

Equating the dimensions, we have

$$[ML^2T^{-2}] = \text{henry} \times \frac{[Q^2]}{[T^2]}$$

$$\Rightarrow \quad \text{henry} = \frac{[ML^2]}{[Q^2]}$$

53 (c) Magnetic field due to straight solenoid, $B = \mu_0 nI$

$$\therefore \quad \mu_0 = \frac{B}{nI} = \frac{[MLT^{-2}]/[AL]}{[L^{-1}A]} = [MLT^{-2}A^{-2}]$$

54 (d) Dimensional formula of angular momentum, $L = [ML^2T^{-1}]$

Torque, $\tau = [ML^2T^{-2}]$

$$\Delta Q = KA\left(\frac{T_1 - T_2}{L}\right)\Delta t$$

Coefficient of thermal conductivity,

$$K = [MLT^{-3}K^{-1}]$$

Gravitational constant, $G = [M^{-1}L^3T^{-2}]$

Thus, gravitational constant has negative dimension in mass.

55 (a) As, we know

$[e] = [AT]$, $[\varepsilon_0] = [M^{-1}L^{-3}T^4A^2]$, $[h] = [ML^2T^{-1}]$ and $[c] = [LT^{-1}]$

$$\text{So,} \left[\frac{e^2}{4\pi\varepsilon_0 hc}\right] = \left[\frac{A^2T^2}{M^{-1}L^{-3}T^4A^2 \times ML^2T^{-1} \times LT^{-1}}\right] = [M^0L^0T^0]$$

56 (c) As, $y = B[T^3]$

So, $[L] = B[T^3]$

$\Rightarrow \quad B = [LT^{-3}]$

57 (b) Intensity of radiation is energy flowing per second per unit area, i.e.

$$[\text{Intensity}] = \frac{[\text{Energy}]}{[\text{Time}]\,[\text{Area}]} = \frac{[ML^2T^{-2}]}{[T][L^2]} = [ML^0T^{-3}]$$

58 (d) Given, $T \propto p^a d^b E^c$

We have

$$[M^0L^0T] = [ML^{-1}T^{-2}]^a [ML^{-3}]^b [ML^2T^{-2}]^c$$

On comparing dimensions of similar terms, we have

$$[M^0L^0T] = k[M^{a+b+c}L^{-a-3b+2c}T^{-2a-2c}]$$

On comparing powers of M, we have

$$0 = a + b + c \quad \ldots(i)$$

On comparing powers of L, we have

$$0 = -a - 3b + 2c \quad \ldots(ii)$$

On comparing powers of T, we have

$$1 = -2a - 2c \quad \ldots(iii)$$

On solving Eqs. (i), (ii) and (iii), we have

$$a = -\frac{5}{6},\ b = \frac{1}{2},\ c = \frac{1}{3}$$

59 (b) The electric field intensity due to conducting infinite sheet is $E = \frac{\sigma}{\varepsilon}$.

Hence, option (b) is correct.

60 (c) Magnetic force, $\mathbf{F} = q(\mathbf{v} \times \mathbf{B})$

or $\quad F = qvB\sin\theta$

$$\therefore \quad [B] = \left[\frac{F}{qv}\right] = \frac{[MLT^{-2}]}{[AT][LT^{-1}]} = [MT^{-2}A^{-1}]$$

61 (d) Dimensions of Planck's constant

$$= [ML^2T^{-1}]$$

Dimensions of gravitational constant

$$= [M^{-1}L^3T^{-2}]$$

Dimensions of Bulk modulus

$$= [ML^{-1}T^{-2}]$$

Dimensions of coefficients of viscosity

$$= [ML^{-1}T^{-1}]$$

$A \rightarrow R,\ B \rightarrow S,\ C \rightarrow P,\ D \rightarrow Q$

62 (b) Rate of heat flow, $\frac{\Delta Q}{\Delta t} = \frac{T - T_0}{\frac{1}{K}\frac{l}{A}}$

$$[K] = \frac{[ML^2T^{-2}][L]}{[L^2][Q][T]} = [MLT^{-3}Q^{-1}]$$

63 (a) Relative density of a fluid

$$= \frac{\text{Density of fluid}}{\text{Density of water}}$$

As the density of any substance has same units, hence relative density is dimensionless.

64 (b) Energy, $E \propto [F]^a[A]^b[T]^c$

Writing the dimensions on both sides, we have

$$[ML^2T^{-2}] = k[MLT^{-2}]^a[LT^{-2}]^b[T]^c$$

$$[ML^2T^{-2}] = k[M^aL^{a+b}T^{-2a-2b+c}]$$

Taking dimensional balance of equation into consideration and equating the dimensions of both sides, we get

$$a = 1 \quad \ldots(i)$$

$$a + b = 2 \quad \ldots(ii)$$

$$-2a - 2b + c = -2 \quad \ldots(iii)$$

On solving Eqs. (i), (ii) and (iii), we get

$$a = 1,\ b = 1,\ c = 2$$

$$\therefore \quad [E] = [FAT^2]$$

65 (d) Dimensions of

$$\frac{ab^2}{c^3d} = \frac{[M][L^2]}{[T^3][A]} = \frac{[ML^2T^{-2}]}{[AT]} = \frac{\text{Work}}{\text{Charge}} = \text{Electric potential}$$

66 (a) Self-inductance,

$$L = \frac{e}{\Delta I/\Delta t} = e\frac{\Delta t}{\Delta I}$$

$$\therefore \quad \text{Unit of } L = \frac{\text{volt-second}}{\text{ampere}} = \frac{\text{(joule/coulomb) second}}{\text{ampere}} = \frac{\text{newton - metre - second}}{\text{coulomb-ampere}}$$

$$\Rightarrow \text{Unit of } L = \frac{\text{newton-metre}}{\text{ampere}^2}$$

$$\therefore \quad [L] = \frac{[MLT^{-2}][L]}{[A^2]} = [ML^2T^{-2}A^{-2}]$$

67 (c) As, $\mu = \frac{\text{Velocity of light in vacuum}}{\text{Velocity of light in medium}}$

The refractive index μ is dimensionless, so each term on right hand side is dimensionless.

Hence, $\frac{B}{\lambda^2}$ is also dimensionless.

This implies that dimensions of B will have the dimensions of λ^2, i.e. of area.

68 (d) Given, $F = at + bt^2$

Only similar quantities can be equated, hence dimensions of the terms on both sides of the equation must be same.

$$[MLT^{-2}] = a[T] \Rightarrow a = [MLT^{-3}]$$

Similarly, $[MLT^{-2}] = b[T]^2$

$$\Rightarrow \quad b = [MLT^{-4}]$$

02

Motion in a Straight line

Quick Review

Rest

If the position of an object does not change w.r.t. its surrounding or with the passage of time, it is said to be at rest. e.g. Book lying on the table, a person sitting on a chair, etc.

Motion

- If the position of an object is continuously changing w.r.t. its surrounding, then it is said to be in the **state of motion**.
- On the basis of the number of co-ordinates required to specify the object, motion of object can be classified as

  (*i*) **One-dimensional Motion** The motion of an object is considered as 1-D (one-dimensional), if only one co-ordinate is needed to specify the position of the object at any time.

  (*ii*) **Two-dimensional Motion** The motion of an object is considered as 2-D (two-dimensional), if two co-ordinates are needed to specify the position of the object at any time. In 2-D motion, the object moves in a plane.

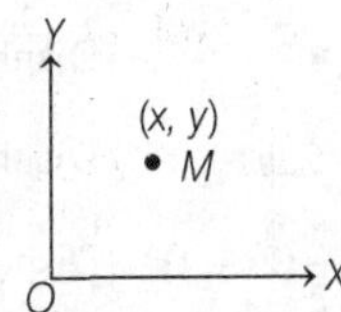

  (*iii*) **Three-dimensional Motion** The motion of an object is considered as 3-D (three-dimensional), if all the three co-ordinates are needed to specify the position of the object.

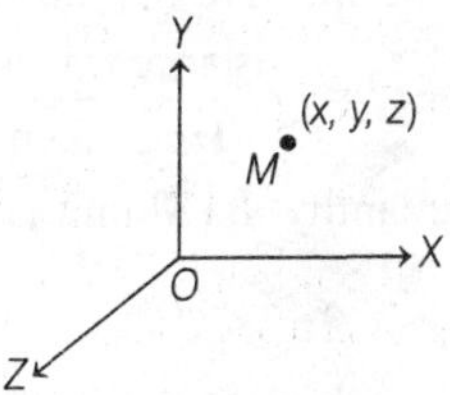

Scalar and Vector Quantities

Physical quantities are studied under two heads, scalars and vectors. Both types of quantity can be defined as follows

(*i*) **Scalar Quantity** If only the magnitude is required to specify a physical quantity, that physical quantity is known as scalar quantity. e.g. Mass, length, time, speed, etc.

(*ii*) **Vector Quantity** If magnitude as well as direction both are required to specify a physical quantity, that physical quantity is known as vector quantity. e.g. Displacement, velocity, acceleration, etc.

Distance

The total length of the path covered by the object in a given time interval is known as its distance or path length travelled. It is a scalar quantity. Its unit is metre (m).

Displacement

- The change in position of an object in a particular direction is termed as displacement, i.e. the minimum difference between the final and initial positions of the object in a given time. It is denoted by Δx. Mathematically, it is represented by

$$\text{Displacement}, \quad \Delta x = x_2 - x_1$$

where, x_1 and x_2 are the initial and final positions of the object, respectively. It is a vector quantity. Its unit is metre.

- Displacement of motion may be zero but path length or distance can never be zero.
- Displacement may be positive, negative or zero.

Uniform Motion in a Straight Line

A body is said to be in a uniform motion, if it travels equal distances in equal interval of time along a straight line.

Non-uniform Motion in a Straight Line

- A body is in non-uniform motion, if it travels equal displacement in unequal intervals of time.
- During the non-uniform motion, the speed of the body or its direction of motion or both change with time.

Speed

The path length or the distance covered by an object divided by the time taken by the object to cover that distance is called the speed of that object.

$$\text{Speed} = \frac{\text{Distance travelled}}{\text{Time taken}}$$

Speed is a scalar quantity. Its SI unit is ms^{-1}.

Average Speed

Average speed of an object is defined as the total distance travelled divided by the total time taken.

$$\text{Average speed, } v_{av} = \frac{\text{Total distance travelled}}{\text{Total time taken}}$$

Instantaneous Speed

- Speed at an instant is defined as the limit of the average speed as the time interval (Δt) becomes infinitesimally small or approaches to zero.
- Mathematically, instantaneous speed at any instant of time (t) is expressed as

$$\text{Instantaneous speed, } s_i = \lim_{\Delta t \to 0} \frac{\Delta s}{\Delta t} \quad \text{or} \quad s_i = \frac{ds}{dt}$$

where, ds is the distance covered in time dt.

Velocity

The rate of change in position or displacement of an object with time is called the velocity of that object.

$$\text{Velocity} = \frac{\text{Displacement}}{\text{Time}}$$

It is a vector quantity. Its unit is ms^{-1}.

Average Velocity

Average velocity of a body is defined as the change in position or displacement $(\Delta \mathbf{x})$ divided by the time interval (Δt) in which that displacement occurs.

Average velocity of body is given by

$$\mathbf{v}_{av} = \frac{\Delta \mathbf{x}}{\Delta t} = \frac{\mathbf{x}_2 - \mathbf{x}_1}{t_2 - t_1}$$

Instantaneous Velocity

- Velocity at an instant is defined as the limit of average velocity as the time interval (Δt) becomes infinitesimally small or approaches to zero.
- Mathematically, instantaneous velocity at an instant of time (t) is given by

$$\mathbf{v}_i = \lim_{\Delta t \to 0} \frac{\Delta \mathbf{x}}{\Delta t} \quad \text{or} \quad \mathbf{v}_i = \frac{d\mathbf{x}}{dt}$$

where, dx is displacement for time dt.

Acceleration

The time rate of change of velocity is known as acceleration.

$$\text{Acceleration} = \frac{\text{Change in velocity}}{\text{Time taken}}$$

It is a vector quantity. Its unit is ms^{-2}.

Average Acceleration

The average acceleration is the ratio of the change in velocity to the time taken to undergo this change.

$$\mathbf{a}_{av} = \frac{\mathbf{v}(t_2) - \mathbf{v}(t_1)}{t_2 - t_1} = \frac{\Delta \mathbf{v}}{\Delta t}$$

Instantaneous Acceleration

Instantaneous acceleration is the acceleration at any instant of time or at any given point.

$$\mathbf{a} = \lim_{\Delta t \to 0} \frac{\Delta \mathbf{v}}{\Delta t} = \frac{d\mathbf{v}}{dt}$$

Note If we simply call velocity or speed or acceleration, it means instantaneous one, respectively.

Equations of Uniformly Accelerated Motion

Motion of a body moving with constant acceleration can be expressed by following equations

(i) $\mathbf{v} = \mathbf{u} + \mathbf{a}t$ (Velocity-time equation)

(ii) $\mathbf{s} = \mathbf{u}t + \frac{1}{2}\mathbf{a}t^2$ (Displacement-time equation)

(iii) $\mathbf{v}^2 = \mathbf{u}^2 + 2\mathbf{as}$ (Displacement-velocity equation)

(iv) $\mathbf{s}_{nth} = \mathbf{u} + \frac{\mathbf{a}}{2}(2n-1)$ (Displacement in nth second)

where, $\mathbf{v}$ = final velocity, $\mathbf{u}$ = initial velocity, $\mathbf{a}$ = acceleration, t = time and $\mathbf{s}$ = displacement.

Equations of Motion for Object Falling Under Gravity

When the object fall under the influcnce of gravity, its motion is uniformly accelerated motion. Hence, equations of motion are applicable in this case also.

- For upward motion, i.e. an object is thrown vertically upwards

$$v = u - gt,\ h = ut - \frac{1}{2}gt^2$$

and $\quad v^2 = u^2 - 2gh.$

Note In upward motion, g is taken as negative.

- For downward motion, i.e. an object is thrown vertically downwards

$$v = u + gt,\ h = ut + \frac{1}{2}gt^2$$

and $\quad v^2 = u^2 + 2gh.$

Note In downward motion, g is taken as positive.

- If an object is dropped (from some height)

$$v = gt$$

$$h = \frac{1}{2}gt^2$$

$$v^2 = 2gh$$

Note If an object is dropped from some height, then initial velocity is taken as zero.

- For fast calculations in objective problems remember the following results
  - (*i*) Maximum height attained by a particle, thrown upward from ground, $h = \frac{u^2}{2g}$
  - (*ii*) Velocity of particle at the time of striking the ground, when released $(u = 0)$ from a height h, $v = \sqrt{2gh}$
  - (*iii*) Time of collision with ground, $t = \sqrt{\frac{2h}{g}}$

Graphs in One-dimensional Motion

There are three types of graphs representing motion in one dimension

(*i*) Position-time graph (*s-t*)
(*ii*) Velocity-time graph (*v-t*)
(*iii*) Acceleration-time graph (*a-t*)

The tabular forms of *s-t*, *v-t* and *a-t* graphs are given for one-dimensional motion with uniform velocity or with constant acceleration.

Note • Area under *v-t* graph gives the value at displacement covered in given time.

• Area under the acceleration-time (a -t) graph between t_1 to t_2 gives the change in velocity, i.e.
$v_2 - v_1 =$ Area under *a-t* graph
$= \int_{t_1}^{t_2} a \cdot dt$

Different Cases	*s-t* Graph	*v-t* Graph	*a-t* Graph	Slope of *v-t* Graph
At rest	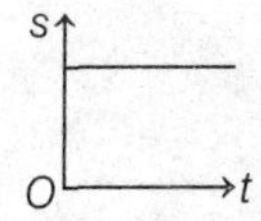	—	—	—
Uniform motion	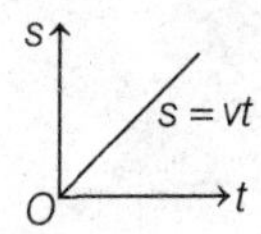 $s = vt$	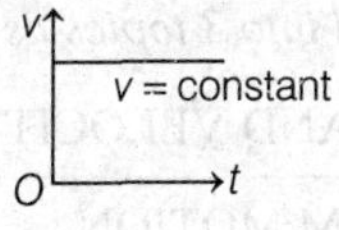 v = constant	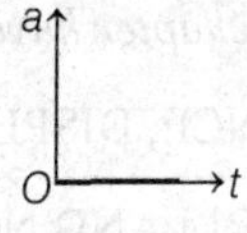	Slope = Zero
Uniformly accelerated motion with $u = 0$, $s = 0$ at $t = 0$.	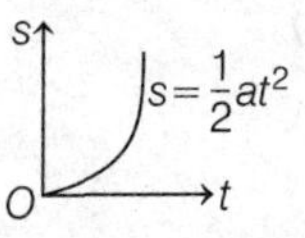 $s = \frac{1}{2}at^2$	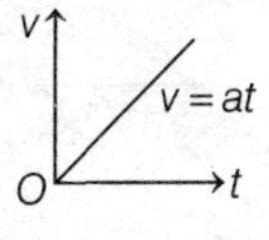 $v = at$	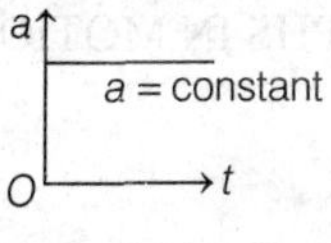 a = constant	Slope is positive
Uniformly accelerated motion with $u \neq 0$ but $s = 0$ at $t = 0$.	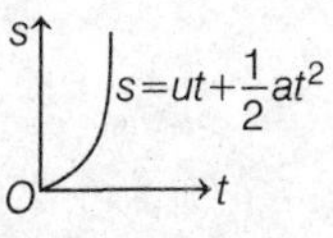 $s = ut + \frac{1}{2}at^2$	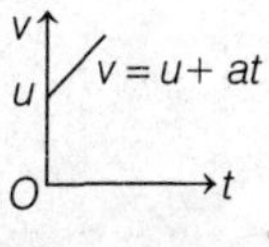 $v = u + at$	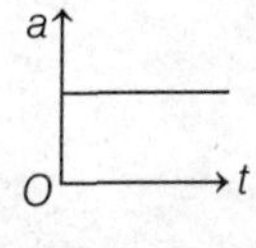	Slope is positive
Uniformly retarded motion	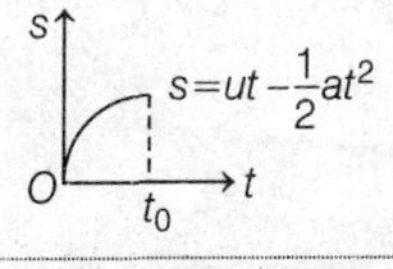 $s = ut - \frac{1}{2}at^2$	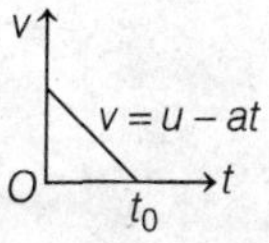 $v = u - at$	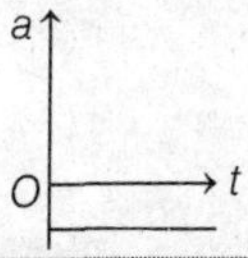	Slope is negative

Different Cases	*s-t* Graph	*v-t* Graph	*a-t* Graph	Slope of *v-t* Graph
Non-uniform accelerated motion	—			Slope is positive
Non-uniform decelerated motion	—			Slope is first increase, then decreases
A body falling freely under gravity				Slope is negative
A body is projected vertically upwards				Slope is negative

Non-Uniformly Accelerated Motion

When particle is not uniformly accelerated, i.e. acceleration of particle is not constant or acceleration is a function of time, then the following relations hold for one-dimensional motion

(*i*) $v = \dfrac{ds}{dt}$

(*ii*) $a = \dfrac{dv}{dt} = \dfrac{dv}{ds} \times \dfrac{ds}{dt} = v\dfrac{dv}{ds}$

(*iii*) $ds = vdt$

(*iv*) $dv = adt$ or $vdv = ads$

Topical Practice Questions

All the exam questions of this chapter have been divided into 3 topics as listed below

Topic 1

Distance, Displacement and Velocity

2019

1 A person travelling in a straight line moves with a constant velocity v_1 for certain distance x and with a constant velocity v_2 for next equal distance. The average velocity v is given by the relation **[NEET]**

(a) $\frac{1}{v} = \frac{1}{v_1} + \frac{1}{v_2}$ (b) $\frac{2}{v} = \frac{1}{v_1} + \frac{1}{v_2}$

(c) $\frac{v}{2} = \frac{v_1 + v_2}{2}$ (d) $v = \sqrt{v_1 v_2}$

2 Find the average velocity when a particle complete the circle of radius 1m in 10 s. **[JIPMER]**

(a) 2 ms^{-1} (b) 3.14 ms^{-1}

(c) 6.28 ms^{-1} (d) Zero

2018

3 A runner starts from O and goes to O following path $OQRO$ in 1 h. What is net displacement and average speed? **[JIPMER]**

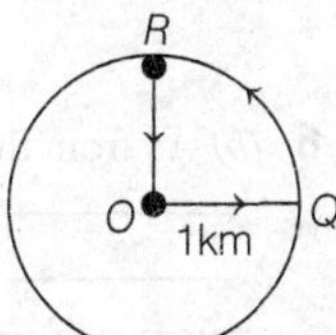

(a) 0, 3.57 kmh^{-1} (b) 0, 0 kmh^{-1}

(c) 0, 2.57 kmh^{-1} (d) 0, 1 kmh^{-1}

2017

4 Preeti reached the metro station and found that the escalator was not working. She walked up the stationary escalator in time t_1. On other days, if she remains stationary on the moving escalator, then the escalator takes her up in time t_2. The time taken by her to walk up on the moving escalator will be **[NEET]**

(a) $\frac{t_1 + t_2}{2}$ (b) $\frac{t_1 t_2}{t_2 - t_1}$ (c) $\frac{t_1 t_2}{t_2 + t_1}$ (d) $t_1 - t_2$

5 Which of the following statements is true for a car moving on the road? **[Manipal]**

(a) With respect to the frame of reference attached to the ground, the car is at rest.

(b) With respect to the frame of reference attached to the person sitting in the car, the car is at rest.

(c) With respect to the frame of reference attached to the person outside the car, the car is at rest.

(d) None of the above

2014

6 A car covers the first half of the distance between the two places at 40 kmh^{-1} and another half at 60 kmh^{-1}. The average speed of the car is **[UK PMT]**

(a) 40 km/h (b) 48 km/h

(c) 50 km/h (d) 60 km/h

7 A ball is thrown vertically upwards after reaching a maximum height h returns to the starting point after a time of 10 s. Its displacement is **[Kerala CEE]**

(a) h (b) $2h$

(c) $10h$ (d) $20h$

(e) zero

2013

8 Which of the following can be zero, when a particle is in motion for sometime? **[WB JEE]**

(a) Distance (b) Displacement

(c) Speed (d) None of these

2011

9 A body is moving with velocity 30 ms^{-1} towards east. After 10 s, its velocity becomes 40 ms^{-1} towards north. The average acceleration of the body is **[CBSE AIPMT]**

(a) 7 ms^{-2} (b) $\sqrt{7}$ ms^{-2}

(c) 5 ms^{-2} (d) 1 ms^{-2}

10 The displacement of a car is given as – 240 m, here, negative sign indicates **[CBSE AIPMT]**

(a) direction of displacement

(b) negative path length

(c) position of car is at point whose coordinate is – 120

(d) no significance of negative sign

2010

11 The sign (+ ve or – ve) of the average velocity depends only upon **[BHU]**

(a) the sign of displacement

(b) the initial position of the object

(c) the final position of the object

(d) None of the above

12 A wheel completes 2000 revolutions to cover the 9.5 km distance, then the diameter of the wheel is **[JCECE]**

(a) 1.5 km (b) 1.5 m

(c) 7.5 cm (d) 7.5 m

13 Select the incorrect statements and mark the correct option given below. **[JCECE]**

I. Average velocity is path length divided by the time interval.

II. In general, speed is greater than the magnitude of the velocity.

III. A particle moving in a given direction with a non-zero velocity can have zero speed.

IV. The magnitude of an average velocity is the average speed.

(a) II and III (b) I and IV
(c) I, III and IV (d) All of these

2009

14 A cyclist moving on a circular track of radius 40 m completes half a revolution in 40 s. Its average velocity is **[JCECE]**

(a) zero (b) 2 ms^{-1} (c) $4\pi\text{ ms}^{-1}$ (d) $8\pi\text{ ms}^{-1}$

2008

15 A particle moving in a straight line covers half the distance with speed of 3 ms^{-1}. The other half of the distance is covered in two equal time intervals with speed of 4.5 ms^{-1} and 7.5 ms^{-1}, respectively. The average speed of the particle during this motion is **[Kerala CEE]**

(a) 4 ms^{-1} (b) 5 ms^{-1} (c) 5.5 ms^{-1} (d) 4.8 ms^{-1}
(e) 6 ms^{-1}

2007

16 A car moves from X to Y with a uniform speed v_u and returns to Y with a uniform speed v_d. The average speed for this round trip is **[CBSE AIPMT]**

(a) $\dfrac{2v_d v_u}{v_d + v_u}$ (b) $\sqrt{v_u v_d}$

(c) $\dfrac{v_d v_u}{v_d + v_u}$ (d) $\dfrac{v_u + v_d}{2}$

Answers

1 (b)	2 (d)	3 (a)	4 (c)	5 (b)	6 (b)	7 (e)	8 (b)	9 (c)	10 (a)
11 (a)	12 (b)	13 (d)	14 (b)	15 (a)	16 (a)				

Explanations

1 *(b)* For distance x, the person moves with constant velocity v_1 and for another x distance, he moves with constant velocity of v_2, then

Total distance travelled,

$$D = x + x = 2x$$

Total time taken,

$$T = t_1 + t_2 = \frac{x}{v_1} + \frac{x}{v_2}\left[\because t = \frac{\text{Distance}}{\text{Velocity}}\right]$$

Average velocity,

$$v_{av} = \frac{\text{total distance}}{\text{total time}} = \frac{D}{T}$$

$$v = \frac{2x}{\frac{x}{v_1} + \frac{x}{v_2}} = \frac{2}{\frac{1}{v_1} + \frac{1}{v_2}} \quad [\because v_{av} = v]$$

$$\Rightarrow \frac{2}{v} = \frac{1}{v_1} + \frac{1}{v_2}$$

2 *(d)* When a particle completes one revolution in circular motion, then average displacement travelled by particle is zero.

Hence, average velocity

$$= \frac{\text{average displacement}}{\Delta t}$$

$$= \frac{0}{\Delta t} = 0$$

3 *(a)* ∵ Runner starts from O and goes to O, so net displacement is zero.

∵ Average speed

$$= \frac{\text{Total distance}}{\text{Total time}} = \frac{OQ + QR + RO}{\text{Total time}}$$

$$= \frac{1\text{ km} + (2\pi r)(1/4) + 1\text{ km}}{1\text{h}}$$

$$= 2 + \frac{\pi}{2} = 3.57\text{ kmh}^{-1}$$

4 *(c)* Speed of walking $= \dfrac{h}{t_1} = v_1$

Speed of escalator $= \dfrac{h}{t_2} = v_2$

Time taken when she walks over moving escalator

$$t = \frac{h}{v_1 + v_2}$$

$$\Rightarrow \frac{1}{t} = \frac{v_1}{h} + \frac{v_2}{h} = \frac{1}{t_1} + \frac{1}{t_2}$$

$$\Rightarrow t = \frac{t_1 t_2}{t_1 + t_2}$$

5 *(b)* For a car in motion, if we describe this event w.r.t. a frame of reference attached to the person sitting inside the car, the car will appear to be at rest as the person inside the car (observer) is also moving with same velocity and in the same direction as car.

6 *(b)* As from the question,

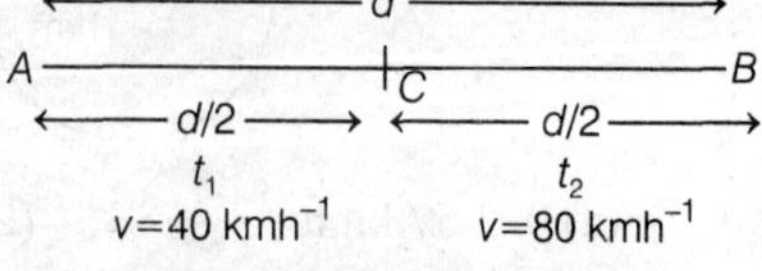

Average speed of the car v_{av} is given by

$$\frac{\text{Total distance travelled by the car }(d)}{\text{Total time taken }(t_1 + t_2)} \quad \text{...(i)}$$

So, now time taken in 1st half of the distance,

$$t_1 = \text{Time} = \frac{\text{Distance}}{\text{Velocity}} = \frac{d}{2 \times 40}$$

$$(\therefore \text{distance} = \frac{d}{2} \text{ and velocity} = 40\text{ kmh}^{-1})$$

$$\Rightarrow t_1 = \frac{d}{80}$$

and time taken for 2nd half, t_2

$$= \frac{d}{2 \times \text{velocity}} \quad (\because \text{distance} = \frac{d}{2} \text{ and velocity} = 60\text{ kmh}^{-1})$$

So, $t_2 = \dfrac{d}{2 \times 60} = \dfrac{d}{120}$

Now, average velocity,

$$v_{av} = \frac{d}{\frac{d}{80} + \frac{d}{120}} \quad \text{[from Eq. (i)]}$$

$$= \frac{d \times 80 \times 120}{200d} = 48 \text{ kmh}^{-1}$$

7 *(e)* The position of an object is always expressed w.r.t. some reference point. If the initial position of an object w.r.t. a reference point is s_1 and after sometime, it changes to s_2, then the magnitude of the displacement of the object is $s_2 - s_1$. But here, object moves back to s_1. So, its displacement is zero. $(\because s_1 = s_2 = h)$

8 *(b)* Displacement of a particle may be zero, because final position of the particle may coincide with its initial position.

9 *(c)* Average acceleration

$$= \frac{\text{Change in velocity}}{\text{Total time}}$$

$$a = \frac{|\mathbf{v}_f - \mathbf{v}_i|}{\Delta t} = \frac{\sqrt{30^2 + 40^2}}{10}$$

$$= \frac{\sqrt{900 + 1600}}{10} = 5 \text{ ms}^{-2}$$

10 *(a)* The displacement of a car is given as –240 m, here negative sign indicates the direction of displacement.

11 *(a)* Since, average velocity,

$$\mathbf{v} = \frac{\Delta x}{\Delta t} = \frac{\text{Displacement}}{\text{Time-interval}}$$

Thus, average velocity depends on the displacement and hence it depends on the sign of the displacement.

12 *(b)* Distance covered in n revolutions is

$$n \cdot \pi D = l$$

$$\Rightarrow \quad 2000\pi D = 9500$$

Given, $n = 2000$,

and distance, $l = 9500$ m

So, $D = \frac{9500}{2000 \times \pi} = 1.5$ m

13 *(d)* I. Average velocity $= \frac{\text{Displacement}}{\text{Time taken}}$

$$v_{av} = \frac{\Delta r}{\Delta t}$$

II. For a given time interval, Distance $\geq$ | Displacement |

i.e. average speed may be greater than or equal to average velocity

$\therefore$ Average speed $\geq$ | Average velocity |

III. A particle moving in a given direction with a non-zero velocity cannot have zero speed.

IV. In general, average speed is not equal to the magnitude of average velocity.

14 *(b)* As given, $R = 40$ m and $t = 40$ s

Here, net displacement is equal to the diameter of circular track,

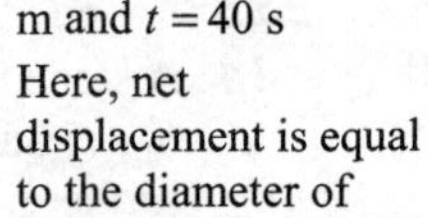

i.e. Displacement $= 2R$

Average velocity

$$= \frac{\text{Displacement}}{\text{Time taken}} = \frac{2R}{t} = \frac{2 \times 40}{40} = 2 \text{ ms}^{-1}$$

15 *(a)* If t_1 and $2t_2$ are the time taken by particle to cover first and second half distance, respectively

$$t_1 = \frac{x/2}{3} = \frac{x}{6}$$

and $\quad x_1 = 4.5t_2$ and $x_2 = 7.5t_2$

As, $\quad x_1 + x_2 = \frac{x}{2}$

So, $4.5t_2 + 7.5t_2 = \frac{x}{2} \Rightarrow t_2 = \frac{x}{24}$

Total time, $t = t_1 + 2t_2 = \frac{x}{6} + \frac{x}{12} = \frac{x}{4}$

$$\therefore u_{av} = \frac{\text{Total distance}}{\text{total time}} = \frac{x/2 + x/2}{x/4}$$

So, average speed $= 4 \text{ ms}^{-1}$.

16 *(a)* Average speed $= \frac{\text{Distance travelled}}{\text{Time taken}}$

Let t_1 and t_2 be times taken by the car to go from X to Y and then from Y to X, respectively.

Then, $t_1 + t_2 = \frac{XY}{v_u} + \frac{XY}{v_d}$

$$= XY\left(\frac{v_u + v_d}{v_u v_d}\right)$$

Total distance travelled

$$= XY + XY = 2XY$$

Therefore, average speed of the car for this round trip is

$$v_{av} = \frac{2XY}{XY\left(\frac{v_u + v_d}{v_u v_d}\right)}$$

or $v_{av} = \frac{2v_u v_d}{v_u + v_d}$

Topic 2

Uniform and Non-uniform Motion

2019

1 Speeds of a particle at 3rd and 8th second are 20 ms^{-1} and zero respectively, then average acceleration between 3rd and 8th second will be **[JIPMER]**

(a) 3 ms^{-2} (b) 4 ms^{-2}
(c) 5 ms^{-2} (d) 6 ms^{-2}

2018

2 A toy car with charge q moves on a frictionless horizontal plane surface under the influence of a uniform electric field **E**. Due to the force q**E**, its velocity increases from 0 to 6 ms^{-1} in one second duration. At that instant, the direction of the field is reversed. The car continues to move for two more seconds under the influence of this field. The average velocity and the average speed of the toy car between 0 to 3 s are respectively **[NEET]**

(a) 1 ms^{-1}, 3.5 ms^{-1}
(b) 1 m/s, 3 m/s
(c) 2 ms^{-1}, 4 ms^{-1}
(d) 1.5 ms^{-1}, 3 ms^{-1}

3 **Assertion** A body is momentarily at rest at the instant, if it reverse the direction.
Reason A body cannot have acceleration, if its velocity is zero at a given instant of time. **[AIIMS]**
(a) Assertion and Reason both are correct and Reason is correct explanation of Assertion.
(b) Assertion and Reason both are correct but Reason is not the correct explanation of Assertion.
(c) Assertion is correct but Reason is incorrect.
(d) Assertion is incorrect but Reason is correct.

4 Velocity is given by $v = 4t(1-2t)$, then find the value of time at which velocity is maximum. **[AIIMS]**
(a) 0.25 s (b) 1 s (c) 0.45 s (d) 4 s

5 A ball is thrown upwards with a speed u from a height h above the ground. The time taken by the ball to hit the ground is **[JIPMER]**
(a) $\sqrt{2h/g}$ (b) $\sqrt{8h/g}$
(c) $\frac{\sqrt{u^2+2gh}}{g}$ (d) $\frac{u}{g}+\sqrt{\frac{2h}{g}}$

2017

6 The x and y co-ordinates of the particle at any time are $x = 5t - 2t^2$ and $y = 10t$ respectively, where x and y are in metres and t in seconds. The acceleration of the particle at $t = 2$s is **[NEET]**
(a) 0 (b) 5 m/s^2 (c) -4 m/s^2 (d) -8 m/s^2

7 A body is projected vertically upwards. The times corresponding to height h while ascending and while descending are t_1 and t_2, respectively. Then, the velocity of projection will be (take g as acceleration due to gravity) **[JIPMER]**
(a) $\frac{g\sqrt{t_1t_2}}{2}$ (b) $\frac{g(t_1+t_2)}{2}$ (c) $g\sqrt{t_1t_2}$ (d) $g\frac{t_1t_2}{(t_1+t_2)}$

2016

8 Two cars P and Q start from a point at the same time in a straight line and their positions are represented by $x_P(t) = at + bt^2$ and $x_Q(t) = ft - t^2$. At what time do the cars have the same velocity? **[NEET]**
(a) $\frac{a-f}{1+b}$ (b) $\frac{a+f}{2(b-1)}$ (c) $\frac{a+f}{2(1+b)}$ (d) $\frac{f-a}{2(1+b)}$

2015

9 A particle of unit mass undergoes one-dimensional motion such that its velocity varies according to $v(x) = \beta x^{-2n}$, where β and n are constants and x is the position of the particle. The acceleration of the particle as a function of x is given by **[AIPMT]**
(a) $-2n\beta^2 x^{-2n-1}$ (b) $-2n\beta^2 x^{-4n-1}$
(c) $-2\beta^2 x^{-2n+1}$ (d) $-2n\beta^2 e^{-4n+1}$

2014

10 A particle moves with constant acceleration along a straight line starting from rest. The percentage increase in its displacement during the 4th second compared to that in the 3rd second is **[WB JEE]**
(a) 33% (b) 40% (c) 66% (d) 77%

11 A body of mass 10 kg is moving with a constant velocity of 10 ms^{-1}. When a constant force acts for 4 s on it, it moves with a velocity 2 ms^{-1} in the opposite direction. The acceleration produced in it is **[OJEE]**
(a) 3 ms^{-2} (b) -3 ms^{-2}
(c) 0.3 ms^{-2} (d) -0.3 ms^{-2}

12 A particle starts moving from rest with uniform acceleration. It travels a distance x in first 2 s and distance y in the next 2 s, then **[EAMCET]**
(a) $y = 3x$ (b) $y = 4x$ (c) $y = x$ (d) $y = 2x$

13 A body starts from rest and moves with constant acceleration for t sec. It travels a distance x_1 in first half of time and x_2 in next half of time, then **[KCET]**
(a) $x_2 = x_1$ (b) $x_2 = 2x_1$
(c) $x_2 = 3x_1$ (d) $x_2 = 4x_1$

2013

14 A stone falls freely under gravity. It covers distances h_1, h_2 and h_3 in the first 5 s, the next five second and the further next 5s, respectively. The relation between h_1, h_2 and h_3 is **[NEET]**
(a) $h_1 = 2h_2 = 3h_3$ (b) $h_1 = \frac{h_2}{3} = \frac{h_3}{5}$
(c) $h_2 = 3h_1$ and $h_3 = 3h_2$ (d) $h_1 = h_2 = h_3$

2012

15 The motion of a particle along a straight line is described by equation $x = 8 + 12t - t^3$, where x is in metre and t is in second. The retardation of the particle, when its velocity becomes zero **[CBSE AIPMT]**
(a) 24 ms^{-2} (b) zero
(c) 6ms^{-2} (d) 12ms^{-2}

16 A particle moves along the X-axis. The position x of a particle w.r.t. time from origin given by $x = b_0 + b_1t + b_2t^2$. The acceleration of particle is **[AIIMS]**
(a) b_0 (b) b_1 (c) b_2 (d) $2b_2$

17 A particle is travelling along a straight line OX. The distance x (in metre) of the particle from O at a time t is given by $x = 37 + 27t - t^3$, where t is time in second. The distance of the particle from O when it comes to rest is **[WB JEE]**
(a) 81 m (b) 91 m
(c) 101 m (d) 111 m

18 From the top of a tower, 80 m high from the ground, a stone is thrown in the horizontal direction with a velocity of 8 ms^{-1}. The stone reaches the ground after a time t and falls at a distance of d from the foot of the tower, then the time t and distance d are given respectively by (assuming, $g = 10 ms^{-2}$) **[WB JEE]**

(a) 6 s, 64 m (b) 6 s, 48 m (c) 4 s, 32 m (d) 4 s, 16 m

2010

19 A body starts from rest with a uniform acceleration. If its velocity after n second is v, then its displacement in the last 2 s is **[WB JEE]**

(a) $\frac{2v(n+1)}{n}$ (b) $\frac{v(n+1)}{n}$

(c) $\frac{v(n-1)}{n}$ (d) $\frac{2v(n-1)}{n}$

20 A stone falls freely from rest and the total distance covered by it in the last second of its motion equals the distance covered by it in the first three seconds of its motion. The stone remains in the air for **[WB JEE]**

(a) 6 s (b) 5 s (c) 7 s (d) 4 s

21 A body falls freely from the top of a tower. It covers 36% of the total height in the last second before striking the ground level. The height of the tower is **[Haryana PMT]**

(a) 50 m (b) 75 m

(c) 100 m (d) 123 m

22 From the top of a tower, a particle is thrown vertically downwards with a velocity of 10 ms^{-1}. The ratio of distances covered by it in the 3rd and 2nd second of its motion is (take, $g = 10 ms^{-2}$) **[Punjab PMET]**

(a) 5 : 7 (b) 7 : 5

(c) 3 : 6 (d) 6 : 3

23 A body A is thrown up vertically from the ground with a velocity v_0 and another body B is simultaneously dropped from a height H. They meet at a height $H/2$, if v_0 is equal to **[AMU]**

(a) $\sqrt{2gH}$ (b) $\sqrt{gH}$ (c) $\frac{1}{2}\sqrt{gH}$ (d) $\sqrt{\frac{2g}{H}}$

24 The ratios of the distance travelled in successive intervals of time by a body falling from rest are **[AMU]**

(a) 1 : 3 : 5 : 7 : 9 : ... (b) 2 : 4 : 6 : 8 : 10 : ...

(c) 1 : 4 : 7 : 10 : 13 : ... (d) None of these

2009

25 A car starts from rest and accelerates uniformly to a speed of 180 kmh^{-1} in 10 s. The distance covered by the car in this time interval is **[Kerala CEE]**

(a) 500 m (b) 250 m (c) 100 m

(d) 200 m (e) 150 m

26 A stone is thrown vertically upwards. When the stone is at a height equal to the half of its maximum height, its speed will be 10 ms^{-1}, then the maximum height attained by the stone is (take, $g = 10 ms^{-2}$) **[Punjab PMET]**

(a) 5 m (b) 150 m

(c) 20 m (d) 10 m

2008

27 The distance travelled by a particle starting from rest and moving with an acceleration $\frac{4}{3}$ ms^{-2}, in the third second is **[CBSE AIPMT]**

(a) 6 m (b) 4 m

(c) $\frac{10}{3}$ m (d) $\frac{19}{3}$ m

28 A particle moves in a straight line with a constant acceleration. It changes its velocity from 10 ms^{-1} to 20 ms^{-1} while passing through a distance 135 m in t s. The value of t (in second) is **[CBSE AIPMT]**

(a) 10 (b) 1.8

(c) 12 (d) 9

29 A parachutist after bailing out falls 50 m without friction. When parachute opens, it decelerates at 2 ms^{-2}. He reaches the ground with a speed of 3 ms^{-1}. At what height, did he bail out? **[AIIMS]**

(a) 91 m (b) 182 m

(c) 293 m (d) 111 m

30 A car starting from rest accelerates at the rate f through a distance s, then continues at a constant speed for time t and then decelerates at the rate $f/2$ to come to rest. If the total distance travelled is 15 s, then **[AIIMS]**

(a) $s = ft$ (b) $s = \frac{1}{6} ft^2$

(c) $s = \frac{1}{72} ft^2$ (d) $s = \frac{1}{4} ft^2$

31 An automobile travelling with a speed of 60 kmh^{-1}, can brake to stop within a distance of 20 m. If the car is going twice as fast, i.e. 120 kmh^{-1}, the stopping distance will be **[BHU]**

(a) 20 m (b) 40 m

(c) 60 m (d) 80 m

32 If the velocity of a particle is $v = At + Bt^2$, where A and B are constants, then the distance travelled by it between 1s and 2s is **[NEET]**

(a) $3A + 7B$ (b) $\frac{3}{2} A + \frac{7}{3} B$

(c) $\frac{A}{2} + \frac{B}{3}$ (d) $\frac{3}{2} A + 4B$

33 A car moving with a speed of 50 kmh^{-1} can be stopped by brakes after atleast 6 m. If the same car is moving at a speed of 100 kmh^{-1}, the minimum stopping distance is **[MP PMT]**

(a) 12 m (b) 18 m
(c) 24 m (d) 6 m

34 A boy standing at the top of a tower of 20 m height drops a stone. Assuming $g = 10 \, ms^{-2}$, the velocity with which it hits the ground is **[CBSE AIPMT]**

(a) 20 ms^{-1} (b) 40 ms^{-1}
(c) 5 ms^{-1} (d) 10 ms^{-1}

2007

35 The position x of a particle with respect to time t along X-axis is given by $x = 9t^2 - t^3$, where x is in metre and t in sec. What will be the position of this particle when it achieves maximum speed along the $+X$- direction? **[CBSE AIPMT]**

(a) 32 m (b) 54 m
(c) 81 m (d) 24 m

36 A ball thrown vertically upwards with an initial velocity of 1.4 ms^{-1} returns in 2 s. The total displacement of the ball is **[Manipal]**

(a) 22.4 cm (b) zero
(c) 44.8 m (d) 33.6 m

37 A particle moving along X-axis has acceleration f, at time t is given by $f = f_0\left(1 - \frac{t}{T}\right)$, where f_0 and T are constants. The particle at $t = 0$ has zero velocity. In the time interval between $t = 0$ and the instant when $f = 0$, the particle's velocity (v_x) is **[CBSE AIPMT]**

(a) $f_0 T$ (b) $f_0 T^2$
(c) $f_0^2 T^2$ (d) $\frac{1}{2} f_0 T$

38 A man throws balls with the same speed vertically upwards one after the other at an interval of 2s. What should be the speed of the throw, so that more than two balls are in the sky at any time? (Take, $g = 9.8 \, ms^{-2}$) **[AFMC]**

(a) Any speed less than 19.6 ms^{-1}
(b) Only with speed 19.6 ms^{-1}
(c) More than 19.6 ms^{-1}
(d) Atleast 9.8 ms^{-1}

39 Two bodies A (of mass 1 kg) and B (of mass 3 kg) are dropped from heights of 16 m and 25 m, respectively. The ratio of the time taken by them to reach the ground is **[Manipal]**

(a) 5/4 (b) 12/5
(c) 5/12 (d) 4/5

40 When a bullet is fired at a target, its velocity decreases by half, after penetrating 30 cm into it. The additional thickness, that it will penetrate before coming to rest is **[Kerala CEE]**

(a) 30 cm (b) 40 cm (c) 10 cm (d) 50 cm
(e) 20 cm

41 A body is moving with a uniform acceleration covers 200 m in the first 2 s and 220 m in the next 4 s. Find the value of velocity in ms^{-1} after 7 s. **[J&K CET]**

(a) 10 (b) 15 (c) 20 (d) 30

42 The acceleration of a particle is increasing linearly with time t as bt. The particle starts from the origin with an initial velocity v_0. The distance travelled by the particle in time t will be **[AMU]**

(a) $v_0 t + \frac{1}{3} bt^2$ (b) $v_0 t + \frac{1}{3} bt^3$
(c) $v_0 t + \frac{1}{6} bt^3$ (d) $v_0 t + \frac{1}{2} bt^2$

43 A conveyor belt is moving horizontally at a speed of 4 ms^{-1}. A box of mass 20 kg is gently laid on it. It takes 0.1 s for the box to come to rest. If the belt continues to move uniformly, then the distance moved by the box on the conveyor belt is **[AMU]**

(a) zero (b) 0.2 m
(c) 0.4 m (d) 0.8 m

44 A particle moving with a uniform acceleration travels 24 m and 64 m in the first two consecutive intervals of 4 s each. Its initial velocity will be **[BCECE]**

(a) 5 ms^{-1} (b) 3 ms^{-1} (c) 1 ms^{-1} (d) 4 ms^{-1}

2006

45 The displacement of a particle starting from rest (at $t = 0$) is given by

$$s = 6t^2 - t^3$$

The time in second at which the particle will obtain zero velocity again is **[AIIMS]**

(a) 2 (b) 4 (c) 6 (d) 8

46 A body falls from a height $h = 200$ m. The ratio of distance travelled in each 2 s, during $t = 0$ to 6 s of the journey is **[Manipal]**

(a) 1 : 4 : 9 (b) 1 : 2 : 4
(c) 1 : 3 : 5 (d) 1 : 2 : 3

47 From the top of a tower a stone is thrown up and reaches the ground in time $t_1 = 9$ s. A second stone is thrown down with the same speed and reaches the ground in time $t_2 = 4$ s. A third stone is released from rest and reaches the ground in time t_3, which is equal to **[Kerala CEE]**

(a) 6.5 s (b) 6 s (c) $\frac{5}{36}$ s (d) 65 s
(e) 64 s

48 A ball is thrown upwards, it takes 4 s to reach back to the ground. Find the value of its initial velocity. **[RPMT]**
(a) 30 ms^{-1} (b) 10 ms^{-1}
(c) 40 ms^{-1} (d) 20 ms^{-1}

49 A ball is thrown from height h and another from $2h$. The ratio of time taken by the two balls to reach the ground is **[MP PMT]**
(a) $1:\sqrt{2}$ (b) $\sqrt{2}:1$ (c) 2 : 1 (d) 1 : 2

50 A car accelerates from rest at a constant rate for first 10 s and covers a distance x. It covers a distance y in next 10 s at the same acceleration. Then, which of the following is true? **[Punjab PMET]**
(a) $x = 3y$ (b) $y = 3x$ (c) $x = y$ (d) $y = 2x$

51 The velocity of a particle at an instant is 10 ms^{-1}. After 3 s its velocity will become 16 ms^{-1}. The velocity at 2 s, before the given instant would have been **[AMU]**
(a) 6 ms^{-1} (b) 4 ms^{-1} (c) 2 ms^{-1} (d) 1 ms^{-1}

52 A body is projected vertically upwards with a velocity u. It crosses a point in its journey at a height h twice just after 1 s and 7 s. The value of u in ms^{-1} is (take, $g = 10\ ms^{-2}$) **[EAMCET]**
(a) 50 (b) 40 (c) 30 (d) 20

53 A metro train starts from rest and in 5 s achieves 108 kmh^{-1}. After that it moves with constant velocity and comes to rest after travelling 45 m with uniform retardation. If total distance travelled is 395 m, find total time of travelling. **[DUMET]**
(a) 12.2 s (b) 15.3 s (c) 9 s (d) 17.2 s

54 The distance covered by an object (in metre) in given by $s = 8t^3 - 7t^2 + 5t$, find its speed at $t = 2$ sec **[Manipal]**
(a) 76 ms^{-1} (b) 72 ms^{-1} (c) 86 ms^{-1} (d) 82 ms^{-1}

2005

55 The displacement x of a particle varies with time t as $x = ae^{-\alpha t} + be^{\beta t}$, where a, b, α and β are positive constants. The velocity of the particle will **[CBSE AIPMT]**
(a) go on decreasing with time
(b) be independent of α and β
(c) drop to zero when $\alpha = \beta$
(d) go on increasing with time

56 When a ball is thrown up vertically with velocity v_0, it reaches a maximum height of h. If one wishes to triple the maximum height, then the ball should be thrown with velocity **[AIIMS]**
(a) $\sqrt{3}v_0$ (b) $3v_0$
(c) $9v_0$ (d) $3/2\ v_0$

57 If a car at rest, accelerates uniformly and attains a speed of 72 kmh^{-1} in 10 s, then it covers a distance of **[BHU]**
(a) 50 m (b) 100 m
(c) 200 m (d) 400 m

58 The velocity of bullet is reduced from 200 ms^{-1} to 100 ms^{-1} while travelling through a wooden block of thickness of 10 cm. The retardation assuming to be uniform, will be **[RPMT]**
(a) $15 \times 10^4\ ms^{-2}$ (b) $13.5 \times 10^4\ ms^{-2}$
(c) $12 \times 10^4\ ms^{-2}$ (d) None of these

59 A man is 45 m behind the bus, when the bus start accelerating from rest with acceleration 2.5 ms^{-2}. With what minimum velocity should the man start running to catch the bus? **[J&K CET]**
(a) 12 ms^{-1} (b) 14 ms^{-1}
(c) 15 ms^{-1} (d) 16 ms^{-1}

60 A particle moves along X-axis as $x = 4(t-2) + a(t-2)^2$. Which of the following is true? **[J&K CET]**
(a) The initial velocity of particle is 4
(b) The acceleration of particle is $2a$
(c) The particle is at origin at $t = 0$
(d) None of the above

61 From the top of a tower two stones, whose masses are in the ratio 1 : 2 are thrown on straight up with an initial speed u and the second straight down with the same speed u. Then, neglecting air resistance **[KCET]**
(a) the heavier stone hits the ground with a higher speed
(b) the lighter stone hits the ground with a higher speed
(c) Both the stones will have the same speed when they hit the ground
(d) the speed can't be determined with the given data

62 A particle moves along Y-axis in such a way that its y-coordinate varies with time t according to the relation $y = 3 + 5t + 7t^2$. The initial velocity and acceleration of the particle are respectively **[BCECE]**
(a) 14 ms^{-1}, $-5\ ms^{-2}$
(b) 19 ms^{-1}, $-9\ ms^{-2}$
(c) $-14\ ms^{-1}$, $-5\ ms^{-2}$
(d) 5 ms^{-1}, 14 ms^{-2}

63 An object travels North with a velocity of 10 ms^{-1} and then speeds upto a velocity of 25 ms^{-1} in 5 s. The acceleration of the object in these 5 s is **[JCECE]**
(a) 12 ms^{-2} in North direction
(b) 3 ms^{-2} in North direction
(c) 15 ms^{-2} in North direction
(d) 3 ms^{-2} in South direction

Answers

1 (b)	2 (b)	3 (c)	4 (a)	5 (c)	6 (c)	7 (b)	8 (d)	9 (b)	10 (b)
11 (b)	12 (a)	13 (c)	14 (b)	15 (d)	16 (d)	17 (b)	18 (c)	19 (d)	20 (b)
21 (d)	22 (b)	23 (b)	24 (a)	25 (b)	26 (d)	27 (c)	28 (d)	29 (c)	30 (c)
31 (d)	32 (b)	33 (c)	34 (a)	35 (b)	36 (b)	37 (d)	38 (c)	39 (d)	40 (c)
41 (a)	42 (c)	43 (b)	44 (c)	45 (b)	46 (c)	47 (b)	48 (d)	49 (a)	50 (b)
51 (a)	52 (b)	53 (d)	54 (a)	55 (d)	56 (a)	57 (b)	58 (a)	59 (c)	60 (b)
61 (c)	62 (d)	63 (b)							

Explanations

1 *(b)* Time interval between 8th and 3rd second,

$$\Delta t = 8 - 3 = 5\text{ s},\ \text{i.e. } \Delta t = 5\text{s}$$

Change in velocity,

$$\Delta v = 20 - 0 = 20\text{ ms}^{-1}$$

∴ Average acceleration

$$= \frac{\Delta v}{\Delta t} = \frac{20}{5} = 4\text{ ms}^{-2}$$

2 *(b)* According to the question, For the time duration $0 < t < 1\text{s}$, the velocity increase from 0 to 6 ms^{-1}. As the direction of field has been reversed, for $1 < t < 2\text{s}$, the velocity firstly decreases from 6 ms^{-1} to 0. Then, for $2 < t < 3\text{s}$; as the field strength is same; the magnitude of acceleration would be same, but velocity increases from 0 to -6 ms^{-1}.

⟵ $0<t<1$s ⟶ B ⟵ $1<t<2$s ⟶
A • $v=0$ a $v = 6\text{ ms}^{-1}$ −a C $v=0$
D $v=-6\text{ ms}^{-1}$ −a
⟵ $2<t<3$s ⟶

Acceleration of the car

$$|a| = \left|\frac{v-u}{t}\right| = \frac{6-0}{1} = 6\text{ms}^{-2}$$

The displacement of the particle is given as

$$s = ut + \frac{1}{2}at^2$$

For $t = 0$ to $t = 1$ s,

$$u = 0, a = +6\text{ ms}^{-2}$$

$$\Rightarrow \quad s_1 = 0 + \frac{1}{2} \times 6 \times (1)^2 = 3\text{ m}$$

For $t = 1$ s to $t = 2$ s,

$$u = 6\text{ ms}^{-1}, a = -6\text{ ms}^{-2}$$

$$\Rightarrow s_2 = 6 \times 1 - \frac{1}{2} \times 6 \times (1)^2$$

$$= 6 - 3 = 3\text{m}$$

For $t = 2$ s to $t = 3$ s,

$$u = 0, a = -6\text{ ms}^{-1}$$

$$\Rightarrow s_3 = 0 - \frac{1}{2} \times 6 \times (1)^2 = -3\text{ m}$$

∴ Net displacement,

$$s = s_1 + s_2 + s_3$$
$$= 3\text{ m} + 3\text{ m} - 3\text{ m}$$
$$= 3\text{ m}$$

Hence, average velocity

$$= \frac{\text{Net displacement}}{\text{Total time}}$$

$$= \frac{3}{3} = 1\text{m s}^{-1}$$

Total distance travelled, $d = 9$m

Hence, average speed

$$= \frac{\text{Total distance}}{\text{Total time}} = \frac{9}{3} = 3\text{ m s}^{-1}$$

Alternate Method

Given condition can be represented through graph also as shown below.

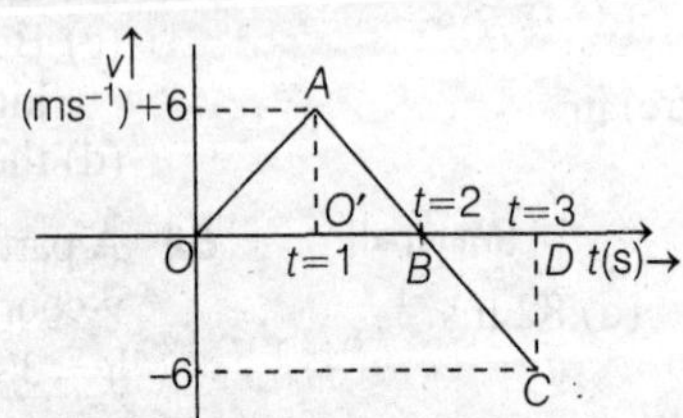

∴ Displacement in three seconds
= Area under the graph
= Area of ΔOAO′ + Area of ΔAO′B − Area of ΔBCD

$$= \frac{1}{2} \times 1 \times 6 + \frac{1}{2} \times 1 \times 6 - \frac{1}{2} \times 6 \times 1$$

$$= 3\text{m}$$

$$\therefore \text{Average velocity} = \frac{3}{3} = 1\text{ms}^{-1}.$$

Total distance travelled, $d = 9$m

$$\therefore \text{Average speed} = \frac{9}{3} = 3\text{ms}^{-1}$$

3 *(c)* When a particle is released from rest position under gravity, then $v = 0$, but $a \neq 0$.

4 *(a)* To find value of time at which velocity is maximum, taking differentiation of v with respect to time

$$\Rightarrow \quad \frac{dv}{dt} = 0$$

Given, $\quad v = 4t(1-2t)$

$$v = 4t - 8t^2$$

$$\Rightarrow \quad \frac{d}{dt}(4t - 8t^2) = 0$$

$$\Rightarrow 4 - 16t = 0$$

$$\Rightarrow \quad t = \frac{1}{4}\text{ s} = 0.25\text{ s}$$

Again taking differentiation, we get

$$\Rightarrow \quad \frac{d^2v}{dt^2} = -16 < 0$$

So, at $t = 0.25$ s velocity is maximum.

5 *(c)* Time taken to reach the highest point from the height h is obtained from equation, $v = u - gt$

$$\therefore \quad 0 = u - gt \text{ or } t = \frac{u}{g}$$

Height attained above h is obtained from

$$v^2 - u^2 = 2(-g)h_1$$

$$\text{or } 0 - u^2 = 2(-g)h_1 \text{ or } h_1 = \frac{u^2}{2g}$$

$$\text{Total height, } h_2 = \left[h_1 + h = \frac{u^2}{2g} + h\right]$$

Time taken to hit the ground is obtained

$$\text{from} \quad h_2 = ut + \frac{1}{2}at^2$$

$$\text{or} \quad \frac{u^2}{2g} + h = 0 + \frac{1}{2}gt^2$$

$$\therefore \text{Total time taken, } t = \sqrt{\frac{(u^2 + 2gh)}{g}}$$

6 *(c)* Given, $x = 5t - 2t^2$

Velocity of the particle,

$$v_x = \frac{dx}{dt} = \frac{d}{dt}(5t - 2t^2) = 5 - 4t$$

Acceleration, $a_x = \frac{d}{dt} v_x = -4\ \text{ms}^{-2}$

Also, $y = 10t$

Velocity, $v_y = \frac{dy}{dt} = 10$

$\therefore$ Acceleration $a_y = \frac{dv_y}{dt} = 0$

$\therefore$ Net acceleration of the particle,

$$\mathbf{a}_{\text{net}} = a_x\hat{\mathbf{i}} + a_y\hat{\mathbf{j}}$$

$$= (-4\ \text{ms}^{-2})\ \hat{\mathbf{i}} + 0\hat{\mathbf{j}}$$

or $\mathbf{a}_{\text{net}} = -4\ \hat{\mathbf{i}}\ \text{ms}^{-2}$

7 *(b)* Let v be initial velocity of vertical projection and t be the time taken by the body to reach a height h from ground.

Here, $u = u, a = -g, s = h, t = t$

Using, $s = ut + \frac{1}{2}at^2$, we have

$$h = ut + \frac{1}{2}(-g)t^2$$

or $gt^2 - 2ut + 2h = 0$

$$\therefore \quad t = \frac{2u \pm \sqrt{4u^2 - 4g \times 2h}}{2g}$$

$$= \frac{u \pm \sqrt{u^2 - 2gh}}{g}$$

It means t has two values, i.e.

$$t_1 = \frac{u + \sqrt{u^2 - 2gh}}{g}$$

$$t_2 = \frac{u - \sqrt{u^2 - 2gh}}{g}$$

$$t_1 + t_2 = \frac{2u}{g} \text{ or } u = \frac{g(t_1 + t_2)}{2}$$

8 *(d)* Velocity of each car is given by

$$v_P = \frac{dx_P(t)}{dt} = a + 2bt$$

and $v_Q = \frac{dx_Q(t)}{dt} = f - 2t$

It is given that, $v_P = v_Q$

$\Rightarrow a + 2bt = f - 2t \Rightarrow t = \frac{f - a}{2(b + 1)}$

9 *(b)* Given, $v(x) = \beta x^{-2n}$

$$a = \frac{dv(x)}{dt} = \frac{dx}{dt} \cdot \frac{dv}{dx}$$

$$\Rightarrow \quad a = v\frac{dv}{dx} = (\beta x^{-2n})(-2n\beta x^{-2n-1})$$

$$\Rightarrow \quad a = -2n\beta^2 x^{-4n-1}$$

10 *(b)* We know that,

$$s_{\text{nth}} = u + \frac{1}{2}a(2n - 1)$$

$$s_{\text{3rd}} = 0 + \frac{1}{2}a(2 \times 3 - 1) = \frac{5}{2}a \text{ (for } n = 3\text{ s)}$$

$$s_{\text{4rd}} = 0 + \frac{1}{2}a(2 \times 4 - 1) = \frac{7}{2}a \text{ (for } n = 4\text{ s)}$$

So, the percentage increase

$$= \frac{s_{\text{4th}} - s_{\text{3rd}}}{s_{\text{3rd}}} \times 100$$

$$= \frac{\frac{7}{2}a - \frac{5}{2}a}{\frac{5}{2}a} \times 100 = \frac{\frac{2a}{2}}{\frac{5}{2}a} \times 100$$

$$= 2 \times 20 = 40\%$$

11 *(b)* Given, $u = 10\ \text{ms}^{-1}$, time, $t = 4$ s and $v = -2\ \text{ms}^{-1}$

From $v = u + at$

$\Rightarrow -2 = 10 + a \times 4$

$\Rightarrow a = -3\ \text{ms}^{-2}$

12 *(a)* The distance covered in 2 s,

$$x = \frac{1}{2}a(2)^2 = 2a$$

The distance covered in next 2 s,

$$y = \frac{1}{2}a(4)^2 - \frac{1}{2}a(2)^2 = 6a$$

Now, $x/y = \frac{2a}{6a} = \frac{1}{3} \Rightarrow y = 3x$

13 *(c)*

A (0,0) — x_1 — C — x_2 — B

$u=0$ ⟵ $t/2$ ⟶ ⟵ $t/2$ ⟶

$a =$ constant

Let A be the origin point, from equation of motion,

$$x = ut + \frac{1}{2}at^2 = \frac{1}{2}at^2 \qquad (\because u = 0)$$

where, x is the position of the particle.

For point C, $x_1 = \frac{1}{2}a(t/2)^2$

$$\Rightarrow \quad x_1 = \frac{1}{8}at^2 \qquad \text{...(i)}$$

As, $x_2 = x - x_1 = \frac{1}{2}at^2 - \frac{1}{8}at^2$

$$= \frac{3}{8}at^2 = 3\left(\frac{1}{8}at^2\right)$$

Hence, $x_2 = 3x_1$

14 *(b)* As, $h_1 = \frac{1}{2}gt^2$

In 5 s, $h_1 = \frac{1}{2}g \times (5)^2 = \frac{25g}{2}$

In next 5 s,

$$h_2 = \frac{1}{2}g \times 10^2 - \frac{1}{2}g(5)^2 = 50g - \frac{25g}{2}$$

$$= \frac{100g - 25g}{2} = \frac{75g}{2}$$

In other next 5 s,

$$h_3 = \frac{1}{2}g \times (15)^2 - \frac{1}{2}g(10)^2$$

$$= \frac{225g}{2} - 50g$$

$$= \frac{125g}{2}$$

Now, $h_1 : h_2 : h_3 = \frac{25g}{2} : \frac{75g}{2} : \frac{125g}{2} = 1 : 3 : 5$

15 *(d)* Given, $x = 8 + 12t - t^3$, $v = \frac{dx}{dt}$

and $a = \frac{dv}{dt}$

So, $v = 12 - 3t^2$ and $a = -6t$

At $t = 2$s, $v = 0$ and $a = -12\ \text{m/s}^2$

So, retardation of the particle is $12\ \text{ms}^{-2}$.

16 *(d)* Position of particle,

$$x = b_0 + b_1 t + b_2 t^2$$

Velocity, $v = \left(\frac{dx}{dt}\right) = b_1 + 2b_2 t$

Acceleration, $|\mathbf{a}| = \frac{d^2x}{dt^2} = 2b_2$

17 *(b)* Given, $x = 37 + 27t - t^3$

$$v = \frac{dx}{dt} = 27 - 3t^2$$

According to the question,

$$\frac{dx}{dt} = v = 0$$

$\Rightarrow 27 - 3t^2 = 0$

Here, $t = 3$s

$$x = 37 + 27 \times 3 - (3)^3 = 91\ \text{m}$$

18 *(c)* Given, $h = 80$ m, $v = 8\ \text{ms}^{-1}$ and $g = 10\ \text{ms}^{-2}$

Here, $h = \frac{1}{2}gt^2$

$\Rightarrow 80 = \frac{1}{2} \times 10 \times t^2 \Rightarrow t = 4$ s

$\therefore x = vt = 8 \times 4 = 32$ m

19 *(d)* As, $v = 0 + na$

$$\Rightarrow a = \frac{v}{n} \Rightarrow s_n = \frac{1}{2}an^2$$

Distance travelled in $(n - 2)$ second,

$$s_{n-2} = \frac{1}{2}a(n - 2)^2$$

So, distance travelled in the last 2 s,

$$s_n - s_{n-2} = \frac{1}{2}an^2 - \frac{1}{2}a(n-2)^2$$

$$= \frac{a}{2}[n^2 - (n-2)^2]$$

$$= \frac{a}{2}[n + (n-2)][n - (n-2)]$$

$$= 2a(n-1) = \frac{2v(n-1)}{n}$$

20 *(b)* Given, the stone falls from rest, so $u = 0$

Now, distance covered in the last second is equal to the distance covered in the first three seconds of the motion.

Thus, $s_3 = s_l$

$$\Rightarrow \quad s_3 = 0 + \frac{1}{2}gt^2$$

$$= \frac{1}{2} \times 10 \times (3)^2 \quad [\because g = 10\ \text{ms}^{-2}]$$

$$= \frac{1}{2} \times 10 \times 9 = 45$$

$$\Rightarrow \quad s_l = 45 = u + (2n-1) \times \frac{10}{2}$$

$$\Rightarrow \quad n = 5\text{s}$$

21 *(d)* Let the height of tower be h and the body takes time n to reach the ground when it falls freely.

$$\therefore \quad h = \frac{1}{2}gn^2 \quad \text{...(i)}$$

In the last second, i.e. in n th second the body travels $0.36h$.

So, in $(n-1)$ s, it travels,

$$1h - 0.36h = 0.64h$$

From Eq. (i), $0.64h = \frac{1}{2}g(n-1)^2$

$$\Rightarrow \quad \frac{0.64}{2}gn^2 = \frac{1}{2}g(n^2 + 1 - 2n)$$

$$\Rightarrow \quad \frac{64}{100}n^2 = n^2 + 1 - 2n$$

$$\Rightarrow \quad 64n^2 = 100n^2 + 100 - 200n$$

$$\Rightarrow \quad 36n^2 - 200n + 100 = 0$$

$$\Rightarrow \quad 9n^2 - 50n + 25 = 0$$

$$\Rightarrow \quad 9n^2 - 45n - 5n + 25 = 0$$

$$\Rightarrow \quad 9n(n-5) - 5(n-5) = 0$$

$$\Rightarrow \quad (9n-5)(n-5) = 0$$

$\Rightarrow 9n - 5 = 0$ or $n = 5/9$ s (impossible)

So, $n - 5 = 0$ or $n = 5$ s

From Eq. (i) $h = \frac{1}{2} \times 9.8 \times 25$

$$h = 12.5 \times 9.8$$

$$= 122.5 \simeq 123\ \text{m}$$

22 *(b)* Distance covered in 3rd second,

$$s_{3\text{rd}} = 10 + \frac{10}{2}(2 \times 3 - 1) = 35\ \text{m}$$

Distance covered in 2nd second,

$$s_{2\text{nd}} = 10 + \frac{10}{2}(2 \times 2 - 1) = 25\ \text{m}$$

$$\Rightarrow \quad \frac{s_{3\text{rd}}}{s_{2\text{nd}}} = \frac{35}{25} = \frac{7}{5}$$

23 *(b)* Suppose the two bodies A and B meet at time t, at a height $\frac{H}{2}$ from the ground.

For B, $u = 0$

H $H/2$

For A, $v = 0$

For body B, $u = 0$,

$$h = \frac{H}{2}$$

$$\Rightarrow \quad h = ut + \frac{1}{2}gt^2$$

$$\text{Hence,} \quad \frac{H}{2} = \frac{1}{2}gt^2 \quad \text{...(i)}$$

For body A, $u = v_0$, $h = \frac{H}{2}$

$$\Rightarrow \quad h = ut - \frac{1}{2}gt^2$$

$$\text{Hence,} \quad \frac{H}{2} = v_0t - \frac{1}{2}gt^2 \quad \text{...(ii)}$$

So, from Eqs. (i) and (ii), we get

$$v_0t - \frac{1}{2}gt^2 = \frac{1}{2}gt^2 \quad \Rightarrow \quad v_0t = gt^2$$

$$\Rightarrow \quad t = \frac{v_0}{g}$$

Now putting this value in Eq. (i), we get

$$\frac{H}{2} = \frac{1}{2}g \times \frac{v_0^2}{g^2} \quad \Rightarrow \quad H = \frac{v_0^2}{g}$$

$$\Rightarrow \quad v_0 = \sqrt{gH}$$

24 *(a)* As, we know distance travelled in n th second is

$$s_{n\text{th}} = u + \frac{1}{2}g(2n-1), \quad \text{(where, } u = 0\text{)}$$

So, for $n = 1, 2, 3, \ldots\ldots$

$$s_1 = \frac{1}{2}g(2-1) = \frac{1}{2}g$$

Similarly, $s_2 = \frac{3g}{2}$, $s_3 = \frac{5g}{2}$

$$\Rightarrow s_1 : s_2 : s_3 : s_4 = 1 : 3 : 5 : 7 : \ldots..$$

25 *(b)* Speed, $v = 180\ \text{kmh}^{-1} = 50\ \text{ms}^{-1}$ and time, $t = 10$ s

$\therefore$ Acceleration of the car,

$$a = \frac{v-u}{t} = \frac{50-0}{10} = 5\ \text{ms}^{-2}$$

Thus, the distance covered by the car,

$$s = \frac{1}{2}at^2 = \frac{1}{2} \times 5 \times (10)^2 = 250\ \text{m}$$

26 *(d)* Let u be the initial velocity and h be the maximum height attained by the stone.

So, $v_1^2 = u^2 - 2gh_1$

$$\therefore \quad (10)^2 = u^2 - 2 \times 10 \times \frac{h}{2}$$

$$\left(\because h_1 = \frac{h}{2}, v_1 = 10\ \text{ms}^{-1}\right)$$

$$\Rightarrow \quad 100 = u^2 - 10h \quad \text{...(i)}$$

Again at height h, $v_2^2 = u^2 - 2gh$

$$\Rightarrow \quad 0^2 = u^2 - 2 \times 10 \times h \quad (\because v_2 = 0)$$

$$\Rightarrow \quad u^2 = 20h \quad \text{...(ii)}$$

So, from Eqs. (i) and (ii), we have

$$100 = 10h$$

$$\Rightarrow h = 10\ \text{m}$$

27 *(c)* Distance travelled by the particle in nth second,

$$s_{n\text{th}} = u + \frac{1}{2}a(2n-1)$$

where, u is initial speed and a is acceleration of the particle.

Given, $n = 3, u = 0, a = \frac{4}{3}\ \text{ms}^{-2}$

Putting these values, we get

$$s_{3\text{rd}} = 0 + \frac{1}{2} \times \frac{4}{3} \times (2 \times 3 - 1)$$

$$= \frac{4}{6} \times 5 = \frac{10}{3}\ \text{m}$$

28 *(d)* Let u and v be the initial and final velocities of particle and a and s be the constant acceleration and distance covered by it.

From third equation of motion,

$$v^2 = u^2 + 2as$$

Given, $v = 20\ \text{ms}^{-1}$, $u = 10\ \text{ms}^{-1}$ and $s = 135$ m

Putting these values, we get

$$\Rightarrow (20)^2 = (10)^2 + 2a \times 135$$

$$a = \frac{300}{2 \times 135} = \frac{10}{9}\ \text{ms}^{-2}$$

Now, using 1st equation of motion,

$$v = u + at$$

$$\Rightarrow \quad t = \frac{v-u}{a} = \frac{20-10}{(10/9)} = \frac{10 \times 9}{10} = 9\ \text{s}$$

29 *(c)* Parachute bails out at height H from ground.

Velocity at A, $v = \sqrt{2gh}$

$= \sqrt{2 \times 9.8 \times 50}$ (given)

$= \sqrt{980}\ \text{ms}^{-1}$

The velocity at ground, $v_1 = 3\ \text{ms}^{-1}$ (given)

Acceleration, $a = -2\ \text{ms}^{-2}$ (given)

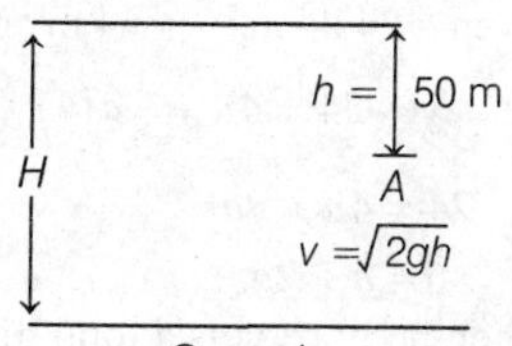

$$\therefore\ H - h = \frac{v^2 - v_1^2}{2 \times 2} = \frac{980 - 9}{4}$$

$$= \frac{971}{4} = 242.75$$

$$\therefore\ H = 242.75 + h$$

$$= 242.75 + 50 \approx 293\ \text{m}$$

30 *(c)* The velocity-time graph for the given situation can be drawn as below

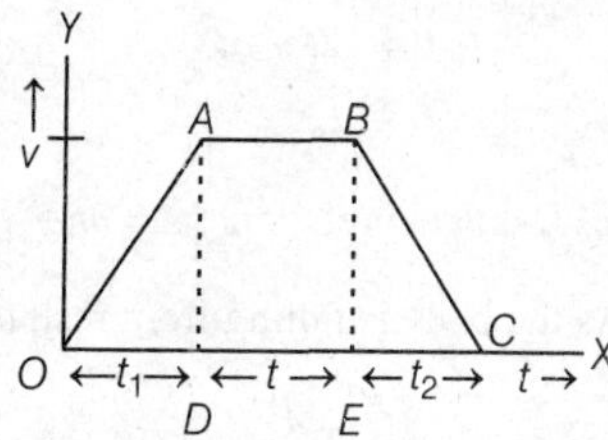

Magnitudes of slope of $OA = f$ and slope of $BC = \frac{f}{2}$

$$\Rightarrow\ v = ft_1 = \frac{f}{2}t_2\ \Rightarrow\ t_2 = 2t_1$$

In graph, area of ΔOAD gives distance

$$s_1 = \frac{1}{2} f t_1^2 = s \quad \ldots\text{(i)}$$

Area of rectangle $ABED$ gives distance travelled in time t,

$$s_2 = (ft_1)t$$

Distance travelled in time t_2,

$$s_3 = \frac{1}{2} f(2t_1)^2$$

Thus, $s_1 + s_2 + s_3 = 15\ \text{s}$

$$\Rightarrow\ s + (ft_1)\,t + ft_1^2 = 15\ \text{s}$$

$$s + (ft_1)\,t + 2s = 15\ \text{s}\ \left(\because s = \frac{1}{2} ft_1^2\right)$$

$$(ft_1)\,t = 12\ \text{s} \quad \ldots\text{(ii)}$$

From Eqs. (i) and (ii), we have

$$\frac{12s}{s} = \frac{(ft_1)t}{\frac{1}{2}(ft_1)t_1}$$

$$\Rightarrow\ t_1 = \frac{t}{6}$$

From Eq. (i), we get

$$s = \frac{1}{2} f(t_1)^2 = \frac{1}{2} f\left(\frac{t}{6}\right)^2 = \frac{1}{72} ft^2$$

31 *(d)* The braking retardation will remain same and assumed to be constant, let it be a.

From the third equation of motion, $v^2 = u^2 + 2as$

***Case* I** When final velocity is zero and initial velocity is 60 km/h then

$$0 = \left(60 \times \frac{5}{18}\right)^2 - 2a \times s_1$$

$$\text{or}\ \ s_1 = \frac{(60 \times 5/18)^2}{2a}$$

***Case* II** Also, when initial velocity is 120 km/h then

$$0 = \left(120 \times \frac{5}{18}\right)^2 - 2a \times s_2$$

$$\text{or}\ \ s_2 = \frac{(120 \times 5/18)^2}{2a}$$

$$\therefore\ \frac{s_1}{s_2} = \frac{1}{4}$$

$$\Rightarrow\ s_2 = 4s_1 = 4 \times 20 = 80\ \text{m}$$

32 *(b)* Velocity of the particle is given as

$$v = At + Bt^2$$

where, A and B are constants.

$$\Rightarrow\ \frac{dx}{dt} = At + Bt^2 \quad \left[\because v = \frac{dx}{dt}\right]$$

$$\Rightarrow\ dx = (At + Bt^2)dt$$

Integrating both sides, we get

$$\int_{x_1}^{x_2} dx = \int_1^2 (At + Bt^2)dt$$

$$\Rightarrow\ \Delta x = x_2 - x_1$$

$$= A\int_1^2 t\,dt + B\int_1^2 t^2 dt$$

$$= A\left[\frac{t^2}{2}\right]_1^2 + B\left[\frac{t^3}{3}\right]_1^2$$

$$= \frac{A}{2}(2^2 - 1^2) + \frac{B}{3}(2^3 - 1^3)$$

$\therefore$ Distance travelled between 1s and 2s,

$$\Delta x = \frac{A}{2} \times (3) + \frac{B}{3}(7)$$

$$= \frac{3A}{2} + \frac{7B}{3}$$

33 *(c)* Given, $v_1 = 0$, $u_1 = 50\ \text{kmh}^{-1}$, $v_2 = 0$, $u_2 = 100\ \text{kmh}^{-1}$, $s_1 = 6$ m and $s_2 = ?$

We know that, $v_1^2 = u_1^2 + 2as_1$

$$0 = \left(50 \times \frac{5}{18}\right)^2 + 2a \times 6$$

$$\Rightarrow\ a = -16\ \text{ms}^{-2}$$

Again, $v_2^2 = u_2^2 + 2as_1$

$$0 = \left(100 \times \frac{5}{18}\right)^2 - 16 \times 2 \times s_2$$

$$\Rightarrow\ s_2 = \frac{(100 \times 5)^2}{18 \times 18 \times 32} \approx 24\ \text{m}$$

34 *(a)* Given, $g = 10\ \text{ms}^{-2}$, $h = 20$ m and $u = 0$

We have, $v = \sqrt{2gh}$

$$= \sqrt{2 \times 10 \times 20} = \sqrt{400}$$

$$= 20\ \text{ms}^{-1}$$

35 *(b)* The position x of a particle w.r.t. to time t along X-axis

$$x = 9t^2 - t^3 \quad \ldots\text{(i)}$$

Differentiating Eq. (i) w.r.t. time, we get

$$\text{Speed, } v = \frac{dx}{dt} = \frac{d}{dt}(9t^2 - t^3)$$

$$\Rightarrow\ v = 18t - 3t^2 \quad \ldots\text{(ii)}$$

Again differentiating Eq. (ii) w.r.t. time, we get

$$\text{Acceleration, } a = \frac{dv}{dt} = \frac{d}{dt}(18t - 3t^2)$$

$$\Rightarrow\ a = 18 - 6t \quad \ldots\text{(iii)}$$

Now, when speed of particle is maximum, its acceleration is zero.

$$a = 0\ \Rightarrow\ 18 - 6t = 0$$

$$\Rightarrow\ t = 3\ \text{s}$$

Putting in Eq. (i), we obtain position of particle at that time

$$x = 9(3)^2 - (3)^3 = 9(9) - 27$$

$$= 81 - 27 = 54\ \text{m}$$

36 *(b)* Displacement can be defined as the distance between initial and final positions of the ball. Since, the ball returns back to its initial position, then displacement is zero.

37 *(d)* Acceleration,

$$f = f_0\left(1 - \frac{t}{T}\right) \quad \left(\because f = \frac{dv}{dt}\right)$$

$$\Rightarrow\ dv = f_0\left(1 - \frac{t}{T}\right)dt \quad \ldots\text{(i)}$$

Integrating Eq. (i) on both sides, we get

$$\int dv = \int f_0\left(1 - \frac{t}{T}\right)dt$$

$$\Rightarrow \quad v = f_0 t - \frac{f_0}{T} \cdot \frac{t^2}{2} + C \quad \text{...(ii)}$$

where, C is constant of integration.

Now, when $t = 0$, $v = 0$, so, from Eq. (ii), we get

$$C = 0$$

$$\therefore \quad v = f_0 t - \frac{f_0}{T} \cdot \frac{t^2}{2} \quad \text{...(iii)}$$

As, $f = f_0\left(1 - \frac{t}{T}\right)$

When $f = 0, 0 = f_0\left(1 - \frac{t}{T}\right)$

As, $f_0 \neq 0$, so $1 - \frac{t}{T} = 0 \Rightarrow t = T$

Substituting $t = T$ in Eq. (iii), then,

$$\text{Velocity, } v_x = f_0 T - \frac{f_0}{T} \cdot \frac{T^2}{2}$$

$$= f_0 T - \frac{f_0 T}{2} = \frac{1}{2} f_0 T$$

38 *(c)* Time taken by ball to reach maximum height,

$$v = u - gT$$

At maximum height, final speed is zero, i.e. $v = 0$, so $u = gT$.

In 2s, $u = 2 \times 9.8 = 19.6 \text{ ms}^{-1}$

If a man throws the ball with velocity of 19.6 ms^{-1}, then after 2 s it will reach the maximum height. When he throws 2nd ball, 1st is at the top. When he throws third ball, 1st will come to ground and 2nd will go at the top. Therefore, only 2 balls are in air. If he wants to keep more than 2 balls in air he should throw the ball with a speed greater than 19.6 ms^{-1}.

39 *(d)* For free fall, from a height, $u = 0$ (initial velocity).

By second equation of motion,

$$h = ut + \frac{1}{2}gt^2 = 0 + \frac{1}{2}gt^2$$

$$\Rightarrow \quad \frac{h_1}{h_2} = \left(\frac{t_1}{t_2}\right)^2$$

Given, $h_1 = 16$ m, $h_2 = 25$ m

$$\therefore \quad \frac{t_1}{t_2} = \sqrt{\frac{h_1}{h_2}} = \sqrt{\frac{16}{25}} = \frac{4}{5}$$

40 *(c)* Let the velocity of the bullet when it strikes the target is v cm s^{-1}.

After penetrating 30 cm, velocity becomes half, i.e. $\frac{v}{2}$.

From equation, $v^2 = u^2 + 2as$

$$\therefore \quad \left(\frac{v}{2}\right)^2 = v^2 + 2a \times 30$$

$$\Rightarrow \quad -60a = v^2 - \frac{v^2}{4}$$

$$\Rightarrow \quad -60a = \frac{3v^2}{4}$$

$$\Rightarrow \quad a = -\frac{v^2}{80} \text{ cms}^{-2}$$

Let the bullet further penetrates s' cm before coming to rest, therefore

$$v'^2 = u'^2 + 2as'$$

$$\Rightarrow \quad 0 = \left(\frac{v}{2}\right)^2 + 2\left(-\frac{v^2}{80}\right)s'$$

$$\Rightarrow \quad \frac{v^2 s'}{40} = \frac{v'}{4} \Rightarrow s' = 10 \text{ cm}$$

41 *(a)* Let, initial velocity = u and acceleration = a

In Ist case, $s_1 = ut_1 + \frac{1}{2}at_1^2$

$$200 = 2u + 2a$$

$$(\because t_1 = 2\text{s and } s_1 = 200 \text{ m})$$

$$u + a = 100 \quad \text{...(i)}$$

In IInd case, $s_2 = ut_2 + \frac{1}{2}at_2^2$

$$420 = 6u + 18a$$

$$(\because t_2 = 2 + 4 = 6 \text{ s and } s_2 = 220 \text{ m})$$

$$3a + u = 70 \quad \text{...(ii)}$$

Solving Eqs. (i) and (ii), we get

$$a = -15 \text{ ms}^{-2} \text{ and } u = 115 \text{ ms}^{-1}$$

$$\therefore \quad v = u + at = 115 - 15 \times 7 = 10 \text{ ms}^{-1}$$

42 *(c)* According to the question,

$$\frac{dv}{dt} = bt \Rightarrow dv = bt\,dt$$

$$\Rightarrow \quad v = \frac{bt^2}{2} + k_1$$

At $t = 0$, $v = v_0 \Rightarrow k_1 = v_0$

We get $v = \frac{1}{2}bt^2 + v_0$

Now, $\frac{dx}{dt} = \frac{1}{2}bt^2 + v_0$

$$\Rightarrow \quad x = \frac{1}{2}\frac{bt^3}{3} + v_0 t + k_2$$

At $t = 0, x = 0 \Rightarrow k_2 = 0$

$$\Rightarrow \quad x = \frac{1}{6}bt^3 + v_0 t$$

43 *(b)* From first equation of motion,

$$v = u + at$$

Given $u = 4 \text{ ms}^{-1}$, $v = 0$ and $t = 0.1$ s

So, $0 = 4 + a \times (0.1)$

$$a = -40 \text{ms}^{-2}$$

and $v^2 = u^2 + 2as$

$$(0)^2 = (4)^2 + 2(-40)s$$

$$0 = 16 - 80s$$

$$s = \frac{16}{80} \text{ or } s = 0.2 \text{m}$$

44 *(c)* By equation of motion, we have

$$s = ut + \frac{1}{2}at^2$$

where, s is displacement, u is initial velocity, a is acceleration and t is time.

Given, $s_1 = 24$ m, $s_2 = 64$ m and $t = 4$ s

We have, $24 = 4u + \frac{1}{2}a(4)^2$

$$\Rightarrow \quad 24 = 4u + 8a$$

$$\Rightarrow \quad 6 = u + 2a \quad \text{...(i)}$$

When body travels a total distance of $24 + 64 = 88$ m in 8 s, we get

$$88 = 8u + \frac{1}{2}a(8)^2 \Rightarrow 88 = 8u + 32a$$

$$\Rightarrow \quad 11 = u + 4a \quad \text{...(ii)}$$

On solving Eqs. (i) and (ii), we get

$$u = 1 \text{ ms}^{-1}$$

45 *(b)* Given, $s = 6t^2 - t^3$

$$\text{Velocity, } v = \frac{ds}{dt} = 12t - 3t^2$$

If velocity is zero, then

$$0 = 12t - 3t^2$$

$$\Rightarrow \quad t = 4 \text{s}$$

46 *(c)* Using the relation, $s = ut + \frac{1}{2}gt^2$

As the body is falling from rest, $u = 0$

$$s = \frac{1}{2}gt^2$$

Suppose the distance travelled in $t = 2$ s, $t = 4$ s, $t = 6$ s are s_2, s_4 and s_6, respectively.

Now, $s_2 = \frac{1}{2}g(2)^2 = 2g$

$$\Rightarrow \quad s_4 = \frac{1}{2}g(4)^2 = 8g$$

$$s_6 = \frac{1}{2}g(6)^2 = 18g$$

Hence, the distance travelled in first two seconds,

$$(s_i)_2 = s_2 - s_0 = 2g$$

$$(s_m)_2 = s_4 - s_2 = 8g - 2g = 6g$$

$$(s_f)_2 = s_6 - s_4 = 18g - 8g = 10g$$

Now, the ratios becomes

$$= 2g : 6g : 10g = 1 : 3 : 5$$

47 *(b)* Taking downward motion of the first stone from A to ground, we have

$$h = -ut_1 + \frac{1}{2}gt_1^2 \quad \text{...(i)}$$

Taking downward motion of second stone from A to ground, we have

$$h = ut_2 + \frac{1}{2}gt_2^2 \quad \dots(ii)$$

Third stone $h = \frac{1}{2}gt_3^2 \quad \dots(iii)$

Multiplying Eq. (i) by t_2 and Eq. (ii) by t_1 and adding, we get

$$h(t_1 + t_2) = \frac{1}{2}gt_1t_2(t_1 + t_2)$$

$$\Rightarrow \quad h = \frac{1}{2}gt_1t_2 \quad \dots(iv)$$

From Eqs. (iii) and (iv), we get

$$t_3^2 = t_1t_2$$

or $t_3 = \sqrt{t_1t_2}$

$= \sqrt{9 \times 4}$ (given)

$= 6$ s

48 *(d)* Since, the ball is thrown upwards and it reaches back, so time to reach maximum height is half of total time, i.e. $t_{max} = 2$ s.

Also, speed at maximum height is zero, so

$$0 = u - gt_{max} \quad (\because v = 0)$$

$$\Rightarrow \quad u = gt_{max} = 10 \times 2 = 20 \text{ ms}^{-1}$$

$(\because g = 10 \text{ ms}^{-1})$

49 *(a)* For first ball, $h = 0 \times t_1 + \frac{1}{2}gt_1^2$

$$\Rightarrow \quad t_1 = \sqrt{\frac{2h}{g}} \quad \dots(i)$$

For second ball, $2h = 0 \times t_2 - \frac{1}{2}gt_2^2$

$$\Rightarrow \quad t_2 = \sqrt{\frac{4h}{g}} \quad \dots(ii)$$

From Eqs. (i) and (ii), we get

$$t_1 : t_2 = 1 : \sqrt{2}$$

50 *(b)* By equation of motion, we have

$$s = ut + \frac{1}{2}at^2$$

where, u is initial velocity, t is time, a is acceleration.

Since, car accelerates from rest $u = 0$, $t = 10$ s

$$\therefore \quad s = 0 + \frac{1}{2} \times a \times (10)^2 = 50a \quad \dots(i)$$

$$\Rightarrow a = \frac{s}{50}$$

Also, $v = u + at$

where, v is final velocity.

$\therefore$ Velocity after 10 s is

$$v = 0 + a \times 10$$

$$\Rightarrow \quad v = 10a = 10 \times \frac{s}{50} \quad \dots(ii)$$

In next 10 s, car moves with constant acceleration and with initial velocity.

$$\therefore s' = vt + \frac{1}{2}at^2$$

$$= \frac{s}{50} \times 10 \times 10 + \frac{1}{2} \times \frac{s}{50} \times 100 = 3s$$

Given, $s = x$ and $s' = y$

$\therefore \quad y = 3x$

51 *(a)* At time t, velocity of particle is $v_t = 10 \text{ ms}^{-1}$, $v_{t+3} = 16 \text{ ms}^{-1}$ and $v_{t-2} = v_x$

From equation of motion,

$$v = u + at$$

$$\Rightarrow \quad v_t = 0 + at$$

$$\Rightarrow \quad t = \left(\frac{10}{a}\right) \quad \dots(i)$$

$$\Rightarrow \quad v_{t+3} = u + a(t+3)$$

$$\Rightarrow \quad 16 = 0 + \left(\frac{10}{a} + 3\right)a = 3a + 10$$

$$\Rightarrow \quad a = 2 \text{ ms}^{-2}$$

and $t = 5$ s [from Eq. (i)]

Now, $v_{t-2} = u + a(t-2) = 2(t-2)$

$$\Rightarrow \quad v_x = v_{t-2} = 6 \text{ ms}^{-1}$$

52 *(b)* The projectile of the body is shown in the figure. In the upward journey, the body is at A at $t = 1$ s and in downward journey it is at A at $t = 7$ s.

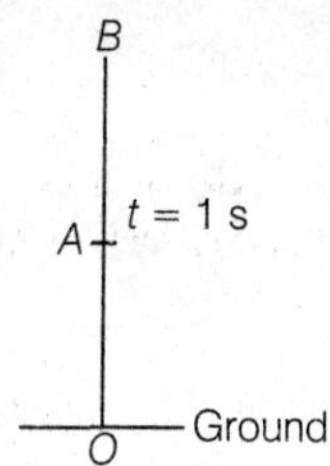

Hence, we can conclude that during upward journey, the body will be at B at $t = 4$ s.

Thus, $v = u - gt$

$$0 = u - 10 \times 4 \quad (\because v = 0)$$

$$\Rightarrow \quad u = 40 \text{ ms}^{-1}$$

53 *(d)* Given, $v = 108 \text{ kmh}^{-1} = 30 \text{ ms}^{-1}$ and $t = 5$ s

From first equation of motion,

$$v = u + at$$

$$\Rightarrow \quad 30 = 0 + a \times 5 \quad (\because u = 0)$$

$$\Rightarrow \quad a = 6 \text{ ms}^{-2}$$

So, distance travelled by metro train in 5 s,

$$s_1 = \frac{1}{2}at^2$$

$$= \frac{1}{2} \times (6) \times (5)^2 = 75 \text{ m}$$

Distance travelled before coming to rest $= 45$ m

So, from third equation of motion,

$$0^2 = (30)^2 - 2a' \times 45\, a'$$

$$a' = \frac{30 \times 30}{2 \times 45} = 10 \text{ ms}^{-2}$$

Time taken in travelling 45 m,

$$t_3 = \frac{30}{10} = 3 \text{ s}$$

Now, total distance $= 395$ m

i.e. $75 + s' + 45 = 395$ m

$$\Rightarrow \quad s' = 395 - (75 + 45) = 275 \text{ m}$$

$$\therefore \quad t_2 = \frac{275}{30} = 9.2 \text{ s}$$

Hence, total time taken in whole journey

$$= t_1 + t_2 + t_3$$

$$= 5 + 9.2 + 3 = 17.2 \text{ s}$$

54 *(a)* We know that,

$$v = \frac{ds}{dt}$$

Here, $s = 8t^3 = -7t^2 + 5t$

$$\Rightarrow v = \frac{ds}{dt} = 24t^2 - 14t + 5$$

$\because$ At $t = 2$ s,

$$v = 24(2)^2 - 14(2) + 5 = 76 \text{ms}^{-1}$$

55 *(d)* Given, $x = ae^{-\alpha t} + be^{\beta t}$

So, velocity, $v = \frac{dx}{dt} = -a\alpha e^{-\alpha t} + b\beta e^{\beta t}$

$$= A + B$$

where, $A = -a\alpha e^{-\alpha t}$ and $B = b\beta e^{\beta t}$.

The value of term $A = -a\alpha e^{-\alpha t}$ decreases and of term $B = b\beta e^{\beta t}$ increases with increase in time. As a result, velocity goes on increasing with time.

56 *(a)* As, $v^2 = u^2 - 2gh \Rightarrow u^2 \propto h$

Hecne, $\frac{u_1}{u_2} = \sqrt{\frac{h_1}{h_2}}$

$$\Rightarrow \quad \frac{v_0}{u_2} = \sqrt{\frac{h}{3h}} \quad \text{(given)}$$

$$\Rightarrow \quad u_2 = \sqrt{3}v_0$$

57 *(b)* Given, $u = 0$, $v = 72 \text{ kmh}^{-1} = 20 \text{ ms}^{-1}$ and $t = 10$ s

The first equation of motion,

$$v = u + at$$

$\Rightarrow \quad 20 = 0 + a \times 10$

$\Rightarrow \quad a = 2 \text{ ms}^{-2}$

The second equation of motion,

$$s = ut + \frac{1}{2}at^2$$

$$= 0 \times 10 + \frac{1}{2} \times 2 \times (10)^2$$

$$= 100 \text{ m}$$

58 *(a)* Given, initial velocity, $u = 200 \text{ ms}^{-1}$, final velocity, $v = 100 \text{ ms}^{-1}$ and distance, $s = 10 \text{ cm} = 0.1 \text{ m}$

Using the relation of equation of motion,

$$v^2 = u^2 + 2as$$

$$\Rightarrow a = \frac{v^2 - u^2}{2s} = \frac{(100)^2 - (200)^2}{2 \times 0.1}$$

$$= \frac{10000 - 40000}{2 \times 0.1}$$

$$= \frac{-300000}{2}$$

$\Rightarrow \quad a = -150000 \text{ ms}^{-2}$

$\Rightarrow \quad a \simeq 15 \times 10^4 \text{ ms}^{-2}$

The minus (negative) sign denotes retardation.

59 *(c)* In order that the man catches the bus, let his minimum velocity be v, then from equation of motion

$$v^2 = u^2 + 2as$$

We have $u = 0$ (initial velocity),

$$a = 2.5 \text{ ms}^{-2}$$

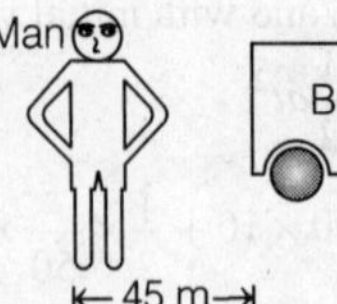

Given, $s = 45$ m

$\therefore \quad v^2 = 2 \times 2.5 \times 45$

$\Rightarrow \quad v = \sqrt{225} = 15 \text{ ms}^{-1}$

60 *(b)* Rate of change of displacement is velocity $\left(v = \frac{dx}{dt}\right)$.

Given, $x = 4(t-2) + a(t-2)^2$

Using, $\frac{d}{dx}x^n = nx^{n-1}$

We have, $v = \frac{dx}{dt} = 4 + 2a(t-2)$

At $t = 0$, $v = 4(1 - a)$

Acceleration, $a' = \frac{d^2x}{dt^2} = 2a$

61 *(c)*

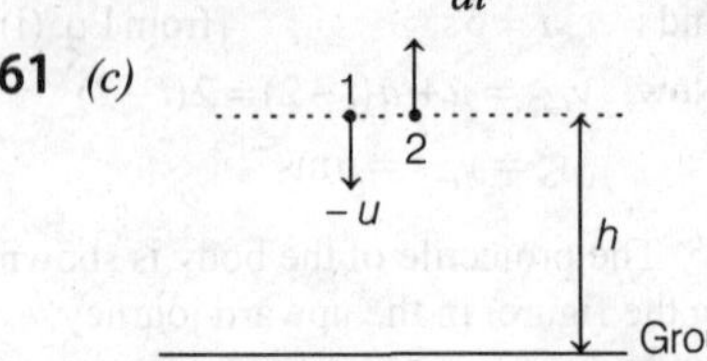

Applying equation of motion for both particles 1 and 2

For particle 1, $v^2 = u^2 + 2as$

$\Rightarrow \quad v_1^2 = (-u)^2 - 2gh$

$v_1^2 = u^2 - 2gh$ ...(i)

For particle 2, $v_2^2 = u^2 - 2gh$ ...(ii)

Hence, $v_1 = v_2$

Both the stones will have same speed when they hit the ground.

62 *(d)* Given, $y = 3 + 5t + 7t^2$

Velocity v is defined as the rate of change of displacement, also using $\frac{d}{dx}x^n = nx^{n-1}$, we have

$$v = \frac{dy}{dt} = 5 + 14t$$

Initial velocity at $t = 0$ is

$$v = 5 \text{ ms}^{-1}$$

Also, acceleration, $a = \frac{d^2y}{dt^2} = 14 \text{ ms}^{-2}$

63 *(b)* Acceleration, $a = \frac{\Delta v}{\Delta t} = \frac{v_2 - v_1}{\Delta t}$

Given, $v_1 = 10 \text{ ms}^{-1}$, $v_2 = 25 \text{ ms}^{-1}$

and $\Delta t = 5$ s

$\therefore \quad a = \frac{25 - 10}{5} = 3 \text{ ms}^{-2}$

in North direction.

Topic 3
Graphs in Motion

2017

1 What will be the a versus x graph for the following graph?

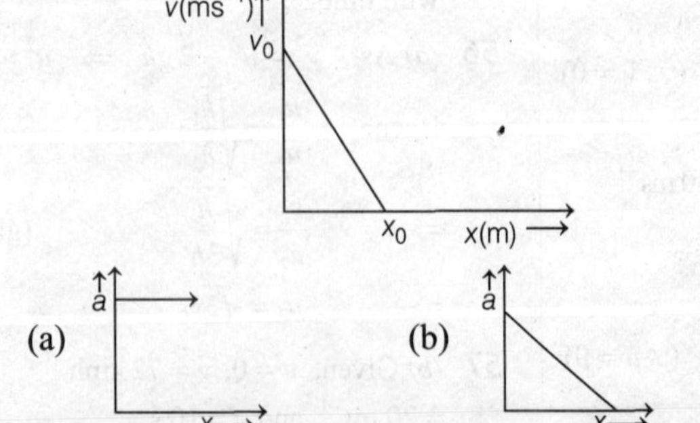

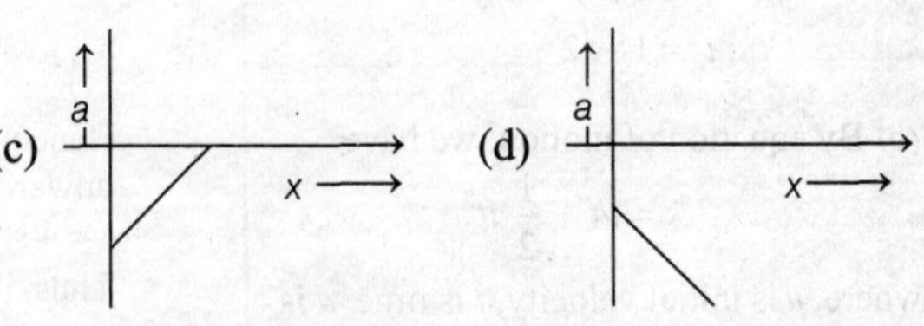

[AIIMS]

2014

2 The acceleration of a moving body is found from the **[Kerala CEE]**

(a) area under velocity - time graph

(b) area under displacement - time graph

(c) slope of distance - time graph

(d) slope of velocity - time graph

(e) area under acceleration - time graph

2013

3 If the figure below represents a parabola, identify the physical quantities representing Y and X for constant acceleration. **[KCET]**

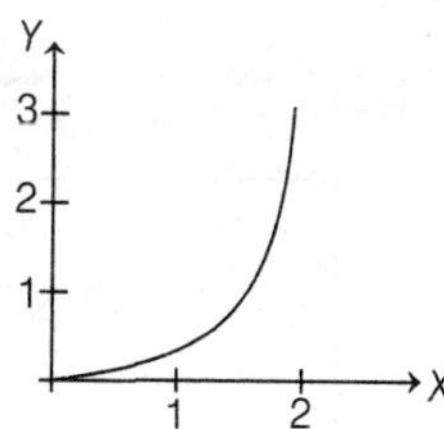

(a) $X =$ time, $Y =$ velocity
(b) $X =$ velocity, $Y =$ time
(c) $X =$ time, $Y =$ displacement
(d) $X =$ time, $Y =$ acceleration
(e) $X =$ velocity, $Y =$ displacement

4 The speed-time graph of a particle moving along a solid curve is shown below. The distance traversed by the particle from $t = 0$ s to $t = 3$ s is **[DUMET]**

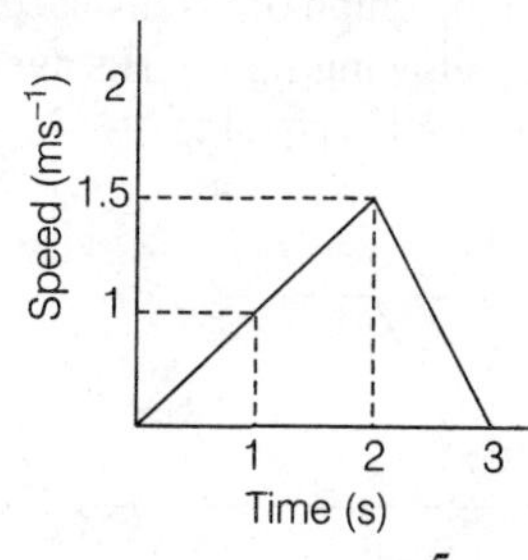

(a) 5 m (b) $\frac{5}{2}$ m
(c) $\frac{10}{3}$ m (d) 2 m

5 The displacement-time graph of two moving particles make angles of 30° and 45° with the X-axis. The ratio of their velocities is **[KCET]**

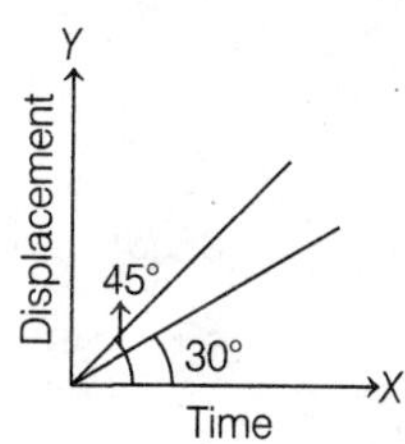

(a) $\sqrt{3}:2$ (b) $1:1$
(c) $1:2$ (d) $1:\sqrt{3}$

2010

6 Which of the following graphs cannot possibly represent one-dimensional motion of a particle? **[AMU]**

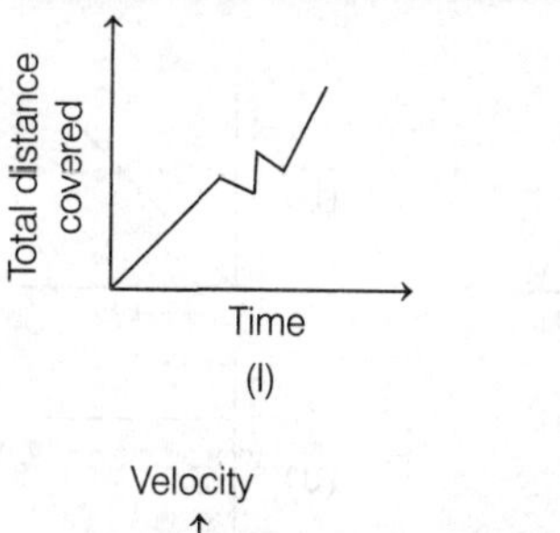

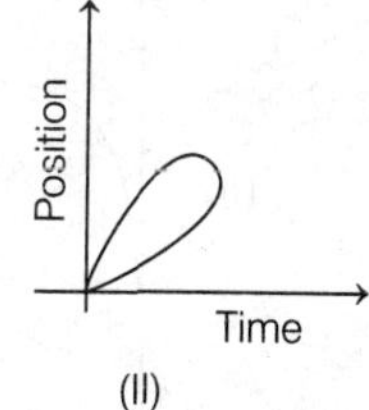

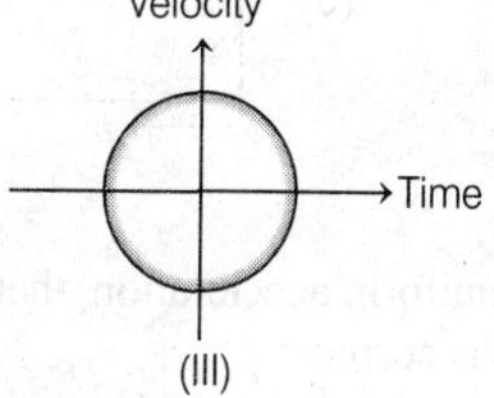

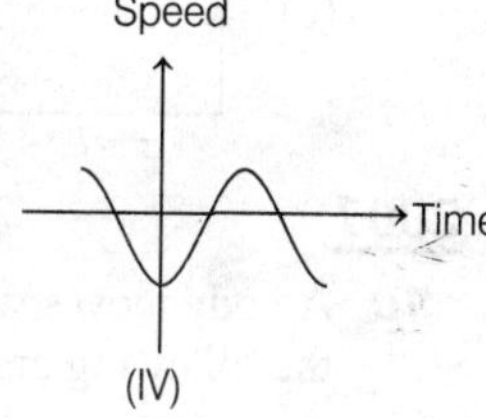

(a) I and II (b) II and III
(c) II and IV (d) All of these

2009

7 Figs. (I) and (II) show the displacement-time graphs of two particles moving along the X-axis. We can say that **[UP CPMT, Punjab PMET]**

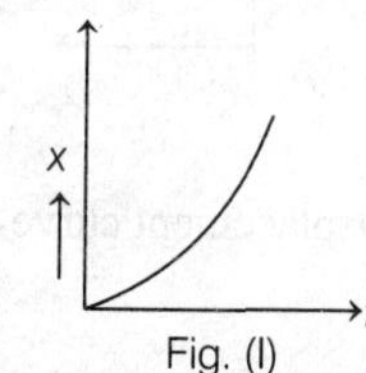

Fig. (I)

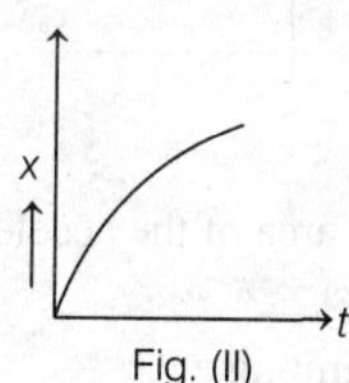

Fig. (II)

(a) both the particles are having an uniformly accelerated motion
(b) both the particles are having an uniformly retarded motion
(c) particle (I) is having an uniformly accelerated motion while particle (II) is having an uniformly retarded motion
(d) particle (I) is having an uniformly retarded motion while particle (II) is having an uniformly accelerated motion

8 Area under the velocity-time curve over a given interval of time represents **[Kerala CEE]**

(a) acceleration (b) momentum
(c) velocity (d) displacement
(e) kinetic energy

2008

9 A body starts from rest and moves with uniform acceleration. Which of the following graphs represent its motion? **[J&K CET]**

(a) 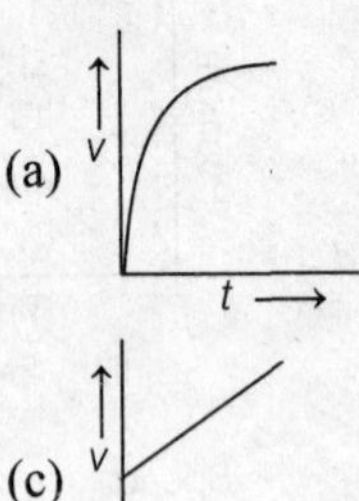

(b) 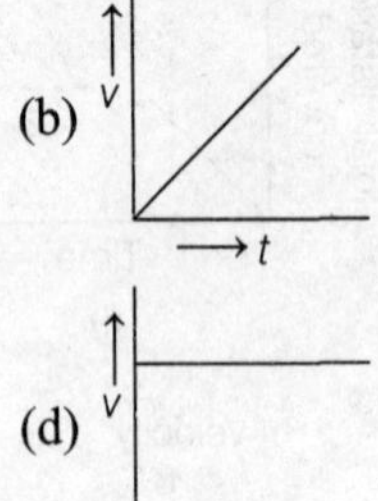

(c) 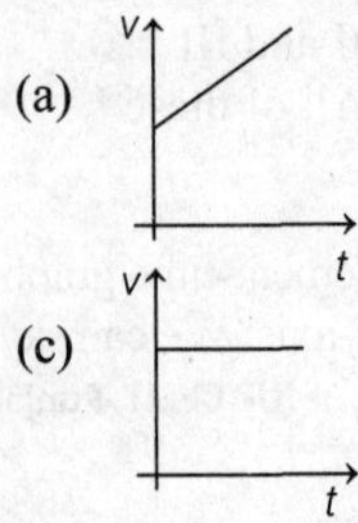

(d) 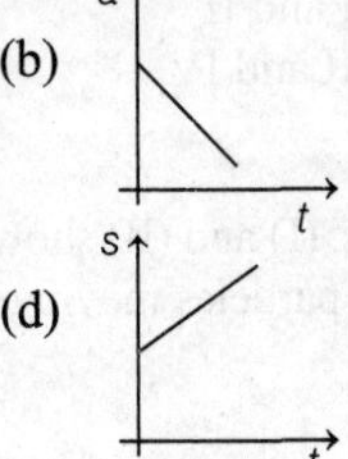

2007

10 A body moves with uniform acceleration, then which of the following graphs is correct? **[DUMET]**

(a) v–t graph (b) a–t graph (c) v–t graph (d) s–t graph

2006

11 The area of the acceleration-displacement curve of a body gives **[AFMC]**

(a) impulse
(b) change in momentum per unit mass
(c) change in kinetic energy per unit mass
(d) total change in energy

12 Consider the given velocity-time graph. It represents the motion of **[Kerala CEE]**

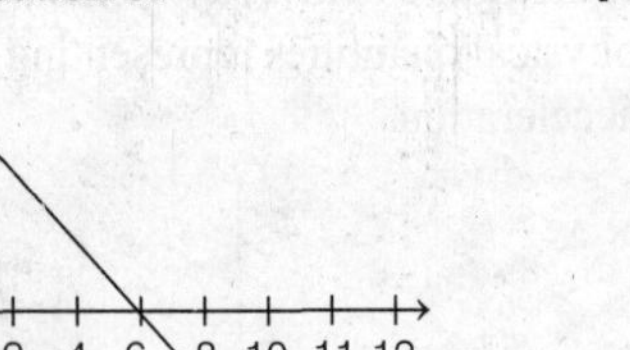

(a) a projectile projected vertically upward, from a point
(b) an electron in the hydrogen atom
(c) a car with constant acceleration along a straight road
(d) a bullet fired horizontally from the top of a tower
(e) an object in the positive direction with decreasing speed

13 A boy begins to walk eastward along a street in front of his house and the graph of his displacement from home is shown in the following figure. His average speed for the whole time interval is equal to **[BHU]**

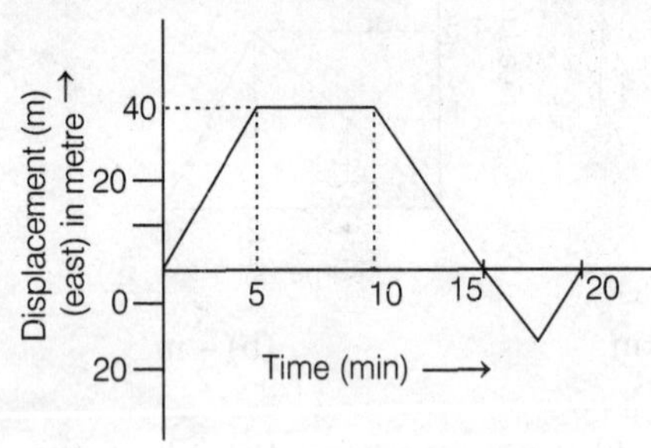

(a) 8 m min^{-1} (b) 6 m min^{-1}
(c) $\frac{8}{3} \text{ m min}^{-1}$ (d) 2 m min^{-1}

Answers

1 (c)	2 (d)	3 (c)	4 (b)	5 (d)	6 (d)	7 (c)	8 (d)	9 (b)	10 (a)
11 (c)	12 (a)	13 (b)							

Explanations

1 *(c)* Equation of given line, ~when velocity is plotted against position with intercept.

Here, slope $= -v_0/x_0$,

$$v = -\frac{v_0 x}{x_0} + v_0 \quad \dots \text{(i)}$$

(–ve, the sign signifies that the slope is decreasing)

On differentiating with respect to t,

$$\frac{dv}{dt} = -\frac{v_0}{x_0}\frac{dx}{dt} + 0$$

or $$a = -\frac{v_0}{x_0} v \quad \dots \text{(ii)}$$

Putting value of v from Eq. (i) in Eq. (ii), we get

$$a = -\frac{v_0}{x_0}\left[-\frac{v_0}{x_0}x + v_0\right]$$

$$= \frac{v_0^2}{x_0^2}x - \frac{v_0^2}{x_0}$$

This equation shows at $x = 0$,

$a = -\frac{v_0^2}{x_0}$ = constant and at $a = 0$, $x = x_0$.

So, option (c) is correct.

2 (d) The acceleration of a moving body is found from the slope of velocity-time graph.

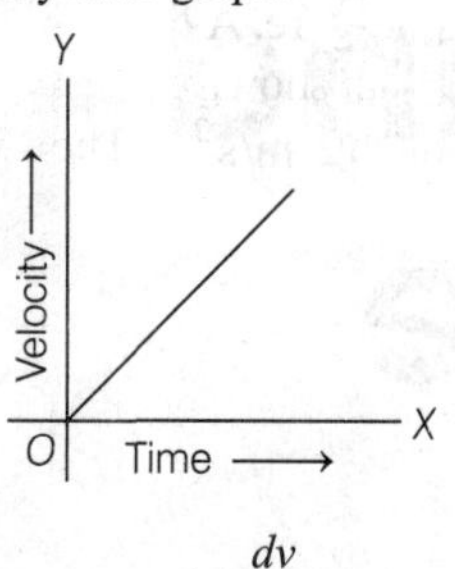

$$a = \frac{dv}{dt}$$

= slope of v-t curve

3 (c) Since, body has uniform acceleration, so velocity of particle is increasing with time.

Hence, this is displacement-time graph with X as time axis and Y as displacement axis.

$\because \; s = ut + \frac{1}{2}at^2 \qquad (\because u = 0)$

$$s = \frac{at^2}{2}$$

$\Rightarrow s \propto t^2$ (parabola)

(given, a = constant)

4 (b)

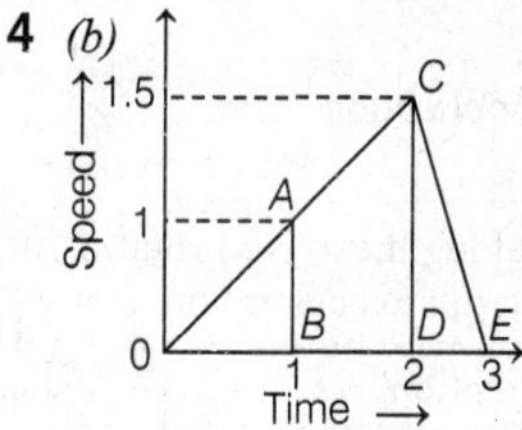

Distance travelled by the particle,

s = Area under the curve

$= s_{01} + s_{12} + s_{23}$

s = Area of ΔOAB

+ Area of trapezium $ABCD$

+ Area of ΔDCE

$= \frac{1}{2} \times OB \times AB + \frac{1}{2}(AB + CD) \times BD + \frac{1}{2} \times DE \times DC$

$= \frac{1}{2} \times (1-0) \times 1 + \frac{1}{2} \times (1+1.5) \times (2-1) + \frac{1}{2} \times (3-2) \times 1.5$

$= \frac{1}{2} + \frac{1}{2} \times 2.5 + \frac{1}{2} \times 1.5$

[$\because$ area of triangle $= \frac{1}{2} \times$ base $\times$ height

and area of trapezium $= \frac{1}{2} \times$ (sum of parallel sides) $\times$ height]

$= \frac{1}{2}(1 + 2.5 + 1.5) = \frac{1}{2} \times 5 = \frac{5}{2}$ m

5 (d) By the definition, the slope of displacement-time graph is velocity.

i.e. $\qquad v = \tan\theta$

$\therefore \quad \frac{v_1}{v_2} = \frac{\tan\theta_1}{\tan\theta_2} = \frac{\tan 30°}{\tan 45°} \Rightarrow \frac{v_1}{v_2} = \frac{1}{\sqrt{3}}$

6 (d) Graph (I) does not represent the one-dimensional motion, because total distance covered by a particle always increases with time.

Graph (II) and Graph (III) do not represent the one-dimensional motion, because at a particular time, there cannot be two values of position or velocity.

Graph (IV) is not possible, because speed can never be negative.

7 (c) Slope of x-t [i.e. displacement-time] curve gives acceleration.

Hence, for curve I, slope of curve is positive.

$\therefore$ Slope of curve $= \frac{d^2x}{dt^2} = \frac{dv}{dt}$ = positive

$\Rightarrow$ It represents uniformly accelerated motion.

For curve II, slope of curve is negative.

$\therefore$ Slope of curve $= \frac{d^2x}{dt^2} = \frac{dv}{dt}$ = negative

$\Rightarrow$ It represents uniformly retarded motion.

8 (d) Area under a v-t [i.e. velocity-time] curve represent displacement.

9 (b) We know that, acceleration,

$$a = \frac{dv}{dt}$$

As, $\quad a$ = constant

Then, $\frac{dv}{dt}$ = constant

$\Rightarrow \qquad v = kt$

This equation shows a straight line passing through origin.

10 (a) An object is said to be moving with a uniform acceleration, if its velocity changes by equal amounts in equal intervals of time.

The velocity-time graph of uniformly accelerated motion is a straight line inclined to time axis. Acceleration of an object in a uniformly accelerated motion in one-dimension is equal to the slope of the velocity-time graph with time axis.

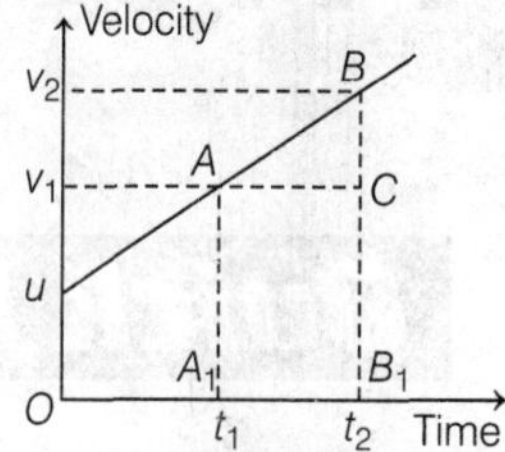

11 (c) Area of acceleration-displacement curve gives change in kinetic energy per unit mass.

$$\frac{1}{2}m(v^2 - u^2) = Fs = \frac{mdv}{dt} \times s$$

$$\therefore \quad \frac{\text{Change in kinetic energy}}{\text{Mass}} = \frac{dv}{dt} \times s$$

12 (a) In this graph, a particle has some positive non-zero velocity $(+v_0)$ at $t = 0$, after that it decrease continuously to zero and then negative. So such variation only matches with option (a). No such behaviour of v-t graph seen in other options.

13 (b) Given,

Distance from 0 to 5s = 40 m

Distance from 5 to 10s = 0

Distance from 10 to 15 s = 60 m

Distance from 15 to 20 s = 20 m

So, net distance = 40 + 0 + 60 + 20

= 120 m

Total time taken = 20 min

Hence, average speed

$= \frac{\text{Distance (m)}}{\text{Time (min)}}$

$= \frac{120}{20} = 6 \text{ m min}^{-1}$

03

Vector Analysis and Motion in a Plane

Quick Review

Scalar

These are the physical quantities which have only magnitude but no direction. It is specified completely by a single number, along with the proper unit. e.g. Temperature, mass, length, time, work, etc.

Vector

These are the physical quantities which have both magnitudes and directions. It is specified by giving its magnitude by a number and its direction. e.g. Displacement, acceleration, velocity, etc

Different Types of Vectors

S.No.	Types of Vectors	Description
(i)	**Polar vectors**	These are the vectors which have a starting point or a point of application. e.g. Displacement, force, etc.
(ii)	**Axial vectors**	These are the vectors which represent rotational effect and act along the axis of rotation in accordance with right hand screw rule. e.g. Angular velocity, angular acceleration, etc.
(iii)	**Equal vectors**	These are the vectors which have equal magnitude and same direction.
(iv)	**Parallel vectors**	These are the vectors which have same direction and magnitude may equal or different.
(v)	**Anti-parallel vectors**	These are the vectors which have opposite direction and magnitude may equal or different.
(vi)	**Collinear vectors**	These are the vectors which act along same line, i.e. vectors lying in the same line. Angle between them can be zero or 180°.
(vii)	**Zero vector**	A vector having zero magnitude is known as zero vector. Its direction is not specified and hence it is arbitrary. It is represented by **0**.
(viii)	**Unit vector**	A vector whose magnitude is unit and points in a particular directions is called unit vector. It is represented by $\hat{\mathbf{A}}$ (*A* cap or *A* hat). The unit vector along the direction of **A** is $\hat{\mathbf{A}} = \dfrac{\mathbf{A}}{\lvert\mathbf{A}\rvert}$, $\therefore$ $\mathbf{A} = \hat{\mathbf{A}}\,\lvert\mathbf{A}\rvert$, where $\mathbf{A} = A_x\hat{\mathbf{i}} + A_y\,\hat{\mathbf{j}} + A_z\hat{\mathbf{k}}$ and $\lvert\mathbf{A}\rvert = \sqrt{A_x^2 + A_y^2 + A_z^2}$.
(ix)	**Coplanar vectors**	These are the vectors which always lie in the same plane.
(x)	**Negative vector**	If the direction of a vector is reversed, the sign of the vector is reversed. It is called negative vector of the original vector.

Addition of Vectors

Vectors can be added by following two methods

1. Triangle Law of Vectors Addition

If two vectors acting at a point are represented in magnitude and direction by the two sides of a triangle taken in one order, then their resultant is represented by the third side of the triangle taken in the opposite order.

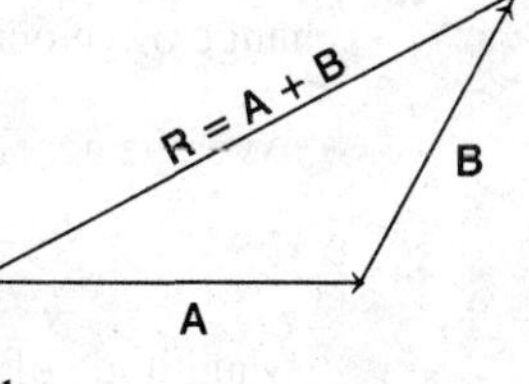

2. Parallelogram Law of Vectors Addition

If two vectors acting at a point are represented in magnitude and direction by the two adjacent sides of a parallelogram draw from a point, then their resultant is represented in magnitude and direction by the diagonal of the parallelogram drawn from the same point.

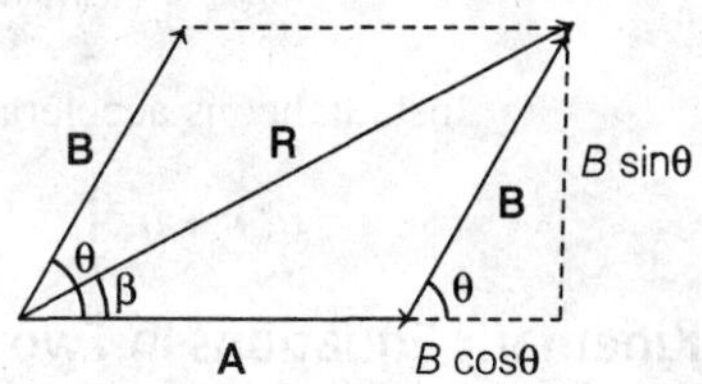

Resultant of vectors **A** and **B** is given by

$$R = \sqrt{A^2 + B^2 + 2AB\cos\theta}$$

If the resultant vector **R** subtends an angle β with vector **A**, then

$$\tan\beta = \frac{B\sin\theta}{A + B\cos\theta}$$

Resolution of a Vector into Rectangular Components

- If any vector **A** subtends an angle θ with *X*-axis, then its
  horizontal component, $A_x = A\cos\theta$
  vertical component, $A_y = A\sin\theta$
  magnitude of vector, $A = \sqrt{A_x^2 + A_y^2}$

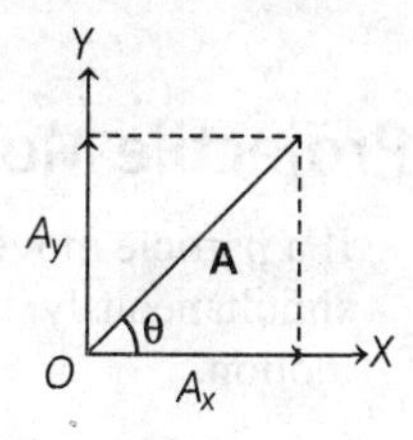

$$\tan\theta = \frac{A_y}{A_x}$$

$$\Rightarrow \quad \text{Angle, } \theta = \tan^{-1}\left(\frac{A_y}{A_x}\right)$$

- **In case of three-dimensional space**
  Magnitude of vector $\mathbf{A} = \sqrt{A_x^2 + A_y^2 + A_z^2}$
  This vector **A**, makes an angle of

$$\alpha = \cos^{-1}\left(\frac{A_x}{A}\right) \text{ with } X\text{-axis}$$

$$\beta = \cos^{-1}\left(\frac{A_y}{A}\right) \text{ with } Y\text{-axis}$$

$$\gamma = \cos^{-1}\left(\frac{A_z}{A}\right) \text{ with } Z\text{-axis}$$

Subtraction of Vectors

Subtraction of a vector **B** from a vector **A** is defined as the addition of vector −**B** (negative of vector **B**) to vector **A**.

Thus, $\mathbf{A} + (-\mathbf{B}) = \mathbf{A} - \mathbf{B}$

Multiplication of a Vector

(*i*) **By a Real Number** When a vector **A** is multiplied by a real number *n*, then its magnitude becomes *n* times but direction and unit remains unchanged.

(*ii*) **By a Scalar** When a vector **A** is multiplied by a scalar *S*, then its magnitude becomes *S* times and unit is the product of units of **A** and *S* but direction remains same as that of vector **A**.

Scalar or Dot Product of Two Vectors

The scalar product of two vectors is equal to the product of their magnitudes and the cosine of the smaller angle between them.

$$\mathbf{A}\cdot\mathbf{B} = AB\cos\theta$$

- Scalar product of orthogonal unit vectors

$$\hat{\mathbf{i}}\cdot\hat{\mathbf{i}} = \hat{\mathbf{j}}\cdot\hat{\mathbf{j}} = \hat{\mathbf{k}}\cdot\hat{\mathbf{k}} = 1$$

and $$\hat{\mathbf{i}}\cdot\hat{\mathbf{j}} = \hat{\mathbf{j}}\cdot\hat{\mathbf{k}} = \hat{\mathbf{k}}\cdot\hat{\mathbf{i}} = 0$$

- Scalar product in cartesian coordinates

$$\mathbf{A}\cdot\mathbf{B} = (A_x\hat{\mathbf{i}} + A_y\hat{\mathbf{j}} + A_z\hat{\mathbf{k}})\cdot(B_x\hat{\mathbf{i}} + B_y\hat{\mathbf{j}} + B_z\hat{\mathbf{k}})$$
$$= A_xB_x + A_yB_y + A_zB_z$$

Vector or Cross Product of Two Vectors

The vector product of two vectors is equal to the product of their magnitudes and the sine of the smaller angle between them.

$$\mathbf{A}\times\mathbf{B} = AB\sin\theta\,\hat{\mathbf{n}}$$

- Vector product of orthogonal unit vectors

$$\hat{\mathbf{i}}\times\hat{\mathbf{i}} = \hat{\mathbf{j}}\times\hat{\mathbf{j}} = \hat{\mathbf{k}}\times\hat{\mathbf{k}} = 0$$
$$\hat{\mathbf{i}}\times\hat{\mathbf{j}} = -\hat{\mathbf{j}}\times\hat{\mathbf{i}} = \hat{\mathbf{k}},\ \hat{\mathbf{j}}\times\hat{\mathbf{k}} = -\hat{\mathbf{k}}\times\hat{\mathbf{j}} = \hat{\mathbf{i}}$$

and $$\hat{\mathbf{k}}\times\hat{\mathbf{i}} = -\hat{\mathbf{i}}\times\hat{\mathbf{k}} = \hat{\mathbf{j}}.$$

- Vector product in cartesian coordinates

$$\mathbf{A}\times\mathbf{B} = (A_x\hat{\mathbf{i}} + A_y\hat{\mathbf{j}} + A_z\hat{\mathbf{k}})\times(B_x\hat{\mathbf{i}} + B_y\hat{\mathbf{j}} + B_z\hat{\mathbf{k}})$$

$$= \begin{vmatrix} \hat{\mathbf{i}} & \hat{\mathbf{j}} & \hat{\mathbf{k}} \\ A_x & A_y & A_z \\ B_x & B_y & B_z \end{vmatrix}$$

$$= (A_yB_z - A_zB_y)\hat{\mathbf{i}} - (A_xB_z - B_xA_z)\hat{\mathbf{j}} + (A_xB_y - A_yB_x)\hat{\mathbf{k}}$$

Division of Vectors by Scalars

The division of vector **A** by a non-zero scalar m is defined as the multiplication of **A** by $1/m$. In this, the unit of resultant vector is the division of unit **A** and m.

Motion in a Plane

Motion in plane is called as motion in two-dimensions, e.g. projectile motion and circular motion. For the analysis of such motion our reference will be made of an origin and two coordinate axes X and Y.

Terms Related to Motion in a Plane

Few terms related to motion in a plane are given below

(i) **Position Vector** A vector that extends from a reference point to the point at which particle is located is called position vector.

Position vector is given by $\mathbf{r} = x\hat{\mathbf{i}} + y\hat{\mathbf{j}}$.

Direction of this position vector **r** is given by the angle θ with X-axis where, $\tan\theta = y/x$.

- In three-dimensions, the position vector is represented as $\mathbf{r} = x\hat{\mathbf{i}} + y\hat{\mathbf{j}} + z\hat{\mathbf{k}}$.

(ii) **Displacement Vector** The displacement vector is a vector which gives the position of a point with reference to a point other than the origin of the coordinate system.

Magnitude of displacement vector,

$$|\Delta\mathbf{r}| = \sqrt{(\Delta x)^2 + (\Delta y)^2} = \sqrt{(x_2 - x_1)^2 + (y_2 - y_1)^2}$$

Direction of the displacement vector $\Delta\mathbf{r}$ is given by

$$\tan\theta = \frac{\Delta y}{\Delta x}$$

- In three-dimensions, the displacement can be represented as $\Delta\mathbf{r} = (x_2 - x_1)\hat{\mathbf{i}} + (y_2 - y_1)\hat{\mathbf{j}} + (z_2 - z_1)\hat{\mathbf{k}}$

(iii) **Velocity Vector** Velocity of an object in motion is defined as the ratio of displacement and the corresponding time interval taken by the object.

- Average velocity, $\mathbf{v}_{av} = \dfrac{\Delta\mathbf{r}}{\Delta t} = \dfrac{\mathbf{r}_2 - \mathbf{r}_1}{t_2 - t_1}$

In the component forms

$$\mathbf{v}_{av} = \frac{\Delta x}{\Delta t}\hat{\mathbf{i}} + \frac{\Delta y}{\Delta t}\hat{\mathbf{j}} = \Delta v_x\hat{\mathbf{i}} + \Delta v_y\hat{\mathbf{j}}$$

- Instantaneous velocity, $\mathbf{v} = \lim_{\Delta t \to 0} \dfrac{\Delta\mathbf{r}}{\Delta t} = \dfrac{d\mathbf{r}}{dt}$

$$v = \frac{dx}{dt}\hat{\mathbf{i}} + \frac{dy}{dt}\hat{\mathbf{j}} \Rightarrow v = v_x\hat{\mathbf{i}} + v_y\hat{\mathbf{j}}$$

Magnitude of instantaneous velocity, $|\mathbf{v}| = \sqrt{v_x^2 + v_y^2}$.

(iv) **Acceleration Vector** It is defined as the rate of change of velocity.

- Average acceleration, $\mathbf{a}_{av} = \dfrac{\Delta v}{\Delta t} = \dfrac{\Delta v_x}{\Delta t}\hat{\mathbf{i}} + \dfrac{\Delta v_y}{\Delta t}\hat{\mathbf{j}}$

$$\mathbf{a}_{av} = a_{(av)x}\hat{\mathbf{i}} + a_{(av)y}\hat{\mathbf{j}}$$

Magnitude of average acceleration is given by

$$|\mathbf{a}_{av}| = \sqrt{(a_{(av)x})^2 + (a_{(av)y})^2}$$

- Instantaneous acceleration, $\mathbf{a} = \lim_{\Delta t \to 0} \dfrac{\Delta\mathbf{v}}{\Delta t} = \dfrac{d\mathbf{v}}{dt}$

$$\Rightarrow \mathbf{a} = a_x\hat{\mathbf{i}} + a_y\hat{\mathbf{j}}$$

Kinematic Equations in Two dimensions

(i) $\mathbf{v}\cdot\mathbf{v} = \mathbf{u}\cdot\mathbf{u} + 2\mathbf{a}\cdot\mathbf{r}$

Along X-axis	Along Y-axis
$v_x^2 = u_x^2 + 2a_x x$	$v_y^2 = u_y^2 + 2a_y y$

(ii) $\mathbf{v} = \mathbf{u} + \mathbf{a}t$

Along X-axis	Along Y-axis
$v_x = u_x + a_x t$	$v_y = u_y + a_y t$

(iii) $\mathbf{r} = \mathbf{r}_0 + \mathbf{u}_0 t + \frac{1}{2}\mathbf{a}t^2$

Along X-axis	Along Y-aixs
$x = x_0 + u_x t + \frac{1}{2}a_x t^2$	$y = y_0 + u_y t + \frac{1}{2}a_y t^2$

Projectile Motion

If a particle moves in horizontal as well as vertical motion simultaneously, the motion of particle is known as projectile motion.

Suppose an object is projected from point O with velocity (u), making an angle (θ) with the horizontal direction OX, such that $x_0 = 0$ and $y_0 = 0$, when $t = 0$. Then

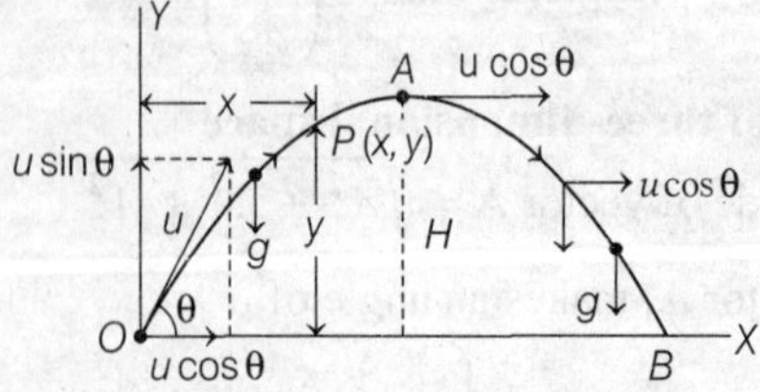

- **Equation of Trajectory** $y = x\tan\theta - \left(\dfrac{1}{2}\dfrac{g}{u^2\cos^2\theta}\right)x^2$

This equation represents a parabola and is known as equation of trajectory of a projectile.

- **Time of Flight** It is defined as the total time for which the projectile remains in air.

  It is given by $T = \dfrac{2u \sin \theta}{g}$

- **Maximum Height** It is defined as the maximum vertical height covered by projectile.

  It is given by $H = \dfrac{u^2 \sin^2 \theta}{2g}$

- **Horizontal Range** It is defined as the maximum distance covered in horizontal distance.

  It is given by $R = \dfrac{u^2 \sin 2\theta}{g}$

Different Cases of Projectile Motion

Projectile from the Ground

Position of Angle (θ)	Equation of Motion (y)	Time of Flight (T)	Maximum Height (H)	Horizontal Range (R)
At an angle with horizontal	$x \tan\theta - \left(\dfrac{gx^2}{2u^2 \cos^2\theta}\right)$	$\dfrac{2u\sin\theta}{g}$	$\dfrac{u^2 \sin^2\theta}{2g}$	$\dfrac{u^2 \sin 2\theta}{g}$
At an angle with vertical	$x \cot\theta - \left(\dfrac{gx^2}{2u^2 \sin^2\theta}\right)$	$\dfrac{2u\cos\theta}{g}$	$\dfrac{u^2 \cos^2\theta}{2g}$	$\dfrac{u^2 \sin 2\theta}{g}$

Projectile from a Point above the Ground

Direction of Projection	Equation of Motion	Time of Flight (T)	Horizontal Range (R)
Horizontally from a height	$y = \dfrac{1}{2}\left(\dfrac{gx^2}{u^2}\right)$	$\sqrt{\dfrac{2h}{g}}$	$u\sqrt{\dfrac{2h}{g}}$
Upward from a height	$x = u\cos\theta t$ $-h = u\sin\theta t - \dfrac{1}{2}gt^2$	$\dfrac{u\sin\theta}{g} \pm \sqrt{\dfrac{u^2 \sin^2\theta}{g^2} + \dfrac{2h}{g}}$	$(u\cos\theta)T$
Downward from a height	$-h = (-u\sin\theta)t - \dfrac{1}{2}gt^2$	$-\dfrac{u\sin\theta}{g} \pm \sqrt{\dfrac{u^2 \sin^2\theta}{g^2} + \dfrac{2h}{g}}$	$(u\cos\theta)T$

Note • Horizontal range is maximum, when it is thrown at an angle of 45° with horizontal and given by $h_{max} = u^2/g$.
• For angle of projection at θ and $(90° - \theta)$, the horizontal range is same.

Circular Motion

- It is the movement of particles along the circumference of a circle.
- The **uniform circular motion** is that in which the particle is moving at a constant speed on circular path.
- The **non-uniform circular motion** is that in which the particles move with variable speed on its circular path.

Variables in Circular Motion

(*i*) **Angular Displacement** It is the angle subtended by the position vector at the centre of the circular path.

Angular displacement, $\Delta\theta = \Delta s / r$

where, Δs is the arc length and r is the radius.

(*ii*) **Angular Velocity** The time rate of change of angular displacement $(\Delta\theta)$ is called angular velocity.

Angular velocity, $\omega = \Delta\theta / \Delta t$

Angular velocity is a vector quantity.

- **Relation between linear velocity (v) and angular velocity (ω) is given by**

$$v = r\omega$$

(*iii*) **Angular Acceleration** The rate of change of angular velocity is called angular acceleration.

Angular acceleration,

$$\alpha = \lim_{\Delta t \to 0} \frac{\Delta\omega}{\Delta t} = \frac{d\omega}{dt} = \frac{d^2\theta}{dt^2}$$ Its SI unit is rad/s^2 and dimensional formula is $[T^{-2}]$.

Acceleration in a circular motion has two components as given below

(a) **Tangential acceleration** is the change in magnitude of linear velocity and act along tangent to the circular path. It is given by

$$\alpha_T = r\alpha$$

(b) **Radial acceleration** is the change in direction of linear velocity and acts along the radius towards the centre of circle. It is given by

$$\alpha_r = \frac{v^2}{r} = \omega^2 r$$

It is also called **centripetal acceleration.**

- **Relation between linear acceleration (*a*) and angular acceleration (α)**

$$a = r\alpha, \text{ where } r = \text{radius.}$$

- **Relation between angular acceleration (α) and linear velocity (*v*)**

$$\alpha = \frac{v^2}{r}$$

Relative Velocity

- The time rate of change of relative position of one object with respect to another is called relative velocity.
- When two bodies are moving along the same line, then relative velocity is given in two ways as

(*i*) $|\mathbf{v}_{AB}|$ = velocity of *A* with respect to *B* (in magnitude)

$= |v_A - v_B|$ (when bodies are moving along same direction).

(*ii*) $|\mathbf{v}_{AB}| = |v_A + v_B|$ (when bodies are moving toward each other).

- When the motion is in a plane, then the relative velocity is given by

$$|\mathbf{v}_{AB}| = \sqrt{v_A^2 + v_B^2 - 2v_A v_B \cos\theta}$$

where, $\mathbf{v}_A$ and $\mathbf{v}_B$ = velocity of *A* and *B* w.r.t. ground.

- It is used to solve following problems

(*i*) For **rain-man** problems

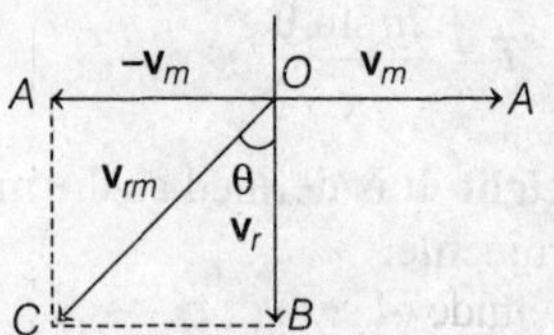

(a) $|\mathbf{v}_{rm}|$ = relative velocity of rain w.r.t man

$$= \sqrt{v_r^2 + v_m^2}$$

(b) The angle at which the man should hold umbrella to save himself from wetting is

$$\theta = \tan\left(\frac{v_m}{v_r}\right)$$

(*ii*) For **river-boat or man** problems

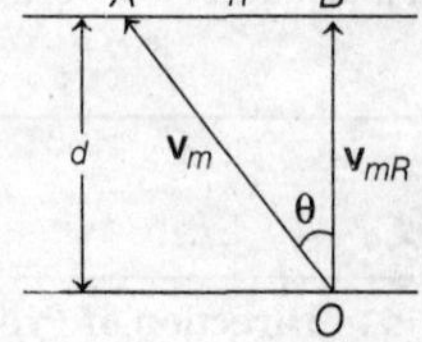

(a) $|\mathbf{v}_{mR}|$ = relative velocity of man w.r.t river

$$= \sqrt{v_m^2 - v_R^2}$$

(b) The angle for crossing the river over shortest distance,

$$\theta = \tan^{-1}\left(\frac{v_r}{\sqrt{v_m^2 - v_R^2}}\right)$$

(c) The time taken for crossing the river over shortest distance,

$$t = \frac{d}{\sqrt{v_m^2 + v_R^2}}$$

(d) To cross the river in shortest possible time, the man should swim perpendicular to the bank and the time taken is

$$t = \frac{\sqrt{x^2 + d^2}}{\sqrt{v_m^2 + v_R^2}}$$

Topical Practice Questions

All the exam questions of this chapter have been divided into 5 topics as listed below

Topic 1

Vectors

2016

1 If the magnitude of sum of two vectors is equal to the magnitude of difference of the two vectors, the angle between these vectors is **[NEET]**

(a) 90° (b) 45° (c) 180° (d) 0°

2014

2 The angle θ between the vector $\mathbf{p} = \hat{\mathbf{i}} + \hat{\mathbf{j}} + \hat{\mathbf{k}}$ and unit vector along X-axis is **[MHT CET]**

(a) $\cos^{-1}\left(\frac{1}{\sqrt{3}}\right)$ (b) $\cos^{-1}\left(\frac{1}{\sqrt{2}}\right)$

(c) $\cos^{-1}\left(\frac{\sqrt{3}}{2}\right)$ (d) $\cos^{-1}\left(\frac{1}{2}\right)$

3 Consider three vectors $\mathbf{A} = \hat{\mathbf{i}} + \hat{\mathbf{j}} - 2\hat{\mathbf{k}}$, $\mathbf{B} = \hat{\mathbf{i}} - \hat{\mathbf{j}} + \hat{\mathbf{k}}$ and $\mathbf{C} = 2\hat{\mathbf{i}} - 3\hat{\mathbf{j}} + 4\hat{\mathbf{k}}$. A vector $\mathbf{X}$ of the form $\alpha\mathbf{A} + \beta\mathbf{B}$ (α and β are numbers) is perpendicular to $\mathbf{C}$. The ratio of α and β is **[WB JEE]**

(a) 1 : 1 (b) 2 : 1

(c) – 1:1 (d) 3:1

4 Two equal vectors have a resultant equal to either of the two. The angle between them is **[UK PMT]**

(a) 90° (b) 60°

(c) 120° (d) 0°

5 Which of the following is not a vector quantity? **[KCET]**

(a) Weight (b) Nuclear spin

(c) Momentum (d) Potential energy

6 A force $\mathbf{F} = 5\hat{\mathbf{i}} + 2\hat{\mathbf{j}} - 5\hat{\mathbf{k}}$ acts on a particle whose position vector is $\mathbf{r} = \hat{\mathbf{i}} - 2\hat{\mathbf{j}} + \hat{\mathbf{k}}$. What is the torque about the origin? **[KCET]**

(a) $8\hat{\mathbf{i}} + 10\hat{\mathbf{j}} + 12\hat{\mathbf{k}}$ (b) $8\hat{\mathbf{i}} + 10\hat{\mathbf{j}} - 12\hat{\mathbf{k}}$

(c) $8\hat{\mathbf{i}} - 10\hat{\mathbf{j}} - 12\hat{\mathbf{k}}$ (d) $10\hat{\mathbf{i}} - 10\hat{\mathbf{j}} - \hat{\mathbf{k}}$

2013

7 The square of resultant of two equal forces is three times their product. Angle between the forces is **[UP CPMT]**

(a) π (b) $\pi/2$

(c) $\pi/4$ (d) $\pi/3$

2012

8 Three vectors satisfy the relation $\mathbf{A} \cdot \mathbf{B} = 0$ and $\mathbf{A} \cdot \mathbf{C} = 0$, then $\mathbf{A}$ is parallel to **[AFMC]**

(a) $\mathbf{C}$ (b) $\mathbf{B}$

(c) $\mathbf{B} \times \mathbf{C}$ (d) $\mathbf{B} \cdot \mathbf{C}$

9 If $\mathbf{a} = 2\hat{\mathbf{i}} - 3\hat{\mathbf{j}} + \hat{\mathbf{k}}$ and $\mathbf{b} = 3\hat{\mathbf{i}} + \hat{\mathbf{j}} - 2\hat{\mathbf{k}}$, then the cosine of angle θ between them is equal to **[UP CPMT]**

(a) 5/14 (b) 1/7

(c) 3/14 (d) 1/14

10 If $\mathbf{a} \cdot \mathbf{b} = |\mathbf{a} \times \mathbf{b}|$, then the angle θ between $\mathbf{a}$ and $\mathbf{b}$ will be

(a) 60° (b) 45°

(c) 75° (d) 90° **[OJEE]**

11 If $\mathbf{A} = \mathbf{B} + \mathbf{C}$ have scalar magnitudes of 5, 4, 3 units respectively, then the angle between $\mathbf{A}$ and $\mathbf{C}$ is **[WB JEE]**

(a) $\cos^{-1}(3/5)$ (b) $\cos^{-1}(4/5)$

(c) $\pi/2$ (d) $\sin^{-1}(4/5)$

2011

12 Given, $\mathbf{A} = 2\hat{\mathbf{i}} + 3\hat{\mathbf{j}}$ and $\mathbf{B} = \hat{\mathbf{i}} + \hat{\mathbf{j}}$. The component of vector $\mathbf{A}$ along vector $\mathbf{B}$ is **[Karala CEE]**

(a) $\frac{1}{\sqrt{2}}$ (b) $\frac{3}{\sqrt{2}}$ (c) $\frac{5}{\sqrt{2}}$ (d) $\frac{7}{\sqrt{2}}$

(e) None of these

13 If vectors $\hat{\mathbf{i}} - 3\hat{\mathbf{j}} + 5\hat{\mathbf{k}}$ and $\hat{\mathbf{i}} - 3\hat{\mathbf{j}} - a\hat{\mathbf{k}}$ are equal vectors, then the value of a is **[Kerala CEE]**

(a) 5 (b) 2

(c) – 3 (d) 4

(e) – 5

14 Which of the following is correct relation between an arbitrary vector $\mathbf{A}$ and vector $\mathbf{O}$? **[DUMET]**

(a) $\mathbf{A} + \mathbf{O} + \mathbf{A} \times \mathbf{O} = \mathbf{A}$ (b) $\mathbf{A} + \mathbf{O} + \mathbf{A} \times \mathbf{O} \neq \mathbf{A}$

(c) $\mathbf{A} + \mathbf{O} + \mathbf{A} \times \mathbf{O} = \mathbf{O}$ (d) None of these

15 The value of λ for which two vectors $\mathbf{a} = 5\hat{\mathbf{i}} + \lambda\hat{\mathbf{j}} + \hat{\mathbf{k}}$ and $\mathbf{b} = \hat{\mathbf{i}} - 2\hat{\mathbf{j}} + \hat{\mathbf{k}}$ are perpendicular to each other is **[WB JEE]**

(a) 2 (b) – 2

(c) 3 (d) – 3

16 For any two vectors $\mathbf{A}$ and $\mathbf{B}$, if $\mathbf{A} \cdot \mathbf{B} = |\mathbf{A} \times \mathbf{B}|$, the magnitude of $\mathbf{C} = \mathbf{A} + \mathbf{B}$ is equal to **[Haryana PMT]**

(a) $\sqrt{A^2 + B^2}$ (b) $A + B$

(c) $\sqrt{A^2 + B^2 + \frac{AB}{\sqrt{2}}}$ (d) $\sqrt{A^2 + B^2 + \sqrt{2}\,AB}$

17 Find the torque of force, $\mathbf{F} = -3\hat{\mathbf{i}} + 2\hat{\mathbf{j}} + \hat{\mathbf{k}}$ acting at the point $\mathbf{r} = 8\hat{\mathbf{i}} + 2\hat{\mathbf{j}} + 3\hat{\mathbf{k}}$. **[AMU]**

(a) $14\hat{\mathbf{i}} - 38\hat{\mathbf{j}} + 16\hat{\mathbf{k}}$ (b) $4\hat{\mathbf{i}} + 4\hat{\mathbf{j}} + 6\hat{\mathbf{k}}$

(c) $-14\hat{\mathbf{i}} + 38\hat{\mathbf{j}} - 16\hat{\mathbf{k}}$ (d) $-4\hat{\mathbf{i}} - 17\hat{\mathbf{j}} + 22\hat{\mathbf{k}}$

18 At what angle must the two forces $(x+y)$ and $(x-y)$ act, so that the resultant may be $(\sqrt{x^2+y^2})$? [JCECE]

(a) $\cos^{-1}\left[-\frac{(x^2+y^2)}{2(x^2-y^2)}\right]$ (b) $\cos^{-1}\left[-\frac{2(x^2-y^2)}{x^2+y^2}\right]$

(c) $\cos^{-1}\left[-\frac{(x^2+y^2)}{(x^2-y^2)}\right]$ (d) $\cos^{-1}\left[-\frac{(x^2-y^2)}{(x^2+y^2)}\right]$

2010

19 If $\mathbf{a}+\mathbf{b}=\mathbf{c}$ and $a+b=c$, then the angle included between $\mathbf{a}$ and $\mathbf{b}$ is [WB JEE]

(a) 90° (b) 180° (c) 120° (d) 0°

2009

20 There are N-coplanar vectors each of magnitude V. Each vector is inclined to the preceding vector at angle $\frac{2\pi}{N}$. What is the magnitude of their resultant? [AIIMS]

(a) V/N (b) V
(c) Zero (d) N/V

21 If $\mathbf{a}_1$ and $\mathbf{a}_2$ are two non-collinear unit vectors and if $|\mathbf{a}_1+\mathbf{a}_2|=\sqrt{3}$, then the value of $(\mathbf{a}_1-\mathbf{a}_2)\cdot(2\mathbf{a}_1+\mathbf{a}_2)$ is [Haryana PMT, Punjab PMET]

(a) 2 (b) 3/2 (c) 1/2 (d) 1

22 $\mathbf{A}$ is a vector with magnitude A, then the unit vector $\hat{\mathbf{a}}$ in the direction of vector $\mathbf{A}$ is [J&K CET]

(a) $A\mathbf{A}$ (b) $\mathbf{A}\cdot\mathbf{A}$ (c) $\mathbf{A}\times\mathbf{A}$ (d) $\frac{\mathbf{A}}{A}$

23 Given, two vectors $\mathbf{A}=-4\hat{\mathbf{i}}+4\hat{\mathbf{j}}+2\hat{\mathbf{k}}$ and $\mathbf{B}=2\hat{\mathbf{i}}-\hat{\mathbf{j}}-\hat{\mathbf{k}}$. The angle made by $(\mathbf{A}+\mathbf{B})$ with $\hat{\mathbf{i}}+2\hat{\mathbf{j}}-4\hat{\mathbf{k}}$ is [Punjab PMET]

(a) 30° (b) 45°
(c) 60° (d) 90°

24 The condition under which vectors $(\mathbf{a}+\mathbf{b})$ and $(\mathbf{a}-\mathbf{b})$ should be at right angles to each other is [AMU]

(a) $\mathbf{a}\neq\mathbf{b}$ (b) $\mathbf{a}\cdot\mathbf{b}=0$
(c) $|\mathbf{a}|=|\mathbf{b}|$ (d) $\mathbf{a}\cdot\mathbf{b}=1$

25 Three forces $\mathbf{A}=(\hat{\mathbf{i}}+\hat{\mathbf{j}}+\hat{\mathbf{k}})$, $\mathbf{B}=(2\hat{\mathbf{i}}-\hat{\mathbf{j}}+3\hat{\mathbf{k}})$ and $\mathbf{C}$ acting on a body to keep it in equilibrium, then $\mathbf{C}$ is [EAMCET]

(a) $-(3\hat{\mathbf{i}}+4\hat{\mathbf{k}})$ (b) $-(4\hat{\mathbf{i}}+3\hat{\mathbf{k}})$
(c) $3\hat{\mathbf{i}}+4\hat{\mathbf{j}}$ (d) $2\hat{\mathbf{i}}-3\hat{\mathbf{k}}$

2007

26 The sides of a parallelogram are represented by vectors $\mathbf{p}=5\hat{\mathbf{i}}-4\hat{\mathbf{j}}+3\hat{\mathbf{k}}$ and $\mathbf{q}=3\hat{\mathbf{i}}+2\hat{\mathbf{j}}-\hat{\mathbf{k}}$. Then, the area of the parallelogram is [Kerala CEE]

(a) $\sqrt{684}$ sq units (b) $\sqrt{72}$ sq units
(c) 171 sq units (d) 72 sq units
(e) $\sqrt{191}$ sq units

27 Vector which is perpendicular to $(a\cos\theta\hat{\mathbf{i}}+b\sin\theta\hat{\mathbf{j}})$ is [J&K CET]

(a) $b\sin\theta\hat{\mathbf{i}}-a\cos\theta\hat{\mathbf{j}}$ (b) $\frac{1}{a}\sin\theta\hat{\mathbf{i}}-\frac{1}{b}\cos\theta\hat{\mathbf{j}}$
(c) $5\hat{\mathbf{k}}$ (d) All of these

28 If $\mathbf{A}=2\hat{\mathbf{i}}+3\hat{\mathbf{j}}-\hat{\mathbf{k}}$ and $\mathbf{B}=-\hat{\mathbf{i}}+3\hat{\mathbf{j}}+4\hat{\mathbf{k}}$, then projection of $\mathbf{A}$ on $\mathbf{B}$ will be [Punjab PMET]

(a) $\frac{3}{\sqrt{13}}$ (b) $\frac{3}{\sqrt{26}}$ (c) $\sqrt{\frac{3}{26}}$ (d) $\sqrt{\frac{3}{13}}$

29 Given, two vectors $\mathbf{A}=-\hat{\mathbf{i}}+2\hat{\mathbf{j}}-3\hat{\mathbf{k}}$, $\mathbf{B}=4\hat{\mathbf{i}}-2\hat{\mathbf{j}}+6\hat{\mathbf{k}}$. The angle made by $(\mathbf{A}+\mathbf{B})$ with X-axis [EAMCET]

(a) 30° (b) 45°
(c) 60° (d) 90°

2006

30 Which of the following statement is true? [J&K CET]

(a) When the coordinate axes are translated the components of a vector in a plane change.
(b) When the coordinate axes are rotated through some angle, components of the vector change but the vector's magnitude remains constant.
(c) Sum of $\mathbf{a}$ and $\mathbf{b}$ is $\mathbf{R}$, if the magnitude of $\mathbf{a}$ alone is increased, angle between $\mathbf{b}$ and $\mathbf{R}$ decreases.
(d) The cross product of $3\hat{\mathbf{i}}$ and $4\hat{\mathbf{j}}$ is 12.

31 Of the vectors given below, the parallel vectors are

$\mathbf{A}=6\hat{\mathbf{i}}+8\hat{\mathbf{j}}$ $\quad\mathbf{B}=210\hat{\mathbf{i}}+280\hat{\mathbf{k}}$

$\mathbf{C}=0.3\hat{\mathbf{i}}+0.4\hat{\mathbf{j}}$ and $\mathbf{D}=3.6\hat{\mathbf{i}}+6\hat{\mathbf{j}}+4.8\hat{\mathbf{k}}$ [EAMCET]

(a) $\mathbf{A}$ and $\mathbf{B}$ (b) $\mathbf{A}$ and $\mathbf{C}$ (c) $\mathbf{A}$ and $\mathbf{D}$ (d) $\mathbf{C}$ and $\mathbf{D}$

2005

32 If the angle between the vectors $\mathbf{A}$ and $\mathbf{B}$ is θ, the value of the product $(\mathbf{B}\times\mathbf{A})\cdot\mathbf{A}$ is equal to [CBSE AIPMT]

(a) $BA^2\cos\theta$ (b) $BA^2\sin\theta$
(c) $BA^2\sin\theta\cos\theta$ (d) zero

33 If a vector $2\hat{\mathbf{i}}+3\hat{\mathbf{j}}+8\hat{\mathbf{k}}$ is perpendicular to the vector $4\hat{\mathbf{j}}-4\hat{\mathbf{i}}+\alpha\hat{\mathbf{k}}$, then the value of α is [CBSE AIPMT]

(a) -1 (b) $\frac{1}{2}$
(c) $-\frac{1}{2}$ (d) 1

34 If $|\mathbf{A}\times\mathbf{B}|=\sqrt{3}\mathbf{A}\cdot\mathbf{B}$, then the value of $|\mathbf{A}+\mathbf{B}|$ is [CBSE AIPMT]

(a) $(A^2+B^2+AB)^{1/2}$
(b) $\left(A^2+B^2+\frac{AB}{\sqrt{3}}\right)^{1/2}$
(c) $A+B$
(d) $(A^2+B^2+\sqrt{3}AB)^{1/2}$

35 Minimum numbers of unequal vectors which can give zero resultant are [AFMC]
(a) two (b) three
(c) four (d) more than four

36 The vectors from origin to the points A and B are $\mathbf{A} = 3\hat{\mathbf{i}} - 6\hat{\mathbf{j}} + 2\hat{\mathbf{k}}$ and $\mathbf{B} = 2\hat{\mathbf{i}} + \hat{\mathbf{j}} - 2\hat{\mathbf{k}}$, respectively. The area of the ΔOAB is [BHU]
(a) $\frac{5}{2}\sqrt{17}$ (b) $\frac{2}{5}\sqrt{17}$ (c) $\frac{3}{5}\sqrt{17}$ (d) $\frac{5}{3}\sqrt{17}$

37 Which of the following is incorrect? [Haryana PMT]
(a) $\mathbf{a}\cdot(\mathbf{b}+\mathbf{c}) = \mathbf{b}\cdot\mathbf{a} + \mathbf{a}\cdot\mathbf{c}$
(b) $\mathbf{a}\times(\mathbf{b}+\mathbf{c}) = (\mathbf{a}\times\mathbf{c}) + (\mathbf{a}\times\mathbf{b})$
(c) $\mathbf{a}\times(\mathbf{b}\cdot\mathbf{c}) = (\mathbf{a}\times\mathbf{b})\cdot(\mathbf{a}\times\mathbf{c})$
(d) $(\mathbf{b}\cdot\mathbf{c})\,\mathbf{a} = \mathbf{a}\,(\mathbf{c}\cdot\mathbf{b})$

38 Angle (in rad) made by the vector $\sqrt{3}\,\hat{\mathbf{i}} + \hat{\mathbf{j}}$ with the X-axis is [EAMCET]
(a) $\pi/6$ (b) $\pi/4$ (c) $\pi/3$ (d) $\pi/2$

Answers

1 (a)	2 (a)	3 (a)	4 (c)	5 (d)	6 (a)	7 (d)	8 (c)	9 (d)	10 (b)
11 (a)	12 (c)	13 (e)	14 (a)	15 (c)	16 (d)	17 (d)	18 (a)	19 (d)	20 (c)
21 (c)	22 (d)	23 (d)	24 (c)	25 (a)	26 (a)	27 (d)	28 (b)	29 (b)	30 (b)
31 (b)	32 (d)	33 (c)	34 (a)	35 (b)	36 (a)	37 (c)	38 (a)		

Explanations

1 *(a)* Suppose two vectors are **P** and **Q**.
It is given that
$$|\mathbf{P}+\mathbf{Q}| = |\mathbf{P}-\mathbf{Q}|$$
Let angle between **P** and **Q** is ϕ.
$$\therefore\ P^2 + Q^2 + 2PQ\cos\phi = P^2 + Q^2 - 2PQ\cos\phi$$
$$\Rightarrow 4PQ\cos\phi = 0$$
$$\Rightarrow \cos\phi = 0 \quad [\because P, Q \neq 0]$$
Hence, $\cos\phi = \cos\frac{\pi}{2}$
$$\Rightarrow \phi = \frac{\pi}{2} = 90^\circ$$

2 *(a)* Given the angle between
$$\mathbf{p} = \hat{\mathbf{i}} + \hat{\mathbf{j}} + \hat{\mathbf{k}}$$
and X-axis, $\mathbf{x} = \hat{\mathbf{i}}$ can be determine by
$$\cos\theta = \frac{\mathbf{p}\cdot\mathbf{x}}{|\mathbf{p}||\mathbf{x}|} = \frac{(\hat{\mathbf{i}}+\hat{\mathbf{j}}+\hat{\mathbf{k}})\cdot(\hat{\mathbf{i}})}{\sqrt{1^2+1^2+1^2}\cdot\sqrt{1^2}} = \frac{1}{\sqrt{3}}$$
$$\therefore \quad \theta = \cos^{-1}\left(\frac{1}{\sqrt{3}}\right)$$

3 *(a)* Vector **X** of the form $\alpha\mathbf{A} + \beta\mathbf{B}$.
i.e. $\mathbf{X} = \alpha\mathbf{A} + \beta\mathbf{B}$
Given, $\mathbf{A} = \hat{\mathbf{i}} + \hat{\mathbf{j}} - 2\hat{\mathbf{k}}$,
$\mathbf{B} = \hat{\mathbf{i}} - \hat{\mathbf{j}} + \hat{\mathbf{k}}$
and $\mathbf{C} = 2\hat{\mathbf{i}} - 3\hat{\mathbf{j}} + 4\hat{\mathbf{k}}$

Putting these values, we get
$$= \alpha(\hat{\mathbf{i}} + \hat{\mathbf{j}} - 2\hat{\mathbf{k}}) + \beta(\hat{\mathbf{i}} - \hat{\mathbf{j}} + \hat{\mathbf{k}})$$
$$\mathbf{X} = \hat{\mathbf{i}}(\alpha+\beta) + \hat{\mathbf{j}}(\alpha-\beta) + \hat{\mathbf{k}}(-2\alpha+\beta)$$
As vector **X** is perpendicular to **C**, i.e. $\mathbf{X}\cdot\mathbf{C} = 0$
$$[\hat{\mathbf{i}}(\alpha+\beta) + \hat{\mathbf{j}}(\alpha-\beta) + \hat{\mathbf{k}}(-2\alpha+\beta)]\cdot[2\hat{\mathbf{i}} - 3\hat{\mathbf{j}} + 4\hat{\mathbf{k}}] = 0$$
$$\Rightarrow 2(\alpha+\beta) - 3(\alpha-\beta) + 4(-2\alpha+\beta) = 0$$
$$\Rightarrow 2\alpha + 2\beta - 3\alpha + 3\beta - 8\alpha + 4\beta = 0$$
$$\Rightarrow -9\alpha + 9\beta = 0$$
or $\alpha = \beta$
$$\Rightarrow \frac{\alpha}{\beta} = \frac{1}{1}$$
or $\alpha : \beta = 1 : 1$

4 *(c)* Let two vectors are **A** and **B**, inclined at an angle θ.

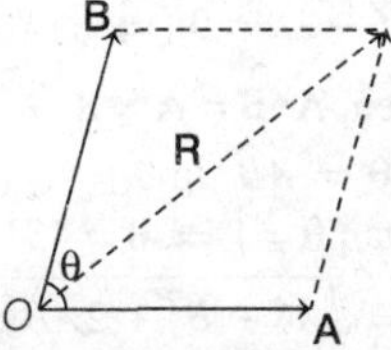

Resultant of the two vectors **A** and **B**,
$$|\mathbf{R}| = \sqrt{|\mathbf{A}|^2 + |\mathbf{B}|^2 + 2|\mathbf{A}||\mathbf{B}|\cos\theta} \quad \ldots\text{(i)}$$

Let, $|\mathbf{A}| = |\mathbf{B}| = a$
According to the question, $|\mathbf{R}| = a$
From Eq. (i),
$$a = \sqrt{a^2 + a^2 + 2aa\cos\theta}$$
$$\Rightarrow a^2 = a^2 + a^2 + 2a^2\cos\theta$$
$$\Rightarrow 2a^2\cos\theta = -a^2$$
$$\Rightarrow \cos\theta = -1/2$$
$$\Rightarrow -\cos\theta = 1/2$$
$$\Rightarrow \cos(180^\circ - \theta) = \cos 60^\circ$$
$$\Rightarrow \theta = 120^\circ$$

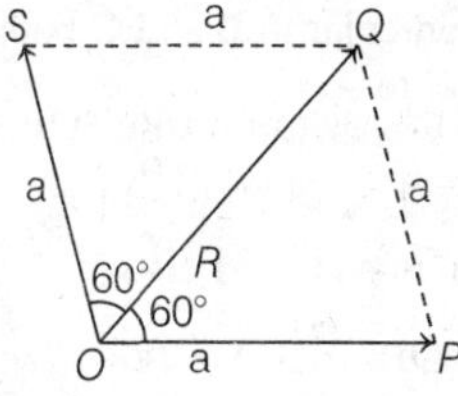

Geometrically,
$$\angle SOP = 120^\circ$$

5 *(d)* Potential energy is not a vector quantity. It has magnitude but no direction, whereas weight = mg where, g is vector, nuclear spin has direction and momentum is mv, where v has direction.

6 *(a)* Given, $\mathbf{F} = 5\hat{\mathbf{i}} + 2\hat{\mathbf{j}} - 5\hat{\mathbf{k}}$
and $\mathbf{r} = \hat{\mathbf{i}} - 2\hat{\mathbf{j}} + \hat{\mathbf{k}}$
We know that, torque, $\tau = \mathbf{r}\times\mathbf{F}$

So, torque about the origin will be given by

$$\tau = \begin{vmatrix} \hat{\mathbf{i}} & \hat{\mathbf{j}} & \hat{\mathbf{k}} \\ 1 & -2 & 1 \\ 5 & 2 & -5 \end{vmatrix}$$

$= \hat{\mathbf{i}}\,(10-2) - \hat{\mathbf{j}}\,(-5-5) + \hat{\mathbf{k}}\,(2+10)$

$= 8\hat{\mathbf{i}} + 10\hat{\mathbf{j}} + 12\,\hat{\mathbf{k}}$

7 *(d)* Let θ be the angle between vectors **P** and **Q** whose resultant is **R**.

Given, $P = Q$

and $R^2 = 3PQ = 3P^2$

As, $R^2 = P^2 + Q^2 + 2PQ\cos\theta$

$\therefore\quad 3P^2 = P^2 + P^2 + 2P^2\cos\theta$

$\Rightarrow\quad 3P^2 - 2P^2 = 2P^2\cos\theta$

$\Rightarrow\quad P^2 = 2P^2\cos\theta$

$\Rightarrow\quad 1 = 2\cos\theta$

$\Rightarrow\quad \cos\theta = \dfrac{1}{2}$

$\Rightarrow\quad \cos\theta = \cos 60^\circ$

$\therefore\quad \theta = 60^\circ = \dfrac{\pi}{3}$

8 *(c)* Since, $\mathbf{A}\cdot\mathbf{B} = 0$

$\Rightarrow\quad \mathbf{A} \perp \mathbf{B}$

$\mathbf{A}\cdot\mathbf{C} = 0 \Rightarrow \mathbf{A} \perp \mathbf{C}$

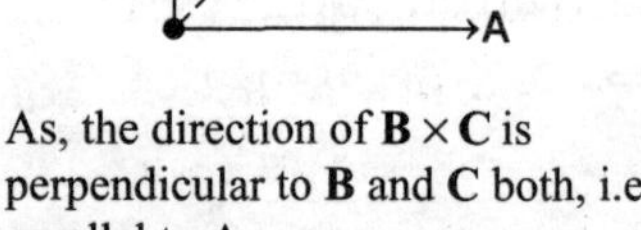

As, the direction of $\mathbf{B}\times\mathbf{C}$ is perpendicular to **B** and **C** both, i.e. parallel to **A**.

9 *(d)* As, $\mathbf{a}\cdot\mathbf{b} = ab\cos\theta$

Given, $\mathbf{a} = 2\hat{\mathbf{i}} - 3\hat{\mathbf{j}} + \hat{\mathbf{k}}$

and $\mathbf{b} = 3\hat{\mathbf{i}} + \hat{\mathbf{j}} - 2\hat{\mathbf{k}}$

$\Rightarrow (2\hat{\mathbf{i}} - 3\hat{\mathbf{j}} + \hat{\mathbf{k}})\cdot(3\hat{\mathbf{i}} + \hat{\mathbf{j}} - 2\hat{\mathbf{k}})$

$= ab\cos\theta$

$\Rightarrow 6 - 3 - 2 = \sqrt{(4+9+1)(9+1+4)}\cos\theta$

$\Rightarrow 1 = \sqrt{14\times 14}\,\cos\theta$

$\Rightarrow\quad 1 = 14\cos\theta$

$\therefore\quad \cos\theta = \dfrac{1}{14}$

10 *(b)* Given, $\mathbf{a}\cdot\mathbf{b} = |\mathbf{a}\times\mathbf{b}|$

$\Rightarrow ab\cos\theta = ab\sin\theta$

$(\because \mathbf{a}\cdot\mathbf{b} = ab\cos\theta \text{ and } \mathbf{a}\times\mathbf{b} = ab\sin\theta)$

$\Rightarrow\quad \dfrac{\sin\theta}{\cos\theta} = \dfrac{ab}{ab} = 1$

$\Rightarrow\quad \tan\theta = 1$

$\Rightarrow\quad \tan\theta = \tan 45^\circ$

$\therefore\quad \theta = 45^\circ$

11 *(a)* Here, triangle *OMN* is given with vectors **A, B** and **C** are its adjacent sides.

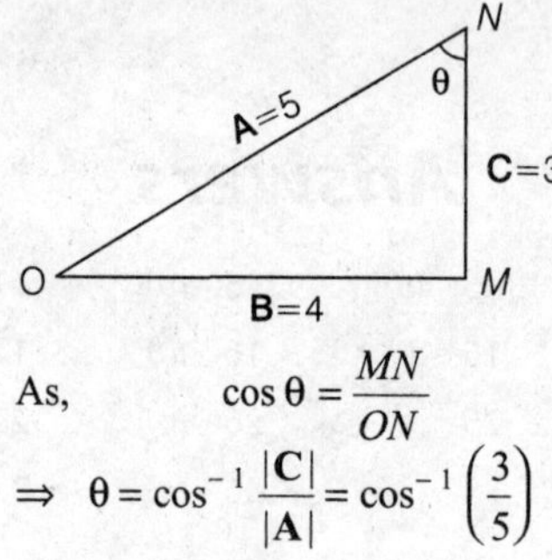

As, $\cos\theta = \dfrac{MN}{ON}$

$\Rightarrow\quad \theta = \cos^{-1}\dfrac{|\mathbf{C}|}{|\mathbf{A}|} = \cos^{-1}\left(\dfrac{3}{5}\right)$

12 *(c)* The component of vector **A** along vector **B** would be equal to

$$\mathbf{A}\cdot\frac{\mathbf{B}}{|\mathbf{B}|} = (2\hat{\mathbf{i}} + 3\hat{\mathbf{j}})\cdot\frac{(\hat{\mathbf{i}} + \hat{\mathbf{j}})}{|\hat{\mathbf{i}} + \hat{\mathbf{j}}|}$$

$$= (2\hat{\mathbf{i}} + 3\hat{\mathbf{j}})\cdot\frac{(\hat{\mathbf{i}} + \hat{\mathbf{j}})}{\sqrt{2}}$$

$$= \frac{(2+3)}{\sqrt{2}} = \frac{5}{\sqrt{2}}$$

13 *(e)* Given vectors, $\mathbf{A} = \hat{\mathbf{i}} - 3\hat{\mathbf{j}} + 5\hat{\mathbf{k}}$

and $\mathbf{B} = \hat{\mathbf{i}} - 3\hat{\mathbf{j}} - a\hat{\mathbf{k}}$

According to the problem both vectors are equal, then $\mathbf{A} = \mathbf{B}$, so that the value of $a = -5$.

14 *(a)* The correct relation is

$$\mathbf{A} + \mathbf{O} + \mathbf{A}\times\mathbf{O} = \mathbf{A}$$

where, **O** is a null vector.

15 *(c)* For two vectors **a** and **b** to be perpendicular, $\mathbf{a}\cdot\mathbf{b} = 0$.

Thus, $(5\hat{\mathbf{i}} + \lambda\hat{\mathbf{j}} + \hat{\mathbf{k}})\cdot(\hat{\mathbf{i}} - 2\hat{\mathbf{j}} + \hat{\mathbf{k}}) = 0$

$5(\hat{\mathbf{i}}\cdot\hat{\mathbf{i}}) - 2\lambda\,(\hat{\mathbf{j}}\cdot\hat{\mathbf{j}}) + 1\,(\hat{\mathbf{k}}\cdot\hat{\mathbf{k}}) = 0$

$\Rightarrow\quad 5 - 2\lambda + 1 = 0$

$\Rightarrow\quad 6 - 2\lambda = 0 \;\Rightarrow\; \lambda = 3$

16 *(d)* Given, $\mathbf{A}\cdot\mathbf{B} = \mathbf{A}\times\mathbf{B}$

$AB\cos\theta = AB\sin\theta$

$\Rightarrow\quad \tan\theta = 1 \Rightarrow \theta = 45^\circ$

$\therefore\quad \mathbf{C} = \sqrt{A^2 + B^2 + 2AB\cos 45^\circ}$

$= \sqrt{A^2 + B^2 + \sqrt{2}\,AB}$

17 *(d)* Given, $\mathbf{F} = -3\hat{\mathbf{i}} + 2\hat{\mathbf{j}} + \hat{\mathbf{k}}$

and $\mathbf{r} = 8\hat{\mathbf{i}} + 2\hat{\mathbf{j}} + 3\hat{\mathbf{k}}$

Torque of the force, $\tau = \mathbf{r}\times\mathbf{F}$

$$\text{So, } \tau = \begin{vmatrix} \hat{\mathbf{i}} & \hat{\mathbf{j}} & \hat{\mathbf{k}} \\ 8 & 2 & 3 \\ -3 & 2 & 1 \end{vmatrix}$$

$= \hat{\mathbf{i}}\,(2-6) - \hat{\mathbf{j}}\,(8+9) + \hat{\mathbf{k}}\,(16+6)$

$= -4\hat{\mathbf{i}} - 17\hat{\mathbf{j}} + 22\hat{\mathbf{k}}$

18 *(a)* As we know that, for the resultant vectors *R*,

$$R^2 = A^2 + B^2 + 2AB\cos\theta$$

On substituting,

$$A = (x+y),\ B = (x-y)$$

and $R = \sqrt{x^2 + y^2}$

We get, $\theta = \cos^{-1}\left[-\dfrac{(x^2+y^2)}{2\,(x^2-y^2)}\right]$

19 *(d)* Given, $\mathbf{a} + \mathbf{b} = \mathbf{c}$

and $c = a + b$

$\Rightarrow\ a + b = \sqrt{a^2 + b^2 + 2ab\cos\theta}$

$\Rightarrow\ a^2 + b^2 + 2ab = a^2 + b^2 + 2ab\cos\theta$

$\Rightarrow\quad \cos\theta = 1 \Rightarrow \theta = 0^\circ$

20 *(c)* Since, each of *N*-coplanar vector is inclined at $\dfrac{2\pi}{N}$ to the preceding, hence they will form a closed polygon. Therefore, their resultant must be zero.

i.e. let $N = 4$, then $\theta = \dfrac{2\pi}{4} = \dfrac{\pi}{2} = 90^\circ$

Hence,

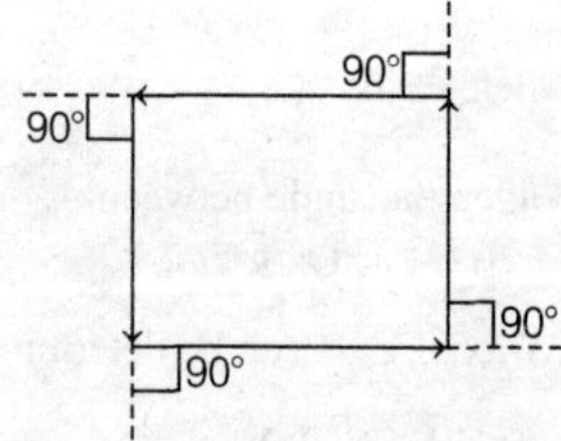

$\Rightarrow$ Square resultant = Zero

21 *(c)* Since, a_1 and a_2 are non-collinear unit vectors.

$\therefore\quad a_1 = a_2 = 1$ and $|\mathbf{a}_1 + \mathbf{a}_2| = \sqrt{3}$

$\Rightarrow\quad a_1^2 + a_2^2 + 2a_1a_2\cos\theta = (\sqrt{3})^2$

$\Rightarrow 1 + 1 + 2\cos\theta = 3$

$\Rightarrow\quad \cos\theta = \dfrac{1}{2}$

Now, $(\mathbf{a}_1 - \mathbf{a}_2)\cdot(2\mathbf{a}_1 + \mathbf{a}_2)$

$= 2a_1^2 - a_2^2 - a_1a_2\cos\theta$

$= 2 - 1 - \dfrac{1}{2} = \dfrac{1}{2}$

22 *(d)* Unit vector of **A** is

$$\hat{\mathbf{a}} = \frac{\mathbf{A}}{|\mathbf{A}|} = \frac{\mathbf{A}}{A}$$

23 *(d)* Given, $\mathbf{A} = -4\hat{\mathbf{i}} + 4\hat{\mathbf{j}} + 2\hat{\mathbf{k}}$

and $\mathbf{B} = 2\hat{\mathbf{i}} - \hat{\mathbf{j}} - \hat{\mathbf{k}}$

Let angle made by $(\mathbf{A} + \mathbf{B})$ with $\hat{\mathbf{i}} + 2\hat{\mathbf{j}} - 4\hat{\mathbf{k}}$ is θ, then

$$\cos\theta = \frac{(\mathbf{A}+\mathbf{B})\cdot(\hat{\mathbf{i}} + 2\hat{\mathbf{j}} - 4\hat{\mathbf{k}})}{|\mathbf{A}+\mathbf{B}|\cdot|\hat{\mathbf{i}} + 2\hat{\mathbf{j}} - 4\hat{\mathbf{k}}|}$$

$$= \frac{(-2\hat{\mathbf{i}} + 3\hat{\mathbf{j}} + \hat{\mathbf{k}})\cdot(\hat{\mathbf{i}} + 2\hat{\mathbf{j}} - 4\hat{\mathbf{k}})}{\sqrt{14}\times\sqrt{21}}$$

$$= 0$$

$$\cos\theta = 0 \Rightarrow \theta = 90°$$

24 *(c)* The dot product of two vectors should be equal to zero, i.e.

$$(\mathbf{a} + \mathbf{b})\cdot(\mathbf{a} - \mathbf{b}) = 0$$

$$\Rightarrow \quad \mathbf{a}^2 - \mathbf{b}^2 = 0$$

$$\therefore \quad |\mathbf{a}| = |\mathbf{b}|$$

25 *(a)* Three forces **A**, **B** and **C** are acting on a body which is in equilibrium position, then

$$\mathbf{A} + \mathbf{B} + \mathbf{C} = 0$$

$$\Rightarrow (\hat{\mathbf{i}} + \hat{\mathbf{j}} + \hat{\mathbf{k}}) + (2\hat{\mathbf{i}} - \hat{\mathbf{j}} + 3\hat{\mathbf{k}}) + \mathbf{C} = 0 \quad \text{(given)}$$

or $$(3\hat{\mathbf{i}} + 4\hat{\mathbf{k}}) + \mathbf{C} = 0$$

$$\therefore \quad \mathbf{C} = -(3\hat{\mathbf{i}} + 4\hat{\mathbf{k}})$$

26 *(a)* Area of a parallelogram $= |\mathbf{a}\times\mathbf{b}|$

where, **a** and **b** are sides of parallelogram.

Given, $\mathbf{a} = \mathbf{p} = 5\hat{\mathbf{i}} - 4\hat{\mathbf{j}} + 3\hat{\mathbf{k}}$

and $\mathbf{b} = \mathbf{q} = 3\hat{\mathbf{i}} + 2\hat{\mathbf{j}} - \hat{\mathbf{k}}$

$$\therefore \quad \mathbf{a}\times\mathbf{b} = \begin{vmatrix} \hat{\mathbf{i}} & \hat{\mathbf{j}} & \hat{\mathbf{k}} \\ 5 & -4 & 3 \\ 3 & 2 & -1 \end{vmatrix}$$

$$\Rightarrow \mathbf{a}\times\mathbf{b} = \hat{\mathbf{i}}\,(4-6) - \hat{\mathbf{j}}\,(-5-9) + \hat{\mathbf{k}}\,(10+12)$$

$$\Rightarrow \quad \mathbf{a}\times\mathbf{b} = -2\hat{\mathbf{i}} + 14\hat{\mathbf{j}} + 22\hat{\mathbf{k}}$$

Thus, $|\mathbf{a}\times\mathbf{b}| = \sqrt{(2)^2 + (14)^2 + (22)^2}$

$$= \sqrt{684}\text{ sq units}$$

27 *(d)* From definition of dot product of vectors, we have

$$\mathbf{x}\cdot\mathbf{y} = xy\cos\theta$$

When $\theta = 90° \Rightarrow \cos 90° = 0$

then $\mathbf{x}\cdot\mathbf{y} = 0$

Given, $\mathbf{x} = a\cos\theta\,\hat{\mathbf{i}} + b\sin\theta\,\hat{\mathbf{j}}$

and $\mathbf{y} = b\sin\theta\,\hat{\mathbf{i}} - a\cos\theta\,\hat{\mathbf{j}}$

$$\therefore \mathbf{x}\cdot\mathbf{y} = (a\cos\theta\hat{\mathbf{i}} + b\sin\theta\hat{\mathbf{j}})\cdot(b\sin\theta\hat{\mathbf{i}} - a\cos\theta\hat{\mathbf{j}})$$

or $$\mathbf{x}\cdot\mathbf{y} = ab\sin\theta\cos\theta - ab\sin\theta\cos\theta = 0$$

Also, $$[a\cos\theta\hat{\mathbf{i}} + b\sin\theta\hat{\mathbf{j}}]\cdot[\frac{1}{a}\sin\theta\hat{\mathbf{i}} - \frac{1}{b}\cos\theta\hat{\mathbf{j}}] = 0$$

and $$[a\cos\theta\hat{\mathbf{i}} + b\sin\theta\hat{\mathbf{j}}]\cdot 5\hat{\mathbf{k}} = 0$$

Thus, we see that all the vector given in the options are perpendicular to the vector $(a\cos\theta\mathbf{i} + b\sin\theta\mathbf{j})$.

Hence option (d) is correct.

28 *(b)* Given, $\mathbf{A} = 2\hat{\mathbf{i}} + 3\hat{\mathbf{j}} - \hat{\mathbf{k}}$

and $\mathbf{B} = -\hat{\mathbf{i}} + 3\hat{\mathbf{j}} + 4\hat{\mathbf{k}}$

As, $$|\mathbf{A}| = \sqrt{(2)^2 + (3)^2 + (-1)^2} = \sqrt{4+9+1} = \sqrt{14}$$

and $$|\mathbf{B}| = \sqrt{(-1)^2 + 3^2 + 4^2} = \sqrt{1+9+16} = \sqrt{26}$$

$$\therefore \quad \mathbf{A}\cdot\mathbf{B} = 2\,(-1) + 3\times 3 + (-1)(4) = 3$$

The projection of **A** on **B** (i.e. $A\cos\theta$)

$$= \frac{\mathbf{A}\cdot\mathbf{B}}{|\mathbf{B}|} = \frac{3}{\sqrt{26}}$$

29 *(b)* Given, $\mathbf{A} = -\hat{\mathbf{i}} + 2\hat{\mathbf{j}} - 3\hat{\mathbf{k}}$

and $\mathbf{B} = 4\hat{\mathbf{i}} - 2\hat{\mathbf{j}} + 6\hat{\mathbf{k}}$

The resultant vector,

$$(\mathbf{A}+\mathbf{B}) = (-\hat{\mathbf{i}} + 2\hat{\mathbf{j}} - 3\hat{\mathbf{k}}) + (4\hat{\mathbf{i}} - 2\hat{\mathbf{j}} + 6\hat{\mathbf{k}}) = (3\hat{\mathbf{i}} + 3\hat{\mathbf{k}})$$

The angle made by $(\mathbf{A}+\mathbf{B})$ with X-axis

$$\tan\theta = \frac{3}{3} = 1$$

$$\therefore \quad \theta = 45°$$

30 *(b)* When the coordinate axes are rotated through some angle, components of the vector change but the vector's magnitude remains constant.

Translation of coordinate axes does not change its components but change the magnitude. As, $\mathbf{R} = \mathbf{a} + \mathbf{b}$, so angle between **b** and **R** is $\tan\phi = \frac{a\sin\theta}{b + a\cos\theta}$,

if a increased then ϕ = increase

cross product $\mathbf{X} = 3\hat{\mathbf{i}}\times 4\hat{\mathbf{j}} = 12\hat{\mathbf{k}}$

31 *(b)* Given vectors,

$$\mathbf{A} = 6\hat{\mathbf{i}} + 8\hat{\mathbf{j}}$$

$$\mathbf{B} = 210\hat{\mathbf{i}} + 280\hat{\mathbf{k}}$$

$$\mathbf{C} = 0.3\hat{\mathbf{i}} + 0.4\hat{\mathbf{j}} = \frac{1}{20}(6\hat{\mathbf{i}} + 8\hat{\mathbf{j}})$$

and $\mathbf{D} = 3.6\hat{\mathbf{i}} + 6\hat{\mathbf{j}} + 4.8\hat{\mathbf{k}}$

Hence, it is clear that **A** and **C** are parallel and we can write as

$$\mathbf{C} = \frac{1}{20}\mathbf{A}$$

because parallel vectors have same direction but magnitude may or may not be same.

32 *(d)* As, $(\mathbf{B}\times\mathbf{A})\cdot\mathbf{A} = (BA\sin\theta\,\hat{\mathbf{n}})\cdot\mathbf{A}$

Here, $\hat{\mathbf{n}}$ is perpendicular to both **A** and **B**.

So, $(BA\sin\theta)\,(\hat{\mathbf{n}}\cdot A) = 0$

$$\Rightarrow \quad (\mathbf{B}\times\mathbf{A})\cdot\mathbf{A} = 0$$

33 *(c)* Given, $\mathbf{a} = 2\hat{\mathbf{i}} + 3\hat{\mathbf{j}} + 8\hat{\mathbf{k}}$

and $\mathbf{b} = 4\hat{\mathbf{j}} - 4\hat{\mathbf{i}} + \alpha\hat{\mathbf{k}} = -4\hat{\mathbf{i}} + 4\hat{\mathbf{j}} + \alpha\hat{\mathbf{k}}$

Given, $\mathbf{a}\perp\mathbf{b} \Rightarrow \mathbf{a}\cdot\mathbf{b} = 0$

$$\Rightarrow (2\hat{\mathbf{i}} + 3\hat{\mathbf{j}} + 8\hat{\mathbf{k}})\cdot(-4\hat{\mathbf{i}} + 4\hat{\mathbf{i}} + \alpha\hat{\mathbf{k}}) = 0$$

$$\Rightarrow -8 + 12 + 8\alpha = 0$$

$$\Rightarrow \quad 8\alpha = -4$$

$$\therefore \quad \alpha = -\frac{4}{8} = -\frac{1}{2}$$

34 *(a)* Given, $|\mathbf{A}\times\mathbf{B}| = \sqrt{3}\mathbf{A}\cdot\mathbf{B}$

but $|\mathbf{A}\times\mathbf{B}| = |\mathbf{A}|\,|\mathbf{B}|\sin\theta = AB\sin\theta$

and $\mathbf{A}\cdot\mathbf{B} = |\mathbf{A}|\,|\mathbf{B}|\cos\theta = AB\cos\theta$

Make these substitution in Eq. (i), we get

$$AB\sin\theta = \sqrt{3}\,AB\cos\theta$$

or $$\tan\theta = \sqrt{3}$$

$$\therefore \quad \theta = 60°$$

The addition of vectors **A** and **B** can be given by the law of parallelogram

$$\therefore |\mathbf{A}+\mathbf{B}| = \sqrt{A^2 + B^2 + 2AB\cos 60°}$$

$$= \sqrt{A^2 + B^2 + 2AB\times\frac{1}{2}}$$

$$= (A^2 + B^2 + AB)^{1/2}$$

35 *(b)* By triangle law of vectors, minimum three vectors are required to give zero resultant, for vectors having unequal magnitude.

36 *(a)* According to the question, the figure can be drawn as

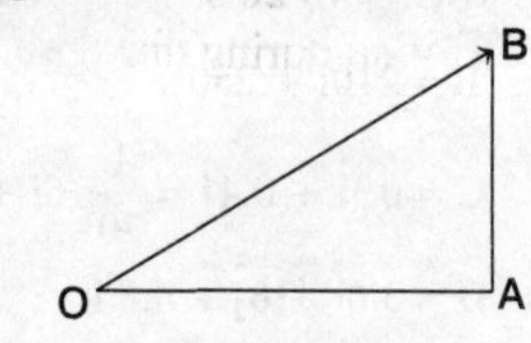

Now, area of the $\Delta\, OAB$

$$= \frac{1}{2}|\mathbf{OA} \times \mathbf{OB}|$$

Given that, $\mathbf{OA} = 3\hat{\mathbf{i}} - 6\hat{\mathbf{j}} + 2\hat{\mathbf{k}}$

and $\mathbf{OB} = 2\hat{\mathbf{i}} + \hat{\mathbf{j}} - 2\hat{\mathbf{k}}$

$$\therefore \text{ Area, } \Delta = \frac{1}{2}\begin{vmatrix} \hat{\mathbf{i}} & \hat{\mathbf{j}} & \hat{\mathbf{k}} \\ 3 & -6 & 2 \\ 2 & 1 & -2 \end{vmatrix}$$

$$= \frac{1}{2}[(12-2)\hat{\mathbf{i}} - (-6-4)\hat{\mathbf{j}} + (3+12)\hat{\mathbf{k}}]$$

$$= \frac{1}{2}[10\hat{\mathbf{i}} + 10\hat{\mathbf{j}} + 15\hat{\mathbf{k}}]$$

$$= \frac{1}{2} \times \sqrt{100+100+225}$$

$$= \frac{1}{2}\sqrt{425} = \frac{5\sqrt{17}}{2}$$

37 *(c)* Here, **a** is a vector but $(\mathbf{b} \cdot \mathbf{c})$ is scalar quantity and the cross product between a vector and a scalar is undefined. Hence LHS of option (c) is not correct.

38 *(a)* Given, $\mathbf{A} = \sqrt{3}\hat{\mathbf{i}} + \hat{\mathbf{j}}$

and $\mathbf{B} = \hat{\mathbf{i}}$ (unit vector along X-axis)

Now, $\mathbf{A} \cdot \mathbf{B} = (\sqrt{3}\,\hat{\mathbf{i}} + \hat{\mathbf{j}}) \cdot \hat{\mathbf{i}}$

$$= \sqrt{3} + 0 = \sqrt{3}$$

$$(\because \hat{\mathbf{i}} \cdot \hat{\mathbf{i}} = 1, \hat{\mathbf{j}} \cdot \hat{\mathbf{i}} = 0)$$

Also, $|\mathbf{A}| = \sqrt{(\sqrt{3})^2 + (1)^2}$

$$= \sqrt{3+1} = 2$$

$$|\mathbf{B}| = \sqrt{(1)^2} = 1$$

$\because AB \cos\theta = \mathbf{A} \cdot \mathbf{B}$, where θ is the angle between vector **A** and X-axis

$$\cos\theta = \frac{\mathbf{B} \cdot \mathbf{A}}{AB}$$

$$= \frac{\sqrt{3}}{2} = \cos\frac{\pi}{6}$$

$$\Rightarrow \quad \theta = \frac{\pi}{6} \text{ rad}$$

Topic 2

Terms Related to Motion in a Plane

2019

1 When an object is shot from the bottom of a long smooth inclined plane kept at an angle 60° with horizontal, it can travel a distance x_1 along the plane. But when the inclination is decreased to 30° and the same object is shot with the same velocity, it can travel x_2 distance. Then $x_1 : x_2$ will be **[NEET]**

(a) $\sqrt{2}:1$ (b) $1:\sqrt{3}$
(c) $1:2\sqrt{3}$ (d) $1:\sqrt{2}$

2017

2 The x and y-coordinates of a particle moving in a plane are given by $x(t) = a\cos(pt)$ and $y(t) = b\sin(pt)$, where $a, b\,(< a)$ and p are positive constants of appropriate dimensions and t is time. Then, which of the following is not true? **[JIPMER]**

(a) The path of the particle is an ellipse.
(b) Velocity and acceleration of the particle are perpendicular to each other at $t = \frac{\pi}{2p}$.
(c) Acceleration of the particle is always directed towards a fixed point.
(d) Distance travelled by the particle in time interval between $t = 0$ and $t = \frac{\pi}{2p}$ is a.

3 A block is dragged on a smooth plane with the help of a rope which moves with a velocity v as shown in the figure. The horizontal velocity of the block is

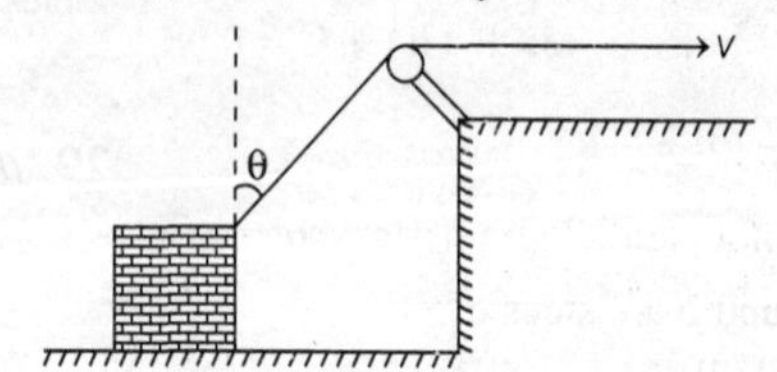

[AIIMS]

(a) $\frac{v}{\sin\theta}$ (b) $v\sin\theta$
(c) $\frac{v}{\cos\theta}$ (d) $v\cos\theta$

2016

4 A particle moves, so that its position vector is given by $\mathbf{r} = \cos\omega t\,\hat{\mathbf{x}} + \sin\omega t\,\hat{\mathbf{y}}$, where ω is a constant. Which of the following is true? **[NEET]**

(a) Velocity and acceleration both are parallel to **r**.
(b) Velocity is perpendicular to **r** and acceleration is directed towards to origin.
(c) Velocity is perpendicular to **r** and acceleration is directed away from the origin.
(d) Velocity and acceleration both are perpendicular to **r**.

2014

5 A particle is moving such that its position coordinates (x, y) are $(2m, 3m)$ at time $t = 0$, $(6m, 7m)$ at time $t = 2$ s and $(13m, 14m)$ at time $t = 5$ s. Average velocity vector (v_{av}) from $t = 0$ to 5 s is **[CBSE AIPMT]**

(a) $\frac{1}{5}(13\hat{\mathbf{i}} + 14\hat{\mathbf{j}})$ (b) $\frac{7}{3}(\hat{\mathbf{i}} + \hat{\mathbf{j}})$

(c) $2(\hat{\mathbf{i}} - \hat{\mathbf{j}})$ (d) $\frac{11}{5}(\hat{\mathbf{i}} + \hat{\mathbf{j}})$

2008

6 A car travels 6 km towards the north at an angle 45° to the east and then travels distance of 4 km towards the north at an angle 135° to the east. How far is the point from the starting point? What angle does the straight line joining its initial and final positions makes with the east? **[AIIMS]**

(a) $\sqrt{50}$ km and $\tan^{-1}(5)$

(b) 10 km and $\tan^{-1}(\sqrt{5})$

(c) $\sqrt{52}$ km and $\tan^{-1}(5)$

(d) $\sqrt{52}$ km and $\tan^{-1}(\sqrt{5})$

7 A proton in a cyclotron changes its velocity from 30 kms^{-1} the north of 40 kms^{-1} in 20 s. What is the magnitude of average acceleration during this time? **[Manipal]**

(a) 2.5 kms^{-2}

(b) 12.5 kms^{-2}

(c) 22.5 kms^{-2}

(d) 32.5 kms^{-2}

8 Two forces of 12 N and 8 N act upon a body. The resultant force on the body has a maximum value of **[Manipal]**

(a) 4 N (b) zero

(c) 20 N (d) 8 N

2005

9 The position vector of a particle is

$$\mathbf{r} = (a\cos\omega t)\hat{\mathbf{i}} + (a\sin\omega t)\hat{\mathbf{j}}.$$

The velocity vector of the particle is **[Punjab PMET]**

(a) parallel to position vector

(b) perpendicular to position vector

(c) directed towards the origin

(d) directed away from the origin

Answers

1 (b)	2 (d)	3 (a)	4 (b)	5 (d)	6 (c)	7 (a)	8 (c)	9 (b)

Explanations

1 *(b)* The motion of object shot in two cases can be depicted as below

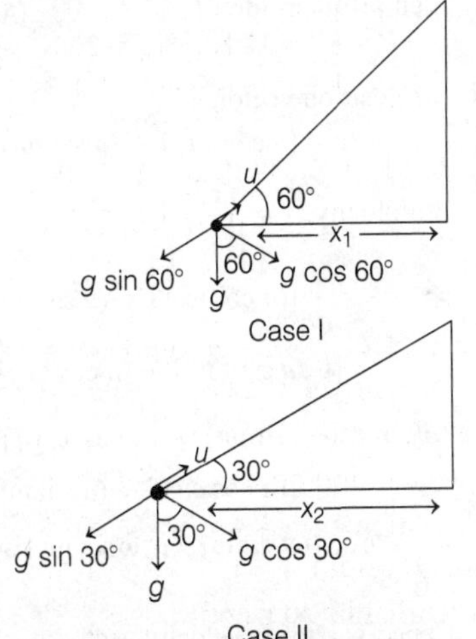

Using third equation of motion,

$$v^2 = u^2 - 2gh \quad \dots (i)$$

As the object stops finally, so

$$v = 0$$

For inclined motion,

$$g = g\sin\theta \text{ and } h = x$$

Substituting these values in Eq. (i), we get

$$\Rightarrow \quad u^2 = 2g\sin\theta\, x$$

$$\Rightarrow \quad x = \frac{u^2}{2g\sin\theta}$$

For case (I) $x_1 = \frac{u^2}{2g\sin 60°}$

For case (II) $x_2 = \frac{u^2}{2g\sin 30°}$

$$\Rightarrow \frac{x_1}{x_2} = \frac{u^2}{2g\sin 60°} \times \frac{2g\sin 30°}{u^2}$$

$$= \frac{1}{2} \times \frac{2}{\sqrt{3}} = \frac{1}{\sqrt{3}} \text{ or } 1 : \sqrt{3}$$

2 *(d)* Given, $x = a\cos(pt)$, $y = b\sin(pt)$

$$\therefore \frac{x^2}{a^2} + \frac{y^2}{b^2} = 1, \text{ i.e. equation of ellipse}$$

Now, $\mathbf{r} = x\hat{\mathbf{i}} + y\hat{\mathbf{j}}$

$$= a\cos(pt)\,\hat{\mathbf{i}} + b\sin(pt)\hat{\mathbf{j}}$$

$$\mathbf{v} = \frac{d\mathbf{r}}{dt} = -pa\sin(pt)\,\hat{\mathbf{i}} + pb\cos(pt)\hat{\mathbf{j}}$$

$$\mathbf{a} = \frac{d\mathbf{v}}{dt} = -p^2a\cos(pt)\,\hat{\mathbf{i}} - p^2b\sin(pt)\hat{\mathbf{j}}$$

At $t = \frac{\pi}{2p}$

$$\mathbf{v} = -pa\hat{\mathbf{i}} \text{ and } \mathbf{a} = -p^2b\hat{\mathbf{j}}$$

v perpendicular to a.

Also, $a = -p^2b$, i.e. directed towards a fixed point as p and b are positive constants.

As, $v = \frac{dr}{dt} \Rightarrow \Delta r = \int^{\frac{\pi}{2p}} v\,dt$

$\Rightarrow \Delta r = [a \cos(pt)\hat{\mathbf{i}} + b\sin(pt)\hat{\mathbf{j}}]_0^{\frac{\pi}{2p}}$

$= -a\hat{\mathbf{i}} + b\hat{\mathbf{j}}$

So, $|\mathbf{r}| = \sqrt{a^2 + b^2}$

3 (a) Let at any instant of time, the length AB be l, here angle θ and length l vary with time, then using Pythagoras theorem in ΔABC

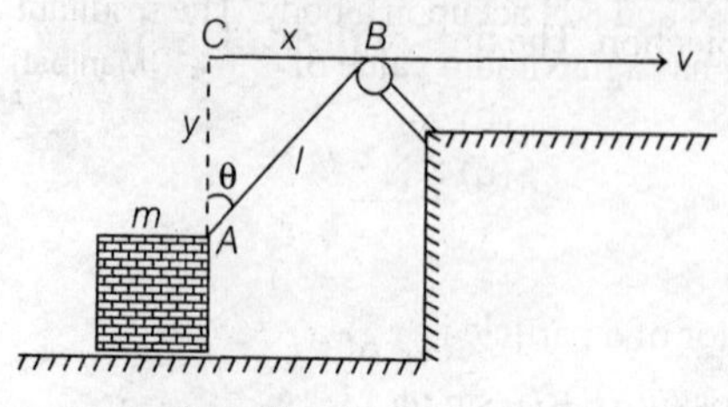

$$x^2 + y^2 = l^2$$

Differentiating both sides w.r.t t, we get

or $\quad 2x\dfrac{dx}{dt} + 2y\dfrac{dy}{dt} = 2l\dfrac{dl}{dt}$

As, there is no vertical motion of the block, so

$$\frac{dy}{dt} = 0, \frac{dx}{dt} = v_x$$

and $\quad \dfrac{dl}{dt} = v$

$\therefore \quad 2xv_x = 2lv$

or $\quad v_x = \dfrac{l}{x}v$

or $\quad v_x = \dfrac{v}{\left(\dfrac{x}{l}\right)} = \dfrac{v}{\sin\theta}$

4 (b) Position vector of the particle is given by

$$\mathbf{r} = \cos\omega t\hat{\mathbf{x}} + \sin\omega t\hat{\mathbf{y}}$$

where, ω is a constant.

Velocity of the particle,

$$\mathbf{v} = \frac{d\mathbf{r}}{dt} = \frac{d}{dt}(\cos\omega t\hat{\mathbf{x}} + \sin\omega t\hat{\mathbf{y}})$$

$$= (-\sin\omega t)\,\omega\hat{\mathbf{x}} + (\cos\omega t)\,\omega\hat{\mathbf{y}}$$

$$= -\omega(\sin\omega t\,\hat{\mathbf{x}} - \cos\omega t\,\hat{\mathbf{y}})$$

Acceleration of the particle,

$$\mathbf{a} = \frac{d\mathbf{v}}{dt} = \frac{d}{dt}[-\omega\sin\omega t\,\hat{\mathbf{x}} + \omega\cos\omega t\,\hat{\mathbf{y}}]$$

$$= -\omega^2\cos\omega t\,\hat{\mathbf{x}} - \omega^2\sin\omega t\,\hat{\mathbf{y}}$$

$$= -\omega^2(\cos\omega t\,\hat{\mathbf{x}} - \sin\omega t\hat{\mathbf{y}})$$

$\Rightarrow \quad \mathbf{a} = -\omega^2\mathbf{r} = \omega^2(-\mathbf{r})$

Assuming the particle as P, then its position vector is directed as shown in the diagram.

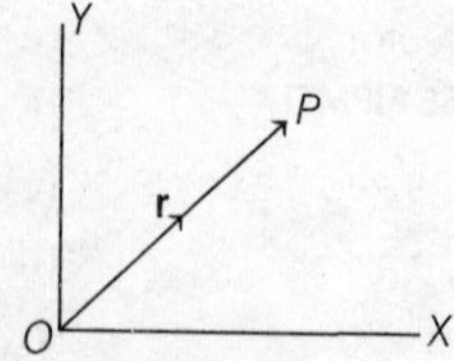

Therefore, acceleration is directed toward $-\mathbf{r}$, i.e. is towards O (origin). Now, we have

$$\mathbf{v}\cdot\mathbf{r} = -\omega(\sin\omega t\,\hat{\mathbf{x}} - \cos\omega t\,\hat{\mathbf{y}})\cdot(\cos\omega t\,\hat{\mathbf{x}} + \sin\omega t\,\hat{\mathbf{y}})$$

$$= -\omega[\sin\omega t\cdot\cos\omega t + 0 + 0 - \sin\omega t\cdot\cos\omega t]$$

$$= -\omega(0) = 0 \qquad [\because \hat{\mathbf{x}} \perp \hat{\mathbf{y}}]$$

$\Rightarrow \quad \mathbf{v} \perp \mathbf{r}$

Thus, velocity is perpendicular to $\mathbf{r}$.

5 (d) Average velocity vector,

$$\mathbf{v}_{av} = \frac{\text{net displacement}}{\text{time taken}}$$

$$= \frac{(13-2)\,\hat{\mathbf{i}} + (14-3)\,\hat{\mathbf{j}}}{5} \text{ (given)}$$

$$= \frac{11\hat{\mathbf{i}} + 11\hat{\mathbf{j}}}{5} = \frac{11}{5}(\hat{\mathbf{i}} + \hat{\mathbf{j}})$$

6 (c) Given, $s_1 = 6$ km, $S_2 = 4$ km and $\theta = 45°$

Net movement along x-direction,

$$s_x = (s_1 - S_2)\cos\theta\hat{\mathbf{i}}$$

$$s_x = (6-4)\cos 45°\,\hat{\mathbf{i}}$$

$$= 2 \times \frac{1}{\sqrt{2}} = \sqrt{2} \text{ km}$$

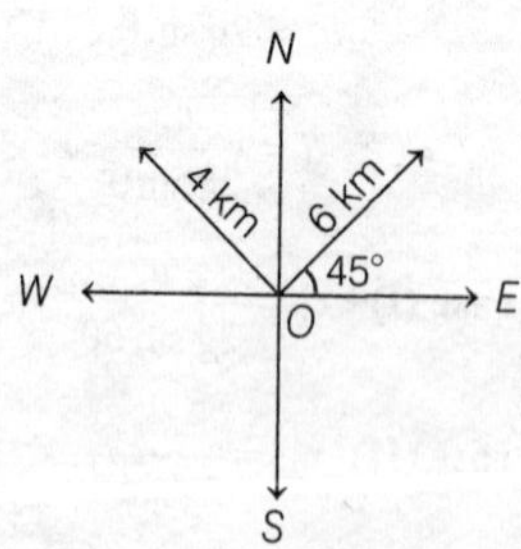

Net movement along y-direction,

$$s_y = (s_1 + s_2)\cos\theta\hat{\mathbf{j}}$$

$$s_y = (6+4)\sin 45°\,\hat{\mathbf{j}}$$

$$= 10 \times \frac{1}{\sqrt{2}} = 5\sqrt{2} \text{ km}$$

Net movement from starting point (O in the diagram),

$$|s| = \sqrt{s_x^2 + s_y^2} = \sqrt{(\sqrt{2})^2 + (5\sqrt{2})^2}$$

$$= \sqrt{52} \text{ km}$$

The tangent of angle which resultant makes with the east direction,

$$\tan\theta = \frac{y\text{-component}}{x\text{-component}} = \frac{5\sqrt{2}}{\sqrt{2}}$$

$\Rightarrow \quad \theta = \tan^{-1}(5)$

7 (a) Given, $v_1 = 30 \text{ kms}^{-1}$,

$v_2 = 40 \text{ kms}^{-1}$

and $\Delta t = 20$ s

Change in velocity

$$= \sqrt{(40)^2 + (30)^2} = 50 \text{ kms}^{-1}$$

$$\text{Average acceleration} = \frac{50}{20} = 2.5 \text{ kms}^{-2}$$

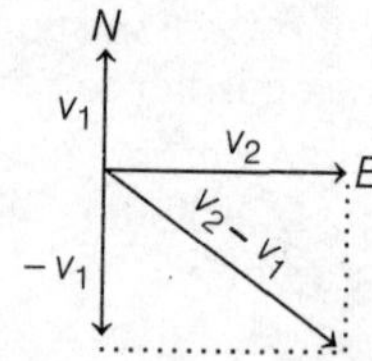

8 (c) When the two forces of 12 N and 8 N act upon a body, the resultant force on the body has maximum value. When two forces are in same direction, then resultant force

$$= 12 \text{ N} + 8 \text{ N} = 20 \text{ N}$$

9 (b) Position vector,

$$\mathbf{r} = (a\cos\omega t)\,\hat{\mathbf{i}} + (a\sin\omega t)\,\hat{\mathbf{j}}$$

$\therefore$ Velocity, $\mathbf{v} = \dfrac{d\mathbf{r}}{dt}$

$\Rightarrow \quad = \dfrac{d}{dt}[(a\cos\omega t)\,\hat{\mathbf{i}} + (a\sin\omega t)\,\hat{\mathbf{j}}]$

$$= [(-a\sin\omega t)\,\hat{\mathbf{i}} + (a\cos\omega t)\hat{\mathbf{j}}]\,\omega$$

$\therefore \mathbf{v}\cdot\mathbf{r} = [(-a\sin\omega t)\hat{\mathbf{i}} + (a\cos\omega t)\,\hat{\mathbf{j}}]\,\omega\cdot[(a\cos\omega t)\,\hat{\mathbf{i}} + (a\sin\omega t)\,\hat{\mathbf{j}}]$

$$= -a^2\omega\cos\omega t\sin\omega t + a^2\omega\sin\omega t\cos\omega t$$

$$= 0$$

Hence $\mathbf{v} \perp \mathbf{r}$, i.e. velocity vector is perpendicular to position vector.

Topic 3

Projectile Motion

2019

1 Two bullets are fired horizontally and simultaneously towards each other from roof tops of two buildings 100 m apart and of same height of 200 m with the same velocity of 25 ms^{-1}. When and where will the two bullets collides? ($g = 10 ms^{-2}$) **[NEET (Odisha)]**

(a) After 2s at a height 180 m
(b) After 2s at a height of 20 m
(c) After 4s at a height of 120 m
(d) They will not collide

2018

2 **Assertion** The maximum height of projectile is always 25% of the maximum range.
Reason For maximum range, projectile should be projected at 90°. **[AIIMS]**

(a) Both Assertion and Reason are correct and Reason is the correct explanation of Assertion.
(b) Both Assertion and Reason are correct and Reason is not the correct explanation of Assertion.
(c) Assertion is correct but Reason is incorrect.
(d) Assertion is incorrect but Reason is correct.

3 What is the range of a projectile thrown with velocity 98 ms^{-1} with angle 30° from horizontal? **[JIPMER]**

(a) $490\sqrt{3}$ m (b) $245\sqrt{3}$ m
(c) $980\sqrt{3}$ m (d) 100 m

2017

4 **Assertion** When $\theta = 45°$ or 135°, the value of R remains the same, only the sign changes.
Reason $R = \frac{u^2 \sin 2\theta}{g}$ **[AIIMS]**

(a) Both Assertion and Reason are correct and Reason is the correct explanation of Assertion.
(b) Both Assertion and Reason are correct and Reason is not the correct explanation of Assertion.
(c) Assertion is correct but Reason is incorrect.
(d) Assertion is incorrect but Reason is correct.

2014

5 If the angle of projection of a projector with same initial velocity exceed or fall short of 45° by equal amount α, then the ratio of horizontal ranges is **[Kerala CEE]**

(a) 1 : 2 (b) 1 : 3 (c) 1 : 4 (d) 1 : 1
(e) $1 : \sqrt{2}$

6 A cricket ball thrown across a field is at heights h_1 and h_2 from the point of projection at times t_1 and t_2 respectively after the throw. The ball is caught by a fielder at the same height as that of projection. The time of flight of the ball in this journey is **[WB JEE]**

(a) $\left(\frac{h_1 t_2^2 - h_2 t_1^2}{h_1 t_2 - h_2 t_1}\right)$ (b) $\left(\frac{h_1 t_2^2 - h_2 t_1^2}{h_1 t_1 - h_2 t_2}\right)$
(c) $\left(\frac{h_1 t_2^2 + h_2 t_1^2}{h_1 t_2 + h_2 t_1}\right)$ (d) None of these

7 For an object thrown at 45° to the horizontal, the maximum height H and horizontal range R are related as **[UK PMT]**

(a) $R = 16H$ (b) $R = 8H$
(c) $R = 4H$ (d) $R = 2H$

8 A body is projected horizontally from the top of a tower with a velocity of 10 ms^{-1}. If it hits the ground at an angle of 45°, then the vertical component of velocity when it hits ground (in ms^{-1}) is **[EAMCET]**

(a) $10\sqrt{2}$ (b) $5\sqrt{2}$
(c) 5 (d) 10

9 A body is projected with an angle θ. The maximum height reached is h. If the time of flight is 4 s and $g = 10 ms^{-2}$, then value of h is **[EAMCET]**

(a) 40 m (b) 20 m (c) 5 m (d) 10 m

2013

10 The velocity of a projectile at the initial point A is $(2\hat{i} + 3\hat{j}) ms^{-1}$. Its velocity (in ms^{-1}) at point B is **[NEET]**

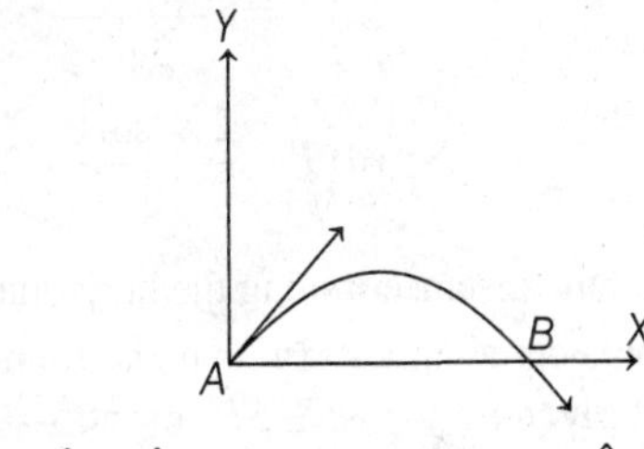

(a) $-2\hat{i} - 3\hat{j}$ (b) $-2\hat{i} + 3\hat{j}$
(c) $2\hat{i} - 3\hat{j}$ (d) $2\hat{i} + 3\hat{j}$

11 An aeroplane is flying horizontally with a velocity of 600 kmh^{-1} and at a height of 1960 m. When it is vertically above a point A on the ground, a bomb is released from it. The bomb strikes the ground at point B. The distance AB is **[Manipal]**

(a) 1200 km (b) 0.33 km
(c) 33.3 km (d) 3.33 km

12 An arrow is shot into air. Its range is 200 m and its time of flight is 5 s. If $g = 10\ ms^{-2}$, then horizontal component of velocity of the arrow is **[KCET]**

(a) $12.5\ ms^{-1}$ (b) $25\ ms^{-1}$
(c) $31.25\ ms^{-1}$ (d) $40\ ms^{-1}$

2012

13 The horizontal range and the maximum height of a projectile are equal. The angle of projection of the projectile is **[CBSE AIPMT]**

(a) $\theta = \tan^{-1}\left(\frac{1}{4}\right)$ (b) $\theta = \tan^{-1}(4)$
(c) $\theta = \tan^{-1}(2)$ (d) $\theta = 45°$

14 The equation of trajectory of a projectile is $y = 10x - \left(\frac{5}{9}\right)x^2$. If we assume $g = 10\ ms^{-2}$, then the range of projectile (in metre) is **[AFMC]**

(a) 36 (b) 24 (c) 18 (d) 9

2011

15 A missile is fired for maximum range with a initial velocity of $20\ ms^{-1}$. If $g = 10\ ms^{-2}$, the range of the missile is **[CBSE AIPMT]**

(a) 50 m (b) 60 m
(c) 20 m (d) 40 m

16 If a person can throw a stone to maximum height of h metre vertically, then the maximum distance through which it can be thrown horizontally by the same person is **[WB JEE]**

(a) $\frac{h}{2}$ (b) h (c) $2h$ (d) $3h$

17 If a projectile is launched with velocity v_0 making an angle θ with X-axis, then its time of flight T is **[J&K CET]**

(a) $T = \frac{v_0^2 \sin 2\theta}{g}$ (b) $T = \frac{v_0^2 \sin^2 \theta}{2g}$
(c) $T = \frac{v_0^2}{g}$ (d) $T = \frac{2v_0 \sin \theta}{g}$

18 The height y and the distance x along the horizontal plane of a projectile on a certain planet (with no surrounding atmosphere) are given by $y = 8t - 5t^2$ m and $x = 6t$ m, where t is in seconds. The velocity with which the projectile is projected is **[KCET]**

(a) $6\ ms^{-1}$ (b) $8\ ms^{-1}$ (c) $10\ ms^{-1}$ (d) $14\ ms^{-1}$

19 The horizontal range of a projectile fired at an angle of 15° is 50 m. If it is fired with the same speed at an angle of 45°, its range will be **[Manipal]**

(a) 60 m (b) 71 m (c) 100 m (d) 141 m

2010

20 For a projectile, $(\text{range})^2$ is 48 times of $(\text{maximum height})^2$ obtained. Find the angle of projection. **[CBSE AIPMT]**

(a) 60° (b) 30° (c) 45° (d) 75°

21 A particle of mass m is projected with a velocity v at an angle of 60° with horizontal. When the particle is at its maximum height, the magnitude of its angular momentum about the point of projection is **[AFMC]**

(a) zero (b) $\frac{3mv^3}{16g}$ (c) $\frac{\sqrt{3}\,mv^3}{16g}$ (d) $\frac{3mv^3}{8g}$

22 **Assertion** Generally, the path of a projectile from the earth is parabolic but it is elliptical for projectile going to a very large height.

Reason The path of a projectile is independent of the gravitational force of the earth. **[AFMC]**

(a) Both Assertion and Reason are correct and Reason is the correct explanation of Assertion.
(b) Both Assertion and Reason are correct but Reason is not the correct explanation of Assertion.
(c) Assertion is correct but Reason is incorrect.
(d) Assertion is incorrect but Reason is correct.

23 Which of the following is the graph between the horizontal velocity (u_x) of a projectile and time (t), when it is projected from the ground? **[UP CPMT]**

(a) 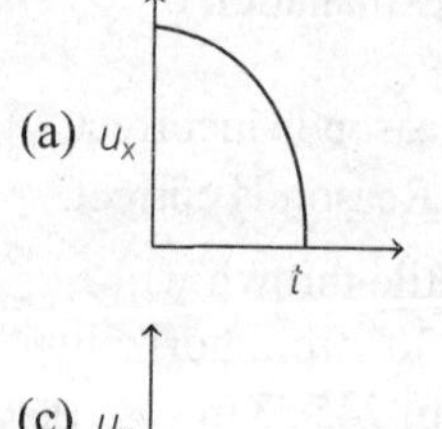

(b) 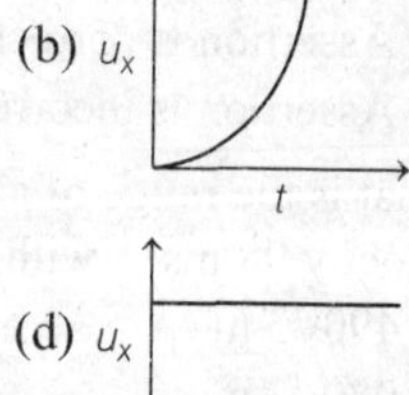

(c) u_x vs t

(d) u_x vs t

24 A cart is moving horizontally along a straight line with constant speed $30\ ms^{-1}$. A projectile is to be fired from the moving cart in such a way that it will return to the cart after the cart has moved 80 m. At what speed (relative to the cart) must the projectile be fired? (Take, $g = 10\ ms^{-2}$) **[BVP]**

(a) $10\ ms^{-1}$ (b) $10\sqrt{8}\ ms^{-1}$
(c) $40/3\ ms^{-1}$ (d) None of these

25 The relation between the time of flight of a projectile T_f and the time to reach the maximum height t_m is **[Kerala CEE]**

(a) $T_f = 2t_m$ (b) $T_f = t_m$
(c) $T_f = \frac{t_m}{2}$ (d) $T_f = \sqrt{2}\,(t_m)$
(e) $T_f = \frac{t_m}{\sqrt{2}}$

26 A body is projected with a speed u ms^{-1} at an angle β with the horizontal. The kinetic energy at the highest point is (3/4)th of the initial kinetic energy. The value of β is **[WB JEE]**
(a) 30° (b) 45° (c) 60° (d) 120°

27 A ball is projected horizontally with a velocity of 5 ms^{-1} from the top of a building 19.6 m high. How long will the ball take to hit the ground? **[WB JEE]**
(a) $\sqrt{2}$ s (b) 2 s (c) $\sqrt{3}$ s (d) 3 s

28 A particle is projected with a velocity v such that its range on the horizontal plane is twice the greatest height attained by it. The range of the projectile is (where, g is acceleration due to gravity) **[Haryana PMT]**
(a) $\frac{4v^2}{5g}$ (b) $\frac{4g}{5v^2}$ (c) $\frac{v^2}{g}$ (d) $\frac{4v^2}{\sqrt{5g}}$

2008

29 A projectile can have the same range R for two angles of projection. If t_1 and t_2 be the times of flights in the two cases, then the product of the two times of flights is proportional to **[AIIMS]**
(a) R^2 (b) $\frac{1}{R^2}$ (c) $\frac{1}{R}$ (d) R

30 The maximum height attained by a projectile is increased by 5%. Keeping the angle of projection constant, what is the percentage increase in horizontal range? **[BHU]**
(a) 5% (b) 10% (c) 15% (d) 20%

31 A ball is projected from the ground at an angle θ with the horizontal. After 1 s, it is moving at an angle 45° with the horizontal and after 2 s it is moving horizontally. What is the velocity of projection of the ball? **[Manipal]**
(a) $10\sqrt{3}$ ms^{-1} (b) $20\sqrt{3}$ ms^{-1}
(c) $10\sqrt{5}$ ms^{-1} (d) $20\sqrt{2}$ ms^{-1}

32 A boy playing on the roof of a 10 m high building throws a ball with a speed of 10 ms^{-1} at an angle of 30° with the horizontal. How far from the throwing point will the ball be at the height of 10 m from the ground?
(Take, $g = 10$ ms^{-2}, $\sin 30° = 1/2$ and $\cos 30° = \sqrt{3}/2$)
(a) 5.20 m (b) 4.33 m **[RPMT]**
(c) 2.60 m (d) 8.66 m

33 For angles of projection of a projectile at angles $(45° - \theta)$ and $(45° + \theta)$, the horizontal ranges described by the projectile are in the ratio of **[Haryana PMT]**
(a) 1 : 1 (b) 2 : 3 (c) 1 : 2 (d) 2 : 1

34 A body is projected at an angle θ with respect to horizontal direction with velocity u. The maximum range of the body is **[J&K CET]**
(a) $R = \frac{u^2 \sin 2\theta}{g}$ (b) $R = \frac{u^2 \sin^2 \theta}{2g}$
(c) $R = \frac{u^2}{g}$ (d) $R = u^2 \sin \theta$

35 A body is projected horizontally with velocity 196 ms^{-1} from height 400 m. What is the time to reach the ground?
(a) 5 s (b) 9 s **[DUMET]**
(c) 15 s (d) 20 s

36 A projectile is projected at an angle 60° with horizontal with speed 10 ms^{-1}. The minimum radius of curvature of trajectory described by the projectile is **[DUMET]**
(a) 2.55 m (b) 2 m
(c) 10 m (d) None of these

37 Two stones are projected with the same speed but making different angles with the horizontal. Their horizontal ranges are equal. The angle of projection of one is $\pi/3$ and the maximum height reached by it is 102 m. Then, the maximum height reached by other in metre **[BCECE]**
(a) 336 (b) 224
(c) 56 (d) 34

2007

38 During projectile motion, the horizontal velocity **[UP CPMT]**
(a) first increases, then decreases
(b) first decreases, then increases
(c) always increases
(d) always constant

39 The maximum height attained by a projectile when thrown at an angle θ with the horizontal is found to be half the horizontal range. Then, θ is equal to **[KCET]**
(a) $\tan^{-1}(2)$ (b) $\frac{\pi}{6}$
(c) $\frac{\pi}{4}$ (d) $\tan^{-1}\left(\frac{1}{2}\right)$

40 A body is projected at such angle that the horizontal range is three times the greatest height. The angle of projection is
(a) 42°8′ (b) 53°7′ **[BCECE]**
(c) 33°7′ (d) 25°8′

41 A bullet fired at an angle of 30° with the horizontal hits the ground 3 km away. By adjusting its angle of projection, can one hope to hit a target 5 km away? Assume the muzzle speed to the same and the air resistance is negligible.
(a) Possible to hit a target 5 km away **[BCECE]**
(b) Not possible to hit a target 5 km away
(c) Prediction is not possible
(d) None of the above

42 A projectile is thrown in the upward direction making an angle of 60° with the horizontal direction with a velocity of 147 ms^{-1}. Then, the time after which its inclination with the horizontal is 45°, is **[JCECE]**
(a) 15 s (b) 10.98 s
(c) 5.49 s (d) 2.745 s

2006

43 A stone is just released from the window of a moving train along a horizontal straight track. The stone will hit the ground following **[JCECE]**

(a) straight path (b) circular path
(c) parabolic path (d) hyperbolic path

44 Two bodies are projected from ground with equal speed $20\ \text{ms}^{-1}$ from the same position in the same vertical plane to have equal range but at different angles above the horizontal. If one of the angle is 30°, then the sum of their maximum heights is (assume, $g = 10\ \text{ms}^{-2}$) **[J&K CET]**

(a) 400 m (b) 20 m (c) 30 m (d) 40 m

45 Two stones are projected with same velocity v at an angle θ and $(90° - \theta)$. If H and H_1 are the greatest heights in the two paths, then what is the relation between R, H and H_1? **[AMU]**

(a) $R = 4\sqrt{HH_1}$ (b) $R = \sqrt{HH_1}$
(c) $R = HH_1$ (d) None of these

46 A tennis ball rolls off the top of a stair-case way with a horizontal velocity $u\ \text{ms}^{-1}$. If the steps are b metre wide and h meter high, the ball will hit the edge of the nth step, if **[J&K CET]**

(a) $n = \dfrac{2hu}{gb^2}$ (b) $n = \dfrac{2hu^2}{gb^2}$ (c) $n = \dfrac{2hu^2}{gb}$ (d) $n = \dfrac{hu^2}{gb^2}$

47 A projectile is fired making an angle 2θ with horizontal with velocity $4\ \text{ms}^{-1}$. At any instant it makes an angle θ, then its velocity is **[JCECE]**

(a) $4\cos\theta$ (b) $4(2\cos\theta - \sec\theta)$
(c) $2(\sec\theta + 4\cos\theta)$ (d) $4(\sec\theta + \cos\theta)$

2005

48 A bullet is fired from the gun with a speed of $1000\ \text{ms}^{-1}$ in order to hit a target $s = 100$ m away. At what height above the target should be gun be aimed? (the resistance of air is negligible and $g = 10\ \text{ms}^{-2}$) **[MP PMT]**

(a) 23 cm (b) 15 cm
(c) 9 cm (d) 5 cm

49 A stone thrown at an angle θ to the horizontal reaches a maximum height H, then the time of flight of stone will be **[Punjab PMET]**

(a) $\sqrt{\dfrac{2H}{g}}$ (b) $2\sqrt{\dfrac{2H}{g}}$
(c) $\dfrac{2\sqrt{2H\sin\theta}}{g}$ (d) $\dfrac{\sqrt{2H\sin\theta}}{g}$

50 At the height 80 m, an aeroplane is moved with $150\ \text{ms}^{-1}$. A bomb is dropped from it so as to hit a target. At what distance from the target should the bomb be dropped? (Take, $g = 10\ \text{ms}^{-2}$) **[Punjab PMET]**

(a) 605.3 m (b) 600 m
(c) 80 m (d) 230 m

51 Two bodies are thrown up at angles of 45° and 60° respectively, with the horizontal. If both bodies attain same vertical height, then ratio of velocities with which these are thrown is **[DUMET]**

(a) $\sqrt{2/3}$ (b) $2/\sqrt{3}$
(c) $\sqrt{3/2}$ (d) $\sqrt{3}/2$

Answers

1 (a)	2 (c)	3 (a)	4 (a)	5 (d)	6 (a)	7 (c)	8 (d)	9 (b)	10 (c)
11 (d)	12 (d)	13 (b)	14 (c)	15 (d)	16 (c)	17 (d)	18 (a)	19 (c)	20 (b)
21 (b)	22 (c)	23 (d)	24 (c)	25 (a)	26 (a)	27 (b)	28 (a)	29 (d)	30 (a)
31 (c)	32 (d)	33 (a)	34 (c)	35 (b)	36 (a)	37 (d)	38 (d)	39 (a)	40 (b)
41 (b)	42 (c)	43 (c)	44 (b)	45 (a)	46 (b)	47 (b)	48 (d)	49 (b)	50 (b)
51 (c)									

Explanations

1 *(a)* Given, distance between the two buildings, $d = 100$ m

Height of each tower, $h = 200$ m

Speed of each bullet, $v = 25\ \text{ms}^{-1}$

The situation can be shown as below

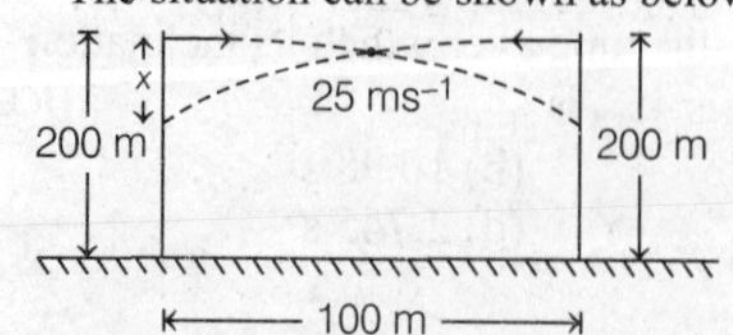

where, x be the vertical distance travelled from the top of the building and t be the time at which they collide.

As two bullets are fired toward each other, so their relative velocity will be

$$v_{rel} = 25 - (-25)$$
$$= 50\ \text{ms}^{-1}$$

Then, time, $t = \dfrac{d}{v_{rel}} = \dfrac{100}{50} = 2$ s

The distance or height at which they collide is calculated from equation of motion,

$$x = ut + \frac{1}{2}at^2$$

The bullet is initially a rest, i.e. $u = 0$ and as it is moving under the effect of gravity $a = -g$, so

$$x = -\frac{1}{2}gt^2$$

$$x = -\frac{1}{2} \times 10(2)^2 = -20 \text{ m}$$

The negative sign shows that the bullets will collide 20 m below the top of tower, i.e. at a height of $(200 - 20) = 180$ m from the ground after 2 s.

2 *(c)* To obtain maximum range, angle of projection must be 45°, i.e. $\theta = 45°$.

$$R_{max} = \frac{u^2 \sin(2 \times 45°)}{g} = \frac{u^2}{g}$$

$$\because \; H_{max} = \frac{u^2 \sin^2 45°}{2g} = \frac{u^2}{4g} = \frac{R_{max}}{4}$$

So, H_{max} is 25% of R_{max}.

3 *(a)* Given, $u = 98 \text{ ms}^{-1}$ and $\theta = 30°$

$\because$ Range of a projectile,

$$R = \frac{u^2 \sin(2\theta)}{g}$$

$$R = \frac{98 \times 98 \times \sin 60°}{9.8}$$

$$R = 490\sqrt{3} \text{ m}$$

4 *(a)* Horizontal range, $R = \frac{u^2 \sin 2\theta}{g}$

When $\theta = 45°$, maximum horizontal range,

$$R_{max} = \frac{u^2}{g} \sin 90° = \frac{u^2}{g}$$

When $\theta = 135°$, maximum horizontal range,

$$R = \frac{u^2}{g} \sin 270° = \frac{-u^2}{g}$$

Negative sign implies opposite direction.

5 *(d)* Given that, $\theta_1 = 45° + \alpha$

$$\theta_2 = 45° - \alpha$$

Let, $u_1 = u_2 = u, \; \frac{R_1}{R_2} = ?$

$$\text{Range, } R_1 = \frac{u^2 \sin 2\theta_1}{g}$$

$$= \frac{u^2 \sin 2(45 + \alpha)}{g} = \frac{u^2 \cos 2\alpha}{g} \quad \ldots(\text{i})$$

$$\text{Similarly, range, } R_2 = \frac{u^2 \sin 2\theta_2}{g}$$

$$= \frac{u^2 \sin 2(45° - \alpha)}{g} = \frac{u^2 \cos 2\alpha}{g} \quad \ldots(\text{ii})$$

So, the ratio of horizontal ranges, dividing Eqs. (i) and (ii) will be

$$\frac{R_1}{R_2} = \frac{\frac{u^2 \cos 2\alpha}{g}}{\frac{u^2 \cos 2\alpha}{g}} = \frac{1}{1}$$

$$\frac{R_1}{R_2} = \frac{1}{1}, \; R_1 : R_2 = 1:1$$

6 *(a)* For vertical motions,

$$h_1 = u \sin \theta t_1 - \frac{1}{2} g t_1^2 \quad (\text{for } h_1)$$

$$\Rightarrow \; t_1 = \frac{h_1 + \frac{1}{2} g t_1^2}{u \sin \theta} \quad \ldots(\text{i})$$

$$\text{and } \; h_2 = u \sin \theta t_2 - \frac{1}{2} g t_2^2 \quad (\text{for } h_2)$$

$$\Rightarrow \; t_2 = \frac{h_2 + \frac{1}{2} g t_2^2}{u \sin \theta} \quad \ldots(\text{ii})$$

On dividing Eq. (i) by Eq. (ii), we get

$$\frac{t_1}{t_2} = \frac{\left(h_1 + \frac{1}{2} g t_1^2\right) / u \sin \theta}{\left(h_2 + \frac{1}{2} g t_2^2\right) / u \sin \theta}$$

$$\Rightarrow \; h_1 t_2 - h_2 t_1 = \frac{g}{2} (t_1 t_2^2 - t_1^2 t_2) \quad \ldots(\text{iii})$$

The time of flight of the ball,

$$T = \frac{2u \sin \theta}{g} = \frac{2}{g} (u \sin \theta)$$

$$= \frac{2}{g} \left(\frac{h_1 + \frac{1}{2} g t_1^2}{t_1} \right) \quad [\text{from Eq. (i)}]$$

$$= \frac{2}{t_1} \left(\frac{h_1}{g} + \frac{t_1^2}{2} \right)$$

$$= \frac{h_1}{t_1} \times \frac{2}{g} + t_1 = \frac{h_1}{t_1} \times \left(\frac{t_1 t_2^2 - t_1^2 t_2}{h_1 t_2 - h_2 t_1} \right) + t_1$$

[from Eq. (iii)]

$$= \frac{h_1 t_1 t_2^2 - h_1 t_1^2 t_2 + h_1 t_1^2 t_2 - h_2 t_1^3}{t_1 (h_1 t_2 - h_2 t_1)}$$

$$= \left(\frac{h_1 t_2^2 - h_2 t_1^2}{h_1 t_2 - h_2 t_1} \right)$$

7 *(c)* As we know that, maximum height of a projectile is given by

$$H_{max} = \frac{u^2 \sin^2 \theta}{2g}$$

where, u = initial velocity of projectile,

g = acceleration due to gravity

and θ = angle of projection = 45°

As from question,

$$H_{max} = \frac{u^2 \sin^2 45°}{2g} = \frac{u^2}{4g} \quad \ldots(\text{i})$$

$(\theta = 45°)$

Now, range of a projectile is given by

$$R_{max} = \frac{u^2 \sin 2\theta}{g}$$

As from question,

$$R = \frac{u^2 \sin(2 \times 45°)}{g}$$

$$\Rightarrow \quad R = \frac{u^2 \sin 90°}{g} = \frac{u^2}{g} \quad \ldots(\text{ii})$$

On dividing Eq. (i) by Eq. (ii), we get

$$\frac{H_{max}}{R} = \frac{u^2}{4g} \times \frac{g}{u^2} = \frac{1}{4}$$

$$\Rightarrow \quad R = 4H_{max} = 4H$$

8 *(d)* The component of velocities are shown below

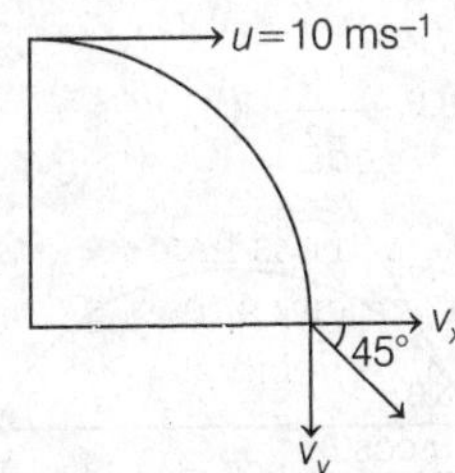

($\because$ horizontal component remains constant)

Now, $\tan \theta = \tan 45° = \frac{v_y}{v_x} = \frac{v_y}{10}$

$$\Rightarrow \quad v_y = 10 \text{ ms}^{-1}$$

9 *(b)* The projectile is shown below

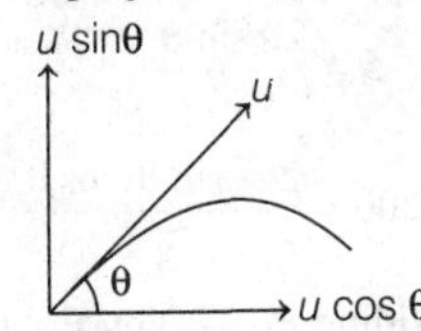

As, $t = \frac{2u \sin\theta}{g} \Rightarrow 4 = \frac{2u \sin\theta}{g}$

$$\Rightarrow \quad \frac{u \sin \theta}{g} = 2 \quad \ldots(\text{i})$$

The height of projectile,

$$h = \frac{u^2 \sin^2 \theta}{2g} = \frac{4g^2}{2g} \quad [\text{from Eq.(i)}]$$

$$\Rightarrow \quad h = 20 \text{ m}$$

10 (c) From the figure the x-component remains unchanged, while the y-component is reverse. Then, the velocity at point B is $(2\hat{i} - 3\hat{j})$ ms^{-1}.

11 (d) From equation of motion,

$$h = \frac{1}{2} gt^2$$

Given, $u = 600$ kmh^{-1} and $h = 1960$ m

$$\Rightarrow \quad t = \sqrt{\frac{2 \times 1960}{9.8}} = 20 \text{ s}$$

$$\therefore \quad s = ut$$

$$= 600 \times \frac{20}{60 \times 60} = 3.33 \text{ km}$$

12 (d) Range is the product of horizontal component of velocity and time of flight.

Let body be projected at an angle θ with the horizontal at velocity u, then its time of flight is

$$T = \frac{2u \sin\theta}{g} \quad \ldots(\text{i})$$

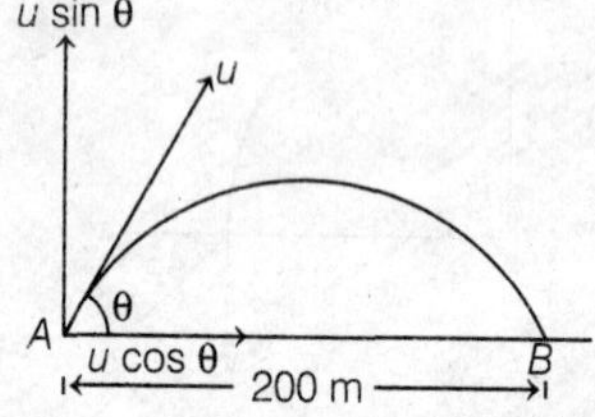

Also, horizontal range,

$$R = u \cos\theta \times T$$

$$\Rightarrow \quad R = \frac{u \cos\theta \times 2u \sin\theta}{g} \quad \ldots(\text{ii})$$

Given, $T = 5$ s and $R = 200$ m

From Eqs. (i) and (ii), we get

$$5 = \frac{2u \sin\theta}{g} \quad \ldots(\text{iii})$$

$$\text{and} \quad 200 = \frac{2u^2 \sin\theta \cos\theta}{g} \quad \ldots(\text{iv})$$

On dividing Eq. (iv) by Eq. (iii), we get the horizontal component of velocity,

$$u \cos\theta = \frac{200}{5} = 40 \text{ ms}^{-1}$$

13 (b) Given, range R = Height H

Now, range, $R = \dfrac{u^2 (2 \sin\theta \cos\theta)}{g}$

and height, $H = \dfrac{u^2 \sin^2\theta}{2g}$.

Hence, $\dfrac{u^2 (2 \sin\theta \cos\theta)}{g} = \dfrac{u^2 \sin^2\theta}{2g}$

$$2 \cos\theta = \frac{\sin\theta}{2}$$

$$\Rightarrow \quad \tan\theta = 4 \quad \Rightarrow \quad \theta = \tan^{-1}(4)$$

14 (c) Equation of projectile,

$$y = 10x - \left(\frac{5}{9}\right) x^2 \quad \ldots(\text{i})$$

Standard equation of trajectory is

$$y = x \tan\theta - \frac{g}{2u^2 \cos^2\theta} \cdot x^2 \quad \ldots(\text{ii})$$

On comparing, Eq. (i) and (ii), we get

$$\tan\theta = 10 \text{ and } \frac{g}{2u^2 \cos^2\theta} = \frac{5}{9}$$

or $10u^2 \cos^2\theta = 9g$

$$\Rightarrow \quad u^2 \cos^2\theta = 9 \quad (\because g = 10 \text{ ms}^{-2})$$

Range of projectile,

$$R = \frac{2u^2 \sin\theta \cos\theta}{g} = \frac{2u^2 \tan\theta \cos^2\theta}{g}$$

$$(\because \sin\theta = \tan\theta \cos\theta)$$

$$= \frac{2 (u^2 \cos^2\theta) \cdot \tan\theta}{g}$$

$$= \frac{2 \times 9 \times 10}{10} = 18 \text{ m}$$

15 (d) For maximum range of projectile, θ will be 45° by the law of projectile motion.

$$\therefore \quad R_{max} = \frac{u^2}{g}$$

Given, $u = 20$ ms^{-1}

and $g = 10$ ms^{-2}

$$\therefore \quad R_{max} = \frac{(20)^2}{10} = \frac{400}{10} = 40 \text{ m}$$

16 (c) Using the equation of motion, we get

$$h = \frac{u^2}{2g}$$

Thus, $\quad u^2 = 2gh$

So, the maximum horizontal distance would be given by

$$R_{max} = \frac{u^2}{g} \text{ (when, } \theta = 45°)$$

Hence, $\quad R_{max} = 2h$

17 (d) Time of flight, $T = \dfrac{2v_0 \sin\theta}{g}$

18 (c) Given, $y = 8t - 5t^2 \quad \ldots(\text{i})$

$x = 6t \quad \ldots(\text{ii})$

We know that, $x = (u \cos\theta)\, t \quad \ldots(\text{iii})$

On comparing with Eq. (ii), we get

$$u \cos\theta = 6$$

and $y = (u \sin\theta)\, t - \dfrac{1}{2} gt^2$

Comparing with Eq. (i), we get

$$u \sin\theta = 8$$

$$\Rightarrow \quad u = \sqrt{(u\cos\theta)^2 + (u\sin\theta)^2}$$

$$= \sqrt{36 + 64} = 10 \text{ ms}^{-1}$$

19 (c) Given, $R = 50$ m, $\theta_1 = 15°$ and $\theta_2 = 45°$

We know that, range, $R = \dfrac{u^2 \sin 2\theta}{g}$

$$\therefore \quad R = \frac{u^2 \sin 2\theta_1}{g}$$

Here, $50 = \dfrac{u^2 \sin 2 \times 15°}{g}$

or $\dfrac{u^2}{g} = \dfrac{50}{\sin 30°} = \dfrac{50}{1/2} = 100$

$$\Rightarrow \quad R = \frac{u^2 \sin 2\theta_2}{g}$$

$$\Rightarrow \quad R = \frac{u^2 \sin 2 \times 45°}{g} = \frac{u^2}{g} = 100 \text{ m}$$

20 (b) As shown in figure, distance OB is the range R is given as $R = \dfrac{u^2 \sin 2\alpha}{g}$.

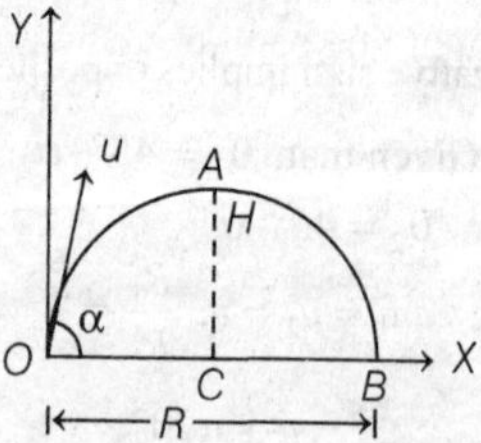

Maximum height of projectile,

$$H = \frac{u^2 \sin^2\alpha}{2g}$$

Now, it is given that,

$$(\text{range})^2 = 48 \times (\text{maximum height})^2$$

$$\therefore \quad \left(\frac{u^2 \sin 2\alpha}{g}\right)^2 = 48 \left(\frac{u^2 \sin^2\alpha}{2g}\right)^2$$

$$\frac{u^2 \sin 2\alpha}{g} = 4\sqrt{3} \left(\frac{u^2 \sin^2\alpha}{2g}\right)$$

$\Rightarrow \quad \frac{2 \sin \alpha \cos \alpha}{4\sqrt{3}} = \frac{\sin^2 \alpha}{2}$

$\Rightarrow \quad \tan \alpha = \frac{4}{4\sqrt{3}} = \frac{1}{\sqrt{3}}$

$\Rightarrow \quad \alpha = 30°$

21 *(b)* Maximum height, $H = \frac{v^2 \sin^2 60°}{2g}$

$= \frac{v^2}{2g} \times \frac{3}{4} \quad \left(\because \sin 60° = \frac{\sqrt{3}}{2}\right)$

$= \frac{3v^2}{8g}$

Momentum of particle at highest point,

$p = mv \cos 60° = \frac{mv}{2}$

Angular momentum $= pH$

($\because$ angle between p and H is 90°)

$= \frac{mv}{2} \times \frac{3v^2}{8g} = \frac{3mv^3}{16g}$

22 *(c)* Upto ordinary heights, the change in the distance of a projectile from the centre of the earth is negligible compared to the radius of the earth.

Hence, the projectile moves under a nearly uniform gravitational force and its path is parabolic. But for the projectiles moving up to a large height, the gravitational force decreases and hence the path of the projectile becomes elliptical.

23 *(d)* Graph between horizontal velocity and time in a projectile motion is a straight line parallel to the time axis as the horizontal velocity remains constant (equal to $u \cos \theta$) with time.

24 *(c)* As seen from the cart, the projectile moves vertically upward and comes back. The time taken by cart to cover 80 m,

$t = \frac{s}{v} = \frac{80}{30} = \frac{8}{3}$ s

For a projectile going upward,

$a = -g = -10 \text{ ms}^{-2}, v = 0$

and $\quad t = \frac{8/3}{2} = \frac{4}{3}$ s

$\therefore \quad v = u + at$

$\Rightarrow \quad 0 = u - 10 \times \frac{4}{3}$

$\Rightarrow \quad u = \left(\frac{40}{3}\right) \text{ms}^{-1}$

25 *(a)* Time of flight is 2 times that of time taken to reach the maximum height, i.e. $T_f = 2t_m$.

26 *(a)* As the vertical component of the velocity at highest point is zero.

$u_y = 0, \; u_x = u\cos\beta$

The kinetic energy at the highest point will be equal to $\frac{1}{2} m (u \cos \beta)^2$

$K - = \frac{1}{2} mu^2 \cos^2 \beta$

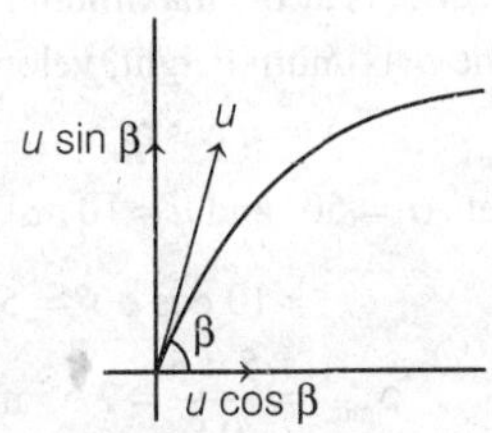

The initial kinetic energy is the maximum kinetic energy.

So, $\text{KE} = K \cos^2 \beta$,

where $K = \frac{1}{2} mu^2$.

Thus, $K \cos^2 \beta = \frac{3}{4} K$

$\Rightarrow \quad \cos \beta = \frac{\sqrt{3}}{2} \Rightarrow \beta = 30°$

27 *(b)* The time taken to hit the ground is given by

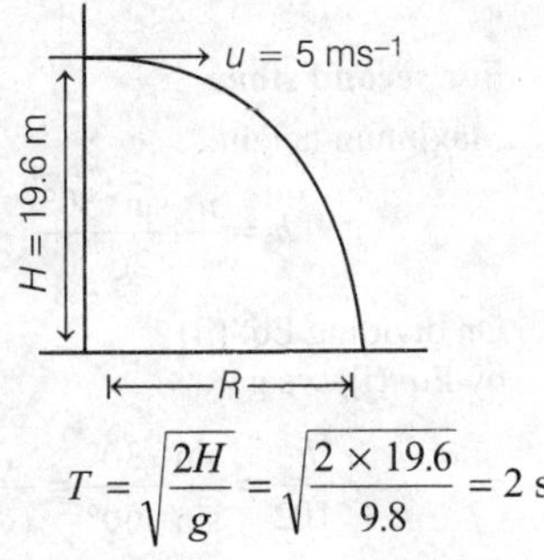

$T = \sqrt{\frac{2H}{g}} = \sqrt{\frac{2 \times 19.6}{9.8}} = 2$ s

28 *(a)* Given, $R = 2H$

We know that, $R = 4H \cot \theta$

$\Rightarrow \quad \cot \theta = \frac{1}{2}$

which implies $\sin \theta = \frac{2}{\sqrt{5}}$

and $\quad \cos \theta = \frac{1}{\sqrt{5}}$

$\therefore$ Range of projectile,

$R = \frac{2v^2 \sin \theta \cos \theta}{g}$

$= \frac{2v^2}{g} \times \frac{2}{\sqrt{5}} \times \frac{1}{\sqrt{5}}$

$= \frac{4v^2}{5g}$

29 *(d)* In both cases, the time of flights

$t_1 = \frac{2u \sin \theta}{g}$ ...(i)

and $\quad t_2 = \frac{2u \sin (90° - \theta)}{g}$

$= \frac{2u \cos \theta}{g}$ ...(ii)

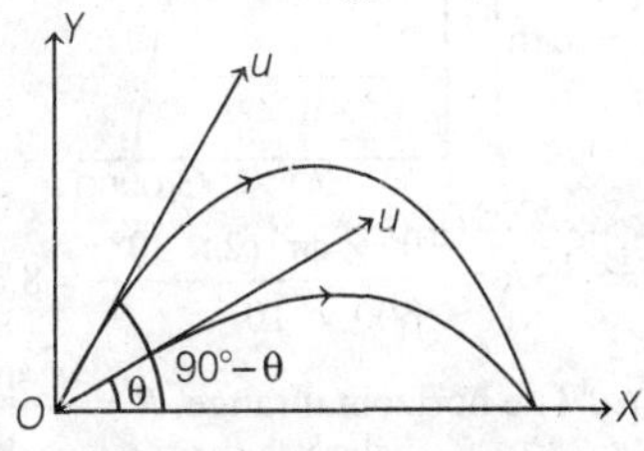

From Eqs. (i) and (ii), we get

$t_1 t_2 = \frac{4u^2 \sin \theta \cos \theta}{g^2} = \frac{2R}{g}$

$\Rightarrow t_1 t_2 \propto R$

30 *(a)* Let h be the maximum height attained by the projectile, then

$h = \frac{u^2 \sin^2 \theta}{2g}, \quad R = \frac{u^2 \sin 2\theta}{g}$

$\therefore \quad \frac{R}{h} = \frac{u^2 \sin 2\theta}{g} \Big/ \frac{u^2 \sin^2 \theta}{2g}$

$= \frac{2 \sin \theta \cos \theta}{(\sin^2 \theta)/2} = 4 \cot \theta$

Therefore, $\quad \frac{\Delta R}{R} = \frac{\Delta h}{h}$

Hence, percentage increase in R = percentage increase in height $h = 5\%$

31 *(c)* Suppose, the angle made by the instantaneous velocity with the horizontal be α. Then,

$\tan \alpha = \frac{v_y}{v_x} = \frac{u \sin \theta - gt}{u \cos \theta}$

Given, $\alpha = 45°$, when $t = 1$ s (i.e. $\tan 45° = 1$)

and $\quad \alpha = 0°$, when $t = 2$ s, (i.e. $\tan 0° = 0$)

This gives $u \cos\theta = u \sin\theta - g$ ...(i)

and $\quad u \sin \theta - 2g = 0$ ...(ii)

On solving Eqs. (i) and (ii), we have

$u \sin \theta = 2g$

$u \cos \theta = g$

$\Rightarrow \quad u = \sqrt{5}g = 10\sqrt{5} \text{ ms}^{-1}$

32 *(d)* The ball will be at point P when it is at a height of 10 m from the ground. So, we have to find distance OP, which can be calculated direct considering it is a projectile on a level OX at a height h from the horizontal level.

$$OP = R = \frac{u^2 \sin 2\theta}{g}$$

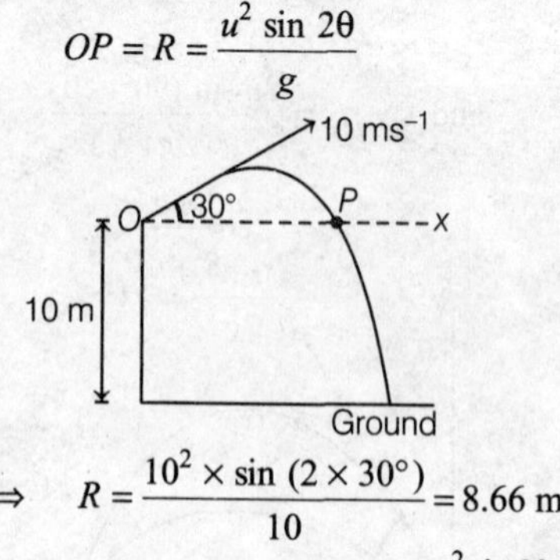

$$\Rightarrow \quad R = \frac{10^2 \times \sin(2 \times 30°)}{10} = 8.66 \text{ m}$$

33 (a) The horizontal range, $R = \frac{u^2 \sin 2\theta}{g}$

$$\Rightarrow \quad R_1 = \frac{u^2 \sin 2(45° + \theta)}{g}$$

$$\Rightarrow \quad R_1 = \frac{u^2 \sin (90° + 2\theta)}{g}$$

$$R_1 = \frac{u^2 \cos 2\theta}{g} \quad \ldots\text{(i)}$$

Also, $R_2 = \frac{u^2 \sin 2(45° - \theta)}{g}$

$$\Rightarrow \quad R_2 = \frac{u^2 \sin (90° - 2\theta)}{g}$$

$$R_2 = \frac{u^2 \cos 2\theta}{g} \quad \ldots\text{(ii)}$$

From Eqs. (i) and (ii), we get

$$\Rightarrow \quad \frac{R_1}{R_2} = 1:1$$

34 (c) As, $R = \frac{u^2 \sin 2\theta}{g}$

At $\theta = 45°$, the horizontal angle R will be maximum

$$\therefore \quad R_{\max} = \frac{u^2}{g}$$

35 (b) Given, $u = 196 \text{ ms}^{-1}$ and $h = 400$ m

As, $t = \sqrt{\frac{2h}{g}} = \sqrt{\frac{2 \times 400}{10}} = 4\sqrt{5} \simeq 9$ s

36 (a) The radius of curvature is given by

$$\rho = \frac{mv^3}{|\mathbf{F} \times \mathbf{v}|} = \frac{mv^3}{Fv \sin\theta} = \frac{mv^3}{mg\, v \sin\theta} \quad (\because F = mg)$$

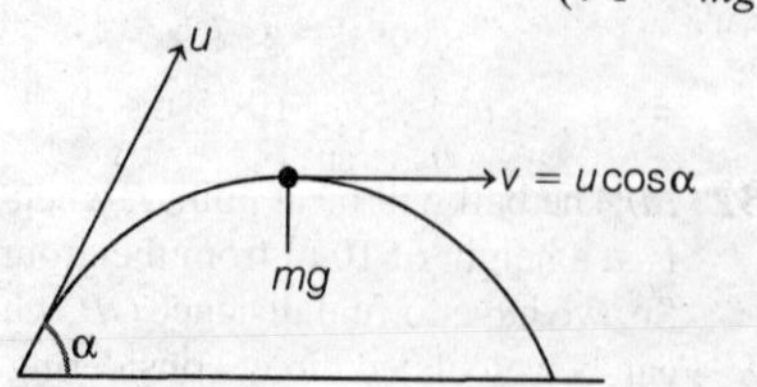

$$\Rightarrow \quad \rho = \frac{v^2}{g \sin\theta}$$

$$\therefore \quad \rho_{\min} = \frac{v^2}{g (\sin\theta)_{\max}}$$

$$\therefore \quad \rho_{\min} = v^2/g \quad \ldots\text{(i)}$$

$$[\because (\sin\theta)_{\max} = 1]$$

i.e. $\theta = 90°$ is possible only when the projectile is at the maximum height.

At the maximum height, velocity,

$$v = u \cos\alpha$$

Given, $\alpha = 60°$ and $u = 10 \text{ ms}^{-1}$

$$= 10 \cos 60° = 5 \text{ ms}^{-1}$$

$$\therefore \quad \rho_{\min} = \frac{5 \times 5}{9.8} = 2.55 \text{ m}$$

[from Eq. (i)]

37 (d) We know that if two stones have same horizontal range, then this implies that both are projected at θ and $(90° - \theta)$.

Given, $\theta = \frac{\pi}{3} = 60°$

$$\therefore \quad 90° - \theta = 90° - 60° = 30°$$

For first stone

Maximum height,

$$h_1 = 102 = \frac{u^2 \sin^2 60°}{2g} \text{ (given)} \ldots\text{(i)}$$

For second stone

Maximum height,

$$h_2 = \frac{u^2 \sin^2 30°}{2g} \quad \ldots\text{(ii)}$$

On dividing Eq. (ii) by Eq. (i), we get

$$\Rightarrow \quad \frac{h_2}{102} = \frac{\sin^2 30°}{\sin^2 60°} = \frac{(1/2)^2}{(\sqrt{3}/2)^2}$$

$$\therefore \quad h_2 = 102 \times \frac{1/4}{3/4} = 34 \text{ m}$$

38 (d) During projectile motion, horizontal velocity always remains constant.

$$u_x = u \cos\theta$$

39 (a) Maximum height,

$$H = \frac{u^2 \sin^2\theta}{2g} \quad \ldots\text{(i)}$$

$$\text{Range, } R = \frac{u^2 \sin 2\theta}{g} \quad \ldots\text{(ii)}$$

Given, $H = \frac{R}{2}$

$$\Rightarrow \quad \frac{u^2 \sin^2\theta}{2g} = \frac{u^2\, 2\sin\theta \cos\theta}{2g}$$

[from Eqs. (i) and (ii)]

$$\Rightarrow \sin\theta = 2\cos\theta \Rightarrow \tan\theta = 2$$

$$\therefore \quad \theta = \tan^{-1}(2)$$

40 (b) Given, $R = 3H$

$$\therefore \quad \frac{u^2 \sin 2\theta}{g} = 3 \times \frac{u^2 \sin^2\theta}{2g}$$

Also, $\sin 2\theta = 2\sin\theta\cos\theta$

$$\therefore \quad \frac{u^2\, 2\sin\theta\cos\theta}{g} = 3 \times \frac{u^2 \sin^2\theta}{2g}$$

$$\Rightarrow \quad 2\cos\theta = 1.5 \sin\theta$$

$$\Rightarrow \quad \tan\theta = \frac{2}{1.5} = 1.33 \Rightarrow = 53°7'$$

Hence, angle of projection is $53°7'$.

41 (b) Horizontal range,

$$R = \frac{u^2 \sin 2\theta}{g} \quad \ldots\text{(i)}$$

For maximum horizontal range, $\sin 2\theta = 1$

$$\therefore \quad R_{\max} = \frac{u^2}{g} \quad \ldots\text{(ii)}$$

Given, $R = 3$ km and $\theta = 30°$

$\therefore$ From Eq. (i), we get

$$\frac{u^2}{g} = \frac{R}{\sin 2\theta} = \frac{3}{\sin 60°}$$

$$= \frac{3 \times 2}{\sqrt{3}} = \sqrt{3} \times 2$$

$$\therefore \quad \frac{u^2}{g} = 3.464 \text{ km}$$

Hence, maximum range with velocity of projection u cannot be more than 3.464 km. Hence, it is not possible to hit a target 5 km away.

42 (c) Given, $u = 147 \text{ ms}^{-1}, \theta_1 = 60°$

and $\theta_2 = 45°$

Horizontal component of velocity at angle 60° = Horizontal component of velocity at 45°

i.e. $u \cos 60° = v \cos 45°$

$$\Rightarrow \quad 147 \times \frac{1}{2} = v \times \frac{1}{\sqrt{2}}$$

$$\Rightarrow \quad v = \frac{147}{\sqrt{2}} \text{ ms}^{-1}$$

Vertical component of $u = u \sin 60°$

$$= \frac{147\sqrt{3}}{2} \text{ ms}^{-1}$$

Vertical component of $v = v \sin 45°$

$$= \frac{147}{\sqrt{2}} \times \frac{1}{\sqrt{2}} = \frac{147}{2} \text{ ms}^{-1}$$

But, from equation of motion

$$v_y = u_y + at$$

$$\therefore \quad \frac{147}{2} = \frac{147\sqrt{3}}{2} - 9.8t$$

$$\Rightarrow \quad 9.8t = \frac{147}{2}(\sqrt{3} - 1)$$

$$\therefore \quad t = 5.49 \text{ s}$$

43 (c) Stone will follow the parabolic path.

44 (b) As range of two projectiles are same, so the angle of projections must be complementary, i.e.

$\theta_1 = 30°$ and $\theta_2 = 90° - \theta_1 = 60°$

The maximum height of projectile is given by

$$h = \frac{u^2 \sin^2\theta}{2g}$$

Given, $u = 20 \text{ ms}^{-1}$

$$\therefore \text{For } \theta = 30°, \; h_1 = \frac{(20)^2 \sin^2 30°}{2 \times 10}$$

$$= \frac{400 \times 1}{2 \times 10 \times 4} = 5 \text{ m}$$

Similarly, for $\theta = 60°$,

$$h_2 = \frac{(20)^2 \sin^2 60°}{2 \times 10}$$

$$= \frac{400 \times 3}{2 \times 10 \times 4} = 15 \text{ m}$$

$\therefore$ Sum of maximum heights

$$= h_1 + h_2$$
$$= 5 + 15$$
$$= 20 \text{m}$$

45 (a) Range of projectile,

$$R = \frac{2u^2 \sin\theta \cos\theta}{g} \quad \ldots\text{(i)}$$

$$\text{Height, } H = \frac{u^2 \sin^2\theta}{2g} \quad \ldots\text{(ii)}$$

$$\text{Also, } H_1 = \frac{u^2 \sin^2(90° - \theta)}{2g} \quad \ldots\text{(iii)}$$

$$= \frac{u^2 \cos^2\theta}{2g}$$

$$\text{Then, } HH_1 = \frac{u^2 \sin^2\theta u^2 \cos^2\theta}{2g \times 2g} \quad \ldots\text{(iv)}$$

From Eq. (i), we get

$$R^2 = \frac{4u^2 \sin^2\theta u^2 \cos^2\theta \times 4}{2g \times 2g}$$

$$R = \sqrt{16HH_1} \quad \text{[from Eq. (iv)]}$$

$$\Rightarrow R = 4\sqrt{HH_1}$$

46 (b) Since, $nh = \frac{1}{2}gt^2$

$$\Rightarrow \quad t = \sqrt{\left(\frac{2nh}{g}\right)} \quad \ldots\text{(i)}$$

Horizontal distance travelled by ball

$$nb = ut, \; nb = u\sqrt{\left(\frac{2nh}{g}\right)} \quad \ldots\text{(ii)}$$

Squaring Eq. (ii), we get

$$n^2b^2 = \frac{u^2 2nh}{g} \Rightarrow n = \frac{2u^2h}{gb^2}$$

47 (b) Let v be the velocity when projected with angle θ, then equating the horizontal velocities in both the cases, we get
(horizontal velocities remains same during projectile)

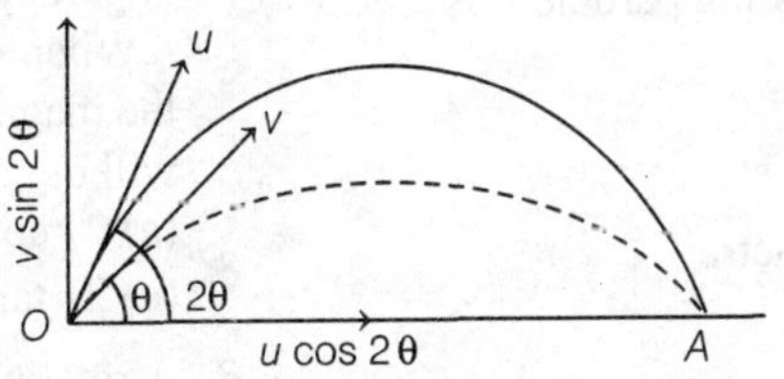

$$v\cos\theta = u\cos 2\theta$$

$$\Rightarrow \quad v = \frac{u\cos 2\theta}{\cos\theta}$$

$$\text{As,} \quad \sec\theta = \frac{1}{\cos\theta}$$

$$\therefore \quad v = u\cos 2\theta \sec\theta$$

Using $\cos 2\theta = 2\cos^2\theta - 1$

Given, $u = 4 \text{ ms}^{-1}$, we get

$$v = 4(2\cos^2\theta - 1)\sec\theta$$

$$\Rightarrow \quad v = 4(2\cos\theta - \sec\theta)$$

48 (d) The time taken to cover the horizontal distance of 100 m from the gun to the target is given by

$$t = \frac{100}{1000} = 0.1 \text{ s}$$

[$\because$ given, $v = 1000 \text{ ms}^{-1}$]

During this time, the bullet will fall down vertically under gravity.

Now, $h = ut + \frac{1}{2}gt^2$ gives

$$h = 0 + \frac{1}{2} \times 10 \times (0.1)^2$$

$$= 5 \times 0.01 = 0.05 \text{ m} = 5 \text{ cm}$$

49 (b) Maximum height,

$$H = \frac{u^2 \sin^2\theta}{2g} \quad \ldots\text{(i)}$$

Time of flight, $T = \frac{2u\sin\theta}{g}$

$$\text{or} \quad u\sin\theta = \frac{Tg}{2} \quad \ldots\text{(ii)}$$

From Eqs. (i) and (ii), we get

$$H = \frac{1}{2g}\left(\frac{Tg}{2}\right)^2$$

$$\Rightarrow \quad H = \frac{T^2g^2}{8g}$$

$$\Rightarrow \quad T^2 = \frac{8H}{g}$$

$$\Rightarrow \quad T = 2\sqrt{\left(\frac{2H}{g}\right)}$$

50 (b) According to the question,

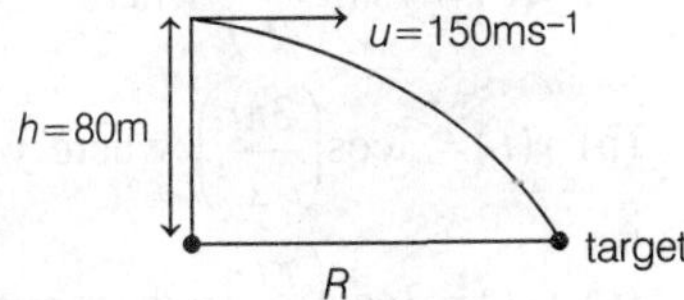

$$\text{As,} \quad t = \sqrt{\left(\frac{2h}{g}\right)}$$

$$t = \sqrt{\left(\frac{2 \times 80}{10}\right)} = 4 \text{ s}$$

Horizontal velocity of bomb $= 150 \text{ ms}^{-1}$.

Horizontal distance covered by bomb $= 150 \times 4 = 600$ m

Hence, the bomb should be dropped 600 m before the target.

51 (c) According to the question, heights of both bodies are equal.

$$\Rightarrow \quad \frac{u_1^2 \sin^2\theta_1}{2g} = \frac{u_2^2 \sin^2\theta_2}{2g}$$

$$\text{or} \quad \frac{u_1}{u_2} = \frac{\sin\theta_2}{\sin\theta_1} = \frac{\sin 60°}{\sin 45°} = \frac{\sqrt{3}/2}{1/\sqrt{2}} = \sqrt{\frac{3}{2}}$$

Topic 4

Uniform and Non-Uniform Circular Motion

2019

1 Two particles A and B are moving in uniform circular motion in concentric circles of radii r_A and r_B with speed v_A and v_B respectively. Their time period of rotation is the same. The ratio of angular speed of A to that of B will be **[NEET]**

(a) $v_A : v_B$ (b) $r_B : r_A$
(c) 1 : 1 (d) $r_A : r_B$

2 The radius of circle, the period of revolution, initial position and sense of revolution are indicated in the below figure. **[NEET]**

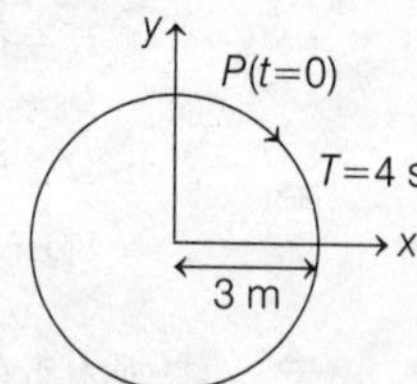

y-projection of the radius vector of rotating particle P is

(a) $y(t) = 4\sin\left(\frac{\pi t}{2}\right)$, where y is in metre

(b) $y(t) = 3\cos\left(\frac{3\pi t}{2}\right)$, where y is in metre

(c) $y(t) = 3\cos\left(\frac{\pi t}{2}\right)$, where y is in metre

(d) $y(t) = -3\cos 2\pi t$, where y is in metre

3 A particle starting from rest, moves in a circle of radius r. It attains a velocity of v_0 ms^{-1} in the nth round. Its angular acceleration will be **[NEET (Odisha)]**

(a) $\frac{v_0}{n}$ rads^{-2} (b) $\frac{v_0^2}{2\pi nr^2}$ rads^{-2}

(c) $\frac{v_0^2}{4\pi nr^2}$ rads^{-2} (d) $\frac{v_0^2}{4\pi nr}$ rads^{-2}

4 An electron is moving in a circle of radius 2m with speed of 4 ms^{-1}. Find the acceleration of the electron. **[AIIMS]**

(a) 8 ms^{-2} (b) 4 ms^{-2}
(c) 16 ms^{-2} (d) 10 ms^{-2}

2016

5 In the given figure, $a = 15$ ms^{-2} represents the total acceleration of a particle moving in the clockwise direction in a circle of radius $R = 2.5$ m at a given instant of time. The speed of the particle is **[NEET]**

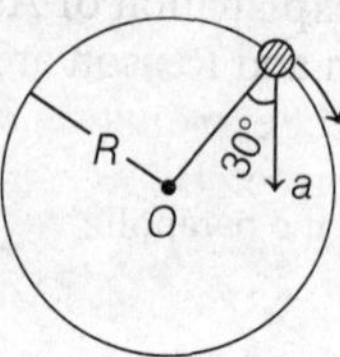

(a) 4.5 ms^{-1} (b) 5.0 ms^{-1}
(c) 5.7 ms^{-1} (d) 6.2 ms^{-1}

2014

6 If the length of second's hand of a clock is 10 cm, the speed of its tip (in cms^{-1}) is nearly **[Kerala CEE]**

(a) 2 (b) 0.5
(c) 1.5 (d) 3
(e) 1

7 A particle is moving uniformly in a circular path of radius r. When it moves through an angular displacement θ, then the magnitude of the corresponding linear displacement will be **[WB JEE]**

(a) $2r\cos(\theta/2)$ (b) $2r\cot(\theta/2)$
(c) $2r\tan(\theta/2)$ (d) $2r\sin(\theta/2)$

8 A rotating wheel changes angular velocity from 1800 rpm to 3000 rpm in 20 s. What is the angular acceleration assuming to be uniform? **[KCET]**

(a) 60π rad s^{-2} (b) 90π rad s^{-2}
(c) 2π rad s^{-2} (d) 40π rad s^{-2}

2013

9 A ball is moving in a circular path of radius 5 m. If tangential acceleration at any instant is 10 ms^{-2} and the net acceleration makes an angle 30° with the centripetal acceleration, then the instantaneous speed is **[AIIMS]**

(a) $50\sqrt{3}$ ms^{-1} (b) 9.3 ms^{-1}
(c) 6.6 ms^{-1} (d) 5.4 ms^{-1}

10 A car is travelling with linear velocity v on a circular road of radius R. If its speed is increasing at the rate of a ms^{-2}, then the net acceleration will be **[AIIMS]**

(a) $\frac{v^2}{R} + a$ (b) $\frac{v^2}{R} - a$

(c) $\sqrt{(v^2/R)^2 + a^2}$ (d) $\sqrt{(v^2/R)^2 - a^2}$

2012

11 **Assertion** Two similar trains are moving along the equatorial line with the same speed but in opposite directions. They will exert equal pressure on the rails.

Reason In a uniform circular motion, the magnitude of acceleration remains constant but the direction continuously changes. [AIIMS]

(a) Both Assertion and Reason are correct and Reason is the correct explanation of Assertion.
(b) Both Assertion and Reason are correct but Reason is not the correct explanation of Assertion.
(c) Assertion is correct but Reason is incorrect.
(d) Assertion is incorrect but Reason is correct.

2011

12 A particle moves in a circle of radius 5 cm with constant speed and time period 0.2π s. The acceleration of the particle is [CBSE AIPMT]

(a) 25 ms^{-2} (b) 36 ms^{-2} (c) 5 ms^{-2} (d) 15 ms^{-2}

13 A wheel is rotating at 900 rpm about its axis. When the power is cut off, it comes to rest in 1 min. The angular retardation (in rads^{-2}) is [AFMC]

(a) $\pi/2$ (b) $\pi/4$ (c) $\pi/6$ (d) $\pi/8$

14 The angular speed of flywheel making 360 rev/min is [UP CPMT]

(a) 12π rads^{-1} (b) 6π rads^{-1}
(c) 3π rad^{-1} (d) 2π rads^{-1}

15 A particle is moving with a constant speed v in a circle. What is the magnitude of average velocity after half rotation? [WB JEE]

(a) $2v$ (b) $2\frac{v}{\pi}$ (c) $\frac{v}{2}$ (d) $\frac{v}{2\pi}$

16 The centre of a wheel rolling on a plane surface moves with a speed v_0. A particle on the rim of the wheel at the same level as the centre will be moving at speed [VITEEE]

(a) zero (b) v_0 (c) $\sqrt{2}\,v_0$ (d) $2v_0$

17 The motor of an engine is rotating about its axis with an angular velocity of 100 rev min^{-1}. It comes to rest in 15 s after being switched off, assuming constant angular deceleration. What is the number of revolutions made by it before coming to rest? [VITEEE]

(a) 12.5 (b) 40 (c) 32.6 (d) 15.6

2009

18 The acceleration of an object moving with speed v in a circle of radius r is [Kerala CEE]

(a) $\frac{v^2}{r}$, towards the centre (b) $\frac{v}{r}$, away from the centre
(c) $\frac{v}{r^2}$, away from the centre (d) $\frac{v}{r}$, towards the centre
(e) $\frac{v}{r^2}$, towards the centre

19 A car moves on a circular road. It describes equal angles about the centre in equal intervals of time. Which of the following statements about the velocity of the car is true? [Punjab PMET]

(a) Magnitude of velocity is not constant.
(b) Both magnitude and direction of velocity change.
(c) Velocity is directed towards the circle.
(d) Magnitude of velocity is constant but direction changes.

2008

20 A particle is moving along a circular path of radius 5 m with a uniform speed 5 ms^{-1}. What will be the average acceleration when the particle completes half revolution? [BHU]

(a) Zero (b) 10 ms^{-2}
(c) 10π ms^{-2} (d) $(10/\pi)$ ms^{-2}

21 In uniform circular motion of a particle, [Kerala CEE]

(a) velocity is constant but acceleration is variable
(b) velocity is variable but acceleration is constant
(c) Both speed and acceleration are constants
(d) speed is constant but acceleration is variable
(e) Both speed and acceleration are variables

22 A body moving along a circular path of radius R with velocity v, has centripetal acceleration a. If its velocity is made equal to $2v$, then its centripetal acceleration is [J&K CET]

(a) $4a$ (b) $2a$
(c) $a/4$ (d) $a/2$

2007

23 A car runs at a constant speed on a circular track of radius 100 m, taking 62.8 s for every circular lap. The average velocity and average speed for each circular lap respectively are [MP PMT]

(a) 0, 0 (b) 0, 10 ms^{-1}
(c) 10 ms^{-1}, 10 ms^{-1} (d) 10 ms^{-1}, 0

24 A cosmonaut is orbiting around the earth in a spacecraft at an altitude $h = 630$ km with a speed of 8 kms^{-1}. If the radius of the earth is 6400 km, the acceleration of the cosmonaut is [MP PMT]

(a) 9.10 ms^{-2} (b) 9.80 ms^{-2} (c) 1.00 ms^{-2} (d) 9.88 ms^{-2}

25 What is the angular velocity of the earth? [OJEE]

(a) $\frac{2\pi}{86400}$ rads^{-1} (b) $\frac{2\pi}{3600}$ rads^{-1}
(c) $\frac{2\pi}{24}$ rads^{-1} (d) $\frac{2\pi}{6400}$ rads^{-1}

26 A stone tied to one end of rope and rotated in a circular motion. If the string suddenly breaks, then the stone travels [J&K CET]

(a) in perpendicular direction
(b) in direction of centrifugal force
(c) towards centripetal force
(d) in tangential direction

2006

27 A spaceman, in training is rotated in a seat at the end of a horizontal arm of length 5 m. If he can withstand accelerations upto 9 g, then what is the maximum number of revolutions per second permissible? (Take, $g = 10\ ms^{-2}$) **[UP CPMT]**

(a) 13.5 rps (b) 1.35 rps
(c) 0.675 rps (d) 6.75 rps

28 An electric fan has blades of length 30 cm as measured from the axis of rotation. If the fan is rotating at 1200 rpm, the acceleration of a point on the tip of the blade is about **[MHT CET]**

(a) 1600 ms^{-2} (b) 4740 ms^{-2}
(c) 2370 ms^{-2} (d) 5055 ms^{-2}

29 If a_r and a_t represent radial and tangential accelerations respectively, the motion of a particle will be uniformly circular if **[Manipal]**

(a) $a_r = 0$ and $a_t = 0$ (b) $a_r = 0$ but $a_t \neq 0$
(c) $a_r \neq 0$ but $a_t = 0$ (d) $a_r \neq 0$ and $a_t \neq 0$

30 The angular velocity of second hand of a clock is **[RPMT]**

(a) $\left(\frac{\pi}{6}\right)$ rad s^{-1} (b) $\left(\frac{\pi}{60}\right)$ rad s^{-1}
(c) $\left(\frac{\pi}{30}\right)$ rad s^{-1} (d) $\left(\frac{\pi}{15}\right)$ rad s^{-1}

31 A body is moving in a circular path with acceleration a. If its velocity gets doubled, then find the ratio of acceleration after and before the change. **[RPMT]**

(a) 1 : 4 (b) $\frac{1}{4}$: 1
(c) 2 : 1 (d) 4 : 1

32 A particle is moving in a circle of radius r with a constant speed v. The change in velocity after the particle has travelled a distance equal to $\left(\frac{1}{8}\right)$th of the circumference of the circle is **[EAMCET]**

(a) zero (b) 0.5000 v
(c) 0.765 v (d) 0.125 v

33 A cyclist starts from the centre O of a circular park of radius 1 km, reaches the edge P of the park, then cycles along the circumference and returns to the centre along QO as shown in the figure. If the round trip takes 10 min, the net displacement (in metre) and average speed of the cyclist (in kmh^{-1}) are **[J&K CET]**

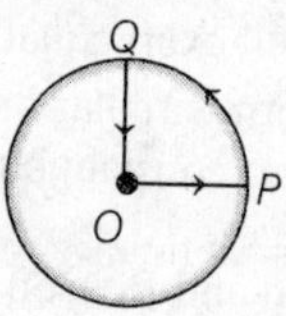

(a) 0, 1 (b) $\frac{\pi + 4}{2}$, 0
(c) 21.4, $\frac{\pi + 4}{2}$ (d) 0, 21.4

2005

34 A stone tied to the end of a string of 1 m long is whirled in a horizontal circle with a constant speed. If the stone makes 22 revolutions in 44 s, then what is the magnitude and direction of acceleration towards centre? **[CBSE AIPMT]**

(a) $\frac{\pi^2}{4}$ ms^{-2} and direction along the radius towards the centre
(b) π^2 ms^{-2} and direction along the radius away from centre
(c) π^2 ms^{-2} and direction along the radius towards the centre
(d) π^2 ms^{-2} and direction along the tangent to the circle

35 What determines the nature of the path followed by the particle? **[AFMC]**

(a) Speed (b) Velocity
(c) Acceleration (d) Both (b) and (c)

36 Angular velocity of hour hand of a watch is **[MHT CET]**

(a) $\frac{\pi}{43200}$ rad s^{-1} (b) $\frac{\pi}{30}$ rad s^{-1}
(c) $\frac{\pi}{21600}$ rad s^{-1} (d) $\frac{\pi}{1800}$ rad s^{-1}

37 A stone tied to one end of spring 80 cm long is whirled in a horizontal circle with a constant speed. If stone makes 14 revolutions in 25 s, the magnitude of acceleration of stone is **[RPMT]**

(a) 850 cm s^{-2} (b) 996 cm s^{-2}
(c) 720 cm s^{-2} (d) 650 cm s^{-2}

Answers

1 (c)	2 (c)	3 (c)	4 (a)	5 (c)	6 (e)	7 (d)	8 (c)	9 (b)	10 (c)
11 (d)	12 (c)	13 (a)	14 (a)	15 (b)	16 (c)	17 (a)	18 (a)	19 (d)	20 (d)
21 (c)	22 (a)	23 (b)	24 (a)	25 (a)	26 (d)	27 (c)	28 (b)	29 (c)	30 (c)
31 (d)	32 (c)	33 (d)	34 (c)	35 (d)	36 (c)	37 (b)			

Explanations

1 (c) The angular speed of a particle in a uniform circular motion is given by

$$\omega = \frac{\text{angle of circle}}{\text{Time}}$$

$$\omega = \frac{2\pi}{T},$$ where T is the time period of rotation.

For particle A, $\omega_A = \dfrac{2\pi}{T_A}$ ...(i)

For particle B, $\omega_B = \dfrac{2\pi}{T_B}$ ...(ii)

from Eqs. (i) and (iii), we get

$$\therefore \frac{\omega_A}{\omega_B} = \frac{2\pi}{T_A} \times \frac{T_B}{2\pi} = \frac{T_B}{T_A}$$

$$= \frac{1}{1} \text{ or } 1:1 [\because T_A = T_B \text{ (given)}]$$

2 (c) Let O be the centre of circle, then at $t = 0$, the displacement y is maximum and have value 3 m.

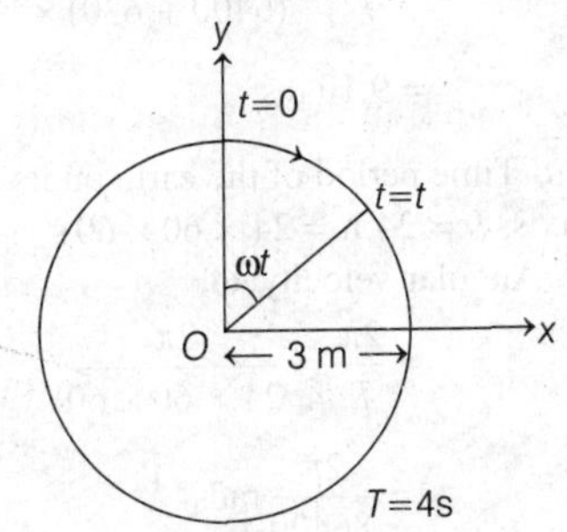

As, the general equation of displacement of a particle will be in the form

$$y = A\cos\omega t$$

Given, $A = 3$ m, $T = 4$ s

Then, $\omega = \dfrac{2\pi}{T} = \dfrac{2\pi}{4}$ [given, $T = 4$ s]

$$= \frac{\pi}{2}$$

$$\therefore \quad y = 3\cos\left(\frac{\pi}{2}t\right) \text{ (in metre)}$$

3 (c) From third equation of motion, for circular motion,

$$\omega^2 - \omega_0^2 = 2\alpha\theta \quad \text{...(i)}$$

where, ω = final angular velocity of particle,

ω_0 = initial angular velocity,

α = angular acceleration

and θ = angular displacement.

Here, $\omega = \dfrac{v_0}{r}$ rads^{-1}

(where, r radius of the circle),

$\omega_0 = 0$ (initially particle is at rest)

and $\theta = 2\pi n$ (for n rounds)

Substituting these values in Eq. (i), we get

$$\left(\frac{v_0}{r}\right)^2 - 0 = 2\alpha(2\pi n)$$

$$\Rightarrow \quad \alpha = \frac{v_0^2}{4\pi n r^2} \text{ rads}^{-2}$$

4 (a) Given, radius of circular path,

$$r = 2\text{ m}$$

Speed of circular path, $v = 4$ ms^{-1}

Acceleration of electron moving on circular path with constant speed is equal to centripetal acceleration.

$\therefore$ Acceleration of electron (a)

= Centripetal acceleration

$$a = \frac{v^2}{r} = \frac{4^2}{2} = 8 \text{ ms}^{-2}$$

5 (c) Centripetal acceleration of a particle moving on a circular path is given by $a_C = v^2/R$

Given, $a = 15$ ms^{-2}, $R = 2.5$ cm

and $\theta = 30°$

In the given figure,

$$a_C = a\cos 30° = 15\cos 30° \text{ ms}^{-2}$$

$$\Rightarrow \quad \frac{v^2}{R} = 15\cos 30°$$

$$\Rightarrow \quad v^2 = R\times 15\times\frac{\sqrt{3}}{2} = 2.5\times 15\times\frac{\sqrt{3}}{2}$$

$$\therefore \quad v = 5.7 \text{ ms}^{-1}$$

6 (e) We know that,

$$\omega = 2\pi \text{ rad in } 60\text{ s} = \frac{\pi}{30} \text{ rad s}^{-1}$$

$$\therefore \quad v = r\omega = 10\times\frac{\pi}{30} = \frac{\pi}{3} \text{ cms}^{-1}$$

$(\because r = 10$ cm$)$

$$= \frac{3.14}{3} \text{ cms}^{-1} = 1.046 \cong 1 \text{ cm s}^{-1}$$

7 (d) The figure is shown as below

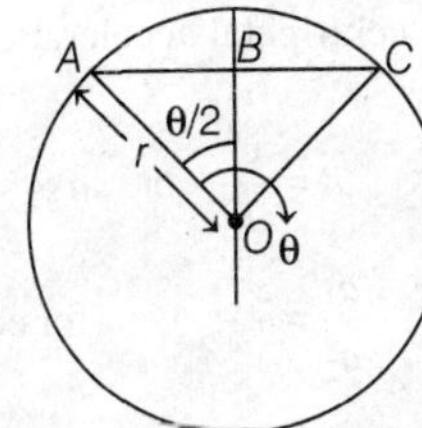

In ΔAOB, $\sin\dfrac{\theta}{2} = \dfrac{AB}{AO}$ $(\because AO = r)$

$$AB = AO\sin\frac{\theta}{2} \Rightarrow AB = r\sin\frac{\theta}{2}$$

$$AC = AB + BC$$

$$AC = r\sin\frac{\theta}{2} + r\sin\frac{\theta}{2} \quad (\because AB = BC)$$

$$AC = 2r\sin\frac{\theta}{2}$$

So, the magnitude of the corresponding linear displacement will be $2r\sin\dfrac{\theta}{2}$.

8 (c) We know that, $\omega = 2\pi n$

$$\therefore \quad \omega_1 = 2\pi n_1$$

Given, $n_1 = 1800$ rpm

$n_2 = 3000$ rpm and $\Delta t = 20$ s

$$\Rightarrow \quad \omega_1 = 2\pi\times\frac{1800}{60} = 2\pi\times 30$$

$$= 60\pi \text{ rads}^{-1}$$

Similarly, $\omega_2 = 2\pi n_2 = 2\pi\times\dfrac{3000}{60}$

$$= 2\pi\times 50 = 100\pi \text{ rads}^{-1}$$

If the angular velocity of a rotating wheel about an axis is changed by change in angular velocity in a time interval Δt, then the angular acceleration of rotating wheel about that axis is given by

$$\alpha = \frac{\text{change in angular velocity}}{\text{time interval}}$$

$$= \frac{\omega_2 - \omega_1}{\Delta t} = \frac{100\pi - 60\pi}{20}$$

$$= \frac{40\pi}{20} = 2\pi \text{ rad s}^{-2}$$

9 (b) Given, $a_t = 10$ ms^{-2}, $r = 5$ m

and $\theta = 30°$

From relation, $\tan\theta = \dfrac{a_t}{a_c} = \dfrac{a_t}{v^2/r}$,

$$v^2 = \frac{a_t r}{\tan\theta} = \frac{10\times 5}{\tan 30°} = 50\sqrt{3}$$

$$= 50\times 1.732 = 86.6$$

$$\therefore \quad v = \sqrt{86.6} = 9.3 \text{ ms}^{-1}$$

10 (c) Given speed is increasing at the rate of a ms^{-2}.

So, linear acceleration = a

and tangential acceleration = v^2/R

Hence, net acceleration = $\sqrt{\left(\dfrac{v^2}{R}\right)^2 + a^2}$

11 (d) Due to earth axial rotation, the speed of the trains relative to the earth will be different and hence the centripetal forces on them as given by $\left(mg - \frac{mv^2}{r}\right)$ and $\left(mg + \frac{mv^2}{r}\right)$ will be different. So, they will exert different pressure on the rails.

Also, the magnitude of acceleration at every point of a circular path is same but its direction changes continuously.

12 (c) Given, $r = 5\text{ cm} = 5 \times 10^{-2}\text{ m}$

and $T = 0.2\pi$ s

We know that, acceleration, $a = r\omega^2$

$$= \frac{4\pi^2}{T^2} r \qquad \left[\because \omega = \frac{2\pi}{T}\right]$$

$$= \frac{4 \times \pi^2 \times 5 \times 10^{-2}}{(0.2\pi)^2} = 5\text{ ms}^{-2}$$

13 (a) As, $\omega = \omega_0 + \alpha t$

Here, $\omega_0 = 900\text{ rpm} = \frac{(2\pi \times 900)}{60}\text{ rads}^{-1}$,

$\omega = 0$ and $t = 60$ s

So, $0 = \frac{2\pi \times 900}{60} - \alpha \times 60$

$$\alpha = \frac{2\pi \times 900}{60 \times 60} = \frac{\pi}{2}$$

14 (a) Given, rpm = 360

We know that, $1\text{ rpm} = 2\pi\text{ rad min}^{-1}$

$= (2\pi/60)\text{ rads}^{-1}$

Hence, for 360 rpm, we have

$$360\text{ rpm} = \frac{2\pi}{60} \times 360 = 12\pi\text{ rads}^{-1}$$

15 (b) It is given that a particle is moving with a constant speed v in the circle, so the time taken to cover the complete circle would be equal to $T = \frac{2\pi r}{v}$, hence the time taken to cover half the rotation would be equal to

$$T_{1/2} = \frac{2\pi r}{2v} = \frac{\pi r}{v}.$$

Hence the magnitude of average velocity after half rotation would be equal to $v_{av} = \frac{2r}{\pi r/v} = \frac{2v}{\pi}$

16 (c) As, in case of pure rolling,

$$v_{P_0} = r\omega = (\sqrt{2}R)\omega = \sqrt{2}v_0$$

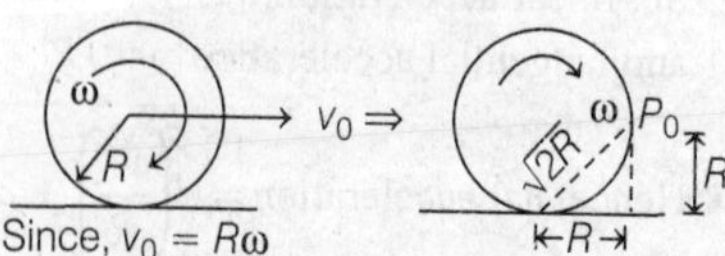

Since, $v_0 = R\omega$

17 (a) Given, $\omega = 0$, $\omega_0 = 100\text{ revmin}^{-1}$ and $t = 15$ s

From equation of motion (angular),

$$0 = \omega_0 - \alpha t \Rightarrow \alpha = \frac{\omega_0}{t}$$

$$= \frac{(100 \times 2\pi)/60}{15} = 0.69\text{ rad s}^{-2}$$

Now, angle rotated before coming to rest is given by

$$\theta = \frac{\omega_0^2}{2\alpha}$$

$$= \frac{\left(\frac{100 \times 2\pi}{60}\right)^2}{2 \times 0.7} \qquad (\because \omega^2 = \omega_0^2 + 2\alpha\theta)$$

$= 78.25$ rad

$\therefore$ Number of revolutions $= \frac{\theta}{2\pi} = 12.5$

18 (a) An object moving with speed v in a circle of radius r has an acceleration towards the centre of the circle. This acceleration is called centripetal acceleration which is given as

$$a = \frac{v^2}{r}$$

(towards the centre of the circle)

19 (d) As body covers equal angles in equal time intervals, so magnitude of velocity is constant, but the direction changes.

20 (d) When the particle completes half revolution, change in velocity

$$\Delta v = [5 - (-5)] = 10\text{ ms}^{-1}$$

Time taken to complete the half revolution,

$$t = \frac{\pi r}{v} = \frac{\pi \times 5}{5} = \pi\text{ s}$$

Thus, average acceleration,

$$a_{av} = \frac{\Delta v}{t} = \frac{10}{\pi}\text{ ms}^{-2}$$

21 (c) In a uniform circular motion, speed of particle is constant. Therefore, tangential acceleration is zero but radial acceleration remains constant in magnitude but its direction changes as particle moves in circular path.

22 (a) The centripetal acceleration is given by

$$a = \frac{v^2}{R} \text{ or } a \propto v^2$$

or $\frac{a_1}{a_2} = \frac{v_1^2}{v_2^2}$ (for constant R)

$\therefore$ $\frac{a_1}{a_2} = \frac{v^2}{(2v)^2} = \frac{1}{4}$ (as $a_1 = a$)

or $a_2 = 4a$

23 (b) On a circular path in completing one turn, the distance travelled is $2\pi r$ while displacement is zero.

Hence, average velocity

$$= \frac{\text{displacement}}{\text{time interval}} = \frac{0}{t} = 0$$

Given, $r_1 = 100$ cm and $t = 62.8$ s

Also, average speed

$$= \frac{\text{distance}}{\text{time interval}}$$

$$= \frac{2\pi r}{t} = \frac{2 \times 3.14 \times 100}{62.8} = 10\text{ ms}^{-1}$$

24 (a) Given, $v = 8\text{ kms}^{-1} = 8000\text{ ms}^{-1}$,

$r = (6400 + 630)$ km

$= (6400 + 630) \times 1000$ m

$$a = \frac{v^2}{r} = \frac{(8000)^2}{(6400 + 630) \times 1000}$$

$= 9.10\text{ ms}^{-2}$

25 (a) Time period of the earth on its own axis, $T = 24\text{ h} = 24 \times 60 \times 60$ s

$\therefore$ Angular velocity, ω

$$= \frac{2\pi}{T} = \frac{2\pi}{24 \times 60 \times 60}$$

$$= \frac{2\pi}{86400}\text{ rads}^{-1}$$

26 (d) If the string suddenly breaks, the centripetal force will be zero as the tension of string become zero but the tangential force will be present due to tangential velocity, so the stone travels in tangential direction.

27 (c) In circular motion, necessary centripetal force to the man is provided by effective weight of man.

$\therefore$ $m \times 9g = mr\omega^2 = mr \times 4\pi^2 n^2$

Given, $r = 5$ m

$\Rightarrow$ $n = \sqrt{\frac{9g}{4\pi^2 r}}$

$\Rightarrow$ $n = \sqrt{\frac{9 \times 10}{4 \times (3.14)^2 \times 5}}$

$= 0.675\text{ rev s}^{-1}$ or hertz (Hz)

28 (b) Acceleration of a point at the tip of the blade

= centripetal acceleration

$= \omega^2 R = (2\pi f)^2 R$

Given, $R = 30$ cm and $f = 1200$ rpm

$$= \left(2 \times \frac{22}{7} \times \frac{1200}{60}\right)^2 \times \frac{30}{100}$$

$$= 4741.22 \text{ m s}^{-2}$$

This value is closer to 4740 ms^{-2}

29 (c) If $a_r \neq 0$ but $a_t = 0$, then motion is a uniform circular.
If $a_r \neq 0$ and $a_t \neq 0$, then motion is a non-uniform circular.

30 (c) Angular velocity,

$$\omega = \frac{\Delta\theta}{\Delta t} = \frac{2\pi}{60} \text{ rad s}^{-1}$$

$$\Rightarrow \quad = \frac{\pi}{30} \text{ rad s}^{-1}$$

31 (d) Centripetal acceleration,
$a = v^2/r$,

$$\therefore \quad \frac{a_2}{a_1} = \left(\frac{v_2}{v_1}\right)^2 = \left(\frac{2v_1}{v_1}\right)^2 = 4:1$$

$(\because v_2 = 2v_1)$

32 (c) Angle traversed by the particle in (1/8)th of the circumference of the circle

$$= \left(\frac{1}{8}\right)\frac{2\pi r}{r} = \frac{\pi}{4} = 45°$$

So, change in velocity,

$$\Delta v = \sqrt{v^2 + v^2 - 2v^2 \cos 45°}$$

$$= \sqrt{2v^2 - 2v^2 \times \frac{1}{\sqrt{2}}}$$

$$= v\sqrt{2 - \sqrt{2}} = 0.765\, v$$

33 (d) Average speed

$$= \frac{\text{Total distance travelled}}{\text{Total time taken}}$$

$$= \frac{OP + PQ + QO}{10} \text{ km min}^{-1}$$

$$= \frac{1 + \frac{\pi}{2} \times 1 + 1}{10} = \frac{\pi + 4}{20} \times 60$$

$$= 21.4 \text{ km h}^{-1}$$

$\therefore$ Net displacement = 0

34 (c) Given, $r = 1$ m, $n = 22$ and $t = 44$ s

Since, speed is constant throughout the motion, so it is a uniform circular motion, therefore its radial acceleration, is

$$a = r\omega^2$$

$$= r\left(\frac{2\pi n}{t}\right)^2 = r \times \frac{4\pi^2 n^2}{t^2}$$

$$= \frac{1 \times 4 \times \pi^2 \times (22)^2}{(44)^2} = \pi^2 \text{ ms}^{-2}$$

along the radius towards the centre.

35 (d) The nature of path is decided by velocity and acceleration. Velocity is ratio of displacement to time. It is a vector quantity possessing both magnitude and direction. When velocity of a particle changes, the particle is said to undergo an acceleration.

The instantaneous acceleration is the derivative of the velocity with respect to time. Acceleration is also a vector quantity, possessing both magnitude and direction. Depending on variation of velocity and acceleration, the path could be a straight line, circle or a parabola.

36 (c) As, angular velocity

$$= \frac{\text{angle traced}}{\text{time taken}} \text{ by hour hand.}$$

Time period of hour hand is 12 h in which it traced 2π angle, so

$$\omega = \frac{2\pi}{12} \text{ rad h}^{-1}$$

$$\Rightarrow \quad = \frac{2\pi}{12 \times 60 \times 60} \text{ rad s}^{-1}$$

$$\Rightarrow \quad = \frac{\pi}{21600} \text{ rad s}^{-1}$$

37 (b) Given, radius of the horizontal circle
$r = 80$ cm = 0.80 m, $n = 14$ and $t = 25$s
Angular speed of revolution of the stone,

$$\omega = \frac{2\pi n}{t} = 2\pi\left(\frac{n}{t}\right)$$

$$\omega = 2 \times \frac{22}{7} \times \left(\frac{14}{25}\right) = \frac{88}{25} \text{ rads}^{-1}$$

$\because$ Magnitude of centripetal acceleration

$$= r\omega^2$$

$$= 80 \times \left(\frac{88}{25}\right)^2 = 992 \text{ cms}^{-2}$$

Hence, option (b) is close to the result.

Topic 5

Relative Velocity

2019

1 The speed of a swimmer in still water is 20 ms^{-1}. The speed of river water is 10 ms^{-1} and is flowing due east. If he is standing on the south bank and wishes to cross the river along the shortest path the angle at which he should make his strokes w.r.t. north is given by **[NEET]**

(a) 0° (b) 60°, west (c) 45°, west (d) 30°, west

2 A ship A is moving westwards with a speed of 10 km h^{-1} and a ship B 100 km South of A, is moving northwards with a speed of 10 km h^{-1}. The time after which the distance between them becomes shortest is **[CBSE AIPMT]**

(a) 0 h (b) 5 h
(c) $5\sqrt{2}$ h (d) $10\sqrt{2}$ h

2014

3 At time $t = 0$, two bodies A and B are at the same point. A moves with constant velocity v and B starts from rest and moves with constant acceleration. Relative velocity of B with respect to A, when the bodies meet each other is **[EAMCET]**

(a) $\frac{v}{2}$ (b) $\frac{v}{3}$ (c) v (d) $2v$

4 A car moves from A to B with a speed of 30 kmh^{-1} and from B to A with a speed of 20 kmh^{-1}. What is the average speed of the car? **[KCET]**

(a) 25 kmh^{-1} (b) 24 kmh^{-1} (c) 50 kmh^{-1} (d) 10 kmh^{-1}

2008

5 A train of 150 m length is going towards north direction at a speed of 10 ms^{-1}. A parrot flies at a speed of 5 ms^{-1} towards south direction parallel to the railway track. The time taken by parrot to cross the train is equal to **[BHU]**

(a) 12 s (b) 8 s (c) 15 s (d) 10 s

6 Rain is falling vertically downwards with a velocity of 4 kmh^{-1}. A man walks in the rain with a velocity of 3 kmh^{-1}. The raindrops will fall on the man with a velocity of **[BHU]**

(a) 1 kmh^{-1} (b) 3 kmh^{-1} (c) 4 kmh^{-1} (d) 5 kmh^{-1}

7 A man is walking due east at the rate of 2 kmh^{-1}. The rain appears to him to come down vertically at the rate of 2 kmh^{-1}. The actual velocity and direction of rainfall with the vertical, respectively are **[EAMCET]**

(a) $2\sqrt{2}$ kmh^{-1}, 45° (b) $\frac{1}{\sqrt{2}}$ kmh^{-1}, 30°

(c) 2 kmh^{-1}, 0° (d) 1 kmh^{-1}, 90°

8 Police is chasing the thief 50 m ahead. In 10 s, distance between them reduces by 6 m. What is distance between them in 25 s? **[DUMET]**

(a) 10 m (b) 25 m (c) 35 m (d) 20 m

2006

9 A police jeep is chasing with velocity of 45 kmh^{-1}, a thief in another jeep moving with velocity 153 kmh^{-1}. Police fires a bullet with muzzle velocity of 180 ms^{-1}. The velocity with which bullet will strike the car of the thief, is **[Manipal]**

(a) 150 ms^{-1} (b) 27 ms^{-1} (c) 450 ms^{-1} (d) 250 ms^{-1}

2005

10 A river is flowing from west to east with a speed of 5 m min^{-1}. A man can swim in still water with a velocity 10 m min^{-1}. In which direction, should the man swim so as to take the shortest possible path to go to the south? **[BHU]**

(a) 30° east of south
(b) 60° east of south
(c) 60° west of south
(d) 30° west of north

11 How long will a passenger sitting at the window of a train travelling at a speed of 54 kmh^{-1} see a train, passing by in the opposite directions with a speed of 36 kmh^{-1}, if the length of the second train is 150 m? **[Haryana PMT]**

(a) 10 s (b) 6 s (c) 6 min (d) 8 min

12 A boat moves with a speed of 5 kmh^{-1} relative to water in a river flowing with a speed of 3 kmh^{-1} and having a width of 1 km. The time taken in back and forth trip is **[J&K CET]**

(a) 5 min (b) 60 min
(c) 20 min (d) 30 min

Answers

1 (d)	2 (b)	3 (c)	4 (b)	5 (d)	6 (d)	7 (a)	8 (c)	9 (a)	10 (a)
11 (b)	12 (d)								

Explanations

1 *(d)* Given, speed of river, $v_R = 10\,ms^{-1}$

Speed of swimmer in still water, $v_{SN} = 20\,ms^{-1}$.

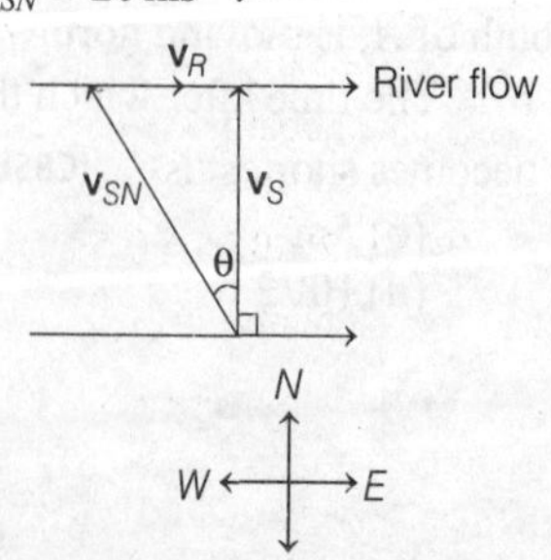

For the shortest path to cross the river, he should swim at an angle (90° + θ) with the stream flow. From the figure above, $\mathbf{v}_{SN} = \mathbf{v}_R + \mathbf{v}_S$

So, angle θ is given by

$$\sin\theta = \left|\frac{\mathbf{v}_R}{\mathbf{v}_{SN}}\right| = \frac{10}{20} = \frac{1}{2}$$

$$\Rightarrow \quad \theta = 30°$$

As the river is flowing in east direction, so he should swim towards west.

2 *(b)* It is clear from the diagram that the shortest distance between the ship A and B is PQ.

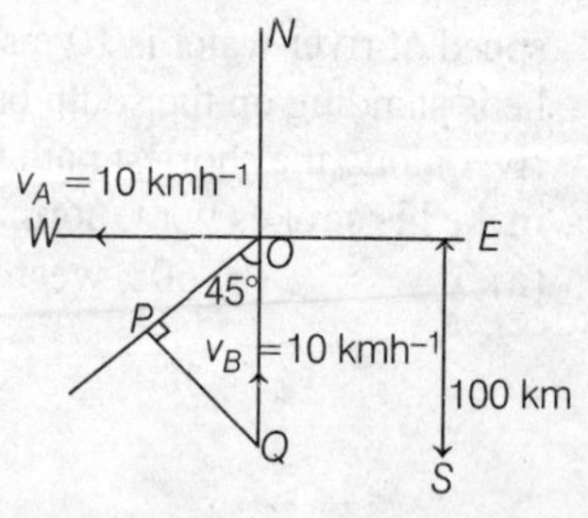

Here, $\sin 45° = \dfrac{PQ}{OQ}$

$\Rightarrow \quad PQ = 100 \times \dfrac{1}{\sqrt{2}} = 50\sqrt{2}$ m

Also, $v_{AB} = \sqrt{v_A^2 + v_B^2} = \sqrt{10^2 + 10^2}$

$= 10\sqrt{2}$ kmh^{-1}

So, time taken for them to reach shortest path is

$$t = \frac{PQ}{v_{AB}} = \frac{50\sqrt{2}}{10\sqrt{2}} = 5 \text{ h}$$

3 (c) $A \rightarrow v_A$ (constant velocity), $B \rightarrow a$ (constant acceleration)

Let C be the fixed point at which both A and B meet in time t

Now, $s = v_A t$ and $v_B = at$

$A \rightarrow v_A = v$

$B \rightarrow a$ O ——— C   ← s →

$$s = \frac{1}{2}at^2 = v_A t$$

$$a = \frac{2v_A}{t}$$

$\Rightarrow \quad v_B = at = 2v_A$

Relative velocity

$\Rightarrow \quad v_{BA} = v_B - v_A = 2v_A - v_A = v_A$

$\Rightarrow \quad v_{BA} = v \qquad (\because v_A = v)$

where, v_{BA} = velocity of B w.r.t. A

4 (b) A ——→ 30 kmh^{-1} ——— B, 20 kmh^{-1} ←——

v_{AB} = speed of car from A to B

i.e. $\quad v_{AB} = 30$ kmh^{-1}

v_{BA} = speed of car from B to A

i.e. $\quad v_{BA} = 20$ kmh^{-1}

Hence, $v_{\text{av}} = \dfrac{2v_{AB}v_{BA}}{v_{AB} + v_{BA}} = \dfrac{2 \times 30 \times 20}{30 + 20}$

$= 24$ kmh^{-1}

5 (d) Given, $l = 150$ m, $v_1 = 10$ ms^{-1}

and $v_2 = 5$ ms^{-1}

Relative velocity of the parrot w.r.t. the train

$= [10 - (-5)]$ ms^{-1} = 15 ms^{-1}

Time taken by the parrot to cross the train, $t = \dfrac{s}{v} = \dfrac{150}{15} = 10$ s

6 (d) Relative velocity of man w.r.t. rain,

$\mathbf{v}_{rm} = \mathbf{v}_r - \mathbf{v}_m = 3\hat{\mathbf{i}} - 4\hat{\mathbf{j}}$

$\therefore |\mathbf{v}_{rm}| = \sqrt{(3)^2 + (-4)^2}$

$= \sqrt{9 + 16} = \sqrt{25} = 5$ kmh^{-1}

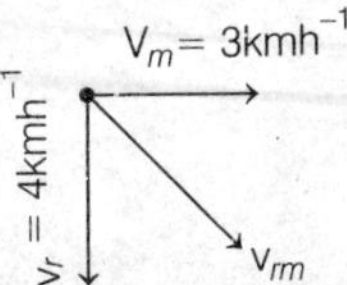

7 (a) Given, velocity of man,

$v_m = 2$ kmh^{-1}

and velocity of rain, $v_r = 2$ kmh^{-1}

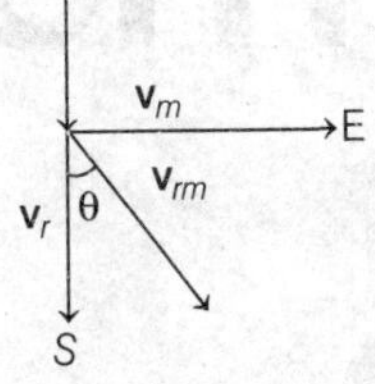

Then, actual velocity,

$v_{rm} = \sqrt{v_m^2 + v_r^2} = \sqrt{(2)^2 + (2)^2}$

$= \sqrt{4 + 4} = 2\sqrt{2}$ kmh^{-1}

The direction of rainfall with the horizontal (east),

$$\sin\theta = \frac{v_m}{v_{rm}} = \frac{2}{2\sqrt{2}} = \frac{1}{\sqrt{2}}$$

$$\theta = \sin^{-1}\left(\frac{1}{\sqrt{2}}\right) \Rightarrow \theta = 45°$$

Thus, direction of rainfall with the vertical is 45°.

8 (c) Let relative velocity police and thief be v, then

$v \times 10 = 6 \Rightarrow v = 0.6$ ms^{-1}

So, distance between them in 25 s

$= 50 - 0.6 \times 25 = 35$ m

9 (a) The relative velocity of thief's jeep with respect to police jeep

$= 153 - 45 = 108$ kmh^{-1}

$= 108 \times \dfrac{5}{18} = 30$ ms^{-1}

Therefore, striking speed = relative speed of bullet with respect to thief's car = 180 − 30 = 150 ms^{-1}

10 (a) Let the swimmer swims at an angle θ with the vertical.

From figure, $\sin\theta = \dfrac{v_r}{v_m}$

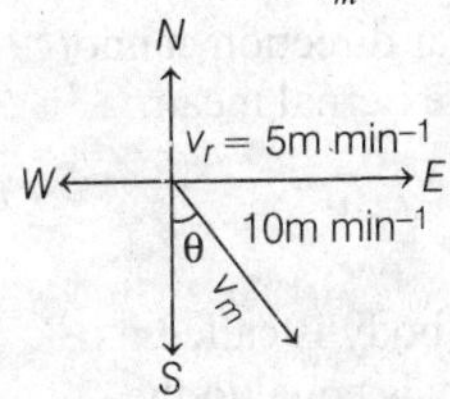

where, v_r is velocity of river and v_m is velocity of man.

Given, $v_r = 5$ m min^{-1},

$v_m = 10$ m min^{-1}

$\therefore \quad \sin\theta = \dfrac{5}{10} = \dfrac{1}{2}$

$\Rightarrow \quad \theta = 30°$

The component 10 sin θ of swimmer's velocity will cancel the velocity of river and the swimmer takes the shortest distance to the south. Therefore, direction is 30° east of south.

11 (b) Given, $v_1 = 54$ kmh^{-1},

$v_2 = 36$ kmh^{-1}

and $\quad s = 150$ m

Relative speed of first train w.r.t. second train

$= (54 + 36)$ kmh^{-1}

$= 90 \times \dfrac{5}{18}$ ms^{-1}

$= 25$ ms^{-1}

Time duration to pass second train

$= \dfrac{150}{25} = 6$ s

12 (d) Time taken by the boat to reach the other side is

$$\text{time} = \frac{\text{distance}}{\text{relative speed}}$$

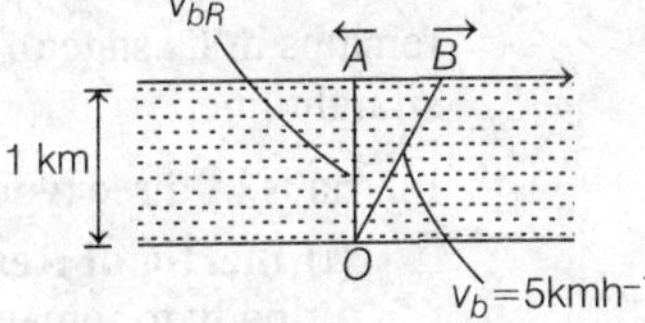

Relative speed,

$v_{bR} = \sqrt{v_b^2 - v_R^2}$

$= \sqrt{5^2 - 3^2}$

$= \sqrt{16} = 4$ kmh^{-1}

$\therefore \quad T = \dfrac{1 \text{ km}}{4 \text{ kmh}^{-1}}$

$= 0.25$ h

To come back, boat takes the same time hence total time is

$T' = 2 \times 0.25 = 0.5$ h

$\therefore \quad (1 \text{ h} = 60 \text{ minp})$

$\therefore \quad 0.5 \text{ h} = 30$ min

04

Laws of Motion

Quick Review

Force

Force is the external agent (a push or pull) which changes or tends to change the state of rest or uniform motion of a body in a straight line.

Impulsive Force

A force which acts on a body for a short interval of time and produces a large change in momentum is called an impulsive force.

Inertia

It is the inherent property of a body by virtue of which it remains in its state of rest or of uniform motion in a straight line.

Inertia is of three types

(*i*) **Inertia of Rest** It is defined as the tendency of a body to remain in its position of rest. i.e., A body at rest remains at rest and cannot start moving on its own.

(*ii*) **Inertia of Motion** It is defined as the tendency of a body to remain in its state of uniform motion along a straight line. i.e., A body in uniform motion can neither gets accelerated nor get retarded on its own, also it cannot stop on its own.

(*iii*) **Inertia of Direction** It is defined as inability of a body to change by itself its direction of motion.

e.g. A body moving in a particular direction cannot change its direction without any external mean.

Linear Momentum

The total amount of motion present in a body is called its momentum. Linear momentum of a body is equal to the product of its mass and velocity. It is denoted by p.

Linear momentum, $\mathbf{p} = m\mathbf{v}$.

Its SI unit is kg-m/s and dimensional formula is $[MLT^{-1}]$.

It is a vector quantity and its direction is in the direction of velocity of the body.

Newton's Laws of Motion

Newton gave three laws of motion

(*i*) **Newton's First Law** A body continues to be in the state of rest or uniform motion along a straight line unless acted upon by an external force.

(*ii*) **Newton's Second Law** The rate of change of momentum (p) of a body is equal to the force applied on it.

Thus, $$\mathbf{F} = \frac{\Delta \mathbf{p}}{\Delta t} = m\mathbf{a}$$

(*iii*) **Newton's Third Law** Every action has an equal and opposite reaction.

Note Newton's second law of motion is called real law of motion because first and third laws of motion can be obtained form it.

Frame of Reference

A frame in which observer is present and makes his observation is called frame of reference.

(*i*) **Inertial Frame of Reference** A non-accelerated frame of reference in which Newton's law of motion holds good, called inertial frame of reference.

(*ii*) **Non-inertial Frame of Reference** It is an accelerated frame of reference in which Newton's law of motions are not valid.

Conservation of Linear Momentum

According to law of conservation of linear momentum, total linear momentum of a system of particles remains constant or conserved in the absence of any external force.

i.e. When $\mathbf{F}_{ext} = 0$, $\dfrac{d\mathbf{p}}{dt} = 0$

$$\mathbf{p} = \text{constant}$$

i.e. $\mathbf{p}_{initial} = \mathbf{p}_{final}$

or for n number of particles

$$\mathbf{p}_1 + \mathbf{p}_2 + \mathbf{p}_3 + \ldots \mathbf{p}_n = \text{constant}.$$

- For collision of two bodies, the total momentum before collision remains same as total momentum after collision.
$$m_1 \mathbf{u}_1 + m_2 \mathbf{u}_2 = m_1 \mathbf{v}_1 + m_2 \mathbf{v}_2$$
- Recoil velocity of gun is calculated by, $v_2 = -\dfrac{m_1 v_1}{m_2}$

  where, m_2 = mass of the gun, m_1 = mass of the bullet

  and v_1 = velocity of the bullet.

Impulse

The product of impulsive force and time for which it acts is called impulse.

Impulse, $\mathbf{J} = \mathbf{F}\,t$

Also, $\mathbf{J} = m(\mathbf{v} - \mathbf{u})$

where, v = final velocity and u = initial velocity.

Impulse = Change in momentum

- If force F is applied for duration $(t_2 - t_1)$, then
$$J = \int_{t_1}^{t_2} F dt = \int_{p_i}^{p_f} dp = \Delta p$$
- Impulse is given by the area covered by F-Δt graph.

Equilibrium of Concurrent Forces

- If all the forces working on a body are acting on the same point, then they are said to be concurrent.
- A body under the action of concurrent forces, is said to be in equilibrium, when there is no change in the state of rest or of uniform motin along a straight line.
- When a particle is at rest or moving with constant velocity in an inertial frame of reference, the net force on it, i.e. the vector sum of all the forces acting on it must be zero.

  i.e., $\mathbf{F}_1 + \mathbf{F}_2 + \mathbf{F}_3 = 0$ or $\Sigma \mathbf{F} = 0$

  In component form, $\Sigma F_x = 0$, $\Sigma F_y = 0$, $\Sigma F_z = 0$

Lami's Theorem Three forces P, Q and R are acting on a body be are in equilibrium, if

$$\frac{P}{\sin\alpha} = \frac{Q}{\sin\beta} = \frac{R}{\sin\gamma}$$

Apparent Weight of a Person in a Moving Lift

(*i*) When the lift moves upwards with acceleration a as shown in figure, then net upward force on the man is

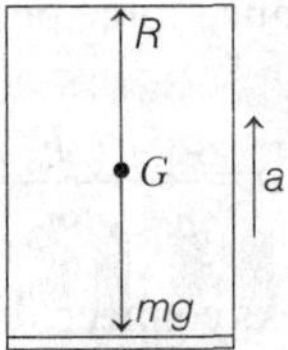

$$R - mg = ma \Rightarrow R = ma + mg,$$

Here R = normal reaction.

Apparent weight, $R = m(g + a)$

So, **when a lift accelerates upwards, the apparent weight of the man inside it increases.**

(*ii*) When the lift move downwards with acceleration a as shown in figure, then net downward force on the man is

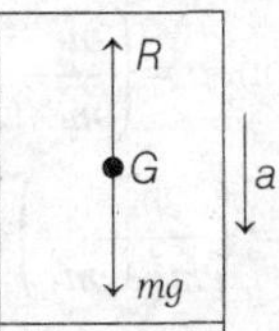

$$mg - R = ma$$

Apparent weight, $R = m(g - a)$

So, **when a lift accelerates downwards, the apparent weight of the man inside it decreases.**

(*iii*) When the lift is at rest or moving with uniform velocity v downward or upward as shown in figure.

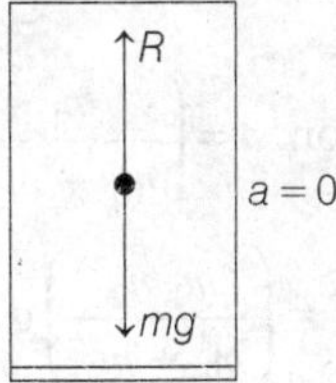

Then, acceleration $a = 0$, so net force on the man is

$$R - mg = m \times 0$$

$$\Rightarrow \quad R = mg$$

or Apparent weight = Actual weight

So, **when the lift is at rest, the apparent weight of the man is his actual weight.**

(*iv*) When the lift falls freely under gravity, if the supporting cable of the lift breaks. Then, $a = g$.

The net downward force on the man is

$$R = m(g - g) \Rightarrow R = 0$$

Thus, **the apparent weight of the man becomes zero.**

Motion of Bodies Connected through Strings

I. Horizontal Motion

(*i*) Motion of blocks in contact

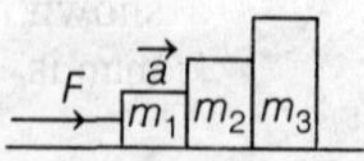

where, F = applied force on the system.

$$\text{Acceleration, } a = \frac{F}{m_1 + m_2 + m_3}$$

(*ii*) Motion of blocks connected by string

$$T = \frac{m_1 F}{m_1 + m_2} \text{ and } a = \frac{F}{m_1 + m_2}$$

II. Objects Attached through Pulleys

(*i*) For two bodies of unequal masses ($m_1 > m_2$) suspended from a pulley

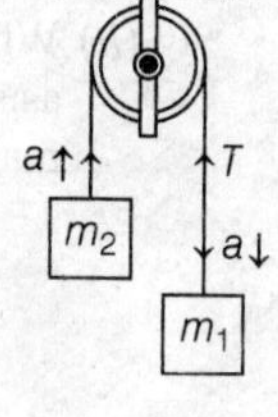

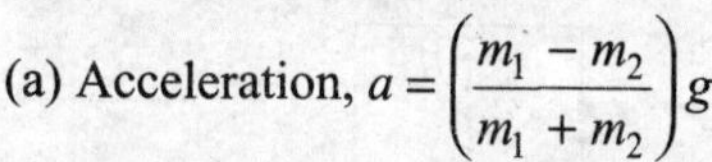

(a) Acceleration, $a = \left(\frac{m_1 - m_2}{m_1 + m_2} \right) g$

(b) Tension, $T = \left(\frac{2m_1 m_2}{m_1 + m_2} \right) g$

(*ii*) For a body (m_2) accelerated on a horizontal smooth surface by a falling body (m_1) through a pulley

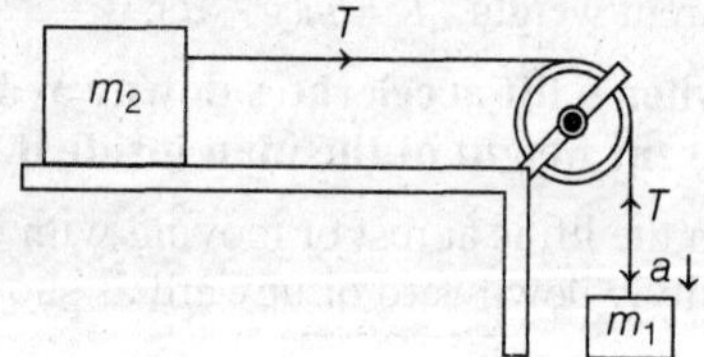

(a) Acceleration, $a = \left(\frac{m_1}{m_1 + m_2} \right) g$

(b) Tension, $T = \left(\frac{m_1 m_2}{m_1 + m_2} \right) g$

(*iii*) For the motion on a smooth inclined plane,

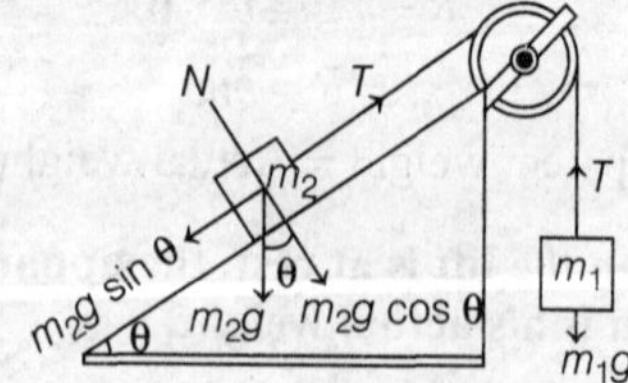

(a) Acceleration, $a = \left(\frac{m_1 - m_2 \sin \theta}{m_1 + m_2} \right) g$

(b) Tension, $T = \frac{m_1 m_2 (1 + \sin \theta) g}{(m_1 + m_2)}$

(*iv*) For a block system and pulley shown in figure, value of the acceleration of the system (if $m_1 + m_2 > m_3$),

$$a = \frac{(m_1 + m_2 - m_3) g}{(m_1 + m_2 + m_3)}$$

$$\text{Tension, } T_1 = \frac{2 m_1 m_3 g}{(m_1 + m_2 + m_3)}$$

$$T_2 = \frac{2 m_3 (m_1 + m_2) g}{(m_1 + m_2 + m_3)}$$

and total tension, $T = 2T_2$

$$= \frac{4 m_3 (m_1 + m_2) g}{(m_1 + m_2 + m_3)}$$

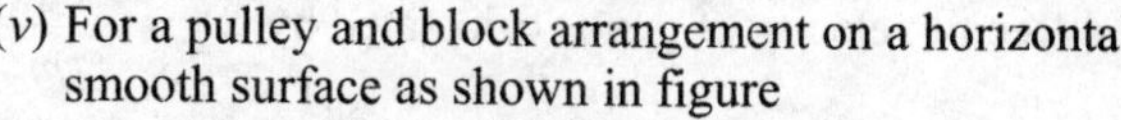

(*v*) For a pulley and block arrangement on a horizontal smooth surface as shown in figure

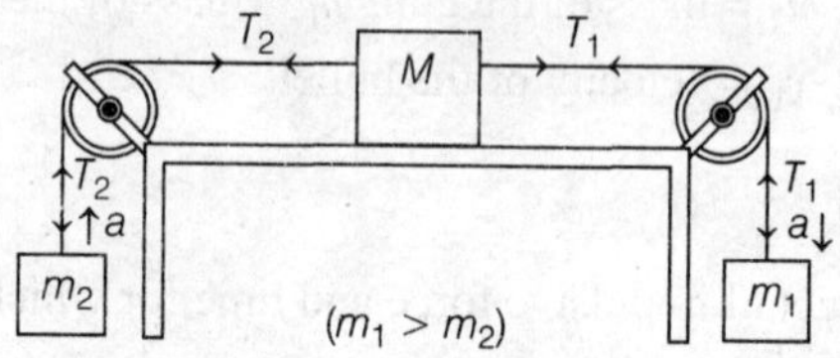

Net acceleration,

$$a = \frac{\text{Net acceleration force}}{\text{Total mass}} = \frac{(m_1 - m_2) g}{(m_1 + m_2 + M)}$$

$$\text{Tension, } T_1 = m_1 (g - a) = \frac{(M + 2m_2) m_1 g}{(M + m_1 + m_2)}$$

$$\text{and } T_2 = m_2 (g + a) = \frac{(M + 2m_1) m_2 g}{(M + m_1 + m_2)}$$

(*vi*) For a pulley and block system on a smooth double inclined plane as shown in figure, we have

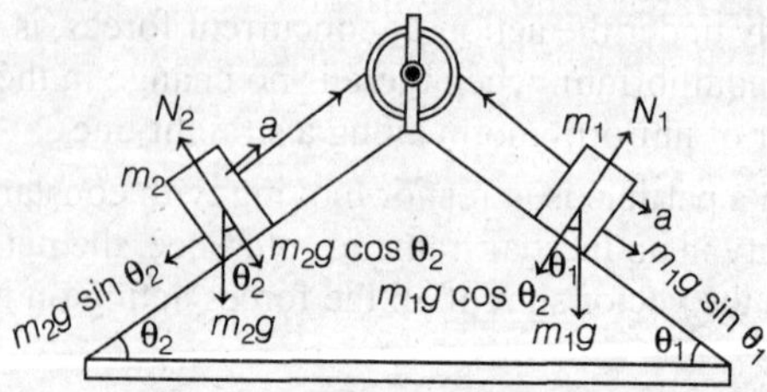

$$\text{Net acceleration, } a = \frac{(m_1 \sin \theta_1 - m_2 \sin \theta_2) g}{(m_1 + m_2)}$$

and tension in string, $T = m_1 (g \sin \theta_1 - a)$

$$= \frac{m_1 m_2 (\sin \theta_1 + \sin \theta_2) g}{(m_1 + m_2)}$$

Motion of a Chain due to its Own Weight

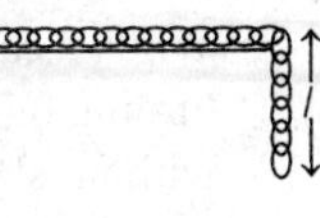

If a chain is placed on the table by some portion hanging in air, then maximum length (l) of chain that can hang in air without sliding is given by $l = \frac{kL}{1+k}$

where, $k = \frac{\text{length hanging from table}}{\text{length lying on the table}}$

and L = total length of chain.

Friction

Whenever a body moves or tends to move over the surface of another body, a force comes into play which acts parallel to the surface of contact and opposes the relative motion. This opposing force is called **friction.**

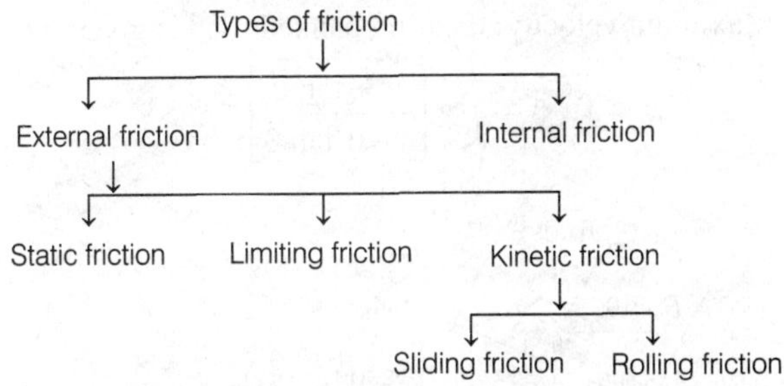

(*i*) **Static Friction** Force of friction which comes into play between two bodies before one body has not actually starts moving over the other is called static friction and it is denoted by f_s.

The static frictional force is given by $f_s \le \mu_s N$, where μ_s is the coefficient of static friction.

(*ii*) **Limiting Friction** Maximum force of static friction which comes into play when a body just starts moving over the surface of another body is called limiting friction. Thus, $f_s \le f_{s\,(\max)}$.

The value of limiting friction ($f_{s(\max)}$) between two given surfaces is directly proportional to the normal reaction (R) between the two surfaces

i.e. $f_{s(\max)} \propto R$ or $f_{s\,(\max)} = \mu_s R$

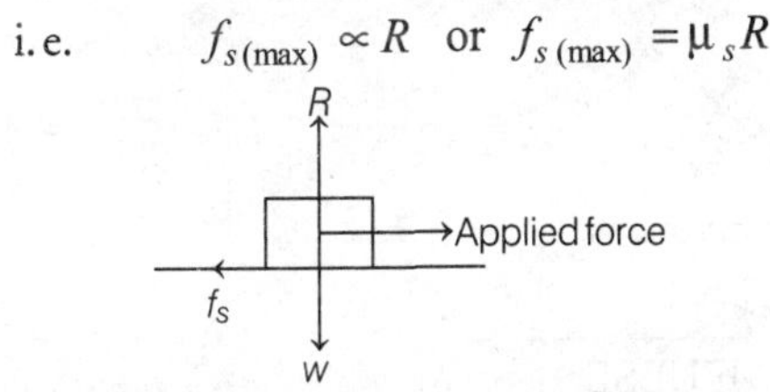

where, $R = w = mg$, m = mass of the block

or $\mu_s = \frac{f_{s(\max)}}{R} = \frac{\text{Limiting friction}}{\text{Normal reaction}}$

The proportionality constant μ_s is called **coefficient of static friction**. It is defined as the ratio of limiting friction to the normal reaction.

(*iii*) **Kinetic Friction** The force of friction that acts between two objects when one object is actually moving over the surface of another is called kinetic friction. Kinetic friction is proportional to the normal force, which presses the two surfaces together.

Mathematically, $f_k \le \mu_k N$, where μ_k is the coefficient of kinetic friction.

Kinetic friction is further divided into following two types, Sliding friction and Rolling friction

- Rolling friction is quite small as compared to sliding friction.
- In rolling, the surfaces at contact do not rub each other.

Angle of Friction

The angle which the resultant of the force of limiting friction and normal reaction makes with the direction of normal reaction is known as angle of friction.

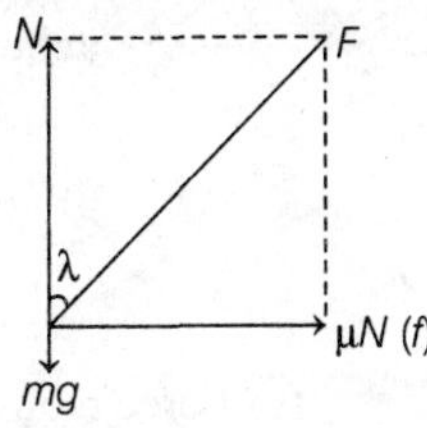

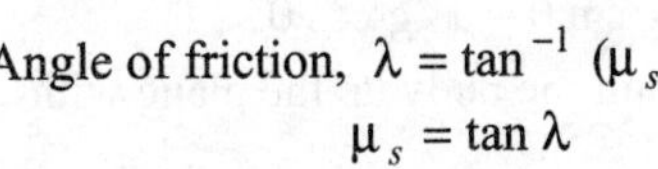

Angle of friction, $\lambda = \tan^{-1}(\mu_s)$

$\mu_s = \tan\lambda$

Angle of Repose

The minimum angle of inclination of plane with the horizontal at which the body placed on the plane just begins to slide down, is known as angle of repose.

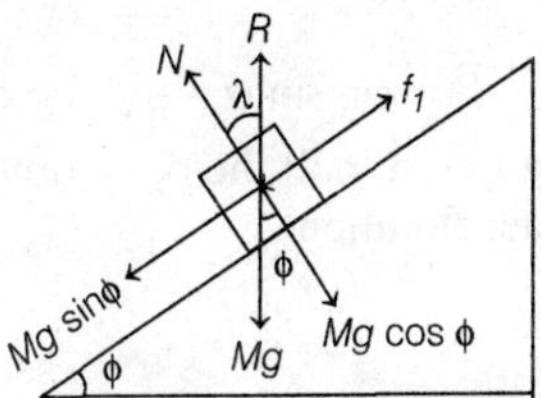

Angle of repose (ϕ) = Angle of friction (λ)

Motion of a Body on Rough Inclined Plane

(*i*) When the angle of inclination is greater than angle of repose and the body is sliding down the rough inclined plane with some acceleration a, then

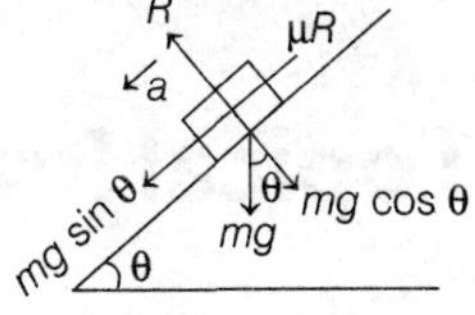

$$a = g\sin\theta - \mu_k g\cos\theta$$

(*ii*) When the angle of inclination α is less than angle of repose and the body is pulled down the plane with uniform velocity by applying an external force P, then

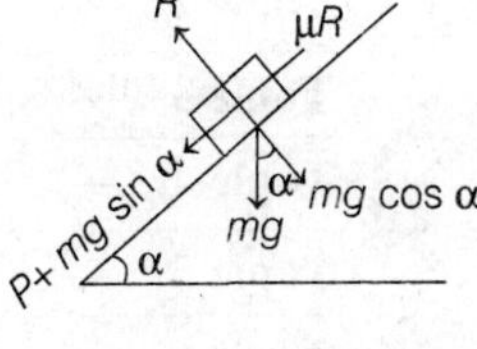

$$P = \mu_k mg\cos\alpha - mg\sin\alpha$$

(*iii*) When the angle of inclination is less than angle of repose and the block is pulled down with certain acceleration *a*, then force is

$$P = \mu mg \cos \alpha - mg \sin \alpha + ma$$

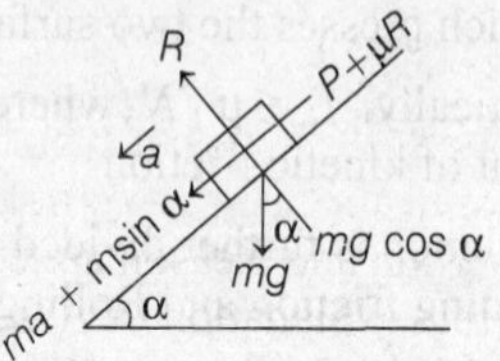

(*iv*) Inclination may be greater than or less than the angle of repose, but the body is projected up the plane with some initial velocity. In this case, the net retardation acting on the body is given by

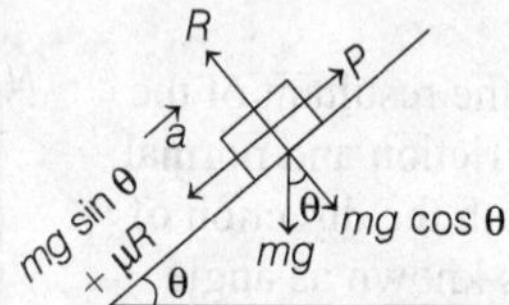

$$a = g \sin \theta + \mu_k g \cos \theta$$

(*v*) Force required to pull the body up the plane with constant velocity

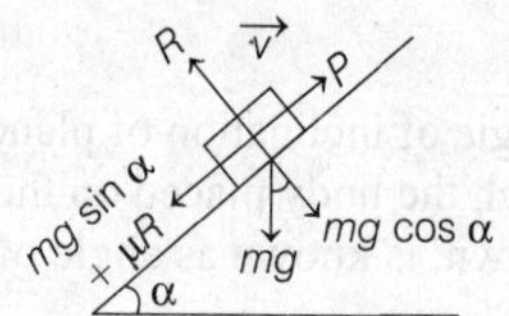

$$P = mg \sin \alpha - \mu_k \; mg \cos \alpha$$

(*vi*) Force required to pull the body up the plane with constant acceleration

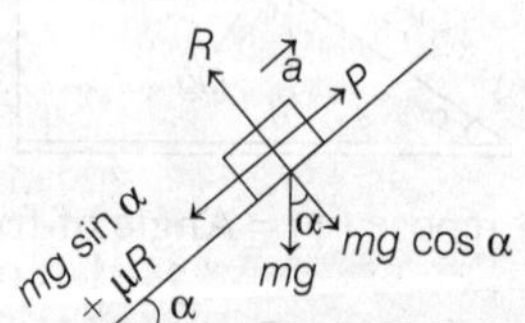

$$P = mg \sin \alpha + (\mu_k mg \cos \alpha) + ma$$

Motion of Car on Level Road

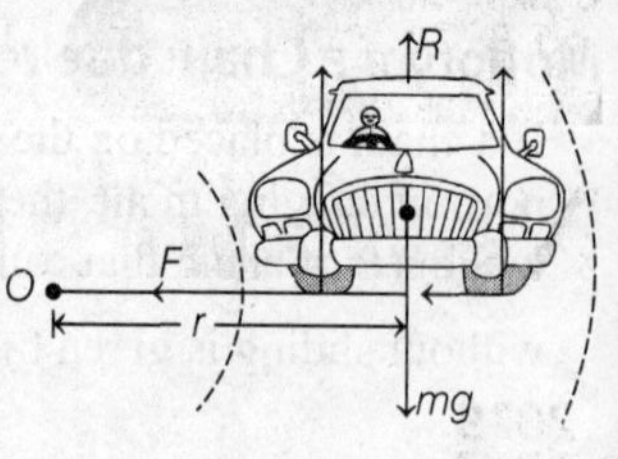

- When a car of mass *m* is turning on the level road without skidding, centripetal force on the car must be equal or less than static friction.

i.e. $F \geq \dfrac{mv_{\max}^2}{r}$ [ω → coefficient of friction]

$$\mu g \geq \frac{mv_{\max}^2}{r} \quad \text{or} \quad v_{\max} \leq \sqrt{\mu . rg}$$

∴ Maximum velocity on a curved road to avoid skidding is

$$v_{\max} = \sqrt{\mu rg}$$

Motion of a Car on Banked Road

- Maximum velocity of car on banked road is given by

$$v_{\max} = \sqrt{rg\left[\frac{\mu + \tan \theta}{1 - \mu \tan \theta}\right]}$$

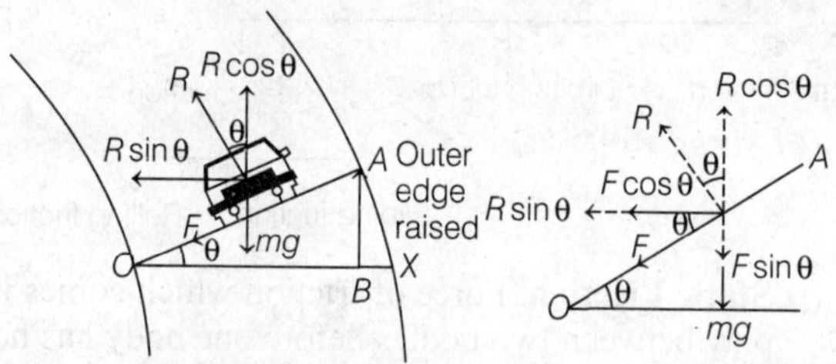

where, θ = inclination of road

and r = radius of turn.

If $\mu = 0$, then $v = \sqrt{rg \tan \theta}$

Bending of Cyclist on Banked Road

In order to take circular turn of radius *r* with speed *v*, the cyclist should bend himself through an angle θ from vertical direction such that $\tan \theta = \dfrac{v^2}{rg}$.

Topical Practice Questions

All the exam questions of this chapter have been divided into 7 topics as listed below

Topic 1
Newton's Laws of Motion

2019

1 **Assertion** A glass ball is dropped on concrete floor can easily get broken compared if it is dropped on wooden floor.

Reason On concrete floor, glass ball will take less time to come to rest. **[AIIMS]**

(a) Both Assertion and Reason are true and Reason is the correct explanation of Assertion.
(b) Both Assertion and Reason are true, but Reason is not the correct explanation of Assertion.
(c) Assertion is true but Reason is false.
(d) Both Assertion and Reason are false.

2018

2 Sand is being dropped on a conveyor belt at the rate of M kgs^{-1}. The force necessary to keep the belt moving with a constant velocity is v ms^{-1} will be

(a) Mv newton (b) $2Mv$ newton
(c) $\frac{Mv}{2}$ newton (d) zero

2014

3 A balloon with mass m is descending down with an acceleration a (where, $a < g$). How much mass should be removed from it so that it starts moving up with an acceleration a? **[CBSE AIPMT]**

(a) $\frac{2ma}{g+a}$ (b) $\frac{2ma}{g-a}$ (c) $\frac{ma}{g+a}$ (d) $\frac{ma}{g-a}$

4 The linear momentum of a particle varies with time t as $p = a + bt + ct^2$. Then, which of the following is correct? **[EAMCET]**

(a) Velocity of particle is inversely proportional to time
(b) Displacement of the particle is independent of time
(c) Force varies with time in a quadratic manner
(d) Force is dependent linearly on time

5 The rate of mass of the gases emitted from rear of a rocket is initially 0.1 kgs^{-1}. If the speed of the gas relative to the rocket is 50 ms^{-1} and mass of the rocket is 2 kg, then the acceleration of the rocket (in ms^{-2}) is **[J&K CET]**

(a) 5 (b) 5.2 (c) 2.5 (d) 25

2013

6 **Assertion** The driver in a vehicle moving with a constant speed on a straight road is in a non-inertial frame of reference.

Reason A reference frame in which Newton's laws of motion are applicable is non-inertial. **[AIIMS]**

(a) Both Assertion and Reason are correct and Reason is the correct explanation of Assertion.
(b) Both Assertion and Reason are correct but Reason is not the correct explanation of Assertion.
(c) Assertion is correct but Reason is incorrect.
(d) Both Assertion and Reason are incorrect.
(e) Assertion is incorrect but Reason is correct.

7 An object of mass 10 kg moves at a constant speed of 10 m/s. A constant force that acts for 4 s on the object, gives it a speed 2 m/s in opposite direction. The force acting on the object is **[WB JEE]**

(a) – 3N (b) – 30 N
(c) 3 N (d) 30 N

2011

8 Diwali rocket is ejecting 50 g of gases/s at a velocity of 400 ms^{-1}. The accelerating force on the rocket will be **[RPMT]**

(a) 22 dyne (b) 20 N (c) 20 dyne (d) 100 N

9 A rocket of mass 1000 kg is to be projected vertically upwards. The gases are exhausted vertically downwards with velocity 100 ms^{-1} with respect to the rocket. What is the minimum rate of burning of fuel, so as to just lift the rocket upwards against the gravitational attraction? (Take, $g = 10$ ms^{-2}) **[AMU]**

(a) 50 kgs^{-1} (b) 100 kgs^{-1}
(c) 200 kgs^{-1} (d) 400 kgs^{-1}

10 In a non-inertial frame, the second law of motion is written as **[DUMET]**

(a) $\mathbf{F} = m\mathbf{a}$ (b) $\mathbf{F} = m\mathbf{a} + \mathbf{F}_p$
(c) $\mathbf{F} = m\mathbf{a} - \mathbf{F}_p$ (d) $\mathbf{F} = 2m\mathbf{a}$

where, $\mathbf{F}_p$ is pseudo-force while $\mathbf{a}$ is the acceleration of the body relative to the non-inertial frame.

2010

11 A 5000 kg rocket is set for vertical firing. The exhaust speed is 800 ms^{-1}. To give an initial upward acceleration of 20 ms^{-2}, the amount of gas ejected per second to supply the needed thrust will be **[JCECE]**

(a) 137.5 kgs^{-1} (b) 185.5 kgs^{-1}
(c) 127.5 kgs^{-1} (d) 187.5 kgs^{-1}

12 A force F_1 of 500 N is required to push a car of mass 1000 kg slowly at constant speed on a levelled road. If a force F_2 of 1000 N is applied, then the acceleration of the car will be **[Manipal]**

(a) zero (b) 1.5 ms^{-2}
(c) 1 ms^{-2} (d) 0.5 ms^{-2}

13 A ball of mass 0.5 kg is moving with a velocity of 2 ms^{-1}. It is subjected to a force of x newton in 2 s. Because of this force, the ball moves with a velocity of 3 ms^{-1}. The value of x is **[Manipal]**

(a) 5 N (b) 8.25 N (c) 0.25 N (d) 1 N

2009

14 A ball hits a vertical wall horizontally at 10 m/s and bounces back at 10 m/s, then **[UP CPMT]**

(a) there is no acceleration because 10 m/s – 10 m/s = 0.
(b) there may be an acceleration because its initial direction is horizontal.
(c) there is an acceleration because there is a momentum change.
(d) even though there is no change in momentum, there is a change in direction. Hence, it has an acceleration.

2008

15 A body of mass 2 kg has an initial velocity of 3 ms^{-1} along OE and it is subjected to a force of 4 N in a direction perpendicular to OE. The distance of body from O after 4 s will be **[Manipal]**

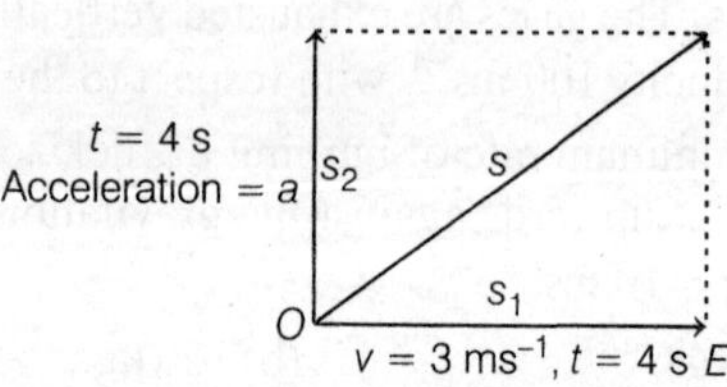

(a) 12 m (b) 20 m
(c) 8 m (d) 48 m

2007

16 When a car moves on a road with uniform speed of 30 kmh^{-1}, then the net resultant force on the car is **[BHU]**

(a) the driving force, drives the car in the direction of propagation of car.
(b) the resistive force, acts opposite to the direction of propagation of car.
(c) zero
(d) None of the above

17 Same force acts on two bodies of different masses 3 kg and 5 kg initially at rest. The ratio of times required to acquire same final velocity is **[Kerala CEE]**

(a) 5 : 3 (b) 25 : 9 (c) 9 : 25 (d) $\sqrt{3}:\sqrt{5}$
(e) 3 : 5

18 A body of mass 0.1 kg attains a velocity of 10 ms^{-1} in 0.1 s. The force acting on the body is **[RPMT]**

(a) 10 N (b) 0.01 N
(c) 0.1 N (d) 100 N

19 Which motion does not require force to maintain it? **[Harayana PMT]**

(a) Uniform circular motion
(b) Elliptical motion
(c) Uniform straight line motion
(d) Projectile motion

20 A machine gun is mounted on a 200 kg vehicle on a horizontal smooth road (friction negligible). The gun fires 10 bullets/s with a velocity of 500 ms^{-1}. If the mass of each bullet of 10 g, what is the acceleration produced in the vehicle? **[BHU]**

(a) 25 cm s^{-2} (b) 30 cm s^{-2}
(c) 50 cm s^{-2} (d) 50 cm s^{-2}

2005

21 The mass of a ship is 2×10^7 kg. On applying a force of 25×10^5 N, it is displaced through 25 m. After the displacement, the speed acquired by the ship will be **[RPMT]**

(a) 12.5 ms^{-1} (b) 5 ms^{-1}
(c) 3.7 ms^{-1} (d) 2.5 ms^{-1}

22 A ball of mass m moves with speed v and it strikes normally with a wall and reflected back normally. If its time of contact with wall is t, then find force exerted by ball on the wall. **[BCECE]**

(a) $\frac{2mv}{t}$ (b) $\frac{mv}{t}$
(c) mvt (d) $\frac{mv}{2t}$

23 A gun fires N bullets per second, each of mass m with velocity v. The force exerted by the bullets on the gun is **[J&K CET]**

(a) vNm (b) $\frac{mv}{N}$
(c) mvN^2 (d) $\frac{mv^2}{N}$

Answers

1 (a)	2 (a)	3 (a)	4 (d)	5 (c)	6 (d)	7 (b)	8 (b)	9 (b)	10 (c)
11 (d)	12 (d)	13 (c)	14 (c)	15 (b)	16 (c)	17 (e)	18 (a)	19 (c)	20 (a)
21 (d)	22 (a)	23 (a)							

Explanations

1 (a) Force exerted by concrete floor is more as compared to wooden floor due to greater change in momentum.

Since on concrete floor, glass ball will take less time to come to rest, so a glass ball is dropped on concrete floor can easily get broken compared to if it is dropped on wooden floor.

Hence, both Assertion and Reason are true and Reason is the correct explanation of Assertion.

2 (a) Force required, $F = \dfrac{d(mv)}{dt}$

$$= v\left(\frac{dm}{dt}\right)$$

As velocity v is constant, hence

$$F = Mv \text{ newton}$$

$$\left(\because \text{given, } M = \frac{dm}{dt}\right)$$

3 (a) When the balloon is descending down with an acceleration a,

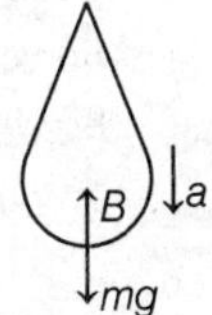

$$mg - B = ma \quad \ldots\text{(i)}$$

where, $B =$ buoyant force.

Here, we should assume that while removing some mass the volume of balloon and hence buoyant force will not change.

Let the new mass of the balloon is m', so

$$B - m'g = m'a \quad \ldots\text{(ii)}$$

On solving Eqs. (i) and (ii), we get

$$mg - m'g = ma + m'a$$

$$\Rightarrow \quad m(g - a) = m'(g + a)$$

$$m' = \frac{m(g - a)}{g + a}$$

So, mass removed, $\Delta m = m - m'$

$$= m\left[1 - \frac{(g - a)}{(g + a)}\right]$$

$$= m\left[\frac{g + a - g + a}{g + a}\right]$$

$$= \frac{2ma}{g + a}$$

4 (d) Given, $p = a + bt + ct^2$

Differentiating with respect to t (time), we get

$$\frac{dp}{dt} = 0 + b + 2ct$$

From Newton's second law of motion,

$$F \propto \frac{dp}{dt}$$

$\Rightarrow$ $F \propto t$, force is dependent linearly on time.

5 (c) As, $a = \dfrac{\Delta v}{\Delta t} = \dfrac{v}{m} \cdot \dfrac{\Delta m}{\Delta t}$

$$\left(\because a = \frac{F}{m} = \frac{1}{m}\frac{\Delta p}{\Delta t} = \frac{v}{m}\frac{\Delta m}{\Delta t}\right)$$

$$\Rightarrow \quad a = \frac{50}{2} \times 0.1 = 2.5 \text{ ms}^{-2}$$

6 (d) A frame (vehicle) which moving with constant speed, i.e. acceleration = 0 is an inertial frame of reference and Newton's laws of motion are applicable in it

Hence, option (d) is correct.

7 (b) From the first equation of motion,

$$v = u + at$$

$$\Rightarrow \quad v - u = at$$

$$\Rightarrow \quad a = \frac{v - u}{t}$$

Given, $u = 10 \text{ m/s}$, $v = -2 \text{ m/s}$ and $t = 4 \text{ s}$.

$$a = \frac{-2 - 10}{4} = -3 \text{ m/s}^2$$

So, force acting on the object

$$F = ma = 10 \times (-3) = -30 \text{ N}$$

8 (b) The accelerating force on the rocket = upward thrust $= \dfrac{\Delta m}{\Delta t} \cdot v$

Given, $\dfrac{\Delta m}{\Delta t} = 50 \times 10^{-3} \text{ kgs}^{-1}$ and

$$v = 400 \text{ ms}^{-1}$$

So, accelerating force

$$= 50 \times 10^{-3} \times 400 = 20 \text{ N}$$

9 (b) The velocity of exhaust gases with respect to the rocket

$$= 100 \text{ ms}^{-1}$$

The minimum force on the rocket to lift it

$$F_{min} = mg = 1000 \times 10$$

$$= 10000 \text{ N}$$

Hence, minimum rate of burning of fuel is given by

$$\frac{dm}{dt} = \frac{F_{min}}{v} = \frac{10000}{100}$$

$$= 100 \text{ kgs}^{-1}$$

10 (c) In a non-inertial frame, the second law of motion is written as $\mathbf{F} = m\mathbf{a} - \mathbf{F}_p$

where, $\mathbf{F}_p$ is the pseudo force while a is the acceleration of the body relative to non-inertial frame.

11 (d) By Newton's second law, we have

$$\mathbf{F} = m\mathbf{a} = m\frac{\Delta \mathbf{v}}{\Delta t} \Rightarrow \mathbf{F} = \mathbf{v}\left(-\frac{\Delta m}{\Delta t}\right)$$

Hence, we have $\dfrac{\Delta m}{\Delta t} v = m(a + g)$

$$[\because a_{net} = (a + g)]$$

Here, mass of the rocket, $m = 5000$ kg

Exhaust speed, $v = 800 \text{ ms}^{-1}$

Acceleration, $a = 20 \text{ ms}^{-2}$

Putting these values in the above equation,

$$\Rightarrow \quad \frac{\Delta m}{\Delta t} \times 800 = 5000\,(10 + 20)$$

$$\therefore \quad \frac{\Delta m}{\Delta t} = \frac{5000 \times 30}{800}$$

$$= 187.5 \text{ kgs}^{-1}$$

12 (d) We know that a force of 500 N does not produce any acceleration as it pushes the car slowly at constant speed. Out of 1000 N force, only 500 N produces acceleration, thus acceleration produced,

$$a = \frac{\text{force}}{\text{mass}} = \frac{500}{1000} = 0.5 \text{ ms}^{-2}$$

13 (c) For a body of mass m on applying a force F for a time Δt, the body suffers a velocity change Δv, then

$$F = ma = m\frac{\Delta v}{\Delta t}$$

$$\Rightarrow \quad F\Delta t = m\Delta v \quad \ldots\text{(i)}$$

So, we have

$$F = x \text{ N}, \Delta t = 2\text{s}, v_1 = 2 \text{ ms}^{-1}$$

$$\Rightarrow \quad v_2 = 3 \text{ ms}^{-1}, m = 0.5 \text{ kg}$$

Substituting these values in Eq. (i), we get

$$\Rightarrow \quad x = \frac{0.5}{2} = 0.25 \text{ N}$$

14 (c) As the ball bounces back with the same speed, so change in momentum, $\Delta p = 2\,mv$

Also, we know that force = rate of change of momentum.

So, force will act on the ball. So, there is an acceleration.

15 *(b)* The acceleration of the body perpendicular to OE is a

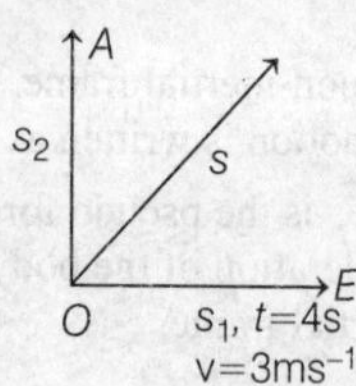

$$a = \frac{F}{m} = \frac{4}{2} = 2 \text{ ms}^{-2}$$

Displacement along OE,

$$s_1 = vt = 3 \times 4 = 12 \text{ m}$$

Displacement perpendicular to OE, i.e. along OA

$$s_2 = \frac{1}{2}at^2 = \frac{1}{2} \times 2 \times (4)^2 = 16 \text{ m}$$

The resultant displacement

$$s = \sqrt{s_1^2 + s_2^2}$$

$$= \sqrt{144 + 256} = 20 \text{ m}$$

16 *(c)* The external force on the body always produces some acceleration in the object. This implies that there is a variable speed. As speed of car (object) is uniform, so there will be no net force on the car.

17 *(e)* From Newton's second law,

$$F = \frac{dp}{dt} = \frac{mv}{t}$$

$$\Rightarrow \quad t = \frac{mv}{F} \Rightarrow t \propto m$$

($\because$ Final velocity and force are same)

Given, $m_1 = 3$ kg, $m_2 = 5$ kg

Hence, $\quad \frac{t_1}{t_2} = \frac{m_1}{m_2}$

$$\Rightarrow \quad \frac{t_1}{t_2} = \frac{3}{5}$$

18 *(a)* As, $\quad F = ma = m \times \frac{\Delta v}{\Delta t}$

Hence, by putting the values

$$= 0.1 \times \frac{10}{0.1} = 10 \text{ N}$$

19 *(c)* When body is moving uniformly along a straight line and there is no force of friction, acceleration/retardation on the body, $a = 0$

$$\therefore \quad F = ma = 0$$

i.e. no external force is required.

For accelerated motion, force is necessary. In uniform circular motion, elliptical motion and projectile motion direction of velocity changes due to which force is imposed.

20 *(a)* Momentum carried by each bullet

$$= Mv$$

$$= 0.010 \times 500 \text{ kg - ms}^{-1}$$

$$= 5 \text{ kg - ms}^{-1}$$

Now, force = change in momentum in 1 s

$$= 5 \times 10 = 50 \text{ N}$$

Hence, acceleration $= \frac{50}{200}$ ms^{-2}

$$= 25 \text{ cm s}^{-2}$$

21 *(d)* According to the Newton's second law of motion,

$$F = ma$$

or $\quad a = \frac{F}{m} = \frac{25 \times 10^5}{2 \times 10^7}$

$$= 12.5 \times 10^{-2} \text{ ms}^{-2}$$

The relation for final velocity is

$$v^2 = u^2 + 2as$$

$$\Rightarrow \quad v^2 = 0 + 2 \times (12.5 \times 10^{-2}) \times 25$$

$$\therefore \quad v = \sqrt{6.25} = 2.5 \text{ ms}^{-1}$$

22 *(a)* Initial velocity of ball = v

When it strikes the wall normally and reflected back, then final velocity = $-v$

Change in velocity = $v - (-v) = 2v$

Force exerted by the ball on the wall is given by Newton's second law, i.e.,

$$F = ma = \frac{m\Delta v}{\Delta t} = \frac{m(2v)}{t} = \frac{2mv}{t}$$

23 *(a)* As, $F = \frac{\Delta p}{\Delta t} = \frac{Nm\,(v-u)}{\Delta t}$

$= Nmv$ (as $u = 0$ and $\Delta t = 1$s)

Topic 2

Conservation of Linear Momentum and Impulse

2019

1 A gun applies a force F on a bullet which is given by $F = (100 - 0.5 \times 10^5\, t)$ N. The bullet emerges out with speed 400 m/s. Then, find out the impulse exerted till force on bullet becomes zero. **[AIIMS]**

(a) 0.2 N-s
(b) 0.3 N-s
(c) 0.1 N-s
(d) 0.4 N-s

2 **Assertion** Even though net external force on a body is zero, momentum need not to conserved.

Reason The internal interaction between particles of a body cancels out momentum of each other. **[AIIMS]**

(a) Both Assertion and Reason are true and Reason is the correct explanation of Assertion.
(b) Both Assertion and Reason are true, but Reason is not the correct explanation of Assertion.
(c) Assertion is true, but Reason is false.
(d) Both Assertion and Reason are false.

2018

3 A force of 10N acts on a body of mass 0.5 kg for 0.25s starting from rest. What is its impulse? **[JIPMER]**

(a) 0.25 N-s (b) 2.5 N-s (c) 0.5 N-s (d) 0.75 N-s

2016

4 A rigid ball of mass m strikes a rigid wall at 60° and gets reflected without loss of speed as shown in the figure. The value of impulse imparted by the wall on the ball will be **[NEET]**

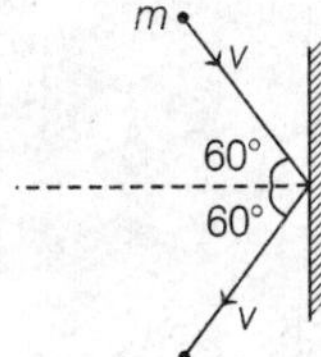

(a) mv (b) $2mv$ (c) $mv/2$ (d) $mv/3$

2014

5 The force F acting on a particle of mass m is indicated by the force-time graph shown below. The change in momentum of the particle over the time interval from zero to 8 s is **[CBSE AIPMT]**

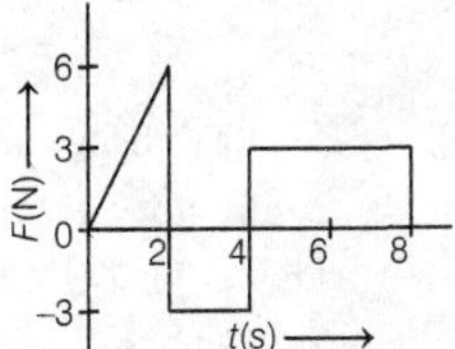

(a) 24 N-s (b) 20 N-s (c) 12 N-s (d) 6 N-s

2012

6 A stone is dropped from a height h. It hits the ground with a certain momentum p. If the same stone is dropped from a height 100% more than previous height, the momentum when it hits the ground will change by **[CBSE AIPMT]**

(a) 68% (b) 41% (c) 200% (d) 100%

7 The force-time (F-t) graph for linear motion of a body initially at rest is shown in figure. The segments shown are circular, the linear momentum gained in 4 s is **[CBSE AIPMT]**

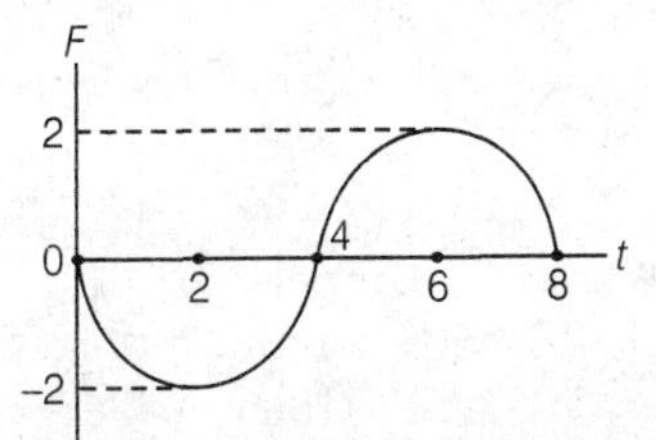

(a) 8 N-s (b) 4π N-s (c) 2π N-s (d) 8π N-s

8 A bullet of mass 10 g is fired from a gun of mass 1 kg with recoil velocity of gun 5 m/s. The muzzle velocity will be **[Manipal]**

(a) 30 km/min (b) 60 km/min
(c) 30 m/s (d) 500 m/s

2008

9. The figure shows the position-time (x-t) graph of one-dimensional motion of a body of mass 0.4 kg. The magnitude of each impulse is **[AIEEE]**

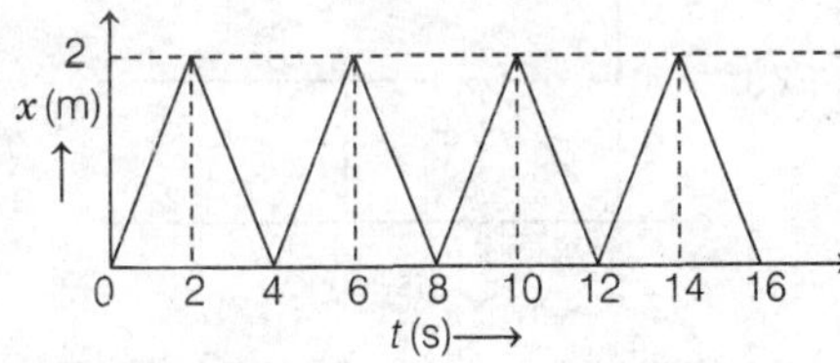

(a) 0.4 N-s (b) 0.8 N-s (c) 1.6 N-s (d) 0.2 N-s

10. A particle of mass 2 kg is initially at rest. A force acts on it whose magnitude changes with the time. The force-time graph is shown below.

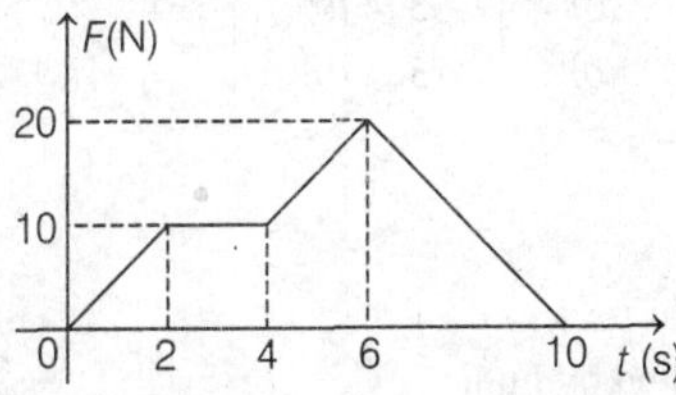

The velocity of the particle after 10 s is **[Kerala CEE]**

(a) 20 ms^{-1} (b) 10 ms^{-1}
(c) 75 ms^{-1} (d) 50 ms^{-1}
(e) 26 m/s

11 The object at rest suddenly explodes into three parts with the mass ratio 2:1:1. The parts of equal masses move at right angles to each other with equal speeds. The speed of the third part after the explosion will be **[EAMCET]**

(a) $2v$ (b) $v/\sqrt{2}$ (c) $v/2$ (d) $\sqrt{2}v$

2006

12 A 0.5 kg ball moving with a speed of 12 ms^{-1} strikes a hard wall at an angle of 30° with the wall. It is reflected with the same speed and at the same angle. If the ball is in contact with the wall for 0.25 s, the average force acting on the wall is **[BHU]**

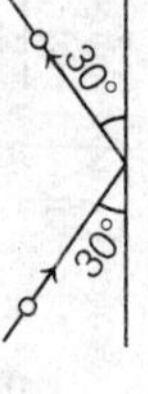

(a) 48 N (b) 24 N (c) 12 N (d) 96 N

13 Impulse is **[J&K CET]**

(a) a scalar
(b) equal to change in the momentum of a body
(c) equal to rate of change of momentum of a body
(d) a force

14 A disc of mass 100 g is kept floating horizontally in air by firing bullets, each of mass 5 g with the same velocity at the same rate of 10 bullets per second. The bullets rebound with the same speed in opposite direction. The velocity of each bullet at the time of impact is **[AMU]**

(a) 196 cm s^{-1} (b) 9.8 cm s^{-1}
(c) 98 cm s^{-1} (d) 980 cm s^{-1}

2005

15 In the figure given, the position-time graph of a particle of mass 0.1 kg is shown. The impulse at $t = 2$s is **[AIIMS]**

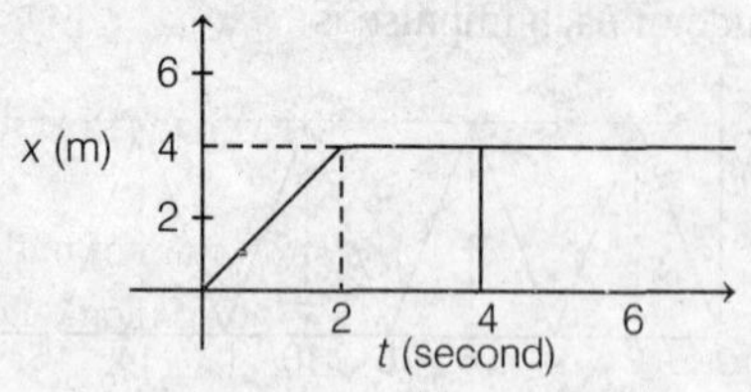

(a) 0.2 kg - ms^{-1} (b) – 0.2 kg - ms^{-1}
(c) 0.1 kg - ms^{-1} (d) – 0.4 kg - ms^{-1}

16 A bullet of mass 0.1 kg is fired with a speed of 100 ms^{-1}. The mass of gun being 50 kg. Then, the velocity of recoil becomes **[Punjab PMET]**

(a) 0.05 ms^{-1} (b) 0.5 ms^{-1}
(c) 0.1 ms^{-1} (d) 0.2 ms^{-1}

17 A force of 10 N acts on a body of mass 20 kg for 10 s. The magnitude of impulse is **[AMU]**

(a) 50 kg - ms^{-1} (b) 100 kg - ms^{-1}
(c) 300 kg - ms^{-1} (d) 1000 kg - ms^{-1}

Answers

1 (c)	2 (d)	3 (b)	4 (a)	5 (c)	6 (b)	7 (c)	8 (d)	9 (b)	10 (d)
11 (b)	12 (b)	13 (b)	14 (d)	15 (a)	16 (d)	17 (b)			

Explanations

1 *(c)* Force applied by gun,

$$F = (100 - 0.5 \times 10^5\, t) \text{ N}$$

Speed of bullet, $v = 400$ m/s,

When $F = 0$, then

$$100 - 0.5 \times 10^5\, t = 0$$

$$\Rightarrow \quad t = 2 \times 10^{-3} \text{ s}$$

Impulse, $I = \int F dt$

$$= \int_0^{2\times 10^{-3}} (100 - 0.5 \times 10^5\, t)\, dt$$

$$= \left[100t - 0.5 \times 10^5 \cdot \frac{t^2}{2}\right]_0^{2\times 10^{-3}}$$

$$= 100 \times 2 \times 10^{-3} - \frac{0.5 \times 10^5}{2} \times 4 \times 10^{-6} - 0$$

$$= 0.2 - 0.1 = 0.1 \text{ N-s}$$

2 *(d)* By Newton's second law of motion, net external force applied on a system is equal to rate of change of momentum.

i.e. $\quad \mathbf{F}_{\text{ext}} = \dfrac{d\mathbf{p}}{dt}$

If $\mathbf{F}_{\text{ext}} = 0$, then

$$\frac{d\mathbf{p}}{dt} = 0$$

$$\Rightarrow \quad p = \text{constant.}$$

i.e. $\mathbf{F}_{\text{ext}} = 0$, then momentum of the system remains conserved.

The internal interaction between particles of a body do not contribute to change in total momentum of body.

Hence both Assertion and Reason are false.

3 *(b)* Given, $F = 10$N, $v_i = 0$, $m = 0.5$ kg and $\Delta t = 0.25$ s

As impulse, $J = p_f - p_i$

Also, $\quad J = F \cdot \Delta t$

$$= 10 \times 0.25 = 2.5$$

$$= 2.5 \text{ N-s}$$

4 *(a)* As we know that, impulse is imparted due to change in perpendicular components of momentum of ball.

$$J = \Delta p = mv_f - mv_i$$

$$= mv \cos 60° - (-mv \cos 60°)$$

$$= 2mv \cos 60°$$

$$= 2mv \times \frac{1}{2} = mv$$

5 *(c)* The area under *F-t* graph gives the change in momentum.

For 0 to 2 s,

$$\Delta p_1 = \frac{1}{2} \times 2 \times 6 = 6 \text{kgms}^{-1}$$

For 2 to 4 s,

$$\Delta p_2 = 2 \times (-3)$$

$$= -6 \text{ kg - ms}^{-1}$$

For 4 to 8 s,

$$\Delta p_3 = (4) \times 3$$

$$= +12 \text{ kg - ms}^{-1}$$

So, total change in momentum for 0 to 8 s

$$\Delta p_{\text{net}} = \Delta p_1 + \Delta p_2 + \Delta p_3 =$$

$$(+6 - 6 + 12) = 12 \text{ kg-m/s} = 12 \text{ N-s}$$

6 *(b)* Velocity, $v = \sqrt{2gh}$ ...(i)

and momentum, $p = mv$ ...(ii)

From Eqs. (i) and (ii), we have

$$p \propto \sqrt{h}$$

Here, $\quad \dfrac{p_2}{p_1} = \sqrt{\dfrac{h_2}{h_1}}$

$$\Rightarrow \quad h_2 = h + h \times \frac{100}{100} = 2h$$

$$\therefore \quad \frac{p_2}{p_1} = \sqrt{\frac{2h}{h}} = \sqrt{2}$$

$$\Rightarrow \quad p_2 = 1.414\, p_1$$

$$\% \text{ change} = \frac{p_2 - p_1}{p_1} \times 100$$

$$= \left(\frac{1.414\, p_1 - p_1}{p_1}\right) \times 100$$

$$= \frac{0.414\, p_1}{p_1} \times 100 = 41\%$$

7 *(c)* Linear momentum gained from 0 to 4 s

= Area enclosed by graph from 0 to 4 s

$$= \frac{\pi r^2}{2} = \frac{\pi\,(2)^2}{2} = 2\pi \text{ N-s}$$

8 (d) Conservation of linear momentum gives $m_1v_1 + m_2v_2 = 0$

$$m_1v_1 = -m_2v_2$$

$$\Rightarrow \quad v_1 = \frac{-m_2v_2}{m_1}$$

Given, $m_1 = 10\text{ g} = \left(\frac{10}{1000}\right)\text{ kg}$,

$m_2 = 1\text{ kg}$ and $v_2 = -5\text{ m/s}$.

$\therefore$ Velocity of muzzle,

$$v_1 = \frac{+1\times5}{10/1000} = 500\text{ m/s}$$

9 (b) From the graph, it is a straight line so it represents uniform motion. Because of impulse direction of velocity changes as can be seen from the slope of the graph.

Initial velocity, $\mathbf{v}_1 = \frac{2}{2} = 1\text{ms}^{-1}$

Final velocity, $\mathbf{v}_2 = \frac{-2}{2} = -1\text{ms}^{-1}$

Hence, $\mathbf{p}_i = m\mathbf{v}_1 = 0.4$ N-s and

$\mathbf{p}_f = m\,\mathbf{v}_2 = -0.4$ N-s

Impulse

$\mathbf{J} = \mathbf{p}_f - \mathbf{p}_i = -0.4 - 0.4 = -0.8$ N-s

$\therefore \quad |\mathbf{J}| = 0.8$ N-s

10. (d) As we know, area under the F-t curve

= change in momentum

or $\frac{1}{2}\times2\times(10) + 2\times10$

$+\frac{1}{2}(10+20)\times2+\frac{1}{2}\times4\times20$

$= m(v-u)$

or $\quad 10+20+30+40 = 2(v-0)$

or $\quad 100 = 2v$

or $\quad v = 50\text{ ms}^{-1}$

11 (b) Let the speed of the third part be v_3. Applying the law of conservation of momentum, we have

$$\sqrt{p_1^2+p_2^2} = p$$

$$\Rightarrow \quad p_1^2+p_2^2 = p^2$$

$$\Rightarrow \quad (m_1v_1)^2 + (m_2v_2)^2 = (m_3v_3)^2$$

$$\Rightarrow \quad (m\times v)^2 + (m\times v)^2 = (2m\times v_3)^2$$

$$\Rightarrow \quad m^2v^2 + m^2v^2 = 4m^2v_3^2$$

$$\Rightarrow \quad 2m^2v^2 = 4m^2v_3^2,$$

$$\Rightarrow \quad v_3 = \frac{v}{\sqrt{2}}$$

12 (b) The vector **OA** represents the momentum of the object before the collision and the vector **OB** that after the collision.

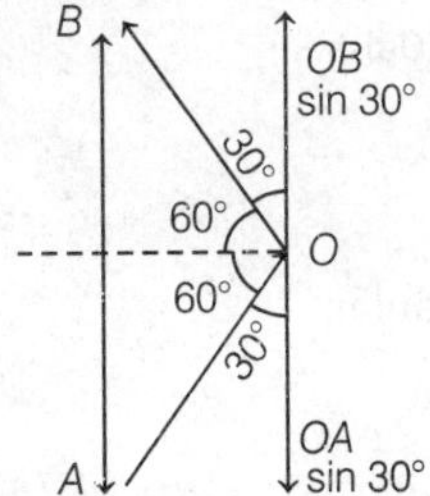

The vector **AB** represents the change in momentum of the object $\Delta\mathbf{p}$. As the magnitude of **OA** and **OB** are equal, the components of **OA** and **OB** along the wall are equal and in the same direction, while those perpendicular to the wall are equal and opposite. Thus, the change in momentum is only due to the change in direction of the perpendicular components.

Hence, $\Delta p = OB\sin30° - (-OA\sin30°)$

$= mv\sin30° - (-mv\sin30°)$

$= 2\,mv\sin30°$

This time rate of change of momentum will appear in the form of average force acting on the wall.

$\therefore \; F\times t = 2\,mv\sin30°$

or $\quad F = \frac{2mv\sin30°}{t}$

Given, $m = 0.5$ kg, $v = 12\text{ ms}^{-1}$,

$t = 0.25$ s, $\theta = 30°$

Hence, $F = \frac{2\times0.5\times12\times\sin30°}{0.25}$

$= 24\text{ N} \quad \left(\sin30° = \frac{1}{2}\right)$

13 (b) The product of impulsive force and time for which it acts is called impulse i.e. $J = F\Delta t = m\Delta v =$ change in momentum of the body.

It is a vector quantity.

14 (d) From the law of conservation of momentum,

total momentum of bullets

= momentum of disc

i.e. $\quad 2m'vn = mg$

where, m' = mass of the bullet

and $\quad m$ = mass of the disc

$\therefore \quad v = \frac{mg}{2m'n} = \frac{100\times980}{2\times5\times10}$

$= 980\text{ cm s}^{-1}$

15 (a) The impulse is given by

I = change in momentum

$= \Delta p = m\Delta v$

$= m\frac{\Delta x}{\Delta t}$

Given, $m = 0.1$ kg,

$\frac{\Delta x}{\Delta t} = \frac{4.0}{2}\text{ ms}^{-1}$

$I = 0.1\times\frac{4}{2}$

$= 0.2\text{ kg-ms}^{-1}$

16 (d) From the law of conservation of momentum, total initial momentum = final momentum

$\Rightarrow \quad m_1u_1 + m_2u_2 = m_1v_1 + m_2v_2$

$\therefore \quad 0.1\times0 + 50\times0$

$= 0.1\times100 + 50(-v_2)$

$\Rightarrow \quad 0 = 10 - 50v_2$

$\therefore \quad v_2 = \frac{10}{50} = 0.2\text{ ms}^{-1}$

17 (b) The impulse of the body is given by

$\mathbf{J} = F\times\Delta t$

$= 10\times10$

$= 100\text{ kg-ms}^{-1}$

Topic 3
Equilibrium of Forces

2019

1 A truck is stationary and has a bob suspended by a light string, in a frame attached to the truck. The truck, suddenly moves to the right with an acceleration of a. The pendulum will tilt **[NEET (Odisha)]**

(a) to the left and the angle of inclination of the pendulum with the vertical is $\sin^{-1}\left(\frac{g}{a}\right)$

(b) to the left and angle of inclination of the pendulum with the vertical is $\tan^{-1}\left(\frac{a}{g}\right)$

(c) to the left and angle of inclination of the pendulum with the vertical is $\sin^{1-}\left(\frac{a}{g}\right)$

(d) to the left and angle of inclination of the pendulum with the vertical is $\tan^{-1}\left(\frac{g}{a}\right)$

2 A particle moving with velocity **v** is acted by three forces shown by the vector triangle PQR.
The velocity of the particle will **[NEET]**

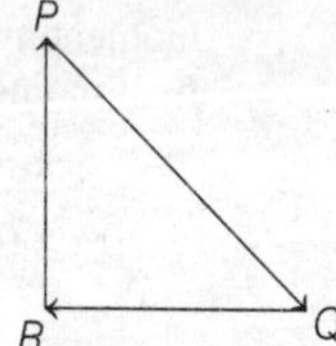

(a) decrease
(b) remain constant
(c) change according to the smallest force QR
(d) increase

2018

3 A mass M is hung with a light inextensible string as shown in the figure. Find the tension of the horizontal string.

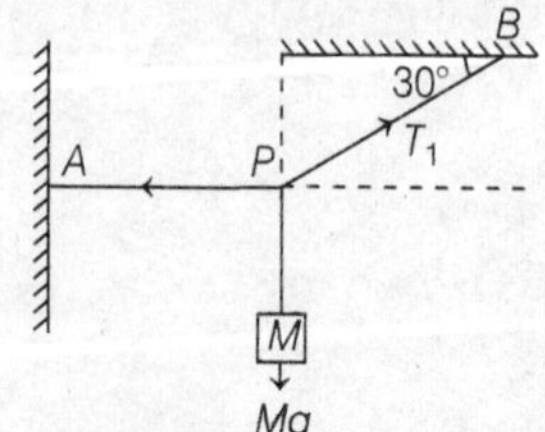

[JIPMER]

(a) $\sqrt{2}\,Mg$ (b) $\sqrt{3}\,Mg$ (c) $2\,Mg$ (d) $3\,Mg$

2012

4 In the figure given, the system is in equilibrium. What is the maximum value that w can have if the friction force on the 40 N block cannot exceed 12.0 N? **[AMU]**

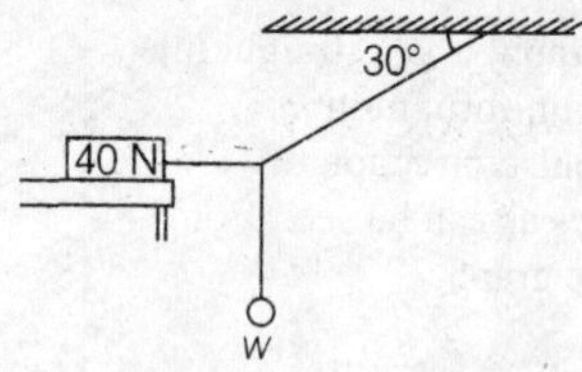

(a) 3.45 N (b) 6.92 N
(c) 10.35 N (d) 12.32 N

2011

5 Two forces in the ratio 1 : 2 act simultaneously on a particle. The resultant of these forces is three times the first force. The angle between them in **[Kerala CEE]**

(a) 0° (b) 60°
(c) 90° (d) 45°
(e) 30°

6 The resultant of two forces acting at an angle of 120° is 10 kg-wt and is perpendicular to one of the forces. That force is **[KCET]**

(a) $10\sqrt{3}$ kg-wt (b) $20\sqrt{3}$ kg-wt
(c) 10 kg-wt (d) $\frac{10}{\sqrt{3}}$ kg-wt

2008

7 Three forces acting on a body are shown in the figure. To have the resultant force only along the y-direction, the magnitude of the minimum additional force needed is **[CBSE AIPMT]**

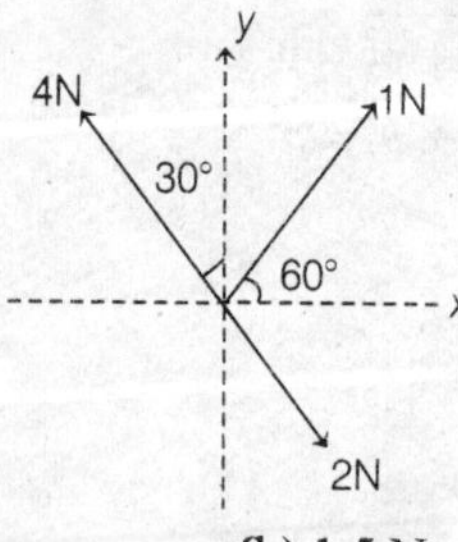

(a) 0.5 N (b) 1.5 N
(c) $\frac{\sqrt{3}}{4}$ N (d) $\sqrt{3}$ N

8 Two equals forces are acting at a point with an angle of 60° between them. If the resultant force is equal to $40\sqrt{3}$ N, the magnitude of each force is **[Kerala CEE]**

(a) 40 N (b) 20 N
(c) 80 N (d) 30 N
(e) 10 N

9 A body of mass 60 kg suspended by means of three strings, P, Q and R as shown in the figure is in equilibrium. The tension in the string P is **[Kerala CEE]**

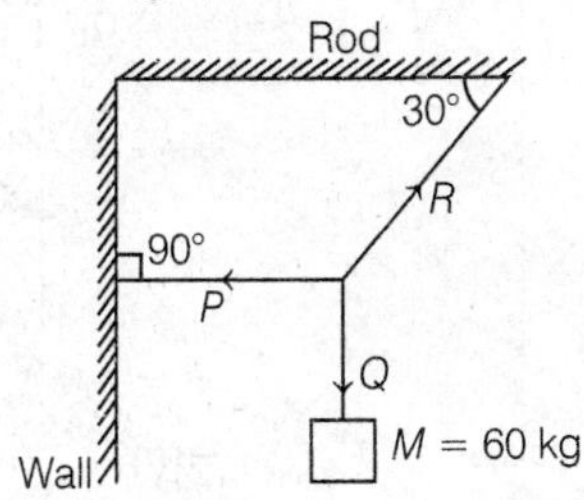

(a) 130.9 g N (b) 60 g N
(c) 50 g N (d) 103.9 g N
(e) 100 g N

10 A body is under the action of two mutually perpendicular forces of 3 N and 4 N. The resultant force acting on the body is **[J&K CET]**

(a) 7 N (b) 1 N
(c) 5 N (d) zero
(e) 10 N

11 A 100 kg gun fires a ball of 1 kg horizontally from a cliff of height 500 m. It falls on the ground at a distance of 400 m from the bottom of the cliff. The recoil velocity of the gun is (take, $g = 10\text{ms}^{-2}$) **[AMU]**

(a) 0.2 ms^{-1} (b) 0.4 ms^{-1}
(c) 0.6 ms^{-1} (d) 0.8 ms^{-1}

2006

12 An explosion breaks a rock into three parts in a horizontal plane. Two of them go off at right angles to each other. The first part of mass 1 kg moves with a speed of 12ms^{-1} and the second part of mass 2 kg moves 8ms^{-1} speed. If the third part flies off with 4ms^{-1} speed, then its mass is

(a) 3 kg (b) 5 kg
(c) 7 kg (d) 17 kg

13 If a street light of mass M is suspended from the end of a uniform rod of length L in different possible patterns as shown in figure, then **[AIIMS]**

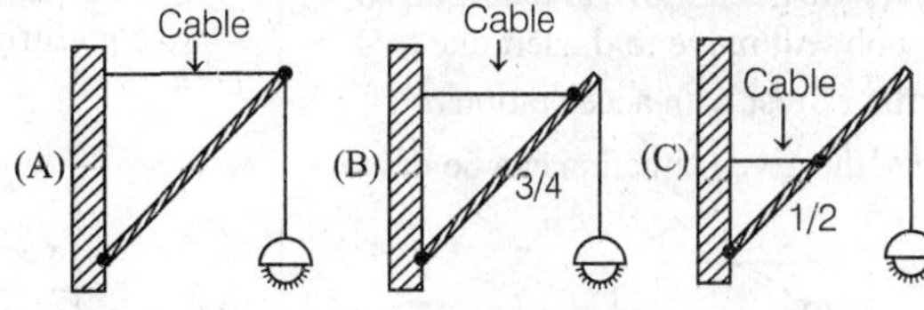

(a) pattern A is more sturdy
(b) pattern B is more sturdy
(c) pattern C is more sturdy
(d) all will have same sturdiness

14 Two particles of equal mass are connected to a rope AB of negligible mass, such that one is at end A and the other dividing the length of the rope in the ratio 1 : 2 from B. The rope is rotated about end B in a horizontal plane. Ratio of the tensions in the smaller part to the other is (ignore effect of gravity) **[J&K CET]**

(a) 4 : 3 (b) 1 : 4 (c) 1 : 2 (d) 1 : 3

15 A weight w is suspended from the mid-point of a rope, whose ends are at the same level. In order to make the rope perfectly horizontal, the force applied to each of its ends must be **[AMU]**

(a) less than w (b) equal to w
(c) equal to $2w$ (d) infinitely large

2005

16 The below figure is the part of a horizontally stretched net. Section AB is stretched with a force of 10 N. The tensions in the sections BC and BF are **[KCET]**

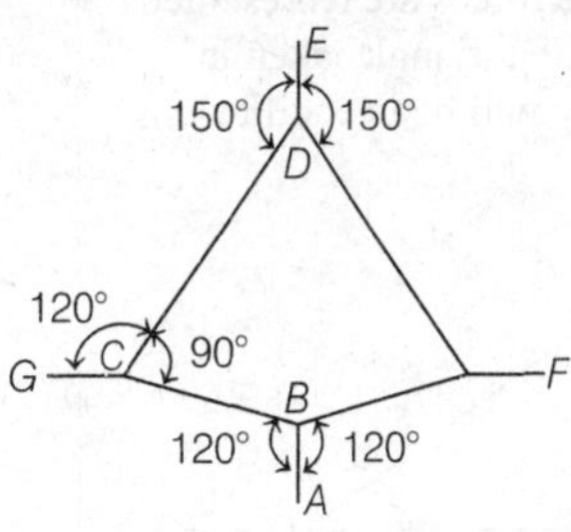

(a) 10 N, 11 N (b) 10 N, 6 N
(c) 10 N, 10 N
(d) cannot be calculated due to insufficient data

Answers

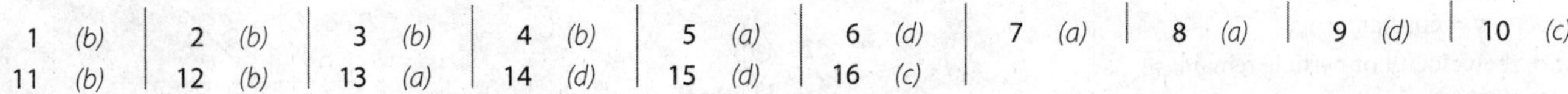

1 (b)	2 (b)	3 (b)	4 (b)	5 (a)	6 (d)	7 (a)	8 (a)	9 (d)	10 (c)
11 (b)	12 (b)	13 (a)	14 (d)	15 (d)	16 (c)				

Explanations

1 *(b)* As the truck move to the right, so the bob will move to the left due to inertia of rest with acceleration a.

Thus, the given situation can be drawn as

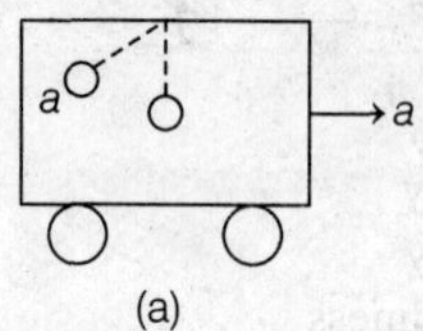

(a)

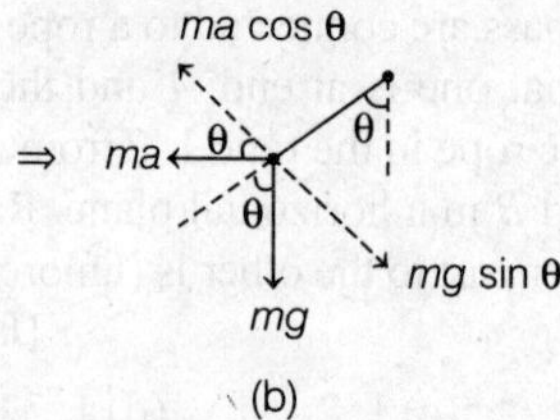

(b)

Now from equilibrium of forces in above digram (b), we get

$$ma\cos\theta = mg\sin\theta$$

$$\Rightarrow \quad \frac{\sin\theta}{\cos\theta} = \frac{ma}{mg}$$

The tangent angle is

$$\tan\theta = \frac{ma}{mg}$$

$$\Rightarrow \quad \theta = \tan^{-1}\left(\frac{a}{g}\right)$$

2 *(b)* As the three forces are represented by three sides of a triangle taken in order, then they will be in equilibrium.

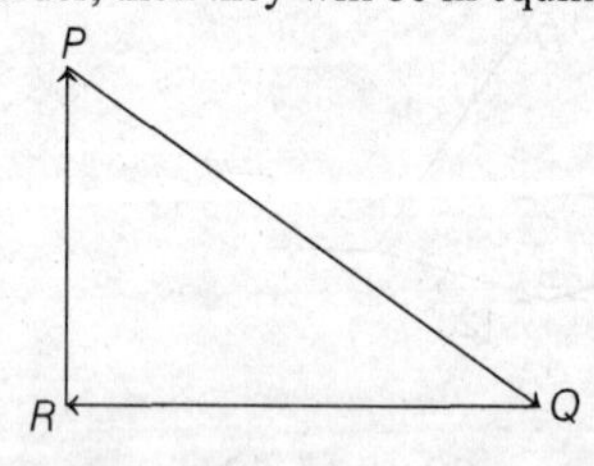

$$\Rightarrow \mathbf{F}_{\text{net}} = \mathbf{F}_{PQ} + \mathbf{F}_{QR} + \mathbf{F}_{RP} = 0$$

$$\mathbf{F}_{\text{net}} = m \times \mathbf{a} = m\frac{d\mathbf{v}}{dt} = 0$$

$$\Rightarrow \quad \frac{d\mathbf{v}}{dt} = 0$$

or $\quad \mathbf{v} = \text{constant}$

So, the velocity of particle remain constant.

3 *(b)* As there is a load at P, so tension in AP and PB will be different. Let these be T_1 and T_2 respectively. For vertical equilibrium of P,

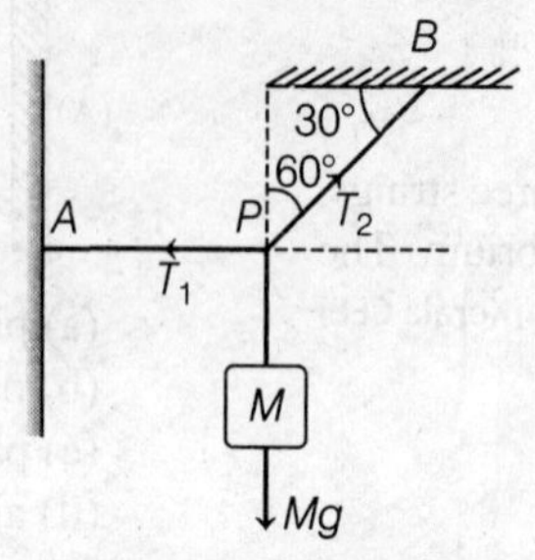

$$T_2 \cos 60° = Mg$$

i.e., $\quad T_2 = 2\,Mg \quad \ldots\text{(i)}$

and for horizontal equilibrium of P,

$$T_1 = T_2 \sin 60° = T_2\,(\sqrt{3}/2)$$

Substituting the value of T_2 from Eq. (i),

$$T_1 = (2Mg) \times (\sqrt{3}/2) = \sqrt{3}\,Mg$$

4 *(b)* For equilibrium at point p,

$$T = T' \cos 30°$$

and $T' \sin 30° = w$

$$T = \mu R = 12\text{ N}$$

$$\therefore \quad 12 = T' \cos 30°$$

$$\Rightarrow \quad T' = \frac{12 \times 2}{\sqrt{3}} = \frac{24}{\sqrt{3}}$$

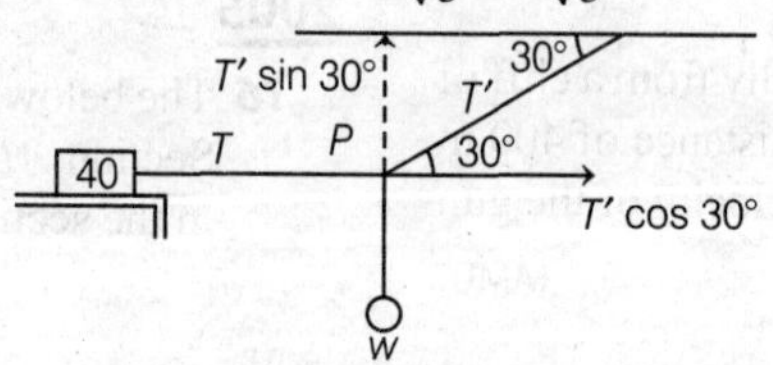

As, $T' \sin 30° = w$

$$\Rightarrow \quad w = \frac{24}{\sqrt{3}} \times \frac{1}{2} = 6.92\text{ N}$$

5 *(a)* Suppose, the forces are of magnitude F and $2F$, then the resultant of these forces is $\quad 3F = F + 2F$

As, $\quad R^2 = P^2 + Q^2 + 2PQ\cos\theta$

So, $\quad 9F^2 = F^2 + 4F^2 + 4F^2\cos\theta$

$$\Rightarrow \quad \cos\theta = 1$$

$$\Rightarrow \quad \theta = 0°$$

6 *(d)* The figure can be drawn as below

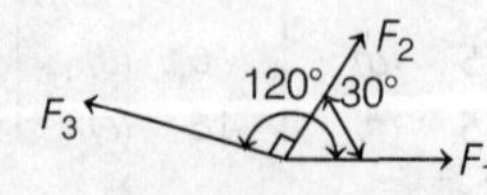

Here, $\quad \tan 30° = \frac{1}{\sqrt{3}}$

$$\Rightarrow \quad \frac{1}{\sqrt{3}} = \frac{x}{10}$$

$$\Rightarrow \quad x = \frac{10}{\sqrt{3}}\text{ kg-wt}$$

7 *(a)* Minimum additional force needed

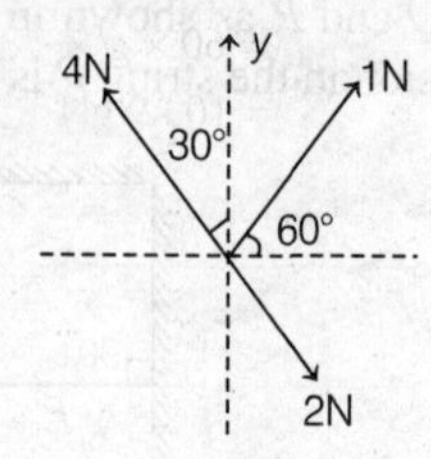

$$F = -(F_{\text{resultant}})_x$$

$$F_{\text{resultant}} = [(4-2)(\cos 30\hat{\mathbf{j}} - \sin 30\hat{\mathbf{i}}) + (\cos 60\hat{\mathbf{i}} + \sin 60\hat{\mathbf{j}})]$$

$$= \left[2\left(\frac{\sqrt{3}}{2}\hat{\mathbf{j}} - \frac{1}{2}\hat{\mathbf{i}}\right) + \left(\frac{1}{2}\hat{\mathbf{i}} + \frac{\sqrt{3}}{2}\hat{\mathbf{j}}\right)\right]$$

$$= \left[\left(\sqrt{3} + \frac{\sqrt{3}}{2}\right)\hat{\mathbf{j}} + \left(-\hat{\mathbf{i}} + \frac{\hat{\mathbf{i}}}{2}\right)\right]$$

$$= \left[-\frac{1}{2}\hat{\mathbf{i}} + \frac{3\sqrt{3}}{2}\hat{\mathbf{j}}\right] = -\frac{\hat{\mathbf{i}}}{2} + \frac{3\sqrt{3}}{2}\hat{\mathbf{j}}$$

$$\Rightarrow \quad F_x = \left(-\frac{\hat{\mathbf{i}}}{2}\right)$$

Hence, $|F| = 0.5\text{ N}$

8 *(a)* Let equal forces $F_1 = F_2 = F$ newton

Angle between the forces, $\quad \theta = 60°$

Resultant force, $\quad R = 40\sqrt{3}\text{ N}$

Now, $R = \sqrt{F_1^2 + F_2^2 + 2F_1F_2\cos\theta}$

$$\therefore 40\sqrt{3} = \sqrt{F^2 + F^2 + 2FF\cos 60°}$$

$$\therefore 40\sqrt{3} = \sqrt{2F^2 + 2F^2 \times \frac{1}{2}}$$

$$\Rightarrow 40\sqrt{3} = \sqrt{3}F \Rightarrow \left(\because \cos 60° = \frac{1}{2}\right)$$

$$\Rightarrow \quad F = 40\text{ N}$$

9 *(d)* The free body diagram of mass M is shown in figure.

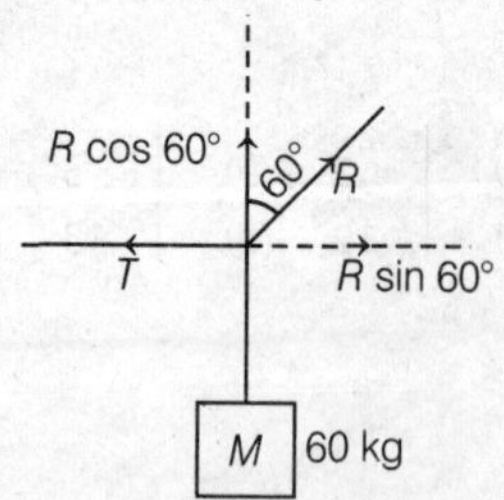

Taking component of forces

$$R\cos\theta = Mg$$

$\Rightarrow R\cos 60° = Mg$ ...(i)

and $R\sin 60° = T$ ...(ii)

By Eqs. (i) and (ii), we get

$$\Rightarrow \tan 60° = \frac{T}{Mg}$$

$$\Rightarrow T = Mg\tan 60°$$

or $T = 60\times g\times\sqrt{3}$

$= 103.9$ gN

10 *(c)* The resultant force will be

$$F_R = \sqrt{F_1^2 + F_1^2 + 2F_1^2 F_2\cos\theta}$$

$$= \sqrt{3^2 + 4^2 + 2\times 3\times 4\cos 90°}$$

$= 5$ N

11 *(b)* Given,

Mass of the gun, $M = 100$ kg

Mass of the ball, $m = 1$ kg

height of the cliff, $h = 500$ m

and $g = 10\,\text{ms}^{-2}$

Time taken by the ball to reach the ground is

$$t = \sqrt{\frac{2h}{g}}$$

$$= \sqrt{\frac{2\times 500\text{ m}}{10\text{ ms}^{-2}}}$$

$= 10$ s

Horizontal distance covered $= ut$

$\therefore\ 400 = u\times 10$

where, u is the velocity of the ball, i.e.

$u = 40\text{ ms}^{-1}$

According to law of conservation of linear momentum, we get

$$0 = Mv + mu$$

$$v = -\frac{mu}{M}$$

$$= -\frac{(1\text{ kg})(40\text{ ms}^{-1})}{100\text{ kg}}$$

$= -0.4\text{ ms}^{-1}$

Negative sign shows that the direction of recoil of the gun is opposite to that of the ball.

12 *(b)* Linear momentum is conserved for such explosion due to internas forces.

Hence, $\mathbf{p}_1 + \mathbf{p}_2 + \mathbf{p}_3 = 0$ $(\because p = mv)$

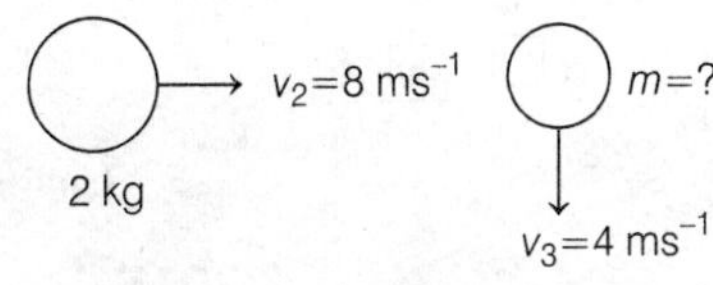

$\therefore\ 1\times 12\hat{\mathbf{i}} + 2\times 8\hat{\mathbf{j}} + \mathbf{p}_3 = 0$

$\Rightarrow\ 12\hat{\mathbf{i}} + 16\hat{\mathbf{j}} + \mathbf{p}_3 = 0$

$\Rightarrow\ \mathbf{p}_3 = -(12\hat{\mathbf{i}} + 16\hat{\mathbf{j}})$

$\therefore\ \mathbf{p}_3 = \sqrt{(12)^2 + (16)^2}$

$= \sqrt{144 + 256}$

$= 20\,\text{kg-ms}^{-1}$

Now, $\mathbf{p}_3 = m_3 v_3$

$$\Rightarrow m_3 = \frac{\mathbf{p}_3}{v_3} = \frac{20}{4} = 5\text{ kg}$$

13 *(a)* For equilibrium of street light, net torque on rod should be zero.

$$mg\times x = T\times y$$

or $T = \dfrac{mgx}{y}$

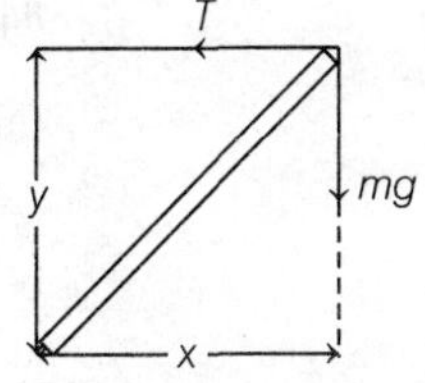

For T to be minimum, y should be maximum.

Hence, pattern A is more sturdy.

14 *(d)* Let x be the distance from A to O and L the the total length of the string. Then, tension or ratio of moments is

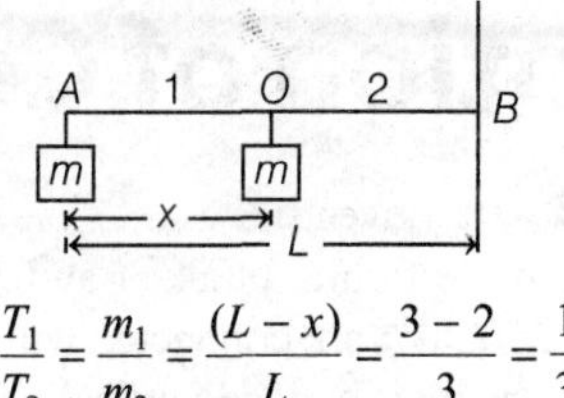

$$\frac{T_1}{T_2} = \frac{m_1}{m_2} = \frac{(L-x)}{L} = \frac{3-2}{3} = \frac{1}{3}$$

15 *(d)* For equilibrium of body,

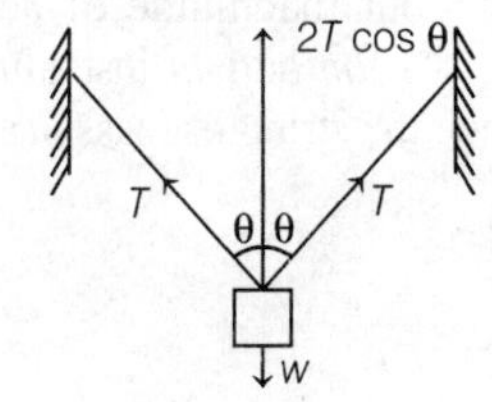

$$w = 2T\cos\theta$$

$$\Rightarrow T = \frac{w}{2\cos\theta}$$

For the string to be horizontal,

$\theta = 90°$

$$\therefore T = \frac{w}{2\cos 90°} \Rightarrow T = \infty$$

16 *(c)* As shown in figure

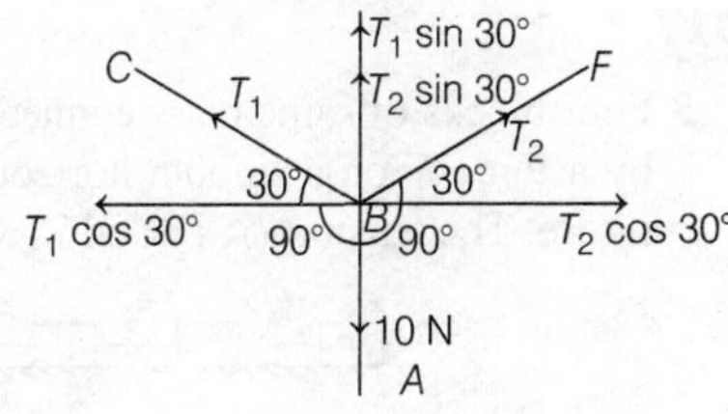

$$T_1\cos 30° = T_2\cos 30°$$

$\therefore\ T_1 = T_2 = T$ (let)

Again, $T_1\sin 30° + T_2\sin 30° = 10$

and $2T\sin 30° = 10$

$$\Rightarrow 2T\cdot\frac{1}{2} = 10$$

$\Rightarrow\ T = 10$ N

Thus, the tension in section BC and BF are 10 N and 10 N respectively.

Topic 4

Motion of Connected Bodies

2018

1 In the figure, block A and B of masses $2m$ and m are connected with a string and system is hanged vertically with the help of a spring. Spring has negligible mass. Find out magnitude of acceleration of masses $2m$ and m just after the instant when the string of mass m is cut **[AIIMS]**

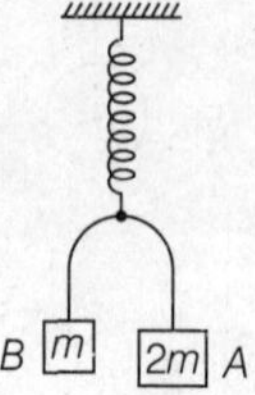

(a) g, g (b) $g, \frac{g}{2}$

(c) $\frac{g}{2}, g$ (d) $\frac{g}{2}, \frac{g}{2}$

2 In the figure, mass of a ball is $\frac{9}{5}$ times mass of the rod. Length of rod is 1 m. The level of ball is same as rod level. Find out time taken by the ball to reach at upper end of rod. **[AIIMS]**

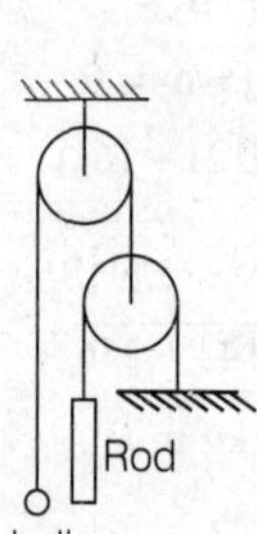

(a) 1.4 s (b) 2.45 s

(c) 3.25 s (d) 5 s

2017

3 Four blocks of same mass connected by strings are pulled by a force F on a smooth horizontal surface as shown in figure. The tension T_1, T_2 and T_3 will be **[AIIMS]**

$F \leftarrow$ m T_1 m T_2 m T_3 m

(a) $T_1 = \frac{1}{4}F, T_2 = \frac{3}{2}F, T_3 = \frac{1}{4}F$

(b) $T_1 = \frac{1}{4}F, T_2 = \frac{1}{2}F, T_3 = \frac{1}{2}F$

(c) $T_1 = \frac{3}{4}F, T_2 = \frac{1}{2}F, T_3 = \frac{1}{4}F$

(d) $T_1 = \frac{3}{4}F, T_2 = \frac{1}{2}F, T_3 = \frac{1}{2}F$

4 Two blocks A and B of masses $3m$ and m respectively are connected by a massless and inextensible string. The whole system is suspended by a massless spring as shown in figure. The magnitudes of acceleration of A and B immediately after the string is cut, are respectively **[NEET]**

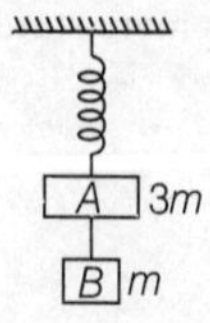

(a) $g, \frac{g}{3}$ (b) $\frac{g}{3}, g$

(c) g, g (d) $\frac{g}{3}, \frac{g}{3}$

5 Two masses 10 kg and 20 kg respectively are connected by a massless spring as shown in figure. A force of 200 N acts on the 20 kg mass. At the instant shown is figure, the 10 kg mass has acceleration of 12 m/s^2. The value of acceleration of 20 kg mass is **[JIPMER]**

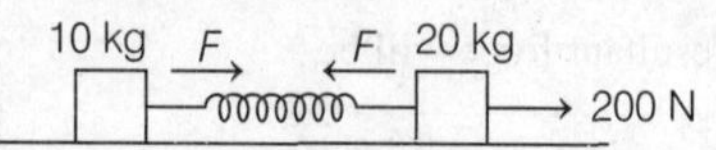

(a) 4 m/s^2 (b) 10 m/s^2 (c) 20 m/s^2 (d) 30 m/s^2

2015

6 Three blocks A, B and C of masses 4 kg, 2 kg and 1 kg respectively, are in contact on a frictionless surface, as shown in the figure. If a force of 14 N is applied on the 4 kg block, then the contact force between A and B is **[AIPMT]**

(a) 2 N (b) 6 N (c) 8 N (d) 18 N

2014

7 A system consists of three masses m_1, m_2 and m_3 connected by a string passing over a pulley P. The mass m_1 hangs freely and m_2 and m_3 are on a rough horizontal table (the coefficient of friction $= \mu$). The pulley is frictionless and of negligible mass. The downward acceleration of mass m_1 is (assume, $m_1 = m_2 = m_3 = m$) **[CBSE AIPMT]**

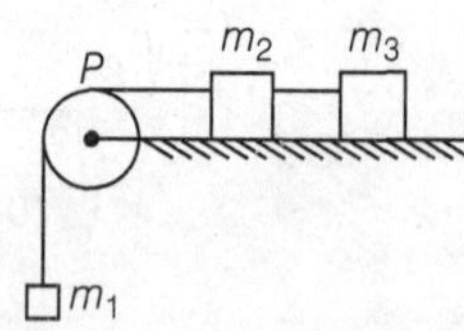

(a) $\frac{g(1-g\mu)}{9}$ (b) $\frac{2g\mu}{3}$

(c) $\frac{g(1-2\mu)}{3}$ (d) $\frac{g(1-2\mu)}{2}$

8 The tension in the string in the pulley system shown in the figure is **[JIPMER]**

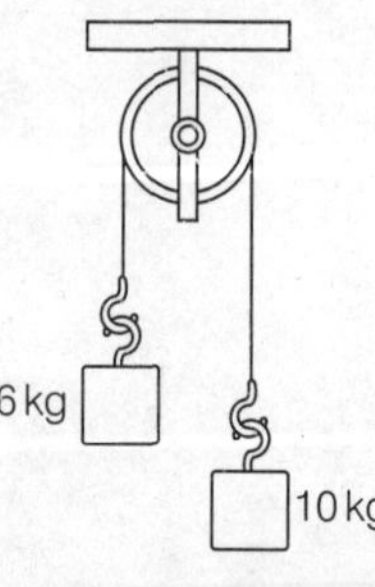

(a) 75 N (b) 80 N

(c) 7.5 N (d) 30 N

9 Three identical blocks of masses $m = 2$ kg are drawn by a force 10.2 N on a frictionless surface. What is the tension (in N) in the string between the blocks B and C ? **[UK PMT]**

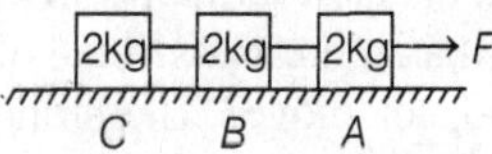

(a) 9.2 (b) 8
(c) 3.4 (d) 9.8

10 Three blocks with masses m, $2m$ and $3m$ are connected by strings as shown in the figure. After an upward force F is applied on block m, the masses move upward at constant speed v. What is the net force on the block of mass $2m$? (g is the acceleration due to gravity) **[NEET]**

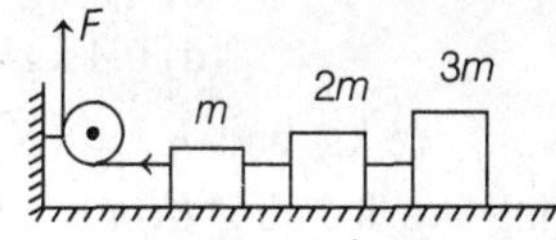

(a) Zero (b) 2 mg
(c) 3 mg (d) 6 mg

2011

11 Two bodies of masses of 4 kg and 6 kg are tied to the ends of a massless string. The string passes over a frictionless pulley. The acceleration of the system is **[Kerala CEE]**

(a) $\frac{g}{2}$ (b) $\frac{g}{3}$ (c) $\frac{g}{5}$ (d) $\frac{g}{10}$
(e) $\frac{g}{4}$

12 Block A of mass 2 kg is placed over block B of mass 8 kg. The combination is placed over a rough horizontal surface. Coefficient of friction between B and the floor is 0.5. Coefficient of friction between the blocks A and B is 0.4. A horizontal force of 10 N is applied on the block B. The force of friction between the blocks A and B is ($g = 10\,\text{ms}^{-2}$) **[KCET]**

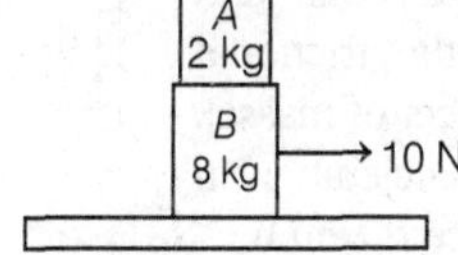

(a) 100 N (b) 40 N
(c) 50 N (d) zero

13 A man of mass 60 kg is riding in a lift. The weight of the man, when the lift is accelerating upwards and downwards at 2 ms^{-2}, are respectively (take, $g = 10\,\text{ms}^{-2}$) **[AMU]**

(a) 720 N and 480 N (b) 480 N and 720 N
(c) 600 N and 600 N (d) None of these

2008

14 Three blocks of masses m_1, m_2 and m_3 kg are placed in contact with each other on a frictionless table. A force F is applied on the heaviest mass m_1, the acceleration of m_3 will be **[BHU]**

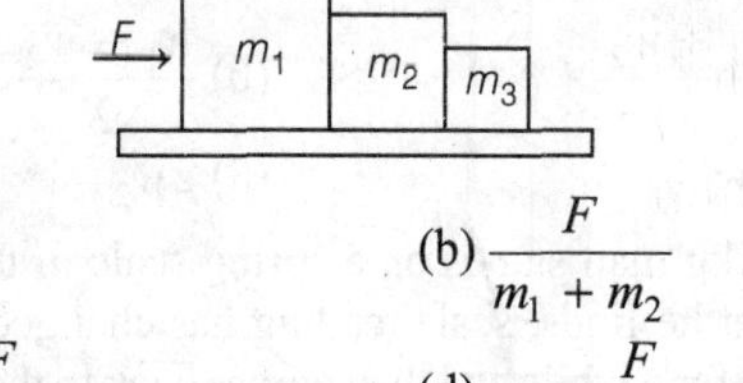

(a) $\frac{F}{m_1}$ (b) $\frac{F}{m_1 + m_2}$
(c) $\frac{F}{m_2 + m_3}$ (d) $\frac{F}{m_1 + m_2 + m_3}$

15 Two blocks of masses 7 kg and 5 kg are placed in contact with each other on a smooth surface. If a force of 6 N is applied on the heavier mass, the force on the lighter mass is **[Kerala CEE]**

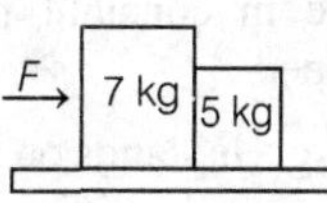

(a) 3.5 N (b) 2.5 N
(c) 7 N (d) 5 N
(e) 6 N

16 Three blocks of masses 2 kg, 3 kg and 5 kg are connected to each other with a light string and are then placed on a frictionless surface as shown in the figure. The system is pulled by a force $F = 10$ N, then tension T_1 is equal to **[Kerala CEE]**

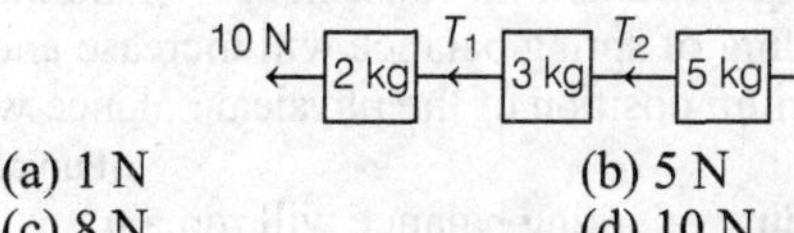

(a) 1 N (b) 5 N
(c) 8 N (d) 10 N

17 A block of mass M is pulled along a horizontal frictionless surface by a rope of mass m. If a force P is applied at the free end of the rope, then the force exerted by the rope on the block is **[RPMT]**

(a) $\frac{Pm}{M + m}$ (b) $\frac{Pm}{M - m}$
(c) P (d) $\frac{PM}{M + m}$

18 A light spring balance changes from the block of the other light spring balance and a block of mass M kg hangs from the former one. Then, the correct statement about the scale reading is **[RPMT]**

(a) Both the scales read M kg each
(b) the scale of the lower one reads M kg and of the upper one zero
(c) the readng of the two scales can be anything but the sum of the readings will be M kg
(d) Both the scales read $M/2$ kg

19 The apparent weight of a person inside a lift is w_1 when lift moves up with a certain acceleration and is w_2 when lift moves down with same acceleration.
The weight of the person when lift moves up with constant speed is **[Punjab PMET]**

(a) $\frac{w_1 + w_2}{2}$ (b) $\frac{w_1 - w_2}{2}$
(c) $2w_1$ (d) $2w_2$

20 A 60 kg man stands on a spring scale in the lift. At some instant he finds, scale reading has changed from 60 kg to 50 kg for a while and then comes back to the original make. What should we conclude? **[AFMC]**

(a) The lift was in constant motion upwards.
(b) The lift was in constant motion downwards.
(c) The lift while in constant motion upwards, is suddenly stopped.
(d) The lift while in constant motion downwards, is suddenly stopped.

21 A man weight 80 kg. He stands on a weighing scale in a lift which is moving upwards with a uniform acceleration of 5 ms^{-2}. What would be the reading on the scale? (take, $g = 10\ ms^{-2}$) **[BHU]**

(a) 800 N (b) 1200 N
(c) Zero (d) 400 N

22 A spring balance and a physical balance are kept in a lift. In these balances, equal masses are placed. If now the lift starts moving upwards with constant acceleration, then

(a) the reading of spring balance will increase and the equilibrium position of the physical balance will disturb. **[Punjab PMET]**
(b) the reading of spring balance will remain unchanged and physical balance will remain in equilibrium.
(c) the reading of spring balance will decrease and physical balance will remain in equilibrium.
(d) the reading of spring balance will increase and the physical balance will remain in equilibrium.

23 A body of mass 8 kg is suspended through two light springs X and Y connected in series as shown in figure. The readings in X and Y respectively are **[Kerala CEE]**

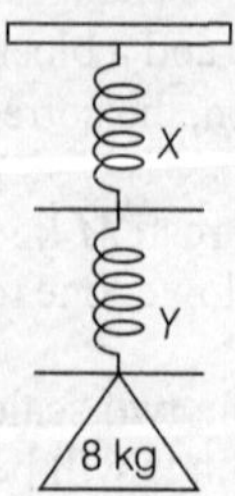

(a) 8 kg, zero (b) zero, 8 kg
(c) 6 kg, 2 kg (d) 2 kg, 6 kg
(e) 8 kg, 8 kg

2007

24 The coefficient of static friction, μ_s between a block A of mass 2 kg and the table as shown in the figure is 0.2. What would be the maximum mass value of block B so that, the two blocks do not move? The string and the pulley are assumed to be smooth and massless (Take, $g = 10\ ms^{-2}$).

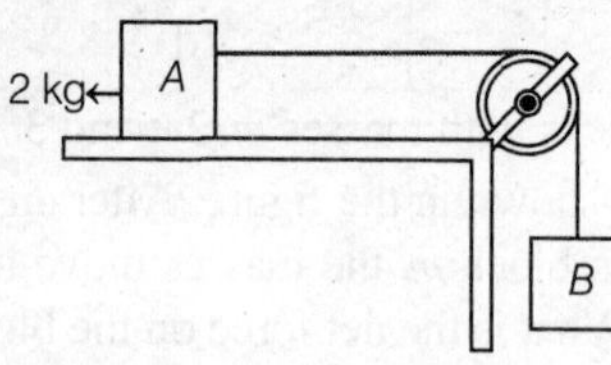

(a) 2.0 kg (b) 4.0 kg **[Manipal]**
(c) 0.2 g (d) 0.4 kg

25 Two masses $m_1 = 5$ kg and $m_2 = 4.8$ kg tied to a string are hanging over a light frictionless pulley. What is the acceleration of the masses, when system is free to move? (Take, $g = 9.8\ ms^{-2}$) **[MP PMT]**

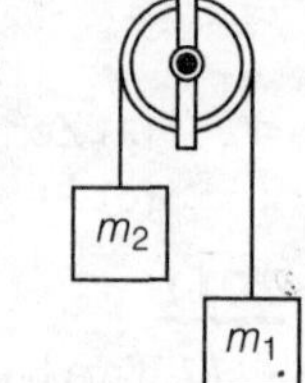

(a) 0.2 ms^{-2} (b) 9.8 ms^{-2}
(c) 5 ms^{-2} (d) 4.8 ms^{-2}

26 A coin is dropped in a lift. It takes time t_1 to reach the floor when lift is stationary. It takes time t_2 when lift is moving up with constant acceleration. Then, **[Punjab PMET]**

(a) $t_1 > t_2$ (b) $t_2 > t_1$ (c) $t_1 = t_2$ (d) $t_1 >> t_2$

27 The mass of a lift is 500 kg. When it ascends with an acceleration of 2 ms^{-2}, the tension in the cable will be (Take, $g = 10\ ms^{-2}$). **[JCECE]**

(a) 6000 N (b) 5000 N
(c) 400 N (d) 1000 N

2006

28 In the given figure the pulley is assumed massless and frictionless. If the frictional force on the object of mass m is f, then its acceleration in terms of the force F will be equal to **[JCECE]**

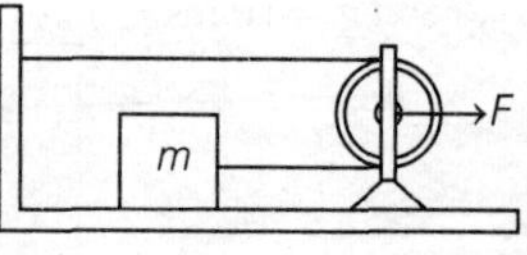

(a) $(F - f)/m$ (b) $\left(\frac{F}{2} - f\right)/m$
(c) $F/2m$ (d) None of these

2005

29 A heavy uniform chain lies on a horizontal top of table. If the coefficient of friction between the chain and the table is 0.25, then the maximum percentage of the length of the chain that can hang over one edge of the table is

(a) 20% (b) 25% **[Manipal]**
(c) 35% (d) 15%

30 Three blocks of masses m_1, m_2 and m_3 are connected by massless strings as shown on a frictionless table. They are pulled with a force of 40 N. If $m_1 = 10$ kg, $m_2 = 6$ kg and $m_3 = 4$ kg, then tension T_2 will be **[AMU]**

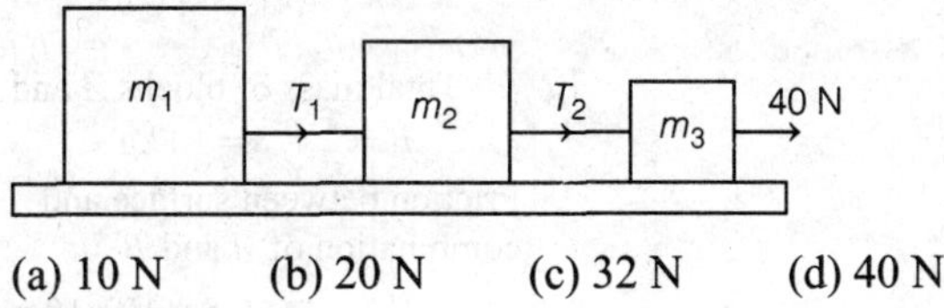

(a) 10 N (b) 20 N (c) 32 N (d) 40 N

31 A person is standing in an elevator. In which situation, he finds himself weightless? **[AIIMS]**

(a) When the elevator moves upward with constant acceleration.
(b) When the elevator moves downward with constant acceleration.
(c) When the elevator moves upward with uniform velocity.
(d) When the elevator moves downward with uniform velocity.

Answers

1 (c)	2 (a)	3 (c)	4 (b)	5 (a)	6 (b)	7 (c)	8 (a)	9 (c)	10 (a)
11 (c)	12 (d)	13 (a)	14 (d)	15 (b)	16 (c)	17 (d)	18 (a)	19 (a)	20 (c)
21 (b)	22 (d)	23 (e)	24 (d)	25 (a)	26 (a)	27 (a)	28 (c)	29 (a)	30 (c)
31 (b)									

Explanations

1 *(c)* When the system is in equilibrium, then the spring force is 3 *mg*. When the string is cut, then net force on block *A*

$= 3\,mg - 2\,mg = mg$

Hence, acceleration of block *A* at that instant

$$a = \frac{\text{force on block } A}{\text{mass of block } A} = \frac{mg}{2\,m} = \frac{g}{2}$$

When string is cut, then block *B* falls freely with an acceleration equal to *g*.

2 *(a)* Let a_1 and a_2 be accelerations of a ball (upward) and rod (downward), respectively.

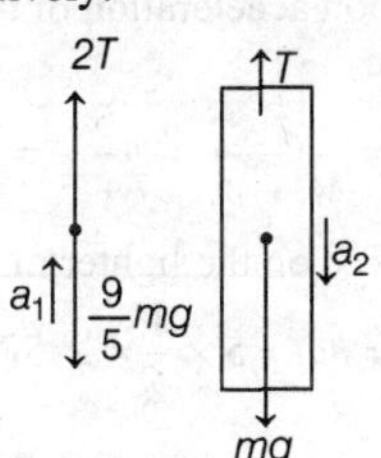

Clearly, from the diagram $2a_1 = a_2$ ...(i)

Now, for the ball

$$2T - \frac{9}{5}mg = \frac{9}{5}ma_1 \quad \text{...(ii)}$$

and for the rod, $mg - T = ma_2$ ...(iii)

On solving Eqs. (i), (ii) and (iii), we get

$$a_1 = \frac{g}{29}\ \text{m/s}^2 \uparrow \text{(upward)}$$

$$a_2 = \frac{2g}{29}\ \text{m/s}^2 \downarrow \text{(downward)}$$

So, acceleration of ball w.r.t. rod

$= a_1 + a_2 = 3g/29$

Now, displacement of ball w.r.t. rod when it reaches the upper end of rod is 1m.

Using equation of motion,

$$s = ut + \frac{1}{2}at^2$$

$$s = 0 + \frac{1}{2} \times \frac{3 \times 10}{29}t^2$$

$$t = \sqrt{58/30} = 1.4 \text{ s (approx)}$$

3 *(c)* Given situation can be represented as,

$$F \leftarrow m_1 \rightarrow T_1 \leftarrow m_2 \rightarrow T_2 \leftarrow m_3 \rightarrow T_3 \leftarrow m_4$$

$$T_1 = \frac{(m_2 + m_3 + m_4)}{m_1 + m_2 + m_3 + m_4} F$$

Given, $m_1 = m_2 = m_3 = m_4 = m$

$$\therefore \quad T_1 = \frac{3}{4}F$$

Similarly, $T_2 = \dfrac{(m_3 + m_4)F}{m_1 + m_2 + m_3 + m_4}$

$$\therefore \quad T_2 = \frac{1}{2}F$$

Also, $T_3 = \dfrac{m_4 F}{m_1 + m_2 + m_3 + m_4}$

$$\Rightarrow \quad T_3 = \frac{1}{4}F$$

4 *(b)* Initially system is in equilibrium with a total weight of $4mg$ over spring.

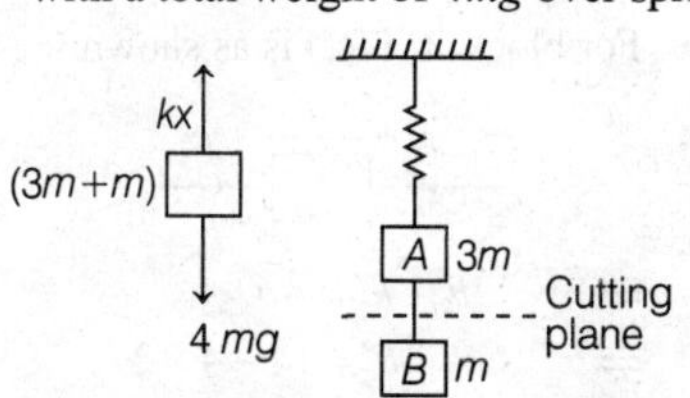

$\therefore \quad kx = 4mg$

When string is cut at the location as shown above.

Free body diagram for *m* is

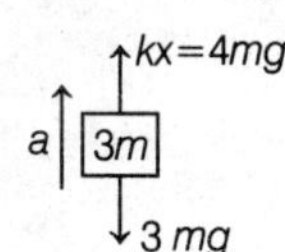

So, force on mass, $m = mg$

$\therefore$ Acceleration of mass $ma_B = g$

For mass 3*m*, free body diagram is

If a_A = acceleration of block of mass 3*m*, then

$$F_{\text{net}} = 4mg - 3mg$$

$$\Rightarrow 3m \cdot a_A = mg \text{ or } a_A = \frac{g}{3}$$

So, accelerations for blocks *A* and *B* are $a_A = \dfrac{g}{3}$ and $a_B = g$

5 *(a)* Equation of motion of mass $m_1 = 10$ kg is

$$F_1 = m_1 a_1 = 10 \times 12 = 120\,\text{N}$$

Force on 10kg mass is 120 N to the right. As action and reaction are equal and opposite, the reactions force F- on 20 kg mass $F = 120$ N to the left.

$\therefore$ Equation of motion of mass

$m_2 = 20$ kg is

$$200 - F = 20\,a_2$$

$$200 - 120 = 20a_2$$

$$20a_2 = 80$$

$$a_2 = \frac{80}{20} = 4\text{ m/s}^2$$

6 *(b)* Given, $m_A = 4$ kg

$m_B = 2$ kg

and $m_C = 1$ kg

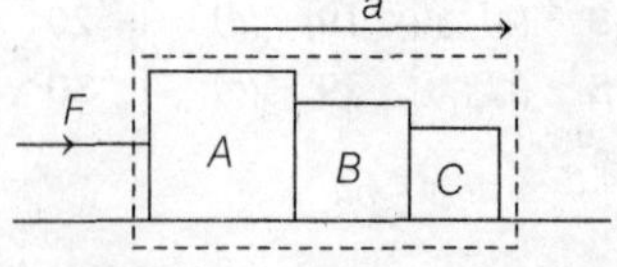

So, total mass, $M = 4 + 2 + 1 = 7$ kg

Now, $F = ma$

$\Rightarrow$ $14 = 7a$

$\Rightarrow$ $a = 2\text{ ms}^{-2}$

For block A, FBD is as shown

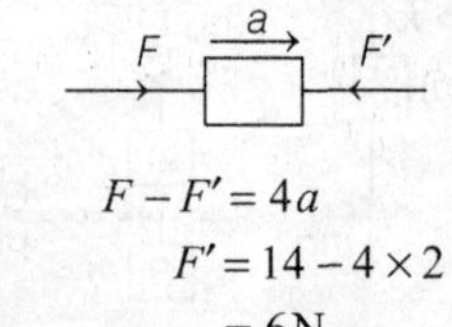

$\Rightarrow$ $F - F' = 4a$

$\Rightarrow$ $F' = 14 - 4 \times 2$

$= 6$N

7 *(c)* First of all consider the forces on the blocks

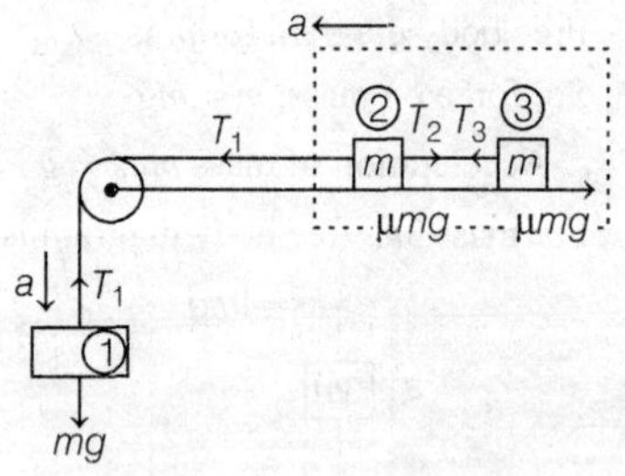

For the Ist block, $[\because m_1 = m_2 = m_3]$

$mg - T_1 = m \times a$ ...(i)

Let us consider 2nd and 3rd block as a system

So, $T_1 - 2\,\mu mg = 2m \times a$ ...(ii)

On solving Eqs. (i) and (ii), we get

$$mg\,(1 - 2\,\mu) = 3m \times a$$

$\Rightarrow$ $a = \frac{g}{3}(1 - 2\,\mu)$

8 *(a)* Equations for the given system

For 10 kg mass,

$10g - T = 10a$ ...(i)

For 6 kg mass, $T - 6g = 6\,a$ ...(ii)

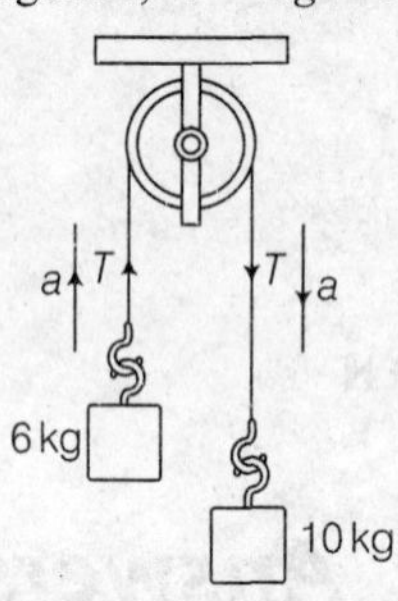

From Eqs. (i) and (ii), we get

$$T = 75\text{N}$$

9 *(c)* Given, $m_1 = m_2 = m_3 = 2$ kg,

$F = 10.2$ N in a frictionless surface as shown in free body diagram.

For body A, $F - T_1 = ma$ ...(i)

For body B, $T_1 - T = ma$ ...(ii)

For body C, $T = ma$ ...(iii)

Adding these equations, $F = 3\,ma$

$$a = \frac{10.2}{3 \times 2} = 1.7\text{ ms}^{-2}$$

From Eq. (iii), we get

$$T = 2 \times 1.7 = 3.4\text{ N}$$

Alternative method

Acceleration can be found as net acceleration of a system, i.e.

$$a = \frac{\text{Total net force}}{\text{Total mass}}$$

$$= \frac{10.2}{(2 + 2 + 2)} = \frac{10.2}{6} = 1.7\text{ m/s}^2$$

So, net tension in string between the blocks B and C is

$$T = m \times a = 2 \times 1.7 = 3.4\text{ N}$$

10 *(a)* Since, all the blocks are moving with constant velocity, then the net force on all blocks will be zero.

Since, $a = 0 \Rightarrow F = 0$

11 *(c)* From the figure,

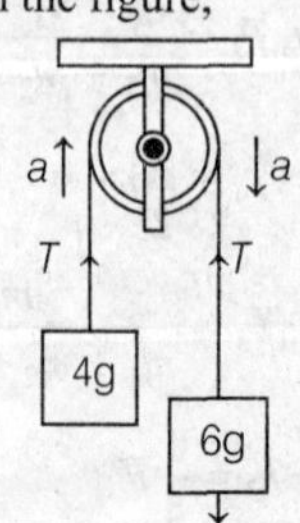

For mass 4 kg, $T - 4g = 4a$ ...(i)

For mass 6 kg, $6g - T = 6a$ ...(ii)

On adding both equations, We get

$$2g = 10\,a$$

$\Rightarrow$ $a = \frac{g}{5}$

12 *(d)* Total mass of blocks A and $B = 2 + 8 = 10$ kg

Friction between surface and combination of A and B

$$F = \mu R = 0.5 \times 10 \times 10 = 50\text{ N}$$

$(\because R = mg)$

Here applied force on box B is 10 N that is less than 50 N. So, the system will be in rest. Because of this there will be no friction between blocks A and B.

13 *(a)* When the lift is accelerating upwards with a constant acceleration a, then the apparent weight,

$$w = m\,(g + a) = 60\,(10 + 2)$$

$$= 60 \times 12 = 720\text{ N}$$

When the lift is accelerating downwards at the rate a, then apparent weight,

$$w' = m(g - a) = 60\,(10 - 2)$$

$$= 60 \times 8 = 480\text{ N}$$

14 *(d)* The acceleration of mass m_3 = common acceleration of the system

$$= \frac{\text{Force applied}}{\text{Total mass}} = \frac{F}{m_1 + m_2 + m_3}$$

15 *(b)* Since, surface is smooth, therefore both the blocks move with same acceleration (say a).

Common acceleration of two blocks system

$$a = \frac{F}{M + m} = \frac{6}{7 + 5} = \frac{1}{2}\text{ ms}^{-2}$$

$\therefore$ Force on the lighter mass,

$$F' = ma = 5 \times \frac{1}{2} = 2.5\text{ N}$$

16 *(c)* Total mass of the system,

$$M = m_1 + m_2 + m_3$$

$$= 2 + 3 + 5 = 10\text{ kg}$$

Force on the system, $F = 10$ N

$\therefore$ Acceleration, $a = \frac{F}{M} = 1\text{ ms}^{-2}$

Now, tension T_1 can be calculated as

$$T_1 = (m_2 + m_3)a$$

$$= 8 \times 1 = 8\text{ N}$$

17 *(d)* Let the acceleration of system (rope + block) is a along the direction of applied force. Then,

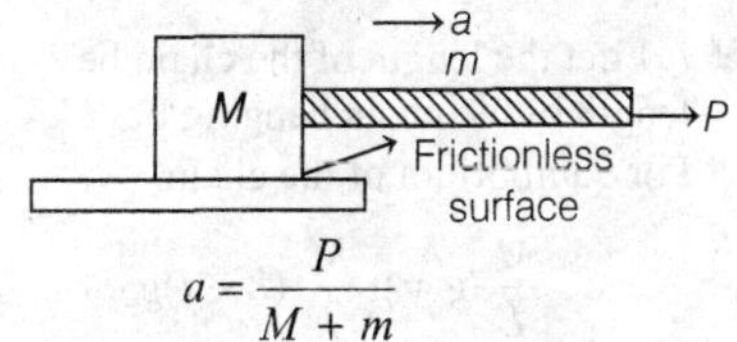

$$a = \frac{P}{M + m}$$

Draw the FBD of block and rope as shown in figure

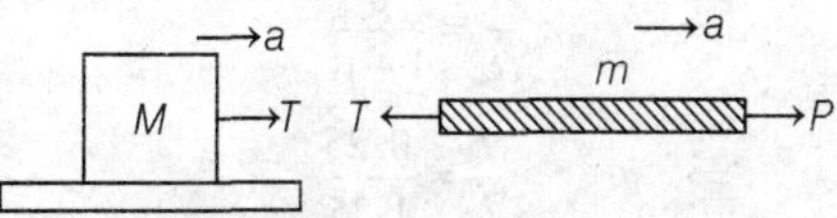

where,
T is the tension.

For block, $T = Ma$

$$\Rightarrow \quad T = \frac{MP}{M + m}$$

18 *(a)* The arrangement is shown in figure

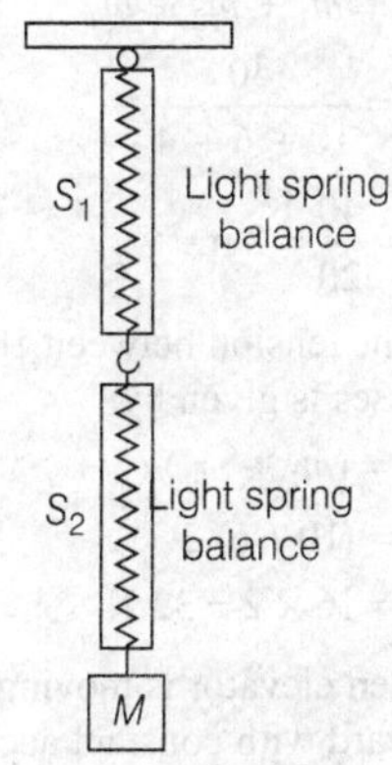

Now, draw the free body diagram of the spring balances and block.

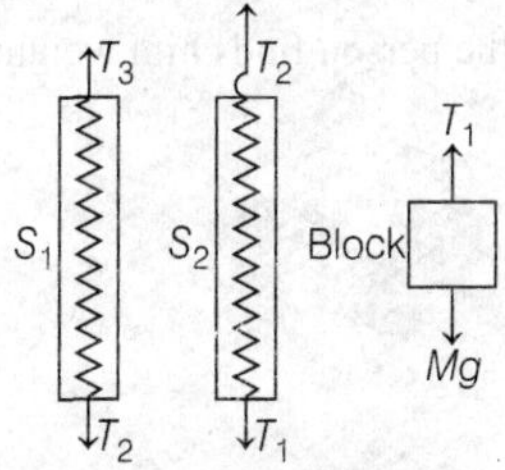

For equilibrium of block,

$$T_1 = Mg$$

where,
T_1 = Reading of spring of S_2

For equilibrium of S_2,

$$T_2 = T_1$$

where,
T_2 = Reading of spring S_1

For equilibrium of S_1,

$$T_2 = T_3$$

Hence, $T_1 = T_2 = Mg$

So, both scales will read M kg.

19 *(a)* When lift moves up with constant acceleration a, then

$$w_1 - mg = ma \quad \text{...(i)}$$

W1, a, m, mg

When lift moves down with constant acceleration a, then

$$mg - w_2 = ma \quad \text{...(ii)}$$

W2, m, a, mg

From Eqs. (i) and (ii), we get

$$w_1 + w_2 = 2mg \quad \text{...(iii)}$$

When lift moves up with constant speed, its acceleration is zero.

So, $$w - mg = 0$$

$$w = mg \quad \text{...(iv)}$$

From Eqs. (iii) and (iv), we get

$$w_1 + w_2 = 2w$$

$$\Rightarrow \quad w = \frac{w_1 + w_2}{2}$$

20 *(c)* For upward accelerations, apparent weight $= m(g + a)$

If lift suddenly stops during upward motion, then apparent weight $= m(g - a)$ because instead of acceleration, we will consider retardation.

In the problem, it is given that scale reading initially was 60 kg and due to sudden jerk reading decreases and finally comes back to the original mark, i.e. 60 kg.

So, we can conclude that lift was moving upwards with constant speed and suddenly stops.

21 *(b)* Mass of man, $M = 80$ kg

Acceleration of lift, $a = 5\ \text{ms}^{-2}$

When lift is moving upwards, the reading of weighting scale will be equal to R.

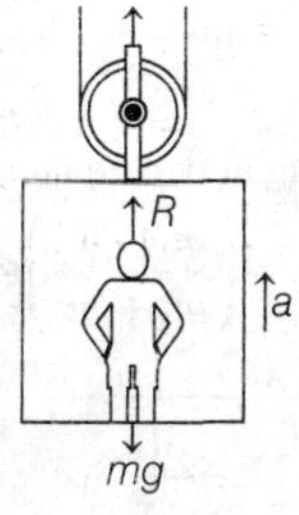

The equation of motion gives

$$R - mg = ma$$

$$\Rightarrow \quad R = mg + ma = m(g + a)$$

$$R = 80\,(10 + 5)$$

$$= 80 \times 15$$

$$= 1200\ \text{N}$$

22 *(d)* In lift, a fictitious force will act downwards. So, the reading of the spring balance will increase. In case of physical balance, the fictitious force will act on both the pans, so the equilibrium is not affected.

23 *(e)* As the springs are light in weight, therefore tension in both springs will be same. So, both springs will show same reading 8 kg.

24 *(d)* Let the mass of the block B is M.

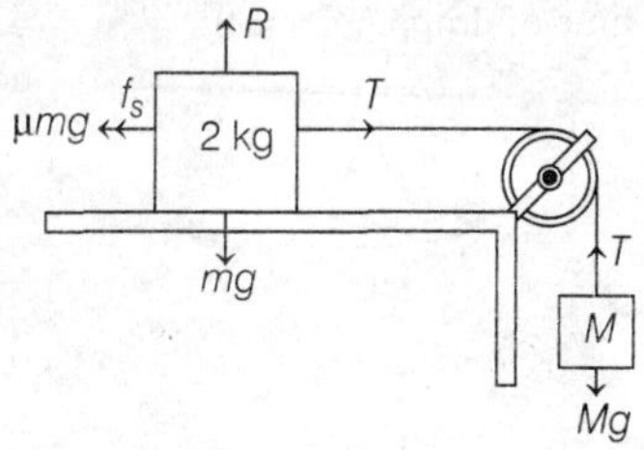

In equilibrium,

$$T - Mg = 0$$

$$\Rightarrow \quad T = Mg \quad \text{...(i)}$$

If blocks do not move, then

$$T = f_s$$

where, f_s = frictional force

$$= \mu_s R = \mu_s mg$$

$\therefore \quad T = \mu_s mg$ ...(ii)

Thus, from Eqs. (i) and (ii), we have

$Mg = \mu_s mg$

$\Rightarrow \quad M = \mu_s m$

Given, $\mu_s = 0.2$, and $m = 2$ kg

$\Rightarrow \quad M = 0.2 \times 2 = 0.4$ kg

25 *(a)* On releasing, the motion of the system will be according to figure.

$m_1g - T = m_1a$ ...(i)

and $T - m_2g = m_2a$ ...(ii)

On solving above equations, we get

$$a = \left(\frac{m_1 - m_2}{m_1 + m_2}\right)g \quad ...(iii)$$

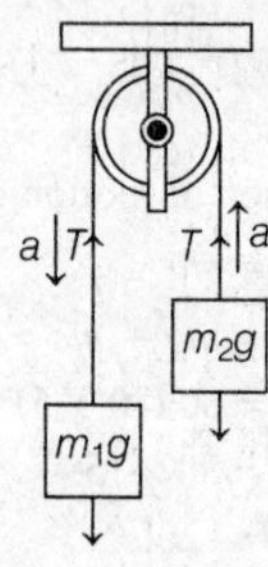

Given, $m_1 = 5$ kg, $m_2 = 4.8$ kg and $g = 9.8 \text{ ms}^{-2}$

$$\therefore \quad a = \left(\frac{5-4.8}{5+4.8}\right) \times 9.8$$

$= 0.2 \text{ ms}^{-2}$

26 *(a)* From equation of motion, we have

$$s = ut + \frac{1}{2}gt^2$$

where, u is initial velocity, t is time, g is acceleration due to gravity. At the time of dropping, $u = 0$

$$\because \quad s = \frac{1}{2}gt_1^2$$

$$\Rightarrow \quad t_1^2 = \frac{2s}{g}$$

When lift moves up,

$$g' = g + a$$

$$s = \frac{1}{2}g' t_2^2$$

$$\Rightarrow \quad t_2^2 = \frac{2s}{g+a}$$

$\Rightarrow \quad t_2^2 < t_1^2$

i.e., $\quad t_2 < t_1$

or $\quad t_1 > t_2$

27 *(a)* By equation of motion,

$T - mg = ma$

$\Rightarrow \quad T = m(g + a)$

Given, $m = 500$ kg, $g = 10 \text{ ms}^{-2}$, and $a = 2 \text{ ms}^{-2}$

$\Rightarrow \quad T = 500\,(10 + 2)$

$= 6000$ N

28 *(c)* To find the acceleration of the block, we will need the tension in the string, that can be obtained by considering the pulley as the system.

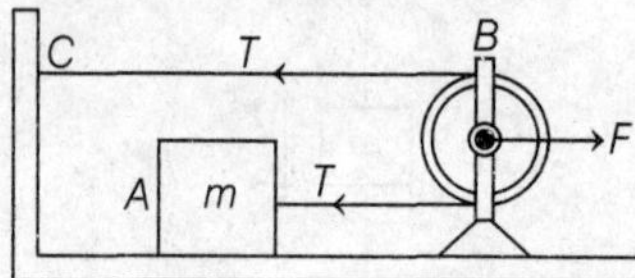

The forces acting on the pulley are

(i) F towards right

(ii) T towards left by the portion BC of the string and

(iii) T towards left by the portion BA of the string. Since, there is no vertical motion. Then, vertical force if any, add to zero.

As the pulley is massless, the equation of motion is

$$F - 2T = 0$$

$$\Rightarrow \quad T = F/2$$

The acceleration of the block is

$$a = \frac{T}{m} = \frac{F}{2m}.$$

29 *(a)* Let the length of the chain be L and length of the chain hanging be 'l',

For equilibrium of the chain,

$$\frac{M}{L}lg = \mu\frac{M}{L}(L-l)g$$

$$\Rightarrow \quad l = (L-l)\mu$$

$$\Rightarrow \quad \frac{l}{L} = \frac{\mu}{1+\mu}$$

$$\Rightarrow \quad \frac{l}{L} = \frac{0.25}{1.25}$$

$$= \left(\frac{1}{5} \times 100\right)\% = 20\%$$

30 *(c)* Since, the table is frictionless, i.e. it is smooth. Therefore, force on the blocks is given by

$$F = (m_1 + m_2 + m_3)a$$

$$\Rightarrow \quad a = \frac{F}{m_1 + m_2 + m_3}$$

$$= \frac{40}{10+6+4}$$

$$= \frac{40}{20} = 2 \text{ ms}^{-2}$$

Now, the tension between 10 kg and 6 kg masses is given by

$$T_2 = (m_1 + m_2)a$$

$= (10 + 6)\,2$

$= 16 \times 2 = 32$ N

31 *(b)* When elevator is moving downward with constant acceleration a, then net weight of the person is given by

$$w' = m(g - a) = 0 \text{ (at } a = g)$$

i.e. the person finds him weightless.

Topic 5
Friction and Its Laws

2019

1 A body of mass m is kept on a rough horizontal surface (coefficient of friction $= \mu$). Horizontal force is applied on the body, but it does not move. The resultant of normal reaction and the frictional force acting on the object is given F, where F is **[NEET (Odisha)]**

(a) $|\mathbf{F}| = mg + \mu\, mg$ (b) $|\mathbf{F}| = \mu mg$

(c) $|\mathbf{F}| \leq mg\sqrt{1+\mu^2}$ (d) $|\mathbf{F}| = mg$

2018

2 Assertion Angle of repose is equal to angle of limiting friction.

Reason When a body is just at the point of motion, the force of friction of this stage is called as limiting friction. **[AIIMS]**

(a) Both Assertion and Reason are correct and Reason is the correct explanation of Assertion.
(b) Both Assertion and Reason are correct but Reason is not the correct explanation of Assertion.
(c) Assertion is correct but Reason is incorrect.
(d) Assertion is incorrect but Reason is correct.

3 Which one of the following statements is incorrect?

(a) Frictional force opposes the relative motion. **[NEET]**
(b) Limiting value of static friction is directly proportional to normal reaction.
(c) Rolling friction is smaller than sliding friction.
(d) Coefficient of sliding friction has dimensions of length.

2017

4 A boy is pushing a ring of mass 3 kg and radius 0.6 m with a stick as shown in figure. The stick applies a force of 3N on the ring and rolls it without slipping with an acceleration of 0.4 m/s^2. Coefficient of friction between stick and ring is $F/10$, then F is given by **[AIIMS]**

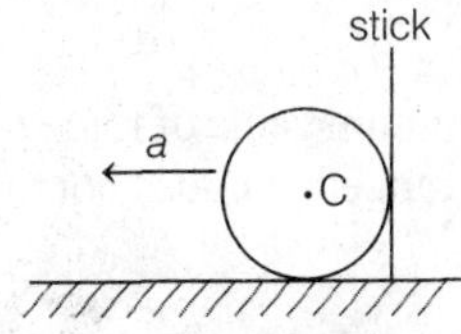

(a) 2 N (b) 4 N
(c) 6 N (d) 3 N

5 A long block A of mass M is at rest on a smooth horizontal surface. A small block B of mass $M/2$ is placed on A at one end and projected along A with some velocity v. The coefficient of friction between the block is μ. Then, the accelerations of blocks A and B before reaching a common velocity will be respectively **[JIPMER]**

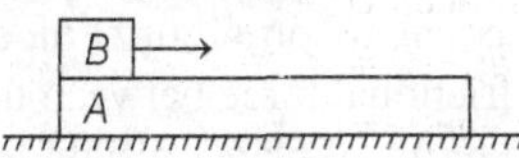

(a) $\frac{\mu g}{2}$ (towards right), $\frac{\mu g}{2}$ (towards left)
(b) μg (towards right), μg (towards left)
(c) $\frac{\mu g}{2}$ (towards right), μg (towards left)
(d) μg (towards right), $\frac{\mu g}{2}$ (towards left)

2012

6 A box of mass 2 kg is placed on the roof of a car. The box would remain stationary until the car attains a maximum acceleration. Coefficient of static friction between the box and the roof of the car is 0.2 and $g = 10$ ms^{-2}.

The maximum acceleration of the car, for the box to remain stationary, is **[WB JEE]**

(a) 8 ms^{-2} (b) 6 ms^{-2} (c) 4 ms^{-2} (d) 2 ms^{-2}

2011

7 An object is moving on a plane surface with uniform velocity 10 ms^{-1} in presence of a force 10 N. The frictional force between the object and the surface is **[DUMET]**

(a) 1 N (b) – 10 N (c) 10 N (d) 100 N

2009

8 A monkey of mass m kg slides down a light rope attached to a fixed spring balance, with an acceleration a. The reading of this balance is w kg, then (g = acceleration due to gravity) **[AIIMS]**

(a) $m = \frac{wg}{g-a}$
(b) $m = w\left(1+\frac{a}{g}\right)$
(c) the force of friction exerted by the rope on the monkey is $m(g-a)$ newton
(d) the tension in the rope is wg newton.

2008

9 A marble block of mass 2 kg lying on ice when given a velocity of 6 ms^{-1} is stopped by friction in 10 s. Then, the coefficient of friction is **[RPMT]**

(a) 0.02 (b) 0.03 (c) 0.06 (d) 0.01

10 Consider a vehicle going on a horizontal road towards East. Neglect any force by the air. The frictional force on the vehicle by the road **[DUMET]**
(a) is zero if the vehicle is moving with a uniform velocity
(b) is towards East if the vehicle is accelerating
(c) must be towards East
(d) must be towards West

11 A man slides down on a telegraphic pole with an acceleration equal to one-fourth of acceleration due to gravity. The frictional force between the man and the pole is equal to, in terms of man's weight w is **[Punjab PMET]**
(a) $\frac{w}{4}$ (b) $\frac{w}{2}$ (c) $\frac{3w}{4}$ (d) w

12 A smooth block is released at rest on a 45° incline and then slides a distance d. The time taken to slide is n times as much to slide on a rough incline, than on a smooth incline. The coefficient of friction is **[AIIMS]**
(a) $\mu_k = 1 - \frac{1}{n^2}$ (b) $\mu_k = \sqrt{1 - \frac{1}{n^2}}$
(c) $\mu_s = 1 - \frac{1}{n^2}$ (d) $\mu_s = \sqrt{1 - \frac{1}{n^2}}$

13 A block of mass 2 kg is placed on the surface of a trolley of mass 20 kg which is on a smooth surface. The coefficient of friction between the block and the surface of the trolley is 0.25. If the horizontal force of 2 N acts on the block, the acceleration of the system in ms^{-2} is (take, $g = 10\ ms^{-2}$) **[Punjab PMET]**
(a) 1.8 (b) 1.0
(c) 0.9 (d) 0.09

2007

14 If coefficient of static friction is μ_s and coefficient of kinetic friction is μ_k, which is correct? **[UP CPMT]**
(a) $\mu_s = \mu_k$ (b) $\mu_s > \mu_k$
(c) $\mu_s < \mu_k$ (d) Cannot predict

15 A force of 49 N is just able to move a block of wood weighing 10 kg on a rough horizontal surface. Its coefficient of friction is **[RPMT]**
(a) 1 (b) 0.7 (c) 0.5 (d) zero

16 With increase of temperature, the frictional force acting between two surfaces **[J&K CET]**
(a) increases (b) remains the same
(c) decreases (d) becomes zero

17 A rough vertical board has an acceleration a so that a 2 kg block pressing against it does not fall. The coefficient of friction between the block and the board should be **[Punjab PMET]**

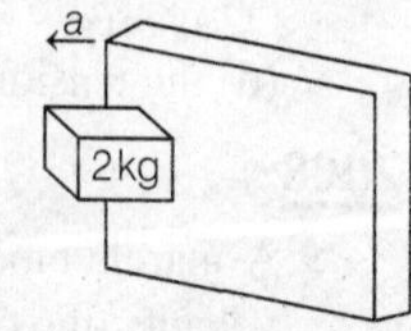

(a) $> g/a$ (b) $< g/a$ (c) $= g/a$ (d) $> a/g$

2006

18 Which of the following statements is not true? **[BHU]**
(a) The coefficient of friction between two surfaces increases as the surface in contact are made rough.
(b) The force of friction acts in the direction opposite to the applied force.
(c) Rolling friction is greater than sliding friction.
(d) The coefficient of friction between wood and wood is less than 1.

19 A block of mass 2 kg rests on a horizontal surface. If a horizontal force of 5 N is applied on the block the frictional force on it is ($\mu_k = 0.4, \mu_s = 0.5$) **[J&K CET]**
(a) 5 N (b) 10 N (c) 8 N (d) zero

20 A body of mass 2 kg is placed on a rough horizontal plane. The coefficient of friction between the body and the plane is 0.2. Then, **[AMU]**
(a) body will move in forward direction, if $F = 5$ N.
(b) body will move in backward direction with an acceleration $0.6\ ms^{-2}$, if force $F = 3$ N.
(c) body will be in rest condition, if $F = 3$ N.
(d) Both (a) and (c) are correct.

21 A block of mass 10 kg is placed on a rough horizontal surface whose coefficient of friction is 0.5. If a horizontal force of 100 N is applied on it, then acceleration of the block will be **[JCECE]**
(a) $10\ ms^{-2}$ (b) $5\ ms^{-2}$ (c) $15\ ms^{-2}$ (d) $0.5\ ms^{-2}$

2005

22 A body is moving along a rough horizontal surface with an initial velocity $6\ ms^{-1}$. If the body comes to rest after travelling a distance 9 m, then the coefficient of sliding friction will be **[Punjab PMET]**
(a) 0.4 (b) 0.2
(c) 0.6 (d) 0.8

23 A cubical block of mass m rests on a rough horizontal surface. μ is the coefficient of static friction between the block and the surface. A force mg acting on the cube at an angle θ with vertical side of the cube pulls the block. If the block is to be pulled along the surface, then the value $\cot(\theta/2)$ should be **[EAMCET]**
(a) less than μ (b) greater than μ
(c) equal to μ (d) not dependent on μ

24 What is the maximum value of force F, such that the block, shown in the arrangement does not move? **[Manipal]**

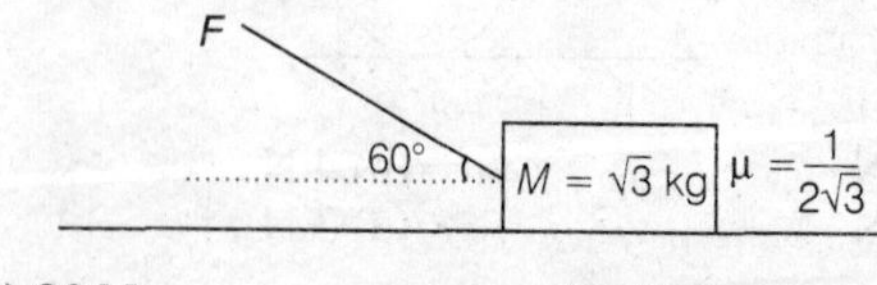

(a) 20 N (b) 10 N
(c) 12 N (d) 15 N

Answers

1 (c)	2 (a)	3 (d)	4 (a)	5 (c)	6 (d)	7 (b)	8 (c)	9 (c)	10 (b)
11 (c)	12 (a)	13 (d)	14 (b)	15 (c)	16 (b)	17 (a)	18 (c)	19 (a)	20 (d)
21 (b)	22 (b)	23 (b)	24 (a)						

Explanations

1 *(c)* The situation can be drawn as

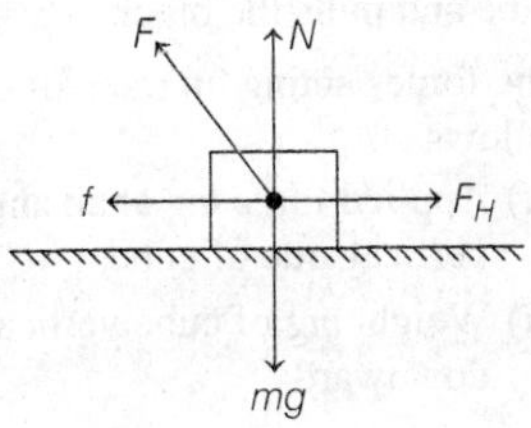

The frictional force, $f = \mu N = \mu mg$ $[\because N = mg]$

From Free body diagram (FBD), the resultant force is

$$|\mathbf{F}| = \sqrt{N^2 + f^2}$$

$$= \sqrt{(mg)^2 + (\mu mg)^2} = mg\sqrt{1+\mu^2}$$

This is the minimum force required to move the object. But as the body is not moving

$$\therefore \quad |\mathbf{F}| \le mg\sqrt{1-\mu^2}$$

2 *(a)* Angle of repose is equal to angle of limiting friction and maximum value of static friction is called the limiting friction.

Hence, option (a) is correct.

3 *(d)* The opposing force that comes into play when one body is actually sliding over the surface of the other body is called sliding friction.

The coefficient of sliding is given as

$$\mu_S = N / F_{\text{sliding}}$$

where, N is the normal reaction and F_{sliding} is the sliding force.

As, the dimensions of N and F_{sliding} are same. Thus, μ_S is a dimensionless quantity. When body is rolling, then it reduces the area of contact of surfaces, hence rolling friction is smaller than sliding friction.

Hence, statment (d) is incorrect.

4 *(a)* Here, mass of ring, $M = 3$ kg

Radius of ring, $r = 0.6$ m

Force applied, $f = 3$ N

Acceleration, $a = 0.4 \text{ m/s}^2$

Coefficient of friction between stick and ring $= F/10$

Now, according to the figure, $f' = Ma$

$$3 - f_s = Ma \text{ or } f_s = 3 - Ma$$

$$= 3 - 3 \times 0.4 = 1.8 \text{ N}$$

Now, taking torque about O, we have

$$f_s R - f_k R = I \cdot \alpha$$

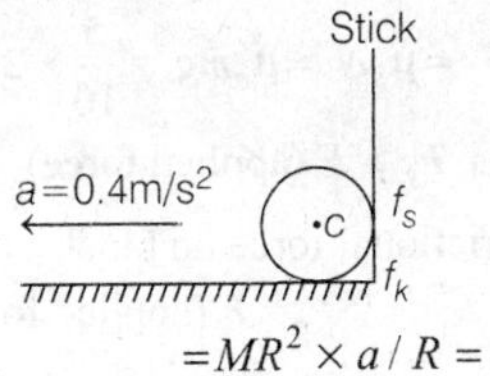

$$= MR^2 \times a / R = MRa$$

$(\because \alpha = \text{angular acceleration} = \frac{a}{R}$ and $I = MR^2)$

or $1.8 \times 0.6 - f_k \times 0.6 = 3 \times 0.6 \times 0.4$

$$f_k = 1.8 - 1.2 = 0.6 \text{ N}$$

If μ is the coefficient of kinetic friction, then

$$f_k = \mu \times 3$$

$$\Rightarrow \quad \mu = \frac{f_k}{3} = \frac{0.6}{3}$$

$$= 0.2 = \frac{2}{10} = \frac{F}{10}$$

Hence, on compairing, we get

$$F = 2 \text{ N}$$

5 *(c)* The force causing the motion of A is frictional force between A and B,

$$\mu M_B g = M_A a_A$$

So, acceleration of A,

$$a_A = \mu\left(\frac{M_B}{M_A}\right)g = \frac{\mu g}{2} \quad \text{(towards right)}$$

Block B experiences frictions force toward left,

$$M_B a_B = \mu M_B g$$

$$\Rightarrow \quad a_B = \mu g \quad \text{(towards left)}$$

6 *(d)* Given, $m = 2$ kg, $\mu = 0.2$

and $g = 10 \text{ m/s}^2$

Here, $ma = \mu mg$

$$\Rightarrow \quad a = \mu g = 0.2 \times 10 = 2 \text{ ms}^{-2}$$

7 *(b)* When an object moves in a plane surface with uniform velocity in the presence of a force, then the frictional force between the object and the surface has opposite value of the present force. So, the frictional force between the object and the surface is -10 N.

8 *(c)* The reading of the spring balance = Tension in the rope

= Force of friction between the rope and monkey

$$= mg - ma = m(g - a) \text{ N}$$

9 *(c)* Let the coefficient of friction be μ, the retardation will be μg. From equation of motion, $v = u + at$

$$\Rightarrow \quad 0 = 6 - \mu g \times 10$$

$$\Rightarrow \quad \mu = \frac{6}{100} = 0.06$$

10 *(b)* When vehicle is moving with uniform velocity, its acceleration is zero and external force applied is zero. Given force of friction is zero. When vehicle is accelerating towards East, force exerted by rear wheels on the ground make force of friction acting in the forward direction, i.e. toward East.

11 *(c)* Man is sliding down the telegraphic pole with acceleration $g/4$. So,

F
g/4
mg

$$mg - F = \frac{mg}{4}$$

$$\Rightarrow \quad F = mg - \frac{mg}{4}$$

$$\Rightarrow \quad F = \frac{3mg}{4} \Rightarrow F = \frac{3w}{4}$$

12 *(a)* When friction is absent

$$a_1 = g \sin\theta$$

$$s_1 = \frac{1}{2} a_1 t_1^2 \quad \ldots\text{(i)}$$

When friction is present, then

$$a_2 = g \sin\theta - \mu_k g \cos\theta$$

$$s_2 = \frac{1}{2} a_2 t_2^2 \quad \ldots\text{(ii)}$$

Since distance traveled is same,

From Eqs. (i) and (ii), we get

$$\frac{1}{2} a_1 t_1^2 = \frac{1}{2} a_2 t_2^2$$

$$\Rightarrow \quad a_1 t_1^2 = a_2 (nt_1)^2 \quad (\because t_2 = nt_1)$$

$\Rightarrow \quad a_1 = n^2 a_2$

$\Rightarrow \quad \dfrac{a_2}{a_1} = \dfrac{g \sin\theta - \mu_k g \cos\theta}{g \sin\theta} = \dfrac{1}{n^2}$

$\Rightarrow \quad \dfrac{g \sin 45° - \mu_k g \cos 45°}{g \sin 45°} = \dfrac{1}{n^2}$

$\Rightarrow \quad 1 - \mu_k = \dfrac{1}{n^2}$ or $\mu_k = 1 - \dfrac{1}{n^2}$

13 *(d)* The force of limiting friction between the block and trolley

$f_L = \mu R = \mu mg$
$= 0.25 \times 2 \times 10 = 5\text{ N}$

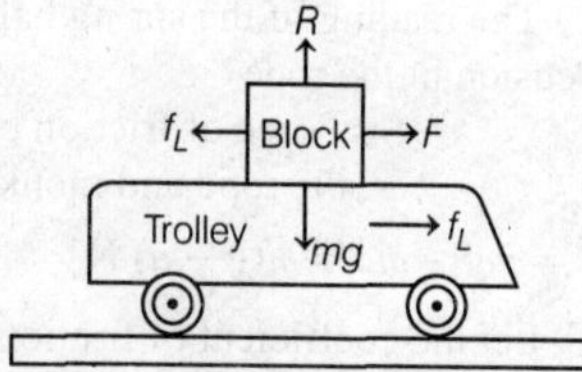

Since, $F = 2\text{N}, F < f_L$

So, both will move together with acceleration

$a_B = a_T = \dfrac{2}{20 + 2}$

$= \dfrac{1}{11} = 0.09 \text{ ms}^{-2}$

14 *(b)* Value of coefficient of static friction (μ_s) is always greater than coefficient of kinetic friction (μ_k), i.e. $\mu_s > \mu_k$.

15 *(c)* For the block to move,

$\therefore \quad F = \mu R \Rightarrow \quad \mu = \dfrac{F}{R} = \dfrac{F}{mg}$

Given, $F = 49\text{ N}, m = 10\text{ kg},$
$g = 9.8 \text{ ms}^{-2}$

$\therefore \quad \mu = \dfrac{49}{10 \times 9.8} = 0.5$

16 *(b)* Frictional force does not depend upon temperature.

17 *(a)* For the limiting condition, upward friction force between board and block will balance the weight of the block,

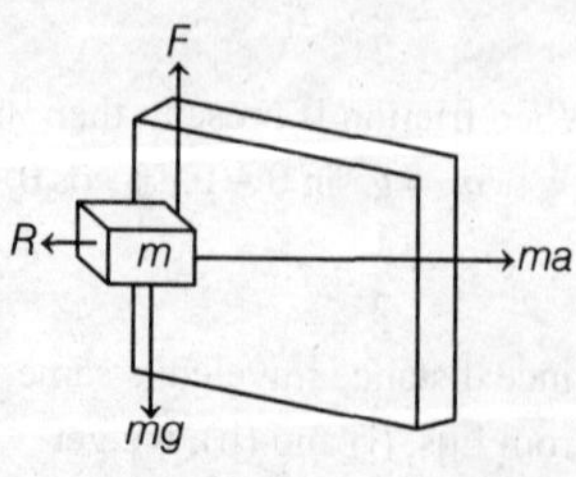

i.e. $\quad F > mg \Rightarrow \quad \mu R > mg$

$\Rightarrow \mu(ma) > mg \quad \Rightarrow \mu > \dfrac{g}{a}$

18 *(c)* Rolling friction is smaller than sliding friction.

19 *(a)* The block diagram is as shown below

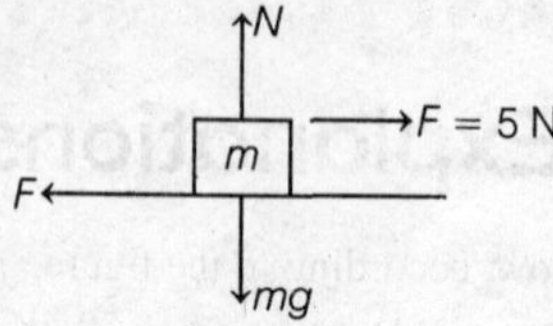

Given, $m = 2\text{kg}, \mu_s = 0.5,$

$F = 5\text{ N}, \mu_k = 0.4$ and $g = 10 \text{ ms}^{-2}$

Static friction is given as

$F_s = \mu_s N = \mu_s mg = \dfrac{5}{10} \times 2 \times 10 = 10\text{ N}$

As, $F_s > F$ (applied force).

Frictional force on block

$= F$ (applied force).

$F = 5\text{ N}$

20 *(d)* For moving the body, applied force should be greater than or equal to limiting friction, (i.e. μN). The limiting friction is

$f_2 = \mu N = \mu mg$
$= 0.2 \times 2 \times 9.8 = 3.92\text{ N}$

(a) Since, applied force $F = 5$ N, so body starts to move in forward direction.
(b) Here, applied force is lesser than limiting friction. So, body does not move.
(c) Body will not move as $F < F_s$. Hence, option (d) is correct.

21 *(b)* Force that produces acceleration is given by

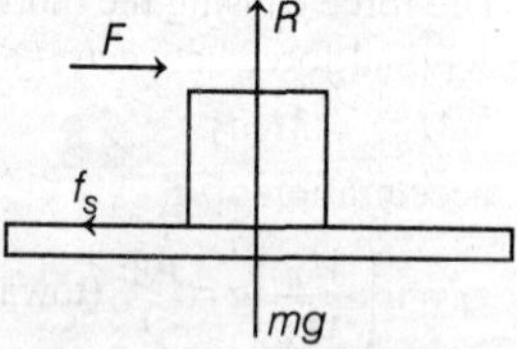

The net force in the direction of F is

$F' = F - f_s$

Given, $F = 100\text{ N}, m = 10\text{kg}$ and $\mu = 0.5$

$f_s = \mu R = 0.5 \times 10 \times 10 = 50\text{N}$

$F' = 100 - 50 = 50\text{ N}$

Also, acceleration,

$a = \dfrac{F'}{m} = \dfrac{50}{10} = 5 \text{ ms}^{-2}$

22 *(b)* Given, $u = 6 \text{ ms}^{-1}, s = 9\text{ m}, v = 0$

By third equation of motion,

$v^2 = u^2 - 2as$

$\Rightarrow (6)^2 - 2 \times a \times 9 = 0$

$18a = 36$

$\Rightarrow \quad a = 2 \text{ ms}^{-2}$

Coefficient of sliding friction is given by

$\mu = a/g = \dfrac{2}{10} = 0.2$

23 *(b)* A force mg acts on a cube of mass m at angle θ with the vertical side of cube and pulls the block.

The forces acting on the block are as follows :

(i) Applied force mg at an angle θ with vertical side of cube.
(ii) Weight mg of cube vertically downward.

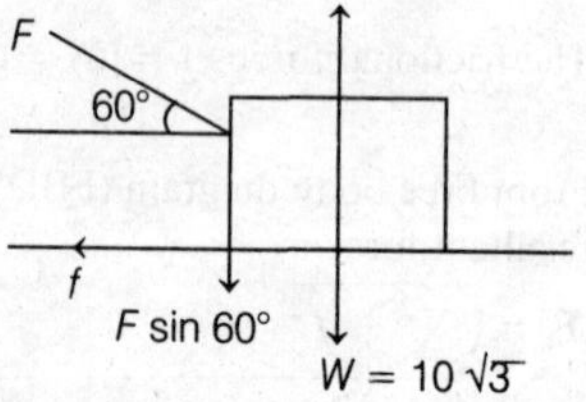

(iii) Reaction of surface vertically upward.
(iv) Friction force f.

Resolving the components of mg along horizontal and vertical, i.e. $mg \sin\theta$ and $mg \cos\theta$.

Component $mg \sin\theta$ moves the block in forward direction. From this, we have

have $\quad mg \sin\theta > f \quad$ ...(i)

Also, $\quad mg \cos\theta + R = mg$

or $\quad R = mg(1 - \cos\theta)$

and $\quad f = \mu R = \mu mg(1 - \cos\theta) \quad$ ...(ii)

From Eqs. (i) and (ii), we have

$mg \sin\theta > \mu mg(1 - \cos\theta)$

$\sin\theta > \mu(1 - \cos\theta)$

$\Rightarrow 2 \sin\theta/2 \cos\theta/2 > \mu 2 \sin^2\theta/2$

$\Rightarrow \quad \dfrac{\cos\theta/2}{\sin\theta/2} > \mu$

$\Rightarrow \quad \cot\theta/2 > \mu$

24 *(a)* As friction, $f = \mu R$

From the diagram given below

$F \cos 60° = \mu(w + F \sin 60°) \quad$ ...(i)

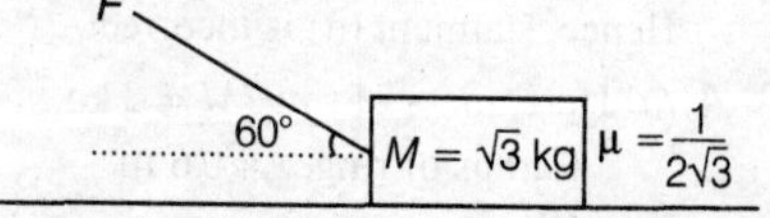

Substituting $\mu = \dfrac{1}{2\sqrt{3}}$ and $w = 10\sqrt{3}$ in Eq. (i), we get $F = 20$ N.

Topic 6

Motion on Rough Surfaces (Plane & Inclined)

2018

1 A wooden wedge of mass M and inclination angle (α) rest on a smooth floor. A block of mass m is kept on wedge. A force F is applied on the wedge as shown in the figure such that block remains stationary with respect to wedge. So, magnitude of force F is **[AIIMS]**

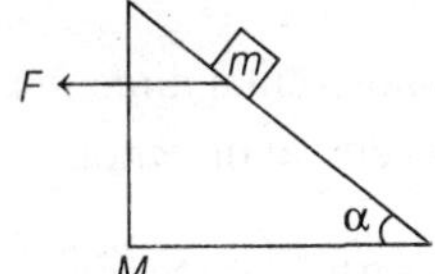

(a) $(M+m)g\tan\alpha$ (b) $g\tan\alpha$
(c) $mg\cos\alpha$ (d) $(M+m)g\operatorname{cosec}\alpha$

2 A piece of ice slides down a rough inclined plane at 45° inclination in twice the time that it takes to slide down an identical but frictionless inclined plane. What is the coefficient of friction between ice and incline? **[AIIMS]**

(a) $\frac{3}{7\cot\theta}$ (b) $\frac{4}{7\cot\theta}$ (c) $\frac{3}{4\cot\theta}$ (d) $\frac{7}{9\cot\theta}$

3 A body of mass 5 kg is suspended by a spring balance on an inclined plane as shown in figure.

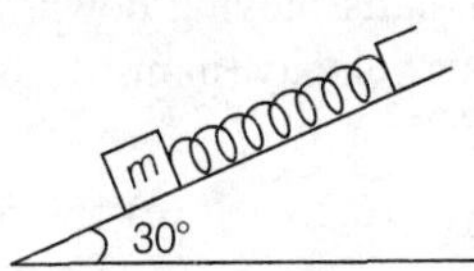

So, force applied on spring balance is **[AIIMS]**

(a) 50 N (b) 25 N (c) 500 N (d) 10 N

4 A block of mass m is placed on a smooth inclined wedge ABC of inclination θ as shown in the figure. The wedge is given an acceleration a towards the right. The relation between a and θ for the block to remain stationary on the wedge is **[NEET]**

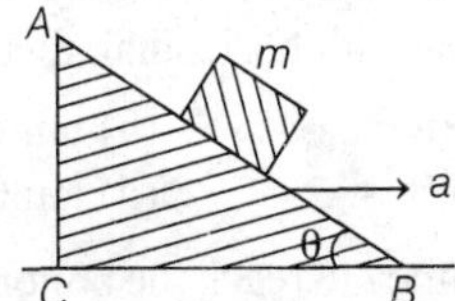

(a) $a=g\cos\theta$ (b) $a=\frac{g}{\sin\theta}$
(c) $a=\frac{g}{\operatorname{cosec}\theta}$ (d) $a=g\tan\theta$

2017

5 A box of mass 8 kg is placed on a rough inclined plane of inclination 30°. Its downward motion can be prevented by applying a horizontal force F, then value of F for which friction between the block and the incline surface is minimum, is **[JIPMER]**

(a) $\frac{80}{\sqrt{3}}$ (b) $40\sqrt{3}$ (c) $\frac{40}{\sqrt{3}}$ (d) $80\sqrt{3}$

6 A body of mass 5×10^{-3} kg is launched upon a rough inclined plane making an angle of 30° with the horizontal. Obtain the coefficient of friction between the body and the plane if the time of ascent is half of the time of descent. **[AIIMS]**

(a) 0.346 (b) 0.921 (c) 1.926 (d) 2.912

7 The upper half of an inclined plane of inclination θ is perfectly smooth while the lower half rough. A block starting from rest at the top of the plane will again come to rest at the bottom if the coefficient of friction between the block and the lower half of the plane is given by **[JIPMER]**

(a) $\mu=2\tan\theta$ (b) $\mu=\tan\theta$
(c) $\mu=2/(\tan\theta)$ (d) $\mu=1/\tan\theta$

2014

8 A wooden block of mass 8 kg slides down an inclined plane of inclination 30° to the horizontal with constant acceleration 0.4 m/s^2. The force of friction between the block and the inclined plane is (Take, $g=10\,\text{m/s}^2$) **[MHT CET]**

(a) 12.2 N (b) 24.4 N
(c) 36.8 N (d) 48.8 N

9 To determine the coefficient of friction between a rough surface and a block, the surface is kept inclined at 45° and the block is released from rest. The block takes a time t in moving a distance d. The rough surface is then replaced by a smooth surface and the same experiment is repeated. The block now takes a time $t/2$ in moving down the same distance d. The coefficient of friction is **[WB JEE]**

(a) 3/4 (b) 5/4 (c) 1/2 (d) $1/\sqrt{2}$

10 A body of mass m is placed on a rough surface with coefficient of friction μ, inclined at θ. If the mass is in equilibrium, then **[KCET]**

(a) $\theta=\tan^{-1}\mu$ (b) $\theta=\tan^{-1}\left(\frac{1}{\mu}\right)$
(c) $\theta=\tan^{-1}\frac{m}{\mu}$ (d) $\theta=\tan^{-1}\frac{\mu}{m}$

2013

11 A smooth inclined plane is inclined at an angle θ with the horizontal. A body starts from rest and slides down the inclined surface, then the time taken by the body to reach the bottom is **[CBSE AIPMT]**

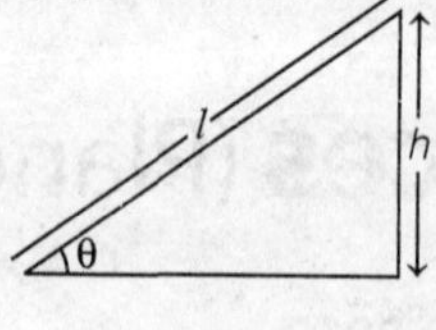

(a) $\sqrt{\frac{2h}{g}}$ (b) $\sqrt{\frac{2l}{g}}$

(c) $\frac{1}{\sin\theta}\sqrt{\frac{2h}{g}}$ (d) $\sin\theta\sqrt{\frac{2h}{g}}$

2012

12 A body of mass 100 g is sliding from an inclined plane of inclination 30°. What is the frictional force, if $\mu = 0.7$? **[CBSE AIPMT]**

(a) $0.7\sqrt{\frac{2}{3}}$ N (b) $\frac{0.7\sqrt{2}}{3}$ N

(c) $0.7\sqrt{3}$ N (d) $\frac{0.7\sqrt{3}}{2}$ N

13 Three blocks of masses $m_1 = 2.0\,\text{kg}$, $m_2 = 4.0\,\text{kg}$ and $m_3 = 6.0$ kg are connected by strings on a frictionless inclined plane of 60°, as shown in the figure. A force $F = 120$ N is applied upward along the incline to the uppermost block, causing an upward movement of the blocks. The connecting cords are light. The values of tensions T_1 and T_2 in the cords are **[AMU]**

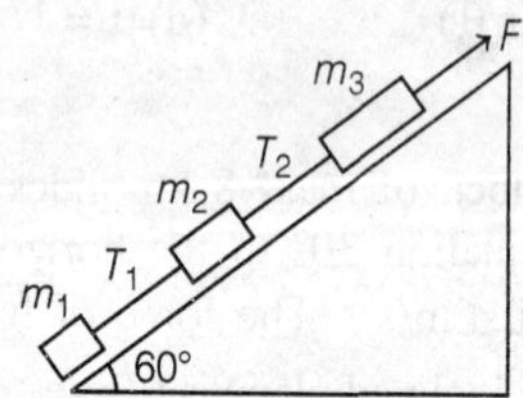

(a) $T_1 = 20\,\text{N}, T_2 = 60\,\text{N}$ (b) $T_1 = 60\,\text{N}, T_2 = 60\,\text{N}$

(c) $T_1 = 30\,\text{N}, T_2 = 50\,\text{N}$ (d) $T_1 = 20\,\text{N}, T_2 = 100\,\text{N}$

2011

14 A cubical block rests on an inclined plane of coefficient of friction $\mu = 1/\sqrt{3}$. What should be the angle of inclination so that the block just slides down the inclined plane? **[J&K CET]**

(a) 30° (b) 60°

(c) 45° (d) 90°

2008

15 A body of mass M starts sliding down on the inclined plane, where the critical angle is $\angle ACB = 30°$ as shown in figure. The kinetic friction will be **[DUMET]**

(a) $Mg/\sqrt{3}$ (b) $\sqrt{3}\,Mg$

(c) $\sqrt{3}$ (d) None of these

16 A body of mass 10 kg is lying on a rough plane inclined at an angle of 30° to the horizontal and the coefficient of friction is 0.5. The minimum force required to pull the body up the plane is **[EAMCET]**

(a) 914 N (b) 91.4 N

(c) 9.14 N (d) 0.914 N

17 Two fixed frictionless inclined plane making an angle 30° and 60° with the vertical are shown in the figure. Two blocks A and B are placed on the two planes. What is the relative vertical acceleration of A with respect to B? **[AIEEE]**

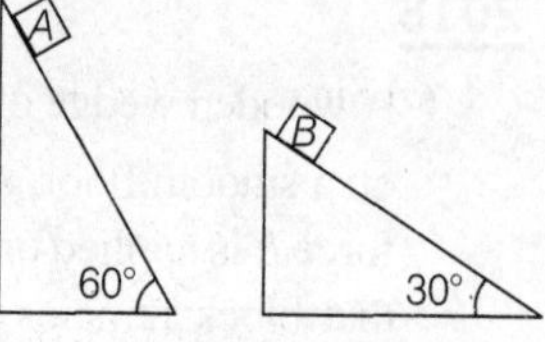

(a) 4.9 ms^{-2} in horizontal direction

(b) 9.8 ms^{-2} in vertical direction

(c) zero

(d) 4.9 ms^{-2} in vertical direction

2007

18 An object is kept on a smooth inclined plane of length l and of height 1 m. The horizontal acceleration to be imparted to the inclined plane so that the object is stationary relative to incline is **[RPMT]**

(a) $g\sqrt{l^2 - 1}$ (b) $g(l^2 - 1)$ (c) $\frac{g}{\sqrt{l^2 - 1}}$ (d) $\frac{g}{l^2 - 1}$

2006

19 A block of wood of 1 kg resting on an inclined plane of angle 30°, just starts moving down. If the coefficient of friction is 0.2, its velocity (in ms^{-1}) after 5 s is (Take, $g = 10\,\text{ms}^{-2}$) **[EAMCET]**

(a) 12.75 (b) 16.35 (c) 18.25 (d) 20

2005

20 If the coefficient of friction of a plane inclined at 45° is 0.5. Then, acceleration of a body sliding freely on it will be **[RPMT]**

(a) $\frac{9.8}{2\sqrt{2}}\,\text{ms}^{-2}$ (b) $\frac{9.8}{\sqrt{2}}\,\text{ms}^{-2}$ (c) 9.8 ms^{-2} (d) 4.8 ms^{-2}

21 The force required to just move a body up an inclined plane is double the force required to just prevent it from sliding down. If θ is the angle of friction and ϕ is the angle which the plane makes with horizontal, then **[Haryana PMT]**

(a) $\tan\phi = 2\tan\theta$ (b) $\tan\phi = 3\tan\theta$

(c) $\tan\phi = \tan\theta$ (d) $\tan\theta = 3\tan\phi$

22 A body takes time t to reach the bottom of an inclined plane of angle θ with the horizontal. If the plane is made rough, time taken now is $2t$. The coefficient of friction of the rough surface is **[DUMET]**

(a) $\frac{3}{4}\tan\theta$ (b) $\frac{2}{3}\tan\theta$ (c) $\frac{1}{4}\tan\theta$ (d) $\frac{1}{2}\tan\theta$

Answers

1 (a)	2 (c)	3 (b)	4 (d)	5 (a)	6 (a)	7 (a)	8 (c)	9 (a)	10 (a)
11 (c)	12 (d)	13 (a)	14 (a)	15 (a)	16 (b)	17 (b)	18 (c)	19 (b)	20 (a)
21 (b)	22 (a)								

Explanations

1 *(a)* Since, $F = (M + m)a$ ...(i)

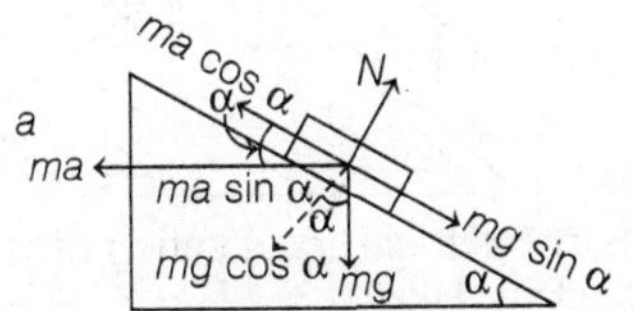

Normal $N = (mg\cos\alpha + ma\sin\alpha)$

So, apply pseudo force on the block by observing it from the wedge.

Now, as in free body diagram of block, we get

$$ma\cos\alpha = mg\sin\alpha$$

$$\Rightarrow \quad a = g\frac{\sin\alpha}{\cos\alpha}$$

$$\Rightarrow \quad a = g\tan\alpha \quad \text{...(ii)}$$

Now, from Eqs. (i) and (ii), we get

$$F = (M + m)g\tan\alpha$$

2 *(c)* Given, $\theta = 45°$,

$$s_1 = s_2,\ u = 0$$

On the rough incline,

$a_1 = g(\sin\theta - \mu\cos\theta)$, t_1 = time taken

On the frictionless incline,

$$a_2 = g\sin\theta$$

t_2 = time taken, $t_1 = 2t_2$

As, $\quad s = ut + \frac{1}{2}at^2$

So, $\quad s_1 = 0 + \frac{1}{2}g(\sin\theta - \mu\cos\theta)t_1^2$

and, $\quad s_2 = 0 + \frac{1}{2}g\sin\theta t_2^2$

As $s_1 = s_2$,

$$\frac{1}{2}g(\sin\theta - \mu\cos\theta)t_1^2 = \frac{1}{2}g\sin\theta t_2^2$$

$$\Rightarrow \quad \frac{\sin\theta - \mu\cos\theta}{\sin\theta} = \frac{t_2^2}{t_1^2}$$

$$\Rightarrow \quad 1 - \mu\cot\theta = \frac{t_2^2}{(2t_2)^2}$$

$$\Rightarrow \quad 1 - \mu\cot\theta = 1/4$$

$$\Rightarrow \quad \mu\cot\theta = 1 - \frac{1}{4} = \frac{3}{4}$$

$$\therefore \quad \mu = \frac{3}{4\cot\theta}$$

3 *(b)* Acceleration of the body down the rough inclined plane $= g\sin\theta$.

$\therefore$ Force applied on spring balance

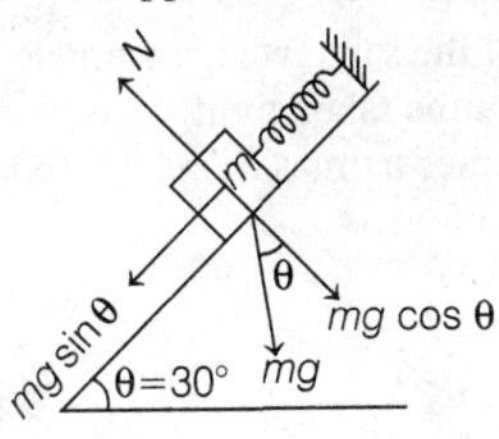

$$= mg\sin\theta = 5 \times 10 \times \sin 30°$$

$$= 5 \times 10 \times \frac{1}{2} = 25\ \text{N}$$

4 *(d)* According to the question, the free body diagrom of the given condition will be

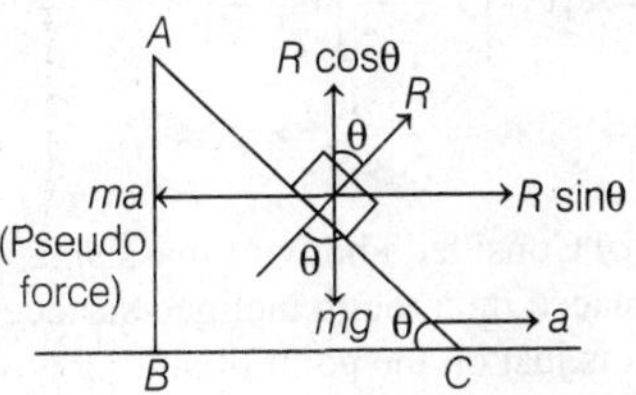

Since, the wedge is accelerating towards right with a, thus a pseudo force acts in the left direction in order to keep the block stationary. As, the system is in equilibrium.

$$\therefore \quad \Sigma F_x = 0 \quad \text{or} \quad \Sigma F_y = 0$$

$$\Rightarrow \quad R\sin\theta = ma \quad \text{...(i)}$$

Similarly, $\quad R\cos\theta = mg \quad$ ...(ii)

Dividing Eq. (i) by Eq (ii), we get

$$\frac{R\sin\theta}{R\cos\theta} = \frac{ma}{mg}$$

$$\Rightarrow \quad \tan\theta = \frac{a}{g} \quad \text{or} \quad a = g\tan\theta$$

$\therefore$ The relation between a and g for the block to remain stationary on the wedge is $a = g\tan\theta$.

5 *(a)* For friction to be minimum,

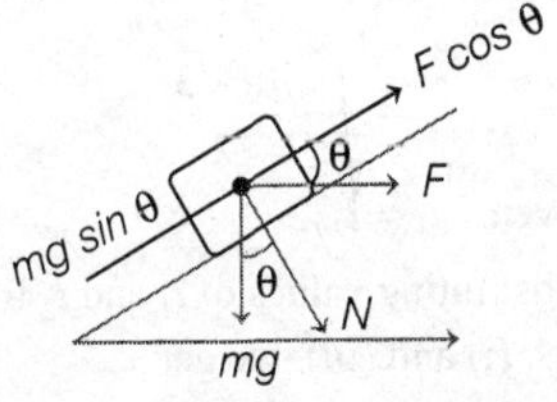

$$F\cos\theta = mg\sin\theta$$

$$F = mg\tan\theta$$

$$= \frac{80}{\sqrt{3}}$$

6 *(a)* According to question, the situation can be shown as

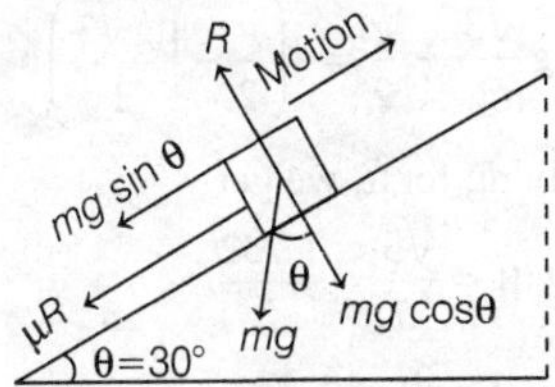

Case 1 For body projected up the plane

$$v = 0$$

$$\Rightarrow \quad v^2 = u^2 - 2a_1s$$

i.e. $\quad 0 = u^2 - 2a_1s$

$$\therefore \quad u = \sqrt{2a_1s}$$

Also, $\quad v = u - a_1t$

i.e. $\quad 0 = u - a_1t_1$

$$\Rightarrow \quad t_1 = u/a_1$$

$$\therefore \quad t_1 = \frac{\sqrt{2a_1s}}{a_1} = \sqrt{\frac{2s}{a_1}} \quad \text{... (i)}$$

Retardation, $a_1 = \dfrac{\mu R + mg\sin 30°}{m}$

As, $\quad R = mg\cos 30°$

$$a_1 = \frac{\mu mg\cos 30° + mg\sin 30°}{m}$$

$$= \mu g\frac{\sqrt{3}}{2} + \frac{g}{2} \quad \text{... (ii)}$$

Case 2 For body coming down the plane,

$$s = ut + \frac{1}{2} a_2 t_2^2$$

$\Rightarrow \quad u = 0$

$$t_2 = \sqrt{2s / a_2} \qquad \dots \text{(iii)}$$

Downward acceleration,

$$a_2 = \frac{mg \sin 30° - \mu R}{m} = \frac{mg \sin 30° - \mu mg \cos 30°}{m}$$

$$= \frac{g}{2} - \frac{\mu g \sqrt{3}}{2} \qquad \dots \text{(iv)}$$

Given, $t_1 = t_2/2$

Substituting values of t_1 and t_2 from Eqs. (i) and (iii), we get

$$\sqrt{\frac{2s}{a_1}} = \frac{1}{2}\sqrt{\frac{2s}{a_2}}$$

Now, squaring both sides, we get

$$a_1 = 4a_2 \qquad \dots \text{(v)}$$

Substituting values of a_1 and a_2 from Eqs. (ii) and (iv) in Eq. (v), we get

$$\mu g \frac{\sqrt{3}}{2} + \frac{g}{2} = 4\left(\frac{g}{2} - \frac{\mu g \sqrt{3}}{2}\right)$$

Solving for μ, we get

$$\mu = \frac{\sqrt{3}}{5} = \frac{1.732}{5}$$

$\Rightarrow \quad \mu = 0 \cdot 346$

7 *(a)* Suppose length of plane is *L*. When block descends the plane, rise in kinetic energy = fall in potential energy

$= mg \, L \sin\theta$

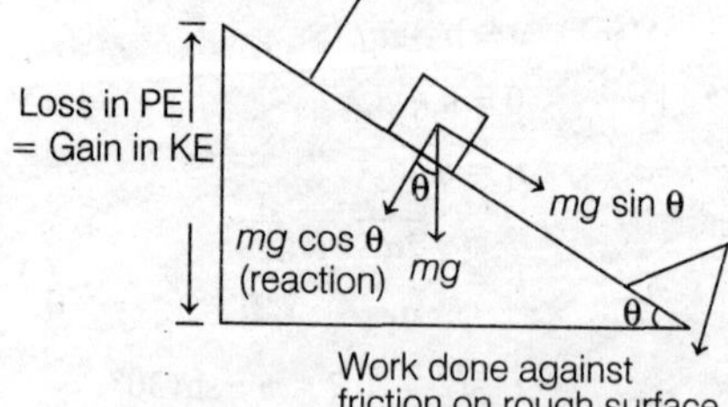

Work done by friction

$= \mu \times (\text{reaction}) \times \text{distance}$

$= 0 + \mu \, (mg \cos\theta) \times (L/2)$

$= \mu \, (mg \cos\theta) \times (L/2)$

Now, work done = change in KE

$$mgL \sin\theta = \mu \, (mg \cos\theta) \times (L/2)$$

$\Rightarrow \quad \tan\theta = \mu/2$

$\therefore \quad \mu = 2\tan\theta$

8 *(c)* Here, $mg \sin \theta - f = ma$

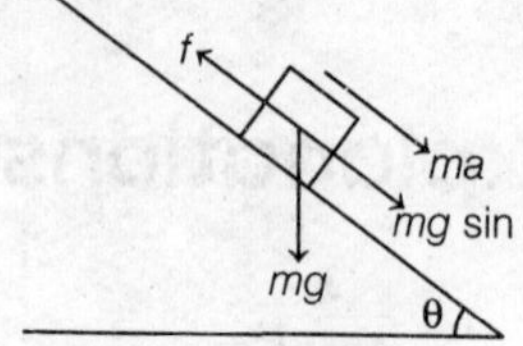

$\Rightarrow mg \sin \theta - ma = f$

$\Rightarrow 8 \times 10 \sin 30° - 8 \times 0.4 = f$

$\Rightarrow \quad 40 - 3.2 = f \Rightarrow \quad f = 36.8 \text{ N}$

9 *(a)* If the same wedge is made rough, then time taken by it to come down becomes *n* times more. The coefficient of friction.

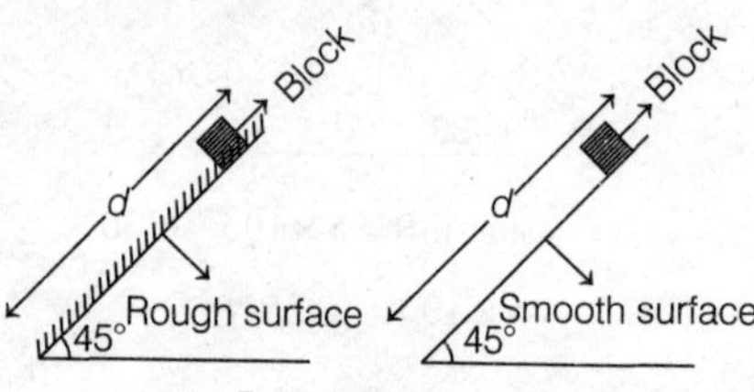

$$\mu = \left[1 - \frac{1}{n^2}\right] \tan \theta$$

$$\Rightarrow \mu = \left[1 - \frac{1}{2^2}\right] \tan 45°$$

$$\Rightarrow \quad \mu = \frac{4-1}{4} \Rightarrow \mu = \frac{3}{4}$$

10 *(a)* Consider a body of mass *m* is placed on a rough inclined surface and it is just on the point of sliding down, with coefficient of friction μ inclined at angle θ as shown in figure.

At the equilibrium point *O*,

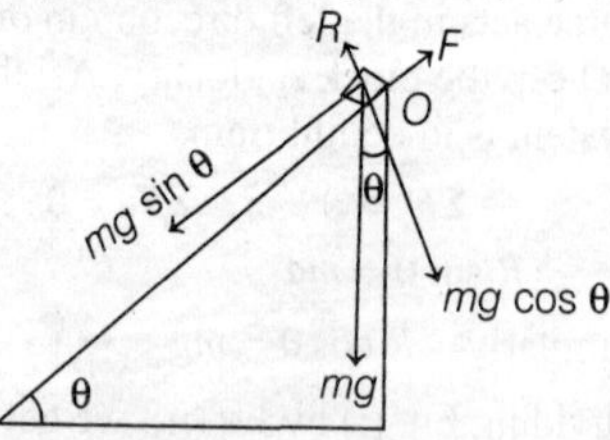

In case of limiting condition,

$$F = mg \sin \theta \qquad \dots \text{(i)}$$

Normal force, $R = mg \cos \theta \qquad \dots \text{(ii)}$

Now, comparing Eqs. (i), (ii), we get

$$\frac{F}{R} = \frac{mg \sin \theta}{mg \cos \theta}$$

($\because$ force of friction $F = \mu R$)

$\Rightarrow \mu = \tan \theta \Rightarrow \theta = \tan^{-1} (\mu)$

This is maximum value of θ for mass *m* to be at rest. For smaller θ, body will be at rest, i.e. in equilibrium

So, angle of repose, i.e. $\theta = \tan^{-1} \mu$.

11 *(c)* Acceleration due to gravity along inclined $g' = g \cos (90° - \theta) = g \sin \theta$

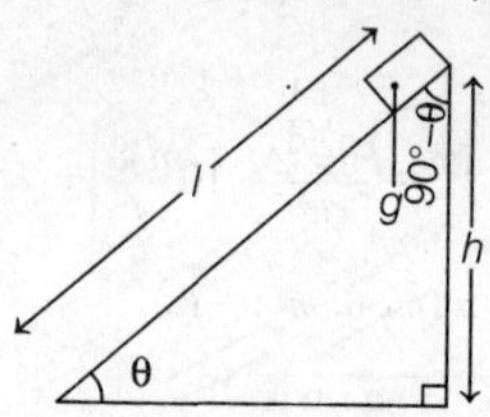

$\therefore$ Time taken, $t = \sqrt{\frac{2s}{g'}} = \sqrt{\frac{2l}{g \sin \theta}}$

But $\quad \sin \theta = \frac{h}{l} \quad \Rightarrow \quad l = \frac{h}{\sin \theta}$

Hence, $\quad t = \sqrt{\frac{2}{g \sin \theta} \cdot \frac{h}{\sin \theta}}$

$\Rightarrow \quad t = \frac{1}{\sin \theta}\sqrt{\frac{2h}{g}}$

12 *(d)* Fricti on force, $F = \mu mg \cos \theta$

$= 0.7 \times 100 \times 10^{-3} \times 10 \cos 30°$

$= 0.7 \times \frac{\sqrt{3}}{2} = \frac{0.7\sqrt{3}}{2} \text{N}$

13 *(a)* The free body diagram are given below

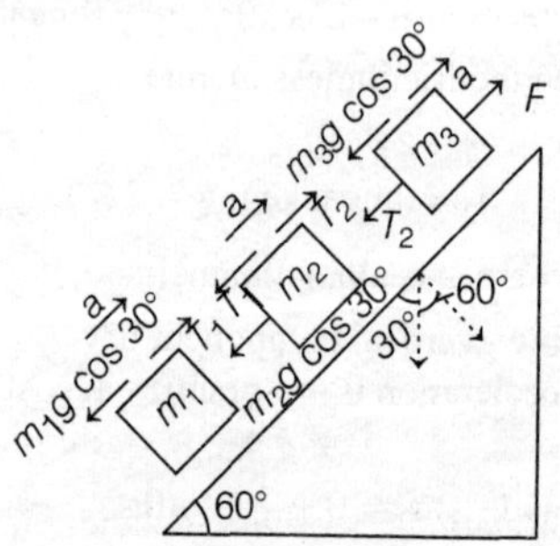

For the motion of mass m_1,

$$T_1 - m_1 g \cos 30° = m_1 a \qquad \dots \text{(i)}$$

For the motion of mass m_2,

$$T_2 - T_1 - m_2 g \cos 30° = m_2 a \qquad \dots \text{(ii)}$$

and for the motion of mass m_3,

$$F - T_2 - m_3 g \cos 30° = m_3 a \qquad \dots \text{(iii)}$$

Adding Eqs. (i), (ii) and (iii), we get

$$F - (m_1 + m_2 + m_3) g \cos 30° = (m_1 + m_2 + m_3) a$$

$$\Rightarrow \quad \frac{F}{m_1 + m_2 + m_3} - g \cos 30° = a$$

$$\Rightarrow \quad \frac{120}{12} - 10 \times \frac{\sqrt{3}}{2} = a$$

$$\Rightarrow \quad a = 10\left(1 - \frac{\sqrt{3}}{2}\right)$$

Now, $T_1 = m_1 (a + g \cos 30°)$

$$= 2\left(10 - \frac{10\sqrt{3}}{2} + 10\frac{\sqrt{3}}{2}\right) = 20 \text{ N}$$

$$T_2 = a (m_1 + m_2) + (m_1 + m_2) g \cos 30°$$
$$= 6 \times 10 = 60 \text{ N}$$

14 *(a)* As, $\tan \theta = \mu$

$$\Rightarrow \quad \tan \theta = 1/\sqrt{3}$$

$$\Rightarrow \quad \tan \theta = \tan 30°$$

Angle of inclination, $\theta = 30°$

15 *(a)* As, coefficient of friction = tangent angle of repose

$\Rightarrow \quad \mu = \tan \theta$

$$= \tan 30° = \frac{1}{\sqrt{3}}$$

Therefore, kinetic friction

$$= Mg \times \frac{1}{\sqrt{3}} = \frac{Mg}{\sqrt{3}}$$

16 *(b)* For equilibrium of body on the inclined plane,

$$F = mg (\sin \theta + \mu \cos \theta)$$
$$= 10 \times 9.8 (\sin 30° + 0.5 \cos 30°)$$
$$= 91.4 \text{ N}$$

17 *(d)* As equation along the inclined plane.

$$mg \sin\theta = ma$$

$$\therefore \quad a = g \sin\theta$$

where, a is along the inclined plane.

Now, vertical component of acceleration is

$$a' = g \sin^2\theta.$$

$\therefore$ Relative vertical acceleration of A with respect to B is

$$a'_A - a'_B =$$

$$g (\sin^2 60° - \sin^2 30°) = \frac{g}{2} = 4.9 \text{ ms}^{-2}$$

(in vertical direction)

18 *(c)* Here, $\sin \theta = \frac{1}{l}$ (from the figure)

When horizontal acceleration is imparted to the inclined plane, then a pseudo acceleration acts on the object.

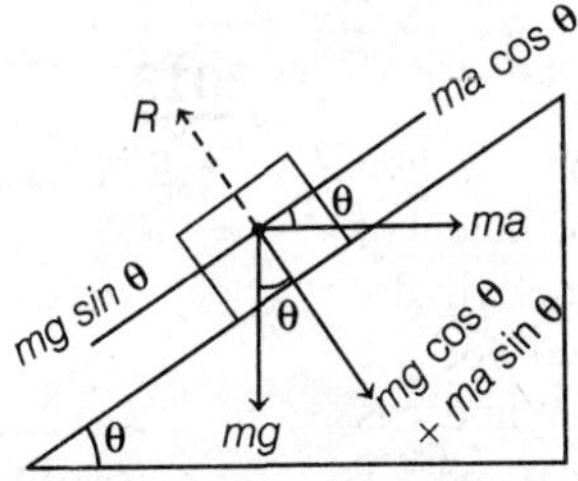

For equilibrium of body on the inclined plane,

$$ma \cos \theta = mg \sin \theta$$

$$\Rightarrow \quad a = g \tan \theta = g\frac{1}{\sqrt{l^2 - 1}}$$

$$\Rightarrow \quad a = \frac{g}{\sqrt{l^2 - 1}}$$

19 *(b)* Acceleration of block down the plane is given by

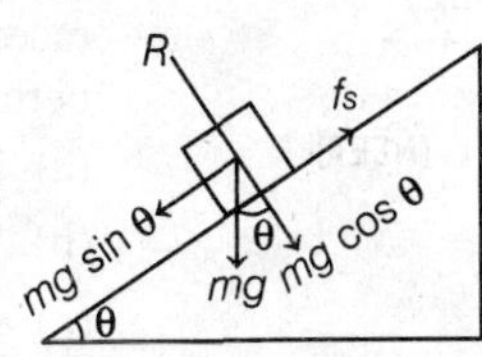

For the motion of body along the incline,

$$a = \frac{\mu mg \cos \theta - mg \sin \theta}{m}$$

(as, $R = mg \cos \theta$ and $f_s = \mu R$)

$$= 0.2 \times 10 \times \cos 30° - 10 \times \sin 30°$$

$$= 2 \times \frac{\sqrt{3}}{2} - 10 \times \frac{1}{2}$$

$$= 3.278$$

From the equation of motion,

$$v = u - at$$

Velocity after 5 s,

$$v = 0 + 3.278 \times 5$$
$$= 16.35 \text{ ms}^{-1}$$

20 *(a)* The acceleration of the body sliding on the inclined plane is given by

$$a = g (\sin \theta - \mu \cos \theta)$$
$$= 9.8 (\sin 45° - 0.5 \cos 45°)$$
$$= 9.8\left(\frac{1}{\sqrt{2}} - 0.5 \times \frac{1}{\sqrt{2}}\right) = \frac{9.8}{2\sqrt{2}} \text{ ms}^{-2}$$

21 *(b)* According to the question,

$$mg (\sin \phi + \mu \cos \phi)$$
$$= 2mg (\sin \phi - \mu \cos \phi)$$

$\Rightarrow \tan \phi = 3\mu$

As, $\quad \mu = \tan \theta$

So, $\tan \phi = 3 \tan \theta$

22 *(a)* The free body diagram shows the various forces acting on the block. When plane is frictionless, then acceleration, $a = g \sin \theta$.

Let time taken is t_1. Since, body starts from rest, initial velocity $u = 0$

$$\therefore \quad s = ut + \frac{1}{2}at_1^2$$

$$\Rightarrow \quad s = \frac{1}{2}g \sin \theta t_1^2$$

$$\Rightarrow \quad t_1 = \sqrt{\frac{2s}{g \sin \theta}}$$

When the plane is made rough, then acceleration $a = g (\sin \theta - \mu \cos \theta)$, where μ is coefficient of friction.

$$t_2 = \sqrt{\frac{2s}{g (\sin \theta - \mu \cos \theta)}}$$

Given, $t_2 = 2t_1$

$$\therefore \quad \sqrt{\frac{2s}{g (\sin \theta - \mu \cos \theta)}} = 2\sqrt{\frac{2s}{g \sin \theta}}$$

$$\frac{1}{\sin \theta - \mu \cos \theta} = \frac{4}{\sin \theta}$$

$$\Rightarrow \quad \sin \theta = 4 \sin \theta - 4 \mu \cos \theta$$

$$\Rightarrow \quad 4\mu \cos \theta = 3 \sin \theta$$

$$\Rightarrow \quad \mu = \frac{3}{4} \tan \theta$$

Topic 7

Dynamics of Circular Motion

2019

1 A block of mass 10 kg is in contact against the inner wall of a hollow cylindrical drum of radius 1 m. The coefficient of friction between the block and the inner wall of the cylinder is 0.1. The minimum angular velocity needed for the cylinder to keep the block stationary when the cylinder is vertical and rotating about its axis, will be $(g = 10 \, m/s^2)$ **[NEET]**

(a) $\frac{10}{2\pi}$ rad/s (b) 10 rad/s

(c) 10π rad/s (d) $\sqrt{10}$ rad/s

2017

2 One end of the string of length l is connected to a particle of mass m and the other end is connected to a small peg on a smooth horizontal table. If the particle moves in circle with speed v, the net force on the particle (directed towards center) will be (T represents the tension in the string) **[NEET]**

(a) T (b) $T + \frac{mv^2}{l}$

(c) $T - \frac{mv^2}{l}$ (d) zero

2016

3 A car is negotiating a curved road of radius R. The road is banked at angle θ. The coefficient of friction between the tyres of the car and the road is μ_s. The maximum safe velocity on this road is **[NEET]**

(a) $\sqrt{gR\left(\frac{\mu_s + \tan\theta}{1 - \mu_s \tan\theta}\right)}$ (b) $\sqrt{\frac{g}{R}\left(\frac{\mu_s + \tan\theta}{1 - \mu_s \tan\theta}\right)}$

(c) $\sqrt{\frac{g}{R^2}\left(\frac{\mu_s + \tan\theta}{1 - \mu_s \tan\theta}\right)}$ (d) $gR^2\left(\frac{\mu_s + \tan\theta}{1 - \mu_s \tan\theta}\right)$

2014

4 A person is driving a vehicle at a uniform speed of $5 \, ms^{-1}$ on a level curved track of radius 5 m. The coefficient of static friction between tyres and road is 0.1. Will the person slip while taking the turn with the same speed? (Take, $g = 10 \, ms^{-2}$.) **[KCET]**

(a) A person will slip, if $v^2 = 5 \, m^2s^{-2}$

(b) A person will slip, if $v^2 > 5 \, m^2s^{-2}$

(c) A person will slip, if $v^2 < 5 \, m^2s^{-2}$

(d) A person will not slip, if $v^2 > 5 \, m^2s^{-2}$

2013

5 A car of mass 1000 kg moves on a circular track of radius 20 m. If the coefficient of fricition of 0.64, then the maximum velocity with which the car can move is **[WB JEE]**

(a) 22.4 m/s (b) 5.6 m/s

(c) 11.2 m/s (d) None of these

2012

6 A car of mass 1000 kg negotiates a banked curve of radius 90 m on a frictionless road. If the banking angle is 45°, the speed of the car is **[CBSE AIPMT]**

(a) $20 \, ms^{-1}$ (b) $30 \, ms^{-1}$

(c) $5 \, ms^{-1}$ (d) $10 \, ms^{-1}$

7 A circular race track of radius 300 m is banked at an angle of 15°. If the coefficient of friction between the wheels of the race car and the road is 0.2. Find optimum speed of the race car to avoid wear and tear on its tyres and maximum permissible speed to avoid slipping. **[AMU]**

(a) $v_o = 48 \, ms^{-1}$ and $v_{max} = 60 \, ms^{-1}$

(b) $v_o = 28.1 \, ms^{-1}$ and $v_{max} = 38.1 \, ms^{-1}$

(c) $v_o = 62.2 \, ms^{-1}$ and $v_{max} = 73.4 \, ms^{-1}$

(d) None of the above

2011

8 A car is moving in a circular horizontal track of radius 10.0 m with a constant speed of $10.0 \, ms^{-1}$. A plumb bob is suspended from the roof of the car by a light rigid rod of length 10.0 m. The angle made by the rod with the track is (take, $g = 10 \, ms^{-2}$) **[AFMC]**

(a) zero (b) 30°

(c) 45° (d) 60°

2008

9 Assertion A body of mass 1 kg is making 1 rps in a circle of radius 1 m. Centrifugal force acting on it is $4\pi^2$ N.

Reason Centrifugal force is given by $F = \frac{mv^2}{r}$. **[AIIMS]**

(a) Both Assertion and Reason are correct and Reason is the correct explanation of Assertion.

(b) Both Assertion and Reason are correct but Reason is not the correct explanation of Assertion.

(c) Assertion is correct but Reason is incorrect.

(d) Both Assertion and Reason are incorrect.

10 A cyclist is travelling with velocity v on a banked curved road of radius R. The angle θ through which the cyclist leans inwards is given by **[J&K CET]**

(a) $\tan\theta = \frac{Rg}{v^2}$ (b) $\tan\theta = v^2 Rg$

(c) $\tan\theta = \frac{v^2 R}{R}$ (d) $\tan\theta = \frac{v^2}{Rg}$

11 Assertion (A) A ball connected to a string is in circular motion on a frictionless horizontal table and is in equilibrium.

Reason (R) Magnitude of the centripetal force is equal to the magnitude of the tension in the string. **[EAMCET]**

(a) Both A and R are correct and R is the correct explanation of A
(b) Both A and R are correct but R is not the correct explanation of A
(c) A is correct but R is incorrect
(d) A is incorrect but R is correct

2007

12 A 500 kg car takes a round turn of radius 50 m with a velocity of 36 kmh^{-1}. The centripetal force is **[MHT CET]**

(a) 250 N (b) 750 N
(c) 1000 N (d) 1200 N

13 A motorcycle is going on an overbridge of radius R. The driver maintains a constant speed. As the motorcycle is ascending on the overbridge, the normal force on it **[JCECE]**

(a) increases (b) decreases
(c) remains the same (d) fluctuates erratically

2006

14 Angle of banking for a vehicle speed of 10 ms^{-1} for a radius of curvature 10 m is (assume, $g = 10\ ms^{-2}$) **[J&K CET]**

(a) 30° (b) $\tan^{-1}\left(\frac{1}{2}\right)$ (c) 60° (d) 45°

15 Two stones of masses m and $2m$ are whirled in horizontal circles, the heavier one in a radius $\frac{r}{2}$ and the lighter one in radius r. The tangential speed of lighter stone is n times that of the value of heavier stone when they experience same centripetal forces. The value of n is **[CBSE AIPMT]**

(a) 2 (b) 3 (c) 4 (d) 1

2005

16 The angle of banking is independent of **[MHT CET]**

(a) speed of vehicle
(b) radius of curvature of road
(c) height of inclination
(d) None of the above

17 A small body of mass m slides without friction from the top of a hemisphere of radius r. The point at which the body will be detached from the surface of hemisphere is **[Haryana PMT]**

(a) $\frac{r}{3}$ (b) $\frac{r}{2}$

(c) $\frac{2}{3}r$ (d) $2r$

18 A particle describes a horizontal circle in a conical funnel whose inner surface is smooth with speed of 0.5 ms^{-1}. What is the height of the plane of circle from vertex of the funnel? **[J&K CET]**

(a) 0.25 m (b) 2 cm
(c) 4 cm (d) 2.5 cm

19 A ball of mass 0.25 kg attached to the ends of a string of length 1.96 m is rotating in a horizontal circle. The string will break, if tension is more than 25 N. What is the maximum velocity with which the ball can be rotated? **[AMU]**

(a) 3 ms^{-1} (b) 5 ms^{-1}
(c) 9 ms^{-1} (d) 14 ms^{-1}

20 A coin placed on a rotating turn table just slips, if it is placed at a distance of 8 cm from the centre. If angular speed of the turn table is doubled, then it will just slip at a distance of **[DUMET]**

(a) 1 cm (b) 2 cm (c) 4 cm (d) 8 cm

21 A particle is moving in a circle of radius R with constant speed v. If radius is doubled, then its centripetal force to keep the same speed gets **[BCECE]**

(a) twice as great as before (b) half
(c) one-fourth (d) remains constant

22 A car is racing on a circular track of 180 m radius with a speed of 32 ms^{-1}. What should be the banking angle of the road to avoid chances of skidding of the vehicle at this speed without taking into consideration the friction between the tyres and the road? **[JCECE]**

(a) 45° (b) 60°
(c) 30° (d) 15°

Answers

1	(b)	2	(a)	3	(a)	4	(b)	5	(c)	6	(b)	7	(b)	8	(c)	9	(a)	10	(d)
11	(a)	12	(c)	13	(a)	14	(d)	15	(a)	16	(c)	17	(c)	18	(d)	19	(d)	20	(b)
21	(b)	22	(c)																

Explanations

1 (b) Given, mass of cylinder $m = 10$ kg, radius of cylinder, $r = 1$ m and coefficient of friction, $\mu = 0.1$.

The given situation can be as shown in the figure given below

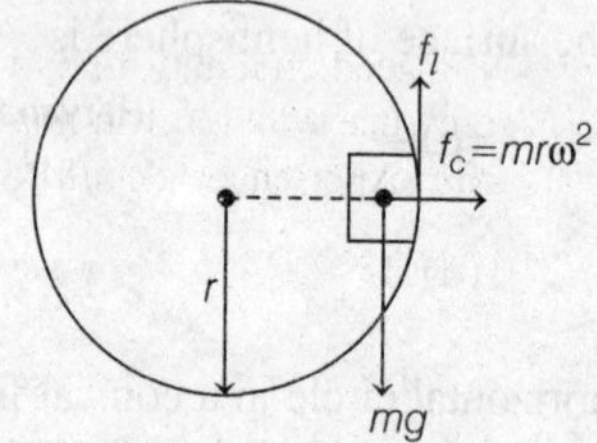

From the above figure, it can be concluded that the block will be stationary when the limiting friction (f_l) is equal to or greater than the downward force or weight of block, i.e.

$$f_l \geq mg \quad \ldots(i)$$

Also, the magnitude of limiting friction between two bodies is directly proportional to the normal reaction (N) between them, i.e.

$$f_l \propto N \text{ or } f_l = \mu N \quad \ldots(ii)$$

From Eqs. (i) and (ii), we get

$$\mu N \geq mg \text{ or } \mu(mr\omega^2) \geq mg \quad [\because N = mr\omega^2]$$

$$\Rightarrow \quad \omega \geq \sqrt{\frac{g}{r\mu}}$$

Thus, the minimum angular velocity is

$$\omega_{\min} = \sqrt{\frac{g}{r\mu}} = \sqrt{\frac{10}{1 \times 0.1}} = 10 \text{ rad/s}$$

2 (a) Consider the string of length l connected to a particle as shown in the figure

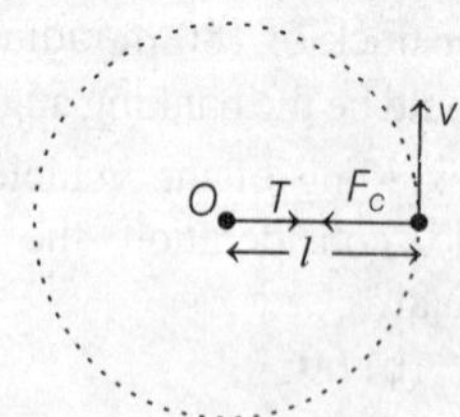

Speed of the particle is v. As, the particle is in uniform circular motion, net force on the particle must be equal to centripetal force which is provided by the tension (T).

$\therefore$ Net force = Centripetal force = Tension in string

$$\Rightarrow \quad \frac{mv^2}{l} = T$$

3 (a) According to question, a car is negotiating a curved road of radius R. The road is banked at angle θ and the coefficient of friction between the tyres of car and the road is μ_s. So, this given situation can be drawn as shown in figure below.

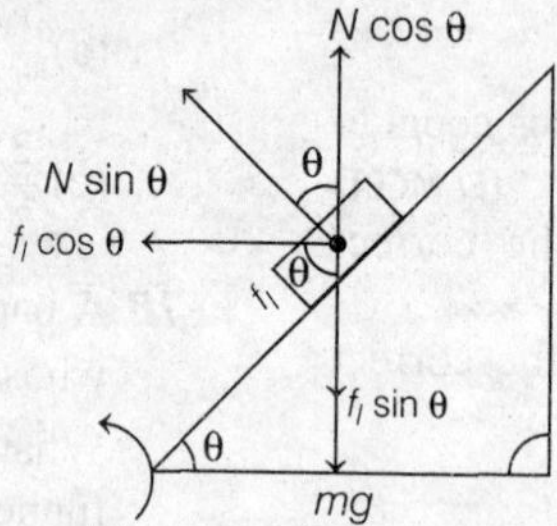

Considering the case of vertical equilibrium.

$$N \cos\theta = mg + f_l \sin\theta$$

$$\Rightarrow \quad mg = N \cos\theta - f_l \sin\theta \quad \ldots(i)$$

Considering the case of horizontal equilibrium,

$$N \sin\theta + f_l \cos\theta = \frac{mv^2}{R} \quad \ldots(ii)$$

Divide Eqs. (i) and (ii), we get

$$\frac{v^2}{Rg} = \frac{\sin\theta + \mu_s \cos\theta}{\cos\theta - \mu_s \sin\theta} \quad (f_l \propto \mu_s)$$

$$\Rightarrow \quad v = \sqrt{Rg\left(\frac{\sin\theta + \mu_s \cos\theta}{\cos\theta - \mu_s \sin\theta}\right)}$$

$$\Rightarrow \quad v = \sqrt{Rg\left(\frac{\tan\theta + \mu_s}{1 - \mu_s \tan\theta}\right)}$$

4 (b) We know that,

$$F = \frac{mv^2_{\max}}{r} \quad \ldots(i)$$

and

$$F = \mu_s mg \quad \ldots(ii)$$

From the Eqs. (i) and (ii) for maximum speed of vehicle

$$\mu_s mg \geq \frac{mv^2_{\max}}{r}$$

where,

$v_{\max}$ = maximum velocity of vehicle

Given,

$\mu_s = 0.1$, $r = 5$ m and $g = 10 \text{ ms}^{-2}$

$$v_{\max} = \sqrt{\mu_s rg}$$

$$v^2_{\max} = 0.1 \times 5 \times 10 = 5 \text{ m}^2\text{s}^{-2}$$

So, person or vehicle will slip, if

$$v^2 > 5 \text{ m}^2\text{s}^{-2}$$

5 (c) Maximum velocity of the car is given by

$$v = \sqrt{\mu rg}$$

Given, $\mu = 0.64$ and $r = 20$ m

$$\therefore \quad v = \sqrt{0.64 \times 20 \times 10} = \sqrt{0.64 \times 200} = \sqrt{128} = 11.2 \text{ m/s}$$

6 (b) The angle of banking, $\tan\theta = \dfrac{v^2}{rg}$

Given, $\theta = 45°$, $r = 90$ m and $g = 10 \text{ m/s}^2$

$$\therefore \quad \tan 45° = \frac{v^2}{90 \times 10}$$

$$\Rightarrow \quad v = \sqrt{90 \times 10 \times \tan 45°}$$

Speed of car, $v = 30$ m/s

7 (b) Here, $\mu_s = 0.2$, $R = 300$ m, $\theta = 15°$

$$v_o \text{ (optimal velocity)} = \sqrt{gR \tan\theta} = \sqrt{9.8 \times 300 \times \tan 15°} = 28.1 \text{ ms}^{-1}$$

and

$$v_{\max} = \sqrt{\frac{gR(\mu_s + \tan 15°)}{1 - \mu_s \tan 15°}} = \sqrt{\frac{9.8 \times 300\,(0.2 + 2 - \sqrt{3})}{1 - 0.2\,(2 - \sqrt{3})}} = 38.1 \text{ ms}^{-1}$$

8 (c) If angle of banking is θ, then

$$\tan\theta = \frac{mv^2/r}{mg} \Rightarrow \tan\theta = \frac{v^2}{rg}$$

Given, $v = 10$, $r = 10$ m and $g = 10 \text{ ms}^{-2}$

So, $\tan\theta = \dfrac{(10)^2}{10 \times 10} = 1$

$$\therefore \quad \theta = 45°$$

9 (a) From relation, the centrifugal force,

$$F = \frac{mv^2}{r} = \frac{m\,(r\omega)^2}{r} = mr\omega^2 = mr\,(2\pi\nu)^2 = 4\pi^2\, mr\nu^2 = 4\pi^2 \times 1 \times 1 \times 1^2 = 4\pi^2 \text{ N}$$

10 (d) The angle made by cyclist with the vertical is given by

$$\tan\theta = \frac{v^2}{Rg}$$

where, v = speed of cycle and R = radius of circular track.

11 *(a)* In a circular motion, the direction of resultant force is towards centre and its magnitude is

$$F = \frac{mv^2}{r}$$

or $$F = mr\omega^2$$

Thus, a centripetal force of magnitude $\frac{mv^2}{r}$ which is equal to the tension in string is needed to keep the particle moving in a circle with constant speed.

12 *(c)* Given, $m = 500\,\text{kg}$

$$v = 36\,\text{kmh}^{-1} = 36 \times \frac{5}{18}\,\text{ms}^{-1}$$

$$= 10\,\text{ms}^{-1} \text{ and } r = 50\,\text{m}$$

Now, the centripetal force,

$$F = \frac{mv^2}{r} = \frac{500 \times (10)^2}{50} = 1000\text{ N}$$

13 *(a)* Reaction of normal force on the motorcyclist

$$Mg\cos\theta - N = \frac{Mv^2}{R}$$

or $$N = Mg\cos\theta - \frac{Mv^2}{R}$$

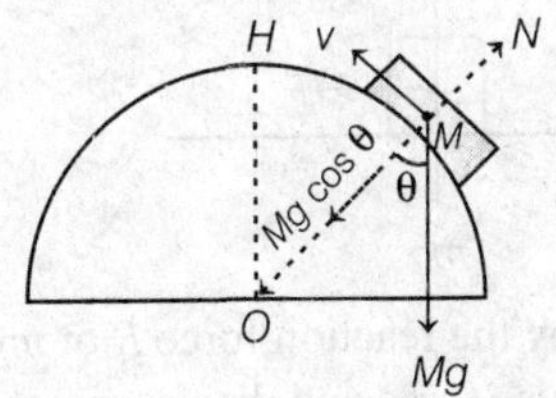

As the motorcyclist moves upward on the bridge, θ decreases and therefore N increases and becomes maximum at the highest point (i.e. point H in the diagram).

14 *(d)* As, $\tan\theta = \frac{v^2}{rg}$

$$\therefore \quad \tan\theta = \frac{10 \times 10}{10 \times 10} = 1$$

$$\Rightarrow \quad \theta = 45°$$

15 *(a)* Given, that two stones of masses m and $2m$ are whirled in horizontal circles, the heavier one in a radius $r/2$ and lighter one in radius r as shown in figure.

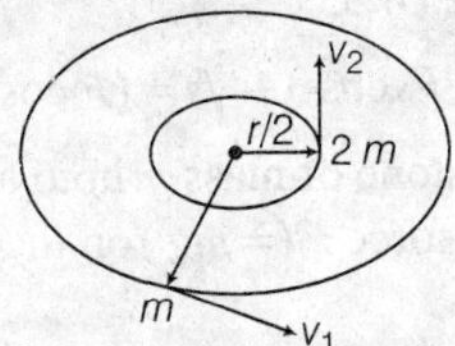

As, lighter stone in n times that of the value of heavier stone when they experience same centripetal forces, we get

$$(F_c)_{\text{heavier}} = (F_c)_{\text{lighter}}$$

$$\Rightarrow \quad \frac{2m(v)^2}{(r/2)} = \frac{m(nv)^2}{r} \Rightarrow n^2 = 4 \Rightarrow n = 2$$

16 *(c)* As, angle of banking of road is given as, $\tan\theta = \frac{v^2}{rg}$, i.e. it does not depend upon height of inclination.

17 *(c)* When released from top with zero velocity block leaves contact at

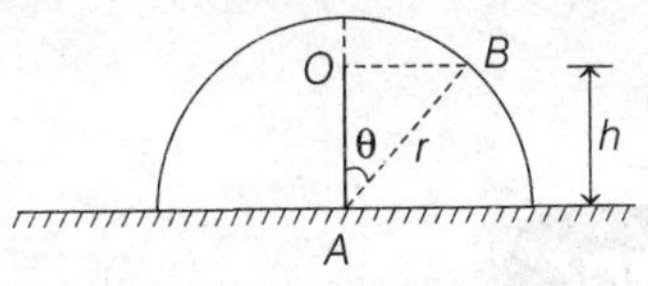

$$\cos\theta = \frac{2}{3}$$

$\because$ In ΔAOB,

$$\cos\theta = \frac{OA}{AB} \Rightarrow \cos\theta = \frac{h}{r}$$

$$\therefore \quad h = r\cos\theta = \frac{2r}{3}$$

18 *(d)* Equating the vertical forces, we get

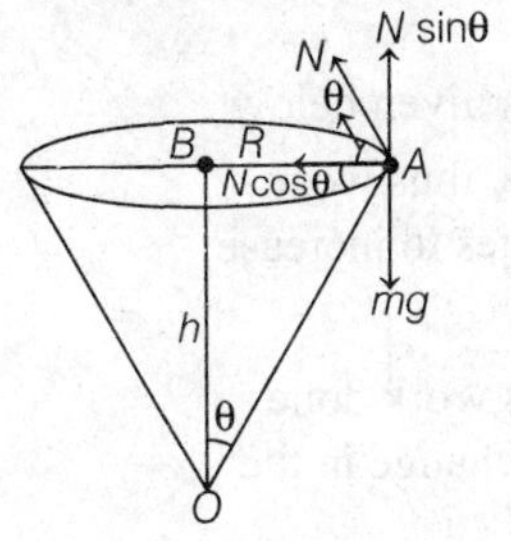

From the diagram for the equilibrium of a particle A

$$N\sin\theta = mg \quad \text{...(i)}$$

and $$\frac{mv^2}{R} = N\cos\theta \quad \text{...(ii)}$$

$$\therefore \quad \tan\theta = \frac{Rg}{v^2} \quad \text{...(iii)}$$

Also, in ΔOAB

$$\tan\theta = \frac{R}{h} \quad \text{...(iv)}$$

On equating Eqs. (iii) and (iv), we get

$$h = \frac{v^2}{g}$$

$$\Rightarrow \quad h = \frac{(0.5)^2}{10} = 0.025\text{ m} = 2.5\text{ cm}$$

19 *(d)* The centripetal force,

$$F = \frac{mv^2}{r}$$

$$\Rightarrow \quad v^2 = \frac{Fr}{m}$$

$$\Rightarrow \quad v^2 = \frac{25 \times 1.96}{0.25} = 196$$

$$\therefore \quad v = \sqrt{196} = 14\,\text{ms}^{-1}$$

20 *(b)* A body placed on a non-inertial frame of reference which is rotating about its axis, experiences a centrifugal force.

It is given by

$$F = mr\omega^2$$

where, r is radius of circle, m is mass and ω is angular speed.

$$\therefore \quad \frac{F_1}{F_2} = \frac{r_1\omega_1^2}{r_2\omega_2^2}$$

Since, $F_1 = F_2$

$$\Rightarrow \quad r_1\omega_1^2 = r_2\omega_2^2$$

$$\Rightarrow \quad r_2 = \frac{r_1\omega_1^2}{\omega_2^2}$$

Given, $r_1 = 8\text{ cm}, \omega_1 = \omega$ and $\omega_2 = 2\omega$

$$\therefore \quad r_2 = \frac{8 \times \omega^2}{(2\omega)^2} = \frac{8}{4} = 2\text{ cm}$$

21 *(b)* The centripetal force,

$$F = \frac{mv^2}{R}$$

$$\Rightarrow \quad F \propto \frac{1}{R}$$

or $$F \propto \frac{1}{R_1}$$

and $$F_2 \propto \frac{1}{R_2}$$

$$\Rightarrow \quad \frac{F_2}{F_1} = \frac{R_1}{R_2}$$

Given, $R_2 = 2R_1$

$$\therefore \quad \frac{F_2}{F_1} = \frac{R_1}{2R_1} = \frac{1}{2}$$

or $$F_2 = \frac{F_1}{2}$$

22 *(c)* As, $\tan\theta = \frac{v^2}{rg}$

$$\Rightarrow \quad \tan\theta = \frac{(32)^2}{180 \times 9.8}$$

$$\therefore \quad \theta = 30°$$

05

Work, Energy and Power

Quick Review

Work

Work done by a force on the body is equal to the scalar (or dot product) product of force and displacement of the body in the direction of force.

It is expressed as $W = \mathbf{F} \cdot \mathbf{s} = Fs\cos\theta$

where, θ = angle between the force (**F**) and displacement (**s**).

- It can be positive, negative or zero as given below
  - (*i*) If θ is acute, $\cos\theta$ will be **positive**, thus work done will be positive and force tries to increase the speed of the body.
  - (*ii*) If θ is 90°, $\cos\theta$ will be **zero**, thus work done will be zero and there will be no change in the speed of the body due to force.
  - (*iii*) When a body moves in a circle, the work done by the centripetal force is always zero as $\mathbf{F} \perp \mathbf{s}$, hence $\theta = 90°$,

    $W = Fs\cos 90° = 0$
  - (*iv*) If θ is greater than 90° (up to 180°), $\cos\theta$ is **negative**. Hence, W is negative and force tries to decrease the speed of the body.
- If the force is constant, work done is independent of the actual path taken by the particle.
- Total work done within the two limits of displacements x_1 and x_2 by a variable force is given by
$$W = \int_{x_1}^{x_2} F\,dx$$

Some Particular Cases of Work Done

(*i*) If an object moves on a rough surface, then

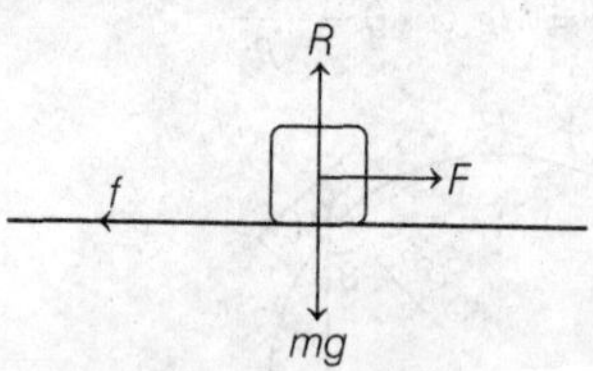

(a) Work done by the reaction force R or mg is $W_1 = 0$, because force and displacement are perpendicular to each other.

(b) Work done by the pulling force F,
$$W_2 = Fs\cos 0° = Fs$$

(c) Work done by the frictional force,
$$W_3 = fs\cos 180° = -fs$$

(d) Net work done (W_{net}) due to all these forces,
$$W_{net} = W_1 + W_2 + W_3$$
$$= 0 + Fs - fs = (F - f)s$$

where, f = force of friction.

If the angle between the force and displacement is θ, then for displacement s, net work done (W),
$$W_{net} = Fs\cos\theta - fs = (F\cos\theta - f)s$$

(*ii*) A labourer lift a stone of mass m upto a height h, then he applies a force $F(= mg)$ on the stone upwards.

Therefore, work done (W) by him,

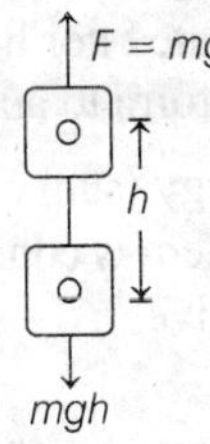

$$W = Fh\cos 0° = Fh = mgh$$

However, work done (W_g) by gravitational force,

$$W_g = mgh\cos 180° = -mgh$$

Work done by Conservative and Non-Conservative Forces

- Work done by or against the conservative force on a body is independent of the path followed by the body. Examples of conservative forces are, field forces such as gravitational, electric, magnetic and spring forces.
- Work done by or against the non-conservative force in a moving body depends on the path between initial and final positions.
  Examples of non-conservative forces are, natural opposing forces like friction, viscous forces, etc.

Work Done by a Spring Force

- Spring force, $F_s = -kx$, where k is a force constant or spring constant or stiffness of the spring and x is the extension or compression in the length of the spring.
- Following are the various cases for the work done by spring force
  (*i*) If x is positive, then spring force F_s is in opposite direction of pulling force F or opposite to the displacement. The work done on the object by the applied force = $(1/2)\,kx^2$ and work done on the object by the spring force, $W = -(1/2)\,kx^2$
  (*ii*) If $x = 0$, $F_s = 0$, so $W = 0$.
  (*iii*) If x is negative and F_s is positive. In this situation, force F_s and displacement x are in opposite direction. Therefore, work done on the object by the spring force is $W = -(1/2)\,kx^2$ and work done on the spring by the applied force is $W = (1/2)kx^2$.
- In the figure given below, the graph between the spring force F_s and x is plotted. If in compression of the spring from x_m to $x = 0$, the spring force and direction of displacement is same, then work done,

$$W = \frac{1}{2}kx_m^2 = \text{area of } MNO$$

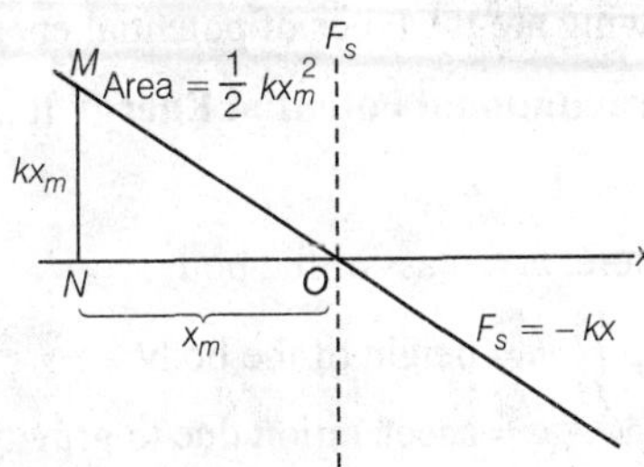

- If the external force is in opposite direction to the spring force, then in expansion from x_1 to x_2. Work done W by the spring force F_s on the object,

$$W = \int_{x_1}^{x_2} F_s dx = \int_{x_1}^{x_2}(-kx)\,dx = -\frac{1}{2}k(x_2^2 - x_1^2)$$

- Work done W by the external force F_{app} on the spring,

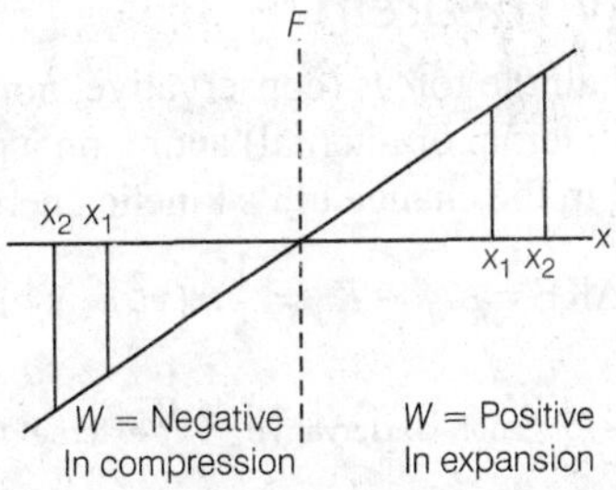

$$W' = \int_{x_1}^{x_2} F_{app}dx = \int_{x_1}^{x_2} kx\,dx = +\frac{1}{2}k(x_2^2 - x_1^2)$$

Therefore, $\quad W' = -W$

Energy

- The capacity or ability to do work is known as energy.
- Energy can exist in various forms such as mechanical energy (sum of potential and kinetic energy), sound energy, heat energy, nuclear energy, etc.

Various Types of Mechanical Energy

(*i*) **Kinetic Energy** The energy possessed by virtue of its motion is called kinetic energy.

- It is expressed as

$$\text{KE} = \frac{1}{2}mv^2,$$

where, m = mass of the body

and $\quad v$ = velocity of the body.

- Relation between kinetic energy and linear momentum is expressed as $K = \dfrac{p^2}{2m}$.

(*ii*) **Potential Energy** It is the energy possessed by a body or system by virtue of its position of configuration.

Following are the types of potential energy

(a) **Gravitational Potential Energy** It is expressed as

$$U = mgh$$

where, m = mass of the body,

h = height of the body

and g = acceleration due to gravity.

(b) **Elastic Potential Energy** It is expressed as

$$U = \frac{1}{2}kx^2$$

where, k = spring constant

and x = compression or expansion in the spring.

Work-Energy Theorem

Work done by all the forces (conservative, non-conservative, external or internal) acting on a particle or an object is equal to the change in its kinetic energy.

Thus, $W_{net} = \Delta KE = K_f - K_i = \frac{1}{2}m(v_f^2 - v_i^2)$

$$\Rightarrow W_{conservative} + W_{non\text{-}conservative} + W_{external\ force} = \Delta KE$$

Application of Work-Energy Theorem for Motion in Vertical Circle

When a body tied to a string is moving in a vertical circle, then the velocities and tension at different positions are given in table below, according to the diagram

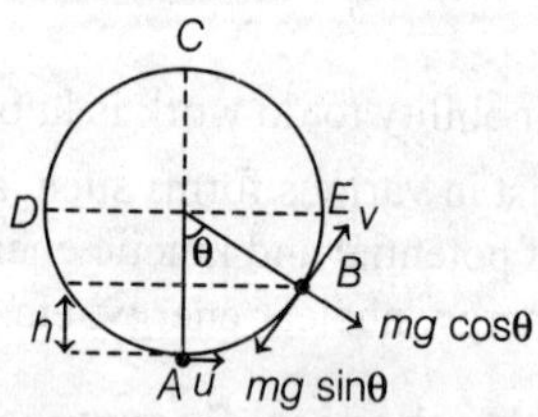

Position of the Body	Velocity	Tension (*T*)
At lowest point (*A*)	$\sqrt{5gL}$	6 *mg*
At highest point (*C*)	$\sqrt{gL}$	0
At horizontal position (*E* or *D*)	$\sqrt{3gL}$	3 *mg*
At any angle θ (*B*)	$\sqrt{3gL + 2gL\cos\theta}$	$\frac{mv^2}{r} + mg\cos\theta$

Law of Conservation of Energy

Energy can neither be created nor be destroyed, it can only be transformed from one form to another form.

The total mechanical energy (sum of kinetic energy and potential energy) of a system is conserved, if the forces acting on it, are conservative.

Power

The time rate at which the work is done by the force is said to be the power due to that force.

$$P = \frac{\Delta W}{\Delta t}$$

$$\Rightarrow \quad P = \frac{dW}{dt}$$

where, work is expressed in terms of variable t time.

Also, $P = \mathbf{F} \cdot \mathbf{v} = Fv\cos\theta$

where, F = force applied on the body

and v = velocity of the body.

If the force and velocity of a body are at right angle, then power delivered will be zero.

Collision

- It is an isolated event, in which two or more colliding bodies exert strong forces on each other for a short duration of time.
- It is of two types, elastic and inelastic collision.
- For every type of collision, linear momentum of colliding body or system is conserved,

  i.e. $m_1\mathbf{u}_1 + m_2\mathbf{u}_2 = m_1\mathbf{v}_1 + m_2\mathbf{v}_2$

  where, m_1 and m_2 = masses of the body which undergo collision,

  $\mathbf{u}_1$ = initial velocity of the body of mass m_1,

  $\mathbf{u}_2$ = initial velocity of the body of mass m_2,

  $\mathbf{v}_1$ = final velocity of the body of mass m_1

  and $\mathbf{v}_2$ = final velocity of the body of mass m_2.
- But kinetic energy of the colliding body and system is conserved in elastic collision only.
- **Coefficient of Restitution (*e*)** It is the ratio of relative velocity of separation after collision to the relative velocity of approach before collision. It is expressed as

  $$e = \frac{|\mathbf{v}_2 - \mathbf{v}_1|}{|\mathbf{u}_1 - \mathbf{u}_2|}, \text{ where } 0 \le e \le 1.$$
- For elastic collision, $e = 1$ and for inelastic collision, $0 < e < 1$.

- For bodies with masses m_1 and m_2 respectively, following are the important relations for head-on collision.

When collision is elastic,

Final velocities for m_1, i.e.

$$v_1 = \frac{(m_1 - m_2)}{m_1 + m_2} u_1 + \frac{2m_2 u_2}{m_1 + m_2}$$

and for m_2, $v_2 = \frac{2m_1 u_1}{m_1 + m_2} + \frac{(m_2 - m_1)}{m_1 + m_2}$

(*ii*) When collision is inelastic

(a) Final velocities for m_1,

$$v_1 = \left(\frac{m_1 - em_2}{m_1 + m_2}\right) u_1 + \left(\frac{(1+e)m_2}{m_1 + m_2}\right) u_2$$

and for m_2, $v_2 = \left(\frac{(1+e)m_1}{m_1 + m_2}\right) u_1 + \left(\frac{m_2 - em_1}{m_1 + m_2}\right) u_2$

(b) Loss in kinetic energy,

$$\Delta K_{\text{loss}} = \frac{1}{2} \frac{m_1 m_2}{(m_1 + m_2)} (u_1 - u_2)^2 (1 - e^2)$$

- If after collision, approaching bodies move with a common velocity, i.e. $e = 0$ (get stuck with one another), then collision is said to be **perfectly inelastic.**
- For **perfectly elastic oblique collision,**

Along X-axis, $m_1 u_1 + m_2 u_2 = m_1 v_1 \cos\theta + m_2 v_2 \cos\phi$

Along Y-axis, $0 = m_1 v_1 \sin\theta - m_2 v_2 \sin\phi$

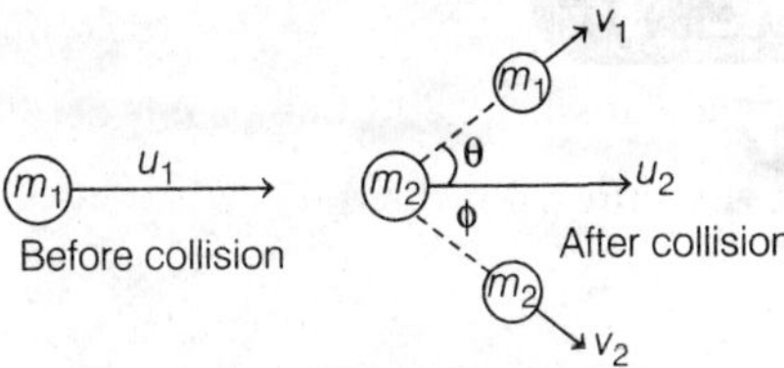

- If two bodies of equal masses undergo perfectly elastic oblique collision then scattering angle $\theta + \phi = \frac{\pi}{2}$ and $u_1^2 = v_1^2 + v_2^2$.

Rebounding of a Ball on Collision with Floor

(*i*) Speed of the ball after n th rebound,

$$v_n = e^n v_0 = e^n \sqrt{2gh}$$

(*ii*) Height covered by the ball after nth rebound,

$$h_n = e^{2n} h$$

(*iii*) Total distance covered s by the ball before it stops bouncing, $s = h\left(\frac{1+e^2}{1-e^2}\right)$

where, h = height of the ball dropped from ground

and e = coefficient of restitution.

Topical Practice Questions

All the exam questions of this chapter have been divided into 5 topics as listed below

Topic 1
Work

2019

1 A force $F = 20 + 10y$ acts on a particle in y-direction, where F is in newton and y is in metre. Work done by this force to move the particle from $y = 0$ to $y = 1$ m is **[NEET]**

(a) 5 J (b) 25 J (c) 20 J (d) 30 J

2018

2 When a rubber band is stretched by a distance x, it exerts a restoring force of magnitude $F = ax + bx^2$, where a and b are constants. The work done in stretching the unstretched rubber band by L is **[JEE Main]**

(a) $aL^2 + bL^3$ (b) $\frac{1}{2}(aL^2 + bL^3)$

(c) $\frac{aL^2}{2} + \frac{bL^3}{3}$ (d) $\frac{1}{2}\left(\frac{aL^2}{2} + \frac{bL^3}{3}\right)$

3 If a machine perform 4000 J output work and 1000 J is inside loss due to friction, then find the efficiency. **[JIPMER]**

(a) 80% (b) 30%

(c) 25% (d) 60%

2017

4 A spring of force constant k is cut into lengths of ratio 1 : 2 : 3. They are connected in series and the new force constant is k'. If they are connected in parallel and force constant is k'', then $k' : k''$ is **[NEET]**

(a) 1 : 6 (b) 1 : 9

(c) 1 : 11 (d) 1 : 14

5 A particle acted upon by constant forces $4\hat{\mathbf{i}} + \hat{\mathbf{j}} - 3\hat{\mathbf{k}}$ and $3\hat{\mathbf{i}} + \hat{\mathbf{j}} - \hat{\mathbf{k}}$ is displaced from the point $\hat{\mathbf{i}} + 2\hat{\mathbf{j}} + 3\hat{\mathbf{k}}$ to the point $5\hat{\mathbf{i}} + 4\hat{\mathbf{j}} + \hat{\mathbf{k}}$. The total work done by the forces in SI unit is **[Kerala CEE]**

(a) 20 (b) 40 (c) 50 (d) 30

(e) 35

6 A force $\mathbf{F} = -k(y\hat{\mathbf{i}} + x\hat{\mathbf{j}})$ where k is a positive constant, acts on a particle moving in the x-y plane. Starting from the origin, the particle is taken along the positive X-axis to the point $(a, 0)$ and then parallel to the Y-axis to the point (a, a). The total work done by the force on the particle is **[AIIMS]**

(a) $-2ka^2$ (b) $2ka^2$

(c) $-ka^2$ (d) ka^2

7 A spring stores 1 J of energy for a compression of 1 mm. The additional work to be done to compress it further by 1 mm is **[Kerala CEE]**

(a) 1 J (b) 2 J

(c) 3 J (d) 4 J

(e) 0.5 J

8 **Assertion** A spring of force constant k is cut into two pieces having lengths in the ratio 1 : 2. The force constant of series combination of the two parts is $3k/2$.

Reason The spring connected in series are represented by $k = k_1 + k_2$ **[AIIMS]**

(a) Both Assertion and Reason are correct and Reason is the correct explanation of Assertion.

(b) Both Assertion and Reason are correct but Reason is not the correct explanation of Assertion.

(c) Assertion is correct but Reason is incorrect.

(d) Both Assertion and Reason are incorrect.

2015

9 Force of 50 N acting on a body at an angle θ with horizontal. If 150 J work is done by displacing it 3 m, then θ is **[OJEE]**

(a) 60° (b) 30°

(c) 0° (d) 45°

2014

10 A string of length L and force constant k is stretched to obtain extension l. It is further stretched to obtain extension l_1. The work done in second stretching is **[MHT CET]**

(a) $\frac{1}{2}kl_1(2l + l_1)$ (b) $\frac{1}{2}kl_1^2$

(c) $\frac{1}{2}k(l^2 + l_1^2)$ (d) $\frac{1}{2}k(l_1^2 - l^2)$

2013

11 A uniform force of $(3\hat{\mathbf{i}} + \hat{\mathbf{j}})$ N acts on a particle of mass 2 kg. Hence, the particle is displaced from position $(2\hat{\mathbf{i}} + \hat{\mathbf{k}})$ m to position $(4\hat{\mathbf{i}} + 3\hat{\mathbf{j}} - \hat{\mathbf{k}})$ m. The work done by the force on the particle is **[NEET]**

(a) 9 J (b) 6 J

(c) 13 J (d) 15 J

12 How much work must be done by a force on 50 kg body in order to accelerate it from rest to 20 ms^{-1} in 10 s? **[UP CPMT]**

(a) 10^{-3} J (b) 10^4 J

(c) 2×10^3 J (d) 4×10^4 J

13 The vessels A and B of equal volume and weight are immersed in water to depth h. The vessel A has an opening at the bottom through which water can enter. If the work done in immersing A and B are W_A and W_B respectively, then **[WB JEE]**

(a) $W_A = W_B$ (b) $W_A < W_B$
(c) $W_A > W_B$ (d) None of these

14 A particle is displaced from a position $(2\hat{\mathbf{i}} - \hat{\mathbf{j}} + \hat{\mathbf{k}})$ to another position $(3\hat{\mathbf{i}} + 2\hat{\mathbf{j}} - 2\hat{\mathbf{k}})$ under the action of the force $(2\hat{\mathbf{i}} + \hat{\mathbf{j}} - \hat{\mathbf{k}})$. The work done by the force in an arbitrary unit is **[Manipal]**

(a) 8 (b) 10
(c) 12 (d) 16

2011

15 Force F on a particle moving in a straight line varies with distance d as shown in the figure. The work done on the particle during its displacement of 12 m is **[CBSE AIPMT]**

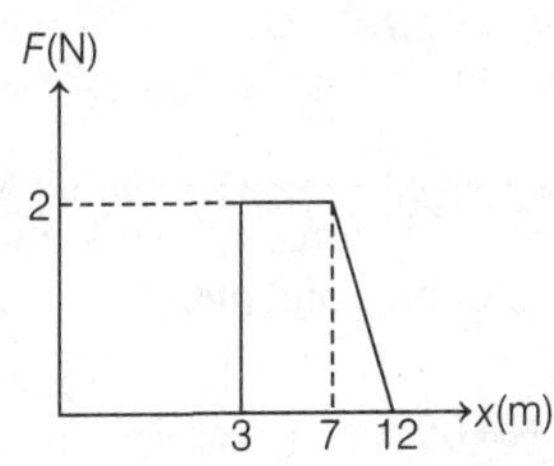

(a) 21 J (b) 26 J
(c) 13 J (d) 18 J

16 A person is holding a bucket by applying a force of 10 N. He moves a horizontal distance of 5m and then climbs up a vertical distance of 10m. Find the total work done by him. **[Manipal]**

(a) 50 J (b) 150 J (c) 100 J (d) 200 J

17 A moon of mass m orbits a planet of mass M in a perfectly circular orbit of radius R, with a force of gravitational attraction between the two bodies of F_g. How much work is done on the moon by the planet during a single orbit of the moon? **[CBSE AIPMT]**

(a) 0 (b) $F_g R$ (c) $F_g 2\pi R$ (d) $F_g \pi R^2$

18 Applied force *versus* position graph of an object is given below. Find the work done by the forces on the object. **[AIIMS]**

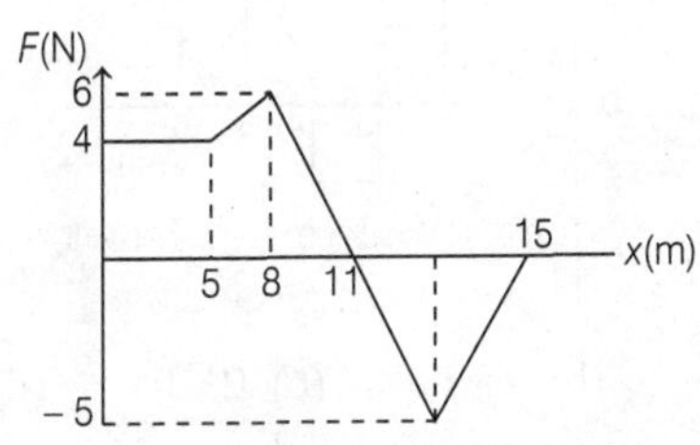

(a) 30 J (b) 34 J (c) 33 J (d) 20 J

19 A gardener pushes a lawn roller through a distance 20 m. If he applies a force of 20 kg-wt in a direction inclined at 60° to the ground, the work done by him is **[J&K CET]**

(a) 1960 J (b) 196 J
(c) 1.96 J (d) 196 kJ

20 A force $\mathbf{F} = -(y\hat{\mathbf{i}} + x\hat{\mathbf{j}})$ acts on a particle moving in the X-Y plane. Starting from the origin, the particle is taken along the positive X-axis to the point $(2a, 0)$ and then parallel to the Y-axis to the point $(2a, 2a)$. The total work done on the particle is **[AMU]**

(a) $-4a^2$ (b) $-2a^2$ (c) $4a^2$ (d) $2a^2$

21 The work done by an applied variable force, $F = x + x^3$ from $x = 0$ m to $x = 2$ m, where x is displacement, is **[DUMET]**

(a) 6 J (b) 8 J (c) 10 J (d) 12 J

2010

22 A plate of mass m, length b and breadth a is initially lying on a horizontal floor with length parallel to the floor and breadth perpendicular to the floor. The work done to rotate and lie on its breadth is **[CBSE AIPMT]**

(a) $mg\left[\frac{b}{2}\right]$ (b) $mg\left[a + \frac{b}{2}\right]$

(c) $mg\left[\frac{b-a}{2}\right]$ (d) $mg\left[\frac{b+a}{2}\right]$

23 A force F acting on an object varies with distance x as shown here. The force is in newton and x is in metre. The work done by the force in moving the object from $x = 0$ m to $x = 6$ m is **[BVP]**

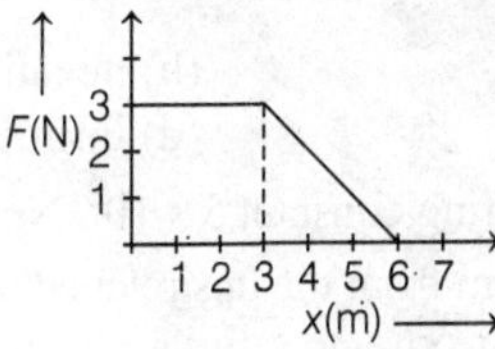

(a) 4.5 J (b) 13.5 J (c) 9 J (d) 18 J

2009

24 If W_1, W_2 and W_3 are the work done in moving a particle from A and B along three different paths 1, 2 and 3 respectively (as shown) in the gravitational field of a point mass M, the relation between W_1, W_2 and W_3 is **[AMU]**

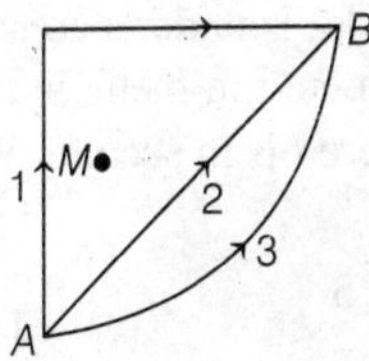

(a) $W_1 > W_2 > W_3$ (b) $W_1 = W_2 = W_3$
(c) $W_1 < W_2 < W_3$ (d) $W_2 > W_1 > W_3$

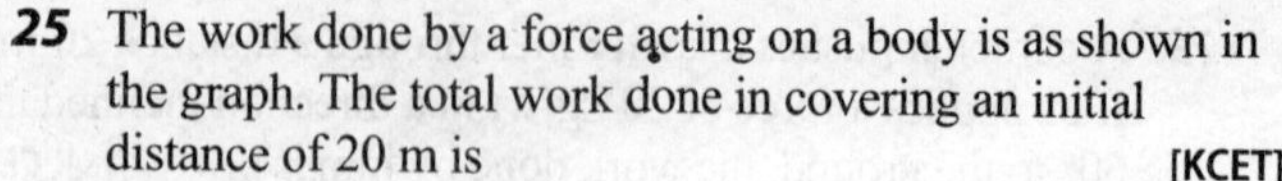

25 The work done by a force acting on a body is as shown in the graph. The total work done in covering an initial distance of 20 m is **[KCET]**

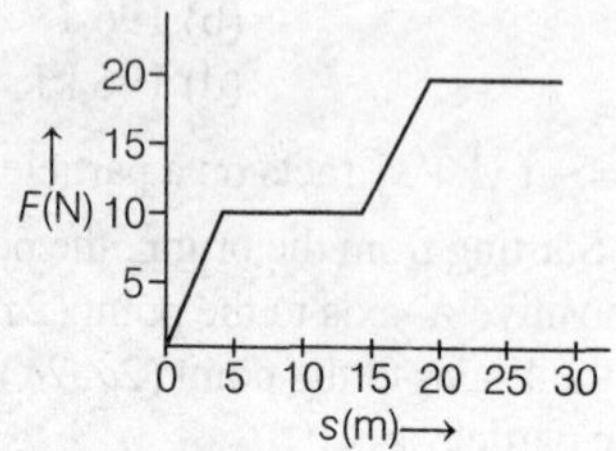

(a) 225 J (b) 200 J (c) 400 J (d) 175 J

2008

26 A particle of mass 100 g is thrown vertically upwards with a speed of 5 ms^{-1}. The work done by the force of gravity during the time, the particle goes up is **[UP CPMT]**

(a) – 0.5 J (b) – 1.25 J (c) 1.25 J (d) 0.5 J

27 When the bob of a simple pendulum swings, the work done by tension in the string is **[BHU]**

(a) > 0 (b) < 0 (c) zero (d) maximum

28 A block of mass $m = 2$ kg is pulled by a force $F = 40$ N upwards through a height $h = 2$ m. Find the work done on the block by the applied force F and its weight mg. (Take, $g = 10\text{ ms}^{-2}$) **[EAMCET]**

(a) 80 J, – 45 J (b) 40 J, 35 J
(c) zero, 0.25 J (d) 80 J, – 40 J

29 The work done by a particle moving with a velocity of 0.7 c (where, c is the velocity of light) in empty space free of electromagnetic field and far away from all matter is **[Manipal]**

(a) positive (b) negative
(c) zero (d) infinite

30 A spring of spring constant $5 \times 10^3\ \text{Nm}^{-1}$ is stretched initially by 5 cm from the unstretched position. Then, the work required to stretch it further by another 5 cm is **[MP PMT]**

(a) 12.50 N-m (b) 18.75 N-m
(c) 25.00 N-m (d) 6.25 N-m

31 300 J of work is done in sliding a 2 kg block up an inclined plane of height 10 m (taking, $g = 10\text{ ms}^{-2}$). Work done against friction is **[RPMT]**

(a) 200 J (b) 100 J (c) zero (d) 1000 J

32 A body of mass 3 kg is under a constant force which causes a displacement s in metre in it, given by the relation $s = (1/3)t^2$, where t is in second. Work done by the force in 2 s is **[Haryana PMT]**

(a) $\frac{5}{19}$ J (b) $\frac{3}{8}$ J (c) $\frac{8}{3}$ J (d) $\frac{19}{5}$ J

33 When a spring is stretched by a distance x, it exerts a force, given by $F = (-5x - 16x^3)$ N. The work done, when the spring is stretched from 0.1 m to 0.2 m is **[BCECE]**

(a) 8.7×10^{-2} J (b) 12.2×10^{-2} J
(c) 8.7×10^{-1} J (d) 12.2×10^{-1} J

2007

34 A vertical spring with force constant k is fixed on a table. A ball of mass m at a height h above the free upper end of the spring falls vertically on the spring, so that the spring is compressed by a distance d. The net work done in the process is **[CBSE AIPMT]**

(a) $mg(h+d) + \frac{1}{2}kd^2$

(b) $mg(h+d) - \frac{1}{2}kd^2$

(c) $mg(h-d) - \frac{1}{2}kd^2$

(d) $mg(h-d) + \frac{1}{2}kd^2$

35 A body moves a distance of 10 m along a straight line under an action of 5 N force. If, work done is 25 J, then angle between the force and direction of motion of the body will be **[BCECE]**

(a) 75° (b) 60° (c) 45° (d) 30°

2006

36 The work done by a force, $\mathbf{F} = (-6x^3)\hat{\mathbf{i}}$ N, in displacing a particle from $x = 4$ m to $x = -2$ m is **[Kerala CEE]**

(a) 360 J (b) 240 J (c) – 240 J (d) – 360 J
(e) 408 J

2005

37 A ball of mass m moves with speed v and strikes a wall having infinite mass and it returns with same speed, then the work done by the ball on the wall is **[Punjab PMET]**

(a) zero (b) mv J (c) m/v J (d) v/m J

38 The relationship between the force F and position x of a body is as shown in figure. The work done in displacing the body from $x = 1$ m to $x = 5$ m will be **[KCET]**

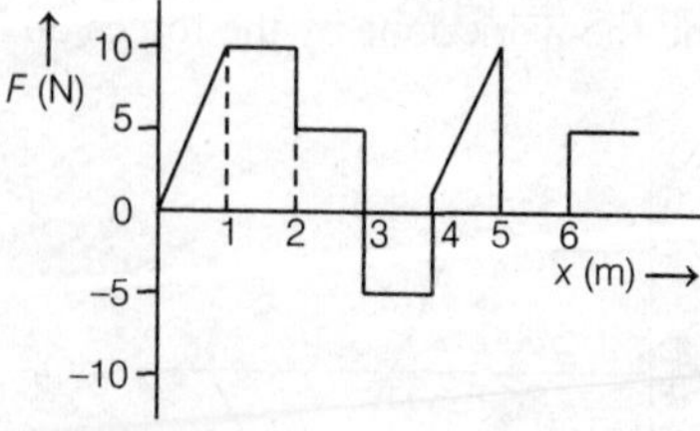

(a) 30 J (b) 15 J (c) 25 J (d) 20 J

Answers

1 (b)	2 (c)	3 (a)	4 (c)	5 (b)	6 (c)	7 (c)	8 (d)	9 (c)	10 (d)
11 (a)	12 (b)	13 (b)	14 (a)	15 (c)	16 (c)	17 (a)	18 (b)	19 (a)	20 (a)
21 (a)	22 (c)	23 (b)	24 (b)	25 (b)	26 (b)	27 (c)	28 (d)	29 (c)	30 (b)
31 (b)	32 (c)	33 (a)	34 (b)	35 (b)	36 (d)	37 (a)	38 (b)		

Explanations

1 *(b)* Work done by a force F, which is variable in nature in moving a particle from y_1 to y_2 is given by

$$W = \int_{y_1}^{y_2} F \cdot dy \quad \ldots \text{(i)}$$

Given, force, $F = 20 + 10y$, $y_1 = 0$ and $y_2 = 1\,\text{m}$

Substituting the given values in Eq. (i), we get

$$W = \int_0^1 (20 + 10y)dy = \left[20y + \frac{10y^2}{2}\right]_0^1$$

$$= 20(1-0) + 5(1-0)^2 = 25\,\text{J}$$

$\therefore$ Work done will be 25 J.

2 *(c)* We know that change in potential energy of a system corresponding to a conservative internal force as,

$$U_f - U_i = -W = -\int_i^f \text{F} \cdot dr$$

Given that, $F = ax + bx^2$

We know that work done in stretching the rubber band by L is given by

$$|dW| = |Fdx|$$

$$\Rightarrow \quad |W| = \int_0^L (ax + bx^2)\,dx$$

$$= \left[\frac{ax^2}{2}\right]_0^L + \left[\frac{bx^3}{3}\right]_0^L$$

$$= \left[\frac{aL^2}{2} - \frac{a \times (0)^2}{2}\right] + \left[\frac{b \times L^3}{3} - \frac{b \times (0)^3}{3}\right]$$

Hence, $|W| = \dfrac{aL^2}{2} + \dfrac{bL^3}{3}$

3 *(a)* $\because$ Efficiency $= \dfrac{W_o}{W_i} \times 100$

Given, $W_o = 4000\,\text{J}$

and $W_i = 4000 + 1000 = 5000\text{J}$

$\because$ Efficiency $(\eta) = \dfrac{4000}{5000} \times 100$

$$\eta = 80\%$$

4 *(c)* When the spring is cut into pieces, they will have the new force constant. The spring is divided into 1 : 2 : 3 ratio.

When the pieces are connected in series, the resultant force constant

$$\frac{1}{k'} = \frac{1}{k_1} + \frac{1}{k_2} + \frac{1}{k_3}$$

$$\frac{1}{k'} = \frac{1}{x} + \frac{1}{2x} + \frac{1}{3x} \Rightarrow k' = \frac{6x}{11}$$

In parallel, the net force constant,

$$k'' = x + 2x + 3x = 6x$$

The required ratio $\dfrac{k'}{k''} = \dfrac{6x/11}{6x} = 1:11$

5 *(b)* Work done, $W = F \cdot ds$

$= (F_1 + F_2) \cdot (s_2 - s_1)$

$= \{(4\hat{\mathbf{i}} + \hat{\mathbf{j}} - 3\hat{\mathbf{k}}) + (3\hat{\mathbf{i}} + \hat{\mathbf{j}} - \hat{\mathbf{k}})\}$
$\{(5\hat{\mathbf{i}} + 4\hat{\mathbf{j}} + \hat{\mathbf{k}}) - (\hat{\mathbf{i}} + 2\hat{\mathbf{j}} + 3\hat{\mathbf{k}})\}$

$= (7\hat{\mathbf{i}} + 2\hat{\mathbf{j}} - 4\hat{\mathbf{k}}) \cdot (4\hat{\mathbf{i}} + 2\hat{\mathbf{j}} - 2\hat{\mathbf{k}})$

$= 28 + 4 + 8 = 40\,\text{J}$

6 *(c)* Given, $\mathbf{F} = -k(y\hat{\mathbf{i}} + x\hat{\mathbf{j}})$

As, $W = \int \mathbf{F} \cdot d\mathbf{r}$

So, $W = -k\int (y\hat{\mathbf{i}} + x\hat{\mathbf{j}}) \cdot (dx\hat{\mathbf{i}} + dy\hat{\mathbf{j}})$

$\Rightarrow \quad W = -k\int (ydx + xdy)$

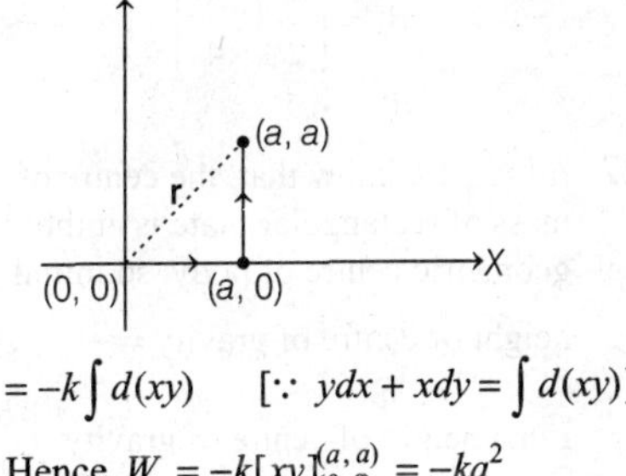

$= -k\int d(xy) \quad [\because ydx + xdy = \int d(xy)]$

Hence, $W = -k[xy]_{(0,0)}^{(a,a)} = -ka^2$

7 *(c)* Given, $W_1 = 1\,\text{J}$

and $x = 1 \times 10^{-3}\,\text{m}$

Work done to compress it 1 mm,

$$W_1 = \frac{1}{2}kx_1^2 \Rightarrow 1 = \frac{1}{2} \times k \times (1 \times 10^{-3})^2$$

$\Rightarrow k = 2 \times 10^6$

Work done to compress it further by 1 mm,

$$W_2 = \frac{1}{2}kx_2^2$$

$$= \frac{1}{2} \times 2 \times 10^6 \times (1 \times 10^{-3} + 1 \times 10^{-3})^2$$

$$W_2 = 4 \times 10^{-6} \times 10^6 = 4\,\text{J}$$

The additional work done

$$= W_2 - W_1 = 4 - 1 = 3\,\text{J}$$

8 *(d)* As we know, $k = \dfrac{F}{l} \Rightarrow k \propto \dfrac{1}{l}$

$$\Rightarrow \quad \frac{k_2}{k_1} = \frac{l_1}{l_2} = \frac{1}{2}$$

$$k_1 = 2k, k_2 = k$$

In series, $\dfrac{1}{k'} = \dfrac{1}{k_1} + \dfrac{1}{k_2} = \dfrac{1}{2k} + \dfrac{1}{k} = \dfrac{3}{2k}$

$$\because \quad k' = \frac{2k}{3}$$

So, both Assertion and Reason are incorrect.

9 *(c)* Given, $F = 50\,\text{N}$, $W = 150\,\text{J}$ and $s = 3\,\text{m}$

Work done, $W = Fs\cos\theta$

$$150 = 50 \times 3 \times \cos\theta$$

$$\cos\theta = \frac{150}{150} = 1 \Rightarrow \theta = 0°$$

10 *(d)* Work done in stretching a string to obtain an extension l,

$$W_1 = \frac{1}{2}kl^2$$

Similarly, work done in stretching a string to obtain an extension l_1 is,

$$W_2 = \frac{1}{2}kl_1^2$$

$\therefore$ Work done in second case, W

$$= W_2 - W_1 = \frac{1}{2}k(l_1^2 - l^2)$$

11 *(a)* Given, force, $\mathbf{F} = (3\hat{\mathbf{i}} + \hat{\mathbf{j}})\,\text{N}$,

$\mathbf{r}_1 = (2\hat{\mathbf{i}} + \hat{\mathbf{k}})\,\text{m}$

and $\mathbf{r}_2 = (4\hat{\mathbf{i}} + 3\hat{\mathbf{j}} - \hat{\mathbf{k}})\,\text{m}$

$\therefore$ Displacement, $\mathbf{s} = \mathbf{r}_2 - \mathbf{r}_1$

$= (4\hat{\mathbf{i}} + 3\hat{\mathbf{j}} - \hat{\mathbf{k}}) - (2\hat{\mathbf{i}} + \hat{\mathbf{k}})$

$= (2\hat{\mathbf{i}} + 3\hat{\mathbf{j}} - 2\hat{\mathbf{k}})\,\text{m}$

$\therefore$ Work done, $W = \mathbf{F} \cdot \mathbf{s}$

$= (3\hat{\mathbf{i}} + \hat{\mathbf{j}}) \cdot (2\hat{\mathbf{i}} + 3\hat{\mathbf{j}} - 2\hat{\mathbf{k}})$

$[\because \hat{\mathbf{i}} \cdot \hat{\mathbf{i}} = \hat{\mathbf{j}} \cdot \hat{\mathbf{j}} = \hat{\mathbf{k}} \cdot \hat{\mathbf{k}} = 1]$

$= 3 \times 2 + 3 + 0 = 6 + 3 = 9\,\text{J}$

12 (b) Given, $m = 50\text{ kg}$, $v = 20\text{ ms}^{-1}$

and $t = 10\text{ s}$

As, equation of motion, $v = u + at$

$\Rightarrow \quad 20 = 0 + a \times 10$

$20 = a \times 10 \Rightarrow a = 2\text{ m/s}^2$

Now, distance $s = ut + \frac{1}{2}at^2$

$\Rightarrow s = 0 + \frac{1}{2} \times 2 \times 10 \times 10$ or $s = 100\text{ m}$

Hence, $W = F \cdot s = ma \cdot s$

$= 50 \times 2 \times 100 = 10^4\text{ J}$

13 (b) Because water enters into the vessel A, it becomes heavier. Gravity helps it to sink. External work required for immersing A is obviously less than that for immersing B.

Hence, $W_A < W_B$.

14 (a) Work done, $W = \mathbf{F} \cdot \mathbf{r}$

$= (2\hat{\mathbf{i}} + \hat{\mathbf{j}} - \hat{\mathbf{k}}) \cdot [(3\hat{\mathbf{i}} + 2\hat{\mathbf{j}} - 2\hat{\mathbf{k}}) - (2\hat{\mathbf{i}} - \hat{\mathbf{j}} + \hat{\mathbf{k}})]$ (given)

$= (2\hat{\mathbf{i}} + \hat{\mathbf{j}} - \hat{\mathbf{k}}) \cdot (\hat{\mathbf{i}} + 3\hat{\mathbf{j}} - 3\hat{\mathbf{k}})$

$W = 2 + 3 + 3 = 8$ unit

15 (c) As, work done = Area under (F-x) graph

$= 2 \times (7 - 3) + \frac{1}{2} \times 2 \times (12 - 7)$

$= 8 + \frac{1}{2} \times 10 = 8 + 5 = 13\text{ J}$

16 (c) Given $F = 10\text{ N}$, $s = 5\text{m}$ and $\theta = 90°$(for horizontal motion)

$\therefore$ Work done, $W_1 = Fs\cos\theta$

$= 10 \times 5 \times \cos 90° = 0$

For vertical, motion, $\theta = 0°$, $s = 10\text{ m}$

$\therefore$ Work done, $W_2 = Fs\cos\theta$

$= 10 \times 10 \times \cos 0° = 100\text{ J}$

$\therefore$ Total work done,

$W = W_1 + W_2 = (0 + 100)\text{ J}$

$= 100\text{ J}$

17 (a) For an orbiting moon, the gravitational force is perpendicular to the displacement, hence work done by gravitational force is zero.

i.e. $\quad W = F_g s\cos 90° = 0$

18 (b) As, work done

= area under f-x graph.

So, work done between 0 to 5 m,

$W_1 = (4)(5) = 20\text{ J}$

Work done between 5 to 8 m,

$$W_2 = \frac{(6+4)}{2} \times 3 = 15\text{ J}$$

Work done between 8 to 11 m,

$$W_3 = \frac{1}{2}(6)(3) = 9\text{ J}$$

Work done between 11 to 15 m,

$$W_4 = \frac{1}{2}(-5)(4) = 10\text{ J}$$

$\therefore W_{\text{net}} = W_1 + W_2 + W_3 + W_4 = 34\text{ J}$

19 (a) Given, $F = 20\text{ kg-wt} = 20 \times 9.8\text{ N}$,

$\theta = 60°$ and $s = 20\text{ m}$

$\therefore$ Work done, $W = Fs\cos\theta$

$= 20 \times 9.8 \times 20 \times \cos 60° = 1960\text{ J}$

20 (a) We know that, work done $= \mathbf{F} \cdot \mathbf{s}$

Work done is independent of path followed,

$\mathbf{F} = [y\hat{\mathbf{i}} + x\hat{\mathbf{j}}]$

$\mathbf{s} = [2a, 2a] - [0, 0]$

$= (2a - 0), (2a - 0) = (2a, 2a)$

$\mathbf{F} = -[y\hat{\mathbf{i}} - x\hat{\mathbf{j}}] = 2a\hat{\mathbf{i}} + 2a\hat{\mathbf{j}}$

$\mathbf{F} \cdot \mathbf{s} = -[2a\hat{\mathbf{i}} + 2a\hat{\mathbf{j}}] \cdot [2a\hat{\mathbf{i}} + 2a\hat{\mathbf{j}}]$

$= -\sqrt{(4a^2)^2 + (4a^2)^2} = -4a^2$

21 (a) Given, $F = x + x^3$

and $\quad x = 0$ to $x = 2\text{ m}$

We know that, work done, $W = \int F dx$

$$\Rightarrow \quad W = \int_0^2 (x + x^3)dx$$

$$\Rightarrow \quad W = \left[\frac{x^2}{2} + \frac{x^4}{4}\right]_0^2$$

$$W = \left[\frac{4}{2} + \frac{16}{4}\right]$$

$W = 6\text{ J}$

22 (c) As, we know that, the centre of mass of rectangular plate is at the geometric centre of body, so initial height of centre of gravity $= \frac{a}{2}$

Final height of centre of gravity $= \frac{b}{2}$

$$\text{Work done} = mg\left[\frac{b}{2} - \frac{a}{2}\right] = mg\left[\frac{b-a}{2}\right]$$

$(\because W = mgh)$

23 (b) Work done in moving the object when displaced from $x = 0$ to $x = 6$ m is

W = area of square + area of triangle

$W = 3 \times 3 + \frac{1}{2} \times 3 \times 3$ (from graph)

$= 9 + 4.5 = 13.5\text{ J}$

24 (b) Gravitational force is conservative force work done by or against the force in moving a body depends only on the initial and final positions of the body and not on the nature of path followed by it.

So, $\quad W_1 = W_2 = W_3$

25 (b) Work done, W = Area $ABCEFDA$

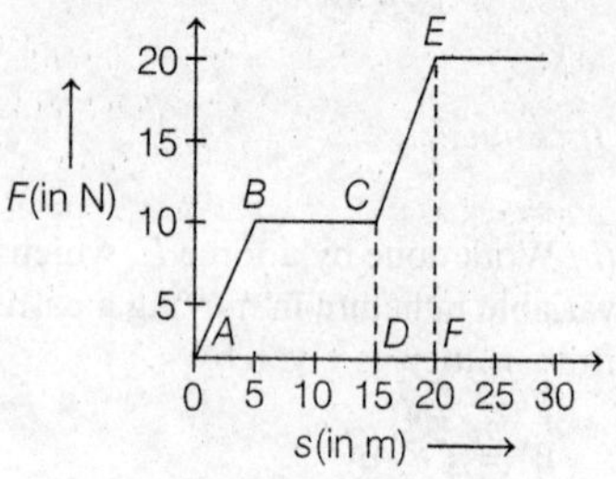

= Area $ABCD$ + Area $CEFD$

$= \frac{1}{2} \times (15 + 10) \times 10 + \frac{1}{2} \times (10 + 20) \times 5$

$= 125 + 75 = 200\text{ J}$

26 (b) The height (h) traversed by a particle while going up is

$$h = \frac{u^2}{2g} = \frac{25}{2 \times 9.8}$$

$v = 0$

$u = 5\text{ ms}^{-1}$

$100\text{ g} = 0.1\text{ kg}$

Work done by the gravity force,

$W = mgh$

$$= 0.1 \times g \times \frac{25}{2 \times 9.8}\cos 180°$$

(angle between the force and displacement is 180°)

$\therefore \; W = -0.1 \times \frac{25}{2} = -1.25\text{ J}$

27 (c) As, tension in the string is along the radius of circular path and the displacement of the bob is along the circumference of the path.

Hence, again **F** and **s** are at 90° and so $W = 0$.

28 (d) Given, $m = 2\text{ kg}$, $F = 40\text{ N}$ and $h = 2\text{ m}$

As $\quad$ weight $= mg = 2 \times 10 = 20\text{ N}$

Work done by the applied force,

$W_F = Fh\cos 0°$

As the angle between force and displacement is 0°, therefore work done by applied force,

$W_F = 40 \times 2 \times 1 = 80\text{ J}$

Similarly, work done by its weight,

$W_{mg} = mg \times h \times \cos 180°$

$= 20 \times 2 \times -1 = -40\text{ J}$

29 *(c)* Acceleration of the particle,

$$a = \frac{dv}{dt} = \frac{d}{dt}(0.7\ c) = 0\ (\because c = \text{constant})$$

Force on the particle, $F = ma = 0$

Thus, work done by a particle will be zero.

30 *(b)* Given, $k = 5 \times 10^3\ \text{Nm}^{-1}$

and $x_1 = x_2 = 5\ \text{cm} = 5 \times 10^{-2}\ \text{m}$

Work done, $W_1 = \frac{1}{2}kx_1^2$

$$= \frac{1}{2} \times 5 \times 10^3 \times (5 \times 10^{-2})^2 = 6.25\ \text{J}$$

Work done in stretching the spring by 10 cm, i.e. 5 cm + 5 cm

$$W_2 = \frac{1}{2}k(x_1 + x_2)^2$$

$$= \frac{1}{2} \times 5 \times 10^3 (5 \times 10^{-2} + 5 \times 10^{-2})^2$$

$$= 25\ \text{J}$$

Net work done, W_{net}

$$= W_2 - W_1 = 25 - 6.25$$

$$= 18.75\ \text{J} = 18.75\ \text{N-m}$$

31 *(b)* Net work done in sliding a body up to a height h on an inclined plane = Work done against the gravitational force + Work done against the frictional force

$\Rightarrow \quad W = W_g + W_f \quad \ldots\text{(i)}$

But $\quad W = 300\ \text{J}$

Given, $m = 2$ kg and $h = 10$ m

$$W_g = mgh = 2 \times 10 \times 10 = 200\ \text{J}$$

Putting these values in Eq. (i), we get

$$300 = 200 + W_f$$

$\Rightarrow \quad W_f = 300 - 200 = 100\ \text{J}$

32 *(c)* As, work done

= force × displacement

i.e. $\quad W = F \times s \quad \ldots\text{(i)}$

But from Newton's second law, we have

force = mass × acceleration

i.e. $\quad F = ma \quad \ldots\text{(ii)}$

Hence, from Eqs. (i) and (ii), we get

$$W = mas = m\left(\frac{d^2s}{dt^2}\right)s \ \ldots\text{(iii)} \left(\because a = \frac{d^2s}{dt^2}\right)$$

Now, we have $\quad s = \frac{1}{3}t^2$

$$\therefore \quad \frac{d^2s}{dt^2} = \frac{d}{dt}\left[\frac{d}{dt}\left(\frac{1}{3}t^2\right)\right]$$

$$= \frac{d}{dt} \times \left(\frac{2}{3}t\right) = \frac{2}{3}$$

Hence, Eq. (iii) becomes

$$W = \frac{2}{3}ms = \frac{2}{3}m \times \frac{1}{3}t^2 = \frac{2}{9}mt^2$$

Given, $m = 3$ kg, $t = 2$ s

$$\therefore \quad W = \frac{2}{9} \times 3 \times (2)^2 = \frac{8}{3}\ \text{J}$$

33 *(a)* Given, $F = (-5x - 16x^3)$ N

$\Rightarrow \quad F = -(5 + 16x^2)x \quad \ldots\text{(i)}$

As, $\quad F_s = -kx \quad \ldots\text{(ii)}$

Now from Eqs. (i) and (ii), we get

$$k = 5 + 16x^2$$

Therefore, work done in stretching the spring from position x_1 to x_2 is

$$W = \frac{1}{2}k_2x_2^2 - \frac{1}{2}k_1x_1^2$$

We have $x_1 = 0.1$ m and $x_2 = 0.2$ m.

$$\therefore \quad W = \frac{1}{2}[5 + 16(0.2)^2](0.2)^2$$

$$- \frac{1}{2}[5 + 16(0.1)^2](0.1)^2$$

$$= 2.82 \times 4 \times 10^{-2} - 2.58 \times 10^{-2}$$

$$= 8.7 \times 10^{-2}\ \text{J}$$

34 *(b)* Situation is shown in the figure. When mass m falls vertically on the spring, then the spring is compressed by a distance d.

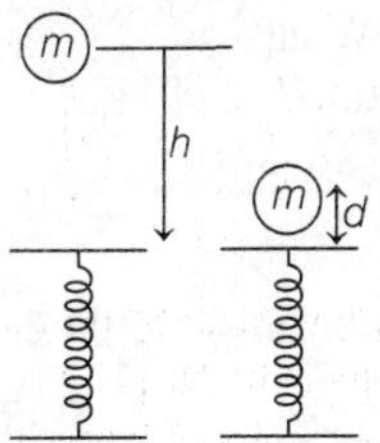

Hence, net work done (W_{net}) in the process is

W = Potential energy stored in the spring + Loss of potential energy of mass $= mg(h + d) - \frac{1}{2}kd^2$

35 *(b)* Work is measured by the product of the applied force and the displacement of the body in the direction of the force.

Work = Force × Displacement

$$W = (F \cos\theta) \times \Delta s$$

Given, $W = 25$ J,

$F = 5$ N

and $\quad \Delta s = 10$ m

$$\therefore \quad \cos\theta = \frac{W}{F \cdot \Delta s}$$

$$= \frac{25}{5 \times 10} = \frac{1}{2}$$

$$\Rightarrow \quad \theta = \cos^{-1}\left(\frac{1}{2}\right) = 60°$$

Hence, angle between the force and the direction of the body is 60°.

36 *(d)* As, work done $= \int F \cdot dx$

Given, $\quad \mathbf{F} = -(6x^3)\hat{\mathbf{i}}$ N

$$\therefore \quad W = -\int_{-2}^{4} 6x^3 dx,$$

$$\Rightarrow \quad W = -6\left[\frac{x^4}{4}\right]_{-2}^{4}$$

$$\Rightarrow \quad W = -\frac{6}{4}[(4)^4 - (-2)^4]$$

$$= -\frac{6}{4}[256 - 16]$$

$$= -1.5 \times 240$$

Hence, $W = -360$ J

37 *(a)* As, work done = force × displacement

As, there is no displacement produced in the wall, so work done by the ball on the wall is zero.

Alternative Method As, there is no change in kinetic energy of the ball, so according to work-energy theorem, work done should be zero.

38 *(b)* As, work done = area enclosed by F-x graph from x = im to $x = 5m$

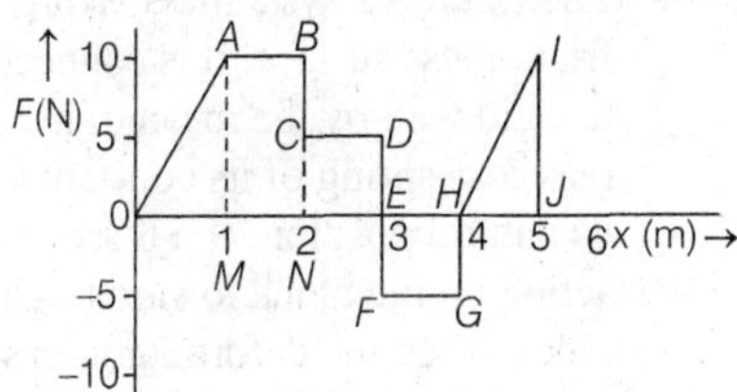

= Area of $ABNM$ + area of $CDEN$ − area of $EFGH$ + area of HIJ

$$= 1 \times 10 + 1 \times 5 - 1 \times 5 + \frac{1}{2} \times 1 \times 10$$

$$= 10 + 5 - 5 + 5 = 15\ \text{J}$$

Topic 2

Energy

2019

1 Initially spring in its natural length, now a block at mass 0.25 kg is released, then find out the value of maximum force by system on the floor. **[AIIMS]**

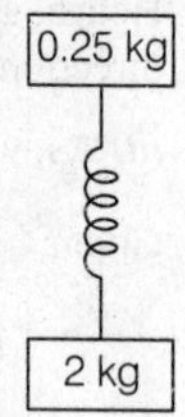

(a) 15 N (b) 20 N (c) 25 N (d) 30 N

2 When a block of mass M is suspended by a long wire of length L, the length of the wire becomes $(L+l)$. The elastic potential energy stored in the extended wire is **[NEET]**

(a) MgL (b) $\frac{1}{2}Mgl$ (c) $\frac{1}{2}MgL$ (d) Mgl

3 The rate of decrease of kinetic energy is $9.6\ \text{Js}^{-1}$. Find the magnitude of force acting on particle when its speed is $3\ \text{ms}^{-1}$. **[JIPMER]**

(a) 3.2 N (b) 4.8 N (c) 2.4 N (d) 5.6 N

2018

4 Kinetic energy of a particle is increased by 4 times. What will be the relation between initial and final momentum? **[JIPMER]**

(a) $p_2 = 2p_1$ (b) $p_2 = p_1/2$
(c) $p_2 = p_1$ (d) $p_2 = 4p_1$

2017

5 The figure shows a mass m on a frictionless surface. It is connected to rigid wall by the mean of a massless spring of its constant k. Initially, the spring is at its natural position. If a force of constant magnitude starts acting on the block towards right, then the speed of the block when the deformation in spring is x, will be **[AIIMS]**

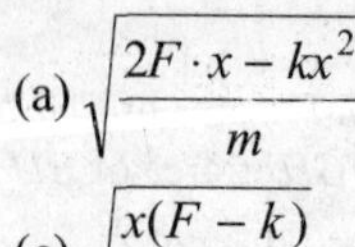

(a) $\sqrt{\frac{2F\cdot x - kx^2}{m}}$ (b) $\sqrt{\frac{F\cdot x - kx^2}{m}}$

(c) $\sqrt{\frac{x(F-k)}{m}}$ (d) $\sqrt{\frac{F\cdot x - kx^2}{2m}}$

6 A skier starts from rest at point A and slides down the hill without turning or breaking. The friction coefficient is μ. When he stops at point B, his horizontal displacement is s. What is the height difference between points A and B? (The velocity of the skier is small, so that the additional pressure on the snow due to the curvature can be neglected. Neglect also the friction of air and the dependence of μ on the velocity of the skier.) **[JIPMER]**

(a) $h = \mu s$ (b) $h = \frac{\mu}{s}$
(c) $h = 2\mu s$ (d) $h = \mu s^2$

7 A person of weight 70 kg wants to loose 7 kg by going up and down 12m high stairs. Assume he burns twice as much fat while going up than going down. If 1 kg of fat is burnt on expending 9000 k-cal. How many times must he go up and down to reduce his 7 kg weight?(Take, $g = 10\ \text{ms}^{-2}$) **[AIIMS]**

(a) 18×10^3 times (b) 24×10^3 times
(c) 30×10^3 times (d) 21×10^3 times

2015

8 A load of mass m falls from a height h on the scale pan hung from a spring as shown in figure. If the spring constant is k and mass of the scale pan is zero and the mass m does not bounce relative to the pan, then the amplitude of vibration is **[AIIMS]**

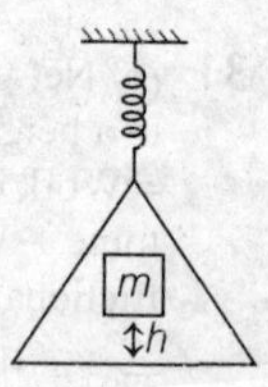

(a) mg (b) $mg/k\sqrt{1+2hk/mg}$

(c) $\frac{mg}{k}+\frac{mg}{k}\sqrt{\frac{1+2hk}{mg}}$ (d) None of these

2013

9 Two bodies of masses m and $2m$ have equal kinetic energies. The ratio of their linear momenta is **[KCET]**

(a) 1 (b) $\frac{1}{2}$ (c) $\frac{1}{\sqrt{2}}$ (d) 2

10 **Assertion** According to the law of conservation of mechanical energy, change in potential energy is equal and opposite to the change in kinetic energy.

Reason Mechanical energy is not conserved. **[AIIMS]**

(a) Both Assertion and Reason are correct and Reason is the correct explanation of Assertion.
(b) Both Assertion and Reason are correct but Reason is not the correct explanation of Assertion.
(c) Assertion is correct but Reason is incorrect
(d) Both Assertion and Reason are incorrect.
(e) Assertion is incorrect but Reason is correct.

2012

11 The graph of kinetic energy (K) of a body *versus* velocity (v) is represented as **[UP CPMT]**

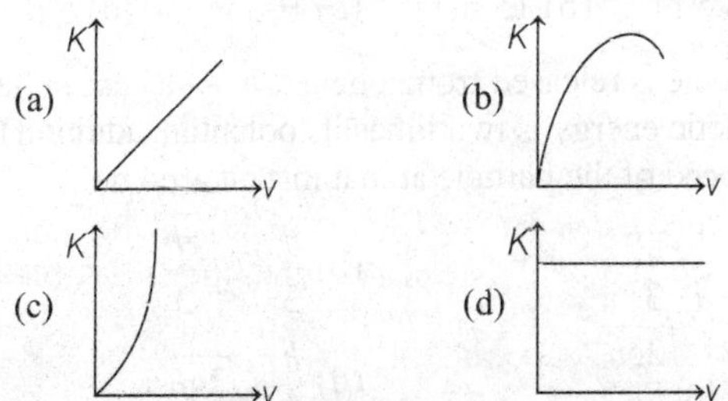

12 A particle is projected from the ground with a kinetic energy E at an angle of 60° with the horizontal. Its kinetic energy at the highest point of its motion will be **[WB JEE]**

(a) $\frac{E}{\sqrt{2}}$ (b) $\frac{E}{2}$ (c) $\frac{E}{4}$ (d) $\frac{E}{8}$

2011

13 Two bodies of masses 4 kg and 5 kg are moving with equal momentum. Then, the ratio of their respective kinetic energies is **[Kerala CEE]**

(a) 4 : 5 (b) 2 : 1 (c) 1 : 3 (d) 5 : 4
(e) 1 : 2

14 A body of mass 5 kg is thrown vertically up with a kinetic energy of 490 J. The height at which the kinetic energy of the body becomes half of the original value is **[KCET]**
(acceleration due to gravity = 9.8 ms^{-2})

(a) 5 m (b) 2.5 m
(c) 10 m (d) 12.5 m

2010

15 A particle which is constrained to move along the x-axis, is subjected to a force in the same direction which varies with the distance x of the particle from the origin is $F(x) = -kx + ax^3$. Here, k and a are positive constants. For $x \geq 0$, the functional from of the potential energy $U(x)$ of the particle is **[Manipal]**

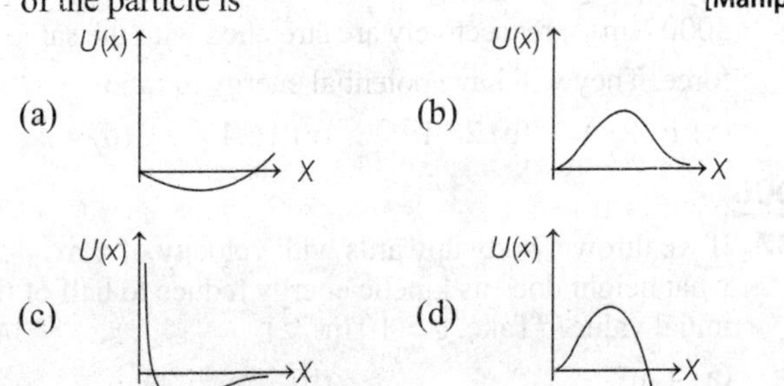

16 A particle of mass 2 mg moves with constant speed and is found to pass two points 5.0 m apart in a time interval of 5 ms. Find the kinetic energy of the particle. **[AMU]**

(a) 1 J (b) 2 J (c) 3 J (d) 4 J

17 A body is projected horizontally with a velocity of $u \text{ ms}^{-1}$ at an angle β with the horizontal. The kinetic energy at the highest point is (3/4)th of the initial kinetic energy. The value of β is **[WB JEE]**

(a) 30° (b) 45° (c) 60° (d) 120°

18 The graph below represents the potential energy U as a function of position r for a particle of mass m. If the particle is released from rest at position r_0, what will its speed be at position $3r_0$? **[CBSE AIPMT]**

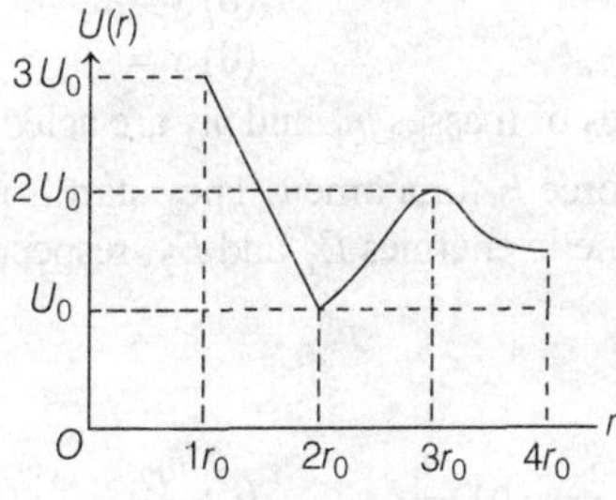

(a) $\sqrt{\frac{3U_0}{m}}$ (b) $\sqrt{\frac{4U_0}{m}}$ (c) $\sqrt{\frac{2U_0}{m}}$ (d) $\sqrt{\frac{6U_0}{m}}$
(e) The particle will never reach position $3r_0$

19 For a moving particle (mass m, velocity v) having a momentum p, which one of the following correctly describes the kinetic energy of the particle? **[J&K CET]**

(a) $\frac{p^2}{2m}$ (b) $\frac{p}{2m}$ (c) $\frac{v^2}{2m}$ (d) $\frac{v}{2m}$

20 An open water tight railway wagon of mass 5×10^3 kg coasts at an initial velocity of 1.2 ms^{-1} without friction on a railway track. Rain falls vertically downwards into the wagon. What change occurs in kinetic energy of the wagon, when it has collected 10^3 kg of water? **[AFMC]**

(a) 900 J (b) 300 J (c) 600 J (d) 1200 J

2009

21 A particle of mass m at rest is acted upon by a force P for a time t. Its kinetic energy after an interval t is **[Manipal]**

(a) $\frac{P^2t^2}{m}$ (b) $\frac{P^2t^2}{2m}$ (c) $\frac{P^2t^2}{3m}$ (d) $\frac{Pt}{2m}$

22 If the linear momentum of a body is increased by 50%, then the kinetic energy of that body increases by **[KCET]**

(a) 100% (b) 125% (c) 225% (d) 25%

2008

23 A body is thrown vertically up with certain initial velocity. The potential and kinetic energies of the body are equal at a point P in its path. If the same body is thrown with double the velocity upwards, the ratio of potential and kinetic energies of the body when it crosses the same point is **[Punjab PMET]**

(a) 1 : 1 (b) 1 : 4 (c) 1 : 7 (d) 1 : 8

24 In the figure shown, a ball of mass 1 kg is rolled with a kinetic energy of 330 J. It reaches R through the path PQR. Find the speed of the ball at R, if its potential energy at P is zero [AMU]

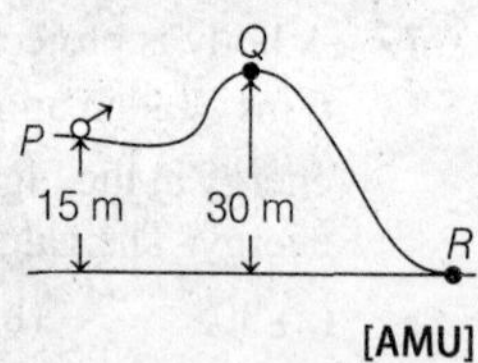

(a) 52 m/s (b) 45 m/s (c) 40 m/s (d) 31 m/s

25 Potential energy of a particle is to α coordinate by equation $x^2 - 2x$ will be equilibrium at [MP PET]

(a) $x = 0.5$ (b) $x = 2$
(c) $x = 1$ (d) $x = 4$

26 Two bodies of masses m_1 and m_2 are acted upon by constant force F for a time t. They start from rest and acquire kinetic energies E_1 and E_2, respectively. Then, $\frac{E_1}{E_2}$ is [KCET]

(a) $\frac{\sqrt{m_1 m_2}}{m_1 + m_2}$ (b) $\frac{m_1}{m_2}$ (c) $\frac{m_2}{m_1}$ (d) 1

27 A particle moves in a straight line with retardation proportional to its displacement. Its loss of kinetic energy for any displacement x is proportional to [JCECE]

(a) x^2 (b) e^x (c) x (d) $\log_e x$

2007

28 A free α-particle and a free proton, which are separated by a distance of 10^{-10} m are released. The KE of α-particle when at infinite separation is [AFMC]

(a) 46×10^{-19} J
(b) 23×10^{-19} J
(c) 36.8×10^{-19} J
(d) 9.2×10^{-19} J

29 A spherical ball of mass 20 kg is stationary at the top of a hill of height 100 m. It rolls down a smooth surface to the ground, then climbs up another hill of height 30 m and finally rolls down to a horizontal base at a height of 20 m above the ground. The velocity attained by the ball is [AIIMS]

(a) 40 ms^{-1} (b) 20 ms^{-1}
(c) 10 ms^{-1} (d) $10\sqrt{30}$ ms^{-1}

30 Two bodies A and B having masses in the ratio of 3 : 1 possess the same kinetic energy. The ratio of linear momentum of B to A is [UP CPMT]

(a) 1 : 3 (b) 3 : 1
(c) $1 : \sqrt{3}$ (d) $\sqrt{3} : 1$

31 A cubical vessel of height 1 m is full of water. What is the amount of work done in pumping water out of the vessel? (take, $g = 10\,ms^{-2}$) [WB JEE]

(a) 1250 J (b) 5000 J
(c) 1000 J (d) 2500 J

32 A bread gives 21 kJ energy to a boy of mass 40 kg. If the efficiency is 28%, then the height that can be climbed by him using this energy is [BHU]

(a) 22.5 m (b) 15 m (c) 10 m (d) 5 m

33 A particle is released from a height h. At a certain height, its kinetic energy is two times its potential energy. Height and speed of the particle at that instant are [BVP]

(a) $\frac{h}{3}, \sqrt{\frac{2gh}{3}}$ (b) $\frac{h}{3}, 2\sqrt{\frac{gh}{3}}$
(c) $\frac{2h}{3}, \sqrt{\frac{2gh}{3}}$ (d) $\frac{h}{3}, \sqrt{2gh}$

34 A particle of mass m_1 is moving with a velocity v_1 and another particle of mass m_2 is moving with a velocity v_2. Both of them have the same momentum but their different kinetic energies are E_1 and E_2, respectively. If $m_1 > m_2$, then [MP PMT]

(a) $E_1 < E_2$ (b) $\frac{E_1}{E_2} = \frac{m_1}{m_2}$
(c) $E_1 > E_2$ (d) $E_1 = E_2$

35

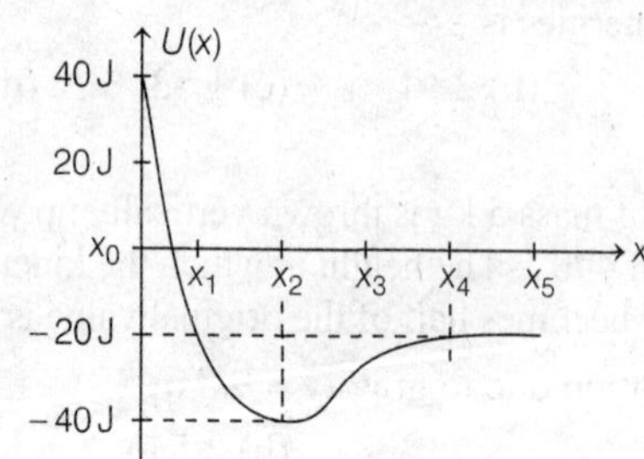

The potential energy function $U(x)$ is associated with a conservative force F and described by the graph given above. If a particle being acted upon by this force has a kinetic energy of 1.0 J at position x_0. What is the particle's kinetic energy at position x_4? [AIIMS]

(a) 60 J (b) 7.0 J
(c) 2.0 J (d) –7.0 J

36 Two springs of spring constant 1500 Nm^{-1} and 3000 Nm^{-1}, respectively are stretched with the same force. They will have potential energy in ratio [BCECE]

(a) 1 : 2 (b) 2 : 1 (c) 1 : 4 (d) 4 : 1

2006

37 If we throw a body upwards with velocity of 4 ms^{-1}, at what height does its kinetic energy reduce to half of the initial value? (Take, $g = 10\,ms^{-2}$) [AFMC]

(a) 4 m (b) 2 m
(c) 1 m (d) 0.4 m

38 If the kinetic energy of a body is increased two times, its momentum will [RPET]

(a) half (b) remain unchanged
(c) be doubled (d) increase $\sqrt{2}$ times

39 A steel ball of mass 5 g is thrown downwards with velocity 10 ms^{-1} from height 19.5 m. It penetrates sand by 50 cm. The change in mechanical energy will be (take, $g = 10\ ms^{-2}$) **[DUMET]**

(a) 1 J (b) 1.25 J
(c) 1.51 J (d) 1.75 J

40 Which of the following graphs shows variation of the elastic potential energy (U) with displacement position x? **[J&K CET]**

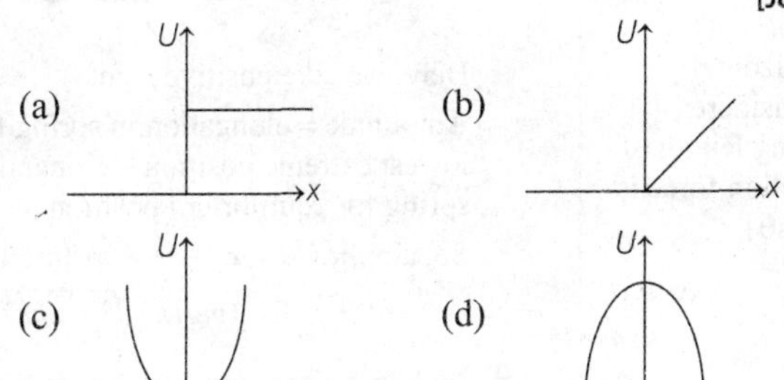

2005

41 A machine which is 75% efficient, uses 12 J of energy in lifting 1 kg mass through a certain distance. The mass is then allowed to fall through the same distance. The velocity at the end of its fall is **[BHU]**

(a) $\sqrt{12}\ ms^{-1}$ (b) $\sqrt{18}\ ms^{-1}$
(c) $\sqrt{24}\ ms^{-1}$ (d) $\sqrt{32}\ ms^{-1}$

42 When a man increases his speed by 2 ms^{-1}, he finds that his kinetic energy is doubled, the original speed of the man is **[DUMET]**

(a) $2(\sqrt{2}-1)\ ms^{-1}$ (b) $2(\sqrt{2}+1)\ ms^{-1}$
(c) 4.5 ms^{-1} (d) None of these

43 An apple gives 20 kJ energy to a boy. How much height can he climb by using this energy, if his efficiency is 20%? (Mass of boy = 40 kg) **[RPMT]**

(a) 22.5 m (b) 15 m (c) 10 m (d) 5 m

Answers

1 (c)	2 (b)	3 (a)	4 (a)	5 (a)	6 (a)	7 (d)	8 (b)	9 (c)	10 (d)
11 (c)	12 (c)	13 (d)	14 (a)	15 (d)	16 (a)	17 (a)	18 (c)	19 (a)	20 (c)
21 (b)	22 (b)	23 (b)	24 (d)	25 (c)	26 (c)	27 (a)	28 (d)	29 (a)	30 (c)
31 (b)	32 (b)	33 (b)	34 (a)	35 (b)	36 (b)	37 (d)	38 (d)	39 (b)	40 (c)
41 (b)	42 (b)	43 (c)							

Explanations

1 *(c)* If x be the compression in the spring, when a block of 0.25 kg is released.

From energy conservation,

Potential energy of spring

= Potential energy of block

$$\frac{1}{2}kx^2 = mgx$$

where, k is force constant of spring.

$$kx = 2\,mg$$
$$= 2 \times 0.25\,g$$
$$kx = 0.5\,g$$

i.e. Force applied by the spring on the block,

$$F = kx$$
$$\Rightarrow \quad F = 0.5\,g$$

From Free body diagram,

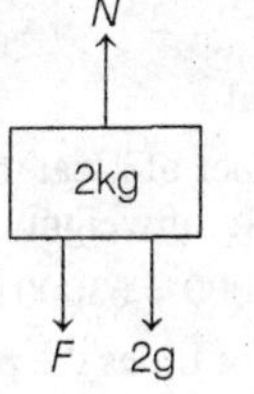

$\therefore$ Maximum force by system on the floor,

$$N = F + 2g$$
$$= 0.5\,g + 2g = 2.5g$$
$$(\because g = 10\ ms^{-2})$$
$$= 25\ N$$

2 *(b)* In stretching a wire, the work done against internal restoring force is stored as elastic potential energy in wire and given by

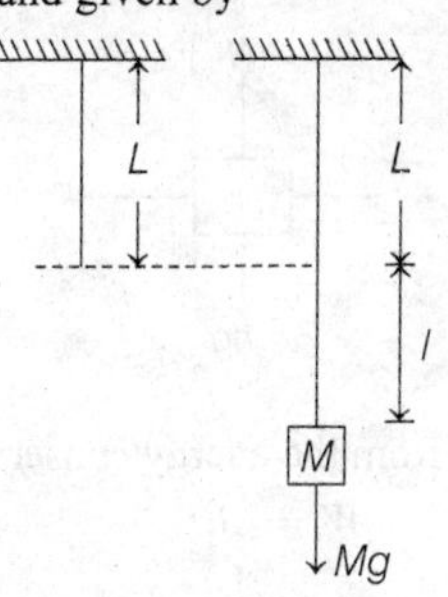

$$U = W = \frac{1}{2} \times \text{Force } (F) \times \text{Elongation } (l)$$
$$= \frac{1}{2}Fl = \frac{1}{2} \times Mg \times l = \frac{1}{2}Mgl$$

3 (a) Given, rate of decrease in kinetic energy,

$$\frac{dK}{dt} = 9.6\ \text{Js}^{-1}$$

When speed, $v = 3\ \text{ms}^{-1}$, then force $F = ?$

Kinetic energy, $K = \frac{1}{2}mv^2$

Differentiating with respect to t, we get

$$\frac{dK}{dt} = \frac{1}{2}m2v\frac{dv}{dt} = vm\frac{dv}{dt}$$

$$= vm\frac{dp}{dt}$$

$$\frac{dK}{dt} = vF \quad \left[\because \text{force, } F = m\frac{dp}{dt}\right]$$

$$\therefore \quad F = \frac{1}{v}\cdot\frac{dK}{dt}$$

$$= \frac{1}{3}\times 9.6$$

$$= 3.2\ \text{N}$$

4 (a) Relation between kinetic energy and momentum is

$$p_1 = \sqrt{2mK_1}$$

$\because$ Kinetic energy is increased by 4 times, then

$$K_2 = 4K_1$$

Hence, $p_2 = \sqrt{2mK_2} = \sqrt{2m(4K_1)}$

$$p_2 = 2\sqrt{2mK_1}$$

or $\quad p_2 = 2p_1$

5 (a) Free body diagram of block is shown below

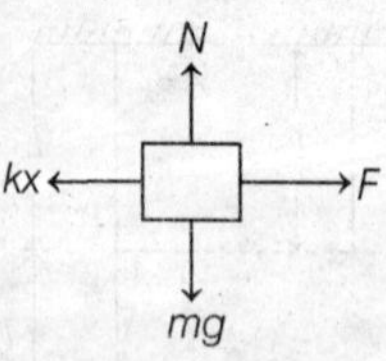

Now, from the energy conservation,

$$W = \Delta K$$

$$\Rightarrow W_F + W_{sp} = \frac{1}{2}mv^2$$

$$\Rightarrow F\cdot x - \frac{1}{2}kx^2 = \frac{1}{2}mv^2$$

$$\therefore \quad v = \sqrt{\frac{2F\cdot x - kx^2}{m}}$$

6 (a) According to question, the situation is shown in the figure

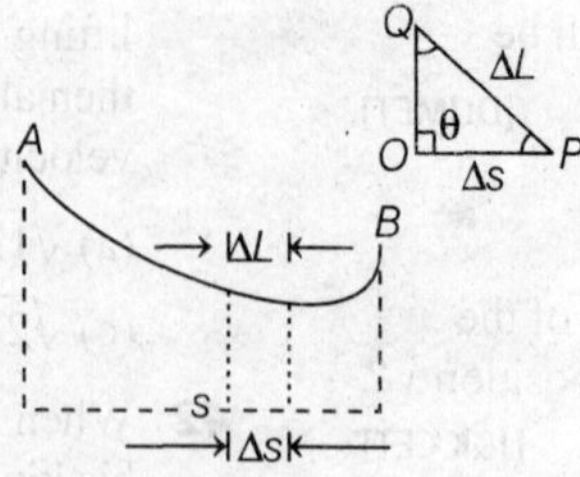

For a sufficiently, safe-horizontal displacement Δs can be considered straight. If the corresponding length of path element is ΔL, the friction force is given by $\Delta F = \mu mg(\Delta L\cos\theta)$

From ΔOPQ,

$$\cos\theta = \frac{\Delta s}{\Delta L}$$

So, $\Delta F = \mu mg\Delta L\left(\frac{\Delta s}{\Delta L}\right) = \mu mg\Delta s$

Adding up, we find that along the whole path, the total work done by the friction force is μmgs. By energy conservation, this must equals to the decrease mgh in potential energy of skier.

$$\therefore \quad \mu mgs = mgh$$

Hence, $\quad h = \mu s$

7 (d) Given, $m = 70$ kg, $g = 10\ \text{ms}^{-2}$ and

$$h = 12\ \text{m}$$

In going up and down once.

Number of k-cals burnt $= \left(mgh + \frac{mgh}{2}\right)$

$$= \frac{3}{2}mgh = \frac{3}{2}\times\frac{70\times 10\times 12}{4.2\times 1000}$$

$$= 3\ \text{k-cal}$$

Total number of k-cal to be burnt for loosing 7 kg of weight

$$= 7\times 9000 = 63000\ \text{k-cal}$$

$\therefore$ Number of times the person has to go up and down the stairs

$$= \frac{63000}{3} = 21000$$

$$= 21\times 10^3\ \text{times}$$

8 (b) Given, spring constant $= k$

From law of conservation of energy,

$$mgh = \frac{1}{2}kx_0^2 - mgx_0$$

where, x_0 is maximum elongation in spring and mgx_0 is the potential energy due to elongation.

$$\Rightarrow \frac{1}{2}kx_0^2 - mgx_0 - mgh = 0$$

$$\Rightarrow x_0^2 - \frac{2mg}{k}x_0 - \frac{2mg}{k}h = 0$$

$$x_0 = \frac{\frac{2mg}{k} \pm \sqrt{\left(\frac{2mg}{k}\right)^2 + 4\times\frac{2mg}{k}h}}{2}$$

Here, we take positive sign.

Amplitude = elongation in spring for lowest extreme position − elongation in spring for equilibrium position

So, amplitude $= x_0 - x_1 \quad [\because x_1 = 0]$

$$= (mg/k)\sqrt{1 + 2hk/mg}$$

9 (c) Kinetic energy is the energy possessed by a body due to its velocity.

$$K = \frac{1}{2}mv^2 \quad \text{...(i)}$$

where, m is its mass

Momentum (p)

$$= \text{mass } (m) \times \text{velocity } (v) \text{ ...(ii)}$$

From Eqs. (i) and (ii), we get

$$p = \sqrt{2mK} = p \propto \sqrt{m}$$

Given, $\quad m_1 = m$, and $m_2 = 2m$

$$\therefore \quad \frac{p_1}{p_2} = \frac{1}{\sqrt{2}}$$

10 (d) According to the law of conservation of mechanical energy, for conservative forces, the sum of kinetic energy and potential energy remains constant and throughout the motion it is independent of time. This is the law of conservation of mechanical energy, i.e. KE + PE = total energy = constant.

Hence, both Assertion and Reason are incorrect.

11 (c) As we know that, $\text{KE} = \frac{1}{2}mv^2$

So, kinetic energy is directly proportional to the square of velocity.

$$K \propto v^2$$

As this equation resembles equation of parabola as m is constant, hence option (c) represents a parabola.

12 (c) At ground, kinetic energy,

$$E = \frac{1}{2}mu^2$$

At highest point, $u_x \neq 0$ and $u_y = 0$

So, $E' = \frac{1}{2} m(u \cos 60°)^2 \quad (\because \theta = 60°)$

$$\Rightarrow E' = \frac{E}{4}$$

13 (d) As, $KE = \frac{p^2}{2m}$

The kinetic energy is inversely proportional to the mass of the body, while momentums are equal, so

$$KE \propto \frac{1}{m}$$

Hence, $\frac{KE_1}{KE_2} = \frac{m_2}{m_1} = \frac{5}{4}$

14 (a) Given, $m = 5$ kg, $(KE)_i = 490$ J and $(KE)_f = 245$ J

By the law of conservation of energy,

$(KE)_i = (KE)_f + mgh$

$490 = 245 + 5 \times 9.8 \times h$

$$h = \frac{490 - 245}{5 \times 9.8} = \frac{245}{49} = 5 \text{ m}$$

15 (d) We know that,

$$F = \frac{dU}{dx}$$

$$\Rightarrow \quad dU = -F \cdot dx$$

$$\Rightarrow \quad U = -\int_0^x (-kx + ax^3)\, dx$$

$$\Rightarrow \quad U = \frac{kx^2}{2} - \frac{ax^4}{4}$$

$\therefore$ We get, $U = 0$ at $x = 0$

and $\quad x = \sqrt{\frac{2k}{a}}$

Also we get,

$U =$ negative for $x > \sqrt{\frac{2k}{a}}$

From the given function, we can see that $F = 0$ at $x = 0$ i.e. slope of U-x graph is zero at $x = 0$.

Hence, option (d) is correct.

16 (a) Given, mass $= 2$ mg $= 2 \times 10^{-6}$ kg,

Distance = 5.0 m

and time, $t = 5$ ms $= 5 \times 10^{-3}$ s

Now, velocity

$$= \frac{\text{distance}}{\text{time}} = \frac{5}{5 \times 10^{-3}} \text{ m/s}$$

$= 1000$ m/s

and $KE = \frac{1}{2} mv^2$

$$= \frac{1}{2} \times 2 \times 10^{-6} (10^3)^2 = 1 \text{ J}$$

17 (a) The kinetic energy at the highest point would be equal to $\frac{1}{2} m(u \cos\beta)^2$ as the vertical component of the velocity is zero.

$$\Rightarrow \quad KE = \frac{1}{2} mu^2 \cos^2\beta$$

u sin β, u, β, u cos β

The initial kinetic energy (K) is the maximum kinetic energy.

So, $\quad KE = K \cos^2\beta$

Given, $\quad K \cos^2\beta = \frac{3}{4} K$

$$\Rightarrow \quad \cos\beta = \frac{\sqrt{3}}{2}$$

So, $\quad \beta = 30°$

18 (c) According to the law of conservation of energy,

$$U_i + K_i = U_f + K_f \quad \text{...(i)}$$

So, by putting the values in Eq. (i),

$$3U_0 + 0 = 2U_0 + \frac{1}{2} mv^2$$

$$\Rightarrow \quad v = \sqrt{\frac{2U_0}{m}}$$

19 (a) Kinetic energy of a particle,

$$K = \frac{1}{2} mv^2$$

or $K = \frac{p^2}{2m}$, where p is the momentum.

$(\because p = mv)$

20 (c) If v' is the final velocity of the wagon, then applying the principle of conservation of linear momentum, we get

$$\Rightarrow \quad mv = m'v'$$

where m, v' are final mass and velocity of wagon.

Given, $m = 5 \times 10^3$ kg, $v = 1.2 \text{ ms}^{-1}$

and $m' = (5 \times 10^3 + 10^3)$ kg

$\Rightarrow 5 \times 10^3 \times 1.2 = (5 \times 10^3 + 10^3) \times v'$

$$v' = 1 \text{ ms}^{-1}$$

Change in $KE = \frac{1}{2} m'v'^2 - \frac{1}{2} mv^2$

$$= \frac{1}{2}(6 \times 10^3) \times 1^2 - \frac{1}{2}(5 \times 10^3) \times (1.2)^2 = 600 \text{ J}$$

21 (b) Given, force, $P = ma$

As the kinetic energy, $K = \frac{1}{2} mv^2$

$$= \frac{1}{2}\frac{m^2(v^2)}{m} = \frac{1}{2}\frac{m^2a^2t^2}{m}$$

$(\because v = at, \text{ as } u = 0)$

$$= \frac{P^2t^2}{2m} \quad (\because P = ma)$$

22 (b) Kinetic energy of the body,

$$K = \frac{p^2}{2m}$$

Since the mass remains constant, so $K \propto p^2$.

So, $\frac{K_2}{K_1} = \frac{p_2^2}{p_1^2} = \left[\frac{150}{100}\right]^2 = \frac{9}{4}$

Thus, $\left(\frac{K_2}{K_1} - 1\right) \times 100 = \left(\frac{9}{4} - 1\right) \times 100$

$= 125\%$

23 (b) In the first case, at a point P, its kinetic and potential energies are equal, i.e.

v, P, PE = KE, h, O, Ground

$$\frac{1}{2} mv^2 = mgh \Rightarrow h = \frac{v^2}{2g} \quad \text{...(i)}$$

In the second case, when body's velocity is $2v$, then at the same point P. The ratio of potential and kinetic energy is

$$\frac{PE}{KE} = \frac{mg \times \frac{v^2}{2g}}{\frac{1}{2} m(2v)^2} = \frac{1}{4}$$

24 (d) Given, mass of ball = 1.0 kg

KE = 330 J

To find, speed of ball at R

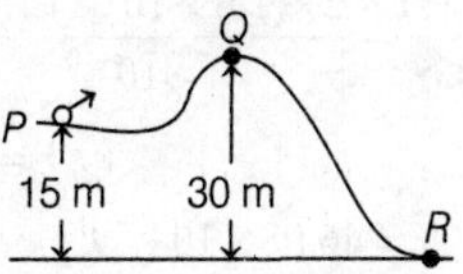

According to conservation of energy,

$$(KE)_{at\ P} + (PE)_{at\ P} = (KE)_{at\ R} = (PE)_{at\ R}$$

$$\frac{1}{2}mv_1^2 + mgh = \frac{1}{2}mv_2^2 + 0$$

$$330 + 1 \times 10 \times 15 = \frac{1}{2} \times 1 \times v^2$$

$$2(330 + 150) = v^2$$

$$960 = v^2$$

$$\Rightarrow \quad v = 31\ m/s$$

25 *(c)* Given, the potential energy of particle, $U = x^2 - 2x$

For stable equilibrium position, $\frac{dU}{dx} = 0$

$\Rightarrow 0 = 2x - 2, \Rightarrow x = 1$

Hence, $0 = \frac{d}{dx}(x^2 - 2x)$

26 *(c)* Momentum acquired by the bodies,

$$p_1 = p_2 = Ft$$

Now, their kinetic energies,

$$E_1 = \frac{p^2}{2m_1} \text{ and } E_2 = \frac{p^2}{2m_2}$$

$$\therefore \quad \frac{E_1}{E_2} = \frac{m_2}{m_1}$$

27 *(a)* From given information $a = -kx$, where a is the acceleration, x is the displacement and k is a proportionality constant.

$$\frac{v\,dv}{dx} = -kx$$

$$\Rightarrow \quad v\,dv = -kx\,dx$$

Let for any displacement from 0 to x, the velocity changes from v_0 to v.

$$\Rightarrow \quad \int_{v_0}^{v} v\,dv = -\int_0^x kx\,dx$$

$$\Rightarrow \quad \frac{v^2 - v_0^2}{2} = -\frac{kx^2}{2}$$

$$\Rightarrow m\left(\frac{v^2 - v_0^2}{2}\right) = -\frac{mkx^2}{2}$$

$$\Rightarrow \quad \Delta K \propto x^2$$

(ΔK is loss in kinetic energy)

28 *(d)* As, kinetic energy of both α-particle and proton

= potential energy of the two particles

$$= \frac{(2e)(e)}{4\pi\varepsilon_0 r} = \frac{2 \times (1.6 \times 10^{-19})^2 \times 9 \times 10^9}{10^{-10}}$$

$(\because r = 10^{-10}\ m)$

$$= 46.08 \times 10^{-19}\ J$$

If the initial momentum of two particles system is zero, their final momentum must also be zero.

$\therefore$ Numerical value of the momentum of each particle $= p$

$$\text{KE of proton} = \frac{p^2}{2m} = E \text{ (say)}$$

Kinetic energy of α-particle

$$= \frac{p^2}{2(4m)} = \frac{E}{4}$$

Total kinetic energy

$$= E + \frac{E}{4} = 46.08 \times 10^{-19}\ J$$

$$\therefore \quad E = \frac{4}{5} \times 46 \times 10^{-19}\ J$$

$$= 36.8 \times 10^{-19}\ J$$

$$\therefore \text{KE of } \alpha\text{-particle} = \frac{36.8 \times 10^{-19}}{4}$$

$$= 9.2 \times 10^{-19}\ J$$

29 *(a)* According to the law of conservation of energy,

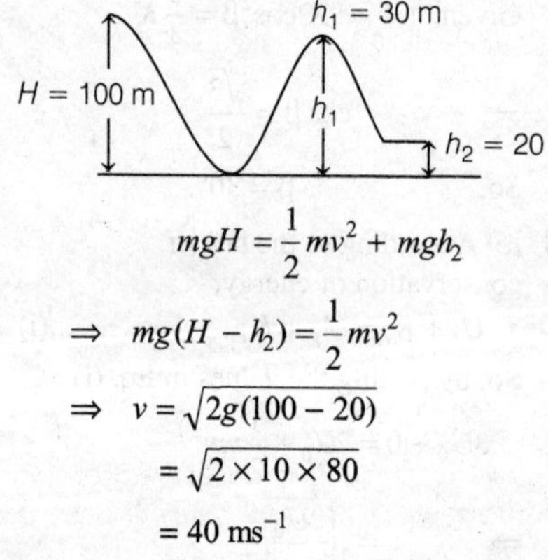

$$mgH = \frac{1}{2}mv^2 + mgh_2$$

$$\Rightarrow \quad mg(H - h_2) = \frac{1}{2}mv^2$$

$$\Rightarrow \quad v = \sqrt{2g(100 - 20)}$$

$$= \sqrt{2 \times 10 \times 80}$$

$$= 40\ ms^{-1}$$

30 *(c)* Kinetic energy of the body is given by

$$E_K = \frac{1}{2}mv^2 \quad \text{...(i)}$$

and linear momentum, $p = mv$ ...(ii)

From Eqs. (i) and (ii), we get

$$E_K = \frac{m^2v^2}{2m} = \frac{p^2}{2m}$$

$$\therefore \quad p = \sqrt{2mE_K}$$

When $E_{K_1} = E_{K_2}$

$$\Rightarrow \quad \frac{p_1^2}{2m_1} = \frac{p_2^2}{2m_2}$$

$$\text{or} \quad \frac{p_1}{p_2} = \sqrt{\frac{m_1}{m_2}}$$

$$\Rightarrow \quad \frac{p_1}{p_2} = \sqrt{\frac{3}{1}} \quad \text{(given)}$$

$$\text{or} \quad \frac{p_2}{p_1} = \frac{1}{\sqrt{3}}$$

31 *(b)* The total volume of water in vessel,

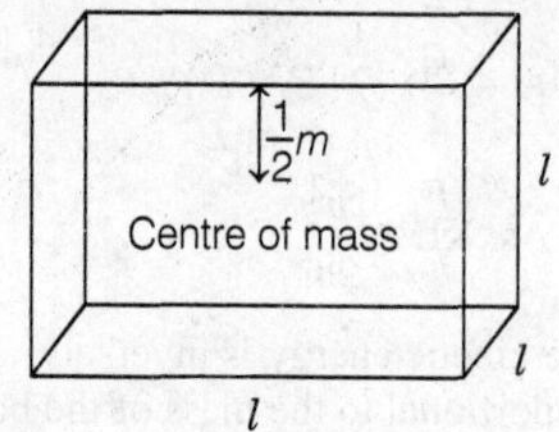

$$V = l^3 = 1\ m^3$$

Given, $m = 1 \times 1000 = 1000$ kg

From conservation of energy,

$$W = mgh = 1000 \times 10 \times \frac{1}{2} = 5000\ J$$

32 *(b)* In order to climb a height h, the boy utilizes potential energy $= mgh$

In order to climb, he will use the efficient energy.

Also, $\quad 1\ kJ = 10^3\ J$

Energy of one bread $= 21\ kJ = 21 \times 10^3\ J$

Efficiency of boy = 28%

Hence, energy consumed by the boy,

$$E = \frac{28}{100} \times 21000 = 5880\ J \quad \text{...(i)}$$

From the law of conservation of energy, this energy is utilized in giving potential energy mgh, where g is the acceleration due to gravity.

$$\therefore \quad mgh = 40 \times 9.8 \times h \quad \text{...(ii)}$$

Equating Eqs. (i) and (ii), we have

$$40 \times 9.8 \times h = 5880$$

$$\Rightarrow \quad h = \frac{5880}{40 \times 9.8} = 15\ m$$

33 *(b)* Total mechanical energy $= mgh$.

As given, $\frac{KE}{PE} = \frac{2}{1}$

$$\Rightarrow \quad KE = \frac{2}{3}mgh \text{ and } PE = \frac{1}{3}mgh$$

Height from the ground at this instant, $h' = \frac{h}{3}$

Speed of particle at this instant,

$$v = \sqrt{2g(h - h')}$$

$$= \sqrt{2g\left(\frac{2h}{3}\right)} = 2\sqrt{\frac{gh}{3}}$$

34 (a) Kinetic energy, $E = \frac{p^2}{2m}$

or $p = \sqrt{2mE}$

$\therefore \quad \frac{p_1}{p_2} = \sqrt{\frac{m_1 E_1}{m_2 E_2}}$

But it is given that, $p_1 = p_2$

$\therefore \quad m_1 E_1 = m_2 E_2$

$\Rightarrow \quad \frac{E_1}{E_2} = \frac{m_2}{m_1} \quad \ldots(i)$

Now, if $m_1 > m_2$

$\Rightarrow \quad \frac{m_1}{m_2} > 1 \quad \ldots(ii)$

Thus, Eqs. (i) and (ii) give

$E_1/E_2 < 1 \Rightarrow E_1 < E_2$

35 (b) According to law of conservation of energy,

$U_i + K_i = U_f + K_f$

where, U_i, K_i are initial PE and KE of a particle at x_0 and U_f, K_f are final PE and KE of particle at x_4.

So, $4.0 + 1.0 = -2.0 + K_f \Rightarrow K_f = 7.0\,J$

36 (b) The work done in pulling the string is stored as potential energy in the spring,

$U = \frac{1}{2}kx^2 \quad \ldots(i)$

where, k is spring constant and x is distance through which it is pulled.

Also for spring, force $\propto$ displacement

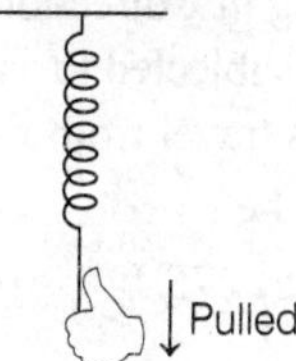

$\Rightarrow F = kx$

where, k is spring constant.

Putting, $x = \frac{F}{k}$ in Eq. (i), we get

$U = \frac{1}{2}k\left(\frac{F}{k}\right)^2 = \frac{F^2}{2k} \quad \ldots(ii)$

Given, $k_1 = 1500\,Nm^{-1}$

and $k_2 = 3000\,Nm^{-1}$

$\therefore \quad \frac{U_1}{U_2} = \frac{k_2}{k_1} = \frac{3000}{1500} = \frac{2}{1}$

or $U_1 : U_2 = 2:1$

37 (d) Initial kinetic energy of the body

$= \frac{1}{2}Mv^2 = \frac{1}{2}M(4)^2 = 8M$

Let at height h, the kinetic energy reduces to half, i.e. it becomes $4M$. It is also equal to potential energy.

Hence, $Mgh = 4M$

or $h = \frac{4}{g} = \frac{4}{10} = 0.4$ m

38 (d) Kinetic energy of particle,

$K = \frac{p_1^2}{2m}$

$p_1^2 = 2mK$

When kinetic energy $= 2K$

$p_2^2 = 2m \times 2K,$

$\Rightarrow \quad p_2^2 = 2p_1^2,$

$\Rightarrow \quad p_2 = \sqrt{2}p_1$

39 (b) The change in mechanical energy,

$\Delta U = mg(h+x) + \frac{1}{2}mv^2$

Given, $m = 5g = 0.005$ kg, $h = 19.5$ m

$x = 50$ cm $= 0.5$ m, $v = 10\,ms^{-1}$

and $g = 10\,ms^{-2}$.

$\therefore \quad \Delta U = 0.005 \times 10(19.5 + 0.5) + \frac{1}{2} \times 0.005 \times (10)^2$

$\Delta U = 0.005 \times 10 \times 20 + \frac{1}{2} \times 0.005 \times 100$

$= 1.25$ J

40 (c) The variation of elastic potential energy (U) with displacement (x) is given as $U = \frac{1}{2}kx^2 \Rightarrow U \propto x^2$

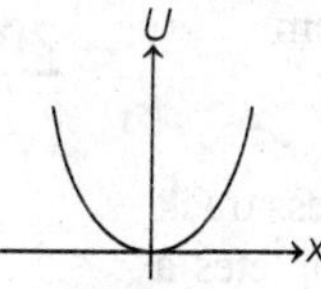

Hence, parabolic graph is obtained.

41 (b) Potential energy of the mass at a height above the surface is given by

$= \frac{75}{100} \times 12 = 9$ J $\quad \ldots(i)$

Now, KE of the mass at the end of fall

$= \frac{1}{2}mv^2 \quad \ldots(ii)$

Applying the law of conservation of energy,

$\frac{1}{2}mv^2 = 9$

$\Rightarrow \quad v = \sqrt{\frac{2 \times 9}{m}} = \sqrt{\frac{18}{1}}$

$= \sqrt{18}\,ms^{-1}$

42 (b) Man possesses kinetic energy, because of its velocity (v).

When m is mass of man, then

$K = \frac{1}{2}mv^2$

Given, $v_1 = v$, $m_1 = m_2 = m$

$v_2 = (v+2)\,ms^{-1}$

When $K_2 = 2K_1$

Then, $\frac{K_1}{K_2} = \frac{v_1^2}{v_2^2}$

$\Rightarrow \quad \frac{K_1}{2K_1} = \frac{v^2}{(v+2)^2}$

$\Rightarrow \quad v^2 - 4v - 4 = 0$

[$\because$ From above equation, $v = \frac{-b \pm \sqrt{b^2 - 4ac}}{2a}$

$a = 1, b = -4, c = -4$]

This gives,

$v_1 = \frac{4 + \sqrt{16+16}}{2}$

$= \frac{4 + \sqrt{32}}{2}$

$= 2(\sqrt{2}+1)\,ms^{-1}$

$v_1 = 2(\sqrt{2}+1)\,ms^{-1}$

43 (c) Energy of one apple $= 20 \times 10^3$ J

Efficiency of the boy $= 20\% = 0.20$

Mass of the boy, $m = 40$ kg

Here the actual energy consumed by the boy is given by

$0.2 \times 20000 = 4000$ J $\quad \ldots(i)$

and the energy consumed by the boy in climbing h metre height is given by

$= mgh = 40 \times 9.8 \times h$ J $\quad \ldots(ii)$

Equating Eqs. (i) and (ii), we get

$40 \times 9.8 \times h = 4000$ J

$h = \frac{4000}{40 \times 9.8} = 10$ m

Topic 3

Work-Energy Theorem and Vertical Circle

2019

1 An object of mass 500 g, initially at rest acted upon by a variable force whose x component varies with x in the manner shown. The velocities of the object a point $x = 8$ m and $x = 12$ m, would be the respective values of (nearly) **[NEET (Odisha)]**

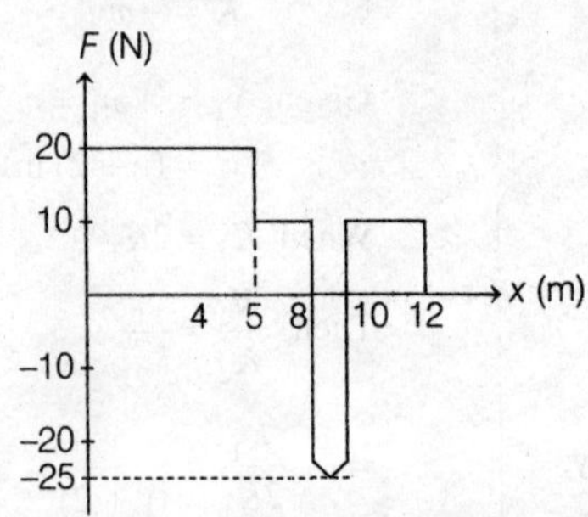

(a) 18 ms^{-1} and 24.4 ms^{-1} (b) 23 ms^{-1} and 24.4 ms^{-1}
(c) 23 ms^{-1} and 20.6 ms^{-1} (d) 18 ms^{-1} and 20.6 ms^{-1}

2 A mass m is attached to a thin wire and whirled in a vertical circle. The wire is most likely to break when **[NEET]**

(a) the wire is horizontal
(b) the mass is at the lowest point
(c) inclined at an angle of 60° from vertical
(d) the mass is at the highest point

3 Find the maximum radius of circle, so that the block can complete the circular motion. **[JIPMER]**

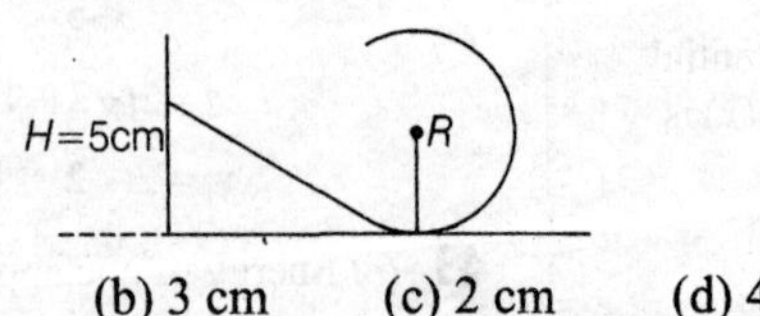

(a) 5 cm (b) 3 cm (c) 2 cm (d) 4 cm

2018

4 A body initially at rest and sliding along a frictionless track from a height h (as shown in the figure) just completes a vertical circle of diameter $AB = D$. The height h is equal to **[NEET]**

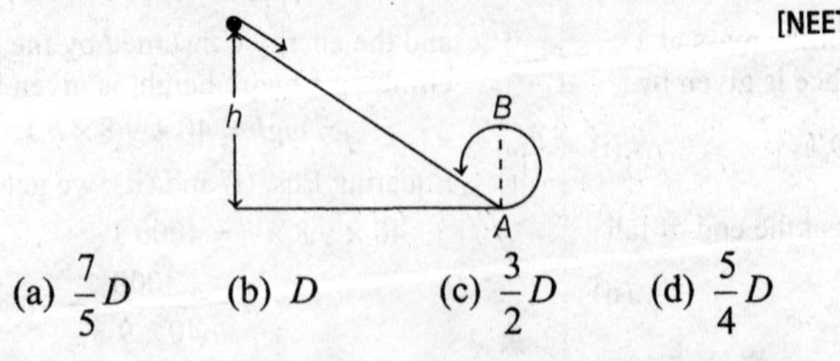

(a) $\frac{7}{5}D$ (b) D (c) $\frac{3}{2}D$ (d) $\frac{5}{4}D$

2017

5 **Assertion** For looping a vertical loop of radius, r the minimum velocity at lowest point should be $\sqrt{5gr}$.

Reason In this event, the velocity at the highest point will be zero. **[AIIMS]**

(a) Both Assertion and Reason are correct and Reason is the correct explanation of Assertion.
(b) Both Assertion and Reason are correct but Reason is not the correct explanation of Assertion.
(c) Assertion is correct but Reason is incorrect.
(d) Both Assertion and Reason are incorrect.

2016

6 What is the minimum velocity with which a body of mass m must enter a vertical loop of radius R, so that it can complete the loop? **[NEET]**

(a) $\sqrt{2gR}$ (b) $\sqrt{3gR}$
(c) $\sqrt{5gR}$ (d) $\sqrt{gR}$

7 A particle of mass 10 g moves along a circle of radius 6.4 cm with a constant tangential acceleration. What is the magnitude of this acceleration, if the kinetic energy of the particle becomes equal to 8×10^{-4} J by the end of the second revolution after the beginning of the motion? **[NEET]**

(a) 0.15 ms^{-2} (b) 0.18 ms^{-2} (b) 0.2 ms^{-2} (d) 0.1 ms^{-2}

2015

8 A block of mass 10 kg, moving in x-direction with a constant speed of 10 ms^{-1}, is subjected to a retarding force $F = 0.1x$ Jm^{-1} during its travel from $x = 20$ m to 30 m. Its final kinetic energy will be **[CBSE AIPMT]**

(a) 475 J (b) 450 J (c) 275 J (d) 250 J

2012

9 One end of a string of length 1.0 m is tied to a body of mass 0.5 kg. It is whirled in a vertical circle with angular frequency 4 $rads^{-1}$. The tension in the string when the body is at the lower most point of its motion will be equal to
(take, $g = 10$ ms^{-2}) **[AMU]**

(a) 3 N (b) 5 N (c) 8 N (d) 13 N

2011

10 A body of mass 6 kg is acted upon by a force which causes a displacement in it given by $x = \frac{t^2}{4}$ m, where t is the time in second. The work done by the force in 2 s is **[WB JEE]**

(a) 12 J (b) 9 J (c) 6 J (d) 3 J

11 A can filled with water is revolved in a vertical circle of radius 4 m, so that the water does not fall down. The time period for a revolution is about **[JCECE]**

(a) 2 s (b) 4 s (c) 8 s (d) 10 s

12 A stone of mass m is tied to a string and is moved in a vertical circle of radius r making n rev/min. The total tension in the string when the stone is at the lowest point is **[VITEEE]**

(a) mg (b) $m(g + \pi n r^2)$

(c) $m(g + nr)$ (d) $m\left(g + \frac{\pi^2 n^2 r}{900}\right)$

2010

13 A 10 kg mass moves 3.0 m against a retarding force shown in the figure. If the force is zero at the beginning, then how much kinetic energy is changed? **[VMMC]**

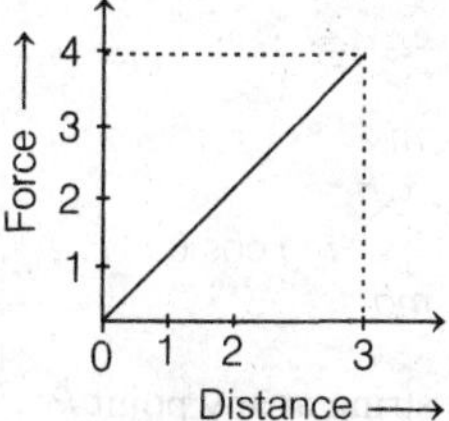

(a) 6 J (b) – 6 J
(c) 12 J (d) – 12 J

2009

14 A stone is attached to one end of a string and rotated in a vertical circle. If string breaks at the position of maximum tension, it will break at **[PMET]**

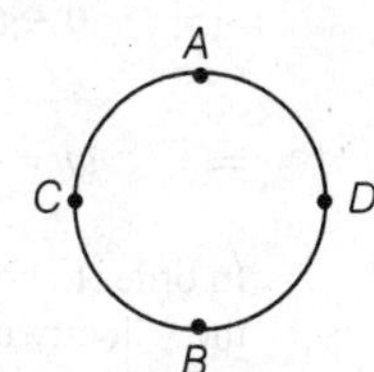

(a) A (b) B (c) C (d) D

2008

15 A body of mass 10 kg initially at rest acquires velocity 10 ms^{-1}. What is the work done? **[DUMET]**

(a) – 500 J (b) 500 J
(c) 50 J (d) –50 J

16 Consider a drop of rain water having mass 1 g falling from a height of 1 km. It hits the ground with a speed of 50 ms^{-1}. Take, g constant with a value of 10 ms^{-2}. The work done by the (i) gravitational force and (ii) resistive force of air is **[NEET]**

(a) (i) –10 J and (ii) – 8.25 J
(b) (i) 1.25 J and (ii) – 8.25 J
(c) (i) 100 J and (ii) 8.75 J
(d) (i) 10 J and (ii) – 8.75 J

17 A body of mass 1 kg is rotating in a vertical circle of radius 1 m. What will be the difference in its kinetic energy at the top and bottom of the circle? (Take, $g = 10$ ms^{-2}) **[Manipal]**

(a) 10 J (b) 20 J (c) 30 J (d) 50 J

18 A ball of mass 0.6 kg attached to a light inextensible string rotates in a vertical circle of radius 0.75 m such that it has speed of 5 ms^{-1} when the string is horizontal. Tension in string when it is horizontal on other side is (take, $g = 10$ ms^{-2}) **[Punjab PMET]**

(a) 30 N (b) 26 N (c) 20 N (d) 6 N

19 A particle is moving in a vertical circle. The tensions in the string when passing through two positions at angles 30° and 60° from vertical (lowest position) are T_1 and T_2 respectively, then **[Punjab PMET]**

(a) $T_1 = T_2$ (b) $T_2 > T_1$
(c) $T_1 > T_2$
(d) tension in the string always remains the same

20 According to the work-energy theorem, the work done by the net force on a particle is equal to the change in its **[Kerala CEE]**

(a) kinetic energy (b) potential energy
(c) linear momentum (d) angular momentum
(e) acceleration

21 A body is just being revolved in a vertical circle of radius R with a uniform speed. The string breaks when the body is at the highest point. The horizontal distance covered by the body after the string breaks is **[MP PMT]**

(a) $2R$ (b) R (c) $R\sqrt{2}$ (d) $4R$

2007

22 An open knife edge of mass m is dropped from a height h on a wooden floor. If the blade penetrates s into the wood, the average resistance offered by the wood to the blade is **[AMU]**

(a) Mg (b) $Mg\left(\frac{h}{s}\right)$

(c) $Mg\left(1-\frac{h}{s}\right)$ (d) $Mg\left(1+\frac{h}{s}\right)^2$

23 A stone is tied to a string of length l and is whirled in a vertical circle with the other end of the string at the centre. At a certain instant of time, the stone is at its lowest position and has a speed u. The magnitude of the change in velocity of string when horizontal (g being acceleration due to gravity) is **[Manipal]**

(a) $\sqrt{2(u^2 - gl)}$ (b) $\sqrt{u^2 - gl}$

(c) $u - \sqrt{u^2 - 2gl}$ (d) $\sqrt{2gl}$

2006

24 A particle accelerating uniformly has velocity v at time t_1. What is work done in time t? **[DUMET]**

(a) $\frac{1}{2}\left(\frac{mv^2}{t_1^2}\right)t^2$ (b) $\frac{1}{2}\left(\frac{mv}{t_1}\right)^2 t^2$

(c) $\left(\frac{mv^2}{t_1^2}\right)t^2$ (d) $\left(\frac{2mv^2}{t_1^2}\right)t^2$

Answers

1 (c)	2 (b)	3 (c)	4 (d)	5 (c)	6 (c)	7 (d)	8 (a)	9 (d)	10 (d)
11 (b)	12 (d)	13 (b)	14 (b)	15 (b)	16 (d)	17 (b)	18 (c)	19 (c)	20 (a)
21 (a)	22 (b)	23 (a)	24 (a)						

Explanations

1 *(c)* The area under the force-displacement curve give the amount of work done.

From work-energy theorem,

$$W = \Delta KE \quad \ldots(i)$$

$\therefore$ At $x = 8$ m,

$$W = \text{Area } ABDO + \text{Area } CEFD = 20 \times 5 + 10 \times 3 = 130 \text{ J}$$

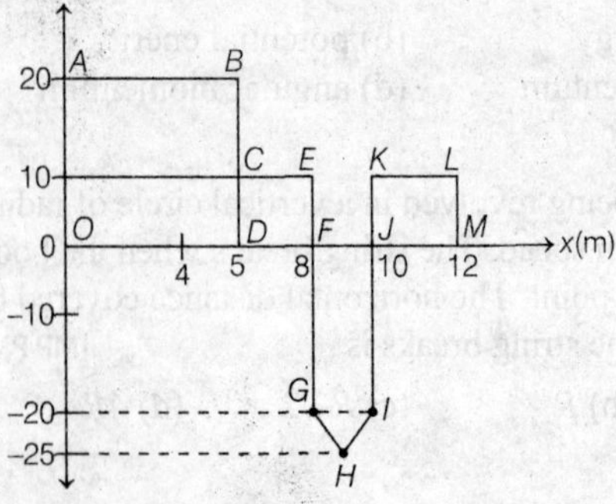

Given, $m = 500 \text{ g} = 500 \times 10^{-3}$ kg

Using Eq. (i), we get

$$\Rightarrow 130 = \frac{1}{2}mv^2 = \frac{1}{2} \times 500 \times 10^{-3} \times v^2$$

$$\Rightarrow v = 2\sqrt{130} = 22.8 \text{ ms}^{-1} \approx 23 \text{ ms}^{-1}$$

At $x = 12$ m,

$W = \text{Area } ABDO + \text{Area } CEFD + \text{Area } FGHIJ + \text{Area } KLMJ$

$$W = 20 \times 5 + 10 \times 3 + (-20 \times 2) + \left(\frac{1}{2} \times -5 \times 2\right) + 10 \times 2$$

[$\because$ Area $FGHIJ$ = Area $FGIJ$ + Area GHI]

$$= 100 + 30 - 40 - 5 + 20 = 105 \text{ J}$$

Using Eq. (i), we get

$$\therefore \quad 105 = \frac{1}{2} \times 500 \times 10^{-3} \times v^2$$

$$\Rightarrow \quad v = 2\sqrt{105} \simeq 20.6 \text{ ms}^{-1}$$

2 *(b)* Let the mass m which is attached to a thin wire and is whirled in a vertical circle is shown in the figure below

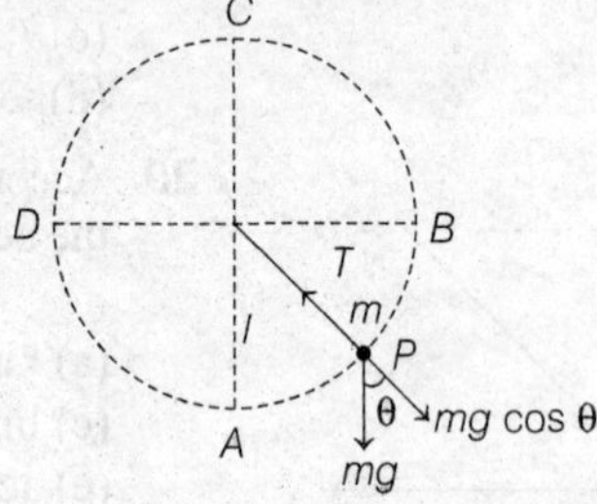

The tension in the string at any point P be T.

According to Newton's law of motion, in equilibrium, net force towards the centre = centripetal force

$$\Rightarrow T - mg\cos\theta = \frac{mv^2}{l}$$

where, l = length of wire and v = linear velocity of the particle whirling in a circle.

$$\Rightarrow \quad T = mg\cos\theta + \frac{mv^2}{l}$$

At point $A, \theta = 0°$

$$\Rightarrow \quad T_A = mg + \frac{mv^2}{l}$$

At point $B, \theta = 90°$

$$\Rightarrow \quad T_B = \frac{mv^2}{l}$$

At point $C, \theta = 180°$

$$\Rightarrow \quad T_C = -mg + \frac{mv^2}{l}$$

At point $D, \theta = 90°$

$$\Rightarrow \quad T_D = T_B = \frac{mv^2}{l}$$

So, from the above analysis, it can be concluded that the tension is maximum at point A, i.e. the lowest point of circle, So chance of breaking is maximum.

3 *(c)* From energy conservation,

$$mgH = \frac{1}{2}mv^2$$

$$\Rightarrow v^2 = 2gH \text{ or } v = \sqrt{2gH} \quad \ldots(i)$$

To complete circular loop, minimum speed at bottom point should be

$$v_{\min} = \sqrt{5gR} \quad \ldots(ii)$$

From Eqs. (i) and (ii), we get

$$\sqrt{2gH} \geq \sqrt{5gR}$$

$$\Rightarrow \quad R \leq \frac{2H}{R}$$

$$\Rightarrow \quad R_{\max} = \frac{2H}{R} = \frac{2(5)}{5} = 2 \text{ cm}$$

4 *(d)* If a body is moving on a frictionless surface, then its total mechanical energy remains conserved.

According to the conservation of mechanical energy,

$$(\text{TE})_{\text{initial}} = (\text{TE})_{\text{final}}$$

$$\Rightarrow (\text{KE})_i + (\text{PE})_i = (\text{KE})_f + (\text{PE})_f$$

$$0 + mgh = \frac{1}{2}mv_A^2 + 0$$

$$\Rightarrow \quad gh = \frac{v_A^2}{2} \quad \text{or} \quad h = \frac{v_A^2}{2g} \quad \ldots(i)$$

In order to complete the vertical circle, the velocity of the body at point A should be

$$v_A = v_{\min} = \sqrt{5gR}$$

where, R is the radius of the body.

Here, $R = \frac{AB}{2} = \frac{D}{2}$

$$\Rightarrow \quad v_{\min} = v_A = \sqrt{\frac{5}{2}gD}$$

Substituting the value of v_A in Eq. (i), we get

$$h = \frac{\left(\sqrt{\left(\frac{5}{2}gD\right)}\right)^2}{2g} = \frac{5gD}{2 \times 2g} = \frac{5}{4}D$$

5 *(c)* At the lowest point of a vertical circle, the minimum velocity at bottom

$$v_{\min} = \sqrt{5gr}$$

Velocity at highest point $(v) = \sqrt{gr}$

So, Assertion is correct but Reason is incorrect.

6 *(c)* According to question, we have

Let the tension at point A be T_A, so from Newton's law

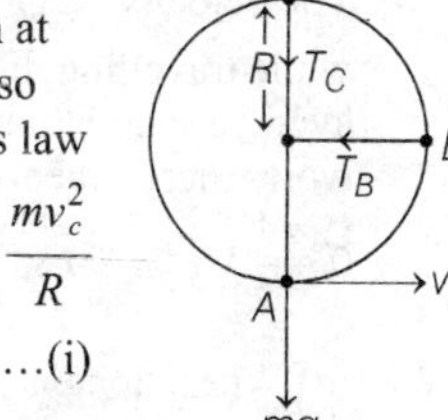

$$T_A - mg = \frac{mv_c^2}{R} \quad \text{...(i)}$$

KE at point

$$A = \frac{1}{2}mv_c^2$$

Energy at point C

$$= \frac{1}{2}mv_c^2 + mg \times 2R \quad \text{...(ii)}$$

Applying Newton's second law at point C,

$$T_c + mg = \frac{mv_c^2}{R}$$

To complete the loop $T_c \geq 0$

$$\text{So, } mg = \frac{mv_c^2}{R} \Rightarrow v_c = \sqrt{gR} \quad \text{...(iii)}$$

From Eqs. (ii) and (iii) by conservation of energy,

$$\frac{1}{2}mv_0^2 = \frac{1}{2}mv_c^2 + 2mgR$$

$$\Rightarrow mv_0^2 = mgR + 2mgR \times 2 \quad (\because v_c = \sqrt{gR})$$

$$\Rightarrow v_0^2 = gR + 4gR$$

$$\Rightarrow v_0 = \sqrt{5gR}$$

7 *(d)* Given, mass of particle,

$$m = 0.01 \text{ kg}.$$

Radius of circle along which particle is moving, $r = 6.4$ cm and initial kinetic energy, $K_i = 0$.

$\because$ Final kinetic energy of particle,

$$K_f = 8 \times 10^{-4} \text{ J}$$

$$\Rightarrow \frac{1}{2}mv^2 = 8 \times 10^{-4} \text{ J}$$

$$\Rightarrow v^2 = \frac{16 \times 10^{-4}}{0.01} = 16 \times 10^{-2} \quad \text{...(i)}$$

As, it is given that kinetic energy of particle is equal to 8×10^{-4} J by the end of second revolution after the beginning of motion of particle. It means, its intial velocity (u) is 0 ms^{-1} at this moment.

$\because$ By Newton's third equation of motion, $v^2 = u^2 + 2a_t s$

$$\Rightarrow v^2 = 2a_t s \quad \text{or} \quad v^2 = 2a_t(4\pi r)$$

{$\because$ particle covers 2 revolutions}

$$\Rightarrow a_t = \frac{v^2}{8\pi r} = \frac{16 \times 10^{-2}}{8 \times 3.14 \times 6.4 \times 10^{-2}}$$

{$\because$ from Eq. (i), $v^2 = 16 \times 10^{-2}$}

$$\therefore a_t = 0.1 \text{ ms}^{-2}$$

Alternative Method

By applying work-energy theorem, Change in KE = Work done by all forces.

Hence, $K_f - K_i = F \times s + 0$

because work done by all forces include work done by tangential force and work done by centripetal force.

$$8 \times 10^{-4} - 0 = m \times a \times (2 \times 2\pi R)$$

$$a = \frac{8 \times 10^{-4}}{4 \times \frac{22}{7} \times 6.4 \times 10^{-2} \times 0.01}$$

$$= 0.099 = 0.1 \text{ ms}^{-2}$$

8 *(a)* From work-energy theorem,

Work done = Change in KE

$$\Rightarrow W = K_f - K_i$$

$$\Rightarrow K_f = W + K_i = \int_{x_1}^{x_2} F x\, dx + \frac{1}{2}mv^2$$

$$= \int_{20}^{30} (-0.1.x\, dx) + \frac{1}{2} \times 10 \times 10^2$$

$$= -0.1\left[\frac{x^2}{2}\right]_{20}^{30} + 500$$

$$= -0.05\,[30^2 - 20^2] + 500$$

$$= -0.05\,[900 - 400] + 500$$

$$\Rightarrow K_f = -25 + 500 = 475 \text{ J}$$

9 *(d)* Given, $r = 1$ m,

$m = 0.5$ kg

and $\omega = 4$ rads^{-1}

As, the tension in the string,

$$T = m\omega^2 r + mg$$

$$= 0.5 \times (4)^2 \times 1 + 0.5 \times 10$$

$$= 13 \text{ N}$$

10 *(d)* From the question, we see that, the mass of the body is 6 kg and the displacement is given by $x = \frac{t^2}{4}$ m. So, the velocity would be equal to

$$v = \frac{dx}{dt} = \frac{t}{2}.$$

Thus, velocity at time $t = 0$, $v(0) = 0$ and velocity at time $t = 2$ s, $v(2) = \frac{2}{2} = 1$.

Hence, the initial kinetic energy would be equal to $(\text{KE})_i = \frac{1}{2}m[v(0)]^2 = 0$ and similarly the final kinetic energy would be

$$(\text{KE})_f = \frac{1}{2}m[v\,(2)]^2 = \frac{1}{2} \times 6 \times (1)^2 = 3$$

So, we see that the work done by the force is equal to

$$W = (\text{KE})_f - (\text{KE})_i = 3 - 0 = 3 \text{ J}.$$

11 *(b)* When a body is set to revolve on a circular path, it is acted upon by a centripetal force directed towards the centre. Water will not fall, if weight of water is balanced by centripetal force.

Therefore,

$$mg = \frac{mv^2}{r} \Rightarrow v^2 = rg \quad \text{... (i)}$$

Circumference of a circle is $2\pi r$.

$$\text{Time for a revolution} = \frac{2\pi r}{v} \quad \text{... (ii)}$$

The speed of can at the top of circle to just complete the vertical circle is $\sqrt{rg}$.

i.e. $v = \sqrt{rg}$

On putting the value of v from Eqs. (i) and (ii) we get

$$T = \frac{2\pi r}{\sqrt{rg}} = 2\pi\sqrt{\frac{r}{g}}$$

$$= 2 \times 3.14\sqrt{\frac{4}{10}} \quad (\because r = um)$$

$$= 2 \times 3.14 \times \frac{2}{3.16} \approx 4 \text{ s}$$

12 *(d)* Tension at lowest point,

$$T_{\text{net}} = mg + \frac{mv^2}{r}$$

$$= mg + mr\omega^2$$

$$= mg + mr\left(\frac{2\pi n}{60}\right)^2 \quad \text{(given)}$$

$$= m\left(g + \frac{\pi^2 n^2 r}{900}\right)$$

13 *(b)* According to the work-energy theorem,

Loss in kinetic energy = Work done

= Area of F-s curve

$$= \frac{1}{2} \times \text{base} \times \text{perpendicular}$$

$$= -\frac{1}{2} \times 3 \times 4 = -6 \text{ J}$$

14 *(b)* The body is describing a vertical circle,

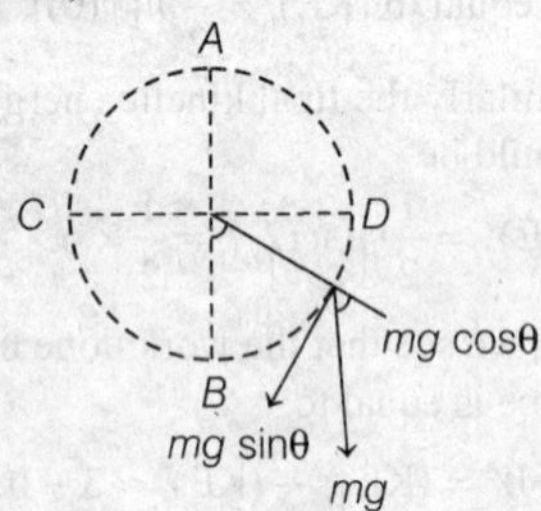

$\therefore\ T - mg\cos\theta = \dfrac{mv^2}{l}$

$\Rightarrow T = mg\cos\theta + \dfrac{mv^2}{l}$

Tension is maximum when $\cos\theta = 1$ and velocity is maximum. Both conditions are satisfied at $\theta = 0°$, i.e. at lowest point B.

15 *(b)* Given, $m = 10\text{ kg}, u = 0$ and $v = 10\text{ ms}^{-1}$

By work-energy theorem,

$W = \Delta K = \dfrac{1}{2} \times 10 \times (10)^2 - 0 = 500\text{ J}$

16 *(d)* Given, $m = 1\text{ kg} = 10^{-3}$ kg, $h = 1\text{ km} = 10^3$ m, $v = 50\text{ ms}^{-1}$ and $g = 10\text{ ms}^{-2}$

By work-energy theorem, we have change in energy = work done by all of the forces. Work done by grventational force,

$W_g = mgh$

$= 10^{-3} \times 10 \times 1 \times 10^3 = 10\text{J}$

Now, from work-energy theorm, we have

$\Delta K = W_{\text{gravity}} + W_{\text{air reistance}}$

$\Rightarrow \dfrac{1}{2} \times mv2 = mg + W_{\text{air resistance}}$

$\Rightarrow W_{\text{air resistance}} = \dfrac{1}{2}mv^2 - mgh$

$= 10^{-3}\left(\dfrac{1}{2} time\ 50 \times 50 - 10^3\right) = -8.75\text{ J}$

17 *(b)* Kinetic energy is the energy possessed by a body of mass m due to its velocity v, $\text{KE} = \dfrac{1}{2}mv^2$

Velocity at the top is $\sqrt{gr}$ and that at the bottom is $\sqrt{5gr}$. Hence, required difference in kinetic energy

$\Delta\text{KE} = \dfrac{1}{2}m_1v_1^2 - \dfrac{1}{2}mv_2^2$

$= \dfrac{1}{2}m(5gr - gr) = 2gmr$

Given, $g = 10\text{ ms}^{-2}$, $m = 1\text{ kg}$

and $r = 1\text{ m}$

$= 2 \times 10 \times 1 \times 1 = 20\text{ J}$

18 *(c)* Tension in the string when it makes angle θ with the vertical,

$T = \dfrac{mv^2}{r} + mg\cos\theta$

When the string is horizontal, $\theta = 90°$

$\therefore T = \dfrac{mv^2}{r} + mg \times 0 = \dfrac{mv^2}{r}$

Given, $m = 0.6$ kg , $r = 0.75$ m

and $v = 5\text{ ms}^{-1}$

$= \dfrac{0.6 \times (5)^2}{0.75} = 20\text{ N}$

19 *(c)* $T = \dfrac{mv^2}{r} + mg\cos\theta$

Taking the tensions at two values of θ,

For $\theta = 30°$, $T_1 = \dfrac{mv^2}{r} + mg\cos 30°$

$= \dfrac{mv^2}{r} + \dfrac{\sqrt{3}mg}{2}\left(\because \cos 30° = \dfrac{\sqrt{3}}{2}\right)$

For $\theta = 60°$, $T_2 = \dfrac{mv^2}{r} + mg\cos 60°$

$= \dfrac{mv^2}{r} + \dfrac{mg}{2} \quad \left(\because \cos 60° = \dfrac{1}{2}\right)$

$\therefore\ T_1 > T_2$

20 *(a)* According to the work-energy theorem, work done by a force in displacing a body on a horizontal level measures the change in its kinetic energy.

21 *(a)* As, the body just completes the circular path, hence critical speed at the highest point, $v_H = \sqrt{gR}$ which is totally horizontal. As, the string breaks at the highest point, hence from here onward the body will follow parabolic path. Time taken by the body to reach the ground,

$t = \sqrt{\dfrac{2h}{g}} = \sqrt{\dfrac{2 \times 2R}{g}}$

Hence, horizontal distance covered by the body

$= v_H \times t = \sqrt{gR} \times \sqrt{\dfrac{4R}{g}} = 2R$

22 *(b)* Velocity at the time when knife edge strikes wooden floor is $\sqrt{2gh}$.

The velocity $\sqrt{2gh}$ is reduced to zero while travelling distance s. If F is the average retardation, then by work-energy theorem, we have

$0 - \dfrac{1}{2}Mv^2 = -Fs \Rightarrow F = Mg\dfrac{h}{s}$

23 *(a)* When stone is at its lowest position, it has only kinetic energy, given by

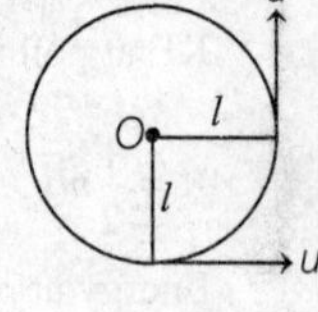

$K = \dfrac{1}{2}mu^2$

At a horizontal position, it has energy,

$E = U + K = \dfrac{1}{2}mu'^2 + mgl$

According to the law of conservation of energy, $K = E$

$\therefore\ \dfrac{1}{2}mu^2 = \dfrac{1}{2}mu'^2 + mgl$

$\Rightarrow \dfrac{1}{2}mu'^2 = \dfrac{1}{2}mu^2 - mgl$

$\Rightarrow \quad u'^2 = u^2 - 2gl$

$\Rightarrow \quad u' = \sqrt{u^2 - 2gl} \quad \ldots\text{(i)}$

The velocities vectorially given below

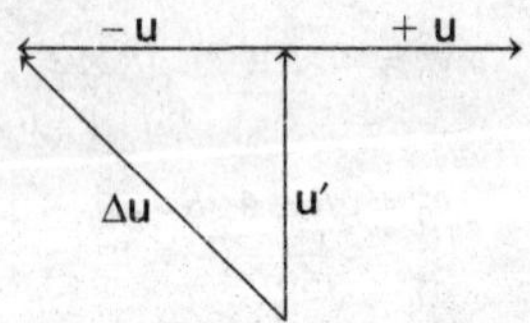

So, the magnitude of change in velocity,

$|\Delta\mathbf{u}| = |\mathbf{u}| = \sqrt{u'^2 + u^2 + 2u'u\cos 90°}$

$|\Delta\mathbf{u}| = \sqrt{u'^2 + u^2} = \sqrt{2(u^2 - gl)}$

[from Eq. (i)]

24 *(a)* Velocity of the particle accelerating uniformly in time t_1,

$v = at_1 \Rightarrow a = \dfrac{v}{t_1} \quad \ldots\text{(i)}$

Velocity of the particle after time t,

$v' = at = \dfrac{vt}{t_1} \quad$ [from Eq. (i)]

According to the work-energy theorem,

Work done by all the forces = Change in KE

i.e. $W = \Delta K$ or $W = \dfrac{1}{2}mv'^2 - 0$

$= \dfrac{1}{2}m\left(\dfrac{vt}{t_1}\right)^2 = \dfrac{1}{2}\left(\dfrac{mv^2}{t_1^2}\right)t^2$

Topic 4

Power

2018

1 1000 N force is required to lift a hook and 10000 N force is requires to lift a load slowly. Find power required to lift hook with load with speed $v = 0.5\ \text{ms}^{-1}$. **[JIPMER]**

(a) 5 kW (b) 1.5 kW (c) 5.5 kW (d) 4.5 kW

2016

2 A body of mass 1 kg begins to move under the action of a time dependent force $\mathbf{F} = (2t\hat{\mathbf{i}} + 3t^2\hat{\mathbf{j}})$ N, where $\hat{\mathbf{i}}$ and $\hat{\mathbf{j}}$ are unit vectors along X and Y-axes. What power will be developed by the force at the time (t)? **[NEET]**

(a) $(2t^2 + 4t^4)$ W (b) $(2t^3 + 3t^4)$ W
(c) $(2t^3 + 3t^5)$ W (d) $(2t + 3t^3)$ W

2014

3 A body is initially at rest. It undergoes one dimensional motion with constant acceleration. The power delivered to it at a time t is proportional to **[UK PMT]**

(a) $t^{1/2}$ (b) t
(c) $t^{3/2}$ (d) t^2

4 If two persons A and B take 2 s and 4 s, respectively to lift an object to the same height h, then the ratio of their powers is **[Kerala CEE]**

(a) 1 : 2 (b) 1 : 1 (c) 2 : 1 (d) 1 : 3
(e) 3 : 1

5 If a machine gun fires n bullets per second each with kinetic energy K, then the power of the machine gun is **[Kerala CEE]**

(a) nK^2 (b) $\frac{K}{n}$ (c) n^2K (d) nK
(e) $\frac{n}{K}$

2013

6 A machine is delivering constant power to drive a body along a straight line. What is the relation between the distance travelled by the body against time? **[WB JEE]**

(a) $s^2 \propto t^3$ (b) $s^2 \propto t^{-3}$
(c) $s^3 \propto t^2$ (d) $s \propto t^3$

7 A car of mass m starts from rest and accelerates, so that the instantaneous power delivered to the car has a constant magnitude P_0. The instantaneous velocity of this car is proportional to **[CBSE AIPMT]**

(a) $t^2 P_0$ (b) $t^{1/2}$
(c) $t^{-1/2}$ (d) $t / \sqrt{m}$

8 The machine gun fires 240 bullets per minute. If the mass of each bullet is 10 g and the velocity of the bullets is $600\ \text{ms}^{-1}$, the power (in kW) of the gun is **[AFMC]**

(a) 43200 (b) 432
(c) 72 (d) 7.2

2011

9 A box is moved along a straight line by a machine delivering constant power. The distance moved by the body in time t is proportional to **[WB JEE]**

(a) $t^{\frac{1}{2}}$ (b) $t^{\frac{3}{4}}$
(c) $t^{\frac{3}{2}}$ (d) t^2

2010

10 A tap supplies water at 22° C, a man takes 1L of water per min at 37° C from the geyser. The power of the geyser is

(a) 525 W (b) 1050 W **[BVP]**
(c) 1775 W (d) 2100 W

11 A body of mass 10 kg moves with a velocity $2\ \text{ms}^{-1}$ along a circular path of radius 8 m. The power produced by the body will be **[Manipal]**

(a) $10\ \text{Js}^{-1}$ (b) $98\ \text{Js}^{-1}$
(c) $49\ \text{Js}^{-1}$ (d) zero

12 A car of mass 1000 kg accelerates uniformly from rest to a velocity of $54\ \text{kmh}^{-1}$ in 5 s. The average power of the engine during this period in watt is (neglect friction).

(a) 2000 W (b) 22500 W **[VMMC]**
(c) 5000 W (d) 2250 W

2008

13 Water falls from a height of 60 m at the rate of $15\ \text{kgs}^{-1}$ to operate a turbine. The losses due to frictional forces are 10% of energy. How much power is generated by the turbine? (Take, $g = 10\ \text{ms}^{-2}$) **[CBSE AIPMT]**

(a) 8.1 kW (b) 10.2 kW
(c) 12.3 kW (d) 7.9 kW

14 An object of mass m moves horizontally, increasing in speed from 0 to v in a time t. The power necessary to accelerate the object during this time period is **[Manipal]**

(a) $\frac{mv^2 t}{2}$ (b) $\frac{mv^2}{2}$
(c) $2mv^2$ (d) $\frac{mv^2}{2t}$

15 A particle of mass m is moving in a circular path of constant radius r such that centripetal acceleration, a_c varying with time is $a_c = k^2rt^2$, where k is a constant. What is the power delivered to the particle by the force acting on it? [BHU]

(a) $2mkr^2t$ (b) mkr^2t^2
(c) mk^2r^2t (d) mk^2rt^2

16 An engine pumps up 100 kg of water through a height of 10 m in 5 s. Given that the efficiency of engine is 60%. If $g = 10\text{ ms}^{-2}$, the power of the engine is [BCECE]

(a) 3.3 kW (b) 0.33 kW
(c) 0.033 kW (d) 33 kW

2006

17 In 2 min, the energy dissipated by a lamp is 3000 J. Find the power of the lamp. [CBSE AIPMT]

(a) 20 W (b) 25 W
(c) 10 W (d) 24 W

18 An engineer claims to have made an engine delivering 10 kW power with fuel consumption of 1 gs^{-1}. The calorific value of fuel is 2 kcal g^{-1}. This claim is [MHT CET]

(a) valid
(b) invalid
(c) dependent on engine design
(d) dependent on load

19 A body of mass 2 kg is projected at 20 ms^{-1} at an angle 60° above the horizontal. Power due to the gravitational force at its highest point is [J&K CET]

(a) 200 W (b) $100\sqrt{3}$ W
(c) 50 W (d) zero

2005

20 A man does a given amount of work in 10 s. Another man does the same amount of work in 20 s. The ratio of the output power of first man to the second man is [J&K CET]

(a) 1 (b) 1/ 2
(c) 2/1 (d) None of these

21 A particle of mass m is driven by a machine that delivers a constant power k watts. If the particle starts from rest, the force on the particle at time t is [AIIMS]

(a) $\sqrt{\dfrac{mk}{2}}\,t^{-1/2}$ (b) $\sqrt{mk}\,t^{-1/2}$

(c) $\sqrt{2mk}\,t^{-1/2}$ (d) $\dfrac{1}{2}\sqrt{mk}\,t^{-1/2}$

22 A quarter horse power motor runs at a speed of 600 rpm. Assuming 40% efficiency, the work done by the motor in one rotation will be [Manipal]

(a) 7.46 J (b) 7400 J
(c) 7.46 erg (d) 74.6 J

Answers

1 (c)	2 (c)	3 (b)	4 (c)	5 (d)	6 (a)	7 (b)	8 (d)	9 (c)	10 (b)
11 (d)	12 (b)	13 (a)	14. (d)	15 (c)	16 (a)	17 (b)	18 (b)	19 (a)	20 (c)
21 (a)	22 (a)								

Explanations

1 (c) Net force required to lift a hook and load, $F_{net} = 1000 + 10000 = 11000$ N

$\because$ Power required to the lift hook,
$$P = \frac{W}{t}$$
We know that, $W = F_{net}d$
$$\therefore\ P = \frac{F_{net}d}{t} = F_{net}\left(\frac{d}{t}\right) = F_{net}v \qquad \left[\because v = \frac{d}{t}\right]$$
or $P = 11000 \times 0.5 = 5500\text{ W} = 5.5\text{ kW}$

2 (c) According to question, a body of mass 1 kg begins to move under the action of time dependent force,
$$\mathbf{F} = (2t\hat{\mathbf{i}} + 3t\hat{\mathbf{j}})\text{N}$$
where, $\hat{\mathbf{i}}$ and $\hat{\mathbf{j}}$ are unit vectors along X and Y-axes.

$$\because\quad \mathbf{F} = m\mathbf{a} \Rightarrow \mathbf{a} = \frac{\mathbf{F}}{m}$$
$$\Rightarrow \mathbf{a} = \frac{(2t\hat{\mathbf{i}} + 3t^2\hat{\mathbf{j}})}{1} \quad \{\because m = 1\text{ kg}\}$$
$$\Rightarrow \mathbf{a} = (2t\hat{\mathbf{i}} + 3t^2\hat{\mathbf{j}})\text{ ms}^{-2}$$
$\because$ Acceleration, $a = \dfrac{dv}{dt} \Rightarrow dv = a\,dt$

Integrating both sides, we get
$$\int dv = \int a\,dt = \int (2t\hat{\mathbf{i}} + 3t^2\hat{\mathbf{j}})dt$$
$$\mathbf{v} = t^2\hat{\mathbf{i}} + t^3\hat{\mathbf{j}}$$
$\because$ Power developed by the force at the time t will be given as
$$P = \mathbf{F}\cdot\mathbf{v} = (2t\hat{\mathbf{i}} + 3t^2\hat{\mathbf{j}}).(t^2\hat{\mathbf{i}} + t^3\hat{\mathbf{j}})$$
$$= (2t.t^2 + 3t^2.t^3)$$
$$P = (2t^3 + 3t^5)\text{ W}$$

3 (b) Let a body of mass m initially at rest attains velocity v after a time t as shown in the figure.

$t = 0$ → a → $t = t$; $v = 0$, $v = v$

The constant force F produces a constant acceleration a.

We know that, power is the rate of doing work.

So, for instantaneous displacement dx, we can write
$$P = \frac{dW}{dt} = \mathbf{F}\cdot\left(\frac{d\mathbf{x}}{dt}\right) = \mathbf{F}\cdot\mathbf{v}$$
where, $\mathbf{v}$ is instantaneous velocity.

For one-dimensional forward motion, we can write

$\mathbf{F} \cdot \mathbf{v} = |\mathbf{F}||\mathbf{v}| \cos 0° = (F)(v)$

So, power delivered to the block by the force F at any time t is

$$P = (F)(v) \quad \ldots(i)$$

Now, by equation of motion along x

$$v_x = u_x + a_x t$$

$\Rightarrow \quad v = 0 + at$

$\Rightarrow \quad v = at \quad \ldots(ii)$

From Eqs. (i) and (ii), we get

$P = (F)(at) = (ma)(at) \quad [\because F = ma]$

$= (ma^2)t \Rightarrow P \propto t$

[given, ma^2 = constant]

4 (c) Given, $t_1 = 2$ s, $t_2 = 4$ s

and $h_1 = h_2 = h$

As, $P_A = \dfrac{mgh_1}{t_1}$ and $P_B = \dfrac{mgh_2}{t_2} \ldots(i)$

$\Rightarrow P_A : P_B = \dfrac{mgh_1/t_1}{mgh_2/t_2}$

$= \left(\dfrac{h_1}{h_1}\right)\left(\dfrac{t_2}{t_1}\right) = \dfrac{t_2}{t_1} = \dfrac{4}{2} = \dfrac{2}{1}$

$\Rightarrow P_A : P_B = 2:1$

5 (d) The power of the machine gun

$= \dfrac{\text{total work done}}{\text{time}} = \dfrac{n \cdot \frac{1}{2}mv^2}{t}$

$= n \cdot \dfrac{1}{2}\dfrac{mv^2}{t} \quad \left(\because K = \dfrac{1}{2}mv^2, t = 1\text{ s}\right)$

$\therefore$ The power of the machine gun $= nK$

6 (a) As dimensions of power $= [\text{ML}^2\text{T}^{-3}]$ = constant

$\therefore \quad \left[\dfrac{\text{ML}^2}{\text{T}^3}\right]$ = constant

$\therefore \quad [\text{L}^2] \propto [\text{T}^3]$ or $s^2 \propto t^3$

7 (b) As, $P_0 = Fv = \left(m\dfrac{dv}{dt}\right)v = mv\dfrac{dv}{dt}$

$\Rightarrow P_0 \cdot dt = mvdv$

Integrating both sides, we get

$\int_0 P_0\, dt = \int mv\, dv$

$\Rightarrow \quad P_0 t = \dfrac{mv^2}{2}$

$\Rightarrow \quad v^2 = \dfrac{2P_0 t}{m} \Rightarrow v \propto t^{1/2}$

8 (d) Given, $n = 240, = 4$ bullets per second, $m = 10\text{ g} = 10 \times 10^{-3}$ kg,

$t = 1$ s and $v = 600\text{ ms}^{-1}$

Work done by the gun

= Total kinetic energy of the bullets

$= n\dfrac{1}{2}mv^2 = 4 \times \dfrac{1}{2} \times 10 \times 10^{-3} \times (600)^2$

$= 2 \times 10 \times 10^{-3} \times 600 \times 600$

$\therefore$ Power of gun $= \dfrac{\text{Work done}}{\text{Time taken}}$

$= \dfrac{2 \times 10 \times 10^{-3} \times 600 \times 600}{1}$

$= 7.2$ kW

9 (c) We are given that, a box is moved along a straight line by a machine under constant power.

So, we have power, $P = Fv = mav$

$P = m\dfrac{dv}{dt}v$ or $\int v dv = \int \dfrac{P}{m} dt$

$\Rightarrow \quad \dfrac{v^2}{2} = \dfrac{Pt}{m} \Rightarrow v = \sqrt{\dfrac{2P}{m}t}$

$\Rightarrow \quad \dfrac{dx}{dt} = \sqrt{\dfrac{2P}{m}t} \quad \left[\because v = \dfrac{dx}{dt}\right]$

$\Rightarrow \quad \int dx = \sqrt{\dfrac{2P}{m}} \int t^{1/2} dt$

$\Rightarrow \quad x = \sqrt{\dfrac{2P}{m}} \dfrac{t^{3/2}}{3/2}$

$\Rightarrow \quad x \propto t^{3/2}$

10 (b) Given, $T_1 = 22°$C, $T_2 = 37°$C,

$\Delta T = T_2 - T_1 = (37 - 22)°$C

and $m = 1$ L of water per min,

i.e. $t = 60$ s

As, power, $P = \dfrac{W}{t} = \dfrac{m \times s \times \Delta T}{t}$

(where, s = specific heat of water)

$= \dfrac{1 \times 4200 \times (37 - 22)}{60}$

$= 1050$ W

11 (d) Given, $m = 10$ kg, $v = 2\text{ms}^{-1}$ and $R = 8$ m

As, force, $F_c = \dfrac{mv^2}{R} = \dfrac{10 \times (2)^2}{8} = 5$ N

Power is defined as the rate of change of energy in a system or the time rate of doing work.

$\Rightarrow \quad P = \dfrac{dE}{dt} = \dfrac{dW}{dt}$

Also, work = force $\cdot$ displacement

$= F \cdot d = F \cdot d \cos\theta$

Since, for circular motion, displacement is zero and $\theta = 90°$.

So, $\quad W = 0$

Hence, power is also zero.

12 (b) Given, $m = 100$ kg, $v = 54\text{ kmh}^{-1}$

$= \dfrac{54 \times 5}{18} = 15\text{ ms}^{-1}$ and $t = 5$ s

From equation of motion, velocity,

$v = u + at$

$\Rightarrow a = \dfrac{15 - 0}{5} = 3\text{ ms}^{-2}$

Hence, $P_{av} = \dfrac{1}{2}Fv = \dfrac{1}{2}mav$

$= \dfrac{1}{2} \times 1000 \times 3 \times 15$

$= 22500$ W

13 (a) As, losses are 10%, so efficiency is 90%.

Power generated by the turbine

$P_{gen} = P_i \times \dfrac{90}{100} = \dfrac{Mgh}{t} \times \dfrac{90}{100}$

Given, $\dfrac{M}{t} = 15\text{ kg s}^{-1}$,

$g = 10\text{ ms}^{-2}$ and $h = 60$ m.

Putting the given values, we get

$\therefore \quad P_{gen} = (15 \times 10 \times 60) \times \dfrac{90}{100}$

$= 8.1$ kW

14 (d) Power, $P = \dfrac{W}{t}$

Since, $\quad K_i$ = initial KE = 0

K_f = final KE $= \dfrac{1}{2}mv^2$

From work-energy theorem,

Work done = Change in KE

$\therefore \quad P = \dfrac{K_f - K_i}{t} = \dfrac{\frac{1}{2}mv^2 - 0}{t}$

$\Rightarrow \quad P = \dfrac{mv^2}{2t}$

15 (c) Centripetal acceleration,

$a_c = \dfrac{v^2}{r} = k^2rt^2$

$\Rightarrow \quad v^2 = k^2r^2t^2$

As, $\quad \text{KE} = \dfrac{1}{2}mv^2$

So, KE $= \dfrac{1}{2}mk^2r^2t^2$

According to work-energy theorem, change in kinetic energy is equal to the work done.

$\therefore \quad W = \dfrac{1}{2}mk^2r^2t^2$

Thus, power delivered to the particle,

$$P = \frac{dW}{dt} = \frac{d}{dt}\left(\frac{1}{2}mk^2r^2t^2\right) = mk^2r^2t$$

16 (a) Efficiency of engine, $\eta = 60\%$

Thus, power $= \dfrac{\text{work / time}}{\eta}$

$$= \frac{100}{60} \times \frac{mgh}{t}$$

Given, $m = 100$ kg, $h = 10$ m, $t = 5$ s

and $g = 10 \text{ ms}^{-2}$

Applying power $= \dfrac{mgh}{t}$

Hence, power $= \dfrac{100}{60} \times \dfrac{100 \times 10 \times 10}{5}$

$= 3.3 \times 10^3 \text{W} = 3.3$ kW

17 (b) Given, $t = 2$ min $= 120$ s

and $W = 3000$ J

Power, $P = \dfrac{W}{t} = \dfrac{3000}{120}$

$\therefore \quad P = 25$ W

18 (b) Given, $P_{\text{output}} = 10$ kW

Now, $P_{\text{input}} = 2 \times 10^3 \text{ calg}^{-1} \times 1 \text{ g s}^{-1}$

$= 2 \times 10^3 \text{ cal s}^{-1}$

$= 2 \times 10^3 \times 4.2 \text{ Js}^{-1}$

$= 8.4$ kW

As, $P_{\text{output}} > P_{\text{input}}$, hence the claim given in question is never possible. Since, energy is always conserved.

19 (a) Power (P) is given as

$$P = \mathbf{F} \cdot \mathbf{v} = Fv\cos\theta$$

where, F is the force, v is the velocity and θ is the angle between F and v.

$$P = mgv\cos\theta \quad [\because F = mg]$$

Given, $m = 2$ kg, $v = 20 \text{ ms}^{-1}$

and $\theta = 60°$

$\Rightarrow \quad P = 2 \times 20 \times 10 \times \cos 60°$

or $\quad P = 2 \times 20 \times 10 \times \dfrac{1}{2}$

$\Rightarrow \quad P = 200$ W

20 (c) The rate of doing work is defined as power.

i.e. Power $= \dfrac{\text{Work done}}{\text{Time}}$

$$\therefore \quad \frac{P_1}{P_2} = \frac{W_1/t_1}{W_2/t_2}$$

Given, $t_1 = 10$ s, $t_2 = 20$ s, $W_1 = W_2$

$$\therefore \quad \frac{P_1}{P_2} = \frac{t_2}{t_1} = \frac{2}{1}$$

21 (a) As the machine delivers a constant power

So $F \cdot v =$ constant $= k$ (watts)

$$\Rightarrow \quad m\frac{dv}{dt} \cdot v = k \quad \left[\because F = \frac{mdv}{dt}\right]$$

$$\Rightarrow \quad \int v dv = \frac{k}{m}\int dt$$

$$\Rightarrow \quad \frac{v^2}{2} = \frac{k}{m}t \Rightarrow v = \sqrt{\frac{2k}{m}t}$$

Now, force on the particle is given by

$$F = m\frac{dv}{dt} = m\frac{d}{dt}\left(\frac{2kt}{m}\right)^{\frac{1}{2}}$$

$$= \sqrt{2km} \cdot \left(\frac{1}{2}t^{-\frac{1}{2}}\right) = \sqrt{\frac{mk}{2}} \cdot t^{-\frac{1}{2}}$$

22 (a) Given, power

$$= \frac{1}{4}\text{HP} = \frac{1}{4} \times 746$$

$= 186.5$ W

$(\because 1 \text{ HP} = 746 \text{ W})$

Power used to do work $= 40\% \times 186.5$

$$= \frac{40}{100} \times 186.5$$

$\Rightarrow \quad P = 74.6$ W

Speed $= 600$ rpm

$= \dfrac{600}{60} = 10$ rps

$= 2\pi\,(10) \text{ rads}^{-1}$

$= 20\pi \text{ rads}^{-1}$

We have, $40\% \times P = \dfrac{W}{t}$

$$\Rightarrow \quad 74.6 = \frac{W}{2\pi \times \dfrac{1}{20\pi} \text{ rotations}}$$

$\Rightarrow \quad W = 7.46$ J

Topic 5
Collision

2019

1 Body A of mass $4m$ moving with speed u collides with another body B of mass $2m$ at rest. The collision is head-on and elastic in nature. After the collision, the fraction of energy lost by the colliding body A is **[NEET]**

(a) $\dfrac{8}{9}$ (b) $\dfrac{4}{9}$ (c) $\dfrac{5}{9}$ (d) $\dfrac{1}{9}$

2 An object flying in air with velocity $(20\hat{\mathbf{i}} + 25\hat{\mathbf{j}} - 12\hat{\mathbf{k}})$ suddenly breaks in two pieces whose masses are in the ratio 1 : 5. The smaller mass flies off with a velocity $(100\hat{\mathbf{i}} + 35\hat{\mathbf{j}} + 8\hat{\mathbf{k}})$. The velocity of the larger piece will be **[NEET (Odisha)]**

(a) $4\hat{\mathbf{i}} + 23\hat{\mathbf{j}} - 8\hat{\mathbf{k}}$ (b) $-100\hat{\mathbf{i}} - 35\hat{\mathbf{j}} - 8\hat{\mathbf{k}}$

(c) $20\hat{\mathbf{i}} + 15\hat{\mathbf{j}} - 80\hat{\mathbf{k}}$ (d) $-20\hat{\mathbf{i}} - 15\hat{\mathbf{j}} - 80\hat{\mathbf{k}}$

3 A body of mass 5×10^3 kg moving with speed 2 ms^{-1} collides with a body of mass 15×10^3 kg inelastically and sticks to it. Then, loss in kinetic energy of the system will be **[AIIMS]**

(a) 7.5 kJ (b) 15 kJ

(c) 10 kJ (d) 5 kJ

4 **Assertion** There is no loss in energy in elastic collision.

Reason Linear momentum is conserved in elastic collision. **[AIIMS]**

(a) If both assertion and reason are true and reason is the correct explanation of assertion.

(b) If both assertion and reason are true, but reason is not the correct explanation of assertion.

(c) If assertion is true, but reason is false.

(d) If both assertion and reason are false.

5 A particle of mass 5*m* at rest suddenly breaks on its own into three fragments. Two fragments of mass *m* each move along mutually perpendicular direction with each speed *v*. The energy released during the process is **[NEET (Odisha)]**

(a) $\frac{3}{5}mv^2$ (b) $\frac{5}{3}mv^2$ (c) $\frac{3}{2}mv^2$ (d) $\frac{4}{3}mv^2$

6 One object of mass 20 kg is moving with speed 10 ms^{-1} in west direction another object of mass 10 kg is moving with 15 ms^{-1} in north direction. Both collide and stick together. Choose the correct alternative. **[JIPMER]**

(a) There kinetic energy is conserved as it is inelastic collision.
(b) There kinetic energy is conserved as it is elastic collision.
(c) There momentum is conserved as it is inelastic collision.
(d) There momentum is conserved as it is elastic collision.

7 Two objects of mass *m* each moving with speed *u* ms^{-1} collide at 90°, then final momentum is (assume collision is inelastic) **[JIPMER]**

(a) *mu* (b) 2 *mu* (c) $\sqrt{2}\,mu$ (d) $2\sqrt{2}\,mu$

2018

8 A moving block having mass *m*, collides with another stationary block having mass 4*m*. The lighter block comes to rest after collision. When the initial velocity of the lighter block is *v*, then the value of coefficient of restitution (*e*) will be **[NEET]**

(a) 0.8 (b) 0.25 (c) 0.5 (d) 0.4

9 Body of mass *M* is much heavier than the other body of mass *m*. The heavier body with speed *v* collides with the lighter body which was at rest initially elastically. The speed of lighter body after collision is **[AIIMS]**

(a) 2 *v* (b) 3 *v* (c) *v* (d) $\frac{v}{2}$

10 **Assertion** Two particles moving in the same direction do not lose all their energy in completely inelastic collision.

Reason Principle of conservation of momentum holds true for all kinds of collisions. **[AIIMS]**

(a) Both Assertion and Reason are correct and Reason is the correct explanation of Assertion.
(b) Both Assertion and Reason are correct but Reason is not the correct explanation of Assertion.
(c) Assertion is correct but Reason is incorrect.
(d) Assertion is incorrect but Reason is correct.

11 A ball of 0.5 kg collided with wall at 30° and bounced back elastically. The speed of ball was 12ms^{-1}. The contact remained for 1s. What is the force applied by wall on ball? **[JIPMER]**

(a) $12\sqrt{3}$ N (b) $\sqrt{3}$ N (c) $6\sqrt{3}$ N (d) $3\sqrt{3}$ N

2017

12 A block *C* of mass *m* is moving with velocity v_0 and collides elastically with block *A* of mass *m* and connected to another block *B* of mass 2*m* through spring of spring constant *k*. What is the value of *k*, if x_0 is compression of spring when, velocity of *A* and *B* is same? **[JIPMER]**

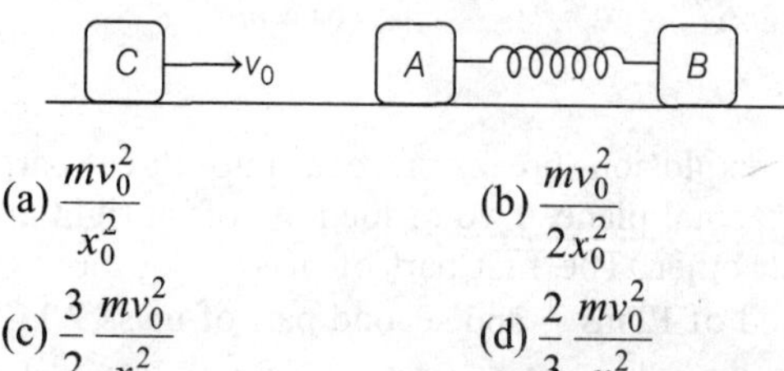

(a) $\frac{mv_0^2}{x_0^2}$ (b) $\frac{mv_0^2}{2x_0^2}$
(c) $\frac{3}{2}\frac{mv_0^2}{x_0^2}$ (d) $\frac{2}{3}\frac{mv_0^2}{x_0^2}$

13 A body of mass 4kg moving with velocity 12 ms^{-1} collides with another body of mass 6kg at rest. If two bodies stick together after collision, then the loss of kinetic energy of system is **[AIIMS]**

(a) zero (b) 288 J (c) 172.8 J (d) 144 J

2016

14 A bullet of mass 10 g moving horizontal with a velocity of 400 ms^{-1} strikes a wood block of mass 2 kg which is suspended by light inextensible string of length 5 m. As result, the centre of gravity of the block found to rise a vertical distance of 10 cm. The speed of the bullet after it emerges of horizontally from the block will be **[NEET]**

(a) 100 ms^{-1} (b) 80 ms^{-1}
(c) 120 ms^{-1} (d) 160 ms^{-1}

15 Two identical balls *A* and *B* having velocities of 0.5 ms^{-1} and -0.3 ms^{-1} respectively collide elastically in one dimension. The velocities of *B* and *A* after the collision respectively will be **[NEET]**

(a) -0.5 ms^{-1} and 0.3 ms^{-1}
(b) 0.5 m/s^{-1} and -0.3 ms^{-1}
(c) -0.3 ms^{-1} and 0.5 ms^{-1}
(d) 0.3 ms^{-1} and 0.5 ms^{-1}

2015

16 Two particles of masses m_1 and m_2 move with initial velocities u_1 and u_2. On collision, one of the particle gets excited to higher level, after absorbing energy ε. If final velocities of particles be v_1 and v_2, then we must have **[CBSE AIPMT]**

(a) $m_1^2 u_1 + m_2^2 u_2 - \varepsilon = m_1^2 v_1 + m_2^2 v_2$
(b) $\frac{1}{2}m_1 u_1^2 + \frac{1}{2}m_2 u_2^2 = \frac{1}{2}m_1 v_1^2 + \frac{1}{2}m_2 v_2^2 - \varepsilon$
(c) $\frac{1}{2}m_1 u_1^2 + \frac{1}{2}m_2 u_2^2 - \varepsilon = \frac{1}{2}m_1 v_1^2 + \frac{1}{2}m_2 v_2^2$
(d) $\frac{1}{2}m_1^2 u_1^2 + \frac{1}{2}m_2^2 u_2^2 + \varepsilon = \frac{1}{2}m_1^2 v_1^2 + \frac{1}{2}m_2^2 v_2^2$

2014

17 A body of mass $4m$ is lying in xy-plane at rest. It suddenly explodes into three pieces. Two pieces each of mass m move perpendicular to each other with equal speeds v. The total kinetic energy generated due to explosion is

(a) mv^2 (b) $(3/2)\,mv^2$ **[CBSE AIPMT]**
(c) $2mv^2$ (d) $4\,mv^2$

2013

18 An explosion breaks a rock into three parts in a horizontal plane. Two of them go off at right angles to each other. The first part of mass 1 kg moves with a speed of 12 ms^{-1} and second part of mass 2 kg moves with 8 ms^{-1} speed. If the third part lies off which 4 ms^{-1} speed, then its mass is **[NEET]**

(a) 3 kg (b) 5 kg (c) 7 kg (d) 17 kg

19 A ball of mass m elastically collides with a wall with velocity v, then change in its momentum is equal to

(a) $2\,m$ (b) $2\,mv$ **[KCET]**
(c) $8\,mv$ (d) zero

2012

20 A spherical ball A of mass 4 kg, moving in a straight line strikes another spherical ball B of mass 1 kg at rest. After the collision, A and B move with velocities v_1 ms^{-1} and v_2 ms^{-1}, respectively making angles of 30° and 60° with respect to the original direction of motion of A. The ratio v_1 / v_2 will be **[WB JEE]**

(a) $\frac{\sqrt{3}}{4}$ (b) $\frac{4}{\sqrt{3}}$
(c) $\frac{1}{\sqrt{3}}$ (d) $\sqrt{3}$

21 Two spheres A and B of masses, m_1 and m_2, respectively collide. A is at rest initially and B is moving with velocity v along X-axis. After collision, B has a velocity $v/2$ in a direction perpendicular to the original direction. The mass A moves after collision in the direction **[CBSE AIPMT]**

(a) same as that of B
(b) opposite to that of B
(c) $\theta = \tan^{-1}\,(1/2)$ to the X-axis
(d) $\theta = \tan^{-1}\left(\frac{-1}{2}\right)$ to the X-axis

2011

22 If two bodies stick together after collision and move as a single body, the collision is said to be **[J&K CET]**

(a) perfectly inelastic (b) elastic
(c) inelastic (d) perfectly elastic

23 A bullet of mass m moving with velocity v strikes a suspended wooden block of mass M. If the block rises to a height h, then initial velocity of the block will be **[Haryana PMT]**

(a) $\sqrt{2gh}$ (b) $\frac{M+m}{m}\sqrt{gh}$
(c) $\frac{m}{M+m}\,2gh$ (d) $\frac{M+m}{M}\sqrt{2gh}$

24 A particle of mass m_1 moves with velocity v_1 and collides with another particle at rest of equal mass. The velocity of the second particle after the elastic collision is **[DUMET]**

(a) $2v_1$ (b) v_1 (c) $-v_1$ (d) 0

2010

25 A ball falls from a height of 20 m on the floor and rebounds to a height of 5 m. Time of contact is 0.02 s. Find the acceleration during impact. **[Manipal]**

(a) 1200 ms^{-2} (b) 1000 ms^{-2}
(c) 2000 ms^{-2} (d) 1500 ms^{-2}

2009

26 In a head-on elastic collision of a very heavy body moving at v with a light body at rest, then velocity of the heavy body after collision is **[KCET]**

(a) v (b) $2v$
(c) zero (d) $v/2$

27 A body of mass 2 kg makes an elastic collision with another body at rest and continues to move in the original direction with one-fourth its original speed. The mass of the second body which collides with the first body is **[Manipal]**

(a) 2 kg (b) 1.2 kg
(c) 3 kg (d) 1.5 kg

2008

28 A shell of mass 200 g is ejected from a gun of mass 4 kg by an explosion that generates 1.05 kJ of energy. The initial velocity of the shell is **[CBSE AIPMT]**

(a) 100 ms^{-1} (b) 80 ms^{-1}
(c) 40 ms^{-1} (d) 120 ms^{-1}

29 For a system to follow the law of conservation of linear momentum during a collision, the condition is **[AFMC]**

(i) total external force acting on the system is zero.
(ii) total external force acting on the system is finite and time of collision is negligible.
(ii) total internal force acting on the system is zero.

(a) Only (i) (b) Only (ii)
(c) Only (iii) (d) Only (i) or (ii)

30 **Assertion** Quick collision between two bodies is more violent than a slow collision; even when the initial and final velocities are identical.

Reason The momentum is greater in first case. [AIIMS]

(a) Both Assertion and Reason are correct and Reason is the correct explanation of Assertion.
(b) Both Assertion and Reason are correct but Reason is not the correct explanation of Assertion.
(c) Assertion is correct but Reason is incorrect.
(d) Both Assertion and Reason are incorrect.

31 In the figure, pendulum bob on left side is pulled a side to a height h from its initial position. After it is released it collides with the right pendulum bob at rest, which is of same mass. After the collision, the two bobs stick together and rise to a height [Punjab PMET]

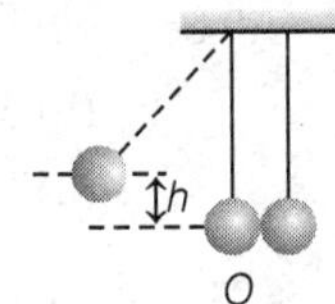

(a) $\frac{3h}{4}$ (b) $\frac{2h}{3}$
(c) $\frac{h}{2}$ (d) $\frac{h}{4}$

32 A sphere of mass m moving with constant velocity u, collides with another stationary sphere of same mass. If, e is the coefficient of restitution, the ratio of the final velocities of the first and second spheres is [Punjab PMET]

(a) $\frac{1+e}{1-e}$ (b) $\frac{1-e}{1+e}$ (c) $\frac{e}{1-e}$ (d) $\frac{1+e}{e}$

33 Two balls of same mass each m are moving with same velocities, v on a smooth surface as shown in figure. If all collisions between the masses and with the wall are perfectly elastic, the possible number of collisions between the bodies and wall together is [EAMCET]

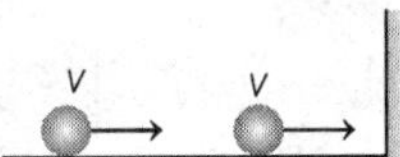

(a) 1 (b) 2
(c) 3 (d) infinity

34 A body of mass m strikes another body at rest of mass $\frac{m}{9}$.

Assuming the impact to be inelastic, the fraction of the initial kinetic energy transformed into heat during the contact is [EAMCET]

(a) 0.1 (b) 0.2 (c) 0.5 (d) 0.64

2007

35 A bomb of mass 3.0 kg explodes in air into two pieces of masses 2.0 kg and 1.0 kg. The smaller mass goes at a speed of 80 ms^{-1}. The total energy imparted to the fragments is

(a) 1.07 kJ (b) 2.14 kJ [UP CPMT]
(c) 2.4 kJ (d) 4.8 kJ

36 A body from height h is dropped. If the coefficient of restitution is e, then calculate the height achieved after one bounce. [UP CPMT]

(a) $h_1 = e^2 h$ (b) $h_1 = e^4 h$
(c) $h_1 = eh$ (d) $h_1 = \frac{h}{e}$

37 A body of mass m moving with velocity v makes a head-on collision with another body of mass $2m$ which is initially at rest. The loss of kinetic energy of the colliding body (mass m) is [Punjab PMET]

(a) (1/ 2) of its initial kinetic energy
(b) (1/ 9) of its initial kinetic energy
(c) (8/ 9) of its initial kinetic energy
(d) (1/ 4) of its initial kinetic energy

38 For inelastic collision between two spherical rigid bodies,

(a) the total kinetic energy is conserved [MP PMT]
(b) the linear momentum is not conserved
(c) the total mechanical energy is not conserved
(d) the linear momentum is conserved

39 A bomb of 12 kg explodes into two pieces of masses 4 kg and 8 kg. The velocity of 8 kg mass is 6 ms^{-1}. The kinetic energy of the other mass is [UP CPMT]

(a) 348 J (b) 332 J
(c) 324 J (d) 288 J

40 A body of mass m_1 collides elastically with another body of mass m_2 at rest. If the velocity of m_1 after collision becomes 2/3 times of its initial velocity, the ratio of their masses, is [J&K CET]

(a) 1 : 5 (b) 5 : 1
(c) 5 : 2 (d) 2 : 5

41 A stationary bomb explodes into two parts of masses in the ratio of 1 : 3. If the heavier mass moves with a velocity 4 ms^{-1}, what is the velocity of the lighter part? [J&K CET]

(a) 12 ms^{-1} opposite to heavier mass
(b) 12 ms^{-1} in the direction of heavier mass
(c) 6 ms^{-1} opposite to heavier mass
(d) 6 ms^{-1} in the direction of heavier mass

2006

42 Which of the following is not an example of perfectly inelastic collision? **[AMU]**

(a) A bullet fired into a block if bullet gets embedded into block
(b) Capture of electrons by an atom
(c) A man jumping on to a moving boat
(d) A ball bearing striking another ball bearing

43 A bullet of mass 20 g and moving with 600 ms^{-1} collides with a block of mass 4 kg hanging with the string. What is velocity of bullet when it comes out of block, if block rises to height 0.2 m after collision? **[DUMET]**

(a) 200 ms^{-1} (b) 150 ms^{-1} (c) 400 ms^{-1} (d) 300 ms^{-1}

44 In two separate collisions, the coefficients of restitutions, e_1 and e_2 are in the ratio 3 : 1. In the first collision, the relative velocity of approach is twice the relative velocity of separation. Then, the ratio between the relative velocity of approach and relative velocity of separation in the second collision is **[EAMCET]**

(a) 1 : 6 (b) 2 : 3 (c) 3 : 2 (d) 6 : 1

2005

45 A bomb of mass 30 kg at rest explodes into two pieces of masses 18 kg and 12 kg. The velocity of 18 kg mass is 6 ms^{-1}. The kinetic energy of the other mass is **[CBSE AIPMT]**

(a) 256 J (b) 486 J
(c) 524 J (d) 324 J

46 A shell of mass 20 kg at rest explodes into two fragments wose masses are in the ratio 2 : 3. The smaller fragment moves with a velocity of 6 ms^{-1}. The kinetic energy of the larger fragment is **[KCET]**

(a) 96 J (b) 216 J (c) 144 J (d) 360 J

47 A body of mass m is moving towards east and another body of equal mass and speed is moving towards the north. If after collision both stick together, then their speed after collision would be **[DUMET]**

(a) v (b) $v/2$
(c) $\sqrt{2}v$ (d) $v/\sqrt{2}$

48 A ball falling freely from a height of 4.9 ms^{-1} hits a horizontal surface. If $e = 3/4$, then the ball will hit the surface second time after **[DUMET]**

(a) 0.5 s (b) 1.5 s
(c) 3.5 s (d) 3.4 s

49 A moving body of mass m and velocity 3 kmh^{-1} collides with a body at rest and of mass $2m$ and then sticks to it. Now the combined mass starts to move, then the combined velocity will be **[RPMT]**

(a) 4 kmh^{-1} (b) 3 kmh^{-1}
(c) 2 kmh^{-1} (d) 1 kmh^{-1}

50 A body of 1 kg mass explodes into three fragments. The ratio of their masses is 1 : 1 : 3. The fragments of same mass move perpendicular to each other with speed 30 ms^{-1}, while the heavier part remains in the initial direction. The speed of heavier part is **[BCECE]**

(a) $10/\sqrt{2}$ ms^{-1} (b) $10\sqrt{2}$ ms^{-1}
(c) $20\sqrt{2}$ ms^{-1} (d) $30\sqrt{2}$ ms^{-1}

51 A body of mass 4 kg moving with velocity 12 ms^{-1} collides with another body of mass 6 kg at rest. If two bodies stick together after collision, then the loss of kinetic energy of system is **[J&K CET]**

(a) zero (b) 288 J
(c) 172.8 J (d) 144 J

Answers

1 (a)	2 (a)	3 (a)	4 (b)	5 (d)	6 (c)	7 (c)	8 (b)	9 (a)	10 (a)
11 (c)	12 (d)	13 (c)	14 (c)	15 (c)	16 (c)	17 (b)	18 (b)	19 (b)	20 (a)
21 (c)	22 (a)	23 (a)	24 (b)	25 (d)	26 (a)	27 (b)	28 (a)	29 (a)	30 (a)
31 (d)	32 (b)	33 (c)	34 (a)	35 (d)	36 (a)	37 (c)	38 (d)	39 (d)	40 (b)
41 (a)	42 (d)	43 (a)	44 (d)	45 (b)	46 (a)	47 (d)	48 (b)	49 (d)	50 (b)
51 (c)									

Explanations

1 (a) The given situation of collision can be drawn as

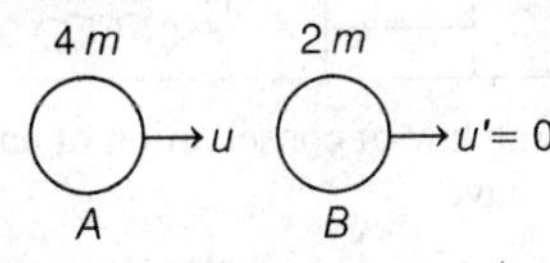

Before collision

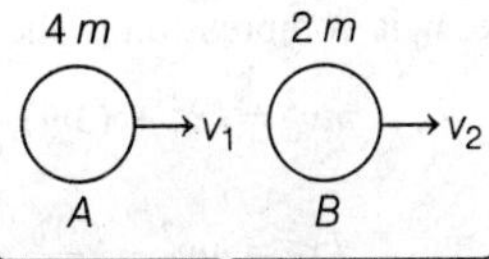

After collision

Applying conservation of linear momentum,

Initial momentum of system = Final momentum of system

$$\Rightarrow (4m)u + (2m)u' = (4m)v_1 + (2m)v_2$$

$$4mu + (2m) \times 0 = 4mv_1 + 2mv_2$$

or $\quad 2u = 2v_1 + v_2 \qquad \ldots \text{(i)}$

The kinetic energy of A before collision,

$$\text{KE}_A = \frac{1}{2}(4m)u^2 = 2mu^2$$

Kinetic energy of B before collision,

$(\text{KE})_B = 0$

The kinetic energy of A after collision ,

$$(\text{KE}')_A = \frac{1}{2}(4m)v_1^2 = 2mv_1^2$$

Kinetic energy of B after collision,

$$(\text{KE}')_B = \frac{1}{2}(2m)v_2^2 = mv_2^2$$

As, initial kinetic energy of the system = final kinetic energy of the system

$$\Rightarrow (\text{KE}')_A + (\text{KE}')_B = (\text{KE}')_A + (\text{KE}')_B$$

$$2mu^2 + 0 = 2mv_1^2 + mv_2^2$$

$$2mu^2 = 2mv_1^2 + mv_2^2$$

or $\quad 2u^2 = 2v_1^2 + v_2^2 \qquad \ldots \text{(ii)}$

Solving Eqs. (i) and (ii), we get

$$v_1 = \frac{1}{3}u \text{ and } v_2 = \frac{4}{3}u$$

or the final velocity of A can be directly calculated by using the formula.

The velocity after collision is given by

$$v_1 = \left(\frac{m_1 - m_2}{m_1 + m_2}\right)u_1 + \frac{2m_2u_2}{m_1 + m_2}$$

$$= \left(\frac{4m - 2m}{4m + 2m}\right)u + \frac{2(2m) \times 0}{(4m + 2m)} \qquad [\because u_2 = u' = 0]$$

$$= \frac{2m}{6m}u = \frac{1}{3}u$$

$\therefore$ Net decreases in kinetic energy of A,

$$\Delta\text{KE} = (\text{KE})_A - (\text{KE}')_A$$

$$= 2mu^2 - 2mv_1^2$$

$$= 2m(u^2 - v_1^2)$$

Substituting the value of v_1, we get

$$\Delta\text{KE} = 2m\left(u^2 - \frac{u^2}{9}\right) = \frac{16\,mu^2}{9}$$

$\therefore$ The fractional decreases in kinetic energy is

$$\frac{\Delta\text{KE}}{(\text{KE})_A} = \frac{16mu^2}{9} \times \frac{1}{2mu^2} = \frac{8}{9}$$

2 (a) Let m be the mass of an object flying with velocity v in air. When it split into two pieces of masses in ratio 1 : 5, the mass of smaller piece is $m/6$ and of bigger piece is $\frac{5m}{6}$.

This situation can be interpreted diagrammatically as below

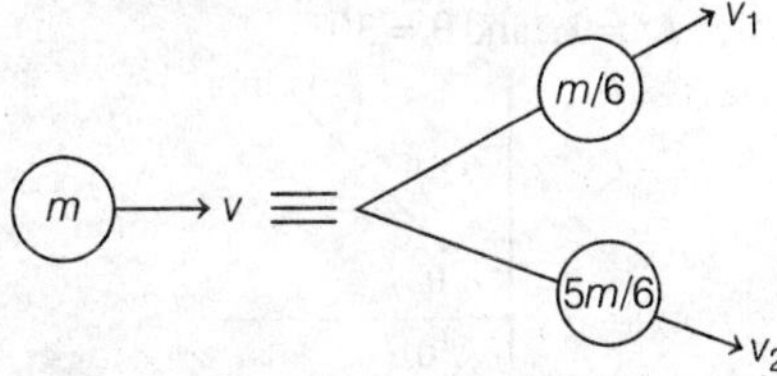

As the object breaks in two pieces, so the momentum of the system will remains conserved, i.e. the total momentum (before breaking) = total momentum (after breaking)

$$m\mathbf{v} = \frac{m}{6}\mathbf{v}_1 + \frac{5m}{6}\mathbf{v}_2$$

$$\Rightarrow \quad \mathbf{v} = \frac{\mathbf{v}_1}{6} + \frac{5\mathbf{v}_2}{6} \qquad \ldots\text{(i)}$$

Given, $\mathbf{v} = 20\hat{\mathbf{i}} + 25\hat{\mathbf{j}} - 12\hat{\mathbf{k}}$

and $\quad \mathbf{v}_1 = 100\hat{\mathbf{i}} + 35\hat{\mathbf{j}} + 8\hat{\mathbf{k}}$

Putting these values in Eq. (i), we get

$$= \frac{(100\hat{\mathbf{i}} + 35\hat{\mathbf{j}} + 8\hat{\mathbf{k}})}{6} + \frac{5\mathbf{v}_2}{6}$$

$$\Rightarrow \quad = (120\hat{\mathbf{i}} + 150\hat{\mathbf{j}} - 72\hat{\mathbf{k}})$$

$$= (100\hat{\mathbf{i}} + 35\hat{\mathbf{j}} + 8\hat{\mathbf{k}}) + 5\mathbf{v}_2$$

$$\Rightarrow \quad \mathbf{v}_2 = \frac{1}{5}(20\hat{\mathbf{i}} + 115\hat{\mathbf{j}} - 80\hat{\mathbf{k}})$$

$$= 4\hat{\mathbf{i}} + 23\hat{\mathbf{j}} - 16\hat{\mathbf{k}}$$

3 (a) Given, mass of body,

$$m_1 = 5 \times 10^3 \text{ kg}$$

Velocity, $v_1 = 2 \text{ ms}^{-1}$

and mass of another body

$$m_2 = 15 \times 10^3 \text{ kg}$$

For perfectly inelastic collision ($e = 0$), Loss in kinetic energy of system,

$$\Delta E_K = \frac{1}{2} \cdot \frac{m_1m_2}{m_1 + m_2} \times v_1^2$$

$$= \frac{1}{2} \times \frac{5 \times 10^3 \times 15 \times 10^3}{5 \times 10^3 + 15 \times 10^3} \times 2^2$$

$$= 7.5 \times 10^3 \text{ J} = 7.5 \text{ kJ}$$

4 (b) In elastic collision, total energy, kinetic energy and momentum remain conserved, therefore no loss in energy occurs in elastic collision.

Hence, both Assertion and Reason are correct but Reason is not the correct explanation of Assertion.

5 (d) The particle of mass $5m$ breaks in three fragments of mass m, m and $3m$ respectively. Two fragments of mass m each move in perpendicular direction with velocity v and the left fragment will move in a direction with velocity $\mathbf{v}'$ such that the total momentum of the system must remain conserved.

By law of conservation of momentum,

$$5m \times 0 = mv\hat{\mathbf{i}} + mv\hat{\mathbf{j}} + 3m\mathbf{v}'$$

$$\Rightarrow \quad \mathbf{v}' = -\frac{v}{3}\hat{\mathbf{i}} - \frac{v}{3}\hat{\mathbf{j}}$$

$$\therefore \quad |\mathbf{v}'| = \sqrt{\left(-\frac{v}{3}\right)^2 + \left(-\frac{v}{3}\right)^2}$$

$$= \frac{v\sqrt{2}}{3}$$

$\therefore$ Energy released,

$$E = \frac{1}{2}mv^2 + \frac{1}{2}mv^2 + \frac{1}{2} \times 3m\left(\frac{v\sqrt{2}}{3}\right)^2$$

$$= mv^2 + \frac{mv^2}{3} = \frac{4}{3}mv^2$$

6 *(c)* When object of mass 20 kg is moving with speed $10\ \text{ms}^{-1}$ in west direction collide with object of mass 10 kg and stick together, hence it is perfectly inelastic collision. In inelastic collision, only momentum is conserved.

7 *(c)* Speed of objects $= u\ \text{ms}^{-1}$

Since, both objects collide with 90°.

Hence, by the law of conservation of momentum,

Total moment before collision

= Total momentum after collision

$$|mu\hat{\mathbf{i}} + mu\hat{\mathbf{j}}| = p_f$$

$$\sqrt{m^2u^2 + m^2u^2} = p_f$$

$$\Rightarrow \quad p_f = \sqrt{2}\, mu$$

8 *(b)* Since, the collision mentioned is an elastic head-on collision. Thus, according to the law of conservation of linear momentum, we get

$$m_1u_1 + m_2u_2 = m_1v_1 + m_2v_2$$

where, m_1 and m_2 are the masses of the two blocks, respectively, u_1 and u_2 are their initial velocities and v_1 and v_2 are their final velocities, respectively.

Given, $m_1 = m, m_2 = 4m$

$u_1 = v, u_2 = 0$

and $v_1 = 0$

$mv + 4m \times 0 = 0 + 4mv_2$

$\Rightarrow \quad mv = 4mv_2$

or $\quad v_2 = \dfrac{v}{4}$ ...(i)

As, the coefficient of restitution is given as

$$e = \frac{\text{relative velocity of separation after collision}}{\text{relative velocity of approach}}$$

$$= -\frac{v_2 - v_1}{u_2 - u_1} = -\frac{\frac{v}{4} - 0}{0 - v} \quad \text{[from Eq. (i)]}$$

$= 1/4$

$\therefore \; e = 0.25$

9 *(a)* From conservation of momentum,

$Mv + m \times 0 = Mv_1 + mv_2$

$\Rightarrow M(v - v_1) = mv_2$ ...(i)

Again, from the conservation of kinetic energy (as collision is of elastic nature)

$$\frac{1}{2}Mv^2 + \frac{1}{2}m \times 0 = \frac{1}{2}Mv_1^2 + \frac{1}{2}mv_2^2$$

$\Rightarrow \quad M(v^2 - v_1^2) = mv_2^2$ ...(ii)

On solving Eqs. (i) and (ii), we get

$$\frac{M(v - v_1)}{M(v + v_1)(v - v_1)} = \frac{mv_2}{mv_2^2}$$

$v_2 = v + v_1$ ...(iii)

Now, solving Eqs. (i) and (iii), we get

$$v_1 = \frac{(M - m)v}{(M + m)} \quad \text{and} \quad v_2 = \frac{2Mv}{(M + m)}$$

As $\quad M >> m$

So, $\quad v_1 = v$ and $v_2 = 2v$

Hence, velocity of ligter body $(m)$is $2v$.

10 *(a)* If two particles are initially moving in the same direction, then their resultant momentum will not be zero. Therefore, their resultant momentum cannot be zero after a completely inelastic collision.

As, kinetic energy is directly proportional to the square of the momentum, hence kinetic energy cannot be zero. This implies, not all the energy in inelastic collision is lost.

So, both Assertion and Reason are correct and Reason is the correct explanation of Assertion.

11 *(c)* Given, $m = 0.5$ kg, $v = 12\ \text{ms}^{-1}$, $\Delta t = 1$ s and $\theta = 30°$

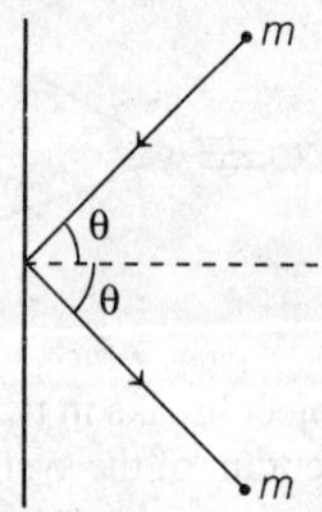

Force applied by wall on ball,

$$F = \frac{\Delta p}{\Delta t} \text{ or } F = \frac{(p_f)_H - (p_i)_H}{\Delta t}$$

$\because$ In this elastic collision, final and initial velocity will be same but direction change.

$(p_f)_H = mv\cos\theta$

and $(p_i)_H = -mv\cos\theta$

$$\because F = \frac{mv\cos\theta + mv\cos\theta}{\Delta t}$$

$$F = \frac{2mv\cos\theta}{\Delta t}$$

$$F = \frac{2 \times 0.5 \times 12 \times \cos 30°}{1}$$

$$F = 6\sqrt{3}\ \text{N}$$

12 *(d)* Using the law of conservation of linear momentum, we have

$$mv_0 = mv + 2mv \Rightarrow v = v_0/3$$

m m 2m
C →v_0 A B

Using law of conservation of energy, we have

$$\frac{1}{2}mv_0^2 = \frac{1}{2}kx_0^2 + \frac{1}{2}(3m)v^2$$

where, x_0 is compression in the string.

$$\therefore \quad mv_0^2 = kx_0^2 + (3m)\frac{v_0^2}{9}$$

$$\Rightarrow \quad kx_0^2 = mv_0^2 - \frac{mv_0^2}{3}$$

$$\Rightarrow \quad kx_0^2 = \frac{2mv_0^2}{3}$$

$$\therefore \quad k = \frac{2mv_0^2}{3x_0^2}$$

13 *(c)* Loss of KE $= \dfrac{1}{2}m_1u_1^2 - \dfrac{m_1^2u_1^2}{2(m_1 + m_2)}$

$$= \frac{m_1m_2u_1^2}{2(m_1 + m_2)}$$

Given, $m_1 = 4\,\text{kg}, u_1 = 12\ \text{ms}^{-1}$,

$m_2 = 6$ kg and $u_2 = 0$

$$\therefore \quad \Delta\text{KE} = \frac{1}{2}\frac{4 \times 6}{(4 + 6)}(12)^2$$

$$= \frac{1}{2} \times \frac{24}{10} \times (12)^2$$

$$= \frac{12}{10} \times 144$$

$= 172.8$ J

14 *(c)* Given, $m_1 = 10\ \text{g} = 0.01$ kg,

$u_1 = 400\ \text{ms}^{-1}$, $m_2 = 2$ kg

and $h = 10\ \text{cm} = 0.1$ m

According to the law of conservation of momentum,

$$p_i = p_f \Rightarrow m_1u_1 = m_2v + m_1v'$$

$\Rightarrow (0.01) \times 400 + 0 = 2v + (0.01)v'$ ...(i)

Also velocity v of the block just after the collision is

$v = \sqrt{2gh} = \sqrt{2 \times 10 \times 0.1} = \sqrt{2}$ ...(ii)

From Eqs. (i) and (ii), we have

$$4 + 0 = 2\sqrt{2} + 0.01v'$$

$$4 = 2.8 + 0.01v'$$

$$v' = 1.2/0.01 \Rightarrow 120\ \text{ms}^{-1}$$

Speed of bullet, $v' = 120\ \text{ms}^{-1}$

15 (*c*) As, we know in a elastical collision of two identical bodies, i.e. $m_A = m_B$, the particles mutually exchange their velocities.

So, $(v_i)_A = 0.5\,\text{ms}^{-1}$

and $(v_i)_B = -0.3\,\text{ms}^{-1}$.

After collision,

$(v_f)_A = -0.3\,\text{ms}^{-1}$

and $(v_f)_B = 0.5\,\text{ms}^{-1}$.

16 (*c*) Total initial energy

$$= \frac{1}{2}m_1u_1^2 + \frac{1}{2}m_2u_2^2$$

Since, after collision one particle absorb energy ε.

∴ Total final energy

$$= \frac{1}{2}m_1v_1^2 + \frac{1}{2}m_2v_2^2 + \varepsilon$$

From conservation of energy,

$$\frac{1}{2}m_1u_1^2 + \frac{1}{2}m_2u_2^2 = \frac{1}{2}m_1v_1^2 + \frac{1}{2}m_2v_2^2 + \varepsilon$$

$$\Rightarrow \frac{1}{2}m_1u_1^2 + \frac{1}{2}m_2u_2^2 - \varepsilon = \frac{1}{2}m_1v_1^2 + \frac{1}{2}m_2v_2^2$$

17 (*b*) The situation is shown

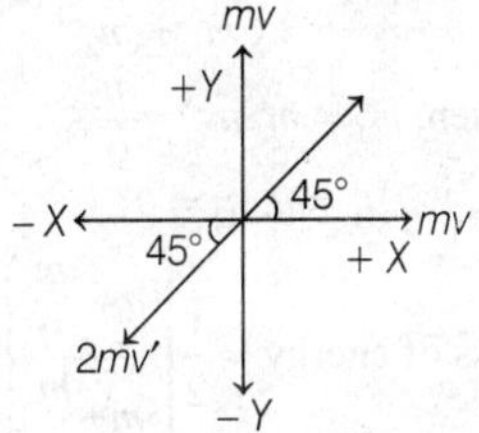

According to question, the third part of mass $2m$ will move as shown in the figure, because the total momentum of the system after explosion must remain zero. Let the velocity of third part is v', then from the conservation of momentum

$\sqrt{2}mv$ = Resultant momenta of two small masses

$$\Rightarrow \sqrt{2}\,(mv) = (2m) \times v'$$

$$\Rightarrow v' = \frac{v}{\sqrt{2}}$$

So, total kinetic energy generated by the explosion

$$= \frac{1}{2}mv^2 + \frac{1}{2}mv^2 + \frac{1}{2}(2m)\,v'^2$$

$$= mv^2 + m \times \left(\frac{v}{\sqrt{2}}\right)^2$$

$$= mv^2 + \frac{mv^2}{2} = \frac{3}{2}mv^2$$

18 (*b*) Given, $m_1 = 1\,\text{kg}$, $v_1 = 12\,\text{ms}^{-1}$,

$m_2 = 2\,\text{kg}$, $v_2 = 8\,\text{ms}^{-1}$, $\theta_3 = 4\,\text{ms}^{-1}$

and $m_3 = ?$

We have $\mathbf{p}_1 + \mathbf{p}_2 + \mathbf{p}_3 = 0$

$$\therefore\ 1 \times 12\hat{\mathbf{i}} + 2 \times 8\hat{\mathbf{j}} + \mathbf{p}_3 = 0 \quad [\because p = mv]$$

$$\Rightarrow 12\hat{\mathbf{i}} + 16\hat{\mathbf{j}} + \mathbf{p}_3 = 0$$

$$\Rightarrow \mathbf{p}_3 = -(12\hat{\mathbf{i}} + 16\hat{\mathbf{j}})$$

$$\therefore\ p_3 = \sqrt{(12)^2 + (16)^2} = \sqrt{144 + 256} = 20\ \text{kg-ms}^{-1}$$

Now, $p_3 = m_3v_3$

$$\Rightarrow m_3 = \frac{p_3}{v_3} = \frac{20}{4} = 5\,\text{kg}$$

19 (*b*) Let the direction in which ball is moving be taken as positive, after collision with the wall the direction of velocity is reversed.

Hence, change in momentum is (initial momentum - final momentum).

$$= mv - (-mv) = 2\,mv$$

20 (*a*) The situation of collision is given as below. Along *Y*-axis, momentum remains as zero.

Conservation of momentum in perpendicular direction,

$$4v_1 \sin 30° = v_2 \sin 60°$$

$$\Rightarrow \frac{v_1}{v_2} = \frac{\sqrt{3}}{4}$$

21 (*c*)

According to law of conservation of linear momentum along *X*-axis, we get

$$m_1 \times 0 + m_2 \times v = m_1v' \cos\theta$$

$$m_2v = m_1v' \cos\theta$$

or $$\cos\theta = \frac{m_2v}{m_1v'} \quad \text{...(i)}$$

According to law of conservation momentum along *Y*-axis, we get

$$m_1 \times 0 + m_2 \times 0 = -m_1v' \sin\theta + m_2\frac{v}{2}$$

$$\frac{m_2v}{2} = m_1v' \sin\theta$$

$$\sin\theta = \frac{m_2v}{2m_1v'} \quad \text{...(ii)}$$

from Eqs. (i) and (ii), we get

$$\tan\theta = \frac{1}{2}$$

or $\theta = \tan^{-1}\left(\frac{1}{2}\right)$ to the *X*-axis.

22 (*a*) If two bodies stick together after collision and move as a single body, the collision is said to be perfectly inelastic.

23 (*a*) Final kinetic energy of te block along wit te bullet wen te bullet strikes

$$= \frac{1}{2}(m + M)v^2$$

Due to tis kinetic energy te block will rise to a height *h*. Its potential energy $= (m + M)\,gh$

So, by the law of conservation of energy, $\frac{1}{2}(M + m)v^2 = (M + m)gh$

$$\Rightarrow v = \sqrt{2gh}$$

24 (*b*) Given, mass $m_1 = m_2$,

velocity, $u_1 = v_1$ and $u_2 = 0$

For elastic collision,

$$v_2 = \left(\frac{m_2 - m_1}{m_1 + m_2}\right)u_2 + \frac{2m_1u_1}{m_1 + m_2}$$

After putting the given values, we get

$$v_2 = \frac{2m_1v_1}{2m_1}$$

$$\Rightarrow v_2 = v_1$$

25 (*d*) According to Newton's second law of motion, the force acting on a body is equal to the rate of change of momentum during the impact

$$F = \frac{\Delta p}{\Delta t}$$

Also, $F = ma \Rightarrow ma = \frac{p_2 - p_1}{\Delta t}$

$$\Rightarrow a = \frac{mv_2 - (-mv_1)}{m\Delta t} = \frac{v_2 + v_1}{\Delta t}$$

Given, $h_2 = 20$ m, $h_1 = 5$ m

and $\Delta t = 0.02$ s

$$a = \sqrt{2g \times h_2} + \sqrt{2g \times h_1}$$

So, $a = \frac{\sqrt{2 \times 10 \times 20} + \sqrt{2 \times 10 \times 5}}{0.02}$

$(\because v = \sqrt{2gh})$

$$= \frac{20 + 10}{0.02} = 1500 \text{ ms}^{-2}$$

26 *(a)* In such collision, velocity of heavy body after the collision is

$$v_f = \left(\frac{M - m}{M + m}\right) v \quad [\because M >> m]$$

So, $v_f = \frac{M}{M} v = v$

27 *(b)* Let initial velocity of first body be u.

For second body, initial velocity, $u_2 = 0$ (at rest),

Mass of first body, $m_1 = 2$ kg,

Mass of second body $= m_2$ and $v_1 = \frac{u}{4}$

Law of conservation of linear momentum gives

$$m_1u_1 + m_2u_2 = m_1v_1 + m_2v_2$$

$$\Rightarrow 2u + 0 = 2\left(\frac{u}{4}\right) + m_2v_2$$

$$\Rightarrow m_2v_2 = \frac{3u}{2} \quad \text{...(i)}$$

Conservation of kinetic energy gives

$$\frac{1}{2}m_1u_1^2 + \frac{1}{2}m_2u_2^2 = \frac{1}{2}m_1v_1^2 + \frac{1}{2}m_2v_2^2$$

$$\Rightarrow \frac{1}{2}m_1u + \frac{1}{2}m_2(0) = \frac{1}{2}m_1\left(\frac{u}{4}\right)^2 + \frac{1}{2}m_2v_2^2$$

$$\Rightarrow m_2v_2^2 = \frac{15u^2}{8} \quad \text{...(ii)}$$

From Eqs. (i) and (ii), we get

$$m_2 = 1.2 \text{ kg.}$$

28 *(a)* Law of conservation of momentum yields $m_1v_1 + m_2v_2 = 0$

Given, $m_1 = 4$ kg,

$m_2 = 200$ g $= 0.2$ kg

and $E = 1.05$ kJ

$= 1050$ J

$$\Rightarrow 4v_1 + (0.2)v_2 = 0 \quad \text{...(i)}$$

Law of conservation of energy yields,

$$\frac{1}{2}m_1v_1^2 + \frac{1}{2}m_2v_2^2 = 1050$$

$$\Rightarrow \frac{1}{2} \times 4v_1^2 + \frac{1}{2} \times 0.2 \times v_2^2 = 1050$$

or $2v_1^2 + 0.1\, v_2^2 = 1050$ ...(ii)

Solving Eqs. (i) and (ii), we have

$$v_2 = 100 \text{ ms}^{-1}$$

29 *(a)* From Newton's second law,

$$F = \frac{dp}{dt}$$

If $F = 0$, then $\frac{dp}{dt} = 0$

$\Rightarrow p =$ constant

Thus, if total external force acting on the system is zero during collision, then the linear momentum of the system remains conserved.

30 *(a)* As momentum, $p = mv$ or $p \propto v$, i.e. momentum is directly proportional to its velocity, so the momentum is greater in a quicker collision between two bodies than in slower one.

Hence, due to greater momentum quicker collision between two bodies will be more violent even initial and final velocities are identical.

31 *(d)* When bob A strikes the bob B, then

$$mu = (m + m)v'$$

$$\Rightarrow v' = \frac{u}{2} \quad \text{...(i)}$$

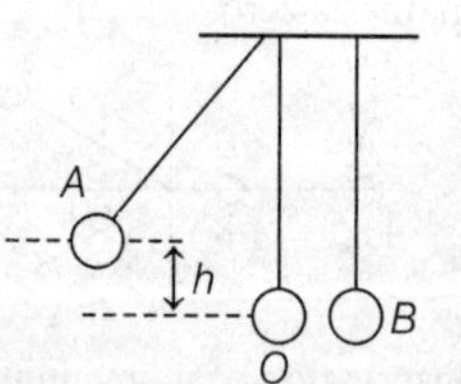

The potential energy of A at height h gets converted into kinetic energy of this mass, at point O, i.e.

$$mgh = \frac{1}{2}mu^2$$

$\Rightarrow u = \sqrt{2gh}$ [from Eq. (i)]

$$\therefore v' = \frac{\sqrt{2gh}}{2} = \sqrt{\frac{gh}{2}}$$

Let the combined mass moves to a height h', then total mass $= 2m$

Then, $2mgh' = \frac{1}{2}(2m)v'^2$

$$\Rightarrow gh' = \frac{gh}{4} \Rightarrow h' = \frac{h}{4}$$

32 *(b)* Let v_1, v_2 be the final velocities of the two spheres. Applying the law of conservation of linear momentum,

$mu = m(v_1 + v_2)$ or $v_1 + v_2 = u$ ...(i)

Again the coefficient of restitution is given by

$$e = \frac{v_2 - v_1}{u}$$

$$\Rightarrow v_2 - v_1 = eu \quad \text{...(ii)}$$

Solving Eqs. (i) and (ii), we get

$$v_1 = \frac{u}{2}(1 - e)$$

and $v_2 = \frac{u}{2}(1 + e)$

$$\Rightarrow \frac{v_1}{v_2} = \frac{1 - e}{1 + e}$$

33 *(c)* The speeds of balls remain unchanged after collisions. Then, there are only three collisions between balls and wall together, which are as

(i) Second ball collide with wall and reverse its direction.

(ii) Collision between first and second ball.

(iii) Second ball collide with wall again.

34 *(a)* The loss in kinetic energy which is transformed into heat

$$= \frac{1}{2}\left(\frac{m_1m_2}{m_1 + m_2}\right)(u_1 - u_2)^2$$

Given, $m_1 = m$, $m_2 = \frac{m}{9}$,

$u_1 = u$, $u_2 = 0$

$$\text{Loss of energy} = \frac{1}{2}\left(\frac{m \times \frac{m}{9}}{m + \frac{m}{9}}\right) \times (u - 0)^2$$

$$= \frac{1}{2}\frac{m}{10}u^2$$

Now, initial kinetic energy $= \frac{1}{2}mu^2$

Required fraction

$$= \frac{\text{loss in kinetic energy}}{\text{initial kinetic energy}}$$

$$= \frac{\frac{1}{2}\frac{m}{10}u^2}{\frac{1}{2}mu^2}$$

$$= \frac{1}{10} = 0.1$$

35 *(d)* From the law of conservation of momentum, when no external force acts upon a system of two (or more) bodies, then the total momentum of the system remains constant.

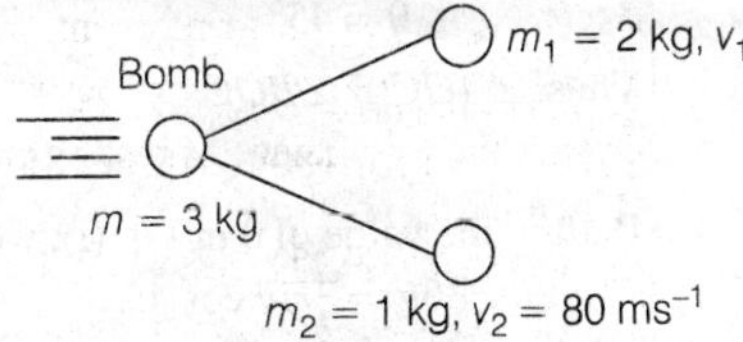

Momentum before explosion

= Momentum after explosion

Since, bomb is initially at rest, its velocity is zero.

Hence, $mv = m_1v_1 + m_2v_2$

$$3 \times 0 = 2v_1 + 1 \times 80$$

$$\Rightarrow \quad v_1 = -\frac{80}{2} = -40 \text{ ms}^{-1}$$

Total energy, $KE = \frac{1}{2}m_1v_1^2 + \frac{1}{2}m_2v_2^2$

$$= \frac{1}{2} \times 2 \times (-40)^2 + \frac{1}{2} \times 1 \times (80)^2$$

$= 1600 + 3200 = 4800$ J $= 4.8$ kJ

36 (a) When a body falls from a height h, it strikes the ground with a velocity, $u = \sqrt{2gh}$. Let it rebounds with a velocity v and rise to a height h_1. Therefore, $v = \sqrt{2gh_1}$

$$e = \frac{v}{u} = \sqrt{\left(\frac{h_1}{h}\right)}$$

If the successive heights to which the body rebounds again and again are $h_2, h_3, \ldots$, then

$$e = \sqrt{\frac{h_1}{h}} = \sqrt{\frac{h_2}{h_1}} = \sqrt{\frac{h_3}{h_2}} = \cdots$$

Clearly, $h_1 = e^2h$, $h_2 = e^4h \ldots$ and so on.

Similarly, after nth rebound, $h_n = e^{2n}h$ and $h_1 = e^2h$.

37 (c) Given, $m_2 = 2m$, $m_1 = m$

$$u_1 = v, \quad u_2 = 0$$

Final velocity of first body in collision,

$$v_1 = \left(\frac{m_1 - m_2}{m_1 + m_2}\right)u_1 + \left(\frac{2m_2}{m_1 + m_2}\right)u_2$$

$$\Rightarrow v_1 = \left(\frac{m - 2m}{m + 2m}\right)u_1 + \left(\frac{2 \times 2m}{m + 2m}\right) \times 0$$

$$\Rightarrow v_1 = -\frac{v}{3} \qquad (\because u_2 = 0)$$

Initial kinetic energy $= \frac{1}{2}mv^2$

Kinetic energy after collision is given by

$$\frac{1}{2}m\left(-\frac{v}{3}\right)^2 = \frac{1}{2}m\left(\frac{v^2}{9}\right)$$

$\therefore$ Change in kinetic energy

$$= \frac{1}{2}m\left(v^2 - \frac{v^2}{9}\right) = \frac{8}{9}\left(\frac{1}{2}mv^2\right)$$

$$= \frac{8}{9} \times \text{initial kinetic energy}$$

38 (d) In an inelastic collision, the particles do not regain their shape and size completely after collision. Some fraction of mechanical energy is retained by the colliding particles in the form of deformation as potential energy.

Thus, the kinetic energy of particles no longer remains conserved. However, in the absence of external forces, law of conservation of linear momentum still holds good.

39 (d) As, the initial momentum of the bomb was zero, therefore after explosion the two parts should possess numerically equal momentum, i.e.

$m_Av_A = m_Bv_B$

where, m_A, v_A and m_Bv_B are masses velocity of each piece.

$$\Rightarrow \quad 4v_A = 8 \times 6 \Rightarrow v_A = 12 \text{ ms}^{-1}$$

Kinetic energy of the other mass,

$$(KE)_A = \frac{1}{2}m_Av_A^2 = \frac{1}{2} \times 4 \times (12)^2$$

$= 288$ J

40 (b) For elastic collision,

$$v_1 = \left(\frac{m_1 - m_2}{m_1 + m_2}\right)u_1 + \left(\frac{2m_2}{m_1 + m_2}\right)u_2$$

If the second ball is at rest, i.e. $u_2 = 0$, then

$$v_1 = \left(\frac{m_1 - m_2}{m_1 + m_2}\right)u_1$$

Given, $v_1 = \frac{2}{3}u_1$

$$\Rightarrow \quad \frac{2}{3}u_1 = \left(\frac{m_1 - m_2}{m_1 + m_2}\right)u_1$$

$$\Rightarrow \quad 2m_1 + 2m_2 = 3m_1 - 3m_2$$

$$\Rightarrow \quad m_1 = 5m_2 \Rightarrow \frac{m_1}{m_2} = \frac{5}{1}$$

41 (a) The ratio of masses $= 1:3$

Therefore, $m_1 = x$ kg, $m_2 = 3x$ kg

Applying law of conservation of momentum, $m_1v_1 + m_2v_2 = 0$

$$\Rightarrow x \times v_1 + 3x \times 4 = 0$$

$$\Rightarrow \quad v_1 = -12 \text{ ms}^{-1}$$

Therefore, velocity of lighter mass is opposite to that of heavier mass.

42 (d) Whenever there is a collision between two bodies, the total momentum of the bodies remains conserved. If after the collision of two bodies, the total kinetic energy of the bodies remains the same as it was before collision, then it a perfectly elastic collision.

A ball bearing striking another ball bearing is an example of elastic collision. If two bodies stick together after the collision, then the collision is said to be perfectly inelastic collision.

Options (a), (b) and (c) are examples of perfectly inelastic collisions.

43 (a) According to the law of conservation of linear momentum,

$$m_1v = m_1v_1 + m_2v_2$$

where, v is the velocity of bullet before the collision, v_1 is velocity of the bullet after the collision and v_2 is the velocity of block.

Given, $m_1 = 20$ g $= 0.02$ kg,

$v = 600$ ms^{-1}, $m_2 = 4$ kg

and $\quad h = 0.2$ m

$\therefore \quad 0.02 \times 600 = 0.02v_1 + 4v_2$

$(\because v_2 = \sqrt{2gh} = \sqrt{2 \times 10 \times 0.2} = 2\text{ms}^{-1})$

$$\Rightarrow \quad 0.02v_1 = 12 - 8$$

$$\Rightarrow \quad v_1 = \frac{4}{0.02} = 200 \text{ ms}^{-1}$$

44 (d) The coefficient of restitution,

$$e = \frac{\text{velocity of separation}}{\text{velocity of approach}}$$

$$\therefore \quad e_1 = \frac{(v_{\text{separation}})_1}{(v_{\text{approach}})_1} = \frac{1}{2}$$

$$\text{and} \quad e_2 = \frac{(v_{\text{separation}})_2}{(v_{\text{approach}})_2}$$

$$\text{But} \quad \frac{e_1}{e_2} = \frac{3}{1} \Rightarrow \frac{e_2}{e_1} = \frac{1}{3}$$

$$\Rightarrow \quad e_2 = e_1 \times \frac{1}{3}$$

$$\therefore \quad \frac{(v_{\text{separation}})_2}{(v_{\text{approach}})_2} = \frac{1}{2} \times \frac{1}{3}$$

$$\Rightarrow \quad \frac{(v_{\text{approach}})_2}{(v_{\text{separation}})_2} = \frac{6}{1}$$

45 (b) Applying law of conservation of linear momentum,

$$m_1u_1 = m_2u_2$$

Given, $m_1 = 18$ kg, $m_2 = 12$ kg

$u_1 = 6\ \text{ms}^{-1}$, $u_2 = ?$

$\therefore \quad 18 \times 6 = 12u_2$

$\Rightarrow \quad u_2 = \dfrac{18 \times 6}{12} = 9\ \text{ms}^{-1}$

Thus, kinetic energy of 12 kg mass

$K_2 = \dfrac{1}{2}m_2u_2^2 = \dfrac{1}{2} \times 12 \times (9)^2$

$= 6 \times 81 = 486$ J

46 (a) Total mass of the shell = 20 kg

Ratio of the masses of the fragments = 2 : 3

Masses of the fragments are 8 kg and 12 kg.

Now, according to the law of conservation of momentum

$$m_1v_1 = m_2v_2$$

$\Rightarrow \quad 8 \times 6 = 12 \times v \Rightarrow v = 4\ \text{ms}^{-1}$

$\therefore$ Kinetic energy $= \dfrac{1}{2}mv^2$

$= \dfrac{1}{2} \times 12 \times (4)^2 = 96$ J

47 (d) In inelastic collision, most of the kinetic energy of the body is lost in the form heat. Thus, in inelastic collision kinetic energy is not conserved but total energy and momentum are still conserved.

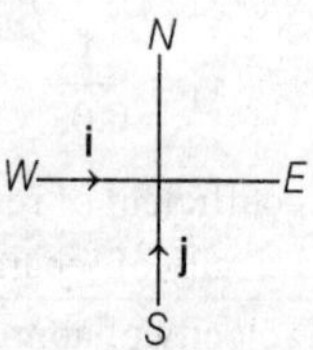

Hence, we have $mv\hat{\mathbf{i}} + mv\hat{\mathbf{j}} = 2mv'$

$\Rightarrow \quad |2mv'| = m|v\hat{\mathbf{i}} + v\hat{\mathbf{j}}|$

$\Rightarrow \quad 2mv' = m\sqrt{v^2 + v^2}$

$\Rightarrow \quad v' = \dfrac{v\sqrt{2}}{2} = \dfrac{v}{\sqrt{2}}$

48 (b) From equation of motion,

$$v^2 = u^2 + 2gh$$

where, v is final velocity, u is initial velocity and h is height,

Given, $h = 4.9$ m, $g = 9.8\ \text{ms}^{-2}$

and $u = 0$

So, $v = \sqrt{2gh}$

$= \sqrt{2 \times 9.8 \times 4.9} = 9.8\ \text{ms}^{-1}$

Coefficient of restitution (e) of an object is a unique fractional value representing the ratio of relative velocities before and after an impact.

$\therefore \quad v' = \dfrac{3}{4} \times 9.8$

Time taken from first bounce to second bounce,

$t = \dfrac{2v'}{g} \Rightarrow t = 2 \times \dfrac{3}{4} \times 9.8 \times \dfrac{1}{9.8} = 1.5$ s

49 (d) Mass of the body, $m_1 = m$

Velocity of the first body, $u_1 = 3\ \text{kmh}^{-1}$

Mass of second body at rest, $m_2 = 2m$

Velocity of second body, $u_2 = 0$

After combination, total mass of the body, $M = m + 2m = 3m$

Now, from the law of conservation of momentum, $m_1u_1 + m_2u_2 = Mv$

$3mv = m \times 3 + 2m \times 0 \quad [\because M = 3m]$

$\Rightarrow \quad v = 1\ \text{kmh}^{-1}$

50 (b) Let u be the velocity and θ is the direction of the third piece as shown below

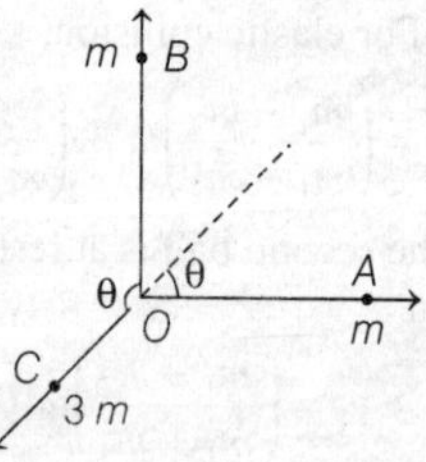

Equating the moment of the system along OA and OB to zero, we get

$m \times 30 - 3m \times v\cos\theta = 0 \quad \ldots\text{(i)}$

and $m \times 30 - 3m \times v\sin\theta = 0 \quad \ldots\text{(ii)}$

These give, $3mv\cos\theta = 3mv\sin\theta$ or $\cos\theta = \sin\theta$

$\therefore \quad \theta = 45°$

Thus, $\angle AOC = \angle BOC$

$= 180° - 45° = 135°$

Putting the value of θ in Eq. (i), we get

$30m = 3mv\cos 45°$

$= \dfrac{3mv}{\sqrt{2}}$

$\therefore \quad v = 10\sqrt{2}\ \text{ms}^{-1}$

The third piece will move with a velocity of $10\sqrt{2}\ \text{ms}^{-1}$ in a direction making an angle of 135° with either of the pieces.

51 (c) In an inelastic collision, kinetic energy is not conserved but the total energy and momentum remains conserved.

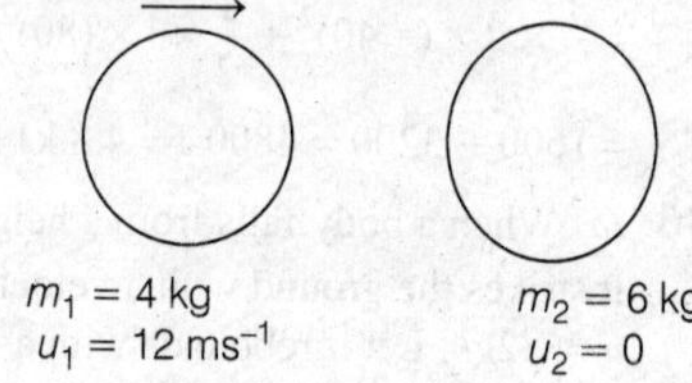

Momentum before collision = Momentum after collision

$$m_1u_1 + m_1u_2 = m_1v_1 + m_2v_2$$

$\Rightarrow \quad 4 \times 12 = (4 + 6)v$

$\Rightarrow \quad v = 4.8\ \text{ms}^{-1}$

Kinetic energy before collision

$= \dfrac{1}{2}m_1u_1^2$

$= \dfrac{1}{2} \times 4 \times (12)^2 = 288$ J

Kinetic energy after collision

$= \dfrac{1}{2}(m_1 + m_2)v^2$

$= \dfrac{1}{2}(4 + 6)(4.8)^2 = 115.2$ J

$\therefore$ Loss in kinetic energy of system

$= 288\ \text{J} - 115.2\ \text{J}$

$= 172.8$ J

06

System of Particles and Rotational Motion

Quick Review

Rigid Body

The body whose particles maintain the same relative positions w.r.t. other particles of the same body even under the action of external unbalanced force is known as rigid body.

Rotational Motion

In rotation motion about a fixed axis, every particle of the rigid body moves in a circle which lies in a plane perpendicular to the axis and has its centre on the axis. Every point in the rotating rigid body has the same angular velocity at any instant of the time.

Pure Translation Motion

In pure translation motion, every particle of the body moves with the same velocity at any instant of time.

Centre of Mass

Centre of mass of a system is the point that behaves as whole mass of the system is concentrated on it. For rigid bodies, centre of mass is independent of the state of the body, i.e. whether it is in rest or in accelerated motion, centre of mass will remain same.

- Centre of mass of a two particles system,

$$x_{CM} = \frac{m_1 x_1 + m_2 x_2}{m_1 + m_2}$$

Similarly, x_{CM} for n particles system,

$$x_{CM} = \frac{m_1 x_1 + m_2 x_2 + \dots\dots + m_n x_n}{m_1 + m_2 + \dots\dots + m_n} = \frac{\sum_{i=1}^{n} m_i x_i}{\sum_{i=1}^{n} m_i}$$

- Velocity of centre of mass (n-particles system),

$$\mathbf{v} = \frac{m_1 \mathbf{v}_1 + m_2 \mathbf{v}_2 + \dots + m_n \mathbf{v}_n}{m_1 + m_2 + \dots + m_n}$$

- Acceleration of centre of mass,

$$\mathbf{a} = \frac{m_1 \mathbf{a}_1 + m_2 \mathbf{a}_2 + \dots + m_n \mathbf{a}_n}{m_1 + m_2 + \dots + m_n}$$

- Momentum of centre of mass,

$$\mathbf{p} = \frac{m_1 \mathbf{p}_1 + m_2 \mathbf{p}_2 + \dots + m_n \mathbf{p}_n}{m_1 + m_2 + \dots + m_n}$$

Position of Centre of Mass of Symmetrical Bodies

Three points given below are, which are very important regarding the centre of mass of symmetrical bodies

(*i*) For the bodies symmetrical about both the axes (X or Y) or all the three axes (X, Y, Z), the centre of mass will lie at point of intersection of symmetrical axes.

(*ii*) The bodies which are symmetrical about one axis, then centre of mass will lie on that axis. Determine only that coordinate about which there is symmetry.

(*iii*) If an arrangement or body is not symmetrical about any axis, then determine all the required coordinates.

Centre of mass of some symmetrical bodies are given in a table below

Name of Body	Figure	Position of COM
Uniform sphere (hollow or solid)	C	Centre of the sphere
Uniform circular ring	C	Centre of the ring
Uniform circular disc	C	Centre of the disc
Uniform rod	C	Centre of the rod
A plane square lamina	C	Point of intersection of diagonals
Triangular lamina	C	Point of intersection of the medians
Rectangular cubical block	C	Point of intersection of the diagonal
Cylinder (Hollow or Solid)	C	Middle point of the axis of the cylinder
Cone or pyramid	h, C, $h/4$	On the axis of the cone at a distant $3h/4$ from the vertex, where h is the height of the cone.
Uniform semi-circular wire	C, $\frac{2R}{\pi}$, $O \leftarrow R \rightarrow$, (0, 0)	Coordinates $\left(0, \frac{2R}{\pi}\right)$ or $(0, 0.64R)$ of CM
Uniform semi-circular plate or disc	C, $\left(0, \frac{4R}{3\pi}\right)$, (0, 0) $O \leftarrow R \rightarrow$	Coordinates $\left(0, \frac{4R}{3\pi}\right)$ or $(0, 0.42R)$ of CM

Torque

The turning effect of the force about the axis rotation is called torque or moment of force.

Mathematically, it is expressed as

$$\text{Torque, } \boldsymbol{\tau} = \mathbf{r} \times \mathbf{F}$$

The magnitude of torque $|\tau|$ is

$$\tau = rF \sin\theta = Fr\sin\theta$$

$$\tau = Fr_\perp$$

where, $r_\perp$ is the perpendicular distance of the line of action of $\mathbf{F}$ from a point.

If the body is rotating counter clockwise, then the torque is taken **positive** otherwise **negative**.

Angular Momentum

Angular momentum (L) can be defined as **moment of linear momentum** about a point.

The angular momentum of a particle of mass m moving with velocity $\mathbf{v}$ (having a linear momentum $\mathbf{p} = m\mathbf{v}$) about a point O is defined by the following vector product.

$$\mathbf{L} = \mathbf{r} \times \mathbf{p}$$

or angular momentum, $\mathbf{L} = m(\mathbf{r} \times \mathbf{v})$

$$\mathbf{L} = mrv \sin\theta$$

where, θ = angle between $\mathbf{r}$ and $\mathbf{v}$.

$\mathbf{L}$ can be represented as $\mathbf{L} = rp \sin\theta = rp_\perp$

where, $p_\perp$ $(p\sin\theta)$ is the component of $\mathbf{p}$ in a direction perpendicular to $\mathbf{r}$.

and $\qquad \mathbf{L} = pr\sin\theta = pr_\perp$

where, $r_\perp$ is the perpendicular distance of the linear momentum vector ($\mathbf{p}$) from origin.

- **Relation between Torque and Angular Momentum**
  Rate of change of angular momentum is equal to the torque applied.

  Rate of change of angular momentum, $\frac{d\mathbf{L}}{dt} = \tau$

Torque and Angular Momentum for a System of Particles

For a system of particles or a rigid body with n-particles, the total angular momentum of the system is the vector sum of the angular momenta of the individual particles.

$$\mathbf{L} = \mathbf{L}_1 + \mathbf{L}_2 + \mathbf{L}_3 + \dots + \mathbf{L}_n = \sum_{i=1}^{n} \mathbf{L}_i$$

Differentiating the above expression with time, we get

$$\frac{d\mathbf{L}}{dt} = \sum_{i=1}^{n} \frac{d\mathbf{L}_i}{dt}$$

But $\sum_{i=1}^{n} \frac{d\mathbf{L}_i}{dt}$ is the net torque on the system, so $\frac{d\mathbf{L}}{dt} = \tau_{\text{net}}$.

Above expression shows **Newton's second law** for system of particles which state that the net external torque τ_{net} acting on a system of particles is equal to the time rate of change of the system's total angular momentum L.

Conservation of Angular Momentum

Without any external torque, angular momentum of a system of particles remain constant. This is known as the conservation of angular momentum.

If $\tau_{ext} = 0 \quad \Rightarrow \quad L_{initial} = L_{final}$

If L is constant, then its all three components will also be constant.

i.e. L_x = constant, L_y = constant and L_z = constant.

Equilibrium of a Rigid Body

A rigid body is said to be in equilibrium, if both of its linear momentum and angular momentum are not changing with time.

Rotational Equilibrium Only

If the net torque acting on the rigid body is zero but net force is non-zero, then rigid body is in rotational equilibrium only.

Translational Equilibrium Only

If the net force acting on the rigid body is zero but net torque is non-zero, then rigid body is in translational equilibrium only.

Couple

A pair of equal and opposite forces with parallel lines of action are known as a couple. A couple produces rotation without translation.

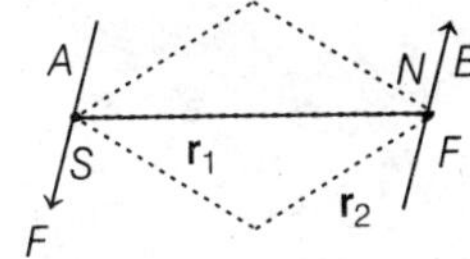

Let a couple with forces – F and F acting at A and B points with position vectors $\mathbf{r}_1$ and $\mathbf{r}_2$ with respect to some origin O.

The moment of couple = total torque

$$= \mathbf{r}_1 \times (-\mathbf{F}) + \mathbf{r}_2 \times \mathbf{F}$$

$$= \mathbf{r}_2 \times \mathbf{F} - \mathbf{r}_1 \times \mathbf{F} = (\mathbf{r}_2 - \mathbf{r}_1) \times \mathbf{F}$$

Principle of Moment

When an object is in rotational equilibrium, then algebraic sum of all torques acting on it is zero. Clockwise torques are taken **negative** and anti-clockwise torques are taken **positive**.

Centre of Gravity

If a body is supported on a point such that total gravitational torque about this point is zero, then this point is called centre of gravity of the body.

Moment of Inertia

The property of a body by virtue of which it opposes the torque tending to change its state of rest or of uniform rotation about an axis is called **rotational inertia** or **moment of inertia.**

- For a very simple case, the moment of inertia of a single particle about an axis is given by

$$I = mr^2$$

where, m is the mass of the particle and r is distance from the axis under consideration.

- The moment of inertia of a system of particles about an axis is given by

$$I = \sum_i m_i r_i^2$$

where, r_i is the perpendicular distance from the axis of the ith particle, which has a mass m_i.

Radius of Gyration

The radius of gyration of a body about a given axis is the perpendicular distance of a point from the axis at which the whole mass of the body could be concentrated without any change in the moment of inertia of the body about that axis.

If a body has mass M and radius of gyration is k, then moment of inertia,

$$I = Mk^2 \quad \Rightarrow \quad k = \sqrt{I/M}$$

where, k is radius of gyration.

Radius of gyration is also defined as the root mean square value of distance of all the particles about the axis of rotation.

i.e. $$k = \sqrt{\frac{r_1^2 + r_2^2 + r_3^2 + \ldots + r_n^2}{n}}$$

Theorem of Parallel Axes

It states that, moment of inertia of a rigid body about any axis is equal to its moment of inertia about a parallel axis through its centre of mass plus the product of the mass of the body and the square of the perpendicular distance between the two axes.

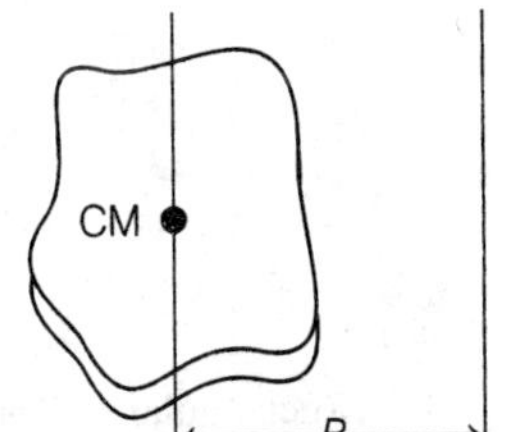

Two such axes are shown in figure for a body of mass M. If R is the distance between the axes and I_{CM} and I are the respective moments of inertia about these axes, then

$$I = I_{CM} + MR^2$$

Theorem of Perpendicular Axes

It states that, the moment of inertia of a plane lamina about an axis perpendicular to its plane is equal to the sum of the moments of inertia of the lamina about any two mutually perpendicular axes in its plane and intersecting each other at the point, where the perpendicular axis passes through it.

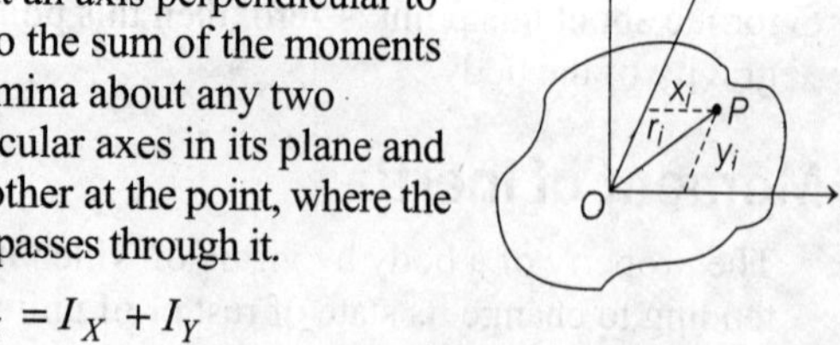

$$I_Z = I_X + I_Y$$

Let X and Y axes be chosen in the plane of the body and Z-axis perpendicular to this plane, three axes being mutually perpendicular, then according to the theorem

$$I_Z = I_X + I_Y$$

where, I_X, I_Y and I_Z are the moments of inertia about the X, Y and Z-axes respectively.

Moment of Inertia of Simple Geometrical Objects

S.No.	Name of Body	Axis of Rotation	Figure	Moment of Inertia	Radius of Gyration (k)	k^2/R^2
1.	Thin circular ring, radius R	(i) About an axis passing through CG and perpendicular to its plane	R	MR^2	R	1
		(ii) About its diameter		$\frac{1}{2}MR^2$	$\frac{R}{\sqrt{2}}$	$\frac{1}{2}$
2.	Circular disc, radius R	(i) Perpendicular to disc at centre	R	$\frac{1}{2}MR^2$	$\frac{R}{\sqrt{2}}$	$\frac{1}{2}$
		(ii) About its diameter		$\frac{1}{4}MR^2$	$\frac{R}{2}$	$\frac{1}{4}$
3.	Long uniform thin rod	(i) About an axis passing through its centre of mass and perpendicular to the rod	L	$\frac{ML^2}{12}$	$\frac{L}{\sqrt{12}}$	
		(ii) About an axis passing through its edge and perpendicular to the rod	L	$\frac{ML^2}{3}$	$\frac{L}{\sqrt{3}}$	
4.	Rectangular lamina	Passing through the centre of mass and perpendicular to the plane.	b, l	$\frac{M}{12}[l^2 + b^2]$	$\sqrt{\frac{l^2 + b^2}{12}}$	

S.No.	Name of Body	Axis of Rotation	Figure	Moment of Inertia	Radius of Gyration (k)	k^2/R^2
5.	Hollow cylinder, radius R	(*i*) About its own axis		MR^2	R	1
		(*ii*) Tangential (Generator)		$2MR^2$	$\sqrt{2}R$	2
		(*iii*) About an axis passing through its CG and perpendicular to its own axis		$M\left[\frac{L^2}{12}+\frac{R^2}{2}\right]$	$\sqrt{\frac{L^2}{12}+\frac{R^2}{2}}$	
		(*iv*) About the diameter of one of faces of the cylinder		$M\left[\frac{L^2}{3}+\frac{R^2}{2}\right]$	$\sqrt{\frac{L^2}{3}+\frac{R^2}{2}}$	
6.	Solid cylinder	(*i*) About its own axis		$\frac{1}{2}MR^2$	$\frac{R}{\sqrt{2}}$	$\frac{1}{2}$
		(*ii*) Tangential (Generator)		$\frac{3}{2}MR^2$	$\sqrt{\frac{3}{2}}R$	$\frac{3}{2}$
		(*iii*) About an axis passing through its CG and perpendicular to its own axis		$M\left[\frac{L^2}{12}+\frac{R^2}{4}\right]$	$\sqrt{\frac{L^2}{12}+\frac{R^2}{4}}$	
		(*iv*) About the diameter of one of the faces of the cylinder		$M\left[\frac{L^2}{3}+\frac{R^2}{4}\right]$	$\sqrt{\frac{L^2}{3}+\frac{R^2}{4}}$	

S.No.	Name of Body	Axis of Rotation	Figure	Moment of Inertia	Radius of Gyration (k)	k^2/R^2
7.	Spherical shell	(i) About its diametric axis	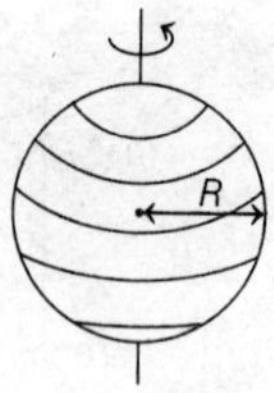 R	$\frac{2}{3}MR^2$	$\sqrt{\frac{2}{3}}R$	$\frac{2}{3}$
		(ii) About a tangential axis	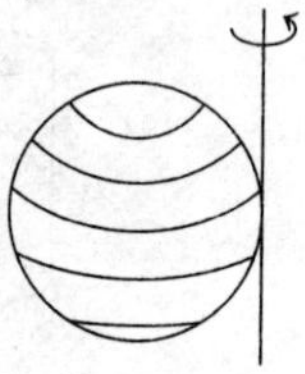	$\frac{5}{3}MR^2$	$\sqrt{\frac{5}{3}}R$	$\frac{5}{3}$
8.	Solid sphere, radius R	(i) About its diametric axis	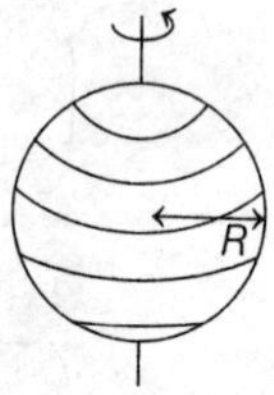 R	$\frac{2}{5}MR^2$	$\sqrt{\frac{2}{5}}R$	$\frac{2}{5}$
		(ii) About a tangential axis	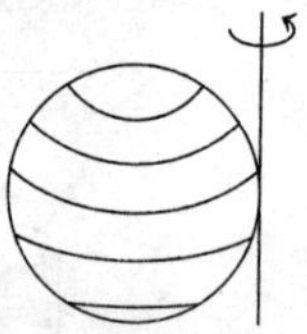	$\frac{7}{5}MR^2$	$\sqrt{\frac{7}{5}}R$	$\frac{7}{5}$
9.	Hollow sphere of inner radius R_1 and outer radius R_2	(i) About its diametric axis	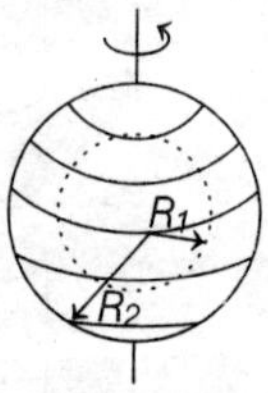 R1 R2	$\frac{2}{5}M\left[\frac{R_2^5 - R_1^5}{R_2^3 - R_1^3}\right]$		
		(ii) Tangential	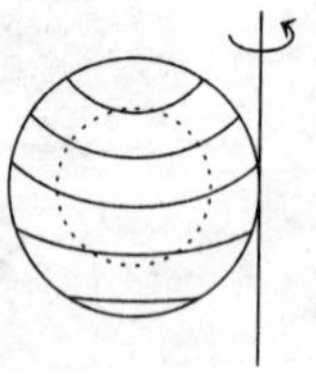	$\frac{2}{5}M\left[\frac{R_2^5 - R_1^5}{R_2^3 - R_1^3}\right] + MR_2^2$		

Rotational Kinetic Energy

The energy due to rotational motion of a body is known as rotational kinetic energy.

$$\text{Rotational KE} = \frac{1}{2} I\omega^2$$

where, ω = angular velocity of particles and I = moment of inertia.

Kinematic Equation of Rotational Motion

The kinematic equations for rotational motion with uniform angular acceleration are given below

(*i*) $\omega = \omega_0 + \alpha t$ (*ii*) $\theta = \omega_0 t + \frac{1}{2}\alpha t^2$

(*iii*) $\omega^2 - \omega_0^2 = 2\alpha(\theta - \theta_0)$

where, θ_0 and ω_0 are initial angular displacement and angular velocity, θ and ω are final angular displacement and angular velocity and α is angular acceleration.

Some Important Formula

- Instantaneous power in rotational motion, $P = \tau\omega$.
- Relation between torque and angular acceleration, $\tau = I\alpha$.

Dynamics of Rotational Motion about a Fixed Axis

From the given table, we compare linear motion and rotational motion about a fixed axis, i. e. Z-axis.

Comparison of Translational and Rotational Motion

Pure translation	Pure rotational
Position, x	Angular position, θ
Velocity, $v = \frac{dx}{dt}$	Angular velocity, $\omega = \frac{d\theta}{dt}$
Acceleration, $a = \frac{dv}{dt}$	Angular acceleration, $\alpha = \frac{d\omega}{dt}$
Mass, m	Rotational inertia, I
Newton's second law, $F = ma$	Newton's second law, $\tau = I\alpha$
Work done, $W = \int F\,dx$	Work done, $W = \int \tau\,d\theta$
Kinetic energy, $K = \frac{1}{2}mv^2$	Kinetic energy, $K = \frac{1}{2}I\omega^2$
Power, $P = Fv$	Power, $P = \tau\omega$
Linear momentum, $p = mv$	Angular momentum, $L = I\omega$

Rolling Motion

When a body performs translation motion as well as rotational motion, then this type of motion is known as rolling motion.

- **Kinetic Energy of Rolling Motion** A body rotating about its axis with angular velocity ω and its centre of mass moving with velocity v_{CM}, then kinetic energy of rolling is given as

$$KE_{\text{rolling}} = KE_{\text{translational}} + KE_{\text{rotational}}$$

$$= \frac{1}{2}Mv_{CM}^2 + \frac{1}{2}I\omega^2$$

- Various physical quantities of a body, rolling on an inclined plane without slipping are listed below

(*i*) Acceleration of the body,

$$a = \frac{g\sin\theta}{1 + \frac{k^2}{R^2}}$$

where, θ = angle of inclination.

(*ii*) Velocity of the body when it reaches the bottom,

$$v = \sqrt{\frac{2gh}{1 + \frac{k^2}{R^2}}}$$

(*iii*) Time taken by a rolling body to reach the bottom,

$$t = \frac{1}{\sin\theta}\sqrt{\frac{2h(1 + k^2/R^2)}{g}}$$

- A body with smaller value of k^2/R^2 will take less time to reach the bottom.
- Change in kinetic energy due to rolling $(v_2 > v_1)$

$$= \frac{1}{2}m\left(1 + \frac{k^2}{R^2}\right)(v_2^2 - v_1^2)$$

Topical Practice Questions

All the exam questions of this chapter have been divided into 6 topics as listed below

Topic 1

Position and Motion of Centre of Mass

2018

1 Three bodies having masses 5 kg, 4 kg and 2 kg is moving at the speed of 5 ms^{-1}, 4 ms^{-1} and 2 ms^{-1} respectively along X-axis. The magnitude of velocity of centre of mass is **[AIIMS]**

(a) 1.0 ms^{-1} (b) 4 ms^{-1} (c) 0.9 ms^{-1} (d) 1.3 ms^{-1}

2017

2 Two masses of 6 and 2 unit are at positions $(6\hat{\mathbf{i}} - 7\hat{\mathbf{j}})$ and $(2\hat{\mathbf{i}} + 5\hat{\mathbf{j}} - 8\hat{\mathbf{k}})$, respectively. The coordinates of the centre of mass are **(JIPMER)**

(a)(2,–5,3) (b) (5,–5, –3)
(c)(5,–4,–2) (d) (5,–4,–4)

2014

3 The position of centre of mass of a system of particles does not depend upon the **[Kerala CEE]**

(a) mass of particles
(b) symmetry of the body
(c) position of the particles
(d) relative distance between the particles
(e) nature of particles

2012

4 Three masses are placed on the X-axis, 300 g at origin, 500 g at $x = 40$ cm and 400 g at $x = 70$ cm. The distance of the centre of mass from the origin is **[CBSE AIPMT]**

(a) 40 cm (b) 45 cm
(c) 50 cm (d) 30 cm

5 Two persons of masses 55 kg and 65 kg respectively, are at the opposite ends of a boat. The length of the boat is 3.0 m and weighs 100 kg. The 55 kg man walks up to the 65 kg man and sits with him. If the boat is in still water, the centre of mass of the system shifts by **[CBSE AIPMT]**

(a) 3.0 m (b) 2.3 m
(c) zero (d) 0.75 m

2011

6 In the diagram shown below, m_1 and m_2 are the masses of two particles and x_1 and x_2 are their respective distances from the origin O. The centre of mass of the system is **[J&K CET]**

(a) $\dfrac{m_1x_2 + m_2x_2}{m_1 + m_2}$ (b) $\dfrac{m_1 + m_2}{2}$

(c) $\dfrac{m_1x_1 + m_2x_2}{m_1 + m_2}$ (d) $\dfrac{m_1m_2 + x_1x_2}{m_1 + m_2}$

2010

7 The centre of mass of a system of three particles of masses 1 g, 2 g and 3 g is taken as the origin of a coordinate system. The position vector of a fourth particle of mass 4 g such that the centre of mass of the four particles system lies at the point (1, 2, 3) is $\alpha(\hat{\mathbf{i}} + 2\hat{\mathbf{j}} + 3\hat{\mathbf{k}})$, where α is a constant.

The value of α is **[AMU]**

(a) $\frac{10}{3}$ (b) $\frac{5}{2}$ (c) $\frac{1}{2}$ (d) $\frac{2}{5}$

8 A block of mass m slides with velocity v along a frictionless level surface towards a block of mass 4 m initially at rest. The velocity of centre of mass is **[AMU]**

(a) $v/5$ (b) $v/4$
(c) $5v/2$ (d) $(4/5)v$

9 The centre of mass of three particles of masses 1 kg, 2 kg and 3 kg is at (3, 3, 3) with reference to a fixed coordinate system. Where should a fourth particle of mass 4 kg be placed, so that the centre of mass of the system of all particles shifts to a point (1, 1, 1)? **[JCECE]**

(a) (–1, – 1, – 1) (b) (–2, – 2, – 2)
(c) (2, 2, 2) (d) (1, 1, 1)

2008

10 Two bodies of different masses of 2 kg and 4 kg moving with velocities 2 ms^{-1} and 10 ms^{-1} towards each other, due to mutual gravitational attraction. What is the velocity of their centre of mass? **[BHU]**

(a) 5 ms^{-1} (b) 6 ms^{-1}
(c) 8 ms^{-1} (d) zero

11 A system consisting of two masses connected by a massless rod lies along the X-axis. A 0.4 kg mass is at a distance $x = 2$ m while a 0.6 kg mass is at a distance $x = 7$ m. The x-coordinate of the centre of mass is **[Kerala CEE]**

(a) 5 m (b) 3.5 m
(c) 4.5 m (d) 4 m
(e) 3 m

12 Identify the correct statement for the rotational motion of a rigid body. **[J&K CET]**

(a) Individual particles of the body do not undergo accelerated motion.
(b) The centre of mass of the body remains unchanged.
(c) The centre of mass of the body moves uniformly in a circular path.
(d) Individual particles and centre of mass of the body undergo an accelerated motion.

2007

13 Four point masses P, Q, R and S with respective masses 1 kg, 1 kg, 2 kg and 2 kg form the corners of a square of side a. The centre of mass of the system will be farthest from **[Kerala CEE]**

(a) P only (b) R and S (c) R only (d) P and Q
(e) P and R

2006

14 A small disc of radius 2 cm is cut from a disc of radius 6 cm. If the distance between their centres is 3.2 cm, what is the shift in the centre of mass of the disc? **[AFMC]**

(a) 0.4 cm (b) 2.4 cm
(c) 1.8 cm (d) 1.2 cm

15 A straight rod of length L has one of its ends at the origin and the other at $x = L$. If the mass per unit length of the rod is given by Ax, here A is constant, then where is its centre of mass?

(a) $L/3$ (b) $L/2$
(c) $2L/3$ (d) $3L/4$ **[BHU]**

16 Find the velocity of centre of mass of the system shown in the figure. **[AMU]**

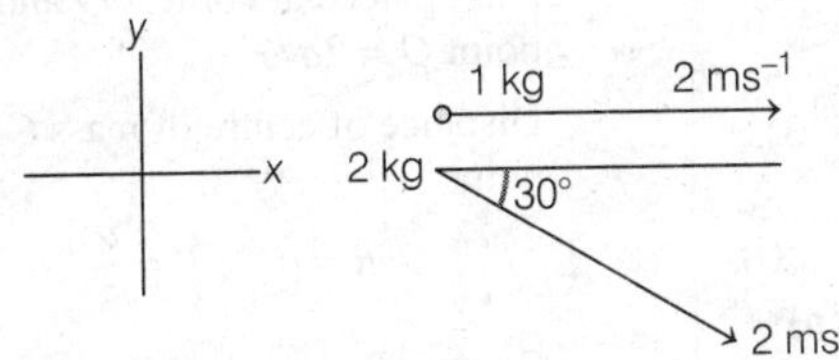

(a) $\left(\frac{2+2\sqrt{3}}{3}\right)\hat{\mathbf{i}} - \frac{2}{3}\hat{\mathbf{j}}$ (b) $4\hat{\mathbf{i}}$

(c) $\left(\frac{2-2\sqrt{3}}{3}\right)\hat{\mathbf{i}} - \frac{1}{3}\hat{\mathbf{j}}$ (d) None of these

17 Three identical spheres of mass m each are placed at the corners of an equilateral triangle of side 2 m. Taking one of the corners as the origin, the position vector of the centre of mass is **[J&K CET]**

(a) $\sqrt{3}(\hat{\mathbf{i}} - \hat{\mathbf{j}})$ (b) $\frac{\hat{\mathbf{i}}}{\sqrt{3}} + \hat{\mathbf{j}}$

(c) $\frac{\hat{\mathbf{i}} + \hat{\mathbf{j}}}{3}$ (d) $\hat{\mathbf{i}} + \frac{\hat{\mathbf{j}}}{\sqrt{3}}$

18 Four particles, each of mass 1 kg are placed at the corners of a square $OABC$ of side 1 m. O is at the origin of the coordinate system. OA and OC are aligned along positive X-axis and positive Y-axis, respectively. The position vector of the centre of mass is (in metre) **[EAMCET]**

(a) $\hat{\mathbf{i}} + \hat{\mathbf{j}}$ (b) $\frac{1}{2}(\hat{\mathbf{i}} + \hat{\mathbf{j}})$ (c) $(\hat{\mathbf{i}} - \hat{\mathbf{j}})$ (d) $\frac{1}{2}(\hat{\mathbf{i}} - \hat{\mathbf{j}})$

2005

19 A cricket bat is cut at the location of its centre of mass as shown. Then, **[Kerala CEE]**

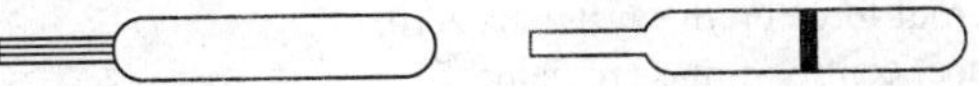

(a) the two pieces will have the same mass
(b) the bottom piece will have larger mass
(c) the handle piece will have larger mass
(d) mass of handle piece is double the mass of bottom piece
(e) None of the above

20 Three particles each of mass 1 kg are placed at the corners of a right angled triangle AOB, O being the origin of the coordinate system (OA and OB along positive x-direction and positive y-direction). If $OA = OB = 1$ m, the positive vector of the centre of mass (in metre) is **[EAMCET]**

(a) $\frac{\hat{\mathbf{i}} + \hat{\mathbf{j}}}{3}$ (b) $\frac{\hat{\mathbf{i}} - \hat{\mathbf{j}}}{3}$ (c) $\frac{2(\hat{\mathbf{i}} + \hat{\mathbf{j}})}{3}$ (d) $(\hat{\mathbf{i}} - \hat{\mathbf{j}})$

Answers

1 (b)	2 (c)	3 (e)	4 (a)	5 (c)	6 (c)	7 (b)	8 (a)	9 (b)	10 (d)
11 (a)	12 (c)	13 (d)	14 (a)	15 (b)	16 (a)	17 (d)	18 (b)	19 (b)	20 (a)

Explanations

1 (b) As, we know

$$v_{CM} = \frac{m_1v_1 + m_2v_2 + m_3v_3}{m_1 + m_2 + m_3}$$

Given, $m_1 = 5$ kg, $v_1 = 5\text{ ms}^{-1}$,

$m_2 = 4$ kg, $v_2 = 4\text{ ms}^{-1}$, $m_3 = 2$ kg

and $v_3 = 2\text{ ms}^{-1}$.

So, by putting the values,

$$v_{CM} = \frac{5\times5+4\times4+2\times2}{5+4+2} = \frac{25+16+4}{11}$$

$$\therefore \quad v_{CM} = \frac{45}{11} = 4.09 \approx 4\text{ ms}^{-1}$$

2 (c) Given, masses, $m_1 = 6$ unit and $m_2 = 2$ unit

Positions $= 6\hat{\mathbf{i}} - 7\hat{\mathbf{j}}$ and $2\hat{\mathbf{i}} + 5\hat{\mathbf{j}} - 8\hat{\mathbf{k}}$

To find centre of mass,

$$x_{CM} = \frac{m_1x_1 + m_2x_2}{m_1 + m_2} = \frac{6\times6+2\times2}{6+2} = \frac{36+4}{8} = 5\hat{\mathbf{i}}$$

$$y_{CM} = \frac{m_1y_1 + m_2y_2}{m_1 + m_2} = \frac{6\times(-7)+2\times(+5)}{6+2} = \frac{-42+10}{8} = -4\hat{\mathbf{j}}$$

$$z_{CM} = \frac{m_1z_1 + m_2z_2}{m_1 + m_2} = \frac{6\times(0)+2\times(-8)}{2+6} = \frac{-16}{8} = -2\hat{\mathbf{k}}$$

$\therefore$ Centre of mass lies on $5\hat{\mathbf{i}} - 4\hat{\mathbf{j}} - 2\hat{\mathbf{k}}$..

3 (e) The position of centre of mass ($\mathbf{r}_{CM}$) of a system of particles does not depend upon the nature of particles.

$$\mathbf{r}_{CM} = \frac{\Sigma m_i \mathbf{r}_i}{\Sigma m_i}$$

4 (a) Given, $m_1 = 300$ g, $x_1 = 0$ cm (origin), $m_2 = 500$ g, $x_2 = 40$ cm, $m_3 = 400$ g and $x_3 = 70$ cm

Distance of the centre of mass from the origin,

$$x_{CM} = \frac{m_1x_1 + m_2x_2 + m_3x_3}{m_1 + m_2 + m_3}$$

$$x_{CM} = \frac{300(0) + 500(40) + 400(70)}{300 + 500 + 400}$$

$$x_{CM} = \frac{20000 + 28000}{1200} = \frac{48000}{1200}$$

$$\Rightarrow x_{CM} = 40 \text{ cm}$$

5 (c) Here, on the entire system, net external force on the system is zero. Hence, centre of mass remains unchanged.

$$\because \quad F_{ext} = \mu A_{CM}$$

$$\Rightarrow \quad F_{ext} = 0 \text{ or } A_{CM} = 0$$

6 (c) The centre of mass of the system is given by

O — m_1 — m_2, with x_1 and x_2 marked from O.

$$x = \frac{m_1x_1 + m_2x_2}{m_1 + m_2}$$

7 (b) The coordinates (x, y, z) of masses 1 g, 2 g, 3 g and 4 g are

$(x_1 = 0, y_1 = 0, z_1 = 0)$

$(x_2 = 0, y_2 = 0, z_2 = 0)$

$(x_3 = 0, y_3 = 0, z_3 = 0)$

[$\because$ Centre of mass of particles 1g,2g and 3g is at origin]

$(x_4 = \alpha, y_4 = 2\alpha, z_4 = 3\alpha)$

$$x_{CM} = \frac{m_1x_1 + m_2x_2 + m_3x_3 + m_4x_4}{m_1 + m_2 + m_3 + m_4}$$

$$x_{CM} = \frac{4\alpha}{1 + 2 + 3 + 4} = \frac{4\alpha}{10}$$

$$\Rightarrow 1 = \frac{4\alpha}{10} \Rightarrow \alpha = \frac{5}{2} \qquad [\because x_{CM} = 1]$$

$$y_{CM} = \frac{m_1y_1 + m_2y_2 + m_3y_3 + m_4y_4}{m_1 + m_2 + m_3 + m_4}$$

$$\Rightarrow \quad 2 = \frac{4 \times 2\alpha}{10}$$

$$\Rightarrow \quad \alpha = \frac{20}{8} = \frac{5}{2}$$

$$z_{CM} = \frac{m_1z_1 + m_2z_2 + m_3z_3 + m_4z_4}{m_1 + m_2 + m_3 + m_4}$$

$$\Rightarrow \quad 3 = \frac{4 \times 3\alpha}{10}$$

$$\Rightarrow \quad \alpha = \frac{5}{2}$$

8 (a) Given, $m_1 = m, v_1 = v$

$m_2 = 4m$, and $v_2 = 0$

As $$v_{CM} = \frac{m_1v_1 + m_2v_2}{m_1 + m_2}$$

So, $$v_{CM} = \frac{m \times v + 4m \times 0}{m + 4m} = \frac{v}{5}$$

9 (b) Centre of mass of a solid body is given by

$$x_{CM} = \frac{\sum_{i=1}^{n} \Delta m_i x_i}{\sum_{j=1}^{n} \Delta M_j}, \quad y_{CM} = \frac{\sum_{i=1}^{n} \Delta m_i y_i}{\sum_{j=1}^{n} \Delta M_j}$$

$$z_{CM} = \frac{\sum_{i=1}^{n} \Delta m_i z_i}{\sum_{j=1}^{n} \Delta M_j}$$

Let us consider masses 1g,2g and 3g are placed at point (3,3,3). Since, this point is centre of mass of these particles.

$$1 \times x_1 + 2 \times x_2 + 3 \times x_3 = (1 + 2 + 3)3$$

As, $x_1 = x_2 = x_3 = 3$

$$x_1 + 2x_2 + 3x_3 = 18 \qquad \text{...(i)}$$

$$x_{CM} = y_{CM} = z_{CM} = 1 \quad \text{(given)}$$

$$1(1 + 2 + 3 + 4) = x_1 + 2x_2 + 3x_3 + 4x_4 \text{ ...(ii)}$$

Solving Eqs. (i) and (ii), we get

$$4x_4 = 10 - 18$$

$$\Rightarrow \quad x_4 = -2$$

Similarly, $y_4 = -2, z_4 = -2$

The fourth particle must be placed at the point (–2, – 2, – 2).

10 (d) As gravitational forces of attraction are mutual and internal. So, centre of mass is not affected (in the absence of external force). Velocity of centre of mass is zero.

$$\mathbf{F}_{ext} = \mathbf{a}\, m_{CM}$$

11 (a) The x-coordinate of centre of mass is given by

$$x = \frac{m_1x_1 + m_2x_2}{m_1 + m_2}$$

Given, $m_1 = 0.4$ kg, $x_1 = 2$ m,

$m_2 = 0.6$ kg and $x_2 = 7$ m.

Hence, $$x = \frac{0.4 \times 2 + 0.6 \times 7}{0.4 + 0.6} = \frac{5}{1}$$

$= 5$ m

12 (c) In rotational motion of a rigid body, the centre of mass of the body moves uniformly in a circular path. Whereas individual particle undergo accelerated motion, Hence, option (c) is correct.

13 (d) Centre of mass C_1 from point P

$$= \frac{1 \times 0 + 2 \times a}{1 + 2} = \frac{2a}{3}$$

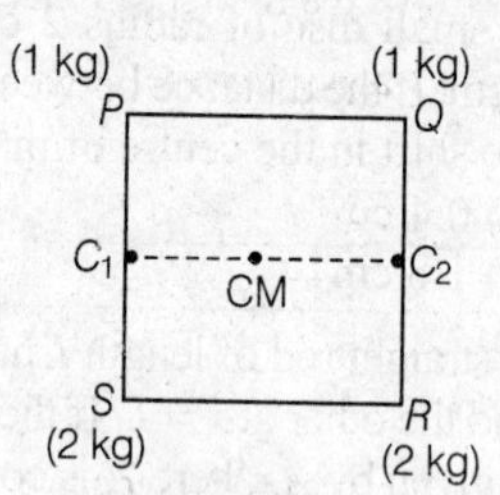

Therefore, distance of centre of mass C_1 from point S

$$= a - \frac{2a}{3} = \frac{a}{3}$$

Similarly, centre of mass C_2 of point mass placed at corners Q and R, from point $Q = 2a/3$

Distance of centre of mass C_2 from point

$$R = a - \frac{2a}{3} = \frac{a}{3}$$

Centre of mass of all four point masses is at the mid-point of the line joining C_1 and C_2, which is farthest from points P and Q.

14 (a)

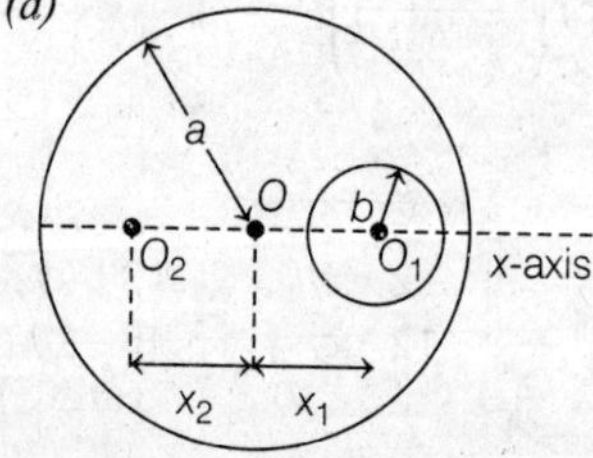

Let radius of complete disc is a and that of small disc is b. Also, let centre of mass now shifts to O_2 at a distance x_2 from original centre.

The position of new centre of mass is given by

$$x_{CM} = \frac{-\sigma\pi b^2 x_1}{\sigma\pi a^2 - \sigma\pi b^2}$$

where, σ = mass per unit area.

Given, $a = 6$ cm, $b = 2$ cm

and $x_1 = 3.2$ cm

Hence,

$$x_{CM} = \frac{-\sigma \times \pi(2)^2 \times 3.2}{\sigma \times \pi \times (6)^2 - \sigma \times \pi \times (2)^2}$$

$$= -\frac{12.8\pi}{32\pi} = -0.4 \text{ cm}$$

Negative sign indicates the shift from the centre.

15 *(b)* Let the mass of an element (dm) of length dx of the rod located at a distance x away from left end is $\frac{M}{L}dx$.

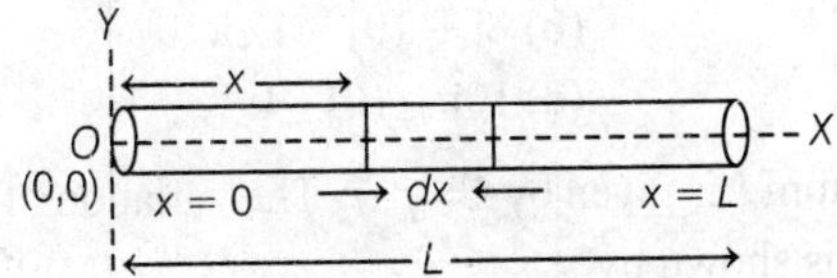

The x-coordinate of the centre of mass is given by

$$x_{CM} = \frac{1}{M}\int x\,dm = \frac{1}{M}\int_0^L x\left(\frac{M}{L}dx\right)$$

$$= \frac{1}{L}\left(\frac{x^2}{2}\right)_0^L = \frac{L}{2}$$

The y-coordinate is

$$y_{CM} = \frac{1}{M}\int y\,dm = 0$$

and similarly, $z_{CM} = 0$

Hence, the centre of mass is at $\left(\frac{L}{2}, 0, 0\right)$ or at the middle point of the rod, i.e. at $\frac{L}{2}$.

16 *(a)* Given, $m_1 = 1$ kg, $\mathbf{v}_1 = 2\hat{\mathbf{i}}$, $m_2 = 2$ kg and $\mathbf{v}_2 = 2\cos 30°\,\hat{\mathbf{i}} - 2\sin 30°\,\hat{\mathbf{j}}$

As, $\mathbf{v}_{CM} = \dfrac{m_1\mathbf{v}_1 + m_2\mathbf{v}_2}{m_1 + m_2}$

So, v_{CM}

$$= \frac{1\times 2\hat{\mathbf{i}} + 2(2\cos 30°\,\hat{\mathbf{i}} - 2\sin 30°\,\hat{\mathbf{j}})}{1+2}$$

$$\Rightarrow \mathbf{v}_{CM} = \frac{2\hat{\mathbf{i}} + 2\sqrt{3}\,\hat{\mathbf{i}} - 2\hat{\mathbf{j}}}{3}$$

$$= \left(\frac{2+2\sqrt{3}}{3}\right)\hat{\mathbf{i}} - \frac{2}{3}\hat{\mathbf{j}}$$

17 *(d)* The x-coordinate of centre of mass is

$$\bar{x} = \frac{\Sigma m_i x_i}{\Sigma m_i}$$

$$= \frac{m_O x_O + m_A x_A + m_B x_B}{m_O + m_A + m_B}$$

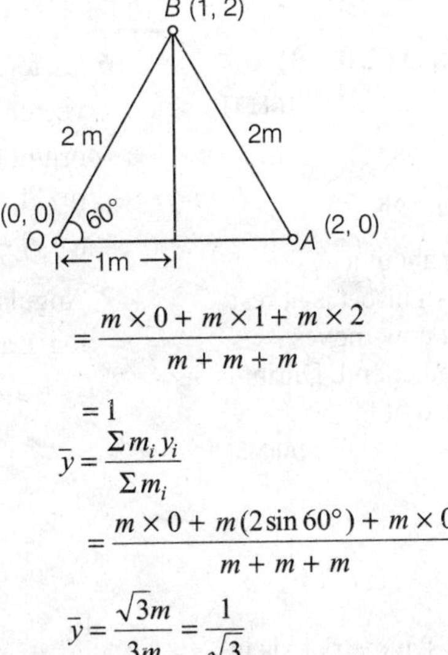

$$= \frac{m\times 0 + m\times 1 + m\times 2}{m+m+m}$$

$$= 1$$

$$\bar{y} = \frac{\Sigma m_i y_i}{\Sigma m_i}$$

$$= \frac{m\times 0 + m(2\sin 60°) + m\times 0}{m+m+m}$$

$$\bar{y} = \frac{\sqrt{3}m}{3m} = \frac{1}{\sqrt{3}}$$

Position vector of centre of mass is $\left(\hat{\mathbf{i}} + \frac{\hat{\mathbf{j}}}{\sqrt{3}}\right)$.

18 *(b)* We can show the situation as

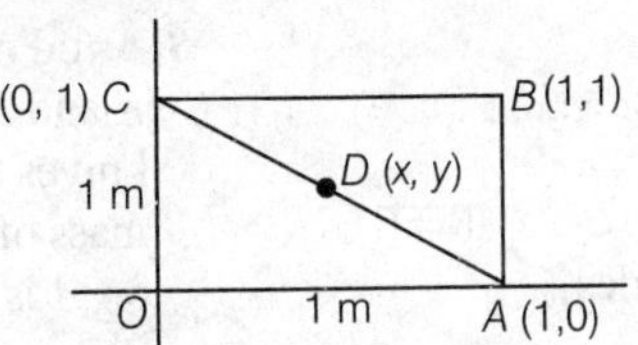

The centre of mass of square is at point $D(x, y)$.

The position coordinates of point D

$$(x, y) \equiv \left[\frac{0+1+1+0}{1+1+1+1}, \frac{0+1+1+0}{1+1+1+1}\right]$$

$$\equiv \left(\frac{1}{2}, \frac{1}{2}\right)$$

$$\because x_{CM} = \frac{m_O x_O + m_A x_A + m_B x_B + m_C x_C}{m_O + m_A + m_B + m_C}$$

Hence, position vector of centre of mass D is

$$= x\hat{\mathbf{i}} + y\hat{\mathbf{j}} = \frac{1}{2}\hat{\mathbf{i}} + \frac{1}{2}\hat{\mathbf{j}}$$

$$= \frac{1}{2}(\hat{\mathbf{i}} + \hat{\mathbf{j}})$$

19 *(b)* Centre of mass is the point where the weighted relative position of the distributed mass sums to zero. The centre of mass of the bat is near the bottom end of the bat, which shows more mass at bottom.

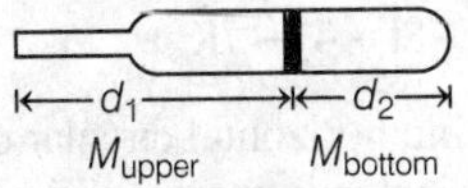

As, $M_{upper} d_1 = M_{bottom} d_2$

$\because \quad d_1 > d_2$

$\Rightarrow \quad M_{bottom} > M_{upper}$

20 *(a)* Three particles each of mass 1 kg are placed at the three corners of a right angled triangle.

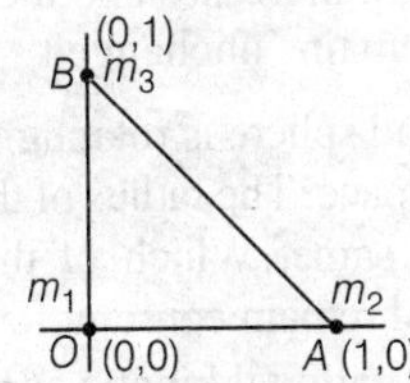

Given, $m_1 = m_2 = m_3 = 1$

$(x_1, y_1) = (0, 0), (x_2, y_2) = (1, 0),$

$(x_3, y_3) = (0, 1), (x_{CM}, y_{CM}) = ?$

$$x_{CM} = \frac{m_1x_1 + m_2x_2 + m_3x_3}{m_1 + m_2 + m_3}$$

$$\Rightarrow x_{CM} = \frac{1\times 0 + 1\times 1 + 1\times 0}{1+1+1} = \frac{1}{3}$$

$$y_{CM} = \frac{m_1y_1 + m_2y_2 + m_3y_3}{m_1 + m_2 + m_3}$$

$$\Rightarrow y_{CM} = \frac{1\times 0 + 1\times 0 + 1\times 1}{1+1+1} = \frac{1}{3}$$

$$\therefore \quad \mathbf{r}_{CM} = x_{CM}\hat{\mathbf{i}} + y_{CM}\hat{\mathbf{j}}$$

$$= \frac{1}{3}\hat{\mathbf{i}} + \frac{1}{3}\hat{\mathbf{j}}$$

$$\Rightarrow \mathbf{r}_{CM} = \frac{\hat{\mathbf{i}} + \hat{\mathbf{j}}}{3}$$

Topic 2

Torque, Couple and Angular Momentum

2018

1 The moment of the force $\mathbf{F} = 4\hat{\mathbf{i}} + 5\hat{\mathbf{j}} - 6\hat{\mathbf{k}}$ at $(2, 0, -3)$, about the point $(2, -2, -2)$ is given by **[NEET]**

(a) $-7\hat{\mathbf{i}} - 8\hat{\mathbf{j}} - 4\hat{\mathbf{k}}$ (b) $-4\hat{\mathbf{i}} - \hat{\mathbf{j}} - 8\hat{\mathbf{k}}$

(c) $-8\hat{\mathbf{i}} - 4\hat{\mathbf{j}} - 7\hat{\mathbf{k}}$ (d) $-7\hat{\mathbf{i}} - 4\hat{\mathbf{j}} - 8\hat{\mathbf{k}}$

2 A thin horizontal circular disc is rotating about a vertical axis passing through its centre. An insect is at rest at a point near the rim of disc. The insect now moves along a diameter of the disc to reach its other end. During the journey of the insect, the angular speed of the disc **[AIIMS]**

(a) continuously decreases
(b) continuously increases
(c) first increases and then decreases
(d) remains unchanged

3 A solid sphere is rotating freely about its symmetry axis in free space. The radius of the sphere is increased keeping its mass same. Which of the following physical quantities would remain constant for the sphere? **[NEET]**

(a) Rotational kinetic energy
(b) Moment of inertia
(c) Angular velocity
(d) Angular momentum

2017

4 Which of the following statements are correct? **[NEET]**

I. Centre of mass of a body usually coincides with the centre of gravity of the body.
II. Centre of mass of a body is the point at which the total gravitational torque on the body is zero.
III. A couple on a body produce both translational and rotational motion in a body.
IV. Mechanical advantage greater than one means that small effort can be used to lift a large load.

(a) II and IV (b) I and II
(c) II and III (d) III and IV

5 A constant torque of 3.14 N-m is exerted on a pivoted wheel. If the angular acceleration of the wheel is 4π rad s^{-2}, then the moment of inertia of the wheel is

(a) 0.25 kg-m^2 (b) 2.5 kg-m^2 **[J&K CET]**
(c) 4.5 kg-m^2 (d) 25 kg-m^2

2016

6 A force $\mathbf{F} = 5\hat{\mathbf{i}} + 2\hat{\mathbf{j}} - 5\hat{\mathbf{k}}$ acts on a particle whose position vector is $\mathbf{r} = \hat{\mathbf{i}} - 2\hat{\mathbf{j}} + \hat{\mathbf{k}}$. What is the torque about the origin? **[KCET]**

(a) $8\hat{\mathbf{i}} + 10\hat{\mathbf{j}} + 12\hat{\mathbf{k}}$ (b) $8\hat{\mathbf{i}} + 10\hat{\mathbf{j}} - 12\hat{\mathbf{k}}$
(c) $8\hat{\mathbf{i}} - 10\hat{\mathbf{j}} - 8\hat{\mathbf{k}}$ (d) $10\hat{\mathbf{i}} - 10\hat{\mathbf{j}} - \hat{\mathbf{k}}$

7 Angular momentum L is given by $L = p \cdot r$. The variation of $\log L$ and $\log p$ is shown by **[AMU]**

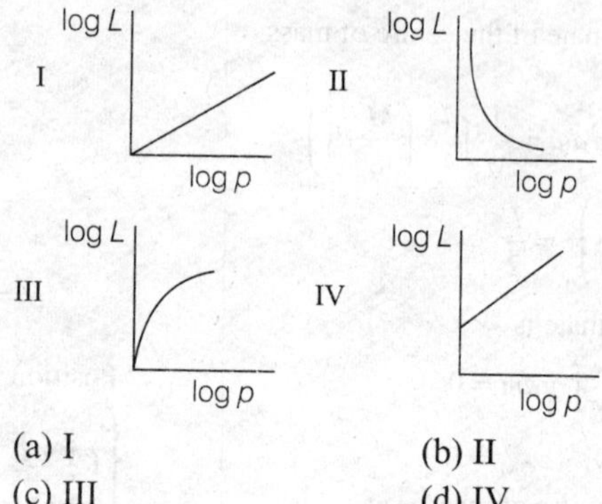

(a) I (b) II
(c) III (d) IV

2015

8 A rod of weight w is supported by two parallel knife edges A and B and is in equilibrium in a horizontal position. The knives are at a distance d from each other. The centre of mass of the rod is at distance x from A. The normal reaction on A is **[CBSE AIPMT]**

(a) $\dfrac{wx}{d}$ (b) $\dfrac{wd}{x}$
(c) $\dfrac{w(d-x)}{x}$ (d) $\dfrac{w(d-x)}{d}$

2012

9 A circular platform is mounted on a frictionless vertical axle. Its radius $r = 2$ m and its moment of inertia about the axle is 200 kg-m^2. It is initially at rest. A 50 kg man stands on the edge of the platform and begins to walk along the edge at the speed of 1 ms^{-1} relative to the ground. Time taken by the man to complete one revolution is **[CBSE AIPMT]**

(a) π s (b) $\dfrac{3\pi}{2}$ s
(c) 2π s (d) $\dfrac{\pi}{2}$ s

2011

10 The instantaneous angular position of a point on a rotating wheel is given by the equation $\theta(t) = 2t^3 - 6t^2$. The torque on the wheel becomes zero at **[CBSE AIPMT]**
(a) $t = 0.5$ s (b) $t = 0.25$ s (c) $t = 2$ s (d) $t = 1$ s

11 A force $F = 2.0$ N acts on a particle P in the x-z plane. The force F is parallel to X-axis. The particle P (as shown in the figure) is at a distance 3 m and the line joining P with the origin makes angle 30° with the X-axis. The magnitude of torque on P w.r.t. origin O (in N-m) is **[AMU]**

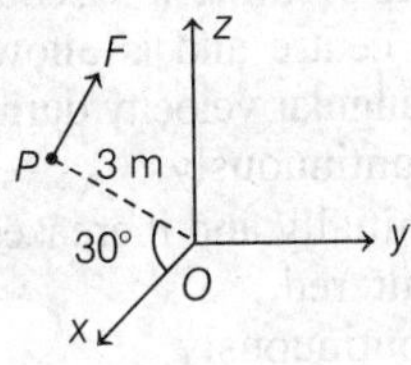

(a) 2 (b) 3
(c) 4 (d) 5

2010

12 A small object of mass m is attached to a light string which passes through a hollow tube. The tube is hold by one hand and the string by the other. The object is set into rotation in a circle of radius R and velocity v. The string is then pulled down, shortening the radius of path of r. What is conserved? **[UP CPMT]**
(a) Angular momentum
(b) Linear momentum
(c) Kinetic energy
(d) None of the above

13 A particle of mass m is projected with a velocity v making an angle of 45° with the horizontal. The magnitude of angular momentum of the projectile about an axis of projection when the particle is of maximum height h is **[BVP]**
(a) zero (b) $\frac{mv^3}{4\sqrt{2}g}$
(c) $\frac{mv^2}{\sqrt{2g}}$ (d) $m(2gh^3)$

14 A particle with the position vector **r** has linear momentum **p**. Which of the following statements is true in respect of its angular momentum **L** about the origin? **[Kerala CEE]**
(a) **L** acts along **p**.
(b) **L** acts along **r**.
(c) **L** is maximum when **p** and **r** are parallel.
(d) **L** is maximum when **p** is perpendicular to **r**.
(e) **L** is minimum when **p** is perpendicular to **r**.

2007

15 A uniform rod AB of length l and mass m is free to rotate about point A. The rod is released from rest in the horizontal position. Given that the moment of inertia of the rod about A is $\frac{ml^2}{3}$, the initial angular acceleration of the rod will be **[CBSE AIPMT]**

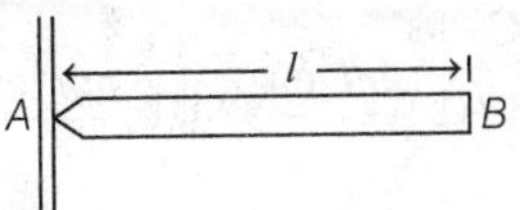

(a) $\frac{2g}{3l}$ (b) $mg\frac{l}{2}$ (c) $\frac{3}{2}gl$ (d) $\frac{3g}{2l}$

16 A particle of mass m moves in the xy- plane with a velocity v along the straight line AB. If the angular momentum of the particle with respect to origin O is L_A when it is at A and L_B when it is at B, then

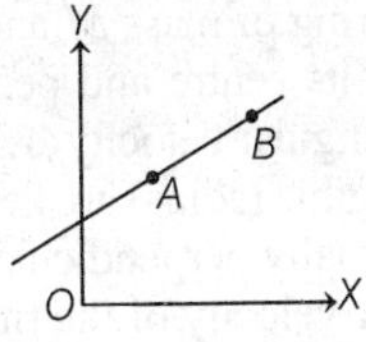

[CBSE AIPMT]
(a) $L_A > L_B$
(b) $L_A = L_B$
(c) the relationship between L_A and L_B depends upon the slope of the line AB
(d) $L_A < L_B$

17 Let **F** be the force acting on a particle having position vector **r** and τ be the torque of this force about the origin. Then, **[DCE]**
(a) $\mathbf{r} \cdot \tau = 0$ and $\mathbf{F} \cdot \tau \neq 0$ (b) $\mathbf{r} \cdot \tau \neq 0$ and $\mathbf{F} \cdot \tau = 0$
(c) $\mathbf{r} \cdot \tau \neq 0$ and $\mathbf{F} \cdot \tau \neq 0$ (d) $\mathbf{r} \cdot \tau = 0$ and $\mathbf{F} \cdot \tau = 0$

18 A wheel having moment of inertia 2 kg -m^2 about its vertical axis, rotates at the rate of 60 rpm about this axis. The torque which can stop the wheel's rotation in one minute would be **[Manipal]**
(a) $\frac{2\pi}{15}$ Nm^{-1} (b) $\frac{\pi}{12}$ Nm^{-1} (c) $\frac{\pi}{15}$ Nm^{-1} (d) $\frac{\pi}{18}$ Nm^{-1}

19 A particle is projected with a speed v at 45° with the horizontal. The magnitude of angular momentum of the projectile about the point of projection when the particle is at its maximum height h is **[Kerala CEE]**
(a) zero (b) $\frac{mvh^2}{\sqrt{2}}$ (c) $\frac{mv^2h}{2}$ (d) $\frac{mvh^3}{\sqrt{2}}$
(e) $\frac{mvh}{\sqrt{2}}$

20 If the torque of the rotational motion will be zero, then the constant quantity will be **[BVP]**
(a) angular momentum
(b) linear momentum
(c) angular acceleration
(d) centripetal acceleration

21 A thin rod of mass m and length $2l$ is made to rotate about an axis passing through its centre and perpendicular to it. If its angular velocity changes from 0 to ω in time t, the torque acting on it is **[AMU]**

(a) $\frac{ml^2\omega}{12t}$ (b) $\frac{ml^2\omega}{3t}$ (c) $\frac{ml^2\omega}{t}$ (d) $\frac{4ml^2\omega}{3t}$

2006

22 A particle of mass $(m) = 5$ units is moving with a uniform speed $v = 3\sqrt{2}$ units in the xoy - plane along the line $y = x + 4$. The magnitude of the angular momentum of the particle about the origin is **[Manipal]**

(a) 60 units (b) $40\sqrt{2}$ units
(c) zero (d) 7.5 units

23 A thin circular ring of mass M and radius R rotates about an axis through its centre and perpendicular to its plane, with a constant angular velocity ω. Four small spheres each of mass m (negligible radius) are kept gently to the opposite ends of two mutually perpendicular diameters of the ring. The new angular velocity of the ring will be **[Kerala CEE]**

(a) 4ω (b) $\frac{M}{4m}\omega$

(c) $\left(\frac{M+4m}{M}\right)\omega$ (d) $\left(\frac{M}{M-4m}\right)\omega$

(e) $\left(\frac{M}{M+4m}\right)\omega$

24 A disc of mass 2 kg and radius 0.2 m is rotating with angular velocity 30 rad s^{-1}. What is angular velocity, if a mass of 0.25 kg is put on periphery of the disc? **[DUMET]**

(a) 24 rad s^{-1} (b) 36 rad s^{-1}
(c) 15 rad s^{-1} (d) 26 rad s^{-1}

2005

25 A horizontal platform is rotating with uniform angular velocity around the vertical axis passing through its centre. At some instant of time, a viscous fluid of mass m is dropped at the centre and is allowed to spread out and finally fall, the angular velocity during this period **[AIIMS]**

(a) decreases continuously
(b) decreases initially and increases again
(c) remains unaltered
(d) increases continuously

26 **Assertion** For a system of particles under central force field, the total angular momentum is conserved.
Reason The torque acting on such a system is zero. **[AIIMS]**

(a) Both Assertion and Reason are correct and Reason is the correct explanation of Assertion.
(b) Both Assertion and Reason are correct but Reason is not the correct explanation of Assertion.
(c) Assertion is correct but Reason is incorrect.
(d) Both Assertion and Reason are incorrect.

Answers

1 (d)	2 (c)	3 (d)	4 (b)	5 (a)	6 (d)	7 (d)	8 (d)	9 (c)	10 (d)
11 (b)	12 (a)	13 (b)	14 (d)	15 (d)	16 (b)	17 (d)	18 (c)	19 (e)	20 (a)
21 (b)	22 (a)	23 (e)	24 (a)	25 (b)	26 (a)				

Explanations

1 *(d)* Moment of force is defined as the cross product of the force and the force arm.

Given, $\mathbf{F} = 4\hat{\mathbf{i}} + 5\hat{\mathbf{j}} - 6\hat{\mathbf{j}}$,
$\mathbf{r}_1 = 2\hat{\mathbf{i}} + 0\hat{\mathbf{j}} - 3\hat{\mathbf{k}}$
and $\mathbf{r}_2 = 2\hat{\mathbf{i}} - 2\hat{\mathbf{j}} - 2\hat{\mathbf{k}}$

Moment of force $= \mathbf{r} \times \mathbf{F} = (\mathbf{r}_2 - \mathbf{r}_1) \times \mathbf{F}$

$= [(2\hat{\mathbf{i}} - 2\hat{\mathbf{j}} - 2\hat{\mathbf{k}}) - (2\hat{\mathbf{i}} + 0\hat{\mathbf{j}} - 3\hat{\mathbf{k}})] \times [4\hat{\mathbf{i}} + 5\hat{\mathbf{j}} - 6\hat{\mathbf{k}}]$

$= [0\hat{\mathbf{i}} + 2\hat{\mathbf{j}} - 1\hat{\mathbf{k}}] \times [4\hat{\mathbf{i}} + 5\hat{\mathbf{j}} - 6\hat{\mathbf{k}}]$

$$= \begin{vmatrix} \hat{\mathbf{i}} & \hat{\mathbf{j}} & \hat{\mathbf{k}} \\ 0 & 2 & -1 \\ 4 & 5 & -6 \end{vmatrix}$$

$= \hat{\mathbf{i}}[(-6\times 2) - (-1\times 5)]$
$- \hat{\mathbf{j}}[(-6\times 0) - (-1\times 4)] + \hat{\mathbf{k}}[(0\times 5) - 2\times 4]$
$= -7\hat{\mathbf{i}} - 4\hat{\mathbf{j}} - 8\hat{\mathbf{k}}$

2 *(c)* Moment of inertia of the insect disc system, $\text{MI} = \frac{1}{2}MR^2 + mx^2$

where, m = mass of insect and x = distance of insect from centre.

Clearly, as the insect moves along the diameter of the disc. Moment of inertia first decreases and then increases.

By conservation of angular momentum, angular speed first increases and then decreases.

3 *(d)* As, we know that external torque,

$$\tau_{ext} = \frac{dL}{dt}$$

where, L is the angular momentum.

Since, in the given condition,

$$\tau_{ext} = 0 \Rightarrow \frac{dL}{dt} = 0$$

or L = constant

Hence, when the radius of the sphere is increased keeping its mass same, only the angular momentum remains constant. But other quantities like moment of inertia, rotational kinetic energy and angular velocity changes.

4 *(b)* Usually, the centre of gravity coincides with the centre of mass for bodies, when the gravitational field is uniform for bodies of small height. Since, the gravitational force can be taken to be centered or confined at the centre of gravity of body, so the torque of gravitational force about the centre of gravity must be zero.

A couple always produces the rotation without translation. Mechanical advantage is the ratio of the force produced by a machine to the force applied on it. It is used in assessing the performance of a machine So, option (b) is correct.

5 (a) Given, $\tau_{ext} = 3.14$ N-m

and $\alpha = 4\pi$ rads^{-2}

As, $\tau_{ext} = I\alpha$

So, $I = \frac{\tau_{ext}}{d} = \frac{3.14}{4\pi} = \frac{1}{4} = 0.25$ kg-m^2

6 (a) Given, $\mathbf{F} = 5\hat{\mathbf{i}} + 2\hat{\mathbf{j}} - 5\hat{\mathbf{k}}$

and $\mathbf{r} = \hat{\mathbf{i}} - 2\hat{\mathbf{j}} + \hat{\mathbf{k}}$

We know that, $\tau = \mathbf{r} \times \mathbf{F}$

So, torque about the origin will be given by

$$= \begin{vmatrix} \hat{\mathbf{i}} & \hat{\mathbf{j}} & \hat{\mathbf{k}} \\ 1 & -2 & 1 \\ 5 & +2 & -5 \end{vmatrix}$$

$= \hat{\mathbf{i}}(10-2) - \hat{\mathbf{j}}(-5-5) + \hat{\mathbf{k}}(2+10)$

$= 8\hat{\mathbf{i}} + 10\hat{\mathbf{j}} + 12\hat{\mathbf{k}}$

7 (d) Angular momentum, $L = rp$

Taking log on both sides, we get

$\log_e L = \log_e p + \log_e r$

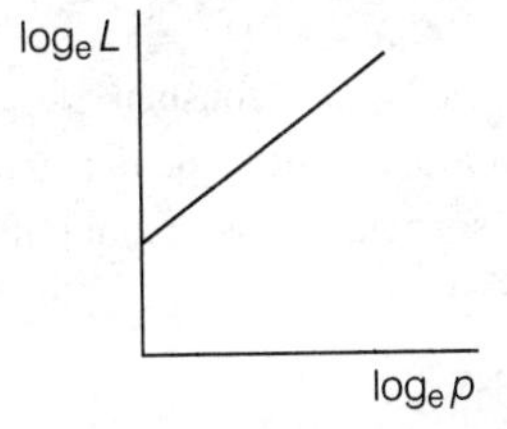

$\therefore$ The graph is drawn between $\log_e L$ and $\log_e p$ is a straight line, which is not pass through the origin.

8 (d) As the weight w balances the normal reactions.

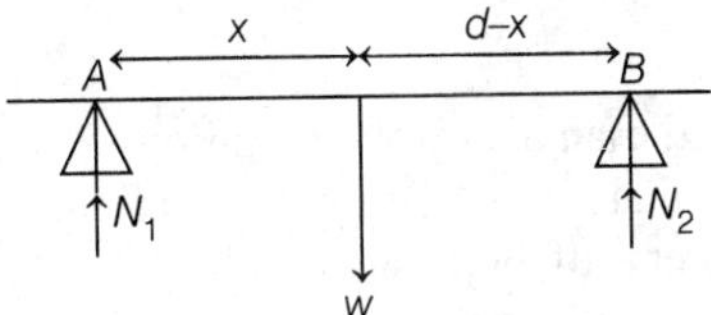

So, $w = N_1 + N_2$ ...(i)

Now balancing torque about the COM, i.e. anti-clockwise momentum = clockwise momentum

$\Rightarrow N_1 x = N_2(d-x)$

Putting the value of N_2 from Eq. (i), we get

$N_1 x = (w - N_1)(d-x)$

$\Rightarrow N_1 x = wd - wx - N_1 d + N_1 x$

$\Rightarrow N_1 d = w(d-x)$

$\Rightarrow N_1 = \frac{w(d-x)}{d}$

9 (c) Given, $r = 2$ m, $I = 200$ kg-m^2,

$m = 50$ kg and $v = 1$ ms^{-1}

On conservating angular momentum,

$I\omega = mvr$

$\Rightarrow 200 \times \omega = 50 \times 1 \times 2$

or $\omega = \frac{1}{2}$ rads^{-1}

Linear velocity, $v = r\omega = 1$ ms^{-1}

Time taken, $t = \frac{2\pi r}{1-(-1)} = \frac{2\pi r}{2}$

$= \pi r = 2\pi$ s $\left(\because t = \frac{2\pi}{\omega}\right)$

10 (d) According to question, torque,

$\tau = I\alpha = 0$

it means that $\alpha = 0$

or $\alpha = \frac{d^2\theta}{dt^2} = 0$

Given, $\theta(t) = 2t^3 - 6t^2$

So, $\frac{d\theta}{dt} = 6t^2 - 12t$

$\frac{d^2\theta}{dt} = 12t - 12 \quad \left(\because \alpha = \frac{d^2\theta}{dt^2} = 0\right)$

$12t - 12 = 0 \Rightarrow t = 1$ s

11 (b) As, torque,

$\tau = F \cdot r \sin\theta = 2 \times 3 \times \sin 30°$ (given)

$\Rightarrow \tau = 6 \times \frac{1}{2} = 3$ N-m

12 (a) In the absence of external torque, angular momentum remains constant whereas linear momentum and kinetic energy changes.

13 (b) Maximum height attained

$= \frac{v^2 \sin^2\theta}{2g} = \frac{v^2 \sin^2 45°}{2g} = \frac{v^2}{4g}$ $(\because \theta = 45°)$

At highest point, momentum

$= mv\cos 45° = \frac{mv}{\sqrt{2}}$

Angular momentum

$= \frac{mv}{\sqrt{2}} \times \frac{v^2}{4g} = \frac{mv^3}{4\sqrt{2}g}$

14 (d) We know that, $\mathbf{L} = \mathbf{r} \times \mathbf{p}$.

Angular momentum $\mathbf{L}$ is maximum when $\mathbf{p}$ is perpendicular to $\mathbf{r}$.

15 (d) The moment of inertia of the uniform rod about an axis through one end and perpendicular to its length is

$$I = \frac{ml^2}{3}$$

where, m is mass of rod and l is length.

Torque ($\tau = I\alpha$) acting on centre of gravity of rod is given by

$\tau = mg\frac{l}{2}$ or $I\alpha = mg\frac{l}{2}$

or $\frac{ml^2}{3}\alpha = mg\frac{l}{2}$ or $\alpha = \frac{3g}{2l}$

16 (b) From the definition of angular momentum,

$\mathbf{L} = \mathbf{r} \times \mathbf{p} = rmv \sin\phi(-\hat{\mathbf{k}})$

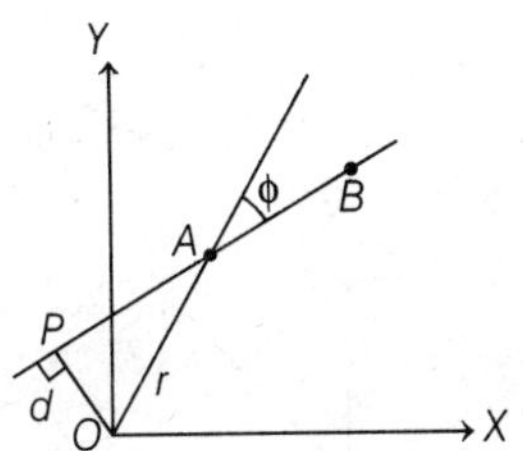

Therefore, the magnitude of L is $L = mvr\sin\phi = mvd$, where $d = r\sin\phi$ is the distance of closest approach of the particle to the origin. As d is same for both the particles, hence, $L_A = L_B$.

17 (d) We know that, $\tau = r \times F$

where, τ is perpendicular to both r and F.

So, $\mathbf{r} \cdot \tau$ as well as, $\mathbf{F} \cdot \tau$ has to be zero.

18 (c) Given, $I = 2$ kg-m^2,

$\omega_0 = \frac{60}{60} \times 2\pi$ rad s^{-1}, $\omega = 0$ and $t = 60$ s

The torque required to stop the wheel's rotation is

$\tau = I\alpha = I\left(\frac{\omega_0 - \omega}{t}\right)$

$\therefore \tau = \frac{2 \times 2\pi \times 60}{60 \times 60} = \frac{\pi}{15}$ Nm^{-1}

19 (e) When a particle is projected with a speed v at 45° with the horizontal, then the velocity of the projectile at maximum height,

$v' = v\cos 45° = \frac{v}{\sqrt{2}}$

Angular momentum of the projectile about the point of projection is

$= mv'h$

$= m\frac{v}{\sqrt{2}}h = \frac{mvh}{\sqrt{2}}$

20 (a) As, torque, $\tau = \frac{dL}{dt}$

If $\tau = 0$, then L = constant

Hence, option (a) is correct.

21 (b) Since, $\tau = I\alpha$

So, $\tau = \left(\frac{m(2l)^2}{12}\right)\left(\frac{\omega}{t}\right) \quad \left(\because I = \frac{ml^2}{12}\right)$

or $\tau = \frac{m \times 4l^2 \times \omega}{12 \times t}$

or $\tau = \frac{4ml^2\omega}{12t} = \frac{ml^2\omega}{3t}$

22 (a) Momentum of the particle

$= \text{Mass} \times \text{Velocity}$

$= (5) \times (3\sqrt{2}) = 15\sqrt{2}$ (given)

The direction of momentum in the XOY plane is given by

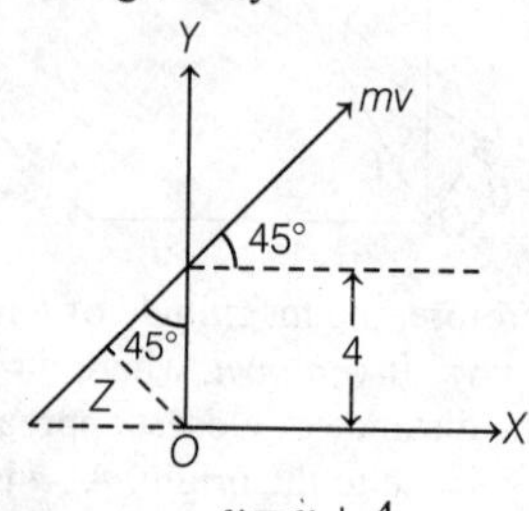

$y = x + 4$

Slope of the line $= 1 = \tan\theta$

$\theta = 45°$

Intercept of its straight line = 4

Length of the perpendicular Z from the origin of the straight line

$= 4\sin 45° = \frac{4}{\sqrt{2}} = 2\sqrt{2}$

Angular momentum = Momentum × Perpendicular length

$= 15\sqrt{2} \times 2\sqrt{2} = 60$ units

23 (e) According to conservation of angular momentum,

$I\omega = \text{constant}$

i.e. we can write,

$I_1\omega_1 = I_2\omega_2$

or $MR^2\omega = (M + 4m)R^2\omega_2$

or $\omega_2 = \left(\frac{M}{M + 4m}\right)\omega$

24 (a) If no external torque acts on a system of particles, then angular momentum of the system remains constant, i.e. $\tau = 0$

$\Rightarrow \frac{dL}{dt} = 0 \Rightarrow L = I\omega = \text{constant}$

$\Rightarrow I_1\omega_1 = I_2\omega_2$

$\Rightarrow \frac{1}{2}Mr^2\omega_1 = \frac{1}{2}(M + 2m)r^2\omega_2 \quad \text{...(i)}$

Given, $M = 2$ kg, $m = 0.25$ kg, $r = 0.2$ m and $\omega_1 = 30$ rad s^{-1}.

Hence, after putting the given values in Eq. (i), we get

$\frac{1}{2} \times 2 \times (0.2)^2 \times 30$

$= \frac{1}{2} \times (2 + 2 \times 0.25)(0.2)^2 \times \omega_2$

or $1.2 = 0.05\omega_2$ or $\omega_2 = 24$ rad s^{-1}

25 (b) Law of conservation of angular momentum gives

$I\omega = \text{constant} \quad \text{...(i)}$

When viscous liquid dropped at the centre of horizontal table and it is made to spread out, then its moment of inertia increases. From Eq. (i), its angular velocity decreases. But when it starts falling then its moment of inertia starts decreasing and so its angular velocity increases again.

26 (a) When a body rotates about an axis under the action of an external torque τ, then the rate of change of angular momentum of the body is equal to the torque, i.e. $\frac{dJ}{dt} = \tau$

If external torque is zero ($\tau = 0$), then

$\frac{dJ}{dt} = 0 \Rightarrow dJ = 0$

$\Rightarrow J = \text{constant}$

As torque is zero, due to central forces. Thus, angular momentum remains conserved.

Topic 3

Moment of Inertia

2019

1 Two discs having mass ratio 1 : 2 and diameter ratio 2 : 1, then find the ratio of moment of inertia. **[JIPMER]**

(a) 2 : 1 (b) 1 : 1

(c) 1 : 2 (d) 2 : 3

2018

2 Find ratio of radius of gyration of a disc and ring of same radii at their tangential axis in plane. **[JIPMER]**

(a) $\sqrt{\frac{5}{6}}$ (b) $\sqrt{\frac{5}{3}}$

(c) 1 (d) $\frac{2}{3}$

2017

3 ABC is right angled triangular plane of uniform thickness. The sides are such that $AB > BC$ as shown in figure. I_1, I_2, I_3 are moments of inertia about AB, BC and AC, respectively. Then, which of the following relations is correct? **[JIPMER]**

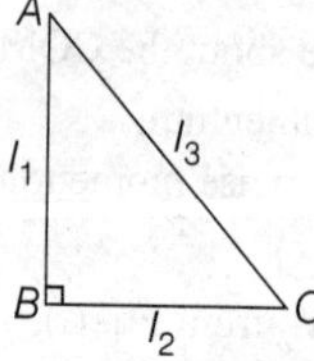

(a) $I_1 = I_2 = I_3$ (b) $I_2 > I_1 > I_3$

(c) $I_3 < I_2 < I_1$ (d) $I_3 > I_1 > I_2$

2016

4 From a disc of radius R and mass M, a circular hole of diameter R, whose rim passes through the centre is cut. What is the moment of inertia of the remaining part of the disc about a perpendicular axis, passing through the centre? **[NEET]**

(a) $13\ MR^2/32$ (b) $11\ MR^2/32$
(c) $9\ MR^2/32$ (d) $15\ MR^2/32$

2016

5 A light rod of length l has two masses m_1 and m_2 attached to its two ends. The moment of inertia of the system about an axis perpendicular to the rod and passing through the centre of mass is **[NEET]**

(a) $\frac{m_1 m_2}{m_1 + m_2} l^2$ (b) $\frac{m_1 + m_2}{m_1 m_2} l^2$
(c) $(m_1 + m_2)l^2$ (d) $\sqrt{m_1 m_2}\, l^2$

2015

6 Three identical spherical shells, each of mass m and radius r are placed as shown in figure. Consider an axis XX', which is touching to two shells and passing through diameter of third shell. Moment of inertia of the system consisting of these three spherical shells about XX' axis is **[CBSE]**

(a) $\frac{11}{5} mr^2$ (b) $3\ mr^2$ (c) $\frac{16}{5} mr^2$ (d) $4\ mr^2$

2014

7 Moment of inertia of ring about its diameter is I. The moment of inertia of the same ring about that axis perpendicular to its plane and passing through centre is **[KCET]**

(a) $\frac{I}{2}$ (b) $2I$ (c) $\frac{I}{4}$ (d) $4I$

2013

8 Moment of inertia of a disc about an axis which is tangent and parallel to its plane is I. Then, the moment of inertia of disc about a tangent but perpendicular to its plane will be **[MHT CET]**

(a) $\frac{3I}{4}$ (b) $\frac{5I}{6}$ (c) $\frac{3I}{2}$ (d) $\frac{6I}{5}$

9 Assertion Two circular discs of equal mass and thickness made of different materials, will have same moment of inertia about their central axes of rotation.

Reason Moment of inertia depends upon the distribution of mass in the body. **[AIIMS]**

(a) Both Assertion and Reason are correct and Reason is the correct explanation of Assertion.
(b) Both Assertion and Reason are correct but Reason is not correct explanation of Assertion.
(c) Assertion is correct but Reason is incorrect.
(d) Assertion is incorrect but Reason is correct.

10 Moment of inertia of circular loop of radius R about the axis of rotation parallel to horizontal diameter at a distance $R/2$ from it is **[WB JEE]**

(a) MR^2 (b) $(1/2)MR^2$
(c) $2MR^2$ (d) $(3/4)MR^2$

11 A rod of length L is composed of a uniform length $(1/2)\ L$ of wood whose mass in m_w and a uniform length $(1/2)\ L$ of brass whose mass is m_b. The moment of inertia I of the rod about an axis perpendicular to the rod and through its centre is equal to **[AMU]**

(a) $(m_w + m_b)L^2/12$
(b) $(m_w + m_b)L^2/6$
(c) $(m_w + m_b)L^2/3$
(d) $(m_w + m_b)L^2/2$

2011

12 The moment of inertia of a thin uniform rod of mass M and length L about an axis passing through its mid-point and perpendicular to its length is I_0. Its moment of inertia about an axis passing through one of its ends and perpendicular to its length is **[CBSE AIPMT]**

(a) $I_0 + ML^2/4$ (b) $I_0 + 2ML^2$
(c) $I_0 + ML^2$ (d) $I_0 + ML^2/2$

13 Moment of inertia of a hollow cylinder of mass M and radius r about its own axis is **[Kerala CEE]**

(a) $\frac{2}{3} Mr^2$ (b) $\frac{2}{5} Mr^2$
(c) $\frac{1}{3} Mr^2$ (d) $\frac{1}{2} Mr^2$
(e) Mr^2

14 One solid sphere A and another hollow sphere B are of same mass and same outer redius. Their moments of inertia about their diameters are respectively, I_A and I_B such that **[J&K CET]**

(a) $I_A = I_B$ (b) $I_A > I_B$
(c) $I_A < I_B$ (d) None of these

2010

15 The ratio of the radii of gyration of a circular disc and a circular ring of the same radii about a tangential axis perpendicular to plane of disc or ring is **[AFMC]**

(a) $1:2$ (b) $\sqrt{5}:\sqrt{6}$ (c) $2:3$ (d) $\frac{\sqrt{3}}{2}$

16 The moment of inertia of two equal masses each of mass m at separation L connected by a rod of mass M, about an axis passing through centre and perpendicular to length of rod is **[VMMC]**

(a) $\frac{(M + 3m)L^2}{12}$ (b) $\frac{(M + 6m)L^2}{12}$
(c) $\frac{ML^2}{4}$ (d) $\frac{ML^2}{12}$

17 If the moment of inertia of a disc about an axis tangential and parallel to its surface be I, then what will be the moment of inertia about the axis tangential but perpendicular to the surface? **[VMMC]**

(a) $\frac{6}{5}I$ (b) $\frac{3}{4}I$

(c) $\frac{3}{2}I$ (d) $\frac{5}{4}I$

18 The moment of inertia of a circular disc of radius 2 m and mass 1 kg about an axis passing through the centre of mass but perpendicular to the plane of the disc is 2 kg-m^2. Its moment of inertia about an axis parallel to this axis but passing through the edge of the disc is (see the given figure). **[KCET]**

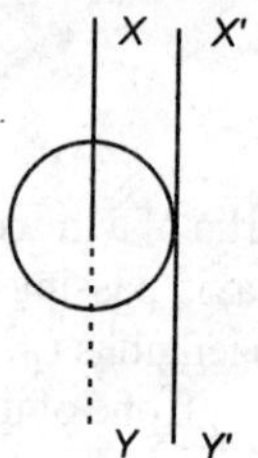

(a) 8 kg-m^2 (b) 4 kg-m^2

(c) 10 kg-m^2 (d) 6 kg-m^2

2008

19 A thin rod of length L and mass M is bent at its mid-point into two halves, so that the angle between them is 90°. The moment of inertia of the bent rod about an axis passing through the bending point and perpendicular to the plane defined by the two halves of the rod is **[CBSE AIPMT]**

(a) $\frac{ML^2}{24}$ (b) $\frac{ML^2}{12}$

(c) $\frac{ML^2}{6}$ (d) $\frac{\sqrt{2}ML^2}{24}$

20 For the given uniform square lamina $ABCD$, whose centre is O. **[AIIMS]**

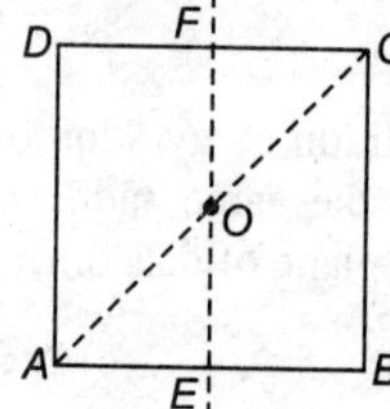

(a) $\sqrt{2}I_{AC} = I_{EF}$

(b) $I_{AD} = 3I_{EF}$

(c) $I_{AD} = 4I_{EF}$

(d) $I_{AC} = \sqrt{2}I_{EF}$

21 Two spheres of equal masses, one of which is a thin spherical shell and the other a solid, have the same moment of inertia about their respective diameters. The ratio of their radii will be **[MHT CET]**

(a) 5 : 7 (b) 3 : 5 (c) $\sqrt{3}:\sqrt{5}$ (d) $\sqrt{3}:\sqrt{7}$

22 The radius of gyration of a rod of length L and mass M about an axis perpendicular to its length and passing through a point at a distance $L/3$ from one of its ends is **[Punjab PMET]**

(a) $\frac{\sqrt{7}}{6}L$ (b) $\frac{L^2}{9}$

(c) $\frac{L}{3}$ (d) $\frac{\sqrt{5}}{2}L$

23 The moment of inertia of a rod of mass M, length l about an axis perpendicular to it through one end is **[J&K CET]**

(a) $Ml^2/12$ (b) $(2/3)Ml^2$

(c) $(3/2)Ml^2$ (d) $Ml^2/3$

24 Two identical rods of mass M and length l are lying in a horizontal plane at an angle α. The moment of inertia of the system of two rods about an axis passing through O and perpendicular to the plane of the rods is **[J&K CET]**

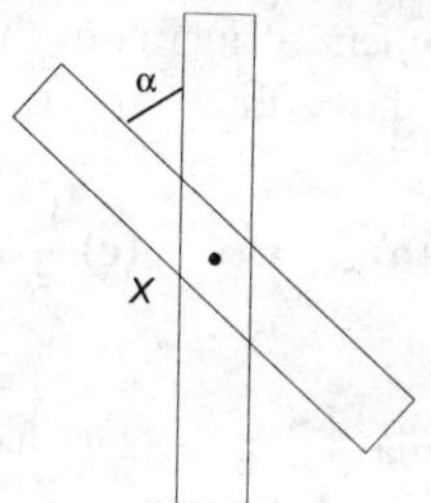

(a) $Ml^2/3$ (b) $Ml^2/12$

(c) $Ml^2/4$ (d) $Ml^2/6$

25 Two identical concentric rings each of mass m and radius R are placed perpendicularly. What is the moment of inertia about axis of one of the rings? **[DUMET]**

(a) $(3/2)MR^2$ (b) $2MR^2$

(c) $3MR^2$ (d) $(1/4)MR^2$

2007

26 The moment of inertia of a rod about an axis through its centre and perpendicaular to it is $\frac{1}{12}ML^2$ (where, M is the mass and L is the length of the rod). The rod is bent in the middle, so that two halves make an angle 60°. Now the moment of inertia about the same axis is **[RPET]**

(a) $ML^2/18$ (b) $ML^2/12$

(c) $ML^2/20$ (d) $ML^2/8\sqrt{3}$

27 Three particles, each of mass m gram are situated at the vertices of an equilateral triangle ABC of side l cm (as shown in the figure). The moment of inertia of the system about a line AX perpendicular to AB and in the plane of ABC, in g-cm^2 units will be **[MP PMT]**

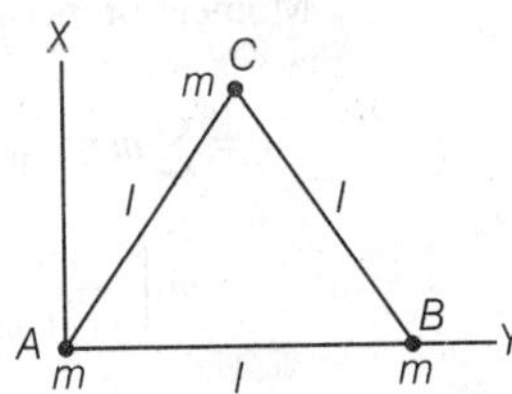

(a) $(3/4)\,ml^2$ (b) $2\,ml^2$
(c) $(5/4)\,ml^2$ (d) $(3/2)\,ml^2$

2006

28 Three rings each of mass M and radius R are arranged as shown in figure. The moment of inertia of the system about the axis XX' will be **[CBSE AIPMT]**

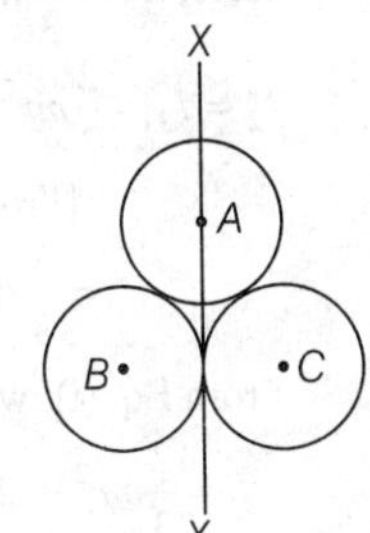

(a) $(7/2)MR^2$ (b) $3R^2$
(c) $(3/2)MR^2$ (d) $5MR^2$

29 The moment of inertia of a solid sphere about an axis passing through centre of gravity is $(2/5)MR^2$, then its radius of gyration about a parallel axis at a distance $2R$ from first axis is **[MHT CET]**

(a) $5R$ (b) $\sqrt{\frac{22}{5}}R$
(c) $\frac{5}{2}R$ (d) $\sqrt{\frac{12}{5}}R$

30 Five particles of each mass 2 kg are attached to the rim of a circular disc of radius 0.1 m and negligible mass. Moment of inertia of the system about the axis passing through the centre of the disc and perpendicular to its place is **[Manipal]**

(a) 1 kg-m^2 (b) 0.1 kg-m^2
(c) 2 kg-m^2 (d) 0.2 kg-m^2

31 A uniform circular disc of radius R lies in the xy-plane with its centre coinciding with the origin of the coordinate system. Its moment of inertia about an axis lying in the xy-plane, parallel to the X-axis and passing through a point on the Y-axis at a distance $y = 2R$ is I_1. Its moment of inertia about an axis lying in a plane perpendicular to xy-plane passing through a point on the X-axis at a distance $x = d$ is I_2. If $I_1 = I_2$, the value of d is **[EAMCET]**

(a) $\frac{\sqrt{19}}{2}R$ (b) $\frac{\sqrt{17}}{2}R$ (c) $\frac{\sqrt{15}}{2}R$ (d) $\frac{\sqrt{13}}{2}R$

2005

32 Out of the given bodies (of same mass) for which the moment of inertia will be maximum, about the axis passing through its centre of gravity and perpendicular to its plane? **[RPMT]**

(a) Disc of radius a
(b) Ring of radius a
(c) Square lamina of side $2a$
(d) Four rods of length $2a$ making a square

33 **Assertion** I_S and I_H are the moments of inertia about the diameters of a solid and thin walled hollow sphere respectively. If the radii and the masses of the above spheres are equal, $I_H > I_S$.

Reason In solid sphere, the mass is continuously and regularly distributed about the centre whereas the mass, to a large extent, is concentrated on the surface of hollow sphere. **[EAMCET]**

(a) Both Assertion and Reason are correct and Reason is the correct explanation of Assertion.
(b) Both Assertion and Reason are true but Reason is not the correct explanation of Assertion.
(c) Assertion is correct but Reason is incorrect.
(d) Both Assertion and Reason are incorrect.

Answers

1 (a)	2 (a)	3 (b)	4 (a)	5 (a)	6 (d)	7 (b)	8 (d)	9 (a)	10 (d)
11 (a)	12 (a)	13 (e)	14 (c)	15 (d)	16 (b)	17 (a)	18 (d)	19 (b)	20 (c)
21 (c)	22 (c)	23 (d)	24 (d)	25 (a)	26 (b)	27 (c)	28 (a)	29 (b)	30 (b)
31 (c)	32 (d)	33 (a)							

Explanations

1 (a) Given, mass ratio of two discs,

$$m_1 : m_2 = 1:2, \text{ i.e. } \frac{m_1}{m_2} = \frac{1}{2}$$

and diameter ratio $\frac{d_1}{d_2} = \frac{2}{1} \Rightarrow \frac{r_1}{r_2} = \frac{2}{1}$

$\therefore$ Ratio of their moment of inertia,

$$\frac{I_1}{I_2} = \frac{\frac{m_1 r_1^2}{2}}{\frac{m_2 r_2^2}{2}} = \frac{m_1}{m_2} \cdot \left(\frac{r_1}{r_2}\right)^2 = \frac{1}{2}\left(\frac{2}{1}\right)^2 = \frac{2}{1}$$

$\therefore \qquad I_1 : I_2 = 2:1$

2 (a) For disc, moment of inertia about the diameter, $I_d = mr^2/4$

and moment of inertia about the tangential axis,

$$I_{\text{disc}} = I_d + mr^2$$

$$I_{\text{disc}} = \frac{mr^2}{4} + mr^2 = \frac{5mr^2}{4}$$

Let the radius of gyration of disc is k_{disc}.

$$I_{\text{disc}} = mk_{\text{disc}}^2$$

$$\frac{5mr^2}{4} = mk_{\text{disc}}^2$$

$$k_{\text{disc}}^2 = \sqrt{\frac{5}{4}}r$$

For ring, moment of inertia about the diameter,

$$I_a = \frac{mr^2}{2}$$

and moment of inertia about the tangential axis

$$I_{\text{ring}} = I_a + mr^2 = \frac{mr^2}{2} + mr^2 = \frac{3}{2}mr^2$$

Let the radius of gyration of ring is k_{ring}.

$$I_{\text{ring}} = mk_{\text{ring}}^2$$

$$\frac{3}{2}mr^2 = mk_{\text{ring}}^2$$

$$k_{\text{ring}} = \sqrt{\frac{3}{2}}r$$

$$\Rightarrow \quad \frac{k_{\text{disc}}}{k_{\text{ring}}} = \frac{\sqrt{\frac{5}{4}}r}{\sqrt{\frac{3}{2}}r} = \sqrt{\frac{5}{6}}$$

3 (b) The moment of inertia of a body about an axis depends not only on the mass of the body but also on the distribution of mass about the axis. For a given body, mass is same, so it will depend only on the distribution of mass about the axis. The mass is farthest from axis BC so I_2 is maximum, mass is nearest to axis AC so I_3 is minimum.

Hence, the correct sequence will be $I_2 > I_1 > I_3$.

4 (a) Considering the information given in the question, let us draw the figure

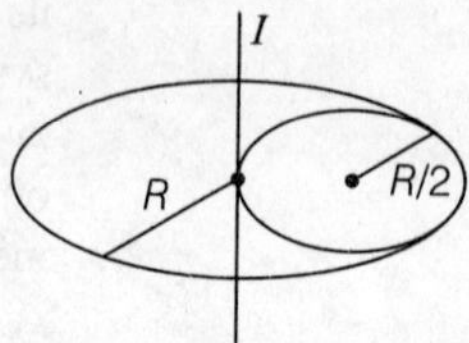

If the above figure is considered, then moment of inertia of disc will be given as

$$I = I_{\text{remain}} + I_{(R/2)}$$

$$\Rightarrow \quad I_{\text{remain}} = I - I_{(R/2)} \qquad \text{...(i)}$$

The mass of smaller disc cut out

$$m_{R/2} = \frac{M}{(\text{area of bigger disc})} \text{(area of smaller disc)}$$

$$= \frac{M}{\pi R^2}\left(\frac{\pi R^2}{4}\right) \Rightarrow m_{R/2} = \frac{M}{4}$$

$\because$ Moment of inertia of a disc,

$$I = \frac{(\text{mass})(\text{radius})^2}{2}$$

Putting the values in Eq. (i), we get

$$= \frac{MR^2}{2} - \left[\frac{(M/4)(R/2)^2}{2} + \frac{M}{4}\left(\frac{R}{2}\right)^2\right]$$

$$= \frac{MR^2}{2} - \left[\frac{MR^2}{32} + \frac{MR^2}{16}\right]$$

$$= \frac{MR^2}{2} - \left[\frac{MR^2 + 2MR^2}{32}\right]$$

$$= \frac{MR^2}{2} - \frac{3MR^2}{32} = \frac{16MR^2 - 3MR^2}{32}$$

$$\therefore \qquad I_{\text{remain}} = \frac{13MR^2}{32}$$

5 (a) COM of m_1 and m_2 masses lies at O

and $r = \frac{m_1 r_1 + m_2 r_2}{m_1 + m_2}$, then

$$m_1 r_1 = m_2 r_2 \qquad \text{...(i)}$$

and $\qquad r_1 + r_2 = l \qquad$ ...(ii)

From Eqs. (i) and (ii), we get

$$r_1 = \frac{m_2 l}{m_1 + m_2} \text{ and } r_2 = \frac{m_1 l}{m_1 + m_2}$$

$\therefore$ Moment of inertia of the point masses about the given axis is

$$I = \sum m_i r_i^2 \Rightarrow I = m_1 r_1^2 + m_2 r_2^2$$

$$= m_1\left(\frac{m_2 l}{m_1 + m_2}\right)^2 + m_2\left(\frac{m_1 l}{m_1 + m_2}\right)^2$$

$$= \frac{m_1 m_2 l^2}{(m_1 + m_2)}$$

6 (d) The total moment of inertia of the system is

$$I = I_1 + I_2 + I_3 \text{ ...(i)}$$

Here, $I_1 = \frac{2}{3}mr^2$

$$I_2 = I_3 = \frac{2}{3}mr^2 + mr^2$$

[From parallel axis theorem]

$$= \frac{5}{3}mr^2$$

From Eq. (i), we get

$$I = \frac{2}{3}mr^2 + 2 \times \frac{5}{3}mr^2 = mr^2\left(\frac{2}{3} + \frac{10}{3}\right)$$

$$I = 4mr^2$$

7 (b) For a ring, $I_z = MR^2$

From perpendicular axis theorem,

$$I_x + I_y = I_z \qquad \text{...(i)}$$

Given, $I_x = I_y = I$

From Eq. (i), we get

$$2I = I_z$$

8 (d) The moment of inertia of the disc about an axis parallel to its plane is

$$I_t = I_d + MR^2$$

$$\Rightarrow \qquad I = \frac{1}{4}MR^2 + MR^2$$

$$\left(\because I_d = \frac{1}{4}MR^2\right)$$

$$= \frac{5}{4}MR^2 \text{ or } MR^2 = \frac{4I}{5} \qquad \text{...(i)}$$

Now, moment of inertia about a tangent perpendicular to its plane is

$$I' = \frac{1}{2}MR^2 + MR^2$$

$$\Rightarrow \quad I' = \frac{3}{2}MR^2 = \frac{3}{2} \times \frac{4}{5}I = \frac{6}{5}I$$

[$\because$ by using Eq. (i)]

9 (a) The moment of inertia is given by $I = \Sigma mr^2$.
The moment of inertia depends on the mass and distribution of mass w.r.t. the axis of rotation in the body, so that moment of inertia of two circular discs having equal mass and thickness made of different material will be same.

10 (d) Applying theorem of parallel axes,

$$I = I_{CM} + M\left(\frac{R}{2}\right)^2$$

$$[\because I_{CM} = \frac{1}{2}MR^2]$$

$$\Rightarrow \quad I = \frac{1}{2}MR^2 + \frac{MR^2}{4} \Rightarrow I = \frac{3}{4}MR^2$$

11 (a) Moment of inertia of wood rod about one end,

$$M_1 = m_w \times \frac{(L/2)^2}{3} = m_w \frac{L^2}{12}$$

Moment of inertia of brass rod about one end,

$$M_2 = m_b \times \frac{(L/2)^2}{3} = m_b \times \frac{L^2}{12}$$

Total moment of inertia,

$$M = M_1 + M_2$$

$$= m_w \frac{L^2}{12} + m_b \times \frac{L^2}{12}$$

$$= (m_w + m_b)\frac{L^2}{12}$$

12 (a) According to parallel axes theorem, we have

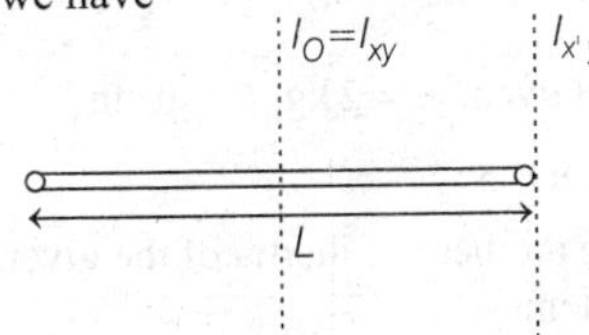

$$I_{x'y'} = I_{xy} + Md^2 = I_0 + M\left(\frac{L}{2}\right)^2$$

$$\Rightarrow I_{x'y'} = I_0 + \frac{ML^2}{4}$$

13 (e) Moment of inertia of a hollow cylinder about its axis $= Mr^2$.

14 (c) Let same mass and same outer radii of solid sphere and hollow sphere be M and R, respectively. The moment of inertia of solid sphere A about its diameter,

$$I_A = \frac{2}{5}MR^2 \quad \text{...(i)}$$

The moment of inertia of hollow sphere (spherical shell) B about its diameter,

$$I_B = \frac{2}{3}MR^2 \quad \text{...(ii)}$$

It is clear from Eqs. (i) and (ii), we get $I_A < I_B$

15 (d) Radius of gyration, $K = \sqrt{\frac{I}{m}}$

As, $$K_{\text{disc}} = \sqrt{\frac{\frac{1}{2}mR^2 + mR^2}{m}} = \sqrt{\frac{3}{2}}R$$

$$K_{\text{ring}} = \sqrt{\frac{mR^2 + mR^2}{m}} = \sqrt{2}R$$

So, $$\frac{K_{\text{disc}}}{K_{\text{ring}}} = \frac{\sqrt{\frac{3}{2}}}{\sqrt{2}} = \frac{\sqrt{3}}{2}$$

16 (b) Moment of inertia of a rod about XY,

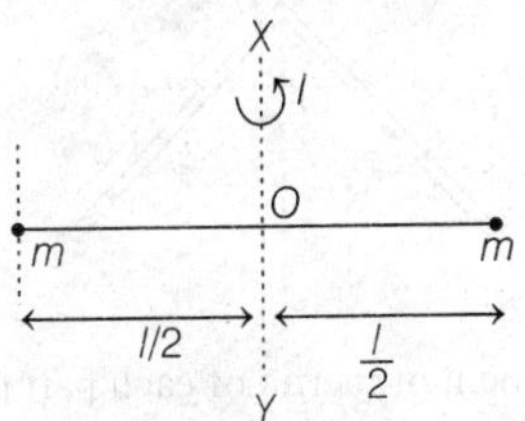

$$I_1 = \frac{ML^2}{12}$$

and $$I_2 = m\left(\frac{L}{2}\right)^2 + m\left(\frac{L}{2}\right)^2 = \frac{mL^2}{2}$$

$$\therefore \quad I = I_1 + I_2 = \frac{ML^2}{12} + \frac{mL^2}{2}$$

$$= \frac{(M + 6m)L^2}{12}$$

17 (a) Moment of inertia I of a disc about a tangent to surface and parallel,

$$I = \frac{5}{4}MR^2$$

or $$MR^2 = (4/5)I$$

Moment of inertia I of disc about the tangent perpendicular to plane,

$$I' = \frac{3}{2}MR^2$$

$$\Rightarrow \quad I' = \frac{3}{2}\left(\frac{4}{5}I\right) = \frac{6}{5}I$$

18 (d) According to parallel axes theorem,

$$I_{X'Y'} = I_{XY} + MR^2$$

Given, $I_{XY} = 2\,\text{kgm}^{-2}$, $M = 1\,\text{kg}$ and $R = 2\,\text{m}$.

$$\Rightarrow \quad I_{XY} = 2 + (1)(2)^2 = 6\,\text{kg-m}^2$$

19 (b) Since, rod is bent at the middle, so each part of it will have same length $\left(\frac{L}{2}\right)$ and mass $\left(\frac{M}{2}\right)$ as shown in figure.

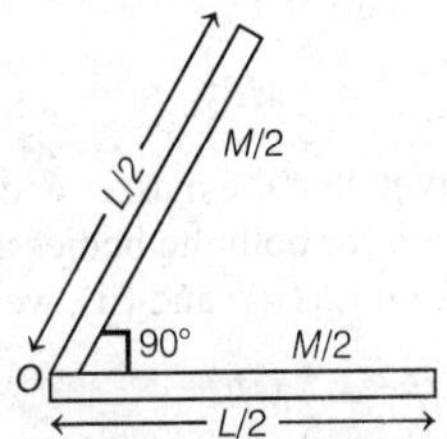

Moment of inertia of each part through its one end

$$= \frac{1}{3}\left(\frac{M}{2}\right)\left(\frac{L}{2}\right)^2$$

Hence, net moment of inertia through its middle point O,

$$I = \frac{1}{3}\left(\frac{M}{2}\right)\left(\frac{L}{2}\right)^2 + \frac{1}{3}\left(\frac{M}{2}\right)\left(\frac{L}{2}\right)^2$$

$$= \frac{1}{3}\left(\frac{ML^2}{8} + \frac{ML^2}{8}\right) = \frac{ML^2}{12}$$

20 (c) Let the each side of square lamina is d.

So, $I_{EF} = I_{GH}$ (due to symmetry)

and $I_{AC} = I_{BD}$ (due to symmetry)

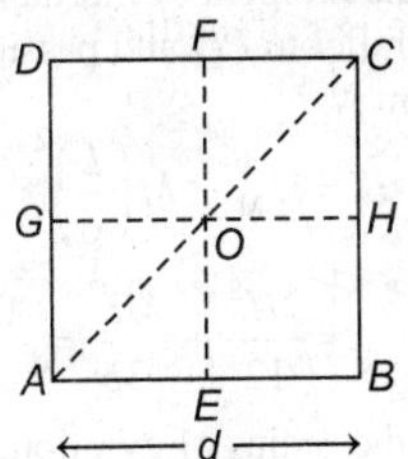

Now, according to the perpendicular axes theorem,

$$I_{AC} + I_{BD} = I_0$$

or $$2I_{AC} = I_0 \quad \text{...(i)}$$

and $$I_{EF} + I_{GH} = I_0$$

or $$2I_{EF} = I_0 \quad \text{...(ii)}$$

From Eqs. (i) and (ii), we get $I_{AC} = I_{EF}$

From parallel axis theorem,

$$\therefore \quad I_{AD} = I_{EF} + \frac{md^2}{4}$$

$$= \frac{md^2}{12} + \frac{md^2}{4} \quad \left(\text{as } I_{EF} = \frac{md^2}{12}\right)$$

So, $$I_{AD} = \frac{md^2}{3} = 4I_{EF}$$

21 (c) Let the radii of the thin spherical shell and the solid sphere are R_1 and R_2, respectively.
Then, the moment of inertia of the spherical shell about its diameter

$$I = \frac{2}{3}MR_1^2 \quad \text{...(i)}$$

and the moment of inertia of the solid sphere is given by

$$I = \frac{2}{5}MR_2^2 \quad \text{...(ii)}$$

It is given that the masses and moment of inertia for both the bodies are equal, then from Eqs. (i) and (ii), we get

$$\frac{2}{3}MR_1^2 = \frac{2}{5}MR_2^2$$

$$\Rightarrow \frac{R_1^2}{R_2^2} = \frac{3}{5} \Rightarrow \frac{R_1}{R_2} = \sqrt{\frac{3}{5}}$$

$$\Rightarrow R_1 : R_2 = \sqrt{3} : \sqrt{5}$$

22 (c) Moment of inertia of the rod about a perpendicular axis PQ passing through centre of mass C, $I_{CM} = ML^2/12$.

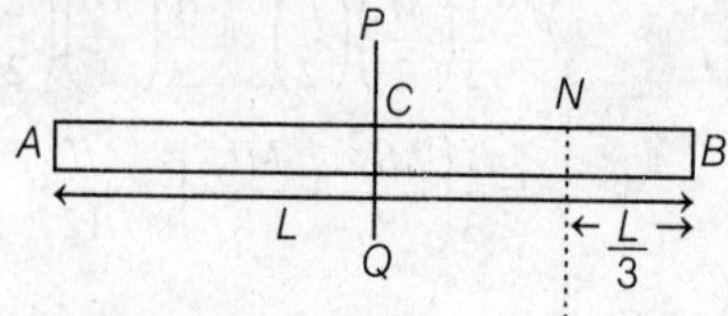

Let N be the point which divides the length of rod AB in ratio 1 : 3. This point will be at a distance $L/6$ from C. Thus, the moment of inertia I' about an axis parallel to PQ and passing through the point N.

$$I' = I_{CM} + M\left(\frac{L}{6}\right)^2$$

$$= \frac{ML^2}{12} + \frac{ML^2}{36} = \frac{ML^2}{9}$$

If k be the radius of gyration, then

$$k = \sqrt{\frac{I'}{M}} = \sqrt{\frac{L^2}{9}} = \frac{L}{3}$$

23 (d) For the rod of mass M and length l,

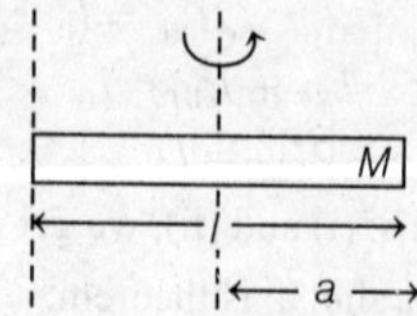

Moment of inertia of rod, $I = \frac{Ml^2}{12}$

Using the parallel axes theorem,

$$I' = I + Ma^2$$

with $a = l/2$, we get

$$I' = \frac{Ml^2}{12} + M\left(\frac{l}{2}\right)^2 = \frac{Ml^2}{3}$$

24 (d) The angle between the rods will not make any difference, hence

$$I = I_1 + I_2$$

$$= \frac{Ml^2}{12} + \frac{Ml^2}{12} = \frac{Ml^2}{6}$$

where, $I_1 = I_2 =$ moment of inertia of rod of length L and mass M about an axis passing through its centre of mass and perpendicular to the rod.

25 (a) Since, the axis of two rings are also perpendicular to each other, therefore applying the perpendicular axis theorem

$$I = MR^2 + \frac{1}{2}MR^2 = \frac{3}{2}MR^2$$

26 (b) Since, rod is bent at the middle, so each part of it will have same length $\left(\frac{L}{2}\right)$ and mass $\left(\frac{M}{2}\right)$ as shown in figure.

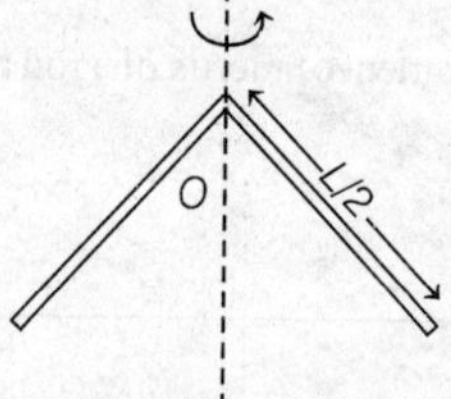

Moment of inertia of each part through its one end

$$= \frac{1}{3}\left(\frac{M}{2}\right)\left(\frac{L}{2}\right)^2$$

Hence, net moment of inertia through its middle point O is

$$I = \frac{1}{3}\left(\frac{M}{2}\right)\left(\frac{L}{2}\right)^2 + \frac{1}{3}\left(\frac{M}{2}\right)\left(\frac{L}{2}\right)^2$$

$$= \frac{1}{3}\left[\frac{ML^2}{8} + \frac{ML^2}{8}\right] = \frac{ML^2}{12}$$

27 (c) Moment of inertia of the system about AX is given by

$$I_{AX} = m_A r_A^2 + m_B r_B^2 + m_C r_C^2$$

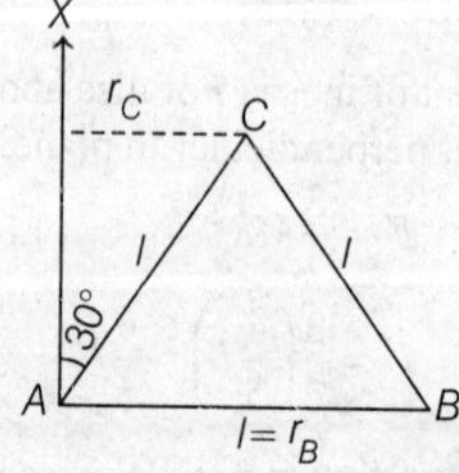

Moment of inertia

$$= m(0)^2 + m(l)^2 + m(l \sin 30°)^2$$

$$= ml^2 + \frac{ml^2}{4} = \frac{5}{4}ml^2$$

28 (a) The axis XX' is a diameter for ring A but this is a tangent in the plane of ring for ring B and ring C.

$$\therefore \quad I = I_A + I_B + I_C$$

As, $I_B = I_C = \frac{3}{2}MR^2$

tangential to rim and parallel to diameter

So, $$I = \frac{1}{2}MR^2 + \frac{3}{2}MR^2 + \frac{3}{2}MR^2$$

$$= \frac{7}{2}MR^2$$

29 (b) Moment of inertia,

$$I = Mk^2$$

$$\Rightarrow \quad k = \sqrt{\left(\frac{I}{M}\right)}$$

where, M is the total mass of the body.

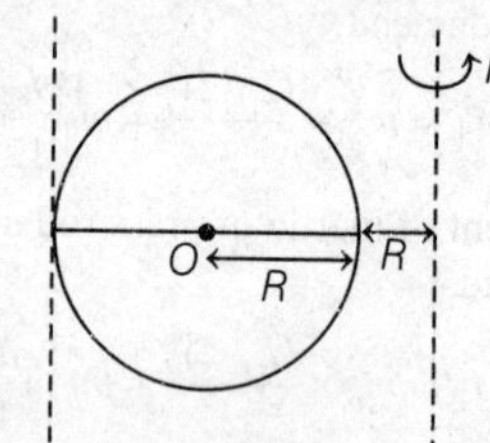

According to theorem of parallel axis,

$$I = I_{CG} + M(2R)^2$$

where, I_{CG} is moment of inertia about an axis through centre of gravity.

$$\therefore \quad I = \frac{2}{5}MR^2 + 4MR^2 = \frac{22}{5}MR^2$$

or $$Mk^2 = \frac{22}{5}MR^2 \Rightarrow k = \sqrt{\frac{22}{5}}R$$

30 (b) Given, $m = 2$ kg, $R = 0.1$ m and $n = 5$

The moment of inertia of the given system

= moment of inertia of disc + moment of inertia of particles

Since, the mass of the disc is negligible, therefore moment of inertia of the system

= moment of inertia of particles

$= nmR^2$

$= 5 \times 2 \times (0.1)^2 = 0.1 \text{ kg-m}^2$

31 (c) Moment of inertia,

$$I_1 = \frac{MR^2}{4} + M(2R)^2$$

$$= \frac{MR^2}{4} + 4MR^2 = \frac{17MR^2}{4}$$

Moment of inertia,

$$I_2 = \frac{MR^2}{2} + Md^2$$

Given, $I_1 = I_2$

$$\therefore \quad \frac{17MR^2}{4} = \frac{MR^2}{2} + Md^2$$

$$\Rightarrow \quad Md^2 = \frac{17}{4}MR^2 - \frac{MR^2}{2}$$

$$\Rightarrow \quad d^2 = \frac{15}{4}R^2 = \frac{\sqrt{15}}{2}R$$

32 (d) For disc, $I = \frac{1}{2}ma^2$

For ring, $I = ma^2$

For square of side $2a$,

$$I = \frac{M}{12}[(2a)^2 + (2a)^2] = \frac{2}{3}Ma^2$$

For square of rod of length $2a$,

$$I = 4\left[M\frac{(2a)^2}{12} + Ma^2\right]$$

$$\Rightarrow \quad I = \frac{16}{3}Ma^2$$

Hence, moment of inertia is maximum for square of four rods.

33 (a) The moment of inertia of solid sphere about its diameter,

$$I_S = \frac{2}{5}MR^2$$

The moment of inertia of a thin walled hollow sphere about its diameter is

$$I_H = \frac{2}{5}M\frac{(R_2^5 - R_1^5)}{(R_2^3 - R_1^3)}$$

where, R_1 and R_2 are its internal and external radii

Since, $\left[\frac{R_2^5 - R_1^5}{R_2^3 - R_1^3}\right] > R^2$

$$\therefore \quad I_H > I_S$$

The reason is that in solid sphere the whole mass is uniformly and continuously distributed about its centre in whole volume while in hollow sphere the mass is distributed on the surface of sphere.

Topic 4

Rotational Energy and Power

2017

1 Two discs of same moment of inertia rotating about their regular axis passing through centre and perpendicular to the plane of disc with angular velocities ω_1 and ω_2. They are brought into contact face to face coinciding the axis of rotation. The expression for loss of energy during this process is **[NEET]**

(a) $\frac{1}{2}I(\omega_1 + \omega_2)^2$ (b) $\frac{1}{4}I(\omega_1 - \omega_2)^2$

(c) $I(\omega_1 - \omega_2)^2$ (d) $\frac{I}{8}(\omega_1 - \omega_2)^2$

2 A uniform rod of length l is free to rotate in a vertical plane about a fixed horizontal axis through B. The rod begins rotating from rest from its unstable equilibrium position. When it has turned through an angle θ, its angular velocity ω is given by **[JIPMER]**

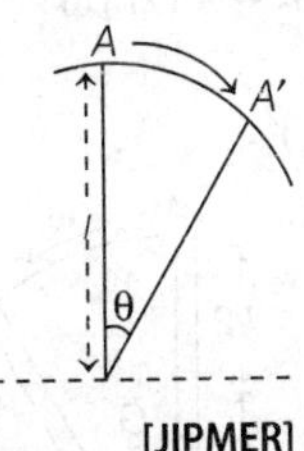

(a) $\sqrt{\left(\frac{6g}{l}\right)}\sin\frac{\theta}{2}$ (b) $\sqrt{\left(\frac{6g}{l}\right)}\cos\frac{\theta}{2}$

(c) $\sqrt{\left(\frac{6g}{l}\right)}\sin\theta$ (d) $\sqrt{\left(\frac{6g}{l}\right)}\cos\theta$

2016

3 Two rotating bodies A and B of masses m and $2m$ with moments of inertia I_A and I_B $(I_B > I_A)$ have equal kinetic energy of rotation. If L_A and L_B be their angular momentum respectively, then **[NEET]**

(a) $L_A = \frac{L_B}{2}$ (b) $L_A = 2L_B$ (c) $L_B > L_A$ (d) $L_A > L_B$

4 A solid sphere of mass m and radius R is rotating about its diameter. A solid cylinder of same mass and same radius is also rotating about its geometrical axis with an angular speed twice that of the sphere. The ratio of their kinetic energies of rotation $(E_{sphere} / E_{cylinder})$ will be **[NEET]**

(a) 2 : 3 (b) 1 : 5 (c) 1 : 4 (d) 3 : 1

2014

5 Two bodies have their moments of inertia I and $2I$, respectively about their axis of rotation. If their kinetic energies of rotation are equal, their angular velocity will be in the ratio **[UK PMT]**

(a) 2:1 (b) 1:2 (c) $\sqrt{2}:1$ (d) $1:\sqrt{2}$

6 A body having a moment of inertia about its axis of rotation equal to 3 kg-m^2 is rotating with angular velocity of 3 rad s^{-1}. Kinetic energy of this rotating body is same as that of a body of mass 27 kg moving with a velocity v. The value of v is **[KCET]**

(a) 1 ms^{-1} (b) 0.5 ms^{-1} (c) 2 ms^{-1} (d) 1.5 ms^{-1}

2010

7 A body of mass 10 kg moves with a velocity of $2\ \text{ms}^{-1}$ along a circular path of radius 8 m. The power produced by the body will be **[Manipal]**

(a) $10\ \text{Js}^{-1}$ (b) $98\ \text{Js}^{-1}$
(c) $49\ \text{Js}^{-1}$ (d) zero

8 A person, with outstretched arms, is spinning on a rotating stool. He suddenly brings his arms down to his sides. Which the following is true about his kinetic energy K and angular momentum L? **[AMU]**

(a) Both K and L increase
(b) Both K and L remain unchanged
(c) K remains constant, L increases
(d) K increases but L remains constant

2008

9 Circular disc of mass 2 kg and radius 1 m is rotating about an axis perpendicular to its plane and passing through its centre of mass with a rotational kinetic energy of 8 J. The angular momentum in (J-s) is **[EAMCET]**

(a) 8 (b) 4
(c) 2 (d) 1

2007

10 The moment of inertia of a flywheel having kinetic energy 360 J and angular speed of $20\ \text{rad s}^{-1}$ is **[Kerala CEE]**

(a) $18\ \text{kg-m}^2$ (b) $1.8\ \text{kg-m}^2$
(c) $2.5\ \text{kg-m}^2$ (d) $9\ \text{kg-m}^2$
(e) $0.9\ \text{kg-m}^2$

11 A thin metal disc of radius of 0.25 m and mass 2 kg starts from rest and rolls down on an inclined plane. If its rotational kinetic energy is 4 J at the foot of inclined plane, then the linear velocity at the same point, is in ms^{-1} **[J&K CET]**

(a) 2 (b) $2\sqrt{2}$ (c) $2\sqrt{3}$ (d) $3\sqrt{2}$

2005

12 Two bodies have their moments of inertia I and $2I$ respectively about their axis of rotation. If their kinetic energies of rotation are equal, their angular momenta will be in the ratio **[CBSE AIPMT]**

(a) $1:2$ (b) $\sqrt{2}:1$ (c) $2:1$ (d) $1:\sqrt{2}$

13 A stick of length L and mass M lies on a frictionless horizontal surface on which it is free to move in any way. A ball of mass m moving with speed v collides elastically with the stick as shown in figure below. If after the collision, the ball comes to rest, then what should be the mass of the ball? **[JIPMER]**

L
m

(a) $m = 2M$ (b) $m = M$ (c) $m = M/2$ (d) $m = M/4$

14 An object of mass m is attached to light string which passes through a hollow tube. The object is set into rotation in a horizontal circle of radius r_1. If the string is pulled shortening the radius to r_2, the ratio of new kinetic energy to the original kinetic energy is **[JCECE]**

(a) $\left(\frac{r_2}{r_1}\right)^2$ (b) $\left(\frac{r_1}{r_2}\right)^2$ (c) $\frac{r_1}{r_2}$ (d) $\frac{r_2}{r_1}$

Answers

1 (b)	2 (a)	3 (c)	4 (b)	5 (c)	6 (a)	7 (d)	8 (d)	9 (b)	10 (b)
11 (b)	12 (d)	13 (d)	14 (b)						

Explanations

1. *(b)* When no external torque acts on system, then angular momentum of system remains constant.

Angular momentum before contact

$$= I_1\omega_1 + I_2\omega_2$$

Angular momentum after the discs brought into contact

$$= I_{\text{net}}\,\omega = (I_1 + I_2)\,\omega$$

So, final angular speed of system,

$$\omega = \frac{I_1\omega_1 + I_2\omega_2}{I_1 + I_2}$$

Now, to calculate loss of energy, we subtract initial and final energies of system.

Loss of energy

$$= \frac{1}{2}I\omega_1^2 + \frac{1}{2}I\omega_2^2 - \frac{1}{2}(2I)\,\omega^2$$

$$= \frac{1}{4}I(\omega_1 - \omega_2)^2$$

2. *(a)* When the rod rotates through an angle θ, the centre of gravity falls through a distance h.

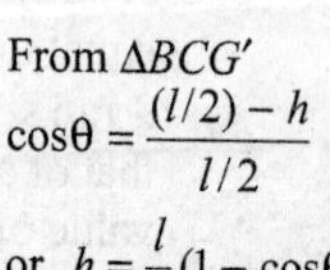

From $\Delta BCG'$

$$\cos\theta = \frac{(l/2) - h}{l/2}$$

or $h = \frac{l}{2}(1 - \cos\theta)$

Decrease in PE $= mg\frac{l}{2}(1-\cos\theta)$ ...(i)

The decrease in PE is equal to the kinetic energy of rotation

$$(\text{KE})_{\text{rotational}} = \frac{1}{2}I\omega^2 = \frac{1}{2}\left(\frac{ml^2}{3}\right)\omega^2 \quad \text{...(ii)}$$

$$\left[\because I = \frac{ml^2}{3}\right]$$

From Eqs. (i) and (ii), we get

$$\frac{1}{2}\left(\frac{ml^2}{3}\right)\omega^2 = mg\frac{l}{2}(1-\cos\theta)$$

$$\Rightarrow \qquad \omega = \sqrt{\frac{6g}{l}}\sin\frac{\theta}{2}$$

3. *(c)* As we know that, the kinetic energy of a rotating body,

$$KE = \frac{1}{2}I\omega^2 = \frac{1}{2}\frac{I^2\omega^2}{I} = \frac{L^2}{2I}$$

Also, angular momentum, $L = I\omega$

Thus, $K_A = K_B$

$$\Rightarrow \frac{1}{2}\frac{L_A^2}{I_A} = \frac{1}{2}\frac{L_B^2}{I_B} \Rightarrow \left(\frac{L_A}{L_B}\right)^2 = \frac{I_A}{I_B}$$

$$\Rightarrow \frac{L_A}{L_B} = \sqrt{\frac{I_A}{I_B}} \Rightarrow L \propto \sqrt{I}$$

$$\therefore L_A < L_B \quad [\because I_B > I_A]$$

4 *(b)* KE of a rotating rigid body,

$$KE = \frac{1}{2}I\omega^2$$

$\therefore$ KE of sphere,

$$K_s = \frac{1}{2}I\omega_1^2 = \frac{1}{2}\cdot\frac{2}{5}mR^2\omega_1^2 = \frac{1}{5}mR^2\omega_1^2 \quad \left[\because I = \frac{2}{5}mR^2\right]$$

KE of cylinder,

$$K_C = \frac{1}{2}\cdot\frac{1}{2}mR^2\omega_2^2 = \frac{1}{4}mR^2\omega_2^2 \quad \left[\because I = \frac{1}{2}mR^2\right]$$

$$\therefore \frac{K_S}{K_C} = \frac{\frac{mR^2\omega_1^2}{5}}{\frac{mR^2\omega_2^2}{4}} = \frac{4}{5}\frac{\omega_1^2}{\omega_2^2}$$

$$= \frac{4}{5}\frac{\omega_1^2}{(2\omega_1)^2} = \frac{1}{5}$$

(given, $\omega_2 = 2\omega_1$)

5 *(c)* Consider two bodies A and B are having moment of inertia I and $2I$.

$K_A =$ Kinetic energy of rotation for the body $A = \frac{1}{2}I\omega_A^2$

and $K_B =$ Kinetic energy of rotation for the body $B = \frac{1}{2}(2I)\omega_B^2$

where, ω_A is angular speed of the body A and ω_B is angular speed of the body B.

According to the question, $K_A = K_B$

$$\Rightarrow \frac{1}{2}I\omega_A^2 = \frac{1}{2}(2I)\omega_B^2$$

$$\Rightarrow \omega_A^2 = 2\omega_B^2$$

$$\Rightarrow \left(\frac{\omega_A}{\omega_B}\right)^2 = 2 \Rightarrow \frac{\omega_A}{\omega_B} = \sqrt{2}$$

$$\Rightarrow \omega_A : \omega_B = \sqrt{2} : 1$$

6 *(a)* We know that, kinetic energy,

$$K = \frac{1}{2}mv^2 = \frac{1}{2}I\omega^2$$

Given, $m = 27$ kg (mass of the body),

$\omega = 3\ \text{rads}^{-1}$ (angular velocity)

and $I = 3\ \text{kg-m}^2$ (moment of inertia).

$$\Rightarrow mv^2 = I\omega^2 \Rightarrow v^2 = \frac{I\omega^2}{m}$$

$$v^2 = \frac{3\times 3^2}{27} \Rightarrow v^2 = \frac{27}{27} = 1$$

$$\Rightarrow v = \sqrt{1} = 1\ \text{ms}^{-1}$$

7. *(d)* Power is defined as the rate of change of energy in a system or the time rate of doing work.

$$P = \frac{dE}{dt} = \frac{dW}{dt}$$

Also, work = force × displacement

$= F \times d$

In a circular motion, displacement is zero, therefore

$$P = \frac{d}{dt}(F \times d) = \frac{d}{dt}(0) = 0$$

8 *(d)* If the person on rotating suddenly brings his arms down to his sides, then his kinetic energy increases due to increase in its angular velocity and angular momentum L remains constant.

9 *(b)* Rotational kinetic energy

$$= \frac{1}{2}I\omega^2 = 8\ \text{J}$$

$$\Rightarrow \frac{1}{2}\times\frac{1}{2}mr^2\omega^2 = 8$$

$(\because m = 2$ kg and $r = 1$ m$)$

or $\frac{1}{4}\times 2\times(1)^2\omega^2 = 8$

or $\omega^2 = 16$

or $\omega = 4\ \text{rad s}^{-1}$

Angular momentum,

$$L = I\omega = \frac{1}{2}mr^2\omega$$

$$= \frac{1}{2}\times 2\times(1)^2\times 4$$

$= 4$ J-s

10 *(b)* Rotational kinetic energy of flywheel, $K = 360$ J and angular speed of flywheel,

$$\omega = 20\ \text{rad s}^{-1}$$

Rotational kinetic energy, $K = \frac{1}{2}I\omega^2$

$\therefore$ Moment of inertia,

$$I = \frac{2K}{\omega^2} = \frac{2\times 360}{(20)^2} = 1.8\ \text{kg - m}^2$$

11 *(b)* Rotational kinetic energy $= (1/2)I\omega^2$

$$\therefore \text{Rotational KE} = \frac{1}{2}\left(\frac{1}{2}mr^2\right)\frac{v^2}{r^2} \quad \left(\text{where, } I = \frac{1}{2}mr^2\right)$$

Given, KE = 4 J, $r = 0.25$ m

and $m = 2$ kg

$$4 = \frac{1}{2}\left(\frac{1}{2}(2)r^2\right)\frac{v^2}{r^2}$$

$$\Rightarrow v^2 = 8$$

$$\Rightarrow v = 2\sqrt{2}\ \text{ms}^{-1}$$

12 *(d)* Rotational kinetic energy remains same.

i.e. $\frac{1}{2}I_1\omega_1^2 = \frac{1}{2}I_2\omega_2^2$

or $\frac{1}{2I_1}(I_1\omega_1)^2 = \frac{1}{2I_2}(I_2\omega_2)^2$

$$\Rightarrow \frac{L_1^2}{I_1} = \frac{L_2^2}{I_2} \text{ or } \frac{L_1}{L_2} = \sqrt{\frac{I_1}{I_2}}$$

But $I_1 = I, I_2 = 2I$

$$\Rightarrow \frac{L_1}{L_2} = \sqrt{\frac{I}{2I}} = \frac{1}{\sqrt{2}}$$

$$\Rightarrow L_1 : L_2 = 1 : \sqrt{2}$$

13 *(d)* Applying the law conservation of momentum,

$$mv = MV$$

$$\Rightarrow V = \frac{mv}{M} \quad \text{...(i)}$$

By conservation of angular momentum,

$$\frac{mv(L)}{2} = \left(\frac{ML^2}{12}\right)\omega$$

$$\Rightarrow \omega = \frac{6mv}{ML} \quad \text{...(ii)}$$

As the collision is elastic, we have

$$\frac{1}{2}mv^2 = \frac{1}{2}MV^2 + \frac{1}{2}\left(\frac{mL^2}{12}\right)\omega^2 \quad \text{...(iii)}$$

Substituting the values from Eqs. (i) and (ii) in Eq. (iii), we get

$$m = M/4$$

14 *(b)* Kinetic energy (K) of rotation is

$$K = (1/2)I\omega^2$$

where, $\omega = v/r$, r is radius of circle.

$$\therefore K = \frac{1}{2}I\left(\frac{v^2}{r^2}\right) \Rightarrow \frac{K_1}{K_2} = \frac{r_2^2}{r_1^2}$$

$$\Rightarrow \frac{K_2}{K_1} = \frac{r_1^2}{r_2^2} = \left(\frac{r_1}{r_2}\right)^2$$

Topic 5

Dynamics of Rotational Motion

2019

1 If object starts from rest and covers angle of 60 rad in 10 s in circular motion, then magnitude of angular acceleration will be **[JIPMER]**

(a) 1.2 rad s^{-2} (b) 1.5 rad s^{-2}
(c) 2 rad s^{-2} (d) 2.5 rad s^{-2}

2 A solid cylinder of mass 2 kg and radius 4 cm is rotating about its axis at the rate of 3 rpm. The torque required to stop after 2π revolutions is **[NEET]**

(a) 2×10^{-3} N-m (b) 12×10^{-4} N-m
(c) 2×10^{6} N-m (d) 2×10^{-6} N-m

2017

3 A rope is wound around a hollow cylinder of mass 3 kg and radius 40 cm. What is the angular acceleration of the cylinder, if the rope is pulled with a force of 30 N? **[NEET]**

(a) 25 ms^{-2} (b) 0.25 rad s^{-2}
(c) 25 rad s^{-2} (d) 5 ms^{-2}

2016

4 A uniform circular disc of radius 50 cm at rest is free to turn about an axis which is perpendicular to its plane and passes through its centre. It is subjected to a torque which produces a constant angular acceleration of 2.0 rad s^{-2}. Its net acceleration in ms^{-2}, at the end of 2.0 s is *a* approximately **[NEET]**

(a) 7.0 (b) 6.0 (c) 3.0 (d) 8.0

2015

5 A mass *m* moves in a circle on a smooth horizontal plane with velocity v_0 at a radius R_0. The mass is attached to a string which passes through a smooth hole in plane as shown.

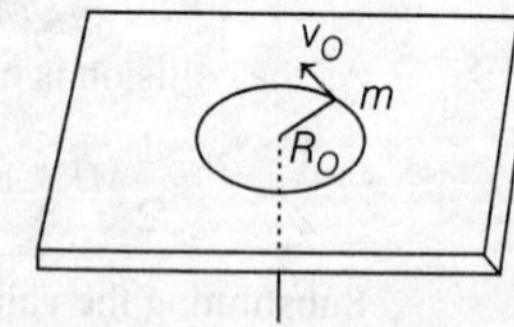

The tension in the string is increased gradually and finally *m* moves in a circle of radius $R_0/2$. The final value of the kinetic energy is **[CRSE AIPMT]**

(a) mv_0^2 (b) $\frac{1}{4}mv_0^2$ (c) $2mv_0^2$ (d) $\frac{1}{2}mv_0^2$

2014

6 A rotating wheel changes angular speed from 1800 rpm to 3000 rpm to 20 s. What is the angular acceleration assuming to be uniform? **[KCET]**

(a) 60π rad s^{-2} (b) 90π rad s^{-2}
(c) 2π rad s^{-2} (d) 40π rad s^{-2}

2008

7 A wheel has angular acceleration of 3.0 rad s^{-2} and an initial angular speed of 2.00 rad s^{-1}. In a time of 2 s, it has rotated through an angle (in rad) of **[AIIMS]**

(a) 6 (b) 10 (c) 12 (d) 4

8 When a ceiling fan is switched OFF, its angular velocity reduces to half its initial value after it completes 36 rotations. The number of rotations it will make further before coming to rest is (assuming angular retardation to be uniform) **[Kerala CEE]**

(a) 10 (b) 20 (c) 18 (d) 12
(e) 16

2007

9 A ring and a disc of different masses are rotating with the same kinetic energy. If we apply a retarding torque τ on the ring, it stops after completing *n* revolutions in all. If same torque is applied to the disc, how many revolutions would it complete in all before stopping? **[Manipal]**

(a) $4n$ (b) $2n$
(c) n (d) $n/2$

10 A tube of length *L* is filled completely with an incompressible liquid of mass *M* and closed at both the ends. The tube is then rotated in a horizontal plane about one of its ends with a uniform angular velocity ω. The force exerted by the liquid at the other end is **[MP PMT]**

(a) $\frac{ML\omega^2}{2}$ (b) $\frac{ML^2\omega}{2}$ (c) $ML\omega^2$ (d) $\frac{ML^2\omega^2}{2}$

2006

11 A particle performs uniform circular motion with an angular momentum *L*. If the frequency of particle motion is doubled and its kinetic energy is halved, the angular momentum becomes **[AMU]**

(a) $2L$ (b) $4L$
(c) $\frac{L}{2}$ (d) $\frac{L}{4}$

Answers

1 (a)	2 (d)	3 (c)	4 (d)	5 (c)	6 (c)	7 (b)	8 (d)	9 (c)	10 (a)
11 (d)									

Explanations

1 *(a)* Given, initial angular velocity of object, $\omega_0 = 0$

Angular displacement, $\theta = 60$ rad

and $\Delta t = 10$ s

From equation of rotational motion,

$$\theta = \omega_0 t + \frac{1}{2}\alpha t^2$$

$$60 = 0 \times t + \frac{1}{2} \times \alpha \times 10^2$$

$$\Rightarrow \quad \alpha = \frac{60}{50}$$

$$\Rightarrow \quad \alpha = 1.2 \text{ rads}^{-2}$$

2 *(d)* Given, mass of cylinder, $m = 2$ kg

Radius of cylinder, $r = 4$ cm $= 4 \times 10^{-2}$ m

Rotational velocity, $\omega = 3$ rpm

$= 3 \times \frac{2\pi}{60} = \frac{\pi}{10}$ rads^{-1} and $\theta = 2\pi \times$ revolution $= 2\pi \times 2\pi = 4\pi^2$ rad.

The work done in rotating an object by an angle θ from rest is given by

$W = \tau\theta$

As the cylinder is brought to rest, so the work done will be negative.

According to work-energy theorem,

Work done

= Change in rotational kinetic energy

$$-\tau\theta = \frac{1}{2}I\omega_f^2 - \frac{1}{2}I\omega_i^2 = \frac{1}{2}I(\omega_f^2 - \omega_i^2)$$

$$\Rightarrow \quad \tau = \frac{I(-\omega_i^2)}{2\theta} \quad [\because \omega_f = 0]$$

$$= \frac{1}{2}\left(\frac{1}{2}mr^2\right)\frac{\omega_i^2}{\theta}$$

$$\left[I = \frac{1}{2}mr^2 \text{(for cylinder)}\right]$$

$$= \frac{1}{4}mr^2\frac{\omega^2}{\theta} \quad [\because \omega_i = \omega]$$

$$= \frac{1}{4} \times 2 \times (4 \times 10^{-2})^2 \times \left(\frac{\pi}{10}\right)^2 \times \frac{1}{4\pi^2}$$

$$= \frac{1}{4} \times 2 \times 16 \times 10^{-4} \times \frac{\pi^2}{100} \times \frac{1}{4\pi^2}$$

$$= \frac{2}{100} \times 10^{-4} = 2 \times 10^{-6} \text{ N-m}$$

3 *(c)* Torque (τ) acting on a body and angular acceleration (α) produced in it are related as

$$\tau = I\alpha$$

Consider a hollow cylinder, around which a rope is wounded.

Torque acting on the cylinder due to the force F is $\tau = Fr$.

Now, we have

$$\tau = I\alpha$$

where, I = moment of inertia of the cylinder about the axis through the centre

$$\Rightarrow \quad I = mr^2$$

Given, $F = 30$ N, $m = 3$ kg and $r = 40$ cm $= 40 \times 10^{-2}$ m

Angular acceleration,

$$\alpha = \frac{\tau}{I} = \frac{Fr}{mr^2}$$

$$= \frac{F}{mr} = \frac{30}{3 \times 40 \times 10^{-2}}$$

$$= \frac{100}{4} = 25 \text{ rads}^{-2}$$

4. *(d)* According to given question, a uniform circular disc of radius 50 cm at rest is free to turn about an axis having perpendicular to its plane and passes through its centre. This situation can be shown by the figure given below

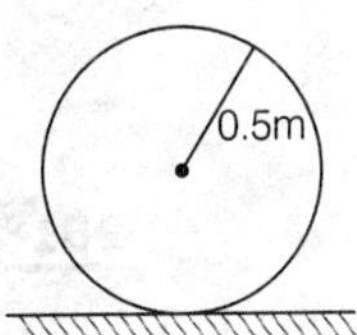

$\therefore$ Angular acceleration,

$$\alpha = 2 \text{ rad s}^{-2} \text{ (given)}$$

Angular speed, $\omega = \alpha t = 4$ rad s^{-1}

$\because$ Centripetal acceleration,

$$a_c = \omega^2 r = (4)^2 \times 0.5 = 16 \times 0.5$$

$$a_c = 8 \text{ ms}^{-2}$$

$\because$ Linear acceleration at the end of 2s,

$$a_t = \alpha r = 2 \times 0.5$$

$$\Rightarrow \quad a_t = 1 \text{ ms}^{-2}$$

Therefore, the net acceleration at the end of 2.0 s is given by

$$a = \sqrt{a_c^2 + a_t^2}$$

$$a = \sqrt{(8)^2 + (1)^2} = \sqrt{65}$$

$$\Rightarrow a \approx 8 \text{ ms}^{-2}$$

5. *(c)* Conserving angular momentum,

$$L_i = L_f$$

$$\Rightarrow mv_0R_0 = mv'\left(\frac{R_0}{2}\right) \text{(given)}$$

$$\Rightarrow \quad v' = 2v_0$$

So, final kinetic energy of the particle,

$$K_f = \frac{1}{2}mv'^2 = \frac{1}{2}m(2v_0)^2$$

$$= 4\frac{1}{2}mv_0^2 = 2mv_0^2$$

6. *(c)* We know that,

$$\omega = 2\pi n$$

$$\Rightarrow \quad \omega_1 = 2\pi n_1$$

where, $n_1 = 1800$ rpm, $n_2 = 3000$ rpm

and $\Delta t = 20$ s.

So, $\omega_1 = 2\pi \times \frac{1800}{60} = 2\pi \times 30 = 60\pi$

Similarly, $\omega_2 = 2\pi n_2 = 2\pi \times \frac{3000}{60}$

$$= 2\pi \times 50 = 100\,\pi$$

If the angular velocity of a rotating wheel about an axis changes by change in angular velocity in a time interval Δt, then the angular acceleration of rotating wheel about that axis is

$$\alpha = \frac{\text{Change in angular velocity}}{\text{Time interval}}$$

$$\alpha = \frac{\omega_2 - \omega_1}{\Delta t}$$

$$\Rightarrow \alpha = \frac{100\pi - 60\pi}{20}$$

$$\alpha = \frac{40\pi}{20} = 2\pi \text{ rad s}^{-2}$$

7 *(b)* The kinematical equation for angular motion is

$$\theta = \omega_0 t + \frac{1}{2}\alpha t^2$$

Given, $\alpha = 3.0$ rad s^{-2},

$\omega_0 = 2.0$ rad s^{-1} and $t = 2$ s

Hence, $\theta = 2 \times 2 + \frac{1}{2} \times 3 \times (2)^2$

or $\theta = 4 + 6 = 10$ rad

8 *(d)* We know that, $\omega^2 = \omega_0^2 + 2\alpha\theta_n$

where, ω is final angular velocity, ω_0 is initial angular velocity, α is angular retardation and θ_n is the angle turned in number of rotations.

Given, for Ist case, final angular velocity,

$$\omega = \frac{\omega_0}{2} \text{ and } \theta = 36 \times 2\pi$$

$$\therefore \quad \frac{\omega_0^2}{4} = \omega_0^2 + 2\alpha \times 36 \times 2\pi$$

or $$-\frac{3\omega_0^2}{4} = 144\pi\alpha$$

or $$\alpha = -\frac{3\omega_0^2}{4 \times 144\pi}$$

Negative sign signifies angular retardation.

Again, for the IInd case,

$$\omega_i = \frac{\omega_0}{2} \text{ and } \omega_f = 0$$

So, $$0 = \frac{\omega_0^2}{4} - 2 \times \frac{3\omega_0^2}{4 \times 144\pi} \times \theta'$$

$$\theta' = \frac{\omega_0^2 \times 4 \times 144\pi}{4 \times 2 \times 3\omega_0^2} = 24\pi$$

Hence, number of rotations it makes before coming to rest is

$$n = \frac{\theta'}{2\pi} = \frac{24\pi}{2\pi} = 12$$

9. *(c)* Because kinetic energy K_R and retarding torque τ are same, therefore in accordance with the relation

Los in kinetic energy

$$= \text{Work done by torque}$$
$$= \tau\theta = \tau 2\pi n$$

So, both the ring and the disc stop after completing equal number of revolutions *n*.

10 *(a)* Let the length of a small element of tube be *dx*. Mass of this element

$$dm = \frac{M}{L} dx$$

dx, ω, F ⟶, ⟵ F + dF, r

where, *M* is the mass of filled liquid and *L* is the length of tube.

Force on this element,

$$dF = dm \times x\omega^2$$

$$\int_0^F dF = \frac{M}{L}\omega^2 \int_0^L x\,dx$$

or $$F = \frac{M}{L}\omega^2\left(\frac{L^2}{2}\right) = \frac{ML\omega^2}{2}$$

or $$F = \frac{1}{2}ML\omega^2$$

11 *(d)* $\because$ Angular momentum,

$$L = mvr = mr^2\omega \quad \text{...(i)}$$

Also, kinetic energy, $K = \frac{1}{2}mv^2$

or $$K = \frac{1}{2}m(r\omega)^2 = \frac{1}{2}mr^2\omega^2$$

$$\Rightarrow \quad K = \frac{1}{2}(mr^2\omega)\omega = \frac{L\omega}{2}$$

[$\because$ from Eq. (i)]

$$\Rightarrow \quad L = \frac{2K}{\omega}$$

Given, $\omega' = 2\omega$

or $K' = \frac{1}{2}K$

Hence, new angular momentum,

$$L' = \frac{2K'}{\omega'} = \frac{2\left(\frac{1}{2}K\right)}{2\omega} = \frac{L}{4}$$

Topic 6

Rolling Motion

2019

1 A sphere pure rolls on a rough inclined plane with initial velocity 2.8 ms^{-1}. Find the maximum distance on the inclined plane. **[AIIMS]**

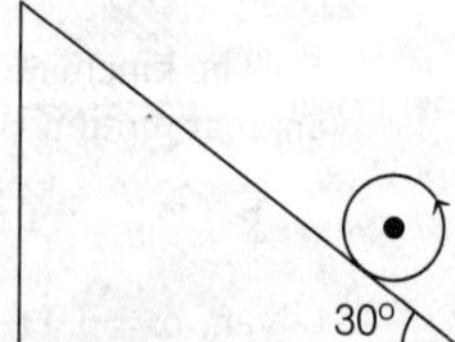

(a) 2.74 m (b) 5.48 m (c) 1.38 m (d) 3.2 m

2 A disc of radius 2 m and mass 100 kg rolls on a horizontal floor. Its centre of mass has speed of 20 cms^{-1}. How much work is needed to stop it? **[NEET]**

(a) 30 kJ (b) 2 J (c) 1 J (d) 3 J

3 A solid cylinder of mass 2 kg and radius 50 cm rolls up an inclined plane of angle inclination 30°. The centre of mass of cylinder has speed of 4 ms^{-1}. The distance travelled by the cylinder on the inclined surface will be (take, $g = 10\,\text{ms}^{-2}$) **[NEET (Odisha)]**

(a) 2.2 m (b) 1.6 m (c) 1.2 m (d) 2.4 m

2018

4 A solid sphere is in rolling motion. In rolling motion, a body possesses translational kinetic energy (K_t) as well as rotational kinetic energy (K_r) simultaneously. The ratio $K_t : (K_t + K_r)$ for the sphere is **[NEET]**

(a) 10 : 7 (b) 5 : 7
(c) 7 : 10 (d) 2 : 5

2017

5 A bicycle wheel rolls without slipping on a horizontal floor. Which one of the following is true about the motion of points on the rim of the wheel, relative to the axis at the wheel's centre? **[JIPMER]**

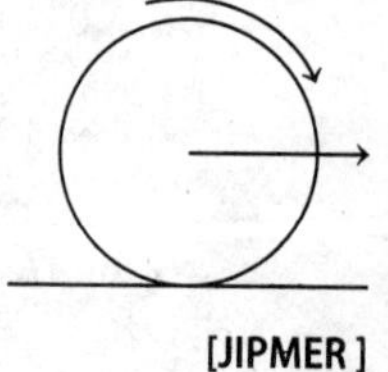

(a) Points near the top move faster than points near the bottom
(b) Points near the bottom move faster than points near the top
(c) All points on the rim move with the same speed
(d) All points have the velocity vectors that are pointing in the radial direction towards the centre of the wheel

6 **Assertion** The total kinetic energy of a rolling solid sphere is the sum of translational and rotational kinetic energies.

Reason For all solid bodies, total kinetic energy is always twice of translational kinetic energy. **[AIIMS]**

(a) Both Assertion and Reason are correct and Reason is the correct explanation of Assertion.
(b) Both Assertion and Reason are correct but Reason is not the correct explanation of Assertion.
(c) Assertion is correct but Reason is incorrect.
(d) Both Assertion and Reason are incorrect.

7 A thin hollow sphere of mass *m* is completely filled with a liquid of mass *m*. When the sphere rolls with a velocity *v*, kinetic energy of the system is (neglect friction) **[AIIMS]**

(a) $(1/2)mv^2$ (b) mv^2
(c) $(4/3)mv^2$ (d) $(4/5)mv^2$

8 A cylinder rolls up an inclined plane, reaches some height and then rolls down (without slipping throughout these motions). The directions of the frictional force acting on the cylinder are **[JIPMER]**

(a) up the incline while ascending and down the incline while descending
(b) up the incline while ascending as well as descending
(c) down the incline while ascending and up the incline while descending
(d) down the incline while ascending as well as descending

2016

9 A disc and a sphere of same radius but different masses roll off on two inclined planes of the same altitude and length. Which one of the two objects gets to the bottom of the plane first? **[NEET]**

(a) Sphere
(b) Both reach at the same time
(c) Depends on their masses
(d) Disc

2014

10 A uniform solid spherical ball is rolling down a smooth inclined plane from a height *h*. The velocity attained by the ball when it reaches the bottom of the inclined plane is *v*. If the ball is now thrown vertically upwards with the same velocity *v*, the maximum height to which the ball will rise is **[WB JEE]**

(a) $5h/8$ (b) $3h/5$
(c) $5h/7$ (d) $7h/9$

2013

11 A small object of uniform density rolls up a curved surface with an initial velocity v'. It reaches upto a maximum height of $3v^2/4g$ with respect to the initial position. The object is **[NEET]**

(a) ring (b) solid sphere
(c) hollow sphere (d) disc

2011

12 A solid sphere of mass *M* rolls without slipping on an inclined plane of inclination θ. What should be the minimum coefficient of friction, so that the sphere rolls down without slipping? **[NEET]**

(a) $\frac{2}{5}\tan\theta$ (b) $\frac{2}{7}\tan\theta$ (c) $\frac{5}{7}\tan\theta$ (d) $\tan\theta$

2010

13 When a uniform solid sphere and a disc of the same mass and of the same radius roll down an inclined smooth plane from rest to the same distance, then the ratio of the times taken by them is **[Haryana PMT]**

(a) $15:14$ (b) $15^2:14^2$
(c) $\sqrt{14}:\sqrt{15}$ (d) $14:15$

2008

14 **Assertion** The velocity of a body at the bottom of an inclined plane of given height is more when it slides down the plane, compared to when it rolling down the same plane.

Reason In rolling down, a body acquires both, kinetic energy of translation and rotation. **[AIIMS]**

(a) Both Assertion and Reason are correct and Reason is the correct explanation of Assertion.
(b) Both Assertion and Reason are correct but Reason is not the correct explanation of Assertion.
(c) Assertion is correct but Reason is incorrect.
(d) Both Assertion and Reason are incorrect.

15 A solid cylinder is rolling down on an inclined plane of angle θ. The coefficient of static friction between the plane and cylinder is μ_s. Then, condition for the cylinder not to slip is **[J&K CET]**

(a) $\tan\theta \geq 3\mu_s$ (b) $\tan\theta > 3\mu_s$
(c) $\tan\theta \leq 3\mu_s$ (d) $\tan\theta < 3\mu_s$

2006

16 A solid cylinder rolls down an inclined plane of height 3 m and reaches the bottom of plane with angular velocity of $2\sqrt{2}$ rad s^{-1}. The radius of cylinder must be (take, $g = 10\ \text{ms}^{-2}$) **[Kerala CEE]**

(a) 5 cm (b) 0.5 cm (c) $\sqrt{10}$ cm (d) $\sqrt{5}$ m
(e) 10 cm

2005

17 A drum of radius *R* and mass *M*, rolls down without slipping along an inclined plane of angle θ. The frictional force **[CBSE AIPMT]**

(a) converts translational energy to rotational energy
(b) dissipates energy as heat
(c) decreases the rotational motion
(d) decreases the rotational and translational motion

18 At any instant, a rolling body may be considered to be in pure rotation about an axis through the point of contact. This axis is translating forward with speed **[JCECE]**

(a) equal to centre of mass
(b) zero
(c) twice of centre of mass
(d) None of the above

19 A coin is of mass 4.8 kg and radius 1 m rolling on a horizontal surface without sliding with angular velocity 600 rot $\min^{-1}$. What is total kinetic energy of the coin?

(a) 360 J (b) $1440\pi^2$ J **[Manipal]**
(c) $4000\pi^2$ J (d) $600\pi^2$ J

20 A body is rolling down an inclined plane. If KE of rotation is 40% of KE in translatory state, then the body is a **[DUMET]**

(a) ring (b) cylinder (c) hollow ball (d) solid ball

21 A ball rolls without slipping. The radius of gyration of the ball about an axis passing through its centre of mass is k. If radius of the ball be R, then the fraction of total energy associated with its rotational energy will be **[BHU]**

(a) $\frac{k^2}{k^2+R^2}$ (b) $\frac{R^2}{k^2+R^2}$
(c) $\frac{k^2+R^2}{R^2}$ (d) $\frac{k^2}{R^2}$

22. A solid sphere is rolling on a frictionless surface, shown in figure with a translational velocity v ms^{-1}. If it is to climb the inclined surface, then v should be **[AIIMS]**

(a) $\geq\sqrt{\frac{10}{7}gh}$ (b) $\geq\sqrt{2gh}$
(c) $2gh$ (d) $\frac{10}{7}gh$

Answers

1 (c)	2 (d)	3 (d)	4 (b)	5 (a)	6 (c)	7 (c)	8 (b)	9 (a)	10 (c)
11 (d)	12 (b)	13 (c)	14 (b)	15 (c)	16 (d)	17 (a)	18 (a)	19 (b)	20 (d)
21 (a)	22 (a)								

Explanations

1 *(c)* Given, initial velocity of sphere, $u = 2.8\ \text{ms}^{-1}$

Acceleration on the inclined plane,

$$a = \frac{g\sin\theta}{1+\frac{k^2}{R^2}} \quad \text{...(i)}$$

where, k and R are the radius of gyration and radius of sphere, respectively.

Moment of inertia of sphere,

$$I = mk^2 = \frac{2}{5}mR^2$$

$$\frac{k^2}{R^2} = \frac{2}{5} \quad \text{...(ii)}$$

From Eqs. (i) and (ii), we have

$$a = \frac{g\sin 30°}{1+\frac{2}{5}} \quad [\because \theta = 30°, \text{given}]$$

$$= \frac{5g}{14} = \frac{25}{7}\ \text{ms}^{-2} \quad [\because g = 10\ \text{ms}^{-2}]$$

If s be the maximum distance travelled by the sphere, then at maximum distance, $v = 0$.

$\therefore$ From equation of motion,

$$v^2 = u^2 - 2as$$

$$0 = u^2 - 2as$$

$$\Rightarrow \quad s = \frac{u^2}{2a} = \frac{(2.8)^2 \times 7}{2 \times 25}$$

$$= 1.09\ \text{m} \simeq 1.38\ \text{m}$$

2 *(d)* Given, radius, $R = 2$ m

Mass, $m = 100$ kg

and v_{CM} (velocity centre of mass).

$$= v = 20\ \text{cms}^{-1}$$

$$= 20 \times 10^{-2}\ \text{ms}^{-1}$$

Then, according to work energy theorem, the work done in stopping the disc is equal to the change in its kinetic energy, i.e.

$$W = (\text{KE})_f - (\text{KE})_i \quad \text{...(i)}$$

As, the disc stops at the end, so final velocity is zero.

Thus, $(\text{KE})_f = 0$

Since, the disc is rolling so, its initial kinetic energy would have both rotational and translational kinetic energy component.

$$(\text{KE})_i = (\text{KE})_r + (\text{KE})_t$$

$$= \frac{1}{2}I\omega^2 + \frac{1}{2}mv^2$$

$$= \frac{1}{2}\left(\frac{1}{2}mR^2\right)\omega^2 + \frac{1}{2}mv^2$$

$$\left[\because \text{for disc, } I = \frac{1}{2}mR^2\right]$$

$$= \frac{1}{4}mR^2\omega^2 + \frac{1}{2}mv^2$$

$$= \frac{1}{4}mR^2\frac{v^2}{R^2} + \frac{1}{2}mv^2 \quad [\because v = r\omega]$$

$$= \frac{3}{4}mv^2$$

$$\therefore W = |\text{KE}_i| = \frac{3}{4}mv^2 \quad [\text{from Eq. (i)}]$$

Substituting the given values, we get

$$W = \frac{3}{4} \times 100 \times (20 \times 10^{-2})^2$$

$$= \frac{3}{4} \times 400 \times 100 \times 10^{-4} = 3\ \text{J}$$

3 *(d)* When a body rolls, i.e. have rotational motion, the total kinetic energy of the system will be

$$KE = \frac{1}{2}mv^2\left(1+\frac{k^2}{R^2}\right)$$

where, m = mass of body, v = velocity and k = radius of gyration.

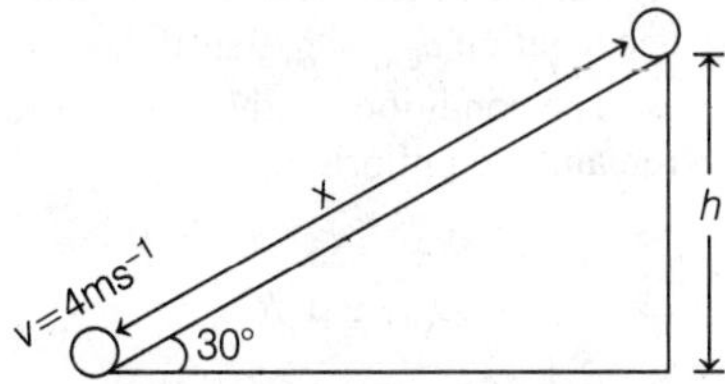

Given, $m = 2$ kg, $\theta = 30°$ and $v = 4$ ms^{-1}

Let h be the height of the inclined plane, then from law of conservation of energy,

$$KE = PE$$

$$\frac{1}{2}mv^2\left(1+\frac{k^2}{R^2}\right) = mgh$$

Substituting the given values in the above equation, we get

$$\frac{1}{2}\times 2\times 16\left(1+\frac{1}{2}\right) = 2\times 10\times h$$

$$\left[\because \text{ for cylinder } \frac{k^2}{R^2} = \frac{1}{2}\right]$$

$$\Rightarrow \quad 8\times\frac{3}{2} = 10\,h \Rightarrow h = 1.2 \text{ m}$$

From the above diagram, $\sin\theta = \frac{h}{x}$

$$\Rightarrow x = \frac{h}{\sin\theta} = \frac{1.2}{\sin 30°}$$

$$= 1.2\times 2 = 2.4 \text{ m} \quad \left[\because \sin 30° = \frac{1}{2}\right]$$

4 *(b)* Translational kinetic energy of a rolling body is

$$K_t = \frac{1}{2}mv_{CM}^2 \quad \ldots(i)$$

Total kinetic energy of a rolling body

$= K_r + K_t$ = Rotational KE + Translational KE

$$= \frac{1}{2}I\omega^2 + \frac{1}{2}mv_{CM}^2 \quad \ldots(ii)$$

For a solid sphere, moment of inertia about its diametric axis, $I = \frac{2}{5}mR^2$

Substituting the value of I in Eq. (ii), we get

$$K_r + K_t = \frac{1}{2}\left(\frac{2}{5}mR^2\right)\omega^2 + \frac{1}{2}mv_{CM}^2$$

$$= \frac{1}{2}\left(\frac{2}{5}mR^2\right)\left(\frac{v_{CM}}{R}\right)^2 + \frac{1}{2}mv_{CM}^2$$

$$[\because v_{CM} = R\omega]$$

$$= \frac{1}{5}mv_{CM}^2 + \frac{1}{2}mv_{CM}^2$$

$$= \left(\frac{1}{5}+\frac{1}{2}\right)mv_{CM}^2$$

$$= \frac{7}{10}mv_{CM}^2 \quad \ldots(iii)$$

$$\therefore \text{ Ratio, } \frac{K_t}{K_t+K_r} = \frac{\frac{1}{2}mv_{CM}^2}{\frac{7}{10}mv_{CM}^2}$$

$$= \frac{1}{2}\times\frac{10}{7} = \frac{5}{7}$$

$$\therefore \quad K_t : (K_t + K_r) = 5:7$$

5 *(a)* Velocity of the particle at Q,

$v_Q = r\omega = R\omega$

Velocity of the particle at P,

$v_P = r\omega = (2R)\omega = 2v_Q$

Hence, points near the top move faster than points near the bottom.

6 *(c)* The kinetic energy of a rolling solid sphere

$$= K_{trans} + K_{rot}$$

$$= \frac{1}{2}mv^2 + \frac{1}{2}I\omega^2$$

$$= \frac{1}{2}mv^2 + \frac{1}{2}\times\frac{2}{5}mR^2\omega^2 \quad \left[\because \omega = \frac{v}{R}\right]$$

$$= \frac{1}{2}mv^2 + \frac{1}{5}mv^2 = 7/10\,mv^2$$

Hence, total kinetic energy is sum of translation and rotational kinetic energies.

For different solid bodies, total kinetic energy is not always twice of translation kinetic energy. Hence, Assertion is correct but Reason is incorrect.

7 *(c)* Total kinetic energy (KE) of the system

= KE (translational) + KE (rotational)

$$= \frac{1}{2}(2m)v^2 + \frac{1}{2}I\,\omega^2$$

$$= \frac{1}{2}(2m)v^2 + \frac{1}{2}\left(\frac{2}{3}mR^2\right)\frac{v^2}{R^2}$$

$$= \frac{1}{2}(2m)v^2 + \frac{1}{3}mv^2 = \frac{4}{3}mv^2$$

8 *(b)* The direction of the frictional force will be up the inclined plane in both the motions. The friction acts opposite to the relative motion of the point of contact on ground. In both cases, the force acting on the point of cylinder in contact with the plane is $mg\sin\theta$. As there is pure rolling, the velocity and acceleration of the point of contact must be zero, so friction acts upwards along the inclined plane in both the motions (ascending or descending).

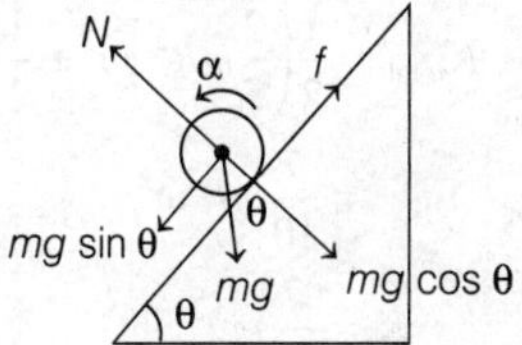

9 *(a)* Acceleration of an object rolling down an inclined plane is given by

$$a = \frac{g\sin\theta}{1+I/mr^2}$$

where, θ = angle of inclination of the inclined plane,

m = mass of the object

and I = moment of inertia about the axis through centre of mass.

For disc, $\frac{I}{mr^2} = \frac{1/2\,mr^2}{mr^2} = \frac{1}{2}$

For solid sphere,

$$\frac{I}{mr^2} = \frac{2/5mr^2}{mr^2} = \frac{2}{5}$$

For hollow sphere,

$$\frac{I}{mr^2} = \frac{2/3mr^2}{mr^2} = \frac{2}{3}$$

$$\therefore \quad a_{disc} = \frac{g\sin\theta}{1+\frac{1}{2}} = \frac{2}{3}g\sin\theta$$

$$= 0.66\,g\sin\theta$$

$$a_{solid\ sphere} = \frac{g\sin\theta}{1+\frac{2}{5}} = \frac{5}{7}g\sin\theta$$

$$= 0.71\,g\sin\theta$$

$$a_{hollow\ sphere} = \frac{g\sin\theta}{1+\frac{2}{3}} = \frac{3}{5}g\sin\theta$$

$$= 0.6\,g\sin\theta$$

Clearly, $a_{solid\ sphere} > a_{disc} > a_{hollow\ sphere}$

Type of sphere is not mentioned in the question. Therefore, we will assume the given sphere as solid sphere.

$$\therefore \quad a_{solid\ sphere} > a_{disc}$$

10 *(c)* Total kinetic energy of a body which is rolling without slipping is given by

$$K_{total} = K_{rot} + K_{trans}$$
$$= \frac{1}{2}I\omega^2 + \frac{1}{2}mv^2$$

For a solid spherical ball,

$$I = (2/5)mR^2$$

and $v = R\omega$ (along to diameter)

where, R is the radius of the spherical ball.

$$\text{So, } K_{total} = \frac{1}{2}\left(\frac{2}{5}mR^2\right)\omega^2 + \frac{1}{2}mR^2\omega^2$$
$$= \frac{7}{10}mR^2\omega^2$$
$$K = \frac{7}{10}mv^2$$

Potential energy = Kinetic energy

$$mgh = \frac{7}{10}mv^2$$
$$\Rightarrow \quad v^2 = \frac{10}{7}gh \quad \ldots(i)$$

For vertical projection,

$$v^2 = u^2 + 2gh'$$
$$\Rightarrow \quad \frac{10}{7}gh = 0 + 2gh'$$
$$\Rightarrow \quad h' = \frac{5}{7}h$$

11 *(d)* As, velocity of body,

$$v = \sqrt{\frac{2gh}{1 + K^2/r^2}}$$

$$\text{Given, } h = \frac{3v^2}{4g}$$

$$\Rightarrow \quad v^2 = \frac{2gh}{1 + \frac{K^2}{r^2}} = \frac{2g3v^2}{4g\left(1 + \frac{K^2}{r^2}\right)}$$
$$= \frac{6gv^2}{4g\left(1 + \frac{K^2}{r^2}\right)}$$
$$1 = \frac{3}{2\left(1 + K^2/r^2\right)}$$
$$\Rightarrow \quad 1 + \frac{K^2}{r^2} = \frac{3}{2}$$
$$\text{or} \quad \frac{K^2}{r^2} = \frac{3}{2} - 1 = \frac{1}{2}$$
$$K^2 = (1/2)r^2 \quad \text{(Equation of disc)}$$

Hence, the object is disc.

12 *(b)* This is a case of rolling on rough inclined plane force of friction in this case will be backward.

$$\text{Hence, } a = \frac{Mg\sin\theta - f}{M} \quad \ldots(i)$$
$$\text{and } \alpha = \frac{fR}{I} \quad \ldots(ii)$$

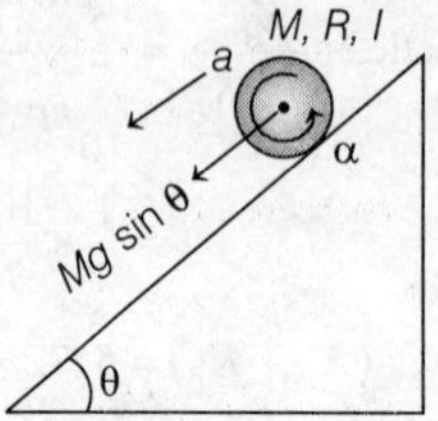

For pure rolling to take place,

$$a = R\alpha \quad \ldots(iii)$$

Solving Eqs. (i), (ii) and (iii), we get

$$f = \frac{Mg\sin\theta}{1 + \frac{MR^2}{I}} \quad \ldots(iv)$$

Further, the force of friction calculated in Eq. (iv) for pure rolling to take place should be less than or equal to the maximum friction $\mu Mg\cos\theta$.

$$\text{or} \quad \frac{Mg\sin\theta}{1 + \frac{MR^2}{I}} \le \mu\, Mg\cos\theta$$
$$\left[\because I = \frac{2}{5}MR^2\right]$$
$$\Rightarrow \quad \mu_{min} \le \frac{\tan\theta}{1 + \frac{MR^2}{I}} = \frac{\tan\theta}{1 + \frac{5}{2}} = \frac{2}{7}\tan\theta$$

13 *(c)* Time taken is given by

$$t = \frac{1}{\sin\theta}\sqrt{\frac{2h}{g}\left(1 + \frac{K^2}{R^2}\right)}$$
$$\therefore \quad \frac{t_S}{t_D} = \sqrt{\frac{1 + (K^2/R^2)_S}{1 + (K^2/R^2)_D}}$$
$$\left[\because \left(\frac{K}{R}\right)_S = \sqrt{\frac{2}{5}} \text{ and } \left(\frac{K}{R}\right)_D = \frac{1}{\sqrt{2}}\right]$$
$$= \sqrt{\frac{1 + (2/5)}{1 + (1/2)}} = \sqrt{\frac{14}{15}}$$
$$= \sqrt{14} : \sqrt{15}$$

14 *(b)* In sliding down, the entire potential energy of a body is converted only into translational energy. While in rolling motion, some part of potential energy is converted into kinetic energy of rotation and rest into kinetic energy of translation. Therefore, in sliding motion, the velocity acquired by the body is more.

Hence, the velocity of a body at the bottom of an inclined plane is more when it slides as compared to rolls. So, option (b) is correct.

15 *(c)* For the rolling of a solid cylinder acceleration $a_{CM} = g/3\sin\theta$

$\therefore$ The condition for the cylinder to remain in equilibrium

$$\Rightarrow \quad F_{CM} \le F_s$$
$$\Rightarrow \quad Ma_{CM} \le \mu_s R$$
$$\Rightarrow \quad \frac{1}{3}Mg\sin\theta \le Mg\cos\theta \cdot \mu_s$$

The cross-sectional view of a cylinder under influence of force is given below

$$\mu_s \ge (1/3)\tan\theta$$
$$\text{or} \quad \tan\theta \le 3\mu_s$$

16 *(d)* The relation between the linear velocity (v) and the angular velocity (ω) is

$$v = r\omega$$
$$\Rightarrow \quad r = v/\omega$$

From the equation of motion,

$$v^2 = u^2 + 2gh$$

When $u = 0$, $h = 3$ m, $g = 10$ ms^{-2}, $\omega = 2\sqrt{2}$ rad s^{-1}

$$v = \sqrt{2 \times 10 \times 3}$$
$$\Rightarrow \quad v = \sqrt{60} \text{ ms}^{-1}$$
$$\therefore \quad r = \frac{\sqrt{60}}{2\sqrt{2}} = \frac{\sqrt{30} \times \sqrt{2}}{2\sqrt{2}}$$
$$\Rightarrow \quad r = \sqrt{\frac{30}{4}} \approx \sqrt{5} \text{ m}$$

17 *(a)* When a body rolls down without slipping along an inclined plane of inclination θ, it suffers loss in gravitational potential energy, which provide translational energy due to frictional force into rotational energy.

18 *(a)* Since, in this case instantaneous axis of rotation is always below the centre of mass. This is possible only when point of contact moves with a velocity equal to the centre of mass.

19 *(b)* Angular velocity is given by

$$\omega = 600 \text{ rot min}^{-1}$$
$$= \frac{600 \times 2\pi}{60} \text{ rad s}^{-1}$$
$$= 20\pi \text{ rad s}^{-1}$$

Kinetic energy of coin which is due to rotation and translation is

$$K = \text{(KE) rotation} + \text{(KE) translation}$$

$$K = \frac{1}{2}I\omega^2 + \frac{1}{2}mv^2$$

$$= \frac{1}{2} \times \frac{1}{2}mr^2\omega^2 + \frac{1}{2}m(r\omega)^2$$

Given, $m = 4.8\,\text{kg}$ and $r = 1\,\text{m}$

$$= \frac{1}{4} \times 4.8 \times (1)^2(20\pi)^2 + \frac{1}{2} \times 4.8 \times (20\pi \times 1)^2$$

$$= 480\pi^2 + 960\pi^2 = 1440\pi^2 \text{J}$$

20 (*d*) KE of rotation is 40% of KE in translatory

$$(\text{KE})_{\text{rot}} = 40\% \times (\text{KE})_{\text{trans}}$$

$$\frac{1}{2}I\omega^2 = \frac{40}{100} \times \frac{1}{2}mv^2$$

$$\Rightarrow \quad I\omega^2 = \frac{2}{5}m(\omega r)^2 \quad [\because v = \omega r]$$

$$\Rightarrow \quad I = \frac{2}{5}mr^2$$

where, I is moment of inertia.

Thus, the body is a solid sphere (solid ball).

21 (*a*) Kinetic energy of rotation,

$$K_{\text{rot}} = \frac{1}{2}I\omega^2 = \frac{1}{2}Mk^2\frac{v^2}{R^2} \quad \left(\because \omega = \frac{v}{R}\right)$$

where, k is radius of gyration.

Kinetic energy of translation,

$$K_{\text{trans}} = (1/2)Mv^2$$

Thus, total energy,

$$E = K_{\text{rot}} + K_{\text{trans}}$$

$$= \frac{1}{2}Mk^2\frac{v^2}{R^2} + \frac{1}{2}Mv^2$$

$$= \frac{1}{2}Mv^2\left(\frac{k^2}{R^2} + 1\right) = \frac{1}{2}\frac{Mv^2}{R^2}(k^2 + R^2)$$

Hence, $$\frac{K_{\text{rot}}}{K_{\text{total}}} = \frac{\frac{1}{2}Mk^2\frac{v^2}{R^2}}{\frac{1}{2}\frac{Mv^2}{R^2}(k^2 + R^2)} = \frac{k^2}{k^2 + R^2}$$

22 (*a*) According to energy conservation,

Potential energy

= Translational kinetic energy + Rotational kinetic energy

$$\Rightarrow mgh = \frac{1}{2}mv^2 + \frac{1}{2}I\omega^2$$

$$= \frac{1}{2}mv^2 + \frac{1}{2}\left(\frac{2}{5}mR^2\right)\cdot\frac{v^2}{R^2}$$

[$\because$ $I = (2/5)mR^2$ for a solid sphere]

$$\text{or} \quad mgh = \frac{1}{2}mv^2 + \frac{1}{5}mv^2$$

$$= \frac{7}{10}mv^2$$

$$\Rightarrow \quad v = \sqrt{\frac{10}{7}gh}.$$

Hence, to climb the inclined surface v should be $\geq \sqrt{\frac{10}{7}gh}$.

Gravitation

Quick Review

Every body in this universe attracts other bodies towards itself with a force called force of gravitation, thus gravitation is the phenomena of mutual attraction between two bodies.

Newton's Law of Gravitation

- If F is the force of attraction between the two bodies of masses m and M distance r apart, then by Newton's law of gravitation and it is given by $F = \dfrac{GMm}{r^2}$

  where, G = gravitational constant

  $= 6.67 \times 10^{-11}\,\text{Nm}^2\text{kg}^{-2}$.

  Dimensional formula of G is $[\text{M}^{-1}\text{L}^3\text{T}^{-2}]$.
- This force is conservative in nature.
- According to principle of superposition of gravitational forces, the resultant force F acting on a particle due to number of point masses is equal to the vector sum of forces exerted by the individual masses on given particle and given as

$$\mathbf{F}_R = -Gm_1\left[\frac{m_2}{r_{12}^2}\mathbf{r}_{21} + \frac{m_3}{r_{13}}\mathbf{r}_{31} + \ldots + \frac{m_n}{r_{1n}}\mathbf{r}_{n1}\right]$$

  where, $\mathbf{r}_{n_1}$ = unit vector pointing from m_n to m_1.

Acceleration Due to Gravity

- The force of gravity acting on a body of unit mass placed near the surface of earth is known as acceleration due to gravity, which is denoted by g and given as

$$g = \frac{F}{m} = \frac{GM}{R^2} = \frac{4}{3}\pi G\rho R$$

  where, M = mass of the earth, R = radius of the earth and ρ = mean density of the earth.

  Its average value on the earth surface is $9.8\ \text{ms}^{-2}$
- The weight of a body of mass m on earth's surface is given by $w = mg$.

Variations in the Value of g

- If ω is the angular velocity of rotation of earth about its own axis, then acceleration due to gravity at any place on earth is given as

$$g' = g - R\omega^2\cos^2\lambda$$

  where, λ is the latitude of that place.

  (*i*) At equator $\lambda = 0°$, then

  $\therefore \quad g' = g - R\omega^2$

  (*ii*) At poles $\lambda = 90°$, then

  $\therefore \quad g' = g$

  $\Rightarrow \quad g'_{\text{pole}} - g'_{\text{equator}} = R\omega^2$

  Thus, value of g' increases from equator to poles as latitude increases.
- The value of g at height h from earth's surface is given by

$$g' = \frac{g}{\left(1+\frac{h}{R}\right)^2} \text{ or } g' \approx g\left(1-\frac{2h}{R}\right)$$

  Therefore, g decreases with height.
- The value of g at depth d below earth's surface is given by

$$g' = g\left(1-\frac{d}{R}\right)$$

  Therefore, g decreases with depth and becomes zero at earth's centre.
- The value of acceleration due to gravity at poles and equator is also given respectively as

$$g_p = \frac{GM}{R_p^2} \text{ and } g_{eq} = \frac{GM}{R_{eq}^2}$$

  where, R_p and R_{eq} are radius of earth at poles and equator respectively.

  As, $\quad R_p < R_{eq}$

  $\therefore \quad g_p > g_{eq}$

  Thus, the value of g is minimum at the equator and maximum at the poles.

Gravitational Field

- The space around a body in which any other body experiences a force of attraction is called the gravitational field of the first body.
- The intensity of gravitational field at a point is given by

$$I \text{ or } E = \frac{F}{m} = \frac{GM}{r^2}$$

where, r = distance of unit mass from centre of body.

Gravitational Field Intensity due to Different Bodies

Shape of Body	Outside the Surface $(r > R)$	On the Surface $(r = R)$	Inside the Surface $(r < R)$	*I versus r* graph
Solid sphere	$I = \frac{GM}{r^2}$	$I = \frac{GM}{R^2}$	$I = \frac{GMr}{R^3}$	$I = \frac{GM}{R^2}$; $I \propto r$; $I \propto \frac{1}{r^2}$; $r < R$; $r > R$; O; R; r
Spherical shell	$I = \frac{GM}{r^2}$	$I = \frac{GM}{R^2}$	$I = 0$	$\frac{GM}{R^2}$; $I \propto \frac{1}{r^2}$; $I = 0$; O; R; r

Note Due to a circular ring, the value of I at a point on its axis is $\frac{GMr}{(R^2 + r^2)^{3/2}}$. However, its value at the centre of ring is zero.

Gravitational Potential

Gravitational potential at a point in the gravitational field is defined as the amount of work done in bringing a body of unit mass from infinity to that point without acceleration.

i.e. $$V = -\frac{W}{m}$$

- Its SI unit is Jkg^{-1} and dimensional formula is $[M^0L^2T^{-2}]$.
- Relation between gravitational field and potential is given as

$$V = -\int I \cdot dr$$

- Gravitational potential at a point due to system of point masses

$$V = -\left[\frac{Gm_1}{r_1} + \frac{Gm_2}{r_2} + \ldots + \frac{Gm_n}{r_n}\right]$$

Gravitational Potential due to Different Bodies

Shape of Body	Outside the Surface $(r > R)$	On the Surface $r = R$	Inside the Surface $(r < R)$	*I versus r* graph
Solid sphere	$V = -\frac{GM}{r}$	$V = -\frac{GM}{R}$	$V = -\frac{GM}{2R}\left[3 - \frac{r^2}{R^2}\right]$	$-1.5\frac{GM}{R}$; $-\frac{GM}{R}$; Parabolic; Hyperbolic; O; R; r; V
Spherical shell	$V = -\frac{GM}{r}$	$V = -\frac{GM}{R}$	$V = -\frac{GM}{R}$	$-\frac{GM}{R}$; O; R; r; V

Note Due to a circular ring, the value of potential at a point on its axis is $-\frac{GM}{\sqrt{R^2 + r^2}}$ and at the centre of ring is $-\frac{GM}{R}$.

Gravitational Potential Energy

Gravitational potential energy of a body at a point is the amount of work done in bringing a given body from infinity to a point against the gravitational force.

- If m_1 and m_2 are two masses separated by infinite distance, then gravitational potential energy of the system when they are brought to a separation of r is given by

$$U = -\frac{Gm_1 m_2}{r}$$

where, the negative sign indicates that the two bodies are attracting each other.

- If three particles of masses m_1, m_2 and m_3 are kept at three corners of an equilateral triangle of the side d, then gravitational potential energy of the system

$$U = -\frac{G}{d}(m_1 m_2 + m_2 m_3 + m_3 m_1)$$

Variation of Gravitational Potential Energy on Earth

- If a body of mass m is kept on surface of earth, then its gravitational potential energy is given by

$$\text{PE} = -\frac{GMm}{R}$$

- If a body is at a height h above surface of the earth, then its gravitational potential energy is given by

$$\text{PE} = -\frac{GMm}{R+h}$$

- Work done in lifting a body from surface of the earth to height h, is given by

$$W = \text{change in PE} = mgh\left(\frac{R}{R+h}\right)$$

If $h << R$, then

$$W = mgh.$$

Escape Velocity

The minimum velocity with which a body should be projected from the surface of earth, so that it escapes (free) from earth's gravitational field.

It is given by

$$v_e = \sqrt{2gR} = \sqrt{\frac{2GM}{R}} = \sqrt{\frac{8}{3}\pi GR^2\rho}$$

(*i*) On the surface of the earth,

$$v_e = 11.2 \text{ km s}^{-1}$$

(*ii*) On the surface of the moon,

$$v_e = 2.5 \text{ km s}^{-1}$$

Kepler's Laws of Planetary Motion

There are three scientific laws describing the motion of planets around the sun as given below

(*i*) **First law** All planets move around the sun in elliptical orbits with the sun at one focus.

(*ii*) **Second law** The area swept by the line joining the sun and the planet per unit time is constant.

i.e., $$\frac{dA}{dt} = \frac{1}{2}rv = \text{constant} = \frac{L}{2m}$$

where, L = angular momentum of sun planet system and m = mass of planet.

(*iii*) **Third law** The square of the time taken to complete the orbit (T) is proportional to the cube of the semi-major axis (a) of the elliptical orbit.

Mathematically, $T^2 \propto a^3$

or $$\frac{T^2}{a^3} = \text{constant}$$

Earth Satellites

They are objects which revolve around the earth. Moon is only natural satellite of earth. Some important terms about earth satellite are given below

Orbital Velocity of Satellite

A satellite (natural and artificial) is a small body, which constantly revolves around a planet (much larger than satellite).

- When a satellite rotates around the earth, the gravitational force due to earth provides the necessary centripetal force for its orbital motion.
- Thus, orbital velocity is the velocity required to put the satellite into its orbit around the earth and given as

$$v_o = \sqrt{\frac{GM}{r}} = \sqrt{\frac{gR^2}{r}} = \sqrt{\frac{gR^2}{(R+h)}}$$

where, h = height of satellite above earth's surface

- When satellite is close of the earth's surface, i.e. $h << R$ or $r \simeq R$, then

$$v_o = \sqrt{\frac{GM}{R}} = \sqrt{gR}$$

- Orbital angular velocity of satellite is also given as

$$\omega_o = \sqrt{\frac{g}{R}} = \sqrt{\frac{GM}{R^3}}$$

- Critical velocity of the satellite near the earth's surface in terms of density of the earth is given by

$$v_c = \sqrt{\frac{4}{3}G\pi R^3\rho}$$

- **Relation between orbital velocity and escape velocity is given as**

$$v_e = \sqrt{2}\, v_o$$

Time Period of Revolution of Satellite

- It is the time taken by a satellite to complete one revolution around the earth. It is given by

$$T = \frac{2\pi r}{v_o} = 2\pi\sqrt{\frac{r^3}{GM}} = 2\pi\sqrt{\frac{r^3}{gR^2}} \qquad \left[\because g = \frac{GM}{R^2}\right]$$

- When satellite is close to earth, i.e. $r \simeq R$, then

$$T = 2\pi\sqrt{\frac{R}{g}}$$

Height of Satellite

From the relation of time period, the height of a satellite from earth surface can be calculated as

$$h = \left(\frac{T^2 gR^2}{4\pi^2}\right)^{\frac{1}{3}} - R$$

Energy of Satellite

- When a satellite revolves around a planet in its orbit, its possesses both potential energy and kinetic energy. These are given below

(*i*) Potential energy of satellite, $U = -\dfrac{GMm}{r}$

(*ii*) Kinetic energy of satellite, $K = \dfrac{1}{2} mv_0^2 = \dfrac{GMm}{2r}$

(*iii*) Total energy of satellite, $E = U + K = -\dfrac{GMm}{2r} = -K$

- Variation of energy of satellite with distance can be represented by graph as below

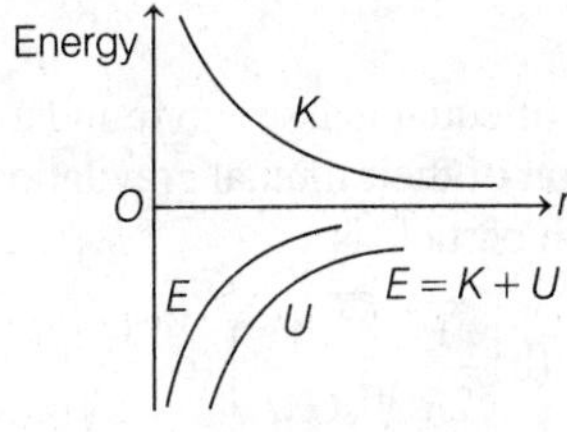

- **Binding energy** of a satellite is the energy required to remove the satellite from its orbit to the infinity. It is given by

$$\text{BE} = -E = \frac{GMm}{2r}$$

Angular Momentum of Satellite

- During motion of satellite around a planet, the angular momentum remains conserved and given by

$$L = mv_0 r = \sqrt{m^2 GMr}$$

Types of Satellites

Depending upon the plane of rotation, there are two types of satellites as given below

(*i*) The satellites which revolve around the earth's equatorial plane are called **geo-stationary satellites.**

They have same time period as that of earth.

Geo-stationary satellites are used for communication purpose such as electromagnetic waves.

(*ii*) The satellites which revolves around the poles of earth in a north-south direction are called **polar** or **sun synchronous satellite**.

Uses of Satellites

These satellites have been used for various purposes, some of these are

- used in spying work for military purpose.
- to know the exact shape and dimensions of the earth.
- to take astronomical observations in the absence of atmospheric disturbances.
- to study topography of the moon, the venus and the mars.

Weightlessness in a Satellite

When a satellite, which does not produce its own gravity moves around the earth in a circular orbit under the action of gravity.

The surface of satellite does not exert any force on the body, hence its apparent weight is zero.

Topical Practice Questions

All the exam questions of this chapter have been divided into 4 topics as listed below

Topic 1

Newton's Law of Gravitation

2017

1 Two astronauts are floating in gravitation free space after having lost contact with their spaceship. The two will **[NEET]**
(a) keep floating at the same distance between them
(b) move towards each other
(c) move away from each other
(d) will become stationary

2 A solid sphere of mass M and radius R has a spherical cavity of radius $\frac{R}{2}$ such that the centre of cavity is at a distance $R/2$ from the centre of the sphere. A point mass m is placed inside the cavity at a distance $R/4$ from the centre of sphere. The gravitational pull between the sphere and the point mass m is **[BVP]**
(a) $\frac{11GMm}{R^2}$ (b) $\frac{14GMm}{R^2}$ (c) $\frac{GMm}{2R^2}$ (d) $\frac{GMm}{R^2}$

2015

3 Two spherical bodies of masses M and $5M$ and radii R and $2R$ are released in free space with initial separation between their centres equal to $12R$. If they attract each other due to gravitational force only, then the distance covered by the smaller body before collision is **[AIPMT]**
(a) $2.5R$ (b) $4.5R$ (c) $7.5R$ (d) $1.5R$

2014

4 The force of gravitation is **[UK PMT]**
(a) repulsive (b) electrostatic
(c) conservative (d) non-conservative

2013

5 If there was a reduction in gravitational effect, then which of the following forces do you think would change in some respect? **[Manipal]**
(a) Magnetic force (b) Electrostatic force
(c) Viscous force (d) Archimedes uplift

6 If the distance between the sun and the earth is increased by three times, then attraction between two will **[WB JEE]**
(a) remain constant (b) decrease by 63%
(c) increase by 63% (d) decrease by 89%

2011

7 A body projected vertically from the earth reaches a height equal to earth's radius before returning to the earth. The power exerted by the gravitational force is greatest **[CBSE AIPMT]**
(a) at the instant just before the body hits the earth
(b) it remains constant all through
(c) at the instant just after the body is projected
(d) at the highest position of the body

8 One can easily weigh the earth by calculating the mass of the earth by using the formula (in usual notation) **[AMU]**
(a) $\frac{G}{g}R_e^2$ (b) $\frac{g}{G}R_e^2$ (c) $\frac{g}{G}R_e$ (d) $\frac{G}{g}R_e^3$

2010

9 Three equal masses of 1 kg each are placed at the vertices of an equilateral ΔPQR and a mass of 2 kg is placed at the centroid O of the triangle which is at a distance of $\sqrt{2}$ m from each of the vertices of the triangle. The force, (in newton) acting on the mass of 2 kg is **[AMU]**
(a) 2 (b) $\sqrt{2}$ (c) 1 (d) zero

10 Which of the following statements about the gravitational constant is true? **[WB JEE]**
(a) It is a force.
(b) It has no unit.
(c) It has same value in all systems of unit.
(d) It does not depend on the nature of the medium in which the bodies are kept.

11 Two balls, each of radius R, equal mass and density are placed in contact, then the force of gravitation between them is proportional to **[DCE]**
(a) $F \propto \frac{1}{R^2}$ (b) $F \propto R$ (c) $F \propto R^4$ (d) $F \propto \frac{1}{R}$

2009

12 Two particles of equal masses go round a circle of radius R under the action of their mutual gravitational attraction. The speed v of each particle is **[AIIMS]**
(a) $\sqrt{\left(\frac{GM}{2R}\right)}$ (b) $\frac{1}{2R}\sqrt{\left(\frac{1}{GM}\right)}$ (c) $\frac{1}{2}\sqrt{\left(\frac{GM}{R}\right)}$ (d) $\sqrt{\left(\frac{4GM}{R}\right)}$

2007

13 Two spheres of masses m and M are situated in air and the gravitational force between them is F. The space around the masses is now filled with a liquid of specific gravity 3. The gravitational force will now be **[BHU]**
(a) $\frac{F}{3}$ (b) $\frac{F}{9}$ (c) $3F$ (d) F

Answers

1 (b)	2 (b)	3 (c)	4 (c)	5 (d)	6 (d)	7 (a)	8 (b)	9 (d)	10 (d)
11 (c)	12 (c)	13 (d)							

Explanations

1 *(b)* In gravitation free space, there is no external gravity. Due to masses of the astronauts, there will be small gravitational attractive force between them. Thus, these astronauts will move towards each other.

2 *(b)* To calculate the force of attraction on the point mass m. We should calculate the force due to the solid sphere and subtract from this the force which the mass of the hollow sphere would have exerted on m, i.e.

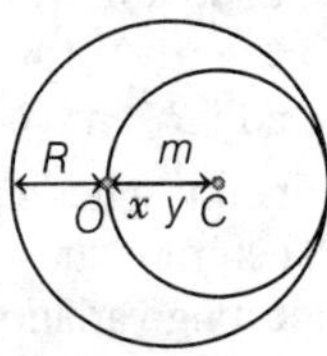

$$F = \frac{GmM}{x^2} - \frac{GmM'}{y^2}$$

$[\because x = R/4, x + y = R/2]$

Since, mass, $M = \left(\frac{4}{3}\right)\pi R^3 \rho$

and $M' = \frac{4}{3}\pi\left(\frac{R}{2}\right)^3 \rho = \frac{M}{8}$

$$\therefore F = \frac{GMm}{(R/4)^2} - \frac{Gm(M/8)}{(R/4)^2} = \frac{14GmM}{R^2}$$

3 *(c)* Suppose the smaller body covers a distance x before collision, then

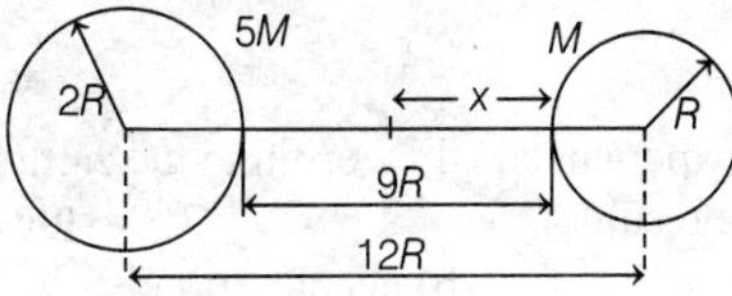

As, gravitational force,

$$F = \frac{GM\,5M}{(12R - x)^2}$$

Now, acceleration of smaller body,

$$a_{\text{small}} = \frac{F}{M} = \frac{G5M}{(12R - x)^2}$$

Similarly, $a_{\text{big}} = \frac{F}{5M} = \frac{GM}{(12R - x)^2}$

As, we know, $s = ut + \frac{1}{2}at^2 \quad [\because u = 0]$

$$\Rightarrow x = \frac{1}{2}a_{\text{small}}t^2 = \frac{1}{2}\frac{5GM}{(12R - x)^2}t^2 \quad \ldots\text{(i)}$$

$$\Rightarrow (9R - x) = \frac{1}{2}a_{\text{big}}t^2 = \frac{1}{2}\frac{GM}{(12R - x)^2}t^2 \quad \ldots\text{(ii)}$$

From Eqs. (i) and (ii), we get

$$\frac{x}{9R - x} = \frac{5}{1}$$

$\Rightarrow \quad 6x = 45R$

$\Rightarrow \quad x = 7.5\,R$

4 *(c)* As the work done by the gravitational force F in closed path is zero. So, it is conservative in nature, i.e. work done by the body is independent of path followed.

5 *(d)* Magnetic, electrostatic and viscous force will not be affected by reduction in gravitational force. Only Archimedes uplift (which is loss in weight equal to the weight of liquid displaced by the immersed part of body) will change.

6 *(d)* As we know,

$$F = \frac{Gm_1m_2}{r^2} \text{ and } F' = \frac{Gm_1m_2}{(3r)^2} = \frac{F}{9} \quad \text{(given)}$$

per cent decrease in force

$$= \left(\frac{F - F'}{F}\right) \times 100 = \frac{8}{9} \times 100 = 89\%$$

7 *(a)* As we know that, power exerted,

$$P = \mathbf{F} \cdot \mathbf{v} = |\mathbf{F}|\ |\mathbf{v}| \cos\theta$$

where, F = magnitude of force,
v = magnitude of velocity
and θ = angle between force & velocity.

So, just before the body hits the earth, θ is zero, so $\mathbf{F}$ and $\mathbf{v}$ are maximum.

So, power is maximum.

8 *(b)* Force, $F = G\frac{M_e m}{R_e^2}$

$$mg = G\frac{M_e m}{R_e^2} \quad (\because F = mg)$$

$$\Rightarrow \quad g = \frac{GM_e}{R_e^2} \Rightarrow M_e = \frac{gR_e^2}{G}$$

9 *(d)* Given, $OP = OQ = OR = \sqrt{2}$ m (given)

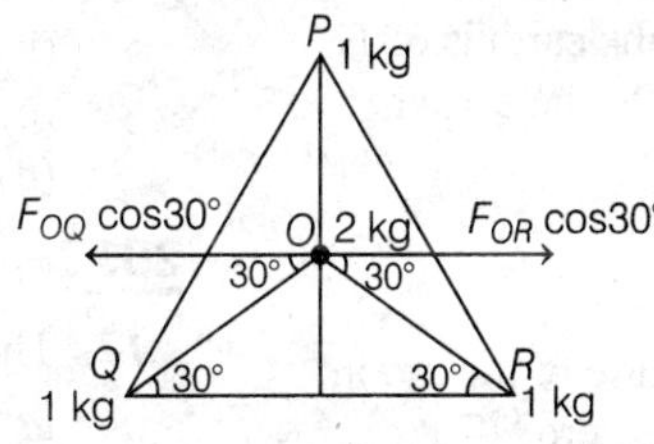

The gravitational force on mass 2 kg due to mass 1 kg at P,

$$F_{OP} = G\frac{2 \times 1}{(\sqrt{2})^2} \quad (\text{along } OP)$$

Similarly, $F_{OQ} = G\frac{2\times1}{(\sqrt{2})^2}$ (along OQ)

and $F_{OR} = G\frac{2 \times 1}{(\sqrt{2})^2}$ (along OR)

$F_{OQ} \cos 30°$ and $F_{OR} \cos 30°$ are equal and acting in opposite directions, hence cancel out each other. Then, the resultant force on the mass 2 kg at O,

$$F = F_{OP} - (F_{OQ} \sin 30° + F_{OR} \sin 30°)$$

$$\Rightarrow F = G - \left(\frac{G}{2} + \frac{G}{2}\right) \Rightarrow F = 0 \text{ (zero)}$$

10 *(d)* Gravitational constant does not depend on the nature of the medium in which the bodies are kept.Its unit is N-m^{2}kg^{-2}.

11 *(c)* Let masses of two balls are $m_1 = m_2 = m$ (given) and the density be ρ. Distance between their centres $= AB = 2R$.

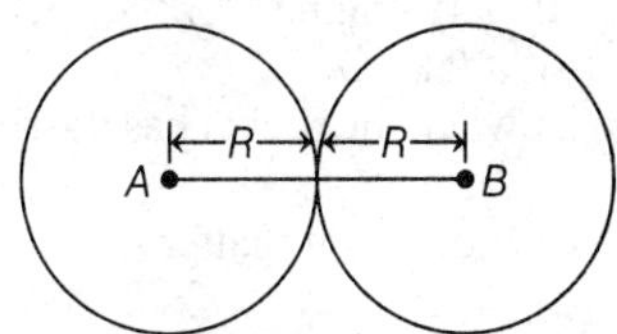

Thus, the magnitude of the gravitational force F that two balls separated by a distance $2R$ exert on each other is

$$F = G\frac{(m)\,(m)}{(2R)^2} = G\frac{m^2}{4R^2}$$

$$= G\frac{\left(\frac{4}{3}\pi R^3 \rho\right)^2}{4R^2} \quad \left[\because m = \frac{4}{3}\pi R^3 \rho\right]$$

$$\Rightarrow \quad F = \frac{4}{9}\pi^2 G \rho^2 R^4$$

$$\therefore \quad F \propto R^4$$

12 *(c)* Two particles A and B each of mass m move in a circular path of radius R. Then, gravitational force between them provides the necessary centripetal force,

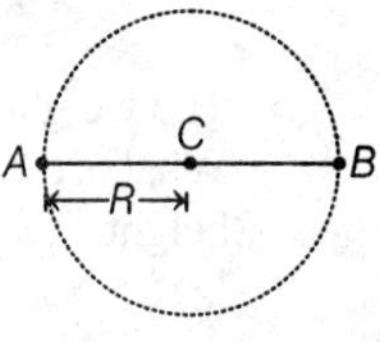

i.e. $\frac{mv^2}{R} = \frac{GMm}{(2R)^2} \Rightarrow v = \frac{1}{2}\sqrt{\left(\frac{GM}{R}\right)}$

13 *(d)* According to Newton's law of gravitation, the force between two spheres is given by $F = \frac{GMm}{r^2}$

From the relation, we can say that the gravitational force does not depend on the medium between two spheres, hence it remains same F.

Topic 2

Acceleration due to Gravity

2019

1 A body weighs 200 N on the surface of the earth. How much will it weigh half way down to the centre of the earth ? **[NEET]**
(a) 200 N (b) 250 N (c) 100 N (d) 150 N

2 A space rocket is intended to leave the earth's gravitational field. The fuel in its main engine is a little less than the amount that is necessary and an auxiliary engine, (only capable of operating for a short time) has to be used as well. When it is best to switch ON, the auxiliary engine **[JIPMER]**
(a) at take OFF
(b) when the rocket has nearly stopped with respect to the earth.
(c) It does not matter
(d) Cannot say

3 Find gravitational field at a distance of 2000 km from the centre of earth. (Given $R_{earth} = 6400\,\text{km}$, $r = 2000\,\text{km}$, $M_{earth} = 6\times 10^{24}$ kg) **[AIIMS]**
(a) $1.53\ \text{ms}^{-2}$ (b) $7.12\ \text{ms}^{-2}$
(c) $3.06\ \text{ms}^{-2}$ (d) $1.8\ \text{ms}^{-2}$

2018

4 R is the radius of earth, ω is its angular velocity and g_p is the value of g at the poles. The effective value of g at a latitude $\lambda = 60°$ is **[JIPMER]**
(a) $g_p - \frac{1}{4}R\omega^2$ (b) $g_p + \frac{1}{4}R\omega^2$
(c) $g_p - \frac{1}{2}R\omega^2$ (d) $g_p + \frac{1}{2}R\omega^2$

5 The weight of a body on the surface of the earth is 63 N. What is the gravitational force on it due to the earth at a height equal to half the radius of the earth? **[AIIMS]**
(a) 35 N (b) 28 N
(c) 18 N (d) 40 N

6 At what distance (in metre) from the centre of the moon, the intensity of gravitational field will be zero? (Take, mass of earth and moon as 5.98×10^{24} kg and 7.35×10^{22} kg respectively and the distance between moon and earth is 3.855×10^{8} m.) **[JIPMER]**
(a) zero (b) 3.85×10^{7} (c) 8×10^{8} (d) 3.46×10^{8}

2017

7 The acceleration due to gravity at a height 1 km above the earth is the same as at a depth d below the surface of earth. Then **[NEET]**
(a) $d = \frac{1}{2}$ km (b) $d = 1$ km (c) $d = \frac{3}{2}$ km (d) $d = 2$ km

8 The planets with radii R_1 and R_2 have densities ρ_1, ρ_2 respectively. Their atmospheric pressures are p_1 and p_2 respectively. Therefore, the ratio of masses of their atmospheres, neglecting variation of g within the limits of atmosphere is **[JIPMER]**
(a) $\rho_1 R_2 p_1 / \rho_2 R_1 p_2$ (b) $p_1 R_2 \rho_2 / pP_2 R_1 \rho_1$
(c) $p_1 R_1 \rho_1 / p_2 R_2 \rho_2$ (d) $p_1 R_1 \rho_2 / p_2 R_2 \rho_1$

2016

9 Starting from the centre of the earth having radius R, the variation of g (acceleration due to gravity) is shown by **[NEET]**

(a)
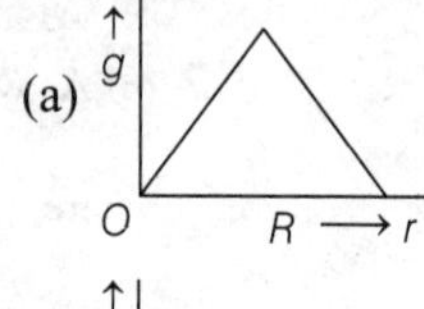

(b)
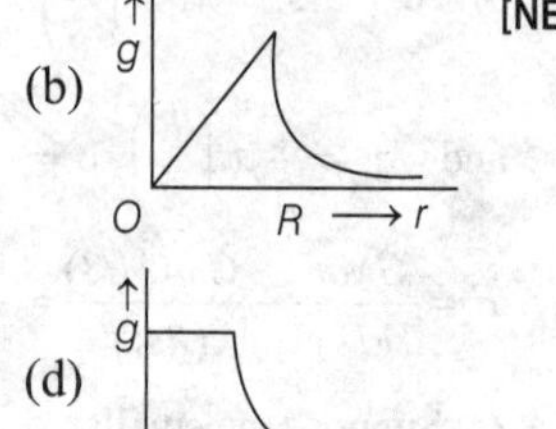

(c)
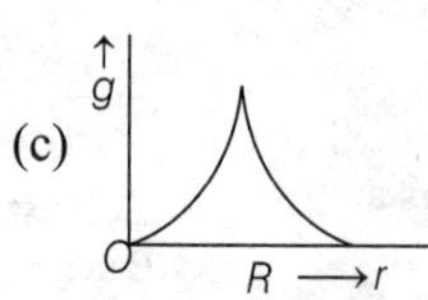

(d)

2013

10 Weightlessness experienced while orbiting the earth in spaceships, is the result of **[UP CPMT]**
(a) inertia (b) acceleration
(c) zero gravity (d) centre of gravity

11 What will happen to the weight of the body at the south-pole, if the earth stops rotating about its polar axis? **[KCET]**
(a) No change
(b) Increases
(c) Decreases but not become zero
(d) Reduces to zero

2012

12 The height at which the weight of a body becomes (1/16)th, its weight on the surface of earth (radius R) is **[CBSE AIPMT]**
(a) $5R$ (b) $15R$ (c) $3R$ (d) $4R$

13 The imaginary angular velocity of the earth for which the effective acceleration due to gravity at the equator shall be zero is equal to (take, $g = 10\ \text{ms}^{-2}$ for the acceleration due to gravity, if the earth were at rest and radius of earth equal to 6400 km.) **[AMU]**
(a) $1.25\times 10^{-3}\ \text{rads}^{-1}$ (b) $2.50\times 10^{-3}\ \text{rads}^{-1}$
(c) $3.75\times 10^{-3}\ \text{rads}^{-1}$ (d) $5.0\times 10^{-3}\ \text{rads}^{-1}$

2011

14 What will be the acceleration due to gravity at a depth d, where g is acceleration due to gravity on the surface of earth? **[UP CPMT]**

(a) $\frac{g}{\left[1+\frac{d}{R}\right]^2}$ (b) $g\left[1-\frac{2d}{R}\right]$ (c) $\frac{g}{\left[1-\frac{d}{R}\right]^2}$ (d) $g\left[1-\frac{d}{R}\right]$

15 The height vertically above the earth's surface at which the acceleration due to gravity becomes 1% of its value at the surface is **[WB JEE]**

(a) $8R$ (b) $9R$ (c) $10R$ (d) $20R$

16 Which of the following graphs shows the variation of acceleration due to gravity g with depth h from the surface of the earth? **[DUMET]**

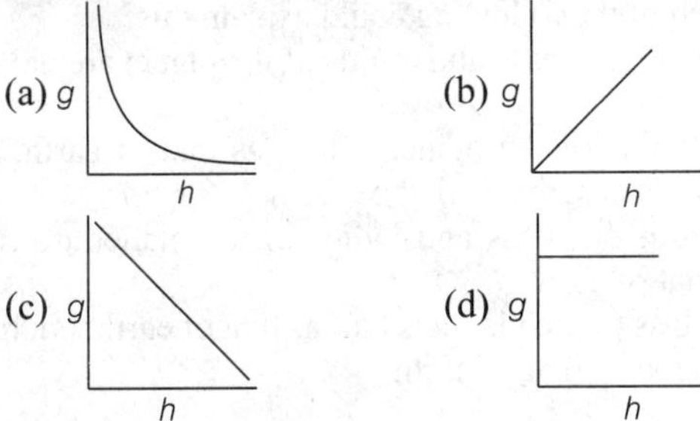

17 At what altitude (h) above the earth's surface would the acceleration due to gravity be one-fourth of its value at the earth's surface? **[DUMET]**

(a) $h = R$ (b) $h = 4R$
(c) $h = 2R$ (d) $h = 16R$

18 The mass of the moon is $(1/81)$th of the earth but gravitational pull is $(1/6)$th of the earth. It is due to the fact that **[Haryana PMT]**

(a) the radius of the moon is $(81/6)$th of the earth
(b) the radius of the earth is $(9/\sqrt{6})$th of the moon
(c) moon is the satellite of the earth
(d) None of the above

2010

19 The ratio of the accelerations due to gravity at the bottom of a deep mine and that on the surface of the earth is 978/980. Find the depth of the mine, if the density of the earth is uniform throughout and the radius of the earth is 6300 km. **[VMMC]**

(a) 12.86 km (b) 13.0 km
(c) 25.38 km (d) 90.9 km

2009

20 At what height above the surface of earth, the value of acceleration due to gravity would be half of its value on the surface of earth? (take, radius of the earth is 6400 km)

(a) 2561 km (b) 2650 km **[AIIMS]**
(c) 3200 km (d) 9800 km

2008

21 A planet has same density and same acceleration due to gravity as of earth and universal gravitational constant G is twice of earth. The ratio of their radii is **[Manipal]**

(a) 1 : 4 (b) 1 : 5
(c) 1 : 2 (d) 3 : 2

22 Two planets have radii r_1 and r_2 and densities d_1 and d_2, respectively. Then, the ratio of accelerations due to gravity on them is **[Kerala CEE]**

(a) $r_1 d_1 : r_2 d_2$ (b) $r_1 d_2 : r_2 d_1$
(c) $r_1^2 d_1 : r_2^2 d_2$ (d) $r_1 d_1^2 : r_2 d_2^2$
(e) $r_1^2 d_2 : r_2^2 d_1$

23 If g is the acceleration due to gravity on the surface of the earth, its value at a height equal to double the radius of the earth is **[J&K CET]**

(a) g (b) $\frac{g}{2}$ (c) $\frac{g}{3}$ (d) $\frac{g}{9}$

2007

24 The density of newly discovered planet is twice that of earth. The acceleration due to gravity at the surface of the planet is equal to that at the surface of the earth. If the radius of the earth is R, then the radius of the plane would be **[AFMC]**

(a) $2R$ (b) $4R$ (c) $\frac{1}{4}R$ (d) $\frac{1}{2}R$

25 The acceleration due to gravity on the planet A is 9 times the acceleration due to gravity on planet B. A man jumps to a height of 2 m on the surface of A. What is the height of jump by the same person on the planet B? **[BHU]**

(a) 6 m (b) 2/3 m (c) 2/9 m (d) 18 m

26 If the radius of earth is R ,then the height h at which the value of g becomes one-fourth, will be **[BCECE]**

(a) $\frac{R}{8}$ (b) $\frac{3R}{8}$
(c) $\frac{3R}{4}$ (d) $\frac{R}{2}$

27 The speed of earth's rotation about its axis is ω . Its speed is increased to x times to make the effective acceleration due to gravity equal to zero at the equator. Then, x is equal to **[JCECE]**

(a) 1 (b) 8.5
(c) 17 (d) 34

2006

28 Acceleration due to gravity at earth's surface is g ms^{-2}. Find the effective value of gravity at a height of 32 km from sea level $(R_e = 6400\,\text{km})$. **[MP PMT]**

(a) $0.5\,g$ ms^{-2} (b) $0.99\,g$ ms^{-2}
(c) $1.01\,g$ ms^{-2} (d) $0.90\,g$ ms^{-2}

2005

29 Imagine a new planet having the same density as that of earth but it is 3 times bigger than the earth in size. If the acceleration due to gravity on the surface of earth is g and that on the surface of the new planet is g', then **[CBSE AIPMT]**

(a) $g' = 3g$ (b) $g' = \frac{g}{9}$
(c) $g' = 9g$ (d) $g' = 27g$

30 If the rotational speed of earth is increased, then weight of a body at the equator **[AMU]**

(a) increases (b) decreases
(c) becomes double (d) does not change

31 The depth at which the value of acceleration due to gravity becomes $1/n$ times the value at the surface is (R be the radius of the earth) **[Kerala CEE]**

(a) R/n (b) R/n^2 (c) $R\frac{(n-1)}{n}$ (d) $\frac{Rn}{(n-1)}$
(e) Rn

32 The ratio of acceleration due to gravity at a height $3R$ above earth's surface to the acceleration due to gravity on the surface of the earth is (R = radius of earth) **[MHT CET]**

(a) $\frac{1}{9}$ (b) $\frac{1}{4}$ (c) $\frac{1}{16}$ (d) $\frac{1}{3}$

33 Assuming earth to be sphere of uniform density, what is the value of acceleration due to gravity at a point 100 km below the earth surface? (Given, $R = 6380 \times 10^3$ m) **[RPMT]**

(a) 3.10 ms^{-2} (b) 5.06 ms^{-2}
(c) 7.64 ms^{-2} (d) 9.66 ms^{-2}

34 The weight of an object at earth's surface is 700 g-wt. What will be its weight at the surface of a planet whose radius is 1/2 and mass is 1/7 of that of the earth? **[RPMT]**

(a) 200 g-wt
(b) 400 g-wt
(c) 50 g-wt
(d) 300 g-wt

35 An astronaut on a strange planet finds that acceleration due to gravity is twice as that on the surface of earth. Which of the following could explain this? **[KCET]**

(a) Both the mass and radius of the planet are half as that of earth
(b) Radius of the planet is half as that of earth, but the mass is same as that of earth
(c) Both the mass and radius of the planet are twice as that of earth
(d) Mass of the planet is half as that of earth, but radius is same as that of earth

Answers

1 (c)	2 (a)	3 (c)	4 (a)	5 (b)	6 (b)	7 (d)	8 (d)	9 (b)	10 (c)
11 (a)	12 (c)	13 (a)	14 (d)	15 (b)	16 (c)	17 (a)	18 (b)	19 (a)	20 (b)
21 (c)	22 (a)	23 (d)	24 (d)	25 (d)	26 (b)	27 (c)	28 (b)	29 (a)	30 (b)
31 (c)	32 (c)	33 (d)	34 (b)	35 (a)					

Explanations

1 *(c)* Given, weight of the body,

$$w = 200 \text{ N}$$

As we know, $w = mg$, where m is the mass of the body and g ($\approx 10 \text{ ms}^{-2}$) is acceleration due to gravity of the body at the surface of the earth.
Since, mass m remains constant irrespective of the position of the body on the earth. However, g is not constant and its value at a depth d below the earth's surface is given as

$$g' = g\left(1 - \frac{d}{R}\right) \quad \text{... (i)}$$

where, R is the radius of the earth.
Multiplying m on both sides of Eq. (i), we get

$$mg' = mg\left(1 - \frac{d}{R}\right)$$

Thus, the weight of the body at half way down $\left(\text{i.e. } d = \frac{R}{2}\right)$ to the centre of the earth is

$$mg' = 200 \times \left(1 - \frac{R/2}{R}\right)$$

$$= 200\left(1 - \frac{1}{2}\right) = 200 \times \frac{1}{2} = 100$$

$\therefore$ The body will weigh 100 N half way down to the centre of the earth.

2 *(a)* For a space rocket, most of its thrust is required during take OFF. The rocket combustion causes fuel to burn and result in decrease of weight, which causes further acceleration using less fuel. So it is best to switch ON the auxiliary engine at take OFF.

3 *(c)* Given, radius of earth, $R_e = 6400$ km

Distance from centre of earth,

$$r = 2000 \text{ km}$$

Distance from the surface of earth,

$$d = R_e - r$$
$$= 6400 - 2000$$
$$= 4400 \text{ km}$$
$$= 4.4 \times 10^6 \text{ m}$$

If g' be the gravitation field below the surface of earth at a depth d, then

$$g' = g\left(1 - \frac{d}{R_e}\right) = 9.8\left(1 - \frac{4.4 \times 10^6}{6.4 \times 10^6}\right)$$

$[\because g = 9.8 \text{ ms}^{-2}]$

$$= 9.8 \times 0.3125 = 3.06 \text{ ms}^{-2}$$

4 *(a)* The acceleration due to gravity at a latitude λ is

$$g' = g - R\omega^2 \cos^2 \lambda$$

At the poles, $\lambda = 90°$

$$\therefore \quad g' = g = g_p$$

For $\lambda = 60°$,

$$g' = g_p - R\omega^2 \cos^2 \lambda$$

or $$g' = g_p - R\omega^2 \cos^2 60°$$

$$= g_p - R\omega^2 \left(\frac{1}{2}\right)^2$$

$$= g_p - \frac{1}{4} R\omega^2$$

5 (b) Given, $h = \frac{R_e}{2}$

Acceleration due to gravity at altitude h is given by

$$g' = \frac{g}{\left(1 + \frac{h}{R_e}\right)^2} = \frac{g}{\left(1 + \frac{R_e/2}{R_e}\right)^2}$$

$$= \frac{g}{\left(1 + \frac{1}{2}\right)^2} = \frac{g}{\left(\frac{3}{2}\right)^2} = \frac{4g}{9} \quad \text{...(i)}$$

Weight of the body at the earth's surface,

$$w = mg = 63 \text{ N} \quad \text{...(ii)}$$

Weight of the body at altitude,

$$h = \frac{R_e}{2}$$

$$w' = mg' = \frac{4}{9} mg \quad \text{...(iii)}$$

Using Eqs. (ii) and (iii), we get

$$w' = \frac{4}{9} \times 63 = 28 \text{ N}$$

6 (b) Given, $M_e = 5.98 \times 10^{24}$ kg, $M_m = 7.35 \times 10^{22}$ kg and $r = 3.855 \times 10^8$ m

Let x be the distance of the point from the centre of earth where gravitational intensity is zero. Therefore,

$$\frac{GM_e}{x^2} = \frac{GM_m}{(3.85 \times 10^8 - x)^2}$$

or $$\frac{x}{3.85 \times 10^8 - x} = \sqrt{\frac{M_e}{M_m}}$$

$$= \sqrt{\frac{5.98 \times 10^{24}}{7.35 \times 10^{22}}} \cong 9$$

or $$\frac{x}{9} + x = 3.85 \times 10^8$$

or $$x = 9 \times 3.85 \times 10^8 / 10$$

$$= 3.46 \times 10^8 \text{ m}$$

Distance from moon

$$= 3.85 \times 10^8 - 3.46 \times 10^8$$

$$= 3.9 \times 10^7 \text{ m}$$

$$\cong 3.85 \times 10^7 \text{ m}$$

7 (d) Acceleration due to gravity at height h above earth's surface

$$g_h = g\left(1 - \frac{2h}{R}\right) \quad [\because h << R]$$

Acceleration due to gravity at depth d below earth's surface

$$g_d = g\left(1 - \frac{d}{R}\right)$$

Given, $h = 1$ km and $g_d = g_h$

or $$g\left(1 - \frac{d}{R}\right) = g\left(1 - \frac{2h}{R}\right)$$

$$\Rightarrow \quad d = 2h$$

or $$d = 2 \text{ km}$$

8 (d) Acceleration due to gravity,

$$g = \frac{GM}{R^2} = \frac{4}{3}\pi\rho GR$$

$$\left[\because \rho = \frac{M}{V} \text{ and } V = \frac{4}{3}\pi R^3\right]$$

$$\therefore \quad \frac{g_1}{g_2} = \frac{\rho_1 R_1}{\rho_2 R_2} \quad \text{...(i)}$$

Atmospheric pressure can be given by

$$p = \frac{w}{S} \quad \text{...(ii)}$$

where, w = weight of atmosphere,

and S = surface area of the planet.

From $w = mg$, we get

$$\frac{m_1}{m_2} = \frac{w_1 g_2}{w_2 g_1}$$

$$\therefore \quad \frac{m_1}{m_2} = \frac{p_1 S_1 g_2}{p_2 S_2 g_1} \quad \text{[From Eq. (ii)]}$$

$$= \frac{p_1 \cdot (4\pi R_1^2)}{p_2 (4\pi R_2^2)} \frac{\rho_2 R_2}{\rho_1 R_1}$$

[From Eq. (i)]

$$= \frac{p_1 R_1 \rho_2}{p_2 R_2 \rho_1}$$

9 (b) Acceleration due to gravity at a depth d below the surface of the earth is given by

$$g_{\text{depth}} = g_{\text{surface}}\left(1 - \frac{d}{R}\right)$$

$$= g_{\text{surface}}\left[\frac{R-d}{R}\right]$$

$$= d_{\text{surface}}\left(\frac{r}{R}\right)$$

Also, for a point at height h above surface,

$$g_{\text{height}} = g_{\text{surface}}\left[\frac{R^2}{(R+h)^2}\right]$$

Therefore, we can say that value of g increases from centre to maximum at the surface and then decreases as depicted in graph (b).

10 (c) Weightlessness experienced while orbiting the earth in spaceships is the result of zero gravity because the surface does not exert any force on the body.

By Newton's law,

$$\frac{GMm}{r^2} - R = ma$$

$$\Rightarrow \quad \frac{GMm}{r^2} - R = m\left(\frac{GM}{r^2}\right)$$

$$\Rightarrow \quad R = 0$$

Since, reaction force by the surface of spaceship is zero, so body will experience weightlessness. This happens in zero gravity region and also from, $w = mg$, when $g = 0$, then $w = 0$.

11 (a) As weight of the body at pole is mg and g is not affected by the rotation of earth at poles. So, there is no change in weight of body.

12 (c) According to the question,

$$\text{Weight, } mg' = \frac{1}{16} mg$$

$$\frac{GMm}{(R+h)^2} = \frac{1}{16}\frac{GMm}{R^2}$$

$$\Rightarrow \quad \frac{1}{(R+h)^2} = \frac{1}{16R^2}$$

$$\Rightarrow \quad \frac{R}{R+h} = \frac{1}{4}$$

$$\Rightarrow \quad \frac{R+h}{R} = 4$$

$$\therefore \quad R = \frac{h}{3} \text{ or } h = 3R$$

13 (a) Acceleration due to gravity,

$$g' = g - \omega^2 R \cos^2 \lambda$$

At equator, $\lambda = 0°$

$$g = \omega^2 R$$

$$\Rightarrow \omega = \sqrt{\frac{g}{R}} = \sqrt{\frac{10}{6400 \times 10^3}} \quad \text{(given)}$$

$$= 1.25 \times 10^{-3} \text{ rad s}^{-1}$$

14 (d) Acceleration due to gravity at the surface of the earth,

$$g = \frac{GM}{R^2} = \frac{4}{3}\pi\rho GR \quad \text{...(i)}$$

where, ρ is the density of earth.

Acceleration due to gravity at depth d from surface of the earth

$$g' = \frac{4}{3}\pi\rho G (R - d) \quad \text{...(ii)}$$

From Eqs. (i) and (ii), we get

$$g' = g\left[1 - \frac{d}{R}\right]$$

15 (b) Acceleration due to gravity at a height h from earth's surface,

$$g' = \frac{GM}{(R+h)^2}$$

Given, $g' = 1\%$ of $g = \frac{g}{100}$

$$\Rightarrow \frac{g}{100} = \frac{GM}{(R+h)^2}$$

$$\frac{(R+h)^2}{100} = \frac{GM}{g}$$

or $\frac{(R+h)^2}{100} = R^2 \quad \left[\because g = \frac{GM}{R^2}\right]$

or $R + h = 10R$

$h = 9R$

where, R is the radius of the earth.

16 (c) Acceleration due to gravity at depth h from the surface of the earth,

$$g_h = \frac{4}{3}\pi\rho G(R-h) = \frac{4}{3}\pi\rho GR - \frac{4}{3}\rho Gh$$

$$\Rightarrow g_h = K - K'h \quad \text{...(i)}$$

where, $K = \frac{4}{3}\pi\rho GR$ and $K' = \frac{4}{3}\pi\rho G$ which are constant terms.

Now comparing Eq. (i) to generalised equation of straight line, $y = mx + c$ where, $m =$ negative.

Hence, the correct option is (c).

17 (a) Given, $g' = \frac{g}{4}$

We know that, acceleration due to gravity at height h from the surface of the earth,

$$g' = g\left[\frac{R}{R+h}\right]^2$$

Hence, $\frac{g}{4} = g\left[\frac{R}{R+h}\right]^2 \quad \left(\because g' = \frac{g}{4}\right)$

$$\Rightarrow \frac{R}{R+h} = \frac{1}{2}$$

$$\Rightarrow R + h = 2R \Rightarrow h = R$$

where, R is the radius of the earth.

18 (b) Gravitational pull depends upon acceleration due to gravity on that planet.

$$M_m = \frac{1}{81}M_e, g_m = \frac{1}{6}g_e \quad \text{(given)}$$

As $g = \frac{GM}{R^2}$,

so $g \propto \frac{M}{R^2}$

$$\Rightarrow \frac{R_e}{R_m} = \left[\frac{M_e}{M_m} \times \frac{g_m}{g_e}\right]^{1/2} = \left[81 \times \frac{1}{6}\right]^{1/2}$$

$$\therefore R_e = \frac{9}{\sqrt{6}}R_m$$

19 (a) Given, $\frac{g'}{g} = \frac{978}{980}$ and $R = 6300$ km

Ratio of accelerations due to gravity,

$$\frac{g'}{g} = \frac{978}{980} = 1 - \frac{d}{R}$$

$$\Rightarrow \frac{d}{R} = 1 - \frac{978}{980} = \frac{2}{980}$$

$$\Rightarrow d = \frac{2R}{980} = \frac{2 \times 6300}{980}$$

$$= 12.86 \text{ km}$$

20 (b) The ratio,

$$\frac{g'}{g} = \frac{R^2}{(R+h)^2} = \frac{1}{2}$$

$$\Rightarrow R + h = \sqrt{2}R$$

$$\Rightarrow h = (\sqrt{2} - 1)R$$

$$\Rightarrow h = (0.414) \times 6400 \quad \text{(given)}$$

$$\therefore h = 2650 \text{ km}$$

21 (c) Acceleration due to gravity at earth's surface is given by

$$g = \frac{GM}{R^2} \quad \text{...(i)}$$

Since, the earth is assumed to be spherical in shape, its mass is

$$M = \text{volume} \times \text{density} = \frac{4}{3}\pi R^3\rho$$

Given, $\rho_e = \rho_p = \rho, G_p = 2G_e$

$$\therefore \frac{g_e}{g_p} = \frac{G_e\left(\frac{4}{3}\pi R_e^3\right)\rho \times R_p^2}{R_e^2 \times G_p\left(\frac{4}{3}\pi R_p^3\right)\rho}$$

$$1 = \frac{G_e R_e^3 \times R_p^2}{R_e^2 \times R_p^3 \times 2G_e} \quad (\because G_p = 2G_e)$$

$$1 = \frac{R_e}{2R_p}$$

$$\Rightarrow \frac{R_p}{R_e} = \frac{1}{2}$$

22 (a) Acceleration due to gravity,

$$g = \frac{GM}{r^2}$$

$$= \frac{G}{r^2} \times \frac{4}{3}\pi r^3 d = \frac{4}{3}\pi dGr$$

$$\Rightarrow g \propto dr$$

Hence, $\frac{g_1}{g_2} = \frac{d_1 r_1}{d_2 r_2}$

23 (d) Acceleration due to gravity at a height h from the surface of the earth,

$$g' = g\frac{1}{(1 + h/R)^2}$$

Given, $h = 2R$

$$\therefore g' = g\frac{1}{(1+2)^2}$$

$$\Rightarrow g' = \frac{g}{9}$$

24 (d) The acceleration due to gravity on an object of mass m,

$$g = \frac{F}{m}$$

But from Newton's law of gravitation,

$$F = \frac{GMm}{R^2}$$

where, M is the mass of the earth and R is the radius of earth.

$$\therefore g = \frac{GMm/R^2}{m} = \frac{GM}{R^2}$$

Given, $\rho_p = 2\rho_e$

Also, $g_p = g_e$

$$\Rightarrow \frac{GM_p}{R_p^2} = \frac{GM_e}{R_e^2}$$

$$\Rightarrow \frac{G \times \frac{4}{3}\pi R_p^3\rho_p}{R_p^2} = \frac{G \times \frac{4}{3}\pi R_e^3\rho_e}{R_e^2}$$

$$\Rightarrow R_p\rho_p = R_e\rho_e$$

$$\Rightarrow R_p \times 2\rho_e = R_e\rho_e$$

$$\therefore R_p = \frac{R_e}{2} = \frac{R}{2}$$

25 (d) It is given that, acceleration due to gravity on plane A is 9 times the acceleration due to gravity on planet B, i.e.

$$g_A = 9g_B \quad \text{...(i)}$$

From third equation of motion,

$v^2 = 2gh$

At planet A, $h_A = \frac{v^2}{2g_A}$ ...(ii)

At planet B, $h_B = \frac{v^2}{2g_B}$ ...(iii)

Dividing Eq. (ii) by Eq. (iii), we have

$$\frac{h_A}{h_B} = \frac{g_B}{g_A}$$

From Eq. (i),

$$\frac{h_A}{h_B} = \frac{g_B}{9g_B} = \frac{1}{9} \quad [\because g_A = 9g_B]$$

$$h_B = 9h_A = 9 \times 2 = 18\text{m}$$

$(\because h_A = 2\text{ m})$

26 *(b)* The value of acceleration due to gravity at a height h above the surface of the earth is given by

$$g' = \frac{g}{\left(1+\frac{h}{R}\right)^2}$$

where, R is radius of earth.

When h is negligible compared to R, we have

$$g' = g\left(1+\frac{h}{R}\right)^{-2} = g\left(1-\frac{2h}{R}\right)$$

Given, $g' = \frac{g}{4}$

So, $\frac{g}{4} = g\left(1-\frac{2h}{R}\right)$

$\Rightarrow \frac{1}{4} = 1 - \frac{2h}{R}$

$\Rightarrow \frac{2h}{R} = \frac{3}{4}$

$\Rightarrow h = \frac{3R}{8}$

27 *(c)* Earth rotates about its own axis in 24 h.

So, $T = 24 \times 60 \times 60$ s

So, angular speed of earth about its own axis,

$$\omega = \frac{2\pi}{T} = \frac{2\pi}{24 \times 60 \times 60} \text{ rad s}^{-1}$$

At equator, $g' = g - R_e\omega^2$

$\Rightarrow 0 = g - R_e\omega'^2$

$\Rightarrow \omega' = \sqrt{\frac{g}{R_e}} = \frac{2\pi}{84.6 \times 60}$

($\because T = 84.6 \times 60$ s at equator)

$\therefore \frac{\omega'}{\omega} = \frac{24 \times 60 \times 60}{84.6 \times 60} \approx 17$

$\Rightarrow \omega' = 17\omega$

So, value of x is 17.

28 *(b)* For height h, above the earth's surface ($h = 32$ km),

$$g' = g\left(1-\frac{2h}{R_e}\right)$$

$$= g\left(1-\frac{64}{6400}\right)$$

($\because R_e = 6400$ km)

$$= g(1-0.01) = 0.99\, g \text{ ms}^{-2}$$

29 *(a)* The acceleration due to gravity on the new planet can be found using the relation,

$$g = \frac{GM}{R^2} \quad \text{...(i)}$$

But $M = \frac{4}{3}\pi R^3\rho$, where ρ is density.

Thus, Eq. (i) becomes

$$g = \frac{G \times \frac{4}{3}\pi R^3\rho}{R^2} = G \times \frac{4}{3}\pi R\rho$$

$\Rightarrow g \propto R$

$\therefore \frac{g'}{g} = \frac{R'}{R}$

$\Rightarrow \frac{g'}{g} = \frac{3R}{R}$

$\Rightarrow \frac{g'}{g} = 3 \Rightarrow g' = 3g$

30 *(b)* The acceleration due to gravity at the equator is given by

$$g' = g - R_e\omega^2$$

According to the question, the rotational speed or angular velocity is increased, so the amount of $R_e\omega^2$ will increase. Therefore, the acceleration due to gravity (g') on equator will decrease which will cause the weight of body to decrease.

31 *(c)* At depth d from earth's surface,

$$g' = g\left(1-\frac{d}{R}\right)$$

Given, $g' = \frac{g}{n}$

So, $\frac{g}{n} = g\left(1-\frac{d}{R}\right)$

$\Rightarrow \frac{1}{n} = 1 - \frac{d}{R}$

$\Rightarrow \frac{d}{R} = 1 - \frac{1}{n} = \frac{(n-1)}{n}$

$\Rightarrow d = \frac{R(n-1)}{n}$

32 *(c)* The value of acceleration due to gravity changes with height (i.e. altitude). If g' is the acceleration due to gravity at height h above the surface of earth, then

$$g' = \frac{GM}{(R+h)^2}$$

But $g = \frac{GM}{R^2}$

$\Rightarrow \frac{g'}{g} = \frac{GM}{(R+h)^2} \times \frac{R^2}{GM} = \frac{R^2}{(R+h)^2}$

$\Rightarrow \frac{g'}{g} = \frac{R^2}{(R+3R)^2}$ $[\because h = 3R]$

$\Rightarrow \frac{g'}{g} = \frac{1}{16}$

33 *(d)* Given, $d = 100$ km $= 100 \times 10^3$ m and $R = 6380 \times 10^3$ m

Acceleration due to gravity below the earth's surface is given by

$$g' = g\left(1-\frac{d}{R}\right)$$

$\Rightarrow g' = 9.8\left[1-\frac{100\times 10^3}{6380\times 10^3}\right]$

$= 9.8\left[1-\frac{1}{63.8}\right]$

$= 9.8 \times \frac{62.8}{63.8} = 9.66 \text{ ms}^{-2}$

34 *(b)* Weight at earth's surface $w = mg$

Acceleration due to gravity at earth's surface, $g = \frac{GM_e}{R_e^2}$

For planet, $g' = \frac{GM_p}{R_p^2} = \frac{GM_e/7}{(R_e/2)^2}$

$= \frac{4}{7}\frac{GM_e}{R_e^2} = \frac{4}{7}g$

Given, $M_p = M_e/7$ and $R_p = \frac{R_e}{2}$

$\therefore$ Weight at the surface of planet $= mg'$

$= m\left(\frac{4g}{7}\right)$

$= \frac{4}{7}mg = \frac{4}{7} \times 700$

$= 400$ g-wt

35 Acceleration due to gravity on the surface of the planet is

$$g_p = \frac{GM_p}{R_p^2}$$

Given, $M_p = \frac{M_e}{2}$ and $R_p = \frac{R_e}{2}$

$\therefore g_p = \frac{G(M_e/2)}{(R_e/2)^2} = \frac{2GM_e}{R_e} = 2g_e.$

Topic 3

Gravitational Potential Energy and Escape Velocity

2019

1 The work done to raise a mass m from the surface of the earth to a height h, which is equal to the radius of the earth, is **[NEET]**

(a) $2mgR$ (b) $\frac{1}{2}mgR$ (c) $\frac{3}{2}mgR$ (d) mgR

2 Assuming that the gravitational potential energy of an object at infinity is zero, the change in potential energy (final – initial) of an object of mass m, when taken to a height h from the surface of earth (of radius R) is given by **[NEET (Odisha)]**

(a) $-\frac{GMm}{R+h}$ (b) $\frac{GMmh}{R(R+h)}$

(c) mgh (d) $\frac{GMm}{R+h}$

3 If escape velocity on earth surface is $11.1\ \text{kmh}^{-1}$, then find the escape velocity on moon surface. If mass of moon is $\frac{1}{81}$ times of mass of earth and radius of moon is $\frac{1}{4}$ times radius of earth. **[JIPMER]**

(a) $2.46\ \text{kmh}^{-1}$ (b) $3.46\ \text{kmh}^{-1}$

(c) $4.4\ \text{kmh}^{-1}$ (d) None of these

2017

4 A spaceship is launched into a circular orbit close to earth's surface. What additional velocity has now to be imparted to the spaceship in the orbit to overcome the gravitational pull? (Radius of earth = 6400 km and $g = 9.8\ \text{ms}^{-2}$) **[AIIMS]**

(a) $3.28\ \text{kms}^{-1}$ (b) $12\ \text{kms}^{-1}$

(c) $10\ \text{kms}^{-1}$ (d) $40\ \text{kms}^{-1}$

5 What is the maximum height attained by a body projected with a velocity equal to one-third of the escape velocity from the surface of the earth? (Radius of the earth = R) **[AIIMS]**

(a) $R/2$ (b) $R/3$ (c) $R/5$ (d) $R/8$

2016

6 At what height from the surface of earth, the gravitation potential and the value of g are $-5.4\times10^{7}\ \text{Jkg}^{-2}$ and $6.0\ \text{ms}^{-2}$ respectively? (Take, the radius of earth as 6400 km.) **[NEET]**

(a) 1600 km (b) 1400 km (c) 2000 km (d) 2600 km

7 The ratio of escape velocity at earth (v_e) to the escape velocity at a planet (v_p) whose radius and mean density are twice as that of earth is **[JIPMER]**

(a) $1:2\sqrt{2}$ (b) $1:4$ (c) $1:\sqrt{2}$ (d) $1:2$

2014

8 A body of mass m is raised to a height $10R$ from the surface of the earth, where R is the radius of the earth. The increase in potential energy is (G = universal constant of gravitation, M = mass of the earth and g = acceleration due to gravity) **[MHT CET]**

(a) $\frac{GMm}{11R}$ (b) $\frac{GMm}{10R}$ (c) $\frac{mgR}{11G}$ (d) $\frac{10GMm}{11R}$

9 A mass of 6×10^{24} kg is to be compressed in a sphere in such a way that the escape velocity from the sphere is 3×10^{8} m/s. What should be the radius of the sphere? (Take, $G = 6.67\times10^{-11}\ \text{Nm}^2/\text{kg}^2$) **[JCECE]**

(a) 9 km (b) 9 m (c) 9 cm (d) 9 mm

10 Dependence of intensity of gravitational field (E) of earth with distance (r) from centre of earth is correctly represented by **[CBSE AIPMT]**

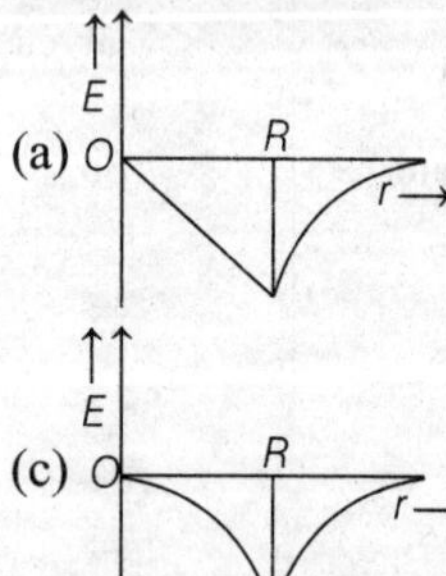

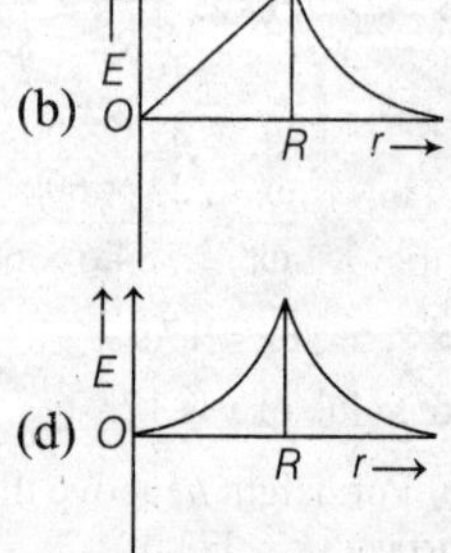

2013

11 A body of mass m taken from the earth's surface to the height equal to twice the radius (R) of the earth. The change in potential energy of body will be **[NEET]**

(a) $mg\,2R$ (b) $\frac{2}{3}mgR$ (c) $3mgR$ (d) $\frac{1}{3}mgR$

12 Infinite number of bodies, each of mass 2 kg are situated on X-axis at distance 1 m, 2 m, 4 m, 8 m,... respectively from the origin. The resulting gravitational potential due to this system at the origin will be **[NEET]**

(a) $-G$ (b) $-\frac{8}{3}G$ (c) $-\frac{4}{3}G$ (d) $-4G$

2012

13 Which one of the following plots represents the variation of gravitational field on a particle with distance r due to a thin spherical shell of radius R? (r is measured from the centre of the spherical shell). **[CBSE AIPMT]**

(a) 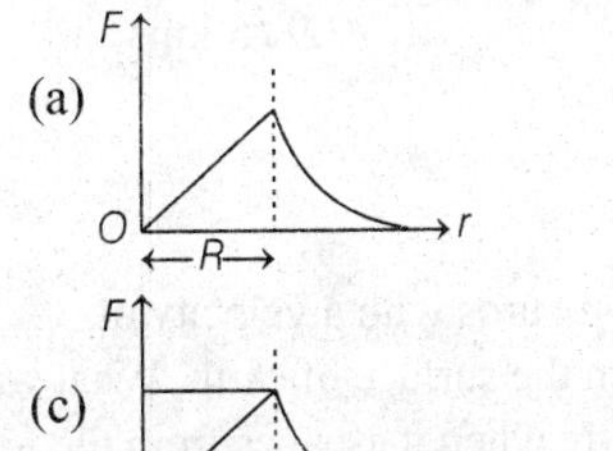
(b) 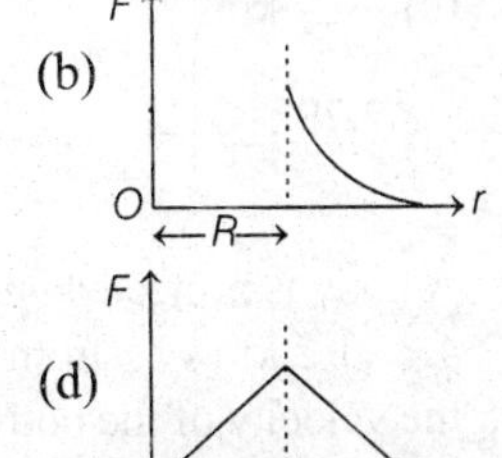
(c)
(d)

14 If g is the acceleration due to gravity on the surface of the earth, the gain in potential energy of an object of mass m raised from the earth's surface to a height equal to the radius R of the earth is **[WB JEE]**

(a) $\frac{mgR}{4}$ (b) $\frac{mgR}{2}$ (c) mgR (d) $2mgR$

15 The escape speed of a body from the surface of earth (radius of earth = R_e) is **[Kerala CEE]**

(a) $\sqrt{gR_e}$ (b) $\sqrt{\frac{gR_e}{2}}$ (c) gR_e (d) $\sqrt{2gR_e}$
(e) $2gR_e$

16 The escape velocity of a body on the surface of earth is $11.2\ \text{kms}^{-1}$. If the earth's mass increases to twice its present value and the radius of the earth becomes half, then the escape velocity would become **[J&K CET]**

(a) $5.6\ \text{kms}^{-1}$ (b) $11.2\ \text{kms}^{-1}$
(c) $44.8\ \text{kms}^{-1}$ (d) $22.4\ \text{kms}^{-1}$

2010

17 Two planets A and B have the same material density. If the radius of A is twice that of B, then the ratio of escape velocity $\frac{v_A}{v_B}$ is **[UP CPMT]**

(a) 2 (b) $\sqrt{2}$
(c) $\frac{1}{\sqrt{2}}$ (d) $\frac{1}{2}$

18 A particle is fired with a speed of $20\ \text{kmh}^{-1}$. The speed with which it will move in intersteller space is (take escape velocity, $v_e = 8\sqrt{2}\ \text{kmh}^{-1}$) **[UP CPMT]**

(a) $16.5\ \text{kmh}^{-1}$ (b) $11.2\ \text{kmh}^{-1}$
(c) $10\ \text{kmh}^{-1}$ (d) $8.8\ \text{kmh}^{-1}$

19 The escape velocity for the earth is v_e. The escape velocity for a planet whose radius is (1/4)th the radius of the earth and mass half that of the earth is **[UP CPMT]**

(a) $\frac{v_e}{\sqrt{2}}$ (b) $\sqrt{2}v_e$ (c) $2v_e$ (d) $\frac{v_e}{2}$

20 The change in the gravitational potential energy when a body of mass m is raised to a height nR above the surface of the earth is (where, R is the radius of the earth) **[WB JEE]**

(a) $\left(\frac{n}{n+1}\right)mgR$ (b) $\left(\frac{n}{n-1}\right)mgR$
(c) $nmgR$ (d) $\frac{mgR}{n}$

21 The energy required to move a satellite of mass m from an orbit of radius $2R$ to $3R$ around earth of mass M is **[Kerala CEE]**

(a) $\frac{GMm}{12R}$ (b) $\frac{GMm}{R}$ (c) $\frac{GMm}{8R}$ (d) $\frac{GMm}{2R}$
(e) $\frac{GMm}{3R}$

2009

22 If both the mass and radius of earth decreases by 1%, then the value of **[Haryana PMT]**

I. acceleration due to gravity would increase by 1%.
II. acceleration due to gravity would decrease by 1%
III. escape velocity from earth's surface would decrease by 1%.
IV. the gravitational potential energy of a body on earth's surface will remain unchanged.

(a) I and III (b) I and IV
(c) II and IV (d) III and IV

23 The maximum vertical distance through which a full dressed astronaut can jump on the earth is 0.5 m. Estimate the maximum vertical distance through which he can jump on the moon, which has a mean density $\left(\frac{2}{3}\right)$rd that of the earth and radius one-quarter that of the earth. **[VMMC]**

(a) 1.5 m (b) 3 m (c) 6 m (d) 7.5 m

2008

24 A particle of mass 10 g is kept on the surface of a uniform sphere of mass 100 kg and radius 10 cm. Find the work to be done against the gravitational force between them, to take the particle far away from the sphere.
(Take, $G = 6.67 \times 10^{-11}\ \text{Nm}^2\text{kg}^{-2}$) **[AIIMS]**

(a) 13.34×10^{-10} J (b) 3.33×10^{-10} J
(c) 6.67×10^{-9} J (d) 6.67×10^{-10} J

25 Two bodies of masses m_1 and m_2 are initially at rest at infinite distance apart. They are then allowed to move towards each other under mutual gravitational attraction. Their relative velocity of approach at a separation distance r between them is **[AIIMS]**

(a) $\left[2G\frac{(m_1 - m_2)}{r}\right]^{1/2}$ (b) $\left[\frac{2G}{r}(m_1 + m_2)\right]^{1/2}$
(c) $\left[\frac{r}{2G(m_1 m_2)}\right]^{1/2}$ (d) $\left[\frac{2G}{r}m_1 m_2\right]^{1/2}$

26 The earth is assumed to be a sphere of radius R. A platform is arranged at a height R from the surface of the earth. The escape velocity of a body from this platform is $f v_e$, where v_e is its escape velocity from the surface of the earth. The value of f is **[Haryana PMT]**

(a) $\sqrt{2}$ (b) $\frac{1}{\sqrt{2}}$ (c) $\frac{1}{3}$ (d) $\frac{1}{2}$

27 The mass of the earth is 6.00×10^{24} kg and that of the moon is 7.40×10^{22} kg. The constant of gravitation $G = 6.67 \times 10^{-11}$ N-m^{2}kg^{-2}. The potential energy of the system is -7.79×10^{28} J. The mean distance between the earth and the moon is **[JCECE]**

(a) 3.80×10^8 m (b) 3.37×10^6 m
(c) 7.60×10^4 m (d) 1.90×10^2 m

2007

28 An asteroid of mass m is approaching earth, initially at a distance of $10R_e$ with speed v_i. It hits the earth with a speed v_f (R_e and M_e are radius and mass of earth), then **[AIIMS]**

(a) $v_f^2 = v_i^2 + \frac{2Gm}{M_e R}\left(1 - \frac{1}{10}\right)$

(b) $v_f^2 = v_i^2 + \frac{2GM_e}{R_e}\left(1 + \frac{1}{10}\right)$

(c) $v_f^2 = v_i^2 + \frac{2GM_e}{R_e}\left(1 - \frac{1}{10}\right)$

(d) $v_f^2 = v_i^2 + \frac{2Gm}{R_e}\left(1 - \frac{1}{10}\right)$

29 The escape velocity of a body from the earth is v_e. If the radius of earth contracts to $(1/4)$th of its value, keeping the mass of the earth constant, then the escape velocity will be **[J&K CET]**

(a) doubled (b) halved (c) tripled (d) unaltered

2006

30 If a spherical shell is cut into two pieces along a chord as shown in figure and point P and Q have gravitational intensities I_P and I_Q respectively, then **[DUMET]**

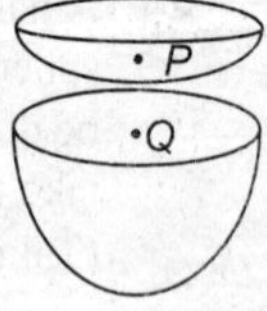

(a) $I_P > I_Q$ (b) $I_P = I_Q = 0$
(c) $I_P = I_Q \neq 0$ (d) $I_P < I_Q$

31 What is the escape velocity for a body on the surface of a planet on which the acceleration due to gravity is $(3.1)^2$ ms^{-2} and whose radius is 8100 km? **[Kerala CEE]**

(a) 2790 km s^{-1} (b) 27.9 km s^{-1}
(c) $\frac{27.9}{\sqrt{5}}$ kms^{-1} (d) $27.9\sqrt{5}$ kms^{-1}
(e) $\frac{2.79}{\sqrt{5}}$ km s^{-1}

32 A body is projected upwards with a velocity of 4×11.2 km s^{-1} from the surface of earth. What will be the velocity of the body when it escapes from the gravitational pull of earth? **[MHT CET]**

(a) 11.2 km s^{-1} (b) 2×11.2 km s^{-1}
(c) 3×11.2 km s^{-1} (d) $\sqrt{15} \times 11.2$ km s^{-1}

2005

33 There are two planets and the ratio of radius of the two planets is K but ratio of acceleration due to gravity of both planets is g. What will be the ratio of their escape velocity? **[BHU]**

(a) $(Kg)^{1/2}$ (b) $(Kg)^{-1/2}$
(c) $(Kg)^2$ (d) $(Kg)^{-2}$

34 At what temperature, hydrogen molecules will escape from the earth's surface? (Take, radius of earth $= 6.4 \times 10^6$ m, mass of hydrogen molecule $= 0.34 \times 10^{-26}$ kg, Boltzmann constant $= 1.38 \times 10^{-23}$ JK^{-1} and acceleration due to gravity $= 9.8$ ms^{-2}) **[AMU]**

(a) 10 K (b) 10^2 K
(c) 10^3 K (d) 10^4 K

35 Escape velocity from a planet is v_e. If its mass is increased to 8 times and its radius is increased to 2 times, then the new escape velocity would be **[DUMET]**

(a) v_e (b) $\sqrt{2}v_e$
(c) $2v_e$ (d) $2\sqrt{2}v_e$

36 A body is projected vertically upwards from the surface of a planet of radius r with a velocity equal to (1/3)rd the escape velocity for the planet. The maximum height attained by the body is **[JCECE]**

(a) $R/2$ (b) $R/3$
(c) $R/5$ (d) $R/9$

Answers

1 (b)	2 (b)	3 (a)	4 (a)	5 (d)	6 (d)	7 (a)	8 (d)	9 (d)	10 (b)
11 (b)	12 (d)	13 (b)	14 (b)	15 (d)	16 (d)	17 (a)	18 (a)	19 (b)	20 (a)
21 (a)	22 (b)	23 (b)	24 (d)	25 (b)	26 (b)	27 (a)	28 (c)	29 (a)	30 (c)
31 (c)	32 (d)	33 (a)	34 (d)	35 (c)	36 (d)				

Explanations

1 (b) As we know, the potential energy of body of mass m on the surface of earth is

$$U_1 = -\frac{GMm}{R} \quad \dots \text{(i)}$$

where, G = gravitational constant, M = mass of earth and R = radius of earth.

When the mass is raised to a height h from the surface of the earth, then the potential energy of the body becomes

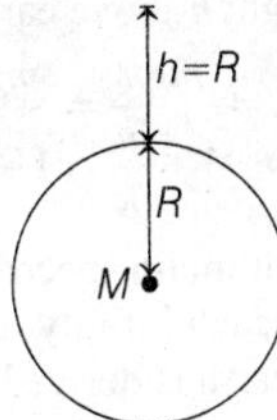

$$U_2 = -\frac{GMm}{(R+h)}$$

Here, $h = R$ (given)

$$\Rightarrow \quad U_2 = -\frac{GMm}{2R} \quad \dots \text{(ii)}$$

Thus, the change in potential energy, $\Delta U = U_2 - U_1$

Substituting the values from Eqs. (i) and (ii), we get

$$\Delta U = -\frac{GMm}{2R} + \frac{GMm}{R}$$

$$= \frac{GMm}{2R} = \frac{gR^2m}{2R} \quad \left[\because g = \frac{GM}{R^2}\right]$$

$$= \frac{mgR}{2}$$

Thus, the work done in raising the mass to a height R is equals to $\frac{mgR}{2}$.

2 (b) The gravitational potential energy of an object placed at earth's surface is

$$U_1 = -\frac{GMm}{R} \quad \dots \text{(i)}$$

where, G = gravitational constant, M = Mass of earth, m = mass of object and R = radius of the earth.

The negative sign in the above relation indicates that it is the work done in bringing the object from infinity to a distance R.

The gravitational potential energy of object at a height h above the surface of earth is

$$U_2 = -\frac{GMm}{(R+h)} \quad \dots \text{(ii)}$$

So, the change in potential energy is

$$\Delta U = U_2 - U_1 = -\frac{GMm}{R+h} - \left(-\frac{GMm}{R}\right)$$

[From Eq. (i) and (ii)]

$$= -GMm\left[\frac{1}{(R+h)} - \frac{1}{R}\right]$$

$$= -GMm\left(-\frac{h}{R(R+h)}\right)$$

$$= \frac{GMmh}{R(R+h)}$$

3 (a) Given, Escape velocity on the surface of earth, $v_e = 11.1$ km/h

i.e. $\quad v_e = \sqrt{2gR_e}$

$$v_e = \sqrt{\frac{2GM_e}{R_e}}$$

Mass of moon, $M_m = \frac{M_e}{81}$

Radius of moon, $R_m = \frac{R_e}{4}$

$\therefore$ Escape velocity on the surface of moon

$$v_m = \sqrt{\frac{2G\,M_m}{R_m}} = \sqrt{\frac{2G\,\frac{Me}{81}}{\frac{R_e}{4}}}$$

$$= \frac{2\sqrt{2}}{9}\sqrt{\frac{GM_e}{R_e}}$$

$$= \frac{2}{9}\sqrt{\frac{2GM_e}{R_e}} = \frac{2}{9}v_e$$

$$= \frac{2}{9} \times 11.1 = 2.46 \text{ km h}^{-1}$$

4 (a) The orbital velocity of space ship in circular orbit, $v_o = \sqrt{\frac{GM}{r}}$

If space ship is very close to earth surface, then r = radius of earth (R)

$$\therefore \quad v_o = \sqrt{\frac{GM}{R}} = \sqrt{\frac{R^2g}{R}} = \sqrt{Rg}$$

$$\left(\text{since, } g = \frac{GM}{R^2}\right)$$

Here, $R = 6400$ km $= 6.4 \times 10^6$ m

and $\quad g = 9.8 \text{ms}^{-2}$

$$\therefore \quad v_0 = \sqrt{6.4 \times 10^6 \times 9\cdot 8}$$

$$= 7.92 \times 10^3 \text{m/s}$$

$$= 7.92 \text{ km s}^{-1}$$

The escape velocity of spaceship

$$v_e = \sqrt{(2Rg)} = \sqrt{2}\,v_0$$

$$= \sqrt{2} \times 7.92 = 11.20 \text{ km s}^{-1}$$

$\therefore$ Additional velocity required

$$= 11.20 - 7.92$$

$$= 3.28 \text{ km s}^{-1}$$

Therefore, velocity 3.28 km/s must be added to orbital velocity to spaceship to overcome the gravitational pull.

5 (d) From conservation of energy,

$$\frac{1}{2}mv_1^2 - \frac{GM_em}{R} = \frac{1}{2}mv_2^2 - \frac{GM_em}{R+H}$$

Here, $v_2^2 = 0$ (At maximum height)

$$\therefore \quad \frac{1}{2}mv_1 - \frac{GM_em}{R} = -\frac{GM_em}{R+H}$$

Solving, we get

$$H = \frac{R}{\frac{2gR}{v_1^2} - 1} = \frac{R}{\frac{v_e^2}{v_1^2} - 1}$$

$$[\because v_e = \sqrt{2gR}]$$

where, v_e is escape velocity.

Here, $\quad v = \frac{1}{3}v_e \Rightarrow \frac{v_e}{v} = 3$

$$\therefore \quad H = \frac{R}{9-1} = \frac{R}{8}$$

6 (d) Gravitational potential at some height h from the surface of the earth is given by

$$V = -\frac{GM}{R+h} \quad \dots \text{(i)}$$

And acceleration due to gravity at some height h from the earth surface can be given as

$$g' = \frac{GM}{(R+h)^2} \quad \dots \text{(ii)}$$

From Eqs. (i) and (ii), we get

$$\frac{|V|}{g'} = \frac{GM}{(R+h)} \times \frac{(R+h)^2}{GM}$$

$$\Rightarrow \quad \frac{|V|}{g'} = R + h \quad \text{(iii)}$$

Given, $V = -5.4 \times 10^7$ J-kg^{-2}

$g' = 6.0 \text{ ms}^{-2}$ and

radius of earth, $R = 6400$ km.

Substitute these values in Eq. (iii), we get

$$\frac{5.4 \times 10^7}{6.0} = R + h$$

$$\Rightarrow \quad 9 \times 10^6 = R + h$$

$\Rightarrow \quad h = (9 - 6.4) \times 10^6 = 2.6 \times 10^6$ m

$\Rightarrow \quad h = 2600$ km

7 (a) Since, the escape velocity of earth can be given as

$$v_e = \sqrt{2gR} = R\sqrt{\frac{8}{3}\pi G\rho}$$

$$\left[\because g = \frac{4}{3}\pi G\rho R\right]$$

[ρ = density of earth]

$$\Rightarrow \quad v_e = R\sqrt{\frac{8}{3}\pi G\rho} \quad \ldots(i)$$

As it is given that, the radius and mean density of planet are twice as that of earth. So, escape velocity at planet will be

$$v_p = 2R\sqrt{\frac{8}{3}\pi G 2\rho} \quad \ldots(ii)$$

Divide Eq. (i) by Eq. (ii), we get

$$\frac{v_e}{v_p} = \frac{R\sqrt{\frac{8}{3}\pi G\rho}}{2R\sqrt{\frac{8}{3}\pi G 2\rho}}$$

$$\Rightarrow \quad \frac{v_e}{v_p} = \frac{1}{2\sqrt{2}}$$

8 (d) Potential energy at the earth's surface

$$V = \frac{-GMm}{R}$$

Potential energy at a height h above the earth's surface

$$V_h = \frac{-GMm}{(R+h)}$$

$\therefore$ Change in potential energy

$$V_h - V = \frac{-GMm}{(R+h)} - \left(-\frac{GMm}{R}\right)$$

$$= \frac{GMmh}{R(R+h)}$$

Substituting, $h = 10R$ in Eq. (i), we get

$$\Delta PE = \frac{GMm \times 10R}{R(R+10R)} = \frac{10\,GMm}{11R}$$

9 (d) Let escape velocity be v_e, then kinetic energy is

$$KE = \frac{1}{2}mv_e^2 \quad \ldots(i)$$

and escape energy $= + \dfrac{GM_e m}{R_e} \quad \ldots(ii)$

Equating Eqs. (i) and (ii), we get

$$\frac{1}{2}mv_e^2 = \frac{GM_e m}{R_e}$$

$$\Rightarrow \quad v_e = \sqrt{\frac{2GM_e}{R_e}}$$

$$\Rightarrow \quad R = \frac{2GM_e}{v_e^2}$$

Given, $G = 6.67 \times 10^{-11}$ Nm^2 / kg,

$M_e = 6 \times 10^{24}$ kg and $v_e = 3 \times 10^8$ m/s^2

$$\text{So, } R = \frac{2 \times 6.67 \times 10^{-11} \times 6 \times 10^{24}}{(3 \times 10^8)^2}$$

$$= 8.89 \times 10^{-3}$$

$$R \approx 9 \times 10^{-3} \text{ m} = 9 \text{ mm}$$

10 (b) Dependence of gravitational field (E) with distance is depicted properly in option (a) because at centre $r = 0$,

$$\therefore \quad E = \frac{GM}{R^2} = 0$$

For a point outside the earth $R > R$

$$E = \frac{GM}{r^2} \Rightarrow E \propto \frac{1}{r^2}$$

and at the surface of earth $r = R$

$$E = \frac{GM}{R^2}$$

Inside the eath, $r < R$

$$E = \frac{GMr}{R^3} \Rightarrow E \propto r$$

11 (b) Change in potential energy,

$$\Delta U = -\frac{GMm}{R+2R} - \left(\frac{-GMm}{R}\right)$$

$(\because h = 2R)$

$$= -\frac{GMm}{3R} + \frac{GMm}{R} = \frac{2GMm}{3R}$$

$$\left[\because g = \frac{GM}{R^2}\right]$$

$$= \frac{2}{3}mgR$$

12 (d) As we know,

$$V = -\frac{GM}{r} = -G2\sum_{i=1}^{\infty}\frac{1}{r_i}, \quad [\because M = 2\text{kg}]$$

So, the resulting gravitational potential,

$$V = -2G\left(\frac{1}{1} + \frac{1}{2} + \frac{1}{4} + \frac{1}{8} \ldots\right)$$

$$= -2G\left(1 + \frac{1}{2} + \frac{1}{2^2} + \frac{1}{2^3} \ldots\right)$$

$$\Rightarrow \quad V = -2G\left(1 - \frac{1}{2}\right)^{-1}$$

$$\Rightarrow \quad V = \frac{-2G}{\left(1 - \frac{1}{2}\right)} = \frac{-2G}{\frac{1}{2}} = -4G$$

13 (b) Among the four plots, option (b) is the correct one, because in case of spherical shell.

Gravitational field inside the surface $r < R$ field, $F = 0$ upto $r = R$. But at $r = R$, it becomes equal to $\dfrac{GM}{R^2}$ and at $r > R$, it will be equal to $\dfrac{GM}{r^2}$, where r = distance of mass from centre of body.

14 (b) The change in potential energy on going height h above earth surface,

$$\Delta PE = \frac{mgh}{1 + \frac{h}{R}} = \frac{mgR}{1 + \frac{R}{R}} = \frac{mgR}{2}$$

15 (d) The minimum speed required for an object to reach infinity, i.e to escape from the earth is derived by

$$\frac{1}{2}mv_e^2 = \frac{GM_e m}{R}.$$

From earth's surface,

$$v_e = \sqrt{\frac{2GM_e}{R}}$$

$$\Rightarrow \quad v_e = \sqrt{2gR_e}$$

16 (d) Escape velocity,

$$v_e = \sqrt{\frac{2GM}{R}} = \sqrt{\frac{2G \times 2M}{R/2}} = 2\sqrt{\frac{2GM}{R}}$$

$$= 2 \times 11.2 \text{ km s}^{-1}$$

$$= 22.4 \text{ km s}^{-1}$$

17 (a) Escape velocity is given by

$$v_e = \sqrt{\frac{2GM}{R}} = \sqrt{\frac{2G}{R} \times \frac{4}{3}\pi R^3\rho}$$

$$\Rightarrow \quad v_e = R\sqrt{\frac{8}{3}\pi G\rho}$$

$$\Rightarrow \quad v \propto R$$

$$\therefore \quad \frac{v_A}{v_B} = \frac{R_A}{R_B} = 2 \quad [\because R_A = 2R_B]$$

18 (a) Using law of conservation of energy,

$$\frac{1}{2}mv^2 = \frac{1}{2}m[(20)^2 - v_e^2]$$

Here, escape velocity $v_e = 8\sqrt{2}$ kmh^{-1}

$$\therefore \quad v^2 = (20)^2 - (8\sqrt{2})^2$$

$$= 400 - 128 = 272$$

So, $\quad v = 16.5$ kmh^{-1}

19 (b) Escape velocity of a body from the earth's surface, $v_e = \sqrt{\dfrac{2GM_e}{R_e}} \quad \ldots(i)$

So, from the question, $M_p = \frac{M_e}{2}$ and

$$R_p = \frac{R_e}{4}$$

Putting these values in Eq. (i), we get

$$v'_e = \sqrt{\frac{2G \times M_e \times 4}{2R_e}} = \sqrt{2} v_e$$

20 (a) Gravitational potential energy of mass m at earth's surface,

$$U_e = -\frac{GMm}{R}$$

Gravitational potential energy of same mass at a height nR from the earth's surface,

$$U_h = -\frac{GMm}{(R + nR)} = -\frac{GMm}{R(n+1)}$$

Thus, magnitude of the change in gravitational potential energy,

$$\Delta U = U_h - U_e = \frac{GMm}{R}\left\{1 - \frac{1}{(n+1)}\right\}$$

$$= \left(\frac{n}{n+1}\right)\frac{GMm}{R} = \left(\frac{n}{n+1}\right) mgR$$

$$(\because GM = gR^2)$$

21 (a) Energy required = Total energy (final) – Total energy (initial)

$$= \left[\frac{-GMm}{2(3R)}\right] - \left[\frac{-GMm}{2(2R)}\right]$$

$$= \frac{GMm}{4R} - \frac{GMm}{6R} = \frac{GMm}{12R}$$

22 (b) If both the mass and radius of the earth decreases by 1%, the value of acceleration due to gravity,

$$g' = \frac{G(0.99M_e)}{(0.99R_e)^2}$$

$$\approx 1.01 \frac{GM_e}{R_e^2} = 1.01\, g$$

So, g would increase by

$$(1.01 - 1) \times 100\% = 1\%$$

New escape velocity would be

$$v'_e = \sqrt{\frac{2 \times 0.99\, M_e G}{0.99\, R_e}}$$

$$= \sqrt{\frac{2GM_e}{R_e}} = v_e$$

So, it will remain unchanged.

Also, gravitational potential energy

$$= \frac{Gm(0.99\, M_e)}{0.99\, R_e}$$

$$= -\frac{GM_e m}{R_e}$$

Hence, it will also remain same.

23 (b) On moon, $g_m = \frac{4}{3}\pi G R_m P_m$

$$= \frac{4}{3}\pi G\left(\frac{R}{4}\right)\left(\frac{2\rho}{3}\right)$$

$$= \frac{1}{6}\left(\frac{4}{3}\pi G R\rho\right)$$

$$= \frac{1}{6} g$$

Work done in jumping will be same,

i.e. $mg \times 0.5 = m \times \left(\frac{g}{6}\right) h_1$

$$\Rightarrow \quad h_1 = 0.5 \times 6$$

$$= 3.0 \text{ m}$$

24 (d) Given, $M = 100$ kg, $m = 10g$

$$= 10 \times 10^{-3} \text{kg}$$

$$= 10^2 \text{kg}$$

and $r = 10\text{cm} = 0.1\text{m}$

As gravitational potential energy,

$$U_i = -\frac{GMm}{r}$$

So, $U_i = -\frac{6.67 \times 10^{-11} \times 100 \times 10^{-2}}{0.1}$

$$\Rightarrow U_i = -\frac{6.67 \times 10^{-11}}{0.1}$$

$$= -6.67 \times 10^{-10} \text{J}$$

Hence, $W = -U_i$

$$= +6.67 \times 10^{-10} \text{J}$$

25 (b) Let velocities of these masses at r distance from each other be v_1 and v_2 respectively.

By the law of conservation of momentum,

$$m_1 v_1 - m_2 v_2 = 0$$

$$\Rightarrow \quad m_1 v_1 = m_2 v_2 \quad \ldots\text{(i)}$$

By the law of conservation of energy,

Change in PE = Change in KE

$$\frac{Gm_1 m_2}{r} = \frac{1}{2} m_1 v_1^2 + \frac{1}{2} m_2 v_2^2$$

$$\Rightarrow \frac{m_1^2 v_1^2}{m_1} + \frac{m_2^2 v_2^2}{m_2} = \frac{2Gm_1 m_2}{r} \quad \ldots\text{(ii)}$$

On solving Eqs. (i) and (ii)

$$v_1 = \sqrt{\frac{2Gm_2^2}{r(m_1 + m_2)}}$$

and $v_2 = \sqrt{\frac{2Gm_1^2}{r(m_1 + m_2)}}$

$$\therefore \quad v_{\text{app}} = |v_1| + |v_2|$$

$$= \sqrt{\frac{2G}{r}(m_1 + m_2)}$$

26 (b) At a platform at a height h, energy = binding energy of sphere

$$\Rightarrow \frac{1}{2} m v'^2_e = \frac{GMm}{R+h}$$

$$\Rightarrow \quad v'_e = \sqrt{\frac{2\,GM}{R+h}} = \sqrt{\frac{2\,GM}{2R}}$$

$$(\because h = R)$$

But at surface of earth, $v_e = \sqrt{\frac{2GM}{R}}$

As given, $v'_e = f v_e$

Hence, $\sqrt{\frac{2GM}{2R}} = f\sqrt{\frac{2GM}{R}}$

or $\frac{1}{2R} = \frac{f^2}{R} \Rightarrow f = \frac{1}{\sqrt{2}}$

27 (a) Given, $U = -7.79 \times 10^{28}$ J

$$G = 6.67 \text{ N-m}^2\text{kg}^{-2}$$

$$m = 6 \times 10^{24} \text{ kg}$$

and $M = 7.40 \times 10^{22}$ kg

Potential energy of the system,

$$U = \frac{-GMm}{R}$$

$$\Rightarrow -7.79 \times 10^{28} = \frac{-6.67 \times 10^{-11} \times 7.4 \times 10^{22} \times 6 \times 10^{24}}{R}$$

$$R = \frac{-6.67 \times 10^{-11} \times 7.4 \times 10^{22} \times 6 \times 10^{24}}{-7.79 \times 10^{28}}$$

$$\Rightarrow R = 3.8 \times 10^8 \text{ m}$$

28 (c) Applying law of conservation of energy for asteroid at a distance $10\, R_e$ and at earth's surface,

$$K_i + U_i = K_f + U_f \quad \ldots\text{(i)}$$

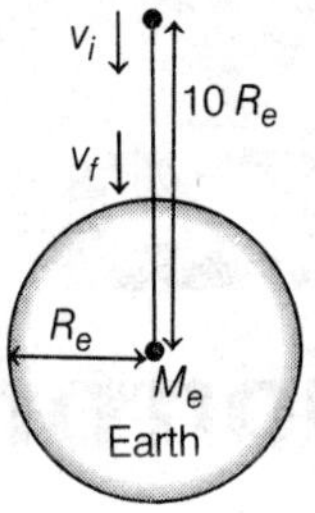

Now, $K_i = \frac{1}{2} m v_i^2$

and $U_i = -\frac{GM_e m}{10R_e}$

$K_f = \frac{1}{2} m v_f^2$ and $U_f = -\frac{GM_e m}{R_e}$

On substituting these values in Eq. (i), we get

$$\frac{1}{2} m v_i^2 - \frac{GM_e m}{10R_e} = \frac{1}{2} m v_f^2 - \frac{GM_e m}{R_e}$$

$$\frac{1}{2}mv_f^2 = \frac{1}{2}mv_i^2 + \frac{GM_em}{R_e} - \frac{GM_em}{10R_e}$$

$$\Rightarrow \quad v_f^2 = v_i^2 + \frac{2GM_e}{R_e} - \frac{2GM_e}{10R_e}$$

$$\therefore \quad v_f^2 = v_i^2 + \frac{2GM_e}{R_e}\left(1 - \frac{1}{10}\right)$$

29 (a) Escape velocity, $v_e = \sqrt{\frac{2\,GM}{R}}$

If $R' = \frac{R}{4}$ (given)

$$\Rightarrow \quad v_e' = 2\sqrt{\frac{2GM}{R}}$$

Since, G and M are constant, hence $v'_e = 2v_e$

30 (c) We know that inside a spherical shell gravitational field intensity at any point is zero, hence

$$I_P + I_Q = 0$$

$$\Rightarrow \quad I_P = I_Q \neq 0$$

31 (c) Escape velocity, $v_e = \sqrt{2gR}$

Given, $g = (3.1)^2 \text{ms}^{-2}$

$R = 8100$ km $= 8100 \times 10^3$ m

$$\therefore \quad v_e = \sqrt{2 \times (3.1)^2 \times 8100 \times 10^3}$$

$$v_e = 12.5 \times 10^3 \text{ms}^{-1} \approx \frac{27.9}{\sqrt{5}} \text{ kms}^{-1}$$

32 (d) Initial KE of the body $= \frac{1}{2}mv^2$

Here, $v = 4 \times 11.2 \text{ kms}^{-1}$

So, KE $= \frac{1}{2} \times \text{m}\,(4 \times 11.2)^2 = 16 \times \frac{1}{2}mv_e^2$

As $\frac{1}{2}mv_e^2$ energy is used up in coming out from the gravitational pull of the earth, so final KE should be $15 \times \frac{1}{2}mv_e^2$.

Hence, $\frac{1}{2}mv'^2 = 15 \times \frac{1}{2}mv_e^2$

$$\therefore \quad v'^2 = 15v_e^2$$

$$\Rightarrow \quad v = \sqrt{15}v_e = \sqrt{15} \times 11.2 \text{ kms}^{-1}$$

33 (a) Escape velocity, $v_e = \sqrt{2g_eR}$

where, g_e is acceleration due to gravity and R is radius.

Given, $\frac{R_1}{R_2} = K, \frac{g_1}{g_2} = g$

$$\Rightarrow \quad \frac{v_1}{v_2} = \frac{\sqrt{g_1R_1}}{\sqrt{g_2R_2}} = \sqrt{Kg}$$

$$\Rightarrow \quad \frac{v_1}{v_2} = (Kg)^{\frac{1}{2}}$$

34 (d) The root mean square velocity of gas is

$$v_{\text{rms}} = \sqrt{\frac{3kT}{m}} \quad \ldots\text{(i)}$$

Escape velocity of the gas molecules is

$$v_e = \sqrt{2gR_e} \quad \ldots\text{(ii)}$$

As the root mean square velocity of gas molecules must be equal to the escape velocity.

$\therefore$ From Eqs. (i) and (ii), we get

$$\sqrt{\frac{3kT}{m}} = \sqrt{2gR_e}$$

$$\Rightarrow \quad T = \frac{2gR_em}{3k}$$

$$\Rightarrow T = \frac{2 \times 9.8 \times 6.4 \times 10^6 \times 0.34 \times 10^{-26}}{3\,(1.38 \times 10^{-23})}$$ [given]

$= 10^4$K

Therefore, 10^4K is the temperature at which hydrogen molecules will escape from earth's surface.

35 (c) Escape velocity of a body on earth surface is given by

$$v_e = \sqrt{\frac{2GM}{R}}$$

where, G is gravitational constant, M is mass of planet and R is radius.

When $M' = 8M, R' = 2R$, then

$$\Rightarrow \quad v_e' = \sqrt{\frac{2G(8M)}{(2R)}} = 2\sqrt{\frac{2GM}{R}}$$

$$\Rightarrow \quad v_e' = 2v_e$$

36 (d) Let h be the maximum height attained, then from the law of equation of motion

$$v^2 = u^2 + 2gh$$

When $u = 0$

$$\Rightarrow \quad v = \sqrt{2gh}$$

Given, $v = \frac{v_e}{3}$, where, $v_e = \sqrt{2gR}$

$$\Rightarrow \quad \sqrt{2gh} = \frac{1}{3}\sqrt{2gR}$$

On squaring both sides of equation, we get

$$h = \frac{R}{9}$$

Topic 4

Motion of Satellite and Kepler's Laws of Planetary Motion

2019

1 The time period of a geo-stationary satellite is 24 h, at a height $6R_E$ (R_E is the radius of earth) from surface of earth. The time period of another satellite whose height is 2.5 R_E from surface will be **[[NEET (Odisha)]**

(a) $6\sqrt{2}$ h (b) $12\sqrt{2}$ h (c) $\frac{24}{2.5}$ h (d) $\frac{12}{2.5}$ h

2 A planet of radius R has a time period of revolution T. Find time period of a planet of radius $9R$? **[JIPMER]**

(a) $3\sqrt{3}\,T$ (b) $9T$

(c) $27T$ (d) $9\sqrt{3}\,T$

2018

3 The kinetic energies of a planet in an elliptical orbit about the sun, at positions A, B and C are K_A, K_B and K_C, respectively. AC is the major axis and SB is perpendicular to AC at the position of the sun S as shown in the figure. Then **[NEET]**

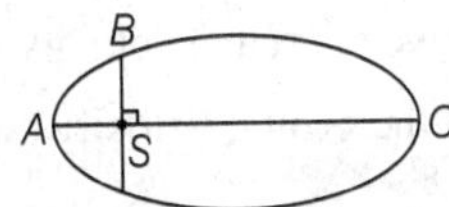

(a) $K_B < K_A < K_C$
(b) $K_A > K_B > K_C$
(c) $K_A < K_B < K_C$
(d) $K_B > K_A > K_C$

4 Two satellites A and B revolve round the same planet in coplanar circular orbits lying in the same plane. Their periods of revolutions are 1 h and 8 h, respectively. The radius of the orbit of A is 10^4 km. The speed of B is relative to A, when they are closed in km/h is **[AIIMS]**

(a) $3\pi \times 10^4$ (b) zero
(c) $2\pi \times 10^4$ (d) $\pi \times 10^4$

5 A planet is revolving around the sun in a circular orbit with a radius r. The time period is T. If the force between the planet and star is proportional to $r^{-3/2}$, then the square of time period is proportional to **[AIIMS]**

(a) $r^{3/2}$ (b) r^2 (c) r (d) $r^{5/2}$

2016

6 A satellite of mass m is orbiting the earth (of radius R) at a height h from its surface. The total energy of the satellite in terms of g_0, if the value of acceleration due to gravity at the earth's surface is g_0 **[NEET]**

(a) $\frac{mg_0R^2}{2(R+h)}$ (b) $-\frac{mg_0R^2}{2(R+h)}$
(c) $\frac{2mg_0R^2}{R+h}$ (d) $-\frac{2mg_0R^2}{R+h}$

7 Kepler's third law states that square of period of revolution (T) of a planet around the sun, is proportional to third power of average distance r between the sun and planet, i.e. $T^2 = Kr^3$, here K is constant.
If the masses of the sun and planet are M and m respectively, then as per Newton's law of gravitation force of attraction between them is
$F = \frac{GMm}{r^2}$, here G is gravitational constant. **[AIPMT]**
The relation between G and K is described as

(a) $GK = 4\pi^2$ (b) $GMK = 4\pi^2$
(c) $K = G$ (d) $K = \frac{I}{G}$

2014

8 An artificial satellite moves in a circular orbit around the earth. Total energy of the satellite is given by E. The potential energy of the satellite is **[WB JEE]**

(a) $-2E$ (b) $2E$
(c) $\frac{2E}{3}$ (d) $-\frac{2E}{3}$

9 What is a period of revolution of the earth satellite? Ignore the height of satellite above the surface of the earth.
Given,
(i) The value of gravitational acceleration, $g = 10\,\text{ms}^{-2}$.
(ii) Radius of the earth, $R_E = 6400$ km. (take, $\pi = 3.14$)

(a) 85 min (b) 156 min **[KCET]**
(c) 83.73 min (d) 90 min

10 At a height H from the surface of earth, the total energy of a satellite is equal to the potential energy of a body of equal mass at a height $3R$ from the surface of the earth (R = radius of the earth). The value of H is **[EAMCET]**

(a) R (b) $\frac{4R}{3}$ (c) $3R$ (d) $\frac{R}{3}$

11 Keeping the mass of the earth as constant, if its radius is reduced to $\frac{1}{4}$ th of its initial value, then the period of revolution of the earth about its own axis and passing through the centre, (in hours) is (assume the earth to be a solid sphere and its initial period of rotation as 24 h) **[EAMCET]**

(a) 12 (b) 3
(c) 6 (d) 1.5

2013

12 The largest and the shortest distances of the earth from the sun are r_1 and r_2. Its distance from the sun when it is at the perpendicular to the major axis of the orbit drawn from the sun is **[UP CPMT]**

(a) $\frac{r_1 + r_2}{4}$ (b) $\frac{r_1 r_2}{r_1 + r_2}$
(c) $\frac{2r_1 r_2}{r_1 + r_2}$ (d) $\frac{2r_1}{r_1 + r_2}$

13 Two satellites A and B go around a planet P in circular orbits having radius $4R$ and R, respectively. If the speed of satellite A is $3v$, then the speed of satellite B will be **[Manipal]**

(a) $6v$ (b) $9v$
(c) $3v$ (d) None of these

2012

14 A geostationary satellite is orbiting the earth at a height of $5R$ above the surface of the earth, R being the radius of the earth. The time period of another satellite (in hours) at a height of $2R$ from the surface of the earth is **[CBSE AIPMT]**

(a) 5 (b) 10
(c) $6\sqrt{2}$ (d) $6/\sqrt{2}$

15 A satellite is launched into a circular orbit of radius R around the earth. A second satellite is launched into an orbit of radius $4R$. The ratio of their respective periods is **[Kerala CEE]**

(a) 4 : 1 (b) 1 : 8
(c) 8 : 1 (d) 1 : 4
(e) 1 : 2

16 Consider a satellite orbiting the earth as shown in the figure below. Let L_a and L_p represent the angular momentum of the satellite about the earth when at aphelion and perihelion, respectively. Consider the following relations, **[AMU]**

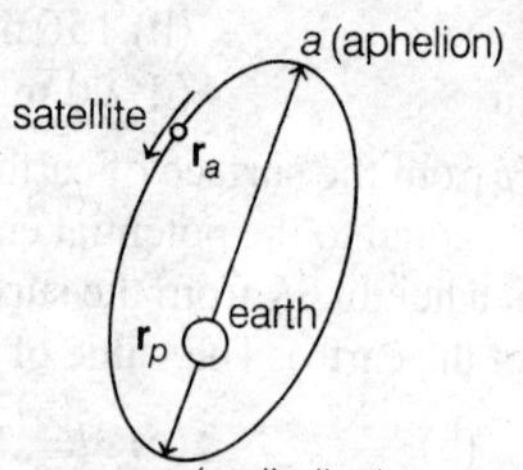

I. $\mathbf{L}_a = \mathbf{L}_p$ II. $\mathbf{L}_a = -\mathbf{L}_p$
III. $\mathbf{r}_a \times \mathbf{L}_a = \mathbf{r}_p \times \mathbf{L}_p$

Which of the above relations is/are true?
(a) Only I (b) Only II
(c) Only III (d) I and III

17 Average distance of the earth from the sun is L_1. If one year of the earth = D days, one year of another planet whose average distance from the sun is L_2 will be **[WB JEE]**

(a) $D\left(\frac{L_2}{L_1}\right)^{1/2}$ days (b) $D\left(\frac{L_2}{L_1}\right)^{3/2}$ days
(c) $D\left(\frac{L_2}{L_1}\right)^{2/3}$ days (d) $D\left(\frac{L_2}{L_1}\right)$ days

2011

18 The time period T of the moon of planet mars (mass M_m) is related to its orbital radius R (G = Gravitational constant) as **[Kerala CEE]**

(a) $T^2 = \frac{4\pi^2 R^3}{GM_m}$ (b) $T^2 = \frac{4\pi^2 GR^3}{M_m}$
(c) $T^2 = \frac{2\pi R^3 G}{M_m}$ (d) $T^2 = 4\pi M_m GR^3$
(e) $T^2 = GM_m R^3$

19 Two satellites of mass m and $9m$ are orbiting a planet in orbits of radius R. Their periods of revolution will be in the ratio of **[KCET]**

(a) 9:1 (b) 3:1
(c) 1 : 1 (d) 1 : 3

2010

20 By what percent, the energy of a satellite has to be increased to shift it from an orbit of radius r to $\frac{3}{2}r$? **[UP CPMT]**

(a) 15% (b) 20.3%
(c) 66.7% (d) 33.33%

21 The relation between escape velocity (v_e) from the surface of the earth and the orbital velocity (v_o) is **[Kerala CEE]**

(a) $\sqrt{2}v_e = v$ (b) $v_e = \sqrt{2}v_o$
(c) $v_e = 2v_o$ (d) $4v_e = 3v_o$
(e) $v_e = \sqrt{3}v_o$

22 A research satellite of mass 200 kg circles the earth in an orbit of average radius $\frac{3R}{2}$, where R is the radius of earth. Assuming the gravitational pull on a mass of 1 kg on the earth's surface to be 10 N, the pull on the satellite will be **[VMMC]**

(a) 880 N (b) 889 N
(c) 885 N (d) 892 N

2009

23 The period of revolution of an earth's satellite close to surface of earth is 90 min. The time period of another satellite in an orbit at a distance of four times the radius of earth from its surface will be **[AIIMS]**

(a) $90\sqrt{9}$ min (b) 270 min
(c) 720 min (d) 360 min

2008

24 A satellite in a circular orbit of radius R has a period of 4 h. Another satellite with orbital radius $3R$ around the same planet will have a period (in hour) **[AFMC]**

(a) 16 (b) 4 (c) $4\sqrt{27}$ (d) $4\sqrt{8}$

25 A synchronous relay satellite reflects TV signals and transmits TV programme from one part of the world to the other, because its **[Manipal]**

(a) period of revolution is greater than the period of rotation of the earth about its axis
(b) period of revolution is less than the period of rotation of the earth about its axis
(c) period of revolution is equal to the period of rotation of the earth about its axis
(d) mass is less than the mass of earth

26 Two satellites of earth, S_1 and S_2, are moving in the same orbit. The mass of S_1 is four times the mass of S_2. Which one of the following statements is true? **[MHT CET]**

(a) The time period of S_1 is four times that of S_2
(b) The potential energies of earth and satellite in the two cases are equal.
(c) S_1 and S_2 are moving with the same speed
(d) The kinetic energies of the two satellites are equal

27 The time period of a satellite of earth is 5 h. If the separation between the earth and the satellite is increased to 4 times the previous value, then the new time period will become **[RPMT]**

(a) 10 h (b) 80 h (c) 40 h (d) 20 h

2007

28 The earth moves in an elliptical orbit with the sun S at one of foci as shown in the figure. Its rotational kinetic energy is maximum at the point **[UP CPMT]**

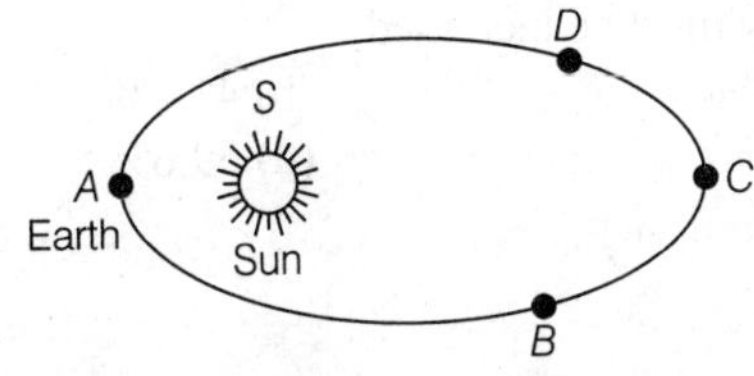

(a) A (b) B
(c) C (d) D

29 The satellite of mass m revolving in a circular orbit of radius r around the earth has kinetic energy E. Then, its angular momentum will be **[Kerala CEE]**

(a) $\sqrt{\frac{E}{mr^2}}$ (b) $\frac{E}{2mr^2}$
(c) $\sqrt{2Emr^2}$ (d) $\sqrt{2Emr}$
(e) $\sqrt{\frac{E}{2mr^2}}$

30 A body is orbiting around earth at a mean radius which is two times as greater as the parking orbit of a satellite, the period of body is **[BCECE]**

(a) 4 days (b) 16 days
(c) $2\sqrt{2}$ days (d) 64 days

2006

31 For a satellite moving in an orbit around the earth, the ratio of kinetic energy to potential energy is **[AFMC]**

(a) 2 (b) $\frac{1}{2}$ (c) $\frac{1}{\sqrt{2}}$ (d) $\sqrt{2}$

32 The minimum energy required to launch a m kg satellite from earth's surface in a circular orbit at an altitude of $2R$, R is the radius of earth, will be **[AMU]**

(a) $3mgR$ (b) $\frac{5}{6}mgR$ (c) $2mgR$ (d) $\frac{1}{5}mgR$

33 A satellite moving on a circular path of radius r around the earth has a time period T. If its radius slightly increases by Δr, the change in its time period is **[AMU]**

(a) $\frac{3}{2}\left(\frac{T}{r}\right)\Delta r$ (b) $\left(\frac{T}{r}\right)\Delta r$
(c) $\frac{3}{2}\left(\frac{T^2}{r^2}\right)\Delta r$ (d) None of these

34 Suppose the gravitational force varies inversely as the nth power of the distance. The time period of a planet in circular orbit of radius R around sun will be proportional to **[DUMET]**

(a) $R^{(n-1)/2}$ (b) $R^{(n+1)/2}$
(c) R^{n-1} (d) R^{n+1}

35 The radius of the orbit of a planet is two times that of the earth. The time period of planet is **[MP PMT]**

(a) 4.2 T (b) 2.8 T
(c) 5.6 T (d) 8.4 T

36 Near earth's surface, time period of a satellite is 4 h. Find its time period at height $4R$ from the centre of earth. **[RPMT]**

(a) 32 h (b) $\left(\frac{1}{8\sqrt[3]{2}}\right)$ h
(c) $8\sqrt[3]{2}$ h (d) 16 h

37 Radius of orbit of satellite of earth is R. Its kinetic energy is proportional to **[RPMT]**

(a) $\frac{1}{R}$ (b) $\frac{1}{\sqrt{R}}$
(c) R (d) $\frac{1}{R^{3/2}}$

38 The time period of an artificial satellite in a circular orbit is independent of **[J&K CET]**

(a) the mass of the satellite
(b) radius of the orbit
(c) mass of the earth and radius of the earth
(d) None of the above

2005

39 Two planets are revolving around the earth with velocities v_1 and v_2 and in radii r_1 and r_2 ($r_1 > r_2$), respectively. Then, **[BHU]**

(a) $v_1 = v_2$ (b) $v_1 > v_2$
(c) $v_1 < v_2$ (d) $\frac{v_1}{r_1} = \frac{v_2}{r_2}$

40 The orbital velocity of an artificial satellite in a circular orbit just above the earth's surface is v_o. The orbital velocity of a satellite orbiting at an altitude of half of the radius, is **[AMU]**

(a) $\frac{3}{2}v_o$ (b) $\frac{2}{3}v_o$
(c) $\sqrt{\frac{2}{3}}v_o$ (d) $\sqrt{\frac{3}{2}}v_o$

41 The earth revolves around the sun in one year. If the distance between them becomes double, then the new time period of revolution will be **[AMU]**

(a) $4\sqrt{2}$ yr (b) $2\sqrt{2}$ yr
(c) 4 yr (d) 8 yr

42 A planet revolves in elliptical orbit around the sun. The linear speed of the planet will be maximum at **[Manipal]**

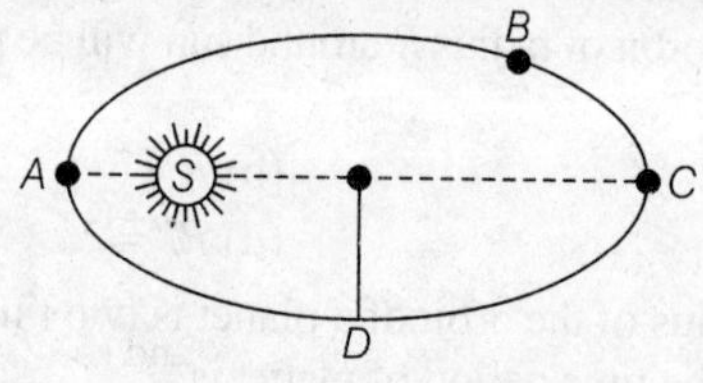

(a) A (b) B (c) C (d) D

43 When earth moves round the sun, the quantity which remains constant is **[BCECE]**

(a) angular velocity (b) kinetic energy
(c) potential energy (d) areal velocity

44 A satellite moves in a circle around the earth. The radius of this circle is equal to one-half of the radius of the moon's orbit. The satellite completes one revolution in **[J&K CET]**

(a) $\frac{1}{2}$ lunar month (b) $\frac{2}{3}$ lunar month
(c) $2^{-3/2}$ lunar month (d) $2^{3/2}$ lunar month

45 A geostationary satellite is revolving around the earth. To make it escape from gravitational field of earth, its velocity must be increased **[J&K CET]**

(a) 100% (b) 41.4%
(c) 50% (d) 59.6%

Answers

1 (a)	2 (c)	3 (b)	4 (d)	5 (d)	6 (b)	7 (b)	8 (a)	9 (c)	10 (a)
11 (a)	12 (c)	13 (a)	14 (c)	15 (b)	16 (a)	17 (b)	18 (a)	19 (c)	20 (d)
21 (b)	22 (b)	23 (c)	24 (c)	25 (c)	26 (c)	27 (c)	28 (a)	29 (c)	30 (c)
31 (b)	32 (b)	33 (a)	34 (b)	35 (b)	36 (a)	37 (a)	38 (a)	39 (c)	40 (c)
41 (b)	42 (a)	43 (d)	44 (c)	45 (b)					

Explanations

1 (a) From Kepler's third law, the time period of revolution of satellite around earth is

$$T^2 \propto r^3 \quad \text{or} \quad T \propto r^{3/2} \quad \dots\text{(i)}$$

where, r is the radius of satellite's orbit.

Here, $r_1 = 6R_E + R_E, T_1 = 24$ h

$r_2 = 2.5R_E + R_E, T_2 = ?$

where, R_e = radius of earth.

So, from Eq. (i), we get

$$\frac{T_1}{T_2} = \left(\frac{r_1}{r_2}\right)^{3/2}$$

$$\frac{24}{T_2} = \left(\frac{6R_E + R_E}{2.5R_E + R_E}\right)^{3/2} = \left(\frac{7}{3.5}\right)^{3/2}$$

$$\Rightarrow T_2 = \frac{24}{(2)^{3/2}} = \frac{24}{2\sqrt{2}} = \frac{12}{\sqrt{2}} = 6\sqrt{2}\text{ h}$$

2 (c) By Kepler's third law of planetory motion,

$$\frac{T_1}{T_2} = \left(\frac{a_1}{a_2}\right)^{3/2}$$

Given, $T_1 = T, a_1 = R, T_2 = ?, a_2 = 9R$

$$\therefore \quad \frac{T}{T_2} = \left(\frac{R}{9R}\right)^{3/2}, \quad \frac{T}{T_2} = \left[\left(\frac{1}{3}\right)^2\right]^{3/2}$$

$$\frac{T}{T_2} = \frac{1}{27} \Rightarrow T_2 = 27T$$

3 (b) According to the question,

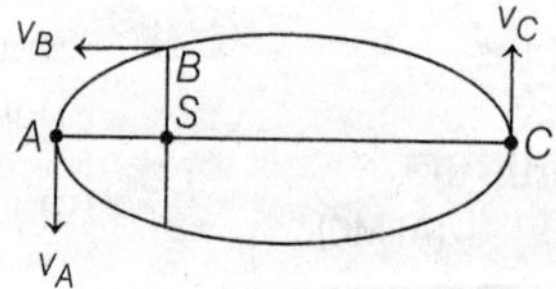

The figure above shows an ellipse traced by a planet around the sun S. The closed point A is known as perihelion and the farthest point C is known as aphelion .

Since, as per the Kepler's second law of area, that the planet will move slowly ($v_{\min}$) only, when it is farthest from the sun and more rapidly ($v_{\max}$), when it is nearest to the sun.

Thus, $\quad v_A = v_{\max}, v_C = v_{\min}$

Therefore, we can write

$$v_A > v_B > v_C \quad \dots\text{(i)}$$

Kinetic energy of the planet at any point is given as, $K = \frac{1}{2}mv^2$

Thus, at A,

$$K_A = \frac{1}{2}mv_A^2$$

At B, $\quad K_B = \frac{1}{2}mv_B^2$

At C, $\quad K_C = \frac{1}{2}mv_C^2$

From Eq. (i), we can write

$$K_A > K_B > K_C$$

4 (d) Given, $T_A > 1\text{h}, T_B = 8\text{h}$

and $\quad r_A = 10^4\text{km}$

From Kepler's law,

$$\frac{T_A^2}{T_B^2} = \frac{r_A^3}{r_B^3}$$

$$\Rightarrow \quad \frac{1^2}{8^2} = \frac{(10^4)^3}{r_B^3}$$

$$\Rightarrow \quad r_B^3 = 64 \times (10^4)^3$$

$$\therefore \quad r_B = 4 \times 10^4 \text{ km}$$

Speed of satellite A,

$$v_A = \frac{2\pi r_A}{T_A} \quad [\because v = \omega r]$$

$$= \frac{2\pi \times 10^4}{1}$$
$$= 2\pi \times 10^4 \text{ km/h}$$

Speed of satellite B,

$$v_B = \frac{2\pi r_B}{T_B} = \frac{2\pi \times 4 \times 10^4}{8}$$
$$= \pi \times 10^4 \text{ km/h}$$

The speed of B relative to A when they are closed.

$$v_{BA} = v_A - v_B$$
$$= 2\pi \times 10^4 - \pi \times 10^4$$
$$= \pi \times 10^4 \text{ km/h}$$

5 *(d)* As, force, $F = \frac{GMm}{r^{3/2}} = m\omega^2 r$

$$\Rightarrow \frac{GMm}{r^{3/2}} = \frac{4\pi^2 mr}{T^2} \quad \left[\because T = \frac{2\pi}{\omega}\right]$$

$$\Rightarrow T^2 = \left(\frac{4\pi^2}{GM}\right) \cdot r^{5/2} \Rightarrow T^2 \propto r^{5/2}$$

6 *(b)* $\because$ Total energy of a satellite at height h is

$$= \text{KE} + \text{PE} = \frac{GMm}{2(R+h)} - \frac{GMm}{(R+h)}$$
$$= \frac{-GMm}{2(R+h)} = \frac{-GMmR^2}{2R^2(R+h)}$$
$$= \frac{-mg_0R^2}{2(R+h)} \quad \left(\because g_0 = \frac{GM}{R^2}\right)$$

7 *(b)* The gravitational force of attraction between the planet and sun provide the centripetal force

i.e. $$\frac{GMm}{r^2} = \frac{mv^2}{r}$$
$$v = \sqrt{\frac{GM}{r}}$$

The time period of planet will be,

$$T = \frac{2\pi r}{v}$$

$$\Rightarrow T^2 = \frac{4\pi^2 r^2}{\frac{GM}{r}} = \frac{4\pi^2 r^3}{GM} \quad \text{...(i)}$$

Also from Kepler's third law,

$$T^2 = kr^3 \quad \text{...(ii)}$$

From Eqs. (i) and (ii), we get

$$\frac{4\pi^2 r^3}{GM} = kr^3$$
$$\Rightarrow GMK = 4\pi^2$$

8 *(a)* We know that, the potential energy of the satellite

$$U = -\frac{GM_e m}{R_e}$$

The kinetic energy of the satellite,

$$K = \frac{1}{2}\frac{GM_e m}{R_e}$$

The total energy $E = U + K$

$$= -\frac{GM_e m}{R_e} + \frac{1}{2}\frac{GM_e m}{R_e}$$
$$= -\frac{1}{2}\frac{GM_e m}{R_e}$$
$$\Rightarrow 2E = -\frac{GM_e m}{R_e} \Rightarrow -2E = U$$

So, potential energy $= -2$ (total energy)

$$\Rightarrow \text{PE} = -2E$$

9 *(c)* Given, $R_e = 6400 \text{ km} = 6.4 \times 10^6 \text{m}$
$\pi = 3.14$ and $g = 10 \text{ m/s}^2$.

We know that, the period of revolution of the earth satellite

$$T = 2\pi\sqrt{\frac{(R_e + h)^3}{gR_e^2}}$$

[if $h << R_e$, then $(R_e + h = R_e)$]

$$\text{So, } T = 2\pi\sqrt{\frac{R_e^3}{gR_e^2}}$$
$$= 2\pi\sqrt{\frac{R_e}{g}} = 2 \times 3.14\sqrt{\frac{6.4 \times 10^6}{10}}$$
$$= 2 \times 3.14 \times 0.8 \times 10^3$$
$$= 5.024 \times 10^3 = 5024 \text{ s}$$
$$= 83.73 \text{ min}$$

10 *(a)* We know that, the total energy of the satellite is

$$E = -\frac{1}{2}\frac{GM_e m}{R}$$

At a height H from the surface of the earth, the total energy of the satellite,

$$E = -\frac{1}{2}\frac{G M_e m}{R + H} \quad \text{...(i)}$$

and the potential energy,

$$U = -\frac{GM_e m}{R + 3R} = -\frac{GM_e m}{4R} \quad \text{...(iii)}$$

According to the question, $E = U$

$$\Rightarrow E = U - \frac{1}{2} \cdot \frac{GM_e m}{R + H} = -\frac{GM_e m}{4R}$$
$$\Rightarrow \frac{1}{2R + 2H} = \frac{1}{4R}$$
$$\Rightarrow 2H = 4R - 2R$$
$$\Rightarrow H = R$$

11 *(a)* As we know that,

$$\text{Time period, } (T) = 2\pi\sqrt{\frac{R_e}{g}} \quad \text{...(i)}$$

So, if $R' = \frac{R_e}{4}$

$$\Rightarrow T' = 2\pi\sqrt{\frac{R_e}{4g}} \quad \text{...(ii)}$$

From Eqs. (i) and (ii), we get

$$\frac{T}{T'} = \frac{2\pi\sqrt{\frac{R_e}{g}}}{2\pi\sqrt{\frac{R_e}{g}}} \times 2$$
$$\Rightarrow T' \times 2 = 24$$
$$\Rightarrow T' = \frac{24}{2} = 12 \text{ h}$$

12 *(c)* The equation of general conic is

$$\frac{1}{r} = \frac{1}{l}(1 + e\cos\theta)$$

where, e is eccentricity.

For ellipse, turning points are at $\theta = 0°$ and $\theta = 180°$ giving $r_{min} = r_2$ and $r_{max} = r_1$ respectively.

$$\therefore \frac{1}{r_2} = \frac{1}{l}(1 - e) \quad \text{...(i)}$$

$$\text{and} \quad \frac{1}{r_1} = \frac{1}{l}(1 + e) \quad \text{...(ii)}$$

From Eqs. (i) and (ii), we get

$$\Rightarrow \frac{1}{r_1} + \frac{1}{r_2} = \frac{2}{l}$$
$$\Rightarrow l = \frac{2r_1r_2}{r_1 + r_2}$$

13 *(a)* Gravitational force of attraction provides the necessary centripetal force

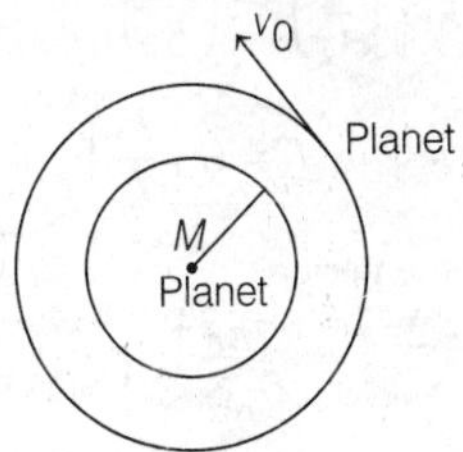

Let M be mass of planet and R is its radius, then the gravitational force provides the necessary centripetal force.

$$F = \frac{GMm}{r^2} = \frac{mv_0^2}{r}$$
$$\Rightarrow v_0 = \sqrt{\frac{GM}{r}}$$

So, $v_0 \propto \sqrt{\frac{1}{r}}$

Given, $v_A = 3v, r_A = 4R$ and $r_B = R$

$\Rightarrow \frac{3v}{v_B} = \sqrt{\frac{R}{4R}} = \frac{1}{2}$

$\Rightarrow v_B = 6v$

14 *(c)* From Kepler's third law,

$T^2 \propto r^3$

Hence, $T_1^2 \propto r_1^3$ and $T_2^2 \propto r_2^3$

So, $\frac{T_2^2}{T_1^2} = \frac{r_2^3}{r_1^3} = \frac{(R+2R)^3}{(R+5R)^3} = \frac{(3R)^3}{(6R)^3}$

$\Rightarrow \frac{T_2}{T_1} = \frac{1}{2\sqrt{2}}$ $(\because T_1 = 24\text{ h})$

$\therefore T_2 = \frac{24}{2\sqrt{2}} = 6\sqrt{2}$

15 *(b)* We have,(from Kepler's law)

$T^2 \propto R^3$

Given, $R_1 = r$ and $R_2 = 4r$

$\therefore \frac{T_1^2}{T_2^2} = \frac{(r)^3}{(4r)^3}$ or $\frac{T_1}{T_2} = \frac{1}{8}$

Hence, the ratio will be 1 : 8.

16 *(a)* Using the law of conservation of angular momentum,

Angular momentum of planet at p = Angular momentum of planet at a

$\Rightarrow L_p = L_a$

$\Rightarrow r_a > r_p$

$\Rightarrow \mathbf{r}_a \times \mathbf{L}_a > \mathbf{r}_p \times \mathbf{L}_p$

17 *(b)* According to Kepler's law, $T^2 \propto R^3$

Given, $R_1 = L_1, R_2 = L_2$ and period of earth around sun, $T_1 = D$ days.

$\left(\frac{T}{T_1}\right)^2 = \left(\frac{R_2}{R_1}\right)^3$

So, $T = D\left(\frac{L_2}{L_1}\right)^{3/2}$

18 *(a)* Time period,

$T = \frac{2\pi r}{v_0} = \frac{2\pi R}{\sqrt{\frac{GM_m}{R}}}$ $\left(\because v_0 = \sqrt{\frac{GM}{R}}\right)$

$\Rightarrow T^2 = \frac{4\pi^2 R^3}{GM_m}$

19 *(c)* $\because$ As we know,

From Kepler's law, time period of satellite is $T^2 = \frac{4\pi^2 R^3}{GM}$

$T_{\text{sat}} = 2\pi\sqrt{\frac{(R+h)^2}{GM_e}}$

As two satellites of masses m and $9m$ are orbiting a planet of radius R, their time periods will remain same i.e. in the ratios 1 : 1, because time period of satellite does not depend on its mass.

20 *(d)* Binding energy of satellite in the first case is $= \frac{GMm}{2r}$

where, r is the radius of orbit.

In second case,

$\text{BE} = \frac{GMm}{2 \times (3r/2)}$

$\therefore \Delta E = \frac{GMm}{r}\left(\frac{1}{2} - \frac{1}{3}\right) = \frac{GMm}{6r}$

per cent increase in energy of a satellite

$= \frac{GMm/6r}{GMm/2r} \times 100$

$= \frac{2}{6} \times 100 = 33.33\%$

21 *(b)* We know that, relation between orbital velocity and escape velocity,

$v_o = \sqrt{gR_e}$ ...(i)

$\Rightarrow v_e = \sqrt{2gR_e}$ ...(ii)

$\Rightarrow \frac{v_o}{v_e} = \sqrt{\frac{gR_e}{2gR}} \Rightarrow \frac{v_o}{v_e} = \frac{1}{\sqrt{2}}$

$\Rightarrow v_e = \sqrt{2}v_o$

22 *(b)* Given, $m' = 200$ kg, $m = 1$ kg and $r = 3R/2$

On earth, $mg = 10$ N

$\Rightarrow 1 \times g = 10 \Rightarrow g = 10\text{ ms}^{-2}$

Now, $g' = g\frac{R^2}{r^2} = 10 \times \frac{R^2}{(3R/2)^2} = \frac{40}{9}$

Pull on satellite $= m'g'$

$= 200 \times \frac{40}{9} = 889$ N

23 *(c)* Given, $R' = 4R$ and $T = 90$ min

From Kepler's law, $T^2 \propto R^3$

$\Rightarrow T \propto R^{3/2}$

$\Rightarrow \frac{T'}{T} = \left(\frac{R'}{R}\right)^{3/2} \Rightarrow \frac{T'}{T} = \left(\frac{4R}{R}\right)^{3/2}$

$= (4)^{3/2} = (2^2)^{3/2} = 2^3 = 8$

$\therefore T' = 8T = 8 \times 90 = 720$ min

24 *(c)* According to Kepler's third law,

$T^2 \propto R^3 \Rightarrow \frac{T_2}{T_1} = \left(\frac{R_2}{R_1}\right)^{3/2}$

$\therefore \frac{T_2}{T_1} = \left(\frac{3R}{R}\right)^{3/2} \Rightarrow \frac{T_2}{T_1} = \sqrt{27}$

$\therefore T_2 = \sqrt{27}T_1 = \sqrt{27} \times 4 = 4\sqrt{27}$ h

25 *(c)* The period of revolution of a synchronous relay satellite is equal to the period of rotation of earth about its axis. This makes it possible to reflect TV signals and transmits TV programme from one part of the world to the other.

26 *(c)* The orbitial velocity of satellite is

$v_0 = \sqrt{\frac{GM}{r}}$

Thus, it is independent of mass of satellite, so the velocity of both will be same whereas potential energy and kinetic energy of a satellite depends on its mass.

27 *(c)* Given , $T = 5$ h and $r^1 = 4r$

According to Kepler's law,

$T^2 \propto r^3 \Rightarrow 5^2 \propto r^3$ ...(i)

and $(T')^2 \propto (4r)^3$ ...(ii)

From Eqs. (i) and (ii), we get

$\frac{25}{(T')^2} = \frac{r^3}{64r^3}$

$\therefore T' = \sqrt{1600} = 40$ h

28 *(a)* The earth revolves around the sun once in a year. In order to find the rotational kinetic energy about the sun, we may treat the earth as a point mass of moment of inertia I. If ω is angular velocity of earth, then

$K_{\text{rot}} = \frac{1}{2}I\omega^2$

In planetary motion, angular momentum remains conserved. At A, the moment of inertia is least, so angular speed is maximum. So at A, rotational kinetic energy is maximum.

29 *(c)* If m is the mass and v is the orbital velocity of the satellite, then its kinetic energy,

$E = \frac{1}{2}mv^2$

$\Rightarrow Em = \frac{1}{2}m^2v^2$

$\Rightarrow m^2v^2 = 2Em$

$\Rightarrow mv = \sqrt{2Em}$ ...(i)

If r is the radius of the orbit of the satellite, then its angular momentum

$L = mvr$

Using Eq. (i),

$L = (\sqrt{2Em})r = \sqrt{2Emr^2}$

30 (c) By Kepler's third law of planetary motion,

We have, $T^2 \propto a^3$

Given, $T_1 = 1$ day (geostationary)

$a_1 = a,\ a_2 = 2a$

$$\therefore \quad \frac{T_1^2}{T_2^2} = \frac{a_1^3}{a_2^3}$$

$$\Rightarrow \quad T_2^2 = \frac{a_2^3}{a_1^3} T_1^2 = \frac{(2a)^3}{a^3} \times 1 = 8$$

$$T_2 = 2\sqrt{2} \text{ days}$$

31 (b) Potential energy of satellite,

$$U = -\frac{GM_e m}{R_e}$$

where, R_e is radius of earth, M_e is the mass of earth, m is the mass of satellite and G is the gravitational constant.

$$|U| = \frac{GM_e m}{R_e}$$

Kinetic energy of satellite

$$(K) = \frac{1}{2}\frac{GM_e m}{R_e}$$

$$\text{So,} \quad \frac{K}{U} = \frac{1}{2}\frac{GM_e m}{R_e} \times \frac{R_e}{GM_e m} = \frac{1}{2}$$

32 (b) Minimum required energy

$$= TE_f - PE_i$$

$$= \frac{-GMm}{2(R + 2R)} - \left(\frac{-GMm}{R}\right)$$

$$= \frac{GMm}{R}\left(-\frac{1}{6} + 1\right)$$

$$= \frac{5}{6}\frac{GMm}{R}$$

$$= \frac{5}{6}\frac{gR^2 \times m}{R}$$

$$= \frac{5}{6} mgR$$

33 (a) According to Kepler's law,

$$T^2 \propto r^3$$

$$\Rightarrow \quad T = kr^{3/2}$$

$$\Rightarrow \quad \frac{dT}{dr} = \frac{3}{2} kr^{1/2}$$

$$\Rightarrow \quad \frac{dT}{dr} = \frac{3}{2}\left(\frac{T}{r}\right) \quad \left[\because kr^{1/2} = \frac{T}{r}\right]$$

$$\Rightarrow \quad \frac{\Delta T}{\Delta r} = \frac{3}{2}\left(\frac{T}{r}\right)$$

$$\therefore \quad \Delta T = \frac{3}{2}\left(\frac{T}{r}\right)\Delta r$$

34 (b) Given, gravitational force, $F = \frac{GMm}{R^n}$

$$\left[\because F \propto \frac{1}{R^n}\right]$$

Gravitational force will provide the necessary centripetal force to the planet, i.e.

centripetal force = gravitational force

$$\text{i.e.,} \quad \frac{mv^2}{R} = \frac{GMm}{R^n}$$

$$\Rightarrow \quad v = \sqrt{\frac{GM}{R^{n-1}}}$$

Time period of planet in circular orbit of radius R around sun will be

$$T = \frac{2\pi R}{v}$$

$$\Rightarrow \quad T = \frac{2\pi R}{\sqrt{\frac{GM}{R^{n-1}}}} = \frac{2\pi}{\sqrt{GM}} R^{1 + \left(\frac{n-1}{2}\right)}$$

$$\Rightarrow \quad T = \frac{2\pi}{\sqrt{GM}} R^{\frac{n+1}{2}} \Rightarrow T \propto R^{\frac{(n+1)}{2}}$$

35 (b) Applying Kepler's third law,

$$T^2 \propto R^3$$

$$\therefore \quad \left(\frac{T_1}{T_2}\right)^2 = \left(\frac{R_1}{R_2}\right)^3 = \left(\frac{R}{2R}\right)^3$$

$$\Rightarrow \quad \frac{T}{T_2} = \left(\frac{1}{2}\right)^{3/2}$$

$$\Rightarrow \quad T_2 = (2)^{3/2} T \text{ or } T_2 = 2.8\,T$$

36 (a) We know that,

$$T^2 \propto R^3$$

$$\therefore \quad \left(\frac{T_2}{T_1}\right)^2 = \left(\frac{R_2}{R_1}\right)^3 \Rightarrow \frac{T_2}{4} = \left(\frac{4R}{R}\right)^{3/2}$$

$$[\because R_2 = 4R]$$

$$\Rightarrow \quad T_2 = 4 \times 8 = 32 \text{ h}$$

37 (a) Kinetic energy of the satellite,

$$KE = \frac{1}{2} mv_0^2 \quad \text{...(i)}$$

$$\text{where,} \quad v_0 = \sqrt{\left(\frac{GM}{R}\right)}$$

Now, putting the value of v_0 in Eq. (i), we get

$$KE = \frac{1}{2} m \left(\sqrt{\left(\frac{GM}{R}\right)}\right)^2 = \frac{1}{2}\frac{mGM}{R}$$

$$\text{Hence,} \quad KE \propto \frac{1}{R}$$

38 (a) The time period of an artificial satellite is given by

$$T = 2\pi\sqrt{\frac{(R_e + h)^3}{gR_e^2}}$$

where, R_e is radius of earth and h the height of satellite.

From the above formula, it is clear that time period of revolution does not depend upon the mass of the satellite.

39 (c) The gravitational force exerted on the planet is

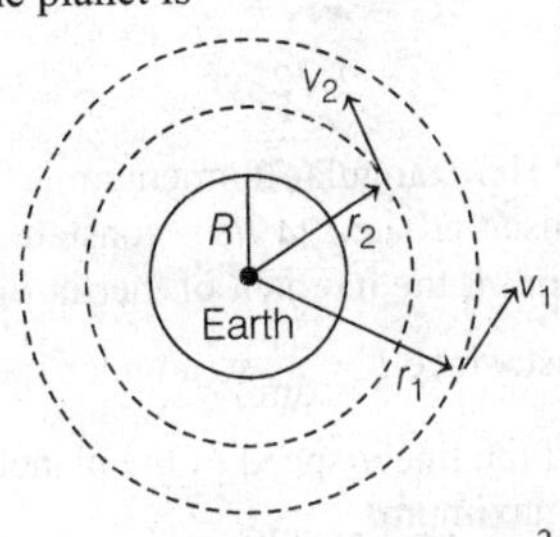

$$F_1 = \frac{GMm}{r_1^2} = \frac{gR^2 m}{r_1^2}$$

$$\text{where,} \quad GM = gR^2$$

$$\text{Similarly} \quad F_2 = \frac{GMm}{r_2^2} = \frac{gR^2 m}{r_2^2}$$

This gravitational force provides the necessary centripetal force, hence we have

$$\frac{gR^2 m}{r_1^2} = \frac{mv_1^2}{r_1} \Rightarrow v_1^2 = \frac{gR^2}{r_1}$$

$$\Rightarrow \quad v_1 = \sqrt{\frac{gR^2}{r_1}} \quad \text{...(i)}$$

$$\text{Similarly,} \quad v_2 = \sqrt{\frac{gR^2}{r_2}} \quad \text{...(ii)}$$

Taking ratio of (i) and (ii),

$$\therefore \quad \frac{v_1}{v_2} = \sqrt{\frac{r_2}{r_1}}$$

$$\therefore \quad v_2 > v_1 \quad (\text{given, } r_1 > r_2)$$

40 (c) Given, $R_1 = R_e$ and

$$R_2 = R_e + \frac{R_e}{2} = \frac{3}{2} R_e$$

The orbital velocity of satellite is

$$v_o = \sqrt{\frac{GM_e}{R}} \Rightarrow v_o \propto \sqrt{\frac{1}{R}}$$

$$\text{Now} \quad \frac{v_1}{v_2} = \sqrt{\frac{R_2}{R_1}} = \sqrt{\frac{3R_e}{2R_e}} = \sqrt{\frac{3}{2}}$$

$$v_2 = \sqrt{\frac{2}{3}}\, v_1 = \sqrt{\frac{2}{3}}\, v_o \; (\because v_1 = v_o)$$

41 *(b)* Given, $T_1 = 1\,\text{yr}$,

$R_1 = R, R_2 = 2R$

According to Kepler's third law of planetary motion, $T^2 \propto R^3$

where, R is the distance between earth and sun.

$$\therefore \quad = \left(\frac{R}{2R}\right)^3 = \frac{1}{8}$$

$$\Rightarrow \quad \frac{T_1}{T_2} = \frac{1}{2\sqrt{2}}$$

$$\Rightarrow \quad T_2 = 2\sqrt{2}\,T_1$$

$$= 2\sqrt{2}\ \text{yr}$$

42 *(a)* Here, angular momentum is conserved, i.e. $L = I\omega$ = constant. At point A, the moment of inertia I is least, since $I \propto \frac{l}{\omega}$, so angular speed and the linear speed of the planet at A is maximum.

43 *(d)* When earth moves round the sun, then according to Kepler's second law, the radius vector drawn from the sun to earth, sweeps out equal areas in equal time, i.e. its areal velocity (or the area swept out by it per unit time) is constant. While in such motion, angular velocity, kinetic energy and potential energy change.

44 *(c)* Time period of revolution of a satellite is

$$T = 2\pi\sqrt{\frac{r^3}{gR^2}}$$

Given, T_m = Time period of moon = 1 lunar month,

$r_m = a$

$$T = 2\pi\sqrt{\frac{(a)^3}{gR^2}} \quad \ldots\text{(i)}$$

For satellite $T_s = 2\pi\sqrt{\frac{(a/2)^3}{gr^2}}$ ...(ii)

$[\because r_s = a/2]$

From Eqs. (i) and (ii),

$$\frac{T_m}{T_s} = \sqrt{\frac{a^3}{(a/2)^3}} = 2^{3/2}$$

$$\Rightarrow \quad T_s = 2^{-3/2}\ \text{lunar month}$$

45 *(b)* Orbital velocity, $v_o = \sqrt{gR_e}$

Escape velocity, $v_e = \sqrt{2gR_e}$

where, R_e is radius of earth.

$$\text{Increase Percentage} = \frac{v_e - v_o}{v_o} \times 100$$

$$= \frac{\sqrt{2gR_e} - \sqrt{gR_e}}{\sqrt{gR_e}} \times 100$$

$$= (\sqrt{2} - 1) \times 100$$

$$= (1.414 - 1) \times 100$$

$$= 41.4\%$$

08

Mechanical Properties of Solids

Quick Review

Elastic and Plastic behaviour of Materials

- Whenever a force is applied on a body, then it tends to change the size or shape of the body.
- The property of a body by virtue of which it tends to regain its original size and shape when the applied force is removed, is known as **elasticity** and the deformation caused is known as **elastic deformation**.
- Those substances which do not have a tendency to regain their shape and hence gets permanently deformed are called **plastic** and this property is called **plasticity**.

Stress

- The restoring force per unit cross-sectional area set up within the body is called stress.

$$\text{Stress} = \frac{\text{Restoring force}}{\text{Area of cross-section}} = \frac{F}{A}$$

- In SI system, unit of stress is N/m^2 or pascal (Pa).
- In general, there are three types of stresses as given below
  (*i*) **Longitudinal Stress** When the stress is normal to the surface of object, then it is known as longitudinal stress. It is of two types
    (a) **Tensile Stress** If the stress produced in an object is due to increase in its length, then it is called tensile stress.
    (b) **Compressive Stress** If the stress produced in an object is due to decrease in its length, then it is called compressive stress.
  (*ii*) **Volumetric Stress** The restoring force acting per unit area inside the object opposing change in volume is called volumetric stress.
  (*iii*) **Shearing Stress** When a force is applied on an object along the tangential direction of the surface of the object, then stress produced in the object is called shearing stress.

Breaking Stress

- The minimum stress after which the wire breaks is called breaking stress.
- A wire of length l will break due to its own weight, when $l = \dfrac{\text{Breaking stress}}{dg}$

  where, d = density of material of wire
  and g = acceleration due to gravity.

Strain

- Strain is defined as the ratio of change in shape of an object to the original shape.

$$\text{Strain} = \frac{\text{Change in configuration of the object}}{\text{Original configuration of the object}}$$

- It is a pure number and has no unit.
- The three types of stresses results in three types of strain as given below
  (*i*) **Longitudinal Strain** (S_L) It is the change in length per unit length of the wire on application of force, i.e.

$$S_L = \frac{\text{Change in length}}{\text{Original length}} = \frac{\Delta L}{L}$$

  (*ii*) **Bulk or Volume Strain** (S_V) It is the change in volume per unit volume of the object on application of force, i.e.

$$S_V = \frac{\text{Change in volume}}{\text{Original volume}} = \frac{\Delta V}{V}$$

(*iii*) **Shearing Strain (S_S)** It is the ratio of displacement of the upper surface to the distance between two layers, i.e.

$$S_S = \frac{\text{Relative displacement of a layer}}{\text{Distance between two layers}} = \tan\theta$$

where, θ = shearing angle.

- Also, shearing strain = $2 \times$ longitudinal strain and volume strain = $3 \times$ longitudinal strain.

Hooke's Law

- This law states that, for small deformations, the stress and strain are proportional to each other.
  Thus, stress $\propto$ strain
  stress = $k \times$ strain
  where, k is a proportionality constant which is known as **modulus of elasticity.**
- The SI unit of modulus of elasticity is Nm^{-2}.
- Depending on the types of stresses and strains, there are three modulii of elasticity as given below
  (*i*) **Young's Modulus** It is the ratio of longitudinal stress to the corresponding strain for small change in length and it is expressed as $Y = \frac{FL}{Al} = \frac{MgL}{\pi r^2 l}$.
  where, M = mass of the body, A = area of the body, l = change in the length due to the strain and L = length of the body.
  (*ii*) **Bulk Modulus** It is the ratio of volume stress to the corresponding volume strain in the material for small value of strain and it is given by $K = \frac{F/A}{-\Delta V/V} = -\frac{Vdp}{dV}$.
  where, dp = change in pressure
  and dV = change in volume.
- Compressibility $= \frac{1}{\text{Bulk modulus } (K)} = \frac{dV}{Vdp}$
- Gases have two types of bulk modulus as given below
  (a) **Isothermal Bulk Modulus** under isothermal condition, bulk modulus is equal to pressure of gas, i.e.
  $K_i = p$ (pressure of the gas)
  (b) **Adiabatic Bulk Modulus** Under adiabatic condition, bulk modulus is equal to γ times pressure, i.e.
  $$K_a = \gamma p \qquad \left(\gamma = \frac{C_p}{C_V}\right)$$
  where, γ = heat capacity ratio.
  Also, $K_a = \gamma K_i$

(*iii*) **Modulus of Rigidity** It is the ratio of shearing stress to the shearing strain for small strain in a body, which is given as $\eta = \frac{F}{A\theta}$, where, θ = shearing angle.

- Young's modulus and modulus of rigidity are defined for solids only while bulk modulus is defined for all solids, liquids and gases.
- For perfectly rigid body, we have
  $Y = \infty$, $K = \infty$ and $\eta = \infty$.

Poisson's ratio

It is the ratio of transverse or lateral contraction strain to longitudinal contraction strain in the direction of stretching force. It is expressed as

$$\sigma = \frac{\text{Lateral contraction strain}}{\text{Longitudinal contraction strain}} = \frac{d/D}{l/L}$$

where, d = change in diameter and D = original diameter, l = change in length and L = original length.

- Theoretical limits of Poisson's ratio are -1 and 0.5, while the practical limits are 0 and 0.5.
- Relations between Y, K, η and σ as given below
  (*i*) $K = \frac{Y}{3(1-2\sigma)}$ (*ii*) $\eta = \frac{Y}{2(1+\sigma)}$ (*iii*) $\sigma = \frac{(3K-2\eta)}{2(3K+\eta)}$
  (*iv*) $Y = \frac{9\eta K}{3K+\eta}$ (*v*) $\frac{9}{Y} = \frac{3}{\eta} + \frac{1}{K}$

Applications of Modulus of Elasticity

If a beam is fixed at its ends and loaded with weight at its middle, then depression at the centre is given as

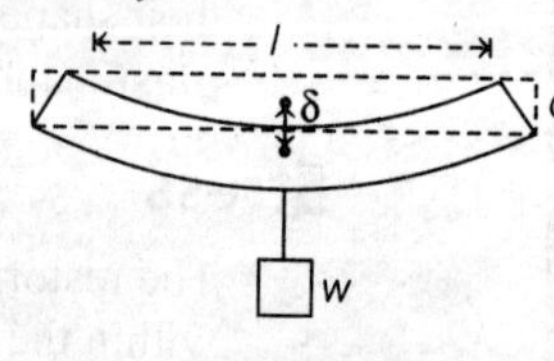

$$\delta = \frac{Mg\,l^3}{4bd^3\,Y}$$

where, Y = Young's modulus, l = length of beam, b = breadth of beam and d = thickness of beam.

- If a rubber ball of volume V is taken to a depth h in water, then decrease in its volume is given as $dV = \frac{hdgV}{K}$.

Factors Affecting Elasticity

Elasticity of any material is affected due to many factors as given below

- Due to **hammering** and rolling, the elasticity of material increases.
- Due to **annealing** (heating and slow cooling), the elasticity of material decreases.
- With rise in **temperature**, the elasticity decreases.
- Due to **impurity**, the elasticity can be increased or decreased.

Stress-Strain Curve

- A typical stress-strain curve for a metal is as shown in figure

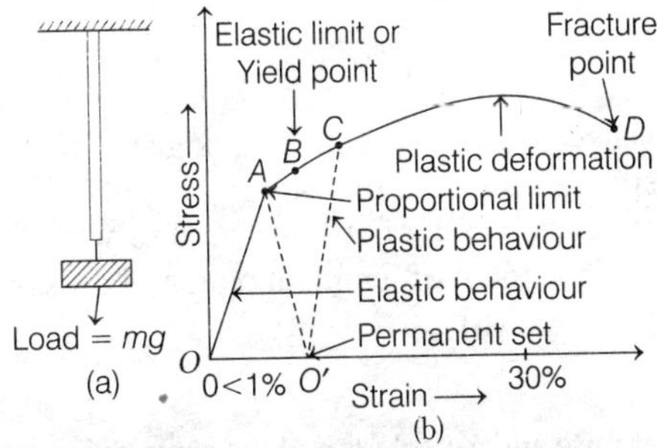

- In the region O to A, stress is found proportional to strain. Thus, Hooke's law is fully obeyed in this region and body regain its original shape.
- Point A is known as point of proportional limit.
- In the region from A to B, stress and strain are not proportional, but the body still returns to its original shape and size.
- The point B is yield point (also called elastic limit) and corresponding stress is yield stress (σ_y).
- If stress increases beyond point B, the strain further increases, but on removing the strain wire does not regain its original length.
- Beyond point C, for a small stress, the strain produced is large upto point D. The wire will break at point D called fracture point of wire.

Thermal Stress and Strain

- The strain and stress produced by heating a material is called the thermal strain and stress, respectively which are given as

$$\text{Thermal strain} = \frac{\Delta l}{l} = \alpha t$$

where, α = thermal coefficient of linear expansion
and t = increase in temperature.

$$\text{Thermal stress} = \frac{F}{A} = Y\alpha\Delta t$$

- If a metal cube is heated, then pressure applied on the cube to prevent its expansion is

$$p = K\gamma_V \, dt$$

where, γ_V = coefficient of volume expansion
and dt = rise in temperature.

Elastic Potential Energy Stored in a Stretched Wire

- The work done in stretching a wire against the interatomic forces is stored as the elastic potential energy.
  (*i*) Potential energy or work done per unit volume is given by

$$u = \frac{W}{V} = \frac{1}{2} \times \text{stress} \times \text{strain}$$

$$= \frac{1}{2} \times Y \times (\text{strain})^2 = \frac{1}{2Y} \times (\text{stress})^2 \left[\because Y = \frac{\text{stress}}{\text{strain}}\right]$$

  (*ii*) Work done in stretching a wire is expressed as

$$W = \frac{1}{2} \times F \times l$$

  where, F = stretching force
  and l = elongation produced.

  (*iii*) If the force acting on the body is increased from F_1 to F_2 within the elastic limit, then

$$W = \frac{(F_1 + F_2)}{2} \times \text{extension.}$$

- **Interatomic Force Constant** It is the ratio of interatomic force to that of change in interatomic distance, i.e. $k = \frac{F}{\Delta r}$

Also, $k = Yr_0$

where, Y = Young's modulus
and r_0 = distance between two atoms.

- A wire is suspended from a rigid support. If a torque(τ) is applied at free end of the wire, so that it experiences a twist of θ radian, then

$$\text{Work done} = \frac{1}{2}\tau\theta^2$$

Topical Practice Questions

All the exam questions of this chapter have been divided into 4 topics as listed below

Topic 1

Stress and Strain

2011

1 A stress of 6×10^6 Nm^{-2} required for breaking a material. The density ρ of the material is 3×10^3 kg m^{-3}. If the wire is to break under its own weight, the length of the wire made of that material should be (take, $g = 10\,\text{ms}^{-2}$) **[Manipal]**

(a) 20 m (b) 200 m
(c) 100 m (d) 2000 m

2010

2 If the angle of shear is 30° for a cubical body and the change in length is 250 cm, then the original length of cube is **[Manipal]**

(a) 4.9 m (b) 5.5 m
(c) 5.3 m (d) 4.3 m

3 To break a wire of 1 m length, minimum 40 kg weight is required. Then, the wire of the same material of double radius and 6 m length will require breaking weight **[Haryana PMT]**

(a) 80 kg-wt (b) 240 kg-wt
(c) 200 kg-wt (d) 160 kg-wt

4 Which statement is true about breaking stress? **[KCET]**

(a) It depends on length of wire.
(b) It depends on area of cross-scction of wire.
(c) It is independent of length and area of cross-scction
(d) Both (a) and (b)

2008

5 A copper wire and a steel wire of the same diameter and length are joined end-to-end and a force is applied which stretches their combined length by 1 cm. Then, the two wires will have **[Manipal]**

(a) the same stress and strain
(b) the same stress but different strains
(c) the same strain but different stresses
(d) different stresses and strains

6 The breaking force for a wire of diameter D of a material is F. The breaking force for a wire of the same material of diameter $2D$ is **[AMU]**

(a) F (b) $2F$ (c) $\frac{F}{4}$ (d) $4F$

2005

7 Shearing stress is related to **[Punjab PMET]**

(a) length (b) volume (c) shape (d) area

Answers

1 (b)	2 (d)	3 (d)	4 (c)	5 (b)	6 (d)	7 (c)

Explanations

1 *(b)* The minimum stress after which the wire breaks, i.e.

$$\text{Stress} = \frac{\text{Force}}{\text{Area}} = \frac{mg}{A}$$

$$= \frac{V\rho g}{A} = \frac{LA\rho g}{A} = L\rho g$$

Given, stress $= 6\times 10^6$ Nm^{-2},

$\rho = 3\times 10^3$ kgm^{-3}

and $g = 10$ ms^{-2}

$$L = \frac{\text{Stress}}{\rho g} = \frac{6\times 10^6}{3\times 10^3\times 10}$$

$$= 2\times 10^2 = 200\,\text{m}$$

2 *(d)* Given, angle of shear. $\theta = 30°$

Change in length, $\Delta L = 250\,\text{cm} = 2.5\,\text{m}$

As, shear strain, $\tan\theta = \frac{\Delta L}{L}$

$$\Rightarrow \quad \tan 30° = \frac{2.5}{L}$$

$$L = 2.5\sqrt{3} = 4.33\,\text{m}$$

3 *(d)* Breaking force

= Breaking stress

× Area of cross-section of wire

∴ Breaking force $\propto r^2$

(breaking stress is constant)

If radius becomes doubled, then breaking force will become 4 times, i.e. $40\times 4 = 160$ kg-wt.

4 *(c)* Breaking stress is independent of length and area of cross-section of wire and depends on the nature of material and its temperature.

5 *(b)* As, same force is applied to each wire having equal area of cross- section, so stress is same but extensions will be different for wires as they are of different materials. So, same stress but different strains are there.

6 *(d)* Breaking stress $= \frac{\text{Breaking force}}{\text{Area}}$ = Constant

$$\therefore \quad \frac{F}{\left(\frac{\pi D^2}{4}\right)} = \frac{F'}{\pi D^2}$$

or $$\frac{4F}{\pi D^2} = \frac{F'}{\pi D^2}$$

$$\Rightarrow \quad F' = 4F$$

7 *(c)* Shearing stress is related to the shape of the material.

Topic 2

Hooke's Law : Young's, Bulk and Rigidity Modulus

2019

1 Two wire of same material having radius in ratio 2 : 1 and lengths in ratio 1 : 2. If same force is applied on them, then ratio of their change in length will be **[JIPMER]**

(a) 1 : 1 (b) 1 : 2
(c) 1 : 4 (d) 1 : 8

2018

2 If compressibility of a material is 4×10^{-5} per atm, pressure is 100 atm and volume is 100 cm^3, then find the value of ΔV. **[JIPMER]**

(a) 0.4 cm^3 (b) 0.8 cm^3
(c) 0.6 cm^3 (d) 0.2 cm^3

3 Two wires are made of the same material and have the same volume. The first wire has cross-sectional area A and the second wire has cross-sectional area $3A$. If the length of the first wire is increased by Δl on applying a force F, how much force is needed to stretch the second wire by the same amount? **[NEET]**

(a) $4F$ (b) $6F$ (c) $9F$ (d) F

2017

4 The bulk modulus of a spherical object is B. If it is subjected to uniform pressure p, the fractional decrease in radius is **[NEET]**

(a) $\frac{p}{B}$ (b) $\frac{B}{3p}$ (c) $\frac{3p}{B}$ (d) $\frac{p}{3B}$

2014

5 A rubber cord 10 m is suspended vertically. How much does it stretch under its own weight (density of rubber is 1500kg m^{-3}, $Y = 5\times10^8$ Nm^{-2} and $g = 10$ ms^{-2})? **[EANEET]**

(a) 15×10^{-4} m (b) 7.5×10^{-4} m
(c) 12×10^{-4} m (d) 25×10^{-4} m

6 The pressure on an object of bulk modulus B undergoing hydraulic compression due to a stress exerted by surrounding fluid having volume strain $\left(\frac{\Delta V}{V}\right)^2$ is **[J&K CET]**

(a) $B^2\left(\frac{\Delta V}{V}\right)$ (b) $B\left(\frac{\Delta V}{V}\right)^2$ (c) $\frac{1}{B}\left(\frac{\Delta V}{V}\right)$ (d) $B\left(\frac{\Delta V}{V}\right)$

2013

7 A beam of metal supported at the two ends is loaded at the centre. The depression at the centre is proportional to **[WB JEE]**

(a) Y^2 (b) Y (c) $\frac{1}{Y}$ (d) $\frac{1}{Y^2}$

8 A 5 m aluminium wire ($Y = 7\times10^{10}$ Nm^{-2}) of diameter 3 mm supports a 40 kg mass. In order to have the same elongation in a copper wire ($Y = 12\times10^{10}$ Nm^{-2}) of the same length under the same weight, the diameter should be in mm **[KCET]**

(a) 1.75 (b) 2.0 (c) 2.3 (d) 5.0

9 The following four wires are made of the same material. Which of these will have the largest extension when the same tension is applied? **[NEET]**

(a) Length = 50 cm, diameter = 0.5 mm
(b) Length = 100 cm, diameter = 1 mm
(c) Length = 200 cm, diameter = 2 mm
(d) Length = 300 cm, diameter = 3 mm

10 A copper wire and a steel wire of the same length and same cross-section are joined end to end to form a composite wire. The composite wire is hung from a rigid support and a load is suspended from the other end. If the increase in length of the composite wire is 2.4 mm, then the increase in lengths of steel and copper wires are (take, $Y_{Cu} = 10\times10^{10}$ Nm^{-2}, $Y_{Steel} = 2\times10^{11}$ Nm^{-2}) **[EAMCET]**

(a) 1.2 mm, 1.2 mm (b) 0.6 mm, 1.8 mm
(c) 0.8 mm, 1.6 mm (d) 0.4 mm, 2.0 mm

2011

11 The ratio of tensile stress to the longitudinal strain is defined as **[J&K CET]**

(a) Bulk modulus (b) Young's modulus
(c) shear modulus (d) compressibility

2010

12 The Young's modulus of brass and steel are respectively 1.0×10^{11} Nm^{-2} and 2.0×10^{11} Nm^{-2}. A brass wire and a steel wire of the same length are extended by 1 mm each under the same force. If radii of brass and steel wires are R_B and R_S respectively, then **[AFMC]**

(a) $R_S = \sqrt{2}R_B$ (b) $R_S = \frac{R_B}{\sqrt{2}}$
(c) $R_S = 4R_B$ (d) $R_S = \frac{R_B}{2}$

13 When a weight of 10 kg is suspended from a copper wire of length 3 m and diameter 0.4 mm, its length increases by 2.4 cm. If the diameter of the wire is doubled, then the extension in its length will be **[VMMC]**

(a) 7.6 cm (b) 4.8 cm (c) 1.2 cm (d) 0.6 cm

2009

14 The Young's modulus of the material of a wire is equal to the **[Kerala CEE]**

(a) stress required to increase its length four times
(b) stress required to produce unit strain
(c) strain produced in it
(d) half the strain produced in it
(e) stress acting on it

2008

15 The adjacent graph shows the extension (Δl) of a wire of length 1 m suspended from the top of a roof at one end with a load w connected to the other end. If the cross-sectional area of the wire is $10^{-6}\ m^2$, calculate the Young's modulus of the material of the wire. **[AIIMS]**

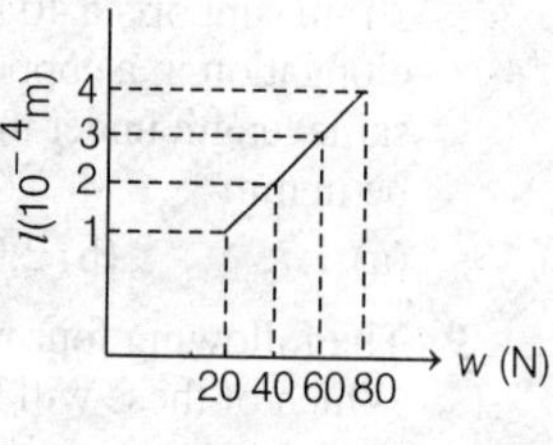

(a) $2\times10^{11}\ Nm^{-2}$ (b) $2\times10^{-11}\ Nm^{-2}$
(c) $3\times10^{-12}\ Nm^{-2}$ (d) $2\times10^{-13}\ Nm^{-2}$

16 A stress of $3.18\times10^{8}\ Nm^{-2}$ is applied to a steel rod of length 1 m along its length, its Young's modulus is $2\times10^{11}\ Nm^{-2}$. Then, the elongation produced in the rod (in mm) is **[J&K CET]**

(a) 3.18 (b) 6.36 (c) 5.18 (d) 1.59

17 A uniform plank of Young's modulus Y is moved over a smooth horizontal surface by a constant horizontal force F. The area of cross-section of the plank is A. The compression strain on the plank in the direction of the force is **[Punjab PMET]**

(a) F/AY (b) $2F/AY$ (c) $\frac{1}{2}(F/AY)$ (d) $3F/AY$

2007

18 An iron rod of length 2 m and cross-sectional area of $50\ mm^2$ is stretched by 0.5 mm, when a mass of 250 kg is hung from its lower end. Young's modulus of iron rod is **[BHU]**

(a) $19.6\times10^{20}\ Nm^{-2}$ (b) $19.6\times10^{18}\ Nm^{-2}$
(c) $19.6\times10^{10}\ Nm^{-2}$ (d) $19.6\times10^{15}\ Nm^{-2}$

19 According to Hooke's law of elasticity, if stress is increased, then the ratio of stress to strain **[MHT CET]**

(a) becomes zero (b) remains constant
(c) decreases (d) increases

20 A particular force (F) applied on a wire increases its length by 2×10^{-3} m. To increase the wire's length by 4×10^{-3} m the applied force will be **[J&K CET]**

(a) $4F$ (b) $3F$ (c) $2F$ (d) F

21 Which one of the following statements is wrong? **[BHU]**

(a) Young's modulus for a perfectly rigid body is zero.
(b) Bulk modulus is relevant for solids, liquids and gases.
(c) The Young modulus and shear modulus are relevant for solids.
(d) The stretching of a coil spring is determined by its shear modulus

22 The Young's modulus of the material of the wire of length L and radius r is $Y\ Nm^{-2}$. If the length is reduced to $L/2$ and radius $r/2$, the Young's modulus will be **[AMU]**

(a) $Y/2$ (b) Y (c) $2Y$ (d) $4Y$

2006

23 The increase in pressure required to decrease the 200 L volume of a liquid by 0.004% (in kPa) is (take, bulk modulus of the liquid = 2100 MPa) **[MHT CET]**

(a) 8.4 (b) 84 (c) 92.4 (d) 168

24 To what depth below the surface of sea should a rubber ball be taken as to decrease its volume by 0.1% ? (Take, density of sea water = 1000 kgm^{-3}, Bulk modulus of rubber = $9\times10^{8}\ Nm^{-2}$ and acceleration due to gravity = 10 ms^{-2}.) **[Kerala CEE]**

(a) 9 m (b) 18 m (c) 180 m (d) 90 m
(e) 900 m

25 For a wire of length L, maximum change in length under stress condition is 2 mm. What is the change in length under same conditions when length of wire is halved? **[Punjab PMET]**

(a) 1 mm (b) 2 mm (c) 4 mm (d) 8 mm

26 When a sphere is taken to bottom of sea 1 km deep, it contracts by 0.01%. The bulk modulus of elasticity of the material of sphere is (take, density of water = 1 $g\,cm^{-3}$) **[AMU]**

(a) $9.8\times10^{10}\ Nm^{-2}$ (b) $10.2\times10^{10}\ Nm^{-2}$
(c) $0.98\times10^{10}\ Nm^{-2}$ (d) $8.4\times10^{10}\ Nm^{-2}$

27 A mass of 6.5 kg in hanging from the ends of a 60 cm long steel wire ($Y = 2\times10^{11}$ Pa) with area of cross-section 0.05 cm^2. When it is revolving in a vertical circle it has an angular velocity of 2 revolutions per second, at the bottom of the circle. Approximate elongation of the wire (in metre) when the mass is at its lowest point of the trajectory is **[EAMCET]**

(a) 8×10^{-4} (b) 4×10^{-4} (c) 8×10^{-5} (d) 4.8×10^{-5}

2005

28 The area of cross-section of a wire of length 1.1m is 1 mm^2. It is loaded with 1 kg, if Young's modulus of copper is $1.1\times10^{11}\ Nm^{-2}$, then the increase in length will be (if $g = 10\ ms^{-2}$) **[UP CPMT]**

(a) 0.01 mm (b) 0.075 mm (c) 0.1 mm (d) 0.15 mm

Answers

1 (d)	2 (a)	3 (c)	4 (d)	5 (a)	6 (b)	7 (c)	8 (c)	9 (a)	10 (c)
11 (b)	12 (b)	13 (d)	14 (b)	15 (a)	16 (d)	17 (a)	18 (c)	19 (b)	20 (c)
21 (a)	22 (b)	23 (b)	24 (d)	25 (a)	26 (a)	27 (d)	28 (c)		

Explanations

1. (*d*) Given, ratio of radius of two wires,

$$\frac{r_1}{r_2} = \frac{2}{1}$$

and ratio in their lengths,

$$\frac{l_1}{l_2} = \frac{1}{2}$$

When same force is applied on them, then ratio change in their lengths,

$$\frac{\Delta l_1}{\Delta l_2} = ?$$

We know that, Young's modulus,

$$Y = \frac{Fl}{A\Delta l}$$

$$\Rightarrow \quad \Delta l = \frac{Fl}{AY}$$

$$\Delta l \propto \frac{l}{A}$$

$$\therefore \quad \frac{\Delta l_1}{\Delta l_2} = \frac{l_1}{A_1} / \frac{l_2}{A_2} = \frac{l_1 A_2}{l_2 A_1}$$

$$\Rightarrow \quad \frac{\Delta l_1}{\Delta l_2} = \frac{l_1}{l_2} \cdot \frac{r_2^2}{r_1^2} = \frac{1}{2} \cdot \left(\frac{1}{2}\right)^2 = \frac{1}{8}$$

2 (*a*) Given, $\beta = 4 \times 10^{-5}$ per atm,

$$p = 100 \text{ atm}$$

and $V = 100 \text{ cm}^3$

$$= 100 \times 10^{-6} \text{ m}^3$$

$\because$ Compressibility $= \dfrac{1}{\text{Bulk modulus of elasticity}}$

$$\beta = \frac{1}{\dfrac{\Delta p}{\dfrac{V}{\Delta V}}} = \frac{\Delta V}{\Delta p V}$$

$$\therefore \Delta V = \beta(\Delta p V)$$

$$= 4 \times 10^{-5}(100 \times 100 \times 10^{-6})$$

$$= 0.4 \times 10^{-6} \text{m}^3 = 0.4 \text{ cm}^3$$

3 (*c*) According to the question,

For wire 1 Area of cross-section $= A_1$,

Force applied $= F_1$

and increase in length $= \Delta l$.

From the relation of Young's modulus of elasticity,

$$Y = \frac{Fl}{A\Delta l}$$

Substituting the values for wire 1 in the above relation, we get

$$\Rightarrow \quad Y_1 = \frac{F_1 l_1}{A_1 \Delta l} \quad \text{...(i)}$$

For wire 2 Area of cross-section $= A_2$

Force applied $= F_2$

increase in length $= \Delta l$

$$\text{Similarly}, Y_2 = \frac{F_2 l_2}{A_2 \Delta l} \quad \text{...(ii)}$$

$\because$ Volume, $V = Al$ or $l = \dfrac{V}{A}$

Substituting the value of l in Eqs. (i) and (ii), we get

$$Y_1 = \frac{F_1 V}{A_1^2 \Delta l} \text{ and } Y_2 = \frac{F_2 V}{A_2^2 \Delta l}$$

As it is given that the wires are made up of same material,

i.e. $Y_1 = Y_2$

$$\Rightarrow \quad \frac{F_1 V}{A_1^2 \Delta l} = \frac{F_2 V}{A_2^2 \Delta l}$$

$$\Rightarrow \quad \frac{F_1}{F_2} = \frac{A_1^2}{A_2^2} = \frac{A^2}{9A^2} = \frac{1}{9}$$

$(\because A_1 = A \text{ and } A_2 = 3A)$

or $F_2 = 9F_1 = 9F$ (given, $F_1 = F$)

4 (*d*) The object is spherical and the bulk modulus is represented by B. It is the ratio of normal stress to the volumetric strain.

$$\text{Hence,} \quad B = \frac{F/A}{\Delta V/V} \quad \left(\because p = \frac{F}{A}\right)$$

$$\Rightarrow \quad \frac{\Delta V}{V} = \frac{p}{B} \Rightarrow \left|\frac{\Delta V}{V}\right| = \frac{p}{B}$$

Here, p is applied pressure on the object and $\dfrac{\Delta V}{V}$ is volume strain.

Fractional decreases in volume,

$$\frac{\Delta V}{V} = 3\frac{\Delta R}{R} \quad [\because V = \frac{4}{3}\pi R^3]$$

Volume of the sphere decreases due to the decrease in its radius, hence

$$\frac{\Delta V}{V} = \frac{3\Delta R}{R} = \frac{p}{B} \Rightarrow \frac{\Delta R}{R} = \frac{p}{3B}$$

5 (*a*) Given $L = 10$ m, $d = 1500 \text{ kgm}^{-3}$

$Y = 5 \times 10^8 \text{ Nm}^{-2}$ and $g = 10 \text{ ms}^{-2}$.

Elongation in rubber cord,

$$l = \frac{L^2 dg}{2Y} = \frac{(10)^2 \times 1500 \times 10}{2 \times 5 \times 10^8}$$

$$= 15 \times 10^{-4}$$

6 (*b*) Given, volume strain $= \left(\dfrac{\Delta V}{V}\right)^2$

$$B = \frac{\text{Normal stress}}{\text{Volume strain}} = \left|\frac{p}{-(\Delta V/V)^2}\right|$$

$$\Rightarrow \quad p = B\left(\frac{\Delta V}{V}\right)^2$$

where, p = normal stress

and $-\dfrac{\Delta V}{V}$ = volume strain.

7 (*c*) Depression in the beam at the middle due to load w is,

$$\delta = \frac{wl^3}{4Ybd^3} \text{ or } \delta \propto \frac{1}{Y}$$

where b, d = breadth and thickness of slab, l = length and Y = Young's modulus of slab.

8 (*c*) Ratio of stress to strain is a constant. When strain is small, the ratio of the longitudinal stress to the corresponding longitudinal strain is called Young's modulus (Y) of the material of the body.

As we know,

$$Y = \frac{\text{stress}}{\text{strain}} = \frac{F/A}{l/L} = \frac{F \cdot L}{\pi r^2 l}$$

Given, $Y_1 = 7 \times 10^{10} \text{N/m}^2$,

$$Y_2 = 12 \times 10^{10} \text{N/m}^2$$

$$r_1 = \frac{D_1}{2} = \frac{3}{2} \text{ mm}$$

and $r_2 = \dfrac{D_2}{2}$

$\therefore$ Taking ratio of Young's modulus and putting given values, we get

$$\frac{Y_2}{Y_1} = \left(\frac{D_1}{D_2}\right)^2 \Rightarrow \frac{12 \times 10^{10}}{7 \times 10^{10}} = \left(\frac{3}{D_2}\right)^2$$

$$\Rightarrow \quad \frac{3}{D_2} = \sqrt{\frac{12}{7}}$$

$$\Rightarrow \quad D_2 = 3\sqrt{\frac{7}{12}} \approx 2.3 \text{mm}$$

9 (a) As, change in length,

$$\Delta L = \frac{FL}{AY}$$

$$\Rightarrow \quad \Delta L = \frac{4FL}{\pi D^2 Y} \quad \left[\because A = \frac{\pi D^2}{4}\right]$$

$$\text{or} \quad \Delta L \propto \frac{L}{D^2}$$

As $(\text{diameter})^2$ is in the denominator of the expression, hence value of ΔL will be maximum for option (a).

After calculating ΔL, for values of lengths 50 cm, 100 cm, 200 cm and 300 cm, the elongations come as follows

$(20000)_{\text{for length 50 cm}}$
$> (10000)_{\text{for length 100 cm}}$
$> (50000)_{\text{for length 200 cm}}$
$> (3333)_{\text{for length 300 cm}}$.

10 (c) Let the increase in length of steel and copper wires be Δl_1 and Δl_2, respectively.

Given, $Y_{\text{steel}} = 2 \times 10^{11}\ \text{Nm}^{-2}$
$= 20 \times 10^{10}\ \text{Nm}^{-2}$

and $Y_{\text{Cu}} = 10 \times 10^{10}\ \text{Nm}^{-2}$

We know that,

$$Y_{\text{steel}} = \frac{F/A}{\Delta l_1 / l}$$

$$\Rightarrow \quad 20 \times 10^{10} = \frac{Fl}{\Delta l_1 \cdot A} \quad \ldots \text{(i)}$$

$$\text{and} \quad Y_{\text{Cu}} = \frac{F/A}{\Delta l_2 / l}$$

$$\Rightarrow \quad 10 \times 10^{10} = \frac{F \cdot l}{\Delta l_2 / A} \quad \ldots \text{(ii)}$$

Dividing Eq. (i) by Eq. (ii), we get

$$\frac{20 \times 10^{10}}{10 \times 10^{10}} = \frac{F \cdot l / \Delta l_1 \cdot A}{F \cdot l / \Delta l_2 \cdot A}$$

$$\frac{2}{1} = \frac{\Delta l_2}{\Delta l_1}$$

$$\Delta l_2 = 2\Delta l_1 \quad \ldots \text{(iii)}$$

But $\Delta l_1 + \Delta l_2 = 2.4$ mm (given)

$\Delta l_1 + 2\Delta l_1 = 2.4$ mm [from Eq.(iii)]

$3\Delta l_1 = 2.4$ mm

$\Delta l_1 = 0.8$ mm

and $\Delta l_2 = 1.6$ mm

So, $\Delta l_1, \Delta l_2 = 0.8$ mm, 1.6 mm

11 (b) Young's modulus is defined as the ratio of tensile stress to the longitudinal strain whereas ratio of volume stress to volume strain is known as bulk modulus of elasticity (B). The reciprocal of bulk modulus is known as compressibility and ratio of shearing stress to shearing strain is called shear modulus.

Hence, option (b) is the correct option.

12 (b) Increase in length,

$$\Delta L = \frac{FL}{YA} = \frac{FL}{Y\pi R^2}$$

As F, L and ΔL are same, hence

$$YR^2 = \text{constant.}$$

$$\therefore 2.0 \times 10^{11} R_S^2 = 1.0 \times 10^{11} R_B^2$$

$$\Rightarrow \quad R_S = \frac{R_B}{\sqrt{2}}$$

13 (d) As, $l \propto \dfrac{1}{r^2}$ $\left(\because l = \dfrac{FL}{YA}\right)$

(where, l = length of wire and r = radius of wire)

$$\Rightarrow \quad \frac{l_2}{l_1} = \left(\frac{r_1}{r_2}\right)^2 = \left(\frac{1}{2}\right)^2 \text{ (given)}$$

$$l_2 = \frac{l_1}{4} = \frac{2.4}{4} = 0.6 \text{ cm}$$

$(\because l_1 = 2.4 \text{ cm})$

14 (b) According to Hooke's law,

stress $\propto$ strain

$\Rightarrow$ stress $= Y \times$ strain

where, Y is Young's modulus.

For unit strain, Young's modulus is equal to the stress.

15 (a) From the graph, $l = 10^{-4}$m,

$F = 20$ N

$A = 10^{-6}\text{m}^2$, $L = 1$ m

$$\therefore \quad Y = \frac{FL}{Al} = \frac{20 \times 1}{10^{-6} \times 10^{-4}}$$

$$= 20 \times 10^{10} = 2 \times 10^{11} \text{Nm}^{-2}$$

16 (d) Given, $F = 3.18 \times 10^8\ \text{Nm}^{-2}$

$L = 1\,\text{m}$, $A = (L)^2 = (1)^2\text{m}^2 = 1\ \text{m}^2$

and $Y = 2 \times 10^{11}\ \text{Nm}^{-2}$

$= (1)^2\text{m}^2 = 1\,\text{m}^2$

$$\text{Young's modulus, } Y = \frac{FL}{A\Delta l}$$

$$\Rightarrow \quad \Delta l = \frac{FL}{AY} = \frac{3.18 \times 10^8 \times 1}{2 \times 10^{11}}$$

$$= 1.59 \times 10^{-3}\text{m} = 1.59 \text{ mm}$$

17 (a) As, $Y = \dfrac{F/A}{\text{Strain}} \Rightarrow \text{Strain} = \dfrac{F}{AY}$

18 (c) Young's modulus of material of the body is given by

$$Y = \frac{\text{longitudinal stress}}{\text{longitudinal strain}} = \frac{MgL}{Al}$$

Putting the numerical values, we have

$L = 2$ m, $A = 50\ \text{mm}^2 = 50 \times 10^{-6}\text{m}^2$

$l = 0.5\ \text{mm} = 0.5 \times 10^{-3}\text{m}$, $M = 250$ kg

$$\therefore \quad Y = \frac{250 \times 9.8 \times 2}{50 \times 10^{-6} \times 0.5 \times 10^{-3}}$$

$$= 19.6 \times 10^{10}\ \text{Nm}^{-2}$$

19 (b) As, $E = \dfrac{\text{stress}}{\text{strain}} = \text{constant}$

Hence, if stress is increased the strain increases, thus the ratio of stress to strain remains constant for a material.

20 (c) Young's modulus,

$$Y = \frac{F/A}{l/L} = \frac{F \times L}{A \times l}$$

Since, Y, L and A remain same.

$$F \propto l,$$

$$\frac{F_1}{F_2} = \frac{l_1}{l_2} \Rightarrow \frac{F}{F_2} = \frac{2 \times 10^{-3}}{4 \times 10^{-3}}$$

$[\because F_1 = F]$

$$\Rightarrow \quad F_2 = 2F$$

21 (a) For a perfectly rigid body, Young's modulus is infinite.

Thus, statement (a) is wrong while all other are correct.

22 (b) Young's modulus depends upon the nature of material and is independent of the dimensions of the material. Hence, it is constant for a material, so it will remain same.

23 (b) As, bulk modulus,

$$B = \frac{\text{normal stress}}{\text{volumetric strain}}$$

$$B = \frac{\Delta p}{-\Delta V / V} \quad \ldots \text{(i)}$$

Here, negative sign shows that volume is decreased, when pressure is increased.

Given, $B = 2100$ MPa

$= 2100 \times 10^6$ Pa and $V = 200$ L

$$\Delta V = 200 \times \frac{0.004}{100} = 0.008 \text{ L}$$

Substituting these values in Eq. (i), we get

$$2100 \times 10^6 = \frac{\Delta p}{\left(\frac{0.008}{200}\right)}$$

$$\Rightarrow \quad \Delta p = 84 \text{ kPa}$$

24 (d) As, bulk modulus,

$$B = \frac{\text{normal stress}}{\text{volume strain}} = \frac{p}{-\Delta V / V}$$

Given, $\dfrac{\Delta V}{V} = \dfrac{0.1}{100}$, $B = 9 \times 10^8\ \text{Nm}^{-2}$

$d = 100\ \text{kgm}^{-3}$ and $g = 10\text{ms}^{-2}$

$p = hdg = h \times 1000 \times 10$

$\therefore \quad \frac{-\Delta V}{V} B = p = hdg \Rightarrow h = -\frac{B\Delta V}{Vdg}$

$h = -\frac{9 \times 10^8 \times 0.1}{1000 \times 100 \times 10} = -90 \text{ m}$

25 *(a)* Young's modulus,

$Y = \frac{\text{Longitudinal stress}}{\text{Longitudinal strain}}$

$Y = \frac{F/A}{l/L}$ where F is force, A is area, l is change in length and L is original length.

In first case, $\quad Y = \frac{F/A}{2/L} \quad$ ...(i)

In second case, $\quad Y = \frac{F/A}{l/L/2} \quad$ ...(ii)

Equating Eqs. (i) and (ii), we get

$\frac{L}{2} = \frac{L/2}{l}$

$\Rightarrow \quad l = 1 \text{ mm}$

26 *(a)* Bulk modulus, $B = \frac{\Delta p}{\frac{-\Delta V}{V}}$

Given, $h = 1 \text{ km} = 10^3$ m,

$\rho = 1 \text{ gcm}^{-3}$

and $\quad \frac{-\Delta V}{V} = \frac{0.01}{100} = 10^{-4}$

where, Δp = pressure of water.

$= 10^3 \times 1 \times 10^3 \times 9.8$

$= 9.8 \times 10^6$

$B = \frac{9.8 \times 10^6}{10^{-4}} = 9.8 \times 10^{10} \text{Nm}^{-2}$

27 *(d)* Forces acting on the mass are (i) the tension (T) and (ii) the weight (w).

At the lowest point,

$T - w = \frac{mv^2}{r}$

or $\quad T = mg + mr\omega^2$

$(\because v = r\omega \text{ and } w = mg)$

Given, $m = 6.5$ kg, $r = 60$ cm $= 0.60$ m,

$Y = 2 \times 10^{11}$ Pa,

$A = 0.05 \text{ cm}^2 = 0.05 \times 10^{-4} \text{ m}^2$

and $\omega = 2$ rev/s

$\Rightarrow \quad T = 6.5 \times 9.8 + 6.5 \times 0.60 \times (2)^2$

$= 63.7 + 15.6 = 79.3 \text{ N}$

We have, $Y = \frac{TL}{Al}$

$\Rightarrow l = \frac{TL}{AY} = \frac{79.3 \times 0.60}{0.05 \times 10^{-4} \times 2 \times 10^{11}}$

$= 4.8 \times 10^{-5} \text{ m}$

28 *(c)* Given, $L = 1.1$ m,

$A = 1 \text{ mm}^2 = 10^{-6}$ m,

$Y = 1.1 \times 10^{11} \text{ Nm}^{-2}$,

$m = 1$ kg and $g = 10 \text{ ms}^{-2}$

Increase in length,

$l = \frac{mgL}{AY} = \frac{1 \times 10 \times 1.1}{10^{-6} \times 1.1 \times 10^{11}}$ m

$= 0.1$ mm

Topic 3

Poisson's Ratio, Stress-Strain Curve and Thermal Stress

2019

1 The stress-strain curves are drawn for two different materials X and Y. It is observed that the ultimate strength point and the fracture point are close to each other for material X but are far apart for material Y. We can say that materials X and Y are likely to be (respectively) **[NEET (Odisha)]**

(a) ductile and brittle (b) brittle and ductile
(c) brittle and plastic (d) plastic and ductile

2016

2 The stress-strain graph of a material is shown in the figure. The region in which the material is elastic is **[J & KCET]**

(a) OA (b) OB (c) OC (d) AC

2014

3 A metal rod is fixed rigidly at two ends so as to prevent its thermal expansion. If L, α and Y respectively denote the length of the rod, coefficient of linear thermal expansion and Young's modulus of its material, then for an increase in temperature of the rod by ΔT, the longitudinal stress developed in the rod is **[AMU]**

(a) inversely proportional to α
(b) inversely proportional to Y
(c) directly proportional to $\Delta T / Y$
(d) independent of L

2012

4 **Assertion** Soft steel can be made red hot by continued hammering on it, but hard steel cannot.

Reason Energy transfer in case of soft is large as in hard steel. **[AIIMS]**

(a) Both Assertion and Reason are correct and Reason is the correct explanation of the Assertion.
(b) Both Assertion and Reason are correct but Reason is not the correct explanation of the Assertion.
(c) Assertion is correct but Reason is incorrect.
(d) Assertion is incorrect but Reason is correct.

5 A material has Poisson's ratio 0.50. If a uniform rod of it suffers a longitudinal strain of 2×10^{-3}, then the percentage change in volume is **[WB JEE]**

(a) 0.6 (b) 0.4 (c) 0.2 (d) zero

2010

6 For a given material, the Young's modulus is 2.4 times that of rigidity modulus, then Poisson's ratio is **[Manipal]**

(a) 0.2 (b) 0.4 (c) 1.2 (d) 2.4

2008

7 When a rod is heated but prevented from expanding, the stress developed is independent of **[Manipal]**

(a) material of the rod (b) rise in the temperature
(c) length of the rod (d) None of these

8 When a wire is subjected to a force along its length, its length increases by 0.4% and its radius decreases by 0.2%. Then, the Poisson's ratio of the material of the wire is **[EAMCET]**

(a) 0.8 (b) 0.5 (c) 0.2 (d) 0.1

2007

9 Two rods of different materials with coefficients of linear thermal expansion α_1, α_2 and Young's modulii Y_1 and Y_2 respectively are fixed between two rigid walls. They are heated to have same increase in temperature. If the rods do not bend and $\alpha_1 : \alpha_2 = 2:3$, then the thermal stresses developed in two rods will be equal when $Y_1 : Y_2$ is equal to **[EAMCET]**

(a) 2 : 3 (b) 2 : 5 (c) 3 : 2 (d) 5 : 2

2006

10 There is no change in the volume of a wire due to change in its length on stretching. The Poisson's ratio of the material of the wire is **[MHT CET]**

(a) 0.50 (b) – 0.50 (c) 0.25 (d) – 0.25

11 If longitudinal strain for a wire is 0.03 and its Poisson's ratio is 0.5, then its lateral strain is **[J&K CET]**

(a) 0.003 (b) 0.0075
(c) 0.015 (d) 0.4

2005

12 If a wire having initial diameter of 2 mm produced the longitudinal strain of 0.1%, then the final diameter of wire is $(\sigma = 0.5)$ **[MHT CET]**

(a) 2.002 mm (b) 1.999 mm
(c) 1.998 mm (d) 2.001 mm

13 In case of steel wire or a metal wire, the elastic limit is reached when **[Manipal]**

(a) the wire just break
(b) the load is more than the weight of wire
(c) elongation is inversely proportional to the tension
(d) None of the above

14 Which of the following substances has the highest elasticity? **[KCET]**

(a) Sponge (b) Steel
(c) Rubber (d) Copper

15 For most of the material, Young's modulus (Y) and rigidity modulus (G) are related as **[UK PMT]**

(a) $G = 3Y$ (b) $G = \frac{Y}{3}$
(c) $G = \frac{3}{2}Y$ (d) $G = \frac{Y}{8}$

16 A body subjected to strain several times will not obey Hooke's law due to **[Punjab PMET]**

(a) yield point
(b) permanent state
(c) elastic fatigue
(d) breaking stress

Answers

1 (b)	2 (a)	3 (d)	4 (c)	5 (d)	6 (a)	7 (c)	8 (b)	9 (c)	10 (a)
11 (c)	12 (b)	13 (d)	14 (b)	15 (b)	16 (a)				

Explanations

1 (b) The stress-strain curve for a material is shown in figure

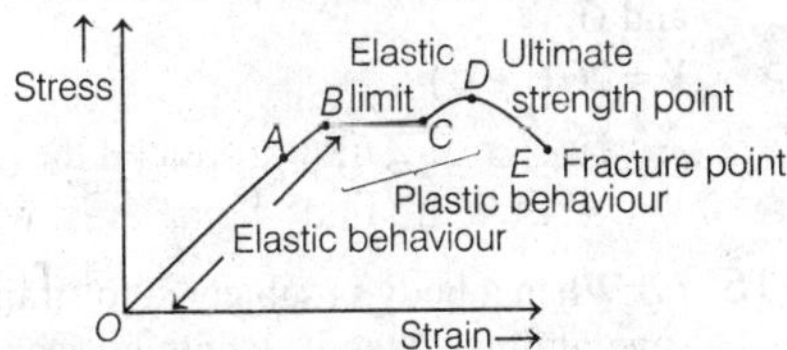

This curve specifies the behaviour of material.

For the material X, as the distance between strength point X and fracture point is small, so it is brittle and will break easily on the application of some extra stress after point D.

For material Y, as the distance between strength point and fracture point is large, so it is a ductile material and can withstand for some extra stress beyond point D.

2 (a) According to Hooke's law, stress is found proportional to strain in the given curve upto point A, which is known as point of proportional limit.

Material in this region OA shows the elastic behaviour (material regains its original dimension only when load applied is less than or equal to certain elastic limit).

3 (d) Longitudinal stress $= Y\alpha\Delta T$

where, ΔT = change in temperature,
α = coefficient of linear thermal expansion
and Y = Young's modulus of its material.

So, the longitudinal stress developed in the rod is directly proportional to $Y \cdot \Delta T$ and independent of length.

4 (c) Soft steels are highly ductile and malleable compared to hard steels which are brittle. Hence, hard steels have very small range of plastic extensions compared to ductile materials in stress-strain curve.

The rise in temperature of the soft steel means transferring energy into a system by work which appears as an increase in the internal energy of the system. The softness results in a deformation of the steel under blow of the hammer. Thus, the point of application of the force is displaced by the hammer and positive work is done on the steel. With the hard steel, less deformation occurs, (as it is less ductile) thus there is less displacement of point of application of the force.

As soft steel is better in absorbing energy from hammer, hence its temperature rises rapidly.

5 (d) Given, Poisson's ratio, $\sigma = 0.50$

Longitudinal strain,

$$\frac{\Delta L}{L} = 2\times10^{-3}$$

As Poisson's ratio,

$$\sigma = \frac{\text{Lateral strain}}{\text{Longitudinal strain}} = \frac{-\Delta D/D}{\Delta L/L}$$

$$\Rightarrow \Delta D/D = -\sigma\times\frac{\Delta L}{L}$$

$$= -0.5\times2\times10^{-3} = -1\times10^{-3}$$

Change in volume,

$$\frac{\Delta V}{V} = \frac{2\Delta R}{R} + \frac{\Delta L}{L} \quad [\because V = \pi R^2 L]$$

$$\Rightarrow \frac{\Delta V}{V} = \frac{2\Delta D}{D} + \frac{\Delta L}{L}$$

$$= -2\times1\times10^{-3} + 2\times10^{-3}$$

$$= 0$$

$\therefore$ % change in volume is zero.

6 (a) The fractional change in the transverse length is proportional to the fractional change in the longitudinal length. The constant of proportionality is called Poisson's ratio. In terms of Young's modulus and rigidity modulus, it is given by

$$\sigma = -\frac{\Delta d/d}{\Delta L/L} = \frac{Y}{2\eta} - 1$$

Given, $Y = 2.4\eta$

$$\therefore \quad \sigma = \frac{2.4\eta}{2\eta} - 1 = 0.2$$

7 (c) Initial length of the rod,

$$L_t = L_0(1 - \alpha\Delta\theta)$$

$$\Rightarrow \quad \Delta L = L_t - L_0 = L_0\alpha\Delta\theta \quad \ldots(\text{i})$$

If the same rod of length L_0 is subjected to stress along its length, then extension in length can be calculated by Hooke's law.

$$Y = \frac{\text{stress}}{\text{strain}} = \frac{\text{stress}}{\Delta L/L_0} = \frac{L_0\times\text{stress}}{\Delta L}$$

$$\therefore \quad \Delta L = \frac{L_0\times\text{stress}}{Y} \quad \ldots(\text{ii})$$

If the rod is prevented from expanding, we have

$$L_0\alpha\Delta\theta = \frac{L_0\times\text{stress}}{Y}$$

$\therefore$ Stress $= Y\alpha\Delta\theta$ (independent of L_0)

8 (b) Poisson's ratio σ is the ratio of fractional change in diameter to fractional change in length.

Thus, $$\sigma = \frac{\Delta r/r}{\Delta l/l} \quad \ldots(\text{i})$$

where, r is the radius of the wire.

Given, $\frac{\Delta r}{r} = 0.2$ and $\frac{\Delta l}{l} = 0.4$

Putting these values in Eq. (i), we get

$$\therefore \quad \sigma = \frac{0.2}{0.4}$$

$$= 0.5$$

9 (c) Thermal stress $= Y\times$ Strain

or $\quad S = Y\varepsilon = Y\alpha t$

where,
α = coefficient of linear thermal expansion
and Y = Young's modulus.

Given, $S_1 = S_2$

$$\Rightarrow Y_1\alpha_1 t = Y_2\alpha_2 t$$

$$\Rightarrow \frac{Y_1}{Y_2} = \frac{\alpha_2}{\alpha_1} = \frac{3}{2} \quad [\because \alpha_1 : \alpha_2 = 2:3]$$

Thus, $Y_1 : Y_2 = 3:2$

10 (a) Poisson's ratio,

$$\sigma = \frac{\text{Lateral strain}}{\text{Longitudinal strain}} = -\frac{\Delta R/R}{\Delta l/l}$$

$$= \frac{dD/D}{dl/l} \quad [\text{where, } D = \text{diameter}]$$

Let D be the diameter and V be the volume.

Then, $$V = \pi D^2 L/4 \quad \ldots(\text{i})$$

There is no change in volume.

Differentiating Eq. (i),

$$\therefore \quad 0 = \frac{\pi 2D}{4}dDL + \frac{\pi D^2}{4}dL$$

$$\Rightarrow \quad \frac{(dD/D)}{(dL/L)} = -0.5$$

$\therefore$ Poisson's ratio, $\sigma = 0.5$

11 (c) Poisson's ratio,

$$\sigma = \frac{\text{Lateral strain}}{\text{Longitudinal strain}}$$

Given, $\sigma = 0.5$

and longitudinal strain = 0.03

$\therefore$ Lateral strain $= 0.5\times0.03 = 0.015$

12 (b) Poisson's ratio,

$$\sigma = \frac{\text{Lateral strain}}{\text{Longitudinal strain}} = -\frac{\Delta R/R}{\Delta l/l}$$

$$\sigma = -\frac{\Delta R}{R}\times\frac{l}{\Delta l}$$

or $|\sigma| = \frac{\Delta R}{R} \times \frac{l}{\Delta l}$

$\therefore \frac{\Delta R}{R} = |\sigma|\left(\frac{\Delta l}{l}\right)$

Given, $d = 2$ mm,

$\frac{\Delta l}{l} = 0.1\% = \frac{0.1}{100}$

and $\sigma = 0.5$

$\Rightarrow \Delta R = 0.5 \times \frac{0.1}{100} \times \left(\frac{2 \times 10^{-3}}{2}\right)$

$= 0.0005$ mm

$\therefore$ Final radius $= R - \Delta R$

$= 1$ mm $- 0.0005$ mm

$= 0.9995$ mm

Final diameter $= 2 \times 0.9995$ mm

$= 1.9990$ mm

13. *(d)* In case of steel wire or metal wire, for elastic limit to reach none of the above three options are correct. Elastic limit means the maximum value of strain for which a body shows elastic property.
In Hooke's law, a proportionality exists between stress and only small strains. Iron is a ductile material, it has a widely separated fracture point (the point where the wire breaks) from the elastic limit. Moreover elongation is directly proportional to the tension, hence none of the options are correct. It can be explained with the help of stress-strain curve also.

14 *(b)* Out of the given substances, steel has greater value of stress-strain ratio. Therefore, steel has highest elasticity.

15 *(b)* We know that, relation between Y and G,

$Y = 2G(1+\sigma)$

$G = \frac{Y}{2(1+\sigma)} \Rightarrow G = \frac{Y}{3}$ $(\because \sigma_{max} = 0.5)$

16 *(a)* When a body is subjected to strain several times, then its length goes on increasing rapidly, i.e. the material of body flows like a viscous fluid and it acquires yield point after which it does not obey Hooke's law.

Topic 4

Elastic Potential Energy Stored in a Stretched Wire

2010

1 Wires A and B are made from the same material. A has twice the diameter and three times the length of B. If the elastic limits are not reached, when each is stretched by the same tension, the ratio of energy stored in A to that in B is
(a) 2 : 3 (b) 3 : 4 (c) 3 : 2 (d) 6 : 1 **[BVP]**

2008

2 When a metal wire elongates by hanging a load Mg on it, the gravitational potential energy of mass M decreases by Mgl. This energy appears **[Manipal]**
(a) as elastic potential energy completely
(b) as thermal energy completely
(c) half as elastic potential energy and half as thermal energy
(d) as kinetic energy of the load completely

2007

3 If the tension on a wire is removed at once, then **[AFMC]**
(a) it will break
(b) its temperature will reduce
(c) there will be no change in its temperature
(d) its temperature increases

4 A wire is suspended by one end. At the other end, a weight equivalent to 20 N force is applied. If the increase in length is 1 mm, the increase in the energy of the wire will be **[BHU]**
(a) 0.01 J (b) 0.02 J (c) 0.04 J (d) 1.00 J

5 If in a wire of Young's modulus Y, longitudinal strain X is produced, then the potential energy stored in its unit volume will be **[MHT CET]**
(a) $0.5YX^2$ (b) $0.5Y^2X$ (c) $2YX^2$ (d) YX^2

2006

6 Young's modulus of the material of a wire is Y. On pulling the wire by a force F, the increase in its length is x. The potential energy of the stretched wire is **[BHU]**
(a) $\frac{1}{2}Fx$ (b) $\frac{1}{2}Yx$ (c) $\frac{1}{2}Fx^2$ (d) None of these

2005

7 The energy stored per unit volume in copper wire, which produces longitudinal strain of 0.1% is (take, $Y = 1.1 \times 10^{11}$ Nm^{-2}) **[MHT CET]**
(a) 11×10^3 Jm^{-3} (b) 5.5×10^3 Jm^{-3}
(c) 5.5×10^4 Jm^{-3} (d) 11×10^4 Jm^{-3}

8 Two wires of same material and same diameter have lengths in the ratio 2 : 5. They are stretched by same force. The ratio of work done in stretching them is **[EAMCET]**
(a) 5 : 2 (b) 2 : 5 (c) 1 : 3 (d) 3 : 1

9 A 1 m long steel wire of cross-sectional area 1 mm^2 is extended by 1 mm. If $Y = 2 \times 10^{11}$ Nm^{-2}, then the work done is **[DUMET]**
(a) 0.1 J (b) 0.2 J (c) 0.3 J (d) 0.4 J

Answers

1 (b)	2 (c)	3 (d)	4 (a)	5 (a)	6 (a)	7 (c)	8 (b)	9 (a)

Explanations

1 *(b)* As, $U = \frac{1}{2}Fl = \frac{F^2L}{2AY}$ $\left(\because l = \frac{FL}{AY}\right)$

$\Rightarrow \quad U \propto \frac{L}{r^2}$ (F and Y are constant)

Given, $L_A = 3L_B$ and $r_A = 2r_B$

$$\Rightarrow \frac{U_A}{U_B} = \left[\frac{L_A}{L_B}\right] \times \left[\frac{r_B}{r_A}\right]^2$$

$$= 3 \times \left(\frac{1}{2}\right)^2 = \frac{3}{4}$$

2 *(c)* When a metal wire elongates by hanging a load Mg on it.

Decrease in potential energy of the load $= Mgl$, where l = elongation in metal wire.

Elastic potential energy stored in stretched wire $= \frac{1}{2} \times Mgl$

Difference of Mgl and $\frac{1}{2}Mgl$ appears as thermal energy in the stretched wire.

$\therefore$ Energy appearing as thermal energy

$$= Mgl - \frac{1}{2}Mgl$$

$$= \frac{1}{2}Mgl$$

3 *(d)* Due to tension, intermolecular distance between atoms is increased and therefore potential energy of the wire is increased and with the removal of force, interatomic distance is reduced and so, it decreases the potential energy. This change in potential energy appears as heat in the wire thereby increasing its temperature.

4 *(a)* Increase in energy, ΔU

$$= \frac{1}{2}Fl = \frac{1}{2}wl \quad (\because F = w)$$

Given, $w = 20\,\text{N}$,

$$l = 1\,\text{mm} = 1 \times 10^{-3}\ \text{m}$$

$$\Rightarrow \Delta U = \frac{1}{2} \times 20 \times 1 \times 10^{-3} = 0.01\ \text{J}$$

5 *(a)* Elastic potential energy per unit volume,

$$U = \frac{1}{2} \times \text{stress} \times \text{strain}$$

From definition of Young's modulus of wire,

$$Y = \frac{\text{stress}}{\text{strain}}$$

$\Rightarrow$ Stress = $Y \times$ Strain

Given, strain = X

and Young's modulus = Y

$\Rightarrow$ Stress = YX

$$\therefore \quad U = \frac{1}{2}YX^2$$

$$\Rightarrow \quad U = 0.5\,YX^2$$

6 *(a)* When a wire is stretched through a length, then work has to be done, this work is stored in the wire in the form of elastic potential energy. Potential energy of stretched wire is

$$U = \frac{1}{2}Fx$$

7 *(c)* Elastic potential energy per unit volume of the wire,

$$U = \frac{1}{2} \times \text{stress} \times \text{strain}$$

$$= \frac{1}{2} \times (\text{Young's modulus} \times \text{strain}) \times \text{strain}$$

$$= \frac{1}{2} \times (Y) \times (\text{strain})^2$$

Given, $\quad Y = 1.1 \times 10^{11}\ \text{Nm}^{-2}$

and $\quad$ strain $= 0.1\,\% = \frac{0.1}{100}$

$$\therefore \quad U = \frac{1}{2} \times 1.1 \times 10^{11} \times \left(\frac{0.1}{100}\right)^2$$

$$= 5.5 \times 10^4\,\text{Jm}^{-3}$$

8. *(b)* Stretching force, $F = \frac{YA}{L} \cdot l$

Here, both wires are of same material (i.e. same Y), same diameter (i.e. same A) and are stretched by same force.

So, $\quad \frac{l_1}{L_1} = \frac{l_2}{L_2}$

$$\therefore \quad \frac{l_1}{l_2} = \frac{L_1}{L_2} = \frac{2}{5}$$

Work done, $\quad W = \frac{1}{2}YA\frac{l^2}{L}$

Ratio of work done,

$$\frac{W_1}{W_2} = \left(\frac{l_1}{l_2}\right)^2 \cdot \frac{L_2}{L_1}$$

$$= \left(\frac{2}{5}\right)^2 \cdot \left(\frac{5}{2}\right) = \frac{2}{5}$$

$$= 2:5$$

9 *(a)* Young's modulus, $Y = \frac{F/A}{l/L}$

$$\Rightarrow \quad F = \frac{YA}{L}l$$

Now, work done

$$W = \int dW = \int F \times dl$$

$$= \int_0^l \frac{YA}{L}\,l\,dl = \frac{1}{2}YA\frac{l^2}{L} \quad \ldots \text{(i)}$$

Given, $A = 1\ \text{mm}^2 = 10^{-6}\text{m}$, $l = 1\,\text{mm}$

$= 10^{-3}$ m, $Y = 2 \times 10^{11}\text{Nm}^{-2}$

and $L = 1$ m

Putting these values in Eq. (i), we get

$$\therefore W = \frac{1}{2} \times 2 \times 10^{11} \times 10^{-6} \times (10^{-3})^2$$

$$= 0.1\ \text{J}$$

09

Mechanical Properties of Fluids

Quick Review

- The basic property of a fluid is that it can flow.
- The fluid does not have any resistance to change of its shape. Thus, the shape of a fluid is governed by the shape of its container.

Fluid Pressure

- Pressure exerted by the fluid on the bottom and walls of water bodies is called fluid pressure which is expressed as

  $p_{\text{total}} = p_0 \text{(atmospheric pressure)} + \rho gh.$

  where, atmospheric pressure (p_0) = pressure exerted by the earth's atmosphere.
- **Gauge pressure** is the excess pressure above the atmospheric pressure.
- **Absolute pressure** is the net pressure or sum of atmospheric pressure and gauge pressure. It is expressed as

  Absolute pressure = Gauge pressure + Atmospheric pressure.
- The pressure difference between the two points in a liquid column, $\Delta p = hdg$.
- If a block of mass (m) and area (A) floats over fluid surface, fluid pressure at the base of the vessel is expressed as

$$p = p_0 + \rho gh + \frac{mg}{A}$$

  where, h = height of the liquid and ρ = density of liquid.

Density and Relative Density

- Density of a substance is defined as mass per unit volume of the substance. It is expressed as

$$\text{Density, } \rho = \frac{\text{Mass } (m)}{\text{Volume } (V)}$$

- Relative density or specific gravity of a substance is the ratio of density of liquid or substance to density of water at 4°C.
- If two liquids of densities ρ_1 and ρ_2 having masses m_1 and m_2, respectively are mixed together, then the density of mixture is given by

$$\rho = \frac{m_1 + m_2}{\left(\frac{m_1}{\rho_1} + \frac{m_2}{\rho_2}\right)}$$

  If $m_1 = m_2$, then

$$\rho = \frac{2\rho_1\rho_2}{\rho_1 + \rho_2} = \text{Harmonic mean of } \rho_1 \text{ and } \rho_2.$$

- If two liquids of densities ρ_1 and ρ_2 having volumes V_1 and V_2 are mixed, then the density of the mixture is given by

$$\rho = \frac{\rho_1 V_1 + \rho_2 V_2}{V_1 + V_2}$$

  If $V_1 = V_2$, then

$$\rho = \frac{\rho_1 + \rho_2}{2} = \text{Arithmetic mean of } \rho_1 \text{ and } \rho_2.$$

Pascal's Law

This law states that, pressure applied to an enclosed fluid is transmitted undiminished to every point of the fluid and the walls of the containing vessel.

Archimedes' Principle

According to this principle, the loss of weight of a body submerged in a fluid is equal to the weight of the fluid displaced, which can be expressed as

$$\rho_s g V_s = \rho_f g V_p$$

where ρ_s, ρ_f are densities of body and fluid respectively and V_s and V_p are volume of body and part submerged respectively.

Flow of Fluids

- If the velocity of fluid particles at any time does not vary with time, the flow is said to be **steady** or **streamline flow**. The path followed by a fluid particle is known as **streamlines**.
- Velocity of particles in streamline is along the tangent to the curve at that point.
- The flow of fluid in which velocity of all particles crossing a given point is not same and the motion of the fluid is irregular is called **turbulent flow**.
- If the liquid flows over a horizontal surface in the form of layers of different velocities, then the flow of liquid is called **laminar flow**.

Equation of Continuity

- When an incompressible fluid flows in streamlined motion through a non-uniform cross-section, then mass flow rate is same at every section of the tube.
- It can be expressed as

$$Av = \text{constant}$$

where, A = area of cross-section

and v = velocity of flow.

or $$v \propto \frac{1}{A}$$

- Generalised continuity equation for liquids having densities ρ_1 and ρ_2 can be expressed as

$$\rho_1 A_1 v_1 = \rho_2 A_2 v_2$$

where,

A_1, A_2 = areas of non-uniform cross-sections of a tube and v_1, v_2 = velocities of flow across A_1 and A_2.

Bernoulli's Theorem

- It is a general expression relating pressure difference between two points in a pipe to both KE change (velocity changes) and PE change.
- It states that the sum of pressure energy per unit volume, kinetic energy per unit volume and potential energy per unit volume of an incompressible, non-viscous fluid in a streamlined irrotational flow remains constant at every cross-section throughout the liquid flow.
- Bernoulli's equation is given by

$$p + \frac{1}{2}\rho v^2 + \rho g h = \text{constant}$$

where,

p = pressure,

$\frac{1}{2}\rho v^2$ = kinetic energy per unit volume

and $\rho g h$ = potential energy per unit volume.

- If the fluid is flowing through a horizontal tube, two ends of the tube are at the same level. i.e., $h = 0$.

$$p + \frac{1}{2}\rho v^2 = \text{constant}$$

For fluid at rest,

$$p_1 - p_2 = \rho g (h_2 - h_1)$$

Applications Based on Bernoulli's Theorem

- **Venturimeter** is a device (based on Bernoulli's theorem) used to measure flow speed in a pipe. The pressure difference in this device is measured as

$$p_1 - p_2 = \frac{1}{2}\rho v_1^2 \left(\frac{A_1^2}{A_2^2} - 1 \right)$$

and velocity of flow, $v_1 = \sqrt{\dfrac{2gh}{\left(\dfrac{A_1}{A_2}\right)^2 - 1}}$ $[\because p_1 - p_2 = h\rho g]$

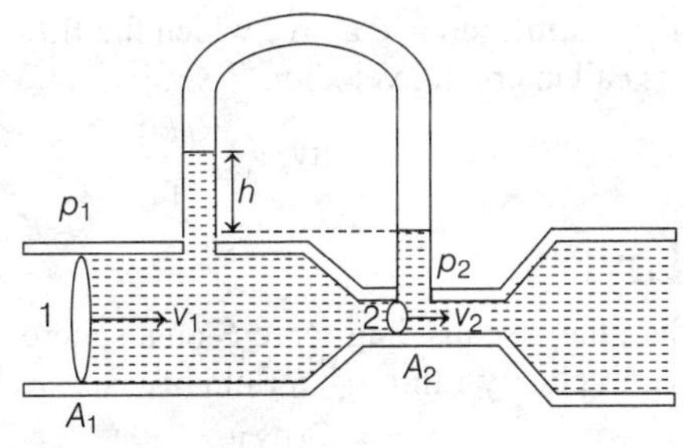

- **Velocity of Efflux** It is the velocity of the liquid coming out from the side of a container through a small hole is given by $v = \sqrt{2gh}$

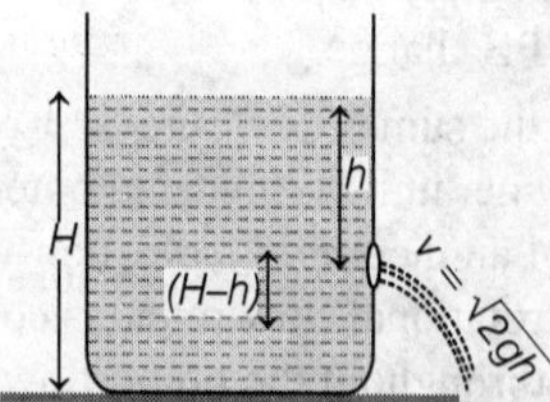

where, h = depth of the hole below the free surface.

- The time taken by the liquid to reach the base level in above case is given by

$$t = \sqrt{\frac{2(H-h)}{g}}$$

where, H = height of free surface from bottom initially.

Viscous Force or Viscosity

- The internal frictional force in a fluid which opposes the relative motion between the two layers of the fluid is known as viscous force.

  The tendency of fluids to oppose the relative motion of its layers is called **viscosity of fluid**.

  Viscous force, $F = -\eta A \dfrac{dv}{dy}$

  where, η = coefficient of viscosity,

  A = area of layer of fluid in contact

  and $\dfrac{dv}{dy}$ = velocity gradient between the layers.

- The viscosity of fluids decrease with increase in temperature and *vice-versa*.
- The viscosity of gases increase with increase in temperature.

Critical Velocity

The limiting value of velocity of flow of liquid upto which the flow is **streamlined** and above which the flow becomes turbulent is called critical velocity.

$$\text{Critical velocity, } v_C = \frac{k\eta}{\rho r}$$

Stokes' Law

It states that, the viscous drag force F on a sphere of radius r moving with velocity v through a fluid of viscosity is

$$F = 6\pi\eta rv$$

Terminal Velocity

Terminal velocity is the maximum constant velocity with which a small sphere falls from rest through a large column of viscous liquid. It is expressed as

$$v_T = \frac{2}{9}\frac{r^2(\rho - \sigma)g}{\eta}$$

where, r = radius of the body,

ρ = density of material of the body, σ = density of fluid and η = coefficient of viscosity.

Reynolds' Number

The onset of turbulence in a fluid is determined by a dimensionless parameter called the Reynolds' number which is given by

$$R_e = \frac{\rho v d}{\eta}$$

where, d is a typical geometrical length associated with the fluid flow and the other symbols have their usual meanings.

Poiseuille's Formula

It relates the volume of liquid coming out through capillary tube with other parameters of capillary,

$$V = \frac{\pi p R^4}{8\eta L}$$

where, V = volume of liquid coming out from the tube per second,

L = length of the capillary tube,

R = radius of the capillary tube,

p = pressure difference across the tube

and η = coefficient of viscosity.

Surface Tension

- Surface tension is the property of liquid at rest by virtue of which a liquid surface tends to occupy a minimum surface area and behaves like a stretched membrane.
- Surface tension can be defined as the force acting per unit length of an imaginary line drawn on the liquid surface. Direction of this force is perpendicular to the line and tangential to the liquid surface.

$$T = \frac{F}{L}$$

where, F = force acting on one side of imaginary line of length L.

- **Force due to Surface Tension** On different bodies having different shapes are shown in the table given below

Body having Different Shapes	Force Required to Lift a Body from the Surface of Water
A thin wire	$F = T \times 2l$ where, l = length of a thin wire and T = surface tension.
A rectangular plate	$F = 2T(l + b)$ where, l, b = length and breadth of rectangular plate.
A circular plate or disc	$F = T \times 2\pi r$ where, r = radius of the plate or disc.
Ring	$F = 2\pi(r_1 + r_2)T$ where, r_1 and r_2 = inner and outer radii.
Two glass plates of area A, containing a liquid film of thickness d between them.	$F = \frac{2TA}{d}$

Surface Energy

The surface energy may be defined as the amount of work done in increasing the area of the surface film through unity.

It is expressed as

$$\text{Surface energy} = \frac{\text{Work done in increasing surface area}}{\text{Increase in surface area}}$$

Different cases of work done by droplets or soap bubbles

(*i*) Work done to increase the area of surface film by A is

$$W = T \times A$$

(*ii*) Work done in blowing a soap bubble of radius r

$$W = 8\pi r^2 T$$

(*iii*) Work done in splitting a big liquid drop of radius R into n small identical drops of radius r

$$W = 4\pi TR^2(n^{1/3} - 1)$$

(*iv*) Work done in combining n small identical drops of radius r to form a big drop of radius R

$$W = 4\pi T(nr^2 - R^2)$$

Excess Pressure

- It is the difference of pressure between two sides of the liquid surface in a drop or bubble due to surface tension.
- Different cases of excess pressure in liquid drop and soap bubbles are given in tabular form below

Different Cases	Excess Pressure
In a liquid drop of radius r	$p = \frac{2T}{r}$ where, T = surface tension of liquid drop
A soap bubble of radius r	$p = \frac{4T}{r}$
Soap bubble of radius r, when it is inside a liquid	$p = \frac{2T}{r}$

- Different cases where droplets or soap bubbles coalesce given below

(*i*) If two droplets of radii r_1 and r_2 in vacuum coalesce under isothermal conditions, then the radius of the big drop is given by

$$r = \sqrt[3]{r_1^3 + r_2^3}$$

(*ii*) If two soap bubbles of radii r_1 and r_2 $(r_1 > r_2)$ are in contact with each other, then the radius of curvature of their interface is given by

$$r = \frac{r_1 r_2}{r_1 - r_2}$$

(*iii*) If two soap bubbles of radii r_1 and r_2 combine in vacuum to form a single bubble of radius r under isothermal condition, then

$$r = \sqrt{r_1^2 + r_2^2}$$

(*iv*) The radii of the two limbs of a U-tube are r_1 and r_2. A liquid of density ρ and surface tension T is poured in it. The difference between the levels of the liquid is given by

$$h = \frac{2T}{\rho g}\left(\frac{1}{r_1} - \frac{1}{r_2}\right)$$

Angle of Contact

- It is the angle between the tangent to the liquid surface at the point of contact and the solid surface inside the liquid.
- If angle of contact is acute, then liquid's surface is **concave.**
- If angle of contact is obtuse, then liquid surface in capillary tube is **convex.**

Capillarity

- The phenomena of rise or fall of a liquid in the capillary is called capillarity.
- Capillary rise or fall of a liquid,

$$h = \frac{2T\cos\theta}{r\rho g}$$

where,

h = height of liquid column in capillary,
T = surface tension of the liquid,
g = acceleration due to gravity,
θ = angle of contact

and r = radius of the capillary tube & ρ is the density of the liquid.

- Weight of the water in capillary tube

$$= mg = 2\pi rT\cos\theta$$

- Using capillary tube, surface tension of liquid which wets solid, can be determined by the formula

$$T = \frac{hr\rho g}{2\cos\theta}$$

- The liquids for which angle of contact is obtuse, falls in the capillary (do not rise).
- A capillary tube is vertically dipped in a liquid. The height of the liquid in tube is h and the total set up is kept in a lift, then
  (*i*) If lift is moving up with acceleration a, then height of the liquid in the tube, $h_1 = h\ (g/g+a)$.
  (*ii*) If lift is moving down with acceleration a, then height of the liquid in the tube, $h_1 = h\,(g/g-a)$.
- A capillary tube is vertically dipped in a liquid. The height of the liquid in tube is h, then
  (*i*) If total set up is taken to height H above the ground, then the height of the liquid in the tube,

$$h_1 = \frac{hR}{R-2H}$$

  (*ii*) If total set up is taken to depth d below the ground, then the height of the liquid in tube,

$$h_1 = \frac{hR}{R-d}$$

where, R = radius of the earth.

Topical Practice Questions

All the exam questions of this chapter have been divided into 6 topics as listed below

Topic 1

Fluid Pressure and Density

2015

1 The approximate depth of an ocean is 2700 m. The compressibility of water is $45.4 \times 10^{-11}\ \text{Pa}^{-1}$ and density of water is $10^3\ \text{kg/m}^3$. What fractional compression of water will be obtained at the bottom of the ocean? **[AIPMT]**

(a) 0.8×10^{-2} (b) 1.0×10^{-2}
(c) 1.2×10^{-2} (d) 1.4×10^{-2}

2014

2 A bubble is at the bottom of the lake of depth *h*. As the bubble comes to sea level, its radius increases three times. If atmospheric pressure is equal to *l* metre of water column, then *h* is equal to **[UK PMT]**

(a) $26\,l$ (b) l
(c) $25\,l$ (d) $30\,l$

2012

3 $4\ \text{m}^3$ of water is to be pumped to a height of 20 m and forced into a reservoir at a pressure of $2 \times 10^5\ \text{N/m}^2$. The work done by the motor is
(external pressure $= 10^5\ \text{N/m}^2$) **[UP CPMT]**

(a) 8×10^5 J (b) 16×10^5 J
(c) 12×10^5 J (d) 32×10^5 J

2011

4 A cubical vessel of height 1 m is full of water. What is the amount of work done in pumping water out of the vessel? (Take, $g = 10\ \text{ms}^{-2}$) **[WB JEE]**

(a) 1250 J (b) 5000 J
(c) 1000 J (d) 2500 J

2010

5 Three liquids of equal masses are taken in three identical cubical vessels *A*, *B* and *C*. Their densities are ρ_A, ρ_B and ρ_C, respectively but $\rho_A < \rho_B < \rho_C$. The force exerted by the liquid on the base of the cubical vessel is **[KCET]**

(a) maximum in vessel *C*
(b) minimum in vessel *C*
(c) the same in all the vessels
(d) maximum in vessel *A*

6 A closed compartment containing gas is moving with some acceleration in horizontal direction. Neglect effect of gravity. Then, the pressure in the compartment is **[JCECE]**

(a) same everywhere (b) lower in front side
(c) lower in rear side (d) lower in upper side

2008

7 A common hydrometer reads specific gravity of liquids. Compared to the 1.6 mark of the stem, the mark 1.5 will be **[AMU]**

(a) upwards
(b) downwards
(c) in the same place
(d) may be upward or downward depending upon the hydrometer

2006

8 By sucking through a straw, a student can reduce the pressure in his lungs to 750 mm of Hg. Using the straw, he can drink water from a glass upto a maximum depth of (density $= 13.6\ \text{gcm}^{-3}$) **[AIIMS]**

(a) 10 cm (b) 75 cm (c) 13.6 cm (d) 1.36 cm

2005

9 From the figure given below, the correct observation is

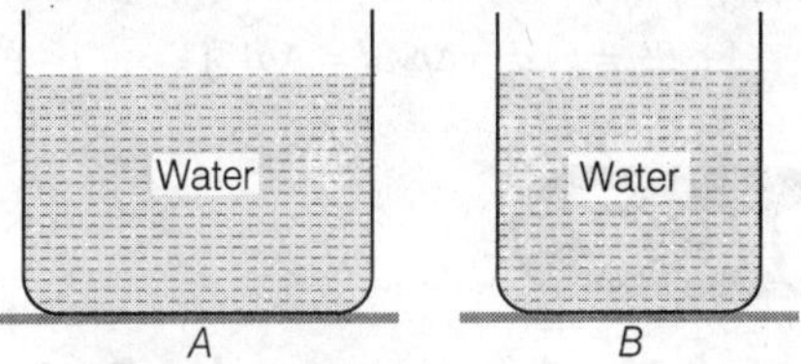

[KCET]

(a) the pressure on the bottom of tank *A* is greater than at the bottom of *B*
(b) the pressure on the bottom of the tank *A* is smaller than at the bottom of *B*
(c) the pressure depends on the shape of the container
(d) the pressure on the bottom of *A* and *B* is the same

10 An adulterated sample of milk has a density of $1032\ \text{kgm}^{-3}$, while pure milk has a density of $1080\ \text{kgm}^{-3}$. The volume of pure milk in a sample of 10 L of adulterated milk is **[JCECE]**

(a) 0.5 L (b) 1 L (c) 2 L (d) 4 L

Answers

1 (c)	2 (a)	3 (c)	4 (b)	5 (c)	6 (b)	7 (a)	8 (c)	9 (d)	10 (d)

Explanations

1 (c) Given, $d = 2700$ m, $\rho = 10^3$ kg/m^3

Compressibility

$= 45.4 \times 10^{-11}$ per pascal

The pressure at the bottom of an ocean is given by

$p = \rho g d = 10^3 \times 10 \times 2700 = 27 \times 10^6$ Pa

So, fractional compression

= compressibility × pressure

$= 45.4 \times 10^{-11} \times 27 \times 10^6 = 1.2 \times 10^{-2}$

2 (a) Assuming temperature constant.

As from the Boyle's law,

$pV =$ constant

So, from the two cases at h depth and at the surface,

$$p_1V_1 = p_2V_2 \quad \text{...(i)}$$

where, p_1 = pressure at h depth,

V_1 = volume at h depth,

p_2 = pressure at surface

and V_2 = volume at surface.

$\Rightarrow \quad p_1 = (h + l)\rho g, \; V_1 = \frac{4}{3}\pi r^3$

$p_2 = l\rho g, \; V_2 = \frac{4}{3}\pi(3r)^3$

Putting these values in Eq. (i), we get

So, $(h + l) = 27l \Rightarrow h = 26\,l$

3 (c) Work done by motor = Change in gravitational potential energy + Work done against external pressure

$= mgh + \Delta pV$

$[\because W = F \cdot d = \Delta pAd = \Delta pV]$

$= V\rho gh + \Delta pV = 4 \times 10^3 \times 10 \times 20 + (2 \times 10^5 - 1 \times 10^5) \times 4$

$= 8 \times 10^5 + 4 \times 10^5 = 12 \times 10^5$ J

4 (b) The volume of water contained in the vessel would be equal to $V = l^3 = (1\text{m})^3 = 1\text{m}^3$. Assuming water to be pure, so the density of water would be equal to $d = 1000$ kg/m^3, hence the mass of water contained in the vessel would be equal to $m = Vd = 1000$ kg.

Thus, the work done would be equal to

$W = mgh = 1000 \times 10 \times \frac{1}{2} = 5000$ J

Here, h is the height of centre of mass from the bottom of vessel.

5 (c) Force exerted by the liquid on the base of the vessel is $F = mg$

$\Rightarrow \quad F \propto m$

Here, $\quad m_A = m_B = m_C$

$\therefore \quad F_A = F_B = F_C$

6 (b) The pressure on the rear side would be more due to fictitious force (acting in the opposite direction of acceleration) on the rear face.

On application of force,

Since $m_1 > m_2$, hence pressure ($p = F/A = mg/A$) is more on rear side.

where, m_1 = mass on rear side,

m_2 = mass on front size.

Consequently, the pressure in the front side would be lowered.

7 (a) In hydrometer, lower density mark is upwards and higher density mark is downwards.

8 (c) Pressure difference between lungs of student and atmosphere

= (760 − 750) mm of Hg.

Water pressure = Atmospheric pressure

i.e. $\quad hdg = 10$ mm of Hg = 1 cm of Hg

or $\quad h \times 1 = 1 \times 13.6 = 13.6$ cm

9 (d) Pressure applied by liquid column, $p = hdg$

i.e. the pressure depends on the height of liquid column not on its size or shape, so pressure at the bottom of A and B is the same.

10 (d) Mass of adulterated milk,

$M_A = 1032 \times 10 \times 10^{-3} = 10.32$ kg

$\Rightarrow$ Mass of water $= \rho_w V_w = M_A - M_P$

where, M_P = mass of pure milk.

$\Rightarrow 10^3(10 \times 10^{-3} - V_P) = 10.32 - 1080V_P$

$\Rightarrow \quad 10 - 10^3V_P = 10.32 - 1080V_P$

$\Rightarrow \quad 80V_P = 0.32$

$\Rightarrow \quad V_P = \frac{0.32}{80} \times 1000 = 4$ L

Topic 2

Pascal's Law and Archimedes' Principle

2019

1 In a U-tube as shown in the figure, water and oil are in the left side and right side of the tube, respectively. The heights from the bottom for water and oil columns are 15 cm and 20 cm, respectively. The density of the oil is (take, $\rho_{water} = 1000$ kg/m^3) **[NEET (Odisha)]**

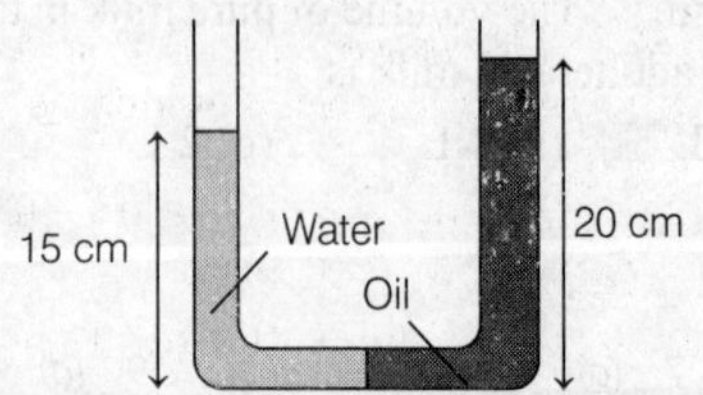

(a) 1200 kg/m^3 (b) 750 kg/m^3
(c) 1000 kg/m^3 (d) 1333 kg/m^3

2018

2 Find density of ethyl alcohol. **[JIPMER]**

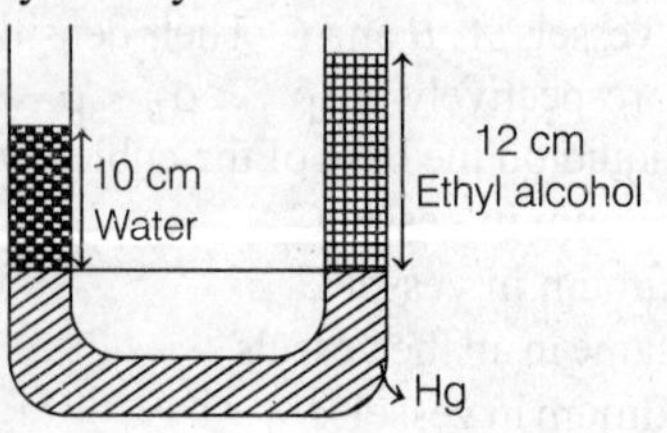

(a) 0.83 gcm^{-3} (b) 0.5 gcm^{-3}
(c) 1.83 gcm^{-3} (d) 0.12 gcm^{-3}

3 A solid floats with 1/4 th of its volume above the surface of water, the density of the solid is **[JIPMER]**

(a) 750 kg m^{-3} (b) 650 kg m^{-3}
(c) 560 kg m^{-3} (d) 450 kg m^{-3}

2017

4 An ice-berg of density 900 kgm^{-3} is floating in water of density 1000 kgm^{-3}. The percentage of volume of ice-berg outside the water is **[JIPMER]**
(a) 20% (b) 35% (c) 10% (d) 11%

5 A U-tube with both ends open to the atmosphere, is partially filled with water. Oil, which is immiscible with water, is poured into one side until it stands at a distance of 10 mm above the water level on the other side. Meanwhile the water rises by 65 mm from its original level (see diagram). The density of the oil is **[NEET]**

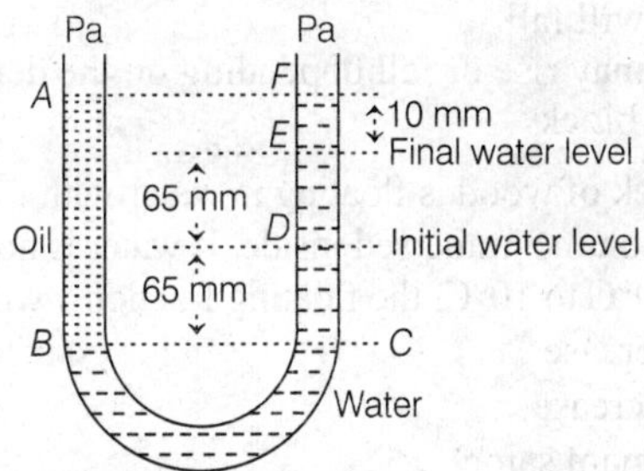

(a) 650 kg m^{-3} (b) 425 kg m^{-3}
(c) 800 k g m^{-3} (d) 928 kg m^{-3}

2016

6 Two non-mixing liquids of densities ρ and $n\rho$ $(n > 1)$ are put in a container. The height of each liquid is h. A solid cylinder of length L and density d is put in this container. The cylinder floats with its axis vertical and length pL $(p < 1)$ in the denser liquid. The density d is equal to
(a) $\{2+(n+1)p\}\rho$ (b) $\{2+(n-1)p\}\rho$ **[NEET]**
(c) $\{1+(n-1)p\}\rho$ (d) $\{1+(n+1)p\}\rho$

2014

7 A wooden block is floating on water kept in a beaker. 40% of the block is above the water surface. Now, the beaker is kept inside a lift that starts going upward with acceleration equal to $g/2$. The block will then **[WB JEE]**
(a) sink
(b) float with 10% above the water surface
(c) float with 40% above the water surface
(d) float with 70% above the water surface

2013

8 A body floats with one-third of its volume outside water and 3 / 4 of its volume outside another liquid. The density of other liquid is **[WB JEE]**
(a) $\frac{9}{4}$ g/cc (b) $\frac{4}{9}$ g/cc (c) $\frac{8}{3}$ g/cc (d) $\frac{3}{8}$ g/cc

9 A 10 cm^3 cube floats in water with a volume of 4 cm^3 remaining above the surface. The density of the material from which the cube is made, is **[Manipal]**
(a) 0.6 g cm^{-3} (b) 1 g cm^{-3}
(c) 0.4 g cm^{-3} (d) 0.24 g cm^{-3}

2011

10 A stone of relative density K is released from rest on the surface of a lake. If viscous effects are ignored, the stone sinks in water with an acceleration of **[WB JEE]**
(a) $g(1-K)$ (b) $g(1+K)$
(c) $g\left(1-\frac{1}{K}\right)$ (d) $g\left(1+\frac{1}{K}\right)$

11 A hydraulic system is used to lift a 2000 kg vehicle in an auto-garage. If the vehicle is kept on a piston of area 0.55m^2 and a force is applied to a piston of area 0.03m^2. What is the minimum force that must be applied to lift the vehicle?
(a) 1160N (b) 2000N (c) 2010N (d) 1069N

12 A body floats in water with 40% of its volume outside water. When the same body floats in an oil, 60% of its volume remains outside oil. The relative density of oil is
(a) 0.9 (b) 1 **[WB JEE]**
(c) 1.2 (d) 1.5

13 A block of wood floats in water with $\left(\frac{4}{5}\right)$th of its volume submerged. If the same block just floats in a liquid, the density of the liquid is (in kgm^{-3}) **[Kerala CEE]**
(a) 1250 (b) 600 (c) 400 (d) 800
(e) 750

2010

14 A liquid X of density 3.36 g/cm^3 is poured in a U-tube in right arm with height 10 cm, which contains Hg. Another liquid Y is poured in left arm with height 8 cm. Upper levels of X and Y are same. What is the density of Y? **[Manipal]**

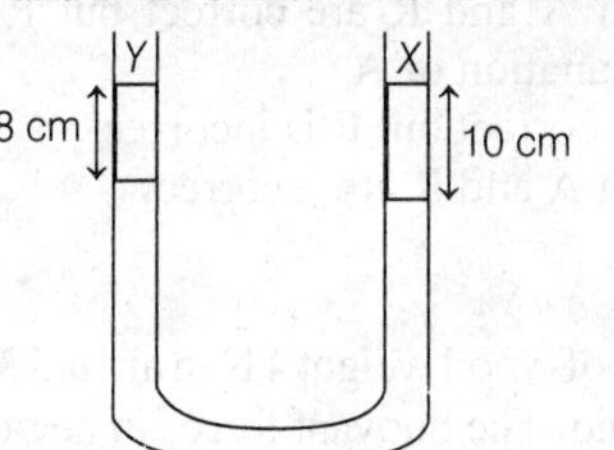

(a) 0.8 g/cc (b) 1.2 g/cc
(c) 1.4 g/cc (d) 1.6 g/cc

2009

15 **Assertion** (A) A ship floats higher in the water on a high pressure day than on a low pressure day.
Reason (R) Floating of ship in the water is not possible because of buoyancy force which is present due to pressure difference. **[AIIMS]**
(a) Both A and R are correct and R is the correct explanation of A
(b) Both A and R are correct but R is not the correct explanation of A
(c) A is correct but R is incorrect
(d) Both A and R are incorrect

2008

16 A body floats in water with one-third of its volume above the surface of water. If it is placed in oil, it floats with half of its volume above the surface of the oil. The specific gravity of the oil is **[Kerala CEE]**

(a) $\frac{5}{3}$ (b) $\frac{4}{3}$ (c) $\frac{3}{2}$ (d) 1

(e) 3/4

17 An ice block floats in a liquid whose density is less than water. A part of block is outside the liquid. When whole of ice has melted, the liquid level will **[AMU]**

(a) rise (b) go down

(c) remain same (d) first rise then go down

18 A body weighs 50 g in air and 40 g in water. How much would it weigh in a liquid of specific gravity 1.5? **[KCET]**

(a) 30 g (b) 35 g (c) 65 g (d) 45 g

19 A cube made of material having a density of 0.9×10^3 kgm^{-3} floats between water and a liquid of density 0.7×10^3 kgm^{-3}, which is immiscible with water. What part of the cube is immersed in water? **[Manipal]**

(a) $\frac{1}{3}$ (b) $\frac{2}{3}$ (c) $\frac{3}{4}$ (d) $\frac{3}{7}$

2007

20 **Assertion** (A) Taking into account the fact that any object which floats must have an average density less than that of water, during world war I, a number of cargo vessels were made of concrete. **[AIIMS]**

Reason (R) Concrete cargo vessels were filled with air.

(a) Both A and R are correct and R is the correct explanation of A

(b) Both A and R are correct but R is not the correct explanation of A

(c) A is correct but R is incorrect

(d) Both A and R are incorrect

2006

21 A block of wood weight 4 N in air and 3 N, when immersed in a liquid. The buoyant force (in newton) is **[Kerala CEE]**

(a) zero (b) 1 (c) $\frac{3}{4}$ (d) $\frac{4}{3}$

(e) 7

22 A large ship can float but a steel needle sinks because of **[Punjab PMET]**

(a) viscosity (b) surface tension

(c) density (d) None of these

23 If there were no gravity, which of the following will not be there for a fluid? **[KCET]**

(a) Viscosity (b) Surface tension

(c) Pressure

(d) Archimedes' upward thrust

24 A ball whose density is 0.4×10^3 kgm^{-3} falls into water from a height of 9 cm. To what depth does the ball sink? **[EAMCET]**

(a) 9 cm (b) 6 cm

(c) 4.5 cm (d) 2.25 cm

25 A rectangular block is 5 cm × 5 cm × 10 cm in size. The block is floating in water with 5 cm side vertical. If it floats with 10 cm side vertical, what change will occur in the level of water? **[MHT CET]**

(a) No change

(b) It will rise

(c) It will fall

(d) It may rise or fall depending on the density of block

26 A block of wood is floating in water with fraction x of the total volume immersed inside. If water is now heated from 0°C to 10°C, the floating fraction x will **[MP PMT]**

(a) increase

(b) decrease

(c) remain same

(d) first decrease and then increase

27 An open U-tube contains mercury. When 11.2 cm of water is poured into one of the arms of the tube, how high does the mercury rise in the other arm from its initial level? **[BCECE]**

(a) 0.56 cm (b) 1.35 cm

(c) 0.41 cm (d) 2.32 cm

2005

28 A ball is floating on the surface of water with half the volume submerged. If the ball has a radius of 12 cm, what is the buoyancy force on the ball due to water? **[AIIMS]**

(a) 33 N (b) 35 N

(c) 25 N (d) 40 N

29 A candle of diameter d is floating on a liquid in a cylindrical container of diameter D $(D >> d)$ as shown in figure. If it is burning at the rate of 2 cm h^{-1}, then the top of the candle will **[AIIMS]**

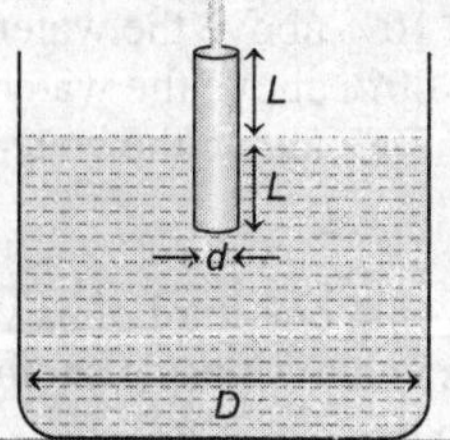

(a) remain at the same height

(b) fall at the rate of 1 cmh^{-1}

(c) fall at the rate of 2 cmh^{-1}

(d) go up at the rate of 1 cmh^{-1}

Answers

1 (b)	2 (a)	3 (a)	4 (c)	5 (d)	6 (c)	7 (b)	8 (c)	9 (a)	10 (c)
11 (d)	12 (d)	13 (d)	14 (a)	15 (d)	16 (b)	17 (b)	18 (b)	19 (b)	20 (b)
21 (b)	22 (d)	23 (d)	24 (b)	25 (a)	26 (d)	27 (c)	28 (b)	29 (b)	

Explanations

1 *(b)* According to Pascal's law
''Pressure applied to an enclosed fluid is transmitted undiminished to every point of the fluid and the walls of the containing vessel.''
In the given situation as shown in the figure below

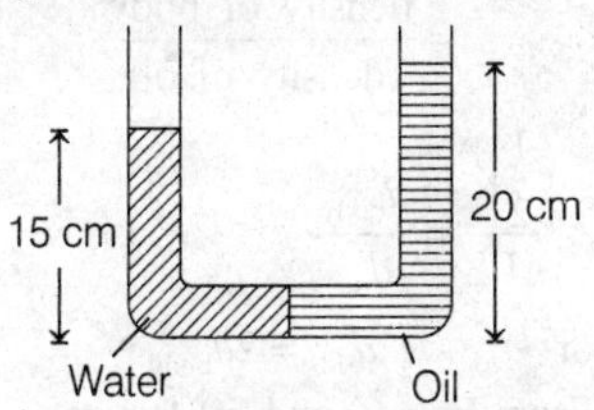

Pressure due to water column of height 15 cm = Pressure due to oil column of height 20 cm

$$\Rightarrow \quad h_w\rho_w g = h_o\rho_o g$$

$$15\rho_w = 20\rho_o \quad \Rightarrow \quad \rho_o = \frac{15}{20}\rho_w$$

$$\Rightarrow \quad \rho_o = \frac{15}{20} \times 1000$$

$(\because$ given, $\rho_w = 1000\,\text{kg m}^{-3})$

$$= 750\,\text{kgm}^{-3}$$

2 *(a)* Pressure at left hand of a U-tube,

$$p_1 = p_0 + \rho_1 g h_1 = p_0 + \rho_1 10\,(10\times10^{-2})$$

or $\quad p_1 = p_0 + \rho_1$

Pressure at right hand of a U-tube,

$$p_2 = p_0 + \rho_2 g h_2 = p_0 + \rho_2 10(12\times10^{-2})$$

or $\quad p_2 = p_0 + 1.2\,\rho_2$

The mercury column in both arms of U-tube are at same level, therefore pressure in both arms will be same.

or $p_1 = p_2 \quad \Rightarrow \quad p_0 + \rho_1 = p_0 + 1.2\rho_2$

$\therefore$ Density of ethyl alcohol,

$$\rho_2 = \frac{\rho_1}{1.2} = \frac{1000}{1.2} = 833.3\,\text{kgm}^{-3}$$

$$= 0.83\,\text{gcm}^{-3}$$

3 *(a)* Let V and ρ be volume and density of solid respectively and ρ' be the density of water,

i.e. $\quad \rho' = 10^3\,\text{kgm}^{-3}$

Weight of body $= V\rho g$

Volume of solid body outside water $= V/4$

$\therefore$ Volume of solid body inside water

$$= V - V/4 = 3V/4$$

Weight of water displaced by solid

$$= \frac{3V}{4} \times 10^3 \times g$$

As solid body is floating, then

Weight of body = Weight of water displaced by it

$$V\rho g = \frac{3V}{4} \times 10^3 g$$

$$\Rightarrow \quad \rho = \frac{3}{4} \times 1000 = 750\,\text{kg m}^{-3}$$

4 *(c)* Let the volume of ice-berg is V and its density is ρ. If this ice-berg floats in water with volume V_{in} inside it, then

$V_{in}\,\sigma g = V\rho g$

$$\Rightarrow V_{in} = \left(\frac{\rho}{\sigma}\right)V$$

$$\Rightarrow V_{out} = V - V_{in} = \left(\frac{\sigma - \rho}{\sigma}\right)V$$

$$= \left(\frac{1000 - 900}{1000}\right)V = \frac{V}{10}$$

$$\Rightarrow \frac{V_{out}}{V} = 0.1 = 10\%$$

5 *(d)* Pressure of two points lie in the same horizontal level should be same and $p = hdg$.

Both ends of the U-tube are open, so the pressure on both the free surfaces must be equal,

i.e. $\quad p_1 = p_2$

$h_{oil} \cdot S_{oil}\, g = h_{water} \cdot S_{water} \cdot g$

where, S_{oil} = specific density of oil.

$$\Rightarrow \quad S_{oil} = \frac{h_{water} \cdot S_{water} \cdot g}{h_{oil} \cdot g}$$

From figure,

$$S_{oil} = \frac{(65 + 65) \times 1000}{(65 + 65 + 10)} = 928\,\text{kgm}^{-3}$$

6 *(c)* According to question, the situation can be drawn as following.

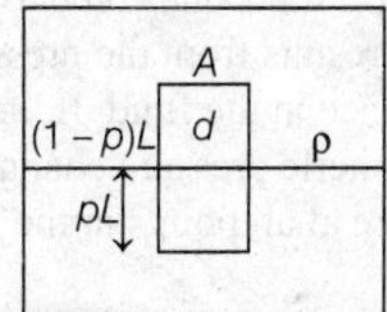

Applying Archimedes' principle,

Weight of cylinder

$$= (\text{Upthrust})_1 + (\text{Upthrust})_2$$

i.e. $ALdg = (1 - p)\,LA\rho g + (pLA)\,n\rho g$

$$\Rightarrow \quad d = (1 - p)\,\rho + pn\rho$$

$$= \rho - p\rho + n\,p\rho$$

$$= \rho + (n - 1)\,p\rho$$

$$= \rho\,[1 + (n - 1)\,p]$$

7 *(b)* According to Archimedes' principle, weight of the wooden block = weight of the liquid displaced

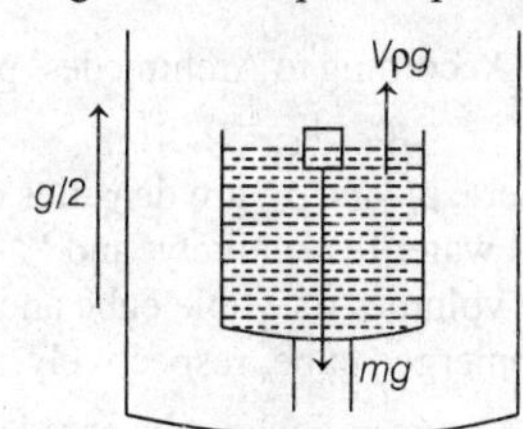

$$\Rightarrow \quad mg = \left(\frac{60}{100}\right)V \times \rho_l \times g$$

$$= \frac{3}{5}V \times \rho_l \times g \qquad \ldots\text{(i)}$$

[Here, V = total volume of block, ρ_l = density of liquid]

When beaker is kept in a lift, then net weight of the block

$$= mg + mg/2$$

$$= \frac{3mg}{2} \qquad \left[\because R - mg = \frac{mg}{2}\right]$$

Again, for float condition,

Net weight of the block = Buoyant force

$$\Rightarrow \frac{3mg}{2} = V_i \times \rho_l \times g \qquad \ldots\text{(ii)}$$

Here, V_i = volume of block inside liquid.

From Eqs. (i) and (ii), we have

$$\left(\frac{3}{2}\right) \times \frac{3}{5}(V \times \rho_l \times g) = V_i \times \rho_l \times g$$

or $\quad V_i = \dfrac{9}{10}V$

So, volume of the block above liquid

$$= \frac{1}{10}V = 10\%\text{ of total volume.}$$

8 (c) Let V be the volume of a body and ρ its density, then by law of floatation in water

$$V\rho g = \frac{2}{3}V \times \rho_w g \quad ...(i)$$

$$\left[\because \frac{2}{3}V \text{ is immersed in water of density } \rho_w\right]$$

Similarly, in a liquid,

$$V\rho g = \frac{1}{4}V \times \rho_l g \quad ...(ii)$$

[∵ mass is same in both the cases]

From Eqs. (i) and (ii), we get

$$\frac{2}{3}V\rho_w g = \frac{1}{4}V\rho_l g$$

$$\Rightarrow \frac{\rho_l}{\rho_w} = \left(\frac{2}{3}\right) \times \left[\frac{4}{1}\right]$$

$$\Rightarrow \frac{\rho_l}{\rho_w} = \frac{8}{3}$$

$$\Rightarrow \rho_l = \frac{8}{3} \text{ g/cc } (\because \rho_w = 1 \text{ g/cc})$$

9 (a) According to Archimedes' principle,

$$\rho_C g V_C = \rho_w g V_{CS}$$

where, ρ_C and ρ_w are densities of cube and water respectively; and V_C and V_{CS} are volumes of whole cube and submerged cube, respectively.

$$\Rightarrow \frac{\text{Volume of cube submerged}}{\text{Total volume of cube}} = \frac{\text{Density of cube material}}{\text{Density of water}}$$

$$\Rightarrow \frac{10-4}{10} = \frac{d}{1}$$

$$\Rightarrow d = \frac{6}{10} = 0.6 \text{ g cm}^{-3}$$

10 (c) The net force acting on the stone of mass (m) in a downward direction would be equal to $F = V\sigma g - V\rho g$, where the force acting downwards would be equal to $V\sigma g$ due to its weight and the force acting upwards would be equal to $V\rho g$ due to the buoyant force. Hence, we get

$V\rho g$ ↑, a ↓, $mg = V\sigma g$

$$F = V\sigma g - V\rho g = V\sigma g\left(1 - \frac{\rho}{\sigma}\right)$$

where, σ = density of stone and ρ = density of liquid.

$$= mg\left(1 - \frac{\rho}{\sigma}\right) = mg\left(1 - \frac{1}{K}\right)$$

Thus, $$a = g\left(1 - \frac{1}{K}\right)$$ [$\because F = ma$]

11 (d) We know, $p_1 = p_2$

$$\Rightarrow \frac{F_1}{A_1} = \frac{F_2}{A_2} \Rightarrow F_1 = \left(\frac{A_1}{A_2}\right)F_2$$

$$\Rightarrow F_1 = \left(\frac{0.03}{0.55}\right)(2000 \times 9.8)$$

$$\Rightarrow F_1 \simeq 1069 \text{ N}$$

12 (d) Using the law of buoyancy, we have $V\sigma g = 0.6 V\sigma_1 g$, for the part of body inside water and $V\sigma g = 0.4 V\sigma_2 g$, for the part of body inside oil, hence we get

$$0.6 V\sigma_1 g = 0.4 V\sigma_2 g$$

$$1 = \frac{0.6\sigma_1}{0.4\sigma_2}$$

So, we have $\frac{\sigma_2}{\sigma_1} = \frac{6}{4}$

$$= \frac{3}{2} = 1.5$$

13 (d) Applying Archimedes' principle, submerged part = replaced water

$$\Rightarrow \frac{4}{5}h\rho_w g = h \times \rho_\lambda \times g$$

where, ρ_w = density of water and ρ_λ = density of liquid.

$$\therefore \rho_\lambda = \frac{4}{5} \times \rho_w$$

$$= \frac{4}{5} \times 1000$$

$$\Rightarrow \rho_\lambda = 800 \text{ kgm}^{-3}$$

14 (a) As shown in figure, in the two arms of a tube atmospheric pressure remains same on surface pp'. Hence,

$$8 \times \rho_Y \times g + 2 \times \rho_{Hg} \times g = 10 \times \rho_X \times g$$

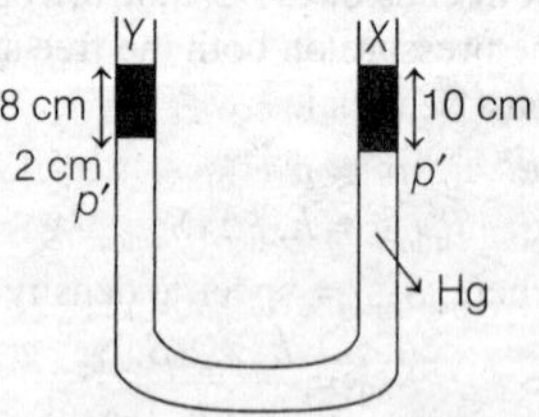

$$\therefore 8\rho_Y + 2 \times 13.6 = 10 \times 3.36$$

$$\text{or} \quad \rho_Y = \frac{33.6 - 27.2}{8} = 0.8 \text{ g/cc}$$

15 (d) The level of floating of a ship in the water is unaffected by the atmospheric pressure. It depends on buoyancy force which results from the pressure difference in the fluid. If the atmospheric pressure changes, the pressure at all points in the water changes by same amount keeping pressure difference in the water same.

16 (b) Initially in water,

$$\frac{\text{volume of body immersed in water}}{\text{volume of body}} = \frac{\text{density of body}}{\text{density of water}}$$

$$\therefore \frac{2/3V}{V} = \frac{d_{body}}{d_{water}}$$

$$\text{or} \quad d_{body} = \frac{2}{3}d_{water} \quad ...(i)$$

In oil, $$\frac{\text{volume of body immersed in oil}}{\text{volume of body}} = \frac{\text{density of body}}{\text{density of oil}}$$

$$\therefore \frac{\frac{1}{2}V}{V} = \frac{d_{body}}{d_{oil}}$$

$$\text{or} \quad d_{oil} = 2d_{body} \quad ...(ii)$$

From Eqs. (i) and (ii), we get

$$\text{or } d_{oil} = 2 \times \frac{2}{3}d_{water}$$

Therefore, specific gravity of oil

$$\frac{d_{oil}}{d_{water}} = \frac{\frac{4}{3} \times d_{water}}{d_{water}}$$

$$= \frac{4}{3} \quad \left[\because \text{Specific gravity} = \frac{\text{Density of substance}}{\text{Density of water}}\right]$$

17 (b) Ice is lighter than water. When ice melts, the volume occupied by water is less than that of ice, due to which the level of water goes down.

18 (b) $$\frac{\sigma_l}{\sigma_w} = \frac{\text{upthrust on body in liquid}}{\text{upthrust on body in water}}$$

$$\frac{1.5}{1} = \frac{x}{(50-40)\text{ g}}$$

$$\Rightarrow x = 15 \text{ g}$$

∴ Upthrust on body in liquid = 15 g

Weight of the body = 50 g

Hence, body will weigh (50 − 15) = 35 g in the liquid.

19 (b) Let l = side of the cube,

x = side of cube immersed in water

and $l - x$ = side of cube immersed in liquid.

According to law of floatation,

$$l^3 \times 0.9 \times 10^3 \times g = (l^2 \times x) \times 1000 \text{ g} + l^2(l - x) \times 0.7 \times 10^3 g$$

$$[\because V_1\rho_1 g = V_2\rho_2 g]$$

$\Rightarrow \quad l \times 0.9 = x + (l - x) \times 0.7$

or $\quad 0.3x = 0.2l \quad$ or $\quad \frac{x}{l} = \frac{2}{3}$

20 (b) The density of concrete ofcourse is more than that of water and a block of concrete will sink like a stone, if dropped into water. Concrete cargo were filled with air and as such, average density of cargo vessels

$$= \frac{\text{Mass of concrete} + \text{Mass of air}}{\text{Volume of concrete} + \text{Volume of air}}$$

It follows that the average density of cargo vessels must be less than that of water. As a result, the concrete cargo vessels did not sink.

21 (b) From Archimedes' principle, the buoyant force is

$F = 4\text{ N} - 3\text{ N} = 1\text{N}$

22 (d) A large ship can float but a steel needle sinks, this concept is explained by Archimedes' principle which states that when a body is fully or partially submerged in a fluid, a buoyant force from the surrounding fluid acts on the body. The force is directed upward and has a magnitude equal to the weight of the fluid that has been displaced by the body. Hence, a large ship can float but a needle sinks.

23 (d) Archimedes' upward thrust ($V\rho g$) will be absent for a fluid, if there were no gravity.

24 (b) Given, density of ball,

$d = 0.4 \times 10^3 \text{ kg m}^{-3}$

Height above the surface of water,

$h = 9$ cm

Velocity acquired by ball at the moment, it reaches surface,

$$v_0 = \sqrt{2gh}$$

$[\because v^2 = u^2 + 2gh \text{ and } u = 0]$

From law of conservation of energy,

Loss in KE = Work done by the net upward force in water

$$\Rightarrow \frac{1}{2}mv_0^2 = V(\rho_w - d)g \times x$$

Here, ρ_w = density of water,

x = depth to which ball sink

and V = volume of water.

$$\Rightarrow \frac{(V \times d)v_0^2}{2} = V(\rho_w - d)g \times x$$

$$\Rightarrow d\left(\frac{2gh}{2}\right) = (\rho_w - d)gx$$

$$\Rightarrow x = \frac{dh}{\rho_w - d} = \frac{0.4 \times 10^3 \times 9}{(1 \times 10^3 - 0.4 \times 10^3)}$$

$$= \frac{0.4}{0.6} \times 9 = 6 \text{ cm}$$

25 (a) By the law of floatation, we know that a body will float in a liquid, when its weight w is equal to the weight w' of the liquid displaced by the immersed part of the body. But this does not necessarily indicate that the body will be in equilibrium.

A body will be in equilibrium only, if the resultant of all the forces and couples acting on the body is zero. If w and w' act along different lines, they will form a couple which will tend to rotate the body.

Thus, a floating body can be in equilibrium, if no couple acts on it. It will be so, if the line of action of w and w' is along the same vertical straight line.

Here, in both the situations, as the mass of floating block remains same, hence according to principle of floatation mass of volume of water displaced also remains same. Hence, water level will remain same in both the cases.

26 (d) Floating fraction or immersed fraction

$$= \frac{\text{density of wood}}{\text{density of water}}$$

When water is heated from 0°C to 10°C, density of water first increases upto 4°C and then decreases due to anomalous expansion of water. Therefore, floating fraction will first decrease because density of water increases and then increase because density of water decreases.

27 (c) On pouring water on left side, mercury rises x cm (say) from its previous level in the right limb of U-tube creating a difference of levels of mercury by $2x$ cm. Equating pressures at A and B, we get

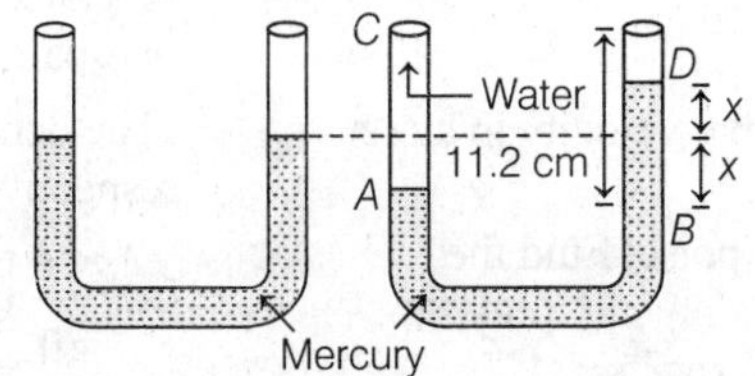

$$p_A = p_B$$

$$\therefore 11.2 \times 10^{-2} \times \rho_{\text{water}} \times g = 2x \times \rho_{\text{mercury}} \times g$$

$$\Rightarrow 11.2 \times 10^{-2} \times 1000 \text{ kgm}^{-3} = 2x \times 13600 \text{kgm}^{-3}$$

$$\Rightarrow \quad x = \frac{11.2 \times 10^{-2} \times 1000 \text{ m}}{2 \times 13600}$$

$$= 0.41 \text{ cm}$$

28 (b) Buoyant force, $F = mg$

where, m = mass of water.

Given, $V_w = \frac{1}{2}V_b$

where, V_w = volume of water displaced and V_b = volume of ball.

$$\Rightarrow \quad V_w = \frac{1}{2}\left(\frac{4}{3}\pi r^3\right)$$

$$= \frac{2}{3}\pi(0.12)^3$$

$[\because r = 12 \text{ cm} = 0.12 \text{ m}]$

$\therefore \quad F = \rho V_w g$

(where, ρ = density of water)

$$= 1000 \times \frac{2}{3}\pi(0.12)^3 \times 9.8$$

$$= 35 \text{ N}$$

29 (b) Weight of candle

= Weight of liquid displaced

i.e. $\quad V\rho g = V'\rho' g$

or $\left(\pi\frac{d^2}{4} \times 2L\right)\rho = \left(\pi\frac{d^2}{4}L\right)\rho'$

or $\quad \frac{\rho}{\rho'} = \frac{1}{2}$

Let,

x = length of burnt part of candle,

ρ = density of wax

and ρ' = density of liquid.

Since, candle is burning at the rate of 2 cm per hour, then after an hour, it will remain $(2L - 2)$ cm.

$\therefore \quad (2L - 2)\rho = (L - x)\rho'$

or $\quad \frac{\rho}{\rho'} = \frac{L - x}{2(L - 1)}$

So, $\quad \frac{1}{2} = \frac{L - x}{2(L - 1)}$

or $\quad L - 1 = L - x$

$\Rightarrow \quad x = 1$ cm

Thus, it falls at the rate of 1 cm h^{-1}.

Topic 3

Fluid Flow, Bernoulli's Theorem and Stokes' Law

2019

1 If a small orifice is made at a height of 0.25 m from the ground, the horizontal range of water stream will be

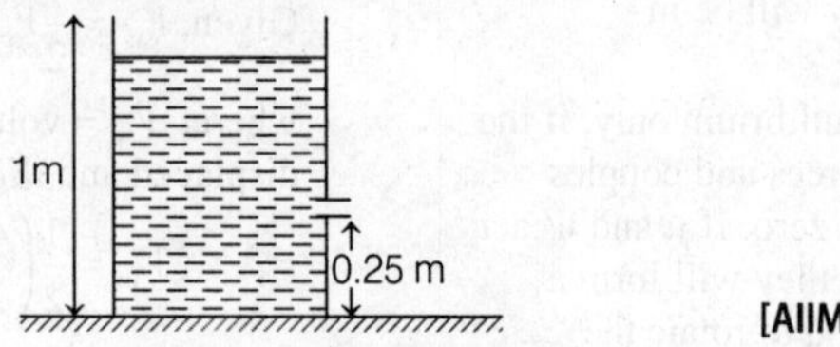

[AIIMS]

(a) 46.5 cm (b) 56.6 cm
(c) 76.6 cm (d) 86.6 cm

2 Two small spherical metal balls, having equal masses, are made from materials of densities ρ_1 and ρ_2 ($\rho_1 = 8\rho_2$) and have radii of 1 mm and 2 mm, respectively. They are made to fall vertically (from rest) in viscous medium whose coefficient of viscosity equals η and whose density is $0.1\,\rho_2$. The ratio of their terminal velocities would be [NEET (Odisha)]

(a) $\frac{79}{72}$ (b) $\frac{19}{36}$
(c) $\frac{39}{72}$ (d) $\frac{79}{36}$

3 Determine the pressure difference in tube of non-uniform cross-sectional area as shown in figure. [AIIMS]
$\Delta p = ?$, $d_1 = 5\,\text{cm}$, $v_1 = 4\text{m/s}$, $d_2 = 2\,\text{cm}$, $v_2 = ?$

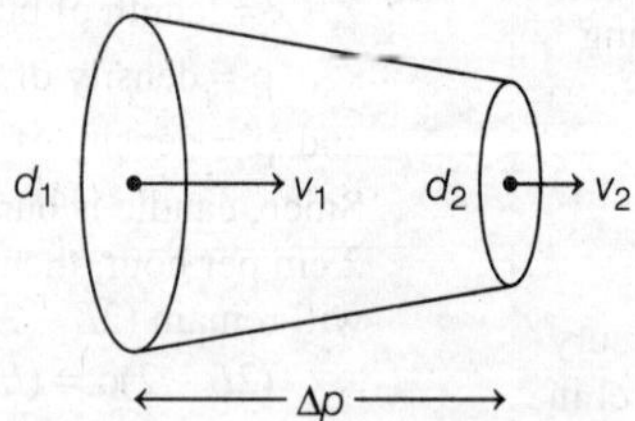

(a) 304200 Pa (b) 304500 Pa
(c) 302500 Pa (d) 303500 Pa

2018

4 A rain drop of radius 0.3 mm has a terminal velocity in air 1 ms^{-1}. The viscosity of air is 18×10^{-5} poise. Find the viscous force on the rain drops. [JIPMER]

(a) 2.05×10^{-7} N (b) 1.018×10^{-7} N
(c) 1.05×10^{-7} N (d) 2.058×10^{-7} N

5 At what speed will the velocity of a stream of water be equal to 20 cm of mercury column? (Take, $g = 10\,\text{ms}^{-2}$) [JIPMER]

(a) 6.4 ms^{-1} (b) 7.3756 ms^{-1}
(c) 6.4756 ms^{-1} (d) None of these

6 Water flows through a horizontal pipe of variable cross-section at the rate of 20 L min^{-1}. What will be the velocity of water at a point where diameter is 4 cm? [JIPMER]

(a) 0.2639 ms^{-1} (b) 0.5639 ms^{-1}
(c) 0.4639 ms^{-1} (d) 0.3639 ms^{-1}

7 A small sphere of radius r falls from rest in a viscous liquid. As a result, heat is produced due to viscous force. The rate of production of heat when the sphere attains its terminal velocity, is proportional to [NEET]

(a) r^5 (b) r^2 (c) r^3 (d) r^4

2017

8 A liquid is allowed into a tube of truncated cone shape. Identify the correct statement from the following. [JIPMER]

(a) The speed is high at the wider end and low at the narrow end.
(b) The speed is low at the wider end and high at the narrow end.
(c) The speed is same at both ends in a streamline flow.
(d) The liquid flows with uniform velocity in the tube.

2014

9 A small metal sphere of radius a is falling with a velocity v through a vertical column of a viscous liquid. If the coefficient of viscosity of the liquid is η, then the sphere encounters an opposing force of [WB JEE]

(a) $6\pi\eta a^2 v$ (b) $\frac{6\eta v}{\pi a}$ (c) $6\pi\eta a v$ (d) $\frac{\pi\eta v}{6a^3}$

2013

10 What is the velocity v of a metallic ball of radius r falling in a tank of liquid at the instant when its acceleration is one-half that of a freely falling body?
(The densities of metal and of liquid are ρ and σ, respectively and the viscosity of liquid is η) [Manipal]

(a) $\frac{r^2 g}{9\eta}(\rho - 2\sigma)$ (b) $\frac{r^2 g}{9\eta}(2\rho - \sigma)$
(c) $\frac{r^2 g}{9\eta}(\rho - \sigma)$ (d) $\frac{2r^2 g}{9\eta}(\rho - \sigma)$

2011

11 In the case of a sphere falling through a viscous medium, it attains terminal velocity, when **[J&K CET]**
(a) viscous force plus buoyant force becomes equal to force of gravity
(b) viscous force is zero
(c) viscous force plus force of gravity becomes equal to buoyant force
(d) buoyant force becomes equal to force of gravity

12 A vertical tank with depth H is full with water. A hole is made on one side of the walls at a depth h below the water surface. At what distance from the foot of the wall does the emerging stream of water strike the foot? **[DUMET]**
(a) $\sqrt{h(H-h)}$ (b) $2\sqrt{h(H-h)}$
(c) $2(H-h)\sqrt{h/(H-h)}$ (d) $\sqrt{2h/(H-h)}$

2010

13 Water is in streamline flows along a horizontal pipe with non-uniform cross-section. At a point in the pipe, where the area of cross-section is 10 cm^2, the velocity of water is 1 ms^{-1} and the pressure is 2000 Pa. The pressure at another point, where the cross-sectional area is 5 cm^2 is **[KCET]**
(a) 4000 Pa (b) 2000 Pa
(c) 1000 Pa (d) 500 Pa

14 Two raindrops of same radius r falling with terminal velocity v merge and from a bigger drop of radius R. The terminal velocity of the bigger drop is **[VMMC]**
(a) $v\dfrac{R}{r}$ (b) $v\dfrac{R^2}{r^2}$
(c) v (d) $2v$

15 Two solid spheres of same metal but of mass M and $8M$ fall simultaneously on a viscous liquid and their terminal velocities are v and nv, then value of n is **[WB JEE]**
(a) 16 (b) 8
(c) 4 (d) 2

2009

16 The working of venturimeter is based on **[Kerala CEE]**
(a) Torricelli's law
(b) Pascal's law
(c) Bernoulli's theorem
(d) Archimedes' principle
(e) Stokes' law

17 Water flows along a horizontal pipe whose cross-section is not constant. The pressure is 1 cm of Hg where the velocity is 35 cm s^{-1}. At a point, where the velocity is 65 cm s^{-1}, the pressure will be **[UP CPMT]**
(a) 0.89 cm of Hg (b) 8.9 cm of Hg
(c) 0.5 cm of Hg (d) 1 cm of Hg

18 In a streamline flow, **[Manipal]**
(a) the speed of a particle always remains same
(b) the velocity of a particle always remains same
(c) the kinetic energies of all particles arriving at a given point are the same
(d) the moments of all the particles arriving at a given point are the same

2008

19 If the terminal speed of a sphere of gold (density $= 19.5\text{ kgm}^{-3}$) is 0.2 ms^{-1} in viscous liquid (density $= 1.5\text{ kgm}^{-3}$), find the terminal speed of a sphere of silver (density $= 10.5\text{ kgm}^{-3}$) of the same size in the same liquid. **[AIIMS]**
(a) 0.4 ms^{-1} (b) 0.133 ms^{-1}
(c) 0.1 ms^{-1} (d) 0.2 ms^{-1}

20 Water is filled in a tank to a height of 3 m. An orifice is made at a height 52.5 cm from bottom of tank. The ratio of the cross-sectional area of the orifice and the tank is 0.1. The square of the speed of the liquid coming out from the orifice is (take, $g = 10\text{ ms}^{-2}$) **[AIIMS]**
(a) $50\text{ m}^2\text{s}^{-2}$ (b) $50.5\text{ m}^2\text{s}^{-2}$
(c) $51\text{ m}^2\text{s}^{-2}$ (d) $52\text{ m}^2\text{s}^{-2}$

21 A rectangular vessel when full of water, takes 10 min to be emptied through an orifice in its bottom. How much time will it take to be emptied when half filled with water? **[AFMC]**
(a) 9 min (b) 7 min
(c) 5 min (d) 3 min

22 An air bubble of radius 1 cm rises from the bottom portion through a liquid of density 1.5 g cc^{-1} at a constant speed of 0.25 cms^{-1}. If the density of air is neglected, the coefficient of viscosity of the liquid is approximately (in Pa). **[AFMC]**
(a) 13000 (b) 1300
(c) 130 (d) 13

23 To get the maximum flight, a ball must be thrown as **[BHU]**
(a) 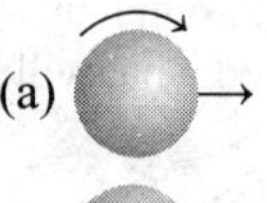 (b) 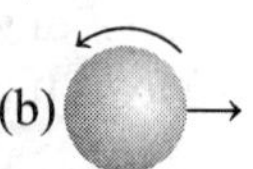
(c) (d) Any of (a), (b) and (c)

24 In the figure, the velocity v_3 will be

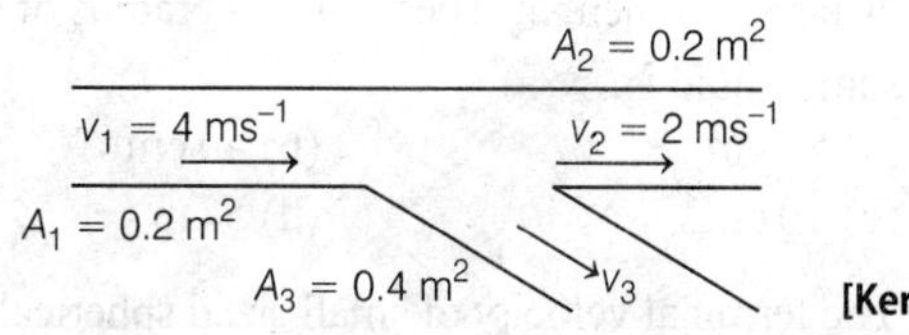

[Kerala CEE]
(a) zero (b) 4 ms^{-1} (c) 1 ms^{-1} (d) 3 ms^{-1}
(e) 2 ms^{-1}

25 A uniformly tapering vessel is filled with a liquid of density 900 kgm^{-3}. The force that acts on the base of the vessel due to the liquid is (take, $g = 10 \, ms^{-2}$) [AMU]

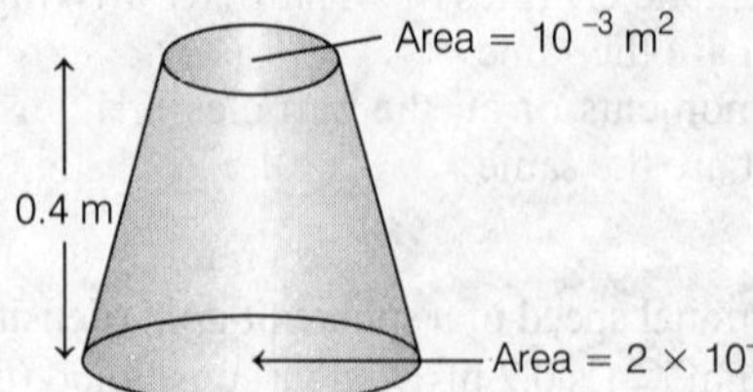

(a) 3.6 N (b) 7.2 N (c) 9 N (d) 14.4 N

26 A solid sphere falls with a terminal velocity v in CO_2 gas. If it is allowed to fall in vacuum, then [EAMCET]
(a) terminal velocity of sphere = v
(b) terminal velocity of sphere < v
(c) terminal velocity of sphere > v
(d) sphere never attain terminal velocity

27 At what speed, the velocity head of water is equal to pressure head of 40 cm of Hg? [BCECE]
(a) 10.3 ms^{-1} (b) 2.8 ms^{-1} (c) 5.6 ms^{-1} (d) 8.4 ms^{-1}

2007

28 When a body falls in air, the resistance of air depends to a great exient on the shape of the body. Three different shapes are given. Identify the combination of air resistances which truely represents the physical situation. (The cross-sectional areas are the same) [AIIMS]

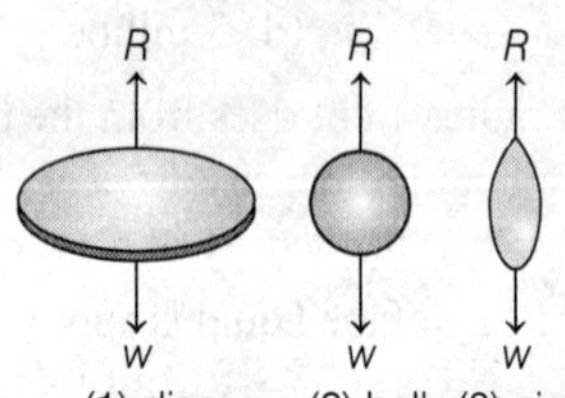

(a) 1< 2< 3 (b) 2< 3< 1
(c) 3< 2< 1 (d) 3< 1< 2

29 Two equal drops of water are falling through air with a steady velocity v. If the drops coalesced what will be the new velocity? [AFMC]
(a) $(2)^{1/3} v$ (b) $(2)^{3/2} v$
(c) $(2)^{2/3} v$ (d) $(2)^{1/4} v$

30 Speed of a ball of 2 cm radius in a viscous liquid is 20 cms^{-1}. Then, the speed of 1 cm radius of ball in the same liquid is [BHU]
(a) 80 cms^{-1} (b) 40 cms^{-1}
(c) 10 cms^{-1} (d) 5 cms^{-1}

31 The terminal velocity of small sized spherical body of radius r falling vertically in a viscous liquid is given by the following proportionality [AMU]
(a) $1/r^2$ (b) $1/r$ (c) r (d) r^2

32 The reading of a manometer fitted to a closed tap is $3.5 \times 10^5 \, Nm^2$. If the valve is opened, the reading of the manometer falls to $3 \times 10^5 \, Nm^{-2}$. The velocity of water is [AMU]
(a) 1 ms^{-1} (b) 10 ms^{-1}
(c) 100 ms^{-1} (d) 0.1 ms^{-1}

33 The cylindrical tube of a spray pump has a cross-section of 8cm^2, one end of which has 40 fine holes each of area $10^{-8} \, m^2$. If the liquid flows inside the tube with a speed of 0.15 m min^{-1}, the speed with which the liquid is ejected through the holes is [KCET]
(a) 50 ms^{-1} (b) 5 ms^{-1}
(c) 0.05 ms^{-1} (d) 0.5 ms^{-1}

34 A cylindrical vessel of 90 cm height is kept filled upto the brim. It has four holes 1, 2, 3, 4 which are respectively at heights of 20 cm, 30 cm, 45 cm and 50 cm from the horizontal floor PQ. The water falling at the maximum horizontal distance from the vessel comes from [EAMCET]
(a) hole number 4 (b) hole number 3
(c) hole number 2 (d) hole number 1

35 A hole is in the bottom of the tank having water. If total pressure at the bottom is 3 atm (1 atm = $10^5 \, Nm^{-2}$), then velocity of water flowing from hole is [Manipal]
(a) $\sqrt{400}$ ms^{-1} (b) $\sqrt{600}$ ms^{-1}
(c) $\sqrt{60}$ ms^{-1} (d) None of these

2006

36 According to Bernoulli's equation,

$$\frac{p}{\rho g} + h + \frac{1}{2}\frac{v^2}{g} = \text{constant}$$

The terms $A\left(=\frac{p}{\rho g}\right)$, $B(=h)$ and $C\left(=\frac{v^2}{2g}\right)$ are generally called respectively [AFMC]
(a) gravitational head, pressure head and velocity head
(b) gravity, gravitational head and velocity head
(c) pressure head, gravitational head and velocity head
(d) gravity, pressure and velocity head

37 Blood is flowing at the rate of 200 cm^3s^{-1} in a capillary of cross-sectional area 0.5 m^2. The velocity of flow (in mms^{-1}) is [Kerala CEE]
(a) 0.1 (b) 0.2
(c) 0.3 (d) 0.4
(e) 0.5

38 An atomiser is based on the application of [Punjab PMET]
(a) Torricelli's theorem
(b) Bernoulli's theorem
(c) Archimedes' principle
(d) principle of continuity

39 The speeds of air-flow on the upper and lower surfaces of a wing of an aeroplane are v_1 and v_2, respectively. If A is the cross-sectional area of the wing and ρ is the density of air, then the upward lift is **[EAMCET]**

(a) $\frac{1}{2}\rho A(v_1 - v_2)$

(b) $\frac{1}{2}\rho A(v_1 + v_2)$

(c) $\frac{1}{2}\rho A(v_1^2 - v_2^2)$

(d) $\frac{1}{2}\rho A(v_1^2 + v_2^2)$

40 When the temperature increases, the viscosity of **[J&K CET]**

(a) gas decreases and liquid increases
(b) gas increases and liquid decreases
(c) gas and liquid increases
(d) gas and liquid decreases

41 Water flows steadily through a horizontal pipe of variable cross-section. If the pressure of water is p at a point, where flow speed is v, the pressure at another point, where the flow of speed is $2v$, is (take, density of water as ρ) **[J&K CET]**

(a) $p - \frac{3\rho v^2}{2}$ (b) $p - \frac{\rho v^2}{2}$ (c) $p - \frac{3\rho v^2}{4}$ (d) $p - \rho v^2$

2005

42 A given shaped glass tube having uniform cross-section is filled with water and is mounted on a rotatable shaft as shown in figure. If the tube is rotated with a constant angular velocity ω, then **[AIIMS]**

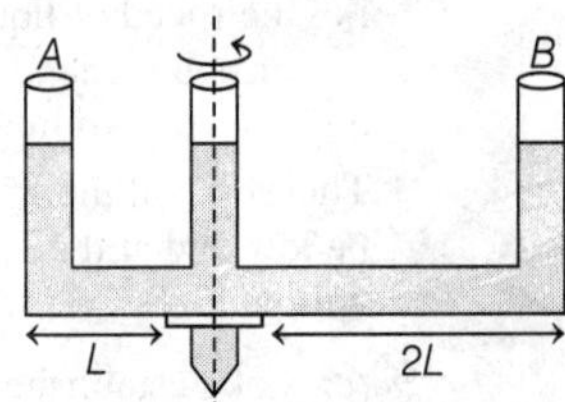

(a) water levels in both sections A and B go up
(b) water level in section A goes up and that in B comes down
(c) water level in section A comes down and that in B it goes up
(d) water levels remain same in both sections

43 **Assertion** (A) For Reynolds' number $R_e > 2000$, the flow of fluid is turbulent.

Reason (R) Inertial forces are dominant compared to the viscous forces at such high Reynolds' numbers. **[AIIMS]**

(a) Both A and R are correct and R is the correct explanation of A
(b) Both A and R are correct but R is not the correct explanation of A
(c) A is correct but R is incorrect
(d) Both A and R are incorrect

44 An incompressible fluid flows steadily through a cylindrical pipe, which has radius $2r$ at point A and radius r at B further along the flow direction. If the velocity at point A is v, its velocity at point B is **[Kerala CEE]**

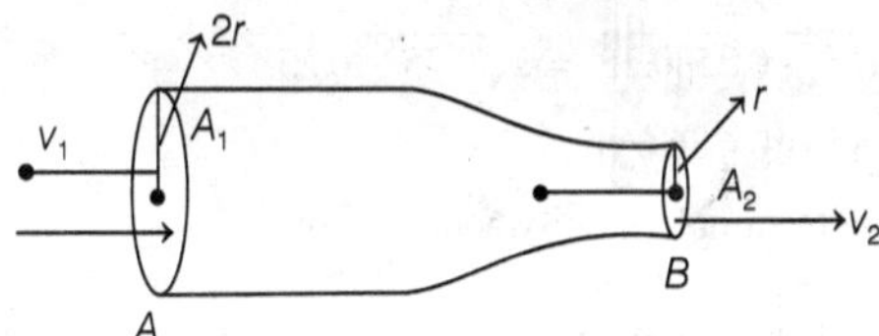

(a) $2v$ (b) v (c) $v/2$ (d) $4v$
(e) $8v$

45 Water is flowing in a pipe of diameter 4 cm with a velocity 3 ms^{-1}. The water then enters into a pipe of diameter 2 cm. The velocity of water in the other pipe is **[BCECE]**

(a) 3 ms^{-1} (b) 6 ms^{-1} (c) 12 ms^{-1} (d) 8 ms^{-1}

46 A viscous fluid is flowing through a cylindrical tube. The velocity distribution of the fluid is best represented by the diagram. **[BCECE]**

(a)  (b) 

(c)  (d) None of these

47 A container with square base of side a is filled up to a height H with a liquid. A hole is made at a depth h from the free surface of water. With what acceleration the container must be accelerated, so that the water does not come out? **[J&K CET]**

(a) g (b) $\frac{g}{2}$ (c) $\frac{2gH}{2}$ (d) $\frac{2gh}{a}$

Answers

1 (d)	2 (d)	3 (b)	4 (b)	5 (b)	6 (a)	7 (a)	8 (b)	9 (c)	10 (a)
11 (a)	12 (b)	13 (d)	14 (b)	15 (c)	16 (c)	17 (a)	18 (c)	19 (c)	20 (a)
21 (b)	22 (c)	23 (b)	24 (c)	25 (b)	26 (d)	27 (a)	28 (c)	29 (c)	30 (d)
31 (d)	32 (b)	33 (b)	34 (b)	35 (a)	36 (c)	37 (d)	38 (b)	39 (c)	40 (b)
41 (a)	42 (d)	43 (a)	44 (d)	45 (c)	46 (c)	47 (a)			

Explanations

1 *(d)* Given, height of small orifice from ground $(h) = 0.25$ m

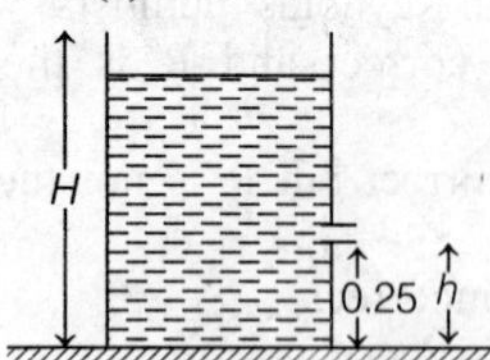

Total height of water tank, $H = 1$ m

$\therefore$ Range of water stream,

$$R = 2\sqrt{h(H-h)}$$
$$= 2\sqrt{(H-0.25)(0.25)}$$
$$= 2\sqrt{(1-0.25)0.25} = 2\sqrt{0.75 \times 0.25}$$
$$= 0.866 \text{ m} = 86.6 \text{ cm}$$

2 *(d)* The terminal velocity achieved by ball in a viscous fluid is

$$v_t = \frac{2(\rho-\sigma)r^2 g}{9\eta}$$

where, ρ = density of metal of ball,

σ = density of viscous medium,

r = radius of ball and η = coefficient of viscosity of medium.

Terminal velocity of first ball,

$$v_{t_1} = \frac{2(\rho_1-\sigma)r_1^2 g}{9\eta}$$
$$= \frac{2(8\rho_2-\sigma)r_1^2 g}{9\eta} \quad \text{...(i)} \; [\because \rho_1 = 8\rho_2]$$

Similarly, for second ball,

$$v_{t_2} = \frac{2(\rho_2-\sigma)r_2^2 g}{9\eta} \quad \text{...(ii)}$$

From Eqs. (i) and (ii), we get

$$\frac{v_{t_1}}{v_{t_2}} = \frac{2(8\rho_2-\sigma)r_1^2 g}{2(\rho_2-\sigma)r_2^2 g} \times \frac{9\eta}{9\eta}$$
$$= \left(\frac{8\rho_2-0.1\rho_2}{\rho_2-0.1\rho_2}\right)\left(\frac{r_1}{r_2}\right)^2 \quad \text{...(iii)}$$
$$[\because \sigma = 0.1\rho_2]$$

Here, $r_1 = 1$ mm and $r_2 = 2$ mm

Substituting these values in Eq. (iii), we get

$$\Rightarrow \frac{v_{t_1}}{v_{t_2}} = \left(\frac{7.9\rho_2}{0.9\rho_2}\right)\left(\frac{1}{2}\right)^2 = \frac{79}{36}$$

3 *(b)* Given, diameter of tube at first end, $d_1 = 5$ cm

$$\therefore \text{Radius}, r_1 = \frac{d_1}{2} = 2.5 \text{ cm}$$
$$= 2.5 \times 10^{-2} \text{ m}$$

Diameter of tube at second end,

$$d_2 = 2 \text{ cm}$$

$$\therefore \text{Radius}, r_2 = \frac{d_2}{2} = 1 \text{ cm} = 10^{-2} \text{ cm}$$

Velocity of fluid at first end, $v_1 = 4$ m/s

By the principle of continuity,

$$A_1 v_1 = A_2 v_2$$
$$\pi r_1^2 v_1 = \pi r_2^2 v_2$$
$$(2.5 \times 10^{-2})^2 \times 4 = (10^{-2})^2 \cdot v_2$$
$$\Rightarrow \quad v_2 = 25 \text{ m/s}$$

From Bernoulli's theorem,

$$p_1 + \frac{1}{2}\rho v_1^2 = p_2 + \frac{1}{2}\rho v_2^2$$
$$p_1 - p_2 = \frac{1}{2}\rho(v_2^2 - v_1^2)$$
$$= \frac{1}{2} \times 10^3 (25^2 - 4^2)$$

$[\because$ density of water, $\rho = 10^3 \text{ kg/m}^3]$

$$= 304500 \text{ Pa}$$

4 *(b)* Here,

$r = 0.3$ mm $= 0.3 \times 10^{-3}$ m, $v = 1 \text{ ms}^{-1}$

$\eta = 18 \times 10^{-5}$ poise

$= 18 \times 10^{-6}$ decapoise

Viscous force, $F = 6\pi\eta r v$

$$= 6 \times \frac{22}{7} \times (18 \times 10^{-6}) \times (0.3 \times 10^{-3}) \times 1$$
$$= 1.018 \times 10^{-7} \text{ N}$$

5 *(b)* Here, velocity head = 20 cm of Hg

$= 20 \times 13.6$ cm of water

As, velocity head $= v^2/2g$

$$\therefore \quad 20 \times 13.6 = \frac{v^2}{2 \times 1000}$$
$$v = \sqrt{20 \times 13.6 \times 2 \times 1000}$$
$$= 737.56 \text{ cms}^{-1} = 7.3756 \text{ ms}^{-1}$$

6 *(a)* Volume of the water flowing per second, $V = 20 \text{ L min}^{-1}$

$$= \frac{20 \times 1000}{60 \times (100)^3} \text{m}^3\text{s}^{-1} = \frac{1}{3} \times 10^{-3} \text{m}^3\text{s}^{-1}$$

Radius of the pipe,

$$r = \frac{4}{2} = 2 \text{ cm} = 0.02 \text{ m}$$

Area of cross-section,

$$A = \pi r^2 = \frac{22}{7} \times (0.02)^2 \text{ m}^2$$

Let v be the velocity of the flow of water at the given point. Clearly, $V = Av$

$$\text{or} \quad \frac{1}{3} \times 10^{-3} = \frac{22}{7} \times (0.02)^2 \times v$$
$$v = \frac{7 \times 10^{-3}}{3 \times 22 \times (0.02)^2} \simeq 0.2639 \text{ ms}^{-1}$$

7 *(a)* The rate of heat generation is equal to the rate of work done by the viscous force which in turn is equal to its power.

Rate of heat produced,

$$\frac{dQ}{dt} = F \times v_T$$

where, F is the viscous force and v_T is the terminal velocity.

As, $\quad F = 6\pi\eta r v_T$

$$\Rightarrow \quad \frac{dQ}{dt} = 6\pi\eta r v_T \times v_T = 6\pi\eta r v_T^2 \quad \text{...(i)}$$

From the relation for terminal velocity,

$$v_T = \frac{2}{9} \cdot \frac{r^2(\rho-\sigma)}{\eta} g, \text{ we get}$$
$$v_T \propto r^2 \quad \text{...(ii)}$$

From Eq. (ii), we can rewrite Eq. (i) as

$$\frac{dQ}{dt} \propto r \cdot (r^2)^2 \text{ or } \frac{dQ}{dt} \propto r^5$$

8 *(b)* For an incompressible liquid equation of continuity,

$$Av = \text{constant}$$
$$\text{or} \quad A \propto \frac{1}{v}$$

where,

A = area of cross-section of tube and v = speed of liquid.

So, the speed of liquid flow is not uniform, but changes with area of cross-section of tube.

Therefore, at the wider end speed will be low and at the narrow end speed will be high.

9 *(c)* Stoke established that, if a sphere of radius a moves with velocity v through a fluid of viscosity η, the viscous force opposing the motion of the sphere is $F = 6\pi\eta a v$.

10 *(a)* Net force on the ball = downward force − upward force $= \frac{mg}{2}$

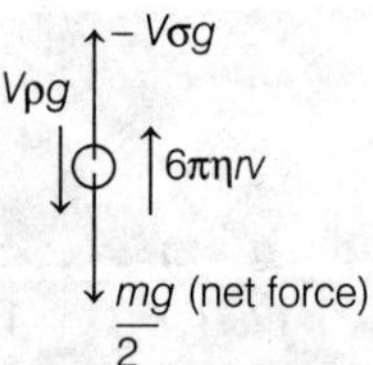

$$\frac{4}{3}\pi r^3(\rho-\sigma)g - 6\pi\eta r v = \frac{mg}{2}$$

$$\frac{4}{3}\pi r^3(\rho-\sigma)g - 6\pi\eta r v = \frac{1}{2}\left(\frac{4}{3}\pi r^3\rho\right)g$$

$$r^2(\rho-\sigma)g - \frac{9}{2}\eta v = \frac{1}{2}r^2\rho g$$

$$\frac{9}{2}v\eta = r^2(\rho-\sigma)g - \frac{1}{2}r^2\rho g$$

$$= \frac{1}{2}r^2\rho g - r^2\sigma g$$

$$\frac{9}{2}v\eta = \frac{1}{2}r^2 g(\rho - 2\sigma)$$

$$\Rightarrow \quad v = \frac{r^2 g}{9\eta}(\rho - 2\sigma)$$

11 *(a)* The sphere falling through a viscous medium accelerates initially due to gravity. As the velocity increases, the retarding viscous force also increases. Finally, when viscous force plus buoyant force becomes equal to force due to gravity, the net force and hence acceleration becomes zero.

Then, it descends with constant terminal velocity.

12 *(b)* Time taken by water to reach the foot,

$$t = \sqrt{\frac{2(H-h)}{g}}$$

Velocity of water coming out of hole,

$$v = \sqrt{2gh}$$

$\therefore$ Emerging stream of water strike the foot, $x = v \times t$

$$= \sqrt{2gh} \times \sqrt{\frac{2(H-h)}{g}} = 2\sqrt{h(H-h)}$$

13 *(d)* According to equation of continuity,

$A_1 v_1 = A_2 v_2 \Rightarrow 10 \times 1 = 5 \times v_2$

$\Rightarrow v_2 = 2\ \text{ms}^{-1}$

From Bernoulli's theorem,

$$\frac{p_1}{\rho} + \frac{v_1^2}{2} = \frac{p_2}{\rho} + \frac{v_2^2}{2}$$

$$\left[\because p + \frac{1}{2}\rho v^2 = \text{constant and } h_1 = h_2\right]$$

$$\frac{2000}{1000} + \frac{1^2}{2} = \frac{p_2}{1000} + \frac{2^2}{2}$$

$$\Rightarrow \quad p_2 = 500\ \text{Pa}$$

14 *(b)* Terminal velocity, $v = \frac{2}{9}\frac{r^2(\rho-\sigma)g}{\eta}$

$$\therefore \quad v \propto r^2$$

$$\Rightarrow \quad \frac{v}{V} = \frac{r^2}{R^2} \Rightarrow V = \frac{vR^2}{r^2}$$

15 *(c)* The terminal velocity is given by $v \propto r^2$, where(r = radius of the sphere). The mass of the sphere can be given by

$$m = \frac{4}{3}\pi r^3\rho$$

Thus, $m \propto r^3$

So, according to the question,

$$\frac{m_1}{m_2} = \frac{1}{8} = \left(\frac{r_1}{r_2}\right)^3 \Rightarrow \frac{r_1}{r_2} = \frac{1}{2}$$

and since, $\frac{v_1}{v_2} = \left(\frac{r_1}{r_2}\right)^2 = \left(\frac{1}{2}\right)^2 = \frac{1}{4}$

$$\frac{v}{nv} = \frac{1}{4} \Rightarrow n = 4$$

16 *(c)* Venturimeter is a device used to measure the rate of flow of a liquid through a pipe. It is an application of Bernoulli's principle. It is also called flow meter or venture tube.

17 *(a)* In horizontal pipe,

$$p_1 + \frac{1}{2}\rho v_1^2 = p_2 + \frac{1}{2}\rho v_2^2 \quad \text{... (i)}$$

Here,

$p_1 = \rho_m g h_1 = 13600 \times 9.8 \times 10^{-2}$,

$p_2 = 13600 \times 9.8 \times h$

$\rho = 1000\ \text{kgm}^{-3}$, $v_1 = 35 \times 10^{-2}\ \text{ms}^{-1}$,

$v_2 = 65 \times 10^{-2}\ \text{ms}^{-1}$

$\therefore$ From Eq. (i), we get

$$13600 \times 9.8 \times 10^{-2} + \frac{1}{2} \times 1000 \times (0.35)^2$$

$$= 13600 \times 9.8 \times h + \frac{1}{2} \times 1000 \times (0.65)^2$$

After solving, we get

$h = 0.89$ cm of Hg

18 *(c)* The path taken by a fluid particle under a steady flow is a streamline flow. The flow of the fluid is said to be steady, if at a given point, the velocity of each passing fluid particle remains constant in time, i.e. kinetic energy of all particles arriving at a given point is the same.

19 *(c)* Terminal speed of spherical body in a viscous liquid is given by

$$v_T = \frac{2r^2(\rho-\sigma)g}{9\eta}$$

where, ρ = density of substance of body and σ = density of liquid.

From given data

$$\frac{v_T(\text{Ag})}{v_T(\text{Gold})} = \frac{\rho_{\text{Ag}} - \sigma_l}{\rho_{\text{Gold}} - \sigma_l}$$

$$\Rightarrow \quad v_T(\text{Ag}) = \left(\frac{10.5 - 1.5}{19.5 - 1.5}\right) \times 0.2$$

$$= \frac{9}{18} \times 0.2 = 0.1\ \text{ms}^{-1}$$

20 *(a)* Let A = cross-section of tank,

a = cross-section of hole

V = velocity with which level decreases and v = velocity of efflux.

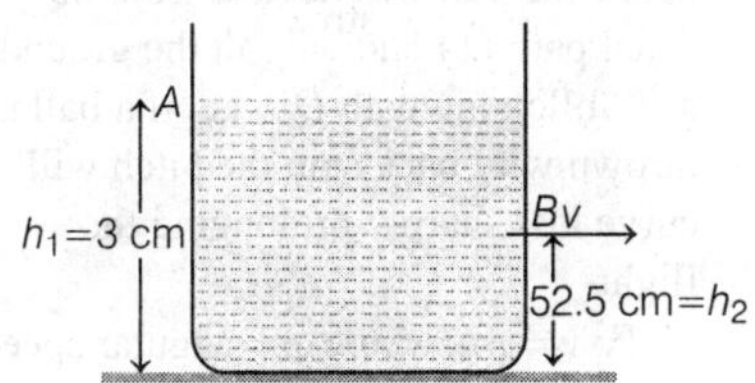

From equation of continuity, $av = AV$

$$\Rightarrow \quad V = \frac{av}{A} \quad \text{...(i)}$$

By using Bernoulli's theorem for energy per unit volume.

Energy per unit volume at point A

= Energy per unit volume at point B

$$p_0 + \rho g h_1 + \frac{1}{2}\rho V^2 = p_0 + \rho g h_2 + \frac{1}{2}\rho v^2$$

$$\Rightarrow \rho g(h_1 - h_2) = \frac{1}{2}\rho(v^2 - V^2)$$

Substituting the value of V from Eq. (i), we get

$$\Rightarrow \quad v^2 = \frac{2g(h_1 - h_2)}{1 - (a/A)^2}$$

$$= \frac{2 \times 10 \times (3 - 0.525)}{1 - (0.1)^2}$$

$$= 50\ \text{m}^2\text{s}^{-2}$$

21 *(b)* If A_0 is the area of orifice at the bottom below the free surface and A that of vessel, time t taken to be emptied the tank,

$$t = \frac{A}{A_0}\sqrt{\frac{2H}{g}}$$

$$\therefore \quad \frac{t_1}{t_2} = \sqrt{\frac{H_1}{H_2}} \Rightarrow \frac{t}{t_2} = \sqrt{2}$$

$$\therefore \quad t_2 = \frac{t}{\sqrt{2}} = \frac{10}{\sqrt{2}} \approx 7\ \text{min}$$

22 *(c)* Terminal velocity,

$$v = \frac{2}{9}\frac{r^2\rho g}{\eta} \Rightarrow \eta = \frac{2}{9}\cdot\frac{r^2\rho g}{v}$$

$$= \frac{2}{9}\frac{(1 \times 10^{-2})^2 \times (1.5 \times 10^3) \times 9.8}{0.25 \times 10^{-2}}$$

$$= 130\ \text{Pa}$$

23 (b) If a ball is moving from left to right and also spinning about a horizontal axis in anti-clockwise direction of motion, then relative to the ball air will be moving from right to left. The resultant velocity of air above and below the ball will be $(v + r\omega)$ and $(v - r\omega)$, respectively.

So, according to Bernoulli's principle, due to this difference of pressure an upward force will act on the ball and hence the ball will deviate from its usual path OA and will hit the ground at B following path OB, i.e. if a ball is thrown with back spin the pitch will curve less sharply prolonging the flight.

[$\because v = r\omega$, where ω = angular speed]

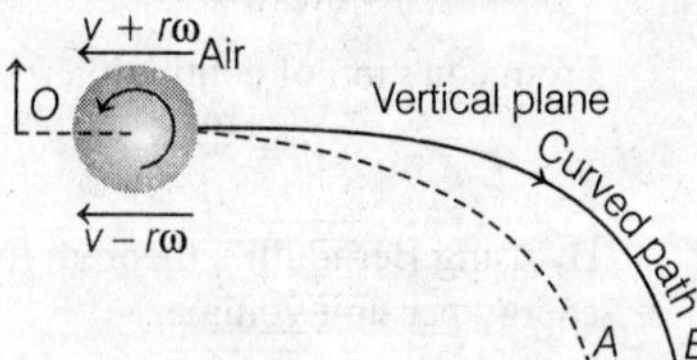

F = force which acts on ball due to difference of pressure.

24 (c) From principle of continuity,

$$A_1v_1 = A_2v_2 + A_3v_3$$

$$\Rightarrow \quad 0.2 \times 4 = 0.2 \times 2 + 0.4v_3$$

$$\Rightarrow \quad 0.4v_3 = 0.8 - 0.4 = 0.4$$

or $\quad v_3 = 1 \text{ ms}^{-1}$

25 (b) Pressure of liquid column $= h\rho g$

$$p = 0.4 \times 900 \times 10 \text{ Nm}^{-2}$$

Force on the base

$$= p \times \text{area} = p \times 2 \times 10^{-3} \text{m}^2$$

$$= 0.4 \times 900 \times 10 \times 2 \times 10^{-3} \text{N}$$

$$= 7.2 \text{ N}$$

26 (d) The terminal velocity of the sphere

$$v = \frac{2}{9}\frac{r^2(\rho - \sigma)g}{\eta}$$

$$\Rightarrow \quad v = 0$$

In vacuum, there is no upthrust. Hence, the sphere never attains terminal velocity in vacuum.

27 (a) Bernoulli's equation for flowing liquid be written as

$$p + \frac{1}{2}\rho v^2 + \rho g h = \text{constant} \quad \text{...(i)}$$

Here, p = pressure energy per unit volume of liquid,
ρ = density of liquid (water),
h = height of liquid column,
v = velocity of liquid,
and g = acceleration due to gravity.

Dividing the Eq. (i) by ρg, we have

$$\frac{p}{\rho g} + \frac{v^2}{2g} + h = \text{constant}$$

In this expression, $\frac{v^2}{2g}$ is velocity head and $\frac{p}{\rho g}$ is pressure head.

It is given that

Velocity head = Pressure head

i.e. $\quad \frac{v^2}{2g} = \frac{p}{\rho g}$ or $v^2 = \frac{2p}{\rho}$

or $\quad v^2 = \frac{2 \times 13.6 \times 10^3 \times 40 \times 10^{-2} \times 9.8}{10^3}$

$\therefore \quad v = 10.3 \text{ ms}^{-1}$

28 (c) Fig. 3 is streamlined, so air resistance of it will be minimum. For Fig.1, surface area is maximum, so air resistance for it is maximum.

Hence, correct sequence is 3 < 2 < 1.

29 (c) Let r be the radius of the each drop. The terminal velocity of drop will be given by

$$v = \frac{2}{9}\frac{r^2(\rho - \sigma)g}{\eta} \quad \text{...(i)}$$

where, ρ is density of drop and σ is density of viscous medium of coefficient of viscosity η.

When two drops each of radius r coalesce to form a new drop, then the radius of coalesced drop will be

$$\frac{4}{3}\pi r^3 \times 2 = \frac{4}{3}\pi R^3$$

$$\Rightarrow \quad R = (2)^{1/3} r$$

Hence, new terminal velocity of coalesced drop will be

$$v' = \frac{2}{9}\left[\frac{(2^{1/3} r)^2(\rho - \sigma)g}{\eta}\right] \quad \text{...(ii)}$$

From Eqs. (i) and (ii), we get

$$\frac{v'}{v} = (2)^{2/3}$$

or $\quad v' = (2)^{2/3} v$

30 (d) Terminal velocity,

$$v = \frac{2}{9}\frac{r^2(\rho - \sigma)g}{\eta} \Rightarrow v \propto r^2$$

Here, $v_1 = 20 \text{ cm s}^{-1}$, $r_1 = 2$ cm, $r_2 = 1$ cm

$$\therefore \quad \frac{v_1}{v_2} = \left(\frac{r_1}{r_2}\right)^2 \text{ and } \frac{20}{v_2} = \frac{(2)^2}{(1)^2}$$

$$\Rightarrow \quad v_2 = 20/4 = 5 \text{ cm s}^{-1}$$

31 (d) According to formula,

$$v = \frac{2r^2(\rho - \sigma)g}{9\eta}$$

Hence, $\quad v \propto r^2$

32 (b) According to Bernoulli's theorem,

$$p_1 + \frac{1}{2}\rho v_1^2 = p_2 + \frac{1}{2}\rho v_2^2$$

$$\Rightarrow \quad \frac{1}{2}\rho v_2^2 = (p_1 - p_2) + \frac{1}{2}\rho v_1^2$$

$$= (p_1 - p_2) \quad (\because v_1 = 0)$$

$$\Rightarrow \quad v_2 = \sqrt{\frac{2(p_1 - p_2)}{\rho}}$$

$$\Rightarrow \quad v_2 = \sqrt{\frac{2 \times (3.5 \times 10^5 - 3 \times 10^5)}{10^3}}$$

$$\Rightarrow \quad v_2 = 10 \text{ ms}^{-1}$$

33 (b) According to equation of continuity, av = constant

$\therefore$ For tube, $(8 \times 10^{-4}) \times \left(\frac{0.15}{60}\right) = a_1v_1$

For holes, $\quad (40 \times 10^{-8}) \times v = a_2v_2$

As, $\quad a_2v_2 = a_1v_1$

$$\therefore \quad 40 \times 10^{-8} \times v = \frac{8 \times 10^{-4} \times 0.15}{60}$$

$$\Rightarrow \quad v = \frac{8 \times 10^{-4} \times 0.15}{40 \times 10^{-8} \times 60} = 5 \text{ ms}^{-1}$$

34 (b) Horizontal range will be maximum when

$$h = \frac{H}{2} = \frac{90}{2} = 45 \text{ cm},$$

i.e. hole number 3

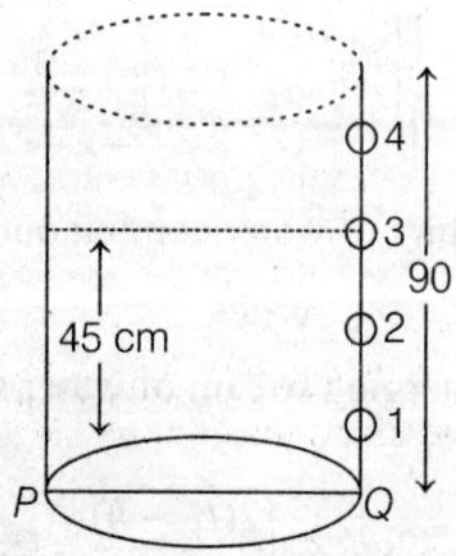

35 (a) Let height of water column in the tank be h.

Total pressure (p) = atmospheric pressure (p_0) + pressure due to water column in tank (p')

$\therefore p' = p - p_0 = 3 - 1 = 2$ atm

or $\quad h\rho g = 2 \times 10^5$

or $\quad h \times 10^3 \times 10 = 2 \times 10^5$

or $\quad h = 20$ m

Hence, velocity of water coming from hole, i.e. velocity of efflux is

$$v = \sqrt{2gh} = \sqrt{2 \times 10 \times 20} = \sqrt{400} \text{ ms}^{-1}$$

36 (c) According to Bernoulli's theorem, in case of steady flow of incompressible and non-viscous liquid through a tube of non-uniform cross-section, the sum of the pressure, the potential energy per unit volume and the kinetic energy per unit volume is same at every point in the tube, i.e.

$$p + \rho g h + \frac{1}{2}\rho v^2 = \text{constant}$$

Dividing this expression by ρg, we have

$$\frac{p}{\rho g} + \frac{v^2}{2g} + h = \text{constant}$$

In this expression $\frac{p}{\rho g}$ is called the 'pressure head', $\frac{v^2}{2g}$ the 'velocity head' and h the 'gravitational head'.

37 (d) By the equation of continuity, we have

$$Av = \text{rate of flow } (R)$$

Given, $R = 200 \text{ cm}^3\text{s}^{-1}$, $A = 0.5 \text{ m}^2$

or $A = 0.5 \times (10^3)^2 \text{mm}^2$

and $R = 200 \times (10)^3 \text{mm s}^{-1}$.

$$\therefore \quad v = \frac{200 \times (10)^3}{0.5 \times 10^6}$$

$$= 400 \times 10^{-6} \times 10^3$$

$$= 0.4 \text{ mms}^{-1}$$

38 (b) Bernoulli's theorem states that when an incompressible and non-viscous liquid flows in a streamlined motion from one place to another, then at every point its total energy per unit volume is conserved. Atomiser is based on this principle.

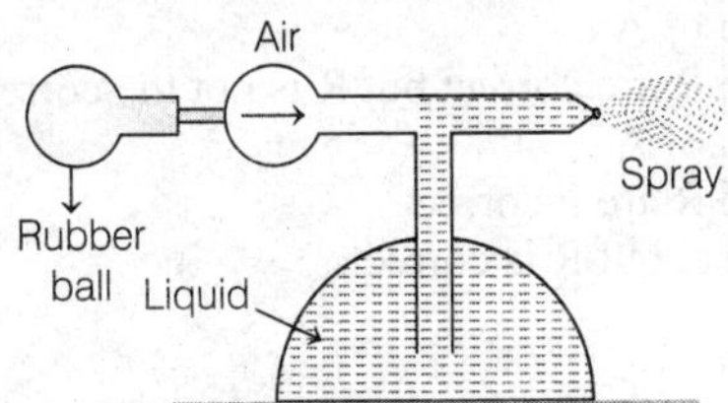

When the rubber ball is squeezed, it sends a stream of air which passes over the tube. The velocity is very large in the constricted part, so that pressure in that part is lowered. Consequently, liquid rises in the tube and is mixed with air and comes out in the form of fine spray.

39 (c) Due to the specific shape of wings when the aeroplane runs, air passes at higher speed over it as compared to its lower surface. This difference of air speeds above and below the wings, in accordance with Bernoulli's principle, creates a pressure difference, due to which an upward force called 'dynamic lift' acts on the plate.

$\therefore$ Upward lift = pressure difference × area of wing $\quad [\because F = p \times A]$

From Bernoulli's equation,

$$p_1 + \frac{1}{2}\rho v_1^2 = p_2 + \frac{1}{2}\rho v_2^2$$

$$\because \quad p_2 - p_1 = \frac{1}{2}\rho(v_1^2 - v_2^2)$$

Hence, upward lift $= \frac{1}{2}\rho A\,(v_1^2 - v_2^2)$

40 (b) Viscosity in gases arises principally from the molecular diffusion that transports momentum between layers of flow. For gases, viscosity increases as temperature increases, while in liquids, the additional force between molecules become important, hence viscosity tends to fall as temperature increases.

41 (a) From Bernoulli's equation, the sum of all forms of energy in a fluid flowing along an enclosed path (a streamline) is same at any two points in the path. Therefore,

$$p + \frac{1}{2}\rho v_1^2 = p' + \frac{1}{2}\rho v_2^2$$

Given, $v_2 = 2v$, $v_1 = v$

$$\therefore \quad p + \frac{1}{2}\rho v^2 = p' + \frac{1}{2}\rho(2v)^2$$

$$\Rightarrow \quad p' = p - \frac{3}{2}\rho v^2$$

42 (d) There is no effect of rotation on levels of water in two limbs. This is because each limb is under vertical pressure due to atmosphere only (p_0). Hence, water levels remain same in both sections.

43 (a) It is established from experiments that flow is steady or laminar when Reynold's number is less than about 2000, wherein the region between 2000 to 3000, the flow is unstable, i.e. may change from laminar to turbulent or *vice-versa*. This case arises only when inertial forces are dominant compared to viscous force.

44 (d) From continuity equation,

$$A_1 v_1 = A_2 v_2$$

or $\frac{v_1}{v_2} = \frac{A_2}{A_1} = \frac{\pi r_2^2}{\pi r_1^2}$

or $v_2 = \frac{r_1^2}{r_2^2} \times v_1$

or $v_2 = \frac{(2r)^2}{(r)^2} \times v = 4v$

45 (c) According to principle of continuity,

$$Av = \text{constant}$$

or $A_1 v_1 = A_2 v_2$

or $\pi r_1^2 v_1 = \pi r_2^2 v_2$

Given, $r_1 = 4/2 \text{ cm} = 0.02 \text{ m}$

$r_2 = 2/2 \text{ cm} = 0.01 \text{ m}$

$\Rightarrow v_1 = 3 \text{ ms}^{-1}$

$$\pi(0.02)^2 \times 3 = \pi(0.01)^2 v_2$$

or $v_2 = \left(\frac{0.02}{0.01}\right)^2 \times 3$

$$= 12 \text{ ms}^{-1}$$

46 (c) Figure shows the flow speed profile for laminar flow of a viscous fluid in a long cylindrical pipe. The speed is greatest along the axis and zero at the pipe walls.

47 (a) Bernoulli's theorem is a form of conservation of energy, hence we have

$$p_0 + H\rho g + \frac{1}{2}\rho v_1^2 = p_0 + (H - h)\rho g + \frac{1}{2}\rho v_2^2$$

Solving above equation, we get

$$\frac{1}{2}\rho v_1^2 = -h\rho g + \frac{1}{2}\rho v_2^2$$

$$\Rightarrow \quad v_1^2 + 2gh = v_2^2$$

$$\Rightarrow \quad v_1^2 - v_2^2 = -2gh \quad \text{...(i)}$$

If $u = 0$ (free fall)

$$v^2 - u^2 = -2gh$$

$$\Rightarrow \quad v^2 = -2gh$$

So, from Eq. (i),

$$v_2^2 = 0 \Rightarrow v_2 = 0$$

Water will not come out.

When vessel is accelerated down with an acceleration g (free fall), then pseudo acceleration g will be vertically upwards and effective value of g is zero. Hence, water will not flow.

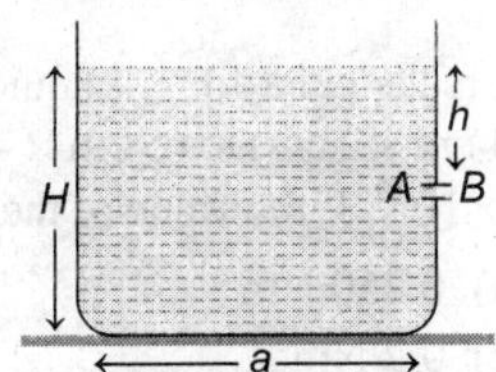

Topic 4

Surface Tension and Surface Energy

2019

1 **Assertion** (A) Sometimes insects can walk on water.
Reason (R) The gravitational force on insect is balanced by force due to surface tension. **[AIIMS]**
(a) Both A and R are correct and R is the correct explanation of A
(b) Both A and R are correct but R is not the correct explanation of A
(c) Both A and R are incorrect
(d) A is incorrect but R is correct

2 **Assertion** (A) Water drops take spherical shape when falling freely.
Reason (R) Water has minimum surface tension among all liquids. **[AIIMS]**
(a) Both A and R are correct and R is the correct explanation of A
(b) Both A and R are correct but R is not the correct explanation of A
(c) Both A and R are incorrect
(d) A is incorrect but R is correct

3 In an isothermal process, 2 water drops of radius 1 mm are combined to form a bigger drop. Find the energy change in this process, if $T = 0.1$ N/m. **[AIIMS]**
(a) 1 μJ (b) 0.5 μJ (c) 0.25 μJ (d) 0.75 μJ

2018

4 The work done in blowing a soap bubble of surface tension 0.06 Nm^{-1} from 2 cm radius to 5 cm radius is **[JIPMER]**
(a) 0.004168 J (b) 0.003168 J
(c) 0.003158 J (d) 0.004568 J

2017

5 Two soap bubbles coalesce. It is noticed that, whilst joined together, the radii of the two bubbles are a and b where $a > b$. Then, the radius of curvature of interface between the two bubbles will be **[JIPMER]**
(a) $a - b$ (b) $a + b$
(c) $\frac{ab}{(a-b)}$ (d) $\frac{ab}{(a+b)}$

2016

6 A rectangular film of liquid is extended from $(4 \text{ cm} \times 2 \text{ cm})$ to $(5 \text{ cm} \times 4 \text{ cm})$. If the work done is 3×10^{-4} J, the value of the surface tension of the liquid is **[NEET]**
(a) 0.250 Nm^{-1} (b) 0.125 Nm^{-1}
(c) 0.2 Nm^{-1} (d) 8.0 Nm^{-1}

2014

7 A certain number of spherical drops of a liquid of radius r coalesce to form a single drop of radius R and volume V. If T is the surface tension of the liquid, then **[CBSE AIPMT]**
(a) energy $= 4V(1/r - 1/R)$ is released
(b) energy $= 3VT(1/r + 1/R)$ is absorbed
(c) energy $= 3VT(1/r - 1/R)$ is released
(d) energy is neither released nor absorbed

8 A drop of some liquid of volume 0.04 cm^3 is placed on the surface of a glass slide. Then, another glass slide is placed on it in such a way that the liquid forms a thin layer of area 20 cm^2 between the surfaces of the two slides. To separate the slides a force of 16×10^5 dyne has to be applied normal to the surfaces. The surface tension of the liquid is (in dyne cm^{-1}) **[WB JEE]**
(a) 60 (b) 70
(c) 80 (d) 90

9 Under isothermal condition, energy E is supplied to a soap bubble of surface tension σ and radius r, to double the radius of the soap bubble. The value of E is **[EAMCET]**
(a) $16\pi r^2\sigma$ (b) $24\pi r^2\sigma$
(c) $8\pi r^2\sigma$ (d) $12\pi r^2\sigma$

2013

10 **Assertion** (A) A small drop of mercury is spherical but bigger drops are oval in shape.
Reason (R) Surface tension of liquid decreases with increase in temperature. **[AIIMS]**
(a) Both A and R are correct and R is the correct explanation of A
(b) Both A and R are correct but R is not the correct explanation of A
(c) Both A and R are incorrect
(d) A is incorrect but R is correct

2012

11 A liquid drop of diameter D breaks into 27 small drops of equal size. If the surface tension of the liquid is σ, then change in surface energy is **[AFMC]**
(a) $\pi D^2\sigma$ (b) $2\pi D^2\sigma$
(c) $3\pi D^2\sigma$ (d) $4\pi D^2\sigma$

12 If T is the surface tension of a liquid, the energy needed to break a liquid drop of radius R into 64 drops is **[Kerala CEE]**
(a) $6\pi R^2 T$ (b) $\pi R^2 T$
(c) $12\pi R^2 T$ (d) $8\pi R^2 T$
(e) $4\pi R^2 T$

2008

13 A frame made of metallic wire enclosing a surface area A is covered with a soap film. If the area of the frame of metallic wire is reduced by 50%, the energy of the soap film will be changed by **[UP CPMT]**
(a) 100% (b) 75% (c) 50% (d) 25%

14 A liquid drop of radius R breaks into 64 tiny drops each of radius r. If the surface tension of the liquid is T, then the gain in energy is **[Punjab PMET]**
(a) $48\pi R^2 T$ (b) $12\pi r^2 T$ (c) $96\pi R^2 T$ (d) $192\pi r^2 T$

15 The potential energy of a molecule on the surface of a liquid compared to one inside the liquid is **[MHT CET]**
(a) zero (b) lesser (c) equal (d) greater

2007

16 The radius R of the soap bubble is doubled under isothermal condition. If T be the surface tension of soap bubble, the required surface energy in doing so is given by **[Punjab PMET]**
(a) $32\pi R^2 T$ (b) $24\pi R^2 T$
(c) $8\pi R^2 T$ (d) $4\pi R^2 T$

17 Two drops of equal radius coalesce to form a bigger drop. What is ratio of surface energy of bigger drop to smaller one? **[MHT CET]**
(a) $2^{1/2}:1$ (b) $1:1$
(c) $2^{2/3}:1$ (d) None of these

18 A wire of length l metre made of a material of specific gravity 8 is floating horizontally on the surface of water. If it is not wet by water, the maximum diameter of the wire (in millimetre) upto which it can continue to float is (surface tension of water is $T = 70 \times 10^{-3}\ \text{Nm}^{-1}$) **[MP PMT]**
(a) 1.5 (b) 1.1
(c) 0.75 (d) 0.55

19 Two glass plates are separated by water. If surface tension of water is 75 dyne cm^{-1} and area of each plate wetted by water is $8\ \text{cm}^2$ and the distance between the plates is 0.12 mm, then the force applied to separate the two plates is **[JCECE]**
(a) 10^2 dyne (b) 10^4 dyne
(c) 10^5 dyne (d) 10^6 dyne

2005

20 When a drop splits up into a number of drops, then **[UP CPMT]**
(a) area increases
(b) volume increases
(c) energy is absorbed
(d) energy is liberated

21 Work done in forming a liquid drop of radius R is W_1 and that of radius $3R$ is W_2. The ratio of work done is **[MHT CET]**
(a) 1 : 3 (b) 1 : 2
(c) 1 : 4 (d) 1 : 9

Answers

1 (a)	2 (c)	3 (b)	4 (b)	5 (c)	6 (b)	7 (c)	8 (c)	9 (a)	10 (b)
11 (b)	12 (c)	13 (c)	14 (d)	15 (d)	16 (b)	17 (c)	18 (b)	19 (c)	20 (c)
21 (d)									

Explanations

1 *(a)* Sometimes, insects can walk on the surface of water due to surface tension, when legs of insects are not being wet. In this situation, the gravitational force on insect is balanced by force due to surface tension.

Hence, both Assertion and Reason are correct and Reason is the correct explanation of Assertion.

2 *(c)* Surface tension is responsible for the shape of tiny water drops when falling freely in the absence of other forces like gravity, shape of water drops is spherical because droplets of water tend to be pulled into a spherical shape by the cohesive forces of the surface layer.

In the presence of gravity, the shape of heavy water drops is not spherical when falling freely. It is oval shaped surface tension of methyl alcohol is lower than surface tension of water.

Hence, water does not have minimum surface tension among all liquids.

Therefore, both Assertion and Reason are incorrect.

3 *(b)* Given, surface tension of water,

$$T = 0.1\ \text{N/m}$$

Radius of small drops,

$$r = 1\ \text{mm} = 10^{-3}\ \text{m}$$

If R be the radius of bigger drops, then volume remains conserved.

i.e. $$V_1 = V_2$$

$$\frac{4}{3}\pi R^3 = 2 \times \frac{4}{3}\pi r^3$$

$$R^3 = 2r^3 = 2\cdot(10^{-3})^3$$

$$\therefore \quad R = 2^{1/3} \times 10^{-3}\ \text{m}$$

$\therefore$ Change in energy during isothermal combination,

$$\Delta E = T \cdot \Delta A$$
$$= T[A_2 - A_1]$$
$$= 0.1[2 \times 4\pi r^2 - 4\pi R^2]$$
$$= 0.1 \times 4\pi[2r^2 - R^2]$$
$$= 0.4\pi[2 \times 10^{-6} - 2^{2/3} \times 10^{-6}]$$
$$= 0.4\pi \times 10^{-6} \times 0.41$$
$$= 0.52 \times 10^{-6}\ \text{J}$$
$$= 0.52\ \mu\text{J} \simeq 0.5\ \mu\text{J}$$

4 *(b)* Here, $S = 0.06\ \text{Nm}^{-1}$,

$r_1 = 2\ \text{cm} = 0.02\ \text{m}, r_2 = 5\ \text{cm} = 0.05\ \text{m}$

Since, bubble has two surfaces.

Initial surface area of the bubble

$= 2 \times 4\pi r_1^2 = 2 \times 4\pi\ (0.02)^2$

$= 32\pi \times 10^{-4} m^2$

Final surface area of the bubble

$= 2 \times 4\pi r_2^2 = 2 \times 4\pi (0.05)^2$

$= 200\pi \times 10^{-4} m^2$

Increase in surface area

$= 200\pi \times 10^{-4} - 32\pi \times 10^{-4}$

$= 168\pi \times 10^{-4} m^2$

$\therefore$ Work done = Surface tension (S) × Increase in surface area

$= 0.06 \times 168\pi \times 10^{-4} = 0.003168$ J

5 (c) According to given figure,

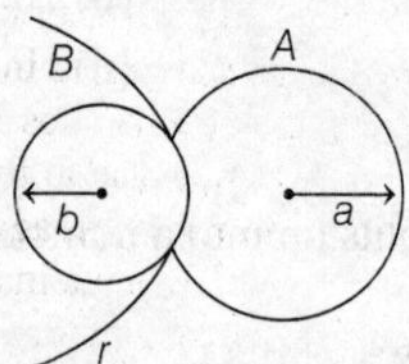

Let the radius of curvature of the common internal film surface of the double bubble formed by two bubbles be r. Excess of pressure as compared to atmosphere inside A is $(4T / a)$. In double bubble, the pressure difference between A and B on either side of the common surface

$$= \frac{4T}{b} - \frac{4T}{a}$$

This will be equal to $(4T / r)$.

$$\therefore \quad \frac{4T}{r} = \frac{4T}{b} - \frac{4T}{a}$$

$$\text{or} \quad \frac{1}{r} = \left(\frac{1}{b} - \frac{1}{a}\right) = \frac{a-b}{ba}$$

$$\text{or} \quad r = \frac{ab}{a-b}$$

6 (b) Increase in surface energy
= Work done = Increase in area × Surface tension

$\therefore$ Increase in surface area,

$\Delta A = (5 \times 4 - 4 \times 2) \times 2$ ($\because$ film has two surfaces)

$= (20 - 8) \times 2\ cm^2 = 24\ cm^2$

$= 24 \times 10^{-4}\ m^2$

So, work done, $W = T \cdot \Delta A$

$3 \times 10^{-4} = T \times 24 \times 10^{-4}$

$$\therefore \quad T = \frac{1}{8} = 0.125 \text{ N/m}$$

7 (c) Here, if the surface area changes, it will change the surface energy as well. If the surface area decreases, it means that energy is released and *vice-versa*.

Change in surface energy

$= \Delta A \times T$ ...(i)

Let we have n number of drops initially.

So, $\Delta A = 4\pi R^2 - n(4\pi r^2)$ ...(ii)

Volume is constant.

So, $n\frac{4}{3}\pi r^3 = \frac{4}{3}\pi R^3 = V$ ...(iii)

From Eqs. (ii) and (iii), we get

$$\Delta A = \frac{3}{R}\left(\frac{4\pi}{3} \times R^3\right) - \frac{3}{r}\left(n\frac{4}{3}\pi r^3\right)$$

$$= \frac{3}{R} \times V - \frac{3}{r}V$$

$$\Rightarrow \quad \Delta A = 3V\left(\frac{1}{R} - \frac{1}{r}\right) = \text{negative value}$$

As $R > r$, so ΔA is negative. It means that surface area is decreased, so energy must be released.

Energy released

$$= \Delta A \times T = -3VT\left(\frac{1}{r} - \frac{1}{R}\right)$$

Above expression shows the magnitude of energy released.

8 (c) Let thickness of layer be x.

So, volume V = Area × x

$V = A \times x$

$\Rightarrow \quad x = V / A$

$\Rightarrow \quad 2r = \frac{V}{A}$ ($\because x = 2r$)

$\Rightarrow \quad r = \frac{V}{2A}$ ...(i)

and $\quad \Delta p = \frac{T}{r}$

We know that

$F = \Delta p \times A = (T / r) \times A$

$F = \frac{T}{(V / 2A)} \times A$ [from Eq. (i)]

$\Rightarrow \quad T = \frac{F \times V}{2A^2}$

where, $F = 16 \times 10^5$ dyne, $V = 0.04\ cm^3$ and $A = 20\ cm^2$.

$$T = \frac{16 \times 10^5 \times 0.04}{2 \times 20^2}$$

$$= \frac{8 \times 10^5 \times 4}{20^2 \times 100} = \frac{8 \times 10^5 \times 4}{400 \times 100}$$

$= 8 \times 10^5 \times 10^{-4} = 80$ dyne/cm

$= 80$ dynecm^{-1}

9 (a) The energy of soap bubbles (when radius = r)

E = surface area of soap bubble × surface tension

$E = 4\pi r^2 \sigma$

Now, radius becomes double.

Then, the value of $E = 4\pi(2r)^2\sigma$

$= 16\pi r^2 \sigma$

10 (b) In a small drop, the force due to surface tension is very large as compared to its weight and hence it is spherical in shape. A big drop becomes oval in shape due to its large weight.

The surface tension of liquid decreases with increase of temperature because cohesive forces decrease with an increase of molecular thermal activity.

11 (b) Work done, $W = T \times \Delta A$

We know that, work done in splitting n liquid drops,

$W = 4\pi\sigma R^2[n^{1/3} - 1]$

$= 4\pi\sigma\left[\frac{D}{2}\right]^2[(27)^{1/3} - 1]$

$= \pi D^2\sigma\,[(27)^{1/3} - 1] = 2\pi D^2\sigma$

12 (c) Total volume of 64 drop = Volume of big drop

$$64 \times \frac{4}{3}\pi r^3 = \frac{4}{3}\pi R^3$$

$\Rightarrow \quad R^3 = 64r^3$

$R = 4r$

$\Rightarrow \quad r = \frac{R}{4}$

Energy of big drop, $E_1 = T \times 4\pi R^2$

Energy of 64 drops, $E_2 = 64(T \times 4\pi r^2)$

$$= 64\left[T \times 4\pi\left(\frac{R}{4}\right)^2\right] = 16\pi TR^2$$

$\therefore$ Energy needed to break a drop into 64 drops,

$\Delta W = E_2 - E_1 = 12\pi R^2 T$

13 (c) Surface energy = Surface tension × Surface area

$E = T \times 2A$

New surface energy,

$$E_1 = T \times 2\left(\frac{A}{2}\right) = T \times A$$

% decrease in surface energy

$$= \frac{E - E_1}{E} \times 100$$

$$= \frac{2TA - TA}{2TA} \times 100 = 50\%$$

14 (d) Volume of big drop = 64 × volume of tiny drop

or $\frac{4}{3}\pi R^3 = 64 \times \frac{4}{3}\pi r^3$ or $R = 4r$

So, the gain in surface energy
= work done in splitting a liquid drop of radius R into n identical drops

$= 4\pi TR^2(n^{1/3} - 1)$

$= 4\pi T(4r)^2(64^{1/3} - 1) = 192\pi r^2 T$

15 *(d)* When the surface area of a liquid is increased, molecules from the interior of the liquid rise to the surface. As these molecules reach the surface work is done against the cohesive force. This work is stored in the molecules in the form of potential energy. Thus, the potential energy of the molecules lying on the surface is greater than that of the molecules in the interior of the liquid.

16 *(b)* Initial surface energy,

$U_1 = 2 \times 4\pi R^2 T = 8\pi R^2 T$

[$\because$ Soap bubble has 2 free surfaces]

Final surface energy,

$$U_2 = 2 \times 4\pi (2R)^2 T = 32\pi R^2 T$$

Hence, required energy

$$= 32\pi R^2 T - 8\pi R^2 T = 24\pi R^2 T$$

17 *(c)* Volume remains constant after coalescing.

Thus, $\frac{4}{3}\pi R^3 = 2 \times \frac{4}{3}\pi r^3$

where, R is radius of bigger drop and r is radius of each smaller drop.

$\therefore \quad R = 2^{1/3} r$

Now, surface energy per unit surface area is the surface tension. So,

Surface energy,

$$W = T\Delta A$$

or $\quad W = 4\pi R^2 T$

Therefore, surface energy of bigger drop

$W_1 = 4\pi (2^{1/3} r)^2 T = (2^{2/3}) 4\pi r^2 T$

Surface energy of smaller drop

$$W_2 = 4\pi r^2 T$$

Hence, required ratio, $W_1 / W_2 = 2^{2/3} : 1$

18 *(b)* $T \cdot l = V\rho g$ or $T \cdot l = \pi r^2 l \rho g$

or $\quad T = \pi r^2 \rho g$

$70 \times 10^{-3} = 3.14 \times r^2 \times 8 \times 10^{-3} \times 9.8$

or $r^2 = \dfrac{70 \times 10^{-3}}{3.14 \times 8 \times 10^{-3} \times 9.8} = 0.28$

$\Rightarrow r = \sqrt{0.28} = 0.53$

$\therefore$ Maximum diameter of the wire

$= 2r = 2 \times 0.53 \approx 1.1$ m

19 *(c)* The shape of water layer between the two plates is shown in the figure. Thickness d of the film

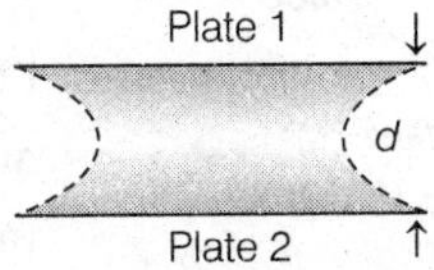

$= 0.12$ mm $= 0.012$ cm

Radius R of the cylindrical face $= \dfrac{d}{2}$

Pressure difference across the surface

$$= \frac{T}{R} = \frac{2T}{d}$$

Area of each plate wetted by water

$$= A = 8 \text{cm}^2$$

Force F required to separate the two plates is given by

$F =$ pressure difference $\times$ area

$$= \frac{2T}{d} A \qquad \text{...(i)}$$

Putting the given values in Eq. (i), we get

$$F = \frac{2 \times 75 \times 8}{0.012} = 10^5 \text{dyne}$$

20 *(c)* When a drop of liquid is split into a large number of drops, the surface area of the liquid increases. In this process, the molecules from the interior of the liquid rise to the surface of the drops, doing work against the cohesive force. This results in a decrease in the internal energy because energy is absorbed. Consequently, the temperature of the drop falls.

21 *(d)* Work done, $W = T \times 4\pi R^2$

$$\Rightarrow \quad \frac{W_1}{W_2} = \frac{T \times 4\pi R^2}{T \times 4\pi (3R)^2}$$

$$= \frac{T \times 4\pi R^2}{T \times 36\pi R^2} = \frac{1}{9}$$

$\therefore \quad W_1 : W_2 = 1 : 9$

Topic 5

Excess Pressure (Pressure Difference)

2013

1 A soap bubble in air (two surfaces) has surface tension 0.03 Nm^{-1}. Find the gauge pressure inside a bubble of diameter 30 mm. **[KCET]**

(a) 2 Pa (b) 8 Pa (c) 16 Pa (d) 10 Pa

2012

2 A bubble of 8 mm diameter is formed in the air. The surface tension of soap solution is 30 dyne/cm. The excess pressure inside the bubble is **[AFMC]**

(a) 150 dyne/cm^2 (b) 300 dyne/cm^2

(d) 3×10^3 dyne/cm^2 (d) 12 dyne/cm^2

2011

3 If R is the radius of a soap bubble and S its surface tension, then the excess pressure inside it, is **[J&K CET]**

(a) $2S/R$ (b) $3S/R$

(c) $4S/R$ (d) S/R

2010

4 A uniform long tube is bent into a circle of radius R and it lies in vertical plane. Two liquids of same volume but densities ρ and δ fill half the tube. The angle θ is **[WB JEE]**

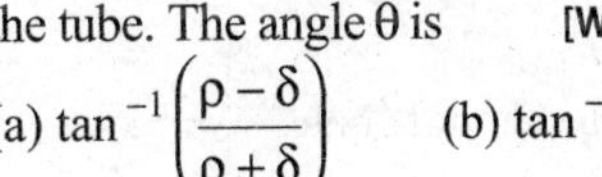

(a) $\tan^{-1}\left(\dfrac{\rho - \delta}{\rho + \delta}\right)$ (b) $\tan^{-1}\left(\dfrac{\rho}{\delta}\right)$

(c) $\tan^{-1}\left(\dfrac{\delta}{\rho}\right)$ (d) $\tan^{-1}\left(\dfrac{\rho + \delta}{\rho - \delta}\right)$

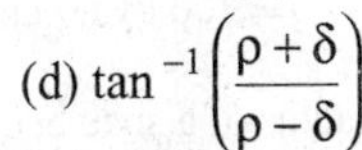

2009

5 Excess of pressure in a gas bubble of radius r in a liquid is (liquid gas interface surface tension is S) **[Kerala CEE]**

(a) $\dfrac{4S}{r}$ (b) $\dfrac{S}{r}$ (c) $\dfrac{3S}{r}$ (d) $\dfrac{2S}{r}$

(e) $\dfrac{S}{2r}$

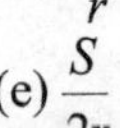

2008

6 Two soap bubbles have radii in the ratio of 2 : 1. What is the ratio of excess pressures inside them? [AMU]

(a) 1 : 2 (b) 1 : 4
(c) 2 : 1 (d) 4 : 1

7 A water drop is divided into 8 equal droplets. The pressure difference between the inner and outer side of the big drop will be [BHU]

(a) same as for smaller droplet
(b) 1/2 of that for smaller droplet
(c) 1/4 of that for smaller droplet
(d) twice that for smaller droplet

8 Find the difference of air pressure between the inside and outside of a soap bubble 5 mm in diameter, if the surface tension is $1.6\ \text{Nm}^{-1}$. [Manipal]

(a) $2560\ \text{Nm}^{-2}$ (b) $3720\ \text{Nm}^{-2}$
(c) $1208\ \text{Nm}^{-2}$ (d) $10132\ \text{Nm}^{-2}$

9 The radius of a spherical drop of water is 1 mm. If surface tension of water be $70\times10^{-3}\ \text{Nm}^{-1}$, the pressure difference inside and outside the drop will be [Haryana PMT]

(a) $70\ \text{Nm}^{-2}$ (b) $140\ \text{Nm}^{-2}$
(c) $280\ \text{Nm}^{-2}$ (d) zero

10 The excess pressure in a bubble of radius R of a gas in a liquid of surface tension S is [J&K CET]

(a) $\frac{2S}{R}$ (b) $\frac{2R}{S}$
(c) $\frac{2S}{R^2}$ (d) $\frac{2R^2}{S}$

2007

11 The excess of pressure inside the first soap bubble is three times that inside the second bubble. The ratio of volume of the first to that of the second bubble is [Kerala CEE]

(a) 1 : 3 (b) 1 : 9 (c) 1 : 27 (d) 9 : 1
(e) 27 : 1

12 A soap bubble A of radius 0.03 and another bubble B of radius 0.04 m are brought together, so that the combined bubble has a common interface of radius r, then the value of r is [BCECE]

(a) 0.24 m (b) 0.48 m
(c) 0.12 m (d) None of these

13 Two liquid drops have diameters of 1 cm and 1.5 cm. The ratio of excess of pressures inside them is [J&K CET]

(a) 1 : 1 (b) 5 : 3 (c) 2 : 3 (d) 3 : 2

2006

14 What should be the pressure inside a small air bubble of 0.1 mm radius situated just below the water surface? (Take, surface tension of water $=7.2\times10^{-2}\ \text{Nm}^{-1}$ and atmospheric pressure $=1.013\times10^5\ \text{Nm}^{-2}$) [EAMCET]

(a) $2.012\times10^5\ \text{Nm}^{-2}$ (b) $2.012\times10^4\ \text{Nm}^{-2}$
(c) $1.027\times10^5\ \text{Nm}^{-2}$ (d) $1.027\times10^4\ \text{Nm}^{-2}$

2005

15 If two soap bubbles of equal radii r coalesce, then the radius of curvature of interface between two bubbles will be [J&K CET]

(a) r (b) zero (c) infinity (d) $\frac{1}{2r}$

Answers

1 (b)	2 (b)	3 (c)	4 (a)	5 (d)	6 (a)	7 (b)	8 (a)	9 (b)	10 (a)
11 (c)	12 (c)	13 (d)	14 (c)	15 (c)					

Explanations

1 (b) Gauge pressure $= 4T/R$

$$= \frac{4\times0.03}{(30/2)\times10^{-3}} = 8\ \text{Pa}$$

2 (b) The excess pressure inside the bubble,

$$\Delta p = \frac{4T}{r} = \frac{4\times30}{0.4} = 300\ \text{dyne/cm}^2$$

3 (c) If R is the radius of a soap bubble and S its surface tension, then the excess pressure inside it is $4S/R$.

4 (a) From the figure, we have

$$\delta gR(\cos\theta+\sin\theta) = \rho gR(\cos\theta-\sin\theta)$$

[equating pressure at junction]

$$\Rightarrow \delta\cos\theta + \delta\sin\theta = \rho\cos\theta - \rho\sin\theta$$

$$\Rightarrow \sin\theta(\delta+\rho) = \cos\theta(\rho-\delta)$$

$$\Rightarrow \tan\theta = \frac{\rho-\delta}{\rho+\delta}$$

$$\Rightarrow \theta = \tan^{-1}\left(\frac{\rho-\delta}{\rho+\delta}\right)$$

5 (d) An air bubble inside a liquid is similar to a liquid drop in air. It has only one free spherical surface. Hence, excess pressure is given by $p = 2S/r$

6 (a) Excess pressure inside the bubble is given by, $p = 4T/r$

Then, $p_1 = 4T/r_1$ ...(i)

$p_2 = 4T/r_2$ ...(ii)

From Eqs. (i) and (ii), we have

$$\frac{p_1}{p_2} = \frac{4T/r_1}{4T/r_2} = \frac{r_2}{r_1} = \frac{1}{2}$$

7 (b) Volume of big drop = Volume of 8 droplets

i.e. $\frac{4}{3}\pi R^3 = 8\times\frac{4}{3}\pi r^3 \Rightarrow r = \frac{R}{2}$

For smaller drop,

$$\Delta p_s = \frac{2T}{r} = \frac{2T}{R/2} = \frac{4T}{R}$$

For bigger drop,

$$\Delta p_b = \frac{2T}{R} = \frac{1}{2}\Delta p_s$$

8 (a) The excess pressure p of bubble in air is given by,

$$p=\frac{4T}{R}=\frac{4\times1.6}{2.5\times10^{-3}}=2560\ \text{Nm}^{-2}$$

9 (b) The excess pressure p is given by $p=2T/R$

where, T is surface tension and R is radius of bubble.

Given, $T=70\times10^{-3}\text{Nm}^{-1}$, $R=1\text{ mm}=10^{-3}\text{m}$

$$\therefore\ p=\frac{2\times70\times10^{-3}}{10^{-3}}=140\ \text{Nm}^{-2}$$

10 (a) Excess pressure inside a bubble of radius R inside a liquid $=2S/R$, where S is the surface tension of the liquid.

11 (c) Excess pressure inside a soap bubble,

$$p=\frac{4T}{R}\quad\text{or}\quad\frac{p_1}{p_2}=\frac{R_2}{R_1}$$

Given, $p_1=3p_2$

$$\therefore\ \frac{3p_2}{p_2}=\frac{R_2}{R_1}\quad\text{or}\quad\frac{R_1}{R_2}=\frac{1}{3}$$

Therefore, ratio of volumes of bubbles

$$\frac{V_1}{V_2}=\frac{(4/3)\pi R_1^3}{(4/3)\pi R_2^3}=\frac{R_1^3}{R_2^3}=\left(\frac{1}{3}\right)^3=\frac{1}{27}$$

$$\therefore\ V_1:V_2=1:27$$

12 (c) Let the radius of curvature of the common internal film surface of the double bubble formed by two bubbles A and B be r.

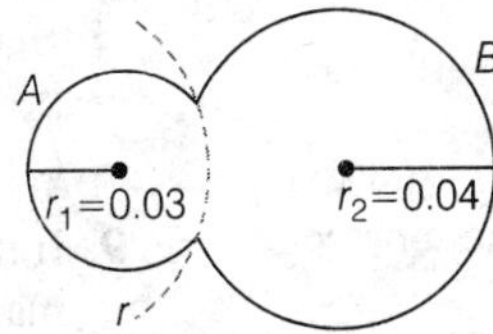

Excess pressure as compared to atmosphere inside A is given by

$$p_1=\frac{4T}{r_1}=\frac{4T}{0.03}$$

Excess pressure inside B is given by,

$$p_2=\frac{4T}{r_2}=\frac{4T}{0.04}$$

In the double bubble, the pressure difference between A and B on either side of the common surface is given by

$$\frac{4T}{0.03}-\frac{4T}{0.04}=\frac{4T}{r}$$

$$\Rightarrow\ \frac{1}{0.03}-\frac{1}{0.04}=\frac{1}{r}$$

$$\Rightarrow\ r=\frac{0.03\times0.04}{0.01}=0.12\text{ m}$$

13 (d) Excess pressure inside a liquid drop,

$$\Delta p=2T/R$$

where, T is surface tension and R is radius of liquid drop.

$$\therefore\ \frac{\Delta p_1}{\Delta p_2}=\frac{R_2}{R_1}=\frac{0.75}{0.50}\Rightarrow\frac{\Delta p_1}{\Delta p_2}=\frac{3}{2}$$

14 (c) The excess pressure inside the air bubble is given by

$$p_2-p_1=2T/R$$

$\therefore$ Pressure inside the air bubble,

$$p_2=p_1+(2T/R)$$

where, $p_1=$ atmospheric pressure.

Substituting the values, we have

$$p_2=(1.013\times10^5)+\frac{2\times7.2\times10^{-2}}{10^{-4}}=1.027\times10^5\ \text{Nm}^{-2}$$

15 (c) Let radius of curvature of the common internal film surface of the double bubble formed be r'. Then, excess pressure as compared to atmosphere inside A is $\frac{4T}{r_1}$ and B is $\frac{4T}{r_2}$.

The pressure difference is given by

$$\frac{4T}{r_1}-\frac{4T}{r_2}=\frac{4T}{r'}$$

$$\Rightarrow\ r'=\frac{r_1r_2}{r_2-r_1}$$

Given, $r_1=r_2=r\Rightarrow r'=r^2/0=\infty$

Topic 6

Angle of Contact and Capillarity

2016

1 Three liquids of densities ρ_1, ρ_2 and ρ_3 (with $\rho_1>\rho_2>\rho_3$), having the same value of surface tension T, rise to the same height in three identical capillaries. The angles of contact θ_1, θ_2 and θ_3 obey **[NEET]**

(a) $\frac{\pi}{2}>\theta_1>\theta_2>\theta_3\geq0$

(b) $0\leq\theta_1<\theta_2<\theta_3<\frac{\pi}{2}$

(c) $\frac{\pi}{2}<\theta_1<\theta_2<\theta_3<\pi$

(d) $\pi>\theta_1>\theta_2>\theta_3>\frac{\pi}{2}$

2014

2 A 20 cm long capillary tube is dipped in water. The water rises upto 8 cm. If the entire arrangement is put in a freely falling elevator, the length of water column in the capillary tube will be **[UK PMT]**

(a) 4 cm (b) 20 cm (c) 8 cm (d) 10 cm

2013

3 The wettability of a surface by a liquid depends primarily on the **[NEET]**

(a) viscosity (b) surface tension (c) density

(d) angle of contact between the surface of solid and the liquid

2012

4 **Assertion** (A) The water rises higher in a capillary tube of small diameter than in the capillary tube of large diameter.

Reason (R) Height through which liquid rise in capillary tube is inversely proportional to the diameter of capillary tube. **[AIIMS]**

(a) Both A and R are correct and R is the correct explanation of A
(b) Both A and R are correct but R is not the correct explanation of A
(c) A is correct but R is incorrect
(d) A is incorrect but R is correct

2010

5 Two capillary of lengths L and $2L$ and of radii R and $2R$ are connected in series. The net rate of flow of fluid through them will be (given rate of the flow through single capillary, $X = \frac{\pi R^4}{8\eta L}$) **[JCECE]**

(a) $\frac{8}{9}X$ (b) $\frac{9}{8}X$
(c) $\frac{5}{7}X$ (d) $\frac{7}{5}X$

2008

6 A liquid does not wet the solid surface, if the angle of contact is **[Punjab PMET]**

(a) zero (b) equal to 45°
(c) smaller than 90° (d) greater than 90°

7 A capillary tube is taken from the earth to the surface of the moon. The rise of the liquid column on the moon (acceleration due to gravity on the earth is 6 times that of the moon) is **[EAMCET]**

(a) six times that on the earth's surface
(b) $\frac{1}{6}$ that on the earth's surface
(c) equal to that on the earth's surface
(d) zero

2007

8 A capillary tube is attached horizontally to a constant head arrangement. If the radius of the capillary tube is increased by 10%, then the rate of flow of liquid will change nearly by **[AFMC]**

(a) +10% (b) +46%
(c) −10% (d) −40%

9 If the length of tube is less and cannot accommodate the maximum rise of liquid, then **[AFMC]**

(a) liquid will form fountain
(b) liquid will not rise
(c) the meniscus will adjust itself, so that the water does not spill
(d) None of the above

10 Water rises in plant fibres due to **[KCET]**

(a) capillarity (b) viscosity
(c) fluid pressure (d) osmosis

11 The meniscus of mercury in a capillary glass tube, is **[J&K CET]**

(a) concave (b) plane
(c) cylindrical (d) convex

2005

12 Water rises in a capillary tube to a certain height such that the upward force due to surface tension is balanced by 75×10^{-4} N force due to the weight of the liquid. If the surface tension of the water is 6×10^{-2} Nm^{-1}, the inner circumference of the capillary must be **[KCET]**

(a) 1.25×10^{-2} m
(b) 0.50×10^{-2} m
(c) 6.5×10^{-2} m
(d) 12.5×10^{-2} m

13 Water rises upto height h in a capillary tube of certain diameter. This capillary tube is replaced by similar tube of half the diameter. Now, the water will rise to the height of **[Kerala CEE]**

(a) $4h$ (b) $3h$
(c) $2h$ (d) h
(e) $\frac{1}{2}h$

Answers

1 (b)	2 (b)	3 (d)	4 (a)	5 (a)	6 (d)	7 (a)	8 (b)	9 (c)	10 (a)
11 (d)	12 (d)	13 (c)							

Explanations

1 (b) According to ascent formula for capillary tube, $h = \frac{2T\cos\theta}{\rho g r}$

$$\therefore \quad \frac{\cos\theta_1}{\rho_1} = \frac{\cos\theta_2}{\rho_2} = \frac{\cos\theta_3}{\rho_3}$$

Thus, $\cos\theta \propto \rho$

As, $\rho_1 > \rho_2 > \rho_3$

$$\therefore \quad \cos\theta_1 > \cos\theta_2 > \cos\theta_3$$
$$0 \le \theta_1 < \theta_2 < \theta_3 < \pi/2$$

2 (b) Consider the situation where a capillary tube is dipped in water of density ρ.

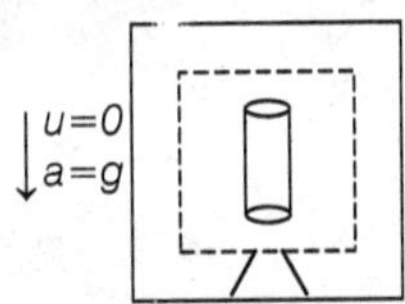

Net force on the liquid due to surface tension will be upward and is balanced by the downward force of the weight

$$w = \pi r^2 h\rho g = \text{weight of liquid}$$

As, $2\pi r S\cos\theta =$ Net force due to surface tension

$$\Rightarrow \quad \pi r^2 h\rho g = 2\pi r S\cos\theta$$

where, S is surface tension and θ is the contact angle.

$$\Rightarrow h = \frac{2S\cos\theta}{r\rho g} \Rightarrow h \propto \frac{1}{g}$$

where, g is acceleration due to gravity. When the entire arrangement is falling with an acceleration g.

$$g_{\text{eff}} = g - g = 0$$

Hence, $h' \propto \frac{1}{g_{\text{eff}}} = \frac{1}{0} = \infty$

Hence, there is an overflow in the capillary tube. As length of the capillary tube is l.

$$\Rightarrow \quad h' = l = 20 \text{ cm}$$

3 (d) The wettability of a surface by a liquid depends primarily on the angle of contact between the surface of solid and liquid surface.

The liquid does not wet the solid surface, if the angle of contact is obtuse, i.e. greater than 90° and wets when angle of contact is acute, i.e. less than 90°.

4 (a) The height of capillary rise is inversely proportional to radius (or diameter) of capillary tube,

$$h \propto \frac{1}{r}$$

So, for smaller value of r, the value of h is higher.

i.e. the water rises higher in a capillary tube of small diameter than in a capillary tube of large diameter.

5 (a) Fluid resistance is given by $R = \frac{8\eta L}{\pi r^4}$

When two capillary tubes of same size are joined in series, then equivalent fluid resistance is

$$R_{\text{eq}} = R_1 + R_2$$
$$= \frac{8\eta L}{\pi R^4} + \frac{8\eta \times 2L}{\pi (2R)^4} = \left[\frac{8\eta L}{\pi R^4} \times \frac{9}{8}\right]$$

Equivalent resistance becomes 9/8 times, so rate of flow will be $\frac{8}{9}X$.

6 (d) A liquid does not wet the solid surface, if the angle of contact is obtuse, i.e. greater than 90°. In this case, cohesive forces will be greater than adhesive forces and so the liquid does not wet the surface of solid.

7 (a) By the relation, $h = \frac{2T\cos\theta}{rdg}$

where, $r =$ radius of capillary tube,
$h =$ rise or fall of the liquid,
$g =$ acceleration due to gravity
and $d =$ density of the liquid.

$$\therefore \quad h \propto \frac{1}{g} \Rightarrow \frac{h_2}{h_1} = \frac{g_1}{g_2}$$

According to the question,

On earth, $h_1 = h, g_1 = g$

On moon, $h_2 = ?\ g_2 = g/6$

$$\frac{h_2}{h} = \frac{g}{g/6} \Rightarrow h_2 = 6h$$

Hence, the rise of the liquid column on the moon becomes six times that on the earth's surface.

8 (b) Volume of liquid flowing through capillary per second is given by

$$V = \frac{\pi p r^4}{8\eta l}$$

$$\Rightarrow \quad V \propto r^4$$

$$\Rightarrow \quad \frac{V_2}{V_1} = \left(\frac{r_2}{r_1}\right)^4$$

$$\therefore \quad V_2 = V_1\left(\frac{110}{100}\right)^4 = V_1(1.1)^4 = 1.4641\text{ V}$$

$$\therefore \quad \frac{\Delta V}{V} = \frac{V_2 - V_1}{V}$$

$$\Rightarrow \quad = \frac{1.4641\,V - V}{V} = 0.46 \text{ or } 46\%$$

9 (c) If the length of the tube h' is less than h, it is found that the liquid does not overflow. In a tube of insufficient length, the liquid rises upto the top of the tube and increases the radius of curvature of its meniscus to a value R', i.e. smaller the length h' of the tube, greater will be the radius of curvature R' of the meniscus, but the liquid will never overflow.

10 (a) The rise or fall of liquids in vertical capillary tubes is called capillarity. Water in plant fibres rises due to same phenomenon.

11 (d) The meniscus of mercury in a capillary glass tube is convex because in case of mercury, the adhesive force between solids and liquids molecules is less than the cohesive force between liquid-liquid molecules.

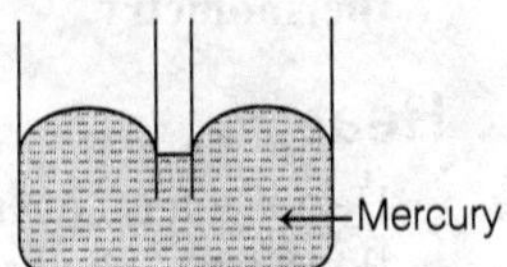

The angle of contact between mercury and clean glass is 137°.

12 (d) $6 \times 10^{-2} \times \text{Circumference} = \text{Force}$

$$\therefore \text{Circumference} = \frac{75 \times 10^{-4}}{6 \times 10^{-2}}$$
$$= 12.5 \times 10^{-2}\text{m}$$

13 (c) According to Jurin's law, the rise in capillary tube is inversely proportional to the radius of capillary tube.

or $h \propto \frac{1}{r}$ or $\frac{h_2}{h_1} = \frac{r_1}{r_2} = \frac{d_1}{d_2}$

Given, $d_2 = d_1/2$

$$\therefore \quad \frac{h_2}{h_1} = \frac{d_1}{d_1/2} = 2 \text{ or } h_2 = 2h_1 = 2h$$

10

Thermal Properties of Matter

Quick Review

Temperature and Heat

Temperature

Temperature is the property of a state of matter by virtue of which we predict the hotness or coldness of a body relative to some body. The devices which are used to measure the temperature are termed as **thermometers**, while the science related to measurement of temperature is termed as **thermometry**.

Heat

Heat is a form of energy called thermal energy which flows from a higher temperature body (hotter) to a lower temperature body (colder) when they are placed in contact.

Measurement of Temperature

The measurement of temperature is done by some specified scales as given below

Different Scales to Measure the Temperature

Name of Scale	Measuring Unit	Freezing or ice point (Lower fixed point)	Boiling or steam point (Upper fixed point)
Celsius scale	Degree centigrade (°C)	0°C	100°C
Fahrenheit scale	Degree Fahrenheit (°F)	32°F	212°F
Reaumur scale	Degree Reaumur (°R)	0° R	80°R
Kelvin scale	Kelvin (K)	273.15 K	373.15 K

To convert the temperature of one scale to another, the following relation is used

$$\frac{\text{Temperature on one scale} - \text{LFP (ice point)}}{\text{UFP (steam point)} - \text{LFP (ice point)}}$$

$$= \frac{\text{Temperature on other scale} - \text{LFP (ice point)}}{\text{UFP (steam point)} - \text{LFP (ice point)}}$$

- Relation between C, F and K temperature scales is given below

$$\frac{C}{5} = \frac{F-32}{9} = \frac{K-273}{5}$$

Thermometers

The thermometers work on the thermometric property, i.e. the property which changes with temperature like any physical quantity such as length, volume, pressure and resistance, etc., which varies linearly with a certain range of temperature.

Let X denote the thermometric physical quantity and X_0, X_{100} and X_t be its values at 0°C, 100°C and t°C, respectively. Then,

$$\text{temperature, } t = \left(\frac{X_t - X_0}{X_{100} - X_0}\right) \times 100°\text{C}$$

Thermal Expansion

When matter is heated without any change in its state, it usually expands. This phenomena of expansion of matter on heating is called thermal expansion. There are three types of thermal expansions

1. Expansion of Solids

Three types of expansion takes place in solid as given below

(*i*) **Linear Expansion** The expansion in length of a body due to increase in its temperature is called the **linear expansion**.

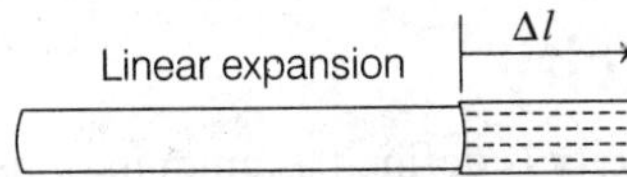

Increase in length, $l_2 = l_1 (1 + \alpha \Delta t)$

where, l_1 and l_2 are initial and final lengths, Δt = change in temperature and α = coefficient of linear expansion.

Coefficient of linear expansion,

$$\alpha = \frac{\Delta l}{l \times \Delta t}$$

where, l = real length

and Δl = change in length

and Δt = change in temperature.

The coefficient of linear expansion of a material of a solid rod is defined as increase in length per unit original length per degree rise in temperature. Its unit is $°C^{-1}$ or K^{-1}.

(*ii*) **Superficial Expansion** The expansion in the area of a surface due to increase in its temperature is called **area expansion**.

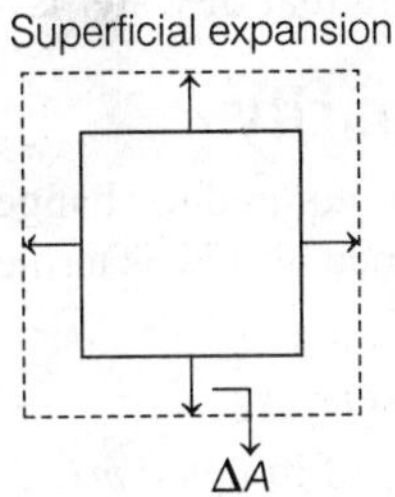

Increase in area,

$$A_2 = A_1 (1 + \beta \Delta t)$$

where, A_1 and A_2 are initial and final areas and β is a coefficient of superficial expansion.

Coefficient of superficial expansion,

$$\beta = \frac{\Delta A}{A \times \Delta t}$$

where, A = area,

ΔA = change in area

and Δt = change in temperature.

The coefficient of area expansion of metal sheet is defined as the increase in its surface area per unit original surface area per degree rise in its temperature. Its unit is $°C^{-1}$ or K^{-1}.

(*iii*) **Cubical Expansion** The expansion in the volume of an object due to increase in its temperature is known as cubical or **volume expansion**.

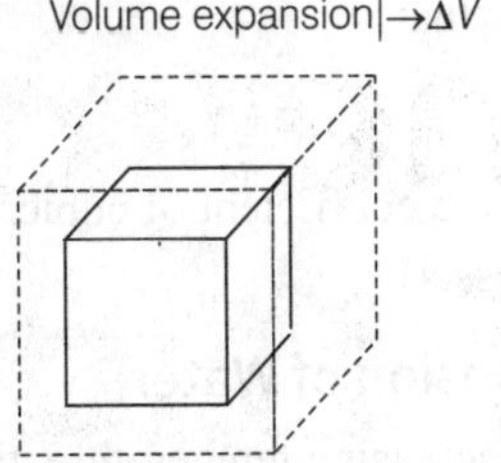

Increase in volume, $V_2 = V_1 (1 + \gamma \Delta t)$

where, V_1 and V_2 are initial and final volumes and γ is a coefficient of cubical expansion.

The coefficient of cubical expansion, $\gamma = \dfrac{\Delta V}{V \times \Delta t}$

where, V = real volume, ΔV = change in volume and Δt = change in temperature.

The coefficient of volume (cubical) expansion of a substance is defined as the increase in volume per unit original volume per degree rise in its temperature. Its unit is $°C^{-1}$ or K^{-1}.

- Relation between coefficients of linear, superficial and cubical expansions $\beta = 2\alpha$ and $\gamma = 3\alpha$ or $\alpha : \beta : \gamma = 1 : 2 : 3$

2. Expansion of Liquids

Liquids do not have linear and superfical expansion but these only have volumetric expansion.

Since, liquids are always heated in a vessel, so initially on heating the system (liquid + vessel), the level of liquid in vessel falls (as vessel expands more since it absorbs heat and liquid expands less) but later on, it starts rising due to faster expansion of the liquid. Thus, liquids have two coefficients of volume expansion

(*i*) **Apparent Expansion of Liquids** When expansion of the container containing liquid, on heating is not taken into account, then observed expansion is called apparent expansion of liquids.

Coefficient of apparent expansion of a liquid

$$(\gamma_a) = \frac{\text{apparent (or observed) increase in volume}}{\text{original volume} \times \text{change in temperature}}$$

(*ii*) **Real Expansion of Liquids** When expansion of the container, containing liquid, on heating is also taken into account, then observed expansion is called real expansion of liquids.

Coefficient of real expansion of a liquid

$$(\gamma_r) = \frac{\text{real increase in volume}}{\text{original volume} \times \text{change in temperature}}$$

Both γ_r and γ_a are measured in $^\circ C^{-1}$.

We can show that

$$\gamma_r = \gamma_a + \gamma_g$$

where, γ_g is the coefficient of cubical expansion of the container (vessel).

Anomalous Expansion of Water

Generally, with increasing temperature, the volume expansion coefficient of liquids is about ten times greater than that of solids. Water is an exception to this rule. From 0°C to 4°C water contracts and beyond 4°C, it expands. Thus, density of water reaches a maximum value of 1000 kgm^{-3} at 4°C.

3. Thermal Expansion of Gases

On heating, gases expand more than solids or liquids and equal volumes of different gases expands equally, when heated by the same amount.

All gases have coefficient of volume expansion γ_V with volume variation given by $V = V_0(1+\gamma_V \Delta\theta)$

and pressure variation is given by $p = p_0\,(1+\gamma_p \Delta\theta)$

Variation of Density with Temperature

Most substances expand when they are heated, i.e. volume of a given mass of a substance increases on heating, so density decreases. Hence $\rho \propto \frac{1}{V}$, $\rho' = \rho(1+\gamma\Delta T)^{-1}$, as γ is small

$$(1+\gamma\Delta T)^{-1} \approx 1-\gamma\Delta T$$

$$\rho' \approx \rho(1-\gamma\Delta T)$$

Thermal Strain and Thermal Stress

When a metal rod whose ends are rigidly fixed so as to prevent the rod from expansion or contraction, undergoes a change in temperature, thermal strains and thermal stresses are developed in the rod.

If a rod of length l is heated by a temperature ΔT, then increase in length of rod should have been $\Delta l = l\alpha\Delta T$.

But due to being fixed at ends rod does not expand and a compressive thermal strain is developed in it whose value is

$$\text{Thermal (compressive) strain} = \frac{\Delta l}{l} = \alpha\,\Delta T$$

Here, α = linear expansion coefficient of the material of rod. Due to this strain, a thermal stress is developed in the rod having a value.

Thermal stress = $Y \times$ Thermal strain = $Y\alpha\Delta T$

Thermal stress = $Y\alpha\Delta T$

Here, Y = Young's modulus of the material of given rod. If A be the cross-section area of the rod, then force exerted by the rod on the supports will be $F = Y\alpha\Delta T A$.

Heat Capacity

The heat capacity is defined as amount of heat needed to change the temperature by unity, i. e. 1° C, it is denoted by S and having SI unit JK^{-1}.

$$\text{Heat capacity, } S = \frac{\Delta Q}{\Delta T}$$

where, ΔQ = heat absorbed or rejected by body

and ΔT = change in temperature.

Specific Heat Capacity

- The quantity of heat Q required to change the temperature of a mass m of certain material by ΔT, is approximately proportional to the product of m and ΔT, i.e.

$$Q \propto m\Delta T \text{ or } Q = ms\,\Delta T$$

where, s = specific heat capacity of the material.

- Specific heat capacity can have any value from 0 to ∞. For some substances under particular situations, it can have negative values also. Specific heat of ice is 500 cal/kg °C and that of water is 1000 cal/kg°C.

Molar Heat Capacity

The amount of heat required to change the temperature of unit mole of substance by 1°C is termed as its molar heat capacity.

$$C = Q/\mu\Delta T$$

where, μ = number of moles = m/M

Types of molar specific heat capacity are as follows

(*i*) Molar specific heat capacity at constant pressure (C_p) is expressed as

$$C_p = \left[\frac{\Delta Q}{\Delta T}\right]_{p=\text{constant}}$$

(*ii*) Molar specific heat capacity at constant volume (C_V)

$$C_V = \left(\frac{\Delta Q}{\Delta T}\right)_{V=\text{constant}}$$

- Relation between specific heat and molar heat capacity can be expressed as $C = Ms$

where, C = molar heat capacity,

M = molecular mass of the substance

and s = specific heat capacity.

Calorimetry

It is the branch of science which deals with the measurement of heat.

When a body at higher temperature is brought in contact with another body at lower temperature, then the heat flows from the body kept at higher temperature to the body kept at lower temperature till the both bodies acquire the same temperature.

Principle of calorimetry is expressed as

Heat lost by hotter body = Heat gained by colder body

$$m_1 s_1 \Delta T = m_2 s_2 \Delta T$$

where, m_1 = mass of hot body,

m_2 = mass of cold body,

s_1 = specific heat of hot body

and s_2 = specific heat of cold body.

Change of State

The process of converting one state of a substance into another state is known as change of state of a substance or matter.

Matter generally exists in three states

(*i*) Solid (*ii*) Liquid (*iii*) Gas

These states can be changed into one another by absorbing heat or rejecting heat. The process is so called the change of state. The temperature of a substance remains constant during change of state.

Triple Point of Water

The values of pressure and temperature at which water coexists in equilibrium in all three states of matter, i.e. ice, water and vapour is called triple point of water.

Triple point of water is 273 K temperature and 0.46 cm of mercury pressure.

Latent Heat

The amount of heat transferred per unit mass during the change of state of a substance without any change in its temperature is called latent heat of the substance for particular change.

$$Q \propto m \Rightarrow Q = mL$$

where, L = latent heat of the material.

There are two types of latent heat of materials

(*i*) **Latent Heat of Fusion or Melting** It is the quantity of heat required to change the state of a substance from solid to liquid state at its melting point. It is denoted by L_f.

Latent heat of fusion,

$$L_f = \frac{Q}{m}$$

Its SI unit is Jkg^{-1}.

(*ii*) **Latent Heat of Vaporisation** It is the quantity of heat required to change the state of unit mass of a substance from liquid to vapour state at its boiling point. It is denoted by L_V.

Latent heat of vaporisation, $L_V = \frac{Q}{m}$ and its SI unit is Jkg^{-1}.

Heat Transmission

Heat can be transferred from one part of system to another. It is called heat transmission. There are three methods of heat transmission, Conduction, Convection and Radiation.

Conduction

In solids, heat is transmitted from higher temperature to lower temperature without actual movements of the particles. This mode of transmission of heat is called conduction.

- **Thermal Conductivity** The ability of material to conduct the heat through it, is known as thermal conductivity.

  The amount of heat flow in a conducting rod,

$$Q = \frac{KA\,\Delta\theta t}{l}$$

where, K = coefficient of thermal conductivity,

A = area of cross-section,

l = length of rod,

$\Delta\theta$ = temperature difference between the ends of the rod

and t = time.

The SI unit of K is $\text{Wm}^{-1}\ \text{K}^{-1}$ and its dimensional formula is $[\text{MLT}^{-3}\theta^{-1}]$.

- The rate of flow of heat is known as **thermal** or **heat current**. It is denoted by H.

$$H = \frac{KA\Delta\theta}{l}$$

- **Thermal resistance** is given by

$$R = \frac{\Delta\theta}{H} = \frac{l}{KA}$$

Its SI unit is K/W and its dimensional formula is $[\text{M}^{-1}\text{L}^{-2}\ \text{T}^{3}\theta^{-1}]$.

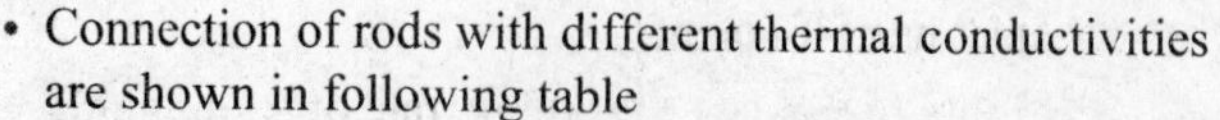

- Connection of rods with different thermal conductivities are shown in following table

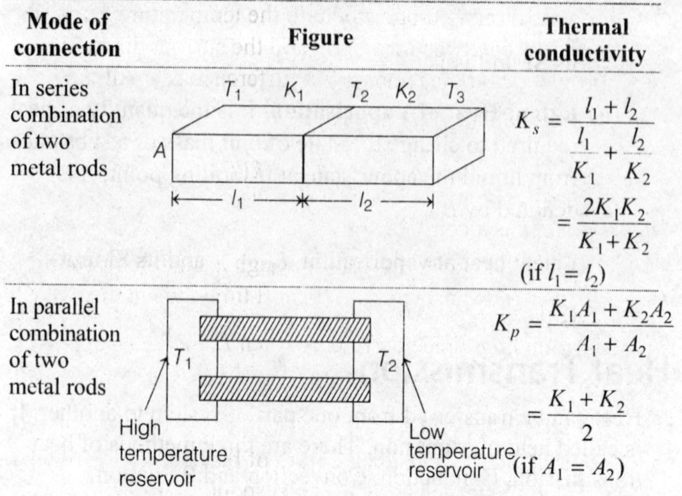

Mode of connection	Figure	Thermal conductivity
In series combination of two metal rods	T_1 K_1 T_2 K_2 T_3; A; l_1, l_2	$K_s = \dfrac{l_1 + l_2}{\dfrac{l_1}{K_1} + \dfrac{l_2}{K_2}}$ $= \dfrac{2K_1K_2}{K_1+K_2}$ (if $l_1 = l_2$)
In parallel combination of two metal rods	T_1, T_2; High temperature reservoir; Low temperature reservoir	$K_p = \dfrac{K_1A_1 + K_2A_2}{A_1 + A_2}$ $= \dfrac{K_1 + K_2}{2}$ (if $A_1 = A_2$)

Note If temperature of common interface of the series combination be T, then it can be expressed as $T = \dfrac{K_1T_1 + K_2T_2}{K_1 + K_2}$

Convection

The process of heat transmission in which the particles of the fluid (liquid or gas) move is called convection.

Land breeze, see-breeze and trade wind are formed due to convection.

Radiation

The process of heat transmission in the form of electromagnetic waves, is called radiation.

Radiation do not require any medium for propagation. It propagates without heating the intervening medium. The heat energy transferred by radiation is called radiant energy. Heat from the sun reaches the earth by radiation.

Reflectance or Reflecting Power

The ratio of the amount of thermal radiations reflected by a body in a given time to the total amount of thermal radiations incident on the body in that time is called reflectance or reflecting power of the body.

It is denoted by r.

Absorptance or Absorbing Power

The ratio of the amount of thermal radiations absorbed by a body in a given time to the total amount of thermal radiations incident on the body in that time is called abscrptance or absorbing power of the body. It is denoted by a.

Transmittance or Transmitting Power

The ratio of the amount of thermal radiations transmitted by the body in a given time to the total amount of thermal radiations incident on the body in that time is called transmittance or transmitting power of the body. It is denoted by t.

Relation among reflecting power, absorbing power and transmitting power

$$r + a + t = 1$$

If body does not transmit any heat radiations, then $t = 0$

$$\therefore \quad r + a = 1$$

- r, a and t all are the pure ratio, so they have no unit and dimensions.
- For perfect reflector, $r = 1$, $a = 0$ and $t = 0$.
- For perfect absorber, $a = 1$, $r = 0$ and $t = 0$ (perfect black body).
- For perfect transmitter, $t = 1$, $a = 0$ and $r = 0$.

Emissive Power

Emissive power of a body at a particular temperature is the total amount of thermal energy emitted per unit time per unit area of the body for all possible wavelengths.

It is denoted by e_λ, $e_\lambda = \dfrac{1}{A} \cdot \dfrac{d\theta}{dt}$

Emissivity

Emissivity of a body at a given temperature is equal to the ratio of the total emissive power of the body (e_λ) to the total emissive power of a perfectly black body (E_λ) at that temperature.

Emissivity, $\varepsilon = \dfrac{e_\lambda}{E_\lambda}$

Perfectly Black Body

A body which absorbs completely the radiations of all wavelengths incident on it, is called a perfectly black body.

For a perfectly black body, emissive power $(E_\lambda) = 1$

Lamp black is 96% black and platinum black is about 98% black.

Kirchhoff's Law of Radiation

This law states that, the ratio of emissive power to absorptive power is same for all surfaces at the same temperature and is equal to the emissive power of a perfectly black body at that temperature.

Mathematically, $\dfrac{e_1}{a_1} = \dfrac{e_2}{a_2} = \cdots = E$

Stefan's Law

According to this law, the emissive power of a perfectly black body (energy emitted by a black body per unit surface area per unit time) is directly proportional to the fourth power of its absolute temperature.

Mathematically, $E \propto T^4$

or $E = \sigma T^4$

where, σ is a constant known as the Stefan's constant. Value of σ is $5.67 \times 10^{-8}\ \text{Wm}^{-2}\text{K}^{-4}$.

- The total radiant energy Q emitted by a body of surface area A in time t is given by

$$Q = Ate = At\varepsilon\sigma T^4$$

- The radiant power (P), i.e. energy radiated by a body per unit time is given by

$$P = \frac{Q}{t} = A\varepsilon\sigma T^4$$

- If a body at temperature T is surrounded by another body at temperature T_0 (where, $T_0 < T$), then Stefan's law is modified as

$$E = \sigma(T^4 - T_0^4)$$

and $$e = \varepsilon\sigma(T^4 - T_0^4)$$

Newton's Law of Cooling

- According to this law of cooling, rate of cooling of a body is directly proportional to the temperature difference between the body and the surroundings provided that the temperature difference is small.

Mathematically,

$$-\frac{dT}{dt} \propto (T - T_0) \quad \text{or} \quad -\frac{dT}{dt} = k(T - T_0)$$

where, k is a constant.

- If a body cools by radiation through a small temperature difference from T_1 to T_2 in a short time t when the surrounding temperature is T_0, then $T = k\left(\frac{T_1 + T_2}{2} - T_0\right)$

Wien's Displacement Law

This law states that as temperature of black body T increases, the wavelength λ_m corresponding to the maximum emission decreases such that $\lambda_m \propto \frac{1}{T}$

or $$\lambda_m T = b$$

where, b is known as Wien's constant and its value is 2.89×10^{-3} m-K.

Topical Practice Questions

All the exam questions of this chapter have been divided into 6 topics as listed below

Topic 1

Thermometry

2017

1 Mercury boils at 367°C. However, mercury thermometers are made such that they can measure temperature upto 500°C. This is done by **[JIPMER]**

(a) maintaining vacuum aboves mercury column in the stem of the thermometer
(b) filling nitrogen gas at high pressure above the mercury column
(c) filling oxygen gas at high pressure above the mercury column
(d) filling nitrogen gas at low pressure above the mercury column

2014

2 A scientist proposes a new temperature scale in which the ice point is 25 X (X is the new unit of temperature) and the steam point is 305 X. The specific heat capacity of water in this new scale is (in $Jkg^{-1}X^{-1}$) **[WB JEE]**

(a) 4.2×10^3 (b) 3.0×10^3 (c) 1.2×10^3 (d) 1.5×10^3

2013

3 Two thermometers are constructed in the same way except that one has a spherical bulb and the other a cylindrical bulb, which one will respond quickly to temperature changes? **[WB JEE]**

(a) Spherical bulb thermometer
(b) Cylindrical bulb thermometer
(c) Both equally
(d) None of the above

2012

4 If a thermometer reads freezing point of water as 20°C and boiling point as 150°C, how much thermometer read when the actual temperature is 60°C? **[AFMC]**

(a) 98°C (b) 10°C (c) 40°C (d) 60°C

5 In a mercury thermometer, the ice point (lower fixed point) is marked as 10° and the steam point (upper fixed point) is marked as 130°. At 40°C temperature, what will this thermometer read? **[WB JEE]**

(a) 78° (b) 66° (c) 62° (d) 58°

2011

6 Two temperature scales A and B are related by $\frac{A-42}{110}=\frac{B-72}{220}$. At which temperature two scales have the same readings? **[WB JEE]**

(a) – 42° (b) – 72°
(c) + 12° (d) – 40°

2010

7 Oxygen boils at – 183° C. This temperature is approximately in Fahrenheit is **[CG PMT]**

(a) – 329° F (b) – 261° F
(c) – 215° F (d) – 297° F

2009

8 If absolute zero is –273.15°C on Celsius temperature scale, then the absolute zero on the Fahrenheit scale is **[BVP]**

(a) – 227.15° F (b) – 453.15° F
(c) – 459.67° F (d) – 491.67° F

2008

9 On a new scale of temperature (which is linear) and called the W scale, the freezing and boiling points of water are 39°W and 239°W, respectively. What will be the temperature on the new scale, corresponding to a temperature of 39°C on the Celsius scale? **[CBSE AIPMT]**

(a) 78°W (b) 117°W (c) 200°W (d) 139°W

2006

10 The temperature of a body is 95°F, what will be reduction at Celsius scale? **[BHU]**

(a) 7°C (b) 65°C
(c) 63°C (d) 35°C

2005

11 A faulty thermometer has its fixed point marked as 5° and 95°C. The temperature of a body as measured by the faulty thermometer is 59°C. The correct temperature of the body on Celsius scale is **[Haryana PMT]**

(a) 40°C (b) 60°C (c) 20°C (d) 30°

Answers

1 (b)	2 (d)	3 (b)	4 (a)	5 (d)	6 (c)	7 (d)	8 (c)	9 (b)	10 (d)
11 (b)									

Explanations

1 *(b)* If we fill nitrogen gas at a high pressure above mercury level, the boiling point of mercury is increased which can extend to the range upto 500° C.

2 *(d)* Given, 305 X − 25 X =100°C

($\because$ X is the new unit of temperature)

$$(305-25)\text{ X} = 100°\text{ C}$$

$$\Rightarrow \quad 1°\text{C} = 2.8\text{ X}$$

The specific heat capacity of water

$$= 4200\,\frac{\text{J}}{\text{kg°C}}$$

$$= 4200 \times \frac{\text{J}}{\text{kg} \times 2.8\text{ X}}$$

$$= 1500\text{ J/kg-X}$$

$$= 1.5 \times 10^3\text{ J kg}^{-1}\text{X}^{-1}$$

3 *(b)* Cylindrical bulb thermometer has more area as compared to spherical one, so the heat received by the cylindrical bulb is more, which will make it indicate change in temperature, more quickly.

4 *(a)* Temperature on any scale can be converted into other scale by

$$\frac{\lambda - \text{LFP}}{\text{UFP} - \text{LFP}} = \text{constant for all scales}$$

$$\frac{x-20}{150-20} = \frac{60}{100} \Rightarrow x = 98°\text{C}$$

5 *(d)* $\dfrac{x-10}{130-10} = \dfrac{40}{100}$

$$\Rightarrow 100x - 1000 = 4800$$

$$\Rightarrow \quad 100x = 5800$$

$$\Rightarrow \quad x = 58°$$

6 *(c)* We are given the relation between the temperature scale A and B as $\dfrac{A-42}{110} = \dfrac{B-72}{220}$, so for the two scales to have the same reading,

$A = B$ and so, $\dfrac{A-42}{110} = \dfrac{A-72}{220}$

$$\Rightarrow \quad \frac{A-42}{1} = \frac{A-72}{2}$$

$$\Rightarrow 2A - 84 = A - 72$$

$$\Rightarrow 2A - A = 84 - 72$$

$$\Rightarrow \quad A = 12°$$

7 *(d)* $\dfrac{C}{5} = \dfrac{F-32}{9}$

$$\Rightarrow -\frac{183}{5} = \frac{F-32}{9}$$

$$\Rightarrow \quad F = -297.4°\text{F} \approx -297°\text{F}$$

8 *(c)* Celsius and Kelvin scales are related as $\dfrac{C}{5} = \dfrac{F-32}{9}$

$$\Rightarrow \frac{-273.15}{5} = \frac{F-32}{9}$$

$$\Rightarrow \quad F = -459.67°\text{F}$$

9 *(b)* In general, whenever we compare any known scale to any unknown scale, then we follow the equation

$$\frac{\text{(Temperature on known scale)} - \text{(LFP for known scale)}}{(\text{UFP} - \text{LFP})_{\text{known}}} = \frac{\text{(Temperature on unknown scale)} - \text{(LFP for unknown scale)}}{(\text{UFP} - \text{LFP})_{\text{unknown}}}$$

$$\Rightarrow \quad \frac{39-0}{100-0} = \frac{t-39}{239-39}$$

$$\Rightarrow \quad t = 117°\text{ W}$$

Note LFP→ Lower Fixed Point
UFP→ Upper Fixed Point

10 *(d)* The relation between Celsius scale and Fahrenheit scale is

$$T_F = 32 + \frac{9}{5}T_C$$

$$\Rightarrow \quad T_C = \frac{5}{9}(T_F - 32)$$

Given, $T_F = 95°\text{F}$

$$\therefore \quad T_C = 5/9(95-32) = 35°\text{C}$$

11 *(b)* x be the temperature measured by faulty thermometer

$$\therefore \quad \frac{C-0}{100} = \frac{x - \text{lower fixed point}}{\text{Number of divisions between the two fixed points}}$$

$$\Rightarrow \quad \frac{C}{100-0} = \frac{59-5}{95-5}$$

$$\Rightarrow \quad \frac{C}{100} = \frac{54}{90} \Rightarrow C = 60°\text{C}$$

Topic 2

Thermal Expansion

2019

1 A copper rod of 88 cm and an aluminium rod of unknown length have their increase in length independent of increase in temperature. The length of aluminium rod is **[NEET (National)]**

(a) 113.9 cm (b) 88 cm (c) 68 cm (d) 6.8 cm

2 The wooden wheel of radius R is made of two semicircular parts (see figure). The two parts are held together by a ring made of a metal strip of cross-sectional area S and length L. L is slightly less than $2\pi R$. To fit the ring on the wheel, it is heated so that its temperature rises by ΔT and it just steps over the wheel. As it cools down to surrounding temperature, it presses the semicircular parts together. If the coefficient of linear expansion of the metal is α and its Young's modulus is Y, the force that one part of the wheel applies on the other part is **[JIPMER]**

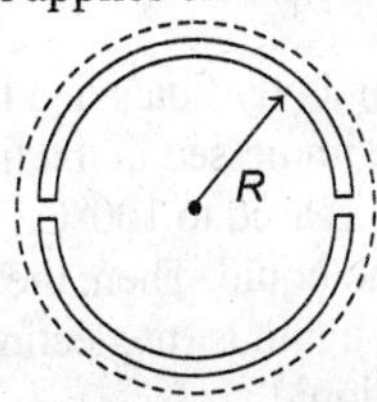

(a) $2\pi SY\alpha\Delta T$ (b) $SY\alpha\Delta T$
(c) $\pi SY\alpha\Delta T$ (d) $2SY\alpha\Delta T$

2018

3 The coefficient of volume expansion of glycerine is $49 \times 10^{-5} \,°C^{-1}$. What is the fractional change in density for a 30° C rise in temperature? **[JIPMER]**

(a) 0.0155 (b) 0.0145
(c) 0.0255 (d) 0.0355

4 How much should the temperature of a brass rod be increased so as to increase its length by 1%? (Take, α for brass is $0.00002°C^{-1}$) **[JIPMER]**

(a) 300°C (b) 400°C
(c) 500° C (d) 550° C

2017

5 The coefficient of cubical expansion of mercury is 0.00018/°C and that of brass 0.00006 /°C. If a barometer having a brass scale were to read 74.5 cm at 30°C, find the true barometric height at 0°C. The scale is supposed to be correct at 15°C. **[AIIMS]**

(a) 74.122 cm (b) 79.152 cm
(c) 42.161 cm (d) 142.39 cm

2016

6 Coefficient of linear expansion of brass and steel rods are α_1 and α_2. Lengths of brass and steel rods are l_1 and l_2 respectively. If $(l_2 - l_1)$ is maintained same at all temperatures, which one of the following relations holds good? **[NEET]**

(a) $\alpha_1 l_2^2 = \alpha_2 l_1^2$ (b) $\alpha_1^2 l_2 = \alpha_2^2 l_1$
(c) $\alpha_1 l_1 = \alpha_2 l_2$ (d) $\alpha_1 l_2 = \alpha_2 l_1$

2014

7 The length of a steel rod is 5 cm longer than that of a brass rod. If this difference in their lengths is to remain the same at all temperatures, then the length of brass rod will be (coefficient of linear expansion for steel and brass are 12×10^{-6}/° C and 18×10^{-6}/° C respectively) **[EAMCET]**

(a) 20 cm (b) 15 cm
(c) 5 cm (d) 10 cm

8 In anomalous expansion of water, at what temperature, the density of water is maximum? **[KCET]**

(a) 4°C (b) < 4°C
(c) > 4°C (d) 10° C

2012

9 A non-conducting body floats in a liquid at 20° C with 2/3 of its volume immersed in the liquid. When liquid temperature is increased to 100°C, 3/4 of body's volume is immersed in the liquid. Then, the coefficient of real expansion of the liquid is (neglecting the expansion of container of the liquid) **[AIIMS]**

(a) $15.6 \times 10^{-4} \,°C^{-1}$ (b) $156 \times 10^{-4} \,°C^{-1}$
(c) $1.56 \times 10^{-4} \,°C^{-1}$ (d) $0.156 \times 10^{4} \,°C^{-1}$

10 When the temperature of a rod increases from t to $t + \Delta t$, its moment of inertia increases from I to $I + \Delta I$. If α be the coefficient of linear expansion of the rod, then the value of $\Delta I / I$ is **[Kerala CEE]**

(a) $2\alpha\Delta t$ (b) $\alpha\Delta t$ (c) $\frac{\alpha\Delta t}{2}$ (d) $\frac{\Delta t}{\alpha}$
(e) $\frac{\Delta t}{2\alpha}$

2010

11 A clock with a metal pendulum beating seconds keeps correct time at 0° C. If it loses 12.5 s a day at 25°C, the coefficient of linear expansion of metal pendulum is **[AIIMS]**

(a) $\frac{1}{86400}$ /°C (b) $\frac{1}{43200}$ /°C
(c) $\frac{1}{14400}$ /°C (d) $\frac{1}{28800}$ /°C

12 There are two spheres of same radius and material at same temperature but one being solid while the other hollow. Which sphere will expand more if they are heated to same temperature? **[OJEE]**

(a) Hollow sphere (b) Solid sphere
(c) Both will expand equally (d) None of these

13 An ideal gas is initially at temperature T and volume V. Its volume is increased by ΔV due to an increase in temperature ΔT, pressure remaining constant. The physical quantity $\delta = \frac{\Delta V}{V\Delta T}$ varies with temperature as **[EAMCET]**

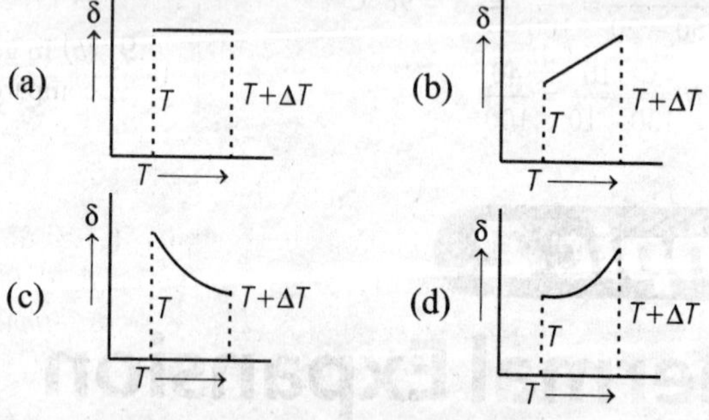

14 The coefficient of real expansion of mercury is 0.18×10^{-3} C^{-1}. If the density of mercury at 0° C is 13.6 g / cc, its density at 473 K will be **[Manipal]**

(a) 13.12 g/cc (b) 13.65 g/cc
(c) 13.51 g/cc (d) 13.22 g/cc

2009

15 The volume of mercury in the bulb of a thermometer is 10^{-6} m^3. The area of cross-section of the capillary tube is 2×10^{-7} m^2. If the temperature is raised by 100° C, the increase in the length of the mercury column is (Take, $\gamma_{Hg} = 18 \times 10^{-5}$/° C) **[EAMCET]**

(a) 18 cm (b) 0.9 cm (c) 9 cm (d) 1.8 cm

16 There is some change in length when a 33000 N tensile force is applied on a steel rod of area of cross-section 10^{-3} m^2. The change of temperature required to produce the same elongation, if the steel rod is heated, is (the modulus of elasticity is 3×10^{11} Nm^{-2} and the coefficient of linear expansion of steel is 1.1×10^{-5} °C^{-1}) **[BITSAT]**

(a) 20°C (b) 15°C (c) 10°C (d) 0°C

17 A bimetallic strip consists of brass and iron when it is heated it bends into an arc with brass on the convex and iron on the concave side of the arc. This happens, because **[BCECE]**

(a) brass has a higher specific heat capacity than iron
(b) density of brass is more than that of iron
(c) it is easier to bend an iron strip than a brass strip of the same size
(d) brass has a higher coefficient of linear expansion than iron

2008

18 What fraction of the volume of a glass flask must be filled with mercury, so that the volume of the empty space may be the same at all temperatures?
(Take, $\alpha_{glass} = 9 \times 10^{-6}/°C, \gamma_{Hg} = 18.9 \times 10^{-5}/°C$) **[Punjab PMET]**

(a) $\frac{1}{2}$ (b) $\frac{1}{7}$
(c) $\frac{1}{4}$ (d) $\frac{1}{5}$

19 A clock which keeps correct time at 20°C is subjected to 40°C. If coefficient of linear expansion of the pendulum is $12 \times 10^{-6}/°C$. How much will it gain or loss in time?

(a) 10.3 s/day (b) 20.6 s/day **[Punjab PMET]**
(c) 5 s/day (d) 20 min/day

20 A 2 L glass flask contains some mercury. It is found that at all temperatures the volume of the air inside the flask remains the same. The volume of the mercury inside the flask is (α for glass $= 9 \times 10^{-6}/°C, \gamma$ for mercury $= 1.8 \times 10^{-4}/°C$) **[EAMCET]**

(a) 1500 cc (b) 150 cc (c) 3000 cc (d) 300 cc

2007

21 Coefficient of cubical expansion of water is zero at **[AMU]**

(a) 0°C (b) 4°C (c) 15.5 °C (d) 100°C

2006

22 A bimetallic strip consists of metals X and Y. It is mounted rigidly at the base as shown. The metal X has a higher coefficient of expansion compared to that for metal Y. When bimetallic strip is placed in a cold bath, **[AIIMS]**

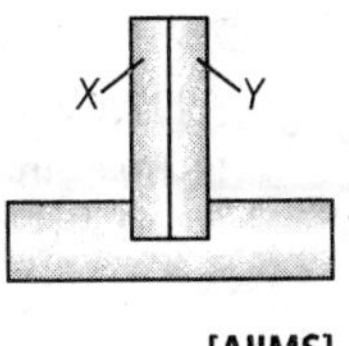

(a) it will bend towards the right
(b) it will bend towards the left
(c) it will not bend but shrink
(d) it will neither bend nor shrink

23 A vertical column 50 cm long at 50°C balances another column of same liquid 60 cm long at 100°C. The coefficient of absolute expansion of the liquid is **[Manipal]**

(a) 0.005/°C (b) 0.0005/°C
(c) 0.002/°C (d) 0.0002/°C

24 The coefficient of apparent expansion of a liquid when determined using two different vessels A and B are γ_1 and γ_2, respectively. If the coefficient of linear expansion of vessel A is α. The coefficient of linear expansion of the vessel B is **[Haryana PMT]**

(a) $\frac{\alpha\gamma_1\gamma_2}{\gamma_1 + \gamma_2}$ (b) $\frac{\gamma_1 - \gamma_2}{2\alpha}$
(c) $\frac{\gamma_1^{\tau} - \gamma_2}{3} + \alpha$ (d) $\frac{\gamma_1 - \gamma_2}{3} + \alpha$

2005

25 A beaker is completely filled with water at 4°C. It will overflow, if **[Punjab PMET]**

(a) heated above 4°C
(b) cooled below 4°C
(c) Both heated and cooled above and below 4°C respectively
(d) None of the above

26 Two uniform metal rods of lengths l_1 and l_2 and linear coefficients of expansions α_1 and α_2, respectively are connected to form a single rod of length $(l_1 + l_2)$. When the temperature of the combined rod is raised by $t°$ C, the length of each rod increases by the same amount. Then, $\left(\frac{\alpha_2}{\alpha_1 + \alpha_2}\right)$ is **[EAMCET]**

(a) $\frac{l_1}{l_1 + l_2}$ (b) $\frac{l_1 + l_2}{l_1}$ (c) $\frac{l_2}{l_1 + l_2}$ (d) $\frac{l_1 + l_2}{l_2}$

Answers

1 (c)	2 (d)	3 (b)	4 (c)	5 (a)	6 (c)	7 (d)	8 (a)	9 (a)	10 (a)
11 (a)	12 (a)	13 (c)	14 (a)	15 (c)	16 (c)	17 (d)	18 (b)	19 (a)	20 (d)
21 (b)	22 (b)	23 (a)	24 (d)	25 (c)	26 (c)				

Explanations

1 (c) Due to change in temperature, the thermal strain produced in a rod of length L is given by

$$\frac{\Delta L}{L} = \alpha\,\Delta T \Rightarrow \Delta L = L\,\alpha\,\Delta T$$

where, l = original length of rod and α = coefficient of linear expansion of solid rod.

As the change in length (Δl) of the given two rods of copper and aluminium are independent of temperature change, i.e. ΔT is same for both copper and aluminium.

$$L_{\text{Cu}}\alpha_{\text{Cu}} = L_{\text{Al}}\alpha_{\text{Al}} \quad \text{... (i)}$$

Here, $\alpha_{\text{Cu}} = 1.7 \times 10^{-5}\ \text{K}^{-1}$

$\alpha_{\text{Al}} = 2.2 \times 10^{-5}\ \text{K}^{-1}$

and $L_{\text{Cu}} = 88$ cm

Substituting the given values in Eq. (i), we get

$$L_{\text{Al}} = \frac{\alpha_{\text{Cu}}L_{\text{Cu}}}{\alpha_{\text{Al}}} = \frac{1.7 \times 10^{-5} \times 88}{2.2 \times 10^{-5}} \simeq 68 \text{ cm}$$

2 (d) Elongation due to change in temperature.

$$\Delta l = L\alpha\Delta T \quad \text{...(i)}$$

where,

α = coefficient of linear expansion which is compensated by elastic strain, when temperature becomes normal, i.e.

$$\Delta l = \frac{TL}{YS} \quad \text{...(ii)}$$

From Eqs. (i) and (ii), we get

$$\frac{TL}{YS} = L\alpha\Delta T$$

$$\Rightarrow \quad T = YS\alpha\Delta T$$

At equilibrium, force exerted by one-half on other,

$$F = 2T = 2YS\alpha\Delta T$$

3 (b) Here, $\gamma = 49 \times 10^{-5}\,{}^\circ\text{C}^{-1}$,

$$\Delta T = 30^\circ\text{C}$$

$$V' = V + \Delta V = V(1 + \gamma\Delta T)$$

$$\therefore \quad V' = V\,(1 + 49 \times 10^{-5} \times 30)$$

$$= 1.0147\text{V}$$

$$\because \quad \rho = \frac{m}{V} \text{ and } \rho' = \frac{m}{V'} = \frac{m}{1.0147\,V}$$

$$= 0.9855\,\rho$$

Hence, fractional change in density

$$= \frac{\rho - \rho'}{\rho} = \frac{\rho - 0.9855\,\rho}{\rho} = 0.0145$$

4 (c) Here, $\Delta T = ?, \dfrac{\Delta L}{L} = \dfrac{1}{100}$,

$$\alpha = 0.00002^\circ\ \text{C}^{-1}$$

As, $\quad \Delta L = \alpha L\Delta T$

$$\therefore \quad \alpha\,\Delta T = \frac{\Delta L}{L}$$

or $\quad \Delta T = \dfrac{\Delta L}{L\alpha} = \dfrac{1}{100 \times 0.00002}$

$$\Delta T = \frac{10^5}{2 \times 10^2} = 500^\circ\text{C}$$

5 (a) As, $\alpha_{\text{brass}} = \dfrac{\gamma_{\text{brass}}}{3} = \dfrac{0.00006}{3}$

$$= 0.00002 = 2 \times 10^{-5}/^\circ\text{C}$$

The brass scale is true at 15°C, therefore at 30°, its graduations will increase in length and so observed reading will be less than actual reading at 30°.

$\therefore$ The change in reading,

$$\Delta l = l\alpha_{\text{brass}}(\Delta T)$$
$$= 74.5 \times 2 \times 10^{-5}(30 - 15)$$
$$= 0.02235 \text{ cm}$$

$\therefore$ Actual reading at 30°C,

$$l_{30} = l_{\text{observed}} + \Delta l$$
$$= 74.5 + 0.02235$$
$$= 74.522 \text{ cm}$$

Assuming area of cross-section to be constant, we have

$$V_0\rho_0 = V_{30}\rho_{30}$$

or $\quad ah_0\rho_0 = ah_{30}\rho_{30}$

Therefore, true height at 0°C,

$$h_0 = h_{30}\frac{\rho_{30}}{\rho_0} = \frac{h_{30}}{(1 + \gamma_{\text{Hg}}\Delta T)}$$

$$= \frac{74.522}{1 + 0.00018 \times 30} = \frac{74.522}{1.0054}$$

$$= 74.122 \text{ cm}$$

6 (c) According to question,

Coefficient of linear expansion of brass $= \alpha_1$

Coefficient of linear expansion of steel $= \alpha_2$

Length of brass and steel rods are l_1 and l_2, respectively.

As given difference increase in length $(l_2' - l_1')$ is same for all temperature.

So, $\quad l_2' - l_1' = l_2 - l_1$

$$\Rightarrow l_2(1 + \alpha_2\Delta t) - l_1\,(1 + \alpha_1\Delta t) = l_2 - l_1$$

$$\Rightarrow \quad l_2\alpha_2 = l_1\alpha_1$$

7 (d) Given, $L_{\text{St}} - L_{\text{Br}} = 5$ cm,

$$L_{\text{St}} = L,\ L_{\text{Br}} = (L - 5) \text{ cm}$$

$$\alpha_{\text{St}} = 12 \times 10^{-6}/^\circ\text{C},$$

$$\alpha_{\text{Br}} = 18 \times 10^{-6}/^\circ\text{C}$$

We know that, $\alpha_{\text{St}} = \Delta L_{\text{St}}/L_{\text{St}} \times t_1$

$$12 \times 10^{-6} = \frac{\Delta L}{L \times t} \quad \text{...(i)}$$

$$\alpha_{\text{Br}} = \frac{\Delta L_{\text{Br}}}{L_{\text{Br}} \times t_2}$$

$$18 \times 10^{-6} = \frac{\Delta L}{(L - 5) \times t} \quad \text{...(ii)}$$

Dividing Eq. (i) by Eq , (ii), we get

$$\frac{12 \times 10^{-6}}{18 \times 10^{-6}} = \frac{\Delta L/L \times t}{\Delta L/(L - 5) \times t}$$

$$\Rightarrow \quad \frac{2}{3} = \frac{L - 5}{L}$$

$$2L = 3L - 15$$

$$\Rightarrow \quad L = 15$$

So, $\quad L_{\text{Br}} = L - 5 = 15 - 5 = 10$ cm

8 (a) When cooled from room temperature, liquid water becomes dense, like other substances, but at approximately 4°C (39° F), pure water reaches its maximum density. If it is cooled further, it expands to become less dense.

9 (a) Coefficient of real expansion,

$$\gamma_R = \frac{V_2 - V_1}{V_1(t_2 - t_1)}$$

Here, $\quad V_2 = \dfrac{3}{4}, V_1 = \dfrac{2}{3}$

and $(t_2 - t_1) = (100 - 20) = 80^\circ$C

$$\therefore \quad \gamma_R = \frac{\left(\frac{3}{4} - \frac{2}{3}\right)}{\frac{2}{3}(80)} = \frac{1}{640}$$

$$= 15.6 \times 10^{-4}\,{}^\circ\text{C}^{-1}$$

10 (a) Moment of inertia of a rod, $I = \dfrac{Ml^2}{12}$

On differentiating w.r.t. l, we get

$$dI = \frac{M}{12}2l\,dl$$

$$\therefore \quad \frac{dI}{I} = \frac{\frac{M}{12}2l\,dl}{\frac{Ml^2}{12}}$$

$$\Rightarrow \quad \frac{dI}{I} = 2\frac{dl}{l} = 2\alpha\Delta t$$

11 (*a*) Number of second lost in a day,

$$\Delta t = \frac{1}{2}\alpha\, \Delta\theta \times 86400$$

The coefficient of linear expansion of metal pendulum,

$$\alpha = \frac{2\Delta t}{\Delta\theta \times 86400} = \frac{2\times 12.5}{25\times 86400} = \frac{1}{86400}/\,°\text{C}$$

12 (*a*) If same amount of heat is given to both the solid and hollow spheres having same radii and temperature, hollow sphere will expand more. As, hollow sphere has lesser mass, its rise in temperature will be more because $\Delta T = \frac{Q}{MC}$, but apparently it seems for both are having same expansion coefficient (γ) as both of them are of same material.

Change in volume, $\Delta V = \gamma V \Delta T$

As ΔT is more for hollow sphere, so it will expand more.

13 (*c*) From ideal gas equation,

$$pV = RT \quad \ldots \text{(i)}$$

or $$p\Delta V = R\Delta T \quad \ldots \text{(ii)}$$

Dividing Eq. (ii) by Eq. (i), we get

$$\frac{\Delta V}{V} = \frac{\Delta T}{T}$$

$$\Rightarrow \quad \frac{\Delta V}{V\Delta T} = \frac{1}{T} = \delta \quad \left[\because \delta = \frac{\Delta V}{V\Delta T}\right]$$

So, the graph between δ and T will be

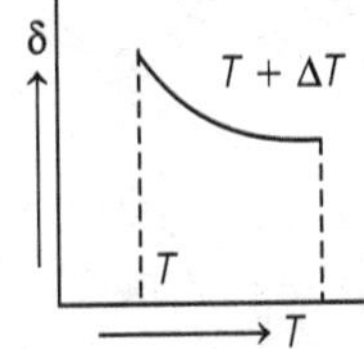

14 (*a*) Here, $t_1 = 0°\text{C} = 273\text{K}$, $t_2 = 473\text{K}$

$$\gamma_r = 0.18\times 10^{-3}\,\text{C}^{-1}$$

$$d_1 = 13.6\,\text{g/cc},\ d_2 = ?$$

$$d_2 = \frac{d_1}{1+\gamma_r(\Delta t)} = \frac{13.6}{1+0.18\times 10^{-3}\times(473-273)}$$

$$\Rightarrow \quad d_2 = \frac{13.6}{1.036} = 13.12\,\text{g/cc}$$

15 (*c*) By cubical expansion relation,

$$\Delta V = V \times \gamma\Delta T$$

where, γ = coefficient of cubical expansion,

$$V = 10^{-6}\text{m}^3 = \text{initial volume}$$

$$\gamma = 18\times 10^{-5}/°\text{C}$$

$$\Delta T = 100°\text{C}$$

$$\Delta V = 10^{-6}\times 18\times 10^{-5}\times 10^2 = 18\times 10^{-9}\ \text{m}^3$$

Since, $\Delta V = A\times \Delta l$

$\therefore \quad 18\times 10^{-9} = 2\times 10^{-7}\times \Delta l$

or $\quad 9\times 10^{-2} = \Delta l$

or $\quad \Delta l = 9$ cm

16 (*c*) Modulus of elasticity $= \frac{\text{Force}}{\text{Area}}\times\frac{l}{\Delta l}$

$$\Rightarrow 3\times 10^{11} = \frac{33000}{10^{-3}}\times\frac{l}{\Delta l}$$

$$\Rightarrow \quad \frac{\Delta l}{l} = \frac{33000}{10^{-3}}\times\frac{1}{3\times 10^{11}} = 11\times 10^{-5}$$

Change in length, $\frac{\Delta l}{l} = \alpha\,\Delta T$

where, α = coefficient of linear expansion

Δl = charge in length and l = original length.

So, $11\times 10^{-5} = 1.1\times 10^{-5}\times\Delta T$

$$\Rightarrow \quad \Delta T = 10\,\text{K or } 10°\text{C}$$

17 (*d*) Two strips of equal lengths but of different materials (different coefficient of linear expansion α) when joined together, is called bimetallic strip. This strip has the characteristic property of bending on heating due to unequal linear expansion of the two metals. The brass side bends on outer side (convex side) due to greater α and iron bends on inner side (concave side) due to smaller α.

18 (*b*) If V is the volume of glass flask, V_L of mercury and V_A of air in it,

$$V = V_L + V_A$$

Now, as with change in temperature volume of air remains constant, the expansion of mercury will be equal to that of the glass flask, i.e.

$$\Delta V = \Delta V_L$$

or $V\gamma_G\Delta\theta = V_{\text{Hg}}\,\gamma_{\text{Hg}}\,\Delta\theta$ (as $\Delta V = V\gamma\Delta\theta$)

or $$\frac{V_{\text{Hg}}}{V} = \frac{\gamma_G}{\gamma_{\text{Hg}}}$$

$$= \frac{3\times 9\times 10^{-6}}{18.9\times 10^{-5}} \quad (\because \gamma_G = 3\alpha_G)$$

$$= \frac{1}{7}$$

19 (*a*) Time period, $T = 2\pi\sqrt{\frac{l}{g}}$

Fractional change,

$$\frac{\Delta T}{T} = \frac{1}{2}\frac{\Delta l}{l} = \frac{1}{2}\alpha\,\Delta\theta$$

$$= \frac{1}{2}\times 12\times 10^{-6}(40-20)$$

$$= 12\times 10^{-5}$$

$$\Delta T = T\times 12\times 10^{-5}$$

$$= 24\times 60\times 60\times 12\times 10^{-5}$$

$$= 10.3\ \text{s day}^{-1}$$

20 (*d*) It is given that the volume of air in the flask remains the same. This means that the expansion in volume of the vessel (ΔV_v) is exactly equal to the volume expansion of mercury (ΔV_m),

i.e. $\quad \Delta V_v = \Delta V_m$

or $\quad V_v\gamma_v\Delta T = V_m\gamma_m\Delta T$

$$\therefore \quad V_m = \frac{V_v\gamma_v}{\gamma_m} = \frac{V_v\times 3\alpha_G}{\gamma_m}$$

$$(\because \gamma_v = 3\alpha_G)$$

$$\Rightarrow \quad V_m = \frac{2000\times 3\times 9\times 10^{-6}}{1.8\times 10^{-4}}$$

$$V_m = 300\ \text{cc}$$

21 (*b*) Coefficient of cubical expansion of water at 4°C is zero, because the density of water at 4°C is maximum.

22 (*b*) The metal X has a higher coefficient of expansion compared to that for metal Y so on placing bimetallic strip in a cold bath, X will shrink more than Y. Hence, the strip will bend towards the left.

23 (*a*) $\frac{h_1}{h_2} = \frac{\rho_2}{\rho_1} = \frac{(1+\gamma\theta_1)}{(1+\gamma\theta_2)}$

$$\left[\because \rho = \frac{\rho_0}{(1+\gamma\theta)}\right]$$

$$\Rightarrow \quad \frac{50}{60} = \frac{1+50\gamma}{1+100\gamma} \Rightarrow r = 0.005/°\text{C}$$

24 (*d*) $\gamma_{\text{real}} = \gamma_{\text{app}} + \gamma_{\text{vessel}},\ \gamma_{\text{vessel}} = 3\alpha$

For vessel A, $\gamma_{\text{real}} = \gamma_1 + 3\alpha$

For vessel B, $\gamma_{\text{real}} = \gamma_2 + 3\alpha_B$

Hence, $\quad \gamma_1 + 3\alpha = \gamma_2 + 3\alpha_B$

$$\Rightarrow \quad \alpha_B = \frac{\gamma_1-\gamma_2}{3} + \alpha$$

25 (c) Certain substances do not expand but contract when heated within a certain range of temperature and water is such a substance. Density of water is maximum at 4°C, so its volume is minimum at this temperature. If water is heated above 4°C, its volume increases. Also, on cooling below 4°C its volume increases instead of decreasing, this is known as anomalous expansion of water. Since, volume increases in both cases, so water will overflow.

26 (c) Initial length of I rod = l_1

Initial length of II rod = l_2

Linear coefficient of I rod = α_1

Linear coefficient of II rod = α_2

If temperature of combined rod increases by t°C, then increase in length in I rod is given by

$$\Delta l_1 = l_1 / \alpha_1 t$$

Increase in length of II rod is given by

$$\Delta l_2 = \frac{l_2}{\alpha_2 t} \quad \text{and} \quad \Delta l_1 = \Delta l_2$$

$$\therefore \quad \frac{l_1}{\alpha_1 t} = \frac{l_2}{\alpha_2 t} \Rightarrow \frac{l_1}{\alpha_1} = \frac{l_2}{\alpha_2}$$

$$\Rightarrow \frac{\alpha_1}{\alpha_2} = \frac{l_1}{l_2}$$

$$\Rightarrow \frac{\alpha_1}{\alpha_2} + 1 = \frac{l_1}{l_2} + 1$$

$$\Rightarrow \frac{\alpha_1 + \alpha_2}{\alpha_2} = \frac{l_1 + l_2}{l_2}$$

$$\Rightarrow \frac{\alpha_2}{\alpha_1 + \alpha_2} = \frac{l_2}{l_1 + l_2}$$

Topic 3

Specific Heat Capacity, Calorimetry and Latent Heat

2019

1 1g of water, of volume 1 cm^3 at 100°C is converted into steam at same temperature under normal atmospheric pressure = ($\simeq 1 \times 10^5$ Pa). The volume of steam formed equals 1671 cm^3. If the specific latent heat of vaporisation of water is 2256 J/g, the change in internal energy is **[NEET (Odisha)]**

(a) 2423 J (b) 2089 J (c) 167 J (d) 2256 J

2014

2 Steam at 100° C is passed into 20 g of water at 10° C. When water acquires a temperature of 80° C, the mass of water present will be [Take, specific heat of water = 1 calg^{-1} ° C^{-1} and latent heat of steam = 540 calg^{-1}] **[AIPMT]**

(a) 24 g (b) 31.5 g (c) 42.5 g (d) 22.5 g

3 A 10 W electric heater is used to heat a container filled with 0.5 kg of water. It is found that the temperature of water and container rises by 3K in 15 min. The container is then emptied, dried and filled with 2 kg of oil. The same heater now raises the temperature of container oil system by 2K in 20 min. Assume there is no heat loss in the process and the specific heat of water 4200 J kg^{-1} K^{-1}, the specific heat of oil in the same limit is equal to **[WB JEE]**

(a) 1.50×10^3 (b) 2.55×10^3 (c) 3.00×10^3 (d) 2.10×10^3

4 A block of ice of mass 50 kg is sliding on a horizontal plane. It starts with speed 5 m/s and stop 3 after moving through some distance. The mass of ice that has melted due to friction between the block and the surface is (assuming that no energy is lost and latent heat of fusion of ice is 80 cal/g, J = 4.2 J/cal) **[WB JEE]**

(a) 2.86 g (b) 3.86 g (c) 0.86 g (d) 1.86 g

2012

5 4320 cal of heat is supplied to 100 g of ice at 0°C. If the latent heat of fusion of ice is 80 cal g^{-1} and latent heat of vaporisation of water is 540 cal g^{-1}, the final amount of water, thus obtained and its temperature respectively are **[WB JEE]**

(a) 8 g and 100°C (b) 100 g and 100°C
(c) 92 g and 1000°C (d) 82 g and 100°C

2011

6 A solid material is supplied with heat at constant rate and the temperature of the material changes as shown. From the graph, the false conclusion drawn is **[Kerala CEE]**

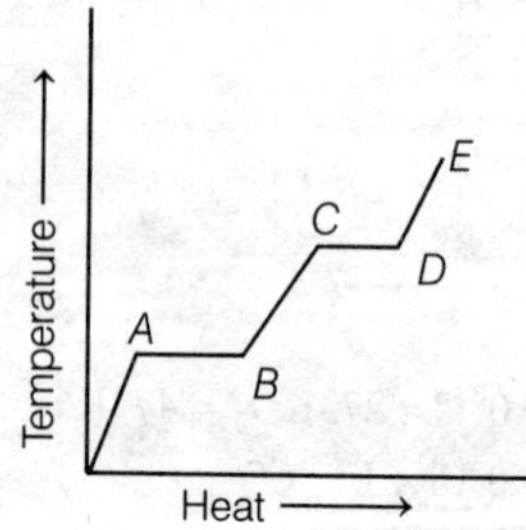

(a) AB and CD of the graph represent phase changes
(b) AB represents the change of state from solid to liquid
(c) latent heat of fusion is twice the latent heat of vaporisation
(d) CD represents change of state from liquid to vapour
(e) latent heat of vaporisation is twice the latent heat of fusion

2010

7 0.3 kg of hot coffee, which is at 70° C, is poured into a cup of mass 0.12 kg. Find the final equilibrium temperature. (Take, room temperature as 20° C, $s_{\text{coffee}} = 4080$ J/kg-K and $s_{\text{cup}} = 1020$ J/kg-K). **[UP CPMT]**

(a) 45.5°C (b) 55.5°C
(c) 65.5°C (d) 40.5°C

8 Certain amount of heat is given to 100 g of copper to increase its temperature by 21° C. If the same amount of heat is given to 50 g of water, then the rise in its temperature is (Take, specific heat capacity of copper $= 400 \text{ Jkg}^{-1} \text{ K}^{-1}$ and that for water $= 4200 \text{ Jkg}^{-1} \text{ K}^{-1}$) **[Kerala CEE]**

(a) 4° C (b) 5.25° C
(c) 8° C (d) 6° C
(e) 10.5°C

9 If 70 cal of heat is required to raise the temperature of 2 mol of an ideal gas at constant pressure from 30° C to 35° C, then the amount of heat required to raise the temperature of same gas through same range at constant volume is **[Punjab PMT]**

(a) 50 cal (b) 70 cal
(c) 60 cal (d) 65 cal

10 Two bodies at different temperatures are mixed in a calorimeter. Which of the following quantities remains conserved? **[Punjab PMT]**

(a) Sum of the temperatures of the two bodies
(b) Total heat of the two bodies
(c) Total internal energy of the two bodies
(d) Internal energy of each body

11 A lead bullet of unknown mass is fired with a speed of 180 ms^{-1} into a tree in which it stops. Assuming that in this process two-third of heat produced goes into the bullet and one-third into wood. The temperature of the bullet rises by (Take, specific heat of lead = 0.120 J/ g°C) **[EAMCET]**

(a) 140° C (b) 106° C
(c) 90° C (d) 100° C

12 A block of ice at temperature – 20° C is slowly heated and converted to steam at 100° C. Which of the following diagrams is most appropriate? **[WB JEE]**

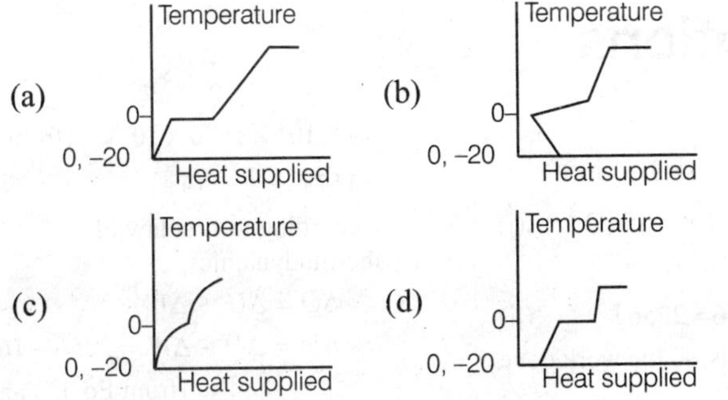

2009

13 Equal masses of two liquids A and B contained in vessels of negligible heat capacity are supplied heat at the same rate. The temperature-time graphs for the two liquids are shown below.

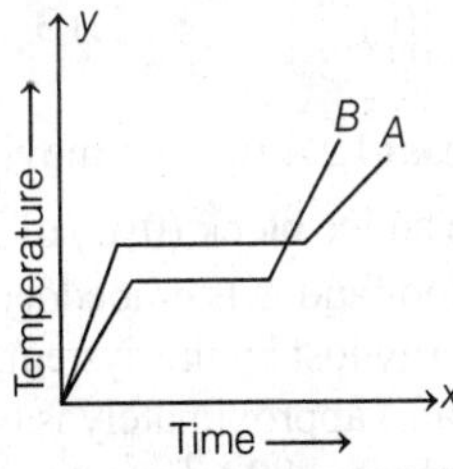

If s represents specific heat and L represents latent heat of liquid, then **[AIIMS]**

(a) $s_A > s_B, L_A < L_B$ (b) $s_A > s_B, L_A > L_B$
(c) $s_A < s_B, L_A < L_B$ (d) $s_A < s_B, L_A > L_B$

14 19 g of water at 30° C and 5 g of ice at –20° C are mixed together in a calorimeter. What is the final temperature of the mixture?
(Take, specific heat of ice = $0.5 \text{ cal g}^{-1} (°\text{C})^{-1}$ and latent heat of fusion of ice = 80 cal g^{-1}) **[KCET]**

(a) 0° C (b) – 5° C
(c) 5° C (d) 10° C

15 0.1 m^3 of water at 80°C is mixed with 0.3 m^3 of water at 60° C. The final temperature of the mixture is **[KCET]**

(a) 65° C (b) 70° C
(c) 60° C (d) 75° C

16 The sprinkling of water reduces slightly the temperature of a closed room, because **[JCECE]**

(a) temperature of water is less than that of the room
(b) specific heat of water is high
(c) water has large latent heat of vaporisation
(d) water is a bad conductor of heat

2008

17 A lead bullet of initial temperature 27°C and speed $v \text{ km h}^{-1}$ penetrates into a solid object and melts. If 50% of the kinetic energy is used to heat it, the value of v (in km h^{-1}) is (for lead melting point = 600 K, latent heat of fusion = $2.5 \times 10^4 \text{ Jkg}^{-1}$, specific heat = $125 \text{ Jkg}^{-1}\text{K}^{-1}$) **[EAMCET]**

(a) 3600 (b) 1800 (c) 1200 (d) 1000

2007

18 Work done in converting one gram of ice at –10°C into steam at 100°C is **[J&K CET]**

(a) 3045 J (b) 6056 J (c) 721 J (d) 616 J

2006

19 In an energy recycling process, X gram of steam at 100°C becomes water at 100°C which converts Y gram of ice at 0°C into water at 100°C. The ratio of X and Y will be **[AMU]**

(a) $\frac{1}{3}$ (b) $\frac{2}{3}$ (c) 3 (d) 2

20 A bullet of mass 10×10^{-3} kg moving with a speed of 20 ms^{-1} hits an ice block (0°C) of 990 g kept at rest on a frictionless floor and gets embedded in it. If ice takes 50% of kinetic energy lost by the system, the amount of ice melted (in gram) approximately is (1 cal = 4.25) (Latent heat of ice = 80 cal/g) **[EAMCET]**

(a) 6 (b) 3 (c) 6×10^{-3} (d) 3×10^{-3}

21 The following figure represents the temperature *versus* time plot for a given amount of a substance when heat energy is supplied to it at a fixed rate and at a constant pressure.

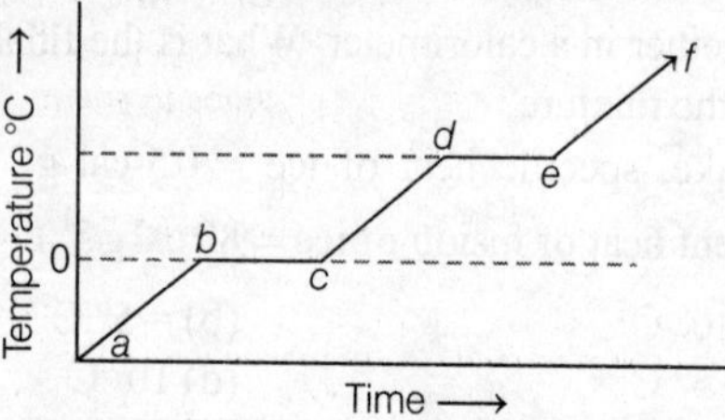

Which part of the above plot represent a phase change? **[BCECE]**

(a) *a* to *b* and *e* to *f* (b) *b* to *c* and *c* to *d*
(c) *d* to *e* and *e* to *f* (d) *b* to *c* and *d* to *e*

2005

22 **Assertion** In pressure-temperature (*p*-*T*) phase diagram of water, the slope of the melting curve is found to be negative.

Reason Ice contracts on melting to water. **[AIIMS]**

(a) Both Assertion and Reason are correct and Reason is the correct explanation of Assertion.
(b) Both Assertion and Reason are correct but Reason is not the correct explanation of Assertion.
(c) A is correct but Reason is incorrect.
(d) Both Assertion and Reason are incorrect.

23 2 g of water condenses when passed through 40 g of water initially at 25°C. The condensation of steam raises the temperature of water to 54.3°C. What is the latent heat of steam? **[J&K CET]**

(a) 540 cal g^{-1} (b) 536 cal g^{-1}
(c) 270 cal g^{-1} (d) 480 cal g^{-1}

24 Calculate the amount of heat (in calorie) required to convert 5 g of ice at 0°C to steam at 100°C. **[DUMET]**

(a) 3100 (b) 3200 (c) 3600 (d) 4200

25 Hailstorm at 0°C falls from a height of 1 km on an insulating surface converting whole of its kinetic energy into heat. What part of it will melt? (take, latent heat of ice = $3.34 \times 10^5 \text{ Jkg}^{-1}$, $g = 10 \text{ ms}^{-2}$) **[DUMET]**

(a) $\frac{1}{33}$ (b) $\frac{1}{8}$
(c) $\frac{3}{3} \times 10^{-4}$ (d) All of it will melt

26 A 42 kg block of ice moving on rough horizontal surface stops due to friction, after sometime. If the initial velocity of the decelerating block is 4 ms^{-1}, the mass of ice (in kg) that has melted due to the heat generated by the friction is
(Take, latent heat of ice = $3.36 \times 10^5 \text{ J kg}^{-1}$) **[EAMCET]**

(a) 1×10^{-3} (b) 1.5×10^{-3}
(c) 2×10^{-3} (d) 2.5×10^{-3}

Answers

1 (b)	2 (d)	3 (b)	4 (d)	5 (a)	6 (c)	7 (c)	8 (a)	9 (a)	10 (c)
11 (c)	12 (a)	13 (d)	14 (c)	15 (a)	16 (c)	17 (b)	18 (a)	19 (a)	20 (d)
21 (d)	22 (a)	23 (a)	24 (c)	25 (a)	26 (a)				

Explanations

1 *(b)* Given, mass of water, $m = 1\text{g}$

Volume of 1 g of water

$= 1 \text{ cm}^3 = 10^{-6} \text{ m}^3$

Volume of 1 g of steam $= 1671 \text{ cm}^3$

$= 1671 \times 10^{-6} \text{ m}^3$

Pressure, $p = 1 \times 10^5$ Pa

Latent heat of vaporisation of water,

$L = 2256$ J/g

Change in volume,

$\Delta V = (1671 - 1) \times 10^{-6} \text{ m}^3$

$= 1670 \times 10^{-6} \text{ m}^3$ ...(i)

Heat supplied, $\Delta Q = mL$

$= 1 \times 2256 = 2256 \text{J}$ ...(ii)

As the steam expands, so the work done in expansion is

$\Delta W = p\Delta V$

$= 1 \times 10^5 \times 1670 \times 10^{-6}$ [from Eq. (i)]

$= 167 \text{J}$ ...(iii)

According to first law of thermodynamics,

$\Delta Q = \Delta U + \Delta W$

$\Rightarrow \Delta U = \Delta Q - \Delta W = 2256 - 167$ [from Eq. (ii) and (iii)]

$= 2089$ J

2 (d) Heat lost by system = Heat gain by water.

Let m' be amount of heat converted into water

$\Rightarrow \quad m'L + m's\Delta t_1 = ms\Delta t_2$

$\Rightarrow \quad m'(100-80) + m' \times 540$

$= 20 \times 1 \times (80-10)$

$\left[\begin{array}{l}\text{where, } L = \text{latent heat} = 540 \text{ calg}^{-1} \\ \text{and } s = \text{specific heat} = 1 \text{ cal g}^{-1}\,{}^\circ\text{C}^{-1}\end{array}\right]$

$\Rightarrow \quad m' = \dfrac{20 \times 70}{560} = 2.5 \text{ g}$

Now, net water = $20 + 2.5 = 22.5$ g

3 (b) As we know, work done by an electric heater,

i.e. $m_1 s_1 \,\Delta t + m_2 s_2 \,\Delta t$ = work done

So, $\quad m_1 s_1 \Delta t + m_2 s_2 \Delta t = P_1 t_1$

where, $m_1 = 0.5$ kg,

Specific heat $s_1 = 4200$ J/kg-K,

$\Delta t = \Delta t_1 = \Delta t_2 = 3$K,

$P_1 = P_2 = 10$ W,

$t_1 = 15 \times 60 = 900$ s,

s_2 = specific heat capacity of container.

So, $0.5 \times 4200 \times (3-0) + m_2 s_2 \times (3-0)$

$= 10 \times 15 \times 60$

$2100 \times 3 + m_2 s_2 \times 3 = 9000$

$m_2 s_2 = \dfrac{9000-6300}{3} = 900$

Similarly, in the case of oil,

$m_1 s_o \Delta t + m_2 s_2 \Delta t = P_2 t_2$

where, s_o = specific heat capacity of oil

$P_1 = P_2 = 10$ W

$2 \times s_o \times 2 + 900 \times 2 = 10 \times 20 \times 60$

$4s_o + 1800 = 12000$

$s_o = 2550$

$= 2.55 \times 10^3 \text{ J kg}^{-1} \text{ K}^{-1}$

4 (d) Given, $m = 50$ kg, $v = 5 \text{ ms}^{-1}$,

$L = 80$ cal/g, $J = 4.2$ J/cal and $m = ?$

Heat lost, i.e. Q_1 = work done,

K = kinetic energy

i.e. $Q_1 = \dfrac{1}{2}mv^2 = \dfrac{1}{2} \times 50 \times 5^2 = 625$ J

and heat gained, i.e.

$Q_2 = m' \times L$

$= 80 \times m' \times 4.2$

$\because \quad Q_1 = Q_2$

$625 = m' \times 8 \times 42$

$m' = 1.86$ g

5 (a) Heat required to convert ice into water at 100° C.

$Q = m \times L + ms\Delta T = 18000$ cal

Amount of heat left = 4320 cal

$m \times L = 4320$

$\Rightarrow \quad m \times 540 = 4320$

$\Rightarrow \quad m = 8$ g

Temperature obtained = 100° C or boiling point of water (steam) = 100° C

6 (c) First of all, AB and CD according to the graph represent change of state, from ice to water and water to steam respectively. Secondly, latent heat of fusion of ice is less than latent heat of vaporisation of steam.

In horizontal portions of AB and CD, temperature remains same showing change of state. Latent heat of vaporisation is greater than latent heat of fusion.

Hence, options (a), (b), (d), (e) are all correct. Only option (c) is incorrect.

7 (c) Let T be the final equal temperature.

Heat lost by coffee = Heat gained by the cup

$m_{\text{coffee}} \times s_{\text{coffee}} \times \Delta T_1 = m_{\text{cup}} \times s_{\text{cup}} \times \Delta T_2$

$\Rightarrow 0.3 \times s_{\text{coffee}} \times (70 - T)$

$= 0.12 \times s_{\text{cup}} \times (T - 20)$

$\Rightarrow 0.3 \times 4080 (70 - T)$

$= 0.12 \times 1020 \times (T - 20)$

$\Rightarrow \quad 10(70 - T) = T - 20$

$\Rightarrow \quad T = 65.5°$ C

8 (a) The amount of heat supplied is given by the relation, $\quad Q = mc\Delta T$

Here, $m = 100 \text{ g} = 0.1$kg,

$c = 400$J/kg-K,

$\Delta T = 21$K for copper

Thus, $\quad Q = 0.1 \times 400 \times 21 = 840$ J

Hence, $840 = 0.05 \times 4200 \times \Delta T$

$\Rightarrow \quad \Delta T = 4$°C

9 (a) From $\Delta Q = 2\, C_p (\Delta T)$,

$70 = 2 \times C_p \times (35 - 30)$

$C_p = 70/10 = 7$ cal/mol°C

$C_V = C_p - R = 7 - 2 = 5$ cal/mol° C

$\Delta Q' = nC_V(\Delta T) = 2 \times 5 \times 5 = 50$ cal

10 (c) Due to the temperature difference heat transfer is taking place from one body to another and no external source is supplying energy to the bodies, thus total internal energy of the two bodies remains conserved although individually it changes.

11 (c) Since, specific heat of lead is given in joule. Specific heat of lead

$= 0.120$ J/g°C

$= 120$ J/kg °C

The two-third of head produced goes into the bullet.

So, $\quad m \times s \times \Delta\theta = \dfrac{2}{3} \times \dfrac{1}{2} mv^2$

$\Rightarrow \quad \Delta\theta = \dfrac{v^2}{3 \times s} = \dfrac{180 \times 180}{3 \times 120} = 90$°C

12 (a) The ice at –20 °C converts to ice at 0°C, thus having an increase in temperature. On further heating, ice at 0°C is converted into water at 0°C, thus the temperature remaining constant, a change of phase occurs. Water at 0°C when heated changes to water at 100°C which results an increase of temperature. So, water at 100°C changes to steam, i.e. change of phase.

13 (d) It is clear from the graph, $ab > cd$.

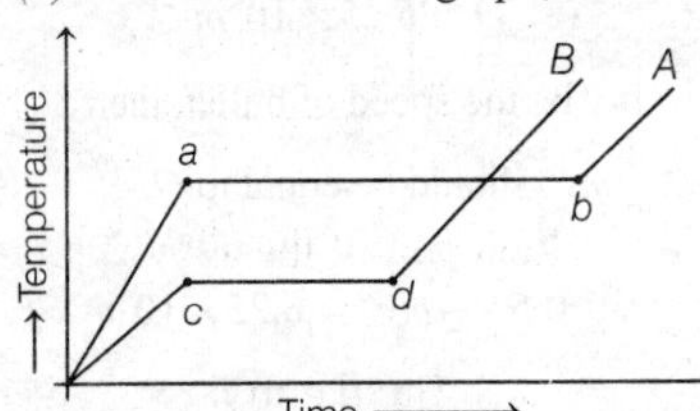

$\Rightarrow$ Latent heat of liquid $A(L_A)$ > Latent heat of liquid $B(L_B)$

and $\quad s_A < s_B \quad [\because$ Slope $A >$ Slope $B]$

14 (c) Let the final temperature of mixture be t°C.

s_w = specific heat of water,

s_i = specific heat of ice.

Heat lost by water in calorie,

$H_1 = 19 \times 1 \times (30 - t) = 570 - 19t$

Heat taken by ice,

$H_2 = ms_i\Delta t + mL + ms_w t$

$= 5 \times (0.5)20 + 5 \times 80 + 5 \times 1 \times t$

According to the principle of calorimetry, $H_1 = H_2$

$5 \times (0.5) \times 20 + 5 \times 80 + 5t = 570 - 19t$

$\Rightarrow \quad 24t = 570 - 450 = 120$

$\Rightarrow \quad t = 5°$ C

15 (a) Let the temperature of the mixture be t°C.

$\therefore$ Heat lost = Heat gain

$0.1 \times 10^3 \times (80° - t) = 0.3 \times 10^3 \times (t - 60°)$

$$\frac{1}{3}=\frac{t-60}{80-t}$$

$\Rightarrow$ $80-t=3t-180$

$4t=180+80$

$\Rightarrow$ $t=\frac{260}{4}=65°C$

16 (c) Evaporation causes cooling. As the latent heat of vaporisation of water is large, it will absorb lots of heat from the room and hence the temperature of the room will decrease.

17 (b) Heat energy required to just melt the bullet,

$$Q=Q_1+Q_2 \quad \ldots (i)$$

Here, $Q_1=ms\Delta\theta$ ($\because$ 600 K = 327° C)

$=m\times125\times(327-27)$

$=3.75\times10^4 m$

$Q_2=mL=m\times2.5\times10^4$

$=2.5\times10^4 m$

Putting the value of Q_1 and Q_2 in Eq. (i), we get

$$Q=6.25\times10^4 m$$

If v be the speed of bullet, then 50% of $\frac{1}{2}mv^2$ should be equal to Q.

$\therefore$ $0.5\times\frac{1}{2}mv^2=6.25\times10^4 m$

$\Rightarrow$ $v=\sqrt{\frac{6.25\times10^4\times2}{0.5}}=500\text{ ms}^{-1}$

$=1800\text{ km h}^{-1}$

18 (a) Given, $m=1$ g

To convert $-10°$C ice to 0° C ice,

$Q_1=mS_{ice}$
$\Delta t=1\times(0.5)\times[0-(-10)]=5$ cal

To convert 0°C ice to 0° C water,

$Q_2=mL_{ice}=1\times80=80$ cal

To convert 0°C water to 100° C water,

$Q_3=mS_w\Delta t=1\times1\times100=100$ cal

To convert 100°C water to steam 100°C,

$Q_4=mL_w=1\times540=540$ cal

$\therefore$Total work done,

$Q=Q_1+Q_2+Q_3+Q_4$

$=725\text{ cal}=725\times4.2$ J

$\therefore$ $Q=3045$ J

19 (a) Specific heat of water

$=4200\text{ J kg K}^{-1}$

Specific latent heat of fusion

$=3.36\times10^5\text{ J kg}^{-1}$

Specific latent heat of vaporisation

$=22.68\times10^5\text{J kg}^{-1}$

$\therefore$ $Q_1=X\times10^{-3}\times22.68\times10^5$

Also $Q_2=Y\times10^{-3}\times3.36\times10^5$
$+Y\times10^{-3}\times4200\times100$

$\therefore Q_1-Q_2\Rightarrow\frac{X}{Y}=\frac{7.56}{22.68}=\frac{1}{3}$

20 (d) Kinetic energy of bullet $=\frac{1}{2}mv^2$

$=\frac{1}{2}\times10\times10^{-3}\times20\times20$

$=2\text{ J}=\frac{2}{4.2}$ cal

Heat gained by ice to melt

$=\frac{2}{4.2}\times\frac{50}{100}$

$\Rightarrow$ $mL=\frac{1}{4.2}$

$\Rightarrow$ $m=\frac{1}{4.2\times80}$ g

$\approx3\times10^{-3}$g

21 (d) At 0°C from b to c, temperature of matter does not change but its state changes.

Similarly, from d to e, state of matter changes without changing temperature. Hence, b to c and d to e show phase changes.

22 (a) In pressure-temperature (p-T) phase diagram of water, the negative slope is due to the change of phase. This corresponds to liquids which contract on melting (like ice).

Therefore, both Assertion and Reason are correct and Reason is the correct explanation of Assertion.

23 (a) Heat required to raise the temperature of 40 g of water from 25°C to 54.3°C, is equivalent to the sum of heat required to condense the steam.

$\therefore$Heat required to raise the temperature of water by t°C

$=m_1c\Delta t_1 \quad \ldots$(i)

where, c is specific heat of water and m is the mass. Heat required to condense steam

$=m_2L+m_2c\Delta t_2 \quad \ldots$(ii)

Equating Eqs. (i) and (ii), we get

$m_2L+m_2c\Delta t_2=m_1c\Delta t_1$

Given, $m_2=2$ g,

$\Delta t_2=(100-54.3)°\text{C}=45.7°$C

$m_1=40$ g,

$\Delta t_1=(54.3-25)°\text{C}=29.3°$C

$c=1\text{ cal g}^{-1}$

$\Rightarrow 2\times L+2\times1\times45.7=40\times1\times29.3$

$\Rightarrow$ $2L+91.4=1172$

$\Rightarrow$ $L=540.3\text{ cal g}^{-1}$

24 (c) Total heat required = heat required to convert ice into water at 0° C(Q_1) + heat required to increase the temperature of water upto 100° C(Q_2) + heat required to convert water into steam at 100° C(Q_3).

$\therefore$ $Q_1=mL=5\times80=400$ cal

$Q_2=ms\Delta t$

$=5\times1\times(100-0)=500$ cal

$Q_3=mL=5\times540=2700$ cal

$\therefore$ $Q=Q_1+Q_2+Q_3$

$=400+500+2700$

$=3600$ cal

25 (a) Let k be the fraction of ice that melts.

Hence, potential energy = $k\times$ latent heat

i.e., $mgh=k\,mL$

$\Rightarrow$ $k=\frac{gh}{L}=\frac{10\times1000}{3.34\times10^5}\approx\frac{1}{33}$

26 (a) Initial mass of ice block,

$m=42$ kg

Initial velocity of ice block,

$u=4\text{ ms}^{-1}$

Final velocity of ice block, $v=0$

Let retardation be a. Using third equation of motion, we get

$v^2=u^2-2as$

$\Rightarrow$ $2as=u^2-v^2$

$\Rightarrow$ $as=\frac{u^2-v^2}{2}=\frac{(4)^2-(0)^2}{2}$

$=8\text{ m}^2\text{s}^{-2}$

Heat generated = Work done against friction

$Q=F\times s$

$Q=m\times a\times s$

$Q=42\times8$

$Q=336$ J

Due to this heat, let M kg of ice melts.

So, $Q=ML$

$\Rightarrow$ $M=\frac{Q}{L}=\frac{336}{3.36\times10^5}$ kg

$M=1\times10^{-3}$ kg

Topic 4

Thermal Conduction and Convection

2019

1 A deep rectangular pond of surface area A, containing water (density $= \rho$, specific heat capacity $= s$), is located in a region where the outside air temperature is a steady value at the $-26°C$. The thickness of the frozen ice layer in this pond, at a certain instant is x.
Taking the thermal conductivity of ice as K, and its specific latent heat of fusion as L, the rate of increase of the thickness of ice layer, at this instant would be given by **[NEET (Odisha)]**

(a) $26K/\rho r(L-4s)$ (b) $26K/(\rho x^2 - L)$
(c) $26K/(\rho xL)$ (d) $26K/\rho r(L+4s)$

2 The unit of thermal conductivity is **[NEET (National)]**

(a) $J\,m^{-1}\,K^{-1}$ (b) $W\,m\,K^{-1}$
(c) $W\,m^{-1}\,K^{-1}$ (d) $J\,m\,K^{-1}$

2017

3 Two rods A and B of different materials are welded together as shown in figure. Their thermal conductivities are K_1 and K_2. The thermal conductivity of the composite rod will be **[NEET]**

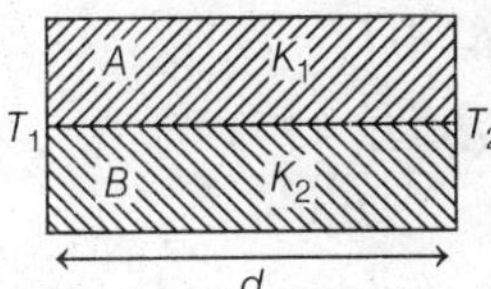

(a) $\frac{K_1+K_2}{2}$ (b) $\frac{3(K_1+K_2)}{2}$
(c) K_1+K_2 (d) $2(K_1+K_2)$

2016

4 Two identical bodies are made of a material for which the heat capacity increases with temperature. One of these is at 100°C, while the other one is at 0°C. If the two bodies are brought into contact, then assuming no heat loss, the final common temperature is **[NEET]**

(a) 50°C
(b) more than 50°C
(c) less than 50°C but greater than 0°C
(d) 0°C

2014

5 Same quantity of ice is filled in each of the two metal containers P and Q having the same size, shape and wall thickness but make of different materials. The containers are kept in identical surroundings. The ice in P melts completely in time t_1, whereas in Q takes a time t_2. The ratio of thermal conductivities of the materials of P and Q is

(a) $t_2 : t_1$ (b) $t_1 : t_2$ **[WB JEE]**
(c) $t_1^2 : t_2^2$ (d) $t_2^2 : t_1^2$

6 Two identical rods are connected between two containers. One of them is at 100°C. If rods are connected in parallel, then the rate of melting of ice is g_1 g/s.
If they are connected in series, then the rate is g_2 g/s. The ratio g_2/g_1 is **[UK PMT]**

(a) 2 (b) 4 (c) 1/2 (d) 1/4

7 Two rods of lengths d_1 and d_2 and coefficients of thermal conductivities K_1 and K_2 are kept in end to end contact with each other. The equivalent thermal conductivity is

(a) $K_1d_1+K_2d_2$ (b) K_1+K_2 **[UK PMT]**
(c) $\frac{K_1d_1+K_2d_2}{d_1+d_2}$ (d) $(d_1+d_2)/\left(\frac{d_1}{K_1}+\frac{d_2}{K_2}\right)$

2013

8 For a certain thermocouple, if the temperature of the cold junction is 0° C, the neutral temperature and inversion temperatures are 285° C and 570° C, respectively. If the cold junction is brought to 10° C, then the new neutral and inversion temperatures are respectively **[Manipal]**

(a) 285° C and 560° C (b) 285° C and 570° C
(c) 295° C and 560° C (d) 275° C and 560° C

2012

9 A slab of stone of area 0.36 m^2 and thickness 0.1 m is exposed on the lower surface of steam at 100° C. A block of ice at 0° C rests on the upper surface of the slab. In one hour, 4.8 kg of ice is melted. The thermal conductivity of slab is (Take, latent heat of fusion of ice $= 3.36\times 10^5$ J kg^{-1}) **[CBSE AIPMT]**

(a) 1.24 J/m/s/° C (b) 1.29 J/m/s/° C
(c) 2.05 J/m/s/° C (d) 1.02 J/m/s/° C

10 Two slabs A and B of different materials but of the same thickness are joined end to end to form a composite slab. The thermal conductivities of A and B are K_1 and K_2, respectively. A steady temperature difference of 12° C is maintained across the composite slab. If $K_1 = \frac{K_2}{2}$, the temperature difference across slab A is **[AIIMS]**

(a) 4° C (b) 6° C
(c) 8° C (d) 10° C

11 The temperature of hot and cold end of 20 g long rod in thermal steady state are at 100° C and 20° C respectively temperature of the centre of the rod is **[AFMC]**

(a) 50° C (b) 60° C (c) 40° C (d) 30° C

2011

12 Three identical rods A, B and C are placed end to end. A temperature difference is maintained between the free ends of A and C. The thermal conductivity of B is thrice that of C and half of that of A. The effective thermal conductivity of the system will be (K_A is the thermal conductivity of rod A) **[KCET]**

(a) $\frac{1}{3}K_A$ (b) $3K_A$ (c) $2K_A$ (d) $\frac{2}{3}K_A$

2010

13 A cylindrical metallic rod in thermal contact with two reservoirs of heat as its two ends conducts an amount of heat Q in time t. The metallic rod is melted and the material is formed into a rod of half the radius of the original rod. What is the amount of heat conducted by the new rod when placed in thermal contact with the two reservoirs in time t? **[CBSE AIPMT]**

(a) $\frac{Q}{4}$ (b) $\frac{Q}{16}$ (c) $2Q$ (d) $\frac{Q}{2}$

14 The thermal conductivity of a material in CGS system is 0.4. In steady state, the rate of flow of heat 10 cal/s-cm^2, then the thermal gradient will be **[CG PMT]**

(a) 10° C/cm (b) 12° C/cm (c) 25° C/cm (d) 20° C/cm

15 In the diagram, a system of two metals of equal lengths and of same cross-sectional area are joined together.

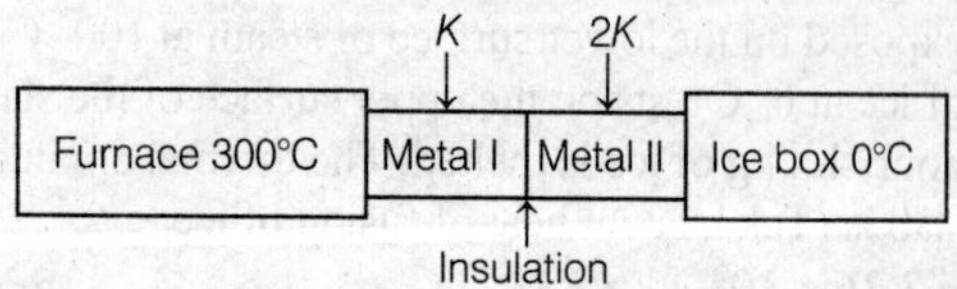

The coefficient of thermal conductivities of the metals are K and $2K$, respectively. If the furnace temperature at one end is 300° C and ice box temperature at the other end is 0° C, then the junction temperature is **[Manipal]**

(a) 100° C (b) 125° C
(c) 150° C (d) 200° C

16 Two slabs are of the thicknesses d_1 and d_2. Their thermal conductivities are K_1 and K_2, respectively. They are in series. The free ends of the combination of these two slabs are kept at temperatures θ_1 and θ_2. Assume $\theta_1 > \theta_2$. The temperature θ of their common junction is **[KCET]**

(a) $\frac{K_1\theta_1 + K_2\theta_2}{\theta_1 + \theta_2}$ (b) $\frac{K_1\theta_1 d_1 + K_2\theta_2 d_2}{K_1 d_2 + K_2 d_1}$

(c) $\frac{K_1\theta_1 d_2 + K_2\theta_2 d_1}{K_1 d_2 + K_2 d_1}$ (d) $\frac{K_1\theta_1 + K_2\theta_2}{K_1 + K_2}$

17 A body of length 1 m having cross-sectional area 0.75 m^2 has heat flow through it at the rate of 6000 J/s. Then, find the temperature difference, if $K = 200\,\text{Jm}^{-2}\text{K}^{-1}$. **[Gujarat CET]**

(a) 20° C (b) 40° C
(c) 80° C (d) 100° C

2009

18 The two ends of a rod of length L and a uniform cross-sectional area A are kept at two temperatures T_1 and T_2 ($T_1 > T_2$). The rate of heat transfer $\frac{dQ}{dt}$ through the rod in a steady state is given by **[CBSE AIPMT]**

(a) $\frac{dQ}{dt} = \frac{KL(T_1 - T_2)}{A}$

(b) $\frac{dQ}{dt} = \frac{K(T_1 - T_2)}{LA}$

(c) $\frac{dQ}{dt} = KLA(T_1 - T_2)$

(d) $\frac{dQ}{dt} = \frac{KA(T_1 - T_2)}{L}$

19 A cylinder of radius r and of thermal conductivity K_1 is surrounded by a cylindrical shell of inner radius r and outer radius $2r$ made of a material of thermal conductivity K_2. The effective thermal conductivity of the system is **[AFMC]**

(a) $\frac{1}{3}(K_1 + 2K_2)$ (b) $\frac{1}{2}(2K_1 + 3K_2)$

(c) $\frac{1}{3}(3K_2 + 2K_1)$ (d) $\frac{1}{4}(K_1 + 3K_2)$

20 Three rods of same dimensions have thermal conductivities $3K$, $2K$ and K. They are arranged as shown below

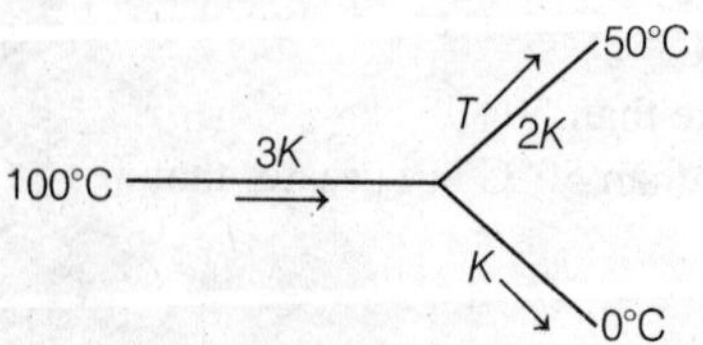

What will be the temperature T of the junction? **[EAMCET]**

(a) $\frac{200}{3}$ °C (b) $\frac{100}{3}$ °C (c) 75 °C (d) $\frac{50}{3}$ °C

2008

21 Ice starts freezing in a lake with water at 0°C when the atmospheric temperature is – 10° C. If the time taken for 1 cm of ice to be formed is 12 min, the time taken for the thickness of the ice to change from 1 cm to 2 cm will be [BHU]

(a) 12 min
(b) less than 12 min
(c) more than 12 min but less than 24 min
(d) more than 24 min

22 The coefficient of thermal conductivity of copper is 9 times that of steel. In the composite cylindrical bar shown in the figure, what will be the temperature at the junction of copper and steel? [KCET]

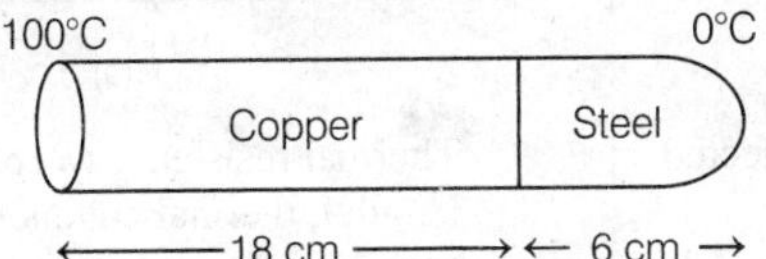

(a) 75°C (b) 67°C (c) 25°C (d) 33°C

23 The temperature of the two outer surfaces of a composite slab, consisting of two materials having coefficients of thermal conductivities K and $2K$ and thicknesses x and $4x$ respectively, are T_2 and T_1 ($T_2 > T_1$). The rate of heat transfer through the slab, in a steady state is $\left[\frac{A(T_2 - T_1)K}{x}\right] f$, with f equals to [JCECE]

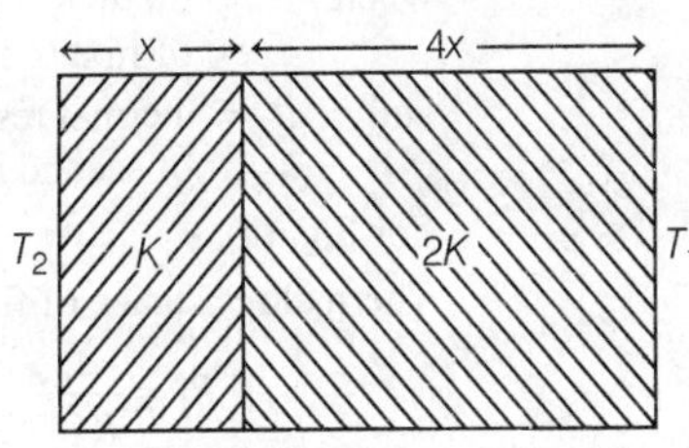

(a) 1 (b) 1/2
(c) 2/3 (d) 1/3

2007

24 Consider a composite slab consisting of two different materials having equal thickness and thermal conductivities K and $2K$, respectively. The equivalent thermal conductivity of the slab is [BHU]

(a) $3K$ (b) $\frac{4}{3}K$ (c) $\frac{2}{3}K$ (d) $\sqrt{2}K$

25 Two identical rods AC and CB made of two different metals having thermal conductivities in the ratio 2 : 3 are kept in contact with each other at the end C as shown in the figure. A is at 100°C and B is at 25°C. Then, the junction C is at [KCET]

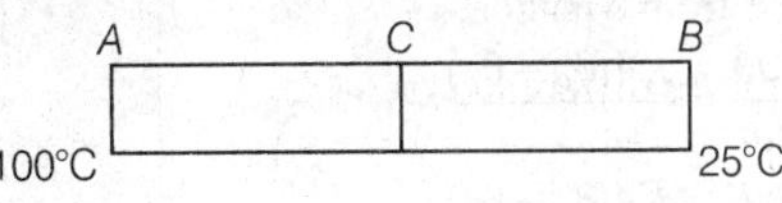

(a) 55°C (b) 60°C
(c) 75°C (d) 50°C

26 The ratio of the coefficient of thermal conductivity of two different materials is 5 : 3. If the thermal resistance of the rods of same thickness of these materials is same, then the ratio of the length of these rods will be [BCECE]

(a) 3 : 5 (b) 5 : 3
(c) 3 : 4 (d) 3 : 2

2006

27 Which of the following circular rods, (given radius r and length l) each made of the same material and whose ends are maintained at the same temperature will conduct most heat? [AFMC]

(a) $r = 2r_0, l = 2l_0$ (b) $r = 2r_0, l = l_0$
(c) $r = r_0, l = l_0$ (d) $r = r_0, l = 2l_0$

2005

28 Two rods of same material have same length and area. The heat ΔQ flows through them for 12 min when they are joint side by side. If now both the rods are joined in parallel, then the same amount of heat ΔQ will flow in [BHU]

(a) 24 min (b) 3 min (c) 12 min (d) 6 min

29 Three rods identical area of cross-section and made from the same metal from the sides of an isosceles triangle ABC, right angled at B.

The points A and B are maintained at temperatures T and $\sqrt{2}T$, respectively. In the steady state, the temperature of the point C is T_C.

Assuming that only heat conduction takes place, T_C/T is equal to [UP CPMT]

(a) $\frac{1}{(\sqrt{2}+1)}$ (b) $\frac{3}{(\sqrt{2}+1)}$
(c) $\frac{1}{2(\sqrt{2}-1)}$ (d) $\frac{1}{\sqrt{3}(\sqrt{2}-1)}$

Answers

1 (c)	2 (c)	3 (a)	4 (b)	5 (a)	6 (d)	7 (d)	8 (a)	9 (a)	10 (c)
11 (b)	12 (a)	13 (b)	14 (c)	15 (a)	16 (c)	17 (b)	18 (d)	19 (d)	20 (a)
21 (d)	22 (a)	23 (d)	24 (b)	25 (a)	26 (b)	27 (b)	28 (b)	29 (b)	

Explanations

1 *(c)* Given, $\theta_0 = 0°\,C, \theta_1 = -26°\,C$

The rate of increase of thickness can be calculated from equation,

$$\frac{d\theta}{dt} = \frac{KA(\theta_0 - \theta_1)}{x}$$

$$\Rightarrow \quad \frac{\rho A dx L}{dt} = \frac{KA(\theta_0 - \theta_1)}{x}$$

$$\Rightarrow \quad \frac{dx}{dt} = \frac{KA(\theta_0 - \theta_1)}{\rho A x L}$$

$$= \frac{K[0-(-26)]}{\rho x L} = \frac{26K}{\rho x L}$$

2 *(c)* The rate of heat flow through a conductor of length L and area of cross-section A is given by

$$\frac{dQ}{dt} = KA\frac{\Delta T}{L} \text{ J/s or watt}$$

where, K = coefficient of thermal conductivity

and ΔT = change in temperature.

$$\Rightarrow \quad K = \frac{L}{A\,\Delta T}\frac{dQ}{dt}$$

$$\therefore \text{Unit of } K = \frac{\text{metre}}{(\text{metre})^2 \times \text{kelvin}} \times \text{watt}$$

$$= \text{Wm}^{-1}\text{K}^{-1}$$

3 *(a)* In parallel arrangement of n rods, equivalent thermal conductivity is given by

$$K_{eq} = \frac{K_1A_1 + K_2A_2 + \ldots + K_nA_n}{A_1 + A_2 + \ldots + A_n}$$

If rods are of same area, then

$$K_{eq} = \frac{K_1 + K_2 + \ldots + K_n}{n}$$

Now, in the question, it is not given that rods are of same area. But we can judge that from given diagram.

$\therefore$ Equivalent thermal conductivity of the system of two rods,

$$\Rightarrow \quad K_{eq} = \frac{K_1 + K_2}{2}$$

4 *(b)* Heat lost by first body = Heat gained by second body.

Body at 100°C temperature has greater heat capacity than body at 0°C, so final temperature will be closer to 100°C. So, $T_c > 50°\,C$.

5 *(a)* We know that, relation between the temperature gradient (TG) and thermal conductivity (K),

$$\frac{dQ}{dt} = -KA\frac{d\theta}{dx} = -KA \times (\text{TG})$$

i.e. $\quad \text{TG} \propto \frac{1}{K} \quad \left(\frac{dQ}{dt} = \text{constant}\right)$

or $\quad K \propto \frac{1}{t} \Rightarrow K_1 \propto \frac{1}{t_1} \quad \ldots(i)$

$K_2 \propto 1/t_2 \quad \ldots(ii)$

From Eqs. (i) and (ii), we get

$$\frac{K_1}{K_2} = \frac{1/t_1}{1/t_2}$$

$$\Rightarrow \quad K_1 : K_2 = t_2 : t_1$$

6 *(d)* According to the question,

When two identical rods are connected in parallel,

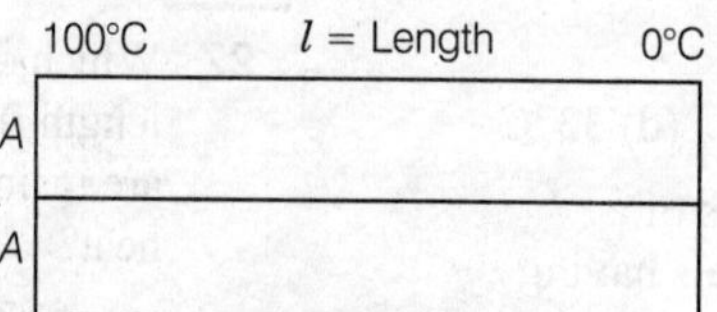

So, rate of heat transfer is given by

$$\frac{dQ}{dT} = \frac{2KA(T_1 - T_2)}{l}$$

$$= \frac{2KA\,(100-0)}{l} = \frac{200KA}{l}$$

where, net area = $2A$

K = thermal conductivity constant,

T_1 = temperature at one end,

T_2 = temperature at other end

and l = length of rod.

As, $\frac{dQ}{dT}$ is rate of heat transfer $= \frac{mL}{T}$

So, $\quad g_1 = \frac{dQ}{dT} = \frac{Q}{T}$

$$\Rightarrow \quad \left(\frac{m}{T}\right)L = \frac{200\,KA}{l}$$

So, for parallel connection,

$$\frac{m}{T} = g_1 \text{ g/s} = \frac{200KA}{Ll} \quad \ldots(i)$$

Similarly, for series connection

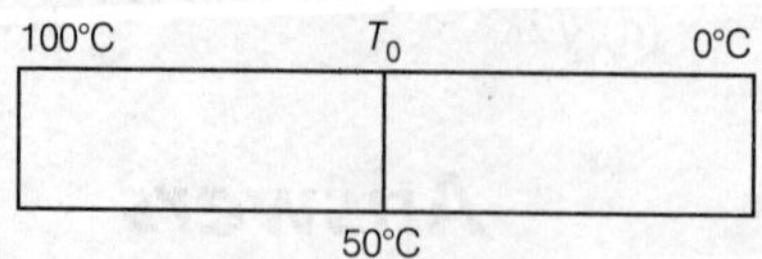

So, $100° - T_0 = T_0 - 0 \Rightarrow 2T_0 = 100°$

$\Rightarrow \quad T_0 = 50°\,C$

So, $\quad \frac{dQ}{dT} = \left(\frac{m}{l}\right)L = \frac{KA\,(50-0)}{l}$

and it can be written as

$$g_2(\text{g/s}) = \frac{KA\,50}{lL} \quad \ldots(ii)$$

Dividing Eq. (i) and Eq. (ii), we get

$$\frac{g_1}{g_2} = \frac{200}{50} = 4 \Rightarrow \frac{g_2}{g_1} = \frac{1}{4}$$

7 *(d)* Consider the diagram, where two rods are connected end to end (series).

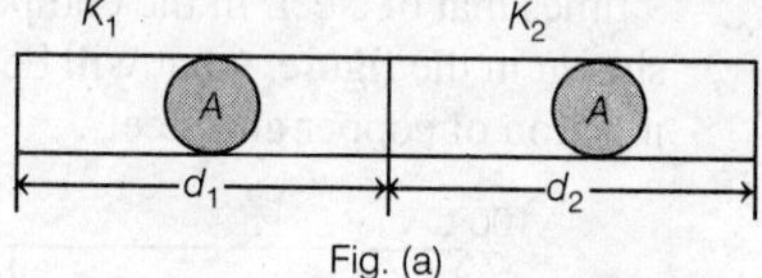

Fig. (a)

Thermal resistance (R) of a rod of length l, thermal conductivity K and area of cross-section A is given by

$$R = l\,/\,KA$$

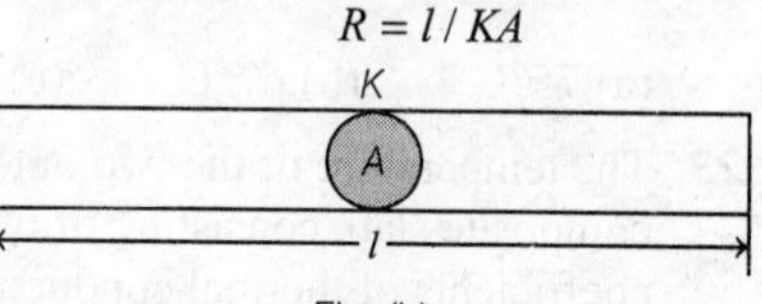

Fig. (b)

When rods are connected in series,

R_{eq} = equivalent thermal resistance $= R_1 + R_2 \quad \ldots(i)$

where, R_1 = thermal resistance of first rod

and R_2 = thermal resistance of second rod.

For Fig. (a),

Thermal resistance of first rod,

$$R_1 = \frac{d_1}{K_1A}$$

where, A is area of cross-section of each rod. Similarly, thermal resistance of second rod, $R_2 = \frac{d_2}{K_2A}$

Now, from Fig. (a),

$$R_{eq} = \frac{d_1}{K_1A} + \frac{d_2}{K_2A}$$

$$\Rightarrow \quad \frac{L_{eq}}{K_{eq}A_{eq}} = \frac{d_1}{K_1A} + \frac{d_2}{K_2A} \quad \ldots(ii)$$

where, L_{eq} = equivalent length of rod,

K_{eq} = equivalent thermal conductivity

A_{eq} = equivalent area of cross-section.

For series connection,

L_{eq} = equivalent length $= d_1 + d_2$

equivalent cross-sectional area = A

Now, from Fig. (b),

$$\frac{d_1 + d_2}{(K_{eq})(A)} = \frac{d_1}{K_1 A} + \frac{d_2}{K_2 A}$$

$$\Rightarrow \frac{d_1 + d_2}{K_{eq}} = \frac{d_1}{K_1} + \frac{d_2}{K_2}$$

$$\Rightarrow K_{eq} = \left(\frac{K_1 K_2}{K_2 d_1 + K_1 d_2}\right)(d_1 + d_2)$$

$$= \frac{d_1 + d_2}{\frac{d_1}{K_1} + \frac{d_2}{K_2}}$$

[Dividing numerator and denominator by $K_1 K_2$]

Equivalent thermal conductivity,

$$K_{eq} = \frac{d_1 + d_2}{\left(\frac{d_1}{K_1} + \frac{d_2}{K_2}\right)}$$

8 *(a)* Neutral temperature remains same.

Inversion temperature,

$T_i = 2T_n - T_c = 2 \times 285 - 10 = 560°C$

9 *(a)* $\frac{\delta Q}{\delta t} = \frac{KA}{L}(T_1 - T_2)$

$$\Rightarrow Q = \frac{KA}{L}(T_1 - T_2)t$$

$\because Q = mL_f$

$$\therefore \frac{KA}{L}(T_1 - T_2)t = mL_f$$

$$\Rightarrow K = \frac{mL_f \times L}{A(T_1 - T_2)t}$$

$$K = \frac{4.8 \times 3.36 \times 10^5 \times 0.1}{0.36 \times 100 \times 3600} = \frac{4.8 \times 3.36}{0.36 \times 36}$$

$= 1.24$ J/m/s/°C

10 *(c)* Given situation can be shown in figure as

P Q R
100°C
T_P A (K_1) B (K_2) T_R
L L

Rate of heat flow through rod is given as

$$\frac{dQ}{dt} = \frac{\Delta T}{l/KA} = \frac{KA(\Delta T)}{l}$$

As, rate of heat flow is same for all sections

$$\left(\frac{dQ}{dT}\right)_{PQ} = \left(\frac{dQ}{dT}\right)_{PR}$$

$$\left(\frac{100 - T_Q}{\frac{L}{K_1 A}}\right) = \left(\frac{T_P - T_R}{\frac{L}{K_1 A} + \frac{L}{K_2 A}}\right)$$

$$\frac{(100 - T_Q)}{\frac{1}{K_1}} = \frac{12}{\frac{1}{K_1} + \frac{1}{2K_1}}$$

$$(100 - T_Q) = \frac{2.12}{3} = 8$$

$T_P - T_Q = 8°C$

11 *(b)*

A C B
100°C T_0 20°C
L

Rate of heat flow through the rod is given as

$$\frac{dQ}{dt} = \frac{KA(\Delta t)}{L} \quad ...(i)$$

As, $\left(\frac{dQ}{dt}\right)_{AC} = \left(\frac{dQ}{dt}\right)_{CB}$

$$\frac{KA(100 - T_0)}{L/2} = \frac{KA\,(T_0 - 20)}{L/2}$$

$\Rightarrow 2T_0 = 120°,$

$\Rightarrow T_0 = 60°C$

12 *(a)* Given, $K_B = K_A/2$

and $K_B = 3K_C$

$\therefore K_C = K_A/6$

A	B	C

Rods are in series form, so

$$\frac{L}{K} = \frac{l_1}{K_A} + \frac{l_2}{K_B} + \frac{l_3}{K_C}$$

$(\because l = l_1 = l_2 = l_3)$

$$\frac{3l}{K} = \frac{l}{K_A} + \frac{l}{K_A/2} + \frac{l}{K_A/6}$$

or $\frac{3l}{K} = \frac{9l}{K_A}$ or $K = \frac{K_A}{3}$

13 *(b)* In steady state, the amount of heat flowing from one face to the other face in time t is given by $Q = \frac{KA(\theta_1 - \theta_2)t}{l}$

where, K is the coefficient of thermal conductivity of material of rod.

$$\Rightarrow \frac{Q}{t} \propto \frac{A}{l} \propto \frac{r^2}{l} \quad ...(i)$$

As the metallic rod is melted and the material is formed into a rod of half the radius,

$V_1 = V_2$

$$\pi r_1^2 l_1 = \pi r_2^2 l_2 \Rightarrow l_1 = \frac{l_2}{4} \quad ...(ii)$$

Now, from Eqs. (i) and (ii), we get

$$\frac{Q_1}{Q_2} = \frac{r_1^2}{l_1} \times \frac{l_2}{r_2^2} = \frac{r_1^2}{l_1} \times \frac{4l_1}{(r_1/2)^2}$$

$[\because Q_1 = Q]$

$$\Rightarrow Q_1 = 16Q_2 \Rightarrow Q_2 = \frac{Q}{16}$$

14 *(c)* We know, $\frac{\Delta Q}{\Delta t} = \frac{KA\Delta\theta}{\Delta x}$

Thermal gradient,

$$\frac{\Delta\theta}{\Delta x} = \frac{(\Delta Q/\Delta t)}{k} = \frac{10}{0.4} = 25° \text{ C/cm}$$

15 *(a)* Temperature of interface,

$$\theta = \frac{K_1\theta_1 l_2 + K_2\theta_2 l_1}{K_1 l_2 + K_2 l_1}$$

$$= \frac{2K \times 0 \times l + K \times 300 \times l}{Kl + 2Kl}$$

$$= \frac{300Kl}{3Kl} \Rightarrow \theta = 100°C$$

16 *(c)* For first slab,

θ_1 θ θ_2
K_1 K_2
d_1 d_2

Heat current, $H_1 = \frac{K_1(\theta_1 - \theta)A}{d_1}$

For second slab,

Heat current, $H_2 = \frac{K_2(\theta - \theta_2)A}{d_2}$

As slabs are in series, $H_1 = H_2$

$$\therefore \frac{K_1(\theta_1 - \theta)A}{d_1} = \frac{K_2(\theta - \theta_2)A}{d_2}$$

$$\Rightarrow \theta = \frac{K_1\theta_1 d_2 + K_2\theta_2 d_1}{K_2 d_1 + K_1 d_2}$$

17 *(b)* The rate of heat flow, $\frac{Q}{t} = \frac{KA\Delta\theta}{l}$

$$\Rightarrow 6000 = \frac{200 \times 0.75 \times \Delta\theta}{1}$$

$$\Delta\theta = \frac{6000 \times 1}{200 \times 0.75} = 40°C$$

18 *(d)* Heat current, $\frac{dQ}{dt} = \frac{T_1 - T_2}{L/KA}$

$$\Rightarrow \frac{dQ}{dt} = \frac{KA(T_1 - T_2)}{L}$$

19 *(d)* Both the cylinders are in parallel, for the heat flow from one end as shown

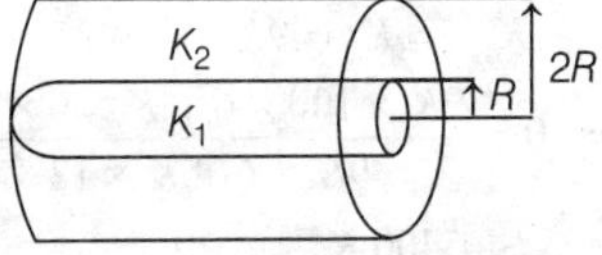

Hence $K_{eq} = \frac{K_1 A_1 + K_2 A_2}{A_1 + A_2}$

where, A = area of cross-section of inner cylinder = πR^2

and A_2 = area of cross-section of cylindrical shell

$$= \pi\{(2R)^2 - (R)^2\} = 3\pi R^2$$

$$\Rightarrow \quad K_{eq} = \frac{K_1(\pi R^2) + K_2(3\pi R^2)}{\pi R^2 + 3\pi R^2}$$

$$= \frac{1}{4}(K_1 + 3K_2)$$

20 *(a)*

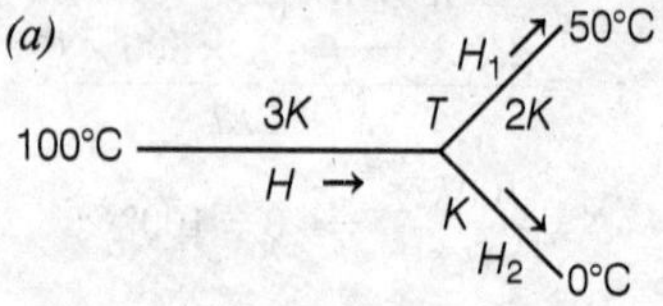

Rate of flow of heat,

$$H = H_1 + H_2$$

$$\frac{3K(T-100)A}{l} = \frac{2K(50-T)A}{l} + \frac{K(0-T)A}{l}$$

$$3(T-100) = 2(50-T) + (0-T)$$

$$3T - 300 = 100 - 2T - T$$

$$6T = 400$$

$$\Rightarrow \quad T = \frac{400}{6} = \frac{200}{3}\,°\text{C}$$

21 *(d)* Time taken by ice to grow by thickness y,

$$t = \frac{\rho L}{2K\theta}y^2$$

Hence, time intervals to change thickness from 0 to y, from y to $2y$ and so on will be in the ratios

$$\Delta t_1 : \Delta t_2 : \Delta t_3 :: (1^2 - 0^2) : (2^2 - 1^2) : (3^2 - 2^2)$$

or $\Delta t_1 : \Delta t_2 : \Delta t_3 :: 1 : 3 : 5$

According to the question,

$$\Delta t_1 = 12 \text{ min}$$

Hence, $\Delta t_2 = 3\Delta t_1 = 3 \times 12$ min $= 36$ min

22 *(a)* Temperature of interface,

$$\theta = \frac{K_1\theta_1 l_2 + K_2\theta_2 l_1}{K_1 l_2 + K_2 l_1}$$

Given, $K_{Cu} = 9K_s$

So, if $K_s = K_1 = K$, then

$$K_{Cu} = K_2 = 9K$$

$$\Rightarrow \theta = \frac{9K \times 100 \times 6 + K \times 0 \times 18}{9K \times 6 + K \times 18}$$

$$\theta = \frac{5400\,K}{72\,K} = 75°\text{C}$$

23 *(d)* Let the temperature of common interface be T °C.

Rate of heat flow,

$$H = \frac{Q}{t} = \frac{KA\,\Delta T}{l}$$

$$\therefore \quad H_1 = \left(\frac{Q}{t}\right)_1 = \frac{2KA(T - T_1)}{4x}$$

$$\Rightarrow H_2 = \left(\frac{Q}{t}\right)_2 = \frac{KA(T_2 - T)}{x}$$

In steady state, the rate of heat flow should be same in whole system, i.e.

$$H_1 = H_2$$

$$\Rightarrow \quad \frac{2KA(T-T_1)}{4x} = \frac{KA(T_2 - T)}{x}$$

$$\Rightarrow \quad \frac{T - T_1}{2} = T_2 - T$$

$$\Rightarrow \quad T - T_1 = 2T_2 - 2T$$

$$\Rightarrow \quad T = \frac{2T_2 + T_1}{3} \quad \ldots\text{(i)}$$

Hence, heat flow from composite slab is

$$H = \frac{KA(T_2 - T)}{x}$$

$$H = \frac{KA}{x}\left(T_2 - \frac{2T_2 + T_1}{3}\right)$$

$$= \frac{KA}{3x}(T_2 - T_1) \quad \ldots\text{(ii)}$$

According to question,

$$H = \left[\frac{A(T_2 - T_1)K}{x}\right]f \quad \ldots\text{(iii)}$$

By comparing Eqs. (ii) and (iii), we get

$$\Rightarrow \quad f = \frac{1}{3}$$

24 *(b)* The quantity of heat flowing through a slab in time t,

$$Q = \frac{KA\Delta\theta}{l}$$

For same heat flow through each slab and composite slab, we have

$$\frac{K_1A(\Delta\theta_1)}{l} = \frac{K_2A(\Delta\theta_2)}{l} = \frac{K'A(\Delta\theta_1 + \Delta\theta_2)}{2l}$$

or $\quad K_1\Delta\theta_1 = K_2\Delta\theta_2 = \frac{K'}{2}(\Delta\theta_1 + \Delta\theta_2) = C$ (say)

So, $\quad \Delta\theta_1 = \frac{C}{K_1}, \Delta\theta_2 = \frac{C}{K_2}$

and $\quad (\Delta\theta_1 + \Delta\theta_2) = \frac{2C}{K'}$

or $\quad \frac{C}{K_1} + \frac{C}{K_2} = \frac{2C}{K'}$

or $\quad C\left(\frac{K_1 + K_2}{K_1K_2}\right) = \frac{2C}{K'}$

$$\therefore \quad K' = \frac{2K_1K_2}{K_1 + K_2}$$

Given, $K_1 = K$ and $K_2 = 2K$

So, $\quad K' = \frac{2K \times 2K}{K + 2K} = \frac{4K^2}{3K} = \frac{4K}{3}$

25 *(a)* Let the temperature of the junction be θ.

Heat flow through the rod is given by

$$Q = \frac{KA(\theta_1 - \theta_2)t}{d}$$

Here, $K_1(100 - \theta) = K_2(\theta - 25)$

$$\Rightarrow \quad \frac{K_1}{K_2} = \frac{\theta - 25}{100 - \theta}$$

But $\quad \frac{K_1}{K_2} = \frac{2}{3}$

$$\therefore \quad \frac{2}{3} = \frac{\theta - 25}{100 - \theta}$$

or $\quad 3\theta - 75 = 200 - 2\theta$

$$\Rightarrow \quad 5\theta = 275$$

$$\therefore \quad \theta = 55°\text{C}$$

26 *(b)* The thermal resistance of a rod of length l, area of cross-section A and thermal conductivity K, is $R = \frac{l}{KA}$

Given, thermal resistance of rods is equal, therefore also $A_1 = A_2$

$$\frac{l_1}{K_1A_1} = \frac{l_2}{K_2A_2}$$

$$\Rightarrow \quad \frac{l_1}{K_1} = \frac{l_2}{K_2}$$

$$\Rightarrow \quad \frac{l_1}{l_2} = \frac{K_1}{K_2} = \frac{5}{3}$$

27 *(b)* Heat conduction through a rod is given by

$$H = \frac{\Delta Q}{\Delta t} = KA\left(\frac{T_1 - T_2}{l}\right)$$

$$\Rightarrow \quad H \propto \frac{r^2}{l} \quad \ldots\text{(i)}$$

(a) When $r = 2r_0$, $l = 2l_0$

$$H \propto \frac{(2r_0)^2}{2l_0}$$

$$\Rightarrow \quad H \propto \frac{2r_0^2}{l_0}$$

(b) When $r = 2r_0, l = l_0$

$$H \propto \frac{(2r_0)^2}{l_0} \Rightarrow H \propto \frac{4r_0^2}{l_0}$$

(c) When $r = r_0, l = l_0 \Rightarrow H \propto \frac{r_0^2}{l_0}$

(d) When $r = r_0, l = 2l_0 \Rightarrow H \propto \frac{r_0^2}{2l_0}$

It is obvious that heat conduction will be more in case (b).

28 (b) $\frac{Q}{t} = \frac{KA\Delta\theta}{l} = \frac{\Delta\theta}{(l/KA)} = \frac{\Delta\theta}{R}$

(R = thermal resistance)

$\Rightarrow t \propto R$ ($\because Q$ and $\Delta\theta$ are same)

$\Rightarrow \frac{t_p}{t_s} = \frac{R_p}{R_s} = \frac{R/2}{2R} = \frac{1}{4}$

$\Rightarrow t_p = \frac{t_s}{4} = \frac{12}{4} = 3$ min

29 (b) Because $T_B > T_A$

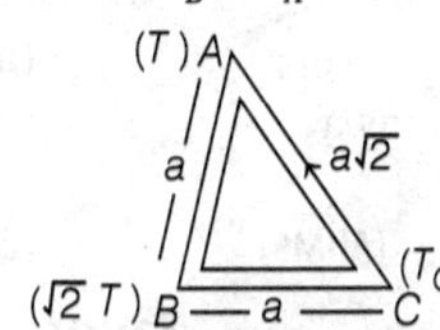

$\Rightarrow$ Heat will flow B to A *via* two paths

(*i*) B to A

(*ii*) and along BCA rate of flow of heat in path BCA will be same,

i.e. $\left[\frac{Q}{t}\right]_{BC} = \left[\frac{Q}{t}\right]_{CA}$

$$\Rightarrow \frac{K(\sqrt{2}T - T_C)A}{a} = \frac{K(T_C - T)A}{\sqrt{2}a}$$

$$\Rightarrow \frac{T_C}{T} = \frac{3}{1+\sqrt{2}}$$

Topic 5

Radiation I (Kirchhoff's Law and Black Body)

2013

1 A piece of red glass when heated in dark to red hot state will appear to be **[KCET]**

(a) white (b) red
(c) green (d) invisible

2010

2 **Assertion** (A) Like light radiation, thermal radiations are also electromagnetic radiation.

Reason (R) The thermal radiations require no medium for propagation. **[AIIMS]**

(a) Both A and R are correct and R is the correct explanation of A
(b) Both A and R are correct but R is not the correct explanation of A
(c) A is correct but R is incorrect
(d) Both A and R are incorrect

3 For an opaque body coefficient of transmission is **[MHT CET]**

(a) zero (b) 1
(c) 0.5 (d) ∞

4 The thermal radiation from a hot body travels with a velocity of **[Kerala CEE]**

(a) 330 ms^{-1} (b) 2×10^8 ms^{-1}
(c) 1200 ms^{-1} (d) 230 ms^{-1}
(e) 3×10^8 ms^{-1}

5 In which process, the rate of transfer of heat is maximum? **[MGIMS]**

(a) Conduction
(b) Radiation
(c) Convection
(d) In all three heat is transferred with the same speed

6 Which of the following statements does not hold good for thermal radiation? **[JCECE]**

(a) The wavelength changes when it travels from one medium to another
(b) The frequency changes when it travels from one medium to another
(c) The speed changes when it travels from one medium to another
(d) They travel in straight line in a given medium

2009

7 "Good emitters are good absorbers" is a statement concluded from **[Haryana PMT, CG PMT]**

(a) Newton's law of cooling
(b) Stefan's law of radiation
(c) Prevost's theory
(d) Kirchhoff's law

2008

8 Which of the following is more close to a black body? **[Haryana PMT]**

(a) Black board paint (b) Green leaves
(c) Black holes (d) Red roses

2007

9 We consider the radiation emitted by the human body. Which of the following statements is true? **[BHU]**

(a) The radiation is emitted during the summers and absorbed during the winters.
(b) The radiation emitted lies in the ultraviolet region and hence is not visible.
(c) The radiation emitted in the infrared region.
(d) The radiation is emitted only during the day.

10 The temperature at which a black body ceases to radiate energy, is [J&K CET]

(a) 0 K (b) 273 K
(c) 30 K (d) 100 K

2006

11 Three objects coloured black, grey and white can withstand hostile conditions upto 2800°C. These objects are thrown into a furnace where each of them attains a temperature of 2000°C. Which object will glow brightest? [AIIMS]

(a) The white object
(b) The black object
(c) All glow with equal brightness
(d) Gray object

12 **Assertion** (A) Perspiration from human body helps in cooling the body.

Reason (R) A thin layer of water on the skin enhances its emissivity. [AIIMS]

(a) Both A and R are correct and R is the correct explanation of A
(b) Both A and R are correct but R is not the correct explanation of A
(c) A is correct but R is incorrect
(d) Both A and R are incorrect

13 A perfect black body is one whose emissive power is [J&K CET]

(a) maximum (b) zero
(c) unity (d) minimum

14 A hot and a cold body are kept in vacuum separated from each other. Which of the following causes decrease in temperature of the hot body? [Punjab PMET]

(a) Radiation
(b) Convection
(c) Conduction
(d) Temperature remains unchanged

2005

15 **Assertion** A body that is a good radiator is also a good absorber of radiation at a given wavelength.

Reason According to Kirchhoff's law, the absorptivity of a body is equal to its emissivity at a given wavelength. [AIIMS]

(a) Both Asssertion and Reason are correct and Reason is the correct explanation of Asssertion
(b) Both Asssertion and R are correct but Reason is not the correct explanation of Asssertion
(c) Asssertion is correct but Reason is incorrect
(d) Both Asssertion and Reason are incorrect

16 The absorptivity of a black body is equal to

(a) 2 (b) 1 (c) 3 (d) 4

Answers

1 (c)	2 (b)	3 (a)	4 (e)	5 (b)	6 (b)	7 (d)	8 (c)	9 (c)	10 (a)
11 (b)	12 (c)	13 (c)	14 (a)	15 (a)	16 (b)				

Explanations

1 *(c)* From Kirchhoff's law at a definite temperature and for a given wavelength, the ratio of the emissive power to the absorptive power for different surface is same.

i.e. $e_\lambda / a_\lambda = E_\lambda$

When red glass is heated in a dark room to a red hot state, it will appear green, because according to Kirchhoff's law the emissive power of red glass will be maximum for green light.

2 *(b)* Light radiations and thermal radiations both belong to electromagnetic spectrum. Light radiation belongs to visible, while thermal radiation belongs to infrared region of EM spectrum.

Also, EM radiations require no medium for propagation.

Therefore, both Assertion and Reason are correct but Reason is not the correct explanation of Assertion.

3 *(a)* An opaque body does not transmit any radiation, hence transmission of coefficient of an opaque body is zero.

4 *(e)* Thermal radiation belongs to infrared region of electromagnetic wave, which travels at speed of 3×10^8 m/s.

5 *(b)* The rate of heat transfer is maximum in radiation in the form of electromagnetic radiations.

6 *(b)* Thermal radiations are electromagnetic radiation and its frequency does not change when it travels from one medium to another.

7 *(d)* Kirchhoff's law of radiation states that the ratio of emissive power to absorptive power is same for all surfaces at the same temperature and is equal to the emissive power of a perfectly black body at that temperature.

8 *(c)* Black holes are more closer to a black body as all the radiations come in contact to black hole is being absorbed by it.

9 *(c)* The heat radiation emitted by the human body is the infrared radiation. Their wavelength is of the order of 7.9×10^{-7} m to 10^{-3}m which is in the range of infrared region.

10 *(a)* The temperature at which a black body ceases to radiate energy is 0 K.

11 *(b)* An ideal black body absorbs all the radiations incident upon it and has an emissivity equal to 1. If a black body and an identical another body are kept at the same temperature, then the black body will radiate maximum power. Hence, the black object at a temperature of 2000°C, will glow brightest.

12 (c) Perspiration involves exchange of heat from body to surrounding. Water takes heat from the body and cools it down. However a thin layer of water on the skin will decrease rather than increase it emissivity.

So, Assertion is correct but Reason is incorrect.

13. (c) A black body is an object that absorbs all electromagnetic radiation that falls on to it. No radiation passes through it and none is reflected. Hence, its emissive power is unity.

14. (a) Convection and conduction mode of heat transfer require physical medium and contact between the bodies to transfer heat but radiation does not require any medium. As they transfer heat as electromagnetic waves/radiation. Thus, the cold body will get warmer and the hot body will get colder.

15. (a) According to Kirchhoff's law at a given wavelength, the absorptivity of a body is equal to its emissivity. Also a body which is a good radiator, is also a good absorber of radiation or a poor reflector.

Therefore, both Assertion and Reason are correct and Reason is the correct explanation of Assertion.

16. (b) The absorptivity of a black body is equal to unity.

Topic 6

Radiation II

(Wien's Law, Stefan's Law and Newton's Law of Cooling)

2019

1 An object kept in a large room having air temperature of 25°C takes 12 min to cool from 80°C to 70°C.

The time taken to cool for the same object from 70°C to 60°C would be nearly **[NEET (Odisha)]**

(a) 10 min (b) 12 min
(c) 20 min (d) 15 min

2 Calculate radiation power for sphere whose temperature is 227°C, radius 2 m and emissivity 0.8. **[AIIMS]**

(a) 142.5 kW (b) 1500 W
(c) 1255 W (d) 1575 W

3 If temperature of sun = 6000 K, radius of sun is 7.2×10^5 km, radius of earth = 6000 km and distance between earth and sun = 15×10^7 km. Find intensity of light on earth. **[AIIMS]**

(a) 19.2×10^{16} (b) 12.2×10^{16}
(c) 18.3×10^{16} (d) 9.2×10^{16}

2018

4 The power radiated by a black body is P and it radiates maximum energy at wavelength λ_0. If the temperature of the black body is now changed, so that it radiates maximum energy at wavelength $\frac{3}{4}\lambda_0$, the power radiated by it becomes nP. The value of n is **[NEET]**

(a) $\frac{256}{81}$ (b) $\frac{4}{3}$ (c) $\frac{3}{4}$ (d) $\frac{81}{256}$

2017

5 A spherical black body with a radius of 12 cm radiates 450 W power at 500 K. If the radius were halved and the temperature doubled, the power radiated (in watt) would be

(a) 225 (b) 450 (c) 1000 (d) 1800 **[NEET]**

2016

6 A black body is at a temperature of 5760 K. The energy of radiation emitted by the body at wavelength 250 nm is U_1, at wavelength 500 nm is U_2 and that at 1000 nm is U_3. Wien's constant, $b = 2.88 \times 10^6$ nmK. Which of the following is correct? **[NEET]**

(a) $U_3 = 0$ (b) $U_1 > U_2$ (c) $U_2 > U_1$ (d) $U_1 = 0$

7 A body cools from a temperature $3T$ to $2T$ in 10 min. The room temperature is T. Assume that Newton's law of cooling is applicable. The temperature of the body at the end of next 10 min will be **[NEET]**

(a) $\frac{7}{4}T$ (b) $\frac{3}{2}T$ (c) $\frac{4}{3}T$ (d) T

2015

8 On observing light from three different stars P, Q and R, it was found that intensity of violet colour is maximum in the spectrum of P, the intensity of green colour is maximum in the spectrum of R and the intensity of red colour is maximum in the spectrum of Q. If T_P, T_Q and T_R are the respective absolute temperatures of P, Q and R, then it can be concluded from the above observations that

(a) $T_P > T_Q > T_R$ (b) $T_P > T_R > T_Q$ **[AIPMT]**
(c) $T_P < T_R < T_Q$ (d) $T_P < T_Q < T_R$

2014

9 Certain quantity of water cools from 70°C to 60°C in the first 5 min and to 54°C in the next 5 min. The temperature of the surrounding is **[CBSE AIPMT]**

(a) 45°C (b) 20°C
(c) 42°C (d) 10°C

2013

10 Which of the following is the λ_m - T graph for a perfectly black body? **[AIIMS]**

(a) 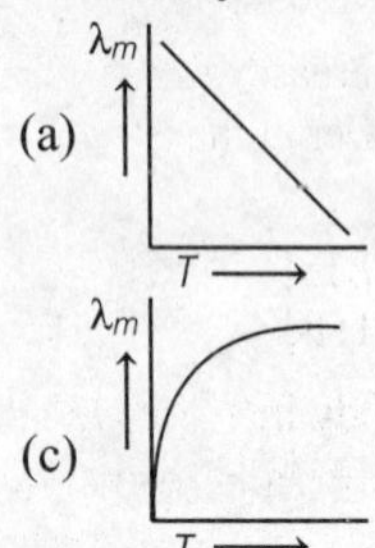

(b) 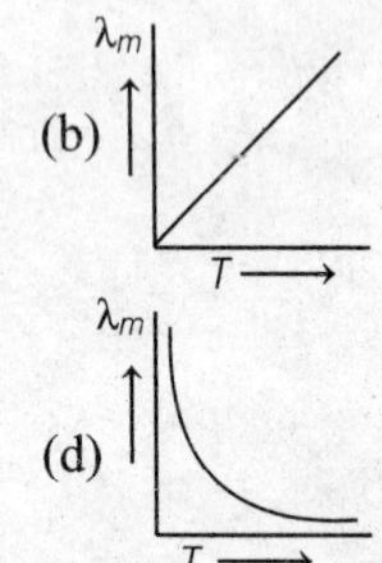

(c) (d)

11 A cup of tea cools from 80°C to 60°C in 1 min. The ambient temperature is 30°C. In next 1 min, its temperature will be **[AIIMS]**

(a) 40°C (b) 45°C
(c) 48°C (d) 42°C

12 The total radiant energy per unit area, normal to the direction of incidence, received at a distance R from the centre of a star of radius r, whose outer surface radiates as a black body at a temperature T kelvin is given by **[CBSE AIPMT]**

(a) $\frac{\sigma r^2 T^4}{R^2}$ (b) $\frac{\sigma r^2 T^4}{4\pi r^2}$
(c) $\frac{\sigma r^4 T^4}{r^4}$ (d) $\frac{4\pi\sigma r^2 T^4}{R^2}$

13 A piece of iron is heated in a flame. It first becomes dull red, then becomes reddish yellow and finally turns to white out. The correct explanation for the above observations is possible by using **[NEET]**

(a) Stefan's law
(b) Wien's displacement law
(c) Kirchhoff's law
(d) Newton's law of cooling

14 A body cools from 50° C to 49°C in 5 s. How long will it take cool from 40°C to 39°C ? (Assume temperature of surroundings to be 30°C and Newton's law of cooling is valid) **[WB JEE]**

(a) 2.5 s (b) 10 s
(c) 20 s (d) 5 s

15 Let there be four particles having colours blue, red, black and white. When they are heated together and allowed to cool, which article will cool at the earliest? **[KCET]**

(a) Blue (b) Red (c) Black (d) White

2012

16 If the radius of a star is R and it acts as a black body, what would be the temperature of the star, in which the rate of energy production is Q? **[CBSE AIPMT]**

(a) $Q/4\pi R^2\sigma$ (b) $(Q/4\pi R^2\sigma)^{-1/2}$
(c) $(4\pi R^2 Q/\sigma)^{1/4}$ (d) $(Q/4\pi R^2\sigma)^{1/4}$

2010

17 A thin square steel plate with each side equal to 10 cm is heated by a blacksmith. The rate of radiated energy by the heated plate is 1134 W. The temperature of the hot steel plate is (Stefan's constant, $\sigma = 5.67\times10^{-8}$ Wm^{-2}K^{-4}, emissivity of the plate = 1) **[BHU]**

(a) 1000 K (b) 1189 K (c) 2000 K (d) 2378 K

18 A hot body at temperature T losses heat to the surrounding temperature T_S by radiation. If the difference in temperature is small, then the rate of loss of heat by the hot body is proportional to **[Manipal]**

(a) $(T - T_s)$ (b) $(T - T_s)^2$
(c) $(T - T_s)^{1/2}$ (d) $(T - T_s)^4$

19 A body takes 5 min to cool from 80°C to 70°C . To cool from 80° C to 60° C, it will take (Room temperature = 40° C) **[OJEE]**

(a) 5 min (b) 10 min
(c) 12 min (d) 14 min

20 Experimental investigations show that the intensity of solar radiation is maximum for a wavelength 480 nm in the visible region. Estimate the surface temperature of the sun. (Take, Wien's constant, $b = 2.88\times10^{-3}$ mK.) **[WB JEE]**

(a) 4000 K (b) 6000 K
(c) 8000 K (d) 10^6 K

21 Hot water cools from 60° C to 50° C in the first 10 min and to 42° C in the next 10 min. Then, the temperature of the surroundings is **[KCET]**

(a) 20° C (b) 30° C
(c) 15° C (d) 10° C

22 A black body has a wavelength of λ at temperature 2000 K. Its corresponding wavelength at temperature 3000 K will be **[JIPMER]**

(a) $\frac{2\lambda}{3}$ (b) $\frac{3\lambda}{2}$ (c) $\frac{4\lambda}{9}$ (d) $\frac{9\lambda}{4}$

23 According to Newton's law of cooling, the rate of cooling of a body is proportional to $(\Delta\theta)^n$, where $\Delta\theta$ is the difference of the temperature of the body and the surroundings and n is equal to **[MGIMS]**

(a) 2 (b) 3 (c) 4 (d) 1

24 A chef, on finding his stove out of order, decides to boil the water for his wife's coffee by shaking it in a thermos flask. Suppose that he uses tap water at 15° C and that the water falls 30 m each shake, the chef making 30 shakes each minute. Neglecting any loss of thermal energy by the flask, how long must he shake the flask until the water reaches 100° C? **[VMMC]**

(a) 2.25×10^3 min (b) 3.97×10^3 min
(c) 4.03×10^3 min (d) 5.25×10^3 min

25 A body cools in 7 min from 60°C to 40°C. What time (in min) does it take to cool from 40°C to 28°C, if surrounding temperature is 10°C ? (Assume, Newton's law of cooling is valid) **[CG PMT]**

(a) 3.5 (b) 14 (c) 7 (d) 10

26 Two black metallic spheres of radius 4 m, at 2000 K and 1 m, at 4000 K will have ratio of energy radiation as **[AFMC]**

(a) 1:1 (b) 4:1
(c) 1:4 (d) 2:1

27 The sphere of radii 8 cm and 2 cm are cooling. Their temperatures are 127°C and 527°C, respectively. Find the ratio of energy radiated by them in the same time. **[MHT CET]**

(a) 0.06 (b) 0.5 (c) 1 (d) ∞

28 At 273° C, the emissive power of a perfect black body is R. What is its value at 0° C? **[Manipal]**

(a) $\frac{R}{4}$ (b) $\frac{R}{16}$
(c) $\frac{R}{2}$ (d) None of these

29 **Assertion** As temperature of a black body is raised, wavelength corresponding to maximum energy reduces.
Reason Higher temperature would mean higher energy and hence higher wavelength. **[VMMC]**

(a) Both Assertion and Reason are correct and Reason is the correct explanation of A.
(b) Both Assertion and Reason are correct but R is not the correct explanation of A.
(c) Assertion is correct but Reason is incorrect.
(d) Both Assertion and Reason are incorrect.

30 Using which of the following instruments, the temperature of the sun can be determined? **[CG PMT]**

(a) Platinum thermometer
(b) Gas thermometer
(c) Pyrometer
(d) Vapour pressure thermometer

2009

31 The tungsten filament of an electric lamp has a surface area A and a power rating P. If the emissivity of the filament is ε and σ is Stefan's constant, the steady temperature of the filament will be **[AFMC]**

(a) $T=\left(\frac{P}{A\varepsilon\sigma}\right)^4$ (b) $T=\left(\frac{P}{A\varepsilon\sigma}\right)$
(c) $T=\left(\frac{A\varepsilon\sigma}{P}\right)^{\frac{1}{4}}$ (d) $T=\left(\frac{P}{A\varepsilon\sigma}\right)^{\frac{1}{4}}$

32 If temperature of a black body increases from – 73°C to 327°C, then ratio of emissive power at these two temperatures is **[OJEE]**

(a) 27:1 (b) 81:1
(c) 1:27 (d) 1:81

33 The temperature of a radiating body increases by 30%. Then, the increase in the amount of radiation emitted will be approximately **[Kerala CEE]**

(a) 185% (b) 285%
(c) 325% (d) 245%
(e) 130%

34 The surface temperature of the stars is determined using **[KCET]**

(a) Planck's law
(b) Wien's displacement law
(c) Rayleigh-Jeans law
(d) Kirchhoff's law

35 The amount of heat energy radiated by a metal at temperature T is E. When the temperature is increased to $3T$, energy radiated is **[KCET]**

(a) $81E$ (b) $9E$
(c) $3E$ (d) $27E$

36 A black body at 227°C radiates heat at the rate of 7 cal $cm^{-2}s^{-1}$. At a temperature of 727°C, the rate of heat radiated in the same units will be **[CBSE AIPMT]**

(a) 60 (b) 50
(c) 112 (d) 80

37 For a black body at temperature 727° C, its radiating power is 60 W and temperature of surrounding is 227°C. If the temperature of the black body is changed to 1227°C, then its radiating power will be **[UP CPMT]**

(a) 120 W (b) 240 W
(c) 304 W (d) 320 W

38 The wavelength of the radiation emitted by a body depends upon **[BCECE]**

(a) the nature of its surface
(b) the area of its surface
(c) the temperature of its surface
(d) All the above factors

39 A black body of mass 34.38 g and surface area 19.2 cm^2 is at an initial temperature of 400 K. It is allowed to cool inside an evacuated enclosure kept at constant temperature 300 K. The rate of cooling is 0.04 °C/s. The specific heat of body is (Stefan's constant, $\sigma = 5.73 \times 10^{-8}$ Jm^{-2} K^{-4}) **[MGIMS]**

(a) 2800 J/kg-K (b) 2100 J/kg-K
(c) 1400 J/kg-K (d) 1200 J/kg-K

2008

40 Two solid spheres A and B made of the same material have radii r_A and r_B, respectively. Both the spheres are cooled from the same temperature under the conditions valid for Newton's law of cooling. The ratio of the rate of change of temperature A and B is **[AFMC]**

(a) $\frac{r_A}{r_B}$ (b) $\frac{r_B}{r_A}$ (c) $\frac{r_A^2}{r_B^2}$ (d) $\frac{r_B^2}{r_A^2}$

41 Which of the following statements is true/correct? **[MHT CET]**

(a) During clear nights, the temperature rises steadily upward near the ground level.
(b) Newton's law of cooling, an approximate form of Stefan's law, is valid only for natural convection.
(c) The total energy emitted by a black body per unit time per unit area is proportional to the square of its temperature in the Kelvin scale.
(d) Two spheres of the same material have radii 1 m and 4 m and temperatures 4000 K and 2000 K, respectively. The energy radiated per second by the first sphere is greater than that radiated per second by the second sphere.

42 A hot liquid is filled in a container and kept in a room of temperature of 25°C. The liquid emits heat at the rate of 200 Js^{-1} when its temperature is 75°C. When the temperature of the liquid becomes 40°C, the rate of heat loss (in Js^{-1}) is **[Kerala CEE]**

(a) 160 (b) 140 (c) 80 (d) 60
(e) 40.5

43 A black body at 1227°C emits radiations with maximum intensity at a wavelength of 5000 Å. If the temperature of the body is increased by 1000°C, the maximum intensity will be observed at **[Haryana PMT]**

(a) 4000 Å (b) 5000 Å
(c) 6000 Å (d) 3000 Å

44 Wien's displacement law for emission of radiation can be written as **[J&K CET]**

(a) λ_{max} is proportional to absolute temperature (T)
(b) λ_{max} is proportional to square of absolute temperature (T^2)
(c) λ_{max} is inversely proportional to absolute temperature (T)
(d) λ_{max} is inversely proportional to square of absolute temperature (T^2)

(λ_{max} = wavelength whose energy density is greatest)

45 The power of a black body at temperature 200 K is 544 W. Its surface area is **[Punjab PMET]**

(Take, $\sigma = 5.67 \times 10^{-8}$ Wm^{-2} K^{-4})

(a) 6×10^{-2} m^2 (b) 6 m^2
(c) 6×10^{-6} m^2 (d) 6×10^2 m^2

46 A body cools from 80°C to 64°C in 5 min and same body cools from 80°C to 52°C in 10 min, what is the temperature of the surrounding? **[DUMET]**

(a) 24°C (b) 28°C
(c) 22°C (d) 25°C

47 If a black body emits 0.5 J of energy per second when it is at 27°C, then the amount of energy emitted by it when it is at 627°C will be **[KCET]**

(a) 40.5 J (b) 162 J
(c) 13.5 J (d) 135 J

48 Two circular discs A and B with equal radii are blackened. They are heated to same temperature and are cooled under identical conditions. What inference do you draw from their cooling curves? **[BCECE]**

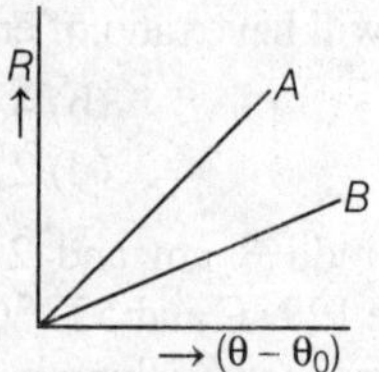

(a) A and B have same specific heats
(b) Specific heat of A is less
(c) Specific heat of B is less
(d) Nothing can be said

49 Assuming the sun to have a spherical outer surface of radius r, radiating like a black body at temperature $t°$ C, the power received by a unit surface, (normal to the incident rays) at a distance R from the centre of the sun is **[JCECE]**

(a) $\frac{4\pi r^2 \sigma t^4}{R^2}$ (b) $\frac{r^2 \sigma (t + 273)^4}{4\pi R^2}$
(c) $\frac{16\pi^2 r^2 \sigma t^4}{R^2}$ (d) $\frac{r^2 \sigma (t + 273)^4}{R^2}$

where, σ is the Stefan's constant.

2007

50 Two friends A and B are waiting for another friend for tea. A took the tea in a cup and mixed the cold milk and then waits. B took the tea in the cup and then mixed the cold milk when the friend comes. Then, the tea will be hotter in the cup of **[AFMC]**

(a) A
(b) B
(c) tea will be equally hot in both cups
(d) friend's cup

51 A sphere and a cube of same material and same volume are heated upto same temperature and allowed to cool in the same surroundings. The ratio of the amounts of radiation emitted will be **[Manipal]**

(a) 1 : 1 (b) $\frac{4}{3}\pi:1$

(c) $\left(\frac{\pi}{6}\right)^{1/3}:1$ (d) $\frac{1}{2}\left(\frac{4\pi}{3}\right)^{2/3}:1$

52 A planet having average surface temperature T_0 at an average distance d from the sun. Assuming that the planet receives radiant energy from the sun only and it loses radiant energy only from the surface and neglecting all other atmospheric effects we conclude **[AMU]**

(a) $T_0 \propto d^2$ (b) $T_0 \propto d^{-2}$

(c) $T_0 \propto d^{1/2}$ (d) $T_0 \propto d^{-1/2}$

53 The surface temperature of the sun which has maximum energy emission at 500 nm is 6000 K. The temperature of a star which has maximum energy emission at 400 nm will be **[KCET]**

(a) 8500 K (b) 4500 K
(c) 7500 K (d) 6500 K

2006

54 Newton's law of cooling holds good only, if the temperature difference between the body and the surroundings is **[MHT CET]**

(a) less than 10°C (b) more than 10°C
(c) less than 100°C (d) more than 100°C

55 A black body at a temperature T radiates energy at E. If the temperature falls to $\frac{T}{2}$, the radiated energy will be **[J&K CET]**

(a) $\frac{E}{4}$ (b) $\frac{E}{2}$

(c) $2E$ (d) $\frac{E}{16}$

56 The surface temperature of the sun is T kelvin and the solar constant for a plate is S. The sun subtends an angle θ at the planet. Then, **[AMU]**

(a) $S \propto T^4$ (b) $S \propto T^2$

(c) $S \propto \theta^2$ (d) $S \propto \theta$

57 A body cools from 75°C to 70°C to time t_1, from 70°C to 65°C in time t_2 and from 65°C to 60°C in time t_3, then

(a) $t_3 > t_2 > t_1$
(b) $t_1 > t_2 > t_3$ **[JCECE]**
(c) $t_2 > t_1 = t_3$
(d) $t_1 > t_2 < t_3$

2005

58 **Assertion** (A) For higher temperatures, the peak emission wavelength of a black body shifts to lower wavelengths.

Reason (R) Peak emission wavelengths of a black body is proportional to the fourth-power of temperature. **[AIIMS]**

(a) Both A and R are correct and R is the correct explanation of A
(b) Both A and R are correct but R is not the correct explanation of A
(c) A is correct but R is incorrect
(d) Both A and R are incorrect

59 A body at a temperature of 727°C and has surface area 5 cm^2, radiates 300 J of energy each minute. The emissivity is (given, Boltzmann constant $= 5.67\times 10^{-8}$ Wm^{-2}K^{-4}) **[Manipal]**

(a) $e = 0.18$ (b) $e = 0.02$ (c) $e = 0.2$ (d) $e = 0.15$

60 A hot liquid kept in a beaker cools from 80°C to 70°C in 2 min. If the surrounding temperature to 30°C, then the time of cooling of the same liquid from 60°C to 50°C is

(a) 240 s (b) 360 s (c) 480 s **[Kerala CEE]**
(d) 216 s (e) 264 s

61 A black body is heated from 27°C to 927°C. The ratio of radiations emitted will be **[MP PMT]**

(a) 1 : 256 (b) 1 : 64 (c) 1 : 16 (d) 1 : 4

62 A black body at temperature 10^4 K radiates maximum energy at wavelength 500 Å. If the temperature is increased 10 times, the maximum energy would be radiated at wavelength equal to **[Haryana PMT]**

(a) 50000 Å (b) 500 Å (c) 50 Å (d) 5 Å

63 The spectral energy distribution of a star is maximum at twice temperature as that of the sun. The total energy radiated by the star is **[J&K CET]**

(a) twice as that of the sun (b) same as that of the sun
(c) sixteen times as that of the sun
(d) one-sixteenth of the sun

64 Two bodies of same shape, same size and same radiating power have emissivities 0.2 and 0.8. The ratio of their temperatures is **[EAMCET]**

(a) $\sqrt{3}:1$ (b) $\sqrt{2}:1$ (c) $1:\sqrt{5}$ (d) $1:\sqrt{8}$

65 A piece of blue glass heated to a high temperature and a piece of red glass at room temperature, are taken inside a dimly lit room, then **[KCET]**

(a) the blue piece will look blue and red will look as usual
(b) red looks brighter red and blue looks ordinary blue
(c) blue shines brighter or compared to the red piece
(d) both the pieces will look equally red

Answers

1 (d)	2 (a)	3 (a)	4 (a)	5 (d)	6 (c)	7 (b)	8 (b)	9 (a)	10 (d)
11 (c)	12 (a)	13 (b)	14 (b)	15 (b)	16 (d)	17 (b)	18 (a)	19 (c)	20 (b)
21 (d)	22 (a)	23 (d)	24 (c)	25 (c)	26 (a)	27 (c)	28 (b)	29 (c)	30 (c)
31 (d)	32 (d)	33 (a)	34 (b)	35 (a)	36 (c)	37 (d)	38 (c)	39 (c)	40 (b)
41 (b)	42 (d)	43 (d)	44 (c)	45 (b)	46 (a)	47 (a)	48 (b)	49 (d)	50 (a)
51 (c)	52 (d)	53 (c)	54 (a)	55 (d)	56 (a)	57 (a)	58 (c)	59 (a)	60 (d)
61 (a)	62 (c)	63 (c)	64 (b)	65 (c)					

Explanations

1 (d) When the object cool from 80°C to 70°C in 12 min, then from Newton's law of cooling,

$$\frac{80^\circ - 70^\circ}{12} = \frac{1}{K}\left(\frac{80^\circ + 70^\circ}{2} - 25^\circ\right)$$

$$[\because T_0 = 25^\circ \text{ C}]$$

$$\frac{5}{6} = \frac{1}{K}50 \qquad \ldots\text{(i)}$$

Similarly, when object cool from 70°C to 60°C, we get

$$\frac{70^\circ - 60^\circ}{t} = \frac{1}{K}\left(\frac{70^\circ + 60^\circ}{2} - 25^\circ\right)$$

$$\frac{10}{t} = \frac{1}{K}40 \qquad \ldots\text{(ii)}$$

Divide Eq. (i) by Eq. (ii), we get

$$\frac{5}{6} \times \frac{t}{10} = \frac{50}{40}$$

$$\Rightarrow \quad t = \frac{5}{4} \times 12 = 15 \text{ min}$$

2 (a) Temperature of sphere, $T = 227^\circ$ C

$= 273 + 227 = 500$ K

Radius, $r = 2$ m

Emissivity, $e = 0.8$

$\therefore$ Radiation power of sphere

= Radiated energy per second

$= \sigma AeT^4$

$= 5.67 \times 10^{-8} \times 4\pi \times 2^2 \times 0.8 \times (500)^4$

$= 142502.6$ W

$= 142.5$ kW

3 (a) Given, temperature of sun,

$T_S = 6000$ K

Radius of sun,

$R_s = 7.2 \times 10^5 \text{ km} = 7.2 \times 10^8$ m

Radius of earth,

$R_e = 6000 \text{ km} = 600 \times 10^3$ m

Distance between earth and sun,

$d = 15 \times 10^7 \text{ km} = 15 \times 10^{10}$ m

Intensity of light on the earth,

$$I = \frac{\text{Total energy emitted by sun}}{4\pi d^2} \times (\pi R_e^2)$$

$$= \frac{\sigma(T_s^4 \cdot 4\pi R_s^2 \times \pi R_e^2)}{4\pi d^2}$$

$$= \frac{\sigma T_s^4 R_s^2 \times \pi R_e^2}{d^2}$$

$$= \frac{5.67 \times 10^{-8} \times (6000)^4 \times (7.2 \times 10^8)^2 \times 3.14 \times (6000 \times 10^3)^2}{(15 \times 10^{10})^2}$$

$= 19.2 \times 10^{16}$

4 (a) According to Wien's law,

$\lambda_{(\max)} \propto 1/T$

i.e. $\lambda_{(\max)} T = $ constant

where, $\lambda_{(\max)}$ is the maximum wavelength of the radiation emitted at temperature T.

$$\therefore \quad \lambda_{(\max)_1} T_1 = \lambda_{(\max)_2} T_2$$

$$\text{or} \quad \frac{T_1}{T_2} = \frac{\lambda_{(\max)_2}}{\lambda_{(\max)_1}} \qquad \ldots\text{(i)}$$

Here $\lambda_{(\max)_1} = \lambda_0$ and $\lambda_{(\max)_2} = \frac{3}{4}\lambda_0$

Substituting the above values in Eq. (i), we get

$$\frac{T_1}{T_2} = \frac{\frac{3}{4}\lambda_0}{\lambda_0} = \frac{3}{4} \quad \text{or} \quad \frac{T_1}{T_2} = \frac{3}{4} \qquad \ldots\text{(ii)}$$

As we know that, from Stefan's law, the power radiated by a body at temperature T is given as

$$P = \sigma AeT^4$$

i.e. $P \propto T^4$

($\because$ the quantity σAe is constant for a body)

$$\Rightarrow \quad \frac{P_1}{P_2} = \frac{T_1^4}{T_2^4} = \left(\frac{T_1}{T_2}\right)^4$$

From Eq. (i), we get

$$\frac{P_1}{P_2} = \left(\frac{3}{4}\right)^4 = \frac{81}{256}$$

Given, $P_1 = P$ and $P_2 = nP$

$$\Rightarrow \quad \frac{P_1}{P_2} = \frac{P}{nP} = \frac{81}{256} \quad \text{or} \quad n = \frac{256}{81}$$

5 (d) Radiated power of a black body,

$P = \sigma AT^4$

where, A = surface area of the body,

T = temperature of the body

and σ = Stefan's constant.

When radius of the sphere is halved, new area, $A' = A/4$

$\therefore$ Power radiated,

$$P' = \sigma\left(\frac{A}{4}\right)(2T)^4 = \frac{16}{4} \cdot (\sigma AT^4)$$

$= 4P = 4 \times 450 = 1800$ W

6 (c) Given, temperature, $T_1 = 5760$ K

Since, it is given that energy of radiation emitted by the body at wavelength 250 nm in U_1, at wavelength 500 nm is U_2 and that at 1000 nm is U_3.

$\because$ According to Wien's law, we get

$$\lambda_m T = b$$

where, b = Wien's constant

$= 2.88 \times 10^6$ nmK

$$\Rightarrow \quad \lambda_m = \frac{b}{T}$$

$$= \frac{2.88 \times 10^6 \text{ nmK}}{5760 \text{ K}} = 500 \text{ nm}$$

$\because \lambda_m$ = wavelength corresponding to maximum energy, so $U_2 > U_1$.

7 (b) According to Newton's law of cooling, $\Delta T = \Delta T_0 e^{-\lambda t}$

$\Rightarrow 3T - 2T = (3T - T) e^{-\lambda \times 10}$ ...(i)

Again for next 10 min,

$$T' - T = (2T) \times e^{-\lambda(20)} \quad ...(ii)$$

From Eqs. (i) and (ii), we get

$$T' - T = (2T)(e^{-\lambda \times 10})^2$$

$$= (2T)\left(\frac{1}{2}\right)^2 = \frac{T}{2}$$

$$\left[\text{from Eq. (i), } e^{-\lambda \times 10} = \frac{1}{2}\right]$$

$$\therefore \quad T' = T + \frac{T}{2} = \frac{3T}{2}$$

8 (b) We know from Wien's displacement law, $\lambda_m T$ = constant

So, $T \propto \frac{1}{\lambda_m}$

As, $\lambda_r > \lambda_g > \lambda_v$

So, $T_r < T_g < T_v$

Given, $P \rightarrow v_{max}$, $Q \rightarrow r_{max}$, $R \rightarrow g_{max}$

Hence, $T_Q < T_R < T_P$

i.e. $T_P > T_R > T_Q$

9 (a) Let temperature of surrounding Q_0 from Newton's law of cooling

Case I $\frac{Q_2 - Q_1}{t} = K\left(\frac{Q_2 + Q_1}{2} - Q_0\right)$

$$\frac{70-60}{5} = (65 - Q_0)K \quad ...(i)$$

Case II $\frac{60-54}{5} = (57 - Q_0)K$ ...(ii)

From Eqs. (i) and (ii), we get

$$\frac{10}{6} = \frac{65 - Q_0}{57 - Q_0}$$

$$\Rightarrow \quad Q_0 = 45°\text{C}$$

10 (d) The equation of Wien's displacement law,

i.e. $\lambda_m T$ = constant

For perfectly black body, $\lambda_m \propto \frac{1}{T}$

So, graph is rectangular hyperbola.

11 (c) $\frac{\theta_1 - \theta_2}{t} = K\left(\frac{\theta_1 + \theta_2}{2} - \theta_0\right)$

$$\therefore \frac{80° - 60°}{1} = K\left(\frac{80° + 60°}{2} - 30°\right)$$

$$20° = K \times 40°$$

$$\Rightarrow \quad K = \frac{1}{2}$$

For next 1 min,

$$\frac{60° - \theta}{1} = \frac{1}{2}\left(\frac{60° + \theta}{2} - 30°\right)$$

$$120° - 2\theta = \frac{60° + \theta - 60°}{2}$$

$$\Rightarrow \quad 240° - 4\theta = \theta$$

$$\Rightarrow \quad \theta = \frac{240°}{5} = 48°\text{C}$$

12 (a) If r is the radius of the star and T its temperature, then the energy emitted by the star per second through the radiation in accordance with Stefan's law will be given by

$$P = A\sigma T^4 = 4\pi r^2 \sigma T^4$$

In reaching a distance R, this energy will spread over a sphere of radius R, so the intensity of radiation will be given by

$$S = \frac{P}{4\pi R^2}$$

$$= \frac{4\pi r^2 \sigma T^4}{4\pi R^2} = \frac{\sigma r^2 T^4}{R^2}$$

13 (b) This can be explain by Wien's displacement law, i.e. $\lambda_m T$ = constant

or $\lambda_m = \frac{\text{constant}}{T}$

When the piece of iron is heated, i.e. temperature increases, λ_m decreases. Thus, maximum intensity of emitted radiation moves towards the shorter wavelength. So, the colour of iron piece will change from longer wavelength (dull red) to shorter wavelength (reddish yellow) and when temperature is further increased the iron piece emitted all wavelength, so colour will become white.

14 (b) From Newton's law of cooling,

$$\frac{\theta_1 - \theta_2}{t} \propto \left(\frac{\theta_1 + \theta_2}{2} - \theta_0\right)$$

where, θ_0 = temperature of surroundings.

$$\therefore \quad \frac{50° - 49°}{t_1} \propto \left(\frac{50° + 49°}{2} - 30°\right) \quad ...(i)$$

and $\frac{40° - 39°}{t_2} \propto \left(\frac{40° + 39°}{2} - 30°\right)$ ...(ii)

Dividing Eq. (i) by Eq. (ii), we get

$$\frac{t_2}{t_1} = \frac{39}{19}$$

$$\Rightarrow \quad t_2 = \frac{39}{19} \times 5 = 10 \text{ s}$$

15 (b) Red colour has maximum wavelength.

From Wien's displacement law, the relation between maximum wavelength λ_m and temperature T is

$$\lambda_m T = \text{constant}$$

which implies longer the wavelength, smaller the temperature. Since, red colour has maximum wavelength, so its temperature will be minimum and hence it will cool at the earliest.

16 (d) From Stefan's law, $E = \sigma T^4$

So, the rate energy production,

$$Q = E \times A$$

$$\Rightarrow \quad Q = \sigma T^4 \times 4\pi R^2$$

Temperature of star, $T = \left(\frac{Q}{4\pi R^2 \sigma}\right)^{1/4}$

17 (b) The rate of radiated energy,

$$E = \varepsilon \sigma A T^4$$

or $1134 = 1 \times 5.67 \times 10^{-8} \times (0.1)^2 T^4$

Temperature, $T = 1189$ K

18 (a) By Stefan's law,

$$\frac{dT}{dt} = \frac{A\varepsilon\sigma}{mc}[T^4 - T_0^4]$$

When the temperature difference between the body and its surrounding is not very large, i.e. $T - T_0 = \Delta T$, then $T^4 - T_0^4$ may be approximated as $4T_0^3 \Delta T$.

Hence, $\frac{dT}{dt} = \frac{A\varepsilon\sigma}{mc} 4T_0^3 \Delta T$

$$\Rightarrow \quad \frac{dT}{dt} \propto \Delta T \quad (\because \Delta T = T - T_S)$$

i.e., if the temperature of the body is not very different from surrounding, rate of cooling is proportional to temperature difference between the body and its surrounding. This law is called Newton's law of cooling.

19 (c) According to Newton's law of cooling,

$$\frac{\theta_1 - \theta_2}{t} = K\left[\frac{\theta_1 + \theta_2}{2} - \theta_0\right]$$

$$\therefore \quad \frac{80° - 70°}{5} = K\left[\frac{80° + 70°}{2} - 40°\right]$$

$$\Rightarrow \quad K = \frac{2}{35}$$

Again, $\frac{80° - 60°}{t} = \frac{2}{35}\left[\frac{80° + 60°}{2} - 40°\right]$

$$\approx 11.55 \approx 12 \text{ min}$$

20 (b) The Wien's radiation law is given by

$$\lambda_m T = b$$

For the given problem,

$$b = 2.88 \times 10^{-3} \text{ mK}$$

Hence, $\lambda_m T = 2.88 \times 10^{-3}$

$$\Rightarrow \quad T = \frac{2.88 \times 10^{-3}}{\lambda_m} = \frac{2.88 \times 10^{-3}}{480 \times 10^{-9}} = 6000 \text{ K}$$

21 (d) According to Newton's law of cooling,

$$\frac{\theta_2 - \theta_1}{t} = K\left[\frac{\theta_1 + \theta_2}{2} - \theta_s\right]$$

where, θ_s is the temperature of the surroundings.

$$\frac{60° - 50°}{10} = K\left[\frac{60° + 50°}{2} - \theta_s\right]$$

$$1 = K[55 - \theta_s] \quad \text{...(i)}$$

Similarly, $\dfrac{50° - 42°}{10} = K(46° - \theta_s)$

$$\frac{8}{10} = K(46° - \theta_s) \quad \text{...(ii)}$$

Dividing Eq. (i) by Eq. (ii), we get

$$\frac{10}{8} = \frac{K(55° - \theta_s)}{K(46° - \theta_s)}$$

$$\Rightarrow \quad \theta_s = 10°\text{C}$$

22 (a) According to Wien's displacement law,

$$\lambda_m T = \text{constant}$$

$$\frac{\lambda_2}{\lambda_1} = \frac{T_1}{T_2}$$

$$\frac{\lambda_2}{\lambda} = \frac{2000}{3000} = \frac{2}{3}$$

or $\quad \lambda_2 = \dfrac{2}{3}\lambda$

23 (d) According to Newton's law of cooling,

$$\frac{dQ}{dt} \propto \Delta\theta$$

But $\quad \dfrac{dQ}{dt} \propto (\Delta\theta)^n \quad$ (given)

$$\therefore \quad n = 1$$

24 (c) Hence, $t = \dfrac{Q}{Rmgh}$

$$= \frac{cm(T_f - T_i)}{Rmgh} = \frac{c(T_f - T_i)}{Rgh}$$

$$= \frac{(4190)(100 - 15)}{(30)(9.8)(0.30)}$$

$$= 4.03 \times 10^3 \text{min}$$

25 (c) From Newton's law of cooling,

$$\frac{\theta_1 - \theta_2}{t} = \left(\frac{\theta_1 + \theta_2}{2} - \theta_0\right)$$

Therefore,

$$\frac{60° - 40°}{7} \propto \left(\frac{60° + 40°}{2} - 10°\right) \quad \text{...(i)}$$

$$\frac{40° - 28°}{t} \propto \left(\frac{40° + 28°}{2} - 10°\right) \quad \text{...(ii)}$$

On solving the Eqs. (i) and (ii), we get $t = 7$ min

26 (a) According to Stefan's law,

$$P = A\varepsilon\sigma T^4$$

$$\because \quad \frac{P_1}{P_2} = \frac{A_1}{A_2} \cdot \frac{T_1^4}{T_2^4} = \left(\frac{R_1}{R_2}\right)^2 \cdot \left(\frac{T_1}{T_2}\right)^4$$

$$(\because A = \pi R^2)$$

$$= \left(\frac{4}{1}\right)^2 \times \left(\frac{2000}{4000}\right)^4 = \frac{1}{1}$$

27 (c) According to Stefan's law, $P = A\varepsilon\sigma T^4$

$$\frac{P_1}{P_2} = \left(\frac{A_1}{A_2}\right)\left(\frac{T_1}{T_2}\right)^4 = \frac{(R_1)^2}{(R_2)^2}\left(\frac{T_1}{T_2}\right)^4$$

$$= \left(\frac{8}{2}\right)^2 \left(\frac{273 + 127}{273 + 527}\right)^4$$

$$= (4)^2 \left(\frac{400}{800}\right)^4 = (4)^2 \left(\frac{1}{2}\right)^4 = 1$$

28 (b) From Stefan's law, the total radiant energy emitted per second per unit surface area of a black body is proportional to the fourth power of the absolute temperature (T) of the body.

$$\therefore \quad E = \sigma T^4$$

where, σ is Stefan's constant.

Given, $\quad E_1 = R$

$\Rightarrow T_1 = 273°\text{C} = 273 + 273 = 546$ K

$$T_2 = 0°\text{C} = 273 \text{ K}$$

$$\therefore \quad \frac{E_1}{E_2} = \frac{T_1^4}{T_2^4}$$

$$\Rightarrow \quad E_2 = \frac{T_2^4}{T_1^4} E_1$$

$$\Rightarrow \quad E_2 = \frac{(273)^4}{(546)^4} R$$

$$\Rightarrow \quad E_2 = \frac{R}{16}$$

29 (c) According to Wien's displacement law, the wavelength corresponding to maximum emission of radiation decreases with increasing temperature, i.e. $\lambda_m \propto \dfrac{1}{T}$, when temperature of a black body is raised, wavelength decreases means its corresponding energy reduces. Hence, the statement given in Reason is contradictory. Hence, option (c) is correct.

30 (c) Pyrometers are the devices used to measure the temperature by measuring the intensity of radiations received from the body.

They are based on the fact that the amount of radiation emitted from a body per unit area per second is directly proportional to the fourth power of temperature, i.e. Stefan's law. These can be used to measure temperature ranging from 800°C to 6000°C.

31 (d) Radiating power of a body of area A, emissivity ε and surface temperature (T) is,

$$P = \sigma\varepsilon A T^4$$

$$\Rightarrow \quad T = \left[\frac{P}{\sigma\varepsilon A}\right]^{1/4}$$

32 (d) Emissive power of a body with surface temperature (T kelvin) is given as $\quad E = \sigma T^4$

Hence, $\dfrac{E_2}{E_1} = \left(\dfrac{T_2}{T_1}\right)^4$

$$= \left(\frac{273 - 73}{273 + 327}\right)^4 = \left(\frac{200}{600}\right)^4$$

$$\therefore E_2 : E_1 = 1 : 81$$

33 (a) Let initial surface temperature be T_0.

From Stefan's law,

$$E_1 = \sigma T_0^4, \text{ i.e. } E \propto T^4$$

As, surface temperature is increased by 30%,

$$E_2 = \sigma\left[T_0 + \frac{30}{100}T_0\right]$$

$$= \sigma T_0 \left(\frac{130}{100}\right)^4$$

$$\frac{E_2}{E_1} = \left(\frac{130}{100}\right)^4 = \frac{E_2 - E_1}{E_1} = \left(\frac{13}{10}\right)^4 - 1$$

$$\frac{\Delta E}{E_1} \times 100 = \left[\left(\frac{13}{10}\right)^4 - 1\right] \times 100$$

Increase in $E = 185.61\% \simeq 185\%$

34 (b) Surface temperature of stars is determined by Wien's displacement law.

As, $T = \frac{b}{\lambda_m}$ where

b = Wien's constant $= 2.898 \times 10^{-3}$ m-K

and $\lambda_m = 4753 \times 10^{-10}$ m

35 (a) From Stefan's law, $E = \sigma T^4$

⇒ Initial surface temperature is T.

As, temperature is increased to $3T$.

$$E_2 = \sigma (3T)^4$$

$$\Rightarrow \quad E_2 = \sigma T^4 (81)$$

$$E_2 = 81 E$$

36 (c) Apply Stefan's law of radiations,

$$E = \sigma T^4$$

$$\frac{E_1}{E_2} = \left(\frac{T_1}{T_2}\right)^4$$

$$\Rightarrow \quad E_2 = 7\left(\frac{273 + 727}{273 + 227}\right)^4$$

$$= \left(\frac{1000}{500}\right)^4 \times 7$$

$$= 112 \text{ cal cm}^{-2}\text{s}^{-2}$$

37 (d) As per modified Stefan's law, if a body at temperature T is surrounded by another body at temperature T_0 (where, $T_0 < T$), then Stefan's law is given as

$$E = \sigma (T^4 - T_0^4)$$

$$\frac{E_2}{E_1} = \frac{(T_2^4 - T_0^4)}{(T_1^4 - T_0^4)}$$

$$\frac{E_2}{E_1} = \left[\frac{(1500)^4 - (500)^4}{(1000)^4 - (500)^4}\right]$$

$$\Rightarrow \quad E_2 = 60\left[\frac{(15)^4 - (5)^4}{(10)^4 - (5)^4}\right]$$

$$= 320 \text{ W}$$

38 (c) The wavelength of radiation emitted by a body depends upon the temperature of its surface. According to Wien's law$\lambda_m T$ = constant, on heating upto ordinary temperatures, only long wavelength (red) radiation is emitted.

As the temperature rises, shorter wavelengths are also emitted in more and more quantity.

Hence, the colour of radiation emitted by the hot wire shifts from red to yellow, then the blue and finally to white.

39 (c) From Stefan's law,

$$mc\frac{dT}{dt} = \sigma(T^4 - T_0^4)A$$

$$\Rightarrow \quad c = \frac{\sigma(T^4 - T_0^4)A}{m\left(\frac{dT}{dt}\right)}$$

$$\Rightarrow c = \frac{\left[\begin{array}{r}(5.73 \times 10^{-8})\,[(400)^4 - (300)^4] \\ \times 19.2 \times 10^{-4}\end{array}\right]}{(34.38 \times 10^{-3}) \times 0.04}$$

$$\Rightarrow c = 1400 \text{ J/kg - K}$$

40 (b) $\frac{4\pi}{3} r^3 \rho c\left(-\frac{dT}{dt}\right) = \sigma 4\pi r^2 (T^4 - T_0^4)$

$$\therefore \quad \left(-\frac{dT}{dt}\right) = \frac{3\sigma}{\rho rc}(T^4 - T_0^4) = H \text{ (say)}$$

Ratio of rates of fall of temperature ,

$$\frac{H_A}{H_B} = \frac{r_B}{r_A}$$

41 (b) Stefan's law,

$$E = Ae\sigma(T^4 - T_0^4)$$

We assume that difference between T, T_0 is very small.

Now, $E = Ae\sigma(T^2 + T_0^2)(T^2 - T_0^2)$

$= Ae\sigma (T^2 + T_0^2)(T + T_0)(T - T_0)$

$= Ae\sigma (T^3 + T^2T_0 + TT_0^2 + T_0^3)(T - T_0)$

Since, we assumed $T \approx T_0$

$$E = Ae\sigma 4T_0^3(T - T_0)$$

$$= k(T - T_0)$$

where, $k = Ae\sigma 4T_0^3$

$$\frac{-dQ}{dt} = 4k(T - T_0)k \quad \left[\because E = -\frac{dQ}{dt}\right]$$

Since, $\frac{dQ}{dt} = ms\frac{d\theta}{dt}$

So, $ms\frac{d\theta}{dt} = k(T - T_0)$

$$\frac{d\theta}{dt} = \frac{-k}{ms}(T - T_0)$$

$$\frac{d\theta}{dt} = K'(T - T_0)$$

Which is Newton's law of cooling, hence Newton's law is a approximate form of Stefan's law of radiation and works well for natural convection.

42 (d) Rate of heat loss $\propto \Delta t$

$$\therefore \quad \frac{\left(\frac{dQ}{dt}\right)_1}{\left(\frac{dQ}{dt}\right)_2} = \frac{(75° - 25°)}{(40° - 25°)}$$

$$\Rightarrow \quad \frac{200}{\left(\frac{dQ}{dt}\right)_2} = \frac{50}{15}$$

$$\therefore \quad \left(\frac{dQ}{dt}\right)_2 = 60 \text{ Js}^{-1}$$

43 (d) According to Wien's law,

$\lambda_m T$ = constant (say b)

where, λ_m is wavelength corresponding to maximum intensity of radiation and T is temperature of the body in kelvin.

$$\therefore \quad \frac{\lambda'_m}{\lambda_m} = \frac{T}{T'}$$

Given, $T = 1227 + 273 = 1500$ K

$$T' = 1227 + 1000 + 273$$

$$= 2500 \text{ K}$$

$$\lambda_m = 5000 \text{ Å}$$

Hence, $\lambda'_m = \frac{1500}{2500} \times 5000 = 3000$ Å

44 (c) Wien's displacement law,

$$\lambda_{max} \cdot T = b$$

where, b = Wien's constant.

$$\therefore \quad \lambda_{max} \propto \frac{1}{T}$$

Thus, λ_{max} is inversely proportional to absolute temperature (T).

45 (b) According to Stefan's law,

$$\frac{Q}{At} = \sigma T^4$$

Here, $\frac{Q}{t} = 544$,

$$T = 200 \text{ K}$$

$$\sigma = 5.67 \times 10^{-8} \text{ Wm}^{-2}\text{K}^{-4}$$

$$\therefore \quad A = \frac{Q}{\sigma t T^4} = \frac{544}{5.67 \times 10^{-8} \times (200)^4}$$

$$= 6 \text{ m}^2$$

46 (a) According to Newton's law of cooling,

$$\frac{80 - 64}{5} = \alpha\left[\frac{80 + 64}{2} - T\right] \quad \ldots\text{(i)}$$

and $\frac{80 - 52}{10} = \alpha\left[\frac{80 + 52}{2} - T\right] \quad \ldots\text{(ii)}$

where, T is the temperature of the surroundings.

Solving Eqs. (i) and (ii), we get

$$T = 24°\text{C}$$

47 (a) $Q_2 = Q_1\left(\frac{T_2}{T_1}\right)^4$

$$= 0.5\left(\frac{900}{300}\right)^4 = 40.5\text{ J}$$

$[\because T_2 = 627 + 273 = 900\text{ K}, T_1 = 27 + 273 = 300\text{ K}]$

48 (b) According to Newton's law of cooling, rate of cooling is given by

$$\left(\frac{-dT}{dt}\right) = \frac{eA\sigma}{mc}(T^4 - T_0^4)$$

where, c is specific heat of material,

$$\left(\frac{-dT}{dt}\right) \propto \frac{1}{c}$$

i.e., rate of cooling varies inversely as specific heat. From the graph, for A, rate of cooling is larger. Therefore, specific heat of A is smaller.

49 (d) From Stefan's law, the rate at which energy is radiated by sun at its surface is

$$P = \sigma \times 4\pi r^2 T^4$$

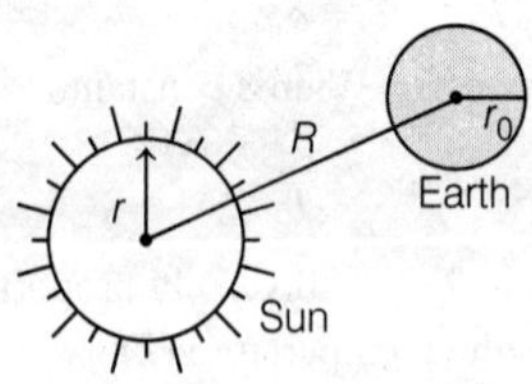

[Sun is a perfectly black body as it emits radiations of all wavelengths and so for it, $e = 1$]

The intensity of this power at earth's surface (under the assumption $R >> r_0$) is

$$I = \frac{P}{4\pi R^2} = \frac{\sigma \times 4\pi r^2 T^4}{4\pi R^2}$$

$$\Rightarrow \quad = \frac{\sigma r^2 T^4}{R^2} = \frac{\sigma r^2 (t + 273)^4}{R^2}$$

50 (a) The rate of heat loss is proportional to the difference in temperature. The difference of temperature between the tea in cup A and the surrounding is reduced, so it losses less heat, the tea in cup B losses more heat because of large temperature difference.

Hence, the tea in cup A will be hotter.

51 (c) Energy radiated per second is given as, $P = A\sigma\varepsilon T^4$

$$P \propto A$$

[As temperature of surface is constant]

$$\frac{P_1}{P_2} = \frac{A_1}{A_2} = \frac{A_s}{A_c}$$

$$\Rightarrow \quad \frac{P_1}{P_2} = \frac{4\pi R^2}{6a^2} \quad \text{...(i)}$$

Also, volume of sphere = volume of cube

$$\frac{4}{3}\pi R^3 = a^3$$

$$\Rightarrow \quad \frac{R}{a} = \left(\frac{3}{4\pi}\right)^{1/3} \quad \text{...(ii)}$$

From Eqs. (i) and (ii), we get

$$\frac{P_1}{P_2} = \left(\frac{\pi}{6}\right)^{1/3}$$

52 (d) Energy received per second by the planet $= \frac{P}{4\pi d^2}(\pi R^2)$

where, P is power radiated by the sun and R is the radius of the planet.

Further, energy radiated per second by the planet according to Stefan's law is $\sigma(4\pi R^2)T_0^4$.

For thermal equilibrium to exist, we get

$$\frac{P}{4\pi d^2}(\pi R^2) = \sigma(4\pi R^2)T_0^4$$

$$\Rightarrow \quad T_0^4 \propto d^{-2}$$

$$\Rightarrow \quad T_0 \propto d^{-1/2}$$

53 (c) By using Wien's displacement law,

$(\lambda_m)_1 T_1 = (\lambda_m)_2 T_2$

$\therefore \; 500 \times 6000 = 400 \times T_2$

$$\Rightarrow \quad T_2 = \frac{500 \times 6000}{400} = 7500\text{ K}$$

54 (a) Newton's law of cooling states that the rate of cooling (R) is directly proportional to temperature difference between body and its surroundings.

$$\frac{-dT}{dt} = k(T - T_0)$$

When temperature difference between the body and surroundings is small, then loss of heat energy from the body is mainly due to the process of convection. In such a case, the rate of cooling of the body is governed by Newton's law of cooling from the given options (a) would be correct.

55 (d) By Stefan's law, $E = \sigma T^4$

(σ = Stefan's constant)

Given, $E_1 = E, T_1 = T, T_2 = T/2$

$$\therefore \quad \frac{E_1}{E_2} = \frac{T_1^4}{T_2^4} \Rightarrow E_2 = \frac{T_2^4}{T_1^4} \cdot E_1$$

$$\Rightarrow \quad E_2 = \frac{(T/2)^4}{T^4} \cdot E = \frac{E}{16}$$

56 (a) Let radius of sun = R and distance of the earth from the sun = d

Power radiated from the sun

$$= (4\pi R^2)\sigma T^4 = P$$

Energy received/area/s = $S = P/4\pi d^2$

$$S = 4\pi R^2 \sigma \frac{T^4}{4\pi d^2} = \sigma T^4 \frac{R^2}{d^2}$$

$$= \frac{1}{4}\sigma T^4 \left(\frac{2R}{d}\right)^2$$

Angle subtended by sun at the earth,

$$\theta = 2R/d$$

$$S = \text{constant} \times T^4 \times \theta^2$$

$$\Rightarrow \quad S \propto T^4$$

57 (a) By Newton's law of cooling,

$$\frac{dH}{dt} = K\left(\frac{\theta_1 + \theta_2}{2} - \theta_0\right)$$

where, θ_0 is temperature of surroundings

and $\frac{\theta_1 + \theta_2}{2}$ is the temperature of body.

Hence, $t_3 > t_2 > t_1$.

58 (c) Figure shows that how the energy of a black body radiation varies with temperature and wavelength. As the temperature of the black body increases, two distinct behaviours are observed.

The first effect is that the peak of the distribution shifts to shorter wavelengths. This shift is found to obey the following relationship called Wien's displacement law.

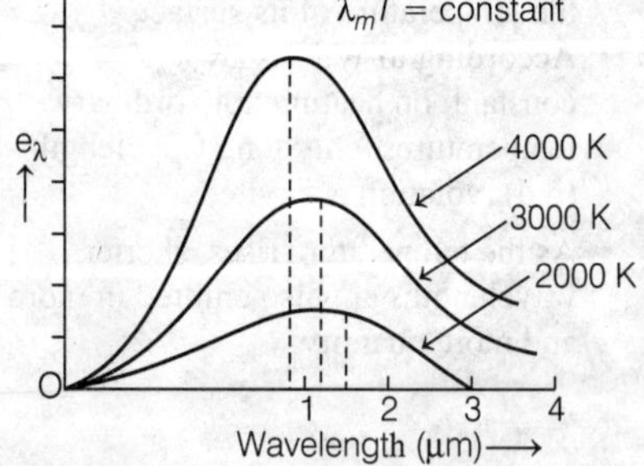

The second effect is that the total amount of energy that the black body emits per unit area per unit time increases with fourth power of absolute temperature T.

Hence, Assertion is correct but Reason is incorrect.

59 *(a)* $Q = EAt = e\sigma(T^4 - T_0^4)At$

where, t = time

and T_0 = temperature of surroundings

When $T > T_0$,

$$Q = e\sigma T^4 At$$

$$300 = e \times (5.67 \times 10^{-8})(1000)^4 (5.00 \times 10^{-4})(60)$$

$$\Rightarrow \quad e = 0.18$$

$$(\because T = 273 + 727 = 1000\text{K})$$

60 *(d)* By Newton's law of cooling,

$$\frac{\theta_1 - \theta_2}{t} \propto \left(\frac{\theta_1 + \theta_2}{2} - \theta_0\right)$$

$$\therefore \quad \frac{80 - 70}{2} \propto \left(\frac{80 + 70}{2} - 30\right) \quad \ldots\text{(i)}$$

and $$\frac{60 - 50}{t} \propto \left(\frac{60 + 50}{2} - 30\right) \quad \ldots\text{(ii)}$$

Dividing Eq. (i) by Eq. (ii), we get

$$\frac{10}{2} \times \frac{t}{10} = \frac{45}{25}$$

$$t = \frac{45 \times 2 \times 10}{10 \times 25}$$

$$= 3.6 \text{ min} = 216 \text{ s}$$

61 *(a)* Here, initial temperature,

$$T_1 = 27°\text{C} = 300 \text{ K}$$

Final temperature,

$$T_2 = 927°\text{C} = 1200 \text{ K}$$

According to Stefan's law, the radiant energy is $E \propto T^4$

Here, $$\frac{E_1}{E_2} = \frac{T_1^4}{T_2^4}$$

$$= \left(\frac{300}{1200}\right)^4 = \left(\frac{1}{4}\right)^4 = \frac{1}{256}$$

Hence, $E_1 : E_2 = 1 : 256$

62 *(c)* By Wien's displacement law,

$$\lambda_1 T_1 = \lambda_2 T_2 \text{ or } \lambda_2 = \lambda_1 T_1 / T_2$$

$$\therefore \lambda_2 = \frac{500 \text{ Å} \times 10^4}{10^5} = 50 \text{ Å}$$

63 *(c)* From Stefan's law of radiation, the total radiant energy emitted per second per unit surface area of a black body is proportional to the fourth power of the absolute temperature (T) of the body.

Therefore, $E = \sigma T^4$

where, σ is Stefan's constant.

Given, $T = 2T_s$

$$\therefore \quad E' = \sigma(2T_s)^4 = 16\sigma T_s^4 = 16E_s$$

Hence, total energy radiated by star is sixteen times as that of the sun.

64 *(b)* Radiating power of a body of area A_1, emissivity e_1 and surface temperature T_1 is

$$P_1 = \sigma e_1 T_1^4 A_1 \quad \ldots\text{(i)}$$

Similarly, radiating power of a body of area A_2, emissivity e_2 and surface temperature T_2 is

$$P_2 = \sigma e_2 T_2^4 A_2 \quad \ldots\text{(ii)}$$

Given, $P_1 = P_2$

and $A_1 = A_2$

$$\sigma e_1 T_1^4 A_1 = \sigma e_2 T_2^4 A_2$$

$$\Rightarrow \quad \left(\frac{T_1}{T_2}\right)^4 = \left(\frac{e_2}{e_1}\right)\left(\frac{A_2}{A_1}\right)$$

$$\frac{T_1}{T_2} = \left(\frac{e_2}{e_1}\right)^{1/4} \cdot 1 \quad (\because A_1 = A_2)$$

Here, $e_1 = 0.2, e_2 = 0.8$

$$\therefore \quad \frac{T_1}{T_2} = \left(\frac{0.8}{0.2}\right)^{\frac{1}{4}}$$

$$= \left(\frac{4}{1}\right)^{\frac{1}{4}} = \left(\frac{2^2}{1^2}\right)^{\frac{1}{4}}$$

$$\frac{T_1}{T_2} = \left(\frac{2}{1}\right)^{1/2} = \sqrt{\frac{2}{1}}$$

$$T_1 : T_2 = \sqrt{2} : 1$$

65 *(c)* According to Stefan's law, the energy emitted by a body per second is directly proportional to the fourth power of the temperature of the body.

Here, the temperature of blue glass is more than that of red glass, so it will look brighter.

11

Thermodynamics

Quick Review

The branch of physics which deals with the study of transformation of heat energy into other forms of energy and *vice-versa* is called **thermodynamics.**

Thermal Equilibrium

A thermodynamical system is said to be in thermal equilibrium when macroscopic variables (like pressure, volume, temperature, mass, composition, etc.) that characterise the system do not change with time.

Zeroth Law of Thermodynamics

According to this law, "Two systems in thermal equilibrium with a third system separately, are also in thermal equilibrium with each other."

Thus, if A and B are separately in equilibrium with C, i.e. if $T_A = T_C$ and $T_B = T_C$, then this implies that $T_A = T_B$, i.e. the systems A and B are also in thermal equilibrium.

By zeroth law, temperature can be defined as the thermodynamic variable that determines whether the two systems in contact will be in thermal equilibrium or not.

Internal Energy, Heat and Work

- **Internal energy** of a system is defined as the total energy of the system due to molecular motion and molecular configuration.
  Internal energy, $U = U_K + U_P$
  where, U_K is internal kinetic energy due to molecular motion and U_P is internal potential energy due to molecular configuration.
- Ideal gas has only internal kinetic energy and no internal potential energy while real gases have both types of internal energy.
- The energy that is exchanged between a system and its surroundings due to temperature difference is called **heat**.
- By **work**, we mean work done by the system or on the system.
  Work done by a thermodynamic system,
  $$W = p \times \Delta V$$
  where, p = pressure and ΔV = change in volume.
- If system expands, then ΔV is positive, so W is positive, hence work is done by the system.
- If system contracts, then ΔV is negative, so W is negative, hence work is done on the system.

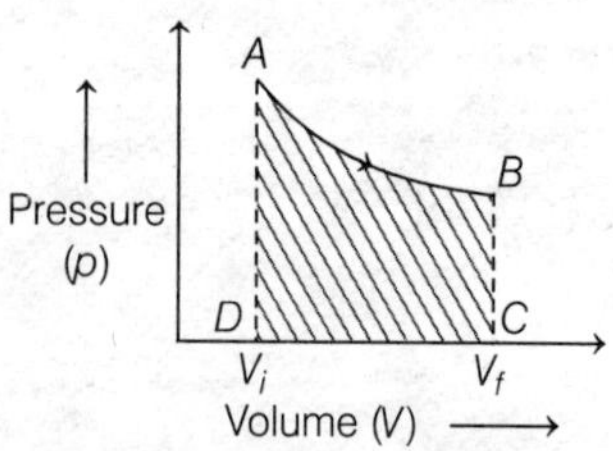

- Work done by a thermodynamic system is equal to the area enclosed between the P-V curve and the volume axis.
- Work done by a thermodynamic system depends not only upon the initial and final states of the system but also depend upon the path followed in the process.

First Law of Thermodynamics

Heat given to a thermodynamic system (ΔQ) is partially utilised in doing work (ΔW) against the surrounding and the remaining part increases the internal energy (ΔU) of the system.

Therefore, $\Delta Q = \Delta U + \Delta W$

In differential form, $dQ = dU + dW$

First law of thermodynamics is a restatement of the principle of conservation of energy.

Thermodynamic Processes

A thermodynamical process is said to take place when some changes occur in the state of a thermodynamic system, i.e. the thermodynamic parameters of the system change with time.

Different Thermodynamical Processes

Name of Process	Description	Form of Ist law of thermodynamics	Equation of State	Work Done	Indicator Diagram
Isochoric process	Volume remains constant, i.e. $\Delta V = 0$.	$\Delta Q = \Delta U$	$\frac{p}{T}$ = constant	$W = 0$	slope = ∞
Isothermal process	Temperature remains constant, i.e. $\Delta T = 0$.	$\Delta Q = \Delta W$	pV = constant	$W = nRT \ln \frac{p_1}{p_2}$	slope = $\frac{-p}{V}$
Isobaric process	Pressure remains constant, i.e. $\Delta p = 0$.	$\Delta Q = \Delta U + \Delta W$	$\frac{V}{T}$ = constant	$W = p(V_2 - V_1)$	slope = 0
Adiabatic process	No exchange of heat, i.e. $\Delta Q = 0$.	$\Delta W = -\Delta U$	$pV^\gamma = TV^{\gamma-1}$ $= p^{1-\gamma}T^\gamma$ = constant, where $\gamma = \frac{C_p}{C_V}$.	$W = \frac{p_1V_1 - p_2V_2}{\gamma - 1}$ $= \frac{nR}{\gamma-1}(T_1 - T_2)$	slope $= -\gamma\frac{p}{V}$
Cyclic process	Change in internal energy is zero, i.e. $\Delta U = 0$.	$\Delta Q = \Delta W$	—	$\Delta W = \Delta Q$	$A(V_1, p_1)$, M, N, $B(V_2, p_2)$, O, D, C

Heat Engine

A heat engine is a device which converts heat energy into mechanical energy. A heat engine consists of three parts

(i) Source of heat at higher temperature (ii) Working substance (iii) Sink of heat at lower temperature.

Thermal efficiency of a heat engine is given by

$$\eta = \frac{\text{Work done / cycle}}{\text{Total amount of heat absorbed / cycle}}$$

$$\eta = 1 - \frac{Q_2}{Q_1} = 1 - \frac{T_2}{T_1}$$

where, Q_1 is heat absorbed from the source, Q_2 is heat rejected to the sink and T_1 and T_2 are temperatures of source and sink.

Refrigerator or Heat Pump

A refrigerator or heat pump is basically a heat engine which runs in reverse direction.

The performance of a refrigerator is expressed by means of **coefficient of performance** β which is defined as the ratio of the heat extracted from the cold body to the work needed to transfer it to the hot body.

i.e. $$\beta = \frac{\text{Heat extracted}}{\text{Work done}} = \frac{Q_2}{W} = \frac{Q_2}{Q_1 - Q_2}$$

Coefficient of performance, $\beta = \frac{Q_2}{Q_1 - Q_2}$

- A perfect refrigerator is one which transfers heat from cold to hot body without doing work. i.e. $W = 0$, so that $Q_1 = Q_2$ and hence $\beta = \infty$.
- Air conditioners are basically refrigerators whose refrigerated space is a room or a building.
- In domestic refrigerator, inside portion acts as a cold reservoir and the surrounding act as hot reservoir.
- Relation between coefficient of performance and efficiency of heat engine, $\beta = \frac{1-\eta}{\eta}$.

Second Law of Thermodynamics

The second law of thermodynamics gives a fundamental limitation to the efficiency of a heat engine and the coefficient of performance of a refrigerator. It says that efficiency of a heat engine can never be unity (or 100%). This implies that heat released to the cold reservoir can never be made zero.

- **Kelvin's Statement** It is impossible to obtain a continuous supply of work from a body by cooling it to a temperature below the coldest of its surroundings.
- **Clausius' Statement** It is impossible to transfer heat from a lower temperature body to a higher temperature body without use of an external agency.
- **Planck's Statement** It is impossible to construct a heat engine that will convert heat completely into work. All these statements are equivalent as one can be obtained from the other.

Reversible and Irreversible Processes

- **Reversible Process** A process which can be reserved in such a way that the system and its surrounding return exactly to their initial states with no other changes in the universe is known as reversible process.
- **Irreversible Process** Any process which is not reversible exactly is an irreversible process.

Carnot's Engine

The reversible engine which operaters between two temperatures of source (T_1) and sink (T_2) is called Carnot heat engine. It is a theoretical engine free from all defects of a practical engine.

As the engine works, the working substance of the engine undergoes a cycle known as Carnot cycle..

Carnot cycle consists of following four strokes

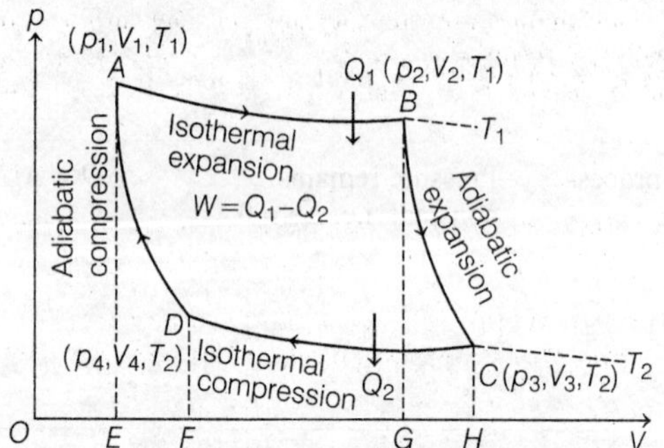

- Work done in first stroke **(Isothermal expansion)** along curve AB,

$$W_1 = \int_{V_1}^{V_2} pdV = RT_1 \log_e\left(\frac{V_2}{V_1}\right) = \text{area of } ABGEA.$$

- Work done in second stroke **(Adiabatic expansion)** along curve BC, $W_2 = \int_{V_2}^{V_3} pdV = \frac{R}{(\gamma - 1)}(T_1 - T_2)$

$$= \text{Area } BCHGB$$

- Work done in third stroke **(Isothermal compression)** along curve CD,

$$W_3 = -\int_{V_3}^{V_4} pdV = -RT_2 \log_e \frac{V_4}{V_3}$$

$$= RT_2 \log_e \frac{V_3}{V_4} = \text{area } CDFHC$$

- Work done in fourth stroke **(Adiabatic compression)** along DA,

$$W_4 = -\int_{V_4}^{V_1} p dV = \frac{-R}{\gamma - 1}(T_2 - T_1)$$

$$= \frac{R}{\gamma - 1}(T_1 - T_2) = \text{area } ADFEA$$

- Efficiency of Carnot engine, $\eta = 1 - \frac{T_2}{T_1}$
- Coefficient of performance of Carnot engine, $\beta = T_2 / T_1 - T_2$

Carnot Theorem

According to Carnot theorem

(*i*) A heat engine working between the two given temperatures T_1 of hot reservoir, i.e. source and T_2 of cold reservoir, i.e. sink cannot have an efficiency more than that of the Carnot engine.

(*ii*) The efficiency of the Carnot engine is independent of the nature of working substance.

Topical Practice Questions

All the exam questions of this chapter have been divided into 3 topics as listed below

Topic 1

First Law of Thermodynamics

2018

1 A sample of 0.1 g of water at 100° C and normal pressure (1.013×10^5 Nm^{-2}) requires 54 cal of heat energy to convert to steam at 100° C. If the volume of the steam produced is 167.1 cc, the change in internal energy of the sample is **[NEET]**

(a) 42.2 J (b) 208.7 J
(c) 104.3 J (d) 84.5 J

2 Assertion In isothermal process, whole of the heat energy supplied to the body is converted into internal energy.

Reason According to the first law of thermodynamics,

$$\Delta Q = \Delta U + \Delta W$$ **[AIIMS]**

(a) Both Assertion and Reason are correct and Reason is the correct explanation of Assertion.
(b) Both Assertion and Reason are correct but Reason is not the correct explanation of Assertion.
(c) Assertion is correct but Reason is incorrect.
(d) Assertion is incorrect but Reason is correct.

3 An ideal gas of mass m in a state A goes to another state B *via* three different processes as shown in figure. If Q_1, Q_2 and Q_3 denote the heat absorbed by the gas along the three paths, then **[AIIMS]**

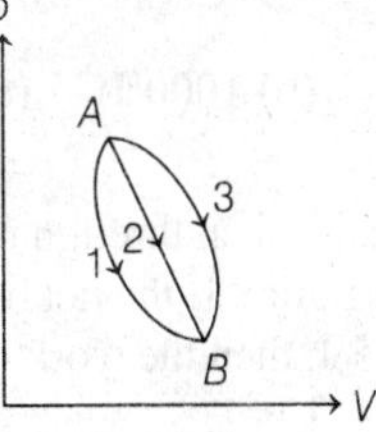

(a) $Q_1 < Q_2 < Q_3$
(b) $Q_1 < Q_2 = Q_3$
(c) $Q_1 = Q_2 > Q_3$
(d) $Q_1 > Q_2 > Q_3$

2017

4 One mole of an ideal diatomic gas undergoes transition from A to B along a path AB as shown below **[AIIMS]**

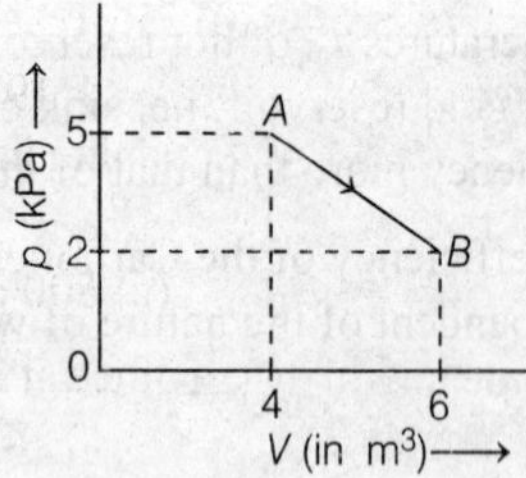

The change in internal energy of the gas during the transition is

(a) 20 kJ (b) – 12 kJ (c) – 20 kJ (d) 20 J

2014

5 The change in internal energy of a thermodynamical system which has absorbed 2 kcal of heat and done 400 J of work is (take, 1 cal = 4.2 J) **[Kerala CEE]**

(a) 2 kJ (b) 8 kJ (c) 3.5 kJ (d) 5.5 kJ (e) 4.2 kJ

2013

6 A gas is taken through the cycle $A \to B \to C \to A$, as shown in figure. What is the net work done by the gas?

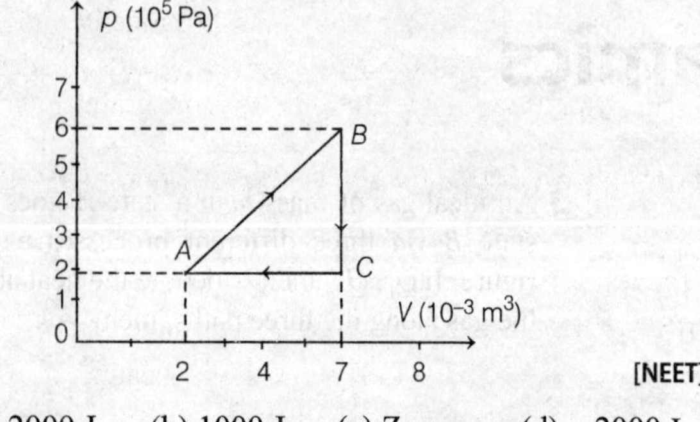

[NEET]

(a) 2000 J (b) 1000 J (c) Zero (d) – 2000 J

7 An ideal gas is taken through the cycle $A \to B \to C \to A$, as shown in figure. If the net heat supplied to the gas in the cycle is 5 J, then the work done by the gas in the process $C \to A$ is **[KCET]**

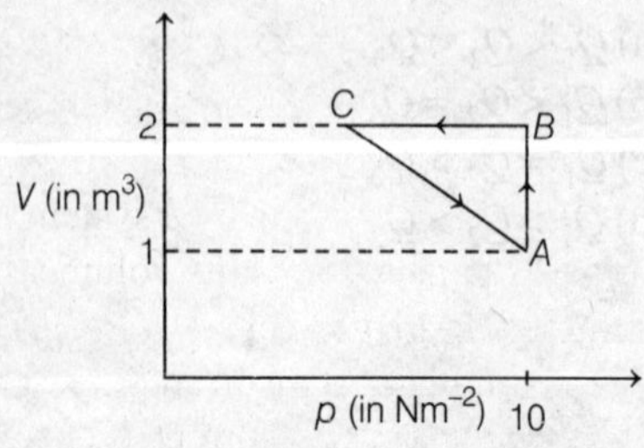

(a) – 5 J (b) – 10 J (c) – 15 J (d) – 20 J

2012

8 An ideal gas goes from state A to state B *via* three different processes as indicated in the p-V diagram. If Q_1, Q_2 and Q_3 indicate the heat absorbed by the three processes and $\Delta U_1, \Delta U_2$ and ΔU_3 indicate the change in internal energy along the three processes respectively, then **[CBSE AIPMT]**

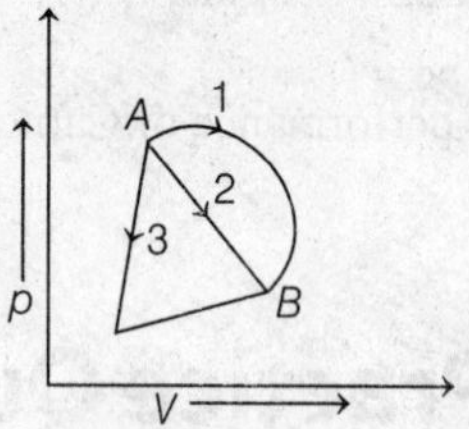

(a) $Q_1 > Q_2 > Q_3$ and $\Delta U_1 = \Delta U_2 = \Delta U_3$
(b) $Q_3 > Q_2 > Q_1$ and $\Delta U_1 = \Delta U_2 = \Delta U_3$
(c) $Q_1 = Q_2 = Q_3$ and $\Delta U_1 > \Delta U_2 > \Delta U_3$
(d) $Q_3 > Q_2 > Q_1$ and $\Delta U_1 > \Delta U_2 > \Delta U_3$

9 A thermodynamic system is taken through the cycle $ABCD$ as shown in figure. Heat rejected by the gas during the cycle is **[CBSE AIPMT]**

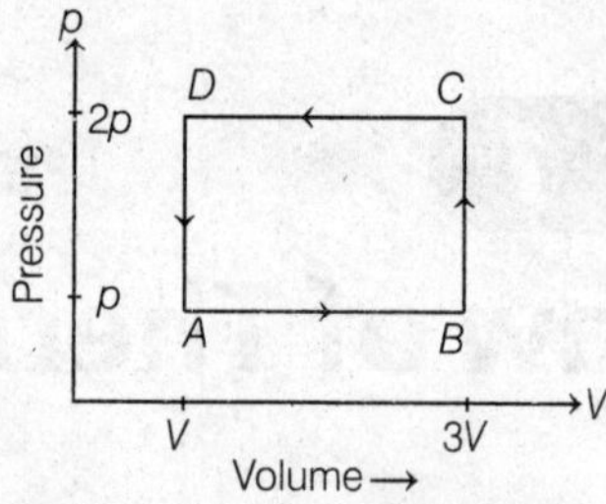

(a) $2pV$ (b) $4pV$
(c) $\frac{1}{2}pV$ (d) pV

2011

10 A perfect gas goes from state A to state B by absorbing 8×10^5 J of heat and doing 6.5×10^5 J of external work. It is now transferred between the same two states in another process in which it absorbs 10^5 J of heat. In the second process, **[AIIMS]**

(a) work done on the gas is 10^5 J
(b) work done on the gas is 0.5×10^5 J
(c) work done by the gas is 10^5 J
(d) work done by the gas is 0.5×10^5 J

11 A cylinder of fixed capacity (of 44.8 L) contains 2 moles of helium gas at STP. What is the amount of heat needed to raise the temperature of the gas in the cylinder by 20° C? (Take, $R = 8.31 \text{J mol}^{-1}\text{K}^{-1}$) **[AMU]**

(a) 996 J (b) 831 J
(c) 499 J (d) 374 J

2010

12 Two rigid boxes containing different ideal gases are placed on table. Box A contains one mole of nitrogen at temperature T_0, while box B contains one mole of helium at temperature $(7/3)\,T_0$. The boxes are then put into thermal contact with each other, and heat flows between them until the gases reach a common final temperature (ignore the heat capacity of boxes). Then, the final temperature of the gases T_f in terms of T_0 is **[AIIMS]**

(a) $T_f = \frac{3}{7}T_0$ (b) $T_f = \frac{7}{3}T_0$ (c) $T_f = \frac{3}{2}T_0$ (d) $T_f = \frac{5}{2}T_0$

13 The state of a thermodynamic system is represented by **[VMMC]**

(a) pressure only
(b) volume only
(c) pressure, volume and temperature
(d) number of moles

2008

14 If Q, E and W denote respectively the heat added, change in internal energy and the work done in a closed cycle process, then **[CBSE AIPMT]**

(a) $W = 0$ (b) $Q = W = 0$ (c) $E = 0$ (d) $Q = 0$

15 An ideal gas is taken through a cyclic thermodynamical process through four steps. The amounts of heat involved in these steps are $Q_1 = 5960$ J, $Q_2 = -5585$ J, $Q_3 = -2980$ J and $Q_4 = 3645$ J, respectively. The corresponding works involved are $W_1 = 2200$ J, $W_2 = -825$ J, $W_3 = -1100$ J and W_4 respectively. The value of W_4 is **[BHU]**

(a) 1315 J (b) 275 J (c) 765 J (d) 675 J

16 An ideal gas is taken around the cycle $ABCA$ as shown in the p-V diagram

The total work done by the gas during the cycle is **[Kerala CEE]**

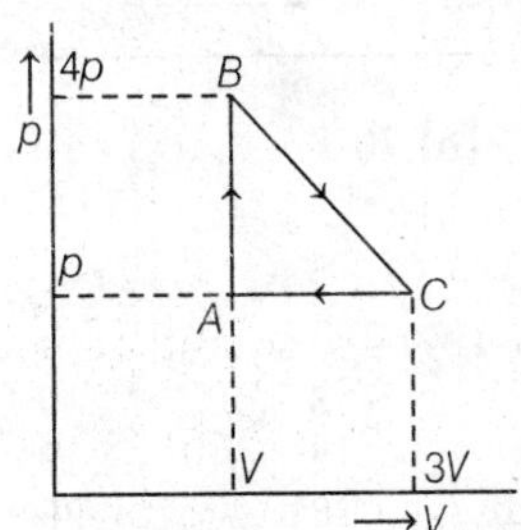

(a) pV (b) $2\,pV$ (c) $4\,pV$ (d) $3\,pV$
(e) $6\,pV$

17 Which of the following parameters does not characterise the thermodynamic state of matter? **[RPMT]**

(a) Temperature (b) Pressure
(c) Work (d) Volume

2007

18 1 cm^3 of water at its boiling point absorbs 540 cal of heat to become steam with a volume of 1671 cm^3. If the atmospheric pressure $= 1.013 \times 10^5$ Nm^{-2} and the mechanical equivalent of heat $= 4.19$ J cal, the energy spent in this process in overcoming intermolecular forces is **[Manipal]**

(a) 540 cal (b) 40 cal (c) 500 cal (d) zero

19 During the melting of a slab of ice at 273 K at atmospheric pressure, **[RPMT]**

(a) positive work is done by the ice-water system on the atmosphere
(b) positive work is done on the ice-water system by the atmosphere
(c) internal energy of ice-water system decreases
(d) None of the above

20 Which of the following is not a state function? **[Haryana PMT]**

(a) Work done at constant pressure
(b) Enthalpy
(c) Work done by conservative force
(d) Work done by non-conservative force

21 Which of the following statements is true? **[J&K CET]**

(a) Internal energy of a gas depends only on the state of the gas.
(b) In an isothermal process, change in internal energy is maximum.
(c) Area under pressure, volume graph equals to heat supplied in any process.
(d) Work done is state dependent but not path dependent.

22 A gas is compressed at a constant pressure of 50 Nm^{-2} from a volume of 10 m^3 to a volume of 4 m^3. Energy of 100 J is thus added to the gas by heating, its internal energy is **[Punjab PMET]**

(a) decreased by 200 J
(b) increased by 100 J
(c) increased by 300 J
(d) increased by 400 J

23 Consider the following two statements and choose the correct answer. **[EAMCET]**

I. If heat is added to a system, its temperature must always increase.
II. If positive work is done by a system in thermodynamic process, its volume must increase.

(a) Both I and II are correct
(b) I is correct, but II is incorrect
(c) II is correct, but I is incorrect
(d) Both I and II are incorrect

24 If 150 J of heat is added to a system and the work done by the system is 110 J, then change in internal energy will be [BCECE]

(a) 40 J (b) 110 J
(c) 150 J (d) 260 J

2006

25 An ideal gas is taken through a cycle $ABCA$ as shown in the p-V diagram. The work done during the cycle is

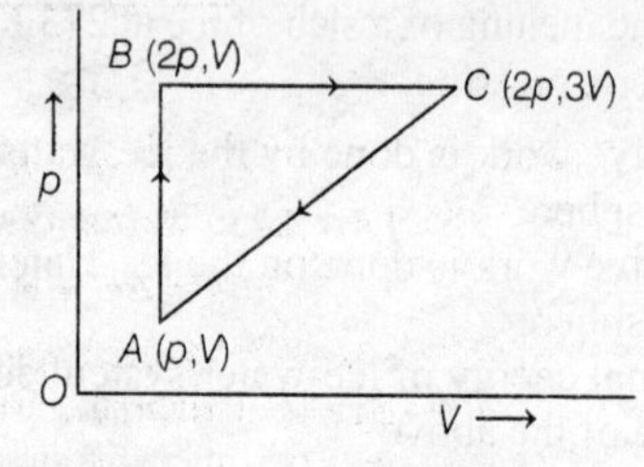

[Kerala CEE]

(a) $\frac{1}{2}pV$ (b) $2pV$
(c) $4pV$ (d) pV
(e) zero

26 In a thermodynamic process, pressure of a fixed mass of a gas is changed in such a manner that the gas molecule gives out 30 J of heat and 10 J of work is done on the gas. If the initial internal energy of the gas is 40 J, then the final internal energy will be [RPMT]

(a) − 20 J (b) 20 J (c) 80 J (d) 3 J

27 An ideal gas after going through a series of four thermodynamic states in order, reaches the initial state again (cyclic process). The amounts of heat and work involved in these states are

$$Q_1 = 6000\text{ J}, Q_2 = -5500\text{ J},$$
$$Q_3 = -3000\text{ J and } Q_4 = 3500\text{ J};$$
$$W_1 = 2500\text{ J}, W_2 = -1000\text{ J},$$
$$W_3 = -1200\text{ J and } W_4 = x\text{ J}.$$

The ratio of net work done by the gas to the total heat absorbed by the gas is η. The value of x and η are nearly

(a) 500, 7.5% (b) 700, 10.5% [EAMCET]
(c) 1000, 21% (d) 1500, 15%

28 If temperature is increased by 1 K at constant volume, then work done on the gas is [JCECE]

(a) $\frac{5}{2}R$ (b) $\frac{3}{2}R$ (c) zero (d) $\frac{1}{2}R$

2005

29 First law of thermodynamics is a consequence of the conservation of [Punjab PMET]

(a) energy (b) charge
(c) heat (d) All of these

30 An ideal monoatomic gas is taken around the cycle $ABCDA$ as shown in the p-V diagram. The work done during the cycle is given by [KCET]

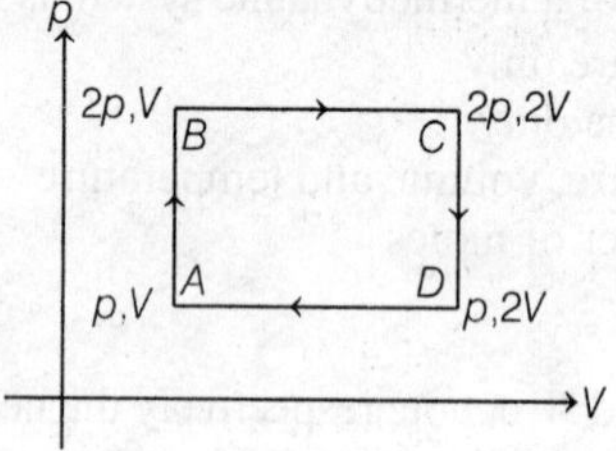

(a) $\frac{1}{2}pV$ (b) pV (c) $2pV$ (d) $4pV$

31 Which is not a path function? [BCECE]

(a) ΔQ (b) $\Delta Q + \Delta W$ (c) ΔW (d) $\Delta Q - \Delta W$

32 The p-V diagram of a system undergoing thermodynamic transformation is shown in figure. The work done by the system in going from $A \to B \to C$ is 30 J and 40 J heat is given to the system. The change in internal energy between A and C is [BCECE]

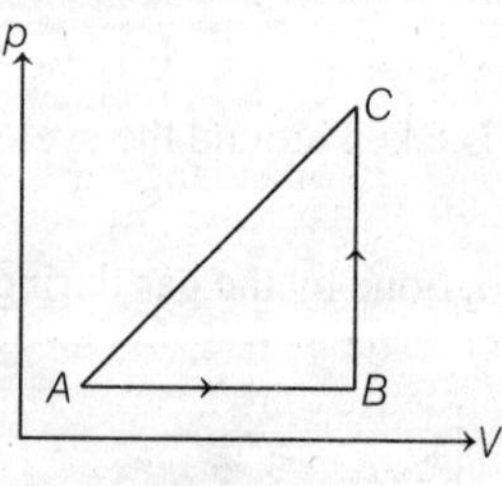

(a) 10 J (b) 70 J (c) 84 J (d) 134 J

Answers

1 (b)	2 (d)	3 (a)	4 (c)	5 (b)	6 (b)	7 (a)	8 (a)	9 (a)	10 (b)
11 (c)	12 (c)	13 (c)	14 (c)	15 (c)	16 (d)	17 (c)	18 (c)	19 (b)	20 (d)
21 (a)	22 (d)	23 (c)	24 (a)	25 (d)	26 (b)	27 (b)	28 (c)	29 (a)	30 (b)
31 (d)	32 (a)								

Explanations

1 (b) According to the question,

heat spent during the conversion of sample of water at 100°C to steam is

$$\Delta Q = 54 \text{ cal}$$
$$= 54 \times 4.18 \text{ J}$$
$$= 225.72 \text{ J}$$

Normal pressure, $p = 1.013 \times 10^5 \text{ Nm}^{-2}$

Net work done during the conversion would be given as

$$\Delta W = p\Delta V = p(V_{\text{steam}} - V_{\text{water}})$$

Here, $V_{\text{steam}} = 167.1 \text{ cc}$

$$= 167.1 \times 10^{-6} \text{ m}^3$$

$$V_{\text{water}} = 0.1 \text{ g} = 0.1 \text{cc}$$
$$= 0.1 \times 10^{-6} \text{ m}^3$$

$$\therefore \quad \Delta W = 1.013 \times 10^5 [(167.1 - 0.1) \times 10^{-6}]$$
$$= 1.013 \times 167 \times 10^{-1}$$
$$= 16.917 \text{ J}$$

Now, by the first law of thermodynamics,

$$\Delta Q = \Delta U + \Delta W$$

where, ΔU is the change in internal energy of the sample.

$$\Rightarrow \quad \Delta U = \Delta Q - \Delta W \quad \ldots \text{(i)}$$

Substituting the values in Eq. (i), we get

$$\Delta U = 225.72 - 16.917$$
$$= 208.7 \text{ J}$$

2 (d) As in isothermal process temperature remains constant internal energy ($\Delta U = 0$), hence there is no change in internal energy of the system. Hence, the energy taken by the gas is utilized by doing work against external pressure.

Hence, whole heat energy given to the body at isothermal process gets converted into work done.

But $\Delta Q = \Delta U + \Delta W$ is first law of thermodynamics, hence Assertion is incorrect but Reason is correct.

3 (a) Initial and final states are same in all the process.

Hence, $\Delta U = 0$ is same for each case.

$$\therefore \quad \Delta Q = \Delta W$$

Area enclosed by curve with volume,

$$\because \quad (\text{Area})_1 < (\text{Area})_2 < (\text{Area})_3$$
$$\therefore \quad Q_1 < Q_2 < Q_3$$

4 (c) For a diatomic gas,

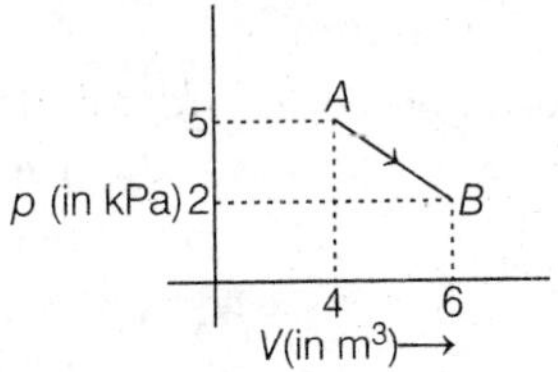

$$C_V = \frac{5}{2}R$$

The change in internal energy of gas from A to B is

$$\Delta U = nC_V dT$$
$$= n\left(\frac{5R}{2}\right)(T_B - T_A)$$
$$= nR\frac{5}{2}\left(\frac{p_B V_B}{nR} - \frac{p_A V_A}{nR}\right)$$
$$= \frac{5}{2}(2 \times 10^3 \times 6 - 5 \times 10^3 \times 4)$$
$$= \frac{5}{2} \times (-8 \times 10^3)$$
$$= -\frac{4 \times 10^4}{2}$$
$$= -20 \text{ kJ}$$

5 (b) According to first law of thermodynamics,

i.e. $Q = \Delta U + W$

$$Q = 2 \text{ kcal}$$
$$= 2000 \times 4.2$$
$$= 8400 \text{ J}$$
$$W = 400 \text{ J}$$
$$8400 = \Delta U + 400$$
$$\Delta U = 8400 - 400$$
$$\Delta U = 8000 \text{ J}$$

So, change in internal energy,

$$\Delta U = 8 \text{ kJ}$$

6 (b) Net work done by the gas = Area enclosed in p-V curve, i.e. area of ΔABC.

$$W_{\text{net}} = \frac{1}{2} \times 5 \times 10^{-3} \times 4 \times 10^5 \text{J}$$
$$= 10^3 \text{ J} = 1000 \text{ J}$$

7 (a) Here, process is cyclic, so change in internal energy is zero.

We know that, work done by gas is given by $W = p\Delta V$, where p is pressure and ΔV is the change in volume.

Total work done by gas is

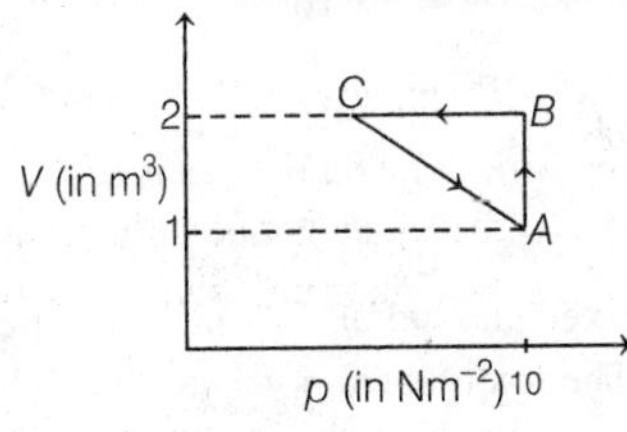

$$W = W_{AB} + W_{BC} + W_{CA} \quad \ldots \text{(i)}$$

First law of thermodynamics,

$$\Delta Q = \Delta U + W \quad \ldots \text{(ii)}$$

where, ΔQ is heat supplied, ΔU is the change in internal energy which is zero and W is the work done.

$$\therefore \quad W_{AB} = p\Delta V = 10(2 - 1) = 10 \text{ J}$$
$$W_{BC} = p\Delta V = 2 \times 0 = 0$$

Hence, Eqs. (i) and (ii) will be written as

$$5 = 0 + (10 + 0 + W_{CA})$$
$$\Rightarrow \quad W_{CA} = -5 \text{J}$$

Work done by the gas in the process

$$C \to A, W_{CA} = -5 \text{ J}$$

8 (a) For all processes 1, 2 and 3

Change in internal energy, i.e.

$$\Delta U = U_B - U_A$$
$$\therefore \quad \Delta U_1 = \Delta U_2 = \Delta U_3$$

Now, $\quad Q = \Delta U + \Delta W$

Now, ΔW = work done by the gas, i.e. area under p-V curve.

As, area (1) > area (2) > area (3)

$$\therefore \quad \Delta W_1 > \Delta W_2 > \Delta W_3$$
$$\therefore \quad Q_1 > Q_2 > Q_3$$

9. (a) For given cyclic process, $\Delta U = 0$

$$\therefore \quad Q = W$$

Also, W = Area enclosed by the curve

$$= AB \times AD$$
$$= (2p - p)(3V - V)$$
$$= p \times 2V$$

$\therefore$ Heat rejected by the gas during the cycle $= 2pV$.

10 (b) According to first law of thermodynamics,

$$dU = dQ - dW$$
$$dU = 8 \times 10^5 - 6.5 \times 10^5$$
$$= 1.5 \times 10^5 \text{ J}$$

In the second process, dU remains the same.

$$\therefore \quad dW = dQ - dU$$
$$= 1\times 10^5 - 1.5\times 10^5$$
$$dW = -0.5\times 10^5 \text{ J} \simeq 0.5\times 10^5 \text{ J}$$

$\therefore$ Work done on the gas is 0.5×10^5 J

11 (c) Since, the volume of cylinder is fixed and helium is a monoatomic gas. The internal energy $= \mu C_V \Delta T$

$$\Rightarrow \quad U = \frac{1}{2} f\mu R\Delta T \left[\because C_V = \frac{1}{2} fR\right]$$
$$U = \frac{1}{2}\times 3\times 2\times 8.31\times 20$$
$$= 498.6 \approx 499 \text{ J} \quad (\because f = 3)$$

12 (c) The system of two rigid boxes is shown in figure

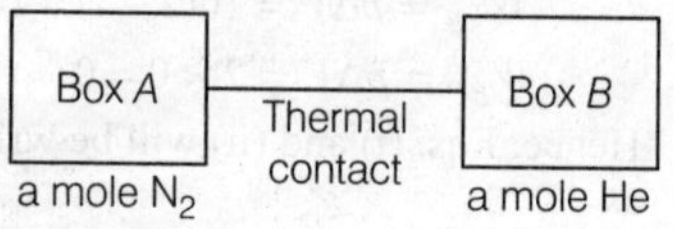

We know that, $\Delta U = \frac{1}{2} f\mu R\Delta T$

$f = 5$ for nitrogen

and $f = 3$ for helium.

Change in internal energy at box A,

i.e. $\Delta U_A = 1\times \frac{5R}{2}(T_f - T_0)$

Change in internal energy at box B,

i.e. $\Delta U_B = 1\times \frac{3R}{2}\left(T_f - \frac{7}{3}T_0\right)$

Now, $\Delta U_A + \Delta U_B = 0$

$$\frac{5R}{2}(T_f - T_0) + \frac{3R}{2}\left(T_f - \frac{7T_0}{3}\right) = 0$$
$$5T_f - 5T_0 + 3T_f - 7T_0 = 0$$
$$\Rightarrow \quad 8T_f = 12T_0$$
$$\Rightarrow \quad T_f = \frac{12}{8}T_0 = \frac{3}{2}T_0$$

13 (c) In thermodynamics, the value of a state variable depends only on the particular state not on the path used to attain that state. Pressure (p), volume (V), temperature (T) and mass (m) are state variables.

14 (c) In a cyclic process, a system starts from one point and ends at the same point. In this case, the change in the internal energy must again be zero and therefore the thermal energy added to the system must be equal the work done during the cycle, i.e., in a cyclic process, $\Delta U = 0$ or $E = 0$.

15 (c) Total amount of heat,

$$\Delta Q = Q_1 + Q_2 + Q_3 + Q_4$$
$$= 5960 - 5585 - 2980 + 3645$$
$$= 1040 \text{ J}$$

Total work done,

$$\Delta W = W_1 + W_2 + W_3 + W_4$$
$$= 2200 - 825 - 1100 + W_4$$
$$= 275 + W_4$$

For a cyclic process,

$$\Delta U = 0, \text{ i.e. } U_f - U_i = 0$$

From first law of thermodynamics,

$$\Delta Q = \Delta U + \Delta W$$
$$1040 = 0 + 275 + W_4 \text{ or } W_4 = 765 \text{ J}$$

16 (d) Work done = Area enclosed by triangle

$$= \frac{1}{2} AB\times AC$$
$$= \frac{1}{2}(4p - p)\times(3V - V)$$
$$= \frac{1}{2}3p\times 2V = 3pV$$

17 (c) Work does not characterise the thermodynamic state of matter, it is a path function giving only relationship between two quantities.

18 (c) Change in volume, i.e.

$$\Delta V = V_2 - V_1$$
$$= 1671 - 1 = 1670 \text{ cm}^3$$
$$= 1670\times 10^{-6} \text{ m}^3$$

Work done by the system,

$$W = p\Delta V$$
$$= 1.013\times 10^5\times 1670\times 10^{-6}$$
$$= 1691.71\times 10^{-1} \text{ J}$$
$$= 169.171 \text{ J}$$

(as, we know 1 cal = 4.2 J)

$$= \frac{169.171}{4.2} = 40.06 \text{ cal}$$

Total energy spent in boiling to overcome intermolecular force $= 540 - 40.06$

$$= 499.93 \text{ cal}$$
$$\approx 500 \text{ cal}$$

19 (b) When a slab of ice at 273 K melts, volume of water formed is less than the volume of ice melted, i.e. volume decreases. Therefore, work done by ice-water system is negative or in other words positive work is done by the atmosphere on the ice-water system.

This increases the internal energy of ice-water system becasue

$$\Delta Q = \Delta U + \Delta W$$

so $\quad \Delta Q + \Delta W = \Delta U$

20 (d) The value of a state function depends only on the particular state, not on the path used to attain that state, while pressure, volume, temperature and mass are state variable but work done by non-conservative force is not a state function.

21 (a) In taking a system from one state to another state by different processes, the heat transferred Q and work done W are different, but their difference $Q - W$ is same for all processes. It gives the internal energy of the system

$$\Delta U = Q - W$$

Thus, internal energy U of a thermodynamic system is a characteristic property of the state of the system, it does not matter how that state has been obtained.

22 (d) Change in volume of a gas,

$$\Delta V = V_2 - V_1$$
$$= 4 - 10 = -6 \text{ m}^3$$

As volume decreases, work is done on the gas and so it is negative

$$W = p\Delta V = 50\times(-6)$$
$$= -300 \text{ J}$$

Heat supplied, $Q = 100$ J

According to first law of thermodynamics, change in internal energy is $\Delta U = Q - W$

$$= 100 - (-300)$$
$$= 400 \text{ J}$$

It means that internal energy increase by 400 J.

23 (c) In cyclic and isothermal processes, energy supplied to a system does not change temperature of the system. If gas expands ($\Delta W = +$ ve), then volume of gas system increases.

24 (a) From the first law of thermodynamics, if an amount of heat Q is given to a system, a part of it is used in increasing the internal energy ΔU of the system and the rest in doing work W by the system.

$$\therefore \quad Q = \Delta U + W$$
$$\Rightarrow \quad \Delta U = Q - W$$
$$\Rightarrow \quad \Delta U = 150 - 110$$
$$= 40 \text{ J}$$

25 (*d*) Work done = Area of ΔABC

$$= \frac{AB \times BC}{2} = \frac{(2p - p) \times (3V - V)}{2} = \frac{p \times 2V}{2} = pV$$

26 (*b*) Given, $dQ = -30$ J

(negative sign appears as the heat is going out from the system)

$$dW = -10 \text{ J}, U_i = 40 \text{ J}$$

Using the relation,

$$dQ = dU + dW$$
$$-30 = (U_f - 40) + (-10)$$
$$U_f = 20 \text{ J}$$

27 (*b*) According to the given problem,

Total heat produced,

$$\Delta Q = Q_1 + Q_2 + Q_3 + Q_4$$
$$= 6000 - 5500 - 3000 + 3500$$
$$\Delta Q = 9500 - 8500 = 1000 \text{ J}$$

Total work done by ideal gas,

$$\Delta W = W_1 + W_2 + W_3 + W_4$$
$$= 2500 - 1000 - 1200 + x$$
$$= 300 + x$$

For cyclic process,

$$U_F = U_I, \Delta U = U_F - U_I = 0$$

So, from first law of thermodynamics,

i.e., $\Delta Q = \Delta U + \Delta W$

We have $1000 = (300 + x) + 0$

i.e., $x = 1000 - 300$

$= 700$ J

Efficiency of a cycle is defined as

$$\eta = \frac{\text{Work done}}{\text{Input heat}} = \frac{\Delta W}{Q_1 + Q_4} = \frac{\Delta Q}{(Q_1 + Q_4)}$$
$$= \frac{1000}{(6000 + 3500)} = \frac{1000}{9500} \times 100$$
$$= 0.105 \times 100 = 10.5\%$$

28 (*c*) Work done on a gas is given by

$$W = p\Delta V$$

where, p is the pressure and ΔV is the change in volume.

Given, $\Delta V = 0$, therefore $W = p \times 0 = 0$.

29 (*a*) As we know that, first law of thermodynamics is a consequences of the conservation of energy.

i.e. $dQ = dU + dW$

where, dQ is heat given to the system, dU is internal energy and dW is work done by the system.

30 (*b*) Work done during the cycle

= Area enclosed by *p*-V graph

= Area of region $ABCD$

$= AD \times CD$

$= (2V - V) \times (2p - p)$

$= pV$

31 (*d*) According to first law of thermodynamics,

i.e., $dQ = dU + dW$

So, heat energy, i.e. dQ is a state function. Hence, $\Delta Q - \Delta W (= dU)$ is not a path function.

32 (*a*) Since, work is done by the system, so it is positive, therefore

$$\Delta W = 30 \text{ J}$$

Heat given to the system,

$$\Delta Q = 40 \text{ J}$$

According to first law of thermodynamics, change in internal energy is given by

$$\Delta U = \Delta Q - \Delta W$$
$$= 40 - 30 = 10 \text{ J}$$

Topic 2
Thermodynamic Processes

2019

1 In which of the following processes, heat is neither absorbed nor released by a system? **[NEET]**

(a) Adiabatic (b) Isobaric
(c) Isochoric (d) Isothermal

2 **Assertion** In adiabatic process, work is independent of path.

Reason In adiabatic process, work done is equal to negative of change in internal energy. **[AIIMS]**

(a) Both Assertion and Reason are correct and Reason is the correct explanation of Assertion.
(b) Both Assertion and Reason are correct but Reason is not the correct explanation of Assertion.
(c) If Assertion is correct but Reason is incorrect.
(d) Both Assertion and Reason are incorrect.

2018

3 The efficiency of an ideal gas with adiabatic exponent γ for the shown cyclic process would be **[JIPMER]**

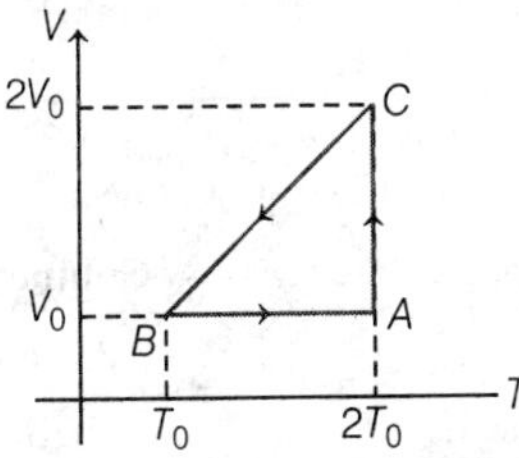

(a) $\dfrac{(2\ln 2 - 1)}{\gamma / (\gamma - 1)}$ (b) $\dfrac{(1 - 1\ln 2)}{\gamma / (\gamma - 1)}$

(c) $\dfrac{(2\ln 2 + 1)}{\gamma / (\gamma - 1)}$ (d) $\dfrac{(2\ln 2 - 1)}{\gamma / (\gamma + 1)}$

2017

4 **Assertion** Molar heat capacity cannot be defined for isothermal process.

Reason In isothermal process, p-V *versus* T graph is a dot. [AIIMS]

(a) Both Assertion and Reason are correct and Reason is the correct explanation of Assertion.
(b) Both Assertion and Reason are correct but Reason is not the correct explanation of Assertion.
(c) Assertion is correct but Reason is incorrect.
(d) Reason is correct but Assertion is incorrect.

5 **Assertion** In adiabatic expansion process, the product of p and V always decreases.

Reason In adiabatic expansion process, work is done by the gas at the cost of internal energy of gas. [AIIMS]

(a) Both Assertion and Reason are correct and Reason is the correct explanation of Assertion.
(b) Both Assertion and Reason are correct but Reason is not the correct explanation of Assertion.
(c) Assertion is correct but Reason is incorrect.
(d) Reason is correct but Assertion is incorrect.

6 p-V plots for two gases during adiabatic process as shown in figure. Plots 1 and 2 should correspond respectively to [JIPMER]

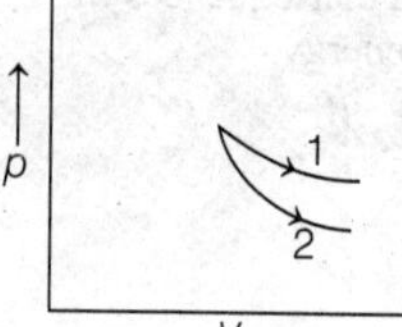

(a) He and O_2
(b) O_2 and He
(c) He and Ar
(d) O_2 and N_2

7 Thermodynamic processes are indicated in the following diagram

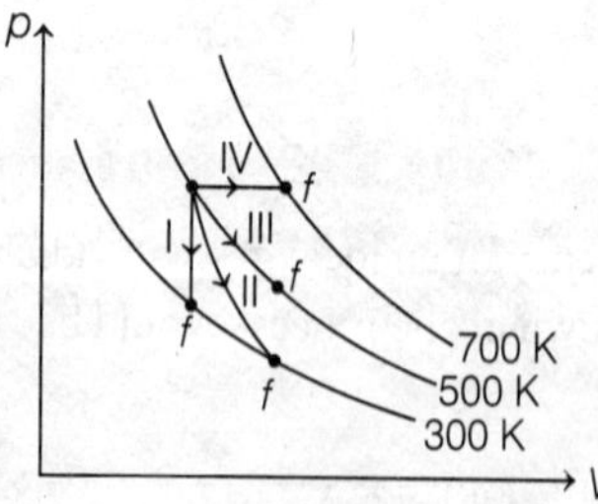

Match the following columns.

	Column I		Column II
P.	Process I	A.	Adiabatic
Q.	Process II	B.	Isobaric
R.	Process III	C.	Isochoric
S.	Process IV	D.	Isothermal

[NEET]

(a) P→ A, Q→ C, R→ D, S→ B
(b) P→ C, Q→ A, R→ D, S→ B
(c) P→ C, Q→ D, R→ B, S→ A
(d) P→ D, Q→ B, R→ A, S→ C

2016

8 A gas is compressed isothermally to half its initial volume. The same gas is compressed separately through an adiabatic process until its volume is again reduced to half. Then [NEET]

(a) compressing the gas through adiabatic process will require more work to be done
(b) compressing the gas isothermally or adiabatically will require the same amount of work
(c) which of the case (whether compression through isothermal or through adiabatic process) requires more work will depend upon the atomicity of the gas
(d) compressing the gas isothermally will require more work to be done

2014

9 A monoatomic gas at a pressure p, having a volume V expands isothermally to a volume $2V$ and then adiabatically to a volume $16V$. The final pressure of the gas is (take, $\gamma = \frac{5}{3}$) [CBSE AIPMT]

(a) $64p$ (b) $32p$ (c) $\frac{p}{64}$ (d) $16p$

10 If for hydrogen $C_p - C_V = m$ and for nitrogen $C_p - C_V = n$, where C_p and C_V refers to specific heat per unit mass respectively at constant pressure and constant volume. The relation between m and n is (molecular weight of hydrogen = 2 and molecular weight of nitrogen = 28) [AIIMS, UP CPMT]

(a) $n = 14m$ (b) $n = 7m$ (c) $m = 7n$ (d) $m = 14n$

11 The p- T relation for an adiabatic expansion is [UK PMT]

(a) $p^{\gamma}T^{\gamma-1}$ = constant (b) $p^{\gamma-1}T^{\gamma}$ = constant
(c) $p^{\gamma}T^{1-\gamma}$ = constant (d) $p^{1-\gamma}T^{\gamma}$ = constant

12 In isochoric process, [UP CPMT]

(a) $\Delta W = 0$ (b) $\Delta U = 0$ (c) $\Delta Q = 0$ (d) $\Delta T = 0$

2013

13 During an adiabatic process, the pressure of a gas is found to be proportional to the cube of its temperature. The ratio of $\frac{C_p}{C_V}$ for the gas is [NEET]

(a) $\frac{4}{3}$ (b) 2 (c) $\frac{5}{3}$ (d) $\frac{3}{2}$

14 The molar specific heats of an ideal gas at constant pressure and volume are denoted by C_p and C_V respectively. If $\gamma = \frac{C_p}{C_V}$ and R is the universal gas constant, then C_V is equal to [NEET]

(a) $\frac{1+\gamma}{1-\gamma}$ (b) $\frac{R}{(\gamma-1)}$ (c) $\frac{(\gamma-1)}{R}$ (d) γR

2012

15 One mole of an ideal gas goes from an initial state A to final state B *via* two processes. It first undergoes isothermal expansion from volume V to $3V$ and then its volume is reduced from $3V$ to V at constant pressure. The correct p-V diagram representing the two processes is **[CBSE AIPMT]**

(a)
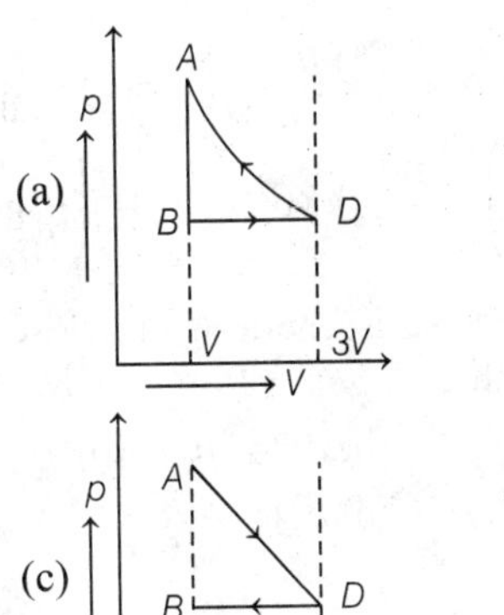

(b)
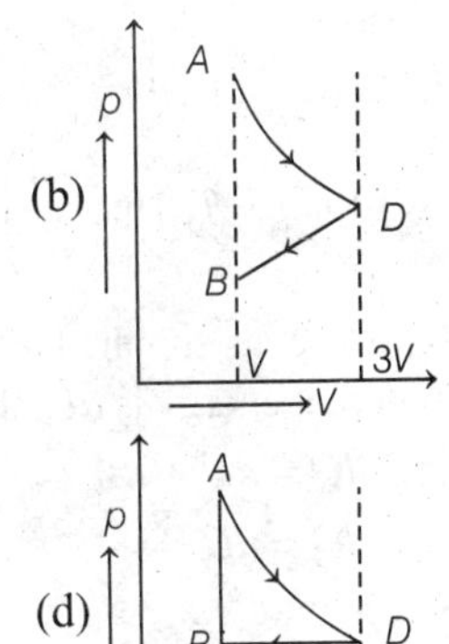

(c)

(d)

16 310 J of heat is required to raise the temperature of 2 mol of an ideal gas at constant pressure from 25°C to 35°C. The amount of heat required to raise the temperature of the gas through the same range at constant volume is **[AFMC]**

(a) 384 J (b) 144 J
(c) 276 J (d) 452 J

17 When an ideal gas in a cylinder was compressed isothermally by a piston, the work done on the gas was found to be 1.5×10^4 J. During the process about **[AFMC]**

(a) 3.6×10^3 cal of heat flowed out from the gas
(b) 3.6×10^3 cal of heat flowed into the gas
(c) 1.5×10^4 cal of heat flowed into the gas
(d) 1.5×10^4 cal of heat flowed out from the gas

2011

18 Ten moles of an ideal gas at constant temperature 600 K is compressed from 100 L to 10 L. The work done in the process is **[AFMC]**

(a) 4.11×10^4 J (b) -4.11×10^4 J
(c) 11.4×10^4 J (d) -11.4×10^4 J

19 Work done per mole in an isothermal change is **[UP CPMT]**

(a) $RT \log_{10} \frac{V_2}{V_1}$ (b) $RT \log_{10} \frac{V_1}{V_2}$
(c) $RT \log_e \frac{V_2}{V_1}$ (d) $RT \log_e \frac{V_1}{V_2}$

20 No heat flows between the system and surroundings, then the thermodynamic process is **[Kerala CEE]**

(a) isothermal (b) isochoric
(c) adiabatic (d) isobaric
(e) cyclic

21 For a certain mass of gas, the isothermal curves between p and V at T_1 and T_2 temperatures are 1 and 2 as shown in figure. Then, **[CMC]**

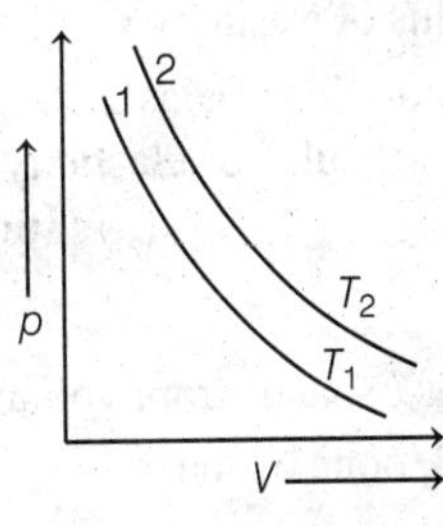

(a) $T_1 = T_2$ (b) $T_1 < T_2$
(c) $T_1 > T_2$
(d) Nothing can be predicted

2010

22 **Assertion** The isothermal curves intersect each other at a certain point.
Reason The isothermal changes take place rapidly, so the isothermal curves have very little slope. **[AIIMS]**

(a) Both Assertion and Reason are correct and Reason is the correct explanation of Assertion.
(b) Both Assertion and Reason are correct but Reason is not the correct explanation of Assertion.
(c) Assertion is correct but Reason is incorrect.
(d) Both Assertion and Reason are incorrect.
(e) Assertion is incorrect but Reason is correct.

23 During an adiabatic expansion, the increase in volume is associated with which of the following possibilities w.r.t. pressure and temperature? **[AMU]**

	Pressure	Temperature		Pressure	Temperature
(a)	increase	increase	(b)	decrease	decrease
(c)	increase	decrease	(d)	decrease	increase

2008

24 A monoatomic gas is suddenly compressed to $(1/8)$th of its initial volume adiabatically. The ratio of its final pressure to the initial pressure is (given, the ratio of the specific heats of the given gas is 5/3) **[AFMC]**

(a) 32 (b) 40/3
(c) 24/5 (d) 8

25 For an adiabatic process, the relation between V and T is given by **[Punjab PMET]**

(a) $TV^{\gamma} =$ constant (b) $T^{\gamma}V =$ constant
(c) $TV^{1-\gamma} =$ constant (d) $TV^{\gamma-1} =$ constant

26 The temperature of the system decreases in the process of **[Punjab PMET]**
(a) free expansion (b) adiabatic expansion
(c) isothermal expansion (d) isothermal compression

27 In which of the processes, does the internal energy of the system remains constant? **[KCET]**
(a) Adiabatic (b) Isochoric (c) Isobaric (d) Isothermal

28 Isobaric modulus of elasticity is equal to **[KCET]**
(a) isochoric modulus of elasticity
(b) isothermal modulus of elasticity
(c) zero (d) infinite

2007

29 A sample of gas expands from volume V_1 to V_2. The amount of work done by the gas is greatest when the expansion is **[AFMC]**
(a) adiabatic (b) isobaric
(c) isothermal (d) equal in all above cases

30 The internal energy of an ideal gas increases during an isothermal process when the gas is **[AFMC]**
(a) expanded by adding more molecules to it
(b) expanded by adding more heat to it
(c) expanded against zero pressure
(d) compressed by doing work on it

31 In an adiabatic change, the pressure and temperature of a monoatomic gas are related with relation $p \propto T^C$, where, C is equal to **[MHT CET]**
(a) $\frac{5}{4}$ (b) $\frac{5}{3}$ (c) $\frac{5}{2}$ (d) $\frac{3}{5}$

32 We consider a thermodynamic system. If ΔU represents the increase in its internal energy and W the work done by the system, which of the following statements is true?
(a) $\Delta U = -W$ an adiabatic process **[MHT CET]**
(b) $\Delta U = W$ an isothermal process
(c) $\Delta U = -W$ an isothermal process
(d) $\Delta U = W$ an adiabatic process

33 At 27°C a gas suddenly compressed such that its pressure becomes $\frac{1}{8}$th of original pressure. The temperature of the gas will be $(\gamma = 5/3)$ **[BCECE]**
(a) −142°C (b) 300 K (c) 327°C (d) 420 K

2006

34 A thermo flask made of stainless steel contains several tiny lead shots. If the flask is quickly shaken up and down several times, the temperature of lead shots **[Kerala CEE]**
(a) increases by adiabatic process
(b) increases by isothermal process
(c) decreases by adiabatic process
(d) remains same
(e) first decreases and then increases

35 If there is a straight line parallel to volume axis in a p-V diagram, then it is a ...... graph. **[RPMT]**
(a) isochoric (b) isobaric
(c) isothermal (d) None of these

36 If the volume of gas is changed from V_1 to V_2 isothermally, then work done is **[JCECE]**
(a) $RT \ln\left(\frac{V_1}{V_2}\right)$ (b) $RT \ln\left(\frac{V_2}{V_1}\right)$
(c) $R(T_2 - T_1)\ln\left(\frac{V_2}{V_1}\right)$ (d) $R(V_2 - V_1)\ln\left(\frac{T_2}{T_1}\right)$

37 If energy is supplied to a gas isochorically, increase in internal energy is dU, then **[JCECE]**
(a) $dQ = dU + dW$ (b) $dQ = dU - dW$
(c) $dQ = dU$ (d) $dQ = -dU$

2005

38 **Assertion** Air quickly leaking out of a balloon becomes cooler. **[AIIMS]**
Reason The leaking air undergoes adiabatic expansion.
(a) Both Assertion and Reason are correct and Reason is the correct explanation of Assertion.
(b) Both Assertion and Reason are correct but Reason is not the correct explanation of Assertion.
(c) Assertion is correct but Reason is incorrect.
(d) Both Assertion and Reason are incorrect.

39 A perfect gas is found to obey the relation $pV^{3/2}$ = constant, during an adiabatic process, if such a gas initially at a temperature T is compressed to half of its initial volume, then its final temperature will be **[BHU]**
(a) $2T$ (b) $4T$
(c) $(2)^{1/2}T$ (d) $2(2)^{1/2}T$

40 One mole of an ideal gas at an initial temperature of T K does $6R$ J of work adiabatically. If the ratio of specific heats of this gas at constant pressure and at constant volume is 5/3, the final temperature of gas will be **[EAMCET]**
(a) $(T + 2.4)$K (b) $(T - 2.4)$K
(c) $(T + 4)$K (d) $(T - 4)$K

41 At 27°C, a motor car tyre has pressure of 2 atm. The temperature at which the tyre suddenly burst will be (take, $\gamma_{air} = 1.4$) **[DUMET]**
(a) 246.1 K (b) 250 K
(c) 290 K (d) 248 K

42 If a cylinder containing a gas at high pressure explodes, the gas undergoes **[BCECE]**
(a) reversible adiabatic change and fall of temperature
(b) reversible adiabatic change and rise of temperature
(c) irreversible adiabatic change and fall of temperature
(d) irreversible adiabatic change and rise of temperature

Answers

1 (a)	2 (a)	3 (a)	4 (c)	5 (a)	6 (b)	7 (b)	8 (a)	9 (c)	10 (d)
11 (d)	12 (a)	13 (d)	14 (b)	15 (d)	16 (b)	17 (a)	18 (d)	19 (c)	20 (c)
21 (b)	22 (e)	23 (b)	24 (a)	25 (d)	26 (b)	27 (d)	28 (c)	29 (b)	30 (a)
31 (c)	32 (a)	33 (a)	34 (a)	35 (b)	36 (b)	37 (c)	38 (a)	39 (c)	40 (d)
41 (a)	42 (c)								

Explanations

1 *(a)* In an adiabatic process, the system is completely insulated from the surroundings. Thus, heat is neither absorbed nor released by the system to the surroundings, so $\Delta Q = 0$.
Sudden processes are adiabatic like bursting of cycle tyre etc.
If the pressure of gas is kept constant, then the process is called isobaric, i.e. $\Delta p = 0$.
If the temperature of the system remains constant, then it is called isothermal process, i.e. $\Delta T = 0$.
If the volume of gas is constant in a system, then it is called isochoric process, i.e. $\Delta V = 0$.

2 *(a)* In adiabatic process, heat transfer to the thermodynamic system is zero, i.e., $Q = 0$.
Hence, by first law of thermodynamics,

$$Q = 0 = \Delta U + W$$

$$\therefore \quad W = -\Delta U$$

So, work done is equal to negative of change in internal energy.
Since, the internal energy is a function of thermodynamic state of the system.
It does not depend on the path, therefore work done is independent of path in adiabatic process.

Hence, both Assertion and Reason are correct and Reason is the correct explanation of Assertion.

3 *(a)* As, we know $W = p\Delta V = nR\Delta T$

$$W_{BC} = -nR(2T_0 - T_0) = -nRT_0$$

and $W_{CA} = +\,2nRT_0 \ln 2$

$$\text{Work done} = W_{CA} + W_{BC} = 2nRT_0 \ln 2 - nRT_0 = nRT_0(2\ln 2 - 1)$$

Also, input heat

$$\Delta Q_{BC} = nC_p \Delta T = \frac{nR\gamma T_0}{\gamma - 1}$$

$$\text{Efficiency} = \frac{\text{Work}}{\text{Input heat}} = \frac{(2\ln 2 - 1)}{\gamma/(\gamma - 1)}$$

4 *(c)* As, molar heat capacity,

$$C = \frac{Q}{m\Delta T} = \frac{Q}{0} = \infty$$

In isothermal process, $\Delta T = 0$, therefore C is not defined further in isothermal process. pV and T both are constants.

5 *(a)* In adiabatic expansion, $\Delta Q = 0$
$\Rightarrow W + \Delta U = 0$, so W = positive and ΔU = negative.
$\therefore U, T$ or product of pV will decrease because $U \propto T \propto pV$.

6 *(a)* Slope of adiabatic process of p-V diagram $\left(\frac{dp}{dV}\right) = \gamma \frac{p}{V}$, i.e. slope $\propto \gamma$
From graph $(\text{slope})_2 > (\text{slope})_1$
$\Rightarrow \quad \gamma_2 > \gamma_1$
γ for monoatomic gas (Ar, He) is greater than γ for diatomic gas (O_2, N_2).

7 *(b)* In isochoric process, the curve is parallel to Y-axis because volume is constant.
Isobaric is parallel to X-axis because pressure is constant.
Along the curve, it will be isothermal because temperature is constant.
Process II is adiabatic.
So, P$\rightarrow$ C, Q$\rightarrow$ A, R$\rightarrow$ D, S$\rightarrow$ B

8 *(a)* The solution of this question can be understood by plotting a p-V graph for the compression of a gas isothermally and adiabatically simultaneously to half of its initial volume, i.e.

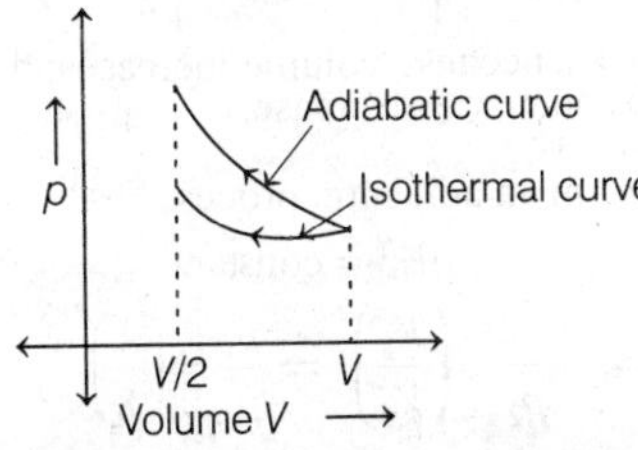

Since, the isothermal curve is less steeper than the adiabatic curve, so area under the p-V curve for adiabatic process has more magnitude than isothermal curve.

Hence, work done in adiabatic process will be more than in isothermal process.

9 *(c)* For isothermal expansion,

$$pV = p'V'$$

i.e., $\quad pV = p' \times 2V \qquad [\because V' = 2V]$

$$p' = \frac{p}{2}$$

For adiabatic expansion,

$$pV^\gamma = \text{constant}$$

$$p'V'^\gamma = p''V''^\gamma$$

$$\frac{p}{2}[2V]^{5/3} = p''[16V]^{5/3} \qquad \left[\because \gamma = \frac{5}{3}\right]$$

$$\Rightarrow \quad p'' = \frac{p}{2}\left[\frac{2V}{16V}\right]^{5/3} = \frac{p}{2}\left[\frac{1}{8}\right]^{5/3}$$

Final pressure of the gas

$$= \frac{p}{2}[0.03125]$$

$$= 0.0156\,p = p/64$$

10 *(d)* For hydrogen,

$$C_p - C_V = \frac{R}{M_{H_2}} = \frac{R}{2},$$

But given that $C_p - C_V = m$

$$m = R/2$$

For nitrogen, $C_p - C_V = n$

$$\therefore \quad n = R/28$$

$$\therefore \quad \frac{m}{n} = \frac{R/2}{R/28} = 14$$

Hence, $\quad m = 14n$

11 *(d)* For an adiabatic process, pressure (p) and volume (V) of the system are related as

$$pV^\gamma = \text{constant} \qquad \ldots\text{(i)}$$

where, γ is the ratio of specific heat capacities at constant pressure and constant volume.
For an ideal gas, $pV = nRT$ (ideal gas equation)

$$\Rightarrow \quad V = \frac{nRT}{p} \qquad \ldots\text{(ii)}$$

From Eqs. (i) and (ii), we get

$$p\left(\frac{nRT}{p}\right)^\gamma = \text{constant}$$

$\Rightarrow \quad p^{1-\gamma}T^{\gamma} = \text{constant}$

[$\because$ number of moles (n) and gas constant (R) are constants]

12 (a) Isochoric process takes place at constant volume. We know that, work done by a system,

$$W = p \times \Delta V$$

where, p is pressure and ΔV is the change in volume.

In an isochoric process, change in volume $\Delta V = 0$, therefore work done $\Delta W = 0$ while $\Delta Q = 0$ in an adiabatic process, ΔU or $\Delta T = 0$ in an isothermal process.

13 (d) According to question, $p \propto T^3$

$$pV = nRT \quad \text{and} \quad p \propto T^3$$

$$p \propto (pV)^3$$

$\Rightarrow p^2V^3 = \text{constant}$

$\Rightarrow pV^{3/2} = \text{constant}, \quad pV^{\gamma} = \text{constant}$

i.e., $\gamma = \frac{3}{2} \qquad \left(\because \gamma = \frac{C_p}{C_V}\right)$

14 (b) As, we know $\gamma = \frac{C_p}{C_V}$ and

$C_p - C_V = R$, then value of molar specific heat of an ideal gas at constant volume, i.e. $C_V = \frac{R}{\gamma - 1}$

15 (d) According to the question, the gas first undergoes isothermal expansion from V to $3V$.

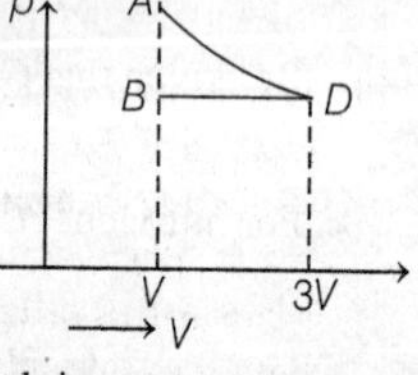

We known that in isothermal expansion, p-V curve is rectangular hyperbola In isobaric compression, which is at constant pressure, hence its p-V curve is parallel to X-axis. From A to D according to the graph its isothermal and from D to B its isobaric.

16 (b) At constant pressure,

Heat required $= nC_p\Delta T$

$\Rightarrow \quad 310 = 2 \times C_p \times (35 - 25)$

$\Rightarrow \quad C_p = \frac{310}{20} = 15.5 \text{ J/mol/K}$

Similarly, at constant volume

Heat required $= nC_V\Delta T$

$= 2(C_p - R) \times (35 - 25)$

$[\because C_p - C_V = R]$

$= 2 \times (15.5 - 8.3) \times 10$

$= 2 \times 7.2 \times 10 = 144 \text{ J}$

17 (a) In isothermal compression, there is always an increase of heat which must flow out the gas.

$$\Delta Q = \Delta U + \Delta W$$

$\Rightarrow \quad \Delta Q = \Delta W \qquad (\because \Delta U = 0)$

$$\Delta Q = 1.5 \times 10^4 \text{ J} = \frac{1.5 \times 10^4}{4.18} \text{ cal}$$

$$= -3.6 \times 10^3 \text{ cal}$$

18 (d) Work done in an isothermal process,

$$W = 2.3026 nRT \log_{10}\left(\frac{V_2}{V_1}\right)$$

$$= 2.3026 \times 10 \times 8.3 \times 600 \log_{10}\left(\frac{10}{100}\right)$$

$$W = -11.4 \times 10^4 \text{ J}$$

19 (c) For isothermal process, work done per mole, i.e. $pV = RT$

$\Rightarrow \quad p = \frac{RT}{V}$

$\therefore \quad W = pdV$

$$= \int_{V_1}^{V_2} \frac{RT}{V} dV = RT \log_e \frac{V_2}{V_1}$$

20 (c) Adiabatic process is a thermodynamic process in which there is no exchange of heat energy between system and surroundings, i.e. $\Delta Q = 0$.

21 (b) In isothermal process, curves between p and V is such that T_2 is farther from the origin than T_1. Therefore, $T_2 > T_1$.

22 (e) To carry out isothermal process, a perfect gas is compressed or allowed to expand very slowly. Isothermal curves never intersect each other as they have very little slope.

23 (b) According to first law of thermodynamics, $\Delta Q = \Delta U + \Delta W$

For an adiabatic process, $\Delta Q = 0$

$\therefore \quad \Delta U = -W$

In adiabatic process,

$$p \propto \frac{1}{V^{\gamma}} \text{ and } T \propto \frac{1}{V^{\gamma-1}}$$

$\gamma > 1$, because volume increases, then p and T will decrease.

24 (a) In an adiabatic process,

$$pV^{\gamma} = \text{constant}$$

$$\Rightarrow \quad \frac{p_1}{p_2} = \left(\frac{V_2}{V_1}\right)^{\gamma} \Rightarrow \frac{p_1}{p_2} = \left(\frac{1}{8}\right)^{5/3}$$

$$\Rightarrow \quad \frac{p_1}{p_2} = \left(\frac{1}{2^3}\right)^{5/3} = \frac{1}{32} \Rightarrow \frac{p_2}{p_1} = 32$$

25 (d) In an adiabatic process,

$pV^{\gamma} = \text{constant}$

Using ideal gas equation,

$$pV = RT$$

$\therefore \quad \left(\frac{RT}{V}\right)V^{\gamma} = \text{constant}$

or $\quad TV^{\gamma-1} = \text{constant}$

(as R is a gas constant)

26 (b) In adiabatic expansion of a gas system, the gas expands so temperature of the system decreases but no flow of heat is there between the system and the surroundings.

27 (d) In isothermal process, the internal energy of the system remains constant. Heat supplied in an isothermal change is used to do work against external surroundings or if the work is done on the system, then equal amount of heat energy will be liberated by the system.

28 (c) As we know, bulk modulus,

$$B = -\frac{\Delta p}{\Delta V / V}$$

For isobaric process, $\Delta p = 0$, so $B = 0$.

29 (b) The p-V diagram for isobaric, isothermal and adiabatic process of an ideal gas is shown in graph below

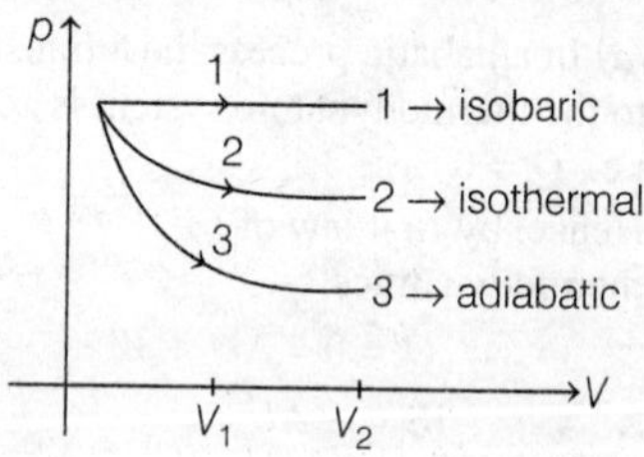

In thermodynamics, for same change in volume, the work done is maximum for the curve having maximum area enclosed with the volume axis.

Area enclosed by the curve $\propto$ (Slope of curve)$^{-1}$

As shown

$$(\text{slope})_{\text{isobaric}} < (\text{slope})_{\text{isothermal}} < (\text{slope})_{\text{adiabatic}}$$

$$\Rightarrow (\text{Area})_{\text{isobaric}} > (\text{Area})_{\text{isothermal}} > (\text{Area})_{\text{adiabatic}}$$

Hence, work done is maximum in isobaric process.

30 (a) Internal energy of an ideal gas is given by

$$U = \frac{f}{2}\mu RT$$

where, f is degree of freedom.

$$= \frac{f}{2}\left(\frac{N}{N_A}\right)RT$$

$\Rightarrow \quad U \propto NT$

In isothermal process, T = constant

$\Rightarrow \quad U \propto N$

i.e., internal energy increases by increasing number of molecules N.

31 (c) For an adiabatic process,

$$pV^{\gamma} = \text{constant} \quad \ldots\text{(i)}$$

Ideal gas relation is $pV = RT$

$$\Rightarrow \quad V = \frac{RT}{p} \quad \ldots\text{(ii)}$$

From Eqs. (i) and (ii), we get

$$p\left(\frac{RT}{p}\right)^{\gamma} = \text{constant} \Rightarrow \frac{T^{\gamma}}{p^{\gamma-1}} = \text{constant}$$

$$p \propto T^{\left(\frac{\gamma}{\gamma-1}\right)} \quad \ldots\text{(iii)}$$

where, γ is ratio of specific heats of the gas.

Given, $\quad p \propto T^{C} \quad \ldots$(iv)

On comparing with Eq. (iii), we have,

$$C = \frac{\gamma}{\gamma-1}$$

For a monoatomic gas, $\gamma = \frac{5}{3}$ we have,

$$C = \frac{\frac{5}{3}}{\frac{5}{3}-1} = \frac{5}{2}$$

32 (a) An isothermal process is a constant temperature process. In this process, T = constant or $\Delta T = 0$.

$$\therefore \quad \Delta U = nC_V\Delta T = 0$$

An adiabatic process is defined as one with no heat transfer into or out of a system. Therefore, $Q = 0$.

From first law of thermodynamics,

$$W = -\Delta U \text{ or } \Delta U = -W$$

33 (a) The relation between temperature T and pressure p is $\frac{T^{\gamma}}{p^{\gamma-1}}$ = constant,

where γ is ratio of specific heats.

Given, $T_1 = 27°\text{C} = 27 + 273$

$= 300\text{ K}, p_1 = p$

$$p_2 = \frac{p}{8}, \gamma = \frac{5}{3}$$

$\therefore$ Ratio of temperature, i.e.

$$\frac{T_1}{T_2} = \left(\frac{p_1}{p_2}\right)^{\frac{\gamma-1}{\gamma}}$$

$$\Rightarrow \quad \frac{T_1}{T_2} = \left(\frac{8}{1}\right)^{\frac{2}{5}} = (8)^{0.4} = 2.297$$

$$\Rightarrow \quad T_2 = \frac{T_1}{2.297} = \frac{300}{2.297} = 130.6\text{ K}$$

$$\approx 131\text{ K}$$

Final temperature of a gas, i.e.

$$T_2 = 131 - 273$$
$$= -142°\text{C}$$

34 (a) The thermo flask system undergoes a change under the condition that no exchange of heat takes place between the system and the surroundings, then such a process is called adiabatic process. Under this condition, if any heat is produced, it does not go out from the system so the temperature of the system is increased, i.e., $\Delta Q = O$.

35 (b) An isobaric process is one in which volume and temperature of system may change but pressure remains constant, i.e. $\Delta p = 0$.

So, it shows a straight line parallel to volume axis in a p-V diagram is isobaric graph.

36 (b) Work done in isothermal process,

$$\text{i.e.} \quad W = \int_{V_1}^{V_2} p\,dV$$

From ideal gas law,

$$pV = RT$$

$$\therefore \quad W = \int_{V_1}^{V_2} \left(\frac{RT}{V}\right) dV$$

$$= RT \int_{V_1}^{V_2} \frac{dV}{V}$$

$$\Rightarrow \quad W = RT \ln\left(\frac{V_2}{V_1}\right)$$

37 (c) Work done by a gas = $p\Delta V$

where, p is pressure and ΔV is the change in volume.

For an isochoric process, $\Delta V = 0$,

$$\therefore \quad dW = p\,dV = 0$$

From first law of thermodynamics,

$$dQ = dU + dW$$

where, $\quad dW = 0$

$$\therefore \quad dQ = dU$$

38 (a) The leaking air of a balloon undergoes adiabatic expansion. In this expansion, due to work done against external pressure, the internal energy of air reduces. Thus, it becomes cooler.

39 (c) From ideal gas equation, we have,

$pV = RT$, where R is gas constant.

Also, given $pV^{3/2}$ = constant

$\therefore$ Putting the value of $p = \frac{RT}{V}$, we have, $\frac{RT}{V} V^{3/2}$ = constant

$$TV^{1/2} = \text{constant}$$

$$T_1V_1^{1/2} = T_2V_2^{1/2}$$

Given, $T_1 = T, V_1 = V, V_2 = \frac{V}{2}$

$$\Rightarrow \quad TV^{1/2} = T_2\left(\frac{V}{2}\right)^{1/2}$$

$\Rightarrow$ Final temperature of an adiabatic process, i.e. $T_2 = (2)^{1/2}T$.

40 (d) Given, initial temperature i.e., $T_1 = TK, n = 1$

Work done, $W = 6R$ J

$$\gamma = \frac{C_p}{C_V} = \frac{5}{3}$$

In adiabatic process,

$$W = \frac{p_1V_1 - p_2V_2}{\gamma - 1}$$

$$= \frac{nR(T_1 - T_2)}{\gamma - 1}$$

$$\Rightarrow 6R = \frac{1 \times R \times (T - T_2)}{\frac{5}{3} - 1}$$

$$6R = \frac{R \times (T - T_2)}{\frac{2}{3}}$$

$$\Rightarrow \quad 6R \times \frac{2}{3} = R\,(T - T_2)$$

$$4 = T - T_2$$

$$\Rightarrow \quad T_2 = (T - 4)\text{ K}$$

$\therefore$ Final temperature of gas,

$$T_2 = (T - 4)\text{K}$$

41 (a) When a system undergoes a sudden change under condition that no exchange of heat takes place between the system and surroundings, then such a process is called adiabatic. So, a tyre bursting suddenly an adiabatic process.

$$p^{1-\gamma}T^{\gamma} = \text{constant}$$

where, γ is ratio of specific heats, p is pressure and T is temperature.

$$\therefore \quad \left(\frac{p_2}{p_1}\right)^{\gamma-1} = \left(\frac{T_2}{T_1}\right)^{\gamma}$$

$$\Rightarrow \quad \left(\frac{1}{2}\right)^{0.4} = \left(\frac{T_2}{300}\right)^{1.4}$$

$\therefore$ $0.4[\log 1 - \log 2]$

$$= 1.4[\log T_2 - \log 300]$$

$$\Rightarrow \quad T_2 = 246.1\text{ K}$$

42 (c) If gas cylinder suddenly explodes in an irreversible adiabatic change, then work done against expansion reduces the temperature of a gas cylinder.

Topic 3

Heat Engine, Second Law of Thermodynamics and Carnot Engine

2019

1 The temperature of food material in refrigerator is 4°C and temperature of environment is 15°C. If Carnot cycle is used in its working gas, then find its Carnot efficiency. [AIIMS]

(a) 0.038
(b) 0.028
(c) 0.053
(d) 0.072

2018

2 A Carnot engine absorbs 6×10^5 cal at 227°C. The work done per cycle by the engine, if its sink is maintained at 127°C is [JIPMER]

(a) 15×10^8 J
(b) 15×10^4 J
(c) 5×10^5 J
(d) 2×10^4 J

3 If the efficiency of an engine is 50% and its work output is 500 J, then find the value of input work. [JIPMER]

(a) 1000 J
(b) 500 J
(c) 100 J
(d) 250 J

4 The efficiency of a heat engine is 1/6. Its efficiency double when the temperature of sink decrease by 62°C, then what is the temperature of source? [JIPMER]

(a) 470 K
(b) 372 K
(c) 542 K
(d) 1042 K

5 The efficiency of an ideal heat engine working between the freezing point and boiling point of water is [NEET]

(a) 6.25%
(b) 20%
(c) 26.8%
(d) 12.5%

2017

6 A Carnot engine having an efficiency of $\frac{1}{10}$ as heat engine, is used as a refrigerator. If the work done on the system is 10 J, then the amount of energy absorbed from the reservoir at lower temperature is [NEET AIPMT]

(a) 1 J
(b) 90 J
(c) 99 J
(d) 100 J

7 The temperature of source and sink of a heat engine are 127°C and 27°C, respectively. An inventor claims its efficiency to be 26%, then [JIPMER]

(a) it is impossible
(b) it is possible with high probability
(c) it is possible with low probability
(d) Data are insufficient

2016

8 The temperature inside a refrigerator is t_2 °C and the room temperature is t_1 °C. The amount of heat delivered to the room for each joule of electrical energy consumed ideally will be [NEET]

(a) $\frac{t_1}{t_1 - t_2}$
(b) $\frac{t_1 + 273}{t_1 - t_2}$
(c) $\frac{t_2 + 273}{t_1 - t_2}$
(d) $\frac{t_1 + t_2}{t_1 + 273}$

9 A refrigerator works between 4°C and 30°C. It is required to remove 600 cal of heat every second in order to keep the temperature of the refrigerated space constant. The power required is (take, 1 cal = 4.2 J) [NEET]

(a) 23.65 W
(b) 236.5 W
(c) 2365 W
(d) 2.365 W

2014

10 A refrigerator extracts heat from water at 0°C and rejects it to room at 24.4°C. The work required by the refrigerator for every 1 kg of water converted into ice is (take, latent heat of ice = 336 kJ/kg) [EAMCET]

(a) 30 kJ
(b) 336 kJ
(c) 11.2 kJ
(d) 24.4 kJ

11 A Carnot engine working between 300 K and 600 K has work output of 800 J/cycle. The amount of heat energy supplied from the source of engine in each cycle is [WB JEE]

(a) 800 J
(b) 1600 J
(c) 3200 J
(d) 6400 J

2013

12 A Carnot engine operates with source at 127°C and sink at 27°C. If the source supplies 40 kJ of heat energy, then the work done by the engine is [AFMC]

(a) 30 kJ
(b) 10 kJ
(c) 4 kJ
(d) 1 kJ

13 An ideal gas heat engine operates in Carnot cycle between 227°C and 127°C. It absorbs 6×10^4 J at high temperature. The amount of heat converted into work is [Manipal]

(a) 1.6×10^4 J
(b) 1.2×10^4 J
(c) 4.8×10^4 J
(d) 3.5×10^4 J

14 Carnot cycle of an ideal gas shown in the figure. Let $W_{a\to b}, W_{b\to c}, W_{c\to d}$ and $W_{d\to a}$ represents the work done by the system during the processes $a \to b, b \to c$, $c \to d$ and $d \to a$ respectively. Consider the following relations **[AMU]**

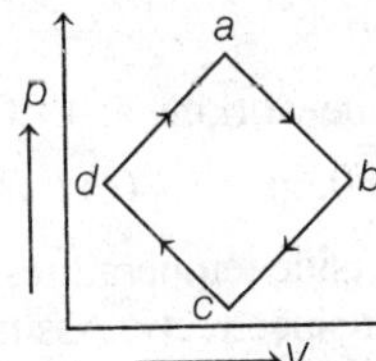

I. $W_{a\to b} + W_{b\to c} + W_{c\to d} + W_{d\to a} > 0$

II. $W_{a\to b} + W_{b\to c} + W_{c\to a} + W_{d\to a} < 0$

III. $W_{a\to b} + W_{c\to d} > 0$

IV. $W_{b\to c} + W_{d\to a} = 0$

Which of the above relations is/are true?

(a) I and III (b) III and IV
(c) I, III and IV (d) II, III and IV

2011

15 The temperature of the sink of a Carnot engine is 27°C and its efficiency is 25%. The temperature of the source is **[J&K CET]**

(a) 227°C (b) 27°C
(c) 327°C (d) 127°C

16 A Carnot engine has efficiency 25%. It operates between reservoirs of constant temperatures with temperature difference of 80 K. What is the temperature of the low temperature reservoir? **[DUMET]**

(a) –25°C (b) 25°C (c) –33°C (d) 33°C

2010

17 Which of the following statements is correct for any thermodynamic system? **[AFMC]**

(a) The internal energy changes in all processes.
(b) Internal energy and entropy are state functions.
(c) The change in entropy can never be zero.
(d) The work done in an adiabatic process is always zero.

18 Choose the incorrect statement from the following.

S1 : The efficiency of a heat engine can be 1, but the coefficient of performance of a refrigerator can never be infinity.

S2 : The first law of thermodynamics is basically the principle of conservation of energy.

S3 : The second law of thermodynamics does not allow several phenomena consistent with the first law.

S4 : A process, whose sole result is the transfer of heat from a colder object to a hotter object is impossible. **[AMU]**

(a) S1 (b) S3
(c) S2 (d) S4

2009

19 The temperature-entropy diagram of a reversible engine cycle is given in the figure. Its efficiency is **[AIIMS]**

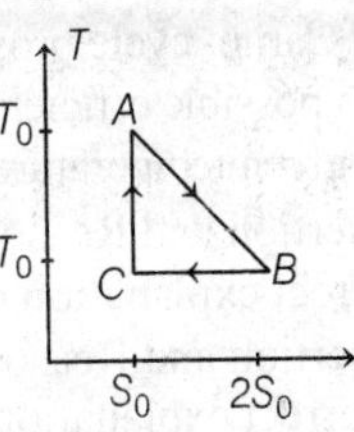

(a) 1/2 (b) 1/4
(c) 1/3 (d) 2/3

20 A Carnot engine takes heat from a reservoir at 627°C and rejects heat to a sink at 27°C. Its efficiency will be **[AFMC]**

(a) 3/5 (b) 1/3
(c) 2/3 (d) 200/209

2008

21 The freezer in a refrigerator is located at the top section, so that **[AFMC]**

(a) the entire chamber of the refrigerator is cooled quickly due to convection
(b) the motor is not heated
(c) the heat gained from the environment is high
(d) the heat gained from the environment is low

22 "Heat cannot by itself flow from a body at lower temperature to a body at higher temperature" is a statement or consequence of **[RPMT]**

(a) second law of thermodynamics
(b) conservation of momentum
(c) conservation of mass
(d) first law of thermodynamics

23 A Carnot engine whose sink is at 300 K has an efficiency of 40%. By how much should the temperature of source be increased so as to increase its efficiency by 50% of original efficiency? **[Haryana PMT]**

(a) 275 K (b) 325 K (c) 250 K (d) 380 K

24 A Carnot engine has an efficiency of 50% at sink temperature 50°C. Calculate the temperature of source. **[BCECE]**

(a) 133°C (b) 143°C
(c) 100°C (d) 373°C

2007

25 A Carnot reversible engine converts 1/6 of heat input into work. When the temperature of the sink is reduced by 62 K, the efficiency of Carnot cycle becomes 1/3. The temperature of the source and sink will be **[BCECE]**

(a) 372 K, 310 K (b) 181 K, 150 K
(c) 472 K, 410 K (d) None of these

2006

26 **Assertion** The Carnot cycle is useful in understanding the performance of heat engines. **[AIIMS]**

Reason The Carnot cycle provides a way of determining the maximum possible efficiency achievable with reservoirs of given temperatures.

(a) Both Assertion and Reason are correct and Reason is the correct explanation of Assertion.
(b) Both Assertion and Reason are correct but Reason is not the correct explanation of Assertion.
(c) Assertion is correct but Reason is incorrect.
(d) Both Assertion and Reason are incorrect.

27 A refrigerator works between 4°C and 30°C. It is required to remove 600 cal of heat every second in order to keep the temperature of the refrigerated space constant.

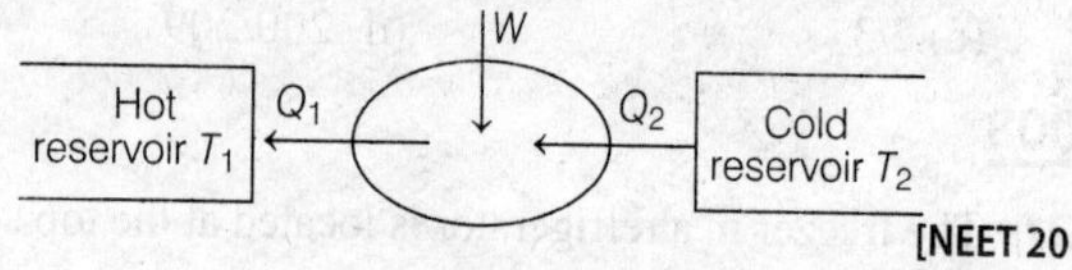

[NEET 2016]

Choose the correct option regarding above refrigerator.
(a) The heat extracted by working substance is Q_2.
(b) The heat released by working substance to hot reservoir is greater than Q_2.
(c) Work done on the system is $Q_1 - Q_2$.
(d) All of the above

28 Efficiency of engine working at 40°C and 20°C is **[MP PMT]**
(a) 0.064% (b) 0.64% (c) 64% (d) 6.4%

29 The inside and outside temperatures of a refrigerator are 273 K and 303K respectively. Assuming that refrigerator cycle is reversible, for every joule of work done the heat delivered to the surroundings will be **[AMU]**
(a) 10 J (b) 20 J (c) 30 J (d) 50 J

2005

30 Carnot engine cannot give 100% efficiency, because we cannot **[AMU]**
(a) eliminate friction (b) find ideal sources
(c) prevent radiation
(d) reach absolute zero temperature

Answers

1 (a)	2 (c)	3 (a)	4 (b)	5 (c)	6 (b)	7 (a)	8 (b)	9 (b)	10 (a)
11 (b)	12 (b)	13 (b)	14 (c)	15 (d)	16 (c)	17 (b)	18 (a)	19 (c)	20 (c)
21 (a)	22 (a)	23 (c)	24 (d)	25 (a)	26 (a)	27 (d)	28 (d)	29 (a)	30 (d)

Explanations

1 *(a)* Given, temperature of food material in refrigerator,

$T_2 = 4°C = 273 + 4 = 277\text{K}$

Temperature of environment,

$T_1 = 15°C$
$= 273 + 15 = 288\text{ K}$

$\therefore$ Carnot efficiency, $\eta = 1 - \dfrac{T_2}{T_1}$

$= 1 - \dfrac{277}{288} = 0.038$

2 *(c)* Here, $Q_1 = 6 \times 10^5$ cal

$T_1 = 227°C = 227 + 273 = 500\text{K}$
$T_2 = 127°C = 127 + 273 = 400\text{K}$

Work done/cycle, $W = ?$

As, $\dfrac{Q_2}{Q_1} = \dfrac{T_2}{T_1}$ or $Q_2 = \dfrac{T_2}{T_1} \times Q_1$

$= \dfrac{400}{500} \times 6 \times 10^5$

$= 4.8 \times 10^5$ cal

As, $W = Q_1 - Q_2$

$= 6 \times 10^5 - 4.8 \times 10^5$

$= 1.2 \times 10^5$ cal

$(\because 1 \text{ cal} = 4.2 \text{ J})$

$= 1.2 \times 10^5 \times 4.2$ J

$\Rightarrow W = 5.04 \times 10^5 \text{ J} \approx 5 \times 10^5$ J

3 *(a)* $\because$ Efficiency of heat engine is

$$\eta = \frac{\text{Work done}}{\text{Heat input}} \times 100$$

or $\dfrac{\eta}{100} = \dfrac{\text{Work done}}{\text{Heat input}} = \dfrac{500}{\text{Heat input}}$

Heat input $= \dfrac{500 \times 100}{50} = 1000$ J

4 *(b)* $\because$ Efficiency of a heat engine,

$$\eta = 1 - \frac{T_2}{T_1} \text{ or } \frac{1}{6} = 1 - \frac{T_2}{T_1}$$

$$\frac{T_2}{T_1} = 1 - \frac{1}{6} = \frac{5}{6}$$

$\Rightarrow$ $T_2 = \dfrac{5T_1}{6}$ ...(i)

According to question, its efficiency is doubled when temperature of sink decreased by 62°C.

$\therefore$ $2\eta = 1 - \dfrac{T_2 - 62}{T_1}$

$\Rightarrow$ $2\left(\dfrac{1}{6}\right) = 1 - \dfrac{\left(\dfrac{5T_1}{6} - 62\right)}{T_1}$ [from Eq. (i)]

$\Rightarrow$ $\dfrac{5T_1}{6} - 62 = T_1\left(1 - \dfrac{2}{6}\right) = \dfrac{2T_1}{3}$

or $\dfrac{5T_1}{6} - \dfrac{2T_1}{3} = 62$

$\Rightarrow$ $\dfrac{T_1}{6} = 62$ or $T_1 = 372$ K

5 *(c)* Efficiency of an ideal heat engine is given as

$$\eta = 1 - \frac{T_2}{T_1}$$

where, T_1 is the temperature of the source and T_2 is the temperature of the sink.

Here, $T_1 = 100 + 273 = 373$ K
$T_2 = 0 + 273 = 273$ K

$\Rightarrow$ $\eta = 1 - \dfrac{273}{373} = \dfrac{373 - 273}{373} = \dfrac{100}{373}$

$= 0.268$

$\therefore \eta\,\% = 0.268 \times 100 = 26.8\,\%$

6 (b) Consider schematic diagram for a Carnot engine as shown below

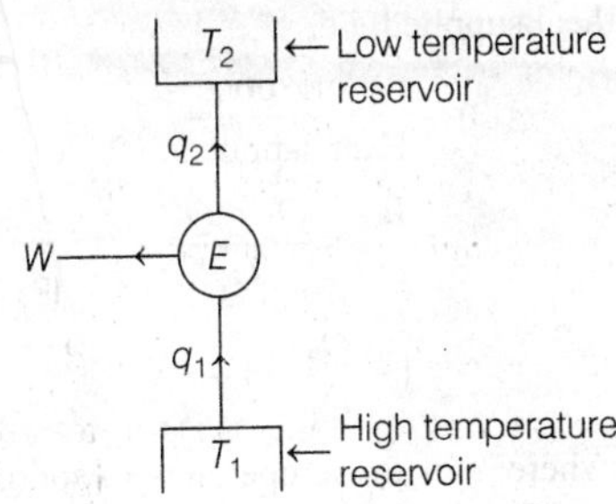

In case of engine, engine efficiency

$$= \frac{\text{work}}{\text{heat absorbed}} = \frac{W}{q_1}$$

$$\therefore \quad \frac{W}{q_1} = \frac{1}{10} \Rightarrow \frac{10}{q_1} = \frac{1}{10}$$

or $\quad q_1 = 100\text{ J}$

When this engine is reversed, it takes in work W and heat q_2 from cold reservoir and ejects 100 J of heat to hot reservoir.

$\therefore \; W + q_2 = q_1$

$\Rightarrow 10 + q_2 = 100$

or $\quad q_2 = 90\text{ J}$

7 (a) Efficiency of heat engine is

$$\eta = 1 - \frac{T_2}{T_1}$$

or $\quad \eta = \frac{T_1 - T_2}{T_1}$

Here, $T_1 = 273 + 127 = 400\text{K}$

$T_2 = 273 + 27 = 300\text{ K}$

$$\therefore \quad \eta = \frac{400 - 300}{400}$$

$$= \frac{100}{400} = 0.25 = 25\%$$

Hence, 26% efficiency is impossible for a given heat engine.

8 (b) For a refrigerator, we know that

$$\frac{Q_1}{W} = \frac{Q_1}{Q_1 - Q_2} = \frac{T_1}{T_1 - T_2}$$

where,

Q_1 = amount of heat delivered to the room,

W = electrical energy consumed,

T_1 = room temperature = $t_1 + 273$

and T_2 = temperature of sink = $t_2 + 273$.

$$\therefore \quad \frac{Q_1}{W} = \frac{t_1 + 273}{t_1 + 273 - (t_2 + 273)}$$

$$\Rightarrow \quad Q_1 = \frac{t_1 + 273}{t_1 - t_2}$$

9 (b) Given, temperature of source,

$T_1 = 30°\text{C} = 30 + 273 = 303\text{ K}$

Temperature of sink,

$T_2 = 4°\text{C} = 4 + 273 = 277\text{ K}$

As, we know that, $\frac{Q_1}{Q_2} = \frac{T_1}{T_2}$

$$\Rightarrow \quad \frac{Q_2 + W}{Q_2} = \frac{T_1}{T_2}$$

$$\{\because W = Q_1 - Q_2\}$$

where, Q_2 is the amount of heat drawn from the sink (at T_2), W is work done on working substance and Q_1 is amount of heat rejected to source (at room temperature T_1).

$$\Rightarrow \quad WT_2 + T_2Q_2 = T_1Q_2$$

$$\Rightarrow \quad WT_2 = T_1Q_2 - T_2Q_2$$

$$\Rightarrow \quad WT_2 = Q_2\,(T_1 - T_2)$$

$$\Rightarrow \quad W = Q_2\left(\frac{T_1}{T_2} - 1\right)$$

$$\Rightarrow \quad W = 600 \times 4.2 \times \left(\frac{303}{277} - 1\right)$$

$$W = 600 \times 4.2 \times \left(\frac{26}{277}\right)$$

$$W = 236.5\text{ J}$$

$$\text{Power} = \frac{\text{Work done}}{\text{Time}}$$

$$= \frac{W}{t} = \frac{236.5}{1} = 236.5\text{W}$$

10 (a) Given, $m = 1\text{ kg}$

$T_1 = 24.4 + 273$

$= 297.4\text{ K}$

$T_2 = 0 + 273 = 273\text{ K}$

$L = 336\text{ kJ/kg}$

Total heat produced per kg of mass

i.e., $\quad Q_2 = mL = 1 \times 336\text{ kJ}$

We know that

$$\frac{Q_1}{Q_2} = \frac{T_1}{T_2}$$

$$\Rightarrow \quad Q_1 = \left(\frac{T_1}{T_2}\right) Q_2$$

$$= \frac{297.4}{273} \times 336$$

$$= \frac{99926.4}{273}\text{ kJ} = 366.0\text{ kJ}$$

Work required by refrigerator,

$$W = Q_1 - Q_2$$

$$= 366 - 336 = 30\text{ kJ}$$

11 (b) The efficiency of Carnot engine is given by

$$\eta = 1 - \frac{T_2}{T_1}$$

Given, $T_1 = 600\text{ K}$ and $T_2 = 300\text{ K}$

$$\therefore \quad \eta = 1 - \frac{300}{600}$$

$$\Rightarrow \quad \eta = 1 - \frac{1}{2}$$

$$\Rightarrow \quad \eta = \frac{1}{2} = 50\%$$

Also, $\quad \eta = \frac{W}{Q} = \frac{800}{Q} = \frac{1}{2}$

Thus, amount of heat supplied from source to engine is

$$Q = 800 \times 2 = 1600\text{ J}$$

12 (b) Efficiency of a Carnot engine,

$$\eta = 1 - \frac{T_2}{T_1}$$

$$= 1 - \frac{(273 + 27)}{(273 + 127)}$$

$$= 1 - \frac{300}{400} = \frac{1}{4}$$

$$\eta = \frac{\text{Work done}}{\text{Heat supplied}}$$

$$\Rightarrow \quad \frac{1}{4} = \frac{W}{40}$$

$$\Rightarrow \quad W = 10\text{ kJ}$$

13 (b) In Carnot cycle of an ideal gas,

$$\frac{W}{Q_1} = \frac{Q_1 - Q_2}{Q_1}$$

or $\quad \frac{W}{Q_1} = 1 - \frac{Q_2}{Q_1}$

or $\quad \frac{W}{Q_1} = 1 - \frac{T_2}{T_1} \quad \left(\because \frac{Q_1}{Q_2} = \frac{T_1}{T_2}\right)$

or $\quad W = Q_1\left(1 - \frac{T_2}{T_1}\right)$

$$\therefore \quad W = 6 \times 10^4\left[1 - \frac{(127 + 273)}{(227 + 273)}\right]$$

or $\quad W = 6 \times 10^4\left(1 - \frac{400}{500}\right)$

$$= 6 \times 10^4 \times \frac{100}{500}$$

$$W = 1.2 \times 10^4\text{ J}$$

14 (c) In Carnot cycle, in order to obtain continuous supply of work, net work done

As, $W_{a \to b}$ is isothermal

$W_{b\to c}$ is adiabatic
$W_{c\to d}$ is isothermal (negative)
$W_{d\to a}$ is adiabatic (negative)
Net work done during the complete cycle,

$$W = W_{a\to b} + W_{b\to c} + (-W_{c\to d}) + (-W_{d\to a})$$

$$W = W_{a\to b} - W_{c\to d}$$

[as $W_{b\to c} = W_{d\to a}$]

i.e. $W_{a\to b} + W_{c\to d} > 0$

$$W_{a\to b} + W_{b\to c} + W_{c\to d} + W_{d\to a} > 0$$

$\because$ $W_{b\to c} = W_{d\to a}$

$\therefore$ $W_{b\to c} + W_{d\to a} = 0$

15 (*d*) Efficiency of a Carnot engine, i.e.

$$\eta = 1 - \frac{T_2}{T_1}$$

$$\frac{25}{100} = 1 - \frac{(273+27)}{T_1}$$

$$\therefore \quad \frac{25}{100} = 1 - \frac{300}{T_1}$$

$$\Rightarrow \quad \frac{300}{T_1} = 1 - \frac{25}{100}$$

$$\frac{300}{T_1} = \frac{100-25}{100}$$

$$\Rightarrow \quad \frac{300}{T_1} = \frac{75}{100}$$

$$T_1 = \frac{300 \times 100}{75}$$

$$\Rightarrow \quad T_1 = 400\text{K}$$

$\therefore$ Temperature of a source, i.e.

$$T_1 = 400 - 273$$

$$= 127°\text{C}$$

16 (*c*) Efficiency of a Carnot engine, i.e.

$$\eta = 1 - \frac{T_2}{T_1} = \frac{T_1 - T_2}{T_1}$$

$$\Rightarrow \quad \frac{25}{100} = \frac{T_1 - (T_1 - 80)}{T_1}$$

$$\Rightarrow \quad \frac{1}{4} = \frac{80}{T_1}$$

$$\Rightarrow \quad T_1 = 320 \text{ K}$$

$$T_1 = 320 - 273$$

$$= 47°\text{C}$$

Temperature of the low temperature reservoir

$$= 47 - 80$$

$$= -33°\text{C}.$$

17 (*b*) Internal energy does not change in isothermal process.

As entropy is a measure of disorder of molecular motlion of system, ΔS can be zero for adiabatic process.

Work done in adiabatic process may be non-zero.

However, internal energy and entropy are state functions.

18 (*a*) Efficency of heat engine,

$$\eta = 1 - \frac{T_2}{T_1}$$

For $\eta = 1$ $\quad (\theta_1 = \infty)$

$\frac{T_2}{T_1}$ should zero that is either, $T_2 = 0\text{ K}$

or $\quad T_1 = \infty \text{ K}$

As source at infinite temperature or sink at 0 K is not attainable.

Therefore, efficiency of heat engine is always less than 1.

19 (*c*) According to the figure,

Heat energy from A to B,

$$Q_1 = T_0S_0 + \frac{1}{2}T_0S_0 = \frac{3}{2}T_0S_0$$

Heat, energy from B to C,

$$Q_2 = T_0(2S_0 - S_0) = T_0S_0$$

Heat energy from C to A

$$Q_3 = 0$$

$$\Rightarrow \quad \eta = \frac{W}{Q_1} = \frac{Q_1 - Q_2}{Q_1}$$

$$= 1 - \frac{Q_2}{Q_1} = 1 - \frac{2}{3} = \frac{1}{3}$$

20 (*c*) Efficiency of a Carnot engine,

$$\eta = 1 - \frac{T_2}{T_1}$$

$$\therefore \quad \eta = 1 - \frac{(27+273)}{(273+627)}$$

$$= 1 - \frac{300}{900} = \frac{600}{900} = \frac{2}{3}$$

21 (*a*) The freezer in a refrigerator is located at the top section, so that the entire chamber of the refrigerator is cooled quickly due to convection.

In convection, transfer of heat takes place by transport of matter in the form of motion of particles.

22 (*a*) Heat cannot flow itself from a body at lower temperature to a body at higher temperature. This corresponds to second law of thermodynamics.

23 (*c*) The efficiency of Carnot engine is defined as the ratio of work done to the heat supplied, i.e.

$$\eta = \frac{\text{Work done}}{\text{Heat supplied}}$$

$$= \frac{W}{Q_1} = \frac{Q_1 - Q_2}{Q_1}$$

$$= 1 - \frac{Q_2}{Q_1} = 1 - \frac{T_2}{T_1} \quad \ldots \text{(i)}$$

where, T_1 is the temperature of source and T_2 is the temperature of sink.

Given, $T_2 = 300$ K, $\eta = 40\% = 0.4$

Putting these values in Eq. (i), we get

$$0.4 = 1 - \frac{300}{T_1}$$

$$\Rightarrow \quad T_1 = \frac{300}{1-0.4} = \frac{300}{0.6} = 500 \text{ K}$$

Let temperature of the source be increased by x K, then efficiency becomes

$$\eta' = 40\% + 50\% \text{ of } \eta$$

$$= \frac{40}{100} + \frac{50}{100} \times 0.4$$

$$= 0.4 + 0.5 \times 0.4 = 0.6$$

$$\text{Hence,} \quad 0.6 = 1 - \frac{300}{500+x}$$

$$\Rightarrow \quad \frac{300}{500+x} = 0.4 \Rightarrow x = 250 \text{ K}$$

24 (*d*) Thermal efficiency of a Carnot engine is given by

$$\eta = 1 - \frac{T_2}{T_1} \quad \ldots \text{(i)}$$

where, T_2 is temperature of sink and T_1 is the temperature of the source.

Here, $\eta = 50\%$, $T_2 = 50°\text{C}$

$= 273 + 50 = 323\text{K}$

Putting these values in Eq. (i), we get

$$\frac{50}{100} = 1 - \frac{323}{T_1}$$

$$\text{or} \quad \frac{323}{T_1} = 1 - \frac{1}{2} = \frac{1}{2}$$

$$\therefore \quad T_1 = 646 \text{ K} = 373°\text{C}$$

25 (*a*) A heat engine is a device which converts heat energy into mechanical energy. The efficiency of heat engine is the fraction of total heat supplied to the engine which is converted into work.

$$\eta = \frac{W}{Q} = 1 - \frac{Q_2}{Q_1} = 1 - \frac{T_2}{T_1}$$

where, T_1 is temperature of source and T_2 is temperature of sink.

Given, $\eta_1 = \frac{1}{6}, \eta_2 = \frac{1}{3}$

$$\therefore \quad \frac{1}{6} = \frac{T_1 - T_2}{T_1} \quad \ldots(i)$$

and $$\frac{1}{3} = \frac{T_1 - (T_2 - 62)}{T_1} \quad \ldots(ii)$$

Solving Eqs. (i) and (ii), we get

$T_1 = 372$ K

and $T_2 = 310$ K

26 (*a*) Carnot engine turns out to be the best at using energy as heat to do useful work. Carnot engine comprises four cycles.

During each cycle of engine, the working substance absorbs energy $|Q_H|$ as heat from a thermal reservoir at constant temperature T_H and discharges energy $|Q_L|$ as heat to a second thermal reservoir at a constant lower temperature T_L, these terms can be used for calculating efficiency of heat engine.

Thus, Carnot cycle provides a way of determining the maximum possible efficiency achievable with reservoirs of given temperature.

27 (*d*) An external work W has to be done to suck heat Q_2 from the cold reservoir and $Q_1 = (Q_2 + W)$ is given to the hot reservoir.

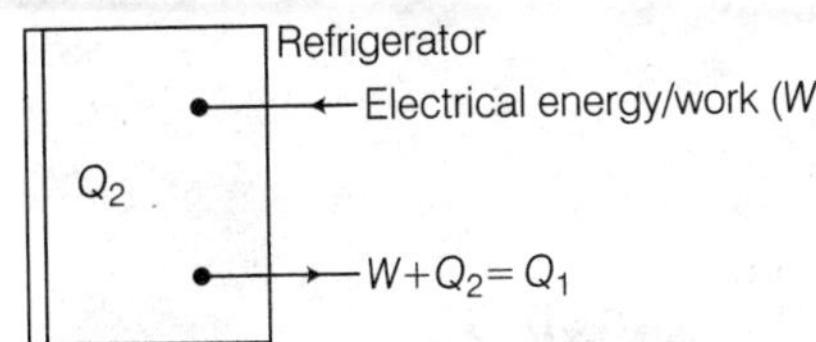

On removal of Q_2 from refrigerator box, temperature of refrigerator interior become lower as compared to outside.

28 (*d*) Efficiency of the engine is given by

$$\eta = \left(1 - \frac{T_2}{T_1}\right) \times 100$$

$$= \left(1 - \frac{273 + 20}{273 + 40}\right) \times 100$$

$$= \left(1 - \frac{293}{313}\right) \times 100$$

$$= 0.064 \times 100$$

$$= 6.4\%$$

29 (*a*) Coefficient of performance,

$$\beta = \frac{Q_2}{W} = \frac{T_L}{T_H - T_L}$$

$$Q_2 = \frac{273 \times 1}{303 - 273} = \frac{273}{30} = 9 \text{ J}$$

Heat delivered to the surroundings,

$$Q_1 = Q_2 + W$$

$$= 9 + 1 = 10 \text{ J}$$

30 (*d*) The efficiency of Carnot engine is

$$\eta = \frac{T_1 - T_2}{T_1} = 1 - \frac{T_2}{T_1} \, (T_1 > T_2)$$

where, T_1 = source temperature

and T_2 = sink temperature.

The value of efficiency of Carnot engine can be 1 or 100%, if the sink temperature (T_2) is at 0 K.

In order to achieve 100%, efficiency $(\eta = 1)$, Q_2 must be equal to 0 which means all the heat from the source is converted to work.

As practically, absolute zero temperature cannot be achieved.

Hence, Carnot engine cannot give 100% efficiency.

12

Kinetic Theory of Gases

Quick Review

Kinetic theory of gases explains the behaviour of gases based on the idea that gas consists of rapidly moving atoms or molecules.

Assumptions of Kinetic Theory of Gases

- A given amount of gas consists of a very large number of molecules (the order of Avogadro's number 10^{23}) and all molecules are identical in all respect.
- The molecules of a gas are in a state of incessant random motion in all directions with different speeds and they move freely in straight lines following Newton's first law.
- The size of a molecule is much smaller than the average separation between the molecules. At ordinary pressure and temperature, the average distance between molecules is about 20 Å, whereas size of a molecule is 2 Å.
- The collision between molecules among themselves or between molecules and walls are perfectly elastic, i.e. total momentum and total kinetic energy of molecules are conserved, however only their velocities will change.
- The molecules exert no force on each other or on the walls of the container except during collision.

Ideal Gas and Real Gas

The gas which follows all the assumptions of kinetic theory of gases is called **ideal gas** but practically no real gas is ideal. However a **real gas** behaves as an ideal gas most closely at low temperature and high pressure.

Pressure Exerted by an Ideal Gas

The pressure exerted by a gas is the result of collisions of gas molecules with the walls of the container. The pressure of the gas is equal to the force exerted per unit area of the walls by the gas.

Pressure of an ideal gas,

$$p=\frac{1}{3}\frac{mn}{V}v_{\text{rms}}^2=\frac{1}{3}\rho v_{\text{rms}}^2 \quad \left[\because \rho=\frac{m}{V}\right]$$

where,

m = mass of molecule of gas,
n = number of molecules,
V = volume of the gas,
ρ = density of the gas

and v_{rms} = root mean square speed of the molecules.

Also, $$p=\frac{2}{3}\left(\frac{1}{2}\rho\bar{v}^2\right)$$

where, $\frac{1}{2}\rho\bar{v}^2$ is average kinetic energy of gas molecules per unit volume.

$$\therefore \quad p = \frac{2}{3}\frac{E_{mol}}{V}$$

where, V is volume of one mole gas which is equal to 22.4 L.

$$E_{mol} = \frac{3}{2}RT \Rightarrow E_{mol} \propto T$$

Note Critical temperature is the temperature at which gases can be liquified.

Ideal Gas Equation

An ideal gas follows ideal gas equation in all the conditions of temperature and pressure.

Ideal gas equation, $pV = nRT = nkT$

where, k = Boltzmann's constant = R/N

$$= 1.38 \times 10^{-23}\ \text{JK}^{-1}.$$

Ideal Gas Laws

Some important gaseous laws are given below

Boyle's Law It states that, for a given mass of a gas at constant temperature, the volume of that mass of gas is inversely proportional to its pressure.

i.e. $$V \propto 1/p$$

$$pV = \text{constant}$$

$$\Rightarrow \quad p_1V_1 = p_2V_2 = p_3V_3 \cdots = \text{constant}$$

Charles' Law It states that, for a given mass of an ideal gas at constant pressure, volume (V) of a gas is directly proportional to its absolute temperature T.

i.e. $$V \propto T$$

$$\Rightarrow \quad \frac{V}{T} = \text{constant}$$

$$\Rightarrow \quad \frac{V_1}{T_1} = \frac{V_2}{T_2} = \frac{V_3}{T_3} \cdots = \text{constant}$$

Gay Lussac's or Pressure Law It states that, for a given mass of an ideal gas at constant volume, pressure (p) of a gas is directly proportional to T.

i.e. $$p \propto T \Rightarrow \frac{p}{T} = \text{constant}$$

$$\Rightarrow \quad \frac{p_1}{T_1} = \frac{p_2}{T_2} = \frac{p_3}{T_3} = \ldots = \text{constant}$$

Pressure of the gas at t°C,

$$p_t = p_0\left(1 + \frac{t}{273.15}\right)$$

where, p_0 is the pressure of gas at 0°C.

Dalton's Law of Partial Pressure It states that, the total pressure of a mixture of non-interacting ideal gases is the sum of partial pressures exerted by individual gases in the mixture.

i.e. $$p = p_1 + p_2 + p_3 + \cdots$$

where, $p_1 = n_1RT/V$ is the pressure of gas 1 would exert at the same condition of volume and temperature, if no other gases are present and $p_2, p_3, \ldots\ldots$ are pressure exert by gas 2, gas 3.... respectively, at the same condition of temperature and pressure.

Graham's Law of Diffusion It states that, the rate of diffusion of a gas is inversely proportional to the square root of its density.

$$r \propto \frac{1}{\sqrt{\rho}}$$

Avogadro's Law It states that, at the same temperature and pressure, equal volume of all gases contain equal number of molecules.

i.e. At the constant temperature and pressure, $N_1 = N_2$

where, N_1 and N_2 are number of molecules present in the same volume of two gases.

The number of molecules in mole of a gas is $N = 6.023 \times 10^{23}$, where N is called Avogadro's number.

Molecular Velocities

Based upon the calculations, there are three main kinds of molecular velocities as given below

(*i*) **Average Velocity** ($\bar{v}$ or v_{av}) It is the arithmetic mean of the velocities of the different molecules of a gas.

Mathematically, $$\bar{v} = \frac{v_1 + v_2 + v_3 + \ldots + v_n}{n}$$

where, $v_1\ v_2\ v_3 \ldots v_n$ are the velocities of the individual molecules and $n = n_1 + n_2 + n_3 \ldots$, are the total number of molecules.

This is related to temperature T of the gas as

$$\bar{v} = \sqrt{\frac{8RT}{\pi M}} = \sqrt{\frac{8p}{\pi\rho}} = \sqrt{\frac{8kT}{\pi m}}$$

(*ii*) **Root Mean Square Velocity** (v or v_{rms}) It is the square root of the mean of the squares of the velocities of the molecules of gas.

Mathematically, $$v_{rms} = \sqrt{\frac{v_1^2 + v_2^2 + v_3^2 + \ldots + v_n^2}{n}}$$

From kinetic gas equation,

$$v_{rms} = \sqrt{\frac{3RT}{M}} = \sqrt{\frac{3kT}{m}} = \sqrt{\frac{3p}{d}}$$

where, p = pressure (RT/V) and d = density (M/V).

(iii) **Most Probable Velocity** (v_{mp} or u_{mp}) It is the velocity, possessed by the largest number of molecules of gas (Maxwell speed distribution law).

From kinetic gas equation,

$$v_{mp} = \sqrt{\frac{2RT}{M}}$$

$$= \sqrt{\frac{2p}{d}} = \sqrt{\frac{2kT}{m}}$$

- The ratio of different molecular velocities is

$$v_{rms} : v_{av} : v_{mp} = \sqrt{3} : \sqrt{\frac{8}{\pi}} : \sqrt{2}$$

$$= \sqrt{3} : \sqrt{2.5} : \sqrt{2}$$

Mean Free Path

The average distance travelled by a molecule between two successive collisions is known as the mean free path of the molecule.

$$\text{Mean free path, } \lambda = \frac{1}{\sqrt{2}\, n\pi d^2}$$

where, d = diameter of each molecule

and n = number of molecules per unit volume.

Relation Between Mean Free Path (λ), Temperature (T) and Pressure (p)

$$\lambda = \frac{kT}{\sqrt{2}\pi d^2 p}$$

Equation of State for a Real Gas

For ideal gases, equation of state is $pV = \mu RT$ and for real gases, equation of state is different as of the ideal one. van der Waals' derived following equation of state for real gases,

$$\left(p + \frac{n^2 a}{V^2}\right)(V - nb) = nRT$$

(for n moles of a gas)

where, a and b are constants called van der Waal's constants.

Degrees of Freedom

The total number of co-ordinates axes of independent quantities required to describe completely the position and configuration of dynamical system (gaseous) is known as number of degrees of freedom of the system. It is represented by f and expressed as $f = 3N - K$

where, N is the number of particles and K is number of co-ordinates of the particles.

Degrees of Freedom for Different Gases According to Atomicity of Gas at Low Temperature

Atomicity of Gas	Translational	Rotational	Total
Monoatomic, e.g. Ar, Ne, Ideal gas etc.	3	0	3
Diatomic, e.g. O_2, Cl_2, N_2 etc.	3	2	5
Triatomic (linear), e.g. CO_2, C_2H_2.	3	2	5
Triatomic (Non-linear) or Polyatomic, e.g. H_2O, NH_3, CH_4.	3	3	6

Law of Equipartition of Energy

For a dynamic system in thermal equilibrium, the total energy is distributed equally amongst all the degrees of freedom and the energy associated with each molecule per degree of freedom is $(1/2)kT$, where k is Boltzmann's constant.

If f be the number of degrees of freedom, the internal energy of 1 mole of the gas will be $\frac{f}{2}RT$ or internal energy of n moles of the gas will be $\frac{n}{2}fRT$.

Thus, internal energy, $U = \frac{n}{2}fRT$.

Specific Heat Capacity

The amount of heat required to change the temperature of unit mass of substance by unity is called specific heat capacity.

$$\text{Specific heat capacity, } C = \frac{1}{m}\frac{\Delta Q}{\Delta T}$$

where, m = mass of substance.

- Heat capacity per mole is called **molar specific heat capacity**.

  $$\text{Molar specific heat capacity, } C = \frac{1}{n}\frac{\Delta Q}{\Delta T}$$

- Molar heat capacity at constant pressure, $C_p = \frac{1}{n}\left(\frac{\Delta Q}{\Delta T}\right)_p$
- Molar heat capacity at constant volume, $C_V = \frac{1}{n}\left(\frac{\Delta Q}{\Delta T}\right)_V$
- For an ideal gas, $C_p - C_V = R$, where R is universal gas constant and this relation is called **Mayer's formula.**
- Ratio of C_p and C_V is represented by γ,

  i.e. $$\gamma = \frac{C_p}{C_V}$$

- In terms of degrees of freedom,

  $$\gamma = 1 + \frac{2}{f}$$

Note Work done in increasing the volume or temperature of a gas is given by $\Delta W = p\Delta V = nR\Delta T$.

Degree of Freedom, Specific Heat and Kinetic Energy for Different Gases

		Monotomic	Diatomic	Triatomic (non-linear)	Triatomic (linear)
Atomicity	A	1	2	3	3
Restriction	B	0	1	3	2
Degree of freedom	$f = 3A - B$	3	5	6	7
Degree of freedom at high temperature	f'	3 (no change)	7	8	9
Molar specific heat at constant volume	$C_V = (f/2)R = R/(\gamma - 1)$	$3/2R$	$5/2R$	$3R$	$7/2\ R$
Molar specific heat at constant pressure	$C_p = [(f/2)+1]R = \gamma R/(\gamma - 1)$	$5/2R$	$7/2R$	$4R$	$9/2\ R$
Ratio of C_p to C_V	$\gamma = C_p / C_V = 1 + (2/f)$	$5/3 \simeq 1.66$	$7/5 \simeq 1.4$	$4/3 \simeq 1.33$	$9/7 \simeq 1.28$
Kinetic energy of 1 mol	$E_{mole} = (f/2)RT$	$(3/2)RT$	$(5/2)RT$	$3RT$	$(7/2)RT$
Kinetic energy of 1 molecule	$E_{molecule} = (f/2)kT$	$(3/2)kT$	$(5/2)kT$	$3kT$	$(7/2)kT$
Kinetic energy of 1g	$E_{gram} = (f/2)rT$	$(3/2)rT$	$(5/2)rT$	$3rT$	$(7/2)rT$

Topical Practice Questions

All the exam questions of this chapter have been divided into 3 topics as listed below

Topic 1

Kinetic Theory of Gases, Gas Laws and Ideal Gas Equation

2019

1 An ideal gas intially at pressure 1 bar is being compressed from 30 m^3 to 10 m^3 volume and its temperature decreases from 320 K to 280 K, then find the value of final pressure of the gas. [AIIMS]

(a) 2.625 bar (b) 3.4 bar
(c) 1.325 bar (d) 4.5 bar

2 **Assertion** NH_3 is liquified more easily than CO_2.
Reason Critical temperature of NH_3 is more than CO_2. [AIIMS]

(a) Both Assertion and Reason are correct and Reason is the correct explanation of Assertion.
(b) Both Assertion and Reason are correct, but Reason is not the correct explanation of Assertion.
(c) Assertion is correct but Reason is incorrect.
(d) Both Assertion and Reason are incorrect.

2017

3 A graph between pressure p (along Y-axis) and absolute temperature T(along X-axis) for equal moles of two gases has been drawn. Given that volume of second gas is more than volume of first gas. Which of the following statements is correct? [JIPMER]

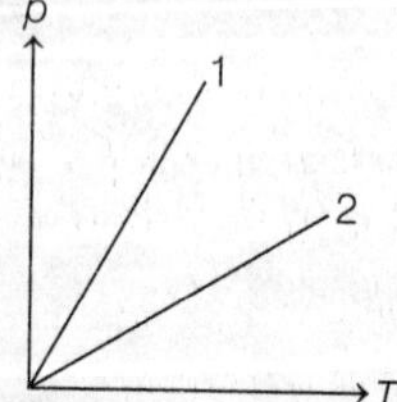

(a) Slope of gas 1 is less than gas 2
(b) Slope of gas 1 is more than gas 2
(c) Both have some slopes
(d) None of the above

4 A given sample of an ideal gas occupies a volume V at a pressure p and absolute temperature T. The mass of each molecule of the gas is m. Which of the following gives the density of the gas? [NEET]

(a) $\frac{p}{kT}$ (b) $\frac{pm}{kT}$
(c) $\frac{p}{kTV}$ (d) mkT

2014

5 Which one of the following is a wrong statement in kinetic theory of gases? [Kerala CEE]

(a) The gas molecules are in random motion.
(b) The gas molecules are perfect elastic spheres.
(c) The volume occupied by the molecules of a gas is negligible.
(d) The force of attraction between the molecules is negligible.
(e) The collision between molecules is inelastic.

2013

6 In the given (V-T) diagram, what is the relation between pressures p_1 and p_2? [NEET]

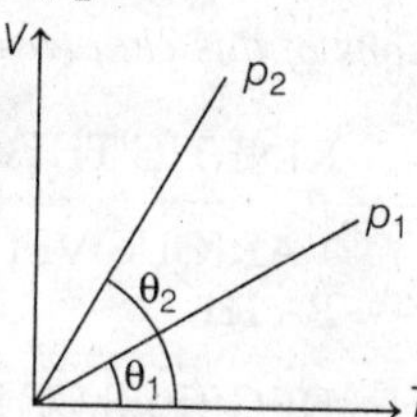

(a) $p_2 = p_1$ (b) $p_2 > p_1$
(c) $p_2 < p_1$ (d) Cannot be predicted

2012

7 A balloon is filled at 27 °C and 1 atm pressure by 500 m^3 He gas. At −3°C and 0.5 atm pressures, the volume of He-gas contained in balloon will be [AIIMS]

(a) 700 m^3 (b) 900 m^3 (c) 1000 m^3 (d) 500 m^3

2011

8 Air inside a closed container is saturated with water vapour. The air pressure is p and the saturated vapour pressure of water is $\bar{p}$. If the mixture is compressed to one-half of its volume by maintaining temperature constant, the pressure becomes [WB JEE]

(a) $2(p + \bar{p})$ (b) $2p + \bar{p}$
(c) $(p + \bar{p})/2$ (d) $p + 2\bar{p}$

9 A perfect gas at 27°C is heated at constant pressure so as to double its volume. The increase in temperature of the gas will be [KCET]

(a) 600°C (b) 327°C (c) 54°C (d) 300°C

2010

10 If pressure of CO_2 (real gas) in a container is given by $p = \frac{RT}{2V - b} - \frac{9}{4b^2}$, then mass of the gas in container is **[AIIMS]**

(a) 11 g (b) 22 g (c) 33 g (d) 44 g

11 A closed vessel contains 8 g of oxygen and 7g of nitrogen. The total pressure is 10 atm at a given temperature. If now oxygen is absorbed by introducing a suitable absorbent, the pressure of the remaining gas (in atm) will be **[BHU]**

(a) 2 (b) 10 (c) 4 (d) 5

12 The figure shows graphs of pressure *versus* density for an ideal gas at two temperatures T_1 and T_2, then **[OJEE]**

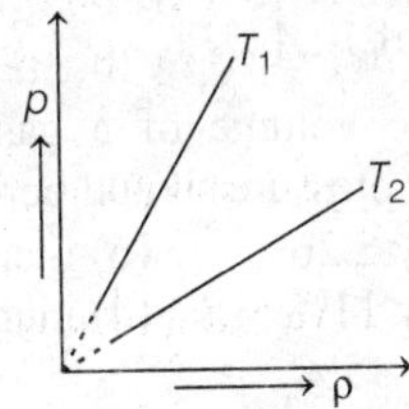

(a) $T_1 > T_2$ (b) $T_1 = T_2$
(c) $T_1 < T_2$ (d) None of these

13 Average momentum of an ideal gas depends upon **[OJEE]**

(a) temperature (b) mass
(c) volume (d) None of these

14 Simple behaviour under all conditions of real gas is governed by the equation **[MP PMT]**

(a) $pV = \mu RT$ (b) $\left(p + \frac{a}{V^2}\right)(V - b) = RT$
(c) $pV =$ constant (d) $pV^\gamma =$ constant

15 Ideal gas and real gas have major difference of **[MP PMT]**

(a) phase transition (b) temperature
(c) pressure (d) None of these

16 Air is filled at 60° C in a vessel of open mouth. The vessel is heated to a temperature T so that (1/4)th part of air escapes. Assuming the volume of the vessel remaining constant, the value of T is **[Haryana PMT]**

(a) 80° C (b) 444° C (c) 333° C (d) 171° C

17 The pressure p for a gas is plotted against its absolute temperature T for two different volumes V_1 and V_2, where $V_1 > V_2$. If p is plotted on Y-axis and T on X-axis, then **[EAMCET]**

(a) the curve for V_1 has greater slope than that for V_2
(b) the curve for V_2 has greater slope than that for V_1
(c) Both curves have same slope
(d) the curves intersect at some point other than $T = 0$

18 The temperature of a gas contained in a closed vessel of constant volume increases by 1° C when the pressure of the gas is increased by 1%. The initial temperature of the gas is **[KCET]**

(a) 100 K (b) 273° C
(c) 100° C (d) 200 K

19 Air is pumped into an automobile tube upto a pressure of 200 kPa in the morning when the air temperature is 22° C. During the day, temperature rises to 42° C and the tube expands by 2 %. The pressure of the air in the tube at this temperature will be approximately **[JCECE]**

(a) 212 kPa (b) 209 kPa (c) 206 kPa (d) 200 kPa

20 The gas in a vessel is subjected to a pressure of 20 atm at a temperature 27° C. The pressure of the gas in a vessel after one-half of the gas is released from the vessel and the temperature of the remainder is raised by 50° C is **[MGIMS]**

(a) 8.5 atm (b) 10.8 atm
(c) 11.7 atm (d) 17 atm

21 Which one of the following is not an assumption in the kinetic theory of gases? **[Manipal]**

(a) The volume occupied by the molecules of the gas is negligible.
(b) The force of attraction between the molecules is negligible.
(c) The collision between molecules are elastic.
(d) All molecules have same speed.

22 A closed compartment containing gas is moving with some acceleration in horizontal direction, then the pressure in the compartment is (neglect effect of gravity) **[JCECE]**

(a) same everywhere (b) lower in front side
(c) lower in rear side (d) lower in upper side

2009

23 By what percentage should the pressure of a given mass of a gas be increased, so as to decrease its volume by 10% at a constant temperature? **[AFMC]**

(a) 5% (b) 7.2%
(c) 12.5% (d) 11.1%

24 When a van der Waals' gas undergoes free expansion, then its temperature **[AFMC]**

(a) decreases
(b) increases
(c) does not change
(d) depends upon the nature of the gas

25 An electron tube was sealed OFF during manufacture at a pressure of 1.2×10^{-7} mm of mercury at 27°C. Its volume is 100 cm^3. The number of molecules that remains in the tube is **[Manipal]**

(a) 2×10^{16} (b) 3×10^{15}
(c) 3.86×10^{11} (d) 5×10^{11}

26 Two monatomic ideal gases A and B occupying the same volume V are at the same temperature T and pressure p. If they are mixed, the resultant mixture has volume V and temperature T. The pressure of the mixture is **[J&K CET]**

(a) p (b) $\frac{p}{2}$
(c) $4p$ (d) $2p$

2008

27 Two vessels A and B having equal volume contain equal masses of hydrogen in A and helium in B at 300 K. Then, mark the correct statement? **[BHU]**

(a) The pressure exerted by hydrogen is half that exerted by helium
(b) The pressure exerted by hydrogen is equal to that exerted by helium
(c) Average KE of the molecule of hydrogen is half the average KE of the molecules of helium
(d) The pressure exerted by hydrogen is twice that exerted by helium

28 At 10°C, the value of the density of a fixed mass of an ideal gas divided by its pressure is x. At 110°C, this ratio is **[CBSE AIPMT]**

(a) x (b) $\frac{383}{283}x$ (c) $\frac{10}{110}x$ (d) $\frac{283}{383}x$

2007

29 The figure below shows the plot of $\frac{pV}{nT}$ *versus* p for oxygen gas at two different temperatures. **[AIIMS]**

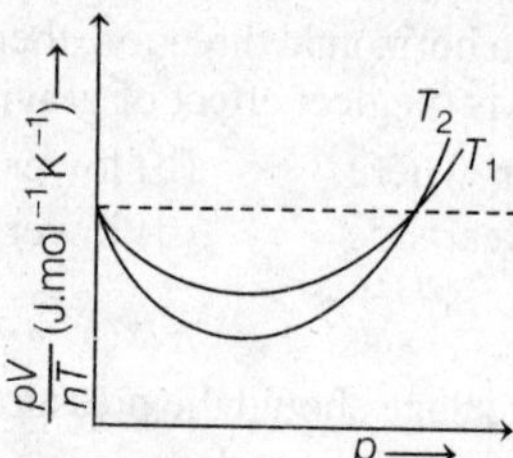

Read the following statements concerning the above curves.

I. The dotted line corresponds to the ideal gas behaviour.

II. The temperatures are related as $T_1 > T_2$.

III. The value of $\frac{pV}{nT}$ at the point, where the curves meet on the Y-axis is the same for all gases.

Which of the above statements is true?

(a) I Only (b) I and III
(c) Both (a) and (b) (d) None of these

30 Temperature remaining constant, the pressure of gas is decreased by 20%. The percentage change in volume **[J&K CET]**

(a) increases by 20% (b) decreases by 20%
(c) increases by 25% (d) decreases by 25%

31 One litre of an ideal gas at 27°C is heated at a constant pressure to the 297°C. Then, the final volume is the approximately **[AMU]**

(a) 1.2 L (b) 1.9 L
(c) 19 L (d) 2.4 L

2006

32 Two balloons are filled, one with pure He gas and the other by air, respectively. If the pressure and temperature of these balloons are same, then the number of molecules per unit volume is **[AFMC]**

(a) more in the He filled balloon
(b) same in both balloons
(c) more in air filled balloon
(d) in the ratio of 1 : 4

33 To decrease the volume of a gas by 5% at constant temperature, the pressure should be **[Kerala CEE]**

(a) decreased by 5.26% (b) increased by 5.26%
(c) decreased by 11% (d) increased by 11%
(e) increased by 15%

34 A closed vessel is maintained at a constant temperature. It is first evacuated and then vapour is injected into it continuously. The pressure of the vapour in the vessel **[MHT CET]**

(a) increases continuously
(b) first increases and then remains constant
(c) first increases and then decreases
(d) None of the above

2005

35 If p is the pressure, V the volume, R the gas constant, k the Boltzmann constant and T the absolute temperature, then the number of molecules in the given mass of the gas is given **[MP PMT]**

(a) $\frac{pV}{RT}$ (b) $\frac{pV}{kT}$ (c) $\frac{pR}{T}$ (d) pV

36 What is the mass of 2 L of nitrogen at 22.4 atm pressure and 273 K? **[J&K CET]**

(a) 28 g (b) 14×22.4 g
(c) 56 g (d) None of these

37 Equation of a gas in the terms of pressure (p), absolute temperature (T) and density (d) is **[EAMCET]**

(a) $\frac{p_1}{T_1 d_1} = \frac{p_2}{T_2 d_2}$ (b) $\frac{p_1 T_1}{d_1} = \frac{p_2 T_2}{d_2}$

(c) $\frac{p_1 d_2}{T_2} = \frac{p_2 d_1}{T_1}$ (d) $\frac{p_1 d_1}{T_1} = \frac{p_1 d_2}{T_2}$

Answers

1 (a)	2 (a)	3 (b)	4 (b)	5 (e)	6 (c)	7 (b)	8 (a)	9 (d)	10 (b)
11 (d)	12 (a)	13 (d)	14 (b)	15 (c)	16 (d)	17 (b)	18 (a)	19 (b)	20 (b)
21 (d)	22 (b)	23 (d)	24 (a)	25 (c)	26 (d)	27 (d)	28 (d)	29 (c)	30 (c)
31 (b)	32 (b)	33 (b)	34 (b)	35 (b)	36 (c)	37 (a)			

Explanations

1 (a) Given, initial pressure of ideal gas,

$$p_1 = 1 \text{ bar} = 1 \text{ Nm}^{-2}$$

Initial volume, $V_1 = 30 \text{ m}^3$

Final volume, $V_2 = 10 \text{ m}^3$

Initial temperature, $T_1 = 320 \text{ K}$

Final temperature, $T_2 = 280 \text{ K}$

Final pressure of gas, $p_2 = ?$

By ideal gas equation,

$$\frac{p_1V_1}{T_1} = \frac{p_2V_2}{T_2}$$

$$\Rightarrow \quad \frac{1 \times 30}{320} = \frac{p_2 \times 10}{280}$$

$$\Rightarrow \quad p_2 = 2.625 \text{ bar}$$

2 (a) A gas can be liquified by applying pressure only when it is cooled below critical temperature. Critical temperature of NH_3 is more than CO_2, i.e. $T_{NH_3} = 405$ K and $T_{CO_2} = 304.1$ K. Therefore, NH_3 is liquified more easily than CO_2. Hence, both Assertion and Reason are correct and Reason is the correct explanation of Assertion.

3 (b) According to ideal gas equation,

$$pV = nRT$$

or $$\frac{p}{T} = \frac{nR}{V}$$

where $\frac{p}{T}$ represents slope of the graph

As, the number of moles are the same for the two gases,

$$\therefore \quad \frac{p}{T} \propto \frac{1}{V}$$

$$\because \quad V_2 > V_1 \text{ (Given)}$$

$\therefore$ (Slope)$_2$ < (Slope)$_1$

or (Slope)$_1$ > (Slope)$_2$

4 (b) We know that,

$$pV = RT$$

$$\Rightarrow \quad V = \frac{RT}{p} \quad \text{...(i)}$$

$$\therefore \text{ Density } (\rho) = \frac{M}{V} = \frac{mN_A}{\frac{RT}{p}} \quad \text{[from Eq. (i)]}$$

$$= \frac{mpN_A}{kN_AT} \quad [R = kN_A]$$

$$\rho = \frac{pm}{kT}$$

5 (e) The kinetic theory of gases assume the collision between molecules as perfectly elastic. So, incorrect statement is that the collision between molecules is inelastic.

6 (c) The slope of the graph $\propto \frac{1}{p}$

or $$p \propto \frac{1}{\tan\theta}$$

$$\because \quad \theta_1 < \theta_2$$

Hence, $p_2 < p_1$

7 (b) As, $$\frac{p_1V_1}{T_1} = \frac{p_2V_2}{T_2}$$

or $$V_2 = \frac{p_1V_1T_2}{p_2T_1}$$

Given, $p_1 = 1$ atm, $V_1 = 500 \text{ m}^3$,

$T_2 = -3°\text{C} = [273 + (-3)]\text{K}$

$= (273 - 3)\text{K}$, $p_2 = 0.5$ atm and

$T_1 = 27°\text{C} = (27 + 273)\text{K}$

$\therefore$ Volume of He,

$$V_2 = \frac{1 \times 500 \times (273 - 3)}{0.5 \times (273 + 27)}$$

$$= \frac{1 \times 500 \times 270}{0.5 \times 300} = 900 \text{ m}^3$$

8 (a) Given that, the air inside a closed container is saturated with water vapour, so if the temperature remains constant, the saturated vapour pressure does not change. Also, pressure will be twice, when volume will be halved.

Hence, pressure of mixture,

$$p' = 2(p + \bar{p}).$$

9 (d) We know that, for perfect gas,

$$V \propto T$$

i.e. $$\frac{V_1}{V_2} = \frac{T_1}{T_2} \quad \text{...(i)}$$

According to the question,

$V_1 = V$, then $V_2 = 2V$ and $T_1 = 300$ K

$$\therefore \quad \frac{1}{2} = \frac{300}{T_2}$$

$$\Rightarrow \quad T_2 = 600 \text{ K}$$

$$\Rightarrow \quad T_2 = 327°\text{C}$$

So, $$\Delta t = 327 - 27 = 300°\text{C}$$

10 (b) van der Waals' gas equation for μ mole of real gas is

$$\left(p + \frac{\mu^2 a}{V^2}\right)(V - \mu b) = \mu RT$$

$$\Rightarrow \quad p = \left(\frac{\mu RT}{V - \mu b}\right) - \frac{\mu^2 a}{V^2}$$

Given equation,

$$p = \left(\frac{RT}{2V - b} - \frac{9}{4b^2}\right)$$

On comparing the given equation with this standard equation, we get

$$\mu = \frac{1}{2}$$

As, $$\mu = \frac{m}{M}$$

where, m = mass of gas and M = molecular weight of the gas.

$$m = \mu M = \frac{1}{2} \times 44 = 22 \text{ g}$$

11 (d) From Dalton's law, final pressure of the mixture of nitrogen and oxygen,

$$p_{mix} = p_1 + p_2$$

$$= \frac{n_1RT}{V} + \frac{n_2RT}{V} \quad \left[\because n = \frac{m}{M}\right]$$

$$= \frac{m_1}{M_1} \cdot \frac{RT}{V} + \frac{m_2}{M_2} \cdot \frac{RT}{V}$$

$$= \frac{8}{32} \cdot \frac{RT}{V} + \frac{7}{28} \cdot \frac{RT}{V} = \frac{RT}{2V}$$

$$10 = RT/2V \quad \text{...(i)}$$

When oxygen is absorbed, then pressure by nitrogen,

$$p = \frac{7}{28} \cdot \frac{RT}{V}$$

$$\Rightarrow \quad p = \frac{RT}{4V} \quad \text{...(ii)}$$

From Eqs. (i) and (ii), we get

Pressure exerted by nitrogen gas,

$$p = 5 \text{ atm}$$

12 (a) As, $$pV = nRT = \frac{m}{M}RT$$

where, M = molecular weight.

$$\Rightarrow \quad \frac{p}{m/V} = \frac{RT}{M}$$

$$\Rightarrow \quad \frac{p}{\rho} = \frac{RT}{M}$$

$$\Rightarrow \quad \frac{p}{\rho} \propto T$$

($\because$ for a given gas M is constant)

Temperature is directly proportional to the slope of p-ρ graph, so $T_1 > T_2$.

13 (d) The average momentum of an ideal gas molecules before and after striking the wall of container is **p** and −**p**, respectively considering elastic collisions, according to kinetic theory of gases assumptions.

Hence, average momentum,

$$\mathbf{p}_{av} = \frac{\mathbf{p} + (-\mathbf{p})}{2} = 0$$

[$\because$ average velocity of an ideal gas is zero]

Thus, for any temperature, mass and volume the average momentum of the gas will be zero. So, it does not depend upon any of these parameters.

14 (b) Real gas behaviour is governed by van der Waals' equation given as

$$\Rightarrow \quad \left(p+\frac{a}{V^2}\right)(V-b)=RT$$

[for one mole of gas]

15 (c) No attractive or repulsive force acts between gas molecules in an ideal gas whereas for a real gas intermolecular force exists. Molecules do not exert that force on the wall which they would have exerted in the absence of intermolecular force.

Therefore, the observed pressure p of the gas will be less than that present in the absence of intermolecular force. Thus, the observed pressure for an ideal gas is more as compared for real gas. So, ideal and real gas have major difference of pressure.

16 (d) For open mouth vessel, pressure is constant.

Volume is also given constant.

Hence, from $pV=\mu RT=\left(\frac{m}{M}\right)RT$

$$\Rightarrow \quad T \propto \frac{1}{m}$$

$$\Rightarrow \quad \frac{T_1}{T_2}=\frac{m_2}{m_1}$$

$\therefore \left(\frac{1}{4}\right)$ th part escapes, so remaining mass in the vessel, $m_2=\frac{3}{4}m_1$

$$\Rightarrow \quad \frac{(273+60)}{T}=\frac{3/4m_1}{m_1}$$

$[\because T_1=60°C=(60+273)K]$

$$\Rightarrow \quad T=444\text{ K}$$

$$=(444-273)°C$$

$$=171°C$$

17 (b) Pressure *versus* temperature diagram is given below

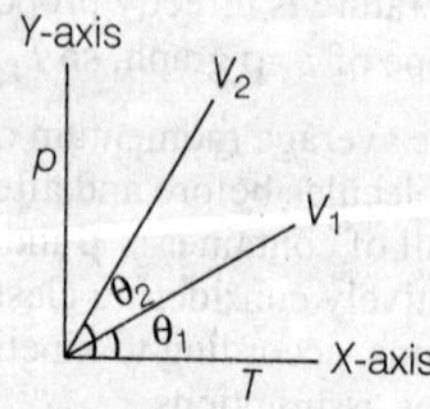

Given, $V_1 > V_2$

From ideal gas equation,

$$pV=nRT$$

$$\Rightarrow \quad \frac{p}{T}=\frac{nR}{V} \quad \text{or} \quad \frac{p}{T}\propto\frac{1}{V}$$

Slope of curve $=\tan\theta=\frac{p}{T}\propto\frac{1}{V}$

$$\Rightarrow \quad \left(\frac{p_1}{T_1}\right)<\left(\frac{p_2}{T_2}\right) \quad [\because V_1>V_2]$$

$$\Rightarrow \quad \tan\theta_1<\tan\theta_2$$

or slope of curve for V_1 is less than that for V_2.

18 (a) According to Gay Lussac's law,

$$p\propto T$$

$$\therefore \quad \frac{dp}{p}\times100=\frac{dT}{T}\times100$$

$$\left[\because \frac{dp}{p}\times100=1\right]$$

$$\Rightarrow \quad 1=\frac{1}{T}\times100 \Rightarrow T=100\text{ K}$$

19 (b) The ideal gas law is the equation of state of an ideal gas. The state of an amount of gas is determined by its pressure, volume and temperature. The equation has the form $pV=\mu RT$, where p is the pressure, V is the volume, μ is the number of moles, R is the universal gas constant and T is the temperature.

$$\therefore \quad p_1V_1/T_1=p_2V_2/T_2 \quad \text{...(i)}$$

Given, $p_1=200$ kPa, $V_1=V$,

$T_1=273+22=295$ K,

$V_2=V+2\%V=V+\frac{2V}{100}$

$=V+0.02V=1.02V$

$T_2=273+42=315$ K

Putting these values in Eq. (i), we get

$$\Rightarrow \quad \frac{200\times V}{295}=\frac{p_2\times1.02V}{315}$$

$$\Rightarrow \quad p_2=\frac{200\times315}{295\times1.02}\approx 209\text{ kPa}$$

20 (b) Given, $p=20$ atm,

$T_1=27°C=(27+273°)K=300$ K

and $T_2=50°C=(50+273)K=323K$

As, $pV=\mu RT=\frac{m}{M}RT$

$$pV=\frac{m}{M}RT_1$$

$$\Rightarrow \quad 20\times V=\frac{m}{M}\times R\times300 \quad \text{...(i)}$$

When $m=m/2$ and $p=p'$, then

$$pV=\frac{m}{M}RT_2$$

As, $$p'\times V=\left(\frac{m/2}{M}\right)R\times323 \quad \text{...(ii)}$$

From Eqs. (i) and (ii), we get

$$p'\approx=\frac{323}{30}\approx10.8\text{ atm}$$

21 (d) All molecules have same speed. This statement is true but this is not an assumption of kinetic theory of gases.

22 (b) The pressure on the rear side would be more due to fictitious force (acting in the opposite direction of real acceleration) on the rear face. Consequently, the pressure in the front side would be lowered.

23 (d) From ideal gas equation,

$$pV=\mu RT$$

At constant temperature,

$$pV=\text{constant}$$

i.e. $pV=c$

Hence, $p_1V_1=p_2V_2$ ...(i)

Given, $V_2=V_1-\frac{10}{100}V_1=(0.90)V_1$

Form Eq. (i),

$$p_2=\frac{p_1V_1}{V_2}=\frac{p_1V_1}{0.90\,V_1}=\frac{p_1}{0.90}$$

$$\Rightarrow \quad \frac{p_2}{p_1}=\frac{1}{0.90}=\frac{10}{9}$$

$$\frac{p_2-p_1}{p_1}=\frac{10-9}{9}=\left(\frac{1}{9}\right)$$

Therefore, % increase in pressure

$$=\frac{100\%}{9}=11.1\%$$

24 (a) When a van der Waals' gas (real gas) undergoes free expansion, then its temperature decreases.

25 (c) From ideal gal equation,

$$pV=\mu RT$$

Given, $p=1.2\times10^{-7}$ mm

$=1.2\times10^{-7}\times10^{-3}\text{m}=1.2\times10^{-10}\text{m}$,

$T=27°C=(27+273)K$ and

$V=100\text{ cm}^3=10^{-4}\text{ m}^3$

$\Rightarrow 1.2\times10^{-7}\times133.322\times10^{-4}$

$=\mu\times8.31\times(273+27)$

$\therefore$ Number of moles, $\mu=6.42\times10^{-13}$

Hence, number of molecules

$=6.42\times10^{-13}\times6.02\times10^{23}$

$=3.86\times10^{11}$

26 (d) As, $\frac{p_1V_1}{T_1}=\frac{p_{mix}\times V_{mix}}{T_{mix}}$

Given, $T_1=T_{mix}=T$

and $V_1=V+V$, $V_{mix}=V$

$$\therefore \quad \frac{p\times2V}{T}=\frac{p_{mix}\times V}{T}$$

$$\Rightarrow \quad p_{mix}=2p$$

27 (d) As, $pV = nRT$

$$\Rightarrow \quad p_{H_2} = \frac{m}{M_{H_2}} \cdot \frac{RT}{V}$$

and $p_{He} = \frac{m}{M_{He}} \cdot \frac{RT}{V}$

$$\therefore \quad \frac{p_{H_2}}{p_{He}} = \frac{M_{He}}{M_{H_2}} = \frac{4}{2} = 2$$

$[\because M_{H_2} = 2 \text{ and } M_{He} = 4]$

$$\Rightarrow \quad p_{H_2} = 2p_{He}$$

The pressure exerted by hydrogen is twice that exerted by helium.

28 (d) In terms of density, ideal gas can be written as,

$pM_0 = dRT$ [where, d = density of gas]

$$\Rightarrow \quad \frac{d}{p} = \frac{M_0}{RT} \quad \Rightarrow \quad \frac{d}{p} \propto \frac{1}{T}$$

or $\frac{d_1/p_1}{d_2/p_2} = \frac{T_2}{T_1} = \frac{383}{283}$

$\left[\because T_2 = 110°C = 383 \text{ K and } T_1 = 10°\text{ C} = 283 \text{ K}\right]$

$$\Rightarrow \quad \frac{x}{(d_2/p_2)} = \frac{383}{283} \quad \left[\because \frac{d_1}{p_1} = x \text{ (given)}\right]$$

or $(d_2/P_2) = x \times \left(\frac{283}{383}\right)$

29 (c)

I. The dotted line in the diagram shows that there is no deviation in the value of $\frac{pV}{nT}$ for different temperatures T_1 and T_2 for increasing pressure, so this gas behaves ideally. Hence, dotted line corresponds to ideal gas behaviour.

II. At high temperature, the deviation of the gas is less and at low temperature the deviation of gas is more. In the graph, deviation for T_2 is greater than for T_1. Thus, $T_1 > T_2$.

III. Since, the two curves intersect at dotted line at same point, so the value of $\frac{pV}{nT}$ at that point on the Y-axis is same for all gases.

30 (c) According to Boyle's law,

$$p_1V_1 = p_2V_2$$

As, the pressure is decreased by 20%,

therefore $p_2 = \frac{80}{100} p_1$

$$\Rightarrow \quad p_1V_1 = \frac{80}{100} p_1V_2$$

$$\Rightarrow \quad V_1 = \frac{80}{100} V_2$$

$\therefore$ Percentage increase in volume

$$= \frac{V_2 - V_1}{V_1} \times 100$$

$$= \frac{100 - 80}{80} \times 100$$

$$= 25\%$$

31 (b) By Charles' law,

$$\frac{V_1}{V_2} = \frac{T_1}{T_2}$$

So, $V_2 = \frac{V_1T_2}{T_1}$

Given, $V_1 = 1$ L,

$T_1 = 27°\text{ C} = (27 + 273)$ K and

$T_2 = 297°\text{ C} = (297 + 273)$ K

Putting these values, we get

$$\therefore \quad V_2 = 1 \times \frac{(297 + 273)}{(27 + 273)}$$

$$= \frac{570}{300} = 1.9 \text{ L}$$

32 (b) Ideal gas equation can be written as

$$pV = \mu RT \quad \text{...(i)}$$

In this equation,

μ = number of moles of the gas,

p = pressure of the gas,

V = volume of the gas,

R = universal gas constant

and T = temperature of the gas.

From Eq. (i), we have

$$\mu/V = p/RT = \text{constant}$$

So, at constant pressure and temperature, both balloons will contain equal number of molecules (i.e. mole) per unit volume.

33 (b) By Boyle's law,

$$pV = RT$$

$$\therefore \quad p_1V_1 = p_2V_2$$

($\because$ temperature = constant)

Given, $V_1 = V$,

$V_2 = V - 5\%V = V - \frac{5}{100}V$

$$\Rightarrow \quad pV = p_2\left(V - \frac{5}{100}V\right)$$

$$\Rightarrow \quad pV = p_2\left(\frac{95}{100}V\right) \Rightarrow p_2 = \frac{20}{19}p$$

Increase in pressure

$$= \left(\frac{20}{19} - 1\right) \times 100$$

$$= \frac{1}{19} \times 100 = 5.26\%$$

34 (b) Total pressure inside the container is given as

$$p = \frac{1}{3}\frac{mN}{V} v^2_{rms}$$

$$p \propto m \quad \text{...(i)}$$

(when volume and temperature are constant)

From Eq. (i), pressure first increases and then becomes constant.

35 (b) From ideal gas equation,

$$pV = NkT$$

where, k is the Boltzmann's constant, p is the pressure, V is the volume, T is the absolute temperature and N is the number of molecules.

Hence, number of molecules in given mass of gas, $N = pV/kT$.

36 (c) From ideal gas equation,

$$pV = \mu RT$$

where, p is the pressure, V is the volume, R is the universal gas constant, T is the temperature and μ is the number of moles.

$$\therefore \quad \mu = \frac{pV}{RT} \quad \text{...(i)}$$

Given, pressure $p = 22.4$ atm

$= 22.4 \times 1.01 \times 10^5 \text{ Nm}^{-2}$

$V = 2\text{L} = 2 \times 10^{-3} \text{m}^3$

$R = 8.31 \text{ J mol}^{-1} - \text{K}^{-1}$

$T = 273$ K

Putting these values in Eq. (i), we get

$$\therefore \quad \mu = \frac{22.4 \times 1.01 \times 10^5 \times 2 \times 10^{-3}}{8.31 \times 273}$$

$$= 1.99 \approx 2$$

Since, $\mu = \frac{\text{Mass}}{\text{Molecular weight}}$

$\Rightarrow$ Mass $= \mu \times$ Molecular weight

$= 2 \times 28 = 56$ g

37 (a) Gas equation, pV/T = constant

$= R$ (for 1 mol of gas)

$$\Rightarrow \quad \frac{p_1V_1}{T_1} = \frac{p_2V_2}{T_2}$$

If m is the mass of a gas and d_1 & d_2 are its density at absolute temperatures T_1K and T_2K respectively, then

$V_1 = m/d_1$ and $V_2 = m/d_2$

$$\therefore \quad \frac{p_1}{T_1}\left(\frac{m}{d_1}\right) = \frac{p_2}{T_2}\left(\frac{m}{d_2}\right)$$

$$\Rightarrow \quad \frac{p_1}{T_1 d_1} = \frac{p_2}{T_2 d_2}$$

Topic 2

Various Velocities & Kinetic Energy of Gas and Mean Free Path

2019

1 Increase in temperature of a gas filled in a container would lead to **[NEET]**
(a) increase in its kinetic energy
(b) decrease in its pressure
(c) decrease in intermolecular distance
(d) increase in its mass

2018

2 At what temperature will the rms speed of oxygen molecules become just sufficient for escaping from the earth's atmosphere? **[NEET]**
(Take, mass of oxygen molecule, $m = 2.76 \times 10^{-26}$ kg and Boltzmann's constant, $k_B = 1.38 \times 10^{-23}$ J K^{-1})
(a) 5.016×10^4 K (b) 8.326×10^4 K
(c) 2.508×10^4 K (d) 1.254×10^4 K

2016

3 The molecules of a given mass of a gas have rms velocity of 200 ms^{-1} at 27°C and 1.0×10^5 Nm^{-2} pressure. When the temperature and pressure of the gas are respectively, 127°C and 0.05×10^5 Nm^{-2}, the rms velocity of its molecules in ms^{-1} is **[NEET]**
(a) $\frac{400}{\sqrt{3}}$ (b) $\frac{100\sqrt{2}}{3}$ (c) $\frac{100}{3}$ (d) $100\sqrt{2}$

2014

4 A gas is compressed isothermally. The rms velocity of its molecules **[MHT CET]**
(a) increases (b) decreases
(c) first increases and then decreases
(d) remains the same

5 The mean free path of molecules of a gas (radius) is inversely proportional to **[CBSE AIPMT]**
(a) r^3 (b) r^2 (c) r (d) $\sqrt{r}$

2013

6 Critical temperature of CO_2 is 31.2°C. In summer, the room temperature is 40° C, then **[AIIMS]**
(a) CO_2 cannot be liquified
(b) CO_2 can be liquified with increase of pressure
(c) CO_2 can be liquified with decrease of pressure
(d) CO_2 can be liquified, if temperature of CO_2 is decreased below 31.2° C

2011

7 The mean free path of collision of gas molecules varies with its diameter (d) of the molecules as **[DUMET]**
(a) d^{-1} (b) d^{-2} (c) d^{-3} (d) d^{-4}

2010

8 The velocity of 4 gas molecules are given by 1 kms^{-1}, 3 kms^{-1}, 5 kms^{-1} and 7 kms^{-1}. Calculate the difference between average and rms velocity. **[MHT CET]**
(a) 0.338 (b) 0.438 (c) 0.583 (d) 0.683

9 At what temperature will the oxygen molecules have the same root mean square speed as hydrogen molecules at 300 K? **[OJEE]**
(a) 1600 K (b) 2400 K (c) 3200 K (d) 4800 K

10 Average velocity of an ideal gas molecule is **[OJEE]**
(a) proportional to $\sqrt{T}$ (b) proportional to T^2
(c) proportional to T^3 (d) zero

11 At what temperature is the rms velocity of a hydrogen molecule equal to that of an oxygen molecule at 47° C? **[Manipal]**
(a) 80 K (b) −73 K
(c) 3 K (d) 20 K

12 The temperature of an ideal gas is increased from 120 K to 480 K. If at 120 K, the root mean square speed of gas molecules is v, then at 480 K, it will be **[WB JEE]**
(a) $4v$ (b) $2v$ (c) $v/2$ (d) $v/4$

13 The temperature at which the velocity of oxygen will be half that of hydrogen at NTP is **[BCECE]**
(a) 1092° C (b) 1492° C (c) 273 K (d) 819° C

14 Nitrogen (N_2) is in equilibrium state at $T = 421$ K. The value of most probable velocity v_{mp} is **[BCECE]**
(a) 400 ms^{-1} (b) 421 ms^{-1} (c) 500 ms^{-1} (d) 600 ms^{-1}

15 **Assertion** If a gas container in motion is suddenly stopped, the temperature of the gas rises.
Reason The kinetic energy of ordered mechanical motion is converted into the kinetic energy of random motion of gas molecules. **[AIIMS]**
(a) Both Assertion and Reason are correct and Reason is the correct explanation of Assertion.
(b) Both Assertion and Reason are correct but Reason is not the correct explanation of Assertion.
(c) Assertion is correct but Reason is incorrect.
(d) Both Assertion and Reason are incorrect.

16 The kinetic energy of 1 g molecule of a gas at normal temperature and pressure is ($R = 8.31$ Jmol K^{-1}) **[BHU]**

(a) 1.3×10^2 J (b) 2.7×10^2 J
(c) 0.56×10^4 J (d) 3.4×10^3 J

17 The temperature at which the mean kinetic energy of the molecules of gas is one-third of the mean kinetic energy of its molecules at 180° C is

(a) – 122° C (b) – 90° C **[MGIMS]**
(c) 60° C (d) 151° C

2009

18 To what temperature should the hydrogen at 327° C be cooled at constant pressure, so that the root mean square velocity of its molecules becomes half of its previous value?

(a) – 123° C (b) 123° C **[MHT CET]**
(c) – 100° C (d) 0° C

19 The average velocity of the molecules in a gas in equilibrium is **[MGIMS]**

(a) proportional to $\sqrt{T}$ (b) proportional to T
(c) proportional to T^2 (d) equal to zero

20 A sealed container with negligible coefficient of volumetric expansion contains helium (a monatomic gas). When it is heated from 300 K to 600 K, the average kinetic energy of helium atoms is **[UP CPMT]**

(a) halved (b) unchanged
(c) doubled (d) increased by factor $\sqrt{2}$

21 If at the same temperature and pressure, the densities of two diatomic gases are d_1 and d_2, respectively. The ratio of mean kinetic energy per molecule of gases will be **[MGIMS]**

(a) 1 : 1 (b) $d_1 : d_2$
(c) $\sqrt{d_1} : \sqrt{d_2}$ (d) $\sqrt{d_2} : \sqrt{d_1}$

2008

22 If average velocity becomes 4 times, then what will be the effect on rms velocity at that temperature? **[BCECE]**

(a) 1.4 times (b) 4 times
(c) 2 times (d) 1/4 times

23 **Assertion** Mean free path of a gas molecules varies inversely as density of the gas.

Reason Mean free path varies inversely as pressure of the gas. **[AIIMS]**

(a) Both Assertion and Reason are correct and Reason is the correct explanation of Assertion.
(b) Both Assertion and Reason are correct but Reason is not the correct explanation of Assertion.
(c) Assertion is correct but Reason is incorrect.
(d) Both Assertion and Reason are incorrect.

2007

24 At what temperature, the kinetic energy of a gas molecule is half of the value at 27°C ? **[Kerala CEE]**

(a) 13.5°C (b) 150°C (c) 75 K (d) 13.5 K
(e) – 123° C

2006

25 **Assertion** The root mean square and most probable speeds of the molecules in a gas are the same.
Reason The Maxwell distribution for the speed of molecules in a gas is symmetrical. **[AIIMS]**

(a) Both Assertion and Reason are correct and Reason is the correct explanation of Assertion.
(b) Both Assertion and Reason are correct but Reason is not the correct explanation of Assertion.
(c) Assertion is correct but Reason is incorrect.
(d) Both Assertion and Reason are incorrect.

26 When temperature of an ideal gas is increased from 27°C to 227°C, its rms speed is changed from 400 ms^{-1} to v_s. Then v_s is **[Manipal]**

(a) 516 ms^{-1} (b) 450 ms^{-1} (c) 310 ms^{-1} (d) 746 ms^{-1}

27 If at NTP velocity of sound in a gas is 1150 ms^{-1}, then the rms velocity of gas molecules at NTP is (take, $R = 8.3$ J mol^{-1} K^{-1}, $C_p = 4.8$ cal mol^{-1} K^{-1}) **[AMU]**

(a) 1600 ms^{-1} (b) 1532.19 ms^{-1}
(c) 160 ms^{-1} (d) zero

28 The temperature of H_2 at which the rms velocity of its molecules is seven times, the rms velocity of the molecules of nitrogen gas at 300 K is **[AMU]**

(a) 2100 K (b) 1700 K (c) 1350 K (d) 1050 K

29 Some gas at 300 K is enclosed in a container. Now, the container is placed on a fast moving train while the train is in motion, the temperature of the gas **[MHT CET]**

(a) rises above 300 K (b) falls below 300 K
(c) remains unchanged (d) becomes unsteady

2005

30 The ratio of root mean square velocities of O_3 and O_2 is **[BVP]**

(a) 1 : 1 (b) 2 : 3
(c) 3 : 2 (d) $\sqrt{2} : \sqrt{3}$

31 The temperature, at which the rms velocity of hydrogen is four times of its value at NTP is **[MHT CET]**

(a) 819°C (b) 1092°C (c) 4368°C (d) 4095°C

32 If mass of He is 4 times that of hydrogen, then mean velocity of He is **[Punjab PMET]**

(a) 2 times of H-mean value
(b) (1/2) times of H-mean value
(c) 4 times of H-mean value
(d) same as H-mean value

Answers

1 (a)	2 (b)	3 (a)	4 (d)	5 (b)	6 (a)	7 (b)	8 (c)	9 (d)	10 (d)
11 (d)	12 (b)	13 (d)	14 (c)	15 (a)	16 (d)	17 (a)	18 (a)	19 (a)	20 (c)
21 (a)	22 (b)	23 (b)	24 (e)	25 (d)	26 (a)	27 (b)	28 (d)	29 (c)	30 (d)
31 (d)	32 (b)								

Explanations

1 *(a)* The kinetic energy of gas molecules is given by

$$\text{KE} = \frac{3}{2}RT$$

$$\Rightarrow \quad \text{KE} = \frac{3}{2}RT$$

$$\Rightarrow \quad \text{KE} \propto T$$

Thus, increase in temperature, would increase the kinetic energy of molecules.

Option (b) is incorrect as increase in temperature will lead to increase in pressure as $p \propto T$. Other options (c) and (d) are also incorrect as molecular distance increases while mass remains the same for increase in the temperature.

2 *(b)* The minimum velocity with which the body must be projected vertically upwards, so that it could escape from the earth's atmosphere, is its escape velocity (v_e).

As, $v_e = \sqrt{2gR}$

Substituting the value of g (9.8 ms^{-2}) and radius of earth ($R = 6.4 \times 10^6$ m),

we get $v_e = \sqrt{2 \times 9.8 \times 6.4 \times 10^6}$

$$\cong 11.2 \text{ km s}^{-1} = 11200 \text{ m s}^{-1}$$

Let the temperature of molecule be T when it attains v_e.

According to the question, $v_{\text{rms}} = v_e$

where, v_{rms} is the rms speed of the oxygen molecule.

$$\Rightarrow \quad \sqrt{\frac{3k_BT}{m_{O_2}}} = 11.2 \times 10^3$$

or $$T = \frac{(11.2 \times 10^3)^2 (m_{O_2})}{(3k_B)}$$

Substituting the given values, i.e.

$$k_B = 1.38 \times 10^{-23} \text{ JK}^{-1}$$

and $m_{O_2} = m = 2.76 \times 10^{-26}$ kg

We get $$T = \frac{(11.2 \times 10^3)^2 (2.76 \times 10^{-26})}{(3 \times 1.38 \times 10^{-23})}$$

$$= 8.326 \times 10^4 \text{ K}$$

3 *(a)* Given, $v_{\text{rms}} = 200 \text{ ms}^{-1}$,

$T_1 = 27°\text{C} = (27 + 273) \text{ K} = 300 \text{ K}$,

$p_1 = 10^5 \text{ Nm}^{-2}$

$T_2 = 400 \text{ K}$, $p_2 = 0.05 \times 10^5 \text{ Nm}^{-2}$

As, rms velocity of gas molecules,

$$\because \quad v_{\text{rms}} \propto \sqrt{T} \quad \left(\because v_{\text{rms}} = \sqrt{\frac{3RT}{m}}\right)$$

For two different cases,

$$\Rightarrow \quad \frac{(v_{\text{rms}})_1}{(v_{\text{rms}})_2} = \sqrt{\frac{T_1}{T_2}}$$

$$\Rightarrow \quad \frac{200}{(v_{\text{rms}})_2} = \sqrt{\frac{300}{400}} = \sqrt{\frac{3}{4}}$$

$$\Rightarrow \quad (v_{\text{rms}})_2 = \frac{2}{\sqrt{3}} \times 200$$

$$= \frac{400}{\sqrt{3}} \text{ ms}^{-1}$$

4 *(d)* The root mean square velocity of a gas molecule is given by

$$v_{\text{rms}} = \sqrt{\frac{3RT}{M}}$$

Gas is compressed isothermally, so T remains constant and hence root mean square velocity will remain same.

5 *(b)* Mean free path,

$$\lambda = \frac{1}{\sqrt{2}\pi n d^2}$$

$$\Rightarrow \quad \lambda \propto \frac{1}{r^2}$$

where, d = diameter of the molecule and n = number of molecules per unit volume.

6 *(a)* Gases cannot be liquified above critical temperature, however large the pressure may be hence CO_2 cannot be liquified.

7 *(b)* Mean free path of gas molecules,

$$\lambda = \frac{\lambda_1 + \lambda_2 + \cdots + \lambda_n}{n}$$

$$\Rightarrow \quad \lambda = \frac{1}{\sqrt{2}\pi n d^2}$$

$$\therefore \quad \lambda \propto d^{-2}$$

8 *(c)* Given, $N = 4$, $v_1 = 1 \text{ kms}^{-1}$, $v_2 = 3 \text{ kms}^{-1}$, $v_3 = 5 \text{ kms}^{-1}$ and $v_4 = 7 \text{ kms}^{-1}$

The average velocity,

$$v_{\text{av}} = \frac{v_1 + v_2 + v_3 + \cdots + v_n}{N}$$

$$= \frac{1 + 3 + 5 + 7}{4} = 4 \text{ kms}^{-1}$$

Root mean square velocity,

$$v_{\text{rms}} = \sqrt{\frac{v_1^2 + v_2^2 + v_3^2 + v_4^2 + \cdots + v_n^2}{N}}$$

$$= \sqrt{\frac{1 + (3)^2 + (5)^2 + (7)^2}{4}}$$

$$= \sqrt{21} = 4.583 \text{ kms}^{-1}$$

Difference between average velocity and root mean square velocity $= 4.583 - 4 = 0.583 \text{ km s}^{-1}$

9 *(d)* As, $v_{\text{rms}} = \sqrt{\dfrac{3RT}{M}}$

$$\Rightarrow \quad T \propto M$$

($\because v_{\text{rms}}$ and R are constants)

$$\Rightarrow \quad \frac{T_{O_2}}{T_{H_2}} = \frac{M_{O_2}}{M_{H_2}}$$

$$\Rightarrow \quad \frac{T_{O_2}}{300} = \frac{32}{2} \quad \text{(given)}$$

$$\therefore \quad T_{O_2} = 4800 \text{ K}$$

10 *(d)* Average velocity of an ideal gas molecule is collectively assumed to be zero.

11 *(d)* We know that, $v_{\text{rms}} = \sqrt{\dfrac{3RT}{M}}$

In the given problem, v_{rms} and R are constants.

$$\frac{T}{M} = \text{constant}$$

$$\frac{T_H}{M_H} = \frac{T_O}{M_O}$$

$$\left[\because M_H = 2, M_O = 32 \atop T_O = 47°\text{C} = 320 \text{ K}\right]$$

$$\Rightarrow \quad \frac{T_H}{2} = \frac{273 + 47}{32}$$

$\Rightarrow \quad \dfrac{T}{2} = \dfrac{320}{32} = 10$

$\therefore \quad T = 20\,\text{K}$

12 *(b)* The root mean square velocity is given by

$$v_{rms} = \sqrt{\frac{3RT}{M}}$$

So, $\dfrac{v_1}{v_2} = \sqrt{\dfrac{T_1}{T_2}}$

(where, M is a constant)

Given, $T_1 = 120\,\text{K}, T_2 = 480\,\text{K}, v_1 = v$

So, $\dfrac{v}{v_2} = \sqrt{\dfrac{120}{480}} = \sqrt{\dfrac{1}{4}} = \dfrac{1}{2}$

$\Rightarrow \quad v_2 = 2v$

13 *(d)* Given, $v_{O_2} = \dfrac{1}{2} v_{H_2}$

$\therefore \quad \sqrt{\dfrac{3RT}{32}} = \dfrac{1}{2}\sqrt{\dfrac{3R \times 273}{2}}$

$\left(\because v_{rms} = \sqrt{\dfrac{3RT}{\text{molecular weight}}}\right)$

$\Rightarrow \quad \dfrac{T}{32} = \dfrac{273}{8}$ or $T = 4 \times 273$

or $\quad T = 1092\,\text{K}$

$= 1092 - 273 = 819\,°\text{C}$

14 *(c)* Most probable velocity,

$$v_{mp} = \sqrt{\frac{2RT}{m}} = \sqrt{\frac{2 \times 8.31 \times 421}{28 \times 10^{-3}}}$$

$[m_{N_2} = 28\,\text{gmol}^{-1} = 28 \times 10^{-3}\,\text{kgmol}^{-1}]$

$= 499.89 = 500\,\text{ms}^{-1}$

15 *(a)* The motion of the container is known as the ordered motion of the gas and *zig-zag* motion of gas molecules within the container is called disordered/Random motion, like brownian motion. When the container suddenly stops, ordered kinetic energy gets converted into disordered kinetic energy which increases the temperature of the gas.

16 *(d)* If nothing is said about gas, then we should calculate the translational kinetic energy.

$$E_{trans} = \frac{3}{2}RT$$

$= \dfrac{3}{2} \times 8.31 \times (273 + 0)$

$= 3.4 \times 10^3\,\text{J}$

17 *(a)* Given, $K_1 = K, K_2 = K/3$, $T_1 = 180°\text{C} = (180 + 273)\text{K}$

Kinetic energy of a gas is directly proportional to its temperature.

$\therefore \quad \dfrac{K_1}{K_2} = \dfrac{T_1}{T_2} \Rightarrow \dfrac{K}{K/3} = \dfrac{273 + 180}{T_2}$

$\Rightarrow \quad 3 = \dfrac{453}{T_2} \Rightarrow T_2 = 151\text{K}$

$T_2 = 151 - 273 = -122°\text{C}$

18 *(a)* rms speed, $v_{rms} = \sqrt{\dfrac{3RT}{M}}$

$\Rightarrow \quad v_{rms_1} = \sqrt{\dfrac{3RT_1}{M}}$

and $\quad v_{rms_2} = \sqrt{\dfrac{3RT_2}{M}}$

Given, $T_1 = 327°\text{C} = (327 + 273)\text{K}$

Now, $\dfrac{v_{rms_1}}{v_{rms_2}} = \sqrt{\dfrac{T_1}{T_2}} \Rightarrow \dfrac{v}{\frac{v}{2}} = \sqrt{\dfrac{600}{T_2}}$

$\Rightarrow \quad T_2 = \dfrac{600}{4} = 150\,\text{K}$

$= 150 - 273 = -123°\text{C}$

19 *(a)* Average speed of gas is given as

$$v_{av} = \sqrt{\frac{8}{\pi} \cdot \frac{RT}{M}}$$

Hence, $v_{av} \propto \sqrt{T}$

20 *(c)* As, kinetic energy of gas is given as

$$K = \frac{1}{2}mv_{rms}^2 = \frac{3}{2}RT$$

$\Rightarrow \quad K \propto T \Rightarrow \dfrac{K_2}{K_1} = \dfrac{T_2}{T_1}$

$\Rightarrow \quad K_2 = K_1\left(\dfrac{T_2}{T_1}\right)$

$\Rightarrow \quad K_2 = K_1\left(\dfrac{600}{300}\right)$ (given)

$\Rightarrow \quad K_2 = 2K_1$

21 *(a)* At a given temperature (T), all the ideal gas molecules no matter what their masses have the same average translational kinetic energy.

i.e. $\quad E = \dfrac{3}{2}kT$

So, E does not depend upon density (as mass $= \rho V$)

$$\frac{E_1}{E_2} = 1:1$$

22 *(b)* According to kinetic theory of gases, average velocity,

$$v_{av} = \sqrt{\frac{8RT}{M\pi}} \quad \text{...(i)}$$

According to kinetic theory of gases, root mean square velocity,

$$v_{rms} = \sqrt{\frac{3RT}{M}} \quad \text{...(ii)}$$

From Eqs. (i) and (ii), we get

$$v_{av} = \sqrt{\left(\frac{8}{3\pi}\right)}\, v_{rms} = 0.92\, v_{rms} \quad \text{...(iii)}$$

Therefore, $\dfrac{v_{av}}{v_{rms}} = \text{constant}$

Hence, root mean square velocity will also become 4 times, while the average velocity becomes 4 time of initial one.

23 *(b)* The mean free path of a gas molecule is the average distance between two successive collisions. It is represented by λ.

$$\lambda = \frac{k_B T}{\sqrt{2}\pi\sigma^2 p}$$

Here, $\sigma =$ density of molecule

and $\quad k_B =$ Boltzmann's as constant.

Hence, mean free path varies inversely with the density of the gas. It can be easily proved that the mean free path varies directly with the temperature and inversely with the pressure of the gas.

24 *(e)* Kinetic energy of a gas molecule

$$E = \frac{3}{2}RT$$

where, R is universal gas constant.

$\therefore \quad E \propto T \Rightarrow \dfrac{E_1}{E_2} = \dfrac{T_1}{T_2}$

Given, $E_1 = E, E_2 = E/2$, $T_1 = 27°\text{C} = (27 + 273)\,\text{K}$ and $T_2 = ?$

$\Rightarrow \quad \dfrac{E}{(E/2)} = \dfrac{300}{T_2}$

$T_2 = 150\,\text{K}$

or $\quad T_2 = 150 - 273 = -123°\text{C}$

25 *(d)* Root mean square speed of molecules in a gas is defined as the square root of mean of the squares of the speed of different molecules,

i.e. $\quad v_{rms} = \sqrt{\dfrac{(v_1^2 + v_2^2 + \cdots)}{N}}$

or $\quad v_{rms} = \sqrt{\dfrac{3RT}{M}}$

(according to kinetic theory of gases)

while most probable speed is the speed which maximum number of molecules in a gas have at constant temperature and is given by

$$v_{mp} = \sqrt{2RT/M}$$

It is obvious that, $v_{rms} > v_{mp}$.

Also, Maxwell distribution for the speed of molecules in a gas is asymmetrical.

26 *(a)* We know that, rms speed is directly proportional to square root of temperature.

$$v_{rms} \propto \sqrt{T}$$

Hence, $\frac{v_{rms(1)}}{v_{rms(2)}} = \sqrt{\frac{T_1}{T_2}}$

Given, $T_1 = 27°C = (27 + 273)$ K, $T_2 = 227°C = (227 + 273)$ K, $v_{rms(1)} = 400 \text{ ms}^{-1}$ and $v_s = v_{rms(2)} = ?$

$\Rightarrow \frac{400}{v_{rms(2)}} = \frac{\sqrt{27+273}}{\sqrt{227+273}} = \sqrt{\frac{300}{500}}$

$\Rightarrow v_{rms(2)} = v_s = \sqrt{\frac{500}{300}} \times 400$

$= 1.29 \times 400$

$= 516.39 \text{ ms}^{-1} \simeq 516 \text{ ms}^{-1}$

27 *(b)* As we know,

$R = \frac{8.3}{4.2} \text{ cal g mol}^{-1}\text{K}^{-1}$

and $C_V = C_p - R$

$= \left(4.8 - \frac{8.3}{4.2}\right) = 2.824$

Also, $\gamma = \frac{C_p}{C_V} = \frac{4.8}{2.824} = 1.69$

Since, $v = \sqrt{\left(\frac{3}{\gamma}\right)} v_s = \sqrt{\frac{3}{1.69}} \times 1150$

$= 1532.19 \text{ ms}^{-1}$

28 *(d)* As, $v_{rms} = \sqrt{\frac{3RT}{M}}$

$\Rightarrow \frac{v_1}{v_2} = \sqrt{\frac{T_1}{M_1} \times \frac{M_2}{T_2}}$

$\Rightarrow \frac{v_H}{v_N} = \sqrt{\frac{T_H}{M_H} \times \frac{M_N}{T_N}}$

$\Rightarrow 7 = \sqrt{\frac{T_H \times 28}{2 \times 300}}$ (given)

or $49 = \frac{T_H \times 28}{600}$

$\therefore T_H = \frac{49 \times 600}{28} = 1050$ K

29 *(c)* When container is placed on fast moving train, then there is no effect on the random speed of molecules in the container, therefore temperature of the gas remains unchanged.

30 *(d)* As, $v_{rms} = \sqrt{\frac{3RT}{M}}$

$\Rightarrow v_{rms} \propto \frac{1}{\sqrt{M}}$

$\frac{(v_{rms})_{O_3}}{(v_{rms})_{O_2}} = \sqrt{\frac{M_{O_2}}{M_{O_3}}} = \sqrt{\left(\frac{32}{48}\right)} = \sqrt{2} : \sqrt{3}$

31 *(d)* Root mean square velocity is defined as the square root of the mean of the squares of the random velocities of the individual molecules of a gas. Maxwell's speed distribution law states that,

$$v_{rms} = \sqrt{\left(\frac{3kT}{m}\right)}$$

$\Rightarrow v_{rms} \propto \sqrt{T}$

$\therefore \frac{v_{rms_1}}{v_{rms_2}} = \sqrt{\frac{T_1}{T_2}}$

$\Rightarrow \frac{4}{1} = \sqrt{\frac{T'}{273}}$ (given)

$T' = 4368 \text{ K} = 4095°C$

32 *(b)* We have,

$\frac{\bar{v}_H}{\bar{v}_{He}} = \sqrt{\frac{M_{He}}{M_H}} = \sqrt{\left(\frac{4}{1}\right)} = \frac{2}{1}$

Thus, $\bar{v}_{He} = \frac{1}{2}\bar{v}_H$

Topic 3

Degrees of Freedom, Law of Equipartition of Energy and Specific Heat Capacity

2019

1 The value of $\gamma\left(=\frac{C_p}{C_V}\right)$, for hydrogen, helium and another ideal diatomic gas X (whose molecules are not rigid but have an additional vibrational mode), are respectively equal to **[NEET (Odisha)]**

(a) $\frac{7}{5}, \frac{5}{3}, \frac{9}{7}$ (b) $\frac{5}{3}, \frac{7}{5}, \frac{9}{7}$ (c) $\frac{5}{3}, \frac{7}{5}, \frac{7}{5}$ (d) $\frac{7}{5}, \frac{5}{3}, \frac{7}{5}$

2 If 7 g N_2 is mixed with 20 g Ar, the $\frac{C_p}{C_V}$ of mixture will be **[AIIMS]**

(a) $\frac{17}{6}$ (b) $\frac{11}{7}$ (c) $\frac{17}{11}$ (d) $\frac{17}{13}$

3 In an isobaric process, the work done by a di-atomic gas is 10 J, the heat given to the gas will be **[AIIMS]**

(a) 35 J (b) 30 J
(c) 45 J (d) 60 J

4 **Assertion** Vibrational degree of freedom of a di-atomic gas molecule appears at every high temperature.

Reason Di-atomic gas has two vibrational degree of freedom in one direction. **[AIIMS]**

(a) Both Assertion and Reason are correct and Reason is the correct explanation of assertion.
(b) Both Assertion and Reason are correct but Reason is not the correct explanation of Assertion.
(c) Assertion is correct, but Reason is incorrect.
(d) Both Assertion and Reason are incorrect.

2018

5 The volume (V) of a monoatomic gas varies with its temperature (T), as shown in the graph. The ratio of work done by the gas, to the heat absorbed by it, when it undergoes a change from state A to state B, is **[NEET]**

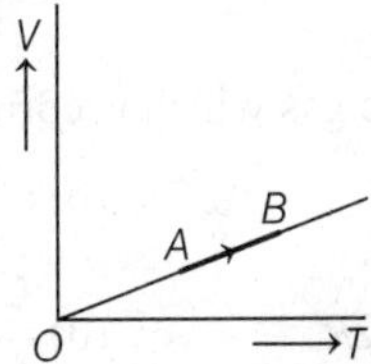

(a) 1/3 (b) 2/3
(c) 2/5 (d) 2/7

6 A gas consisting of a rigid di-atomic molecules was initially under standard condition. Then, gas was compressed adiabatically to one-fifth of its initial volume. What will be the mean kinetic energy of a rotating molecule in the final state? **[AIIMS]**

(a) 1.44 J (b) 4.55 J
(c) 787.98×10^{-23} J (d) 757.3×10^{-23} J

2017

7 **Assertion** The molecules of a monoatomic gas has three degrees of freedom.

Reason The molecules of di-atomic gas has five degrees of freedom. **[NEET]**

(a) Both Assertion and Reason are correct and Reason is the correct explanation of Assertion.
(b) Both Assertion and Reason are correct but Reason is not the correct explanation of Assertion.
(c) Assertion is correct but Reason is incorrect.
(d) Both Assertion and Reason are incorrect.

8 A gas mixture consists of 2 moles of O_2 and 4 moles of Ar at temperature T. Neglecting all vibrational modes, the total internal energy of the system is **[NEET]**

(a) 4 RT (b) 15 RT
(c) 9 RT (d) 11 RT

2016

9 One mole of an ideal monoatomic gas undergoes a process described by the equation pV^3 = constant. The heat capacity of the gas during this process is **[NEET]**

(a) $\frac{3}{2}R$ (b) $\frac{5}{2}R$ (c) $2R$ (d) R

2015

10 The ratio of the specific heats $\frac{C_p}{C_V} = \gamma$ in terms of degrees of freedom (n) is given by **[AIPMT]**

(a) $\left(1+\frac{1}{n}\right)$ (b) $\left(1+\frac{n}{3}\right)$ (c) $\left(1+\frac{2}{n}\right)$ (d) $\left(1+\frac{n}{2}\right)$

2013

11 The amount of heat energy required to raise the temperature of 1 g of helium at NTP, from T_1 K to T_2 K is **[NEET]**

(a) $\frac{3}{8}N_a k_B (T_2 - T_1)$ (b) $\frac{3}{2}N_a k_B (T_2 - T_1)$
(c) $\frac{3}{4}N_a k_B (T_2 - T_1)$ (d) $\frac{3}{4}N_a k_B \left(\frac{T_2}{T_1}\right)$

2010

12 The value of C_V for O_2 is $\frac{5}{2}R$, with increase in temperature, It becomes $\frac{7}{2}R$ due to **[OJEE]**

(a) translational motion (b) rotational motion
(c) vibrational motion (d) None of these

13 10 mol of an ideal monatomic gas at 10° C is mixed with 20 mol of another monatomic gas at 20° C. Then, the temperature of the mixture is **[DUMET]**

(a) 15.5° C (b) 15° C (c) 16° C (d) 16.6° C

2009

14 At ordinary temperature, the molecules of an ideal gas have only translational and rotational kinetic energies. At high temperatures they may also have vibrational energy. As a result of this at higher temperature, **[UP CPMT]**

(a) $C_V = \frac{3}{2}R$ for a monoatomic gas
(b) $C_V > \frac{3}{2}R$ for a monoatomic gas
(c) $C_V < \frac{5}{2}R$ for a diatomic gas
(d) $C_V = \frac{5}{2}R$ for a diatomic gas

2008

15 A given mass of a gas is compressed isothermally until its pressure is doubled. It is then allowed to expand adiabatically until its original volume is restored and its pressure is then found to be 0.75 of its initial pressure. The ratio of the specific heat of the gas is approximately **[AFMC]**

(a) 1.20 (b) 1.41
(c) 1.67 (d) 1.83

16 If quantity of heat 1163.4 J supplied to one mole of nitrogen gas, at room temperature and at constant pressure, then the rise in temperature is **[Kerala CEE]**

(a) 54 K (b) 28 K (c) 65 K (d) 8 K
(e) 40 K

17 The molar specific heat at constant pressure of an ideal gas is (7/2)R. The ratio of specific heat at constant pressure to that at constant volume is **[Haryana PMT]**

(a) 7/5 (b) 8/7 (c) 5/7 (d) 9/7

18 For a gas molecule with 6 degrees of freedom, the law of equipartition of energy gives the following relation between the molecular specific heat (C_V) and gas constant (R) **[J&K CET]**

(a) $C_V = R/2$ (b) $C_V = R$
(c) $C_V = 2R$ (d) $C_V = 3R$

19 For an ideal gas **[J&K CET]**

(a) C_p is less than C_V (b) C_p is equal to C_V
(c) C_p is greater than C_V (d) $C_p = C_V = 0$

20 If γ is the ratio of specific heats and R is the universal gas constant, then the molar specific heat at constant volume C_V is given by **[KCET]**

(a) γR (b) $\frac{(\gamma - 1)R}{\gamma}$
(c) $\frac{R}{\gamma - 1}$ (d) $\frac{\gamma R}{\gamma - 1}$

21 How much heat energy in joules must be supplied to 14 g of nitrogen at room temperature to raise its temperature by 40° C at constant pressure? (Molecular weight of N_2 = 28 g and R = constant) **[EAMCET]**

(a) $50\ R$ (b) $60\ R$
(c) $70\ R$ (d) $80\ R$

2007

22 If 310 J of heat is required to raise the temperature of 2 moles of an ideal gas at constant pressure from 25°C to 35°C. The amount of heat required to raise the temperature of the gas through the same range at constant volume is **[KCET]**

(a) 384 J (b) 144 J
(c) 276 J (d) 452 J

23 The gases carbon monoxide (CO) and nitrogen at the same temperature have kinetic energies E_1 and E_2, respectively. Then, **[MHT CET]**

(a) $E_1 = E_2$ (b) $E_1 > E_2$
(c) $E_1 < E_2$ (d) None of these

2006

24 For monoatomic gas which is correct ? **[JCECE]**

(a) $C_V = \frac{3}{5}R$ (b) $C_p = \frac{5}{2}R$
(c) $C_p - C_V = 2R$ (d) $\frac{C_p}{C_V} = \frac{3}{5}$

2005

25 Two cylinders fitted with pistons contain equal amounts of an ideal diatomic gas at 300 K. The piston of A is free to move, while that of B is held fixed. The same amount of heat is given to the gas in each cylinder. If the rise in temperature of gas in A is 30 K, then rise in temperature of gas in B is **[AMU]**

(a) 30 K (b) 18 K (c) 50 K (d) 42 K

26 Two perfect gases at absolute temperatures T_1 and T_2 are mixed. There is no loss of energy. The temperature of mixture of masses of molecules are m_1 and m_2 and the number of molecules in the gases are n_1 and n_2 respectively, is **[Haryana PMT]**

(a) $\frac{T_1 + T_2}{2}$ (b) $\frac{n_1T_1 + n_2T_2}{n_1 + n_2}$
(c) $\frac{n_1T_2 + n_2T_1}{n_1 + n_2}$ (d) $\sqrt{T_1T_2 / n_1n_2}$

Answers

1 (a)	2 (c)	3 (a)	4 (b)	5 (c)	6 (c)	7 (b)	8 (d)	9 (d)	10 (c)
11 (a)	12 (c)	13 (d)	14 (a)	15 (b)	16 (e)	17 (a)	18 (d)	19 (c)	20 (c)
21 (c)	22 (b)	23 (a)	24 (b)	25 (d)	26 (b)				

Explanations

1 *(a)* The Poisson's ratio,

$$\gamma = \frac{C_p}{C_V} \quad \dots(i)$$

where, C_p = molar heat capacity constant pressure and C_V = molar heat capacity at constant volume

Also, $C_p = C_V + R$ (from Mayer's relation)

$$C_V = \frac{f}{2}R$$

where, f = degree of freedom.

$$\Rightarrow \quad C_p = \left(\frac{f}{2} + 1\right)R$$

So, Eq. (i) becomes,

$$\Rightarrow \quad \gamma = 1 + \frac{2}{f}$$

For hydrogen gas, which is diatomic, the degree of freedom is 5 (3 translational, 2 rotational).

$$\therefore \quad \gamma = 1 + \frac{2}{5} = \frac{7}{5}$$

For helium gas, which is monoatomic, the degree of freedom is 3 (3 translational only).

$$\therefore \quad \gamma = 1 + \frac{2}{3} = \frac{5}{3}$$

The diatomic gas X also have vibrational motion, so degree of freedom is 7 (3 translational, 2 rotational and 2 vibrational).

$$\therefore \quad \gamma = 1 + \frac{2}{7} = \frac{9}{7}$$

2 *(c)* For N_2 gas, degree of freedom [for di-atomic gas]

$$\therefore \quad C_{V_1} = \frac{f}{2} \cdot R = \frac{5}{2}R$$

and $$C_{p_1} = C_{V_1} + R = \frac{7}{2}R$$

Amount of N_2 gas, $m_1 = 7$ g

$\therefore$ Number of moles of N_2,

$$n_1 = \frac{m_1}{28} = \frac{7}{28}$$

$$n_1 = \frac{1}{4}$$

For Ar gas, degree of freedom, $f = 3$

$$\therefore \quad C_{V_2} = \frac{3}{2}R$$

$$\therefore \quad C_{p_2} = C_{V_2} + R = \frac{3}{2}R + R = \frac{5}{2}R$$

Amount of Ar gas, $m_2 = 20$ g

$\therefore$ Number of moles of Ar gas,

$$n_2 = \frac{m_2}{40} = \frac{20}{40} = \frac{1}{2}$$

$$\therefore (C_p)_{\text{mix}} = \frac{n_1 C_{p_1} + n_2 C_{p_2}}{n_1 + n_2} = \frac{\frac{1}{4} \times \frac{7}{2}R + \frac{1}{2} \times \frac{5}{2}R}{\frac{1}{4} + \frac{1}{2}} = \frac{17R}{6}$$

$$(C_V)_{\text{mix}} = \frac{n_1 C_{V_1} + n_2 C_{V_2}}{n_1 + n_2} = \frac{\frac{1}{4} \times \frac{5}{2}R + \frac{1}{2} \times \frac{3}{2}R}{\frac{1}{4} + \frac{1}{2}} = \frac{11R}{6}$$

$$\therefore \left(\frac{C_p}{C_V}\right)_{\text{mix}} = \gamma_{\text{mix}} = \frac{\frac{17R}{6}}{\frac{11R}{6}} = \frac{17}{11}$$

3 *(a)* Given, for isobaric process, Work done by a di-atomic gas

By ideal gas equation, at constant pressure,

$$p\Delta V = nR\Delta T \quad \ldots \text{(i)}$$

$\therefore$ Work done, $W = p\,\Delta V$

$$W = nR\Delta T \quad \ldots \text{(ii)}$$

At constant pressure, heat given to gas is given by

$$Q = nC_p\Delta T \quad \ldots \text{(iii)}$$

where,

C_p = specific heat at constant pressure.

From Eqs. (ii) and (iii), we get

$$\frac{W}{Q} = \frac{nR\Delta T}{nC_p\,\Delta T} = \frac{R}{C_p} = \frac{R}{\frac{(f+2)R}{2}}$$

$$\left[\because C_p = \frac{(f+2)R}{2}\right]$$

$$\frac{W}{Q} = \frac{2}{f+2}$$

$[\because W = 10\text{ J (given)}]$

$$\frac{10}{Q} = \frac{2}{5+2}$$

[For di-atomic gas, $f = 5$]

$$\Rightarrow \quad Q = 35\text{ J}$$

4 *(b)* There are two vibrational degree of freedom of di-atomic gas molecules at high temperature. Hence, vibrational degree of freedom of a di-atomic gas molecule appears at every high temperature because vibration in gas molecules is directly proportional to the square root of its temperature.

Hence, both Assertion and Reason are correct but Reason is not the correct explanation of Assertion.

5 *(c)* According to the given graph, volume $(V) \propto$ temperature (T)

or $$\frac{V}{T} = \text{constant}$$

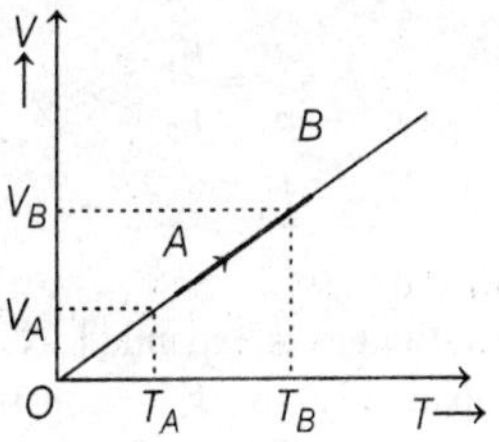

Thus, the process is isobaric.

$\therefore$ Work done, $\Delta W = p\Delta V$

$$= nR\Delta T = nR(T_B - T_A) \ldots \text{(i)}$$

Heat absorbed,

$$\Delta Q = nC_p\Delta T = nC_p(T_B - T_A) \quad \ldots \text{(ii)}$$

As, $C_p = \dfrac{\gamma R}{\gamma - 1}$, $\left(\text{where, } \gamma = 1 + \dfrac{2}{f}\right)$

For a monoatomic gas, $f = 3$

$$\Rightarrow \quad C_p = \left(R + \frac{3}{2}R\right) = \frac{5}{2}R$$

Substituting the value of C_p in Eq. (ii), we get

$$\Delta Q = n\left(\frac{5}{2}R\right)(T_B - T_A)$$

Hence, $$\frac{\Delta W}{\Delta Q} = \frac{nR(T_B - T_A)}{n\left(\frac{5}{2}R\right)(T_B - T_A)} = \frac{2}{5}$$

6 *(c)* For di-atomic gas, $\gamma = 1.4 = \frac{7}{5}$

At standard condition, $T = 27°\text{C} = 300\text{ K}$

For adiabatic process,

$$TV^{\gamma-1} = \text{constant}$$

$$T_1V_1^{\gamma-1} = T_2V_2^{\gamma-1}$$

$$(300)V_1^{\frac{7}{5}-1} = T_2\left(\frac{V_1}{5}\right)^{\frac{7}{5}-1} \quad \text{(given)}$$

$$\Rightarrow T_2 = \frac{300 \times V_1^{2/5}}{V_1^{\frac{2}{5}} \times \left(\frac{1}{5}\right)^{2/5}} = \frac{300}{5^{\frac{-2}{5}}} = 300 \times 5^{2/5}$$

$$= 300 \times 1.903 = 571$$

Mean kinetic energy of rotating molecules

$$= kT = 1.38 \times 10^{-23} \times 571$$

$$= 787.98 \times 10^{-23}\text{ J}$$

7 *(b)* A monoatomic gas molecules like He consists of single atom. It can have translational motion in any direction in space.

Thus, it has three translational degree of freedom $f = 3$ (all translational). It can also rotate but due to its small moment of inertia rotational kinetic energy is neglected.

The molecules of a diatomic gas (like O_2, CO_2, H_2) cannot only move body, but also rotate about any one of the three coordinates.

Hence, it can have two rotational degree of freedom.

Thus, a diatomic molecule has 5 degree of freedom i.e. 3 translational and 2 rotational.

8 (d) Total internal energy of system
= Internal energy of oxygen molecules
+ Internal energy of argon molecules

$$= \frac{f_1}{2} n_1 RT + \frac{f_2}{2} n_2 RT$$
$$= \frac{5}{2} \times 2RT + \frac{3}{2} \times 4RT$$
$$= 11RT$$

9 (d) As we know that, for polytropic process of index α,

Specific heat capacity, $C_V + \frac{R}{1-\alpha}$

$\because$ Process, $pV^3 = \text{constant}$

$\Rightarrow \alpha = 3$

$$\therefore \quad C = C_V + \frac{R}{1-\alpha} = \frac{fR}{2} + \frac{R}{1-3}$$

For monoatomic gas, $f = 3$

$$\Rightarrow \quad C = \frac{3R}{2} - \frac{R}{2} = R$$

10 (c) The specific heat of gas at constant volume in terms of degree of freedom n is

$$C_V = \frac{n}{2} R$$

Also, $C_p - C_V = R$

So, $C_p = \frac{n}{2} R + R = R\left(1 + \frac{n}{2}\right)$

Now, $\gamma = \frac{C_p}{C_V} = \frac{R\left(1+\frac{n}{2}\right)}{\frac{n}{2}R} = \left(1 + \frac{2}{n}\right)$

11 (a) We know that,

$$Q = \frac{f}{2} nR\Delta T = \frac{f}{2} \frac{m}{M} k_B N_a \Delta T$$
$$\left[\text{where, } k_B = \frac{R}{N_a}\right]$$

where, f = degree of freedom.
Amount of heat required,

$$Q = \frac{3}{2} \times \frac{1}{4} \times k_B N_a \Delta T$$

$\left[\because f = 3, m = \text{given mass} = 1\text{g and } M = \text{molecular mass} = 4 \text{ (for He)}\right]$

$$= \frac{3}{8} k_B N_a (T_2 - T_1)$$

where, k_B is Boltzmann constant and N_a is Avogadro's number.

12 (c) Oxygen is a di-atomic gas and hence has 5 degrees of freedom 3 translational and 2 rotational.
As the heat is given to oxygen C_V increases from $\frac{5R}{2}$ to $\frac{7R}{2}$.
Hence, internal energy ($\Delta U = nC_V\Delta T$) increases. With the increase in internal energy, the atoms within the molecule may also vibrate with respect to each other. In such cases, the molecule will have an additional degree of freedom due to their vibrational motion.

13 (d) Temperature of the mixture is given by

$$T = \frac{n_1 T_1 + n_2 T_2}{n_1 + n_2}$$

Given, $n_1 = 10$ mol, $n_2 = 20$ mol,
$T_1 = 10°\text{C}$ and $T_2 = 20°\text{C}$

$$= \frac{10 \times 10 + 20 \times 20}{10 + 20}$$
$$= \frac{500}{30} \approx 16.6°\text{C}$$

14 (a) The degree of freedom for diatomic gas and polyatomic at room temperature is f but at higher temperature their degree of freedom are increased by one due to vibrational motion of molecule.
But for monoatomic gas it is constant.
Hence, for monoatomic gas

$$C_V = \frac{3}{2} R$$

where, C_V = molar heat capacity at constant volume.

15 (b) In isothermal process, temperature of the gas remains constant, so the gas obeys Boyle's law.

i.e. $\quad p \propto \frac{1}{V}$

$$\Rightarrow \quad \frac{p_2}{p_1} = \frac{V_1}{V_2}$$
$$\Rightarrow \quad \frac{2p}{p} = \frac{V_1}{V_2}$$
$$\therefore \quad \frac{V_1}{V_2} = 2 \quad \ldots\text{(i)}$$

Now, the gas is expanded adiabatically, so $pV^\gamma = \text{constant}$

$$\frac{p_1}{p_2} = \left(\frac{V_2}{V_1}\right)^\gamma$$
$$\Rightarrow \quad \frac{2p}{0.75p} = \left(\frac{1}{2}\right)^\gamma$$

Taking log on both sides, we get

$$\log\left(\frac{8}{3}\right) = -\gamma \log 2$$
$$\Rightarrow \log 8 - \log 3 = -\gamma \log 2$$
$$\therefore \quad \gamma = -1.41$$

Hence, the ratio of specific heat of gas is 1.41 involve.

16 (e) Heat given to the gas at room temperature and at constant pressure.

$$Q = nC_p\Delta T$$

Given, $Q = 1163.4$ J

$$\Rightarrow \quad 1163.4 = 1 \times \frac{7}{2} R \times \Delta T$$
$$\left(\because C_p = \frac{7}{2} R \text{ for diatomic gas}\right)$$
$$\Rightarrow \quad \Delta T = \frac{2 \times 1163.4}{7 \times 8.31}$$
$$(\because R = 8.31 \text{ J mol}^{-1}\text{K}^{-1})$$

$\therefore$ Rise in temperature, $\Delta T = 40$ K

17 (a) Molar specific heat at constant pressure, $C_p = \frac{7}{2} R$

Mayer's relation can be written as

$$C_p - C_V = R$$
$$\Rightarrow \quad C_V = C_p - R$$
$$= \frac{7}{2} R - R = \frac{5}{2} R$$

Hence, required ratio is

$$\gamma = \frac{C_p}{C_V} = \frac{\left(\frac{7}{2}\right)R}{\left(\frac{5}{2}\right)R} = \frac{7}{5}$$

18 (d) Specific heat at constant volume (C_V) and degree of freedom (f) are related as

$$\because \quad C_V = \frac{f}{2} R$$
$$C_V = \frac{6}{2} R \quad \text{(given)}$$
$$\Rightarrow \quad C_V = 3R$$

19 (c) From $C_V = \frac{1}{2} fR = \frac{1}{2} \times 6R = 3R$

(for polyatomic gas)

and $\quad C_p - C_V = R$

$$C_p = R + 3R = 4R$$

Hence, C_p is always greater than C_V

i.e. $\quad C_p > C_V$

20 (c) From the Mayer's formula,

$$C_p - C_V = R \quad \ldots\text{(i)}$$

Also, $\quad \gamma = \frac{C_p}{C_V}$

$$\Rightarrow \quad \gamma C_V = C_p \quad \ldots\text{(ii)}$$

On substituting Eq. (ii) in Eq. (i), we get

$$\gamma C_V - C_V = R$$
$$C_V(\gamma - 1) = R$$
$$\Rightarrow \quad C_V = \frac{R}{\gamma - 1}$$

21 (c) Heat supplied at constant pressure,

$$Q = nC_p\,\Delta T$$

Given, $\Delta T = 40°\text{C}$

$$C_p = \frac{7}{2}R \quad \text{(for diatomic gases)}$$

Number of moles, $n = \frac{14}{28} = \frac{1}{2}$

$$\Rightarrow \quad Q = \frac{1}{2} \times \frac{7}{2} R \times 40 = 70R$$

22 (b) At constant pressure, heat required

$$= nC_p\Delta T$$

Given, $n = 2$, heat required = 310 J,

$\Delta T = T_2 - T_1 = (35 - 25)\,°\text{C}$

$$\Rightarrow \quad 310 = 2 \times C_p \times (35 - 25)$$

$$\Rightarrow \quad C_p = \frac{310}{20} = 15.5 \text{ J mol}^{-1}\text{ K}^{-1}$$

Similarly, at constant volume,

heat required $= nC_V\Delta T$

$$= 2(C_p - R) \times (35 - 25)$$

$$(\because C_p - C_V = R)$$

$$= 2 \times (15.5 - 8.3) \times 10$$

$$= 2 \times 7.2 \times 10 = 144 \text{ J}$$

23 (a) The gases carbon monoxide (CO) and nitrogen (N_2) are diatomic, so both have equal kinetic energy $\frac{5}{2}kT$, i.e.

$$E_1 = E_2$$

24 (b) Specific heat at constant volume,

$$C_V = \frac{f}{2}R$$

and specific heat at constant pressure,

$$C_p = \left(\frac{f}{2} + 1\right)R$$

For monatomic gas, $f = 3$

$$\therefore \quad C_V = \frac{3}{2}R$$

$$\text{and} \quad C_p = \left(\frac{3}{2} + 1\right)R = \frac{5}{2}R$$

From Mayer's formula,

$$C_p - C_V = R$$

$$\therefore \quad \frac{5}{2}R - \frac{3}{2}R = R$$

$$\text{and} \quad \gamma = \frac{C_p}{C_V} = \frac{5/2}{3/2} = \frac{5}{3}$$

25 (d) In cylinder A, heat is supplied at constant pressure while in cylinder B heat is supplied at constant volume.

$$\therefore \quad (\Delta Q)_A = nC_p(\Delta T)_A \quad \text{...(i)}$$

$$\text{and} \quad (\Delta Q)_B = nC_V(\Delta T)_B \quad \text{...(ii)}$$

Given, $(\Delta Q)_A = (\Delta Q)_B$

$$\therefore \quad (\Delta T)_B = \frac{C_p}{C_V}(\Delta T)_A$$

$$= 1.4 \times 30$$

$$\left(\because \frac{C_p}{C_V} = 1.4 \text{ for di-atomic gas}\right)$$

$$= 42.0 \text{ K}$$

26 (b) We know that, $E = \frac{3}{2}nkT$

where, k = Boltzmann's constant.

$$\therefore \quad \frac{3}{2}n_1kT_1 + \frac{3}{2}n_2kT_2 = \frac{3}{2}(n_1 + n_2)\,kT$$

$$\Rightarrow \quad T = \frac{n_1T_1 + n_2T_2}{(n_1 + n_2)}$$

13

Oscillations

Quick Review

Periodic Motion

A motion which repeats itself over and over again after a regular interval of time is called a **periodic motion.** e.g., revolution of planets around the sun, rotation of the earth about its polar axis etc.

The function which are used to represent periodic motion are called **periodic functions**.

One of the simplest periodic function is given by

$$f(t) = A\cos\omega t$$

Oscillatory Motion

A motion in which a body moves back and forth repeatedly about a fixed point (called mean position) is called **oscillatory** or **vibratory motion**.

Simple Harmonic Motion

Simple Harmonic Motion (SHM) is that type of oscillatory motion in which the particle moves to and fro about a fixed point under a restoring force whose magnitude is directly proportional to its displacement and directed towards mean position, i.e.

$$F \propto -y \text{ or } F = -ky$$

where, k is a positive constant called **force constant** or **spring factor**.

- Mathematically a SHM can be expressed as

$$y = A\sin\omega t = A\sin\frac{2\pi}{T}t$$

or

$$y = A\cos\omega t = A\cos\frac{2\pi}{T}t$$

where, y = displacement from mean position at time t,
A = amplitude or maximum displacement,
ω = angular frequency and T = time period.

- If initial phase is ϕ, then displacement in SHM is

$$y = A\sin(\omega t + \phi)$$

and

$$y = A\cos(\omega t + \phi).$$

Velocity in SHM

The velocity of particle executing SHM is defined as the time rate of change of its displacement at particular instant.

$$v = \omega\sqrt{A^2 - y^2}$$

- When the particle is at the mean position i.e., $x = 0$, then its velocity is maximum.

$\therefore \quad v_{max} = \omega A \quad$ (maximum velocity)

- When the particle is at the extreme position, i.e., $x = \pm A$, then its velocity is zero.

$$v = \omega\sqrt{A^2 - A^2} = 0$$

Therefore, the velocity of a particle executing SHM is zero at the either of its extreme positions.

Acceleration in SHM

The acceleration of SHM at an instant is defined as the time rate of change of velocity at that instant.

$$a = -\omega^2 y$$

- When the particle is at the mean position i.e., $x = 0$, then acceleration is zero.

$\therefore \quad a_{\text{mean position}} = 0 \quad$ (minimum acceleration)

- When the particle is at the extreme position i.e., $x = A$, then acceleration is maximum.

$\therefore \quad a_{\text{(extreme position)}} = -\omega^2 A$

(maximum acceleration)

Displacement, Velocity and Acceleration of a Body Executing SHM

Displacement $y(t) = A \cos \omega t$	**Velocity $v(t) = -\omega A \sin \omega t$**	**Acceleration $a(t) = -\omega^2 A \cos \omega t$**
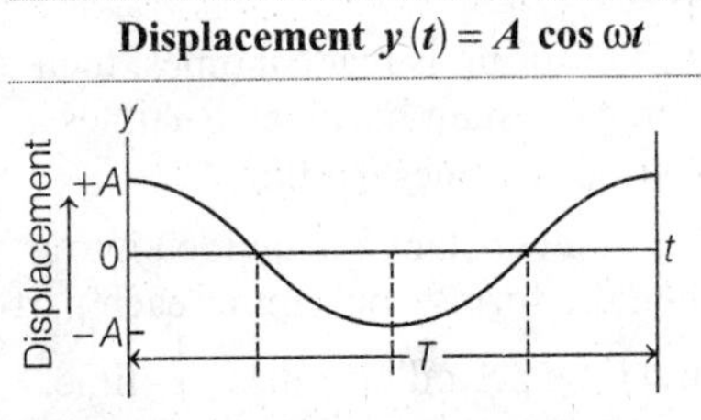	y Velocity +ωA 0 –ωA t⟶	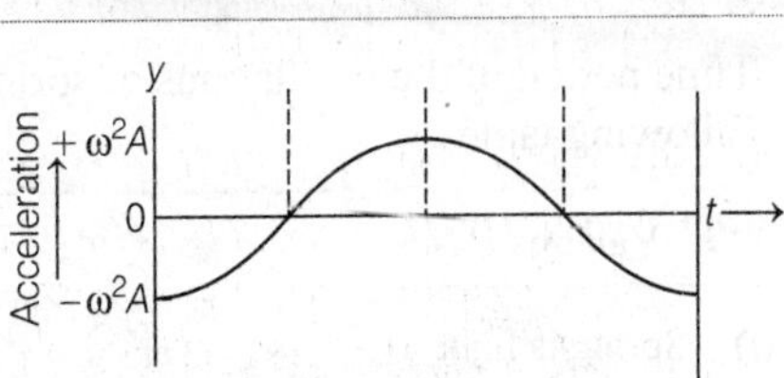
Sinusoidal in nature, y varies from $-A$ to A. It has zero phase difference.	Sinusoidal in nature, $v(t)$ varies from $-\omega A$ to ωA. It has a phase difference of $\frac{\pi}{2}$ w.r.t. $y(t)$	Sinusoidal in nature, $a(t)$ varies from $-\omega^2 A$ to $\omega^2 A$. It has a phase difference of π w.r.t. $y(t)$.

Force Law in SHM

It states that simple harmonic motion is the motion executed by a particle subjected to a force, which is proportional to the displacement of the particle and is always directed towards the mean position.

Restoring force, $F = -m\omega^2 y = -ky$

here, $\omega = \sqrt{\frac{k}{m}}$

$\because \quad \omega = \frac{2\pi}{T} = \sqrt{\frac{k}{m}}$

$\therefore$ Time period, $T = 2\pi\sqrt{\frac{m}{k}} = 2\pi\sqrt{\frac{\text{inertia factor}}{\text{spring factor}}}$

For linear SHM,

$$T = 2\pi\sqrt{\frac{\text{displacement}}{\text{acceleration}}}$$

Energy in SHM

- If a particle of mass m executes SHM, then at a displacement y from mean position, the particle possesses potential and kinetic energy.
- At any displacement y,

  (*i*) Potential energy, $U = \frac{1}{2} m\omega^2 y^2 = \frac{1}{2} ky^2$

  (*ii*) Kinetic energy,

  $$K = \frac{1}{2} m\omega^2 (A^2 - y^2) = \frac{1}{2} k(A^2 - y^2)$$

  (*iii*) Total energy,

  $$E = U + K = \frac{1}{2} m\omega^2 A^2 = 2\pi^2 m\nu^2 A^2$$

- At mean position, kinetic energy is maximum and potential energy is zero.
- At extreme position, potential energy is maximum and kinetic energy is zero.
- The time period of potential and kinetic energies is $T/2$.
- The frequency of oscillation of potential energy and kinetic energy is twice as that of displacement or velocity or acceleration.

System Executing SHM

A spring block system and simple pendulum come under SHM.

Simple Pendulum

A simple pendulum, in practice, consists of a heavy but small sized metallic bob suspended by a light, inextensible and flexible string.

The motion of a simple pendulum is simple harmonic whose time period and frequency are given by

$$T = 2\pi\sqrt{\frac{l}{g}} \text{ and } \nu = \frac{1}{2\pi}\sqrt{\frac{g}{l}}$$

- If a pendulum of length l at temperature $\theta°$ C has a time period T, then on increasing the temperature by $\Delta\theta°$ C its time period changes to $T \times \Delta T$.

  where, $\frac{\Delta T}{T} = \frac{1}{2}\alpha \cdot \Delta\theta$

- If the length of a simple pendulum is increased to such an extent that $l \to \infty$, i.e., $l >> R$, then its time period is

  $$T = 2\pi\sqrt{R/g} = 84.6 \text{ min}$$

  where, R = radius of the earth.

Spring Mass System

If the mass is once pulled so as to stretch the spring and released, the spring pendulum oscillates simple harmonically having time period and frequency.

$$T = 2\pi\sqrt{\frac{m}{k}} \text{ and } \nu = \frac{1}{2\pi}\sqrt{\frac{k}{m}}$$

Angular frequency, $\omega = \sqrt{\frac{k}{m}}$

The mechanical energy E of the oscillator is given by

$$E(t) = \frac{1}{2} kA^2 e^{-bt/m}$$

Time period of the oscillations of spring-mass system are shown in following table

Various Cases		Figures
(*i*) Spring is light	$T = 2\pi\sqrt{\frac{m}{k}}$	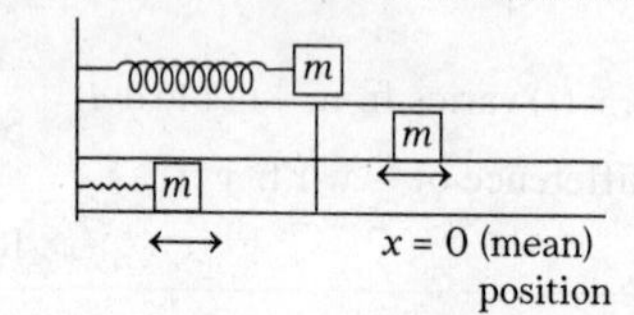
(*ii*) Spring is not light but has mass m_s	$T = 2\pi\sqrt{\frac{m + \frac{1}{3}m_s}{k}}$	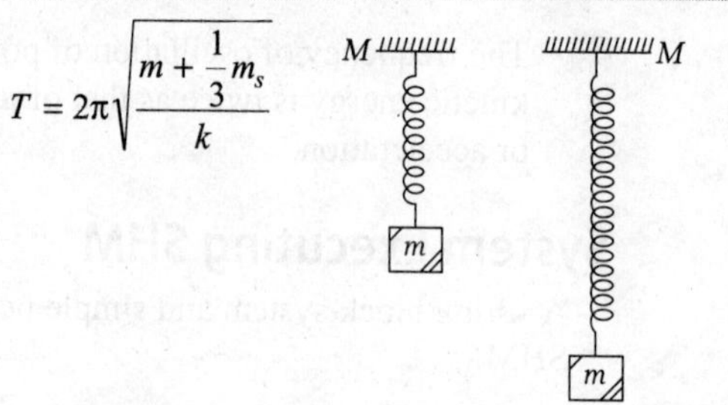
(*iii*) Spring connected with two masses (m_1 and m_2)	$T = 2\pi\sqrt{\frac{\mu}{k}}$	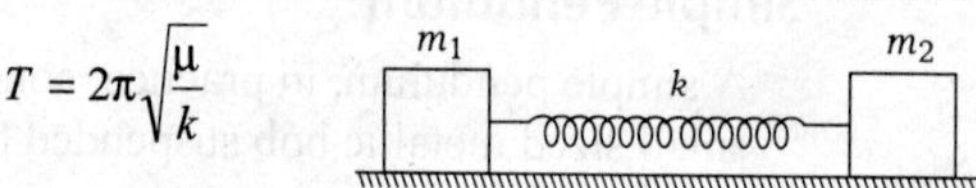
(*iv*) Springs with spring constants (k_1 and k_2) connected in series	$T = 2\pi\sqrt{\frac{m}{k_s}}$ $= 2\pi\sqrt{\frac{m(k_1 + k_2)}{k_1 k_2}}$	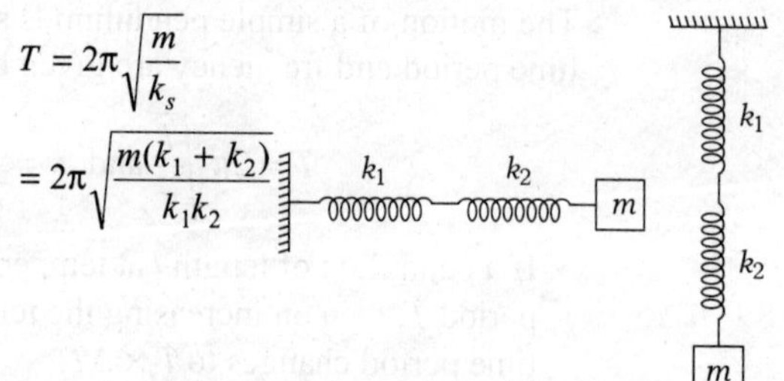
(*v*) Spring connected in parallel	$T = 2\pi\sqrt{\frac{m}{k_p}}$ $= 2\pi\sqrt{\frac{m}{k_1 + k_2}}$	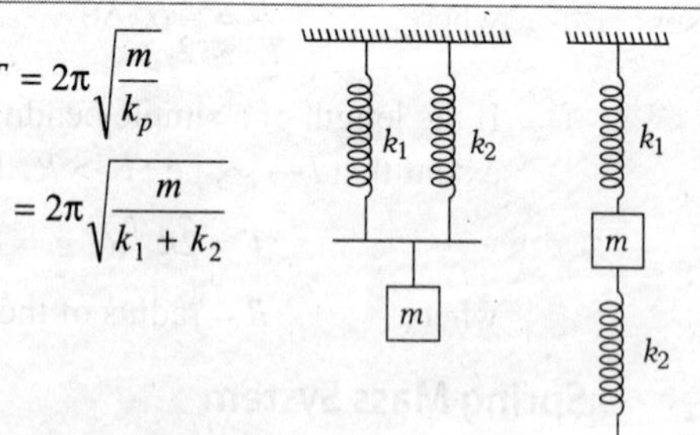

where, $\mu = \frac{m_1 m_2}{m_1 + m_2}$ = reduced mass of the system, $k_s = \frac{k_1 k_2}{k_1 + k_2}$

and $k_p = k_1 + k_2$.

Important Points Regarding Spring Block System

(*i*) If the length of the spring is made n times, then the effective force constant becomes $1/n$ times and the time period becomes $\sqrt{n}$ times.

(*ii*) If a spring of spring constant k is divided into n equal parts, then the spring constant of each part becomes nk and time period becomes $\frac{1}{\sqrt{n}}$ times.

(*iii*) The force constant of a stiffer spring is higher than that of a soft spring.

Simple Harmonic Motion in Special Cases

The time period of SHM due to the motion of incompressible and non-viscous liquid in U-tube is given as

$$T = 2\pi\sqrt{\frac{h}{g}}$$

where, h = height of undisturbed liquid in each limb and $L = 2h$ = total length of liquid column.

- The time period of a ball performing SHM in hemispherical bowl is expressed as

$$T = 2\pi\sqrt{\frac{R - r}{g}}$$

where, R and r are radii of bowl and ball.

- The time period of a ball executing SHM in a tunnel through the earth is expressed as

$$T = 2\pi\sqrt{\frac{R}{g}}$$

where, R = radius of earth.

- The time period of an elastic wire executing SHM, due to the restoring force $F = -AY\left(\frac{\Delta l}{l}\right)$ is expressed as

$$T = 2\pi\sqrt{\frac{ml}{AY}}$$

and $k = \frac{YA}{l}$

where, Y = Young's modulus,
l = length of wire, Δl = elongation
and A = area of cross-section.

Undamped and Damped Oscillations

When a simple harmonic system oscillates with a constant amplitude which does not change with time, its oscillations are called **undamped oscillations**.

When a simple harmonic system oscillates with a decreasing amplitude with time, its oscillations are called **damped oscillations**.

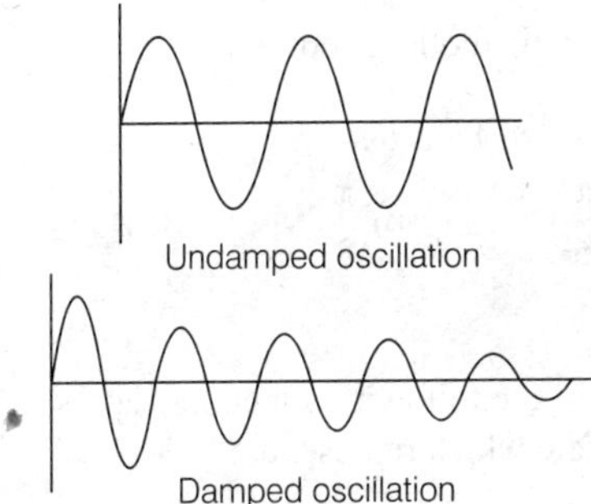

Undamped oscillation

Damped oscillation

Amplitude of damped oscillations $A = A_0 e^{-\gamma t}$

Energy of damped oscillations $E = E_0 e^{-2\gamma t}$

where, γ = damping coefficient $= \frac{b}{2m}$, where m is the mass of body undergoing damped oscillations.

Damping force $F_d = -bv$

where, b = damped constant and v = velocity of oscillation.

Equation of damped oscillation

$$m\frac{d^2y}{dt^2} + b\frac{dy}{dt} + ky = 0$$

Displacement of damped oscillations

$$y = y_m e^{-bt/2m} \sin(\omega' t + \phi)$$

where, ω' = angular frequency of damped oscillations

$$= \sqrt{\omega_0^2 - (b/2m)^2}$$

Free and Forced Oscillations

A body capable of oscillating is said to be executing **free oscillations,** if it vibrates with its own natural frequency without the help of any external periodic force.

When a body oscillates with the help of an external periodic force with a frequency different from the natural frequency of the body, these oscillations are called **forced oscillations.**

Resonance

When a body oscillates with its own natural frequency ν_0, with the help of an external periodic force whose frequency ν_d is equal to the natural frequency of the body, the oscillations of the body are called resonance.

Condition for resonance, $\nu_0 = \nu_d$.

Superposition of SHM

A simple harmonic motion is produced when a force (called restoring force) proportional to the displacement acts on a particle. If a particle is acted upon by two such forces, the resultant motion of the particle is a combination of two simple harmonic motions. Suppose the two individual motions are represented by

$$y_1 = A_1 \sin \omega t$$

and $$y_2 = A_2 \sin(\omega t + \phi)$$

Both the simple harmonic motions have same angular frequency ω.

Resultant amplitude is expressed as

$$A = \sqrt{a_1^2 + a_2^2 + 2a_1 a_2 \cos \phi}$$

Topical Practice Questions

All the exam questions of this chapter have been divided into 5 topics as listed below

Topic 1

Displacement and Phase in SHM

2019

1 The distance covered by a particle undergoing SHM in one time period is (amplitude = A) [NEET (Odisha)]

(a) zero (b) A (c) $2A$ (d) $4A$

2 The displacement of a particle executing simple harmonic motion is given by $y = A_0 + A \sin \omega t + B \cos \omega t$ [NEET]
Then, the amplitude of its oscillation is given by

(a) $\sqrt{A^2 + B^2}$ (b) $\sqrt{A_0^2 + (A+B)^2}$
(c) $A + B$ (d) $A_0 + \sqrt{A^2 + B^2}$

2017

3 The displacement of a particle along the X-axis is given by $x = a \sin^2 \omega t$. The motion of the particle corresponds to

(a) simple harmonic motion of frequency ω / π [JIPMER]
(b) simple harmonic motion of frequency $3\omega/2\pi$
(c) non-simple harmonic motion
(d) simple harmonic motion of frequency $\omega / 2\pi$

2014

4 A body oscillates with SHM according to the equation (in SI unit), $x = 5 \cos \left(2\pi t + \frac{\pi}{4}\right)$. Its instantaneous displacement at $t = 1$ s is [Kerala CEE]

(a) $\frac{\sqrt{2}}{5}$ m (b) $\frac{1}{\sqrt{3}}$ m (c) $\frac{1}{\sqrt{2}}$ m (d) $\frac{1}{2}$ m
(e) $\frac{5}{\sqrt{2}}$ m

5 Estimate the time taken by the oscillating pendulum to shift from $x = 0$ to $A/2$, where A is the amplitude. [WB JEE]

(a) $\frac{T}{4}$ (b) $\frac{T}{12}$ (c) $\frac{T}{2}$ (d) $\frac{T}{16}$

6 Two pendulums have time period T and $5T/4$. They start SHM at the same time from the mean position. What will be the phase difference between them after the bigger pendulum completed one oscillation? [UP CPMT]

(a) 45° (b) 90° (c) 60° (d) 30°

7 The amplitude of a particle executing SHM is 4 cm. At the mean position, the speed of the particle is 16 cm/s. The distance of the particle from the mean position at which the speed of the particle becomes $8\sqrt{3}$ cm/s will be [AFMC]

(a) $2\sqrt{3}$ cm (b) $\sqrt{3}$ cm
(c) 1 cm (d) 2 cm

8 What is the phase difference between two simple harmonic motions represented by $x_1 = A \sin \left(\omega t + \frac{\pi}{6}\right)$ and $x_2 = A \cos \omega t$? [WB JEE]

(a) $\frac{\pi}{6}$ (b) $\frac{\pi}{3}$ (c) $\frac{\pi}{2}$ (d) $\frac{2\pi}{3}$

2011

9 Out of the following functions representing motion of a particle which represents SHM [CBSE AIPMT]

I. $y = \sin \omega t - \cos \omega t$
II. $y = \sin^3 \omega t$
III. $y = 5 \cos \left(\frac{3\pi}{4} - 3\omega t\right)$
IV. $y = 1 + \omega t + \omega^2 t^2$

(a) Only IV does not represent SHM
(b) I and III
(c) I and II
(d) Only I

10 The motion which is not simple harmonic is [Kerala CEE]

(a) vertical oscillations of a spring
(b) motion of simple pendulum
(c) motion of a planet around the sun
(d) oscillation of liquid column in a U-tube
(e) vertical oscillation of a wooden plank floating in a liquid

11 The amplitude and the time period in a SHM is 0.5 cm and 0.4 s respectively. If the initial phase is $\pi/2$ rad, then the equation of SHM will be [MHT CET]

(a) $y = 0.5 \sin 5\pi t$ (b) $y = 0.5 \sin 4\pi t$
(c) $y = 0.5 \sin 2.5\pi t$ (d) $y = 0.5 \cos 5\pi t$

12 $x(t) = A \cos(\omega t + \phi)$ is the equation of simple harmonic motion. In this equation, ϕ is called [J&K CET]

(a) phase constant (b) frequency
(c) amplitude (d) displacement

13 A particle executing a simple harmonic motion has a period of 6 s. The time taken by the particle to move from the mean position to half the amplitude, starting from the mean position is [KCET]

(a) $\frac{3}{2}$ s (b) $\frac{1}{2}$ s
(c) $\frac{3}{4}$ s (d) $\frac{1}{4}$ s

2010

14 Two simple harmonic motions are represented by

$$y_1 = 5[\sin 2\pi t + \sqrt{3}\cos 2\pi t]$$

and $$y_2 = 5\sin\left(2\pi t + \frac{\pi}{4}\right)$$

The ratio of their amplitudes is **[KCET]**

(a) 1:1 (b) 2:1 (c) 1:3 (d) $\sqrt{3}:1$

15 Two simple harmonic motions A and B are given respectively by the following equations **[CG PMT]**

$$y_1 = a\sin\left(\omega t + \frac{\pi}{6}\right),$$

$$y_2 = a\sin\left(\omega t + \frac{3\pi}{6}\right)$$

The phase difference between the waves is

(a) $\frac{\pi}{2}$ (b) $\frac{\pi}{6}$ (c) $\frac{\pi}{3}$ (d) zero

2009

16 A block is resting on a piston which is moving vertically with SHM of period 1 s. At what amplitude of motion, will the block and piston separate? **[UP CPMT]**

(a) 0.2 m (b) 0.25 m
(c) 0.3 m (d) 0.35 m

17 The phase difference between the instantaneous velocity and acceleration of a particle executing simple harmonic motion is **[AIIMS]**

(a) 0.5π (b) π (c) $0.707\,\pi$ (d) zero

18 The displacement equation of a simple harmonic oscillator is given by **[MHT CET]**

$$y = A\sin\omega t - B\cos\omega t$$

The amplitude of the oscillator will be

(a) $A - B$ (b) $A + B$
(c) $\sqrt{A^2 + B^2}$ (d) $(A^2 + B^2)$

2006

19 The motion of a particle varies with time according to the relation **[BHU]**

$$y = a(\sin\omega t + \cos\omega t)$$

(a) the motion is oscillatory but not SHM
(b) the motion is SHM with amplitude a
(c) the motion is SHM with amplitude $a\sqrt{2}$
(d) the motion is SHM with amplitude $2a$

20 Two particles execute SHM of the same amplitude and frequency along the same straight line. If they pass one another when going in opposite directions, each time their displacement is half their amplitude, the phase difference between them is **[MHT CET]**

(a) $\frac{\pi}{3}$ (b) $\frac{\pi}{4}$
(c) $\frac{\pi}{6}$ (d) $\frac{2\pi}{3}$

21 A particle executes SHM, its time period is 16 s. If it passes through the centre of oscillation, then its velocity is 2 ms^{-1} at time 2 s. The amplitude will be **[AMU]**

(a) 7.2 m (b) 4 cm
(c) 6 cm (d) 0.72 cm

2005

22 Which of the following functions represent a simple harmonic oscillation? **[AIIMS]**

(a) $\sin\omega t - \cos\omega t$ (b) $\sin^2\omega t$
(c) $\sin\omega t + \sin 2\omega t$ (d) $\sin\omega t - \sin 2\omega t$

23 The displacement of a particle performing simple harmonic motion is given by $x = 8\sin\omega t + 6\cos\omega t$, where distance is in cm and time is in second. The amplitude of motion is **[MHT CET]**

(a) 10 cm (b) 2 cm
(c) 14 cm (d) 3.5 cm

24 The minimum phase difference between two simple harmonic oscillations, **[MHT CET]**

$$y_1 = (1/2)\sin\omega t + (\sqrt{3}/2)\cos\omega t,$$
$$y_2 = \sin\omega t + \cos\omega t \text{ is}$$

(a) $\frac{7\pi}{12}$ (b) $\frac{\pi}{12}$ (c) $-\frac{\pi}{6}$ (d) $\frac{\pi}{6}$

25 Which of the following is not characteristic of simple harmonic oscillation? **[Kerala CEE]**

(a) The motion is periodic
(b) The motion is along straight line about the mean position
(c) The acceleration of the particle is directed towards the extreme positions
(d) The oscillations are responsible for the energy transportation
(e) The period is given by $T = 2\pi\sqrt{\frac{m}{k}}$, where the symbols have usual meaning

Answers

1 (d)	2 (a)	3 (c)	4 (e)	5 (b)	6 (b)	7 (d)	8 (b)	9 (b)	10 (c)
11 (d)	12 (a)	13 (b)	14 (b)	15 (c)	16 (b)	17 (a)	18 (c)	19 (c)	20 (d)
21 (a)	22 (a)	23 (a)	24 (b)	25 (c)					

Explanations

1 *(d)* In a simple harmonic motion (SHM) the particle oscillates about its mean position on a straight line.

The particle moves from its mean position (O) to an extreme position (P) and then return to its mean position covering same distance of A.

Then by the conservative force, it is moved in opposite direction to a point Q by distance A and then back to mean position covering a distance of A. This comprises of one time period as shown below

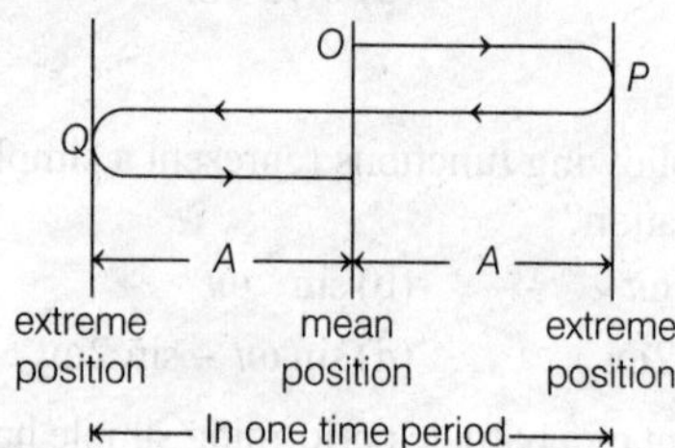

Hence, in one time period it covers a distance of

$$x = OP + PO + OQ + QO$$
$$= A + A + A + A = 4A$$

2 *(a)* The displacement of given particle is

$$y = A_0 + A\sin\omega t + B\cos\omega t \quad \dots \text{(i)}$$

The general equation of SHM can be given as

$$x = a\sin\omega t + b\cos\omega t \quad \dots \text{(ii)}$$

So, from Eqs. (i) and (ii), we can say that A_0 be the value of mean position, at which $y = 0$.

$\therefore$ Amplitude,

$$R = \sqrt{A^2 + B^2 + 2AB\cos\theta}$$

As two function sine and cosine have phase shift to 90°.

$$\therefore \quad R = \sqrt{A^2 + B^2} \quad [\because \cos 90° = 0]$$

3 *(c)* For a SHM, $\dfrac{d^2x}{dt^2} = -\omega^2 x \quad \dots$(i)

According question,

$$x = a\sin^2\omega t$$

Differentiating w.r.t t,

$$\frac{dx}{dt} = 2a\omega\sin\omega t\cos\omega t$$
$$= a\omega 2\sin\omega t\cos\omega t$$
$$= a\omega\sin 2\omega t$$

Again differentiating w.r.t t,

$$\frac{d^2x}{dt^2} = 2a\omega^2\cos 2\omega t$$

or $\quad \dfrac{d^2x}{dt^2} = 2a\omega^2(1 - 2\sin^2\omega t)$

$$\Rightarrow \quad \frac{d^2x}{dt^2} = 2a\omega^2 - 4a\omega^2\sin^2\omega t$$
$$= 2a\omega^2 - 4\omega^2 x \quad \dots \text{(ii)}$$

From Eqs. (i) and (ii), the motion of particle is non-simple harmonic motion.

4 *(e)* Given, $x = 5\cos\left(2\pi t + \dfrac{\pi}{4}\right)$

(where, x is a displacement)

$$\Rightarrow \quad x = 5\cos\left(2\pi + \frac{\pi}{4}\right) \quad (\text{at } t = 1\text{ s})$$

$$[\because \cos(360° + \theta) = \cos\theta]$$

$$\Rightarrow \quad x = 5\cos\frac{\pi}{4} \Rightarrow x = 5 \times \frac{1}{\sqrt{2}}$$

$$\therefore \quad x = \frac{5}{\sqrt{2}}\text{ m}$$

5 *(b)* Initial position at $t = 0$ is $x = 0$

The equation of SHM, $x = A\sin\omega t$

When, $\quad x = \dfrac{A}{2}$

$$\frac{A}{2} = A\sin\omega t$$

$$\Rightarrow \quad \sin\omega t = \frac{1}{2} = \sin\frac{\pi}{6}$$

$$\omega t = \frac{\pi}{6}$$

$$t = \frac{\pi}{6\omega} = \frac{\pi \times T}{6 \times 2\pi}$$

$$\Rightarrow \quad t = \frac{T}{12}$$

6 *(b)* When bigger pendulum of time period $(5T/4)$ completes one vibration, the smaller pendulum will complete $(5/4)$ vibrations. It means the smaller pendulum will be leading, the bigger pendulum by phase corresponding to $T/4$ sec $= \pi/2$ rad $= 90°$.

7 *(d)* At mean position, velocity is maximum $v_{\max} = \omega a$

$$\Rightarrow \quad \omega = \frac{v_{\max}}{a} = \frac{16}{4} = 4$$

$$\therefore \quad v = \omega\sqrt{a^2 - y^2}$$

$$\Rightarrow \quad 8\sqrt{3} = 4\sqrt{4^2 - y^2}$$

$$192 = 16(16 - y^2)$$

$$\Rightarrow \quad 12 = 16 - y^2$$

$$\Rightarrow \quad y = 2\text{ cm}$$

8 *(b)* Given, $x_1 = A\sin\left(\omega t + \dfrac{\pi}{6}\right)$

and $\quad x_2 = A\cos\omega t$

$$\therefore \quad x_2 = A\sin\left(\omega t + \frac{\pi}{2}\right)$$

Phase difference,

$$\Delta\phi = \phi_2 - \phi_1$$

$$\Rightarrow \quad \Delta\phi = \frac{\pi}{2} - \frac{\pi}{6}$$

$$\Rightarrow \quad \Delta\phi = \frac{3\pi - \pi}{6} = \frac{\pi}{3}$$

9 *(b)* For a simple harmonic motion,

$$\frac{d^2y}{dt^2} \propto -y$$

Hence, equation $y = \sin\omega t - \cos\omega t$

and $\quad y = 5\cos\left(\dfrac{3\pi}{4} - 3\omega t\right)$

are satisfying this condition but equation $y = 1 + \omega t + \omega^2 t^2$ is not periodic and $y = \sin^3\omega t$ is periodic but not SHM.

10 *(c)* The motion of planets around the sun is periodic but not simple harmonic motion. Simple harmonic motion is a special simplified case that assumes some effect that restores thing to middle position.

11 *(d)* $y = a\sin(\omega t + \phi)$

$$= a\sin\left(\frac{2\pi}{T}t + \phi\right)$$

$$\Rightarrow \quad y = 0.5\sin\left(\frac{2\pi}{0.4}t + \frac{\pi}{2}\right)$$

$$y = 0.5\sin\left(5\pi t + \frac{\pi}{2}\right)\text{s}$$

$$= 0.5\cos 5\pi t$$

12 *(a)* Given, $x(t) = A\cos(\omega t + \phi)$

where, ϕ is the phase constant.

whereas $x(t)$, A and ω represent instantaneous displacement, amplitude and angular velocity respectively.

13 *(b)* Equation for simple harmonic motion,

$$y = a\sin\left(\frac{2\pi}{T}\right)t$$

$$\Rightarrow \quad \frac{a}{2} = a\sin\left(\frac{2\pi}{T}\right)t \quad \left(\because y = \frac{a}{2}\right)$$

$$\Rightarrow \quad \frac{2\pi}{T}t = \frac{\pi}{6} \Rightarrow t = \frac{T}{12} = \frac{6}{12} = \frac{1}{2}\text{ s}$$

14 (b) Given, $y_1 = 5[\sin 2\pi t + \sqrt{3}\cos 2\pi t]$

$$= 10\left[\frac{1}{2}\sin 2\pi t + \frac{\sqrt{3}}{2}\cos 2\pi t\right]$$

$$= 10\left[\cos\frac{\pi}{3}\sin 2\pi t + \sin\frac{\pi}{3}\cos 2\pi t\right]$$

$$= 10\left[\sin\left(2\pi t + \frac{\pi}{3}\right)\right]$$

$\Rightarrow \quad A_1 = 10$ unit

Similarly, $y_2 = 5\sin\left(2\pi t + \frac{\pi}{4}\right)$

$\Rightarrow \quad A_2 = 5$ unit

Hence, $\frac{A_1}{A_2} = \frac{10}{5} = \frac{2}{1}$

15 (c) Phase difference, $\Delta\phi = \phi_1 - \phi_2$

$$= \frac{3\pi}{6} - \frac{\pi}{6} \Rightarrow = \frac{2\pi}{6} = \frac{\pi}{3}$$

16 (b) When maximum force just exceeds the weight of the body, then weight kept on the system will separate from the piston

$\therefore \quad mg = m\omega^2 y$

$\Rightarrow \quad y = \frac{g}{\omega^2} \quad [\because a_{max} = \omega^2 y]$

Given, $g = 9.8 \text{ ms}^{-2}, \omega = 2\pi$

$\Rightarrow \quad y = \frac{9.8}{(2\pi)^2} = 0.25 \text{ m}$

17 (a) The displacement equation of particle executing SHM is

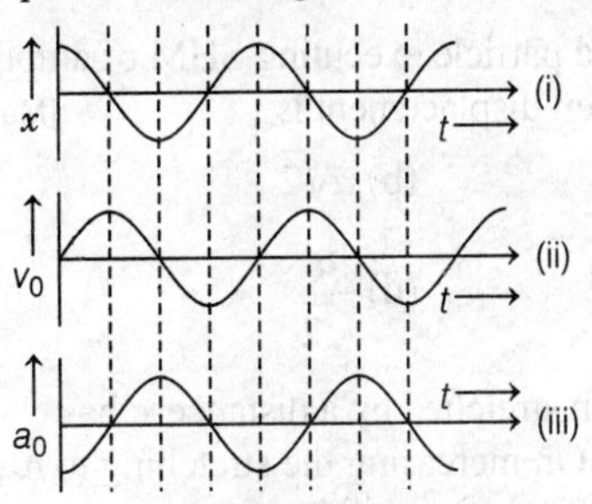

$$x = a\cos(\omega t + \phi) \quad \text{...(i)}$$

Velocity,

$$v = \frac{dx}{dt} = -a\omega\sin(\omega t + \phi) \quad \text{...(ii)}$$

Acceleration,

$$A = \frac{dv}{dt} = -a\omega^2\cos(\omega t + \phi) \quad \text{...(iii)}$$

Fig. (i) is a plot of Eq. (i) with $\phi = 0$. Fig. (ii) shows Eq. (ii) also with $\phi = 0$. Fig. (iii) is a plot of Eq. (iii). It should be noted that in the figures the curve of v is shifted (to the left) from the curve of x by one-quarter period $\left(\frac{1}{4}T\right)$.

Similarly, the acceleration curve of A is shifted (to the left) by $\frac{1}{4}T$ relative to the velocity curve of v. This implies that velocity is 90°, i.e. 0.5 π out of phase with the displacement and the acceleration is 90° (0.5π) out of phase with the velocity but 180° (π) out of phase with displacement.

18 (c) Displacement equation,

$$y = A\sin\omega t - B\cos\omega t$$

Let, $A = a\cos\theta$ and $B = a\sin\theta$

So, $A^2 + B^2 = a^2$

$\Rightarrow \quad a = \sqrt{A^2 + B^2}$

Then, $y = a\cos\theta\sin\omega t - a\sin\theta\cos\omega t$

$$y = a\sin(\omega t - \theta)$$

which is the equation of simple harmonic oscillator.

The amplitude of the oscillator,

$$a = \sqrt{A^2 + B^2}.$$

19 (c) The equation of particle varying with time is

$$y = a(\sin\omega t + \cos\omega t)$$

$$\Rightarrow y = a\sqrt{2}\left(\frac{1}{\sqrt{2}}\sin\omega t + \frac{1}{\sqrt{2}}\cos\omega t\right)$$

$$\Rightarrow y = a\sqrt{2}\left(\cos\frac{\pi}{4}\sin\omega t + \sin\frac{\pi}{4}\cos\omega t\right)$$

$$\Rightarrow y = a\sqrt{2}\sin\left(\omega t + \frac{\pi}{4}\right) \quad \text{...(i)}$$

This is the equation of simple harmonic motion with amplitude $a\sqrt{2}$.

20 (d) Equation of simple harmonic wave is $y = A\sin(\omega t + \phi)$

Here, $y = \frac{A}{2}$

$\therefore \quad A\sin(\omega t + \phi) = \frac{A}{2}$

So, $\delta = \omega t + \phi = \frac{\pi}{6}$ or $\frac{5\pi}{6}$

So, the phase difference of the two particles when they are crossing each other at $y = \frac{A}{2}$ in opposite directions are

$$\delta = \delta_1 - \delta_2$$

$$= \frac{5\pi}{6} - \frac{\pi}{6} = \frac{2\pi}{3}$$

21 (a) Given, $v = 2$ m/s, $T = 16$ s and $t = 2$ s

As the velocity, $v = A\,\omega\cos\omega t$

$\Rightarrow \quad 2 = A \cdot \frac{2\pi}{16} \cdot \cos\frac{2\pi}{16} \cdot 2 \quad \left[\because \omega = \frac{2\pi}{T}\right]$

$\Rightarrow \quad A = \frac{16\sqrt{2}}{\pi} = 7.2 \text{ m}$

22 (a) Let $y = \sin\omega t - \cos\omega t$

$$\frac{dy}{dt} = \omega\cos\omega t + \omega\sin\omega t$$

$$\frac{d^2y}{dt^2} = -\omega^2\sin\omega t + \omega^2\cos\omega t$$

$\Rightarrow \quad a = -\omega^2(\sin\omega t - \cos\omega t)$

$\Rightarrow \quad a = -\omega^2 y \Rightarrow a \propto -y$

Thus, it is a simple harmonic motion. This condition does not satisfied with other functions.

23 (a) Here, $x = 8\sin\omega t + 6\cos\omega t$

So, $a_1 = 8$ cm and $a_2 = 6$ cm

$\therefore$ Amplitude of motion,

$$A = \sqrt{A_1^2 + A_2^2} = \sqrt{8^2 + 6^2}$$

$\Rightarrow \quad A = \sqrt{64 + 36} = \sqrt{100} = 10$ cm

24 (b) Here, $y_1 = \frac{1}{2}\sin\omega t + \frac{\sqrt{3}}{2}\cos\omega t$

$$= \cos\frac{\pi}{3}\sin\omega t + \sin\frac{\pi}{3}\cos\omega t$$

$\therefore \quad y_1 = \sin\left(\omega t + \frac{\pi}{3}\right)$

Similarly, $y_2 = \sqrt{2}\sin\left(\omega t + \frac{\pi}{4}\right)$

$\therefore$ Phase difference,

$$\Delta\phi = \phi_1 - \phi_2 = \frac{\pi}{3} - \frac{\pi}{4} = \frac{\pi}{12}$$

25 (c) The acceleration of a particle executing SHM is always directed towards the mean position.

Topic 2

Velocity, Acceleration and Energy of SHM

2019

1 Average velocity of a particle executing SHM in one complete vibration is **[NEET]**

(a) $A\omega$ (b) $\frac{A\omega^2}{2}$ (c) zero (d) $\frac{A\omega}{2}$

2018

2 A particle doing SHM having amplitude 5cm, mass 0.5 kg and angular frequency 5 rad/s is at 1cm from mean position. Find potential energy and kinetic energy. **[JIPMER]**

(a) KE $= 6.25\times10^{-4}$ J, PE $= 150\times10^{-3}$ J
(b) KE $= 150\times10^{-4}$ J, PE $= 6.25\times10^{-4}$ J
(c) KE $= 6.25\times10^{-4}$ J, PE $= 6.25\times10^{-4}$ J
(d) KE $= 150\times10^{-3}$ J, PE $= 150\times10^{-4}$ J

2014

3 The oscillation of a body on a smooth horizontal surface is represented by the equation, $x = A\cos\omega t$
where, x = displacement at time t
ω = frequency of oscillation

Which one of the following graphs shows correctly the variation of a with t? **[CBSE AIPMT]**

(a) 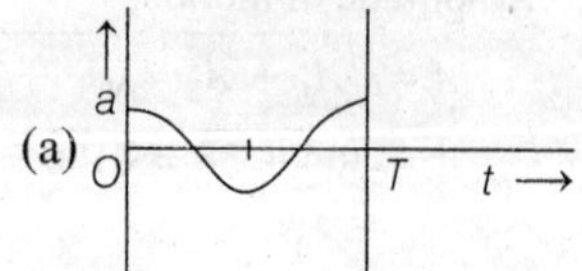

(b) 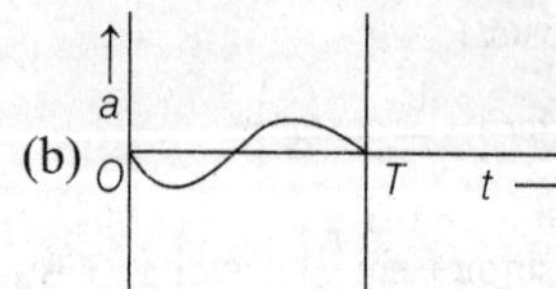

(c) 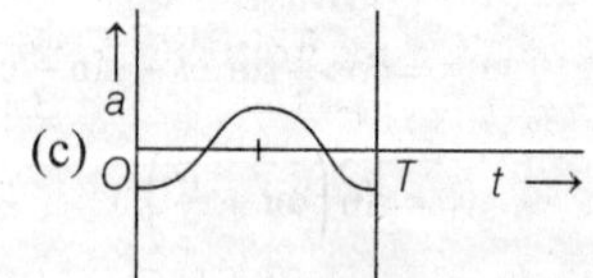

(d) 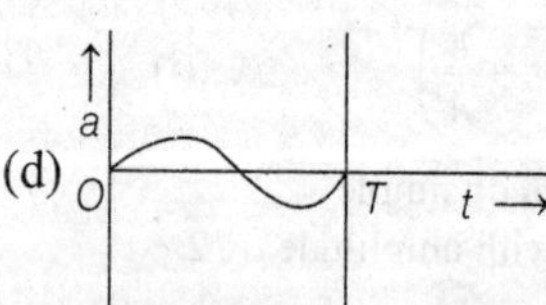

Here, a = acceleration at time t
T = time period

4 When the displacement of a particle executing simple harmonic motion is half its amplitude, the ratio of its kinetic energy to potential energy is **[Kerala CEE]**

(a) 1 : 3 (b) 2 : 1 (c) 3 : 1
(d) 1 : 2 (e) 2 : 3

5 The displacement of a particle having SHM is $x = 10\sin\left[10xt + \frac{x}{4}\right]$ m and its angular frequency.

(a) $6x$ (b) $8x$
(c) $2x$ (d) $10x$

6 When a particle executing SHM oscillates with a frequency ν, then the kinetic energy of the particle **[WB JEE]**

(a) changes periodically with a frequency of ν
(b) changes periodically with a frequency of 2ν
(c) changes periodically with a frequency of ν/2
(d) remains constant

7 If a body is executing simple harmonic motion and its current displacement is $\sqrt{3}/2$ times the amplitude from its mean position, then the ratio between potential energy and kinetic energy is **[EAMCET]**

(a) 3 : 2 (b) 2 : 3 (c) $\sqrt{3}:1$ (d) 3 : 1

8 A 10 kg metal block is attached to a spring of spring constant 1000 Nm^{-1}. A block is displaced from equilibrium position by 10 cm and released. The maximum acceleration of the block is **[KCET]**

(a) 10 ms^{-2} (b) 100 ms^{-2} (c) 200 ms^{-2} (d) 0.1 ms^{-2}

9 A body of mass 1 kg is executing simple harmonic motion. Its displacement y (cm) at t seconds is given by $y = 6\sin\left(100t + \frac{\pi}{4}\right)$. Its maximum kinetic energy is **[MPPMT]**

(a) 6 J (b) 18 J (c) 24 J (d) 36 J

2013

10 The KE and PE of a particle executing SHM of amplitude a will be equal, when displacement is **[Manipal]**

(a) $\frac{a}{2}$ (b) $a\sqrt{2}$
(c) $2a$ (d) $\frac{a}{\sqrt{2}}$

11 A long spring, when stretched by a distance x, has potential energy U. On increasing the stretching to nx, the potential energy of the spring will be **[WB JEE]**

(a) $\frac{U}{n}$ (b) nU
(c) n^2U (d) $\frac{U}{n^2}$

2012

12 A body is executing simple harmonic motion with an angular frequency of 2 rad s^{-1}. The velocity of the body at 20 mm displacement, when the amplitude of the motion is 60 mm is **[Manipal]**

(a) 131 mms^{-1} (b) 118 mms^{-1}
(c) 113 mms^{-1} (d) 90 mms^{-1}

13 The displacement of a particle executing SHM is given by $y = 0.25 \sin 200t$ cm. The maximum speed of the particle is [MHT CET]

(a) 200 cms^{-1} (b) 100 cms^{-1}
(c) 50 cms^{-1} (d) 5.25 cms^{-1}

14 The length of the second pendulum is decreased by 0.3 cm when it is shifted to Chennai from London. If the acceleration due to gravity at London is 981 cm/s^2, the acceleration due to gravity at Chennai is (assume $\pi^2 = 10$) [Manipal]

(a) 981 cm/s^2 (b) 978 cm/s^2
(c) 984 cm/s^2 (d) 975 cm/s^2

15 For a body performing SHM, at a distance $A/\sqrt{2}$, the correct relation between KE and PE will be [OJEE]

(a) KE is equal to PE (b) KE is 2 times of PE
(c) KE is 3 times of PE (d) KE is half of PE

16 When a spring is stretched by 10 cm, the potential energy stored is E. When the spring is stretched by 10 cm more, the potential energy stored in the spring becomes [WB JEE]

(a) $2E$ (b) $4E$ (c) $6E$ (d) $10E$

17 U is the PE of an oscillating particle and F is the force acting on it at a given instant. Which of the following is true? [MHT CET]

(a) $\frac{U}{F} + x = 0$ (b) $\frac{2U}{F} + x = 0$
(c) $\frac{F}{U} + x = 0$ (d) $\frac{F}{2U} + x = 0$

18 For a particle in SHM, if the amplitude of the displacement is a and the amplitude of velocity is v, the amplitude of acceleration is [MHT CET]

(a) va (b) $\frac{v^2}{a}$ (c) $\frac{v^2}{2a}$ (d) $\frac{v}{a}$

19 The average acceleration of a particle performing SHM over one complete oscillation is [MHT CET]

(a) $\frac{\omega^2 A}{2}$ (b) $\frac{\omega^2 A}{\sqrt{2}}$
(c) zero (d) $A\omega^2$

20 In SHM, the acceleration is ahead of velocity by a phase angle [OJEE]

(a) $0°$ (b) $\pi/2$ (c) π (d) 2π

21 A particle is executing linear simple harmonic motion of amplitude A. At what displacement, is the energy of the particle half potential and half kinetic? [WB JEE]

(a) $\frac{A}{4}$ (b) $\frac{A}{2}$
(c) $\frac{A}{\sqrt{2}}$ (d) $\frac{A}{\sqrt{3}}$

22 The maximum velocity of a particle in SHM is v. If the amplitude is doubled and the time period of oscillation decreased to $\frac{1}{3}$ of its original value, the maximum velocity becomes [WB JEE]

(a) $18v$ (b) $12v$ (c) $6v$ (d) $3v$

23 The total energy of the body executing simple harmonic motion (SHM) is E. Then, the kinetic energy when the displacement is half of the amplitude is [CG PMT]

(a) $\frac{E}{2}$ (b) $\frac{E}{4}$ (c) $\frac{3E}{4}$ (d) $\frac{\sqrt{3}E}{4}$

24 A particle is vibrating in a simple harmonic motion with an amplitude of 4 cm. At what displacement from the equilibrium position, is its energy half potential and half kinetic? [VMMC]

(a) 1 cm (b) $\sqrt{2}$ cm
(c) 3 cm (d) $2\sqrt{2}$ cm

2009

25 Which one of the following equations of motion represents simple harmonic motion? [CBSE AIPMT]

(a) Acceleration $= -k_0 x + k_1 x^2$
(b) Acceleration $= -k(x + a)$
(c) Acceleration $= k(x + a)$
(d) Acceleration $= kx$

where, k, k_0, k_1 and a are all positive.

26 A particle is executing linear simple harmonic motion. The fraction of the total energy that is potential, when its displacement is 1/4 of the amplitude is [J&K CET]

(a) $\frac{1}{16}$ (b) $\frac{1}{8}$ (c) $\frac{1}{2}$ (d) $\frac{1}{4}$

27 A particle performing SHM has time period $2\pi/\sqrt{3}$ and path length 4 cm. The displacement from mean position at which acceleration is equal to velocity is [MHT CET]

(a) zero (b) 0.5 cm (c) 1 cm (d) 1.5 cm

28 A body executing linear simple harmonic motion has a velocity of 3 ms^{-1} when its displacement is 4 cm and a velocity of 4 ms^{-1} when its displacement is 3 cm. What is the amplitude of oscillation? [BCECE]

(a) 5 cm (b) 7.5 cm
(c) 10 cm (d) 12.5 cm

29 A simple performs SHM about $n = 0$ with an amplitude a and time period T. What is the speed of the pendulum at $x = A/2$? [Manipal]

(a) $\frac{\sqrt{3}AT}{n}$ (b) $\frac{\sqrt{3}A\pi}{T}$
(c) $\frac{\sqrt{2}A\pi}{T}$ (d) $\frac{\sqrt{5}A\pi}{T}$

30 A particle is executing SHM. Then, the graph of velocity as a function of displacement is a/an **[Manipal]**

(a) straight line (b) circle
(c) ellipse (d) hyperbola

2008

31 Two simple harmonic motions of angular frequency 100 and 1000 rad s^{-1} have the same displacement amplitude. The ratio of their maximum accelerations is **[CBSE AIPMT]**

(a) 1 : 10 (b) $1:10^2$ (c) $1:10^3$ (d) $1:10^4$

32 A point performs simple harmonic oscillation of period T and the equation of motion is given by $x = a\sin(\omega t + \pi/6)$. After the elapse of what fraction of the time period the velocity of the point will be equal to half of its maximum velocity? **[CBSE AIPMT]**

(a) $\frac{T}{8}$ (b) $\frac{T}{6}$
(c) $\frac{T}{3}$ (d) $\frac{T}{12}$

33 A body executes simple harmonic motion. The potential energy (PE), the kinetic energy (KE) and total energy (TE) are measured as function of displacement X. Which of the following statements is true? **[RPMT]**

(a) KE is maximum, when $x = 0$
(b) TE is zero, when $x = 0$
(c) KE is maximum, when x is maximum
(d) PE is maximum, when $x = 0$

34 If a body is executing simple harmonic motion, then **[J&K CET]**

(a) at extreme positions, the total energy is zero
(b) at equilibrium position, the total energy is in the form of potential energy
(c) at equilibrium positions, the total energy is in the form of kinetic energy
(d) at extreme positions, the total energy is infinite

35 The displacement of a particle of mass 3 g executing simple harmonic motion is given by $Y = 3\sin(0.2t)$ in SI units. The kinetic energy of the particle at a point which is at a distance equal to 1/3 of its amplitude from its mean position is **[Punjab PMET]**

(a) 12×10^3 J (b) 25×10^{-3} J
(c) 0.48×10^{-3} J (d) 0.24×10^{-3} J

2007

36 The particle executing simple harmonic motion has a kinetic energy $K_0\cos^2\omega t$. The maximum values of the potential energy and the total energy are respectively. **[CBSE AIPMT]**

(a) 0 and $2K_0$ (b) $\frac{K_0}{2}$ and K_0
(c) K_0 and $2K_0$ (d) K_0 and K_0

37 The potential energy of a simple harmonic oscillator when the particle is half way to its end point is **[BHU]**

(a) $\frac{1}{4}E$ (b) $\frac{1}{2}E$ (c) $\frac{2}{3}E$ (d) $\frac{1}{8}E$

(where, E is the total energy)

38 Which one of the following statements is true for the speed v and the acceleration a of a particle executing simple harmonic motion? **[Manipal]**

(a) Where v is maximum, a is maximum
(b) Value of a is zero, whatever may be the value of v
(c) When v is zero, a is zero
(d) When v is maximum, a is zero

39 In SHM restoring force is $F = -kx$, where k is force constant, x is displacement and A is amplitude of motion, then total energy depends upon **[MHT CET]**

(a) k, A and M (b) k, x, M
(c) k, A (d) k, x

40 A particle executes SHM with a period of 8 s and amplitude 4 cm. Its maximum speed in cm s^{-1}, is **[J&K CET]**

(a) π (b) $\frac{\pi}{2}$ (c) $\frac{\pi}{3}$ (d) $\frac{\pi}{4}$

2006

41 Amplitude of a pendulum is 60 mm and angular velocity is 2 rad s^{-1}. Find its velocity, if its displacement is 20 mm **[RPMT]**

(a) 120 mm s^{-1} (b) 113 mm s^{-1}
(c) 115 mm s^{-1} (d) 125 mm s^{-1}

42 A particle executing SHM has amplitude 0.01 m and frequency 60 Hz. The maximum acceleration of particle is **[MP PMT]**

(a) $60\pi^2$ ms^{-2} (b) $80\pi^2$ ms^{-2}
(c) $120\pi^2$ ms^{-2} (d) $144\pi^2$ ms^{-2}

43 A simple harmonic oscillator has amplitude A, angular velocity ω and mass m. Then, average energy in one time period will be **[Haryana PMT]**

(a) $\frac{1}{4}m\omega^2A^2$ (b) $\frac{1}{2}m^2\omega^2A^2$
(c) $m\omega^2A^2$ (d) zero

44 If a particle executes SHM with angular velocity 3.5 rad s^{-1} and maximum acceleration 7.5 ms^{-2}, then the amplitude of oscillation will be **[DUMET]**

(a) 0.80 m (b) 0.69 m
(c) 0.41 m (d) 0.61 m

45 A body executing SHM has velocity 10 cm s^{-1} and 7 cm s^{-1}, when its displacements from the mean position are 3 cm and 4 cm respectively.
The length of path is **[DUMET]**

(a) 10 cm (b) 9.5 cm
(c) 4 cm (d) 11.36 cm

46 When the kinetic energy of a body executing SHM is 1/3 of the potential energy. The displacement of the body is x per cent of the amplitude, where x is **[RPMT]**

(a) 33 (b) 87
(c) 67 (d) 50

2005

47 In simple harmonic motion, maximum velocity is at **[Punjab PMET]**

(a) extreme positions
(b) half of extreme positions
(c) equilibrium positions
(d) between extreme and equilibrium positions

48 Consider the following statements.
The total energy of a particle executing simple harmonic motion depends on its **[BCECE]**

(I) amplitude
(II) period
(III) displacement, of these statements

(a) I and II are correct
(b) II and III are correct
(c) I and III are correct
(d) I, II and III are correct

49 The maximum velocity of a simple harmonic motion represented by $y = 3\sin\left(100\,t + \frac{\pi}{6}\right)$ m is given by **[BCECE]**

(a) 300 ms^{-1} (b) $\frac{3\pi}{6}$ ms^{-1} (c) 100 ms^{-1} (d) $\frac{\pi}{6}$ ms^{-1}

50 A simple pendulum performs simple harmonic motion about $x = 0$ with an amplitude a and time period T. The speed of the pendulum at $x = a/2$ will be **[CBSE AIPMT]**

(a) $\frac{\pi a\sqrt{3}}{2T}$ (b) $\frac{\pi a}{T}$ (c) $\frac{3\pi^2 a}{T}$ (d) $\frac{\pi a\sqrt{3}}{T}$

51 A coin is placed on a horizontal platform which undergoes vertical simple harmonic motion of angular frequency (ω). The amplitude of oscillation is gradually increased. The coin will leave contact with the platform for the first time **[AIIMS]**

(a) at the mean position of the platform
(b) for an amplitude of $\frac{g}{\omega^2}$
(c) for an amplitude of $\frac{g^2}{\omega^2}$
(d) at the highest position of the platform

Answers

1 (c)	2 (b)	3 (a)	4 (a)	5 (d)	6 (b)	7 (d)	8 (a)	9 (b)	10 (d)
11 (c)	12 (b)	13 (b)	14 (b)	15 (a)	16 (b)	17 (b)	18 (b)	19 (c)	20 (b)
21 (c)	22 (c)	23 (c)	24 (d)	25 (b)	26 (a)	27 (c)	28 (a)	29 (b)	30 (c)
31 (b)	32 (d)	33 (a)	34 (c)	35 (c)	36 (d)	37 (a)	38 (d)	39 (c)	40 (a)
41 (b)	42 (d)	43 (a)	44 (d)	45 (b)	46 (b)	47 (c)	48 (a)	49 (a)	50 (d)
51 (b)									

Explanations

1 *(c)* The average velocity of a particle executing simple harmonic motion (SHM) is

$$v_{av} = \frac{\text{Total displacement}}{\text{Time interval}} = \frac{x_f - x_i}{T}$$

where, x_f and x_i are the initial and final position of the particle executing SHM.

As, in vibrational motion, the particle executes SHM about its mean position. So, after one complete vibration of the particle, it will reaches its initial position, i.e.

Displacement, $x_f - x_i = 0$

$\therefore$ $v_{av} = \frac{0}{T}$

Hence, the average velocity is zero.

2 *(b)* Given, $m = 0.5$ kg, $\omega = 5$ rad/s,

$$x = 10^{-2}\text{m}$$
$$A = 5 \times 10^{-2}\text{m}$$

$\because$ Potential energy, $PE = \frac{1}{2} m\omega^2 x^2$

or $PE = \frac{1}{2} \times 0.5 \times (5)^2 \times (10^{-2})^2$

$= \frac{25}{4} \times 10^{-4}\ \text{J} = 6.25 \times 10^{-4}\ \text{J}$

$\because$ Kinetic energy, $KE = \frac{1}{2} m\omega^2 (A^2 - x^2)$

or $K = \frac{1}{2} \times 0.5 \times (5)^2 (25 - 1) \times 10^{-4}$

$= 150 \times 10^{-4}$ J

3 *(a)* We can find the correct graph by putting different values of t in the given expression $x = A\cos\omega t$

If $t = 0$, then $x = +A$

If $t = \frac{T}{4}$, then $x = 0$

If $t = \frac{T}{2}$, then $x = -A$

We can see that only graph (a) will satisfy the above results.

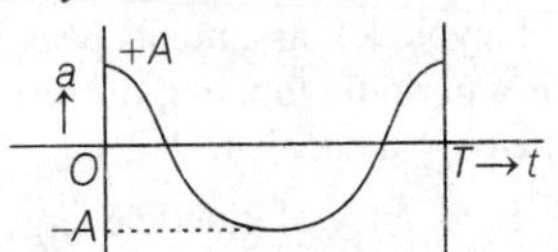

4 *(a)* For simple harmonic motion, the displacement,

$$x = A\cos\omega t$$

$\Rightarrow$ $\frac{A}{2} = A\cos\omega t$ $\left(\because x = \frac{A}{2}\right)$

$\cos\omega t = \frac{1}{2} \Rightarrow \omega t = 30°$

We know that kinetic energy,

$$KE = \frac{1}{2} mv^2$$

$$= \frac{1}{2} m\omega^2 A^2 \sin^2 \omega t$$

$$(\because v = - A\omega \sin \omega t) \quad \ldots(i)$$

Potential energy, $PE = \frac{1}{2} m\omega^2 x^2$

$$= \frac{1}{2} m\omega^2 A^2 \cos^2 \omega t \quad \ldots(ii)$$

$$\Rightarrow \frac{KE}{PE} = \frac{\frac{1}{2} m\omega^2 A^2 \sin^2 \omega t}{\frac{1}{2} m\omega^2 A^2 \cos^2 \omega t} = \tan^2 \omega t$$

$$= \tan^2(30^\circ) = \left(\frac{1}{\sqrt{3}}\right)^2 = \frac{1}{3}$$

So, KE : PE = 1 : 3

5 *(d)* Given, $x = 10 \sin\left[10\,xt + \frac{x}{4}\right]$

By comparing $\omega = 10\,x$

because equation of SHM

$\Rightarrow x(t) = A \cos(\omega t + \phi)$

6 *(b)* We know that, kinetic energy,

$$K = \frac{1}{2} mv^2$$

where, $v = \frac{dy}{dt} = \omega A \cos \omega t$

So, $K = \frac{1}{2} m\omega^2 A^2 \cos^2 \omega t$

Kinetic energy *versus* time graph is given below

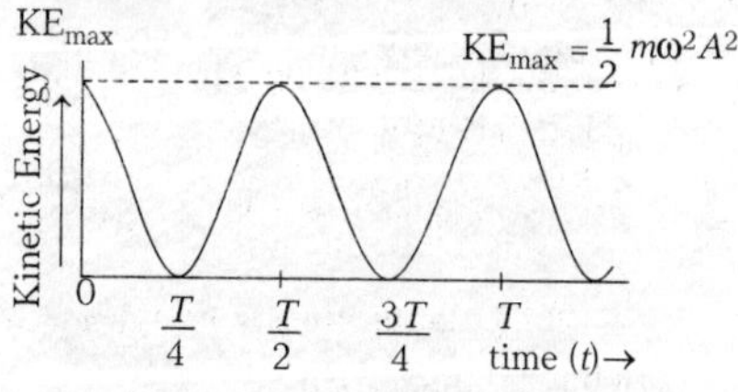

From the graph, it is clear that at $t = 0$, $T/2$, T, etc. KE has its maximum value.

For $x = \pm A$ or $t = \frac{T}{4}, \frac{3T}{4}$, the KE has its minimum value. Clearly, twice in each cycle KE assume its peak values. It is a periodic function of time, the time period equals to $T/2$.

i.e. Frequency of kinetic energy,

$$v' = \frac{1}{T/2} = \frac{2}{T} = 2v \quad \left[\because v = \frac{1}{T}\right]$$

7 *(d)* The current displacement is $\frac{\sqrt{3}}{2}$ times the amplitude.

i.e., $y = \frac{\sqrt{3}}{2} A$

We know that potential energy of a body in SHM is given by

$$U = \frac{1}{2} m\omega^2 y^2$$

where, m and ω are constant.

$$U = \frac{1}{2} m\omega^2 \left(\frac{\sqrt{3}}{2} A\right)^2 = \frac{1}{2} m\omega^2 \times \frac{3A^2}{4} \quad \ldots(i)$$

Similarly, kinetic energy of a body in SHM is given by

$$K = \frac{1}{2} m\omega^2 (A^2 - y^2)$$

$$\Rightarrow K = \frac{1}{2} m\omega^2 \left(A^2 - \frac{3A^2}{4}\right) = \frac{1}{2} m\omega^2 \frac{A^2}{4} \quad \ldots(ii)$$

So, the ratio of PE and KE

$$PE : KE = \frac{1}{2} m\omega^2 \times \frac{3A^2}{4} : \frac{1}{2} m\omega^2 \frac{A^2}{4} = 3:1$$

8 *(a)* We know that in spring SHM, the restoring force is proportional to displacement,

$$F = - m\omega^2 y \quad \ldots(i)$$

$$F = - ky \quad \ldots(ii)$$

where, k = force constant of the spring

$m = 10$ kg, $A = 10$ cm $= 0.1$ m,

$k = 1000$ N/m

Comparing the both equations, we get

$$\omega^2 = \frac{k}{m} \Rightarrow \omega = \sqrt{\frac{k}{m}} = \sqrt{\frac{1000}{10}}$$

$$\Rightarrow \quad = 10 \text{ rad/s}$$

and acceleration in SHM,

$$a_{max} = - \omega^2 \cdot y = - 10^2 \times (0.1)$$

$$= - 10 \text{ m/s}^2 \simeq 10 \text{ ms}^{-2}$$

9 *(b)* $a = 6$ cm, $\omega = 100$ rad s^{-1}

$$K_{max} = \frac{1}{2} m\omega^2 a^2$$

$$= \frac{1}{2} \times 1 \times (100)^2 \times (6 \times 10^{-2})^2 = 18 \text{ J}$$

10 *(d)* As per question, KE = PE

$$\frac{1}{2} m\omega^2 (a^2 - y^2) = \frac{1}{2} m\omega^2 y^2$$

$$\therefore \quad y = \frac{a}{\sqrt{2}}$$

11 *(c)* Potential energy of the spring,

$$U = \frac{1}{2} kx^2 \quad \ldots(i)$$

and $U' = \frac{1}{2} k(nx)^2$

$$\Rightarrow U' = n^2 \frac{1}{2} kx^2$$

$$\Rightarrow U' = n^2 U \quad \text{[From Eq. (i)]}$$

12 *(c)* $v = \omega\sqrt{A^2 - x^2}$

$$= 2\sqrt{(60)^2 - (20)^2}$$

$$= 113 \text{ mms}^{-1}$$

13 *(c)* $v_{max} = \omega A$

$$= (200)(0.25) = 50 \text{ cm s}^{-1}$$

14 *(b)* As, $L_1 = \frac{g_1 T^2}{4\pi^2} = \frac{g_1}{\pi^2} \left[\because T = 2\pi\sqrt{\frac{l}{g}}\right]$

and $L_2 = \frac{g_2 T^2}{4\pi^2} = \frac{g_2}{\pi^2}$

Since, length is decreased, g_2 is less than g_1.

$$\therefore \quad L_1 - L_2 = \frac{g_1 - g_2}{\pi^2}$$

$$\Rightarrow (L_1 - L_2)\pi^2 = g_1 - g_2$$

$$\Rightarrow 0.3 \times 10 = g_1 - g_2$$

$$\Rightarrow g_2 = 981 - 3 = 978 \text{ cm/s}^2$$

15 *(a)* Potential energy of body

$$= \frac{1}{2} m\omega^2 y^2$$

PE at $y = \frac{A}{\sqrt{2}} = \frac{1}{2} m\omega^2 \left(\frac{A}{\sqrt{2}}\right)^2$

$$\Rightarrow \quad = \frac{1}{4} m\omega^2 A^2$$

Kinetic energy of body

$$= \frac{1}{2} m\omega^2 (A^2 - y^2)$$

KE at $y = \frac{A}{\sqrt{2}} = \frac{1}{2} m\omega^2 \left[A^2 - \left(\frac{A}{\sqrt{2}}\right)^2\right]$

$$= \frac{1}{4} m\omega^2 A^2$$

Hence, KE is equal to PE.

16 *(b)* For 1st situation,

$$E = \frac{1}{2} k(10 \times 10^{-2})^2 \quad \ldots(i)$$

For 2nd situation,

$$E' = \frac{1}{2} k(20 \times 10^{-2})^2 \quad \ldots(ii)$$

On comparing Eqs. (i) and (ii), we get

$$E' = 4E$$

17 *(b)* The potential energy, $U = \frac{1}{2} kx^2$

$$2U = kx^2 \Rightarrow 2U = - Fx \ (\because F = - kx)$$

or $\frac{2U}{F} = - x$ or $\frac{2U}{F} + x = 0$

18 *(b)* We know that, $v_{max} = a\omega$ and

Maximum acceleration $= \omega^2 a \ [\because x = a]$

$$= \left(\frac{v}{a}\right)^2 a = \frac{v^2}{a}$$

19 (c) The average acceleration of a particle performing SHM over one complete oscillation is zero. Because acceleration is a function of sine and average value of sin for 1 complete oscillation = 0.

20 (b) In SHM, the acceleration is ahead of velocity by a phase angle $\frac{\pi}{2}$.

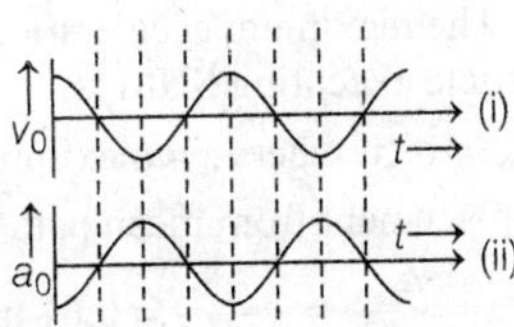

$$x = A\sin\omega t$$

Velocity, $v = A\omega \sin\left(\omega t + \frac{\pi}{2}\right)$

and the acceleration,

$$a = A\omega^2 \sin(\omega t + \pi)$$

where, A = amplitude.

21 (c) The total energy of a particle executing SHM

$$= \frac{1}{2}m\omega^2 A^2$$

The PE of the particle at a distance x from the equilibrium position

$$= \frac{1}{2}m\omega^2 x^2$$

From the question,

$$\frac{1}{2}m\omega^2 x^2 = \frac{1}{2}\left(\frac{1}{2}m\omega^2 A^2\right)$$

$$\Rightarrow \quad x^2 = \frac{A^2}{2} \Rightarrow x = \frac{A}{\sqrt{2}}$$

22 (c) Maximum velocity,

$$v_{max} = A\omega \qquad \ldots(i)$$

$$\omega = \frac{2\pi}{T} \qquad \ldots(ii)$$

From Eqs. (i) and (ii), we get

$$v_{max} = \frac{2\pi A}{T}$$

Thus, $v \propto \frac{A}{T} \Rightarrow \frac{v_1}{v_2} = \frac{A_1}{A_2} \times \frac{T_2}{T_1}$

$$= \frac{1}{2} \times \frac{1}{3} = \frac{1}{6}$$

$$\Rightarrow \quad v_2 = 6v_1 = 6v \qquad (\because v_1 = v)$$

23 (c) Total energy in SHM,

$E = \frac{1}{2}m\omega^2 a^2$, (where, a = amplitude)

Kinetic energy, $K = \frac{1}{2}m\omega^2(a^2 - y^2)$

$$\Rightarrow \quad K = E - \frac{1}{2}m\omega^2 y^2$$

When $y = \frac{a}{2}$ (given)

$$\Rightarrow \quad K = E - \frac{1}{2}m\omega^2\left(\frac{a^2}{4}\right) = E - \frac{E}{4}$$

$$K = 3E/4$$

24 (d) Let x be the point, where KE = PE

Hence, $\frac{1}{2}m\omega^2(a^2 - x^2) = \frac{1}{2}m\omega^2 x^2$

$$2x^2 = a^2, x = \frac{a}{\sqrt{2}}$$

$$\Rightarrow \quad x = \frac{4}{\sqrt{2}} = 2\sqrt{2} \text{ cm}$$

25 (b) We know that, the acceleration of particle executing SHM at a displacement x from the mean position is given by, $a = -k(x + a)$.

26 (a) For SHM, potential energy $= \frac{1}{2}m\omega^2 y^2$, where y = displacement from mean position.

and total energy $= \frac{1}{2}m\omega^2 A^2$

where, A = amplitude of SHM

Therefore, fraction of potential energy with respect to total energy

$$= \frac{\frac{1}{2}m\omega^2 y^2}{\frac{1}{2}m\omega^2 A^2}$$

$$\Rightarrow \quad = \frac{y^2}{A^2} = \frac{\left(\frac{1}{4}A\right)^2}{A^2} \qquad \left(\text{As, } y = \frac{1}{4}A\right)$$

$$= \frac{1}{16}$$

27 (c) Given, $T = \frac{2\pi}{\sqrt{3}}$

Path length,

$$l = 4 \text{ cm}$$

$$\Rightarrow A = \frac{4}{2} = 2 \text{ cm}$$

Now,

$$v = \omega\sqrt{A^2 - x^2} \text{ and } a = \omega^2 x$$

where, x = displacement of particle executing SHM, at any time.

According to the question,

$$\omega\sqrt{A^2 - x^2} = \omega^2 x$$

$$\Rightarrow \quad A^2 - x^2 = \omega^2 x^2$$

$$\Rightarrow \quad 2^2 - x^2 = 3x^2$$

$$\left(\because T = \frac{2\pi}{\sqrt{3}} \text{ and } \omega = \frac{2\pi}{\frac{2\pi}{\sqrt{3}}} = \sqrt{3}\right)$$

$$\Rightarrow \quad 4x^2 = 4 \Rightarrow |x| = 1 \text{ cm}$$

28 (a) Velocity of SHM, $v = \omega\sqrt{a^2 - y^2}$

$$\Rightarrow \quad 9 = \omega^2[a^2 - 16] \qquad \ldots(i)$$

Similarly, $16 = \omega^2[a^2 - 9] \qquad \ldots(ii)$

On dividing Eq. (ii) by Eq. (i), we get

$$\frac{16}{9} = \frac{[a^2 - 9]}{[a^2 - 16]}$$

$$\Rightarrow \quad a^2 = 25$$

$$\therefore \quad a = 5 \text{ cm}$$

29 (b) Velocity of oscillating body,

$$v = \omega\sqrt{A^2 - x^2}$$

At $x = \frac{A}{2}$, $v = \omega\sqrt{A^2 - \left(\frac{A^2}{4}\right)}$

$$= \frac{\sqrt{3}A\omega}{2} = \frac{\sqrt{3}A\pi}{T}$$

30 (c) From the relation, $v^2 = \omega^2(a^2 - x^2)$

$$\Rightarrow \quad v^2 + \omega^2 x^2 = \omega^2 a^2$$

$$\Rightarrow \quad \frac{v^2}{a^2\omega^2} + \frac{x^2}{a^2} = 1$$

which is the equation of an ellipse.

31 (b) Acceleration of simple harmonic motion is $a_{max} = -\omega^2 A$

$$\Rightarrow \quad \frac{(a_{max})_1}{(a_{max})_2} = \frac{\omega_1^2}{\omega_2^2}$$

(as A remains same)

$$\Rightarrow \quad \frac{(a_{max})_1}{(a_{max})_2} = \frac{(100)^2}{(1000)^2} = \left(\frac{1}{10}\right)^2 = 1:10^2$$

32 (d) Writing the given equation of a point performing SHM,

$$x = a\sin\left(\omega t + \frac{\pi}{6}\right) \qquad \ldots(i)$$

Differentiating Eq. (i), w.r.t. time, we obtain

$$v = \frac{dx}{dt} = a\omega\cos\left(\omega t + \frac{\pi}{6}\right)$$

It is given that, $v = \frac{a\omega}{2}$, so that

$$\frac{a\omega}{2} = a\omega\cos\left(\omega t + \frac{\pi}{6}\right)$$

$$\Rightarrow \quad \frac{1}{2} = \cos\left(\omega t + \frac{\pi}{6}\right)$$

$$\Rightarrow \quad \cos\frac{\pi}{3} = \cos\left(\omega t + \frac{\pi}{6}\right)$$

$$\Rightarrow \quad \frac{\pi}{3} = \omega t + \frac{\pi}{6} \Rightarrow \omega t = \frac{\pi}{6}$$

$$\Rightarrow \quad t = \frac{\pi}{6\omega} = \frac{\pi \times T}{6 \times 2\pi} = \frac{T}{12}$$

Thus, at $\frac{T}{12}$ velocity of the point will be equal to half of its maximum velocity.

33 (a) At $x = 0$, kinetic energy is maximum and potential energy is minimum (from principle of conservation of total mechanical energy).

34 (c) At equilibrium position, potential energy of the body is zero. So, the total energy at equilibrium position is completely kinetic energy.

35 (c) Equation of SHM, $Y = 3\sin(0.2t)$

Comparing with $Y = A\sin\omega t$, we have

$$A = 3\text{ m}, \omega = 0.2\text{ s}^{-1}$$

Mass of the particle $= 3\text{ g} = 3\times10^{-3}$kg

Therefore, kinetic energy of the particle is

$$K = \frac{1}{2}m\omega^2(A^2 - x^2)$$

$$= \frac{1}{2}\times3\times10^{-3}\times(0.2)^2(3^2-1^2)\left(\because x = \frac{A}{3}\right)$$

$$K = 0.48\times10^{-3}\text{ J}$$

36 (d) In simple harmonic motion, the total energy of the particle is constant at all instants which is totally kinetic when particle is passing through the mean position and is totally potential when particle is passing through the extreme positions.

The variation of PE and KE with time is shown in figure by dotted parabolic curve and solid parabolic curve, respectively.

Figure indicates that maximum values of total energy, KE and PE of SHM are equal.

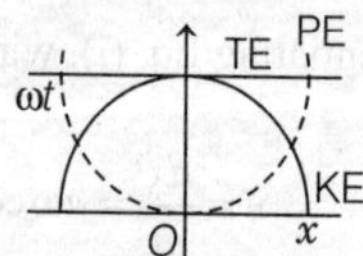

Now, $E_K = K_0\cos^2\omega t \Rightarrow (E_K)_{max} = K_0$

So, $(E_P)_{max} = K_0$ and $(E)_{Total} = K_0$

37 (a) In SHM, total energy = potential energy + kinetic energy

When the particle is half-way to its end point i.e. at half of its amplitude, then

$$y = A/2$$

Hence, potential energy

$$U = \frac{1}{2}m\omega^2\left(\frac{A}{2}\right)^2 = \frac{1}{4}\left(\frac{1}{2}m\omega^2A^2\right)$$

$$\Rightarrow \quad U = \frac{E}{4}$$

38 (d) In simple harmonic motion, the displacement equation is,

$$y = A\sin\omega t$$

where, A is amplitude of the motion.

Velocity, $v = \frac{dy}{dt} = A\omega\cos\omega t$

$$\Rightarrow \quad v = A\omega\sqrt{1-\sin^2\omega t}$$

Acceleration, $v = \omega\sqrt{A^2 - y^2}$ ...(i)

$$a = \frac{dv}{dt} = \frac{d}{dt}(A\omega\cos\omega t)$$

$$\Rightarrow \quad a = -A\omega^2\sin\omega t$$

$$a = -\omega^2 y \quad \text{...(ii)}$$

When $y = 0, v = A\omega = v_{max}$

$\Rightarrow a = 0 = a_{min}$

When $y = A, v = 0 = v_{min}$

$\Rightarrow a = -\omega^2A = a_{max}$

Hence, it is clear that when v is maximum, then a is minimum, i.e. zero or *vice-versa*.

39 (c) In SHM, the total energy = potential energy + kinetic energy $\Rightarrow E = U + K$

$$\Rightarrow \quad = \frac{1}{2}m\omega^2x^2 + \frac{1}{2}m\omega^2(A^2 - x^2)$$

$$= \frac{1}{2}m\omega^2A^2$$

where, k = force constant $= m\omega^2$.

Thus, total energy depends on k and A.

40 (a) For a particle executing SHM

$$v_{max} = A\omega$$

$$\Rightarrow \quad v_{max} = 4\times\frac{2\pi}{T}$$

$$\Rightarrow \quad v_{max} = 4\times\frac{2\pi}{8} = \pi\text{ cm s}^{-1}$$

41 (b) In SHM, velocity, $v = \omega\sqrt{a^2 - y^2}$

$$\Rightarrow \quad = 2\sqrt{(60)^2 - (20)^2}$$

$$\Rightarrow \quad = 113.14\text{ mm s}^{-1}$$

$$\simeq 113\text{ mm s}^{-1}$$

42 (d) Maximum acceleration of particle

$$= A\omega^2 = A(2\pi f)^2$$

$$\Rightarrow \quad = 4A\pi^2f^2$$

$$= 4\times0.01\times\pi^2\times(60)^2$$

$$(\because A = 0.01\text{ m})$$

$$\Rightarrow \quad = 144\pi^2\text{ m s}^{-2}$$

43 (a) Average energy in a time period,

$$U_{av} = \frac{\int_0^T U\,dt}{\int_0^T dt} = \frac{1}{T}\int_0^T U\,dt$$

$$= \frac{1}{2T}\int_0^T m\omega^2A^2\cos^2(\omega t + \phi)dt$$

$$= \frac{1}{2T}\cdot m\omega^2A^2\int_0^T\frac{1+\cos2(\omega t+\phi)}{2}dt$$

$$= \frac{1}{2T}\cdot m\omega^2A^2\cdot\left[\frac{T}{2} + 0\right]$$

$$= \frac{1}{4}m\omega^2A^2$$

44 (d) The maximum acceleration for a particle executing SHM is

$a_{max} = \omega^2x$, where x = maximum displacement from mean path

$$\therefore \quad x = \frac{a_{max}}{\omega^2} = \frac{7.5}{(3.5)^2} = 0.61\text{ m}$$

45 (b) The velocity (v) of a body in SHM changes with displacement (y) as follows

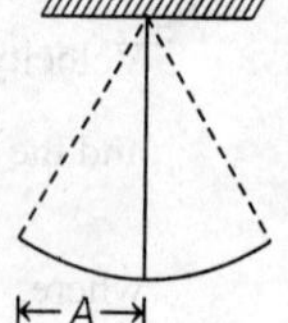

where, A is amplitude and ω is angular speed.

Given, $v_1 = 10\text{ cms}^{-1}$, $v_2 = 7\text{ cms}^{-1}$

$y_1 = 3$ cm and $y_2 = 4$ cm.

$$\therefore \quad \frac{v_2}{v_1} = \sqrt{\frac{A^2 - y_2^2}{A^2 - y_1^2}}\left[\because v = \omega\sqrt{A^2 - y^2}\right]$$

$$\Rightarrow \quad \frac{7}{10} = \sqrt{\frac{A^2 - 16}{A^2 - 9}}$$

$$\Rightarrow \quad A = 4.77\text{ cm}$$

Length of path, $2A = 2\times4.77 \approx 9.5$ cm

46 (b) The relation for kinetic energy of SHM

$$\text{KE} = \frac{1}{2}m\omega^2(A^2 - y^2) \quad \text{...(i)}$$

Potential energy, $U = \frac{1}{2}m\omega^2y^2$ ...(ii)

Now, for the condition of question and from Eqs. (i) and (ii), we get

$$\frac{1}{2}m\omega^2(A^2 - y^2) = \frac{1}{3}\times\frac{1}{2}m\omega^2y^2$$

$$\Rightarrow \quad \frac{4}{6}m\omega^2y^2 = \frac{1}{2}m\omega^2A^2$$

$$\Rightarrow \quad y^2 = \frac{3}{4}A^2$$

$$\Rightarrow \quad y = \frac{A}{2}\sqrt{3} = 0.866\text{ A}$$

$\approx 87\%$ of amplitude

47 (c) In SHM, velocity, $v = \omega\sqrt{A^2 - y^2}$

Therefore, velocity is maximum when $y = 0$, i.e. at equilibrium position, velocity will be maximum.

48 (a) Potential energy of particle in SHM,

$$U = \frac{1}{2}m\omega^2 x^2$$

$$\Rightarrow \quad U = \frac{1}{2}m(2\pi f)^2 x^2$$

$$\Rightarrow \quad U = 2\pi^2 m f^2 x^2 \quad \ldots(i)$$

Kinetic energy of particle in SHM,

$$K = \frac{1}{2}m\omega^2(A^2 - x^2)$$

$$\Rightarrow K = 2\pi^2 m f^2 (A^2 - x^2) \quad \ldots(ii)$$

Hence, total energy

$$E = K + U$$
$$= 2\pi^2 m f^2 x^2 + 2\pi^2 m f^2 (A^2 - x^2)$$
$$= 2\pi^2 m f^2 A^2$$
$$= \frac{2\pi^2 m A^2}{T^2} \quad \left(\because T = \frac{1}{f}\right)$$

Thus, it is obvious that total energy of particle executing simple harmonic motion depends on amplitude (A) and period (T).

49 (a) The given equation is written as

$$y = 3\sin\left(100t + \frac{\pi}{6}\right)\text{m} \quad \ldots(i)$$

The general equation of simple harmonic motion is written as

$$y = A\sin(\omega t + \phi) \quad \ldots(ii)$$

Equating Eqs. (i) and (ii), we get

$$A = 3,\ \omega = 100$$

Maximum velocity,

$$v = A\omega$$
$$= 3 \times 100 = 300\ \text{ms}^{-1}$$

50 (d) As we know that the speed of particle executing SHM is given by

$$v = \omega\sqrt{a^2 - x^2} \text{ and } \omega = \frac{2\pi}{T}$$

where, x = displacement

$$\Rightarrow \quad v = \frac{2\pi}{T}\sqrt{a^2 - \left(\frac{a}{2}\right)^2} \quad (\text{at } x = a/2)$$

$$\Rightarrow \quad v = \frac{2\pi}{T}\left(\frac{\sqrt{3}a}{2}\right) = \frac{\sqrt{3}\pi a}{T}$$

51 (b) As the amplitude is increased, the maximum acceleration of the platform (along with coin as long as they doesn't get separated) increases.

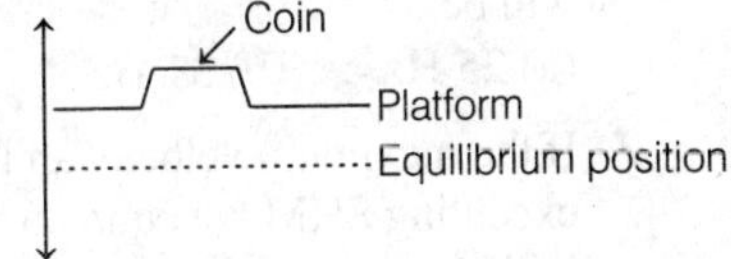

If we draw the free body diagram for coin at one of the extreme positions as shown, below

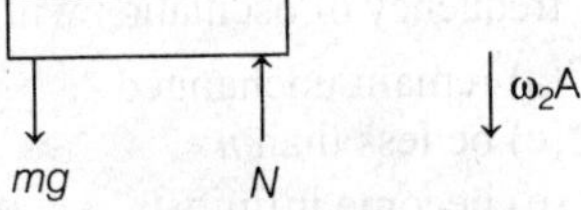

Then, from Newton's law

$$mg - N = m\omega^2 A$$

For loosing contact with the platform,

$$N = 0$$

So, $$A = \frac{g}{\omega^2}$$

Topic 3

Time Period and Frequency

2018

1 A block of rectangular size of mass m and area of cross-section A, floats in a liquid of density ρ. If we give a small vertical displacement from equilibrium, it undergoes SHM with time period T, then **[AIIMS]**

(a) $T^2 \propto \frac{1}{\rho}$ (b) $T^2 \propto \rho$ (c) $T^2 \propto m^{-1}$ (d) $T^2 \propto \frac{1}{A^{-2}}$

2 $Y = 5\sin\frac{\pi}{2}(100t - 2x)$, what is time period? **[JIPMER]**

(a) 0.04 s (b) 1 s (c) 0.06 s (d) 0.02 s

2017

3 A particle executes linear simple harmonic motion with an amplitude of 3 cm. When the particle is at 2 cm from the mean position, the magnitude of its velocity is equal to that of its acceleration. Then, its time period in seconds is **[NEET]**

(a) $\frac{\sqrt{5}}{\pi}$ (b) $\frac{\sqrt{5}}{2\pi}$ (c) $\frac{4\pi}{\sqrt{5}}$ (d) $\frac{2\pi}{\sqrt{3}}$

2015

4 A particle is executing SHM along a straight line. Its velocities at distances x_1 and x_2 from the mean positions are v_1 and v_2, respectively. Its time period is **[CBSE]**

(a) $2\pi\sqrt{\frac{x_1^2 + x_2^2}{v_1^2 + v_2^2}}$ (b) $2\pi\sqrt{\frac{x_2^2 - x_1^2}{v_1^2 - v_2^2}}$

(c) $2\pi\sqrt{\frac{v_1^2 + v_2^2}{x_1^2 + x_2^2}}$ (d) $2\pi\sqrt{\frac{v_1^2 - v_2^2}{x_1^2 - x_2^2}}$

2014

5 A block resting on the horizontal surface executes SHM in horizontal plane with amplitude A. The frequency of oscillation for which the block just starts to slip is (μ = coefficient of friction and g = gravitational acceleration) **[MHT CET]**

(a) $\frac{1}{2\pi}\sqrt{\frac{\mu g}{A}}$ (b) $\frac{1}{4\pi}\sqrt{\frac{\mu g}{A}}$ (c) $2\pi\sqrt{\frac{A}{\mu g}}$ (d) $4\pi\sqrt{\frac{A}{\mu g}}$

2013

6 Frequency of oscillation of a body is 7 Hz when force F_1 is applied and 24 Hz when F_2 is applied. If both forces F_1 and F_2 are applied together, then frequency of oscillation will be

(a) 25 Hz (b) 31 Hz (c) 17 Hz (d) 24 Hz

7 If the maximum velocity and acceleration of a particle executing SHM are equal in magnitude, the time period will be **[UP CPMT]**

(a) 1.57 s (b) 3.17 s (c) 6.28 s (d) 12.56 s

8 A simple pendulum of frequency n falls freely under gravity from certain height from the ground level. Its frequency of oscillation will **[Kerala CEE]**

(a) remain unchanged (b) be greater than n
(c) be less than n (d) become zero
(e) become infinity

9 A particle executing simple harmonic motion has a time period of 4 s. After how much interval of time from $t = 0$ will its displacement be half of its amplitude? **[KCET]**

(a) $\frac{1}{3}$ s (b) $\frac{1}{2}$ s (c) $\frac{2}{3}$ s (d) $\frac{1}{6}$ s

2012

10 The displacement equation of a body performing SHM is given as $y = 200\sin\left(180\pi t + \frac{\pi}{4}\right)$. The time period of body is **[MPPMT]**

(a) $\frac{1}{65}$ s (b) $\frac{1}{50}$ s (c) $\frac{1}{90}$ s (d) $\frac{1}{80}$ s

2011

11 A particle of mass m is located in a one-dimensional potential field, where potential energy is given by $V(x) = A(1 - \cos px)$, where A and p are constants. The period of small oscillations of the particle is **[WB JEE]**

(a) $2\pi\sqrt{\frac{m}{Ap}}$ (b) $2\pi\sqrt{\frac{m}{Ap^2}}$ (c) $2\pi\sqrt{\frac{m}{A}}$ (d) $\frac{1}{2\pi}\sqrt{\frac{Ap}{m}}$

12 A harmonic oscillation is represented by $y = 0.34\cos(3000t + 0.74)$. Find its frequency.

(a) $\frac{1000}{\pi}$ (b) $\frac{1500}{\pi}$ (c) $\frac{750}{\pi}$ (d) $\frac{3000}{\pi}$

13 **Asertion** (A) Water in a U-tube executes SHM, the time period for mercury filled upto the same height in te U-tube be greater than that in case of water.

Reason (R) The amplitude of an oscillating pendulum goes on increasing. **[AIIMS]**

(a) Both A and R are correct and R is the corret explanation of A
(b) Bot A and R are correct but R is not the correct explanation of A
(c) A is correct but R is incorrect
(d) Both A and R are incorrect

2010

14 A body is executing SHM when its displacement from the mean position are 4 cm and 5 cm, it has velocity 10 cms^{-1} and 8 cms^{-1}, respectively. Its periodic time t is **[AFMC]**

(a) $\frac{2\pi}{3}$ s (b) π s
(c) $\frac{3\pi}{2}$ s (d) 2π s

15 A body is executing SM of amplitude 1 m. Its velocity wile passing through the mean position, is 10 m/s. Find its frequency.

(a) 1.442 Hz (b) 1.592 Hz
(c) 1.322 Hz (d) 1.132 Hz

16 A verticle U-tube of iniform cross section contains water upto a heignt of 20 cm. Calculate the time period of the oscillation of water when it is disturbed **[AFMC]**

(a) 0.11 s (b) 0.25 s
(c) 0.40 s (d) 0.9 s

17 The equation of a particle executing SHM is $\frac{2d^2x}{dt^2} + 32x = 0$. Then, the time period of the body is **[OJEE]**

(a) zero (b) $\pi / 2$
(c) π (d) 2π

18 A 8 kg body performs SHM of amplitude 30 cm. The restoring force is 60 N when the displacement is 30 cm. Find its time period.

(a) 1.432 s (b) 1.256 s
(c) 2.424 s (d) 2.412 s

19 The time period of the variation of potential energy of a particle executing SHM with period T is **[Kerala CEE]**

(a) $\frac{T}{4}$ (b) T (c) $2T$ (d) $\frac{T}{2}$
(e) $\frac{T}{3}$

20 The motion of a particle executing SHM in one dimension is described by $x = -0.3\sin\left(t + \frac{\pi}{4}\right)$, where x is in metre and t in second. The frequency of oscillation in Hz is **[DUMET]**

(a) 3 (b) $\frac{1}{2\pi}$
(c) $\frac{\pi}{2}$ (d) $\frac{1}{\pi}$

2009

21 Two bodies performing SHM are expressed as $y_1 = 50\sin\left(100\pi t + \frac{\pi}{3}\right)$ and $y_2 = 10\sin\left(50\pi t + \frac{\pi}{6}\right)$. The difference of their oscillating frequency is **[MHT CET]**

(a) 5 Hz (b) 50 Hz (c) 20 Hz (d) 25 Hz

22 A body executes simple harmonic motion under the action of force F_1 with a time period $\frac{4}{5}$ s. If the force is changed to F_2 it executes simple harmonic motion with time period $\frac{3}{5}$ s. If both forces F_1 and F_2 act simultaneously in the same direction on the body then, its time period will be **[AFMC]**

(a) $\frac{12}{25}$ s (b) $\frac{24}{25}$ s
(c) $\frac{35}{24}$ s (d) $\frac{15}{12}$ s

23 The periodic time of a particle doing simple harmonic motion is 4 s. The time taken by it to go from its mean position to the maximum displacement (amplitude) is **[MHT CET]**

(a) 2 s (b) 1 s
(c) $\frac{2}{3}$ s (d) $\frac{1}{3}$ s

24 The motion of a particle executing SHM is given by $x = 0.01 \sin 100\pi (t + 0.05)$, where x is in metre and t in second. The time period of motion (in second) is **[MGIMS]**

(a) 0.01 (b) 0.02
(c) 0.1 (d) 0.2

2008

25 The function $\sin^2 \omega t$ represents **[AIIMS]**

(a) a periodic but not simple harmonic motion with a period $2\pi/\omega$
(b) a periodic but not simple harmonic motion with a period π/ω
(c) a simple harmonic motion with a period $2\pi/\omega$
(d) a simple harmonic motion with a period π/ω

26 A particle of mass m is executing oscillations about the origin on the X-axis. Its potential energy is $U(x) = k[x]^3$, where k is a positive constant. If the amplitude of oscillation is a, then its time period T is **[AIIMS]**

(a) proportional to $\frac{1}{\sqrt{a}}$ (b) independent of a
(c) proportional to $\sqrt{a}$ (d) proportional to $a^{3/2}$

27 The magnitude of maximum acceleration is π times that of maximum velocity of a simple harmonic oscillator. The time period of the oscillator in second is **[Punjab PMET]**

(a) 4 (b) 2
(c) 1 (d) 0.5

2007

28 A particle executes simple harmonic oscillation with an amplitude a. The period of oscillation is T. The minimum time taken by the particle to travel half of the amplitude from the equilibrium position is **[CBSE AIPMT, JIPMER]**

(a) $\frac{T}{4}$ (b) $\frac{T}{8}$ (c) $\frac{T}{12}$ (d) $\frac{T}{2}$

29 The maximum displacement of the particle executing SHM is 1 cm and the maximum acceleration is $(1.57)^2$ cm s^{-2}. Its time period is **[AMU]**

(a) 0.25 s (b) 4.0 s
(c) 1.57 s (d) 3.14 s

2006

30 A rectangular block of mass m and area of cross-section A floats in a liquid of density ρ. If it is given a small vertical displacement from equilibrium it undergoes oscillation with a time period T. Then, **[CBSE AIPMT]**

(a) $T \propto \sqrt{\rho}$ (b) $T \propto \frac{1}{\sqrt{A}}$
(c) $T \propto \frac{1}{\rho}$ (d) $T \propto \frac{1}{\sqrt{m}}$

31 A particle executes simple harmonic motion with a frequency f. The frequency with which the potential energy oscillates is **[AMU]**

(a) f (b) $f/2$
(c) $2f$ (d) None of these

32 A particle executes SHM of amplitude 25 cm and time period 3 s. What is the minimum time required for the particle to move between two points 12.5 cm on either side of the mean position? **[BCECE]**

(a) 0.5 s (b) 1.0 s
(c) 1.5 s (d) 2.0 s

Answers

1 (a)	2 (a)	3 (c)	4 (b)	5 (a)	6 (a)	7 (c)	8 (d)	9 (a)	10 (c)
11 (d)	12 (b)	13 (d)	14 (b)	15 (b)	16 (d)	17 (b)	18 (b)	19 (d)	20 (b)
21 (d)	22 (a)	23 (b)	24 (b)	25 (b)	26 (a)	27 (b)	28 (c)	29 (b)	30 (b)
31 (d)	32 (a)								

Explanations

1 (a) According to the law of floatation, weight of the retangular block ↓

= buoyant force ↑

$\Rightarrow mg = v \times \rho \times g$

Now, volume of rectangular block

= length × breadth × height

$= l \times b \times h = l \times A$

(because $A = b \times h$)

At equilibrium, $mg = Al\rho g$

$\Rightarrow \quad m = A\rho l$

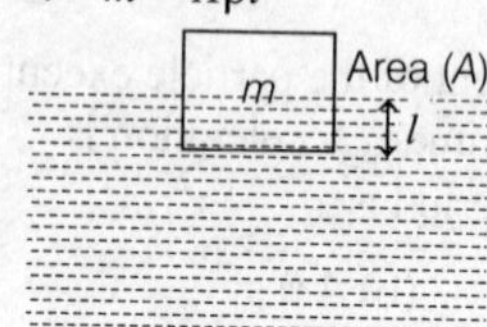

where, l = length of part immersed in liquid.

When it is given in downward displacement y, restoring force (upward direction) on block is

$$F = -[A(l+y)\rho g - mg]$$
$$= -[A(l+y)\rho g - Al\rho g]$$
$$= -A\rho g y$$

i.e. $F \propto -y$ or $a \propto -y$, so it executes SHM (inertia factor).

Mass of block = m

Spring factor = $A\rho g$

Time period $= 2\pi\sqrt{\dfrac{\text{Inertia factor}}{\text{Spring factor}}}$

$$T = 2\pi\sqrt{\frac{m}{A\rho g}}$$

$$\Rightarrow T^2 \propto \frac{m}{A\rho}$$

2 (a) Given that,

$$Y = 5\sin(50\pi t - \pi x) \quad \text{...(i)}$$

Equation of displacement,

$$Y = A\sin(\omega t - kx) \quad \text{...(ii)}$$

After comparing with Eqs. (i) and (ii),

$$\omega = 50\pi$$

$\because$ Time period, $T = \dfrac{2\pi}{\omega} = \dfrac{2\pi}{50\pi} = 0.04$ s

3 (c) Magnitude of velocity of particle when it is at displacement x from mean position

$$= \omega\sqrt{A^2 - x^2}$$

Also, magnitude of acceleration of particle in SHM

$$= \omega^2 x$$

Given, when $x = 2$ cm

$$|\mathbf{v}| = |\mathbf{a}|$$

$$\Rightarrow \omega\sqrt{A^2 - x^2} = \omega^2 x$$

$$\Rightarrow \omega = \frac{\sqrt{A^2 - x^2}}{x} = \frac{\sqrt{9-4}}{2}$$

$\Rightarrow$ Angular velocity, $\omega = \dfrac{\sqrt{5}}{2}$

$\therefore$ Time period of motion,

$$T = \frac{2\pi}{\omega} = \frac{4\pi}{\sqrt{5}} \text{ s}$$

4 (b) Let A be the amplitude of oscillation, then

$$v_1^2 = \omega^2(A^2 - x_1^2) \quad \text{...(i)}$$
$$v_2^2 = \omega^2(A^2 - x_2^2) \quad \text{...(ii)}$$

Subtracting Eq. (ii) from Eq. (i), we get

$$v_1^2 - v_2^2 = \omega^2(x_2^2 - x_1^2)$$

$$\Rightarrow \omega = \sqrt{\frac{v_1^2 - v_2^2}{x_2^2 - x_1^2}}$$

$$\Rightarrow \frac{2\pi}{T} = \sqrt{\frac{v_1^2 - v_2^2}{x_2^2 - x_1^2}}$$

$$\Rightarrow T = 2\pi\sqrt{\frac{x_2^2 - x_1^2}{v_1^2 - v_2^2}}$$

5 (a) When restoring force will become equal to the frictional force, block will start to slip.

$\therefore$ Restoring force = Frictional force

$$\Rightarrow kA = \mu mg \quad [\because F_{\text{rest}} = -kx] \text{...(i)}$$

Now, frequency, $f = \dfrac{1}{2\pi}\sqrt{\dfrac{k}{m}}$

From Eq. (i), we get

$$f = \frac{1}{2\pi}\sqrt{\frac{\mu g}{A}}$$

6 (a) According to question, $F_1 = -k_1 x$ and $F_2 = -k_2 x$

$$\therefore n_1 = \frac{1}{2\pi}\sqrt{\frac{k_1}{m}} = 7 \text{ Hz} \quad \text{...(i)}$$

$$n_2 = \frac{1}{2\pi}\sqrt{\frac{k_2}{m}} = 24 \text{ Hz} \quad \text{...(ii)}$$

Now, $F = F_1 + F_2 = -(k_1 + k_2)x$

$\therefore$ Frequency of oscillation,

$$n = \frac{1}{2\pi}\sqrt{\frac{k_1 + k_2}{m}}$$

$$= \frac{1}{2\pi}\sqrt{\frac{4\pi^2 n_1^2 m + 4\pi^2 n_2^2 m}{m}}$$

$$= \frac{2\pi}{2\pi}\sqrt{n_1^2 + n_2^2} = \sqrt{7^2 + 24^2}$$

$$= 25 \text{ Hz}$$

7 (c) According to the question,

$|v_{\max}| = |a_{\max}|$, i.e. $\omega A = \omega^2 A$

$$\Rightarrow \omega = 1 = \frac{2\pi}{T} \quad \therefore T = 2\pi$$

$$\Rightarrow T = 2 \times 3.14$$

$$\Rightarrow T = 6.28 \text{ s}$$

8 (d) For freely falling case, the effective value of g is zero, so that frequency of oscillation will be zero.

As, $\quad f = \dfrac{1}{2\pi}\sqrt{\dfrac{g_{\text{eff}}}{\lambda}}$

$$\Rightarrow f = \frac{1}{2\pi}\sqrt{\frac{0}{\lambda}}$$

$$\therefore f = 0$$

9 (a) The displacement equation for SHM is $y = A\sin\omega t'$

where, ω is angular velocity $\left(\omega = \dfrac{2\pi}{T}\right)$ and A the amplitude.

Given, $\quad y = \dfrac{A}{2},\ t' = \dfrac{t}{4}$

$$\frac{A}{2} = A\sin\frac{2\pi t}{4}$$

$$\Rightarrow \frac{1}{2} = \sin\frac{\pi t}{2}$$

$$\therefore \sin\frac{\pi}{6} = \sin\frac{\pi t}{2}$$

$$\Rightarrow \frac{\pi}{6} = \frac{\pi t}{2}$$

$$\Rightarrow t = \frac{1}{3} \text{ s}$$

10 (c) Given, $y = 200\sin\left(100\pi t + \dfrac{\pi}{4}\right)$

Comparing with equation of SHM

$$y = a\sin(\omega t + \phi),$$

we get $\omega = 180\pi$

$$\frac{2\pi}{T} = 180\pi$$

$$T = \frac{2\pi}{180\pi} = \frac{1}{90} \text{ s}$$

11 (b) We are given that a particle of mass m is located in a one-dimensional potential field and the potential energy is given by $V(x) = A(1 - \cos px)$.

So, we can find the force experienced by the particle as

$$F = -\frac{dV}{dx} = -Ap\sin px$$

For small oscillations, we have

$$F \approx -Ap^2x \quad [\because \sin px \simeq px]$$

Hence, the acceleration would be given by

$$a = \frac{F}{m} = -\frac{Ap^2}{m}x$$

Also, we know that

$$a = \frac{F}{m} = -\omega^2 x$$

So, $\omega = \sqrt{\frac{Ap^2}{m}}$

$\Rightarrow \quad T = \frac{2\pi}{\omega} = 2\pi\sqrt{\frac{m}{Ap^2}}$

12 *(b)* Given $y = 0.34\cos(3000t + 0.74)$

On compare, $y = a\cos(\omega t + \phi)$

angular frequency, $\omega = 3000$ rad/s

and frequency, $v = \frac{\omega}{2\pi} = \frac{3000}{2\pi}$

$$v = \frac{1500}{\pi}$$

13 *(d)* The period of the liquid executing SHM in a U-tube does not depend upon the density of the liquid. Therefore, time period will be the same, when mercury is filled upto the same height as the water in the U-tube.

Now, as the pendulum oscillates, it drags air along with it. Therefore, its kinetic energy is dissipated in overcoming viscous drag due to air and hence, its amplitude goes on decreasing.

14 *(b)* For a body executing SHM, velocity,

$$v = \sqrt{\omega^2(A^2 - y^2)}$$

We have,

$$10^2 = \omega^2(A^2 - 4^2)$$

and $\quad 8^2 = \omega^2(A^2 - 5^2)$

So, $\quad 10^2 - 8^2 = \omega^2(5^2 - 4^2) = (3\omega)^2$

$\Rightarrow \quad 6 = 3\omega$

$\Rightarrow \quad \omega = 2$

Since, time period, $t = \frac{2\pi}{\omega}$

$\therefore \quad t = \frac{2\pi}{2} = \pi$ s

15 *(b)* Here, $a = 1$ m, $v_{max} = 10$ m/s

$$v_{max} = a\omega = 2\pi va$$

So frequency, $v = \frac{v_{max}}{2\pi a}$

$$v = \frac{10 \times 7}{2 \times 22 \times 1} = 1.592 \text{ Hz}$$

16 *(d)* The length of the liquid column

$$L = 2 \times 20 = 40 \text{ cm}$$

Time period, $T = 2\pi\sqrt{\frac{l}{2g}}$

$$T = 2\pi\sqrt{\frac{40}{2 \times 980}}$$

$$T = \frac{2\pi}{7} = 0.898 \simeq 0.9 \text{ s}$$

17 *(b)* The equation of SHM is given by

$$\frac{d^2x}{dt^2} + 16x = 0$$

On comparing with standard equation $\frac{d^2x}{dt^2} + \omega^2 x = 0$, we get

$\therefore \quad \omega^2 = 16 \Rightarrow \omega = 4$

$\Rightarrow \quad T = \frac{2\pi}{\omega} = \frac{2\pi}{4} = \frac{\pi}{2}$

18 *(b)* As the body performs SHM, hence

angular frequency, $\omega = \sqrt{\frac{k}{m}}$

But for SHM $F = -kx$, hence

$$k = \frac{F}{x} = \frac{60}{30 \times 10^{-2}} = 200$$

Substituting $k = 200$, we get

$$\omega = \sqrt{\frac{200}{8}} = \frac{10}{2} = 5 \text{ rad/s}$$

Time period, $T = \frac{2\pi}{\omega} = \frac{2 \times 22}{7 \times 5}$

$$= \frac{44}{35} = 1.256 \text{ s}$$

19 *(d)* In a complete cycle of SHM, potential energy varies for half the cycle and kinetic energy varies for the other half of the cycle.

Thus, for a time period T, the potential energy varies for time of $\frac{T}{2}$.

20 *(b)* We have, $x = -0.3\sin\left(t + \frac{\pi}{4}\right)$

Comparing with the general equation

$$x = x_0\sin(\omega t + \phi)$$

where, x_0 = maximum displacement

So, $\quad x_0 = 0.3, \quad \omega = 1, \quad \phi = \frac{\pi}{4}$

Hence, $\quad 2\pi f = 1 \Rightarrow f = 1/2\pi$

21 *(d)* $y_1 = 50\sin\left(100\pi t + \frac{\pi}{3}\right)$

$$y_2 = 10\sin\left(50\pi t + \frac{\pi}{6}\right)$$

Comparing with general equation of SHM

$y = a\sin(\omega t + \phi)$, we have

$$\omega_1 = 100\pi \text{ and } \omega_2 = 50\pi$$

$$2\pi f_1 = 100\pi \Rightarrow f_1 = 50 \text{ Hz}$$

$$\omega_2 = 50\pi$$

$$\Rightarrow 2\pi f_2 = 50\pi \Rightarrow f_2 = 25 \text{ Hz}$$

$$\therefore \quad f_1 - f_2 = 50 - 25 = 25 \text{ Hz}$$

22 *(a)* The required time period would be given by

$$T = T_1 \times T_2$$

[$\because$ Time period is multiplicative]

$$= \frac{4}{5} \times \frac{3}{5} = \frac{12}{25} \text{ s}$$

23 *(b)* The time taken by particle to go from mean position to extreme positions would be

$$\frac{T}{4} = \frac{4\text{s}}{4} = 1 \text{ s}$$

24 *(b)* Given, SHM is

$$x = 0.01\sin 100\pi(t + 0.05).$$

On comparing with $x = A\sin(\omega t + \phi)$

We get $\quad \omega = 100\pi$

Now, time period

$$T = \frac{2\pi}{\omega} = \frac{2\pi}{100\pi} = \frac{1}{50} = 0.02 \text{ s}$$

25 *(b)* Here, $y = \sin^2 \omega t$

$$\frac{dy}{dt} = 2\omega\sin\omega t\cos\omega t$$

$$= \omega\sin 2\omega t$$

$\Rightarrow \quad \frac{d^2y}{dt^2} = 2\omega^2\cos 2\omega t$

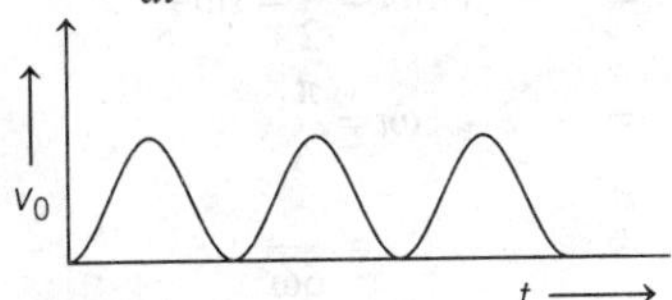

For SHM, $\frac{d^2y}{dt^2} \propto -y$

Hence, function is not SHM, but periodic.

From the v-t graph, time period is

$$t = \frac{\pi}{\omega}$$

26 *(a)* Given, $\quad U(x) = k[x]^3$

$\Rightarrow \quad F = -\frac{dU}{dx}$

$$F = -3k[x]^2 \quad \ldots(\text{i})$$

Also, for SHM $x = a\sin\omega t$

and $\frac{d^2x}{dt^2} + \omega^2 x = 0$

Acceleration, $a = \frac{d^2x}{dt^2} = -\omega^2 x$

$\Rightarrow F = ma = m\frac{d^2x}{dt^2} = -m\omega^2 x$ ...(ii)

From Eqs. (i) and (ii), we get

$$\omega = \sqrt{\frac{3kx}{m}}$$

$$\Rightarrow T = \frac{2\pi}{\omega} = 2\pi\sqrt{\frac{m}{3kx}}$$

$$= 2\pi\sqrt{\frac{m}{3k(a\sin\omega t)}}$$

$$\Rightarrow T \propto \frac{1}{\sqrt{a}}$$

27 *(b)* As, maximum acceleration = maximum velocity × π

i.e. $\omega^2 A = \pi\omega A$

where, A is amplitude and ω is angular velocity,

$\Rightarrow \omega = \pi$

$\Rightarrow \frac{2\pi}{T} = \pi$

$\Rightarrow T = 2$ s

28 *(c)* Let displacement equation of particle executing SHM is $y = a\sin\omega t$. As particle travels half of the amplitude from the equilibrium position, so

$$y = \frac{a}{2}$$

Therefore, $\frac{a}{2} = a\sin\omega t$

$\Rightarrow \sin\omega t = \frac{1}{2} = \sin\frac{\pi}{6}$

$\Rightarrow \omega t = \frac{\pi}{6}$

$\Rightarrow t = \frac{\pi}{6\omega}$

$\Rightarrow t = \frac{\pi}{6\left(\frac{2\pi}{T}\right)}$ $\left(\text{as } \omega = \frac{2\pi}{T}\right)$

$\Rightarrow t = \frac{T}{12}$ $(A = 1\text{cm})$

Hence, the particle travels half of the amplitude from equilibrium in $\frac{T}{12}$ s.

29 *(b)* Maximum acceleration $= A\omega^2$

$\Rightarrow \left(\frac{\pi}{2}\right)^2 = 1\left(\frac{2\pi}{T}\right)^2$ $\left(\because 1.57 = \frac{\pi}{2}\right)$

$\Rightarrow \frac{\pi^2}{4} = \frac{4\pi^2}{T^2}$

$\Rightarrow T^2 = \frac{4 \times 4\pi^2}{\pi^2}$

$\Rightarrow T^2 = 16$

$\therefore T = 4$ s

30 *(b)* Let block is displaced through x metre, then weight of displaced water or upthrust (upwards)

$= -Ax\rho g$ $[\because f = mg = (Ax\rho)g]$

where, A is area of cross-section of the block and ρ is its density. This must be equal to force (= ma) applied, where m is mass of the block and a is acceleration.

$\therefore ma = -Ax\rho g$

$\Rightarrow a = -\frac{A\rho g}{m}x = -\omega^2 x$

A m x mg

This is the equation of simple harmonic motion. Time period of oscillation,

$$T = \frac{2\pi}{\omega} = 2\pi\sqrt{\frac{m}{A\rho g}}$$

$$\Rightarrow T \propto \frac{1}{\sqrt{A}} \left[\because T = 2\pi\sqrt{\frac{\text{displacement}}{\text{acceleration}}}\right]$$

31 *(d)* In one time period, the potential energy changes its value from maximum to minimum and minimum to maximum four times. So, frequency should be four times.

32 *(a)* In order to find the time taken by the particle from – 12.5 cm to + 12.5 cm on either side of mean position, we will find the time taken by particle to go from $x = -12.5$ cm to $x = 0$ and to go from $x = 0$ to $x = +12.5$ cm.

12.5 cm 12.5 cm
m
25 cm 25 cm
x=0

Let the equation of motion be

$$x = A\sin\omega t$$

First, the particle moves from

$$x = -12.5 \text{ cm to } x = 0$$

$\therefore 12.5 = 25\sin\omega t$ $(\because A = 25 \text{ cm})$

$\Rightarrow \frac{1}{2} = \sin\omega t$

$\Rightarrow \omega t = \frac{\pi}{6}$

$$t = \pi/6\omega$$

Similarly, to go from position $x = 0$ to $x = 12.5$ cm

$$\omega t = \frac{\pi}{6}$$

$\Rightarrow t = \frac{\pi}{6\omega}$

∴ Total time taken from $x = -12.5$ cm to $x = 12.5$ cm

$$t = \frac{\pi}{6\omega} + \frac{\pi}{6\omega} = \frac{\pi}{3\omega}$$

$$= \frac{\pi}{3\left(\frac{2\pi}{T}\right)} = \frac{T}{6}$$

$$= \frac{3}{6} = 0.5 \text{ s}$$

Topic 4

System Executing SHM

(Simple Pendulum and Spring Mass System)

2018

1 A pendulum is hung from the roof of a sufficiently high building and is moving freely to and fro like a simple harmonic oscillator. The acceleration of the bob of the pendulum is 20 m/s^2 at a distance of 5 m from the mean position. The time period of oscillation is **[NEET]**

(a) 2 s (b) π s
(c) 2π s (d) 1 s

2011

2 Two simple pendulums first of bob mass M_1 (bob A) and length L_1, second of bob mass M_2 (bob B) and length L_2. $M_2 = M_1$ and $L_1 = 2L_2$. If the vibrational energies of both are same. Then, which is correct? **[AIIMS]**

(a) Amplitude of B is greater than A
(b) Amplitude of B is smaller than A
(c) Amplitude will be same
(d) None of the above

3 The mass and diameter of a planet are twice those of the earth. The period of oscillation of pendulum on this planet will be (if it is a second's pendulum on earth) **[AIIMS]**

(a) $1/\sqrt{2}$ s (b) $2\sqrt{2}$ s
(c) 2 s (d) 1/2 s

4 **Assertion** (A) The percentage change in time period is 1.5%. If the length of simple pendulum increases by 3%.
Reason (R) Time period is directly proportional to length of pendulum. **[AIIMS]**

(a) Both A and R are correct and R is the correct explanation of A.
(b) Both A and R are correct but R is not the correct explanation of A.
(c) A is correct but R is incorrect.
(d) Both A and R are incorrect.

5 A clock S is based on oscillation of a spring and a clock P is based on pendulum motion . Both clocks run at the same rate on the earth. On a planet having the same density as earth but twice the radius **[AFMC]**

(a) S will run faster than P
(b) P will run faster than S
(c) both will run at the same rate as on the earth
(d) both will run at the same rate which will be different from that on the earth

6 The time period of a simple pendulum of length L as measured in an elevator descending with acceleration $g/3$ is **[BHU]**

(a) $2\pi\sqrt{\frac{3L}{2g}}$ (b) $\pi\sqrt{\frac{3L}{g}}$ (c) $2\pi\sqrt{\frac{3L}{g}}$ (d) $2\pi\sqrt{\frac{2L}{3g}}$

7 A pendulum has time period T in air when it is made to oscillate in water, it acquired a time period $T' = \sqrt{2}T$. The density of the pendulum bob is equal to (Take density of water = 1) **[Haryana PMT]**

(a) $\sqrt{2}$ (b) 2
(c) $2\sqrt{2}$ (d) None of these

8 A pendulum is made to hang from the ceiling of an elevator. It has period of T s (for small angles). The elevator is made to accelerate upwards with 10 m/s^2. The period of the pendulum now will be (Take, $g = 10\ m/s^2$) **[DUMET]**

(a) $T\sqrt{2}$ (b) infinite
(c) $T/\sqrt{2}$ (d) zero

9 If pendulum bob on a 2 m string is displaced 60° from the vertical and then released. What is the speed of the bob as it passes through the lowest point in its path? **[VMMC]**

(a) $\sqrt{2}\ ms^{-1}$ (b) $\sqrt{2 \times 9.8}\ ms^{-1}$
(c) 4.43 ms^{-1} (d) $1/\sqrt{2}\ ms^{-1}$

10 Two pendulums of lengths 100 cm and 121 cm start vibrating. At some instant the two are at the mean position in the same phase. After how many vibrations of the longer pendulum will the two be in the same phase at the mean position again? **[MGIMS]**

(a) 10 (b) 11 (c) 20 (d) 21

2010

11 In the figure, S_1 and S_2 are identical springs. The oscillation frequency of the mass m is f. If one spring is removed, the frequency will become **[VMMC]**

A B
m
S_1 S_2

(a) f (b) $2f$ (c) $\sqrt{2}f$ (d) $\frac{1}{\sqrt{2}}f$

12 An iron ball of mass M is hanged from the ceiling by a spring with a spring constant k. It executes a SHM with a period P. If the mass of the ball is increased by four times, the new period will be **[DUMET]**

(a) $4P$ (b) $\frac{P}{4}$ (c) $2P$ (d) P

2009

13 As shown in figure, a simple harmonic motion oscillator having identical four springs has time period **[BVP]**

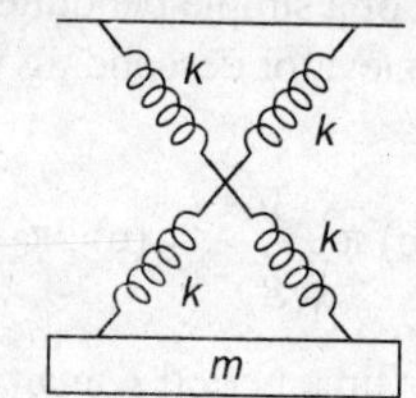

(a) $T = 2\pi\sqrt{\frac{m}{4k}}$ (b) $T = 2\pi\sqrt{\frac{m}{2k}}$

(c) $T = 2\pi\sqrt{\frac{m}{k}}$ (d) $T = 2\pi\sqrt{\frac{2m}{k}}$

14 Two masses m_1 and m_2 are suspended together by a massless spring of force constant k, as shown in figure. When the masses are in equilibrium, mass m_1 is removed without disturbing the system. The angular frequency of oscillation of mass m_2 is **[BCECE]**

m_1
m_2

(a) $\sqrt{\frac{k}{m_2}}$ (b) $\sqrt{\frac{k}{m_1}}$ (c) $\sqrt{\frac{k\,m_1}{m_2^2}}$ (d) $\sqrt{\frac{k\,m_2}{m_1^2}}$

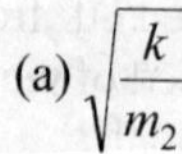

15 If a simple pendulum oscillates with an amplitude of 50 mm and time period of 2 s, then its maximum velocity is **[MHT CET]**

(a) $0.10\ \text{ms}^{-1}$ (b) $0.15\ \text{ms}^{-1}$ (c) $0.8\ \text{ms}^{-1}$ (d) $0.26\ \text{ms}^{-1}$

16 If the length of second's pendulum is increased by 2%, then in a day the pendulum **[Kerala CEE]**

(a) loses 764 s (b) loses 924 s
(c) gains 236 s (d) loses 864 s
(e) gains 346 s

17 Maximum time period of any simple pendulum on the earth is **[BVP]**

(a) 180.5 min (b) 100 min (c) 90.5 min (d) 1.5 min

18 A simple pendulum is executing SHM with a period of 6 s between two extreme positions B and C about a point O. If the length of the arc BC is 10 cm, how long will the pendulum take the move from position C to a position D towards O exactly midway between C and O? **[EAMCET]**

(a) 0.5 s (b) 1 s (c) 1.5 s (d) 3 s

19 A clock pendulum made of invar has a period of 0.5 s at 20°. If the clock is used in a climate where the temperature averages 30°C, how much time does the clock lose in each oscillation? (for invar $\alpha = 9 \times 10^{-7}/°\text{C}$ and $g =$ constant) **[EAMCET]**

(a) 2.25×10^{-6} s (b) 2.5×10^{-7} s
(c) 5×10^{-7} s (d) 1.125×10^{-6} s

20 A simple pendulum is made by attaching a 1 kg bob to a 5 m long copper wire. Its period is T. Now, if 1 kg bob is replaced by 10 kg bob, the period of oscillations **[MGIMS]**

(a) remains T
(b) becomes greater than T
(c) becomes less than T
(d) Any of above depends on locality

21 The length of a second's pendulum is **[MGIMS]**

(a) 99.8 cm (b) 99 cm
(c) 100 cm (d) None of these

22 A pendulum suspended from the ceiling of a train has a period T when the train is at rest. When the train accelerates with a uniform acceleration a, the period of oscillation will **[MGIMS]**

(a) increase
(b) decrease
(c) remain unaffected
(d) become infinite

2008

23 The time period of a simple pendulum of infinite length is [take, $g = 9.8\ \text{m/s}^2$ and radius of earth $(R_e) = 6400\ \text{km}$] **[MHT CET]**

(a) 86.4 min (b) 84.6 min
(c) infinite (d) zero

24 A hollow sphere is filled with water through the small hole in it. It is then hung by a long thread and made to oscillate. As the water slowly flow out of the hole at the bottom, the period of oscillation will **[MHT CET]**

(a) continuously decrease
(b) continuously increase
(c) first decrease, then increase
(d) first increase, then decrease

25 A heavy small-sized sphere is suspended by a string of length l. The sphere rotates uniformly in a horizontal circle with the string making an angle θ with the vertical. Then, the time period of this conical pendulum is **[Manipal]**

(a) $t = 2\pi\sqrt{\frac{l}{g}}$ (b) $t = 2\pi\sqrt{\frac{l\sin\theta}{g}}$

(c) $t = 2\pi\sqrt{\frac{l\cos\theta}{g}}$ (d) $t = 2\pi\sqrt{\frac{l}{g\cos\theta}}$

26 A spring of force constant k is cut into two pieces such that one piece is double the length of the other. The force constant of the longer piece will be **[Kerala CEE]**

(a) $1.5\ k$ (b) $3\ k$ (c) $2k$ (d) $\frac{2}{3}k$
(e) $\frac{1}{3}k$

27 A simple pendulum has a time period T_1 on the surface of earth of radius R. When taken to a height of R above the earth's surface, its time period is T_2. Then, the ratio T_2/T_1 is **[Kerala CEE]**

(a) $\frac{1}{\sqrt{2}}$ (b) $\sqrt{2}$ (c) 2 (d) 4
(e) $\frac{1}{2}$

28 The length of a simple pendulum executing simple harmonic motion is increased by 21%. The percentage increase in the time period of the pendulum of increased length is **[RPMT]**

(a) 11% (b) 21% (c) 42% (d) 10.5%

29 A mass M is suspended from a spring of negligible mass. The spring is pulled a little and then released so that the mass executes SHM of time period T. If the mass is increased by m, the time period becomes $5T/3$, then the ratio of m/M is **[RPMT]**

(a) $\frac{3}{5}$ (b) $\frac{25}{9}$ (c) $\frac{16}{9}$ (d) $\frac{5}{3}$

30 The angular amplitude of a simple pendulum is θ_0. The maximum tension in its string will be **[BCECE]**

(a) $mg\ (1-\theta_0)$ (b) $mg\ (1+\theta_0)$
(c) $mg\ (1-\theta_0^2)$ (d) $mg\ (1+\theta_0^2)$

31 Time period of a simple pendulum of length l is T_1 and time period of a uniform rod of the same length l pivoted about one end and oscillating in a vertical plane is T_2. Amplitude of oscillations in both the cases is small. Then, T_1/T_2 is **[BCECE]**

(a) $\frac{1}{\sqrt{3}}$ (b) 1 (c) $\sqrt{\frac{4}{3}}$ (d) $\sqrt{\frac{3}{2}}$

32 A girl swings on a cradle in sitting position. If she stands, the time period of cradle **[EAMCET]**

(a) decreases (b) increases
(c) remains constant
(d) first increases, then it remains constant

33 A simple pendulum is suspended from the ceiling of a lift. When the lift is at rest its time period is T. With what acceleration should the lift be accelerated upwards in order to reduce its period to $T/2$? (g is acceleration due to gravity). **[KCET]**

(a) $2\ g$ (b) $3\ g$ (c) $4\ g$ (d) g

2007

34 A bob of simple pendulum executes SHM in water with a period T. The period of oscillation of the bob in air is T_0. The relation between T and T_0 is [take, density of bob $(\rho) = \frac{400}{3}\ \text{kg/m}^3$] **[KCET]**

(a) $T_0 = T^2$ (b) $T_0 = 2T$ (c) $T = T_0$ (d) $T = 2T_0$

35 The time period of a simple pendulum in a stationary van is T. The time period of a mass attached to a spring is also T. The van accelerates at the rate $5\ \text{ms}^{-2}$. If the new time periods of the pendulum and spring be T_p and T_s respectively, then **[AFMC]**

(a) $T_p = T_s$ (b) $T_p > T_s$
(c) $T_p < T_s$ (d) Cannot be predicted

36 One body is suspended from a spring of length l, spring constant k and has time period T. Now if spring is divided in two equal parts which are joined in parallel and the same body is suspended from this arrangement, then new time period of body is **[UP CPMT]**

(a) $\frac{3T}{4}$ (b) T (c) $2T$ (d) $\frac{T}{2}$

37 A pendulum of length 1 m is released from $\theta = 60°$. The rate of change of speed of the bob at $\theta = 30°$ is (Take, $g = 10\ \text{ms}^{-2}$) **[AFMC]**

(a) $10\ \text{ms}^{-2}$ (b) $7.5\ \text{ms}^{-1}$ (c) $5\ \text{ms}^{-2}$ (d) $5\sqrt{3}\ \text{ms}^{-2}$
(e) $2.5\ \text{ms}^{-2}$

38 A simple pendulum has a time period T in vacuum. Its time period when it is completely immersed in a liquid of density one-eighth of the density of material of the bob is **[Kerala CEE]**

(a) $\sqrt{\frac{7}{8}}T$ (b) $\sqrt{\frac{5}{8}}T$ (c) $\sqrt{\frac{3}{8}}T$ (d) $\sqrt{\frac{8}{7}}T$
(e) $\sqrt{\frac{8}{5}}T$

39 A body of mass 20 g connected to spring of constant k executes simple harmonic motion with a frequency of $\left(\frac{5}{\pi}\right)$ Hz. The value of spring constant is **[Kerala CEE]**

(a) $4\ \text{Nm}^{-1}$ (b) $3\ \text{Nm}^{-1}$ (c) $2\ \text{Nm}^{-1}$ (d) $5\ \text{Nm}^{-1}$
(e) $2.5\ \text{Nm}^{-1}$

40 If k_s and k_p respectively are effective spring constants in series and parallel combination of springs as shown in figure, find $\frac{k_s}{k_p}$. **[Haryana PMT]**

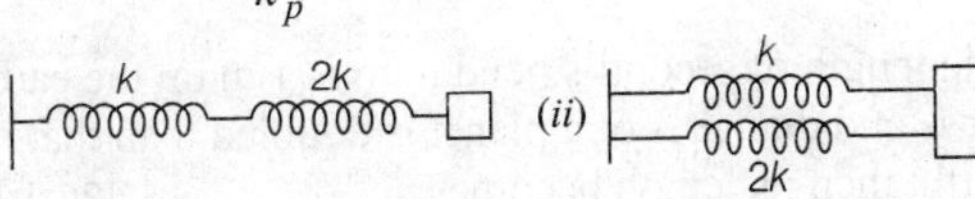

(a) $\frac{9}{2}$ (b) $\frac{3}{7}$ (c) $\frac{2}{9}$ (d) $\frac{7}{3}$

41 A uniform spring of force constant k is cut into two pieces whose lengths are in the ratio of 1 : 2. What is the force constant of second piece in terms of k? **[J&K CET]**

(a) $\frac{k}{2}$ (b) $\frac{2k}{2}$ (c) $\frac{3k}{2}$ (d) $\frac{4k}{2}$

42 To make the frequency double of a spring oscillator, we have to **[Punjab PMET]**

(a) reduce the mass to one-fourth
(b) quadruple the mass
(c) double the mass
(d) half the mass

43 What is the velocity of the bob of a simple pendulum at its mean position, if it is able to rise to vertical height of 10 cm? (Take, $g = 9.8 \text{ ms}^{-2}$) **[BCECE]**

(a) 2.2 ms^{-1} (b) 1.8 ms^{-1}
(c) 1.4 ms^{-1} (d) 0.6 ms^{-1}

2006

44 A spring balance has a scale that reads 0 to 50 kg. The length of the spring is 20 cm. A body suspended from this spring when displaced and released. Oscillates with period of 0.60 s. What is the weight of the body? **[J&K CET]**

(a) 22.40 kg (b) 22.35 kg
(c) 25.30 kg (d) 22.36 kg

45 What is the effect on the time period of a simple pendulum, if the mass of the bob is doubled? **[Kerala CEE]**

(a) Halved (b) Doubled
(c) Becomes eight times (d) Becomes zero
(e) No effect

46 Choose the correct statement. **[J&K CET]**

(a) Time period of a simple pendulum depends on amplitude.
(b) Time shown by a spring watch varies with acceleration due to gravity.
(c) In a simple pendulum time period varies linearly with the length of the pendulum.
(d) The graph between length of the pendulum and time period is a parabola.

47 Time period of a spring mass system is T. If this spring is cut into two parts whose lengths are in the ratio 1 : 3 and the same mass is attached to the longer part, the new time period will be **[J&K CET]**

(a) $\sqrt{\frac{3}{2}}T$ (b) $\frac{T}{\sqrt{3}}$
(c) $\frac{\sqrt{3}T}{2}$ (d) $\sqrt{3}T$

48 The length of second's pendulum is 1 m on the earth. If mass and diameter of a planet is doubled than that of the earth, then its length becomes **[Punjab PMET]**

(a) 1 m (b) 2 m
(c) 0.5 m (d) 4 m

49 What effect occurs on the frequency of a pendulum, if it is taken from the earth's surface to deep into a mine? **[Punjab PMET]**

(a) Increases
(b) Decreases
(c) First increases, then decreases
(d) No effect

50 A body of mass 5 kg executes SHM of amplitude of 0.5 m. If the force constant is 100 N/m, calculate its time period. **[J & K CET]**

(a) 1.41 (b) 0.46
(c) 0.40 (d) 0.37

51 A 8 kg body perform SHM amplitude 30 cm. The restoring force is 60 N, when the displacement is 30 cm. Find its time period. **[J & K CET]**

(a) 1.236 (b) 1.256 (c) 1.212 (d) 1.846

2005

52 If the length of a pendulum is made 9 times and mass of the bob is made 4 times, then the value of time period becomes **[BHU]**

(a) $3T$ (b) $\frac{3}{2T}$ (c) $4T$ (d) $2T$

53 The masses and length of two simple pendulums are given as respectively m_A, m_B and l_A, l_B. If frequency of A is double that of B, then relation between l_A and l_B is given as **[UP CPMT]**

(a) $l_A = \frac{l_B}{2}$ (b) $l_A = 2l_B$
(c) $l_A = \frac{4}{l_B}$ (d) $l_A = \frac{l_B}{4}$.

54 The simple pendulum acts as second's pendulum on earth. Its time on a planet, whose mass and diameter are twice that of the earth is **[MHT CET]**

(a) $\sqrt{2}$ s (b) $2\sqrt{2}$ s (c) 2s (d) $\frac{1}{\sqrt{2}}$ s

55 A simple pendulum of length l and mass (bob) m is suspended vertically. The string makes an angle θ with the vertical. The restoring force acting on the pendulum is **[MHT CET]**

(a) $mg \tan\theta$ (b) $-mg \sin\theta$
(c) $mg \sin\theta$ (d) $-mg \cos\theta$

56 A point mass m is suspended at the end of a massless wire of length L and cross-section area A. If Y is the Young's modulus for the wire, then the frequency of oscillations for the SHM along the vertical line is **[MHT CET]**

(a) $\frac{1}{2\pi}\sqrt{\frac{YA}{mL}}$ (b) $2\pi\sqrt{\frac{mL}{YA}}$ (c) $\frac{1}{\pi}\sqrt{\frac{YA}{mL}}$ (d) $\pi\sqrt{\frac{mL}{YA}}$

57 A simple pendulum is taken from the equator to the pole. Its period **[Kerala CEE]**

(a) decreases
(b) increases
(c) remains the same
(d) decreases and then increases
(e) becomes infinity

58 The resultant spring constant of the system of springs shown below **[Kerala CEE]**

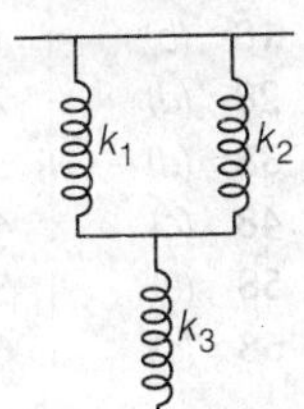

(a) $\frac{(k_1+k_2)}{k_1+k_2+k_3}$ (b) $\frac{(4k_1+2k_2)(k_3)}{k_1+k_2+k_3}$

(c) $\frac{k_1+k_2}{2(k_1+k_2+k_3)}$ (d) $\frac{k_1k_2k_3}{k_1+k_2+k_3}$

(e) $\frac{(k_1+k_2)(k_3)}{k_1+k_2+k_3}$

59 Two simple pendulums of lengths 1.44 m and 1 m start swinging together. After how many vibrations will they again start swinging together? **[J&K CET]**

(a) 5 oscillations of smaller pendulum
(b) 6 oscillations of smaller pendulum
(c) 4 oscillations of bigger pendulum
(d) 6 oscillations of bigger pendulum

60 Two pendulums begin to swing simultaneously. If the ratio of the frequency of oscillations of the two is 7 : 8, then the ratio of lengths of the two pendulums will be **[J&K CET]**

(a) 7 : 8 (b) 8 : 7
(c) 49 : 64 (d) 64 : 49

61 A spring has length l and spring constant k. If spring is divided in two equal parts, then spring constant of each part is **[Punjab PMET]**

(a) k (b) $\frac{k}{2}$ (c) $2k$ (d) $4k$

62 The amplitude of an oscillating simple pendulum is 10 cm and its time period is 4 s. Its speed after 1 s, when it passes through its equilibrium position is **[AMU]**

(a) zero (b) 2.0 ms^{-1} (c) 0.3 ms^{-1} (d) 0.4 ms^{-1}

63 A simple second pendulum is mounted in a rocket. Its time period will decrease when the rocket is **[AMU]**

(a) moving up with uniform velocity
(b) moving up with uniform acceleration
(c) moving down with uniform acceleration
(d) moving around the earth in geostationary orbit

64 Two simple pendulums whose lengths are 100 cm and 121 cm are suspended side by side. Their bobs are pulled together and then released. After how many minimum oscillations of the longer pendulum, will be the two be in phase again? **[DUMET]**

(a) 11 (b) 10 (c) 21 (d) 20

65 A heavy brass sphere is hung from a weightless inelastic spring and as a simple pendulum its time period of oscillation is T. When the sphere is immersed in a non-viscous liquid of density 1/10 that of brass, it will act as a simple pendulum of period **[JCECE]**

(a) T (b) $\frac{10}{9}T$

(c) $\sqrt{\left(\frac{9}{10}\right)}T$ (d) $\sqrt{\left(\frac{10}{9}\right)}T$

66 The period of oscillation of a simple pendulum of constant length at surface of the earth is T. Its time period inside a mine will be **[KCET]**

(a) cannot be compared
(b) equal to T
(c) less than T
(d) more than T

67 The period of oscillation of a simple pendulum of length l suspended from the roof of a vehicle, which moves without friction down an inclined plane of inclination α, is given by **[WB JEE]**

(a) $2\pi\sqrt{\frac{l}{g\cos\alpha}}$ (b) $2\pi\sqrt{\frac{l}{g\sin\alpha}}$

(c) $2\pi\sqrt{\frac{l}{g}}$ (d) $2\pi\sqrt{\frac{l}{g\tan\alpha}}$

68 A simple harmonic oscillator consists of a particle of mass m and an ideal spring with spring constant k. The particle oscillates with a time period T. The spring is cut into two equal parts. If one part oscillates with the same particle, the time period will be **[AIIMS]**

(a) $2T$ (b) $\sqrt{2}T$

(c) $\frac{T}{\sqrt{2}}$ (d) $\frac{T}{2}$

69 One-fourth length of a spring of force constant k is cut away. The force constant of the remaining spring will be **[AFMC]**

(a) $\frac{3}{4}k$ (b) $\frac{4}{3}k$

(c) k (d) $4k$

70 A body of mass 500 g is attached to a horizontal spring of spring constant $8\pi^2$ Nm^{-1}. If the body is pulled to a distance of 10 cm from its mean position, then its frequency of oscillation is **[Kerala CEE]**

(a) 2 Hz (b) 4 Hz
(c) 8 Hz (d) 0.5 Hz
(e) 4π Hz

Answers

1 (b)	2 (b)	3 (b)	4 (c)	5 (b)	6 (a)	7 (b)	8 (c)	9 (b)	10 (a)
11 (d)	12 (c)	13 (c)	14 (a)	15 (b)	16 (d)	17 (d)	18 (b)	19 (a)	20 (a)
21 (b)	22 (b)	23 (b)	24 (d)	25 (c)	26 (a)	27 (c)	28 (d)	29 (c)	30 (d)
31 (d)	32 (a)	33 (b)	34 (d)	35 (c)	36 (d)	37 (c)	38 (d)	39 (c)	40 (c)
41 (a)	42 (a)	43 (c)	44 (d)	45 (e)	46 (d)	47 (b)	48 (c)	49 (b)	50 (a)
51 (b)	52 (a)	53 (d)	54 (b)	55 (b)	56 (a)	57 (a)	58 (e)	59 (a)	60 (d)
61 (c)	62 (a)	63 (b)	64 (b)	65 (d)	66 (d)	67 (a)	68 (c)	69 (b)	70 (a)

Explanations

1 (b) The acceleration of particle/body executing SHM at any instant (at position x) is given as

$$a = -\omega^2 x$$

where, ω is the angular frequency of the body.

$$\Rightarrow \quad |a| = \omega^2 x \quad \ldots\text{(i)}$$

Here, $x = 5\text{m}, |a| = 20\,\text{ms}^{-2}$

Substituting the given values in Eq. (i), we get

$$20 = \omega^2 \times 5$$

$$\Rightarrow \quad \omega^2 = \frac{20}{5} = 4$$

or $\quad \omega = 2\text{ rad s}^{-1}$

As, we know that

time period, $T = 2\pi/\omega \quad \ldots\text{(ii)}$

$\therefore$ Substituting the value of ω in Eq. (ii), we get

$$T = \frac{2\pi}{2} = \pi\text{ s}$$

2 (b) Frequency, $n = \frac{1}{2\pi}\sqrt{\frac{g}{l}}$

$$\Rightarrow \quad n \propto \frac{1}{\sqrt{l}}$$

$$\Rightarrow \quad \frac{n_1}{n_2} = \sqrt{\frac{l_2}{l_1}} = \sqrt{\frac{L_2}{2L_2}}$$

$$\Rightarrow \quad \frac{n_1}{n_2} = \frac{1}{\sqrt{2}}$$

$$\Rightarrow \quad n_2 = \sqrt{2}\,n_1$$

$$\Rightarrow \quad n_2 > n_1$$

Energy, $E = \frac{1}{2}m\omega^2 A^2 = 2\pi^2 m n^2 A^2$

and $\quad A^2 \propto \frac{1}{mn^2} \quad (\because E \text{ is same})$

$$\therefore \quad \frac{A_1^2}{A_2^2} = \frac{m_2 n_2^2}{m_1 n_1^2}$$

Given, $n_2 > n_1$ and $m_1 = m_2$

$$\Rightarrow \quad A_1 > A_2.$$

So, amplitude of bob B is smaller than bob A.

3 (b) Gravity, $g = \frac{GM}{R^2}$ (G is constant)

$$\therefore \quad \frac{g_{\text{earth}}}{g_{\text{planet}}} = \frac{M_e}{M_p} \times \frac{R_p^2}{R_e^2}$$

$$\Rightarrow \quad \frac{g_e}{g_p} = \frac{2}{1}$$

Also, $\quad T \propto \frac{1}{\sqrt{g}} \Rightarrow \frac{T_e}{T_p} = \sqrt{\frac{g_p}{g_e}}$

$$\Rightarrow \quad \frac{2}{T_p} = \sqrt{\frac{1}{2}} \Rightarrow T_p = 2\sqrt{2}\text{ s}$$

4 (c) Time period of simple pendulum of length l is

$$T = 2\pi\sqrt{l/g}$$

$$\Rightarrow \quad T \propto \sqrt{l}$$

Hence, time period of simple pendulum is inversely proportional to square root to length of pendulum.

$$\therefore \quad \frac{\Delta T}{T} = \frac{1}{2}\frac{\Delta l}{l} \quad [\because g = \text{constant}]$$

$$\frac{\Delta T}{T} = \frac{1}{2} \times 3 = 1.5\%$$

5 (b) Acceleration due to gravity,

$$g = \frac{GM}{R^2} = \frac{G \times \frac{4}{3}\pi R^3 \rho}{R^2} = \frac{4}{3}\pi G \rho R$$

$$\Rightarrow \quad g \propto R$$

For pendulum clock, g will increase on the planet so time period will decrease. But for spring clock, it will not change. Hence, P will run faster than S.

6 (a) The effective acceleration in a lift descending with acceleration $\frac{g}{3}$ is

$$g_{\text{eff}} = g - \frac{g}{3} = \frac{2g}{3}$$

Time period of simple pendulum,

$$\therefore \quad T = 2\pi\sqrt{\frac{L}{g_{\text{eff}}}} = 2\pi\sqrt{\frac{L}{2g/3}}$$

$$\Rightarrow \quad T = 2\pi\sqrt{\frac{3L}{2g}}$$

7 (b) The effective acceleration of a bob in water, $g' = g\left[1 - \frac{\sigma}{\rho}\right]$, where, σ and ρ are the densities of water and the bob, respectively. Since, the periods of oscillation of the bob in air and water are given as

$$T = 2\pi\sqrt{\frac{l}{g}} \text{ and } T' = 2\pi\sqrt{\frac{l}{g'}}$$

$$\therefore \quad \frac{T}{T'} = \sqrt{\frac{g'}{g}} = \sqrt{\frac{g\left(1 - \frac{\sigma}{\rho}\right)}{g}}$$

$$\frac{T}{T'} = \sqrt{1 - \frac{\sigma}{\rho}} = \sqrt{1 - \frac{1}{\rho}} \quad [\because \sigma = 1]$$

Putting $\frac{T}{T'} = \frac{1}{\sqrt{2}}$

We obtain, $\frac{1}{2} = 1 - \frac{1}{\rho} \Rightarrow \rho = 2$

8. (c) When the elevator is at rest, its time period is given by

$$T = 2\pi\sqrt{\frac{l}{g}} = 2\pi\sqrt{\frac{l}{10}}$$

When the elevator accelerates upwards, its time period becomes

$$T' = 2\pi\sqrt{\frac{l}{g + a}} = 2\pi\sqrt{\frac{l}{10 + 10}}$$

$$[\because T - mg = ma \Rightarrow T = m(g + a)]$$

$$= 2\pi\sqrt{\frac{l}{20}} = 2\pi\sqrt{\frac{l}{10}} \times \frac{1}{\sqrt{2}} = \frac{T}{\sqrt{2}}$$

9 (b) Velocity of bob, $v = \sqrt{2gl(1 - \cos\theta)}$

[using $v^2 = u^2 + 2gh$]

$$v = \sqrt{2 \times 9.8 \times 2 \times (1 - \cos 60°)}$$

$$v = \sqrt{2 \times 9.8}\text{ ms}^{-1}$$

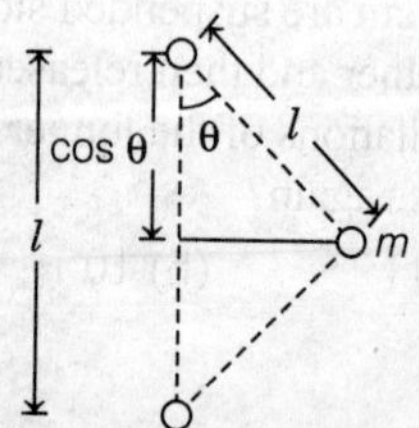

10 (a) Let the two pendulums are in same phase, after n vibrations of the longer pendulum. In this time, the shorter pendulum will complete $(n+1)$ vibrations.

$$\therefore\ n \times 2\pi\sqrt{\frac{l_2}{g}} = (n+1)2\pi\sqrt{\frac{l_1}{g}}$$

$$n \times 2\pi\sqrt{\frac{121}{g}} = (n+1)2\pi\sqrt{\frac{100}{g}}$$

$$11n = 10(n+1) \Rightarrow n = 10$$

11 (d) For the given figure,

$$f = \frac{1}{2\pi}\sqrt{\frac{k_{eq}}{m}} \quad \text{...(i)}$$

$$f = \frac{1}{2\pi}\sqrt{\frac{2k}{m}}$$

If one spring is removed, then $k_{eq} = k$

and $$f' = \frac{1}{2\pi}\sqrt{\frac{k}{m}} \quad \text{...(ii)}$$

From Eqs. (i) and (ii), we get

$$\frac{f}{f'} = \sqrt{2} \Rightarrow f' = \frac{1}{\sqrt{2}}f$$

12 (c) The time period of the iron ball would be given by,

$$P = 2\pi\sqrt{\frac{M}{K}}$$

So, if mass of the ball is increased to 4 times of its initial mass, then the new period becomes

$$P' = 2\pi\sqrt{\frac{4M}{K}} = 2P$$

13 (c) As equivalent spring constant when joined in series,

$$k_s = \frac{k \times k}{k+k} = \frac{k}{2}$$

Now, the springs are in parallel this equivalent.

Spring constant, $k_p = \frac{k}{2} + \frac{k}{2} = k$

Thus, overall k does not change and time period will remain same as

$$T = 2\pi\sqrt{m/k}$$

14 (a) The angular frequency after removing the mass m_1 of m_2 is given by

$$\omega = \sqrt{\frac{k}{m_2}} \text{ (as system is undisturbed)}$$

15 (b) As amplitude

$= 50\text{ mm} = 50 \times 10^{-3}\text{ m}$

Time period, $T = \frac{2\pi}{\omega}$

$$\Rightarrow \omega = \frac{2\pi}{T} = \frac{2\pi}{2} = \pi\text{ rad/s}$$

Now, maximum velocity $= \omega A$

$$= \pi \times 50 \times 10^{-3}$$

$$= (3.14) \times 50 \times 10^{-3} \simeq 0.15\text{ ms}^{-1}$$

16 (d) As time period, $T = 2\pi\sqrt{l/g}$

$$\Rightarrow \frac{\Delta T}{T} = \frac{1}{2}\left(\Delta\frac{l}{l}\right) = \frac{1}{2} \times 2 = 1\%$$

$\therefore$ Loses in seconds in a day

$$= \frac{24 \times 3600}{100}$$

$$= 36 \times 24 = 864\text{ s}$$

17 (d) The maximum time period of any pendulum on the earth is 1.5 min.

18 (b) As time period, $T = 6$ s

Time to come from D to C or C to D

$$= \frac{T}{4} - \frac{T}{12} = \frac{T}{6} = \frac{6}{6} = 1\text{ s}$$

19 (a) Time period of simple pendulum,

$$T = 2\pi\sqrt{\frac{l}{g}}, \quad \frac{\Delta T}{T} = \frac{1}{2}\frac{\Delta l}{l}$$

But at temperature $\theta°$C, increase in length of pendulum,

$$\frac{\Delta l}{l} = \alpha\Delta\theta$$

$$\therefore \frac{\Delta T}{T} = \frac{1}{2}\alpha\Delta\theta$$

$$\Rightarrow \frac{\Delta T}{T} = \frac{1}{2} \times 9 \times 10^{-7} \times (30 - 20)$$

$$= \frac{1}{2} \times 9 \times 10^{-7} \times 10$$

$$= 4.5 \times 10^{-6}$$

or $$\Delta T = 4.5 \times 10^{-6} \times 0.5$$

$$= 2.25 \times 10^{-6}\text{ s}$$

20 (a) Time period of a simple pendulum,

$$T = 2\pi\sqrt{\frac{l}{g}}$$

It is independent of the mass of the bob. Therefore, time period of the pendulum will remain T.

21 (b) Time period of second pendulum

$$T = 2\text{s}$$

$$2\pi\sqrt{\frac{l}{g}} = 2 \text{ [where, } l = \text{length of second pendulum]}$$

$$\pi^2\frac{l}{g} = 1$$

$$\Rightarrow l = \frac{g}{\pi^2} = \frac{9.8}{\pi^2} \quad [g = 9.8\text{ m/s}^2]$$

$$= 0.9929\text{ m} = 99.29\text{ cm} \simeq 99\text{ cm}$$

22 (b) When train accelerates, the effective value of g increases (i.e. resultant of g and a)

Also, the time period, $T \propto \frac{1}{\sqrt{g_{\text{effective}}}}$

So, time period will decreases, while $g_{\text{effective}}$ increases.

23 (b) Radius of earth, $R_e = 6400$ km

$= 6.4 \times 10^6$ m, $g = 9.8\text{ m/s}^2$

Time period of simple pendulum of infinte length,

$$T = 2\pi\sqrt{\frac{R_e}{g}} = 2 \times 3.14\sqrt{\frac{6.4 \times 10^6}{9.8}}$$

$$= 5076\text{ s} = 84.6\text{ min}$$

24 (d) The time period of the pendulum,

$$T = 2\pi\sqrt{l/g} \Rightarrow T \propto \sqrt{l}$$

Initially, the centre of mass CM of the sphere is at the centre of the sphere. As the water slowly flows out of the hole at the bottom, the CM of the liquid (hollow sphere) first goes on downward and then upward. Hence, the effective length of the pendulum first increases and then decreases.

25 (c) Radius of circular path in the horizontal plane

$$\Delta DAB, r = l\sin\theta$$

Resolving T along the vertical and horizontal directions, we get

$$T\cos\theta = Mg \quad \text{...(i)}$$

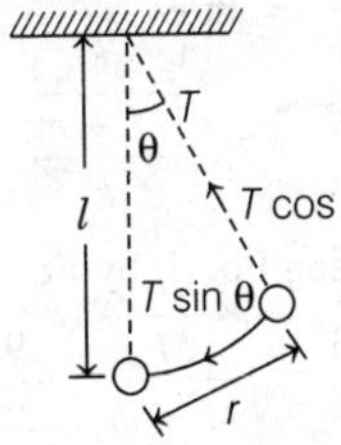

$$T\sin\theta = Mr\omega^2 = M(l\sin\theta)\omega^2$$

$$\Rightarrow \quad T = Ml\omega^2 \quad \text{...(ii)}$$

On dividing Eq. (ii) by Eq. (i), we get

$$\frac{1}{\cos\theta} = \frac{l\omega^2}{g} \Rightarrow \omega^2 = \frac{g}{l\cos\theta}$$

$$\therefore \text{ Time period, } t = \frac{2\pi}{\omega} = 2\pi\sqrt{\frac{l\cos\theta}{g}}$$

26 (a) As, $l_1 + l_2 = l$

$$\Rightarrow l_1 + 2l_1 = l \text{ or } l_1 = \frac{l}{3}$$

Also, $$l_2 = l - l_1 = l - \frac{l}{3} = \frac{2l}{3}$$

Again, $k \propto \frac{1}{l}$

$$\Rightarrow \quad \frac{k_2}{k} = \frac{l}{l_2} = \frac{l}{2l/3} = \frac{3}{2}$$

$$\Rightarrow \quad k_2 = \frac{3}{2}k = 1.5k$$

27 *(c)* As, time period, $T \propto \sqrt{l/g}$

$$\Rightarrow \quad \frac{T_1}{T_2} = \sqrt{\frac{g_2}{g_1}} \quad \ldots\text{(i)}$$

If $g_1 = g$, then

$$g_2 = \frac{g}{\left(1+\frac{h}{R}\right)^2} = \frac{g}{\left(1+\frac{R}{R}\right)^2} \quad (\text{as } h = R)$$

$$\therefore \quad g_2 = \frac{g}{4}$$

On putting these values in Eq. (i), we obtain

$$\frac{T_1}{T_2} = \sqrt{\frac{g/4}{g}} = \sqrt{\frac{1}{4}} = \frac{1}{2}$$

$$\Rightarrow \quad \frac{T_2}{T_1} = 2$$

28 *(d)* As, $T = 2\pi\sqrt{\frac{l}{g}} \Rightarrow \frac{\Delta T}{T} = \frac{1}{2}\frac{\Delta l}{l}$

Given, $\frac{\Delta l}{l} = 21\%$

$$\Rightarrow \quad \frac{\Delta T}{T} = \frac{1}{2} \times 21\% = 10.5\%$$

29 *(c)* Time period, $T = 2\pi\sqrt{\frac{M}{k}} \quad \ldots\text{(i)}$

and $T' = 2\pi\sqrt{\frac{M+m}{k}}$

$$\Rightarrow \quad \frac{5T}{3} = 2\pi\sqrt{\frac{M+m}{k}} \quad \ldots\text{(ii)}$$

On dividing Eq. (i) by Eq. (ii), we have

$$\frac{3}{5} = \sqrt{\frac{M}{M+m}}, \quad \frac{9}{25} = \frac{M}{M+m}$$

$$\Rightarrow \quad 9M + 9m = 25M \Rightarrow 16M = 9m$$

$$\frac{m}{M} = \frac{16}{9}$$

30 *(d)* The simple pendulum at angular amplitude θ_0 is shown in figure

In ΔOCB, $\cos\theta = \frac{l-h}{l}$

Maximum tension in the string is

$$T_{max} = mg + \frac{mv^2}{l} \quad \ldots\text{(i)}$$

When bob of the pendulum comes from A to B, it covers a vertical distance h

$$\therefore \quad \cos\theta_0 = \frac{l-h}{l}$$

$$\Rightarrow \quad h = l(1-\cos\theta_0) \quad \ldots\text{(ii)}$$

Also, during B to A, potential energy of bob converts into kinetic energy,

i.e. $$mgh = \frac{1}{2}mv^2$$

$$\therefore \quad v = \sqrt{2gh} \quad \ldots\text{(iii)}$$

Thus, using Eqs. (i), (ii) and (iii), we obtain

$$T_{max} = mg + \frac{2mg}{l}l(1-\cos\theta_0)$$

$$= mg + 2mg\left[1 + \frac{\theta_0^2}{2}\right]$$

$$= mg\,(1 + \theta_0^2)$$

31 *(d)* Time period of simple pendulum is given by $T_1 = 2\pi\sqrt{\frac{l}{g}}$

and time period of a uniform rod in given position is given by

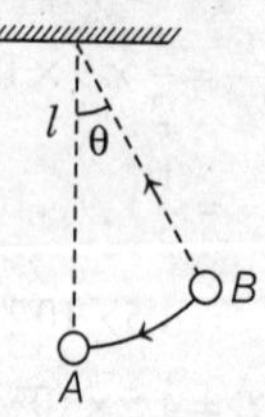

$$T_2 = 2\pi\sqrt{\frac{\text{Inertia factor}}{\text{Spring factor}}}$$

Here, inertia factor = moment of inertia of rod at one end

$$\frac{ml^2}{12} + \frac{ml^2}{4} = \frac{ml^2}{3}$$

Spring factor = Restoring torque per unit angular displacement

$$= mg \times \frac{l}{2}\frac{\sin\theta}{\theta}$$

$$= mg\frac{l}{2} \quad \left[\begin{array}{l}\text{if } \theta \text{ is small,}\\ \sin\theta \simeq \theta\end{array}\right]$$

$$\therefore \quad T_2 = 2\pi\sqrt{\frac{ml^2/3}{mgl/2}} = 2\pi\sqrt{\frac{2}{3}\frac{l}{g}}$$

Hence, $$\frac{T_1}{T_2} = \sqrt{\frac{3}{2}}$$

32 *(a)* Time period, $T = 2\pi\sqrt{\frac{l}{g}}$

where, l is the length of simple pendulum.

On standing the effective length of the pendulum measured from the point of suspension decreases. Hence, the time period of cradle decreases.

33 *(b)* Time period of simple pendulum is given by

$$T = 2\pi\sqrt{\frac{l}{g}} \quad \ldots\text{(i)}$$

When the lift is moving up with an acceleration a, then time period becomes

$$T' = 2\pi\sqrt{\frac{l}{g+a}}$$

Here, $$T' = \frac{T}{2}$$

$$\Rightarrow \quad \frac{T}{2} = 2\pi\sqrt{\frac{l}{g+a}} \quad \ldots\text{(ii)}$$

On dividing Eq. (ii) by Eq. (i), we get

$$a = 3g$$

34 *(d)* Given, $\rho_{bob} = \frac{400}{3}$ kg/m^3

and $\rho_{water} = 1000$ kg/m^3

If g' be the gravitational acceleration in water, then

$$g' = \left(1 - \frac{\rho_{water}}{\rho_{bob}}\right)g = \left(1 - \frac{1000 \times 3}{4000}\right)g = \frac{g}{4}$$

$$\therefore \quad T = 2\pi\sqrt{\frac{L}{g'}}$$

$$= 2\pi\sqrt{\frac{4L}{g}} \quad \left[g' = \frac{g}{4}\right]$$

$$= 2 \times 2\pi\sqrt{\frac{L}{g}} = 2T_0$$

35 *(c)* Time period of simple pendulum placed in a van accelerating at the rate of a ms^{-2} is given by

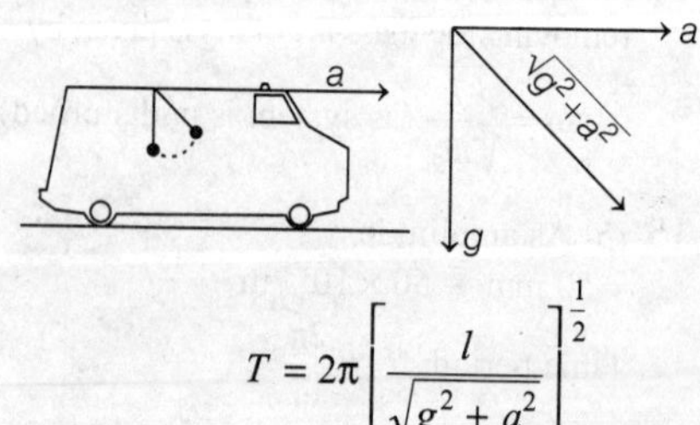

$$T = 2\pi\left[\frac{l}{\sqrt{g^2 + a^2}}\right]^{\frac{1}{2}}$$

However, the time period of mass attached to the spring is

$$T = 2\pi\sqrt{\left(\frac{m}{k}\right)}$$

It is independent of g as well as a. Hencc, when the van accelerates, the time period of the simple pendulum decreases and that of spring remains unchanged.

Hence, $\quad T_p < T \quad$ and $\quad T_s = T$

i.e. $\quad T_p < T_s$

36 *(d)* When spring of spring constant k is divided in two equal parts, then spring constant of each part becomes $2k$.

$\therefore$ Spring constant in parallel combination, $k' = 2k + 2k = 4k$

$$\therefore T' = 2\pi\sqrt{\frac{m}{k'}} = 2\pi\sqrt{\frac{m}{4k}} = \frac{1}{2}.2\pi\sqrt{\frac{m}{k}}$$

$$= \frac{1}{2}.T = \frac{T}{2}$$

37 *(c)* For a simple pendulum, time period,

$$T = 2\pi\sqrt{\frac{l}{g}} \Rightarrow \frac{2\pi}{T} = \sqrt{\frac{g}{l}}$$

$$\therefore \quad \omega = \sqrt{\frac{g}{l}}, \quad \omega^2 = \frac{g}{l} \quad \text{...(i)}$$

Amplitude when angular displacement is 60°

$$= \frac{2\pi l}{360°} \times 60° = \frac{2\pi l}{6}$$

Therefore, displacement when angular displacement is 30°

$$= \frac{1}{2}\left(\frac{2\pi l}{6}\right), \quad y = \frac{\pi l}{6} \quad \text{...(ii)}$$

Acceleration, $a = -\omega^2 y$

Using Eqs. (i) and (ii), we get

$$a = -\frac{g}{l} \times \frac{\pi l}{6} = -\frac{10 \times 3.14}{6}$$

$$= -5.2 \text{ ms}^{-2} \simeq 5 \text{ ms}^{-2}$$

38 *(d)* Let l be the length of simple pendulum, V be the volume and ρ be the density of the material of bob.

$\therefore$ Density of the liquid $= \frac{\rho}{8}$

Time period of simple pendulum in vacuum, $T = 2\pi\sqrt{\frac{l}{g}}$

When the simple pendulum is completely immersed in a liquid, then forces acting on bob are

(i) $V\rho g$, in downward direction

(ii) $V\frac{\rho}{8}g$, in upward direction

Therefore, the resultant force acting on bob in downward direction

$$= V\rho g - V\frac{\rho}{8}g = \frac{7V\rho g}{8}$$

Therefore, effective value of g in liquid is $\frac{7}{8}g$.

$$\therefore \text{ Time period, } T' = 2\pi\sqrt{\frac{l}{(7g/8)}} = \sqrt{\frac{8}{7}}\,T$$

39 *(c)* Mass, $m = 20 \text{ g} = 0.02 \text{ kg}$

Frequency, $f = \frac{5}{\pi}$ Hz

Time period of a loaded spring, $T = 2\pi\sqrt{m/k}$

Frequency, $f = \frac{1}{2\pi}\sqrt{\frac{k}{m}}$

$$\frac{5}{\pi} = \frac{1}{2\pi}\sqrt{\frac{k}{0.02}} \text{ or } 10 = \sqrt{\frac{k}{0.02}}$$

$$\text{or} \quad 100 = \frac{k}{0.02} \Rightarrow k = 2 \text{ Nm}^{-1}$$

40 *(c)* In the arrangement shown in Fig. (i), the two springs are in series. The effective spring constant k_s of this arrangement is

$$\frac{1}{k_s} = \frac{1}{k} + \frac{1}{2k} \text{ or } \frac{1}{k_s} = \frac{2+1}{2k} = \frac{3}{2k}$$

$$\Rightarrow \quad k_s = \frac{2k}{3}$$

In the arrangement shown in Fig. (ii), the two springs are in parallel. The effective spring constant k_p of this arrangement is

$$k_p = k_1 + k_2$$

$$\Rightarrow \quad = k + 2k = 3k$$

$$\therefore \quad \frac{k_s}{k_p} = \frac{2k/3}{3k} = \frac{2}{9}$$

41 *(a)* Let the force constant of 2nd piece be k_2

As, $\quad k \propto \frac{1}{l}$

$$\Rightarrow \quad \frac{k_1}{k_2} = \frac{l_2}{l_1} \Rightarrow \frac{k}{k_2} = \frac{2l/3}{l/3}$$

$$\Rightarrow \quad k_2 = \frac{k}{2} \quad (\because k_1 = k)$$

42 *(a)* The frequency of spring oscillator is

$$\nu = \frac{1}{2\pi}\sqrt{\left(\frac{k}{m}\right)}$$

$$\Rightarrow \quad \nu \propto \sqrt{\left(\frac{1}{m}\right)}$$

Hence, $\quad \frac{\nu_1}{\nu_2} = \sqrt{\left(\frac{m_2}{m_1}\right)}$

$$\text{or} \quad \frac{m_2}{m_1} = \left(\frac{\nu_1}{\nu_2}\right)^2 = \left(\frac{\nu}{2\nu}\right)^2 = \frac{1}{4}$$

$$\Rightarrow \quad m_2 = \frac{m_1}{4}$$

43 *(c)* The bob possess kinetic energy at its mean position which gets converted to potential energy at height h. But the total energy remains conserved in accordance with principle of conservation of total mechanical energy.

KE = PE

Let velocity of bob at mean position is v and m be its mass, then

$$\frac{1}{2}mv^2 = mgh$$

$$\Rightarrow \quad v = \sqrt{2gh}$$

Putting $g = 9.8 \text{ ms}^{-2}$, $h = 0.1$ m

$$\therefore \quad v = \sqrt{2 \times 9.8 \times 0.1} = 1.4 \text{ ms}^{-1}$$

44 *(d)* $m = 50$ kg, $y = 20$ cm,

$T = 0.6$ (second)

$$F = mg = 50 \times 98 \text{ N}$$

$$K = \frac{F}{y} = 2450 \text{ N/m}$$

$$T = 2\pi\sqrt{\frac{m}{k}} \text{ or } 0.6 = 2\pi\sqrt{\frac{m}{2450}}$$

$$m = 22.36 \text{ kg}$$

$\therefore$ weight of the body $= mg$

$$= 22.36 \times 9.8$$

$$= 219.1 \text{ N} = 22.36 \text{ kg}$$

45 *(e)* The time period of a simple pendulum is $T = 2\pi\sqrt{\frac{l}{g}}$

where, l is length of suspension of pendulum, g is acceleration due to gravity. From the above expression, it is clear that time period of a simple pendulum is not dependent on the mass of bob, hence no effect.

46 *(d)* The relation between time period (T) and length of pendulum (l) is

$$T = 2\pi\sqrt{l/g}$$

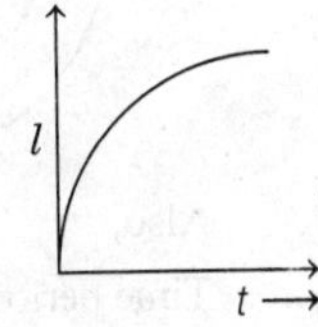

On squaring and rearranging the terms, we get

$$T^2 = 4\pi^2 \frac{l}{g}$$

which is general equation ($y^2 = 4ax$) of a parabola.

47 (b) The spring mass system oscillates in SHM, its time period is given by

$$T = 2\pi\sqrt{m/k}$$

When spring is cut into ratio 1 : 3, the new time constant is $k' = 3k$

$$\therefore \quad \frac{T}{T'} = \sqrt{\frac{3k}{k}}$$

$$\Rightarrow \quad T' = \frac{T}{\sqrt{3}}$$

48 (c) The motion of the bob is simple harmonic, hence its time period is given by

$$T = 2\pi\sqrt{\frac{\text{displacement}}{\text{acceleration}}} = 2\pi\sqrt{\frac{l}{g}}$$

Also, if the periodic time of a pendulum is 2 s, then it is called a second's pendulum.

Also, $g = GM/R^2$

where, M is mass and R is radius.

$$\therefore \quad T = 2\pi\sqrt{\frac{R^2 l}{GM}} = 2 \quad \text{...(i)}$$

Second's pendulum on other planet is

$$2 = 2\pi\sqrt{\frac{4R^2 l'}{G(2M)}} \quad \text{...(ii)}$$

From Eqs. (i) and (ii), we have

$$\frac{R^2 l}{GM} = \frac{4R^2 l'}{G(2M)}$$

$$\Rightarrow \quad l' = 0.5 \text{ m} \quad [\because l = 1 \text{ m}]$$

49 (b) On going below depth h from the surface of the earth. The value of g' below is given by $g' = g\left(1 - \frac{h}{R_e}\right)$, hence, g decreases.

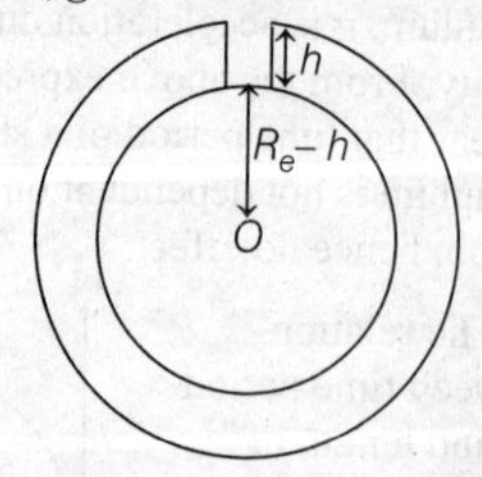

Also,

Time period, $T = \dfrac{1}{\text{Frequency } (n)}$

and $T = 2\pi\sqrt{\dfrac{l}{g}}$

where, l is length of pendulum.

$$\therefore \quad \frac{1}{n} = 2\pi\sqrt{\frac{l}{g\left(1 - \frac{h}{R_e}\right)}}$$

Since, $n \propto g$, and g decreases therefore frequency also decreases.

50 (a) Given $m = 5$ kg, $k = 100$ N/m and $A = 0.5$ m.

$$T = 2\pi\sqrt{\frac{m}{k}}$$

$$T = 2\pi\sqrt{\frac{5}{100}}$$

$$\Rightarrow \quad T = 1.41 \text{ s}$$

51 (b) Given, $m = 8$ kg, $a = 30$ cm

$F = 60$ N and $y = 0.30$ m

$$F = -Ky$$

$$K = \frac{-F}{y} = \frac{-60}{0.30} = -200 \text{ N/m}$$

$$\omega = \sqrt{\frac{K}{m}} = \sqrt{\frac{200}{8}} = 5\text{s}^{-1}$$

$$T = \frac{2\pi}{\omega} = \frac{2 \times 22}{7 \times 5} = \frac{44}{35} = 1.256$$

52 (a) The periodic time of a simple pendulum is given by

$$T = 2\pi\sqrt{\frac{l}{g}}$$

where, l is length of pendulum, g is acceleration due to gravity.

Given, $T_1 = T, l_1 = l, l_2 = 9l$

$$\therefore \quad \frac{T_1}{T_2} = \sqrt{\frac{l_1}{l_2}} = \sqrt{\frac{1}{9}} = \frac{1}{3}$$

$$\Rightarrow \quad T_2 = 3T_1 = 3T$$

53 (d) The frequency is given as

$$n = \frac{1}{2\pi}\sqrt{\frac{g}{l}} \Rightarrow n \propto \frac{1}{\sqrt{l}}$$

$$\text{So,} \quad \frac{n_A}{n_B} = \sqrt{\frac{l_B}{l_A}}$$

$$\Rightarrow \quad \frac{2n}{n} = \sqrt{\frac{l_B}{l_A}}$$

$$\Rightarrow \quad l_A = \frac{l_B}{4}$$

54 (b) Second's pendulum is that simple pendulum whose time period of vibration is two second. The bob of such pendulum while oscillating passes through the mean position after every one second.

Now, time period of simple pendulum is given by

$$T = 2\pi\sqrt{\left(\frac{l}{g}\right)} \Rightarrow T \propto \frac{1}{\sqrt{g}} \quad \text{...(i)}$$

but $g = \dfrac{GM}{R^2}$ (on the earth)

but $g' = \dfrac{G(2M)}{4R^2}$ (on the planet)

$$= \frac{1}{2}\frac{GM}{R^2} = \frac{g}{2}$$

Eq. (i) gives

$$\frac{T'}{T} = \frac{\sqrt{g}}{\sqrt{g'}} = \sqrt{2}$$

or $T' = \sqrt{2}T$

$= 2\sqrt{2}$ s (given, $T = 2$ s)

55 (b) When the bob is displaced to position P through a small angle θ from the vertical, then various forces acting on the bob at P are

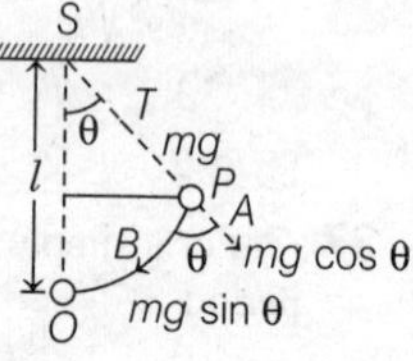

(i) the weight mg of the bob acting vertically downwards.

(ii) the tension T in the string acting along PS. Resolving mg into two rectangular components, we get

(a) $mg\cos\theta$ acts along PA, opposite to tension T

(b) $mg\sin\theta$ acts along PB, tangent to the arc OP and directed towards O.

If the string neither slackens nor breaks but remains taut, then

$$T = mg\cos\theta$$

The force $mg\sin\theta$ tends to bring the bob back to its mean position O.

$\therefore$ Restoring force acting on the bob is

$$F = -mg\sin\theta$$

56 (a) In this case, stress $= \dfrac{mg}{A}$ and strain $= \dfrac{l}{L}$ (where, l is extension)

Now, Young's modulus Y is given by

$$Y = \frac{\text{Stress}}{\text{Strain}} = \frac{mg/A}{l/L}$$

$$mg = \frac{YAl}{L} \quad (\because mg = kl)$$

$$\text{So,} \quad kl = \frac{YAl}{L} \Rightarrow k = \frac{YA}{L}$$

Now, frequency is given by

$$n = \frac{1}{2\pi}\sqrt{\frac{k}{m}} = \frac{1}{2\pi}\sqrt{\left(\frac{YA}{mL}\right)}$$

57 (a) Time period of pendulum is given by

$$T = 2\pi\sqrt{\frac{l}{g}} \text{ or } T \propto \frac{1}{\sqrt{g}}$$

If simple pendulum is taken from the equator to the pole, acceleration due to gravity increases. Hence, time period of pendulum decreases

$[\because g_{pole} > g_{equator}]$

58 (e) The first two springs are in parallel, so their equivalent spring constant

$$k' = k_1 + k_2$$

Now, this combination is in series with the third spring, so their equivalent spring constant

$$k = \frac{k' \times k_3}{k' + k_3} = \frac{(k_1 + k_2)(k_3)}{k_1 + k_2 + k_3}$$

59 (a) Given, $l_1 = 1.44$ m, $l_2 = 1$ m

Now, the ratio of time periods of two pendulums, $\frac{T_1}{T_2} = \frac{\sqrt{1.44}}{\sqrt{1}} = 1.2$

Now, the ratio is positive integer. So, 1.2 would be the integers after multiplied (atleast) by 5.
Thus, required answer will be 5 oscillations.

60 (d) The frequency of oscillation of pendulum of length l is given by

$$n = \frac{1}{2\pi}\sqrt{\frac{g}{l}}$$

Given, $n_1 : n_2 = 7 : 8$, then

$$\frac{n_1}{n_2} = \sqrt{\frac{l_2}{l_1}} \Rightarrow \frac{7}{8} = \sqrt{\frac{l_2}{l_1}}$$

On squaring, we get $\frac{l_1}{l_2} = \frac{64}{49}$

61 (c) Spring constant, $k = F/l$

If spring is divided into two equal parts, then length l will become half.

So, the spring constant will become double, i.e. will become $2k$.

62 (a) Given, $A = 10\text{ cm} = 0.1\text{ m}, T = 4$ s, $t = 1$ s.

Speed of oscillating simple pendulum is given by

$$v = \frac{dy}{dt} = v = A\omega\cos\omega t$$

(as $y = A\sin\omega t$)

$$= A \times \frac{2\pi}{T}\cos\left(\frac{2\pi}{T}t\right)$$

$$= \frac{2\pi \times 0.1}{4}\cos\left(\frac{2\pi \times 1}{4}\right)$$

$$= \frac{2\pi \times 0.1}{4}\cos\frac{\pi}{2} = 0$$

63 (b) The time period of simple pendulum is

$$T = 2\pi\sqrt{\frac{l}{g}} \Rightarrow T \propto \frac{1}{\sqrt{g}}$$

T will decrease, when g increases and g will increase when rocket moves up with a uniform acceleration.

64 (b) The time period of a simple pendulum is $T = 2\pi\sqrt{l/g}$

$$\therefore \frac{T_1}{T_2} = \sqrt{\frac{l_1}{l_2}}$$

(where, l is length of pendulum)

Given, $l_1 = 100$ cm, $l_2 = 121$ cm

$$\Rightarrow \frac{T_2}{T_1} = \sqrt{\frac{121}{100}} = \frac{11}{10}$$

In a given time, shorter pendulum will make one oscillation more than the longer.

Let after n oscillations, the pendulums are in same phase, then

$$n \times 11 = (n+1) \times 10 \Rightarrow n = 10$$

65 (d) The time period of a pendulum in air,

$$T = 2\pi\sqrt{l/g} \quad \text{...(i)}$$

l being the length of simple pendulum.

In liquid, effective weight of sphere

w' = weight of bob in air – upthrust

$$\Rightarrow \rho V g_{eff} = mg - m'g$$

$$= \rho Vg - \rho' Vg = (\rho - \rho')Vg$$

where, ρ' = density of sphere

ρ = density of liquid.

$$\therefore g_{eff} = \left(\frac{\rho - \rho/10}{\rho}\right)g = \frac{9}{10}g$$

Thus, $$T' = 2\pi\sqrt{\frac{l}{g_{eff}}} = 2\pi\sqrt{\frac{l}{\frac{9}{10}g}}$$

$$\frac{T'}{T} = \sqrt{\frac{10}{9}} \Rightarrow T' = \sqrt{\frac{10}{9}}T$$

66 (d) Value of g decreases on going below the earth's surface. The time period (T) of a simple pendulum of length l and acceleration due to gravity g is given by

$$T = 2\pi\sqrt{\frac{l}{g}} \quad \text{...(i)}$$

$$\Rightarrow T \propto \frac{1}{\sqrt{g}}$$

Let mine be at a depth h below the surface of the earth having radius R, then

$g' = g\left(1 - \frac{h}{R}\right)$, Hence, g decreases

Therefore, from Eq. (i), T increases.

67 (a) We are given that the simple pendulum of length l is hanging from the roof of a vehicle which is moving down the frictionless inclined plane. So, its acceleration is $g\sin\alpha$. Since, vehicle is accelerating a pseudo force $m(g\sin\alpha)$ will act on bob of pendulum which cancel the $\sin\alpha$ component of weight of the bob.

Hence, we can say that the effective acceleration would be equal to

$$g_{eff} = g\cos\alpha$$

Now, the time period of oscillation is given by

$$T = 2\pi\sqrt{\frac{l}{g_{eff}}} = 2\pi\sqrt{\frac{l}{g\cos\alpha}}$$

68 (c) Mass of the particle = m

Spring constant = k

Time period of oscillator, $T = 2\pi\sqrt{\frac{m}{k}}$

As $k \propto \frac{1}{l}$

(where, l is the length of spring)

$$\because k' = 2k$$

$$\therefore T' = 2\pi\sqrt{\frac{m}{2k}} = \frac{1}{\sqrt{2}}T$$

69 (b) By using, $k \propto \frac{1}{l}$

Since, one-fourth length is cut away, so remaining length is $\frac{3}{4}$ th, hence, k becomes $\frac{4}{3}$ times, i.e. $k' = \frac{4}{3}k$.

70 (a) The stretched spring oscillates in accordance with the Hooke's law which goes as

$$\frac{1}{2}mv^2 = \frac{1}{2}kx^2 \Rightarrow \omega^2 = \frac{k}{m} \quad \left[\because \omega = \frac{v}{x}\right]$$

$$\Rightarrow f = \frac{1}{2\pi}\sqrt{\frac{k}{m}} = \frac{1}{2\pi}\sqrt{\frac{8\pi^2}{0.5}} = 2\text{Hz}$$

Topic 5

Free, Damped, Forced Oscillations & Resonance and Superposition of SHM

2015

1 When two displacements represented by $y_1 = a\sin(\omega t)$ and $y_2 = b\cos(\omega t)$ are superimposed, the motion is **[CBSE AIPMT]**

(a) not a simple harmonic

(b) simple harmonic with amplitude $\frac{a}{b}$

(c) simple harmonic with amplitude $\sqrt{a^2 + b^2}$

(d) simple harmonic with amplitude $\frac{(a+b)}{2}$

2014

2 The displacement of a particle in a periodic motion is given by $y = 4\cos^2(t/2)\sin(1000t)$. This displacement may be considered as the result superposition of n independent harmonic oscillations. Here, n is **[WB JEE]**

(a) 1 (b) 2

(c) 3 (d) 4

2009

3 Two simple harmonic motions are given by $x = A\sin(\omega t + \delta)$ and $y = A\sin\left(\omega t + \delta + \frac{\pi}{2}\right)$ act on a particle simultaneously, then the motion of particle will be **[UP CPMT]**

(a) circular anti-clockwise

(b) elliptical anti-clockwise

(c) elliptical clockwise

(d) circular clockwise

4 If the differential equation given by

$$\frac{d^2y}{dt^2} + 2k\frac{dy}{dt} + \omega^2 y = F_0 \sin pt$$

describes the oscillatory motion of body in a dissipative medium under the influence of a periodic force, then the state of maximum amplitude of the oscillation is a measure of **[CG PMT]**

(a) free vibration (b) damped vibration

(c) forced vibration (d) resonance

2007

5 In case of a forced vibration, the resonance wave becomes very sharp when the **[BHU]**

(a) applied periodic force is small

(b) quality factor is small

(c) damping force is small

(d) restoring force is small

2006

6 A particle is executing two different simple harmonic motions, mutually perpendicular, of different amplitudes and having phase difference of $\pi/2$. The path of the particle will be **[Manipal]**

(a) circular (b) straight line

(c) parabolic (d) elliptical

7 During the phenomenon of resonance **[DUMET]**

(a) the amplitude of oscillation becomes large

(b) the frequency of oscillation becomes large

(c) the time period of oscillation becomes large

(d) All of the above

8 The equation of a damped simple harmonic motion is $m\frac{d^2x}{dt^2} + b\frac{dx}{dt} + kx = 0$. Then, the angular frequency of oscillation is **[Manipal]**

(a) $\omega' = \left(\frac{k}{m} - \frac{b^2}{4m^2}\right)^{1/2}$ (b) $\omega' = \left(\frac{k}{m} - \frac{b}{4m}\right)^{1/2}$

(c) $\omega' = \left(\frac{k}{m} - \frac{b^2}{4m}\right)^{1/2}$ (d) $\omega' = \left(\frac{k}{m} - \frac{b^2}{4m^2}\right)$

Answers

1 (c)	2 (c)	3 (d)	4 (d)	5 (c)	6 (d)	7 (a)	8 (a)

Explanations

1. *(c)* Given, $y_1 = a\sin\omega t$

$$y_2 = b\cos\omega t = b\sin\left(\omega t + \frac{\pi}{2}\right)$$

The resultant displacement is given by

$$y = y_1 + y_2 = \sqrt{a^2 + b^2}\,\sin(\omega t + \phi)$$

Hence, the motion of superimposed wave is simple harmonic with amplitude $\sqrt{a^2 + b^2}$.

2 *(c)* Given, $y = 4\cos^2\left(\frac{t}{2}\right)\sin(1000t)$

$$= 2\times 2\cos^2\left(\frac{t}{2}\right)\cdot\sin(1000t)$$

$$\left[\because 2\cos^2\frac{t}{2} = (1 + \cos t)\right]$$

$$= 2(1 + \cos t)\sin(1000t)$$
$$= 2\sin(1000t) + 2\cos t\cdot\sin(1000t)$$
$$= 2\sin(1000t) + 2\sin(1000t)\cdot\cos t$$
$$= 2\sin(1000t) + \sin(1000t + t) + \sin(1000t - t)$$

$[\because 2\sin A\cdot\cos B = \sin(A + B) + \sin(A - B)]$

$$= 2\sin(1000t) + \sin(1001t) + \sin(999t)$$

So, $n = 3$

($\because$ above equation shows three inside independent oscillations)

3 *(d)* Given, $x = A\sin(\omega t + \delta)$ ...(i)

and $y = A\sin\left(\omega t + \delta + \frac{\pi}{2}\right)$

$= A\cos(\omega t + \delta)$ ...(ii)

On squaring and adding Eqs. (i) and (ii), we get

$$x^2 + y^2 = A^2[\sin^2(\omega t + \delta) + \cos^2(\omega t + \delta)]$$

$$\Rightarrow x^2 + y^2 = A^2$$

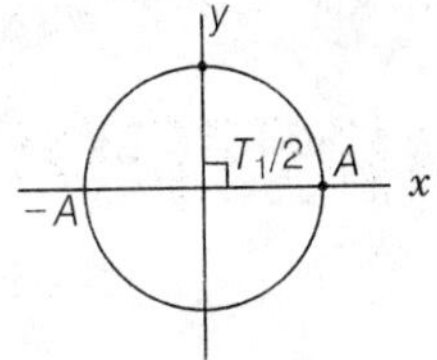

which is the equation of a circle.

Now, At $(\omega t + \delta) = 0, x = 0, y = 0$
At $(\omega t + \delta) = \pi/2, x = A, y = 0$
At $(\omega t + \delta) = \pi, x = 0, y = -A$
At $(\omega t + \delta) = 3\pi/2, x = -A, y = 0$
At $(\omega t + \delta) = 2\pi, x = A, y = 0$

From the above data, the motion of a particle is a circle transversed in clockwise direction.

4 *(d)* The differential equation,

$$\frac{d^2y}{dt^2} + 2k\frac{dy}{dt} + \omega^2 y = F_0\sin pt$$

shows oscillatory motion (forced). The state of maximum amplitude of the oscillation is the measure of resonance.

5 *(c)* In resonant vibrations of a body, the frequency of external force applied on the body is equal to its natural frequency. If on increasing and decreasing the frequency of external force from the natural frequency by a factor, the amplitude of vibrations reduces very much. In this case, sharp resonance will take place.

But if it reduces by a small factor, then flat resonance will take place. The sharp and flat resonance will depend on damping present in the body executing resonant vibrations. Less the damping, greater will be sharpness.

6 *(d)* If the equations of two mutually perpendicular SHM of same frequency be

$x = a_1\sin\omega t$ and $y = a_2\sin(\omega t + \phi)$

General equation of Lissajous' figure is

$$\frac{x^2}{a_1^2} + \frac{y^2}{a_2^2} - \frac{2xy}{a_1a_2}\cos\phi = \sin^2\phi$$

When $\phi = \frac{\pi}{2}$, then $\frac{x^2}{a_1^2} + \frac{y^2}{a_2^2} = 1$

which represents the path of ellipse.

7 *(a)* During the phenomenon of resonance, the amplitude of oscillation becomes large. Because applied frequency is equal to natural frequency.

8 *(a)* Damping force, $F_d = -bv$

where, b = damped constant,

v = velocity of oscillation and

$\omega_0 = 2\pi\nu_0 = 2\pi.\frac{1}{2\pi}\sqrt{\frac{k}{m}} = \sqrt{\frac{k}{m}}$, where

ω_0 = angular frequency of free oscillation.

Displacement of damped oscillator is given by

$$x = x_m e^{-bt/2m}\sin(\omega' t + \phi),$$

where, ω' = angular frequency of damped oscillator.

$$\therefore \quad \omega' = \sqrt{\omega_0^2 - \left(\frac{b}{2m}\right)^2} = \sqrt{\frac{k}{m} - \frac{b^2}{4m^2}}$$

14

Waves

Quick Review

Wave Motion

A wave motion is a means of transferring energy and momentum from one point to another without actual transport of matter between two points.

Important properties of medium for wave motion are given below

(*i*) The medium must possesses **inertia** so that its particles can store kinetic energy.

(*ii*) In order to make the particles return to their original position after getting disturbed, the medium must possesses **elasticity**.

(*iii*) There should be **minimum frictional force** between the particles of medium.

Characteristics of Wave Motion

(*i*) In a wave motion, the disturbance travels through the medium due to repeated periodic oscillations of the particles of the medium about their mean positions.

(*ii*) The energy is transferred from one place to another without any actual transfer of the particles of the medium.

(*iii*) There is a continuous phase difference between two successive particles because each particle receives disturbance a little later than its preceding particle.

(*iv*) The velocity of a wave is different from the velocity with which the particles vibrate simple harmonically about their mean positions.

(*v*) In a given medium, the wave velocity remains constant, while the particle velocity changes continuously during its vibration about the mean position.

The particle's velocity is maximum at the mean position and zero at the extreme position.

(*vi*) For the propagation of a mechanical wave, the medium must possesses the properties of inertia, elasticity as well as friction.

Definitions Related to the Wave Motion

Some important definitions related to the wave motion are given below

(*i*) **Amplitude** The maximum displacement suffered by the particles of the medium from their mean position is called amplitude.
It is denoted by A.

(*ii*) **Time Period** The time in which a particle of the medium completes one vibration to and fro about its mean position, is known as time period of a wave. It is denoted by T.

(*iii*) **Frequency** The number of waves produced per unit time in the given medium, is known as frequency of a wave. It is denoted by ν.

(*iv*) **Wavelength** The distance covered by a wave during the time in which a particle of medium completes one vibration about its mean motion, is known as wavelength of a wave. It is denoted by λ.

(*v*) **Wave Number** The number of waves present in a unit distance along the direction of propagation is known as wave number. It is equal to the reciprocal of wavelength (λ). It is denoted by $\bar{\nu}$.

$$\therefore \quad \bar{\nu} = \frac{1}{\lambda}$$

The SI unit of wave number is m^{-1}.

(*vi*) **Phase** The position of a point in time on a waveform is known as the phase of a wave. Phase can also be expressed as relative displacement between two corresponding peaks of a waveform.

(*vii*) **Path Difference** The difference in the path traversed by the two waves, measured in the terms of wavelength of the associated waves is called path difference.

(*viii*) **Speed of a Wave** Wave speed is a measure of how fast a wave travels. It is calculated as a ratio of how far a wave travels to the time taken by the wave to travel that distance.

Mechanical Waves

Waves which requires a material medium for their propagation are known as mechanical waves. Mechanical waves can be further categorised as

(*i*) **Transverse Wave** In this type of wave, the particles of the medium oscillate perpendicular to the direction of propagation of wave in the form of crests and troughs.

(*ii*) **Longitudinal Wave** In this type of wave, the particles of the medium oscillate about their mean position along the direction of wave propagation in the form of compressions and rarefactions.

Sound Waves

Sound is a form of energy which produces a sensation of hearing in our ears. Sound waves are longitudinal in nature.

Speed of a Longitudinal (Sound) Wave in a Medium

- Speed of sound wave (v) in a medium (for solids, liquids and gases) are expressed below

(*i*) For solids, $v = \sqrt{\frac{Y}{\rho}}$

where, Y = Young's modulus and ρ = density of solid.

(*ii*) For liquids, $v = \sqrt{\frac{B}{\rho}}$

where, B = bulk modulus of elasticity.

(*iii*) For gases, $v = \sqrt{\frac{p}{\rho}}$ where, p = pressure exerted by gas.

This is also known as **Newton's formula**. For gases, bulk modulus is equal to pressure of the gas.

- The modification of Newton's formula is referred to as the **Laplace correction** which is expressed as $v = \sqrt{\frac{\gamma p}{\rho}}$

where, γ = adiabatic constant = $\frac{C_p}{C_V}$

and C_p, C_V = specific heat capacities of gas at constant pressure and constant volume.

- For a gas, $\frac{v_{\text{rms}}}{v_{\text{sound}}} = \frac{\sqrt{3p/\rho}}{\sqrt{\gamma p/\rho}} = \sqrt{\frac{3}{\gamma}}$

- Speed of sound can be compared as follows

$$v_{\text{solid}} > v_{\text{liquid}} > v_{\text{gas}}$$

Factors Affecting the Speed of Sound

Factors that affect the speed of sound in air are as follows

(*i*) **Effect of Temperature** The velocity of sound in air increases roughly by 0.61 ms^{-1} with per degree centigrade rise in temperature. It means sound travels faster in warm air.

$$v = \sqrt{\frac{\gamma RT}{M}}$$

where, R = universal gas constant, M = molecular mass of gas and T = absolute temperature.

(*ii*) **Effect of Pressure** It is not effected by the pressure change, if the temperature of the gas remains constant.

(*iii*) **Effect of Humidity** Its speed in moist-air is slightly greater than dry air.

(*iv*) **Effect of Frequency** Its speed in air is independent of its frequency.

Characteristics of Sound

Sound has following three characteristics

(*i*) **Loudness** It is related to the intensity $\left(\frac{\text{energy}}{\text{time} \times \text{area}}\right)$ of sound and is measured in the unit 'bel' as

$$L_1 - L_2 = 10 \log_{10} \frac{I}{I_0}$$

where, I is the intensity of sound to be measured and I_0 is a constant reference intensity 10^{-12} Wm^{-2}.

(*ii*) **Pitch** It is related to the frequency of sound. A shrill or sharp sound has high frequency, hence higher pitch and a grave or dull sound has low frequency, hence lower pitch.

(*iii*) **Quality** The property of sound due to which difference between two sounds can be made is quality of sound.

Progressive Wave

A transverse or longitudinal wave that travel from one point of the medium to another is called a progressive wave.

Displacement relation for a wave travelling in $+X$ direction is given by

$$y = A \sin\left\{2\pi\left(\frac{t}{T} - \frac{x}{\lambda}\right) \pm \phi\right\}$$

while displacement relation for a wave travelling in $-X$ direction is given by

$$y = A \sin\left\{2\pi\left(\frac{t}{T} + \frac{x}{\lambda}\right) \pm \phi\right\}$$

- In terms of speed of wave (v), above relation can be written as

  For $+X$ direction, $y = A \sin\left\{\frac{2\pi}{\lambda}(vt - x) \pm \phi\right\}$

  For $-X$ direction, $y = A \sin\left\{\frac{2\pi}{\lambda}(vt + x) \pm \phi\right\}$

  In the above equation, v represent speed of wave.
- Other forms of displacement relation for progressive waves are

$$y = A \sin\{(\omega t \pm kx) \pm \phi\}$$
$$= A \sin\{k(vt \mp x) \pm \phi\}$$
$$= A \sin\left\{\omega\left(t \mp \frac{x}{v}\right) \pm \phi\right\}$$

Here, $\omega = \frac{2\pi}{T}$ is the angular frequencies and

$k = \frac{2\pi}{\lambda} = \frac{\omega}{v}$,

where λ is wavelength, v is wave velocity and k is called **angular wave number** or **propagation constant.**

- The relation between the phase difference, path difference and time difference of a plane progressive wave is represented as

  Phase difference $(\Delta\phi) = \frac{2\pi}{\lambda} \times$ Path difference (x)

- Particle velocity and acceleration in plane progressive harmonic wave

  As particle displacement, $y = A \sin(\omega t - kx)$

  $\therefore$ Particle velocity, $v = \frac{dy}{dt} = A\omega \cos(\omega t - kx)$

  Again differentiating the above equation, we get

  Particle acceleration,

$$a = \frac{d^2 y}{dt^2} = -A\omega^2 \sin(\omega t - kx) = -\omega^2 y$$

Energy in Wave

- **Energy density** (u) is the total mechanical energy per unit volume of the medium in a wave. It is expressed as

$$u = \frac{1}{2}\rho\omega^2 A^2$$

  where, A = amplitude of wave, ω = angular frequency and ρ = density.
- **Intensity** (I) is the flow of energy per unit cross-section of the medium (string) in unit time is expressed as

$$I = \frac{1}{2}\rho\omega^2 A^2 v \text{ or } \frac{P}{4\pi d^2}$$

  where, d = distance from line source.
- **Power** (P) is the instantaneous rate at which energy is transferred along the medium (string) is expressed as

$$P = \frac{1}{2}\rho\omega^2 A^2 SV$$

  where, ρ = density of the medium.

Principle of Superposition of Waves

- According to this principle, resultant displacement at any point is the vector sum of the displacement produced by the two waves when they travel simultaneously in a medium.

  i.e. $y = y_1 + y_2$

  where, y_1 and y_2 are displacement of particles at a particular time due to two waves.
- In superposition when two waves of same frequency (or wavelength) superimpose, interference of waves is seen as result.
- Resultant displacement will be represented as

$$y = y_1 + y_2 = A \sin(\omega t + \phi)$$

  where, $A = \sqrt{A_1^2 + A_2^2 + 2A_1 A_2 \cos\phi}$

  and $\tan\theta = \frac{A_2 \sin\phi}{A_1 + A_2 \cos\phi}$.
- $A = A_1 + A_2 = A_{\max}$ is known as **constructive interference**, where phase difference $\phi = 0°$ or $2n\pi$ $(n = 1, 2, 3, \ldots)$.
- $A = A_1 \sim A_2 = A_{\min}$ is known as **destructive interference**, where phase difference $\phi = (2n - 1)\pi$ $(n = 1, 2, 3, \ldots)$.
- Resultant intensity, $I = I_1 + I_2 + 2\sqrt{I_1 I_2} \cos\phi$

  where, I_1, I_2 = intensities due to two waves,

$$I_{\max} = I_1 + I_2 + 2\sqrt{I_1 I_2}$$

  and

$$I_{\min} = I_1 + I_2 - 2\sqrt{I_1 I_2}.$$

Beats

- The alternate rise and fall of sound at a given position, when two sound waves of slightly different frequencies or amplitudes superimpose at a given point is called beats.
- **Beat frequency** Number of beats formed per second are expressed as $(\nu_1 \sim \nu_2)$, i.e. either $(\nu_1 - \nu_2)$ or $(\nu_2 - \nu_1)$ where ν_1, ν_2 are frequencies of two sound waves.
- **Beat Period** It is the reciprocal of beat frequency expressed as

$$T = \frac{1}{\nu_1 - \nu_2}$$

- Essential condition for hearing beats is that $(\nu_1 \sim \nu_2)$ should not exceed 10.

Reflection of Waves

- When a progressive wave travelling through a medium reaches a rigid boundary, it gets reflected and the phenomena is called reflection of waves.

If equation of incident travelling wave is

$$y_i(x, t) = a \sin(kx - \omega t)$$

At a rigid boundary, the reflected wave is given by

$$y_r(x, t) = a \sin(kx + \omega t + \pi) = -a \sin(kx + \omega t)$$

- Different result related to reflection of waves are given in tabular form

Wave property	Reflection	Transmission (Refraction)
v	does not change	changes
f, T, ω	do not change	do not change
λ, k	do not change	change
A, I	change	change
ϕ	$\Delta\phi = 0$, from a rarer medium	does not change
	$\Delta\phi = \pi$, from a denser medium	

Stationary/Standing Waves

These waves are produced when two harmonic waves of equal frequency and amplitude travelling through a medium (string) in opposite directions superimpose on each other.

Stationary Waves in Organ Pipes

Its representation of frequency and wavelengths for both closed and open organ pipes are shown in tabular form below

Types of Organ Pipes	Vibrating in *n*th Mode: Frequency (f_n)	Wavelength (λ_n)	Figures
Closed	$f_n = (2n-1) f_1$ for n th overtone $f_n = (2n+1) f_1$ $f_1 = \frac{v}{4L}$ Ratio of overtones is 3 : 5 : 7:	$\lambda_n = \frac{4L}{(2n-1)}$	$(2n-1)\frac{n\lambda}{4}$; A_1, A_2, A_3, A_4, N_1, N_2, N_3, N_4 Position of nodes is $0, \frac{\lambda}{2}, \lambda, \frac{3\lambda}{2}, \ldots\ldots$ Position of anti-nodes is $0, \frac{\lambda}{4}, \frac{3\lambda}{4}, \frac{5\lambda}{4}, \ldots\ldots$
Open	$f_n = nf_1$, where f_1 = fundamental frequency. $f_1 = \frac{v}{2L}$ Ratio of overtones is 2 : 3 : 4 : 5 :	$\lambda_n = \frac{2L}{n}$	A_1, A_2, A_3, A_4, N_1, N_2, N_3; $l = \frac{n\lambda_n}{(n-1)}$ Position of nodes is $\frac{\lambda}{4}, \frac{3\lambda}{4}, \frac{5\lambda}{4}, \ldots\ldots$ Position of anti-nodes is $0, \frac{\lambda}{2}, \lambda, \frac{3\lambda}{2}, \ldots\ldots$

End Correction (e) As the anti-node is not formed exactly at open end of organ pipe an end correction must be applied to get true frequency. It is expressed as

(*i*) For closed organ pipe,

$$f_1 = \frac{v}{4(L+e)} \qquad (e = 0.6r)$$

where, r = radius of the pipe.

(*ii*) For open organ pipe,

$$f_2 = \frac{v}{2(L+2e)} \qquad (e = 1.2r)$$

Vibration of Stretched String

For a string tied at both ends, transverse wave is set up, whose speed is given by

$$v = \sqrt{\frac{T}{\mu}}$$

where, μ = mass per unit length of string

= volume of unit length × density.

Wavelength of stretched string in its nth mode can be expressed in generalised form as

$$\lambda = \frac{2L}{n}, n = 1, 2, 3, \ldots$$

and corresponding frequency,

$$f = \frac{nv}{2L} = \frac{v}{\lambda_n}$$

where, L = length of stretched string

and velocity $v_{nth} = \frac{n}{2l} = \sqrt{\frac{T}{\mu}} = nf_1$ and is known as nth harmonic or $(n-1)$ th overtone.

Vibration of Composite Strings

Suppose two strings of different materials and lengths are joined end to end and tied between clamps as shown in figure. Now after plucking, stationary waves are established only at those frequencies which matches with any one harmonic of both the independent string S_1 and S_2.

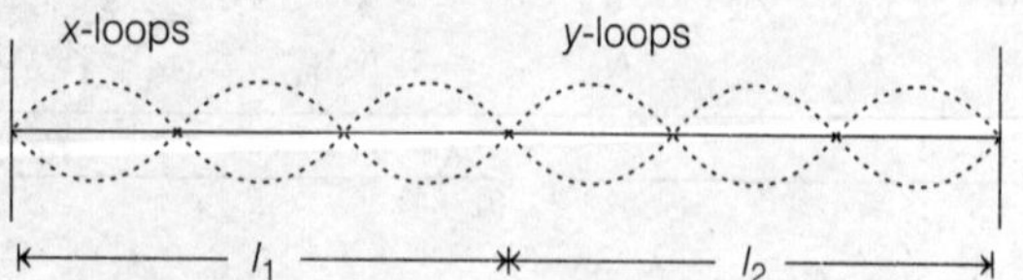

As the frequency of the wave in both strings must be same, so

$$\frac{x}{2l_1}\sqrt{\frac{T}{m_1}} = \frac{y}{2l_2}\sqrt{\frac{T}{m_2}}$$

$$\Rightarrow \quad \frac{x}{y} = \frac{l_1}{l_2}\sqrt{\frac{m_1}{m_2}} = \frac{l_1}{l_2}\sqrt{\frac{\rho_1}{\rho_2}}$$

(if radius is equal for both strings.)

Doppler's Effect

If a wave source and a receiver are moving relative to each other, the frequency observed by receiver is different from the actual source frequency. This phenomena is known as doppler's effect.

For different situations of the source and the observer, the apparent frequencies observed due to doppler's effect are tabulated as follows

Observer (*o*)	Source (*s*)	Apparent frequency
$\rightarrow v_o$	Stationary ($v_s = 0$)	$f_a = \left(\frac{v+v_o}{v}\right) f_o$
$v_o \leftarrow$	Stationary ($v_s = 0$)	$f_a = \left(\frac{v-v_o}{v}\right) f_o$
Stationary ($v_o = 0$)	$\rightarrow v_s$	$f_a = \left(\frac{v}{v+v_s}\right) f_o$
Stationary ($v_o = 0$)	$v_s \leftarrow$	$f_a = \left(\frac{v}{v-v_s}\right) f_o$
$\rightarrow v_o$	$\rightarrow v_s$	$f_a = \left(\frac{v+v_o}{v+v_s}\right) f_o$
$v_o \leftarrow$	$\rightarrow v_s$	$f_a = \left(\frac{v-v_o}{v+v_s}\right) f_o$
$\rightarrow v_o$	$v_s \leftarrow$	$f_a = \left(\frac{v+v_o}{v-v_s}\right) f_o$
$v_o \leftarrow$	$v_s \leftarrow$	$f_a = \left(\frac{v-v_o}{v-v_s}\right) f_o$

where,
f_o = original frequency of sound wave,
f_a = apparent frequency, v = speed of sound in medium,
v_s = speed of source and v_o = speed of observer.

Special Cases of Doppler's effect

(*i*) If a source of sound is moving towards a stationary cliff a wall, then apparent frequency of sound heard by the stationary observer directly from the source

$$f' = \left(\frac{v}{v+v_s}\right)f \quad \text{(source is moving away)}$$

Apparent frequency of reflected sound heard by stationary observer, $f' = \left(\frac{v}{v-v_s}\right)f$

(*ii*) Sound source and observer are moving in a direction making an angle with the line joining them

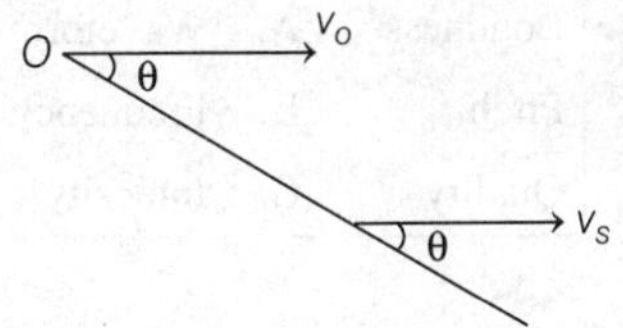

Apparent frequency, $f' = \left(\frac{v+v_o\cos\theta}{v+v_o\sin\theta}\right)f$

(*iii*) When source is rotating about an observer, then

$$f_{\max} = \left(\frac{v}{v-v_s}\right)f$$

and $$f_{\min} = \left(\frac{v}{v+v_s}\right)f.$$

If observer is at the centre of circle, then there will no change in the frequency of sound heard.

(*iv*) If observer is rotating around a source, then

$$f_{\max} = \left(\frac{v+v_o}{v}\right)f$$

and $$f_{\min} = \left(\frac{v-v_o}{v}\right)f.$$

Topical Practice Questions

All the exam questions of this chapter have been divided into 6 topics as listed below

Topic 1

Basic of Mechanical Waves

2018

1 If speed of sound in air is 340 m/s and in water is 1480 m/s. If frequency of sound is 1000 kHz, then find the value of wavelength in water. **[JIPMER]**

(a) 2.96 mm (b) 1.48 mm
(c) 0.74 mm (d) 1 mm

2014

2 Identify the correct statement. **[Kerala CEE]**

(a) Transverse wave can propagate in gases.
(b) Transverse wave consists of compressions and rarefactions.
(c) Longitudinal wave can propagate in solids, liquids and gases.
(d) In a longitudinal wave, particles of the medium vibrate perpendicular to the direction of propagation.
(e) In a longitudinal wave, the higher density corresponds to rarefactions.

3 The speed of sound in air **[Kerala CEE]**

(a) decreases with temperature
(b) increases with pressure
(c) increases with humidity
(d) decreases with pressure
(e) increases with density

2013

4 Which of the following is different from others? **[WB JEE]**

(a) Wavelength (b) Velocity
(c) Frequency (d) Amplitude

5 When a certain volume of water is subjected to increase of 100 kPa pressure, the volume of water decreases by 0.005%. The speed of sound in water must be **[UP CPMT]**

(a) 140 m/s (b) 300 m/s
(c) 1400 m/s (d) 5000 m/s

6 Oxygen is 16 times heavier than hydrogen. Equal volumes of hydrogen and oxygen are mixed. The ratio of speed of sound in the mixture to that in hydrogen is **[Manipal]**

(a) $\sqrt{8}$ (b) $\sqrt{2/17}$
(c) $\sqrt{1/8}$ (d) $\sqrt{32/17}$

7 A sound has an intensity of $2\times10^{-8}\ \mathrm{W/m^2}$. Its intensity level (in decibel) is ($\log_{10} 2 = 0.3$) **[WB JEE]**

(a) 23 (b) 3
(c) 43 (d) 4.3

2011

8 Each of the properties of sound in Column I primarily depends on one of the quantities in Column II. Select the correct answer (matching Column I with Column II) as per code given below the columns. **[Haryana PMT, CG PMT]**

	Column I		Column II
P.	Loudness	A.	Waveform
Q.	Pitch	B.	Frequency
R.	Quality	C.	Intensity

Codes

	P	Q	R		P	Q	R
(a)	A	B	C	(b)	C	B	A
(c)	B	C	A	(d)	B	A	C

9 The intensity level of a sound wave is defined by an arbitrary scale. The zero of the scale is taken at the sound wave intensity **[BCECE]**

(a) $1\times10^{-10}\ \mathrm{Wm^2}$ (b) $1\times10^{-12}\ \mathrm{Wm^2}$
(c) $1\times10^{-14}\ \mathrm{Wm^2}$ (d) $1\times10^{-16}\ \mathrm{Wm^2}$

10 A theatre of volume $100\times40\times10\,\mathrm{m^3}$ can accommodate 1000 visitors. The reverberation time of the theatre when empty is 8.5 s. If the theatre is now filled with 500 visitors, occupying the front-half seats, the reverberation time changes to 6.2 s. The average absorption coefficient of each visitor is nearly **[EAMCET]**

(a) 0.6 (b) 0.5
(c) 0.45 (d) 0.7

11 A sound absorber attenuates the sound level by 20 dB. The intensity decreases by a factor of **[JIPMER]**

(a) 1000 (b) 10000
(c) 10 (d) 100

2009

12 The pressure variations in the propagation of sound waves in gaseous medium are **[Kerala CEE]**

(a) adiabatic (b) isothermal
(c) isobaric (d) isochoric
(e) cyclic

13 When a wave undergoes refraction, **[J&K CET]**

(a) its frequency changes
(b) its amplitude changes
(c) its velocity changes
(d) Both amplitude and frequency change

14 The temperature at which the speed of sound in air becomes doubled of its value at 0°C is **[VMMC]**

(a) 1092°C (b) 819 K (c) 819°C (d) 546°C

15 Sound waves transfer **[KCET]**

(a) only energy not momentum
(b) energy
(c) momentum
(d) Both (b) and (c)

16 A stationary point source of sound emits sound uniformly in all directions in a non-absorbing medium. Two points *P* and *Q* are at a distance of 4 m and 9 m respectively from the source. The ratio of amplitudes of the waves at *P* and *Q* is **[KCET]**

(a) $\frac{3}{2}$ (b) $\frac{4}{9}$ (c) $\frac{2}{3}$ (d) $\frac{9}{4}$

2008

17 The time of reverberation of a room *A* is one second. What will be the time (in second) of reverberation of a room, having all the dimensions double of those of room *A*? **[Haryana PMT]**

(a) 2 (b) 4 (c) 1/2 (d) 1

18 Reverberation time does not depend upon **[BCECE]**

(a) temperature (b) volume of room
(c) size of window (d) carpet and curtain

19 How many times more intense is a 60 dB sound than a 30 dB sound? **[KCET]**

(a) 1000 (b) 2 (c) 100 (d) 4

20 **Assertion** The change in air pressure affects the speed of sound.

Reason The speed of sound in gases is proportional to the square of pressure. **[AIIMS]**

(a) Both Assertion and Reason are correct and Reason is the correct explanation of Assertion
(b) Both Assertion and Reason are correct but Reason is not the correct explanation of Assertion
(c) Assertion is correct but Reason is incorrect
(d) Both Assertion and Reason are incorrect

2007

21 The intensity of sound increases at night due to **[AFMC]**

(a) increase in density of air
(b) decrease in density of air
(c) low temperature
(d) None of the above

22 Sound waves are not transmitted over a long distance, because **[MHT CET]**

(a) they are absorbed by the atmosphere
(b) they have constant frequency
(c) the height of antenna required should be very high
(d) velocity of sound waves is very less

23 The gas having average speed four times as that of SO_2 (molecular mass 64) is **[MHT CET]**

(a) He (molecular mass 4)
(b) O_2 (molecular mass 32)
(c) H_2 (molecular mass 2)
(d) CH_4 (molecular mass 16)

24 Which one of the following statements is true? **[MP PMT]**

(a) Both light and sound waves in air are transverse.
(b) The sound waves in air are longitudinal while the light waves are transverse.
(c) Both light and sound waves in air are longitudinal.
(d) Both light and sound waves can travel in vacuum.

25 The speed of sound waves in a gas **[J&K CET]**

(a) does not depend upon density of the gas
(b) depend upon changes in pressure
(c) does not depend upon temperature
(d) depends upon density of the gas

26 A boat at anchor is rocked by waves of velocity 25 ms^{-1} having crests 100 m apart. They reach the boat once every **[AMU]**

(a) 4.0 s (b) 8.0 s
(c) 2.0 s (d) 0.25 s

27 Compressional wave pulses are sent to the bottom of sea from a ship and the echo is heard after 2 s. If bulk modulus of elasticity of water is 2×10^9 Nm^{-2} and mean temperature is 4°C, the depth of the sea will be **[BCECE]**

(a) 1014 m (b) 1414 m
(c) 2828 m (d) None of these

2006

28 When sound waves travel from air to water, which one of the following remains constant? **[Manipal]**

(a) Time period (b) Frequency
(c) Velocity (d) Wavelength

29 Velocity of sound waves in air is 330 ms^{-1}. For a particular sound in air, a path difference of 40 cm is equivalent to a phase difference of 1.6 π. The frequency of the wave is **[Manipal]**

(a) 165 Hz (b) 150 Hz
(c) 660 Hz (d) 330 Hz

30 The velocity of sound is *v* at 273 K. The temperature at which it is 2*v* is **[Kerala CEE]**

(a) 2×273 K (b) 4×273 K
(c) 8×273 K (d) 16×273 K
(e) $\sqrt{2} \times 273$ K

31 Distance between successive compression and rarefaction is 1 m and velocity of sound is 360 ms^{-1}. Find frequency of the sound wave. **[RPMT]**

(a) 180 Hz (b) 45 Hz
(c) 120 Hz (d) 90 Hz

32 A bomb explodes on the moon. How long will it take for the sound to reach the earth? **[Punjab PMET]**

(a) 10 s (b) 1000 s
(c) 1 day (d) None of these

2005

33 The ratio of velocity of sound in hydrogen and oxygen at STP is **[KCET]**

(a) 16 : 1 (b) 8 : 1
(c) 4 : 1 (d) 2 : 1

34 A particle on the trough of a wave at any instant will come to the mean position after a time (T = time period) **[KCET]**

(a) $T/2$ (b) $T/4$
(c) T (d) $2T$

35 Sound travels faster after rain than on a dry day because **[Haryana PMT]**

(a) the temperature of the atmosphere increases after rain
(b) the density of air increases after rain
(c) the humidity in the air increases after rain
(d) None of the above

Answers

1 (b)	2 (c)	3 (c)	4 (d)	5 (c)	6 (b)	7 (c)	8 (b)	9 (b)	10 (d)
11 (d)	12 (a)	13 (c)	14 (c)	15 (d)	16 (d)	17 (a)	18 (a)	19 (a)	20 (d)
21 (a)	22 (a)	23 (a)	24 (b)	25 (d)	26 (a)	27 (b)	28 (b)	29 (c)	30 (b)
31 (a)	32 (d)	33 (c)	34 (b)	35 (c)					

Explanations

1 *(b)* Given, $v_w = 1480$ m/s,

$f = 1000$ kHz

Speed, $v_w = f\lambda$

$$\therefore \quad \lambda = \frac{v_w}{f} = \frac{1480}{1000 \times 10^3} = 1.480 \text{ mm}$$

2 *(c)* The correct statement is longitudinal wave can propagate in solids, liquids and gases. Transverse wave does not require medium to travel, it consists of crests and troughs. In a longitudinal wave, particles of the medium vibrate to the direction of propagation of wave. In longitudinal wave, higher density corresponds to compressions.

Hence, options (a), (b), (d) and (e) are incorrect.

3 *(c)* The velocity of sound in a gas or air is given by

$$v = \sqrt{\frac{\gamma p}{\rho}} = \sqrt{\frac{\gamma RT}{M}} \quad \text{...(i)}$$

where symbols have their usual meaning.

Thus, from Eq. (i), we can conclude that

$$v \propto \sqrt{\frac{p}{\rho}}$$

As the pressure of gas or air increases, then density also increases and hence p/ρ remain constants. So, velocity of sound is independent of pressure.

Also, $v \propto \sqrt{T}$, so with rise in temperature, velocity of sound decreases.

Also, $v \propto \frac{1}{\sqrt{\rho}}$, so with increase in density, the velocity of sound decreases. With increase in humidity, density of air decreases. So, with rise in humidity, velocity of sound increases.

Hence, option (c) is correct.

4 *(d)* Amplitude is independent of wavelength, velocity and frequency of oscillation.

Because, velocity (v) = frequency (f) × wavelength (λ), hence these are related with each other. Whereas amplitude is the maximum displacement suffered by the particles of the medium from mean position.

5 *(c)* Volume elasticity,

$$|B| = \frac{\Delta p}{\Delta V/V} = \frac{100 \times 10^3}{0.005/100} = 2 \times 10^9$$

$$\text{Speed of sound, } v = \sqrt{\frac{B}{d}} = \sqrt{\frac{2 \times 10^9}{10^3}} = 1.4 \times 10^3 = 1400 \text{ m/s}$$

6 *(b)* Let one mole of each gas has same volume as V. When they are mixed, then density of mixture is

$$\rho_{\text{mixture}} = \frac{\text{Mass of } O_2 + \text{Mass of } H_2}{\text{Volume of } O_2 + \text{Volume of } H_2} = \frac{32+2}{V+V} = \frac{34}{2V} = \frac{17}{V}$$

Also, $\rho_{H_2} = \frac{2}{V}$

$$\text{Now, velocity} = \left(\frac{\gamma p}{\rho}\right)^{1/2}$$

or $v \propto \frac{1}{\sqrt{\rho}}$

$$\frac{v_{\text{mixture}}}{v_{H_2}} = \sqrt{\left(\frac{\rho_{H_2}}{\rho_{\text{mixture}}}\right)} = \sqrt{\left(\frac{2/V}{17/V}\right)} = \sqrt{\left(\frac{2}{17}\right)}$$

7 *(c)* We know that, intensity level in decibel,

$$L = 10 \log_{10}\left(\frac{I}{I_0}\right)$$

$$\therefore L = 10 \log_{10}\left(\frac{2 \times 10^{-8}}{10^{-12}}\right)$$

$$(\because I_0 = 12^{-12} \text{ W/m}^2)$$

$$L = 10 \log_{10}(2 \times 10^4)$$

$$L = 10 [\log_{10} 2 + \log_{10}(10)^4]$$

$L = 10\,(4.3)$ $L = 43$ decibel

8 *(b)* **Loudness of sound** is a subjective term describing the strength of sound. It is related to sound intensity.

Pitch of sound may be generally characterised by frequency. The perceived pitch of a sound is just the ear's response to frequency, i.e. for most practical purpose, the pitch is just frequency.

Quality of sound depends upon the waveform which produces it.

P → C, Q → B, R → A

9 *(b)* Sound intensity is defined as the sound power per unit area. Many sound intensity measurements are made relative to a standard threshold of hearing intensity

$$I_0 = 10^{-12}\ \text{Wm}^2$$

$$\Rightarrow \quad I_0 = 1\times 10^{-12}\ \text{Wm}^2$$

10 *(d)* Number of visitors = 1000

Volume of theatre = $100 \times 40 \times 10\ \text{m}^3$

***Case* I** Volume acquired by one visitor

$$= \frac{100\times 40\times 10}{1000} = 40\ \text{m}^3$$

Reverberation time = 8.5 s

***Case* II** Volume acquired by one visitor

$$= \frac{100\times 40\times 10}{500} = 80\ \text{m}^3$$

Reverberation time = 6.2 s

The average absorption coefficient,

$$\eta = \frac{40\times 8.5}{80\times 6.2}$$

$$= \frac{85}{124} \approx 0.7$$

11 *(d)* We know that,

$$\beta = 10\log\left(\frac{I}{I_0}\right)$$

$$\beta_1 = 10\log\left(\frac{I_1}{I_0}\right)$$

$$\beta_2 = 10\log\left(\frac{I_2}{I_0}\right)$$

$$\beta_2 - \beta_1 = 20$$

$$\Rightarrow \quad 10\log\left(\frac{I_2}{I_0}\right) - 10\log\left(\frac{I_1}{I_0}\right) = 20$$

$$\Rightarrow \quad 10\log\left(\frac{I_2}{I_1}\right) = 20$$

$$I_2 = 100 I_1$$

12 *(a)* When a sound wave propagates in a gaseous medium, the pressure varies in an adiabatic process.

13 *(c)* When a wave undergoes refraction, then its velocity changes.

14 *(c)* Speed, $v \propto \sqrt{T}$

$$\therefore \quad \frac{2v}{v} = \sqrt{\frac{T_2}{T_1}}$$

$$\Rightarrow \quad 2 = \sqrt{\frac{T_2}{T_1}}$$

$$\Rightarrow \quad 4 = \frac{T_2}{T_1}$$

$$\Rightarrow \quad T_2 = 4T_1 = 4\times 273 = 1092\ \text{K}$$

$$\therefore \quad T_2 = 1092 - 273 = 819°\text{C}$$

15 *(d)* Sound waves transfer both energy and momentum.

16 *(d)* In a non-absorbing medium when a wave travels in three-dimensional space, then amplitude varies inversely with distance.

i.e. $$A \propto \frac{1}{r}$$

So, $$\frac{A_P}{A_Q} = \frac{r_Q}{r_P} = \frac{9}{4}$$

17 *(a)* Sabine's formula for reverberation time,

$$T = \frac{0.16V}{\alpha S}$$

where, V is volume of hall in m^3,

α = absorption coefficient

and S = surface area of room.

$$\therefore \quad \frac{T'}{T} = \frac{V'}{S'} \times \frac{S}{V} = \frac{8V}{V} \times \frac{S}{4S}$$

$$= \frac{8}{4} = 2$$

Hence, $T' = 2T = 2\times 1 = 2$ s

18 *(a)* Reverberation depends upon the size of the room, opening of the room, i.e. window size and also the material inside room but does not depend upon the temperature of the room.

19 *(a)* We know that,

$$L = 10\log_{10}\left(\frac{I}{I_0}\right)$$

$$\therefore \quad 60 = 10\log_{10}\left(\frac{I_1}{I_0}\right)$$

$$\Rightarrow \quad \frac{I_1}{I_0} = 10^6 \quad \ldots(\text{i})$$

Similarly, $$30 = 10\log_{10}\left(\frac{I_2}{I_0}\right)$$

$$\Rightarrow \quad \frac{I_2}{I_0} = 10^3 \quad \ldots(\text{ii})$$

Dividing Eq. (i) by Eq. (ii), we get

$$\frac{I_1}{I_2} = 1000$$

20 *(d)* The speed of sound in gaseous medium is given by

$$v = \sqrt{\frac{\gamma p}{\rho}} \quad \ldots(\text{i})$$

At constant temperature,

$$pV = \text{constant} \quad \ldots(\text{ii})$$

If V is the volume of one mole of a gas, then density of gas

$$\rho = \frac{M}{V}$$

or $$V = \frac{M}{\rho}$$

where, M is the molecular weight of the gas.

∴ Eq. (ii) becomes,

$$\frac{pM}{\rho} = \text{constant}$$

or $\frac{p}{\rho}$ = constant, as M is a constant.

Therefore from Eq. (i), we have,

$$v = \text{constant} \times \sqrt{\gamma}$$

Thus, change in air pressure does not affect the speed of sound.

21 *(a)* At night, amount of carbon dioxide in atmosphere increases which raises the density of atmosphere. Since, intensity is directly proportional to density, so intensity of sound is more at night.

22 *(a)* There are several factors which affects the propagation of sound. These are geometric spreading, atmospheric effects and surfaces effects. There are two mechanisms by which acoustic energy is absorbed by the atmosphere. These are molecular relaxation and viscosity effects. The amount of absorption depends on the temperature and humidity of the atmosphere.

23 *(a)* Average speed v_{av} of gas molecules is inversely proportional to the square root of the absolute temperature T of the gas

$$v_{av} = \sqrt{\frac{8RT}{\pi M}}$$

where, R is gas constant and M be the molecular weight.

Given, $v_1 = v$, $M_1 = 64$, $v_2 = 4v$

$$\therefore \quad \frac{v_1}{v_2} = \sqrt{\frac{M_2}{M_1}}$$

$$\Rightarrow \quad \frac{v}{4v} = \sqrt{\frac{M_2}{64}}$$

$$\Rightarrow \quad M_2 = \frac{64}{16} = 4$$

Hence, the gas is helium (molecular mass 4).

24 *(b)* In a longitudinal wave, the particles of the medium oscillate about their mean or equilibrium position along the direction of propagation of the wave itself. Sound waves are longitudinal in nature. In transverse wave, the particles of the medium oscillate about their mean or equilibrium position at right angles to the direction of propagation of wave itself. Light wave being electromagnetic are transverse waves.

25 *(d)* Speed of sound is independent of changes in pressure, it depends upon density of the gas.

Because, speed of sound in a gas,

$v = \sqrt{\frac{rp}{\rho}}$, means $v \propto \sqrt{p}$, but actually it is not, so because $\frac{p}{\rho} = \frac{RT}{M}$ = constant at constant temperature.

26 *(a)* The required relation can be given as

$$v = n\lambda$$

Given, $v = 25 \text{ ms}^{-1}$

and $\lambda = 100$ m

$$\therefore \quad 25 = n \times 100$$

$$\Rightarrow \quad n = \frac{25}{100} = \frac{1}{4} = 0.25$$

Then, $T = \frac{1}{n} = \frac{1}{0.25} = 4$ s

27 *(b)* The speed of sound (longitudinal waves) in water is given by

$$v = \sqrt{\frac{B}{d}}$$

where, B is bulk modulus of water and d is density.

Given, $B = 2 \times 10^9 \text{ Nm}^{-2}$,

$$d = 10^3 \text{kgm}^{-3}$$

$$\therefore \quad v = \sqrt{\frac{2 \times 10^9}{10^3}} = 1.414 \times 10^3$$

$$= 1414 \text{ ms}^{-1}$$

When sound travels back to the observer, it cover's twice the distance. So, time of echo is given by

$$t = \frac{2d}{v}$$

$$\therefore \quad d = \frac{tv}{2}$$

$$= \frac{1414 \times 2}{2} = 1414 \text{ m}$$

28 *(b)* We know that frequency is independent of refraction, therefore when sound waves travel from air to water, the frequency remains constant.

29 *(c)* Phase difference of 1.6π corresponds to path difference of 40 cm. Hence, phase difference of 2π will correspond to a path difference of 50 cm, i.e. $\lambda = 50$ cm or 0.5 m.

$$\therefore \quad n = \frac{v}{\lambda} = \frac{330}{0.5} = 660 \text{ Hz}$$

30 *(b)* Velocity of sound is given by

$$v = \sqrt{\frac{3RT}{M}}$$

$$\Rightarrow \quad v \propto \sqrt{T}$$

Given, $T_1 = 273$ K, $v_1 = v$, $v_2 = 2v$

$$\therefore \quad \frac{v_1}{v_2} = \sqrt{\frac{T_1}{T_2}}$$

$$\Rightarrow \quad v_2 = \sqrt{\frac{T_2}{T_1}} v_1$$

$$2v = \sqrt{\frac{T_2}{273}} v$$

$$\Rightarrow \quad T_2 = 4 \times 273 \text{ K}$$

31 *(a)* $\lambda = 2d = 2$ m

$$\nu = \frac{v}{\lambda} = \frac{360 \text{ ms}^{-1}}{2 \text{ m}} = 180 \text{ Hz}$$

32 *(d)* The radius of moon and acceleration due to gravity at its surface both are smaller compared to earth. Therefore, the escape velocity at the moon is 2.38 kms^{-1}. At the temperature of moon, the average velocity of gas molecules greater than this.

Therefore, gas molecules cannot stay at moon. Hence, there is no atmosphere around the moon. Since, sound waves need a medium for propagation, therefore sound produced by the bomb explosion will never reach the earth.

33 *(c)* Velocity of sound, $v = \sqrt{\frac{\gamma RT}{M}}$

$$\therefore \quad \frac{v_H}{v_O} = \sqrt{\frac{M_O}{M_H}}$$

$$= \sqrt{\frac{16}{1}} = 4 : 1$$

34 *(b)* The time taken by the particle to come to mean position from the trough $= \frac{T}{4}$

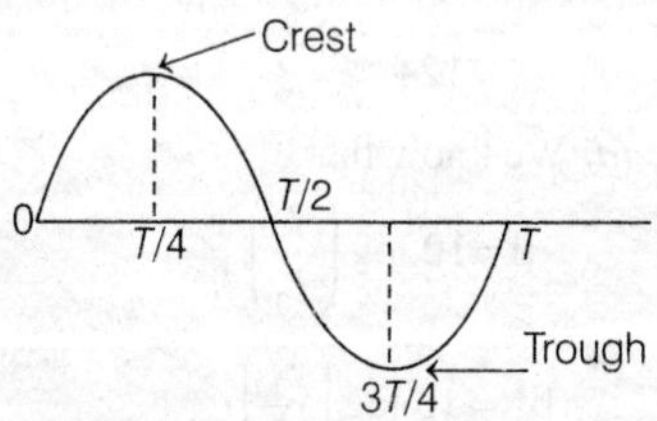

35 *(c)* The speed of sound will become higher as the humidity in the air increases after rain.

Because, $v = \frac{\sqrt{\gamma p}}{\rho}$, density of moist air is less than density of dry air.

Topic 2
Progressive Waves

2014

1 When a wave travels in a medium, displacement of a particle is given by $y = a\sin 2\pi(bt - cx)$, where a, b, c are constants. The maximum particle velocity will be twice the wave velocity, if **[MHT CET]**

(a) $b = ac$ (b) $b = \frac{1}{ac}$

(c) $c = \pi a$ (d) $c = \frac{1}{\pi a}$

2 The displacement y of a particle in a medium can be expressed as $y = 10^{-6}\sin\left(100t + 20x + \frac{\pi}{4}\right)$, where t is in second and x in metre. The speed of the wave is **[UK PMT]**

(a) 2000 m/s (b) 5 m/s
(c) 20 m/s (d) 5π m/s

2013

3 A wave travelling in the positive x-direction having displacement along y-direction 1 m, wavelength 2π m and frequency of $(1/\pi)$ Hz is represented by **[NEET]**

(a) $y = \sin(x - 2t)$ (b) $y = \sin(2\pi x - 2\pi t)$
(c) $y = \sin(10\pi x - 20\pi t)$ (d) $y = \sin(2\pi x + 2\pi t)$

4 A wave pulse in a thin string is incident on a thick string as shown in the figure. If joint is at P, then the form of reflected and transmitted pulses is **[AIIMS]**

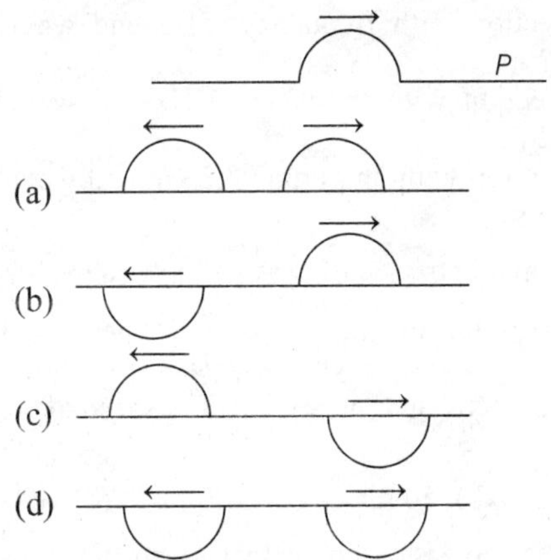

5 Which of the following equations represents a wave travelling along Y-axis? **[KCET]**

(a) $y = A\sin(kx - \omega t)$
(b) $x = A\sin(ky - \omega t)$
(c) $y = A\sin ky \cos \omega t$
(d) $y = A\cos ky \sin \omega t$

2012

6 A progressive wave moving along x-axis is represented by $y = A\sin\left[\frac{2\pi}{\lambda}(vt - x)\right]$. The wavelengths (λ) at which the maximum particle velocity is 3 times, the wave velocity is **[WB JEE]**

(a) $\frac{A}{3}$ (b) $\frac{2A}{3\pi}$ (c) $\left(\frac{3}{4}\right)\pi A$ (d) $\left(\frac{2}{3}\right)\pi A$

7 The equation of a simple harmonic progressive wave is given by $y = A\sin(100\pi t - 3x)$. Find the distance between 2 particles having a phase difference of $\frac{\pi}{3}$. **[MHT CET]**

(a) $\frac{\pi}{9}$ m (b) $\frac{\pi}{18}$ m (c) $\frac{\pi}{6}$ m (d) $\frac{\pi}{3}$ m

8 In sine wave, minimum distance between 2 particles always having same speed is **[MHT CET]**

(a) $\frac{\lambda}{2}$ (b) $\frac{\lambda}{4}$ (c) $\frac{\lambda}{3}$ (d) λ

9 A wave equation which gives the displacement along the direction is given by $y = 0.001\sin(100t + x)$, where x and y are in metre and t is in second. This equation represents a wave **[Manipal]**

(a) travelling with a velocity of 100 m/s in the negative x-direction
(b) travelling with a velocity of $50/\pi$ m/s in the positive x-direction
(c) of wavelength 1 m
(d) of frequency $\frac{100}{\pi}$ Hz

10 The equation of longitudinal wave represented as $y = 20\cos\pi(50t - x)$ cm, then its wavelength is **[Manipal]**

(a) 120 cm (b) 50 cm (c) 2 cm (d) 5 cm

2011

11 A man stands in a narrow, steep-sided valley. When he shouts, he hears two echoes, one after 1 s and other after 2 s. If the velocity of sound in air is 330 m/s, the width of the valley is **[MGIMS]**

(a) 330 m (b) 495 m (c) 660 m (d) 990 m

2009

12 Angle between wave velocity and particle velocity of a transverse wave is **[OJEE]**

(a) 90° (b) 60° (c) 0° (d) 120°

13 A wave motion is described by $y(x, t) = a\sin(kx - \omega t)$. Then, the ratio of the maximum particle velocity to the wave velocity is [WB JEE]

(a) ka (b) $\frac{\omega}{k}$ (c) $\frac{d\omega}{dk}$ (d) $\frac{x}{l}$

14 A longitudinal wave is represented by $x = x_0 \sin 2\pi(nt - x/\lambda)$. The maximum particle velocity will be four times the wave velocity, if [WB JEE]

(a) $\lambda = \frac{\pi x_0}{4}$ (b) $\lambda = 2\pi x_0$ (c) $\lambda = \frac{\pi x_0}{2}$ (d) $\lambda = 4\pi x_0$

15 The equation of a progressive wave is $y = 4\sin(4\pi t - 0.04 + \pi/3)$, where x is in metre and t is in second. The velocity of the wave is [WB JEE]

(a) 100π m/s (b) 50π m/s (c) 25π m/s (d) π m/s

16 In the case of a travelling wave, the reflection at a rigid boundary will take place with a phase change of [J&K CET]

(a) $\frac{\pi}{2}$ rad (b) $\frac{\pi}{4}$ rad (c) π rad (d) $\frac{\pi}{6}$ rad

17 Equation of a progressive wave is given by $y = 0.2\cos\pi\left(0.04t + 0.02x - \frac{\pi}{6}\right)$. The distance is expressed in cm and time in second. What will be the minimum distance between two particles having the phase difference of $\pi/2$? [VMMC]

(a) 4 cm (b) 8 cm (c) 25 cm (d) 12.5 cm

18 Two points on a travelling wave having frequency 500 Hz and velocity 300 m/s are 60° out of phase, then the minimum distance between the two points is [VMMC]

(a) 0.2 (b) 0.1 (c) 0.5 (d) 0.4

19 The longitudinal wave can be observed in [DUMET]

(a) elastic media (b) inelastic media
(c) Both (a) and (b) (d) None of these

20 A wave equation which gives the displacement along y-direction is given by $y = 10^{-4}\sin(60t + x)$, where x and y are in metre and t is time in second. This represents a wave [AIIMS]

(a) travelling with a velocity of 300 ms^{-1} in the –ve x-direction
(b) of wavelength π metre
(c) of frequency $\frac{30}{\pi}$ Hz
(d) of amplitude 10^4 m travelling along the positive x-direction

21 The equation of a wave is $y = 5\sin\left(\frac{t}{0.04} - \frac{x}{4}\right)$, where x is in cm and t is in second. The maximum velocity of the wave will be [JIPMER]

(a) 1 ms^{-1} (b) 2 ms^{-1} (c) 1.5 ms^{-1} (d) 1.25 ms^{-1}

22 $y = 3\sin\pi\left(\frac{t}{2} - \frac{x}{4}\right)$ represents an equation of a progressive wave, where t is in second and x is in metre. The distance travelled by the wave in 5 s is [KCET]

(a) 8 m (b) 10 m (c) 5 m (d) 32 m

23 The equation of a wave travelling on a string is $y = 4\sin\left[\frac{\pi}{2}\left(8t - \frac{x}{8}\right)\right]$, where x, y are in cm and t is in second. The velocity of the wave is [VMMC]

(a) 64 cm/s in $-x$-direction (b) 32 cm/s in $-x$-direction
(c) 32 cm/s in $+x$-direction (d) 64 cm/s in $+x$-direction

24 The equation $y = 4 + 2\sin(6t - 3x)$ represents a wave motion, then wave speed and amplitude, respectively are [AIIMS]

(a) wave speed 1 unit, amplitude 6 units
(b) wave speed 2 units, amplitude 2 units
(c) wave speed 4 units, amplitude 1/2 unit
(d) wave speed 1/2 unit, amplitude 5 units

25 The path difference between the two waves $y_1 = a_1\sin\left(\omega t - \frac{2\pi x}{\lambda}\right)$ and $y_2 = a_2\cos\left(\omega t - \frac{2\pi x}{\lambda} + \phi\right)$ is [Manipal]

(a) $\frac{\lambda}{2\pi}\phi$ (b) $\frac{\lambda}{2\pi}\left(\phi + \frac{\pi}{2}\right)$
(c) $\frac{2\pi}{\lambda}\left(\phi - \frac{\pi}{2}\right)$ (d) $\frac{2\pi}{\lambda}\phi$

2008

26 The wave described by $y = 0.25\sin(10\pi x - 2\pi t)$, where x and y are in metre and t in second, is a wave travelling along the [CBSE AIPMT]

(a) $-x$-direction with frequency 1 Hz
(b) $+x$-direction with frequency π Hz and wavelength $\lambda = 0.2$ m
(c) $+x$-direction with frequency 1 Hz and wavelength $\lambda = 0.2$ m
(d) $-x$-direction with amplitude 0.25 m and wavelength $\lambda = 0.2$ m

27 The equation of a transverse wave on a stretched string is given by $y = 0.05\sin 2\pi\left(\frac{t}{0.002} - \frac{x}{0.1}\right)$, where x and y are expressed in metre and t in second. The speed of the wave is [EAMCET]

(a) 100 ms^{-1} (b) 50 ms^{-1} (c) 200 ms^{-1} (d) 400 ms^{-1}

28 A transverse wave is described by the equation $y = y_0\sin 2\pi\left(ft - \frac{X}{\lambda}\right)$. The maximum particle velocity is equal to four times the wave velocity, if [MH CET]

(a) $\lambda = \frac{\pi y_0}{4}$ (b) $\lambda = \frac{\pi y_0}{2}$
(c) $\lambda = \pi y_0$ (d) $\lambda = 2\pi y_0$

29 In a sinusoidal wave, the time required for a particular point to move from maximum displacement to zero displacement is 0.17 s. The frequency of the wave is **[Manipal]**

(a) 1.47 Hz (b) 0.36 Hz (c) 0.73 Hz (d) 2.94 Hz

30 A transverse wave propagating along x-axis is represented by $y(x,t) = 8\sin\left(0.5\pi x - 4\pi t - \frac{\pi}{4}\right)$ where, x is in metre and t is in second. The speed of the wave is **[Haryana PMT]**

(a) 4π ms^{-1} (b) 0.5π ms^{-1} (c) $\frac{\pi}{4}$ ms^{-1} (d) 8 ms^{-1}

31 Pressure variation in a mechanical wave depends upon as **[DUMET]**

(a) $\propto$ (intensity)$^{1/2}$ (b) independent of intensity

(c) $\propto \frac{1}{\text{intensity}}$ (d) None of these

32 The equation of a simple harmonic wave is given by $y = 6\sin 2\pi(2t - 0.1x)$, where x and y are in mm and t is in seconds. The phase difference between two particles 2 mm apart at any instant is **[KCET]**

(a) 18° (b) 36° (c) 54° (d) 72°

2007

33 The power of a sound from the speaker of a radio is 20 mW. By turning the knob of the volume control, the power of the sound is increased to 400 mW. The power increase in decibels as compared to the original power is **[Punjab PMET]**

(a) 13 dB (b) 10 dB

(c) 20 dB (d) 800 dB

34 Three progressive waves A, B and C are shown in the figure. **[UP CPMT]**

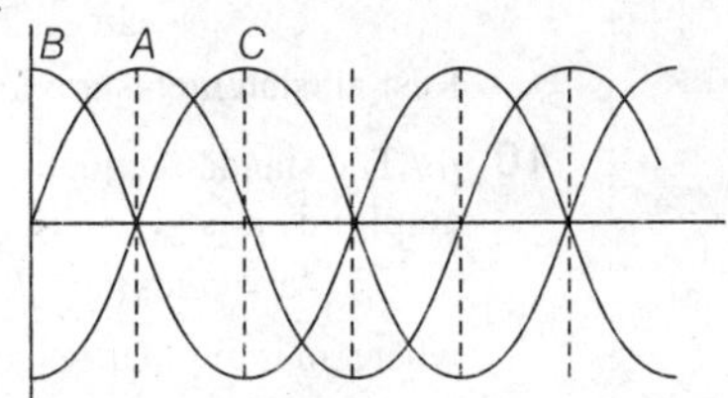

With respect to A, the progressive wave

(a) B lags by $\frac{\pi}{2}$ and C leads by $\frac{\pi}{2}$

(b) B lags by π and C leads by π

(c) B leads by $\frac{\pi}{2}$ and C lags by $\frac{\pi}{2}$

(d) B leads by π and C lags by π

35 The phase difference between two waves represented by

$$y_1 = 10^{-6}\sin[100t + (x/50) + 0.5]\,\text{m}$$

and $$y_2 = 10^{-6}\cos[100t + (x/50)]\,\text{m}$$

where x is expressed in metre and t is expressed in second, is approximately **[Manipal]**

(a) 1.07 rad (b) 2.07 rad (c) 0.5 rad (d) 1.5 rad

36 Two waves are given by $y_1 = \cos(4t - 2x)$ and $y_2 = \sin\left(4t - 2x + \frac{\pi}{4}\right)$. The phase difference between the two waves is **[Kerala CEE]**

(a) $\frac{\pi}{4}$ (b) $\frac{-\pi}{4}$ (c) $\frac{3\pi}{4}$ (d) $\frac{\pi}{2}$ (e) $\frac{3\pi}{2}$

37 Which of the following expressions is that of a simple harmonic progressive wave? **[MP PMT]**

(a) $a\sin\omega t$ (b) $a\sin\omega t\cos kx$

(c) $a\sin(\omega t - kx)$ (d) $a\cos kx$

38 The maximum particle velocity in a wave motion is half the wave velocity. Then, the amplitude of the wave is equal to **[KCET]**

(a) $\frac{\lambda}{4\pi}$ (b) $\frac{2\lambda}{\pi}$ (c) $\frac{\lambda}{2\pi}$ (d) λ

2006

39 A point source emits sound equally in all directions in a non-absorbing medium. Two points P and Q are at distance of 2 m and 3 m respectively from the source. The ratio of the intensities of the waves at P and Q is **[AIIMS]**

(a) 9 : 4 (b) 2 : 3 (c) 3 : 2 (d) 4 : 9

40 The distance between two points differing in phase by 60° on a wave having wave velocity 360 ms^{-1} and frequency 500 Hz is **[KCFET]**

(a) 0.36 m (b) 0.18 m (c) 0.48 m (d) 0.12 m

41 If the equation of a progressive wave is given as $y = a\sin\pi\left[\frac{t}{2} - \frac{x}{4}\right]$, where x is in metre and t is in second, then the distance through which the wave moves in 8 s is

(a) 2 m (b) 16 m (c) 4 m (d) 8 m **[RPMT]**

42 When a wave travels in a medium, particles displacement is given by the equation $y = 0.03\sin\pi(2t - 0.01x)$, where x and y are in metre and t is in second. The wavelength of the wave is **[RPMT]**

(a) 200 m (b) 100 m (c) 20 m (d) 10 m

43 Equation of progressive wave is **[J&K CET]**

$$y = A\sin\left(10\pi x + 11\pi t + \frac{\pi}{3}\right),$$

(a) its wavelength is 0.2 units

(b) it is travelling in the positive x-direction

(c) wave velocity is 1.5 units

(d) time period of SHM is 1 s

44 A wave equation is given by $y = 4\sin\left[\pi\left(\frac{t}{5} - \frac{x}{9} + \frac{1}{6}\right)\right]$, where x is in centimetre and t is in second. Which of the following is true? **[DUMET]**

(a) $\lambda = 18$ cm (b) $v = 4$ ms^{-1}

(c) $a = 0.4$ m (d) $f = 50$ Hz

Answers

1 (d)	2 (b)	3 (a)	4 (b)	5 (b)	6 (d)	7 (a)	8 (a)	9 (a)	10 (c)
11 (b)	12 (a)	13 (a)	14 (c)	15 (a)	16 (c)	17 (c)	18 (b)	19 (a)	20 (c)
21 (d)	22 (b)	23 (d)	24 (b)	25 (b)	26 (c)	27 (b)	28 (b)	29 (a)	30 (d)
31 (a)	32 (d)	33 (a)	34 (c)	35 (a)	36 (b)	37 (c)	38 (a)	39 (a)	40 (d)
41 (b)	42 (a)	43 (a)	44 (a)						

Explanations

1 *(d)* Given, $y = a \sin 2\pi\,(bt - cx)$

On comparing with general equation

$$y = r \sin\left[\frac{2\pi t}{T} - \frac{2\pi}{\lambda}x\right], \text{ we get}$$

$$\frac{2\pi}{T} = \omega = 2\pi b \Rightarrow T = \frac{1}{b}$$

$$r = a \text{ and } \lambda = \frac{1}{c}$$

Maximum particle velocity, $\omega r = 2\pi ba$

Wave velocity, $v = \frac{\lambda}{T} = \frac{b}{c}$

Given, maximum particle velocity $= 2 \times$ wave velocity

$$2\pi ba = 2 \times \frac{b}{c} \Rightarrow c = \frac{1}{\pi a}$$

2 *(b)* The displacement is given by

$$y = 10^{-6} \sin\left(100t + 20x + \frac{\pi}{4}\right)$$

Comparing with standard equation,

$$y = a \sin(\omega t + kx + \phi)$$

$$\omega = 100 \text{ rad s}^{-1}, k = 20$$

where, ω is angular frequency and k is angular wave number

Now, $k = \frac{2\pi}{\lambda} = \frac{2\pi v}{\lambda v} = \frac{\omega}{v} = 20$

$$\Rightarrow \quad v = \frac{\omega}{20} = \frac{100}{20} = 5 \text{ m/s}$$

So, the speed of the wave is 5 m/s.

3 *(a)* Given, $a = 1$ m, $\lambda = 2\pi$ and $f = (1/\pi)$Hz

We know, $k = \frac{2\pi}{\lambda}$ and $\omega = 2\pi f$

As, $y = a \sin(kx - \omega t)$

$$= \sin\left(\frac{2\pi}{2\pi} \times x - 2\pi \times \frac{1}{\pi}t\right)$$

$$= \sin(x - 2t)$$

4 *(b)* The reflected and transmitted pulses are rightly shown in Fig. (b).

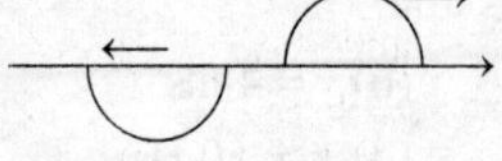

5 *(b)* The given equation is

$$x = A \sin(ky - \omega t)$$

which represents a wave travelling along Y-axis, where A is its amplitude.

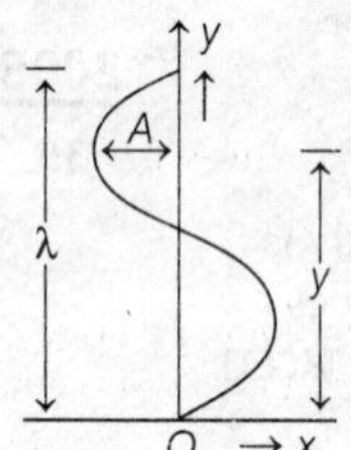

6 *(d)* Progressive wave,

$$y = A \sin\left[\frac{2\pi}{\lambda}(vt - x)\right]$$

Particle velocity, $(v_p)_{\max} = \frac{2\pi v}{\lambda} A$

According to question,

$$(v_p)_{\max} = 3v = \frac{2\pi v}{\lambda} A \Rightarrow \lambda = \frac{2\pi}{3} A$$

7 *(a)* Given, $y = A \sin(100\pi t - 3x)$

The general equation,

$$y = A \sin(\omega t - kx)$$

$$\therefore \quad k = 3$$

and $k = \frac{2\pi}{\lambda}$ or $\lambda = \frac{2\pi}{k} = \frac{2\pi}{3}$

Phase difference, $\phi = \frac{\pi}{3}$

$$\Rightarrow \quad \frac{2\pi}{\lambda} \cdot x = \frac{\pi}{3}$$

$$\text{or} \quad x = \frac{\pi}{3} \times \frac{\lambda}{2\pi}$$

$$\Rightarrow \quad x = \frac{\pi}{3} \times \frac{2\pi}{3 \times 2\pi} = \frac{\pi}{9} \text{ m}$$

8 *(a)* The representation of sine wave is shown as below

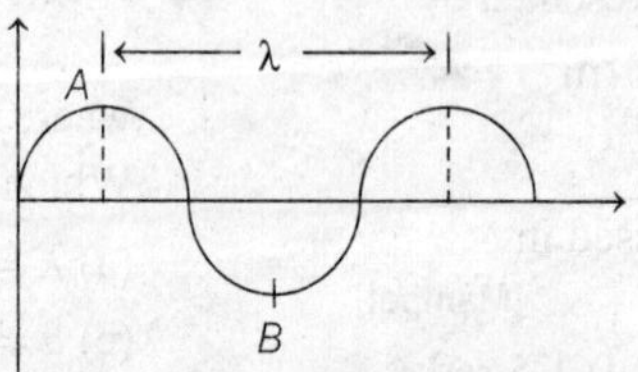

Particle velocity,

$$v_p = \frac{dy}{dt} = \text{slope of wave at that point.}$$

As slope at A and B is zero, hence, their velocities at A and B will be same. The distance between A and B is $\frac{\lambda}{2}$.

9 *(a)* The standard equation of a wave travelling with amplitude a in the negative x-direction with angular velocity ω is given by

$$y = a \sin(\omega t + kx) \quad \ldots(\text{i})$$

where, k is a wave number.

We compare the given equation with the standard equation, where $a = 0.001$ m, $\omega = 100 \text{ rads}^{-1}$ and $k = 1$

Velocity, $v = \frac{\omega}{k} = \frac{100}{1} = 100$ m/s

Wavelength, $\lambda = \frac{2\pi}{k} = \frac{2\pi}{1} = 2\pi$

Frequency, $\nu = \frac{\omega}{2\pi} = \frac{100}{2\pi}$

Rest all statements are incorrect.

10 *(c)* The standard equation of a wave of amplitude a is given by

$$y = a \cos(\omega t - kx) \quad \ldots(\text{i})$$

where, ω is angular velocity, k is the wave number and t is the time.

Comparing with given equation, we get $k = \pi$.

Wavelength, $\lambda = \frac{2\pi}{k} = \frac{2\pi}{\pi} = 2$ cm

11 *(b)* Let s_1 and s_2 be the distances of man from either side of valley, then

$$2s_1 = vt_1 \text{ and } 2s_2 = vt_2$$

$$\Rightarrow 2(s_1 + s_2) = v(t_1 + t_2)$$

$$\Rightarrow \quad s_1 + s_2 = \frac{v(t_1 + t_2)}{2}$$

$$\therefore \; d = s_1 + s_2 = \frac{330 \times (1 + 2)}{2}$$

$$\Rightarrow d = \frac{330 \times 3}{2} = 495 \text{ m}$$

12 *(a)* In a transverse wave, the particles of the medium vibrate about their mean positions in a direction perpendicular to the direction of wave propagation.

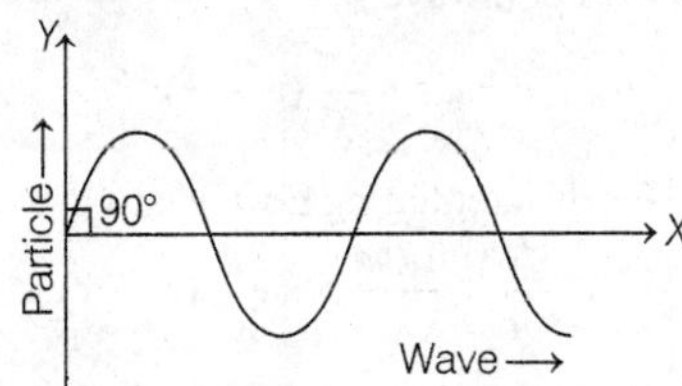

Here, the particle velocity is given by $\frac{dy}{dt}$ and wave velocity is given by $\frac{dx}{dt}$.

Hence, the angle between particle velocity and wave velocity in a transverse wave is $\frac{\pi}{2}$ or 90°.

13 *(a)* Maximum particle velocity

$(v_p)_{max} = a\omega$ and wave velocity, $v = \frac{\omega}{k}$

$\therefore$ Ratio $= \frac{(v_p)_{max}}{v} = \frac{a\omega k}{\omega} = ka$

14 *(c)* The longitudinal wave is given by

$$x = x_0 \sin[2\pi(nt - x/\lambda)]$$
$$= x_0 \sin\left(2\pi nt - \frac{2\pi}{\lambda}x\right)$$

Here, we compare the given equation with the equation

$$x = x_0 \sin(\omega t \pm kx)$$

The maximum particle velocity

$$= A\omega = x_0(2\pi n)$$

Wave velocity $= n\lambda$

From the question,

$$2\pi n x_0 = 4n\lambda \Rightarrow \lambda = \frac{\pi}{2}x_0$$

15 *(a)* The equation of the progressive wave is given as

$y = 4\sin(4\pi t - 0.04x + \pi/3)$.

The velocity of the wave would be equal to

$$v = \frac{\omega}{k} = \frac{4\pi}{0.04} = 100\pi \text{ m/s}$$

16 *(c)* In the case of travelling wave, the reflection at a rigid boundary will take place with a phase change of π rad.

17 *(c)* Comparing with

$y = a\cos(\omega t + kx - \phi)$,

we get $k = \frac{2\pi}{\lambda} = 0.02\pi$

$\Rightarrow \quad \lambda = 100$ cm

Also it is given that, phase difference between particles $\Delta\phi = \frac{\pi}{2}$.

Hence, path difference between them

$$\Delta x = \frac{\lambda}{2\pi} \times \Delta\phi = \frac{\lambda}{2\pi} \times \frac{\pi}{2} = \frac{\lambda}{4} = \frac{100}{4}$$
$$= 25 \text{ cm}$$

18 *(b)* As, $v = n\lambda$

$$\therefore \quad \lambda = \frac{v}{n} = \frac{300}{500} = \frac{3}{5} \text{ m}$$

Now, phase difference

$$= \frac{2\pi}{\lambda} \times \text{path difference}$$

$$\therefore \quad 60° = \frac{2\pi}{\lambda} \times \text{path difference}$$

$$\Rightarrow \frac{60° \times \pi}{180°} = \frac{2\pi \times 5}{3} \times \text{path difference}$$

$$\Rightarrow \text{Path difference} = \frac{3 \times 60° \times \pi}{2\pi \times 5 \times 180°} = 0.1$$

19 *(a)* The longitudinal wave can be observed in elastic media. Because elasticity in necessary for propagation, i.e. in order to make the particles return to their original position after getting disturbed, the medium must possess elasticity.

20 *(c)* Angular velocity, $\omega = 2\pi f$

or $\quad 60 = 2\pi f$

$\therefore$ Frequency, $f = \frac{30}{\pi}$ Hz

21 *(d)* Given, equation of wave,

$$y = 5\sin\left(\frac{t}{0.04} - \frac{x}{4}\right)$$

The standard equation of a wave in the given form is

$$y = a\sin\left(\omega t - \frac{2\pi x}{\lambda}\right)$$

Comparing the given equation with the standard equation, we get

$$a = 5 \text{ and } \omega = \frac{1}{0.04} = 25$$

Therefore, maximum velocity of particles of the medium,

$$v_{max} = a\omega = 5 \times 25 = 125 \text{ cms}^{-1}$$
$$= 1.25 \text{ ms}^{-1}$$

22 *(b)* $y = 3\sin\pi\left(\frac{t}{2} - \frac{x}{4}\right)$

$$\Rightarrow y = 3\sin 2\pi\left(\frac{t}{4} - \frac{x}{8}\right)$$

Comparing with

$y = A\sin 2\pi\left(\frac{t}{T} - \frac{x}{\lambda}\right)$, we get

$$\frac{1}{T} = \frac{1}{4} \Rightarrow v = \frac{1}{4}$$

and $\frac{1}{\lambda} = \frac{1}{8} \Rightarrow \lambda = 8$

Now, velocity of wave

$$= v\lambda = \frac{1}{4} \times 8 = 2 \text{ m/s}$$

$\therefore$ Distance travelled by the wave in 5s

$$= 5 \times 2 = 10 \text{ m}$$

23 *(d)* Given, $y = 4\sin\left(4\pi t - \frac{\pi x}{16}\right)$

where, $\omega = 4\pi$ and $k = \frac{\pi}{16}$

$$\therefore \quad v = \frac{\omega}{k} = \frac{4\pi}{\frac{\pi}{16}} = 64 \text{ cm/s}$$

(in +x-direction)

24 *(b)* The shape of the wave is shown in the figure

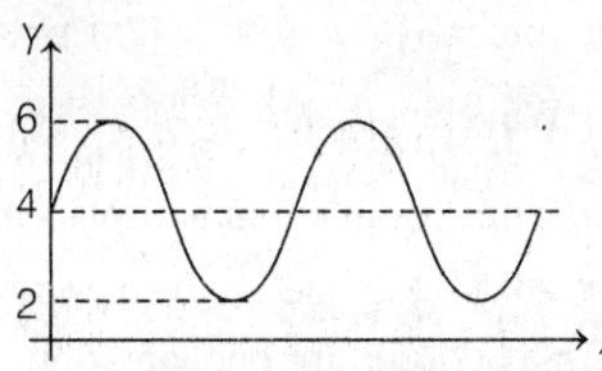

From this graph, we see that amplitude of wave is 2 units.

Wave speed,

$$v = \frac{\text{Coefficient of } t}{\text{Coefficient of } x} = \frac{6}{3} = 2 \text{ units}$$

25 *(b)* Here,

$$y_1 = a_1\sin\left(\omega t - \frac{2\pi}{\lambda}x\right) \quad \text{...(i)}$$

and $y_2 = a_2\cos\left(\omega t - \frac{2\pi x}{\lambda} + \phi\right)$

$$\Rightarrow \quad y_2 = a_2\sin\left(\omega t - \frac{2\pi x}{\lambda} + \phi + \frac{\pi}{2}\right) \quad \text{...(ii)}$$

From Eqs. (i) and (ii), we get the phase difference between two waves is

$$\phi = \phi + \frac{\pi}{2}$$

Now, phase difference

$$= \frac{2\pi}{\lambda} \times (\text{path difference})$$

$\Rightarrow$ Path difference

$$= \frac{\lambda}{2\pi} \times (\text{phase difference})$$

$$\Rightarrow \text{Path difference} = \frac{\lambda}{2\pi}\left(\phi + \frac{\pi}{2}\right)$$

26 *(c)* Writing the given wave equation,

$$y = 0.25\sin(10\pi x - 2\pi t) \quad \text{...(i)}$$

The minus (–) between ($10\pi x$) and ($2\pi t$) implies that the wave is travelling along positive x-direction.

Now, comparing Eq. (i) with standard wave equation

$$y = a\sin(kx - \omega t) \quad \text{...(ii)}$$

We have

$$a = 0.25\text{ m}, \omega = 2\pi,\ k = 10\pi\text{ m}$$

$\therefore \quad \frac{2\pi}{T} = 2\pi \Rightarrow f = 1\text{ Hz}$

Also, $\lambda = \frac{2\pi}{k} = \frac{2\pi}{10\pi} = 0.2\text{ m}$

Therefore, the wave is travelling along positive x-direction with frequency 1 Hz and wavelength 0.2 m.

27 *(b)* Speed of wave

$$= \frac{\text{Coefficient of } t}{\text{Coefficient of } x} = \frac{\frac{2\pi}{0.002}}{\frac{2\pi}{0.1}} = 50\text{ ms}^{-1}$$

28 *(b)* We have, $(v_P)_{max} = 4v$

or $y_0\omega = 4(f\lambda)$ or $y_0(2\pi f) = 4f\lambda$

$\therefore$ Wavelength, $\lambda = \frac{\pi y_0}{2}$

29 *(a)* Time for maximum displacement,

$t = 0.17$ s

Time period T for one vibration

$= 4t = 4 \times 0.17 = 0.68$ s

$$\text{Frequency} = \frac{1}{\text{Time period }(T)}$$

$$= \frac{1}{0.68} = 1.47\text{ Hz}$$

30 *(d)* The given equation is

$$y(x, t) = 8.0 \sin\left(0.5\pi x - 4\pi t - \frac{\pi}{4}\right) \quad \ldots(i)$$

The standard wave equation can be written as

$$y = a\sin(kx - \omega t + \phi) \quad \ldots(ii)$$

Comparing the Eqs. (i) and (ii), we have

$k = 0.5\pi, \omega = 4\pi$

$\therefore$ Speed of transverse wave,

$$v = \frac{\omega}{k} = \frac{4\pi}{0.5\pi} = 8\text{ ms}^{-1}$$

31 *(a)* Amplitude of pressure variation,

$$p_m = BkA$$

and intensity of wave, $I \propto A^2$

So, $\quad p_m \propto (I)^{1/2}$

i.e. Pressure variation $\propto$ (Intensity)$^{1/2}$

32 *(d)* From the given equation, $k = 0.2\pi$

$\Rightarrow \quad \frac{2\pi}{\lambda} = 0.2\pi \Rightarrow \lambda = 10$ mm

$$\Delta\phi = \frac{2\pi}{\lambda}\Delta x = \frac{2\pi}{10} \times 2$$

$$= \frac{2\pi}{5} = \frac{2 \times 180°}{5} = 72°$$

33 *(a)* We know that, $P \propto I$

$$\Rightarrow \quad \frac{P_1}{P_2} = \frac{I_1}{I_2} \quad \ldots(i)$$

$\therefore \quad L_1 = 10\log_{10}\left(\frac{I_1}{I_0}\right)$

and $\quad L_2 = 10\log_{10}\left(\frac{I_2}{I_0}\right)$

So, $L_2 - L_1 = 10\log_{10}\left(\frac{I_2}{I_1}\right)$

$= 10\log_{10}\left(\frac{P_2}{P_1}\right)$ [from Eq. (i)]

$= 10\log_{10}\left(\frac{400}{20}\right)$

$= 10\log_{10} 20 = 13$ dB

34 *(c)* Equations of waves A, B and C are respectively

$$y_A = A\sin\omega t,\ y_B = A\sin\left(\omega t + \frac{\pi}{2}\right)$$

and $y_C = A\sin\left(\omega t - \frac{\pi}{2}\right)$

Therefore, w.r.t. A, the progressive wave B leads by $\frac{\pi}{2}$ and C lags by $\frac{\pi}{2}$.

35 *(a)* The given waves equations are

$y_1 = 10^{-6}\sin[100t + (x/50) + 0.5]$ m

and $y_2 = 10^{-6}\cos[100t + (x/50)]$m

$\Rightarrow y_2 = 10^{-6}\sin\left[100t + (x/50) + \frac{\pi}{2}\right]$m

$$\left[\because \sin\left(\frac{\pi}{2} + \theta\right) = \cos\theta\right]$$

Hence, the phase difference between the waves is

$$\Delta\phi = \left(\frac{\pi}{2} - 0.5\right)\text{rad} = \left(\frac{3.14}{2} - 0.5\right)\text{rad}$$

$$= (1.57 - 0.5)\text{ rad} = 1.07\text{ rad}$$

36 *(b)* Equations of waves,

$$y_1 = \cos(4t - 2x) = \sin\left(4t - 2x + \frac{\pi}{2}\right)$$

and $\quad y_2 = \sin\left(4t - 2x + \frac{\pi}{4}\right)$

Therefore, phase difference between the two waves is

$$\Delta\phi = \left(4t - 2x + \frac{\pi}{4}\right) - \left(4t - 2x + \frac{\pi}{2}\right)$$

$$= \frac{\pi}{4} - \frac{\pi}{2} = -\frac{\pi}{4}$$

37 *(c)* General equation of wave motion should be represented by

$$y = f(ax \pm bt) \text{ or } f(at \pm bx)$$

When y is a sine or cosine function such as

$$y = a\sin(\omega t - kx)$$

or $\quad y = a\cos(\omega t - kx)$

It is called simple harmonic progressive wave.

38 *(a)* For a wave,

$$y = a\sin\frac{2\pi}{\lambda}(vt - x) \quad \ldots(i)$$

On differentiating Eq. (i) w.r.t. t, we get

$$\frac{dy}{dt} = \frac{2\pi va}{\lambda}\cos\frac{2\pi}{\lambda}(vt - x)$$

Now, maximum velocity is obtained, when $\cos\frac{2\pi}{\lambda}(vt - x) = 1$

$$\therefore \quad v_{max} = \left(\frac{dy}{dt}\right)_{max} = \frac{2\pi va}{\lambda}$$

But $\quad v_{max} = \frac{v}{2}$ (given)

$\Rightarrow \quad \frac{v}{2} = \frac{2\pi va}{\lambda}$

$\Rightarrow \quad a = \frac{\lambda}{4\pi}$

39 *(a)* The average power per unit area that is incident perpendicular to the direction of propagation is called the intensity, i.e.

$$I = \frac{P}{4\pi r^2} \Rightarrow I \propto \frac{1}{r^2}$$

$$\Rightarrow \quad \frac{I_1}{I_2} = \left(\frac{r_2}{r_1}\right)^2$$

Here, $r_1 = 2$ m, $r_2 = 3$ m

$$\therefore \quad \frac{I_1}{I_2} = \left(\frac{3}{2}\right)^2 = \frac{9}{4} = 9:4$$

40 *(d)* Phase angle, $\Delta\phi = \frac{2\pi}{\lambda}\cdot\Delta x$

The distance between two points,

$$\Delta x = \frac{(\Delta\phi)(\lambda)}{2\pi} = \frac{(\Delta\phi)(v/f)}{2\pi}$$

$$= \frac{(\pi/3)(360/500)}{2\pi} = 0.12\text{ m}$$

41 *(b)* Given, $y = a\sin\pi\left[\frac{t}{2} - \frac{x}{4}\right]$

Comparing it with standard equation,

$$y = a\sin\pi\left[\frac{2t}{T} - \frac{2x}{vT}\right]$$

$\Rightarrow \quad \frac{2}{T} = \frac{1}{2}$ or $T = 4$ s

and $\quad \frac{2}{vT} = \frac{1}{4}$

$\Rightarrow \quad v = \frac{8}{T} = \frac{8}{4} = 2\text{ ms}^{-1}$

So, distance travelled by wave in 8 s

$= v \times t = 2 \times 8 = 16$ m

42 (a) Here, displacement equation is

$$y = 0.03 \sin \pi (2t - 0.01x) \quad \ldots\text{(i)}$$

The standard equation is

$$y = a \sin 2\pi \left(\frac{t}{T} - \frac{x}{\lambda}\right) \quad \ldots\text{(ii)}$$

Comparing the given Eq. (i) with standard Eq. (ii), we have

$$\frac{2}{\lambda} = 0.01$$

or $\lambda = \frac{2}{0.01}$

$= 200$ m

43 (a) The standard equation is

$$y = a \sin 2\pi \left(\frac{t}{T} - \frac{x}{\lambda} + \phi\right) \quad \ldots\text{(i)}$$

Dividing and multiplying the given equation by 2π, we get

$$y = a \sin 2\pi \left(\frac{10}{2}x + \frac{11}{2}t + 1/6\right) \ldots\text{(ii)}$$

On comparing Eqs. (i) and (ii), we get

$\lambda = 2/10 = 0.2$ units

44 (a) The given equation will be written as

$$y = 4 \sin\left[\pi\left(\frac{t}{5} - \frac{x}{9} + \frac{1}{6}\right)\right] \quad \ldots\text{(i)}$$

The standard wave equation can be written as

$$y = a \sin (\omega t - kx + \phi)$$

$$\Rightarrow y = a \sin\left(\frac{2\pi}{T}t - \frac{2\pi}{\lambda}\cdot x + \phi\right) \ldots\text{(ii)}$$

Comparing Eqs. (i) and (ii), we get

Amplitude, $a = 4$ cm $= 0.04$ m

Frequency, $f = \frac{1}{T} = \frac{1}{10}$ Hz $= 0.1$ Hz

Wavelength, $\lambda = 2 \times 9 = 18$ cm

Velocity, $v = f\lambda$

$= 0.1 \times 18 = 1.8 \text{ cm s}^{-1}$

Topic 3

Interference and Superposition of Waves

2014

1 Sound waves are passing through two routes-one in straight path and the other along a semi-circular path of radius r and are again combined into one pipe and superposed as shown in the figure. If the velocity of sound waves in the pipe is v, then frequencies of resultant waves of maximum amplitude will be multiples integral of **[WB JEE]**

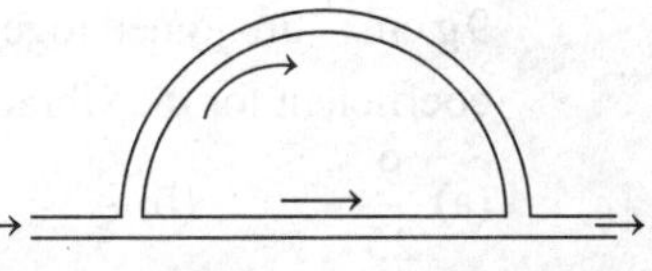

(a) $\frac{v}{r(\pi - 2)}$ (b) $\frac{v}{r(v-1)}$

(c) $\frac{2v}{r(\pi - 1)}$ (d) $\frac{v}{r(\pi + 1)}$

2013

2 Two waves having the intensities in the ratio of 9 : 1 produce interference. The ratio of maximum to minimum intensity is equal to **[UP CPMT]**

(a) 10 : 8 (b) 9 : 1 (c) 4 : 1 (d) 2 : 1

3 **Assertion** It is not possible to have interference between the waves produced by two violins.

Reason For interference of two waves, the phase difference between the waves must remain constant. **[AIIMS]**

(a) Both Assertion and Reason are correct and Reason is the correct explanation of Assertion

(b) Both Assertion and Reason are correct but Reason is not the correct explanation of Assertion

(c) Assertion is correct but Reason is incorrect

(d) Assertion is incorrect but Reason is correct

2011

4 Two waves are represented by the equations $y_1 = a \sin (\omega t + kx + 0.57)$ m and $y_2 = a \cos (\omega t + kx)$ m, where x is in metre and t is in second. The phase difference between them is **[CBSE AIPMT]**

(a) 1.25 rad (b) 1.57 rad (c) 0.57 rad (d) 1.0 rad

5 Two sound waves travel in the same direction in a medium. The amplitude of each wave is A and the phase difference between the two waves is 120°. The resultant amplitude will be **[Kerala CEE]**

(a) $\sqrt{2}A$ (b) $2A$ (c) $3A$ (d) $4A$

(e) A

6 A plane progressive wave is given by

$$y = 2\cos 6.284(330t - x).$$

What is period of the wave? **[WB JEE]**

(a) $\frac{1}{330}$ s (b) $2\pi \times 330$ s

(c) $(2\pi \times 330)^{-1}$ s (d) $\frac{6.284}{330}$ s

2010

7 Two waves $y_1 = A_1 \sin (\omega t - \beta_1)$ and $y_2 = A_2 \sin (\omega t - \beta_2)$ superimpose to form a resultant wave, whose amplitude is **[UP CPMT]**

(a) $\sqrt{A_1^2 + A_2^2 + 2A_1A_2 \cos (\beta_1 - \beta_2)}$

(b) $\sqrt{A_1^2 + A_2^2 + 2A_1A_2 \sin (\beta_1 - \beta_2)}$

(c) $A_1 + A_2$

(d) $|A_1 + A_2|$

8 Two waves are passing through a region in the same direction at the same time. If the equations of these waves are $y_1 = a\sin\frac{2\pi}{\lambda}(vt - x)$ and $y_2 = b\sin\frac{2\pi}{\lambda}[(vt - x) + x_0]$, then the amplitude of the resulting wave for $x_0 = (\lambda/2)$ is [Manipal]

(a) $|a - b|$ (b) $a + b$
(c) $\sqrt{a^2 + b^2}$ (d) $\sqrt{a^2 + b^2 + 2ab\cos x}$

9 Two sound waves, each of amplitude A and frequency ω, superpose at a point with phase difference of $\frac{\pi}{2}$. The amplitude and frequency of the resultant wave are respectively [BCECE]

(a) $\frac{A}{\sqrt{2}}, \frac{\omega}{2}$ (b) $\frac{A}{\sqrt{2}}, \omega$ (c) $\sqrt{2}A, \frac{\omega}{2}$ (d) $\sqrt{2}A, \omega$

10 Two coherent sources of different intensities sound waves which interfere. The ratio of maximum intensity to the minimum intensity is 25. The intensities of the sources are in the ratio [JCECE]

(a) 25 : 1 (b) 5 : 1 (c) 9 : 4 (d) 25 : 16

2009

11 When a stationary wave is formed, then its frequency is [Manipal]

(a) same as that of the individual waves
(b) twice that of the individual waves
(c) half that of the individual waves
(d) $\sqrt{2}$ that of the individual waves

12 If the phase difference between two sound waves of wavelength λ is 60º, the corresponding path difference is [Kerala CEE]

(a) $\frac{\lambda}{6}$ (b) $\frac{\lambda}{2}$ (c) 2λ (d) $\frac{\lambda}{4}$
(e) $\frac{6}{\lambda}$

13 When two sinusoidal waves moving at right angle to each other superimpose, they produce [Haryana PMT, CG PMT]

(a) beats (b) interference
(c) stationary waves (d) Lissajous figure

14 Four light sources produce the following four waves

I. $y_1 = a\sin(\omega t + \phi_1)$ II. $y_2 = a\sin 2\omega t$
III. $y_3 = a'\sin(\omega t + \phi_2)$ IV. $y_4 = a'\sin(3\omega t + \phi)$

Superposition of which two waves give rise to interference? [EAMCET]

(a) I and II (b) II and III
(c) I and III (d) III and IV

2008

15 Two waves having intensities 25 : 9 produce interference. The ratio maximum to minimum intensity is equal to [AMU]

(a) 10 : 8 (b) 9 : 1
(c) 16 : 1 (d) 2 : 1

16 Two periodic waves of intensities I_1 and I_2 pass through a region at the same time in the same direction. The sum of the maximum and minimum intensities is [MHT CET]

(a) $I_1 + I_2$ (b) $(\sqrt{I_1} + \sqrt{I_2})^2$
(c) $(\sqrt{I_1} - \sqrt{I_2})^2$ (d) $2(I_1 + I_2)$

17 Ratio of intensities of two waves is given by 9 : 1, then the ratio of their amplitudes is [MP PMT]

(a) 9 : 1 (b) 1 : 9 (c) 3 : 1 (d) 2 : 1

2007

18 A pulse of a wave train travels along a stretched string and reaches the fixed end of the string. It will be reflected back with [MHT CET]

(a) a phase change of 180° with velocity reversed
(b) the same phase as the incident pulse with no reversal of velocity
(c) a phase change of 180° with no reversal of velocity
(d) the same phase as the incident pulse but with velocity reversed

2006

19 Two strings with mass per unit length of 25 g cm^{-1} and 9 g cm^{-1} are joined together in series. The reflection coefficient for the vibration waves are [MHT CET]

(a) $\frac{9}{25}$ (b) $\frac{3}{5}$ (c) $\frac{1}{16}$ (d) $\frac{9}{16}$

20 Two waves represented by the following equations, are travelling in the same medium

$$y_1 = 5\sin 2\pi(75t - 0.25x)$$
and
$$y_2 = 10\sin 2\pi(150t - 0.50x).$$

The intensity $\frac{I_2}{I_1}$ of two waves is [MP PMT]

(a) 8 : 1 (b) 2 : 1 (c) 4 : 1 (d) 16 : 1

21 A particle is executing two different simple harmonic motions, mutually perpendicular of different amplitudes and having phase difference of $\pi/2$. The path of the particle will be [RPMT]

(a) circular (b) straight line
(c) parabolic (d) elliptical

2005

22 The ratio of intensities of two waves is 16 : 9. If they produce interference, then the ratio of maximum and minimum will be [AFMC]

(a) 4 : 3 (b) 49 : 1 (c) 64 : 27 (d) 81 : 49

23 The phenomena arising due to the superposition of waves is/are [AMU]

(a) beats (b) stationary waves
(c) Lissajous figure (d) All of these

24 The two waves of the same frequency moving in the same direction given rise to **[DUMET]**
(a) beats (b) interference
(c) stationary waves (d) None of these

25 The displacement of a particle executing periodic motion is given by $y = 4\cos^2(t/2)\sin(1000t)$. This expression may be considered to be a result of superposition of **[BHU]**
(a) two waves (b) three waves
(c) four waves (d) five waves

26 Equations of motion in the same direction are given by

$$y_1 = 2a\sin(\omega t - kx)$$
and
$$y_2 = 2a\sin(\omega t - kx - \theta).$$

The amplitude of the medium particle will be **[Manipal]**
(a) $2a\cos\theta$ (b) $\sqrt{2a}\cos\theta$
(c) $4a\cos\frac{\theta}{2}$ (d) $\frac{\sqrt{2a}\cos\theta}{2}$

Answers

1 (a)	2 (c)	3 (a)	4 (d)	5 (e)	6 (a)	7 (a)	8 (a)	9 (d)	10 (c)
11 (c)	12 (a)	13 (d)	14 (c)	15 (c)	16 (d)	17 (c)	18 (c)	19 (c)	20 (c)
21 (d)	22 (b)	23 (d)	24 (b)	25 (b)	26 (c)				

Explanations

1 *(a)* Path difference $= (\pi r - 2r)$
$$= (\pi - 2)r = n\lambda$$
$$\Rightarrow \lambda = \frac{(\pi - 2)r}{n}$$

where, $v = f \times \lambda \Rightarrow f = \frac{v}{\lambda}$

f = frequency
$$\Rightarrow f = \left[\frac{v}{(\pi - 2)r}\right] n$$

So, frequency is multiple integral of $\left[\frac{v}{(\pi - 2)r}\right]$

2 *(c)* We have,
$$\frac{I_1}{I_2} = \frac{a_1^2}{a_2^2} = \frac{9}{1}$$
$$\Rightarrow \frac{a_1}{a_2} = \sqrt{\frac{9}{1}} \Rightarrow \frac{a_1}{a_2} = \frac{3}{1}$$

Then, $\frac{I_{max}}{I_{min}} = \frac{(a_1 + a_2)^2}{(a_1 - a_2)^2}$
$$= \frac{(3+1)^2}{(3-1)^2} = \frac{(4)^2}{(2)^2} = \frac{16}{4} = \frac{4}{1}$$

Then, $I_{max} : I_{min} = 4:1$

3 *(a)* Since, the initial phase difference between the two waves coming from different violins change, therefore the waves produced by two different violins do not interfere because two waves interfere only when the phase difference between them remains constant throughout.

4 *(d)* Given, $y_1 = a\sin(\omega t + kx + 0.57)$ m
and $y_2 = a\cos(\omega t + kx)$ m
$$\Rightarrow y_2 = a\sin\left(\frac{\pi}{2} + \omega t + kx\right) \text{ m}$$

Phase difference,
$$\Delta\phi = \phi_2 - \phi_1$$
$$= \frac{\pi}{2} - 0.57 = 1.57 - 0.57$$
$$= 1 \text{ rad}$$

5 *(e)* The resultant amplitude is
$$R = \sqrt{P^2 + Q^2 + 2PQ\cos\theta}$$

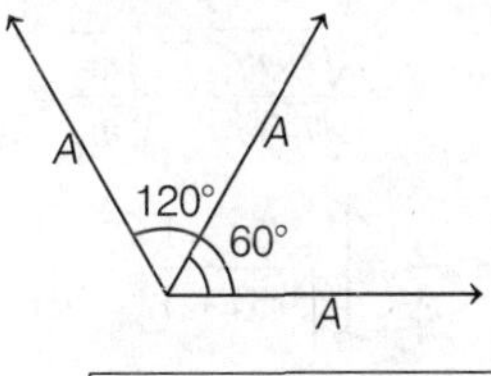

$$= \sqrt{A^2 + A^2 + 2A^2\cos 120^\circ} = A$$

6 *(a)* We have the progressive wave equation is given by
$$y = 2\cos 6.284\,(330t - x)$$
$$= 2\cos 2\pi\,(330t - x)$$
$$= 2\cos(2\pi \times 330\,t - 2\pi x)$$
$$\omega = 2\pi \times 330$$

and time period, $T = \frac{2\pi}{\omega} = \frac{1}{330}$ s

7 *(a)* Phase difference between the two waves is
$$\phi = (\omega t - \beta_2) - (\omega t - \beta_1) = (\beta_1 - \beta_2)$$
$\therefore$ Resultant amplitude,
$$A = \sqrt{A_1^2 + A_2^2 + 2A_1A_2\cos(\beta_1 - \beta_2)}$$

8 *(a)* Let ϕ_1 and ϕ_2 represent angles of the first and second waves, then
$$\phi_2 = \frac{2\pi}{\lambda}[(vt - x) + x_0]$$
and $\phi_1 = \frac{2\pi}{\lambda}(vt - x)$

But $x_0 = \frac{\lambda}{2} \Rightarrow \phi_2 - \phi_1 = \pi$

Hence, phase difference $\phi = \pi$, so amplitude of the resultant wave is
$$R = \sqrt{a^2 + b^2 + 2ab\cos\phi}$$
$$= \sqrt{a^2 + b^2 + 2ab\cos\pi}$$
$$= \sqrt{(a-b)^2} = a - b$$
$$\therefore R = |a - b|$$

9 *(d)* Let $y_1 = A\sin(\omega t)$
and $y_2 = A\sin\left(\omega t + \frac{\pi}{2}\right)$

Resultant amplitude
$$R^2 = A^2 + A^2 + 2A^2\cos\left(\frac{\pi}{2}\right)$$
$$\Rightarrow R^2 = 2A^2 + 2A^2 \times 0$$
$$\Rightarrow R^2 = 2A^2$$
$$\Rightarrow R = \sqrt{2}A$$

However, both will have the same frequency ω on superimposing.

10 (c) Let a_1 and a_2 be amplitudes of the two waves. For maximum intensity,

$$I_{max} = (a_1 + a_2)^2$$

For minimum intensity,

$$I_{min} = (a_1 - a_2)^2$$

Given, $$\frac{I_{max}}{I_{min}} = \frac{25}{1} = \frac{(a_1 + a_2)^2}{(a_1 - a_2)^2}$$

$$\Rightarrow \quad \frac{a_1 + a_2}{a_1 - a_2} = \frac{5}{1} \Rightarrow \frac{a_1}{a_2} = \frac{3}{2}$$

$$\therefore \quad \frac{I_1}{I_2} = \frac{a_1^2}{a_2^2} = \left(\frac{3}{2}\right)^4 = \frac{9}{4} = 9:4$$

11 (c) When a stationary wave is formed, then its frequency is half that of the individual waves.

12 (a) Phase difference

$$= \frac{2\pi}{\lambda} \text{(Path difference)}$$

$$\Rightarrow \quad \frac{\pi}{3} = \frac{2\pi}{\lambda} \text{(Path difference)}$$

$$\Rightarrow \text{Path difference} = \frac{\lambda}{6}$$

13 (d) Lissajous figure is a pattern produced by the intersection of two sinusoidal waves, the axis of which are at right angles to each other.

14 (c) For interference phenomenon, we know that when two waves of equal frequency propagate in same medium and same direction, then interference phenomenon takes place.

Here, waves, $y_1 = a \sin(\omega t + \phi_1)$ and $y_3 = a' \sin(\omega t + \phi_2)$ have equal frequency, hence they will produce interference.

15 (c) $$\frac{I_1}{I_2} = \frac{a_1^2}{a_2^2} = \frac{25}{9}$$

$$\Rightarrow \quad \frac{a_1}{a_2} = \sqrt{\frac{25}{9}} \Rightarrow \frac{a_1}{a_2} = \frac{5}{3}$$

$$\therefore \quad \frac{I_{max}}{I_{min}} = \frac{(a_1 + a_2)^2}{(a_1 - a_2)^2} = \frac{(5+3)^2}{(5-3)^2}$$

$$= \frac{(8)^2}{(2)^2} = \frac{64}{4} = \frac{16}{1}$$

$$I_{max} : I_{min} = 16:1$$

16 (d) Resultant intensity of two periodic wave is given by

$$I = I_1 + I_2 + 2\sqrt{I_1 I_2} \cos\delta$$

where, δ is the phase difference between the waves.

For maximum intensity, $\delta = 2n\pi$, where, $n = 0, 1, 2, \ldots$ etc.

Therefore, for zero order maxima, $\cos\delta = 1$

$$I_{max} = I_1 + I_2 + 2\sqrt{I_1 I_2}$$

$$= (\sqrt{I_1} + \sqrt{I_2})^2$$

For minimum intensity,

$$\delta = (2n-1)\pi, \text{ where, } n = 1, 2, \ldots \text{ etc.}$$

So, for first order minima, $\cos\delta = -1$

$$I_{min} = I_1 + I_2 - 2\sqrt{I_1 I_2} = (\sqrt{I_1} - \sqrt{I_2})^2$$

Therefore, $I_{max} + I_{min}$

$$= (\sqrt{I_1} + \sqrt{I_2})^2 + (\sqrt{I_1} - \sqrt{I_2})^2$$

$$= 2(I_1 + I_2)$$

17 (c) Given, $\frac{I_1}{I_2} = \frac{9}{1}$ ...(i)

We know that, $I \propto a^2$

So, $$\frac{I_1}{I_2} = \left(\frac{a_1}{a_2}\right)^2 \Rightarrow \frac{9}{1} = \left(\frac{a_1}{a_2}\right)^2$$

$$\Rightarrow \quad \sqrt{\frac{9}{1}} = \frac{a_1}{a_2} \Rightarrow \frac{a_1}{a_2} = \frac{3}{1}$$

$$\therefore \quad a_1 : a_2 = 3:1$$

18 (c) A pulse of a wave train when travels along a stretched string and reaches the fixed end of the string, then it will be reflected back to the same medium and the reflected ray suffers a phase change of π with the incident wave but wave velocity after reflection does not change.

19 (c) Let I_r and I_i represent the intensities of reflected and incident waves respectively, then

$$\frac{I_r}{I_i} = \left(\frac{\mu - 1}{\mu + 1}\right)^2$$

where, $\mu = \frac{v_1}{v_2}$

$$\Rightarrow \quad v = \frac{\sqrt{T/m_1}}{\sqrt{T/m_2}} = \sqrt{\frac{m_2}{m_1}} = \sqrt{\frac{25}{9}} = \frac{5}{3}$$

$$\therefore \quad \frac{I_r}{I_i} = \left[\frac{(5/3) - 1}{(5/3) + 1}\right]^2 = \frac{1}{16}$$

20 (c) We know that,

Intensity $\propto$ (Amplitude)^2

Hence, $\frac{I_1}{I_2} = \frac{a_1^2}{a_2^2}$

Here, $a_1 = 5, a_2 = 10$

$$\Rightarrow \quad \frac{I_1}{I_2} = \frac{5 \times 5}{10 \times 10} = \frac{1}{4}$$

So, $I_2 / I_1 = 4/1$

21 (d) As the different amplitudes are mutually perpendicular which have phase difference of $\frac{\pi}{2}$, therefore particle will follow elliptical path.

22 (b) Since, $\frac{I_1}{I_2} = \frac{16}{9} = \frac{a_1^2}{a_2^2}$

$$\Rightarrow \quad \frac{a_1}{a_2} = \sqrt{\frac{16}{9}} = \frac{4}{3}$$

$$\Rightarrow \quad a_1 = \frac{4}{3} a_2$$

$$\therefore \quad \frac{I_{max}}{I_{min}} = \frac{(a_1 + a_2)^2}{(a_1 - a_2)^2} = \frac{\left(\frac{4}{3}a_2 + a_2\right)^2}{\left(\frac{4}{3}a_2 - a_2\right)^2}$$

$$= 49:1$$

23 (d) Beats, stationary waves, Lissajous figure all correspond to the phenomena of superposition of waves.

24 (b) The supreme position of waves in which two waves of same frequency (or same wavelength) travelling along same path superimpose each other is called interference of waves.

25 (b) $y = 4\cos^2(t/2)\sin(1000t)$

$$= 2[2\cos^2(t/2)\sin(1000t)]$$

$$= 2(1 + \cos t)\sin(1000t)$$

$$= 2\sin(1000t) + 2\sin(1000t)\cos t$$

$$= 2\sin(1000t) + \sin(1001t) + \sin(999t)$$

Thus, given wave represents the superposition of three waves.

26 (c) The equations of motion are

$$y_1 = 2a\sin(\omega t - kx)$$

and $y_2 = 2a\sin(\omega t - kx - \theta)$.

Now, the equation of resultant wave is given by

$$y = y_1 + y_2 = 2a\sin(\omega t - kx) + 2a\sin(\omega t - kx - \theta)$$

$$\Rightarrow y = 2a\left[2\sin\left(\frac{\omega t - kx + \omega t - kx - \theta}{2}\right) \times \cos\left\{\frac{\omega t - kx - (\omega t - kx - \theta)}{2}\right\}\right]$$

$$\Rightarrow y = 4a\cos\frac{\theta}{2}\sin\left(\omega t - kx - \frac{\theta}{2}\right) \quad \text{...(i)}$$

Now, comparing Eq. (i) with $y = A\sin(\omega t - kx)$, we have

Resultant amplitude, $A = 4a\cos\frac{\theta}{2}$.

Topic 4
Beats

2018

1 When two tuning forks A and B are sounded together, x beat/s are heard. Frequency of A is n. Now when one prong of fork B is loaded with a little wax, the number of beats decreases. The frequency of fork B is **[JIPMER]**

(a) $n+x$ (b) $n-x$ (c) $n+2x$ (d) $n-2x$

2 **Assertion** To hear different beats, difference of the frequencies of two sources should be less than 10.

Reason More the number of beats more in the confusion. **[AIIMS]**

(a) Both Assertion and Reason are correct and Reason is the correct explanation of Assertion.
(b) Both Assertion and Reason are correct and Reason is not the correct explanation of Assertion.
(c) Assertion is correct but Reason is incorrect.
(d) Assertion is incorrect but Reason is correct.

2016

3 Three sound waves of equal amplitudes have frequencies $(n-1), n, (n+1)$. They superimpose to give beats. The number of beats produced per second will be

(a) 1 (b) 4 (c) 3 (d) 2 **[NEET]**

2013

4 A source of unknown frequency gives 4 beats/s when sounded with a source of known frequency 250 Hz. The second harmonic of the source of unknown frequency gives five beats per second when sounded with a source of frequency 513 Hz. The unknown frequency is **[NEET]**

(a) 254 Hz (b) 246 Hz (c) 240 Hz (d) 260 Hz

5 Two sound waves of slightly different frequencies propagating in the same direction produce beats due to

(a) interference (b) diffraction **[UP CPMT]**
(c) reflection (d) refraction

6 If v_1 and v_2 are the frequencies of two tuning forks, then the beat frequency is **[J&K CET]**

(a) $\frac{v_1}{v_2}$ (b) v_1+v_2 (c) $\frac{v_2}{v_1}$ (d) v_1-v_2

2011

7 Two tuning forks A and B, produce notes of frequencies 258 Hz and 262 Hz. An unknown note sounded with A produces certain beats. When the same note is sounded with B, the beat frequency gets doubled. The unknown frequency is **[KCET]**

(a) 250 Hz (b) 252 Hz (c) 254 Hz (d) 245 Hz

2010

8 A tuning fork of frequency 512 Hz makes 4 beats/s with the vibrating string of a piano. The beat frequency decreases to 2 beats/s when the tension in the piano string is slightly increased. The frequency of the piano string before increasing the tension was **[CBSE AIPMT]**

(a) 510 Hz (b) 514 Hz
(c) 516 Hz (d) 508 Hz

9 A fork A has frequency 2% more than the standard fork and B has a frequency 3% less than the frequency of same standard fork. The forks A and B when sounded together produced 6 beats/s. The frequency of fork A is **[AIIMS]**

(a) 116.4 Hz (b) 120 Hz
(c) 122.4 Hz (d) 238.8 Hz

10 Two instruments having stretched strings are being played in unison. When the tension in one of the instruments is increased by 1%, 3 beats are produced in 2 s. The initial frequency of vibration of each wire is **[BHU]**

(a) 600 Hz (b) 300 Hz (c) 200 Hz (d) 150 Hz

11 The frequencies of two tuning forks A and B are respectively, 1.5% more and 2.5% less than that of the tuning fork C. When A and B are sounded together, 12 beats are produced in 1 s. The frequency of the tuning fork C is **[Kerala CEE]**

(a) 200 Hz (b) 240 Hz (c) 360 Hz (d) 300 Hz
(e) 400 Hz

12 5 beats/s are produced on blowing together two closed organ pipes of the same diameter but of different lengths. If shorter pipe is of 10 cm length and speed of sound in air is 300 m/s, length of other pipe is **[VMMC]**

(a) 10.06 cm (b) 11.22 cm
(c) 16 cm (d) 14 cm
(e) None of these

13 A sound wave travels with a velocity of 300 ms^{-1} through a gas. 9 beats are produced in 3 s when two waves pass through it simultaneously. If one of the waves has 2 m wavelength, the wavelength of the other wave is

(a) 1.98 m (b) 2.04 m **[EAMCET]**
(c) 2.00 m (d) 1.99 m

14 A disc of a siren containing 60 holes rotates at a constant speed of 360 rpm. The emitted sound is in unison with a tuning fork of frequency **[MGIMS]**

(a) 10 Hz (b) 360 Hz
(c) 216 Hz (d) 60 Hz

15 Each of the two strings of length 51.6 cm and 49.1 cm are tensioned separately by 20 N force. Mass per unit length of both the strings is same and equal to 1 gm^{-1}. When both the strings vibrate simultaneously, the number of beats is **[CBSE AIPMT]**

(a) 4 (b) 7 (c) 8 (d) 3

2009

16 A closed organ pipe and an open organ pipe of same length produce 2 beats/s while vibrating in their fundamental modes. The length of the open organ pipe is halved and that of closed pipe is doubled. Then, the number of beats produced per second while vibrating in the fundamental mode is **[KCET]**

(a) 2 (b) 6 (c) 8 (d) 7

17 Beats are produced by two waves given by $y_1 = a\sin 2000\pi t$ and $y_2 = a\sin 2008\pi t$. The number of beats heard per second is **[MHT CET]**

(a) zero (b) one (c) four (d) eight

18 Three sound waves of equal amplitudes have frequencies $(\nu - 1)$, ν, $(\nu + 1)$. They superpose to produce beats. The number of beats produced per second will be **[BCECE]**

(a) ν (b) $\nu/2$ (c) 2 (d) 1

19 Two waves are represented by $y_1 = 4\sin 404\pi t$ and $y_2 = 3\sin 400\pi t$. Then, **[BCECE]**

(a) beat frequency is 4 Hz and the ratio of maximum to minimum intensity is 49 : 1
(b) beat frequency is 2 Hz and the ratio of maximum to minimum intensity is 49 : 1
(c) beat frequency is 2 Hz and the ratio of maximum to minimum intensity is 1 : 49
(d) beat frequency is 4 Hz and the ratio of maximum to minimum intensity is 1 : 49

2008

20 A tuning fork A produces 4 beats s^{-1} with another tuning fork B of frequency 320 Hz. On filling one of the prongs of A, 4 beats s^{-1} are again heard when sounded with the same fork B. Then, the frequency of the fork A before filling is **[AFMC, JCECE]**

(a) 328 Hz (b) 316 Hz
(c) 324 Hz (d) 320 Hz

21 Two sound waves with wavelength 5.0 m and 5.5 m respectively, each propagate in a gas with velocity 330 ms^{-1}. We expect the following number of beats per second **[Haryana PMT]**

(a) 12 (b) zero (c) 1 (d) 6

22 Beats are produced by frequencies f_1 and f_2 $(f_1 > f_2)$. The duration of time between two successive maxima or minima is equal to **[J&K CET]**

(a) $\frac{1}{f_1 + f_2}$ (b) $\frac{2}{f_1 - f_2}$ (c) $\frac{2}{f_1 + f_2}$ (d) $\frac{1}{f_1 - f_2}$

23 Number of beats between A and B is 5 and between B and C is 3. Beat frequency between A and C may be **[DUMET]**

(a) 1 (b) 2
(c) 8 (d) None of these

24 The frequencies of three tuning forks A, B and C have a relation $n_A > n_B > n_C$. When the forks A and B are sounded together, the number of beats produced is n_1. When A and C are sounded together the number of beats produced is n_2, then the number of beats produced when B and C are sounded together is **[EAMCET]**

(a) $n_1 + n_2$ (b) $\frac{n_1 + n_2}{2}$
(c) $n_2 - n_1$ (d) $n_1 - n_2$

2007

25 Which of the following is true regarding beats? **[UP CPMT]**

(a) Frequency different, amplitude same
(b) Frequency same, amplitude same
(c) Frequency same, amplitude different
(d) None of the above

2006

26 Two tuning forks P and Q when set vibrating, give 4 beats s^{-1}. If a prong of the fork P is filled, the beats are reduced to 2 s^{-1}. What is frequency of P, if that of Q is 250 Hz? **[AIIMS]**

(a) 246 Hz (b) 250 Hz
(c) 254 Hz (d) 252 Hz

27 Choose the correct statement. **[J&K CET]**

(a) Beats are due to destructive interference.
(b) Maximum beat frequency audible to a human being is 20.
(c) Beats are as a result of Doppler's effect.
(d) Beats are due to superposition of two waves of nearly equal frequencies.

28 When a tuning fork produces sound waves in air, which one of the following is same in the material of tuning fork as well as in air? **[Punjab PMET]**

(a) Wavelength (b) Frequency
(c) Velocity (d) Amplitude

29 A tuning fork of frequency 100 when sound together with another tuning fork of unknown frequency produces 2 beats per second. On loading the tuning fork whose frequency is not known and sounded together with the same tuning fork produces one beat, then the frequency of the unknown tuning fork is **[AIIMS]**

(a) 102 (b) 98 (c) 99 (d) 101

30 The frequency of a tuning fork is 256 Hz. The velocity of sound in air 344 ms^{-1}. The distance travelled (in metre) by the sound during the time in which the tuning fork completes 32 vibrations, is **[EAMCET]**

(a) 21 (b) 43 (c) 86 (d) 129

2005

31 Two vibrating tuning forks produce progressive waves given by $y_1 = 4\sin 500\pi t$ and $y_2 = 2\sin 506\pi t$. Number of beats produced per minute is **[CBSE AIPMT]**

(a) 360 (b) 180
(c) 3 (d) 60

32 There are 26 tuning forks arranged in the decreasing order of their frequencies. Each tuning fork gives 3 beats with the next. The first one is octave of the last. What is the frequency of 18th tuning fork? **[BHU]**

(a) 100 Hz (b) 99 Hz
(c) 96 Hz (d) 103 Hz

33 Three sources of equal intensities with frequencies 400, 401 and 402 vibration per second are sounded together. The number of beat per second is **[J&K CET]**

(a) zero (b) 1
(c) 2 (d) 4

Answers

1 (a)	2 (b)	3 (a)	4 (a)	5 (a)	6 (d)	7 (c)	8 (d)	9 (c)	10 (b)
11 (d)	12 (a)	13 (b)	14 (b)	15 (b)	16 (d)	17 (c)	18 (c)	19 (b)	20 (b)
21 (d)	22 (d)	23 (b)	24 (c)	25 (a)	26 (a)	27 (d)	28 (b)	29 (b)	30 (b)
31 (b)	32 (b)	33 (c)							

Explanations

1 (a) Frequency of B can be $n + x$ or $n - x$.

When B is loaded with wax, its frequency will decrease. So if its original frequency is $(n + x)$, then beat frequency will decrease.

2 (b) According to the property of persistence of hearing the impression of a sound heard perists on our mind for $\frac{1}{10}$ s. To hear distinct beats, time interval between two successive beats should be greater than $\frac{1}{10}$ s. Hence, difference in two frequencies must be less than 10Hz.

Frequency of 10 Hz means 10 beats per second, i.e. if the number of beats is more than 10, then they will not be audible or more is the confusion.

3 (a) As we know that,

Beat frequency $= f_1 \sim f_2$

$= n - (n-1) = 1$

and similarly for n and $n+1$

Beat frequency $= n + 1 - n = 1$

4 (a) For 2nd harmonic, the frequency and beats are given below in the diagram.

Here, the exact frequency may be determined by loading method.

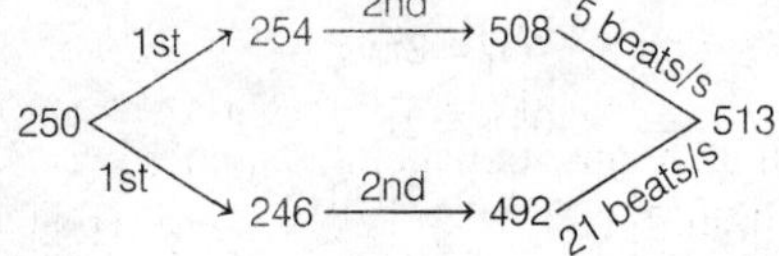

The frequency of unknown tunning fork can be $(250 + 4 = 254$ Hz) or $(250 - 4 = 246$Hz)

Hence, to produce 5 beats per second from source frequency of 513 Hz, the unknown frequency should be 254 Hz.

5 (a) Beats are produced on account of interference of sound waves of slightly different frequencies.

6 (d) The number of beats produced per second is called beat frequency.

It is expressed as $\nu = \nu_1 - \nu_2$.

7 (c) Given, $n_A = 258$ Hz and

$n_B = 262$ Hz

If it produces x beats with 258 and $2x$ with 262, then

$$262 - (258 - x) = 2x$$
$$\Rightarrow 262 - 258 + x = 2x$$
$$\Rightarrow x = 4$$

Therefore, unknown frequency is

$$n = 258 - x = 254 \text{ Hz.}$$

8 (d) Let f_1 be frequency of tuning fork and f_2 be frequency of piano string.

Now, $|f_1 - f_2| = 4$ Hz

$\therefore f_1 = 512$ Hz, so f_2 is 508 Hz.

On increasing tension, frequency f_1 is increased and beat frequency decreases, so f_2 is 508 Hz before increasing tension.

9 (c) The frequency of A,

$$n_A = n + \frac{2}{100}n$$

and the frequency of B,

$$n_B = n - \frac{3}{100}n$$

According to the question,

$$n_A - n_B = 6$$

$$\Rightarrow \left(n + \frac{2}{100}n\right) - \left(n - \frac{3}{100}n\right) = 6$$

$$\Rightarrow \frac{5}{100}n = 6$$

$$\Rightarrow n = \frac{600}{5} = 120 \text{ Hz}$$

The frequency of A

$$n_A = \left(n + \frac{2}{100}n\right)$$
$$= 120 + \frac{2}{100} \times 120$$
$$= 122.4 \text{ Hz}$$

10 (b) Initial frequency of vibration,

$$\nu \propto \sqrt{T}$$

When the tension in one of the instruments is increased by 1%, then

$$\nu' \propto \sqrt{1 + \frac{1}{100}}$$

$$\therefore \frac{\nu'}{\nu} = \left(1 + \frac{1}{100}\right)^{1/2} = 1 + \frac{1}{200}$$

$$\Rightarrow \frac{\nu' - \nu}{\nu} = \frac{1}{200}$$

$$\Rightarrow \frac{3}{2\nu} = \frac{1}{200} \quad \left[\because \nu' - \nu = \frac{3 \text{ beats}}{2\text{s}}\right]$$

$$\Rightarrow \nu = 300 \text{ Hz}$$

11 (*d*) Let the frequency of tuning fork C is x Hz. The frequency of tuning fork A is

$$x + \frac{1.5}{100}x = 1.015x$$

The frequency of tuning fork B is

$$x - \frac{2.5}{100}x = 0.975x$$

Beat frequency of tuning fork A and B is $1.015x - 0.975x = 0.04x$

Thus, $0.04x = 12$

$\Rightarrow \quad x = \frac{12}{0.04} = 300\text{ Hz}$

12 (*a*) $m = n_1 - n_2 = \frac{v}{4}\left[\frac{1}{l_1} - \frac{1}{l_2}\right]$

$\Rightarrow \quad 5 = \frac{300 \times 100}{4}\left[\frac{1}{l_1} - \frac{1}{l_2}\right]$

$\frac{1}{l_1} - \frac{1}{l_2} = \frac{20}{300 \times 100} \Rightarrow \frac{1}{1500}$

$\frac{1}{l_2} = \frac{1}{10} - \frac{1}{1500} \Rightarrow \frac{149}{1500}$

$\Rightarrow \quad l_2 = \frac{1500}{149} = 10.06\text{ cm}$

13 (*b*) Frequency, $f = \frac{9}{3} = 3\text{ Hz}$

$$f = v\left[\frac{1}{\lambda_1} - \frac{1}{\lambda_2}\right]$$

$\Rightarrow \quad 3 = 300\left[\frac{1}{2} - \frac{1}{\lambda_2}\right]$

$\Rightarrow \quad \frac{1}{100} = \frac{1}{2} - \frac{1}{\lambda_2}$

$\Rightarrow \quad \frac{1}{\lambda_2} = \frac{1}{2} - \frac{1}{100}$

$\Rightarrow \quad \frac{1}{\lambda_2} = \frac{50-1}{100} = \frac{49}{100}$

$\Rightarrow \quad \lambda_2 = \frac{100}{49} = 2.04\text{ m}$

14 (*b*) Speed $= 360$ rev/min

$= \frac{360}{60}$ rev/s $= 6$ rev/s

$\therefore$ Frequency $= 6 \times 60 = 360$ Hz

15 (*b*) The number of beats will be the difference of frequencies of the two strings.

Frequency of first string,

$$f_1 = \frac{1}{2l_1}\sqrt{\frac{T}{m}}$$

$$= \frac{1}{2 \times 51.6 \times 10^{-2}}\sqrt{\frac{20}{10^{-3}}}$$

$= 137.03$ Hz

Similarly, frequency of second string

$$f_2 = \frac{1}{2 \times 49.1 \times 10^{-2}}\sqrt{\frac{20}{10^{-3}}}$$

$= 144.01$ Hz

Number of beats $= f_2 - f_1$

$= 144 - 137$

$= 7$ beats

16 (*d*) Given, $f_o - f_c = 2 \quad \ldots$(i)

Frequency of fundamental mode for a closed organ pipe, $f_c = \frac{v}{4L_c}$

Similarly, frequency of fundamental mode for an open organ pipe,

$$f_o = \frac{v}{2L_o}$$

Given, $L_c = L_o$

$\Rightarrow \quad f_o = 2f_c \quad \ldots$(ii)

From Eqs. (i) and (ii), we get

$f_o = 4\text{Hz}$ and $f_c = 2\text{Hz}$

When the length of an open pipe is halved, its frequency of fundamental mode is

$$f_o' = \frac{v}{2[L_o/2]} = 2f_o$$

$= 2 \times 4$ Hz $= 8$ Hz

When the length of the closed pipe is doubled, its frequency of fundamental mode,

$$f_o' = \frac{v}{4(2L_c)} = \frac{1}{2}f_c$$

$= \frac{1}{2} \times 2 = 1$ Hz

Hence, number of beats produced per second is

$$f_o' - f_c' = 8 - 1 = 7$$

17 (*c*) Here, $y_1 = a\sin 2000\,\pi t$

and $\quad y_2 = a\sin 2008\,\pi t$

Comparing with $y = a\sin\omega t$, we have

$\omega_1 = 2000\,\pi$

$\Rightarrow \quad 2\pi f_1 = 2000\pi$

$\Rightarrow \quad f_1 = 1000$ Hz

and $\quad \omega_2 = 2008\pi$

$\Rightarrow \quad 2\pi f_2 = 2008\,\pi$

$\Rightarrow \quad f_2 = 1004$ Hz

$\therefore$ Beat frequency $= |f_1 - f_2|$

$= |1004 - 1000|$

$= 4$ Hz

Thus, number of beats heard per second is 4.

18 (*c*) If $(\nu - 1)$, ν, $(\nu + 1)$ be the frequencies of the three waves and a be the amplitude of each, then

$y_1 = a\sin 2\pi\,(\nu - 1)t$,

$y_2 = a\sin 2\pi\,\nu t$

and $\quad y_3 = a\sin 2\pi\,(\nu + 1)t$

Resultant displacement due to all three waves is

$y = y_1 + y_2 + y_3$

$= a\sin 2\pi\nu t + a[\sin 2\pi\,(\nu - 1)t + \sin 2\pi(\nu + 1)t]$

$= a\sin 2\pi\nu t + a[2\sin 2\pi\,\nu t\cos 2\pi t]$

$= a[2\cos 2\pi t + 1]\sin 2\pi\nu t$

$= a'\sin 2\pi\,\nu t$

where, $a' = a[1 + 2\cos 2\pi t]$

So, $\quad I \propto (a')^2 \propto a^2(1 + 2\cos 2\pi t)^2$

For I to be maximum or minimum,

$$\frac{dI}{dt} = 0$$

$\Rightarrow \quad \frac{d}{dt}(1 + 2\cos 2\pi t)^2 = 0$

i.e. $\quad 2(1 + 2\cos\pi t)(2\sin 2\pi t) \times 2\pi = 0$

Either $\quad \sin 2\pi t = 0$

or $\quad 1 + 2\cos 2\pi t = 0$

So, if $1 + 2\cos 2\pi t = 0$

$\Rightarrow \quad 2\pi t = 2\pi n \pm \frac{2\pi}{3}$

where, $n = 0, 1, 2, \ldots$

$$t = \frac{1}{3}, \frac{2}{3}, \frac{4}{3}, \frac{5}{3}, \ldots$$

and for these values of t,

$$\cos 2\pi t = -\left(\frac{1}{2}\right), I = 0,$$

i.e. I is minimum and if $\sin 2\pi t = 0$

$2\pi t = n\pi$, $n = 0, 1, 2, \ldots$

$\Rightarrow \quad t = 0, \frac{1}{2}, 1, \frac{3}{2}, 2, \ldots$

$\therefore$ I is therefore $9a^2, a^2, 9a^2, a^2$.

i.e. intensity is maximum (with two different values)

i.e. number of beats per second is two.

19 (*b*) Given, $y_1 = 4\sin 404\pi t$

and $y_2 = 3\sin 400\pi t$

Comparing with equation

$$y = A\sin\omega t$$

$\therefore \quad \omega_1 = 404\pi,\ \omega_2 = 400\pi$

$A_1 = 4,\ A_2 = 3$

$\because \quad \omega_1 = 2\pi\nu_1$

$\Rightarrow \quad 404\pi = 2\pi\nu_1$

$\Rightarrow \quad \nu_1 = 202$ Hz

$\because \quad \omega_2 = 2\pi\nu_2$

$\Rightarrow \quad 400\pi = 2\pi\nu_2$

$\Rightarrow \quad \nu_2 = 200\,\text{Hz}$

Beat frequency $= \nu_1 - \nu_2$

$= 202 - 200 = 2\,\text{Hz}$

$$\frac{I_{max}}{I_{min}} = \left(\frac{A_1 + A_2}{A_1 - A_2}\right)^2 = \left(\frac{4+3}{4-3}\right)^2 = \left(\frac{7}{1}\right)^2 = \frac{49}{1}$$

20 *(b)* There are 4 beats between A and B, therefore the possible frequencies of A are 316 or 324, i.e. (320 ± 4) Hz.

When the prong of A is filled, its frequency becomes greater than the original frequency. If we assume that original frequency of A is 324, then on filling its frequency will be greater than 324. The beats between A and B will be more than 4.

But it is given that, the beats are again 4, therefore, 324 is not possible.

Therefore, required frequency must be 316 Hz. This is true because on filing the frequency may increase so as to give 4 beats with B of frequency 320 Hz.

21 *(d)* Let $\lambda_1 = 5.0$ m, $v = 330\ \text{ms}^{-1}$ and $\lambda_2 = 5.5$ m

The relation between frequency, wavelength and velocity is given by

$$v = n\lambda$$

$$\Rightarrow \quad n = \frac{v}{\lambda} \quad \ldots\text{(i)}$$

The frequency corresponding to wavelength λ_1,

$$n_1 = \frac{v}{\lambda_1} = \frac{330}{5.0} = 66\ \text{Hz}$$

The frequency corresponding to wavelength λ_2,

$$n_2 = \frac{v}{\lambda_2} = \frac{330}{5.5} = 60\ \text{Hz}$$

Hence, number of beats per second

$= n_1 - n_2 = 66 - 60 = 6$

22 *(d)* The time-interval between two successive beats

$$T = \frac{1}{\text{Beat frequency}} = \frac{1}{f_1 - f_2}$$

23 *(b)* Number of beats between A and B, $n_1 = 5$

Number of beats between B and C, $n_2 = 3$

Hence, number of beats between A and C,

$$n_3 = n_1 - n_2 = 5 - 3 = 2$$

24 *(c)* When A and B are sounded together the number of beats $= n_1$

When A and C are sounded together the number of beats $= n_2$

So, the number of beats produced when B and C are sounded together $= n_2 - n_1$

25 *(a)* When two sound waves of slightly different frequencies and equal amplitude travelling along the same direction superimpose at a point give rise to beats.

26 *(a)* There are four beats between P and Q, therefore the possible frequencies of P are 246 or 254 (i.e. 250 ± 4) Hz.

When the prong of P is filled, its frequency becomes greater than the original frequency.

If we assume that the original frequency of P is 254, then on filling its frequency will be greater than 254. The beats between P and Q will be more than 4. But it is given that the beats are reduced to 2, therefore, 254 is not possible.

Therefore, the required frequency must be 246 Hz. This is true, because on filling the frequency may increase to 248, giving 2 beats with Q of frequency 250 Hz.

27 *(d)* Beats are the periodic and repeating fluctuation heard when two sound waves of nearly equal frequencies interfere with one another.

28 *(b)* Speed of sound depends on pressure, temperature, humidity and motion of air.

While there is no effect of frequency on the speed of sound. Sound waves of different frequencies travel with the same speed in air although their wavelengths in air are different.

29 *(a)* Unknown frequency may be 102 Hz or 98 Hz. On loading this tuning fork, its frequency will decrease. Suppose they become 101 Hz or 97 Hz. With 100 Hz, beat frequency will be 1 Hz or 3 Hz. Given frequency is 1 Hz. Hence, unknown frequency should be 102 Hz.

30 *(b)* Wavelength of sound,

$$\lambda = \frac{v}{n} = \frac{344}{256}\ \text{m}$$

So, distance travelled by the sound in 32 vibrations is

$$s = 32\lambda = 32 \times \frac{344}{256} = 43\ \text{m}$$

31 *(b)* Here, $y_1 = 4 \sin 500\pi t$ and $y_2 = 2 \sin 506\,\pi t$

Comparing with $y = a \sin \omega t$ we have

$\omega_1 = 500\pi$

$\Rightarrow \quad 2\pi f_1 = 500\pi$

$\Rightarrow \quad f_1 = 250$ Hz and $\omega_2 = 506\pi$

$\Rightarrow \quad 2\pi f_2 = 506\pi$

$\Rightarrow \quad f_2 = 253$ Hz

Now, beats produced per second

$|f_1 - f_2| = 3$

Beats produced per minute

$= 3 \times 60 = 180$

32 *(b)* Frequency of two consecutive forks is 3.

$\therefore \quad f = f_1 + (n-1)(d)$ (arithmetic progression)

Given, $f_1 = 2f$, $n = 26$ and $d = -3$

$\therefore \quad f = 2f + (26-1)(-3)$

$\Rightarrow \quad f = 75$ Hz

Frequency of 18th tuning fork is

$f_{18} = f_1 + (18-1)(-3)$

$\Rightarrow \quad = 2 \times 75 + 17 \times (-3)$

$= 150 - 51$

$= 99$ Hz

33 *(c)* Beats are the periodic and repeating fluctuations heard in the intensity of sound, when two sound waves of very similar frequencies interfere with one another.

Beats = Difference in frequencies.

Maximum number of beats per second

$= 402 - 400 = 2$

Topic 5

Stationary Waves : Vibrations of Strings and Organ Pipes

2019

1 A string wave equation is given by $y = 0.002\sin(300t - 15x)$ and mass density is ($\mu = 0.1$ kg/m). Then, find the tension force in the string. **[AIIMS]**

(a) 30 N (b) 20 N (c) 40 N (d) 45 N

2 If the speed of sound in air is 330 m/s, then find the number of tones present in an open organ pipe of length 1 m whose frequency is ≤ 1000 Hz. **[AIIMS]**

(a) 2 (b) 4 (c) 8 (d) 6

3 A tuning fork with frequency 800 Hz produces resonance in a resonance column tube with upper end open and lower end closed by water surface. Successive resonance are observed at length 9.75 cm, 31.25 cm and 52.75 cm. The speed of sound in air is **[NEET (Odisha)]**

(a) 500 ms^{-1} (b) 156 ms^{-1}
(c) 344 ms^{-1} (d) 172 ms^{-1}

2018

4 An organ pipe open on both ends in the nth harmonic is in resonance with a source of 1000 Hz. The length of pipe is 16.6 cm and speed of sound in air is 332 m/s. Find the value of n. **[JIPMER]**

(a) 3 (b) 2 (c) 1 (d) 4

5 A steel rod 100 cm long is damped at into middle. The fundamental frequency of longitudinal vibrations of the rod are given to be 2.53 kHz. What is the speed of sound in steel? **[AIIMS]**

(a) 6.2 kms^{-1} (b) 5.06 kms^{-1}
(c) 7.23 kms^{-1} (d) 7.45 kms^{-1}

6 The fundamental frequency in an open organ pipe is equal to the third harmonic of a closed organ pipe. If the length of the closed organ pipe is 20 cm, the length of the open organ pipe is **[NEET]**

(a) 12.5 cm (b) 8 cm (c) 13.3 cm (d) 16 cm

7 A tuning fork is used to produce resonance in a glass tube. The length of the air column in this tube can be adjusted by a variable piston. At room temperature of 27° C, two successive resonances are produced at 20 cm and 73 cm of column length. If the frequency of the tuning fork is 320 Hz, the velocity of sound in air at 27° C is **[NEET]**

(a) 350 ms^{-1} (b) 339 ms^{-1} (c) 330 ms^{-1} (d) 300 ms^{-1}

2017

8 The two nearest harmonics of a tube closed at one end and open at other end are 220 Hz and 260 Hz. What is the fundamental frequency of the system? **[NEET]**

(a) 10 Hz (b) 20 Hz (c) 30 Hz (d) 40 Hz

2016

9 The fundamental frequency of a closed organ pipe of length 20 cm is equal to the second overtone of an organ pipe open at both the ends. The length of organ pipe open at both the ends is **[NEET]**

(a) 80 cm (b) 100 cm (c) 120 cm (d) 140 cm

10 A uniform rope of length L and mass m_1 hangs vertically from a rigid support. A block of mass m_2 is attached to the free end of the rope. A transverse pulse of wavelength λ_1 is produced at the lower end of the rope. The wavelength of the pulse when it reaches the top of the rope is λ_2. The ratio λ_2/λ_1 is **[NEET]**

(a) $\sqrt{\frac{m_1 + m_2}{m_2}}$ (b) $\sqrt{\frac{m_2}{m_1}}$

(c) $\sqrt{\frac{m_1 + m_2}{m_1}}$ (d) $\sqrt{\frac{m_1}{m_2}}$

2015

11 An air column, closed at one end and open at the other, resonates with a tuning fork when the smallest length of the column is 50 cm. The next larger length of the column resonating with the same tuning fork is **[NEET]**

(a) 100 cm (b) 150 cm
(c) 200 cm (d) 66.7cm

2014

12 If n_1, n_2 and n_3 are the fundamental frequencies of three segments into which a string is divided, then the original fundamental frequency n of the string is given by **[CBSE AIPMT]**

(a) $\frac{1}{n} = \frac{1}{n_1} + \frac{1}{n_2} + \frac{1}{n_3}$

(b) $\frac{1}{\sqrt{n}} = \frac{1}{\sqrt{n_1}} + \frac{1}{\sqrt{n_2}} + \frac{1}{\sqrt{n_3}}$

(c) $\sqrt{n} = \sqrt{n_1} + \sqrt{n_2} + \sqrt{n_3}$

(d) $n = n_1 + n_2 + n_3$

13 The number of possible natural oscillations of air column in a pipe closed at one end of length 85 cm whose frequencies lie below 1250 Hz are (take, velocity of sound = 340 ms^{-1}) **[CBSE AIPMT]**

(a) 4 (b) 5 (c) 7 (d) 6

14 A whistle whose air column is open at both ends has a fundamental frequency of 5100 Hz. If the speed of sound in air is 340 ms^{-1}, then the length of the whistle, in cm is **[WB JEE]**

(a) 5/3 (b) 10/3 (c) 5 (d) 20/3

15 A closed pipe and an open pipe of same length produce 2 beats, when they are set into vibration simultaneously in their fundamental mode. If the length of the open pipe is halved and that of closed pipe is doubled, and if they are vibrating in the fundamental mode, then the number of beats produced is **[EAMCET]**

(a) 4 (b) 7
(c) 2 (d) 8

16 A pipe of 30 cm long open at both the ends produces harmonics. Which harmonic mode of pipe resonates at 1.1 kHz source? (Take, speed of sound in air = 330 ms^{-1}) **[KCET]**

(a) Fifth harmonic (b) Fourth harmonic
(c) Third harmonic (d) Second harmonic

17 A metallic wire of 1 m length has a mass of 10×10^{-3} kg. If a tension of 100 N is applied to a wire, then what is the speed of transverse wave? **[KCET]**

(a) 100 ms^{-1} (b) 10 ms^{-1} (c) 200 ms^{-1} (d) 0.1 ms^{-1}

2013

18 If we study the vibration of a open pipe at both ends, then which of the following statements is not true? **[NEET]**

(a) Open end will be anti-node.
(b) Odd harmonics of the fundamental frequency will be generated.
(c) All harmonics of the fundamental frequency will be generated.
(d) Pressure change will be maximum at both ends.

19 **Assertion** Velocity of particles while crossing mean position (in stationary waves) from maximum at anti-nodes to zero at nodes.

Reason Amplitude of vibration at anti-nodes is maximum and at nodes, the amplitude is zero and all particles between two successive nodes cross the mean position together. **[AIIMS]**

(a) Both Assertion and Reason are correct and Reason is the correct explanation of Assertion
(b) Both Assertion and Reason are correct but Reason is not the correct explanation of Assertion
(c) Assertion is correct but Reason is incorrect
(d) Both Assertion and Reason are incorrect
(e) Assertion is incorrect but Reason is correct

20 What is the fractional change in tension necessary in a sonometer of fixed length to produce a note one octave lower than before? **[UP CPMT]**

(a) $\frac{1}{4}$ (b) $\frac{1}{2}$
(c) $\frac{2}{3}$ (d) $\frac{3}{4}$

2012

21 A transverse wave propagating on a stretched string of linear density 3×10^{-4} kg-m^{-1} is represented by the equation $y = 0.2 \sin (15x + 60t)$
where, x is in metres and t is in seconds. The tension in the string (in newton) is **[AFMC]**

(a) 0.24 (b) 0.48
(c) 1.20 (d) 1.80

22 The frequency of the first overtone of a closed pipe of length l_1 is equal to that of the first overtone of an open pipe of length l_2. The ratio of their lengths ($l_1 : l_2$) is **[WB JEE]**

(a) 2 : 3 (b) 4 : 5
(c) 3 : 5 (d) 3 : 4

2011

23 **Assertion** The fundamental frequency of an open organ pipe increases as the temperature is increased.

Reason As the temperature increases, the velocity of sound increases more rapidly than length of the pipe. **[AIIMS]**

(a) Both Assertion and Reason are correct and Reason is the correct explanation of the Assertion
(b) Both Assertion and Reason are correct but Reason is not the correct explanation of Assertion
(c) Assertion is correct but Reason is incorrect
(d) Both Assertion and Reason are incorrect

24 Two Cu wires of radii R_1 and R_2 are such that ($R_1 > R_2$). Then, which of the following is true? **[MHT CET]**

(a) Transverse wave travels faster in thicker wire
(b) Transverse wave travels faster in thinner wire
(c) Travels with the same speed in both the wires
(d) Does not travel

25 In the fundamental mode, time taken by the wave to reach the closed end of the air filled pipe is 0.01 s. The fundamental frequency is **[MHT CET]**

(a) 25 (b) 12.5 (c) 20 (d) 15

26 n_1 is the frequency of the pipe closed at one end and n_2 is the frequency of the pipe open at both ends. If both are joined end to end, find the fundamental frequency of closed pipe so formed. **[MHT CET]**

(a) $\frac{n_1 n_2}{n_2 + 2n_1}$ (b) $\frac{n_1 n_2}{2n_2 + n_1}$
(c) $\frac{n_1 + 2n_2}{n_2 2n_1}$ (d) $\frac{2n_1 + n_2}{n_2 n_1}$

27 The fundamental frequencies of an open and a closed tube, each of same length l with v as the speed of sound in air, respectively are **[Manipal]**

(a) $\frac{v}{2l}$ and $\frac{v}{l}$ (b) $\frac{v}{l}$ and $\frac{v}{2l}$

(c) $\frac{v}{2l}$ and $\frac{v}{4l}$ (d) $\frac{v}{4l}$ and $\frac{v}{2l}$

28 A cylindrical tube closed at one end contains air. It produces the fundamental note of frequency 512 Hz. If the tube is opened at both ends, then the fundamental frequency that can be excited is **[Manipal]**

(a) 256 Hz (b) 512 Hz (c) 1024 Hz (d) 128 Hz

29 An air column in a pipe which is closed at one end, will be in resonance with the vibrating body of frequency 166 Hz, if the length of the air column is **[Manipal]**

(a) 0.5 m (b) 1.0 m (c) 1.5 m (d) 2.0 m

30 In a stationary wave, all the particles **[OJEE]**

(a) on either side of a node vibrate in same phase
(b) in the region between two nodes vibrate in same phase
(c) in the region between two anti-nodes vibrate in same phase
(d) of the medium vibrate in same phase

31 Air is blown at the mouth of an open tube of length 25 cm and diameter 2 cm. If the velocity of sound in air is 330 ms^{-1}, then the emitted frequencies (in Hz) are **[Kerala CEE]**

(a) 660, 1320, 2640 (b) 660, 1000, 3300
(c) 302, 664, 1320 (d) 330, 990 1690
(e) 330, 660, 990

32 The fundamental frequency of a closed pipe is 220 Hz. If $\left(\frac{1}{4}\right)$th of the pipe is filled with water, then the frequency of the first overtone of the pipe now is **[Haryana PMT]**

(a) 220 Hz (b) 440 Hz (c) 880 Hz (d) 1760 Hz

33 A pipe opened at both ends produces a note of frequency f_1. When the pipe is kept with $\left(\frac{3}{4}\right)$th of its length in water, it produces a note of frequency f_2. The ratio $\frac{f_1}{f_2}$ is **[BCECE]**

(a) $\frac{3}{4}$ (b) $\frac{4}{3}$ (c) $\frac{1}{2}$ (d) 2

34 A stretched string of length l fixed at both ends can sustain stationary waves of wavelength λ given by **[CG PMT]**

(a) $\lambda = \frac{n^2}{2l}$ (b) $\lambda = \frac{l^2}{2n}$

(c) $\lambda = \frac{2l}{n}$ (d) $\lambda = 2ln$

(Here, n is a integer)

35 Two vibrating strings of the same material but lengths L and $2L$ have radii $2r$ and r respectively. They are stretched under the same tension. Both the strings vibrate in their fundamental modes, the one of length L with frequency ν_1 and the other with frequency ν_2. The ratio ν_1/ν_2 is **[JIPMER]**

(a) 2 (b) 4
(c) 3 (d) 1

36 A wire under tension vibrates with a fundamental frequency of 600 Hz. If the length of the wire is doubled, the radius is halved and the wire is made to vibrate under one-ninth the tension. Then, the fundamental frequency will become **[KCET]**

(a) 200 Hz (b) 300 Hz (c) 600 Hz (d) 400 Hz

37 A piston of filled in cylindrical pipe is pulled as shown in the figure. A tuning fork is sounded at open end and loudest sound is heard at open length 13 cm, 41 cm and 69 cm. The frequency of tuning fork, if velocity of sound is 350 ms^{-1}, is **[DUMET]**

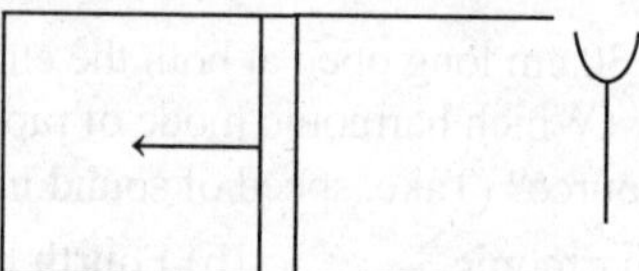

(a) 1250 Hz (b) 625 Hz (c) 417 Hz (d) 715 Hz

38 A uniform wire of length L, diameter D and density ρ is stretched under a tension T. The correct relation between its fundamental frequency f, the length L and the diameter D is **[KCET]**

(a) $f \propto \frac{1}{LD}$ (b) $f \propto \frac{1}{L\sqrt{D}}$

(c) $f \propto \frac{1}{D^2}$ (d) $f \propto \frac{1}{LD^2}$

39 Standing waves are formed on a string when interference occurs between two waves having **[MGIMS]**

(a) the same amplitude travelling in the same direction with no phase difference between them
(b) the same amplitude, travelling in the opposite direction with no phase difference between them
(c) different amplitudes travelling in the same direction
(d) different amplitudes travelling in the opposite direction

2009

40 A wave in a string has an amplitude of 2 cm. The wave travels in the +ve direction of x-axis with a speed of 128 ms^{-1} and it is noted that 5 complete waves fit in 4 m length of the string. The equation describing the wave is **[BSE AIPMT]**

(a) $y = 0.02 \sin(7.85x + 1005t)$
(b) $y = 0.02 \sin(15.7x - 2010t)$
(c) $y = 0.02 \sin(15.7x + 2010t)$
(d) $y = 0.02 \sin(7.85x - 1005t)$

41 A resonance in an air column of length 40 cm resonates with a tuning fork of frequency 450 Hz. Ignoring end correction, the velocity of sound in air is **[AIIMS]**

(a) 1020 ms^{-1} (b) 720 ms^{-1}
(c) 620 ms^{-1} (d) 820 ms^{-1}

42. A closed organ pipe of length 1.2 m vibrates in its first overtone mode. The pressure variation is maximum at **[AIIMS]**

(a) 0.4 m from the open end
(b) 0.4 m from the closed end
(c) Both (a) and (b)
(d) 0.8 m from the open end

43 In a resonance pipe, the first and second resonances are obtained at depths 22.7 cm and 70.2 cm, respectively. What will be the end correction? **[MHT CET]**

(a) 1.05 cm (b) 115.5 cm
(c) 92.5 cm (d) 113.5 cm

44 Fundamental frequency of pipe is 100 Hz and other two frequencies are 300 Hz and 500 Hz, then **[MHT CET]**

(a) pipe is open at both the ends
(b) pipe is closed at both the ends
(c) one end is open and another end is closed
(d) None of the above

45 In a closed organ pipe, the first resonance occurs at 50 cm. At what length of pipe, the second resonance will occur?

(a) 150 cm (b) 50 cm **[OJEE]**
(c) 100 cm (d) 200 cm

46 A sonometer wire supports a 4 kg load and vibrates in fundamental mode with a tuning fork of frequency 416 Hz. The length of the wire between the bridges is now doubled. In order to maintain fundamental mode, the load should be changed to **[Kerala CEE]**

(a) 1 kg (b) 2 kg
(c) 4 kg (d) 8 kg
(e) 16 kg

47 Damping on sharpness or resonance has

(a) no effect **[Haryana PMT, CG PMT]**
(b) more damping, sharper resonance
(c) less damping, sharper resonance
(d) less damping, less sharp resonance

48 In a stationary wave represented by $y = 2a\cos kx \sin \omega t$, the intensity at a certain point is maximum when

(a) $\cos kx$ is maximum **[Haryana PMT, CG PMT]**
(b) $\cos kx$ is minimum
(c) $\sin \omega t$ is maximum
(d) $\sin \omega t$ is minimum

49 A sound wave with frequency 256 Hz falls normally on a perfectly reflecting wall. The shortest distance from the wall at which the air particles will have maximum amplitude of vibrations is nearly (velocity of sound in air is 336 ms^{-1}) **[J&K CET]**

(a) 32.8 cm (b) 50 cm (c) 65.8 cm (d) 25 cm

50 Which of the following functions does not represent a stationary wave? Here a, b and c are constants. **[BCECE]**

(a) $y = a\cos bx \sin ct$
(b) $y = a\sin bx \cos ct$
(c) $y = a\sin (bx + ct)$
(d) $y = a\sin (bx + ct) + a\sin (bx - ct)$

51 A cylindrical tube open at both the ends has a fundamental frequency of 390 Hz in air. If $\left(\frac{1}{4}\right)$th of the tube is immersed vertically in water, then the fundamental frequency of air column is **[KCET]**

(a) 260 Hz (b) 130 Hz
(c) 390 Hz (d) 520 Hz

52 A cylindrical tube, open at both ends emits a fundamental frequency f in air. The tube is dipped vertically in water, so that half of it is in water. The fundamental frequency of air column is now **[MGIMS]**

(a) $f/2$ (b) $3f/4$ (c) f (d) $2f$

53 The end correction of a resonance column is 1.0 cm. If the shortest length resonating with the tuning fork is 15.0 cm, the next resonating length will be **[MGIMS]**

(a) 31 cm (b) 45 cm
(c) 46 cm (d) 47 cm

54 If λ_1, λ_2 and λ_3 are the wavelengths of the waves giving resonance with the fundamental, first and second overtones respectively of a closed organ pipe. Then, the ratio of wavelengths $\lambda_1 : \lambda_2 : \lambda_3$ is **[UP CPMT]**

(a) 1 : 3 : 5 (b) 1 : 2 : 3
(c) 5 : 3 : 1 (d) $1 : \frac{1}{3} : \frac{1}{5}$

2008

55 An organ pipe P closed at one end vibrates in its first harmonic. Another organ pipe Q open at both ends vibrates in its third harmonic. When both are in resonance with a tuning fork, the ratio of the length of P to that of Q is **[Kerala CEE]**

(a) $\frac{1}{2}$ (b) $\frac{1}{4}$ (c) $\frac{1}{6}$ (d) $\frac{1}{8}$
(e) $\frac{1}{3}$

56 A string is hanging from a rigid support. A transverse pulse is excited at its free end. The speed at which the pulse travels a distance x is proportional to **[Kerala CEE]**

(a) x (b) $\frac{1}{x}$
(c) $\frac{1}{\sqrt{x}}$ (d) x^2
(e) $\sqrt{x}$

57 A metal wire of mass per unit length of 9.8 gm^{-1} is stretched with a tension of 10 kW between two rigid supports 1 m apart. The wire passes at its middle point between the poles of a permanent magnet and it vibrates in resonance when carrying an alternating current of frequency n. The frequency n of the alternating source is **[MHT CET]**

(a) 50 Hz (b) 100 Hz (c) 200 Hz (d) 25 Hz

58 A uniform wire of linear density 0.004 kgm^{-1} when stretched between two rigid supports with a tension 3.6×10^2 N, resonates with a frequency of 420 Hz. The next harmonic frequency with which the wire resonates is 490 Hz. The length of the wire (in metre) is **[Punjab PMET]**

(a) 1.41 (b) 2.14
(c) 2.41 (d) 3.14

59 To increase the frequency by 20%, the tension in the string vibrating on a sonometer has to be increased by **[Punjab PMET]**

(a) 44% (b) 33%
(c) 22% (d) 11%

60 Two strings of the same material and the same area of cross-section are used in sonometer experiment. One is loaded with 12 kg and the other with 3 kg. The fundamental frequency of the first string is equal to the first overtone of the second string. If the length of the second string is 100 cm, then the length of the first string is **[EAMCET]**

(a) 300 cm (b) 200 cm
(c) 100 cm (d) 50 cm

61 A string vibrates with a frequency of 200 Hz. When its length is doubled and tension is altered, it begins to vibrate with a frequency of 300 Hz. The ratio of the new tension to the original tension is **[KCET]**

(a) 9 : 1 (b) 1 : 9
(c) 3 : 1 (d) 1 : 3

62 A standing wave having 3 nodes and 2 anti-nodes is formed between two atoms having a distance 1.21 Å between them. The wavelength of the standing wave is **[MHT CET]**

(a) 1.21 Å (b) 1.42 Å
(c) 6.05 Å (d) 3.63 Å

63 A wave represented by the equation $y = a\cos(kx - \omega t)$ is superposed with another wave to form a stationary wave such that the point $x = 0$ is a node. The equation for the other wave is **[Kerala CEE]**

(a) $y = a\cos(kx + \omega t)$ (b) $y = a\sin(kx + \omega t)$
(c) $y = -a\sin(kx + \omega t)$ (d) $y = -a\sin(kx - \omega t)$
(e) $y = -a\cos(kx + \omega t)$

64 A segment of wire vibrates with fundamental frequency of 450 Hz under a tension of 9 kg-wt. Then, tension at which the fundamental frequency of the same wire becomes 900 Hz is **[J&K CET]**

(a) 36 kg-wt (b) 27 kg-wt
(c) 18 kg-wt (d) 72 kg-wt

65 A tuning fork of frequency 340 Hz is vibrated just above the tube of 120 cm height. Water is poured slowly in the tube. What is the minimum height of water necessary for the resonance? (Take, speed of sound in air = 340 ms^{-1}) **[Punjab PMET]**

(a) 45 cm (b) 30 cm
(c) 40 cm (d) 25 cm

66 A stretched wire of length 110 cm is divided into three segments whose frequencies are in ratio 1 : 2 : 3. Their length must be **[Punjab PMET]**

(a) 20 cm, 30 cm, 60 cm
(b) 60 cm, 30 cm, 20 cm
(c) 60 cm, 20 cm, 30 cm
(d) 30 cm, 60 cm, 20 cm

67 A glass tube is open at both the ends. A tuning fork of frequency f resonates with the air column inside the tube. Now, the tube is placed vertically inside water so that half the length of the tube is filled with water. Now, the air column inside the tube is in unison with another fork of frequency f'. Then, **[KCET]**

(a) $f' = f$ (b) $f' = 4f$
(c) $f' = 2f$ (d) $f' = \frac{f}{2}$

2006

68 A closed organ pipe of length 20 cm is sounded with tuning fork in resonance. What is the frequency of tuning fork? (Take, speed of sound = 332 ms^{-1}) **[AFMC]**

(a) 300 Hz (b) 350 Hz
(c) 375 Hz (d) 415 Hz

69 Two closed organ pipes A and B have the same length. A is wider than B. They resonate in the fundamental mode at frequencies n_A and n_B respectively, then **[BHU]**

(a) $n_A = n_B$ (b) $n_A > n_B$
(c) $n_A < n_B$ (d) Either (b) or (c) depending on the ratio of their diameters

70 A closed organ pipe and an open organ pipe are tuned to the same fundamental frequency. What is the ratio of their lengths? **[Manipal]**

(a) 1 : 2 (b) 2 : 1
(c) 2 : 3 (d) 4 : 3

71 Two stretched strings of same material are vibrating under same tension in fundamental mode. The ratio of their frequencies is 1 : 2 and ratio of the length of the vibrating segments is 1 : 4, then the ratio of the radii of the strings is **[Kerala CEE]**

(a) 2 : 1 (b) 4 : 1
(c) 3 : 2 (d) 8 : 1
(e) 4 : 5

72 To increase the frequency from 100 Hz to 400 Hz, the tension in the string has to be changed by **[KCET]**

(a) 4 times (b) 16 times
(c) 2 times (d) None of these

73 A string has tension T. For tripling the frequency, the tension in string will become **[DUMET]**

(a) $3T$ (b) $\frac{T}{9}$
(c) $\frac{T}{\sqrt{3}}$ (d) $9T$

74 A uniform string of length 1.5 m has two successive harmonics of frequencies 70 Hz and 84 Hz. The speed of the wave in the string (in ms^{-1}) is **[EAMCET]**

(a) 84 (b) 42
(c) 21 (d) 10.5

75 When the length of the vibrating segment of a sonometer wire is increased by 1%, the percentage change in its frequency is **[KCET]**

(a) $\frac{100}{101}$ (b) $\frac{99}{100}$
(c) 1 (d) 2

2005

76 If the length of an open organ pipe is 33.3 cm, then the frequency of fifth overtone is ($v_{sound} = 333\ ms^{-1}$) **[MHT CET]**

(a) 3000 Hz (b) 1500 Hz
(c) 2500 Hz (d) 1250 Hz

77 In an open organ pipe of length 1 m, what is the harmonic of resonance obtained with a tuning fork of frequency 480 Hz? **[J&K CET]**

(a) First (b) Second
(c) Third (d) Fourth

78 The fundamental frequency of a sonometer wire is n. If its radius is doubled and its tension becomes half, the material of the wire remains same, then the new fundamental frequency will be **[BCECE]**

(a) n (b) $\frac{n}{\sqrt{2}}$ (c) $\frac{n}{2}$ (d) $\frac{n}{2\sqrt{2}}$

79 In open organ pipe, if fundamental frequency is n, then the other frequencies are **[BCECE]**

(a) $n, 2n, 3n, 4n$ (b) $n, 3n, 5n$
(c) $n, 2n, 4n, 8n$ (d) None of these

80 Two instruments having stretched strings are being played in unison. When the tension of one of the instruments is increased by 1%, 3 beats are produced in 2 s. The initial frequency of vibration of each wire is **[JCECE]**

(a) 300 Hz (b) 500 Hz
(c) 1000 Hz (d) 400 Hz

81 In an experiment with sonometer, a tuning fork of frequency 256 Hz resonates with a length of 25 cm and another tuning fork resonates with a length of 16 cm. Tension of the string remaining constant, the frequency of the second tuning fork is **[KCET]**

(a) 163.84 Hz (b) 400 Hz
(c) 320 Hz (d) 204.8 Hz

Answers

1 (c)	2 (d)	3 (c)	4 (c)	5 (b)	6 (c)	7 (b)	8 (b)	9 (c)	10 (a)
11 (b)	12 (a)	13 (d)	14 (b)	15 (b)	16 (d)	17 (a)	18 (d)	19 (b)	20 (d)
21 (b)	22 (d)	23 (a)	24 (b)	25 (a)	26 (a)	27 (c)	28 (c)	29 (a)	30 (d)
31 (a)	32 (c)	33 (c)	34 (c)	35 (d)	36 (a)	37 (b)	38 (a)	39 (b)	40 (d)
41 (b)	42 (a)	43 (a)	44 (c)	45 (a)	46 (e)	47 (c)	48 (a)	49 (a)	50 (c)
51 (a)	52 (c)	53 (d)	54 (d)	55 (c)	56 (e)	57 (a)	58 (b)	59 (a)	60 (c)
61 (a)	62 (a)	63 (e)	64 (a)	65 (a)	66 (b)	67 (a)	68 (d)	69 (c)	70 (a)
71 (d)	72 (b)	73 (d)	74 (b)	75 (c)	76 (a)	77 (c)	78 (d)	79 (a)	80 (a)
81 (b)									

Explanations

1 (c) Given, wave equation,
$y = 0.002 \sin(300t - 15x)$

Mass density, $\mu = 0.1 \text{ kg/m}$

Comparing the given wave equation with $y = a\sin(\omega t - kx)$, we have

$\omega = 300, k = 15$

$\therefore$ Velocity of wave,

$$v = \frac{\omega}{k} = \frac{300}{15} = 20 \text{ m/s}$$

Wave speed in string is also given by

$$v = \sqrt{\frac{T}{\mu}}$$

where, T = tension in the string
and μ = mass per unit length of string

$$\therefore \quad 20 = \sqrt{\frac{T}{0.1}}$$

$$\Rightarrow \quad 400 = \frac{T}{0.1}$$

$$\Rightarrow \quad T = 40 \text{N}$$

2 (d) Given, speed of sound, $v = 330$ m/s

Length of open organ pipe, $l = 1$ m

Frequency, $f = 1000$ Hz

For open organ pipe,

Fundamental frequency,

$$f_0 = \frac{v}{2l} = \frac{330}{2 \times 1} = 165 \text{Hz}$$

$\therefore$ Number of tones present in the open organ pipe

$$= \frac{f}{f_0} = \frac{1000}{165}$$

$$= 6.06 \simeq 6$$

3. (c) For vibrating tuning fork over a resonance tube, the first resonance is obtained at the length

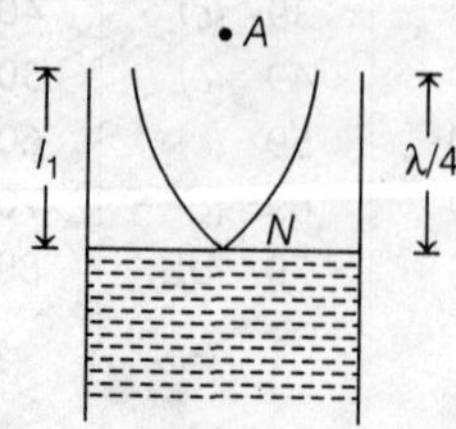

$$l_1 = \frac{\lambda}{4} \quad \text{...(i)}$$

and for second resonance,

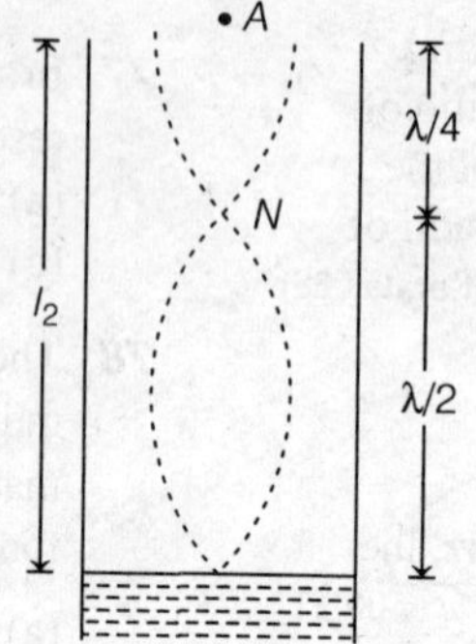

$$l_2 = \frac{\lambda}{4} + \frac{\lambda}{2} = \frac{3\lambda}{4} \quad \text{...(ii)}$$

From Eqs. (i) and (ii), we get

$$l_2 - l_1 = \frac{3\lambda}{4} - \frac{\lambda}{4} = \frac{\lambda}{2}$$

$$\Rightarrow \lambda = 2(l_2 - l_1)$$

$$\Rightarrow \quad v = 2f(l_2 - l_1) \quad \text{...(iii)}$$

$$\left(\because \lambda = \frac{v}{f}\right)$$

Here, $f = 800$ Hz, $l_1 = 9.75$ cm and $l_2 = 31.25$ cm

Substituting the given values in Eq. (iii), we get

$$\Rightarrow v = 2 \times 800(31.25 - 9.75)$$

$$= 34400 \text{ cm/s} = 344 \text{ ms}^{-1}$$

4 (c) Given, $f = 1000$ Hz, $v = 332$ m/s, $l = 16.6 \text{ cm} = 16.6 \times 10^{-2}$ m

Frequency in an organ pipe open on both ends,

$$f = \frac{nv}{2l} \quad \text{or} \quad n = \frac{2fl}{v}$$

$$\text{or} \quad n = \frac{2 \times 1000 \times 16.6 \times 10^{-2}}{332} = 1$$

5 (b) In fundamental mode,

$$l = 2\left(\frac{\lambda}{4}\right) = \frac{\lambda}{2}$$

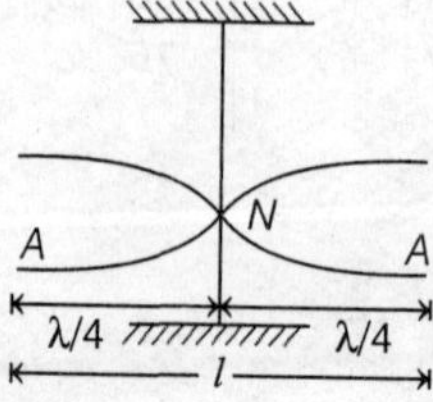

$$\Rightarrow \quad \lambda = 2l \quad \text{...(i)}$$

Given, $l = 100$ cm,

$\nu = 2.53 \text{ kHz} = 2.53 \times 10^3$ Hz

We know that,

$$v = \nu\lambda$$

$$= \nu \times 2l \quad \text{[from Eq. (i)]}$$

$$= 2.53 \times 10^3 \times 2 \times 100 \times 10^{-2}$$

$$= 5.06 \times 10^3 \text{ ms}^{-1}$$

$$= 5.06 \text{ kms}^{-1}$$

6 (c) Fundamental frequency for an open organ pipe is given as

$$f_1 = \frac{v}{2L}$$

where, L is the length of the open organ pipe.

Third harmonic for a closed organ pipe is given as

$$f' = \frac{3v}{4L'}$$

where, L' is the length of closed organ pipe.

According to the question,

$$f = f'$$

$$\frac{v}{2L} = \frac{3v}{4L'} \Rightarrow L = \frac{2}{3}L'$$

Given, $L' = 20$ cm

$$\Rightarrow L = \frac{2}{3} \times 20 \text{ cm} = \frac{40}{3} \text{ cm} = 13.3 \text{ cm}$$

7 (b) For first resonance, $l_1 = \dfrac{\lambda}{4}$

For second resonance, $l_2 = \dfrac{3\lambda}{4}$

$$\therefore (l_2 - l_1) = \frac{3\lambda}{4} - \frac{\lambda}{4}$$

$$\text{or} \quad \lambda = 2(l_2 - l_1) \quad \text{...(i)}$$

As, velocity of sound wave is given as

$$v = \nu\lambda$$

where, ν is the frequency.

$$\Rightarrow \quad v = \nu[2(l_2 - l_1)] \quad \text{...(ii)}$$

[from Eq. (i)]

Here, $\nu = 320$ Hz,

$l_2 = 0.73$ m, $l_1 = 0.20$ m (given)

Putting the values in Eq. (ii), we get

$$v = 2[320(0.73 - 0.20)]$$

$$= 2 \times 320 \times 0.53$$

$$= 339.2 \text{ms}^{-1} \simeq 339 \text{ ms}^{-1}.$$

8 *(b)* Frequency of nth harmonic in an closed end tube,

$$f = \frac{(2n-1)v}{4l} \quad n = 1, 2, 3, \ldots$$

Also, only odd harmonics exists in a closed end tube.

Now, given two nearest harmonics are of frequency 220 Hz and 260 Hz.

$$\therefore \quad \frac{(2n-1)v}{4l} = 220 \text{ Hz} \quad \ldots\text{(i)}$$

Next harmonic occurs at

$$\frac{(2n+1)v}{4l} = 260 \text{ Hz} \quad \ldots\text{(ii)}$$

On subtracting Eq. (i) from Eq. (ii), we get

$$\frac{\{(2n+1)-(2n-1)\}v}{4l} = 260 - 220$$

$$2\left(\frac{v}{4l}\right) = 40$$

$$\Rightarrow \quad \frac{v}{4l} = 20 \text{ Hz}$$

$\therefore$ Fundamental frequency of the system

$$= \frac{v}{4l} = 20 \text{ Hz}$$

9 *(c)* The fundamental frequencies of closed and open organ pipe are given as

$$\nu_c = \frac{v}{4l} \quad \text{and} \quad \nu_o = \frac{v}{2l'}$$

Given, the second overtone (i.e. third harmonic) of open pipe is equal to the fundamental frequency of closed pipe

i.e $\quad 3\nu_o = \nu_c$

$$\Rightarrow \quad 3\frac{v}{2l'} = \frac{v}{4l}$$

$$\Rightarrow \quad l' = 6l = 6 \times 20 = 120 \text{ cm}$$

10 *(a)* According to question, we have,

Wavelength of transverse pulse

$$\lambda = \frac{v}{f} \quad \ldots\text{(i)}$$

where, v = velocity of the wave and f = frequency of the wave.

As we know, $\nu = \sqrt{\frac{T}{\mu}} \quad \ldots\text{(ii)}$

where, T = tension in the string or rope and μ = mass per unit length of the rope.

From Eqs. (i) and (ii), we get

$$\lambda = \frac{1}{f}\sqrt{\frac{T}{\mu}}$$

$$\Rightarrow \quad \lambda \propto \sqrt{T}$$

So for two different cases, we get

$$\frac{\lambda_2}{\lambda_1} = \sqrt{\frac{T_2}{T_1}} = \sqrt{\frac{m_1 + m_2}{m_2}}$$

11 *(b)* The smallest length of the air column is associated with fundamental mode of vibration of the air column as shown in the diagram

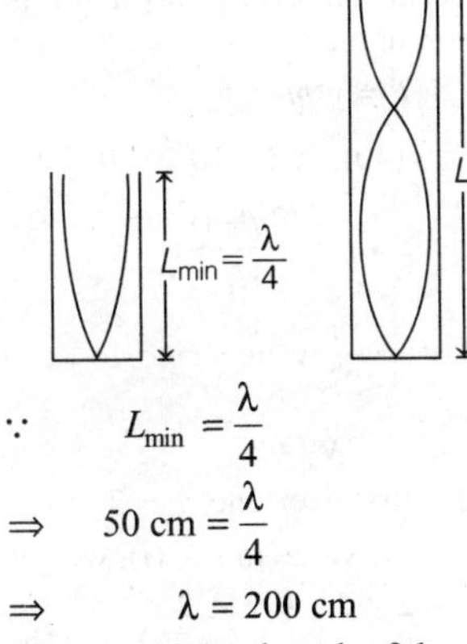

$$\because \quad L_{min} = \frac{\lambda}{4}$$

$$\Rightarrow \quad 50 \text{ cm} = \frac{\lambda}{4}$$

$$\Rightarrow \quad \lambda = 200 \text{ cm}$$

The next higher length of the air column is

$$L = \frac{\lambda}{4} + \frac{\lambda}{2} = \frac{\lambda + 2\lambda}{4} = \frac{3\lambda}{4}$$

$$= \frac{3}{4} \times 200 = 150 \text{ cm}$$

12 *(a)* From law of length, the frequency of vibrating string is inversely proportional to its length, i.e.

$$n \propto \frac{1}{l} \quad \text{or} \quad nl = \text{constant (say } k)$$

or $\quad nl = k$ or $l = \frac{k}{n}$

The segments of string of length $l_1, l_2, l_3 \ldots$ have frequencies $n_1, n_2, n_3, \ldots$ Total length of string is l.

So $\quad l = l_1 + l_2 + l_3 + \ldots$.

$$\therefore \quad \frac{k}{n} = \frac{k}{n_1} + \frac{k}{n_2} + \frac{k}{n_3} + \ldots .$$

or $\quad \frac{1}{n} = \frac{1}{n_1} + \frac{1}{n_2} + \frac{1}{n_3} + \ldots .$

13 *(d)* For a pipe closed at one end

$$f_n = n\left(\frac{v}{4l}\right) = n\left[\frac{340}{4 \times 85 \times 10^{-2}}\right]$$

$$= n[100]$$

Here, n is an odd number, so for the given condition n can go upto $n = 11$ because for $n = 13$ condition will not be valid.

Because, the given frequencies should lie below 1250 Hz.

$$n = 1, 3, 5, 7, 9, 11$$

So, number of possible natural oscillations could be 6.

14 *(b)* For an open pipe, the frequency,

$$f = \frac{v}{2l} \Rightarrow 5100 = \frac{340}{2 \times l}$$

$$l = \frac{340}{5100 \times 2}$$

$$\Rightarrow \quad l = \frac{2}{30 \times 2} = \frac{1}{30} \text{ m}$$

$$l = \frac{100}{30} = \frac{10}{3} \text{ cm}$$

15 *(b)* For fundamental mode (closed organ pipe), $n_1 = \frac{v}{4l} \quad \ldots\text{(i)}$

and for open organ pipe,

$$n_2 = \frac{v}{2l} \quad \ldots\text{(ii)}$$

According to the question,

$$n_2 - n_1 = 2 \text{(beats)}$$

$$\frac{v}{2l} - \frac{v}{4l} = 2 \Rightarrow \frac{2v - v}{4l} = 2$$

$$\Rightarrow \quad v = 8l \quad \ldots\text{(iii)}$$

When length of open organ pipe is halved and that of closed organ pipe is doubled, then let the two produce n beats,

$$\Rightarrow \quad \frac{v}{l} - \frac{v}{8l} = n$$

$$\Rightarrow \quad \frac{8v - v}{8l} = n \Rightarrow \frac{7v}{8l} = n$$

$$\Rightarrow \quad n = \frac{7(8l)}{8l} = 7$$

16 *(d)* According to the mode of vibration of air column in an open organ pipe,

First mode of vibration,

$$\nu_1 = \frac{v}{2l} \quad \ldots\text{(i)}$$

where, ν_1 = frequency of vibration,

v = speed of sound

and $\quad l$ = length of organ pipe

The frequency of n th mode of vibration,

$$\nu_n = n \times \nu_1 = n \times \left(\frac{v}{2l}\right) \quad \ldots\text{(ii)}$$

[From Eq. (i)]

Given, $\nu_n = 1.1 \text{ kHz} = 1100 \text{ Hz}$

$v = 330 \text{ ms}^{-1}$

$l = 30 \text{ cm} = 0.30 \text{ m}$

Putting these values in Eq. (ii), we get

$$1100 = n \times \left(\frac{330}{2 \times 0.30}\right)$$

$$\Rightarrow \quad n = \frac{1100 \times 2 \times 0.30}{330}$$

$$\Rightarrow \quad n = \frac{660}{330} = 2$$

So, second harmonic mode of pipe resonates.

17 (a) We know that, linear mass density is defined as a measure of mass per unit of length.

$\therefore$ Linear mass density,

$$\mu = \frac{\text{Mass}}{\text{Length}} = \frac{10 \times 10^{-3}}{1}$$

$$= 10 \times 10^{-3} \text{ kg/m}$$

$\therefore$ The speed of transverse wave,

$$v = \sqrt{\frac{T}{\mu}} = \sqrt{\frac{100}{10 \times 10^{-3}}} = \sqrt{10 \times 10^{3}}$$

$$= 1 \times 10^{2} = 100 \text{ ms}^{-1}$$

where, μ = volume per unit $\times$ density.

18 (d) Statement (d) is not true, because at the open ends change in pressure will be zero because velocity is proportional to λ.

19 (b) Stationary wave is represented as shown in figure. It is quite clear from figure that at nodes the amplitude is zero and velocity of particle is also zero and at anti-nodes the amplitude is maximum, so that the velocity of particle is also maximum and all particles cross mean position between two successive nodes.

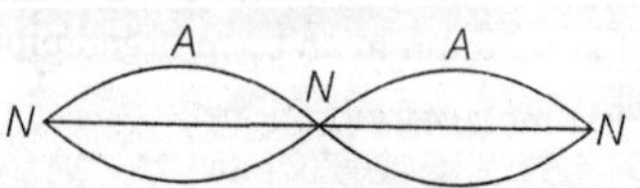

20 (d) From the relation,

$$n = \frac{1}{2l}\sqrt{\frac{T}{m}} \quad \text{...(i)}$$

$$\frac{n}{2} = \frac{1}{2l}\sqrt{\frac{T'}{m}} \quad \text{...(ii)}$$

From Eqs. (i) and (ii), we get

$$\Rightarrow \quad \frac{T'}{T} = \frac{1}{4}$$

$$\Rightarrow \quad 1 - \frac{T'}{T} = 1 - \frac{1}{4}$$

$$\therefore \quad \frac{T - T'}{T} = \frac{3}{4}$$

21 (b) Equation of wave,

$$y = 0.2 \sin (1.5x + 60t)$$

Comparing with standard equation,

$$y = A \sin (kx + \omega t), \text{ we get}$$

$$k = 1.5 \quad \text{and} \quad \omega = 60$$

$\therefore$ Velocity of wave,

$$v = \frac{\omega}{k} = \frac{60}{1.5} = 40 \text{ m/s}$$

$$\Rightarrow \quad v = \sqrt{\frac{T}{m}}$$

where, m is linear density and T is tension in the string.

So, $\quad T = v^2 m$

$$= (40)^2 \times 3 \times 10^{-4} = 0.48 \text{ N}$$

22 (d) Here, $\nu_1 = \frac{(2n-1)}{4l_1} v$

$$\nu_2 = \frac{n}{2l_2} v$$

Given, $\quad \nu_1 = \nu_2 \quad$ ...(i)

and for first overtone, $n = 2$

Putting the value in Eq. (i), we get

$$\frac{2 \times 2 - 1}{4l_1} v = \frac{2}{2l_2} v$$

$$\frac{3v}{4l_1} = \frac{2v}{2l_2}$$

So, the ratio of lengths $\frac{l_1}{l_2} = \frac{3}{4}$

23 (a) The fundamental frequency of an open organ pipe is $n = \frac{v}{2l}$. As temperature increases, both v and l increase but v increase more rapidly than l. Hence, the fundamental frequency increases as the temperature increases.

24 (b) The velocity of a transverse wave,

$$v = \sqrt{\frac{T}{\rho A}}$$

$$\Rightarrow \quad v \propto \frac{1}{\sqrt{A}}$$

$$\Rightarrow \quad v \propto \frac{1}{R} \quad [\because A = \pi R^2]$$

Because the velocity of wave depends on the radius. So, transverse wave travels faster in thinner wire.

25 (a) In the fundamental mode,

Frequency, $\quad n = \frac{v}{\lambda} \Rightarrow n = \frac{v}{4l}$

$$\Rightarrow \quad n = \frac{l}{t \times 4l} \quad \left[\because v = \frac{l}{t}\right]$$

$$\Rightarrow \quad n = \frac{1}{0.01 \times 4} \text{ [for } l = 1\text{m]}$$

$$\Rightarrow \quad n = 25$$

26 (a) Fundamental frequency of closed pipe,

$$n_1 = \frac{v}{4l_1}$$

$$\Rightarrow \quad l_1 = \frac{v}{4n_1}$$

Fundamental frequency of open pipe,

$$n_2 = \frac{v}{2l_1}$$

$$\Rightarrow \quad l_2 = \frac{v}{2n_2}$$

When both pipes are joined, then length of closed pipe

$$l = l_1 + l_2$$

$$\frac{v}{4n} = \frac{v}{4n_1} + \frac{v}{2n_2}$$

$$\Rightarrow \quad \frac{1}{2n} = \frac{1}{2n_1} + \frac{1}{n_2}$$

$$\Rightarrow \quad \frac{1}{2n} = \frac{n_2 + 2n_1}{2n_1 n_2} \Rightarrow n = \frac{n_1 n_2}{n_2 + 2n_1}$$

27 (c)

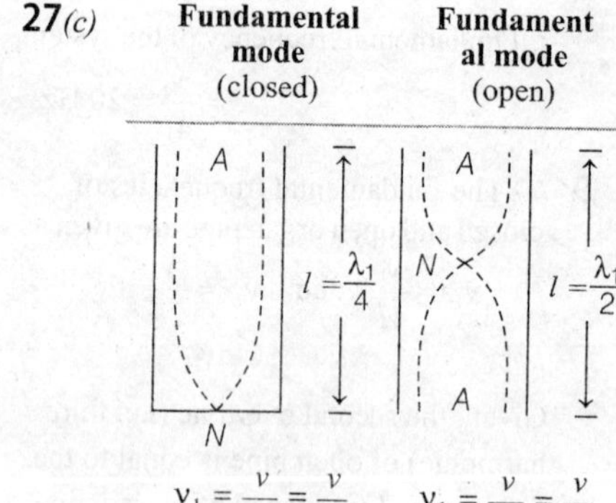

28 (c) Let l be the length of pipe, v is the speed of sound, then the fundamental note or first harmonic of closed tube,

$$n_1 = \frac{v}{4l}$$

Closed tube Open tube

For open tube, $\quad n_2 = \frac{v}{2l}$

$$\Rightarrow \quad n_2 = 2n_1$$

Given, $\quad n_1 = 512$ Hz

$$n_2 = 2n_1 = 2 \times 512 = 1024 \text{ Hz}$$

29 (a) When air is blown at the open end of a closed pipe, a longitudinal wave travels in the air of the pipe from open end to closed end.

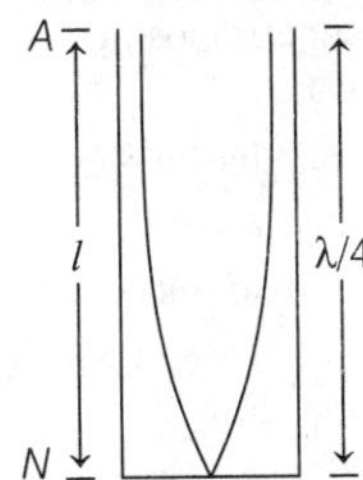

When λ is the wavelength and l be the length of pipe and n is the frequency of note emitted and v is the velocity of sound in air, then

$$n = \frac{v}{\lambda} \text{(fundamental note)}$$

Given, $n = 166$ Hz, $v = 332$ m/s

$$\therefore \quad \lambda = \frac{332}{166} = 2 \text{ m}$$

But, $\lambda = 4l$

$$\Rightarrow \quad l = \frac{\lambda}{4} = \frac{2}{4} = 0.5 \text{ m}$$

30 (d) Phase is expressed as relative displacement between two corresponding peaks of a waveform. In stationary wave, at any instant the phase of all particles between two successive nodes is the same, but phase of particles on one side of node is opposite to the phase of particles on the other side of node, i.e. phase difference between any two particles can be either 0 or π.

In this wave pattern, amplitude varies from point to point, but each element of the string (medium) oscillates with the some angular frequency or time period.

31 (a) Given, $l = 25$ cm, $d = 2$ cm and $v = 330 \text{ ms}^{-1}$

We know that, for open pipe, $f = \frac{nv}{2L}$

For $n = 1$, $f_1 = \frac{v}{2L}$

$$= \frac{330}{2 \times 25 \times 10^{-2}} = 660 \text{ Hz.}$$

Similarly for $n = 2, 3, 4$, etc. f_2, f_3 and f_4 will be 1320 Hz, 1980Hz and 2640Hz.

Hence correct option is (a).

32 (c) Fundamental frequency of closed pipe

$$n = \frac{v}{4l} = 220 \text{ Hz}$$

$$\Rightarrow \quad v = 220 \times 4l \quad \ldots\text{(i)}$$

If $\left(\frac{1}{4}\right)$th of the pipe is filled with water, then remaining length of air column is $\frac{3l}{4}$.

Now, fundamental frequency

$$= \frac{v}{4\left(\frac{3l}{4}\right)} = \frac{v}{3l}$$

First overtone

$$= 3 \times \text{fundamental frequency}$$

$$= 3 \times \frac{v}{3l} = \frac{3 \times 220 \times 4l}{3l} \quad \text{[from Eq(i)]}$$

$$= 880 \text{ Hz}$$

33 (c) For open pipe, $f_1 = \frac{v}{2l}$

and for closed pipe,

$$f_2 = \frac{v}{4 \times \left(\frac{l}{4}\right)} = \frac{v}{l} = 2f_1$$

$$\Rightarrow \quad \frac{f_1}{f_2} = \frac{1}{2}$$

34 (c) If number of loops in string is n, then

$$l = \frac{n\lambda}{2}$$

$$\therefore \quad \lambda = \frac{2l}{n}$$

35 (d) Fundamental frequency,

$$\nu = \frac{1}{2l}\sqrt{\frac{T}{m}} = \frac{1}{2l}\sqrt{\frac{T}{\rho r^2}} \quad \left[\because \rho = \frac{m}{r^2}\right]$$

$$\Rightarrow \nu \propto \frac{1}{lr}$$

$$\therefore \quad \frac{\nu_1}{\nu_2} = \frac{l_2 r_2}{l_1 r_1}$$

$$= \frac{2L \times r}{L \times 2r} = 1$$

36 (a) Frequency of wire,

$$f = \frac{1}{2lr}\sqrt{\frac{T}{\pi\rho}}$$

$$\therefore \quad \frac{f_1}{f_2} = \frac{l_2}{l_1} \times \frac{r_2}{r_1} \times \sqrt{\frac{T_1}{T_2}}$$

$$\Rightarrow \quad \frac{600}{f_2} = \frac{2}{1} \times \frac{1}{2} \times \sqrt{\frac{T}{T/9}}$$

$$\frac{600}{f_2} = 3$$

$$\Rightarrow \quad f_2 = \frac{600}{3} = 200 \text{ Hz}$$

37 (b) In a closed organ pipe in which length of air-column can be increased or decreased. The first resonance occurs at $\lambda/4$ and second resonance occurs at $3\lambda/4$.

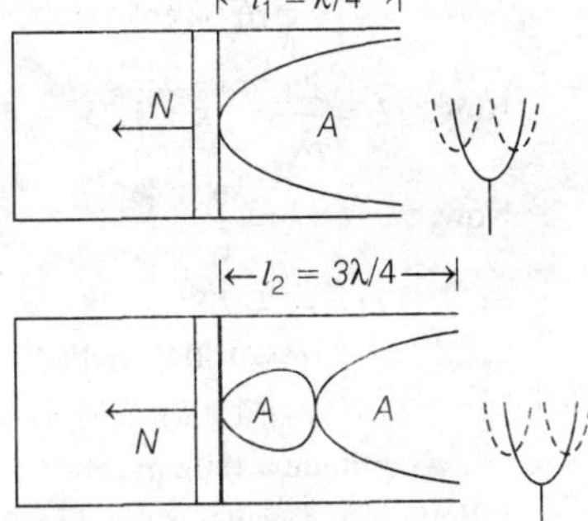

Thus, at first resonance

$$\frac{\lambda}{4} = 13 \quad \ldots\text{(i)}$$

and at second resonance

$$\frac{3\lambda}{4} = 41 \quad \ldots\text{(ii)}$$

Subtracting Eq. (i) from Eq. (ii), we have

$$\frac{3\lambda}{4} - \frac{\lambda}{4} = 41 - 13$$

$$\Rightarrow \quad \frac{\lambda}{2} = 28$$

$$\Rightarrow \quad \lambda = 56 \text{ cm}$$

Hence, frequency of tuning fork

$$n = \frac{v}{\lambda} = \frac{350}{56 \times 10^{-2}}$$

$$= 625 \text{ Hz}$$

38 (a) The fundamental frequency,

$$f = \frac{1}{2L}\sqrt{\frac{T}{\mu}}$$

$$f = \frac{1}{2L}\sqrt{\frac{T}{\rho\pi\frac{D^2}{4}}}$$

$$= \frac{1}{LD}\sqrt{\frac{T}{\pi\rho}}$$

$$\Rightarrow \quad f \propto \frac{1}{LD}$$

39 (b) When two identical transverse or longitudinal, progressive waves travel in a bounded medium with the same speed and same amplitude, but in opposite directions with no phase difference, then by their superposition a new type of wave is produced which appears stationary in the medium. Thus, it is called stationary or standing wave.

40 (d) In 4 m length, 5 complete waves fit, so, in 1 m length 1.25 complete wave fits.

$$\therefore \quad \frac{1}{\lambda} = 1.25$$

Now, $k = \frac{2\pi}{\lambda} = 2\pi \times 1.25 = 7.85$

Now, $k = \frac{\omega}{v}$

$$\Rightarrow \quad \omega = kv = 7.85 \times 128$$

$$\Rightarrow \quad \omega = 1004.8 \text{ rad/s} \simeq 1005 \text{ rad/s}$$

Amplitude = 0.02 m

$\therefore$ Equation of wave in + x-direction,

$$y = (0.02) \sin (7.85x - 1005t)$$

41 (b) In the first position of resonance, let length of air column is l,

$$l_1 = \frac{\lambda}{4}$$

$$\Rightarrow \quad \lambda = 4l_1$$

$$\Rightarrow \quad \lambda = 4 \times (0.4)$$

$$\Rightarrow \quad \lambda = 1.6 \text{ m}$$

Velocity of sound in air,

$$v = f\lambda = 450 \times 1.6 = 720 \text{ ms}^{-1}$$

42 (a) In closed organ pipe, open end of the pipe behaves as an anti-node and a node is formed at the closed end in first overtone mode or third harmonics for $n = 2$

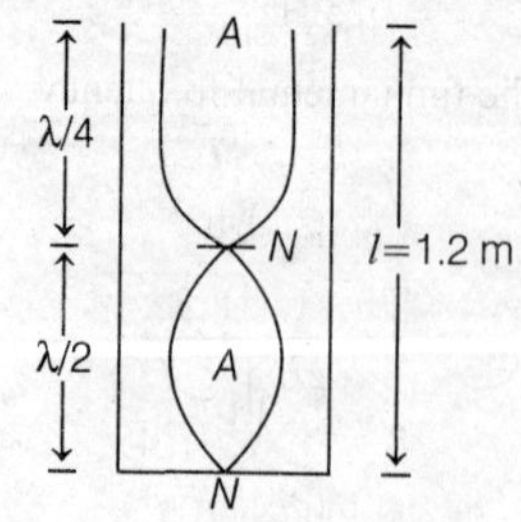

$$\Rightarrow \quad l = \frac{3\lambda}{4}$$

$$\Rightarrow \quad \frac{\lambda}{4} = \frac{l}{3} = \frac{1.2}{3} = 0.4 \text{ m}$$

Pressure variation will be maximum displacement nodes, i.e. at 0.4 m from the open end.

43 (a) End correction (e) can be calculated by relation

$$e = \frac{(l_2 - 3l_1)}{2}$$

where, l_1 and l_2 are depth at first and second resonance.

$$\Rightarrow \quad e = \frac{70.2 - 3 \times 22.7}{2} = 1.05 \text{ cm}$$

44 (c) $\because n_1 : n_2 : n_3 = 1 : 3 : 5$, which is possible when pipe is closed at one end and open at other end.

45 (a) First resonance occurs at 50 cm, so

$$l_1 = \lambda/4$$

$$\Rightarrow \quad \lambda = 4l_1 = 4 \times 50 = 200 \text{ cm}$$

Now, length of closed organ pipe at second resonance,

$$l_2 = \frac{3\lambda}{4}$$

$$\Rightarrow \quad l_2 = \frac{3 \times 200}{4} = 150 \text{ cm}$$

46 (e) Frequency in fundamental mode,

$$n = \frac{1}{2L}\sqrt{\frac{T}{\mu}}$$

where, $T = Mg$ = tension in string.

If length (L) becomes double, then mass (M) will be 4 times to maintain fundamental mode.

Then, the new load = 4 × 4 = 16 kg

47 (c) Less damping will result in sharper resonance.

48 (a) $y = 2a \cos kx \sin \omega t$

Comparing with equation

$y = A \sin \omega t$, we get

Amplitude of standing wave,

$$A = 2a \cos kx$$

Intensity at a certain point will be maximum when amplitude is maximum.

$\Rightarrow \quad \cos kx$ is maximum.

49 (a) Given, $f = 256$ Hz

$$v_{\text{sound}} = 336 \text{ ms}^{-1}$$

$$\lambda = \frac{v}{f} = \frac{336}{256} = 1.3125 \text{ m} = 131.25 \text{ cm}$$

The distance between a node (N) and adjoining anti-node $= \frac{\lambda}{4} = \frac{131.25}{4}$ = 32.8 cm. Hence, the shortest distance from the wall at which the air particles will have maximum amplitude of vibration is 32.8 cm.

50 (c) Two superimposing waves are as incident wave,

$$y_1 = a \sin (\omega t - kx)$$

and reflected wave,

$$y_2 = a \sin (\omega t + kx)$$

Then, by principle of superposition,

$$y = y_1 + y_2 = a[\sin (\omega t - kx) + \sin (\omega t + kx)]$$

$$\Rightarrow \quad y = 2a \cos kx \sin \omega t$$

Therefore, option (c) does not represent a stationary wave.

51 (a) Fundamental frequency,

open tube, $n = \frac{v}{2l} = 390$ Hz.

When $\left(\frac{1}{4}\right)$th of the tube is immersed in water, then it will be open at one end with its new length, i.e. $l' = \frac{3l}{4}$.

$\therefore$ New fundamental frequency will be

$$n' = \frac{v}{4l'} = \frac{v}{4\left(\frac{3l}{4}\right)}$$

$$\Rightarrow \quad n' = \frac{v}{3l} = \frac{2}{3}\left(\frac{v}{2l}\right) = \frac{2}{3} \times 390$$

$$\Rightarrow \quad n' = 260 \text{ Hz}$$

52 (c) For an open organ tube, fundamental frequency $f = \frac{v}{2l}$. When tube is half immersed in water, the organ tube becomes closed and length of vibrating air column becomes half, i.e. $l/2$.

$\therefore$ New fundamental frequency,

$$f' = \frac{v}{4\left(\frac{l}{2}\right)} = \frac{v}{2l} = f$$

53 (d) $\frac{\lambda}{4} = l_1 + e$

and $\frac{3\lambda}{4} = l_2 + e$

$$\Rightarrow \quad \frac{l_2 + e}{l_1 + e} = 3$$

$$l_2 + e = 3l_1 + 3e$$

$$\Rightarrow \quad l_2 = 3l_1 + 2e = 3 \times 15 + 2 \times 1.0 = 47 \text{ cm}$$

54 (d) According to the question,

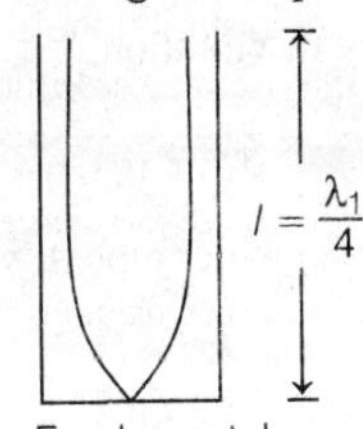

Fundamental overtone

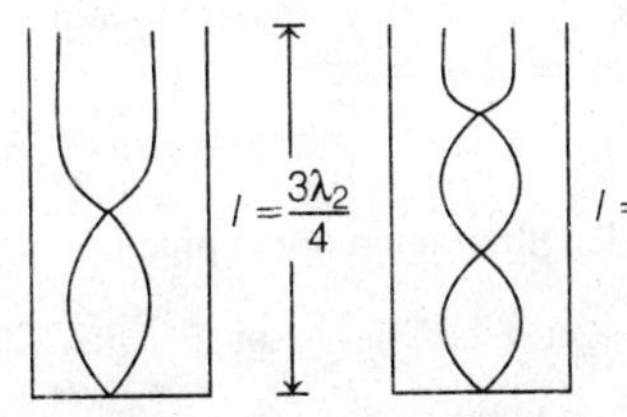

First overtone Second overtone

$$l = \frac{\lambda_1}{4} \Rightarrow \lambda_1 = 4l$$

$$l = \frac{3\lambda_2}{4} \Rightarrow \lambda_2 = \frac{4l}{3}$$

$$l = \frac{5\lambda_3}{4} \Rightarrow \lambda_3 = \frac{4l}{5}$$

$$\therefore \quad \lambda_1 : \lambda_2 : \lambda_3 = 4l : \frac{4l}{3} : \frac{4l}{5}$$

$$= 1 : \frac{1}{3} : \frac{1}{5}$$

55 (c) First harmonic of closed organ pipe of length l_1,

$f = \frac{v}{4l_1}$, v being velocity of sound.

Third harmonic of open organ pipe of length l_2, $f' = \frac{3v}{2l_2}$.

Therefore, in resonance condition

$$f = f'$$

or $$\frac{v}{4l_1} = \frac{3v}{2l_2}$$

or $$\frac{l_1}{l_2} = \frac{1}{6}$$

56 (e) Speed of transverse pulse,

$$v = \sqrt{\frac{T}{\mu}}$$

where, μ is mass of string per unit length.

For a transverse pulse,

$$T = \mu x g$$

$$\therefore \quad v = \sqrt{\frac{\mu x g}{\mu}}$$

$$\Rightarrow \quad v \propto \sqrt{x}$$

57 (a) The wire will vibrate with the same frequency as that of source. This can be considered as an example of forced vibration.

Given, $m = 9.8 \times 10^{-3} \text{kgm}^{-1}$

and $T = 10 \times 10^3 \times 9.8 \times 10^{-3}$ N $= 98$ N

Frequency of wire,

$$n = \frac{1}{2L}\sqrt{\left(\frac{T}{m}\right)}$$

$$= \frac{1}{2 \times 1}\sqrt{\left(\frac{98}{9.8 \times 10^{-3}}\right)}$$

$$= 50 \text{ Hz}$$

58 (b) $$n = \frac{1}{2l}\sqrt{\frac{T}{m}}$$

$$\Rightarrow \quad 490 - 420 = \frac{1}{2l}\sqrt{\frac{3.6 \times 10^2}{0.004}}$$

$$\Rightarrow \quad 70 = \frac{1}{2l} \times 300$$

$$\Rightarrow \quad l = \frac{300}{2 \times 70} = 2.14 \text{ m}$$

59 (a) We know that, $v \propto \sqrt{T}$

Let tension has to be increased by x%, then

$$\frac{v + 20\% \text{ of } v}{v} = \sqrt{\frac{T + x\% \text{ of } T}{T}}$$

$$\Rightarrow \quad \frac{6}{5} = \sqrt{\left(1 + \frac{x}{100}\right)}$$

$$\Rightarrow \quad \frac{36}{25} = 1 + \frac{x}{100}$$

or $$x = 44\%$$

Thus, tension has to be increased by 44%.

60 (c) The frequency of the sonometer,

$$n = \frac{1}{2l}\sqrt{\frac{T}{m}}$$

$$\Rightarrow \quad n = \frac{1}{2l}\sqrt{\frac{Mg}{\pi r^2 d}}$$

$$(\because T = Mg, m = \pi r^2 d)$$

$$\Rightarrow \quad n_1 = \frac{1}{2l_1}\sqrt{\frac{M_1 g}{\pi r^2 d}}$$

and $$n_2 = \frac{2}{2l_2}\sqrt{\frac{M_2 g}{\pi r^2 d}}$$

From the question,

$$n_1 = n_2$$

$$\frac{l_2}{l_1} = 2\sqrt{\frac{M_2}{M_1}}$$

$$\Rightarrow \quad \frac{100}{l_1} = 2\sqrt{\frac{3}{12}} = 2\sqrt{\frac{1}{4}}$$

$$\Rightarrow \quad = 2 \times \frac{1}{2}$$

$$\therefore \quad l_1 = 100 \text{ cm}$$

61 (a) $$\nu = \frac{1}{2l}\sqrt{\frac{T}{m}}$$

$$\Rightarrow \quad \nu \propto \frac{\sqrt{T}}{l}$$

$$\Rightarrow \quad \sqrt{T} \propto \nu \cdot l$$

Given, $\nu_1 = 200$ Hz, $\nu_2 = 300$ Hz, $l_1 = l$ and $l_2 = 2l$

$$\Rightarrow \quad \frac{T_2}{T_1} = \left[\frac{\nu_2}{\nu_1}\right]^2 \left[\frac{l_2}{l_1}\right]^2$$

$$= \left[\frac{300}{200}\right]^2 \left[\frac{2l}{l}\right]^2 = \frac{9}{1}$$

62 (a) The given standing wave is shown in the figure, where N represents node and A represents anti-node.

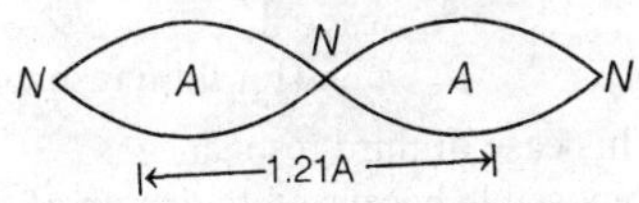

As length of one loop or segment is $\lambda/2$, so length of 2 segments is $2(\lambda/2)$.

$$\therefore \quad 2\frac{\lambda}{2} = 1.21 \text{ Å}$$

$$\Rightarrow \quad \lambda = 1.21 \text{ Å}$$

63 (e) The equation of given wave is

$$y = a\cos(kx - \omega t)$$

The other possible wave having opposite directions is

$$y' = -a\cos(kx + \omega t)$$

Therefore, equation of stationary wave is

$$y_s = y + y'$$

$$= a\cos(kx - \omega t) - a\cos(kx + \omega t)$$

$$= 2a \sin kx \cdot \sin \omega t$$

At $x = 0$,

$$y_s = 2a \sin 0 \cdot \sin \omega t = 0$$

Therefore, a node is formed at $x = 0$.

Hence, the other possible wave equation is

$$y = -a\cos(kx + \omega t)$$

64 (a) Fundamental frequency,

$$n = \frac{1}{2l}\sqrt{\frac{T}{m}}$$

i.e. $$n \propto \sqrt{T}$$

$\therefore \quad \dfrac{n_1}{n_2} = \sqrt{\dfrac{T_1}{T_2}}$

Given, $n_1 = 450$ Hz, $n_2 = 900$ Hz, $T_1 = 9$ kg-wt, $T_2 = ?$

$\Rightarrow \quad \dfrac{450}{900} = \sqrt{\dfrac{9}{T_2}}$

$\Rightarrow \quad T_2 = 36$ kg-wt

65 *(a)* Using relation $v = n\lambda$,

$$\lambda = \frac{v}{n} = \frac{340}{340} = 1 \text{ m}$$

If length of resonance columns are l_1, l_2 and l_3, then

$$l_1 = \frac{\lambda}{4} = \frac{1}{4} \text{ m} = \frac{100}{4} \text{ cm} = 25 \text{ cm}$$

(for first resonance)

$$l_2 = 3\frac{\lambda}{4} = \frac{3}{4} \text{ m} = \frac{3 \times 100}{4} \text{ cm} = 75 \text{ cm}$$

(for second resonance)

$$l_3 = \frac{5\lambda}{4} = \frac{5}{4} \text{ m} = \frac{5 \times 100}{4} \text{ cm} = 125 \text{ cm}$$

(for third resonance)

This case of third resonance is impossible because total length of the tube is 120 cm. So, minimum height of water

$$= 120 - 75 = 45 \text{ cm}$$

66 *(b)* Given, $l_1 + l_2 + l_3 = 110$ cm

and $n_1 l_1 = n_2 l_2 = n_3 l_3$

$n_1 : n_2 : n_3 :: 1 : 2 : 3$

$\therefore \quad \dfrac{n_1}{n_2} = \dfrac{1}{2} = \dfrac{l_2}{l_1} \Rightarrow l_2 = \dfrac{l_1}{2}$

and $\quad \dfrac{n_1}{n_3} = \dfrac{1}{3} = \dfrac{l_3}{l_1} \Rightarrow l_3 = \dfrac{l_1}{3}$

$\therefore l_1 + \dfrac{l_1}{2} + \dfrac{l_1}{3} = 110$

So, $\quad l_1 = 60$ cm, $l_2 = 30$ cm

and $\quad l_3 = 20$ cm

67 *(a)* For fundamental frequency of vibration of air column,

$$l = \frac{\lambda}{2} \Rightarrow \lambda = 2l$$

Frequency, $f = \dfrac{v}{\lambda}$

$$\Rightarrow \quad f = \frac{v}{2l} \qquad \text{...(i)}$$

When tube is placed inside water with half length immersed in water, then

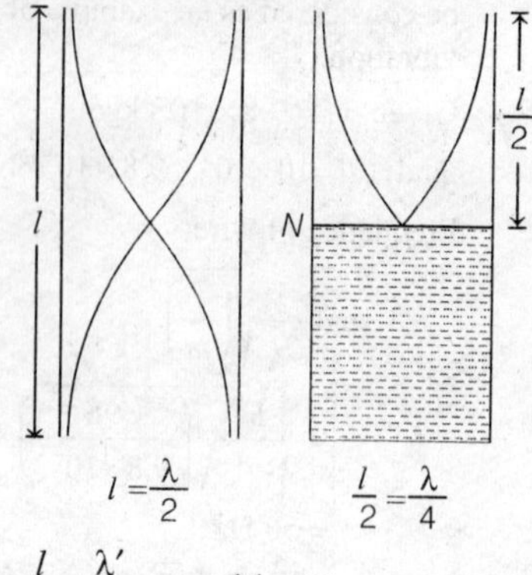

$$\frac{l}{2} = \frac{\lambda'}{4} \Rightarrow \lambda' = 2l$$

$$\text{Frequency, } f' = \frac{v}{\lambda'} = \frac{v}{2l} \qquad \text{...(ii)}$$

From Eqs. (i) and (ii), we get

$$f' = f$$

68 *(d)* If we adjust the length of air-column in closed organ pipe as such its any natural frequency equals to the frequency of tuning fork, then the amplitude of forced vibrations of air-column increases very much. This is the state of resonance.

At first resonance,

$$l = \frac{\lambda}{4} \Rightarrow \lambda = 4l$$

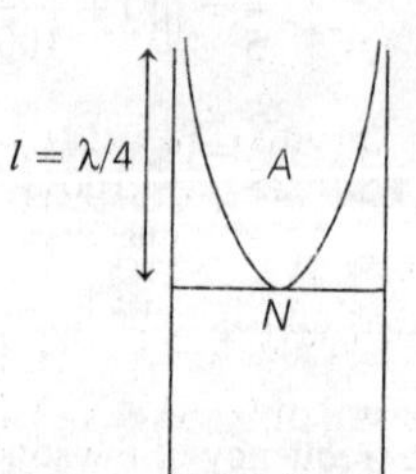

So, frequency of tuning fork,

$$f = \frac{v}{\lambda} = \frac{v}{4l}$$

Given, $l = 20$ cm $= 0.2$ m

and $\quad v = 332 \text{ ms}^{-1}$

Hence, frequency,

$$f = \frac{332}{4 \times 0.2} = 415 \text{ Hz}$$

69 *(c)* In closed organ pipe, first resonance occurs at $\lambda/4$, so in fundamental mode of vibration of organ pipe

$$\frac{\lambda}{4} = (l + 0.3d)$$

where, $0.3d$ is necessary end correction.

Frequency of vibration,

$$n = \frac{v}{\lambda} = \frac{v}{4(l + 0.3d)}$$

As l is same, wider pipe A will resonate at a lower frequency, i.e. $n_A < n_B$.

70 *(a)* Avoiding end correction, the length of closed organ pipe is

$$l_1 = \frac{\lambda_1}{4}$$

or $\quad \lambda_1 = 4l_1$

The length of open organ pipe is

$$l_2 = \frac{\lambda_2}{2} \quad \text{or} \quad \lambda_2 = 2l_2$$

Here, $\quad n_1 = n_2$

(according to the question)

$$\frac{v}{\lambda_1} = \frac{v}{\lambda_2}$$

$\Rightarrow \quad \dfrac{v}{4l_1} = \dfrac{v}{2l_2}$

$\therefore \quad l_1 : l_2 = 1 : 2$

71 *(d)* Frequency, $n = \dfrac{1}{2l}\sqrt{\dfrac{T}{\pi r^2 d}}$

where, l is the length, T is tension, r is the radius and d is the density.

Given, $\quad \dfrac{n_1}{n_2} = \dfrac{1}{2}, \dfrac{l_1}{l_2} = \dfrac{1}{4}$

$\Rightarrow \quad \dfrac{n_1}{n_2} = \dfrac{l_2}{l_1}\sqrt{\dfrac{r_2^2}{r_1^2}}$

$\Rightarrow \quad \left(\dfrac{n_1 l_1}{n_2 l_2}\right)^2 = \dfrac{r_2^2}{r_1^2}$

$\Rightarrow \quad \dfrac{r_1}{r_2} = \dfrac{n_2 l_2}{n_1 l_1} = 2 \times 4 = 8 : 1$

72 *(b)* As, $n \propto \sqrt{T}$

$\therefore T \propto n^2$ and $T' \propto (4n)^2$

Tension in the string, $T' = 16T$.

73 *(d)* The frequency of a string,

$f = \dfrac{1}{2l}\sqrt{\dfrac{T}{\mu}}$ where, μ is mass per unit length of strings and T is tension in the string.

$\therefore \quad f \propto \sqrt{T}$

$\Rightarrow \quad T \propto f^2$

$\Rightarrow \quad \dfrac{T_2}{T_1} = \left(\dfrac{f_2}{f_1}\right)^2$

Given, $f_1 = f,\ f_2 = 3f$ and $T_1 = T$

$$\therefore \quad \frac{T_2}{T} = \left(\frac{3f}{f}\right)^2$$

$$\Rightarrow \quad T_2 = 9T$$

74 (b) Fundamental frequency of string = HCF of the successive harmonics of frequencies 70 Hz and 84 Hz

$$\therefore \quad n = 14 \text{ Hz}$$

$$\Rightarrow \quad \frac{v}{2l} = 14$$

Speed, $v = 2 \times 1.5 \times 14$

$$= 42 \text{ ms}^{-1}$$

75 (c) The frequency of sonometer wire,

$$n = \frac{1}{2l}\sqrt{\frac{T}{m}}$$

Taking logarithm and differentiating the above relation, we get

$$\frac{\Delta n}{n} = \frac{\Delta l}{l} + \frac{1}{2}\frac{\Delta T}{T} + \frac{1}{2}\frac{\Delta m}{m}$$

$$\therefore \quad \frac{\Delta n}{n} = \frac{\Delta l}{l} + 0 + 0 = 1\%$$

Hence, frequency will decrease by 1%.

76 (a) The frequency of vibration in open organ pipe for first mode is given by

$$\nu_1 = \frac{v}{\lambda_1} = \frac{v}{2L}$$

or $$\nu_1 = \frac{v}{2L}$$

This is the lowest frequency of vibration and is called the fundamental frequency. The note or sound of this frequency is called fundamental note or first harmonic.
Similarly for $n = 2$,

$$\nu_2 = \frac{2v}{2L} = 2\nu_1$$

For $n = 3$,

$$\nu_3 = \frac{3v}{2L} = 3\nu_1$$

In general, the frequency of vibration in nth normal mode of vibration in open organ pipe would be

$$\nu_n = n\nu_1$$

Hence, frequency of fifth overtone

$= 6 \times$ fundamental frequency.

$$= 6 \times \frac{v}{2L} = \frac{6 \times 333}{2 \times 33.3 \times 10^{-2}}$$

$$= 3000 \text{ Hz}$$

77 (c) For an open organ pipe of length l, the frequency n is given by

$$n = n'\frac{v}{2l}$$

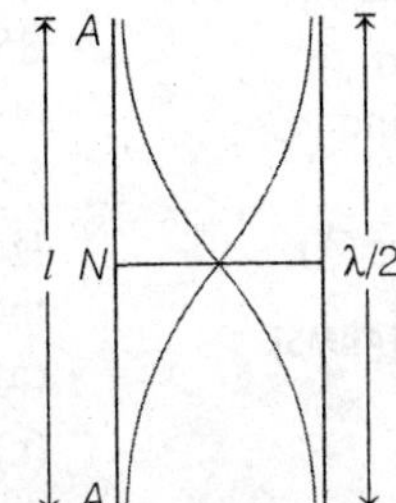

where, v is velocity of sound and n' is the overtone. frequency

Given, $n = 480$ Hz and $l = 1$ m,

and $v = 330 \text{ ms}^{-1}$

$$n' = \frac{n(2l)}{v} = \frac{480 \times 2 \times 1}{330}$$

$$= 2.9 \approx 3$$

Hence, this is the second overtone or third harmonic.

78 (d) Frequency of sonometer wire is given by

$$n = \frac{1}{2l}\sqrt{\frac{T}{m}}$$

where, m is mass of string per unit length and T is tension in the string.
Also, $m = \pi r^2 d$
where, r being radius of string and d is the density of material of string.

So, $$n = \frac{1}{2l}\sqrt{\frac{T}{\pi r^2 d}}$$

$$\Rightarrow \quad n \propto \frac{\sqrt{T}}{r}$$

$$\Rightarrow \quad \frac{n_1}{n_2} = \sqrt{\frac{T_1}{T_2}} \times \left(\frac{r_2}{r_1}\right)$$

Given, $T_2 = \frac{T_1}{2},\ r_2 = 2r$ and $n_1 = n$

Hence, $$\frac{n}{n_2} = \sqrt{2} \times 2$$

$$\Rightarrow \quad n_2 = \frac{n}{2\sqrt{2}}$$

79 (a) In an open organ pipe, both ends of the pipe are open. There are pressure nodes (or displacement anti-nodes) at both ends. In open organ pipe at both ends, the natural frequencies of oscillation form a harmonic series that includes all integral multiples of the fundamental frequency, i.e. all even and odd harmonics are present.
Therefore, if fundamental frequency is n, then other frequencies are n, $2n, 3n, 4n, \ldots$.

80 (a) The frequency of vibration,

$$n = \frac{1}{2l}\sqrt{\frac{T}{m}} \quad \ldots\text{(i)}$$

Given, $n' = n + \frac{3}{2}$

and $T' = T + \frac{T}{100} = \frac{101T}{100}$

$$n' = \frac{1}{2l}\sqrt{\frac{T'}{m}}$$

$$\therefore \quad n + \frac{3}{2} = \frac{1}{2l}\sqrt{\frac{101T}{100m}}$$

$$\Rightarrow \quad n + \frac{3}{2} = 1.005 \times \frac{1}{2l}\sqrt{\frac{T}{m}} \quad \ldots\text{(ii)}$$

From Eqs. (i) and (ii), we get

$$n + \frac{3}{2} = 1.005 \times n$$

$$\therefore \quad n = 300 \text{ Hz}$$

81 (b) For sonometer,

$$n \propto \frac{1}{l}$$

$$\therefore \quad \frac{n_1}{n_2} = \frac{l_2}{l_1}$$

Given, $n_1 = 256$ Hz, $l_1 = 25$ cm and $l_2 = 16$ cm

$$\Rightarrow \quad \frac{256}{n_2} = \frac{16}{25}$$

$$n_2 = \frac{256 \times 25}{16} = 400 \text{ Hz}$$

Topic 6
Doppler's Effect

2019

1 Two sources of sound S_1 and S_2 are moving towards and away from a stationary observer with the same speed respectively. Observer detects 3 beats per second. Find the value of speed of sources (approximately) (take, $f_1 = f_2 = 500\,\text{Hz}$ and speed of sound in air $= 330\,\text{ms}^{-1}$). **[AIIMS]**

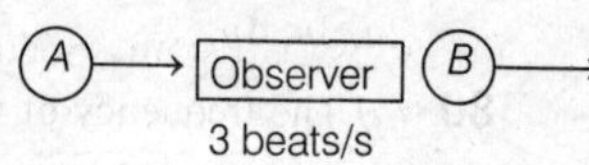

(a) $1\,\text{ms}^{-1}$ (b) $2\,\text{ms}^{-1}$
(c) $3\,\text{ms}^{-1}$ (d) $4\,\text{ms}^{-1}$

2017

2 The driver of a car travelling with speed $30\,\text{ms}^{-1}$ towards a hill sounds a horn of frequency 600 Hz. If the velocity of sound in air is $330\,\text{ms}^{-1}$, the frequency of reflected sound as heard by driver is **[AIIMS]**

(a) 550 Hz (b) 555.5Hz
(c) 720 Hz (d) 500 Hz

3 Two cars moving in opposite directions approach each other with speed of $22\,\text{ms}^{-1}$ and $16.5\,\text{ms}^{-1}$ respectively. The driver of the first car blows a horn having a frequency 400 Hz. The frequency heard by the driver of the second car is (take, velocity of sound $= 340\,\text{ms}^{-1}$) **[NEET]**

(a) 350 Hz (b) 361 Hz
(c) 411 Hz (d) 448 Hz

2016

4 A siren emitting a sound of frequency 800 Hz moves away from an observer towards a cliff at a speed of $15\,\text{ms}^{-1}$. Then, the frequency of sound that the observer hears in the echo reflected from the cliff is (take, velocity of sound in air $= 330\,\text{ms}^{-1}$) **[NEET]**

(a) 800 Hz (b) 838 Hz
(c) 885 Hz (d) 765 Hz

2014

5 A speeding motorcyclist sees traffic jam ahead of him. He slows down to $36\,\text{kmh}^{-1}$. He finds that traffic has eased and a car moving ahead of him at $18\,\text{kmh}^{-1}$ is honking at a frequency of 1392 Hz. If the speed of sound is $343\,\text{ms}^{-1}$, then the frequency of the honk as heard by him will be

(a) 1332 Hz (b) 1372 Hz **[CBSE AIPMT]**
(c) 1412 Hz (d) 1454 Hz

6 A car is moving with a speed of $72\,\text{kmh}^{-1}$ towards a roadside source that emits sound at a frequency of 850 Hz. The car driver listens to the sound while approaching the source and again while moving away from the source after crossing it. If the velocity of sound is $340\,\text{ms}^{-1}$, then the difference of the two frequencies, the driver hears, is

(a) 50 Hz (b) 85 Hz **[WB JEE]**
(c) 100 Hz (d) 150 Hz

7 A train is approaching towards a platform with a speed of $10\,\text{ms}^{-1}$, while blowing a whistle of frequency 340 Hz. What is the frequency of whistle heard by a stationary observer on the platform? (Take, speed of sound $= 340\,\text{ms}^{-1}$) **[KCET]**

(a) 330 Hz (b) 350 Hz
(c) 340 Hz (d) 360 Hz

8 The driver of a car travelling with speed of $30\,\text{ms}^{-1}$ towards a hill, sounds a horn of frequency 600 Hz. If the velocity of sound in air is $330\,\text{ms}^{-1}$, then the frequency of the reflected sound as heard by driver is **[UK PMT]**

(a) 500 Hz (b) 550 Hz
(c) 555.5 Hz (d) 720 Hz

2013

9 A train approaches stationary observer, the velocity of train being $(1/20)$ th of the velocity of sound. A sharp blast is blown with the whistle of the engine at equal intervals of a second. The interval between the successive blasts as heard by the observer **[UP CPMT, KCET]**

(a) $\frac{1}{20}$ s (b) $\frac{1}{2}$ min
(c) $\frac{19}{20}$ s (d) $\frac{19}{20}$ min

10 A train is moving at $30\,\text{ms}^{-1}$ in still air. The frequency of the locomotive whistle is 500 Hz and the speed of sound is $345\,\text{ms}^{-1}$. The apparent wavelength of sound in front of and behind the locomotive are respectively **[Manipal]**

(a) 0.80 m, 0.63 m (b) 0.63 m, 0.80 m
(c) 0.50 m, 0.85 m (d) 0.63 m, 0.75 m

11 The law applicable for determining the apparent change in frequency when a source and an observer are in motion is

(a) Doppler's law (b) Huygens' law **[WB JEE]**
(c) Newton's law (d) Galileo's law

2012

12 A train is moving at a speed of 200 ms^{-1} towards a stationary object, emits a sound of frequency 1000 Hz. Some of the sound reaching the object gets reflected back to the train as echo. The frequency of the echo as detected by the driver of the train is (take, speed of sound in air is 300 ms^{-1}) **[CBSE AIPMT]**

(a) 3500 Hz (b) 4000 Hz
(c) 5000 Hz (d) 3000 Hz

13 A train approaching a railway platform with a speed of 20 ms^{-1} starts blowing the whistle. Speed of sound in air is 340 ms^{-1}. If the frequency of the emitted sound from the whistle is 640 Hz, the frequency of sound to a person standing on the platform will appear to be **[WB JEE]**

(a) 600 Hz (b) 640 Hz (c) 680 Hz (d) 720 Hz

2011

14 A source of sound S is moving with a velocity of 50 ms^{-1} towards a stationary observer. The observer measures the frequency of the source as 1000 Hz. What will be the apparent frequency of the source when it is moving away from the observer after crossing him? (the velocity of the sound in the medium is 350 ms^{-1}). **[AIIMS]**

(a) 750 Hz (b) 857 Hz (c) 1143 Hz (d) 1333 Hz

15 A band playing music at a frequency f is moving towards a wall at a speed v_b. A motorist is following the band with a speed v_m. If v be the speed of the sound, the expression for beat frequency heard by motorist is **[AFMC, BHU]**

(a) $\frac{v+v_m}{v+v_b} f$ (b) $\frac{v+v_m}{v-v_b} f$

(c) $\frac{2v_b(v+v_m)}{v^2-v_b^2} f$ (d) $\frac{2v_m(v+v_b)}{v^2-v_m^2} f$

16 A source of sound is travelling at (100/3) ms^{-1} along a road, towards a point A. When the source is 3 m away from A, a person standing at a point O on a road perpendicular of frequency ν'. The distance of O from A at that time is 4 m. If the original frequency is 640 Hz, then the value of ν' is (take, velocity of sound = 340 ms^{-1}) **[BHU]**

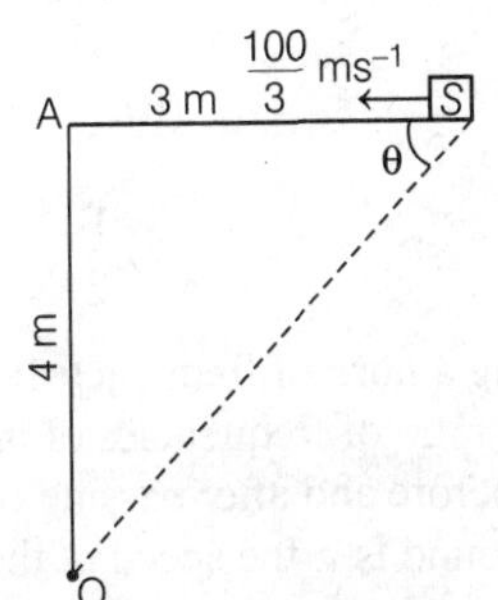

(a) 620 Hz (b) 680 Hz (c) 720 Hz (d) 840 Hz

17 A source of sound moves towards an observer with a velocity 108 kmh^{-1} and the observer also moves towards the source with the velocity 5 kmh^{-1}, then the velocity of sound is **[UP CPMT]**

(a) 320 ms^{-1} (b) 330 ms^{-1}
(c) 340 ms^{-1} (d) Data insufficient

18 Two sources are at a finite distance apart. They emit sound of wavelength λ. An observer situated between them on line joining the sources, approaches towards one source with speed u, then number of beats heard per second by observer will be **[UP CPMT]**

(a) $\frac{2u}{\lambda}$ (b) $\frac{u}{\lambda}$ (c) $\frac{u}{2\lambda}$ (d) $\frac{\lambda}{u}$

19 A train is moving with a constant speed along a circular track. The engine of the train emits a sound of frequency f. The frequency heard by the guard at rear end of the train is **[UP CPMT]**

(a) less than f
(b) equal to f
(c) greater than f
(d) may be greater than, less than or equal to f depending on the factors like speed of train, length of train and radius of circular track

20 Due to Doppler's effect, the shift in wavelength observed is 0.1 Å, for a star producing wavelength 6000 Å. The velocity of recession of star will be **[BCECE]**

(a) 2.5 kms^{-1} (b) 10 kms^{-1} (c) 5 kms^{-1} (d) 20 kms^{-1}

21 A source of sound is approaching an observer with speed of 30 ms^{-1} and the observer is approaching the source with a speed of 60 ms^{-1}. Then, the fractional change in the frequency of sound is (take, speed of sound in air = 330 ms^{-1}) **[Manipal]**

(a) $\frac{1}{3}$ (b) $\frac{3}{10}$
(c) $\frac{2}{5}$ (d) $\frac{2}{3}$

22 Two tuning forks A and B having a frequency of 500 Hz each are placed with B to the right of A. An observer is between the forks and is moving towards B with a speed of 25 ms^{-1}. The speed of sound is 345 ms^{-1} and the wind speed is 5 ms^{-1} from A to B. Calculate the difference in the two frequencies heard by the observer. **[Manipal]**

(a) 72.5 Hz (b) 55.6 Hz
(c) 76.2 Hz (d) 80.9 Hz

23 Two cars are moving on two perpendicular roads towards a crossing with uniform speeds of 72 kmh^{-1} and 36 kmh^{-1}. If first car blows horn of frequency 280 Hz, then the frequency of horn heard by the driver of second car when line joining the car makes angle of 45° with the roads, will be **[Manipal]**

(a) 321 Hz (b) 298 Hz (c) 289 Hz (d) 280 Hz

24 An observer moves towards a stationary sources of sound, with a velocity one-fifth of the velocity of sound. What is the percentage increase in the apparent frequency? **[OJEE]**

(a) 5% (b) 20%
(c) Zero (d) 0.5%

25 Two cars A and B approach a stationary observer from opposite sides as shown in figure. Observer hears no beats. If the frequency of the horn of the car B is 504 Hz, the frequency of horn of car A will be **[VMMC]**

(a) 529.2 Hz (b) 295.2 Hz
(c) 440.5 Hz (d) 259.2 Hz
(e) None of these

26 A sounding source of frequency 500 Hz moves towards a stationary observer with a velocity 30 ms^{-1}. If the velocity of sound in air is 330 ms^{-1}, then find the frequency heard by the observer. **[VMMC]**

(a) 500 Hz (b) 550 Hz
(c) 355 Hz (d) 55.5 Hz
(e) None of these

27 A source of sound producing wavelength of 50 cm is moving away from stationary observer with (1/5)th speed of sound. Then, what is the wavelength of sound heard by observer? **[EAMCET]**

(a) 70 cm (b) 55 cm (c) 40 cm (d) 60 cm

28 Two trains are moving towards each other with speeds of 20 ms^{-1} and 15 ms^{-1} relative to the ground. The first train sounds a whistle of frequency 600 Hz, the frequency of the whistle heard by a passenger in the second train before the train meet, is (take, the speed of sound in air is 340 ms^{-1}) **[JCECE]**

(a) 600 Hz (b) 585 Hz
(c) 645 Hz (d) 666 Hz

29 A bat flies at a steady speed of 4 ms^{-1} emitting a sound of $f = 90\times10^3$ Hz. It is flying horizontally towards a vertical wall. The frequency of the reflected sound as detected by the bat will be (take, velocity of sound in air is 330 ms^{-1}) **[KCET]**

(a) 88.1×10^3 Hz (b) 87.1×10^3 Hz
(c) 92.1×10^3 Hz (d) 89.1×10^3 Hz

30 A vehicle with a horn of frequency n is moving with a velocity of 30 ms^{-1} in a direction perpendicular to the straight line joining the observer and the vehicle. The observer receives the sound to have a frequency $n+n_1$, then (take, sound velocity in air is 300 ms^{-1}) **[KCET]**

(a) $n_1 = 10n$ (b) $n_1 = 0$
(c) $n_1 = 0.1n$ (d) $n_1 = -0.1n$

31 A stationary police car sounds a siren with a frequency of 990 Hz. If the speed of sound is 330 ms^{-1}, an observer, driving towards the car with a speed of 33 ms^{-1}, will hear a frequency of **[MGIMS]**

(a) 891 Hz (b) 900 Hz
(c) 1089 Hz (d) 1100 Hz

2008

32 When both the listener and source are moving towards each other, then which of the following is true regarding frequency and wavelength of wave observed by the observer? **[BCECE]**

(a) More frequency, less wavelength
(b) More frequency, more wavelength
(c) Less frequency, less wavelength
(d) More frequency, constant wavelength

33 A body is moving forward and backward and change in frequency observed by the body of a source is 2%. What is velocity of the body? (take, speed of sound is 300 ms^{-1}.) **[DUMET]**

(a) 6 ms^{-1} (b) 2 ms^{-1}
(c) 2.5 ms^{-1} (d) 3 ms^{-1}

34 With what velocity should an observer approach a stationary sound source, so that the apparent frequency of sound should appear double the actual frequency? **[KCET]**

(a) $\frac{v}{2}$ (b) $3v$
(c) $2v$ (d) v

2007

35 An observer moves towards a stationary source of sound with a speed (1/5)th of the speed of sound. The wavelength and frequency of the source emitted are λ and f, respectively. The apparent frequency and wavelength recorded by the observer are respectively **[BHU]**

(a) $f, 1.2\lambda$ (b) $0.8f, 0.8\lambda$
(c) $1.2f, 1.2\lambda$ (d) $1.2f, \lambda$

36 A car is moving towards a high cliff. The car driver sounds a horn of frequency f. The reflected sound heard by the driver has a frequency $2f$. If v be the velocity of sound, then the velocity of the car in the same velocity units, will be **[Manipal]**

(a) $\frac{v}{\sqrt{2}}$ (b) $\frac{v}{3}$
(c) $\frac{v}{4}$ (d) $\frac{v}{2}$

37 A car sounding a horn of frequency 1000 Hz passes an observer. The ratio of frequencies of the horn noted by the observer before and after passing of the car is 11 : 9. If the speed of sound is v, the speed of the car is **[RPMT]**

(a) $\frac{1}{10}v$ (b) $\frac{1}{2}v$ (c) $\frac{1}{5}v$ (d) v

38 The difference between the apparent frequency of a source of sound as perceived by the observer during its approach and recession is 2% of the frequency of the source. If the speed of sound in air is 300 ms^{-1}, then the velocity of the source is **[Punjab PMET]**

(a) 1.5 ms^{-1} (b) 12 ms^{-1}
(c) 6 ms^{-1} (d) 3 ms^{-1}

39 An engine moving towards a wall with a velocity 50 ms^{-1} emits a note of 1.2 kHz. Speed of sound in air is 350 ms^{-1}. The frequency of the note after reflection from the wall as heard by the driver of the engine is **[KCET]**

(a) 2.4 kHz (b) 0.24 kHz
(c) 1.6 kHz (d) 1.2 kHz

2006

40 A source is approaching a stationary observer with velocity (1/10) th that of sound. Ratio of observed and real frequencies will be **[RPMT]**

(a) $\frac{9}{10}$ (b) $\frac{11}{10}$
(c) $\frac{10}{11}$ (d) $\frac{10}{9}$

41 A motorcar is approaching towards a crossing with a velocity of 72 kmh^{-1}. The frequency of sound of its horn as heard by a policeman standing on the crossing is 260 Hz. The frequency of horn is **[J&K CET]**

(a) 200 Hz (b) 244 Hz
(c) 150 Hz (d) 80 Hz

42 An astronaut is approaching the Moon. He sends out a radio signal of frequency 5000 MHz and the frequency of echo is different from that of the original frequency by 100 kHz. His velocity of approach with respect to the Moon is **[AMU]**

(a) 2 km s^{-1} (b) 3 km s^{-1}
(c) 4 km s^{-1} (d) 5 km s^{-1}

43 If a source approaches and recedes from observer with same velocity, then the ratio of frequencies (apparent) is 6 : 5, then velocity of source is (take, $v_s = 330\ ms^{-1}$) **[JCECE]**

(a) 20 ms^{-1} (b) 10 ms^{-1}
(c) 30 ms^{-1} (d) 33 ms^{-1}

2005

44 A person is observing two trains one coming towards him and other leaving with the same velocity 4 ms^{-1}. If their whistling frequencies are 240 Hz each, then the number of beats per second are heard by the person will be (if velocity of sound is 320 ms^{-1}) **[BHU]**

(a) 3 (b) 6 (c) 9 (d) zero

45 A vehicle with horn of frequency ν is moving with a velocity of 30 ms^{-1} in a direction perpendicular to the line joining the observer and the vehicle. The observer perceives the sound to have a frequency $(\nu + \nu_1)$. If the sound velocity in air is 300 ms^{-1}, then **[AMU]**

(a) $\nu_1 = 0$ (b) $\nu_1 = 0.1\nu$
(c) $\nu_1 = -0.1\nu$ (d) $\nu_1 = 10\nu$

46 A source of sound and an observer are approaching each other with the same speed, which is equal to (1/10) times the speed of sound. The apparent relative change in the frequency of the source is **[EAMCET]**

(a) 22. 2% increase (b) 22. 2% decrease
(c) 18. 2% decrease (d) 18. 2% increase

47 The apparent frequency of a note is 200 Hz, when a listener is moving with a velocity of 40 ms^{-1} towards a stationary source. When he moves away from the same source with the same speed, the apparent frequency of the same note is 160 Hz. The velocity of sound in air (in ms^{-1}) is **[KCET]**

(a) 340 (b) 330
(c) 360 (d) 320

Answers

1 (a)	2 (c)	3 (d)	4 (b)	5 (c)	6 (c)	7 (a)	8 (d)	9 (c)	10 (d)
11 (a)	12 (c)	13 (c)	14 (a)	15 (a)	16 (b)	17 (d)	18 (a)	19 (b)	20 (c)
21 (b)	22 (a)	23 (b)	24 (b)	25 (a)	26 (b)	27 (d)	28 (d)	29 (c)	30 (b)
31 (c)	32 (a)	33 (d)	34 (d)	35 (d)	36 (b)	37 (a)	38 (d)	39 (c)	40 (d)
41 (b)	42 (b)	43 (c)	44 (b)	45 (a)	46 (a)	47 (c)			

Explanations

1 *(a)* Given, frequency of sound produced source S_1 and S_2 i.e, $f_1 = f_2 = 500\text{ Hz}$

Speed of sound in air, $v = 330\text{ ms}^{-1}$

Beats = 3 Hz

If v_s be the speed of source, when first source is moving towards the observer and f_1' be apparent frequency heard by the observer, then

$$f_1' = \frac{v}{v - v_s} \times f_1 = \frac{330}{330 - v_s} \times 500$$

When second source is moving away from the observer and f_2' be apparent frequency heard by the observer, then

$$f_2' = \frac{v}{v + v_s} \times f_2 = \frac{330}{330 + v_s} \times 500$$

$\therefore$ Beats $= f_1' - f_2' = 3$

$$\Rightarrow \frac{330}{330 - v_s} \times 500 - \frac{330}{330 + v_s} \times 500 = 3$$

$$\Rightarrow \frac{500 \times 2v_s \times 330}{(330)^2 - v_s^2} = 3$$

Since, $v_s^2 << (330)^2$

$$\Rightarrow \frac{500 \times 2v_s \times 330}{(330)^2} = 3$$

$$\Rightarrow v_s = 0.99 \approx 1\text{ ms}^{-1}$$

2 *(c)* When the sound is reflected from the cliff, it approaches the driver of the car. Therefore, the driver acts as an observer and both sources (car) and observer are moving.

In this case, the apparent frequency heard by the driver (observer),

$$f' = f\left(\frac{v + v_o}{v - v_o}\right)$$

Given, $f = 600\text{ Hz}$, $v = 330\text{ ms}^{-1}$

$v_o = 30\text{ ms}^{-1}$

$$f' = 600\left(\frac{330 + 30}{330 - 30}\right)$$

$$= 720\text{ Hz}$$

3 *(d)* When both source and observer are moving towards each other, apparent frequency is given by

$$f_a = f_0\left(\frac{v + v_o}{v - v_s}\right)$$

where,

f_o = original frequency of source = 400 Hz,

v_s = speed of source = 22ms^{-1},

v_o = speed of observer = 16.5ms^{-1}

and v = speed of sound = 340ms^{-1}.

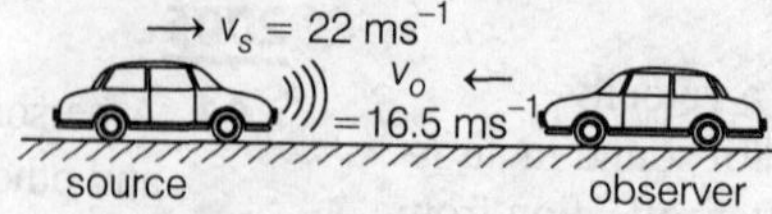

Frequency heard by the driver in the second car,

$$f_a = f_0\left(\frac{v + v_o}{v - v_s}\right) = 400\left(\frac{340 + 16.5}{340 - 22}\right)$$

$$= 448\text{ Hz}$$

4 *(b)* According to question, situation can be drawn as follows

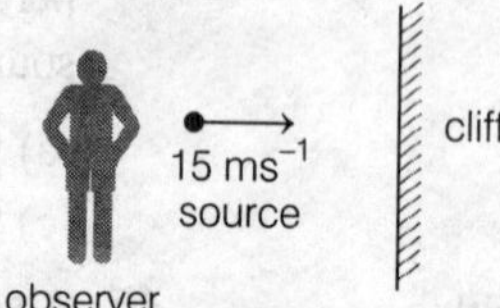

Frequency of sound that the observer hear in the echo reflected from the cliff is given by

$$f' = \left(\frac{v}{v - v_s}\right)$$

where,

f = original frequency of source;

v = velocity of sound

and v_s = velocity of source.

So, $f' = \left(\frac{330}{330 - 15}\right) 800 = 838\text{ Hz}$

5 *(c)* As both observer and source are moving, we can use the formula of apparent frequency as

⟶ 36 kmh^{-1} ⟶ 18 kmh^{-1}

f=1392 Hz

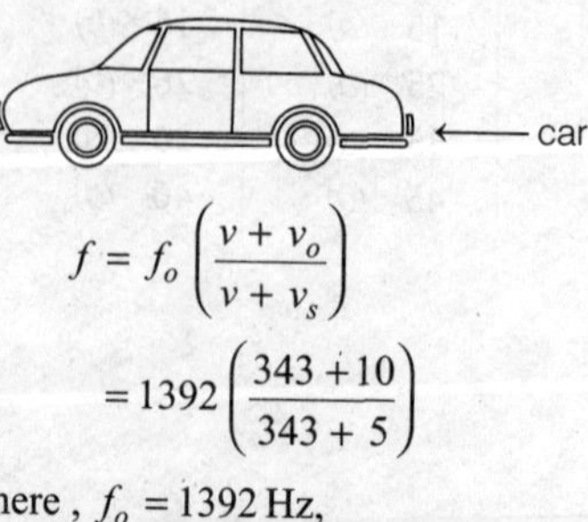

$$f = f_o\left(\frac{v + v_o}{v + v_s}\right)$$

$$= 1392\left(\frac{343 + 10}{343 + 5}\right)$$

where, $f_o = 1392\text{ Hz}$,

$v_o = 36 \times \frac{5}{18} = 10\text{ m/s}$,

$v_s = 18 \times \frac{5}{18} = 5\text{m/s}$

and $v = 343\text{ ms}^{-1}$

$$\Rightarrow f = 1392\left(\frac{353}{348}\right) = 1412\text{ Hz}$$

6 *(c)* By Doppler's effect, when observer is moving with velocity v_o towards a source at rest, then approach frequency is

$$n_{\text{approach}} = n\left(\frac{v + v_o}{v}\right)$$

where, $n = 850\text{ Hz}$, $v = 340\text{ ms}^{-1}$,

$v_0 = 72\text{ km h}^{-1} = 20\text{ ms}^{-1}$

$$n_{\text{approach}} = 850\left(\frac{340 + 20}{340}\right)$$

Similarly, when observer is moving away from source, then

$$n_{\text{separation}} = n\left(\frac{v - v_o}{v}\right)$$

$$= 850\left(\frac{340 - 20}{340}\right)$$

The difference of the two frequencies, $n_{\text{approach}} - n_{\text{separation}}$

$$= 850\left(\frac{360}{340}\right) - 850\left(\frac{320}{340}\right)$$

$$= \frac{850}{340} \times 40$$

$$= \frac{850}{8.5} = 100\text{ Hz}$$

7 *(a)* Given, $f = 340\text{ Hz}$ (frequency of sound produced by source)

Speed of sound, $v = 340\text{ ms}^{-1}$

Approaching speed of train, $v_s = 10\text{ ms}^{-1}$ and $f' = ?$

We know that when sound source is in motion and observer is stationary, then frequency of whistle heard by observer on platform

$$\Rightarrow f' = f\left(\frac{v}{v + v_s}\right)$$

$$= 340\left(\frac{340}{340 + 10}\right) = \frac{340 \times 340}{350}$$

$$= \frac{340 \times 34}{35} = \frac{11560}{35}$$

$$= 330.28$$

$$\approx 330\text{ Hz}$$

8 (d) Velocity of sound in air,
$v = 330$ m/s

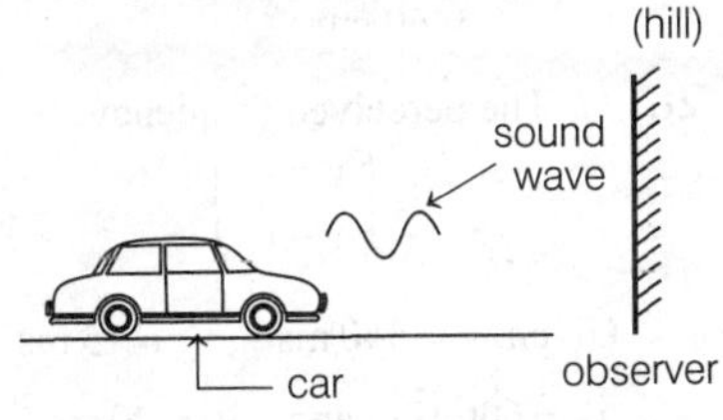

Due to relative motion between source and observer, we will assume Doppler's effect of sound.

Driver as observer and hill as source.

Speed of source, $v_s' = 0$

Speed of the observer (driver)

$= v_o' = 30 \text{ ms}^{-1}$

$\nu_0 = 600$ Hz.

Frequency of source (from hill) is

$$\nu_{a_1} = \nu_0 \frac{v}{v - v'_0}$$

$$= 600 \times \frac{330}{330 - 30} = 660 \text{ Hz.}$$

Apparent frequency observed, ν_2

$$= \left(\frac{v + v_o'}{v - v_s'}\right)\nu_{a_1} = \left(\frac{v + v_o'}{v - 0}\right)\nu_{a_1}$$

$$= \left(\frac{330 + 30}{330}\right)(660 \text{ Hz})$$

$$= \left(\frac{360}{330}\right)(660 \text{ Hz})$$

$= (360)(2)$ Hz

$= 720$ Hz

9 (c) From Doppler's effect, the sound of apparent change in frequency of the source due to a relative motion between source and observer is

$$n' = n\left(\frac{v - v_o}{v - v_s}\right)$$

where, v is velocity of sound, v_o is the velocity of observer and v_s is the velocity of source.

Given, $v_o = 0$ (observer stationary)

$$(v_s)_{20} = \frac{v}{20}$$

$n = 1$ Hz

(as blast is blown at an interval of 1s)

$$\therefore \quad n' = \frac{v}{v - \frac{v}{20}} \times 1 = \frac{20}{19} \text{ Hz}$$

Observed time interval between two successive blasts $= \frac{19}{20}$ s.

10 (d) Apparent wavelength in front of locomotive,

$$\lambda' = \frac{\lambda(v - v_s)}{\nu}$$

or $\lambda' = \frac{v - v_s}{\nu} = \frac{345 - 30}{500} \quad \left(\because \nu = \frac{v}{\lambda}\right)$

$$= \frac{315}{500} = 0.63 \text{ m}$$

Behind locomotive,

$$\lambda'' = \frac{\lambda(v + v_s)}{v} = \frac{v + v_s}{\nu}$$

$$= \frac{345 + 30}{500} = \frac{375}{500} = 0.75 \text{ m}$$

11 (a) Whenever there is a relative motion between a sounding body and a listener, there occurs an apparent change in the pitch of the sounding body. This law is called Doppler's law.

12 (c) From Doppler's shift, we know for this case

$$n' = n\left(\frac{v + v_s}{v - v_s}\right) = 1000\left(\frac{300 + 200}{300 - 200}\right)$$

$$= 1000\left(\frac{500}{100}\right) = 5000 \text{ Hz}$$

13 (c) Given, $v = 340 \text{ ms}^{-1}$, $v_s = 20 \text{ ms}^{-1}$

and $\nu_0 = 640$ Hz

From Doppler's law,

$$\nu = \left(\frac{340}{340 - 20}\right) 640 = 680 \text{ Hz}$$

14 (a) When the source is coming to the stationary observer,

$$n' = \left(\frac{v}{v - v_s}\right) n$$

$$\Rightarrow 1000 = \left(\frac{350}{350 - 50}\right) n$$

or $n = \frac{1000 \times 300}{350}$ Hz

When the source is moving away from the stationary observer.

$$n'' = \left(\frac{v}{v + v_s}\right) n$$

$$= \left(\frac{350}{350 + 50}\right)\left(\frac{1000 \times 300}{350}\right)$$

$= 750$ Hz

15 (a) According to Doppler's effect,

When observer is moving behind the source (band), apparent frequency heard

$$n' = n\left[\frac{v + v_o}{v + v_s}\right]$$

Here, $v_o = v_m \Rightarrow v_s = v_b$

$$\therefore \quad n_1 = \left[\frac{v + v_m}{v + v_b}\right] f$$

The other sound is the echo reaching the observer from the wall and can be regarded as coming from the image of source formed by reflection at the wall. This image is approaching the observer in the direction of sound.

Hence, for reflected sound, frequency heard by motorist

$$n_2 = n\left[\frac{v + v_o}{v + v_s}\right]$$

$$\Rightarrow \quad n_2 = f\left[\frac{v + v_m}{v + v_b}\right]$$

16 (b) Effective value of velocity of source,

$$v_s = \frac{100}{3}\cos\theta$$

By Pythagoras theorem, $\cos\theta = \frac{3}{5}$

$$\therefore \ v_s = \frac{100}{3} \times \frac{3}{5} = 20 \text{ ms}^{-1}$$

$$\nu' = \frac{v}{v - v_s}\nu = \frac{340}{340 - 20} \times 640$$

$= 680$ Hz

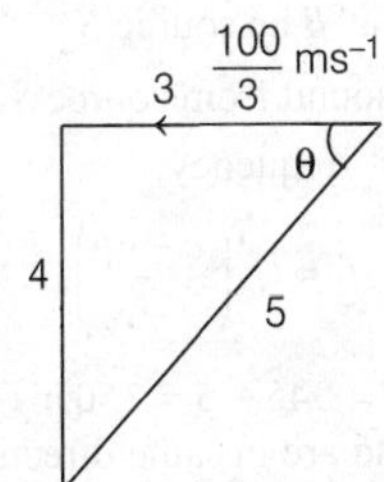

17 (d) The observed and emitted frequencies are required for calculating the velocity of sound.

18 (a) $n_1 = \left(\frac{v + u}{v}\right) n$ and $n_2 = \left(\frac{v - u}{v}\right) n$

Number of beats per second,

$$x = n_1 - n_2 = \left(\frac{v + u}{v}\right) n - \left(\frac{v - u}{v}\right) n$$

$$= \left(\frac{v + u - v + u}{v}\right) n = 2u\left(\frac{n}{v}\right) = \frac{2u}{\lambda}$$

19 (b) Suppose v be the speed of sound.

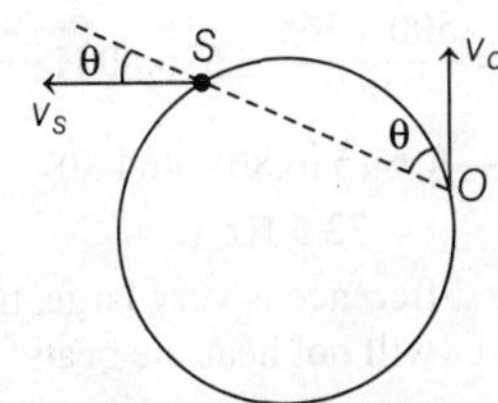

Then, $v = v_o \cos\theta = v_s \cos\theta$

and $f' = f\left(\frac{v + v_o \cos\theta}{v + v_s \cos\theta}\right) = f$

20 (c) The spectral shift, $z = \frac{\lambda - \lambda_0}{\lambda_0}$

Also,

$$z = \frac{\text{Velocity of recession of star}(v)}{\text{Velocity of light}(c)}$$

$\therefore \quad v = \frac{\lambda - \lambda_0}{\lambda_0} \times c = \frac{0.1}{6000} \times 3 \times 10^8$

$= 5000 \text{ ms}^{-1} = 5 \text{ kms}^{-1}$

21 (b) Given, $v_s = 30 \text{ ms}^{-1}$, $v_o = 60 \text{ ms}^{-1}$

Apparent frequency,

$$\nu' = \nu\left[\frac{v + v_o}{v - v_s}\right] = \nu\left[\frac{330 + 60}{330 - 30}\right]$$

$$\nu' = \nu\left[\frac{390}{300}\right]$$

$$\Rightarrow \quad \nu' = \frac{39}{30}\nu$$

$\therefore$ Fractional change in frequency

$$= \frac{\frac{39}{30}\nu - \nu}{\nu} = \frac{9}{30} = \frac{3}{10}$$

22 (a) Let the fork at A be source S_1 and the fork at B be source S_2.

For the sound from source S_1,

Apparent frequency,

$$f_1 = f\left(\frac{c - v_o}{c - v_s}\right) \quad \text{...(i)}$$

where, $c = 345 + 5 = 350 \text{ ms}^{-1}$ as wind and sound are in same direction.

$v_o = +25 \text{ ms}^{-1}$, $v_s = 0$

Put these values in Eq. (i), we get

$$\Rightarrow f_1 = 500\left(\frac{350 - 25}{350 - 0}\right)$$

$= 464.3$ Hz

For the sound from source S_2,

$c = 345 - 5 = 340 \text{ ms}^{-1}$ as wind is opposite to sound $v_s = 0 \text{ ms}^{-1}$,

$v_o = -25 \text{ ms}^{-1}$, then

$$f_2 = f\left(\frac{c - v_o}{c - v_s}\right) = 500\left(\frac{c - (-25)}{c - 0}\right)$$

$$= \frac{500 \times 365}{340} = 536.80 \text{ Hz}$$

$\Rightarrow f_2 - f_1 = (536.80 - 464.30)$

$= 72.5$ Hz

As the difference is very large, the observer will not hear the beats.

23 (b) The component of velocity of source along line joining,

$$v_s = v_1 \cos 45^\circ$$

$$= 36 \times \frac{1}{\sqrt{2}} \text{ kmh}^{-1} = 5\sqrt{2} \text{ ms}^{-1}$$

Component of velocity of observer (second car) along line joining

$$v_o = v_2 \cos 45^\circ = 72 \times \frac{1}{\sqrt{2}} \text{ kmh}^{-1}$$

$$= 10\sqrt{2} \text{ ms}^{-1}$$

$$n' = \frac{v + v_o}{v - v_s} n = \frac{330 + 10\sqrt{2}}{330 - 5\sqrt{2}} \times 280$$

$$= \frac{344}{323} \times 280 = 298 \text{ Hz}$$

24 (b) When the observer is moving towards a stationary source, apparent frequency,

$$\nu' = \nu = \left(\frac{v + v_o}{v}\right) \Rightarrow \nu' = \frac{6}{5}\nu$$

$\therefore$ Change in frequency $= \frac{6}{5}\nu - \nu = \frac{\nu}{5}$

$\therefore$ per cent change = 20%

25 (a) From Doppler's effect, the apparent change in frequency of a wave that is perceived by stationary observer is

$$n' = n_o\left(\frac{v}{v - v_s}\right)$$

where, v is speed of sound.

Since, observer is not hearing any beats, the apparent frequency of the two cars should be equal.

$\therefore \quad n' = n''$

$$504\left(\frac{v}{v - 30}\right) = n\left(\frac{v}{v - 15}\right)$$

$$\therefore \quad n = \frac{(330 - 15) \times 504}{(330 - 30)}$$

$$= \frac{315 \times 504}{300} = 529.2 \text{ Hz}$$

26 (b) Here, $n = 500$ Hz, $v_o = 0$,

$v_s = 30 \text{ ms}^{-1}$, $v = 330 \text{ ms}^{-1}$

$\therefore$ From $n' = n\left(\frac{v - v_o}{v - v_s}\right)$

$$= 500\left(\frac{330}{330 - 30}\right) = 550 \text{ Hz}$$

27 (d) Wavelength, $\lambda' = \lambda\left(\frac{v + v_s}{v}\right)$

$$\lambda' = 50\left(\frac{330 + (330/5)}{330}\right)$$

$$\Rightarrow \lambda' = 50\left(\frac{330 + 66}{330}\right)$$

$$= 50\left(\frac{396}{330}\right) = 50 \times \frac{6}{5}$$

$= 60$ cm

28 (d) The perceived frequency,

$$f' = f_o\left(\frac{v + v_o}{v - v_s}\right)$$

Given, $v = 340 \text{ ms}^{-1}$, $v_o = 15 \text{ ms}^{-1}$, $f_o = 600$ Hz and $v_s = 20 \text{ ms}^{-1}$

$$\Rightarrow f' = 600 \times \left(\frac{340 + 15}{340 - 20}\right) = \frac{355}{320} \times 600$$

$= 666$ Hz

29 (c) Frequency of reflected sound heard by the bat,

$$f' = f\left[\frac{v - (-v_o)}{v - v_s}\right] = f\left[\frac{v + v_o}{v - v_s}\right]$$

$$= f\left[\frac{v + v_b}{v - v_b}\right]$$

Given, $v = 330 \text{ ms}^{-1}$ and $v_b = 4 \text{ ms}^{-1}$.

$= 92.1 \times 10^3$ Hz

$$= \left[\frac{330 + 4}{330 - 4}\right] \times 90 \times 10^3$$

30 (b) Here, apparent distance between source and observer does not change, so the frequency that observer receive, i.e. $n' = n \Rightarrow n_1 = 0$

31 (c) From Doppler's effect, the perceived frequency f' is given by

$$f' = f\left(\frac{v + v_o}{v}\right)$$

Given, $f = 990$ Hz, $v = 330 \text{ ms}^{-1}$ and $v_o = 33 \text{ ms}^{-1}$

$$\therefore \quad f' = 990\left(\frac{330 + 33}{330}\right)$$

$$= 990 \times \frac{363}{330}$$

$= 1089$ Hz

32 (a) According to Doppler's effect, whenever there is a relative motion between a source of sound and listener, the apparent frequency of sound heard by the listener is different from the actual frequency of sound emitted by the source. Let S be source of sound and L is the listener of sound. ν be the actual frequency of sound emitted by the source and λ be the actual wavelength of the sound emitted.

If v is velocity of sound in still air, then $\lambda = v/\nu$

If velocity of listener is v_L and velocity of source is v_S, then apparent frequency of sound waves heard by the listener is

$$\nu' = \frac{v - v_L}{v - v_S} \times \nu$$

Here, both source and listener are approaching each other.

S $\longrightarrow v_S\ (+)$ $\quad v_L(-) \longleftarrow$ L

Then, v_S is positive and v_L is negative.

$$\therefore \quad \nu' = \frac{v - (-v_L)}{v - v_S} \nu = \left(\frac{v + v_L}{v - v_S}\right) \nu$$

i.e. $\nu' > \nu$

Also, $\lambda' < \lambda$

So, listener, listens more frequency and observe less wavelength.

33 *(d)* Here, body is acting as an observer. According to the given case, let u be the velocity of the body, then,

$$\nu_1 = \nu\left(\frac{v - u}{v}\right) \text{ and } \nu_2 = \nu\left(\frac{v + u}{v}\right)$$

$$\therefore \quad \Delta\nu = \nu_2 - \nu_1 = \nu\frac{2u}{v}$$

$$\text{So,} \quad \frac{\Delta\nu}{\nu} \times 100 = \frac{2u}{v} \times 100$$

$$\Rightarrow \quad 2 = \frac{2u}{v} \times 100$$

Given, $v = 300\ \text{ms}^{-1}$

$$\therefore \quad u = \frac{v}{100} = 3\ \text{ms}^{-1}$$

34 *(d)* By using $\nu' = \nu\left[\dfrac{v - v_o}{v - v_s}\right]$

$$\Rightarrow \quad 2\nu = \nu\left[\frac{v - v_o}{v - 0}\right]$$

$$\Rightarrow \quad v_o = -v$$

Negative sign indicates that observer is moving opposite to the direction of velocity of sound.

35 *(d)* When an observer moves towards an stationary source of sound, then apparent frequency heard by the observer increases. The apparent frequency heard in this situation,

$$f' = \left(\frac{v + v_o}{v - v_s}\right) f$$

As source is stationary, hence $v_s = 0$.

$$f' = \left(\frac{v + v_o}{v}\right) f$$

Given, $v_o = \dfrac{v}{5}$

Substituting in the relation for f', we have

$$f' = \left(\frac{v + v/5}{v}\right) f$$

$$= \frac{6}{5} f = 1.2 f$$

Motion of observer does not affect the wavelength reaching the observer, hence wavelength remains λ.

36 *(b)* When the sound is reflected from the cliff, it approaches the driver of the car. Therefore, the driver acts as an observer and both the source (car) and observer are moving.

Hence, apparent frequency heard by the observer (driver) is given by

$$f' = f\left(\frac{v + v_o}{v - v_s}\right) \quad \ldots\text{(i)}$$

where, v_s = velocity of sound

and v_o = velocity of car

Thus, Eq. (i) becomes

$$2f = f\left(\frac{v + v_o}{v - v_o}\right)$$

$$\Rightarrow 2v - 2v_o = v + v_o$$

$$\Rightarrow \quad 3v_o = v$$

$$\Rightarrow \quad v_o = \frac{v}{3}$$

37 *(a)* $n_{\text{before}} = \left(\dfrac{v}{v - v_c}\right) \cdot n$

and $n_{\text{after}} = \left(\dfrac{v}{v + v_c}\right) \cdot n$

$$\frac{n_{\text{before}}}{n_{\text{after}}} = \frac{11}{9} = \left(\frac{v + v_c}{v - v_c}\right) \Rightarrow v_c = \frac{v}{10}$$

38 *(d)* When source approaches the observer, the apparent frequency heard by observer is

$$n' = n\left(\frac{v}{v - v_s}\right) \quad \ldots\text{(i)}$$

where, v_s = speed of source of sound.

During it recession, apparent frequency

$$n'' = n\left(\frac{v}{v + v_s}\right) \quad \ldots\text{(ii)}$$

Accordingly $n' - n'' = \dfrac{2}{100} n$ (given)

$$\therefore \quad n\left(\frac{v}{v - v_s}\right) - n\left(\frac{v}{v + v_s}\right) = \frac{2}{100} n$$

$$\Rightarrow \quad v\left[\frac{v + v_s - v + v_s}{(v - v_s)(v + v_s)}\right] = \frac{2}{100}$$

$$\Rightarrow \quad \frac{2v_s}{(v - v_s)(v + v_s)} = \frac{2}{100}$$

$$\Rightarrow \quad 100\, v_s = v^2 - v_s^2$$

But speed of sound in air,

$$v = 300\ \text{ms}^{-1}$$

$$\therefore \quad 30000\, v_s = (300)^2 - v_s^2$$

$$\Rightarrow v_s^2 + 30000\, v_s - 90000 = 0$$

$$\therefore \quad v_s = \frac{-30000 \pm \sqrt{(30000)^2 + 4 \times 90000}}{2}$$

$$= \frac{-30000 \pm 30006}{2}$$

$$= \frac{6}{2} = 3\ \text{ms}^{-1} \text{ (taking + ve sign only)}$$

39 *(c)* The reflected sound appears to propagate in a direction opposite to that of moving engine. Thus, the source and the observer can be presumed to approach each other with same velocity.

$$\nu' = \frac{\nu(v + v_o)}{(v - v_s)} = \nu\left(\frac{v + v_s}{v - v_s}\right)$$

$$(\because v_o = v_s)$$

Given, $\nu = 1.2$ kHz, $v = 350\ \text{ms}^{-1}$ and $v_s = 50\ \text{ms}^{-1}$

$$\therefore \quad \nu' = 1.2\left(\frac{350 + 50}{350 - 50}\right)$$

$$= \frac{1.2 \times 400}{300}$$

$$= 1.6\ \text{kHz}$$

40 *(d)* From the relation,

$$f' = f_o\left[\frac{v_{\text{sound}} - v_{\text{observer}}}{v_{\text{sound}} - v_{\text{source}}}\right]$$

$v_o = 0$, because observer is stationary

$$\Rightarrow \text{Frequency, } f' = f_o\left[\frac{v}{v - \dfrac{v}{10}}\right]$$

$$= f_o\left[\frac{1}{\dfrac{9}{10}}\right]$$

$$\Rightarrow \quad f'/f_o = 10/9$$

41 (b) From Doppler's effect, perceived frequency,

$$n' = n\left(\frac{v - v_o}{v - v_s}\right)$$

Here, $v_s = 72 \text{ km h}^{-1} = \frac{72 \times 1000}{60 \times 60}$

$= 20 \text{ ms}^{-1}$

$v_o = 0$, $v = 332 \text{ ms}^{-1}$ and $n' = 260$ Hz

$$\therefore \quad 260 = n\left(\frac{332}{332 - 20}\right)$$

$$\therefore \quad n = \frac{260 \times 312}{332}$$

$= 244$ Hz

42 (b) Let the shift in frequency,

$\Delta n = 100 \times 10^3$ Hz

$n = 5000$ MHz $= 5000 \times 10^6$ Hz

and v = relative speed.

Then, $\frac{\Delta n}{n} = \frac{2v}{c}$

$$\Rightarrow \quad v = \frac{\Delta n}{2n}c = \frac{100 \times 10^3 \times 3 \times 10^8}{2 \times 5000 \times 10^6}$$

$= 3000 \text{ ms}^{-1}$

$= 3 \text{ km s}^{-1}$

43 (c) By Doppler's effect, the perceived frequency when source approaches observer,

$$n' = n\left(\frac{v}{v - v_s}\right) \quad \text{...(i)}$$

When source recedes the observer,

$$n'' = n\left(\frac{v}{v + v_s}\right) \quad \text{...(ii)}$$

From Eqs. (i) and (ii), we get

$$\frac{n'}{n''} = \frac{v + v_s}{v - v_s}$$

Given, $v = 330 \text{ ms}^{-1}$

$$\Rightarrow \quad \frac{6}{5} = \frac{330 + v_s}{330 - v_s}$$

$\Rightarrow 1980 - 6v_s = 1650 + 5v_s$

$\Rightarrow \quad 11v_s = 1980 - 1650 = 330$

$$v_s = \frac{330}{11} = 30 \text{ms}^{-1}$$

44 (b) By Doppler's effect of sound, when source is moving towards observer perceived frequency,

$$n' = n\left(\frac{v}{v - v_s}\right)$$

where, v is the velocity of sound and v_s is velocity of source.

Given, $n = 240$ Hz, $v = 320 \text{ ms}^{-1}$ and $v_s = 4 \text{ ms}^{-1}$

$$\therefore \quad n' = 240 \times \frac{320}{320 - 4}$$

$$= 240 \times \frac{320}{316} = 243 \text{ Hz}$$

When source is moving away from observer, perceived frequency,

$$n'' = n\left(\frac{v}{v + v_s}\right)$$

$$= 240 \times \frac{320}{320 + 4}$$

$= 237$ Hz

Number of beats per second (beat frequency)

$= n' - n''$

= difference of the frequency of sound source

$\Rightarrow \quad = 243 - 237 = 6$

45 (a) Actual frequency of horn = ν

Apparent frequency perceived by observer, $\nu = \nu + \nu_1$

Velocity of vehicle, $v_s = 30 \text{ ms}^{-1}$

Velocity of sound in air, $v = 300 \text{ ms}^{-1}$

Doppler's effect of sound is valid only if source and observer are both in relative motion.

As the source is moving in a direction perpendicular to the straight line which joins the observer, hence there is no relative motion between them.

Therefore, Doppler's effect will not occur, thus, $\nu_1 = 0$.

46 (a) Speed of sound = v (say)

Speed of source = speed of observer

$= \frac{v}{10}$ (given)

Let natural frequency of sound = n

Apparent frequency of sound,

$$n' = n\left(\frac{v - v_o}{v - v_s}\right)$$

Since, source is moving in the direction of sound and observer moving towards source, then

$$v_o = -\frac{v}{10} \text{ and } v_s = \frac{v}{10}$$

$$\therefore \quad n' = n\frac{\left(v + \frac{v}{10}\right)}{\left(v - \frac{1}{10}\right)} = \frac{\left(\frac{11v}{10}\right)}{\left(\frac{9v}{10}\right)}$$

$$\Rightarrow \quad n' = \frac{11}{9}n$$

$$\Rightarrow \quad n' - n = \frac{11}{9}n - n = \frac{2}{9}n$$

$$\Rightarrow \quad \frac{n' - n}{n} = \frac{2}{9}$$

$$\therefore \quad \frac{n' - n}{n} \times 100\% = \frac{2}{9} \times 100\%$$

$$= \frac{200}{9}\%$$

= 22.22% increase

47 (c) When listener is moving towards the source, then apparent frequency

$$n' = \left(\frac{v + v_o}{v}\right) \times n$$

Given, $n' = 200$ Hz and $v = 40 \text{ ms}^{-1}$

$$\Rightarrow \quad 200 = \left(\frac{v + 40}{v}\right) \times n \quad \text{...(i)}$$

where, v = velocity of sound in air

n = actual frequency of sound source.

Similarly, when listener is moving away

$$n' = \left(\frac{v - v_0}{v}\right) \times n$$

$$160 = \frac{v - 40}{v} \times n \quad \text{...(ii)}$$

From Eqs. (i) and (ii), we have

$$\frac{200}{160} = \frac{v + 40}{v - 40}$$

$\Rightarrow 5v - 200 = 4v + 160$

$\Rightarrow \quad v = 360 \text{ ms}^{-1}$

15

Electrostatics I

Quick Review

Electric Charges

The intrinsic property of atoms and molecules or elementary particles which give rise to electric force between various objects are known as electric charges.

Some important points related to charges are given below

(*i*) Charge is a scalar quantity and can be of two types : positive and negative. When some electrons are removed from the atom, it acquires a positive charge and when some electrons are added to the atom, it acquires a negative charge.

(*ii*) Like charges repel each other and unlike charges attract each other.

(*iii*) The property which differentiates the two kinds of charges is called the **polarity** of charge. If an object possesses an electric charge, then it is said to be electrified or charged.

(*iv*) 1 coulomb $= 3\times10^9$ esu $= \frac{1}{10}$ emu of charge, where esu is electrostatic unit of charge. Its CGS unit is stat coulomb.

(*v*) The dimensional formula of charge $[q] = [\text{AT}]$.

Basic Properties of Electric Charges

Additivity of Charge If a system consists of n charges $q_1, q_2, q_3 \dots\dots\dots q_n$, then the total charge of the system will be $q_1 + q_2 + q_3 + q_4 + \dots\dots + q_n$.

Quantisation of Charge Charge on any object can be an integral multiple of a smallest charge (e).

$$Q = \pm\, ne$$

where, $n = 1, 2, 3, \dots$ and $e = 1.6\times 10^{-19}$ C.

Conservation of Charge Charge can neither be created nor be destroyed, but can be transferred from one object to another object.

Coulomb's Law of Electrostatics

Force of attraction or repulsion between two stationary point charges are formulated by Coulomb' s law.

According to Coulomb's law, the force of attraction/repulsion between the charges q_1 and q_2 is given by,

$$F = k\frac{q_1 q_2}{r^2} = \frac{1}{4\pi\varepsilon_0}\cdot\frac{q_1 q_2}{r^2}$$

where, ε_0 = permittivity of free space

and $\frac{1}{4\pi\varepsilon_0} = 9\times10^9$ N-m^2/C^2.

Coulomb's Law in Vector Form

In vector form, Coulomb's law can be expressed as

$$F_{12} = \frac{1}{4\pi\varepsilon_0}\frac{q_1 q_2}{r^2}\,\hat{\mathbf{r}}_{21}$$

where,

F_{12} = force on charge q_1 due to q_2

and $\hat{\mathbf{r}}_{21}$ = unit vector points from charge q_2 to q_1.

Similarly, $F_{21} = \frac{1}{4\pi\varepsilon_0}\frac{q_1 q_2}{r^2}\,\hat{\mathbf{r}}_{12}$

Forces Between Multiple Charges : Superposition Principle

According to the principle of superposition, "Total force on a given charge due to number of charges is the vector sum of individual forces acting on that charge due to the presence of other charges".

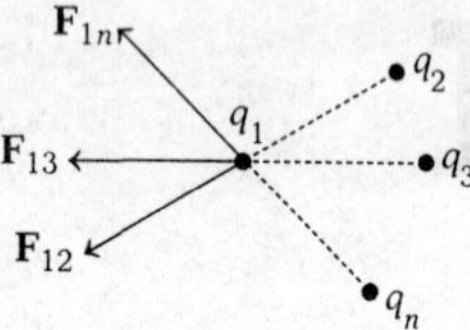

Consider a system of n point charges q_1, q_2, q_3 .....q_n distributed in space. Let the charges be q_2, q_3 ... q_n, exert forces $\mathbf{F}_{12}, \mathbf{F}_{13}, \ldots \mathbf{F}_{1n}$ on charge q_1. The total force on charge q_1 is given by

$$\mathbf{F}_1 = \frac{1}{4\pi\varepsilon_0}\left(\frac{q_1 q_2}{r_{12}^2}\hat{\mathbf{r}}_{12} + \frac{q_1 q_2}{r_{13}^2}\hat{\mathbf{r}}_{13} + \ldots + \frac{q_1 q_2}{r_{1n}^2}\hat{\mathbf{r}}_{1n}\right)$$

Electric Field and Field Strength

- The region surrounding a charge or distribution of charges in which its electrical effects can be observed is called **electric field.**
- The force experienced by a unit positive test charge placed at that point, without disturbing position of source charge is called **electric strength.**

  Electric field strength, $\mathbf{E} = \mathbf{F}/q_0$

  where, q_0 = test charge

  and F = force on positive test charge.
- Electric field at a distance r from a point charge q is expressed as

$$E = \frac{1}{4\pi\varepsilon_0} \cdot \frac{q}{r^2}$$

- Electric field E at a point P due to the systems of charges is given by

$$E(r) = \frac{1}{4\pi\varepsilon_0}\sum_{i=1}^{n}\frac{q_i}{r_i^2}\hat{\mathbf{r}}_i$$

or $$E = \mathbf{E}_1 + \mathbf{E}_2 + \ldots\ldots + \mathbf{E}_n.$$

Electric Field Lines

Imaginary lines drawn through a region of space so that its tangent at that point is the direction of electric field vectors, are called electric field lines.

Different properties of electric field lines are given below

(*i*) Electric field lines start from positive charges and end at negative charges. In the case of a single charge, they may start or end at infinity.

(*ii*) Tangent to any point on electric field lines shows the direction of electric field at that point.

(*iii*) Two field lines can never intersect each other because if they intersect, then two tangents drawn at that point will represent two directions of field at that point, which is not possible.

(*iv*) In a charge free region, electric field lines can be taken to be continuous curves without any breaks.

(*v*) Electric field lines do not form closed loops (because of conservative nature of electric field).

(*vi*) Electric field lines are perpendicular to the surface of a charged conductor.

(*vii*) Electric field lines contract lengthwise to represent attraction between two unlike charges.

(*viii*) Electric field lines exert sideways pressure to represent repulsion between two like charges.

Electric Field due to Continuous Charge Distributions

Electric field due to different types of charge distributions is given by

(*i*) Electric field due to line charge distribution is given by

$$E_L = \frac{1}{4\pi\varepsilon_0}\int_L \frac{\lambda}{r^2}\,dL\,\hat{\mathbf{r}}$$

where, λ = linear charge density, i.e. charge per unit length.

(*ii*) Electric field due to surface charge distribution is given by

$$E_S = \frac{1}{4\pi\varepsilon_0}\int_S \frac{\sigma}{r^2}\,dS\,\hat{\mathbf{r}}$$

where, σ = surface charge density, i.e. charge per unit area.

(*iii*) Electric field due to volume charge distribution is given by

$$E_V = \frac{1}{4\pi\varepsilon_0}\int_V \frac{\rho}{r^2}\,dV\,\hat{\mathbf{r}}$$

where, ρ = volume charge density, i.e. charge per unit volume.

(*iv*) Electric field at distance x from the centre of uniformly charged ring of total charge q on its axis is given by

$$E_x = \left(\frac{1}{4\pi\varepsilon_0}\right)\frac{qx}{(x^2 + R^2)^{3/2}}$$

Electric Dipole

A pair of equal and opposite point charges, that are separated by a short distance is known as electric dipole.

The product of magnitude of one charge and the distance between the charges is called the magnitude of the electric dipole moment p.

$$p = (2a)\,q$$

Electric Field Intensity due to Electric Dipole

Electric field intensity due to an electric dipole in different cases is given below

- Electric field intensity at a point on axial line of dipole,

$$E = \frac{1}{4\pi\varepsilon_0}\frac{2rp}{(r^2 - a^2)^2}$$

where, r = distance of point on axial line from the centre of dipole

and a = half of distance between the charges of dipole.

For short dipole, $E = \frac{1}{4\pi\varepsilon_0}\frac{2p}{r^3}$.

- Electric field intensity at a point on equatorial line of dipole, $E = \frac{1}{4\pi\varepsilon_0}\frac{-p}{(r^2 + a^2)^{3/2}}$

For short dipole, $E = \frac{1}{4\pi\varepsilon_0}\frac{-p}{r^3}$.

- Electric field due to dipole at any point,

$$E = \frac{1}{4\pi\varepsilon_0}\frac{1}{r^3}\sqrt{1 + 3\cos^2\theta}$$

where, θ = angle between the axis of dipole and the line joining the point and centre of dipole.

For axial position, $\theta = 0$.

For equatorial position, $\theta = 90°$.

Dipole in a Uniform Electric Field

When a dipole in kept in a uniform electric field, then no force with on it, i.e. $F_{net} = 0$.

In uniform electric field, a torque is applied on electric dipole whose magnitude is given as

$$\tau = pE\sin\theta \quad \text{or} \quad \boldsymbol{\tau} = \mathbf{p} \times \mathbf{E}$$

where, $\mathbf{p}$ = dipole moment and $\mathbf{E}$ = electric field strength.

- Direction of torque is perpendicular to the plane of paper and inwards.
- When dipole is parallel or anti-parallel to E, then (i.e. $\theta = 0°$, torque is zero and maximum at $\theta = 90°$ or $180°$).
- Work done in rotating the dipole in uniform electric field is given by

$$W = pE\,(\cos\theta_1 - \cos\theta_2)$$

where, θ_1 and θ_2 are initial and final angles between axis of dipole and electric field.

If $\quad \theta_1 = 90°$ and $\theta_2 = \theta$

$\therefore \quad W = -pE\cos\theta$ or $W = -\mathbf{p}\cdot\mathbf{E}$

Dipole in Non-uniform Electric Field

When an electric dipole is placed in a non-uniform electric field, then a resultant force as well as a torque act on it.

Let force on electric dipole = $(qE_1 - qE_2)$, along the direction of greater electric field intensity. Therefore, electric dipole undergoes rotational as well as linear motion.

Electric Flux

Electric flux over an area in an electric field is a measure of the number of field lines crossing a surface. It is denoted by ϕ_E.

Let $\mathbf{E}$ be electric field at the location of the surface element $d\mathbf{S}$. The electric flux through the entire surface is given by

$$\phi_E = \int_S \mathbf{E}\cdot d\mathbf{S} \Rightarrow \phi_E = \int_S E\,dS\cos\theta = E\cos\theta\int_S dS$$

where, θ is smaller angle between $\mathbf{E}$ and $d\,\mathbf{S}$.

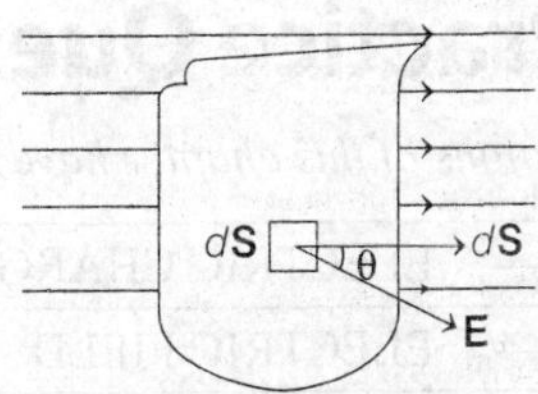

The flux of electric field passing through an area is the dot product of electric field vector and area vector.

$$\phi = \mathbf{E}\cdot\mathbf{S} = ES\cos\theta$$

Gauss's law

According to Gauss' law in electrostatics, "the total electric flux linked with a closed surface is equal to $\frac{1}{\varepsilon_0}$ times the net charge enclosed by that surface."

Thus, $\phi_E = \oint_s \mathbf{E}\cdot d\mathbf{S} = \frac{1}{\varepsilon_0}[Q_{\text{enclosed}}]$

If a charge Q is placed at the centre part of a cube, then electric flux with surface of cube, $\phi = \frac{Q}{\varepsilon_0}$ and electric flux with any one face of cube $= \frac{Q}{6\varepsilon_0}$.

Electric field due to various charged symmetrical bodies can be obtained by applying Gauss's law shown in the following table

Uniformly Charged Symmetrical Bodies	Electric Field	E-r Curve
(i) Infinitely long wire	$E = \frac{\lambda}{2\pi\varepsilon_0 r}$, where λ = line charge density.	
(ii) Infinite plane sheet	$E = \frac{\sigma}{2\varepsilon_0}$, where σ = surface charge density.	
(iii) Conducting sphere or shell of radius R and charge Q	$E = 0$ for $r < R$, $E = \frac{Q}{4\pi\varepsilon_0 R^2}$ for $r = R$ and $E = \frac{Q}{4\pi\varepsilon_0 r^2}$ for $r > R$	
(iv) Conducting cylinder of linear charge density λ and radius R	$E = \frac{\lambda}{2\pi\varepsilon_0 r}$ for $r > R$, $E = \frac{\lambda}{2\pi\varepsilon_0 R}$ for $r = R$ and $E = 0$ for $r < R$	
(v) Non-conducting cylinder	$E = \frac{\lambda r}{2\pi\varepsilon_0 R^2}$ for $r \leq R$	

Topical Practice Questions

All the exam questions of this chapter have been divided into 4 topics as listed below

Topic 1

Electric Charge and Coulomb's Law

2019

1 Two point charges A and B, having charges $+Q$ and $-Q$ respectively, are placed at certain distance apart and force acting between them is F. If 25% charge of A is transferred to B, then force between the charges becomes **[NEET]**

(a) $\frac{9F}{16}$ (b) $\frac{16F}{9}$ (c) $\frac{4F}{3}$ (d) F

2018

2 If point charges $Q_1 = 2\times10^{-7}$ C and $Q_2 = 3\times10^{-7}$ C are at 30 cm separation, then find electrostatic force between them. **[JIPMER]**

(a) 2×10^{-3} N

(b) 6×10^{-3} N

(c) 5×10^{-3} N

(d) 1×10^{-3} N

3 Positive charge Q is distributed uniformly over a circular ring of radius R. A point particle having a mass (m) and a negative charge $-q$ is placed on its axis at a distance x from the centre. Assuming $x < R$, find the time period of oscillation of the particle, if it is released from there [neglect gravity]. **[AIIMS]**

(a) $\left[\frac{16\pi^3\varepsilon_0 R^3 m}{Qq}\right]^{1/2}$ (b) $\left[\frac{8\pi^2\varepsilon_0 R^3}{q}\right]^{1/2}$

(c) $\left[\frac{2\pi^3\varepsilon_0 R^3}{3q}\right]^{1/2}$ (d) None of these

2017

4 A certain charge Q is divided into two parts q and $Q-q$. How the charge Q and q must be related, so that when q and $(Q-q)$ is placed at a certain distance apart experience maximum electrostatic repulsion? **[JIPMER]**

(a) $Q = 2q$ (b) $Q = 3q$
(c) $Q = 4q$ (d) $Q = 4q + c$

5 Suppose the charge of a proton and an electron differ slightly. One of them is $-e$ and the other is $(e + \Delta e)$. If the net of electrostatic force and gravitational force between two hydrogen atoms placed at a distance d (much greater than atomic size) apart is zero, then Δe is of the order (Take, mass of hydrogen, $m_h = 1.67 \times 10^{-27}$ kg) **[NEET]**

(a) 10^{-20} C (b) 10^{-23} C
(c) 10^{-37} C (d) 10^{-47} C

6 Two identical conducting balls A and B have positive charges q_1 and q_2 respectively but $q_1 \neq q_2$. The balls are brought together so that they touch each other and then kept in their original positions. The force between them is **[JIPMER]**

(a) less than that before the balls touched
(b) greater than that before the balls touched
(c) same as that before the balls touched
(d) zero

2014

7 Two charged spheres separated at a distance d exert a force F on each other. If they are immersed in a liquid of dielectric constant $K = 2$, then the force is (if all conditions are same) **[UK PMT]**

(a) $F/2$ (b) F (c) $2F$ (d) $4F$

8 If a charge on the body is 1 nC, then how many electrons are present on the body? **[KCET]**

(a) 1.6×10^{19} (b) 6.25×10^{9}
(c) 6.25×10^{27} (d) 6.25×10^{28}

2013

9 Two pitch balls carrying equal charges are suspended from a common point by strings of equal length, the equilibrium separation between them is r. Now, the strings are rigidly clamped at half the height. The equilibrium separation between the balls now become **[NEET]**

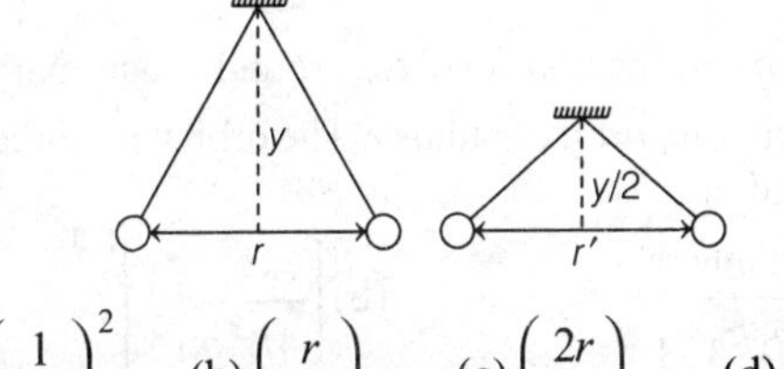

(a) $\left(\frac{1}{\sqrt{2}}\right)^2$ (b) $\left(\frac{r}{\sqrt[3]{2}}\right)$ (c) $\left(\frac{2r}{\sqrt{3}}\right)$ (d) $\left(\frac{2r}{3}\right)$

10 Each of the two point charges are doubled and their distance is halved. Force of interaction becomes n times, where n is

(a) 4 (b) 1 (c) 1/16 (d) 16 **[UP CPMT]**

11 A cylindrical conductor is placed near another positively charged conductor. The net charge acquired by the cylindrical conductor will be **[UP CPMT, KCET]**

(a) positive only (b) negative only
(c) zero (d) either positive or negative

12 Three identical charges are placed at the corners of an equilateral triangle. If the force between any two charges is F, then the net force on each will be **[WB JEE]**

(a) $\sqrt{2}F$ (b) $2F$ (c) $\sqrt{3}F$ (d) $3F$

2012

13 Three charges each of magnitude q are placed at the corners of an equilateral triangle, the electrostatic force on the charge placed at the centre is (each side of triangle is L) **[AFMC]**

(a) zero (b) $\frac{1}{4\pi\varepsilon_0}\cdot\frac{q^2}{L^2}$

(c) $\frac{1}{4\pi\varepsilon_0}\cdot\frac{3q^2}{L^2}$ (d) $\frac{1}{12\pi\varepsilon_0}\cdot\frac{q^2}{L^2}$

14 When a piece of polythene is rubbed with wool, a charge of -2×10^{-7} C is developed on polythene. What is the amount of mass which is transferred to polythene? **[UP CPMT]**

(a) 5.69×10^{-19} kg (b) 6.25×10^{-19} kg
(c) 9.63×10^{-19} kg (d) 11.38×10^{-19} kg

2011

15 A charged oil drop is suspended in uniform field of 3×10^4 Vm^{-1}, so that it neither falls nor rise. The charge on the drop will be (take, the mass of the charge 9.9×10^{-15} kg and $g = 10$ ms^{-2}) **[AIEEE 2004]**

(a) 3.3×10^{-18} C (b) 3.2×10^{-18} C
(c) 1.6×10^{-18} C (d) 4.8×10^{-18} C

16 Four charges equal to $-Q$ are placed at the four corners of a square and a charge q is at its centre. If the system is in equilibrium, the value of q is **[WB JEE]**

(a) $\frac{-Q}{4}(1+2\sqrt{2})$ (b) $\frac{Q}{4}(1+2\sqrt{2})$

(c) $\frac{-Q}{2}(1+2\sqrt{2})$ (d) $\frac{Q}{2}(1+2\sqrt{2})$

17 Charge q_2 of mass m revolves around a stationary charge q_1 in a circular orbit of radius r. The orbital periodic time of q_2 would be **[J&K CET]**

(a) $\left[\frac{4\pi^2 mr^3}{kq_1q_2}\right]^{1/2}$ (b) $\left[\frac{kq_1q_2}{4\pi^2 mr^3}\right]^{1/2}$

(c) $\left[\frac{4\pi^2 mr^4}{kq_1q_2}\right]^{1/2}$ (d) $\left[\frac{4\pi^2 mr^2}{kq_1q_2}\right]^{1/2}$

18 A soap bubble is given negative charge, then its radius will be **[DCE]**

(a) increase (b) decrease

(c) remain changed (d) fluctuate

19 Two identical charged spheres of material density ρ, suspended from the same point by inextensible strings of equal length make an angle θ between the strings. When suspended in a liquid of density σ and the angle θ remains the same. The dielectric constant K of the liquid is **[KCET]**

(a) $\frac{\rho}{\rho-\sigma}$ (b) $\frac{\rho-\sigma}{\rho}$

(c) $\frac{\rho}{\rho+\sigma}$ (d) $\frac{\rho+\sigma}{\rho}$

2010

20 Two positive ions, each carrying a charge q are separated by a distance d. If F is the force of repulsion between the ions, then the number of electrons missing from each ion will be (e being the charge on an electron) **[CBSE AIPMT]**

(a) $\frac{4\pi\varepsilon_0 Fd^2}{e}$ (b) $\sqrt{\frac{4\pi\varepsilon_0 Fe^2}{d^2}}$

(c) $\sqrt{\frac{4\pi\varepsilon_0 Fd^2}{e^2}}$ (d) $\frac{4\pi\varepsilon_0 Fd^2}{e^2}$

21 Two small spheres of masses M_1 and M_2 are suspended by weightless insulating threads of lengths L_1 and L_2. The spheres carry charges Q_1 and Q_2 respectively.

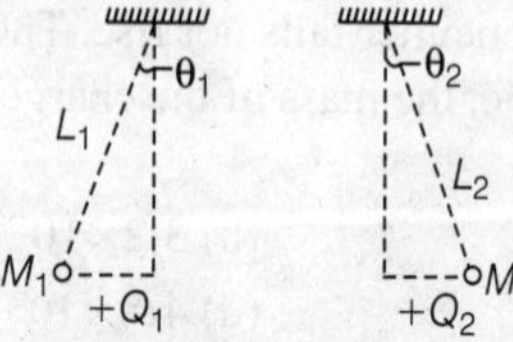

The spheres are suspended such that they are in level with one another and the threads are inclined to the vertical at angles of θ_1 and θ_2 as shown in figure. Which one of the following conditions is essential, if $\theta_1 = \theta_2$? **[UP CPMT]**

(a) $M_1 \neq M_2$ but $Q_1 = Q_2$ (b) $M_1 = M_2$

(c) $Q_1 = Q_2$ (d) $L_1 = L_2$

22 A charged particle of mass 0.003 g is held stationary in space by placing it in a downward direction of electric field of 6×10^4 N/C. Then, the magnitude of charge is **[UP CPMT]**

(a) 5×10^{-4} C (b) 5×10^{-10} C

(c) 5×10^{-6} C (d) 5×10^{-9} C

23 Two copper balls, each weighing 10 g are kept in air 10 cm apart. If one electron from every 10^6 atoms is transferred from one ball to the other, the Coulomb force between them is (atomic weight of copper is 63.5) **[Manipal]**

(a) 2.0×10^{10} N (b) 2.0×10^4 N

(c) 2.0×10^8 N (d) 2.0×10^6 N

24 Among two discs A and B, first has radius 10 cm and charge 10^{-6} C and second has radius 30 cm and charge 10^{-5} C. When they are touched charges on both are q_A and q_B respectively, will be **[Manipal]**

(a) $q_A = 2.75\ \mu C$, $q_B = 3.15\ \mu C$

(b) $q_A = 1.09\ \mu C$, $q_B = 1.53\ \mu C$

(c) $q_A = q_B = 5.5\ \mu C$

(d) None of the above

25 Two charges are at a distance d apart. If a copper plate of thickness $d/2$ is kept between them, the effective force will be **[Manipal]**

(a) $F/2$ (b) zero (c) $2F$ (d) $\sqrt{2F}$

2009

26 The distance between charges 5×10^{-11} C and -2.7×10^{-11} C is 0.2 m. The distance, at which third charge should be placed from second charge in order that it will not experience any force along the line joining the two charges, is **[Manipal]**

(a) 0.44 m (b) 0.65 m (c) 0.556 m (d) 0.350 m

27 When air medium in which two charges kept apart at a distance r is replaced by a dielectric medium of dielectric constant K, the force between the charges is **[J&K CET]**

(a) remain unchanged (b) $1/K$ times

(c) $\frac{1}{K^2}$ times (d) K^2 times

28 Mark the correct option. **[Punjab PMET]**

(a) In electrostatics, there is no motion of charge at all in conductor's bulk.

(b) In electrostatics, there is a motion of charged particle in conductor's bulk.

(c) In electrostatics and current electricity, there is a net motion of charged particles in the bulk of the material of the conductor.

(d) In electrostatics and current electricity, there is no net motion of charged particles in the bulk of the material of the conductor.

29 A ball with charge $-50e$ is placed at the centre of a hollow spherical shell has a net charge of $-50e$. What is the charge on the shell's outer surface? **[DUMET]**
(a) $-50e$ (b) Zero (c) $-100e$ (d) $+100e$

30 If 10^{10} electrons are acquired by a body every second, then the time required for the body to get a total charge of C will be **[DUMET]**
(a) 2h (b) 2 days (c) 2 yr (d) 20 yr

31 A charge q is placed at the centre of the line joining two equal charges, Q. The system of the three charges will be in equilibrium, if q is equal to **[BCECE]**
(a) $-\frac{Q}{2}$ (b) $-\frac{Q}{4}$ (c) $+\frac{Q}{4}$ (d) $+\frac{Q}{2}$

32 A pendulum bob of mass m carrying a charge q is at rest with its string making an angle θ with the vertical in a uniform horizontal electric field E. The tension in the string is **[BCECE]**
(a) $\frac{mg}{\sin\theta}$ and $\frac{qE}{\cos\theta}$ (b) $\frac{mg}{\cos\theta}$ and $\frac{qE}{\sin\theta}$
(c) $\frac{qE}{mg}$ (d) $\frac{mg}{qE}$

33 Two identical charged spheres suspended from a common point by two massless strings of lengths l, are initially at a distance d ($d << l$) apart because of their mutual repulsion. The charges begin to leak from both the spheres at a constant rate. As a result, the spheres approach each other with a velocity v. Then, v varies as a function of the distance x between the sphere, as **[NEET]**
(a) $v \propto x$ (b) $v \propto x^{-1/2}$ (c) $v \propto x^{-1}$ (d) $v \propto x^{1/2}$

34 When 10^{19} electrons are removed from a neutral metal plate, the electric charge on it is **[VMMC]**
(a) -1.6 C (b) $+1.6$ C (c) 10^{+19} C (d) 10^{-19} C

35 Two spherical conductors B and C having equal radii and carrying equal charges in them repel each other with a force F when kept apart at some distance. A third spherical conductor having same radius as that of B but uncharged is brought in contact with B, then brought in contact with C and finally removed away from both. The new force of repulsion between B and C is **[JIPMER]**
(a) $\frac{F}{4}$ (b) $\frac{3F}{4}$ (c) $\frac{F}{8}$ (d) $\frac{3F}{8}$

36 The number of electrons in 2 C of charge is **[JIPMER]**
(a) 5×10^{29} (b) 125×10^{17} (c) 1.6×10^{19} (d) 9×10^{11}

2008

37 A comb rub through one's dry hair attracts small bits of paper. This is due to **[AFMC]**
(a) comb is a good conductor
(b) paper is a good conductor
(c) the atoms is the paper get polarised by the charged comb
(d) the comb possesses magnetic properties

38 A table tennis ball which has been covered with a conducting paint is suspended by a silk thread, so that it hangs between two metal plates. One plate is earthed and the other plate is connected to a high voltage generator, then the ball **[BHU]**
(a) is attracted to the high voltage plate and stays there
(b) hangs without moving
(c) swings backward and forward hitting each plate in turn
(d) is repelled to the earthed plate and stays there

39 Consider a non-spherical conductor shown in the figure which is given a certain amount of positive charge. The charge distributes itself on the surface such that the charge densities are σ_1, σ_2 and σ_3 at the region 1, 2 and 3 respectively. Then **[Kerala CEE]**

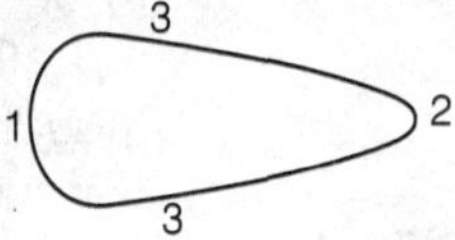

(a) $\sigma_1 > \sigma_2 > \sigma_3$ (b) $\sigma_2 > \sigma_3 > \sigma_1$
(c) $\sigma_3 > \sigma_1 > \sigma_2$ (d) $\sigma_2 > \sigma_1 > \sigma_3$
(e) $\sigma_1 > \sigma_3 > \sigma_2$

40 Three charges 1μC, 1μC and 2μC are kept at the vertices A, B and C of an equilateral triangle ABC of 10 cm side, respectively. The resultant force on the charge at C is **[Punjab PMET]**
(a) 0.9 N (b) 1.8 N (c) 2.72 N (d) 3.12 N

41 What is charge on 90 kg of electrons? **[DUMET]**
(a) 1.58×10^{13} C (b) 2.3×10^{12} C
(c) 2.53×10^{12} C (d) None of these

42 If charge and distance between two charges are reduced to half, then force between them is **[DUMET]**
(a) remain same (b) increases four times
(c) reduce four times (d) None of the above

43 Two identical metal spheres charged with $+12\mu$F and -8μF are kept at a certain distance in air. They are brought into contact and then kept at the same distance. The ratio of the magnitudes of electrostatic forces between them before and after contact is **[KCET]**
(a) 12 : 1 (b) 8 : 1 (c) 24 : 1 (d) 4 : 1

44 A circle of radius a has charge density given by $\lambda = \lambda_0 \cos^2\theta$ on its circumference. What will be the total charge on the circle? **[Guj CET]**
(a) $2\pi a$ (b) Zero
(c) $\pi a \lambda_0$ (d) None of these

45 Electrical force between two point charges is 200 N. If we increase 10% charge on one of the charges and decrease 10% charge on the other, then electrical force between them for the same distance becomes **[Guj CET]**
(a) 198 N (b) 100 N
(c) 200 N (d) 99 N

2007

46 Assertion The lightning conductor at the top of high building has sharp pointed ends. **[AIIMS]**

Reason The surface density of charge at sharp points is very high resulting in setting up of electric wind.

(a) Both Assertion and Reason are correct and Reason is the correct explanation of Assertion
(b) Both Assertion and Reason are correct but Reason is not the correct explanation of Assertion
(c) Assertion is correct but Reason is incorrect
(d) Both Assertion and Reason are incorrect

47 An electron is moving around the nucleus of a hydrogen atom in a circular orbit of radius r. The Coulomb force $\mathbf{F}$ between the two is **[BHU]**

(a) $k\frac{e^2}{r^3}\hat{\mathbf{r}}$ (b) $-k\frac{e^2}{r^3}\hat{\mathbf{r}}$
(c) $k\frac{e^2}{r}\hat{\mathbf{r}}$ (d) $-k\frac{e^2}{r}\hat{\mathbf{r}}$
(where, $k = 1/4\pi\varepsilon_0$)

48 Two identical spheres carrying charges $-9\mu C$ and $5\mu C$, respectively are kept in contact and then separated from each other. Point out true statement from the following. In each sphere **[Kerala CEE]**

(a) 1.25×10^{13} electrons are in deficit
(b) 1.25×10^{13} electrons are in excess
(c) 2.15×10^{13} electrons are in excess
(d) 2.15×10^{13} electrons are in deficit
(e) 1.52×10^{13} electrons are in excess

49 Two identical charges repel each other with a force equal to 10 g-wt, when they are 0.6 m apart in air ($g = 10\text{ ms}^{-2}$). The value of each charge is **[KCET]**

(a) 2 mC (b) 2×10^{-7} C
(c) 2 nC (d) $2\mu C$

50 Two point charges +2C and + 6 C repel each other with a force of 12 N. If a charge of –2C is given to each of these charges, the force will now be **[AMU]**

(a) zero (b) 8 N (attractive)
(c) 8 N (repulsive) (d) None of these

2006

51 Electric charges of $1\mu C$, $-1\mu C$ and $2\mu C$ are placed in air at the corners A, B and C respectively of an equilateral triangle ABC having length of each side 10 cm. The resultant force on the charge at C is **[KCET]**

(a) 0.9 N (b) 1.8 N (c) 2.7 N (d) 3.6 N

52 A pendulum bob carriers a negative charge $-q$. A positive charge $+q$ is held at the point of support. Then, the time period of the bob is **[MHT CET]**

(a) greater than $2\pi\sqrt{L/g}$ (b) less than $2\pi\sqrt{L/g}$
(c) equal to $2\pi\sqrt{L/g}$ (d) equal to $2\pi\sqrt{2L/g}$

53 Two identical spheres with charges $4q$ and $-2q$ kept some distance apart exert a force F on each other. If they are made to touch each other and replaced at their old positions, the force between them will be **[J&K CET]**

(a) $\frac{1}{9}F$ (b) $\frac{1}{8}F$ (c) $\frac{9}{8}F$ (d) $\frac{8}{9}F$

2005

54 Two equal negative charges $-q$ are fixed at the point $(0, a)$ and $(0, -a)$ on the y-axis. A positive charge Q is released from rest at the point $(2a, 0)$ on the x-axis. The charge will **[BHU]**

(a) execute SHM about the origin
(b) move to the origin and remain at rest
(c) move to infinity
(d) execute oscillatory but not SHM

55 A and B are two identical spherical charged bodies, which repel each other with force F, kept at a finite distance. A third uncharged sphere of the same size is brought in contact with sphere B and removed. It is then kept at mid-point of A and B. Find the magnitude of force on C. **[Manipal]**

(a) $F/2$ (b) $F/8$ (c) F (d) Zero

56 Charges $4Q, q$ and Q are placed along x-axis at position $x = 0, x = l/2$ and $x = l$, respectively. Find the value of q, so that force on charge Q is zero. **[DUMET]**

(a) Q (b) $Q/2$ (c) $-Q/2$ (d) $-Q$

Answers

1 (a)	2 (b)	3 (a)	4 (a)	5 (c)	6 (b)	7 (a)	8 (b)	9 (b)	10 (d)
11 (c)	12 (c)	13 (a)	14 (d)	15 (a)	16 (b)	17 (a)	18 (a)	19 (a)	20 (c)
21 (b)	22 (b)	23 (c)	24 (c)	25 (b)	26 (c)	27 (b)	28 (a)	29 (d)	30 (d)
31 (b)	32 (b)	33 (b)	34 (b)	35 (d)	36 (b)	37 (c)	38 (c)	39 (d)	40 (d)
41 (a)	42 (a)	43 (c)	44 (c)	45 (a)	46 (a)	47 (b)	48 (b)	49 (d)	50 (a)
51 (b)	52 (c)	53 (b)	54 (d)	55 (c)	56 (d)				

Explanations

1 (a) The force between two point charges A and B, having charges $+Q$ and $-Q$ respectively is given by

+Q −Q
A B
r

$$F = \frac{kQ_AQ_B}{r^2} = \frac{kQ(-Q)}{r^2} = -\frac{kQ^2}{r^2} \quad \ldots(i)$$

where, $k = \text{constant} = \frac{1}{4\pi\varepsilon_0}$

and r = distance between two charges A and B.

When 25% charge of A is transferred to B, then new amount of charge on A and B respectively become

$$Q'_A = \frac{75}{100}(Q_A) = \frac{3}{4}Q$$

$$Q'_B = \left(\frac{25}{100}Q_A + Q_B\right)$$

$$= \left(\frac{1}{4}Q - Q\right) = \frac{-3}{4}Q$$

So, the force between the two charges now becomes

$$F' = \frac{kQ'_AQ'_B}{r^2} = \frac{k\left(\frac{3Q}{4}\right)\left(-\frac{3}{4}Q\right)}{r^2}$$

$$= \frac{-9kQ^2}{16r^2} = \frac{9}{16}F \quad \text{[from Eq. (i)]}$$

Thus, the new force between the charges is 9/16 times the initial force between the charges.

2 (b) $\because$ Electrostatic force, $F = k\frac{Q_1Q_2}{r^2}$

$$= 9\times10^9 \times \frac{2\times10^{-7}\times3\times10^{-7}}{(30\times10^{-2})^2}$$

$$= 6\times10^{-3}\ \text{N}$$

3 (a) When the negative charge is shifted at a distance x from the centre of the ring along its axis, then force acting on the point charge due to the ring is

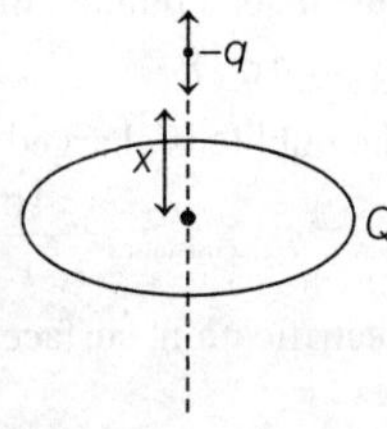

$$F = qE \quad \text{(towards centre)}$$

$$= q\cdot\frac{kQx}{(R^2+x^2)^{3/2}}$$

If $R >> x$, then $R^2 + x^2 \simeq R^2$

and $F = \frac{1}{4\pi\varepsilon_0}\cdot\frac{Qqx}{R^3}$ (towards centre)

Since force on charged particle is acting in opposite direction of electric field, hence acceleration on charged particle towards centre of ring is given by

$$\Rightarrow \quad a = -\frac{F}{m} = -\frac{1}{4\pi\varepsilon_0}\cdot\frac{Qqx}{mR^3}$$

Since, restoring force $F_E \propto -x$, therefore, motion of charged particle will be SHM.

Time period of SHM,

$$T = \frac{2\pi}{\omega} = \left[\frac{16\pi^3\varepsilon_0R^3m}{Qq}\right]^{1/2}$$

But, acceleration, $a = -\omega^2x$

$$-\frac{1}{4\pi\varepsilon_0}\cdot\frac{Qqx}{mR^3} = -\omega^2x$$

$$\Rightarrow \quad \omega = \sqrt{\frac{Qq}{4\pi\varepsilon_0mR^3}}$$

4 (a) The electrostatic force of repulsion between the charge q and $(Q-q)$ at separation r is given by

$$F = \frac{1}{4\pi\varepsilon_0}\cdot\frac{q(Q-q)}{r^2} = \frac{1}{4\pi\varepsilon_0}\cdot\frac{qQ-q^2}{r^2}$$

If F is maximum, then $\frac{\partial F}{\partial q} = 0$

i.e. $\frac{1}{4\pi\varepsilon_0}\cdot\frac{(Q-2q)}{r^2} = 0$

As, $1/4\pi\varepsilon_0r^2$ is constant, therefore

$$Q - 2q = 0 \text{ or } Q = 2q$$

5 (c) Net charge on one H-atom,

$$q = -e + e + \Delta e = \Delta e$$

Net electrostatic repulsive force between two H-atoms,

$$F_r = \frac{kq^2}{d^2} = \frac{k(\Delta e)^2}{d^2}$$

Similarly, net gravitational attractive force between two H-atoms,

$$F_G = \frac{Gm_r^2}{d^2}$$

It is given that,

$$F_r - F_G = 0$$

$$\Rightarrow \frac{K(\Delta e)^2}{d^2} - \frac{Gm_r^2}{d^2} = 0$$

$$\Rightarrow \quad (\Delta e)^2 = \frac{Gm_r^2}{K}$$

$$(\Delta e)^2 = \frac{(6.67\times10^{-11})(1.67\times10^{-27})^2}{9\times10^9}$$

$$\Rightarrow \Delta\varepsilon = 1.437\times10^{-37}\ \text{C}$$

6 (b) According to Coulomb's law, the force of repulsion between them is given by $F = \frac{q_1q_2}{4\pi\varepsilon_0r^2}$

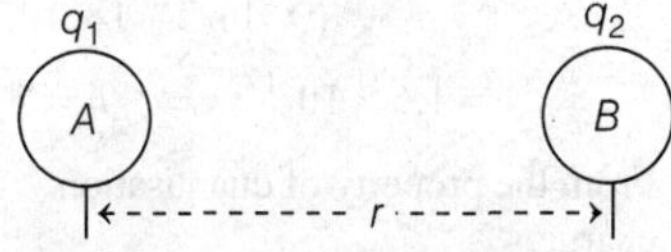

When the charged spheres A and B are brought in contact, each sphere will attain equal charge q'

$$q' = \frac{q_1+q_2}{2}$$

Now, the force of repulsion between them at the same distance r is

$$F' = \frac{q'\times q'}{4\pi\varepsilon_0r^2} = \frac{1}{4\pi\varepsilon_0}$$

$$\frac{\left(\frac{q_1+q_2}{2}\right)\left(\frac{q_1+q_2}{2}\right)}{r^2} = \frac{\left(\frac{q_1+q_2}{2}\right)^2}{4\pi\varepsilon_0r^2}$$

As, $\left(\frac{q_1+q_2}{2}\right)^2 > q_1q_2$

$\therefore \quad F' > F$

7 (a) Consider the situation shown in the diagram.

Sphere Sphere
A B
d

Let charges on sphere A and B be q_1 and q_2, respectively.

Force between the charges placed in air by Coulomb's law (spheres can be assumed as point charges placed at their centres)

$$F_{AB} = k_1\frac{q_1q_2}{d^2} \quad \ldots(i)$$

where, $k_1 = 1/4\pi\varepsilon_0$.

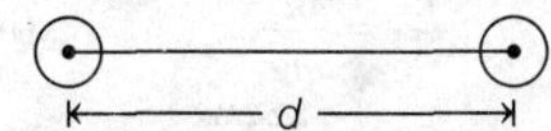

When the spheres are immersed in a liquid, then force between the charges is

$$F'_{AB} = k_1\cdot\frac{q_1\cdot q_2}{K\cdot d^2} = k_1\frac{q_1\cdot q_2}{2d^2} \quad \ldots(ii)$$

where, k is dielectric constant of the liquid $=2$.

On dividing Eqs. (i) and (ii), we get

$$\frac{F_{AB}}{F'_{AB}} = \frac{k_1}{k_1/2} = 2$$

According to question, $F_{AB} = F$

$$\Rightarrow \frac{F}{F'_{AB}} = 2 \Rightarrow F'_{AB} = \frac{F}{2}$$

8 *(b)* Given, $q = 1\text{ nC} = 1 \times 1 \times 10^{-9}$ C

$$(\because 1\text{ nC} = 1 \times 10^{-9}\text{ C})$$

$$e = 1.6 \times 10^{-19} \Rightarrow n = ?$$

From the property of quantisation charge,

$$q = ne \Rightarrow n = \frac{q}{e} = \frac{1 \times 10^{-9}}{1.6 \times 10^{-19}}$$

$$= 0.625 \times 10^{-9} \times 10^{19} = 6.25 \times 10^{9}$$

9 *(b)* For the case I equilibrium of forces,

$$T\cos\theta = mg \quad \text{...(i)}$$

$$T\sin\theta = kq^2/r^2 \quad \text{...(ii)}$$

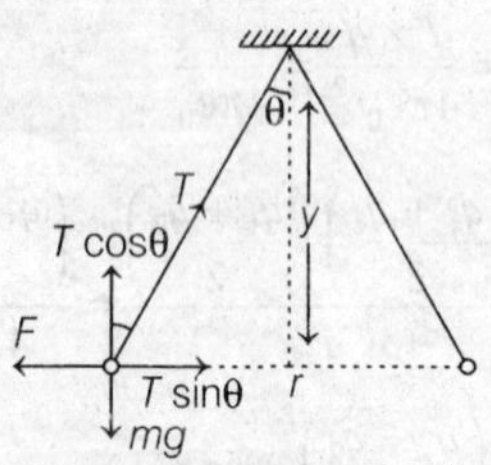

On dividing Eq. (ii) by Eq. (i), we get

$$\frac{T\sin\theta}{T\cos\theta} = \frac{kq^2/r^2}{mg}$$

$$\tan\theta = \frac{kq^2}{r^2 mg}$$

$$\Rightarrow \frac{r}{2y} = \frac{kq^2}{r^2 mg}$$

$$\Rightarrow \frac{r^3}{2y} = \frac{kq^2}{mg} \quad \text{...(iii)}$$

Similar equation as Eq. (iii), we can write for the case II as shown in figure.

$$\Rightarrow \frac{r'^3}{2 \cdot \frac{y}{2}} = \frac{kq^2}{mg}$$

$$\Rightarrow \frac{r'^3}{y} = \frac{kq^2}{mg} \quad \text{...(iv)}$$

From Eqs. (iii) and (iv), we get

$$\frac{r'^3}{y} = \frac{r^3}{2y} \Rightarrow r' = \frac{r}{\sqrt[3]{2}}$$

10 *(d)* From the formula, $F = \frac{1}{4\pi\varepsilon_0}\frac{q_1 q_2}{r^2}$

$$F' = \frac{1}{4\pi\varepsilon_0}\frac{2q_1 \times 2q_2}{(r/2)^2} = \frac{4}{1/4}F = 16F$$

$$nF = 16F \Rightarrow n = 16$$

11 *(c)* Net charge acquired by induction is zero, as there is only transfer of electrons from one part of body to the other.

12 *(c)* Net force on each charge will be

$$F_{\text{net}} = \sqrt{F^2 + F^2 + 2F^2\cos 60^\circ}$$

$$\Rightarrow F_{\text{net}} = \sqrt{2F^2 + 2F^2 \times \frac{1}{2}}$$

$$= \sqrt{2F^2 + F^2}$$

$$\Rightarrow F_{\text{net}} = \sqrt{3F^2} = \sqrt{3}F$$

13 *(a)* In the following figure, since $|\mathbf{F}_A| = |\mathbf{F}_B| = |\mathbf{F}_C|$ and they are equally inclined with each other, so their resultant will be zero.

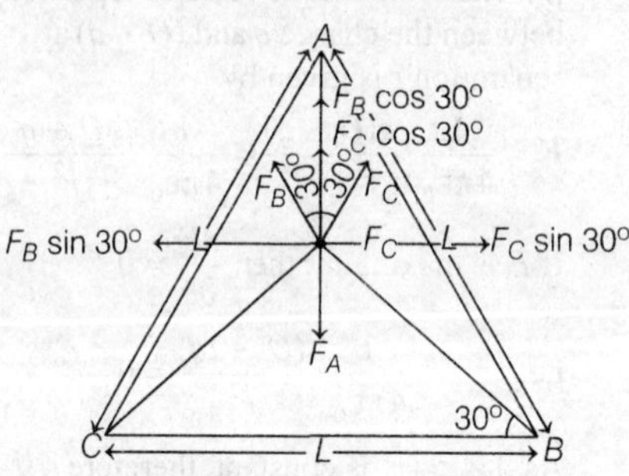

$$F_A = F_B\cos 30^\circ + F_C\cos 30^\circ \text{ and}$$

$$F_B\sin 30^\circ = F_C\sin 30^\circ$$

14 *(d)* Number of electrons transferred, $n = q/e$

Mass transferred to polythene $= m_e \times n$

$$= m_e \times \left(\frac{q}{e}\right)$$

$$= 9.1 \times 10^{-31} \times \left(\frac{2 \times 10^{-7}}{1.6 \times 10^{-19}}\right)$$

$$= 11.38 \times 10^{-19}\text{ kg}$$

15 *(a)* For stationary oil drop,

Force due to electric field = Weight of the oil drop

$$qE = mg \Rightarrow q = \frac{mg}{E}$$

$$q = \frac{9.9 \times 10^{-15} \times 10}{3 \times 10^4}$$

$$= 3.3 \times 10^{-18}\text{ C}$$

16 *(b)* The system is in equilibrium means the force experienced by each charge is zero. It is clear that charge placed at centre would be in equilibrium for any value of q, so we are considering the equilibrium of charge placed at any corner.

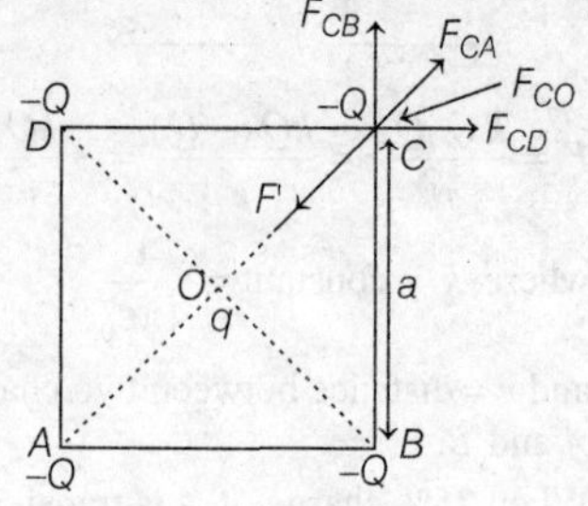

$$F_{CD} + F_{CA}\cos 45^\circ + F_{CO}\cos 45^\circ = 0$$

$$\Rightarrow \frac{1}{4\pi\varepsilon_0}\cdot\frac{(-Q)(-Q)}{a^2} + \frac{1}{4\pi\varepsilon_0}\frac{(-Q)(-Q)}{(\sqrt{2}a)^2} \times \frac{1}{\sqrt{2}} + \frac{1}{4\pi\varepsilon_0}\frac{(-Q)q}{(\sqrt{2}a/2)^2} \times \frac{1}{\sqrt{2}} = 0$$

$$\Rightarrow \frac{1}{4\pi\varepsilon_0}\cdot\frac{Q^2}{a^2} + \frac{1}{4\pi\varepsilon_0}\cdot\frac{Q^2}{2a^2}\cdot\frac{1}{\sqrt{2}} - \frac{1}{4\pi\varepsilon_0}\cdot\frac{2Qq}{a^2} \times \frac{1}{\sqrt{2}} = 0$$

$$\Rightarrow Q + \frac{Q}{2\sqrt{2}} - \sqrt{2}q = 0$$

$$\Rightarrow 2\sqrt{2}Q + Q - 4q = 0$$

$$\Rightarrow 4q = (2\sqrt{2} + 1)Q$$

$$\Rightarrow q = Q/4(2\sqrt{2} + 1)$$

17 *(a)* We have,

$$\frac{1}{4\pi\varepsilon_0}\frac{q_1 q_2}{r^2} = mr\omega^2 = \frac{4\pi^2 mr}{T^2}$$

$$T^2 = \frac{(4\pi\varepsilon_0)r^2(4\pi^2 mr)}{q_1 q_2}$$

$$\Rightarrow T = \left[\frac{4\pi^2 mr^3}{kq_1 q_2}\right]^{1/2}$$

18 *(a)* If σ is the surface tension and r is the radius of soap bubble, then

$$p_{\text{excess}} = 4\sigma/r$$

When the bubble is charged,

$$p_{\text{excess}} = p_{\text{electrostatics}} + \frac{4\sigma}{r}$$

After electrification, surface tension decreases.

This decrease the pressure and increase the radius $\left(p \propto \frac{1}{r}\right)$.

19 (a) $E_r = \frac{F_a}{F_m} = \frac{mg}{(m-m_1)g}$

$= \frac{\rho V}{(\rho - \sigma)V} = \frac{\rho}{(\rho-\sigma)}$

where, ρ = density of sphere,
σ = density of liquid
and V = volume of the liquid.

20 (c) Two positive ions each carrying a charge q are kept at a distance d, then it is found that force of repulsion between them is

$$F = \frac{kqq}{d^2} = \frac{1}{4\pi\varepsilon_0}\frac{q^2}{d^2},$$

where, $q = ne$

$$\therefore\ F = \frac{1}{4\pi\varepsilon_0}\frac{n^2e^2}{d^2} \Rightarrow n = \sqrt{\frac{4\pi\varepsilon_0 Fd^2}{e^2}}$$

21 (b) For sphere 1, in equilibrium

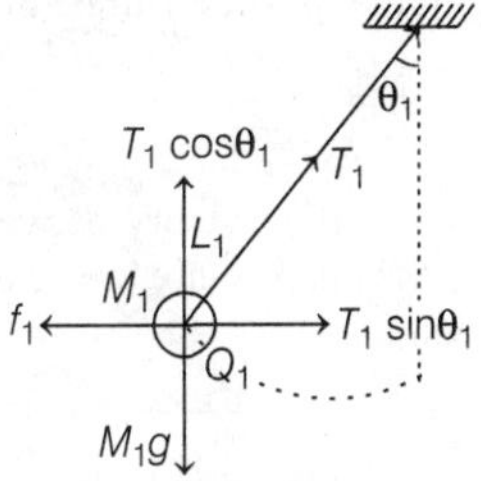

$T_1\cos\theta_1 = M_1g$ and $T_1\sin\theta_1 = F_1$

$\therefore\ \tan\theta_1 = F_1/M_1g$

Similarly for sphere 2,

$\tan\theta_2 = F_2/M_2g$

F is same on both the charges, θ will be same only if their masses M are equal.

22 (b) By using, $qE = mg \Rightarrow q = mg/E$

$= \frac{3\times10^{-6}\times10}{6\times10^4} = \frac{30\times10^{-10}}{6}$

$= 5\times10^{-10}$C

23 (c) Number of electrons,

$$n = \frac{6\times10^{23}}{63.5}\times10\times\frac{1}{10^6} = \frac{6\times10^{18}}{63.5} \quad \text{...(i)}$$

$\because$ According to law of quantisation of charge, $q = ne$ ...(ii)

From Eqs. (i) and (ii), we get

$$q = \frac{6\times10^{18}\times1.6\times10^{-19}}{63.5}$$

$= 1.5\times10^{-2}$C

$$F = \frac{9\times10^9\times1.5\times10^{-2}\times1.5\times10^{-2}}{\left(\frac{10}{100}\right)^2}$$

$= 2.0\times10^8$ N

24 (c) When touched, charge flows from higher potential to lower potential till it equalizes on the two discs.

Given, $q_1 = 10^{-6}$C, $q_2 = 10^{-5}$ C

$$\therefore q = \frac{q_1+q_2}{2} = \frac{10^{-6}+10^{-5}}{2} = 5.5\mu\text{C}$$

25 (b) From Coulomb's law, electric force between two charges is directly proportional to the product of charges and inversely proportional to the square of distance between them.

e.g. $F = k\frac{q_1q_2}{d^2}$

where,

$k = \frac{1}{4\pi\varepsilon_0}$ = proportionality constant.

If a medium is placed between the charges, then $F' = \frac{1}{4\pi\varepsilon_0 K}\frac{q_1q_2}{d^2}$.

Since, medium placed between the charge is a metallic plate, so for it $K = \infty$. Hence, $F' = 0$ (zero).

26 (c)

A —— 0.2 m —— B - - - x - - - C; $q_1 = 5\times10^{-11}$C, $q_2 = -2.7\times10^{-11}$C, q at C

Let a charge q is placed at a point C such that force at C is zero.

$\mathbf{F}_{q_2}$ = force at q due to charge q_2

and $\mathbf{F}_{q_1}$ = force at q due to charge q_1.

As, $\mathbf{F}_{q_1} + \mathbf{F}_{q_2} = 0 \Rightarrow \mathbf{F}_{q_1} = -\mathbf{F}_{q_2}$

or $|\mathbf{F}_{q_1}| = -|\mathbf{F}_{q_2}|$

$$\Rightarrow \frac{1}{4\pi\varepsilon_0}\cdot\frac{q_1q}{(x+0.2)^2} = \frac{1}{4\pi\varepsilon_0}\cdot\frac{qq_2}{x^2}$$

$$\Rightarrow \frac{5\times10^{-11}}{(x+0.2)^2} = \frac{2.7\times10^{-11}}{x^2}$$

$\Rightarrow x = 0.556$ m

27 (b) Force between two charged particles, when air is the medium between them is given as

$$F = \frac{1}{4\pi\varepsilon_0}\cdot\frac{q_1q_2}{r^2}$$

where, q_1 and q_2 are charge on the particles and r is the distance between them.

Now, if a dielectric is inserted between them, the force is given as

$$F' = \frac{1}{4\pi\varepsilon}\cdot\frac{q_1q_2}{r^2} = \frac{1}{4\pi\varepsilon_0 K}\cdot\frac{q_1q_2}{r^2}$$

$= \frac{1}{K}F$ (As, $\varepsilon = K\varepsilon_0$)

28 (a) In electrostatics, charge is uniformly distributed at the surface of the body.

As, there is no motion of the charge in the bulk of the conducting body.

29 (d) The net charge on the outer surface is $-(-50e-50e) = 100e$.

30 (d) 1 electron has a charge of 1.6×10^{-19} C.

10^{10} electrons would have a charge of

$q = ne$

$= 1.6\times10^{-19}\times10^{10}$

$= 1.6\times10^{-9}$ C

Thus in 1s, charge accumulated $= 1.6\times10^{-9}$ C

So, time taken to accumulate 1C

$= \frac{1}{1.6\times10^{-9}}$

$= 0.625\times10^9$ s

$= 173611$ h $= 7233$ days

≈ 20 yr

31 (b) Q at A, q at C (at $l/2$), Q at B; AB = l

$\Rightarrow$ Value of q such that all three charges are in equilibrium.

i.e., F_{net} at B = zero

F_{BA} = force at charge Q due to Q

and F_{BC} = force at charge Q due to q.

$\mathbf{F}_{BA} + \mathbf{F}_{BC} = 0$ or $|\mathbf{F}_{BA}| = |\mathbf{F}_{BC}|$

$$\frac{1}{4\pi\varepsilon_0}\frac{Q^2}{l^2} = \frac{1}{4\pi\varepsilon_o}\frac{Qq}{l^2/4}$$

$\Rightarrow Q = q(4)$

$\Rightarrow q = Q/4$

As, $\mathbf{F}_{BA} = -\mathbf{F}_{BC}$

$\Rightarrow q = \left(-\frac{Q}{4}\right)$

32 (b) For the equilibrium of the bob,

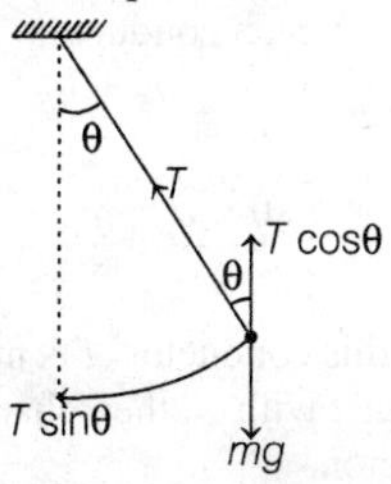

$T\sin\theta = qE$ and $T\cos\theta = mg$

$T = \frac{qE}{\sin\theta}$ and $T = \frac{mg}{\cos\theta}$

33 (b) According to question, two identical charged spheres suspended from a common point by two massless strings of length l.

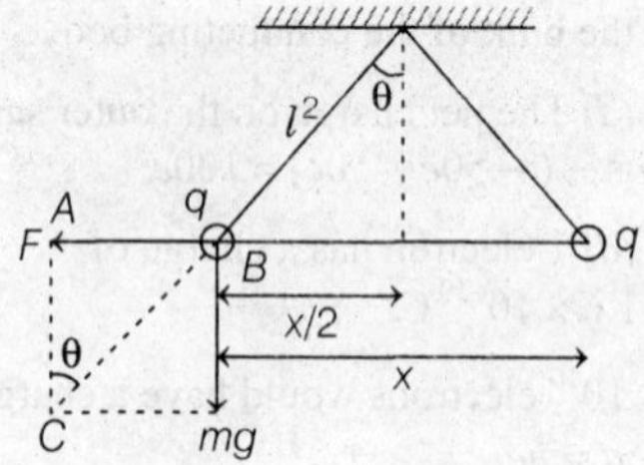

$\because$ In ΔABC,

$$\tan\theta = \frac{F}{mg} \text{ or } \frac{F}{mg} = \tan\theta \quad ...(i)$$

Since, the charges begins to leak from both the spheres at a constant rate. As a result, the spheres approach each other with velocity v.

Therefore, Eq. (i) can be rewritten as

$$\frac{kq^2}{x^2mg} = \frac{x/2}{\sqrt{l^2-(x^2/4)}}$$

$$\Rightarrow \frac{kq^2}{x^2mg} = \frac{x}{2l} \quad [\because x << l]$$

$$\Rightarrow \text{ or } q^2 \propto x^3$$

$$q \propto x^{3/2} \Rightarrow \frac{dq}{dt} \propto \frac{d(x^{3/2})}{dx}\cdot\frac{dx}{dt}$$

$$\Rightarrow \frac{dq}{dt} \propto x^{1/2}\cdot v$$

$$\Rightarrow v \propto \frac{1}{x^{1/2}} \text{ or } v \propto x^{-1/2}$$

34 (b) Charge, $q = ne$

$$\Rightarrow q = 10^{19}\times 1.6\times 10^{-19} = 1.6\text{C}$$

35 (d) Let the spherical conductors B and C have same charge as q. The electric force between them is

$$F = \frac{1}{4\pi\varepsilon_0}\frac{q^2}{r^2}$$

where, r being the distance between them. When third uncharged conductor A is brought in contact with B, then charge on each conductor

$$q_A = q_B = \frac{q_A + q_B}{2}$$

$$= \frac{0+q}{2} = \frac{q}{2}$$

When this conductor A is now brought in contact with C, then charge on each conductor

$$q_A = q_C = \frac{q_A + q_C}{2}$$

$$= \frac{(q/2)+q}{2} = \frac{3q}{4}$$

Hence, electric force acting between B and C is

$$F' = \frac{1}{4\pi\varepsilon_0}\frac{q_Bq_C}{r^2} = \frac{1}{4\pi\varepsilon_0}\frac{(q/2)(3q/4)}{r^2}$$

$$= \frac{3}{8}\left[\frac{1}{4\pi\varepsilon_0}\frac{q^2}{r^2}\right] = \frac{3F}{8}$$

36 (b) Using, $q = ne \Rightarrow 2 = n\times 1.6\times 10^{-19}$

$$\Rightarrow n = \frac{2}{1.6\times 10^{-19}} = 1.25\times 10^{19}$$

$$= 125\times 10^{17} \text{ electrons}$$

37 (c) When a comb rubs through one's dry hair, then comb gets charged and when it comes close to the paper, it induces opposite charges in paper. The field due to the charges in comb, polarises the atoms in the paper. Finally, it attracts the paper.

38 (c) When the other plate is connected to the high voltage generator, the negative charge induced on the ball cause attraction. When it strikes the positive plate, charge distribution again takes place, this causes repulsion. Hence, the ball swings backward and forward hitting each plate in turn.

39 (d) Charge density is inversely proportional to radius of curvature, i.e.

$$\text{Charge density} \propto \frac{1}{\text{Radius of curvature}}$$

Therefore, as shown in figure,

$$\sigma_2 > \sigma_1 > \sigma_3$$

40 (d) The situation is shown in figure. Force on C due to A

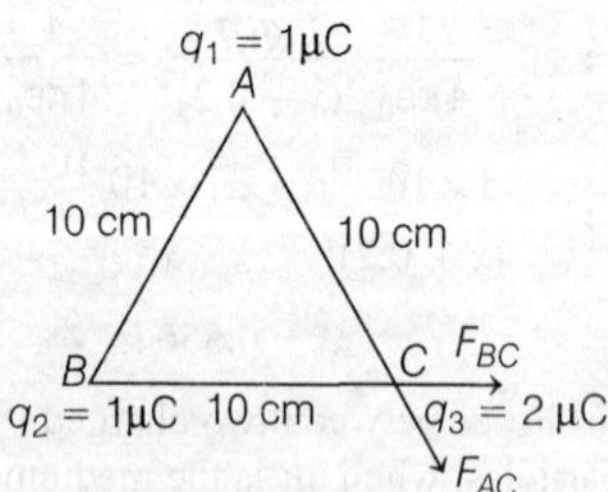

$$F_{AC} = \frac{1}{4\pi\varepsilon_0}\frac{q_Aq_C}{r_{AC}^2}$$

$$= \frac{9\times 10^9\times 1\times 2\times 10^{-12}}{(0.1)^2} = 1.8\text{ N}$$

Similarly, $F_{BC} = 1.8$ N

Hence, net force on C is

$$F = \sqrt{F_{AC}^2 + F_{BC}^2 + 2F_{AC}F_{BC}\cos 60^\circ}$$

$$= \sqrt{(1.8)^2 + (1.8)^2 + 2\times 1.8\times 1.8\times\frac{1}{2}}$$

$$= \sqrt{3(1.8)^2} = \sqrt{3}\times 1.8 = 3.12\text{ N}$$

41 (a) Since, e/m is the charge per kg of electrons, therefore, charge on 90 kg of electrons $= \frac{e}{m}\times 90$

$$= 1.76\times 10^{11}\times 90$$

$$= 1.58\times 10^{13}\text{C}$$

42 (a) As per Coulomb's law, $F = k\frac{q_1q_2}{r^2}$

According to question,

$$F' = k\frac{\left(\frac{q_1}{2}\right)\left(\frac{q_2}{2}\right)}{\left(\frac{r}{2}\right)^2} = k\frac{q_1q_2}{r^2} = F$$

Thus, force between them will remains same.

43 (c) $F_{\text{initial}} = \frac{1}{4\pi\varepsilon_0}\cdot\frac{12\times(-8)}{r^2} = -\frac{1}{4\pi\varepsilon_0}\cdot\frac{96}{r^2}$

Magnitude of force will be given as

$$F = \frac{1}{4\pi\varepsilon_0}\frac{96}{r^2}$$

where, r is the distance between them. When the charges are brought in contact, then

$$q_1 = q_2 = \frac{12-8}{2}$$

$$= \frac{4}{2} = 2\,\mu\text{F}$$

$$\therefore F_{\text{final}} = \frac{1}{4\pi\varepsilon_0}\times\frac{2\times 2}{r^2} = \frac{4}{r^2}\times\frac{1}{4\pi\varepsilon_0}$$

$$= \frac{4}{r^2}\times\frac{1}{4\pi\varepsilon_0}$$

$$\therefore \frac{|F|_{\text{initial}}}{|F|_{\text{final}}} = \frac{96}{4} = 24:1$$

44 (c) Charge density, $\lambda = \lambda_0\cos^2\theta$

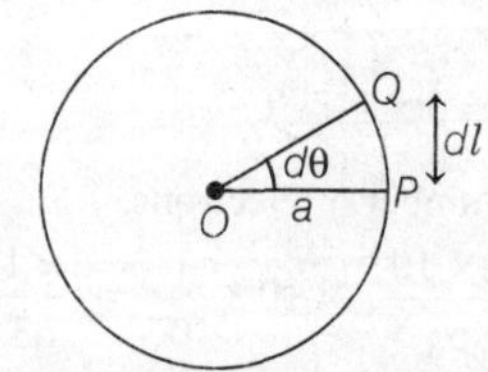

Let PQ be an element of length dl on the circumference of the circle which makes an angle $d\theta$ at the centre of the circle.

Then, the charge on the element is

$$dq = \lambda\times dl$$

$$\Rightarrow dq = \lambda_0\cos^2\theta\cdot dl \quad ...(i)$$

Now, $d\theta = dl/a \Rightarrow dl = a\,d\theta \quad ...(ii)$

Then, from Eqs. (i) and (ii), we get

$$dq = \lambda_0\cos^2\theta\cdot(a\,d\theta)$$

$$\Rightarrow dq = \lambda_0 a\cos^2\theta\cdot d\theta \quad ...(iii)$$

The total charge on the circle [on integrating Eq. (iii) with limit 0 to 2π]

$$q=\int_0^{2\pi}\lambda_0 a\cos^2\theta d\theta$$

$$=\lambda_0 a\int_0^{2\pi}\cos^2\theta d\theta$$

$$\Rightarrow \quad q=\lambda_0 a\int_0^{2\pi}\frac{\cos 2\theta+1}{2}d\theta$$

$$[\because \cos^2\theta=(\cos 2\theta+1)/2]$$

$$\Rightarrow q=\frac{\lambda_0 a}{2}\left[\frac{\sin 2\theta}{2}+\theta\right]_0^{2\pi}$$

$$=\frac{\lambda_0 a}{2}\left[\frac{\sin 4\pi}{2}+2\pi-\frac{\sin 0}{2}-0\right]$$

$$\Rightarrow q=\frac{\lambda_0 a}{2}[0+2\pi-0]$$

$$\Rightarrow q=\pi a\lambda_0$$

45 *(a)* Let two charges be q_1 and q_2 and r be the distance between them, then electrical force,

$$F=\frac{1}{4\pi\varepsilon_0}\cdot\frac{q_1q_2}{r^2}=200\text{ N} \quad \ldots\text{(i)}$$

If q_1 is increased by 10%, then

$$q_1'=\frac{110}{100}q_1$$

and q_2 is decreased by 10%, then

$$q_2'=\frac{90}{100}q_2$$

Then, electrical force between them is

$$F'=\frac{1}{4\pi\varepsilon_0}\cdot\frac{q_1'q_2'}{r^2}$$

$$\Rightarrow \quad F'=\frac{1}{4\pi\varepsilon_0}\frac{\frac{110}{100}q_1\times\frac{90}{100}q_2}{r^2}$$

$$\Rightarrow \quad F'=\frac{1}{4\pi\varepsilon_0}\cdot\frac{q_1q_2}{r^2}\times\frac{99}{100} \quad \ldots\text{(ii)}$$

From Eqs. (i) and (ii), we get

$$F'=200\times\frac{99}{100}$$

$$\Rightarrow \quad F'=198\text{ N}$$

46 *(a)* We know that, surface density of charge is very large on the sharp ends of a conductor. This charge from pointed ends sets up a charged electric wind, to the near by charged clouds.

This charged electric wind comes in contact with the charged clouds and then source of its charge is neutralised, so potential drops between building and clouds.

Hence, chances of lightning on building is reduced. Even if lightning strikes the building, charge is conducted by the lightning conductor to the earth and there is no harm to building.

So, both Assertion and Reason are correct and Reason is the correct explanation of Assertion.

47 *(b)* Let charges on an electron and hydrogen nucleus be q_1 and q_2. The Coulomb's force between them at a distance r is

$$\mathbf{F}=-\frac{1}{4\pi\varepsilon_0}\frac{q_1q_2}{r^2}\hat{\mathbf{r}}$$

Putting, $\frac{1}{4\pi\varepsilon_0}=k$ (given)

$$\mathbf{F}=-k\frac{q_1q_2}{r^2}\hat{\mathbf{r}}$$

Since, the nucleus of hydrogen atom has one proton, so charge on nucleus is e, i.e. $q_2=e$ and also $q_1=e$ for electron.

So $\quad \mathbf{F}=-k\frac{e\cdot e}{r^2}\hat{\mathbf{r}}=-k\frac{e^2}{r^2}\hat{\mathbf{r}}$

but $\quad \hat{\mathbf{r}}=\frac{\hat{\mathbf{r}}}{|\hat{\mathbf{r}}|}=\frac{\hat{\mathbf{r}}}{r}$

Hence, $\quad \mathbf{F}=-k\frac{e^2}{r^2}\cdot\frac{\hat{\mathbf{r}}}{r}=-k\frac{e^2}{r^3}\cdot\hat{\mathbf{r}}$

48 *(b)* Charge on first sphere, $q_1=-9\mu$C

Charge on second sphere, $q_2=5\mu$C

Charges on each sphere after they are kept in contact,

$$q=\frac{q_1+q_2}{2}=\frac{-9+5}{2}$$

$$=-2\mu\text{C}$$

If n electrons are in excess on each sphere, then

$$n=\frac{q}{e}=\frac{2\times10^{-6}}{1.6\times10^{-19}}=1.25\times10^{13}$$

Therefore, 1.25×10^{13} electrons are in excess on each sphere.

49 *(d)* Coulomb's force is given by

$$F=\frac{1}{4\pi\varepsilon_0}\frac{q_1q_2}{r^2}$$

$$\therefore \quad (10\times10^{-3})\times10=\frac{(9\times10^9)\times q^2}{(0.6)^2}$$

$$(\because q_1=q_2=q)$$

or $\quad q^2=\frac{10^{-1}\times0.36}{9\times10^9}=4\times10^{-12}$

$$\Rightarrow \quad q=2\times10^{-6}\text{C}=2\mu\text{C}$$

50 *(a)* On adding −2 C to both, one charge becomes neutral and hence Coulomb's force get equals to zero.

51 *(b)* Let F_A = Force on charge at C due to charge at A

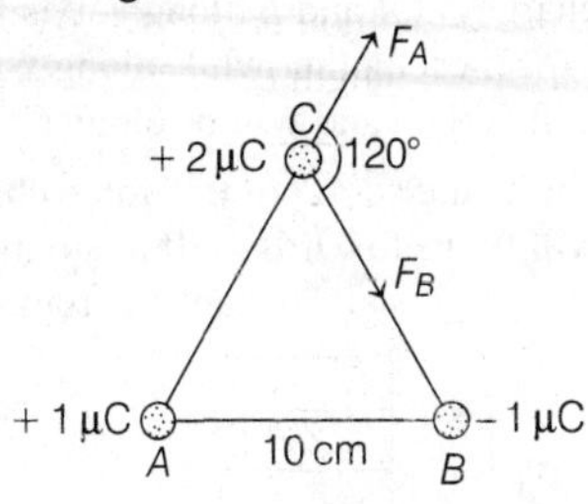

$$\therefore \quad F_A=9\times10^9\times\frac{10^{-6}\times2\times10^{-6}}{(10\times10^{-2})^2}=1.8\text{ N}$$

Similarly, F_B = force on point C due to charge at B

$$=9\times10^9\times\frac{10^{-6}\times2\times10^{-6}}{(10\times10^{-2})^2}=1.8\text{ N}$$

$\therefore$ Net force on C,

$$F_{\text{net}}=\sqrt{(F_A)^2+(F_B)^2+2F_AF_B\cos120^\circ}$$

$$=\sqrt{(1.8)^2+(1.8)^2+2(1.8)(1.8)(-1/2)}$$

$$=1.8\text{ N}$$

52 *(c)* There is no change in the restoring force as the electrostatic forces are the central forces. Negative and positive charges at the two extremities of the string affect tension T which does not affect the restoring force.

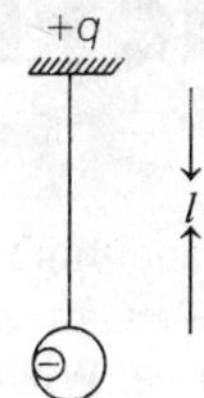

So that, the time period of bob is

$$T=2\pi\sqrt{\frac{L}{g}}$$

53 *(b)* When spheres are touched and separated, charge is

$$q'=\frac{4q-2q}{2}=\frac{2q}{2}=q$$

From Coulomb's law,

$$F=\frac{1}{4\pi\varepsilon_0}\frac{(4q)(-2q)}{r}$$

When made to touch,

$$F'=\frac{1}{4\pi\varepsilon_0}\frac{q^2}{r} \quad \ldots\text{(ii)}$$

From Eqs. (i) and (ii), we get

$$F'=\frac{F}{8}$$

54 *(d)* By symmetry of problem, the components of forces on Q due to charges at A and B along y-axis will cancel each other while along x-axis will add up and will be along CO.

Under the action of this force charge Q will move towards O. If at any time charge Q is at a distance x from O.

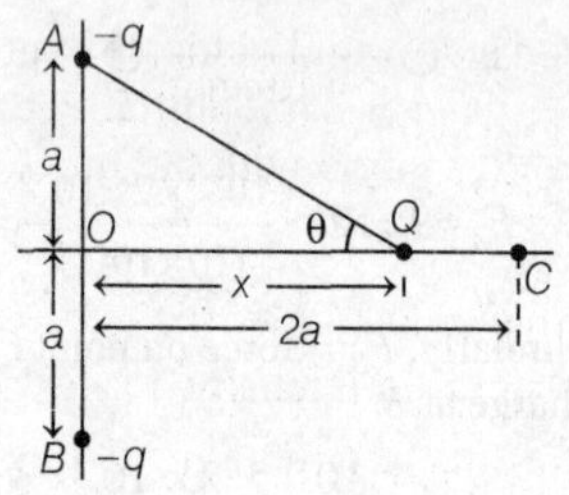

$$F = 2F\cos\theta$$

$$= 2\frac{1}{4\pi\varepsilon_0}\frac{-qQ}{(a^2+x^2)}\times\frac{x}{(a^2+x^2)^{1/2}}$$

i.e. $F = \frac{1}{4\pi\varepsilon_0}\frac{2qQx}{(a^2+x^2)^{3/2}}$

Since, the restoring force F is not linear, motion will be oscillatory (with amplitude $2a$) but not simple harmonic.

55 *(c)* From Coulomb's law, the force of attraction between two charged particles (q), kept at distance r apart is

$$F = \frac{1}{4\pi\varepsilon_0}\frac{q^2}{r^2}$$

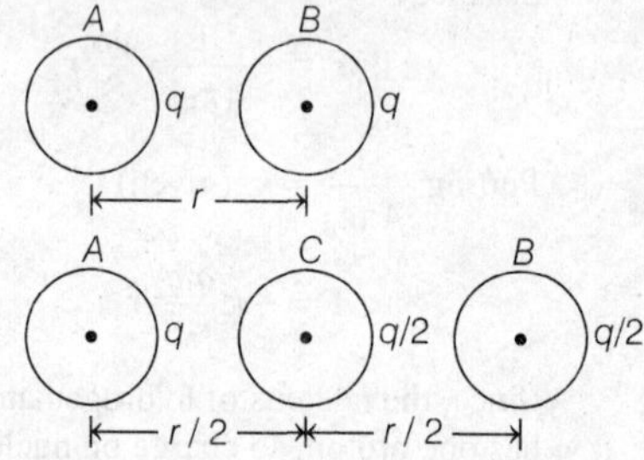

When two identical spheres are brought in contact, then charge on them is equalised, hence total charge on C is equally shared when brought in contact with sphere B having a charge q. Therefore, charge on B and C is $\frac{q}{2}$.

From Coulomb's law, the force on C is

$$F_C = \frac{q\times q/2}{4\pi\varepsilon_0(r/2)^2} - \frac{(q/2)(q/2)}{4\pi\varepsilon_0(r/2)^2}$$

$$= \frac{qq}{4\pi\varepsilon_0 r^2}(2-1) = F$$

56 *(d)* From Coulomb's law, the force acting between two charges (q_1, q_2) separated at a distance r is given by

$$F = \frac{1}{4\pi\varepsilon_0}\frac{q_1 q_2}{r^2}$$

Total force acting on charge Q is

$$F = \frac{1}{4\pi\varepsilon_0}\frac{qQ}{(l/2)^2} + \frac{1}{4\pi\varepsilon_0}\frac{4Q\cdot Q}{(l)^2}$$

According to question, $F = 0$

$$\therefore \quad \frac{1}{4\pi\varepsilon_0}\frac{qQ}{(l/2)^2} + \frac{1}{4\pi\varepsilon_0}\cdot\frac{4Q^2}{(l)^2} = 0$$

$$\Rightarrow \quad q = -Q$$

Topic 2

Electric Field

2019

1 Two parallel infinite line charges with linear charge densities $+\lambda$ C/m and $-\lambda$ C/m are placed at a distance of $2R$ in free space. What is the electric field mid-way between the two line charges? **[NEET]**

(a) $\frac{2\lambda}{\pi\varepsilon_0 R}$ N/C (b) $\frac{\lambda}{\pi\varepsilon_0 R}$ N/C

(c) $\frac{\lambda}{2\pi\varepsilon_0 R}$ N/C (d) Zero

2018

2 An electron falls from rest through a vertical distance h in a uniform and vertically upward directed electric field E. The direction of electric field is now reversed, keeping its magnitude the same. A proton is allowed to fall from rest in it through the same vertical distance h. The time of fall of the electron, in comparison to the time of fall of the proton is **[NEET]**

(a) 10 times greater (b) 5 times greater

(c) smaller (d) equal

2017

3 A positively charged ball hangs from a silk thread. We put a positive test charge q_0 at a point and measure F/q_0, then it can be predicted that the electric field strength E **[JIPMER]**

(a) $> F/q_0$ (b) $= \frac{F}{q}$

(c) $< F/q_0$ (d) Cannot be estimated

2016

4 The electric field strength due to a point charge of 5μC at a distance of 80 cm from the charge is **[UP CPMT]**

(a) 5×10^4 N/C (b) 7×10^4 N/C

(c) 3.5×10^4 N/C (d) 7×10^2 N/C

2015

5 The electric field in a certain region is acting radially outward and is given by $E = Ar$. A charge contained in a sphere of radius a centred at the origin of the field will be given by **[CBSE AIPMT]**

(a) $4\pi\varepsilon_0 Aa^2$ (b) $A\varepsilon_0 a^2$ (c) $4\pi\varepsilon_0 Aa^3$ (d) $\varepsilon_0 Aa^3$

2014

6 Electric field at a point of distance r from a uniformly charged wire of infinite length having linear charge density λ is directly proportional to **[Kerala CEE]**

(a) r^{-1} (b) r (c) r^2 (d) r^{-2}
(e) None of these

7 Two equal and opposite charges of masses m_1 and m_2 are accelerated in a uniform electric field through the same distance. What is the ratio of their accelerations, if their ratio of masses is $m_1/m_2 = 0.5$? **[KCET]**

(a) $\frac{a_1}{a_2} = 0.5$ (b) $\frac{a_1}{a_2} = 1$ (c) $\frac{a_1}{a_2} = 2$ (d) $\frac{a_1}{a_2} = 3$

2013

8 Which one of the following graphs represents the variation of electric field strength E with distance r from the centre of a uniformly charged non-conducting sphere? **[AIIMS]**

(a)
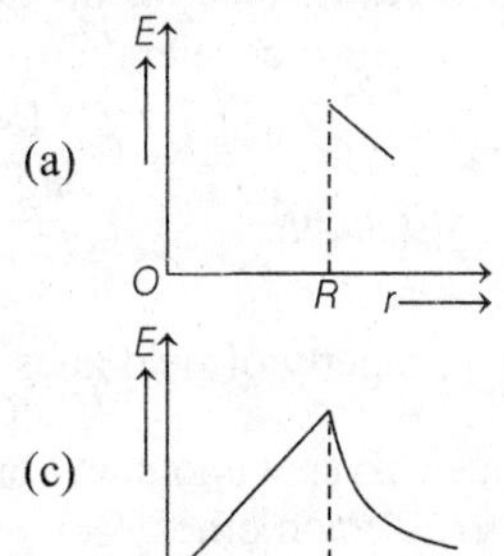

(b)
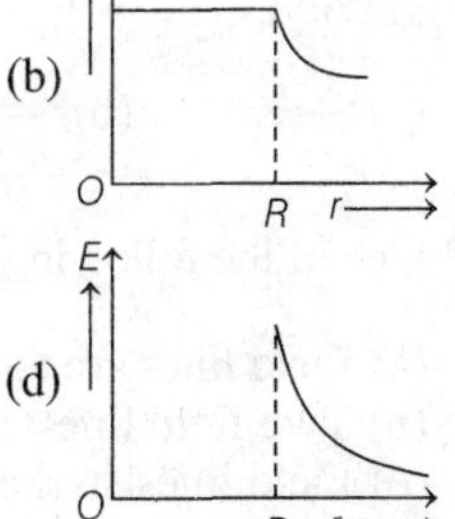

(c)

(d)

9 An electron enters uniform electric field maintained by parallel plates and of value E Vm^{-1} with a velocity v ms^{-1}, the plates are separated by a distance d metre, then acceleration of the electron in the field is **[Manipal]**

(a) $\frac{Ee}{m}$ (b) $\frac{-Ee}{m}$ (c) $\frac{Ee}{md}$ (d) $Ee\frac{d}{m}$

10 The insulation property of air breaks down when the electric field is 3×10^6 V/m. The maximum charge that can be given to a sphere of diameter 5 m is approximately **[WB JEE]**

(a) 2×10^{-2} C (b) 2×10^{-3} C
(c) 2×10^{-4} C (d) 2×10^{-5} C

2012

11 Assertion If the bob of a simple pendulum is kept in a horizontal electric field, its period of oscillation will remain same.

Reason If bob is charged and kept in horizontal electric field, then the time period will be decreased. **[AIIMS]**

(a) Both Assertion and Reason are correct and Reason is the correct explanation of Assertion.
(b) Both Assertion and Reason are correct but Reason is not the correct explanation of Assertion.
(c) Assertion is correct but Reason is incorrect.
(d) Assertion is incorrect but Reason is correct.

12 The unit of physical quantity obtained by the line integral of electric field is **[J&K CET]**

(a) NC^{-1} (b) Vm^{-1} (c) JC^{-1} (d) C^{2}N^{-1}m^{-2}

2010

13 A charged particle is free to move in an electric field. It will travel **[BHU]**

(a) always along a line of force
(b) along a line of force, if its initial velocity is zero
(c) along a line of force, if it has same initial velocity in the direction of an active angle with the line of force
(d) None of the above

14 An electron moving with the speed 5×10^6 m/s is shooted parallel to the electric field of intensity 1×10^3 N/C. Field is responsible for the retardation of motion of electron. Now, evaluate the distance travelled by the electron before coming to rest for an instant. (Mass of $e = 9 \times 10^{-31}$ kg and charge $= 1.6 \times 10^{-19}$ C) **[BHU]**

(a) 7 m (b) 0.7 mm (c) 7 cm (d) 0.7 cm

15 A charged particle of mass m and charge q is released from rest in uniform electric field E. Neglecting the effect of gravity, the kinetic energy of the charged particle after t second is **[BHU]**

(a) $\frac{Eq^2M}{2t^2}$ (b) $\frac{2E^2t^2}{mq}$
(c) $\frac{E^2q^2t^2}{2m}$ (d) $\frac{Eqm}{t}$

16 The electric intensity outside a charged sphere of radius R at a distance $r (r > R)$ is **[MHT CET]**

(a) $\frac{\sigma R^2}{\varepsilon_0 r^2}$ (b) $\frac{\sigma r^2}{\varepsilon_0 R^2}$
(c) $\frac{\sigma r}{\varepsilon_0 R}$ (d) $\frac{\sigma R}{\varepsilon_0 r}$

17 The electric field that can balance a deuteron of mass 3.2×10^{-27} kg is **[MHT CET]**

(a) 19.6×10^{-10} NC^{-1} (b) 19.6×10^{-8} NC^{-1}
(c) 19.6×10^{10} NC^{-1} (d) 19.6×10^{8} NC^{-1}

18 An electron of mass m and charge q is accelerated from rest in a uniform electric field of strength E. The velocity acquired by it as it travels a distance l is **[Manipal]**

(a) $\sqrt{\frac{2Eql}{m}}$ (b) $\sqrt{\frac{2Eq}{ml}}$ (c) $\sqrt{\frac{2Em}{ql}}$ (d) $\sqrt{\frac{Eq}{ml}}$

19 The distance between two charges 6 μC and 15 μC is 2 m. At what point on the line joining the two, the intensity will be zero? **[OJEE]**

(a) At a distance 1 m from 6μC
(b) At a distance 1 m from 15 μC
(c) At a distance 0.77 m from 6 μC
(d) At a distance 0.77 m from 15 μC

20 A particle of mass 2×10^{-3} kg, charge 4×10^{-3} C enters in an electric field of 5 V/m, then its kinetic energy after 10 s is **[OJEE]**

(a) 0.1 J (b) 1 J
(c) 10 J (d) 100 J

21 The figure shows some of the electric field lines corresponding to an electric field. The figure suggests

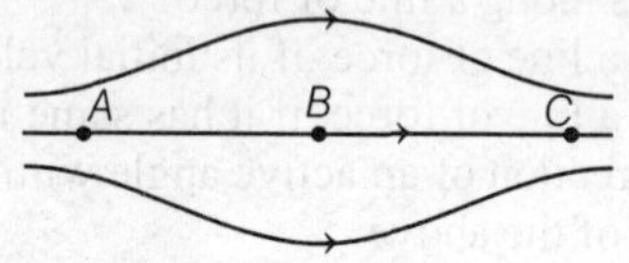

[OJEE]

(a) $E_A > E_B > E_C$.
(b) $E_A = E_B = E_C$
(c) $E_A = E_C > E_B$
(d) $E_A > E_C > E_B$

22 The point charges Q and $-2Q$ are placed some distance apart. If the electric field at the location of Q is E, then the electric field at the location of $-2Q$ will be **[AIIMS]**

(a) $-\frac{E}{2}$ (b) $-\frac{3E}{2}$
(c) $-E$ (d) $-2E$

23 Two point charges $-q$ and $+\frac{q}{2}$ are situated at the origin and at the point $(a, 0, 0)$ respectively. The point along the x-axis where the electric field vanishes is **[Haryana PMT]**

(a) $x = \frac{a}{\sqrt{2}}$ (b) $x = \sqrt{2}a$
(c) $x = \frac{\sqrt{2}a}{\sqrt{2}-1}$ (d) $x = \frac{\sqrt{2}a}{\sqrt{2}+1}$

24 At what distance along the central axis of a uniformly charged plastic disc of radius R is the magnitude of the electric field equal to one-half the magnitude of the field at the centre of the surface of the disc? **[UMMC]**

(a) $\frac{R}{\sqrt{2}}$ (b) $\frac{R}{\sqrt{3}}$
(c) $\sqrt{2}R$ (d) $\sqrt{3}R$

2009

25 If the linear charge density of a cylinder is $4 \mu Cm^{-1}$, then electric field intensity at point 3.6 cm from axis is **[MHT CET]**

(a) 4×10^5 NC^{-1} (b) 2×10^6 NC^{-1}
(c) 8×10^7 NC^{-1} (d) 12×10^7 NC^{-1}

26 The relation between electric field vector **E**, the displacement vector **D** and the polarisation vector **P** for a dielectric placed in electric field **E** is given by **[Haryana PMT, CG PMT]**

(a) $\mathbf{P} = \varepsilon_0 \mathbf{E} + \mathbf{D}$ (b) $\mathbf{P} = \mathbf{D} + \mathbf{E}$
(c) $\mathbf{D} = \varepsilon_0 \mathbf{E} + \mathbf{P}$ (d) $\mathbf{E} = \mathbf{D} + \mathbf{P}$

27 The figure shows electric field E at a distance r in any direction from the origin O. The electric field E is due to **[Haryana PMT, CG PMT]**

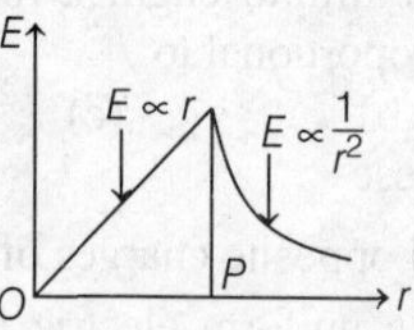

(a) a charged hollow metallic sphere of radius OP with centre at O
(b) a charged solid metallic sphere of radius OP with centre at O
(c) a uniformly charged non-conducting sphere of radius OP with centre at O
(d) a uniformly charged non-conducting hollow sphere of radius OP with centre at O

28 The magnitude of electric field balance an oil drop of mass m, carrying charge q is (g = acceleration due to gravity) **[J&K CET]**

(a) $\frac{q}{m}$ (b) $\frac{mg}{q^2}$ (c) mgq (d) $\frac{mg}{q}$

29 One of the following is not a property of field lines **[DUMET]**

(a) Field lines are continuous curves without any breaks.
(b) Two field lines cannot cross each other.
(c) Field lines start at positive charges and end at negative charges.
(d) They does not form closed loops.

30 An α-particle of mass 6.4×10^{-27} kg and charge 3.2×10^{-19} C is situated in a uniform electric field of 1.6×10^5 Vm^{-1}. The velocity of the particle at the end of 2×10^{-2} m path, when it starts from rest is **[KCET]**

(a) $2\sqrt{3} \times 10^5$ ms^{-1} (b) 8×10^5 ms^{-1}
(c) 16×10^5 ms^{-1} (d) $4\sqrt{2} \times 10^5$ ms^{-1}

31 A oil drop having a mass 4.8×10^{-10} g and charge 24×10^{-18} C stands still between two charged horizontal plates separated by a distance of 1 cm. If now the polarity of the plates is changed, instantaneous acceleration of the drop is (take, $g = 10 ms^{-2}$) **[JCECE]**

(a) 5 ms^{-2} (b) 10 ms^{-2}
(c) 15 ms^{-2} (d) 20 ms^{-2}

32 A charged oil drop is suspended in uniform field of 3×10^4 V/m, so that it neither falls nor rises. The charge on the drop will be (take, the mass of the charge $= 9.9 \times 10^{-15}$ kg and $g = 10 m/s^2$) **[JIPMER]**

(a) 3.3×10^{-18} C (b) 3.2×10^{-18} C
(c) 1.6×10^{-18} C (d) 4.8×10^{-18} C

2008

33 The electric potential at a point in free space due to a charge Q coulomb is $Q \times 10^{11}$ V. The electric field at that point is **[CBSE AIPMT]**

(a) $4\pi\varepsilon_0 Q \times 10^{22}\ \text{Vm}^{-1}$
(b) $12\pi\varepsilon_0 Q \times 10^{20}\ \text{Vm}^{-1}$
(c) $4\pi\varepsilon_0 Q \times 10^{20}\ \text{Vm}^{-1}$
(d) $12\pi\varepsilon_0 Q \times 10^{22}\ \text{Vm}^{-1}$

34 A thin conducting ring of radius R is given a charge $+Q$. The electric field at the centre O of the ring due to the charge on the part AKB of the ring is E. The electric field at the centre due to the charge on the part $ACDB$ of the ring is **[CBSE AIPMT]**

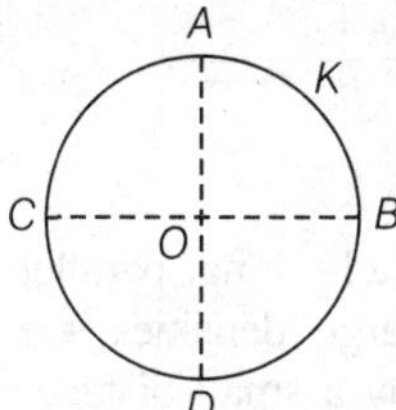

(a) $3E$ along KO (b) E along OK
(c) E along KO (d) $3E$ along OK

35 Charge q is uniformly distributed over a thin half ring of radius R. The electric field at the centre of the ring is **[AIIMS]**

(a) $\dfrac{q}{2\pi^2\varepsilon_0 R^2}$ (b) $\dfrac{q}{4\pi^2\varepsilon_0 R^2}$

(c) $\dfrac{q}{4\pi\varepsilon_0 R^2}$ (d) $\dfrac{q}{2\pi\varepsilon_0 R^2}$

36 Figure below show regular hexagons, with charges at the vertices. In which case, the electric field at the centre zero? **[BHU]**

(a) 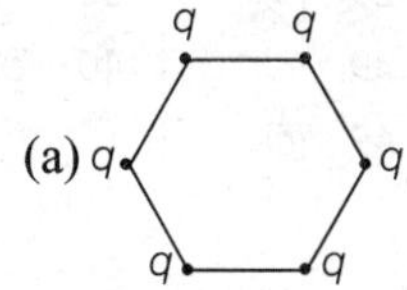

(b) 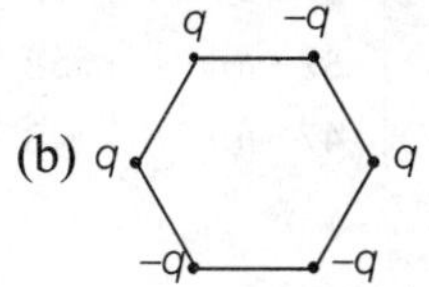

(c) 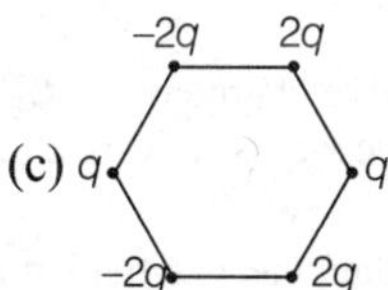

(d) 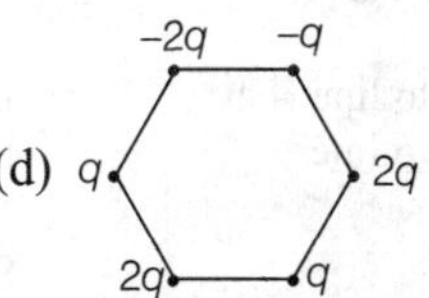

37 How does the electric field (E) between the plates of a charged cylindrical capacitor vary with the distance r from the axis of the cylinder? E **[Manipal]**

(a) $E \propto \dfrac{1}{r^2}$ (b) $E \propto \dfrac{1}{r}$
(c) $E \propto r^2$ (d) $E \propto r$

38 Consider a thin spherical shell of radius R consisting of uniform surface charge density σ. The electric field at a point of distance x from its centre and outside the shell is **[J&K CET]**

(a) inversely proportional to σ
(b) directly proportional to x^2
(c) directly proportional to σ
(d) inversely proportional to x^2

2007

39 Two spheres of radii R_1 and R_2 respectively are charged and joined by a wire. The ratio of electric fields of spheres is **[RPMT]**

(a) $\dfrac{R_2^2}{R_1^2}$ (b) $\dfrac{R_1^2}{R_2^2}$

(c) $\dfrac{R_2}{R_1}$ (d) $\dfrac{R_1}{R_2}$

40 Two unlike charges of the same magnitude Q are placed at a distance d. The intensity of the electric field at the middle point in the line joining the two charges is **[J&K CET]**

(a) zero (b) $\dfrac{8Q}{4\pi\varepsilon_0 d^2}$

(c) $\dfrac{6Q}{4\pi\varepsilon_0 d^2}$ (d) $\dfrac{4Q}{4\pi\varepsilon_0 d^2}$

41 Two parallel plates have equal and opposite charge. When the space between them is evacuated, the electric field between the plates is $2 \times 10^5\ \text{V m}^{-1}$. When the space is filled with dielectric, the electric field becomes $1 \times 10^5\ \text{Vm}^{-1}$. The dielectric constant of dielectric material is **[Punjab PMET]**

(a) 1/2 (b) 1 (c) 2 (d) 3

42 The potential of the electric field produced by point charge at any point (x, y, z) is given by $V = 3x^2 + 5$, where x, y are in metre and V is in volt. The intensity of the electric field at $(-2, 1, 0)$ is **[KCET]**

(a) $+17\ \text{Vm}^{-1}$ (b) $-17\ \text{Vm}^{-1}$
(c) $+12\ \text{Vm}^{-1}$ (d) $-12\ \text{Vm}^{-1}$

43 A point charge q produces an electric field of magnitude $2\ \text{NC}^{-1}$ at a point distance 0.25 m from it. What is the value of charge? **[BVP]**

(a) 1.39×10^{-11} C (b) 1.39×10^{11} C
(c) 13.9×10^{-11} C (d) 13.9×10^{11} C

44 A solid metallic sphere has a charge $+3Q$. Concentric with this sphere is a conducting spherical shell having charge $-Q$. The radius of the sphere is a and that of the spherical shell is $b (b > a)$. What is the electric field at a distance $R (a < R < b)$ from the centre? **[BCECE]**

(a) $\dfrac{4Q}{2\pi\varepsilon_0 R^2}$ (b) $\dfrac{3Q}{4\pi\varepsilon_0 R^2}$ (c) $\dfrac{3Q}{2\pi\varepsilon_0 R^2}$ (d) $\dfrac{Q}{2\pi\varepsilon_0 R}$

2006

45 The spatial distribution of the electric field due to charges (A, B) is shown in figure. Which one of the following statements is correct? **[AIIMS]**

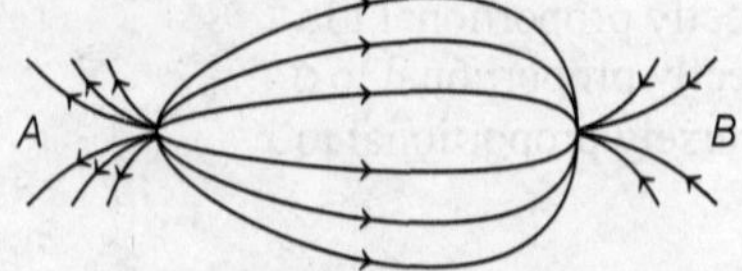

(a) A is positive and B negative $|A| > |B|$
(b) A is negative and B positive $|A| = |B|$
(c) Both are positive but $A > B$
(d) Both are negative but $A > B$

46 A cube has point charges of magnitude $-q$ at all its vertices. Electric field at the centre of the cube is **[RPMT]**

(a) $\frac{1}{4\pi\varepsilon_0}\frac{6q}{3a^2}$ (b) $\frac{1}{4\pi\varepsilon_0}\frac{8q}{a^2}$
(c) zero (d) $\frac{1}{4\pi\varepsilon_0}\frac{-8q}{a^2}$

47 Forces exerted by a uniform electric field on an electron having mass m_e and proton of mass m_p are represented as F_e and F_p respectively are related as **[J&K CET]**

(a) $F_p = F_e$ (b) $\frac{F_e}{F_p} = \frac{m_e}{m_p}$
(c) $\frac{F_e}{F_p} = \frac{m_p}{m_e}$ (d) $\frac{F_e}{F_p} = \frac{m_e^2}{m_p^2}$

48 Which of the following plots represents the variation of the electric field with distance from the centre of a uniformly charged non-conducting sphere of radius R? **[BCECE]**

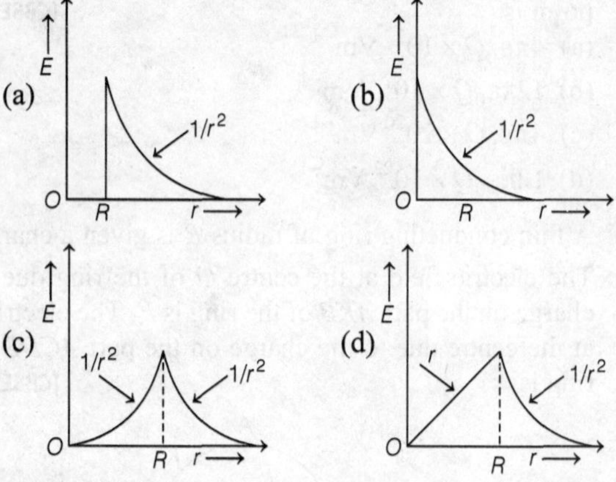

2005

49 Two infinitely long parallel conducting plates having surface charge densities $+\sigma$ and $-\sigma$ respectively, are separated by a small distance. The medium between the plates is vacuum. If ε_0 is the dielectric permittivity of vacuum, then the electric field in the region between the plates is **[AIIMS]**

(a) 0 (b) $\frac{\sigma}{2\varepsilon_0}\,\text{Vm}^{-1}$
(c) $\frac{\sigma}{\varepsilon_0}\,\text{Vm}^{-1}$ (d) $\frac{2\sigma}{\varepsilon_0}\,\text{Vm}^{-1}$

Answers

1 (b)	2 (c)	3 (a)	4 (b)	5 (c)	6 (a)	7 (c)	8 (c)	9 (a)	10 (b)
11 (a)	12 (c)	13 (b)	14 (c)	15 (c)	16 (a)	17 (b)	18 (a)	19 (c)	20 (c)
21 (c)	22 (a)	23 (c)	24 (b)	25 (b)	26 (c)	27 (c)	28 (d)	29 (d)	30 (d)
31 (d)	32 (a)	33 (a)	34 (b)	35 (a)	36 (a)	37 (a)	38 (d)	39 (c)	40 (b)
41 (c)	42 (d)	43 (a)	44 (b)	45 (a)	46 (c)	47 (a)	48 (d)	49 (c)	

Explanations

1 (b) Consider two infinite line charges with linear charge densities $+\lambda$ C/m and $-\lambda$ C/m respectively, which are lying in y-direction as shown in the figure below

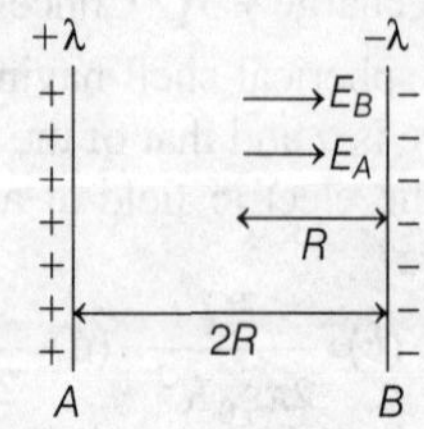

Then, the electric field due to line A at the mid-way between the two line charges, i.e. at R is

$$|\mathbf{E}_A| = \frac{\lambda}{2\pi\varepsilon_0 R}\ \text{N/C} \quad \ldots\text{(i)}$$

which lies along +ve x-axis (outward), i.e. from A to B.

Similarly, the electric field due to line B at the mid-way between the two line charges, i.e. at R is

$$|\mathbf{E}_B| = \frac{\lambda}{2\pi\varepsilon_0 R}\ \text{N/C} \quad \ldots\text{(ii)}$$

Due to negative charge on B, $\mathbf{E}_B$ also lies along +ve x-axis (inward), i.e. from A to B.

So, the resultant electric field at R is given as

$$|\mathbf{E}_R| = |\mathbf{E}_A| + |\mathbf{E}_B|$$

Substituting the values from Eqs. (i) and (ii), we get

$$|\mathbf{E}_R| = \frac{\lambda}{2\pi\varepsilon_0 R} + \frac{\lambda}{2\pi\varepsilon_0 R} = \frac{\lambda}{\pi\varepsilon_0 R}\ \text{N/C}$$

which also lies along the + ve x-axis, i.e. from A to B.

2 (c) Force on a charged particle in the presence of an electric field is given as

$$F = qE \quad \ldots(i)$$

where, q is the charge on the charged particle and E is the electric field.

From Newton's second law of motion, force on a particle with mass m is given as

$$F = ma \quad \ldots(ii)$$

where, a is the acceleration.

From Eqs. (i) and (ii), we get

$$F = ma = qE$$

$$\Rightarrow \quad a = \frac{qE}{m} \quad \ldots(iii)$$

Now, consider that a particle falls from rest through a vertical distance h. Therefore, $u = 0$ and the second equation of motion becomes

$$s = ut + \frac{1}{2}at^2$$

or $h = 0 \times t + \frac{1}{2}at^2 = \frac{1}{2} \times \frac{qE}{m}t^2$ [from Eq. (iii)]

$$\Rightarrow \quad t^2 = \frac{2hm}{qE} \text{ or } t = \sqrt{\frac{2hm}{qE}}$$

Since, the particles given in the question is electron and proton and the quantity $\sqrt{2h/qE}$ (here, $q_p = q_e = e$) for both of them is constant. Thus, we can write

$$t = k\sqrt{m}$$

where, $k = \sqrt{\frac{2h}{qE}}$

or $t \propto \sqrt{m}$

As, mass of proton $(m_p) >>$ mass of electron (m_e).

Thus, the time of fall of an electrons would be smaller than the time of fall of a protons.

3 (a) Due to presence of test charge q_0 in front of positively charged ball, there would be a redistribution of charge on the ball. In the redistribution of charge, there will be less charge on front half surface and more charge on the back half surface. As a result, the net force F between ball and charge will decrease, i.e. the electric field is decreased. Thus, actual electric field will be greater than F/q_0.

4 (b) Given, $q = 5\mu C = 5 \times 10^{-6} C$

$$r = 80 \text{ cm} = 80 \times 10^{-2} \text{ m}$$

Electric field strength,

$$E = \frac{1}{4\pi\varepsilon_0} \cdot \frac{q}{r^2}$$

$$\Rightarrow \quad E = 9 \times 10^9 \times \frac{5 \times 10^{-6}}{(80 \times 10^{-2})^2}$$

$$\Rightarrow \quad E = 7.0 \times 10^4 \text{ N/C}$$

5 (c) Given, $E = Ar \quad \ldots(i)$

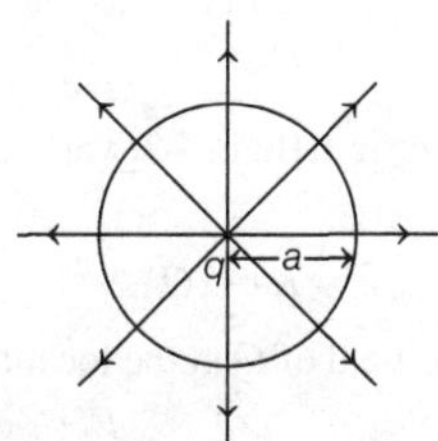

Here, $r = a$

$$\Rightarrow \quad E = \frac{1}{4\pi\varepsilon_0} \cdot \frac{q}{a^2}$$

From Eq. (i),

$$\frac{1}{4\pi\varepsilon_0} \cdot \frac{q}{a^2} = Aa$$

$$\Rightarrow \quad q = 4\pi\varepsilon_0 Aa^3$$

6 (a) We know that, electric field at distance r from an infinitely long line charge is given by

$$E = \frac{\lambda}{2\pi\varepsilon_0 r}$$

$$\Rightarrow \quad \lambda = 2\pi\varepsilon_0 \cdot rE$$

$$E \propto r^{-1}$$

7 (c) We know that,

$$F_1 = q_1E = m_1a_1 \quad \ldots(i)$$

$$F_2 = q_2E = m_2a_2 \quad \ldots(ii)$$

From Eqs. (i) and (ii), we get

$$\frac{a_1}{a_2} = \frac{F_1/m_1}{F_2/m_2} = \frac{F \cdot m_2}{F \cdot m_1} \quad [\because F_1 = F_2]$$

$$\Rightarrow \quad \frac{a_1}{a_2} = \frac{m_2}{m_1} = \frac{1}{0.5} = \frac{10}{5} = 2$$

$$\Rightarrow \quad \frac{a_1}{a_2} = 2 \quad [\because m_1/m_2 = 0.5]$$

8 (c) $\because \; E_{in} \propto r, E_{out} = \frac{k \cdot q}{r^2}$

and $E_{sur} = \text{constant} = k \cdot q/R^2$

Graph (c) correctly represents the variation of electric field intensity due to a uniformly charged non-conducting sphere.

9 (a) We know that, $F = eE$

Therefore, acceleration in electron due to force F

$$a = \frac{F}{m} = \frac{eE}{m}$$

10 (b) The electric field due to charge q on sphere is given by,

$$E = \frac{1}{4\pi\varepsilon_0} \frac{q}{r^2}$$

Given, $E = 3 \times 10^6$ V/m,

$$r = (5/2) \text{ m} = 2.5 \text{m}$$

$$\therefore \quad 3 \times 10^6 = \frac{1}{4\pi\varepsilon_0} \frac{q}{(2.5)^2}$$

$$\Rightarrow 9 \times 10^9 \; q = 6.25 \times 3 \times 10^6$$

$$\therefore \quad q = 2 \times 10^{-3} \text{ C}$$

11 (a) When the bob is placed in an electric field, the time period of simple pendulum will remain same as the bob is not charged. If simple pendulum having charged bob is placed in a horizontal electric field, then the period will be decreased because there will be an increase in restoring force.

So, option (a) is correct. It means that both Assertion and Reason are correct and Reason is the correct explanation of Assertion.

12 (c) The unit of physical quantity obtained by the line integral of electric field is JC^{-1}.

$$\because \quad E = -\frac{dV}{dl}$$

$$\Rightarrow \quad -\int E dl = V = \frac{W}{q}$$

13 (b) Because E point is along the tangent to the lines of force. If initial velocity is zero, then due to the force, it moves in the direction of E.

14 (c) Electric force, $qE = ma$

$$\Rightarrow \quad a = \frac{qE}{m} = \frac{1.6 \times 10^{-19} \times 1 \times 10^3}{9 \times 10^{-31}}$$

$$= \frac{1.6 \times 10^{15}}{9} \text{ ms}^{-2}$$

Given, $u = 5 \times 10^6$ and $v = 0$

$\therefore$ From $v^2 = u^2 - 2as \Rightarrow s = u^2/2a$

$$\therefore \text{ Distance, } s = \frac{(5 \times 10^6)^2 \times 9}{2 \times 1.6 \times 10^{15}}$$

$$= 0.07 \text{ m} = 7 \text{cm}$$

15 (c) When charge q is released in uniform electric field E, then its acceleration $a = \frac{qE}{m}$ (constant)

So, its motion will be uniformly accelerated motion and its velocity after t second is given by

$$v = at = \frac{qE}{m}t$$

The KE of charged particle,

$$\text{KE} = \frac{1}{2}mv^2 = \frac{1}{2}m\left(\frac{qE}{m}t\right)^2 = \frac{q^2E^2t^2}{2m}$$

16 *(a)* The electric intensity outside a charged sphere,

$$E = \frac{kq}{r^2} = \frac{k(\sigma A)}{r^2}$$

$$= \left(\frac{1}{4\pi\varepsilon_0}\right)\frac{\sigma 4\pi R^2}{r^2} = \frac{\sigma R^2}{\varepsilon_0 r^2}$$

17 *(b)* As, $E = \frac{F}{q} = \frac{mg}{q} = \frac{3.2\times10^{-27}\times9.8}{1.6\times10^{-19}}$

$$= 19.6\times10^{-8}\,\text{NC}^{-1}$$

18 *(a)* Here, $u = 0$, $a = \frac{qE}{m}$, $s = l$ and $v = ?$

$$v^2 = u^2 + 2as$$

$$v^2 = 0 + 2\frac{qEl}{m} \Rightarrow v = \sqrt{\frac{2qEl}{m}}$$

19 *(c)* $\mathbf{E}_A$ = Electric field at C due to charge at A and $\mathbf{E}_B$ = Electric field at C due to charge at B.

A C B
2 m
$q_A = 6\mu$C $q_B = 15\mu$C
x 2−x

As per question,

$$\mathbf{E}_A + \mathbf{E}_B = 0 \quad \text{or} \quad |\mathbf{E}_A| = |\mathbf{E}_B|$$

$$\frac{1}{4\pi\varepsilon_0}\frac{q_A}{x^2} = \frac{1}{4\pi\varepsilon_0}\frac{q_B}{(2-x)^2}$$

$$\frac{q_A}{x^2} = \frac{q_B}{(2-x)^2} \Rightarrow \frac{(2-x)^2}{x^2} = \frac{q_B}{q_A}$$

$$\left(\frac{2-x}{x}\right)^2 = \frac{15}{6}$$

$$\Rightarrow \left(\frac{2}{x}-1\right) = \sqrt{\frac{15}{6}} \quad \Rightarrow \quad x = 0.77\text{ m}$$

20 *(c)* Force on a charge placed inside an electric field given as

$$F = qE$$

$$\Rightarrow \quad ma = qE \quad \Rightarrow \quad a = qE/m$$

$$\Rightarrow \quad \frac{dv}{dt} = \frac{qE}{m} \quad \Rightarrow \quad dv = \frac{qE}{m}$$

Integrating with proper limits,

$$\int_0^v dv = \int_0^t \frac{qE}{m}\,dt$$

Now, $v = \frac{1}{m}qE\,(t)$

$$\text{KE} = \frac{1}{2}mv^2 = \frac{1}{2}m\frac{q^2E^2t^2}{m^2}$$

$$= \frac{1}{2}\frac{q^2E^2t^2}{m} = \frac{(4\times10^{-3})^2\times5^2\times10^2}{2\times2\times10^{-3}}$$

$$= 10\text{ J}$$

21 *(c)* Electric field intensity at a particular point is directly proportional to the number of electric line of forces crossing per unit area.

$$E_A = E_B \qquad \ldots\text{(i)}$$

As, density of electric line of force in region A and C are more as compare to B.

Hence, $E_A > E_B \qquad \ldots$(ii)

From Eqs. (i) and (ii), we get

$$E_A = E_C > E_B$$

22 *(a)* Electric field of $-2Q$ at the location of Q_1

$$E = K(-2Q)/r^2$$

Electric field of Q at the location of $-2Q$

$$E' = K\frac{Q}{r^2} = -\frac{E}{2}$$

23 *(c)* Suppose the field vanishes at a distance x, we have

$$\frac{kq}{x^2} = \frac{kq/2}{(x-a)^2}$$

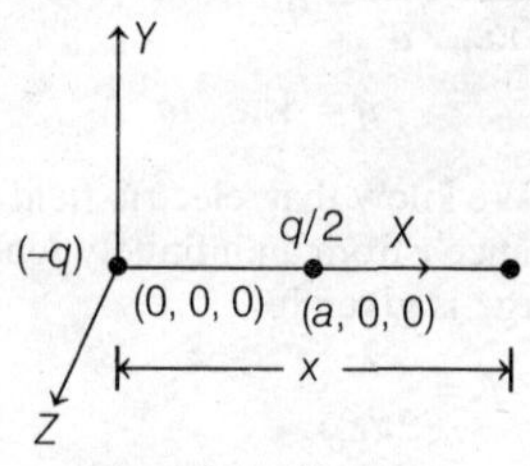

$$\Rightarrow \quad 2(x-a)^2 = x^2$$

$$\Rightarrow \quad \sqrt{2}(x-a) = x$$

$$\Rightarrow \quad (\sqrt{2}-1)x = \sqrt{2}a$$

$$\Rightarrow \quad x = \frac{\sqrt{2}a}{\sqrt{2}-1}$$

24 *(b)* At a point on the axis of uniformly charged disc at a distance x above the centre of the disc, the magnitude of the electric field is

$$E = \frac{\sigma}{2\varepsilon_0}\left[1 - \frac{x}{\sqrt{x^2+R^2}}\right]$$

But $E_c = \frac{\sigma}{2\varepsilon_0}$ such that $\frac{E}{E_c} = \frac{1}{2}$

Then, $1 - \frac{x}{\sqrt{x^2+R^2}} = \frac{1}{2}$

$$\Rightarrow \quad \frac{x}{\sqrt{x^2+R^2}} = \frac{1}{2}$$

Squaring both sides and multiplying by $x^2 + R^2$ to obtain

$$x^2 = \frac{x^2}{4} + \frac{R^2}{4} = \frac{R^2}{3}$$

$$\Rightarrow \quad x = \frac{R}{\sqrt{3}}$$

25 *(b)* Electric field intensity at a point close to the cylinder with linear charge distribution λ is given as

$$E = \frac{\lambda}{2\pi\varepsilon_0}\left(\frac{1}{r}\right) = \frac{1}{4\pi\varepsilon_0}\left(\frac{2\lambda}{r}\right)$$

$$= (9\times10^9)\frac{2\times4\times10^{-6}}{36\times10^{-3}}$$

$$= 2\times10^6\,\text{NC}^{-1}$$

26 *(c)* Relation between electric field vector (**E**), displacement vector (**D**) and polarisation vector (**P**) for a dielectric placed in an electric field is given as $\mathbf{D} = \varepsilon_0\mathbf{E} + \mathbf{P}$.

27 *(c)* Electric field due to a uniformly charged non-conducting sphere of radius R is found to be as,

For a point r (i.e. $r \le R$)

$\Rightarrow \quad E \propto r$

For a point r (i.e. $r > R$)

Hence, $OP = R$

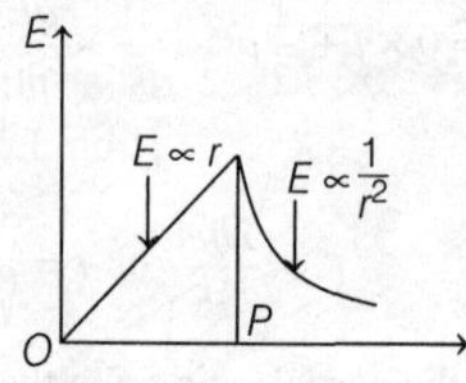

28 *(d)* As per question,

Weight of oil drop = Electrostatic force

$$\Rightarrow \quad mg = qE$$

$$\Rightarrow \quad E = \frac{mg}{q}$$

29 *(d)* Electric lines of force does not form closed loops.

30 *(d)* Force on a charged particle placed in a uniform electric field is given as

$$F = qE \quad \Rightarrow \quad ma = qE \Rightarrow a = qE/m$$

From equation of motion,

$$v^2 = u^2 + 2as = (0)^2 + 2as$$

$$\Rightarrow \quad v = \sqrt{\frac{2qE}{m}s}$$

$$= \sqrt{\frac{2\times3.2\times10^{-19}\times1.6\times10^5\times2\times10^{-2}}{6.4\times10^{-27}}}$$

$$\Rightarrow \quad v = 4\sqrt{2}\times10^5\text{ m/s}$$

31 *(d)* ***Case* I** When oil drop is in equilibrium,

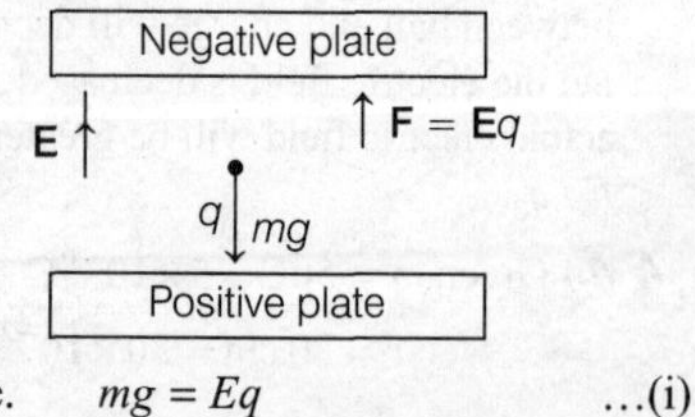

i.e. $\quad mg = Eq \qquad \ldots$(i)

Case II When the polarity are reversed,

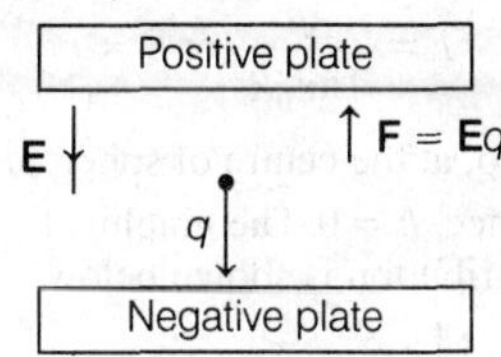

i.e. $mg + Eq = ma$

$ma = 2mg$ [from Eq. (i)]

$a = 2g \Rightarrow a = 20 \text{ ms}^{-2}$

32 (a) In steady state, electric force on drop = weight of drop

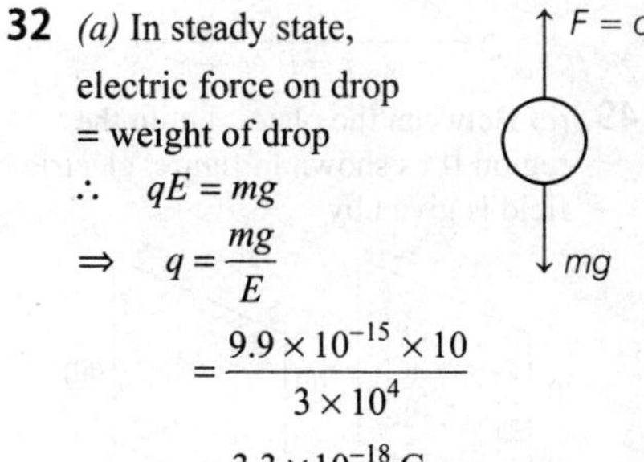

$\therefore \quad qE = mg$

$\Rightarrow \quad q = \frac{mg}{E}$

$= \frac{9.9 \times 10^{-15} \times 10}{3 \times 10^4}$

$= 3.3 \times 10^{-18}$ C

33 (a) At any point, electric potential due to charge Q is

$$V = \frac{1}{4\pi\varepsilon_0} \cdot \frac{Q}{r} \quad \ldots\text{(i)}$$

where, r is the distance of observation point from the charge.

At the same point, electric field is

$$E = \frac{1}{4\pi\varepsilon_0} \cdot \frac{Q}{r^2} \quad \ldots\text{(ii)}$$

Combining Eqs. (i) and (ii), we have

$$E = \frac{4\pi\varepsilon_0 V^2}{Q} = \frac{4\pi\varepsilon_0 \times (Q \times 10^{11})^2}{Q}$$

$= 4\pi\varepsilon_0 Q \times 10^{22} \text{ Vm}^{-1}$

34 (b) As the ring is conducting, so electric field at its centre is zero,

i.e. $\mathbf{E}_{\text{total}} = 0$ or $\mathbf{E}_{AKB} + \mathbf{E}_{ACDB} = 0$

or $\mathbf{E}_{ACDB} = -\mathbf{E}_{AKB}$

or $\mathbf{E}_{ACDB} = -\mathbf{E}$ (along KO)

Therefore, the electric field at the centre due to the charge on the part $ACDB$ of the ring is E along OK.

Alternative Method

As the ring is conducting, so electric field at its centre is zero,

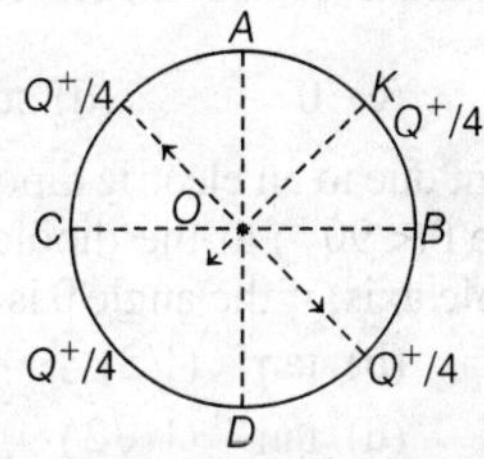

The fields at O due to AC and BD cancel each other.

The field due to CD is acting in the direction OK and equal in magnitude to E due to AKB.

35 (a) From figure, $dl = Rd\theta$

Charge on $dl = \lambda R d\theta \quad \left\{\lambda = \frac{q}{\pi R}\right\}$

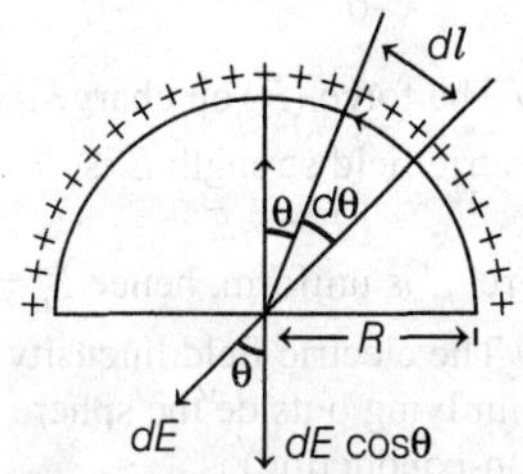

Electric field at centre due to dl is

$$dE = \frac{k \cdot \lambda R d\theta}{R^2}$$

We need to consider only the component $dE\cos\theta$, as the component $dE\sin\theta$ will cancel out.

Total field at centre $= 2\int_0^{\pi/2} dE\cos\theta$

$$= \frac{2k\lambda}{R}\int_0^{\pi/2}\cos\theta d\theta = \frac{2k\lambda}{R} = \frac{q}{2\pi^2\varepsilon_0 R^2}$$

$$\left[\because \lambda = \frac{q}{l} \text{ and } l = 2\pi R\right]$$

36 (a) In the case (a), the fields due to charges at the opposite corners cancel each other. So, in this case, net electric field at the centre will be zero.

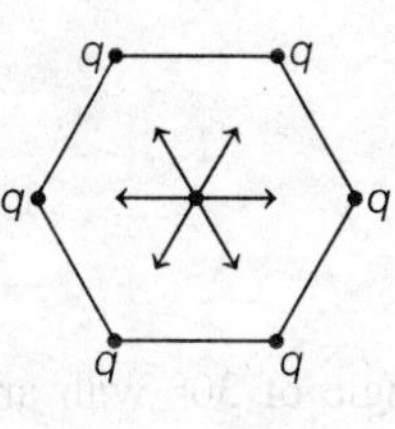

37 (a) Electric field due to outer plate is zero and so the electric field due to inner cylindrical charged conductor varies inversely as the distance from the axis.

38 (d) Electric field at a distance x from the centre

$$E = \frac{1}{4\pi\varepsilon_0}\frac{q}{x^2} \Rightarrow E \propto \frac{1}{x^2}$$

39 (c) When two spheres are joined, charge flows till it equalizes.

Hence, electric potential is same.

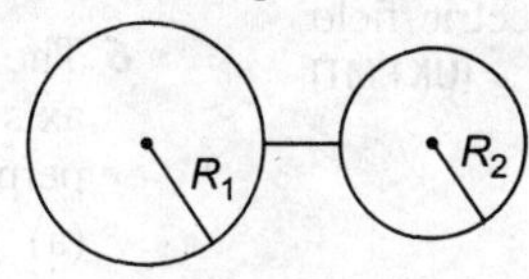

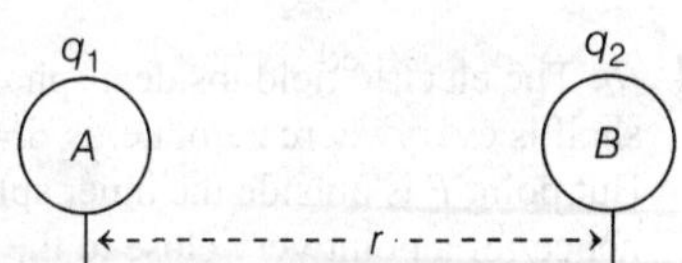

$\therefore \quad V_1 = V_2$

$$\frac{1}{4\pi\varepsilon_0}\frac{q_1}{R_1} = \frac{1}{4\pi\varepsilon_0}\frac{q_2}{R_2}$$

$$\Rightarrow \quad \frac{q_1}{R_1} = \frac{q_2}{R_2} \quad \ldots\text{(i)}$$

Ratio of electric fields, $\frac{E_1}{E_2} = \frac{\frac{1}{4\pi\varepsilon_0}\frac{q_1}{R_1^2}}{\frac{1}{4\pi\varepsilon_0}\frac{q_2}{R_2^2}}$

$$\Rightarrow \quad \frac{E_1}{E_2} = \frac{q_1}{q_2}\left(\frac{R_2}{R_1}\right)^2 \quad \ldots\text{(ii)}$$

or $\frac{E_1}{E_2} = \frac{R_1}{R_2}\left(\frac{R_2}{R_1}\right)^2 = \frac{R_2}{R_1}$

[from Eq. (i)]

40 (b) Two equal and opposite charges are placed at a distance d.

+Q   d/2   –Q
A   B   C
d

Electric field at centre (B) due to $+Q$ charge,

$$E_1 = \frac{1}{4\pi\varepsilon_0}\frac{(Q)}{\left(\frac{d}{2}\right)^2}$$

Similarly, electric field due to $-Q$ charge,

$$E_2 = \frac{1}{4\pi\varepsilon_0}\frac{(Q)}{(d/2)^2}$$

Therefore, net electric field at point

$$E = E_1 + E_2 = \frac{1}{4\pi\varepsilon_0}\frac{4Q}{d^2} + \frac{1}{4\pi\varepsilon_0}\frac{4Q}{d^2}$$

$$= \frac{1}{4\pi\varepsilon_0}\frac{8Q}{d^2}$$

41 (c) $K = \frac{E_{\text{without dielectric}}}{E_{\text{with dielectric}}} = \frac{2 \times 10^5}{1 \times 10^5} = 2$

42 (d) Potential, $(V) = 3x^2 + 5$

Intensity of the electric field

$= \frac{dV}{dx} = 6x$

$= 6(-2)$ (E at $x = -2$) $= -12 \text{ Vm}^{-1}$

43 (a) Electric field, $E = \frac{q}{9\pi\varepsilon_0 r^2}$

$$q = 4\pi\varepsilon_0 r^2 E = \frac{(0.25)^2 \times 2}{9 \times 10^9}$$

$= 1.39 \times 10^{-11}$ C

44 (b) The electric field inside a spherical shell is everywhere zero, i.e. is $E = 0$. But point P is outside the inner sphere, hence for a point very close to the surface the intensity of electric field is given by

$$E = \frac{1}{4\pi\varepsilon_0}\frac{q}{R^2}$$

Given, $q = +3Q$

Therefore, $E = \frac{1}{4\pi\varepsilon_0}\frac{3Q}{R^2}$

45 (a) Electric lines of force usually start (i.e. diverge out) from positive charge and end (i.e. converge) on negative charge or extends to infinity. Thus, A is positive charge and B is negative charge. Also, density of lines at A is more than that at B, i.e. $|A| > |B|$.

46 (c) Clearly, the electric field of each point charge is equal and opposite to the electric field of charge diagonally opposite to it. So, the net electric field at centre of the cube is zero.

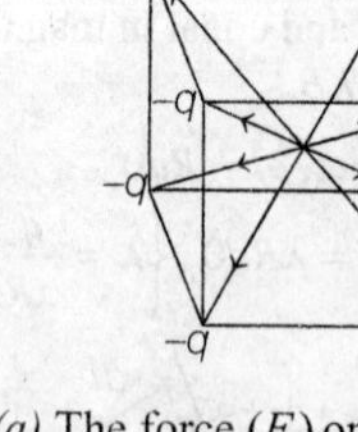

47 (a) The force (F) on charge q due to electric field strength E is

$$F = qE$$

Here, E is uniform, hence $F_p = F_e$.

48 (d) The electric field intensity at a point lying outside the sphere (non-conducting) is

$$E = \frac{1}{4\pi\varepsilon_0}\frac{q}{r^2}$$

where, r is the distance of that point from centre of sphere.

$$\therefore \quad E \propto \frac{1}{r^2} \quad \ldots(i)$$

The electric field intensity at surface of sphere,

$$E = \frac{q}{4\pi\varepsilon_0 R^2} \text{ or } E \propto \frac{1}{R^2} \quad \ldots(ii)$$

where R, being the radius of sphere.

The electric field intensity at a point lying inside the sphere is

$$E = \frac{qr}{4\pi\varepsilon_0 R^3} \text{ or } E \propto r \quad \ldots(iii)$$

Also, at the centre of sphere, $r = 0$.

Hence, $E = 0$. The graphical distribution is shown below

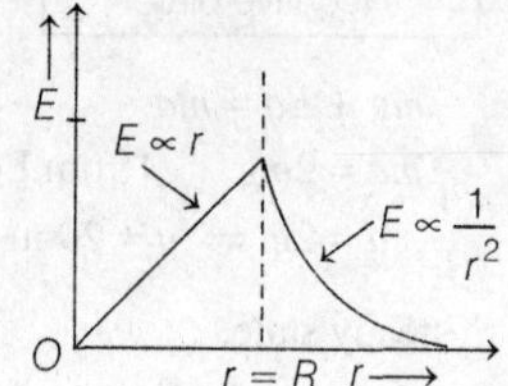

49 (c) Between the plates, i.e. in the region II as shown in figure, electric field is given by

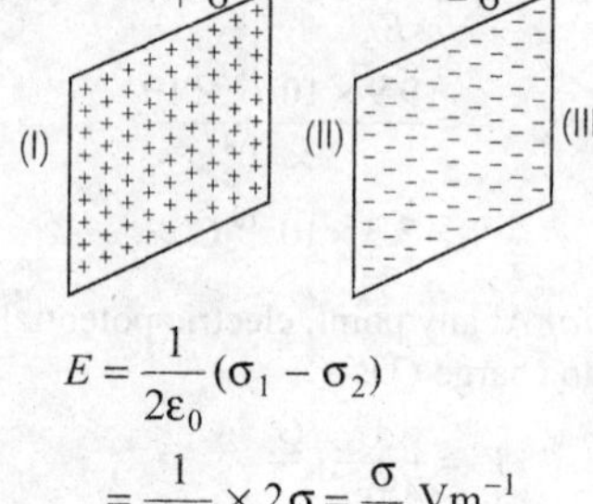

$$E = \frac{1}{2\varepsilon_0}(\sigma_1 - \sigma_2)$$

$$= \frac{1}{2\varepsilon_0} \times 2\sigma = \frac{\sigma}{\varepsilon_0} \text{ Vm}^{-1}$$

Topic 3

Electric Dipole

2016

1 An electric dipole is placed at an angle of 30° with an electric field intensity 2×10^5 N/C. It experiences a torque equal to 4 N-m. The charge on the dipole, if the dipole length is 2 cm, is **[NEET]**

(a) 8 mC (b) 2 mC (c) 5 mC (d) 7 μC

2014

2 An electric dipole of dipole moment **p** is placed in a uniform external electric field **E**. Then, the **[Kerala CEE]**

(a) torque experienced by the dipole is $\mathbf{E} \times \mathbf{p}$
(b) torque is zero, if **p** is perpendicular to **E**
(c) torque is maximum, if **p** is perpendicular to **E**
(d) potential energy is maximum, if **p** is parallel to **E**
(e) potential energy is maximum, if **p** is perpendicular to **E**

3 An electric dipole placed in a non-uniform electric field experiences **[UK PMT]**

(a) both a torque and a net force
(b) only a force but no torque
(c) only a torque but no net force
(d) no torque and no net force

2012

4 An electric dipole of moment p is placed in an electric field of intensity E. The dipole acquires a position such that the axis of the dipole makes an angle θ with the direction of the field.

Assuming that the potential energy of the dipole to be zero when $\theta = 90°$, then the torque and the potential energy of the dipole will respectively be **[CBSE AIPMT]**

(a) $pE \sin\theta, -pE\cos\theta$ (b) $pE\sin\theta, -2pE\cos\theta$
(c) $pE\sin\theta, 2pE\cos\theta$ (d) $pE\cos\theta, -pE\sin\theta$

2011

5 An electric dipole is placed in an uniform electric field with the dipole axis making an angle θ with the direction of the electric field. The orientation of the dipole for stable equilibrium is **[J&K CET]**

(a) $\pi/6$ (b) $\pi/3$ (c) 0 (d) $\pi/2$

6 The electric field at a point due to an electric dipole, on an axis inclined at an angle $\theta (< 90°)$ to the dipole axis, is perpendicular to the dipole axis, if the angle θ is **[KCET]**

(a) $\tan^{-1}(2)$ (b) $\tan^{-1}(1/2)$
(c) $\tan^{-1}(\sqrt{2})$ (d) $\tan^{-1}(1/\sqrt{2})$

2010

7 The electric field and the potential of an electric dipole vary with distance r as [Manipal]

(a) $\frac{1}{r}$ and $\frac{1}{r^2}$ (b) $\frac{1}{r^2}$ and $\frac{1}{r}$

(c) $\frac{1}{r^2}$ and $\frac{1}{r^3}$ (d) $\frac{1}{r^3}$ and $\frac{1}{r^2}$

8 An electric dipole of moment $\mathbf{p}$ is placed in a uniform electric field $\mathbf{E}$. Then, [Kerala CEE]

(i) the torque on the dipole is $\mathbf{p} \times \mathbf{E}$.
(ii) the potential energy of the system is $\mathbf{p} \cdot \mathbf{E}$.
(iii) the resultant force on the dipole is zero.

(a) (i), (ii) and (iii) are correct
(b) (i) and (iii) are correct and (ii) is incorrect
(c) Only (i) is correct
(d) (i) and (ii) are correct and (iii) is incorrect
(e) (i), (ii) and (iii) are incorrect

9 The electric dipole moment of an electron and a proton 4.3 nm apart is [DUMET]

(a) 6.88×10^{-28} C-m (b) 2.56×10^{-29} C^2-m^{-1}

(c) 3.72×10^{-14} C-m^{-1} (d) 1.1×10^{-46} C^2-m

10 Let E_a be the electric field due to a dipole in its axial plane distant l and E_q be the field in the equatorial plane distant l', then the relation between E_a and E_q will be [JCECE]

(a) $E_a = 4E_q$ (b) $E_q = 2E_a$

(c) $E_a = 2E_q$ (d) $E_q = 3E_a$

2008

11 The direction of electric field intensity ($\mathbf{E}$) at a point on the equatorial line of an electric dipole of dipole moment ($\mathbf{p}$) is [Kerala CEE]

(a) along the equatorial line towards the dipole
(b) along the equatorial line away from the dipole
(c) perpendicular to the equatorial line and the opposite to $\mathbf{p}$
(d) perpendicular to the equatorial line and parallel to $\mathbf{p}$
(e) along the axial line in the direction of $\mathbf{p}$

12 An electric dipole of moment $\mathbf{p}$ is lying along a uniform electric field $\mathbf{E}$. The work done in rotating the dipole by 90° is [Haryana PMT]

(a) $\sqrt{2}pE$ (b) $\frac{pE}{2}$ (c) $2pE$ (d) pE

13 An electric dipole has a pair of equal and opposite point charges q and $-q$ are separated by a distance $2x$. The axis of the dipole is defined as [J&K CET]

(a) direction from positive charge to negative charge
(b) direction from negative charge to positive charge
(c) perpendicular to the line joining the two charges drawn at the centre and pointing upward direction
(d) perpendicular to the line joining the two charges drawn at the centre and pointing downward direction

14 The dipole moment of a dipole in an uniform external field $\mathbf{E}$ is $\mathbf{p}$, then the torque (τ) acting on the dipole is [J&K CET]

(a) $\tau = \mathbf{p} \times \mathbf{E}$ (b) $\tau = \mathbf{p} \cdot \mathbf{E}$

(c) $\tau = 2(\mathbf{p} + \mathbf{E})$ (d) $\tau = (\mathbf{p} + \mathbf{E})$

2007

15 Three point charges $+q$, $-2q$ and $+q$ are placed at points $(x = 0, y = a, z = 0)$, $(x = 0, y = 0, z = 0)$ and $(x = a, y = 0, z = 0)$, respectively. The magnitude and direction of the electric dipole moment vector of this charge assembly are [CBSE AIPMT]

(a) $\sqrt{2}qa$ along $+y$-direction
(b) $\sqrt{2}qa$ along the line joining points $(x = 0, y = 0, z = 0)$ and $(x = a, y = a, z = 0)$
(c) qa along the line joining points $(x = 0, y = 0, z = 0)$ and $(x = a, y = a, z = 0)$
(d) $\sqrt{2}qa$ along $+x$-direction

16 An electric dipole consists of two opposite charges each 0.05μC separated by 30 mm. The dipole is placed in an uniform external electric field of 10^6 NC^{-1}. The maximum torque exerted by the field on the dipole is [Kerala CEE]

(a) 6×10^{-3} Nm (b) 3×10^{-3} Nm

(c) 15×10^{-3} Nm (d) 1.5×10^{-3} Nm

(e) 9×10^{-3} Nm

17 An electric dipole coincides on z-axis and its mid-point is on origin of the co-ordinate system. The electric field at an axial point at a distance z from origin is $\mathbf{E}_{(z)}$ and electric field at an equatorial point at a distance y from origin is $\mathbf{E}_{(y)}$.

Here $z = y > a$, so $\left|\frac{\mathbf{E}_{(z)}}{\mathbf{E}_{(y)}}\right| = ..$. [Guj CET]

(a) 1 (b) 4 (c) 3 (d) 2

2006

18 A charge is situated at a certain distance along the axis of an electric dipole experience a force F. If the distance of the charge from the dipole is doubled, then the force acting on it will become [BHU]

(a) $2F$ (b) $\frac{F}{2}$ (c) $\frac{F}{4}$ (d) $\frac{F}{8}$

19 What is the angle between the electric dipole moment and the electric field strength due to it on the equatorial line ? [Punjab PMET]

(a) 0° (b) 90°

(c) 180° (d) None of these

2005

20 The electric field due to an electric dipole at a distance r from its centre in axial position is E. If the dipole is rotated through an angle of 90° about its perpendicular axis, the electric field at the same point will be [J&K CET]

(a) E (b) $\frac{E}{4}$ (c) $\frac{E}{2}$ (d) $2E$

Answers

1 (b)	2 (c)	3 (a)	4 (a)	5 (c)	6 (c)	7 (d)	8 (a)	9 (a)	10 (c)
11 (c)	12 (d)	13 (b)	14 (a)	15 (b)	16 (d)	17 (d)	18 (d)	19 (c)	20 (c)

Explanations

1 *(b)* $\because$ Torque on an electric dipole in an electric field,

$$\tau = \mathbf{p} \times \mathbf{E}$$

$\Rightarrow$ $|\tau| = pE \sin\theta$

where, θ is angle between **E** and **p**.

$\Rightarrow$ $4 = p \times 2 \times 10^5 \times \sin 30$

$\Rightarrow$ $p = 4 \times 10^{-5}$ cm

$\Rightarrow$ $p = q2l$

$\therefore$ $q2l = 4 \times 10^{-5}$

where, $2l = 2\text{ cm} = 2 \times 10^{-2}$ m

$\therefore$ $q = \dfrac{4 \times 10^{-5}}{2 \times 10^{-2}}$

$\Rightarrow$ $2 \times 10^{-3}\text{ C} = 2\text{ mC}$

2 *(c)* Torque on dipole, $\tau = pE\sin\theta$

The direction of torque is perpendicular to the plane of paper inwards, i.e. when the dipole is parallel or anti-parallel to **E** and maximum at $\theta = 90°$. So, torque is maximum, if **p** is perpendicular to **E**.

3 *(a)* Consider the diagram, where an electric dipole is placed in non-uniform electric field.

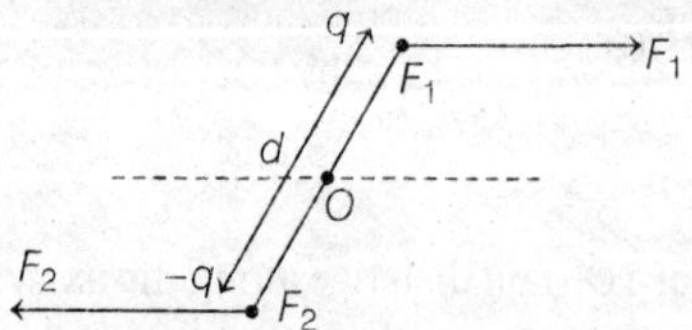

Electric field at the sight of q is E_1 and electric field at the sight of $-q$ is E_2.

F_1 = force on the charge $q = qE_1$

F_2 = force on the charge $-q = -qE_2$

Net force on the dipole,

$$F = F_1 + F_2 = q(E_1 - E_2)$$

$\therefore$ $|E_1| \neq |E_2|$

$\Rightarrow$ $|F| \neq 0$

τ_1 = torque on the dipole due to E_1 $= p \times E_1$ (clockwise)

τ_2 = torque on the dipole due to E_2 $= p \times E_2$ (clockwise)

where, $p = \dfrac{1}{2}qd$ is dipole moment of the dipole.

$$\tau_{net} = \tau_1 + \tau_2 = p \times E_1 + p \times E_2 \neq 0$$

Hence, both torque (τ_{net}) and force (F) act on the dipole.

4 *(a)* Here, torque $\tau = pE\sin\theta$

Potential energy of the dipole,

$$U = -\int \tau\, d\theta = -\int_{\theta_1}^{\theta_2} pE \sin\theta$$

$$= pE[\cos\theta_1 - \cos\theta_2]$$

$$= -pE(\cos 90° - \cos\theta)$$

$$= -pE\cos\theta$$

5 *(c)* For stable equilibrium, the angle θ should be zero.

E; −q +q

$\tau = pE \sin\theta = 0$

6 *(c)* Here, $\alpha + \theta = 90°$

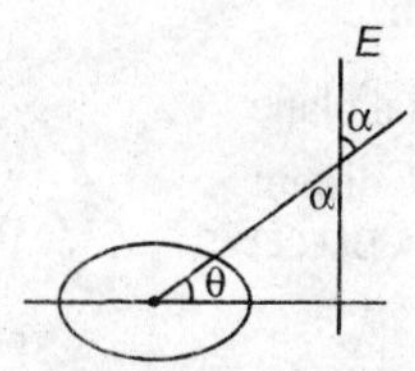

$\Rightarrow$ $\tan\alpha = \dfrac{1}{2}\tan\theta$

$\Rightarrow$ $\tan\theta = 2\tan\alpha = 2\tan(90° - \theta)$

$\Rightarrow$ $\tan^2\theta = 2$

$\Rightarrow$ $\tan\theta = \sqrt{2}$

$\Rightarrow$ $\theta = \tan^{-1}(\sqrt{2})$

7 *(d)* Electric field and electric potential at a general point at a distance r from the centre of the dipole is

$$E_g = \frac{1}{4\pi\varepsilon_0}\frac{p}{r^3}\sqrt{(3\cos^2\theta + 1)}$$

and $$V_g = \frac{1}{4\pi\varepsilon_0}\frac{p\cos\theta}{r^2}$$

8 *(a)* The torque acting on a dipole is given by $\tau = \mathbf{p} \times \mathbf{E}$, the potential energy of the dipole is given by $-U = -\mathbf{p} \cdot \mathbf{E}$ and the resultant force on the dipole is zero.

9 *(a)* The electric dipole moment is equal to $p = 1.6 \times 10^{-19} \times 4.3 \times 10^{-9}$ $[\because p = q \times 2l]$

$$= 6.88 \times 10^{-28}\text{ C-m}$$

10 *(c)* Intensity of electric field at a point on the axis of dipole is given by

$$E_a = \frac{1}{4\pi\varepsilon_0} \cdot \frac{2p}{r^3}\text{ N/C} \quad \text{...(i)}$$

where, p is dipole moment.

Intensity of electric field at a point on the equatorial line of dipole is given below

−q, l, l, +q, r, E_q, p, E_a, r

Now, similarly

$$E_q = \frac{1}{4\pi\varepsilon_0}\frac{p}{r^3}\text{ N/C} \quad \text{...(ii)}$$

From Eqs. (i) and (ii), we get

$$E_a = 2E_q$$

11 *(c)* The magnitudes of electric fields due to the two charges $+q$ and $-q$ are given by

$$E_{+q} = \frac{q}{4\pi\varepsilon_0(r^2 + a^2)}$$

and $$E_{-q} = \frac{q}{4\pi\varepsilon_0(r^2 + a^2)}$$

they are equal. The components normal to dipole axis cancel away, but along dipole axis add up. Hence, the total electric field **E** and **p** is opposite to dipole moment vector **p**.

12 *(d)* When an electric dipole is placed in an electric field **E**, a torque $\tau = \mathbf{p} \times \mathbf{E}$ acts on it. This torque tries to rotated the dipole through an angle θ.

If the dipole is rotated from an angle θ_1 to θ_2, then work done by external force is given by

$$W = pE(\cos\theta_1 - \cos\theta_2) \quad \text{...(i)}$$

Putting $\theta_1 = 0°, \theta_2 = 90°$ in the Eq. (i), we get

$$W = pE(\cos 0° - \cos 90°)$$

$$= pE(1 - 0) = pE$$

13 *(b)* Axis of an electric dipole is always directed from negative charge to the positive charge.

14 *(a)* Torque (τ) acting on the dipole in an uniform external field **E**

τ = Either force × Perpendicular distance

$= qE \times 2a\sin\theta = (q \times 2a) \times E\sin\theta$

$= pE\sin\theta$ or $\tau = \mathbf{p} \times \mathbf{E}$

15 (b) Choose the three coordinate axes as x, y and z and plot the charges with the given coordinates as shown

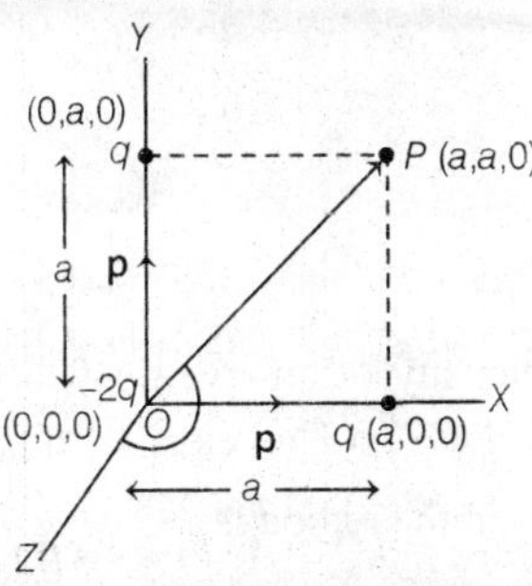

O is the origin at which $-2q$ charge is placed.

The system is equivalent to two dipoles along x and y-directions, respectively. The dipole moments of two dipoles are shown in figure. The resultant dipole moment will be directed along OP, where $P \equiv (a, a, 0)$. The magnitude of resultant dipole moment is

$$p' = \sqrt{p^2 + p^2} = \sqrt{(qa)^2 + (qa)^2}$$

$$= \sqrt{2}qa$$

16 (d) Given, $q = 0.05\mu C = 5 \times 10^{-8}$ C,

$2a = 30$ mm $= 0.03$ m

and $E = 10^6$ NC^{-1}

Torque acting on an electric dipole placed in an uniform electric field,

$$\tau = pE \sin\theta$$

For maximum torque, $\theta = 90°$

$$\therefore \quad \tau_{max} = pE = E(q \times 2a)$$

$$= 10^6 \times 5 \times 10^{-8} \times 0.03$$

$$= 1.5 \times 10^{-3} \text{ N-m}$$

17 (d) The magnitude of electric field at an axial point M at a distance z from the origin is given by

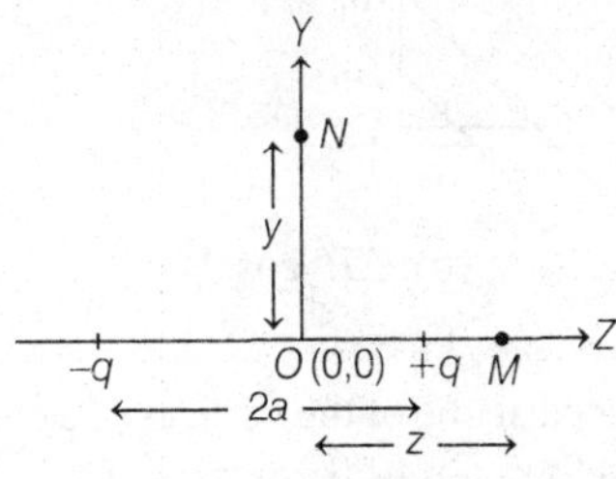

$$|\mathbf{E}_z| = \frac{1}{4\pi\varepsilon_0} \cdot \frac{2pz}{(z^2 - a^2)^2}$$

For $z >> a$,

$$|\mathbf{E}_z| = \frac{2p}{4\pi\varepsilon_0 z^3}$$

and magnitude of electric field at a equatorial point N at a distance y from origin (0, 0) is given by

$$|\mathbf{E}_y| = \frac{p}{4\pi\varepsilon_0 (y^2 + a^2)^{3/2}}$$

For $y >> a$,

$$|\mathbf{E}_y| = \frac{1}{4\pi\varepsilon_0} \cdot \frac{p}{y^3}$$

For $z = y >> a$,

$$\frac{|\mathbf{E}_z|}{|\mathbf{E}_y|} = 2$$

18 (d) The electric field at a point distance r from electric dipole is

$$E = \frac{1}{4\pi\varepsilon_0} \cdot \frac{2p}{r^3} \quad \text{(axial line)}$$

where, p is dipole moment and r is the distance of charge from centre of dipole.

or $$E \propto \frac{1}{r^3}$$

Force on charge,

$$F = QE$$

or $$F \propto \frac{1}{r^3}$$

$$\therefore \quad \frac{F_2}{F_1} = \left(\frac{r_1}{r_2}\right)^3$$

Given, $r_1 = r, r_2 = 2r$

and $F_1 = F$

$$\therefore \quad \frac{F_2}{F} = \left(\frac{r}{2r}\right)^3 = \frac{1}{8}$$

$$\Rightarrow \quad F_2 = \frac{F}{8}$$

19 (c) An electric dipole is a system formed by two equal and opposite point charges placed at a short distance apart.

The product of one charge and the distance between the charges is called electric dipole moment. The electric dipole moment is a vector quantity whose direction is along the axis of the dipole pointing from the negative charge to the positive charge.

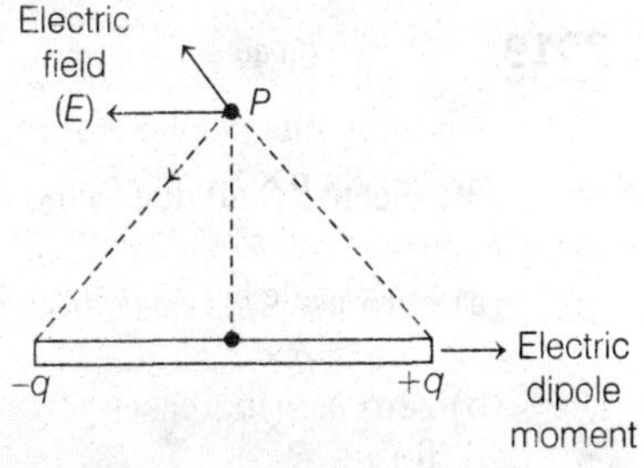

The direction of electric field is from positive charge to negative charge. As it is clear from the figure, the direction of electric field intensity at a point on the equatorial line of the dipole is opposite to the direction of dipole moment. Hence, angle between them is 180°.

20 (c) When a dipole AB of very small length is taken, then for a point P located at a distance r from the axis the electric field is given by

$$E = \frac{1}{4\pi\varepsilon_0} \cdot \frac{2p}{r^3} \quad \text{...(i)}$$

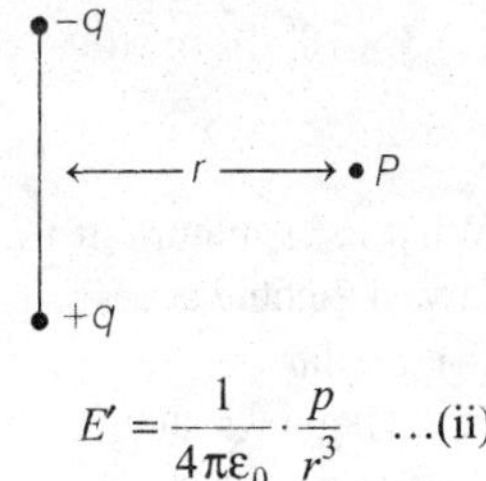

where, p is dipole moment. When dipole is rotated by 90°, then electric field is given by

$$E' = \frac{1}{4\pi\varepsilon_0} \cdot \frac{p}{r^3} \quad \text{...(ii)}$$

From Eqs. (i) and (ii), we get

$$E' = \frac{E}{2}$$

Topic 4

Electric Flux and Gauss' Theorem

2019

1 A hollow metal sphere of radius R is uniformly charged. The electric field due to the sphere at a distance r from the centre **[NEET]**

(a) zero as r increases for $r< R$, decreases as r increases for $r> R$
(b) zero as r increases for $r< R$, increases as r increases for $r> R$
(c) decreases as r increases for $r< R$ and for $r> R$
(d) increases as r increases for $r< R$ and for $r> R$

2 Two metal spheres, one of radius R and the other of radius $2R$ respectively have the same surface charge density σ. They are brought in contact and separated. What will be the new surface charge densities on them? **[NEET Odisha]**

(a) $\sigma_P = \frac{5}{6}\sigma, \ \sigma_Q = \frac{5}{2}\sigma$
(b) $\sigma_P = \frac{5}{2}\sigma, \ \sigma_Q = \frac{5}{6}\sigma$
(c) $\sigma_P = \frac{5}{2}\sigma, \ \sigma_Q = \frac{5}{3}\sigma$
(d) $\sigma_P = \frac{5}{3}\sigma, \ \sigma_Q = \frac{5}{6}\sigma$

3 A sphere encloses an electric dipole with charge $\pm 3 \times 10^{-6}$ C. What is the total electric flux across the sphere? **[NEET Odisha]**

(a) -3×10^{-6} N-m^2/C (b) Zero
(c) 3×10^{6} N-m^2/C (d) 6×10^{-6} N-m^2/C

2014

4 What is the nature of Gaussian surface involved in Gauss' law of electrostatics? **[KCET]**

(a) Scalar (b) Electrical
(c) Magnetic (d) Vector

2013

5 Three charges $q_1, -q_1$ and q_2 are placed as shown in figure, S is a Gaussian surface. Electric field at any point on S is **[AIIMS]**

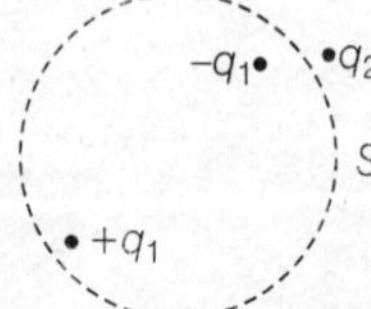

(a) due to q_2 only (b) uniform at all points
(c) zero at all the points (d) due to all the charges

2012

6 In a region, the intensity of an electric field is given by $\mathbf{E} = 2\hat{\mathbf{i}} + 3\hat{\mathbf{j}} + \hat{\mathbf{k}}$ in NC^{-1}. The electric flux through a surface $\mathbf{S} = 10\hat{\mathbf{i}}$ m^2 in the region is **[WB JEE]**

(a) 5 Nm^2 C^{-1} (b) 10 Nm^2 C^{-1}
(c) 15 Nm^2 C^{-1} (d) 20 Nm^2 C^{-1}

2011

7 There exists an electric field of 1 N/C along y-direction. The flux passing through the square of 1 m placed in xy-plane inside the electric field is **[J&K CET]**

(a) 1.0 Nm^{2}C^{-1} (b) 10.0 Nm^{2}C^{-1}
(c) 2.0 Nm^{2}C^{-1} (d) zero

8 A charge Q is enclosed by a Gaussian spherical surface of radius R. If the radius is doubled, then the outward electric flux will **[CBSE AIPMT]**

(a) be reduced to half (b) remain the same
(c) be doubled (d) increase four times

9 A square surface of side L metre in the plane of the paper is placed in a uniform electric field E (volt/metre) acting along the same plane at an angle θ with the horizontal side of the square as shown in figure.

The electric flux linked to the surface in unit of Nm^{2}C^{-1} is **[CBSE AIPMT]**

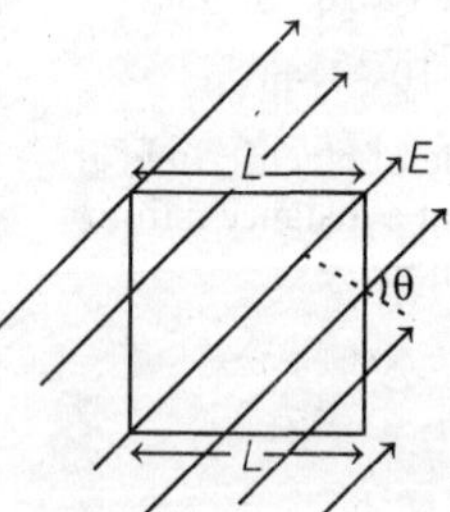

(a) EL^2 (b) $EL^2 \cos\theta$
(c) $EL^2 \sin\theta$ (d) zero

10 A point charge Q is placed at one of the vertices of a cubical block. The electric flux flowing through this cube is **[Manipal]**

(a) $\frac{Q}{6\varepsilon_0}$ (b) $\frac{Q}{4\varepsilon_0}$ (c) $\frac{Q}{8\varepsilon_0}$ (d) $\frac{Q}{\varepsilon_0}$

11 The total electric flux emanating from a closed surface enclosing an α-particle is (e = electronic charge) **[Kerala CEE]**

(a) $2e/\varepsilon_0$ (b) e/ε_0 (c) $e\varepsilon_0$ (d) $\varepsilon_0 e/4$
(e) $4e/\varepsilon_0$

12 The electric flux for Gaussian surface A that encloses the charged particles in free is (given, $q_1 = -14$ nC, $q_2 = 78.85$ nC, $q_3 = -56$ nC) **[MP PMT]**

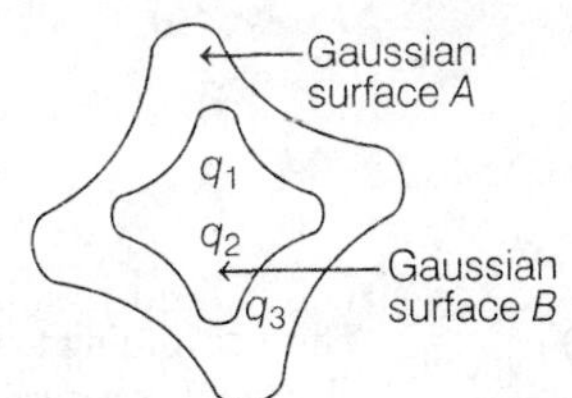

(a) 10^3 Nm^{2}C^{-1} (b) 10^3 CN^{-1}m^{-2}
(c) 6.32×10^3 Nm^{2}C^{-1} (d) 6.32×10^3 CN^{-1}m^{-2}

13 A point charge $+q$ is placed at the centre of a cube of side L. The electric flux emerging from the cube is **[WB JEE]**
(a) $\frac{q}{\varepsilon_0}$ (b) zero (c) $\frac{6qL^2}{\varepsilon_0}$ (d) $\frac{q}{6L^2\varepsilon_0}$

14 The Gaussian surface for calculating the electric field due to a charge distribution is **[J&K CET]**
(a) any surface near the charge distribution
(b) always a spherical surface
(c) a symmetrical closed surface containing the charge distribution, at every point of which electric field has a single fixed value
(d) None of the above

15 If the amount of flux entering and leaving an enclosed surface respectively are ϕ_1 and ϕ_2. The electric charge inside the surface will be **[AIEEE 2003]**
(a) $(\phi_2 - \phi_1)\varepsilon_0$ (b) $(\phi_2 + \phi_1)\varepsilon_0$
(c) $\frac{(\phi_2 - \phi_1)}{\varepsilon_0}$ (d) $\frac{(\phi_2 + \phi_1)}{\varepsilon_0}$

2009

16 The total electric flux through a cube when a charge $8q$ is placed at one corner of the cube is **[Kerala CEE]**
(a) $\varepsilon_0 q$ (b) $\frac{\varepsilon_0}{q}$ (c) $4\pi\varepsilon_0 q$ (d) $\frac{q}{4\pi\varepsilon_0}$
(e) $\frac{q}{\varepsilon_0}$

17 Electric flux emanating through a surface element $d\mathbf{S} = 5\hat{\mathbf{i}}$ placed in an electric field $\mathbf{E} = 4\hat{\mathbf{i}} + 4\hat{\mathbf{j}} + 4\hat{\mathbf{k}}$ is **[J&K CET]**
(a) 10 units (b) 20 units (c) 4 units (d) 16 units

18 A Gaussian sphere encloses an electric dipole within it. The total flux across the sphere is **[JCECE]**
(a) zero
(b) half that due to a single charge
(c) double that due to a single charge
(d) dependent on the position of the dipole

19 Gauss's law is valid for **[DUMET]**
(a) any closed surface
(b) only regular closed surfaces
(c) any open surface
(d) only irregular open surfaces

2008

20 A hollow cylinder has a charge q C within it. If ϕ is the electric flux in unit of voltmeter associated with the curved surface B, the flux linked with the plane surface A in unit of voltmeter will be **[AIIMS]**
(a) $\frac{1}{2}\left(\frac{q}{\varepsilon_0} - \phi\right)$ (b) $\frac{q}{2\varepsilon_0}$ (c) $\frac{\phi}{3}$ (d) $\frac{q}{\varepsilon_0} - \phi$

21 The electric flux through a closed surface area S enclosing charge Q is ϕ. If the surface area is doubled, then the flux is **[J&K CET]**
(a) 2ϕ (b) $\phi/2$ (c) $\phi/4$ (d) ϕ

2007

22 A square surface of side L m is in the plane of the paper. A uniform electric field $\mathbf{E}$ (Vm^{-1}), also in the plane of the paper is limited only to the lower half of the square surface (see figure). The electric flux in SI units associated with the surface is **[CBSE AIPMT]**

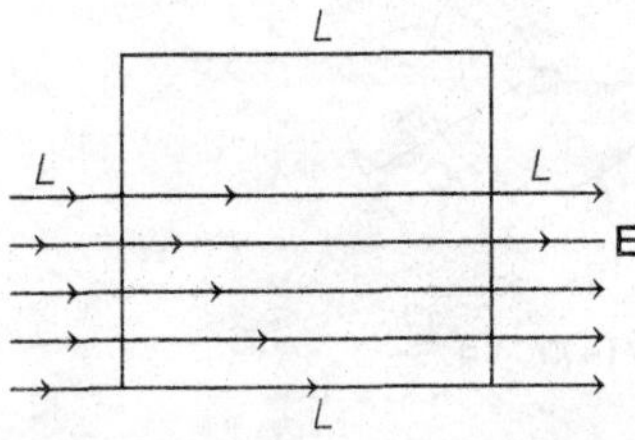

(a) $\frac{EL^2}{(2\varepsilon_0)}$ (b) $\frac{EL^2}{2}$ (c) zero (d) EL^2

23 A charge q is located at the centre of a cube. The electric flux through any face is **[BHU, JIPMER]**
(a) $\frac{\pi q}{6(4\pi\varepsilon_0)}$ (b) $\frac{q}{6(4\pi\varepsilon_0)}$ (c) $\frac{2\pi q}{6(4\pi\varepsilon_0)}$ (d) $\frac{4\pi q}{6(4\pi\varepsilon_0)}$

24 A charge q is placed at the corner of a cube of side a. The electric flux through the cube is **[MHT CET]**
(a) $\frac{q}{\varepsilon_0}$ (b) $\frac{q}{3\varepsilon_0}$ (c) $\frac{q}{6\varepsilon_0}$ (d) $\frac{q}{8\varepsilon_0}$

25 If the electric flux entering and leaving an enclosed surface respectively are ϕ_1 and ϕ_2, the electric charge inside the surface will be **[RPMT, AFMC]**
(a) $(\phi_2 - \phi_1)/\varepsilon_0$ (b) $(\phi_2 + \phi_1)/\varepsilon_0$
(c) $\frac{\phi_1 - \phi_2}{\varepsilon_0}$ (d) $\varepsilon_0(\phi_1 + \phi_2)$

26 If the uniform surface charge density on the infinite plane sheet is σ, then electric field near the surface will be **[Guj CET]**
(a) $\frac{\sigma}{2\varepsilon_0}$ (b) $\frac{3\sigma}{\varepsilon_0}$ (c) $\frac{\sigma}{\varepsilon_0}$ (d) $\frac{2\sigma}{\varepsilon_0}$

Answers

1 (a)	2 (d)	3 (b)	4 (d)	5 (d)	6 (d)	7 (d)	8 (b)	9 (d)	10 (c)
11 (a)	12 (a)	13 (a)	14 (c)	15 (a)	16 (e)	17 (b)	18 (a)	19 (a)	20 (a)
21 (d)	22 (c)	23 (d)	24 (d)	25 (d)	26 (a)				

Explanations

1 *(a)* As the hollow sphere is uniformly charged, so the net charge will appear on the surface of the sphere.

(i) The electric field at a point outside the hollow sphere is

$$\phi = \oint_S \mathbf{E} \cdot d\mathbf{S} = \frac{Q_{\text{enclosed}}}{\varepsilon_0}$$

[from Gauss' law]

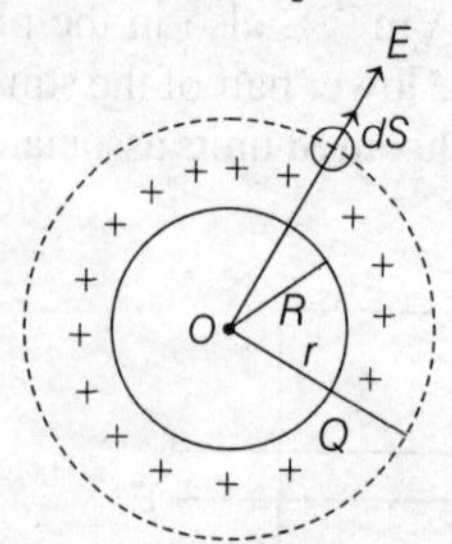

$$\Rightarrow \quad E(4\pi r^2) = \frac{Q}{\varepsilon_0}$$

$$\Rightarrow \quad E = \frac{Q}{4\pi\varepsilon_0 r^2} \Rightarrow E \propto \frac{1}{r^2}$$

(ii) The electric field at the surface $(r = R)$,

$$E = \frac{Q}{4\pi\varepsilon_0 R}$$

(iii) The electric field inside hollow sphere is

$$E = \frac{Q}{4\pi\varepsilon_0 r} = 0 \quad [\because Q_{\text{inside}} = 0]$$

2 *(d)* The surface charge density of a closed surface area having charge Q is given by

$$\sigma = \frac{\text{Charge}}{\text{Area}} = \frac{Q}{\text{A}}$$

or $\quad Q = \sigma\text{A}$

Thus, the charges on sphere P and Q having same charge density as shown in the figure below is given by

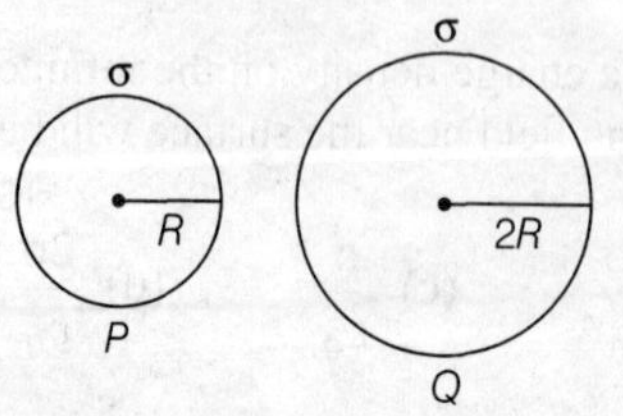

$$Q_P = \sigma \times 4\pi R^2 = 4\pi\sigma R^2 \quad \text{...(i)}$$

$$\text{and } Q_Q = \sigma \times 4\pi(2R)^2 = 16\pi\sigma R^2 \quad \text{...(ii)}$$

When they are brought in contact with each other, the total charge will be

$$Q_t = Q_P + Q_Q$$
$$= 4\pi\sigma R^2 + 16\pi\sigma R^2$$

[from Eqs. (i) and (ii)]

$$= 20\pi\sigma R^2 \quad \text{...(iii)}$$

In connection of two charged conducting bodies, the potential will become same on both, i.e.

$$\frac{Q_P}{4\pi\,\varepsilon_0 R} = \frac{Q_Q}{4\pi\,\varepsilon_0 2R}$$

$$\Rightarrow \quad \frac{Q_P}{R} = \frac{Q_Q}{2R} \Rightarrow \frac{Q_P}{Q_Q} = \frac{1}{2}$$

So, the charges on the sphere P and Q after separation will be distributed as

$$\Rightarrow \quad Q_P' = \frac{1}{3}Q_t \text{ and } Q_Q' = \frac{2}{3}Q_t$$

After separation, the new surface charge densities on P and Q will be

$$\sigma_P = \frac{Q_P'}{\text{Area}} = \frac{1}{3}\frac{Q_t}{\text{Area}}$$

$$= \frac{1}{3}\frac{20\pi\sigma R^2}{4\pi R^2} = \frac{5}{3}\sigma$$

$$\text{and } \sigma_Q = \frac{Q_Q'}{\text{Area}} = \frac{2}{3}\frac{Q_t}{\text{Area}}$$

$$= \frac{2}{3} \times \frac{20\pi\sigma R^2}{4\pi(2R)^2}$$

$$= \frac{2}{3} \times \frac{5}{4}\sigma = \frac{5}{6}\sigma$$

3 *(b)* When a sphere encloses a charged dipole,

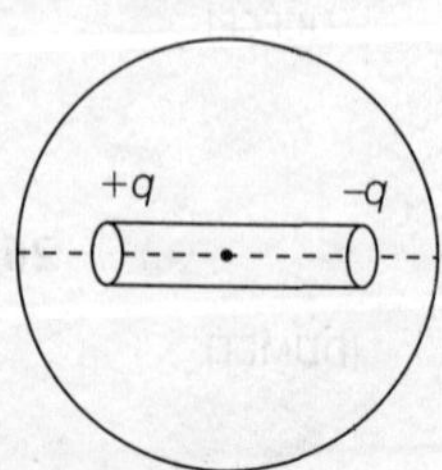

Here, $q = \pm 3 \times 10^{-6}$ C

Thus, according to Gauss's law, the net electric flux across the closed surface is equal to the net charge enclosed by it divided by ε_0, i.e.

$$\phi_E = \frac{q_{\text{in}}}{\varepsilon_0}$$

$$= \frac{+3 \times 10^{-6} - 3 \times 10^{-6}}{\varepsilon_0} = 0$$

Hence, electric flux across the sphere is zero.

4 *(d)* The Gauss' law in electrostatic given a relation between electric flux through any closed hypothetical surface (called a Gaussian surface) and the charge enclosed by the surface. So, the nature of Gaussian surface is vector.

5 *(d)* The electric field at any point on S (Gaussian surface) is due to all the charges but the flux through the S is due to only charges q_2 and $-q_1$ inside the Gaussian surface.

6 *(d)* Given, $\mathbf{E} = (2\hat{\mathbf{k}} + 3\hat{\mathbf{j}} + \hat{\mathbf{k}})\ \text{NC}^{-1}$

and $\quad \mathbf{S} = 10\hat{\mathbf{i}}\ \text{m}^2$

We know that,

Electric flux, $\phi = \mathbf{E} \cdot \mathbf{S}$

$= (2\hat{\mathbf{i}} + 3\hat{\mathbf{j}} + \hat{\mathbf{k}}) \cdot (10\hat{\mathbf{i}}) = 20\ \text{Nm}^2\text{C}^{-1}$

7 *(d)* The flux passing through the square of 1 m placed in xy-plane inside the electric field is zero because number of field lines entering are equal to number of field lines (flux) leaving the surface. So, net flux will be zero, so $E = 0$.

8 *(b)* Total flux $= \dfrac{\text{Net enclosed charge}}{\varepsilon_0}$

Hence, we can say that the electric flux depends only on net enclosed charge by surface. So, flux will remain the same.

9 *(d)* Flux of electric field $\mathbf{E}$ through any area A is defined as $\phi = EA\cos\theta$.

The lines are parallel to the surface.

$\Rightarrow$ Angle between E and $A = 90°$, hence $\phi = 0$.

10 (c) Let ϕ_{total} be the total electric flux and ϕ_{cube} be that of flowing through cube. So, when a point charge Q is placed at one of the vertices of a cubical block, then only (1/8)th part of total flux will pass through this cube, therefore

$$\phi_{cube} = \frac{\phi_{total}}{8} = \frac{Q}{8\varepsilon_0} \quad \left[\because \phi_{total} = \frac{Q}{\varepsilon_0}\right]$$

11 (a) As we know that, charge on α-particle is double to that on electron.

$\because$ By Gauss' theorem, $|\phi_E| = \left|\frac{q}{\varepsilon_0}\right|$

$$\Rightarrow \quad |\phi_E| = \left|\frac{-2e}{\varepsilon_0}\right| = \frac{2e}{\varepsilon_0}$$

12 (a) Flux is due to charges enclosed per ε_0.

$\therefore$ Total flux $= (-14 + 78.85 - 56)\ \text{nC}/\varepsilon_0$

$$= 8.85 \times 10^{-9}\ \text{C} \times \frac{4\pi}{4\pi\varepsilon_0}$$

$$= 8.85 \times 10^{-9} \times 9 \times 10^9 \times 4\pi$$

$$= 1000.4\ \text{Nm}^2/\text{C} \simeq 1000\ \text{Nm}^2\ \text{C}^{-1}$$

13 (a) Since, the charge is placed at the centre of the cube, so the electric flux lines move out equally from all sides of the cube. Thus, the electric flux emerging from the cube is equal to q/ε_0.

14 (c) The Gaussian surface for calculating the electric field due to a charge distribution is a symmetrical closed surface containing the charge distribution, at every point of which electric field has a single fixed value.

15 (a) By Gauss's theorem,

Net flux leaving the enclosed surface

$$= \frac{1}{\varepsilon_0} \times \text{Net charge enclosed}$$

or $\phi_2 - \phi_1 = \frac{1}{\varepsilon_0} \times q$

or $q = (\phi_2 - \phi_1)\varepsilon_0$

16 (e) Total electric flux,

$$\phi = \frac{q_{inside}}{8\varepsilon_0} = \frac{8q}{8\varepsilon_0} = \frac{q}{\varepsilon_0}$$

17 (b) $\phi = \mathbf{E} \cdot d\mathbf{S}$, $\mathbf{E} = 4\hat{\mathbf{i}} + 4\hat{\mathbf{j}} + 4\hat{\mathbf{k}}$

and $\quad d\mathbf{S} = 5\hat{\mathbf{i}}$

$\Rightarrow \quad \phi = (4\hat{\mathbf{i}} + 4\hat{\mathbf{j}} + 4\hat{\mathbf{k}}) \cdot (5\hat{\mathbf{i}})$

$\phi = 20$ units

18 (a) Flux through the Gaussian sphere

$$\phi = \frac{q_{inside}}{\varepsilon_0} = \frac{+q-q}{\varepsilon_0}$$

$\phi = 0$

19 (a) Gauss' law is valid for any closed surface not necessary to be a regular closed surface.

20 (a) Gauss' law states that, the net electric flux through any closed surface is equal to the net charge inside the surface divided by ε_0.

i.e. $\quad \phi_{total} = \frac{q}{\varepsilon_0}$

Let electric flux linked with surfaces A, B and C are ϕ_A, ϕ_B and ϕ_C, respectively.

i.e. $\quad \phi_{total} = \phi_A + \phi_B + \phi_C$

Since, $\quad \phi_C = \phi_A$

$\therefore \quad 2\phi_A + \phi_B = \phi_{total} = \frac{q}{\varepsilon_0}$

or $\quad \phi_A = \frac{1}{2}\left(\frac{q}{\varepsilon_0} - \phi_B\right)$

Hence, $\phi_A = \frac{1}{2}\left(\frac{q}{\varepsilon_0} - \phi\right)$ (given, $\phi_B = \phi$)

21 (d) By Gauss' law, $\phi_E = \frac{q}{\varepsilon_0}$

$\therefore$ Flux will remain same, i.e. ϕ.

[$\because$ flux does not depend upon surface area]

22 (c) $\because$ The angle between area vector **S** and electric field is 90°.

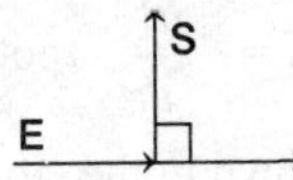

$\therefore$ Flux associated will be

$$\phi_E = \mathbf{E} \cdot d\mathbf{S} = EdS\cos 90° = 0$$

23 (d) From Gauss' law, $\phi = \frac{q}{\varepsilon_0}$

This is the net flux coming out of the cube.

Since, a cube has 6 sides, so electric flux through any face is

$$\phi' = \frac{\phi}{6} = \frac{q}{6\varepsilon_0} = \frac{4\pi q}{6(4\pi\varepsilon_0)}$$

24 (d) According to Gauss' law, the electric flux through a closed surface is equal to $\frac{1}{\varepsilon_0}$ times the net charge enclosed by the surface. Since, q is the charge enclosed by the surface, then the electric flux, $\phi = \frac{q}{\varepsilon_0}$.

If charge q is placed at a corner of cube, it will be divided into 8 such cubes. Therefore, electric flux through the cube is

$$\phi' = \frac{1}{8}\left(\frac{q}{\varepsilon_0}\right)$$

25 (d) Any closed surface is equal to the net charge inside the surface divided by ε_0.

Therefore, $\phi = \frac{q}{\varepsilon_0}$

Let $-q_1$ be the charge, due to which flux ϕ_1 is entering the surface

$$\phi_1 = \frac{-q_1}{\varepsilon_0}$$

or $\quad -q_1 = \varepsilon_0\phi_1$

Let $+q_2$ be the charge, due to which flux ϕ_2 is leaving the surface

$\therefore \quad \phi_2 = \frac{q_2}{\varepsilon_0}$ or $q_2 = \varepsilon_0\phi_2$

So, electric charge inside the surface

$$= q_2 - q_1$$
$$= \varepsilon_0\phi_2 + \varepsilon_0\phi_1$$
$$= \varepsilon_0(\phi_2 + \phi_1)$$

26 (a) Figure shows a portion of a flat thin sheet, infinite in size with constant surface charge density σ (charge per unit area).

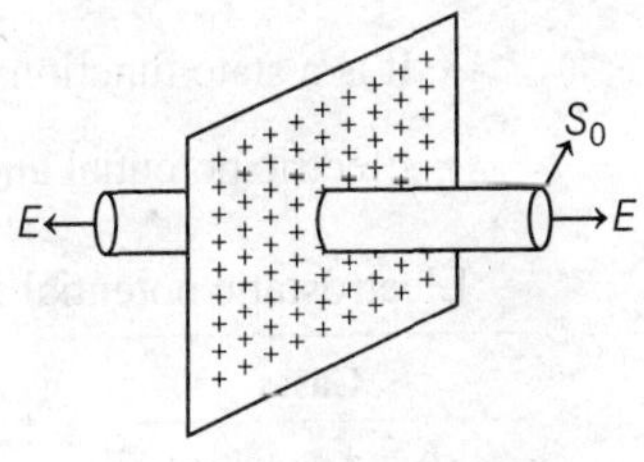

Let us draw a Gaussian surface (a cylinder) with one end on one side and other end on the other side and of cross-sectional area S_0. Field lines will be tangential to the curved surface, so flux passing through this surfaces is zero. At plane surface electric field has same magnitude and perpendicular to surface. Hence, using

$$ES = \frac{q_{in}}{\varepsilon_0}$$

where, S is the surface area of cross-section of cylinder. Since, there are two cross-sectional area, therefore surface area, $S = 2S_0$

$\therefore \quad E(2S_0) = \frac{(\sigma)(S_0)}{\varepsilon_0}$

$\Rightarrow \quad E = \frac{\sigma}{2\varepsilon_0}$

16

Electrostatics II
(Electric Potential and Capacitance)

Quick Review

Electric Potential

- It is the amount of work done in bringing a unit positive test charge from infinity to a point, along any arbitrary path. It is a scalar quantity, expressed as $V = \dfrac{\text{work done } (W)}{\text{charge } (q)}$.
- It is a state function and can have positive, negative or zero value according to the nature of the charge.
- Electric potential and field are related by $E = -\dfrac{dV}{dr}$ (potential decreases in the direction of E).

Electrostatic potential in various cases are shown in the table given below

	Cases	Electric potential	Diagrammatic representation	Graphical representation
(*i*)	A point charge	$V = \dfrac{q}{4\pi\varepsilon_0 r}$		
(*ii*)	A system of charges	$V = V_1 + V_2 + V_3 + \ldots$ $= \dfrac{1}{4\pi\varepsilon_0}\sum_{i=1}^{n}\left(\dfrac{q_i}{r_i}\right)$		
(*iii*)	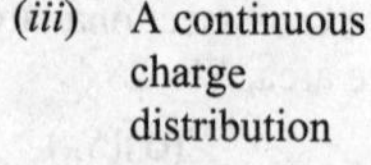 A continuous charge distribution	$V = \int dV = \int \dfrac{dq}{4\pi\varepsilon_0 r}$	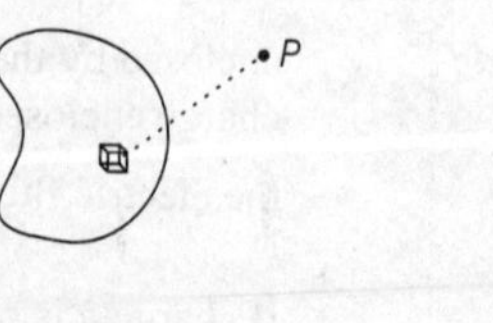	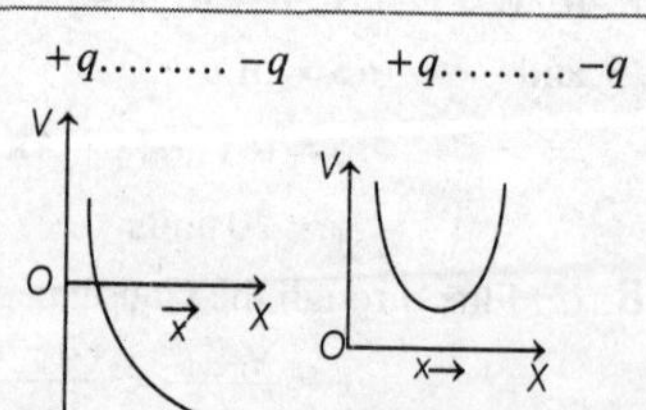

	Cases	Electric potential	Diagrammatic representation	Graphical representation
(iv)	Electric dipole	$V = \frac{1}{4\pi\varepsilon_0}\frac{p\cos\theta}{r^2}$ p = dipole moment		—
(v)	Charged spherical shell of conducting sphere	(a) $V = \frac{Q}{4\pi\varepsilon_0 r}$, for $r > R$ (b) $V = \frac{1}{4\pi\varepsilon_0}\frac{Q}{R}$, for $r = R$ (c) $V = \frac{Q}{4\pi\varepsilon_0 R}$, for $r < R$		
(vi)	Charged shell of non-conducting sphere	At centre, potential $V_{\text{centre}} = \frac{3}{2}\left[\frac{1}{4\pi\varepsilon_0}\cdot\frac{q}{r}\right]$ $= \frac{3}{2}V_{\text{surface}}$		
(vii)	Uniformly charged long thin wire	$V = \frac{\lambda}{2\pi\varepsilon_0}\log_e\left[\frac{\sqrt{r+l^2}-l}{\sqrt{r^2+l^2}+l}\right]$ [where, λ = line charge density $= \frac{dq}{dl}$]		—
(viii)	Uniformly charged ring	$V_{\text{centre}} = \frac{1}{4\pi\varepsilon_0}\cdot\frac{q}{R}$ $V_r = \frac{1}{4\pi\varepsilon_0}\cdot\frac{q}{\sqrt{R^2+r^2}}$		
(ix)	Uniformly charged disc	$V = 2\pi k\sigma\,[R^2 + r^2 - r]$ and at $r = 0, V = \frac{\sigma R}{2\varepsilon_0}$		—

Equipotential Surface

Any surface over which the electric potential is same everywhere is called an equipotential surface. These surfaces for a point charge are concentric spherical surfaces centred at the charge.

The potential of these surfaces are expressed as

$$V = \frac{1}{4\pi\varepsilon_0} \cdot \frac{q}{r}$$

Electrostatic Potential Energy

Electric potential energy of a system of point charges is defined as the total amount of work done in bringing the different charges to their respective positions from infinitely large mutual separations.

It is represented by U and for a system of two point charges q_1 and q_2, $U = \frac{1}{4\pi\varepsilon_0} \cdot \frac{q_1 q_2}{r}$

where, r = distance of separation.

For system of n point charges,

$$U = \frac{k}{2} \sum_{\substack{i,j \\ i \neq j}}^{n} \frac{q_i q_j}{r_{ij}} \quad \left(\text{where, } k = \frac{1}{4\pi\varepsilon_0}\right)$$

Potential energy of charges in an external field for different cases are shown below in tabular form.

	Cases	Potential energy in external field
(i)	Single charge	$U = q \cdot V(r)$
(ii)	A system of two charges	$U = q_1 V(r_1) + q_2 V(r_2) + \frac{q_1 q_2}{4\pi\varepsilon_0 r_{12}}$
(iii)	Dipole	$U = -pE\cos\theta = -\mathbf{p} \cdot \mathbf{E}$ $U = -pE$ (minimum), for $\theta = 0°$ (stable equilibrium). $U = +pE$ (maximum), for $\theta = 180°$ i.e. dipole is in unstable equilibrium.

Conductors and Insulators

Conductors are the materials through which electric charge can flow easily.

Under electrostatic conditions, the conductors have following properties

(i) Inside a conductor, electrostatic field is zero.

(ii) At the surface of a charged conductor, electrostatic field must be normal to the surface at every point.

(iii) The interior of the conductor can have no excess charge in the static situation.

(iv) Electrostatic potential is constant throughout the volume of the conductor and has the same value (as inside) on its surface.

(v) Surface charge density of a conductor could be different at different points.

Insulators are the materials through which electric charge cannot flow, e.g. glass, rubber, wood, etc.

Insulators are also called dielectrics.

Dielectric and Polarisation

- **Dielectrics** Non-conducting (insulating) materials that can produce electric effect without conduction are known as dielectrics.
- Dielectrics are classified based on their behaviour in external field given in tabular form below

Types	Definition	Diagram	Dipole moment
Polar	Centres of positive and negative charges are separated	$E=0$ / $E \neq 0$	$P = 0\ (E = 0)$ $P > 0\ (E \neq 0)$
Non-polar	Centres of positive and negative charges coincide	$E=0$ / $E \neq 0 \to 0$	$P = 0\ (E = 0)$ $P > 0\ (E \neq 0)$

In a dielectric under the effect of an external field, a net dipole moment is induced. Due to molecular dipole moments, a net charge appears on the surface of the dielectric.

Field inside the dielectric gets reduced by

$$\mathbf{E} = |\mathbf{E}_0| - |\mathbf{E}_{\text{in}}|$$

where, E_0 = external electric field between two plates

and E_{in} = electric field inside the dielectric.

E_0, E_{in}, σ_p

Dielectric Constant (K) is expressed as $K = E_0 / E$ which is always > 1.

- **Polarisation** The induced dipole moment developed per unit volume in a dielectric slab on placing it in an electric field is called polarisation. It is denoted by P.

  It is expressed as $P = Np$

  where, p = induced dipole moment acquired by an atom of dielectric K and N = number of atoms per unit volume.
- **Electric susceptibility (χ)** The polarisation density of dielectric slab is directly proportional to the reduced value of the electric field and may be expressed as

  $$P = \chi \varepsilon_0 E_0$$

  where, χ is a constant of proportionality and is called electric susceptibility of the dielectric slab. It is a dimensionless constant.

Note 1. For vacuum, $\chi = 0$ 2. $K = 1 + \chi$

- **Dielectric strength** The maximum electric field that a dielectric can withstand without breakdown is called its dielectric strength.
  Its SI unit is Vm^{-1} and its practical unit is $\mathrm{kV(mm)}^{-1}$.
  For air it is about $3 \times 10^6\ \mathrm{Vm}^{-1}$.

Capacitors and Capacitance

A capacitor is a system of two conductors separated by an insulating medium. The conductors have charges Q and $-Q$ with potential difference $V = V_1 - V_2$ between them.

The electric field in the region between the conductors is proportional to the charge Q.

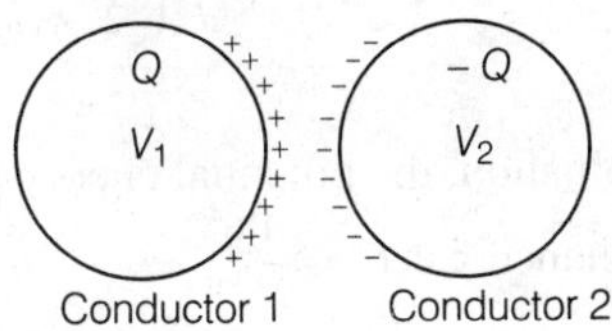

If the potential difference (V) is the work done per unit positive charge in taking a small test charge from the conductor 2 to 1 against the field, then V is proportional to Q and the ratio Q/V is a constant.

$$C = Q/V$$

The constant C is called the capacitance of the capacitor. Capacitance C depends on shape, size and separation of the system of two conductors.

A capacitor with fixed capacitance is symbolically shown as ⊣⊢, while the one with variable capacitance is shown as ⊣̸⊢. In practice, farad is a very big unit, the most common units are its sub-multiples.

$$1\,\mu\mathrm{F} = 10^{-6}\ \mathrm{F},\ 1\,\mathrm{nF} = 10^{-9}\ \mathrm{F}\ \text{and}\ 1\,\mathrm{pF} = 10^{-12}\ \mathrm{F}$$

Capacitance of an Isolated Spherical Conductor

- If charge Q is given to a spherical conductor of radius R, then $C = 4\pi\varepsilon_0 R$
  where, ε_0 = permittivity of the medium.
- If sphere is placed in a medium of dielectric constant K, then $$C = K \times 4\pi\varepsilon_0 R$$
  For air or vacuum, $K = 1$.

Capacity of a Spherical Conductor Enclosed by an Earthed Concentric Spherical Shell

- It consists of two concentric conducting sphere of radii a and b $(a < b)$.
- If inner sphere is given a charge $+Q$ and outer sphere is earthed, then capacitance will be
$$C = 4\pi\varepsilon_0 \left(\frac{ab}{b-a}\right)$$

If outer sphere is given a charge $+Q$ and inner sphere is earthed, then

$$C = 4\pi\varepsilon_0 \left(\frac{b^2}{b-a}\right)$$

Cylindrical Capacitor

It consists of two co-axial cylinders of radii a and b $(a < b)$. Its capacitance is given by

$$C = \frac{2\pi\varepsilon_0 l}{\log_e\left(\frac{b}{a}\right)}$$

where, l = length of cylinder.

Parallel Plate Capacitor

It consists of two parallel metallic plates separated by a small distance as shown

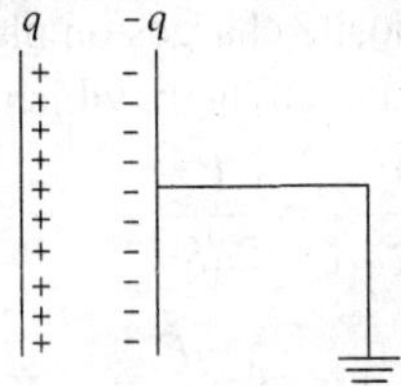

Its capacitance is given by $C = \dfrac{\varepsilon_0 A}{d}$

where, A = area of plates of capacitor

and d = distance between plates.

- The capacitance of parallel plate capacitor varies with the medium between the plates which is shown below
  (*i*) If a dielectric medium of dielectric constant K is filled completely between the plates of capacitor, then
  $$C' = \frac{K\varepsilon_0 A}{d}$$
  (*ii*) If dielectric medium is filled partially between the plates, then
  $$C' = \frac{\varepsilon_0 A}{d - t + \frac{t}{K}}$$
  where, t = thickness of dielectric.
  (*iii*) If a metallic slab of thickness t is inserted between the plates, then
  $$C' = \frac{\varepsilon_0 A}{(d-t)}$$
  (*iv*) If a number of dielectric slabs are inserted between the plates, then
  $$C' = \frac{\varepsilon_0 A}{d - (t_1 + t_2 + t_3 + \dots) + \left(\frac{t_1}{K_1} + \frac{t_2}{K_2} + \frac{t_3}{K_3} + \dots\right)}$$

- If the space between two plates of a parallel plate capacitor is filled with different dielectrics, then their capacitance for various combinations are tabulated as shown below

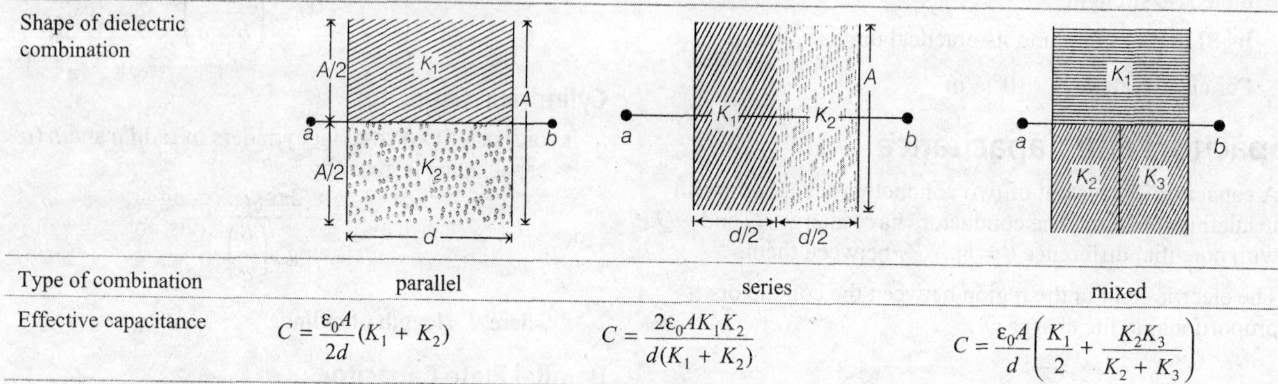

Shape of dielectric combination	(figure)	(figure)	(figure)
Type of combination	parallel	series	mixed
Effective capacitance	$C = \frac{\varepsilon_0 A}{2d}(K_1 + K_2)$	$C = \frac{2\varepsilon_0 A K_1 K_2}{d(K_1 + K_2)}$	$C = \frac{\varepsilon_0 A}{d}\left(\frac{K_1}{2} + \frac{K_2 K_3}{K_2 + K_3}\right)$

Force Between Plates of a Parallel Plate Capacitor

Due to equal and opposite charges on plates of capacitor, an attractive force act between them, which is given by

$$F = \frac{Q^2}{2K\varepsilon_0 A} = \frac{CV^2}{2dK}$$

This force per unit area is $f = \frac{F}{A} = \frac{Q^2}{2K\varepsilon_0 A^2} = \frac{\sigma^2}{2K\varepsilon_0}$

where, $\sigma = \left(\frac{Q}{A}\right)$ = surface charge density.

Energy Stored in a Capacitor

In charging a capacitor, work has to be done against the repulsive electric force. This work done is stored as potential energy in capacitor and given by

$$U = W = \frac{Q^2}{2C} = \frac{1}{2}CV^2$$

Energy density between the plates of a parallel plate capacitor is $E = \frac{U}{V} = \frac{1}{2}\frac{CV^2}{Ad}$

Combination of Capacitors

- There are two common methods of combining capacitors and they are given below

(i) Series Combination

- In this combination, the charge on each capacitor is same (equal to charge given by battery), while potential difference is distributed inversely as the ratio of capacitance, i.e. $V_1 : V_2 : V_3 \ldots = \frac{1}{C_1} : \frac{1}{C_2} : \frac{1}{C_3} : \ldots$
- The equivalent capacitance in this combination is calculated as, $\frac{1}{C_s} = \frac{1}{C_1} + \frac{1}{C_2} + \frac{1}{C_3} + \ldots$
- In this combination, the potential energy varies inversely as the capacitance, i.e. $U \propto \frac{1}{C}$.
- If n identical capacitors are connected in series, then equivalent capacitance and potential on each capacitor respectively are $C_s = \frac{C}{n}$ and $V' = \frac{V}{n}$
- If n identical plates are arranged as shown below, they constitute $(n-1)$ capacitors in series, then equivalent capacitance is

$$C_{eq} = \frac{\varepsilon_0 A}{(n-1)d}$$

(ii) Parallel Combination

- In this combination, potential difference on each capacitor is same (equal to supply voltage), while the charges are distributed in the ratio at capacitance, i.e.

$$Q_1 : Q_2 : Q_3 : \ldots = C_1 : C_2 : C_3 : \ldots$$

- The equivalent capacitance of this combination is calculated as

$$C_p = C_1 + C_2 + C_3 + \ldots$$

- In this combination, the potential energy varies directly as the capacitance, i.e.

$$U \propto C$$

- If n identical capacitors are connected in parallel, then equivalent capacitance and charge on each capacitor are respectively

$$C_p = nC$$

and $$Q' = \frac{Q}{n}$$

- If n identical plates are arranged as shown below, then $(n-1)$ capacitors will be in parallel and their equivalent capacitance is

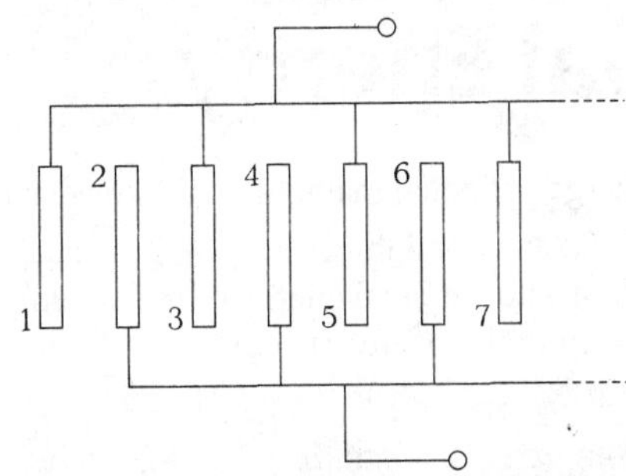

$$C_{eq} = (n-1)C$$

- If C_p is the effective capacitance or capacity of n identical capacitors connected in parallel and C_s is their effective capacitance when connected in series, then $\frac{C_p}{C_s} = n^2$.

Common Potential and Energy Loss on Sharing Charges

- If two capacitors are connected by a wire, then due to potential difference between them, they attain a common potential which can be given as

$$V = \frac{C_1V_1 + C_2V_2}{C_1 + C_2}$$

where, C_1 and C_2 = capacitance of two capacitors and V_1 and V_2 = potential of two capacitors.

- Due to this connection, charges are shared between two capacitors. This causes some loss of energy which can be given as

$$\Delta U = U_i - U_f = \frac{1}{2}\left(\frac{C_1C_2}{C_1 + C_2}\right)(V_1 - V_2)^2$$

Van de Graaff Generator

It is a device which is used for generating high electric potential of the order of ten million volts, for accelerating charged particles to a very high speed.

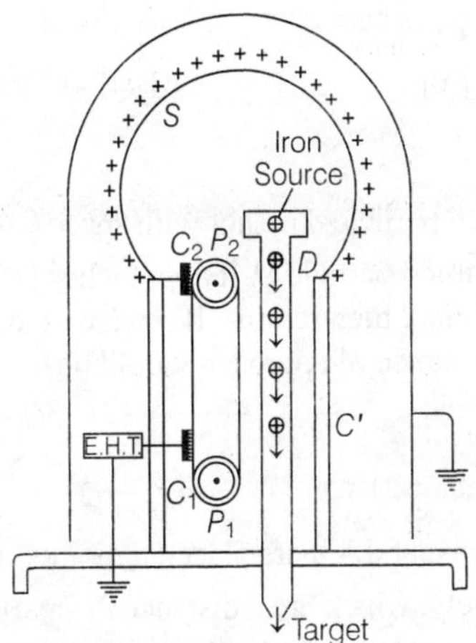

Its working is based on following two points

(*i*) The action of sharp points (corona discharge)

(*ii*) Total charge given to a spherical shell resides on its outer surface.

Topical Practice Questions

All the exam questions of this chapter have been divided into 3 topics as listed below

Topic 1

Electric Potential and Potential Energy

2019

1 Potential difference is given as $V(x) = -x^2 y$ volt. Find electric field at a point (1, 2). **[JIPMER]**

(a) $\hat{\mathbf{i}} + 4\hat{\mathbf{j}}\ \text{Vm}^{-1}$ (b) $-4\hat{\mathbf{i}} - \hat{\mathbf{j}}\ \text{Vm}^{-1}$

(c) $4\hat{\mathbf{i}} + \hat{\mathbf{j}}\ \text{Vm}^{-1}$ (d) $4\hat{\mathbf{i}} - \hat{\mathbf{j}}\ \text{Vm}^{-1}$

2017

2 A charged particle q is shot with speed v towards another fixed charged particle Q. It approaches Q upto a closest distance r and then returns. If q were given a speed $2v$, the closest distance of approach would be **[JIPMER]**

q•——→ v ←——•- - r - - -oQ

(a) r (b) $2r$ (c) $r/2$ (d) $r/4$

3 Charges $+q$ and $-q$ are placed at points A and B respectively, which are a distance $2L$ apart, C is the mid-point between A and B. The work done in moving a charge $+Q$ along the semi-circle CRD is **[AIIMS]**

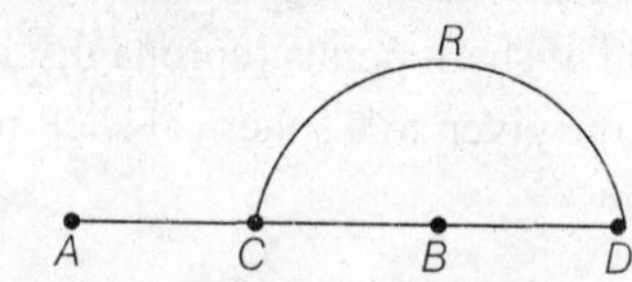

(a) $\dfrac{qQ}{4\pi\varepsilon_0 L}$ (b) $\dfrac{qQ}{2\pi\varepsilon_0 L}$ (c) $\dfrac{qQ}{6\pi\varepsilon_0 L}$ (d) $\dfrac{-qQ}{6\pi\varepsilon_0 L}$

2014

4 A conducting sphere of radius R is given a charge Q. The electric potential and the electric field at the centre of the sphere respectively are **[CBSE AIPMT]**

(a) zero and $\dfrac{Q}{4\pi\varepsilon_0 R^2}$ (b) $\dfrac{Q}{4\pi\varepsilon_0 R}$ and zero

(c) $\dfrac{Q}{4\pi\varepsilon_0 R}$ and $\dfrac{Q}{4\pi\varepsilon_0 R^2}$ (d) Both are zero

5 Two concentric spheres kept in air have radii R and r. They have similar charge and equal surface charge density σ. The electrical potential at their common centre is (ε_0 = permittivity of free space) **[MHT CET]**

(a) $\dfrac{\sigma(R+r)}{\varepsilon_0}$ (b) $\dfrac{\sigma(R-r)}{\varepsilon_0}$

(c) $\dfrac{\sigma(R+r)}{2\varepsilon_0}$ (d) $\dfrac{\sigma(R+r)}{4\varepsilon_0}$

6 Two charges of equal magnitude q are placed in air at a distance $2a$ apart and third charge $-2q$ is placed at mid-point. The potential energy of the system is (ε_0 = permittivity of free space) **[MHT CET]**

(a) $-\dfrac{q^2}{8\pi\varepsilon_0 a}$ (b) $-\dfrac{3q^2}{8\pi\varepsilon_0 a}$ (c) $-\dfrac{5q^2}{8\pi\varepsilon_0 a}$ (d) $-\dfrac{7q^2}{8\pi\varepsilon_0 a}$

7 Consider two concentric spherical metal shells of radii r_1 and r_2 ($r_2 > r_1$). If the outer shell has a charge q and the inner one is grounded, the charge on the inner shell is **[WB JEE]**

(a) $\dfrac{-r_2}{r_1}q$ (b) zero (c) $\dfrac{-r_1}{r_2}q$ (d) $-q$

8 What is the electric potential at a distance of 9 cm from 3 nC? **[KCET]**

(a) 270 V (b) 3 V

(c) 300 V (d) 30 V

9 Work done in carrying an electric charge Q_1 once round a circle of radius R with a charge Q_2 at the centre of the circle is **[EAMCET]**

(a) $\dfrac{Q_1Q_2}{4\pi\varepsilon_0 R}$ (b) ∞ (c) $\dfrac{Q_1Q_2}{4\pi\varepsilon_0 R^2}$ (d) 0

2013

10 A, B and C are three points in a uniform electric field. The electric potential is **[NEET]**

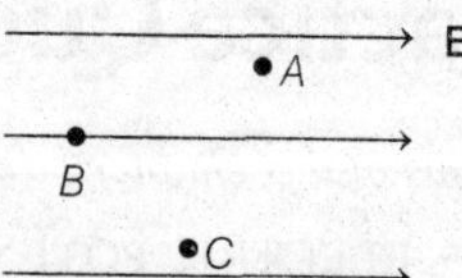

(a) maximum at A

(b) maximum at B

(c) maximum at C

(d) same at all the three points A, B and C

2012

11 Two metallic spheres of radii 1 cm and 3 cm are given charges of -1×10^{-2} C and 5×10^{-2} C, respectively. If these are connected by a conducting wire, the final charge on the bigger sphere is **[CBSE AIPMT]**

(a) 2×10^{-2} C (b) 3×10^{-2} C

(c) 4×10^{-2} C (d) 1×10^{-2} C

12 Four point charges $-Q, -q, 2q$ and $2Q$ are placed, one at each corner of the square. The relation between Q and q for which the potential at the centre of the square is zero, is **[CBSE AIPMT]**

(a) $Q = -q$ (b) $Q = -\frac{1}{q}$ (c) $Q = q$ (d) $Q = \frac{1}{q}$

13 Two equal point charges Q are fixed at $x = -a$ and $x = +a$ on X-axis. Another point charge is placed at the origin. The change in electrical potential energy of Q, when it is displaced by a small amount x along X-axis, is approximately proportional to **[Manipal]**

(a) x (b) x^2 (c) x^3 (d) $\frac{1}{x}$

14 A charge $+q$ is placed at the origin O of XY- axis as shown in the figure. The work done in taking a charge Q from A to B along the straight line AB is **[WB JEE]**

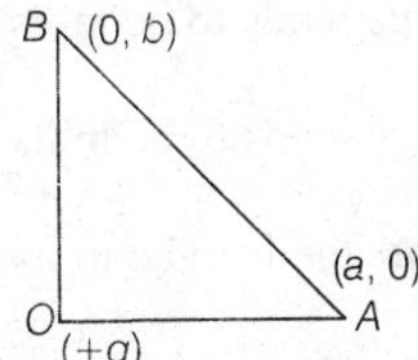

(a) $\frac{qQ}{4\pi\varepsilon_0}\left(\frac{a-b}{ab}\right)$ (b) $\frac{qQ}{4\pi\varepsilon_0}\left(\frac{b-a}{ab}\right)$

(c) $\frac{qQ}{4\pi\varepsilon_0}\left(\frac{b}{a^2}-\frac{1}{b}\right)$ (d) $\frac{qQ}{4\pi\varepsilon_0}\left(\frac{a}{b^2}-\frac{1}{b}\right)$

2011

15 A charge Q is placed at the origin. The electric potential due to this charge at a given point in space is V. The work done by an external force in bringing another charge q from infinity upto the point is **[J&K CET]**

(a) $\frac{V}{q}$ (b) Vq (c) $V + q$ (d) V

16 A hollow metal sphere of radius 10 cm is charged such that the potential on its surface becomes 80 V. The potential at the centre of the sphere is **[J&K CET]**

(a) 80 V (b) 800 V (c) 8 V (d) zero

17 Which of the following is not true? **[EAMCET]**

(a) For a point charge, the electrostatic potential varies as $1/r$

(b) For a dipole, the potential depends on the position vector and dipole moment vector

(c) The electric dipole potential varies as $1/r$ at large distance

(d) For a point charge, the electrostatic field varies as $1/r^2$

18 It is possible to have a positively charged body at **[AIIMS]**

(a) zero potential (b) negative potential

(c) positive potential (d) All of these

19 If an electron is brought towards another electron, then the electric potential energy of the system **[AIIMS]**

(a) increases (b) decreases

(c) become zero (d) remaining the same

2010

20 A ball of mass 1 g and charge 10^{-8} C moves from a point A, where potential is 600 V to the point B, where potential is zero. Velocity of the ball at the point B, is 20 cms^{-1}. The velocity of the ball at the point A will be **[AIIMS]**

(a) 22.8 cms^{-1} (b) 228 cms^{-1}

(c) 16.8 ms^{-1} (d) 168 ms^{-1}

21 The electrostatic potential of a uniformly charged thin spherical shell of charge Q and radius R at a distance r from the centre is **[Manipal]**

(a) $\frac{Q}{4\pi\varepsilon_0 r}$ for points outside and $\frac{Q}{4\pi\varepsilon_0 R}$ for points on surface of the sphere

(b) $\frac{Q}{4\pi\varepsilon_0 r}$ for both points inside and outside the shell

(c) zero for points outside and $\frac{Q}{4\pi\varepsilon_0 r}$ for points inside the shell

(d) zero for both points inside and outside the shell

22 The ionisation potential of mercury is 10.39 V. How far an electron must travel in an electric field of 1.5×10^6 V/m to gain sufficient energy to ionise mercury? **[Manipal]**

(a) $\frac{10.39}{1.6 \times 10^{-19}}$ m (b) $\frac{10.39}{2 \times 1.6 \times 10^{-19}}$ m

(c) $10.39 \times 1.6 \times 10^{-19}$ m (d) $\frac{10.39}{1.5 \times 10^6}$ m

23 Identify the false statement. **[Kerala CEE]**

(a) Inside a charged or neutral conductor, electrostatic field is zero.

(b) The electrostatic field at the surface of the charged conductor must be tangential to the surface at any point.

(c) There is no net charge at any point inside the conductor.

(d) Electrostatic potential is constant throughout the volume of the conductor.

(e) Electric field at the surface of a charged conductor is proportional to the surface charge density.

24 The electric potential on the hollow sphere of radius 1 m is 1000 V. The potential at 1/4 m from the centre of sphere is **[MP PMT]**

(a) 1000 V (b) 500 V

(c) 250 V (d) zero

25 There is a uniform electric field of intensity E which is as shown. How many labelled points have the same electric potential as the fully shaded point? **[KCET]**

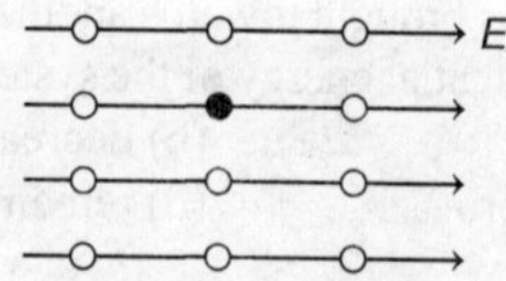

(a) 2 (b) 3
(c) 8 (d) 11

26 If a charged spherical conductor of radius 10 cm has potential V at a point distant 5 cm from its centre, then the potential at a point distant 15 cm from the centre will be **[JCECE]**

(a) $\frac{1}{3}V$ (b) $\frac{2}{3}V$ (c) $\frac{3}{2}V$ (d) $3V$

27 A hollow metal sphere of radius 10 cm is charged, such that the potential on its surface becomes 80 V. The potential at the centre of the sphere is **[Guj CET]**

(a) 80 V (b) 800 V
(c) 8 V (d) zero

28 Figure shows three spherical and equipotential surfaces A, B and C round a point charge q. The potential difference $V_A - V_B = V_B - V_C$. If t_1 and t_2 be the distances between them, then **[JIPMER]**

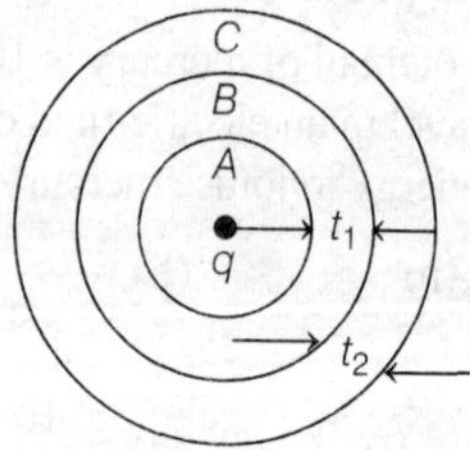

(a) $t_1 = t_1$ (b) $t_1 > t_2$
(c) $t_1 < t_2$ (d) $t_1 \leq t_2$

2009

29 The electric potential at a point (x, y, z) is given by

$$V = -x^2y - xz^3 + 4$$

The electric field **E** at that point is **[CBSE AIPMT]**

(a) $\mathbf{E} = (2xy + z^3)\hat{\mathbf{i}} + x^2\hat{\mathbf{j}} + 3xz^2\hat{\mathbf{k}}$
(b) $\mathbf{E} = 2xy\hat{\mathbf{i}} + (x^2 + y^2)\hat{\mathbf{j}} + (3xz - y^2)\hat{\mathbf{k}}$
(c) $\mathbf{E} = z^3\hat{\mathbf{i}} + xyz\hat{\mathbf{j}} + z^2\hat{\mathbf{k}}$
(d) $\mathbf{E} = (2xy - z^3)\hat{\mathbf{i}} + xy^2\hat{\mathbf{j}} + 3z^2x\hat{\mathbf{k}}$

30 Three concentric spherical shells have radii a, b and $c (a < b < c)$ and have surface charge densities $\sigma, -\sigma$ and σ, respectively. If V_A, V_B and V_C denote the potentials of the three shells for $c = a + b$, we have **[CBSE AIPMT]**

(a) $V_C = V_A \neq V_B$ (b) $V_C = V_B \neq V_A$
(c) $V_C \neq V_B \neq V_A$ (d) $V_C = V_B = V_A$

31 **Assertion** A and B are two conducting spheres of same radius. A being solid and B hollow. Both are charged to the same potential. Then, charge on A = charge on B.

Reason Potentials on both are same. **[AIIMS]**

(a) Both Assertion and Reason are correct and Reason is the correct explanation of Assertion.
(b) Both Assertion and Reason are correct but Reason is not the correct explanation of Assertion.
(c) Assertion is correct but Reason is incorrect.
(d) Both Assertion and Reason are incorrect.

32 n identical mercury droplets charged to the same potential V coalesce to form a single bigger drop. The potential of new drop will be **[AFMC (Manipal)]**

(a) V/n (b) nV
(c) nV^2 (d) $n^{2/3}V$

33 The charge given to any conductor resides on its outer surface, because **[RPMT]**

(a) the free charge tends to be in its minimum potential energy state
(b) the free charge tends to be in its minimum kinetic energy state
(c) the free charge tends to be in its maximum potential energy state
(d) the free charge tends to be in its maximum kinetic energy state

34 Two equal and opposite charge ($+q$ and $-q$) are situated at distance x from each other, the value of potential at very far point will depend upon **[AFMC]**

(a) only on q (b) only on x
(c) on qx (d) on q/x

35 Three point charges $q, -2q$ and $-2q$ are placed at the vertices of an equilateral triangle of side a. The work done by some external force to increase their separation to $2a$ will be **[UP CPMT]**

(a) $\frac{1}{4\pi\varepsilon_0}\frac{2q^2}{a}$ (b) $\frac{1}{4\pi\varepsilon_0}\frac{q^2}{2a}$
(c) $\frac{1}{4\pi\varepsilon_0}\frac{8q}{a^2}$ (d) zero

36 Three charges are placed at the vertex of an equilateral triangle as shown in figure. For what value of Q, the electrostatic potential energy of the system is zero? **[OJEE]**

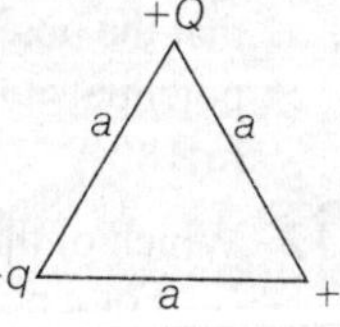

(a) $-q$ (b) $q/2$
(c) $-2q$ (d) $-q/2$

37 The charge q is projected into a uniform electric field E, work done when it moves a distance y is **[OJEE]**

(a) qEy (b) $\frac{qy}{E}$
(c) $\frac{qE}{y}$ (d) $\frac{y}{qE}$

38 Two charged spheres of radii R_1 and R_2 have equal surface charge density. The ratio of their potential is **[OJEE]**

(a) R_1/R_2 (b) R_2/R_1
(c) $(R_1/R_2)^2$ (d) $(R_2/R_1)^2$

39 The mutual electrostatic potential energy between two protons which are at a distance of 9×10^{-15} m, in $_{92}U^{235}$ nucleus is **[J&K CET]**

(a) 1.56×10^{-14} J (b) 5.5×10^{-14} J
(c) 2.56×10^{-14} J (d) 4.56×10^{-14} J

40 Three charges $-q, +Q$ and $+q$ are placed in a straight line as shown. If the total potential energy of the system is zero, then the ratio q/Q is **[J&K CET]**

$-q$ $+Q$ $+q$
$\leftarrow x \rightarrow\leftarrow x \rightarrow$

(a) 2 (b) 5.5 (c) 4 (d) 1.5

41 The electric potential at any point x, y, z in metres is given by $V = 3x^2$. The electric field at a point (2, 0, 1) is **[KCET]**

(a) 12 Vm^{-1} (b) -6 Vm^{-1}
(c) 6 Vm^{-1} (d) -12 Vm^{-1}

2008

42 The work done in bringing a unit positive charge from infinity distance to a point at distance X from a positive charge Q is W. When the potential ϕ at that point is **[J&K CET]**

(a) $\dfrac{WQ}{X}$ (b) W (c) $\dfrac{W}{Q}$ (d) WQ

43 The electric potential inside a conducting sphere **[J&K CET]**

(a) increases from centre to surface
(b) decreases from centre to surface
(c) remains constant from centre to surface
(d) is zero at every point inside

44 A charge Q is placed at each corner of a cube of side a. The potential at the centre of the cube is **[EAMCET]**

(a) $\dfrac{8Q}{\pi\varepsilon_0 a}$ (b) $\dfrac{4Q}{4\pi\varepsilon_0 a}$ (c) $\dfrac{4Q}{\sqrt{3}\pi\varepsilon_0 a}$ (d) $\dfrac{2Q}{\pi\varepsilon_0 a}$

45 A small conducting sphere of radius r is lying concentrically inside a bigger hollow conducting sphere of radius R. The bigger and smaller spheres are charged with Q and $q(Q > q)$ and are insulated from each other. The potential difference between the spheres will be **[KCET]**

(a) $\dfrac{1}{4\pi\varepsilon_0}\left(\dfrac{q}{r}-\dfrac{q}{R}\right)$ (b) $\dfrac{1}{4\pi\varepsilon_0}\left(\dfrac{q}{R}-\dfrac{Q}{r}\right)$

(c) $\dfrac{1}{4\pi\varepsilon_0}\left(\dfrac{q}{r}-\dfrac{Q}{R}\right)$ (d) $\dfrac{1}{4\pi\varepsilon_0}\left(\dfrac{Q}{R}+\dfrac{q}{r}\right)$

46 If 20 J of work has to be done to move an electric charge of 4 C from a point, where potential is 10V to another point, where potential is V volt, find the value of V. **[Guj CET]**

(a) 2 V (b) 70 V
(c) 5 V (d) 15 V

2007

47 In the figure, a proton moves a distance d in a uniform electric field **E** as shown in the figure. Does the electric field do a positive or negative work on the proton ? Does the electric potential energy of the proton increase or decrease? **[AIIMS]**

E
p
$\leftarrow d \rightarrow$

(a) Negative, increase
(b) Positive, decrease
(c) Negative, decrease
(d) Positive, increase

48 In bringing an electron towards another electron, the electrostatic potential energy of the system **[MHT CET]**

(a) decreases (b) increases
(c) remains same (d) becomes zero

49 If a positive charge is shifted from a low potential region to a high potential region, then electric potential energy **[RPMT]**

(a) decreases
(b) increases
(c) remains same
(d) may increase or decrease

50 Electric potential at the centre of a charged hollow metal sphere is **[J&K CET]**

(a) zero
(b) twice as that on the surface
(c) half of that on the surface
(d) same as that on the surface

51 The potential of a large liquid drop when eight liquid drops are combined is 20 V. Then, the potential of each single drop was **[KCET]**

(a) 10 V (b) 7.5 V
(c) 5 V (d) 2.5 V

52 An electric field is spread uniformly in Y-axis. Consider a point A as origin point. The coordinates of point B are equal to (0, 2) m. The coordinates of point C are (2, 0) m. At points A, B and C, electric potentials are V_A, V_B and V_C, respectively. From the following options, which is correct? **[Guj CET]**

(a) $V_A = V_C < V_B$
(b) $V_A = V_B = V_C$
(c) $V_A = V_B > V_C$
(d) $V_A = V_C > V_B$

2006

53 What is not true for equipotential surface for uniform electric field? **[AFMC]**

(a) Equipotential surface is flat
(b) Two equipotential surfaces can cross each other
(c) Electric lines are perpendicular to equipotential surface
(d) Work done is zero

54 Figure shows three points A, B and C in a region of uniform electric field $\mathbf{E}$. The line AB is perpendicular and BC is parallel to the field lines. Then, which of the following holds good? **[BHU]**

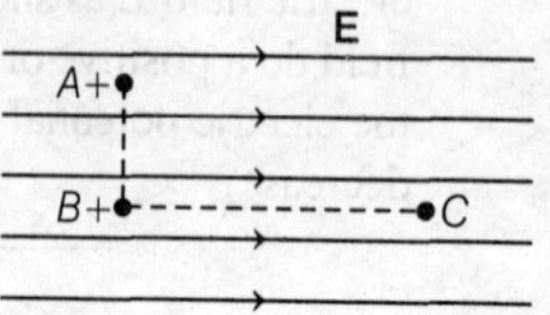

(a) $V_A = V_B = V_C$ (b) $V_A = V_B > V_C$
(c) $V_A = V_B < V_C$ (d) $V_A > V_B = V_C$

where, V_A, V_B and V_C represent the electric potentials at the points A, B and C, respectively.

55 Two electric charges $12 \mu C$ and $-6 \mu C$ are placed 20 cm apart in air. There will be a point P on the line joining these charges and outside the region between them, at which the electric potential is zero. The distance of P from $-6 \mu C$ charge is **[Kerala CEE]**

(a) 0.10 m (b) 0.15 m
(c) 0.20 m (d) 0.25 m
(e) None of these

56 The electrical potential on the surface of a sphere of radius r due to a charge 3×10^{-6} C is 500 V. The intensity of electric field on the surface of the sphere is [Take, $1/4\pi\varepsilon_0 = 9 \times 10^9$ N-m^{2}C^{-2}] (in NC^{-1}) **[EAMCET]**

(a) < 10 (b) > 200
(c) between 10 and 20 (d) < 5

57 The electric potential at the surface of an atomic nucleus $(Z = 50)$ of radius 9×10^{-15} m is **[Guj CET]**

(a) 80 V (b) 8×10^6 V
(c) 9 V (d) 9×10^5 V

2005

58 As per the diagram, a point charge $+q$ is placed at the origin O. Work done in taking another point charge $-Q$ from the point A [coordinates $(0, a)$] to another point B [coordinates $(a, 0)$] along the straight path AB is **[CBSE AIPMT]**

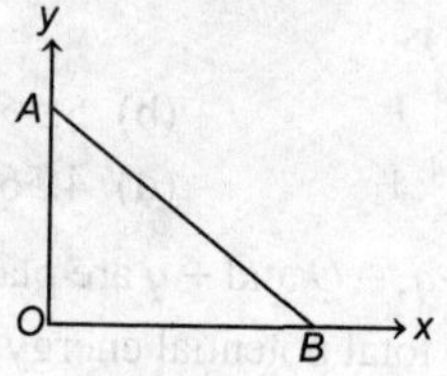

(a) zero (b) $\left(\frac{-qQ}{4\pi\varepsilon_0} \frac{1}{a^2}\right)\sqrt{2}a$
(c) $\left(\frac{qQ}{4\pi\varepsilon_0} \frac{1}{a^2}\right) \cdot \frac{a}{\sqrt{2}}$ (d) $\left(\frac{qQ}{4\pi\varepsilon_0} \frac{1}{a^2}\right)\sqrt{2}a$

59 Two charges q_1 and q_2 are placed 30 cm apart, as shown in the figure. A third charge q_3 is moved along the arc of a circle of radius 40 cm from C to D. The change in the potential energy of the system is $\frac{q_3}{4\pi\varepsilon_0} k$, where k is **[CBSE AIPMT]**

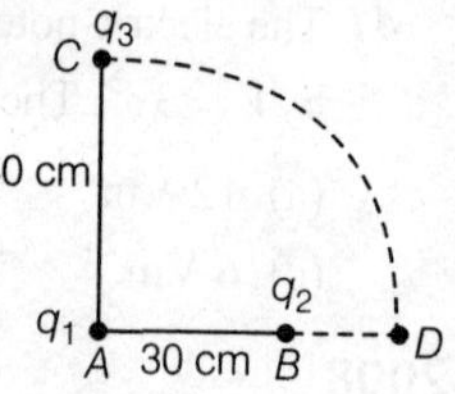

(a) $8q_2$ (b) $8q_1$ (c) $6q_2$ (d) $6q_1$

60 Which of the following is not the property of equipotential surfaces? **[AFMC]**

(a) They do not cross each other
(b) They are concentric spheres for uniform electric field
(c) Rate of change of potential with distance on them is zero
(d) They can be imaginary spheres

61 A solid metal sphere of radius 50 cm carries a charge 25×10^{-10} C. The electrostatic potential at the surface of the sphere will be **[DUMET]**

(a) 25 V (b) 15 V (c) 35 V (d) 45 V

Answers

1 (c)	2 (d)	3 (d)	4 (b)	5 (a)	6 (d)	7 (c)	8 (c)	9 (d)	10 (b)
11 (b)	12 (a)	13 (b)	14 (a)	15 (b)	16 (a)	17 (c)	18 (d)	19 (a)	20 (a)
21 (a)	22 (d)	23 (b)	24 (a)	25 (b)	26 (b)	27 (a)	28 (c)	29 (a)	30 (b)
31 (a)	32 (d)	33 (a)	34 (c)	35 (d)	36 (d)	37 (a)	38 (a)	39 (c)	40 (c)
41 (d)	42 (c)	43 (c)	44 (c)	45 (a)	46 (d)	47 (a)	48 (b)	49 (b)	50 (d)
51 (c)	52 (d)	53 (b)	54 (b)	55 (c)	56 (a)	57 (b)	58 (a)	59 (a)	60 (b)
61 (d)									

Explanations

1 (c) Given, potential difference,

$V(x) = -x^2 y$ volt

$$\therefore \quad \mathbf{E} = -\Delta V$$

$$= -\left[\hat{\mathbf{i}}\frac{\partial}{\partial x}(-x^2y) + \hat{\mathbf{j}}\frac{\partial}{\partial y}(-x^2y)\right]$$

$$= -[-2xy\,\hat{\mathbf{i}} - x^2\hat{\mathbf{j}}] = 2xy\,\hat{\mathbf{i}} + x^2\hat{\mathbf{j}}$$

$$\mathbf{E} \text{ at } (1, 2) = 2\times 1\times 2\,\hat{\mathbf{i}} + 1^2\hat{\mathbf{j}}$$

$$= 4\hat{\mathbf{i}} + \hat{\mathbf{j}}\ \text{Vm}^{-1}$$

2 (d) At closest distance r, the whole kinetic energy of charge q is converted into potential energy.

$$\therefore \quad \frac{1}{2}mv^2 = \frac{1}{4\pi\varepsilon_0}\frac{Q\cdot q}{r}$$

$$\Rightarrow \quad r = \frac{1}{4\pi\varepsilon_0}\cdot\frac{2Q\cdot q}{mv^2}$$

In next case, $r' = \dfrac{1}{4\pi\varepsilon_0}\dfrac{2Qq}{m(2v)^2}$

$$\Rightarrow \quad r' = \frac{1}{4}\left(\frac{1}{4\pi\varepsilon_0}\cdot\frac{2Qq}{mv^2}\right)$$

$$\Rightarrow \quad r' = \frac{r}{4}$$

3 (d) In first case, when charge $+Q$ is situated at C.

+q +Q −q
A C B
|← L →|← L →|

Electric potential energy of system,

$$U_1 = \frac{1}{4\pi\varepsilon_0}\cdot\frac{q(-q)}{2L} + \frac{1}{4\pi\varepsilon_0}\cdot\frac{(-q)Q}{L} + \frac{1}{4\pi\varepsilon_0}\frac{qQ}{L}$$

In second case, when charge $+Q$ is moved from C to D

+q −q +Q
A B D
|← 2L →|← L →|

Electric potential energy of system in this case,

$$U_2 = \frac{1}{4\pi\varepsilon_0}\cdot\frac{q(-q)}{2L} + \frac{1}{4\pi\varepsilon_0}\cdot\frac{qQ}{3L} + \frac{1}{4\pi\varepsilon_0}\cdot\frac{(-q)(Q)}{L}$$

Work done $(\Delta U) = U_2 - U_1$

$$= \left(-\frac{1}{4\pi\varepsilon_0}\cdot\frac{q^2}{2L} + \frac{1}{4\pi\varepsilon_0}\cdot\frac{qQ}{3L} - \frac{1}{4\pi\varepsilon_0}\cdot\frac{qQ}{L}\right) - \left(-\frac{1}{4\pi\varepsilon_0}\cdot\frac{q^2}{2L} - \frac{1}{4\pi\varepsilon_0}\cdot\frac{qQ}{L} + \frac{1}{4\pi\varepsilon_0}\cdot\frac{qQ}{L}\right)$$

$$= \frac{qQ}{4\pi\varepsilon_0}\left[\frac{1}{3L} - \frac{1}{L}\right] = \frac{qQ}{4\pi\varepsilon_0}\frac{(1-3)}{3L}$$

$$= -\frac{2qQ}{12\pi\varepsilon_0 L} = -\frac{qQ}{6\pi\varepsilon_0 L}$$

4 (b) $\mathbf{E}_{\text{inside}} = 0$ and

$$V_{\text{inside}} = V_{\text{surface}} = \frac{1}{4\pi\varepsilon_0}\cdot\frac{Q}{R}$$

$E_{\text{inside}} = 0$, R, Q

5 (a) Potential due to a uniformly charged sphere is

$$V = \frac{1}{4\pi\varepsilon_0}\frac{Q}{R} \quad \text{...(i)}$$

Also, $\sigma = \dfrac{Q}{4\pi R^2} = \dfrac{Q\,\varepsilon_0}{4\pi\varepsilon_0 R^2}$

$$\frac{\sigma R^2}{\varepsilon_0} = \frac{1\times Q}{4\pi\varepsilon_0}$$

$$\Rightarrow \quad \frac{\sigma R}{\varepsilon_0} = \frac{Q}{4\pi\varepsilon_0}\times\frac{1}{R} \quad \text{...(ii)}$$

From Eqs. (i) and (ii), we get $V = \dfrac{\sigma R}{\varepsilon_0}$

Potential due to sphere (1), $V_1 = \dfrac{\sigma R}{\varepsilon_0}$

Potential due to sphere (2), $V_2 = \dfrac{\sigma r}{\varepsilon_0}$

Net potential at centre, $V = V_1 + V_2$

$$= \frac{\sigma}{\varepsilon_0}(R + r)$$

6 (d) Potential energy of the system,

$$U = \frac{1}{4\pi\varepsilon_0}\left[\frac{q_1q_2}{r_{12}} + \frac{q_1q_3}{r_{13}} + \frac{q_2q_3}{r_{23}}\right]$$

$$= \frac{1}{4\pi\varepsilon_0}\left[\frac{q(-2q)}{a} + \frac{q(-2q)}{a} + \frac{qq}{2a}\right]$$

$$= \frac{1}{4\pi\varepsilon_0}\left[\frac{-2q^2}{a} - \frac{2q^2}{a} + \frac{q^2}{2a}\right]$$

$$= \frac{1}{4\pi\varepsilon_0}\left[\frac{-4q^2}{a} + \frac{q^2}{2a}\right] = \frac{-7q^2}{8\pi\varepsilon_0 a}$$

7 (c) Let the charge on the inner shell be q'.

The total charge will be zero.

So, $\dfrac{Kq'}{r_1} + \dfrac{Kq}{r_2} = 0 \qquad (\because r_2 > r_1)$

$$\Rightarrow \quad q' = \frac{-Kq/r_2}{K/r_1} \Rightarrow q' = -\frac{r_1}{r_2}q$$

8 (c) Given, $q = 3\text{ nC} = 3\times 10^{-9}$ C,

$r = 9\text{ cm} = 9\times 10^{-2}$ m

We know that, potential due to point charge is given by

$$V = \frac{1}{4\pi\varepsilon_0}\frac{q}{r} = \frac{9\times 10^9\times 3\times 10^{-9}}{9\times 10^{-2}}$$

$$= 3\times 10^2$$

$$\Rightarrow \quad V = 300\text{ V}$$

9 (d) Electrostatic force is a conservative force, so work done in carrying an electric charge Q_1 once round a circle of radius R with a charge Q_2 at the centre of the circle is zero.

10 (b) The electric field is maximum at B, because electric field is directed along decreasing potential $V_B > V_C > V_A$.

Therefore, electric potential is maximum at point B.

11 (b) Charge flows from high potential to low potential,

Electric potential on smaller sphere = Electric potential on bigger sphere

$$\frac{KQ_1}{3} = \frac{KQ_2}{1}$$

$$\Rightarrow \quad Q_1 = 3Q_2 \quad \text{...(i)}$$

$$Q_1 + Q_2 = 4\times 10^{-2}$$

$$\Rightarrow \quad 4Q_2 = 4\times 10^{-2}$$

$$\Rightarrow \quad Q_2 = 10^{-2}\text{ C} \quad \text{...(ii)}$$

From Eqs. (i) and (ii), we get

The final charge on the bigger sphere,

$$Q_1 = 3\times 10^{-2}\text{ C}$$

12 (a) If potential at centre is zero, then

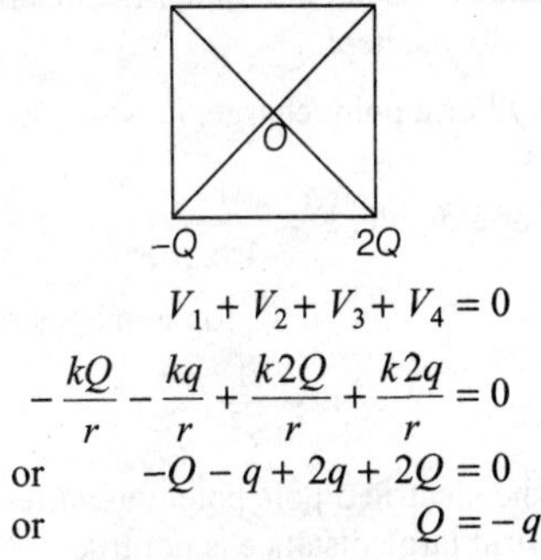

$$V_1 + V_2 + V_3 + V_4 = 0$$

$$-\frac{kQ}{r} - \frac{kq}{r} + \frac{k2Q}{r} + \frac{k2q}{r} = 0$$

or $\quad -Q - q + 2q + 2Q = 0$

or $\quad Q = -q$

13 (b) **Case I** Electric potential energy,

$$U_1 = \frac{1}{4\pi\varepsilon_0}\frac{2Qq}{a}$$

R Q +q
$x = -a$ $x = 0$ $x = +a$

***Case* II** Electric potential energy,

$$U_2 = \frac{1}{4\pi\varepsilon_0} Qq\left(\frac{1}{a+x} + \frac{1}{a-x}\right)$$

Change in potential energy

$$= U_2 - U_1$$

$$= \frac{1}{4\pi\varepsilon_0} Qq\left[\frac{1}{a+x} + \frac{1}{a-x} - \frac{2}{a}\right]$$

$$= \frac{1}{4\pi\varepsilon_0} Qq\left[\frac{a(a-x+a+x) - 2(a^2-x^2)}{(a^2-x^2)a}\right]$$

For $x << a$, $\Delta U = \frac{1}{4\pi\varepsilon_0} Qq \frac{2x^2}{a^3}$

$\Rightarrow \quad \Delta U = x^2$

14 *(a)* We know that,
Work done $= q\Delta V$
and potential,

$$V = \frac{Q}{4\pi\varepsilon_0 r}$$

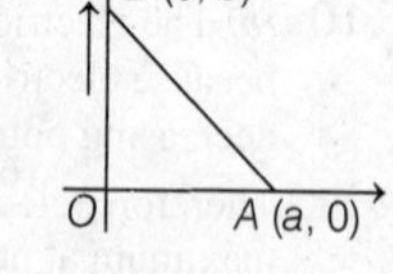

Work done in taking a charge Q from A to B,

$$W = q\left[\frac{Q}{4\pi\varepsilon_0 b} - \frac{Q}{4\pi\varepsilon_0 a}\right] = \frac{Qq}{4\pi\varepsilon_0}\left[\frac{a-b}{ab}\right]$$

15 *(b)* Potential at a point in a field is defined as the amount of work done in bringing a unit positive test charge (q) from infinity to that point along any arbitrary path,

i.e. $\quad V = \frac{W}{q}$

$\therefore$ Work done, $W = qV$

16 *(a)* The potential at the centre of the sphere is 80 V, because it remains same at each point under the metallic hollow sphere.

17 *(c)* For a point charge, $V \propto \frac{1}{r}$

For a dipole, $V = \frac{1}{4\pi\varepsilon_0} \cdot \frac{p}{r^2}$ [on axial position]

i.e. $\quad V \propto \frac{1}{r^2}$

The electric dipole potential varies as $1/r$ at large distance is not true.

18 *(d)* A positively charged body can have positive, negative or zero potential.

When we ground the charged body, potential difference between body and ground is zero but not the charge and same for negatively charged body.

19 *(a)* The work done against the force of repulsion in moving the two charges closer, increases the potential energy of the system.

20 *(a)* By using, $\frac{1}{2}m(v_1^2 - v_2^2) = QV$

$$\frac{1}{2} \times 10^{-3}[v_1^2 - (0.2)^2] = 10^{-8}(600 - 0)$$

$\Rightarrow \quad v_1 = 22.8\ \text{cms}^{-1}$

21 *(a)* If charge on a conducting sphere of radius R is Q, then potential outside the sphere, $V_{out} = \frac{1}{4\pi\varepsilon_0} \frac{Q}{r}$

At the surface of sphere, $V_s = \frac{1}{4\pi\varepsilon_0} \frac{Q}{R}$

22 *(d)* Ionisation potential (V) of mercury is the energy required to strip it of an electron. The electric field strength is given by, $E = \frac{V}{d}$

where, d is distance between plates creating electric field.

Given, $V = 10.39$ V

$E = 1.5 \times 10^6\ \text{Vm}^{-1}$

$\therefore \quad d = \frac{V}{E} = \frac{10.39}{1.5 \times 10^6}$ m

Hence, distance travelled by electron to gain ionisation energy is

$$= \frac{10.39}{1.5 \times 10^6}\ \text{m}$$

23 *(b)* Electrostatic field at the surface of a conductor is perpendicular to the surface.

24 *(a)* Inside the conducting charged sphere, electric field is zero and potential remains constant at all points and equals to potential at the surface. Hence, the potential at 1/4 m from the centre is 1000 V.

25 *(b)* For a uniform electric field, the equipotential surfaces are placed at right angles to the lines of forces. Therefore, only three points have the same electric field potential.

26 *(b)* Potential inside the sphere will be same as that on its surface, i.e.

$$V = V_{surface} = \frac{q}{10}\ \text{volt}$$

$$V_{out} = \frac{q}{15}\ \text{volt}$$

$\therefore \quad \frac{V_{out}}{V} = \frac{2}{3} \Rightarrow V_{out} = \frac{2}{3}V$

27 *(a)* The potential at the centre of the sphere is 80 V, because it remains same at each point under the metallic hollow sphere.

28 *(c)* Potential difference between two equipotential surfaces A and B,

$$V_A - V_B = kq\left(\frac{1}{r_A} - \frac{1}{r_B}\right) = kq\left(\frac{r_B - r_A}{r_A r_B}\right) = \frac{kqt_1}{r_A r_B}$$

or $\quad t_1 = \frac{(V_A - V_B)r_A r_B}{kq}$

$\Rightarrow \quad t_1 \propto r_A r_B$

Similarly, $\quad t_2 \propto r_B r_C$

Since, $r_A < r_B < r_C$, therefore $r_A r_B < r_B r_C$

$\therefore \quad t_1 < t_2$

29 *(a)* Potential gradient relates with electric field according to the following relation, $E = \frac{-dV}{dr}$

Given, $V = -x^2y - xz^3 + 4$

$$\mathbf{E} = -\frac{\partial V}{\partial r} = \left[-\frac{\partial V}{\partial x}\hat{\mathbf{i}} - \frac{\partial V}{\partial y}\hat{\mathbf{j}} - \frac{\partial V}{\partial x}\hat{\mathbf{k}}\right]$$

$$= [(2xy + z^3)\hat{\mathbf{i}} + x^2\hat{\mathbf{j}} + 3xz^2\hat{\mathbf{k}}]$$

30 *(b)* Given, $c = a + b$

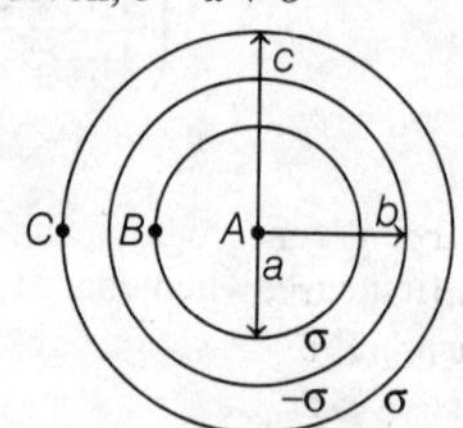

As, potential is given by

$$V = \frac{1}{4\pi\varepsilon_0} \frac{q}{R} = \frac{\sigma}{\varepsilon_0} R$$

Potential at A,

$$V_A = \frac{\sigma}{\varepsilon_0}a - \frac{\sigma}{\varepsilon_0}b + \frac{\sigma}{\varepsilon_0}c = \frac{\sigma}{\varepsilon_0}(a - b + c)$$

$$= \frac{\sigma}{\varepsilon_0}(a - b + a + b) = \frac{2\sigma}{\varepsilon_0}a$$

Potential at B,

$$V_B = \frac{\sigma}{\varepsilon_0}b - \frac{\sigma}{\varepsilon_0}b + \frac{\sigma}{\varepsilon_0}c = \frac{\sigma}{\varepsilon_0}c$$

Potential at C,

$$V_C = \frac{\sigma}{\varepsilon_0}c - \frac{\sigma}{\varepsilon_0}c + \frac{\sigma}{\varepsilon_0}c = \frac{\sigma}{\varepsilon_0}c$$

Hence, $V_B = V_C \neq V_A$ or $V_C = V_B \neq V_A$

31 *(a)* As charge is being distributed on the outer surface of conducting sphere and for hollow sphere also, charge is distributed on outer surface. If both spheres have same potential, then charge will be same, independent of the fact that sphere is hollow or solid,

$$\frac{V_1}{V_2} = \left(\frac{R_2}{R_1}\right)\left(\frac{Q_1}{Q_2}\right)$$

As, $V_1 = V_2$

$R_1 = R_2 \Rightarrow Q_1 = Q_2$

Therefore, both Assertion and reason are correct and Reason is the correct explanation of Assertion.

32 *(d)* As, volume of n identical droplets = volume of bigger droplet

$$\frac{4}{3}\pi r^3 (n) = \frac{4}{3}\pi R^3$$

$$\frac{R^3}{r^3} = n \Rightarrow \frac{R}{r} = n^{1/3}$$

$$\Rightarrow \quad R = rn^{1/3}$$

Let Q be the final charge on the bigger droplet.

By conservation of charge, $nq = Q$

Potential of smaller droplets is

$$V = \frac{1}{4\pi\varepsilon_0}\frac{q}{r}$$

Potential of bigger droplet is

$$V' = \frac{1}{4\pi\varepsilon_0}\frac{Q}{R} = \frac{1}{4\pi\varepsilon_0}\frac{nq}{r(n)^{1/3}}$$

$$V' = n^{1-1/3}\, V = Vn^{2/3}$$

33 *(a)* Charge given to a conductor is uniformly distributed at its outer surface to acquire its minimum potential energy state.

34 *(c)* Electric potential at point P is given as

$$V = \frac{1}{4\pi\varepsilon_0}\frac{qx\cos\theta}{r^2 - \frac{x^2}{4}\cos^2\theta}$$

As, $r >>> x$

Hence, $V \propto qx$

35 *(d)* According to the question, work done in increasing the separation from a to $2a$ is

$$W = U_f - U_i$$

Here, $U_i = \frac{1}{4\pi\varepsilon_0}\left[\frac{q(-2q)}{a} + \frac{q(-2q)}{a} + \frac{(-2q)(-2q)}{a}\right]$

$$= \frac{1}{4\pi\varepsilon_0 a}[-2q^2 - 2q^2 + 4q^2] = 0$$

Similarly, U_f is also zero.

$\Rightarrow \quad U_t - U_i = 0$

Hence, $\quad W = 0$

36 *(d)* Electrostatic potential energy of the given system is given as

$$U = \frac{1}{4\pi\varepsilon_0} \times \frac{1}{a}(Qq + Qq + q^2)$$

Given, $U = 0$

$$\Rightarrow \quad 2Qq = -q^2 \Rightarrow Q = -\frac{q}{2}$$

37 *(a)* Work done is given as

$$dW = \mathbf{F}\cdot d\mathbf{x} = F\,dx\cos\theta$$

For maximum work, $\theta = 0°$

$$dW = F\,dx$$

Force on charge (q) due to uniform electric field is

$$F = qE$$

$$\int_0^W dW = \int_0^y qE dx \Rightarrow W = qEy$$

38 *(a)* Surface charge density is given as

$$\sigma = \frac{Q}{A} = \frac{Q}{4\pi R^2}$$

As, $\sigma_A = \sigma_B$

$$\Rightarrow \frac{Q_1}{4\pi R_1^2} = \frac{Q_2}{4\pi R_2^2}$$

$$\Rightarrow \frac{Q_1}{4\pi\varepsilon_0 R_1^2} = \frac{Q_1}{4\pi\varepsilon_0 R_2^2} \Rightarrow \frac{V_1}{V_2} = \frac{R_1}{R_2}$$

39 *(c)* Electrostatic potential energy,

$$U = \frac{1}{4\pi\varepsilon_0}\cdot\frac{q_1 q_2}{r}$$

Here, $q_1 = q_2 = 1.6 \times 10^{-19}$ C,

$r = 9 \times 10^{-15}$ m

$$\therefore U = \frac{9\times 10^9 \times 1.6\times 10^{-19} \times 1.6 \times 10^{-19}}{9 \times 10^{-15}}$$

$$= 2.56 \times 10^{-14}\text{J}$$

40 *(c)* Potential energy of the system,

$$\frac{-kqQ}{x} - \frac{kQq}{x} - \frac{kq^2}{2x} = 0$$

$$\Rightarrow \frac{-4kqQ + kq^2}{2x} = 0$$

$$\Rightarrow kq^2 = 4\,kQq \Rightarrow q/Q = 4$$

41 *(d)* Electric potential is given in question,

$$V = 3x^2$$

As, $\quad E = -(\partial V/\partial x)$

$$\Rightarrow \quad E = -\left[\frac{\partial}{\partial x}(3x^2)\right] = -6x$$

$$E_{(2,0,1)} = -6(2) = -12\text{ Vm}^{-1}$$

42 *(c)* Potential at a point in a field is defined as the amount of work done in bringing a unit positive test charge, from infinity to that point along any arbitrary path, i.e.

$$V = \frac{W}{q_0} \Rightarrow V = \phi = \frac{W}{Q}$$

$(\because X << \infty)$

43 *(c)* Electric potential inside a conductor is constant and it is equal to that on the surface of the conductor.

44 *(c)* Let V_1 be the potential at the centre of the cube due to one charge.

$$V_1 = \frac{1}{4\pi\varepsilon_0}\frac{Q}{x} \text{ and } x = \frac{a\sqrt{3}}{2}$$

Potential due to all eight corners of the cube

$$\Rightarrow \quad V = 8V_1 = 8\left[\frac{1}{4\pi\varepsilon_0}\frac{Q}{(\sqrt{3}/2)\times a}\right]$$

$$= \frac{16Q}{4\pi\varepsilon_0\sqrt{3}\times a} = \frac{4Q}{a\sqrt{3}\pi\varepsilon_0}$$

45 *(a)* The potential V_1 of smaller sphere is given by

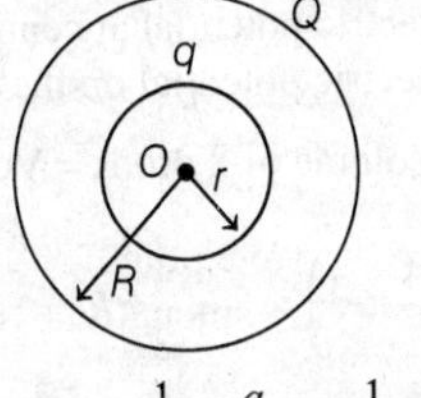

$$V_1 = \frac{1}{4\pi\varepsilon_0}\cdot\frac{q}{r} + \frac{1}{4\pi\varepsilon_0}\cdot\frac{Q}{R} \quad \text{...(i)}$$

The potential V_2 of bigger sphere is given by

$$V_2 = \frac{1}{4\pi\varepsilon_0}\cdot\frac{Q}{R} + \frac{1}{4\pi\varepsilon_0}\cdot\frac{q}{R} \quad \text{...(ii)}$$

So, the potential difference between the plates,

$$V = V_1 - V_2$$

or $\quad V = \frac{1}{4\pi\varepsilon_0}\cdot\frac{q}{r} + \frac{1}{4\pi\varepsilon_0}\cdot\frac{Q}{R} - \frac{1}{4\pi\varepsilon_0}\cdot\frac{Q}{R} - \frac{1}{4\pi\varepsilon_0}\cdot\frac{q}{R}$

$$= \frac{1}{4\pi\varepsilon_0}\cdot\frac{q}{r} - \frac{1}{4\pi\varepsilon_0}\cdot\frac{q}{R}$$

$$= \frac{1}{4\pi\varepsilon_0}\left(\frac{q}{r} - \frac{q}{R}\right)$$

46 *(d)* If we move a charge q from point A to B, then potential difference,

$$V_B - V_A = \frac{W_{AB}}{q} \quad \text{...(i)}$$

Here, $V_B = V, V_A = 10$ V,

$W_{AB} = 20$ J and $q = 4$ C

On putting these values in Eq. (i), we get

$$V - 10 = \frac{20}{4} = 5 \Rightarrow V = 15\ \text{V}$$

47 (a) Since, the proton is moving against the direction of electric field, so work is done by the proton against electric field. It implies that electric field does negative work on the proton.

Again, proton is moving in electric field from a low potential region to a high potential region, hence its potential energy increases.

48 (b) Electrostatic potential energy of system of two electrons,

$$U = \frac{1}{4\pi\varepsilon_0} \cdot \frac{(-e)(-e)}{r} = \frac{1}{4\pi\varepsilon_0} \cdot \frac{e^2}{r}$$

Thus, as r decreases, potential energy U increases.

49 (b) When positive charge is shifted from a low potential to a high potential region, the electric potential energy increases.

50 (d) Electric potential of charged spherical shell, $V = \frac{q}{4\pi\varepsilon_0 R}$ $(0 \le r \le R)$

∴ Electric potential at centre = Electric potential on the surface

51 (c) Volume of 8 drops = Volume of a big drop

$$\therefore \left(\frac{4}{3}\pi r^3\right) \times 8 = \frac{4}{3}\pi R^3$$

$$\Rightarrow 8r^3 = R^3$$

$$\Rightarrow 2r = R \quad \text{...(i)}$$

According to charge conservation,

$$8q = Q \quad \text{...(ii)}$$

Potential of one small drop, $V' = \frac{q}{4\pi\varepsilon_0 r}$

Similarly, potential of big drop,

$$V = \frac{Q}{4\pi\varepsilon_0 R}$$

Now, $\frac{V'}{V} = \frac{q}{Q} \times \frac{R}{r} \Rightarrow \frac{V'}{20} = \frac{q}{8q} \times \frac{2r}{r}$

[from Eqs. (i) and (ii)]

$$\therefore V' = 5\ \text{V}$$

52 (d) Potential decreases in the direction of electric field. Dotted lines are equipotential lines.

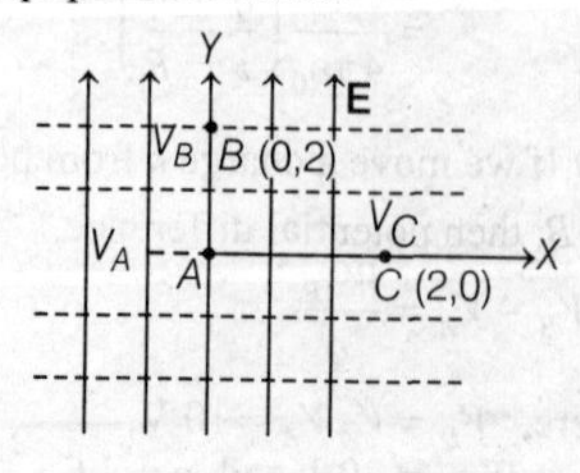

$$\therefore V_A = V_C \text{ and } V_C > V_B$$

53 (b) Equipotential surface for uniform electric field is perpendicular planes to the field as shown in figure.

Option (b) is not true as two equipotential surface cannot cross each other.

54 (b) Electric lines of force constitute electric field. In an electric field, electric lines of force always flow from higher potential to lower potential. Hence, A and B are at a same higher potential and C is at lower potential. Thus, $V_A = V_B > V_C$.

55 (c) Let potential at point P is zero is at x unit from q_2, i.e. $-6\,\mu$C.

$$\Rightarrow V_P = V_A + V_B = 0$$

$$\Rightarrow \frac{1}{4\pi\varepsilon_0} \cdot \frac{q_A}{(20 + x)} = -\frac{1}{4\pi\varepsilon_0} \frac{q_B}{x}$$

$$\frac{12 \times 10^{-6}}{20 + x} = \frac{-(-6 \times 10^{-6})}{x}$$

$$\Rightarrow 2x = 20 + x$$

$$= 20\ \text{cm} = 0.20\ \text{m}$$

56 (a) Electric potential on the surface of sphere, $V_s = \frac{1}{4\pi\varepsilon_0} \cdot \frac{q}{r}$

$$500 = \frac{9 \times 10^9 \times 3 \times 10^{-6}}{r}$$

$$\Rightarrow r = \frac{9 \times 10^9 \times 3 \times 10^{-6}}{500}$$

$$\Rightarrow r = 54\ \text{m}$$

∴ Electric field on the surface,

$$E_s = \frac{1}{4\pi\varepsilon_0} \cdot \frac{q}{R^2} = \frac{V_s}{R} = \frac{500}{54}$$

$$= 9.25 < 10\ \text{NC}^{-1}$$

57 (b) Electric potential at surface,

$$V = \frac{1}{4\pi\varepsilon_0} \frac{q}{R} \quad (\because q = Ze)$$

$$= 9 \times 10^9 \times \frac{50 \times 1.6 \times 10^{-19}}{9 \times 10^{-15}}$$

$$= 8 \times 10^6\ \text{V}$$

58 (a) Potential at A, $V_A = \frac{1}{4\pi\varepsilon_0} \frac{q}{a}$

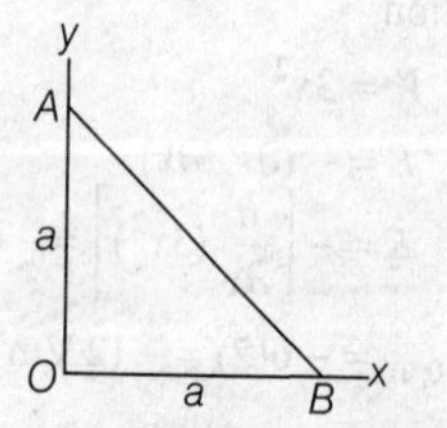

Potential at B, $V_B = \frac{1}{4\pi\varepsilon_0} \frac{q}{a}$

Thus, work done in carrying a test charge $-Q$ from A to B,

$$W = (V_A - V_B)(-Q) = 0$$

59 (a) When charge q_3 is at C, then its potential energy is

$$U_C = \frac{1}{4\pi\varepsilon_0}\left(\frac{q_1 q_3}{0.4} + \frac{q_2 q_3}{0.5}\right)$$

When charge q_3 is at D, then

$$U_D = \frac{1}{4\pi\varepsilon_0}\left(\frac{q_1 q_3}{0.4} + \frac{q_2 q_3}{0.1}\right)$$

Hence, change in potential energy,

$$\Delta U = U_D - U_C = \frac{1}{4\pi\varepsilon_0}\left(\frac{q_2 q_3}{0.1} - \frac{q_2 q_3}{0.5}\right)$$

But $\Delta U = \frac{q_3}{4\pi\varepsilon_0} k$

$$\therefore \frac{q_3}{4\pi\varepsilon_0} k = \frac{1}{4\pi\varepsilon_0}\left(\frac{q_2 q_3}{0.1} - \frac{q_2 q_3}{0.5}\right)$$

$$\Rightarrow k = q_2(10 - 2) = 8q_2$$

60 (b) Any surface over which the electric potential is same everywhere is called an equipotential surface. The electric field and hence lines of force everywhere are at right angles to the equipotential surface. This is so, because there is no potential gradient along any direction parallel to the surface and so no electric field is parallel to the surface.

This means the electric field and hence lines of force are always at right angles to the equipotential surface. Hence, they are not concentric spheres for uniform electric field. They are concentric spheres for an isolated point charge. Options (a), (c) and (d) are properties of equipotential surface.

61 (d) The potential at P is the ratio of the work done in bringing the test charge from infinity to the point P to the magnitude of test charge (q). Thus, the potential at P due to charge $+q$ is given by

$$V = \frac{W}{q_0} = \frac{1}{4\pi\varepsilon_0} \frac{q}{r}\ \text{volt}$$

Given, $r = 50$ cm $= 50 \times 10^{-2}$ m

$q = 25 \times 10^{-10}$ C

$$\therefore V = \frac{9 \times 10^9 \times 25 \times 10^{-10}}{50 \times 10^{-2}}$$

$$= 45\ \text{V}$$

Topic 2
Capacitance and Capacitors

2019

1 In a parallel plate capacitor, the capacity increases, if [MHT CET]
(a) area of the plate is decreased
(b) distance between the plates increases
(c) area of the plate is increased
(d) dielectric constant decrease

2 A capacitor of capacitance 15μF having dielectric slab of $\varepsilon_r = 2.5$, dielectric strength 30 MV/m and potential difference = 30 V. Calculate the area of the plate. [AIIMS]
(a) $6.7\times10^{-4}\ m^2$ (b) $4.2\times10^{-4}\ m^2$
(c) $8.0\times10^{-4}\ m^2$ (d) $9.85\times10^{-4}\ m^2$

3 A parallel plate capacitor is charged. If the plates are pulled apart [DCE]
(a) the capacitance increases
(b) the potential difference increases
(c) the total charge increases
(d) the charge and potential difference remains the same

4 Van de Graaff generator is used to [JIPMER]
(a) create a high potential of range of few million volts
(b) create a low potential of range of few million volts
(c) to de-accelerate projectile; like protons, deuterons, etc.
(d) it cannot be used to study collision experiments in physics

2018

5 The electrostatic force between the metal plates of an isolated parallel plate capacitor C having a charge Q and area A is [NEET]
(a) proportional to square root of the distance between the plates
(b) inversely proportional to the distance between the plates
(c) independent of the distance between the plates
(d) inversely proportional to the distance between the plates

6 If a capacitor having capacitance 2F and plate separation of 0.5 cm will have area [JIPMER]
(a) $1130 cm^2$ (b) $1130 km^2$
(c) $1130 m^2$ (d) None of these

2017

7 A parallel plate capacitor of capacitance 100 pF is to be constructed by using paper sheets of 1 mm thickness as dielectric. If the dielectric constant of paper is 4, the number of circular metal foils of diameter 2 cm each required for the purpose is [VITEEE]
(a) 40 (b) 20 (c) 30 (d) 10

2016

8 A dielectric of dielectric constant K is introduced such that half of its area of a capacitor of capacitance C is occupied by it. The new capacity is [J&K CET]
(a) $2C$ (b) $\frac{C}{2}$
(c) $\frac{(1+K)C}{2}$ (d) $2C(1+K)$

2015

9 A parallel plate air capacitor of capacitance C is connected to a cell of emf V and then disconnected from it. A dielectric slab of dielectric constant K, which can just fill the air gap of the capacitor is now inserted in it. Which of the following is incorrect? [AIPMT]
(a) The potential difference between the plates decreases K times
(b) The energy stored in the capacitor decreases K times
(c) The change in energy stored is $\frac{1}{2}CV^2(1/K-1)$
(d) The charge on the capacity is not conserved

2014

10 Two thin dielectric slabs of dielectric constants K_1 and K_2 $(K_1 < K_2)$ are inserted between the plates of a parallel plate capacitor, as shown in the figure below. The variation of electric field E between the plates with distance d as measured from plate P is correctly shown by [CBSE AIPMT]

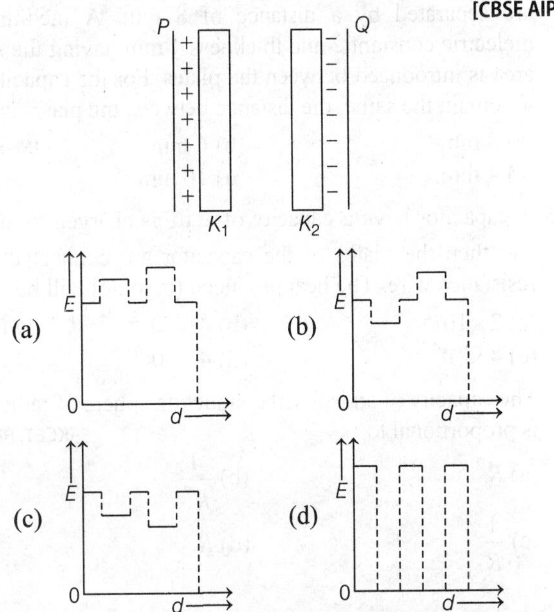

11 The capacitance of two concentric spherical shells of radii R_1 and $R_2 (R_2 > R_1)$ is [EAMCET]

(a) $4\pi\varepsilon_0 R_2$ (b) $4\pi\varepsilon_0 \frac{(R_2 - R_1)}{R_1 R_2}$

(c) $4\pi\varepsilon_0 \frac{R_1 R_2}{(R_2 - R_1)}$ (d) $4\pi\varepsilon_0 R_1$

12 Two capacitors of 10 pF and 20 pF are connected to 200 V and 100 V sources, respectively. If they are connected by the wire, then what is the common potential of the capacitors? [KCET]

(a) 133.3 V (b) 150 V (c) 300 V (d) 400 V

2013

13 A parallel plate capacitor is located horizontally such that one of the plates is submerged in a liquid while the other is above the liquid surface. When plates are charged, the level of liquid [AIIMS]

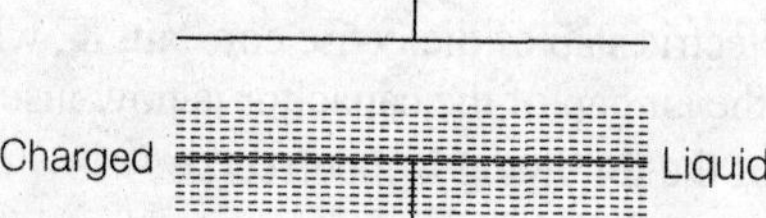

(a) rises
(b) falls
(c) remains unchanged
(d) may rise of fall depending on the amount of charge

14 A capacitor of capacitance C has charge Q and stored energy is W. If the charge is increased to $2Q$, the stored energy will be [UP CPMT]

(a) $\frac{W}{4}$ (b) $\frac{W}{2}$

(c) $2W$ (d) $4W$

15 The plates of a parallel plate capacitor with air as medium are separated by a distance of 8 mm. A medium of dielectric constant 2 and thickness 4 mm having the same area is introduced between the plates. For the capacitance to remain the same, the distance between the plates is [Manipal]

(a) 8 mm (b) 6 mm
(c) 4 mm (d) 10 mm

16 A capacitor having capacity of 2 μF is charged to 200 V and then the plates of the capacitor are connected to a resistance wire. The heat produced (in joule) will be [WB JEE]

(a) 2×10^{-2} (b) 4×10^{-2}
(c) 4×10^{4} (d) 4×10^{10}

17 The capacity of an isolated conducting sphere of radius R is proportional to [KCET, RPMT]

(a) R^2 (b) $\frac{1}{R^2}$

(c) $\frac{1}{R}$ (d) R

2012

18 A parallel plate capacitor has a uniform electric field E in the space between the plates. If the distance between the plates is d and area of each plate is A, the energy stored in the capacitor is [CBSE AIPMT]

(a) $\frac{1}{2}\varepsilon_0 E^2$ (b) $\frac{E^2 Ad}{\varepsilon_0}$

(c) $\frac{1}{2}\varepsilon_0 E^2 Ad$ (d) $\varepsilon_0 EAd$

19 A spherical drop of capacitance 1μF is broken into eight drops of equal radius. Then, the capacitance of each small drop is [AIIMS]

(a) $\frac{1}{2}$μF (b) $\frac{1}{4}$μF (c) $\frac{1}{8}$μF (d) 8 μF

20 Two identical capacitors each of capacitance 5 μF are charged to potentials 2 kV and 1 kV, respectively. Their negative ends are connected together. When the positive ends are also connected together, the loss of energy of the system is [AFMC, KCET]

(a) 160 J (b) zero
(c) 5 J (d) 1.25 J

21 An uncharged capacitor with a solid dielectric is connected to a similar air capacitor charged to a potential of V_0. If the common potential after sharing of charges becomes V, then the dielectric constant of the solid dielectric must be [UP CPMT, VMMC]

(a) $\frac{V_0}{V}$ (b) $\frac{V}{V_0}$

(c) $\frac{(V_0 + V)}{V}$ (d) $\frac{V_0 - V}{V}$

2011

22 Electric potential of earth is taken to be zero because earth is a good [AIIMS]

(a) insulator (b) conductor
(c) semiconductor (d) dielectric

23 When a capacitor is connected to a battery, [AIIMS]

(a) a current flows in the circuit for sometime, then decreases to zero
(b) no current flows in the circuit at all
(c) an alternating current flows in the circuit
(d) None of the above

24 A parallel plate capacitor is connected to a 5 V battery and charged. The battery is then disconnected and a glass slab is introduced between the plates. Then, the quantities that decreases are [KCET]

(a) charge and potential difference
(b) charge and capacitance
(c) capacitance and potential difference
(d) energy stored and potential difference

2010

25 A charged oil drop of mass 2.5×10^{-7} kg is in space between the two plates, each of area 2×10^{-2} m^2 of a parallel plate capacitor. When the upper plate has a charge of 5×10^{-7} C and the lower plate has an equal negative charge, the oil remains stationary. The charge of the oil drop is (Take, $g = 10\,\text{ms}^{-2}$) **[AIIMS]**

(a) 9×10^{-1} C (b) 9×10^{-6} C
(c) 8.85×10^{-13} C (d) 1.8×10^{-14} C

26 Work done in placing a charge of 8×10^{-18} C on a condenser of capacity $100\,\mu$F is **[AFMC]**

(a) 16×10^{-32} J (b) 31×10^{-26} J
(c) 4×10^{-10} J (d) 32×10^{-32} J

27 The capacitance of a parallel plate capacitor with air as medium is $3\,\mu$F. With the introduction of a dielectric medium between the plates, the capacitance becomes $15\,\mu$F. The permittivity of the medium is **[BHU]**

(a) $5\ \text{C}^2\ \text{N}^{-1}\ \text{m}^{-2}$
(b) $15\ \text{C}^2\ \text{N}^{-1}\ \text{m}^{-2}$
(c) $0.44\times10^{-10}\ \text{C}^2\ \text{N}^{-1}\ \text{m}^{-2}$
(d) $8.845\times10^{-11}\ \text{C}^2\ \text{N}^{-1}\ \text{m}^{-2}$

28 A $500\,\mu$F capacitor is charged at the steady rate of $100\,\mu\text{Cs}^{-1}$. How long will it take to raise the potential difference between the plates of the capacitor to 10 V? **[BHU]**

(a) 5 s (b) 10 s
(c) 50 s (d) 100 s

29 Two conducting spheres of radii R_1 and R_2 are charged with charges Q_1 and Q_2, respectively. On bringing them in contact, there is **[BHU]**

(a) no increase in the energy of the system
(b) an increase in the energy of the system, if $Q_1R_2 \neq Q_2R_1$
(c) always a decrease in the energy of the system
(d) a decrease in the energy of the system, if $Q_1R_2 = Q_2R_1$

30 A parallel plate air capacitor of capacitance C_0 is connected to a cell of emf V and then disconnected from it. A dielectric slab of dielectric constant K, which can just fill the air gap of the capacitor, is now inserted in it. Which of the following is incorrect? **[BHU]**

(a) The potential difference between the plates decreases K times
(b) The energy stored in the capacitor decreases K times
(c) The change in energy $\frac{1}{2}C_0V^2(K-1)$
(d) The change in energy $\frac{1}{2}C_0V^2\left(\frac{1}{K}-1\right)$

31 The energy stored in a condenser of capacity C which has been raised to a potential V is given by **[UP CPMT]**

(a) $\frac{1}{2}CV$ (b) $\frac{1}{2}CV^2$ (c) CV (d) $\frac{1}{2VC}$

32 Capacity of a capacitor is $48\,\mu$F. When it is charged from 0.1 C to 0.5 C, change in the energy stored is **[MHT CET]**

(a) 2500 J (b) 2.5×10^{-3} J
(c) 2.5×10^{6} J (d) 2.42×10^{-2} J

33 In a parallel plate capacitor, the capacity increase, if **[MHT CET]**

(a) area of the plate is decreased
(b) distance between the plates increases
(c) area of the plate is increased
(d) dielectric constant decrease

34 The capacitance of a metallic sphere is $1\,\mu$F, then its radius is nearly **[Manipal]**

(a) 1.11 m (b) 10 m (c) 9 km (d) 1.11 cm

35 A capacitor is charged by a battery and the energy stored is U. The battery is now removed and the separation distance between the plates is doubled. The energy stored now is **[Manipal]**

(a) $U/2$ (b) U (c) $2U$ (d) $4U$

36 Energies stored in capacitor and dissipated during charging a capacitor bear a ratio **[MP PMT]**

(a) 1 : 1 (b) 1 : 2
(c) 1 : 1/2 (d) 2 : 1

37 What is the value of capacitance, if the thin metallic plate is introduced between two parallel plates of area A and separated at distance d? **[MP PMT]**

(a) $\frac{\varepsilon_0 A}{d}$ (b) $\frac{2\varepsilon_0 A}{d}$ (c) $\frac{4\varepsilon_0 A}{d}$ (d) $\frac{\varepsilon_0 A}{2d}$

38 What is called electrical energy tank? **[MP PMT]**

(a) Resistor (b) Inductor
(c) Capacitor (d) Motor

39 The radii of the inner and outer spheres of a condenser are 9 cm and 10 cm, respectively. If the dielectric constant of the medium between the two spheres is 6 and charge on the inner sphere is 18×10^{-9} C, then the potential of inner sphere will be, if the other sphere is earthed **[Haryana PMT]**

(a) 180 V (b) 30 V
(c) 18 V (d) 90 V

40 In a parallel plate capacitor, the separation between the plates is 3 mm with air between them. Now, 1 mm thick layer of a material of dielectric constant 2 is introduced between the plates due to which the capacity increases. In order to bring its capacity of the original value, the separation between the plates must be made **[Haryana PMT]**

(a) 1.5 mm (b) 2.5 mm (c) 3.5 mm (d) 4.5 mm

41 The plates in a parallel plate capacitor are separated by a distance d with air as the medium between the plates. In order to increase the capacity by 66%, a dielectric slab of dielectric constant 5 is introduced between the plates. What is the thickness of the dielectric slab? **[EAMCET]**

(a) $d/4$ (b) $d/2$ (c) $5d/8$ (d) d

42 If the energy of a $100\,\mu F$ capacitor charged to 6 kV could all be used to lift a 50 kg mass, then what would be the greatest vertical height through which mass could be raised? **[MGIMS]**

(a) 0.6 mm (b) 3.6 m
(c) 1.2 mm (d) 12 m

43 A charged oil drop of mass 9.75×10^{-15} kg and charge 30×10^{-16} C is suspended in a uniform electric field existing between two parallel plates. The field between the plates is (Take, $g = 10\ ms^{-2}$) **[JCECE]**

(a) $3.25\ Vm^{-1}$ (b) $3000\ Vm^{-1}$
(c) $325\ Vm^{-1}$ (d) $32.5\ Vm^{-1}$

2009

44 **Assertion** Circuit containing capacitors should be handled cautiously even when there is no current.

Reason The capacitors are very delicate and so quickly breakdown. **[AIIMS]**

(a) Both Assertion and Reason are correct but Reason is the correct explanation of Assertion.
(b) Both Assertion and Reason are correct but Reason is not the correct explanation of Assertion.
(c) Assertion is correct but Reason is incorrect.
(d) Both Assertion and Reason are incorrect.

45 The potential energy of a charged parallel plate capacitor is U_0. If a slab of dielectric constant K is inserted between the plates, then the new potential energy will be **[AFMC]**

(a) $\frac{U_0}{K}$ (b) U_0K (c) $\frac{U_0}{K^2}$ (d) U_0^2

46 A capacitor of $10\,\mu F$ is charged to a potential 50 V with a battery. The battery is now disconnected and an additional charge $200\,\mu$ C is given to the positive plate of the capacitor. The potential difference across the capacitor will be **[UP CPMT]**

(a) 100 V (b) 70 V
(c) 80 V (d) 50 V

47 Capacitors are used in electrical circuits where appliances need more **[BVP]**

(a) current (b) voltage
(c) watt (d) resistance

48 If the circumference of a sphere is 2 m, then the capacitance of sphere in water would be **[BVP]**

(a) 2700 pF (b) 2760 pF
(c) 2780 pF (d) 2800 pF

49 If dielectric is inserted in charged capacitor (battery removed), the quantity that remain constant is **[MHT CET]**

(a) capacitance (b) potential
(c) intensity (d) charge

50 Capacitance (in farad) of spherical conductor with radius 1 m is **[Manipal]**

(a) 1.1×10^{-10} (b) 10^{-6}
(c) 9×10^{-9} (d) 10^{-3}

51 Energy stored per unit volume of a parallel plate capacitor having plate area A and plate separation d when charged to a potential of V volt is (air space in between the plates) **[J&K CET]**

(a) $\frac{1}{2}C^2V^2$ (b) $\frac{q^2}{4C}$
(c) $\frac{1}{2}\varepsilon_0\left(\frac{V}{d}\right)$ (d) $\frac{1}{2}\varepsilon_0\left(\frac{V^2}{d^2}\right)$

52 A parallel plate capacitor of plate area A has a charge Q. The force on each plate of the capacitor is **[BCECE]**

(a) $\frac{2Q^2}{\varepsilon_0 A}$ (b) $\frac{Q^2}{\varepsilon_0 A}$
(c) $\frac{Q^2}{2\varepsilon_0 A}$ (d) zero

53 What is the area of the plates of a 3 F parallel plate capacitor, if the separation between the plates is 5 mm? **[MGIMS]**

(a) $1.694 \times 10^9\ m^2$ (b) $4.529 \times 10^9\ m^2$
(c) $9.281 \times 10^9\ m^2$ (d) $12.981 \times 10^9\ m^2$

54 A condenser of capacitance $6\,\mu F$ was originally charged to 10 V. Now, potential difference is made 20 V. The increase in potential energy is **[MGIMS, Punjab PMET]**

(a) 3×10^{-4} J (b) 6×10^{-4} J
(c) 9×10^{-4} J (d) 12×10^{-4} J

55 The outer sphere of a spherical air capacitor is earthed. For increasing its capacitance, **[MGIMS]**

(a) vacuum is created between two spheres
(b) dielectric material is filled between the two spheres
(c) the space between two spheres is increased
(d) the earthing of the outer sphere is removed

2008

56 The energy required to charge a parallel plate condenser of plate separation d and plate area of cross-section A such that the uniform electric field between the plates is E, is **[CBSE AIPMT]**

(a) $\frac{\frac{1}{2}\varepsilon_0 E^2}{Ad}$ (b) $\frac{\varepsilon_0 E^2}{Ad}$
(c) $\varepsilon_0 E^2 Ad$ (d) $\frac{1}{2}\varepsilon_0 E^2 Ad$

57 **Assertion** A parallel plate capacitor is connected across battery through a key. A dielectric slab of dielectric constant K is introduced between the plates. The energy which is stored becomes K times.

Reason The surface density of charge on the plate remains constant or unchanged. [AIIMS]

(a) Both Assertion and Reason are correct but Reason is the correct explanation of Assertion.
(b) Both Assertion and Reason are correct but Reason is not the correct explanation of Assertion.
(c) Assertion is correct but Reason is incorrect.
(d) Both Assertion and Reason are incorrect.

58 The plates of a parallel plate capacitor are not exactly parallel. The surface charge density [Manipal]

(a) is lower at the closer end
(b) will not be uniform
(c) each plate will have the same potential at every point
(d) Both (b) and (c)

59 A sheet of aluminium foil of negligible thickness is introduced between the plates of a capacitor. The capacitance of the capacitor [MP PMT]

(a) decreases
(b) remains unchanged
(c) becomes infinite
(d) increases

60 The capacitance C of a capacitor is [J&K CET]

(a) independent of the charge and potential of the capacitor
(b) dependent on the charge and independent of potential
(c) independent of the geometrical configuration of the capacitor
(d) independent of the dielectric medium between the two conducting surfaces of the capacitor

61 64 small drops of water having same charge and same radius are combined to form one big drop. The ratio of capacitance of big drop to small drop is [Guj CET]

(a) 2 : 1 (b) 1 : 2 (c) 4 : 1 (d) 1 : 4

2007

62 A capacitor of $20\mu F$ charged upto 500 V is connected in parallel with another capacitor of $10\mu F$, which is charged upto 200 V. The common potential is [AFMC]

(a) 250 V (b) 300 V
(c) 400 V (d) 600 V

63 An insulator plate is passed between the plates of a capacitor. Then, current [MP PMT]

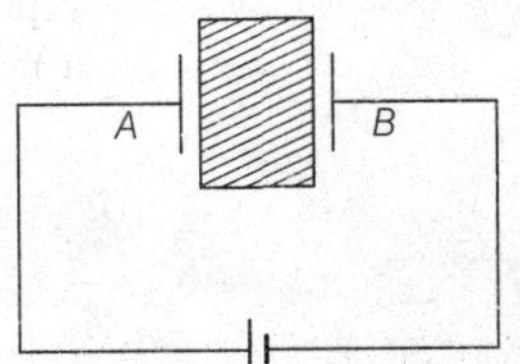

(a) first flows from A to B and then from B to A
(b) first flows from B to A and then from A to B
(c) always flows from B to A
(d) always flows from A to B

64 In a capacitor of capacitance 20 μF, the distance between the plates is 2 mm. If a dielectric slab of width 1 mm and dielectric constant 2 is inserted between the plates, then the new capacitance will be [BCECE]

(a) $22\mu F$ (b) $26.6\mu F$
(c) $52.2\mu F$ (d) $13\mu F$

65 To increase the charge on the plate of a capacitor means to [Guj CET]

(a) decrease the potential difference between the plates
(b) decrease the capacitance of the capacitor
(c) increase the capacitance of the capacitor
(d) increase the potential difference between the plates

66 27 small drops each having charge q and radius r coalesce to form a big drop. How many times charge and capacitance will become? [JCECE]

(a) $3q, 27\ C$ (b) $27q, 3\ C$
(c) $27q, 27\ C$ (d) $3q, 3\ C$

67 A parallel plate condenser with oil (dielectric constant 2) between the plates has capacitance C. If oil is removed, the capacitance of capacitor becomes [MHT CET]

(a) $\sqrt{2C}$ (b) $2C$
(c) $\frac{C}{\sqrt{2}}$ (d) $\frac{C}{2}$

2006

68 A parallel plate air capacitor is charged to a potential difference of V volt. After disconnecting the charging battery, the distance between the plates of the capacitor is increased using an insulating handle. As a result, the potential difference between the plates [CBSE AIPMT, J&K CET]

(a) decreases (b) does not change
(c) becomes zero (d) increases

69 If the plates of a parallel plate capacitor are not equal in area, then quantity of charge [MHT CET]

(a) on the plates will be same but nature of charge will differ
(b) on the plates as well as nature of charge will be different
(c) on the plates will be different but nature of charge will be same
(d) as well as nature of charge will be same

70 A capacitor of capacitance $6\mu F$ is charged upto 100 V. The energy stored in the capacitor is [Manipal]

(a) 0.6 J (b) 0.06 J
(c) 0.03 J (d) 0.3 J

71 700 pF capacitor is charged by 50 V battery. Electrostatic energy is stored by it will be [RPMT]

(a) 17.0×10^{-8} J
(b) 13.0×10^{-9} J
(c) 8.7×10^{-7} J
(d) 6.7×10^{-7} J

72 A capacitor is connected to a cell of emf E having some internal resistance r. The potential difference across the [MP PMT]

(a) cell is $< E$
(b) cell is E
(c) capacitor is $> E$
(d) capacitor is $< E$

73 The plates of a charged condenser are connected to a voltmeter. If the plates are moved apart, the reading of voltmeter will [J&K CET]

(a) increase
(b) decrease
(c) remain unchanged
(d) information is insufficient

74 The potentials of the two plates of capacitors are +10 V and – 10 V. The charge on one of the plates is 40 C. The capacitance of the capacitor is [Punjab PMET]

(a) 2 F (b) 4 F
(c) 0.5 F (d) 0.25 F

75 An air parallel plate capacitor has capacity C. The capacity and distance between plates are doubled when immersed in a liquid, then dielectric constant of the liquid is [Punjab PMET]

(a) 1 (b) 2
(c) 3 (d) 4

76 Energy E is stored in a parallel plate capacitor C_1. An identical uncharged capacitor C_2 is connected to it, kept in contact with it for a while and then disconnected, the energy stored in C_2 is [EAMCET]

(a) $\frac{E}{2}$ (b) $\frac{E}{3}$ (c) $\frac{E}{4}$ (d) zero

77 Two plates (area $= S$) charged to $+q_1$ and $+q_2$ $(q_2 < q_1)$ are brought closer to form a capacitor of capacitance C. The potential difference across the plates is [DUMET]

(a) $\frac{q_1 - q_2}{2C}$ (b) $\frac{q_1 - q_2}{C}$
(c) $\frac{q_1 - q_2}{4C}$ (d) $\frac{2(q_1 - q_2)}{C}$

78 Two capacitors of capacitance C_1 and C_2 are connected in parallel. If a charge Q is given to the combination, the charge gets shared. The ratio of the charge on the capacitor C_1 to the charge on the capacitor C_2 is [Guj CET]

(a) C_1C_2 (b) C_2 / C_1
(c) $C_1 + C_2$ (d) C_1 / C_2

79 The two capacitors C_1 and C_2 are charged to potentials V_1 and V_2 and then connected in parallel. There will be no flow of energy, if [JCECE]

(a) $C_1V_1 = C_2V_2$ (b) $V_1 = V_2$
(c) $C_1 = C_2$ (d) $\frac{C_1}{V_1} = \frac{C_2}{V_2}$

2005

80 An air filled parallel plate condenser has a capacity of 2 pF. The separation of the plates is doubled and the interspace between the plates is filled with wax. If the capacity is increased to 6 pF, the dielectric constant of wax is [KCET]

(a) 2 (b) 3 (c) 4 (d) 6

Answers

1 (c)	2 (a)	3 (b)	4 (a)	5 (c)	6 (b)	7 (d)	8 (c)	9 (d)	10 (b)
11 (c)	12 (a)	13 (a)	14 (d)	15 (d)	16 (b)	17 (d)	18 (c)	19 (a)	20 (d)
21 (d)	22 (b)	23 (a)	24 (d)	25 (c)	26 (d)	27 (c)	28 (c)	29 (d)	30 (c)
31 (b)	32 (a)	33 (c)	34 (c)	35 (c)	36 (d)	37 (a)	38 (c)	39 (b)	40 (c)
41 (b)	42 (b)	43 (d)	44 (c)	45 (b)	46 (b)	47 (a)	48 (d)	49 (d)	50 (a)
51 (d)	52 (c)	53 (a)	54 (c)	55 (b)	56 (c)	57 (c)	58 (d)	59 (b)	60 (c)
61 (c)	62 (c)	63 (b)	64 (b)	65 (d)	66 (b)	67 (d)	68 (d)	69 (a)	70 (c)
71 (c)	72 (b)	73 (a)	74 (a)	75 (d)	76 (c)	77 (a)	78 (d)	79 (b)	80 (d)

Explanations

1 (c) In a parallel plate capacitor, the capacity of capacitor,

$$C = \frac{k\,\varepsilon_0 A}{d}$$

$$\therefore \quad C \propto A$$

So, the capacity of capacitor increases, if area of the plate is increased.

2 (a) Given, capacitance of a capacitor,

$$C = 15\text{ nF} = 15 \times 10^{-9}\text{ F},$$

$$\varepsilon_r = 2.5$$

Electric field, $E = 30 \times 10^6$ V/m

Potential difference, $V = 30$ V

Area of plate = ?

If d be the distance between the plates, then

$$d = \frac{V}{E} = \frac{30}{30 \times 10^6} = 10^{-6}\text{ m}$$

Capacitance of capacitor,

$$C = \frac{\varepsilon_0\,\varepsilon_r A}{d}$$

$$15 \times 10^{-9} = \frac{8.85 \times 10^{-12} \times 2.5 \times A}{10^{-6}}$$

$$\Rightarrow \quad A = 6.7 \times 10^{-4}\text{ m}^2$$

3 (b) The electric field between the plates is given by

$$E = \frac{V}{d} \text{ or } V = Ed \text{ or } V \propto d$$

Hence, if the plate are pulled apart the potential difference increases.

4 (a) Van de Graaff generator is a device used to create a high potential difference of range of few million volts.

5 (c) As we know, the total work in transferring a charge to a parallel plate capacitor is given as

$$W = \frac{Q^2}{2C} \quad \text{... (i)}$$

We can also write a relation for work done as, $W = F \cdot d$ ... (ii)

From Eqs. (i) and (ii), we get

$$W = \frac{Q^2}{2C} = Fd$$

$$\Rightarrow \quad F = \frac{Q^2}{2Cd} \quad \text{...(iii)}$$

As ,the capacitance of a parallel plate capacitor is given as $C = \dfrac{\varepsilon_0 A}{d}$

Substituting the value of C in Eq. (iii), we get

$$F = \frac{Q^2 d}{2\varepsilon_0 A d} = \frac{Q^2}{2\varepsilon_0 A}$$

Thus, it means electrostatic force is independent of the distance between the plates.

6 (b) $\because$ Capacitance of a parallel plate capacitor, $C = \dfrac{\varepsilon_0 A}{d}$

$$\Rightarrow \quad A = \frac{Cd}{\varepsilon_0} = \frac{2 \times 0.5 \times 10^{-2}}{8.854 \times 10^{-12}}$$

$$\Rightarrow \quad A = 1130\text{ km}^2$$

7 (d) The arrangement of n metal plates separated by dielectric acts as parallel combination of $(n-1)$ capacitors.

Therefore, $C = \dfrac{(n-1)\,K\,\varepsilon_0 A}{d}$

Here, $C = 100\text{ pF} = 100 \times 10^{-12}$ F,

$K = 4$, $\varepsilon_0 = 8.85 \times 10^{-12}\text{ C}^2\text{N}^{-1}\text{m}^{-2}$,

$A = \pi r^2 = 3.14 \times (1 \times 10^{-2})^2$

and $d = 1\text{ mm} = 1 \times 10^{-3}$.

$$\therefore 100 \times 10^{-12} = \frac{(n-1) \times 4 \times (8.85 \times 10^{-12}) \times 3.14 \times (1 \times 10^{-2})^2}{1 \times 10^{-3}}$$

or $\quad n = \dfrac{1111.156}{111.156} = 9.99 \approx 10$

8 (c) The dielectric is introduced such that half of its area is occupied by it. In the given case, the two capacitors are in parallel.

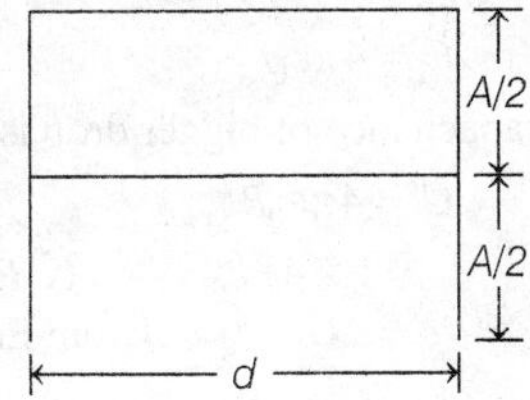

$$\therefore \quad C' = C_1 + C_2$$

But $\quad C_1 = \dfrac{A\varepsilon_0}{2d}$

and $\quad C_2 = \dfrac{KA\varepsilon_0}{2d}$

Thus, $\quad C' = \dfrac{A\varepsilon_0}{2d} + \dfrac{KA\varepsilon_0}{2d}$

$$C' = \frac{C}{2}(1 + K)$$

9 (d) When a parallel plate air capacitor connected to a cell of emf (V), then charge stored will be

$$q = CV \Rightarrow V = q/C$$

Also, energy stored is,

$$U = 1/2CV^2 - q^2/2C$$

As the battery is disconnected from the capacitor, the charge will not be destroyed, i.e. $q' = q$ with introduction of dielectric in gap of capacitor, the new capacitance will be

$$C' = CK \Rightarrow V' = q/C' = q/CK$$

The new energy stored will be

$$U' = \frac{q^2}{2CK}$$

$$\Delta U = U' - U = \frac{q^2}{2C}\left(\frac{1}{K} - 1\right)$$

$$= \frac{1}{2}CV^2\left(\frac{1}{K} - 1\right)$$

10 (b) Graph of (b) will be the right graph of the electric field inside the dielectrics will be less than the electric field outside the dielectrics. The electric field inside the dielectric could not be zero.

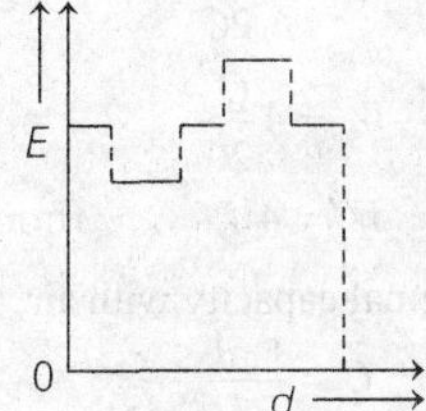

As $K_2 > K_1$, the drop in electric field for K_2 dielectric must be more than K_1.

11 (c) We know that, concentric spherical shells ($R_2 > R_1$),

$$V_{R_1} = \frac{1}{4\pi\varepsilon_0} \cdot \frac{Q}{R_1} \quad \text{...(i)}$$

$$V_{R_2} = \frac{1}{4\pi\varepsilon_0} \cdot \frac{Q}{R_2} \quad \text{...(ii)}$$

$$V = V_{R_1} - V_{R_2} = \frac{1}{4\pi\varepsilon_0} \cdot Q\left(\frac{1}{R_1} - \frac{1}{R_2}\right)$$

If the capacitance of two concentric spherical shell be C, then

$$C = \frac{Q}{V} = \frac{Q}{\dfrac{Q}{4\pi\varepsilon_0}\left(\dfrac{R_2 - R_1}{R_2 R_1}\right)}$$

$$= 4\pi\varepsilon_0 \frac{R_1 R_2}{(R_2 - R_1)}$$

12 (a) Given, $C_1 = 10\text{ pF} = 10\times10^{-12}\text{F}$, $C_2 = 20\text{ pF} = 20\times10^{-12}\text{F}$, $V_1 = 200\text{ V}$ and $V_2 = 100\text{ V}$

We know that, $V_1 = \frac{q_1}{C_1}$ and $V_2 = \frac{q_2}{C_2}$

$\Rightarrow \quad q_1 = V_1C_1 \quad$ ...(i)

$q_2 = V_2C_2 \quad$ ...(ii)

So, common potential of capacitors,

$$V = \frac{q_1+q_2}{C_1+C_2} = \frac{V_1C_1+V_2C_2}{C_1+C_2}$$

$$= \frac{200\times10\times10^{-12}+100\times20\times10^{-12}}{10\times10^{-12}+20\times10^{-12}}$$

$$= \frac{200\times10+100\times20}{10+20}$$

$$= \frac{2000+2000}{30} = \frac{4000}{30} = 133.3\text{ V}$$

13 (a) When plates of the capacitor are charged, opposite charges are induced on water (dielectric), so due to attractive forces, level of liquid rises.

14 (d) From the formula, $W = \frac{Q^2}{2C}$ ... (i)

$\therefore \quad W' = \frac{Q'^2}{2C}$

$W' = \frac{(2Q)^2}{2C} \quad (\because Q' = 2Q)$

$\Rightarrow \quad W' = 4\frac{Q^2}{2C}$

$\Rightarrow \quad W' = 4W \quad$ [from Eq. (i)]

15 (d) Original capacity with air,

$C = \frac{\varepsilon_0A}{d} \quad$ ...(i)

When dielectric plate (medium) of thickness t is introduced between the plates, then capacity becomes

$C' = \frac{\varepsilon_0A}{d'-t\left(1-\frac{1}{K}\right)} \quad$ ...(ii)

But as given, $C' = C \quad$ ...(iii)

where, $t = 4$ mm,

$d = 8$ mm, $K = 2$

From Eqs. (i), (ii) and (iii), we get

$$\frac{\varepsilon_0A}{d} = \frac{\varepsilon_0A}{d'-t\left(1-\frac{1}{K}\right)}$$

$$d = d'-t\left(1-\frac{1}{K}\right)$$

$$d' = d+t\left(1-\frac{1}{K}\right)$$

$$= 8+4\left(1-\frac{1}{2}\right) = 10\text{ mm}$$

Hence, $d' = 10$ mm

16 (b) Heat produced in a wire is equal to the energy stored in capacitor,

$$H = \frac{1}{2}CV^2$$

$$= \frac{1}{2}\times(2\times10^{-6})\times(200)^2$$

$$= 10^{-6}\times200\times200$$

$$= 4\times10^{-2}\text{J}$$

17 (d) On giving a charge q to a conductor, the electric potential of the conductor becomes V. Then, the capacitance of the conductor is

$C = q/V$

Potential on sphere of radius R is

$$V = \frac{1}{4\pi\varepsilon_0}\frac{q}{R}$$

$\Rightarrow \quad C = \frac{q\times4\pi\varepsilon_0R}{q}$

$= 4\pi\varepsilon_0R$

$\Rightarrow \quad C \propto R$

18 (c) Energy density for a parallel plate capacitor $= \frac{1}{2}\varepsilon_0E^2$ and volume $= Ad$

Hence, total energy = energy density × volume

$$= \left(\frac{1}{2}\varepsilon_0E^2\right)\times(Ad)$$

$$= \frac{1}{2}\varepsilon_0E^2Ad$$

19 (a) Let R and r be the radii of bigger and each smaller drop, respectively.

$\therefore \quad \frac{4}{3}\pi R^3 = 8\times\frac{4}{3}\pi r^3$

$\Rightarrow \quad R = 2r \quad$ ...(i)

The capacitance of a smaller spherical drop is

$C = 4\pi\varepsilon_0r \quad$ ...(ii)

The capacitance of bigger drop is

$C' = 4\pi\varepsilon_0R$

$= 2\times4\pi\varepsilon_0r \quad (\because R = 2r)$

$= 2C \quad$ [from Eq. (ii)]

$\therefore \quad C = \frac{C'}{2} = \frac{1}{2}\mu\text{F} \quad (\because C' = 1\mu\text{F})$

20 (d) Loss of energy

$$= \frac{1}{2}\frac{C_1C_2}{(C_1+C_2)}(V_1-V_2)^2$$

$$= \frac{1}{2}\times\frac{5\times5\,(2000-1000)^2}{(5+5)}\times10^{-6}$$

$$= \frac{5\times5\times1000\times1000\times10^{-6}}{2\times10}$$

$$= 1.25\text{ J}$$

21 (d) Common potential,

$$V = \frac{\text{Total charge}}{\text{Total capacitance}}$$

$$V = \frac{C_1V_1+C_2V_2}{C_1+C_2}$$

$\Rightarrow \quad V = \frac{0+CV_0}{KC+C}$

$V = \frac{CV_0}{C(1+K)}$

$\Rightarrow \quad V = \frac{V_0}{1+K}$

$\Rightarrow \quad K+1 = \frac{V_0}{V}$

$\Rightarrow \quad K = \frac{V_0}{V}-1 = \frac{V_0-V}{V}$

The dielectric constant of the solid dielectric, $K = \frac{V_0-V}{V}$

22 (b) Earth is a conducting sphere of large capacitance, $V = q/C$

As, C is very large, so $V \to 0$ for all finite charges.

Hence, earth is a conductor.

23 (a) A current flows in the circuit during the time, the capacitor is charged. After the capacitor gets fully charged, the current stops flowing. It means when a capacitor is connected to a battery, a current flows in the circuit for sometime, then reduces to zero.

24 (d) The quantities, energy stored and potential difference decreases because capacitance increases as

$$U = \frac{1}{2}\frac{q^2}{KC} \text{ and } V = \frac{q}{KC}$$

25 (c) We know that, $qE = mg$

$$\frac{qQ}{\varepsilon_0A} = mg \text{ or } q = \frac{\varepsilon_0A\,mg}{Q}$$

$$= \frac{\left[\begin{array}{r}8.85\times10^{-12}\times2\times10^{-2}\\ \times2.5\times10^{-7}\times10\end{array}\right]}{5\times10^{-7}}$$

$$= 8.85\times10^{-13}\text{C}$$

26 (d) Here, $q = 8\times10^{-18}$ C,

$C = 100\,\mu\text{F} = 10^{-4}\text{F}$

$\therefore \quad V = \frac{q}{C} = \frac{8\times10^{-18}}{10^{-4}}$

$= 8\times10^{-14}$ V

$\therefore$ Work done, $W = \frac{1}{2}qV$

$$= \frac{1}{2}\times8\times10^{-18}\times8\times10^{-14}$$

$$= 32\times10^{-32}\text{ J}$$

27 (c) Capacitance of a parallel plate capacitor with air is $C = \frac{\varepsilon_0 A}{d}$.

Capacitance of a same parallel plate capacitor with the introductory of a dielectric medium, $C' = \frac{K\varepsilon_0 A}{d}$

where, K is the dielectric constant of a medium.

$\therefore \quad \frac{C'}{C} = K \Rightarrow K = \frac{15}{3} = 5$

and $\quad K = \frac{\varepsilon}{\varepsilon_0}$

or $\quad \varepsilon = K\varepsilon_0 = 5 \times 8.854 \times 10^{-12}$

$= 0.44 \times 10^{-10}\ C^2N^{-1}m^{-2}$

28 (c) Charge, $Q = CV = 500\ \mu F \times 10 V$

$= 500 \times 10^{-6} \times 10$

$= 5 \times 10^{-3} C$

Now, $\quad Q = qt$

$\Rightarrow \quad t = Q/q$

$t = \frac{5 \times 10^{-3}}{100 \times 10^{-6}}$

$= \frac{1}{20} \times 1000\ s = 50\ s$

29 (d) Potential, $V_1 = \frac{1}{4\pi\varepsilon_0}\frac{Q_1}{R_1}$

and $\quad V_2 = \frac{1}{4\pi\varepsilon_0}\frac{Q_2}{R_2}$

If $V_1 = V_2$, then $\frac{Q_1}{R_1} = \frac{Q_2}{R_2}$

$\Rightarrow \quad Q_1R_2 = Q_2R_1$

In this case, there will be no flow of charges.

However, if the given spheres have unequal potentials, then the charges shall flow from higher potential to lower potential. Flow of charges shall be accompanied by loss of energy.

30 (c) Initial energy,

$$U_i = \frac{1}{2}C_0V^2$$

When dielectric slab is introduced between plates, then

$$C' = KC_0$$

and $\quad V' = \frac{q}{C'} = \frac{q}{KC_0} = \frac{V}{K}$

Thus, potential difference decreases K times.

Final energy, $U_f = \frac{1}{2}(KC_0)\left(\frac{V}{K}\right)^2$

or $\quad U_f = \frac{1}{K}\left(\frac{1}{2}C_0V^2\right)$

Thus, the energy stored in the capacitor decreases K times.

Change in energy $= U_f - U_i$

$$= \frac{1}{2}C_0V^2\left(\frac{1}{K} - 1\right)$$

Note that this change of energy is negative, i.e. there is a decrease of energy.

Hence, option (c) is incorrect.

31 (b) Energy stored in a capacitor of capacitance C and potential V is $\frac{1}{2}CV^2$.

32 (a) Change in energy,

$$\Delta U = \frac{1}{2}\left(\frac{q_1^2 - q_2^2}{C}\right)$$

$$= \frac{1}{2}\left(\frac{(0.5)^2 - (0.1)^2}{48 \times 10^{-6}}\right)$$

$$= \frac{1}{2}\left(\frac{0.25 - 0.01}{48 \times 10^{-6}}\right)$$

$$= \frac{1}{2}\left(\frac{0.24}{48 \times 10^{-6}}\right) = \frac{1}{2}\left(\frac{10^4}{2}\right)$$

$= 2500$ J

33 (c) In a parallel plate capacitor, the capacity of capacitor,

$$C = K\varepsilon_0 A/d$$

$\Rightarrow \quad C \propto A$

So, the capacity of capacitor increases, if area of the plate is increased.

34 (c) For a spherical capacitor of radius R, the capacitance is given by

$$C = 4\pi\varepsilon_0 R$$

Given, $C = 1\ \mu F = 1 \times 10^{-6} F$

$\Rightarrow \quad R = \frac{C}{4\pi\varepsilon_0}$

$= 9 \times 10^9 \times 1 \times 10^{-6}$ m

$\Rightarrow \quad R = 9 \times 10^3 = 9$ km

35 (c) Energy stored,

$$U = \frac{1}{2}qV$$

As the distance d is increased between the two plates.

Now, stored energy,

$$dU' = \frac{1}{2}qV'$$

$$= \frac{1}{2}q\left(\frac{q}{C}\right) = \frac{1}{2}\frac{q^2 d}{\varepsilon_0 A}$$

$\Rightarrow U' \propto d$, as the separation distance d is doubled the energy stored also becomes 2 times, i.e.

$$U' = 2U$$

36 (d) Half of the energy is dissipated during charging a capacitor.

$\therefore \quad \frac{\text{Energy stored in a capacitor}}{\text{Energy dissipated during charging a capacitor}} = \frac{2}{1}$

37 (a) When a metallic slab is inserted between the plates, capacitance,

$$C = \frac{\varepsilon_0 A}{d - t}$$

Here, $t = 0$ as plate is very thin.

$\therefore \quad C = \frac{\varepsilon_0 A}{d}$

38 (c) Capacitor stores electrical energy, whereas inductor stores magnetic energy. Hence, capacitor is called the electrical energy tank.

39 (b) Given system is a spherical capacitor, so capacitance of system,

$$C = K \times 4\pi\varepsilon_0\left(\frac{r_1r_2}{r_2 - r_1}\right)$$

$$= \frac{6}{9 \times 10^9}\left(\frac{9 \times 10}{1}\right) \times 10^{-2}$$

$= 6 \times 10^{-10}$ F

Now, potential of inner sphere will be equal to potential difference of the capacitor.

$\therefore \quad V = \frac{q}{C} = \frac{18 \times 10^{-9}}{6 \times 10^{-10}} = 30$ V

40 (c) Dielectric constant,

$$K = \frac{t}{t - d'}$$

$\Rightarrow \quad 2 = \frac{1}{1 - d'}$

$\Rightarrow \quad d' = \frac{1}{2}$ mm

$\therefore$ New distance $= 3 + \frac{1}{2} = 3.5$ mm

41 (b) The capacity in air, $C = \varepsilon_0 A/d$

The capacity when dielectric slab of dielectric constant 5 is introduced between the plates,

$$C' = \frac{\varepsilon_0 A}{d - t + \frac{t}{5}}$$

$\therefore \quad \frac{C}{C'} = \frac{d - t + \frac{t}{5}}{d} \quad$ ...(i)

$\Rightarrow \quad C' = \frac{166}{100}C \quad$ ...(ii) (given)

From Eqs. (i) and (ii), we get

$$\therefore \quad \frac{100}{166} = \frac{d - t + \frac{t}{5}}{d} = \frac{d - \frac{4t}{5}}{d}$$

$$\Rightarrow \quad 100\,d = 166d - 166\left(\frac{4t}{5}\right)$$

$$\Rightarrow \quad 166\left(\frac{4t}{5}\right) = 66d$$

$$\Rightarrow \quad t = \frac{66d \times 5}{166 \times 4} = \frac{d}{2}$$

42 (*b*) Energy stored in the capacitor is used in lifting the mass.

$$\therefore \quad mgh = \frac{1}{2}CV^2$$

$$50 \times 9.8 \times h = \frac{1}{2} \times 100 \times 10^{-6} \times (6 \times 10^3)^2$$

$$50 \times 9.8 \times h = \frac{1}{2} \times 100 \times 10^{-6} \times 36 \times 10^6$$

$$\therefore \quad h = \frac{1800}{50 \times 9.8} = 3.6\text{ m}$$

43 (*d*) In equilibrium, $eE = mg$

$$\Rightarrow \quad E = \frac{mg}{e} = \frac{9.75 \times 10^{-15} \times 10}{30 \times 10^{-16}}$$

$$= 32.5\text{ Vm}^{-1}$$

44 (*c*) Circuit containing capacitors should be handled cautiously even, when there is no current, because a capacitor does not completely discharge itself.

If some person handles such a capacitor without discharging it, he may get a severe shock.

Hence, Assertion is correct but Reason is incorrect.

45 (*b*) According to question,

$$U_0 = \frac{1}{2}CV^2$$

where, $C = \frac{\varepsilon_0 A}{d}$

$$\Rightarrow \quad U_0 = \frac{1}{2}\frac{\varepsilon_0 A}{d}V^2$$

Now, new potential energy,

$$U = \frac{1}{2}C_n V^2$$

$$\Rightarrow \quad U = \frac{1}{2}\frac{K\varepsilon_0 A}{d}V^2$$

$$\left(\because \text{ new capacitance, } C_n = \frac{K\varepsilon_0 A}{d}\right)$$

$$U = U_0 K$$

46 (*b*) Given, $V = 50\text{V}$

We know that, $Q = CV$

$$\Rightarrow \quad Q = 10 \times 10^{-6} \times 50 = 500\,\mu\text{C}$$

Now, total charge,

$$Q_T = 500\,\mu\text{C} + 200\,\mu\text{C} = 700\,\mu\text{C}$$

$$\Rightarrow \quad 700\,\mu\text{C} = 10 \times 10^{-6} \times V$$

$$\Rightarrow \quad V = \frac{700}{10} = 70\text{ V}$$

47 (*a*) Capacitors are used in electrical circuit, where appliances need more current.

48 (*d*) Capacitance of a sphere in water is given by

$$C = K4\pi\varepsilon_0 R \quad \text{...(i)}$$

where,

K = dielectric constant of water = 80.1

R = radius of sphere

$$\varepsilon_0 = 8.85 \times 10^{-12}\text{ C}^2/\text{Nm}^2$$

Now, given circumference of sphere = 2 m

$$\Rightarrow \quad 2\pi R = 2$$

$$\Rightarrow \quad R = \frac{2}{2\pi} = \frac{1}{\pi}\text{ metre}$$

Putting this in Eq. (i), we get

$$C = 80.1 \times 4\pi \times 8.85 \times 10^{-12} \times \frac{1}{\pi}$$

$$\approx 2800 \times 10^{-12}\text{F} = 2800\text{ pF}$$

49 (*d*) If dielectric is inserted in charged capacitor (battery removed), the quantity that remains constant is charge.

50 (*a*) $C = 4\pi\varepsilon_0 R = \frac{1}{9 \times 10^9} \times 1$

$$= 1.1 \times 10^{-10}\text{F}$$

51 (*d*) Energy stored per unit volume of a parallel plate capacitor is known as energy density.

$$\sigma = \frac{U}{V} = \frac{\frac{1}{2}CV^2}{Ad} = \frac{1}{2}\frac{CV^2}{Ad} \quad \text{...(i)}$$

Now, we know that,

$$C = \varepsilon_0 A/d$$

Putting the value of C in Eq. (i), we get

$$\sigma = \frac{1}{2}\frac{\varepsilon_0 AV^2}{d} \times \frac{1}{Ad}$$

$$\Rightarrow \quad \sigma = \frac{1}{2}\frac{\varepsilon_0 V^2}{d^2} = \frac{1}{2}\varepsilon_0\left(\frac{V^2}{d^2}\right)$$

52 (*c*) Force on one plate due to another is

$$F = QE = Q \times \frac{\sigma}{2\varepsilon_0}$$

$$= Q\left(\frac{Q}{2A\varepsilon_0}\right) = \frac{Q^2}{2A\varepsilon_0}$$

53 (*a*) Given, capacitance, $C = 3\text{F}$

Separation, $d = 5\text{ mm} = 5 \times 10^{-3}\text{ m}$

We know that, $C = \varepsilon_0 A/d$

where, A = area of capacitor.

$$\Rightarrow \quad A = \frac{Cd}{\varepsilon_0} = \frac{3 \times 5 \times 10^{-3}}{8.85 \times 10^{-12}}$$

$$= 1.694 \times 10^9\text{ m}^2$$

54 (*c*) Potential energy, $U = \frac{1}{2}CV^2$

$$= \frac{1}{2}C(V_2^2 - V_1^2)$$

$$= \frac{1}{2} \times 6 \times 10^{-6}(20^2 - 10^2)$$

$$= 3 \times 10^{-6} \times 300$$

$$= 9 \times 10^{-4}\text{ J}$$

55 (*b*) The capacitance can be increased by two methods, i.e. by increasing the charges and by inserting a dielectric materials between the plates of capacitor. But capacitor here is earthened. So, the only method is to fill dielectric between the two spheres.

56 (*c*) Energy given by the cell,

$$E = CV^2$$

Here, $C = \frac{A\varepsilon_0}{d}$, $V = Ed$

$$\therefore \quad E = \left(\frac{A\varepsilon_0}{d}\right)(Ed)^2 = A\varepsilon_0 E^2 d$$

57 (*c*) If a dielectric slab of dielectric constant K is filled in between the plates of a condenser while charging it, the potential difference between the plates does not change but the capacity becomes K times, therefore

$$V' = V,\ C' = KC.$$

Energy stored in the capacitor,

$$U' = \frac{1}{2}C'V'^2 = \frac{1}{2}(KC)(V^2)$$

$$= \left(\frac{1}{2}CV^2\right)K = KU$$

Thus, energy stored becomes K times.

Surface charge density,

$$\sigma' = \frac{q}{A} = \frac{C'V'}{A}$$

$$= \frac{KCV}{A} = K\frac{q}{A} = K\sigma$$

58 *(d)* Being a conductor, each plate have the same potential at each point. As $E \propto \sigma$, and electric field being the gradient of potential $\left(E = \frac{dV}{dr}\right)$ is highest, where the plates are closest to each other. So, surface charge density is highest at closest end and lowest at far end. Hence, it is not uniform.

59 *(b)* Aluminium is a metal, so when we insert an aluminium foil, equal and opposite charges appear on its two surfaces. Since, it is of negligible thickness, so it will not affect the capacitance.

60 *(c)* Capacitance, $C = Q/V$

For a dielectric media, $C = \varepsilon A/d$

Therefore, capacitance C of a capacitor is independent of the geometrical configuration of the capacitor.

61 *(c)* Let the radius of each small drop be r and the radius of big drop be R. When 64 small drops of water are combined to form one big drop, then the volume remains constant.

So, the volume of 64 small drops = the volume of big drop

i.e. $64 \times \frac{4}{3}\pi r^3 = \frac{4}{3}\pi R^3$

$\Rightarrow \quad 64r^3 = R^3$

$\Rightarrow \quad 4r = R$

$\Rightarrow \quad R = 4r \quad \text{...(i)}$

Now, the capacitance of a spherical conductor is

$$C = 4\pi\varepsilon_0 a$$

(a is the radius of the conductor)

Now, the capacitance of small drop,

$$C_1 = 4\pi\varepsilon_0 r \quad \text{...(ii)}$$

and the capacitance of big drop,

$$C_2 = 4\pi\varepsilon_0 R$$

On putting the value of R from Eq. (i), we get

$$C_2 = 4\pi\varepsilon_0(4r)$$

$\Rightarrow \quad C_2 = 16\pi\varepsilon_0 r \quad \text{...(iii)}$

On dividing Eq. (iii) by Eq. (ii), we get

$$\frac{C_2}{C_1} = \frac{16\pi\varepsilon_0 r}{4\pi\varepsilon_0 r}$$

$\Rightarrow \quad \frac{C_2}{C_1} = \frac{4}{1}$

$\Rightarrow \quad C_2 : C_1 = 4 : 1$

62 *(c)* Common potential,

$$V = \frac{\text{Net charge}}{\text{Net capacitance}}$$

$$= \frac{q_1 + q_2}{C_1 + C_2} = \frac{C_1V_1 + C_2V_2}{C_1 + C_2}$$

Given, $C_1 = 20 \times 10^{-6}$ F

$\Rightarrow \quad V_1 = 500$ V

$\Rightarrow \quad C_2 = 10 \times 10^{-6}$ F

$\Rightarrow \quad V_2 = 200$ V

$\therefore \quad V = \frac{20\times10^{-6}\times500 + 10\times10^{-6}\times200}{30\times10^{-6}}$

$= 400$ V

63 *(b)* As insulator plate is passed between the plates of the capacitor, its capacity increases first and then decreases as the plate slips out. As a result, positive charge on plate A increases first and then decreases, hence current in outer circuit flows from B to A and then from A to B.

64 *(b)* The capacitance C of a capacitor of area A and distance d between plates is given as

$$C = \frac{\varepsilon_0 A}{d}$$

When a dielectric slab of thickness t is placed between the plates, we have

$$C' = \frac{\varepsilon_0 A}{d - t + t/K}$$

Given, $C = 20\,\mu\text{F} = 20 \times 10^{-6}$ F,

$d = 2\text{ mm} = 2 \times 10^{-3}$ m,

$t = 1\text{ mm} = 1 \times 10^{-3}$ m, $K = 2$

$\therefore \quad \frac{C'}{C} = \frac{d}{d - t\left(1 - \frac{1}{K}\right)}$

$$\frac{C'}{C} = \frac{2\times10^{-3}}{2\times10^{-3} - 1\times10^{-3}(1 - 1/2)} = 1.33$$

$\Rightarrow C' = 1.33 \times 20 \times 10^{-6}$

$= 26.6\,\mu$F

65 *(d)* A large amount of charge given to one plate raises its potential to be maximum and so a potential difference is established across the plates of capacitor.

66 *(b)* Let R and r be the radii of bigger and each smaller drop, respectively. In coalescing into a single drop, charge remains conserved.

Charge on bigger drop

= 27 × Charge on smaller drop

i.e. $\quad q' = 27q$

Now, before and after coalescing, volume remains same.

$$\frac{4}{3}\pi R^3 = 27 \times \frac{4}{3}\pi r^3$$

$\therefore \quad R = 3r$

Hence, capacitance of bigger drop,

$$C' = 4\pi\varepsilon_0 R$$

$= 4\pi\varepsilon_0(3r)$

$= 3(4\pi\varepsilon_0 r)$

$= 3C$

67 *(d)* The capacitance of a parallel plate capacitor with dielectric (oil) between its plates is

$$C = K\varepsilon_0 A/d \quad \text{...(i)}$$

When dielectric (oil) is removed, then capacitance,

$$C_0 = \varepsilon_0 A/d \quad \text{...(ii)}$$

Comparing Eqs. (i) and (ii), we get

$$C = KC_0$$

$\Rightarrow \quad C_0 = \frac{C}{K} = \frac{C}{2} \quad (\because K = 2)$

68 *(d)* If the battery is removed after charging, then the charge stored in the capacitor remains constant.

i.e. $\quad q$ = constant

Change in capacitance,

$$C' = \frac{\varepsilon_0 A}{d'}$$

As, $\quad d' > d$

$\therefore \quad C' < C$

Hence, potential difference between the plates,

$$V' = \frac{q}{C'}$$

or $\quad V' \propto \frac{1}{C'}$

As capacitance decreases, so potential difference increases.

69 (a) If the plates of a parallel plate capacitor are not equal in area, then quantity of charge on the plates will be same but nature of charge will different.

70 (c) The energy stored in the capacitor is given by

$$U = \frac{1}{2}CV^2$$

Given, $C = 6 \times 10^{-6}$F, $V = 100$ V

$$\therefore \quad U = \frac{1}{2} \times 6 \times 10^{-6} \times (100)^2$$
$$= 3 \times 10^{-2} \text{ J} = 0.03 \text{ J}$$

71 (c) Capacitance,

$$C = 700\text{pF} = 700 \times 10^{-12} \text{ F}$$

Source voltage, $V = 50$ V

Electrostatic energy is given by

$$E = \frac{1}{2}CV^2$$
$$= 0.5 \times 700 \times 10^{-12} \times (50)^2$$
$$= 8.7 \times 10^{-7} \text{ J}$$

72 (b) When capacitor is fully charged, it draws no current. When no current flows in the circuit, potential difference across the cell = emf of the cell = potential difference across the capacitor, i.e. E.

73 (a) $q = CV$ = constant ...(i)

Capacitance (C) of a parallel plate capacitor is given by

$$C = \frac{\varepsilon_0 A}{d} \quad \text{...(ii)}$$

where, A is area of plates and d the separation between them.

From Eqs. (i) and (ii), we get

$$q = \frac{\varepsilon_0 A}{d} \cdot V = \text{constant}$$

When plates are moved apart, d increases, hence value of C decreases and in order, charge (q) remains constant and V increases.

74 (a) The capacitance of capacitor is

$$C = q/V$$

The potential difference across the parallel plate capacitor is

$$10\text{V} - (-10\text{V}) = 20 \text{ V}$$

$$\therefore \text{Capacitance, } C = \frac{Q}{V} = \frac{40}{20} = 2\text{F}$$

75 (d) Capacity of air parallel plate capacitor,

$$C = \frac{A\varepsilon_0}{d}$$

Capacity of parallel plate capacitor when immersed in liquid and distance is doubled, is

$$C' = \frac{KA\varepsilon_0}{2d}$$

Given, $C' = 2C$

$$\therefore \quad 2C = \frac{K}{2}C \quad \left(\because C = \frac{A\varepsilon_0}{d}\right)$$

or $\quad K = 4$

76 (c) Let capacitance of a parallel plate capacitor, $C_1 = C$

If energy stored in capacitor C_1 is E.

The charge on capacitor, $q = \sqrt{2EC}$

$$\left(\because E = \frac{1}{2}\frac{q^2}{C}\right)$$

When another uncharged capacitor C_2 having same capacitance C is connected to it, then total charge on both capacitor = q.

When disconnected, the charge on each one capacitor,

$$q' = \frac{q}{2} = \frac{\sqrt{2EC}}{2} = \sqrt{\frac{EC}{2}}$$

$\therefore$ Energy stored in C_2,

$$E' = \frac{1}{2}\frac{q'^2}{C} = \frac{1}{2}\frac{EC}{2}\frac{1}{C}$$

$$\Rightarrow \quad E' = \frac{E}{4}$$

77 (a) Capacitance of the parallel plate capacitor is $C = \dfrac{\varepsilon_0 A}{d}$

where, A is area of plates and d is distance between them.

Potential difference across the plates,

$$V = Ed$$

Here, $\quad E = \dfrac{(q_1 - q_2)}{2\varepsilon_0 A}$

$$V = \frac{(q_1 - q_2)d}{2\varepsilon_0 A} = \frac{q_1 - q_2}{2C}$$

78 (d) In parallel combination, they will have common potential.

$$\text{Common potential} = \frac{\text{Total charge}}{\text{Total capacitance}}$$

$$\therefore \quad V = \frac{Q}{C_1 + C_2}$$

$$\text{Charge on } C_1 = C_1 V = \frac{C_1 Q}{C_1 + C_2}$$

$$\text{Charge on } C_2 = C_2 V = \frac{C_2 Q}{C_1 + C_2}$$

$\therefore$ Required ratio

$$= \frac{C_1 Q/(C_1 + C_2)}{C_2 Q/(C_1 + C_2)} = \frac{C_1}{C_2}$$

79 (b) When a conductor of capacitance C is charged, it acquires a potential,

$$V = q/C$$

When connected in parallel, equivalent capacitance of combination is

$$C' = C_1 + C_2$$

Also, energy flow $\left(E = \frac{1}{2}C'V^2\right)$ will not take place, if potential across capacitors is same.

i.e. $\quad V_1 = V_2$

80 (d) Capacitance with air, $C = \dfrac{A\varepsilon_0}{d}$

When interspace between the plates is filled with wax and distance between the plates is doubled, then

$$C' = \frac{KA\varepsilon_0}{2d}$$

or $\quad C' = \left(\dfrac{A\varepsilon_0}{d}\right)\dfrac{K}{2}$

or $\quad C' = C\dfrac{K}{2}$

$\Rightarrow \quad 6 = 2 \times \dfrac{K}{2}$

$\Rightarrow \quad K = 6$

Topic 3

Grouping of Capacitors

2018

1 An infinite number of identical capacitor each of capacitance $1\,\mu F$ are connected as shown in the figure. Then, the equivalent capacitance between A and B is **[AIIMS]**

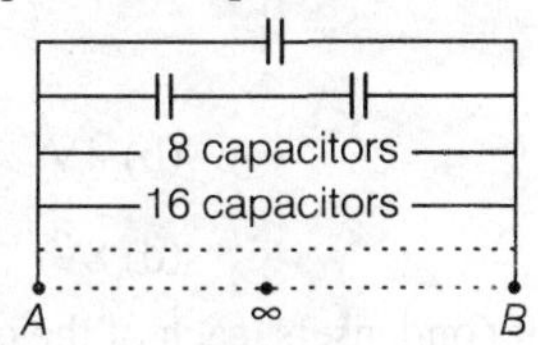

(a) $1\,\mu F$ (b) $\frac{1}{2}\,\mu F$ (c) $2\,\mu F$ (d) ∞

2 Find the capacitance as shown in the figure. **[JIPMER]**

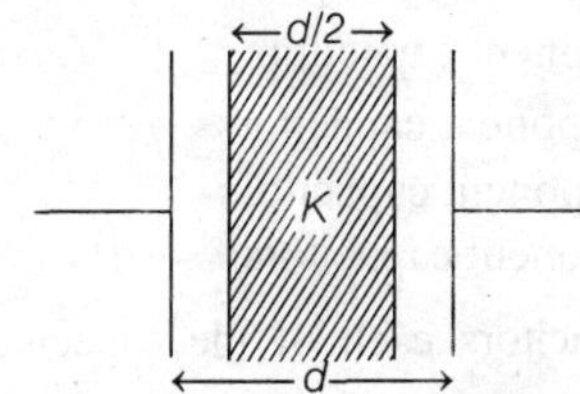

(a) $2KA\varepsilon_0/(K+1)d$ (b) $\frac{2KA\varepsilon_0}{d}$

(c) $(K+1)A\varepsilon_0/2d$ (d) $\frac{2KA\varepsilon_0}{(K^2+1)d}$

2017

3 Two capacitors C and $C/2$ are connected to a battery of V volts, as shown below **[AIIMS]**

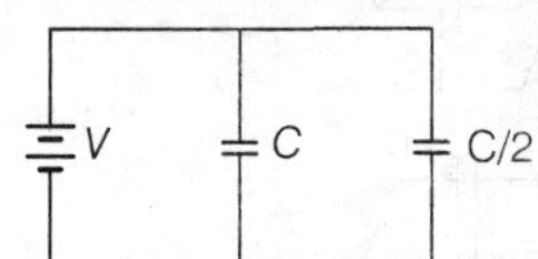

The work done in charging both the capacitor fully is

(a) $2CV^2$ (b) $1/2CV^2$ (c) $3/4CV^2$ (d) $1/4CV^2$

2014

4 In the given figure, the capacitors C_1, C_3, C_4 and C_5 have a capacitance $4\,\mu F$ each. If the capacitor C_2 has a capacitance $10\,\mu F$, then effective capacitance between A and B will be **[UK PMT]**

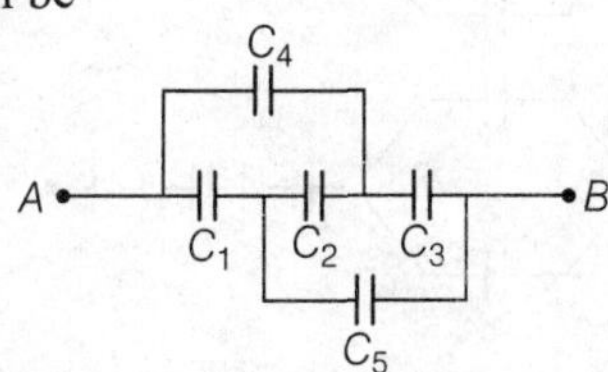

(a) $2\,\mu F$ (b) $4\,\mu F$ (c) $6\,\mu F$ (d) $8\,\mu F$

5 Three capacitors $3\,\mu F$, $6\,\mu F$ and $6\,\mu F$ are conncted in series to a source of 120 V. The potential difference (in volt) across the $3\,\mu F$ capacitor will be **[WB JEE]**

(a) 24 V (b) 30 V (c) 40 V (d) 60 V

2012

6 Effective capacitance between A and B in the figure shown below is (all capacitances are in μF) **[Manipal]**

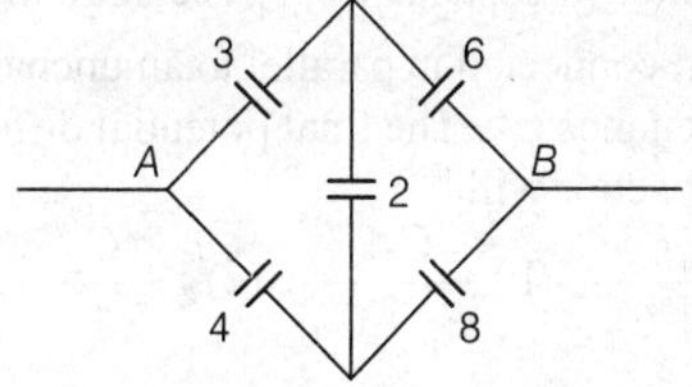

(a) $\frac{3}{14}\,\mu F$ (b) $\frac{14}{3}\,\mu F$ (c) $21\,\mu F$ (d) $23\,\mu F$

7 In the adjoining figure, the potential difference between X and Y is 60 V. The potential difference between the points M and N will be **[WB JEE]**

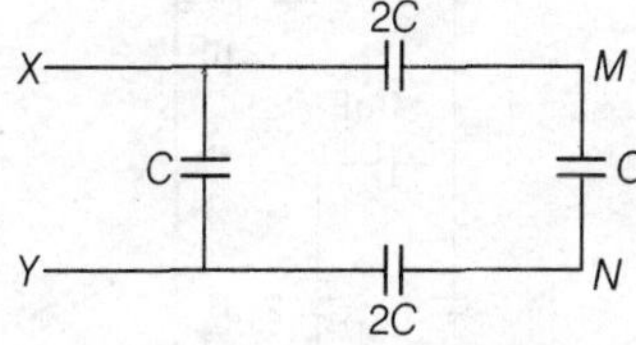

(a) 10 V (b) 15 V (c) 20 V (d) 30 V

8 A parallel plate capacitor with air as the dielectric has capacitance C. A slab of dielectric constant K and having the same thickness as the separation between the plates, is introduced so as to fill one-fourth of the capacitor as shown in the figure. The new capacitance will be **[AFMC]**

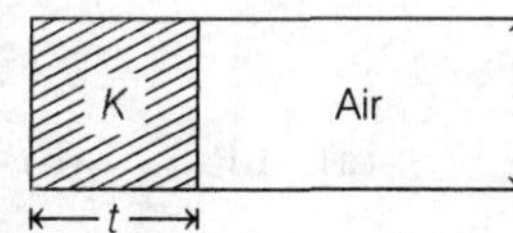

(a) $(K+3)\frac{C}{4}$ (b) $(K+2)\frac{C}{4}$

(c) $(K+1)\frac{C}{4}$ (d) $\frac{KC}{4}$

9 Two capacitors $3\,\mu F$ and $4\,\mu F$ are individually charged across a 6 V battery. After being disconnected from the battery, they are connected together with the negative plate of one attached to the positive plate of the other. What is the final total energy stored? **[AMU]**

(a) 1.26×10^{-4} J (b) 2.57×10^{-4} J

(c) 1.26×10^{-6} J (d) 2.57×10^{-6} J

2011

10 If the equivalent capacitance between points P and Q of the combination of the capacitors shown in figure below is $30\mu F$, the capacitor C is **[J&K CET]**

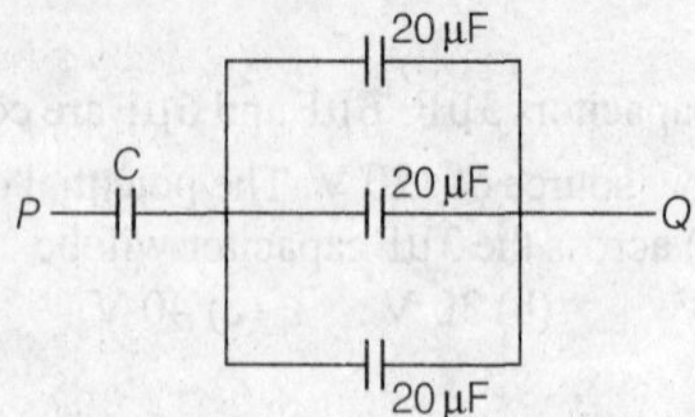

(a) $60\mu F$ (b) $30\mu F$ (c) $10\mu F$ (d) $5\mu F$

11 A capacitor of capacitance C_1 is charge to a potential V and then connected in parallel to an uncharged capacitor of capacitance C_2. The final potential difference across each capacitor will be **[J&K CET]**

(a) $\frac{C_1V}{C_1+C_2}$ (b) $\frac{C_2V}{C_1+C_2}$ (c) $1+\frac{C_2}{C_1}$ (d) $1-\frac{C_2}{C_1}$

12 In the given network, the value of C, so that an equivalent capacitance between points A and B is $3\mu F$, is **[KCET]**

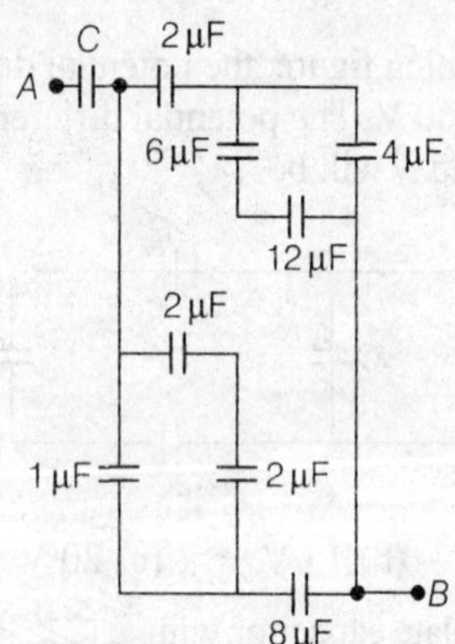

(a) $\frac{1}{2}\mu F$ (b) $\frac{31}{5}\mu F$ (c) $48\,\mu F$ (d) $36\,\mu F$

13 How many $1\mu F$ capacitors must be connected in parallel to store a charge of 1 C with a potential of 110 V across the capacitors? **[DUMET]**

(a) 990 (b) 900 (c) 9090 (d) 909

2010

14 A series combination of n_1 capacitors, each of value C_1 is charged by a source of potential difference $4V$. When another parallel combination of n_2 capacitors, each of value C_2 is charged by a source of potential difference V, it has the same (total) energy stored in it, as the first combination has. The value of C_2, in terms of C_1 is, then **[CBSE AIPMT]**

(a) $\frac{2C_1}{n_1n_2}$ (b) $16\frac{n_1}{n_2}C_1$ (c) $2\frac{n_2}{n_1}C_1$ (d) $\frac{16C_1}{n_1n_2}$

15 In the circuit shown in the figure, the potential difference across the $4.5\mu F$ capacitor is **[AIIMS]**

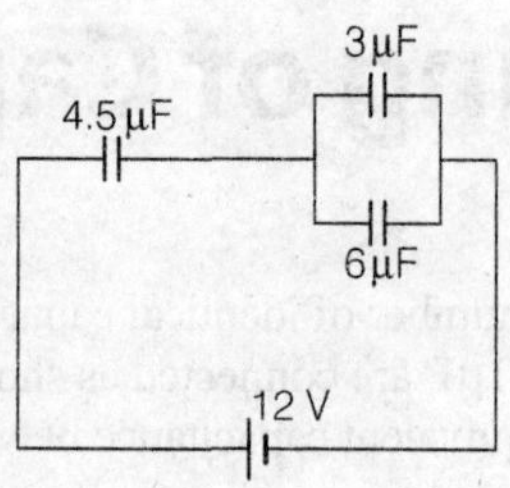

(a) $\frac{8}{3}V$ (b) 4V

(c) 6V (d) 8V

16 A number of condensers, each of the capacitance $1\mu F$ and each one of which gets punctured, if a potential difference just exceeding 500 V is applied, are provided. An arrangement suitable for giving capacitance of $2\mu F$ across which 3000 V may be applied requires atleast **[AFMC]**

(a) 6 component capacitors

(b) 12 component capacitors

(c) 72 component capacitors

(d) 2 component capacitors

17 Seven capacitors each of the capacitance $2\,\mu F$ are be connected in a configuration to obtain an effective capacitance of $10/11\mu F$. Which of the combination(s) shown in figure will achieve the desired result? **[AFMC]**

(a)
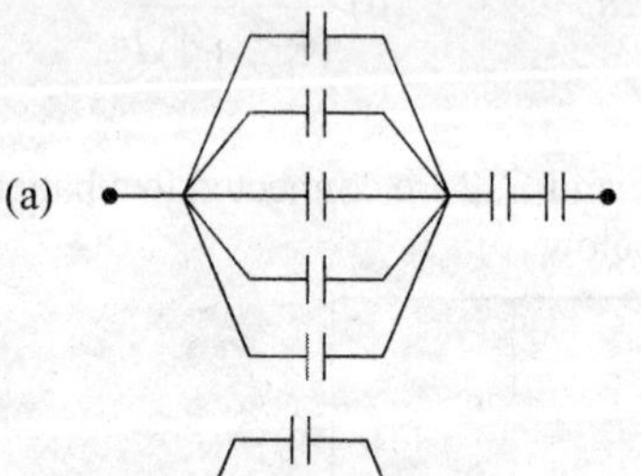

(b)
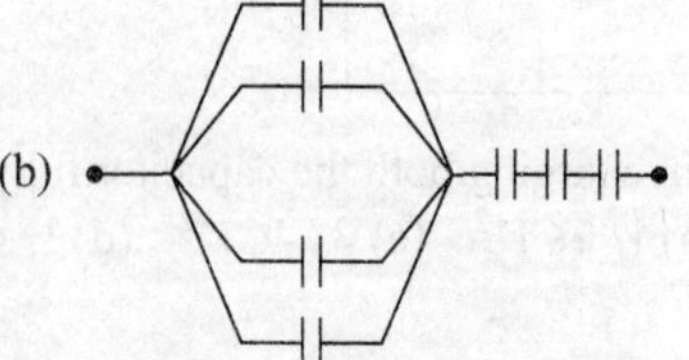

(c)
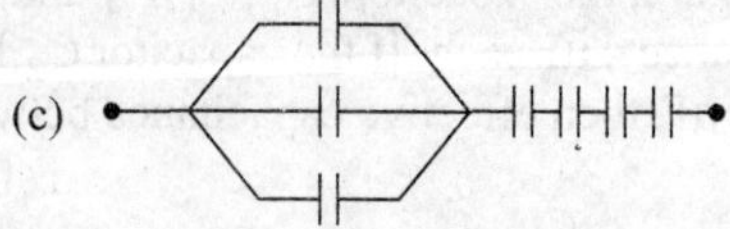

(d)
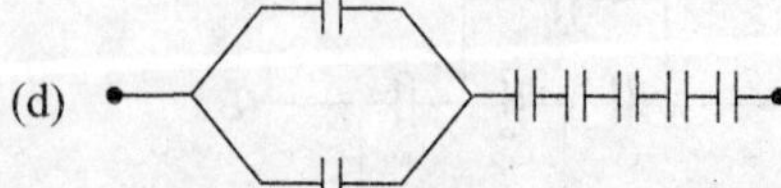

18 In the connections shown in the given figure below, the equivalent capacity between A and B will be **[UP CPMT]**

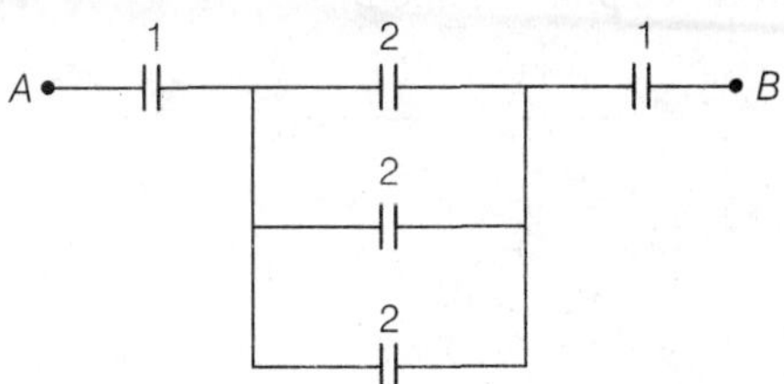

(a) 13/6 (b) 6/13 (c) 6 (d) 13

19 n identical capacitors each of capacitance C when connected in parallel give the effective capacitance 90 μF and when connected in series give 2.5 μF. Then, the values of n and C respectively, are **[Manipal]**
(a) 6 and 15 μF (b) 5 and 18 μF
(c) 15 and 6 μF (d) 18 and 5 μF

20 The number of ways one can arrange three identical capacitors to obtain distinct effective capacitances is
(a) 8 (b) 6
(c) 4 (d) 3 **[Manipal]**

21 Effective capacitance between A and B in the figure shown below is ($C_1 = C_2 = 20\,\mu F, C_3 = C_4 = 10\,\mu F$) **[OJEE]**

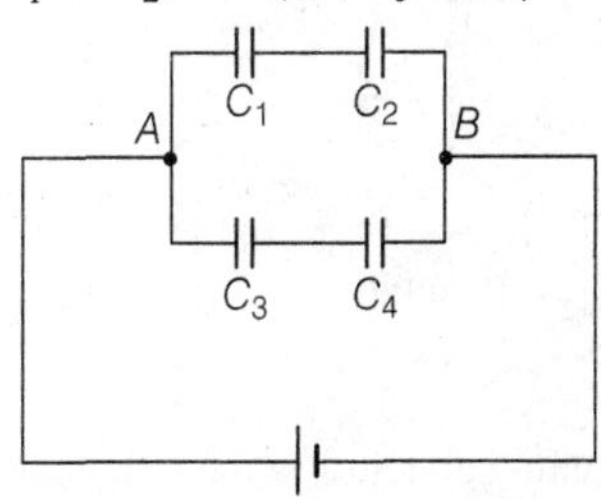

(a) 10 μF (b) 15 μF (c) 20 μF (d) 25 μF

22 In the figure below, the capacitance of each capacitor is 3 μF. The effective capacitance between A and B is **[WB JEE]**

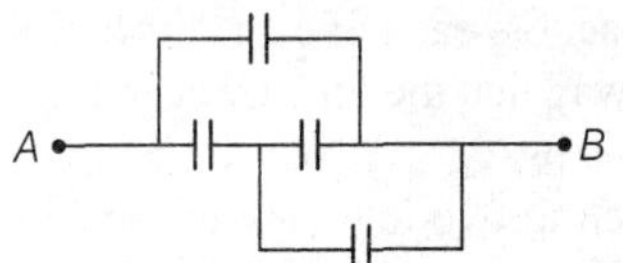

(a) $\frac{3}{4}$ μF (b) 3 μF (c) 6 μF (d) 5 μF

23 The equivalent capacitance between points A and B in the given figure, is **[CG PMT]**

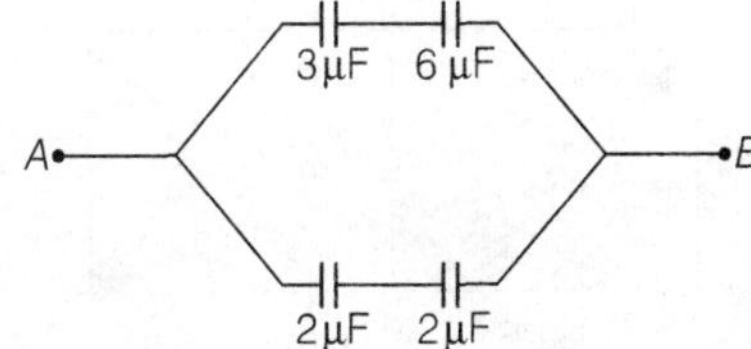

(a) $\frac{36}{13}$ μF (b) 2 μF (c) 1 μF (d) 3 μF

24 Three capacitors of capacitances 1 μF, 2 μF and 4 μF are connected first in a series combination and then in parallel combination. The ratio of their equivalent capacitances will be **[JIPMER]**
(a) 2:49 (b) 49:2 (c) 4:49 (d) 49:4

25 0.2 F capacitor is charged to 600 V by a battery, on removing the battery, it is connected with another parallel plate condenser of 1 F. The potential decreases to **[VMMC]**
(a) 100 V (b) 120 V (c) 300 V (d) 600 V

26 Parallel plate capacitor is constructed using three different dielectric materials as shown in the figure. The parallel plates, across which a potential difference is applied of area A metre^2 and separated by a distance d metre. The capacitance across A and B is **[VMMC]**

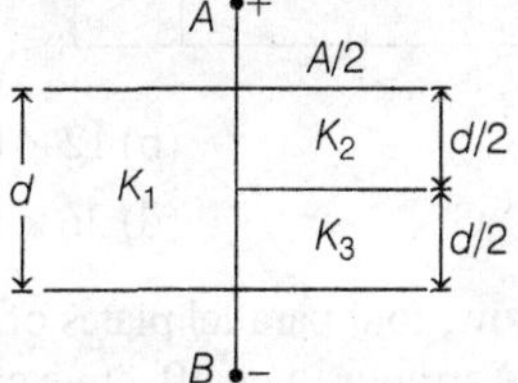

(a) $\frac{\varepsilon_0 A}{d}\left[\frac{K_1}{2} + \frac{K_2 K_3}{K_2 + K_3}\right]$ (b) $\frac{\varepsilon_0 A}{d}\left[\frac{K_1}{2} + \frac{(K_2 + K_3)}{K_2 K_3}\right]$

(c) $\frac{\varepsilon_0 A}{d}\left[\frac{2}{K_1} + \frac{K_2 K_3}{K_2 + K_3}\right]$ (d) $\frac{\varepsilon_0 A}{d}\left[\frac{2}{K_1} + \frac{K_2 + K_3}{K_1 K_3}\right]$

27 Two capacitors, one 4 pF and the other 6 pF, connected in parallel are charged by a 100 V battery. The energy stored in the capacitors is **[MGIMS]**
(a) 1.2×10^{-8} J (b) 2.4×10^{-8} J
(c) 5.0×10^{-8} J (d) 1.2×10^{-6} J

2009

28 Three capacitors each of capacitance C and of breakdown voltage V are joined in series. The capacitance and breakdown voltage of the combination will be **[CBSE AIPMT]**
(a) $\frac{C}{3}, \frac{V}{3}$ (b) $3C, \frac{V}{3}$ (c) $\frac{C}{3}, 3V$ (d) $3C, 3V$

29 Four capacitors of equal capacitance have an equivalent capacitance C_1 when connected in series and an equivalent capacitance C_2 when connected in parallel. The ratio $\frac{C_1}{C_2}$ is **[CBSE AIPMT]**
(a) $\frac{1}{4}$ (b) $\frac{1}{16}$ (c) $\frac{1}{8}$ (d) $\frac{1}{12}$

30 Three capacitors has a capacitance C are connected in parallel to which a capacitor of capacitance C is connected in series. Effective capacitance is 3.75, then capacity of each capacity is **[MHT CET]**
(a) 4 μF (b) 5 μF (c) 6 μF (d) 8 μF

31 The effective capacitance between A and B is [OJEE]

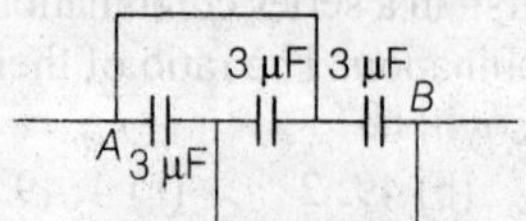

(a) 9μF (b) 3μF
(c) 6μF (d) 1μF

32 The charge deposited on 4 μF capacitor in the circuit is [KCET]

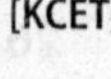
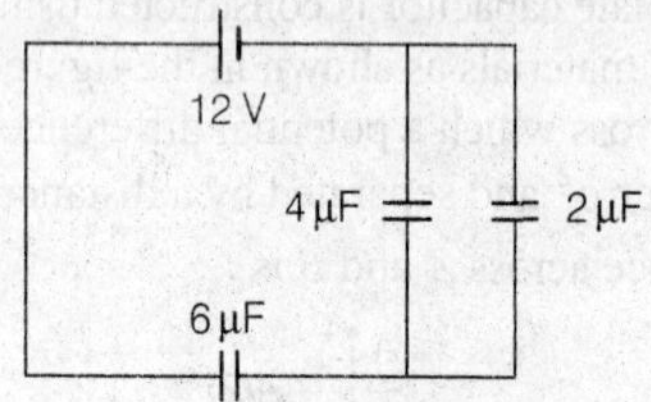

(a) 6×10^{-6} C (b) 12×10^{-6} C
(c) 24×10^{-6} C (d) 36×10^{-6} C

33 In figure below, four parallel plates of equal area A and spacing d are arrange, then effective capacitance between a and b is [BVP, MP PMT]

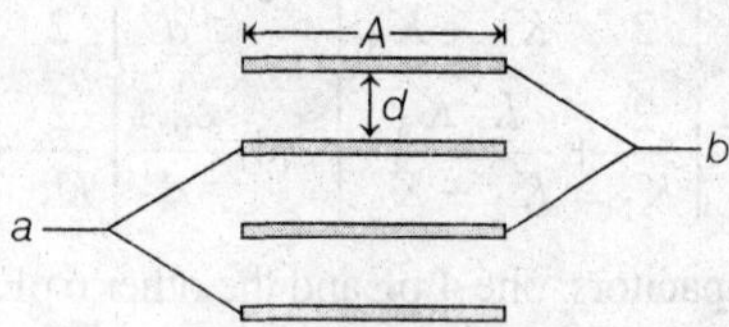

(a) $\frac{\varepsilon_0 A}{d}$ (b) $\frac{2\varepsilon_0 A}{d}$ (c) $\frac{3\varepsilon_0 A}{d}$ (d) $\frac{4\varepsilon_0 A}{d}$

34 A parallel plate air capacitor has a capacitance C. When it is half filled with a dielectric of dielectric constant 5, the percentage increase in the capacitance will be [JCECE]

(a) 400% (b) 66.6% (c) 33.3% (d) 200%

2008

35 Six capacitors each of capacitance of 2 μF are connected as shown in the figure. The effective capacitance between A and B is [Kerala CEE]

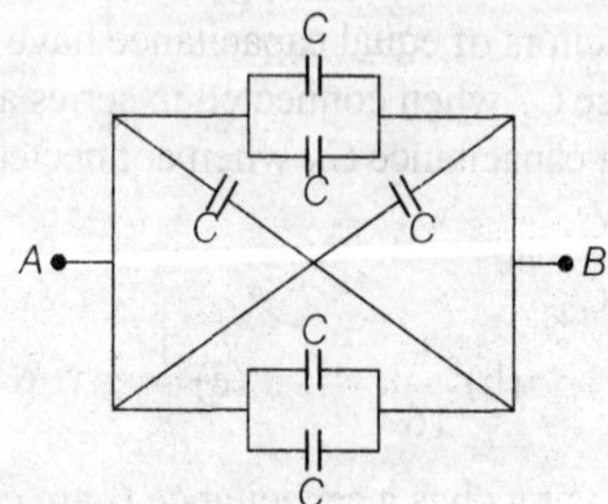

(a) 12 μF (b) 8/3 μF (c) 3 μF (d) 6 μF
(e) $\frac{2}{3}$ μF

36 Four capacitors are connected in a circuit as shown in the following figure. Calculate the effective capacitance between the points A and B. [J&K CET]

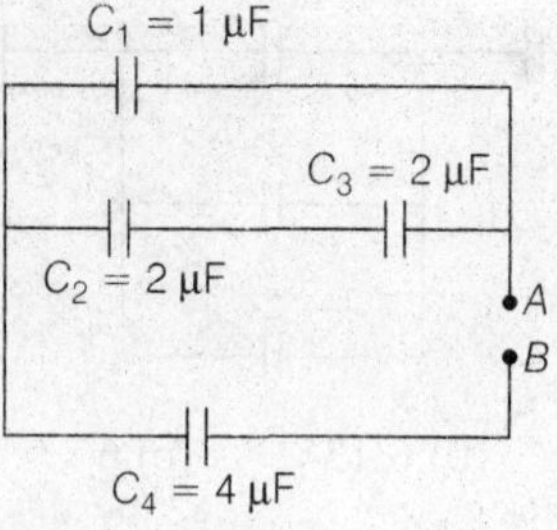

(a) $\frac{4}{3}$ μF (b) $\frac{24}{5}$ μF (c) 9 μF (d) 5 μF

37 How many 6 μF, 200 V condensers are needed to make a condenser of 18 μF, 600 V? [KCET]

(a) 9 (b) 18 (c) 3 (d) 27

38 The total energy stored in the condenser system shown in the figure will be [KCET]

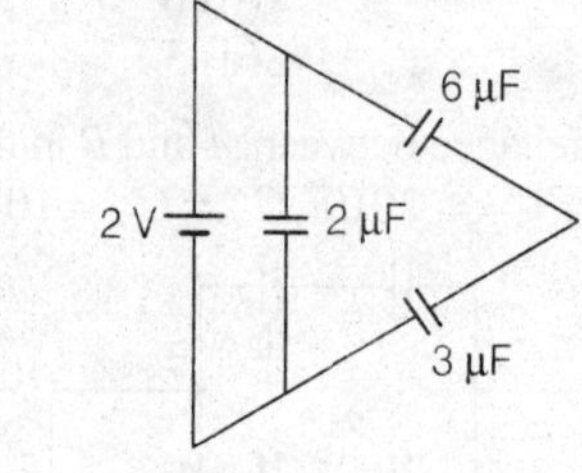

(a) 2 μJ (b) 4 μJ (c) 8 μJ (d) 16 μJ

2007

39 A parallel plate capacitor is made by stacking n equally spaced plates connected alternatively. If the capacitance between any two adjacent plates is C, then the resultant capacitance is [AIIMS]

(a) $(n-1)C$ (b) $(n+1)C$ (c) C (d) nC

40 Three capacitors each of capacity 4μF are to be connected in such a way that the effective capacitance is 6μF. This can be done by [BHU]

(a) connecting two in series and one in parallel
(b) connecting two in parallel and one in series
(c) connecting all of them in series
(d) connecting all of them in parallel

41 In the figure, the equivalent capacitance between A and B is [AMU]

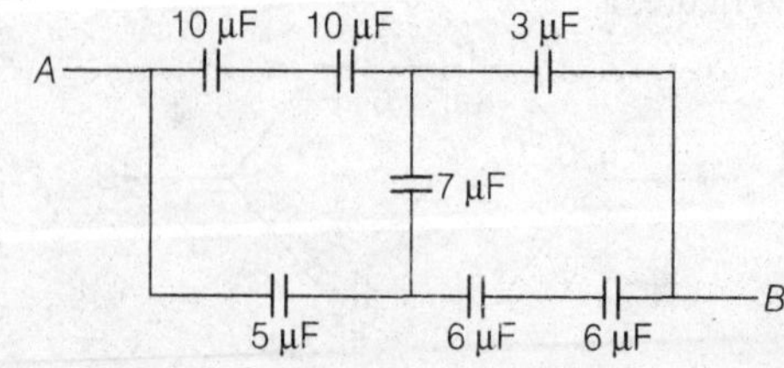

(a) 3.75 μF (b) 5.25 μF (c) 6.5 μF (d) 10.5 μF

42 The equivalent capacity between the points X and Y in the circuit with $C = 1\mu F$ is **[EAMCET]**

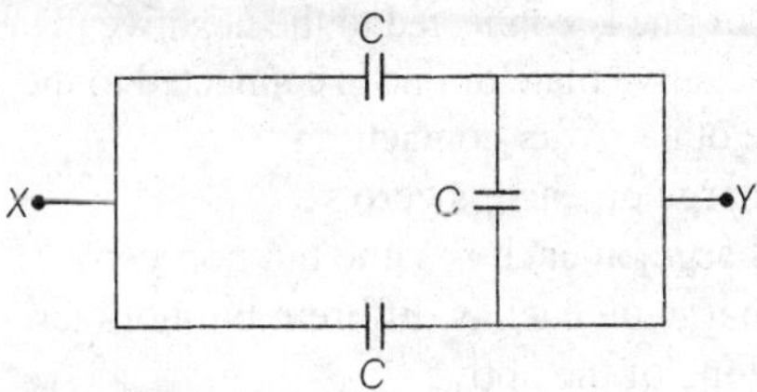

(a) $2\mu F$ (b) $3\mu F$ (c) $1\mu F$ (d) $0.5\mu F$

43 Two condensers, one of capacity C and the other of capacity $(C/2)$ are connected to a V volt battery, as shown below in the figure. The work done in charging fully both the condensers is **[CBSE AIPMT]**

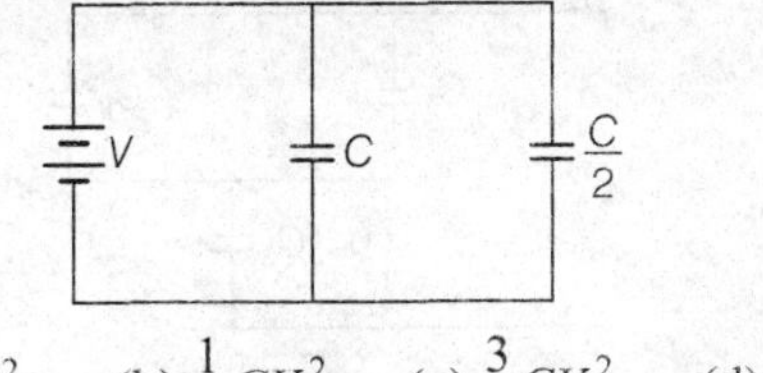

(a) $2CV^2$ (b) $\frac{1}{4}CV^2$ (c) $\frac{3}{4}CV^2$ (d) $\frac{1}{2}CV^2$

44 A dielectric of dielectric constant K is introduced such that half of its area of a capacitor of capacity C is occupied by it. The new capacity is **[J&K CET]**

(a) $2C$ (b) $C/2$
(c) $C/2(1+K)$ (d) $2C(1+K)$

45 Consider a parallel plate capacitor of $10\mu F$ with air filled in the gap between the plates. Now, one-half of the space between the plates is filled with a dielectric of dielectric constant 4, as shown in the figure. The capacity of the capacitor changes to **[Punjab PMET]**

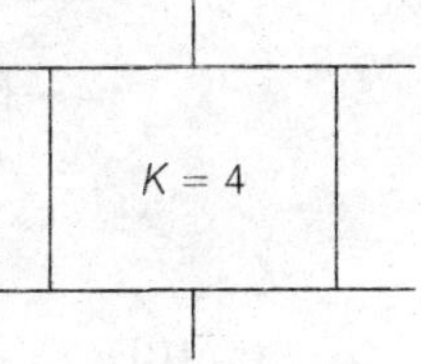

(a) $25\mu F$ (b) $20\mu F$
(c) $40\mu F$ (d) $5\mu F$

2006

46 Five capacitors, each of capacitance value C are connected as shown in the figure. The ratio of capacitance between P and R; and the capacitance between P and Q is

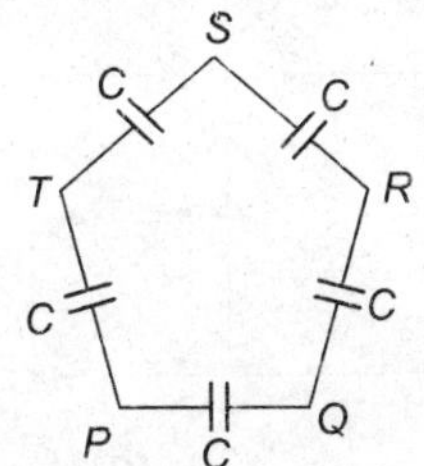

(a) 3 : 1 (b) 5 : 2
(c) 2 : 3 (d) 1 : 1 **[AIIMS]**

47 For circuit, the equivalent capacitance between P and Q is **[AMU, KCET]**

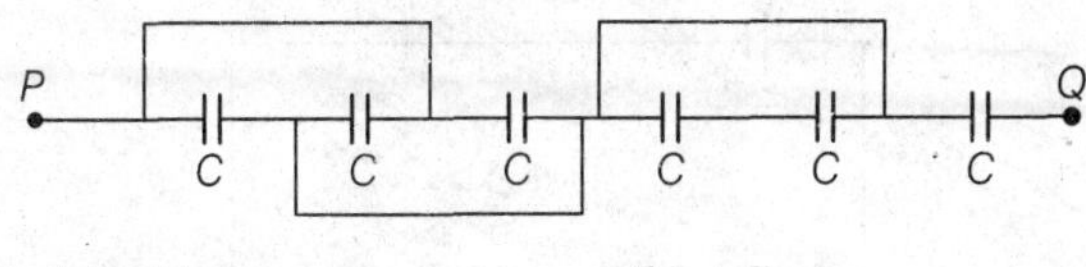

(a) $6C$ (b) $4C$
(c) $\frac{3C}{2}$ (d) $\frac{6C}{11}$

48 A gang capacitor is formed by interlocking a number of plates as shown in figure below. The distance between the consecutive plates is 0.885 cm and the overlapping area of the plates is $5 cm^2$. The capacity of the unit is **[KCET]**

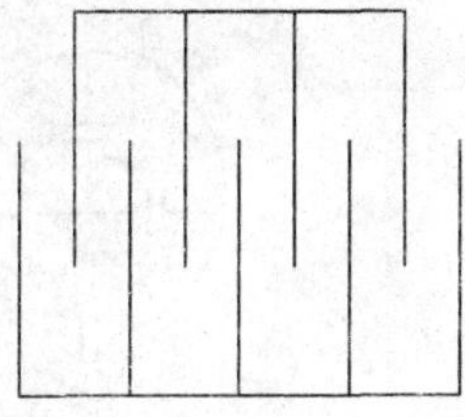

(a) 1.06 pF (b) 4 pF
(c) 6.36 pF (d) 12.72 pF

49 The combined capacitance of the arrangement shown in the figure given below, (in μF) is **[Guj CET]**

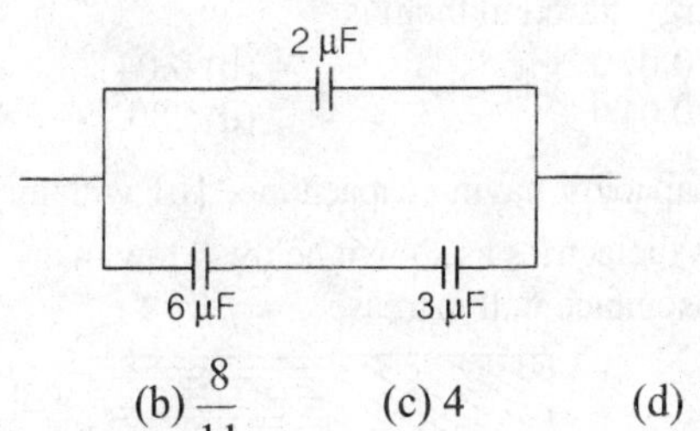

(a) $\frac{30}{11}$ (b) $\frac{8}{11}$ (c) 4 (d) 1

50 What is equivalent capacitance of the network? Each capacitor has $1\mu F$ capacitance. **[JCECE]**

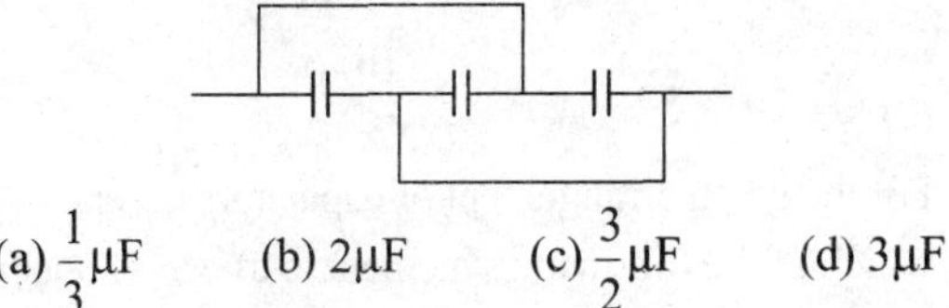

(a) $\frac{1}{3}\mu F$ (b) $2\mu F$ (c) $\frac{3}{2}\mu F$ (d) $3\mu F$

51 A $10\mu F$ capacitor is charged to a potential difference of 1000 V. The terminals of the charged capacitor are disconnected from the power supply and connected to the terminals of an uncharged $6\mu F$ capacitor. What is the final potential difference across each capacitor? **[Kerala CEE]**

(a) 167 V (b) 100 V (c) 625 V (d) 250 V
(e) None of these

52 The charge on capacitors in the following figure is **[Haryana PMT]**

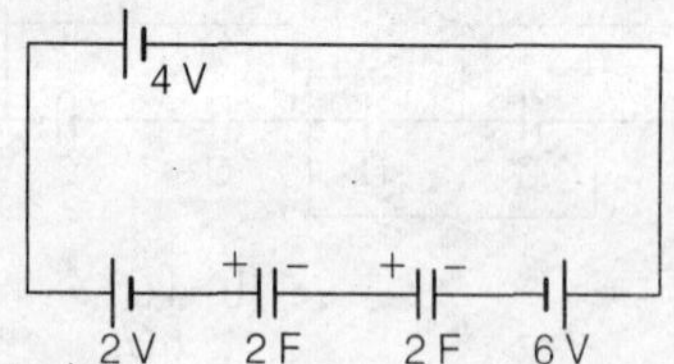

(a) $\frac{32}{3}$ C (b) 8 C
(c) zero (d) ∞

53 If each capacitor of $9\,\mu F$ is arranged as shown in figure below, then the equivalent capacitance between the points A and B is **[Haryana PMT]**

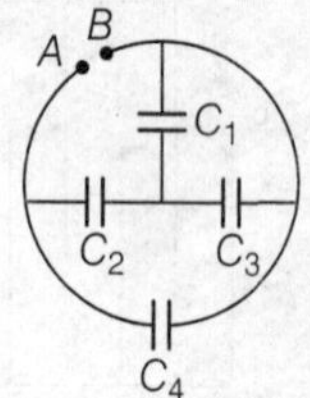

(a) $15\,\mu F$ (b) $18\,\mu F$
(c) $9\,\mu F$ (d) $4.5\,\mu F$

54 Two capacitors each of capacity $2\,\mu F$ are connected in parallel. If they are connected to 100 V battery, then energy stored in them is **[J&K CET]**
(a) 0.02 J (b) 0.04 J
(c) 0.01 J (d) 200 J

55 A capacitor having capacitance $1\,\mu F$ with air, is filled with two dielectrics as shown below. How many times capacitance will increase? **[Punjab PMET]**

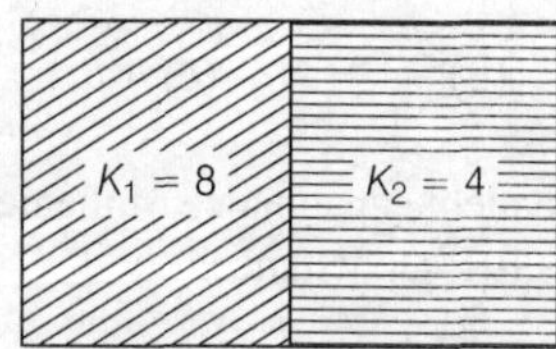

(a) 12 (b) 6
(c) 8/3 (d) 3

56 For the given arrangement of capacitors C_1 and C_2, which of the following statement is true? **[Punjab PMET]**

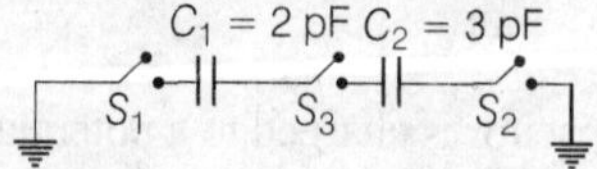

(a) When S_1 and S_3 closed, $V_1 = 30\,V, V_2 = 20\,V$
(b) When S_1 and S_3 closed, $V_1 = V_2 = 0$
(c) When S_1 is closed, $V_1 = 15\,V, V_2 = 20\,V$
(d) When S_3 is closed, $V_1 = V_2 = 20\,V$

57 Across each of two capacitors of capacitance $1\,\mu F$, a potential difference of 10 V is applied. Then, positive plate of one is connected to the negative plate of the other and negative plate of one is connected to the positive plate of the other. After contact, **[DUMET]**
(a) charge on each is zero
(b) charge on each is same but non-zero
(c) charge on each is different but non-zero
(d) None of the above

2005

58 In the given network capacitance $C_2 = 10\,\mu F, C_1 = 5\,\mu F$ and $C_3 = 4\,\mu F$. The resultant capacitance between P and Q will be **[RPMT]**

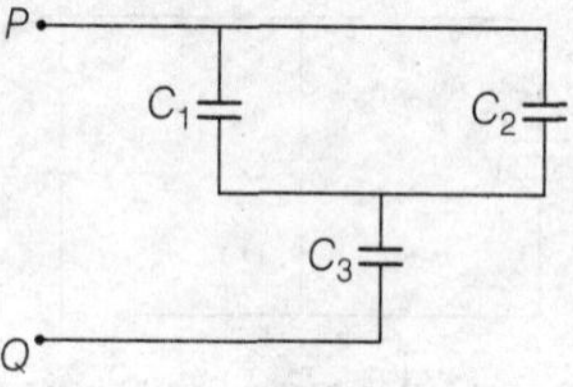

(a) $4.7\,\mu F$ (b) $1.2\,\mu F$
(c) $3.2\,\mu F$ (d) $2.2\,\mu F$

59 The equivalent capacitance between the points A and B in the following circuit is **[BCECE]**

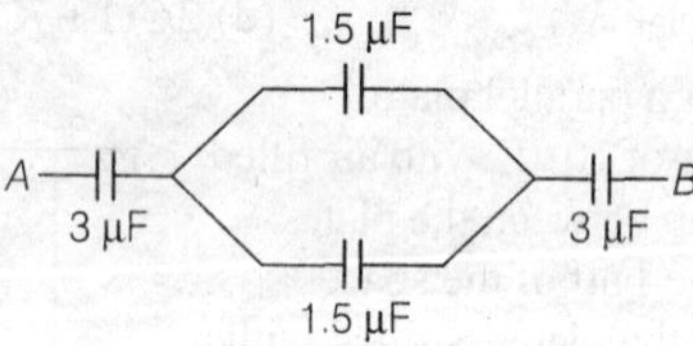

(a) $1\,\mu F$ (b) $2\,\mu F$
(c) $4\,\mu F$ (d) $8\,\mu F$

60 Two identical capacitors C_1 and C_2 of equal capacitance are connected as shown in the circuit. Terminals a and b of the key K are connected to charge capacitor C_1 using battery of emf V volt. Now, disconnecting a and b, the terminals b and c are connected. Due to this, what will be the percentage loss of energy? **[NEET (Odisha)]**

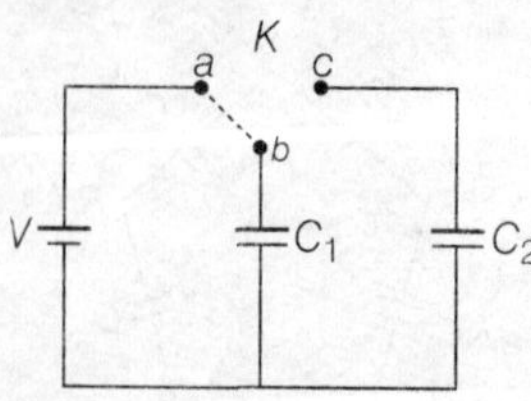

(a) 75% (b) 0%
(c) 50% (d) 25%

61 In the given circuit, find the heat produced between A and B (given $C = 1\mu F$) **[JIPMER]**

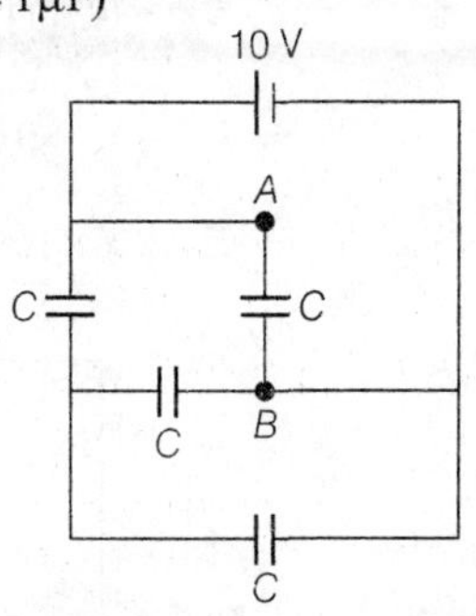

(a) $50\mu J$ (b) $60\mu J$ (c) $70\mu J$ (d) $100\mu J$

62 A capacitor of $2\mu F$ is charged as shown in the figure. When the switch S is turned to position 2, the percentage of its stored energy dissipated is **[NEET]**

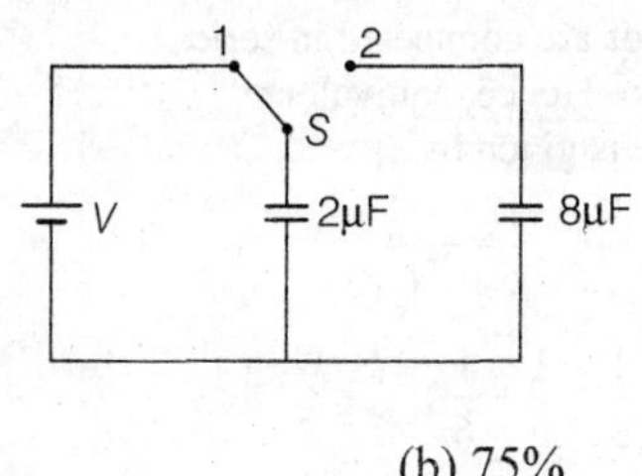

(a) 20% (b) 75%
(c) 80% (d) 0%

Answers

1 (c)	2 (a)	3 (c)	4 (b)	5 (d)	6 (b)	7 (d)	8 (a)	9 (a)	10 (a)
11 (a)	12 (c)	13 (c)	14 (d)	15 (d)	16 (c)	17 (a)	18 (b)	19 (a)	20 (c)
21 (b)	22 (d)	23 (d)	24 (c)	25 (a)	26 (a)	27 (c)	28 (c)	29 (b)	30 (b)
31 (a)	32 (c)	33 (c)	34 (b)	35 (a)	36 (a)	37 (d)	38 (c)	39 (a)	40 (a)
41 (a)	42 (a)	43 (c)	44 (c)	45 (a)	46 (c)	47 (d)	48 (b)	49 (c)	50 (d)
51 (c)	52 (b)	53 (a)	54 (a)	55 (b)	56 (a)	57 (c)	58 (c)	59 (a)	60 (c)
61 (a)	62 (c)								

Explanations

1 *(c)* This combination forms a GP,

$$S = 1 + \frac{1}{2} + \frac{1}{4} + \frac{1}{8} + \ldots\ldots\ldots\ldots\ldots$$

Sum of infinite GP, $S = \frac{a}{1-r}$

$$\Rightarrow S = \frac{1}{1-1/2} = \frac{1}{\frac{1}{2}} = 2$$

Hence, capacitance of combination,

$$C_\infty = 2 \times 1\mu F = 2\mu F$$

2 *(a)* This combination is same as the two capacitors are connected in series and distance between plate of each capacitor is $d/2$. So,

$$C_1 = \frac{K\varepsilon_0 A}{d/2} \quad \text{and}$$

$$C_2 = \frac{\varepsilon_0 A}{d/2}$$

Hence, $C_{net} = \frac{C_1 C_2}{C_1 + C_2}$

$$= \frac{\left(\frac{2K\varepsilon_0 A}{d}\right)\left(\frac{2\varepsilon_0 A}{d}\right)}{\left(\frac{2K\varepsilon_0 A}{d} + \frac{2\varepsilon_0 A}{d}\right)}$$

$$C_{net} = \frac{2KA\varepsilon_0}{(K+1)d}$$

3 *(c)* The two capacitors are in parallel. The equivalent capacitance,

$$C' = C + \frac{C}{2} = \frac{3C}{2}$$

Work done in charging the equivalent capacitor is stored in the form of potential energy,

$$W = U = 1/2C'V^2$$

$$W = \frac{1}{2} \times \frac{3C}{2} \times V^2$$

$$W = \frac{3}{4}CV^2$$

4 *(b)*

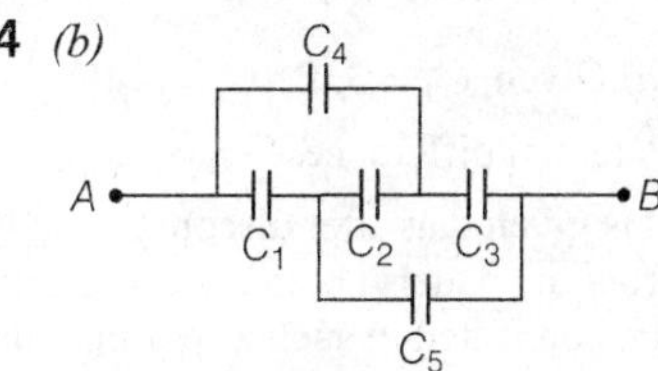

Clearly, the capacitors form Wheatstone bridge arrangement.

$$C_1 = C_3 = C_4 = C_5$$

$$\Rightarrow \frac{C_4}{C_1} = \frac{C_3}{C_5}$$

By symmetry, $q_1 = q_4$, $q_3 = q_5$

Also, $q_1 + q_4 = q_3 + q_5$

$$\Rightarrow q_1 = q_4 = q_5 = q_3$$

$$\Rightarrow q_2 = 0$$

Hence, the bridge is balanced. The point S and T are in the same potential. No charge can accumulate on C_2 which thus become ineffective.

Between A and B, two series combination (C_4, C_3) and (C_1, C_5) are connected in parallel.

Then, effective capacitance,

$$\frac{1}{C'} = \frac{1}{C_1} + \frac{1}{C_5} = \frac{1}{4} + \frac{1}{4}$$

$$\Rightarrow C' = \frac{4}{2} = 2\ \mu F$$

Similarly, $C'' = 2\mu F$

Hence, equivalent capacitance between A and B is

$$C = C' + C''$$

$$= 2 + 2 = 4\mu F$$

Due to balanced Wheatstone bridge arrangement, charge q on C_2 is zero. Hence, net capacitance between A and B will be $4\mu F$.

5 *(d)* Capacitor are connected in series combination. Hence, equivalent capacitance is given by

$$\frac{1}{C}=\frac{1}{C_1}+\frac{1}{C_2}+\frac{1}{C_3}$$

$$\Rightarrow \quad \frac{1}{C}=\frac{1}{3}+\frac{1}{6}+\frac{1}{6}$$

$$\Rightarrow \quad C=\frac{6}{4}=1.5\,\mu F$$

The charge on the capacitor,

$$q=CV$$
$$=1.5\times 120$$
$$=180\,\mu C$$

In the series combination of capacitors, each capacitor have equal charge. Hence, potential difference across the $3\,\mu F$,

$$q=CV$$
$$V=\frac{q}{C}=\frac{180}{3}=60\,V$$

6 *(b)* The points C and D will be at same potentials, since $\frac{3}{6}=\frac{4}{8}$. Therefore, capacitance of $2\,\mu F$ will be ineffective.

So, the equivalent circuit can be shown as the effective capacitance in upper arm in series, is given by

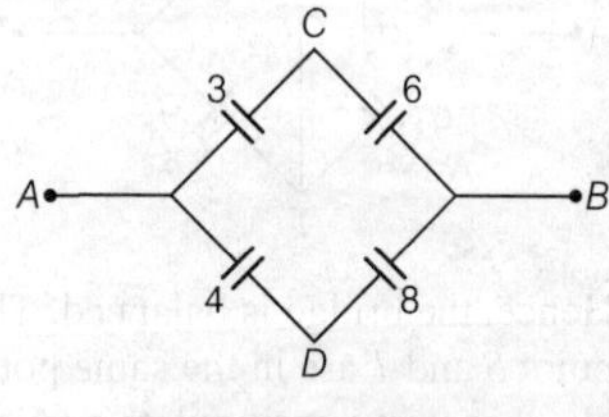

$$C_1=\frac{3\times 6}{3+6}=\frac{18}{9}=2\,\mu F$$

The effective capacitance in lower arm in series, is given by

$$C_2=\frac{4\times 8}{4+8}=\frac{32}{12}=\frac{8}{3}\,\mu F$$

Hence, the resultant capacitance in parallel is given by

$$C=C_1+C_2$$
$$=2+\frac{8}{3}=\frac{14}{3}\,\mu F$$

7 *(d)* Consider the following circuit

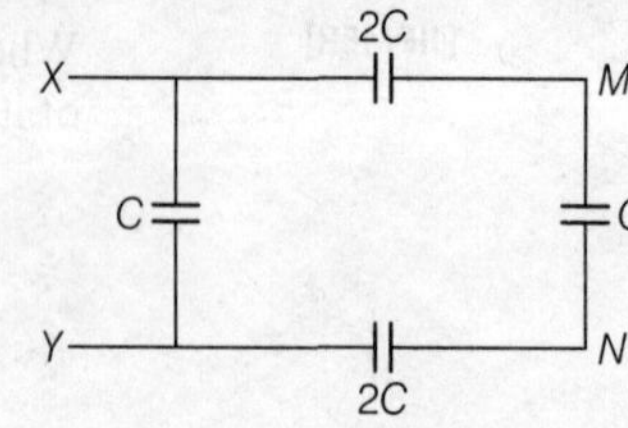

Equivalent circuit can be drawn as

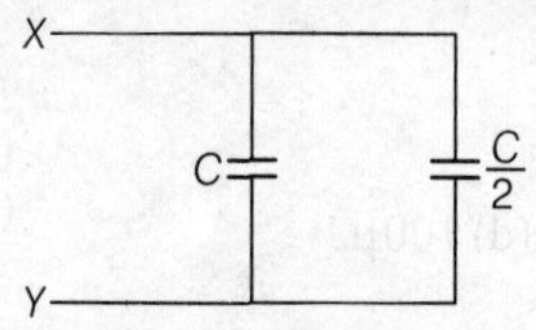

According to the question,

$$V_{XY}=60\,V \Rightarrow V_{C/2}=60\,V$$

We know that, charge (Q) = capacitance $(C)\times$ voltage (V)

$$\therefore \quad \frac{Q_{C/2}}{C/2}=60\,V$$

$$\Rightarrow Q_{C/2}=(60)(C/2)=30C$$

Now $\quad Q_{MN}=Q_{C/2}=30C$

$$\Rightarrow \quad (C_{MN})V_{MN}=30\,C$$
$$\Rightarrow \quad (C)(V_{MN})=30\,C$$
$$\Rightarrow \quad V_{MN}=30\,V$$

8 *(a)* The capacitor with air as the dielectric has capacitance,

$$C_1=\frac{\varepsilon_0}{d}\left(\frac{3A}{4}\right)=\frac{3\varepsilon_0 A}{4d}$$

Similarly, the capacitor with K as the dielectric constant has capacitance,

$$C_2=\frac{\varepsilon_0 K}{d}\left(\frac{A}{4}\right)=\frac{\varepsilon_0 AK}{4d}$$

Since, C_1 and C_2 are in parallel.

$$C_{net}=C_1+C_2$$
$$=\frac{3\varepsilon_0 A}{4d}+\frac{\varepsilon_0 AK}{4d}$$
$$=\frac{\varepsilon_0 A}{d}\left(\frac{3}{4}+\frac{K}{4}\right)=\frac{C}{4}(K+3)$$

9 *(a)* Given, $C_1=3\mu F$, $C_2=4\mu F$

Potential difference, $V=6\,V$

It is given that after disconnection from the battery, both the capacitors are connected in such a way that the negative plate of one capacitor is attached to the positive plate of the other. It means, they are connected in parallel.

$$\Rightarrow C_{eq}=C_1+C_2=(3+4)\,\mu F$$
$$7\mu F=7\times 10^{-6}\,F$$

$\therefore$ Energy stored,

$$E=\frac{1}{2}(C_{eq})V^2=\frac{1}{2}\times 7\times 10^{-6}\times (6)^2$$

$$\Rightarrow E=\frac{1}{2}\times 7\times 10^{-6}\times 36$$

$$\Rightarrow E=1.26\times 10^{-4}\,J$$

10 *(a)*

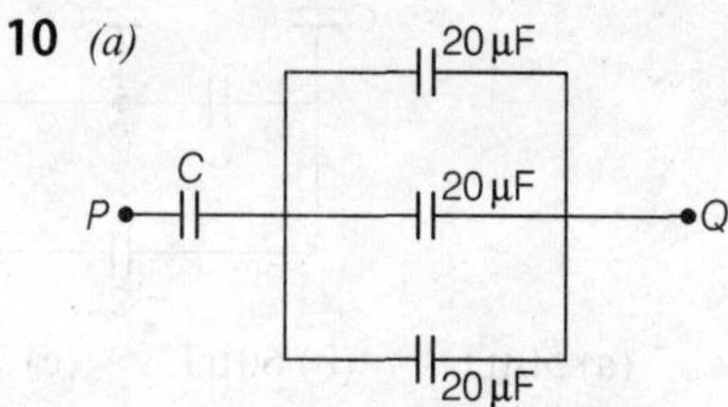

$$C'=C_1+C_2+C_3$$
$$=20+20+20=60\,\mu F$$

$$\frac{1}{C''}=\frac{1}{C}+\frac{1}{60}$$

$$\Rightarrow \quad \frac{1}{30}=\frac{1}{C}+\frac{1}{60}$$

$$\Rightarrow \quad \frac{1}{C}=\frac{1}{30}-\frac{1}{60}$$

$$\Rightarrow \quad \frac{1}{C}=\frac{2-1}{60} \Rightarrow \frac{1}{C}=\frac{1}{60}$$

$$\Rightarrow \quad C=60\,\mu F$$

11 *(a)* If two capacitors having capacitances C_1 and C_2 respectively, are connected in parallel, then

$$C_{eq}=C_1+C_2$$

The final potential difference across each capacitor

$$V'=\frac{C_1 V}{C_1+C_2}$$

12 *(c)* Here, $\frac{\frac{16}{5}C}{\frac{16}{5}+C}=3$

$$\Rightarrow \quad \frac{16}{5}C=\frac{48}{5}+3C$$

$$\Rightarrow \quad \frac{C}{5}=\frac{48}{5}$$

$$\Rightarrow \quad C=48\mu F$$

13 *(c)* Charge, $q=nCV$

$$1=n\times 1\times 10^{-6}\times 110$$

$$n=\frac{1}{110\times 10^{-6}}$$

$$\Rightarrow \quad n=\frac{100000}{11}\approx 9090$$

14 *(d)* ***Case* I** When the capacitors are joined in series,

$$U_{\text{series}} = \frac{1}{2}\frac{C_1}{n_1}(4V)^2$$

***Case* II** When the capacitors are joined in parallel,

$$U_{\text{parallel}} = \frac{1}{2}(n_2C_2)V^2$$

Given, $U_{\text{series}} = U_{\text{parallel}}$

or $\frac{1}{2}\frac{C_1}{n_1}(4V)^2 = \frac{1}{2}(n_2C_2)V^2$

$\Rightarrow \quad C_2 = \frac{16\,C_1}{n_1\,n_2}$

15 *(d)* The total capacity of capacitor,

$$C = \frac{9\times 4.5}{13.5}\,\mu\text{F}$$

or $\quad C = 3\,\mu\text{F}$

Charge, $Q = CV$

$= 3\times 13 = 39\,\mu\text{C}$

Potential difference across $4.5\,\mu\text{F}$

$= \frac{39}{4.5}\text{V} \approx 8\text{V}$

16 *(c)* Minimum number of condensers in each row $= \frac{3000}{500} = 6$

If C_S is capacity of 6 condensers in a row,

$$\frac{1}{C_S} = \frac{1}{1}+\frac{1}{1}+\frac{1}{1}+\frac{1}{1}+\frac{1}{1}+\frac{1}{1} = 6$$

$\Rightarrow C_S = \frac{1}{6}\,\mu\text{F}$

Let there be m such rows in parallel.

Total capacity $= m\times C_S$

$2 = m\times 1/6$

$\Rightarrow \quad m = 12$

Total number of capacitors

$= 6\times 12 = 72$

17 *(a)* For option (a),

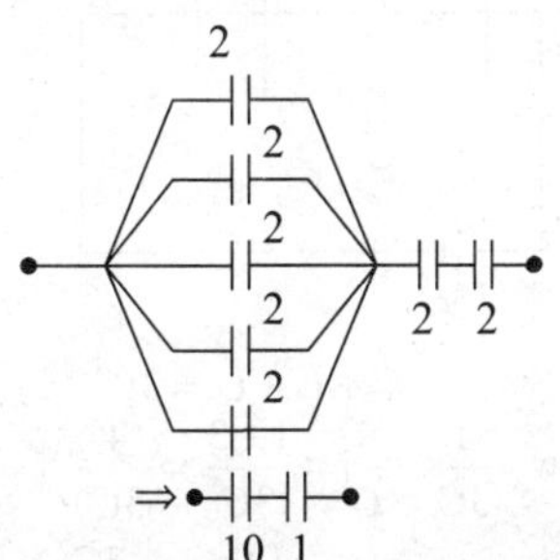

$$C_{\text{eq}} = \frac{10\times 1}{10+1} = \frac{10}{11}\,\mu\text{F}$$

For option (b),

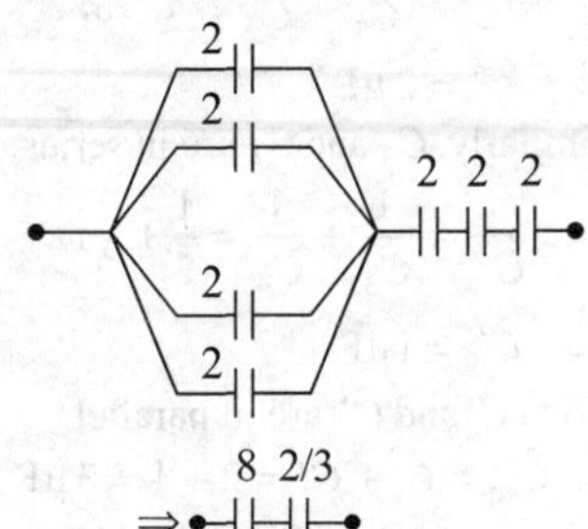

$$C_{\text{eq}} = \frac{8\times 2/3}{8+2/3} = \frac{8}{13}\,\mu\text{F}$$

For option (c),

2 2 2 2 2 2 2

$\Rightarrow$ 6 1/2

$$C_{\text{eq}} = \frac{6\times 1/2}{6+1/2} = \frac{6}{13}\,\mu\text{F}$$

For option (d),

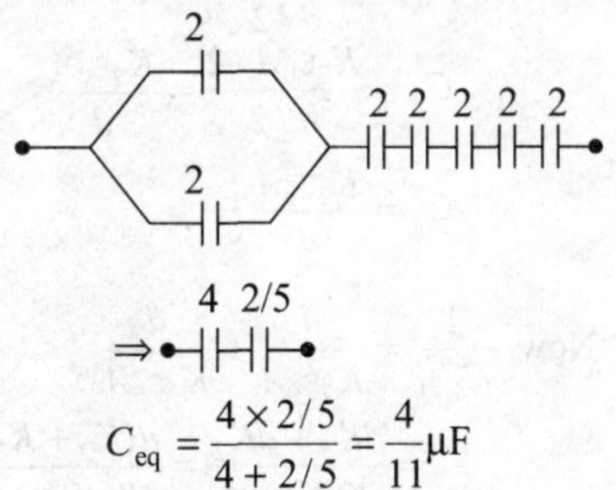

$$C_{\text{eq}} = \frac{4\times 2/5}{4+2/5} = \frac{4}{11}\,\mu\text{F}$$

Hence, combination of option (a) will provide derived result.

18 *(b)*

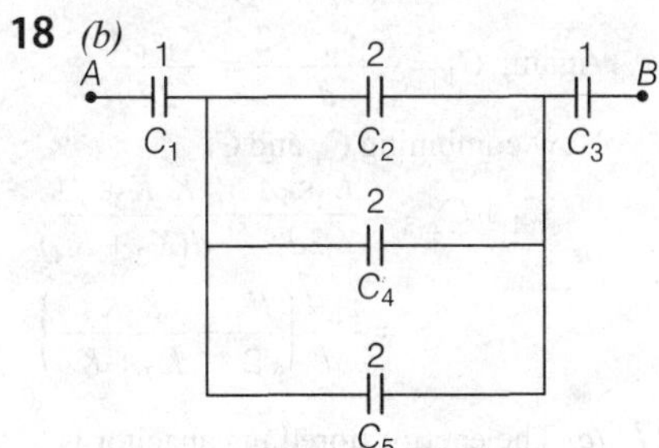

Here, C_2, C_4 and C_5 are in parallel combination.

So, $C_2 + C_4 + C_5 = 2+2+2$

$= 6 = C_{2\text{eq}}$

Now, C_1, C_2 equivalent and C_3 are in series.

So, $\frac{1}{C} = \frac{1}{C_1}+\frac{1}{C_{2\text{eq}}}+\frac{1}{C_3}$

$= 1+\frac{1}{6}+1$

$= \frac{6+1+6}{6} = \frac{13}{6}$

$\therefore \quad C = \frac{6}{13}$

19 *(a)* According to the question,

***Case* I** When capacitors are connected in parallel,

$C_1 + C_2 + C_3 + \cdots + C_n = 90\,\mu\text{F}$

$\Rightarrow \quad nC = 90\,\mu\text{F}$ ...(i)

***Case* II** When capacitors are connected in series,

$$\frac{1}{C_n} = \frac{1}{C_1}+\frac{1}{C_2}+\cdots+\frac{1}{C_n}$$

$$\frac{1}{C_n} = \frac{n\cdot C^{n-1}}{C^n}$$

$\Rightarrow \quad C_n = \frac{C^n}{nC^{n-1}} = 2.5$

$\Rightarrow \quad \frac{C\cdot C^{n-1}}{nC^{n-1}} = 2.5$

$\Rightarrow \quad \frac{C}{n} = 2.5 \Rightarrow C = 2.5n$ ...(ii)

Putting the value of C in Eq. (i), we get

$2.5n^2 = 90$

$\Rightarrow \quad n^2 = \frac{90}{2.5} = \frac{900}{25} = 36$

$\Rightarrow \quad n = 6$

Now, putting the value of n in Eq. (ii), we get

$C = 2.5\times 6 = 15 = 15\,\mu\text{F}$

20 *(c)* The arrangement of three identical capacitors to obtain distinct effective capacitances is 4, i.e.

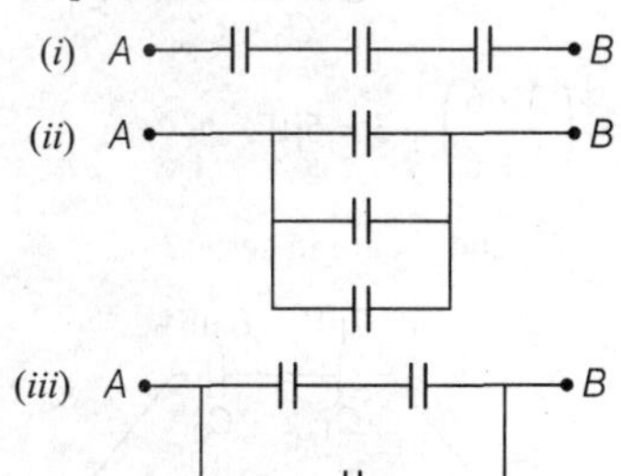

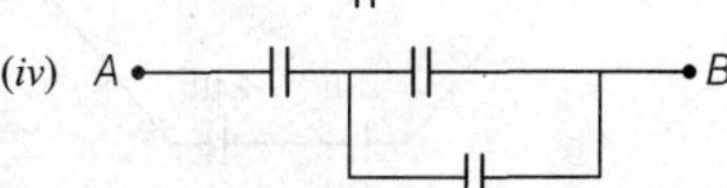

21 *(b)* Here, C_1 and C_2 are in series. Hence, their effective capacitance C' is given by

$$\frac{1}{C'} = \frac{1}{C_1} + \frac{1}{C_2}$$

$$\Rightarrow \frac{1}{C'} = \frac{1}{20} + \frac{1}{20}$$

$$\Rightarrow C' = 10\,\mu F$$

Similarly, $\frac{1}{C''} = \frac{1}{C_3} + \frac{1}{C_4}$

$$\Rightarrow \frac{1}{C''} = \frac{1}{10} + \frac{1}{10}$$

$$\Rightarrow C'' = 5\,\mu F$$

Now, C' and C'' are in parallel.

Hence, resultant capacitance C will be

$$C = C' + C'' = 10 + 5 = 15\,\mu F$$

22 *(d)*

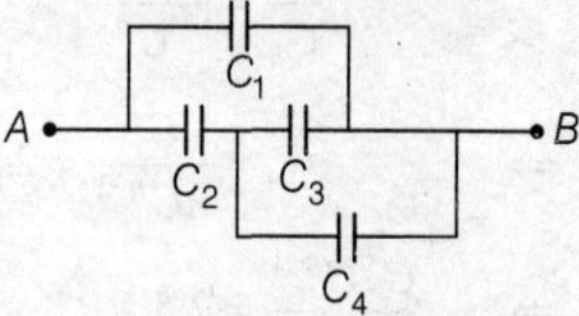

$$C_1 = C_2 = C_3 = C_4 = 3\mu F \text{ (given)}$$

$\because C_4$ and C_3 are in parallel, i.e.

$$C_{eq} = C_4 + C_3 = (3+3)\,\mu F = 6\mu F$$

Now arrangement of capacitors will be as follows

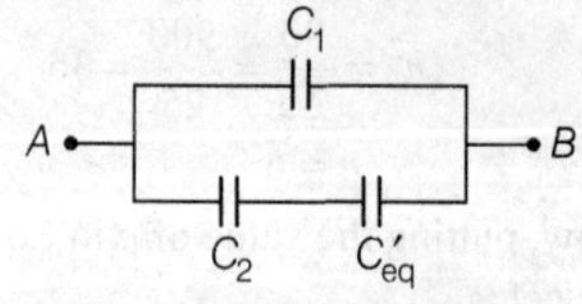

$\because C_1$ is in parallel with the series combination of C_2 and C'_{eq}.

$\therefore C''_{eq}$ between A and B

$$= \frac{(C_2 \times C'_{eq})}{C_2 + C'_{eq}} + C_1$$

$$\Rightarrow \left(\frac{3 \times 6}{3+6}\right) + 3 = 5\mu F$$

23 *(d)* C_1 and C_2 are in series,

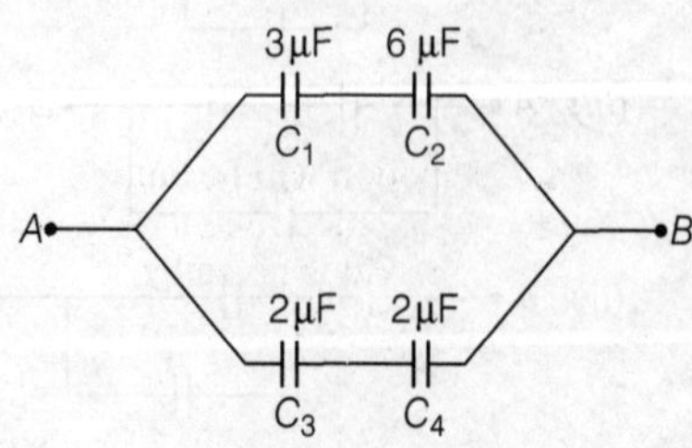

$$\frac{1}{C'} = \frac{1}{C_1} + \frac{1}{C_2} = \frac{1}{3} + \frac{1}{6}$$

$$\Rightarrow C' = 2\,\mu F$$

Similarly, C_3 and C_4 are in series,

$$\frac{1}{C''} = \frac{1}{C_3} + \frac{1}{C_4} = \frac{1}{2} + \frac{1}{2}$$

$$\Rightarrow C'' = 1\,\mu F$$

Now, C' and C'' are in parallel

So, $C_{eq} = C' + C'' = 2 + 1 = 3\,\mu F$

24 *(c)* In series combination,

$$\frac{1}{C_1} = \frac{1}{1} + \frac{1}{2} + \frac{1}{4} = \frac{4+2+1}{4} = \frac{7}{4}$$

$$\Rightarrow C_1 = \frac{4}{7}\,\mu F$$

In parallel combination,

$$C_2 = 1 + 2 + 4 = 7\,\mu F$$

$$\Rightarrow \frac{C_1}{C_2} = \frac{4/7}{7} = \frac{4}{49}$$

25 *(a)* By using charge conservation,

$$0.2 \times 600 = (0.2 + 1)\,V$$

$$\Rightarrow V = \frac{0.2 \times 600}{1.2} = 100\,V$$

26 *(a)* Here, $C_2 = \frac{K_2 \varepsilon_0 A_2}{d/2}$,

$$C_2 = \frac{K_2 \varepsilon_0 A/2}{d/2} = \frac{K_2 \varepsilon_0 A}{d}$$

$$C_3 = \frac{K_3 \varepsilon_0 A}{d}$$

Now, $\frac{1}{C_{2-3}} = \frac{d}{K_2 \varepsilon_0 A} + \frac{d}{K_3 \varepsilon_0 A}$

$$= \frac{dK_3 + dK_2}{K_2 K_3 \varepsilon_0 A} = \frac{d(K_2 + K_3)}{K_2 K_3 \varepsilon_0 A}$$

$$C_{2-3} = \frac{K_2 K_3 \varepsilon_0 A}{d(K_2 + K_3)}$$

Again, $C_1 = \frac{K_1 \varepsilon_0 A/2}{d} = \frac{K_1 \varepsilon_0 A}{2d}$

Now combining C_1 and C_{2-3},

$$C_1 + C_{2-3} = \frac{K_1 \varepsilon_0 A}{2d} + \frac{K_2 K_3 \varepsilon_0 A}{d(K_2 + K_3)}$$

$$= \frac{\varepsilon_0 A}{d}\left(\frac{K_1}{2} + \frac{K_2 K_3}{K_2 + K_3}\right)$$

27 *(c)* The energy stored in capacitor is given by $E = \frac{1}{2} CV^2$.

Resultant capacitance,

$$C' = C_1 + C_2 = 4 + 6 = 10\text{ pF}$$

$$E = \frac{1}{2} \times 10 \times 10^{-12} \times (100)^2 \quad (\because 1\text{pF} = 10^{-12}\text{ F})$$

$$= 5 \times 10^{-8}\text{ J}$$

28 *(c)* Given, capacitance of each capacitor $= C$ and breakdown voltage $= V$

Here, each capacitance can have a maximum charge of CV.

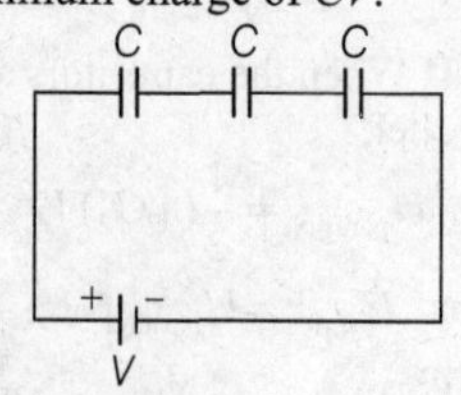

Now, capacitance of series combination is given by

$$\frac{1}{C_{eq}} = \frac{1}{C} + \frac{1}{C} + \frac{1}{C} = \frac{3}{C}$$

$$\Rightarrow C_{eq} = \frac{C}{3}$$

Now, breakdown voltage is given by V'

Then, $CV = \frac{C}{3} V'$

$$\Rightarrow V' = \frac{3CV}{C} = 3V$$

29 *(b)* For series combination of capacitance is given by

$$\frac{1}{C_1} = \frac{1}{C} + \frac{1}{C} + \frac{1}{C} + \frac{1}{C}$$

$$\frac{1}{C_1} = \frac{4}{C}$$

$$\Rightarrow C_1 = \frac{C}{4}$$

Now, parallel combination of capacitances is given by

$$C_2 = C + C + C + C = 4C$$

Now, $\frac{C_1}{C_2} = \frac{C}{4} \times \frac{1}{4C} = \frac{1}{16}$

30 *(b)* According to question, effective capacitance of parallel capacitors

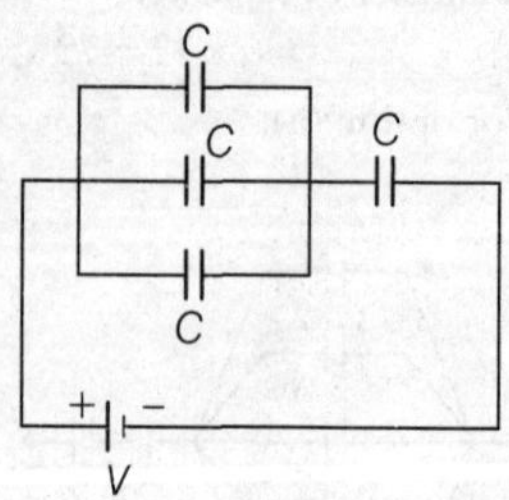

$$= C + C + C = 3C$$

Now, $\frac{1}{3C} + \frac{1}{C} = \frac{1+3}{3C} = \frac{4}{3C}$

$\therefore$ According to question, $\frac{3C}{4} = 3.75$

$$C = \frac{3.75 \times 4}{3} = 5\,\mu F$$

31 (a) Here in the modified figure of question, all the capacitors are in parallel.

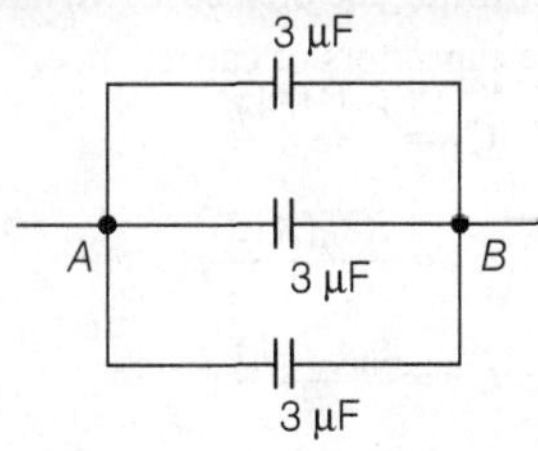

So, effective capacitance is given by

$$C_{AB} = C_1 + C_2 + C_3$$

$$C_{AB} = 3 + 3 + 3 = 9\,\mu F$$

32 (c) Label the figure

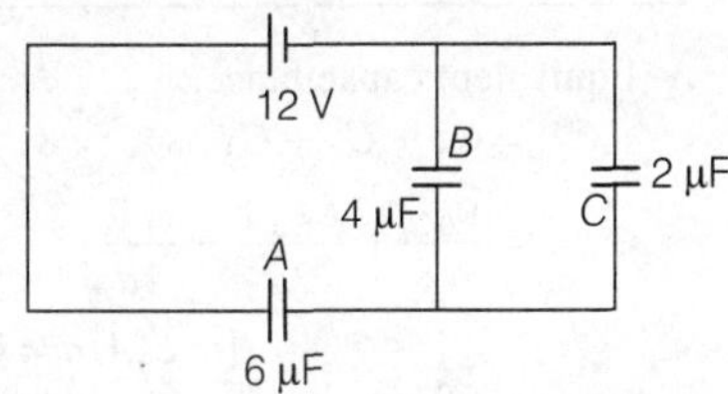

Here, capacitors B and C are in parallel. So, their total capacitance is given by, $4 + 2 = 6\,\mu F$

Now, total capacity of $6\,\mu F$ and capacitor A are in series with respect to battery

$$\therefore \quad \frac{1}{C_T} = \frac{1}{6} + \frac{1}{6} = \frac{2}{6} = \frac{1}{3}$$

$$C_T = 3\,\mu F$$

Now, total charge

$$= C_T V = 3 \times 12 = 36\,\mu C$$

This is the charge on A and also on charge B and C.

Thus, voltage on combination of capacitors B and C, $\frac{Q}{6} = \frac{36}{6} = 6$ V

Now, charge on capacitor B is given by

$$C_B \times V = 4 \times 6$$

$$= 24\mu C = 24 \times 10^{-6}\ C$$

33 (c) Suppose the pair of plates a is connected to positive terminal of the battery and the pair of plate b is connected to negative terminal of the battery. Thus, from figure, we can conclude that, we have three capacitors I, II and III.

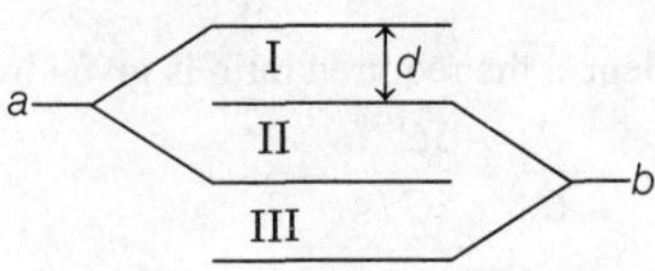

Their positive plates are connected to each other and so are the negative plates. Therefore, these are joined in parallel, i.e.

$$C_p = C_1 + C_2 + C_3 = 3\varepsilon_0 A / d$$

34 (b) Initial capacitance

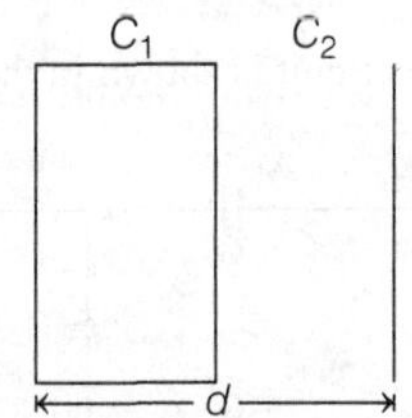

$$C = \varepsilon_0 A / d$$

When it is half filled by a dielectric of dielectric constant K, then

$$C_1 = \frac{K\varepsilon_0 A}{d/2} = 2K\frac{\varepsilon_0 A}{d}$$

$$\text{and } C_2 = \frac{\varepsilon_0 A}{d/2} = \frac{2\varepsilon_0 A}{d}$$

$$\therefore \quad \frac{1}{C'} = \frac{1}{C_1} + \frac{1}{C_2} = \frac{d}{2\varepsilon_0 A}\left(\frac{1}{K} + 1\right)$$

$$= \frac{d}{2\varepsilon_0 A}\left(\frac{1}{5} + 1\right) = \frac{6}{10}\frac{d}{\varepsilon_0 A}$$

$$\Rightarrow C' = 5\varepsilon_0 A / 3d$$

Hence, increase in capacitance

$$= \frac{\frac{5}{3}\frac{\varepsilon_0 A}{d} - \frac{\varepsilon_0 A}{d}}{\varepsilon_0 A / d} \times 100$$

$$= \frac{2}{3} \times 100 = 66.6\%$$

35 (a) All the capacitors are connected in parallel.

Therefore, the effective capacitance between A and B

$$= 6\,C = 6 \times 2 = 12\mu F$$

36 (a) Effective capacitance of C_2 and C_3,

$$\frac{1}{C} = \frac{1}{2} + \frac{1}{2}$$

$$\Rightarrow \quad C = 1\mu F$$

Now, C_1 and C are in parallel, therefore effective capacitance,

$$C' = 1 + 1 = 2\mu F$$

Now, C' and C_4 are in series, therefore effective capacitance between points A and B,

$$\frac{1}{C''} = \frac{1}{2} + \frac{1}{4} = \frac{3}{4}$$

$$\Rightarrow \quad C'' = \frac{4}{3}\,\mu F$$

37 (d) In series arrangement, potential difference is the sum of the individual potential difference of each capacitor, i.e. $V = V_1 + V_2 + V_3 + \cdots$

$$\Rightarrow \quad 600 = x \times 200 \quad \Rightarrow x = 3$$

So, there should be three capacitors in series to obtain the required potential difference.

The equivalent capacitance of the three capacitors in series is

$$\frac{1}{C_{eq}} = \frac{1}{6} + \frac{1}{6} + \frac{1}{6}$$

$$\Rightarrow \quad C_{eq} = 2\mu F$$

Now, we require $18\,\mu F$ capacitance, for this we need 9 such combinations in parallel.

Hence, required condensers $= 9 \times 3 = 27$

38 (c) $6\mu F$ and $3\mu F$ capacitors are in series

$$\therefore \quad \frac{1}{C_1} = \frac{1}{6} + \frac{1}{3}$$

$$\Rightarrow \quad C_1 = 2\mu F$$

C_1 is parallel to $2\mu F$ capacitor

$$\therefore \quad C_{eq} = 2 + 2 = 4\mu F$$

$$\text{Total energy, } U = \frac{1}{2}CV^2 = \frac{1}{2} \times 4 \times (2)^2$$

$$= 8\,\mu J$$

39 (a) Each plate is taking part in the formation of two capacitors except the plates at the ends. These capacitors are in parallel and n plates form $(n - 1)$ capacitors. Thus, equivalent capacitance between A and $B = (n - 1)C$

40 (a)

(a) The network of three capacitors can be shown in the figure below:

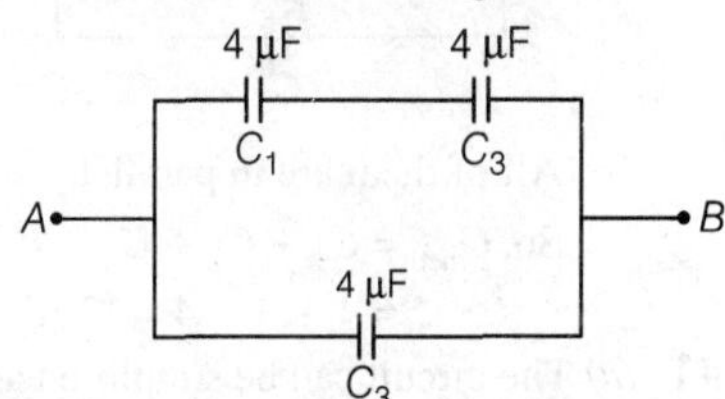

Here, C_1 and C_2 are in series and the combination of two is in parallel with C_3.

$$C_{net} = \frac{C_1 C_2}{C_1 + C_2} + C_3$$

$$= \left(\frac{4 \times 4}{4 + 4}\right) + 4$$

$$= 2 + 4 = 6\mu F$$

(b) The corresponding network can be shown in the figure below

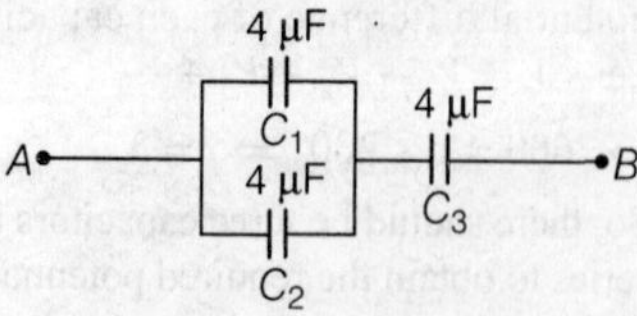

Here, C_1 and C_2 are in parallel and this combination is in series with C_3.

$$\text{So, } C_{net} = \frac{(C_1 + C_2) \times C_3}{(C_1 + C_2) + C_3}$$

$$= \frac{(4+4) \times 4}{(4+4)+4}$$

$$= \frac{32}{12} = \frac{8}{3}\mu F$$

(c) The corresponding network can be shown in the figure below

4 μF 4 μF 4 μF
A — C_1 — C_2 — C_3 — B

All of three are in series, so

$$\frac{1}{C_{net}} = \frac{1}{C_1} + \frac{1}{C_2} + \frac{1}{C_3}$$

$$= \frac{1}{4} + \frac{1}{4} + \frac{1}{4} = \frac{3}{4}$$

$$\Rightarrow C_{net} = \frac{4}{3}\mu F$$

(d) The corresponding network can be shown in the figure below

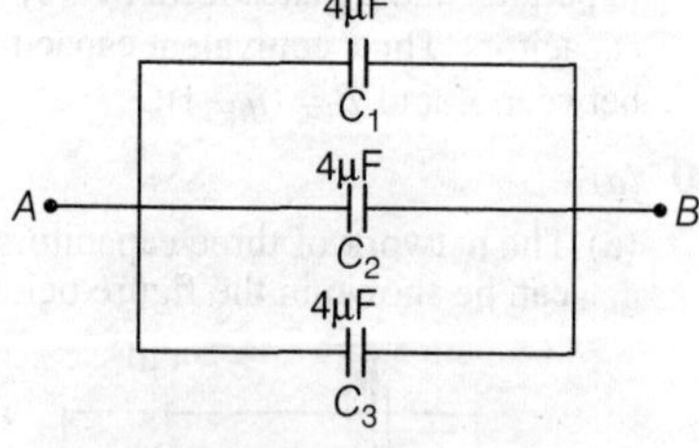

All of them are in parallel.

$$\text{So, } C_{net} = C_1 + C_2 + C_3$$

$$= 4 + 4 + 4 = 12\mu F$$

41 *(a)* The circuit can be simplified as shown in the figure below.

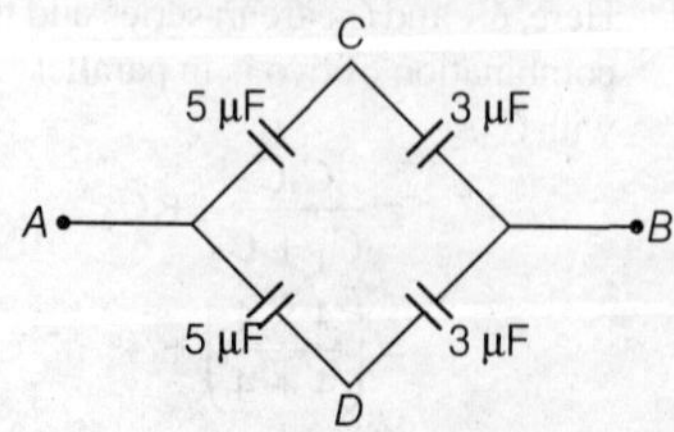

It is a balanced Wheatstone bridge.

$$\Rightarrow C_{AB} = \frac{5 \times 3}{5+3} + \frac{5 \times 3}{5+3}$$

$$\Rightarrow C_{AB} = 2 \times \frac{15}{8}$$

$$= \frac{30}{8} = 3.75\mu F$$

42 *(a)* The circuit is shown in the figure below.

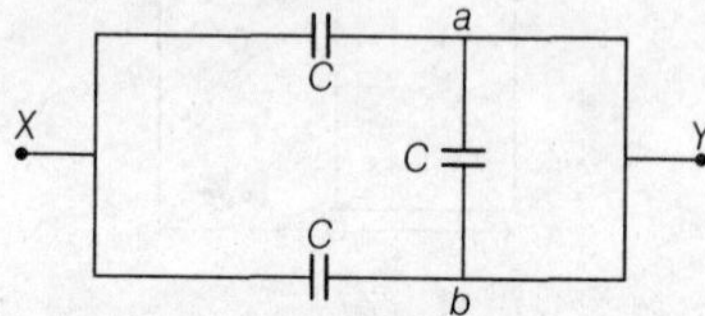

As points a and b are at same potential, so no charge flows through ab.

Hence, capacitance in ab is shorted.

Now, two remaining capacitors are in parallel, hence

$$C_{eq} = C + C = 2C$$

$$= 2 \times 1 = 2\mu F$$

43 *(c)* The two condensers in the circuit are in parallel order, hence

$$C' = C + \frac{C}{2} = \frac{3C}{2}$$

The work done in charging the equivalent capacitor is stored in the form of potential energy.

$$\text{Hence, } W = U = \frac{1}{2}C'V^2$$

$$= \frac{1}{2}\left(\frac{3C}{2}\right)V^2$$

$$= \frac{3}{4}CV^2$$

44 *(c)* The dielectric is introduced such that, half of its area is occupied by it.

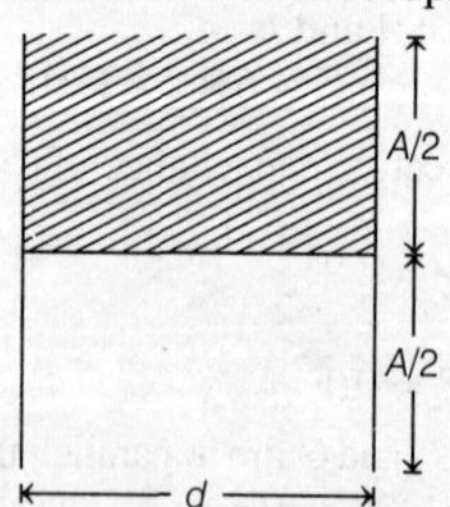

In the given case, the two capacitors are in parallel.

$$\therefore \quad C' = C_1 + C_2$$

$$C_1 = \frac{A\varepsilon_0}{2d} \text{ and } C_2 = \frac{KA\varepsilon_0}{2d}$$

$$\text{Thus, } C' = \frac{A\varepsilon_0}{2d} + \frac{KA\varepsilon_0}{2d} = \frac{C}{2}(1+K)$$

45 *(a)* Initially, the capacitance of capacitor, $C = 10\mu F$

After filling the dielectric, we have these capacitors of capacitance,

$$C_1 = \frac{\varepsilon_0(A/4)}{d}$$

$$C_2 = \frac{K\varepsilon_0(A/2)}{d},$$

$$C_3 = \frac{\varepsilon_0(A/4)}{d}$$

A/4 A/2 A/4
K
d 1 2 3

$\therefore$ Equivalent capacitance,

$$C_{eq} = C_1 + C_2 + C_3$$

$$= \frac{\varepsilon_0 A}{4d} + \frac{K\varepsilon_0 A}{2d} + \frac{\varepsilon_0 A}{4d}$$

$$[\because \varepsilon_0 A/d = C]$$

$$= \frac{10}{4}C = 25\,\mu F$$

46 *(c)* If a source is connected between points P and R, same charge will flow through two capacitors in arms PQ and QR. Similarly, same charge will flow through capacitors in arms PT, TS and SR.

So, equivalent capacitance of right side,

$$C' = \frac{C \times C}{C + C} = \frac{C}{2}$$

and equivalent capacitance of left side,

$$\frac{1}{C''} = \frac{1}{C} + \frac{1}{C} + \frac{1}{C} = \frac{3}{C}$$

$$\Rightarrow \quad C'' = \frac{C}{3}$$

Now, C' and C'' will in parallel combination,

$$\text{Hence, } C_1 = C' + C''$$

$$= \frac{C}{2} + \frac{C}{3} = \frac{5C}{6}$$

Similarly, if a source is connected between points P and Q, then equivalent capacitance,

$$C_2 = C + \frac{C}{4} = \frac{5C}{4}$$

Hence, the required ratio is given by

$$\frac{C_1}{C_2} = \frac{5C/6}{5C/4} = \frac{2}{3}$$

47 (d)

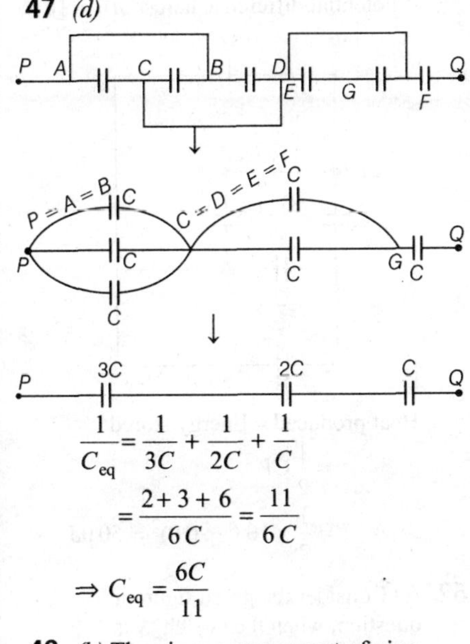

$$\frac{1}{C_{eq}} = \frac{1}{3C} + \frac{1}{2C} + \frac{1}{C}$$

$$= \frac{2+3+6}{6C} = \frac{11}{6C}$$

$$\Rightarrow C_{eq} = \frac{6C}{11}$$

48 (b) The given arrangement of nine plates is equivalent to the parallel combination of 8 capacitors.

The capacity of each capacitor,

$$C = \frac{\varepsilon_0 A}{d}$$

$$= \frac{8.854 \times 10^{-12} \times 5 \times 10^{-4}}{0.885 \times 10^{-2}}$$

$$= 0.5 \text{ pF}$$

Hence, the capacity of 8 capacitors

$$= 8C = 8 \times 0.5 = 4 \text{ pF}$$

49 (c) Capacitors of $6\mu F$ and $3\mu F$ are in series, so

$$C' = \frac{6 \times 3}{6+3} = \frac{18}{9} = 2\mu F$$

Now, C' is in parallel with $2\mu F$ capacitor, so

$$C = C' + 2 = 2 + 2 = 4\mu F$$

50 (d) The given circuit can be rearranged as follows, it consists of three capacitors connected in parallel, hence equivalent resistance of the combination is

$$C' = C_1 + C_2 + C_3.$$

1μF

1μF

A B

1μF

Given, $C' = 1 + 1 + 1 = 3\mu F$

51 (c) The capacitance of system of capacitors,

$$C = C_1 + C_2$$
$$= 10 + 6$$
$$= 16 \ \mu F$$

The charge stored in first capacitor,

$$q = C_1 V$$
$$= 10 \times 1000$$
$$= 10^4 \ \mu C$$

Final potential difference across each capacitor,

$$V' = q/C = 10^4/16 = 625 \text{ V}$$

52 (b) The capacitors are in series, so they will have same charge. Applying Kirchhoff's loop law,

$$-6 + \frac{Q}{2} + \frac{Q}{2} + 2 - 4 = 0$$

$$\therefore \quad Q = 8 \text{ C}$$

53 (a) The arrangement can be redrawn as

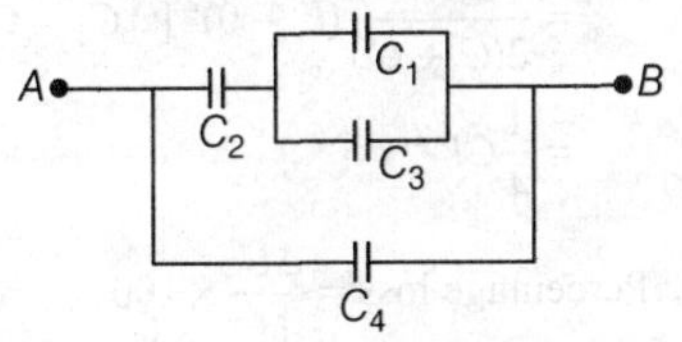

$$\therefore \quad C_{13} = C_1 + C_3$$
$$= 9 + 9 = 18\mu F$$
$$C_{2-13} = \frac{C_2 \times C_{13}}{C_2 + C_{13}}$$
$$= \frac{9 \times 18}{9 + 18} = 6\mu F$$
$$\therefore \quad C = C_{2-13} + C_4$$
$$= 6 + 9 = 15\mu F$$

54 (a) The energy stored is given by

$$E = \frac{1}{2} CV^2$$

When capacitors are connected in parallel, resultant capacitance

$$C' = C_1 + C_2$$
$$= 2\mu F + 2\mu F = 4\mu F$$
$$V = 100 \text{ V}$$
$$\therefore \quad E = \frac{1}{2} \times 4 \times 10^{-6} \times (100)^2$$
$$\Rightarrow \quad E = 0.02 \text{ J}$$

55 (b) Initially the capacitance of capacitor

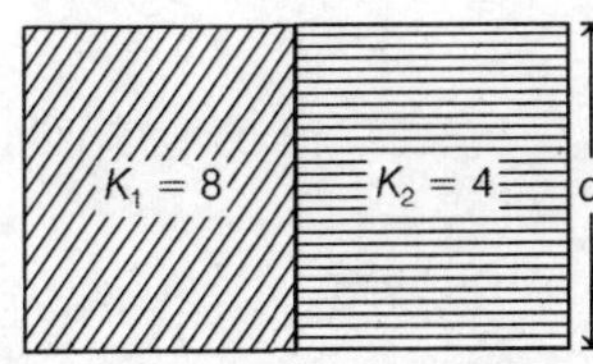

$$C = \frac{\varepsilon_0 A}{d}$$

where, A is area of each plate and d is the separation between the plates.

After filling with dielectrics, we have two capacitors of capacitance,

$$C_1 = \frac{K_1 \varepsilon_0 (A/2)}{d}$$
$$= \frac{8}{2} \frac{\varepsilon_0 A}{d} = \frac{4\varepsilon_0 A}{d} = 4C$$

and
$$C_2 = \frac{K_2 \varepsilon_0 (A/2)}{d}$$
$$= \frac{4}{2} \frac{\varepsilon_0 A}{d}$$
$$= \frac{2\varepsilon_0 A}{d} = 2C$$

Hence, their equivalent capacitance,

$$C_{eq} = C_1 + C_2$$
$$= 4C + 2C = 6C$$

i.e. new capacitance will be six times the original.

56 (a) When S_1 and S_3 are closed, the capacitors C_1 and C_2 are in series arrangement. So, the potential difference developed across capacitors are in the inverse ratio of their capacities.

$$\therefore \quad \frac{V_1'}{V_2'} = \frac{C_2}{C_1} = \frac{3\text{pF}}{2\text{pF}} = \frac{3}{2}$$

and $V_1' + V_2' = V_1 + V_2$

$$= 30 + 20 = 50 \text{ V}$$

We get,

$$V_1' = V_1 = 30 \text{ V}$$

and $\quad V_2' = V_2 = 20 \text{ V}$

57 (c) A capacitor is an arrangement which can store sufficient quantity of charge. Suppose on giving a charge q to a conductor, the electric potential of the conductor becomes V. Then, the capacitance of the conductor is

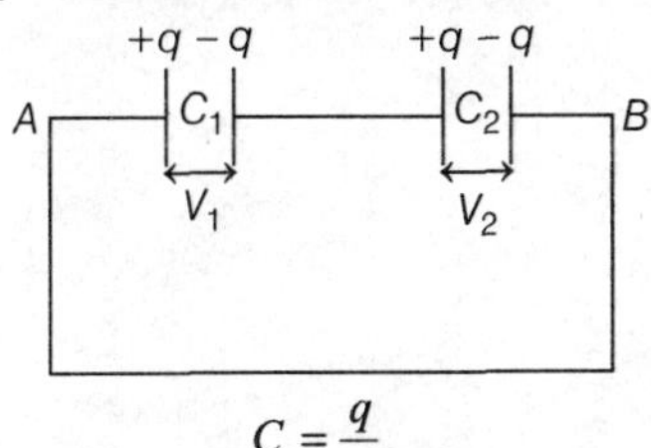

$$C = \frac{q}{V}$$

When two capacitors are connected as given, then charge will be redistributed in the ratio of their capacitance, so charge on each capacitor will be different but non-zero.

58 (c) Seeing in the given circuit C_1 and C_2 are connected in parallel.
Hence, their equivalent capacitance is given by,

$$C_{eq} = C_1 + C_2 = 5 + 10 = 15\mu F$$

As, C_{eq} and C_3 are connected in series. Hence, resultant capacitance between P and Q is given by

$$\frac{1}{C_{PQ}} = \frac{1}{C_{eq}} + \frac{1}{C_3} = \frac{1}{15} + \frac{1}{4} = \frac{19}{60}$$

$$\Rightarrow \quad C_{PQ} = \frac{60}{19} = 3.2\mu F$$

59 (a) The two capacitors each of value $1.5\mu F$ are in parallel, so their equivalent capacitance is given by

$$C_1 = 1.5 + 1.5 = 3\mu F$$

Now, three capacitors each of value $3\mu F$ are in series. Hence, their equivalent capacitance is given by

$$\frac{1}{C} = \frac{1}{3} + \frac{1}{3} + \frac{1}{3}$$

$$\Rightarrow \quad \frac{1}{C} = \frac{3}{3}$$

$$\Rightarrow \quad C = 1\mu F$$

60 (c) When C_1 is connected to voltage source, it is charged to a potential V and this will be stored as a potential energy in the capacitor given by

$$U = \frac{1}{2}CV^2$$

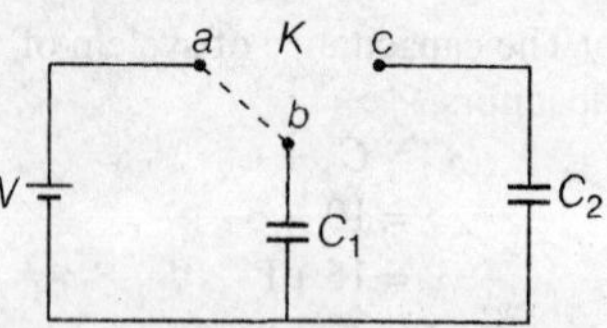

When key is disconnected from battery and b and c are connected, then the charge will be transformed from the capacitor C_1 to capacitor C_2, so

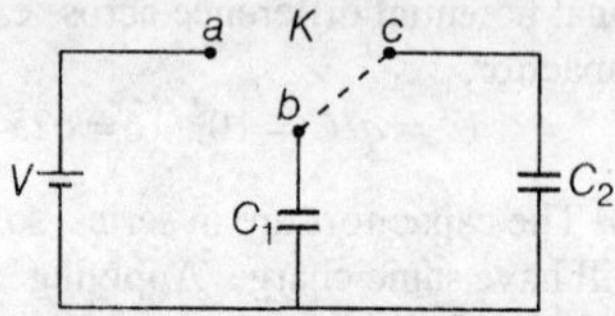

the loss of energy due to redistribution of charge is given by,

$$\Delta U = \frac{C_1C_2}{2(C_1 + C_2)}(V_1 - V_2)^2$$

$$= \frac{C \times C}{2(C + C)}(V - 0)^2 \quad [\because C_1 = C_2]$$

$$= \frac{1}{4}CV^2$$

$$\therefore \text{Percentage loss} = \frac{\Delta U}{U} \times 100$$

$$= \frac{\frac{1}{4}CV^2}{\frac{1}{2}CV^2} \times 100 = 50\%$$

61 (a) Potential drop is zero along an ideal conductor because it has zero resistance.
Potential at point $A = 10$ V
Potential at point $B = 0$ V

$\therefore$ Potential difference across $AB = 10$ V

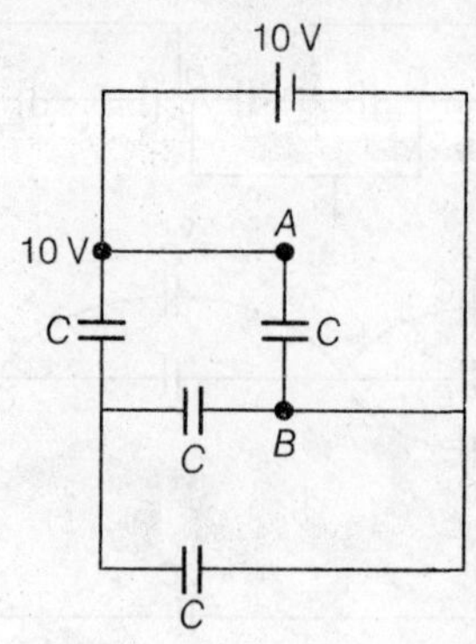

Heat produced = Energy stored

$$= \frac{1}{2}CV^2$$

$$= \frac{1}{2} \times 10^{-6} \times (10)^2 = 50\,\mu J$$

62 (c) Consider the given figure in question, when the switch S is connected to point 1, the initial energy stored in capacitor is $= \frac{1}{2}(2\mu F)V^2$

When the switch S is connected to point 2, energy dissipated on connection across $8\,\mu F$ will be

$$= \frac{1}{2}\left(\frac{C_1C_2}{C_1 + C_2}\right)V^2$$

$$= \frac{1}{2} \times V^2 \times \frac{2\mu F \times 8\mu F}{10\mu F}$$

$$= \frac{1}{2} \times \frac{16\mu F \times V^2}{10}$$

Therefore, % loss of energy

$$= \frac{16}{2 \times 10} \times 100 = 80\%$$

17

Current Electricity

Quick Review

Electric Current

It is the rate of flow of charge through any cross-sectional area of the conductor and given by

$$I = \frac{dq}{dt}$$

For steady flow, $I = Q/t = ne/t$

where, n = number of charge carrier

and e = electronic charge.

If n-particles of charge q moving with velocity v in a unit volume, then current through area A is

$$I = nqvA$$

Current Density

It is the vector having magnitude equal to the current per unit area, i.e. $\mathbf{J} = I/\mathbf{A}$

If area A makes an angle θ with the direction of current, then

$$\mathbf{J} = \frac{I}{A\cos\theta}$$

Electric Currents in Conductors

The electric current in a conductor can be explained by an electron theory. **Free electrons** or **conduction electrons**, carry the charge in the substance from one place to the other. Therefore, the electrical conductivity of a solid substance depends upon the number of free electrons in it.

Drift Velocity

It is the average velocity with which the free electrons in a conductor get drifted towards the positive end of the conductor. It is given by

$$v_d = \frac{e\mathbf{E}}{m}\tau, \quad \text{where } \tau = \text{relaxation time.}$$

Relaxation Time

It is the time interval between two successive collisions of electrons with the positive ions in the metallic lattice. It is given by

$$\tau = \frac{\text{mean free path}}{\text{rms velocity of electron}} = \frac{\lambda}{v_{rms}}$$

With rise in temperature v_{rms} increase, consequently τ decreases.

Mobility

For an electron, it is the drift velocity per unit electric field, i.e. $\mu = \frac{v_d}{\mathbf{E}} = \frac{e\tau}{m}$

Its SI unit is $m^2V^{-1}s^{-1}$.

- **Relation Between Drift Velocity, Electric Current and Current Density** Due to the drift velocity of electrons in a conductor, current flow which is given by $I = neAv_d$. The current density, $J = nev_d$.

Ohm's Law

According to this law, the current flowing through a conductor is directly proportional to the potential difference across its ends, i.e. $I \propto V$ or $V = IR$

where, R is resistance of the conductor.

V-I Characteristics

- For a metallic conductor which obey ohm's law, this characteristic is linear or straight line inclined at an angle θ.

- For substances like gases and semiconductors, which do not obey ohm's law, this characteristic is non-linear.
- At different temperatures, V-I curves are different.

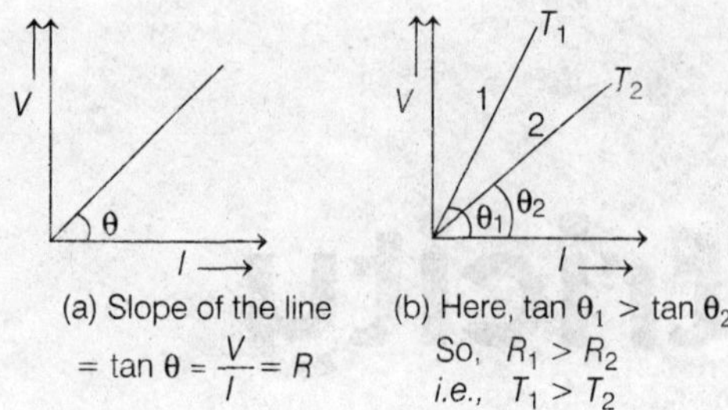

(a) Slope of the line $= \tan\theta = \frac{V}{I} = R$ (b) Here, $\tan\theta_1 > \tan\theta_2$ So, $R_1 > R_2$ i.e., $T_1 > T_2$

Resistance

It is the property of a conductor by virtue of which it opposes the flow of current through it.

From Ohm's law, it is given by $R = \frac{V}{I}$

It depends directly on the length of conductor and inversely on its area of cross-section and also given by $R = \rho\frac{l}{A}$

where, ρ = constant of proportionality called resistivity of material of conductor.

In terms of free electron density (n) and relaxation time (τ), the resistance of a conductor is given by $R = \frac{m}{ne^2\tau}\cdot\frac{l}{A}$.

Resistivity or Specific Resistance

It is the intrinsic property of the substance and independent of the shape and size of conductor. It is given by

$$\rho = \frac{RA}{l}$$

In terms of free electron density (n) and relaxation time (τ), the resistivity is given by

$$\rho = \frac{m}{ne^2\tau}$$

Temperature Dependance of Resistance and Resistivity

- If the temperature of a conductor is changed, its resistance varies according the given relation,

$$R_t = R_0\,(1 + \alpha\,\Delta T)$$

where, R_t and R_0 = resistance at temperature $t°$ C and 0° C, respectively and α = temperature coefficient of conductor.

- Similarly, resistivity also varies as $\rho_t = \rho_0\,(1 + \alpha\,\Delta T)$.
- For metal, α is positive, i.e. their resistivity and resistance increases with temperature rise and for semiconductor, α is negative, i.e. their resistivity and resistance decreases with temperature rise.

Conductance and Conductivity

Conductance is the reciprocal of resistance, i.e. $C = 1/R$.

Its SI unit is Ω^{-1} or siemen.

Conductivity is the reciprocal of resistivity, i.e. $\sigma = 1/\rho$.

Its SI unit is mho m^{-1}.

- **Relation between conductivity, resistivity, electric field and current density**

$$\mathbf{J} = \sigma\mathbf{E} = \mathbf{E}/\rho$$

Colour Coding of Carbon Resistors

The resistance of a carbon resistor can be calculated by the code given on it in the form of coloured strips.

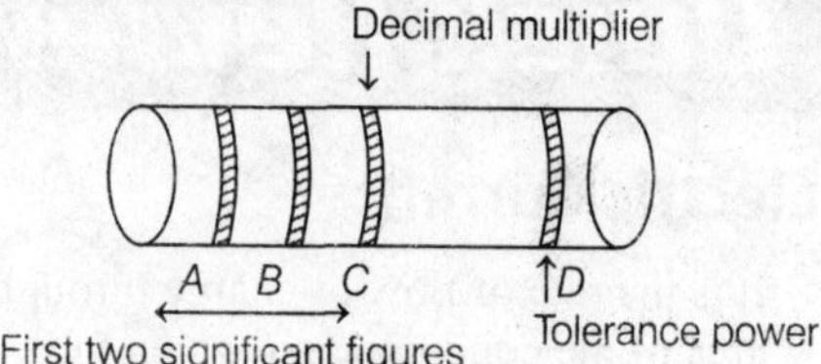

Colour Coding

Colour	Figure	Multiplier
Black	0	1
Brown	1	10^1
Red	2	10^2
Orange	3	10^3
Yellow	4	10^4
Green	5	10^5
Blue	6	10^6
Violet	7	10^7
Grey	8	10^8
White	9	10^9

Tolerance Power

Colour	Gold	Silver	No colour
Tolerance	5%	10%	20%

This colour coding can be easily learned in the sequence "BB ROY Great Britain Very Good Wife".

From colour codes of resistor

$$R = AB \times C \pm D\%$$

Combination of Resistors

1. In Series

(*i*) Equivalent resistance, $R = R_1 + R_2 + R_3$

(*ii*) Current through each resistor is same.

(*iii*) Sum of potential differences across individual resistors is equal to the potential difference applied by the source.

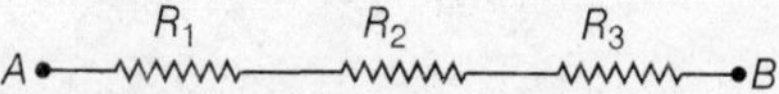

2. In Parallel

(*i*) Equivalent resistance, $\frac{1}{R} = \frac{1}{R_1} + \frac{1}{R_2} + \frac{1}{R_3}$

(*ii*) Potential difference across each resistor is same.

(*iii*) Sum of electric currents flowing through individual resistors is equal to the electric current drawn from the source.

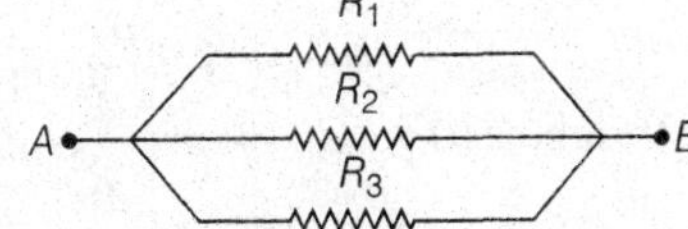

If n identical resistances are first connected in series and then in parallel, the ratio of the equivalent resistance,

$$R_s / R_p = n^2 / 1$$

Electric Cell

It is a device which converts chemical energy into electrical energy. The combination of cell produces a battery.

- **Emf of a Cell** It is the amount of work done in moving a unit positive charge through the whole circuit and given by
$$E = \frac{W}{q}$$
Its SI unit is volt or joule/coulomb.
- **Terminal Potential Difference of a Cell** In a closed circuit, it is the potential difference between the two terminal of the cell. It is given by $V = iR$
Its value is always less than the emf of the cell.
- **Internal Resistance of a Cell** It is the resistance offered by the electrolyte of the cell to the flow of current through it.
In terms of E and V, it is represented as $r = \left(\frac{E}{V} - 1\right) R$
If cell is charging state, then $E = V - ir$.

Grouping of Cells

(*i*) **In Series** If n cells, each of emf e and internal resistance r are connected in series to a resistance R, then equivalent emf

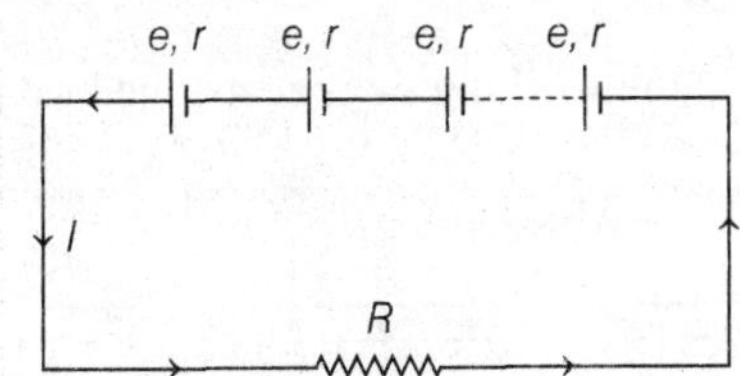

$$e_{eq} = e_1 + e_2 + \ldots + e_n = ne$$

Equivalent internal resistance,

$$r_{eq} = r_1 + r_2 + \ldots + r_n = nr$$

Current in the circuit, $I = \frac{e_{eq}}{(R + r_{eq})} = \frac{ne}{(R + nr)}$

(*ii*) **In Parallel** If n cells, each of emf e and internal resistance r are connected in parallel to resistance R, then equivalent emf, $e_{eq} = e$.

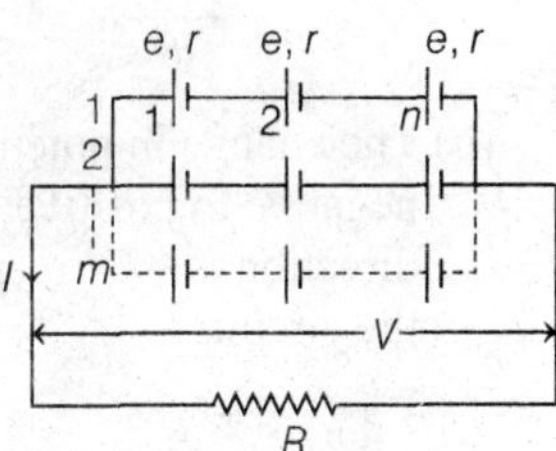

Equivalent internal resistance,

$$\frac{1}{r_{eq}} = \frac{1}{r_1} + \frac{1}{r_1} + \ldots + \frac{1}{r_n} = \frac{n}{r}$$

or $r_{eq} = \frac{r}{n}$

Current in the circuit, $I = \frac{e}{(R + r/n)}$

(*iii*) **In Mixed Grouping** If n identical cells are connected in a row and such m rows are connected in parallel as shown below, then equivalent emf of the combination, $e_{eq} = ne$.

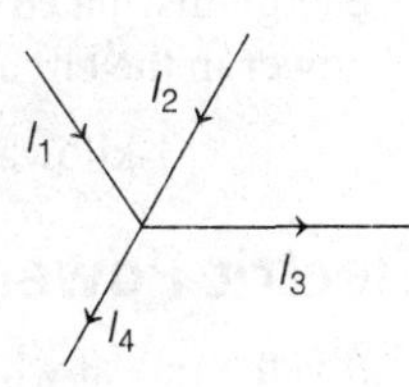

Equivalent internal resistance of the combination,

$$r_{eq} = \frac{nr}{m}$$

Main current flowing through the load,

$$I = \frac{ne}{R + \frac{nr}{m}} = \frac{mne}{mR + nr}$$

Potential difference across load, $V = IR$.

Current from each cell, $I' = \frac{I}{n}$

Potential difference across each cell, $V' = \frac{V}{n}$.

Kirchhoff's Laws

- **Kirchhoff's First Law [Junction or Current Law (KCL)]**
According to this law, "the algebraic sum of currents meeting at the junction is zero". i.e. $\Sigma I = 0$
According to KCL,
$I_1 + I_2 = I_3 + I_4$

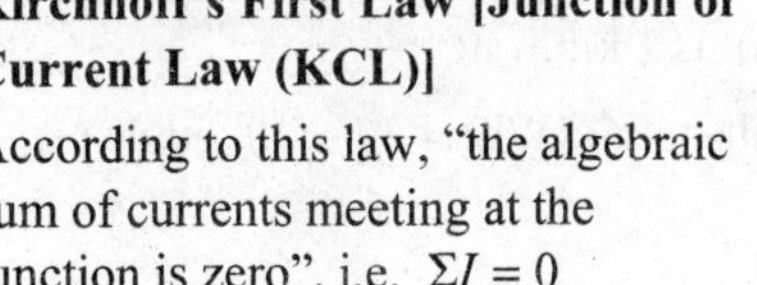

The currents entering a junction are taken positive, while the currents leaving the junction are taken negative.
This law represents conservation of charges.
- **Kirchhoff's Second Law [Loop or Voltage Law (KVL)]**
According to this law, "the algebraic sum of potential differences in a closed loop is zero", i.e. $\Sigma V = 0$
The potential difference across a source is taken negative, when we traverse from negative to positive terminal otherwise positive.

The potential difference across a resistor is taken positive, when we traverse in reverse direction of current otherwise negative.

This law represents conservation of energy.

Sign Convention for the Application of Kirchhoff's Law

For the application of Kirchhoff's laws, the following sign conventions are to be considered

(*i*) The change in potential in traversing a resistance in the direction of current is $-IR$ while in the opposite direction is $+IR$.

(*ii*) The change in potential in traversing an emf source from negative to positive terminal is $+E$, while in the opposite direction is $-E$ irrespective of the direction of current in the circuit.

Electrical Energy

It is the total work done by the source of emf in maintaining the electric current in the given circuit for a specified time. It is given by $E = W = VIt = V^2 t/R$

Its SI unit is joule (J) or watt-second.

Electricity Consumption

To express electrical energy consumed commercially, a special unit **kilowatt-hour** is used in place of joule. It is also called 1 unit of electrical energy.

1 kilowatt hour or 1 unit of electrical energy is the amount of energy dissipated in 1 hour in a circuit, when the electric power in the circuit is 1 kilowatt.

$$1 \text{ kilowatt-hour (kWh)} = 3.6 \times 10^6 \text{ joule (J)}$$

Electric Power

It is the rate at which electrical energy is supplied per unit time to maintain the flow of current in a conductor and given by $P = VI = I^2 R = V^2/R$.

Its SI unit is watt (W) and its commercial unit is horse power (HP), where 1 HP = 746 W

Power Consumption in a Combination of Bulbs

Series Combination of Bulbs

(*i*) Total power consumed is given by

$$\frac{1}{P_{eq}} = \frac{1}{P_1} + \frac{1}{P_2} + \ldots.$$

(*ii*) $P_{consumed}$ (brightness) $\propto V \propto R \propto \frac{1}{P_{rated}}$, i.e. in series combination, bulb of lesser wattage will give more bright light and potential difference appearing across it will be more.

Parallel Combination of Bulbs

(*i*) Total power consumed is given by $P_{total} = P_1 + P_2 + \ldots.$

(*ii*) $P_{consumed}$ (brightness) $\propto P_{rated} \propto I \propto \frac{1}{R}$, i.e. in parallel combination, bulb of greater wattage will give more bright light and more current will pass through it.

Heating Effect of Current

Due to this electrical energy, the current flowing in a conductor is dissipated as heat energy and given by

$$H = E = \frac{V^2 t}{R} \text{ joule} = \frac{V^2 t}{4.2 R} \text{ cal}$$

This relation is called **Joule's law of heating.**

Wheatstone's Bridge

It is an arrangement of four resistances to determine the value of one of unknown resistance, as shown below

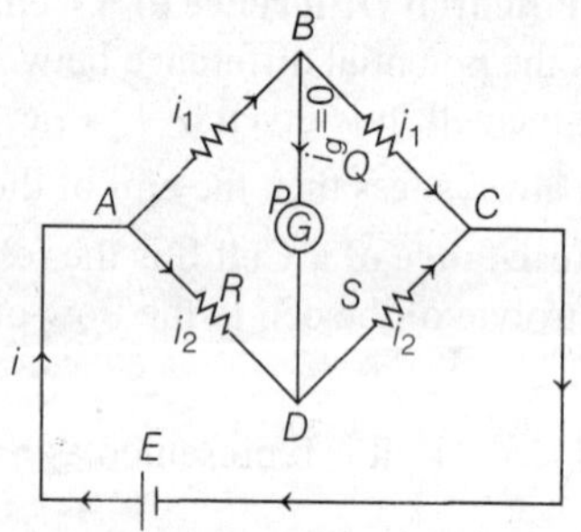

In balanced condition, $P/Q = R/S$

If position of cell and galvanometer is interchanged, this condition will not change.

Meter Bridge

It is based on the working of Wheatstone bridge.

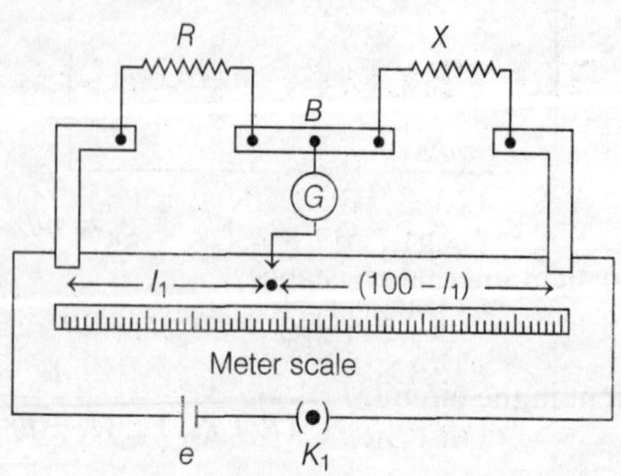

If null point is obtained at length l of meter wise, then

$$\frac{R}{X} = \frac{l}{(100 - l)}$$

where, X = unknown resistance.

It is used for following purpose

(*i*) To measure an unknown resistance.

(*ii*) To compare two unknown resistances.

Potentiometer

It consists of a long resistive wire of length of about 1 m to 10 m.

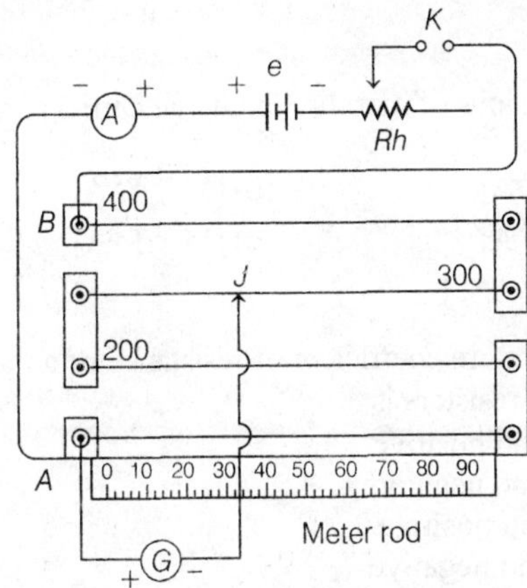

It works on the principle that the fall of potential across any portion is directly proportional to the length of that portion.

The potential gradient, i.e. fall in potential per unit length is given by,

$$k = \frac{V}{L} = \frac{IR}{L} = \frac{E_0 R}{(R_0 + R) L}$$

where,

E_0 = emf of battery

and R_0 = resistance inserted by rheostat.

To Compare the emf's of two Cells using Potentiometer

The arrangement of two cells of emfs e_1 and e_2 which are to be compared is shown in the figure.

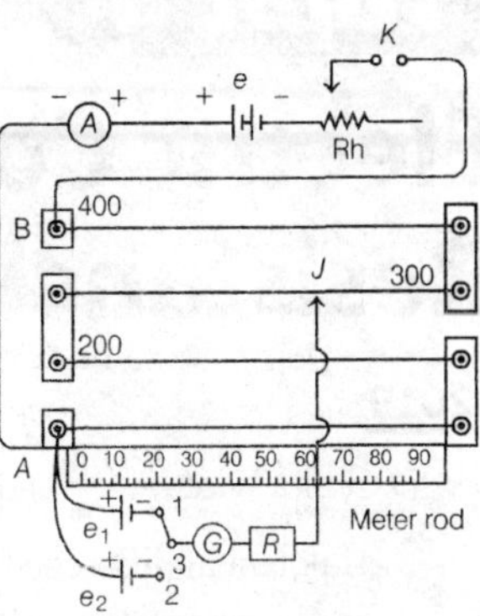

If the plug is put in the gap between 1 and 3, we get

$$e_1 = (x l_1) I \quad \text{...(i)}$$

where, x = resistance per unit length.

Similarly, when the plug is put in the gap between 2 and 3, we get

$$e_2 = (x l_2) I \quad \text{...(ii)}$$

From Eqs. (i) and (ii), we get

or $$\frac{e_1}{e_2} = \frac{l_1}{l_2}$$

Determination of Internal Resistance of a Cell using Potentiometer

The arrangement is shown in figure.

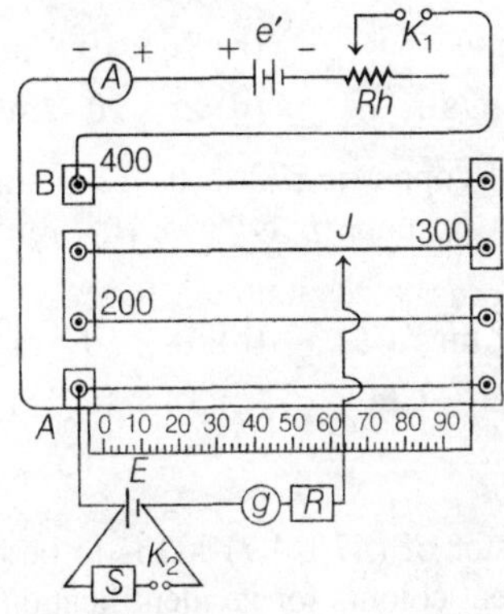

When K_2 is kept out, $e = x l_1 I$

But if by inserting key K_2 and introducing some resistance S (say), then potential difference V is balanced by a length l_2,

where $V = k l_2$.

Internal resistance of cell,

$$r = \frac{e - V}{V} R = \frac{l_1 - l_2}{l_2} R$$

Topical Practice Questions

All the exam questions of this chapter have been divided into 5 topics as listed below

Topic 1

Electric Conduction, Ohm's Law, Resistance and Carbon Resistors

2019

1 For a wire $\frac{R}{l} = \frac{1}{2}$ and length of wire is $l = 5$ cm. If potential difference of 1 V is applied across it, then current through wire will be **[AIIMS]**

(a) 40 A (b) 4 A (c) 25 A (d) 2.5 A

2 A current of 10 A is passing through a metallic wire of cross-sectional area $4 \times 10^{-6}\ m^2$. If the density of the aluminium conductor is 2.7 g/cc considering aluminium gives 1 electron per atom for conduction, then find the drift velocity of the electrons if molecular weight of aluminium is 27 g. **[AIIMS]**

(a) 1.6×10^{-4} m/s (b) 3.6×10^{-4} m/s
(c) 2.6×10^{-4} m/s (d) 1.5×10^{-4} m/s

3 If resistivity of copper is $1.72 \times 10^{-8}\ \Omega$-m and number of free electrons in copper is $8.5 \times 10^{28}\ /\ m^3$. Find the mobility. **[JIPMER]**

(a) $4.25 \times 10^{-3}\ m^2 / C\Omega$ (b) $6.8 \times 10^{-3}\ m^2 / C\Omega$
(c) $8.5 \times 10^{-3}\ m^2 / C\Omega$ (d) $3.4 \times 10^{-3}\ m^2 / C\Omega$

2018

4 A carbon resistor of (47 ± 4.7) kΩ is to be marked with rings of different colours for its identification. The colour code sequence will be **[NEET]**

(a) Yellow - Green - Violet - Gold
(b) Yellow - Violet - Orange - Silver
(c) Violet - Yellow - Orange - Silver
(d) Green - Orange - Violet - Gold

5 $R = 65 \pm 1\,\Omega$, $l = 5 \pm 0.1$ mm and $d = 10 \pm 0.5$ mm. Find error in calculation of resistivity. **[JIPMER]**

(a) 21% (b) 13% (c) 16% (d) 41%

6 A current i is flowing through the wire of diameter (d) having drift velocity of electrons v_d in it. What will be new drift velocity when diameter of wire is made $d/4$? **[JIPMER]**

(a) $4v_d$ (b) $\frac{v_d}{4}$ (c) $16v_d$ (d) $\frac{v_d}{16}$

2017

7 The resistance of a wire is R ohm. If it is melted and stretched to n times its original length, its new resistance will be **[NEET]**

(a) nR (b) $\frac{R}{n}$ (c) n^2R (d) $\frac{R}{n^2}$

2015

8 Across a metallic conductor of non-uniform cross-section, a constant potential difference is applied. The quantity which remain constant along the conductor is **[NEET]**

(a) current density (b) current
(c) drift velocity (d) electric field

2014

9 The dimensions of mobility of charge carriers are **[Kerala CEE]**

(a) $[M^{-2}T^2A]$ (b) $[M^{-1}T^2A]$
(c) $[M^{-2}T^3A]$ (d) $[M^{-1}T^3A]$
(e) $[M^{-1}T^3A^{-1}]$

10 The temperature coefficient of resistance of an alloy used for making resistors is **[Kerala CEE]**

(a) small and positive
(b) small and negative
(c) large and positive
(d) large and negative
(e) zero

11 A wire of resistance 4 Ω is stretched to twice its original length. In the process of stretching, its area of cross-section gets halved. Now, the resistance of the wire is **[EAMCET]**

(a) 8 Ω (b) 16 Ω (c) 1 Ω (d) 4 Ω

12 A carbon film resistor has colour code, green, black, violet and gold. The value of the resistor is **[KCET]**

(a) 50 MΩ (b) 500 MΩ
(c) 500 ± 5% MΩ (d) 500 ± 10% MΩ

2013

13 The resistance R_t of a conductor varies with temperature t as shown in figure. If the variation is represented by $R_t = R_0\,(1 + \alpha t + \beta t^2)$, then **[AIIMS]**

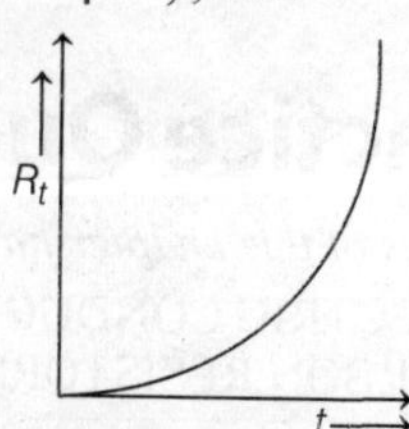

(a) α and β both are negative
(b) α is positive and β is negative
(c) α and β both are positive
(d) α is negative and β is positive

14 A 220 V main supply is connected to a resistance of 100 kΩ. The effective current is **[UP CPMT]**

(a) 2.2 mA (b) $2.2\sqrt{2}$ mA

(c) $\frac{2.2}{\sqrt{2}}$ mA (d) None of these

15 The electrical conductivity of the metal decreases with temperature, because **[WB JEE]**

(a) the energy of the electrons increases with temperature

(b) a metal expands on heating

(c) the atoms of the metal vibrate more at higher temperature

(d) metals have low specific heat

2012

16 Charge passing through a conductor of cross-section area $A = 0.3\ m^2$ is given by $q = 3t^2 + 5t + 2$ in coulomb, where t is in second. What is the value of drift velocity at $t = 2$ s? (Given, $n = 2 \times 10^{25} / m^2$) **[AIIMS]**

(a) 0.77×10^{-5} m/s (b) 1.77×10^{-5} m/s

(c) 2.08×10^{5} m/s (d) 0.57×10^{-5} m/s

2011

17 The masses of the three wires of copper are in the ratio 5 : 3 : 1 and their lengths are in the ratio 1 : 3 : 5. The ratio of their electrical resistances is **[J&K CET]**

(a) 5 : 3 : 1 (b) $\sqrt{125}$: 15 : 1 (c) 1 : 15 : 125 (d) 1 : 3 : 5

2010

18 Two wires of the same material but of different diameters carry the same current I. If the ratio of their diameters is 2 : 1, then the corresponding ratio of their mean drift velocities will be **[AFMC]**

(a) 4 : 1 (b) 1 : 1 (c) 1 : 2 (d) 1 : 4

19 The temperature (T) dependence of resistivity (ρ) of a semiconductor is represented by **[BHU]**

(a) 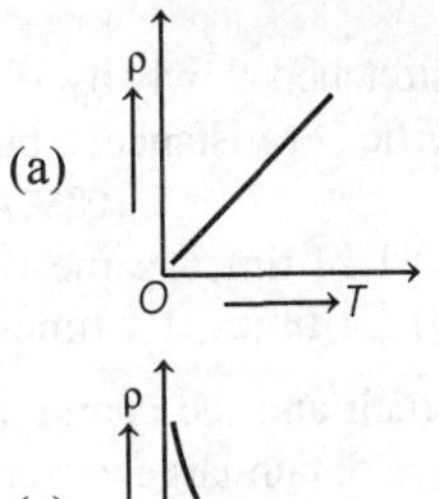

(b) 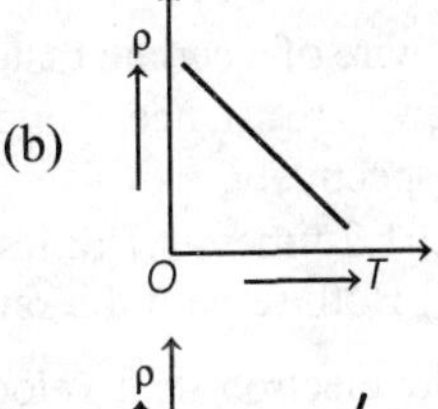

(c) 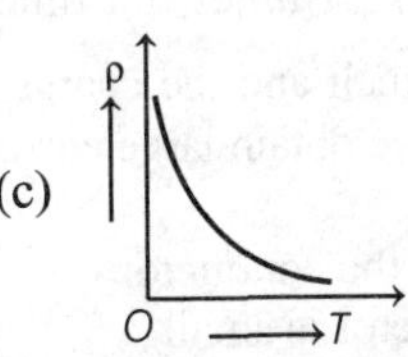

(d) 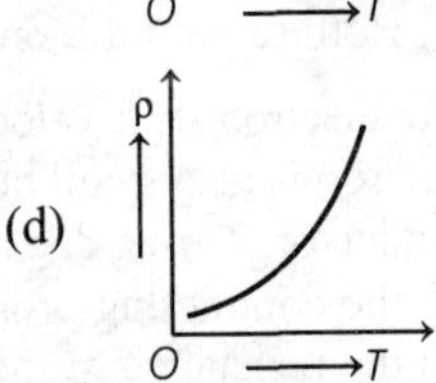

20 Choose the correct statement. **[UP CPMT]**

(a) When we heat a semiconductor, its resistance increases.

(b) When we heat a semiconductor, its resistance decreases.

(c) When we cool a semiconductor, it becomes superconductor.

(d) Resistance of semiconductor is independent of temperature.

21 A conducting wire of cross-sectional area 1 cm^2 has 3×10^{23} charge carriers per metre^3. If the wire carries a current 24 mA, then drift velocity of carriers is **[Manipal]**

(a) $5 \times 10^{-2}\ ms^{-1}$ (b) $0.5\ ms^{-1}$

(c) $5 \times 10^{-3}\ ms^{-1}$ (d) $5 \times 10^{-6}\ ms^{-1}$

22 The mobility of free electrons (charge = e, mass = m and relaxation time = τ) in a metal is proportional to **[Manipal]**

(a) $\frac{e}{m}\tau$ (b) $\frac{m}{e}\tau$

(c) $\frac{e}{m\tau}$ (d) $\frac{m}{e\tau}$

23 The resistance of a wire is 24 Ω. It is so stretched that the length becomes four times, then the new resistance of wire will be **[OJEE]**

(a) 248 Ω (b) 298 Ω

(c) 384 Ω (d) 428 Ω

24 A wire of resistance R is elongated n-fold to make a new uniform wire. The resistance of new wire is **[WB JEE]**

(a) nR (b) n^2R

(c) $2nR$ (d) $2n^2R$

25 Electric field and current density have relation **[MP PMT]**

(a) $\mathbf{E} \propto \mathbf{J}^2$ (b) $\mathbf{E} \propto \mathbf{J}$

(c) $\mathbf{E} \propto \frac{1}{\mathbf{J}^2}$ (d) $\mathbf{E}^2 \propto \frac{1}{\mathbf{J}}$

26 A battery is connected to a uniform resistance wire AB and B is earthed. Which one of the following graphs below shows how the current density J varies along AB? **[Haryana PMT]**

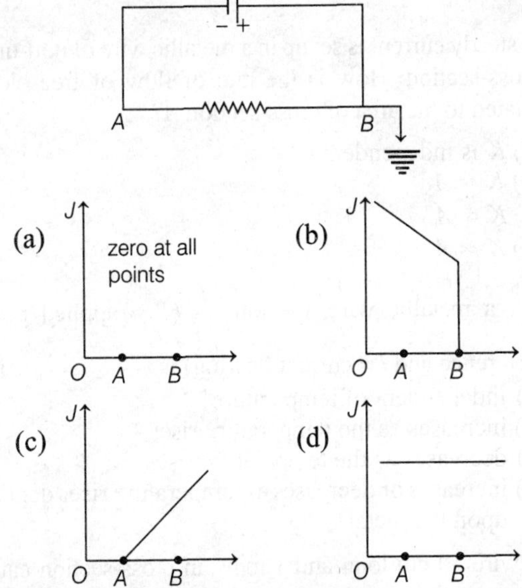

27 The unit of specific conductivity is **[Punjab PMET]**

(a) $\Omega\ cm^{-1}$ (b) $\Omega\ cm^{-2}$

(c) Ω^{-1} cm (d) $\Omega^{-1}\ cm^{-1}$

28 The current-voltage graph for a given metallic wire at two different temperatures T_1 and T_2 is shown in the figure. The temperatures T_1 and T_2 are related as **[EAMCET]**

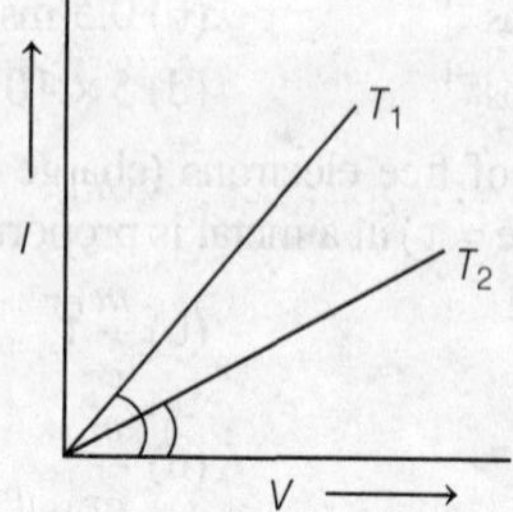

(a) $T_1 > T_2$ (b) $T_1 < T_2$ (c) $T_1 = T_2$ (d) $T_1 > 2T_2$

29 The temperature coefficient of resistance of a wire is 0.00125 / °C. At 300 K temperature, its resistance is 1 Ω. The resistance of the wire will be 2 Ω at **[CG PMT]**

(a) 1154 K (b) 1100 K
(c) 1400 K (d) 1127 K

30 The electrical resistivity of a sample **[MGIMS]**

(a) is proportional to its length
(b) is proportional to the area of cross-section
(c) is inversely proportional to the length
(d) Neither depends on the length nor on the area of cross-section

31 At room temperature, copper has free electron density of 8.4×10^{28} m^{-3}. The electron drift velocity in a copper conductor of cross-sectional area of 10^{-6} m^2 and carrying a current of 5.4 A, will be **[JIPMER]**

(a) 4 ms^{-1} (b) 0.4 ms^{-1} (c) 4 cms^{-1} (d) 0.4 mms^{-1}

2009

32 A steady current is set up in a metallic wire of non-uniform cross-section. How is the rate of flow of free electrons related to the area of cross-section A? **[AIIMS]**

(a) K is independent of A
(b) $K \propto A^{-1}$
(c) $K \propto A$
(d) $K \propto A^2$

33 For a metallic wire, the ratio $\frac{V}{i}$ (V = applied potential difference and i = current flowing) is **[AFMC]**

(a) independent of temperature
(b) increases as the temperature rises
(c) decreases as the temperature rises
(d) increases or decreases as temperature rises depending upon the metal

34 A wire 50 cm long and 1 mm^2 in cross-section carries a current of 4 A when connected to a 2 V battery. The resistivity of the wire is **[AFMC]**

(a) 2×10^{-7} Ω-m (b) 5×10^{-7} Ω-m
(c) 4×10^{-6} Ω-m (d) 1×10^{-6} Ω-m

35 Resistance of a wire at 20°C is 20 Ω and at 500°C is 60 Ω. At what temperature its resistance is 25 Ω? **[OJEE]**

(a) 160°C (b) 250°C (c) 100°C (d) 80°C

36 Which of the following materials is the best conductor of electricity? **[RPMT]**

(a) Platinum (b) Gold (c) Silicon (d) Copper

37 The resistance of a wire at 300 K is found to be 0.3 Ω. If the temperature coefficient of resistance of wire is 1.5×10^{-3} K^{-1}, then the temperature at which the resistance becomes 0.6 Ω is **[KCET]**

(a) 720 K (b) 345 K (c) 993 K (d) 690 K

38 A flash light lamp is marked 3.5 V and 0.28 A. The filament temperature is 425°C. The filament resistance at 0°C is 4 Ω. Then, the temperature coefficient of resistance of the material of the filament is **[EAMCET]**

(a) 8.5×10^{-3} K^{-1} (b) 3.5×10^{-3} K^{-1}
(c) 0.5×10^{-3} K^{-1} (d) 5×10^{-3} K^{-1}

39 The copper having mass of 1kg is drawn into a wire of 1 mm diameter and a wire of 2 mm diameter. The resistance of the two wires will be in the ratio **[CG PMT]**

(a) 2 : 1 (b) 1 : 2
(c) 16 : 1 (d) 4 : 1

40 Nichrome or manganin is widely used in wire bound standard resistors, because of their **[DUMET]**

(a) temperature independent resistivity
(b) very weakly temperature dependent resistivity
(c) strong dependence of resistivity with temperature
(d) mechanical strength

41 The current flowing through a wire depends on time as $I = 3t^2 + 2t + 5$. The charge flowing through the cross-section of the wire in time from $t = 0$ to $t = 2$ s is **[DUMET]**

(a) 22 C (b) 20 C
(c) 18 C (d) 5 C

2008

42 A wire of a certain material is stretched slowly by 10%. Its new resistance and specific resistance become respectively, **[CBSE AIPMT]**

(a) 1.2 times, 1.1 times (b) 1.21 times, same
(c) Both remain the same (d) 1.1 times, 1.1 times

43 The electron drift velocity is small and the charge of the electron is also small but still, we obtain large current in a conductor. This is due to **[AFMC]**

(a) the conducting property of the conductor
(b) the resistance of the conductor is small
(c) the electron number density of conductor is small
(d) the electron number density of conductor is enormous

44 There is current of 40 A in wire of 10^{-6} m^2 area of cross-section. If the number of free electrons per cubic metre is 10^{29}, then the drift velocity is **[BHU]**

(a) 250×10^{-3} ms^{-1} (b) 25.0×10^{-3} ms^{-1}
(c) 2.50×10^{-3} ms^{-1} (d) 1.25×10^{-3} ms^{-1}

45 Which part represents the negative dynamic resistance? **[Manipal]**

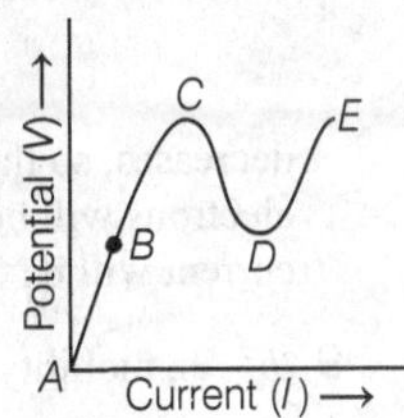

(a) AB (b) BC (c) CD (d) DE

46 A wire of resistance 5.5 Ω is drawn out uniformly so that its length is increased twice, then its new resistance is **[Kerala CEE]**

(a) 44 Ω (b) 42 Ω
(c) 40 Ω (d) 11 Ω
(e) 22 Ω

47 A metal wire is subjected to a constant potential difference. When the temperature of the metal wire increases, then the drift velocity of the electron in it **[KCET]**

(a) increases and thermal velocity of the electron decreases
(b) decreases and thermal velocity of the electron decreases
(c) increases and thermal velocity of the electron increases
(d) decreases and thermal velocity of the electron increases

2007

48 The length of the wire is doubled. Its conductance will be **[AFMC]**

(a) remain unchanged (b) halved
(c) doubled (d) quadrupled

49 An aluminium rod and copper rod are taken such that their lengths are same and their resistances are also same. The specific resistance of copper is half that of aluminium but its density is three times that of aluminium. The ratio of the mass of aluminium rod and that of copper rod will be **[UP CPMT]**

(a) $\frac{1}{6}$ (b) $\frac{2}{3}$ (c) $\frac{1}{3}$ (d) 6

50 The electric resistance of a certain wire of iron is R. If its length and radius are both doubled, then **[Manipal]**

(a) the resistance will be doubled and the specific resistance will be halved
(b) the resistance will be halved and the specific resistance will remain unchanged
(c) the resistance will be halved and specific resistance will be doubled
(d) the resistance and the specific resistance, both will remain unchanged

51 The colour code for a resistor of resistance 3.5 k Ω with 5% tolerance is **[Kerala CEE]**

(a) orange, green, orange and gold
(b) red, yellow, black and gold
(c) orange, green, orange and silver
(d) orange, green, red and silver
(e) orange, green, red and gold

52 For driving current of 2 A for 6 min in a circuit, 1000 J of work is to be done. The emf of the source in the circuit is **[BHU]**

(a) 1.38 V (b) 1.68 V
(c) 2.03 V (d) 3.10 V

2006

53 A certain electrical conductor has a square cross-section, 2.0 mm on a side and is 12 m long. The resistance between its ends is 0.072 Ω. The resistivity of its material is equal to **[BHU]**

(a) 2.4×10^{-6} Ω-m (b) 1.2×10^{-6} Ω-m
(c) 1.2×10^{-8} Ω-m (d) 2.4×10^{-8} Ω-m

54 A potential difference is applied across the ends of a metallic wire. If the potential difference is doubled, the drift velocity will **[MHT CET]**

(a) be doubled (b) be halved
(c) be quadrupled (d) remain unchanged

55 Two copper wires of length l and $2l$ have radii r and $2r$, respectively. What is the ratio of their specific resistances? **[DUMET]**

(a) 1:2 (b) 2:1 (c) 1:1 (d) 1:3

2005

56 The electric field **E**, current density **J** and conductivity σ of a conductor are related as **[Kerala CEE]**

(a) $\sigma = \frac{\mathbf{E}}{\mathbf{J}}$ (b) $\sigma = \frac{\mathbf{J}}{\mathbf{E}}$ (c) $\sigma = \mathbf{JE}$ (d) $\sigma = \frac{1}{\mathbf{JE}}$
(e) $\sigma = \mathbf{J}^2\mathbf{E}$

57 What is the drift velocity of electrons, if the current flowing through a copper wire of 1 mm diameter is 1.1 A? Assume that, each atom of copper contributes one electron. (Take, density of Cu = 9 g cm^{-3} and atomic weight of Cu = 63) **[DUMET]**

(a) 0.3 mm s^{-1} (b) 0.5 mm s^{-1}
(c) 0.1 mm s^{-1} (d) 0.2 mm s^{-1}

Answers

1 (a)	2 (c)	3 (a)	4 (b)	5 (b)	6 (c)	7 (c)	8 (b)	9 (b)	10 (a)
11 (b)	12 (c)	13 (c)	14 (a)	15 (a)	16 (b)	17 (c)	18 (d)	19 (c)	20 (b)
21 (c)	22 (a)	23 (c)	24 (b)	25 (b)	26 (d)	27 (d)	28 (b)	29 (d)	30 (d)
31 (d)	32 (c)	33 (b)	34 (d)	35 (d)	36 (d)	37 (c)	38 (d)	39 (c)	40 (b)
41 (a)	42 (b)	43 (d)	44 (c)	45 (c)	46 (e)	47 (d)	48 (b)	49 (b)	50 (b)
51 (e)	52 (a)	53 (d)	54 (a)	55 (c)	56 (b)	57 (c)			

Explanations

1 (a) Given, for a wire, $\frac{R}{l} = \frac{1}{2}$

Length of wire, $l = 5\text{ cm} = 5 \times 10^{-2}\text{ m}$

$\therefore \quad R = \frac{l}{2} = 2.5 \times 10^{-2}\,\Omega$

Potential difference, $V = 1\text{ V}$

or $\quad IR = 1$

$I = \frac{1}{R} = \frac{1}{2.5 \times 10^{-2}} = \frac{100}{2.5} = 40\text{ A}$

2 (c) Given, current, $I = 10\text{ A}$

Area of cross-section, $A = 4 \times 10^{-6}\text{ m}^2$

Density of conductors,

$\rho = 2.7\text{ g/cc} = 2.7 \times 10^3\text{ kg/m}^3$

Molecular weight of aluminium,

$M_w = 27\text{g} = 27 \times 10^{-3}\text{ kg}$

If n be the total number of electrons in the conductor per unit volume, then

$$n = \frac{\text{Total number of electrons}}{\text{Volume of conductor } (V)}$$

$$= \frac{\text{Number of atoms per mole} \times \text{Number of moles}}{V}$$

$$= \frac{\text{Avogadro number}}{V} \times \left(\frac{M}{M_w}\right)$$

$$= 6 \times 10^{23} \times \frac{\rho}{M_w}$$

$$= 6 \times 10^{23} \times \frac{2.7 \times 10^3}{27 \times 10^{-3}}$$

$\therefore \quad n = 6 \times 10^{28}$

We know that, drift velocity,

$$v_d = \frac{I}{neA}$$

$$= \frac{10}{6 \times 10^{28} \times 1.6 \times 10^{-19} \times 4 \times 10^{-6}}$$

$$= 2.6 \times 10^{-4}\text{ m/s}$$

3 (a) Given, resistivity of copper,

$\rho = 1.72 \times 10^{-8}\,\Omega\text{-m}$

Electrons density, $n = 8.5 \times 10^{28}/\text{m}^3$

$\therefore \quad \text{Mobility } (\mu) = \frac{1}{\rho ne}$

$$= \frac{1}{1.72 \times 10^{-8} \times 8.5 \times 10^{28} \times 1.6 \times 10^{-19}}$$

$$= 4.25 \times 10^{-3}\text{ m}^2/\text{C}\,\Omega$$

4 (b) Given, $R = (47 \pm 4.7)\text{ k}\Omega$

$$= 47 \times 10^3 \pm 10\%\,\Omega$$

As per the colour code for carbon resistors, the colour assigned to numbers.

4-Yellow, 7-Violet, 3-Orange

For ±10% accuracy, the colour is silver. Hence, the bands of colours on carbon resistor in sequence are yellow, violet, orange and silver.

5 (b) Given,

$R = 65\,\Omega, \Delta R = 1\Omega, l = 5 \times 10^{-3}\text{ m},$

$\Delta l = 0.1 \times 10^{-3}\text{ m}, d = 10 \times 10^{-3}\text{ m},$

$\Delta d = 0.5 \times 10^{-3}\text{ m}$

$\because$ Resistivity, $\rho = RA/l$

or $\quad \rho = \frac{R\pi\,(d/2)^2}{l} = \frac{\pi R d^2}{4l}$

$\therefore \quad \frac{\Delta\rho}{\rho} = \frac{\Delta R}{R} + 2\frac{\Delta d}{d} + \frac{\Delta l}{l}$

$\therefore \quad \frac{\Delta\rho}{\rho} = \frac{1}{65} + 2\left(\frac{0.5 \times 10^{-3}}{10 \times 10^{-3}}\right) + \frac{0.1 \times 10^{-3}}{5 \times 10^{-3}}$

or $\quad \frac{\Delta\rho}{\rho} = 0.0153 + 0.1 + 0.02$

or $\quad \frac{\Delta\rho}{\rho} \approx 0.1353$

So, error in calculation of resistivity is 13.5% ≈ 13%.

6 (c) $\because$ Current, $I = nAev_d$ or $v_d \propto \frac{1}{A}$

If diameter of wire is $d/4$, then area will be $A/16$, so new drift velocity $= 16\,v_d$.

7 (c) Volume of material remains same in stretching.

As volume remains same, $A_1 l_1 = A_2 l_2$

Now, $\quad$ given $\quad l_2 = nl_1$

$\therefore \quad$ New area, $A_2 = A_1 l_1 / l_2 = A_1 / n$

Resistance of wire after stretching,

$$R_2 = \rho\frac{l_2}{A_2} = \rho\frac{nl_1}{A_1/n} = \left(\rho\frac{l_1}{A_1}\right)n^2$$

$$= n^2 R \qquad \left[\because R = \left(\rho\frac{l_1}{A_1}\right)\right]$$

8 (b) As the cross-sectional area of the conductor is non-uniform, so current density will be different.

As, $\quad I = JA \qquad \ldots\text{(i)}$

It is clear from Eq. (i), when area increases, the current density decreases, so the number of flow of electrons will be same and thus the current will be constant.

9 (b) As, mobility $= \frac{\text{drift velocity}}{\text{electric field}}$

$$\Rightarrow \quad \mu = \frac{v_d}{E} = \frac{v_d}{\frac{V}{d}} = \frac{v_d\,d}{\left(\frac{W}{q}\right)} = \frac{v_d\,dq}{W}$$

$$= \frac{[\text{metre second}^{-1}]\,[\text{metre}]\,[\text{ampere - second}]}{[\text{kg-metre}^2\text{-second}^{-2}]}$$

$$= \frac{[\text{LT}^{-1}\text{LAT}]}{[\text{ML}^2\text{T}^{-2}]} = [\text{M}^{-1}\text{AT}^2]$$

10 (a) The temperature coefficient of resistance of an alloy used for making resistors is small and positive.

11 (b) By specific resistance, $R = \rho\,\frac{l}{A}$

Given, $R_1 = 4\,\Omega,\ l_1 = l,\ A_1 = A,\ R_2 = ?$

$l_2 = 2l,\ A_2 = A/2,\ \rho = \text{constant}$

$$\therefore \quad \frac{R_1}{R_2} = \frac{\frac{l_1}{A_1}}{\frac{l_2}{A_2}} = \frac{l_1 \times A_2}{l_2 \times A_1}$$

$$\Rightarrow \quad \frac{4}{R_2} = \frac{l \times \frac{A}{2}}{2l \times A}$$

$$\Rightarrow \quad \frac{4}{R_2} = \frac{1}{4} \quad \Rightarrow \quad R_2 = 16\,\Omega$$

12 (c) According to the question, corresponding to the colours of the first and second bands, i.e. green and black, first two significant figures are 5 and 0.

Corresponding to the colour of third band, i.e. violet, the multiplier is 10^7. Therefore, the value of the resistance is $50 \times 10^7\,\Omega$. The gold colour of the fourth band indicates the tolerance of ± 5%.

So, the value of the resistor is written as $50 \times 10^7\,\Omega \pm 5\% = 500 \times 10^6\,\Omega + 5\%$

$$= 500 \pm 5\%\text{ M}\Omega$$

13 (c) Graph indicates that resistance increases with increase in temperature, so α and β both are positive.

14 (a) According to Ohm's law,

$$V = IR \quad \Rightarrow \quad I = \frac{V}{R}$$

Given, $V = 220$ V,

$R = 100\ \text{k}\Omega = 100 \times 10^3 \Omega$

$\therefore \quad I = \dfrac{220}{100 \times 10^3}$

$\Rightarrow \quad I = 2.2 \times 10^{-3}\ \text{A} = 2.2\ \text{mA}$

15 *(a)* The electrical resistance arises due to the collisions of electrons with the lattice and other electrons in their paths. When temperature increases, the electrons move faster due to their increased kinetic energy. Thus, they make more number of collisions thereby, increasing the resistance. As, resistance is inversely proportional to the conductivity. Hence, when the temperature of the metal increases electrical conductivity decreases.

16 *(b)* Cross-sectional area of conductor,

$A = 0.3\ \text{m}^2$

and $\quad n = 2 \times 10^{25}\ \text{m}^{-2}$

Charge, $q = 3t^2 + 5t + 2\text{C}$

Current, $i = \dfrac{dq}{dt} = 6t + 5 = 17\ \text{A}$ $\quad [\because t = 2]$

We also have $\quad i = neAv_d$

Drift velocity, $v_d = \dfrac{i}{neA}$

$= \dfrac{17}{2 \times 10^{25} \times 1.6 \times 10^{-19} \times 0.3}$

$= \dfrac{17}{0.96 \times 10^6}$

$= 1.77 \times 10^{-5}\ \text{m/s}$

17 *(c)* Given, $l_1 : l_2 : l_3 = 1 : 3 : 5 = k$ (say)

$\Rightarrow \quad l_1 = 1k, l_2 = 3k, l_3 = 5k$

$m_1 : m_2 : m_3 = 5 : 3 : 1 = m$ (say)

$\Rightarrow m_1 = 5m, m_2 = 3m, m_3 = 1m$

Resistance, $R = \dfrac{\rho l}{A}$

where, ρ is resistivity of the material of conductor.

So, $R_1 : R_2 : R_3 = \dfrac{l_1}{A_1} : \dfrac{l_2}{A_2} : \dfrac{l_3}{A_3}$

$= \dfrac{l_1^2}{V_1} : \dfrac{l_2^2}{V_2} : \dfrac{l_3^2}{V_3}$

$= \dfrac{l_1^2}{m_1} : \dfrac{l_2^2}{m_1} : \dfrac{l_3^2}{m_3}$ $\quad \left[\because \text{density} = \dfrac{m}{V}\right]$

$= \dfrac{1}{5} : \dfrac{9}{3} : \dfrac{25}{1} = 1 : 15 : 125$

18 *(d)* Given, $\quad D_1 : D_2 = 2 : 1$

Drift velocity, $v_d = \dfrac{I}{nAe} = \dfrac{I \times 4}{n\pi D^2 e}$

where, D is the diameter of the wire

i.e $\quad v_d \propto \dfrac{1}{D^2}$

$\Rightarrow \quad \dfrac{v_{d_1}}{v_{d_2}} = \dfrac{D_2^2}{D_1^2} = \left(\dfrac{1}{2}\right)^2 = \dfrac{1}{4}$

19 *(c)* The resistivity of a semiconductor decreases with increase in temperature exponentially.

20 *(b)* With the rise in temperature, conductivity of semiconductor increases while resistance decreases.

21 *(c)* The current i and area of cross-section A, can be expressed in terms of drift velocity v_d and the moving charges is given as $i = nev_dA$ where, n is number of charge carriers per unit volume (i.e. number density) and e is the charge on the electron (i.e. charge carrier).

Given, $A = 1\ \text{cm}^2 = 1 \times 10^{-4}\ \text{m}^2$,

$n = 3 \times 10^{23}\ \text{m}^{-3}$

and $\quad i = 24\ \text{mA} = 24 \times 10^{-3}\ \text{A}$

$\therefore \quad v_d = \dfrac{i}{neA}$

$= \dfrac{24 \times 10^{-3}}{(3 \times 10^{23})(1.6 \times 10^{-19})(10^{-4})}$

$= 5 \times 10^{-3}\ \text{ms}^{-1}$

22 *(a)* Drift velocity per unit electric field is called mobility of electrons.

i.e. $\quad \mu = \dfrac{v_d}{E} = \dfrac{eE}{Em}\tau$

$\therefore \quad \mu = \dfrac{e\tau}{m}$

23 *(c)* In case of stretching the wire, $R \propto l^2$.

If length becomes 4 times, so resistance becomes 16 times,

i.e $\quad R' = 16 \times 24 = 384\ \Omega$

24 *(b)* The resistance of a wire is directly proportional to the length of the wire. Thus, $R \propto l^2$, when the length increases n-fold, resistance will also increase by n-fold times. Also, since the volume of the wire remains constant, so the area of the wire decreases n-fold. Hence, the net resistance increases to n^2R, as the area is inversely proportional to resistance.

25 *(b)* Electric field E in a conductor of length l and having potential difference V at its ends is given by

$E = \dfrac{V}{l} \Rightarrow V = El \quad$ ...(i)

Also, from Ohm's law, $V = IR \quad$ ...(ii)

From Eqs. (i) and (ii), we get

$V = IR = \dfrac{I\rho l}{A} = El$

$\Rightarrow \quad E = \dfrac{I}{A}\rho$

$\therefore \quad \mathbf{E} = \rho\mathbf{J}$ or $\mathbf{J} = \sigma\mathbf{E}$

where, σ = conductivity and ρ = resistivity or specific resistance of substance. Hence, $\mathbf{E} \propto \mathbf{J}$.

26 *(d)* Wire AB is uniform, so current through wire AB at every point across cross-section will be same. Hence, current density, $J\ (= i/A)$ at every point of the wire will be same.

27 *(d)* Specific conductivity

$= \dfrac{1}{\text{Specific resistance}}$

$= \dfrac{1}{\Omega\text{-cm}} = (\Omega\text{-cm})^{-1}$

28 *(b)* Slope of the I-V curve at any point is equal to reciprocal of resistance at that point.

From the given curve, slope for $T_1 >$ slope for T_2, $\dfrac{1}{R_{T_1}} > \dfrac{1}{R_{T_2}}$

$\Rightarrow \quad R_{T_1} < R_{T_2}$

Also for metallic wire, at higher temperature, resistance will be higher, so

$T_2 > T_1$

29 *(d)* Given, $\alpha = 0.00125\ /°\text{C}$, $R_1 = 1\ \Omega$, $R_2 = 2\ \Omega$, $t_1 = 300\ \text{K} = 27°\ \text{C}$

and $\quad t_2 = T°\ \text{C}$ (say)

As, $\quad R_t = R_0(1 + \alpha t)$

$\Rightarrow \quad \dfrac{R_1}{R_2} = \dfrac{(1 + \alpha t_1)}{(1 + \alpha t_2)}$

$\Rightarrow \quad \dfrac{1}{2} = \dfrac{(1 + 0.00125 \times 27)}{(1 + 0.00125 \times t)}$

$\Rightarrow \quad t = 854°\ \text{C}$

$= (854 + 273)\text{K}$

$= 1127\ \text{K}$

30 *(d)* Specific resistance or resistivity is the intrinsic property of the substance and independent of the shape and size of material. Hence, option (d) is correct.

31 (d) Given, $n = 8.4 \times 10^{28}\ \text{m}^{-3}$, $A = 10^{-6}\ \text{m}^2$ and $i = 5.4$ A

Drift velocity in a copper conductor,

$$v_d = i/neA$$
$$= \frac{5.4}{8.4\times 10^{28} \times 1.6\times 10^{-19} \times 10^{-6}}$$
$$= 0.4\times 10^{-3}\text{ms}^{-1} = 0.4\ \text{mm s}^{-1}$$

32 (c) As, $i = Anev_d$

$$\Rightarrow \frac{dq}{dt} = Anev_d \qquad \left(\because i = \frac{dq}{dt}\right)$$
$$\therefore \frac{dq}{dt} \propto A \Rightarrow K \propto A$$

33 (b) The resistance of a metallic wire at temperature $t°$ C is given by

$$R_t = R_0(1 + \alpha t)$$

where, α is the coefficient of expansion. The resistance of wire increases on increasing the temperature. Also, from ohm's law, the ratio of V/i is equal to R. Hence, on increasing the temperature, the resistance of metallic wire is increased, so the ratio V/i also increases.

34 (d) As, $R = \rho\frac{l}{A}$

$$\because V = IR \Rightarrow R = \frac{V}{I}$$
$$\Rightarrow \frac{V}{I} = \rho\frac{l}{A} \quad \ldots\text{(i)}$$

Putting $V = 2$ V,

$l = 50 \times 10^{-2}$ m,

$I = 4$ A

and $A = 1\times 10^{-6}\ \text{m}^2$, in Eq. (i), we get

$$\rho = \frac{2\times 10^{-6}}{4\times 50\times 10^{-2}} = 1\times 10^{-6}\ \Omega\text{-m}$$

35 (d) Here, $R_0 = 20\ \Omega$, $t_1 = 20°$ C,

$t_2 = 500°$ C and $R_{500} = 60\ \Omega$

$$\Rightarrow \Delta t = t_2 - t_1 = 500 - 20 = 480° \text{C}$$

As, $R_{500} = R_0(1 + \alpha\Delta t)$

$$\Rightarrow 60 = 20[1 + \alpha(480)]$$
$$\therefore \alpha = \frac{1}{240}$$

Now, let the temperature be t.

Then, $R_t = 25\Omega$

$$\because R_t = R_0[1 + \alpha(\Delta t)]$$
$$\Rightarrow 25 = 20\left[1 + \frac{1}{240}\cdot\Delta t\right]$$
$$\Rightarrow \left(\frac{5}{4} - 1\right) = \frac{1}{240}(t - 20)$$
$$\Rightarrow t = 80° \text{C}$$

36 (d) Copper is the best conductor among the given materials.

37 (c) Given, $R_{300} = 0.3\ \Omega$, $R_t = 0.6\ \Omega$

and $t' = 300\ \text{K} = 27°$ C

Temperature coefficient of resistance,

$$\alpha = 1.5\times 10^{-3}\ \text{K}^{-1}$$
$$\therefore R_{300} = R_0(1 + \alpha\times 27)$$
$$\Rightarrow 0.3 = R_0(1 + 1.5\times 10^{-3}\times 27) \quad \ldots\text{(i)}$$

Again, $R_t = R_0(1 + \alpha t)$

$$\Rightarrow 0.6 = R_0(1 + 1.5\times 10^{-3}\times t) \quad \ldots\text{(ii)}$$

Dividing Eq. (ii) by Eq. (i), we get

$$\frac{0.6}{0.3} = \frac{1 + 1.5\times 10^{-3}t}{1 + 1.5\times 10^{-3}\times 27}$$
$$\Rightarrow 2(1 + 1.5\times 10^{-3}\times 27) = 1 + 1.5\times 10^{-3}t$$
$$\Rightarrow 2 + 81\times 10^{-3} = 1 + 1.5\times 10^{-3}t$$
$$\Rightarrow 2 + 0.081 = 1 + 1.5\times 10^{-3}t$$
$$\Rightarrow t = \frac{1.081}{1.5\times 10^{-3}} = 720°\ \text{C} = 993\ \text{K}$$

38 (d) Resistance at 425° C,

$$\Rightarrow R_{425°\text{C}} = \frac{V}{I} = \frac{3.5}{0.28} = \frac{350}{28}\ \Omega$$

As, $R_t = R_0[1 + \alpha\Delta t]$

Here, $\Delta t = 425°$ C, $R_0 = 4\ \Omega$

$$\Rightarrow R_{425°\text{C}} = R_0[1 + \alpha\Delta t] \quad \ldots\text{(i)}$$
$$\Rightarrow \frac{350}{28} = 4[1 + \alpha(425 - 0)] \quad \text{[from Eq. (i)]}$$
$$\Rightarrow \alpha = 5\times 10^{-3}\ \text{K}^{-1}$$

39 (c) Mass of Ist wire $= (\pi r_1^2 l_1)\sigma$

Mass of IInd wire $= (\pi r_2^2 l_2)\sigma$

$$\therefore (\pi r_1^2 l_1)\sigma = (\pi r_2^2 l_2)\sigma$$
$$\Rightarrow \frac{l_1}{l_2} = \left(\frac{r_2}{r_1}\right)^2 \quad \ldots\text{(i)}$$
$$\because \frac{R_1}{R_2} = \frac{\rho\frac{l_1}{A_1}}{\rho\frac{l_2}{A_2}} \quad \ldots\text{(ii)}$$
$$\frac{R_1}{R_2} = \frac{l_1}{l_2}\times\frac{A_2}{A_1} = \frac{l_1}{l_2}\times\left(\frac{r_2}{r_1}\right)^2$$

From Eqs. (i) and (ii), we get

$$= \left(\frac{r_2}{r_1}\right)^2 \times \left(\frac{r_2}{r_1}\right)^2 = \left(\frac{1}{1/2}\right)^4$$
$$= 16:1$$

40 (b) Nichrome and manganin are widely used in wire bound standard resistors, because their resistivity is very weakly dependent on temperature.

41 (a) As, $I = \frac{dq}{dt}$

$$\Rightarrow \int dq = \int_{t_1}^{t_2} I\,dt$$
$$\therefore q = \int_0^2 [3t^2 + 2t + 5]\,dt$$
$$= \frac{3}{3}[t^3]_0^2 + \frac{2}{2}[t^2]_0^2 + 5[t]_0^2$$
$$= 8 + 4 + 10 = 22\ \text{C}$$

42 (b) Original resistance of the wire,

$$R = \frac{\rho l}{A}$$

or $R \propto \frac{l}{A}$ or $R \propto \frac{l^2}{V}$ (as $V = Al$)

and $R' \propto \frac{(l + 10\%\ l)^2}{V}$

Therefore, $\frac{R'}{R} = \frac{\left(l + \frac{10}{100}l\right)^2}{l^2}$

or $\frac{R'}{R} = \frac{\left(\frac{11l}{10}\right)^2}{l^2} = \frac{121}{100}$

or $R' = 1.21R$

But the specific resistance will remain same for same material.

43 (d) When we close a circuit, the electric field is set up in the conductor, with the velocity of light. Due to which current is set up in entire circuit, which does not wait for the electrons to flow from one portion to other. Also in a conductor, the electron number density, i.e. number of electrons per unit volume of a conductor is very large ($\approx 10^{28}\ \text{m}^{-3}$).

So, large current in a conductor is obtained irrespective of their small drift velocity.

44 (c) Drift velocity,

$$v_d = \frac{i}{neA}$$
$$= \frac{40}{10^{29}\times 1.6\times 10^{-19}\times 10^{-6}}$$
$$= 2.50\times 10^{-3}\ \text{ms}^{-1}$$

45 (c) From the given V-I graph, the slope represents the resistance. As the part CD has negative slope, hence it has negative dynamic resistance.

46 (e) Resistance, $R = \frac{\rho l}{A}$ or $R \propto \frac{l}{A}$

or $R \propto \frac{l^2}{V}$ or $R \propto l^2$

(as, $Al = V$ = constant)

$$\Rightarrow \frac{R_2}{R_1} = \left(\frac{l_2}{l_1}\right)^2 = \left(\frac{2l}{l}\right)^2 = 4$$

or $R_2 = 4R_1 = 4 \times 5.5 = 22\ \Omega$

47 (d) With rise in temperature, the thermal velocity of the electron increases due to increase in their thermal energy. As the result, the relaxation time decreases and hence drift velocity of charge carrier will also decrease because drift velocity is proportional to the relaxation time.

48 (b) Conductance is given by $\sigma = \frac{1}{R}$

Substituting $R = \rho\frac{l}{A}$, we get $\sigma = \frac{A}{\rho l}$.

If A is constant, then we have $\sigma \propto \frac{1}{l}$

$$\Rightarrow \frac{\sigma_2}{\sigma_1} = \frac{l_1}{l_2}$$

Substituting, $l_2 = 2l_1$, we get $\sigma_2 = \frac{\sigma_1}{2}$

We see that, conductance will be halved.

49 (b) Resistance of wire of length l and area of cross-section A is

$$R = \rho \cdot \frac{l}{A} \quad \ldots(i)$$

If V is the volume of wire, then

$$R = \rho \cdot \frac{l^2}{V} \quad \ldots(ii)$$

If d is the density and m is the mass of wire, then

$$R = \rho \cdot \frac{l^2 d}{m} \Rightarrow m \propto \rho d$$

$$\therefore \frac{m_{Al}}{m_{Cu}} = \frac{\rho_{Al}}{\rho_{Cu}} \times \frac{d_{Al}}{d_{Cu}} = \frac{2}{1} \times \frac{1}{3} = \frac{2}{3}$$

50 (b) The resistance of wire, $R = \frac{\rho l}{A}$

where, ρ = specific resistance of the wire.

$$\Rightarrow R \propto \frac{l}{A} \Rightarrow R \propto \frac{l}{r^2} \quad (\because A = \pi r^2)$$

$$\therefore \frac{R_1}{R_2} = \frac{l_1}{l_2} \times \frac{r_2^2}{r_1^2} \quad \ldots(i)$$

Given, $l_1 = l, l_2 = 2l, r_1 = r, r_2 = 2r$

and $R_1 = R$

Substituting these values in Eq. (i),

we get $\frac{R}{R_2} = \frac{l}{2l} \times \frac{(2r)^2}{r^2}$

$$\Rightarrow \frac{R}{R_2} = 2 \Rightarrow R_2 = \frac{R}{2}$$

Therefore, resistance will be halved.

Now, the specific resistance of the wire does not depend on the geometry of the wire. Hence, it remains unchanged.

51 (e) As, $R = 3.5\ \text{k}\Omega \pm 5\%$

$$\Rightarrow R = 35 \times 10^2 \pm 5\%$$

As per the colour code for carbon resistors, the colours assigned to numbers, 3 and 5 are orange and green. To the multiplier 10^2 the colour assigned is red. For ±5% accuracy, the colour is gold.

$\therefore$ **Colour code** is orange, green, red, and gold.

52 (a) If i is the current in a wire, then the charge flowing through the wire in t second is $q = it = 2 \times 6 \times 60 = 720$ C

The work done in taking q coulomb (720 C) of charge from one end of wire to other end under a potential difference of V volt (in this case emf) is

$$W = Vq$$

$$\Rightarrow V = \frac{W}{q} = \frac{1000}{720} = 1.38\ \text{V}$$

53 (d) Resistance of a conductor is given by

$$R = \frac{\rho l}{A}$$

$$\therefore \text{Resistivity, } \rho = \frac{RA}{l} \quad \ldots(i)$$

Given, $R = 0.072\ \Omega$,

$A = (2 \times 2)\ \text{mm}^2 = 4 \times 10^{-6}\ \text{m}^2$,

$l = 12$ m

Substituting the given values in Eq. (i), we get

$$\rho = \frac{0.072 \times 4 \times 10^{-6}}{12} = 2.4 \times 10^{-8}\ \Omega\text{-m}$$

54 (a) Drift velocity is given by $v_d = \frac{eE\tau}{m}$

But $E = \frac{V}{l}$

where, l is length of the conductor and V is potential difference applied across the ends of the conductor.

$$\therefore v_d = \frac{eV\tau}{ml} \Rightarrow v_d \propto V$$

So, when the potential difference is doubled, then the drift velocity will be doubled.

55 (c) The specific resistance (ρ) is the characteristic property of the material of conductor. Its value depend upon the material of conductor and its temperature. Its value does not depend on the length and area of cross-section of the conductor.

As, the materials (i.e. copper) of both the wires are same, hence $\rho_1 : \rho_2 = 1:1$.

56 (b) The required relation is $\mathbf{J} = \sigma \mathbf{E}$

or $\sigma = \frac{\mathbf{J}}{\mathbf{E}}$

57 (c) As, $i = neAv_d$

The number of electrons,

$$n = \frac{\text{Avogadro's number}}{\text{Volume of 63 g of copper}}$$

$$= \frac{6.02 \times 10^{23}}{\frac{63 \times 10^{-3}}{9 \times 10^{-3}}} = \frac{6.02 \times 10^{23}}{7}\ \text{cm}^3$$

$$\therefore n = \frac{6.02 \times 10^{29}}{7}\ \text{m}^3$$

$$\because i = neAv_d \text{ or } v_d = \frac{i}{neA}$$

$$= \frac{1.1 \times 7}{\left[6.02 \times 10^{29} \times 1.6 \times 10^{-19} \times \pi \times (0.5 \times 10^{-3})^2\right]}$$

$$= 0.1 \times 10^{-3}\ \text{ms}^{-1} = 0.1\ \text{mm s}^{-1}$$

Topic 2
Combination of Resistors

2019

1 The reading of an ideal voltmeter in the circuit shown is **[NEET (Odisha)]**

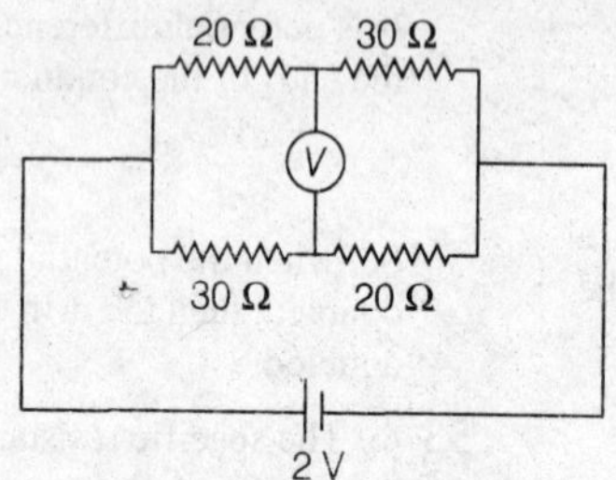

(a) 0.6 V (b) 0 V (c) 0.5 V (d) 0.4 V

2 Find the current in the 8 Ω resistance in the given circuit. **[JIPMER]**

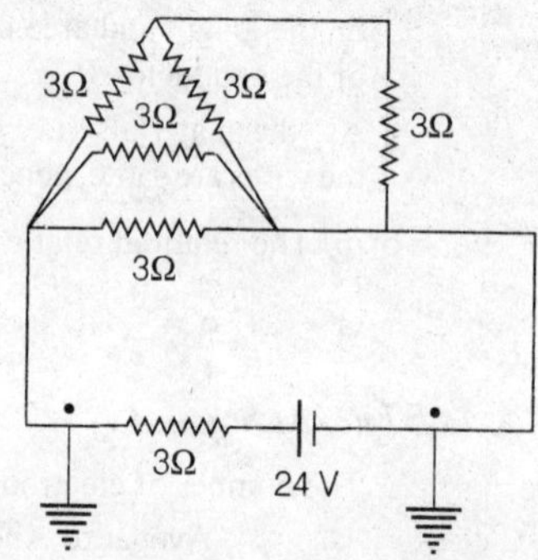

(a) 2 A (b) 3A
(c) 4 A (d) 5 A

3 A circuit contain two resistances R_1 and R_2 are in series. Find the ratio of input voltage to voltage of R_2. **[JIPMER]**

(a) $\dfrac{R_2}{R_1 + R_2}$ (b) $\dfrac{R_1 + R_2}{R_2}$

(c) $\dfrac{R_1 + R_2}{R_1}$ (d) $\dfrac{R_1}{R_1 + R_2}$

4 In the given circuit, find voltage across 12 Ω resistance. **[JIPMER]**

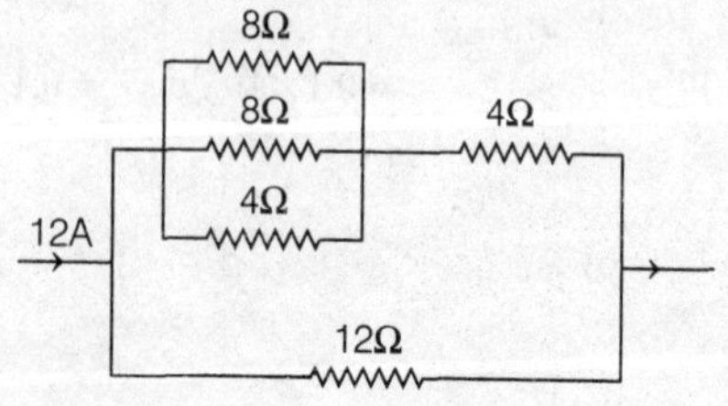

(a) 12 V (b) 36 V
(c) 72 V (d) 48 V

2017

5 Find the value of R_{net} between A and B. **[NEET]**

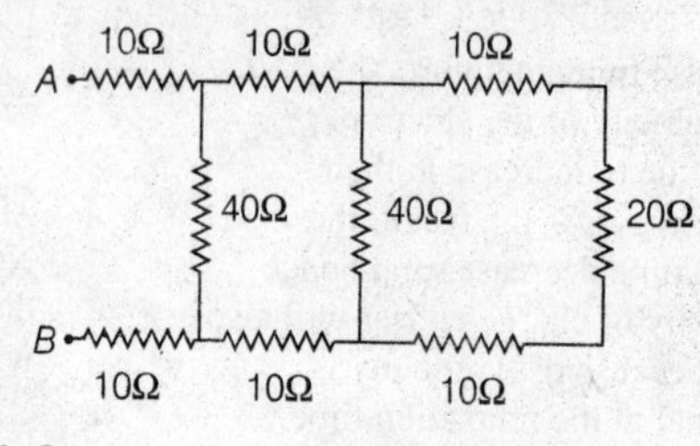

(a) 60 Ω (b) 40 Ω
(c) 70 Ω (d) 20 Ω

6 Find $V_P - V_Q$ in the circuit shown in figure. **[NEET]**

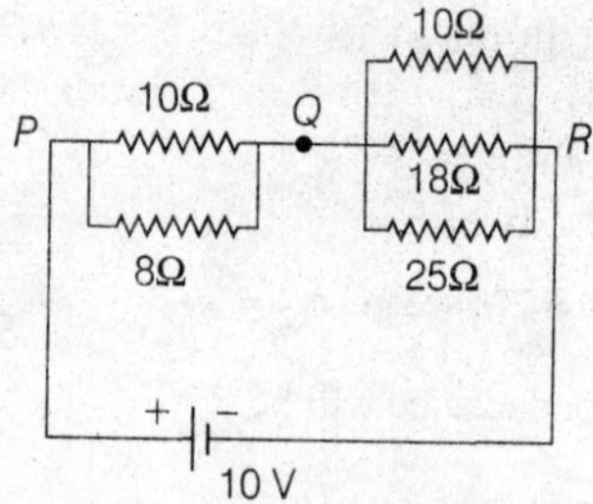

(a) 6.68 V (b) 8 V (c) 4.65 V (d) 7 V

7 Find the value of i in shown figure. **[NEET]**

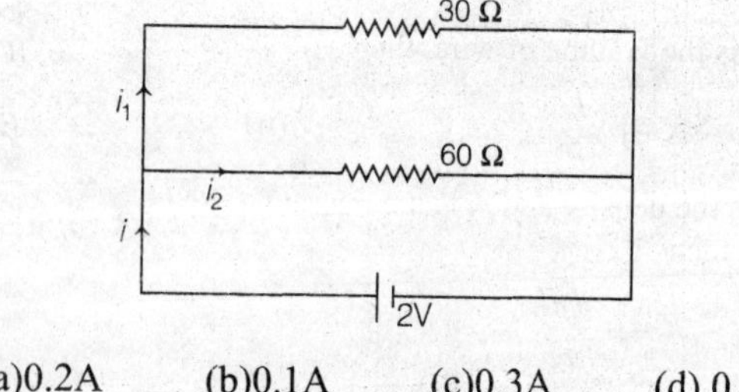

(a)0.2A (b)0.1A (c)0.3A (d) 0.4A

2015

8 A, B and C are voltmeters of resistance R, 1.5 R and 3R respectively as shown in the figure. When some potential difference is applied between X and Y, the voltmeter readings are V_A, V_B and V_C respectively. Then, **[NEET]**

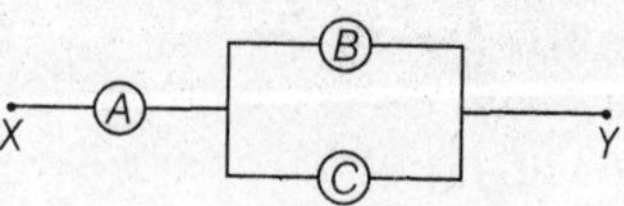

(a) $V_A = V_B = V_C$ (b) $V_A \neq V_B = V_C$
(c) $V_A = V_B \neq V_C$ (d) $V_A \neq V_B \neq V_C$

2014

9 The equivalent resistance of two resistors connected in series is 6 Ω and their parallel equivalent resistance is $\frac{4}{3}$ Ω. What are the values of resistances? **[KCET]**

(a) 4 Ω, 6 Ω (b) 8 Ω, 1 Ω
(c) 4 Ω, 2 Ω (d) 6 Ω, 2 Ω

10 Five resistances are connected as shown in figure. If total current flowing is 0.5 A, then the potential difference $V_A - V_B$ is **[EAMCET]**

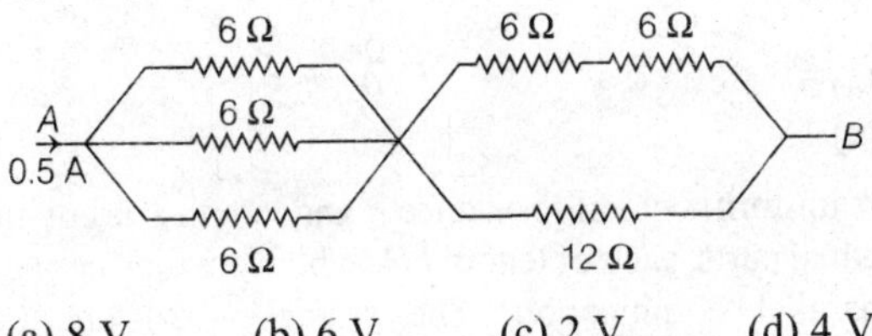

(a) 8 V (b) 6 V (c) 2 V (d) 4 V

2013

11 Four wires each of same length, diameter and material are connected to each other to form a square. If the resistance of each wire is R, then equivalent resistance across the opposite corners is **[UP CPMT]**

(a) R (b) $R/2$ (c) $R/4$ (d) None of these

12 In the given circuit, the equivalent resistance between the points A and B (in ohms) is **[Manipal]**

(a) 9 (b) 11.6 (c) 14.5 (d) 21.2

2012

13 A ring is made of a wire having a resistance $R_0 = 12$ Ω. Find the points A and B as shown in the figure, at which a current carrying conductor should be connected so that the resistance R of the sub-circuit between these points is equal to 8/3 Ω. **[CBSE AIPMT]**

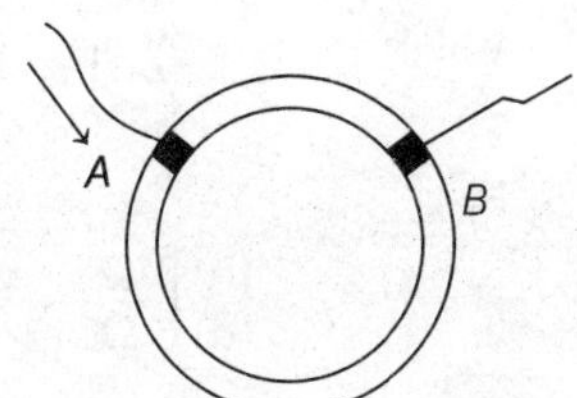

(a) $\frac{l_1}{l_2} = \frac{5}{8}$ (b) $\frac{l_1}{l_2} = \frac{1}{3}$ (c) $\frac{l_1}{l_2} = \frac{3}{8}$ (d) $\frac{l_1}{l_2} = \frac{1}{2}$

14 Resistors of 6 Ω and 12 Ω are connected in parallel. This combination is connected in series with a 10 V battery and 6 Ω resistor. What is the potential difference between the terminals of the 12 Ω resistor? **[AIIMS]**

(a) 4 V (b) 16 V (c) 2 V (d) 8 V

15 Six resistances each of value $r = 6$ Ω are connected between points A, B and C as shown in the figure. If R_1, R_2 and R_3 are the resistances between A and B, between B and C and between A and C respectively, then $R_1 : R_2 : R_3$ will be equal to **[AMU]**

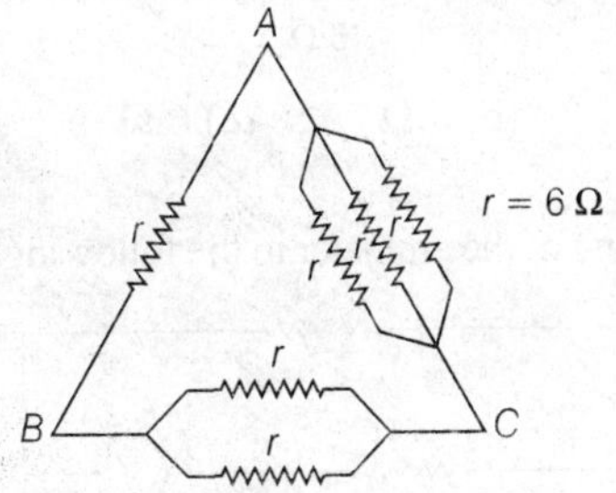

(a) 6 : 3 : 2 (b) 1 : 2 : 3 (c) 5 : 4 : 3 (d) 4 : 3 : 2

16 What current will flow through the 2 kΩ resistor in the circuit shown in the figure? **[WB JEE]**

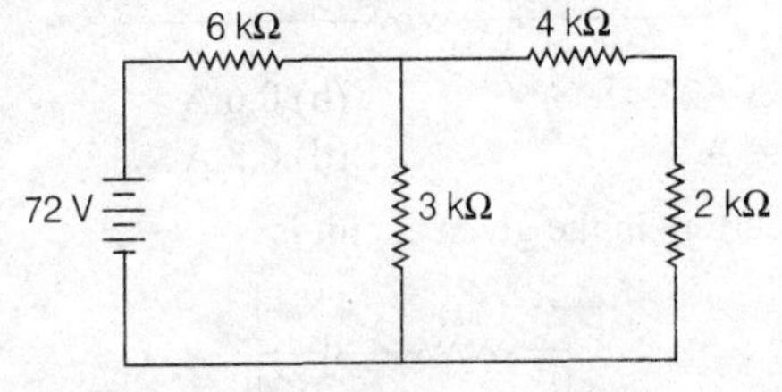

(a) 3 mA (b) 6 mA (c) 12 mA (d) 36 mA

2011

17 The resistance across A and B in the figure below will be **[WB JEE]**

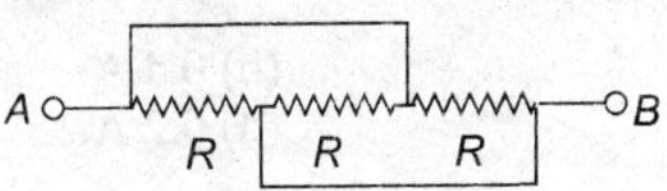

(a) 3R (b) R (c) $\frac{R}{3}$ (d) None of these

2010

18 The effective resistance between points A and C for the network shown in figure is **[OJEE]**

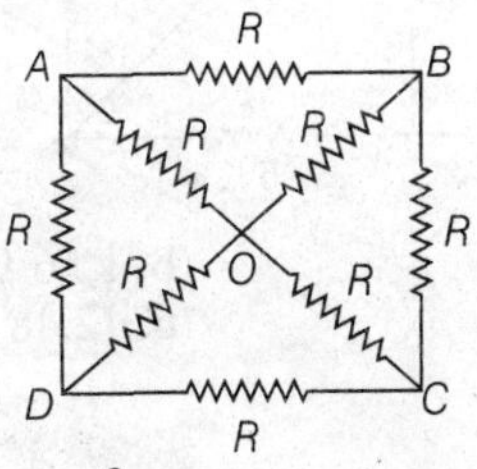

(a) $\frac{2}{3}R$ (b) $\frac{3}{2}R$ (c) 2R (d) $\frac{1}{2R}$

19 Three resistances 5 Ω, 5 Ω and 6 Ω are connected as shown in figure. If the point S divides the resistance 6 Ω into two equal halves, the resistance between points P and S is **[Kerala CEE]**

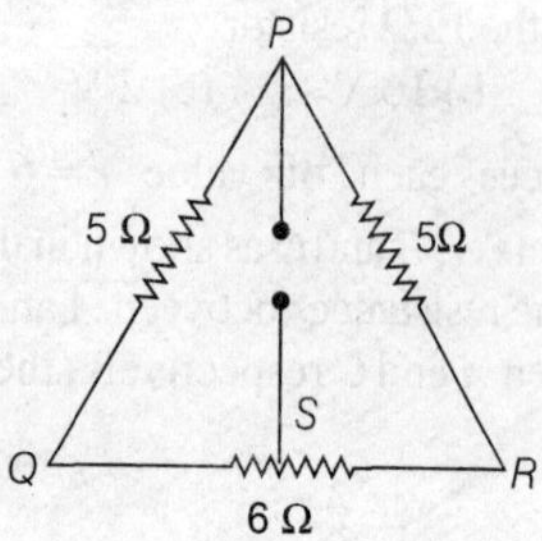

(a) 11 Ω (b) 8 Ω (c) 6 Ω (d) 10 Ω
(e) 4 Ω

20 The reading of the ammeter in the following figure will be

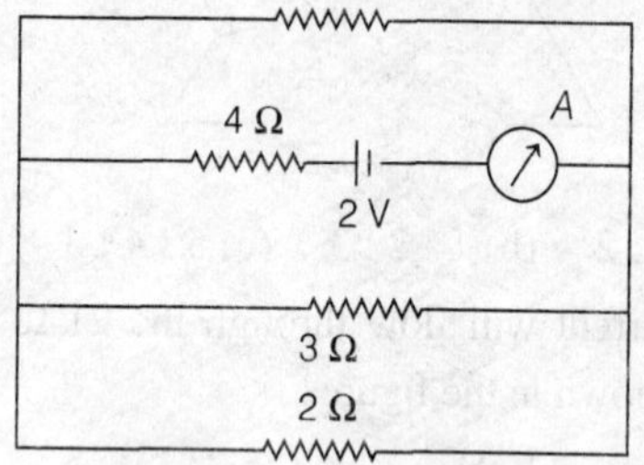

(a) 0.8 A (b) 0.6 A **[WB JEE]**
(c) 0.4 A (d) 0.2 A

21 The current in the given circuit is **[JCECE]**

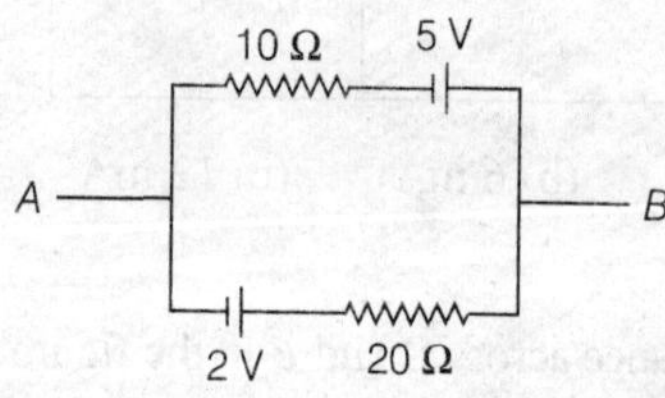

(a) 0.3 A (b) 0.4 A
(c) 0.1 A (d) 0.2 A

22 The equivalent resistance between the points A and B in the following circuit is **[DUMET]**

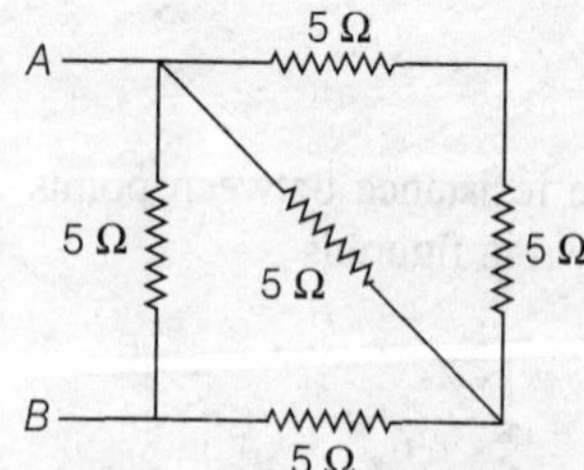

(a) 3.12 Ω (b) 1.56 Ω
(c) 6.24 Ω (d) 12.48 Ω

23 The potential difference (in volt) across the resistance R_3 in the circuit shown in figure, is ($R_1 = 15\ \Omega$, $R_2 = 15\ \Omega$, $R_3 = 30\ \Omega$ and $R_4 = 35\ \Omega$) **[BCECE]**

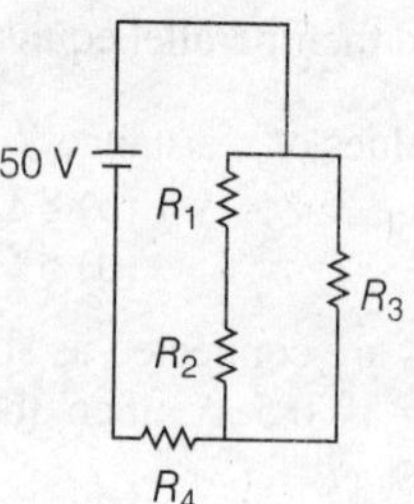

(a) 5 (b) 7.5
(c) 15 (d) 12.5

24 A uniform wire of resistance R and length L is cut into four equal parts, each of length $L/4$, which are then connected in parallel combination. The effective resistance of the combination will be **[JIPMER]**

(a) R (b) $4R$
(c) $\frac{R}{4}$ (d) $\frac{R}{16}$

2009

25 Four resistances 10 Ω, 5 Ω, 7 Ω and 3 Ω are connected so that they form the sides of a rectangle AB, BC, CD and DA, respectively. Another resistance of 10 Ω is connected across the diagonal AC. The equivalent resistance between A and B is **[AFMC]**

(a) 2 Ω (b) 5 Ω
(c) 7 Ω (d) 10 Ω

26 You are given two resistances R_1 and R_2. By using them singly in series and in parallel, you can obtain the resistances of 8 Ω and 1.5 Ω, respectively. The values of R_1 and R_2 are

(a) 1 Ω and 7 Ω (b) 1.5 Ω and 6.5 Ω **[BCECE]**
(c) 3 Ω and 5 Ω (d) 2 Ω and 6 Ω

27 A wire of resistance 12 Ω-m^{-1} is bent to form a complete circle of radius 10 cm. The resistance between its two diametrically opposite points A and B as shown in the figure, is **[CBSE AIPMT]**

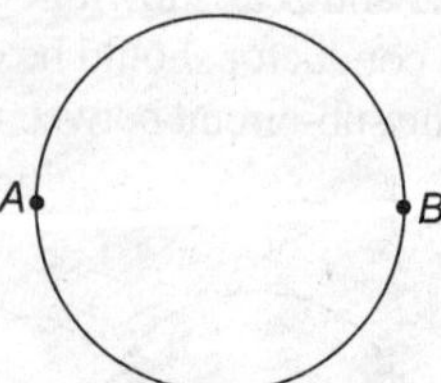

(a) 0.6π Ω (b) 3 Ω
(c) 6π Ω (d) 6 Ω

2008

28 In the circuit shown, the current through the 4 Ω resistor is 1 A when the points P and M are connected to a DC voltage source. The potential difference between the points M and N is **[CBSE AIPMT]**

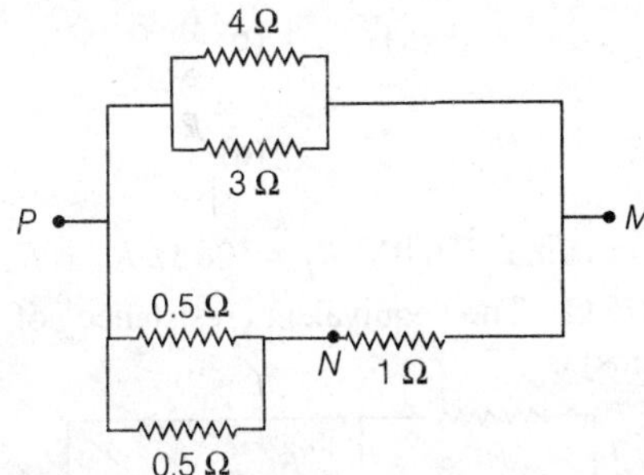

(a) 1.5 V (b) 1.0 V
(c) 0.5 V (d) 3.2 V

29 A piece of wire of resistance R is cut into n equal parts, then these parts are connected in parallel. If the equivalent resistance of the parallel combination is R', then (R/R') is **[BHU]**

(a) $\frac{1}{1}$ (b) $\frac{n}{1}$
(c) $\frac{n^2}{1}$ (d) $\frac{1}{n}$

30 In circuit shown below, the resistances are given in ohm and the battery is assumed ideal with emf equal to 3 V. The voltage across the resistance R_4 is **[J&K CET]**

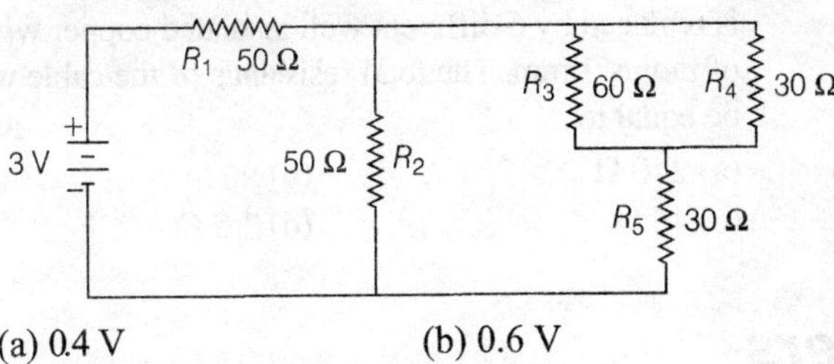

(a) 0.4 V (b) 0.6 V
(c) 1.2 V (d) 1.5 V

31 The equivalent resistance between the points A and B will be (each resistance is of 15 Ω) **[KCET]**

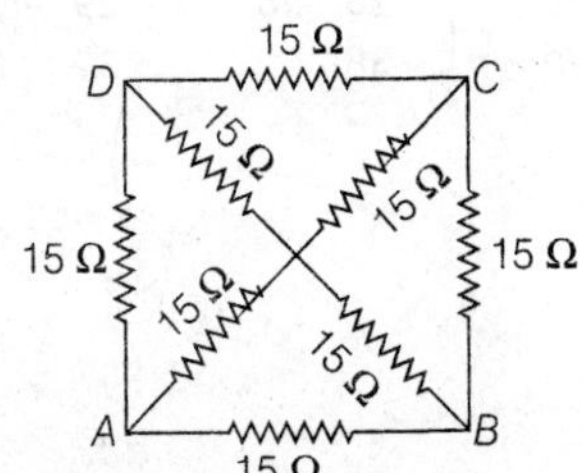

(a) 30 Ω (b) 8 Ω
(c) 10 Ω (d) 40 Ω

2007

32 In the adjoining figure, the equivalent resistance between A and B is **[Kerala CEE]**

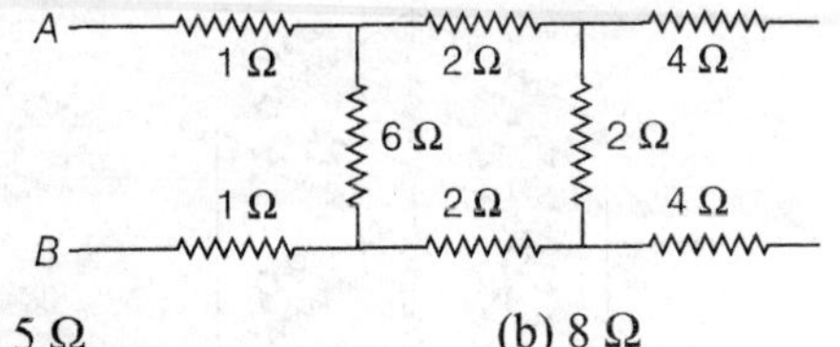

(a) 5 Ω (b) 8 Ω
(c) 2.5 Ω (d) 6.8 Ω
(e) 7.8 Ω

33 For two resistance wires joined in parallel, the resultant resistance is $\frac{6}{5}$ Ω. When one of the resistance wires breaks, the effective resistance becomes 2 Ω. The resistance of the broken wire is **[RPMT]**

(a) $\frac{3}{5}$ Ω (b) 2 Ω
(c) $\frac{6}{5}$ Ω (d) 3 Ω

34 The equivalent resistance between A and B (of the circuit shown) is **[AMU]**

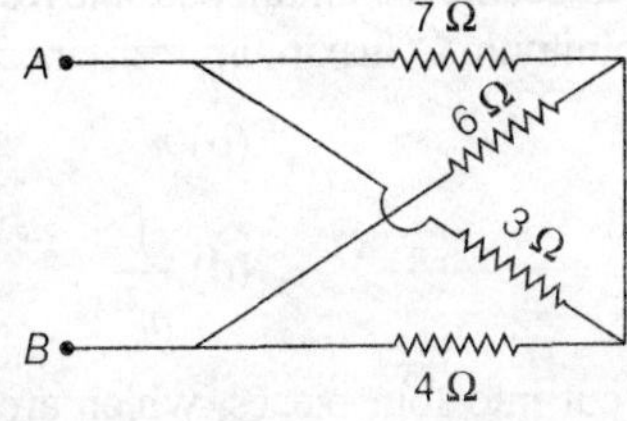

(a) 4.5 Ω (b) 12 Ω
(c) 5.4 Ω (d) 20 Ω

35 In a network as shown in the figure, the potential difference across the resistance $2R$ is (the cell has an emf of E volt and no internal resistance) **[BCECE]**

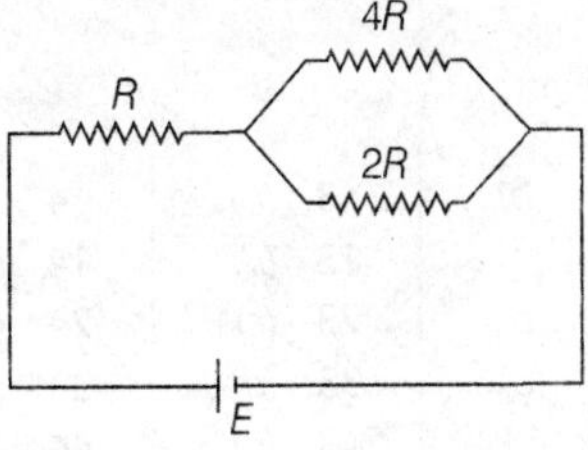

(a) $2E$ (b) $4E/7$
(c) $E/7$ (d) E

36 A copper wire of length 1 m and radius 1 mm is joined in series with an iron wire of length 2 m and radius 3 mm and a current is passed through the wires. The ratio of the current density in the copper and iron wires is **[Punjab PMET]**

(a) 18 : 1 (b) 9 : 1
(c) 6 : 1 (d) 2 : 3

2006

37 The effective resistance across the points A and I is **[Kerala CEE]**

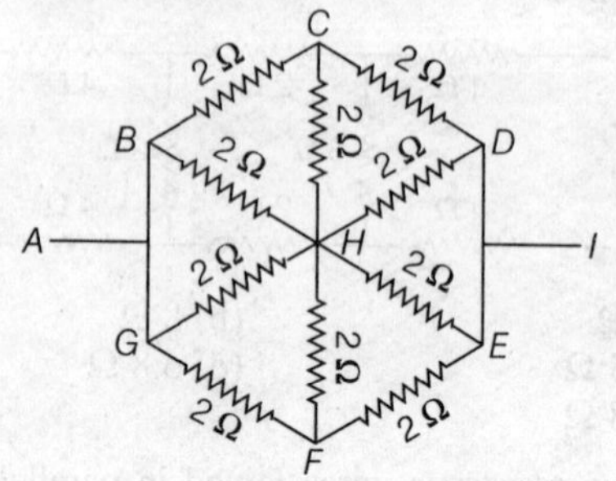

(a) 2 Ω (b) 1 Ω
(c) 0.5 Ω (d) 5 Ω
(e) 10 Ω

38 A wire has resistance 12 Ω. It is bent in the form of a circle. The effective resistance between the two points on any diameter of the circle is **[Haryana PMT]**

(a) 12 Ω (b) 24 Ω
(c) 6 Ω (d) 3 Ω

39 You are given n resistors, each of resistance r. They are first combined to get minimum possible resistance, then they are connected to get the maximum possible resistance. The ratio between minimum to maximum resistance is **[Guj CET]**

(a) $\frac{1}{n}$ (b) n
(c) n^2 (d) $\frac{1}{n^2}$

40 A wire is cut into four pieces, which are put together by sides to obtain one conductor. If the original resistance of wire was R, the resistance of the bundle will be **[Punjab PMET]**

(a) $\frac{R}{4}$ (b) $\frac{R}{8}$ (c) $\frac{R}{16}$ (d) $\frac{R}{32}$

2005

41 When a wire of uniform cross-section a, length l and resistance R is bent into a complete circle, resistance between two of diametrically opposite points will be **[CBSE AIPMT]**

(a) $\frac{R}{4}$ (b) $\frac{R}{8}$
(c) $4R$ (d) $\frac{R}{2}$

42 In the circuit, $E = 6.0\text{V}$, $R_1 = 100\ \Omega$, $R_2 = R_3 = 50\ \Omega$ and $R_4 = 75\ \Omega$. The equivalent resistance of the circuit (in ohms) is **[KCET]**

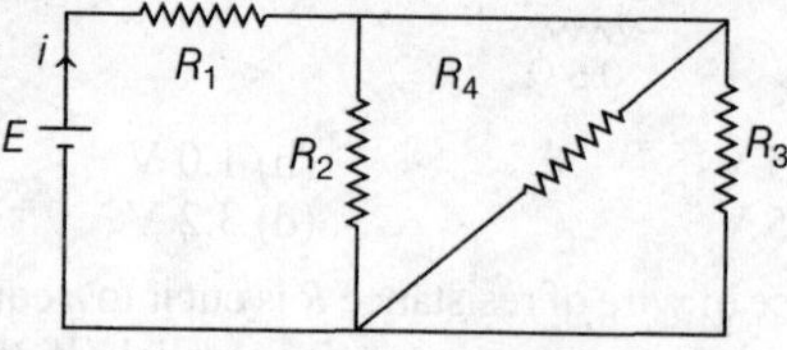

(a) 11.875 (b) 26.31
(c) 118.75 (d) None of these

43 By using only two resistance coils singly, in series or in parallel, one should be able to obtain resistance of 3 Ω, 4 Ω, 12 Ω and 16 Ω. The separate resistances of the coil are **[KCET]**

(a) 3 and 4 (b) 4 and 12
(c) 12 and 16 (d) 16 and 3

44 An electrical cable of copper has just one wire of radius 9 mm and its resistance is 5 Ω. The single wire of the cable is replaced by 6 different well insulated copper wires each of radius 3 mm. The total resistance of the cable will now be equal to **[UP CPMT]**

(a) 270 Ω (b) 90 Ω
(c) 45 Ω (d) 7.5 Ω

Answers

1 (d)	2 (b)	3 (b)	4 (d)	5 (b)	6 (c)	7 (b)	8 (a)	9 (c)	10 (d)
11 (a)	12 (b)	13 (d)	14 (a)	15 (c)	16 (a)	17 (c)	18 (a)	19 (e)	20 (c)
21 (c)	22 (a)	23 (c)	24 (d)	25 (b)	26 (d)	27 (a)	28 (d)	29 (c)	30 (a)
31 (c)	32 (a)	33 (d)	34 (a)	35 (b)	36 (b)	37 (b)	38 (d)	39 (d)	40 (c)
41 (a)	42 (c)	43 (b)	44 (a)						

Explanations

1 (*d*) The given circuit diagram can be drawn as shown below

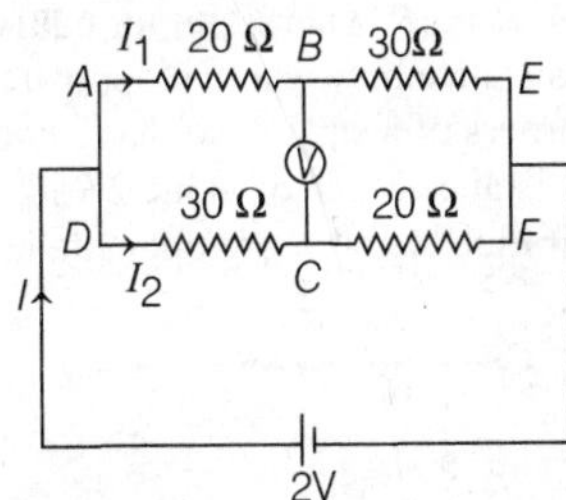

The equivalent resistance of circuit is given by

$$\frac{1}{R_{eq}} = \frac{1}{R_{AE}} + \frac{1}{R_{DF}}$$

$$= \frac{1}{(20+30)} + \frac{1}{(30+20)}$$

$$= \frac{1}{50} + \frac{1}{50} = \frac{2}{50}$$

$\Rightarrow R_{eq} = 25\ \Omega$

The current in circuit, $I = \frac{V}{R} = \frac{2}{25}$ A

As the resistance of two branches is same, i.e. 50Ω.

So, the current $I_1 = I_2$

$$\Rightarrow \quad I = I_1 + I_2$$

$$\frac{2}{25} = 2I_1$$

$$\Rightarrow \quad I_2 = I_1 = \frac{1}{25} \text{A}$$

∴ The voltage across AB,

$$V_1 = I_1 R_1 = \frac{1}{25} \times 20$$

and voltage across CD,

$$V_2 = I_2 R_2 = \frac{1}{25} \times 30$$

∴ Voltmeter reading

$$= V_2 - V_1$$

$$= \frac{30}{25} - \frac{20}{25}$$

$$= \frac{10}{25} = 0.4 \text{ V}$$

2 (*b*) As the other end of 8Ω resistor is grounded, is at zero potential, the potential difference across 8 Ω resistor $= 24 - 0 = 24$ V

So, current in 8Ω resistor,

$$I = \frac{V}{R} = \frac{24-0}{8} = 3\text{A}$$

3 (*b*) The situation is shown in the circuit diagram.

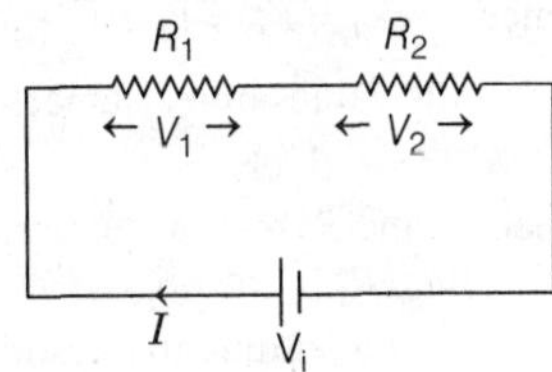

Current flowing through the circuit,

$$I = \frac{V_i}{R_1 + R_2}$$

Voltage across R_2, $V_2 = IR_2$

$$V_2 = \frac{V_i R_2}{R_1 + R_2}$$

$$\Rightarrow \quad \frac{R_1 + R_2}{R_2} = \frac{V_i}{V_2}$$

$$\Rightarrow \quad \frac{V_i}{V_2} = \frac{R_1 + R_2}{R_2}$$

4 (*d*) If R_1 be the equivalent resistance of parallel resistors 8Ω, 8Ω and 4Ω, then

$$\frac{1}{R_1} = \frac{1}{8} + \frac{1}{8} + \frac{1}{4} = \frac{4}{8}$$

$$\Rightarrow \quad R_1 = 2\Omega$$

∴ Total resistance of upper branch,

$R_2 = R_1 + 4 = 2 + 4 = 6\Omega$

Now circuit can be redraw of

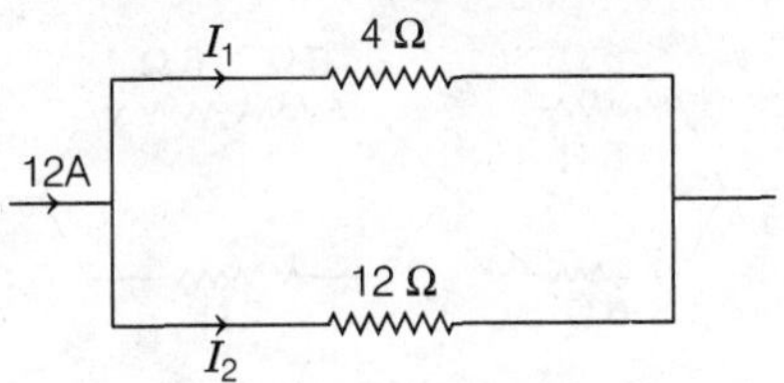

By current division rule, current through 12 Ω resistor, $I_2 = \frac{12 \times 6}{12 + 6}$

$$= 12 \times \frac{1}{3} = 4\text{A}$$

∴ Voltage across 12Ω resistor,

$$V = I_2 R = 4 \times 12 = 48 \text{ V}$$

5 (*b*)

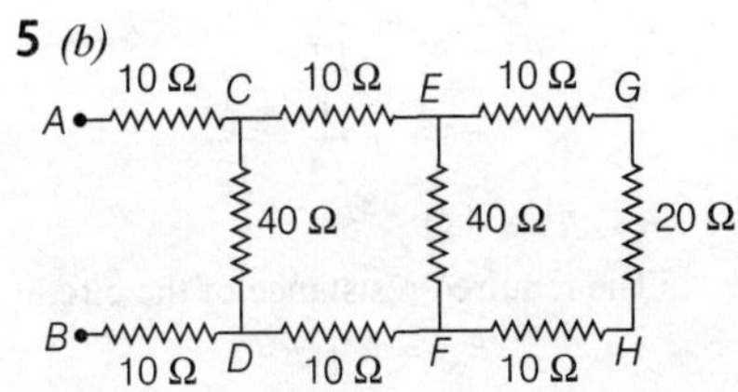

In the circuit, the branch $EGHF$ have three resistances of 10 Ω, 20 Ω and 10 Ω, respectively which are connected in series combination.

So, their equilvalent resistance is given by

$$R_1 = 10 + 20 + 10 = 40\ \Omega$$

This R_1 resistance is parallel with 40 Ω resistance which is connected in the branch EF. So, their equivalent resistance,

$$R_2 = \frac{40 \times 40}{40 + 40} = 20\ \Omega$$

Now, circuit becomes

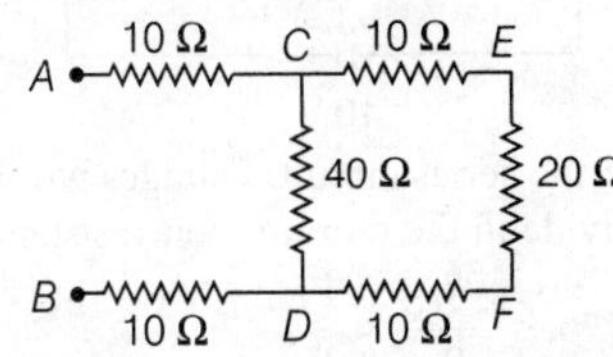

Now, in the branch $CEFD$ 10 Ω, 20 Ω and 10 Ω resistance are connected in series combination their equivalent resistance is given by

$R_3 = 10\ \Omega + 20\ \Omega + 40\ \Omega = 40\ \Omega$

This R_3 is parallel with 40 Ω resistance which is in branch CD. Their equivalent resistance,

$$R_4 = \frac{40 \times 40}{40 + 40} = 20\ \Omega$$

Now, circuit becomes

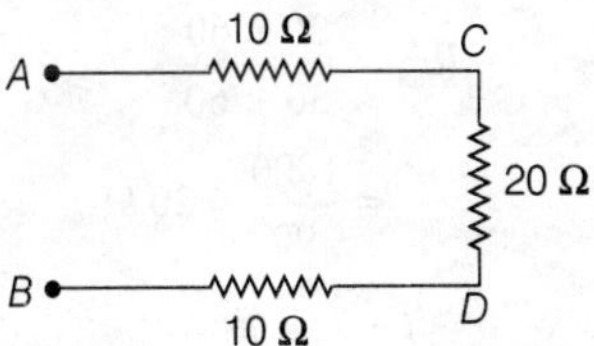

The net resistance between A and B,

$R_{net} = 10 + 20 + 10 = 40\ \Omega$

6 (*c*)

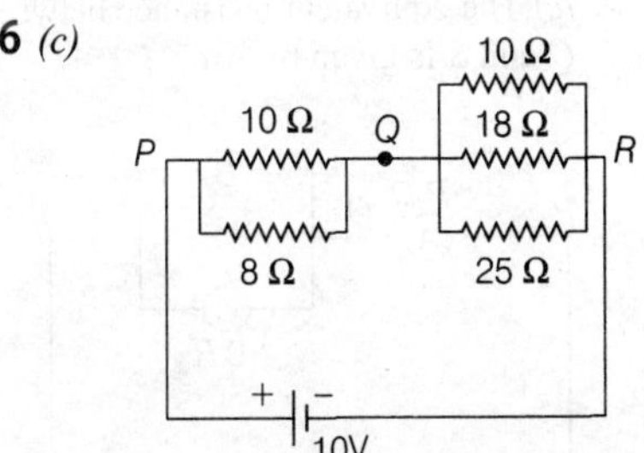

In the given circuit, net resistance between P and Q points is R_{PQ} and net resistance between Q and R points is R_{QR}, then

$$R_{PQ} = \frac{10 \times 8}{10 + 8} = \frac{80}{18} = \frac{40}{9}\ \Omega$$

$$R_{QR} = \frac{10 \times 18 \times 25}{10 \times 18 + 18 \times 25 + 25 \times 10}$$

$$= \frac{4500}{880} = \frac{225}{44}\ \Omega$$

So, circuit will be

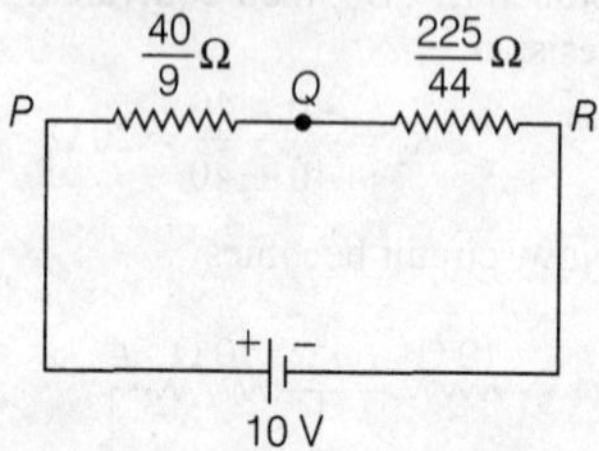

In the series circuit, voltages will be divide in the ratio of their resistance.

$$\therefore \quad \frac{R_{PQ}}{R_{QR}} = \frac{V_{PQ}}{V_{QR}}$$

$$\therefore \quad \frac{\left(\frac{40}{9}\right)}{\left(\frac{225}{44}\right)} = \frac{V_{PQ}}{V_{QR}} \text{ or } \frac{1760}{2025} = \frac{V_{PQ}}{V_{QR}}$$

$$\text{or} \quad \frac{1760}{3785} = \frac{V_{PQ}}{10}$$

$$\Rightarrow \quad V_{PQ} = 4.65 \text{ V}$$

7 *(b)* $\because$ 60 Ω and 30 Ω resistors are connected in parallel. So, their net resistance

$$R_{\text{net}} = \frac{30 \times 60}{30 + 60}$$

$$= \frac{1800}{90} = 20\ \Omega$$

$$\therefore \quad i = \frac{2}{R_{\text{net}}} = \frac{2}{20}$$

$$= 0.1 \text{ A}$$

8 *(c)* The equivalent resistance between Q and S is given by

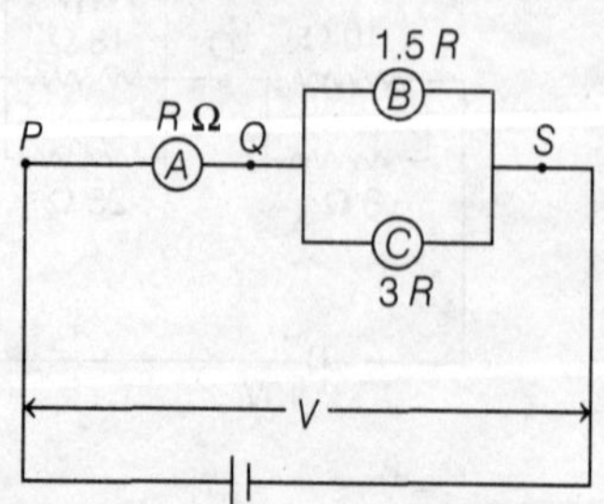

$$\frac{1}{R'} = \frac{1}{1.5R} + \frac{1}{3R} = \frac{2+1}{3R} \Rightarrow R' = R$$

Now, $V_{PQ} = V_A = IR$

Also, $V_{QS} = V_B = V_C = IR$

Hence, $V_A = V_B = V_C$

9 *(c)* Let the values of resistances be R_1 and, R_2 respectively.

When R_1 and R_2 resistances are in series, then $R_1 + R_2 = 6$

(according to question) ...(i)

When R_1 and R_2 resistances are in parallel, then

$$\frac{R_1 R_2}{R_1 + R_2} = \frac{4}{3} \quad \text{...(ii)}$$

From Eqs. (i) and (ii), we get,

$$\frac{R_1 R_2}{6} = \frac{4}{3}$$

$$\Rightarrow \quad R_1 R_2 = 4 \times 2$$

$$\Rightarrow \quad R_1 R_2 = 8 \quad \text{...(iii)}$$

We know that,

$$R_1 - R_2 = \sqrt{(R_1 + R_2)^2 - 4R_1R_2}$$

$$= \sqrt{36 - 4 \times 8}$$

$$\Rightarrow \quad R_1 - R_2 = \sqrt{4}$$

$$\Rightarrow \quad R_1 - R_2 = 2 \quad \text{...(iv)}$$

From Eqs. (i) and (iv), we get

$$R_1 = 4\ \Omega \text{ and } R_2 = 2\ \Omega$$

10 *(d)* Given, 6 Ω, 6 Ω and 6 Ω are in parallel between A and C, so

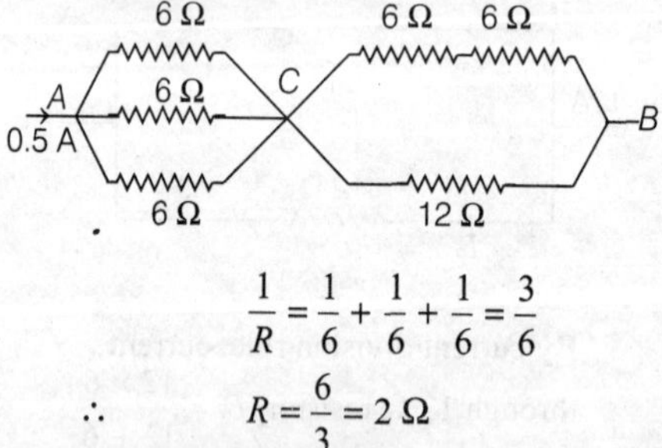

$$\frac{1}{R} = \frac{1}{6} + \frac{1}{6} + \frac{1}{6} = \frac{3}{6}$$

$$\therefore \quad R = \frac{6}{3} = 2\ \Omega$$

Now between C and B, 6 Ω and 6 Ω are in series whose equivalent resistance and 12 Ω are in parallel.

So, $R' = 6 + 6 = 12\Omega$

$$\therefore \quad \frac{1}{R''} = \frac{1}{R'} + \frac{1}{12}$$

$$= \frac{1}{12} + \frac{1}{12} = \frac{2}{12}$$

$$\Rightarrow R'' = 6\ \Omega$$

The required resistance of the circuit,

$$R_{\text{eq}} = R + R''$$

$$= 2 + 6 = 8\ \Omega$$

So, the potential difference,

$$V_A - V_B = iR_{\text{eq}} = 0.5 \times 8 = 4 \text{ V}$$

11 *(a)* The resistance of two arms on the opposite corners of a square is $R + R = 2R$. Therefore, for equivalent resistance between two opposite corners of a square, we have two resistances each of value $2R$ in parallel. A and B are opposite corner.

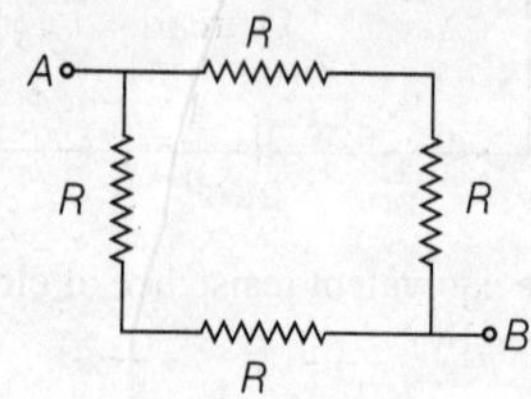

$$\text{So,} \quad \frac{1}{R'} = \frac{1}{2R} + \frac{1}{2R}$$

$$\Rightarrow \quad \frac{1}{R'} = \frac{1+1}{2R} = \frac{2}{2R}$$

$$\therefore \quad R' = R$$

12 *(b)* The given circuit can be redrawn as

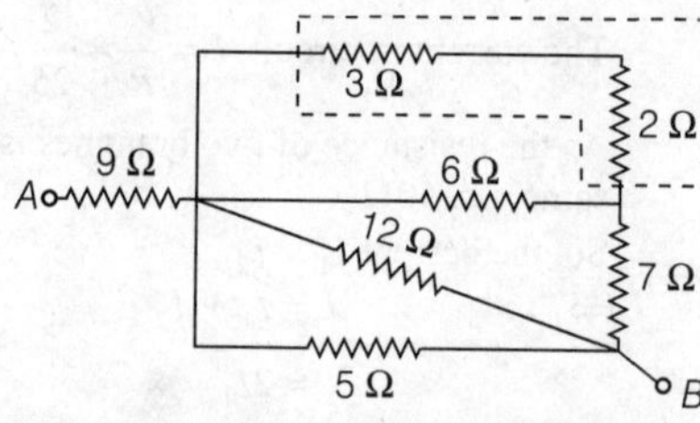

From the above dotted region, 3 Ω and 2 Ω are in series, $R = 3 + 2 = 5\ \Omega$

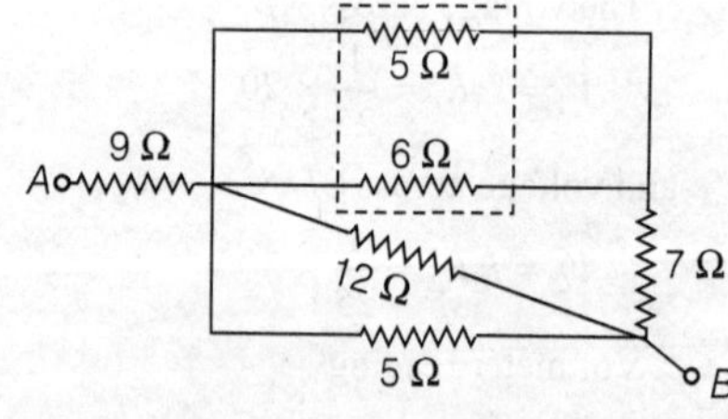

5 Ω and 6 Ω are in parallel, so

$$R = \frac{5 \times 6}{5 + 6} = \frac{30}{11}\ \Omega$$

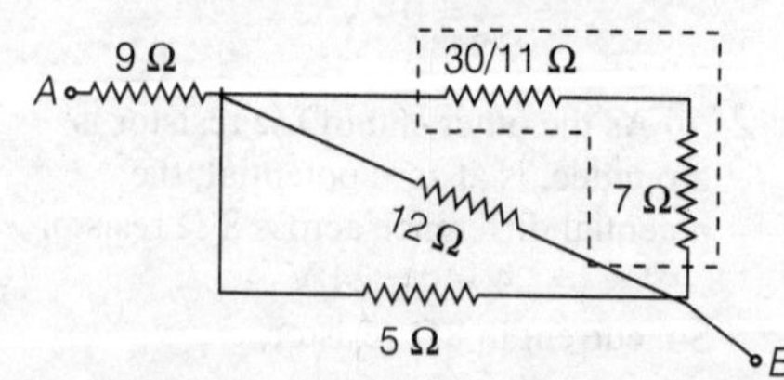

$\frac{30}{11}$ Ω and 7 Ω are in series,

$$R = \frac{30}{11} + 7 = \frac{107}{11}\ \Omega$$

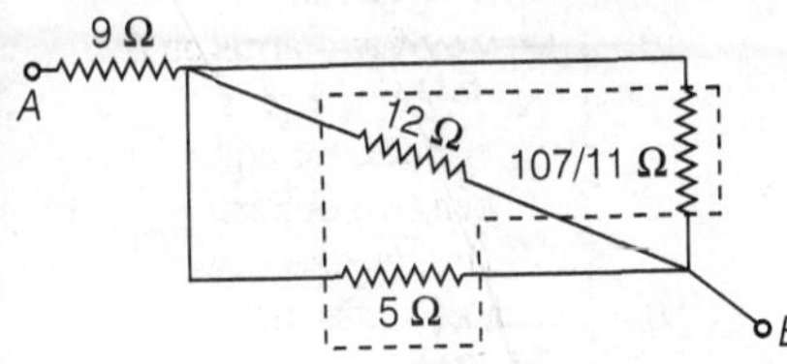

$12\ \Omega$, $\frac{107}{11}\ \Omega$ and $5\ \Omega$ are in parallel.

So, $\frac{1}{R} = \frac{1}{12} + \frac{11}{107} + \frac{1}{5} = 0.386$

$\Rightarrow \quad R = 2.6\ \Omega$

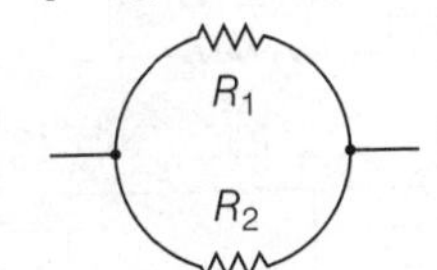

Hence, $R_{eq} = 9 + 2.6 = 11.6\ \Omega$

13 *(d)* Let r be the resistance per unit length of wire, then

$R_s = R_1 + R_2 = rl_1 + rl_2 = r(l_1 + l_2)$ ...(i)

R_1

R_2

When the wire is wound to form a circle, then

$$R_p = \frac{R_1R_2}{R_1 + R_2} = \frac{rl_1 \times rl_2}{rl_1 + rl_2}$$

$$= \frac{rl_1l_2}{l_1 + l_2} \quad \text{...(ii)}$$

Dividing Eq. (i) by Eq. (ii), we get

$$\frac{R_s}{R_p} = \frac{r(l_1 + l_2)}{r(l_1l_2)/(l_1 + l_2)}$$

$$= \frac{(l_1 + l_2)^2}{l_1l_2}$$

$$\Rightarrow \frac{l_1}{l_2} + \frac{l_2}{l_1} + 2 = \frac{R_s}{R_p} = \frac{12}{8/3} = \frac{9}{2}$$

$$\left[\because R_s = 12\Omega \text{ and } R_p = 8/3\Omega\right]$$

If $\quad l_1/l_2 = x$, then

$\Rightarrow \quad x + \frac{1}{x} = \frac{5}{2}$

$\Rightarrow \quad 2x^2 = 2 - 5x = 0$

Solving it, we get

$$x = 2 \text{ or } \frac{1}{2}$$

i.e. $\quad \frac{l_1}{l_2} = 2$ or $\frac{1}{2}$

Hence, option (d) is correct.

14 *(a)* The circuit is shown as below

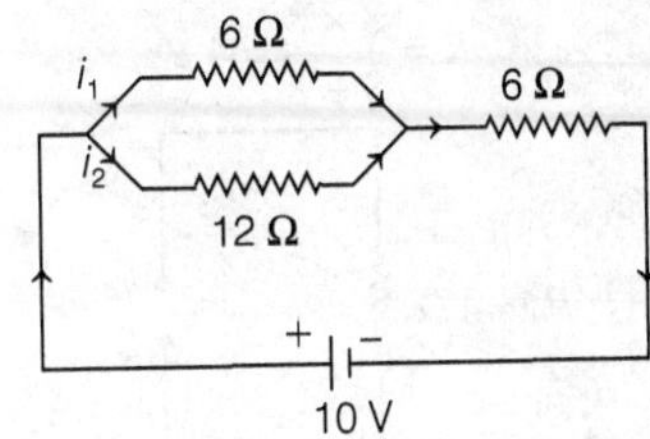

Here, $6\ \Omega$ and $12\ \Omega$ are in parallel.

So, $\quad R = \frac{6 \times 12}{6 + 12} = \frac{6 \times 12}{18} = 4\ \Omega$

Total resistance,

$$R_{eq} = 6 + 4 = 10\ \Omega$$

$\therefore$ Current, $i = \frac{V}{R} = \frac{10}{10} = 1\text{A}$

The current in $12\ \Omega$ resistor is

$$i_2 = i\left(\frac{R_1}{R_1 + R_2}\right) = 1 \times \left(\frac{6}{6 + 12}\right)$$

$\Rightarrow \quad i_2 = \frac{1}{3}$ A

The potential difference in $12\ \Omega$ resistor,

$$V = i_2R = \frac{1}{3} \times 12 = 4\text{ V}$$

15 *(c)* The given circuit can be redrawn as

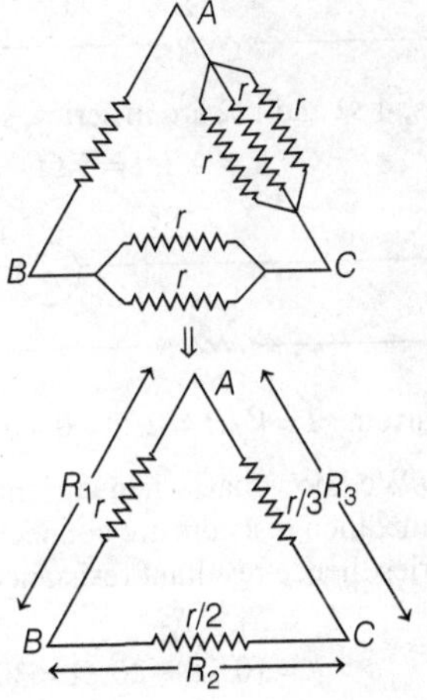

Resistance between A and B,

$$= r \| \left(\frac{r}{3} + \frac{r}{2}\right)$$

$$\Rightarrow \quad R_1 = \frac{(r)\left(\frac{5}{6}r\right)}{r + \frac{5}{6}r} = \frac{5}{11}r$$

Resistance between B and C,

$$R_2 = \frac{r}{2} \| \left(r + \frac{r}{3}\right) = \frac{\frac{r}{2} \times \frac{4r}{3}}{\frac{r}{2} + \frac{4r}{3}} = \frac{4}{11}r$$

Resistance between A and C,

$$R_3 = \frac{r}{3} \| \left(r + \frac{r}{2}\right) = \frac{\frac{r}{3} \times \frac{3r}{2}}{\frac{r}{3} + \frac{3r}{2}}$$

$\therefore \quad R_3 = \frac{3r}{11}$

Hence, $R_1 : R_2 : R_3 = 5 : 4 : 3$

16 *(a)* In the circuit, $4\ \text{k}\Omega$ and $2\ \text{k}\Omega$ are in series whose resistance is in parallel with $3\ \text{k}\Omega$. So, their equivalent resistance is

$$\frac{1}{R_e} = \frac{1}{3} + \frac{1}{6} = \frac{2+1}{6} = \frac{1}{2}$$

$\Rightarrow \quad R_e = 2\ \text{k}\Omega$

$\therefore$ Net resistance of the circuit $= 6 + 2 = 8\ \text{k}\Omega$

Thus, we have

$$I = \frac{72}{8 \times 10^3}$$

$$= 9 \times 10^{-3}\text{A} = 9\text{ mA}$$

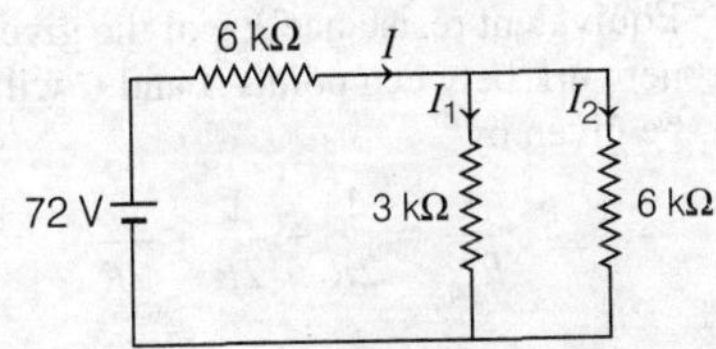

From current dividing rule,

$$I_2 = \left(\frac{3}{3+6}\right)I$$

$$= \left(\frac{3}{3+6}\right)9$$

$\Rightarrow \quad I_2 = 3\text{ mA}$

17 *(c)* Three resistances are in parallel, so the effective resistance could be given as

$$\frac{1}{R_{eff}} = \frac{1}{R} + \frac{1}{R} + \frac{1}{R} = \frac{3}{R}$$

R

A — B

R

R

So, $\quad R_{eff} = R/3$

18 *(a)* As $R_{AB} = R_{AO}$ and $R_{BC} = R_{OC}$, so points O and B will be at same potential and hence resistance R_{OB} becomes ineffective.

Similarly, $R_{AO} = R_{AD}$ and $R_{OC} = R_{DC}$, resistance R_{OD} becomes ineffective.

So, excluding R_{BO} and R_{OD}, the equivalent circuit is shown below

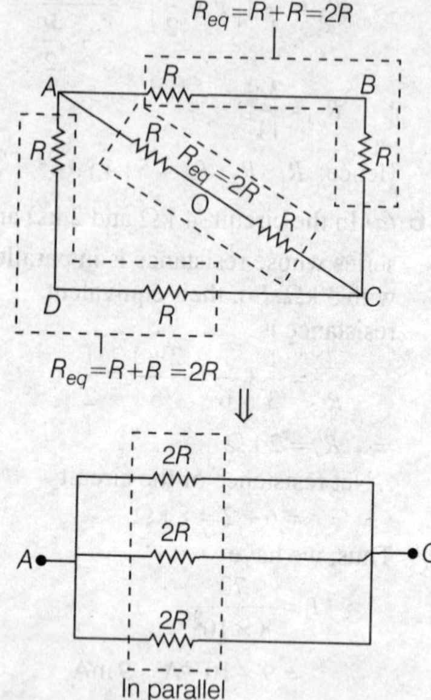

Equivalent resistance R_{eq} of the given network between points A and C will be given by

$$\frac{1}{R_{eq}} = \frac{1}{2R} + \frac{1}{2R} + \frac{1}{2R}$$

i.e. $\quad R_{eq} = \frac{2}{3}R$

19 *(e)* Series transformations of circuit is shown below

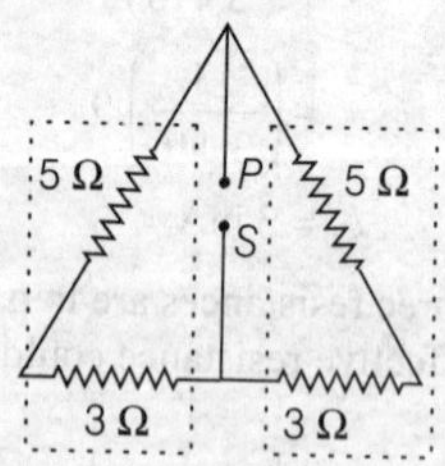

From the above dotted region, 5 Ω and 3 Ω are in series, so $R = 5 + 3 = 8\ \Omega$.

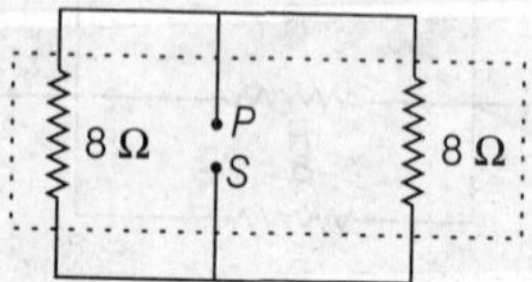

From the above dotted region 8 Ω and 8 Ω are in parallel, so

$$R = \frac{8 \times 8}{8 + 8} = 4\ \Omega$$

The resistance between points P and S is 4 Ω.

$$R_e' = 4\ \Omega$$

20 *(c)* Given circuit is

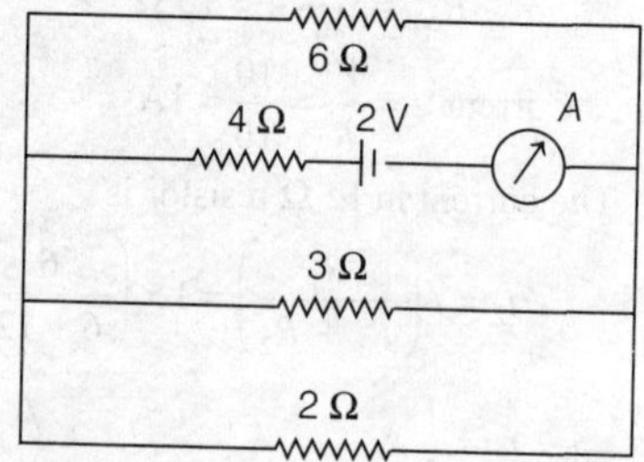

As, 6 Ω, 3 Ω and 2 Ω are in parallel,

so $\frac{1}{R} = \frac{1}{6} + \frac{1}{3} + \frac{1}{2} = \frac{1 + 2 + 3}{6} = 1$

or $\quad R = 1\ \Omega$

As, 4 Ω and 1 Ω are in series, so

$$R = 4 + 1 = 5\ \Omega$$

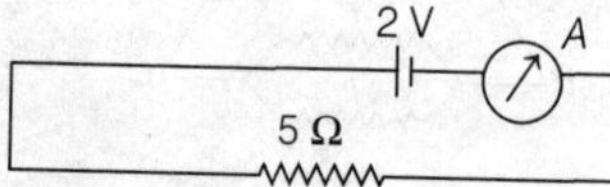

Current, $I = V/R = 2/5 = 0.4$ A

21 *(c)* We know that, when current flow is same, then resistors are connected in series, hence resultant resistance is

$$R' = R_1 + R_2$$
$$= 10\ \Omega + 20\ \Omega = 30\ \Omega$$

Also since, cells are connected in opposite directions, the resultant emf is

$$E = E_1 - E_2$$
$$= 5\text{ V} - 2\text{ V} = 3\text{ V}$$

From Ohm's law, $E = iR$

$$\Rightarrow \quad i = \frac{E}{R} = \frac{3}{30} = 0.1\text{ A}$$

22 *(a)* The circuit can be redrawn as

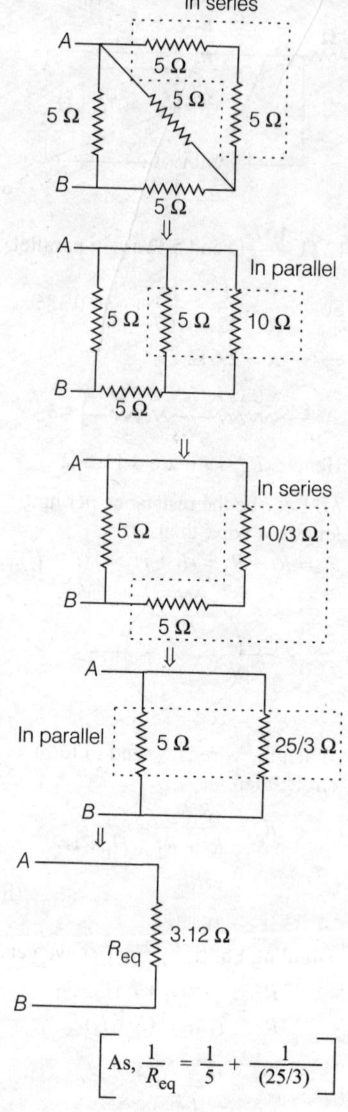

$$\left[\text{As, } \frac{1}{R_{eq}} = \frac{1}{5} + \frac{1}{(25/3)}\right]$$

23 *(c)* Total resistance of the circuit,

$$R = R_4 + \frac{(R_1 + R_2) \times R_3}{(R_1 + R_2) + R_3}$$
$$= 35 + \frac{(15 + 15) \times 30}{(15 + 15) + 30}$$
$$= 35 + \frac{30 \times 30}{30 + 30} = 50\ \Omega$$

Current in circuit, $i = \frac{V}{R} = \frac{50}{50} = 1$ A

Current through R_3, i.e. $i' = i/2 = \frac{1}{2}$ A

Potential difference across R_3

$$= i' \times R_3 = \frac{1}{2} \times 30 = 15\text{ V}$$

24 (d) Resistance, $R = \frac{\rho l}{A}$ or $R \propto l$

$\therefore \quad \frac{R_1}{R_2} = \frac{l_1}{l_2} = \frac{L}{L/4} = 4$

$\Rightarrow \quad R_2 = \frac{R}{4} \quad (\because R_1 = R)$

In parallel combination of such four resistances,

$$\frac{1}{R'} = \frac{1}{R_1} + \frac{1}{R_2} + \frac{1}{R_3} + \frac{1}{R_4}$$

or $\frac{1}{R'} = \frac{1}{R/4} + \frac{1}{R/4} + \frac{1}{R/4} + \frac{1}{R/4}$

$\Rightarrow \quad \frac{1}{R'} = \frac{4}{R} + \frac{4}{R} + \frac{4}{R} + \frac{4}{R}$

$\therefore \quad \frac{1}{R'} = \frac{16}{R} \Rightarrow R' = \frac{R}{16}$

25 (b) The circuit given in the question can be drawn as

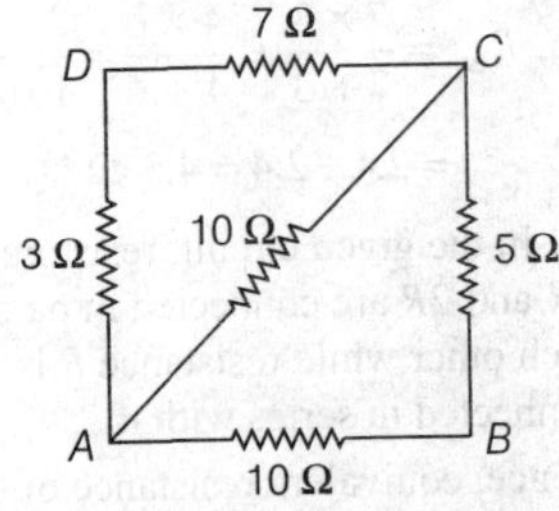

As, 3 Ω resistor and 7 Ω resistor are in series.

Therefore, resultant = 7 + 3 = 10 Ω

This 10 Ω equivalent resistance is in parallel with resistance (10 Ω) in arm *AC*.

$\therefore \quad \frac{1}{R_1} = \frac{1}{10} + \frac{1}{10} \Rightarrow R_1 = 5\ \Omega$

Now, R_1 is in series with resistor (5 Ω) in arm *CB*.

$\therefore \quad R_2 = 5 + 5 = 10\ \Omega$

Again, R_2 is in parallel with resistance (10 Ω) in arm *AB*.

$\therefore \quad \frac{1}{R} = \frac{1}{10} + \frac{1}{10} \Rightarrow R = 5\ \Omega$

26 (d) Let the two resistances be R_1 and R_2, then $R_1 + R_2 = 8\ \Omega$ [in series] ...(i)

and $\frac{R_1R_2}{R_1 + R_2} = 1.5\ \Omega$ [in parallel] ...(ii)

By using Eqs. (i) and (ii), we obtain

$$\frac{R_1R_2}{8} = 1.5$$

$\Rightarrow \quad R_1R_2 = 12$ or $R_2 = \frac{12}{R_1}$

Thus, Eq. (i) becomes,

$$R_1 + \frac{12}{R_1} = 8$$

$\Rightarrow \quad R_1^2 - 8R_1 + 12 = 0$

$R_1(R_1 - 6) - 2(R_1 - 6) = 0$

$\Rightarrow \quad R_1 = 2\ \Omega$ or $6\ \Omega$

This gives, $R_2 = 6\ \Omega$ or $2\ \Omega$ [by Eq. (i)]

27 (a) As, $r = 10$ cm = 0.1 m

Resistance per unit length = $12\ \Omega\text{m}^{-1}$

Length of the wire

= Circumference of circle = $2\pi r$

$\Rightarrow$ As, total resistance, $R = 2\pi r(12)$ ...(i)

$$\frac{1}{R_{eq}} = \frac{1}{R/2} + \frac{1}{R/2} = \frac{4}{R} = \frac{1}{6\pi r}$$

[from Eq. (i)]

$\Rightarrow R_{eq} = 6\pi\ (0.1) = 0.6\ \pi\ \Omega$

28 (d) Potential difference across *PM*,

$V = 4 \times 1 = 4$ V (i.e. across 4 Ω)

Equivalent resistance of lower side arm, $R_{eq} = 1 + \frac{0.5 \times 0.5}{0.5 + 0.5} = 1.25\ \Omega$

Now, the circuit can be shown as

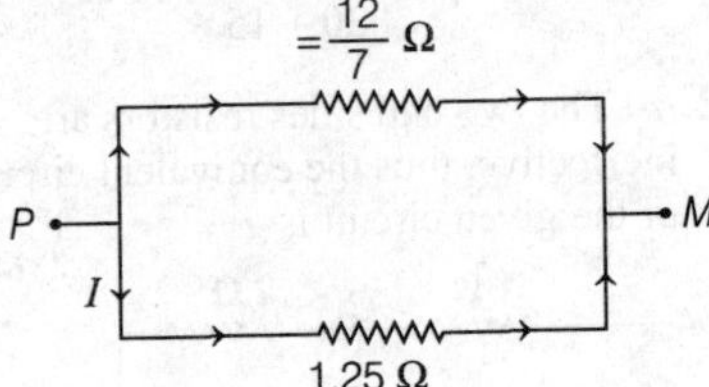

Let current I flows in lower branch, so

$1.25\ I = 4$ V

or $I = \frac{4}{1.25} = 3.2$ A

Therefore, 3.2 A current flows in 1 Ω resistance, hence potential difference between *M* and *N* is

$$V' = 3.2 \times 1 = 3.2 \text{ V}$$

29 (c) Resistance, $R = \frac{\rho l}{A}$

If r is the resistance of one cut part, then

$$r = \frac{\rho(l/n)}{A} = \frac{R}{n}$$

The resistance R' of the parallel combination of resistors is given by

$$\frac{1}{R'} = \frac{1}{r} + \frac{1}{r} + \ldots = \frac{n}{r}$$

$\Rightarrow \quad R' = \frac{r}{n} = \frac{\frac{R}{n}}{n} = \frac{R}{n^2}$

Hence, $\frac{R}{R'} = \frac{n^2}{1}$

30 (a) According to the question, the given circuit is

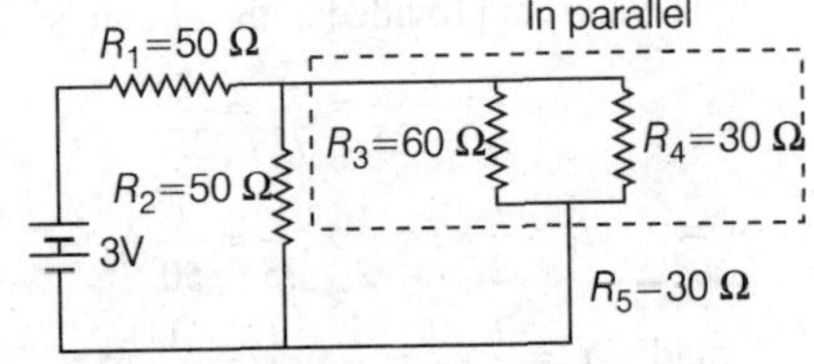

Upper dotted part in parallel, then

$\frac{1}{R} = \frac{1}{30} + \frac{1}{60} = \frac{2+1}{60}$

$\Rightarrow \quad \frac{60}{3} = 20\ \Omega$

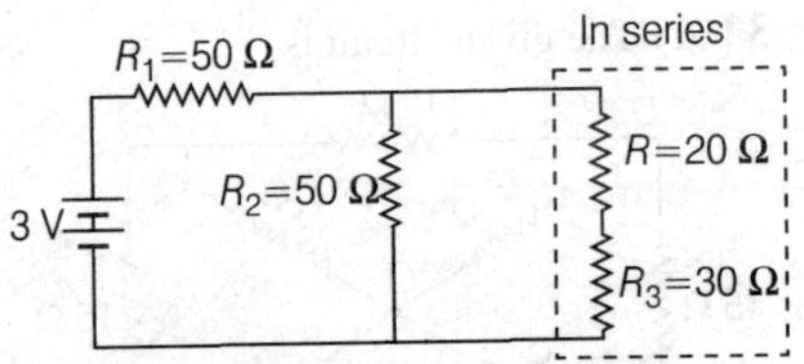

In the figure dotted part in series, then

$R = 30 + 20$

$R = 50\ \Omega$

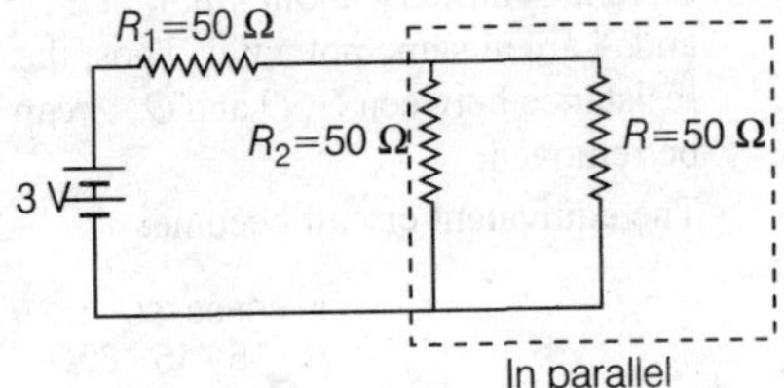

In the figure dotted part in parallel, then

$\frac{1}{R} = \frac{1}{50} + \frac{1}{50} = \frac{2}{50}$

$\Rightarrow \quad R = \frac{50}{2} = 25\ \Omega$

R_1=50 Ω R=25 Ω

In series

3V

Equivalent resistance of the given network,

$$R_{eq} = 75\ \Omega$$

The given circuit can be redrawn as

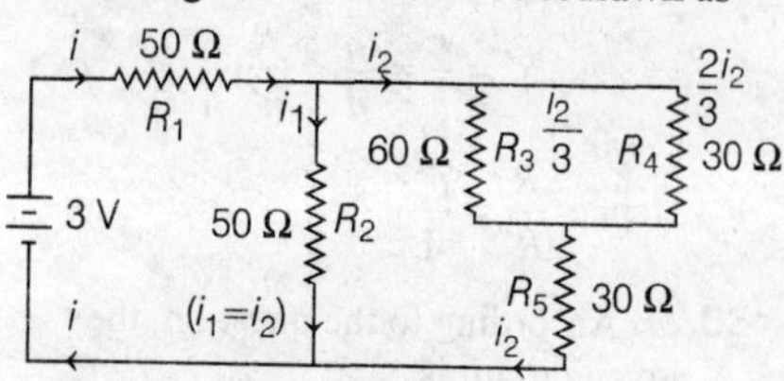

The current provided in the circuit is

$$i = \frac{3}{50+25} = \frac{3}{75} = \frac{1}{25}$$

$$\Rightarrow \quad i_1 = \frac{1}{2} \times i = \frac{1}{2} \times \frac{1}{25} = \frac{1}{50} \text{ A}$$

and $\quad i_2 = \frac{1}{2} \times i = \frac{1}{2} \times \frac{1}{25} = \frac{1}{50} \text{ A}$

Now voltage across R_4,

$$V = \frac{2i_2}{3} \times R_4 = 2 \times \frac{1}{50} \times \frac{1}{3} \times 30$$

$$= \frac{2}{5} = 0.4 \text{ V}$$

31 *(c)* The given circuit is

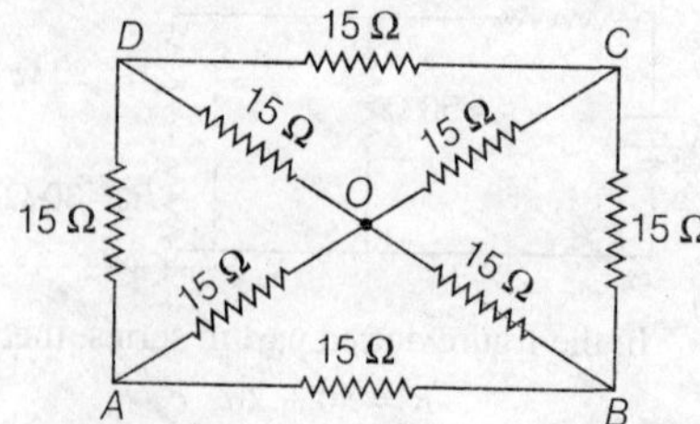

It can be seen that, in the figure that, there is symmetry about DB, that C, O and A are at same potential. Thus, the resistance between C, O and O, A can be removed.

The equivalent circuit becomes

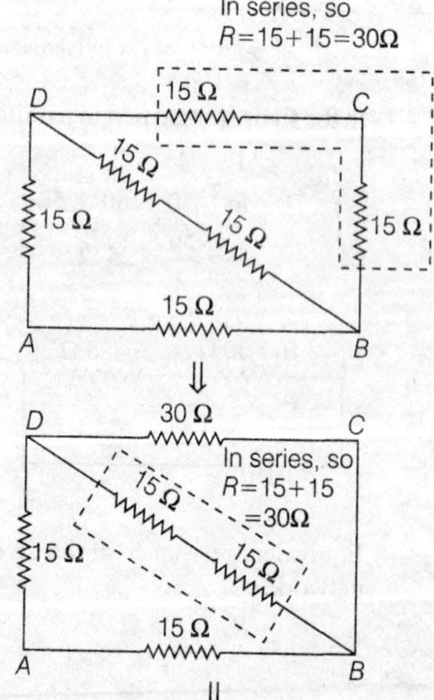

In parallel, so $R = \frac{30 \times 30}{30+30} = 15\ \Omega$

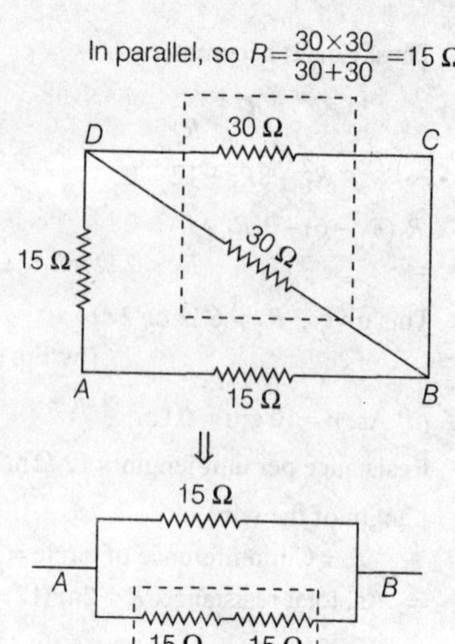

In series, so $R = 15\Omega + 15\Omega = 30\Omega$

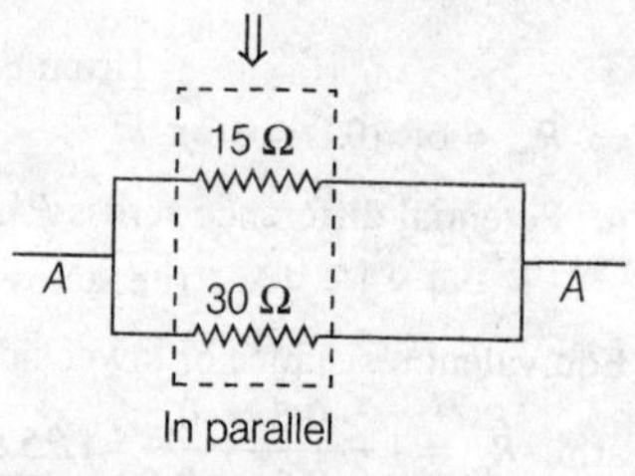

Thus, the resistance between the points A and B will be

$$R_{eq} = \frac{30 \times 15}{30+15} = 10\ \Omega$$

32 *(a)* The two end sides resistors are ineffective, thus the equivalent circuit of the given circuit is

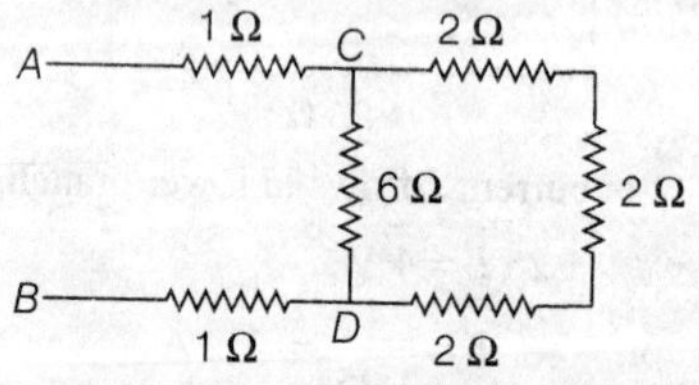

Between points C and D, resistors 2 Ω, 2 Ω and 2 Ω are in series, therefore their equivalent resistance,

$$R' = 2 + 2 + 2 = 6\ \Omega$$

Resistors R' and 6 Ω are in parallel, therefore their equivalent resistance is given by

$$\frac{1}{R''} = \frac{1}{6} + \frac{1}{6}$$

$$\Rightarrow \quad R'' = 3\ \Omega$$

Now, between points A and B, 1 Ω, 3 Ω and 1 Ω are in series. Therefore, resultant resistance,

$$R = 1 + 3 + 1 = 5\ \Omega.$$

33 *(d)* Let R_1 and R_2 be the resistances of two wires. In parallel combination,

$$\frac{R_1 R_2}{R_1 + R_2} = \frac{6}{5} \quad \text{...(i)}$$

If one of the wires breaks, then effective resistance becomes 2 Ω, i.e. $R_1 = 2\ \Omega$.

Substituting in Eq. (i), we have

$$\frac{2R_2}{2 + R_2} = \frac{6}{5}$$

or $\quad 10R_2 = 12 + 6R_2$

$\Rightarrow \quad 4R_2 = 12$

$\Rightarrow \quad R_2 = \frac{12}{4} = 3\ \Omega$

34 *(a)* As, resistances 7 Ω and 3 Ω are in parallel while 6 Ω and 4 Ω are in parallel also both combinations are in series.

So, $R_{eq} = \frac{7 \times 3}{7+3} + \frac{4 \times 6}{4+6} = \frac{21}{10} + \frac{24}{10}$

$$= 2.1 + 2.4 = 4.5\ \Omega$$

35 *(b)* In the given circuit, resistors $4R$ and $2R$ are connected in parallel to each other while resistance R is connected in series with it.

Hence, equivalent resistance of $4R$ and $2R$ resistance is

$$\frac{1}{R'} = \frac{1}{4R} + \frac{1}{2R} = \frac{3}{4R}$$

$$\Rightarrow \quad R' = \frac{4}{3} R$$

Thus, equivalent resistance of overall circuit, $R'' = R + \frac{4}{3} R = \frac{7R}{3}$

Given, emf is E volt, therefore

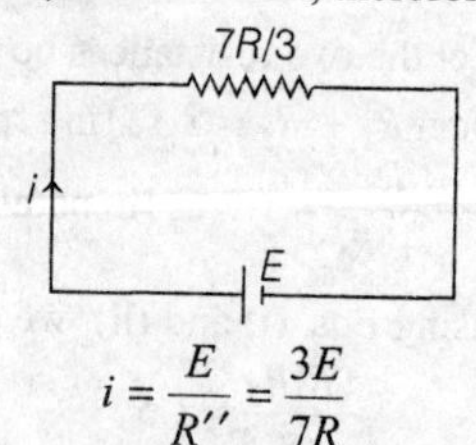

$$i = \frac{E}{R''} = \frac{3E}{7R}$$

Potential difference across R,

$$V = iR = \frac{3E}{7R} \times R = \frac{3E}{7}$$

Potential difference across $2R$,

$$V' = E - \frac{3E}{7} = \frac{4E}{7}$$

36 (b) Current density, $J = \frac{i}{A} = \frac{i}{\pi r^2}$

But the wires are in series, so they have the same current, hence $i_1 = i_2$.

So, $$\frac{J_1}{J_2} = \frac{r_2^2}{r_1^2} = 9:1$$

37 (b) The given circuit is symmetrical about AB, the points X, Y and Z are at same potential.

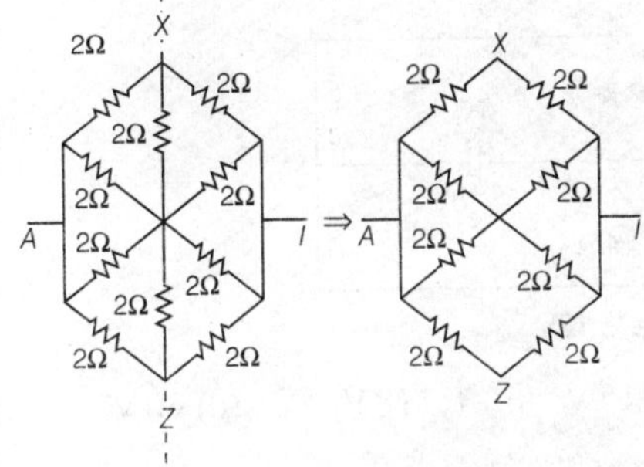

Thus, the given circuit reduces to equivalent resistance of 4 Ω each connected in parallel, as shown below

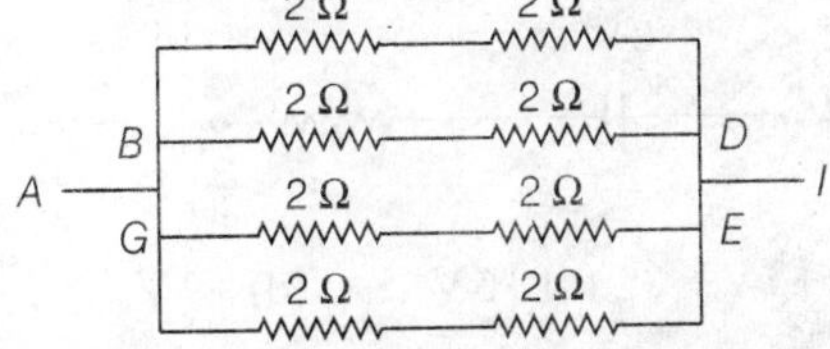

For equivalent resistance of above electrical circuit

$$\frac{1}{R} = \frac{1}{4} + \frac{1}{4} + \frac{1}{4} + \frac{1}{4}$$

$$\Rightarrow \quad \frac{1}{R} = \frac{4}{4}$$

$$\Rightarrow \quad R = 1\,\Omega$$

38 (d) As, resistance offered by $2\pi R$ length of wire = 12 Ω

Resistance offered by πR length of wire $= \frac{12}{2} = 6\,\Omega$

$$\therefore \quad \frac{1}{R_{eq}} = \frac{1}{6} + \frac{1}{6}$$

$$\Rightarrow \quad R_{eq} = 3\,\Omega$$

39 (d) Minimum possible resistance can be found in parallel arrangement and maximum possible resistance can be found in series arrangement.

Thus,

$$\frac{1}{R_{min}} = \frac{1}{R} + \frac{1}{R} + \ldots + n \text{ times} = \frac{n}{R}$$

$$\Rightarrow \quad R_{min} = R/n$$

and $R_{max} = R + R + \ldots + n$ times

$$\Rightarrow \quad R_{max} = nR$$

$$\therefore \quad \frac{R_{min}}{R_{max}} = \frac{R/n}{nR} = \frac{1}{n^2}$$

40 (c) For a wire of length l, area of cross-section A and specific resistance ρ, the resistance is given by

$$R = \frac{\rho l}{A}$$

$$\Rightarrow \quad R \propto l$$

When wire is cut into 4 pieces, then the resistance of each part is

$$R'' \propto \frac{l}{4}$$

$$\Rightarrow \quad R'' = \frac{R}{4}$$

Also, equivalent resistance for parallel combination is

$$\frac{1}{R'} = \frac{1}{R_1} + \frac{1}{R_2} + \frac{1}{R_3} + \frac{1}{R_4}$$

$$\therefore \quad \frac{1}{R'} = \frac{4}{R''}$$

$$= \frac{4 \times 4}{R}$$

$$\Rightarrow \quad R' = \frac{R}{16}$$

41 (a) When wire is bent to form a complete circle, then resistance of each semi-circle $= \frac{R}{2}$

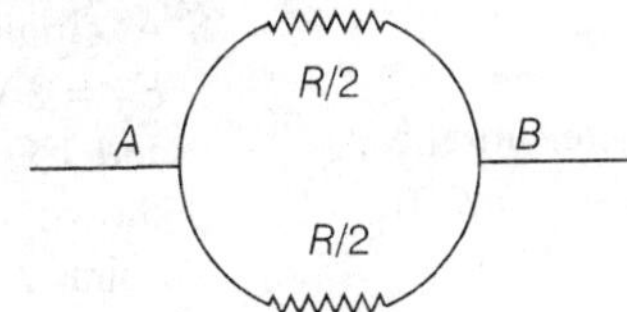

Thus, net resistance in parallel combination of two semi-circular resistances,

$$R' = \frac{\frac{R}{2} \times \frac{R}{2}}{\frac{R}{2} + \frac{R}{2}} = \frac{\frac{R^2}{4}}{R} = \frac{R}{4}$$

42 (c) As, resistors R_2, R_3 and R_4 are in parallel connection, so their equivalent resistance,

$$\frac{1}{R'} = \frac{1}{R_2} + \frac{1}{R_3} + \frac{1}{R_4}$$

$$= \frac{1}{50} + \frac{1}{50} + \frac{1}{75}$$

$$= \frac{3 + 3 + 2}{150} = \frac{8}{150} = \frac{4}{75}$$

$$\Rightarrow \quad R' = \frac{75}{4}\,\Omega$$

$$\therefore \quad R = R_1 + R' = 100 + \frac{75}{4}$$

$$= 118.75\,\Omega$$

43 (b) If we take $R_1 = 4\,\Omega$, $R_2 = 12\,\Omega$, then in series, $R = R_1 + R_2$

$$= 4 + 12 = 16\,\Omega$$

and in parallel,

$$R = \frac{R_1 \times R_2}{R_1 + R_2}$$

$$= \frac{4 \times 12}{4 + 12} = \frac{48}{16} = 3\Omega$$

44 (a) The resistance of a wire of length l and area of cross-section A is given by

$$R = \frac{\rho l}{A}$$

where, ρ is specific resistance.

Also, $A = \pi r^2$, r being radius of wire.

$$\therefore \quad \frac{R_1}{R_2} = \frac{r_2^2}{r_1^2}$$

Given, $r_1 = 9$ mm, $R_1 = 5\,\Omega$

and $r_2 = 3$ mm

$$\therefore \quad \frac{5}{R_2} = \frac{3^2}{9^2}$$

$$\Rightarrow \quad R_2 = 5 \times 9 = 45\,\Omega$$

Equivalent resistance of 6 wires each of resistance R_2 connected in series,

$$R' = 6 \times R_2 = 270\,\Omega$$

Topic 3

Cells & their Combinations and Kirchhoff's Laws

2018

1 A set of n equal resistors, of value R each, are connected in series to a battery of emf E and internal resistance R. The current drawn is I. Now, the n resistors are connected in parallel to the same battery. Then, the current drawn from battery becomes $10I$. The value of n is **[NEET]**

(a) 20 (b) 11 (c) 10 (d) 9

2 A battery consists of a variable number n of identical cells (having internal resistance r each) which are connected in series. The terminals of the battery are short-circuited and the current I is measured. Which of the graphs shows the correct relationship between I and n? **[NEET]**

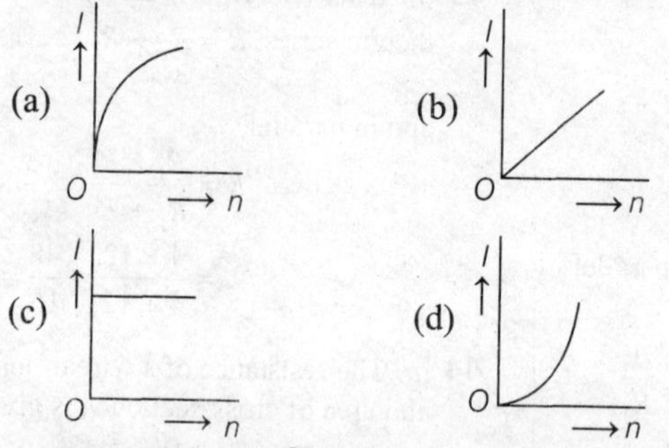

3 **Assertion** Terminal voltage of a cell is greater than emf of cell during charging of the cell. **[AIIMS]**

Reason The emf of a cell is always greater than its terminal voltage.

(a) Both Assertion and Reason are correct and Reason is the correct explanation of Assertion.
(b) Both Assertion and Reason are correct but Reason is not the correct explanation of Assertion.
(c) Assertion is correct but Reason is incorrect.
(d) Assertion is incorrect but Reason is correct.

2017

4 The current passing through the ideal ammeter in the circuit given below is **[KCET]**

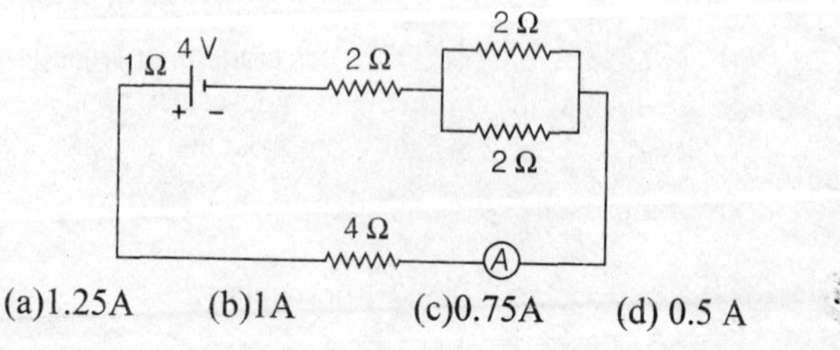

(a) 1.25 A (b) 1 A (c) 0.75 A (d) 0.5 A

5 Two batteries, one of emf 18V and internal resistance 2Ω and the other of emf 12V and internal resistance 1Ω are connected as shown in figure. The voltmeter V will record a reading of **[AIIMS]**

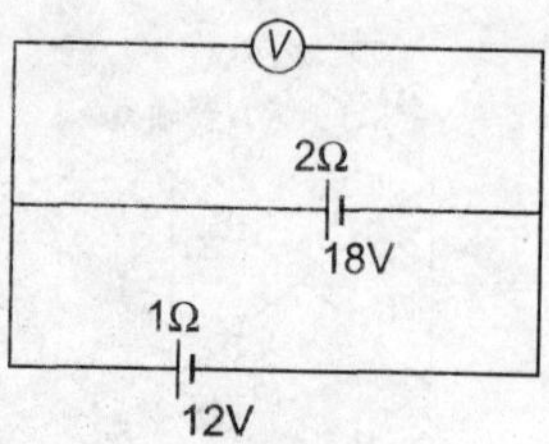

(a) 14 V (b) 15 V (c) 18 V (d) 30 V

2016

6 The potential difference $(V_A - V_B)$ between the points A and B in the given figure is **[NEET]**

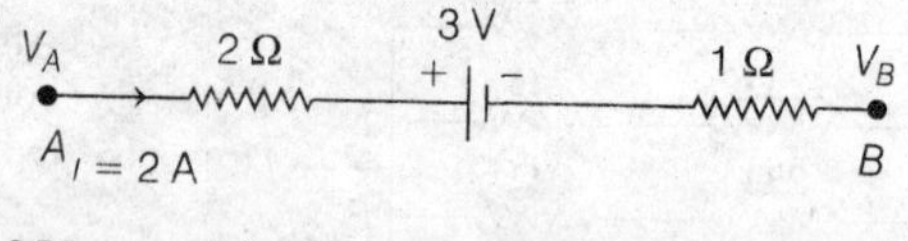

(a) −3 V (b) +3 V (c) +6 V (d) +9 V

2014

7 Four cells, each of emf E and internal resistance r are connected in series across an external resistance R. By mistake, one of the cells is connected in reverse, then the current in the external circuit is **[WB JEE]**

(a) $\frac{2E}{4r+R}$ (b) $\frac{3E}{4r+R}$

(c) $\frac{3E}{3r+R}$ (d) $\frac{2E}{3r+R}$

8 A circuit consists of three batteries of emf $E_1 = 1$ V, $E_2 = 2$ V and $E_3 = 3$ V and internal resistances 1 Ω, 2 Ω and 1 Ω respectively which are connected in parallel as shown in the figure. The potential difference between points P and Q is **[WB JEE]**

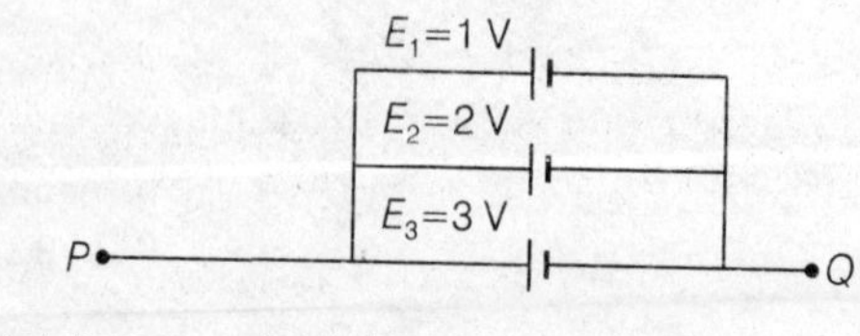

(a) 1.0 V (b) 2.0 V (c) 2.2 V (d) 3.0 V

9 Two resistors of resistances 2 Ω and 6 Ω are connected in parallel. This combination is connected to a battery of emf 2 V and internal resistance 0.5 Ω. What is the current flowing through the battery? **[KCET]**

(a) 4 A (b) $\frac{4}{3}$ A (c) $\frac{4}{17}$ A (d) 1 A

2013

10 In the electric circuit shown, each cell has an emf of 2 V and internal resistance is 1 Ω. The external resistance is 2 Ω. The value of the current I is (in ampere) **[Manipal]**

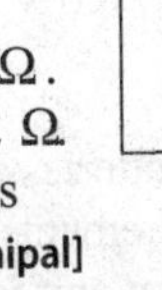

(a) 2 (b) 1.25 (c) 0.4 (d) 1.2

2012

11 A cell having an emf E and internal resistance r are connected across a variable external resistance R. As the resistance R is increased, the plot of potential difference V across R is given by **[CBSE AIPMT]**

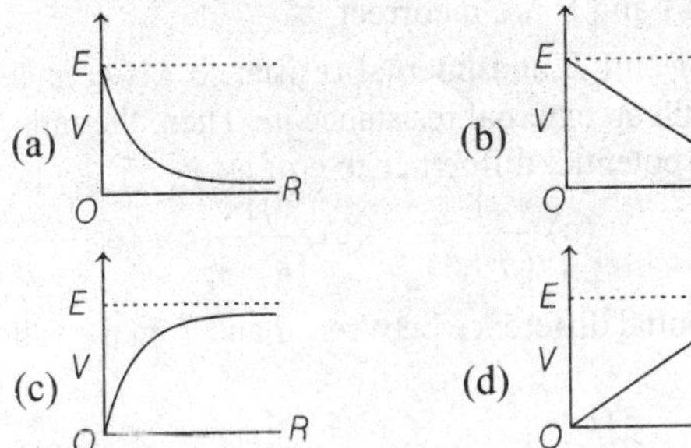

12 In the circuit shown below, the cells A and B have negligible resistance. For $V_A = 12$ V, $R_1 = 500$ Ω and $R = 100$ Ω, the galvanometer (G) shows no deflection. The value of V_B is **[CBSE AIPMT]**

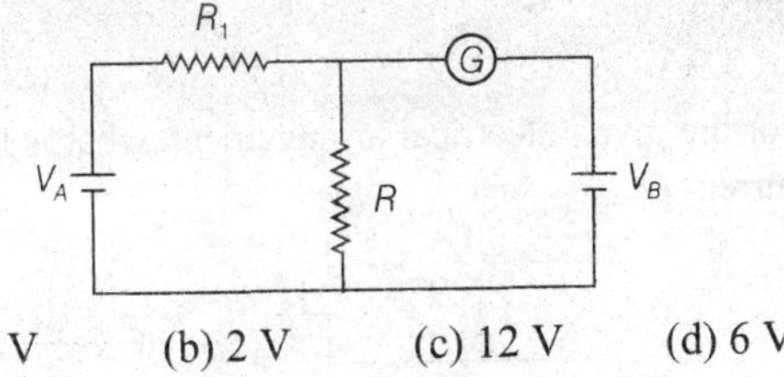

(a) 4 V (b) 2 V (c) 12 V (d) 6 V

13 A current of 2 A flows through a 2 Ω resistor when connected across a battery. The same battery supplies a current of 0.5 A when connected across a 9 Ω resistor. The internal resistance of the battery is **[CBSE AIPMT]**

(a) (1/3) Ω (b) (1/4) Ω (c) 1 Ω (d) 0.5 Ω

2011

14 Two batteries of emfs 2 V and 1 V of internal resistances 1 Ω and 2 Ω respectively are connected in parallel. The effective emf of the combination is **[Kerala CEE]**

(a) $\frac{3}{2}$ V (b) $\frac{5}{3}$ V (c) $\frac{3}{5}$ V (d) 2 V

(e) 5 V

15 Two cells with the same emf E and different internal resistances r_1 and r_2 are connected in series to an external resistance R. What is the value of R, if the potential difference across the first cell is zero? **[WB JEE]**

(a) $\sqrt{r_1 r_2}$ (b) $r_1 + r_2$ (c) $r_1 - r_2$ (d) $\frac{r_1 + r_2}{2}$

16 In the circuit shown below, the currents i_1 and i_2 are **[KCET]**

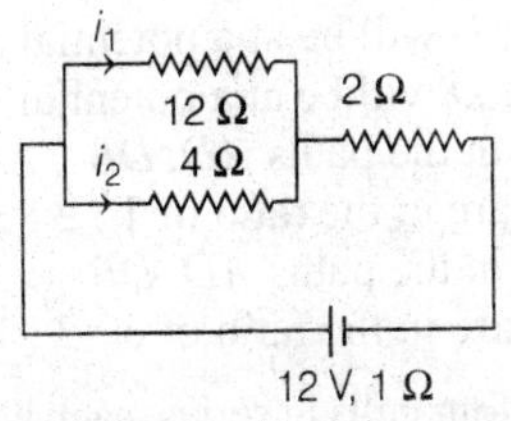

(a) 1.5 A, 0.5 A (b) 0.5 A, 1.5 A
(c) 1 A, 3 A (d) 3 A, 1 A

2010

17 Consider the following two statements.

I. Kirchhoff's junction law follows from the conservation of charge.

II. Kirchhoff's loop law follows from the conservation of energy.

Which of the following is/are correct? **[CBSE AIPMT]**

(a) Both I and II are incorrect
(b) I is correct and II is incorrect
(c) I is incorrect and II is correct
(d) Both I and II are correct

18 Current provided by a battery is maximum, when **[UP CPMT]**

(a) internal resistance is equal to external resistance
(b) internal resistance is greater than external resistance
(c) internal resistance is less than external resistance
(d) None of the above

19 When a resistance R_1 is connected across the terminals of a cell, the current is I_1. When the resistance is changed to R_2, the current is I_2. The internal resistance of the cell is **[OJEE]**

(a) $\frac{I_1 R_1 + I_2 R_2}{I_1 + I_2}$ (b) $\frac{I_1 R_2 + I_2 R_1}{I_1 + I_2}$

(c) $\frac{I_1 R_2 - I_2 R_1}{I_1 - I_2}$ (d) $\frac{I_2 R_2 - I_1 R_1}{I_1 - I_2}$

20 A battery of emf E has an internal resistance r. A variable resistance R is connected to the terminals of the battery. A current I is drawn from the battery. V is the terminal potential difference. If R alone is gradually reduced to zero, then which of the following best describes I and V? **[KCET]**

(a) I approaches zero and V approaches E
(b) I approaches $\frac{E}{r}$ and V approaches zero
(c) I approaches $\frac{E}{r}$ and V approaches E
(d) I approaches infinity and V approaches E

21 In the circuit given below, the points A, B and C are 70 V, zero and 10 V respectively. Then, **[KCET]**

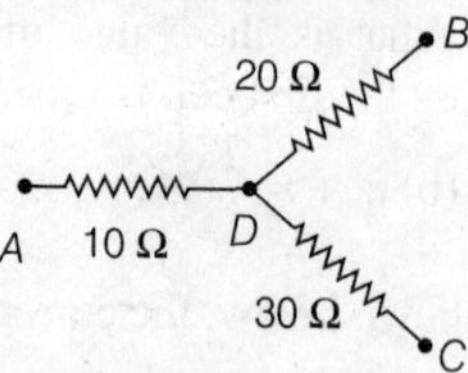

(a) the point D will be at a potential of 60 V
(b) the point D will be at a potential of 20 V
(c) currents in the paths AD, DB and DC are in the ratio of 1 : 2 : 3
(d) currents in the paths AD, DB and DC are in the ratio of 3 : 2 : 1

22 A battery of four cells in series, each having an emf of 1.4V and an internal resistance of 2 Ω is to be used to charge a small 2V accumulator of negligible internal resistance. What is the charging current? **[MGIMS]**

(a) 0.1 A (b) 0.2 A (c) 0.3 A (d) 0.35 A

23 A student measures the terminal potential difference (V) of a cell (of emf ε and internal resistance r) as a function of the current (I) flowing through it. The slope and intercept of the graph between V and I are **[CBSE AIPMT]**

(a) ε and $-r$ (b) $-r$ and ε (c) r and $-$ε (d) $-$ε and r

2009

24 The potential difference across the terminals of a battery is 50 V, when 11 A current is drawn and 60 V, when 1 A current is drawn. The emf and the internal resistance of the battery are **[AFMC]**

(a) 62 V, 2 Ω (b) 63 V, 1 Ω
(c) 61 V, 1 Ω (d) 64 V, 2 Ω

25 See the electrical circuit shown in this figure. Which of the following equations is a correct equation for it? **[AFMC]**

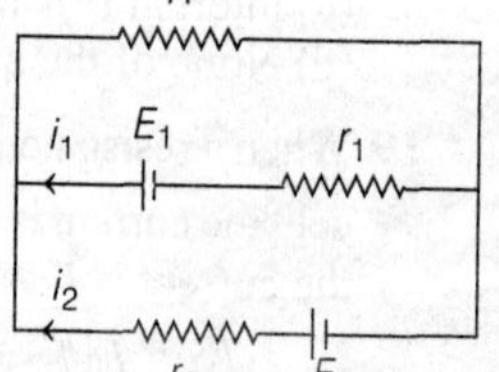

(a) $E_1 - (i_1 + i_2)R - i_1 r_1 = 0$
(b) $E_2 - i_2 r_2 - E_1 - i_1 r_1 = 0$
(c) $-E_2 - (i_1 + i_2)R + i_2 r_2 = 0$
(d) $E_1 - (i_1 + i_2)R + i_1 r_1 = 0$

26 A battery of emf 10 V and internal resistance 3 Ω is connected to a resistor. The current in the circuit is 0.5 A. The terminal voltage of the battery when the circuit is closed is **[JCECE]**

(a) 10 V (b) 0 V
(c) 1.5 V (d) 8.5 V

27 Two cells each of same emf e but of internal resistances r_1 and r_2 are connected in series through an external resistance R. If the potential difference between the ends of the first cell is zero, then what will be the value of R in terms of r_1 and r_2? **[JCECE]**

(a) $r_1 - r_2$ (b) $r_1 + r_2$ (c) $2r_1 - r_2$ (d) $2r_1 + r_2$

28 In the circuit, the potential difference across PQ will be nearest to **[UP CPMT]**

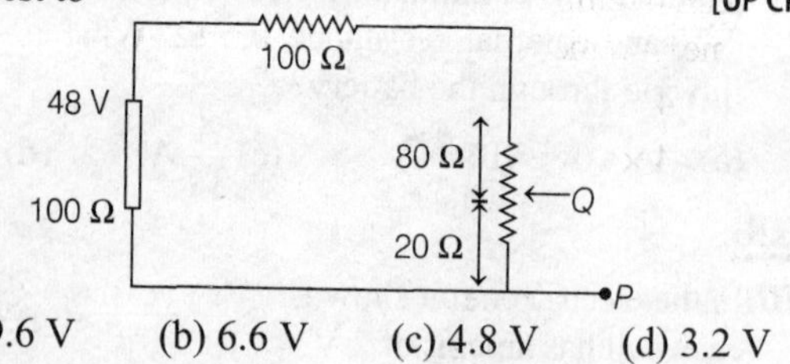

(a) 9.6 V (b) 6.6 V (c) 4.8 V (d) 3.2 V

2008

29 Two non-ideal batteries are connected in parallel. Consider the following statements.

I. The equivalent emf is smaller than either of the two emfs.
II. The equivalent internal resistance is smaller than either of the two internal resistances. **[UP CPMT]**

(a) Both I and II are correct
(b) I is correct but II is incorrect
(c) II is correct but I is incorrect
(d) Both I and II are incorrect

30 A cell of emf E and internal resistance r is connected in series with an external resistance nr. Then, the ratio of the terminal potential difference to emf is **[Manipal]**

(a) $\left(\frac{1}{n}\right)$ (b) $\frac{1}{(n+1)}$ (c) $\frac{n}{(n+1)}$ (d) $\frac{(n+1)}{n}$

31 The potential difference between A and B in the following figure is **[KCET]**

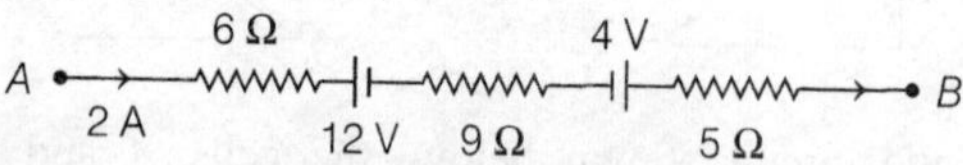

(a) 32 V (b) 48 V (c) 24 V (d) 14 V

32 The internal resistance of a cell of emf 4 V is 0.1 Ω. It is connected to a resistance of 3.9 Ω. The voltage across the cell will be **[Guj CET]**

(a) 3.9 V (b) 2 V (c) 0.1 V (d) 3.8 V

33 For the given electrical arrangement, what is the value of current I? **[DUMET]**

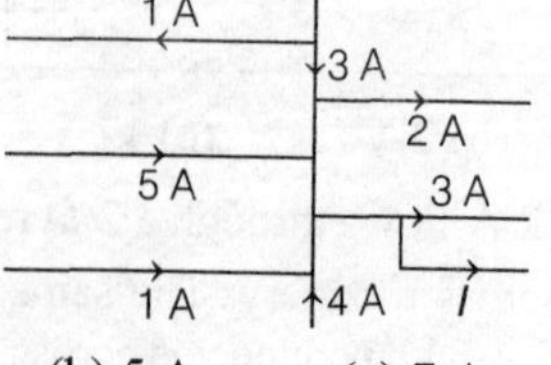

(a) 6 A (b) 5 A (c) 7 A (d) 8 A

2007

34 A cell of emf X is connected across a resistor R. The potential difference across the wire is measured as Y. The internal resistance of the cell should be **[Punjab PMET]**

(a) $X - \frac{Y}{R}$ (b) $(X - Y)\frac{R}{Y}$
(c) $(X - Y)\frac{Y}{R}$ (d) $\frac{(X - Y)}{R}$

35 A voltmeter having a resistance of 998 Ω is connected to a cell of emf 2 V and internal resistance 2 Ω. The error in the measurement of emf will be **[DUMET]**

(a) 4×10^{-1} V (b) 2×10^{-3} V
(c) 4×10^{-3} V (d) 2×10^{-1} V

2006

36 What is the potential drop between points A and C in the following circuit?
(Resistances 1 Ω and 2 Ω are represent the internal resistance of the respective cells). **[BHU]**

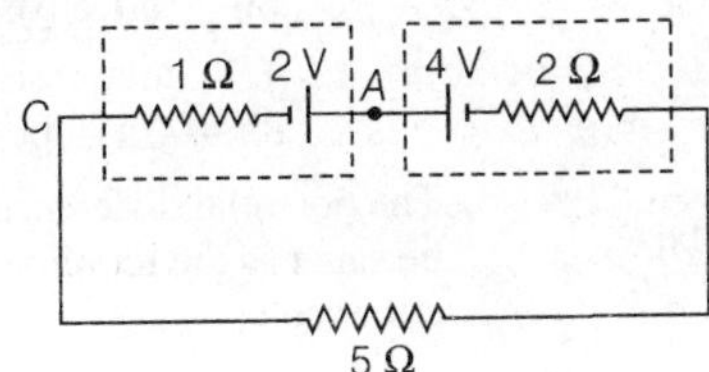

(a) 1.75 (b) 2.25 V (c) $\frac{5}{4}$ V (d) $\frac{4}{5}$ V

37 4 cells each of emf 2 V and internal resistance of 1 Ω are connected in parallel to a load resistor of 2 Ω. Then, the current through the load resistor is **[Kerala CEE]**

(a) 2 A (b) 1.5 A (c) 1 A (d) 0.888 A
(e) 0.75 A

38 In the circuit shown, the value of I (in ampere) is **[KCET]**

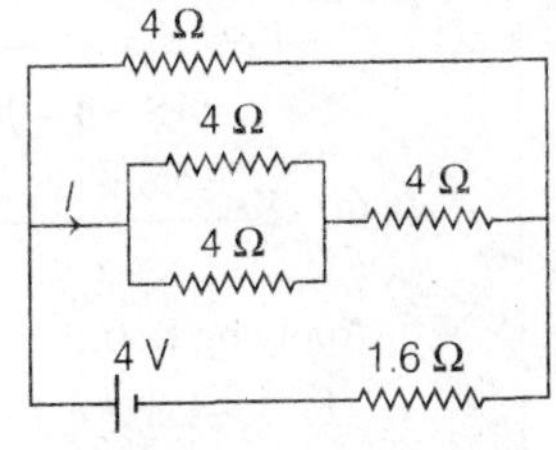

(a) 1 (b) 0.60 (c) 0.4 (d) 1.5

39 A current of 6 A enters one corner P of an equilateral ΔPQR having 3 wires of resistances 2 Ω each and leaves by the corner R. Then, the currents I_1 and I_2 are, respectively **[KCET]**

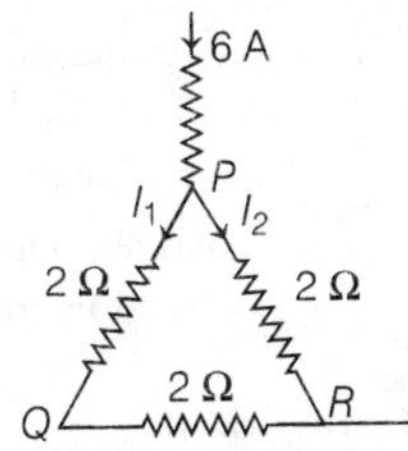

(a) 2 A, 4 A (b) 4 A, 2 A (c) 1 A, 2 A (d) 2 A, 3 A

40 A teacher asked a student to connect N cells each of emf e in series to get a total emf of Ne. While connecting the student, by mistake, reversed by polarity of n cells. The total emf of the resulting series combination is **[EAMCET]**

(a) $e\left(N - \frac{n}{2}\right)$ (b) $e(N - n)$ (c) $e(N - 2n)$ (d) eN

2005

41 What is the current flowing in arm AB? **[AFMC]**

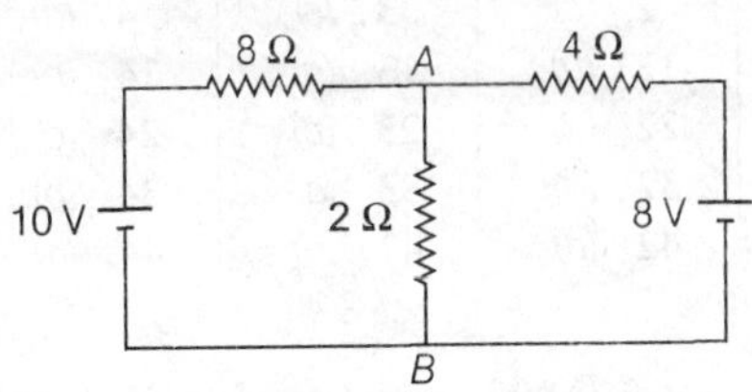

(a) $\frac{35}{4}$ A (b) $\frac{13}{7}$ A (c) $\frac{5}{7}$ A (d) $\frac{7}{5}$ A

42 To draw maximum current from a combination of cells, how should the cells be grouped? **[AFMC]**

(a) Series
(b) Parallel
(c) Mixed
(d) Depends upon the values of external and internal resistance

43 A cell of emf E and internal resistance r is connected with external resistance R. The graph between terminal voltage and current is **[Haryana PMT]**

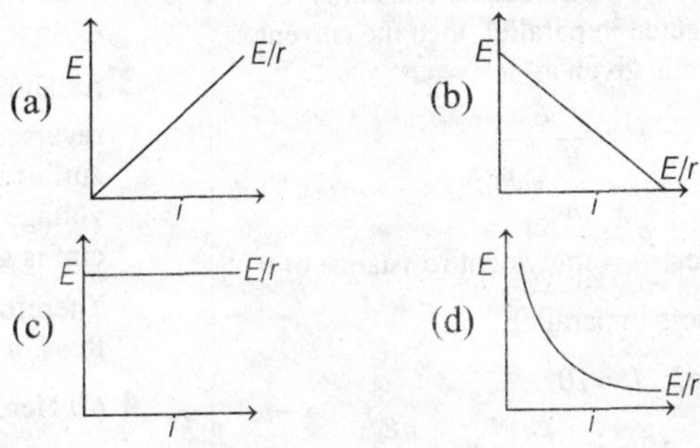

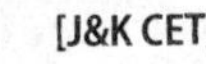

44 The value of current I in figure is **[J&K CET]**

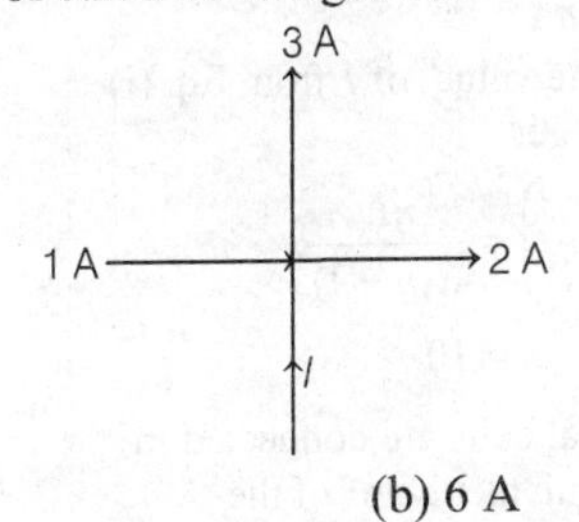

(a) 4 A (b) 6 A
(c) 3 A (d) 5 A

45 The magnitude of I (in ampere) is **[KCET]**

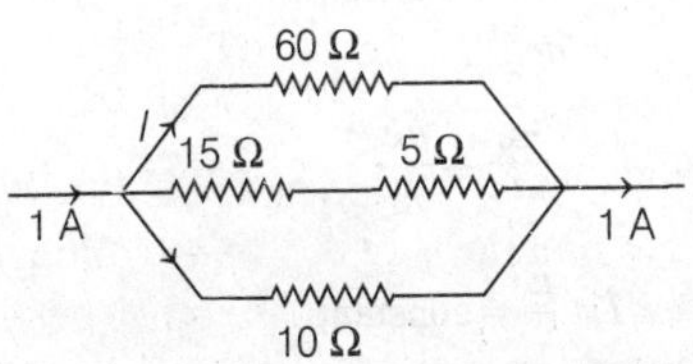

(a) 0.1 (b) 0.3
(c) 0.6 (d) None of these

Answers

1 (c)	2 (c)	3 (c)	4 (d)	5 (a)	6 (d)	7 (a)	8 (b)	9 (d)	10 (d)
11 (c)	12 (b)	13 (a)	14 (b)	15 (c)	16 (b)	17 (d)	18 (d)	19 (d)	20 (b)
21 (d)	22 (d)	23 (b)	24 (c)	25 (a)	26 (d)	27 (a)	28 (d)	29 (c)	30 (c)
31 (b)	32 (a)	33 (d)	34 (b)	35 (c)	36 (b)	37 (d)	38 (c)	39 (a)	40 (c)
41 (b)	42 (d)	43 (b)	44 (a)	45 (a)					

Explanations

1 (c) When n equal resistors of resistances R are connected in series, then the current drawn is given as

$$I = \frac{E}{nR + r}$$

where, nR = equivalent resistance of n resistors in series and r = internal resistance of battery.

Given, $r = R$

$$\Rightarrow \quad I = \frac{E}{nR + R} = \frac{E}{R(n+1)} \quad \ldots \text{(i)}$$

Similarly, when n equal resistors are connected in parallel, then the current drawn is given as

$$I' = \frac{E}{\frac{R}{n} + R}$$

where, $\frac{R}{n}$ = equivalent resistance of n resistors in parallel.

Given, $I' = 10I$

$$\Rightarrow \quad 10I = \frac{E}{\frac{R}{n} + R} = \frac{nE}{(n+1)R} \quad \ldots \text{(ii)}$$

Substituting the value of I from Eq. (i) in Eq. (ii), we get

$$10\left(\frac{E}{R(n+1)}\right) = \frac{nE}{R(n+1)}$$

$$\Rightarrow \quad n = 10$$

2 (c) If n identical cells are connected in series, then equivalent emf of the combination,

$$E_{eq} = nE$$

Equivalent internal resistance,

$$r_{eq} = nr$$

$$\therefore \quad \text{Current, } I = \frac{E_{eq}}{r_{eq}} = \frac{nE}{nr}$$

or $$I = \frac{E}{r} = \text{constant}$$

Thus, current (I) is independent of the number of cells (n) present in the circuit.

Therefore, the graph showing the relationship between I and n would be as shown below

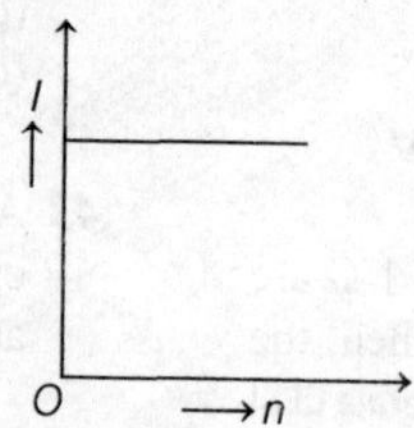

3 (c) During charging, $E = V + ir$ (due to reversed current). In case of charging, emf of a cell is less than its terminal voltage while in case of discharging emf is greater than terminal voltage.

Therefore, Assertion is correct but Reason is incorrect.

4 (d) Here, 2 Ω and 2 Ω are in parallel.

$$\therefore \quad \frac{1}{R} = \frac{1}{2} + \frac{1}{2}$$

$$\Rightarrow \quad R = \frac{2 \times 2}{2 + 2} = 1\,\Omega$$

Now, internal resistance 1 Ω, 2 Ω, 4 Ω and resistance R are in series.

$$\therefore R_{net} = 1\,\Omega + 2\,\Omega + 4\,\Omega + 1\,\Omega = 8\,\Omega$$

Hence, current,

$$I = \frac{V}{R} = \frac{4}{8} = 0.5\text{ A}$$

5 (a) It is clear that the two cells oppose each other, hence the effective emf in closed circuit is 18 − 12 = 6V and net resistance is 1 + 2 = 3Ω (because in the closed circuit the internal resistance of two cells are in series).

The current in circuit will be in direction of arrow shown in figure

$$I = \frac{\text{effective emf}}{\text{total resistance}} = 6/3 = 2\text{A}$$

The potential difference across V will be same as the terminal voltage of either cell

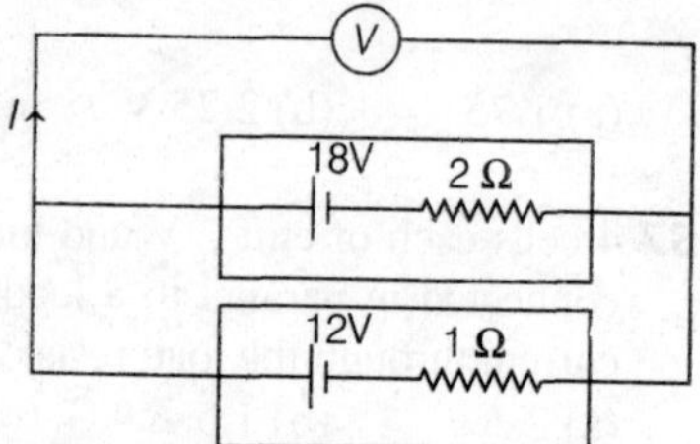

Since, current is drawn from the cell of 18 V, hence

$$V_1 = E_1 - Ir_1 = 18 - (2 \times 2)$$
$$= 18 - 4 = 14\text{V}$$

6 (d) V_A —2A→ 2 Ω + | − (3V) 1 Ω — V_B

Applying KVL,

$$V_A + \Sigma V = V_B + 2 \times 2 + 2 \times 1$$
$$V_A - V_B - 3 = 4 + 2$$
$$V_A - V_B = 9\text{ V}$$

7 (a) Total net emf of the cell

$$= 3E - E = 2E$$

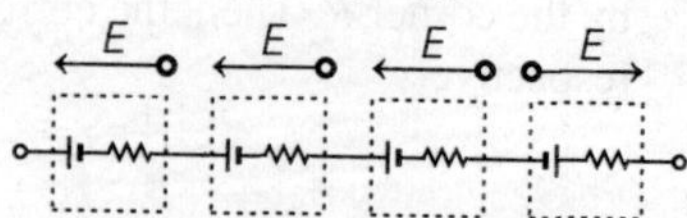

Total internal resistance = $4r$

∴ Total resistance of the circuit

= Total internal resistance + External resistance

$$= 4r + R$$

So, the current in the external circuit,

$$i = \frac{2E}{4r + R} \quad \left(\because i = \frac{V}{R}\right)$$

8 (b) As, the batteries are in parallel, so their resistances 1 Ω, 2 Ω and 1 Ω are in parallel.

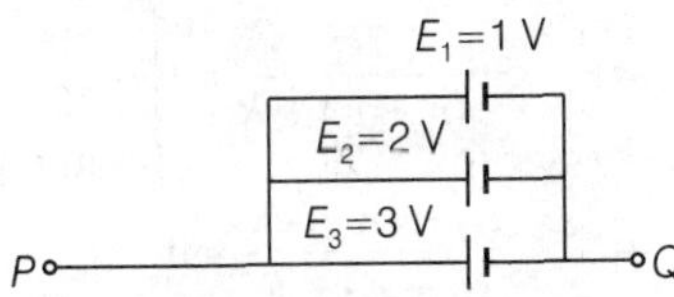

So, the required internal resistance,

$$\frac{1}{r}=\frac{1}{r_1}+\frac{1}{r_2}+\frac{1}{r_1}=\frac{1}{1}+\frac{1}{2}+\frac{1}{1}=\frac{2+1+2}{2}$$

$$\Rightarrow \quad r=\frac{2}{5}\ \Omega$$

The potential difference between points P and Q,

$$E=\frac{\frac{E_1}{r_1}+\frac{E_2}{r_2}+\frac{E_3}{r_3}}{1/r}=\frac{\frac{1}{1}+\frac{2}{2}+\frac{3}{1}}{5/2}=\frac{\frac{2+2+6}{2}}{5/2}=\frac{10/2}{5/2}=\frac{5}{5}\times 2=2\text{ V}$$

9 (d) Given, $R_1=2\ \Omega, R_2=6\ \Omega$, $E=2\text{V}, r=0.5\ \Omega$ and $I=?$

$\because R_1$ and R_2 are in parallel combination,

so $$\frac{1}{R}=\frac{1}{R_1}+\frac{1}{R_2}=\frac{1}{2}+\frac{1}{6}=\frac{3+1}{6}$$

$$\Rightarrow \quad R=\frac{6}{4}=1.5\ \Omega$$

Then, the current in the circuit,

$$I=\frac{E}{r+R}=\frac{2}{0.5+1.5}=\frac{2}{2.0}=1\text{ A}$$

(since internal resistance r is in series with other resistance)

10 (d) $\text{Current}=\frac{\text{Net emf}}{\text{Net resistance}}$

$$\Rightarrow \quad I=\frac{2+2+2}{1+1+1+2}=\frac{6}{5}=1.2\text{ A}$$

11 (c) Here, $E=I(R+r)$

$$\Rightarrow \quad I=\frac{E}{R+r}$$

Also, $E=IR+Ir$

$$\Rightarrow \quad E=V+Ir$$

$$\therefore \quad E=V+\frac{Er}{R+r}$$

$$\Rightarrow \quad V=E-\frac{E}{R+r}\times r=\frac{ER}{R+r}=\frac{E}{1+r/R}$$

So, with the increase in R, the value of V increases exponentially. This is correctly shown in option (c).

12 (b) Applying Kirchhoff's law in loop 1, we get

$500I+100I=12$

So, $$I=\frac{12\times10^{-2}}{6}=2\times10^{-2}\text{ A}$$

Hence, $V_B=100\,(2\times10^{-2})=2\text{ V}$

Remember that at the condition of no deflection of galvanometer, there is no current through it.

13 (a) Current, $i=\frac{E}{R+r}$

$$\Rightarrow \quad 2=\frac{E}{2+r} \quad \ldots\text{(i)}$$

and $$0.5=\frac{E}{9+r} \quad \ldots\text{(ii)}$$

From Eqs. (i) and (ii), we have

$$\frac{2}{0.5}=\frac{9+r}{2+r}$$

$$\Rightarrow \quad 4=\frac{9+r}{2+r}$$

$$4(2+r)=9+r$$

$$\Rightarrow \quad 8+4r=9+r$$

$$\Rightarrow \quad 4r-r=9-8$$

$$\Rightarrow \quad 3r=1\Rightarrow r=\frac{1}{3}\ \Omega$$

14 (b) Equivalent potential in the given parallel circuit is given as

$$E_{eq}=\frac{\frac{E_1}{r_1}+\frac{E_2}{r_2}}{\frac{1}{r_1}+\frac{1}{r_2}}=\frac{E_1r_2+E_2r_1}{r_1+r_2}$$

Here, $E_1=2\text{ V}, E_2=1\text{ V}, r_1=1\ \Omega$

and $r_2=2\ \Omega$

$$\Rightarrow \quad E_{eq}=\frac{2\times2+1\times1}{2+1}=\frac{4+1}{3}=\frac{5}{3}\text{ V}$$

15 (c) Here are two batteries with emf E each and the internal resistances r_1 and r_2, respectively.

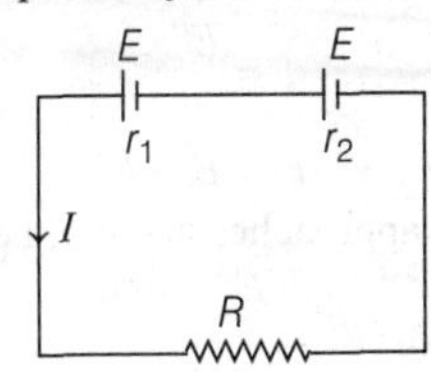

Hence, we have $I(R+r_1+r_2)=2E$

Thus, $$I=\frac{2E}{R+r_1+r_2} \quad \ldots\text{(i)}$$

Now, the potential difference across the first cell would be equal to $V=E-Ir_1$. From the question, $V=0$, hence

$$E=Ir_1=\frac{2Er_1}{R+r_1+r_2} \quad \text{[from Eq. (i)]}$$

Thus, $R+r_1+r_2=2r_1$

Hence, $R=r_1-r_2$.

16 (b) The net resistance,

$$R=\frac{12\times4}{12+4}+2=\frac{48}{16}+2=5\ \Omega$$

Electric current,

$$i=\frac{E}{R+r}=\frac{12}{5+1}=2\text{ A}$$

From current dividing rule,

$$i_2=\left(\frac{12}{12+4}\right)\times2=\frac{3}{4}\times2=1.5\text{ A}$$

and $$i_1=\frac{4}{16}\times2=\frac{1}{2}=0.5\text{A}$$

17 (d) Kirchhoff's first law follows the conservation of charge. Kirchhoff's second law follows the conservation of energy.

18 (d) The current provided by a battery is given by $I=\frac{E}{R+r}$.

Thus, from the relation, if can be seen that the value of I is maximum when $(R+r)$ is minimum, i.e. $R=0$.

19 (d) Let the emf of cell be E and internal resistance be r.

Then, $$I_1=\frac{E}{(r+R_1)}$$

and $$I_2=\frac{E}{(r+R_2)}$$

On dividing the above equations, we get

$$\frac{I_1}{I_2}=\frac{(r+R_2)}{(r+R_1)} \quad \text{or } r=\frac{I_2R_2-I_1R_1}{I_1-I_2}$$

20 *(b)* Current, $I = \dfrac{E}{R + r}$

When R decreases to zero, then

$$I = \frac{E}{r}.$$

Also, $\quad V = E - Ir$

As, R approaches to zero, i.e. I approaches to E/r and V approaches to zero.

21 *(d)* Applying Kirchhoff's law at junction point D, we get

$$I_1 = I_2 + I_3$$

A 70 V
i_1
10 Ω
i_3 i_2
30 Ω D 20 Ω
C B
10 V 0 V

$$\Rightarrow \frac{V_A - V_D}{10} = \frac{V_D - 0}{20} + \frac{V_D - V_C}{30}$$

$$\Rightarrow 70 - V_D = \frac{V_D}{2} + \frac{V_D - 10}{3}$$

$$\Rightarrow \quad V_D = 40\text{ V}$$

$$\therefore \quad i_1 = \frac{70 - 40}{10} = 3\text{ A}$$

$$i_2 = \frac{40 - 0}{20} = 2\text{ A}$$

and $\quad i_3 = \dfrac{40 - 10}{30} = 1\text{ A}$

22 *(d)* The net emf,

$$E_{net} = 4E = 4 \times 1.4 = 5.6\text{ V},$$

$$r_{net} = 4r = 4 \times 2 = 8\ \Omega$$

$$\because \quad E_{net} = I\,r_{net}$$

$$\therefore \quad I = \frac{56}{8 \times 10} = \frac{7}{10} = 0.7\text{ A}$$

Hence, charging current is

$$I = \frac{0.7}{2} = 0.35\text{ A}$$

23 *(b)* As, $V = \varepsilon - ir \Rightarrow V = -ri + \varepsilon$ ...(i)

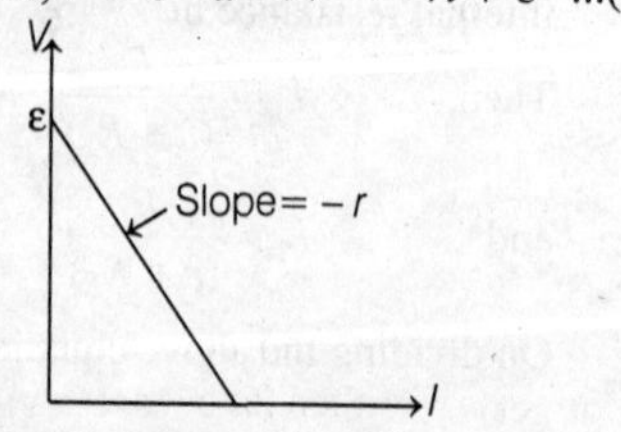

On comparing Eq. (i) with $y = mx + c$, we get

$$m = \text{slope} = -r \text{ and } c = \varepsilon$$

24 *(c)* For a closed circuit cells supplies a constant current in the circuit.

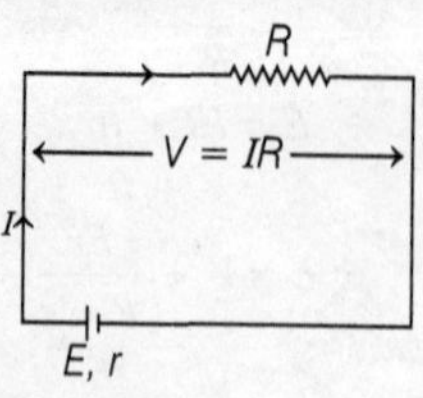

Equation of cell,

$$E = V + Ir$$

For $V = 50$ V and $I = 11$ A

$$\Rightarrow \quad E = 50 + 11r \quad \text{...(i)}$$

Similarly, for $V = 60$ V and $I = 1$ A

$$E = 60 + r \quad \text{...(ii)}$$

From Eqs. (i) and (ii), we get

$$r = 1\ \Omega$$

Substituting the value of r in Eq. (i), we get

$$E = 61\text{ V}$$

25 *(a)* Applying KVL in loop *EBCDE*, then we get

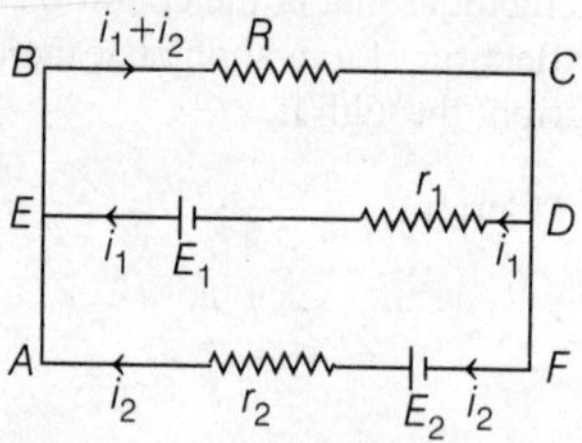

$$E_1 - (i_1 + i_2)R - i_1 r_1 = 0$$

Applying KVL, in loop *AEDFA*, then we get

$$E_2 - i_2 r_2 - E_1 + i_1 r_1 = 0$$

Applying KVL in loop *ABCFA*, then we get

$$E_2 - (i_1 + i_2)R - i_2 r_2 = 0$$

26 *(d)* As, $V = E - Ir \Rightarrow V = 10 - \dfrac{5}{10} \times 3$

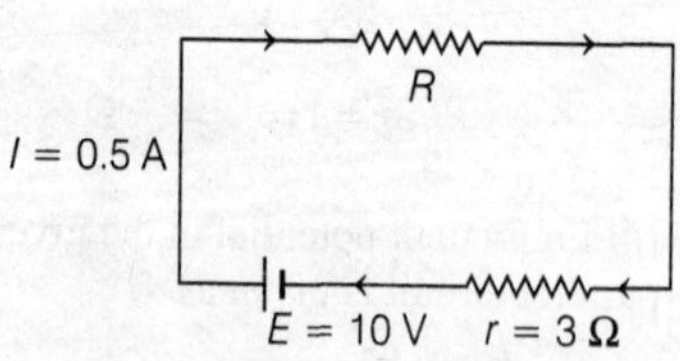

$\therefore$ Terminal potential difference,

$$V = 8.5\text{ V}$$

27 *(a)* Current in the circuit,

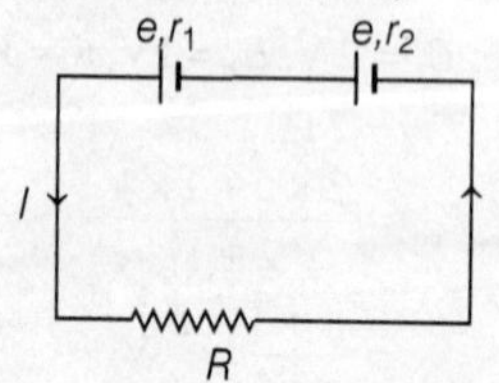

$$I = \frac{2e}{(r_1 + r_2) + R} \quad \text{...(i)}$$

and $\quad e - Ir_1 = 0$

$$\Rightarrow \quad e - \frac{2er_1}{(r_1 + r_2) + R} = 0$$

[from Eq. (i)]

$$\Rightarrow \quad \frac{er_2 - er_1 + eR}{(r_1 + r_2) + R} = 0$$

$$\Rightarrow \quad r_2 - r_1 + R = 0$$

$$\Rightarrow \quad R = (r_1 - r_2)$$

28 *(d)* Potential difference across PQ, i.e. potential difference across the resistance of 20 Ω is

$$V = i \times 20$$

and $i = \dfrac{E}{R + r} = \dfrac{48}{(100 + 100 + 80 + 20)}$

$$= 0.16\text{ A}$$

$$\therefore \ V = 0.16 \times 20 = 3.2\text{ V}$$

29 *(c)* Let emf of two cells be E_1 and E_2 and internal resistances be r_1 and r_2, respectively. In parallel order, we have equivalent emf, $E_{eq} = \dfrac{E_1 r_2 + E_2 r_1}{r_1 + r_2}$ and

equivalent resistance, $R_{eq} = \dfrac{r_1 r_2}{r_1 + r_2}$

If $E_1 = E_2$ and $r_1 = r_2$, then $E_{eq} = E$ and $R_{eq} = r/2$.

So, emf is equal to the emf of any of the cell and internal resistance is less than the internal resistance of any of cell.

Hence, Statement (II) is correct and Statement (I) is incorrect.

30 *(c)* As, $\quad I = \dfrac{E}{r + nr} = \dfrac{E}{r(n+1)}$

$$\Rightarrow \quad V = E - Ir$$

$$= E - \frac{E}{r(n+1)}r = \frac{nE}{n+1}$$

$$\therefore \quad \frac{V}{E} = \frac{n}{n+1}$$

31 *(b)* For the circuit given in question,

$$V_A - (6 \times 2) - 12 - (9 \times 2) + 4 - (5 \times 2) = V_B$$

or $\quad V_A - 12 - 12 - 18 + 4 - 10 = V_B$

or $\quad V_A - V_B = 48\text{ V}$

32 *(a)* The emf of cell, $E = 4$ V

Internal resistance of cell, $r = 0.1\ \Omega$

External resistance, $R = 3.9\ \Omega$

The potential drop across the cell

$$V = E - Ir \quad \text{...(i)}$$

Now, the total resistance of the circuit

$$R' = r + R$$

$\Rightarrow \quad R' = 0.1 + 3.9$

$\Rightarrow \quad R' = 4.0\,\Omega$

Hence, current in the circuit is

$$I = \frac{E}{R'}$$

$$\Rightarrow \quad I = \frac{4}{4} = 1\text{ A}$$

Now, from Eq. (i),

$$V = 4 - 1 \times 0.1$$

$$\Rightarrow \quad V = 4 - 0.1$$

$$\therefore \quad V = 3.9\text{ V}$$

33 *(d)* According to Kirchhoff's Ist law,

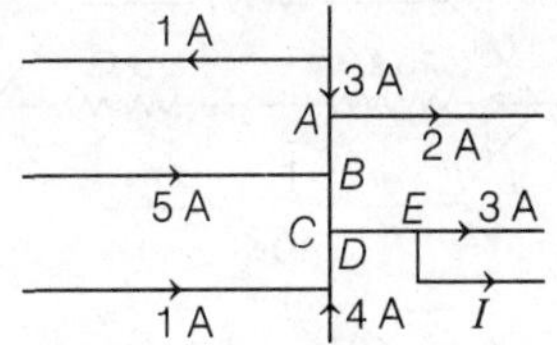

Current at $A = 3 - 2 = 1\text{ A}$

Current at $B = 5 + 1 = 6\text{ A}$

Current at $D = 4 + 1 = 5\text{ A}$

Current at $C = 6 + 5 = 11\text{ A}$

So, $\quad I = 11 - 3 = 8\text{ A}$

34 *(b)* If r is the internal resistance of the cell, then the current through the circuit is given by

$$I = \frac{E}{(R + r)}$$

Substituting $E = X$, we get

$$I = \frac{X}{R + r} \quad \text{...(i)}$$

Now, potential difference across the resistor is given by

$$V = IR$$

Substituting $V = Y$ and $I = \dfrac{X}{R + r}$ [from Eq. (i)]

We get, $\quad Y = \dfrac{XR}{R + r}$

On solving, we get

$$r = \frac{(X - Y)R}{Y}$$

35 *(c)* Current taken from the cell,

$$i = \frac{E}{R + r}$$

Given, $E = 2\text{V}$, $R = 998\,\Omega$ and $r = 2\,\Omega$

$$\therefore \quad i = \frac{2}{998 + 2} = \frac{1}{500}\text{ A}$$

Now, error in value of emf = actual value of emf − measured emf

Here, actual value of emf, $E = 2\text{ V}$

Measured value of emf,

$$V = E - ir = 2 - \frac{1}{500} \times 2$$

$$= 2 - \frac{1}{250}$$

$$\therefore \quad \text{Error} = 2 - \left(2 - \frac{1}{250}\right)$$

$$= \frac{1}{250} = 4 \times 10^{-3}\text{ V}$$

36 *(b)* The emfs E_1 and E_2 are opposing each other. Since, $E_2 > E_1$, so current will flow from right to left.

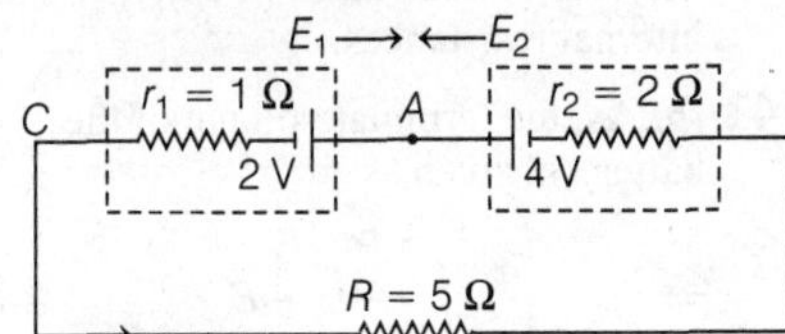

Current in the circuit,

$$i = \frac{\text{net emf}}{\text{total resistance}} = \frac{E_2 - E_1}{R + r_1 + r_2} \quad \text{...(i)}$$

Given, $R = 5\,\Omega, r_1 = 1\,\Omega, r_2 = 2\,\Omega$

$E_1 = 2\text{ V}$ and $E_2 = 4\text{ V}$

On putting the given values in Eq. (i), we get

$$\therefore \quad i = \frac{4 - 2}{5 + 1 + 2} = \frac{2}{8} = 0.25\text{ A}$$

The potential drop between points A and C,

$$V_A - V_C = E_1 + ir_1$$

$$= 2 + 0.25 \times 1 = 2.25\text{ V}$$

37 *(d)* The combined resistance of combination is

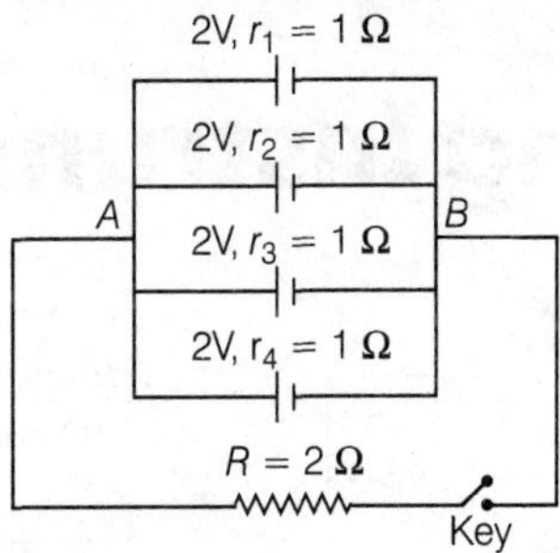

Net resistance,

$$R' = R + \frac{r}{4} = 2 + \frac{1}{4} = \frac{9}{4}$$

and $\quad V = 2\text{ V}$

$$\therefore \quad V = iR$$

$$\Rightarrow \quad i = \frac{V}{R} = \frac{2 \times 4}{9} = \frac{8}{9}$$

$$= 0.888\text{ A}$$

38 *(c)* We can simplify the network in stepwise as shown below

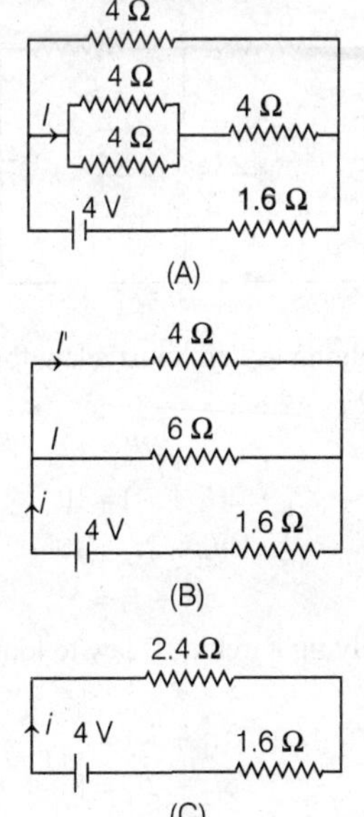

So, net resistance,

$$R = 2.4 + 1.6 = 4.0\,\Omega$$

Therefore, current from the battery,

$$i = \frac{V}{R} = \frac{4}{4} = 1\text{ A} \quad \text{... (i)}$$

Now, from the circuit (B),

$$4I' = 6I$$

$$\Rightarrow \quad I' = \frac{3}{2}I$$

But $\quad i = I + I' = I + \dfrac{3}{2}I = \dfrac{5}{2}I$

$$\Rightarrow \quad 1 = \frac{5}{2}I \quad \text{[from Eq. (i)]}$$

$$\Rightarrow \quad I = 0.4\text{ A}$$

39 *(a)* By Kirchhoff's first law at P,

$$I_1 + I_2 = 6 \quad \text{...(i)}$$

By Kirchhoff's second law to the closed circuit $PQRP$,

$$-2I_1 - 2I_1 + 2I_2 = 0$$

$$\Rightarrow \quad -4I_1 + 2I_2 = 0$$

$$\Rightarrow \quad 2I_1 - I_2 = 0 \quad \text{...(ii)}$$

Adding Eqs. (i) and (ii), we get

$$3I_1 = 6$$

$$\Rightarrow \quad I_1 = 2\text{ A}$$

From Eq. (i),

$$I_2 = 6 - 2 = 4\text{ A}$$

40 *(c)* If polarity on n cells out of N cells is reversed, then $2n$ cells will cancel out each other and equivalent emf

$$= (N - 2n)e$$

41 (b) Let i_1, i_2 be the currents in the two loops of the given circuit, then

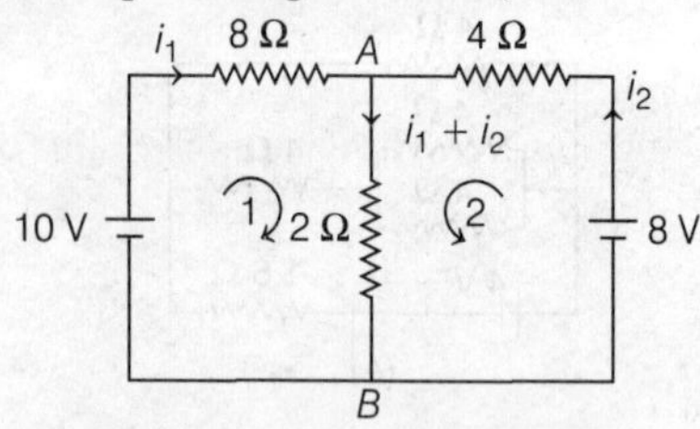

Applying to Kirchhoff's law for loop 1, we get

$$\Sigma iR = V$$

$$\Rightarrow \quad 8i_1 + 2(i_1 + i_2) = 10$$

$$\Rightarrow \quad 10i_1 + 2i_2 = 10$$

$$\Rightarrow \quad 5i_1 + i_2 = 5 \quad \ldots(i)$$

Applying Kirchhoff' law to loop 2, we get

$$4i_2 + 2(i_1 + i_2) = 8$$

$$\Rightarrow \quad 6i_2 + 2i_1 = 8$$

$$\Rightarrow \quad i_1 + 3i_2 = 4 \quad \ldots(ii)$$

From Eqs. (i) and (ii), we get

$$i_1 = \frac{11}{14}\text{ A}$$

and $$i_2 = \frac{15}{14}\text{ A}$$

Hence, current flowing in arm AB is

$$i_1 + i_2 = \frac{11}{14} + \frac{15}{14}$$

$$= \frac{26}{14} = \frac{13}{7}\text{ A}$$

42 (d) Current taken from the combination of n cells each of internal resistance r in series with external resistance R is

$$i = \frac{nE}{nr + R}$$

Similarly, for parallel combination,

$$i = \frac{nE}{r + nR}$$

For mixed grouping of n such cell in m rows with external resistance R is

$$i = \frac{mnE}{mR + nr}$$

It is obvious that maximum current obtained from each combination depends on the values of external and internal resistances.

43 (b) As, the terminal voltage of the battery is given as

$$V = E - ir$$

$$\Rightarrow \quad V = -ir + E \quad \ldots(i)$$

The equation of straight line with slope m and Y intercept c is

$$y = mx + c \quad \ldots(ii)$$

On comparing, Eq. (i) with (ii), we get

$$y = V;\ x = i$$

$$m = -r \text{ and } c = E$$

Thus, current *versus* terminal voltage graph can be plotted as below

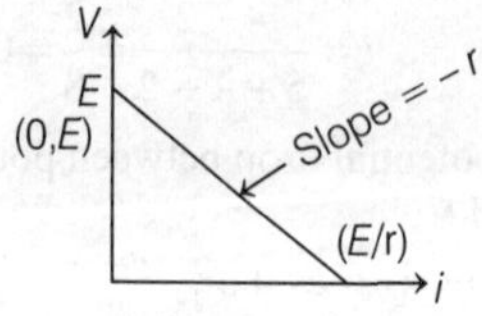

44 (a) From Kirchhoff's first law, in an electric circuit, the algebraic sum of the currents meeting at any junction is zero.

i.e. $$\Sigma i = 0$$

Taking inward direction of current as positive and outward as negative, we have $1\text{ A} - 3\text{ A} - 2\text{ A} + I = 0$

$$\Rightarrow \quad I = 4\text{ A}$$

45 (a) All the resistances are in parallel order, so voltage across them will be equal.

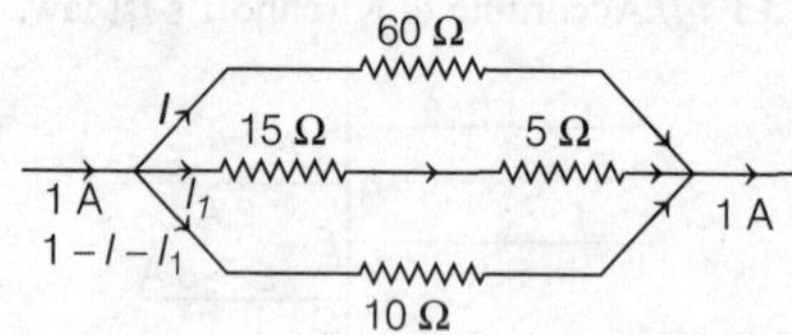

$$\therefore \quad 60I = (15 + 5)I_1$$

$$\Rightarrow \quad 60I = 20I_1$$

$$\Rightarrow \quad I_1 = 3I \quad \ldots(i)$$

Again,

$$(15 + 5)I_1 = 10(1 - I - I_1)$$

$$\Rightarrow \quad 2I_1 = 1 - I - I_1$$

$$\Rightarrow \quad 2(3I) = 1 - I - 3I$$

[from Eq. (i)]

$$\Rightarrow \quad 6I + 4I = 1$$

$$\Rightarrow \quad 10I = 1$$

$$\Rightarrow \quad I = \frac{1}{10} = 0.1\text{ A}$$

Topic 4

Different Measuring Instruments

2019

1 The meter bridge shown in the balance position with $\frac{P}{Q} = \frac{l_1}{l_2}$. If we now interchange the positions of galvanometer and cell, will the bridge work? If yes, that will be balanced condition? **[NEET (Odisha)]**

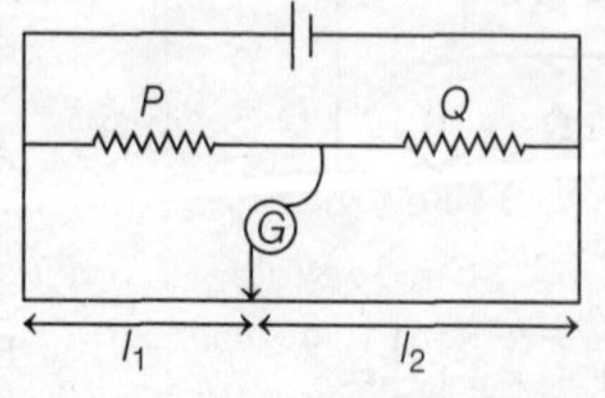

(a) Yes, $\frac{P}{Q} = \frac{l_2 - l_1}{l_2 + l_1}$ (b) No, no null point

(c) Yes, $\frac{P}{Q} = \frac{l_2}{l_1}$ (d) Yes, $\frac{P}{Q} = \frac{l_1}{l_2}$

2 In the circuits shown below, the readings of voltmeters and the ammeters will be **[NEET]**

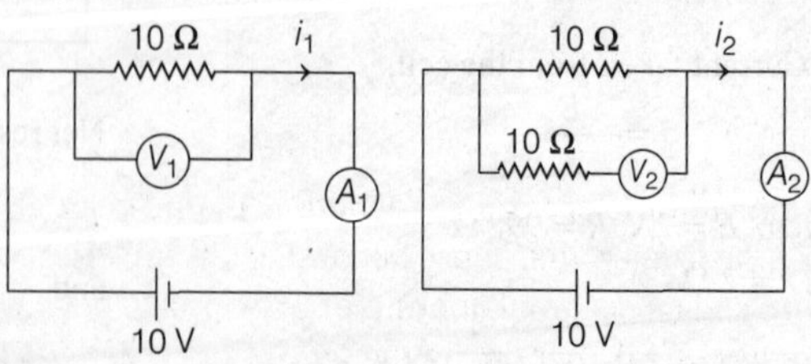

(a) $V_1 = V_2$ and $i_1 > i_2$ (b) $V_1 = V_2$ and $i_i = i_2$

(c) $V_2 > V_1$ and $i_1 > i_2$ (d) $V_2 > V_1$ and $i_1 = i_2$

2018

3 Find current (i) in circuit shown in figure. **[NEET]**

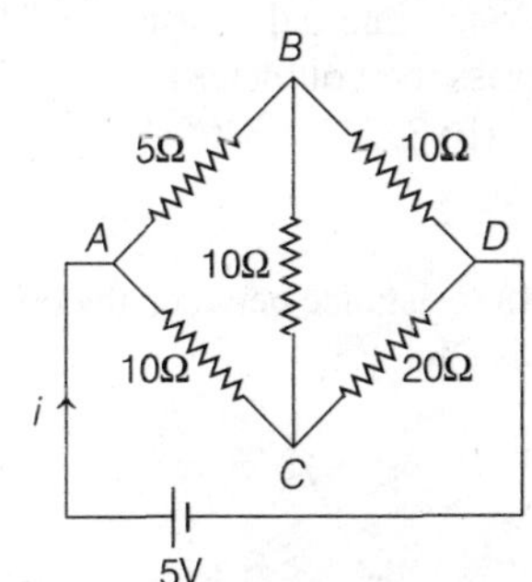

(a) 0.5 A (b) 0.2 A
(c) 1 A (d) 2 A

4 The effective resistance between p and q in given figure is **[AIIMS]**

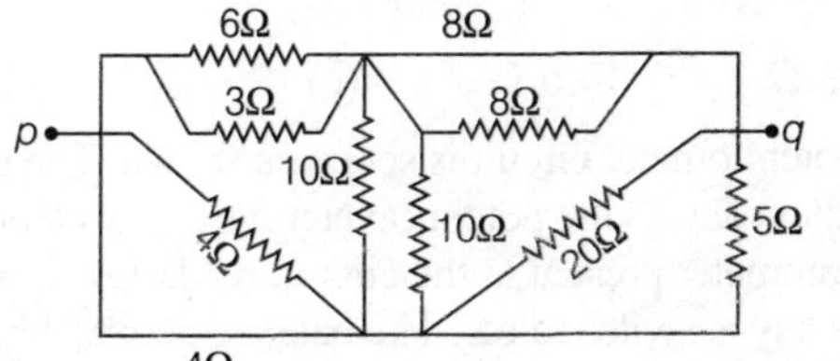

(a) 2Ω (b) 3Ω (c) 5Ω (d) 6Ω

2017

5 Assertion A potentiometer is preferred over that of a voltmeter for measurement of emf of a cell.

Reason Potentiometer does not draw any current from the cell. **[AIIMS]**

(a) Both Assertion and Reason are correct and Reason is the correct explanation of Assertion.
(b) Both Assertion and Reason are correct but Reason is not the correct explanation of Assertion.
(c) Assertion is correct Reason is incorrect.
(d) Assertion is incorrect but Reason incorrect.

2015

6 A potentiometer wire is 100cm long and a constant potential difference is maintained across it. Two cells are connected in series first to support one another and then in opposite direction. The balance points are obtained at 50 cm and 10 cm from the positive end of the wire in the two cases. The ratio of emf is **[NEET]**

(a) 5:4 (b) 3:4
(c) 3:2 (d) 5:1

7 A potentiometer wire has length 4 m and resistance 8Ω. The resistance that must be connected in series with the wire and an accumulator of emf 2V, so as to get a potential gradient 1 mV per cm on the wire is **[NEET 2015]**

(a) 32 Ω (b) 40 Ω
(c) 44 Ω (d) 48 Ω

8 A meter bridge is set up as shown in figure, to determine an unknown resistance X using a standard 10 Ω resistor. The galvanometer shows null point when tapping key is at 52 cm mark. The end-corrections are 1 cm and 2 cm respectively for the ends A and B. The determined value of X is **[IIT JEE]**

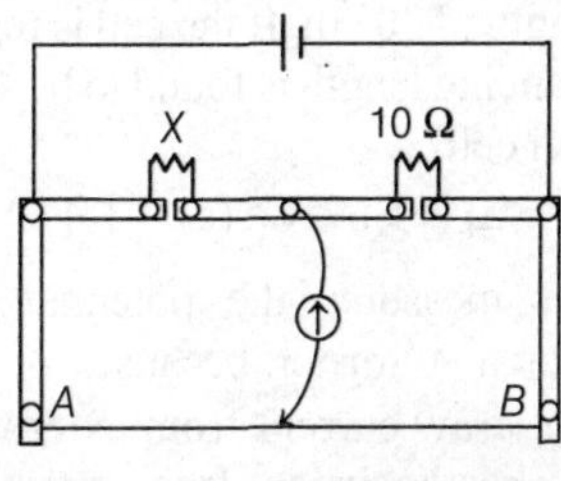

(a) 10.2 Ω (b) 10.6 Ω
(c) 10.8 Ω (d) 11.1 Ω

2014

9 A potentiometer circuit has been set up for finding the internal resistance of a given cell. The main battery, used across the potentiometer wire, has an emf of 2.0 V and a negligible internal resistance. The potentiometer wire itself is 4 m long. When the resistance R, connected across the given cell, has values of (i) infinity and (ii) 9.5 Ω.

The balancing lengths of the potentiometer wire are found to be 3 m and 2.85 m, respectively.

The value of internal resistance of the cell is **[CBSE AIPMT]**

(a) 0.25 Ω (b) 0.95 Ω
(c) 0.5 Ω (d) 0.75 Ω

10 The resistances in the two arms of the meter bridge are 5 Ω and R Ω, respectively. When the resistance R is shunted with an equal resistance, the new balance point is at $1.6\, l_1$. The resistance R is **[CBSE AIPMT]**

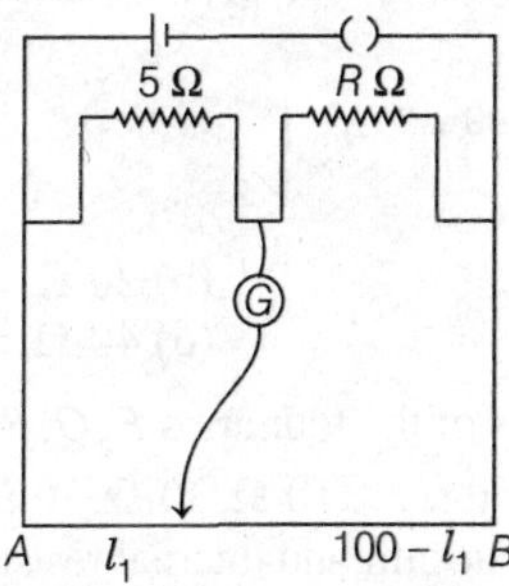

(a) 10 Ω (b) 15 Ω (c) 20 Ω (d) 25 Ω

11 In Wheatstone bridge, three resistors P, Q, R are connected in three arms in order and 4th arm of resistance s, is formed by two resistors s_1 and s_2 connected in parallel. The condition for bridge to be balanced is P/Q **[MHT CET]**

(a) $\frac{R(s_1 + s_2)}{s_1 s_2}$ (b) $\frac{s_1 s_2}{R(s_1 + s_2)}$

(c) $\frac{R s_1 s_2}{(s_1 + s_2)}$ (d) $\frac{(s_1 + s_2)}{R s_1 s_2}$

12 An electron in potentiometer which experiences a force 2.4×10^{-19} N. The length of potentiometer wire is 6 m. The emf of the battery connected across the wire is (electronic charge = 1.6×10^{-19} C) **[MHT CET]**
(a) 6 V (b) 9 V (c) 12 V (d) 15 V

13 In potentiometer experiment of a cell of emf 1.25 V gives balancing length of 30 cm. If the cell is replaced by another cell, then balancing length is found to be 40 cm. What is the emf of second cell? **[KCET]**
(a) $\simeq$ 1.5 V (b) $\simeq$ 1.67 V (c) $\simeq$ 1.47 V (d) $\simeq$ 1.37 V

14 Potentiometer measures the potential difference more accurately than a voltmeter, because **[UK PMT]**
(a) it does not draw current from external circuit
(b) it draws a heavy current from external circuit
(c) it has a wire of high resistance
(d) it has a wire of low resistance

15 In a potentiometer experiment, the balancing with a cell is at length 240 cm. On shunting the cell with a resistance of 2 Ω, the balancing becomes 120 cm. The internal resistance of the cell is **[UK PMT]**
(a) 1 Ω (b) 0.5 Ω (c) 4 Ω (d) 2 Ω

16 If a battery of 6 V is connected to the terminals of 3 m long wire of uniform thickness and resistance of the order of 100 Ω. The difference of potential between the two points separated by 50 cm in the wire will be **[Manipal]**
(a) 1 V (b) 1.5 V (c) 2 V (d) 3 V

2013

17 The equivalent resistance between A and B is **[Manipal, KCET]**

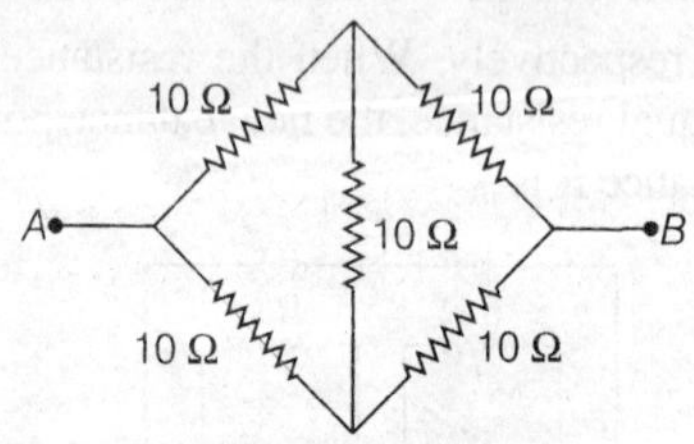

(a) 10 Ω (b) 20 Ω
(c) 30 Ω (d) 40 Ω

18 The resistances of the four arms P, Q, R and S in a Wheatstone bridge are 10 Ω, 30 Ω, 30 Ω and 90 Ω, respectively. The emf and internal resistance of the cell are 7 V and 5 Ω, respectively. If the galvanometer resistance is 50 Ω, then the current drawn from the cell will be
(a) 1.0 A (b) 0.2 A **[NEET]**
(c) 0.1 A (d) 2.0 A

19 A 100 V voltmeter of internal resistance 20 kΩ in series with a high resistance R is connected to 110 V line. The voltmeter reads 5 V, the value of R is **[AIIMS]**
(a) 210 kΩ (b) 315 kΩ
(c) 420 kΩ (d) 4440 kΩ

2012

20 A voltmeter of resistance 998 Ω is connected across a cell of emf 2 V and internal resistance 2Ω. The potential difference across the voltmeter is **[Manipal]**
(a) 1.99 V (b) 3.5 V (c) 5 V (d) 6 V

2011

21 The equivalent resistance between the points A and B in the given circuit is **[J&K CET]**

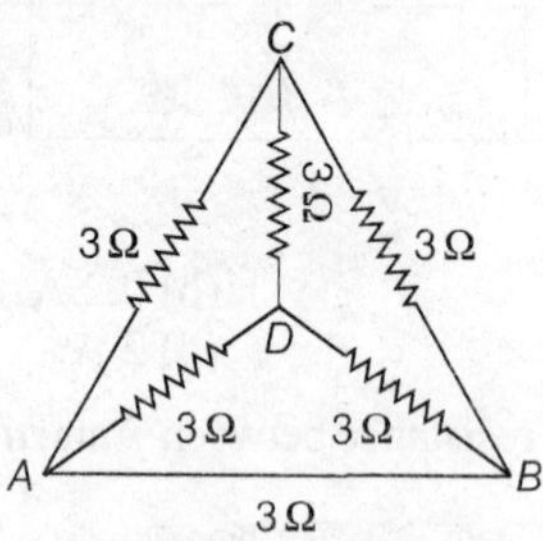

(a) 3 Ω (b) 6 Ω (c) 12 Ω (d) 1.5 Ω

22 A potentiometer circuit is set up as shown. The potential gradient across the potentiometer wire, is k volt/cm and the ammeter present in the circuit, reads 1.0 A, when two way key is switched off. The balance points, when the key between the terminals (i) 1 and 2 and (ii) 1 and 3 is plugged in, are found to be at lengths l_1 cm and l_2 cm, respectively. The magnitudes of the resistors R and X (in ohm) are equal to **[CBSE AIPMT]**

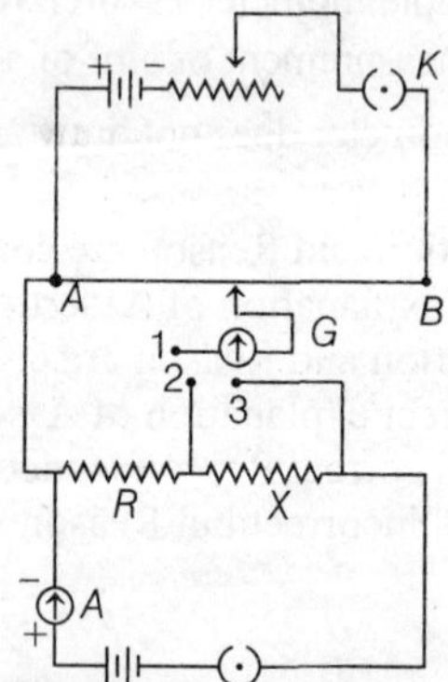

(a) $k(l_2 - l_1)$ and kl_2 (b) kl_1 and $k(l_2 - l_1)$
(c) $k(l_2 - l_1)$ and kl_1 (d) kl_1 and kl_2

23 Two cells of emfs E_1 and $E_2 (E_1 > E_2)$ are connected as shown in figure.

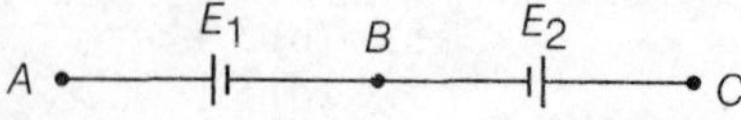

When a potentiometer is connected between A and B, then the balancing length of the potentiometer wire is 300 cm. On connecting the same potentiometer between A and C, the balancing length is 100 cm. The ratio E_1/E_2 is **[AFMC]**
(a) 3 : 1 (b) 1 : 3 (c) 2 : 3 (d) 3 : 2

24 Consider the following statements regarding the network shown in the figure.

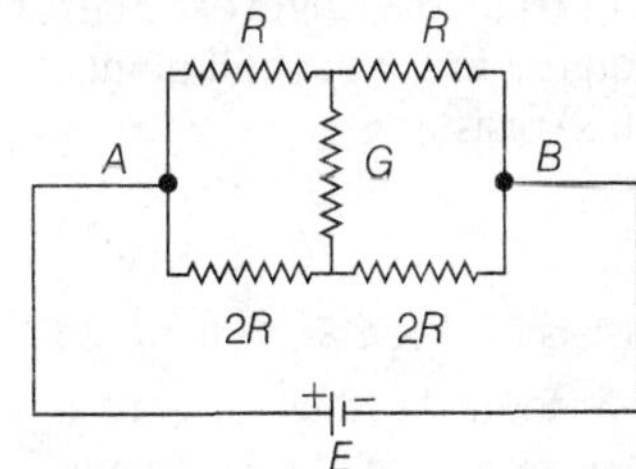

I. The equivalent resistance of the network between points A and B is independent of value of G.

II. The equivalent resistance of the network between points A and B is $\frac{4}{3}R$.

III. The current through G is zero.

Which of the above statements is/are correct? **[KCET]**

(a) Only I (b) Only II
(c) II and III (d) I, II and III

2010

25 The current I drawn from the 5 V source will be **[AFMC]**

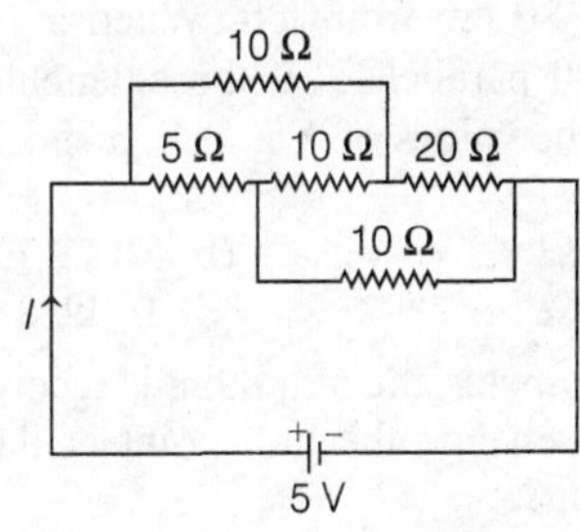

(a) 0.33 A (b) 0.5 A
(c) 0.67 A (d) 0.17 A

26 The equivalent resistance across A and B is **[JIPMER]**

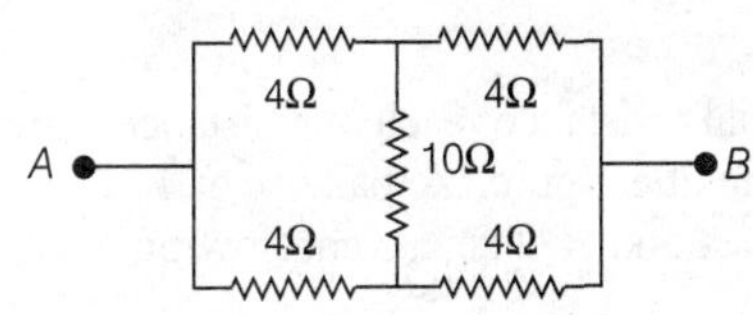

(a) 2 Ω (b) 3 Ω
(c) 4 Ω (d) 5 Ω

27 Five equal resistors, each equal to r are connected as shown in the figure, then the equivalent resistance between points A and B is **[CG PMT]**

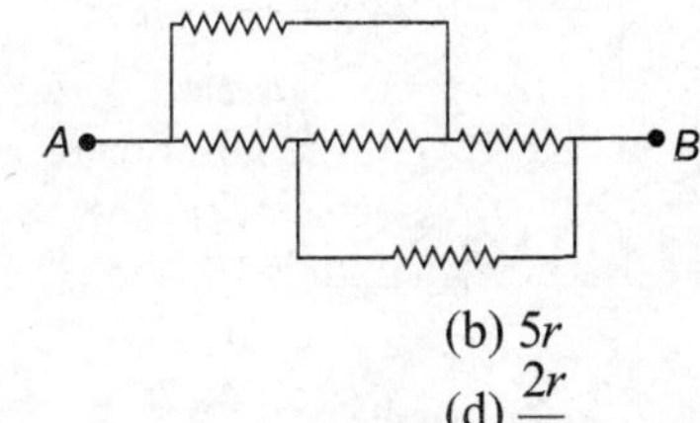

(a) r (b) $5r$
(c) $\frac{r}{5}$ (d) $\frac{2r}{3}$

28 Two resistances are connected in two gaps of a metre bridge. The balance point is 20 cm from the zero end. A resistance of 15 Ω is connected in series with the smaller of the two. The null point shifts to 40 cm. The value of the smaller resistance (in ohm) is **[VMMC]**

(a) 3 (b) 6 (c) 9 (d) 12

29 The length of a wire of a potentiometer is 100 cm and the emf of its standard cell is E volt. It is employed to measure the emf of a battery whose internal resistance is 0.5 Ω. If the balance point is obtained at $l = 30$ cm from the positive end, the emf of the battery is **[MGIMS]**

(a) $\frac{30E}{100.5}$

(b) $\frac{30E}{100-0.5}$

(c) $\frac{30(E-0.5i)}{100}$, where i is the current flow in the potentiometer wire.

(d) $\frac{30E}{100}$

30 Two resistors 400 Ω and 800 Ω are connected in series with a 6 V battery. The potential difference measured by voltmeter of 10 kΩ across 400 Ω resistor is **[BCECE]**

(a) 2 V (b) 1.95 V
(c) 3.8 V (d) 4 V

31 A 10 m long wire of resistance 20 Ω is connected in series with a battery of emf 3 V and a resistance of 10 Ω. The potential gradient along the wire (in V/m) is **[JCECE]**

(a) 0.02 (b) 0.1 (c) 0.2 (d) 1.2

2009

32 Seven resistances are connected as shown in the given figure. The equivalent resistance between A and B is

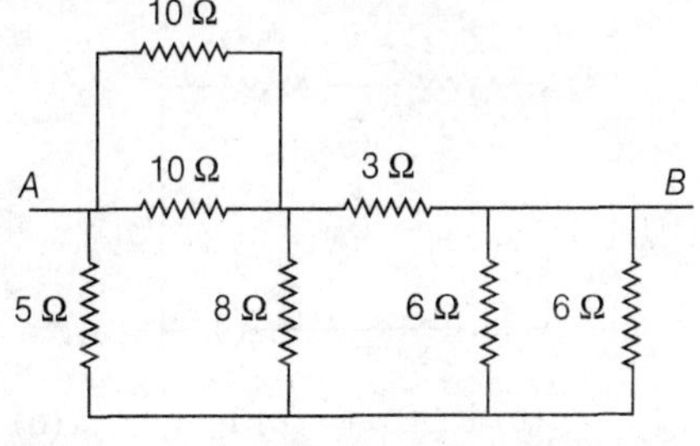

[AFMC]

(a) 3 Ω (b) 4 Ω
(c) 4.5 Ω (d) 15 Ω

33 An ammeter and a voltmeter of resistance R are connected in series to an electric cell of negligible internal resistance. Their readings are A and V, respectively. If another resistance R is connected in parallel with the voltmeter, then **[AFMC]**

(a) Both A and V will increase
(b) Both A and V will decrease
(c) A will decrease and V will increase
(d) A will increase and V will decrease

34 In a potentiometer of one metre length, an unknown emf voltage source is balanced at 60 cm length of potentiometer wire, while a 3V battery is balanced at 45 cm length. Then, the emf of the unknown voltage source is **[AFMC]**

(a) 3 V (b) 2.25 V
(c) 4 V (d) 4.5 V

35 A 2V battery, a 990 Ω resistor and a potentiometer of 2 m length, all are connected in series. If the resistance of potentiometer wire is 10 Ω, then the potential gradient of the potentiometer wire is **[MHT CET]**

(a) 0.05 Vm^{-1} (b) 0.5 Vm^{-1}
(c) 0.01 Vm^{-1} (d) 0.1 Vm^{-1}

36 In a meter bridge experiment, resistances are connected as shown in figure. The balancing length l_1 is 55 cm. Now, an unknown resistance x is connected in series with P and the new balancing length is found to be 75 cm. The value of x is **[Kerala CEE]**

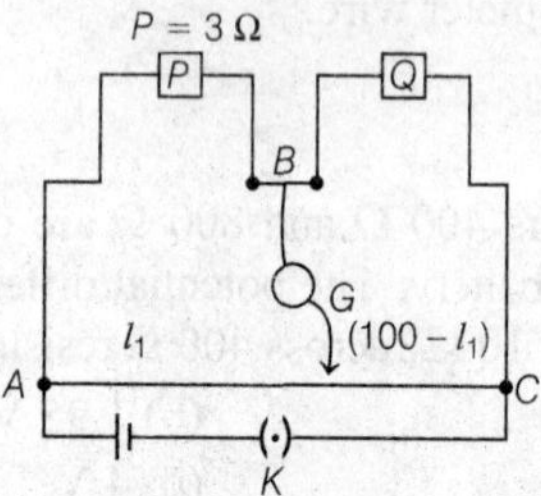

(a) $\frac{54}{13}$ Ω (b) $\frac{20}{11}$ Ω
(c) $\frac{48}{11}$ Ω (d) $\frac{11}{48}$ Ω
(e) 5 Ω

37 If there is no deflection in the galvanometer connected in a circuit shown in figure, then the ratio of lengths AC/CB is **[MGIMS]**

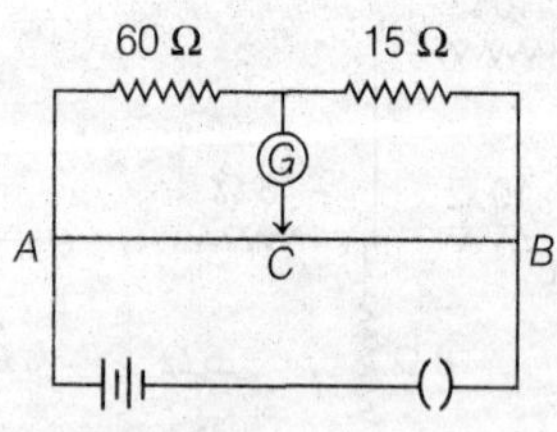

(a) 4 : 1 (b) 1 : 4 (c) 1 : 1 (d) 2 : 1

38 A potentiometer has uniform potential gradient across it. Two cells connected in series (i) to support each other and (ii) to oppose each other are balanced over 6 m and 2 m respectively on the potentiometer wire. The emfs of the cells are in the ratio of **[MGIMS]**

(a) 1 : 2 (b) 1 : 1
(c) 3 : 1 (d) 2 : 1

39 A potentiometer having the potential gradient of 2 Vcm^{-1} is used to measure the difference of potential across a resistance of 10 Ω. If a length of 50 cm of the potentiometer wire is required to get the null points, the current passing through 10 Ω resistor is **[MGIMS]**

(a) 1 (b) 2
(c) 5 (d) 10

40 Three resistances P, Q, R each of 2 Ω and an unknown resistance S form the four arms of a Wheatstone bridge circuit. When resistance of 6 Ω is connected in parallel to S, then the bridge gets balanced. What is the value of S?

(a) 2 Ω (b) 3 Ω **[JIPMER]**
(c) 6 Ω (d) 1 Ω

2008

41 A cell can be balanced against 110 cm and 100 cm of potentiometer wire respectively with and without being short circuited through a resistance of 10 Ω. Its internal resistance is **[CBSE AIPMT]**

(a) 1.0 Ω (b) 0.5 Ω (c) 2.0 Ω (d) zero

42 Two unknown resistances X and Y are connected to left and right gaps of a metre bridge and the balancing point is obtained at 80 cm from left. When a 10 Ω resistance is connected in parallel to X the balancing point is 50 cm from left. The values of X and Y, respectively are **[Punjab PMET]**

(a) 40 Ω, 9 Ω (b) 30 Ω, 7.5 Ω
(c) 20 Ω, 6 Ω (d) 10 Ω, 3 Ω

43 In a potentiometer, the null point is received at 7th wire. If we have to change the null point at the 9th wire, what should we do? **[DUMET]**

(a) Attach a resistance in series with battery
(b) Increase resistance in main circuit
(c) Decrease resistance in main circuit
(d) Decrease applied emf

2007

44 Five equal resistances each of resistance R are connected as shown in the figure. A battery of V volts is connected between A and B. The current flowing in $AFCEB$ will be **[Manipal]**

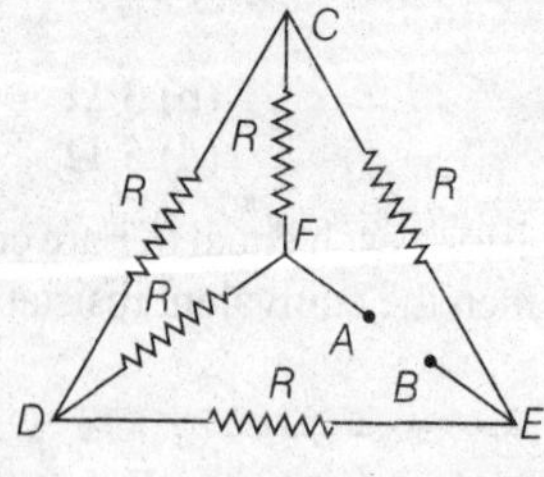

(a) $\frac{3V}{R}$ (b) $\frac{V}{R}$
(c) $\frac{V}{2R}$ (d) $\frac{2V}{R}$

45 A circuit consists of five identical conductors as shown in figure. The two similar conductors are added as indicated by dotted lines. The ratio of resistance before and after addition will be **[RPMT]**

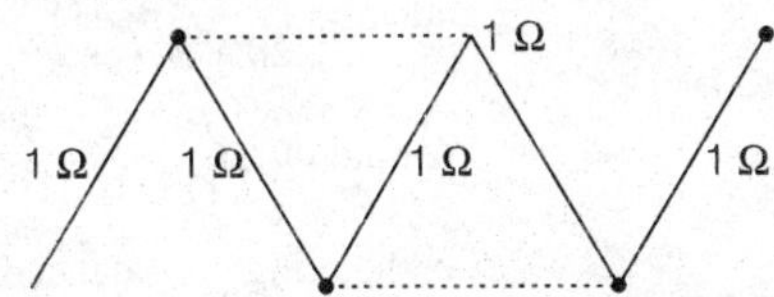

(a) $\frac{7}{5}$ (b) $\frac{3}{5}$ (c) $\frac{5}{3}$ (d) $\frac{6}{5}$

46 In the circuit shown in figure, $P \neq R$ and if the reading of the galvanometer G is same while the switch S is opened or closed, then **[Manipal]**

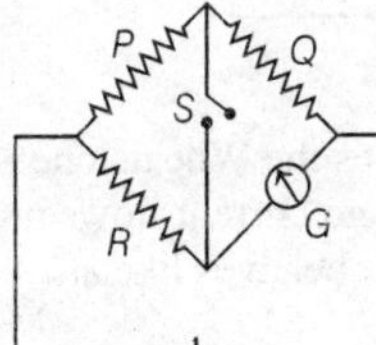

(a) $I_Q = I_R$ (b) $I_R = I_G$
(c) $I_P = I_G$ (d) $I_Q = I_G$

47 A 6 V battery is connected to the terminals of a 3 m long wire of uniform thickness and resistance of 100 Ω. The difference of potential between two points on the wire separated by a distance of 50 cm will be **[Manipal]**

(a) 2 V (b) 3 V (c) 1 V (d) 1.5 V

48 The current in the primary circuit of a potentiometer is 0.2 A. The specific resistance and cross-section of the potentiometer wire are 4×10^{-7} Ω-m and 8×10^{-7} m^2 respectively. The potential gradient will be equal to **[AIEEE]**

(a) 0.2 V/m (b) 1 V/m
(c) 0.3 V/m (d) 0.1 V/m

2005

49 The equivalent resistance between the points P and Q in the network shown in the figure is given by **[BHU]**

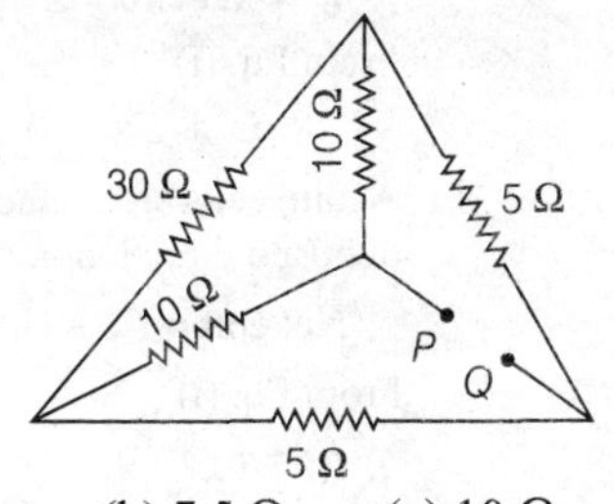

(a) 2.5 Ω (b) 7.5 Ω (c) 10 Ω (d) 12.5 Ω

50 For the network shown in the figure, the value of the current i is **[CBSE AIPMT]**

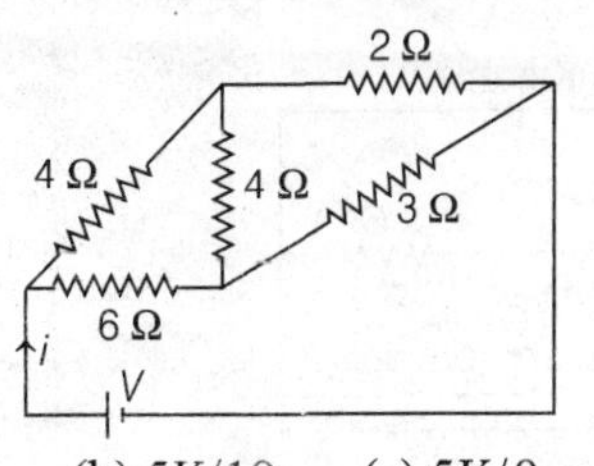

(a) $9V/35$ (b) $5V/18$ (c) $5V/9$ (d) $18V/5$

51 In the Wheatstone's network shown in the figure, the current I in the circuit is **[Kerala CEE]**

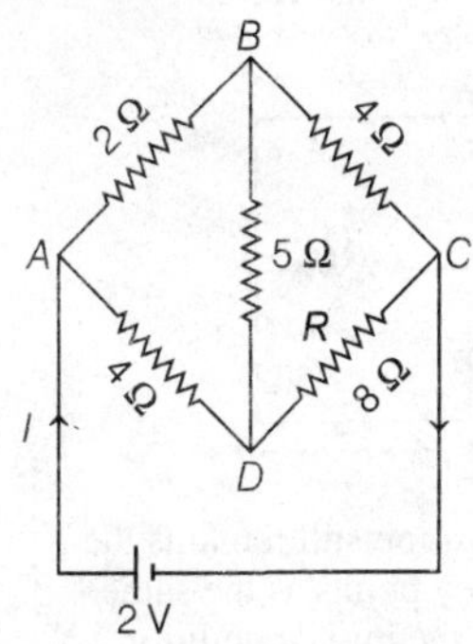

(a) 1 A (b) 2 A
(c) 0.25 A (d) 0.5 A
(e) 0.33 A

52 The figure below shows a 2.0 V potentiometer used for the determination of internal resistance of a 2.5 V cell. The balance point of the cell in the open circuit is 75 cm. When a resistor of 10 Ω is used in the external circuit of the cell, the balance point shifts to 65 cm length of potentiometer wire. The internal resistance of the cell is **[JCECE]**

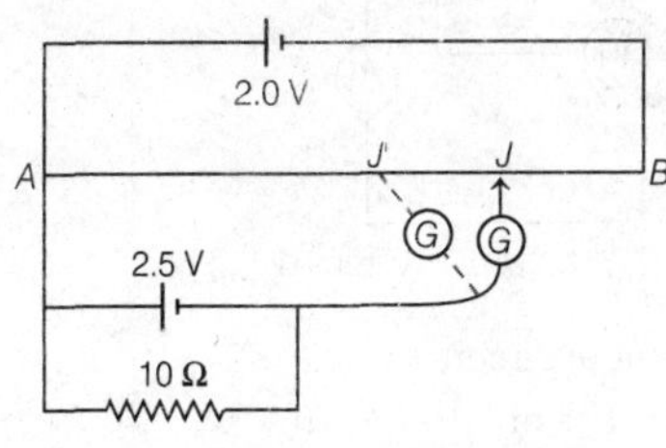

(a) 2.5 Ω (b) 2.0 Ω
(c) 1.54 Ω (d) 1.0 Ω

Answers

1 (d)	2 (b)	3 (a)	4 (b)	5 (a)	6 (c)	7 (a)	8 (b)	9 (c)	10 (b)
11 (a)	12 (b)	13 (b)	14 (a)	15 (d)	16 (a)	17 (a)	18 (b)	19 (c)	20 (a)
21 (d)	22 (b)	23 (d)	24 (d)	25 (b)	26 (c)	27 (a)	28 (c)	29 (d)	30 (b)
31 (c)	32 (b)	33 (a)	34 (c)	35 (c)	36 (c)	37 (a)	38 (c)	39 (d)	40 (b)
41 (a)	42 (b)	43 (b)	44 (c)	45 (c)	46 (b)	47 (c)	48 (d)	49 (b)	50 (b)
51 (d)	52 (c)								

Explanations

1 *(d)* For balanced position in a meter bridge,

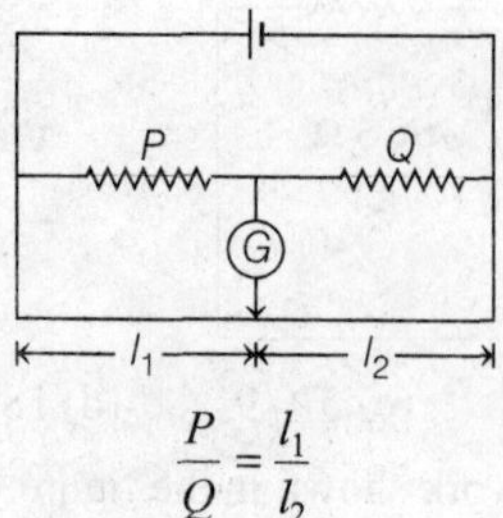

$$\frac{P}{Q} = \frac{l_1}{l_2}$$

Now, if position of G and cell is interchanged,

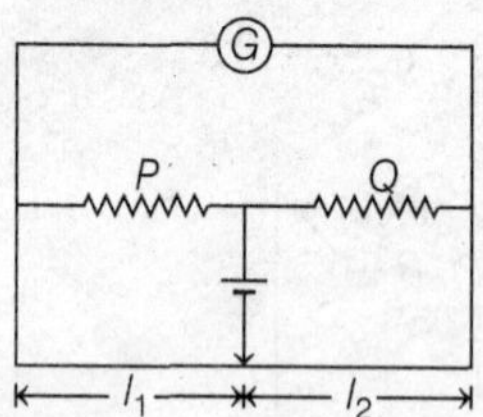

The balance condition still remains the same, if the jockey points as the same point as given in the initial condition, for which there is no deflection in the galvanometer or no current will be drawn from the cell. Thus, the bridge will work as usual and balance condition is same, $P / Q = l_1 / l_2$

2 *(b)* For an ideal voltmeter, the resistance is infinite and for an ideal ammeter, the resistance is zero.

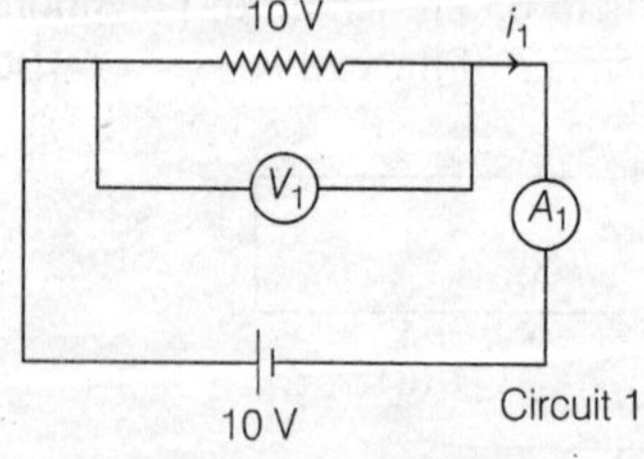

So, the current in circuit 1 is

$$R \times i = V \quad \text{or} \quad 10\, i_1 = 10$$

$$\Rightarrow \quad i_1 = \frac{10}{10} = 1\,\text{A}$$

$$\therefore \quad V_1 = i_1 \times R = 1 \times 10 = 10\,\text{V}$$

Similarly, for circuit 2, the addition of $10\,\Omega$ to voltmeter does not affect the current and hence

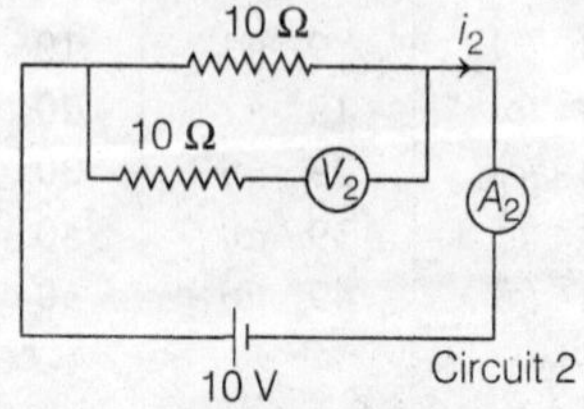

$$10 i_2 = 10 \quad \Rightarrow \quad i_2 = \frac{10}{10} = 1\,\text{A}$$

$$V_2 = i_2 R = 1 \times 10 = 10\,\text{V}$$

$$\therefore \quad V_1 = V_2 \text{ and } i_1 = i_2$$

3 *(a)*

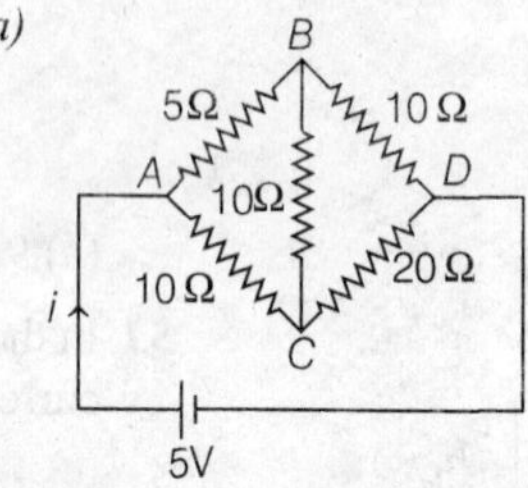

Above circuit satisfies the Wheatstone bridge condition, so no current flows in the branch BC and it behaves like an open circuit.

So, circuit becomes as shown below

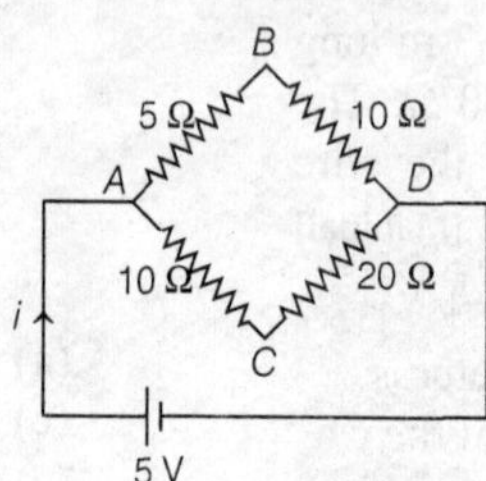

Now, in the above circuit,

$$R_{ABD} = 5 + 10 = 15\,\Omega$$

$$R_{ACD} = 10 + 20 = 30\,\Omega$$

Resistance R_{ABD} and R_{ACD} in parallel, so

$$R_{\text{net}} = \frac{15 \times 30}{30 + 15} = \frac{450}{45} = 10\,\Omega$$

$$\therefore \quad i = \frac{E}{R_{\text{net}}} = \frac{5}{10} = 0.5\,\text{A}$$

4 *(b)* Figure is equivalent to the one shown below. It is a Wheatstone's bridge in which

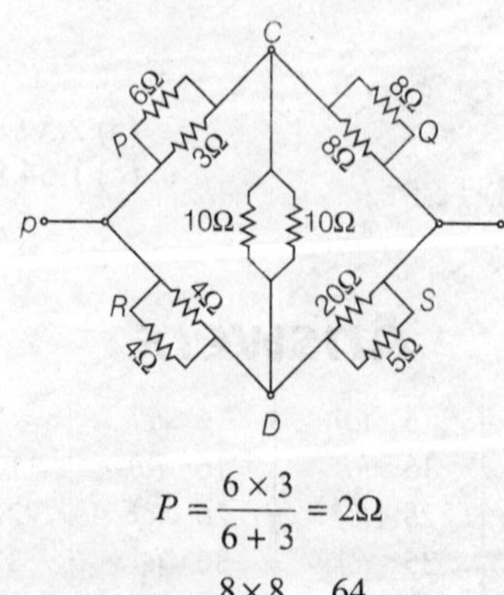

$$P = \frac{6 \times 3}{6 + 3} = 2\Omega$$

$$Q = \frac{8 \times 8}{8 + 8} = \frac{64}{16} = 4\Omega$$

$$R = \frac{4 \times 4}{4 + 4} = \frac{16}{8} = 2\Omega$$

$$\text{and} \quad S = \frac{20 \times 5}{20 + 5} = 4\Omega$$

We find that, $\frac{P}{Q} = \frac{2}{4} = \frac{R}{S}$

i.e. the bridge is balanced and resistance of arm CD is ineffective. Effective resistance between p and q

$$R_{AB} = \frac{(P + Q)(R + S)}{P + Q + R + S} = \frac{(2 + 4)(2 + 4)}{2 + 4 + 2 + 4} = \frac{6 \times 6}{12} = 3\Omega$$

5 *(a)* When a voltmeter is connected across the two terminals of a cell, it draws a small current from the cell, so it measures terminal potential difference between the two terminals of the cell, which is always less than the emf of the cell. On the other hand, when a potentiometer is used for the measurement of emf of cell, it does not draw any current from the cell. Hence, it accurately measures the emf of cell. Thus, a potentiometer is preferred over a voltmeter.

6 *(c)* According to question, emf of the cell is directly proportional to the balancing length, i.e.

$$E \propto l \quad \text{...(i)}$$

Now, in the first case, cells are connected in series to support one another, i.e.

$$\text{Net emf} = E_1 + E_2$$

From Eq. (i),

$$E_1 + E_2 = 50 \quad \text{(given)} \quad \text{...(ii)}$$

Again, cells are connected in series in opposite direction, i.e.

$$\text{Net emf} = E_1 - E_2$$

From Eq. (i),

$$E_1 - E_2 = 10 \quad \text{...(iii)}$$

On dividing Eq. (ii) by Eq. (iii), we get

$$\frac{E_1 + E_2}{E_1 - E_2} = \frac{50}{10}$$

$$\Rightarrow \quad \frac{E_1}{E_2} = \frac{5 + 1}{5 - 1} = \frac{6}{4} = \frac{3}{2}$$

7 *(a)* Given, $l = 4$ m,

R = potentiometer wire resistance $= 8\Omega$

Potential gradient $= \frac{dV}{dr} = 1\,\text{mV/cm}$

So, for 400 cm,

$$\Delta V = 400 \times 1 \times 10^{-3} = 0.4 \text{ V}$$

Let a resistor R_s connected in series, then

$$\Delta V = \frac{V}{R + R_s} \times R$$

$$\Rightarrow \quad 0.4 = \frac{2}{8 + R} \times 8$$

$$\Rightarrow \quad 8 + R = \frac{16}{0.4} = 40$$

$$\Rightarrow \quad R = 32 \ \Omega$$

8 *(b)* Given, standard resistance, $Y = 10\Omega$, balance length, $L_1 = 52$ cm and end corrections, $x_1 = 10$ cm and $x_2 = 2$ cm. Now, balance length, $L_2 = 100 - L_1 = 100 - 52 = 48$ cm.

As, balance condition for meter bridge,

$$\frac{X}{(L_1 + x_1)} = \frac{Y}{(L_2 + x_2)}$$

$$\Rightarrow \quad \frac{X}{(52 + 1)} = \frac{10}{(48 + 2)}$$

$$\Rightarrow \quad x = \frac{10 \times 53}{50} = 10.6\Omega$$

9 *(c)* As, r = internal resistance, then

$$r = R_1 \left(\frac{l - l_1}{l_1} \right)$$

$$\Rightarrow \quad \frac{rl_1}{R_1} = l - l_1 \quad \text{...(i)}$$

Also, $$r = R_2 \left(\frac{l - l_2}{l_2} \right)$$

$$\Rightarrow \quad \frac{rl_2}{R_2} = l - l_2 \quad \text{...(ii)}$$

Subtracting Eq. (i) from Eq. (ii), we get

$$l - l_2 - l + l_1 = r \left[\frac{l_2}{R_2} - \frac{l_1}{R_1} \right]$$

$$l_1 - l_2 = r \left[\frac{l_2}{R_2} - \frac{l_1}{R_1} \right] \quad \text{...(i)}$$

As, $R_1 = \infty$

$\Rightarrow \quad l_1 = 3$ m

and $R_2 = 9.5$

$\Rightarrow \quad l_2 = 2.85$ cm

Putting these values in Eq. (i), we get

$$\Rightarrow (3 - 2.85) = r \left[\frac{2.85}{9.5} - 0 \right]$$

$$\Rightarrow \quad 0.15 = r \left(\frac{2.85}{9.5} \right)$$

$$\Rightarrow \quad r = \frac{0.15 \times 9.5}{2.85}$$

$$\Rightarrow \quad r = 0.5 \ \Omega$$

10 *(b)* There are two cases

***Case* I** For balanced point of meter bridge,

$$\frac{5}{R} = \frac{l_1}{100 - l_1} \quad \text{...(i)}$$

***Case* II** When R is shunted with equal resistance, i.e. R

$$\frac{1}{R'} = \frac{1}{R} + \frac{1}{R}$$

$$\Rightarrow \quad R' = R/2$$

$$\therefore \quad \frac{5}{R/2} = \frac{1.6\, l_1}{100 - 1.6\, l_1} \quad \text{...(ii)}$$

From Eqs. (i) and (ii), we get

$$2\left(\frac{l_1}{100 - l_1} \right) = \frac{1.6\, l_1}{100 - 1.6\, l_1}$$

$$\Rightarrow \quad l_1 = 25 \text{ cm}$$

From Eq. (i), $\dfrac{5}{R} = \dfrac{25}{75}$

$$\Rightarrow \quad R = 15 \ \Omega$$

11 *(a)* Balanced condition for Wheatstone bridge,

$$\frac{P}{Q} = \frac{R}{s} \quad \text{...(i)}$$

where, $$\frac{1}{s} = \frac{1}{s_1} + \frac{1}{s_2}$$

$$\Rightarrow \quad s = \frac{s_1 s_2}{s_1 + s_2} \quad \text{...(ii)}$$

From Eqs. (i) and (ii), we get

$$\frac{P}{Q} = \frac{R(s_1 + s_2)}{s_1 s_2}$$

12 *(b)* Force experienced by electron,

$$F = qE$$

where, E = electric field intensity.

$$\therefore \quad 2.4 \times 10^{-19} = 1.6 \times 10^{-19} E$$

$$\Rightarrow \quad E = 1.5 \text{ N/C}$$

Moreover, E = potential gradient

i.e. $$E = \frac{dV}{dl}$$

$$\Rightarrow \quad E \times l = V$$

$$\Rightarrow \quad V = 1.5 \times 6 = 9 \text{ V}$$

13 *(b)* Given, first balancing length, $l_1 = 30$ cm

Second balancing length, $l_2 = 40$ cm, $E_1 = 1.25$ V and E_2 = ?

So, according to the principle of potentiometer,

$$E_1 = kl_1 \quad \text{...(i)}$$

and $$E_2 = kl_2 \quad \text{...(ii)}$$

$$\because \quad \frac{E_1}{E_2} = \frac{kl_1}{kl_2} \Rightarrow \frac{1.25}{E_2} = \frac{30}{40}$$

$$\Rightarrow \quad E_2 = \frac{1.25 \times 40}{30}$$

$$\Rightarrow \quad E_2 = \frac{5}{3} = 1.666 \text{ V} \simeq 1.67 \text{ V}$$

14 *(a)* Potentiometer measures the potential difference more accurately than a voltmeter because while measuring emf (electromotive force), it does not draw any current from the source of known emf. Potentiometer has its own battery which maintains potential drop across the potentiometer wire.

Driving battery of potentiometer

Potentiometer wire

E r

15 *(d)* Initially, $kl_1 = E - ri = E - r(0) = E$

where, l_1 = balancing length of potentiometer wire = 240 cm.

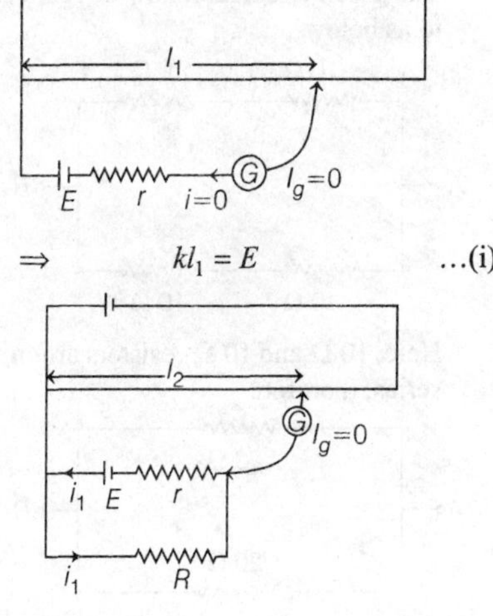

$$\Rightarrow \quad kl_1 = E \quad \text{...(i)}$$

and $kl_2 = E - ri_1 = Ri_1 \Rightarrow i_1 = \dfrac{E}{R + r}$

$$\Rightarrow \quad kl_2 = \frac{RE}{R + r} \quad \text{...(ii)}$$

where, l_2 = balancing length after shunting = 120 cm

and R = shunting resistance = 2 Ω.

Dividing Eq. (i) by Eq. (ii), we get

$$\frac{l_1}{l_2} = \frac{R + r}{R} = 1 + \frac{r}{R}$$

$$\Rightarrow \quad r = R\left(\frac{l_1}{l_2} - 1 \right) \quad \text{...(iii)}$$

Putting all values in Eq. (iii), we get

$$r = \left(\frac{240}{120} - 1\right) \times 2$$
$$= (2-1) \times 2 = 2\ \Omega$$

16 *(a)* Potential drop across 3 m long resistance wire is 6 V.

i.e. $E_1 = 6\text{V}$ and $l_1 = 3$ m,

Also, $l_2 = 50$ cm $= 0.5$ m

As we know that, $E \propto l$

$$\Rightarrow \frac{E_1}{E_2} = \frac{l_1}{l_2} \text{ or } E_2 = E_1 \times \frac{l_2}{l_1}$$

Substituting the given values, we get

$$E_2 = \frac{6 \times 0.5}{3} = 1\text{ V}$$

17 *(a)* The given circuit is in balanced Wheatstone bridge condition. In the given circuit, the ratio of resistances in the opposite arms is same. This implies the current through the middle arm is zero.

$$\therefore \frac{P}{Q} = \frac{10}{10} = \frac{1}{1} \text{ and } \frac{R}{S} = \frac{10}{10} = \frac{1}{1}$$

Hence, bridge is balanced.

The given circuit can now be reduced to as below

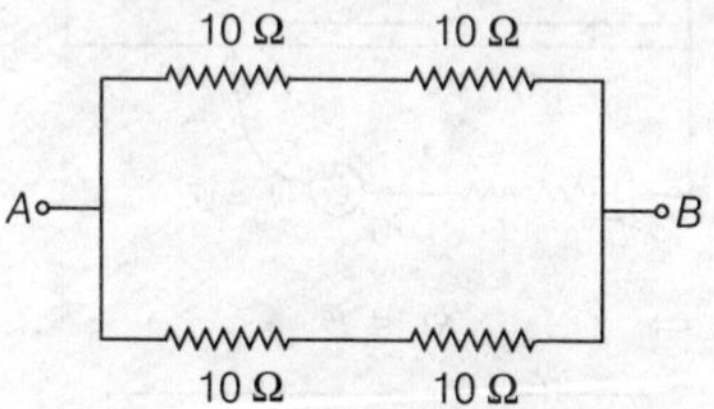

Here, 10 Ω and 10 Ω resistors are in series, therefore

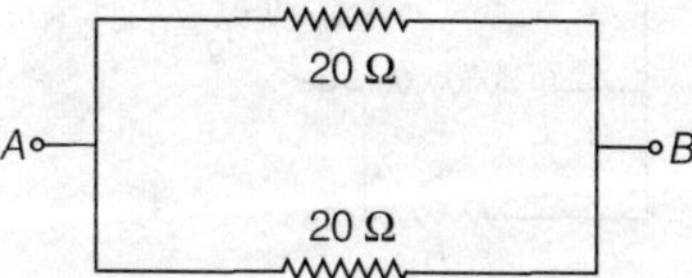

Now, the two 20 Ω resistors are connected in parallel, hence equivalent resistance is

$$\frac{1}{R} = \frac{1}{20} + \frac{1}{20} = \frac{40}{20 \times 20} = \frac{1}{10}$$
$$R = 10\ \Omega$$

18 *(b)* Given, $P = 10\ \Omega$, $Q = 30\ \Omega$, $R = 30\ \Omega$, $S = 90\ \Omega$, $E = 7$ V

$r = 5\ \Omega$, $R = 50\ \Omega$

Since, the given circuit is a balanced Wheatstone bridge.

The effective resistance,

$$R_{\text{eff}} = \frac{(P+Q) \times (R+S)}{(P+Q) + (R+S)}$$

$$R_{\text{eff}} = \frac{40 \times 120}{120 + 40} = \frac{4800}{160} = 30\ \Omega$$

$$\therefore \text{ Current, } I = \frac{7}{(30+5)} = \frac{7}{35} = 0.2\text{ A}$$

$$\left[\because I = \frac{E}{R+r}\right]$$

19 *(c)* The circuit is as shown figure

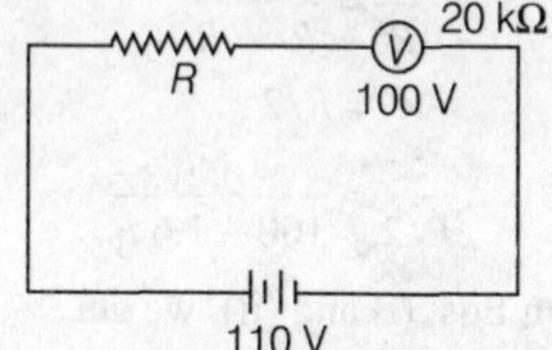

Potential difference across voltmeter $= 5$ V

$\therefore$ Current in the circuit,

$$i = \frac{5}{R_V} = \frac{5}{20 \times 10^3}$$
$$= 0.25 \times 10^{-3}\text{ A}$$

Voltage across R, $V_1 = 110 - 5 = 105$ V

$$\text{Hence, } R = \frac{V_1}{i} = \frac{105}{0.25 \times 10^{-3}}$$
$$= 420 \times 10^3 = 420\text{ k}\Omega$$

20 *(a)* From Ohm's law, current,

$$i = \frac{E}{R+r} = \frac{2}{998+2} = 2 \times 10^{-3}\text{ A}$$

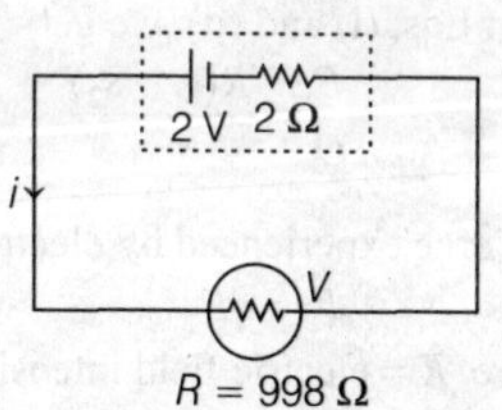

Potential difference across the voltmeter

$$V = iR = (2 \times 10^{-3}) \times 998 = 1.996\text{ V}$$

21 *(d)* The given circuit can be redrawn as

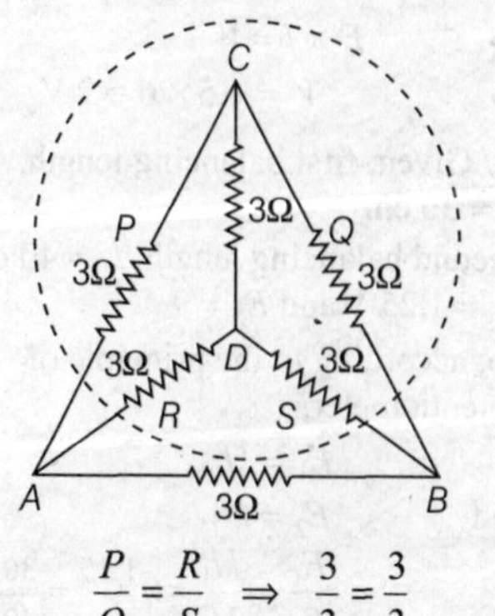

$$\frac{P}{Q} = \frac{R}{S} \Rightarrow \frac{3}{3} = \frac{3}{3}$$

The dotted region represents a balanced Wheatstone bridge. Thus, the current through the arm CD would be zero.

Thus, the resultant resistance of Wheatstone bridge would be

$$\frac{1}{R} = \frac{1}{(3+3)} + \frac{1}{(3+3)}$$

$$\Rightarrow R = \frac{(3+3) \times (3+3)}{(3+3) + (3+3)}$$
$$= \frac{6 \times 6}{6+6} = \frac{36}{12} = 3\ \Omega$$

This R would be parallel with the resistance of arm AB. Hence, the resultant resistance would be

$$R' = \frac{3 \times 3}{3+3} = \frac{9}{6} = 1.5\ \Omega$$

22 *(b)* There are two cases

***Case* I** When switches 1 and 2 are connected.

$$\therefore V_1 = k\,l_1$$
$$\Rightarrow IR = kl_1$$

where, $I = 1\text{A}$

$$\Rightarrow R = k\,l_1$$

***Case* II** When switches 1 and 3 are connected.

$$\therefore V_2 = kl_2$$
$$\Rightarrow I(R+X) = kl_2$$
$$\Rightarrow R + X = k\,l_2$$
$$\Rightarrow X = k(l_2 - l_1)$$

23 *(d)* When potentiometer is connected between A and B, then it measures only E_1 and when connected between A and C, then it measures $E_1 - E_2$.

$$\therefore \frac{E_1}{E_1 - E_2} = \frac{l_1}{l_2}$$
$$\Rightarrow \frac{E_1 - E_2}{E_1} = \frac{l_2}{l_1}$$
$$\Rightarrow 1 - \frac{E_2}{E_1} = \frac{100}{300}$$
$$\Rightarrow \frac{E_2}{E_1} = 1 - \frac{1}{3}$$
$$\Rightarrow \frac{E_2}{E_1} = \frac{2}{3}$$
$$\therefore \frac{E_1}{E_2} = \frac{3}{2}$$

24 *(d)* As in the given circuit, $\frac{R}{R} = \frac{2R}{2R}$

$$\Rightarrow 1 = 1$$

Hence, the circuit is as balanced Wheatstone bridge circuit. So, current through the arm G is zero and the arm G the circuit is assumed to be removed.

Thus, $R_{eff} = \dfrac{(P+Q)(R+S)}{(P+Q+R+S)}$

$\Rightarrow \quad R_{eff} = \dfrac{4}{3}R$

Thus, the equivalent resistance between A and B is independent of value of G.

25 *(b)* The given circuit can be redrawn as

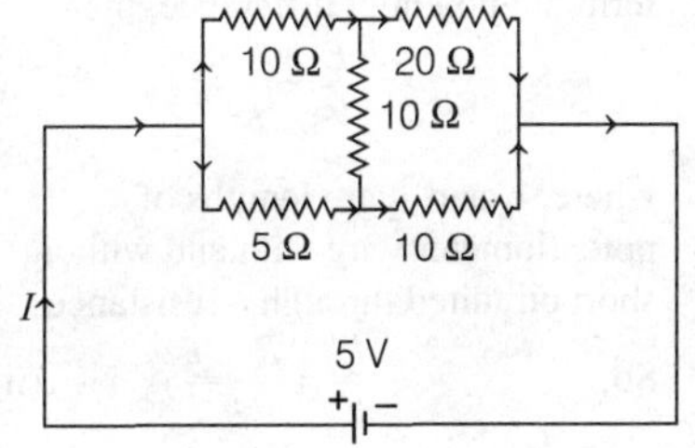

$$\frac{P}{Q} = \frac{R}{S}$$

$$\Rightarrow \quad \frac{10}{20} = \frac{5}{10} \Rightarrow \frac{1}{2} = \frac{1}{2}$$

The circuit shows the balanced condition of Wheatstone bridge and hence no current flows in the middle resistor. So, equivalent circuit would redrawn be as shown below

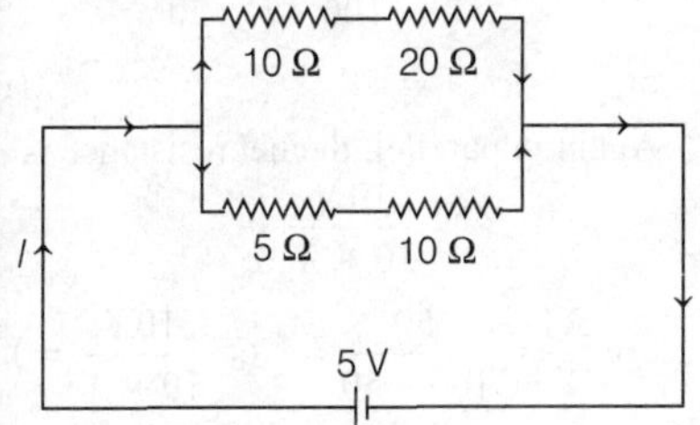

$10\,\Omega$ and $20\,\Omega$ resistances are in series, then $\quad R' = 10\,\Omega + 20\,\Omega = 30\,\Omega$

Similarly, $5\,\Omega$ and $10\,\Omega$ are in series, then $\quad R'' = 15\,\Omega$

Now, R' and R'' are in parallel, then

$$R = \frac{15 \times 30}{15 + 30} = 10\,\Omega$$

So, $\quad I = \dfrac{V}{R} = \dfrac{5}{10} = 0.5\text{ A}$

26 *(c)* The equivalent circuit can be redrawn as

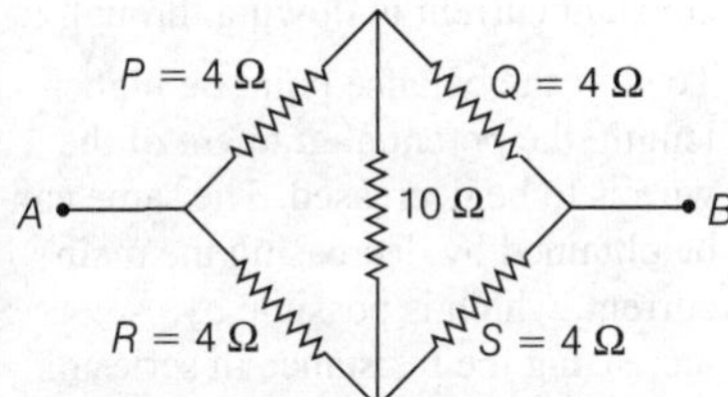

We have $\dfrac{P}{Q} = \dfrac{R}{S}$, i.e. $\dfrac{4}{4} = \dfrac{4}{4}$

So, the given circuit is a balanced Wheatstone bridge. Hence, the equivalent resistance

$$R_{AB} = \frac{(4+4)\times(4+4)}{(4+4)+(4+4)}$$

$$= \frac{8 \times 8}{8 + 8} = \frac{64}{16} = 4\,\Omega$$

27 *(a)* The given figure is in a balanced condition of Wheatstone bridge.

$$\frac{P}{Q} = \frac{R}{S}$$

$$\Rightarrow \quad \frac{r}{r} = \frac{r}{r}$$

Hence, the effective resistance,

$$r_{eq} = \frac{(2r)(2r)}{4r} = r$$

28 *(c)* Let P and Q be the two resistances connected in the two gaps of the metre bridge, such that

The two cases may be appeared

***Case* I** $\quad \dfrac{P}{Q} = \dfrac{20}{100-20} \Rightarrow \dfrac{P}{Q} = \dfrac{1}{4}$

$$\Rightarrow \quad P = \frac{1}{4}Q \quad \ldots\text{(i)}$$

***Case* II** $\quad \dfrac{P+15}{Q} = \dfrac{40}{60}$

$$\Rightarrow \quad P + 15 = \frac{2}{3}Q \quad \ldots\text{(ii)}$$

From Eqs. (i) and (ii), we get $Q = 36$ and the smaller resistance,

$$P = \frac{1}{4}Q = 9\,\Omega$$

29 *(d)* From the principle of potentiometer,

$$V \propto l \quad \text{or} \quad \frac{V}{E} = \frac{l}{L}$$

where, E = emf of cell, l = balance point (30 cm)

L = length of potentiometer wire (100 cm)

or $\quad V = \dfrac{l}{L}E = \dfrac{30 \times E}{100} = \dfrac{30E}{100}$

30 *(b)* Two resistors $400\,\Omega$ and $800\,\Omega$ are connected in series, then total resistance

$$R = 400 + 800 = 1200\,\Omega$$

The current through circuit without voltmeter,

$$I = \frac{V}{R} = \frac{6}{1200} = \frac{1}{200}$$

The current through voltmeter,

$$I_V = \frac{400}{10400}\left(\frac{1}{200}\right) = \frac{1}{5200}$$

Reading in voltmeter,

$$\therefore \quad V = I_V \cdot R_V = \frac{1}{5200} \times 10 \times 1000$$

$$= \frac{100}{52} = 1.95\text{ V}$$

31 *(c)* As, $V = IR \Rightarrow I = \dfrac{V}{R}$

Here, $V = 3$ V,

$$R = (20 + 10)\,\Omega$$

$$\Rightarrow \quad I = \frac{3}{(20+10)} = \frac{3}{30} = \frac{1}{10}\text{ A}$$

Potential gradient $= \left(\dfrac{\Delta V}{\Delta l}\right)$

Potential across $20\,\Omega$ resistance,

$$V' = IR = \frac{1}{10} \times 20 = 2\text{V}$$

$$\therefore \quad \frac{\Delta V}{\Delta l} = \frac{2}{10} = 0.2\text{ V/m}$$

32 *(b)* The given circuit can be redrawn as

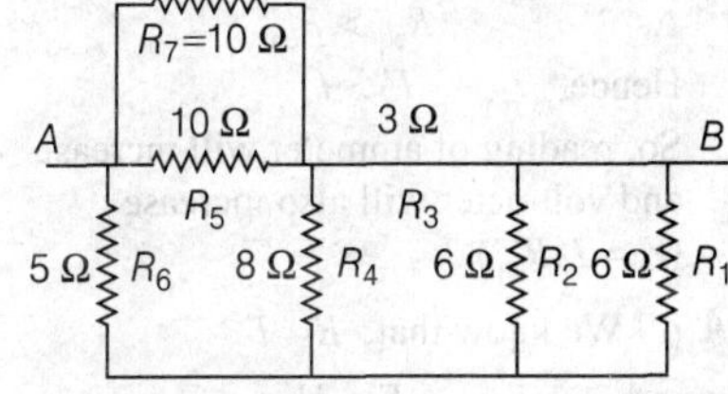

Equivalent resistance of R_1 and R_2 (in parallel) is given by

$$R' = \frac{6 \times 6}{6 + 6} = 3\,\Omega$$

Equivalent resistance of R_5 and R_7 (in parallel) is given by

$$R'' = \frac{10 \times 10}{10 + 10} = 5\,\Omega$$

Now, the circuit is reduced to

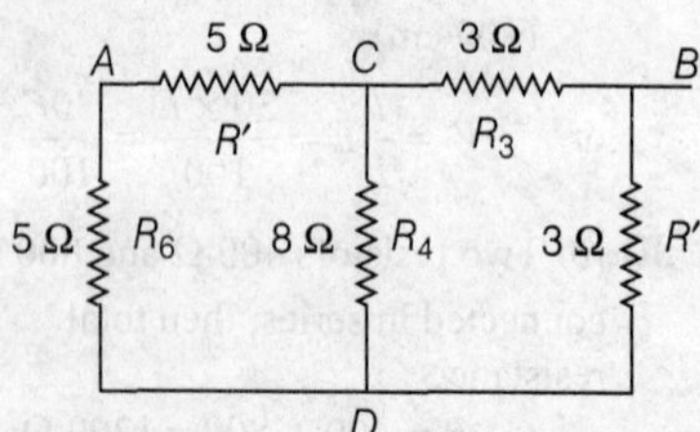

Now, this circuit can be shown as it is balanced Whetstone bridge because the series arm resistance are same. So, it means $\frac{P}{Q} = \frac{R}{S} \Rightarrow \frac{5}{3} = \frac{5}{3} \Rightarrow 1 = 1$

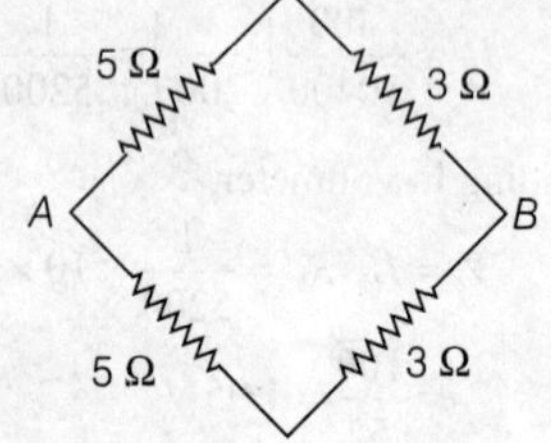

Now, total resistance between AB,

$$R_{AB} = \frac{(5+3)(5+3)}{(5+3)+(5+3)} = \frac{8 \times 8}{8+8} = 4\ \Omega$$

33 *(a)* ***Case* I** $R_{eq} = 2R$

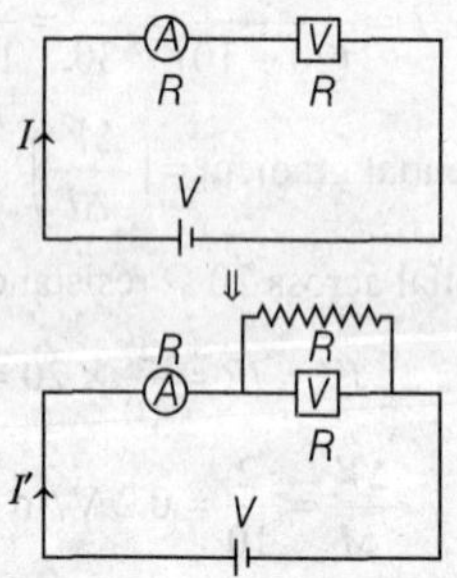

***Case* II** $R'_{eq} = R + R/2 \Rightarrow R'_{eq} = 3R/2$

As $\quad R_{eq} > R'_{eq}$

Hence, $\quad I' > I$

So, reading of ammeter will increase and voltmeter will also increase ($V = I'R'_{eq}$).

34 *(c)* We know that, $E \propto l$

$$E = kl$$

For $l = 60$ cm, $E = k \times 60$ ...(i)

For known emf, i.e. $E = 3$ V

For $l = 45$ cm, $E = k\,45 \Rightarrow 3 = k\,(45)$

$\therefore \quad k = \frac{3}{45}$

From Eq.(i), we get

$$E = \frac{3}{45} \times 60 = 4\ \text{V}$$

35 *(c)* As the current,

$$I = \frac{V}{R} = \frac{2}{990 + 10} = \frac{2}{1000}$$

Now, ΔV = Potential drop across potentiometer $= \frac{2}{1000} \times 10 = \frac{2}{100}$

Also, potential gradient

$$= \frac{\Delta V}{l} = \frac{2}{100 \times 2} = \frac{1}{100} = 0.01\ \text{V/m}$$

36 *(c)* For the balance point of meter bridge

***Case* I** When balancing length is 55 cm

$$\frac{P}{Q} = \frac{l_1}{100 - l_1} \Rightarrow \frac{3}{Q} = \frac{55}{45}$$

$$\Rightarrow \quad Q = \frac{45}{55} \times 3\ \Omega$$

***Case* II** When an unknown resistance x is involved

$$\frac{P + x}{Q} = \frac{l'_1}{100 - l'_1} \Rightarrow \frac{3 + x}{Q} = \frac{75}{25}$$

$$\Rightarrow \quad 3 + x = 3\left(\frac{45}{55}\right) \times 3$$

$$\Rightarrow \quad x = \frac{81}{11} - 3 = \frac{48}{11}\ \Omega$$

37 *(a)* As, galvanometer shows zero deflection. (i.e. balanced condition)

Therefore, $\frac{P}{Q} = \frac{l_1}{l_2}$

$$\Rightarrow \frac{60}{15} = \frac{AC}{CB} \Rightarrow AC : CB = 4 : 1$$

38 *(c)* As, $E \propto l \Rightarrow E = kl$

There are two cases

***Case* I** When $E_1 = kl_1 = k(6)$ ...(i)

***Case* II** When $E_2 = kl_2 = k(2)$ ...(ii)

Dividing Eq. (i) by Eq. (ii), we get

$$\frac{E_1}{E_2} = \frac{6}{2} = 3 : 1$$

39 *(d)* As, k = potential gradient.

Given, $k = 2$ V/cm, $R = 10\ \Omega$ and $l = 50 \times 10^{-2}$ m

As we know that, $E = RI = kl$

$\Rightarrow \quad I = 10$ A

40 *(b)* For balanced condition of Wheatstone bridge circuit,

$$\frac{P}{Q} = \frac{R}{S} \Rightarrow \frac{2}{2} = \frac{2}{\left(\frac{6S}{S+6}\right)} \Rightarrow S = 3\ \Omega$$

41 *(a)* In potentiometer experiment, to find internal resistance of a cell, let E be the emf of the cell and V be the terminal potential difference, then

$$\frac{E}{V} = \frac{l_1}{l_2} \quad \text{...(i)}$$

where, l_1 and l_2 are lengths of potentiometer wire with and without short circuited through a resistance.

So, $$\frac{E}{V} = \frac{R + r}{R} \quad \text{...(ii)}$$

$[\because E = I(R + r)$ and $V = IR]$

From Eqs. (i) and (ii), we get

$$\frac{R + r}{R} = \frac{l_1}{l_2} \text{ or } 1 + \frac{r}{R} = \frac{110}{100}$$

or $\frac{r}{R} = \frac{10}{100}$ or $r = \frac{1}{10} \times 10 = 1\ \Omega$

42 *(b)* Let l be the distance of balancing point from left gap, then

$$\frac{X}{Y} = \frac{l}{100 - l} = \frac{80}{20} = 4$$

or $\quad X = 4Y$ ...(i)

Again in parallel, the net resistance is

$$X' = \frac{10X}{10 + X}$$

So, $\frac{X'}{Y} = \frac{50}{100 - 50} = 1$ or $\frac{10X}{10 + X} = Y$

or $\quad 10X = 10Y + XY$

or $\quad 40Y = 10Y + 4Y^2$ [from Eq. (i)]

This is a quadratic in term of Y, on solving which gives $Y = 7.5\ \Omega$

Putting $Y = 7.5\ \Omega$ in Eq. (i), we get $X = 30\ \Omega$.

43 *(b)* The working of potentiometer is based on the fact that the fall of potential across any portion of the wire is directly proportional to the length of that portion provided the wire is of uniform area of cross-section and a constant current is flowing through it.

To shift the balance point on higher length, the potential gradient of the wire is to be decreased. The same can be obtained by decreasing the main current, which is possible by increasing the resistance in series of potentiometer wire.

44 (c) The given circuit can be redrawn as shown

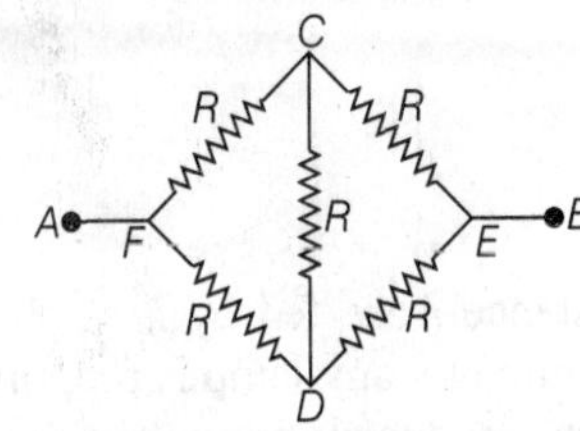

Thus, it is balanced Wheatstone bridge, so resistance in arm CD is ineffective and so current does not flow in this arm.

Net resistance of the circuit is given by

$$\frac{1}{R'} = \frac{1}{(R+R)} + \frac{1}{(R+R)}$$

$$= \frac{1}{2R} + \frac{1}{2R} = \frac{2}{2R} = \frac{1}{R}$$

$$\Rightarrow \quad R' = R$$

So, net current drawn from the battery,

$$i' = \frac{V}{R'} = \frac{V}{R}$$

As from symmetry, upper circuit $AFCEB$ is half of the whole circuit and is equal to $AFDEB$.

So, in both the halves, half of the total current will flow.

Hence, in $AFCEB$, the current flowing is $i = \frac{i'}{2} = \frac{V}{2R}$

45 (c) After adjoining two conductors, the circuit will acquire the form shown in the following figure. From symmetry considerations, we conclude that the central conductor will not be effective in electric charge transfer.

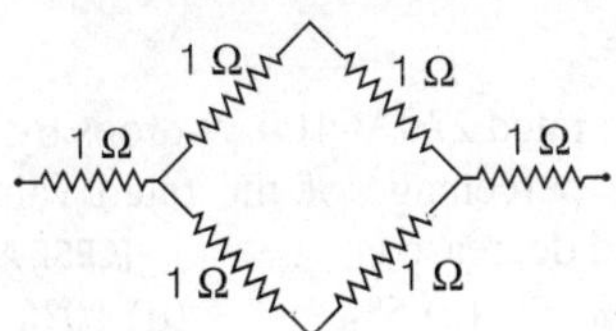

Therefore, if the initial resistance R_1 of circuit was 5 Ω, where resistance of each conductor is 1 Ω, the new resistance of the circuit will become

$$R_2 = 2 + \frac{2}{2} = 3\ \Omega$$

∴ The required ratio of resistance $= \frac{5}{3}$

46 (b) As galvanometer deflection remains unaffected with switch S open or closed, hence the bridge circuit is balanced.

Hence, $\quad I_P = I_Q$ and $I_R = I_G$

However, as $\quad P \neq R$

Hence, $\quad I_P \neq I_R$

47 (c) Total current drawn from the battery $i = \frac{E}{R+r} = \frac{6}{100+0} = 0.06$ A

Resistance of 50 cm wire is

$$R' = \frac{\rho l'}{A} = \left(\frac{\rho}{A}\right) l' = \left(\frac{R}{l}\right) l'$$

$$= \frac{100}{300} \times 50 = \frac{50}{3}\ \Omega$$

Hence, the potential difference between two points on the wires separated by a distance 50 cm is

$$V = iR' = 0.06 \times \frac{50}{3} = 1\ \text{V}$$

48 (d) Given, $I = 0.2$ A, specific resistance, $\rho = 4 \times 10^{-7}$ Ω-m and cross-section area, $A = 8 \times 10^{-7}\ \text{m}^2$.

Potential gradient of a potentiometer,

$$K = \frac{I\rho}{A} = \frac{0.2 \times 4 \times 10^{-7}}{8 \times 10^{-7}}$$

$$= 0.1\ \text{V/m}$$

49 (b) We can show the network as below

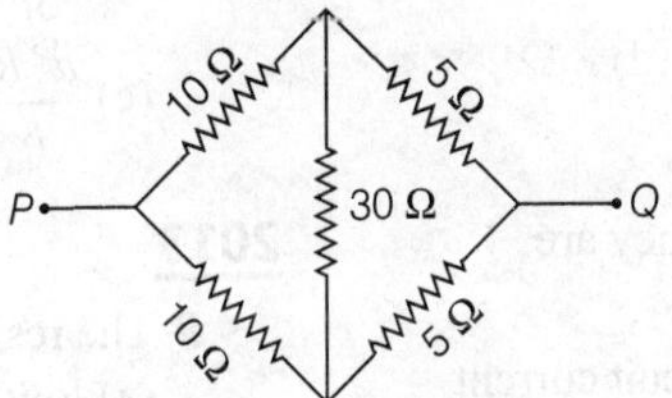

From the circuit diagram, we calculate that, $\frac{10}{5} = \frac{10}{5}$, i.e. $2 = 2$

So, the circuit represents a balanced condition of Wheatstone bridge.

Therefore, no current flows through 30 Ω resistor. Thus, the net resistance in upper arms,

$$R_U = 10 + 5 = 15\ \Omega \quad \text{(series)}$$

The net resistance in lower arms,

$$R_L = 10 + 5 = 15\ \Omega \quad \text{(series)}$$

Hence, equivalent resistance of the network,

$$R = \frac{R_U \times R_L}{R_U + R_L} = \frac{15 \times 15}{15 + 15} = 7.5\ \Omega$$

50 (b) The given circuit resembles to balanced Wheatstone bridge as $\frac{4}{2} = \frac{6}{3}$

Thus, middle arm containing 4 Ω resistance will be ineffective, i.e. no current flow through it.

The equivalent circuit is shown as below

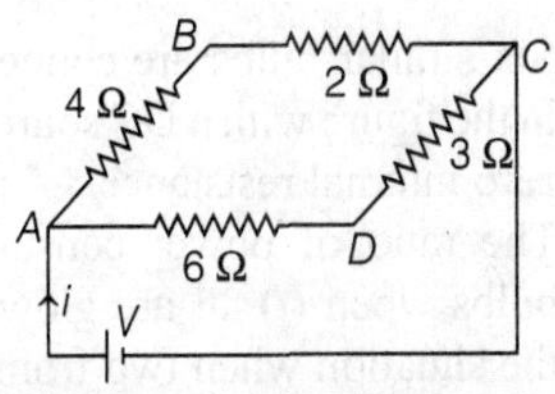

Net resistance between A and C through B, $R' = 4 + 2 = 6\ \Omega$

Net resistance between A and C through D, $R'' = 6 + 3 = 9\ \Omega$

Thus, parallel combination of R' and R'' gives

$$R = \frac{R' \times R''}{R' + R''} = \frac{6 \times 9}{6 + 9}$$

$$= \frac{54}{15} = \frac{18}{5}\ \Omega$$

Hence, current, $i = \frac{V}{R} = \frac{V}{18/5} = \frac{5V}{18}$

51 (d) Since, for balanced condition, $\frac{2}{4} = \frac{4}{8}$, so 5 Ω resistance can be neglected. Therefore, effective resistance,

$$R = \frac{(2+4) \times (4+8)}{(2+4) + (4+8)}$$

$$= \frac{6 \times 12}{6 + 12}$$

$$= \frac{72}{18} = 4\ \Omega$$

So, the current in the circuit,

$$I = \frac{V}{R} = \frac{2}{4} = 0.5\ \text{A}$$

52 (c) For a potentiometer, the internal resistance (r) is given by

$$r = R\left(\frac{l_1}{l_2} - 1\right)$$

Given, $\quad R = 10\ \Omega$, $l_1 = 75$ cm

and $\quad l_2 = 65$ cm

$$\therefore \quad r = 10\left(\frac{75}{65} - 1\right)$$

$$= 10 \times 0.154 = 1.54\ \Omega$$

Topic 5
Heating Effect of Current

2019

1 Six similar bulbs are connected as shown in the figure with a DC source of emf E and zero internal resistance.

The ratio of power consumption by the bulbs when (*i*) all are glowing and (*ii*) in the situation when two from section A and one from section B are glowing, will be **[NEET]**

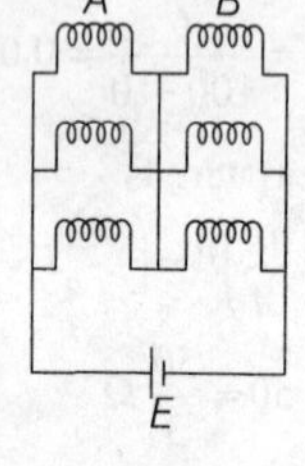

(a) 9 : 4 (b) 1 : 2 (c) 2 : 1 (d) 4 : 9

2 Which of the following acts as a circuit protection device? **[NEET]**

(a) Inductor (b) Switch (c) Fuse (d) Conductor

3 In the given circuit, if power rating of heater is 1000 W at 100 V, find the resistance R in figure so that heater produces power of 62.5 W. **[JIPMER]**

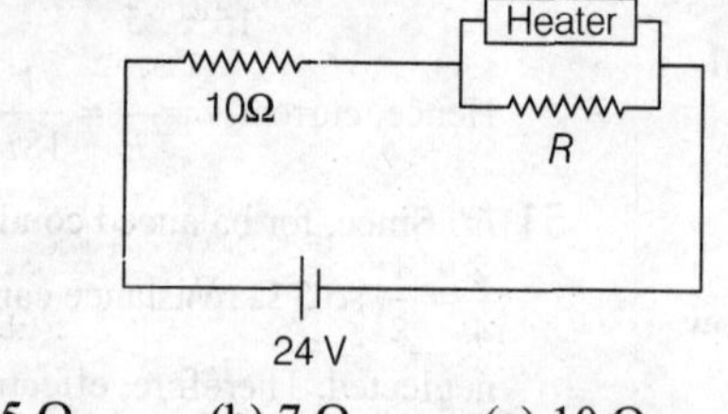

(a) 5 Ω (b) 7 Ω (c) 10 Ω (d) 8 Ω

2018

4 Assertion Bulb generally get fused when they are switched ON or OFF.

Reason When we switch ON or OFF, a circuit current changes in it rapidly. **[AIIMS]**

(a) Both Assertion and Reason are correct and Reason is the correct explanation of Assertion
(b) Both Assertion and Reason are correct but Reason is not the correct explanation of Assertion
(c) Assertion is correct and Reason is incorrect
(d) Assertion is incorrect and Reason is correct

2017

5 You are given resistance wire of length 50 cm and a battery of negligible resistance. In which of the following cases is largest amount of heat generated? **[JIPMER]**

(a) When the wire is connected to the battery directly.
(b) When the wire is divided into two parts and both the parts are connected to the battery in parallel.
(c) When the wire is divided into four parts and all the four parts are connected to the battery in parallel.
(d) When only half of the wire is connected to the battery.

6 N lamps each of resistance r are fed by a machine of resistance R. If light emitted by any lamp is proportional to the square of the heat produced, prove that the most efficient way of arranging them is to place them in parallel arcs, each containing n lamps, where n is the integer nearest to **[NEET]**

(a) $\left(\frac{r}{NR}\right)^{3/2}$ (b) $\left(\frac{NR}{r}\right)^{1/2}$
(c) $(NRr)^{3/2}$ (d) $(NRr)^{1/2}$

2016

7 A filament bulb (500 W, 100 V) is to be used in a 230 V main supply. When a resistance R is connected in series, it works perfectly and the bulb consumes 500 W. The value of R is **[NEET]**

(a) 230 Ω (b) 46 Ω
(c) 26 Ω (d) 13 Ω

8 The charge following through a resistance R varies with time t as $Q = at - bt^2$, where a and b are positive constants. The total heat produced in R is **[NEET]**

(a) $\frac{a^3R}{3b}$ (b) $\frac{a^3R}{2b}$
(c) $\frac{a^3R}{b}$ (d) $\frac{a^3R}{6b}$

2013

9 The resistance of the fuse wire is **[WB JEE]**

(a) low (b) moderate (c) zero (d) very high

2012

10 If voltage across a bulb rated 220 V-100 W drops by 2.5% of its rated value, the percentage of the rated value by which the power would decrease is **[CBSE AIPMT]**

(a) 20% (b) 2.5% (c) 5% (d) 10%

11 The power dissipated in the circuit shown in the figure is 30 W. The value of R is **[CBSE AIPMT]**

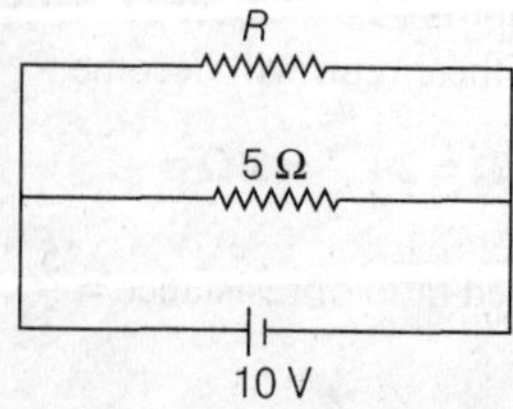

(a) 20 Ω (b) 15 Ω (c) 10 Ω (d) 30 Ω

2011

12 If the power dissipated in the 9 Ω resistor in the circuit shown is 36 W, then the potential difference across the 2 Ω resistor is **[CBSE AIPMT]**

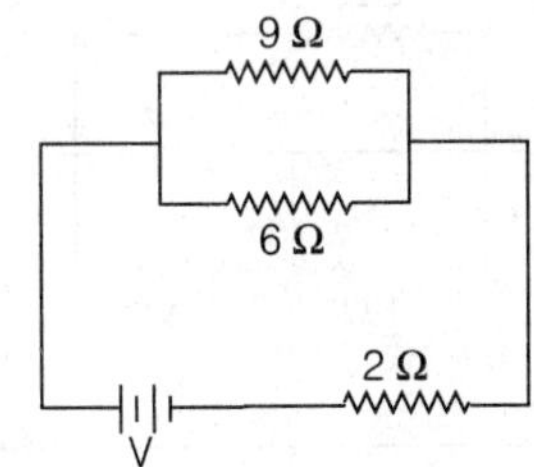

(a) 8 V (b) 10 V
(c) 2 V (d) 4 V

13 The maximum power dissipated in an external resistance R, when connected to a cell of emf E and internal resistance r, will be **[J&K CET]**

(a) $\frac{E^2}{r}$ (b) $\frac{E^2}{2r}$
(c) $\frac{E^2}{3r}$ (d) $\frac{E^2}{4r}$

14 If two bulbs of wattages 25 and 100 W respectively, each rated by 220 V are connected in series with the supply of 440 V, then which bulb will fuse? **[AIIMS]**

(a) 100 W bulb (b) 25 W bulb
(c) Both (a) and (b) (d) None of these

2010

15 There are two electric bulbs of 40 W and 100 W. Which one will be brighter when first connected in series and then in parallel? **[AFMC]**

(a) 40 W in series and 100 W in parallel
(b) 100 W in series and 40 W in parallel
(c) 40 W both in series and parallel will be uniform
(d) 100 W both in series and parallel will be uniform

16 An electric immersion heater of 1.08 kW is immersed in water. After the water has reached a temperature of 100°C, how much time will be required to produce 100 g of steam? **[BHU]**

(a) 50 s (b) 420 s
(c) 105 s (d) 210 s

17 The resistance of the filament of a lamp increases with the increase in temperature. A lamp rated 100 W and 200 V is connected across 220 V power supply. If the voltage drops by 10%, then the power of the lamp will be **[BHU]**

(a) 90 W
(b) more than 81 W
(c) between 90 and 100 W
(d) between 81 and 90 W

18 A factory is served by a 220 V supply line. In a circuit protected by a fuse marked 10 A, the maximum number of 100 W lamps in parallel that can be turned on, is **[Manipal]**

(a) 11 (b) 22
(c) 33 (d) 66

19 Two bulbs consume same power when operated at 200 V and 300 V, respectively. When these bulbs are connected in series across a DC source of 500 V, then **[Haryana PMT]**

(a) ratio of potential differences across them is 3/2
(b) ratio of potential differences across them is 9/4
(c) ratio of powers consumed across them is 4/9
(d) ratio of powers consumed across them is 2/3

20 Consider the diagram in which B_1, B_2 and B_3 are the three identical bulbs connected to a battery of steady emf with key K closed. What happens to the brightness of the bulbs B_1 and B_2 when the key is opened? **[KCET]**

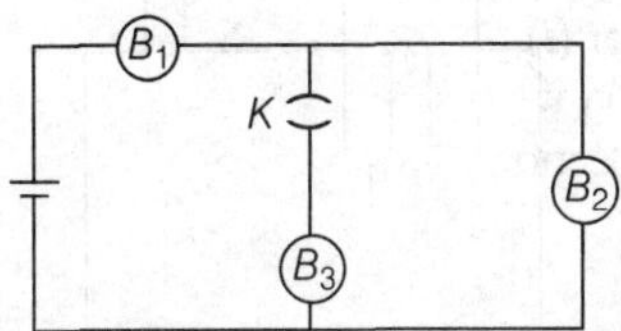

(a) Brightness of the bulb B_1 increases and that of B_2 decreases
(b) Brightness of the bulbs B_1 and B_2 increases
(c) Brightness of the bulb B_1 decreases and B_2 increases
(d) Brightness of the bulbs B_1 and B_2 decreases

21 Two bulbs marked 60 W, 220 V and 100 W, 220 V are connected in series and the series combination is now connected across a 220 V main supply. The power dissipated in the circuit is **[AMU]**

(a) 37.5 W (b) 75 W
(c) 80 W (d) 40 W

22 Two bulbs 40 W and 60 W of rated voltage 240 V are connected in series across a potential difference of 420 V. Which bulb will work at above its rated voltage? **[VMMC]**

(a) 40 W bulb (b) 60 W bulb
(c) Both bulbs will work (d) 20 W bulb

2009

23 Two electric bulbs rated 50 W and 100 V are glowing at full power, when used in parallel with a battery of emf 120 V and internal resistance 10 Ω. The maximum number of bulbs that can be connected in the circuit when glowing at full power, is **[AIIMS]**

(a) 6 (b) 4
(c) 2 (d) 8

24 Two similar heater coils separately take 10 min to boil a certain amount of water. If both coils are connected in series, then time taken to boil the same amount of water will be **[AFMC]**

(a) 15 min (b) 20 min
(c) 7.5 min (d) 25 min

25 A 30 V, 90 W lamp is to be operated on a 120 V DC line. For proper glow, a resistor of ... Ω should be connected in series with the lamp. **[BHU]**

(a) 40 (b) 10
(c) 20 (d) 30

26 Two identical cells each of emf E and internal resistance r are connected in parallel with an external resistance R. To get maximum power developed across R, the value of R is **[OJEE]**

(a) $R = \frac{r}{2}$ (b) $R = r$ (c) $R = \frac{r}{3}$ (d) $R = 2r$

27 Three electric bulbs of 200 W, 200 W and 400 W are shown in figure. The resultant power of the combination is **[OJEE]**

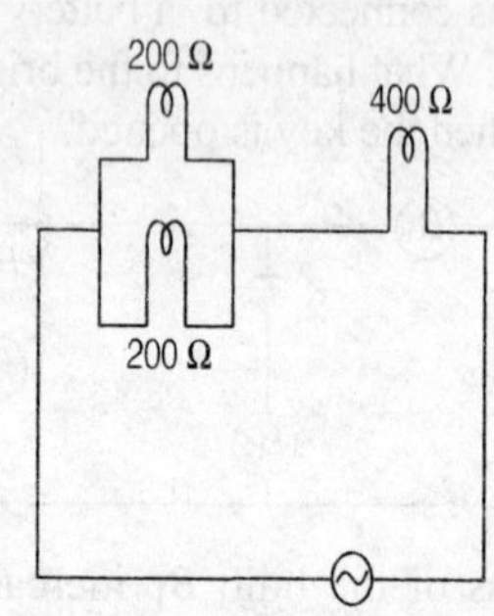

(a) 800 W (b) 400 W
(c) 200 W (d) 600 W

28 An electric bulb rated 220 V, 100 W is connected in series with another bulb rated 220 V, 60 W. If the voltage across the combination is 220 V, the power consumed by the 100 W bulb will be about **[Kerala CEE]**

(a) 25 W (b) 14 W
(c) 60 W (d) 100 W
(e) 80 W

29 160 W, 60 V lamp is connected at 60 V DC supply. The number of electrons passing through the lamp in 1 min is (charge of electron, $e = 1.6 \times 10^{-19}$ C) **[Haryana PMT, CG PMT]**

(a) 10^{19} (b) 10^{21}
(c) 1.6×10^{19} (d) 1.4×10^{20}

30 The tungsten filaments of two electric bulbs are of the same length. If one of them gives 25 W power and the other 60 W power, then **[J&K CET]**

(a) both the filaments are of same thickness
(b) 25 W bulb has thicker filament
(c) 60 W bulb has thicker filament
(d) both the filaments have same cross-section area

31 **Assertion** The power delivered to a light bulb is more just after it is switched ON and the glow of the filament is increasing as compared to when the bulb is glowing steadily, i.e. after sometime of switching ON.
Reason As temperature decreases, resistance of conductor increases. **[AIIMS]**

(a) Both Assertion and Reason are correct and Reason is the correct explanation of Assertion.
(b) Both Assertion and Reason are correct but Reason is not the correct explanation of Assertion.
(c) Assertion is correct but Reason is incorrect.
(d) Both Assertion and Reason are incorrect.

2008

32 A current of 3 A flows through the 2 Ω resistor shown in the circuit. The power dissipated in the 5 Ω resistor is **[CBSE AIPMT]**

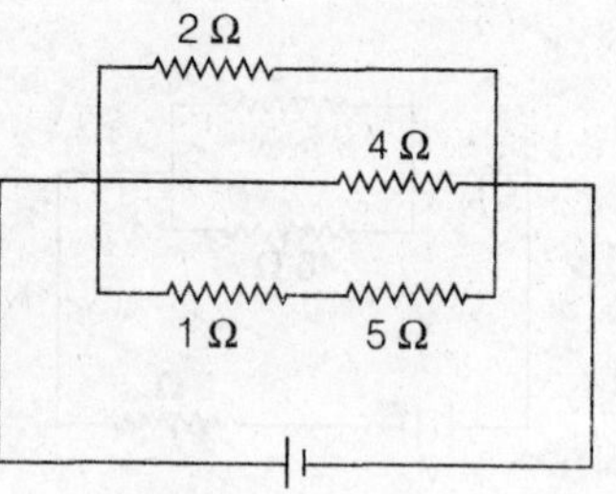

(a) 4 W (b) 2 W (c) 1 W (d) 5 W

33 **Assertion** An electric bulb becomes dim, when an electric heater in parallel circuit is switched ON.
Reason Dimness decreases after sometime. **[AIIMS]**

(a) Both Assertion and Reason are correct and Reason is the correct explanation of Assertion.
(b) Both Assertion and Reason are correct but Reason is not the correct explanation of Assertion.
(c) Assertion is correct but Reason is incorrect
(d) Both Assertion and Reason are incorrect

34 The maximum current that flows in the fuse wire, before it blows out, varies with the radius r as **[BHU]**

(a) $r^{3/2}$ (b) r (c) $r^{2/3}$ (d) $r^{1/2}$

35 The ratio of cross-sectional areas of two conducting wires made up of same material and having same length is 1 : 2. What will be the ratio of heat produced per second in the wires, when same current is flowing in them? **[Guj CET]**

(a) 1 : 4 (b) 2 : 1 (c) $1 : \sqrt{2}$ (d) 1 : 1

36 Two electric bulbs are connected one by one across potential difference V. At that time, power consumed in them are P_1 and P_2 respectively. Now, if potential difference V is applied across series combination of these bulbs, what will be total power consumed? **[Guj CET]**

(a) $\frac{P_1 P_2}{P_1 + P_2}$ (b) $P_1 P_2$ (c) $P_1 + P_2$ (d) $\sqrt{P_1 P_2}$

37 A heater coil working on mains produces 100 cal of heat in a certain time. Now, the heater coil is cut into three equal parts and one part is only used for heating. The quantity of heat produced (in calories) in the same time is **[EAMCET]**

(a) 300 (b) 200 (c) 100/3 (d) 200/3

2007

38 The total power dissipated (in watts) in the circuit shown here is **[CBSE PMT]**

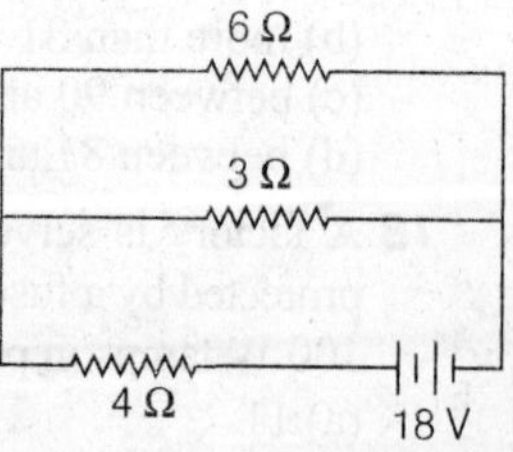

(a) 16
(b) 40
(c) 54
(d) 4

39 The power dissipated across resistance R which is connected across a battery of potential V is P. If the resistance is doubled, then the power decreases by a factor **[UP CPMT]**
(a) $\frac{1}{2}$ (b) 2 (c) $\frac{1}{4}$ (d) 4

40 A battery is charged at a potential of 15 V for 8 H when the current flowing is 10 A. The battery on discharge supplies a current of 5 A for 15 H. The mean terminal voltage during discharge is 14 V. The 'watt-hour' efficiency of the battery is **[Manipal]**
(a) 82.5% (b) 80%
(c) 90% (d) 87.5%

41 When three identical bulbs of 60 W, 200 V rating are connected in series to a 200 V supply, the power drawn by them will be **[Manipal]**
(a) 60 W (b) 180 W
(c) 10 W (d) 20 W

42 A 5 A fuse wire can withstand a maximum power of 1 W in circuit. The resistance of the fuse wire is **[MP PMT]**
(a) 0.2 Ω (b) 5 Ω
(c) 0.4 Ω (d) 0.04 Ω

43 Two bulbs 100 W, 250 V and 200 W, 250 V are connected in parallel across a 500 V line. Then, **[AMU]**
(a) 100 W bulb will be fused
(b) 200 W bulb will be fused
(c) both bulbs will be fused
(d) no bulb will be fused

44 A 2 kW boiler used for 1 h/day consumes the following electrical energy in thirty days **[AMU]**
(a) 60 units (b) 120 units
(c) 15 units (d) 6×10^4 units

2006

45 One filament takes 10 min to heat a kettle and another takes 15 min. If connected in parallel, they combinedly take … min to heat the same kettle. **[RPMT]**
(a) 6 (b) 12.5
(c) 25 (d) 7.5

46 If the electric current in a lamp decreases by 5%, then the power output decreases by **[Guj CET]**
(a) 2.5% (b) 10% (c) 5% (d) 20%

47 If two identical heaters each rated as 1000 W, 220 V are connected in parallel to 220 V, then the total power consumed is **[AMU]**
(a) 200 W (b) 2500 W (c) 250 W (d) 2000 W

2005

48 For ensuring dissipation of same energy in all three resistors (R_1, R_2, R_3) connected as shown in figure, their values must be related as **[AIIMS]**

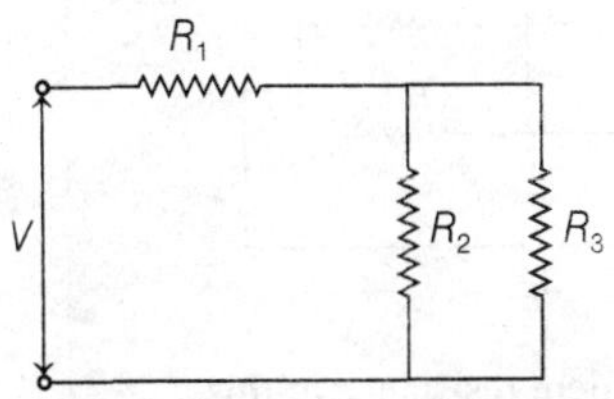

(a) $R_1 = R_2 = R_3$ (b) $R_2 = R_3$ and $R_1 = 4R_2$
(c) $R_2 = R_3$ and $R_1 = \frac{R_2}{4}$ (d) $R_1 = R_2 + R_3$

49 A hot electric iron has a resistance of 80 Ω and is used on a 200 V source. The electrical energy spent, if it is used for 2 h will be **[RPMT]**
(a) 8000 W-h (b) 2000 W-h
(c) 1000 W-h (d) 800 W-h

50 A resistor R has power dissipation P with cell voltage E. The resistor is cut in n equal parts and all parts are connected in parallel with same cell. The new power dissipation is **[Haryana PMT]**
(a) nP (b) nP^2 (c) n^2P (d) n/P

51 Two wires have resistances R and $2R$. When both are joining in series and in parallel, then ratio of heats generated in these situations on applying the same voltage is **[Punjab PMET]**
(a) 2 : 1 (b) 1 : 2 (c) 2 : 9 (d) 9 : 2

52 If percentage change in current through a resistor is 1%, then the change in power through it would be **[DUMET]**
(a) 1% (b) 2% (c) 1.7% (d) 0.5%

53 Three identical bulbs are connected in series and these together dissipate a power P. If the bulbs are connected in parallel, then the power dissipated will be **[DUMET]**
(a) $P/3$ (b) $3P$ (c) $9P$ (d) $P/9$

Answers

1 (a)	2 (c)	3 (a)	4 (a)	5 (c)	6 (b)	7 (c)	8 (d)	9 (d)	10 (c)
11 (c)	12 (b)	13 (d)	14 (b)	15 (a)	16 (d)	17 (d)	18 (b)	19 (c)	20 (c)
21 (a)	22 (a)	23 (c)	24 (b)	25 (d)	26 (a)	27 (c)	28 (b)	29 (b)	30 (c)
31 (c)	32 (d)	33 (b)	34 (a)	35 (b)	36 (a)	37 (a)	38 (c)	39 (a)	40 (d)
41 (d)	42 (d)	43 (c)	44 (a)	45 (a)	46 (b)	47 (d)	48 (c)	49 (c)	50 (c)
51 (c)	52 (b)	53 (c)							

Explanations

1 (a) *Case* **I** When all bulbs are glowing, then the circuit can be realised as shown in the figure below.

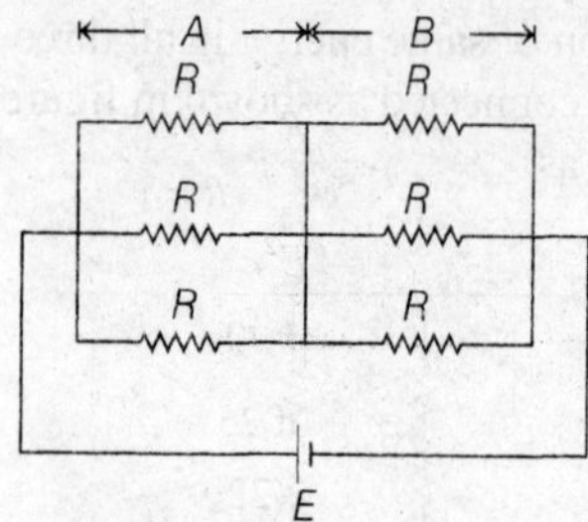

$\therefore$ The equivalent resistance of this circuit is

$$R_{eq} = R_A + R_B$$

As, section A has three parallel resistance, so equivalent resistance,

$$R_A = \frac{R}{3}$$

Similarly, for section B, equivalent resistance, $R_B = \frac{R}{3}$

$$\therefore \quad R_{eq} = \frac{R}{3} + \frac{R}{3} = \frac{2R}{3} \quad \ldots \text{(i)}$$

Thus, power consumed in this circuit,

$$P_1 = \frac{V^2}{R} = \frac{E^2}{R_{eq}} = \frac{3E^2}{2R}$$

[using Eq. (i)] ...(ii)

Case **II** When two from section A and one from section B glow, the circuit can be realised as shown in the figure below.

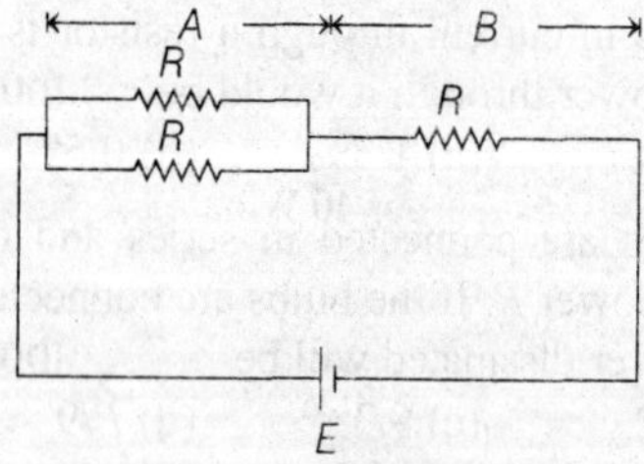

$\therefore$ Equivalent resistance of section A,

$$R_A = \frac{R}{2}$$

and of section B,

$$R_B = R$$

Thus, equivalent resistance of the entire circuit becomes

$$R_{eq} = R_A + R_B = \frac{R}{2} + R = \frac{3R}{2} \quad \ldots \text{(iii)}$$

$\therefore$ Power consumed by this circuit,

$$P_2 = \frac{V^2}{R} = \frac{E^2}{R_{eq}} = \frac{2E^2}{3R}$$

[using Eq. (iii)]... (iv)

So, ratio of power of two cases is obtained from Eqs. (ii) and (iv), we get

$$\frac{P_1}{P_2} = \frac{3E^2}{2R} \times \frac{3R}{2E^2} = \frac{9}{4} \text{ or } 9:4$$

2 (c) Among given devices fuse is used in electric circuit as a protective device.

It helps in preventing excessive amount of current to flow in the circuit or from short circuiting.

It has low melting point and low resistivity, so when excess amount of current flows in the circuit, it melts and break the circuit.

3 (a) Power rating of heater, $P = 1000$ W

Voltage rating of heater, $V = 100$ V

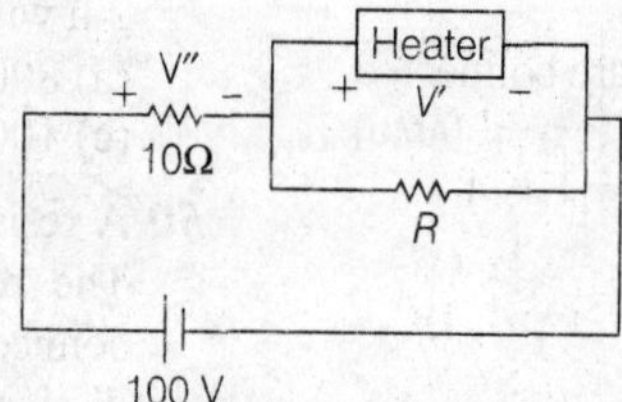

$\therefore$ Resistance of heater,

$$R_1 = \frac{V^2}{P} = \frac{(100)^2}{1000} = 10\ \Omega$$

According to question, power dissipated in heater,

$$P' = 62.5 \text{ W}$$

$\therefore$ Voltage (V') across heater can be calculated as

$$P' = \frac{(V')^2}{R_1} \Rightarrow (V')^2$$

$$= P' \times R_1 = 62.5 \times 10$$

$$\Rightarrow \quad V' = 25 \text{ V (across heater)}$$

$\therefore$ Voltage across 10Ω resistor,

$$V'' = 100 - 25 = 75V$$

Current in 10Ω resistor

$$= \frac{V''}{10} = \frac{75}{10} = 7.5 \text{ A}$$

Current in heater resistor

$$= \frac{V'}{10} = \frac{25}{10} = 2.5 \text{ A}$$

So, current in $R\ \Omega = 7.5 - 2.5 = 5$A

Now, $V = IR$

$$\Rightarrow \quad R = V/I = \frac{25}{5} = 5\ \Omega$$

4 (a) Switching results in high decay/growth rate of current which results in a high current when bulb is turned ON or OFF (due to back emf). So, a bulb is must likely to get fused when it is just turned ON or OFF.

5 (c) Let R be the resistance of the wire

(*i*) The heat generated is $H_1 = \frac{V^2 t}{R}$.

(*ii*) Resistance of each part will be $R/2$. When they are connected in parallel, the resistance will be $R/4$. Hence, $H_2 = 4V^2 t/R$.

(*iii*) In case of four wires connected in parallel, the resistance will be $R/8$.

$$\therefore \quad H_3 = \frac{8V^2 t}{R}$$

(*iv*) $H_4 = \frac{V^2 t}{R/2} = \frac{2V^2 \cdot t}{R}$

Hence, largest amount of heat will be generated in case of four parts connected in parallel.

6 (b) As each arc containing n lamps, hence resistance of each arc $= nr$, number of arcs $= N/n$

Total resistance S is given by

$$\frac{1}{S} = \Sigma \frac{1}{nr} = \frac{N}{n}\left(\frac{1}{nr}\right)$$

$$S = \frac{n^2 r}{N}$$

$\therefore$ Total resistance $= R + S = R + \frac{n^2 r}{N}$

If E is the emf of the machine, current entering the arcs is $E/(R+S)$ and in each arc is $nE/(R+S)N$.

Hence, current passing through each lamp,

$$I = \frac{nE}{N(R + n^2 r/N)}$$

$$= \frac{E}{N}\left[\frac{R}{n} + \frac{nr}{N}\right]^{-1}$$

Now, heat produced per second to the lamps is $H = N_r I^2$

Since, light emitted is proportional to H^2, therefore light produced is maximum when H^2 and hence H is maximum or $\left[\frac{R}{n} + \frac{nr}{N}\right]$ is minimum.

Hence, we can write,

$$\frac{R}{n}+\frac{nr}{N}=\left[\left(\frac{R}{n}\right)^{1/2}-\left(\frac{nr}{N}\right)^{1/2}\right]^2+2\left(\frac{Rr}{N}\right)^{1/2}$$

This is minimum, when

$$\sqrt{\frac{R}{n}}-\sqrt{\frac{nr}{N}}=0$$

or very small or n is closely equal to $(NR/r)^{1/2}$.

7 *(c)* If a rated voltage and power are given, then $P_{rated}=\frac{V_{rated}^2}{R}$

$\therefore$ Current in the bulb, $i=\frac{P}{V}$ $(\because P=Vi)$

$$i=\frac{500}{100}=5\text{ A}$$

$\therefore$ Resistance of bulb,

$$R_b=\frac{100\times100}{500}=20\,\Omega$$

$\because$ Resistance R is connected in series.

$\therefore$ Current, $i=\frac{E}{R_{net}}=\frac{230}{R+R_b}$

$\Rightarrow R+20=\frac{230}{5}=46$

$\therefore \quad R=26\,\Omega$

8 *(d)* Given, charge,

$$Q=at-bt^2 \quad \ldots\text{(i)}$$

$\because$ We know that,

Current, $I=\frac{dQ}{dt}$

So, Eq. (i) can be written as

$$I=\frac{d}{dt}(at-bt^2)$$

$$\Rightarrow \quad I=a-2bt \quad \ldots\text{(ii)}$$

For maximum value of t, till the current exist is given by

$\Rightarrow a-2bt=0$

$$\therefore \quad t=\frac{a}{2b} \quad \ldots\text{(iii)}$$

$\because$ The total heat produced (H) can be given as

$$H=\int_0^t I^2R\,dt$$

$$=\int_0^{a/2b}(a-2bt)^2R\cdot dt \quad \left\{\because t=\frac{a}{2b}\right\}$$

$$=\int_0^{a/2b}(a^2+4b^2t^2-4abt)\,Rdt$$

$$H=\left[a^2t+4b^2\frac{t^3}{3}-\frac{4abt^2}{2}\right]_0^{a/2b}R$$

Solving above equation, we get

$$H=\frac{a^3R}{6b}$$

9 *(d)* A fuse wire should melt when a large current flows through it. Hence, it should have a very high resistance, so that very large amount of heat is produced due to which the fuse wire could melt and break the connectivity of circuit from main supply.

10 *(c)* As power, $P=\frac{V^2}{R}$

For small variation in the value of power,

$$\frac{\Delta P}{P}\times100\%=\frac{2\times\Delta V}{V}\times2\times2.5=5\%$$

Therefore, power would decrease by 5%.

11 *(c)* Here, $R_2=R$

Given, $R_1=5\,\Omega$

and power, $P=30\text{W}$

In parallel combination,

Power, $P=\frac{V^2}{R_1}+\frac{V^2}{R_2}$

$$\Rightarrow \quad \frac{V^2}{R_2}=P-\frac{V^2}{R_1}$$

$$\Rightarrow \quad \frac{10^2}{R}=30-\frac{10^2}{5}$$

or $\quad \frac{100}{R}=30-20 \Rightarrow R=10\,\Omega$

12 *(b)* The power dissipated in resistor of $9\,\Omega$ is

$$P=\frac{V^2}{R} \Rightarrow 36=\frac{V^2}{R}$$

$\Rightarrow \quad V^2=36R$

$\Rightarrow \quad V=\sqrt{36\times9}$

$\Rightarrow \quad V=6\times3=18\text{ V}$

$\therefore$ Total current through circuit is

$$V=IR_{eq} \Rightarrow 18=I\left(\frac{9\times6}{9+6}\right)$$

$$\Rightarrow 18=I\left[\frac{18}{5}\right] \Rightarrow I=5\text{A}$$

Potential across $2\,\Omega$ is

$$V=IR$$

$\Rightarrow \quad V=5(2)=10\text{ V}$

13 *(d)* As, $I=\frac{\text{total emf}}{\text{total resistance}}$

$$\Rightarrow \quad I=\frac{E}{R+r}$$

$$P=I^2R=\frac{E^2}{(R+r)^2}R=\frac{E^2R}{(R-r)^2+4Rr}$$

For power output to be maximum,

$$\frac{dP}{dR}=0$$

which gives $\quad R-r=0$

$\Rightarrow \quad R=r$

$$\therefore \quad P_{max}=\frac{E^2r}{(r+r)^2}=\frac{E^2}{4r}$$

14 *(b)* Resistance of 25 W bulb,

$$R_1=\frac{V^2}{P_1}=\frac{(220)^2}{25}=1936\,\Omega$$

Resistance of 100 W bulb,

$$R_2=\frac{V^2}{P_2}=\frac{(220)^2}{100}=484\,\Omega$$

Series resistance,

$$R=R_1+R_2=2420\,\Omega$$

Current through series combination,

$$I=\frac{440}{2420}=\frac{2}{11}\text{A}$$

$\therefore$ Potential difference across 100 W bulb,

$$V_2=R_2\times I=484\times\frac{2}{11}=88\text{ V}$$

and across 25 W bulb is

$$V_1=R_1\times I=1936\times\frac{2}{11}=352\text{V}$$

Thus, the bulb of 25 W will be fused because it can tolerate only 220 V, while the voltage across it is 352 V.

15 *(a)* As $\frac{R_1}{R_2}=\frac{P_2}{P_1}=\frac{100}{40}=\frac{5}{2}$.

Resistance of 40 W bulb is $\frac{5}{2}$ times than 100 W. In series, $P=i^2R$ and in parallel, $P=\frac{V^2}{R}$. So, 40 W in series and 100 W in parallel will glow brighter.

16 *(d)* Let L be the latent heat of vaporisation of water, the heat required for producing 1 g of steam,

$$L=540\text{ cal}$$

$$=540\times4.2=2268\text{ J}$$

Energy supplied = 1080 Js^{-1}

Time required to boil 100 g of water

$$=540\times4.2\times100/1080$$

$$=210\text{s}$$

17 (*d*) Let the resistance of the lamp filament be R, then $100 = (200)^2/R$.

When the voltage drops, expected power is

$$P = (220 \times 0.9)^2/R'$$

Here, R' will be less than R, because with the rise in temperature resistance will be decrease. Therefore, P is more than $(220 \times 0.9)^2/R = 81\,\text{W}$. But it will not be 90% of earlier value, because fall in temperature is small.

18 (*b*) Current required by each bulb,

$$i = \frac{P}{V} = \frac{100}{220}\,\text{A}$$

If n bulbs are joined in parallel, then

$$ni = i_{\text{fuse}}$$

or $n \times \frac{100}{220} = 10$ or $n = 22$

19 (*c*) As, $P = \frac{V^2}{R} \Rightarrow R = \frac{V^2}{P} \Rightarrow R \propto V^2$

(at constant power)

i.e. $\frac{R_1}{R_2} = \left[\frac{200}{300}\right]^2 = \frac{4}{9}$

When connected in series, potential drop and power consumed are in the ratio of the their resistances.

So, $\frac{P_1}{P_2} = \frac{V_1}{V_2} = \frac{R_1}{R_2} = \frac{4}{9}$

20 (*c*) When key K is opened, bulb B_3 will not draw any current from the source, so that terminal voltage of source increases. Hence, power consumed by bulb B_2 increases, so light of the bulb B_2 becomes more. The brightness of bulb B_1 decreases.

21 (*a*) When connected in series, power dissipated is

$$P_S = \frac{P_1P_2}{P_1 + P_2} = \frac{100 \times 60}{100 + 60}$$

$$= \frac{6000}{160} = 37.5\ \text{W}$$

22 (*a*) Resistance of 40 W bulb

$$= \frac{240 \times 240}{40} = 1440\ \Omega$$

Its safe current $= \frac{240}{1440} = 0.167$ A

Resistance of 60 W bulb

$$= \frac{240 \times 240}{60} = 960\ \Omega$$

Its safe current $= \frac{240}{960} = 0.25$ A

When connected in series to 420 V supply, then the current

$$i = \frac{420}{1440 + 960}$$

$$= \frac{420}{2400} = 0.175\ \text{A}$$

Voltagte across 40 W bulb,

$$V_{40} = 0.175 \times 1440 = 252\text{V}$$

Voltage across 60 W bulb,

$$V_{60} = 0.175 \times 960 = 168\text{V}$$

Thus, 40 W bulb will work at above its rated voltage.

23 (*c*) Resistance of each bulb,

$$R = \frac{V^2}{P} = \frac{(100)^2}{50} = 200\ \Omega$$

In parallel, $R' = \frac{200 \times 200}{400} = 100\Omega$

Power of circuit at 120 V,

$$P' = \frac{(120)^2}{100} = 144\,\text{W}$$

Number of bulbs $= \frac{144}{50} = 2.88$,

i.e. $n = 2$

24 (*b*) Let time taken by coil 1 be t_1 and time taken by coil 2 be t_2.
When both coil are connected in series, then total time $= t_1 + t_2$
Hence, $t = 10 + 10 = 20$ min

$[\because H = I^2Rt]$

25 (*d*) Resistance of the lamp,

$$R = \frac{V^2}{P} = \frac{30 \times 30}{90} = 10\ \Omega$$

Current through the lamp,

$$I = \frac{V}{R} = \frac{30}{10} = 3\,\text{A}$$

For same power dissipation, current through lamp should be same.
When lamp is connected to the 120 V supply, safe resistance of circuit should be

$$R' = \frac{V'}{I} = \frac{120}{3} = 40\ \Omega$$

Resistance required to be connected in series $= R' - R = 40 - 10 = 30\ \Omega$

26 (*a*) Equivalent resistance,

$$R_{\text{eq}} = \frac{r}{2} + R = \frac{r + 2R}{2}$$

$$\therefore \quad I = \frac{2E}{r + 2R}$$

For maximum power consumption, I should be maximum, so denominator is minimum.

For this

$$r + 2R = (\sqrt{r} - \sqrt{2R})^2 + 2\sqrt{r}\sqrt{2R}$$

$$\Rightarrow \sqrt{r} - \sqrt{2R} = 0$$

$$\Rightarrow \quad R = \frac{r}{2}$$

27 (*c*) As, $P' = 200 + 200 = 400$ W

$$\Rightarrow \frac{1}{P_{\text{net}}} = \frac{1}{P'} + \frac{1}{P}$$

$$= \frac{1}{400} + \frac{1}{400} = \frac{2}{400}$$

$$\Rightarrow P_{\text{net}} = 200\ \text{W}$$

28 (*b*) As, $P_s = \frac{V_s^2}{R}$

where, P_s and V_s are specified power.

$$\Rightarrow R_1 = \frac{220 \times 220}{100} \text{ (for 100 W bulb)}$$

and $R_2 = \frac{220 \times 220}{60}$ (for 60 W bulb)

$$R_{\text{eq}} = R_1 + R_2 \simeq 1291\ \Omega$$

Now, power consumed,

$$= \frac{V^2}{R_{\text{eq}}} = \frac{220 \times 220}{1291} = 37.5\ \text{W}$$

Current through circuit,

$$I = \frac{V}{R_{\text{eq}}} = \frac{220}{1291} = 0.17\text{A}$$

Power of 100 W,

$$P_{100} = \frac{V^2}{R} = \frac{I'^2R^2}{R} = I^2R \simeq 14\,\text{W}$$

29 (*b*) As, $P = VI$

$$\Rightarrow \quad I = \frac{160}{60} = \frac{8}{3}\ \text{A}$$

Also, $I = \frac{q}{t} = \frac{ne}{t}$

$$\Rightarrow \quad n = \frac{It}{e} = \frac{8 \times 60}{3 \times 1.6 \times 10^{-19}} = 10^{21}$$

30 (*c*) As, power is given as

$$P = \frac{V^2}{R}.$$

Also, $R = Sl/A$

$$\therefore \quad P = \frac{V^2A}{Sl}$$

Two electric bulb made of same material, same length and also same voltage is applied.

$$P \propto A$$

Hence, bulb produce more power when wire would be thicker.
i.e. 60 W bulb has thicker filament.

31 (c) When the bulb is turned ON, the voltage is applied across a filament which is initially cold, when it is turned ON. Then, the resistance is also low, thus the current flow will be high. Due to this, a large amount of power will be delivered and the glow of the filament would be more. But after sometime of switching ON, the temperature of the filament increases, thereby increasing its resistance. Hence, less amount of current will flow, leading to less power delivered and the glow of the filament would be lesser as compared to before.

32 (d) Voltage across 2 Ω resistance,

$$V = 2 \times 3 = 6\text{ V}$$

So, voltage across lowest arm,

$$V_1 = 6\text{ V}$$

Current across 5 Ω is $I = \frac{6}{1+5} = 1\text{ A}$

Thus, power across 5 Ω,

$$P = I^2R = (1)^2 \times 5$$
$$= 5\text{ W}$$

33 (b) The electric power of a heater is more than that of a bulb.

As $P \propto \frac{1}{R}$, the resistance of heater is less than that of the electric bulb. When a heater connected in parallel to the bulb is switched ON, it draws more current due to its lesser resistance. Consequently, the current through the bulb decreases, so it becomes dim.

When the heater coil becomes sufficiently hot, its resistance becomes more and then it draws a little lesser current. Consequently, the current through the electric bulb recovers.

Hence, dimness of the bulb decreases.

34 (a) If I is the safe current through the fuse wire and h is the rate of loss of heat in steady state, then

$$I^2R = hA$$

$$\Rightarrow \quad I^2\left(\frac{\rho L}{\pi r^2}\right) = h \times 2\pi r L$$

$$\Rightarrow \quad I \propto r^{3/2}$$

35 (b) Given, $\frac{A_1}{A_2} = \frac{1}{2}$

$$i_1 = i_2 = i, \quad l_1 = l_2 = l$$

and $\quad \rho_1 = \rho_2 = \rho$

We know that, heat produced,

$$H = i^2Rt$$

and heat produced per second,

$$H = i^2R \times 1 \quad \left[\text{but, } R = \frac{\rho l}{A}\right]$$

$$\Rightarrow \quad H = i^2\rho\frac{l}{A} \times 1$$

$$\Rightarrow \quad H = \frac{\rho l i^2}{A}$$

So, the ratio of heat produced per second in both the wires

$$\frac{H_1}{H_2} = \left(\frac{\rho_1}{\rho_2}\right)\left(\frac{l_1}{l_2}\right)\left(\frac{i_1^2}{i_2^2}\right) \times \left(\frac{A_2}{A_1}\right)$$

On putting the values, we get

$$\frac{H_1}{H_2} = \frac{\rho}{\rho} \times \frac{l}{l} \times \frac{i^2}{i^2} \times \frac{2}{1} = \frac{2}{1}$$

$$\therefore H_1 : H_2 = 2 : 1$$

36 (a) Let R_1 and R_2 be the resistances of the bulbs.

Power consumed, $P = \frac{V^2}{R}$

So, the power consumed in first bulb is

$$P_1 = \frac{V^2}{R_1} \quad \text{...(i)}$$

and power consumed in second bulb is

$$P_2 = \frac{V^2}{R_2} \quad \text{...(ii)}$$

If these two bulbs are combined in series, so the total resistance of the combination is

$$R = R_1 + R_2$$

Hence, the power consumed in combination is

$$P = \frac{V^2}{(R_1 + R_2)} \quad \text{...(iii)}$$

Now, from Eqs. (i) and (ii),

$$\frac{1}{P_1} + \frac{1}{P_2} = \frac{R_1}{V^2} + \frac{R_2}{V^2} = \frac{R_1 + R_2}{V^2}$$

$$\Rightarrow \quad \frac{1}{P_1} + \frac{1}{P_2} = \frac{1}{V^2/R_1 + R_2}$$

From Eq. (iii), we get

$$\frac{1}{P_1} + \frac{1}{P_2} = \frac{1}{P}$$

$$\Rightarrow \quad \frac{P_2 + P_1}{P_1P_2} = \frac{1}{P} \Rightarrow P = \frac{P_1P_2}{P_1 + P_2}$$

37 (a) Heat, $H = \frac{V^2}{R}$

For the same potential difference, the heat produced per second,

$$H \propto \frac{1}{R}$$

One part of the heater coil has a resistance $R/3$.

Hence, $\frac{H_2}{H_1} = \frac{R_1}{R_2} = \frac{R}{R/3}$

$$\Rightarrow \quad \frac{H_2}{100} = \frac{3R}{R}$$

$$\Rightarrow \quad H_2 = 3 \times 100 = 300\text{ cal}$$

38 (c) The resistances of 6 Ω and 3 Ω are in parallel in the given circuit, their equivalent resistance is

$$\frac{1}{R_1} = \frac{1}{6} + \frac{1}{3} = \frac{1+2}{6} = \frac{1}{2}$$

or $\quad R_1 = 2\,\Omega$

Again, R_1 is in series with 4 Ω resistance, hence

$$R = R_1 + 4 = 2 + 4 = 6\,\Omega$$

Thus, the total power dissipated in the circuit,

$$P = \frac{V^2}{R}$$

Given, $\quad V = 18\text{ V}$ and $R = 6\,\Omega$

$$\Rightarrow \quad P = \frac{(18)^2}{6} = 54\text{ W}$$

39 (a) The rate of dissipation of electric energy is called electric power.

$$W = Vit$$

The electric power dissipated will is given by

$$P = \frac{W}{t} = \frac{Vit}{t} = Vi = \frac{V^2}{R} \quad \text{...(i)}$$

When resistance is doubled, then let electric power be P'.

$$\therefore \quad P' = \frac{V^2}{2R} \quad \text{...(ii)}$$

From Eqs. (i) and (ii), we get,

$$P' = \frac{1}{2}P$$

So, power becomes $\frac{1}{2}$ of initial value.

40 (d) Input energy when the battery is charged

$$= Vit = 15 \times 10 \times 8 = 1200\text{ Wh}$$

Energy released when the battery is discharged

$$= 14 \times 5 \times 15 = 1050\text{ Wh}$$

Hence, efficiency of battery

$$= \frac{\text{energy output}}{\text{energy input}} = \frac{1050}{1200}$$
$$= 0.875 = 87.5\%$$

41 (d) Let R_1, R_2 and R_3 be the resistances of three bulbs, respectively.

In series order, $R = R_1 + R_2 + R_3$

But $R = \frac{V^2}{P}$ and supply voltage in series order is the same as the rated voltage.

$$\therefore \quad \frac{V^2}{P} = \frac{V^2}{P_1} + \frac{V^2}{P_2} + \frac{V^2}{P_3}$$

or $$\frac{1}{P} = \frac{1}{60} + \frac{1}{60} + \frac{1}{60}$$

$$\Rightarrow \quad P = \frac{60}{3} = 20 \text{ W}$$

42 (*d*) As, power, $P = i^2R \Rightarrow R = \frac{P}{i^2}$

Given, $P = 1\text{W}$ and $i = 5\text{A}$

$$\therefore \quad R = \frac{1}{(5)^2} = 0.04\ \Omega$$

43 (*c*) In parallel order, potential difference across each bulb is same and is equal to applied voltage of 500 V which is more than permissible voltage. So, both bulbs will get fused.

44 (*a*) Number of units

$$= \frac{P\text{ (in watt)} \times t\text{ (in hour)}}{1000}$$

$\Rightarrow$ Number of units

$$= \frac{2 \times 10^3 \times 1 \times 30}{1000} = 60 \text{ units}$$

45 (*a*) For first filament,

$$H = \frac{V^2}{R_1} t_1$$

$$\Rightarrow \quad R_1 = \frac{V^2}{H} t_1 \quad \ldots\text{(i)}$$

For second filament,

$$H = \frac{V^2}{R_2} t_2$$

$$\Rightarrow \quad R_2 = \frac{V^2}{H} t_2 \quad \ldots\text{(ii)}$$

When placed in parallel, $H = \frac{V^2}{R_P} t_P$

$$\Rightarrow \quad R_P = \frac{V^2}{H} t_P \quad \ldots\text{(iii)}$$

From Eqs. (i), (ii) and (iii), we get

$$\frac{1}{R_P} = \frac{1}{R_1} + \frac{1}{R_2}$$

$$\Rightarrow \quad \frac{H}{V^2 t_P} = \frac{H}{V^2 t_1} + \frac{H}{V^2 t_2}$$

$$\Rightarrow \quad \frac{1}{t_P} = \frac{1}{10} + \frac{1}{15} \Rightarrow t_P = 6 \text{ min}$$

46 (*b*) Power of lamp, $P = i^2R$

or $$\frac{\Delta P}{P} = 2\frac{\Delta i}{i} = 2 \times 5\% \left[\because \frac{\Delta i}{i} = 5\%\right]$$

$$= 10\% \text{ decrease}$$

47 (*d*) When a single heater (resistance $R_1 = R$) is connected to 220 V, then it will consume a power, $P_1 = 1000$ W, if two such identical heaters are connected in parallel (total resistance $R_2 = R_1/2 = R/2$) to same source, then it will consume power P_2.

Now, $$\frac{P_2}{P_1} = \frac{R_1}{R_2}$$

$$\Rightarrow \quad P_2 = 2P_1 = 2000 \text{ W}$$

48 (*c*) The voltage across R_2 and R_3 is same.

Therefore, for same energy loss according to $H = \frac{V^2}{R} t$, R_2 must be equal to R_3.

i.e. $R_2 = R_3$

Again, the energy is same in all resistances.

$$\therefore \quad i^2 R_1 t = i_1^2 R_2 t \quad \ldots\text{(i)}$$

and $$i_1 = \frac{R_3}{R_2 + R_3} i = \frac{R_3}{R_3 + R_3} i = \frac{1}{2} i$$

$$\ldots\text{(ii)} \; [\because R_2 = R_3]$$

Thus, $$i^2 R_1 t = \frac{i^2}{4} R_2 t$$

[from Eqs. (i) and (ii)]

$$\therefore \quad R_1 = \frac{R_2}{4}$$

49 (*c*) The relation of power is given by

$$P = \frac{V^2}{R} = \frac{(200)^2}{80} = 500 \text{ W}$$

Hence, energy spent

$$= \text{power} \times \text{time}$$

$$= 500 \times 2 = 1000 \text{ W-h}$$

50 (*c*) The resistance of each part $= R/n$

The effective resistance becomes R/n^2.

Since, the battery voltage is constant.

So, $$P \propto \frac{1}{R}$$

$$\Rightarrow \quad \frac{P'}{P} = \frac{R}{R/n^2}$$

$$\Rightarrow \quad P' = n^2 P.$$

51 (*c*) In series combination,

$$R_s = R + 2R = 3R$$

In parallel combination,

$$R_p = \frac{R \times 2R}{R + 2R} = \frac{2R^2}{3R} = \frac{2}{3}R$$

Ratio of heats produced,

$$\frac{H_s}{H_p} = \frac{R_p}{R_s} = \frac{\frac{2}{3}R}{3R} = \frac{2}{9}$$

$$\Rightarrow H_s : H_p = 2 : 9$$

52 (*b*) Maximum percentage error arises due to limit of accuracy of the measured value.

By Joule's law of heating, the power change due to current (i), through resistor (R) is given by

$$P = i^2 R$$

Taking partial differentiation, we have

$$\frac{\Delta P}{P} \times 100 = 2\frac{\Delta i}{i} \times 100 + \frac{\Delta R}{R} \times 100$$

$$\therefore \quad \frac{\Delta P}{P} \times 100 = 2 \times 1\% = 2\%$$

$$\left(\text{given, } \frac{\Delta i}{i} = 1 \text{ and } \frac{\Delta R}{R} = 0\right)$$

53 (*c*) By Joule's law, the power dissipated through a resistor R, having a potential difference V is

$$P = \frac{V^2}{R'}$$

When bulbs are connected in series, then

$$R' = R + R + R = 3R$$

Power dissipated,

$$P = \frac{V^2}{3R} \quad \ldots\text{(i)}$$

When they are connected in parallel, then

$$\frac{1}{R''} = \frac{1}{R} + \frac{1}{R} + \frac{1}{R} = \frac{3}{R}$$

$$\Rightarrow \quad R'' = \frac{R}{3}$$

Power dissipated,

$$P' = \frac{V^2}{R/3} \quad \ldots\text{(ii)}$$

From Eqs. (i) and (ii), we have

$$P' = 9P$$

18

Moving Charges and Magnetism

Quick Review

Magnetic Field

The space in the surrounding of a magnet or a current carrying conductor in which its magnetic influence can be experienced is called **magnetic field**. SI unit of magnetic field is tesla (T) and its CGS unit is gauss (G).

Also, $1\text{ T} = 10^4\text{ G}$

- The direction of magnetic field is found by following rules
  (*i*) Right hand thumb rule (*ii*) Maxwell's cork screw rule

Biot-Savart's Law

According to **Biot-Savart's law**, the magnetic field $d\mathbf{B}$ at a point P due to a current element $Id\mathbf{l}$ is given by

$$d\mathbf{B} = \frac{\mu_0}{4\pi} \cdot \frac{I\,(d\mathbf{l} \times \mathbf{r})}{r^3}$$

where, $\frac{\mu_0}{4\pi}$ is a proportionality constant having a value of 10^{-7} TmA^{-1} in free space.

Applications of Biot-Savart's Law

(*i*) Magnetic Field due to a Current Carrying Conductor

- The magnetic field due to a current carrying wire of finite length at a point P situated at a normal distance r is

$$B = \frac{\mu_0 I}{4\pi r}(\sin\phi_1 + \sin\phi_2)$$

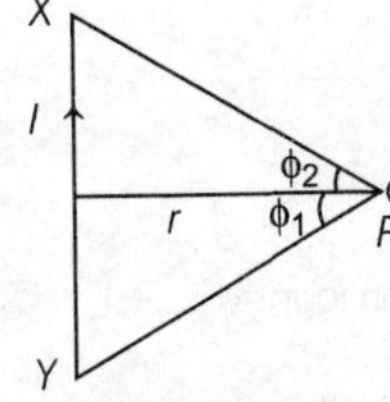

- If point P lies symmetrically on the perpendicular bisector of wire XY, then $\phi_1 = \phi_2 = \phi$ (say) and hence

$$B = \frac{\mu_0 I}{4\pi r} \cdot 2\sin\phi = \frac{\mu_0 I \sin\phi}{2\pi r}$$

- For a wire of infinite length, $\phi_1 = \phi_2 = 90°$ and hence

$$B = \frac{\mu_0 I}{2\pi r}$$

(*ii*) Magnetic Field due to a Current Carrying Circular Loop

- If there is a circular coil of radius R and number of turns N, carrying a current I through the turns, then the magnetic field at the centre of coil is given by

$$B = \frac{\mu_0 NI}{2R}$$

- If there is a circular arc of wire subtending an angle θ at the centre of arc, then the magnetic field at the central point is

$$B = \frac{\mu_0 I}{2R}\left(\frac{\theta}{2\pi}\right)$$

- At a point, situated at a distance r from the centre of a current carrying circular coil along its axial line, the magnetic field is given by

$$B = \frac{\mu_0 NIR^2}{2(R^2 + r^2)^{3/2}}$$

Ampere's Circuital Law

According to **Ampere's circuital law**, the line integral of the magnetic field **B** around any closed path is equal to μ_0 times, the net current I threading through the area enclosed by the closed path.

Mathematically, $\oint \mathbf{B} \cdot d\mathbf{l} = \mu_0 \Sigma I$

Applications of Ampere's Circuital Law

(i) Magnetic Field due to a Straight Current Carrying Wire at different Positions

- At any perpendicular distance, $B = \frac{\mu_0}{4\pi} \frac{i}{r} (\sin\alpha + \sin\beta)$

  where, α and β = angle made by two ends of wire.
- At a point of perpendicular bisector, i.e. $\alpha = \beta = \theta$, then

$$B = \frac{\mu_0}{4\pi} \frac{i}{r} (2\sin\theta)$$

- When wire is of infinite length, i.e. $\alpha = \beta = 90°$, then

$$B = \frac{\mu_0}{4\pi} \left(\frac{2i}{r}\right)$$

(ii) Magnetic Field due to a Cylindrical Wire

- **Outside the Cylinder** $(r > R)$ To find magnetic field outside at point P. Now, we will assume Amperian loops as shown below

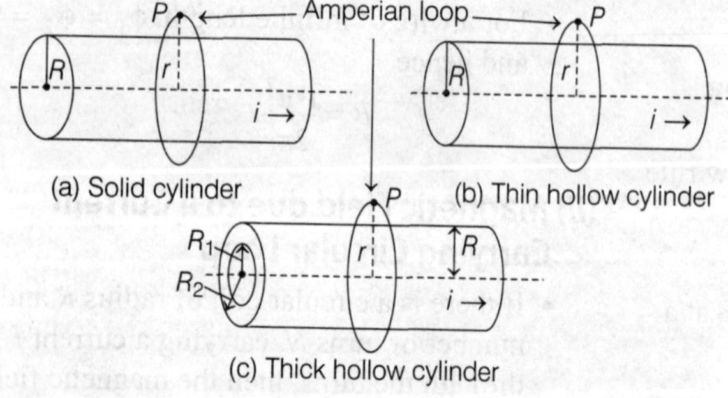

(a) Solid cylinder (b) Thin hollow cylinder (c) Thick hollow cylinder

In all the above cases, magnetic field outside the wire at P,

$$\oint \mathbf{B} \cdot d\mathbf{l} = B(2\pi r) = \mu_0 i \Rightarrow B_{out} = \frac{\mu_0 i}{2\pi r}$$

In all the above cases, $B_{surface} = \frac{\mu_0 i}{2\pi R}$

- **Inside the Hollow Cylinder** $(r < R)$ Magnetic field inside the hollow cylinder is zero because no current is enclosed by Amperian loops as shown below

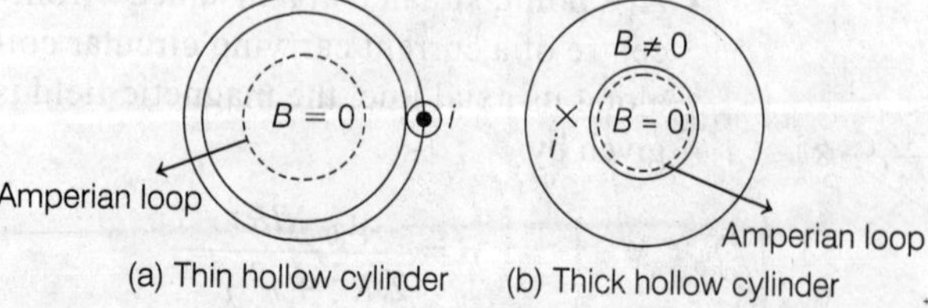

(a) Thin hollow cylinder (b) Thick hollow cylinder

- **Inside the Solid Cylinder** $(r < R)$ Current i' enclosed by Amperian loop is lesser than the total current (i).

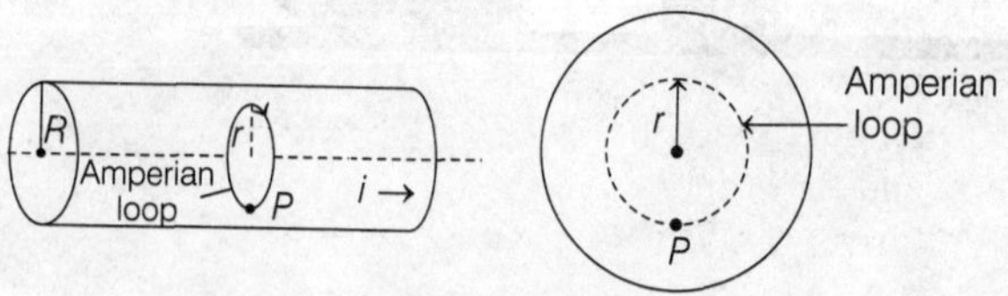

Current density is uniform, i.e. $J = J'$

$$\Rightarrow \quad i' = i \times \frac{A'}{A} = i\left(\frac{r^2}{R^2}\right)$$

Hence, at inside point $\oint \mathbf{B}_{in} \cdot d\mathbf{l} = \mu_0 i' \Rightarrow B_{in} = \frac{\mu_0}{2\pi} \cdot \frac{ir}{R^2}$

- **Inside the Thick Portion of Hollow Cylinder** Current enclosed by the Amperian loop of radius r is given by

$$i' = i \times \frac{A'}{A} = i \times \frac{(r^2 - R_1^2)}{(R_2^2 - R_1^2)}$$

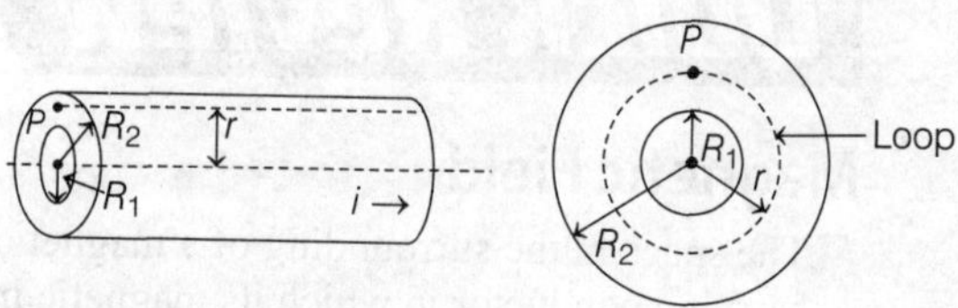

Hence, at point P, $\oint \mathbf{B} \cdot d\mathbf{l} = \mu_0 i'$

$$\Rightarrow \quad B_{in} = \frac{\mu_0 i}{2\pi r} \cdot \frac{(r^2 - R_1^2)}{(R_2^2 - R_1^2)}$$

Variation in Magnetic Field with Radius

- The variation in magnetic field due to infinite long solid cylindrical conductor along its radius is as shown in figure.

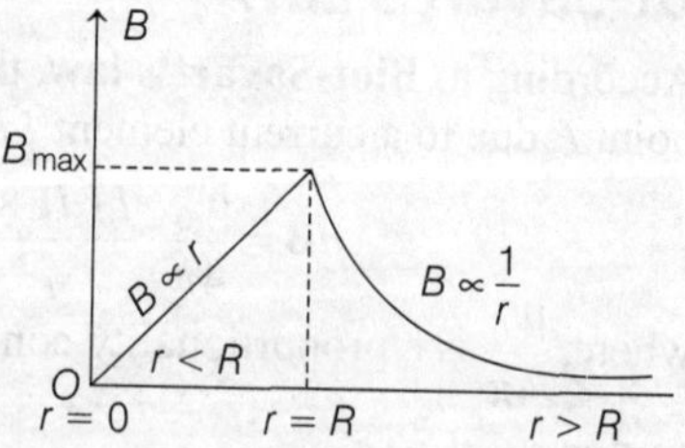

Note That inside the wire $B \to 0$ as $r \to 0$. Also, the magnetic field is continuous at the surface of the wire.

- The variation in magnetic field due to infinite long hollow cylindrical conductor along its radius is as shown in figure.

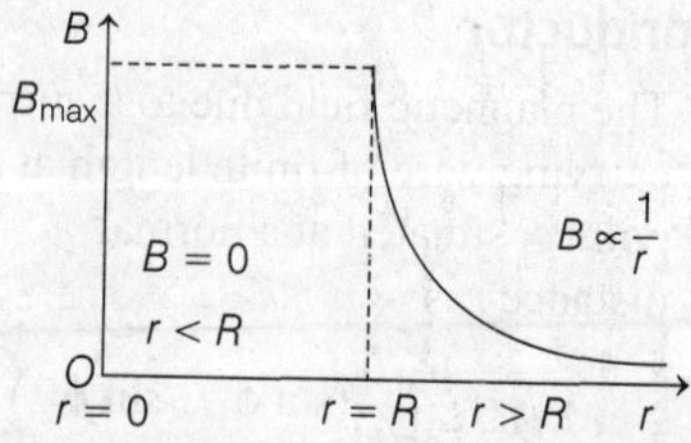

(iii) Magnetic Field due to a Solenoid

(a) **Finite Length Solenoid** If N = total number of turns, l = length of the solenoid and n = number of turns per unit length $= N/l$, then

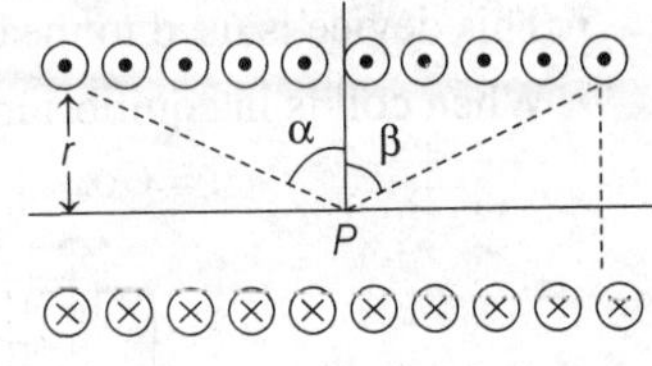

Magnetic field inside the solenoid at point P is given by

$$B = \frac{\mu_0 ni}{2}[\sin\alpha + \sin\beta]$$

(b) **Infinite Length Solenoid** If the solenoid is of infinite length and the point is well inside it.

i.e. $\alpha = \beta = (\pi/2)$.

So, $B_{in} = \mu_0 ni$

If the solenoid is of infinite length and the point is near one end, i.e. $\alpha = 0$ and $\beta = (\pi/2)$, so

$$B_{end} = \frac{1}{2}(\mu_0 ni) \qquad \left(\because B_{end} = \frac{1}{2}B_{in}\right)$$

(c) Variation in magnetic field with distance d from its centre

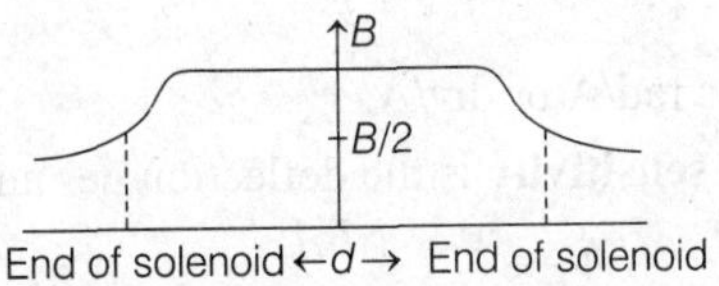

(iv) Magnetic Field due to a Toroid

A toroid can be considered as a ring shaped closed solenoid. Hence, it is like an endless cylindrical solenoid.

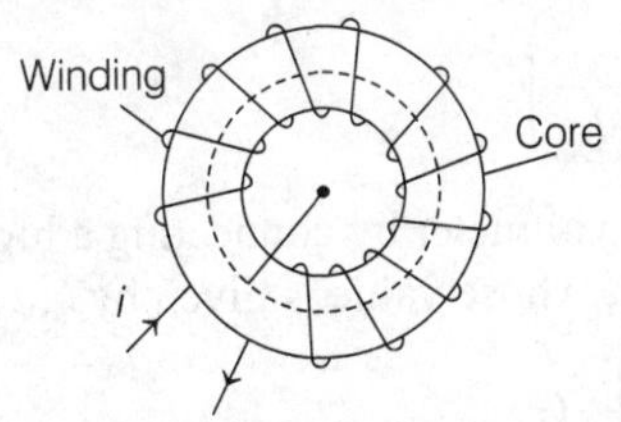

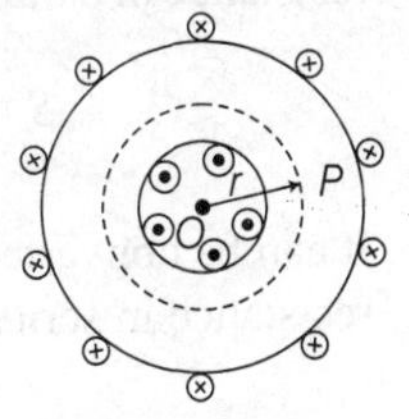

Consider a toroid having n turns per unit length. Magnetic field at a point P in the figure is given as

$$B = \frac{\mu_0 Ni}{2\pi r} = \mu_0 ni$$

where, $n = \frac{N}{2\pi r}$.

(v) Magnetic Field due to an Infinitely Large Carrying Current Sheet

Using Ampere's law, the magnetic field due to a current carrying sheet of infinite length is given by $B = \frac{\mu_0 J}{2}$.

where, J = current density of sheet.

Force on a Moving Charge in a Uniform Magnetic Field

- The magnetic force F_m acting on a charge q moving with a velocity v in a magnetic field B is given by
  $\mathbf{F}_m = q(\mathbf{v} \times \mathbf{B})$
  The direction of force $\mathbf{F}_m$ is given by the rule of vector product.
- The force $\mathbf{F}_m$ is maximum having a value $F_m = qvB$ when $\theta = 90°$, i.e. charged particle is moving in a direction perpendicular to that of magnetic field.
- Depending on the value of θ between $\mathbf{v}$ and $\mathbf{B}$, the particle describes following paths as tabulated below

Value of θ	Type of Path	Radius (r)	Time Period (T)	Frequency (ν)	Angular Frequency (ω)	Pitch (P)
0° or 180°	straight line	—	—	—	—	—
90°	circular	$\frac{mv}{qB}$	$\frac{2\pi m}{qB}$	$\frac{qB}{2\pi m}$	$\frac{qB}{m}$	—
Any angle (other than 0°, 90° or 180°)	helical	$\frac{mv\sin\theta}{qB}$	$\frac{2\pi m}{qB}$	$\frac{qB}{2\pi m}$	—	$v\cos\theta \cdot T$

Lorentz Force : Motion of a Charged Particle is Combined Electric and Magnetic Field

If electric field $\mathbf{E}$ and magnetic field $\mathbf{B}$ are existing at a point, then force on the electric charge q is given by

$\mathbf{F} = q[\mathbf{E} + \mathbf{v} \times \mathbf{B}] = \mathbf{F}_{electric} + \mathbf{F}_{magnetic}$

This force was first given by H. A Lorentz, hence it is called **Lorentz force.**

Here, magnetic force $\mathbf{F}_m = q(\mathbf{v} \times \mathbf{B}) = qvB\sin\theta$ and electric force $\mathbf{F}_e = q\mathbf{E}$.

The direction of magnetic force is same as $\mathbf{v} \times \mathbf{B}$, if charge is positive and opposite to $\mathbf{v} \times \mathbf{B}$, if charge q is negative.

Cyclotron

- It is a device used to accelerate positively charged particles (like, α-particle, deuterons, etc.) to acquire enough energy to carry out nuclear activities.
- The cyclotron frequency is given by $\nu = \frac{Bq}{2\pi m}$.
- The positive ions of charge q and mass m in cyclotron attain maximum energy which is given by

  (i) $E_{max} = \frac{1}{2} \cdot \frac{B^2 q^2 R^2}{m}$

  where, R is the radius of the dees of the cyclotron.

  (ii) $E_{max} = 2n(V_z)$

  where, n is the number of revolutions completed by the positive ions before leaving the dees.

Force on a Current Carrying Conductor in a Magnetic Field

- If a current carrying conductor is placed in a magnetic field, the force experienced by it is given by $\mathbf{F} = \int i(d\mathbf{l} \times \mathbf{B})$.
- In case of a straight conductor, it is given by $F = Bil \sin\theta$
- In case of a closed loop, it is given by $\mathbf{F} = 0$
- Its direction is given by Fleming's left hand rule or Fleming's right hand thumb rule.

Force between Two Parallel Current Carrying Conductor

If two infinitely long parallel conductors carrying the currents I_1 and I_2 respectively and are separated by a distance r, then magnetic force experienced by length l of any one conductor due to the other current carrying conductor is

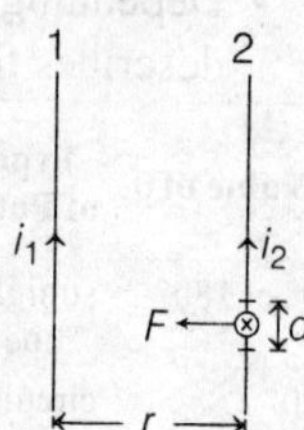

$$F = \frac{\mu_0}{4\pi} \cdot \frac{2I_1I_2}{r} l$$

and force per unit length, $\frac{F}{l} = F_0 = \frac{\mu_0}{4\pi} \cdot \frac{2I_1I_2}{r}$

- The direction of force depends on the direction of current in them as
  (i) attractive, if current flow in same direction.
  (ii) repulsive, if current flow in opposite direction.

Current Carrying Coil

- A current carrying coil is like a bar magnet having magnetic moment $\mathbf{M} = Ni\mathbf{A}$, where A = area of coil.
- Magnetic moment for a revolving electron, $\mathbf{M} = IA = \frac{evr}{2}$.
- Torque on a current carrying loop in a magnetic field, $$\tau = NBiA \sin\theta$$
- In vector form, it is represented as $$\tau = \mathbf{M} \times \mathbf{B}$$

Moving Coil Galvanometer

- This device is used to measure current upto nano ampere.
- When coil is in equilibrium, then the current through it is $$i = G\alpha$$

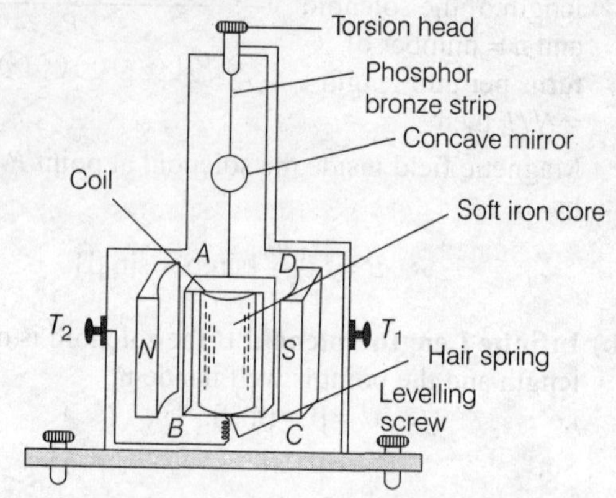

where, $G = \frac{k}{NBA}$ = galvanometer constant

and α = angle of twist due to rotation.

- **Current sensitivity** is the deflection per unit current, i.e. $$I_s = \frac{\theta}{I} = \frac{NAB}{k}$$ Its unit is rad/A or div/A.
- **Voltage sensitivity** is the deflection per unit voltage, i.e. $$V_s = \frac{\theta}{V} = \frac{NBA}{Rk}$$ Its unit is rad/V or div/V.
- It can be converted to an ammeter by connecting a low resistance in parallel or shunt to it, whose value is given by $$S = \left(\frac{I_g}{I - I_g}\right) G$$
- It can be converted to a voltmeter by connecting a high resistance in series, to it, whose value is given by $$R = \left(\frac{V}{I_g}\right) - G$$

Topical Practice Questions

All the exam questions of this chapter have been divided into 4 topics as listed below

Topic 1

Biot-Savart's Law and Ampere's Circuital Law

2019

1 A cylindrical conductor of radius R is carrying a constant current. The plot of the magnitude of the magnetic field B with the distance d from the centre of the conductor, is correctly represented by the figure **[NEET]**

(a) 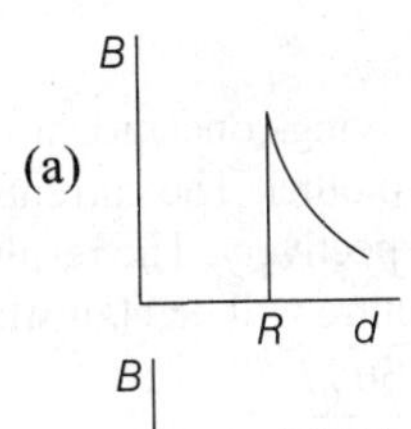

(b) 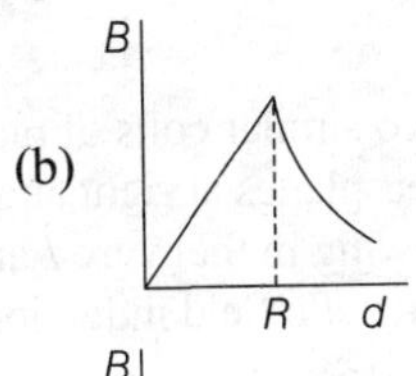

(c) 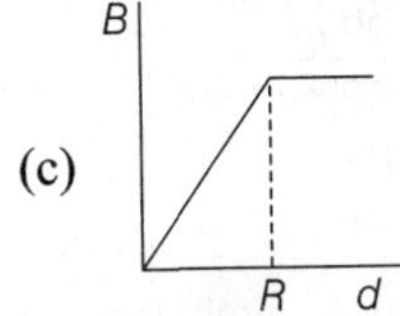

(d) 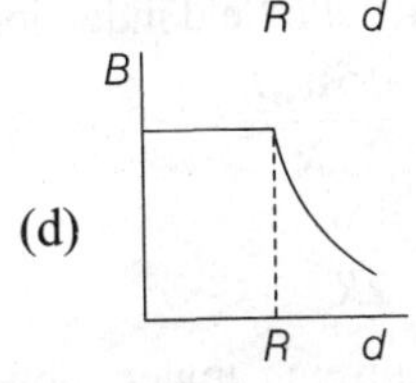

2 Two toroids 1 and 2 have total number of turns 200 and 100 respectively, with average radii 40 cm and 20 cm respectively. If they carry same current i, the ratio of the magnetic fields along the two loops is **[NEET (Odisha)]**

(a) 1 : 1 (b) 4 : 1 (c) 2 : 1 (d) 1 : 2

3 A straight conductor carrying current i splits into two parts as shown in the figure. The radius of the circular loop is R. The total magnetic field at the centre P of the loop is **[NEET (Odisha)]**

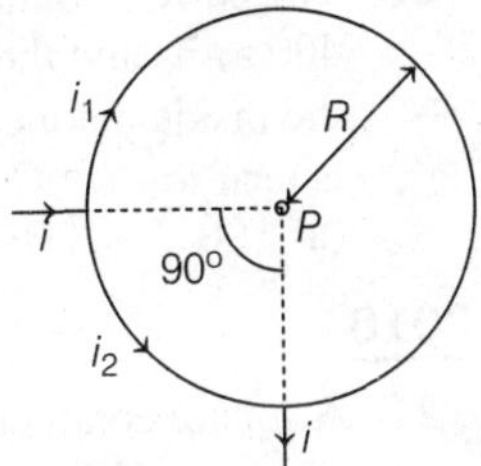

(a) zero

(b) $3\mu_0 i/32R$, outward

(c) $3\mu_0 i/32R$, inward

(d) $\dfrac{\mu_0 i}{2R}$, inward

4 Two circular loops having same radius ($R = 10\,\text{cm}$) and same current $\dfrac{7}{2}$ A are placed along same axis as shown in the figure. If distance between their centres is 10 cm, find the value of net magnetic field at point P. **[AIIMS]**

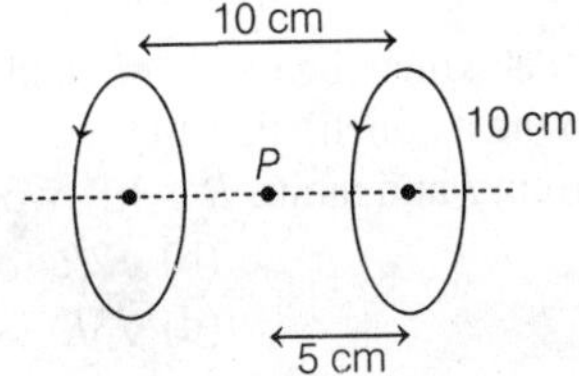

(a) $\dfrac{50\mu_0}{\sqrt{5}}$ T (b) $\dfrac{28\mu_0}{\sqrt{5}}$ T (c) $\dfrac{56\,\mu_0}{\sqrt{5}}$ T (d) $\dfrac{56\mu_0}{\sqrt{3}}$ T

2018

5 A long straight wire, carrying current I is bent at its mid-point to form an angle of 45°. Induction of magnetic field (in tesla) at point P, distant R from point of bending is equal to **[AIIMS]**

(a) $\dfrac{(\sqrt{2}-1)\mu_0 I}{4\pi R}$ (b) $\dfrac{(\sqrt{2}+1)\mu_0 I}{4\pi R}$

(c) $\dfrac{(\sqrt{2}-1)\mu_0 I}{4\sqrt{2}\pi R}$ (d) $\dfrac{(\sqrt{2}+1)\mu_0 I}{4\sqrt{2}\pi R}$

6 An element $dl = dx\,\hat{\mathbf{i}}$ (where, $dx = 1\,\text{cm}$) is placed at the origin and carries a large current $i = 10$ A. What is the magnetic field on the Y-axis at a distance of 0.5 m? **[AIIMS]**

(a) $2\times10^{-8}\,\hat{\mathbf{k}}$T (b) $4\times10^{-8}\,\hat{\mathbf{k}}$T

(c) $-2\times10^{-8}\,\hat{\mathbf{k}}$T (d) $-4\times10^{-8}\,\hat{\mathbf{k}}$T

2017

7 A long wire having a semicircular loop of radius r carries a current i as shown in figure. The magnetic induction at the centre O due to entire wire is **[JIPMER]**

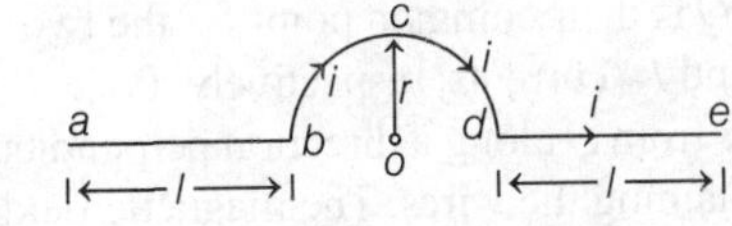

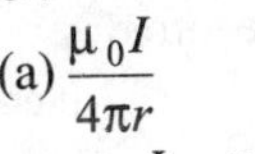

(a) $\dfrac{\mu_0 i}{4r}$ (b) $\dfrac{\mu_0 i^2}{4r}$

(c) $\dfrac{\mu_0 i}{4r^2}$ (d) None of these

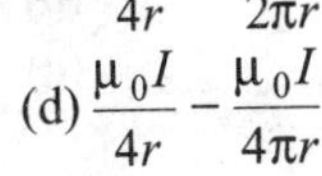

8 In the given figure, what is the magnetic field induction at point O? **[JIPMER]**

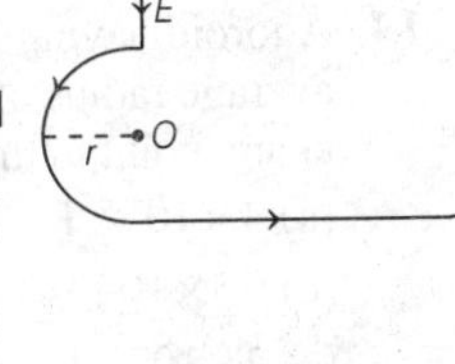

(a) $\dfrac{\mu_0 I}{4\pi r}$ (b) $\dfrac{\mu_0 I}{4r}+\dfrac{\mu_0 I}{2\pi r}$

(c) $\dfrac{\mu_0 I}{4r}+\dfrac{\mu_0 I}{4\pi r}$ (d) $\dfrac{\mu_0 I}{4r}-\dfrac{\mu_0 I}{4\pi r}$

2016

9 A long straight wire of radius a carries a steady current I. The current is uniformly distributed over its cross-section. The ratio of the magnetic fields $\mathbf{B}$ and $\mathbf{B'}$ at radial distances $a/2$ and $2a$ respectively, from the axis of the wire is **[NEET]**

(a) $\dfrac{1}{2}$ (b) 1 (c) 4 (d) $\dfrac{1}{4}$

10 A long wire carrying a steady current is bent into a circular loop of one turn. The magnetic field at the centre of the loop is B. It is then bent into a circular coil of n turns. The magnetic field at the centre of this coil of n turns will be **[NEET]**

(a) nB (b) n^2B (c) $2nB$ (d) $2n^2B$

2015

11 A wire carrying current I has the shape as shown in adjoining figure. Linear parts of the wire are very long and parallel to X-axis while semicircular portion of radius R is lying in yz-plane. Magnetic field at point O is **[NEET]**

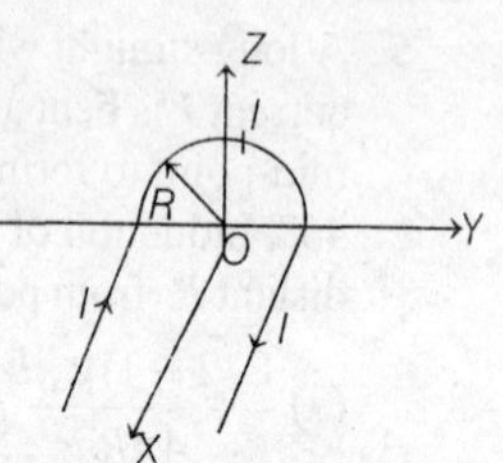

(a) $\mathbf{B} = \frac{\mu_0}{4\pi}\cdot\frac{I}{R}(\pi\hat{\mathbf{i}} + 2\hat{\mathbf{k}})$ (b) $\mathbf{B} = -\frac{\mu_0}{4\pi}\cdot\frac{I}{R}(\pi\hat{\mathbf{i}} - 2\hat{\mathbf{k}})$

(c) $\mathbf{B} = -\frac{\mu_0}{4\pi}\cdot\frac{I}{R}(\pi\hat{\mathbf{i}} + 2\hat{\mathbf{k}})$ (d) $\mathbf{B} = \frac{\mu_0}{4\pi}\cdot\frac{I}{R}(\pi\hat{\mathbf{i}} - 2\hat{\mathbf{k}})$

12 An electron moving in a circular orbit of radius r makes n rotations per second. The magnetic field produced at the centre has magnitude **[NEET]**

(a) $\frac{\mu_0 ne}{2\pi r}$ (b) zero (c) $\frac{\mu_0 n^2 e}{r}$ (d) $\frac{\mu_0 ne}{2r}$

2014

13 Two identical long conducting wires AOB and COD are placed at right angle to each other, with one above other such that O is their common point for the two. The wires carry I_1 and I_2 currents, respectively. Point P is lying at distance d from O along a direction perpendicular to the plane containing the wires. The magnetic field at the point P will be **[CBSE AIPMT]**

(a) $\frac{\mu_0}{2\pi d}\left(\frac{I_2}{I_2}\right)$ (b) $\frac{\mu_0}{2\pi d}(I_1 + I_2)$

(c) $\frac{\mu_0}{2\pi d}(I_1^2 - I_2^2)$ (d) $\frac{\mu_0}{2\pi d}(I_1^2 + I_2^2)^{1/2}$

14 A toroid having 200 turns carries a current of 1A. The average radius of the toroid is 10 cm. The magnetic field at any point in the open space inside the toroid is **[Kerala CEE]**

(a) 4×10^{-3} T (b) zero

(c) 0.5×10^{-3} T (d) 3×10^{-3} T

(e) 2×10^{-3} T

15 A long conducting wire carrying a current I is bent at 120° (see figure). The magnetic field B at a point P on the right bisector of bending angle at a distance d from the bend is (where, μ_0 is the permeability of free space) **[MP PMT]**

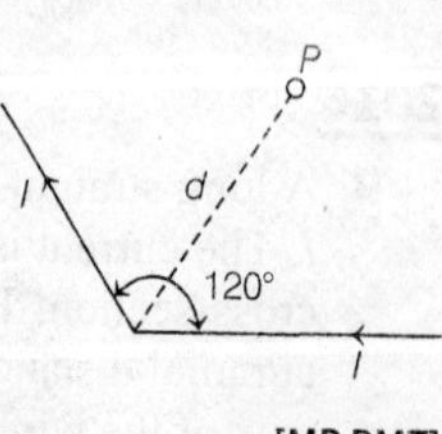

(a) $\frac{2\mu_0 I}{2\pi d}$ (b) $\frac{\mu_0 I}{2\pi d}$ (c) $\frac{\mu_0 I}{\sqrt{3}\pi d}$ (d) $\frac{\sqrt{3}\mu_0 I}{2\pi d}$

16 The magnetic field due to a current carrying circular loop of radius 3 cm at a point on the axis at a distance of 4 cm from the centre is 54 μT. What will be its value at the centre of the loop? **[UK PMT]**

(a) 200 μT (b) 250 μT

(c) 125 μT (d) 75 μT

17 A solenoid has length 0.4 cm, radius 1 cm and 400 turns of wire. If a current of 5 A is passed through this solenoid, what is the magnetic field inside the solenoid? **[KCET]**

(a) 6.28×10^{-4} T (b) 6.28×10^{-3} T

(c) 6.28×10^{-7} T (d) 6.28×10^{-6} T

2013

18 Two similar coils of radius R are lying concentrically with their planes at right angles to each other. The currents flowing in them are I and $2I$, respectively. The resultant magnetic field induction at the centre will be **[AIPMT CBSE]**

(a) $\frac{\sqrt{5}\mu_0 I}{2R}$ (b) $\frac{3\mu_0 I}{2R}$

(c) $\frac{\mu_0 I}{2R}$ (d) $\frac{\mu_0 I}{R}$

19 A current i ampere flows along an infinitely long straight thin walled tube. The magnetic induction at any point inside the tube at a distance r metre from axis is **[AIIMS]**

(a) zero (b) ∞ (c) $\frac{\mu_0 i}{2r}$ (d) $\frac{\mu_0 i}{2\pi r}$

20 The current in the windings on a toroid is 2.0 A. There are 400 turns and the mean circumferential length is 40 cm. If the inside magnetic field is 1.0 T, the relative permeability is near to **[AFMC]**

(a) 100 (b) 200 (c) 300 (d) 400

2010

21 A square conducting loop of side length L carries a current I. The magnetic field at the centre of the loop is **[AIIMS]**

(a) independent of L

(b) proportional to L^2

(c) inversely proportional to L

(d) linearly proportional to L

22 A wire carrying current i and other carrying $2i$ in the same direction produce a magnetic field B at the mid-point. What will be the field when $2i$ current is switched off? **[BHU]**

(a) $B/2$ (b) $2B$ (c) B (d) $4B$

23 The distance at which the magnetic field on axis as compared to the magnetic field at the centre of the coil carrying current I and radius R is 1/8, would be **[MP PMT]**

(a) R (b) $\sqrt{2}R$

(c) $2R$ (d) $\sqrt{3}R$

24 The current in straight wire, if the magnetic field 10^{-6} Wbm^{-2} produced at 0.02 m away from it is **[MP PMT]**

(a) 0.1 A (b) 1 A (c) zero (d) 10 A

25 A winding wire which is used to frame a solenoid can bear a maximum 10 A current. If length of solenoid is 80 cm and its cross-sectional radius is 3 cm, then required length of winding wire is (Take, $B = 0.2$ T) **[Haryana PMT]**

(a) 1.2×10^2 m (b) 4.8×10^2 m
(c) 2.4×10^3 m (d) 6×10^3 m

26 A wire loop $PQRSP$ is constructed by joining two semicircular coils of radii r_1 and r_2 respectively, as shown in the figure. If the current flowing in the loop is i, then the magnetic induction at the point O is **[EAMCET]**

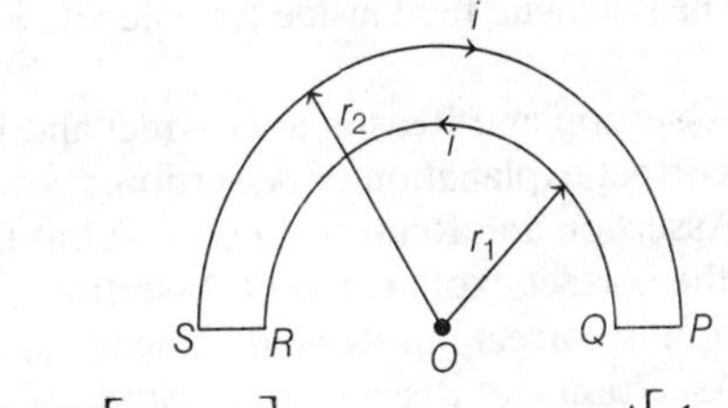

(a) $\frac{\mu_0 i}{4}\left[\frac{1}{r_1}-\frac{1}{r_2}\right]$ (b) $\frac{\mu_0 i}{4}\left[\frac{1}{r_1}+\frac{1}{r_2}\right]$
(c) $\frac{\mu_0 i}{2}\left[\frac{1}{r_1}-\frac{1}{r_2}\right]$ (d) $\frac{\mu_0 i}{2}\left[\frac{1}{r_1}+\frac{1}{r_2}\right]$

27 A helium nucleus makes full rotation in a circle of radius 0.8 m in 2 s. The value of magnetic field B at the centre of the circle, will be (where, μ_0 = permeability constant) **[JCECE]**

(a) $\frac{2\times10^{-19}}{\mu_0}$ (b) $2\times10^{-19}\mu_0$
(c) $10^{-19}\mu_0$ (d) $\frac{10^{-19}}{\mu_0}$

28 A solenoid of 1.5 m length and 4.0 cm diameter possesses 10 turns/cm. A current of 5 A is flowing through it. The magnetic induction at axis inside the solenoid is

(a) $2\pi\times10^{-3}$ T (b) $2\pi\times10^{-5}$ T **[CG PMT, JCECE]**
(c) $2\pi\times10^{-3}$ G (d) $2\pi\times10^{-5}$ G

29 For the magnetic field to be maximum due to a small element of current carrying conductor at a point, the angle between the element and the line joining the element to the given point must be **[VMMC]**

(a) 0° (b) 90° (c) 180° (d) 45°

30 An electric current passes through a long straight copper wire. At a distance 5 cm from the straight wire, the magnetic field is B. The magnetic field at 20 cm from the straight wire would be **[JIPMER]**

(a) $\frac{B}{6}$ (b) $\frac{B}{4}$ (c) $\frac{B}{3}$ (d) $\frac{B}{2}$

31 Two long straight wires are set parallel to each other at separation r and each carries a current i in the same direction. The strength of the magnetic field at any point midway between the two wires is **[BCECE]**

(a) $\frac{\mu_0 i}{\pi r}$ (b) $\frac{2\mu_0 i}{\pi r}$ (c) $\frac{\mu_0 i}{2\pi r}$ (d) zero

32 A solenoid of length 50 cm and a radius of cross-section 1cm has 1000 turns of wire wound over it. If the current carried is 5 A, the magnetic field on its axis, near the centre of the solenoid is approximately (permeability of free space, $\mu_0 = 4\pi\times10^{-7}$ T-mA^{-1}) **[MGIMS]**

(a) 0.63×10^{-2} T (b) 1.26×10^{-2} T
(c) 2.51×10^{-2} T (d) 6.3 T

33 A part of a long wire carrying a current i is bent into a circle of radius r as shown in figure. The net magnetic field at the centre O of the circular loop is **[JCECE]**

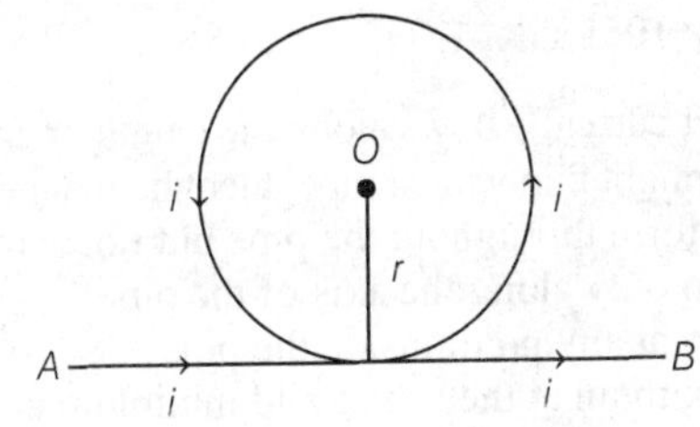

(a) $\frac{\mu_0 i}{4r}$ (b) $\frac{\mu_0 i}{2r}$
(c) $\frac{\mu_0 i}{2\pi r}(\pi+1)$ (d) $\frac{\mu_0 i}{2\pi r}(\pi-1)$

2009

34 A wire is wound in the form of a solenoid of length l and distance d. When a strong current is passed through a solenoid, there is a tendency to **[UP CPMT]**

(a) increase l but decrease d
(b) keep both l and d constant
(c) decrease l but increase d
(d) increase both l and d

35 Which of the following relation represents Biot-Savart's law? **[BVP]**

(a) $d\mathbf{B} = \frac{\mu_0}{4\pi}\cdot\frac{Id\mathbf{l}\times\mathbf{r}}{r}$ (b) $d\mathbf{B} = \frac{\mu_0}{4\pi}\cdot\frac{Id\mathbf{l}\times\mathbf{r}}{\mathbf{r}^2}$
(c) $d\mathbf{B} = \frac{\mu_0}{4\pi}\cdot\frac{Id\mathbf{l}\times\mathbf{r}}{r^3}$ (d) $d\mathbf{B} = \frac{\mu_0}{4\pi}\cdot\frac{Id\mathbf{l}\times\mathbf{r}}{r^4}$

36 Two concentric circular loops of radii R and $2R$ carry currents of $2i$ and i respectively, in opposite sense (i.e. clockwise in one coil and counter clockwise in the other coil). The resultant magnetic field at their common centre is **[Manipal]**

(a) $\mu_0\frac{i}{4R}$ (b) $\mu_0\frac{5i}{4R}$
(c) $\mu_0\frac{3i}{4R}$ (d) $\mu_0\frac{i}{2R}$

37 A straight conductor carrying current I. If the magnetic field at a distance r is 0.4 T, then magnetic field at a distance $2r$ will be **[OJEE]**

(a) 0.4 T (b) 0.1 T
(c) 0.8 T (d) 0.2 T

38 A charge q coulomb makes n revolutions in one second in a circular orbit of radius r. The magnetic field at the centre of the orbit (in $NA^{-1}m^{-1}$) is **[J&K CET]**

(a) $\frac{2\pi rn}{q} \times 10^{-7}$ (b) $\left(\frac{2\pi q}{r}\right) \times 10^{-7}$

(c) $\left(\frac{2\pi q}{nr}\right) \times 10^{-7}$ (d) $\left(\frac{2\pi nq}{r}\right) \times 10^{-7}$

39 Magnetic field at the centre of a coil in the form of a square of side 2 cm carrying a current of 1.414 A is **[J&K CET]**

(a) 8×10^{-5} T (b) 18×10^{-5} T

(c) 1.5×10^{-5} T (d) 6×10^{-5} T

40 A direct current I flows along the length or an infinitely long straight thin walled pipe, then the magnetic field is **[KCET]**

(a) uniform throughout the pipe but not zero
(b) zero only along the axis of the pipe
(c) zero at any point inside the pipe
(d) maximum at the centre and minimum at the edge

41 Two parallel infinitely long current carrying wires are shown in figure. If resultant magnetic field at point A is zero, then determine the value of current I. **[AIIMS]**

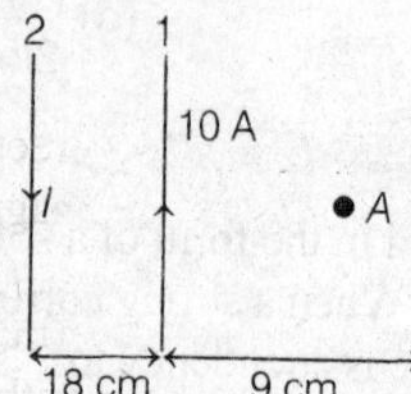

(a) 50 A (b) 15 A (c) 30 A (d) 25 A

42 The magnitude of magnetic induction for a current carrying toroid of uniform cross-section is **[JCECE]**

(a) uniform over the whole cross-section
(b) maximum on the outer edge
(c) maximum on the inner edge
(d) maximum at the centre of cross-section

43 Magnetic field intensity H at the centre of a circular loop of radius r carrying current I ampere is **[CG PMT]**

(a) $\frac{r}{I}$ oersted (b) $\frac{2\pi I}{r}$ oersted

(c) $\frac{I}{2\pi r}$ oersted (d) $\frac{2\pi r}{I}$ oersted

2008

44 Electron revolving with speed v is producing magnetic field B at centre. Find the relation between radius of path, B and v. **[JIPMER]**

(a) $B \propto \frac{v}{r}$ (b) $B \propto \frac{v}{r^2}$

(c) $B \propto \frac{v^2}{r}$ (d) $B \propto \frac{v^2}{r^2}$

45 Two concentric coils each of radius equal to 2π cm are placed at right angles to each other. 3 A and 4 A are the currents flowing in each coil, respectively. The magnetic induction (in Wb m^{-2}) at the centre of the coils will be (Take, $\mu_0 = 4\pi \times 10^{-7}$ Wb A^{-1}m^{-1}). **[AIIMS]**

(a) 12×10^{-5} (b) 10^{-5} (c) 5×10^{-5} (d) 7×10^{-5}

46 **Assertion** The magnetic field produced by a current carrying solenoid is independent of its length and cross-sectional area. **[AIIMS]**

Reason The magnetic field inside the solenoid is uniform.

(a) Both Assertion and Reason are correct and Reason is the correct explanation of Assertion.
(b) Both Assertion and Reason are correct but Reason is not the correct explanation of Assertion.
(c) Assertion is correct but Reason is incorrect.
(d) Both Assertion and Reason are incorrect.

47 Two identical wires A and B have the same length L and carry the same current I. Wire A is bent into a circle of radius R and wire B is bent to form a square of side a. If B_1 and B_2 are the values of magnetic induction at the centre of the circle and the centre of the square respectively, then the ratio B_1/B_2 is **[BHU]**

(a) $\frac{\pi^2}{8}$ (b) $\frac{\pi^2}{8\sqrt{2}}$ (c) $\frac{\pi^2}{16}$ (d) $\frac{\pi^2}{16\sqrt{2}}$

48 A vertical straight conductor carries a current upward. A point P lies to the East of it at a small distance and another point Q lies to the West at the same distance. The magnetic field at P is **[Manipal]**

(a) greater than at Q
(b) same as at Q
(c) less than at Q
(d) greater or less than at Q depending upon the strength of current

49 The magnetic field at the centre of a circular current carrying conductor of radius r is B_c. The magnetic field on its axis at a distance r from the centre is B_a. The value of $B_c : B_a$ will be **[KCET]**

(a) $1:\sqrt{2}$ (b) $1:2\sqrt{2}$ (c) $2\sqrt{2}:1$ (d) $\sqrt{2}:1$

50 Current I is flowing in conductor shaped as shown in the figure. The radius of the curved part is r and the length of straight portion is very large. The value of the magnetic field at the centre O will be **[KCET]**

(a) $\frac{\mu_0 I}{4\pi r}\left(\frac{3\pi}{2}+1\right)$ (b) $\frac{\mu_0 I}{4\pi r}\left(\frac{3\pi}{2}-1\right)$

(c) $\frac{\mu_0 I}{4\pi r}\left(\frac{\pi}{2}+1\right)$ (d) $\frac{\mu_0 I}{4\pi r}\left(\frac{\pi}{2}-1\right)$

51 A circular coil of wire of radius r has N turns and carries a current I. The magnetic induction B at a point on the axis of the coil at a distance $\sqrt{3}r$ from its centre is **[EAMCET]**

(a) $\frac{\mu_0 IN}{4r}$ (b) $\frac{\mu_0 IN}{8r}$ (c) $\frac{\mu_0 IN}{16r}$ (d) $\frac{\mu_0 IN}{32r}$

52 Two concentric circular coils of 10 turns each are situated in the same plane. Their radii are 20 cm and 40 cm and they carry respectively 0.2 A and 0.3 A currents in opposite direction. The magnetic field (in tesla) at the centre is **[BCECE]**

(a) $35\mu_0 / 4$ (b) $\mu_0 / 80$
(c) $7\mu_0 / 80$ (d) $5\mu_0 / 4$

2007

53 A long solenoid carrying a current produces a magnetic field B along its axis. If the current is doubled and the number of turns per cm is halved, the new value of the magnetic field is **[BHU]**

(a) $2B$ (b) $4B$ (c) $B/2$ (d) B

54 The strength of the magnetic field around a long straight wire, carrying current, is **[Kerala CEE]**

(a) same everywhere around the wire at any distance
(b) inversely proportional to the distance from the wire
(c) inversely proportional to the square of the distance from the wire
(d) directly proportional to the square of the distance from the wire
(e) directly proportional to the distance from the wire

55 Two wires A and B are of lengths 40 cm and 30 cm. A is bent into a circle of radius r and B into an arc of radius r. A current I_1 is passed through A and I_2 through B. To have the same magnetic inductions at the centre, the ratio of $I_1 : I_2$ is **[J&K CET]**

(a) 3 : 4 (b) 3 : 5 (c) 2 : 3 (d) 4 : 3

56 A square wire of each side l carries a current I. What is the magnetic field at the mid-point of the square? **[Punjab PMET]**

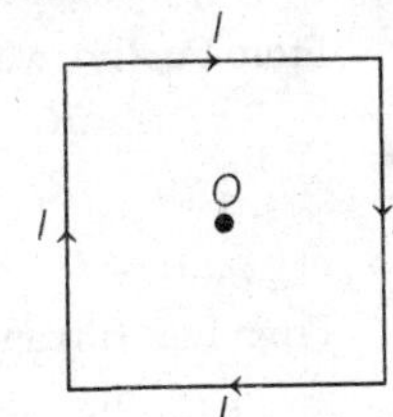

(a) $4\sqrt{2}\frac{\mu_0}{4\pi}\frac{I}{l}$ (b) $8\sqrt{2}\frac{\mu_0}{4\pi}\frac{I}{l}$

(c) $16\sqrt{2}\frac{\mu_0}{4\pi}\frac{I}{l}$ (d) $32\sqrt{2}\frac{\mu_0}{4\pi}\frac{I}{l}$

57 A long solenoid has 20 turns cm^{-1}. The current necessary to produce a magnetic field of 20 mT inside the solenoid is approximately **[AMU]**

(a) 1 A (b) 2 A (c) 4 A (d) 8 A

58 A circular coil carrying a certain current produces a magnetic field B_0 at its centre. The coil is now rewound so as to have 3 turns and the same current is passed through it. The new magnetic field at the centre is **[KCET]**

(a) $B_0/9$ (b) $9B_0$ (c) $B_0/3$ (d) $3B_0$

59 Two identical coils having same number of turns and carrying equal current have common centre and their planes are at right angles to each other. What is the ratio of magnitude of the resultant magnetic field at the centre and magnetic field due to one of the coils at the centre? **[Guj CET]**

(a) $1:\sqrt{2}$ (b) $\sqrt{2}:1$ (c) $1:1$ (d) $2:1$

2006

60 Circular loop of a wire and a long straight wire carry currents I_c and I_e respectively, as shown in figure. Assuming that these are placed in the same plane. The magnetic field will be zero at the centre of the loop when the separation H is **[AIIMS]**

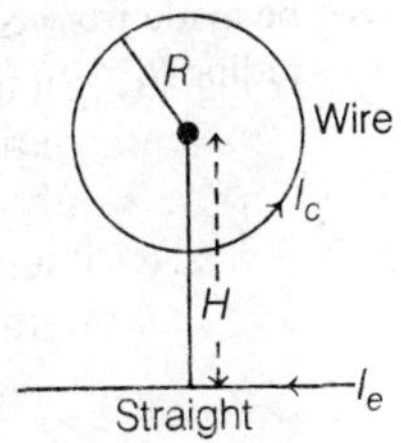

(a) $\frac{I_e R}{I_c \pi}$ (b) $\frac{I_c R}{I_e \pi}$ (c) $\frac{\pi I_c}{I_e R}$ (d) $\frac{I_e \pi}{I_c R}$

61 A wire oriented in the East-West direction carries a current eastward. Direction of the magnetic field at a point to the South of the wire is **[J&K CET]**

(a) vertically down (b) vertically up
(c) North-East (d) South-East

62 In the adjacent figure is shown a closed path P. A long straight conductor carrying a current I passes through O and perpendicular to the plane of the paper. Then, which of the following holds good? **[BCECE]**

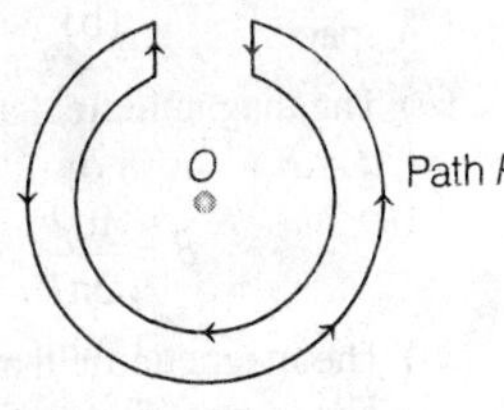

(a) $\int_p \mathbf{B} \cdot d\mathbf{l} = 0$ (b) $\int_p \mathbf{B} \cdot d\mathbf{l} = \mu_0 I$

(c) $\int_p \mathbf{B} \cdot d\mathbf{l} > \mu_0 I$ (d) None of these

2005

63 Two long parallel wires P and Q are both perpendicular to the plane of the paper with distance 5 m between them. If P and Q carry current of 2.5 A and 5 A respectively, in the same direction, then the magnetic field at point half way between the wires is **[Kerala CEE]**

(a) $\frac{\sqrt{3}\mu_0}{2\pi}$ (b) $\frac{\mu_0}{\pi}$ (c) $\frac{3\mu_0}{2\pi}$ (d) $\frac{\mu_0}{2\pi}$

(e) $\frac{\sqrt{3}\mu_0}{\pi}$

Answers

1 (b)	2 (a)	3 (a)	4 (c)	5 (a)	6 (b)	7 (a)	8 (c)	9 (b)	10 (b)
11 (c)	12 (d)	13 (d)	14 (b)	15 (d)	16 (b)	17 (b)	18 (a)	19 (a)	20 (d)
21 (c)	22 (c)	23 (d)	24 (a)	25 (c)	26 (a)	27 (c)	28 (a)	29 (b)	30 (b)
31 (d)	32 (b)	33 (c)	34 (b)	35 (c)	36 (c)	37 (d)	38 (d)	39 (a)	40 (c)
41 (c)	42 (a)	43 (b)	44 (b)	45 (c)	46 (b)	47 (b)	48 (b)	49 (c)	50 (a)
51 (c)	52 (d)	53 (d)	54 (b)	55 (a)	56 (b)	57 (d)	58 (b)	59 (b)	60 (a)
61 (a)	62 (b)	63 (d)							

Explanations

1 *(b)* The cylinder can be considered to be made from concentric circles of radius *R*.

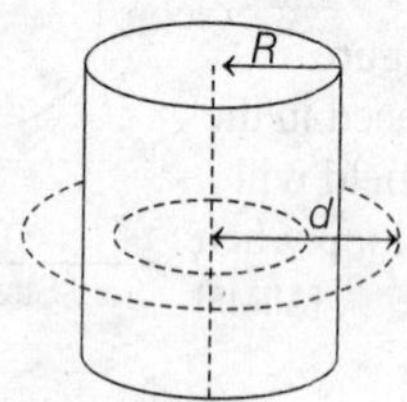

(*i*) The magnetic field at a point outside cylinder, i.e. $d > R$.

From Ampere's circuital law,

$$\oint B \cdot dl = \mu_0 I \Rightarrow B \int dl = \mu_0 I$$

$$B(2\pi d) = \mu_0 I \quad \Rightarrow \quad B = \frac{\mu_0 I}{2\pi d}$$

where, μ_0 = permeability of free space.

(*ii*) The magnetic field at surface, i.e. $d = R$,

$$B = \frac{\mu_0 I}{2\pi R}$$

(*iii*) The magnetic field at inside point. The current for a point inside the cylinder is given by I' = current per unit cross-sectional area of cylinder × cross-section of loop

$$= \frac{I}{\pi R^2} \pi d^2 = \frac{I d^2}{R^2}$$

$$\therefore B = \frac{\mu_0 I'}{2\pi d} = \frac{\mu_0 I d^2}{2\pi R^2 d} = \frac{\mu_0 I}{2\pi R^2} d$$

So, the variation of magnetic field can be plotted as

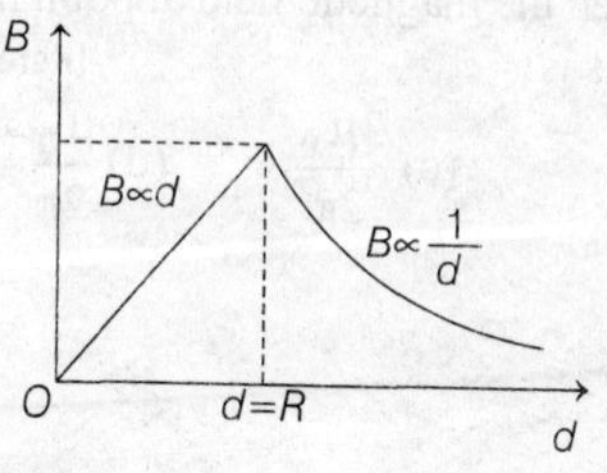

2 *(a)* The magnetic field within the turns of toroid,

$$B = \frac{\mu_0 N I}{2\pi r}$$

where, N = number of turns,

I = current in loops

and r = radius of each turn.

Given, $N_1 = 200$, $N_2 = 100$, $r_1 = 40$ cm, $r_2 = 20$ cm and current I is same, then

$$\frac{B_1}{B_2} = \frac{\mu_0 N_1 I}{2\pi r_1} \times \frac{2\pi r_2}{\mu_0 N_2 I}$$

Substituting the given values in the above relation, we get

$$\frac{B_1}{B_2} = \left(\frac{N_1}{N_2}\right)\left(\frac{r_2}{r_1}\right)$$

$$= \left(\frac{200}{100}\right)\left(\frac{20}{40}\right)$$

$$= 2 \times \frac{1}{2} = 1$$

$$\therefore \quad B_1 : B_2 = 1 : 1$$

3 *(a)* The magnetic field at the centre of an arc subtended at an angle θ is given by

$$B = \frac{\mu_0 i}{2R} \times \frac{\theta}{2\pi}$$

Then, the magnetic field due to larger arc *AB* is

$$B_1 = \frac{\mu_0 i_1}{2R} \times \frac{270}{2\pi} \quad \ldots\text{(i)}$$

which acts in inward direction according to right hand thumb rule.

And magnetic field due to smaller arc *AB* is

$$B_2 = \frac{\mu_0 i_2}{2R} \times \frac{90}{2\pi} \quad \ldots\text{(ii)}$$

which acts in outward direction.

The resultant magnetic field,

$$B_R = B_1 + B_2$$

$$= -\frac{\mu_0 i_1 \times 270}{4\pi R} + \frac{\mu_0 i_2 \times 90}{4\pi R}$$

[from eqs. (i) and (ii)] ...(iii)

which acts in inward direction as $B_1 > B_2$.

Two arcs can also be seen as the two resistances in parallel combination.

So, the potential across them will be same, i.e.

$$V_1 = V_2$$

$$i_1 R_1 = i_2 R_2 \quad \ldots\text{(iv)}$$

where, R_1 and R_2 = resistance of respective segments

The wire is uniform, so

$$\frac{R_1}{R_2} = \frac{L_1}{L_2} = \frac{R \times 270}{R \times 90}$$

[∵ length of arc = radius × angle]

From Eq. (iv), we get

$$\Rightarrow \quad \frac{i_1}{i_2} = \frac{R_2}{R_1} = \frac{90}{270} = \frac{1}{3}$$

or $\quad 3i_1 = i_2 \quad \ldots\text{(v)}$

From Eqs. (iii) and (v), we get

$$B_R = \frac{\mu_0}{4\pi R}(-270 i_1 + 90 i_2)$$

$$= \frac{\mu_0}{4\pi R}[-270 i_1 + 90(3i_1)]$$

$$= \frac{\mu_0}{4\pi R}(-270 i_1 + 270 i_1) = 0$$

4 *(c)* Given, radius of identical circular loops, $\quad R = 10 \text{ cm} = 10^{-1}$ m

Current, $I = \frac{7}{2}$ A

Distance from both circular loop at point P,

$$x_1 = x_2 = x = 5\text{ cm}$$
$$= 5 \times 10^{-2}\text{ m}$$

From figure, according to Maxwell's right hand thumb rule, it is clear that magnetic field will be in same direction by both the coils,

i.e. $B = B_1 + B_2$

$$= \frac{\mu_0 IR^2}{2(R^2 + x^2)^{3/2}} + \frac{\mu_0 IR^2}{2(R^2 + x^2)^{3/2}}$$

$$= \frac{\mu_0 I R^2}{(R^2 + x^2)^{3/2}}$$

$$= \frac{\mu_0 \times 7/2 \times (10^{-1})^2}{[(0.1)^2 + (0.05)^2]^{3/2}}$$

$$= \frac{56}{\sqrt{5}} \mu_0 \text{T}$$

5 *(a)* $\because$ $B\text{ (at }P) = \dfrac{\mu_0 I}{4\pi d}(\cos\theta_1 - \cos\theta_2)$

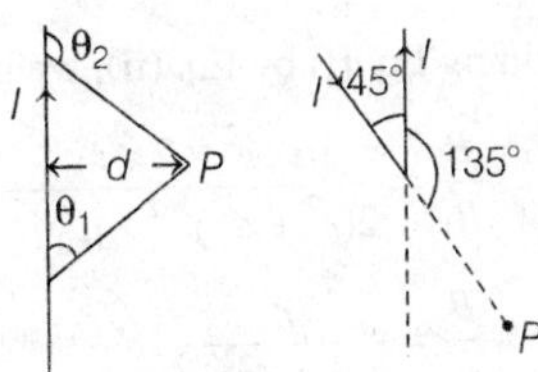

In given case, $d = R\sin 45° = R/\sqrt{2}$

$$\theta_1 = 135°, \theta_2 = 180°$$

$\therefore$ $B\text{ (at }P)$

$$= \frac{\mu_0 I}{4\pi(R/\sqrt{2})}[\cos 135° - \cos 180°]$$

$$= \frac{\mu_0 I}{4\pi R}\sqrt{2}\left[\frac{-1}{\sqrt{2}} - (-1)\right]$$

$$= \frac{\mu_0 I}{4\pi R}\sqrt{2}\left(\frac{\sqrt{2}-1}{\sqrt{2}}\right)$$

or $B\text{ (at }P) = \dfrac{\mu_0 I}{4\pi R}(\sqrt{2} - 1)\text{ T}$

6 *(b)* Here, $dl = dx = 1\text{ cm} = 10^{-2}\text{ m}$,

$$i = 10\text{ A}, r = 0.5\text{ m}$$

$$\therefore \quad dB = \frac{\mu_0}{4\pi}\cdot\frac{i(dl \times r)}{r^3}$$

$$= \frac{\mu_0}{4\pi}\cdot\frac{idl}{r^2}(\hat{\mathbf{i}} \times \hat{\mathbf{j}})$$

$$= \frac{\mu_0}{4\pi}\cdot\frac{idl}{r^2}\hat{\mathbf{k}}$$

$$= \frac{10^{-7} \times 10 \times 10^{-2}}{(0.5)^2}\hat{\mathbf{k}}$$

$$= 4 \times 10^{-8}\hat{\mathbf{k}}\text{T}$$

7 *(a)* According to Biot-Savart's law, the magnetic induction at a point to a current carrying element $i\delta l$ is given by

$$\delta\mathbf{B} = \frac{\mu_0}{4\pi}\cdot\frac{i\delta\mathbf{l} \times \mathbf{r}}{r^3}$$

or $\quad B = \dfrac{\mu_0}{4\pi}\cdot\dfrac{i\delta l\sin\theta}{r^2}$

Directed normal to plane containing $\delta\mathbf{l}$ and $\mathbf{r}$, θ being angle between $\delta\mathbf{l}$ and $\mathbf{r}$.

Field due to semicircular arc

Now, angle between a current element $\delta\mathbf{l}$ of semicircular arc and the radius vector of the element to point c is $\pi/2$. Therefore, the magnitude of magnetic induction B at O due to this element is

$$\delta B = \frac{\mu_0}{4\pi}\cdot\frac{i\delta l\sin\pi/2}{r^2} = \frac{\mu_0 i\delta l}{4\pi r^2}$$

Hence, magnetic induction due to whole semicircular loop is

$$B = \Sigma\delta B = \Sigma\frac{\mu_0}{4\pi}\cdot\frac{i\delta l}{r^2}$$

$$= \frac{\mu_0}{4\pi}\frac{i}{r^2}\Sigma\delta l$$

$$= \frac{\mu_0 i}{4\pi r^2}(\pi r) = \frac{\mu_0 i}{4r}$$

The magnetic field due to ab and de is zero, because $\theta = 0°$ or $180°$. So, net magnetic field is

$$B = \frac{\mu_0 i}{4r}$$

8 *(c)* Magnetic field due to straight wire above O is zero,

i.e. $B_1 = 0$ (since, $\theta = 0°$)

The magnetic field due to semicircular part,

$$B_2 = \left(\frac{\mu_0 nI}{2r}\right) = \frac{\mu_0(1/2)I}{2r} = \frac{\mu_0 I}{4r}$$

The magnetic field due to lower straight portion,

$$B_3 = \frac{\mu_0 I}{4\pi r}(\sin 0° + \sin 90°)$$

$$= \frac{\mu_0 I}{4\pi r} \quad \text{(upward)}$$

Net magnetic field,

$$B = B_1 + B_2 + B_3$$

$$= 0 + \frac{\mu_0 I}{4r} + \frac{\mu_0 I}{4\pi r}$$

$$= \frac{\mu_0 I}{4r} + \frac{\mu_0 I}{4\pi r} \quad \text{(upwards)}$$

9 *(b)* Consider two Amperian loops of radius $a/2$ and $2a$ as shown in the figure. Applying Ampere's circuital law for these loops, we get

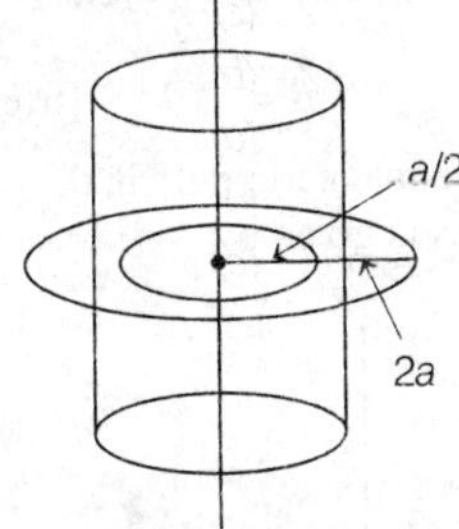

$$\oint \mathbf{B}\cdot d\mathbf{L} = \mu_0 I_{\text{enclosed}}$$

For the smaller loop,

$$B \times 2\pi\frac{a}{2} = \mu_0 \times \frac{I}{\pi a^2} \times \pi\left(\frac{a}{2}\right)^2$$

$$= \mu_0 I \times \frac{1}{4} = \frac{\mu_0 I}{4}$$

$\Rightarrow$ $B = \dfrac{\mu_0 I}{4\pi a}$, at distance $a/2$ from the axis of the wire.

Similarly, for bigger Amperian loop,

$$B' \times 2\pi\,(2a) = \mu_0 I$$

[total current enclosed by Amperian loop is I]

$$\Rightarrow \quad B' = \frac{\mu_0 I}{4\pi a}$$

at distance $2a$ from the axis of the wire.

So, ratio of $\dfrac{B}{B'} = \dfrac{\mu_0 I}{4\pi a} \times \dfrac{4\pi a}{\mu_0 I} = 1$

10 *(b)* A long wire with steady current is bent into a current carrying circle of single turn with radius R.

I I C R

[Here, $2\pi R = l$]

Hence, magnetic field at centre is

$$B = \frac{\mu_0 I}{2R} = \frac{\mu_0 I}{2\left(\dfrac{l}{2\pi}\right)} = \frac{\mu_0 \pi I}{l} \quad \text{...(i)}$$

Now, when wire is bent into a circular loop of n turns.

R' [radius of single loop]

l

$$B' = \frac{\mu_0 nI}{2R'}$$

Here, $n(2\pi R') = l$

$$R' = \frac{l}{2\pi n}$$

$$\Rightarrow \quad B' = \frac{\mu_0 nI}{2l}(2\pi n) = \frac{\mu_0 n^2 \pi I}{l}$$

$$B' = n^2 B \quad \text{[from Eq. (i)]}$$

11 (c) The magnetic field in the different regions is given by

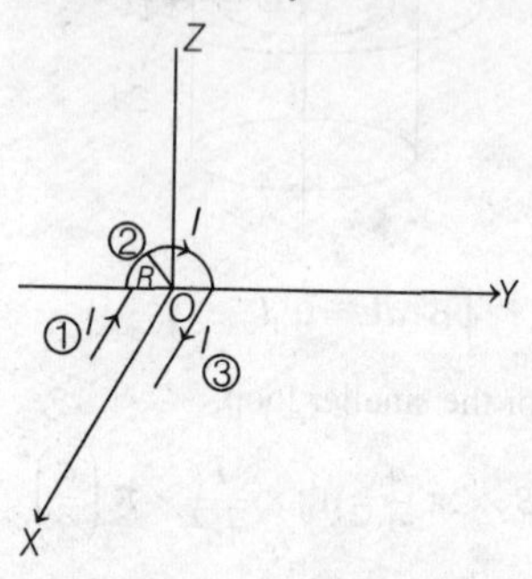

Magnetic field at O due to semi infinite wire, $\mathbf{B}_1 = \frac{\mu_0}{4\pi} \times \frac{I}{R}(-\hat{\mathbf{k}})$

$$\mathbf{B}_3 = \frac{\mu_0 I}{4\pi R}(-\hat{\mathbf{k}})$$

Magnetic field at O due to semi-circular arc in yz-plane,

$$\mathbf{B}_2 = \frac{\mu_0 I}{4R}(-\hat{\mathbf{i}})$$

The net magnetic field at the centre O

$$\mathbf{B} = \mathbf{B}_1 + \mathbf{B}_2 + \mathbf{B}_3$$

$$= \frac{\mu_0 I}{4\pi R}(-2\hat{\mathbf{k}}) + \frac{\mu_0 I}{4R}(-\hat{\mathbf{i}})$$

$$= -\frac{\mu_0 I}{4\pi R}(2\hat{\mathbf{k}} + \pi\hat{\mathbf{i}})$$

$$\therefore \quad \mathbf{B} = \frac{-\mu_0 I}{4\pi R}(\pi\hat{\mathbf{i}} + 2\hat{\mathbf{k}})$$

12 (d) As $I = q/t$

So, for an electron revolving in a circular orbit of radius r

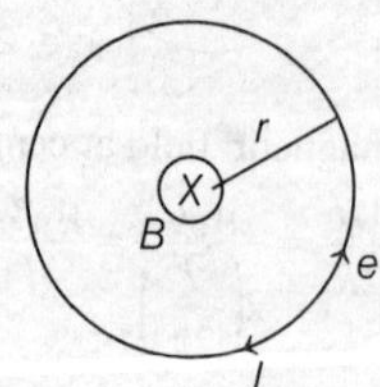

$q = e$ and $t = T$

$$\Rightarrow I = \frac{e}{T} = \frac{e}{2\pi/\omega} = \frac{\omega e}{2\pi} = \frac{2\pi ne}{2\pi} = ne$$

$$[\because \omega = 2\pi n]$$

The magnetic field produced at the centre is

$$B = \frac{\mu_0 I}{2r} = \frac{\mu_0 ne}{2r}$$

13 (d) The given situation can be shown as

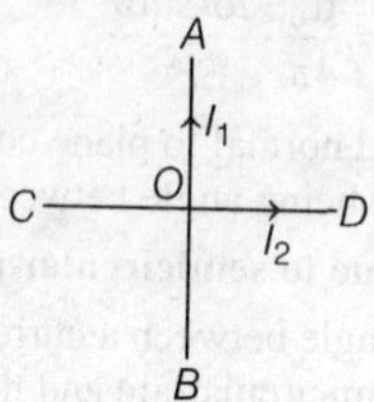

The point P is lying at a distance d along the Z-axis,

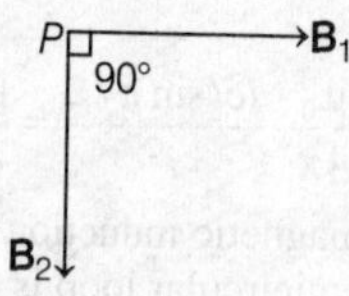

$$|\mathbf{B}_1| = \frac{\mu_0}{2\pi}\frac{I_1}{d} \text{ and } |\mathbf{B}_2| = \frac{\mu_0}{2\pi}\frac{I_2}{d}$$

$$B_{\text{net}} = \sqrt{B_1^2 + B_2^2}$$

$$\Rightarrow \quad B_{\text{net}} = \frac{\mu_0}{2\pi}\cdot\frac{1}{d}(I_1^2 + I_2^2)^{1/2}$$

14 (b) Magnetic field **B** at any point in the open space inside the toroid is zero, because the Ampere loop encloses net current which equals to zero in free space.

15 (d) We know that,

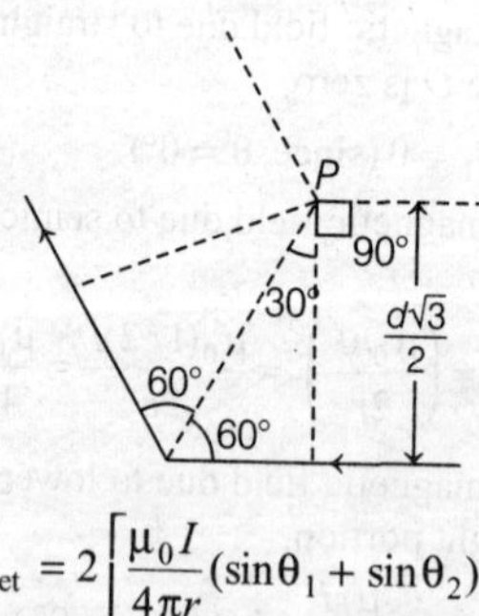

$$B_{\text{net}} = 2\left[\frac{\mu_0 I}{4\pi r}(\sin\theta_1 + \sin\theta_2)\right]$$

$$= 2\left[\frac{\mu_0}{4\pi} \times \frac{I}{\frac{d\sqrt{3}}{2}} \times (\sin 90^\circ + \sin 30^\circ)\right]$$

$$= 2\left[\frac{\mu_0}{4\pi} \times \frac{2I}{d\sqrt{3}} \times \left(1 + \frac{1}{2}\right)\right]$$

$$= 2\left[\frac{\mu_0}{4\pi} \times \frac{2I}{d\sqrt{3}} \times \frac{3}{2}\right] = \frac{\sqrt{3}\,\mu_0 I}{2\pi d}$$

16 (b) As magnetic field at an axis of current carrying loop is given by

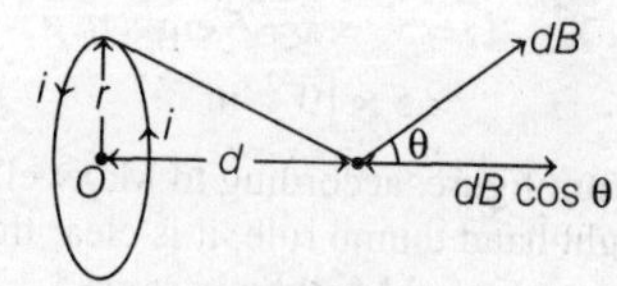

$$B = \frac{\mu_0 i r^2}{2(r^2 + d^2)^{3/2}} \quad \text{...(i)}$$

where, i = current in loop,
r = radius of loop = 3 cm
d = distance on axis = 4 cm,
and B = magnetic field of current carrying loop.

Now, B_1 = magnetic field at centre, $d = 0$

$$\text{Now, } B_1 = \frac{\mu_0 i r^2}{2(r^2 + 0^2)^{3/2}}$$

$$= \frac{\mu_0 i r^2}{2r^3} \quad \text{....(ii)}$$

Dividing Eq. (i) by Eq. (ii), we get

$$\frac{B}{B_1} = \frac{\mu_0 i r^2 \times 2 \times r^3}{2(r^2 + d^2)^{3/2} \times \mu_0 i r^2}$$

$$\Rightarrow \quad \frac{B}{B_1} = \frac{r^3}{(r^2 + d^2)^{3/2}}$$

$$\Rightarrow \quad \frac{B}{B_1} = \frac{(3)^3}{(3^2 + 4^2)^{3/2}}$$

$$\Rightarrow \quad \frac{B}{B_1} = \frac{27}{(25)^{3/2}}$$

$$\Rightarrow \quad \frac{54\mu\text{T}}{B_1} = \frac{27}{5^3}$$

$$B_1 = \frac{54 \times 125}{27}$$

$$\Rightarrow \quad B_1 = 250\,\mu\text{T}$$

17 (b) The magnetic field inside the solenoid is given by

$$B = \mu_0 nI$$

where,
n = number of turns per unit length
and I = current in coil.

Now, we have

$$n = \frac{N}{L} = \frac{400}{0.4 \times 10^{-2}} = 10^5$$

and $\mu_0 = 4\pi \times 10^{-7}$ Tm/A

$$\therefore \quad B = 4 \times 3.14 \times 10^{-7} \times 10^5 \times 5$$

$$= 628 \times 10^{-3}\ \text{T}$$

18 (a) The magnetic field (B) at the centre of circular current carrying coil of radius R and current I is given by

$$B = \frac{\mu_0 I}{2R}$$

Similarly,
if current $= 2I$, then

Magnetic field $= \frac{\mu_0 2I}{2R} = 2B$

So, resultant magnetic field

$$= \sqrt{B^2 + (2B)^2} = \sqrt{5B^2}$$

$$= \sqrt{5}\, B = \sqrt{5}\frac{\mu_0 I}{2R}$$

19 (a) Inside the tube, magnetic field is zero as no current enclosed by Amperean loop.

20 (d) Magnetic field, $B = \frac{\mu_0 \mu_r N i}{2\pi r}$

$$1 = \frac{4\pi \times 10^{-7} \times \mu_r \times 400 \times 2}{40 \times 10^{-2}}$$

$[\because 2\pi r = l]$

$\therefore \mu_r = 400$

21 (c) Magnetic field at the centre due to either arm

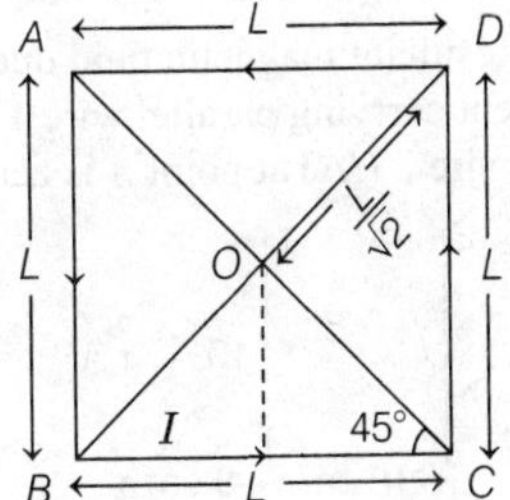

$$B_1 = \frac{\mu_0}{4\pi} \times \frac{I}{(L/2)}[\sin 45° + \sin 45°]$$

$$= \frac{\mu_0}{4\pi} \times \frac{2\sqrt{2}I}{L}$$

Field at centre due to the four arms of the square,

$$B = 4B_1$$

$$= 4\left(\frac{\mu_0}{4\pi} \times \frac{2\sqrt{2}I}{L}\right)$$

$$= \frac{\mu_0}{\pi} \times \frac{2\sqrt{2}I}{L}$$

i.e. $B \propto 1/L$

22 (c) Magnetic field, $B_1 = \frac{\mu_0}{4\pi} \cdot \frac{2i}{R}$

and $B_2 = \frac{\mu_0}{4\pi} \cdot \frac{2 \cdot 2i}{R}$

$$B_2 - B_1 = \frac{\mu_0}{4\pi} \cdot \frac{2i}{R} = B$$

$\therefore \quad B_1 = B - B_2$

Now, $B_2 = 0$, as $I_2 = 0$.

$\therefore \quad B_{net} = B_1 = B$

23 (d) If a coil of radius R is carrying current I, then magnetic field on its axis at a distance x from its centre is given by

$$B_{axis} = \frac{\mu_0}{4\pi} \frac{2\pi I R^2}{(x^2 + R^2)^{3/2}} \quad \text{...(i)}$$

At centre, $B_{centre} = \frac{\mu_0 I}{2R}$ ...(ii)

Dividing Eq. (i) by Eq. (ii), we get

$$\frac{B_{axis}}{B_{centre}} = \frac{\mu_0 I R^2}{2(x^2 + R^2)^{3/2}} \times \frac{2R}{\mu_0 I}$$

$$\Rightarrow \frac{R^3}{(x^2 + R^2)^{3/2}} = \frac{1}{8}$$

$$\text{or} \quad \frac{R}{(x^2 + R^2)^{1/2}} = \frac{1}{2}$$

$$\Rightarrow \quad x = \sqrt{3}R$$

24 (a) In case of straight conductor of infinite length, the magnetic field is given by

$$B = \frac{\mu_0}{4\pi} \times \frac{2i}{a}$$

$$\Rightarrow 10^{-6} = \frac{4\pi \times 10^{-7} \times 2i}{4\pi \times 0.02}$$

$$\Rightarrow 10^{-6} = \frac{10^{-7} \times 2 \times i}{0.02}$$

$$\Rightarrow \quad i = 0.1 \text{ A}$$

25 (c) $B = \frac{\mu_0 N i}{l}$, where N = total number of turns, l = length of the solenoid.

$$\Rightarrow 0.2 = \frac{4\pi \times 10^{-7} \times N \times 10}{0.8}$$

$$\Rightarrow N = \frac{4 \times 10^4}{\pi}$$

Since, N turns are made from the winding wire, so length of the wire $(L) = 2\pi r \times N$

$[\because 2\pi r = \text{length of each turns}]$

$$\Rightarrow L = 2\pi \times 3 \times 10^{-2} \times \frac{4 \times 10^4}{\pi}$$

$$= 2.4 \times 10^3 \text{m}$$

26 (a) In the following figure, magnetic field at O due to sections 1, 2, 3 and 4 are considered as B_1, B_2, B_3 and B_4, respectively.

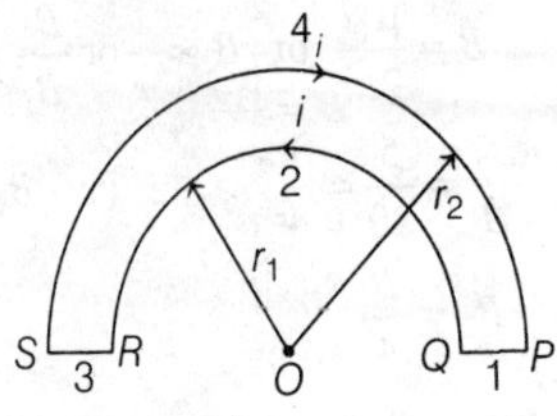

$$B_1 = B_3 = 0$$

$$B_2 = \frac{\mu_0}{4} \cdot \frac{i}{r_1} \quad \text{(vertically upward)}$$

$$B_4 = \frac{\mu_0}{4} \cdot \frac{i}{r_2} \quad \text{(vertically downward)}$$

So, $B_{net} = B_2 - B_4$

$$= \frac{\mu_0}{4}\left(\frac{1}{r_1} - \frac{1}{r_2}\right)i$$

27 (c) The magnetic field at the centre of a circle is given by

$$B = \frac{\mu_0 i}{2r}$$

where, i is current and r is the radius of circle.

Also, $i = \frac{q}{t}$

For helium nucleus, $q = 2e$

$$\therefore \quad i = \frac{2e}{t}$$

$$\text{So,} \quad B = \frac{\mu_0 \cdot 2e}{2rt}$$

$$= \frac{\mu_0 \times 2 \times 1.6 \times 10^{-19}}{2 \times 0.8 \times 2}$$

$$= 10^{-19} \mu_0$$

28 (a) Magnetic field, $B = \mu_0 n i$

$$= 4\pi \times 10^{-7} \times 5 \times 1000$$

$$= 2\pi \times 10^{-3} \text{T}$$

($\because n = 10$ turns/cm or $n = 1000$ turns/m)

29 (b) The magnetic field due to small element conductor of length is given by

$$dB = \frac{\mu_0}{4\pi} \cdot \frac{i\,dl \sin\theta}{r^2}$$

This value will be maximum when

$$\sin\theta = 1 = \sin 90°$$

$$\theta = 90°$$

30 *(b)* The magnetic field at a distance r from the straight wire,

$$B = \frac{\mu_0 i}{2\pi r} \text{ or } B \propto \frac{1}{r} \text{ or } \frac{B_2}{B_1} = \frac{r_1}{r_2}$$

$$\therefore \quad \frac{B_2}{B} = \frac{5}{20} = \frac{1}{4} \qquad (\because B_1 = B)$$

$$\text{or} \quad B_2 = \frac{B}{4}$$

31 *(d)* Magnetic field due to wire A at point P is given as

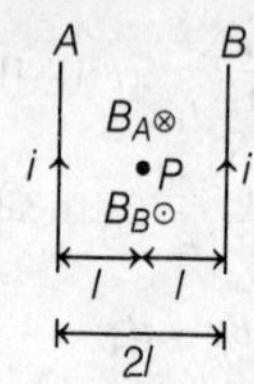

where, $2l = r$.

$$B_A = \frac{\mu_0}{2\pi}\frac{i}{l}$$

$B_A \Rightarrow \otimes$ [perpendicular to plane inward direction]

Magnetic field due to wire (B) at point P is given as

$$B_B = \frac{\mu_0}{2\pi}\frac{i}{l}$$

$$B_B \Rightarrow \odot$$

[perpendicular to plane outward direction]

As, $\quad B_A = B_B$ and $\mathbf{B}_A = -\mathbf{B}_B$

$\therefore$ Net magnetic field $= B$

$$= \mathbf{B}_A + \mathbf{B}_B = 0$$

32 *(b)* The magnetic field is given by

$$B = \mu_0 ni$$

where, $\mu_0 = 4\pi \times 10^{-7} \text{ T - mA}^{-1}$

$$n = \frac{1000}{50 \times 10^{-2}}, i = 5 \text{ A}$$

$$\Rightarrow \quad B = 4\pi \times 10^{-7} \times \frac{1000}{50 \times 10^{-2}} \times 5$$

$$\therefore \quad B = 1.26 \times 10^{-2} \text{T}$$

33 *(c)* The magnitude of the magnetic field at point O due to straight part of wire is

$$B_1 = \frac{\mu_0 i}{2\pi r}$$

B_1 is perpendicular to the plane of the page, directed upwards (right hand palm rule 1).

The field at the centre O due to the current loop of radius r is

$$B_2 = \frac{\mu_0 i}{2r}$$

B_2 is also perpendicular to the page, directed upward (right hand screw rule).

$\therefore$ Resultant field at O is

$$B = B_1 + B_2 = \frac{\mu_0 i}{2r}\left(\frac{1}{\pi} + 1\right)$$

$$= \frac{\mu_0 i}{2\pi r}(\pi + 1)$$

34 *(b)* It has a tendency to keep both l and d constant.

35 *(c)* Biot-Savart's law in vector form is given as

$$d\mathbf{B} = \frac{\mu_0}{4\pi} \cdot \frac{Id\mathbf{l} \times \mathbf{r}}{r^3}$$

36 *(c)* $B_1 = \dfrac{\mu_0 \times 2i}{2 \times R}$

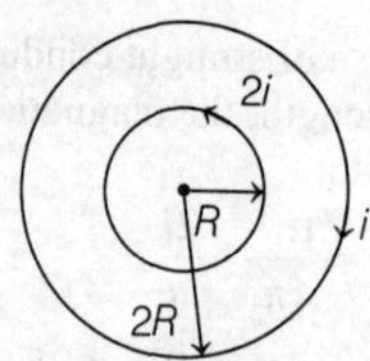

Similarly, $B_2 = \dfrac{\mu_0 i}{4R}$

$$\therefore \quad B_{\text{net}} = \frac{\mu_0 i}{R} - \frac{\mu_0 i}{4R} = \frac{3\mu_0 i}{4R}$$

37 *(d)* B_r is given as

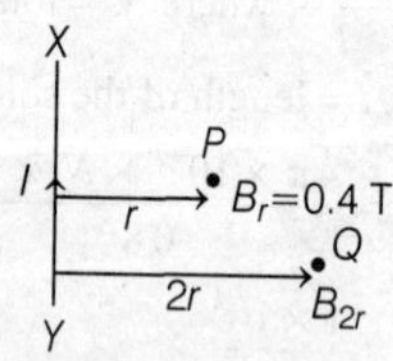

$$B_r = \frac{\mu_0}{2\pi}\frac{I}{d} = \left(\frac{\mu_0}{2\pi}\frac{I}{r}\right) = 0.4 \text{ T}$$

$$B_{2r} = \frac{\mu_0}{2\pi}\frac{I}{d} = \frac{\mu_0}{2\pi}\frac{I}{2r} = \frac{1}{2}\left(\frac{\mu_0}{2\pi}\frac{I}{r}\right)$$

$$B_{2r} = \frac{1}{2}B_r = \frac{1}{2}(0.4) = 0.2 \text{ T}$$

38 *(d)* Current through circular orbit of radius r is given as

$$i = \frac{q'}{t} = \frac{nq}{1} \qquad [\because q' = nq]$$

$$= nq$$

Magnetic field due to a current in a circular orbit at its centre,

$$B_C = \frac{\mu_0}{2}\frac{i}{r}$$

$$B_C = \frac{4\pi \times 10^{-7} nq}{2r} = \left(\frac{2\pi nq}{r}\right) \times 10^{-7}$$

39 *(a)* $B_{\text{centre}} = \dfrac{4 \times \mu_0}{4\pi} \times \dfrac{I}{(a/2)}$

$$(\sin 45° + \sin 45°)$$

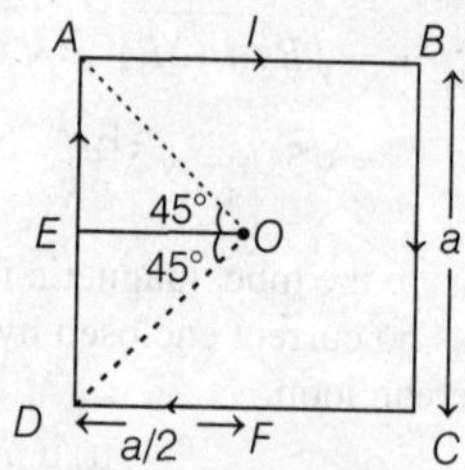

$$= 4 \times \frac{\mu_0}{4\pi} \times \frac{2I}{a} \times \frac{2}{\sqrt{2}} = \frac{\mu_0 I \times 2\sqrt{2}}{\pi a}$$

$$= \frac{4\pi \times 10^{-7} \times 1.414 \times 2 \times \sqrt{2}}{\pi \times 2 \times 10^{-2}}$$

$$= 8 \times 10^{-5} \text{T}$$

40 *(c)* The magnetic field is zero at any point inside the pipe carrying current I.

41 *(c)* Resultant magnetic field due to current carrying parallel wire 1 (10 A) and wire 2 (IA) at point A is zero.

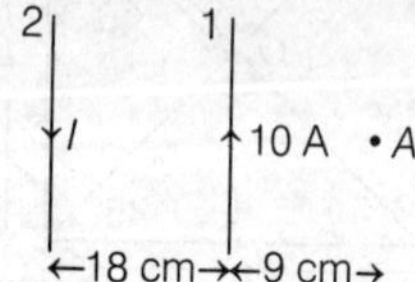

i.e. $\quad B_1 = B_2$

$$\frac{\mu_0 I_1}{2r_1} = \frac{\mu_0 I_2}{2r_2}$$

$$\Rightarrow \quad \frac{I_1}{r_1} = \frac{I_2}{r_2}$$

$$\Rightarrow \quad \frac{10}{9 \times 10^{-2}} = \frac{I}{27 \times 10^{-2}}$$

$$\Rightarrow \quad I = 30 \text{ A}$$

42 *(a)* Magnetic field in case of toroid is uniform over the whole cross-section.

43 *(b)* Magnetic field at the centre of current carrying circular loop,

$$B_C = \frac{\mu_0 I}{2r}$$

As, $\mu_0 = 4\pi \times 10^{-7} \text{ T mA}^{-1}$

$$B_C = \frac{4\pi \times 10^{-7} I}{2r} = \frac{2\pi I}{r} \text{ oersted}$$

44 (b) ∵ Magnetic field at centre, $B = \frac{\mu_0 I}{2r}$

where, $I = \frac{e}{t}$ or $I = \frac{e}{\left(\frac{2\pi r}{v}\right)} = \frac{ev}{2\pi r}$

Hence, $B = \left(\frac{\mu_0}{2r}\right)\left(\frac{ev}{2\pi r}\right) = \frac{\mu_0 ev}{4\pi r^2}$

or $B \propto \frac{v}{r^2}$

45 (c) $B_P = \frac{\mu_0 I_2}{2R}$

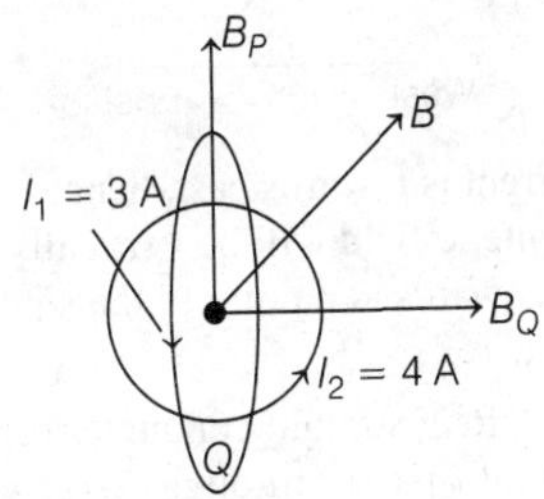

$= \frac{4\pi \times 10^{-7} \times 4}{2 \times 0.02\pi}$

$= 4 \times 10^{-5}$ Wb-m^{-2}

and $B_Q = \frac{\mu_0 I_1}{2R} = \frac{4\pi \times 10^{-7} \times 3}{2 \times 0.02\pi}$

$= 3 \times 10^{-5}$ Wb m^{-2}

∴ $B = \sqrt{B_P^2 + B_Q^2}$

$= \sqrt{(4 \times 10^{-5})^2 + (3 \times 10^{-5})^2}$

$= 5 \times 10^{-5}$ Wb m^{-2}

46 (b) The magnetic field due to a solenoid having n turns/metre and carrying current I is

$B = \frac{\mu_0 nI}{2}$

It is obvious that magnetic field is independent of length and area.

Also, magnetic field is uniform inside the solenoid.

47 (b) We know that,

$B_1 = \frac{\mu_0}{4\pi} \times \frac{2\pi I}{R}$

$= \frac{\mu_0}{4\pi} \times \frac{2\pi I \times 2\pi}{L}$ ...(i)

[∵ $L = 2\pi R$, for circular loop]

and $B_2 = \frac{\mu_0}{4\pi} \times \frac{I}{(a/2)}$

[sin 45°+ sin 45°]×4

where, $a = L/4$

∴ $B_2 = \frac{\mu_0 I}{4\pi L} \times 8 \times 4 \times \left[\frac{1}{\sqrt{2}} + \frac{1}{\sqrt{2}}\right]$

$= \frac{\mu_0 I}{4\pi L} \times \frac{64}{\sqrt{2}}$ ...(ii)

Hence, $\frac{B_1}{B_2} = \left(\frac{\mu_0}{4\pi}\right) \times \frac{4\pi^2 I}{L} \Big/ \frac{\mu_0 I}{4\pi L} \times \frac{64}{\sqrt{2}}$

or $\frac{B_1}{B_2} = \frac{\pi^2}{8\sqrt{2}}$

48 (b) Magnitude of magnetic field at any point due to a straight current carrying conductor depends only on the distance of the point with respect to current carrying conductor but not on the direction. Hence, $B_P = B_Q$ (at same distance).

49 (c) Magnetic field at centre of current carrying coil,

$B_c = \frac{\mu_0 i}{2r}$ ....(i)

Magnetic field at axial point due to a current carrying coil at distance of r

i.e. $d = r$

$B_a = \frac{\mu_0 i r^2}{2(r^2 + d^2)^{3/2}}$

$B_a = \frac{\mu_0 i r^2}{2(2r^2)^{3/2}}$ ....(ii)

Now, $\frac{B_c}{B_a} = \frac{\mu_0 i}{2r} \times \frac{2(2r^2)^{3/2}}{\mu_0 i r^2} = 2\sqrt{2}$

∴ $B_c : B_a = 2\sqrt{2} : 1$

50 (a) Magnetic field at centre due to 3/4th of circular current carrying arc is

$B_Q = \frac{\mu_0}{4\pi} \frac{I}{r}\left(\frac{3\pi}{2}\right) = \frac{3\mu_0 I}{8r}$ ...(i)

Magnetic field at O due to straight wire P is

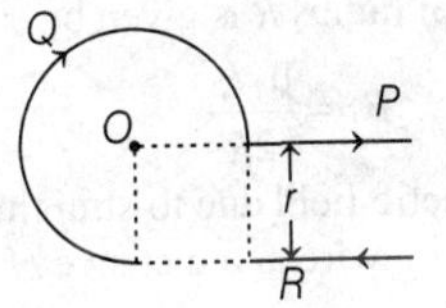

$B_P = 0$ ...(ii)

Now, magnetic field due to straight wire R is

$B_R = \frac{\mu_0}{4\pi} \frac{I}{r}$ [sin 0°+ sin 90°]

$= \frac{\mu_0}{4\pi} \frac{I}{r}$ ...(iii)

∴ $B = B_P + B_Q + B_R$

$= \frac{\mu_0 I}{4\pi r}\left(\frac{3\pi}{2} + 1\right)$

[using Eqs. (i), (ii) and (iii)]

51 (c) The magnetic induction at any point distance x from its centre,

$B = \frac{\mu_0}{4\pi} \cdot \frac{2\pi NIr^2}{(r^2 + x^2)^{3/2}}$ ...(i)

where, r is the radius of the circular coil. Then,

$B = \frac{\mu_0}{4\pi} \frac{2\pi NIr^2}{[r^2 + (\sqrt{3}r)^2]^{3/2}}$

[Given, $x = \sqrt{3}r$]

⇒ $B = \frac{\mu_0}{2} \cdot \frac{NIr^2}{(r^2 + 3r^2)^{3/2}}$

⇒ $B = \frac{\mu_0}{2} \cdot \frac{NIr^2}{(4r^2)^{3/2}}$

⇒ $B = \frac{\mu_0}{2} \cdot \frac{NIr^2}{(2r)^3}$

⇒ $B = \frac{\mu_0}{2} \cdot \frac{NIr^2}{8r^3}$

or $B = \frac{\mu_0 NI}{16r}$

52 (d) Magnetic field at the centre of circular coil of n turns and radius r is given by

$B = \frac{\mu_0 nI}{2r}$

For first coil, $B_1 = \frac{\mu_0 nI_1}{2r_1}$

For second coil, $B_2 = \frac{\mu_0 nI_2}{2r_2}$

Hence, resultant magnetic field at the centre of concentric loop is

$B = \frac{\mu_0 nI_1}{2r_1} - \frac{\mu_0 nI_2}{2r_2}$

Given, $n = 10, I_1 = 0.2$ A,

$r_1 = 20$ cm $= 0.20$ m

$I_2 = 0.3$ A

and $r_2 = 40$ cm $= 0.40$ m

∴ $B = \mu_0\left[\frac{10 \times 0.2}{2 \times 0.20} - \frac{10 \times 0.3}{2 \times 0.40}\right] = \frac{5}{4}\mu_0$

53 (d) Using Ampere's law,

$\oint \mathbf{B} \cdot d\mathbf{l} = \mu_0(I_{net})$ ...(i)

In our case,

I_{net} = (number of turns inside the area) × (current through each turn)

$= (nl)I$

where, n is number of turns per unit length.

Eq. (i) can be written as

$Bl = (\mu_0)(nlI)$

or $\quad B = \mu_0 nI$ or $B \propto nI$

$$\therefore \quad \frac{B_1}{B_2} = \frac{n_1 I_1}{n_2 I_2}$$

Here, $n_1 = n$, $n_2 = \frac{n}{2}$, $I_1 = I$,

$I_2 = 2I$, $B_1 = B$

$$\therefore \quad \frac{B}{B_2} = \frac{n}{n/2} \times \frac{I}{2I} = 1$$

or $\quad B_2 = B$

54 *(b)* The strength of magnetic field around a straight current carrying wire is given by

$$B = \frac{\mu_0}{2\pi} \cdot \frac{I}{r}$$

$$\therefore \quad B \propto \frac{1}{r}$$

Therefore, magnetic field due to a straight current carrying wire is inversely proportional to the distance from the wire.

55 *(a)* For wire *A*, length = 40 cm

It is bent into a circle, so

$\therefore \quad 2\pi r = 40$ or $r = \frac{40}{2\pi}$

Magnetic induction at centre $= \frac{\mu_0 I_1}{2r}$

For wire *B*, length = 30 cm.

It is bent into an arc, so $\theta = 30/r$

Magnetic induction at centre due to circular arc $= \frac{\mu_0 I_2 \theta}{4\pi r}$

Since, $\quad \frac{\mu_0 I_1}{2r} = \frac{\mu_0 I_2 \theta}{4\pi r}$

$$\Rightarrow \quad \frac{I_1}{I_2} = \frac{\theta}{2\pi} = \frac{30 \times 2\pi}{2\pi \times 40} \quad \left[\because r = \frac{40}{2\pi}\right]$$

$$\Rightarrow \quad \frac{I_1}{I_2} = \frac{3}{4}$$

56 *(b)* $B = 4\left[\frac{\mu_0}{4\pi} \cdot \frac{I}{a}(\sin\phi_1 + \sin\phi_2)\right]$

Here, $a = \frac{l}{2}$ and $\phi_1 = \phi_2 = 45°$

$$B = 4 \times \frac{\mu_0}{4\pi} \frac{I}{(l/2)}\left[\frac{1}{\sqrt{2}} + \frac{1}{\sqrt{2}}\right]$$

$$\therefore \quad B = \frac{16}{\sqrt{2}}\left[\frac{\mu_0}{4\pi} \frac{I}{l}\right]$$

$$= 8\sqrt{2}\left(\frac{\mu_0}{4\pi} \cdot \frac{I}{l}\right)$$

57 *(d)* By the formula,

$$B = \mu_0 nI$$

or $\quad 20 \times 10^{-3} = 4\pi \times 10^{-7} \times 2000 \times I$

or $\quad I = \frac{20 \times 10^{-3}}{4\pi \times 10^{-7} \times 2000} = 8\text{A}$

$\Rightarrow \quad I \approx 8\text{ A}$

58 *(b)* The magnetic field produced at the centre of the circular coil carrying current is given by

$$B = \frac{\mu_0 NI}{2r}$$

For one turn, $N = 1$

$$B_0 = \frac{\mu_0 I}{2r}$$

As the coil is rewound

$$r' = \frac{r}{3}, N' = 3$$

$$\therefore \quad B' = \frac{\mu_0 I \times 3}{2 \times \left(\frac{r}{3}\right)} = \frac{9\mu_0 I}{2r} = 9B_0$$

59 *(b)* The coils are placed perpendicular to each other. The magnetic field due to current through each at the centre is *B*. Then, resultant magnetic field due to current through both the coils will be

$$B_r = \sqrt{B^2 + B^2} = \sqrt{2}B$$

Hence, the required ratio will be

$$\frac{B_r}{B} = \frac{\sqrt{2}}{1} = \sqrt{2} : 1$$

60 *(a)* Magnetic field at the centre *O* of the loop of radius *R* is given by

$$B_1 = \frac{\mu_0 I_c}{2R}$$

Magnetic field due to straight current carrying wire at a distance *H*, is given by

$$B_2 = \frac{\mu_0 I_e}{2\pi H}$$

For magnetic field to be zero at the centre of the loop,

$$B_1 = B_2$$

i.e. $\quad \frac{\mu_0 I_c}{2R} = \frac{\mu_0 I_e}{2\pi H} \Rightarrow H = \frac{I_e R}{\pi I_c}$

61 *(a)* According to right hand thumb rule, if the thumb represents the direction of current in a wire, then the curled fingers will represents the direction of magnetic field.

Hence, using right hand thumb rule as per diagram

I West → East

Current is towards east, hence magnetic field will be vertically downwards at a point to the south of the wire.

62 *(b)* A long straight conductor carrying current *I* passes through *O*, then by symmetry, all points of the circular path are equivalent and hence the magnitude of magnetic field should be same at these points.

The circulation of magnetic field along the circle is

$$\oint_p \mathbf{B} \cdot d\mathbf{l} = \mu_0 I \text{ (using Ampere's law)}$$

63 *(d)* $B_1 = \frac{\mu_0 I_1}{2\pi r} = \frac{\mu_0}{2\pi} \times \frac{2.5}{2.5} = \frac{\mu_0}{2\pi}$

$$B_2 = \frac{\mu_0 I_2}{2\pi r} = \frac{\mu_0}{2\pi} \times \frac{5}{2.5} = \frac{2\mu_0}{2\pi}$$

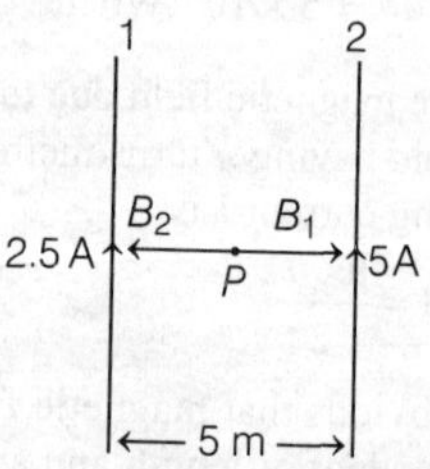

Resultant magnetic field at mid-point *P*,

$$B = B_2 - B_1 = \frac{\mu_0}{2\pi}(2 - 1) = \frac{\mu_0}{2\pi}$$

Topic 2

Motion of a Charged Particle in a Magnetic Field

2019

1 Ionised hydrogen atoms and α-particles with same momenta enters perpendicular to a constant magnetic field B. The ratio of their radii of their paths $r_H : r_\alpha$ will be **[NEET]**

(a) 1 : 2 (b) 4 : 1
(c) 1 : 4 (d) 2 : 1

2 **Assertion** A charge particle is released from rest in magnetic field, then it will move in a circular path.
Reason Work done by magnetic field is non-zero.
(a) Both Assertion and Reason are correct and Reason is the correct explanation of Assertion.
(b) Both Assertion and Reason are correct, but Reason is not the correct explanation of Assertion.
(c) Assertion is correct, but Reason is incorrect.
(d) Both Assertion and Reason are incorrect.

3 A proton is projected with velocity $\mathbf{v} = 2\hat{\mathbf{i}}$ in a region where magnetic field $\mathbf{B} = (\hat{\mathbf{i}} + 3\hat{\mathbf{j}} + 4\hat{\mathbf{k}})\,\mu\text{T}$ and electric field $\mathbf{E} = 10\hat{\mathbf{i}}\,\mu\ \text{Vm}^{-1}$. Then, find out the net acceleration of proton. **[AIIMS]**

(a) 1400 ms^{-2} (b) 700 ms^{-2}
(c) 1000 ms^{-2} (d) 800 ms^{-2}

4 **Assertion** Electron moving perpendicular to **B** will perform circular motion.
Reason Force by magnetic field is perpendicular to velocity. **[AIIMS]**
(a) Both Assertion and Reason are correct and Reason is the correct explanation of Assertion.
(b) Both Assertion and Reason are correct, but Reason is not the correct explanation of Assertion.
(c) Assertion is correct, but Reason is incorrect.
(d) Both Assertion and Reason are incorrect.

5 If two protons are moving with speed $v = 4.5 \times 10^5\ \text{ms}^{-1}$ parallel to each other, then find the value of ratio of electrostatic and magnetic force between them. **[AIIMS]**

(a) 4.4×10^5 (b) 2.2×10^5
(c) 3.3×10^5 (d) 1.1×10^5

6 Ratio of charge on positron to mass of positron (in C kg^{-1}) is approximately **[JIPMER]**

(a) $+2 \times 10^{11}$ (b) $+5 \times 10^{12}$
(c) -2×10^{11} (d) -5×10^{11}

2016

7 An electron is moving in a circular path under the influence of a transverse magnetic field of 3.57×10^{-2} T. If the value of e/m is $1.76 \times 10^{11}\ \text{C kg}^{-1}$, the frequency of revolution of the electron is **[NEET]**

(a) 1 GHz (b) 100 MHz
(c) 62.8 MHz (d) 6.28 MHz

2015

8 The force on a charged particle moving with a velocity v in a magnetic field B is not **[MP PET]**
(a) perpendicular to both v and B
(b) maximum, if v is perpendicular to B
(c) maximum, if v is parallel to B
(d) zero, if v is parallel to B

2014

9 In cyclotron, for a given magnet, radius of the semicircle traced by positive ion is directly proportional to (where, v = velocity of positive ion) **[MHT CET]**

(a) v^{-2} (b) v^{-1} (c) v (d) v^2

10 When a magnetic field is applied on a stationary electron, it **[Kerala CEE]**
(a) remains stationary
(b) spins about its own axis
(c) moves in the direction of the field
(d) moves perpendicular to the direction of the field
(e) moves opposite to the direction of the field

11 A charged particle experiences magnetic force in the presence of magnetic field. Which of the following statement is correct? **[KCET]**
(a) The particle is moving and magnetic field is perpendicular to the velocity
(b) The particle is moving and magnetic field is parallel to the velocity
(c) The particle is stationary and magnetic field is perpendicular to the velocity
(d) The particle is stationary and magnetic field is parallel to the velocity

12 A proton of mass m and charge q is moving in a plane with kinetic energy E. If there exists a uniform magnetic field B, perpendicular to the plane of the motion, the proton will move in a circular path of radius **[WB JEE]**

(a) $\dfrac{2Em}{qB}$ (b) $\dfrac{\sqrt{2Em}}{qB}$ (c) $\dfrac{\sqrt{Em}}{2qB}$ (d) $\dfrac{\sqrt{2Eq}}{qB}$

13 If the velocity of charged particle has both perpendicular and parallel components while moving through a magnetic field, what is the path followed by a charged particle? **[KCET]**

(a) Circular (b) Elliptical (c) Linear (d) Helical

14 A charged particle of mass m and charge q moves along a circular path of radius r that is perpendicular to a magnetic field B. The time taken by the particle to complete one revolution is **[UK PMT]**

(a) $\frac{2\pi mq}{B}$ (b) $\frac{2\pi q^2 B}{m}$

(c) $\frac{2\pi qB}{m}$ (d) $\frac{2\pi m}{qB}$

2013

15 When a proton is released from rest in a room, it starts with an initial acceleration a_0 towards West. When it is projected towards North with a speed v_0, it moves with an initial acceleration $3a_0$ towards West. The electric and magnetic fields in the room are **[NEET]**

(a) $\frac{ma_0}{e}$ West, $\frac{2ma_0}{ev_0}$ up (b) $\frac{ma_0}{e}$ West, $\frac{2ma_0}{ev_0}$ down

(c) $\frac{ma_0}{e}$ East, $\frac{3ma_0}{ev_0}$ up (d) $\frac{ma_0}{e}$ East, $\frac{2ma_0}{ev_0}$ down

16 A uniform electric field and a uniform magnetic field are produced, pointed in the same direction. An electron is projected with its velocity pointing in the same direction, **[AIIMS]**

(a) the electron will turn to its left
(b) the electron will turn to its right
(c) the electron velocity will increase in magnitude
(d) the electron velocity will decrease in magnitude

17 A proton carrying 1 MeV kinetic energy is moving in a circular path of radius R in uniform magnetic field. What should be the energy of an α-particle to describe a circle of same radius in the same field? **[CBSE AIPMT]**

(a) 2 MeV (b) 1 MeV
(c) 0.5 MeV (d) 4 MeV

2011

18 Two particles A and B having equal charges +6C, after being accelerated through the same potential difference, enter a region of uniform magnetic field and describe circular paths of radii 2 cm and 3 cm, respectively. The ratio of mass of A to that of B is **[Kerala CEE]**

(a) 4/9 (b) 9/5
(c) 1/2 (d) 1/3
(e) None of these

19 The path of a charged particle in a uniform magnetic field, when the velocity and the magnetic field are perpendicular to each other is a **[J&K CET]**

(a) circle (b) parabola
(c) helix (d) straight line

20 A proton travelling at 23° w.r.t. the direction of a magnetic field of strength 2.6 mT experiences a magnetic force of 6.5×10^{-17} N. What is the speed of the proton? **[DUMET]**

(a) 2×10^5 ms^{-1} (b) 4×10^5 ms^{-1}
(c) 6×10^5 ms^{-1} (d) 6×10^{-5} ms^{-1}

21 What uniform magnetic field applied perpendicular to a beam of electrons moving at 1.3×10^6 ms^{-1}, is required to make the electrons travel in a circular arc of radius 0.35 m? **[DUMET]**

(a) 2.1×10^{-5} G (b) 6×10^{-5} T
(c) 2.1×10^{-5} T (d) 6×10^{-5} G

2010

22 In the figure given below, the electron enters into a magnetic field. It will deflect in **[JCECE]**

(a) + ve x-direction (b) – ve x-direction
(c) + ve y-direction (d) – ve y-direction

23 A deuteron of kinetic energy 50 keV is describing a circular orbit of radius 0.5 m, in a plane perpendicular to magnetic field B. The kinetic energy of a proton that describes circular orbit of radius 0.5 m in the same plane with the same magnetic field is **[AFMC]**

(a) 200 keV (b) 50 keV (c) 100 keV (d) 25 keV

24 A charged particle enters a magnetic field H with its initial velocity making an angle of 45° with H. The path of the particle will be **[BHU]**

(a) straight line (b) a circle
(c) an ellipse (d) a helix

25 A charged particle moves along a circle under the action of magnetic and electric fields, then this region of space may have **[UP CPMT]**

(a) $E = 0, B = 0$ (b) $E = 0, B \neq 0$
(c) $E \neq 0, B = 0$ (d) $E \neq 0, B \neq 0$

26 Two particles of masses m_a and m_b and same charge are projected in a perpendicular magnetic field. They travel along circular paths of radius r_a and r_b such that $r_a > r_b$. Then, which is true? **[MHT CET]**

(a) $m_a v_a > m_b v_b$ (b) $m_a > m_b$ and $v_a > v_b$
(c) $m_a = m_b$ and $v_a > v_b$ (d) $m_b v_b > m_a v_a$

27 A charged particle moving with velocity 4×10^6 ms^{-1} enters perpendicular to a magnetic field $B = 2$ Wbm^{-2}. It moves in a circular path of radius 2 cm, then charge per unit mass is **[OJEE]**

(a) 10^2 Ckg^{-1} (b) 10^3 Ckg^{-1}
(c) 10^4 Ckg^{-1} (d) 10^8 Ckg^{-1}

28 A charge $+Q$ is moving upwards vertically. It enters a magnetic field directed to North. The force on the charge will be towards **[KCET]**
(a) North (b) South (c) East (d) West

29 A proton enters a magnetic field of flux density 1.5 Wbm^{-2} with a speed of $2 \times 10^7 \ ms^{-1}$ at angle of 30° with the field. The force on a proton will be **[BCECE]**
(a) 0.24×10^{-12} N (b) 2.4×10^{-12} N
(c) 24×10^{-12} N (d) 0.024×10^{-12} N

30 An electron of mass m and charge q is travelling with a speed v along a circular path of radius r at right angles to a uniform magnetic field B. If speed of the electron is doubled and the magnetic field is halved, then resulting path would have a radius of **[JIPMER]**
(a) $r/4$ (b) $r/2$ (c) $2r$ (d) $4r$

31 A particle of mass M and charge Q moving with velocity v describes a circular path of radius R when subjected to a uniform transverse magnetic field of induction B. The work done by the field when the particle completes one full circle is **[MGIMS]**
(a) $\left(\frac{Mv^2}{R}\right) 2\pi R$ (b) zero
(c) $BQ\,2\pi R$ (d) $BQv2\pi R$

32 An electric field of 1500 Vm^{-1} and a magnetic field of 0.40 Wbm^{-2} act on a moving electron. The minimum uniform speed along a straight line, the electron could have is **[CMC]**
(a) $1.6 \times 10^{15} \ ms^{-1}$ (b) $6 \times 10^{-16} \ ms^{-1}$
(c) $3.75 \times 10^3 \ ms^{-1}$ (d) $3.75 \times 10^2 \ ms^{-1}$

2009

33 Work done on electron moving in a solenoid along its axis is equal to **[BVP]**

→ B v
i ooooooooooooooooooo i

(a) zero (b) evB
(c) ilB (d) None of these

34 The magnetic force acting on a charged particle of charge $-2\mu C$ in a magnetic field of 2 T acting in y-direction, when the particle velocity is $(2\hat{i} + 3\hat{j}) \times 10^6 \ ms^{-1}$, is **[CBSE AIPMT]**
(a) 8 N in $-z$-direction (b) 4 N in z-direction
(c) 8 N in y-direction (d) 8 N in z-direction

35 **Assertion** A proton and an alpha particle having the same kinetic energy are moving in circular paths in a uniform magnetic field. The radii of their circular paths will be equal.

Reason Any two charged particles having equal kinetic energies and entering a region of uniform magnetic field **B** in a direction perpendicular to **B**, will describe circular trajectories of equal radii. **[AIIMS]**
(a) Both Assertion and Reason are correct and Reason is the correct explanation of Assertion.
(b) Both Assertion and Reason are correct but Reason is not the correct explanation of Assertion.
(c) Assertion is correct but Reason is incorrect.
(d) Both Assertion and Reason are incorrect.

36 A charged particle with velocity $\mathbf{v} = x\hat{\mathbf{i}} + y\hat{\mathbf{j}}$ moves in a magnetic field $\mathbf{B} = y\hat{\mathbf{i}} + x\hat{\mathbf{j}}$. Magnitude of the force acting on the particle is F. The correct option for F is
I. No force will act on particle, if $x = y$
II. Force will act along Y-axis, if $y < x$
III. Force is proportional to $(x^2 - y^2)$, if $x > y$
IV. Force is proportional to $(x^2 + y^2)$, if $y > x$ **[UP CPMT]**
(a) I and II are correct (b) I and III are correct
(c) II and IV are correct (d) III and IV are correct

37 Four charged particles are projected perpendicularly into the magnetic field with equal speed. Which will have minimum frequency? **[OJEE]**
(a) Proton (b) Electron (c) Li^+ (d) He^+

38 Proton and α-particle are projected perpendicularly in a magnetic field, if both move in a circular path with same speed. Then, the ratio of their radii is **[OJEE]**
(a) 1 : 2 (b) 2 : 1 (c) 1 : 4 (d) 1 : 1

39 The magnetic Lorentz force experienced by a charge q, entering a magnetic field B with a velocity v is **[Kerala CEE]**
(a) $\sqrt{q(\mathbf{B} \times \mathbf{v})}$ (b) $q(\mathbf{B} \times \mathbf{v})$
(c) $q(\mathbf{v} \cdot \mathbf{B})$ (d) $q^2(\mathbf{v} \times \mathbf{B})$
(e) $q(\mathbf{v} \times \mathbf{B})$

40 In a mass spectrometer used for measuring the masses of ions, the ions are initially accelerated by an electric potential V and then made to describe semicircular paths of radius R using a magnetic field B. If V and B are kept constant, then the ratio $\left(\frac{\text{charge on the ion}}{\text{mass of the ion}}\right)$ will be proportional to **[JIPMER]**
(a) $\frac{1}{R}$ (b) $\frac{1}{R^2}$ (c) R^2 (d) R

41 A charged particle enters in a strong perpendicular magnetic field. Then, its kinetic energy **[MGIMS]**
(a) increases
(b) decreases
(c) remains constant
(d) first increases and then becomes constant

42 A cyclotron can accelerate **[MGIMS]**
(a) β-particles (b) α-particles
(c) high velocity gamma rays
(d) high velocity X-rays

43 An α-particle and a deuteron projected with equal kinetic energies describe circular paths of radii r_1 and r_2 respectively, in a uniform magnetic field. The ratio r_1/r_2 is [BCECE]
(a) 1 (b) 2
(c) $\frac{1}{\sqrt{2}}$ (d) $\sqrt{2}$

44 When a positively charged particle enters a uniform magnetic field with uniform velocity, its trajectory can be
(i) a straight line (ii) a circle
(iii) a helix [JCECE]
(a) Only (i) (b) (i) and (ii)
(c) (i) and (iii) (d) (i), (ii) and (iii)

2008

45 A particle of mass m, charge Q and kinetic energy T enters a transverse uniform magnetic field of induction **B**. After 3 s, the kinetic energy of the particle will be [CBSE AIPMT]
(a) $3T$ (b) $2T$ (c) T (d) $4T$

46 A proton, a deuteron and an α-particle with the same kinetic energy enter a region of uniform magnetic field, moving at right angles to B. What is the ratio of the radii of their circular paths? [BHU]
(a) $1:\sqrt{2}:1$ (b) $1:\sqrt{2}:\sqrt{2}$ (c) $\sqrt{2}:1:1$ (d) $\sqrt{2}:\sqrt{2}:1$

47 Under the influence of a uniform magnetic field, a charged particle is moving in a circle of radius R with constant speed v. The time period of the motion [MHT CET]
(a) depends on v and not on R
(b) depends on both R and v
(c) is independent of both R and v
(d) depends on R and not on v

48 Which of the following while in motion cannot be deflected by magnetic field? [MHT CET]
(a) Protons (b) Cathode rays
(c) Alpha particles (d) Neutrons

49 The magnetic force on a charged particle moving in the field does no work, because [J&K CET]
(a) kinetic energy of the charged particle does not change
(b) the charge of the particle remains same
(c) the magnetic force is parallel to velocity of the particle
(d) the magnetic force is parallel to magnetic field

50 Identify the correct statement from the following. [J&K CET]
(a) Cyclotron frequency is dependent on speed of the charged particle.
(b) Kinetic energy of charged particle in cyclotron does not dependent on its mass.
(c) Cyclotron frequency does not depend on speed of charged particle.
(d) Kinetic energy of charged particle in cyclotron is independent of its charge.

51 Frequency of cyclotron does not depend upon [DUMET]
(a) charge (b) mass (c) velocity (d) q/m

52 A proton is moving in a uniform magnetic field B in a circular path of radius a in a direction perpendicular to Z-axis along which field B exists. Calculate the angular momentum, if the charge on proton is e. [BCECE]
(a) Be/a^2 (b) eB^2a (c) a^2eB (d) aeB

2007

53 A man carrying suitable instrument for measuring electric and magnetic field passes by a stationary electron with velocity v. Then, these instruments will note [DCE]
(a) electric field (b) magnetic field
(c) Both (a) and (b) (d) None of these

54 The figure shows three situations when an electron with velocity **v** travels through a uniform magnetic field **B**. In each case, what is the direction of magnetic force on the electron? [AIIMS]

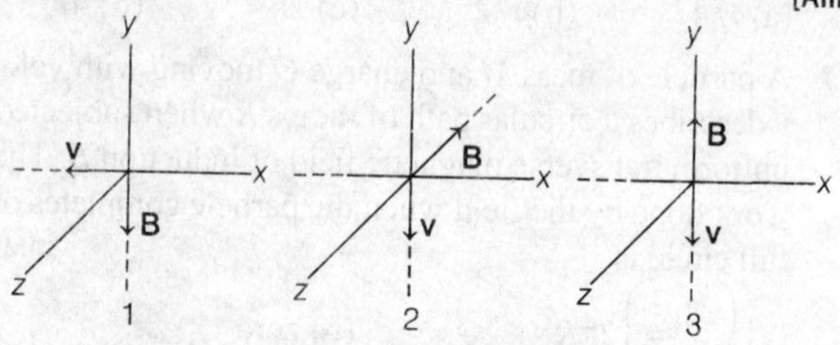

(a) +ve Z-axis, –ve X-axis, +ve Y-axis
(b) –ve Z-axis, –ve X-axis and zero
(c) +ve Z-axis, +ve X-axis and zero
(d) –ve Z-axis, +ve X-axis and zero

55 The path of an electron in a uniform magnetic field may be [AFMC]
(a) circular but not helical
(b) helical but not circular
(c) Neither helical nor circular
(d) Either helical or circular

56 A beam of protons with velocity 4×10^5 ms^{-1} enters a uniform magnetic field of 0.3 T at an angle of 60° to the magnetic field. Find the radius of the helical path taken by the proton beam. [UP CPMT]
(a) 0.2 cm (b) 1.2 cm (c) 2.2 cm (d) 0.122 cm

57 An electron is travelling along the x-direction. It encounters a magnetic field in the y-direction. Its subsequent motion will be [MHT CET]
(a) straight line along the x-direction
(b) a circle in the xz-plane
(c) a circle in the yz-plane
(d) a circle in the xy-plane

58 An electron and a proton enter in a magnetic field perpendicularly. Both have same kinetic energy. Which of the following is correct? [RPMT]
(a) Trajectory of electron is less curved
(b) Trajectory of proton is less curved
(c) Both trajectories are equally curved
(d) Both move on straight line path

59 A charged particle is moving in a magnetic field of strength B perpendicular to the direction of the field. If q and m denote the charge and mass of the particle respectively, then the frequency of rotation of the particle is **[KCET]**

(a) $f=\dfrac{qB}{2\pi m}$ (b) $f=\dfrac{qB}{2\pi m^2}$ (c) $f=\dfrac{2\pi^2 m}{qB}$ (d) $f=\dfrac{2\pi m}{qB}$

60 If velocity of an electron is $(2\hat{\mathbf{i}}+3\hat{\mathbf{j}})\,\text{ms}^{-1}$ and it enters in the magnetic field of $4\hat{\mathbf{k}}$ tesla, then **[Guj CET]**

(a) it will move in the direction of the magnetic field
(b) it will move in the opposite direction to the magnetic field
(c) direction of its velocity will change
(d) its speed will change

2006

61 When a charged particle moving with velocity $\mathbf{v}$ is subjected to a magnetic field of induction $\mathbf{B}$, the force on it is non-zero. This implies that **[CBSE AIPMT]**

(a) angle between $\mathbf{v}$ and $\mathbf{B}$ is necessarily 90°
(b) angle between $\mathbf{v}$ and $\mathbf{B}$ can have any value other than 90°
(c) angle between $\mathbf{v}$ and $\mathbf{B}$ can have any value other than zero and 180°
(d) angle between $\mathbf{v}$ and $\mathbf{B}$ is either zero or 180°

62 A plane metallic sheet is placed with its face parallel to lines of magnetic induction B of a uniform field. A particle of mass m and charge q is projected with a velocity v from a distance d from the plane normal to the lines of induction. Then, the maximum velocity of projection for which the particle does not hit the plate is **[Manipal]**

(a) $\dfrac{2Bqd}{m}$ (b) $\dfrac{Bqd}{m}$ (c) $\dfrac{Bqd}{2m}$ (d) $\dfrac{Bqm}{d}$

63 An electron moves at right angle to a magnetic field of 1.5×10^{-2} T with a speed of $6\times10^{7}\,\text{ms}^{-1}$. If the specific charge of the electron is $1.7\times10^{11}\,\text{Ckg}^{-1}$, the radius of the circular path will be **[Manipal]**

(a) 2.9 cm (b) 3.9 cm (c) 2.35 cm (d) 2 cm

64 An electron revolves in a circle of radius 0.4Å with a speed of $10^{5}\,\text{ms}^{-1}$. The magnitude of the magnetic field, produced at the centre of the circular path due to the motion of the electron, (in Wb m^{-2}) is **[Kerala CEE]**

(a) 0.01 (b) 10 (c) 1 (d) 0.005
(e) 5

65 If velocity of a charged particle is doubled and strength of magnetic field is halved, then radius becomes **[RPMT]**

(a) 8 times (b) 2 times (c) 4 times (d) 3 times

66 A charged particle enters in a uniform magnetic field with a certain speed at right angles to it. In the magnetic field, a change could occur in its **[J&K CET]**

(a) kinetic energy (b) angular momentum
(c) linear momentum (d) speed

67 When deuterium and helium are subjected to an accelerating field simultaneously, then **[KCET]**

(a) both acquire same energy
(b) deuterium accelerates faster
(c) helium accelerates faster
(d) neither of them is accelerated

68 A proton moving vertically downward enters a magnetic field pointing towards North. In which direction proton will deflect? **[DUMET]**

(a) East (b) West
(c) North (d) South

69 A very long straight wire carries a current I. At the instant when a charge $+Q$ at point P has velocity $\mathbf{v}$ as shown, the force on the charge is **[CBSE]**

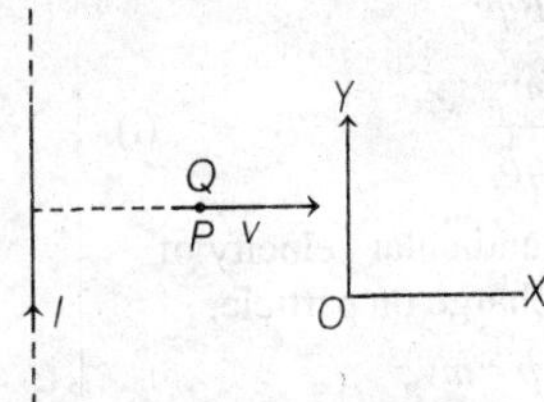

(a) opposite to ox (b) along ox
(c) opposite to oy (d) along oy

2005

70 An electron projected in a perpendicular uniform magnetic field of 3×10^{-3} T, moves in a circle of radius 4 mm. The linear momentum of electron (in kg-ms^{-1}) is **[MHT CET]**

(a) 1.92×10^{-21} (b) 1.2×10^{-24}
(c) 1.92×10^{-24} (d) 1.2×10^{-21}

71 Cyclotron is a device which is used to **[Punjab PMET]**

(a) measure the charge (b) measure the voltage
(c) accelerate protons (d) accelerate electrons

72 A proton is projected with a velocity $10^{7}\,\text{ms}^{-1}$, at right angles to a uniform magnetic field of induction 100 mT. The time (in second) taken by the proton to traverse 90° arc is **[EAMCET]**
(Take, mass of proton $=1.65\times10^{-27}$ kg and charge of proton $=1.6\times10^{-19}$ C)

(a) 0.81×10^{-7} (b) 1.62×10^{-7}
(c) 2.43×10^{-7} (d) 3.24×10^{-7}

73 In a cyclotron if a deuteron can gain an energy of 40 MeV, then a proton can gain an energy of **[DUMET]**

(a) 40 MeV (b) 80 MeV
(c) 20 MeV (d) 60 MeV

74 An electron moving in a uniform magnetic field of induction of intensity $\mathbf{B}$, has its radius directly proportional to **[DUMET]**

(a) its charge (b) magnetic field
(c) speed (d) None of these

Answers

1 (d)	2 (d)	3 (a)	4 (a)	5 (a)	6 (a)	7 (a)	8 (c)	9 (c)	10 (a)
11 (a)	12 (b)	13 (d)	14 (d)	15 (a)	16 (d)	17 (b)	18 (a)	19 (a)	20 (b)
21 (c)	22 (d)	23 (c)	24 (d)	25 (b)	26 (a)	27 (d)	28 (d)	29 (b)	30 (d)
31 (b)	32 (c)	33 (a)	34 (a)	35 (c)	36 (b)	37 (c)	38 (a)	39 (e)	40 (a)
41 (c)	42 (b)	43 (c)	44 (d)	45 (c)	46 (a)	47 (c)	48 (d)	49 (a)	50 (c)
51 (c)	52 (c)	53 (c)	54 (c)	55 (d)	56 (b)	57 (d)	58 (a)	59 (a)	60 (c)
61 (c)	62 (b)	63 (c)	64 (c)	65 (c)	66 (c)	67 (d)	68 (a)	69 (d)	70 (c)
71 (c)	72 (b)	73 (b)	74 (c)						

Explanations

1 *(d)* The centripetal force required for circular motion is provided by magnetic force

$$\Rightarrow \quad \frac{mv_p^2}{r} = Bqv_p$$

$$\Rightarrow \quad r = \frac{mv_p}{qB} \quad \ldots \text{(i)}$$

where, v_p = perpendicular velocity of particle and q = charge on particle.

As, momentum, $p = mv_p$

$$\therefore \quad r = \frac{p}{qB} \quad \text{[from Eq. (i)]}$$

According to the question, moment a of both particle is same.

$$\Rightarrow \quad r \propto \frac{1}{q}$$

For ionised hydrogen atom, $q_H = e$ and for α-particle, $q_\alpha = 2e$

$$\Rightarrow \quad \frac{r_H}{r_\alpha} = \frac{q_\alpha}{q_H} = \frac{2e}{e} = \frac{2}{1} \text{ or } 2:1$$

2 *(d)* When a charge particle of charge (q) is released from rest ($u = 0$) in the uniform magnetic field (B), then magnetic force on the charged particle. $F = Bqu\sin\theta = 0$, because $u = 0$. Therefore, the charge particle will not move on circular path.

In the magnetic field, force on charge particle always acts in perpendicular direction to the direction of velocity of charge particle, therefore work done by magnetic field on charge particle is zero. Hence, Assertion and Reason both are incorrect.

3 *(a)* Given, velocity of proton, $\mathbf{v} = 2\hat{\mathbf{i}}$

Magnetic field, $\mathbf{B} = (\hat{\mathbf{i}} + 3\hat{\mathbf{j}} + 4\hat{\mathbf{k}})\,\mu\text{T}$

Electric field, $\mathbf{E} = 10\hat{\mathbf{i}}\,\mu\ \text{Vm}^{-1}$

Applied Lorentz force on the proton,

$$\mathbf{F} = q\mathbf{E} + q(\mathbf{v} \times \mathbf{B}) = q[\mathbf{E} + (\mathbf{v} \times \mathbf{B})]$$

$$= 1.6 \times 10^{-19}[10 \times 10^{-6}\hat{\mathbf{i}} + 2\hat{\mathbf{i}} \times (\hat{\mathbf{i}} + 3\hat{\mathbf{j}} + 4\hat{\mathbf{k}}) \times 10^{-6}]$$

$$= 1.6 \times 10^{-19} \times 10^{-6}[10\hat{\mathbf{i}} + 6\hat{\mathbf{k}} - 8\hat{\mathbf{j}}]$$

$$\mathbf{F} = 1.6 \times 10^{-25}[10\hat{\mathbf{i}} - 8\hat{\mathbf{j}} + 6\hat{\mathbf{k}}]\text{N}$$

∴ Acceleration of proton,

$$\mathbf{a} = \frac{\mathbf{F}}{m_p} \quad (\because m_p = 1.6 \times 10^{-27}\text{ kg})$$

$$= \frac{1.6 \times 10^{-25}[10\hat{\mathbf{i}} - 8\hat{\mathbf{j}} + 6\hat{\mathbf{k}}]}{1.6 \times 10^{-27}}$$

$$\mathbf{a} = 100[10\hat{\mathbf{i}} - 8\hat{\mathbf{j}} + 6\hat{\mathbf{k}}]$$

$$\therefore a = |\mathbf{a}| = 100\sqrt{10^2 + 8^2 + 6^2}$$

$$= 100 \times 14.14 = 1414\text{ ms}^{-2}$$

$$\simeq 1400\text{ ms}^{-2}$$

4 *(a)* When an electron enters into a uniform magnetic field in perpendicular direction to the direction of magnetic field, then a magnetic force acts on the electron in perpendicular direction of both direction of magnetic field and direction of velocity of electron and direction of force can be determine by Fleming's left hand rule. We know that, when direction of force on a particle is in perpendicular to the direction of velocity, then particle moves in uniform circular motion. Therefore, electron moving perpendicular to magnetic field (**B**) will perform circular motion.

Hence, both Assertion and Reason are correct and Reason is the correct explanation of Assertion.

5 *(a)* Given, speed of proton, $v = 4.5 \times 10^5\text{ ms}^{-1}$

Electrostatic force between two protons,

$$F_e = k\frac{e^2}{r^2} \quad \ldots \text{(i)}$$

Magnetic field produced due to moving proton of speed v,

$$B = \frac{\mu_0}{4\pi}\cdot\frac{ev}{r^2} \quad \ldots \text{(ii)}$$

∴ Magnetic force on the proton,

$$F_m = B\,ev$$

$$= \frac{\mu_0}{4\pi}\cdot\frac{ev}{r^2}\cdot ev \quad \text{[From Eq. (ii)]}$$

$$F_m = \frac{\mu_0}{4\pi}\cdot\frac{e^2v^2}{r^2} \quad \ldots \text{(iii)}$$

From Eqs. (i) and (iii), we get

$$\frac{F_e}{F_m} = \frac{\dfrac{ke^2}{r^2}}{\dfrac{\mu_0}{4\pi}\cdot\dfrac{e^2v^2}{r^2}} = \frac{k \cdot 4\pi}{v^2 \cdot \mu_0}$$

$$\frac{F_e}{F_m} = \frac{9 \times 10^9 \times 4 \times 3.14}{(4.5 \times 10^5)^2 \times 4\pi \times 10^{-7}}$$

$$= 4.4 \times 10^5$$

6 *(a)* Charge on positron, $q = e$

$$= 1.6 \times 10^{-19}\text{ C}$$

Mass of positron (m) = Mass of electron

$$= 9.1 \times 10^{-31}\text{ kg}$$

$$\therefore \quad \frac{q}{m} = \frac{1.6 \times 10^{-19}}{9.1 \times 10^{-31}} = 1.75 \times 10^{11}$$

$$\simeq 2 \times 10^{11}\text{ Ckg}^{-1}$$

7 *(a)* As we know that, radius of a charged particle in a magnetic field B is given by

$$r = \frac{mv}{qB} \quad \ldots \text{(i)}$$

where, r = charge on the particle and v = speed of the particle.

∴ The time taken to complete the circle,

$$T = \frac{2\pi r}{v} \Rightarrow \frac{T}{2\pi} = \frac{m}{qB} \quad \text{[from Eq. (i)]}$$

Here, $q = e$,

$$\frac{e}{m} = 1.76 \times 10^{11}\text{ C kg}^{-1}$$

and $B = 3.57 \times 10^{-2}$ T

$$\Rightarrow \frac{2\pi}{T} = \frac{eB}{m}$$

$$f = \frac{1}{2\pi}\frac{e}{m}B \qquad \left(\because \frac{1}{T} = f\right)$$

$$= \frac{1}{2\pi} \times 1.76 \times 10^{11} \times 3.57 \times 10^{-2}$$

$$= 1.0 \times 10^9 \text{ Hz} = 1 \text{ GHz}$$

8 (c) Force of charged particle,

$$F = qvB\sin\theta$$

Force will be maximum, if $\theta = 90°$ i.e. if v is perpendicular to B.

9 (c) In cyclotron,

Force on charge = Centripetal force

$$\therefore \quad Bqv = \frac{mv^2}{r}$$

$$\Rightarrow \quad r = \frac{mv}{Bq} \Rightarrow r \propto v$$

10 (a) When a magnetic field is applied on a stationary electron, it remains stationary.

Because $F = q(\mathbf{v} \times \mathbf{B})$

If $v = 0 \Rightarrow F = 0$

11 (a) By Fleming's left hand rule, if the particle is moving and magnetic field is perpendicular to the velocity, then the particle experience a force as shown.

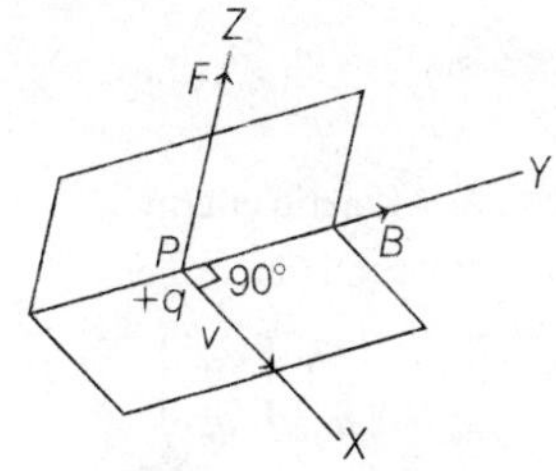

12 (b) Given, kinetic energy = E, mass = m, magnetic field = B and charge = q.

We know that, $F = qvB\sin\theta$

(motion of a charged particle in a uniform magnetic field)

If $\theta = 90°$, then $F = qvB$ ...(i)

We know that centripetal force,

$$F = \frac{mv^2}{r} \quad \text{...(ii)}$$

From Eqs. (i) and (ii), we get

$$qvB = \frac{mv^2}{r}, r = \frac{mv}{qB}$$

$$\left[\because E = \frac{1}{2}mv^2, v = \sqrt{\frac{2E}{m}}\right]$$

$$\therefore \quad r = \frac{m\sqrt{\frac{2E}{m}}}{qB}$$

$$\Rightarrow \quad r = \frac{\sqrt{2Em}}{qB}$$

13 (d) Suppose, the velocity v of the particle entering the magnetic field **B** instead of being perpendicular to **B** makes an angle with it.

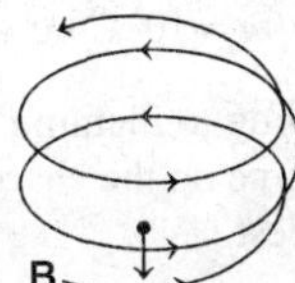

Then, v may be resolved into two components, $v_{||} = v\cos\theta$ parallel to **B** and $v_\perp = v\sin\theta$ perpendicular to **B**.

The component $v_{||}$ gives a linear path and the component $v_\perp$ gives a circular path to the particle. The resultant of these two is a helical path whose axis is parallel to the magnetic field.

14 (d) Consider the diagram, where a charged particle of mass m and charge q moves along a circular path. Anti-clockwise as shown. Magnetic field B is assumed to be into plane of paper and of constant magnitude.

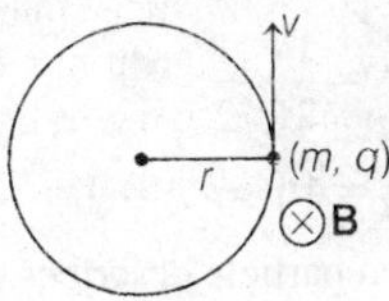

Clearly, centripetal force for the circular movement of the charge will be provided by magnetic Lorentz force ($q\mathbf{v} \times \mathbf{B}$).

$$\text{Hence,} \quad \frac{mv^2}{r} = qvB\sin 90°$$

$$\Rightarrow \quad \frac{mv^2}{r} = qvB$$

$$\Rightarrow \quad r = \frac{mv}{qB} \quad \text{...(i)}$$

T = Time taken to complete one revolution

$$\Rightarrow \quad T = \frac{2\pi}{\omega} = \frac{2\pi}{v/r} = \frac{2\pi r}{v}$$

$$= \frac{2\pi}{v}\left(\frac{mv}{qB}\right) \quad \text{[From Eq. (i)]}$$

$$= \frac{2\pi m}{qB}$$

15 (a) Initial acceleration, $a_0 = \frac{eE}{m}$ ...(i)

$$\Rightarrow \quad E = \frac{a_0 m}{e}$$

$$\therefore \quad \frac{ev_0B + eE}{m} = 3a_0$$

$$\text{or} \quad ev_0B + eE = 3a_0m$$

$$\therefore \quad ev_0B = 3ma_0 - eE$$

$$\Rightarrow \quad = 3ma_0 - ma_0 \quad \text{[from Eq. (i)]}$$

$$\Rightarrow \quad ev_0B = 2ma_0$$

$$\therefore \quad B = \frac{2ma_0}{ev_0}$$

The direction of electric field is along direction of force, hence towards West. The direction of magnetic field is up.

16 (d) As shown in figure,

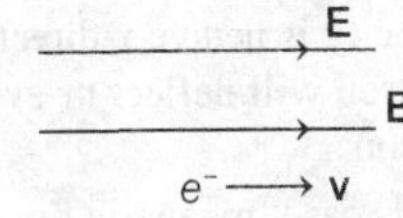

B, **E** and **v** are in same direction.

Due to electric field (**E**), force on e^- will be opposite to its velocity (**v**)

As, angle between **v** and **B** is zero (0°).

Hence, $\mathbf{F}_m = q\mathbf{v} \times \mathbf{B} = qVB\sin\theta = 0$

Hence, electron velocity will decrease in magnitude.

17 (b) Radius of circular path,

$$R = \frac{\sqrt{2m(\text{KE})}}{qB}$$

$$\text{So,} \quad q \propto \sqrt{m(\text{KE})}$$

$$\text{Hence,} \quad \frac{e}{2e} = \sqrt{\frac{(m_p)(1\text{MeV})}{(4m_e)(\text{KE})}}$$

$$\text{or} \quad \frac{1}{4} = \frac{1}{4\text{KE}}$$

Energy of α- particle, $K = 1$ MeV

18 (a) We have,

$$r = \frac{\sqrt{2mqV}}{qB} = \sqrt{\frac{2mV}{qB^2}}$$

$$\frac{r_1}{r_2} = \sqrt{\frac{m_1}{m_2}} \Rightarrow \frac{m_1}{m_2} = \frac{r_1^2}{r_2^2}$$

$$\text{Hence,} \quad \frac{m_1}{m_2} = \frac{(2)^2}{(3)^2} = \frac{4}{9}$$

19 (a) When $\mathbf{v} \perp \mathbf{B}$, charge q performs circular path.

20 (b) Given, $\theta = 23°$,
$B = 2.6\ \text{mT} = 2.6 \times 10^{-3}\ \text{T}$
and $F = 6.5 \times 10^{-17}\ \text{N}$

We know that, $F = qvB\sin\theta$
$6.5 \times 10^{-17} = 1.6 \times 10^{-19} \times v \times 2.6 \times 10^{-3} \times \sin 23°$

$$v = \frac{6.5 \times 10^{-17}}{2.6 \times 10^{-3} \times 1.6 \times 10^{-19} \times 0.39}$$

$\therefore\ v = 4 \times 10^5\ \text{ms}^{-1}$

21 (c) Radius, $r = \dfrac{mv}{qB}$

or $B = \dfrac{mv}{qr} = \dfrac{9.1 \times 10^{-31} \times 1.3 \times 10^6}{1.6 \times 10^{-19} \times 0.35}$
$= 2.1 \times 10^{-5}\ \text{T}$

22 (d) By Fleming's left hand rule, the field is in outward or +ve z-direction and velocity is in +ve x-direction. So, the electron will deflect in +ve y-direction

23 (c) In this case, magnetic force provides necessary centripetal force,

i.e. $qvB = \dfrac{mv^2}{r}$

Radius of path, $r = \dfrac{mv}{Bq} = \dfrac{\sqrt{2mE}}{qB}$

$r = \dfrac{\sqrt{2mE}}{Bq} = \dfrac{\sqrt{2m_1E_1}}{Bq}$

or $E_1 = \dfrac{mE}{m_1} = \dfrac{(2m_1)}{m_1} \times 50\ \text{keV}$
[$\because m = 2m_1$ for deuteron]
$= 100\ \text{keV}$

24 (d) The component of velocity perpendicular to H will make the motion circular, while that parallel to H will make it move along a straight line. The two together will make the motion helical.

25 (b) A charged particle moves in a straight line under the action of an electric field, whereas it moves in a circular path under the action of a magnetic field. Thus, for the particle moving in a circular path, $E = 0$, $B \neq 0$

26 (a) Radius of circular path, $r_a = \dfrac{m_a v_a}{qB}$

and $r_b = \dfrac{m_b v_b}{qB}$

According to question, $r_a > r_b$

$\therefore\ \dfrac{m_a v_a}{qB} > \dfrac{m_b v_b}{qB}$ or $m_a v_a > m_b v_b$

27 (d) For a charged particle, entering perpendicular to a magnetic field will execute a circular path.
Such that,

$$F_m = qvB\sin\theta = mv^2/r$$

$\Rightarrow\ \dfrac{q}{m} = \dfrac{v}{rB\sin\theta}$

$\Rightarrow\ \dfrac{q}{m} = \dfrac{4 \times 10^6}{2 \times 10^{-2} \times 2 \times \sin 90°}$

$\Rightarrow\ q/m = 10^8\ \text{C kg}^{-1}$

28 (d) According to Fleming's left hand rule, the force on the charge will be towards West.

29 (b) Magnetic force,
$F = qvB\sin\theta$
$\therefore\ F = (1.6 \times 10^{-19}) \times (2 \times 10^7) \times (1.5)\sin 30°$

$F = 1.6 \times 10^{-12} \times 2 \times 1.5 \times \dfrac{1}{2}$

$F = 2.4 \times 10^{-12}\ \text{N}$

30 (d) In a perpendicular magnetic field,
Magnetic force = Centripetal force

i.e. $Bqv = \dfrac{mv^2}{r} \Rightarrow r = \dfrac{mv}{Bq}$

$\therefore\ \dfrac{r_1}{r_2} = \dfrac{v_1}{v_2} \times \dfrac{B_2}{B_1}$ (m and q are same)

$\dfrac{r_1}{r_2} = \dfrac{1}{2} \times \dfrac{1}{2}$

$\Rightarrow\ r_2 = 4r_1 \Rightarrow r_2 = 4r$

31 (b) When particle describes circular path in a magnetic field, its velocity is always perpendicular to the magnetic force.

Power, $P = \mathbf{F} \cdot \mathbf{v} = Fv\cos\theta$
Here, $\theta = 90°$
$\therefore\ P = 0$
But $P = \dfrac{W}{t}$
$\Rightarrow\ W = P \times t$
Hence, work done,
$W = 0$ [everywhere]

32 (c) When electron moves in both electric and magnetic fields such that it moves along a straight line, then
$qE = qvB$

$v = \dfrac{E}{B} = \dfrac{1500}{0.40} = 3750\ \text{ms}^{-1}$

$v = 3.75 \times 10^3\ \text{ms}^{-1}$

33 (a) Net force acting on electron is zero as $F_m = evB\sin 0° = 0$

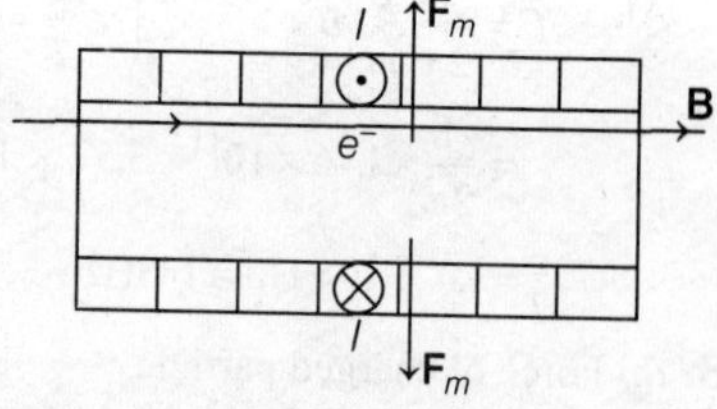

Hence, work done = zero.

34 (a) $q = -2\mu\text{C}$,
$v = (2\hat{\mathbf{i}} + 3\hat{\mathbf{j}}) \times 10^6\ \text{ms}^{-1}$,
$B = 2\text{T}$ along y-direction
$\mathbf{B} = 2\hat{\mathbf{j}}$

$\because$ Magnetic force, $\mathbf{F} = q(\mathbf{v} \times \mathbf{B})$
$= (-2 \times 10^{-6}\text{C})[(2\hat{\mathbf{i}} + 3\hat{\mathbf{j}}) \times 10^6 \times 2\hat{\mathbf{j}}]$
$= (-2 \times 10^{-6})[4(\hat{\mathbf{i}} \times \hat{\mathbf{j}}) \times 10^6]$
[$\because \hat{\mathbf{j}} \times \hat{\mathbf{j}} = 0$]
$= -8\hat{\mathbf{k}} = 8\ \text{N}$ along $-z$-direction

35 (c) As a charged particle enter magnetic field perpendicular

$\dfrac{mv^2}{r} = qvB\sin\theta$

$\Rightarrow\ r = \dfrac{mv}{qB} = \dfrac{\sqrt{2Km}}{qB}$

$r \propto \dfrac{\sqrt{m}}{q}$ [For, $K_1 = K_2$]

where, K = kinetic energy.
Hence, Reason is incorrect.

Also, $\dfrac{r_p}{r_{He}} = \sqrt{\dfrac{m_p}{m_{He}}}\left(\dfrac{q_{He}}{q_p}\right)$

$= \sqrt{\dfrac{1}{4}} \times \dfrac{2}{1} = 1$

$r_p = r_{He}$

$\Rightarrow$ Assertion is correct.

36 (b) $\mathbf{v} = x\hat{\mathbf{i}} + y\hat{\mathbf{j}}$, $\mathbf{B} = y\hat{\mathbf{i}} + x\hat{\mathbf{j}}$
As, $\mathbf{F} = q(\mathbf{v} \times \mathbf{B})$
$\mathbf{F} = q[(x\hat{\mathbf{i}} + y\hat{\mathbf{j}}) \times (y\hat{\mathbf{i}} + x\hat{\mathbf{j}})]$
$= q[x^2(\hat{\mathbf{k}}) - y^2(\hat{\mathbf{k}})]$
$= q(x^2 - y^2)\hat{\mathbf{k}}$
If $x = y \Rightarrow \mathbf{F} = 0$
Also, $x > y$
$\Rightarrow\ F \propto (x^2 - y^2)$

37 (c) As, $r = \frac{mv}{qB}$

Also, T = time period $= \frac{2\pi r}{vB}$

$$= \frac{2\pi mv}{qBv} = \frac{2\pi m}{qB}$$

$$\frac{1}{T} = F = \frac{qB}{2\pi m}$$

$$\Rightarrow \quad F \propto \frac{1}{m}$$

$\Rightarrow Li^+$ has maximum mass, hence Li^+ will have minimum frequency.

38 (a) As, $r = \frac{mv}{qB}$

Here, v and B are constants,

$$r \propto \frac{m}{q}$$

$$\Rightarrow \quad \frac{r_1}{r_2} = \frac{m_1}{m_2}\left(\frac{q_2}{q_1}\right)$$

$$\frac{r_1}{r_2} = \left(\frac{1m}{4m}\right)\left(\frac{2e}{1e}\right)$$

$$\Rightarrow \quad \frac{r_1}{r_2} = \frac{1}{2}$$

39 (e) Magnetic Lorentz force is given as $\mathbf{F} = q(\mathbf{v} \times \mathbf{B})$

40 (a) Magnetic Lorentz force will provide required centripetal force.

Hence, $\frac{mv^2}{R} = qvB$

$$\frac{qB}{mv} = \frac{1}{R}$$

$$\Rightarrow \quad \frac{q}{m} = \frac{1}{R}\left(\frac{v}{B}\right)$$

$$\Rightarrow \quad \left(\frac{q}{m}\right) \propto \frac{1}{R}$$

41 (c) When a charged particle enters a uniform magnetic field perpendicularly, then the charged particle executes circular motion. Such that its velocity changes but speed $|v|$ remains constant. The force on the charged particle $(F_m = qvB)$ only change the direction of v.

Hence, KE is remains constant.

42 (b) Cyclotron can accelerate α-particles (positive charge particle).

43 (c) $\frac{r_1}{r_2} = \sqrt{\frac{m_1}{m_2}\left(\frac{q_2}{q_1}\right)}$

$$\Rightarrow \quad \frac{r_1}{r_2} = \frac{1}{\sqrt{2}}$$

44 (d) When a charged particle (positive) enter a uniform magnetic field with uniform velocity.

$\Rightarrow$ If **B** and **v** are in same direction, F = 0 i.e. path will be straight line.

$\Rightarrow$ If **B** and **v** are perpendicular,

$$\mathbf{F} = q(\mathbf{v} \times \mathbf{B})$$

$$|\mathbf{F}| = qvB\sin\theta = qvB$$

i.e. path will be circular.

$\Rightarrow$ If **B** and **v** have any angle θ [i.e. other than 0° and 90°]

i.e. path will be helix.

45 (c) After passing through a magnetic field, the magnitude of its mass and velocity of the particle remain same, so its energy does not change, i.e. kinetic energy will remain T.

46 (a) At right angle to magnetic field, charged particles move on circular path at which magnetic force provides necessary centripetal force to keep it moving on circular path.

i.e. $\quad qvB = \frac{mv^2}{r}$

$$\therefore \quad r = \frac{mv}{qB} = \sqrt{\frac{2mE}{q^2B^2}}$$

where,

E = kinetic energy of the particle.

$$r_p = \sqrt{\frac{2mE}{e^2B^2}}$$

$$r_d = \sqrt{\frac{2 \times 2m \times E}{e^2B^2}}$$

and $\quad r_a = \sqrt{\frac{2 \times 4m \times E}{(2e)^2 B^2}}$

$$\therefore \quad r_p : r_d : r_a = 1 : \sqrt{2} : 1$$

47 (c) When magnetic field is perpendicular to motion of charged particle, then

centripetal force = magnetic force

i.e. $\quad \frac{mv^2}{R} = Bqv$

or $\quad R = \frac{mv}{Bq}$

Further, time period of the motion,

$$T = \frac{2\pi R}{v} = \frac{2\pi\left(\frac{mv}{Bq}\right)}{v}$$

or $\quad T = \frac{2\pi m}{Bq}$

It is independent of both R and v.

48 (d) The protons, cathode rays and the alpha particles are charged particles, so these are deflected by the magnetic field. But neutrons have no charge, so these are not deflected by magnetic field.

49 (a) The magnetic force on a charged particle moving in the field does no work, because the kinetic energy of the charged particle does not change.

50 (c) Cyclotron frequency,

$$n = \frac{1}{T} = \frac{v}{2\pi r}$$

or $\quad n = \frac{v}{2\pi}\left(\frac{Bq}{mv}\right) \quad \left[\because r = \frac{mv}{Bq}\right]$

or $\quad n = \frac{Bq}{2\pi m}$

Thus, cyclotron frequency does not depend upon the speed of the charged particle.

The maximum kinetic energy of charged particle is

$$E_{max} = \left(\frac{q^2B^2}{2m}\right)r^2$$

Thus, KE depends on both the mass and charge of particle.

51 (c) Frequency of cyclotron,

$$\nu = \frac{1}{T} = \frac{Bq}{2\pi m}$$

which does not depend upon the velocity of particle.

52 (c) Under uniform magnetic field, force evB acts on proton and provides the necessary centripetal force mv^2/a.

$$\therefore \quad \frac{mv^2}{a} = evB$$

or $\quad v = \frac{aeB}{m} \quad \ldots(i)$

Now, angular momentum, $J = r \times p$

Here, $\quad J = a \times mv$

Putting the value of v from Eq. (i), we get

$$J = a \times m\left(\frac{aeB}{m}\right) = a^2eB$$

53 (c) It will measure both electric and magnetic field when he passes by a stationary electron with some velocity v, as there is a relative motion between them.

54 (c) According to Fleming's left hand rule, in Figs. (1) and (2), magnetic force on the electron will be directed in + ve Z-axis and + ve X-axis, respectively. In

Fig. (3), velocity of electron and direction of magnetic field are anti-parallel, so no force will act on electron.

55 *(d)* The path of an electron in a uniform magnetic field is either helical or circular as a centripetal force produces a circular motion perpendicular to the magnetic field B because of force $\mathbf{F} = q(\mathbf{v} \times \mathbf{B})$, where $\mathbf{v}$ is the velocity of electron and q is the charge. If $\mathbf{v}$ and $\mathbf{B}$ are perpendicular to each other, then particle will describe a circle, but if $\mathbf{v}$ is not perpendicular to $\mathbf{B}$, then component of $\mathbf{v}$ along B remains unchanged as the motion along the magnetic field will not be affected by the magnetic field. Hence, motion perpendicular to B will be circular producing helical motion as given below

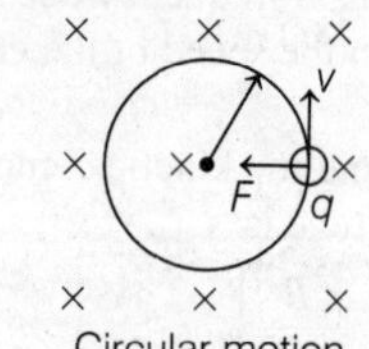

Circular motion

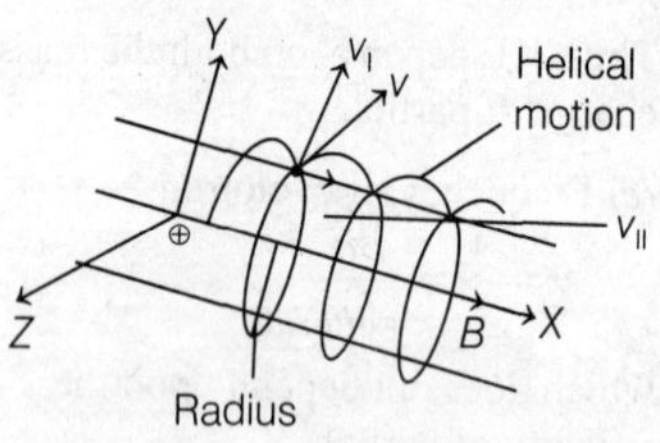

56 *(b)* Radius of the helical path,

$$r = \frac{m(v \sin\theta)}{qB}$$

Given, $m = 1.67 \times 10^{-27}$ kg,

$v = 4 \times 10^5 \text{ms}^{-1}, \theta = 60°$

$q = 1.6 \times 10^{-19}$ C, $B = 0.3$T

$$\therefore\ r = \frac{1.67 \times 10^{-27} \times 4 \times 10^5 \times (\sqrt{3}/2)}{1.6 \times 10^{-19} \times 0.3}$$

$$= 0.012 \text{ m} = 1.2 \text{ cm}$$

57 *(d)* If a particle carrying charge q and moving with velocity $\mathbf{v}$ through a point in magnetic field $\mathbf{B}$ experiences a deflecting force $\mathbf{F}$ given by

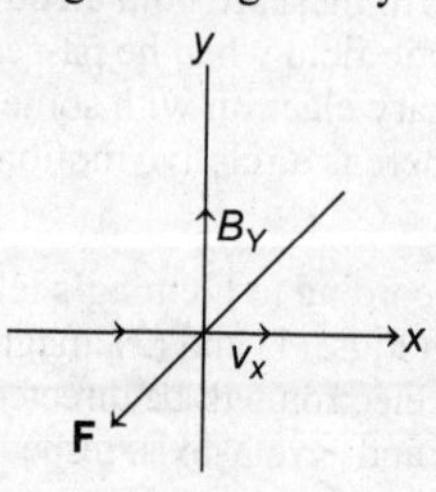

$$\mathbf{F} = q(\mathbf{v} \times \mathbf{B})$$

Here, $q = e$, $\mathbf{v} = v_x \hat{\mathbf{i}}$

and $\mathbf{B} = B_y \hat{\mathbf{j}}$

$$\therefore\quad \mathbf{F} = ev_x B_y (\hat{\mathbf{i}} \times \hat{\mathbf{j}})$$

$$= ev_x B_y \hat{\mathbf{k}}$$

Hence, subsequent motion of the charged particle will be a circle in the xy-plane.

58 *(a)* When a charged particle enters a magnetic field perpendicularly, it moves on a circular path. The required centripetal force is provided by magnetic force.

i.e. Magnetic force = Centripetal force

or $\quad qvB = \dfrac{mv^2}{r}$

$$\therefore\quad r = mv/qB \quad \ldots\text{(i)}$$

Now, kinetic energy of the particle,

$$K = \frac{1}{2}mv^2$$

$$\Rightarrow\quad mv = \sqrt{2mK}$$

Therefore, Eq. (i) becomes

$$r = \frac{\sqrt{2mK}}{qB}$$

or $\quad r \propto \sqrt{m}$

$$\Rightarrow\quad \frac{r_e}{r_p} = \sqrt{\frac{m_e}{m_p}}$$

As $m_e < m_p$, so, $r_e < r_p$.

Hence, trajectory of electron is less curved.

59 *(a)* Lorentz force = Centripetal force

i.e. $\quad Bqv = \dfrac{mv^2}{r}$

or $\quad Bq = m\omega \quad$ (as $v = r\omega$)

or $\quad Bq = m2\pi f \quad (\because\ \omega = 2\pi f)$

$$\therefore\quad f = \frac{Bq}{2\pi m}$$

60 *(c)* Here, $q = -e$, $\mathbf{v} = (2\hat{\mathbf{i}} + 3\hat{\mathbf{j}})\ \text{ms}^{-1}$

and $\mathbf{B} = 4\hat{\mathbf{k}}$ T

$\therefore\ \mathbf{F}_m = q(\mathbf{v} \times \mathbf{B})$

$$= -e[(2\hat{\mathbf{i}} + 3\hat{\mathbf{j}}) \times 4\hat{\mathbf{k}}]$$

$$= -e[8(\hat{\mathbf{i}} \times \hat{\mathbf{k}}) + 12(\hat{\mathbf{j}} \times \hat{\mathbf{k}})]$$

$$= -e[-8\hat{\mathbf{j}} + 12\hat{\mathbf{i}}]$$

$\Rightarrow\ \mathbf{F}_m = 4e[2\hat{\mathbf{j}} - 3\hat{\mathbf{i}}]$N

$\Rightarrow\ \mathbf{F}_m \perp \mathbf{v}$

$\Rightarrow$ Direction of its velocity will change.

61 *(c)* When a charged particle q is moving in a uniform magnetic field $\mathbf{B}$ with velocity $\mathbf{v}$ such that angle between $\mathbf{v}$ and $\mathbf{B}$ be θ, then due to interaction between the magnetic field produced due to moving charge and magnetic field applied, the charge q experiences a force which is given by

$$F = qvB\sin\theta$$

If $\theta = 0°$ or $180°$, then

$$\sin\theta = 0$$

$$\therefore\quad F = qvB\sin\theta = 0$$

Since, force on charged particle is non-zero, so angle between $\mathbf{v}$ and $\mathbf{B}$ can have any value other than zero and 180°.

62 *(b)* The charged particle bends in a circle of radius r.

$$\therefore\quad Bqv\sin\frac{\pi}{2} = \frac{mv^2}{r} \qquad \left(\because\ \sin\frac{\pi}{2} = 1\right)$$

$$\Rightarrow\quad r = \frac{mv}{Bq}$$

The particle does not hit the plate, if $r \le d$

or $\quad \dfrac{mv}{Bq} \le d$

or $\quad v \le \dfrac{Bqd}{m}$

$$\therefore\quad v_{\max} = \frac{Bqd}{m}$$

63 *(c)* The formula for radius of circular path is

$$r = \frac{mv}{eB} = \frac{v}{\left(\frac{e}{m}\right)B} \quad \ldots\text{(i)}$$

Here, $\dfrac{e}{m} = 1.7 \times 10^{11}$ C kg^{-1}

$$\therefore\quad r = \frac{6 \times 10^7}{1.7 \times 10^{11} \times 1.5 \times 10^{-2}}$$

$$= 2.35 \times 10^{-2}\text{m}$$

$$= 2.35 \text{ cm}$$

64 *(c)* Given, $r = 4 \times 10^{-11}$m and

$$v = 10^5 \text{ms}^{-1}$$

$$B = \frac{\mu_0 I}{2r}$$

As, $I = \left(\dfrac{-e}{T}\right) = \dfrac{-e}{\left(\dfrac{2\pi r}{v}\right)} = \dfrac{-ev}{2\pi r}$

$$\therefore\quad B = \left(\frac{\mu_0}{2r}\right)\left(\frac{-ev}{2\pi r}\right) = \frac{-\mu_0 ev}{4\pi r^2}$$

Magnitude of B

$$= \frac{(10^{-7}) \times 1.6 \times 10^{-19} \times 10^5}{16 \times 10^{-22}}$$

$$(\because \mu_0 = 4\pi \times 10^{-7} \text{ TmA}^{-1})$$

$$= \frac{1.6 \times 10}{16}$$

$$= 1 \text{ T or Wb m}^{-2}$$

65 *(c)* $qvB = \frac{mv^2}{r}$

$$\Rightarrow \quad r = \frac{mv}{qB}$$

$$\therefore \quad r' = \frac{m \times 2v}{q \times B/2} = 4r$$

66 *(c)* Force acting on particle due to magnetic field B,

$\mathbf{F} = q(\mathbf{v} \times \mathbf{B}) = qvB\, [\because \theta = 90°]$ ...(i)

and centripetal force,

$$F = \frac{mv^2}{r} \qquad \text{...(ii)}$$

From Eqs. (i) and (ii), we get

$$B = \frac{mv}{rq} = \frac{\text{linear momentum}}{\text{charge}}$$

Since, charge is constant, so change will occur in linear momentum.

67 *(d)* When deuterium and helium are subjected to an accelerating field, neither of them will be accelerated as both of them are neutral. As ions have positive or negative charge, they get accelerated by an electric field or magnetic field moving perpendicular to the field. As, Lorentz force F is exerted due to charge (q), this force cannot be exerted in absence of charge or for neutral particles.

68 *(a)* Proton will represent the direction of current. So, the direction of current is vertically downward.
According to Fleming's left hand rule, if middle finger represents the direction of current and forefinger represents the direction of magnetic field, then thumb will represent the direction of Lorentz force acting on the proton which deflects the proton in East direction.

Alternative Method

Force on proton in magnetic field.

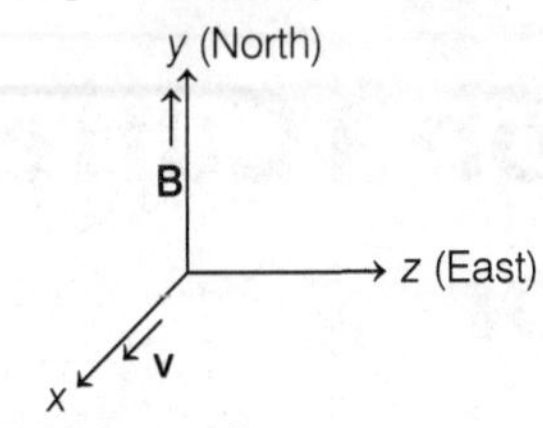

$$\mathbf{F} = q(\mathbf{v} \times \mathbf{B})$$

Given, $\mathbf{v} = v\hat{\mathbf{i}}, \mathbf{B} = B\hat{\mathbf{j}}$

$$\therefore \quad \mathbf{F} = q(v\hat{\mathbf{i}} \times B\hat{\mathbf{j}})$$

$$= qvB\,\hat{\mathbf{k}} \qquad (\because \hat{\mathbf{i}} \times \hat{\mathbf{j}} = \hat{\mathbf{k}})$$

Hence, force will act on the proton in z-direction, i.e. towards East.

69 *(d)* According to Maxwell's cork screw rule, the direction of magnetic field at point P in plane of paper is perpendicular to the plane of paper inwards, i.e. along z-direction.
Now, since charge is moving along x-direction, therefore from Fleming's left hand rule stretching the forefinger in direction of paper inwards the thumb will indicate the direction of force F acting on the charged particle along oy-direction.

Alternative Method

As discussed above, B acts inwards into plane of the paper and v is along OX, hence

$$\mathbf{F} = Q(\mathbf{v} \times \mathbf{B})$$

$$= Q\begin{vmatrix} \hat{\mathbf{i}} & \hat{\mathbf{j}} & \hat{\mathbf{k}} \\ v & 0 & 0 \\ 0 & 0 & -B \end{vmatrix}$$

$$= Q[\hat{\mathbf{i}}(0) - \hat{\mathbf{j}}(-vB) + \hat{\mathbf{k}}(0)]$$

$$= +\hat{\mathbf{j}}QvB$$

i.e. force is along oy-direction.

70 *(c)* $\frac{mv^2}{r} = evB$

$$\Rightarrow \quad r = \frac{mv}{eB}$$

As for a particle in motion, $p = mv$

$$\therefore \quad r = \frac{mv}{eB} = \frac{p}{eB}$$

$$\Rightarrow p = eBr$$

$$\therefore \quad p = 1.6 \times 10^{-19} \times 3 \times 10^{-3} \times 4 \times 10^{-3}$$

$$= 1.92 \times 10^{-24} \text{ kg-ms}^{-1}$$

71 *(c)* Cyclotron is a device which is used to accelerate positively charged particles, e.g. protons, deuterons, etc.

72 *(b)* Velocity of proton, $v = \frac{Bqr}{m}$

where,
r = radius of circular path.
Distance covered by proton to traverse

$90°$ arc $= \frac{1}{4} \times$ circumference

$$d = \frac{1}{4} \times 2\pi r = \frac{\pi r}{2}$$

Time taken by proton to cover distance d,

$$t = \frac{\pi r/2}{v} = \frac{\pi r}{2v} = \frac{\pi}{2}\frac{r}{Bqr/m} = \frac{\pi m}{2Bq} \quad \text{...(i)}$$

Putting, $m = 1.65 \times 10^{-27}$ kg,

$B = 100$ mT $= 100 \times 10^{-3}$ T

and $\quad q = 1.6 \times 10^{-19}$ C, in Eq. (i)

$$\therefore \quad t = \frac{3.14 \times 1.65 \times 10^{-27}}{2 \times 100 \times 10^{-3} \times 1.6 \times 10^{-19}}$$

$$t = 1.62 \times 10^{-7} \text{ s}$$

73 *(b)* $F = qvB = \frac{mv^2}{r}$ = centripetal force

Maximum energy, $E = \frac{1}{2}\frac{B^2q^2r^2}{m}$

Hence, ratio of energy of deuteron and proton is

$$\frac{E_d}{E_p} = \left(\frac{q_d}{q_p}\right)^2 \left(\frac{m_p}{m_d}\right)$$

$$\frac{40}{E_p} = \left(\frac{q}{q}\right)^2 \left(\frac{m}{2m}\right)$$

$$\Rightarrow \quad E_p = 80 \text{ MeV}$$

74 *(c)* The force due to magnetic field acting on the electron of mass m,

$$F = evB \qquad \text{...(i)}$$

The centripetal force is given by

$$F = \frac{mv^2}{r} \qquad \text{...(ii)}$$

where, r is radius of circular path.
Equating Eq. (i) with Eq. (ii), we get

$$F = qvB = \frac{mv^2}{r}$$

$$\Rightarrow \quad r = \frac{mv}{qB}$$

$$\Rightarrow \quad r \propto v$$

Hence, the radius is directly proportional to speed.

Topic 3

Force and Torque on a Current Carrying Conductor

2019

1 A magnetic needle suspended parallel to a magnetic field require $\sqrt{3}J$ of work to turn it through 60°. The torque needed to maintain the needle in this portion will be **[AIIMS]**

(a) $2\sqrt{3}$ J (b) 3 J (c) $\sqrt{3}$ J (d) $\frac{3}{2}$ J

2 α-particle is revolving in a circular path with radius r with speed v, then find the value of magnetic dipole moment. **[AIIMS]**

(a) 2 evr (b) evr (c) 3 evr (d) 4 evr

2018

3 A metallic rod of mass per unit length 0.5 kg m^{-1} is lying horizontally on a smooth inclined plane which makes an angle of 30° with the horizontal. The rod is not allowed to slide down by flowing a current through it, when a magnetic field of induction 0.25 T is acting on it in the vertical direction. The current flowing in the rod to keep it stationary is **[NEET]**

(a) 14.76 A (b) 5.98 A (c) 7.14 A (d) 11.32 A

4 The magnetic moment of an electron orbiting in a circular orbit of radius r with a speed v is equal to **[JIPMER]**

(a) $evr/2$ (b) evr
(c) $er/2v$ (d) None of these

5 A current carrying loop is placed in a uniform magnetic field. The torque acting on it does not depend upon **[JIPMER]**

(a) shape of loop (b) area of loop
(c) value of current (d) magnetic field

2016

6 A square loop $ABCD$ carrying a current i, is placed near and coplanar with a long straight conductor XY carrying a current I, the net force on the loop will be **[NEET]**

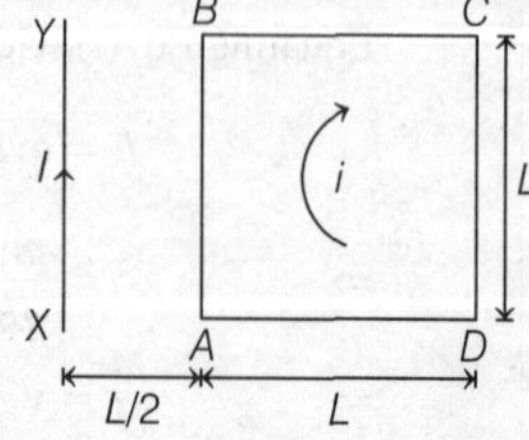

(a) $\frac{\mu_0 Ii}{2\pi}$ (b) $\frac{2\mu_0 IiL}{3\pi}$ (c) $\frac{\mu_0 IiL}{2\pi}$ (d) $\frac{2\mu_0 Ii}{3\pi}$

2014

7 Magnetic induction produced at the centre of a circular loop carrying current is B. The magnetic moment of the loop of radius R is (μ_0 = permeability of free space) **[MHT CET]**

(a) $\frac{BR^2}{2\pi\mu_0}$ (b) $\frac{2\pi BR^3}{\mu_0}$ (c) $\frac{BR^2}{2\pi\mu_0}$ (d) $\frac{2\pi BR^2}{\mu_0}$

8 The ratio of magnetic dipole moment of an electron of charge e and mass m in Bohr's orbit in hydrogen atom to its angular momentum is **[MHT CET]**

(a) $\frac{e}{m}$ (b) $\frac{m}{e}$ (c) $\frac{2m}{e}$ (d) $\frac{e}{2m}$

9 An electron in a circular orbit of radius 0.05 nm performs 10^{16} revolutions per second. The magnetic moment due to this rotation of electron is (in A-m^2) **[WB JEE]**

(a) 2.16×10^{-23} (b) 3.21×10^{-22}
(c) 3.21×10^{-24} (d) 1.26×10^{-23}

10 A circular coil of radius 10 cm and 100 turns carries a current 1 A. What is the magnetic moment of the coil? **[KCET]**

(a) 3.142×10^4 A-m^2 (b) 10^4 A-m^2
(c) 3.14 A-m^2 (d) 3 A-m^2

11 Two thin long conductors separated by a distance d carry currents I_1 and I_2 in the same direction. They exert a force F on each other. Now, the current in one of them is increased to two times and its direction is reversed. The distance is also increased to $3d$. The new value of force between them is **[UK PMT]**

(a) $-2F$ (b) $\frac{F}{3}$ (c) $-\frac{2F}{3}$ (d) $-\frac{F}{3}$

12 A particle with charge q is moving along a circle of radius R with uniform speed v. The associated magnetic moment μ is given by **[EAMCET]**

(a) $\frac{1}{2}v^2R$ (b) $\frac{1}{4}q\,vR$ (c) $\frac{1}{2}qvR$ (d) $\frac{1}{2}q^2vR$

13 A wire of length L metre carrying a current I ampere is bent in the form of a circle. The magnitude of the magnetic moment is **[EAMCET]**

(a) $\frac{L^2I^2}{4\pi}$ (b) $\frac{LI}{4\pi}$ (c) $\frac{L^2I}{4\pi}$ (d) $\frac{LI}{4\pi}$

2013

14 A current loop in a magnetic field **[NEET]**
(a) experiences a torque whether the field is uniform or non-uniform in all orientations
(b) can be in equilibrium in one orientation
(c) can be equilibrium in two orientations, both the equilibrium states are unstable
(d) can be in equilibrium in two orientations, one stable while the other is unstable

15 A small circular flexible loop of wire of radius r carries a current I. It is placed in a uniform magnetic field B. The tension in the loop will be doubled, if **[UP CPMT]**
(a) I is doubled (b) B is halved
(c) r is doubled (d) both B and I are doubled

16 Two parallel wires carrying currents in the same direction attract each other because of **[UP CPMT]**
(a) potential difference between them
(b) mutual inductance between them
(c) electric force between them
(d) magnetic force between them

17 A rectangular loop carrying a current i is situated near a long straight wire such that the wire is parallel to one of the sides of the loop and is in the plane of the loop. If a steady current I is established in the wire as shown in the figure, the loop will **[WB JEE]**

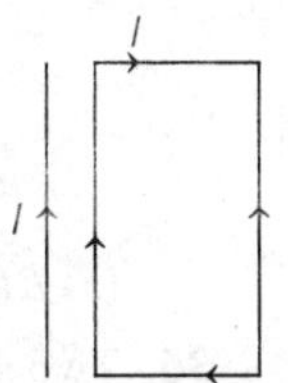

(a) rotate about an axis parallel to the wire
(b) move away from the wire
(c) move towards the wire
(d) remain stationary

2012

18 A straight wire of length 2 m carries a current of 10 A. If this wire is placed in uniform magnetic field of 0.15 T making an angle of 45° with the magnetic field, the applied force on the wire will be **[CBSE AIPMT]**
(a) 1.5 N (b) 3 N (c) $3\sqrt{2}$ N (d) $\frac{3}{\sqrt{2}}$ N

2011

19 A wire of length l is bent in the form of circular coil of some turns. A current i flows through the coil. The coil is placed in a uniform magnetic field B. The maximum torque on the coil can be **[NCERT Exemplar]**
(a) $\frac{iBl^2}{2\pi}$ (b) $\frac{iBl^2}{4\pi}$ (c) $\frac{iBl^2}{\pi}$ (d) $\frac{2iBl^2}{\pi}$

20 A square coil of side 10 cm consists of 20 turns and carries a current of 12 A. The coil is suspended vertically and the normal to the plane of the coil makes an angle of 30° with the direction of a uniform horizontal magnetic field of magnitude 0.80 T. What is the magnitude of torque experienced by the coil? **[NCERT Exemplar]**
(a) 0.96 N-m (b) 2.06 N-m
(c) 0.23 N-m (d) 1.36 N-m

21 Two very long straight parallel wires carry currents i and $2i$ in opposite directions. The distance between the wires is r. At a certain instant of time a point charge q is at a point equidistant from the two wires in the plane of the wires. Its instantaneous velocity v is perpendicular to this plane. The magnitude of the force due to the magnetic field acting on the charge at this instant is **[KCET]**
(a) zero (b) $\frac{3\mu_0}{2\pi}\frac{iqv}{r}$
(c) $\frac{\mu_0}{\pi}\frac{iqv}{r}$ (d) $\frac{\mu_0}{2\pi}\frac{iqv}{r}$

22 The torque required to hold a small circular coil of 10 turns, area 1 mm^2 and carrying a current of $(21/44)$ A in the middle of a long solenoid of 10^3 turns/m carrying a current of 2.5 A with its axis perpendicular to the axis of the solenoid is **[KCET]**

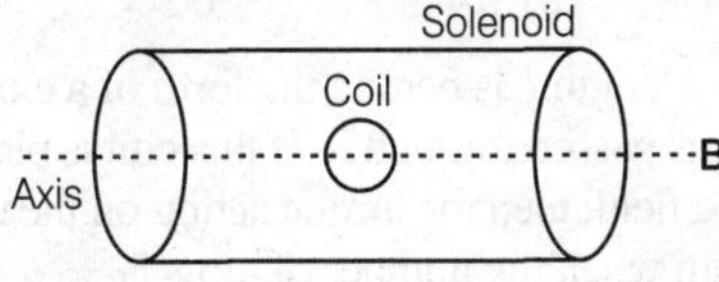

(a) 1.5×10^{-6} N-m (b) 1.5×10^{-8} N-m
(c) $1.5\times10^{+6}$ N-m (d) $1.5\times10^{+8}$ N-m

2010

23 A square current carrying loop is suspended in a uniform magnetic field acting in the plane of the loop. If the force on one arm of the loop is **F**, the net force on the remaining three arms of the loop is **[CBSE AIPMT]**
(a) 3**F** (b) −**F**
(c) −3**F** (d) **F**

24 A coil in the shape of an equilateral triangle of side 0.02 m is suspended from its vertex such that it is hanging in a vertical plane between the pole pieces of permanent magnet producing a uniform field of 5×10^{-2} T. If a current of 0.1 A is passed through the coil, what is the couple acting? **[AIIMS]**
(a) $5\sqrt{3}\times10^{-7}$ N-m
(b) $5\sqrt{3}\times10^{-10}$ N-m
(c) $\frac{\sqrt{3}}{5}\times10^{-7}$ N-m
(d) None of the above

25 **Assertion** Torque on the coil is the maximum when coil is suspended in a radial magnetic field.

Reason The torque tends to rotate the coil on its own axis. **[AIIMS]**
(a) Both Assertion and Reason are correct and Reason is the correct explanation of Assertion.
(b) Both Assertion and Reason are correct but Reason is not the correct explanation of Assertion.
(c) Assertion is correct but Reason is incorrect.
(d) Both Assertion and Reason are incorrect.

26 Magnetic field at the centre of a circular loop of area A is B. The magnetic moment of the loop will be **[AFMC]**

(a) $\frac{BA^2}{\mu_0 \pi}$ (b) $\frac{BA^{3/2}}{\mu_0 \pi}$ (c) $\frac{BA^{3/2}}{\mu_0 \pi^{1/2}}$ (d) $\frac{2BA^{3/2}}{\mu_0 \pi^{1/2}}$

27 Two thin long parallel wires separated by a distance b are carrying a current i ampere each. The magnitude of the force per unit length exerted by one wire on the other, is **[Manipal]**

(a) $\frac{\mu_0 i^2}{b^2}$ (b) $\frac{\mu_0 i}{2\pi b^2}$

(c) $\frac{\mu_0 i}{2\pi b}$ (d) $\frac{\mu_0 i^2}{2\pi b}$

28 The ratio of magnetic field and magnetic moment at the centre of a current carrying circular loop is x. When both the current and radius are doubled, the ratio will be **[WB JEE]**

(a) $x/8$ (b) $x/4$ (c) $x/2$ (d) $2x$

29 A wire of length L is bent in the form of a circular coil and current i is passed through it. If this coil is placed in a magnetic field, then the torque acting on the coil will be maximum when the number of turns is **[Haryana PMT]**

(a) as large as possible (b) any number

(c) 2 (d) 1

30 3 A of current is flowing in a linear conductor having a length of 40 cm. The conductor is placed in a magnetic field of strength 500 G and makes an angle of 30° with direction of the field. It experiences a force of magnitude **[JCECE]**

(a) 3×10^4 N (b) 3×10^2 N

(c) 3×10^{-2} N (d) 3×10^{-4} N

2009

31 A straight wire of mass 200 g and length 1.5 m carries a current of 2 A. It is suspended in mid-air by a uniform horizontal magnetic field **B**. The magnitude of **B** (in tesla) is (assume, $g = 9.8 \text{ ms}^{-2}$) **[JCECE]**

(a) 2 T (b) 1.5 T (c) 0.55 T (d) 0.65 T

32 A conducting rod of length l and mass m is moving down a smooth inclined plane of inclination θ with constant velocity v. A current i is flowing in the conductor in a direction perpendicular to paper inwards. A vertically upwards magnetic field **B** exists in space. Then, magnitude of magnetic field **B** is **[JCECE]**

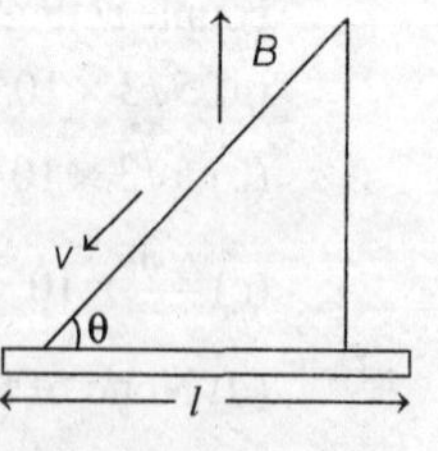

(a) $\frac{mg}{il}\sin\theta$ (b) $\frac{mg}{il}\tan\theta$ (c) $\frac{mg\cos\theta}{il}$ (d) $\frac{mg}{il\sin\theta}$

33 The magnetic dipole moment of current loop i, independent of **[KCET]**

(a) magnetic field in which it is lying

(b) number of turns

(c) area of the loop

(d) current in the loop

2008

34 A closed loop $PQRS$ carrying a current is placed in a uniform magnetic field. If the magnetic forces on segments PS, SR and RQ are F_1, F_2 and F_3 respectively and are in the plane of the paper and along the directions shown, the force on the segment QP is **[CBSE AIPMT]**

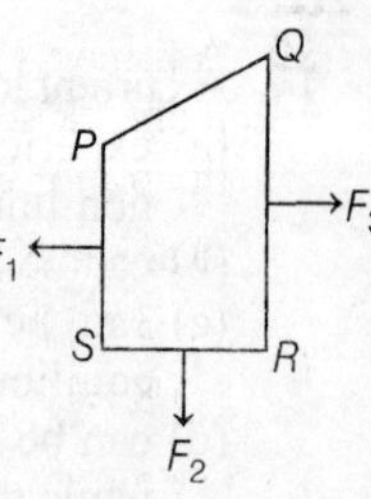

(a) $F_3 - F_1 - F_2$ (b) $\sqrt{(F_3 - F_1)^2 + F_2^2}$

(c) $\sqrt{(F_3 - F_1)^2 - F_2^2}$ (d) $F_3 - F_1 + F_2$

35 A wire PQR is bent as shown in figure and is placed in a region of uniform magnetic field B. The length of $PQ = QR = l$. A current I ampere flows through the wire as shown. The magnitude of the force on PQ and QR will be

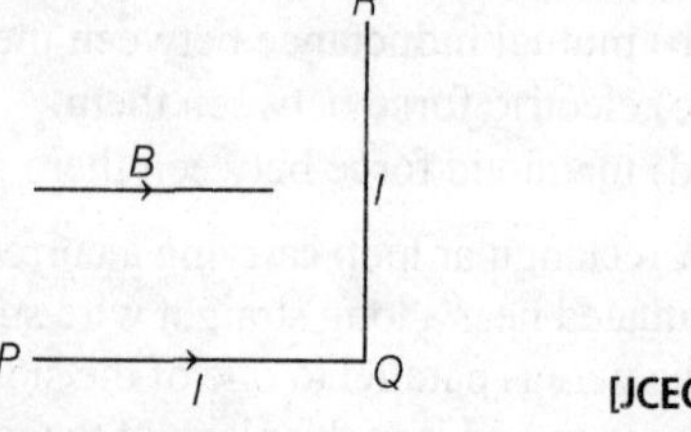

[JCECE, AFMC]

(a) BIl, 0 (b) $2BIl$, 0 (c) 0, BIl (d) 0, 0

36 Two streams of protons move parallel to each other in the same direction. Then, these **[BHU]**

(a) do not interact at all

(b) attract each other

(c) repel each other

(d) get rotated to be perpendicular to each other

37 Consider two straight parallel conductors A and B separated by a distance x and carrying individual currents I_A and I_B, respectively. If the two conductors attract each other, it indicates that **[J&K CET]**

(a) the two currents are parallel in direction

(b) the two currents are anti-parallel in direction

(c) the magnetic lines of induction are parallel

(d) the magnetic lines of induction are parallel to length of conductors

38 The resultant force on the current loop $PQRS$ due to a long current carrying conductor will be **[KCET]**

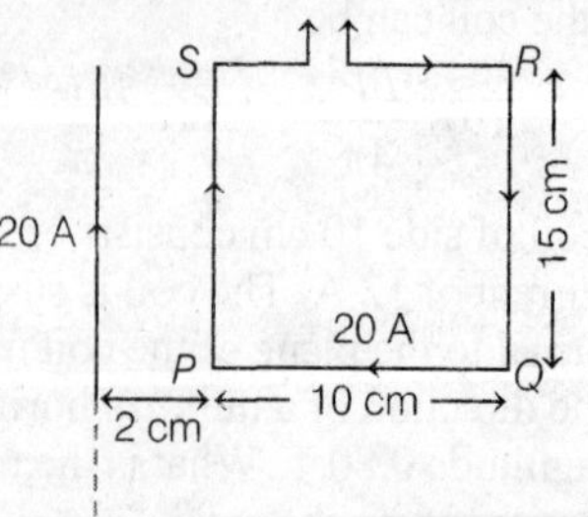

(a) 10^{-4} N (b) 3.6×10^{-4} N

(c) 1.8×10^{-4} N (d) 5×10^{-4} N

2007

39 A proton with energy of 2 MeV enters a uniform magnetic field of 2.5 T normally. The magnetic force on the proton is
(Take, mass of proton to be 1.6×10^{-27} kg) **[Kerala CEE]**
(a) 3×10^{-12} N (b) 8×10^{-10} N
(c) 8×10^{-12} N (d) 2×10^{-10} N
(e) 3×10^{-10} N

40 Two free parallel wires carrying currents in the opposite directions **[J&K CET]**
(a) attract each other
(b) repel each other
(c) do not affect each other
(d) get rotated to be perpendicular to each other

41 A and B are two infinitely long straight parallel conductors. C is another straight conductor of length 1 m kept parallel to A and B as shown in the figure. Then, the force experienced by C is **[KCET]**

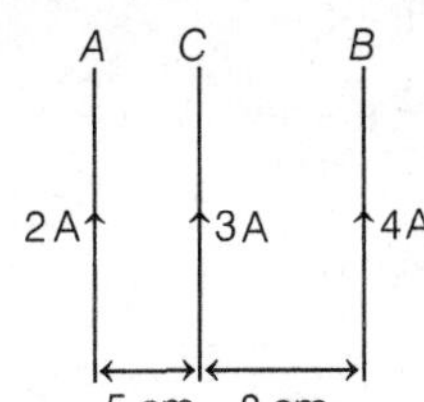

(a) towards A equal to 0.6×10^{-5} N
(b) towards B equal to 5.4×10^{-5} N
(c) towards A equal to 5.4×10^{-5} N
(d) towards B equal to 0.6×10^{-5} N

42 Currents of 10 A and 2 A are passed through two parallel wires A and B respectively, in opposite directions. If the wire A is infinitely long and length of the wire B is 2 m, the force acting on the conductor B which is situated at 10 cm distance from A will be **[Guj CET]**
(a) 5×10^{-5} N (b) $4\pi\times10^{-7}$ N
(c) 8×10^{-5} N (d) $8\pi\times10^{-7}$ N

2006

43 Graph of force per unit length between two long parallel currents carrying conductor and the distance between them is **[J&K CET]**
(a) straight line
(b) parabola
(c) ellipse
(d) rectangular hyperbola

44 A long horizontal rigidly supported wire carries a current $I_a = 96$ A. Directly above it and parallel to it at a distance, another wire of 0.144 N weight per metre carrying a current $I_b = 24$ A, in a direction opposite to that of I_a. If the upper wire is to float in air due to magnetic repulsion, then its distance (in mm) from the lower wire is **[EAMCET]**
(a) 9.6 (b) 4.8
(c) 3.2 (d) 1.6

45 In the given figure, the loop is fixed but straight wire can move. The straight wire will

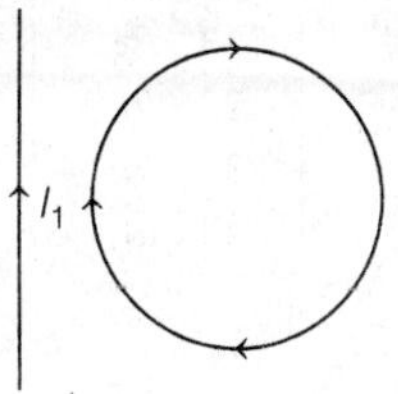

[AMU]

(a) remain stationary
(b) move towards the loop
(c) move away from the loop
(d) rotates about the axis

2005

46 A coil in the shape of an equilateral triangle of side l is suspended between the pole pieces of a permanent magnet such that **B** is in plane of the coil. If due to a current i in the triangle a torque τ acts on it, the side l of the triangle is **[CBSE AIPMT]**
(a) $\frac{2}{\sqrt{3}}\left(\frac{\tau}{BI}\right)^{1/2}$ (b) $\frac{2}{\sqrt{3}}\left(\frac{\tau}{BI}\right)$
(c) $2\left(\frac{\tau}{\sqrt{3}BI}\right)^{1/2}$ (d) $\frac{1}{\sqrt{3}}\frac{\tau}{BI}$

47 Three long, straight and parallel wires carrying currents are arranged as shown in the figure. The wire C which carries a current of 50 A, so placed that it experiences no force. The distance of wire C from wire A is **[UP CPMT]**

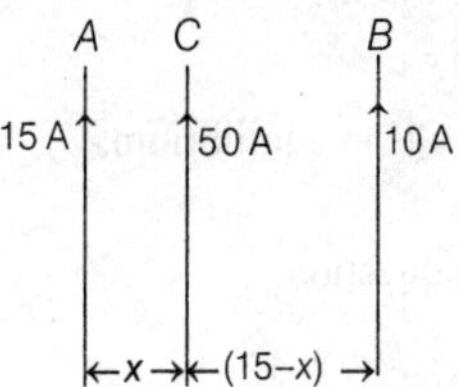

(a) 9 cm (b) 7 cm
(c) 5 cm (d) 3 cm

48 Two parallel wires carrying currents in opposite direction repel each other because of **[UP CPMT]**
(a) potential difference between them
(b) mutual inductance between them
(c) electric force between them
(d) magnetic force between them

49 A circular coil of 20 turns and radius 10 cm is placed in uniform magnetic field of 0.10 T normal to the plane of the coil. If the current in coil is 5 A, then the torque acting on the coil will be **[J&K CET]**
(a) 31.4 N-m (b) 3.14 N-m
(c) 0.314 N-m (d) zero

Answers

1 (b)	2 (b)	3 (d)	4 (a)	5 (a)	6 (d)	7 (b)	8 (d)	9 (d)	10 (c)
11 (c)	12 (c)	13 (c)	14 (d)	15 (a)	16 (d)	17 (c)	18 (d)	19 (b)	20 (a)
21 (a)	22 (b)	23 (b)	24 (a)	25 (b)	26 (d)	27 (d)	28 (a)	29 (d)	30 (c)
31 (d)	32 (b)	33 (a)	34 (b)	35 (c)	36 (c)	37 (a)	38 (d)	39 (c)	40 (b)
41 (d)	42 (c)	43 (d)	44 (c)	45 (b)	46 (c)	47 (a)	48 (d)	49 (d)	

Explanations

1 *(b)* $W = U_f - U_i = MB[\cos 0° - \cos 60°]$

$\Rightarrow \dfrac{MB}{2} = \sqrt{3}$ J

$\Rightarrow MB = 2\sqrt{3}$ J

Torque required,

$\tau = \mathbf{M} \times \mathbf{B} = MB \sin 60°$

$= 2\sqrt{3} \times \dfrac{\sqrt{3}}{2} = 3$ J

2 *(b)* Charge on α-particle, $q = 2e$

Time period of α-particle,

$$T = \frac{2\pi r}{v}$$

∴ Current associated by α-particle,

$$I = \frac{q}{T} = \frac{2e}{\dfrac{2\pi r}{v}} \Rightarrow I = \frac{ev}{\pi r} \quad \text{...(i)}$$

Magnetic dipole moment,

$$\mu = I \cdot A = \frac{ev}{\pi r} \cdot \pi r^2$$

∴ $\mu = evr$

3 *(d)* As, the system is in equilibrium,

$\Sigma F_x = 0$

According to the question,

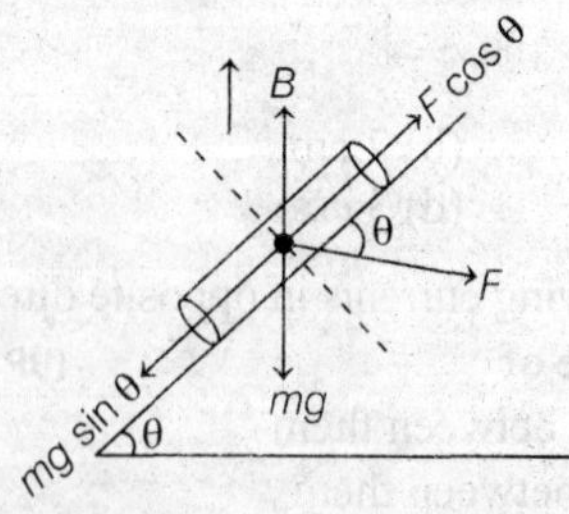

or $mg \sin\theta = F \cos\theta$ ...(i)

where, F is the magnitude of force experienced by the rod when placed in a magnetic field and current I is flowing through it.

But the force experienced by the given rod in a uniform magnetic field is

$F = ILB$

∴ Eq. (i) becomes,

$mg \sin\theta = ILB \cos\theta$

$$\Rightarrow \quad I = \frac{mg \sin\theta}{LB \cos\theta} = \frac{mg}{LB} \tan\theta$$

$$I = \left(\frac{m}{L}\right) \frac{g \tan\theta}{B} \quad \text{...(ii)}$$

Here, $\dfrac{m}{L} = 0.5 \text{ kg m}^{-1}$,

$g = 9.8 \text{ ms}^{-2}, \theta = 30°$,

$B = 0.25$ T

Substituting the given values in Eq. (ii), we get

$$I = \frac{0.5 \times 9.8}{0.25} \tan 30°$$

$$= \frac{0.5 \times 9.8}{0.25} \times \frac{1}{\sqrt{3}}$$

$= 11.32$ A

4 *(a)* Magnetic moment,

$M = NiA$

where, N = number of turns of the current loop and i = current.

Since, the orbiting electron behaves as a current loop of current i, we can write

$$i = \frac{e}{T} = \frac{e}{2\pi r/v} = \frac{ev}{2\pi r}$$

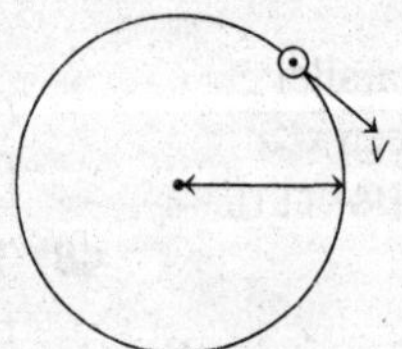

where, A = area of the loop = πr^2.

$$\Rightarrow \quad M = (1)\left(\frac{ev}{2\pi r}\right)(\pi r^2) = \frac{evr}{2}$$

5 *(a)* The torque acting on a current carrying loop is given by

$\tau = MB \cos\theta$

$= NiAB \cos\theta \quad [\because M = NiA]$

where, N = number of turns,

i = current of loop, A = area of loop and B = magnetic field.

Thus, torque does not depends on shape of loop.

6 *(d)* Consider the given figure,

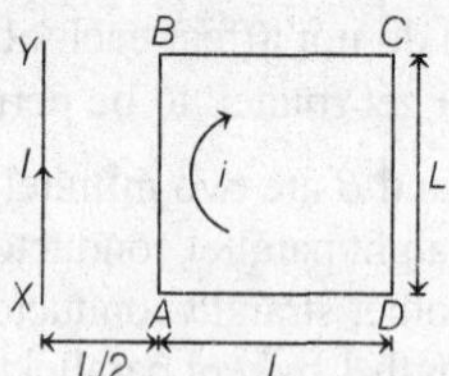

From the above figure, it can be seen that the direction of currents in a long straight conductor XY and arm AB of a square loop $ABCD$ are in the same direction. So, there exist a force of attraction between the two, which will be experienced by AB as

$$F_{BA} = \frac{\mu_0 IiL}{2\pi\left(\dfrac{L}{2}\right)}$$

In the case of XY and arm CD, the direction of currents are in the opposite direction. So, there exist a force of repulsion which will be experienced by CD as

$$F_{CD} = \frac{\mu_0 IiL}{2\pi\left(\dfrac{3L}{2}\right)}$$

Therefore, net force on the loop $ABCD$ will be

$$F_{\text{loop}} = F_{BA} - F_{CD}$$

$$= \frac{\mu_0 IiL}{2\pi}\left[\frac{1}{(L/2)} - \frac{1}{(3L/2)}\right]$$

$$\therefore \quad F_{\text{loop}} = \frac{2\mu_0 iI}{3\pi}$$

7 *(b)* Magnetic moment,

M = Current × Area enclosed by loop

$= I \times A$ ...(i)

Magnetic induction at the centre of circular loop,

$$B = \frac{\mu_0 I}{2R} \Rightarrow I = \frac{2BR}{\mu_0} \quad \text{...(ii)}$$

Here, $A = \pi R^2$ .....(iii)

Substituting Eqs. (ii) and (iii) in Eq. (i), we get

$$M = \frac{2BR}{\mu_0} \times \pi R^2 = \frac{2\pi BR^3}{\mu_0}$$

8 (d) Angular momentum, $L = m_e vr$ ...(i)

Therefore, orbital motion of electron is equivalent to a current,

$$I = e(1/T)$$

Period of revolution of electron is given by

$$T = 2\pi r / v$$

$$\therefore \quad I = e\left(\frac{1}{2\pi r / v}\right) = \frac{ev}{2\pi r}$$

Area of electron orbit, $A = \pi r^2$

Magnetic dipole moment of the atom,

$$M = \frac{ev}{2\pi r} \times \pi r^2 = evr/2$$

Using Eq. (i), we have

$$M = \left(\frac{e}{2m_e}\right)L \text{ or } \frac{M}{L} = \frac{e}{2m}$$

9 (d) Given, $r = 0.05 \text{ nm} = 0.05 \times 10^{-9} \text{m}$ $[\because 1 \text{ nm} = 10^{-9} \text{ m}]$

$$n = 10^{16} \text{ rev/s}$$

$$e = 1.6 \times 10^{-19} \text{ C}$$

We know that, the magnetic moment,

$$M = Ai$$

$$M = \pi r^2 \times ne$$

$$= 3.14 \times (0.05 \times 10^{-9})^2 \times 10^{16} \times 1.6 \times 10^{-19}$$

or $= 1.26 \times 10^{-23} \text{ A-m}^2$

10 (c) Given, radius of coil,

$$r = 10 \times 10^{-2} \text{ m}$$

Number of turns, $N = 100$ turns

Current in coil, $i = 1\text{A}$

and magnetic moment, $M = ?$

By magnetic dipole moment of current loop,

$M = NiA$, where $A = \pi r^2$

$$M = Ni\pi r^2 = 100 \times 1 \times 3.14 \times (10 \times 10^{-2})^2$$

$$= 100 \times 1 \times 3.14 \times 100 \times 10^{-4}$$

$$= 3.14 \text{ A-m}^2$$

11 (c) The situation is shown in the figure.

Given wires are long.

Now, B_1 = magnetic field at I_2 (second wire) due to current in the first wire.

$$= \left[\frac{\mu_0}{2\pi d} I_1\right]$$

The field is perpendicularly inward.

Now, force on the second wire due to first wire,

$$\mathbf{F}_{21} = I_2(\mathbf{l} \times \mathbf{B}_1) \quad \text{(towards left)}$$

$$= I_2 l B_1 \sin 90°$$

$$F_{21} = I_2 l B_1$$

where, l is the length of the wire and d is separation between the two wires.

$$F_{21} = I_2 l \left(\frac{\mu_0 I_1}{2\pi d}\right) - \frac{\mu_0 I_1 I_2 l}{2\pi d}$$

According to question, $|\mathbf{F}_{21}| = F$

$$\Rightarrow \quad F = \frac{\mu_0 I_1 I_2 l}{2\pi d}$$

Now, consider the situation, where the current in first wire is doubled and reversed.

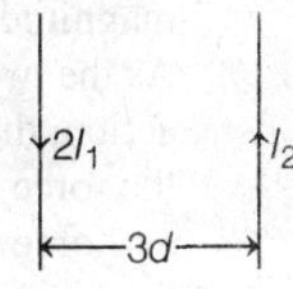

Proceeding as previous case, we can write

$$F' = \frac{\mu_0 (2I_1)(I_2) l}{2\pi d \times 3}$$

Here, force on second wire will be towards right.

$$\text{So,} \quad \frac{F'}{F} = -\left[\frac{\frac{\mu_0 (2I_1)(I_2) l}{2\pi d \times 3}}{\frac{\mu_0 I_1 I_2 l}{2\pi d}}\right]$$

Here, negative sign is due to opposite directions of F' and F.

$$\frac{F'}{F} = -\left[\frac{2I_1 I_2}{3I_1 I_2}\right] = -\frac{2}{3}$$

$$\Rightarrow \quad F' = -\frac{2F}{3}$$

12 (c) As, number of revolutions per second by the charge q is given as

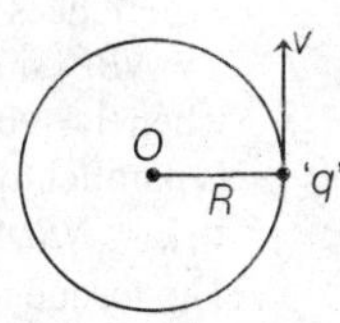

$$N_{\text{per sec}} = \frac{1}{T} = \frac{v}{2\pi R}$$

Current through circular path,

$$i = q(1/T) = vq / 2\pi R$$

Magnetic moment,

$$\mu = iA = \frac{vq}{2\pi R}(\pi R^2) = \frac{1}{2} vqR$$

13 (c) Circumference of circle $= 2\pi R$

$$\therefore \quad 2\pi R = L \Rightarrow R = \left(\frac{L}{2\pi}\right)$$

$$\text{Area,} \quad A = \pi R^2 = \frac{\pi L^2}{4\pi^2} = \frac{L^2}{4\pi}$$

$$\text{Magnetic moment, } M = IA = \frac{IL^2}{4\pi}$$

14 (d) The current loop in a magnetic field is in equilibrium in two orientations. For parallel magnetic field, it is stable and for anti-parallel it is unstable.

15 (a) When a circular flexible loop is placed in a magnetic field, a deflection torque (τ) acts on it, this is given by

$$\tau = MB \sin \theta$$

where, M is dipole moment, B is magnetic field, θ is angle between magnetic field and axis of loop.

Also, $M = IA$, thus when I is doubled, the torque is doubled, hence tension is doubled.

16 (d) Apply Fleming's left hand rule, as shown in the figure. Let the conductor Y carries current i_2, situated in a magnetic field $\mathbf{B}$ perpendicular to its length. It therefore experiences a magnetic force. The magnitude of the force acting on a length l of Y is

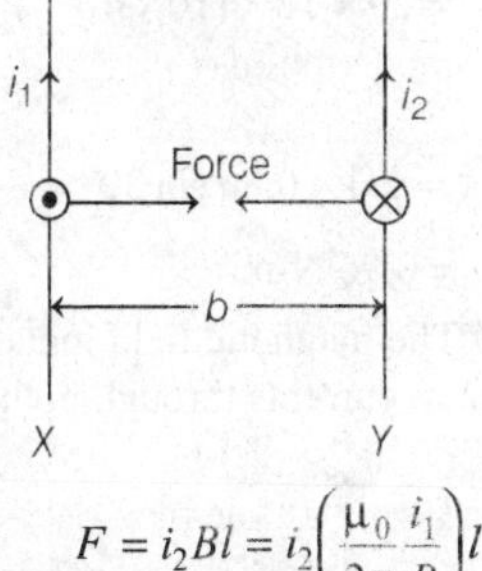

$$F = i_2 Bl = i_2 \left(\frac{\mu_0}{2\pi} \frac{i_1}{R}\right) l$$

From Fleming's left hand rule, the direction of this force is towards X. Similarly, force per unit length on X due to Y acts towards Y. Hence, the conductors attract each other.

17 (c) Wires placed close to each other carry current in the same direction and hence attract. Wires placed far apart carry current in opposite directions and hence repel each other. But here attraction is strong and repulsion is weak. So, loop move towards the wire.

18 (d) Given, $i = 10 \text{ A}$, $B = 0.15 \text{ T}$,

$$\theta = 45° \text{ and } l = 2 \text{ m}$$

Here, $F = ilB \sin \theta = 10 \times 2 \times 0.15 \sin 45°$

$$= \frac{3}{\sqrt{2}} \text{ N}$$

19 (b) Let r be the radius of the coil and n be the number of turns formed, then

$$l = 2\pi rn \text{ or } r = l/2\pi n \quad \text{...(i)}$$

Maximum torque,

$$\tau_{\max} = BniA = Bn\, i\pi r^2$$

$$= B\, ni\pi \times \frac{l^2}{4\pi^2 n^2} = \frac{iBl^2}{4\pi n}$$

Torque will be maximum, if $n = 1$

$$\therefore \quad \tau_{max} = \frac{Bil^2}{4\pi}$$

20 *(a)* Given, side of square coil

$= 10 \text{ cm} = 0.1 \text{ m}$

Number of turns $(n) = 20$

Current in square coil, $I = 12$ A

Angle made by coil, $\theta = 30°$

and magnetic field, $B = 0.80$ T

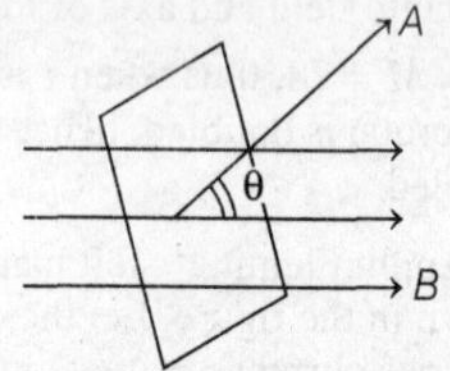

The magnitude of torque experienced by the coil,

$$\tau = NI\,AB \sin\theta$$

$$= 20 \times 12 \times (10 \times 10^{-2})^2 \times 0.80 \times \sin 30°$$

$$\tau = 2.4 \times 0.80 \sin 30° = \frac{2.4 \times 0.80}{2}$$

$$= 0.96 \text{ N-m}$$

21 *(a)* The magnetic field induction at P due to currents through both the wires is

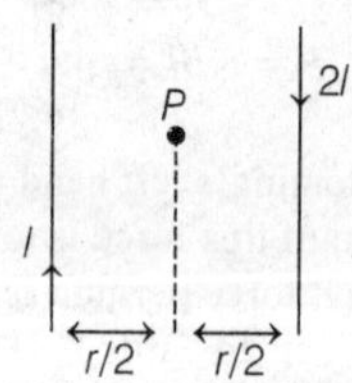

$$B = \frac{\mu_0}{4\pi}\frac{2i}{r/2} + \frac{\mu_0}{4\pi}\frac{2(2i)}{r/2}$$

$$= \frac{\mu_0}{4\pi} \cdot \frac{12i}{r}$$

acting perpendicular to plane of wire inwards. Now, B and v are acting in the same direction, i.e. $\theta = 0°$

Force on charged particle is

$F = qvB \sin\theta = qvB \times 0 = 0.$

22 *(b)* We have, $M = NIA$, $B = \mu_0 nI$

Torque, $\tau = MB$

Here, $\quad \tau = (n_1 I_1 A)(\mu_0 n_2 I_2)$

$$= \left(10 \times \frac{21}{44} \times 10^{-6}\right)\left(4 \times \frac{22}{7} \times 10^{-7} \times 10^3 \times 2.5\right)$$

$$= 1.5 \times 10^{-8} \text{ N-m}$$

23 *(b)* Forces $\mathbf{F}_1$ and $\mathbf{F}_2$ acting on the coil are equal in magnitude and opposite in directions. As the forces $\mathbf{F}_1$and $\mathbf{F}_2$ have the same line of action, their resultant effect on the coil is zero.

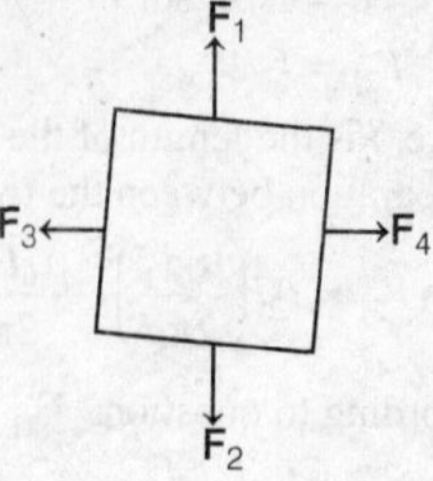

The two forces $\mathbf{F}_3$ and $\mathbf{F}_4$ are equal in magnitude and opposite in directions. As the two forces have different lines of action, they constitute a torque. Thus, if the force on one arc of the loop is $\mathbf{F}$, the net force on the remaining three arms of the loop is $-\mathbf{F}$.

24 *(a)* Torque, $\tau = iAB\sin\theta$,

$i = 0.1$ A, $\theta = 90°$

$$A = \frac{1}{2} \times \text{base} \times \text{height}$$

or $\quad A = \frac{1}{2} a \times \frac{a\sqrt{3}}{2}$

$$= \frac{\sqrt{3}a^2}{4} = \frac{\sqrt{3} \times (0.02)^2}{4}$$

$$= \sqrt{3} \times 10^{-4} \text{m}^2; \theta = 90°$$

$$\tau = 0.1 \times \sqrt{3} \times 10^{-4} \times 5 \times 10^{-2} \sin 90°$$

$$= 5\sqrt{3} \times 10^{-7} \text{ N-m}$$

25 *(b)* When a current carrying loop is placed in a magnetic field, the coil experiences a torque given by $\tau = NBiA\sin\theta$. Torque is maximum when $\theta = 90°$, i.e. the plane of the coil is parallel to the radial field $\tau_{max} = NBiA$.

The torque tends to rotate a coil on its own axis in the magnetic field.

Hence, both Assertion and Reason are correct but Reason is not the correct explanation of Assertion.

26 *(d)* Magnetic field at the centre of circular loop,

$$B = \frac{\mu_0}{4\pi}\frac{2\pi I}{r} = \frac{\mu_0 I}{2r} \Rightarrow I = \frac{2Br}{\mu_0}$$

Also, $A = \pi r^2$ or $r = (A/\pi)^{1/2}$

Magnetic moment, $M = IA = \frac{2Br}{\mu_0} A$

$$= \frac{2BA}{\mu_0} \times \left(\frac{A}{\pi}\right)^{1/2} = \frac{2BA^{3/2}}{\mu_0 \pi^{1/2}}$$

27 *(d)* Let two long parallel thin wires X and Y carry current i and separated by a distance b apart.

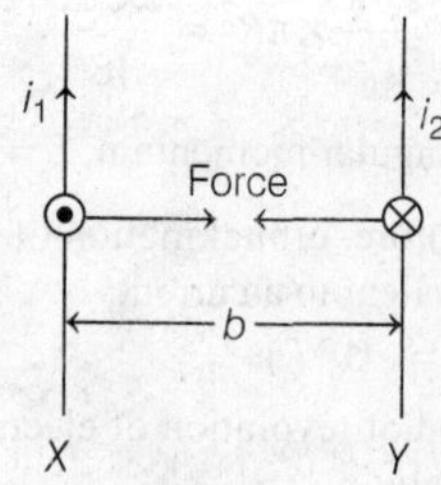

The magnitude of magnetic field B at any point on Y due to current i_1 in X is given by

$$B = \frac{\mu_0}{2\pi}\frac{i_1}{b}$$

The magnitude of force acting on length l of Y is

$$F = i_2 Bl = i_2\left(\frac{\mu_0}{2\pi}\frac{i_1}{b}\right)l$$

Force per unit length is

$$\frac{F}{l} = \frac{\mu_0}{2\pi}\frac{i_1 i_2}{b}$$

Given, $i_1 = i_2 = i$, therefore

$$\frac{F}{l} = \frac{\mu_0}{2\pi} \cdot \frac{i^2}{b}$$

28 *(a)* The magnetic field at the centre of a current carrying loop is given by

$$B = \frac{\mu_0}{4\pi}\left(\frac{2\pi i}{a}\right) = \frac{\mu_0 i}{2a}$$

The magnetic moment at the centre of current carrying loop is given by

$$M = i\,(\pi a^2)$$

Thus, $\frac{B}{M} = \frac{\mu_0 i}{2a} \times \frac{1}{i\pi a^2} = \frac{\mu_0}{2\pi a^3} = x$ [given]

When both the current and the radius are doubled, then ratio becomes

$$\frac{\mu_0}{2\pi(2a)^3} = \frac{\mu_0}{8(2\pi a^3)} = \frac{x}{8}$$

29 *(d)* Maximum torque, $\tau_{max} = MB$

or $\quad \tau_{max} = ni\pi r^2 B$

Let number of turns in length l is n, so

$$l = n(2\pi r)$$

or $\quad r = \frac{l}{2\pi n}$

$$\tau_{max} = \frac{ni\pi Bl^2}{4\pi^2 n^2} = \frac{l^2 iB}{4\pi n_{min}}$$

$\Rightarrow \quad \tau_{max} \propto 1/n_{min}$

$\Rightarrow \quad n_{min} = 1$

30 (c) Force, $F = Bil\sin\theta = Bil\sin 30°$

Given, $B = 500\,\text{G} = 500\times10^{-4}\,\text{T}$,

$i = 3\,\text{A}$

and $l = 40$ cm

$= 40\times10^{-2}$m.

$$F = 500\times10^{-4}\times3\times(40\times10^{-2})\times\frac{1}{2}$$

$= 3\times10^{-2}$N

31 (d) To suspend the wire in mid-air due to magnetic field **B**, the weight of the wire should be balanced by the magnetic force (F_m).

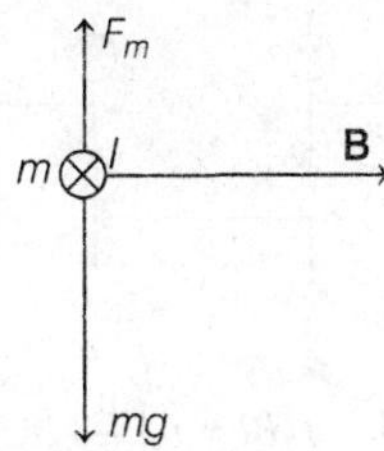

To have F_m opposite to mg (i.e. upward), current should be perpendicular to the plane and inward directed.

[Fleming's right hand rule]

$F_m = mg$ ...(i)

$F_m = Bil$ ...(ii)

From Eqs. (i) and (ii), we get

$$B = mg/il = \frac{200\times10^{-3}\times9.8}{2\times1.5}$$

$= 0.65$ T

32 (b) The situation can be shown as

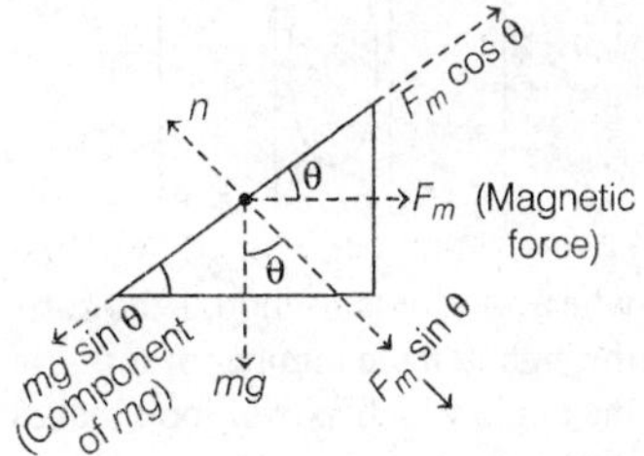

Hence, from figure,

$F_m\cos\theta = mg\sin\theta$ ...(i)

Also, $F_m = Bil$ ...(ii)

From Eqs. (i) and (ii), we get

$$B = \frac{mg}{il}\tan\theta$$

33 (a) Magnetic dipole moment of current loop carrying i current is given as

$\mathbf{u} = i\mathbf{A}$

$\Rightarrow$ $|\mathbf{u}| = i|\mathbf{A}|$

$= iA$ (for single turn)

$= nAi$

(for n number of turns)

Hence, it is independent of magnetic field.

34 (b) The FBD of the loop is shown as

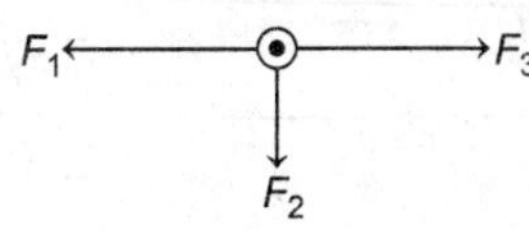

Therefore, force on QP will be equal and opposite to sum of forces on other side.

Thus, $F_{QP} = \sqrt{(F_3 - F_1)^2 + F_2^2}$

Alternative Method

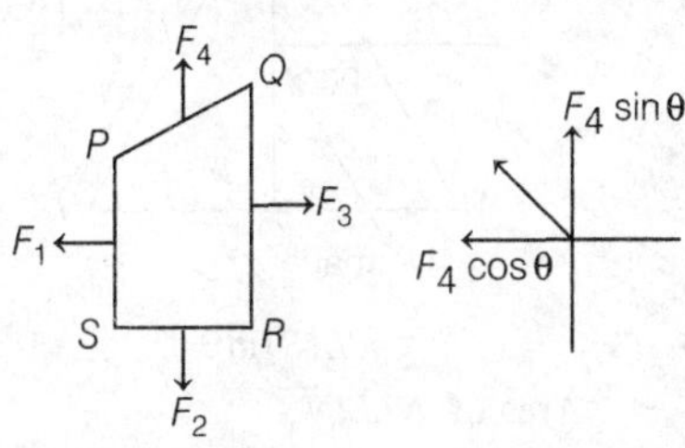

$F_4\sin\theta = F_2$ ...(i)

$F_4\cos\theta = (F_3 - F_1)$ ...(ii)

From Eqs. (i) and (ii), we get

$$F_4 = \sqrt{(F_3 - F_1)^2 + F_2^2}$$

35 (c) The Lorentz force acting on the current carrying conductor in the magnetic field,

$F = IBl\sin\theta$

Since, wire PQ is parallel to the direction of magnetic field, then $\theta = 0$.

$\therefore$ $F_{PQ} = IBl\sin 0° = 0$

Also, wire QR is perpendicular to the direction of magnetic field, then $\theta = 90°$.

$\therefore$ $F_{QR} = IBl\sin 90° = IBl$

36 (c) Proton has positive charge on it. Therefore, two beams of protons parallel to each other will repel due to repulsive force produced between them.

37 (a) The two conductors are attracting each other, which means that currents flowing are parallel in direction.

38 (d) Force on SR and PQ are equal but opposite, so their net force will be zero. Force between two parallel conductors carrying currents I_1 and I_2,

$$F = \frac{\mu_0}{2\pi}\frac{I_1 I_2 l}{r}$$

where, r = distance between two parallel conductors.

$$F_{PS} = \frac{10^{-7}\times2\times20\times20\times15\times10^{-2}}{2\times10^{-2}}$$

$= 6\times10^{-4}$ N

$$F_{QR} = \frac{10^{-7}\times2\times20\times20\times15\times10^{-2}}{12\times10^{-2}}$$

$= 1\times10^{-4}$ N

$F_{\text{net}} = F_{PS} - F_{QR}$

$= 6\times10^{-4} - 1\times10^{-4}$

$= 5\times10^{-4}$ N

39 (c) Energy of proton = 2 MeV

$= 2\times1.6\times10^{-19}\times10^6$

$= 3.2\times10^{-13}$J

Magnetic field, $B = 2.5$ T

Mass of proton, $m = 1.6\times10^{-27}$ kg

Energy of proton, $E = \frac{1}{2}mv^2$

$\therefore$ $v = \sqrt{2E/m}$ ...(i)

Magnetic force on proton,

$F = Bqv\sin 90° = Bqv$

Substituting the value of v from Eq. (i), we get

$$F = Bq\sqrt{\frac{2E}{m}}$$

$$= 2.5\times1.6\times10^{-19}\sqrt{\frac{2\times3.2\times10^{-13}}{1.6\times10^{-27}}}$$

$= 8\times10^{-12}$N

40 (b) The force is attractive, if current in two conductors is in same direction and repulsive, if currents are in opposite directions.

41 (d) The force between the conductors is attractive, if the currents in them are in the same direction and repulsive, if the currents are in opposite directions.

Mutual force between conductors A and C,

$$F_1 = \frac{\mu_0}{2\pi}\frac{I_1I_2l}{r} = \frac{\mu_0}{2\pi}\frac{2\times3\times1}{0.05}$$

$= 2.40\times10^{-5}$N [towards A]

Mutual force between conductors B and C,

$$F_2 = \frac{\mu_0}{2\pi}\times\frac{4\times3\times1}{0.08}$$

$= 3\times10^{-5}$N [towards B]

Hence, the resultant force experienced by C,

$$F = F_2 - F_1$$
$$= (3 - 2.4) \times 10^{-5} \text{N}$$
$$= 0.6 \times 10^{-5} \text{N} \quad \text{[towards } B\text{]}$$

42 *(c)* Force on a conductor of length l carrying current I_2 and placed at a distance r parallel to another infinitely long conductor carrying current I_1 is

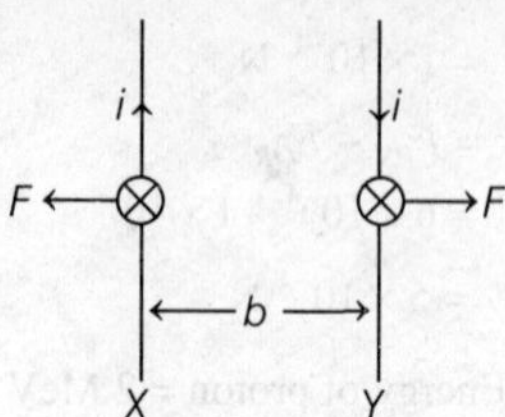

$$F = \frac{\mu_0}{4\pi} \cdot \frac{2 I_1 I_2}{r} l$$

Here, $I_1 = 10$ A,
$I_2 = 2$ A,
$l = 2$ m,
$r = 10$ cm $= 0.1$ m

$$\therefore \quad F = 10^{-7} \times \frac{2 \times 10 \times 2 \times 2}{0.1}$$
$$= 8 \times 10^{-5} \text{N}$$

43 *(d)* The force per unit length between two parallel wires carrying currents i_1 and i_2 separated by a distance R is given by

$$\frac{F}{l} = \frac{\mu_0}{2\pi} \frac{I_1 I_2}{R}$$
$$\Rightarrow \quad \frac{F}{l} \propto \frac{1}{R}$$

Hence, graph between force per unit length and distance between wires is a rectangular hyperbola.

44 *(c)* $\frac{F}{l} = \frac{\mu_0}{4\pi} \frac{2 I_a I_b}{r}$

$$\therefore \quad 0.144 = \frac{10^{-7} \times 2 \times 96 \times 24}{r}$$
$$\therefore \quad r = \frac{10^{-7} \times 2 \times 96 \times 24}{0.144}$$
$$= 3.2 \times 10^{-3} \text{m} = 3.2 \text{ mm}$$

45 *(b)* If we consider a small element dL (shown in figure), the magnetic force on the considered element is towards the straight wire.

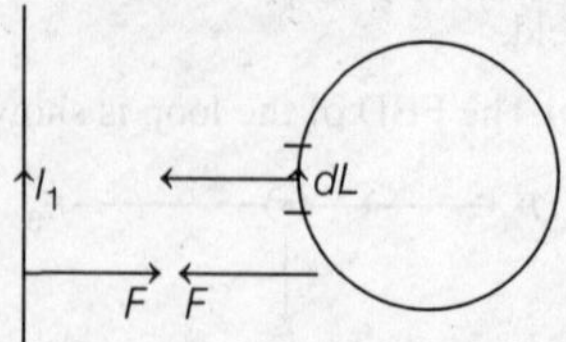

Thus, the wire move toward the loop.

46 *(c)* Torque acting on equilateral triangle in a magnetic field **B** is

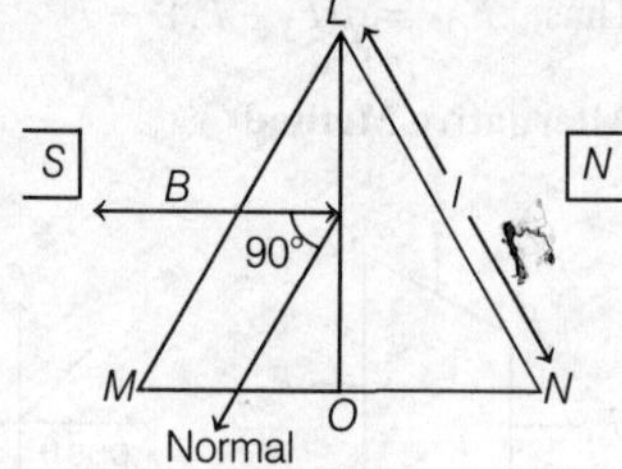

$$\tau = IAB \sin\theta$$

Area of ΔLMN,

$$A = \frac{\sqrt{3}}{4} l^2$$

and $\quad \theta = 90°$

Substituting the given values in the expression for torque, we have

$$\tau = I \times \frac{\sqrt{3}}{4} l^2 B \sin 90° = \frac{\sqrt{3}}{4} I l^2 B$$
$$[\because \sin 90° = 1]$$

$$\text{Hence, } l = 2\left(\frac{\tau}{\sqrt{3} BI}\right)^{1/2}$$

47 *(a)* $\frac{F_{AB}}{l} = \frac{F_{BC}}{l}$

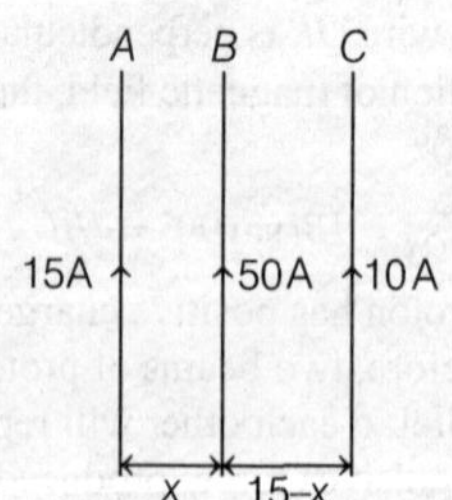

$$\frac{\mu_0}{4\pi} \cdot \frac{2 \times 15 \times 50}{x} = \frac{\mu_0}{4\pi} \times \frac{2 \times 50 \times 10}{(15 - x)}$$
$$\Rightarrow \quad \frac{15}{x} = \frac{10}{(15 - x)}$$
$$\Rightarrow \quad 225 - 15x = 10x$$
$$\Rightarrow \quad 25x = 225$$
$$\text{or} \quad x = 9 \text{ cm}$$

48 *(d)* Let the conductor Y carries current I_2, situated in a magnetic field **B** perpendicular to its length. It therefore experiences a magnetic force, the magnitude of the force acting on a length l of Y is

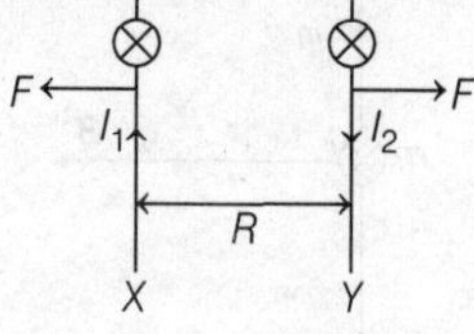

$$F = I_2 B l = I_2 \left(\frac{\mu_0}{2\pi} \frac{I_1}{R}\right) l$$

From Fleming's left hand rule, the direction of this force is away from X. Similarly, force per unit length on X due to Y is directed away from Y. Hence, the conductors repel each other due to magnetic force between them.

49 *(d)* Torque (τ) acting on a loop placed in a magnetic field B is given by

$$\tau = nBIA \sin\theta$$

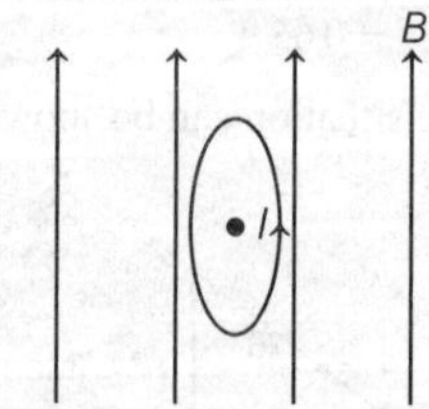

where, A is area of loop, I the current through it, n the number of turns, and θ the angle which axis of loop makes with magnetic field B.

Since, magnetic field B of coil is parallel to the field applied, hence $\theta = 0°$ and $\sin 0° = 0$

$$\therefore \quad \tau = 0$$

Topic 4

Moving Coil Galvanometer

2019

1 A galvanometer of 50 Ω resistance has 25 divisions. A current of 4×10^{-4} A gives a deflection of one division. To convert this galvanometer into a voltmeter having a range of 25V, it should be connected with a resistance of **[JIPMER]**

(a) 2500 Ω as a shunt
(b) 245 Ω as a shunt
(c) 2550 Ω in series
(d) 2450 Ω in series

2018

2 In the adjoining circuit diagram, the readings of ammeter and voltmeter are 2 A and 120 V, respectively. If the value of R is 75 Ω, then the voltmeter resistance will be **[AIIMS]**

(a) 100 Ω
(b) 150 Ω
(c) 300 Ω
(d) 75 Ω

2014

3 In an ammeter, 0.2% of main current passes through the galvanometer. If resistance of galvanometer is G, then the resistance of ammeter will be **[CBSE AIPMT]**

(a) $\frac{1}{499}G$
(b) $\frac{499}{500}G$
(c) $\frac{1}{500}G$
(d) $\frac{500}{499}G$

4 A galvanometer having internal resistance 10 Ω requires 0.01 A for a full scale deflection. To convert this galvanometer to a voltmeter of full scale deflection at 120 V, we need to connect a resistance of **[UK PMT]**

(a) 11990 Ω in series
(b) 11990 Ω in parallel
(c) 12010 Ω in series
(d) 12010 Ω in parallel

5 A galvanometer has a coil of resistance 100 Ω and gives full scale deflection for 30 mA current. If it is to work as a voltmeter of 30 V, the resistance required to be added is **[UK PMT]**

(a) 500 Ω
(b) 900 Ω
(c) 1000 Ω
(d) 1800 Ω

2012

6 A galvanometer coil has a resistance of 15 Ω and gives full scale deflection for a current of 4 mA. To convert it to an ammeter of range 0 to 6 A, **[AFMC]**

(a) 10 mΩ resistance is to be connected in parallel to the galvanometer
(b) 10 mΩ resistance is to be connected in series with the galvanometer
(c) 5 Ω resistance is to be connected in parallel
(d) 2 Ω resistance in series

2010

7 When a resistance of 100 Ω is connected in series with a galvanometer of resistance R, its range is V. To double its range, a resistance of 1000 Ω is connected in series. Find the value of R. **[MHT CET]**

(a) 700 Ω
(b) 800 Ω
(c) 900 Ω
(d) 100 Ω

8 In a galvanometer, 5% of the total current in the circuit passes through it. If the resistance of the galvanometer is G, the shunt resistance S connected to the galvanometer is **[Manipal]**

(a) $19G$
(b) $\frac{G}{19}$
(c) $20G$
(d) $\frac{G}{20}$

9 A moving coil galvanometer is converted into an ammeter reading upto 0.03 A by connecting a shunt of resistance $4r$ across it and into an ammeter reading upto 0.06 A when a shunt of resistance r is connected across it. What is the maximum current which can be sent through this galvanometer, if no shunt is used? **[Haryana PMT]**

(a) 0.01 A
(b) 0.02 A
(c) 0.03 A
(d) 0.04 A

10 A voltmeter of resistance 1000 Ω gives full scale deflection when a current of 100 mA flows through it. The shunt resistance required across it to enable it to be used as an ammeter reading 1 A at full scale deflection is **[Punjab PMET]**

(a) 10000 Ω
(b) 9000 Ω
(c) 222 Ω
(d) 111 Ω

11 The resistance of an ideal voltmeter is **[CG PMT]**

(a) low
(b) high
(c) infinite
(d) zero

12 An ammeter reads upto 1 A. Its internal resistance is 0.81 Ω. To increase the range to 10 A, the value of the required shunt is **[MGIMS]**

(a) 0.03 Ω
(b) 0.3 Ω
(c) 0.9 Ω
(d) 0.09 Ω

13 A galvanometer acting as a voltmeter should have **[JIPMER]**
(a) low resistance in series with its coil
(b) low resistance in parallel with its coil
(c) high resistance in series with its coil
(d) high resistance in parallel with its coil

14 A 36 Ω galvanometer is shunted by resistance of 4 Ω. The percentage of the total current, which passes through the galvanometer is **[JCECE]**
(a) 8% (b) 9%
(c) 10% (d) 91%

15 A galvanometer coil has a resistance of 10 Ω and the ammeter shows full scale deflection for a current of 1 mA. The shunt resistance required to convert the galvanometer into an ammeter of range 0-100 mA is about **[DUMET]**
(a) 10 Ω (b) 1 Ω
(c) 0.1 Ω (d) 0.01 Ω

2009

16 A galvanometer has a resistance of 100 Ω. A potential difference of 100 mV between its terminals gives a full scale deflection. The shunt resistance required to convert it into an ammeter reading upto 5 A is **[AIIMS]**
(a) 0.01 Ω (b) 0.02 Ω
(c) 0.03 Ω (d) 0.04 Ω

17 The seave of a galvanometer of resistance 100 Ω contains 25 divisions. It gives a deflection of one division on passing a current of 4×10^{-4} A. The resistance (in ohm) to be added to it, so that it may become a voltmeter of range 2.5 V is **[UP CPMT]**
(a) 150 (b) 170
(c) 110 (d) 220

18 A galvanometer can be converted into an ammeter by connecting **[Kerala CEE]**
(a) a high resistance in parallel
(b) a very small resistance in series
(c) a very small resistance in parallel
(d) a high resistance in series
(e) a low resistance in series

19 There are three voltmeters of the same range but of resistance 10000 Ω, 8000 Ω and 4000 Ω, respectively. The best voltmeter among these is the one whose resistance is **[Manipal]**
(a) 10000 Ω (b) 8000 Ω
(c) 4000 Ω (d) All are equally good

20 A galvanometer of resistance 20 Ω is to be converted into an ammeter of range 1 A. If a current of 1 mA produces full scale deflection, the shunt required for the purpose is **[Manipal]**
(a) 0.01 Ω (b) 0.05 Ω
(c) 0.02 Ω (d) 0.04 Ω

21 When a galvanometer is shunted by resistance S, its current capacity increases n times. If the same galvanometer is shunted by another resistance S', its current capacity will increase by n', which is given by **[MGIMS]**
(a) $\frac{(n+1)S}{S'}$ (b) $\frac{S(n-1)+S'}{S'}$
(c) $\frac{n+S}{S'}$ (d) $\frac{S(n-1)-S'}{S'}$

22 The resistance of an ammeter is 13 Ω and its scale is graduated for a current upto 100 A. After an additional shunt has been connected to this ammeter, it becomes possible to measure currents upto 750 A by this meter. The value of shunt resistance is **[JIPMER]**
(a) 20 Ω (b) 2 Ω (c) 0.2 Ω (d) 2 kΩ

2008

23 A galvanometer of resistance 50 Ω is connected to a battery of 3 V along with a resistance of 2950 Ω in series. A full scale deflection of 30 divisions is obtained in the galvanometer. In order to reduce this deflection to 20 divisions, the resistance in series should be **[CBSE AIPMT]**
(a) 5050 Ω (b) 5550 Ω
(c) 6050 Ω (d) 4450 Ω

24 The resistance of the shunt required to allow 2% of the main current through the galvanometer of resistance 49 Ω is **[Kerala CEE]**
(a) 1 Ω (b) 2 Ω (c) 0.2 Ω (d) 0.1 Ω
(e) 0.01 Ω

25 A voltmeter of range 2 V and resistance 300 Ω cannot be converted into ammeter of range **[AMU]**
(a) 1 A (b) 1 mA
(c) 100 mA (d) 10 mA

26 The deflection in a moving coil galvanometer falls from 50 divisions to 10 divisions, when a shunt of 12 Ω is connected with it. The resistance of galvanometer coil is **[Guj CET]**
(a) 24 Ω (b) 12 Ω
(c) 6 Ω (d) 48 Ω

2007

27 A galvanometer has resistance of 400 Ω and deflects full scale for current of 0.2 mA through it. The shunt resistance required to convert it into 3 A ammeter is **[RPMT]**
(a) 0.027 Ω (b) 0.054 Ω
(c) 0.0135 Ω (d) None of these

28 A voltmeter has resistance of G ohm and range of V volt. The resistance required in series to convert it into a voltmeter of range nV volt is **[Guj CET]**
(a) $(n-1)G$ (b) nG
(c) $\frac{G}{n}$ (d) $\frac{G}{(n-1)}$

2006

29 A galvanometer having a resistance of 8 Ω is shunted by a wire of resistance 2 Ω. If the total current is 1 A, the part of it passing through the shunt will be **[AFMC]**

(a) 0.25 A (b) 0.8 A
(c) 0.2 A (d) 0.5 A

30 To decrease the range of an ammeter, its resistance need to be increased. An ammeter has resistance R_0 and range I. Which of the following resistance can be connected in series with it to decrease its range to I/n? **[MP PMT]**

(a) $\frac{R_0}{n}$ (b) $\frac{R_0}{(n-1)}$
(c) $\frac{R_0}{(n+1)}$ (d) None of these

31 A galvanometer has a resistance 50 Ω. A resistance of 5 Ω is connected parallel to it. Fraction of the total current flowing through galvanometer is **[J&K CET]**

(a) $\frac{1}{10}$ (b) $\frac{1}{11}$
(c) $\frac{1}{50}$ (d) $\frac{2}{15}$

32 A galvanometer has 30 divisions and a sensitivity of 16 μA/div. It can be converted into a voltmeter to read 3 V by connecting **[Kerala CEE]**

(a) resistance of nearly 6 kΩ in series
(b) 6 kΩ in parallel
(c) 500 Ω in series
(d) it cannot be converted
(e) 6.6 kΩ in series

2005

33 In an ammeter, 10% of main current is passing through the galvanometer. If the resistance of the galvanometer is G, then the shunt resistance (in ohm) is **[KCET]**

(a) $9G$ (b) $G/9$ (c) $90G$ (d) $G/90$

34 If resistance of voltmeter is 10000 Ω and resistance of galvanometer is 2 Ω, then find R when voltmeter reads 12 V and galvanometer reads 0.1 A. **[BCECE]**

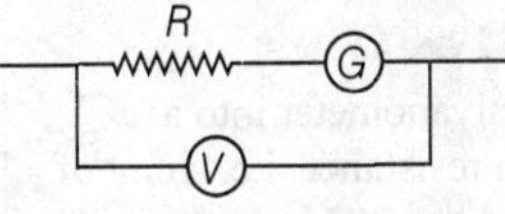

(a) 118 Ω (b) 120 Ω (c) 124 Ω (d) 114 Ω

Answers

1 (d)	2 (c)	3 (a)	4 (a)	5 (b)	6 (a)	7 (c)	8 (b)	9 (b)	10 (d)
11 (c)	12 (d)	13 (c)	14 (c)	15 (c)	16 (b)	17 (a)	18 (c)	19 (a)	20 (c)
21 (b)	22 (b)	23 (d)	24 (a)	25 (b)	26 (d)	27 (a)	28 (a)	29 (b)	30 (b)
31 (b)	32 (a)	33 (b)	34 (a)						

Explanations

1 *(d)* Given, resistance of galvanometer,
$R_g = 50\Omega$
Number of divisions = 25
$I_g = 4 \times 10^{-4} \times 25 = 10^{-2}$ A

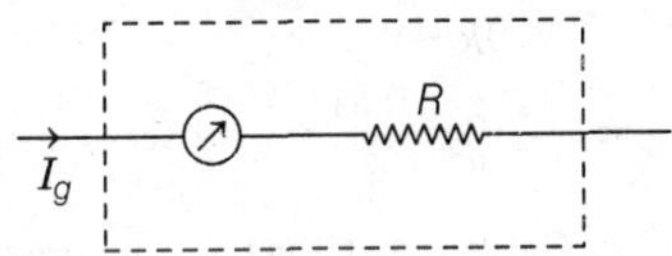

R is the resistance connected in series of galvanometer to convert into voltmeter

$\therefore \; V = I_g (R_g + R)$

$25 = 10^{-2}(50 + R)$

$\Rightarrow R = \frac{25}{10^{-2}} - 50 = 2500 - 50$

$\Rightarrow R = 2450\Omega$ in series.

2 *(c)* $\because V_{PQ} = (I - I_g)R = I_g \cdot G$

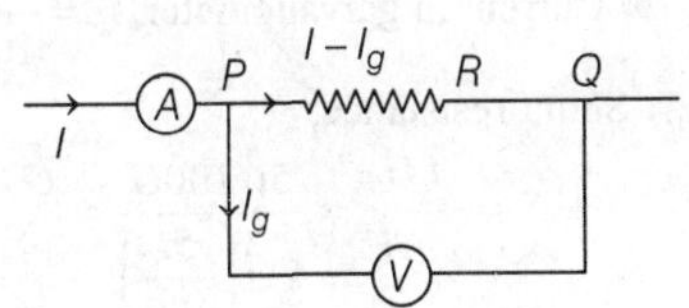

where, G = voltmeter (resistance).

Given, $V_{PQ} = 120$ V, $I = 2$ A,

$R = 75\ \Omega$

$\Rightarrow \quad 120 = (2 - I_g)75$

$\Rightarrow \quad I_g = 0.4$ A

Now, $V_{PQ} = I_g G$

$\Rightarrow \quad G = \frac{120}{0.4} = 300\ \Omega$

3 *(a)* As, $I_G = \frac{2}{1000} I$

Also, $I_r = \left(\frac{G}{G + r}\right) I$

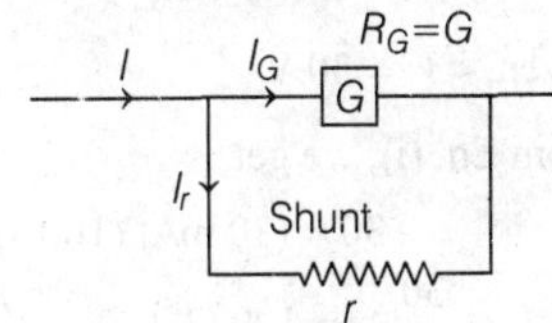

We know that, potential across G and shunt r are same.

$\therefore \quad V_G = V_r$

$\Rightarrow \quad I_G(G) = I_r r$

$\Rightarrow \quad \frac{2IG}{1000} = \frac{GI}{G + r}(r)$

$\Rightarrow \quad 2(G + r) = 1000\, r$

$\Rightarrow \quad G + r = 500\, r$

$\Rightarrow \quad \frac{G}{r} + 1 = 500$

$\Rightarrow \quad G/r = 499$

$\Rightarrow \quad r = \frac{1}{499} G$

4 *(a)* Given, internal resistance, $G = 10\ \Omega$,

Current, $i_g = 0.01$ A

and potential difference, $V = 120$ V

Resistance,

$$R = \frac{V}{i_g} - G$$

$$= \frac{120}{0.01} - 10$$

$$= 12000 - 10$$

$$R = 11990\ \Omega$$

To convert a galvanometer into a voltmeter, high resistance, i.e. shunt of 11990 Ω should connect in series with galvanometer.

5 *(b)* Let R_x resistance be connected in series to convert galvanometer to voltmeter.

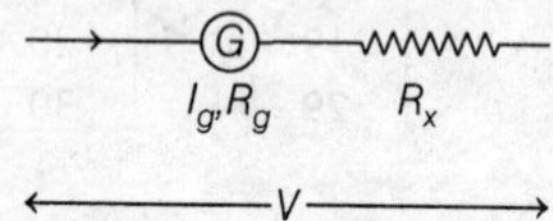

According to the question,

$$R_g = 100\ \Omega, I_g = 30 \text{ mA}$$

Current corresponding to full scale deflection.

Now, we can write

$$V = I_g \times R_g + I_g R_x$$

$$= I_g (R_g + R_x) \quad \dots\text{(i)}$$

Given, $V = 30$ V

From Eq. (i), we get

$$30 = (30 \text{ mA})\ (100\ \Omega + R_x)$$

$$\Rightarrow \quad \frac{30}{(30 \text{mA})} = 100\ \Omega + R_x$$

$$\Rightarrow \quad \frac{30 \text{V}}{30 \times 10^{-3} \text{A}} = 100\ \Omega + R_x$$

$$\Rightarrow \quad 10^3\ \Omega = 100\ \Omega + R_x$$

$$\Rightarrow \quad R_x = 1000\ \Omega - 100\ \Omega$$

$$= 900\ \Omega$$

6 *(a)* To convert a galvanometer into an ammeter, a shunt resistance in parallel is connected to galvanometer.

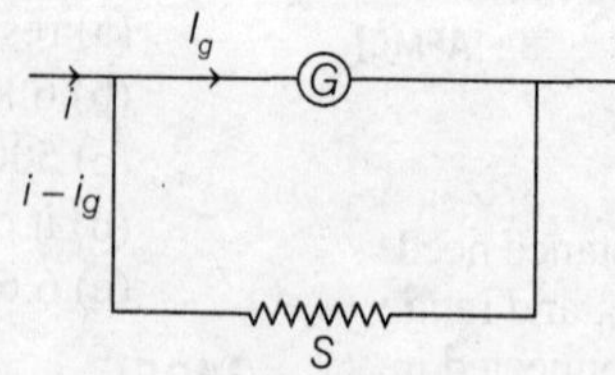

Since, galvanometer G and shunt S are in parallel, hence $i_g G = (i - i_g) S$.

$$\Rightarrow \quad S = \frac{i_g G}{i - i_g} = \frac{4 \times 10^{-3} \times 15}{6 - (4 \times 10^{-3})}$$

$$= \frac{60 \times 10^{-3}}{5.99} = 10 \text{ m}\Omega$$

Hence, 10 mΩ resistance is to be connected in parallel to the galvanometer.

7 *(c)* When a resistance of 100 Ω is connected in series current, then

$$i = \frac{V}{100 + R} \quad \dots\text{(i)}$$

When a resistance of 1000 Ω is connected in series, then its range double.

$$\therefore \quad \text{Current, } i = \frac{2V}{1100 + R} \quad \dots\text{(ii)}$$

From Eqs. (i) and (ii), we get

$$\frac{V}{100 + R} = \frac{2V}{1100 + R}$$

$$\Rightarrow \quad R = 900\ \Omega$$

8 *(b)* Current in galvanometer, $i_g = \frac{5}{100} i$

$\therefore$ Shunt resistance,

$$S = \frac{i_g G}{i - i_g} = \frac{5i/100G}{i - \left(\frac{5i}{100}\right)} = \frac{G}{19}$$

9 *(b)* For an ammeter, $\frac{i_g}{i} = \frac{S}{G + S}$

where, i_g = current in galvanometer.

When $i = 0.03$ A, then shunt resistance, $S = 4r$,

$$\Rightarrow i_g G = (i - i_g) S = (0.03 - i_g) 4r \quad \dots\text{(i)}$$

When $i = 0.06$ A, then shunt resistance, $S = r$

and $\quad i_g G = (0.06 - i_g) r \quad \dots\text{(ii)}$

From Eqs. (i) and (ii), we get

$$0.12 - 4 i_g = 0.06 - i_g$$

$$\Rightarrow \quad i_g = 0.02 \text{ A}$$

10 *(d)* Given, $R = 1000\ \Omega$, $I_g = 100$ mA

$$\therefore \quad V = I_g R = 100 \times 10^{-3} \times 10^3 = 100 \text{ V} \quad \dots\text{(i)}$$

V
I_g $R = 1000\ \Omega$

Voltmeter can use as ammeter by providing a shunt resistance parallel to it.

$$\therefore \quad \text{Voltage, } V = I_g \left(\frac{Rr}{R + r}\right) \quad \dots\text{(ii)}$$

V
I_g
r

From Eqs. (i) and (ii), we get

$$100 = 1 \left(\frac{1000\, r}{1000 + r}\right)$$

$$\Rightarrow 1000 + r = 10r \quad \Rightarrow 9r = 1000$$

$$\Rightarrow \quad r \simeq 111\ \Omega$$

11 *(c)* For an ideal voltmeter, the resistance should be infinite.

12 *(d)* To increase the range of ammeter, we have to connect a small resistance in parallel (shunt), let its value be R.

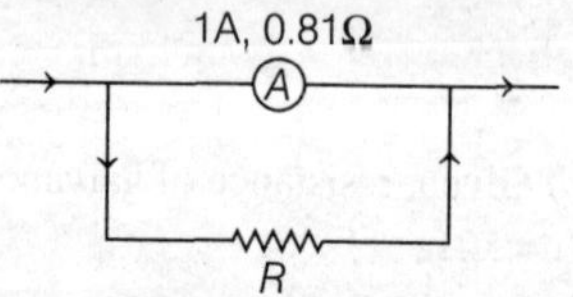

Applying KCL at junction to divide the current, we get

$$9R = 0.81 \times 1$$

$$\Rightarrow \quad R = \frac{0.81}{9} = 0.09\ \Omega$$

13 *(c)* Galvanometer act as a voltmeter when a very high resistance is connected in series with galvanometer.

14 *(c)* When galvanometer is shunted to into an ammeter, then

$$SI = (G + S) I_g$$

$$\frac{I_g}{I} = \frac{S}{G + S}$$

If $G = 36\ \Omega$ and $S = 4\ \Omega$,

then $I_g / I = \frac{1}{10}$

When $I = 100$ A, then $I_g = 10$ A

Percentage of current passes through galvanometer

$$= \frac{10}{100} \times 100 = 10\%$$

15 *(c)* Resistance of galvanometer coil, $R = 10\ \Omega$ and current $= 1$ mA

Range of current is 0-100 mA.

So, the shunt resistance is

$$S = \frac{I_g R}{I - I_g}$$

$$= \frac{1 \times 10^{-3} \times 10}{100 \times 10^{-3} - 1 \times 10^{-3}}$$

$$= \frac{10}{99} = 0.1\Omega$$

16 *(b)* The current required for full scale deflection is

$$i_g = \frac{\text{PD across galvanometer}}{\text{resistance of galvanometer}}$$

$$\Rightarrow \quad i_g = \frac{100 \times 10^{-3}}{100} = 10^{-3}\text{A}$$

The shunt resistance required is

$$S = \left(\frac{i_g}{i - i_g}\right) G = \left(\frac{10^{-3}}{5 - 10^{-3}}\right) \times 100$$

$$= 0.02\ \Omega$$

17 *(a)* The deflection of one division of galvanometer is given by the current $= 4 \times 10^{-4}$A.

$\therefore$ The current sensitivity of galvanometer is $= 4 \times 10^{-4}$ A/div

$\therefore\ i_g$ = Full scale deflection
= Current sensitivity
× Total number of divisions

$$= 4 \times 10^{-4} \times 25 = 10^{-2}\text{ A}$$

Resistance of galvanometer $= 100\ \Omega$

The value of resistance required,

$$R = \frac{V}{i_g} - G = \frac{2.5}{10^{-2}} - 100$$

$$= 250 - 100 = 150\ \Omega$$

18 *(c)* A galvanometer can be converted into ammeter by connecting a shunt or low resistance in parallel with the galvanometer because its resistance needs to be lowered, so that maximum current can pass through it and can give accurate reading.

19 *(a)* Best voltmeter is one with resistance 10000 Ω. As voltmeter with high resistance draw minimum current (or less current) from circuit and gives reading close to the actual current.

20 *(c)* As, $V = I_g R$ ...(i)

and after shunting with resistance, r

$$V = I'_g R' = 1 \times \frac{Rr}{R + r} \quad \text{...(ii)}$$

From Eqs. (i) and (ii), we get

$$1 \times 10^{-3} \times 20 = 1 \times \frac{20r}{20 + r} \quad (\because R = 20)$$

$$\Rightarrow 1000\, r = 20 + r$$

$$\Rightarrow 999r = 20 \quad \Rightarrow \quad r = 0.02\ \Omega$$

21 *(b)* Using the relation, $S = \frac{G}{(n-1)}$

$$\Rightarrow \quad G = S(n-1)$$

and $\quad S' = \frac{G}{(n' - 1)}$

$$\Rightarrow \quad n' = \frac{G + S'}{S'} = \frac{S(n-1) + S'}{S'}$$

22 *(b)* Let i_a be the current flowing through ammeter and i be the total current. So, a current $i - i_a$ will flow through shunt resistance.

Potential difference across ammeter and shunt resistance is same.

i.e. $\quad i_a \times R = (i - i_a) \times S$

or $\quad S = \frac{i_a R}{i - i_a}$ ...(i)

Given, $i_a = 100$ A, $i = 750$ A

and $\quad R = 13\ \Omega$

Hence, $\quad S = \frac{100 \times 13}{750 - 100} = 2\ \Omega$

23 *(d)* The current through the galvanometer,

$$I = \frac{3}{(50 + 2950)} = 10^{-3}\text{ A}$$

i.e. The current for 30 divisions $= 10^{-3}$ A

$\therefore$ Current for 20 divisions

$$= \frac{20}{30} \times 10^{-3}\text{A} = \frac{2}{3} \times 10^{-3}\text{A}$$

For the same deflection to obtain for 20 divisions, let resistance of added resistor is R.

$$\therefore \quad \frac{2}{3} \times 10^{-3} = \frac{3}{(50 + R)}$$

or $\quad R = 4450\ \Omega$

24 *(a)* Shunt required,

$$S = \frac{I_g G}{I - I_g} = \frac{0.02I \times 49}{I - 0.02I} = \frac{0.98I}{0.98I} = 1\ \Omega$$

25 *(b)* As, $I_g = \frac{2}{300}$ A

$$= \frac{2}{300} \times 1000\text{ mA} = \frac{20}{3}\text{ mA}$$

$\therefore \quad I_g = 6.67$ mA

As, range of ammeter cannot be decreased but can be increased only, therefore the instrument cannot be converted to measure the range 1 mA.

26 *(d)* Let the value of current for one division of galvanometer be i.

Then, the current through the ammeter, $I = 50i$

and current through the galvanometer, $I_g = 10i$

We know that, $S = \frac{I_g}{(I - I_g)} G$

$$G = S\left(\frac{I - I_g}{I_g}\right) = 12 \times \left[\frac{50i - 10i}{10i}\right]$$

$$= 12 \times \left[\frac{40i}{10i}\right] = 48\ \Omega$$

27 *(a)* If i is the maximum current, then a part i_g should pass through G and rest $i - i_g$ through S.

Potential across G and S is same, therefore

$$i_g \times G = (i - i_g) \times S$$

$$\Rightarrow \quad S = \frac{i_g G}{i - i_g}$$

Given, $\quad G = 400\ \Omega$,

$i_g = 0.2$ mA $= 0.2 \times 10^{-3}$ A

and $\quad i = 3$ A

$$\therefore \quad S = \frac{0.0002 \times 400}{3 - 0.0002} = 0.027\ \Omega$$

28 *(a)* Resistance required in series,

$$R = \frac{V}{I_g} - G = \frac{nV}{\left(\frac{V}{G}\right)} - G = (n-1)G$$

29 *(b)* Let total current through the parallel combination be I, the current through the galvanometer be I_g and the current through the shunt be $I - I_g$.

The shunted galvanometer is shown in the figure.

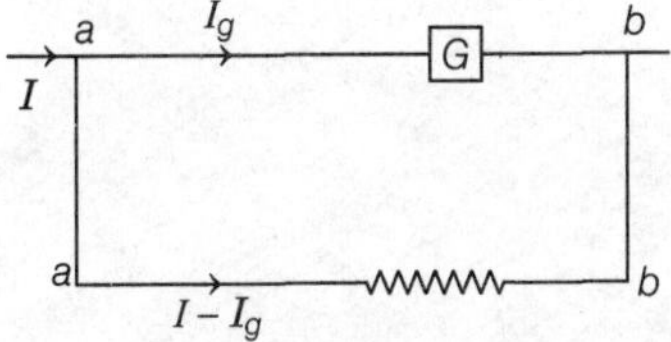

The potential difference, $V_{ab} = (V_a - V_b)$ is the same for both paths, so $I_g G = (I - I_g)S$

$$\Rightarrow I_g(G + S) = IS$$

$$\Rightarrow \frac{I_g}{I} = \frac{S}{S+G}$$

The fraction of current passing through shunt

$$\frac{I - I_g}{I} = 1 - \frac{I_g}{I}$$

$$= 1 - \frac{S}{S+G} = \frac{G}{S+G}$$

$$= \frac{8}{2+8} = \frac{8}{10} = 0.8\text{ A}$$

30 (b) As, I_g = range of ammeter = I

$$\Rightarrow I = I_g = \frac{V}{R_0} = \frac{V(R+r)}{Rr} \quad \text{...(i)}$$

Let R_x be the resistance added and range of ammeter becomes I'_g, then

$$I_g - I'_g = \frac{I_g}{n} = \frac{I}{n} = V\left[\frac{1}{R_0} - \frac{1}{R'_0}\right]$$

where, $R'_0 = R_0 + R_x = \left(\frac{Rr}{R+r} + R_x\right)$

$$\Rightarrow \frac{I}{n} = V\left[\frac{R+r}{Rr} - \frac{(R+r)}{Rr + R_x(R+r)}\right]$$

From Eq. (i), we get

$$\Rightarrow \frac{V(R+r)}{nRr} = V(R+r)\left[\frac{Rr + R_x(R+r) - Rr}{Rr[Rr + R_x(R+r]}\right]$$

$$\Rightarrow \quad R_x = \left(\frac{1}{n-1}\right)R_0$$

31 (b) The galvanometer G and shunt S is connected in parallel, hence potential difference is the same.

$$\therefore \quad i_g \times G = (i - i_g) \times S$$

$$\Rightarrow \frac{i_g}{i - i_g} = \frac{S}{G} = \frac{5}{50} = \frac{1}{10}$$

$$\Rightarrow 10 i_g = i - i_g$$

$$\Rightarrow 11 i_g = i$$

$$\Rightarrow \frac{i_g}{i} = \frac{1}{11}$$

32 (a) Current flowing through the galvanometer,

$$I_g = 16\,\mu\text{A/div} \times 30\text{ div} = 480\,\mu\text{A}$$

The value of resistance in series to the galvanometer is

$$R = \frac{V}{I_g} - G = \frac{3}{480 \times 10^{-6}} - 0$$

$$= 6.25\text{ k}\Omega$$

33 (b) Shunt resistance,

$$S = \frac{I_g G}{I - I_g} = \frac{0.1G}{1 - 0.1} = \frac{G}{9}$$

34 (a) Let current I_g flows through R and G.

For a voltmeter with full scale reading, we have

$$V = I_g(G + R) \text{ or } R = \frac{V}{I_g} - G$$

Given, $G = 2\,\Omega$, $V = 12$ V

and $I_g = 0.1$ A

$$\therefore \quad R = \frac{12}{0.1} - 2 = 120 - 2 = 118\,\Omega$$

19

Magnetism and Matter

Quick Review

Magnet

A magnet is a material or an object that exhibits a strong magnetic field and has a property to attract some specific materials like iron towards it. The magnetic field is invisible but is responsible for properties of a magnet.

Bar Magnet

A bar magnet consists of two equal and non-separable magnetic poles. One pole is designated as north pole (N) and the other as south pole (S). These poles are separated at a small distance but they are not exactly at the ends.

The distance between two poles of a bar magnet is known as **magnetic length of a magnet**.

Its direction is from S-pole of the magnet to N-pole and it is represented by $2l$. It is sometimes also known as **effective length** (L_e) of the magnet and is less than its geometric length (L_g).

N S

L_e

L_g

For a bar magnet, $L_e = \left(\frac{5}{6}\right) L_g$.

Magnetic Field Lines

The magnetic field lines of a magnetic field are the imaginary lines which continuously represent the direction of that magnetic field.

Properties of Magnetic Field Lines

Important properties of magnetic field lines are given below

(*i*) The magnetic field lines of a magnet form closed continuous loops.

(*ii*) The tangent, at any point of a magnetic field line, represents the direction of net magnetic field B at that particular point.

(*iii*) The number of magnetic field lines crossing per unit area is directly proportional to magnitude of magnetic field.

Larger the number of field lines crossing per unit area, the stronger is the magnitude of the magnetic field B.

(*iv*) The magnetic field lines do not intersect each other, for if they did, the direction of the magnetic field would not be unique at the point of intersection.

(*v*) The direction of magnetic field lines is from N to S, if they are outside the magnet and from S to N, if they are inside the magnet.

(*vi*) In case of uniform magnetic field, the magnetic field lines are parallel to each other with equal space between any two lines.

Magnetic Dipole

A magnetic dipole is an arrangement which consists of two magnetic poles of equal and opposite strengths separated at a small distance. A bar magnet, a compass needle etc., are the examples of magnetic dipoles.

Pole Strength

Pole strength can be defined as the strength of a magnetic pole to attract magnetic materials towards itself. It is a scalar quantity and its SI unit is ampere-metre (A-m).

The force between two magnetic poles separated by some distance is given by

$$F = \frac{\mu_0}{4\pi} \cdot \frac{m_1 m_2}{r^2}$$

It is called **Coulomb's law of magnetic force.**

Magnetic Dipole Moment

It is the product of the strength of either of the pole strength and the magnetic length of the magnet. It is represented by **M**.

It is a vector quantity.

−m M→ +m
S N
←2l→

The direction of magnetic dipole moment is same as that of 2l.

Therefore, M = $m(2l)$

Its SI unit is ampere-metre^2 (A-m^2).

Pole Strength and Magnetic Dipole Moment in Special Cases

Special Cases	Figures	Effect on Pole Strength	Formula for New Magnetic Dipole Moment
If bar magnet is cut into two equal pieces such that the length of each piece becomes half.	−m +m, ←2l→; −m+m −m+m, ←l→ ←l→	Remains unchanged	$M' = m \cdot \frac{2l}{2} = \frac{M}{2}$ (becomes half)
If bar magnet is cut into two equal pieces such that the width of each piece becomes half.	−m +m; −m/2 +m/2; −m/2 +m/2; ←2l→	Pole strength of each piece becomes half	$M' = \left(\frac{m}{2}\right)(2l) = \frac{M}{2}$ (becomes half)
If bar magnet is bent in the form of semi-circle.	−m +m, S N, ←2l→; −m +m, ←2r→	Remains unchanged	$M' = m(2r)$ [$\because 2l = \pi r$] $M' = m \times 2\left(\frac{2l}{\pi}\right) = \frac{2M}{\pi}$ $\left(\text{becomes } \frac{2}{\pi} \text{ times}\right)$
When two identical bar magnets are joined perpendicular to each other.	+m, −m +m, S N, −m	Remains unchanged	$M = \sqrt{M_1^2 + M_2^2} = \sqrt{2}M$
When two bar magnets are inclined at an angle θ.	N (+m), M_2, M, (−m) S, θ, φ, S M_1 N, (−m) (+m)	Remains unchanged	Resultant magnetic moment, $M' = \sqrt{M_1^2 + M_2^2 + 2M_1M_2\cos\theta}$ Angle made by resultant magnetic moment (M) with M_1 is given by $\tan\phi = \frac{M_2 \sin\theta}{M_1 + M_2 \cos\theta}$.

Magnetic Field Strength due to a Bar Magnet

The strength of magnetic field at a point due to a bar magnet is defined as the force experienced by a hypothetical unit north pole, placed at that point.

- Magnetic field strength at a point on the axial line of bar magnet, $B = \frac{\mu_0}{4\pi} \frac{2M}{d^3}$

  where, M = magnetic moment of bar magnet

  and d = distance between the point and centre of bar magnet.
- Magnetic field strength at a point on the equatorial line of bar magnet,

  $$B = \frac{\mu_0}{4\pi} \frac{M}{d^3}$$
- Magnetic field strength at any point,

  $$B = \frac{\mu_0}{4\pi} \frac{M}{d^3} \sqrt{1 + 3\cos^2 \theta}$$

  where, θ = angle between the axis of magnet and line joining the point and centre of magnet.
- The magnetic field at a point due to a bar magnet resembles closely to the magnetic field of a current carrying solenoid, so **bar magnet is considered as an equivalent solenoid.**

Torque on a Magnetic Dipole in Uniform Magnetic Field

A magnetic dipole when placed in a uniform magnetic field does not experience any net force. However, it experiences a torque is given by,

$$\tau = \mathbf{M} \times \mathbf{B} = MB \sin \theta$$

where, θ is the angle from magnetic field along which the dipole has been placed.

Work Done by a Magnetic Dipole in Uniform Magnetic Field

Due to the torque, dipole align itself in the direction of field and so some work has to be done to rotate it. This work done is stored as potential energy of the dipole and given by

$$U = W = -\mathbf{M} \cdot \mathbf{B} = -MB \cos \theta$$

Work done in rotating a magnetic dipole in a uniform magnetic field from an initial orientation θ_1 to final orientation θ_2 is given by

$$W = MB (\cos \theta_1 - \cos \theta_2)$$

Oscillations of a Freely Suspended Magnet

When a small bar magnet is suspended in a uniform magnetic field, then torque acting on it makes it oscillate in the uniform magnetic field.

Time period of oscillations, $T = 2\pi \sqrt{\frac{I}{MB}}$

where, I = moment of inertia of magnet

and M = magnetic dipole moment of bar magnet.

Gauss' Law of Magnetism

This law states that, "the surface integral of a magnetic field over a closed surface is zero."

i.e. $$\oint B \cdot dS = 0$$

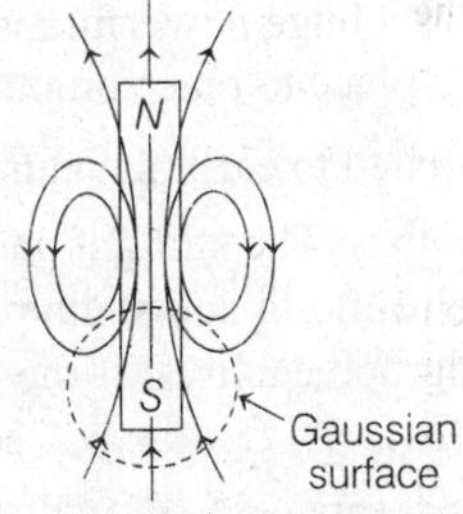

Here, the number of field lines entering the Gaussian surface is same as number of lines leaving the Gaussian surface.

The Electrostatic Analogue : Comparison between an Electric Dipole and a Magnetic Dipole

The behaviour of a magnetic dipole (may be a bar magnet also) is similar to the behaviour of an electric dipole. The only difference is that the electric dipole moment **p** is replaced by magnetic dipole moment **M** and the constant $\frac{1}{4\pi\varepsilon_0}$ is replaced by $\frac{\mu_0}{4\pi}$.

The table gives a comparison between an electric dipole and a magnetic dipole as given below

Physical Quantity to be Compared	Electric Dipole	Magnetic Dipole
Dipole moment	$p = q(2l)$	$M = m(2l)$
Direction of dipole moment	From negative charge to the positive charge.	From south pole to north pole.
Net force in uniform field	0	0
Net torque in uniform field	$\tau = \mathbf{p} \times \mathbf{E}$	$\tau = \mathbf{M} \times \mathbf{B}$

Physical Quantity to be Compared	Electric Dipole	Magnetic Dipole
Field at far away point on the axis	$\frac{1}{4\pi\varepsilon_0}\cdot\frac{2p}{r^3}$ (along **p**)	$\frac{\mu_0}{4\pi}\cdot\frac{2M}{r^3}$ (along **M**)
Field at far away point on perpendicular bisector	$\frac{1}{4\pi\varepsilon_0}\cdot\frac{p}{r^3}$ (opposite to **p**)	$\frac{\mu_0}{4\pi}\cdot\frac{M}{r^3}$ (opposite to **M**)
Potential energy	$U_\theta = -\mathbf{p}\cdot\mathbf{E} = -pE\cos\theta$	$U_\theta = -\mathbf{M}\cdot\mathbf{B} = -MB\cos\theta$
Work done in rotating the dipole	$W_{\theta_1-\theta_2} = pE(\cos\theta_1 - \cos\theta_2)$	$W_{\theta_1-\theta_2} = MB(\cos\theta_1 - \cos\theta_2)$

Note In the table, θ is the angle between electric or magnetic field (**E** or **B**) and dipole moment (**p** or **M**).

Earth's Magnetism

Our earth behaves as a huge powerful magnet and its strength varies from place to place on the earth's surface.

Some definitions related to earth's magnetism are as follows

(*i*) **Geographic Axis** The straight line passing through the geographical north and south poles of the earth is called its geographic axis. It is the axis of rotation of the earth.

(*ii*) **Magnetic Axis** The straight line passing through the magnetic north and south poles of the earth is called the magnetic axis.

(*iii*) **Magnetic Equator** It is the huge circle on the earth perpendicular to the magnetic axis.

(*iv*) **Magnetic Meridian** The vertical plane in the direction of B is called magnetic meridian.

(*v*) **Geographic Meridian** The vertical plane passing through the line joining the geographical north and south poles is called the geographic meridian.

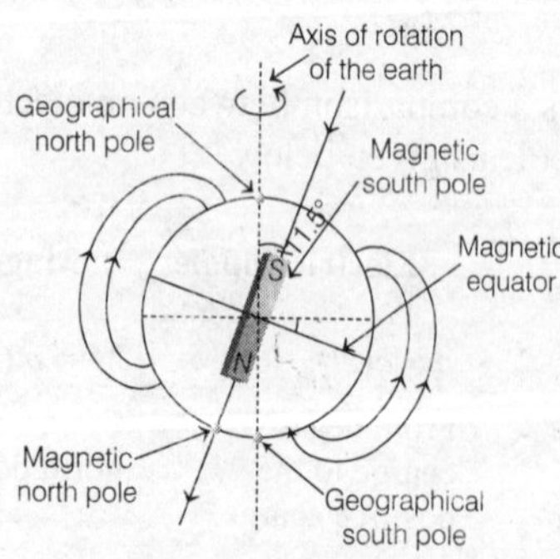

Note Earth's magnetic field varies irregularly from place to place and at a place, it varies with time also.

Elements of Earth's Magnetism

The earth's magnetic field at a place can be completely described by three parameters which are called elements of earth's magnetic field.

These three elements are given below

(*i*) Magnetic Declination or Angle of Declination (α)

At any place, the acute angle between the magnetic meridian and the geographical meridian is called angle of declination (α).

(*ii*) Magnetic Inclination or Angle of Dip (θ)

The angle of dip (θ) at a place is the angle between the direction of Earth's magnetic field (B) and horizontal line in the magnetic meridian. At Earth's magnetic poles, the magnetic field of earth is vertical, i.e. angle of dip is 90°, the freely suspended magnetic needle is vertical there. At magnetic equator, magnetic field is horizontal or angle of dip is 0°.

(*iii*) Horizontal and Vertical Component of Earth's Magnetic Field

Let B_e be the net magnetic field at some point. H and V be the horizontal and vertical components of B_e. Let θ be the angle of dip at some place, then we can see that,

$$H = B_e \cos\theta \quad \text{...(i)}$$

and

$$V = B_e \sin\theta \quad \text{...(ii)}$$

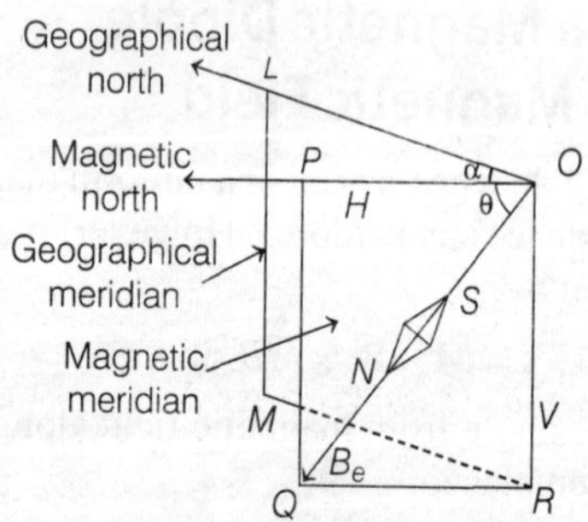

Squaring and adding Eqs. (i) and (ii), we get

$$B_e = \sqrt{H^2 + V^2}$$

Further, dividing Eq. (ii) by Eq. (i), we get

$$\theta = \tan^{-1}\left(\frac{V}{H}\right)$$

By knowing H and θ at some place, we can find B_e and V at that place.

Terms Used in Magnetism

The various terms are used in magnetism as given below

(i) **Magnetic induction (B)** is the number of magnetic field lines passing normally through a cross-sectional area of material. Its SI unit is tesla (T) or weber/metre ^{2} (Wm^{-2}) and CGS unit is gauss (G).
Also, $1T = 10^4$ G

(ii) **Intensity of magnetisation (I)** is the magnetic moment per unit volume of the magnetic substance.
i.e. $I = \frac{M}{V}$.
Its SI unit is Am^{-1}.

(iii) **Magnetic permeability (μ)** is the ratio of the magnetic induction to the magnetic intensity. i.e.
$\mu = \frac{B}{H}$.
Its SI unit is Wb/A-m or TmA^{-1}.

(iv) **Relative magnetic permeability (μ_r)** is the ratio of magnetic permeability of the substance to the permeability of free space and given as
$\mu_r = \frac{\mu}{\mu_0} = \frac{B}{B_0}$.

(v) **Magnetic intensity (H)** is a measure of the capability of external magnetic field to magnetise the given substance and given by $H = \frac{B_0}{\mu_0} = \frac{B}{\mu_0} - I$.
Its SI unit is Am^{-1} and CGS unit is oersted.

(vi) **Magnetic susceptibility (χ_m)** is the ratio of intensity of magnetisation in a substance to the magnetic intensity. i.e. $\chi_m = \frac{I}{H}$

μ_r and χ_m are related as $\mu_r = \chi_m + 1$.

Magnetic Behaviour of Materials

In terms of magnetic behaviour, all substances are categorised in three types; Diamagnetic substances, Paramagnetic substances and Ferromagnetic substances. Their various features are tabulated as follows

Properties	Diamagnetic	Paramagnetic	Ferromagnetic
Definition	These substances when placed in a magnetic field, acquire feeble magnetism opposite to the direction of the magnetic field. 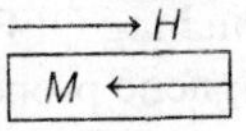 (H →, M ←)	These substances when placed in a magnetic field, acquire feeble magnetism in the direction of the magnetic field. 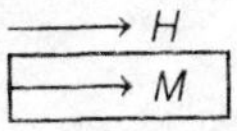 (H →, M →)	These substances when placed in a magnetic field are strongly magnetised in the direction of the field. 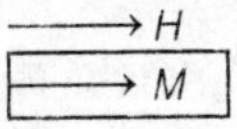 (H →, M →)
Behaviour in a magnetic field	repelled	attracted	strongly attracted
Magnetic moment	zero	non-zero	non-zero
Relative permeability (μ_r)	$\mu_r < 1$	$\mu_r > 1$	$\mu_r >> 1$
Magnetic susceptibility (χ_m)	small and negative	positive	large and positive
Variation of χ_m with temperature	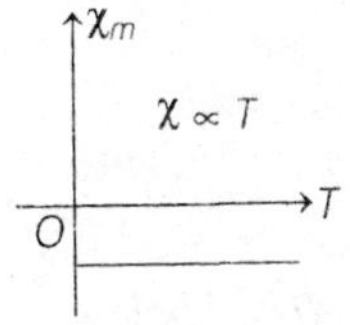 χ_m; $\chi \propto T$; O; T	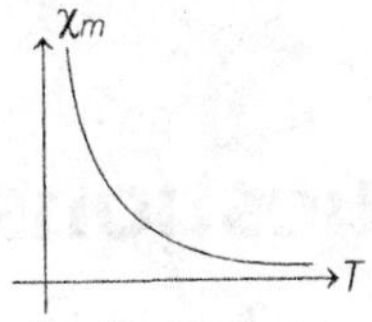 χ_m; T	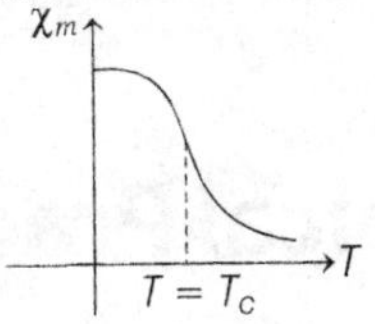 χ_m; $T = T_C$; T
I versus H	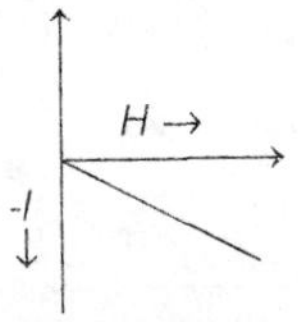 H →; -I ↓	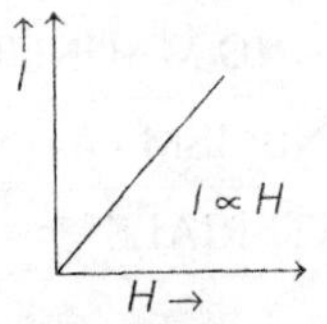 I ↑; $I \propto H$; H →	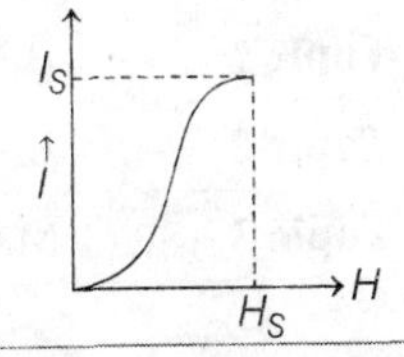 I_S; I ↑; H_S; H
Examples	bismuth, antimony, gold, quartz, water, alcohol, etc.	platinum, aluminium, chromium, air, $CuSo_4$, etc.	iron, nickel, cobalt, steel and their alloys.

Curie's Law

- According to Curie's law, the magnetic susceptibility of paramagnetic material is given by

$$\chi_m = \frac{C}{T}$$

where, C = Curie constant.

- Above Curie temperature, a ferromagnetic substance becomes an ordinary paramagnetic substance whose magnetic susceptibility obeys the Curie-Weiss law and given by $$\chi_m = \frac{C}{T - T_c}$$

where, T_C = Curie temperature and C = constant.

Hysteresis

The phenomenon of the lagging of magnetic induction behind the magnetising field is called hysteresis.

The plot of intensity of magnetisation (I) of ferromagnetic substances *versus* magnetic intensity (H) for a complete cycle of magnetisation and demagnetisation is called **hysteresis loop** or **hysteresis curve**.

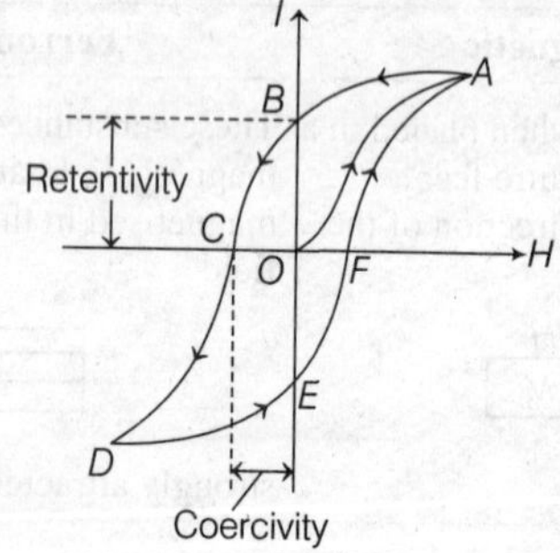

It is clear from the above figure that, if intensity of magnetising field (H) is increased, then the intensity of magnetisation (I) also increases.

Beyond a point, if intensity of magnetising field (H) is increased, then intensity of magnetisation (I) does not increase.

When intensity of magnetising field (H) is decreased, then intensity of magnetisation (I) also decreases, but it lags behind H. Therefore when H becomes zero, I does not reduce to zero, i.e. the curve does not retrace itself.

Now, this value of intensity of magnetisation (I) which is left in the material at $H = 0$, is called **retentivity** or **remanence** (BO).

When the magnetising field is applied in reverse direction and its intensity H, is increased. The material starts demagnetising. The value of magnetising field needed to reduce magnetisation to zero is called **coercivity** (OC).

If reverse magnetising field is increased, further the material becomes saturated. Now, if the magnetising field is reduced after attaining the reverse saturation, the cycle repeats itself.

The area enclosed by the loop represents loss of energy during a cycle of magnetisation and demagnetisation.

Permanent Magnets and Electromagnet

The substance which at room temperature retain their magnetic property are called **permanent magnets.** The electromagnets are the iron core solenoids which show magnetic property when current flows through them, on switching OFF the current, they do not show any magnetic property.

The material used as permanent magnet have high retentivity and high coercivity, while the materials for of construction of **electromagnets** should have high initial permeability and low hysteresis loss.

Topical Practice Questions

All the exam questions of this chapter have been divided into 3 topics as listed below

Topic 1

Bar Magnet and Magnetic Dipole

2016

1 A bar magnet is hung by a thin cotton thread in a uniform horizontal magnetic field and is in equilibrium state. The energy required to rotate it by 60° is W. So, the torque required to keep the magnet in this new position is **[NEET]**

(a) $\frac{W}{\sqrt{3}}$ (b) $\sqrt{3}W$

(c) $\frac{\sqrt{3}W}{2}$ (d) $\frac{2W}{\sqrt{3}}$

2014

2 Following figures show the arrangement of bar magnets in different configurations. Each magnet has magnetic dipole moment m. Which configuration has highest net magnetic dipole moment? **[CBSE AIPMT]**

(a)
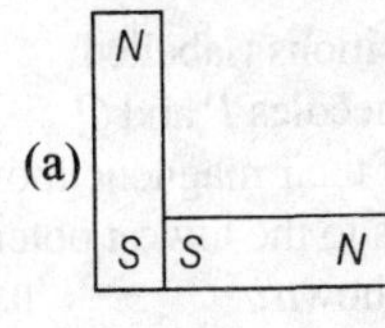

(b)
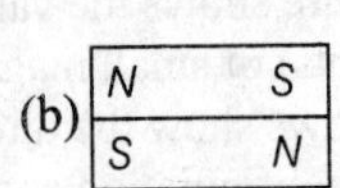

(c)
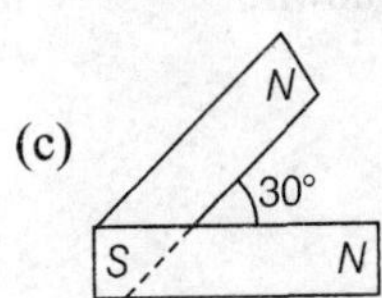

(d)
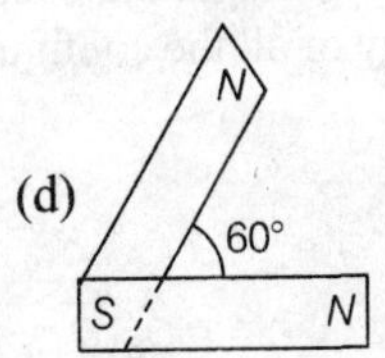

3 A bar magnet of magnetic moment M and pole strength m is cut into two parts of equal lengths. The magnetic moment and pole strength of either part is **[UK PMT]**

(a) $\frac{M}{2}, \frac{m}{2}$ (b) $M, \frac{m}{2}$

(c) $\frac{M}{2}, m$ (d) M, m

2013

4 A north pole of 40 A-m is placed 20 cm apart from a south pole of 80 A-m. Calculate the distance of a point from the south pole on the line joining the two poles where the resultant field due to these poles is zero. **[AIIMS]**

(a) 8.2 cm towards north pole

(b) 8.2 cm away from north pole

(c) 48.2 cm towards north pole

(d) 48.2 cm away from north pole

2012

5 A magnetic needle suspended parallel to a magnetic field requires $\sqrt{3}$ J of work to turn it through 60°. The torque needed to maintain the needle in this position will be **[CBSE AIPMT]**

(a) $2\sqrt{3}$ J (b) 3 J (c) $\sqrt{3}$ J (d) $\frac{3}{2}$ J

2011

6 A magnetic wire of dipole moment 4π A-m^2 is bent in the form of semicircle. The new magnetic moment is **[J&K CET]**

(a) 4π A-m^2 (b) 8 A-m^2

(c) 4 A-m^2 (d) None of these

7 The magnetic field due to short bar magnet of magnetic dipole moment M and length $2l$, on the axis at a distance z (where, $z >> l$) from the centre of the magnet is given by formula **[J&K CET]**

(a) $\frac{\mu_0 M}{4\pi z^3}\hat{\mathbf{M}}$ (b) $\frac{2\mu_0 M}{4\pi z^3}\hat{\mathbf{M}}$

(c) $\frac{4\mu_0 M}{\mu_0 z^3}\hat{\mathbf{M}}$ (d) $\frac{\mu_0 M}{\pi z^3}\hat{\mathbf{M}}$

8 A bar magnet is placed in the position of stable equilibrium in a uniform magnetic field of induction B. If it is rotated through an angle 180°, then the work is **[J&K CET]**

(a) MB (b) $2MB$ (c) $\frac{MB}{2}$ (d) zero

9 If the magnet is cut into four equal parts such that their lengths and breadths are equal. Pole strength of each part is **[MHT CET]**

(a) m (b) $m/2$ (c) $m/4$ (d) $m/8$

2010

10 A bar magnet having a magnetic moment of 2×10^4 JT^{-1} is free to rotate in a horizontal plane. A horizontal magnetic field $B = 6\times10^{-4}$ T exists in the space. The work done in taking the magnet slowly from a direction parallel to the field to a direction 60° from the field is **[CBSE AIPMT]**

(a) 0.6 J (b) 12 J (c) 6 J (d) 2 J

11 A short bar magnet placed with its axis at 30° with a uniform external magnetic field of 0.16 T experiences a torque of magnitude 0.032 J. The magnetic moment of the bar magnet will be **[Punjab PMET]**

(a) 0.23 JT^{-1} (b) 0.40 JT^{-1} (c) 0.80 JT^{-1} (d) zero

12 A bar magnet of length 3 cm has points A and B along its axis at distances of 24 cm and 48 cm on the opposite sides. Ratio of magnetic fields at these points will be **[Punjab PMET]**

A S N B
O
←24 cm→←48 cm→

(a) 8 (b) $1/2\sqrt{2}$ (c) 3 (d) 4

13 The work done in turning a magnet of magnetic moment M by an angle of 90° from the meridian is n times. The corresponding work done to turn it through an angle of 60° is **[BCECE]**

(a) $n = 1/2$ (b) $n = 2$ (c) $n = 1/4$ (d) $n = 1$

14 The magnetic lines of force inside a bar magnet **[MGIMS]**

(a) are from north pole to south pole of the magnet
(b) do not exist
(c) depend upon the area of cross-section of the bar magnet
(d) are from south pole to north pole of the magnet

15 Two small magnets each of magnetic moment 10 A-m^2 are placed in end on position 0.1 m apart from their centres. The force acting between them is **[VMMC]**

(a) 0.6×10^7 N (b) 0.06×10^7 N
(c) 0.6 N (d) 0.06 N

16 Torques τ_1 and τ_2 are required for magnetic needle to remain perpendicular to the magnetic fields B_1 and B_2 at two different places. The ratio B_1/B_2 is **[VMMC]**

(a) $\frac{\tau_2}{\tau_1}$ (b) $\frac{\tau_1}{\tau_2}$
(c) $\frac{\tau_1+\tau_2}{\tau_1-\tau_2}$ (d) $\frac{\tau_1-\tau_2}{\tau_1+\tau_2}$

2009

17 A magnetic needle is kept in a non-uniform magnetic field. It experiences **[AFMC]**

(a) a force only but not a torque
(b) a force and torque both
(c) a torque only but not a force
(d) neither a torque nor a force

18 Two bar magnets having same geometry with magnetic moments M and $2M$ are placed in such a way that their similar poles are on the same side, then its time period of the oscillation is T_1. Now, if the polarity of one of the magnets is reversed, then time period of oscillation is T_2, then **[AIIMS]**

(a) $T_1 < T_2$ (b) $T_1 > T_2$ (c) $T_1 = T_2$ (d) $T_1 = \infty, T_1 = 0$

19 **Assertion** Two short magnets are placed on a cork which floats on water. The magnets are placed such that the axis of one produced bisects the axis of other at right angles. Then, the cork has neither translational nor rotational motion. **[AIIMS]**

Reason Net force on the cork is zero

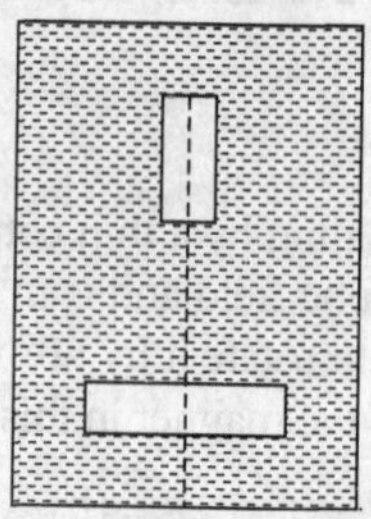

(a) Both Assertion and Reason are correct and Reason is the correct explanation of Assertion.
(b) Both Assertion and Reason are correct but Reason is not the correct explanation of Assertion.
(c) Assertion is correct but Reason is incorrect.
(d) Both Assertion and Reason are incorrect.

20 The mathematical equation for magnetic field lines of force is **[BVP]**

(a) $\nabla \cdot \mathbf{B} = 0$ (b) $\nabla \cdot \mathbf{B} \neq 0$ (c) $\nabla \cdot \mathbf{B} > 0$ (d) $\nabla \cdot \mathbf{B} < 0$

21 The figure shows the various positions (labelled subscripts) of small magnetised needles P and Q. The arrows show the direction of their magnetic moment. Which configuration corresponds to the lowest potential energy of all the configurations shown? **[DUMET]**

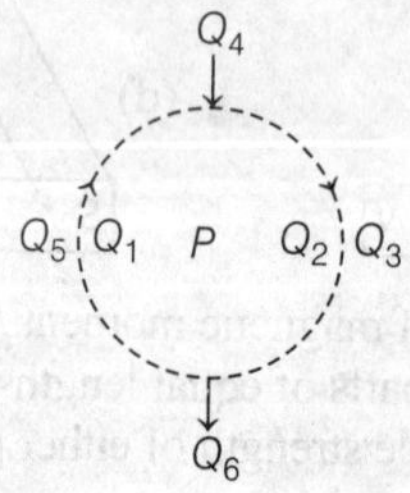

(a) PQ_3 (b) PQ_4 (c) PQ_5 (d) PQ_6

2008

22 A thin rectangular magnet suspended freely has a period of oscillation equal to T. Now, it is broken into two equal halves (each having half of the original length) and one piece is made to oscillate freely in the same field. If its period of oscillation is T'. The ratio of T'/T is **[RPMT]**

(a) $\frac{1}{2\sqrt{2}}$ (b) $\frac{1}{2}$ (c) 2 (d) $\frac{1}{4}$

23 A bar magnet suspended freely in a uniform magnetic field is vibrating with a time period of 3 s. If the field strength is increased to 4 times of the earlier field strength, then the time period (in second) will be **[Punjab PMET]**

(a) 12 (b) 6 (c) 1.5 (d) 0.75

24 A bar magnet of magnetic moment M_1 is axially cut into two equal parts. If these two pieces are arranged perpendicular to each other, the resultant magnetic moment is M_2. Then, the value of M_1 / M_2 is **[Punjab PMET]**

(a) $\frac{1}{2\sqrt{2}}$ (b) 1 (c) $\frac{1}{\sqrt{2}}$ (d) $\sqrt{2}$

25 The effect due to uniform magnetic field on a freely suspended magnetic needle is as follows **[AFMC]**

(a) both torque and net force are present
(b) torque is present but no net force
(c) both torque and net force are absent
(d) net force is present but not torque

26 A thin bar magnet of length $2L$ is bent at the mid-point, so that the angle between them is 60°. The new length of the magnet is **[Manipal]**

(a) $\sqrt{2}\,L$ (b) $\sqrt{3}\,L$ (c) $2L$ (d) L

27 The magnetic moment of a bar magnet of semi-length 20 cm is 4×10^{-6} Am^2. Its pole strength is

(a) 20×10^{-6} Am (b) 10×10^{-6} Am
(c) 80×10^{-6} Am (d) 40×10^{-6} Am

28 A bar magnet of magnetic moment **M**, is placed in a magnetic field of induction **B**. The torque exerted on it is **[Guj CET]**

(a) $\mathbf{M}\times\mathbf{B}$ (b) $-\mathbf{B}\cdot\mathbf{M}$ (c) $\mathbf{M}\cdot\mathbf{B}$ (d) $\mathbf{M}\cdot\mathbf{B}$

2007

29 A bar magnet is oscillating in the earth's magnetic field with a period T. What happens to its period and motion, if its mass is quadrupled? **[BHU]**

(a) Motion remains simple harmonic with time period $= 4T$
(b) Motion remains simple harmonic and period remains nearly constant
(c) Motion remains simple harmonic with time period $= \frac{T}{2}$
(d) Motion remains simple harmonic with time period $= 2T$

30 A long magnet is cut into two equal parts such that the length of each half is same as that of original magnet. If the period of original magnet is T, then the period of new magnet is **[J&K CET]**

(a) T (b) $T/2$
(c) $T/4$ (d) $2T$

31 The time period of a freely suspended bar magnet in a field is 2 s. It is cut into two equal parts along its axis, then the time period is **[J&K CET]**

(a) 4 s (b) 0.5 s (c) 2 s (d) 0.25 s

2006

32 A bar magnet is held at right angle to a uniform magnetic field. The couple acting on the magnet is to be halved by rotating it from this position. The angle of rotation is **[J&K CET]**

(a) 60° (b) 45° (c) 30° (d) 75°

33 The couple acting on a magnet of length 10 cm and pole strength 15 A-m kept in a field of $B = 2\times10^{-5}$ T, at an angle of 30° is **[AMU]**

(a) 1.5×10^{-5} N-m (b) 1.5×10^{-3} N-m
(c) 1.5×10^{-2} Nm (d) 1.5×10^{-6} N-m

34 Two short bar magnets P and Q are arranged such that their centres are on the X-axis and are separated by a large distance. The magnetic axes of P and Q are along X and Y-axes, respectively. At a point R, mid-way between their centres, if B is the magnitude of induction due to Q, the magnitude of total induction at R due to the both magnets is **[EAMCET]**

(a) $3B$ (b) $\sqrt{5}\,B$ (c) $\frac{\sqrt{5}}{2}B$ (d) B

35 Work done in rotating a bar magnet from 0 to angle θ is **[JCECE]**

(a) $MH(1-\cos\theta)$ (b) $\frac{M}{H}(1-\cos\theta)$
(c) $M/H(\cos\theta-1)$ (d) $MH(\cos\theta-1)$

2005

36 The intensity of magnetic field due to an isolated pole of strength m at a point distant r from it will be proportional to **[J&K CET]**

(a) $\frac{m}{r^2}$ (b) mr^2 (c) $\frac{r^2}{m}$ (d) $\frac{m}{r}$

37 For protecting a sensitive equipment from external magnetic field, it should be **[AMU]**

(a) placed inside an iron cane
(b) placed inside an aluminium cane
(c) surrounded with fine copper sheet
(d) wrapped with insulation around it, when passing current through it

Answers

1 (b)	2 (c)	3 (c)	4 (c)	5 (b)	6 (b)	7 (b)	8 (b)	9 (b)	10 (c)
11 (b)	12 (a)	13 (b)	14 (d)	15 (c)	16 (b)	17 (b)	18 (a)	19 (a)	20 (a)
21 (d)	22 (b)	23 (c)	24 (d)	25 (b)	26 (d)	27 (b)	28 (a)	29 (d)	30 (a)
31 (c)	32 (a)	33 (a)	34 (b)	35 (a)	36 (a)	37 (a)			

Explanations

1 *(b)* $\because$ Work done in rotating the magnet, $W = MB(\cos\theta_0 - \cos\theta)$ where, M = magnetic moment of the magnet and B = magnetic field.

Given, $\theta_0 = 0°$ and $\theta = 60°$

$$\because \quad W = MB(\cos 0° - \cos 60°)$$

$$= MB\left(1 - \frac{1}{2}\right)$$

$$\left[\because \cos 0° = 1 \text{ and } \cos 60° = \frac{1}{2}\right]$$

$$= \frac{MB}{2}$$

$$\therefore \quad MB = 2W \qquad \ldots\text{(i)}$$

Torque on a magnet in this position is given by,

$$\tau = \mathbf{M} \times \mathbf{B} = MB\sin\theta$$

$$= 2W \cdot \sin 60° \quad \text{[from Eq. (i)]}$$

$$= 2W \frac{\sqrt{3}}{2} \quad \left[\because \sin 60° = \frac{\sqrt{3}}{2}\right]$$

$$= \sqrt{3}\,W$$

2 *(c)* Magnetic dipole moment is from S to N,

$$m_{\text{net}} = \sqrt{m^2 + m^2 + 2m^2\cos\theta}$$

m_{net} will be maximum, if $\cos\theta$ is maximum. $\cos\theta$ will be maximum when θ will be minimum.

In Fig. (a), $\theta = 90°$, in Fig. (b) it is $180°$, in Fig. (c) it is $30°$ and in Fig. (d) it is $60°$.

So, at $\theta = 30°$, m_{net} will be maximum.

3 *(c)* The bar magnet is shown in the diagram

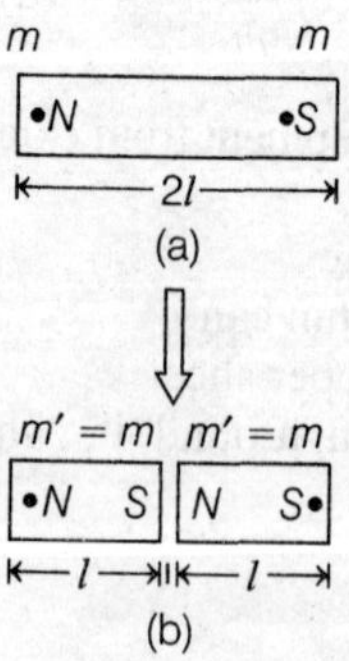

For Figs. (a) and (b), magnetic moment of first part,

$$M = m(2l) = \text{magnetic moment}$$

$$M' = m'(l)$$

$$\text{Now,} \quad \frac{M'}{M} = \frac{m'(l)}{m(2l)} = \frac{1}{2}\left(\frac{m'}{m}\right) \qquad \ldots\text{(i)}$$

When magnet is cut as shown in the diagram, pole strength will not be affected.

$$\text{Hence,} \quad m' = m \Rightarrow \frac{m'}{m} = 1$$

$$\Rightarrow \quad M' = \frac{M}{2} \qquad \text{[from Eq. (i)]}$$

4 *(c)* Let at point P, magnetic field is zero

40 A-m N, 80 A-m S, P, x, 20 cm

$$\therefore \quad \frac{\mu_0}{4\pi}\frac{m_1}{r_1^2} = \frac{\mu_0}{4\pi}\frac{m_2}{r_2^2}$$

$$\frac{40}{x^2} = \frac{80}{(20+x)^2} \qquad \text{[from figure]}$$

$$(20 + x)^2 = 2x^2$$

$$\Rightarrow \quad 20 + x = \sqrt{2}x$$

$$\therefore \quad x = \frac{20}{\sqrt{2} - 1} = 48.2 \text{ cm}$$

(towards north pole)

5 *(b)* In this case, work done,

$$W = MB(\cos\theta_1 - \cos\theta_2)$$

Given, $W = \sqrt{3}$ J,

$$\theta_1 = 0° \text{ and } \theta_2 = 60°$$

$$\sqrt{3} = MB(\cos 0° - \cos 60°)$$

$$= MB\left(1 - \frac{1}{2}\right) = \frac{MB}{2}$$

$$\Rightarrow \quad MB = 2\sqrt{3} \text{ J}$$

$$\text{Torque, } \tau = MB\sin\theta = MB\sin(60°)$$

$$= (2\sqrt{3})(\sqrt{3}/2)$$

$$= 3 \text{ N-m or J}$$

6 *(b)* If length of wire is $2l$, then magnetic moment,

$$M = m \times 2l = 4\pi \text{ A-m}^2 \quad \text{(given)}$$

As wire is bent in the form of semicircle effective distance between the ends is $2r$.

So, new dipole moment, $M' = m \times 2r$

$$\text{As,} \quad \pi r = 2l$$

$$\Rightarrow \quad r = 2l/\pi$$

$$\text{So,} \quad M' = m \times 2 \times \frac{2l}{\pi} = \frac{2}{\pi}(m \times 2l)$$

$$= \frac{2}{\pi}M = \frac{2}{\pi}4\pi = 8 \text{ A-m}^2$$

7 *(b)* Consider a point P located on the axial line of a short bar magnet of magnetic length $2l$ and strength m. Let us find $\mathbf{B}$ at a point P which is at a distance z from the centre of magnet.

Magnetic field at point P due to N-pole,

S, N, 2l, z, P, B, B_2, B_1

$$B_1 = \frac{\mu_0}{4\pi}\left[\frac{m}{(z-l)^2}\right] \text{ along } NP$$

Similarly, magnetic field at point P due to S-pole,

$$B_2 = \frac{\mu_0}{4\pi}\left[\frac{m}{(z+l)^2}\right] \text{ along } PS$$

Net magnetic field at P,

$$B = B_1 - B_2$$

$$= \frac{\mu_0}{4\pi}\left[\frac{m}{(z-l)^2} - \frac{m}{(z+l)^2}\right]$$

$$= \frac{\mu_0}{4\pi}\left[\frac{4mlz}{(z^2 - l^2)^2}\right]$$

$$= \frac{\mu_0}{4\pi}\left[\frac{m \times 2l}{(z^2 - l^2)^2}2z\right]$$

$$B = \frac{\mu_0}{4\pi}\frac{2Mz}{(z^2 - l^2)^2}$$

$$[\therefore M = m(2l)]$$

$$B = \frac{\mu_0}{4\pi}\cdot\frac{2Mz}{z^4} \qquad (\because z >> l)$$

Hence, in vector form, magnetic field at point P due to N-pole can be written as

$$\mathbf{B} = \frac{\mu_0}{4\pi}\frac{2M}{z^3}\hat{\mathbf{M}}$$

where, $\hat{\mathbf{M}}$ = unit vector along magnetic dipole moment.

8 *(b)* We know that,

$$W = MB(\cos\theta_1 - \cos\theta_2)$$

$$\text{As,} \quad \theta_1 = 0° \text{ and } \theta_2 = 180°$$

$$\text{Then,} \quad W = MB(\cos 0° - \cos 180°)$$

$$= 2MB$$

where, M = magnetic dipole moment of bar magnet.

9 *(b)* The situations are shown in figure.

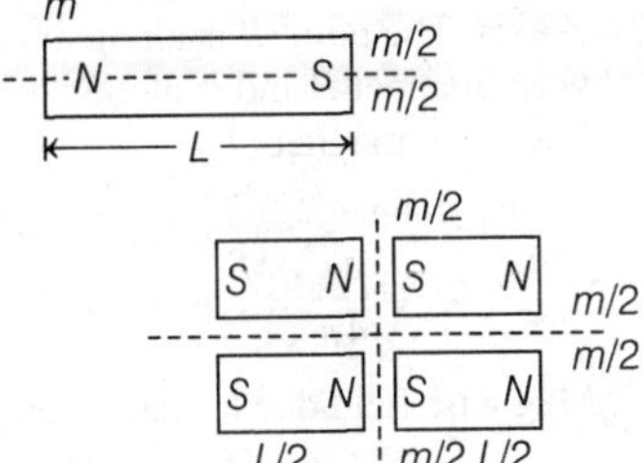

For each part, $m' = \frac{m}{2}$

10 *(c)* Given, magnetic moment,

$M = 2 \times 10^4\ JT^{-1}$

and $B = 6 \times 10^{-4}\ T$

Now, work done in rotating the bar magnet from angular position 0° to 60° (in magnitude).

$W = -\mathbf{M} \cdot \mathbf{B}$

$\Rightarrow W = -\int dW = -\int_0^{60°} M \cdot B \cos\theta\ d\theta$

$= -MB \int_0^{60°} \cos\theta\ d\theta$

$= -MB\ [\cos 60° - \cos 0°]$

$= MB \times 1/2$

$= 2 \times 10^4\ JT^{-1} \times 6 \times 10^{-4}\ T \times \frac{1}{2}$

$= 6\ J$

11 *(b)* Given, $\theta = 30°$, $B = 0.16\ T$

and $\tau = 0.032\ J$

Magnetic moment,

$M = \frac{\tau}{B \sin\theta} = \frac{0.032}{0.16 \times \sin 30°}$

$= 0.40\ JT^{-1}$

12 *(a)* Magnetic field due to a bar magnet at a distance r from the centre of magnet on axial position,

$B = \frac{\mu_0}{4\pi} \cdot \frac{2M}{r^3}$

Given, $l = 3$ cm, $r_1 = 24$ cm

and $r_2 = 48$ cm

Putting these values, we get

$\Rightarrow \quad \frac{B_1}{B_2} = \left(\frac{r_2}{r_1}\right)^3 = \left(\frac{48}{24}\right)^3 = 8$

13 *(b)* Work done,

$W = MB(\cos\theta_1 - \cos\theta_2)$

In first case, $\theta_1 = 0°$ and $\theta_2 = 90°$

$\Rightarrow \quad W_1 = MB\ (\cos 0° - \cos 90°) = MB$

In second case, $\theta_1 = 0°, \theta_2 = 60°$

$\Rightarrow \quad W_2 = MB(\cos 0° - \cos 60°)$

$= MB\left(1 - \frac{1}{2}\right) = \frac{MB}{2}$

Given, $W_1 = nW_2$

$\Rightarrow \quad MB = n\frac{MB}{2}$

$\Rightarrow \quad n = 2$

14 *(d)* In case of a bar magnet, outside it, the magnetic lines of force start from north pole and end on south pole. But inside it, lines of force are from south pole to north pole.

15 *(c)* Magnetic force, $F = \frac{\mu_0}{4\pi} \frac{6M_1M_2}{r^4}$

Given, $\frac{\mu_0}{4\pi} = 10^{-7}, M_1 = M_2$

$= 10\ A\text{-}m^2$ and $r = 0.1\ m$

Putting these values, we get

$\Rightarrow \quad F = 10^{-7} \times \frac{6 \times 10 \times 10}{(0.1)^4}$

$\Rightarrow \quad F = \frac{600 \times 10^{-7}}{0.0001} = 0.6\ N$

16 *(b)* Torque, $\tau = MB\sin\theta$

$\tau_1 = MB_1 \sin 90° = MB_1$

and $\tau_2 = MB_2 \sin 90° = MB_2$

or $\frac{MB_1}{MB_2} = \frac{\tau_1}{\tau_2} \Rightarrow \frac{B_1}{B_2} = \frac{\tau_1}{\tau_2}$

17 *(b)* Magnetic needle kept in a non-uniform magnetic field, experiences a force and torque both.

18 *(a)* Using the formula, for time period,

$T = 2\pi\sqrt{\left(\frac{I}{MH}\right)} \Rightarrow T \propto \frac{1}{\sqrt{M}} \quad \ldots(i)$

When similar poles placed at same side, then

$M_1 = M + 2M = 3M$

So, from Eq. (i)

$T_1 \propto \frac{1}{\sqrt{3M}} \quad \ldots(ii)$

When the polarity of a magnet is reversed, then $M_2 = 2M - M = M$

So, from Eq . (i),

$T_2 \propto \frac{1}{\sqrt{M}} \quad \ldots(iii)$

Now, on dividing Eq. (ii) by Eq. (iii), we get

$\frac{T_1}{T_2} = \frac{\sqrt{M}}{\sqrt{3M}} = \frac{1}{\sqrt{3}}$

$\Rightarrow \quad T_2 = \sqrt{3}T_1$

Hence, $T_1 < T_2$

19 *(a)* We observe that both the magnets exert equal and opposite force/torque on each other.

Hence, net force/torque on cork will be zero. Therefore, the cork has neither translational nor rotational motion.

20 *(a)* The divergence of magnetic field is always zero, i.e. $\nabla \cdot \mathbf{B} = 0$.

21 *(d)* As potential energy is given as

$U = -MB\ (1 - \cos\theta)$

$\Rightarrow \quad U = -MB$

[when $\theta = 0°$, U = minimum]

Hence, **M** amd **B** are parallel to each other for minimum potential energy.

PQ_6 configuration provides $\theta = 0°$

$U_{min} = -MB$

22 *(b)* When a thin rectangular magnet is divided into two equal parts, the magnetic dipole moment,

$M' = \text{pole strength} \times \frac{l}{2} = \frac{M}{2}$

(pole strength remains same)

Also, the mass of magnet becomes half, i.e. $m' = \frac{m}{2}$

Moment of inertia of magnet,

$I = \frac{ml^2}{12}$

New moment of inertia,

$I' = \frac{1}{12}\left(\frac{m}{2}\right)\left(\frac{l}{2}\right)^2 = \frac{ml^2}{12 \times 8}$

$\Rightarrow \quad I' = \frac{I}{8}$

Now, $T = 2\pi\sqrt{\left(\frac{I}{MB}\right)}$

$T' = 2\pi\sqrt{\left(\frac{I'}{M'B}\right)}$

$= 2\pi\sqrt{\left(\frac{I/8}{MB/2}\right)}$

$\therefore \quad T' = \frac{T}{2}$

$\Rightarrow \quad \frac{T'}{T} = \frac{1}{2}$

23 *(c)* As, the time period,

$T = 2\pi\sqrt{\frac{I}{MB}}$

or $T \propto \frac{1}{\sqrt{B}}$

$\Rightarrow \quad \frac{T_2}{T_1} = \sqrt{\frac{B_1}{B_2}}$

or $\frac{T_2}{3} = \sqrt{\frac{1}{4}}$ (given)

or $T_2 = 1.5$ s

24 (d) When a bar magnet is cut axially, new magnetic moment of each part,

$$M = \left(\frac{m}{2}\right) l = \frac{M_1}{2}$$

On placing both the parts perpendicularly, we get

$$M_2 = \sqrt{(M)^2 + (M)^2} = \frac{M}{\sqrt{2}} = \frac{M_1}{\sqrt{2}}$$

$$\Rightarrow \frac{M_1}{M_2} = \sqrt{2}$$

25 (b) When a magnetic needle is placed in a uniform magnetic field, equal and opposite forces act on the poles of the needle (as magnetic dipole) which give rise to a torque but no net force.

26 (d) On bending the magnet, the length of the magnet,

$$AC = AB + BC$$

$$= L \sin\left(\frac{\theta}{2}\right) + L \sin\left(\frac{\theta}{2}\right)$$

$[\because \theta = 60°]$

$$= 2L \sin 30° = 2L \times 1/2 = L$$

27 (b) Given, $M = 4 \times 10^{-6}$ A-m^2

$l = 20$ cm$= \frac{1}{5}$m and $m = ?$

As, $M = m \times 2l$

$$\therefore m = \frac{M}{2l} = \frac{4 \times 10^{-6}}{2 \times 1/5} = 10 \times 10^{-6} \text{A-m}$$

28 (a) When a bar magnet of magnetic moment **M** is placed in a magnetic field of induction **B**, then net force on it is

$$F_R = mB + (-m)B = 0$$

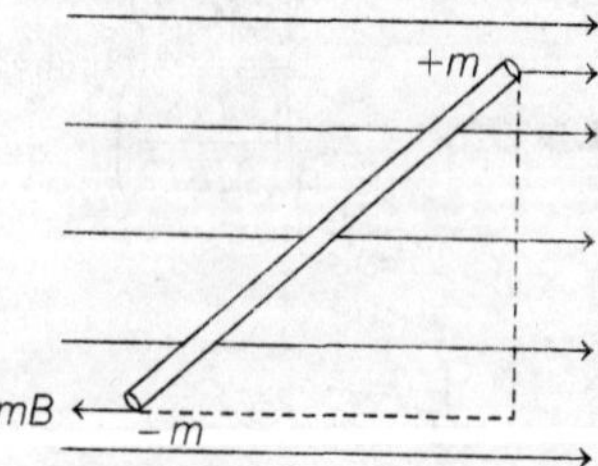

While torque,

$$\tau = mB \times 2l \sin\theta = MB \sin\theta$$

(as, $M = 2ml$)

i.e. $\boldsymbol{\tau} = \mathbf{M} \times \mathbf{B}$

29 (d) Time period,

$$T = 2\pi\sqrt{\left|\frac{\theta}{\alpha}\right|} = 2\pi\sqrt{\frac{I}{MH}}$$

or $T \propto \sqrt{I}$

or $T \propto \sqrt{m}$ $\quad (\because I = ml^2/12)$

$$\Rightarrow \frac{T_1}{T_2} = \sqrt{\frac{m_1}{m_2}}$$

or $\frac{T}{T_2} = \sqrt{\frac{m}{4m}} = \frac{1}{2}$

$\Rightarrow T_2 = 2T$

Thus, motion remains simple harmonic with time period $2T$.

30 (a) Time period, $T = 2\pi\sqrt{\frac{I}{MB}}$

As the magnet is cut into two equal parts along axis, then for each part

$$I' = \frac{I}{2}, \quad M' = \frac{M}{2}$$

$\therefore$ Time period of new magnet,

$$T' = \sqrt{\frac{I'}{M'B}} = \sqrt{\frac{I \times 2}{2 \times M \times B}}$$

$\Rightarrow T' = T$

31 (c) As, time period $T = 2\pi\sqrt{I/MB}$

$$T = 2 \text{ s}, I' = \frac{I}{2}, M' = \frac{M}{2}$$

$\Rightarrow T' = T \Rightarrow T' = 2$ s

32 (a) As, $\tau = MB \sin\theta$

where, $\theta = 90°$

$\Rightarrow \tau = MB$

Given, $\tau_2 = \frac{1}{2}\tau_1$

$\Rightarrow MB \sin\theta = \frac{1}{2} MB$

$\Rightarrow \sin\theta = 1/2 \Rightarrow \theta = 30°$

$\therefore$ Angle of rotation

$= 90° - 30° = 60°$

33 (a) As, $\tau = MB \sin\theta$

Given, $2l = 10$ cm, $m = 15$ A-m

$B = 2 \times 10^{-5}$ T and $\theta = 30°$.

Putting these values, we get

$$= (m \times 2l) \times 2 \times 10^{-5} \sin 30°$$

$$= 15 \times 10 \times 10^{-2} \times 2 \times 10^{-5} \times \frac{1}{2}$$

$$= 1.5 \times 10^{-5} \text{ N-m}$$

34 (b) Since for magnet P, axis lies along X-axis and for magnet Q, axis is along Y-axis. The point R is along axial line w.r.t. magnet P and is along equatorial line w.r.t. magnet Q.

Hence, magnetic field due to magnet Q,

$$B_Q = \frac{\mu_0}{4\pi}\frac{M}{x^3} = B \quad \text{... (i)}$$

Magnetic field due to magnet P,

$$B_P = \frac{\mu_0}{4\pi}\frac{2M}{x^3} = 2B \quad \text{... (ii)}$$

As at point R, magnetic field due to P and Q magnet are perpendicular to each other,

$B_R \Rightarrow$ Net magnetic field at R due to magnet P and Q is given as

$$B_R \Rightarrow \sqrt{B_P^2 + B_Q^2}$$

[from Eqs. (i) and (ii)]

$$= \sqrt{B^2 + (2B)^2}$$

$$= \sqrt{5}\, B$$

35 (a) Work done in rotating a magnet (from angle 0 to θ) is given by

$$W = \int_0^\theta \tau\, d\theta$$

where, τ = torque

and $d\theta$ = angular change.

Also, $\tau = MH \sin\theta$

$$= \int_0^\theta MH \sin\theta d\theta$$

$$= MH \int_0^\theta \sin\theta d\theta$$

$$= MH(-\cos\theta)_0^\theta$$

$$= -MH(\cos\theta - \cos 0)$$

$$= MH(1 - \cos\theta)$$

36 (a) The intensity of magnetic field B due to an isolated pole at a distance r from it is given by $B = \frac{\mu_0}{4\pi} \cdot \frac{m}{r^2}$

$\Rightarrow B \propto \frac{m}{r^2}$

where, m is pole strength.

37 (a) For protecting sensitive equipment from external magnetic field, it must be placed inside a iron cane made from ferromagnetic substance, because there are no magnetic lines of force inside it. Iron is a ferromagnetic substance. Hence, it is used to keep the sensitive equipment.

Topic 2

Earth's Magnetism

2019

1 At a point A on the earth's surface, the angle of dip δ is 25°. At a point B on the earth's surface, the angle of dip δ is – 25°. **[NEET]**

We can interpret that

(a) A is located in the southern hemisphere and B is located in the northern hemisphere

(b) A is located in the northern hemisphere and B is located in the southern hemisphere

(c) A and B are both located in the southern hemisphere

(d) A and B are both located in the northern hemisphere

2 The relations amongst the three elements of earth's magnetic field, namely horizontal component H, vertical component V and dip angle δ are (B_E = total magnetic field) **[NEET (Odisha)]**

(a) $V = B_E \tan\delta, H = B_E$

(b) $V = B_E \sin\delta, H = B_E \cos\delta$

(c) $V = B_E \cos\delta, H = B_E \sin\delta$

(d) $V = B_E, H = Be_E \tan\delta$

2018

3 The horizontal component of the earth's magnetic field at any place is 0.36×10^{-4} Wbm^{-2}. If the angle of dip at that place is 60°, then the value of vertical component of the earth's magnetic field will be (in Wbm^{-2}) **[AIIMS]**

(a) 0.12×10^{-4} (b) 0.24×10^{-4}

(c) 0.40×10^{-4} (d) 0.622×10^{-4}

2017

4 If θ_1 and θ_2 be the apparent angles of dip observed in two vertical planes at right angles to each other, then the true angle of dip θ is given by **[JIPMER]**

(a) $\cot^2\theta = \cot^2\theta_1 + \cot^2\theta_2$

(b) $\tan^2\theta = \tan^2\theta_1 + \tan^2\theta_2$

(c) $\cot^2\theta = \cot^2\theta_1 - \cot^2\theta_2$

(d) $\tan^2\theta = \tan^2\theta_1 - \tan^2\theta_2$

2013

5 At the magnetic pole of earth, the value of angle of dip is **[AIIMS]**

(a) 0° (b) 30°

(c) 45° (d) 90°

6 A circular coil of 5 turns and of 10 cm mean diameter is connected to a voltage source. If the resistance of the coil is 10 Ω, the voltage of the source so as to nullify the horizontal component of earth's magnetic field of 30 A turn m^{-1} at the centre of the coil should be **[UP CPMT, Manipal]**

(a) 6 V, plane of the coil normal to magnetic meridian

(b) 2 V, plane of the coil normal to magnetic meridian

(c) 6 V, plane of the coil along the magnetic meridian

(d) 2 V, plane of the coil along the magnetic meridian

(e) 4 V, plane of the coil normal to magnetic meridian

7 A dip needle in a plane perpendicular to magnetic meridian will remain **[WB JEE]**

(a) vertical

(b) horizontal

(c) in any direction

(d) at any angle of dip to the horizontal

8 In the magnetic meridian of a certain place. The horizontal component of the earths magnetic field is 0.26 and the dip angle 60°. What is the magnetic field of the earth in this location? **[AIIMS]**

(a) 0.48 G (b) 0.50 G (c) 0.60 G (d) 0.52 G

2011

9 The angle which the total magnetic field of earth makes with the surface of the earth is called **[J&K CET]**

(a) declination (b) magnetic meridian

(c) geographic meridian (d) inclination

10 The plane of a dip circle is set in the geographic meridian and the apparent dip is δ_1. It is then set in a vertical plane perpendicular to the geographic meridian. The apparent dip angle is δ_2. The declination θ at the plane is **[Punjab PMET]**

(a) $\theta = \tan^{-1}(\tan\delta_1 \tan\delta_2)$

(b) $\theta = \tan^{-1}(\tan\delta_1 + \tan\delta_2)$

(c) $\theta = \tan^{-1}\left(\frac{\tan\delta_1}{\tan\delta_2}\right)$

(d) $\theta = \tan^{-1}(\tan\delta_1 - \tan\delta_2)$

2010

11 Isogonic lines are those for which **[AFMC]**

(a) declination is the same at all places on the line

(b) angle of dip is the same at the place on the line

(c) the value of horizontal component of earth's magnetic field is the same

(d) All of the above

12 A magnet 10 cm long and having a pole strength 2 A-m is deflected through 30° from the magnetic meridian. The horizontal component of earth's induction is 0.32×10^{-4} T, then the value of deflecting couple is **[UP CPMT]**

(a) 16×10^{-7} Nm (b) 64×10^{-7} Nm
(c) 48×10^{-7} Nm (d) 32×10^{-7} Nm

13 At a certain place, the horizontal component of earth's magnetic field is $\sqrt{3}$ times the vertical component. The angle of dip at that place is **[UP CPMT]**

(a) 30° (b) 60°
(c) 45° (d) 90°

14 A torque of 10^{-5} N-m is required to hold a magnet at 90° with the horizontal component of the earth's magnetic field. The torque required to hold it at 30° will be **[Manipal]**

(a) 5×10^{-6} N-m (b) $\frac{1}{2} \times 10^{-5}$ N-m
(c) $5\sqrt{3} \times 10^{-6}$ N-m (d) Data is insufficient

15 A short bar magnet is arranged with its north pole pointing geographical north. It is found that the horizontal component of earth's magnetic induction (B_H) is balanced by the magnetic induction of the magnet at a point which is at a distance of 20 cm from its centre. The magnetic moment of the magnet is (if $B_H = 4 \times 10^{-5}$ Wbm^{-2}) **[EAMCET]**

(a) 3.2 A-m^2 (b) 1.6 A-m^2
(c) 6.4 A-m^2 (d) 0.8 A-m^2

16 The angle of dip at a place on the earth gives **[VMMC]**

(a) the horizontal component of the earth's magnetic field
(b) the location of geographic meridian
(c) the vertical component of the earth's field
(d) the direction of the earth's magnetic field

2008

17 **Assertion** If a compass needle be kept at magnetic north pole of the earth, the compass needle may stay in any direction. **[AIIMS]**

Reason Dip needle will stay vertical at the north pole of the earth.

(a) Both Assertion and Reason are correct and Reason is the correct explanation of Assertion.
(b) Both Assertion and Reason are correct but Reason is not the correct explanation of Assertion.
(c) Assertion is correct but Reason is incorrect.
(d) Both Assertion and Reason are incorrect.

18 A dip needle arranged to move freely in the magnetic meridian dips at an angle θ. If the vertical plane in which the needle moves is rotated through an angle α to the magnetic meridian, then the needle will dip by an angle **[BHU]**

(a) θ (b) α
(c) more than θ (d) less than θ

19 If the total magnetic field due to the earth is 28 Am^{-1}, then the total magnetic induction due to the earth is **[BHU]**

(a) 28 T (b) 280 A-cm^{-1}
(c) 0.352 G (d) 0.352 T

20 If a magnet is suspended at angle 30° to the magnetic meridian, the dip needle makes angle of 45° with the horizontal. The real dip is **[AMU]**

(a) $\tan^{-1}(\sqrt{3}/2)$ (b) $\tan^{-1}(\sqrt{3})$
(c) $\tan^{-1}\left(\frac{3}{\sqrt{2}}\right)$ (d) $\tan^{-1}\left(\frac{2}{\sqrt{3}}\right)$

21 At a given place on the earth, the angle between the magnetic meridian and the geographic meridian is called **[Guj CET]**

(a) magnetic longitude
(b) magnetic declination
(c) magnetic latitude
(d) magnetic dip

2007

22 A magnetic needle is placed on a cork floating in a still lake in the northern hemisphere. Does the needle together with the cork move towards the north of the lake? **[AFMC]**

(a) Yes (b) No
(c) May or may not move (d) Nothing can be said

23 If $B_H = \frac{1}{\sqrt{3}} B_V$, then find the value of angle of dip (where, symbols have their usual meanings). **[UP CPMT]**

(a) 60° (b) 30°
(c) 45° (d) 90°

24 The time of vibration of a dip needle vibration in the vertical plane in the magnetic meridian is 3 s. When the same magnetic needle is made to vibrate in the horizontal plane, the time of vibration is $3\sqrt{2}$ s. Then, angle of dip will be **[BCECE]**

(a) 90° (b) 60° (c) 45° (d) 30°

2005

25 The dip at a place is δ. For measuring it, the axis of the dip needle is perpendicular to the magnetic meridian. If the axis of the dip needle makes an angle θ with the magnetic meridian, the apparent dip will be given by **[Haryana PMT]**

(a) tan δ cosec θ (b) tan δ sin θ
(c) tan δ cos θ (d) tan δ sec θ

Answers

1 (b)	2 (b)	3 (d)	4 (a)	5 (d)	6 (a)	7 (a)	8 (d)	9 (a)	10 (c)
11 (a)	12 (d)	13 (a)	14 (a)	15 (a)	16 (d)	17 (b)	18 (c)	19 (c)	20 (d)
21 (b)	22 (b)	23 (a)	24 (b)	25 (a)					

Explanations

1 (b) The angle of dip δ is the angle between the horizontal component of earth's magnetic field and the total magnetic field of the earth. Its value is different at different places. It is zero at equator, as the dip needle becomes parallel to horizontal component. It varies from $-90°$ in south pole to $+90°$ in the north pole.

This means the values δ is positive in northern hemisphere and is negative in southern hemisphere.

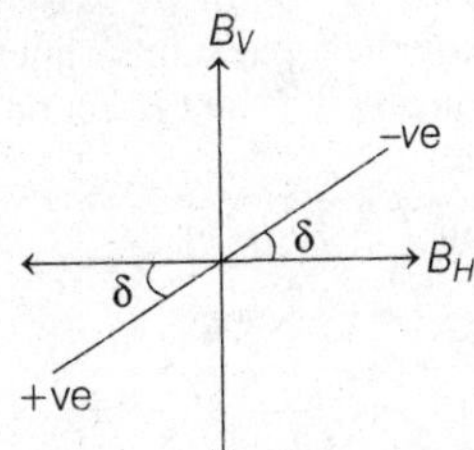

$\therefore$ For point A, $\delta = +25°$, so A lies in the northern hemisphere.

Similarly, for B, $\delta = -25°$, so B lies in the southern hemisphere.

2 (b) Let B_E be the net magnetic field at same point, H and V be the horizontal and vertical components of B_E. Let δ be the angle of dip, which is the angle between direction of earth's magnetic field B_E and horizontal line in the magnetic meridian.

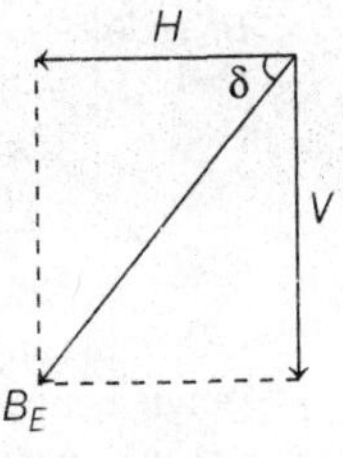

Thus, from figure, we can see that

$$H = B_E \cos\delta$$

and $$V = B_E \sin\delta$$

3 (d) Vertical component of earth's magnetic field,

$$B_V = B_H \tan\delta$$
$$= 0.36 \times 10^{-4} \times \tan 60° \quad \text{(given)}$$
$$= 0.36 \times 10^{-4} \times \sqrt{3} = 0.622 \times 10^{-4}\ \text{T}$$
$$= 0.622 \times 10^{-4}\ \text{Wbm}^{-2}$$

4 (a) Let the B_H and B_V be the horizontal and vertical component of earth's magnetic field B.

$$\tan\theta = \frac{B_V}{B_H} \Rightarrow \cot\theta = \frac{B_H}{B_V} \quad \text{...(i)}$$

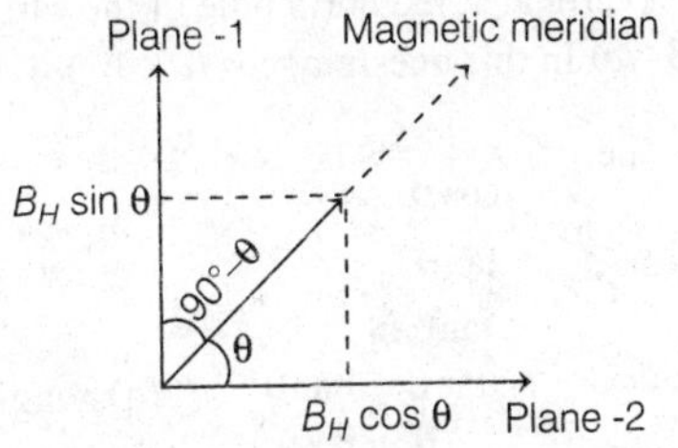

Let plane 1 and 2 be mutually perpendicular planes making angle θ and $(90° - \theta)$ with magnetic meridian. The vertical component of earth's magnetic field remain same in two plane but effective horizontal components in the two planes is given by

$$B_1 = B_H \cos\theta \quad \text{...(ii)}$$

and $$B_2 = B_H \sin\theta \quad \text{...(iii)}$$

Then, $$\tan\theta_1 = \frac{B_V}{B_1} = \frac{B_V}{B_H \cos\theta}$$

$$\cot\theta_1 = \frac{B_H \cos\theta}{B_V} \quad \text{...(iv)}$$

Similarly, $$\Rightarrow \tan\theta_2 = \frac{B_V}{B_2} = \frac{B_V}{B_H \sin\theta}$$

$$\Rightarrow \quad \cot\theta_2 = \frac{B_H \sin\theta}{B_V} \quad \text{...(v)}$$

From Eqs. (iv) and (v), we get

$$\Rightarrow \cot^2\theta_1 + \cot^2\theta_2 = \frac{B_H^2 \cos^2\theta}{B_V^2} + \frac{B_H^2 \sin^2\theta}{B_V^2}$$

$$\Rightarrow \cot^2\theta_1 + \cot^2\theta_2 = \frac{B_H^2}{B_V^2}(\cos^2\theta + \sin^2\theta)$$

$$\Rightarrow \cot^2\theta_1 + \cot^2\theta_2 = \cot^2\theta$$

5 (d) At the earth's magnetic poles, the angle of dip is 90°.

6 (a) Magnetic field of 1 A turn m^{-1}

$$= 4\pi \times 10^{-7}\ \text{T}$$

Field at centre,

$$B = \frac{\mu_0 NI}{2r} = \frac{\mu_0 N}{2r} \times \frac{V}{R}$$

$$V = \frac{2rRB}{\mu_0 N}$$

$$r = 10\ \text{cm} = 10 \times 10^{-2}\ \text{m},\ R = 10\ \Omega$$

and $B = 30$ A turn m^{-1}

$$\therefore \quad V = \frac{2 \times (5 \times 10^{-2}) \times 10 \times (30 \times 4\pi \times 10^{-7})}{(4\pi \times 10^{-7}) \times 5}$$

or $\quad V = 6$ V

To nullify the horizontal component of magnetic field of the earth, plane of the coil should be normal to magnetic meridian.

7 (a) A dip needle in a plane perpendicular to the magnetic meridian will remain vertical as the horizontal component to earth's field is not effective as the axis of rotation of needle lies in the direction of horizontal component of magnetic field.

8 (d) Given, $B_H = 0.26\ \text{G}$, $\delta = 60°$

As, $$B_H = B\cos\delta$$

$$B = \frac{B_H}{\cos\delta} = \frac{0.26\ \text{G}}{\cos 60°} = \frac{0.26\ \text{G}}{0.5}$$

$$B = 0.52\ \text{G}$$

9 (a) The angle which the total magnetic field of the earth makes with the surface of the earth is called declination.

10 (c) Here, $$\tan\delta_1 = \frac{V}{H\cos\theta}$$

$$\tan\delta_2 = \frac{V}{H\cos(90° - \theta)} = \frac{V}{H\sin\theta}$$

$$\Rightarrow \quad \frac{\tan\delta_1}{\tan\delta_2} = \frac{\sin\theta}{\cos\theta} = \tan\theta$$

or $$\theta = \tan^{-1}\left(\frac{\tan\delta_1}{\tan\delta_2}\right)$$

11 (a) Isogonic lines are those lines, which have same angle of declination at all the places on the line.

12 (*d*) As, couple acting on the bar magnet is given as

$$\tau = MB_H \sin\theta$$
$$\tau = (2l)\, m\, B_H \sin\theta$$

Given, $2l = 10\text{ cm} = 10 \times 10^{-2}$ m,

$m = 2$ A-m, $\theta = 30°$ and $B_H = 0.32 \times 10^{-4}$ T

Putting these values, we get

$$\tau = 10 \times 10^{-2}\,(2)\,(0.32 \times 10^{-4}) \times \frac{1}{2}$$
$$\tau = 32 \times 10^{-7}\text{ N-m}$$

13 (*a*) As, angle of dip is given

$$\tan\delta = \frac{B_V}{B_H} = \frac{B_V}{\sqrt{3}B_V} \text{ (given)}$$
$$= \frac{1}{\sqrt{3}}$$
$$\Rightarrow \quad \delta = 30°$$

14 (*a*) The magnet in a magnetic field experiences a torque which rotates the magnet to a position in which the axis of the magnet is parallel to the field.

$$\tau = MB\sin\theta$$

where, M is the magnetic dipole moment, B is the magnetic field and θ is the angle between the two.

Given, $\tau_1 = 10^{-5}$ N-m,

$\theta_1 = 90°$ and $\theta_2 = 30°$.

As we know,

$$\tau_1 = MB\sin 90° \quad \ldots\text{(i)}$$
$$\tau_2 = MB\sin 30° \quad \ldots\text{(ii)}$$

On dividing Eq. (i) by Eq. (ii), we get

$$\frac{\tau_1}{\tau_2} = \frac{10^{-5}}{\tau_2} = \frac{1}{1/2}$$
$$\Rightarrow \quad \tau_2 = \frac{10^{-5}}{2} = \frac{10}{2} \times 10^{-6}$$
$$= 5 \times 10^{-6}\text{ N-m}$$

15 (*a*) As, $B_H = \frac{\mu_0}{4\pi} \cdot \frac{M}{r^3}$

Given, $B_H = 4 \times 10^{-5}\text{ Wbm}^{-2}$,

$r = 20\text{ cm} = 20 \times 10^{-2}$ m

Putting these values, we get

$$\Rightarrow 4 \times 10^{-5} = 10^{-7} \times \frac{M}{(20)^3 \times 10^{-6}}$$
$$M = \frac{(20)^3 \times 4 \times 10^{-5} \times 10^{-6}}{10^{-7}}$$
$$= 3.2\text{ A-m}^2$$

16 (*d*) The dip at a place is defined as the angle made by the direction of the earth's total magnetic field with horizontal direction. So, the angle of dip at a place on the earth gives the direction of the earth's magnetic field.

17 (*b*) We know that at magnetic poles, the horizontal component of the earth's field is zero, only its vertical component exists.

So, as compass needle is free to rotate in horizontal plane and is thus affected by horizontal component only. As $H = 0$, hence compass needle may stay in any direction.

The dip needle rotates in a vertical plane and the angle of dip at poles is 90°. Hence, the dip needle will stand vertical at the north pole of the earth.

18 (*c*) In this question, $\cos\alpha < 1$

i.e. $$\frac{1}{\cos\alpha} > 1$$

or $$\frac{\tan\theta'}{\tan\theta} > 1$$

$$\Rightarrow \quad \tan\theta' > \tan\theta$$
$$\therefore \quad \theta' > \theta$$

i.e. angle of apparent dip θ' is more than angle of actual dip θ.

19 (*c*) Given, $B = 28\text{ Am}^{-1}$

Magnetic induction B is given by

$$B = \mu_0 H = 4\pi \times 10^{-7} \times 28$$
$$= 352 \times 10^{-7}\text{ T} \quad (\because 1\text{ T} = 10^4\text{ G})$$
$$= 0.352\text{ G}$$

20 (*d*) As, $\tan\delta' = \frac{\tan\delta}{\cos\theta} = \frac{\tan 45°}{\cos 30°}$ (given)

$$\tan\delta' = \frac{1}{\sqrt{3}/2} = \frac{2}{\sqrt{3}}$$
$$\Rightarrow \quad \delta' = \tan^{-1}\left(\frac{2}{\sqrt{3}}\right)$$

21 (*b*) The angle between the magnetic meridian and the geographic meridian is called magnetic declination.

22 (*b*) Magnetic needle is a dipole which is in the earth's uniform magnetic field and as a dipole in a uniform field, it does not experience any net force but may experience a couple. So the needle together with the cork will not translate, i.e. not move towards the north of the lake, but will rotate and set itself parallel to the field with its north pole pointing north.

23 (*a*) Magnetic dip or magnetic inclination is given by

$$\tan\delta = B_V / B_H \quad \ldots\text{(i)}$$

where, B_V and B_H are vertical and horizontal components of earth's magnetic field, respectively.

Given, $$B_H = \frac{1}{\sqrt{3}} B_V$$

$$\Rightarrow \quad \frac{B_V}{B_H} = \sqrt{3} \quad \ldots\text{(ii)}$$

From Eqs. (i) and (ii), we get

$$\tan\delta = \sqrt{3} \Rightarrow \delta = 60°$$

24 (*b*) When M is magnetic moment of the magnet, H and V are the horizontal and vertical components of the earth's magnetic field and I is moment of inertia of magnet about its axis of vibration, then the time period of magnet is

$$T = 2\pi\sqrt{I/MH}$$

When horizontal component is taken

$$T' = 2\pi\sqrt{I/MV}$$

(as in vertical plane in magnetic meridian both V and H act on the needle)

Given, $T = 3\sqrt{2}$ s

and $T' = 3$ s

$$\therefore \quad \frac{T'}{T} = \sqrt{\frac{H}{V}}$$
$$\Rightarrow \quad \sqrt{\frac{H}{V}} = \frac{3}{3\sqrt{2}} = \frac{1}{\sqrt{2}}$$

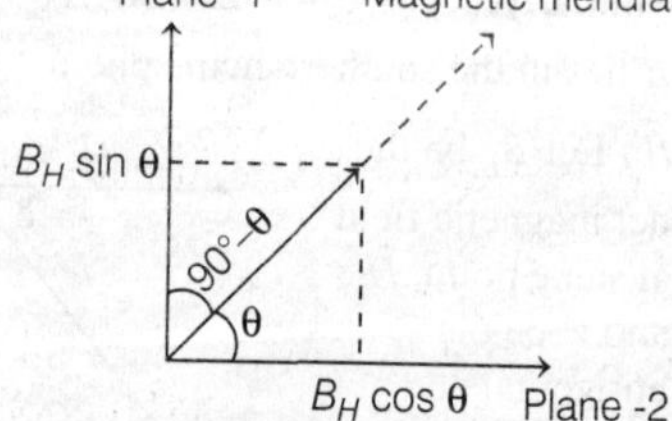

Also, the angle of dip at a place is the angle between the direction of the earth's magnetic field and the horizontal component of magnetic meridian at that place.

$$\therefore \quad \sqrt{\frac{H}{V}} = \sqrt{\cos\phi} = \frac{1}{\sqrt{2}}$$
$$\Rightarrow \quad \cos\phi = \frac{1}{2} \Rightarrow \phi = 60°$$

25 (*a*) As, $\tan\delta = \frac{V}{H}$

and $$\tan\delta_1 = \frac{V}{H\cos(90° - \theta)}$$
$$= \frac{\tan\delta}{\cos(90° - \theta)} = \tan\delta\,\text{cosec}\,\theta$$

Topic 3

Magnetic Materials

2019

1 Coercivity and retentivity of soft iron is **[JIPMER]**

(a) high coercivity, high retentivity
(b) low coercivity, high retentivity
(c) low coercivity, low retentivity
(d) high coercivity, low retentivity

2 **Assertion** Paramagnetic substances get poorly attracted in magnetic field.

Reason Because magnetic dipoles are aligned along external magnetic field weakly. **[AIIMS]**

(a) Both Assertion and Reason are correct and Reason is the correct explanation of Assertion.
(b) Both Assertion and Reason are correct but Reason is not the correct explanation of Assertion.
(c) Assertion is true but Reason is incorrect.
(d) Both Assertion and Reason are incorrect.

2017

3 **Assertion** The magnetism of magnet is due to the spin motion of electrons.

Reason Dipole moment of electron is smaller than that due to orbit motion around nucleus. **[AIIMS]**

(a) Both Assertion and Reason correct and Reason is the correct explanation of Assertion.
(b) Both Assertion and Reason correct but Reason is not the correct explanation of Assertion.
(c) Assertion is correct but Reason is incorrect.
(d) Assertion is incorrect but Reason is correct.

2016

4 The magnetic susceptibility is negative for **[NEET]**

(a) paramagnetic material only
(b) ferromagnetic material only
(c) paramagnetic and ferromagnetic materials
(d) diamagnetic material only

2014

5 The intensity of magnetisation of a bar magnet is 5.0×10^4 Am^{-1}. The magnetic length and the area of cross-section of the magnet are 12 cm and 1 cm^2, respectively. The magnitude of magnetic moment of this bar magnet (in SI unit) is **[WB JEE]**

(a) 0.6 (b) 1.3 (c) 1.24 (d) 2.4

6 A magnetism field of 1500 Am^{-1} produces a magnetic flux of 2.4×10^{-5} Wb in a bar of iron of cross section 0.5 cm^2. Calculate permeability of the iron bar used.

(a) 4×10^{-4} TmA^{-1} (b) 3.2×10^{-4} TmA^{-1}
(c) 2.6×10^{-4} TmA^{-1} (d) 4.2×10^{-4} TmA^{-1}

7 A paramagnetic sample shows a net magnetisation of 0.8 Am^{-1}, when placed in an external magnetic field of strength 0.8 T at a temperature 5 K. When the same sample is placed in an external magnetic field of 0.4 T at a temperature of 20 K, the magnetisation is **[EAMCET]**

(a) 0.8 Am^{-1} (b) 0.8 Am^{-2} (c) 0.1 Am (d) 0.1 Am^{-1}

8 The magnetic susceptibility of a material of a rod is 299 and permeability of vacuum μ_0 is $4\pi \times 10^{-7}$ Hm^{-1}. Absolute permeability of the material of the rod is **[EAMCET]**

(a) 3771×10^{-7} Hm^{-1} (b) 3771×10^{-5} Hm^{-1}
(c) 3770×10^{-6} Hm^{-1} (d) 3771×10^{-8} Hm^{-1}

9 A susceptibility of a certain magnetic material is 400. What is the class of the magnetic material? **[KCET]**

(a) Diamagnetic (b) Paramagnetic
(c) Ferromagnetic (d) Ferroelectric

2013

10 **Assertion** Susceptibility is defined as the ratio of intensity of magnetisation I to magnetic intensity H.

Reason Greater the value of susceptibility, smaller the value of intensity of magnetisation I. **[AIIMS]**

(a) Both Assertion and Reason are correct and Reason is the correct explanation of Assertion.
(b) Both Assertion and Reason are correct but the Reason is not the correct explanation of Assertion.
(c) Assertion is correct but Reason is incorrect.
(d) Both Assertion and Reason are incorrect.

11 A curve between magnetic moment and temperature of magnet is **[AIIMS]**

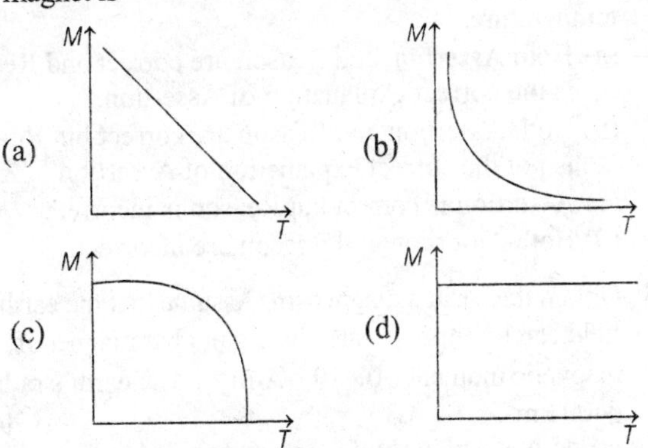

12 An iron rod of 0.2 cm^2 cross-sectional area is subjected to magnetizing field of 1200 Am^{-1}. The susceptibility of iron is 599. Find the value of permeability of rod. **[AIIMS]**

(a) 6.234×10^{-4} TmA^{-1} (b) 7.536×10^{-4} TmA^{-1}
(c) 8.212×10^{-4} TmA^{-1} (d) 4.245×10^{-4} TmA^{-1}

13 A paramagnetic substance of susceptibility 3×10^{-4} is placed in a magnetic field of 4×10^{-4} Am^{-1}. Then, the intensity of magnetisation in the unit of Am^{-1} is **[KCET]**
(a) 1.33×10^{8} (b) 0.75×10^{-8} (c) 12×10^{-8} (d) 14×10^{-8}
(e) 1.2×10^{-8}

2011

14 There are four light-weight-rod samples *A*, *B*, *C* and *D* separately suspended by threads. A bar magnet is slowly brought near each sample and the following observations are noted. **[CBSE AIPMT]**
(i) *A* is feebly repelled. (ii) *B* is feebly attracted.
(iii) *C* is strongly attracted. (iv) *D* remains unaffected.
Which one of the following is true?
(a) *C* is a diamagnetic material
(b) *D* is of a ferromagnetic material
(c) *A* is of a non-magnetic material
(d) *B* is of a paramagnetic material

15 Resultant force acting on a diamagnetic material in a magnetic field is in direction **[J&K CET]**
(a) from stronger to the weaker part of the magnetic field
(b) from weaker to the stronger part of the magnetic field
(c) perpendicular to the magnetic field
(d) in the direction making 60° to the magnetic field

16 The magnetic moment produced in a substance of 1 g is 6×10^{-7} Am^2. If its density is 5 g cm^{-3}, then the intensity of magnetisation (in Am^{-1}) will be **[Haryana PMT]**
(a) 8.3×10^{6} (b) 3.0 (c) 1.2×10^{-7} (d) 3×10^{-6}

2010

17 **Assertion** A paramagnetic sample displays greater magnetisation (for the same magnetising field) when cooled.
Reason The magnetisation does not depend on temperature. **[AIIMS]**
(a) Both Assertion and Reason are correct and Reason is the correct explanation of Assertion.
(b) Both Assertion and Reason are correct but Reason is not the correct explanation of Assertion.
(c) Assertion is correct but Reason is incorrect.
(d) Both Assertion and Reason are incorrect.

18 Obtain the earth's magnetism. Assume that the earth's field can be approximated by a gaint bar magnet of magnetic moment 8.0×10^{22} A-m^2 ? The earth's radius is 6400 km. **[AIPMT]**
(a) 72.9 Am^{-1} (b) 80 Am^{-1} (c) 74.4 Am^{-1} (d) 64 Am^{-1}

19 A magnet of magnetic moment 2.5 A-m^2 weights 66 g. If the density of the material of the magnet is 7500 kg-m^2 find the intensity of magnetisation. **[NEET]**
(a) 2.70×10^{5} Am^{-1} (b) 2.84×10^{5} Am^{-1}
(c) 2.84×10^{-5} Am^{-1} (d) 2.70×10^{-5} Am^{-1}

20 An iron rod of 0.2 cm^2 cross-sectional area is subjected to a magnetising field of 1200 Am^{-1}. The susceptibility of iron is 599. The magnetic flux produced is **[Manipal]**
(a) 0.904 Wb
(b) 1.81×10^{-5} Wb
(c) 0.904×10^{-5} Wb
(d) 5.43×10^{-5} Wb

21 A domain in a ferromagnetic substance is in the form of a cube of side length 1 μm. If it contains 8×10^{10} atoms and each atomic dipole has a dipole moment of 9×10^{-24} A-m^2, then the magnetisation of the domain is **[Kerala CEE]**
(a) 7.2×10^{5} Am^{-1} (b) 7.2×10^{3} Am^{-1}
(c) 7.2×10^{9} Am^{-1} (d) 7.2×10^{12} Am^{-1}
(e) 7.2×10^{18} Am^{-1}

2009

22 If a diamagnetic substance is brought near the North pole or the south pole of a bar magnet, it is **[CBSE AIPMT]**
(a) repelled by both the poles
(b) repelled by the north pole and attracted by the south pole
(c) attracted by the north pole and repelled by the south pole
(d) attracted by both the poles

23 On applying an external magnetic field to a ferromagnetic substance, domains **[MHT CET]**
(a) align in the direction of magnetic field
(b) align in the direction opposite to magnetic field
(c) remain unaffected
(d) None of the above

24 The relative permeability of iron is 6000. Its magnetic susceptibility is **[Kerala CEE]**
(a) 5999 (b) 6001
(c) 6000×10^{-7} (d) 6000×10^{7}
(e) 60

25 A paramagnetic substance is placed in a weak magnetic field and its absolute temperature *T* is increased. As a result, its magnetisation **[BCECE]**
(a) increases in proportional to *T*
(b) decreases in proportional to $1/T$
(c) increases in proportional to T^2
(d) decreases in proportional to $1/T^2$

26 Ferromagnetic materials used in a transformer must have
(a) low permeability and high hysteresis loss **[JCECE]**
(b) high permeability and low hysteresis loss
(c) high permeability and high hysteresis loss
(d) low permeability and low hysteresis loss

27 Relative permeability of iron is 5500, then its magnetic susceptibility will be **[MGIMS]**
(a) 5500×10^{7} (b) 5500×10^{-7}
(c) 5501 (d) 5499

2008

28 Curie temperature is the temperature above which [CBSE AIPMT, MGIMS]
(a) ferromagnetic material becomes paramagnetic material
(b) paramagnetic material becomes diamagnetic material
(c) paramagnetic material becomes ferromagnetic material
(d) ferromagnetic material becomes diamagnetic material

29 Nickel shows ferromagnetic property at room temperature. If the temperature is increased beyond Curie temperature, then it will show [MHT CET]
(a) paramagnetism (b) anti-ferromagnetism
(c) no magnetic property (d) diamagnetism

30 The magnetic susceptibility of paramagnetic materials is [OJEE]
(a) positive but very high
(b) negative but small
(c) negative but very high
(d) positive but small

31 At what temperature iron becomes paramagnetic? [Kerala CEE]
(a) 200°C (b) 400°C (c) 600°C (d) 800°C

32 The magnetic moment of atomic neon is [KCET]
(a) zero (b) $\mu B/2$ (c) μB (d) $3\mu B/2$

33 There are 2.0×10^{24} molecular dipoles in a paramagnetic salt. Each has dipole moment 1.5×10^{-23} A-m^2. Find maximum (saturation) magnetisation in the specimen. [Guj CET]
(a) 200 A-m^2 (b) 50 A-m^2
(c) 20 A-m^2 (d) 30 A-m^2

2007

34 In which type of material, the magnetic susceptibility does not depend on temperature? [AFMC]
(a) Diamagnetic (b) Paramagnetic
(c) Ferromagnetic (d) Ferrite

35 If a magnetic substance is kept in a magnetic field, then which of the following substances is thrown out? [MHT CET]
(a) Paramagnetic (b) Ferromagnetic
(c) Diamagnetic (d) Anti-ferromagnetic

36 The magnetic susceptibility of a paramagnetic substance at –73°C is 0.0060, then its value at –173°C will be [WB JEE]
(a) 0.0030 (b) 0.0120 (c) 0.0180 (d) 0.0045

37 A hydrogen atom is paramagnetic. A hydrogen molecule is [RPMT]
(a) diamagnetic (b) paramagnetic
(c) ferromagnetic (d) None of these

38 A paramagnetic liquid is taken in a U-tube and arranged, so that one of its limbs is kept between pole pieces of the magnet. The liquid level in the limb [J&K CET]
(a) goes down (b) rises up
(c) remains same
(d) first goes down and then rises

39 Curie-Weiss law is obeyed by iron [Punjab PMET]
(a) at Curie temperature only
(b) at all temperatures
(c) below Curie temperature
(d) above Curie temperature

40 Domain formation is the necessary feature of [Guj CET]
(a) ferromagnetism (b) paramagnetism
(c) diamagnetism (d) All of the above

41 Permanent magnet has properties retentivity and coercivity respectively [JCECE]
(a) high-high (b) low-low
(c) low-high (d) high-low

2006

42 **Assertion** Diamagnetic materials can exhibit magnetism.
Reason Diamagnetic materials have permanent magnetic dipole moment. [AIIMS]
(a) Both Assertion and Reason are correct and Reason is the correct explanation of Assertion.
(b) Both Assertion and Reason are correct but R is not the correct explanation of Assertion.
(c) Assertion is correct but Reason is incorrect.
(d) Both Assertion and R are incorrect.

43 A bar magnet has a coercivity 4×10^3 Am^{-1}. It is desired to demagnetise it by inserting it inside a solenoid 12 cm long and having 60 turns. The current by the solenoid should be [BHU]
(a) 8 A (b) 6A (c) 4.5 A (d) 2 A

2005

44 If the magnetic dipole moment of an atom of diamagnetic material, paramagnetic material and ferromagnetic material are denoted by μ_d, μ_p and μ_f respectively, then [CBSE AIPMT]
(a) $\mu_d \neq 0$ and $\mu_f \neq 0$ (b) $\mu_p = 0$ and $\mu_f \neq 0$
(c) $\mu_d = 0$ and $\mu_p \neq 0$ (d) $\mu_d \neq 0$ and $\mu_p = 0$

45 Among the following properties describing diamagnetism identify the property that is wrongly stated. [KCET]
(a) Diamagnetic material do not have permanent magnetic moment.
(b) Diamagnetism is explained in terms of electromagnetic induction.
(c) Diamagnetic materials have a negative susceptibility
(d) The magnetic moment of individual electrons. neutralise each other.

46 The examples of diamagnetic, paramagnetic and ferromagnetic materials are respectively [JCECE]
(a) copper, aluminium, iron (b) aluminium, copper, iron
(c) copper, iron, aluminium (d) aluminium, iron, copper

47 A needle made of bismuth is suspended freely in a magnetic field. The angle which the needle makes with the magnetic field is [JCECE]
(a) 0° (b) 45° (c) 90° (d) 180°

Answers

1 (c)	2 (a)	3 (c)	4 (d)	5 (a)	6 (b)	7 (d)	8 (a)	9 (c)	10 (c)
11 (a)	12 (b)	13 (c)	14 (d)	15 (a)	16 (b)	17 (c)	18 (a)	19 (b)	20 (b)
21 (a)	22 (a)	23 (a)	24 (a)	25 (b)	26 (b)	27 (d)	28 (a)	29 (a)	30 (d)
31 (d)	32 (a)	33 (d)	34 (a)	35 (c)	36 (b)	37 (a)	38 (b)	39 (d)	40 (a)
41 (a)	42 (c)	43 (a)	44 (c)	45 (b)	46 (a)	47 (c)			

Explanations

1 (c) Coercivity and retentivity of soft iron is low, because its magnetisation disappears easily on the removal of external magnetising field.

2 (a) When paramagnetic substances are kept in a external magnetic field, then it develops feeble magnetisation in the direction of external applied magnetic field, i.e. magnetic dipoles are aligned along external magnetic field weakly.

Hence, both Assertion and Reason are correct and Reason is the correct explanation of Assertion.

3 (c) We know that, the magnetism of the magnet is achieved due to the spin motion of electrons. Also, the spinning electrons possess magnetic dipole moment. This dipole moment is much greater than that due to orbital moment of electrons around the nucleus.

So, the Assertion is correct but Reason is incorrect.

4 (d) As we know, the relation between the magnetic permeability and susceptibility of material, i.e.

$$\mu_r = 1 + \chi_m \quad \ldots(i)$$

$\because$ For diamagnetic substances,

$$\mu_r < 1$$

So, according to Eq. (i), the magnetic susceptibility (χ_m) of diamagnetic substance will be negative.

While in the case of para and ferromagnetic substances, magnetic susceptibility is positive.

5 (a) We know that, intensity of magnetisation,

$$I = M/V$$

where, M = magnetic moment,

$$V = \text{volume.}$$

So, $\quad M = IV$

Given, $M = 5\times10^4\ \text{Am}^{-1}$, $I = 12$ cm

$= 12\times10^{-2}$ m and $V = 1\ \text{cm}^2$

$= 1\times(10^{-2})^2 = 1\times10^{-4}$

$= 5.0\times10^4\times12\times10^{-2}\times1\times10^{-4}$

$= 60\times10^4\times10^{-6} = 0.6\ \text{A-m}^2$

6 (b) Given, $H = 1500\ \text{Am}^{-1}$,

$$\phi_B = 2.4\times10^{-5}\ \text{Wb}$$

and $\quad A = 0.5\times10^{-4}\text{m}^2$

Magnetic induction,

$$B = \frac{\phi_B}{A} = \frac{2.4\times10^{-5}}{0.5\times10^{-4}} = 0.48\ \text{Wb m}^{-2}$$

Permeability,

$$m = \frac{B}{H} = \frac{0.48}{1500} = 3.2\times10^{-4}\ \text{TmA}^{-1}$$

7 (d) For paramagnetic sample (Curie's law) $I \propto B/T$

Given, $I_1 = 0.8\ \text{Am}^{-1}$ and $B_1 = 0.8$ T

$$T_1 = 5\ \text{K} \Rightarrow B_2 = 0.4\ \text{T}$$

$$T_2 = 20\ \text{K},\quad I_2 = ?$$

$$\frac{I_1}{I_2} = \frac{B_1/T_1}{B_2/T_2} \Rightarrow \frac{I_1}{I_2} = \frac{B_1\times T_2}{B_2\times T_1}$$

$$\Rightarrow \frac{0.8}{I_2} = \frac{0.8\times20}{0.4\times5}$$

$$\Rightarrow I_2 = \frac{0.4\times5}{20} = 0.1\ \text{Am}^{-1}$$

8 (a) Given, $\chi_m = 299$

$$\mu_0 = 4\pi\times10^{-7}\ \text{Hm}^{-1}, \mu = ?$$

We know that, $\mu = \mu_0(1+\chi_m)$

$$\mu = 4\pi\times10^{-7}\ (1+299)$$

$$= 4\times\frac{22}{7}\times10^{-7}\times300$$

$$= \frac{26400}{7}\times10^{-7}$$

$$= 3771.4\times10^{-7}\ \text{Hm}^{-1}$$

$$\simeq 3771\times10^{-7}\ \text{Hm}^{-1}$$

9 (c) As the value of susceptibility is large and positive, so the class of the magnetic material is ferromagnetic.

10 (c) From the relation, susceptibility of the material is $\chi_m = I/H \Rightarrow \chi_m \propto I$

Thus, it obvious that greater the value of susceptibility of a material greater will be the value of intensity of magnetisation, i.e. more easily it can be magnetised. Therefore, Assertion is correct but Reason is incorrect.

11 (a) With rise in temperature, the magnetism of magnet falls linearly and at critical temperature, it becomes zero.

12 (b) Given, $A = 0.2\ \text{cm}^2$,

$$H = 1200\ \text{Am}^{-1}$$

and $\quad \chi_m = 599$

Permeability, $\mu = \mu_0(1+\chi_m)$

$$= 4\pi\times10^{-7}\ (1+599)$$

$$= 7.536\times10^{-4}\ \text{TmA}^{-1}$$

13 (c) Susceptibility,

$$\chi = \frac{\text{Intensity of magnetisation, } I}{\text{Magnetic field, } B}$$

Given, $\chi = 3\times10^{-4}$

and $\quad B = 4\times10^{-4}\ \text{Am}^{-1}$

or $\quad I = \chi B$

$$\Rightarrow I = 3\times10^{-4}\times4\times10^{-4}$$

$$= 12\times10^{-8}\ \text{Am}^{-1}$$

14 (d) Paramagnetic materials will be feebly attracted, diamagnetic material will be feebly repelled and ferromagnetic material will be strongly attracted towards a magnet.

15 (a) Resultant force acting on a diamagnetic material in a magnetic field is in direction from stronger to the weaker part of the magnetic field.

16 (b) Intensity of magnetisation,

$$I = \frac{M}{V} = \frac{M}{\text{Mass / Density}}$$

Given, mass $= 1\ \text{g} = 10^{-3}\text{kg}$

and density $= 5\text{g cm}^{-3}$

$$= \frac{5\times10^{-3}\text{kg}}{(10^{-2})^3}$$

$$= 5\times10^3\text{kg/m}^3$$

Hence, $\quad I = \frac{6\times10^{-7}\times5\times10^3}{10^{-3}}$

$$= 3.0\ \text{Am}^{-1}$$

17 (c) A paramagnetic sample displays greater magnetisation when cooled. This is because at lower temperature, the tendency to disrupt the alignment of dipoles (due to magnetising field) decreases on account of reduced random thermal motion. Magnetisation depends upon temperature.

18 (a) Given, $m = 8.0\times10^{22}$ A-m^2

Radius of earth, $R = 6400$ km

$= 6.4\times10^6$ m

Magnetisation, $M = \frac{m}{V} = \frac{m}{\frac{4}{3}\pi r^3}$

$$M = \frac{8.0\times10^{22}\times3}{4\times3.14\times(6.4\times10^6)^3}$$

$M = 72.9\text{Am}^{-1}$

19 (b) Volume, $V = \frac{\text{Mass}}{\text{Density}}$

$= \frac{66\times10^{-5}\text{m}^3}{75}$

Magnetisation, $M = \frac{m}{V} = \frac{2.5\times75}{66\times10^{-5}}$

$M = 2.84\times10^5\text{Am}^{-1}$

20 (b) Given, $\chi = 599$, $A = 0.2$ cm^2

$= 0.2\times10^{-4}\text{m}^2$,

$H = 1200\ \text{Am}^{-1}$

As, $\mu = \mu_0(1+\chi)$

or $\mu = 4\pi\times10^{-7}\ (1+599)$

or $\mu = 7.536\times10^{-4}\ \text{TmA}^{-1}$

$B = \mu H = 7.536\times10^{-4}\times1200$ T

$\therefore$ Magnetic flux,

$\phi_B = BA = 7.536\times10^{-4}\times1200\times0.2\times10^{-4}$ Wb

$= 1.81\times10^{-5}$ Wb

21 (a) We know that, magnetisation,

$I = \frac{\text{dipole moment}}{\text{volume}}$

$= \frac{8\times10^{10}\times9\times10^{-24}}{10^{-18}}$ (given)

$= 7.2\times10^5\ \text{Am}^{-1}$

22 (a) The diamagnetic substances are repelled by both the poles of magnet.

23 (a) For ferromagnetic materials when an external magnetic field is applied, the domains are aligned along the direction of magnetic field.

24 (a) As we know that,

$\mu_r = 1+\chi_m$

Given, $\mu_r = 6000$

$\Rightarrow\ 6000 = 1+\chi_m$

$\Rightarrow\ \chi_m = 6000-1 = 5999$

25 (b) For a paramagnetic substance, the intensity of magnetisation of a material is directly proportional to the magnetic intensiy,

As $\mathbf{I}\propto\mathbf{H}\ \Rightarrow\ \mathbf{I} = \chi\mathbf{H}$ ... (i)

Also, from Curie's law,

$\chi\propto\frac{1}{T}$

$\Rightarrow\ \chi = \frac{C}{T}$ ...(ii)

where, T = absolute temperature,

From Eqs. (i) and (ii), we get $I\propto 1/T$.

Thus, I decreases in proportional to $1/T$.

26 (b) Ferromagnetic materials used for transformers must have high permeability and low hysteresis loss.

27 (d) As we know that,

$\mu_r = 1+\chi_m \Rightarrow 5500 = 1+\chi_m$ (given)

$\Rightarrow\ \chi_m = 5500-1 = 5499$

28 (a) Above Curie temperature, a ferromagnetic material becomes paramagnetic material.

29 (a) Nickel shows ferromagnetic property at room temperature. If the temperature is increased beyond Curie temperature, then it will show a paramagnetism.

30 (d) Magnetic susceptibility for paramagnetic material is positive but small.

31 (d) As iron is ferromagnetic but above Curie temperature, it becomes paramagnetic. The Curie temperature for iron is 1043 K [i.e. 770°C]. Hence, above 770°C, iron becomes para-magnetic.

32 (a) Since in neon atom, all the orbitals are filled with electrons of opposite spin and, so net dipole moment of neon atom is zero.
Hence, neon is diamagnetic material.

33 (d) The maximum magnetisation in the specimen

= Number of dipoles × dipole moment

$= 2.0\times10^{24}\times1.5\times10^{-23}$ Am^2 (given)

$= 30$ A-m^2

34 (a) Magnetic susceptibility (χ) is inversely proportional to the absolute temperature and is applicable for paramagnetic and ferromagnetic materials but not for diamagnetic material.

35 (c) Diamagnetic substance is repelled by a magnetic field and hence when a diamagnetic substance is placed inside a magnetic field, it is thrown out.

36 (b) From Curie's law, $\chi\propto T^{-1}$

$\chi = \frac{C}{T}$, where C = constant

$$\frac{\chi_{-173^\circ\text{C}}}{\chi_{-73^\circ\text{C}}} = \frac{T_{-73^\circ\text{C}}}{T_{-173^\circ\text{C}}} = \frac{(273-73)}{(273-173)} = \frac{200}{100} = 2$$

$\chi_{-173^\circ\text{C}} = 2\times(0.0060)$

$\chi_{-173^\circ\text{C}} = 0.0120$

37 (a) Hydrogen atom have unpaired electrons in their orbital and have net magnetic moment and hence it is paramagnetic.

But in hydrogen molecule orbital is filled with two electrons in opposite spin with net dipole moment as zero.

Hence, hydrogen molecule is diamagnetic.

38 (b) When a paramagnetic liquid is taken in U-tube and one arm is placed between the poles of strong magnet, the liquid is feebly attracted by the magnet. Therefore, the level of the solution in the arm rises.

39 (d) Curie-Weiss law is obeyed by iron above Curie temperature.

40 (a) According to Weiss, due to interaction of spin of electrons of one atom with that of neighbouring atoms, a ferromagnetic material gets divided into small regions called domains, each of which is at all times completely magnetised. But the direction of magnetisation varies from domain to **domain**, so that the resultant magnetisation of the material is zero.

41 (a) The materials for a permanent magnet should have high retentivity (so that the magnet is strong) and high coercivity (so that the magnetism is not wiped out by stray magnetic fields).

42 (c) When a diamagnetic substance is placed in a magnetic field, dipole moments are induced in the atom by the applied field but opposite to the direction of applied field. Hence, diamagnetic materials can show magnetism. When external applied magnetic field is removed, these induced magnetic dipole moments vanished.

Hence, diamagnetic material have no permanent magnetic dipole moment.

43 (a) The reversed magnetic field needed to demagnetise the specimen is known as coercivity of the material.

$$B = \mu_0 H$$

$$\Rightarrow \quad \mu_0 ni = \mu_0 H$$

$$\Rightarrow \quad \frac{Ni}{L} = H \qquad \left(\because n = \frac{N}{L}\right)$$

or $$i = \frac{HL}{N} \qquad \dots(i)$$

Given, $H = 4 \times 10^3 \text{ Am}^{-1}$,

$$L = 12 \text{ cm}$$

$$= 12 \times 10^{-2} \text{m}$$

and $N = 60$ turns

Substituting the values in Eq. (i), we get

$$i = \frac{4 \times 10^3 \times 12 \times 10^{-2}}{60} = 8 \text{ A}$$

44 (c) In diamagnetic substances, in each pair of electrons, the spin of both the electrons are in opposite directions. Hence, the electrons of each pair completely cancel the magnetic moment of each other. Thus, the net magnetic moment of each atom of such substances is zero, i.e. $\mu_d = 0$.

The property of paramagnetism is found in those substances whose atoms or molecules have an excess of electrons spinning in same direction. Hence, atoms of paramagnetic substances have permanent magnetic moment, i.e. $\mu_p \neq 0$. The property of ferromagnetism is found in substances which acquire very strong magnetism when placed in an external magnetic field. Like paramagnetic substances each atom of ferromagnetic substances also has permanent magnetic moment, i.e. $\mu_f \neq 0$.

45 (b) Diamagnetism is explained in term of spin motion. The net magnetic moment is zero in them.

Diamagnetic materials have negative susceptibility.

46 (a) Diamagnetic substances when placed in a magnetic field are feebly magnetised in a direction opposite to the magnetising field, e.g. copper. Paramagnetic substances, when placed in a magnetic field get feebly magnetised in a direction of the magnetising field, e.g. aluminium. Ferromagnetic substances when placed in a magnetic field get strongly magnetised in the direction of the magnetising field, e.g. iron.

47 (c) Bismuth is a diamagnetic substance, hence when placed in an external magnetic field, it rotates such that, its axis becomes perpendicular to the magnetic field.

20

Electromagnetic Induction

Quick Review

The phenomenon of generation of current or emf by changing the magnetic fields is known as **Electromagnetic Induction** (EMI). The emf developed in the conductor by the process of EMI is known as **induced emf** and if the conductor is in the form of a closed loop, then the current flowing in the conductor is known as **induced current**.

Magnetic Flux

- The total number of magnetic field lines of force crossing through any surface normally when it is placed in a magnetic field is known as the magnetic flux of that surface.
  Magnetic flux through loop, $\phi_B = \int \mathbf{B} \cdot d\mathbf{S}$

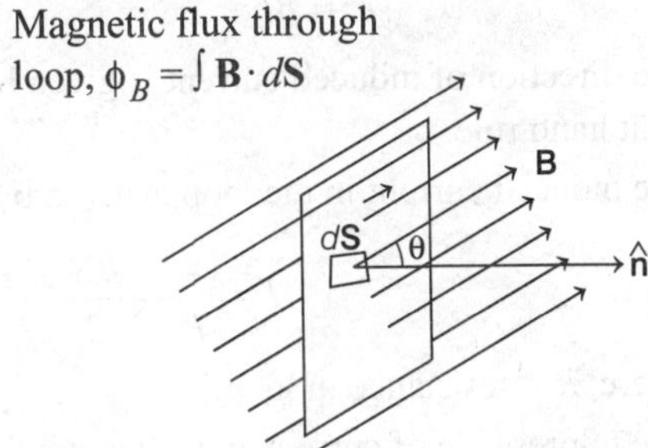

- When the magnetic field is perpendicular to the plane of the loop, then magnetic flux will be
  $$\phi_B = BS = \text{maximum value}$$
- When the magnetic field B is inclined at an angle θ, w.r.t. the normal to the surface, then the magnetic flux becomes
  $\phi_B = \mathbf{B} \cdot \mathbf{S} = |\mathbf{B}||\mathbf{S}|\cos\theta = BS\cos\theta$
  where, θ is smaller angle between **B** and **S**.

Specific Conditions

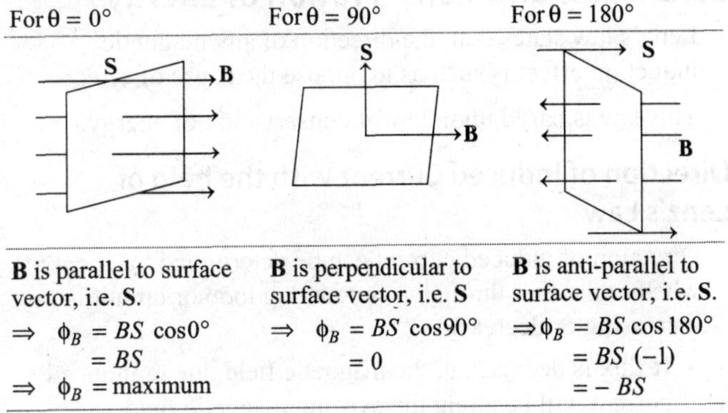

For θ = 0°	For θ = 90°	For θ = 180°
B is parallel to surface vector, i.e. **S**.	**B** is perpendicular to surface vector, i.e. **S**	**B** is anti-parallel to surface vector, i.e. **S**.
$\Rightarrow \phi_B = BS\cos 0° = BS$	$\Rightarrow \phi_B = BS\cos 90° = 0$	$\Rightarrow \phi_B = BS\cos 180° = BS(-1) = -BS$
$\Rightarrow \phi_B = \text{maximum}$		

Faraday's Laws of Electromagnetic Induction

There are two laws of Faraday which are given below

Faraday's First Law

Whenever the amount of magnetic flux linked with a circuit changes, an emf is induced in the circuit.

Faraday's Second Law

The magnitude of the induced emf in a circuit is equal to the rate of change of magnetic flux through the circuit.

Mathematically, Faraday's second law can be expressed as

$$e = \frac{-d\phi_B}{dt}$$

$$\left[\because \text{Rate of change of magnetic flux} = \frac{\phi_2 - \phi_1}{t}\right]$$

In the case of a closely wound coil of N turns, the change of flux associated with each turn is the same.

Therefore, the expression for the total induced emf is given by

$$e = -N\frac{d\phi_B}{dt}$$

Induced Current in a Circuit

- If R is the electrical resistance of the circuit, then induced current in the circuit is given by

$$I = \frac{e}{R} = \frac{1}{R}\left(-\frac{d\phi_B}{dt}\right)$$

Electric charge flown due to induced current,

$$q = I\,dt = -\frac{1}{R}d\phi_B$$

- If induced current is produced in a coil rotated in a uniform magnetic field, then

$$I = \frac{NBA\omega \sin \omega t}{R} = I_0 \sin \omega t$$

where, $I_0 = \frac{NBA\omega}{R}$ = peak value of induced current.

Lenz's Law and Conservation of Energy

Lenz's law states that, the direction of any magnetic induction effect is such as to oppose the cause of effect.

This law is based upon law of conservation of energy.

Direction of Induced Current with the help of Lenz's Law

Direction of induced current can be determined by checking whether the flux through a conducting loop or circuit is increasing or decreasing.

- If flux is decreasing, the magnetic field due to induced current will be along the existing magnetic field.
- If flux is increasing, the magnetic field due to induced current will be opposite to existing magnetic field.

Motional Electromotive Force

Due to motion of conductor in magnetic field, a potential difference is maintained between the ends of the conductor as long as the conductor continues to move through the uniform magnetic field.

This potential difference is called motional electromagnetic force, which is denoted by e and is given by

$$e = Bvl$$

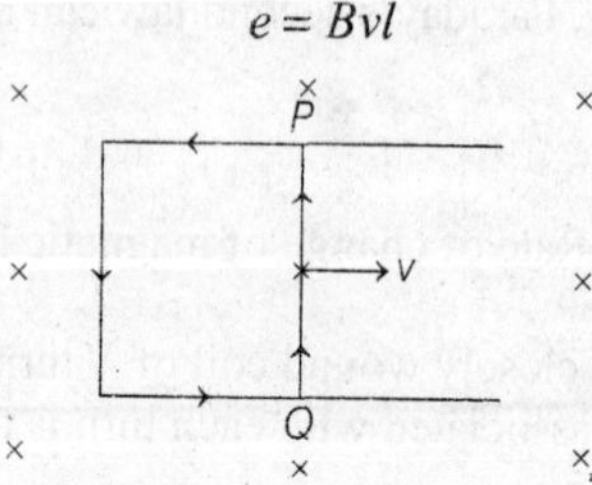

If R is the resistance of the circuit, then current will be written as

$$i = \frac{e}{R} = \frac{Bvl}{R}$$

General Form of Motional emf

To find motional emf for a conductor of any shape moving in a uniform or non-uniform magnetic field, we will consider any small element $d\mathbf{l}$ of a conductor, then the contribution de to the emf is the magnitude of $d\mathbf{l}$ multiplied by the component of $(\mathbf{v}\times\mathbf{B})$ which is parallel to $d\mathbf{l}$, i.e.

$$de = (\mathbf{v}\times\mathbf{B})\cdot d\mathbf{l}$$

$$\Rightarrow \quad e = \oint(\mathbf{v}\times\mathbf{B})\cdot d\mathbf{l}$$

Some important points are related to emf are given below

- When a conducting rod of length l is moving with a uniform magnetic field B, then an induced emf is set up. The magnitude of induced emf will be $|\mathbf{e}| = Blv$.
- If the rod is moving making an angle θ with the direction of magnetic field, then $|\mathbf{e}| = Blv\sin\theta$

  For motion parallel to **B**, i.e. $\mathbf{v} \parallel \mathbf{B}$.

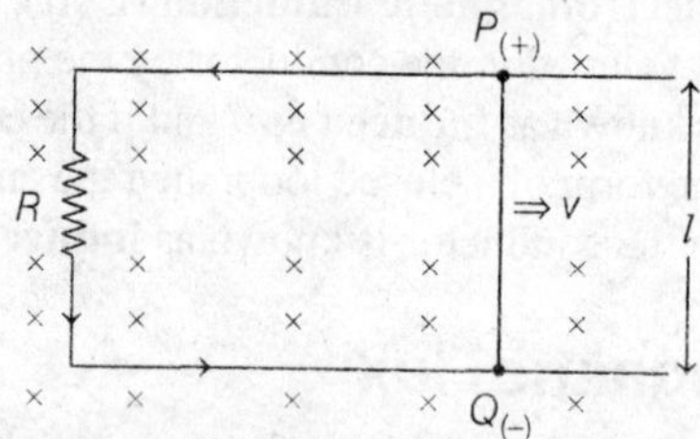

- If a conducting rod moves on two parallel conducting rails, then again an emf is induced whose magnitude is given by

$$|\mathbf{e}| = Blv \qquad [\text{since } \mathbf{v}\perp\mathbf{B}]$$

- The direction of induced current is given by Fleming's right hand rule.
- The induced current in the loop is given by

$$I = \frac{|\mathbf{e}|}{R} = \frac{Blv}{R}$$

where, R = resistance in loop.

- Due to presence of current and magnetic field, arm PQ experiences a magnetic force is given by

$$F = BIl = \frac{B^2l^2v}{R}$$

- The force given above is directed opposite to the velocity of the rod and hence power required to maintain constant speed v, i.e.

$$P = Fv = \frac{B^2l^2v^2}{R}$$

- An emf is induced between the ends of rod when a conducting rod of length l rotates about an axis passing through one of its ends (that end may be fixed) with an angular velocity ω in a plane perpendicular to the magnetic field B and is given by

$$|e| = \frac{1}{2} Bl^2\omega$$

Fleming's Right Hand Thumb Rule to Find the Direction of Induced Current

The direction of motional emf or current can be given by Fleming's right hand thumb rule. If we stretch the thumb, the forefinger and the central finger of right hand in such a way that all are mutually perpendicular to each other and if thumb represents the direction of motion of the conductor and the forefinger represents the direction of magnetic field, then central finger will represent the direction of induced current as shown in figure.

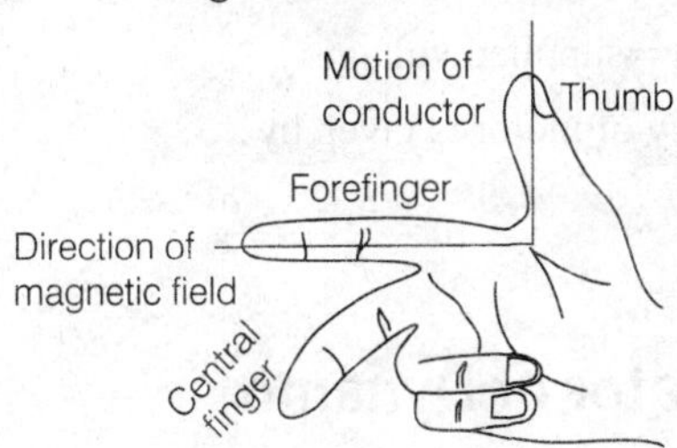

Inductance

Inductance is a scalar quantity which plays same role in an electrical circuit as played by inertia in mechanics. It depends only on the geometry of the coil and intrinsic material properties.

It is the ratio of flux linkage to the current.

$$L = \frac{N\phi}{I} = \frac{NBA}{I} = \frac{\phi_{total}}{I}$$

The SI unit of L is henry (H).

Self-Inductance

- Self-inductance is the property of a coil by virtue of which the coil opposes any change in the strength of current flowing through it by inducing an emf in itself called back emf.
- Induced emf due to self-induction is given by

$$e = -N\frac{d\phi}{dt} = -L\frac{dI}{dt}$$

where, L = coefficient of self-induction.

and given by $L = \frac{N\phi}{i}$.

- When two coils of coefficient of self-inductions L_1 and L_2 are connected as below

(*i*) In series , then

$$L_{eq} = L_1 + L_2$$

(*ii*) In parallel , then

$$L_{eq} = \frac{L_1 L_2}{L_1 + L_2}$$

- For a solenoid coil having length l, total number of turns N and cross-sectional area A, then value of L is

$$L = \frac{\mu_0 N^2 A}{l} = \mu_0 n^2 Al$$

where, $n = N/l$

Energy Stored in an Inductor

- The energy of a capacitor is stored in the electric field between its plates. Similarly, an inductor has the capability of storing energy in its magnetic field. The total energy U is supplied while the current increases from zero to a final value I is

$$U = L\int_0^i IdI = \frac{1}{2}LI^2$$

$$\therefore \quad W = U = \frac{1}{2}LI^2$$

Thus, if $I = 1$ A, then $2W = L$.

Hence, the coefficient of self-inductance is equal to twice the work done in establishing a flow of one ampere current in the circuit.

- Energy stored per unit volume in magnetic field is known as energy density.

$$\therefore \quad \text{Energy density} = \frac{U}{V} = \frac{1}{2}\frac{B^2}{\mu_0}$$

Mutual Inductance

The phenomenon according to which an opposing emf is produced in a coil as a result of change in current or magnetic flux linked with a neighbouring coil is called mutual induction.

Induced emf due to mutual inductance,

In secondary coil, $e_2 = -N_2\frac{d\phi_{B_2}}{dt} = -M\frac{dI_1}{dt}$

Also, $N_2\phi_2 = MI_1$

Its SI unit is henry (H).

- If two coils of self-inductances L_1 and L_2 having mutual inductance M are

(*i*) In series combination, then $L_S = L_1 + L_2 \pm 2M$

(*ii*) In parallel combination, then $L_p = \frac{L_1 L_2 - M^2}{L_1 + L_2 \pm 2M}$

- For a pair of two magnetically coupled coils of self-inductances L_1 and L_2 respectively, the mutual inductance is given by

$$M_{12} = M_{21} = M = k\sqrt{L_1 L_2}$$

where, k = coefficient of coupling and is given as

$$k = \frac{\text{magnetic flux linked in secondary coil}}{\text{magnetic flux linked in primary coil}}$$

- Value of M for different shapes of coils as given below
  (*i*) If coupling coefficient $k = 1$ and medium is a free space or air, value of M for a pair of concentric circular coils is

$$M = \frac{\mu_0 N_1 N_2 \pi r^2}{2R}$$

where, r = radius of the coil (of small radius)
and R = radius of the coil (of larger radius).

  (*ii*) If a pair of two solenoid coils, wound one over the other, then

$$M = \frac{\mu_0 N_1 N_2 A}{l}$$

  (*iii*) If there is a pair of concentric co-planar square coils, then

$$M = \frac{2\sqrt{2}\mu_0 N_1 N_2 a^2}{\pi b}$$

where, a = side of the smaller coil
and b = side of the larger coil.

Eddy Currents

- The currents induced in bulk pieces of conductors when the magnetic flux linked with the conductor changes are known as eddy currents.
- Eddy currents are always produced in a plane which is perpendicular to the direction of magnetic field. Eddy current shows both heating and magnetic effects.
- The magnitude of eddy current is

$$i = \frac{e}{R} = \frac{d\phi / dt}{R}$$

Applications of Eddy Currents

Eddy currents can be used in many ways as given below
(*i*) In electric brakes in trains.
(*ii*) In induction furnace.
(*iii*) In speedometer of automobiles.
(*iv*) In energy meter and dead-beat galvanometer.

DC Motor

- It is an electric machine which converts electrical energy into mechanical energy.
- It is based on the principle that when a current carrying coil is placed in a magnetic field, it experiences a torque, which rotates it.
- Due to rotation of armature coil in the magnetic field, a back emf is induced in the circuit and it is given by

$$e = E - iR$$

where, E = supplied voltage.

- Efficiency of motor is given by

$$\eta = \frac{P_{\text{out}}}{P_{\text{in}}} = \frac{e}{E}$$

AC Generator or Dynamo

- It is an electrical machine which is used to convert mechanical energy into electrical energy.
- It is based on the principle of electromagnetic induction and the emf induced is given by

$$e = -N\frac{d\phi}{dt} = -NBA\omega \sin \omega t$$

$$= e_0 \sin \omega t$$

where, $e_0 = NBA\omega$.

- The current induced in the circuit is given by

$$i' = \frac{e}{R} = \frac{e_0}{R}\sin \omega t$$

$$= i_0 \sin \omega t$$

Topical Practice Questions

All the exam questions of this chapter have been divided into 4 topics as listed below

Topic 1

Magnetic Flux and Faraday's & Lenz's Laws

2019

1 A coil of 800 turns effective area $0.05\ m^2$ is kept perpendicular to a magnetic field 5×10^{-5} T. When the plane of the coil is rotated by 90° around any of its co-planar axis in 0.1 s, the emf induced in the coil will be **[NEET]**

(a) 0.2 V (b) 2×10^{-3} V
(c) 0.02 V (d) 2 V

2 Lenz law is based on principle of conservation of **[JIPMER]**

(a) linear momentum (b) energy
(c) charge (d) mass

2018

3 A system *S* consists of two coils *A* and *B*. The coil *A* carries a steady current *I*. While the coil *B* is suspended nearby as shown in figure. Now, if the system is heated, so as to raise the temperature of two coils steadily, then **[AIIMS]**

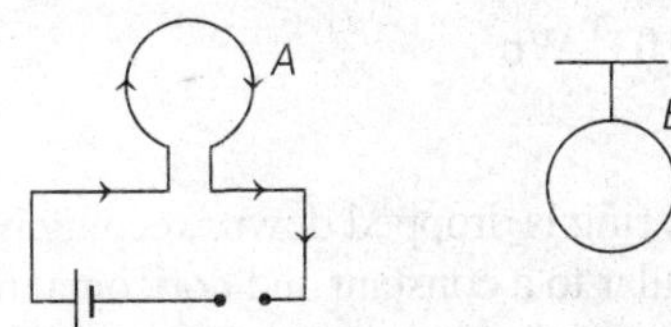

(a) the two coils shows attraction
(b) the two coils shows repulsion
(c) there is no change in the position of the two coils
(d) induced current are not possible in coil *B*

2014

4 The current flows from *A* to *B* as shown in the figure. What is the direction of current in circle? **[UK PMT]**

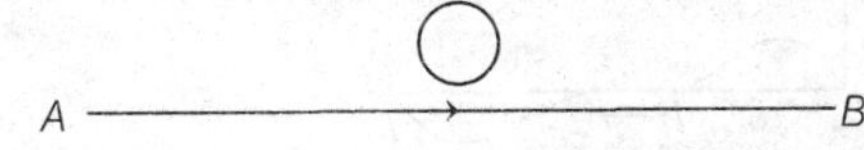

(a) Clockwise (b) Anti-clockwise
(c) Straight line (d) None of these

2013

5 A wire loop is rotated in a magnetic field. The frequency of change of direction of the induced emf is **[NEET]**

(a) once per revolution
(b) twice per revolution
(c) four times per revolution
(d) six times per revolution

2012

6 A coil of resistance 400 Ω is placed in a magnetic field. If the magnetic flux φ (Wb) linked with the coil varies with time *t* (s) as $\phi = 50t^2 + 4$. Current at 2 s is **[CBSE AIPMT]**

(a) 0.5 A (b) 0.1 A (c) 2 A (d) 1 A

7 In a coil of resistance 10 Ω, the induced current developed by changing magnetic flux through it, is shown in figure as a function of time. The magnitude of change in flux through the coil (in weber) is **[CBSE AIPMT]**

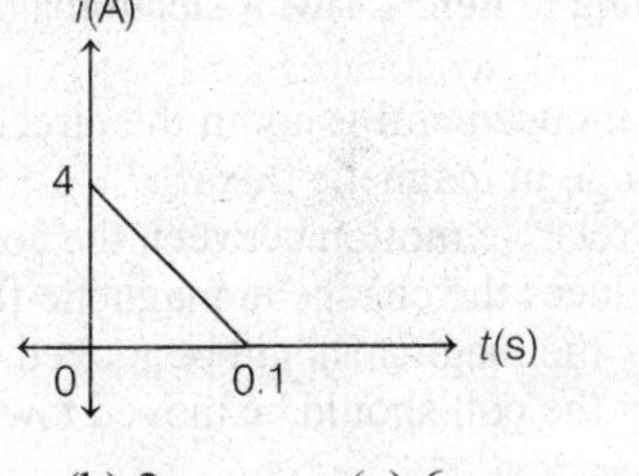

(a) 8 (b) 2 (c) 6 (d) 4

8 The magnetic flux linked with a coil satisfies the relation $\phi = (4t^2 + 6t + 9)$ Wb, where *t* is time in second. The emf induced in the coil at $t = 2$ s is **[CBSE AIPMT]**

(a) 22 V (b) 18 V (c) 16 V (d) 40 V

9 The current *i* in a coil varies with time as shown in the figure. The variation of induced emf with time would be **[AIIMS]**

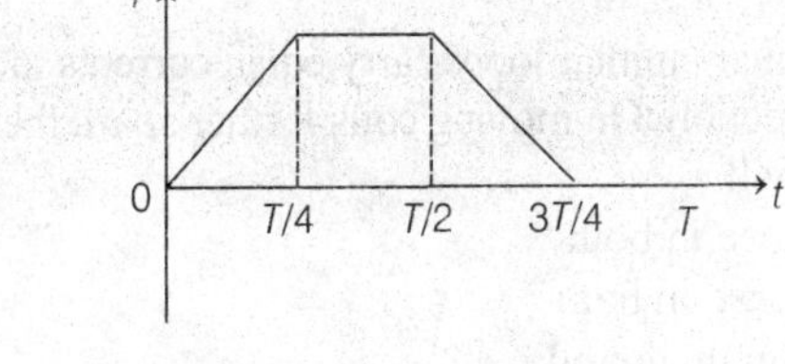

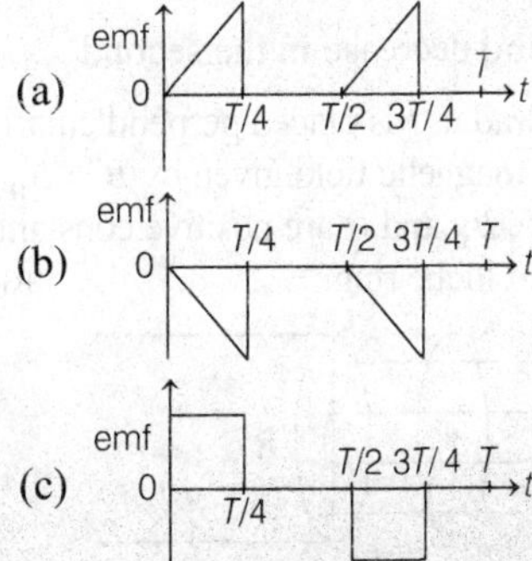

2008

10 A circular disc of radius 0.2 m is placed in a uniform magnetic field of induction $(1/\pi)\,\text{Wbm}^{-2}$ in such a way that its axis makes an angle of 60° with **B**. The magnetic flux linked with the disc is **[CBSE AIPMT]**

(a) 0.02 Wb (b) 0.06 Wb (c) 0.08 Wb (d) 0.01 Wb

11 When a low flying aircraft passes overhead, we sometimes notice a slight shaking of the picture on our TV screen. This is due to **[AFMC]**

(a) diffraction of the signal received from the antenna
(b) interference of the direct signal received by the antenna with the weak signal reflected by the passing aircraft
(c) change of magnetic flux occurring due to the passage of aircraft
(d) vibration created by the passage of aircraft

12 According to Lenz's law of electromagnetic induction, **[J&K CET]**

(a) the induced emf is not in the direction opposing the change in magnetic flux
(b) the relative motion between the coil and magnet produces the change in magnetic flux
(c) only the magnet should be moved towards coil
(d) only the coil should be moved towards magnet

13 The North-pole of a bar magnet is moved towards a coil along the axis passing through the centre of the coil and perpendicular to the plane of the coil. The direction of the induced current in the coil when viewed in the direction of the motion of the magnet is **[EAMCET]**

(a) clockwise
(b) anti-clockwise
(c) no current in the coil
(d) Either clockwise or anti-clockwise

14 Two similar circular loops carry equal currents in the same direction. On moving coils further apart, the electric current will **[KCET]**

(a) increase in both
(b) decrease in both
(c) remain unaltered
(d) increase in one and decrease in the second

15 A conducting ring of radius r is placed perpendicularly inside a time varying magnetic field given by $B = B_0 + \alpha t$, as shown in the figure. B_0 and α are positive constants. Find the emf produced in the ring. **[Guj CET]**

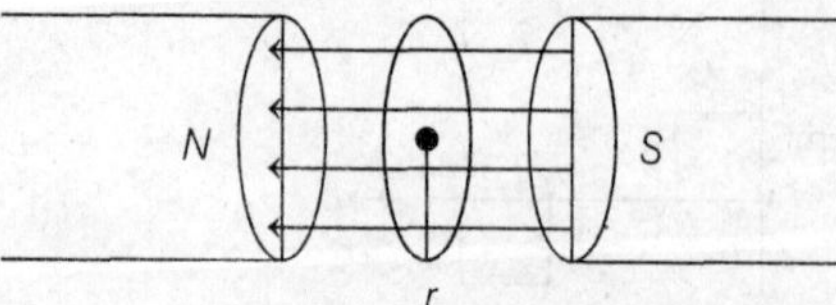

(a) $-\pi\alpha r^2$ (b) $-\pi\alpha r$
(c) $-\pi\alpha^2 r^2$ (d) $-\pi\alpha^2 r$

2007

16 The magnetic flux through a circuit of resistance R changes by an amount $\Delta\phi$ in a time Δt. Then, the total quantity of electric charge Q that passes any point in the circuit during the time Δt is represented by **[Manipal]**

(a) $Q = \frac{1}{R}\cdot\frac{\Delta\phi}{\Delta t}$ (b) $Q = \frac{\Delta\phi}{R}$
(c) $Q = \frac{\Delta\phi}{\Delta t}$ (d) $Q = R\cdot\frac{\Delta\phi}{\Delta t}$

17 Whenever a magnet is moved either towards or away from a conducting coil, an emf is induced, the magnitude of which is independent of **[Kerala CEE]**

(a) the strength of the magnetic field
(b) the speed with which the magnet is moved
(c) the number of turns of the coil
(d) the resistance of the coil
(e) the area of cross-section of the coil

18 A circular coil of diameter 21 cm is placed in a magnetic field of induction 10^{-4} T. The magnitude of flux linked with coil when the plane of coil makes an angle 30° with the field is **[J&K CET]**

(a) 1.44×10^{-6} Wb
(b) 1.732×10^{-6} Wb
(c) 3.1×10^{-6} Wb
(d) 4.2×10^{-6} Wb

2006

19 A metallic ring is dropped down, keeping its plane perpendicular to a constant and horizontal magnetic field. The ring enters the region of magnetic field at $t = 0$ and completely emerges out at $t = T$ s, the current in the ring varies as **[AIIMS]**

(a)
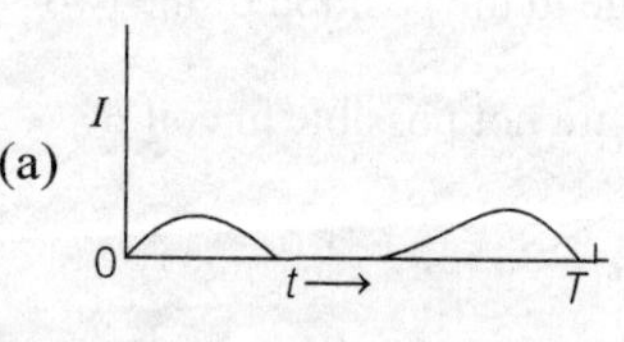

(b)
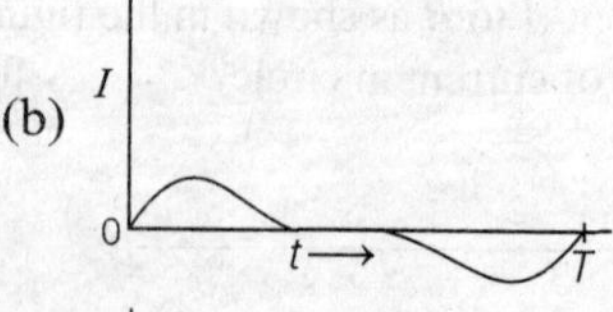

(c)
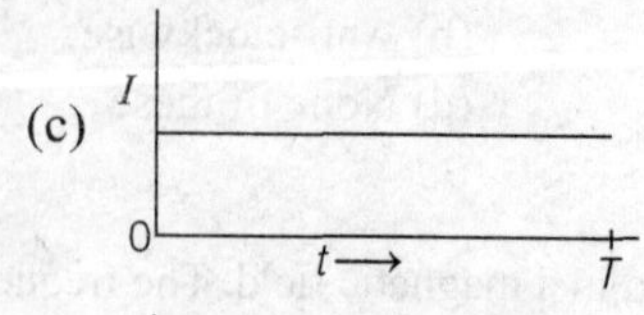

(d)
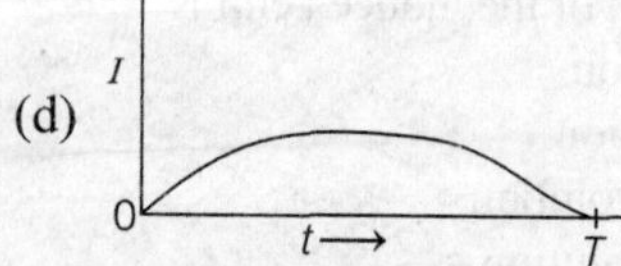

20 The North-pole of a long horizontal bar magnet is being brought closer to a vertical conducting plane along the perpendicular direction. The direction of the induced current in the conducting plane will be [AFMC]
(a) horizontal (b) vertical
(c) clockwise (d) anti-clockwise

21 Induced emf in the coil depends upon [UP CPMT]
(a) conductivity of coil
(b) amount of flux
(c) rate of change of linked flux
(d) resistance of coil

22 A bar magnet is dropped between a current carrying coil. What would be its acceleration? [RPMT]
(a) g downwards
(b) Greater than g downwards
(c) Less than g downwards
(d) Bar will be stationary

23 A coil having 500 turns of square shape, each of side 10 cm is placed normal to a magnetic field which is increasing at $1\ \text{Ts}^{-1}$. The induced emf is [J&K CET]
(a) 0.1 V (b) 0.5 V (c) 1 V (d) 5 V

24 A coil of 1200 turns and mean area of $500\ \text{cm}^2$ is held perpendicular to a uniform magnetic field of induction 4×10^{-4}. The resistance of the coil is 20 Ω. When the coil is rotated through 180° in the magnetic field in 0.1 s, the average electric current (in mA) induced is [EAMCET]
(a) 12 (b) 24 (c) 36 (d) 48

25 There is a uniform magnetic field directed perpendicular and into the plane of the paper. An irregular shaped conducting loop is slowly changing into a circular loop in the plane of the paper. Then, [MHT CET]
(a) current is induced in the loop in the anti-clockwise direction
(b) current is induced in the loop in the clockwise direction
(c) AC is induced in the loop
(d) No current is induced in the loop

26 In a closed circuit of resistance 10 Ω, the change of flux ϕ with respect to time t is given by the equation $\phi = 2t^2 - 5t + 1$, the current at $t = 0.25$ s will be [Guj CET]
(a) 4 A (b) 0.04 A
(c) 0.4 A (d) 1 A

2005

27 As a result of change in the magnetic flux linked to the closed loop shown in the figure, an emf V volt is induced in the loop. The work done (in joule) in taking a charge Q coulomb once along the loop is

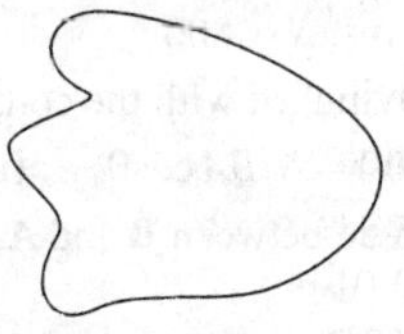

[CBSE AIPMT]
(a) QV (b) zero (c) $2QV$ (d) $QV/2$

28 A magnet is made to oscillate with a particular frequency, passing through a coil as shown in figure. The time variation of the magnitude of emf generated across the coil during one cycle is

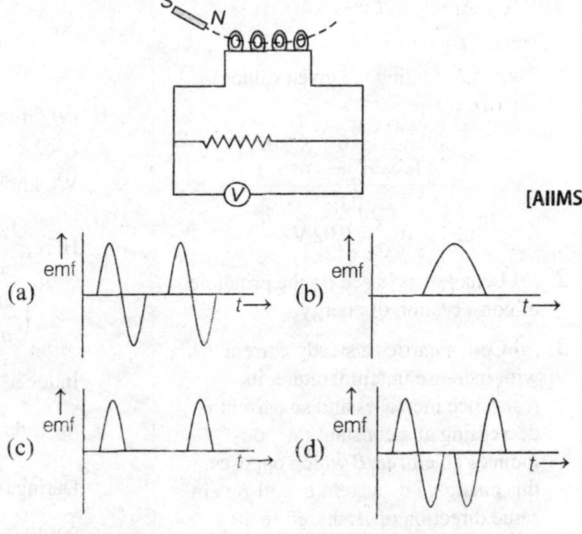

29 The flux associated with coil changes from 1.35 Wb to 0.79 Wb within (1/10) s. Then, the charge produced by the earth coil, if resistance of coil is 7 Ω is [MHT CET]
(a) 0.08 C (b) 0.8 C
(c) 0.008 C (d) 8 C

30 The Lenz's law gives [AMU]
(a) direction of induced current
(b) magnitude of induced emf
(c) magnitude of induced current
(d) magnitude and direction of induced current

Answers

1 (c)	2 (b)	3 (a)	4 (d)	5 (b)	6 (a)	7 (b)	8 (a)	9 (d)	10 (a)
11 (c)	12 (b)	13 (b)	14 (a)	15 (a)	16 (b)	17 (d)	18 (b)	19 (b)	20 (d)
21 (c)	22 (c)	23 (d)	24 (b)	25 (a)	26 (c)	27 (a)	28 (a)	29 (a)	30 (a)

Explanations

1 (c) Given, area of coil, $A = 0.05\,\text{m}^2$, magnetic field, $B = 5 \times 10^{-5}$ T and number of turns, $N = 800$.

The magnetic flux linked with the coil,

$$\phi = N(\mathbf{B} \cdot \mathbf{A}) = N\,BA\cos\theta \quad \dots \text{(i)}$$

where, θ is the angle between **B** and **A**.

The emf induced when the coil is rotated from $\theta_1 = 0°$ to $\theta_2 = 90°$,

$$e = -\frac{\Delta\phi}{\Delta t} = -\frac{\Delta}{\Delta t}(NBA\cos\theta) \quad \text{[using Eq. (i)]}$$

$$= -\frac{NBA}{\Delta t}(\cos\theta_2 - \cos\theta_1) \quad \dots \text{(ii)}$$

Here, $\Delta t = 0.1$ s

Thus, substituting the given values in Eq. (ii), we get

$$e = -\frac{\begin{bmatrix} 800 \times 5 \times 10^{-5} \times 0.05 \\ \times(\cos 90° - \cos 0°) \end{bmatrix}}{0.1}$$

$$= 2000 \times 10^{-5} = 0.02\text{ V}$$

2 (b) Lenz law is based on the principle of conservation of energy.

3 (a) Coil A carries a steady current with increase in temperature, its resistance increases and so current is decreasing at a constant rate, this induces an emf in B which opposes this change, i.e. current in coil B is in same direction of A, therefore they attract to each other.

4 (d) As magnetic field through circle is constant because current through straight wire is constant. Magnetic flux through circle is not changing with time.

$$\Rightarrow \quad \frac{d\phi_B}{dt} = 0$$

$$\Rightarrow \quad |E| = \left|\frac{d\phi_B}{dt}\right| = 0$$

$$\Rightarrow \quad i = \frac{E}{R} = \frac{0}{R} = 0$$

Hence, no current is flowing in circle.

5 (b) A wire loop is rotated in a magnetic field. The frequency of change of direction of the induced emf is twice per revolution. In one half, magnetic flux is decreasing and in other half it is increasing.

6 (a) Induced emf of coil, $E = \left|-\frac{d\phi}{dt}\right|_t$

Given, $\phi = 50t^2 + 4$ and $R = 400\,\Omega$

$$E = \left|-\frac{d\phi}{dt}\right|_{t=2} \Rightarrow = |100\,t|_{t=2} = 200\text{ V}$$

Current in the coil,

$$i = \frac{E}{R} = \frac{200}{400} = \frac{1}{2} = 0.5\text{ A}$$

7 (b) Given, $R = 10\Omega$

$$I = \left|\frac{1}{R}\frac{d\phi}{dt}\right| \Rightarrow |d\phi| = |IR\,dt|$$

Change in flux = Area of triangle × R

$$= \left(\frac{1}{2} \times 4 \times 0.1\right) \times 10$$

$$= 2\text{ Wb}$$

8 (a) Given, $\phi = (4t^2 + 6t + 9)$ Wb and $t = 2$ s

We know that, $|\varepsilon| = \left|\frac{d\phi}{dt}\right|$

Here, $\left|\frac{d\phi}{dt}\right| = |8t + 6|$

$$\Rightarrow \quad \left(\frac{d\phi}{dt}\right)_{t=2} = 8 \times 2 + 6$$

Induced emf in the coil = 22 V

9 (d) Induced emf, $e = -L\frac{di}{dt}$

During 0 to $\frac{T}{4}$, $\frac{di}{dt}$ = constant and positive, so e = negative.

For $\frac{T}{4}$ to $\frac{T}{2}$, $\frac{di}{dt} = 0$, so $e = 0$.

For $T/2$ to $\frac{3T}{4}$, $\frac{di}{dt}$ = constant and negative, so e = positive.

This condition is satisfied only by graph in option (d).

10 (a) The magnetic flux ϕ passing through a plane surface of area A placed in a uniform magnetic field B is given by

$$\phi = BA\cos\theta \quad \dots\text{(i)}$$

where, θ is the angle between the direction of **B** and the normal to the plane **A**.

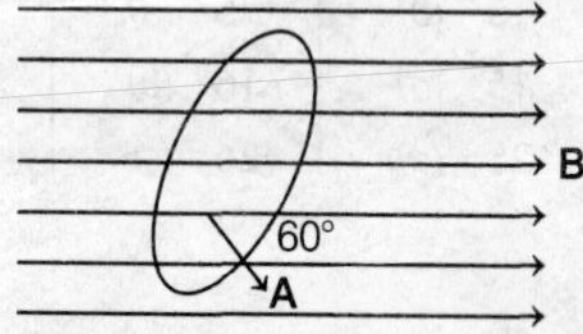

Given, $\theta = 60°$,

$B = (1/\pi)\text{ Wbm}^{-2}$, $A = \pi(0.2)^2$

Putting the values in Eq. (i), we get

$$\therefore \quad \phi = \frac{1}{\pi} \times \pi(0.2)^2 \times \cos 60°$$

$$= (0.2)^2 \times \frac{1}{2} = 0.02\text{ Wb}$$

11 (c) When a low flying aircraft is passing overhead, then it causes a change in magnetic flux and thus causes a disturbance in picture on our TV.

12 (b) According to Lenz's law of electromagnetic induction, the relative motion between the coil and magnet produces the change in magnetic flux.

13 (b) When the North-pole of the magnet is brought towards one end of the coil, the induced current flows in the coil in such a direction that the end of the coil near the magnet becomes a North-pole, which repels the magnet and opposes the motion of the North-pole of the magnet towards the coil, thus direction of induced current is anti-clockwise.

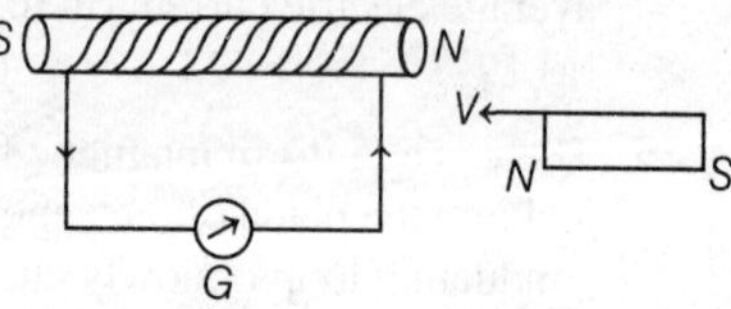

14 (a) On moving the coils further apart initially, the flux linked will be reduced. Then, according to Lenz's law current will increase in both the coils to increase the linked flux.

15 (a) Given, the magnetic field vary with time as

$$B = B_0 + \alpha t \quad \dots\text{(i)}$$

Here, B_0 and α are positive constants.

We know that, the induced emf,

$$e = -\frac{d\phi}{dt} \quad \dots\text{(ii)}$$

and the magnetic flux is given as

$$\phi = BA\cos\theta$$

where, θ is the angle between the magnetic field **B** and area vector of ring **A**.

So, $\quad \theta = 0°$

$$\Rightarrow \quad \phi = BA\cos 0° = BA \quad \dots\text{(iii)}$$

From Eqs. (ii) and (iii), we get

$$e = -\frac{d}{dt}(BA)$$

On putting the value of B from Eq. (i), we get

$$e = -\frac{d}{dt}[(B_0 + \alpha t)A]$$

$$= -A\frac{d}{dt}[B_0 + \alpha t]$$

$$= -A[0 + \alpha] = -A\alpha$$

But $A = \pi r^2$ is the area of ring, where r is the radius of ring.

So, $e = -\pi r^2 \alpha$

$\Rightarrow$ $e = -\pi \alpha r^2$

16 *(b)* From Faraday's second law, emf induced in the circuit

$$|e| = \Delta\phi / \Delta t$$

If R is the resistance of the circuit, then

$$i = \frac{e}{R} = \frac{\Delta\phi}{R\Delta t}$$

Thus, charge passes through the circuit and is given by

$$Q = i \times \Delta t$$

$$\Rightarrow Q = \frac{\Delta\phi}{R\Delta t} \times \Delta t = \frac{\Delta\phi}{R}$$

17 *(d)* Whenever there is relative motion between a magnet and a conducting coil, an emf is induced in the coil,

$$e = -N(d\phi / dt),$$

where, $\phi = BA\cos\theta$,

N = number of turns in coil.

Hence, emf induced does not depend on resistance of coil.

18 *(b)* Given, diameter,

$$d = 21 \text{ cm} = 21 \times 10^{-2} \text{ m}$$

Radius, $r = \frac{21}{2} \times 10^{-2}$ m

Angle between axis of coil and magnetic field,

$$\theta = 90° - 30° = 60°$$

Magnetic field induction,

$$B = 10^{-4} \text{ T}$$

We know that, magnetic flux,

$$\phi = BA\cos\theta$$

$$= 10^{-4} \times \pi r^2 \times \cos 60°$$

$$= 10^{-4} \times \frac{22}{7} \times \frac{21}{2} \times \frac{21}{2} \times 10^{-2} \times 10^{-2} \times \cos 60°$$

$$= 10^{-8} \times \frac{22}{7} \times \frac{21}{2} \times \frac{21}{2} \times \frac{1}{2}$$

$$= 10^{-8} \times \frac{11 \times 3 \times 21}{2 \times 2}$$

$$= 1.732 \times 10^{-6} \text{ Wb}$$

19 *(b)* During free fall, when the ring enters the horizontal field with its plane perpendicular to it, emf is induced in it due to change in magnetic flux. Due to this emf, a current flows in the ring in such a direction that it opposes the change in flux.

When the ring is completely in the magnetic field, there is no change in flux linked with it and thus there is no flow of current in the ring.

Now, when the ring leaves the magnetic field, again the flux changes and thus emf is induced. Due the this emf, the current again flows across it, but in the opposite direction as shown below

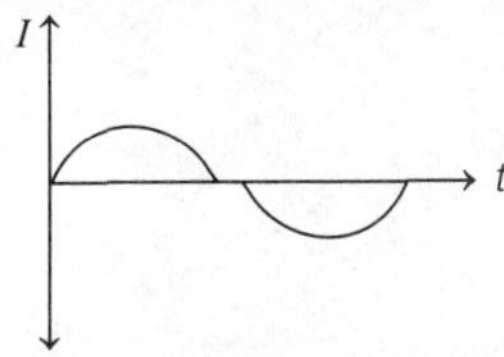

20 *(d)* The induced emf will oppose the motion of the magnet. Applying Lenz's law, the direction of induced current will be anti-clockwise.

21 *(c)* According to Faraday's law, the induced emf in a closed loop equals the time rate of change of magnetic flux through the loop.

i.e. $e = -(d\phi_B / dt)$

Hence, induced emf in a coil depends on the rate of change of flux.

22 *(c)* When a bar magnet is dropped between current carrying coils, then due to change in magnetic flux, induced current will be produced such that it opposes the motion of magnet. So, acceleration of magnet will be less than g in downward direction.

23 *(d)* The magnetic flux through area A placed in magnetic field B,

$$\phi = BA\cos\theta$$

Given, $\theta = 0°$, $N = 500$

and $\phi = BA$.

Now, rate of change of magnetic field per second $= \frac{dB}{dt} = 1 \text{ Ts}^{-1}$

$$A = (10)^2 \text{ cm}^2 = 10^{-2} \text{ m}^2$$

$$\Rightarrow \frac{d\phi}{dt} = \frac{d(BA)}{dt} = \frac{dB}{dt} \cdot A$$

$$\Rightarrow \frac{d\phi}{dt} = 1 \times 10^{-2}$$

By Faraday's law, induced emf

$$e = -N\frac{d\phi}{dt}$$

$$= -500 \times 10^{-2} = -5 \text{ V}$$

$\Rightarrow$ $|e| = 5\text{V}$

24 *(b)* In perpendicular position in a uniform magnetic field, magnetic flux linked with the each turn of coil,

$$\phi_1 = BA$$

On rotating coil through 180°, flux linked,

$$\phi_2 = -BA$$

$\therefore$ Change in magnetic flux,

$$\Delta\phi = \phi_2 - \phi_1 = -2BA$$

So, emf induced in the coil,

$$e = -N\frac{\Delta\phi}{\Delta t} = \frac{2NBA}{\Delta t}$$

where, N is the number of turns in the coil.

Given, $N = 1200$,

$$A = 500 \text{ cm}^2 = 500 \times 10^{-4} \text{ m}^2,$$

$B = 4 \times 10^{-4}$ T, $R = 20\Omega$ and $\Delta t = 0.1$ s.

The current in the coil is given by

$$i = \frac{e}{R} = \frac{2NBA}{R\Delta t}$$

$$= \frac{2 \times 1200 \times 4 \times 10^{-4} \times 500 \times 10^{-4}}{20 \times 0.1}$$

$$= 24 \times 10^{-3} \text{ A} = 24 \text{ mA}$$

25 *(a)* Due to change in the shape of the loop, the magnetic flux linked with the loop increases. Hence, current is induced in the loop in such a direction that it opposes the increases in flux. Therefore, induced current flows in the anti-clockwise direction.

26 *(c)* Given, $\phi = (2t^2 - 5t + 1)$,

$R = 10\Omega$ and $t = 0.25$ s

Induced emf,

$$e = -\frac{d\phi}{dt} = -\frac{d}{dt}(2t^2 - 5t + 1)$$

$$= -(4t - 5)$$

$\therefore$ Current, $i = \frac{e}{R} = -\frac{(4t - 5)}{10}$

At $t = 0.25$ s

$$i = -\frac{(4 \times 0.25 - 5)}{10} = -\frac{(-4)}{10} = 0.4 \text{ A}$$

27 (a) Induced emf

$= \frac{\text{Work done in moving charge}}{\text{Charge}}$

i.e. $V = \frac{W}{Q} \Rightarrow W = VQ$

28 (a) When North-pole of magnet approaches the one face of coil, then the face of the coil becomes a North-pole to oppose this motion and hence current flows anti-clockwise.

Thus, in this case emf is developed in the coil and when it completes one half motion it is momentarily at rest and no emf is present.

While magnet is moving to the other side, South-pole approaches the other face of coil making this face a South-pole. The current now flows in clockwise direction and again an emf is developed in the coil.This variation is shown in Fig. (a).

29 (a) As, $I = \frac{e}{R} = \frac{d\phi}{Rdt}$

$\because e = \frac{d\phi}{dt}$ or $Idt = \frac{d\phi}{R}$

Integrating both sides, we get

$\int Idt = \int \frac{d\phi}{R}$ or $q = \frac{\phi}{R}$

If coil contains N turns, then $q = \frac{N\phi}{R}$

Given, $\phi_1 = 1.35$ Wb, $\phi_2 = 0.79$ Wb, $\Delta\phi = \phi_2 - \phi_1 = (1.35 - 0.79)$ Wb and $R = 7\Omega$.

If there is flux change of $\Delta\phi$, then

$q = \frac{N\Delta\phi}{R} = \frac{1}{7} \times (1.35 - 0.79) = 0.08$ C

30 (d) Lenz's law governs the direction of induced current in electromagnetic induction. Lenz's law states that, the direction of induced current must be in such a way that it opposes the reason because of which it is produced.

Topic 2

Motional EMF

2015

1 A conducting square frame of side a and a long straight wire carrying current I are located in the same plane as shown in the figure. The frame moves to the right with a constant velocity v. The induced emf the frame will be proportional to

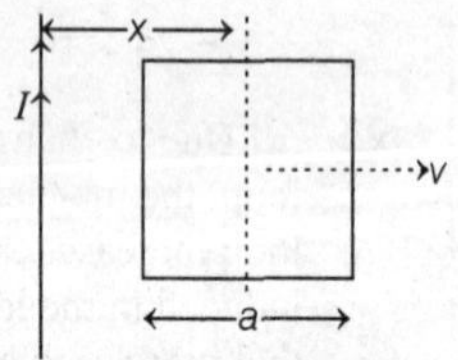

[CBSE AIPMT]

(a) $\frac{1}{x^2}$ (b) $\frac{1}{(2x - a)^2}$

(c) $\frac{1}{(2x + a)^2}$ (d) $\frac{1}{(2x - a)(2x + a)}$

2014

2 A very small circular loop of radius a is initially (at $t = 0$) co-planar and concentric with a much larger fixed circular loop of radius b. A constant current I flows in the larger loop. The smaller loop is rotated with a constant angular speed ω about the common diameter. The emf induced in the smaller loop as a function of time t is [WB JEE]

(a) $\frac{\pi a^2 \mu_0 I}{2b} \omega \cos \omega t$ (b) $\frac{\pi a^2 \mu_0 I}{2b} \omega \sin \omega^2 t^2$

(c) $\frac{\pi a^2 \mu_0 I}{2b} \omega \sin \omega t$ (d) $\frac{\pi a^2 \mu_0 I}{2b} \omega \sin^2 \omega t$

3 A straight conductor of length 0.4 m is moved with a speed of 7 ms^{-1} perpendicular to a magnetic field of intensity 0.9 Wbm^{-2}. The induced emf across the conductor is [UK PMT]

(a) 5.04 V (b) 1.26 V
(c) 2.52 V (d) 25.2 V

2007

4 A wire of length 50 cm moves with a velocity of 300 m min^{-1}, perpendicular to a magnetic field. If the emf induced in the wire is 2 V, then the magnitude of the field (in tesla) is [Kerala CEE]

(a) 2 (b) 5
(c) 0.4 (d) 2.5
(e) 0.8

2005

5 A copper rod of length l is rotated about one end, perpendicular to the uniform magnetic field B with constant angular velocity ω. The induced emf between two ends of the rod is [MHT CET]

(a) $\frac{1}{2} B\omega l^2$ (b) $B\omega l^2$

(c) $\frac{3}{2} B\omega l^2$ (d) $2B\omega l^2$

6 An aeroplane having a wing space of 35 m flies due North with the speed of 90 ms^{-1}. The induced emf between the tips of the wings will be (take, $B = 4 \times 10^{-5}$ T) [RPMT]

(a) 0.013 V (b) 1.26 V
(c) 12.6 V (d) 0.126 V

7 A straight conductor of length 4 m moves at a speed of 10 ms^{-1}. When the conductor makes an angle of 30° with the direction of magnetic field of induction of 0.1 Wb m^{-2}, then induced emf is **[RPMT]**

(a) 8 V (b) 4 V (c) 1 V (d) 2 V

8 Assertion When a conducting wire loop which is inside a uniform magnetic field directed perpendicular to its plane, is moving with uniform velocity, an emf is induced in it.

Reason When the magnetic flux linked with a conducting wire loop changes with time an emf is not induced in the cable. **[EAMCET]**

(a) Both Assertion and Reason are correct and Reason is the correct explanation of Assertion.

(b) Both Assertion and Reason are correct but Reason is not the correct explanation of Assertion.

(c) Assertion is correct but Reason is incorrect.

(d) Both Assertion and Reason are incorrect.

Answers

1 (d)	2 (c)	3 (c)	4 (e)	5 (a)	6 (d)	7 (d)	8 (d)

Explanations

1 *(d)*

Potential difference (induced emf) across PQ,

$$V_P - V_Q = B_1 av = \frac{\mu_0 I}{2\pi\left(x - \frac{a}{2}\right)} av$$

Potential difference (induced emf) across side RS of frame is

$$V_S - V_R = B_2 av = \frac{\mu_0 I}{2\pi\left(x + \frac{a}{2}\right)} av$$

Hence, the net potential difference (induced emf) in the loop will be

$$V_{net} = (V_P - V_Q) - (V_S - V_R)$$

$$= \frac{\mu_0 Iav}{2\pi}\left[\frac{1}{\left(x - \frac{a}{2}\right)} - \frac{1}{\left(x + \frac{a}{2}\right)}\right]$$

$$= \frac{\mu_0 Iav}{2\pi}\left[\frac{a}{\left(x - \frac{a}{2}\right)\left(x + \frac{a}{2}\right)}\right]$$

Thus, $V_{net} \propto \frac{1}{(2x - a)(2x + a)}$

2 *(c)* We know that, $e = NBA\,\omega \sin \omega t$

where, N = number of loops = 1,

$$B = \frac{\mu_0 I}{2b} \text{ N/A-m}$$

and $A = \pi a^2$ m^2.

Putting the values in Eq. (i), we get

$$\therefore \text{Induced emf, } e = \frac{\mu_0 I}{2b}(\pi a^2)\,\omega \sin \omega t$$

$$= \frac{\pi a^2 \mu_0 I}{2b} \cdot \omega \sin \omega t$$

3 *(c)* Consider the diagram, where a conductor AB of length l is moving perpendicular to an inward magnetic field B.

Value of induced emf,

$$|e_{ind}| = |l\,(\mathbf{v} \times \mathbf{B})|$$

$$= lvB \sin\theta = lvB \sin 90° \quad [\because v \perp B]$$

$$e_{ind} = vBl \quad \ldots(i)$$

Given, $v = 7$ ms^{-1}, $l = 0.4$ m

and $B = 0.9$ Wbm^{-2}

Now, putting the values in Eq. (i), we get

$$e_{ind} = 7 \times 0.9 \times 0.4$$

$$= 7\,(0.9)\,(0.4) \text{ V}$$

$$= 2.52 \text{ V}$$

4 *(e)* When a wire of length l moves with a velocity v perpendicular to a magnetic field B, an induced emf is produced in the wire given by

$$e = Blv$$

Given, $l = 50$ cm = 0.5m

$\Rightarrow$ $v = 300$ m min^{-1}

$$= \frac{300}{60} = 5 \text{ ms}^{-1}$$

and $e = 2$ V

Magnetic field,

$$B = \frac{e}{lv} = \frac{2}{0.5 \times 5} = 0.8 \text{ T}$$

5 *(a)* To calculate the emf, we can imagine a closed loop by connecting the centre with any point on the circumference, say P with a resistor. Potential difference across the resistor is then equal to the induced emf. It arises due to separation of charges.

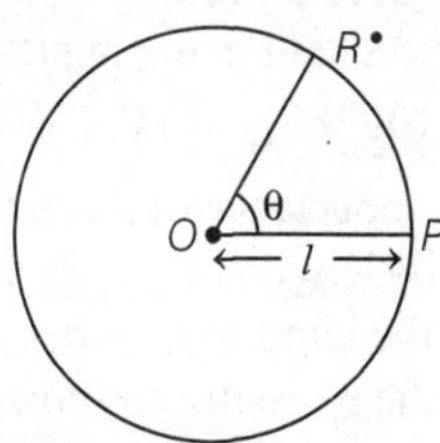

$e = B \times$ (rate of change of area of loop)

If θ is the angle between the rod and the radius of circle at P at time t, the area of the arc formed by the rod and radius is

$$\text{Area } (OPR) = \frac{1}{2} l^2 \theta$$

where, l is radius of the circle.

$$\therefore \quad e = B \times \frac{d}{dt}\left(\frac{1}{2}l^2\theta\right)$$

$$\Rightarrow \quad = \frac{1}{2}B \cdot l^2 \frac{d\theta}{dt} = \frac{1}{2}Bl^2\omega$$

$$(\because \omega = d\theta/dt)$$

6 (d) Given, $B = 4 \times 10^5$ T,

$l = 35$ m and $v = 90 \text{ ms}^{-1}$

The induced emf is given by

$$e = Bvl$$
$$= 4 \times 10^{-5} \times 90 \times 35$$
$$= 0.126 \text{ V}$$

7 (d) Given, $l = 4$ m,

$v = 10 \text{ ms}^{-1}, \theta = 30°$

and $B = 0.1 \text{ Wbm}^{-2}$.

Induced emf is given by

$$e = Bvl \sin\theta$$
$$= 0.1 \times 10 \times 4 \sin 30°$$
$$\Rightarrow \quad e = 2 \text{ V}$$

8 (d) Suppose, a conducting square loop is placed in xy-plane and magnetic field is perpendicular to the xy-plane, i.e. plane of loop. If loop is provided with a uniform velocity the flux through the loop does not change and hence no EMF is induced in the loop.

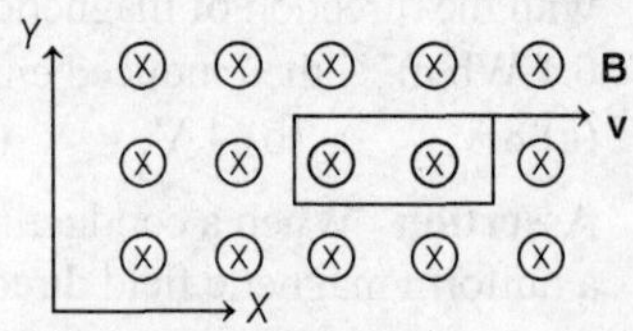

Also, if there is any change in flux through loop. EMF is induced for the loop.

Both Assertion and Reason are incorrect.

Topic 3

Inductance (Self and Mutual Inductance)

2018

1 The magnetic potential energy stored in a certain inductor is 25 mJ, when the current in the inductor is 60 mA. This inductor is of inductance **[NEET]**

(a) 1.389 H (b) 138.88 H
(c) 0.138 H (d) 13.89 H

2016

2 A long solenoid has 1000 turns. When a current of 4A flows through it, the magnetic flux linked with each turn of the solenoid is 4×10^{-3} Wb. The self-inductance of the solenoid is **[NEET]**

(a) 3 H (b) 2 H (c) 1 H (d) 4 H

2013

3 The current in a self-inductance $L = 40$ mH is to be increased uniformly from 1 A to 11 A in 4 ms. The induced emf in the inductor during the process is **[Manipal]**

(a) 100 V (b) 0.4 V (c) 40 V (d) 440 V

4 The inductance of a coil is proportional to **[WB JEE]**

(a) its length
(b) the number of turns
(c) the resistance of coil
(d) the square of the number of turns

2011

5 Two solenoids of equal number of turns have their lengths and the radii in the same ratio 1 : 2. The ratio of their self-inductances will be **[Kerala CEE]**

(a) 1 : 2 (b) 2 : 1 (c) 1 : 1 (d) 1 : 4
(e) 1 : 3

6 What is the self-inductance of solenoid of length 31.4 cm, area of cross-section 10^{-3} m^2 and total number of turns 10^3? **[J&K CET]**

(a) 4 mH (b) 4 H
(c) 40 H (d) 0.4 H

7 What should be the value of self-inductance of an inductor that should be connected to 220 V, 50 Hz supply, so that a maximum current of 0.9 A flows through it? **[J&K CET]**

(a) 11 H (b) 2 H
(c) 1.1 H (d) 5 H

8 Two identical induction coils each of inductance L joined in series are placed very close to each other such that the winding direction of one is exactly opposite to that of the other. What is the inductance?

(a) L^2 (b) $2L$
(c) $L/2$ (d) Zero

2008

9 Two coils are placed close to each other. The mutual inductance of the pair of coils depends upon **[RPMT]**

(a) the rates at which currents are changing in the two coils
(b) relative position and orientation of the two coils
(c) the materials of the wires of the coils
(d) the currents in the two coils

10 When the current changes from +2 A to – 2 A in 0.05 s, an emf of 8V is induced in a coil. The coefficient of self-induction of the coil is **[RPMT]**

(a) 0.2 H (b) 0.4 H
(c) 0.8 H (d) 0.1 H

11 According to phenomenon of mutual inductance, **[J&K CET]**
(a) the mutual inductance does not depend on the geometry of the two coils involved
(b) the mutual inductance depends on the intrinsic magnetic property, like relative permeability of the material
(c) the mutual inductance is independent of the magnetic property of the material
(d) ratio of magnetic flux produced by the coil 1 at the place of the coil 2 and the current in the coil 2 will be different from that of the ratio defined by interchanging the coils

12 X and Y, two metallic coils are arranged in such a way that, when steady change in current flowing in X coil is 4 A, change in magnetic flux associated with coil Y is 0.4 Wb. Mutual inductance of the system of these coils is **[Guj CET]**
(a) 0.2 H (b) 5 H
(c) 0.8 H (d) 0.1 H

13 The induced emf in a secondary coil is 20000 V, when the current breaks in the primary coil. The mutual inductance is 5 H and the current reaches to zero in 10^{-4} s in the primary. The maximum current in the primary before it breaks is **[Punjab PMET]**
(a) 0.1 A (b) 0.4 A
(c) 0.6 A (d) 0.8 A

14 Two coils are wound on the same iron rod, so that the flux generated by one passes through the other. The primary coil has N_p turns in it and when a current 2 A flows through it, the flux in it is 2.5×10^{-4} Wb. If the secondary coil has 12 turns, the mutual inductance of the coils is (assume the secondary coil is in open circuit) **[Punjab PMET]**
(a) 10×10^{-4} H (b) 15×10^{-4} H
(c) 20×10^{-4} H (d) 25×10^{-4} H

2007

15 If coil is open, then L and R become **[MHT CET]**
(a) $\infty, 0$ (b) $0, \infty$ (c) ∞, ∞ (d) 0, 0

16 Two coils of self-inductances 2 mH and 8 mH are placed so close together that the effective flux in one coil is completely linked with the other. The mutual inductance between these coils is **[MP PMT]**
(a) 10 mH (b) 6 mH (c) 4 mH (d) 16 mH

17 The inductance of a coil is $L = 10$ H and resistance $R = 5\,\Omega$. If applied voltage of battery is 10 V and it switches OFF in 1 ms, then find the value of induced emf of inductor.
(a) 2×10^4 V (b) 1.2×10^4 V **[DUMET]**
(c) 2×10^{-4} V (d) None of these

18 A coil of self-inductance 0.5 mH carries a current of 2 A. The energy stored (in joule) is **[Guj CET]**
(a) 1 (b) 0.001 (c) 0.5 (d) 0.05

2006

19 A current $i = 10 \sin(100 \pi t)$ A is passed in first coil, which induces a maximum emf 5π V in second coil. The mutual inductance between the coils is **[Kerala CEE]**
(a) 10 mH (b) 15 mH (c) 25 mH (d) 20 mH
(e) 5 mH

2005

20 In a solenoid, if number of turns is doubled, then self-inductance will become **[AFMC]**
(a) half (b) double
(c) 1/4 times (d) quadruple

21 Two coils have mutual inductance 0.005 H. The current changes in the first coil according to equation $I = I_0 \sin \omega t$, where $I_0 = 10$ A and $\omega = 100\pi$ rad s^{-1}. The maximum value of emf in volt in the second coil is **[RPMT]**
(a) 12π (b) 8π
(c) 5π (d) 2π

22 Two inductors each of inductance L are joined in parallel, then their equivalent inductance will be **[RPMT]**
(a) zero (b) $L/2$
(c) L (d) $2L$

23 For a solenoid having a primary coil of N_1 turns and a secondary coil of N_2 turns, the coefficient of mutual inductance is **[Haryana PMT]**
(a) $\mu_0 \mu_r \dfrac{N_1 N_2}{l}$
(b) $\dfrac{\mu_0 \mu_r N_1 N_2}{Al}$
(c) $\mu_0 \mu_r N_1 N_2 Al$
(d) $\dfrac{\mu_0 \mu_r N_1 N_2 A}{l}$

Answers

1 (d)	2 (c)	3 (a)	4 (d)	5 (a)	6 (a)	7 (d)	8 (b)	9 (b)	10 (d)
11 (b)	12 (d)	13 (b)	14 (b)	15 (b)	16 (c)	17 (a)	18 (b)	19 (e)	20 (d)
21 (c)	22 (b)	23 (d)							

Explanations

1 *(d)* Given, magnetic potential energy stored in an inductor,

$$U = 25 \text{ mJ} = 25 \times 10^{-3} \text{ J}$$

Current in an inductor,

$$i_0 = 60 \text{ mA} = 60 \times 10^{-3} \text{ A}$$

As, the expression for energy stored in an inductor is given as

$$U = \frac{1}{2} L i_0^2 \quad \ldots\text{(i)}$$

where, L is the inductance of the inductor.

Substituting the given values in above Eq. (i), we get

$$(25 \times 10^{-3}) = \frac{1}{2} \times L \times (60 \times 10^{-3})^2$$

$$\Rightarrow \quad L = \frac{2 \times 25 \times 10^{-3}}{3600 \times 10^{-6}} = \frac{500}{36}$$

$$\text{or} \quad L = 13.89 \text{ H}$$

2 *(c)* Given, number of turns of solenoid,

$$N = 1000$$

Current, $i = 4$ A

Magnetic flux, $\phi_B = 4 \times 10^{-3}$ Wb

$\because$ Self-inductance of solenoid is given by

$$L = \phi_B \cdot N / I \quad \ldots\text{(i)}$$

Substitute the given values in Eq. (i), we get

$$L = \frac{4 \times 10^{-3} \times 1000}{4} = 1 \text{ H}$$

3 *(a)* Consider the inductor of inductance L

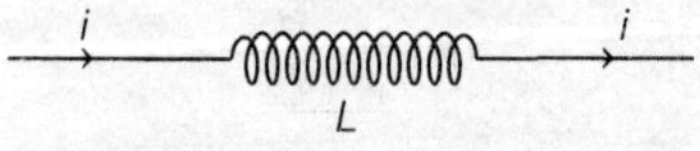

The current flowing through the inductor is i.

Now, we can write,

$$\phi = Li$$

where, ϕ is magnetic flux linked with the inductor.

$$\Rightarrow \quad \left|\frac{d\phi}{dt}\right| = L \frac{di}{dt}$$

Given, $L = 40$ mH

dt = net time difference

$$= t_2 - t_1 = 4 \text{ ms} = \Delta t$$

$$di = i_2 - i_1$$

$$= 11 - 1 = 10 \text{ A} = \Delta i$$

So, $$|\text{emf}| = \left|\frac{d\phi}{dt}\right| = \frac{\Delta\phi}{\Delta t}$$

$$= L \frac{\Delta i}{\Delta t} = (40 \text{ mH}) \frac{(10)\text{A}}{4 \text{ ms}}$$

or Induced emf $= 10 \times 10 = 100$ V

4 *(d)* From the relation, $L = \mu_0 n^2 l A$

$$\Rightarrow \quad L = \mu_0 \frac{N^2}{l} A \quad \left(\because n = \frac{N}{l}\right)$$

$$\Rightarrow \quad L \propto N^2$$

Thus, inductance of a coil is directly proportional to square of number of turns (N).

5 *(a)* Self-inductance, $L = \dfrac{\mu_0 N^2 \pi r^2}{l}$

Given, $r_1 / r_2 = l_1 / l_2 = 1/2$

$$\Rightarrow \quad \frac{L_1}{L_2} = \left(\frac{r_1}{r_2}\right)^2 \left(\frac{l_2}{l_1}\right) = \left(\frac{1}{2}\right)^2 \times \left(\frac{2}{1}\right)$$

$$\Rightarrow \quad \frac{L_1}{L_2} = \frac{1}{2} = 1:2$$

6 *(a)* Given, $A = 10^{-3}$ m^2

$$l = 31.4 \text{ cm} = 31.4 \times 10^{-2} \text{ m}$$

and $N = 10^3$.

Magnetic flux, $\phi = Li \; [\because \phi = B \cdot A]$

$$\Rightarrow \quad N\,BA = Li$$

$$\Rightarrow N\left(\frac{\mu_0 Ni}{l}\right) A = Li \quad \left[\because B = \frac{\mu_0 N}{l} i\right]$$

$$\Rightarrow \quad L = \frac{\mu_0 N^2 A}{l}$$

$$\Rightarrow \quad L = \frac{4\pi \times 10^{-7} \times (10^3)^2 \times 10^{-3}}{31.4 \times 10^{-2}}$$

$$= 4 \text{ mH}$$

7 *(d)* Given, $|e| = 220$ V, $di = 0.9$A and $v = \dfrac{1}{t}$

$$\Rightarrow \quad t = \frac{1}{v} = \frac{1}{50}$$

$$|e| = \frac{Ldi}{dt}$$

$$\Rightarrow \quad 220 = L \times \frac{0.9}{1/50}$$

$$\Rightarrow \quad L = 4.88 = 5 \text{ H}$$

8 *(b)* For two such coils connected oppositely in series,

$$L_{eq} = L_1 + L_2 - 2M$$

But $\quad L_1 = L_2 = L$ and $M = 0$

$$L_{eq} = L + L - 0 = 2L$$

9 *(b)* Mutual inductance of the pair of coils depends on distance between two coils and geometry of two coils, i.e. it depends on relative position and orientation of two coils.

10 *(d)* Given, $e = 8$ V, $i_1 = 2$A, $i_2 = -2$A, $\Delta i = i_2 - i_1 = (-2-2)$A and $dt = 0.05$ s

Induced emf,

$$e = -L\frac{di}{dt} = -L\frac{(-2-2)}{0.05}$$

$$8 = L\frac{(4)}{0.05}$$

$$\Rightarrow \quad L = \frac{8 \times 0.05}{4} = 0.1 \text{ H}$$

11 *(b)* Mutual induction depends upon the magnetic permeability of medium between the coils (μ_r) or nature of material on which two coils are wound.

12 *(d)* We know that, the magnetic flux associated with coil Y is directly proportional to current flowing in X coil.

i.e. $$\phi_Y \propto I_X$$

$$\Rightarrow \quad \phi_Y = MI_X \quad \ldots\text{(i)}$$

where, ϕ_Y = change in magnetic flux in coil Y,

I_X = change in current in coil X

and M = mutual inductance.

Now, given that

$$I_X = 4 \text{ A}$$

$$\Rightarrow \quad \phi_Y = 0.4 \text{ Wb}$$

Then, from Eq. (i)

$$0.4 = M \times 4$$

$$\Rightarrow \quad M = \frac{0.4}{4} = 0.1 \text{H}$$

13 *(b)* Given, $e = 20000$ V, $M = 5$ H and $t = 10^{-4}$ s.

Emf in the coil, $e = \dfrac{Mi_{max}}{t}$

$$\Rightarrow \quad 20000 = 5 \times \frac{i_{max}}{10^{-4}}$$

Current, $$i_{max} = \frac{20000 \times 10^{-4}}{5}$$

$$= 0.4 \text{ A}$$

14 *(b)* Given, $\phi = 2.5 \times 10^{-4}$ Wb,

$i_p = 2$A, and $N = 12$.

Mutual inductance,

$$M = \frac{N_s \phi}{i_p} = \frac{12 \times 2.5 \times 10^{-4}}{2}$$

$$= 15 \times 10^{-4} \text{ H}$$

15 (b) When coil is open, there is no current in it, hence no flux is associated with it, i.e. $\phi = 0$. Also, we know that flux linked with the coil is directly proportional to the current in the coil

i.e. $\phi \propto i$

$\Rightarrow \phi = Li$

where, L is proportionality constant known as self- inductance.

$\therefore L = \phi / i = 0$

Again, since $i = 0$, hence $R = \infty$. $\left[\because R = \frac{e}{i}\right]$

16 (c) When the total flux associated with one coil links with the other, i.e. a case of maximum flux linkage, then

$$M_{12} = \frac{N_2 \phi_{B_2}}{i_1}$$

and $$M_{21} = \frac{N_1 \phi_{B_1}}{i_2}$$

Similarly, $$L_1 = \frac{N_1 \phi_{B_1}}{i_1}$$

and $$L_2 = \frac{N_2 \phi_{B_2}}{i_2}$$

If all the flux of coil 2 links coil 1 and *vice-versa*, then

$$\phi_{B_2} = \phi_{B_1}$$

Since, $M_{12} = M_{21} = M$, hence we have

$$M_{12} M_{21} = M^2 = \frac{N_1 N_2 \phi_{B_1} \phi_{B_2}}{i_1 i_2} = L_1 L_2$$

$$\therefore M_{max} = \sqrt{L_1 L_2}$$

Given, $L_1 = 2\,mH$, $L_2 = 8\,mH$

$$\therefore M_{max} = \sqrt{2 \times 8} = \sqrt{16} = 4\,mH$$

17 (a) Amount of magnetic flux linked with inductor, $\phi = Li$

Now, the emf induced in the inductor is given by

$$e = -\frac{d\phi}{dt} = -\frac{d}{dt}(Li) = -L\frac{di}{dt}$$

$$\Rightarrow |e| = L\frac{di}{dt} = L\frac{\Delta i}{\Delta t}$$

Induced current, $\Delta i = \frac{V}{R} = \frac{10}{5} = 2\,A$

Circuit switches OFF in 1 ms

$\Rightarrow \Delta t = 1 \times 10^{-3}\,s$ and $L = 10\,H$

$\therefore$ Induced emf in inductor,

$$|e| = 10 \times \frac{2}{1 \times 10^{-3}} = 2 \times 10^4\,V$$

18 (b) Energy stored in inductor is given as

$$U = \frac{1}{2} L I^2 \quad \ldots(i)$$

Given, $I = 2\,A, L = 0.5\,mH$
$= 0.5 \times 10^{-3}\,H$

Putting the given value in Eq. (i), we get

$$\therefore U = \frac{1}{2} \times 0.5 \times 10^{-3} \times (2)^2 = 0.001\,J$$

19 (e) From Faraday's law of electromagnetic induction,

$$e = -\frac{Mdi}{dt}$$

$$\Rightarrow M = -\frac{e}{di/dt}$$

Given, $e = 5\pi\,V$
and $i = 10 \sin(100\,\pi t)$.

$$\therefore \left(\frac{di}{dt}\right)_{max} = 10 \cos(100\pi t) \cdot 100\pi$$

$$[\because \cos(100\pi t)_{max} = 1]$$

$$= 10 \times 100\pi$$

$$\Rightarrow M = \left|-\frac{5\pi}{10 \times 100\pi}\right|$$

$$= \left|-5 \times 10^{-3}\right| H = 5\,mH$$

20 (d) For a solenoid of length l, area of cross-section A, having N closely wound turns, the self- inductance of the solenoid is

$$L = \frac{\mu_0 N^2 A}{l}$$

When $N' = 2N$

$$\Rightarrow L' = \frac{\mu_0 (2N)^2 A}{l} = \frac{4\mu_0 N^2 A}{l} = 4L$$

Hence, when number of turns is doubled, then self-inductance becomes quadruple.

21 (c) Given, mutual inductance between two coils, $M = 0.005\,H$,

peak current, $I_0 = 10\,A$,

and angular frequency,

$$\omega = 100\,\pi\,rad\,s^{-1}.$$

Current, $I = I_0 \sin \omega t$

$$\Rightarrow \left|\frac{dI}{dt}\right|_{max} = \frac{d}{dt}(I_0 \sin \omega t) = I_0 \cos \omega t \cdot \omega$$

$$[\because (\cos \omega t)_{max} = 1]$$

$$\Rightarrow \left|\frac{dI}{dt}\right|_{max} = 10 \times 1 \times 100\,\pi$$

$$= 1000\,\pi$$

Hence, induced emf is given by

$$e = M \times \frac{di}{dt}$$

$$= 0.005 \times 1000 \times \pi = 5\pi V$$

22 (b) Inductance of first inductor,

$$L_1 = L$$

Inductance of second inductor,

$$L_2 = L$$

Now, if these inductors are connected in parallel, then their equivalent inductance is

$$\frac{1}{L_{eq}} = \frac{1}{L_1} + \frac{1}{L_2} = \frac{1}{L} + \frac{1}{L} = \frac{2}{L}$$

Hence, $$L_{eq} = \frac{L}{2}$$

23 (d) Coefficient of mutual inductance,

$$M = \frac{\phi}{I_p} = \frac{\mu_0 \mu_r N_1 N_2 A I_p}{l I_p}$$

$$= \frac{\mu_0 \mu_r N_1 N_2 A}{l}$$

where, A and l are the area and length of cross section respectively, I_p = current in primary coil,

N_1 = turns in primary coil and
N_2 = turns in secondary coil.

Topic 4

Applications of EMI (Motor and Dynamo)

2019

1 **Assertion** A metallic surface is moved in and out in magnetic field then emf is induced in it.

Reason Eddy current will be produced in a metallic surface moving in and out of magnetic field. **[AIIMS]**

(a) Both Assertion and Reason are correct and Reason is the correct explanation of Assertion.
(b) Both Assertion and Reason are correct but Reason is not the correct explanation of Assertion.
(c) Assertion is correct but Reason is incorrect.
(d) Both Assertion and Reason are incorrect.

2 In which of the following devices, the eddy current effect is not used? **[NEET]**

(a) Magnetic braking in train
(b) Electromagnet
(c) Electric heater
(d) Induction furnace

2014

3 A dynamo converts **[Kerala CEE]**

(a) mechanical energy into thermal energy
(b) electrical energy into thermal energy
(c) thermal energy into electrical energy
(d) mechanical energy into electrical energy
(e) electrical energy into mechanical energy

2013

4 An electric generator is based on **[WB JEE]**

(a) Faraday's laws of electromagnetic induction
(b) motion of charged particles in electromagnetic field
(c) Newton's laws of motion
(d) fission of uranium by slow neutrons

2012

5 An electric motor runs on DC source of emf 200 V and draws a current 10 A. If the efficiency be 40%, then the resistance of armature is **[UP CPMT, AIPMT]**

(a) 2 Ω (b) 8 Ω (c) 12 Ω (d) 16 Ω

2008

6 **Assertion** An electric motor will have maximum efficiency when back emf becomes equal to half of applied emf.

Reason Efficiency of electric motor depends only on magnitude of back emf. **[AIIMS]**

(a) Both Assertion and Reason are correct and Reason is the correct explanation of Assertion.
(b) Both Assertion and Reason are correct but Reason is not the correct explanation of Assertion.
(c) Assertion is correct but Reason is incorrect.
(d) Both Assertion and Reason are incorrect.

7 At time $t = 0$ s, voltage of an AC generator starts from 0 V and becomes 2 V at time $t = (1/100\,\pi)$ s. The voltage keeps on increasing upto 100 V, after which it starts to decrease. Find the frequency of the generator. **[Guj CET]**

(a) 2 Hz (b) 5 Hz
(c) 100 Hz (d) 1 Hz

2007

8 A six pole generator with fixed field excitation developes an emf of 100 V when operating at 1500 rpm. At what speed must it rotate to develop 120 V? **[AIIMS]**

(a) 1200 rpm (b) 1800 rpm
(c) 1500 rpm (d) 400 rpm

9 Use of eddy currents is done in the following except **[AFMC]**

(a) moving coil galvanometer
(b) electric brakes
(c) induction motor
(d) dynamo

10 Fleming's left and right hand rules are used in **[MHT CET]**

(a) DC motor and AC generator, respectively
(b) DC generator and AC motor, respectively
(c) DC motor and DC generator, respectively
(d) Both rules are same, anyone can be used

11 Results obtained due to eddy currents is **[RPMT]**

(a) high efficiency between coils of transformer
(b) low efficiency between coils of transformer
(c) loss of heat in core of transformer
(d) None of the above

12 When speed of a DC generator decreases, the armature current **[MHT CET]**

(a) increases
(b) decreases
(c) does not change
(d) increases and decreases continuously

Answers

1 (a)	2 (c)	3 (d)	4 (a)	5 (c)	6 (c)	7 (d)	8 (b)	9 (d)	10 (c)
11 (c)	12 (b)								

Explanations

1 *(a)* When a metallic surface is moved in and out in magnetic field, then magnetic flux linked with metallic surface is changed continuously, hence according to Faraday's law of electromagnetic induction, an induced emf is produced. Since, metallic plate behaves as a closed path, therefore an induced current (eddy current) starts flowing in the metallic surface. Hence, Assertion and Reason both are correct and Reason is the correct explanation of Assertion.

2 *(c)* Electric heaters are not based on the eddy current effect. Rather their working is based on Joule's heating effect of current. According to this effect, the passage of an electric current through a resistor produces heat.

However, when a changing magnetic flux is applied to a bulk piece of conducting material, then circulating current is induced in the body of this conductor, which is usually known as eddy currents. This current shows both heating and magnetic effects.

Thus, it is the basic principle behind the working of magnetic braking in train, electromagnet and induction furnace.

3 *(d)* A dynamo converts mechanical energy into electrical energy.

4 *(a)* An electric generator/dynamo is based on Faraday's laws of electromagnetic induction.

5 *(c)* Given, $V = 200\text{V}$, $I = 10$ A and

efficiency $= 40\% = \dfrac{40}{100}$

Input power, $P_i = VI = 200 \times 10$
$= 2000$ W

Output power, $P_o = 40/100 \times 2000$
$= 800$ W

Power loss in heating the armature,

$$P = P_i - P_o$$
$$= 2000 - 800$$
$$P = 1200 \text{ W}$$
$$\therefore \quad I^2R = 1200$$
$$10^2 R = 1200$$
$$\Rightarrow \quad R = 12\,\Omega$$

6 *(c)* Since, the efficiency of an electric motor is given by

$$\eta = \frac{\text{Output power}}{\text{Input power}}$$

From the above relation, it is quite clear that maximum output power corresponds maximum efficiency of motor.

Now, output power is given by

$$eI = \frac{e(E-e)}{R} \quad \text{...(i)}$$

where, $E =$ applied voltage
and $e =$ back emf.

To obtain maximum output power differentiating Eq. (i) with respect to e and equating it to zero.

So, $\dfrac{d}{de}\left[\dfrac{e(E-e)}{R}\right] = 0$

$$\Rightarrow \quad e = \frac{E}{2}$$

Thus, when back emf becomes equal to half of the applied emf, then efficiency of motor will be maximum.

7 *(d)* The produced voltage by an AC generator is 2 V at $t = (1/100\,\pi)$s and maximum produced voltage $(e_0) = 100$ V

We know that, the induced emf produced by an AC generator is

$$e = e_0 \sin \omega t \quad \text{...(i)}$$

Given, $e = 2\text{V}$, $t = (1/100\,\pi)$s

$$\Rightarrow \quad e_0 = 100 \text{ V}$$

On putting the values in Eq. (i), we get

$$2 = 100 \sin \omega \times 1/100\,\pi$$

But the time $(1/100\pi)$s is very small, so the angle ωt is also very small. Therefore, for a small angle, $\sin\theta \approx \theta$

Hence, from Eq. (ii),

$$2 = 100 \times \omega \times 1/100\pi$$
$$\Rightarrow \quad 2\pi = \omega$$
$$\Rightarrow \quad 2\pi = 2\pi n$$

where, $n =$ frequency of the generator.

$$\therefore \quad n = 1 \text{ Hz}$$

8 *(b)* The emf induced is directly proportional to rate at which flux is intercepted which varies directly as the speed of rotation of the generator.

New speed $= \dfrac{120}{100} \times 1500$
$= 1800$ rpm

9 *(d)* Eddy currents is not used in dynamo.

10 *(c)* DC motor is a device which converts electrical energy into mechanical energy. It employs Fleming's left hand rule.

DC generator converts mechanical energy into electrical energy in the farm of DC. It employs Fleming's right hand rule.

11 *(c)* Due to change of magnetic flux, eddy current is produced in the core of transformer. Loss of heat in the core of transformer occurs due to production of eddy current.

12 *(b)* When speed of a DC generator decreases, then rate of change of magnetic flux through armature coil decreases and hence induced emf across armature coil also decreases, i.e armature current decreases.

21

Alternating Current

Quick Review

- The currents whose magnitude and direction changes periodically through a load is known as **alternating currents** and corresponding voltage as **alternating voltage or emf,** which are represented respectively as

$$I = I_0 \sin \omega t, \quad V = V_0 \sin \omega t$$

where, I_0 and V_0 = peak value of current and voltages, respectively and ω = angular frequency.

Some important terms and definitions related to alternating currents are shown in the following table

	Terms	Definitions	Expressed as
(i)	Time period	The time taken to complete one cycle of variations.	$T = 2\pi/\omega$
(ii)	Frequency	The number of cycles completed per second by AC.	$f = \dfrac{1}{T} = \dfrac{\omega}{2\pi}$
(iii)	Average (mean) value of current and voltage	• The mean or average value of AC is that value of direct current or voltage which sends the same amount of charge in a circuit as sent by the given AC in its half cycle. • The average value of alternating quantities over complete cycle is zero.	$I_{av} = \dfrac{1}{T/2}\int_0^{T/2} I\, dt = \dfrac{2}{\pi} I_0 = 0.63\, I_0$ $I_{av} = 63.7\%$ of I_0 The mean value of alternating emf is $E_{av} = \dfrac{2E_0}{\pi} = 0.637 E_0 = 63.7\%$ of E_0
(iv)	The rms value of current or voltage	The root mean square value of AC is the value of direct current which produce same amount of heat as produced by given AC for same time duration of a complete cycle.	$I_{rms} = \dfrac{I_0}{\sqrt{2}} = 0.707\, I_0 = 70.7\%$ of I_0 $E_{rms} = \dfrac{E_0}{\sqrt{2}} = 0.707\, E_0 = 70.7\%$ of E_0
(v)	Phase	**Phase** is a quantity that represents both the instantaneous value and direction of alternating quantity. Its unit is radian.	$I = I_0 \sin(\omega t \pm \phi)$, initial phase = ϕ and instantaneous phase = ωt.
(vi)	Phase difference	**Phase difference** is the difference of phase between voltage and current.	If $V = V_0 \sin(\omega t + \phi_1)$ and $I = I_0 \sin(\omega t + \phi_2)$, phase difference, $\phi = \phi_2 - \phi_1$ (relative to voltage) and $\phi = \phi_1 - \phi_2$ (relative to current).

AC Circuit Elements

- The basic elements of AC circuits are resistor, inductor and capacitor.
- **Reactance** is the opposition offered by inductor or capacitor to the flow of alternating current through it.It is of two types as given below

  (*i*) **Inductive reactance** is the opposition offered by inductive circuit and given by $X_L = \omega L = 2\pi f L$.

  (*ii*) **Capacitive reactance** is the opposition offered by capacitive circuit and given by $X_C = 1/\omega C = 1/2\pi f C$.
- **Impedance** is the opposition offered by AC circuit to the flow of AC through it. Its unit is ohm (Ω).

The various features of these circuit elements are tabulated below (for applied emf $E = E_0 \sin \omega t$)

Circuit element	Instantaneous current	Peak current	Phase difference	Power factor	Power	Phasor diagram	Graph
Resistor only	$I = I_0 \sin \omega t$	$\frac{V_0}{R}$	0°	1	$\frac{V_0 I_0}{2}$	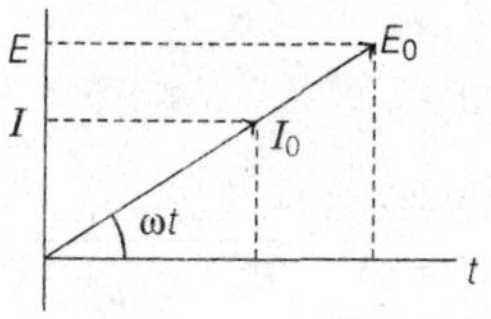	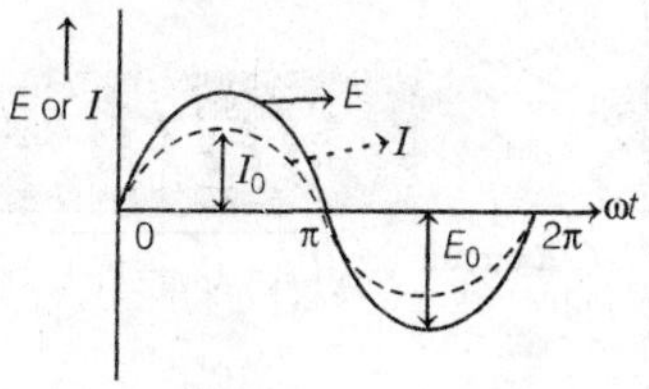
Inductor only	$I = I_0 \sin\left(\omega t - \frac{\pi}{2}\right)$	$\frac{V_0}{X_L}$	90° (current lags the voltage in phase by 90° or π/2)	0	0	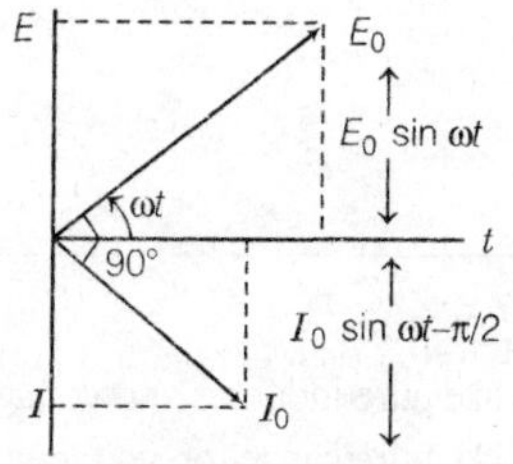	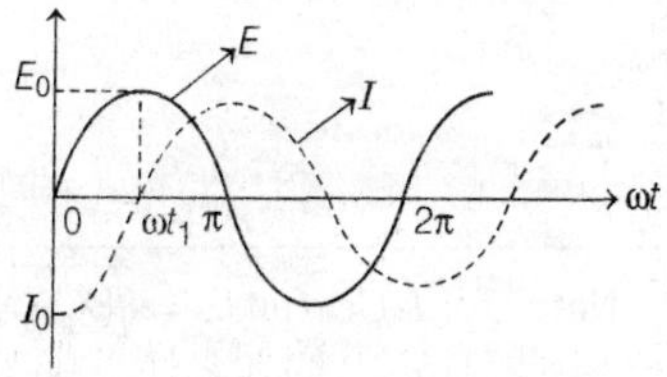
Capacitor only	$I = I_0 \sin\left(\omega t + \frac{\pi}{2}\right)$	$\frac{V_0}{X_C}$	90° (current leads the voltage in phase by 90° or π/2)	0	0	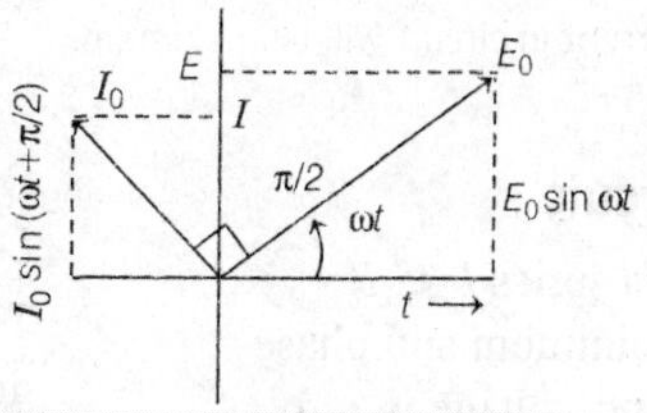	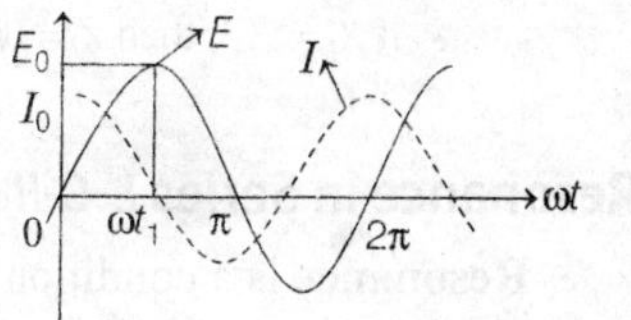

Power in an AC Circuit

- It is the product of voltage and the component of current which is in phase with voltage and given by $P = VI \cos \phi$, where V and I are rms values of voltage and currents.
- **Instantaneous power** of AC is given by $P = VI = V_0 I_0 \sin \omega t \sin(\omega t + \phi)$
- **Average power** of AC is given by $P_{av} = V_{rms} I_{rms} \cos \phi = \frac{1}{2} V_0 I_0 \cos \phi$
- **Power factor** is the cosine of angle of lag or lead or the ratio of resistance and impedance.

  It is given by $\cos \phi = \frac{\text{True power}}{\text{Apparent power}} = \frac{P_{av}}{V_{rms} I_{rms}}$

Series AC Circuit

The circuit elements can be combined in series circuit as given in the table below with their features

Combination	Voltage (V)	Current (I)	Impedance (Z)	Phase difference (ϕ)	Power factor ($\cos\phi$)	Phasor diagram
R-C circuit	$\sqrt{V_R^2 + V_C^2}$	$I_0 \sin(\omega t + \phi)$	$\sqrt{R^2 + X_C^2}$	$\tan^{-1}\frac{X_C}{R}$	$\frac{R}{\sqrt{R^2 + X_C^2}}$	
R-L circuit	$\sqrt{V_R^2 + V_L^2}$	$I_0 \sin(\omega t - \phi)$	$\sqrt{R^2 + X_L^2}$	$\tan^{-1}\frac{X_L}{R}$	$\frac{R}{\sqrt{R^2 + X_L^2}}$	
L-C-R circuit	$\sqrt{V_R^2 + (V_L - V_C)^2}$	$I_0 \sin(\omega t - \phi)$	$\sqrt{R^2 + (X_L - X_C)^2}$	$\tan^{-1}\left(\frac{X_L - X_C}{R}\right)$	$\frac{R}{\sqrt{R^2 + (X_L - X_C)^2}}$	

Note For *L-C* circuit, $Z = \sqrt{(X_L - X_C)^2}$ or $X_L - X_C$

- If $X_L > X_C$, circuit will behave like pure inductor and voltage leads by current by $\pi/2$.
- If $X_L < X_C$, circuit will behave like pure capacitor, voltage lags by current by $\pi/2$.
- If $X_L = X_C$, then $Z = 0$, current in circuit will be maximum.

Resonance in Series *L-C-R* Circuit

- **Resonance** is a condition in a series *L-C-R* circuit, when impedance is minimum and phase difference between current and voltage is zero.

  Then, (ω_r) $X_L = X_C$.

  At resonant frequency,

  $$\omega_0 = \frac{1}{\sqrt{LC}}$$

  or $$f_0 = \frac{1}{2\pi\sqrt{LC}}.$$

  Resonant frequency is independent of resistance.

  At resonating frequency,

  $$Z = R = Z_{\min}$$

  and $$I = \frac{V}{Z} = I_{\max}.$$

- **Quality factor** is a measure of sharpness of the resonance of an *L-C-R* circuit.

  The variation of *Q*-factor in series *L-C-R* circuit with ω is expressed graphically below

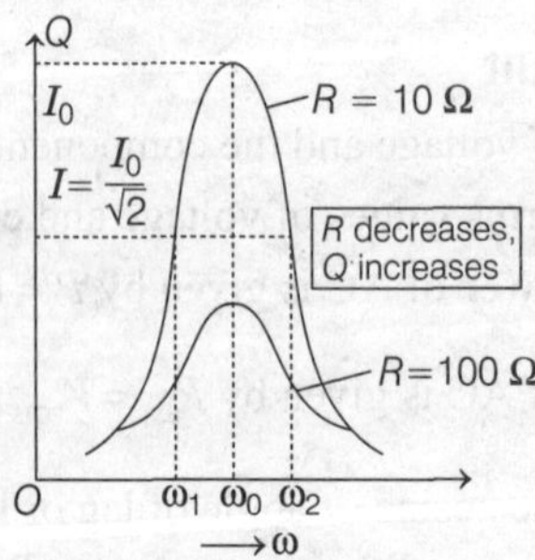

- The quantity ($Q = \omega_0 / 2\Delta\omega$) is the measure of sharpness of resonance, where $\omega_1 - \omega_2 = 2\Delta\omega$ is called bandwidth of the circuit, $\omega_1 = \omega_0 + \Delta\omega$ and $\omega_2 = \omega_0 - \Delta\omega$.

Note
- *Q*-factor denotes the sharpness of tuning.
- Smaller the bandwidth ($\Delta\omega$), the sharper or narrower is the resonance.

Growth and Decay of Current in *L-R* Circuit

Conditions and terms related to *L-R* circuit alongwith its graphs can be shown in tabular form below

Conditions	Currents	Graphs
Growth of current	$I = I_0(1 - e^{-t/\tau_L})$ At $t = 0, I = 0$ At $t = \tau_L$, $I = I_0\left(1 - \frac{1}{e}\right) = 0.63 I_0$ (where, $\tau_L = \frac{L}{R}$ = time constant and $I_0 = \frac{E}{R}$ = maximum current).	
Decay of current	$I = I_0\, e^{-t/\tau_L}$ At $t = 0, I = I_0$ At $t = \tau_L$, $I = \frac{I_0}{e} = 0.37 I_0$	

Note When inductor having resistance is connected to battery, the growth and decay, where $\tau = \frac{L}{R}$ = time constant.

Charging and Discharging of Capacitor

In series *R-C* circuit, this can be shown in table below

Charging	Discharging
(*i*) Charge, $q = q_0(1 - e^{-t/RC})$	$q = q_0 e^{-t/RC}$ ($\tau = RC$ = time constant of circuit)
(*ii*) Potential, $V = V_0(1 - e^{-t/RC})$	$V = V_0 e^{-t/RC}$
(*iii*) Current, $I = \frac{E}{R} e^{(-t/\tau)}$	$I = -I_0 e^{t/\tau}$
(*iv*) At $t = \tau$, $q = q_0\left(1 - \frac{1}{e}\right) = 0.63 q_0$	At $t = \tau$, $q = \frac{q_0}{e} = 0.37 q_0$

(*v*) Graph,

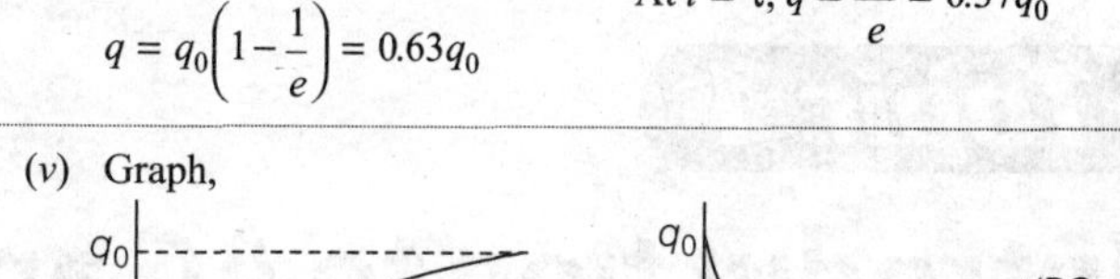
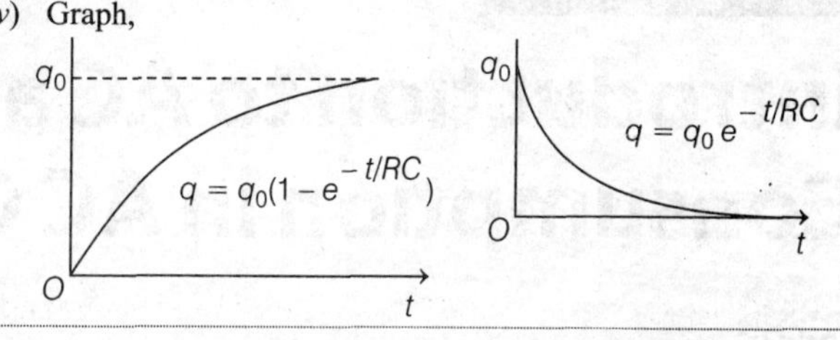

L-C Oscillations

- These are the electrical oscillations of constant amplitude and frequency which are produced when a charged capacitor is allowed to discharge through a non-resistive inductor.
- Terms related to *L-C* oscillations are shown in tabular form below, where $q = q_0 \cos(\omega t + \phi)$ and $I = I_0 \sin(\omega t + \phi)$.

Terms	Equation	Frequency	Electric energy	Magnetic energy
Expressions	$\frac{d^2q}{dt^2} + \frac{1}{LC} q = 0$	$f = \frac{\omega}{2\pi} = \frac{1}{2\pi\sqrt{LC}}$	$U = \frac{q_0^2}{2C}\cos^2(\omega t + \phi)$	$U = \frac{q_0^2}{2C}\sin^2(\omega t + \phi)$

Wattless current is the current which consumes no power for its maintenance in the circuit.

Choke Coil

It is a device having high inductance and negligible resistance.

It is used to control current in AC circuit, so that the power loss can be minimised like in fluorescent tubes.

Transformer

- It is a device which transforms a strong AC at low voltage into a weaker AC at high voltage or *vice-versa* based on the principle of electromagnetic induction.
- For an ideal transformer, $\frac{e_s}{e_p} = \frac{V_s}{V_p} = \frac{N_s}{N_p} = \frac{I_p}{I_s} = k$

where, k is known as the transformation ratio.

- For a step-up transformer $k > 1$ but for a step-down transformer, $k < 1$.
- The efficiency of a transformer is given by

$$\eta = \frac{\text{output power}}{\text{input power}} = \frac{V_s I_s}{V_p I_p}$$

- In a transformer, some power is lost due to following reasons
  (*i*) Heating due to winding resistance and eddy current losses.
  (*ii*) Magnetic flux leakage and hysteresis loss.
- To minimise these losses, the transformer core is made up of a laminated soft iron strips.

Topical Practice Questions

All the exam questions of this chapter have been divided into 4 topics as listed below

Topic 1

Introduction to AC and Power Consumption in AC Circuits

2018

1 An inductor 20 mH, a capacitor 100 μF and a resistor 50 Ω are connected in series across a source of emf $V = 10\sin 314\,t$. The power loss in the circuit is **[AIIMS]**

(a) 2.74 W (b) 0.43 W (c) 0.79 W (d) 1.13 W

2016

2 An inductor 20 mH, a capacitor 50 μF and a resistor 40 Ω are connected in series across a source of emf $V = 10\sin 340\,t$. The power loss in AC circuit is **[NEET]**

(a) 0.67 W (b) 0.76 W (c) 0.89 W (d) 0.51 W

2015

3 A resistance R draws power P when connected to an AC source. If an inductance is now placed in series with the resistance, such that the impedance of the circuit becomes Z the power drawn will be **[AIPMT]**

(a) $P\left(\frac{R}{Z}\right)$ (b) $P\sqrt{\frac{R}{Z}}$ (c) $P\,(R/Z)^2$ (d) P

2014

4 In *L-C-R* series circuit, an alternating emf e and current i are given by the equations $e = 100\sin(100\,t)$ volt.

$$i = 100\sin\left(100\,t + \frac{\pi}{3}\right)\text{ mA}$$

The average power dissipated in the circuit will be **[MHT CET]**

(a) 100 W (b) 10 W (c) 5 W (d) 2.5 W

5 The average power dissipated in AC circuit is 2 W. If a current flowing through a circuit is 2 A, impedance is 1 Ω, then what is the power factor of the circuit? **[KCET]**

(a) 0.5 (b) 1
(c) Zero (d) $1/\sqrt{2}$

6 A hot wire ammeter reads 10 A in an AC circuit. The peak value of the current will be **[KCET]**

(a) $\frac{3}{\pi}$ A (b) $\frac{10}{\sqrt{2}}$ A
(c) $10\sqrt{2}$ A (d) 6π A

2013

7 A coil of self-inductance L is connected in series with a bulb B and AC source. Brightness of the bulb decreases when **[NEET]**

(a) frequency of the AC source is decreased
(b) number of turns in the coil is reduced
(c) a capacitance of reactance $X_C = X_L$ is included in the same circuit
(d) an iron rod is inserted in the coil

2011

8 In an AC circuit, V and I are given by $V = 150\sin(150\,t)$ volt and $I = 150\sin 150\,t + \left(\frac{\pi}{3}\right)$ ampere.

The power dissipated in the circuit is **[KCET]**

(a) 106 W (b) 150 W
(c) 5625 W (d) zero

9 An AC ammeter is used to measure current in a circuit. When a given direct current passes through the circuit, the AC ammeter reads 3A. When another alternating current passes through the circuit, the AC ammeter reads 4A. Then, the reading of this ammeter, if DC and AC flow through the circuit simultaneously, is **[AIIMS]**
(a) 3 A (b) 4 A (c) 7 A (d) 5 A

10 An AC source is 120 V- 60 Hz. The value of voltage after $(1/720)$ s from start will be **[BCECE]**
(a) 20.2 V (b) 42.4 V
(c) 84.8 V (d) 106.8 V

11 Alternating current is transmitted at far off places **[JCECE]**
(a) at high voltage and low current
(b) at high voltage and high current
(c) at low voltage and low current
(d) at low voltage and high current

2008

12 In an AC circuit, the emf (e) and the current (i) at any instant are given respectively by **[CBSE AIPMT]**

$$e = E_0 \sin \omega t \Rightarrow i = I_0 \sin (\omega t - \phi)$$

The average power in the circuit over one cycle of AC is
(a) $\frac{E_0 I_0}{2}$ (b) $\frac{E_0 I_0}{2} \sin \phi$ (c) $\frac{E_0 I_0}{2} \cos \phi$ (d) $E_0 I_0$

13 Alternating current cannot be measured by DC ammeter, because **[Haryana PMT]**
(a) AC cannot pass through DC ammeter
(b) AC changes direction
(c) Average value of current for complete cycle is zero
(d) DC ammeter will get damaged

2007

14 The instantaneous voltage through a device of impedance $20\,\Omega$ is $e = 80 \sin 100\pi t$. The effective value of the current is **[Kerala CEE]**
(a) 3 A (b) 2.828 A
(c) 1.732 A (d) 4 A
(e) $\sqrt{2}$ A

15 For high frequency, capacitor offers **[RPMT]**
(a) more resistance (b) less resistance
(c) zero resistance (d) None of these

16 If the power factor changes from 1/2 to 1/4, then what is the increase in impedance in AC? **[Punjab PMET]**
(a) 20% (b) 50% (c) 25% (d) 100%

2006

17 If impedance is $\sqrt{3}$ times of resistance, then find phase difference. **[RPMT]**
(a) Zero (b) 30°
(c) 60° (d) Data is incomplete

18 If reading of an ammeter is 10 A, then the peak value of current is **[MP PMT]**
(a) $\frac{10}{\sqrt{2}}$ A (b) $\frac{5}{\sqrt{2}}$ A (c) $20\sqrt{2}$ A (d) $10\sqrt{2}$ A

19 An AC is represented by $e = 220 \sin (100\pi) t$ volt and is applied over a resistance of $110\,\Omega$. The heat produced in 7 min is **[Haryana PMT]**
(a) 11×10^3 cal (b) 22×10^3 cal
(c) 33×10^3 cal (d) 25×10^3 cal

20 An alternating voltage $V = V_0 \sin \omega t$ is applied across a circuit. As a result, the current $I = I_0 \sin (\omega t - \pi/2)$ flows in it. The power consumed in the circuit per cycle is **[Guj CET]**
(a) $0.5 V_0 I_0$ W
(b) $0.707 V_0 I_0$ W
(c) $1.919 V_0 I_0$ W
(d) zero

21 If an AC produces same heat as that produced by a steady current of 4 A, then peak value of current is **[JCECE]**
(a) 4 A (b) 1.56 A (c) 5.6 A (d) 1.41 A

22 The potential difference across an instrument in an AC circuit of frequency f is V and the current through it is I such that $V = 5 \cos 2\pi f t$ volt and $I = 2 \sin 2\pi f t$ amp. The power dissipated in the instrument is **[JCECE]**
(a) zero (b) 10 W
(c) 5 W (d) 2.5 W

2005

23 An alternating current is given by $I = I_1 \cos \omega t + I_2 \sin \omega t$ The root mean square current is given by **[AMU, Manipal]**
(a) $\frac{(I_1 + I_2)}{\sqrt{2}}$ (b) $\frac{(I_1 + I_2)^2}{2}$
(c) $\sqrt{\frac{I_1^2 + I_2^2}{2}}$ (d) $\frac{\sqrt{I_1^2 - I_2^2}}{2}$

24 The peak value of AC voltage on a 220 V mains is **[RPMT]**
(a) $240\sqrt{2}$ V (b) $230\sqrt{2}$ V
(c) $220\sqrt{2}$ V (d) $200\sqrt{2}$ V

25 The time taken by an alternating current of 50 Hz in reaching from zero to its maximum value will be **[J&K CET]**
(a) 0.5 s (b) 0.005 s
(c) 0.05 s (d) 5 s

26 The power factor of series L-C-R circuit when at resonance is **[KCET]**
(a) zero
(b) 0.5
(c) 1.0
(d) depends on values of L, C and R

27 The instantaneous values of alternating current and voltages in a circuit given as

$$i = \frac{1}{\sqrt{2}} \sin(100\pi t) \text{ amp}, \; e = \frac{1}{\sqrt{2}} \sin(100\pi t + \pi/3) \text{ volt}$$

The average power (in watts) consumed in the circuit is **[CBSE AIPMT]**

(a) $\frac{1}{4}$ (b) $\frac{\sqrt{3}}{4}$
(c) $\frac{1}{2}$ (d) $\frac{1}{8}$

28 In an electrical circuit R, L, C and AC voltage source are all connected in series. When L is removed from the circuit, the phase difference between the voltage and the current in the circuit is $\pi/3$. If instead C is removed from the circuit, the phase difference is again $\pi/3$. The power factor of the circuit is **[CBSE AIPMT]**

(a) 1/2 (b) $1/\sqrt{2}$
(c) 1 (d) $\frac{\sqrt{3}}{2}$

29 As given in the figure, a series circuit connected across a 200 V, 60 Hz line consists of a capacitor of capacitive reactance 30Ω, a non-inductive resistor of 44 Ω and a coil of inductive reactance 90Ω and resistance 36Ω.

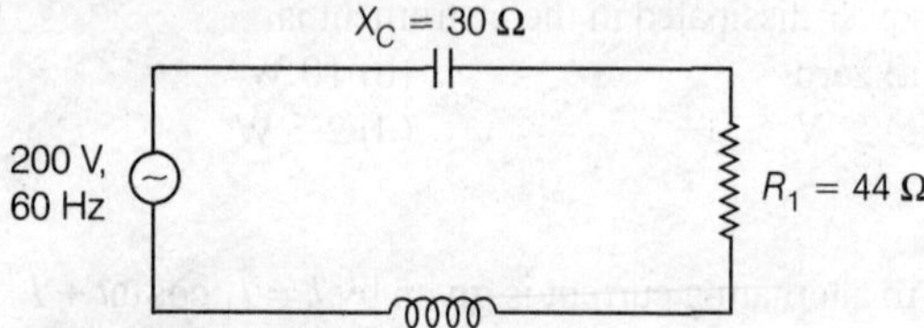

The power dissipated in the coil is **[AMU]**

(a) 320 W (b) 176 W
(c) 144 W (d) 0 W

30 The power factor of an R-L circuit is $1/\sqrt{2}$. If the frequency of AC is doubled, then what will be the power factor? **[AFMC]**

(a) $1/\sqrt{3}$ (b) $1/\sqrt{5}$
(c) $1/\sqrt{7}$ (d) $1/\sqrt{11}$

31 Average power in a L-C-R circuit depends upon **[MHT CET]**

(a) current
(b) phase difference only
(c) emf
(d) current, emf and phase difference

32 A coil of inductive reactance 31 Ω has a resistance of 8 Ω. It is placed in series with a condenser of capacitive reactance 25 Ω. The combination is connected to an AC source of 110 V. The power factor of the circuit is **[MP PMT]**

(a) 0.56 (b) 0.64
(c) 0.80 (d) 0.33

33 The peak value of an alternating current is 5 A and its frequency is 60 Hz. Find its rms value and time taken to reach the peak value of current starting from zero. **[MHT CET]**

(a) 3.536 A, 4.167 ms
(b) 3.536 A, 15 ms
(c) 6.07 A, 10 ms
(d) 2.536 A, 4.167 ms

34 The power dissipated in an AC circuit is zero, if the circuit is **[Kerala CEE]**

(a) purely resistive
(b) purely inductive only
(c) either purely inductive or purely capacitive
(d) purely capacitive only
(e) L-C-R circuit

35 The average power dissipated in a pure capacitance AC circuit is **[J&K CET]**

(a) CV (b) zero (c) $\frac{1}{CV^2}$ (d) $\frac{1}{4}CV^2$

36 Power dissipated in an L-C-R series circuit connected to an AC source of emf e is **[CG PMT]**

(a) $\dfrac{e^2 R}{\left[R^2 + \left(\omega L - \frac{1}{\omega C}\right)^2\right]}$

(b) $\dfrac{e^2 \sqrt{R^2 + \left(\omega L - \frac{1}{\omega C}\right)^2}}{R}$

(c) $\dfrac{e^2 \left[R^2 + \left(\omega L - \frac{1}{\omega C}\right)^2\right]}{R}$

(d) $\dfrac{e^2 R}{\sqrt{R^2 + \left(\omega L - \frac{1}{\omega C}\right)^2}}$

37 The power factor in a circuit connected to an AC power supply has a value which is **[Manipal]**

(a) unity when the circuit contains only inductance
(b) unity when the circuit contains only resistance
(c) zero when the circuit contains an ideal resistance only
(d) unity when the circuit contains an ideal capacitance only

38 For a series L-C-R circuit at resonance, the statement which is not true? **[KCET]**

(a) Peak energy stored by a capacitor = Peak energy stored by an inductor
(b) Average power = Apparent power
(c) Wattless current is zero
(d) Power factor is zero

Answers

1 (c)	2 (d)	3 (a)	4 (d)	5 (a)	6 (c)	7 (d)	8 (c)	9 (d)	10 (c)
11 (a)	12 (c)	13 (c)	14 (b)	15 (b)	16 (d)	17 (c)	18 (d)	19 (b)	20 (d)
21 (c)	22 (a)	23 (c)	24 (c)	25 (b)	26 (c)	27 (d)	28 (c)	29 (a)	30 (b)
31 (d)	32 (c)	33 (a)	34 (c)	35 (b)	36 (a)	37 (b)	38 (d)		

Explanations

1 *(c)* Given, inductance, $L = 20$ mH

$$= 20 \times 10^{-3}\,\text{H}$$

Capacitance, $C = 100\,\mu\text{F} = 100 \times 10^{-6}$ F

Resistance, $R = 50\,\Omega$

$$\text{emf}, V = 10 \sin 314t \quad \ldots\text{(i)}$$

$\because$ The general equation of emf is given as

$$V = V_0 \sin \omega t \quad \ldots\text{(ii)}$$

On comparing Eqs. (i) and (ii), we get

$$V_0 = 10\,\text{V}$$
$$\omega = 314\,\text{rad s}^{-1}$$

The power loss associated with the given AC circuit is given as

$$P = V_{\text{rms}} I_{\text{rms}} \cos\phi$$
$$= V_{\text{rms}}\left(\frac{V_{\text{rms}}}{Z}\right)\left(\frac{R}{Z}\right)$$
$$= \left(\frac{V_{\text{rms}}}{Z}\right)^2 R = \left(\frac{V_0}{\sqrt{2}\cdot Z}\right)^2 R \quad \ldots\text{(i)}$$

$\therefore$ Impedance, $Z = \sqrt{R^2 + (X_L - X_C)^2}$

$$= \sqrt{R^2 + \left(\omega L - \frac{1}{\omega C}\right)^2}$$

$\therefore$ Substituting the given values in the above equation, we get

$$= \sqrt{(50)^2 + \left[(314 \times 20 \times 10^{-3}) - \frac{1}{314 \times 10^{-4}}\right]^2}$$
$$= \sqrt{2500 + [6280 \times 10^{-3} - 0.00318 \times 10^4]^2}$$
$$= \sqrt{2500 + (25.56)^2}$$
$$= 56.15\,\Omega \simeq 56\,\Omega$$

Now, substituting this values in Eq. (i), we get

$$P = \left(\frac{10}{\sqrt{2} \times 56}\right)^2 \times 50 = \frac{100}{2 \times 3136} \times 50$$
$$= 0.79\,\text{W}$$

Thus, the power loss in the circuit is 0.79 W.

2 *(d)* Given, inductance, $L = 20$ mH

Capacitance, $C = 50\,\mu\text{F}$

Resistance, $R = 40\,\Omega$

emf, $V = 10 \sin 340\,t$

$\because$ Power loss in AC circuit will be given as

$$P_{\text{av}} = I_V^2 R = \left[\frac{E_V}{Z}\right]^2 \cdot R = \left(\frac{10}{\sqrt{2}}\right)^2 \cdot 40$$
$$\left[\frac{1}{40^2 + \left(340 \times 20 \times 10^3 - \frac{1}{340 \times 50 \times 10^{-6}}\right)^2}\right]$$
$$= \frac{100}{2} \times 40 \times \frac{1}{1600 + (6.8 - 58.8)^2}$$
$$= \frac{2000}{1600 + 2704} \approx 0.46\,\text{W} \approx 0.51\,\text{W}$$

3 *(a)* When a resistor is connected to an AC source. The power drawn will be of

$$P = V_{\text{rms}} \cdot I_{\text{rms}} = V_{\text{rms}} \cdot \frac{V_{\text{rms}}}{R}$$
$$\Rightarrow \quad V_{\text{rms}}^2 = PR$$

When an inductor is connected in series with the resistor, then the power drawn will be

$$P' = V_{\text{rms}} \cdot I_{\text{rms}} \cos\phi$$

where, ϕ = phase difference.

$$\therefore \quad P' = \frac{V_{\text{rms}}^2}{R} \cdot \frac{R}{Z} = \frac{P \cdot R}{R} \cdot \frac{R}{Z}$$
$$\Rightarrow \quad P' = \frac{P \cdot R}{Z} = P\left(\frac{R}{Z}\right)$$

4 *(d)* Average power,

$$P_{\text{av}} = E_V I_V \cos\phi = \frac{E_0}{\sqrt{2}} \cdot \frac{I_0}{\sqrt{2}} \cos\phi$$
$$= \frac{100\,\text{V}}{\sqrt{2}} \times \frac{100 \times 10^{-3}\,\text{A}}{\sqrt{2}} \cos\frac{\pi}{3}$$
$$= \frac{100 \times 100}{2} \times 10^{-3} \times \frac{1}{2} = 2.5\,\text{W}$$

5 *(a)* Given, average power, $\overline{P} = 2$ W,

$$i_{\text{rms}} = 2\,\text{A}$$

and impedance, $Z = 1\,\Omega$.

Power factor, $(\cos\phi) = ?$

We know that, $\overline{P} = V_{\text{rms}} \times i_{\text{rms}} \cdot \cos\phi$

$$\Rightarrow \quad \overline{P} = i_{\text{rms}}^2\, Z \cdot \cos\phi$$
$$(\because V_{\text{rms}} = i_{\text{rms}} \cdot Z)$$
$$\cos\phi = \frac{P}{i_{\text{rms}}^2 \cdot Z} = \frac{2}{(2)^2 \times 1}$$
$$= \frac{2}{4} = \frac{1}{2} = 0.5$$

6 *(c)* The reading of hot wire ammeter or rms value of current,

$$I_{\text{rms}} = 10\,\text{A}$$

The peak value of the current is given by

$$I_0 = \sqrt{2} \times I_{\text{rms}} = \sqrt{2} \times 10 = 10\sqrt{2}\,\text{A}$$

7 *(d)* As,

$$Z = \sqrt{R^2 + X_L^2} = \sqrt{R^2 + (2\pi f L)^2}$$

and $\quad I = \dfrac{V}{Z}, P = I^2 R$

i.e. with insertion of iron rod $L \uparrow$

$\Rightarrow Z\uparrow, I\downarrow$ and $P\downarrow$

8 *(c)* Given, $V = 150 \sin (150t)$ volt

and $I = 150 \sin (150t + \pi/3)$ ampere

$$\therefore \quad I_0 = 150\,\text{A} \quad \text{and} \quad V_0 = 150\,\text{V}$$

Power, $P = \dfrac{1}{2} V_0 I_0 \cos\phi$

$$= 0.5 \times 150 \times 150 \times \cos 60°$$
$$= 5625\,\text{W}$$

9 *(d)* Quantity of heat liberated in the ammeter of resistance R

(*i*) due to direct current of 3 A

$$= [(3)^2 R / J)]$$

(*ii*) due to alternating current of 4 A

$$= [(4)^2 R / J)]$$

$\therefore$ Total heat produced per second

$$= \frac{(3)^2 R}{J} + \frac{(4)^2 R}{J} = \frac{25R}{J}$$

Let the equivalent alternating current be I virtual ampere, then

$$\frac{I^2 R}{J} = \frac{25R}{J} \Rightarrow I = 5\,\text{A}$$

10 (c) $V = V_0 \sin \omega t \Rightarrow V = V_{rms}\sqrt{2} \sin \omega t$

After, $t = \frac{1}{720}$ s

$$V = 120\sqrt{2} \sin 2\pi f t$$
$$= 120\sqrt{2} \sin\left(2\pi \times 60 \times \frac{1}{720}\right)$$
$$= 120\sqrt{2} \sin\frac{\pi}{6} = 120\sqrt{2} \times \frac{1}{2}$$
$$= 60\sqrt{2} = 84.8 \text{ V}$$

11 (a) Alternating current is transmitted at far off places at high voltage and low current.

12 (c) Given, $e = E_0 \sin \omega t$

and $i = I_0 \sin(\omega t - \phi)$

Instantaneous power, $P_{int} = ei$

$= E_0 I_0 \sin \omega t \sin(\omega t - \phi)$

Average power over one cycle is

$$P_{av} = \frac{1}{T}\sum_0^T P_{int}\, dt$$
$$= \frac{1}{T}\sum_0^T E_0 I_0 \sin \omega t \sin(\omega t - \phi) dt$$
$$= \frac{1}{T} \times E_0 I_0 \sum_0^T (\sin^2 \omega t \cos \phi + \sin \phi \sin \omega t \cos \omega t) dt$$
$$= \frac{E_0 I_0}{T}\left[\cos \phi \times \frac{T}{2} \pm 0\right]$$
$$= \frac{(E_0 I_0 \cos \phi) T/2}{T} = \frac{E_0 I_0 \cos \phi}{2}$$

where, $\cos \phi$ is called the power factor of an AC circuit.

13 (c) The full cycle of alternating current consists of two half cycles. For one-half, current is positive and for second-half, current is negative. Therefore, for an AC cycle, the net value of current average out to zero. While the DC ammeter, reads the average value. Hence, the alternating current cannot be measured by DC ammeter.

14 (b) The instantaneous voltage through the given device, $e = 80 \sin 100\pi t$.

Comparing the given instantaneous voltage with standard instantaneous voltage

$e = e_0 \sin \omega t$, we get

$e_0 = 80$ V

where, e_0 is the peak value of voltage.

Impedance $(Z) = 20\,\Omega$

Peak value of current,

$$I_0 = \frac{e_0}{Z} = \frac{80}{20} = 4 \text{ A}$$

Effective value of current (root mean square value of current),

$$I_{rms} = \frac{I_0}{\sqrt{2}} = \frac{4}{\sqrt{2}} = 2\sqrt{2} = 2.828 \text{ A}$$

15 (b) At a higher frequency, the charge on the capacitor plates will vary more rapidly, so $\left(\frac{dq}{dt}\right)$ will be higher resulting in an increase in the instantaneous current $\left(i = \frac{dq}{dt}\right)$.

This means lower capacitive reactance, i.e. less resistance.

16 (d) Power factor, $\cos \phi = \frac{R}{Z}$

If R is constant, then $\cos \phi \propto \frac{1}{Z}$

$$\therefore \frac{Z_1}{Z_2} = \frac{\cos \phi_2}{\cos \phi_1} = \frac{1/4}{1/2} = \frac{1}{2} \Rightarrow Z_2 = 2Z_1$$

$\therefore$ Percentage change

$$= \frac{2Z_1 - Z_1}{Z_1} \times 100 = 100\%$$

17 (c) From the relation, $\tan \theta = \frac{X_L - X_C}{R}$

where, $X_L - X_C$ is the net impedance of the circuit.

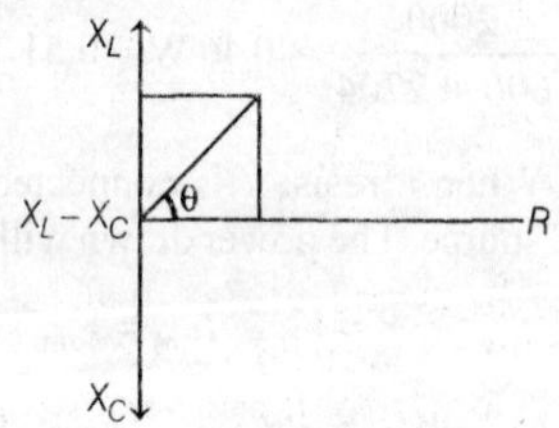

$$\Rightarrow \theta = \tan^{-1}\left(\frac{X_L - X_C}{R}\right) = \tan^{-1}\left(\frac{Z}{R}\right)$$
$$\Rightarrow \theta = \tan^{-1}(\sqrt{3}R/R)$$
$$\Rightarrow \theta = \tan^{-1}(\sqrt{3}) = 60°$$

18 (d) Ammeter reads the root mean square value of current (i_{rms}) which is related to the peak value of current (i_0) by the relation

$$i_{rms} = \frac{i_0}{\sqrt{2}} \Rightarrow i_0 = \sqrt{2} \times i_{rms}$$
$$= \sqrt{2} \times 10 \text{ A} = 10\sqrt{2} \text{ A}$$

19 (b) Heat, $H = \frac{I_{rms}^2 RT}{J}$ cal

$$\left(\because I_{rms} = \frac{I_0}{\sqrt{2}} = \frac{220/110}{\sqrt{2}} = \sqrt{2}\right)$$
$$\therefore H = \frac{(\sqrt{2})^2 \times 110 \times (7 \times 60)}{4.2}$$
$$= 22 \times 10^3 \text{ cal}$$

20 (d) Given, $V = V_0 \sin \omega t$

and $I = I_0 \sin(\omega t - \pi/2)$

It is obvious that current lags behind the voltage by $\pi/2$ in phase.

$\therefore$ Power consumed in the circuit,

$$P = \frac{1}{2} V_0 I_0 \cos \phi$$

But $\phi = \pi/2 = 90°$

$$\therefore P = \frac{1}{2} V_0 I_0 \cos 90° = 0$$

$(\because \cos 90° = 0)$

21 (c) The peak value of current (I_0) is given by, $I_0 = \sqrt{2} I_{rms}$

where, I_{rms} is known as root mean square value of current.

Given, $I_{rms} = 4$ A

$\Rightarrow I_0 = \sqrt{2} \times 4 = 5.6$ A

22 (a) Average power dissipated in an AC circuit is given by, $P = VI \cos \phi$

where, V is voltage, I the current, ϕ the phase difference.

Given, $V = 5 \cos 2\pi f t$

Using $\sin(90° + \theta) = \cos \theta$, we have

$V = 5 \sin[2\pi f t + (\pi/2)]$

and $I = 2 \sin 2\pi f t$

Hence, phase difference between V and I is $\phi = \pi/2$.

$$P = V \cdot I \cos \phi = V \cdot I \cos(\pi/2) = 0$$

23 (c) The equation of AC is

$$I = I_1 \cos \omega t + I_2 \sin \omega t$$

The resultant current is given by

$$I_0 = \sqrt{I_1^2 + I_2^2} \quad \text{...(i)}$$

Hence, the rms current from relation is

$$I_{rms} = \frac{I_0}{\sqrt{2}} = \frac{\sqrt{I_1^2 + I_2^2}}{\sqrt{2}} \quad \text{[from Eq. (i)]}$$
$$= \sqrt{\frac{I_1^2 + I_2^2}{2}}$$

24 (c) Here, rms voltage, $V_{rms} = 220$ V

Using the relation,

$$V_{rms} = \frac{\text{Peak voltage}}{\sqrt{2}} = \frac{V_P}{\sqrt{2}}$$

$\therefore$ Peak value of AC voltage,

$$V_P = 220\sqrt{2} \text{ V}$$

25 (b)

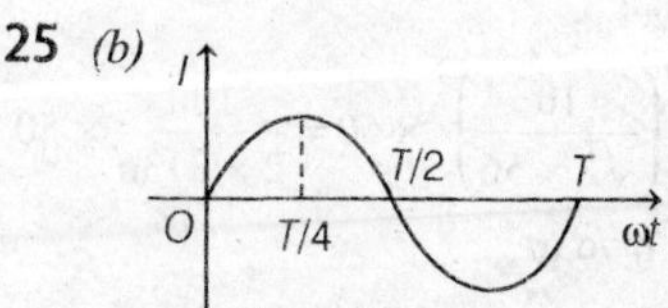

An alternating current is one whose magnitude changes continuously with time between zero and a maximum value and whose direction reverses periodically. The relation between frequency (f) and time (T) is

$$T = \frac{1}{f} = \frac{1}{50} = 0.02 \text{ s}$$

It is clear from the figure, time taken to reach the maximum value is

$$\frac{T}{4} = \frac{0.02}{4} = 0.005 \text{ s}$$

26 (c) At resonance, voltage and current are in phase. Average power of circuit is given by

$$P = E_{\text{rms}} \times I_{\text{rms}} \times \cos\phi$$

where, E_{rms} and I_{rms} are root mean square value of voltage and current and $\cos\phi$ is power factor.
In a series L-C-R circuit at resonance, voltage and current being in same phase, therefore $\phi = 0$.
Hence, power factor $= \cos\phi = \cos 0° = 1$.

27 (d) Given equations are

$$i = \frac{1}{\sqrt{2}} \sin(100\pi t) \text{ amp}$$

and $$e = \frac{1}{\sqrt{2}} \sin(100\pi t + \pi/3) \text{ volt}$$

$\Rightarrow \quad i_0 = \frac{1}{\sqrt{2}}$ and $e_0 = \frac{1}{\sqrt{2}}$

We know that, average power,

$$P_{\text{av}} = V_{\text{rms}} \times i_{\text{rms}} \cos\phi$$

$$= \frac{1}{2} \times \frac{1}{2} \times \cos 60°$$

$(\because i_{\text{rms}} = i_0/\sqrt{2}$ and $V_{\text{rms}} = V_0/\sqrt{2})$

$$= \frac{1}{2} \times \frac{1}{2} \times \frac{1}{2} = \frac{1}{8} \text{ W}$$

28 (c) Here, phase difference

$$\tan\phi = \frac{X_L - X_C}{R}$$

$$\Rightarrow \tan\frac{\pi}{3} = \frac{X_L - X_C}{R}$$

When L is removed, $\tan\frac{\pi}{3} = \frac{X_C}{R} = \sqrt{3}$

$\therefore \quad X_C = \sqrt{3}R \quad$ ...(i)

Similarly, when C is removed

$$\tan\frac{\pi}{3} = \frac{X_L}{R} = \sqrt{3}$$

$\Rightarrow \quad X_L = \sqrt{3}R$

$\Rightarrow \quad X_C = X_L \quad$ ...(ii) [from Eq. (i)]

Now, $\tan\phi = 0$

$\Rightarrow \quad \phi = 0°$

$\therefore$ Power factor, $\cos\phi = \cos 0° = 1$

29 (a)

$X_C = 30\ \Omega$; 200 V, 60 Hz; $R_1 = 44\ \Omega$

$X_L = 90\ \Omega,\ R_2 = 36\ \Omega,\ R_1 = 44\ \Omega$
$X_C = 30\ \Omega,\ V = 200\text{V}$
and total resistance,

$$R = R_1 + R_2 = 44 + 36 = 80\Omega$$

$$Z = \sqrt{R^2 + (X_L - X_C)^2}$$

$$= \sqrt{(80)^2 + (60)^2}$$

$$= \sqrt{6400 + 3600} = 100$$

Current, $I = \frac{V}{Z} = \frac{200}{100} = 2\text{A}$

Power dissipated in the coil,

$$P_{\text{av}} = I^2R = (2)^2 \times 80 = 320 \text{ W}$$

30 (b) Power factor,

$$\cos\phi = \frac{1}{\sqrt{2}} = \frac{R}{\sqrt{R^2 + \omega^2L^2}}$$

This gives, $\omega L = R$.
When ω is doubled, we find,

$$\cos\phi' = \frac{R}{\sqrt{R^2 + 4\omega^2L^2}}$$

$$= \frac{R}{\sqrt{R^2 + 4R^2}} = \frac{1}{\sqrt{5}}$$

31 (d) The average power of an L-C-R circuit, $P_{\text{av}} = V_{\text{rms}}\, i_{\text{rms}} \cos\phi$
Hence, the average power depends upon current, emf and phase difference.

32 (c) Power factor of AC circuit is given by

$$\cos\phi = \frac{R}{Z} \quad \text{...(i)}$$

where, R is resistance employed and Z the impedance of the circuit.

$$Z = \sqrt{R^2 + (X_L - X_C)^2} \quad \text{...(ii)}$$

Eqs. (i) and (ii), meet to give

$$\cos\phi = \frac{R}{\sqrt{R^2 + (X_L - X_C)^2}} \quad \text{...(iii)}$$

Given, $R = 8\ \Omega, X_L = 31\Omega$
and $X_C = 25\ \Omega$

$$\therefore \quad \cos\phi = \frac{8}{\sqrt{(8)^2 + (31 - 25)^2}}$$

$$= \frac{8}{\sqrt{64 + 36}} = \frac{8}{10} = 0.80$$

33 (a) $i_{\text{rms}} = \frac{i_0}{\sqrt{2}} = \frac{5}{\sqrt{2}} = 3.536 \text{ A}$

Time period, $T = \frac{1}{f} = \frac{1}{60} = 0.01675$

$$\therefore \quad t = \frac{T}{4} = 4.16 \text{ ms}$$

34 (c) The power in an AC circuit is given by $P = VI\cos\phi$.
where, ϕ = phase angle between V and I.
Thus, power is zero when $\cos\phi = 0$
$\Rightarrow \phi = 90°$
For both pure inductive and pure capacitive, the phase between current and voltage is 90°. Thus, they have zero power dissipation.

35 (b) Alternating voltage applied to a pure capacitance circuit is $E = E_0 \sin\omega t$
Then, through C, as current leads emf by a phase angle of $\pi/2$.

$$I = I_0 \sin(\omega t + \pi/2) = I_0 \cos\omega t$$

Work done over a complete cycle,

$$W = \int_0^T EI\, dt$$

$$= \int_0^T (E_0 \sin\omega t)(I_0 \cos\omega t)\, dt$$

$$= \frac{E_0I_0}{2} \int_0^T 2\sin\omega t \cos\omega t\, dt$$

$$= \frac{E_0I_0}{2} \int_0^T \sin 2\omega t\, dt$$

$$\Rightarrow W = \frac{E_0I_0}{2}\left[-\frac{\cos 2\omega t}{2\omega}\right]_0^T = \text{zero}$$

Hence, average power dissipated in a pure capacitance AC circuit is zero.

36 (a) Given, $e = e_{\text{rms}}$
Impedance, $Z = \sqrt{R^2 + (\omega L - 1/\omega C)^2}$
Also, $i = \frac{e}{Z}$
Now, power of AC circuit is given by

$$i^2R = \left(\frac{e}{Z}\right)^2 R$$

$$= \frac{e^2}{[\sqrt{R^2 + (\omega L - 1/\omega C)^2}\,]^2} R$$

$$= \frac{e^2R}{[R^2 + (\omega L - 1/\omega C)^2]}$$

37 (b) Power factor, $\cos\phi = \frac{R}{Z}$
When circuit contains only resistance, then $Z = R$

$$\therefore \quad \cos\phi = \frac{R}{R} = 1$$

38 (d) For a series L-C-R circuit at resonance,
Phase difference, $\phi = 0°$
$\Rightarrow$ Power factor $= \cos\phi = 1$

Topic 2

AC Circuits

2019

1 Find resonance frequency in the given circuit

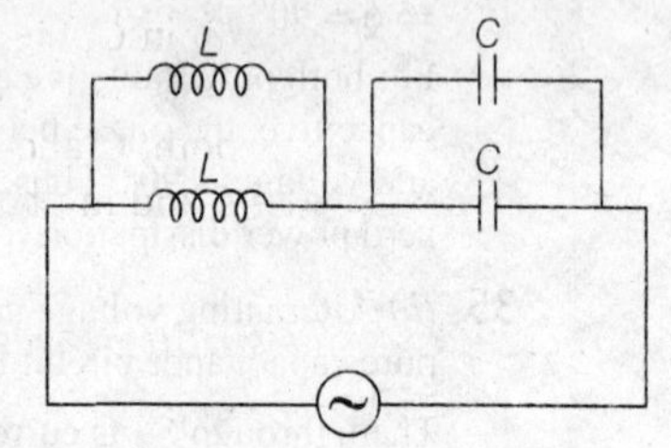

[JIPMER]

(a) $\frac{1}{\sqrt{LC}}$ (b) $\frac{2}{\sqrt{LC}}$ (c) $\frac{1}{2\sqrt{LC}}$ (d) $\frac{4}{\sqrt{LC}}$

2 If maximum energy is stored in a capacitor at $t = 0$, then find the time after which current in the circuit will be maximum. [AIIMS]

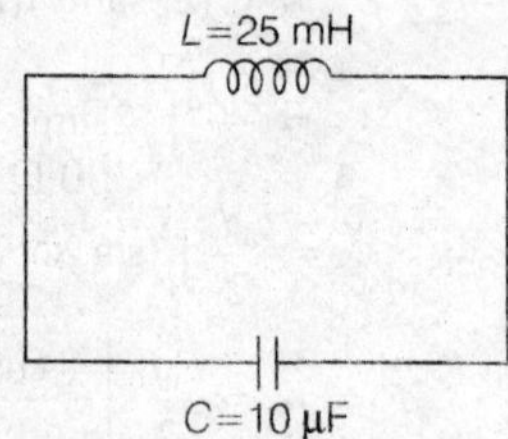

(a) $\frac{\pi}{2}$ ms (b) $\frac{\pi}{4}$ ms (c) π ms (d) 2 ms

3 A circuit when connected to an AC source of 12 V gives a current of 0.2 A. The same circuit when connected to a DC source of 12 V, gives a current of 0.4 A. The circuit is [NEET]

(a) series *L-R* (b) series *R-C*
(c) series *L-C* (d) series *L-C-R*

4 In an *L-C-R* series circuit, source voltage is 120 V and voltage in inductor 50 V and resistance is 40 V, then determine voltage in the capacitor. [AIIMS]

(a) $V_C = 10(5-8\sqrt{2})$ (b) $V_C = 10(5+8\sqrt{2})$
(c) $V_C = 20(5+8\sqrt{2})$ (d) $V_C = 10(5+7\sqrt{2})$

2018

5 In a circuit L, C and R are connected in series with an alternating voltage source of frequency f. The current leads the voltage by 45°. The value of C is [AIIMS]

(a) $\frac{1}{2\pi f(2\pi fL + R)}$ (b) $\frac{1}{\pi f(2\pi fL + R)}$
(c) $\frac{1}{2\pi f(2\pi fL - R)}$ (d) $\frac{1}{\pi f(2\pi fL - R)}$

6 In a series *R-C* circuit shown in figure, the applied voltage is 10 V and the voltage across capacitor is found to be 8V. Then, the voltage across R and the phase difference between current and the applied voltage will respectively be [AIIMS]

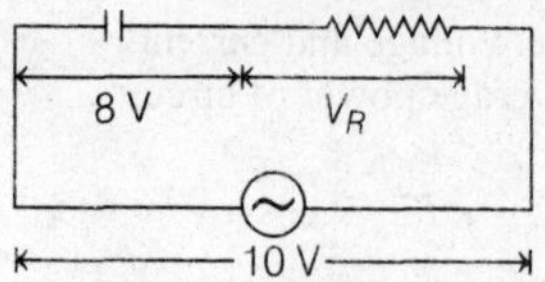

(a) 6 V, $\tan^{-1}\left(\frac{4}{3}\right)$ (b) 3 V, $\tan^{-1}\left(\frac{3}{4}\right)$
(c) 6 V, $\tan^{-1}\left(\frac{5}{3}\right)$ (d) None of these

2017

7 A series *R-C* circuit is connected to AC voltage source. Consider two cases; (A) When C is without a dielectric medium and (B) When C is filled with dielectric of constant 4. The current I_R through the resistor and voltage V_C across the capacitor are compared in two cases. Which of the following is true? [AIIMS]

(a) $I_R^A > I_R^B$ (b) $I_R^A < I_R^B$
(c) $V_C^A < V_C^B$ (d) None of these

2014

8 A 15.0 μF capacitor is connected to a 220 V, 50 Hz source. The capacitive reactance is

(a) 220 Ω (b) 215 Ω
(c) 212 Ω (d) 204 Ω

9 In an *L-C-R* series circuit, the potential difference between the terminals of the inductance is 60 V, between the terminals of the capacitor is 30 V and that across the resistance is 40 V. Then, the supply voltage will be equal to [UK PMT]

(a) 10 V (b) 50 V (c) 70 V (d) 130 V

10 A series *L-C-R* circuit contains inductance 5 mH, capacitance 2 μF and resistance 10 Ω. If a frequency AC source is varied, then what is the frequency at which maximum power is dissipated? [KCET]

(a) $\frac{10^5}{\pi}$ Hz (b) $\frac{10^{-5}}{\pi}$ Hz
(c) $\frac{2}{\pi} \times 10^5$ Hz (d) $\frac{5}{\pi} \times 10^3$ Hz

2013

11 For high frequency L-C circuit, the maximum charge on the capacitor is Q. The charge on the capacitor, when the energy is stored equally between the electric and magnetic fields is **[Manipal]**

(a) $Q/2$ (b) $Q/\sqrt{2}$
(c) $Q/\sqrt{3}$ (d) $Q/3$

2012

12 In the circuit shown below, what will be the readings of the voltmeter and ammeter? (Total impedance of circuit, $Z = 100\,\Omega$) **[JCECE]**

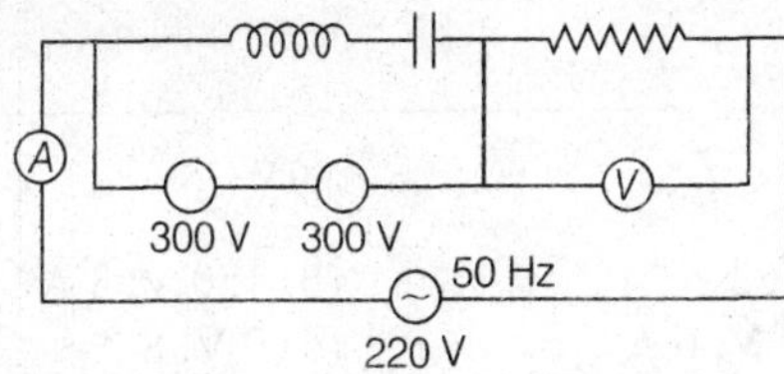

(a) 200 V, 1 A (b) 800 V, 2 A
(c) 100 V, 2 A (d) 220 V, 2.2 A

13 In an AC circuit, an alternating voltage $e = 200\sqrt{2}\sin 100\,t$ volt is connected to a capacitor of capacity $1\,\mu F$. The rms value of the current in the circuit is **[CBSE AIPMT]**

(a) 100 mA (b) 200 mA
(c) 20 mA (d) 10 mA

14 An AC voltage is applied to a resistance R and an inductor L in series. If R and the inductive reactance are both equal to $3\,\Omega$, the phase difference (in rad) between the applied voltage and the current in the circuit is **[CBSE AIPMT]**

(a) $\pi/4$ (b) $\pi/2$ (c) zero (d) $\pi/6$

15 An electron revolves in the path of a circle of radius of 0.5×10^{-10} m at frequency of 5×10^{15} cycles/s. The electric current in the circle is (charge of an electron $= 1.6 \times 10^{-19}$ C) **[AFMC]**

(a) 0.4 mA (b) 0.8 mA (c) 1.2 mA (d) 1.6 mA

16 The capacity of a pure capacitor is 1F. In DC circuits, its effective resistance will be

(a) infinite (b) zero
(c) $1\,\Omega$ (d) $\frac{1}{2}\,\Omega$

17 An L-C-R series circuit is under resonance. If I_m is current amplitude, V_m is voltage amplitude, R is the resistance, Z is the impedance, X_L is the inductive reactance and X_C is the capacitive reactance, then **[J&K CET]**

(a) $I_m = \frac{V_m}{Z}$ (b) $I_m = \frac{V_m}{X_L}$ (c) $I_m = \frac{V_m}{X_C}$ (d) $I_m = \frac{V_m}{R}$

18 In the case of an inductor **[J&K CET]**

(a) voltage lags the current by $\pi/2$
(b) voltage leads the current by $\pi/2$
(c) voltage leads the current by $\pi/3$
(d) voltage leads the current by $\pi/4$

19 When an AC voltage is applied to an L-C-R circuit, which of the following is true? **[DUMET]**

(a) I and V are out of phase with each other in R
(b) I and V are in phase in L with in C, they are out of phase
(c) I and V are out of phase in both, C and L
(d) I and V are out of phase in L and in phase in C

20 In the series L-C-R circuit shown, the impedance is **[KCET]**

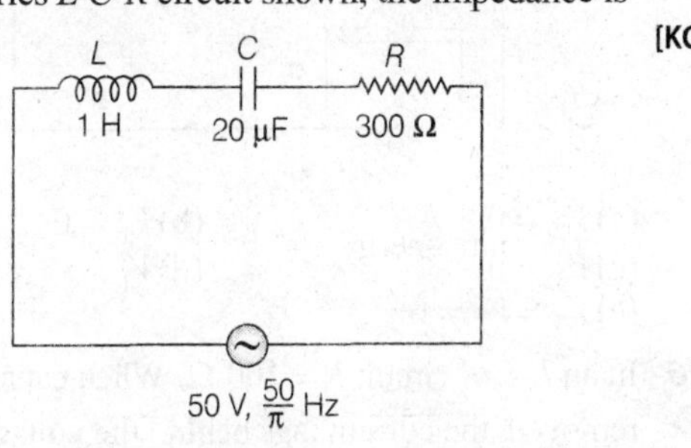

(a) $200\,\Omega$ (b) $100\,\Omega$ (c) $300\,\Omega$ (d) $500\,\Omega$

2010

21 A capacitor of capacitance $1\,\mu F$ is charged to a potential of 1 V. It is connected in parallel to an inductor of inductance 10^{-3} H. The maximum current that will flow in the circuit has the value **[AIIMS]**

(a) $\sqrt{1000}$ mA (b) 1 A
(c) 1 mA (d) 1000 mA

22 **Assertion** For an electric lamp connected in series with a variable capacitor and AC source; its brightness increases with increase in capacitance.

Reason Capacitive reactance decreases with increase in capacitance of capacitor. **[AIIMS]**

(a) Both Assertion and Reason are correct and Reason is the correct explanation of Assertion.
(b) Both Assertion and Reason are correct but Reason is not the correct explanation of Assertion.
(c) Assertion is correct but Reason is incorrect.
(d) Assertion is incorrect but Reason is correct.

23 In an L-R circuit, the value of L is $\left(\frac{0.4}{\pi}\right)$ H and the value of R is $30\,\Omega$. If in the circuit, an alternating emf of 200 V at 50 cycle /s is connected, the impedance of the circuit and current will be **[Manipal]**

(a) $11.4\,\Omega$, 17.5 A (b) $30.7\,\Omega$, 6.5 A
(c) $40.4\,\Omega$, 5 A (d) $50\,\Omega$, 4 A

24 In an *L-C-R* series, AC circuit at resonance, **[Manipal]**
(a) the capacitive reactance is more than the inductive reactance
(b) the capacitive reactance equals the inductive reactance
(c) the capacitive reactance is less than the inductive reactance
(d) the power dissipated is minimum

25 In the figure shown, three AC voltmeters are connected. At resonance, **[Kerala CEE]**

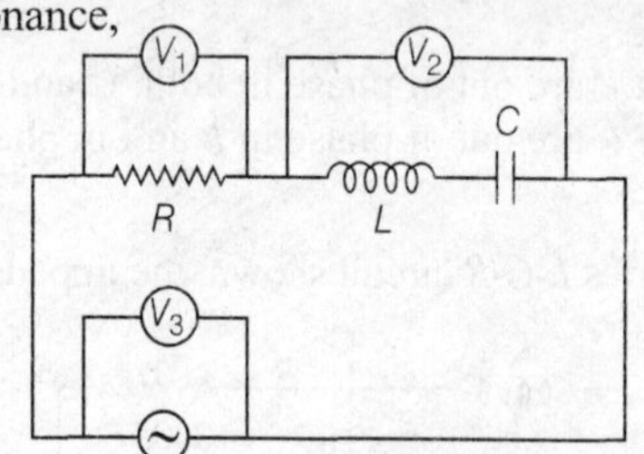

(a) $V_2 = 0$ (b) $V_1 = 0$
(c) $V_3 = 0$ (d) $V_1 = V_2 \neq 0$
(e) $V_3 = V_2 \neq 0$

26 In an *L-C-R* circuit $R = 100\ \Omega$. When capacitance C is removed, the current lags behind the voltage by $\pi / 3$, when inductance L is removed, the current leads the voltage by $\pi / 3$. The impedance of the circuit is **[Haryana PMT]**
(a) 50 Ω (b) 100 Ω (c) 200 Ω (d) 400 Ω

27 An inductor L, a capacitor of 20 μF and a resistor of 10 Ω are connected in series with an AC source of frequency 50 Hz. If the current is in phase with the voltage, then the inductance of the inductor is **[Punjab PMET]**
(a) 2.00 H (b) 0.51 H
(c) 1.5 H (d) 0.99 H

28 An ideal choke draws a current of 8 A when connected to an AC supply of 100 V, 50 Hz. A pure resistor draws a current of 10 A when connected to the same source. The ideal choke and the resistor are connected in series and then connected to the AC source of 150 V, 40 Hz. The current in the circuit becomes **[KCET]**
(a) $\frac{15}{\sqrt{2}}$ A (b) 8 A (c) 18 A (d) 10 A

29 An inductive coil has a resistance of 100 Ω. When an AC signal of frequency 1000 Hz is applied to the coil, the voltage leads the current by 45°. The inductance of the coil is **[BCECE]**
(a) $\frac{1}{10\pi}$ (b) $\frac{1}{20\pi}$
(c) $\frac{1}{40\pi}$ (d) $\frac{1}{60\pi}$

30 An inductor of 1 H is connected across a 220 V, 50 Hz supply. The peak value of the current is approximately
(a) 0.5 A (b) 0.7 A **[BCECE]**
(c) 1 A (d) 1.4 A

31 In the circuit shown in figure neglecting source resistance, the voltmeter and ammeter readings will be respectively, **[JCECE]**

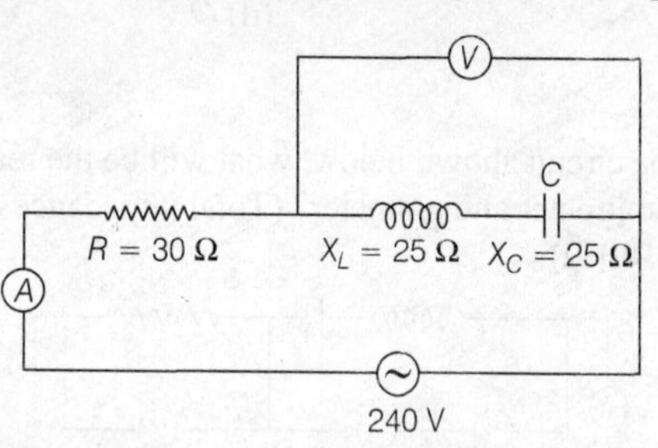

(a) 0 V, 3 A (b) 150 V, 3 A
(c) 150 V, 6 A (d) 0 V, 8 A

32 The impedance of a circuit, when a resistance R and an inductor of inductance L are connected in series in an AC circuit of frequency f, is **[JIPMER]**
(a) $\sqrt{R + 2\pi^2 f^2 L^2}$ (b) $\sqrt{R + 4\pi^2 f^2 L^2}$
(c) $\sqrt{R^2 + 4\pi^2 f^2 L^2}$ (d) $\sqrt{R^2 + 2\pi^2 f^2 L^2}$

33 In a series *L-C-R* circuit, resistance $R = 10\ \Omega$ and the impedance $Z = 10\ \Omega$. The phase difference between the current and the voltage is **[JIPMER]**
(a) 0° (b) 30°
(c) 45° (d) 60°

34 A sinusoidal voltage of peak value 300 V and an angular frequency $\omega = 400$ rad/s is applied to series *L-C-R* circuit, in which $R = 3\ \Omega$, $L = 20$ mH and $C = 625$ μF. The peak current in the circuit is **[MGIMS]**
(a) $30\sqrt{2}$ A (b) 60 A (c) 100 A (d) $60\sqrt{2}$ A

35 A circuit contains a capacitor and inductance each with negligible resistance. The capacitor is initially charged and the charging battery is disconnected. At subsequent time, the charge on the capacitor will **[MGIMS]**
(a) increase exponentially
(b) decrease exponentially
(c) decrease linearly
(d) remain constant

36 An *L-C-R* series circuit consists of a resistance of 10 Ω, a capacitor of reactance 60 Ω and an inductor coil. The circuit is found to resonate when put across a 300 V, 100 Hz supply. The inductance of coil is (Take, $\pi = 3$)
(a) 0.1 H (b) 0.01 H **[MGIMS]**
(c) 0.2 H (d) 0.02 H

2009

37 Two inductors L_1 and L_2 are connected in parallel and a time varying current flows as shown in figure. Then, the ratio of currents i_1/i_2 at any time t is **[AIIMS]**

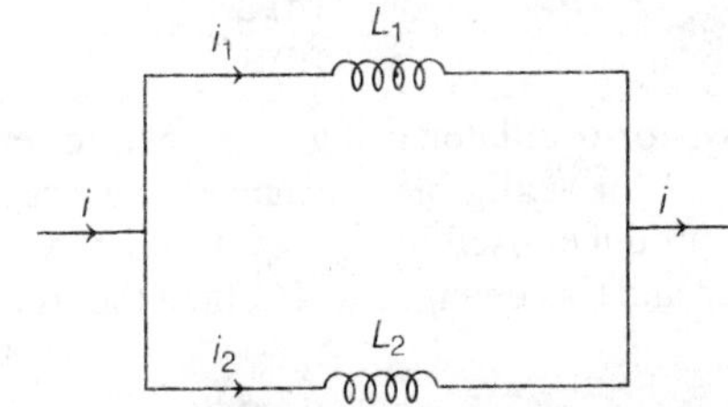

(a) $\frac{L_1}{L_2}$ (b) $\frac{L_2}{L_1}$ (c) $\frac{L_1^2}{(L_1+L_2)^2}$ (d) $\frac{L_2^2}{(L_1+L_2)^2}$

38 An alternating voltage $E = 200\sqrt{2}\sin(100t)$ is connected to 1 μF capacitor through AC ammeter. The reading of ammeter shall be **[MHT CET]**

(a) 10 mA (b) 20 mA (c) 40 mA (d) 80 mA

39 Same current is flowing in two alternating circuits. The first circuit contains only inductance and the other contains only a capacitor. If the frequency of the emf of AC is increased, the effect on the value of the current will be **[MHT CET]**

(a) increases in the first circuit and decreases in the other
(b) increases in both the circuits
(c) decreases in both the circuits
(d) decreases in the first circuit and increases in the second circuit

40 In a pure inductive circuit, current **[Manipal]**

(a) lags behind emf by $\frac{\pi}{2}$
(b) leads the emf by $\frac{\pi}{2}$
(c) lags behind by π
(d) leads the emf by π

41 An alternating current of rms value 10 A is passed through a 12 Ω resistor. The maximum potential difference across the resistor is **[Manipal]**

(a) 20 V (b) 90 V
(c) 169.68 V (d) None of these

42 220 V, 50 Hz AC is applied to a resistor. The instantaneous value of voltage is **[OJEE]**

(a) $220\sqrt{2}\sin 100\pi t$ (b) $220\sin 100\pi t$
(c) $220\sqrt{2}\sin 50\pi t$ (d) $220\sin 50\pi t$

43 In a series resonant circuit, the AC voltage across resistance R, inductor L and capacitor C are 5 V, 10 V and 10 V respectively. The AC voltage applied to the circuit will be **[Guj CET]**

(a) 10 V (b) 25 V (c) 5 V (d) 20 V

44 What is the value of inductance L for which the current is a maximum in a series L-C-R circuit with $C = 10\,\mu F$ and $\omega = 1000\,s^{-1}$? **[MHT CET]**

(a) 100 mH
(b) 1 mH
(c) Cannot be calculated unless R is known
(d) 10 mH

45 The instantaneous values of current and voltage in an AC circuit are given by $I = 6\sin(100\pi t + \pi/4)$, $V = 5\sin(100\pi t - \pi/4)$, then **[J&K CET]**

(a) current leads the voltage by 45°
(b) voltage leads the current by 90°
(c) current leads the voltage by 90°
(d) voltage leads the current by 45°

46 The following series L-C-R circuit, when driven by an emf source of angular frequency 70 k-rad/s, the circuit effectively behaves like **[EAMCET]**

R
L = 1μH
C = 100 μF

(a) purely resistive circuit
(b) series R-L circuit
(c) series R-C circuit
(d) series L-C circuit with $R = 0$

47 An AC voltage is applied to a pure inductor L, drives a current in the inductor. The current in the inductor would be **[DUMET]**

(a) ahead of the voltage by $\pi/2$
(b) lagging the voltage by $\pi/2$
(c) ahead of the voltage by $\pi/4$
(d) lagging the voltage by $3\pi/4$

48 An electric heater rated 220 V and 550 W is connected to AC mains. The current drawn by it is **[KCET]**

(a) 0.8 A (b) 2.5 A (c) 0.4 A (d) 1.25 A

49 A resistor and a capacitor are connected in series with an AC source. If the potential drop across the capacitor is 5 V and that across resistor is 12 V, then applied voltage is **[KCET]**

(a) 13 V (b) 17 V
(c) 5 V (d) 12 V

50 An L-C-R series circuit, connected to a source E, is at resonance. Then, **[BCECE]**

(a) the voltage across R is zero
(b) the voltage across R equals applied voltage
(c) the voltage across C is zero
(d) the voltage across C equals applied voltage

51 A choke is preferred to a resistance for limiting current in AC circuit, because **[JCECE]**

(a) choke is cheap
(b) there is no wastage of power
(c) choke is compact in size
(d) choke is a good absorber of heat

2008

52 From figure shown below, a series L-C-R circuit connected to a variable frequency 200 V source. If $C = 80\mu F$ and $R = 40\,\Omega$, then the source frequency which drive the circuit at resonance is **[VITEEE]**

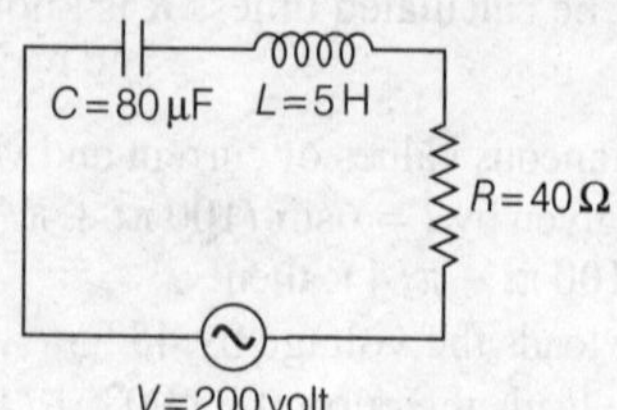

(a) 25 Hz (b) $\frac{25}{\pi}$ Hz (c) 50 Hz (d) $\frac{50}{\pi}$ Hz

53 An AC source of angular frequency ω is fed across a resistor R and a capacitor C in series. The current registered is I. If now the frequency of source is changed to $\omega/3$ (but maintaining the same voltage), the current in the circuit is found to be halved. Calculate the ratio of reactance to resistance at the original frequency ω. **[AIIMS]**

(a) $\sqrt{\frac{3}{5}}$ (b) $\sqrt{\frac{2}{5}}$

(c) $\sqrt{\frac{1}{5}}$ (d) $\sqrt{\frac{4}{5}}$

54 In non-resonant circuit, what will be the nature of the circuit for frequencies higher than the resonant frequency? **[BHU]**

(a) Resistive (b) Capacitive

(c) Inductive (d) None of these

55 A coil has an inductance of 0.7 H and is joined in series with a resistance of 220 Ω. When an alternating emf of 220 V at 50 Hz is applied to it, then the wattless component of the current in the circuit is **[BHU]**

(a) 5 A (b) 0.5 A (c) 0.7 A (d) 7 A

56 What is the value of inductance L for which the current is a maximum in a series L-C-R circuit with $C = 10\,\mu F$ and $\omega = 1000\,s^{-1}$? **[UP CPMT]**

(a) 100 mH

(b) 1 mH

(c) Cannot be calculated unless R is known

(d) 10 mH

57 In an L-C-R series AC circuit, if ω_0 is the resonant angular frequency, then the quality factor (Q-factor) is given by **[Kerala CEE, Manipal]**

(a) $\omega_0 L/C$ (b) $(1/R)\sqrt{\frac{L}{C}}$

(c) $\omega_0 C/R$ (d) $L/\omega_0 R$

(e) L/CR

58 The natural frequency of an L-C circuit is 125000 cycle/s, then the capacitor C is replaced by another capacitor with a dielectric medium of dielectric constant K. In this case, the frequency decreases by 25 kHz. The value of K is **[EAMCET]**

(a) 3.0 (b) 2.1

(c) 1.56 (d) 1.7

59 A transistor-oscillator using a resonant circuit with an inductor L (or negligible resistance) and a capacitor C in series produce oscillations of frequency f. If L is doubled and C is changed to $4C$, then the frequency will be **[Haryana PMT]**

(a) $f/4$ (b) $8f$

(c) $f/2\sqrt{2}$ (d) $f/2$

60 The natural frequency (ω_0) of oscillations in L-C circuit is given by **[J&K CET]**

(a) $\frac{1}{2\pi\sqrt{LC}}$ (b) $\frac{1}{2\pi}\sqrt{LC}$

(c) $\frac{1}{\sqrt{LC}}$ (d) $\sqrt{LC}$

61 In L-C-R series circuit, the resonance condition in terms of capacitive reactance (X_C) and inductive reactance (X_L) is **[J&K CET]**

(a) $X_C + X_L = 0$ (b) $X_C = 0$

(c) $X_L = 0$ (d) $X_C - X_L = 0$

62 A 100 V, AC source of frequency 500 Hz is connected to an L-C-R circuit with $L = 8.1$ mH, $C = 12.5\,\mu F$, $R = 10\,\Omega$ all connected in series as shown in figure. What is the quality factor of circuit? **[BCECE]**

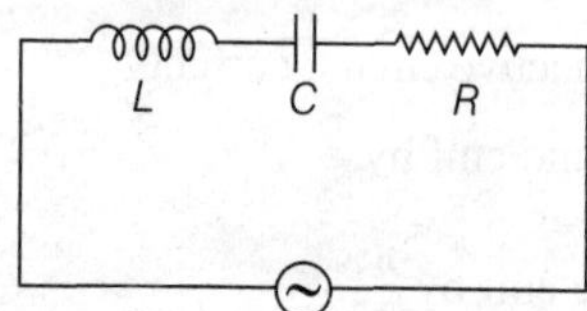

(a) 2.02 (b) 2.5434

(c) 20.54 (d) 200.54

63 In L-C-R resonant circuit, what is the phase angle ϕ? **[DUMET]**

(a) 90° (b) 180°

(c) 0° (d) 60°

64 In R-C circuit, $\omega = 100\,\text{rad s}^{-1}$, $R = 100\,\Omega$, $C = 20\,\mu F$. What is impedance? **[DUMET]**

(a) 510 Ω (b) 200 Ω

(c) 250 Ω (d) 300 Ω

65 In an AC circuit, a resistance of R ohm is connected in series with an inductor of self-inductance L. If phase angle between voltage and current be 45°, then the value of inductive reactance (X_L) will be equal to **[Guj CET]**

(a) R (b) $\frac{R}{8}$ (c) $\frac{R}{4}$ (d) $\frac{R}{2}$

66 A reactance of a 25 μF capacitor at the AC frequency of 4000 Hz is **[KCET]**

(a) $\sqrt{\frac{5}{\pi}}\ \Omega$ (b) 10 Ω
(c) $\frac{5}{\pi}\ \Omega$ (d) $\sqrt{10}\ \Omega$

67 In an *L-C-R* series AC circuit, the voltage across each of the components *L*, *C* and *R* is 50 V. The voltage across the *L-C* combination will be **[JIPMER]**

(a) 50 V (b) $50\sqrt{2}$ V
(c) 100 V (d) zero

2007

68 The figure shows three circuits with identical batteries, inductors and resistance. Rank the circuits according to the currents through the battery just after the switch is closed, greatest first. **[AIIMS]**

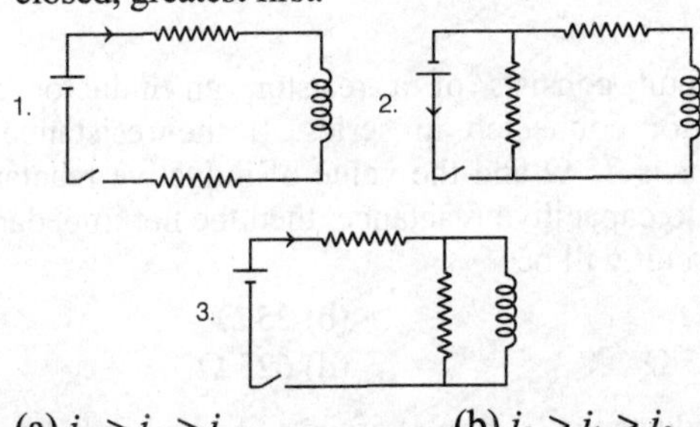

(a) $i_2 > i_3 > i_1$ (b) $i_2 > i_1 > i_3$
(c) $i_1 > i_2 > i_3$ (d) $i_1 > i_3 > i_2$

69 An inductive coil has a resistance of 100 Ω. When an AC signal of frequency 1000 Hz is applied to the coil, the voltage leads the current by 45°. The inductance of the coil is **[AMU]**

(a) $\frac{1}{10\pi}$ (b) $\frac{1}{20\pi}$
(c) $\frac{1}{40\pi}$ (d) $\frac{1}{60\pi}$

70 The reactance of a coil when used in the AC power supply (220 V, 50 Hz) is 50 Ω. The inductance of the coil is nearly **[BHU]**

(a) 0.16 H (b) 0.22 H
(c) 2.2 H (d) 1.6 H

71 An inductor of inductance *L* and resistor of resistance *R* are joined in series and connected by a source of frequency ω. Power dissipated in the circuit is **[UP CPMT]**

(a) $\left(\frac{R^2+\omega^2L^2}{V}\right)$ (b) $\frac{V^2R}{(R^2+\omega^2L^2)}$
(c) $\left(\frac{V}{R^2+\omega^2L^2}\right)$ (d) $\frac{\sqrt{R^2+\omega^2L^2}}{V^2}$

72 In a circuit, the current lags behind the voltage by a phase difference of π / 2, the circuit will contain which of the following? **[MHT CET]**

(a) Only *R* (b) Only *C*
(c) *R* and *C* (d) Only *L*

73 In a choke coil, the reactance X_L and resistance *R* are such that **[RPMT]**

(a) $X_L = R$ (b) $X_L >> R$
(c) $X_L << R$ (d) $X_L = \infty$

74 The inductance of the oscillatory circuit of a radio station is 10 mH and its capacitance is 0.25 μF. Taking the effect of resistance negligible, wavelength of the broadcasted waves will be (Take, velocity of light = 3.0×10^8 ms^{-1} and π = 3.14) **[BCECE]**

(a) 9.42×10^4 m (b) 18.8×10^4 m
(c) 4.5×10^4 m (d) None of these

75 An *L-C-R* series AC circuit is tuned to resonance. The impedance of the circuit is now **[Guj CET]**

(a) *R*
(b) $\left[R^2 + \left(\frac{1}{\omega C} - \omega L\right)^2\right]^{1/2}$
(c) $\left[R^2 + (\omega L)^2 + \left(\frac{1}{\omega C}\right)^2\right]^{1/2}$
(d) $\left[R^2 + \left(\omega L - \frac{1}{\omega C}\right)^2\right]^{1/2}$

76 Resonance frequency of *L-C-R* series AC circuit is f_0. Now, the capacitance is made 4 times, then the new resonance frequency will become **[Guj CET]**

(a) $\frac{f_0}{4}$ (b) $2f_0$ (c) f_0 (d) $\frac{f_0}{2}$

77 An electric bulb has a rated power of 50 W at 100 V. If it is used on an AC source 200 V, 50 Hz, a choke has to be used in series with it. This choke should have an inductance of **[KCET]**

(a) 0.1 mH (b) 1 mH
(c) 0.1 H (d) 1.1 H

78 An inductance of $\left(\frac{200}{\pi}\right)$ mH, a capacitance of $\left(\frac{10^{-3}}{\pi}\right)$ F and a resistance of 10 Ω are connected in series with an AC source 220 V, 50 Hz. The phase angle of the circuit is **[KCET]**

(a) $\frac{\pi}{6}$ (b) $\frac{\pi}{4}$
(c) $\frac{\pi}{2}$ (d) $\frac{\pi}{3}$

2006

79 In a series L-C-R circuit, the frequency of a 10 V, AC voltage source is adjusted in such a fashion that the reactance of the inductor measures 15 Ω and that of the capacitor 11 Ω. If $R = 3\ \Omega$, the potential difference across the series combination of L and C will be **[BHU]**

(a) 8 V (b) 10 V (c) 22 V (d) 52 V

80 In an AC circuit, the current lags behind the voltage by $\pi/3$. The component(s) of the circuit is/are **[MHT CET]**

(a) R and L (b) L and C (c) R and C (d) only R

81 An L-C circuit is in the state of resonance. If $C = 0.1\ \mu F$ and $L = 0.25$ H, neglecting ohmic resistance of circuit, then what is the frequency of oscillations? **[Manipal]**

(a) 1007 Hz (b) 100 Hz (c) 109 Hz (d) 500 Hz

82 A 16μF capacitor is charged to a 20 V potential. The battery is then disconnected and pure 40 mH coil is connected across the capacitor, so that L-C oscillations are setup. The maximum current in the coil is **[Kerala CEE]**

(a) 0.2 A (b) 40 mA (c) 2 A (d) 0.4 A
(e) 0.8 A

83 If a circuit made up of a resistance 1 Ω and inductance 0.01 H; and alternating emf 200 V at 50 Hz is connected, then the phase difference between the current and the emf in the circuit is **[Haryana PMT]**

(a) $\tan^{-1}(\pi)$ (b) $\tan^{-1}\left(\frac{\pi}{2}\right)$
(c) $\tan^{-1}\left(\frac{\pi}{4}\right)$ (d) $\tan^{-1}\left(\frac{\pi}{3}\right)$

84 In L-C-R circuit, $f = \frac{50}{\pi}$ Hz, $V = 50$ V and $R = 300\ \Omega$. If $L = 1$ H and $C = 20\ \mu C$, then voltage across capacitor is **[JCECE]**

(a) zero (b) 20 V
(c) 30 V (d) 50 V

85 What is the ratio of inductive and capacitive reactance in AC circuit? **[Guj CET]**

(a) $\omega^2 LC$ (b) 1 (c) zero (d) $\omega^2 L$

2005

86 In an L-C-R circuit, the capacitance is made 1/4, then what should be change in inductance, so that the circuit remains in resonance? **[BHU]**

(a) 8 times (b) 1/4 times
(c) 2 times (d) 4 times

87 In series L-C-R circuit, the capacitance is changed from C to $2C$. The inductance should be changed from L to ... to obtain same resonance frequency. **[MHT CET]**

(a) $4L$ (b) $L/2$ (c) $L/4$ (d) $2L$

88 An AC source of frequency 50 Hz is connected in series to an inductance of 0.5 H and resistance of 157 Ω. The phase difference between current and voltage is **[Kerala CEE]**

(a) 90° (b) 60°
(c) 75° (d) 45°
(e) 30°

89 The following series resonant L-C-R circuit has a quality factor (Q-factor) 0.4 and a bandwidth of 1.3 kHz. The value of inductance is then **[Kerala CEE]**

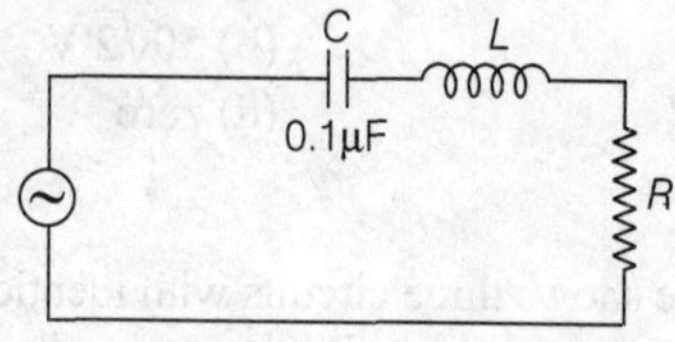

(a) 0.1 H (b) 0.94 H
(c) 2 H (d) 10 H
(e) 5 H

90 A circuit consists of a resistor, an inductor and a capacitor connected in series. If the resistance of a resistor is 25 Ω and the value of inductive reactance is equal to capacitive reactance, then the net impedance of the circuit will be **[AMU]**

(a) 5 Ω (b) 25 Ω
(c) 125 Ω (d) 625 Ω

91 The inductance L (in mH) of the coil which is to be connected in series with a capacitor of 0.3 pF to get an oscillatory frequency of 1 MHz is **[EAMCET]**

(a) 8.44 (b) 84.4
(c) 844 (d) 8440

92 Which of the following combinations should be selected for better tuning of an L-C-R circuit used for communication? **[NEET]**

(a) $R = 20\Omega$, $L = 1.5$ H and $C = 35\ \mu F$
(b) $R = 25\Omega$, $L = 2.5$ H and $C = 45\ \mu F$
(c) $R = 15\Omega$, $L = 3.5$ H and $C = 30\ \mu F$
(d) $R = 25\Omega$, $L = 1.5$ H and $C = 45\ \mu F$

93 An alternating emf given by equation

$$e = 300 \sin [(100\,\pi)t] \text{ volt}$$

is applied to a resistance 100 Ω. The rms current through the circuit is (in ampere) **[EAMCET]**

(a) $3/\sqrt{2}$ (b) $9/\sqrt{2}$
(c) 3 (d) $6/\sqrt{2}$

94 If the capacity of a condenser is 1 F, then its resistance in a DC circuit will be **[J&K CET]**

(a) zero (b) infinity
(c) 1Ω (d) $\frac{1}{2}\ \Omega$

Answers

1 (a)	2 (b)	3 (a)	4 (a)	5 (c)	6 (a)	7 (b)	8 (c)	9 (b)	10 (d)
11 (b)	12 (d)	13 (c)	14 (a)	15 (b)	16 (a)	17 (a)	18 (b)	19 (c)	20 (d)
21 (a)	22 (a)	23 (d)	24 (b)	25 (a)	26 (b)	27 (b)	28 (a)	29 (b)	30 (c)
31 (d)	32 (c)	33 (a)	34 (b)	35 (d)	36 (a)	37 (b)	38 (b)	39 (d)	40 (a)
41 (c)	42 (b)	43 (c)	44 (a)	45 (c)	46 (b)	47 (b)	48 (b)	49 (a)	50 (b)
51 (b)	52 (b)	53 (a)	54 (c)	55 (b)	56 (a)	57 (b)	58 (c)	59 (c)	60 (a)
61 (d)	62 (b)	63 (c)	64 (a)	65 (a)	66 (c)	67 (d)	68 (a)	69 (b)	70 (a)
71 (b)	72 (d)	73 (b)	74 (a)	75 (a)	76 (d)	77 (d)	78 (b)	79 (a)	80 (a)
81 (a)	82 (d)	83 (a)	84 (d)	85 (a)	86 (d)	87 (b)	88 (d)	89 (b)	90 (b)
91 (b)	92 (c)	93 (a)	94 (b)						

Explanations

1 *(a)* In the given circuit diagram, both inductors of inductance L are parallel to each other, hence

$$L_{eq} = \frac{L_1 L_2}{L_1 + L_2} = \frac{L.L}{L+L} = \frac{L}{2}$$

Similarly,

$$C_{eq} = C_1 + C_2 = C + C = 2C$$

$\therefore$ Resonance frequency

$$\omega_r = \frac{1}{\sqrt{L_{eq} \cdot C_{eq}}} = \sqrt{\frac{1}{\frac{L}{2} \cdot 2C}}$$

$$= \sqrt{\frac{1}{LC}} = \frac{1}{\sqrt{LC}}$$

2 *(b)* Given, $L = 25\,\text{mH}$,

$$= 25 \times 10^{-3}\,\text{H}$$

$$C = 10\,\mu\text{F} = 10^{-5}\,\text{F}$$

If T be the time period in L-C oscillation, then

$$T = 2\pi\sqrt{LC}$$

$$= 2\pi\sqrt{25 \times 10^{-3} \times 10^{-5}}$$

$$= \pi \times 10^{-3}\,\text{s} = \pi\,\text{ms}$$

Current in the circuit will be maximum when

$$t = \frac{T}{4} = \frac{\pi}{4}\,\text{ms}$$

3 *(a)* When the circuit is connected to AC source,

Voltage, $V = 12\,\text{V}$

Current, $I = 0.2\,\text{A}$

$\therefore$ Impedance, $Z = \dfrac{V}{I} = \dfrac{12}{0.2} = 60\,\Omega$

When it is connected to DC source,

Voltage, $V = 12\,\text{V}$

Current, $I = 0.4\,\text{A}$

$\Rightarrow$ Resistance,

$$R = \frac{V}{I} = \frac{12}{0.4} = 30\,\Omega$$

As in case of DC supply, the capacitor act as an open circuit and no current flows through the circuit. So, the given circuit will not have capacitor in series combination. Therefore, the circuit should be a series L-R circuit.

4 *(a)* Given, in L-C-R series circuit,

Source voltage (resultant voltage), $V = 120\,\text{V}$

Voltage across inductor, $V_L = 50\,\text{V}$

Voltage across resistor, $V_R = 40\,\text{V}$

In L-C-R series circuit,

$$V = \sqrt{V_R^2 + (V_L - V_C)^2}$$

or $\quad 120 = \sqrt{40^2 + (50 - V_C)^2}$

$$120^2 = 40^2 + (50 - V_C)^2$$

$\Rightarrow (50 - V_C)^2 = 12800$

$\Rightarrow \quad 50 - V_C = 80\sqrt{2}$

$\Rightarrow \quad V_C = 10(5 - 8\sqrt{2})$

5 *(c)* In a L-C-R circuit,

$$\tan\phi = \frac{\omega L - \frac{1}{\omega C}}{R}$$

ϕ being the angle by which the current leads the voltage.

Given, $\phi = 45°$

$$\therefore \tan 45° = \frac{\omega L - \frac{1}{\omega C}}{R}$$

$$\Rightarrow \quad 1 = \frac{\omega L - \frac{1}{\omega C}}{R}$$

$$\Rightarrow \quad R = \omega L - \frac{1}{\omega C}$$

$$\Rightarrow \quad \omega C = \frac{1}{\omega L - R}$$

$$\Rightarrow \quad C = \frac{1}{\omega(\omega L - R)}$$

$$= \frac{1}{2\pi f(2\pi f L - R)}$$

6 *(a)* We know that, for series R-C circuit

$$V^2 = V_C^2 + V_R^2$$

$$100 = 64 + V_R^2$$

$\Rightarrow \quad V_R^2 = 36 \Rightarrow V_R = \sqrt{36} = 6\,\text{V}$

Also, $\quad \tan\phi = \dfrac{V_C}{V_R} \Rightarrow \tan\phi = \dfrac{8}{6}$

$$\tan\phi = \frac{4}{3}$$

$$\therefore \quad \phi = \tan^{-1}\left(\frac{4}{3}\right)$$

7 *(b)* For circuit A,

Impedance, $Z_A = \sqrt{R^2 + \dfrac{1}{\omega^2 C^2}}$

Current in circuit,

$$I_R^A = \frac{V}{\sqrt{R^2 + (1/\omega^2 C^2)}} \quad \text{...(i)}$$

Potential difference across C,

$$V_C^A = I_R^A \times \frac{1}{\omega C} = \frac{V}{\sqrt{(R\omega C)^2 + 1}}$$

For circuit B,

$$\text{Impedance, } Z_B = \sqrt{R^2 + \frac{1}{(4\omega)^2 C^2}}$$

Current in circuit,

$$I_R^B = \frac{V}{\sqrt{R^2 + [1/(4\omega C)^2]}}$$

Potential difference across C,

$$V_C^B = I_R^B \times \frac{1}{4\omega C} = \frac{V}{\sqrt{(4R\omega C)^2 + 1}} \quad \text{... (ii)}$$

Hence, from above Eqs. (i) and (ii), we conclude that because numerator of I_R^B is increased from I_R^A by a factor of 2.

So, $I_R^B > I_R^A$ and $V_C^A > V_C^B$.

8 (c) The capacitive reactance is

$$X_C = \frac{1}{2\pi\nu C}$$

$$= \frac{1}{2\pi\,(50\text{ Hz})(15.0 \times 10^{-6}\text{F})}$$

$$= 212.3\Omega$$

$$\approx 212\Omega$$

9 (b) Given, $V_L = 60\text{ V}, V_C = 30\text{ V}$, $V_R = 40\text{ V}$

According to L-C-R series circuit, we know that

V_R V_L V_C

In phasor diagram, V_C and V_L are in anti-phase to each other due to their 90° leading and lagging relationship with the circuit current I_S.

$V_L - V_C$ V_S θ V_R I_S V_C

So, $V_S = \sqrt{(V_L - V_C)^2 + V_R^2}$

$$= \sqrt{(60-30)^2 + (40)^2}$$

$$= \sqrt{(30)^2 + (40)^2}$$

$$= \sqrt{900 + 1600} = \sqrt{2500}$$

$$= 50\text{ V}$$

10 (d) We know that,

Resonant frequency is given by

$$f_0 = \frac{1}{2\pi\sqrt{LC}}$$

where, $L = 5 \times 10^{-3}$ H

and $C = 2 \times 10^{-6}$ F

$$\therefore \quad f_0 = \frac{1}{2\pi\sqrt{5 \times 10^{-3} \times 2 \times 10^{-6}}}$$

$$= \frac{1}{2\pi\sqrt{10^{-8}}} = \frac{1}{2\pi \times 10^{-4}}$$

$$= \frac{10^4}{2\pi}\text{ Hz} = \frac{5}{\pi} \times 10^3\text{ Hz}$$

11 (b) Energy stored in a capacitor of capacitance C, charge Q is

$$U = \frac{1}{2}\frac{Q^2}{C}$$

Since, energy is stored equally between electric and magnetic fields,

$$E = \frac{1}{2}\left(\frac{1}{2}\frac{Q^2}{C}\right)$$

$$\text{Now,} \quad \frac{Q'^2}{2C} = \frac{1}{2}\cdot\frac{Q^2}{2C} \Rightarrow Q' = \frac{Q}{\sqrt{2}}$$

12 (d) Given, impedance, $Z = 100\ \Omega$

Frequency, $f = 50$ Hz

and voltage, $V = 220$ V.

Voltmeter reading,

$$V_a = \sqrt{V_R^2 + (V_L - V_C)^2}$$

But $V_R = V$ and $V_L = V_C$

$\therefore \quad V_a = 220$ V

Ammeter reading, $I_a = \dfrac{220}{100} = 2.2$ A

13 (c) Given, $e = 200\sqrt{2}\sin 100t$,

$C = 1\mu$F

$$\therefore \quad E_{\text{rms}} = \frac{E_0}{\sqrt{2}} = \frac{200\sqrt{2}}{\sqrt{2}} = 200\text{ V}$$

and $\omega = 100$ rad/s

$$\therefore \quad X_C = \frac{1}{\omega C}$$

$$= \frac{1}{1 \times 10^{-6} \times 100} = 10^4\ \Omega$$

$$\therefore \quad i_{\text{rms}} = \frac{E_{\text{rms}}}{X_C}$$

$$= \frac{200}{10^4} = 2 \times 10^{-2}\text{ A}$$

$$= 20\text{ mA}$$

14 (a) $\tan\phi = \dfrac{X_L}{R} = \dfrac{L\omega}{R}$

$$\Rightarrow \quad \tan\phi = \frac{3\Omega}{3\Omega} \Rightarrow \tan\phi = 1$$

$$\therefore \quad \phi = \tan^{-1}(1)$$

$$\Rightarrow \quad \phi = 45°$$

$$\Rightarrow \quad \phi = \frac{\pi}{4}\text{ rad}$$

15 (b) Current, $i = \dfrac{Q}{T} = Qf \qquad \left(\because f = \dfrac{1}{T}\right)$

$$= 1.6 \times 10^{-19} \times 5 \times 10^{15}$$

$$= 0.8\text{ mA}$$

16 (a) In DC circuits, $f = 0$

$$X_C = \frac{1}{2\pi(0)C} \Rightarrow X_C = \frac{1}{0} = \infty$$

So, the effective resistance will be infinite.

17 (a) Here, $I_m = \dfrac{V_m}{Z}$ is true.

where, $Z = \sqrt{(X_L - X_C)^2 + R^2}$

18 (b) In case of an inductor voltage leads the current by $\dfrac{\pi}{2}$.

19 (c) I and V are out of the phase in both, C and L is true.

20 (d) $X_L = 2\pi fL = 2\pi\left(\dfrac{50}{\pi}\right) \times 1 = 100\ \Omega$

$$X_C = \frac{1}{2\pi fC} = \frac{1}{2\pi\left(\frac{50}{\pi}\right) 20 \times 10^{-6}}$$

$$= 500\ \Omega$$

$$\text{Impedance, } Z = \sqrt{R^2 + (X_C - X_L)^2}$$

$$= \sqrt{(300)^2 + (400)^2}$$

$$= 500\ \Omega$$

21 (a) Charge on the capacitor,

$$q_0 = CV = 1 \times 10^{-6} \times 1 = 10^{-6}\text{ C}$$

Here, $q = q_0 \sin\omega t$

or $I_0 = \omega q_0 =$ maximum current

$$\text{Now, } \omega = \frac{1}{\sqrt{LC}} = \frac{1}{\sqrt{10^{-9}}} = (10^9)^{1/2}$$

$L = 10^{-3}$ H, $C = 10^{-6}$ F

$\therefore \quad I_0 = (10^9)^{1/2} \times (1 \times 10^{-6})$

$= \sqrt{1000}$ mA

22 (a) Capacitive reactance $X_C = \dfrac{1}{\omega C}$.

When capacitance C increases the capacitive reactance decreases. Due to decrease in its values, the current in the circuit will increase $\left(I = \dfrac{E}{\sqrt{R^2 + X_C^2}}\right)$ and hence brightness of source (or electric lamp) will also increase.

23 (d) Given, $X_L = \omega L = 2\pi f L$

$= 2\pi \times 50 \times \dfrac{0.4}{\pi} = 40\ \Omega$

$R = 30\Omega$

$\Rightarrow \quad Z = \sqrt{R^2 + X_L^2}$

$= \sqrt{(30)^2 + (40)^2} = 50\ \Omega$

and $\quad i_{\text{rms}} = \dfrac{V_{\text{rms}}}{Z} = \dfrac{200}{50} = 4$ A

24 (b) The impedance of a series L-C-R circuit is

$Z = \sqrt{(X_L - X_C)^2 + R^2}$

At resonance (series resonant circuit),

$X_L = X_C$

$\Rightarrow \quad Z_{\min} = R$, i.e. circuit behaves as resistive circuit.

25 (a)

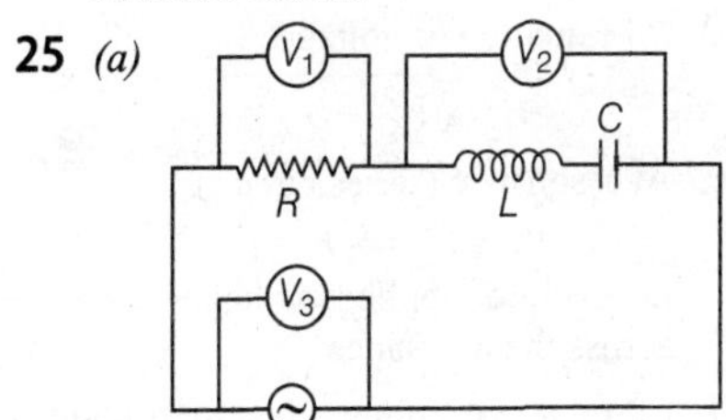

At resonance, $X_L = X_C$, hence $V_2 = 0$.

26 (b) When C is removed, circuit becomes R-L circuit.

Hence, $\quad \tan\dfrac{\pi}{3} = \dfrac{X_L}{R}$ ....(i)

When L is removed, circuit becomes R-C circuit.

Hence, $\quad \tan\dfrac{\pi}{3} = \dfrac{X_C}{R}$ ...(ii)

From Eqs. (i) and (ii), we get $X_L = X_C$, this is the condition of resonance, $Z = R = 100\ \Omega$.

27 (b) In an L-C-R circuit, the current and the voltage are in phase ($\phi = 0$), when

$\tan\phi = \dfrac{\omega L - \dfrac{1}{\omega C}}{R} = 0$

$\Rightarrow \quad \omega L = \dfrac{1}{\omega C} \Rightarrow L = \dfrac{1}{\omega^2 C}$

Here, $\omega = 2\pi f$

$= 2 \times 3.14 \times 50\ \text{s}^{-1} = 314\ \text{s}^{-1}$

and $\quad C = 20\ \mu\text{F} = 20 \times 10^{-6}$ F

$\therefore \quad L = \dfrac{1}{(314\ \text{s}^{-1})^2 \times (20 \times 10^{-6}\text{F})}$

$= 0.51$H

28 (a) Resistance, $R = \dfrac{100}{10} = 10\Omega$

Inductive reactance, $X_L = 2\pi f L$

$\dfrac{100}{8} = 2\pi \times 50 \times L$

$\Rightarrow \quad L = \dfrac{1}{8\pi}$ H

$X_L' = 2\pi f' L$

$= 2\pi \times 40 \times \dfrac{1}{8\pi} = 10\ \Omega$

Impedance of the circuit,

$Z = \sqrt{R^2 + X_L'^2}$

$= \sqrt{(10)^2 + (10)^2}$

$= 10\sqrt{2}\ \Omega$

Current in the circuit,

$i = \dfrac{V}{Z} = \dfrac{150}{10\sqrt{2}} = \dfrac{15}{\sqrt{2}}$ A

29 (b) $\tan\phi = \dfrac{X_L}{R}$

$\therefore \tan 45° = \dfrac{L\omega}{R}$

$\Rightarrow \quad L = \dfrac{R}{\omega}$ $\quad [\because \tan 45° = 1]$

$= \dfrac{100}{2\pi \times 1000}$ $\quad [\because \omega = 2\pi f]$

$= \dfrac{1}{20\,\pi}$

30 (c) Current $(i_0) = E_0 / X_L$

$\Rightarrow i_0 = \dfrac{E_0}{L\omega} = \dfrac{220 \times \sqrt{2}}{1 \times 2\pi \times 50}$

$= \dfrac{220 \times \sqrt{2}}{100\pi} = \dfrac{220 \times \sqrt{2}}{100 \times 3.14} = 1$ A

31 (d) The voltages V_L and V_C are equal and opposite, so voltmeter reading will be zero.

Also, $\quad R = 30\ \Omega$,

$X_L = X_C = 25\ \Omega$

So, $\quad i = \dfrac{V}{\sqrt{R^2 + (X_L - X_C)^2}}$

$= \dfrac{V}{R} = \dfrac{240}{30} = 8$ A

32 (c) In L-R circuit,

Impedance, $Z = \sqrt{R^2 + X_L^2}$

Here, $\quad X_L = \omega L = 2\pi f L$

$\Rightarrow \quad Z = \sqrt{R^2 + 4\pi^2 f^2 L^2}$

33 (a) Impedance,

$Z = \sqrt{R^2 + (X_L - X_C)^2}$

$\therefore \quad 10 = \sqrt{(10)^2 + (X_L - X_C)^2}$

$100 = 100 + (X_L - X_C)^2$

$\Rightarrow \quad X_L - X_C = 0$ ...(i)

Let ϕ is the phase difference between current and voltage.

$\therefore \quad \tan\phi = \dfrac{X_L - X_C}{R}$

$\Rightarrow \quad \tan\phi = \dfrac{0}{R}$ [from Eq. (i)]

$\therefore \quad \phi = 0°$

34 (b) The impedance of the circuit,

$Z = \sqrt{R^2 + (X_L - X_C)^2}$

$\Rightarrow X_L = \omega L = 400 \times 20 \times 10^{-3} = 8\ \Omega$

$X_C = \dfrac{1}{\omega C} = \dfrac{1}{400 \times 625 \times 10^{-6}} = 4\ \Omega$

$Z = \sqrt{(3)^2 + (8-4)^2} = 5$

$\Rightarrow \quad i = \dfrac{E}{Z} = \dfrac{300}{5} = 60$ A

35 (d) When a charged capacitor of negligible resistance is connected with a non-resistive inductor, the charge across it is converted into emf across inductor and then the emf back into the charge on capacitor. This process continues and oscillations are produced called L-C oscillations. Thus, the amount of charge on the capacitor remains same as there is no loss of energy.

36 (a) Given, frequency, $f = 100$ Hz

Angular velocity, $\omega_0 = 2\pi f = 2\pi \times 100$

$\omega_0 = 2 \times 3 \times 100 \quad (\because \pi = 3)$

$= 600$ rad / s

Further $\quad \omega_0 = \dfrac{1}{\sqrt{LC}}$ ....(i)

Also, $\quad X_C = \dfrac{1}{C\omega_0} = 60\ \Omega$

$$\Rightarrow \quad C = \frac{1}{\omega_0 \times 60} = \frac{1}{600 \times 60}$$

$$\Rightarrow \quad C = \frac{1}{36 \times 10^3} \text{F}$$

So, put this values in Eq. (i), we get

$$600 = \frac{1}{\sqrt{L\left(\frac{1}{36 \times 10^3}\right)}}$$

$$\Rightarrow 36 \times 10^4 = \frac{36 \times 10^3}{L}$$

$$\therefore \quad L = \frac{36 \times 10^3}{36 \times 10^4} = \frac{1}{10} = 0.1 \text{ H}$$

37 (*b*) We know that,

$$i_1 = \frac{E_0}{\omega L_1} \cos\omega t \quad \ldots\text{(i)}$$

and $\quad i_2 = \frac{E_0}{\omega L_2} \cos\omega t \quad \ldots\text{(ii)}$

Now, $\quad \frac{i_1}{i_2} = \frac{E_0}{\omega L_1} \cos\omega t \div \frac{E_0}{\omega L_2} \cos\omega t$

$$= \frac{E_0 \cos\omega t}{\omega L_1} \times \frac{\omega L_2}{E_0 \cos\omega t}$$

$$= \frac{\omega L_2}{\omega L_1} = \frac{L_2}{L_1}$$

38 (*b*) Reading of ammeter

$$= I_{\text{rms}} = \frac{V_{\text{rms}}}{X_C} = \frac{V_0 \omega C}{\sqrt{2}}$$

$$= \frac{200\sqrt{2} \times 100 \times (1 \times 10^{-6})}{\sqrt{2}}$$

$$= 2 \times 10^{-2} \text{ A} = 20 \text{ mA}$$

39 (*d*) We know that current in purely inductive circuit and purely capacitive circuit is given by respectively,

$$I_L = \frac{E_0}{\omega L} \sin(\omega t - \pi/2)$$

and $I_C = \frac{E_0}{1/\omega C} \sin(\omega t + \pi/2)$

$$= E_0 \sin(\omega t + \pi/2) \times \omega C$$

Here, ω is the frequency of the alternating current.

Thus, current will decrease in the first circuit and increase in second circuit.

40 (*a*) In a pure inductive circuit, current lags behind the emf by $\frac{\pi}{2}$ or 90°.

41 (*c*) Given, $I_{\text{rms}} = 10\text{A}$

and $\quad R = 12\ \Omega$

$$\therefore \quad E_{\text{rms}} = I_{\text{rms}} \times R$$

$$= 10 \times 12 = 120 \text{ V}$$

Now, maximum potential difference

$$= E_{\text{rms}} \times \sqrt{2} = 120 \times \sqrt{2}$$

$$= 169.68 \text{ V}$$

42 (*b*) We know that, instantaneous voltage,

$$E = E_0 \sin\omega t$$

But $\omega = 2\pi\nu$

$$\therefore \quad E = E_0 \sin 2\pi\nu t \quad \ldots\text{(i)}$$

Given, $\quad E_0 = 220$ V and $\nu = 50$ Hz

On putting these values in Eq. (i), we get

$$E = 220 \sin 2 \times \pi \times 50t$$

$$= 220 \sin 100\pi t$$

43 (*c*) Given, $V_R = 5$ V, $V_L = 10$ V

and $\quad V_C = 10$ V

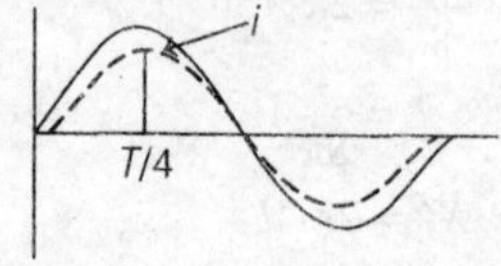

In the *L-C-R* circuit, the AC voltage applied to the circuit will be

$$V = \sqrt{V_R^2 + (V_L - V_C)^2}$$

$$= \sqrt{(5)^2 + (10 - 10)^2} = 5 \text{ V}$$

44 (*a*) Current in *L-C-R* series circuit is given by

$$i = \frac{V}{\sqrt{R^2 + (X_L - X_C)^2}}$$

where, V is rms value of current, R is resistance, X_L is inductive reactance and X_C is capacitive reactance.

For current to be maximum, denominator should be minimum which can be done, if $X_L = X_C$.

This happens in resonance state of the circuit,

i.e. $\quad \omega L = \frac{1}{\omega C} \Rightarrow L = \frac{1}{\omega^2 C} \quad \ldots\text{(i)}$

Given, $\quad \omega = 1000 \text{ s}^{-1}$

and $\quad C = 10\,\mu\text{F} = 10 \times 10^{-6}$ F.

Hence,

$$L = \frac{1}{(1000)^2 \times 10 \times 10^{-6}} = 0.1 \text{ H}$$

$$= 100 \text{ mH}$$

45 (*c*) The phase difference between instantaneous value of I and V is

$$\frac{\pi}{4} - \left(-\frac{\pi}{4}\right) = \frac{\pi}{2}$$

Hence, current leads the voltage by 90°.

46 (*b*) Resonance frequency,

$$\omega_0 = \frac{1}{\sqrt{LC}}$$

$$= \frac{1}{\sqrt{100 \times 10^{-6} \times 1 \times 10^{-6}}}$$

$$= \frac{1}{\sqrt{10^{-10}}} = 10^5 \text{ rad/s}$$

Now, given $\omega = 70$ k-rad/s

$$= 70000 \text{ rad/s}$$

Here, $\quad \omega_0 > \omega$

Thus, the circuit is capacitive dominant circuit. The circuit effectively behaves like series *R-L* circuit.

47 (*b*) In an AC circuit L only, alternating current I lags behind the alternating voltage E by a phase angle of 90°, i.e. by $\pi/2$.

48 (*b*) $\because P = VI \Rightarrow I = \frac{P}{V} = \frac{550}{220} = 2.5$ A

49 (*a*) Let the applied voltage be V volt.

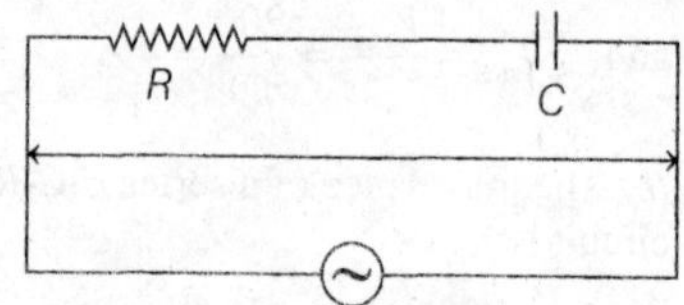

Here, $V_R = 12$ V, $V_C = 5$ V

$$\therefore \quad V = \sqrt{V_R^2 + V_C^2} = \sqrt{(12)^2 + (5)^2}$$

$$= \sqrt{144 + 25} = \sqrt{169} = 13 \text{ V}$$

50 (*b*) Equation of voltage,

$$E = \sqrt{V_R^2 + (V_L - V_C)^2}$$

At resonance (series circuit),

$$V_L = V_C \Rightarrow E = V_R$$

i.e. whole applied voltage appeared across the resistance.

51 (*b*) In an AC circuit, the coil of high inductance and negligible resistance used to control current, is called the choke coil. The power factor of such a coil is given by

$$\cos\phi = \frac{R}{\sqrt{R^2 + \omega^2 L^2}} \approx \frac{R}{\omega L}$$

(as $R << \omega L$)

As $R << \omega L$, $\cos\phi$ is very small. Thus, the power absorbed by the coil is very small. The only loss of energy is due to hysteresis in the iron core, which is much less than the loss of energy in the resistance that can also reduce the current, if placed instead of the choke coil.

52 (b) The impedance (Z) of an R-L-C series circuit is given by

$$Z = \sqrt{R^2 + \left(\omega L - \frac{1}{\omega C}\right)^2}$$

As, frequency of alternating emf applied to the circuit is increased, X_L goes on increasing and X_C goes on decreasing. For a particular value of $\omega = (\omega_r$, say)

$$X_L = X_C$$

i.e. $\omega_r L = \frac{1}{\omega_r C} \Rightarrow \omega_r^2 = \frac{1}{LC}$

or $\omega_r = \frac{1}{\sqrt{LC}} \Rightarrow 2\pi\nu_r = \frac{1}{\sqrt{LC}}$

or $\nu_r = \frac{1}{2\pi\sqrt{LC}}$

$$= \frac{1}{2 \times 3.14 \times \sqrt{5 \times 80 \times 10^{-6}}}$$

$$= \frac{1}{2 \times 3.14\sqrt{(400 \times 10^{-6})}}$$

$$= \frac{1}{2 \times 3.14 \times 2 \times 10^{-2}}$$

$$= \frac{100}{3.14 \times 4} = \frac{25}{3.15} = \frac{25}{\pi} \text{ Hz}$$

53 (a) At angular frequency ω, the current in R-C circuit is given by

$$I_{\text{rms}} = \frac{V_{\text{rms}}}{\sqrt{R^2 + \left(\frac{1}{\omega C}\right)^2}} \quad \ldots\text{(i)}$$

Also, $\frac{I_{\text{rms}}}{2} = \frac{V_{\text{rms}}}{\sqrt{R^2 + \left[\frac{1}{\omega C/3}\right]^2}}$

$$= \frac{V_{\text{rms}}}{\sqrt{R^2 + \frac{9}{\omega^2 C^2}}} \quad \ldots\text{(ii)}$$

From Eqs. (i) and (ii), we get

$$3R^2 = \frac{5}{\omega^2 C^2}$$

$$\Rightarrow \frac{1}{R(\omega C)} = \sqrt{\frac{3}{5}}$$

$$\Rightarrow \frac{X_C}{R} = \sqrt{\frac{3}{5}}$$

54 (c) At resonant frequency,

$$X_L = X_C$$

or $\omega L = \frac{1}{\omega C}$

At frequencies higher than resonance frequencies, $X_L > X_C$

i.e. behaviour is inductive.

55 (b) Wattless component of current

$$= I_V \sin\theta = \frac{E_V}{Z}\sin\theta$$

$$= \frac{220}{\sqrt{R^2 + \omega^2 L^2}} \times \frac{\omega L}{\sqrt{R^2 + \omega^2 L^2}}$$

$$= \frac{220 \times \omega L}{(R^2 + \omega^2 L^2)}$$

$$= \frac{220 \times (2\pi \times 50 \times 0.7)}{(220)^2 + (2\pi \times 50 \times 0.7)^2}$$

$$= \frac{220 \times 220}{(220)^2 + (220)^2} = \frac{1}{2} = 0.5 \text{ A}$$

56 (a) Current in L-C-R series circuit,

$$i = \frac{V}{\sqrt{R^2 + (X_L - X_C)^2}}$$

For current to be maximum, denominator should be minimum which can be done, if

$$X_L = X_C$$

This happens in resonance state of the circuit, i.e.

$$\omega L = \frac{1}{\omega C}$$

or $L = \frac{1}{\omega^2 C}$ …(i)

Given,

$\omega = 1000 \text{ s}^{-1}, C = 10\ \mu\text{F} = 10 \times 10^{-6}\text{F}$

Hence, $L = \frac{1}{(1000)^2 \times 10 \times 10^{-6}}$

$$= 0.1 \text{ H} = 100 \text{ mH}$$

57 (b) Quality factor, $Q = \frac{X_L}{R} = \frac{\omega_0 L}{R}$

At resonance, $\omega_0 = \frac{1}{\sqrt{LC}}$

$$\therefore Q = \frac{L}{R} \times \frac{1}{\sqrt{LC}} = \frac{1}{R}\sqrt{\frac{L}{C}}$$

58 (c) Given frequency,

$$f = \frac{1}{2\pi\sqrt{LC}} \text{ or } f \propto \frac{1}{\sqrt{C}}$$

When capacitor C is replaced by another capacitor C' of dielectric constant K, then

$$C' = KC$$

$$\therefore \frac{f'}{f} = \sqrt{\frac{C}{C'}}$$

or $\frac{125000 - 25000}{125000} = \sqrt{\frac{C}{KC}}$

or $\frac{100}{125} = \frac{1}{\sqrt{K}}$

or $K = \left(\frac{125}{100}\right)^2 = 1.56$

59 (c) In a series L-C circuit, frequency of L-C oscillations is given by

$$f = \frac{1}{2\pi\sqrt{LC}}$$

or $f \propto \frac{1}{\sqrt{LC}}$

$$\Rightarrow \frac{f_1}{f_2} = \sqrt{\frac{L_2 C_2}{L_1 C_1}}$$

Given, $L_1 = L, C_1 = C, L_2 = 2L$, $C_2 = 4C, f_1 = f$

$$\therefore \frac{f}{f_2} = \sqrt{\frac{2L \times 4C}{LC}} = \sqrt{8}$$

$$\Rightarrow f_2 = \frac{f}{2\sqrt{2}}$$

60 (a) Natural frequency is nothing but resonant frequency.

In this case, $X_L = X_C$

$$\Rightarrow \omega_0 L = \frac{1}{\omega_0 C}$$

$$\Rightarrow \omega_0^2 = \frac{1}{LC}$$

$$\Rightarrow \omega_0 = \frac{1}{\sqrt{LC}} \Rightarrow 2\pi f = \frac{1}{\sqrt{LC}}$$

$$\Rightarrow f = \frac{1}{2\pi\sqrt{LC}}$$

61 (d) In an L-C-R circuit in resonance condition,

$$X_L = X_C \text{ or } X_C - X_L = 0$$

62 (b) The Q-factor of series resonant circuit is given as

$$Q = \frac{\text{Voltage across } L \text{ or } C}{\text{Applied voltage (voltage across } R)}$$

$$= \frac{(\omega_r L)i}{Ri} = \frac{\omega_r L}{R}$$

Here, $L = 8.1$ mH, $C = 12.5\ \mu$F, $R = 10\ \Omega$, $f = 500$ Hz

$$\therefore Q = \frac{\omega_r L}{R} = \frac{2\pi f L}{R}$$

$$= \frac{2 \times \pi \times 500 \times 8.1 \times 10^{-3}}{10}$$

$$= 2.5434$$

63 (c) In an L-C-R circuit, phase angle is defined as $\cos\phi = \frac{R}{Z}$

where, $Z = \sqrt{R^2 + (X_L - X_C)^2}$

When circuit is resonant,

$$X_L = X_C \Rightarrow Z = R$$

So, $\cos\phi = \frac{R}{R} = 1, \phi = 0°$

64 (a) Impedance for an R-C circuit is given by

$$Z = \sqrt{R^2 + X_C^2} = \sqrt{R^2 + \left(\frac{1}{\omega C}\right)^2}$$

$$= \sqrt{(100)^2 + \left(\frac{1}{100 \times 20 \times 10^{-6}}\right)^2}$$

$$= \sqrt{10^4 + 25 \times 10^4}$$

$$= 100\sqrt{26} = 510\ \Omega$$

65 (a) The phasor diagram in L-R circuit is given below.

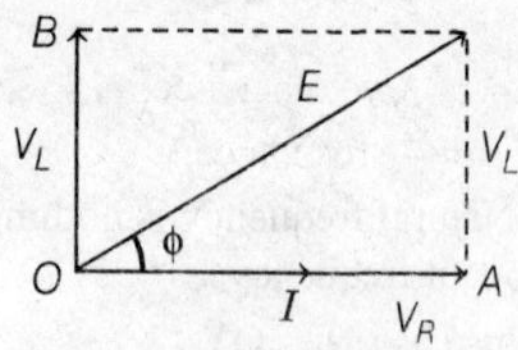

Given, the phase angle between voltage and current

$$\phi = 45°$$

So, $\tan\phi = \frac{V_L}{V_R} = \frac{IX_L}{IR}$

Here, X_L = inductive reactance

$\Rightarrow \tan 45° = \frac{X_L}{R}$

$\Rightarrow 1 = \frac{X_L}{R} \Rightarrow X_L = R$

66 (c) Capacitive reactance,

$$X_C = \frac{1}{2\pi f C}$$

Here, $f = 4000\,\text{Hz}$,

$C = 25 \times 10^{-6}\,\text{F}$

$$= \frac{1}{2\pi \times 4000 \times 25 \times 10^{-6}}$$

$\therefore X_C = \frac{5}{\pi}\,\Omega$

67 (d) In an L-C-R series AC circuit, the voltage across inductor L leads the current by 90° and the voltage across capacitor C lags behind the current by 90°.

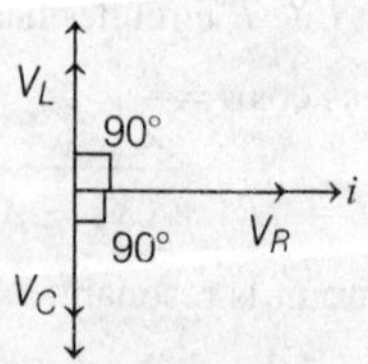

Hence, the voltage across L-C combination will be zero.

68 (a) In circuit (1), on closing the switch, the current in the inductor is zero due to self-induction, i.e. $i_1 = 0$.
In circuit (2), on closing the switch, the current in the inductor is zero due to self-induction.

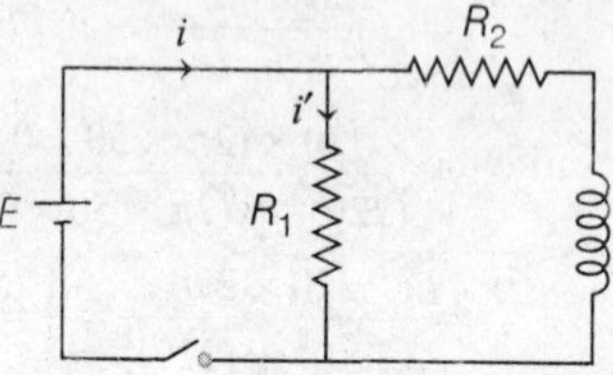

Therefore, $i_2 = i' = \frac{E}{R_1}$

In circuit (3), on closing the switch, the current in the inductor is again zero due to the same reason.

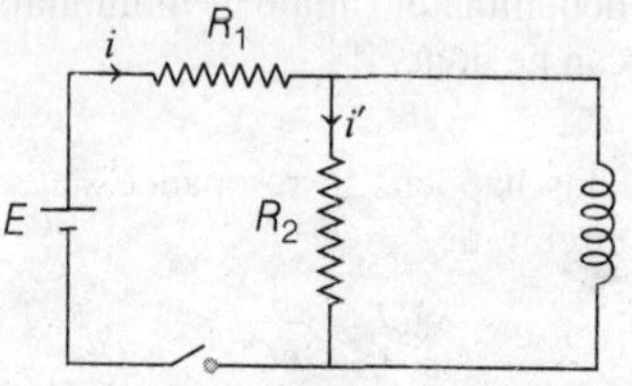

Therefore, $i_3 = i' = \frac{E}{R_1 + R_2}$

Thus, it is obvious that, $i_2 > i_3 > i_1 (= 0)$.

69 (b) $\tan\phi = \frac{X_L}{R}$

$\Rightarrow \tan 45° = \frac{L\omega}{R}$

$\Rightarrow L = \frac{R}{\omega}$ $(\because \tan 45° = 1)$

$$= \frac{100}{2\pi\,(1000)} = \frac{1}{20\pi}$$

70 (a) Reactance of the coil or inductive reactance is given as

$$X_L = \omega L = 2\pi f L$$

where, f is frequency.
Given, $X_L = 50\Omega$, $f = 50\,\text{Hz}$

$\therefore L = \frac{X_L}{\omega} = \frac{X_L}{2\pi f} = \frac{50}{2\pi \times 50}$

$$= \frac{1}{2 \times 3.14} = 0.16\ \text{H}$$

71 (b) $P = VI\cos\phi$

$$= V\left(\frac{V}{Z}\right)\left(\frac{R}{Z}\right) = \frac{V^2R}{Z^2} = \frac{V^2R}{(R^2 + \omega^2L^2)}$$

72 (d) When a circuit contains inductance only, then the current lags behind the voltage by the phase difference of $\frac{\pi}{2}$ or 90°.

73 (b) To decrease current in an AC circuit, choke coil is used. The choke coil has high inductance and negligible resistance, so that the energy loss in the circuit is negligible.
Hence, $X_L >> R$

74 (a) In an L-C circuit, the impedance of circuit is $Z = X_L - X_C$

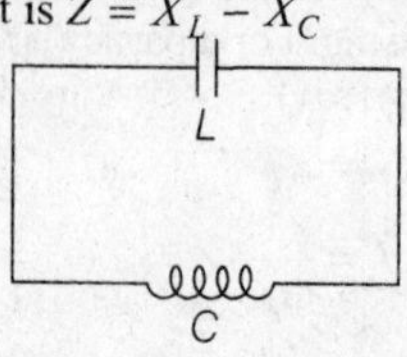

When $X_L = X_C$, then $Z = 0$. In this situation, the amplitude of current in the circuit would be infinite. It will be the condition of electrical resonance and frequency is given by

$$f = \frac{1}{2\pi\sqrt{LC}}$$

$$= \frac{1}{2 \times 3.14 \times \sqrt{10 \times 10^{-3} \times 0.25 \times 10^{-6}}}$$

$$= 3184.7\ \text{cycle s}^{-1}$$

Also, frequency $= \frac{\text{velocity}}{\text{wavelength}}$

$\Rightarrow \lambda = \frac{c}{f} = \frac{3 \times 10^8}{3184.7}$

$$= 9.42 \times 10^4\,\text{m}$$

75 (a) Impedance of L-C-R series circuit is given by

$$Z = \sqrt{R^2 + (X_L - X_C)^2}$$

At resonance, $X_L = X_C \Rightarrow Z = R$

76 (d) In L-C-R series circuit, resonance occurs when

$$X_L = X_C$$

$\Rightarrow \omega L = \frac{1}{\omega C} \Rightarrow \omega^2 = \frac{1}{LC}$

$\Rightarrow \omega = \frac{1}{\sqrt{LC}} \Rightarrow 2\pi f_0 = \frac{1}{\sqrt{LC}}$

$\Rightarrow f_0 = \frac{1}{2\pi\sqrt{LC}}$

$\therefore f_0 \propto \frac{1}{\sqrt{C}}$

When capacitance of the circuit is made 4 times, let its resonant frequency become f_0'.

$\therefore \frac{f_0'}{f_0} = \frac{\sqrt{C}}{\sqrt{4C}}$

or $f_0' = \frac{f_0}{2}$

77 *(d)* Resistance of bulb,

$$R = \frac{V^2}{P} = \frac{(100)^2}{50} = 200\,\Omega$$

Current through bulb,

$$I = \frac{V}{R} = \frac{100}{200} = 0.5\text{A}$$

In a circuit containing inductive reactance (X_L) and resistance (R), impedance (Z) of the circuit is

$$Z = \sqrt{R^2 + \omega^2 L^2} \quad \ldots\text{(i)}$$

Here, $Z = \frac{200}{0.5} = 400\,\Omega$

Now, $X_L^2 = Z^2 - R^2$

$$= (400)^2 - (200)^2$$

$$\Rightarrow (2\pi f L)^2 = 12 \times 10^4$$

$$\therefore \quad L = \frac{2\sqrt{3} \times 100}{2\pi \times 50} = \frac{2\sqrt{3}}{\pi} = 1.1\text{ H}$$

78 *(b)* The phase angle (θ) between I and V is given by

$$\tan\theta = \frac{X_L - X_C}{R} \quad \ldots\text{(i)}$$

where, $X_L = 2\pi f L$

$$= 2\pi \times 50 \times \left[\frac{200}{\pi} \times 10^{-3}\right]$$

$$= 20\,\Omega$$

$$X_C = \frac{1}{2\pi f C} = \frac{1 \times \pi}{2\pi \times 50 \times 10^{-3}}$$

$$= 10\,\Omega \text{ and } R = 10\,\Omega$$

On substituting values of X_L, X_C and R in Eq. (i), we get

$$\tan\theta = \frac{20 - 10}{10} = 1$$

$$\Rightarrow \tan\theta = \tan\frac{\pi}{4} \Rightarrow \theta = \frac{\pi}{4}$$

So, the phase angle of the circuit is $\pi/4$.

79 *(a)* Current through the circuit,

$$i = \frac{V_{\text{rms}}}{\sqrt{R^2 + (X_L - X_C)^2}}$$

Given, $R = 3\Omega$, $X_L = 15\Omega$, $X_C = 11\Omega$ and $V_{\text{rms}} = 10\text{ V}$

$$\therefore \quad i = \frac{10}{\sqrt{(3)^2 + (15-11)^2}}$$

$$= \frac{10}{\sqrt{9+16}} = \frac{10}{5} = 2\text{ A}$$

Since, L, C and R are connected in series combination, then potential difference across R is

$$V_R = iR = 2 \times 3 = 6\text{ V}$$

Across L, $V_L = iX_L = 2 \times 15 = 30\text{ V}$

Across C, $V_C = iX_C = 2 \times 11 = 22\text{ V}$

So, potential difference across series combination of L and C

$$= V_L - V_C = 30 - 22 = 8\text{ V}$$

80 *(a)* Since, current lags behind the voltage in phase by a constant angle, then circuit must contain R and L.

81 *(a)* From the formula, the frequency of oscillation is

$$f = \frac{1}{2\pi\sqrt{LC}} = \frac{1}{2\pi\sqrt{0.25 \times 0.1 \times 10^{-6}}}$$

$$\approx 1007\text{ Hz}$$

82 *(d)* Energy of charged capacitor = Energy generated across inductor coil

$$E = \frac{1}{2}CV^2 = \frac{1}{2}Li^2$$

Given, $C = 16\mu\text{F} = 16 \times 10^{-6}\text{F}$,

$$V = 20\text{ V}$$

and $L = 40\text{ mH} = 40 \times 10^{-3}\text{H}$

$$\therefore \quad \frac{1}{2} \times 16 \times 10^{-6} \times (20)^2$$

$$= \frac{1}{2} \times 40 \times 10^{-3} \times i^2$$

$$\Rightarrow \quad i^2 = \frac{16}{100} \Rightarrow i = 0.4\text{ A}$$

83 *(a)* The phase difference, $\tan\phi = \frac{X_L}{R}$

and $X_L = \omega L = 2\pi f L$

$$= 2\pi \times 50 \times 0.01 = \pi\ \Omega$$

Also, $R = 1\,\Omega \Rightarrow \phi = \tan^{-1}(\pi)$

84 *(d)* For an L-C-R circuit, the impedance (Z) is given by

$$Z = \sqrt{R^2 + (X_L - X_C)^2}$$

where, $X_L = \omega L = 2\pi f L$

and $X_C = \frac{1}{\omega C} = \frac{1}{2\pi f C}$

Given, $f = \frac{50}{\pi}\text{ Hz}$, $R = 300\,\Omega$, $L = 1\text{ H}$

and $C = 20\,\mu\text{C} = 20 \times 10^{-6}\text{C}$.

$$\therefore Z = \sqrt{(300)^2 + \left(2\pi \times \frac{50}{\pi} \times 1 - \frac{1}{2\pi \times \frac{50}{\pi} \times 20 \times 10^{-6}}\right)^2}$$

$$= \sqrt{90000 + (100 - 500)^2}$$

$$= \sqrt{90000 + 160000} = 500\,\Omega$$

Hence, current in circuit is given by

$$i = \frac{V}{Z} = \frac{50}{500} = 0.1\text{ A}$$

Voltage across capacitor,

$$V_C = iX_C = \frac{i}{2\pi f C}$$

$$= \frac{0.1}{2\pi \times \frac{50}{\pi} \times 20 \times 10^{-6}}$$

$$= \frac{0.1 \times 10^6}{100 \times 20} = 50\text{ V}$$

85 *(a)* Inductive reactance, $X_L = \omega L$

Capacitive reactance,

$$X_C = \frac{1}{\omega C}$$

$$\Rightarrow \quad \frac{X_L}{X_C} = \frac{\omega L}{1/\omega C} = \omega^2 LC$$

86 *(d)* The condition for resonance is that the frequency of the applied emf should be equal to the natural frequency of the circuit when the resistance of the circuit is zero.

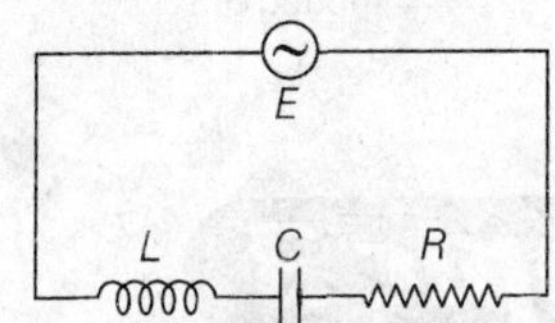

$\therefore$ The frequency, $f = \frac{1}{2\pi}\frac{1}{\sqrt{LC}}$

Given, $C = \frac{C}{4}$, $L_1 = L$

Now, the frequency will be

$$f' = \frac{1}{2\pi}\frac{1}{\sqrt{L_2 \cdot \frac{C}{4}}}$$

Since, $f' = f \Rightarrow L_2 = 4L$

Hence, inductance should be made 4 times.

87 *(b)* At resonance, $X_L = X_C$

i.e. $\omega_r L = \frac{1}{\omega_r C}$ or $\omega_r = \frac{1}{\sqrt{LC}}$

$$\Rightarrow 2\pi f_r = \frac{1}{\sqrt{LC}} \Rightarrow f_r = \frac{1}{2\pi\sqrt{LC}}$$

or $LC = \text{constant}$

(as ν remains same)

$$\therefore \quad \frac{L_2}{L_1} = \frac{C_1}{C_2} \text{ or } \frac{L_2}{L} = \frac{C}{2C}$$

or $L_2 = \frac{L}{2}$

88 (d) $\tan\phi = \frac{X_L}{R} = \frac{\omega L}{R} = \frac{2\pi f L}{R}$

$\Rightarrow \quad \tan\phi = \frac{2 \times 3.14 \times 50 \times 0.5}{157} = 1$

$\Rightarrow \quad \phi = 45°$

89 (b) Quality factor,

$$Q = \frac{\omega}{\omega_2 - \omega_1} = \frac{\omega}{2\pi(f_2 - f_1)}$$

but $\omega = \frac{1}{\sqrt{LC}}$

$$\Rightarrow Q = \frac{1}{2\pi\sqrt{LC}} \times \frac{1}{(f_2 - f_1)}$$

$$0.4 = \frac{1}{2\pi\sqrt{L \times 0.1 \times 10^{-6}}} \times \frac{1}{1.3 \times 10^3}$$

$$\Rightarrow L = \frac{1}{\left[4\pi^2 (0.4 \times 1.3 \times 10^3)^2 \times 0.1 \times 10^{-6}\right]}$$

$= 0.94$ H

90 (b) The impedance of the L-C-R circuit is given by

$$Z = \sqrt{R^2 + (X_L - X_C)^2}$$

or $\quad Z = \sqrt{R^2 + (X_L - X_L)^2} = R \quad (\because X_L = X_C)$

$\therefore \quad Z = 25\,\Omega \quad (\because R = 25\,\Omega)$

91 (b) The frequency of oscillation of L-C circuit is given by

$$f = \frac{1}{2\pi\sqrt{LC}} \text{ or } LC = \frac{1}{4\pi^2 f^2}$$

$$\Rightarrow \quad L = \frac{1}{4\pi^2 f^2 C}$$

Given, $f = 1$ MHz $= 1 \times 10^6$ Hz

$\Rightarrow \quad C = 0.3$ pF $= 0.3 \times 10^{-12}$F

$$\therefore \quad L = \frac{1}{\left[4 \times \frac{22}{7} \times \frac{22}{7} \times (10^6)^2 \times 0.3 \times 10^{-12}\right]}$$

$$= \frac{490}{4 \times 484 \times 3 \times 10^{12} \times 10^{-12}}$$

$= 0.0844$ H $= 84.4$ mH

92 (c) For better tuning, peak of current growth must be sharp. This is ensured by a high value of quality factor Q.

Now, quality factor is given by

$$Q = \frac{1}{R}\sqrt{\frac{L}{C}}$$

From the given options, highest value of Q is associated with $R = 15\,\Omega$, $L = 3.5$ H and $C = 30\,\mu$F.

93 (a) The given equation,

$$e = 300 \sin [(100\pi)\, t] \text{volt} \quad \text{...(i)}$$

We know that,

$$e = e_0 \sin \omega t \quad \text{... (ii)}$$

On comparing Eqs. (i) and (ii), we get

$e_0 = 300$ V

and $\quad R = 100\Omega$

The rms current through the circuit $i_{rms} = ?$

$$i_{rms} = \frac{e_0}{\sqrt{2}R} = \frac{300}{\sqrt{2} \times 100} = \frac{3}{\sqrt{2}}\text{A}$$

94 (b) Capacitive reactance (X_C) is given by $\quad X_C = 1/\omega C$

where, ω is angular frequency and C the capacitance.

Also, $\omega = 2\pi f$, where f is frequency.

In a DC circuit, $f = 0$

$\Rightarrow \quad \omega = 0$

$\Rightarrow \quad X_C = \frac{1}{0} = \infty$

Topic 3

Growth and Decay of Current

2019

1

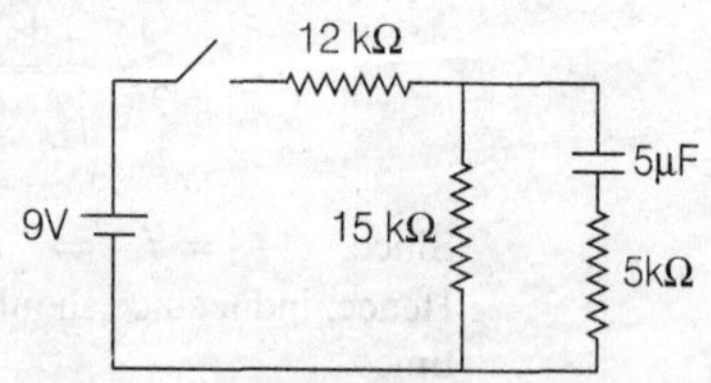

In the given circuit, find charge on capacitor after 1s of opening the switch at $t = \infty$. **[AIIMS]**

(a) $20\, e^{-10}\,\mu$C
(b) $25\, e^{-10}\,\mu$C
(c) $30\, e^{-10}\,\mu$C
(d) $35\, e^{-10}\,\mu$C

2018

2 An ideal coil of 10 H is connected in series with a resistance of 5Ω and a battery of 5 V. After 2 s, after the connection is made, the current flowing (in ampere) in the circuit is **[AIIMS]**

(a) $(1 - e)$
(b) e
(c) e^{-1}
(d) $(1 - e^{-1})$

2016

3 An inductor of inductance $L = 400$ mH and resistors of resistances $R_1 = 4\,\Omega$ and $R_2 = 2\,\Omega$ are connected to battery of emf 12 V as shown in the figure. The internal resistance of the battery is negligible. The switch S is closed at $t = 0$. The potential drop across L as a function of time is **[AIEEE]**

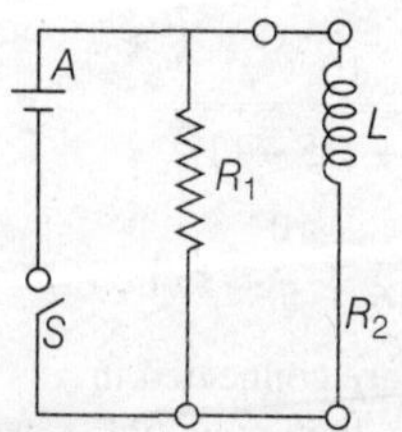

(a) $6e^{-5t}$ V
(b) $\frac{12}{t} e^{-3t}$ V
(c) $6(1 - e^{-t/0.2})$ V
(d) $12e^{-5t}$ V

2010

4 A coil of resistance R and inductance L is connected to a battery of emf e volt. The final current in the coil is **[VMMC]**

(a) $\frac{e}{R}$ (b) $\frac{e}{L}$

(c) $\sqrt{\frac{e}{R^2+L^2}}$ (d) $\sqrt{\frac{eL}{R^2+L^2}}$

2008

5 When the key K is pressed at $t=0$, which of the following statements about the current I in the resistor AB of the given circuit is true? **[AIIMS]**

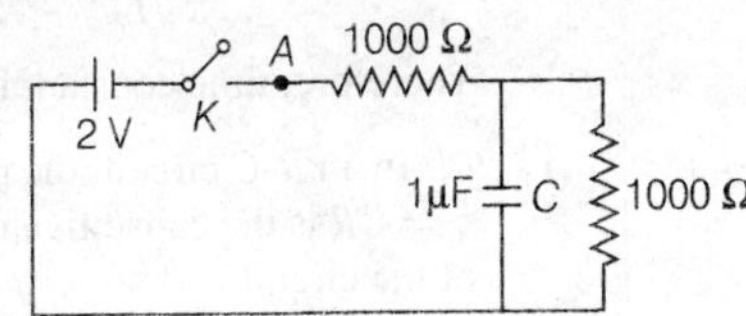

(a) $I = 2\,\text{mA}$ at all t
(b) I oscillates between 1 mA and 2 mA
(c) $I = 1\,\text{mA}$ at all t
(d) At $t=0, I = 2\,\text{mA}$ and with time, it goes to 1 mA

6 A coil of inductance 300 mH and resistance 2 Ω is connected to a source of voltage 2 V. The current reaches half of its steady state value in **[UP CPMT]**

(a) 0.05 s (b) 0.1 s
(c) 0.15 s (d) 0.3 s

2007

7 In an L-R circuit, time constant is that time in which current grows from zero to the value **[RPMT]**

(a) $0.63\, I_0$ (b) $0.50\, I_0$
(c) $0.37\, I_0$ (d) I_0

where, I_0 is steady state current.

8 A coil of 40 H inductance is connected in series with a resistance of 8 Ω and this combination is connected to the terminals of 2 V battery. The inductive time constant of the circuit is (in second) **[EAMCET]**

(a) 40 (b) 20
(c) 5 (d) 0.2

9 The inductive time constant in an electrical circuit is **[CG PMT]**

(a) LR (b) $\frac{L}{R}$ (c) $\sqrt{\frac{L}{R}}$ (d) $\frac{R}{L}$

10 Time constant of L-C circuit is **[BVP]**

(a) $\frac{1}{2\pi LC}$ (b) $\frac{1}{2\pi L^2C^2}$ (c) $\frac{LC}{2\pi}$ (d) $2\pi\sqrt{LC}$

2005

11 In order to obtain time constant of 10 s in an R-C circuit containing a resistance of 10^3 Ω, the capacity of the condenser should be **[DUMET]**

(a) 10 μF (b) 100 μF
(c) 1000 μF (d) 10000 μF

Answers

1 (b)	2 (d)	3 (d)	4 (a)	5 (d)	6 (b)	7 (a)	8 (c)	9 (b)	10 (d)
11 (d)									

Explanations

1 *(b)* At $t \to \infty$, capacitor Works as an open circuit as shown in the figure.

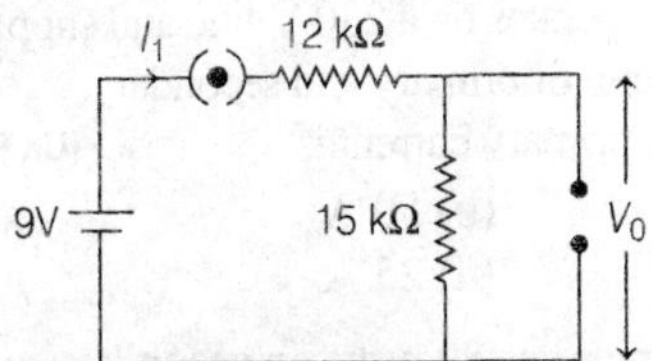

Therefore, current flow in the circuit,

$$I_1 = \frac{9}{(12+15)10^3} = \frac{1}{3}\times 10^{-3}\text{ A}$$

$\therefore\ V_0 = I_1 \times 15 \times 10^3$

$$= \frac{1}{3}\times 10^{-3}\times 15\times 10^3 = 5\text{ V}$$

$\therefore$ Charge on capacitor of 5 μF,

$$q_0 = CV_0 = 5\times 10^{-6}\times 5$$
$$= 25\times 10^{-6}\text{ C} = 25\,\mu\text{C}$$

When switch is open, then capacitor starts discharging across $(5+15 = 20\text{ k}\,\Omega)$ and instantaneous charge on capacitor is given by

$$q = q_0\, e^{-t/RC}$$
$$= 25\, e^{-\frac{1}{20\times 10^3\times 5\times 10^{-6}}} \quad [\because t = 1\text{ s}]$$
$$= 25e^{-10}\,\mu\text{C}$$

2 *(d)* Rise of current in L-R circuit is given by

$$I = I_0(1-e^{-t/\tau})$$

where, $I_0 = \frac{E}{R} = \frac{5}{5} = 1\text{ A}$

Now, $\tau = \frac{L}{R} = \frac{10}{5} = 2\text{ s}$

After 2 s, i.e. at $t = 2$ s

Rise of current, $I = (1-e^{-1})$ A

3 *(d)* $I_1 = \frac{F}{R_1} = \frac{12}{2} = 6\text{ A}$

$$E = L\frac{dI_2}{dt} + R_2\times I_2$$
$$I_2 = I_0(1-e^{-t/t_c})$$
$$\Rightarrow I_0 = \frac{E}{R_2} = \frac{12}{2} = 6\text{ A}$$

$\Rightarrow \quad t_c = \frac{L}{R} = \frac{400 \times 10^{-3}}{2} = 0.2$

$\therefore \quad I_2 = 6(1 - e^{-t/0.2})$

Potential drop across inductor L

$= E - R_2 I_2$

$= 12 - 2 \times 6(1 - e^{-bt})$

$= 12e^{-5t}$ V

4 *(a)* Final current is constant and L plays no role at that instant.

Therefore, $i = e/R$.

5 *(d)* At time, $t = 0$, i.e. when capacitor is charging,

Current, $I = \frac{2}{1000} = 2$ mA

When capacitor is full charged, no current will pass through it, hence current through the circuit,

$I = \frac{2}{2000} = 1$ mA

6 *(b)* The current at any instant is given by

$I = I_0(1 - e^{-Rt/L})$

$\Rightarrow \quad \frac{I_0}{2} = I_0(1 - e^{-Rt/L})$

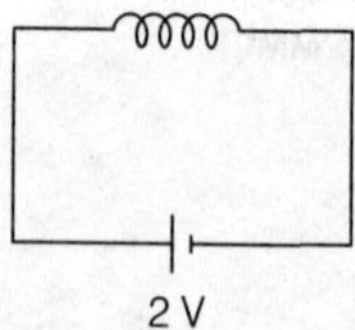

$\Rightarrow \quad \frac{1}{2} = (1 - e^{-Rt/L})$

$\Rightarrow \quad e^{-Rt/L} = 1/2 \Rightarrow \frac{Rt}{L} = \ln 2$

$\therefore \quad t = \frac{L}{R}\ln 2 = \frac{300 \times 10^{-3}}{2} \times 0.693$

$= 150 \times 0.693 \times 10^{-3} = 0.1$ s

7 *(a)* The equation for growth of current in *L-R* circuit is given by

$I = I_0(1 - e^{-t/\tau})$

Here, $\tau\left(= \frac{L}{R}\right)$ is called time constant of the *L-R* circuit.

At a time equal to one time constant, i.e. at $t = \tau$,

$I = I_0(1 - e^{-1})$

or $I = I_0\left(1 - \frac{1}{e}\right)$

or $I = 0.63 I_0$

8 *(c)* Time constant of *L-R* circuit,

$t = \frac{L}{R} = \frac{40}{8} = 5$ s

9 *(b)* $\frac{L}{R}$ has got dimensions of time and is known an inductive time constant.

10 *(d)* For an *L-C* circuit, resonant frequency

$= \frac{1}{2\pi\sqrt{LC}}$

Therefore, time constant is $2\pi\sqrt{LC}$.

11 *(d)* In an *R-C* circuit, the product $\tau_c = CR$ is the capacitive time constant of the circuit.

Given, $\tau_c = 10$ s, $R = 10^3 \Omega$

$\therefore \quad C = \frac{\tau_c}{R}$

$= \frac{10}{10^3} = 10^{-2}$F

$= 10000 \mu$F

Topic 4

Transformer

2019

1 A transformer with turns ratio $\frac{N_1}{N_2} = \frac{50}{1}$ is connected to a 120 V AC supply. If primary and secondary circuit resistances are $1.5\text{k}\Omega$ and 1Ω respectively, then find out power of output. **[AIIMS]**

(a) 5.76 W (b) 11.4 W
(c) 2.89 W (d) 7.56 W

2014

2 A transformer having efficiency of 90% is working on 200V and 3 kW power supply. If the current in the secondary coil is 6 A, then the voltage across the secondary coil and the current in the primary coil respectively, are **[CBSE AIPMT]**

(a) 300 V, 15 A (b) 450 V, 15 A
(c) 450 V, 13.5 A (d) 600 V, 15 A

3 Transformer is used to **[Kerala CEE]**

(a) convert AC to DC voltage
(b) convert DC to AC voltage
(c) obtain desired DC power
(d) obtain desired AC voltage and current
(e) obtain desired DC voltage and current

4 A step-up transformer operates on a 230 V line and supplies a current of 2 A. The ratio of primary and secondary windings is 1 : 25. The primary current is **[UK PMT]**

(a) 12.5 A (b) 50 A
(c) 8.8 A (d) 25 A

5 A step-down transformer has 50 turns on secondary and 1000 turns on primary winding. If a transformer is connected to 220 V, 1 A AC source, then what is output current of the transformer? **[KCET]**

(a) (1/20) A (b) 20A (c) 100A (d) 2A

2013

6 Which quantity is increased in step-down transformer? [UP CPMT]
(a) Current (b) Voltage
(c) Power (d) Frequency

2012

7 A transformer of 100% efficiency has 200 turns in the primary and 40000 turns in secondary. It is connected to a 220 V main supply and secondary feeds to a 100 kΩ resistance. The potential difference per turn is [AIIMS]
(a) 1.1 V (b) 25 V
(c) 18 V (d) 11 V

8 In a step-up transformer, the turns ratio is 1 : 2.
A Leclanche cell (emf = 1.5 V) is connected across the primary. The voltage developed in the secondary would be [UP CPMT]
(a) 3 V (b) 0.75 V
(c) 1.5 V (d) zero

9 A transformer works on the principle of [KCET]
(a) self-induction
(b) electrical inertia
(c) mutual induction
(d) magnetic effect of the electrical current

2011

10 A transformer has 500 primary turns and 10 secondary turns. If the secondary has a resistive load of 15 Ω, the currents in the primary and secondary respectively, are [DUMET]
(a) 0.16A, 3.2×10^{-3} A (b) 3.2×10^{-3} A, 0.16 A
(c) 0.16A, 0.16 A (d) 3.2×10^{-3} A, 3.2×10^{-3} A

2008

11 A transformer is used to light a 100 W and 110 V lamp from a 220 V mains. If the main current is 0.5 A, then the efficiency of the transformer is approximately [UP CPMT]
(a) 30 % (b) 50 % (c) 90 % (d) 10 %

12 The primary and secondary coils of a transformer have 50 and 1500 turns, respectively. If the magnetic flux ϕ linked with the primary coil is given by $\phi = \phi_0 + 4t$, where ϕ is in weber, t is time in second and ϕ_0 is a constant, then the output voltage across the secondary coil is [RPMT]
(a) 90 V (b) 120 V
(c) 220 V (d) 30 V

13 The core of a transformer is laminated because [Haryana PMT]
(a) energy losses due to eddy currents may be minimised
(b) the weight of the transformer may be reduced
(c) rusting of the core may be prevented
(d) ratio of voltages in primary and secondary may be increased

14 In step-up transformer, relation between number of turns in primary (N_p) and number of turns in secondary (N_s) coils is [J&K CET]
(a) N_s is greater than N_p (b) N_p is greater than N_s
(c) N_s is equal to N_p (d) $N_p = 2N_s$

15 A transformer has 1500 turns in the primary coil and 1125 turns in the secondary coil. If the voltage in the primary coil is 200 V, then the voltage in the secondary coil is [EAMCET]
(a) 100 V (b) 150 V
(c) 200 V (d) 250 V

16 A current of 5 A is flowing at 220 V in the primary coil of a transformer. If the voltage produced in the secondary coil is 2200 V and 50% of power is lost, then the current in secondary will be [KCET]
(a) 2.5 A (b) 5 A
(c) 0.25 A (d) 0.5 A

2007

17 A step-down transformer reduces the voltage of a transmission line from 2200 V to 220 V. The power delivered by it is 880 W and its efficiency is 88%. The input current is [KCET]
(a) 4.65 mA (b) 0.045 A
(c) 0.45 A (d) 4.65 A

18 Voltage in the secondary coil of a transformer does not depend upon [BCECE]
(a) frequency of the source
(b) voltage in the primary coil
(c) ratio of number of turns in the two coils
(d) Both (b) and (c)

19 When power is drawn from the secondary coil of the transformer, the dynamic resistance [JCECE]
(a) increases (b) decreases
(c) remains unchanged (d) changes erratically

2006

20 Core of a transformer is made up of [Punjab PMET]
(a) soft iron (b) steel (c) iron (d) alnico

2005

21 The turns ratio of a transformer is given as 2 : 3. If the current through the primary coil is 3 A, thus calculate the current through load resistance. [BHU]
(a) 1 A (b) 4.5 A
(c) 2 A (d) 1.5 A

22 A transformer with efficiency 80% works at 4 kW and 100 V. If the secondary voltage is 200 V, then the primary and secondary currents are respectively, [Kerala CEE]
(a) 40 A, 16 A (b) 16 A, 40 A
(c) 20 A, 40 A (d) 40 A, 20 A
(e) 40 A, 10 A

23 The number of turns in primary and secondary of a transformer are 5 and 10 and mutual inductance of transformer is 25 H. Now, if the number of turns in primary and secondary are 10 and 5, the new mutual inductance will be [RPMT]

(a) 6.25 H (b) 12.5 H
(c) 25 H (d) 50 H

24 Quantity that remains unchanged in a transformer is [J&K CET]

(a) voltage (b) current
(c) frequency (d) None of these

25 If a transformer of an audio amplifier has output impedance 8000 Ω and the speaker has input impedance of 8 Ω, the primary and secondary turns of this transformer connected between the output of amplifier and to loudspeaker should have the ratio [JCECE]

(a) 1000 : 1 (b) 100 : 1 (c) 1 : 32 (d) 32 : 1

26 The coefficient of mutual inductance between the primary and secondary coils of transformer is 5 H. A current of 10 A is cut-off in 0.5 s. The induced emf is [JCECE]

(a) 1 V (b) 10 V (c) 5 V (d) 100 V

Answers

1 (a)	2 (b)	3 (d)	4 (b)	5 (b)	6 (a)	7 (a)	8 (d)	9 (c)	10 (b)
11 (c)	12 (b)	13 (a)	14 (a)	15 (b)	16 (c)	17 (c)	18 (a)	19 (a)	20 (a)
21 (c)	22 (a)	23 (c)	24 (c)	25 (a)	26 (d)				

Explanations

1 (a) Given, turn ratio of a transformer,

$$\frac{N_1}{N_2} = \frac{50}{1}$$

$$\Rightarrow \quad N_1 = 50N_2$$

Since, $\frac{N_1}{N_2} = \frac{V_1}{V_2}$

$$50 = \frac{120}{V_2} \quad [V_1 = 120 \text{ V (given)}]$$

$$\Rightarrow \quad V_2 = \frac{12}{5} \text{ V}$$

Output power at secondary coil,

$$P_s = \frac{V_2^2}{R_2} \quad [R_2 = 1\Omega \text{ (given)}]$$

$$= \frac{\left(\frac{12}{5}\right)^2}{1} = \frac{144}{25}$$

$$= 5.76 \text{ W}$$

2 (b) Initial power = 3 kW= 3000 W

As efficiency is 90%, then final power

$$= 3000 \times \frac{90}{100} = 2700 \text{ W}$$

$$\Rightarrow \quad V_1 I_1 = 3000 \text{ W} \quad \text{...(i)}$$

$$V_2 I_2 = 2700 \text{ W} \quad \text{...(ii)}$$

So, $V_2 = \frac{2700}{6} = \frac{900}{2} = 450 \text{ V}$

and $I_1 = \frac{3000}{200} = 15 \text{ A}$

3 (d) Transformer is used to obtain desired AC voltage and current, because a transformer is a device based on the principle of mutual induction, which is used for converting large AC at low voltage into small current at high voltage and *vice-versa*.

4 (b) As we know that, for transformer,

$$\frac{V_1}{V_2} = \frac{I_2}{I_1} = \frac{N_1}{N_2}$$

where, all the symbols have their usual meanings. (Suffix 1 is for primary and 2 is for the secondary)

$$\Rightarrow \quad \frac{N_1}{N_2} = \frac{1}{25} = \frac{2}{I}$$

where, I = primary side current.

$$I = 50 \text{ A}$$

5 (b) We know that,

Power in the secondary coil = Power in the primary coil

$$V_s \times N_p = V_p \times N_s$$

$$\Rightarrow \quad \frac{N_s}{N_p} = \frac{V_s}{V_p}$$

where,

V_s = voltage across secondary coil,

V_p = voltage across primary coil,

N_p = number of turns is primary coil

and N_s = number of turns in secondary coil.

Given, $N_s = 50$ turns, $N_p = 1000$ turns

$V_p = 220$ V, $I_s = ?$

$$\frac{50}{1000} = \frac{V_s}{220}$$

$$\Rightarrow \quad V_s = \frac{50 \times 220}{1000} = 11 \text{ V}$$

But $V_s I_s = V_p I_p$

$$\Rightarrow 11 \times I_s = 220 \times 1$$

$$I_s = 220/11 = 20 \text{ A}$$

6 (a) In step-down transformer, voltage decreases and corresponding current increases.

7 (a) From transformer ratio,

$$\frac{V_s}{V_p} = \frac{N_s}{N_p}$$

$$\Rightarrow \quad V_s = \frac{V_p \times N_s}{N_p}$$

$$= \frac{220 \times 40000}{200} = 44000 \text{ V}$$

Potential difference per turn is

$$\frac{V_s}{N_s} = \frac{44000}{40000} = 1.1 \text{ V}$$

8 (d) Transformer is an AC device, which work on varying voltage, but Leclanche cell is a DC source with fixed voltage or emf. So, there is no voltage developed across secondary, i.e. it is zero.

9 (c) A transformer works on the principle of mutual induction.

10 (b) We have, $\frac{N_s}{N_p}=\frac{i_p}{i_s} \Rightarrow \frac{10}{500}=\frac{i_p}{i_s}$

$\Rightarrow \quad \frac{i_p}{i_s}=\frac{1}{50} \Rightarrow i_s=50i_p$

This condition is satisfied only when current in primary is 3.2×10^{-3} A and in secondary 0.16 A.

11 (c) Efficiency of transformer,

$$\eta=\frac{\text{Output power}}{\text{Input power}}=\frac{V_sI_s}{V_pI_p}$$

Given, $V_sI_s=100$ W,

$V_p=220$ V, $I_p=0.5$ A

Hence, $\eta=\frac{100}{220\times0.5}=0.90$ or 90%

12 (b) The magnetic flux linked with the primary coil is given by

$$\phi=\phi_0+4t$$

So, voltage across primary coil,

$$V_p=\frac{d\phi}{dt}=\frac{d}{dt}(\phi_0+4t)=4\text{ V}$$

(as $\phi_0=$ constant)

Also, we have,

$N_p=50$ and $N_s=1500$

From relation, $\frac{V_s}{V_p}=\frac{N_s}{N_p}$

$\Rightarrow \quad V_s=V_p\frac{N_s}{N_p}=4\left(\frac{1500}{50}\right)=120$ V

13 (a) When magnetic flux linked with a coil changes, induced emf is produced in it and the induced current flows through the wire forming the coil. These currents look like eddies or whirlpools and likewise are known as eddy currents. They are also known as Focault's current.

These currents oppose the cause of their origin, therefore due to eddy currents, a great amount of energy is wasted in the form of heat energy. If core of transformer is laminated, then their effect can be minimised.

14 (a) In step-up transformer, number of turns in primary coil is less than the number of turns in secondary coil.

i.e. $\frac{N_s}{N_p}>1$

$\Rightarrow \quad N_s>N_p$

15 (b) By the relation, $\frac{N_1}{N_2}=\frac{V_1}{V_2}$

Given, $N_1=1500$ turns,

$N_2=1125$ turns

and $V_1=200$ V

$\therefore \quad \frac{1500}{1125}=\frac{200}{V_2}$

$\Rightarrow \quad V_2=\frac{200\times1125}{1500}=150$ V

16 (c) Given, $V_p=220$ V, $V_s=2200$ V,

$I_p=5$ A and power loss = 50%

Efficiency of transformer (η) is defined as the ratio of output power and input power, i.e.

$$\eta\%=\frac{P_{\text{out}}}{P_{\text{in}}}\times100=\frac{V_sI_s}{V_pI_p}\times100$$

$$50=\frac{2200\times I_s}{220\times5}\times100$$

$\Rightarrow \quad I_s=0.25$ A

17 (c) Efficiency of transformer,

$$\eta=\frac{\text{Output power}}{\text{Input power}}$$

$\Rightarrow \quad \frac{88}{100}=\frac{880}{P_i}$

$\Rightarrow \quad P_i=1000$ W

Input current, $I_i=\frac{P_i}{V_i}=\frac{1000}{2200}=0.45$ A

18 (a) Voltage in the secondary coil of a transformer does not depend upon frequency of the source.

19 (a) When power is drawn from the secondary coil of the transformer, its dynamic resistance increases. This is because the flux of secondary coil reduces the flux of core and thus the back emf decreases. This decreases the current in secondary coil.

20 (a) Soft iron is used for making transformer's cores. Because it has low hysteresis loss.

21 (c) If i_s and i_p be the currents in the primary and secondary coils at any instant and the energy losses be zero, then

Power in secondary coil = Power in primary coil

$$V_s\times i_s=V_p\times i_p$$

$\Rightarrow \quad \frac{i_p}{i_s}=\frac{V_s}{V_p}=\frac{N_s}{N_p}=$ transformer ratio

Given, $\frac{N_p}{N_s}=\frac{2}{3}, i_p=3$ A

$\Rightarrow \quad i_s=\frac{N_p}{N_s}i_p=\frac{2}{3}\times3=2$ A

22 (a) Efficiency, $\eta=\frac{\text{Output power}}{\text{Input power}}$

$\Rightarrow \quad \eta=\frac{V_sI_s}{V_pI_p}$

$\Rightarrow \quad \frac{80}{100}=\frac{200\times I_s}{4000}$

$\Rightarrow \quad I_s=16$ A

Also, $V_pI_p=4000$

$\Rightarrow \quad I_p=\frac{4000}{100}=40$ A

23 (c) Mutual inductance of transformer,

$$M\propto N_1N_2$$

$\Rightarrow \quad \frac{M_1}{M_2}=\frac{N_1N_2}{N'_1N'_2}$

$\Rightarrow \quad \frac{25}{M_2}=\frac{5\times10}{10\times5}$

$\Rightarrow \quad M_2=25$ H

24 (c) Frequency remains unchanged in a transformer, while current and voltage changes.

25 (a) From Faraday's law, the induced emf across primary and secondary is

$$e_p=-N_p\frac{\Delta\phi}{\Delta t},$$

$$e_s=-N_s\frac{\Delta\phi}{\Delta t}$$

Also, $e=iR$

$\therefore \quad \frac{R_p}{R_s}=\frac{N_p}{N_s}$

Given, $R_s=8000\ \Omega, R_p=8\ \Omega$

$\therefore \quad \frac{N_s}{N_p}=\frac{R_s}{R_p}=\frac{8000}{8}$

$=\frac{1000}{1}=1000:1$

26 (d) From Faraday's law of electromagnetic induction, the induced emf e is given by

$$e=-M\frac{di}{dt}$$

Given, $M=5$ H, $di=10$ A, $dt=0.5$ s

$\therefore \quad e=-5\times\frac{10}{0.5}=-100$ V

$|e|=100$ V

22

Electromagnetic Waves

Quick Review

Displacement Current

While applying the Ampere's circuital law to find magnetic field at a point outside a capacitor which connected to a time varying current, Maxwell noticed an inconsistency in Ampere's law. He suggested the existence of an additional current and called it displacement current.

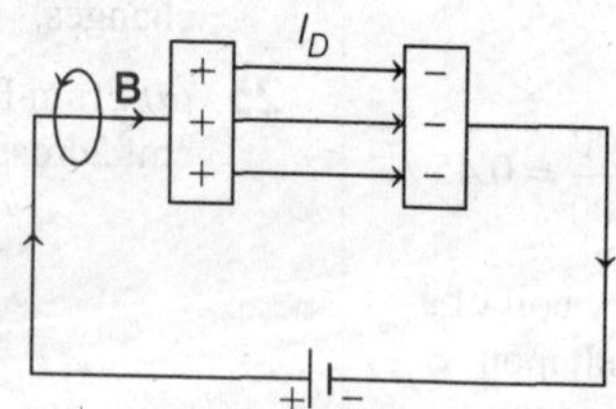

"Displacement current is a current which is produced due to rate of change of electric flux with respect to time".

It is given by $I_D = \varepsilon_0 \dfrac{d\phi_E}{dt}$ ...(i)

According to Ampere's circuital law, we have

$$\oint \mathbf{B} \cdot d\mathbf{l} = \mu_0 I_C \quad \text{...(ii)}$$

where, I_C = current threading through Amperian loop.

- Modified Ampere's circuital law is expressed as

$$\oint \mathbf{B} \cdot d\mathbf{l} = \mu_0 (I_C + I_D)$$

$$= \mu_0 \left(I_C + \varepsilon_0 \frac{d\phi_E}{dt} \right)$$

[from Eqs. (i) and (ii)]

This is also called Ampere-Maxwell law.

Maxwell's Equations

Maxwell's equations are the basic laws of electricity and magnetism. These equations give complete description of all electromagnetic interactions. There are four Maxwell's equations which are explained as below

(i) **Gauss's Law of Electrostatics** This law states that the total electric flux through any closed surface is always equal to $\dfrac{1}{\varepsilon_0}$ times the net charge enclosed by the surface.

It is given by $\oint_S \mathbf{E} \cdot d\mathbf{S} = \dfrac{q}{\varepsilon_0}$.

This equation is called **Maxwell's first equation.**

(ii) **Gauss's Law of Magnetism** This law states that, the net magnetic flux through any closed surface is always zero.

It is given by $\oint \mathbf{B} \cdot d\mathbf{S} = 0$.

This equation is called **Maxwell's second equation.**

(iii) **Faraday's Law of Electromagnetic Induction** This law states that the induced emf produced in a circuit is numerically equal to the rate of change of magnetic flux through it.

It is given by $\oint \mathbf{E} \cdot d\mathbf{l} = -\dfrac{d\phi_B}{dt}$.

This equation is called **Maxwell's third equation.**

(*iv*) **Ampere-Maxwell Law** This law states that the line integral of the magnetic field along a closed path is equal to μ_0 times the total current threading the surface bounded by that closed path.

It is given by

$$\oint \mathbf{B}\cdot d\mathbf{l} = \mu_0\left(I_C + \varepsilon_0 \frac{d\phi_E}{dt}\right) = \mu_0(I_C + I_D)$$

This equation is called **Maxwell's fourth equation.**

Electromagnetic Waves (EM Waves)

Maxwell found that time varying electric and magnetic fields produce Electromagnetic Waves (EMW).

Thus, electromagnetic waves are the waves which are produced due to changing electric field (**E**) and magnetic field (**B**) simultaneously propagating through space such that the two fields are perpendicular to each other and perpendicular to the direction of wave propagation.

- It is represented as

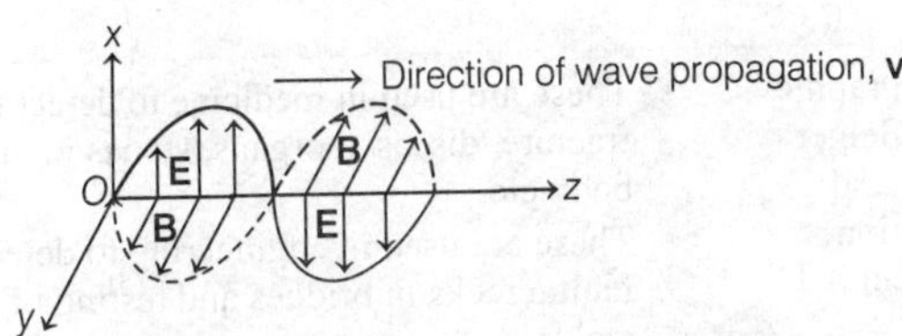

- An electromagnetic wave propagating in z-direction with the oscillating electric field **E** along the x-direction and the oscillating magnetic field **B** along y-direction can be expressed as

$$\mathbf{E}_x = E_0 \sin(kz - \omega t)\hat{\mathbf{i}}$$

and $$\mathbf{B}_y = B_0 \sin(kz - \omega t)\hat{\mathbf{j}}$$

Characterstics of Electromagnetic Waves

Some important characteristics of EM waves are listed as below

(*i*) Light waves are electromagnetic waves.

(*ii*) These waves travel in free space with the speed of light. ($c = 3.0\times10^8\ \text{ms}^{-1}$), where c is given by the relation $c = 1/\sqrt{\mu_0\varepsilon_0}$.

(*iii*) The time varying electric (**E**) and magnetic (**B**) fields are perpendicular to each other.

(*iv*) The variation in electric and magnetic fields occurs simultaneously and the fields acquire their maximum values E_0 and B_0 at the same place and at the same time.

(*v*) Electric and magnetic field vectors are such that $\mathbf{E}\times\mathbf{B}$ (cross product) is always in the direction of propagation of wave.

(*vi*) In free space, the magnitude of electric and magnetic fields in electromagnetic waves are related by $E/B = c$.

(*vii*) The energy in electromagnetic waves is divided equally between electric and magnetic fields.

(*viii*) The electromagnetic waves like other waves carry energy and momentum.

(*ix*) These waves exert pressure (radiation pressure), which is expressed as

$$p = \frac{I}{c}$$

where, I = light intensity.

Electromagnetic Spectrum

The arrangement of electromagnetic waves in increasing or decreasing order of wavelength (λ) or frequency (ν) is called electromagnetic spectrum. The range lies from 10^{-12} m to 10^4 m, i.e. from γ-rays to radio waves.

Various Electromagnetic Waves of Electromagnetic Spectrum with their Features and Uses

	Name of Wave	Frequency Range	Wavelength Range	Production	Detection	Uses
(*i*)	Radio waves	500 kHz to 1000 MHz	> 0.1 m	Rapid acceleration and decelerations of electrons in aerials.	Receiver's aerials.	• These are used in AM (Amplitude Modulation) from 530 kHz to 1710 kHz and ground wave propagation. • These are used in TV waves ranging from 54 MHz to 890 MHz. • These are used in FM (Frequency Modulation) ranging from 88 MHz to 108 MHz.
(*ii*)	Microwaves	1 GHz to 300 GHz	0.1 m to 1 mm	Klystron valve or magnetron valve.	Point contact diodes.	• These are used in RADAR systems for aircraft navigation. • These are used in microwave oven for cooking purpose. • These are used in study of atomic and molecular structures.

	Name of Wave	Frequency Range	Wavelength Range	Production	Detection	Uses
(iii)	Infrared waves (heat waves)	3×10^{11} Hz to 4×10^{14} Hz.	1 mm to 700 nm	Vibration of atoms and molecules	Thermopiles bolometer and infrared photographic film.	• These are used in physical therapy. • These are used in satellites for army purpose. • These are used in weather forecasting.
(iv)	Light rays	4×10^{14} Hz to 7×10^{14} Hz	700 nm to 400 nm	Electrons in atoms emit light, when they move from a higher energy level to a lower energy level.	The eye, photocells and photographic film.	Visible rays are used by the optical organs of humans and animals for three primary purposes given below • To see things, avoid bumping into them and escape danger. • To look for food. • To find other living things with which to copulate so as to prolong the species.
(v)	Ultraviolet rays	10^{14} Hz to 10^{16} Hz	400 nm to 1 nm	Produced by special lamps and very hot bodies, sun. Inner shell electrons in atoms moving from higher energy level to a lower energy level.	Photocells and photographic film	• These are used in burglar alarm. • These are used in checking mineral sample. • These are used to study molecular structure. • To kill germs in water purifiers. • Used in LASER eye surgery.
(vi)	X-rays	3×10^{16} Hz to 3×10^{21} Hz	1 nm to 10^{-3} nm	X-ray tubes or inner shell electrons, bombarding metals by high energy electrons.	Photographic film, Geiger tubes and ionisation chamber.	• These are used in medicine to detect the fracture, diseased organs, stones in the body etc. • These are used in engineering to detect fault, cracks in bridges and testing of welds. • These are used at metro stations to detect metals or explosive material.
(vii)	Gamma (γ) rays	3×10^{18} Hz to 5×10^{22} Hz.	$< 10^{-3}$ nm	Radioactive decay of the nucleus.	Photographic film and ionisation chamber.	• These are used to produce nuclear reactions. • These are used in radio therapy for the treatment of tumour and cancer. • These are used in food industry to kill pathogenic micro-organism.

Topical Practice Questions

All the exam questions of this chapter have been divided into 2 topics as listed below

Topic 1

Properties of Electromagnetic Waves

2019

1 A parallel plate capacitor of capacitance $20\mu F$ is being charged by a voltage source whose potential is changing at the rate of 3 V/s. The conduction current through the connecting wires and the displacement current through the plates of the capacitor would be respectively, **[NEET]**

(a) $60\mu A$, $60\mu A$ (b) $60\mu A$, zero
(c) zero, zero (d) zero, $60\mu A$

2018

2 An EM wave is propagating in a medium with a velocity $\mathbf{v} = v\hat{\mathbf{i}}$. The instantaneous oscillating electric field of this EM wave is along $+Y$-axis. Then, the direction of oscillating magnetic field of electromagnetic wave will be along **[NEET]**

(a) $-y$-direction (b) $+z$-direction
(c) $-z$-direction (d) $-x$-direction

2014

3 The ratio of amplitude of magnetic field to the amplitude of electric field for an electromagnetic wave propagating in vacuum is equal to **[CBSE AIPMT]**

(a) the speed of light in vacuum
(b) reciprocal of speed of light in vacuum
(c) the ratio of magnetic permeability to the electric susceptibility of vacuum
(d) unity

4 In electromagnetic wave, according to Maxwell, changing electric field gives **[MHT CET]**

(a) stationary magnetic field
(b) conduction current
(c) eddy current
(d) displacement current

5 The speed of light in an isotropic medium depends on **[Kerala CEE]**

(a) the nature of the source
(b) nature of the medium
(c) its direction of propagation
(d) its intensity
(e) the motion of the source relative to the medium

6 Light wave is travelling along y-direction. If the corresponding E vector at any time is along the X-axis, the direction of B vector at that time is along **[WB JEE]**

(a) Y-axis (b) X-axis
(c) $+Z$-axis (d) $-Z$-axis

7 A plane electromagnetic wave of frequency 20 MHz travels through a space along x-direction. If the electric field vector at a certain point in space is $6\ Vm^{-1}$, then what is the magnetic field vector at that point? **[KCET]**

(a) 2×10^{-8} T (b) $\frac{1}{2}\times10^{-8}$ T (c) 2 T (d) $\frac{1}{2}$ T

2013

8 There may be a large regions of space where there is no conduction current, but there is only **[WB JEE]**

(a) displacement current due to time varying electric fields
(b) induced current due to time varying electric fields
(c) Both (a) and (b)
(d) Neither (a) nor (b)

9 In an electromagnetic wave, the amplitude of electric and magnetic fields are 100 V/m and 0.265 A/m, respectively. The maximum energy flow is **[KCET]**

(a) $26.5\ W/m^2$ (b) $36.5\ W/m^2$
(c) $46.7\ W/m^2$ (d) $765\ W/m^2$

2011

10 The electric and magnetic fields, associated with an electromagnetic wave, propagating along the $+Z$-axis, can be represented by **[CBSE AIPMT]**

(a) $\mathbf{E} = E_0\ \hat{\mathbf{k}}, \mathbf{B} = B_0\hat{\mathbf{i}}$ (b) $\mathbf{E} = E_0\ \hat{\mathbf{j}}, \mathbf{B} = B_0\ \hat{\mathbf{i}}$
(c) $\mathbf{E} = E_0\ \hat{\mathbf{j}}, \mathbf{B} = B_0\ \hat{\mathbf{k}}$ (d) $\mathbf{E} = E_0\ \hat{\mathbf{i}}, \mathbf{B} = B_0\ \hat{\mathbf{j}}$

11 Dimensions of $\varepsilon_0 \frac{d\phi_E}{dt}$ are same as that of

(a) charge (b) potential
(c) capacitance (d) current

2010

12 Which of the following statements is false for the properties of electromagnetic waves? **[CBSE AIPMT]**

(a) Both electric and magnetic field vectors attain the maxima and minima at the same place and same time.
(b) The energy in electromagnetic wave is divided equally between electric and magnetic vectors.
(c) Both electric and magnetic field vectors are parallel to each other and perpendicular to the direction of propagation of wave.
(d) These waves do not require any material medium for propagation.

13 A plane electromagnetic wave propagating in the x-direction has wavelength of 6.0 mm. The electric field is in the y-direction and its maximum magnitude is 33 Vm^{-1}. The equation for the electric field as a function of x and t is **[AFMC]**

(a) $11 \sin \pi (t - x/c)$
(b) $33 \sin \pi \times 10^{11} (t - x/c)$
(c) $33 \sin \pi (t - x/c)$
(d) $11 \sin \pi \times 10^{11} (t - x/c)$

14 The sun delivers 10^4 W/m^2 of electromagnetic flux to the earth's surface. The total power that is incident on a roof of dimensions (10×10) m^2 will be **[BHU]**

(a) 10^4 W (b) 10^5 W
(c) 10^6 W (d) 10^7 W

15 An electromagnetic wave of frequency, $\nu = 3.0$ MHz passes from vacuum into a dielectric medium with permittivity $\varepsilon = 4.0$, then **[MP PMT]**

(a) wavelength is doubled and the frequency remains unchanged
(b) wavelength is doubled and frequency becomes half
(c) wavelength is halved and frequency remains unchanged
(d) wavelength and frequency both remain unchanged

16 In a free space, electron is placed in the path of a plane electromagnetic wave, it will start moving along **[Manipal]**

(a) centre of earth (b) equator of earth
(c) magnetic field (d) electric field

17 An electromagnetic wave going through vacuum is described by $E = E_0 \sin (kx - \omega t)$ and $B = B_0 \sin (kx - \omega t)$. Which of the following equations is true? **[OJEE]**

(a) $E_0 k = B_0 \omega$
(b) $E_0 \omega = B_0 k$
(c) $E_0 B_0 = \omega k$
(d) None of the above

18 Which one of the following is the property of a monochromatic and plane electromagnetic waves in free space? **[Kerala CEE]**

(a) Electric and magnetic fields have a phase difference of $\pi/2$.
(b) The energy contribution of both electric and magnetic fields are equal.
(c) The direction of propagation is in the direction of $\mathbf{B} \times \mathbf{E}$.
(d) The pressure exerted by the wave is the product of its speed and energy density.
(e) The speed of the wave is B/E.

19 Which is the correct expression of velocity of light? **[MP PMT]**

(a) $\dfrac{1}{\sqrt{\varepsilon_0 \mu_0}}$ (b) $\dfrac{E_0}{B_0}$
(c) $\dfrac{c}{\mu}$ (d) All of these

20 The average magnetic energy density of an electromagnetic wave of wavelength λ travelling in free space is given by **[DUMET]**

(a) $\dfrac{B^2}{2\lambda}$ (b) $\dfrac{B^2}{2\mu_0}$
(c) $\dfrac{2B^2}{\mu_0 \lambda}$ (d) $\dfrac{B}{\mu_0 \lambda}$

21 The speed of electromagnetic waves in vacuum **[KCET]**

(a) increases as we move from γ-rays to radio waves
(b) decreases as we move from γ-rays to radio waves
(c) is same for all the above
(d) None of the above

2009

22 The average electric field of electromagnetic waves in certain region of free space is 9×10^{-4} NC^{-1}. Then, the average magnetic field in the same region is of the order of **[Kerala CEE]**

(a) 27×10^{-4} T (b) 3×10^{-12} T
(c) $\left(\dfrac{1}{3}\right) \times 10^{-12}$ T (d) 3×10^{12} T
(e) $\left(\dfrac{1}{3}\right) \times 10^{12}$ T

23 Which of the following has/have zero average value in a plane electromagnetic wave? **[Kerala CEE]**

(a) Both magnetic and electric fields
(b) Electric field only
(c) Magnetic field only
(d) Magnetic energy
(e) Electric energy

24 An electromagnetic wave has **[Haryana PMT, CG PMT]**

(a) electric vector only
(b) magnetic vector only
(c) electric and magnetic vectors perpendicular to each other
(d) neither the electric vector nor the magnetic vector

25 Suppose that the electric field amplitude of an electromagnetic wave is $E_0 = 120$ N/C and its frequency is $\nu = 50.0$ MHz. The expressions for E will be **[WB JEE]**

(a) $[(120\text{N/C}) \sin \{(1.05 \text{ rad/m})x - (3.14 \times 10^8 \text{ rad/s})t\}]\hat{\mathbf{i}}$
(b) $[(120\text{N/C}) \sin \{(1.05 \text{ rad/m})x - (3.14 \times 10^8 \text{ rad/s})t\}]\hat{\mathbf{k}}$
(c) $[(120\text{N/C}) \sin \{(1.05 \text{ rad/m})x - (3.14 \times 10^8 \text{ rad/s})t\}]\hat{\mathbf{j}}$
(d) $[(120\text{N/C}) \cos \{(1.05 \text{ rad/m})x - (3.14 \times 10^8 \text{ rad/s})t\}]\hat{\mathbf{j}}$

2008

26 **Assertion** The displacement current goes through the gap between the plates of a capacitor when the charge of the capacitor does not change.

Reason The displacement current arises in the region in which the electric field and hence the electric flux does not change with time. [AIIMS]

(a) Both Assertion and Reason are correct and Reason is the correct explanation of Assertion

(b) Both Assertion and Reason are correct but Reason is not the correct explanation of Assertion

(c) Assertion is correct but Reason is incorrect

(d) Both Assertion and Reason are incorrect

2007

27 The electric and magnetic fields of an electromagnetic wave are [CBSE AIPMT]

(a) in phase and parallel to each other

(b) in opposite phase and perpendicular to each other

(c) in opposite phase and parallel to each other

(d) in phase and perpendicular to each other

28 Electromagnetic waves are produced by [UP CPMT]

(a) accelerated charged particle

(b) decelerated charged particle

(c) charge in uniform motion

(d) None of the above

29 A beam of light travelling along X-axis is described by the electric field, $E_y = (600\ \text{Vm}^{-1})\sin\omega(t - x/c)$, then maximum magnetic force on a charge, $q = 2e$, moving along Y-axis with a speed of $3.0 \times 10^7\ \text{ms}^{-1}$ is $(e = 1.6 \times 10^{-19}\ \text{C})$ [UP CPMT]

(a) 19.2×10^{-17} N (b) 1.92×10^{-17} N

(c) 0.192 N (d) None of these

2006

30 A perfectly reflecting mirror has an area of 1 cm^2. Light energy is allowed to fall on it for 1 h at the rate of 10 J/s. The force that acts on the mirror is [MHT CET]

(a) 3.35×10^{-8} N (b) 6.7×10^{-8} N

(c) 1.34×10^{-7} N (d) 2.4×10^{-4} N

31 A parallel plate capacitor is charged to 60μC. Due to a radioactive source, the plate losses charge at the rate of $1.8 \times 10^{-8}\ \text{Cs}^{-1}$. The magnitude of displacement current is [MP PMT]

(a) $1.8 \times 10^{-8}\ \text{Cs}^{-1}$ (b) $3.6 \times 10^{-8}\ \text{Cs}^{-1}$

(c) $4.1 \times 10^{-11}\ \text{Cs}^{-1}$ (d) $5.7 \times 10^{-12}\ \text{Cs}^{-1}$

2005

32 The pressure exerted by an electromagnetic wave of intensity, I (Wm^{-2}) on a non-reflecting surface is [AIIMS]

(a) Ic (b) Ic^2

(c) I/c (d) I/c^2

1 (a)	2 (b)	3 (b)	4 (d)	5 (b)	6 (d)	7 (a)	8. (a)	9 (a)	10 (d)
11 (d)	12 (c)	13 (b)	14 (c)	15 (c)	16 (d)	17 (a)	18 (b)	19 (d)	20 (b)
21 (c)	22 (b)	23 (a)	24 (c)	25 (c)	26 (d)	27 (d)	28 (a)	29 (b)	30 (b)
31 (a)	32 (c)								

Explanations

1 *(a)* Given, $C = 20\mu\text{F} = 20 \times 10^{-6}$ F

and $\frac{dV}{dt} = 3$ V/s

The displacement current in a circuit is given by $I_D = \varepsilon_0 \frac{d\phi}{dt}$

$= \varepsilon_0 \frac{d}{dt}(EA)$ $[\because \phi = EA]$

$= \varepsilon_0 A \frac{d}{dt}\left(\frac{V}{d}\right)$ $[\because V = Ed]$

$= \frac{\varepsilon_0 A}{d}\frac{dV}{dt}$

As the capacitance of a parallel plate capacitor, $C = \frac{\varepsilon_0 A}{d}$

$\therefore \quad I_D = C\frac{dV}{dt}$

Substituting the given values, we get

$I_D = 20 \times 10^{-6} \times 3$

$= 60 \times 10^{-6}\ \text{A} = 60\ \mu\text{A}$

As displacement current is in between the plates of capacitor and conduction current is in the connecting wires which are equal to each other. So,

$I_C = I_D = 60\ \mu\text{A}$

2 *(b)* Here, velocity of EM wave $\mathbf{v} = v\hat{\mathbf{i}}$

Instantaneous oscillating electric field, $\mathbf{E} = E\hat{\mathbf{j}}$

As we know that during the propagation of electromagnetic waves through a medium, oscillating electric and magnetic field vectors are mutually perpendicular to each other and also to the direction of propagation of the wave.

i.e. $\mathbf{E} \times \mathbf{B} = \mathbf{v}$

$\Rightarrow \quad (E\hat{\mathbf{j}}) \times \mathbf{B} = v\hat{\mathbf{i}}$ ...(i)

As we know that, from vector algebra,

$\hat{\mathbf{j}} \times \hat{\mathbf{k}} = \hat{\mathbf{i}}$ ...(ii)

Comparing Eqs. (i) and (ii), we get

$$\mathbf{B} = B\hat{\mathbf{k}},$$

where, B (say) is the magnitude of magnetic field.

Thus, we can say that, the direction of oscillating magnetic field of the EM wave will be along $+z$-direction.

3 *(b)* The ratio of amplitude of magnetic field to the amplitude of electric field for an electromagnetic wave propagating in vacuum is equal to the reciprocal of speed of light in vacuum.

i.e. $\frac{B_0}{E_0} = 1/c$

4 *(d)* According to Maxwell, changing electric field produces displacement current.

$$I_D = \varepsilon_0 \frac{d\phi_E}{dt}$$

5 *(b)* Speed of light in a medium depends on the electric and magnetic properties of the medium or the nature of the medium.

6 *(c)* Electromagnetic radiation is a self propagating wave in space with electric and magnetic components.

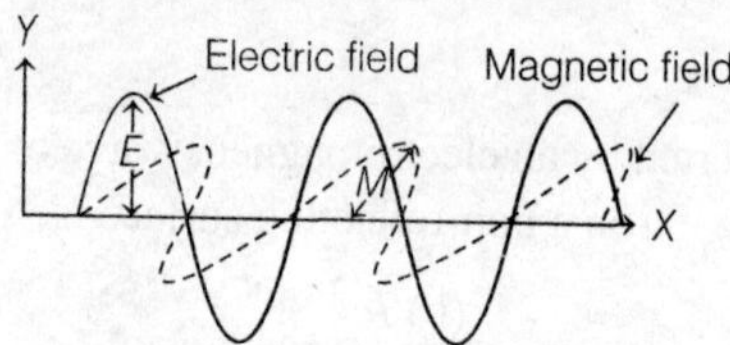

These components oscillate at right angles to each other and to the direction of propagation.

Here, $\mathbf{v} = v\hat{\mathbf{j}}$

$\mathbf{E} = E\hat{\mathbf{i}}$

We know that, $\mathbf{E} \times \mathbf{B} = \mathbf{v}$ ...(i)

$\hat{\mathbf{i}} \times (-\hat{\mathbf{k}}) = \hat{\mathbf{j}}$ ...(ii)

(from vector algebra)

Comparing Eqs. (i) and (ii), we can say that, $\mathbf{B}$ is along $-Z$-axis.

7 *(a)* Magnetic field,

$$B = \frac{E}{c}, \text{ where } c = 3 \times 10^8 \text{ m/s.}$$

$$B = \frac{6}{3 \times 10^8} = 2 \times 10^{-8} \text{ T}$$

8 *(a)* In vast regions of space, where there is no conduction current, there may be displacement current due to varying electric fields in the region.

9 *(a)* Maximum rate of energy flow,

$$S = E_0 H_0$$

Given, $E_0 = 100$ V/m

$H_0 = 0.265$ A/m

$\therefore \quad S = 100 \times 0.265 = 26.5 \text{ W/m}^2$

10 *(d)* In electromagnetic waves, electric vector, magnetic vector and velocity of wave are perpendicular to one another.

Hence,

As $\mathbf{v} = v_0\hat{\mathbf{k}}$

We know, from vector algebra,

$$\hat{\mathbf{i}} \times \hat{\mathbf{j}} = \hat{\mathbf{k}}$$

$\therefore \quad \mathbf{E} = E_0\hat{\mathbf{i}}$

and $\mathbf{B} = B_0\hat{\mathbf{j}}$

11 *(d)* We know that, displacement current,

$$I_D = \varepsilon_0 \frac{d\phi_E}{dt}$$

So, dimensions of $\varepsilon_0 \frac{d\phi_E}{dt}$ are same as that of current.

12 *(c)* The time varying electric and magnetic fields are mutually perpendicular to each other and also perpendicular to direction of propagation of the wave.

13 *(b)* Angular frequency,

$$\omega = 2\pi\nu = \frac{2\pi c}{\lambda}$$

$$= \frac{2\pi \times 3 \times 10^8}{6 \times 10^{-3}}$$

$$= \pi \times 10^{11} \text{ rad s}^{-1}$$

The equation for the electric field, along Y-axis for electromagnetic wave is

$$E_y = E_0 \sin \omega \left(t - \frac{x}{c}\right)$$

$$= 33 \sin \pi \times 10^{11} (t - x/c)$$

14 *(c)* Given, solar constant, $S = 10^4 \text{ W/m}^2$

Area, $A = (10 \times 10) \text{ m}^2$

Total power = Solar constant × Area

$$= 10^4 \times (10 \times 10) = 10^6 \text{ W}$$

15 *(c)* In vacuum, $\varepsilon_0 = 1$, where ε_0 is permittivity in freee space.

In dielectric medium, $\varepsilon = 4$, so refractive index,

$$\mu = \sqrt{\varepsilon/\varepsilon_0}$$

$$= \sqrt{4/1} = 2$$

Wavelength, $\lambda' = \frac{\lambda}{\mu} = \frac{\lambda}{2}$

and wave velocity, $v = \frac{c}{\mu} = \frac{c}{2}$

Hence, it is clear that wavelength and velocity will become half but frequency remains unchanged when the wave is passing through any medium.

16 *(d)* The electron placed in the path of electromagnetic wave will experience force due to electric field vector and not due to magnetic field vector.

Hence, it will move along the electric field.

17 *(a)* As, $\frac{E_0}{B_0} = c$

Also, $k = \frac{2\pi}{\lambda}$

and $\omega = 2\pi\nu$

These relations give $E_0 k = B_0 \omega$.

18 *(b)* The energy in EM waves is divided equally between the electric and magnetic fields.

19 *(d)* The velocity of electromagnetic waves in free space is given by

$$c = \frac{1}{\sqrt{\mu_0 \varepsilon_0}} = \frac{E_0}{B_0}$$

$$= 3 \times 10^8 \text{ ms}^{-1}$$

Moreover in a medium, $v = \frac{c}{\mu}$.

20 *(b)* Energy density of an electromagnetic wave,

$$U = \frac{1}{2} \varepsilon_0 E^2 + \frac{1}{2} \frac{B^2}{\mu_0}$$

So, the magnetic energy density is $\frac{B^2}{2\mu_0}$.

21 *(c)* Speed of electromagnetic waves in vacuum $= \frac{1}{\sqrt{\mu_0 \varepsilon_0}} =$ constant,

so it is same for all of them.

22 *(b)* Given, $E = 9 \times 10^{-9} \text{ NC}^{-1}$

As, $c = E/B$

$$\Rightarrow \quad B = \frac{9 \times 10^{-4}}{3 \times 10^8}$$

$$(\because C = 3 \times 10^8 \text{ ms}^{-1})$$

$$= 3 \times 10^{-12} \text{ T}$$

23 *(a)* Both magnetic and electric fields have zero average value in a plane electromagnetic wave.

24 *(c)* An electromagnetic wave has electric and magnetic vectors perpendicular to each other.

25 (c) Given, $E_0 = 120\text{N/C}, \nu = 50.0\text{MHz}$
$= 50 \times 10^6\text{Hz}$

We know,
$\omega = 2\pi\nu = (2 \times 3.14 \text{ rad})(50 \times 10^6 \text{ Hz})$
$= 3.14 \times 10^8 \text{ rad/s}$

and wave constant,

$$k = \frac{\omega}{c} = \frac{3.14 \times 10^8 \text{ rad/s}}{3 \times 10^8 \text{ m/s}}$$

$= 1.05 \text{ rad/m}$

As it is clear from the option given wave to be propagating along X-axis, then $\mathbf{E}$ is along Y-axis and $\mathbf{B}$ is along Z-axis. Clearly,

$$E = E_0 \sin(kx - \omega t)\,\hat{\mathbf{j}}$$
$$= [(120\text{N/C}) \sin\{(1.05 \text{ rad/m})x - (3.14 \times 10^8 \text{ rad/s})\, t\}]\,\hat{\mathbf{j}}$$

26 (d) The displacement current is given by

$$I_D = \varepsilon_0 \frac{d\phi_E}{dt} = \varepsilon_0 \frac{d}{dt}\left(\frac{q}{\varepsilon_0}\right)$$

$\because$ From Gauss's law, $\phi_E = \dfrac{q}{\varepsilon_0}$

$$\Rightarrow \quad I_0 = \frac{dq}{dt}$$

That is it will happen when charge on capacitor does not remain constant but changes with time.

Also, $\quad I_D = \varepsilon_0 \dfrac{d\phi_E}{dt}$.

Hence, electric flux should also change to have displacement current.

27 (d) As, $\mathbf{E} = E_0 \sin(kx - \omega t)\,\hat{\mathbf{i}}$

$\Rightarrow \quad \mathbf{B} = B_0 \sin(kx - \omega t)\,\hat{\mathbf{j}}$

Hence, electric field and magnetic field are in same phase and perpendicular to each other.

28 (a) The electromagnetic waves are produced by the accelerated charge. The electric and magnetic fields produced by the accelerated charge change with time. Therefore, it radiates electromagnetic waves.

29 (b) Maximum magnetic field is given by $\quad B_0 = \dfrac{E_0}{c}$

Given, $\quad E_0 = 600 \text{ Vm}^{-1}$,
$c = 3 \times 10^8 \text{ ms}^{-1}$
and $\quad v = 3 \times 10^7 \text{ ms}^{-1}$

$$\therefore \quad B_0 = \frac{600}{3 \times 10^8} = 2 \times 10^{-6} \text{ T}$$

Maximum magnetic force imposed on given charge is $F_m = qvB_0 = 2evB_0$
$= 2 \times 1.6 \times 10^{-19} \times 3 \times 10^7 \times 2 \times 10^{-6}$
$= 1.92 \times 10^{-17} \text{N}$

30 (b) Let, E = energy falling on the surface per second = 10 J

Momentum of photons,

$$p = \frac{h}{\lambda} = \frac{h}{(c/\nu)} = \frac{h\nu}{c} = \frac{E}{c}$$

$t = 1 \text{ h}$

On reflection, change in momentum per second = force

$$= \frac{2p}{t} = \frac{2E}{ct} = \frac{2 \times 10}{3 \times 10^8}$$
$$= 6.7 \times 10^{-8} \text{ N}$$

31 (a) Displacement current is given by

$$I_D = \frac{dq}{dt}$$
$$= 1.8 \times 10^{-8} \text{ Cs}^{-1}$$

As current is rate of charge flowing, so value of I_D is given directly here as $1.8 \times 10^{-8} \text{ Cs}^{-1}$.

32 (c) When a surface intercepts electromagnetic radiation, a force and a pressure are exerted on the surface. As the surface is non-reflecting, so it is completely absorbed and in such case the force is, $F = \dfrac{IA}{c}$

The radiation pressure is the force per unit area,

$$p = \frac{F}{A} = \frac{I}{c}$$

where, $\quad c$ = speed of light.

Topic 2

Electromagnetic Spectrum

2014

1 In electromagnetic spectrum, the frequencies of γ-rays, X-rays and ultraviolet rays are denoted by n_1, n_2 and n_3 respectively, then **[MHT CET]**

(a) $n_1 > n_2 > n_3$ (b) $n_1 < n_2 < n_3$
(c) $n_1 > n_2 < n_3$ (d) $n_1 < n_2 > n_3$

2 The electromagnetic waves detected using a thermopile and used in physical therapy are **[Kerala CEE]**

(a) gamma radiations (b) X-rays
(c) ultraviolet radiations (d) infrared radiations
(e) microwave radiations

3 The wavelength of X-rays is in the range **[Guj CET]**

(a) 0.01 Å to 1 Å
(b) 0.001 nm to 1 nm
(c) 0.001 μm to 1 μm
(d) 0.001 cm to 1 cm

4 The wavelength of the short radio waves, microwaves and ultraviolet waves are λ_1, λ_2 and λ_3 respectively. Arrange them in decreasing order. **[Guj CET]**

(a) $\lambda_1, \lambda_2, \lambda_3$ (b) $\lambda_1, \lambda_3, \lambda_2$
(c) $\lambda_3, \lambda_2, \lambda_1$ (d) $\lambda_2, \lambda_1, \lambda_3$

2013

5 The condition under which a microwave oven heats up a food item containing water molecules most efficiently is

(a) the frequency of the microwave must match the resonant frequency of the water molecules **[NEET]**
(b) the frequency of the microwave has no relation with natural frequency of water molecules
(c) microwaves are heat waves, so always produce heating
(d) infrared waves produce heating in a microwave oven

6 If v_γ, v_X and v_M are the speeds of γ-rays, X-rays and microwaves respectively in vacuum, then **[Manipal]**

(a) $v_\gamma > v_M > v_X$ (b) $v_\gamma > v_X > v_M$
(c) $v_\gamma = v_X = v_M$ (d) None of these

2011

7 The electromagnetic wave having the shortest wavelength is **[Kerala CEE]**

(a) X-rays (b) γ-rays
(c) infrared rays (d) microwaves
(e) radio waves

8 The part of the spectrum of the electromagnetic radiation used to cook food is **[J&K CET]**

(a) ultraviolet rays (b) cosmic rays
(c) X-rays (d) microwaves

2010

9 Which of the following waves has the maximum wavelength? **[Haryana PMT]**

(a) X-rays (b) Infrared rays
(c) Ultraviolet rays (d) Radio waves

10 Which of the following shows greenhouse effect? **[JCECE]**

(a) Ultraviolet rays (b) Infrared rays
(c) X-rays (d) None of these

11 The magnetic field of plane electromagnetic wave is given by $B_y = 2\times 10^{-7} \sin (0.5\times 10^3 x + 1.5\times 10^{11} t)$T. This electromagnetic wave is **[DUMET]**

(a) a visible light (b) an infrared wave
(c) a microwave (d) a radio wave

2008

12 Which of the following undergoes largest diffraction?

(a) Infrared ray (b) Radio waves **[Guj CET]**
(c) γ-rays (d) Ultraviolet rays

2007

13 An electromagnetic radiation has an energy of 13.2 keV, then the radiation belongs to the region of **[Kerala CEE]**

(a) visible light (b) ultraviolet
(c) infrared (d) X-ray
(e) microwave

14 All components of the electromagnetic spectrum in vacuum have the same **[KCET]**

(a) energy
(b) velocity
(c) wavelength
(d) frequency

2006

15 We find that the temperature of air decreases as one goes up from the earth's surface, because **[MHT CET]**

(a) the atmospheric pressure drops with height
(b) the earth which radiates waves in the infrared region is the main heat source and temperature drops as we go away from it
(c) the density of air drops with height and the air therefore cannot hold stronger as we go up
(d) winds are stronger as we go up

16 The wavelength of a radio wave of frequency of 1 MHz is **[Haryana PMT]**

(a) 400 m (b) 300 m
(c) 350 m (d) 200 m

2005

17 In the electromagnetic spectrum, the visible spectrum lies between **[JCECE]**

(a) radio waves and microwaves
(b) infrared and ultraviolet rays
(c) microwaves and infrared spectrum
(d) X-rays and gamma rays spectrum

Answers

1 (a)	2 (d)	3 (b)	4 (a)	5 (a)	6 (c)	7 (b)	8 (d)	9 (d)	10 (b)
11 (c)	12 (b)	13 (d)	14 (b)	15 (b)	16 (b)	17 (b)			

Explanations

1 (a) Frequency range of γ-rays

$$\simeq 5\times10^{20} - 3\times10^{19}\,(n_1)$$

Frequency range of X-rays

$$\simeq 3\times10^{19} - 10^{16}(n_2)$$

Frequency range of ultraviolet rays

$$\simeq 10^{16} - 8\times10^{14}(n_3)$$

$\therefore \quad n_1 > n_2 > n_3$

2 (d) The electromagnetic waves detected using a thermopile and used in physical therapy are infrared or heat radiations.

3 (b) X-rays wavelength range

$$= 1\times10^{-12} \text{ m to } 1\times10^{-9} \text{ m}$$
$$= 0.001 \text{ nm to } 1 \text{ nm}$$

4 (a) We know that,
Short radio waves have wavelength range $\lambda_1 = 1\times10^{-1}$ m to 1×10^{4} m

Microwaves wavelength range,

$$\lambda_2 = 1\times10^{-3} \text{ m to } 3\times10^{-1}\text{m}$$

Ultraviolet rays wavelength range,

$$\lambda_3 = 1\times10^{-8} \text{ m to } 4\times10^{-8} \text{ m}$$

So, decreasing order of wavelengths are $\lambda_1, \lambda_2, \lambda_3$.

5 (a) "A microwave oven uses microwaves, which are basically radio waves, to cook food. The commonly used frequency is roughly 2500 MHz (2.5 GHz). Radio waves in this frequency range are absorbed by water, fats and sugars. When absorbed, they are converted directly into heat due to vibration."
Frequency of microwaves matches with the resonant frequency of the water molecules and hence food items with water molecules are effectively heated by microwaves.

6 (c) γ-rays, X-rays and microwaves respectively are electromagnetic waves. They travel with the speed of light in vacuum.
Hence, $\quad v_\gamma = v_X = v_M$

7 (b) The electromagnetic wave having the shortest wavelength is γ-rays.

8 (d) The part of the spectrum of the electromagnctic radiation used to cook food is microwaves.

9 (d) The wavelength order is
$\lambda_{\text{radio waves}} > \lambda_{\text{UV rays}} > \lambda_{\text{IR rays}} > \lambda_{\text{X-rays}}$

10 (b) Infrared rays show green house effect because infrared radiations are trapped by earth atmosphere by and keep the earth warm.

11 (c) We have,
$B_y = 2\times10^{-7} \sin(0.5\times10^3 x + 1.5\times10^{11} t)$
Comparing with the standard equation
$B_y = B_0 \sin(kx + \omega t)$, we get

$$k = 0.5\times10^3$$
$$\Rightarrow \quad \lambda = \frac{2\pi}{k}$$
$$= \frac{2\pi}{0.5\times10^3}$$
$$= 0.01256 \text{ m}$$

The wavelength range of microwaves is 10^{-3} to 0.1 m. The wavelength of this wave lies between 10^{-3} to 0.1 m, so the equation represents a microwave.

12 (b) We know that the diffraction of waves is observed, when size of the obstacle is of the order of wavelength of waves.
Here, the wavelength of radio waves is largest, so the radio waves undergo largest diffraction.

13 (d) Energy of a photon,

$$E = \frac{hc}{\lambda}$$

$\therefore$ Wavelength, $\lambda = \dfrac{hc}{E}$

Given, $E = 13.2$ eV

$$= 13.2\times10^3 \text{ eV}$$
$$= \frac{6.6\times10^{-34}\times3\times10^8}{13.2\times10^3\times1.6\times10^{-19}}$$

$\because \quad h = 6.6\times10^{-34}$ J-s

and $\quad c = 3\times10^8$ ms^{-1}

$$= 0.9375\times10^{-10}\text{m}$$
$$\approx 1\,\text{Å}$$

Wavelength range of X-rays is from 10^{-11} m to 10^{-8} m [i.e. 0.1 Å to 100 Å]
Therefore, the given electromagnetic radiation belongs to the X-ray region of electromagnetic spectrum.

14 (b) All the components of electromagnetic spectrum have same velocity, i.e. 3×10^8 ms^{-1}.

15 (b) The temperature of air decreases as one goes up from the earth's surface, because the earth which radiates in the infrared region is the main heat source and temperature drops as we go away from it.

16 (b) We know that, wavelength,

$$\lambda = \frac{c}{\nu} \qquad (\because c = \nu\lambda)$$

Given, $\quad \nu = 1$ MHz

$$= 1\times10^6 \text{ Hz}$$
$$\therefore \quad \lambda = \frac{3\times10^8}{1\times10^6}$$
$$= 3\times10^2 = 300 \text{ m}$$

17 (b) Electromagnetic waves have wavelengths as small as 30 Fm to as large as 30 km.
The figure shows the electromagnetic spectrum

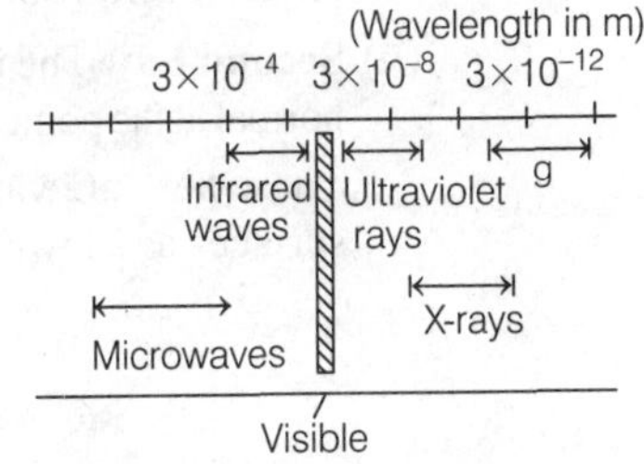

Hence, visible spectrum lies between infrared and ultraviolet rays.

23

Ray Optics and Optical Instruments

Quick Review

Reflection of Light

The returning back of light in the same medium from which it has come after striking a smooth polished surface is called reflection of light. After reflection, velocity, wavelength and frequency of light remains same but intensity decreases.

Laws of Reflection

There are two laws for reflection of light from a smooth reflecting surface

(*i*) **First Law** The angle of incidence is equal to the angle of reflection, i.e. $\angle i = \angle r$.

(*ii*) **Second Law** The incident ray, the reflected ray and the normal at the point of incidence, all lie in the same plane.

These laws are valid for plane as well as curved surfaces as shown in the figure below

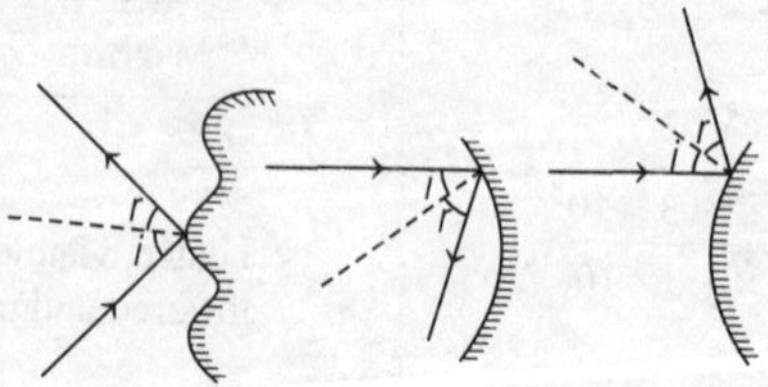

Reflection of Light from a Plane Mirror

- Image formed by a plane mirror is virtual, erect, of same size and at the same distance from the mirror.
- Deviation (δ) produced by a plane mirror and by two inclined plane mirrors can be expressed as

  (*i*) For single reflection, $\delta = (180° - 2i)$.

  (*ii*) For double reflection, $\delta = (360° - 2\theta)$.

- The minimum height of a plane mirror to see object's full size in it is $\frac{H}{2}$, where H = height of the object.
- When two plane mirrors are inclined to each other at an angle θ, multiple images are formed, then number of image formed is given by $\frac{360°}{\theta} = N$ and actual number of image seen is n, where

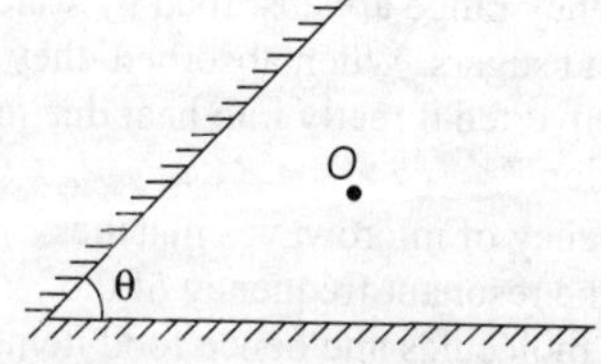

(*i*) $n = N - 1$, if N is even integer.

(*ii*) $n = N$, if N is odd integer and object is not on the bisector of mirrors.

(*iii*) $n = N - 1$, if N is odd integer and object is on the bisector of mirrors.

(*iv*) If $\frac{360°}{\theta} = N$ is a fraction, then the number of images will be equal to its lower boundary of integral part.

Reflection of Light by Spherical Mirrors

- Spherical mirror is a mirror whose reflecting surface is a part of a hollow shpere.
- Spherical mirrors are of two types : concave and convex mirror.

Terms related to spherical mirrors with the expressions and diagrams are shown in following table

Characteristics	Concave Mirror	Convex Mirror
Focus (F)	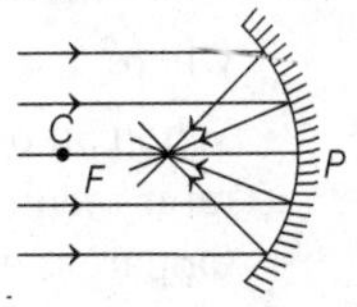	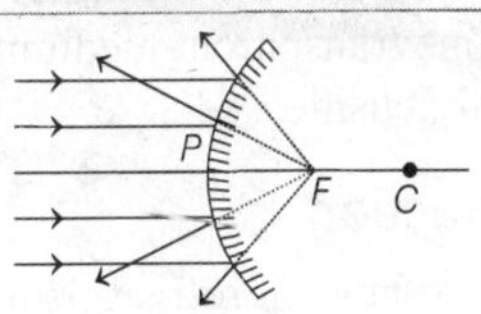
Focal length (f)	$f = -\text{ ve} = \dfrac{-R}{2}$	$f = +\text{ ve} = \dfrac{R}{2}$
Power (P)	$P = -\dfrac{1}{f\text{ (in metre)}}$ $= \dfrac{-100}{f\text{ (in cm)}}$ D For concave mirror, power is negative.	$P = \dfrac{1}{f\text{ (in metre)}}$ $= \dfrac{100}{f\text{ (in cm)}}$ D For convex mirror, power is positive.
Cartesian sign convention	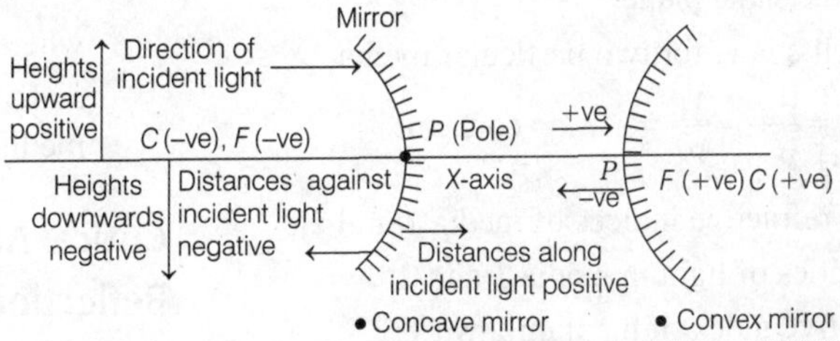	
Mirror formula	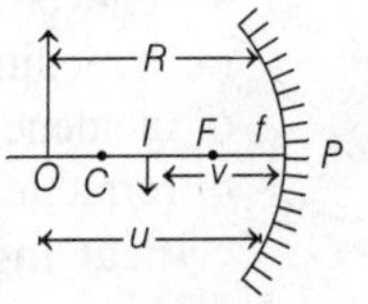 $\dfrac{1}{v} + \dfrac{1}{u} = \dfrac{1}{f}$ where, u and v = distance of object and image from pole of the mirror.	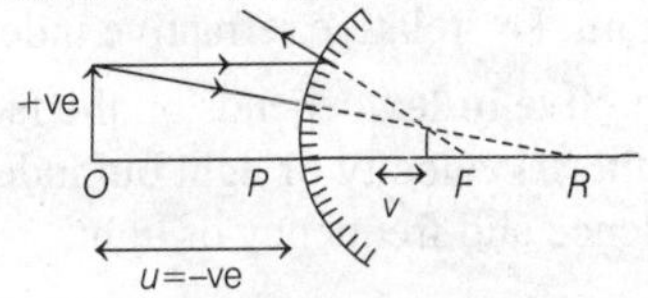 $\dfrac{1}{v} + \dfrac{1}{u} = \dfrac{1}{f}$
Newton's formula	$f^2 = x_1 x_2$ where, x_1 and x_2 are the distances of object and image from the focus of the mirror.	
Linear magnification general equation	$m = \dfrac{h_i}{h_o} = -\dfrac{v}{u} = \dfrac{f}{f-u} = \dfrac{f-v}{f}$ where, h_o and h_i = height of image and object.	For concave mirror, $m \geq 1$. For convex mirror, $m \leq 1$.
Longitudinal magnification • For large object • For small object	$m = \dfrac{\lvert v_1\rvert - \lvert v_2\rvert}{\lvert u_2\rvert - \lvert u_1\rvert}$ $m = \dfrac{dv}{du} = \dfrac{-v^2}{u^2} = -m^2$	
v versus u graph	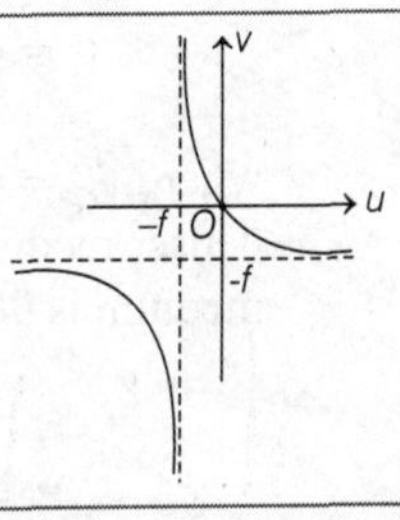	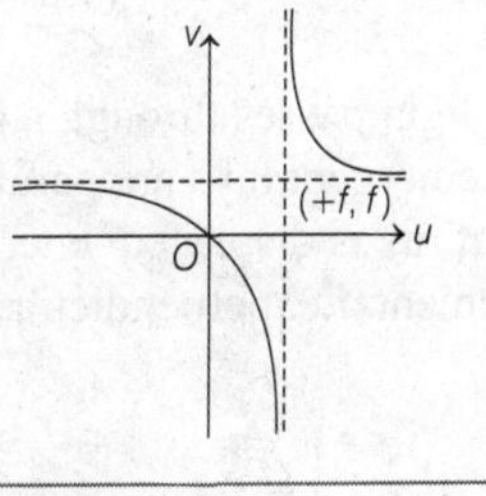

Refraction of Light

It is the phenomena of bending of ray of light when they pass from one transparent medium to another depending on their optical densities.

Laws of Refraction

There are two laws of refraction as follows

(*i*) For two particular media, the ratio of the sine of the angle of incidence to the sine of the angle of refraction is constant.

i.e. $\frac{\sin i}{\sin r} = \text{constant} = \frac{\mu_2}{\mu_1}$

This is known as **Snell's law.**

(*ii*) The incident ray, the reflected ray and the refracted ray, all lie in the same plane.

- According to Snell's law, for two particular media

$$\frac{\sin i}{\sin r} = \frac{\mu_2}{\mu_1} = \frac{v_1}{v_2} = {}_1\mu_2 = \text{constant}$$

where, μ_2, μ_1 = refractive indices of media 1 and 2,

v_2, v_1 = velocities of light in media 1 and 2

and ${}_1\mu_2$ = refractive index of medium 2 w.r.t. medium 1 = relative refractive index.

- **Refractive index** depends on the factors (*i*) wavelength of light (*ii*) velocity of light but independent of angle of incidence and frequency of light.
- **Absolute refractive index** is expressed as $\mu = \frac{c}{v}$, where c = speed of light in vacuum and v is speed of light in medium.
- When light undergoes refraction through several media and finally enters the first medium itself, then it can be expressed as

$${}_1\mu_2 \times {}_2\mu_3 \times {}_3\mu_1 = 1$$

or $${}_2\mu_3 = \frac{{}_1\mu_3}{{}_1\mu_2}$$

where, ${}_1\mu_2$, ${}_2\mu_3$ and ${}_3\mu_1$ are relative refractive indices of media 1, 2 and 3, respectively.

- Refractive index depends on following factors

(*i*) Nature and temperature of media.

(*ii*) Wavelength of light, according to Cauchy's formula

$$\mu = A + \frac{B}{\lambda^2} \quad (\because \text{as } \lambda \text{ increases, } \mu \text{ decreases})$$

- When a light passes through a glass slab, then incident ray and emergent rays are parallel to each other but emergent ray is displaced laterally. The lateral displacement, i.e. perpendicular distance between the incident and emergent ray for a rectangular glass slab is expressed as

$$d = t \sec r \sin (i - r)$$

where, t = thickness of the glass slab and d = lateral shift.

- When an object is in denser medium and observer is in rarer medium, then object appears to be at lesser depth (apparent depth) than its actual depth. The object also appears to be laterally shifted.
- Real and apparent depth have following relationship

$$\frac{\text{real depth } (h)}{\text{apparent depth } (h')} = \mu_{21}$$

i.e. Real depth > Apparent depth

- **Lateral shift**, $y = h - h' = \left(1 - \frac{1}{\mu_{21}}\right) h$

where, h and h' are real and apparent depths and μ_{21} = refractive index of second medium w.r.t. first medium.

Critical Angle and Total Internal Reflection (TIR)

- Whenever a ray of light goes from a denser medium to a rarer medium, it bends away from the normal. The angle of incidence ($\angle i$) in denser medium for which the angle of refraction ($\angle r$) in rarer medium is 90° is called the **critical angle** ($\angle C$).

$$C = \sin^{-1}\left(\frac{\mu_r}{\mu_d}\right)$$

- If the angle of incidence ($\angle i$) in the rarer medium is greater than the critical angle ($\angle C$), then the ray instead of suffering refraction is totally reflected back in the same (denser) medium. This phenomenon is called **total internal reflection**.

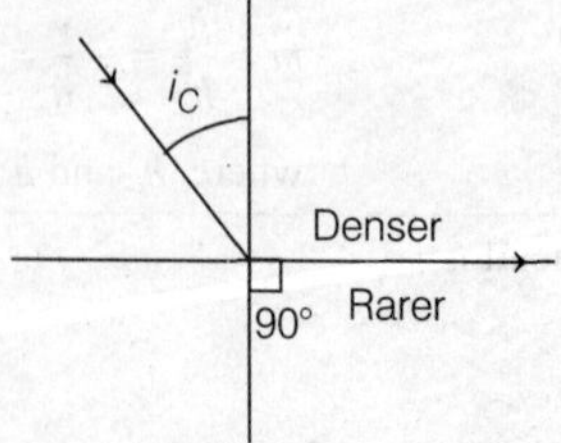

For total internal reflection to take place,

$$\mu = \frac{1}{\sin i_C} = \text{cosec } i_C$$

where, i_C = critical angle, i.e. angle of incidence in denser medium for which the angle of refraction in rarer medium is 90°.

Refraction of Light through Prism

A **prism** is a portion of a transparent medium bounded by two plane faces inclined to each other at a suitable angle.

Refraction of light through a prism is shown in the figure given below

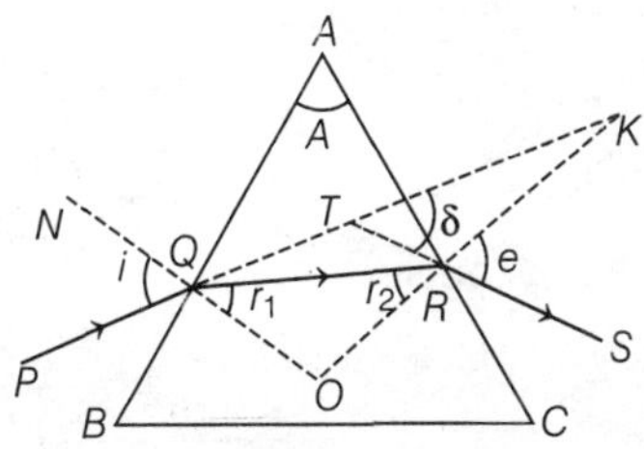

- The angle between emergent ray and incident ray is called angle of deviation (δ).

  $\delta = (i + e) - (r_1 + r_2)$, where $e =$ emergent angle.

  or $\delta = (i + e) - A$, here $A =$ angle of prism.

  For minimum deviation, $\delta_m = (\mu - 1)A$,

  where $\mu =$ refractive index of material of prism.

- **Prism formula** $\mu = \dfrac{\sin\left(\dfrac{A + \delta_m}{2}\right)}{\sin A/2}$

Dispersion of Light through Prism

- Splitting of white light into its seven components of colours, when passes through a prism is known as **dispersion**.
- **Angular dispersion** is expressed as

  $\delta_V - \delta_R = (\mu_V - \mu_R)A$, where, $\delta_V, \delta_R =$ deviations of violet & red light.

  and $\mu_V, \mu_R =$ refractive index of prism for violet & red light.
- The ratio of the angular dispersion to the average deviation, when a white beam of light is passed through a prism is expressed by the following relation

  Dispersive power, $\omega = \dfrac{\mu_V - \mu_R}{\mu - 1} = \dfrac{\delta_V - \delta_R}{\delta}$

  where, $\delta =$ average deviation $= (\mu_Y - 1)A$.
- Deviation of rays of different colours in prism is shown alongside

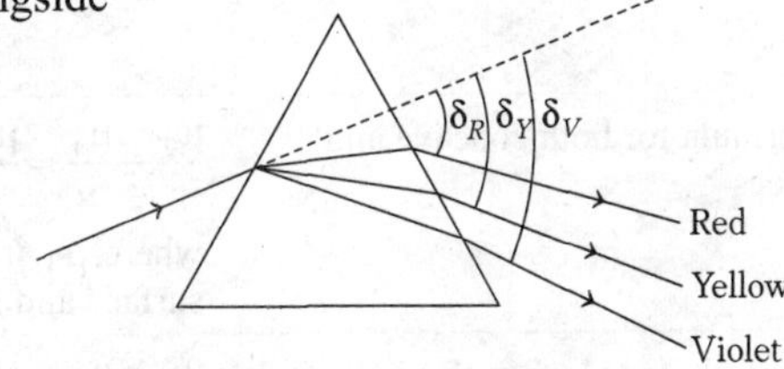

Combination of Prisms

A ray of light passes through the combination of prism is shown as follows

- **Net angular dispersion** $\delta_V - \delta_R = (\mu_V - \mu_R)A - (\mu'_V - \mu'_R)A'$
- **Average deviation** $\delta_Y = (\mu_Y - 1)A - (\mu'_Y - 1)A'$
- **Dispersion without average deviation** $\delta_V - \delta_R = (\mu_Y - 1)A(\omega - \omega')$
- **Average deviation without dispersion** $\delta_Y = (\mu_Y - 1)A\left(1 - \dfrac{\omega}{\omega'}\right)$

Refraction at Spherical Surfaces

- When two transparent media are separated by a spherical surface, light incident on the surface from one side get refracted into the medium on the other side. Spherical surfaces are of two types ; Convex and Concave.
- **Lenses** It is a transparent medium (material) bounded by two surfaces atleast one of which should be spherical.
  Lens are of two types ; Convex lens and Concave lens.

Some basic terms related to lenses are given below

Terms	Convex Lens	Concave Lens
Focus		
• **First Principal Focus** It is a point on the principal axis of lens from which rays emerging (in convex lens) appear to converge or (in concave lens), becomes parallel to principal axis after refraction.	F_1, O, f_1	O, F_1, f_1
• **Second Principal Focus** It is the point on the principal axis at which the rays coming parallel to the principal axis converge (convex lens) or appear to diverge (concave lens) after refraction from the lens.	O, F_2, f_2	F_2, O, f_2

Refraction formula for both concave and convex surfaces	$\frac{\mu_2}{v} - \frac{\mu_1}{u} = \frac{\mu_2 - \mu_1}{R}$ where, μ_1, μ_2 = refractive index of first & second media, R = radius of curvature of spherical surface and u, v = object & image distance.
Refraction formula for plane surface ($R = \infty$)	$\frac{\mu_2}{v} - \frac{\mu_1}{u} = 0$
Lens Maker's formula	$\frac{1}{f} = (\mu - 1)\left(\frac{1}{R_1} - \frac{1}{R_2}\right)$
Magnification	$m = \frac{I}{O} = \frac{v}{u} = \frac{f}{f+u} = \frac{f-u}{f}$
Thin lens formula	$\frac{1}{v} - \frac{1}{u} = \frac{1}{f}$
Power of lens	$P = \frac{1}{f\ (\text{m})}$
Focal length of lens, when it is immersed in liquid	$\frac{f_l}{f_a} = \frac{({}_a\mu_g - 1)}{\left(\frac{{}_a\mu_g}{{}_a\mu_l} - 1\right)}$
Newton's formula	$f^2 = x_1 x_2$, where x_1, x_2 = distance of object and image from first and second principal foci of lens.

- Focal length of convex lens can be determined by the **displacement method.** If an object and a screen are placed at a distance $D\,(> 4f)$ and a lens of focal length f is placed between them.

  For two different position of lens two images (I_1 and I_2) are formed at the screen, then focal length $f = \frac{D^2 - x^2}{4D}$,

  where x = distance between two positions of lens and $f = \frac{x}{m_1 - m_2}$, where $m_1 = \frac{I_1}{O}$, $m_2 = \frac{I_2}{O}$ and size of object, $O = \sqrt{I_1 I_2}$.

Combinations of Lenses

The focal length and power of combination of two or more thin lenses with diagram are shown in following table

	Lenses Separated by a Distance	Lenses are in Contact
Diagrams		
Focal length	$\frac{1}{F} = \frac{1}{f_1} + \frac{1}{f_2} - \frac{x}{f_1 f_2}$	$\frac{1}{F} = \frac{1}{f_1} + \frac{1}{f_2}$
Power	$P = P_1 + P_2 - xP_1P_2$	$P = P_1 + P_2$
Magnification	$m = m_1 \times m_2$	$m = m_1 \times m_2$

Silvering of a Lens

	Type of Lenses	Focal Lengths	Behaves Like
(i)	Plano-convex lens (plane surface is silvered)	$f = \frac{R}{2(\mu - 1)}$	Concave mirror
(ii)	Plano-convex lens (curved surface is silvered)	$f = \frac{R}{2\mu}$	Concave mirror
(iii)	Double-convex (one surface is silvered)	$f = \frac{R}{2(2\mu - 1)}$	Concave mirror
(iv)	Plano-concave lens (plane surface is silvered)	$f = \frac{R}{2(\mu - 1)}$	Convex mirror
(iv)	Plano-concave lens (curved surface is silvered)	$f = \frac{R}{2\mu}$	Convex mirror
(v)	Double-concave lens (one surface is silvered)	$f = \frac{R}{2(2\mu - 1)}$	Convex mirror

Cutting of a Lens

(i) If a symmetrical convex lens of focal length f is cut into two parts along its optical axis (as shown below), then focal length of each part is $2f$.

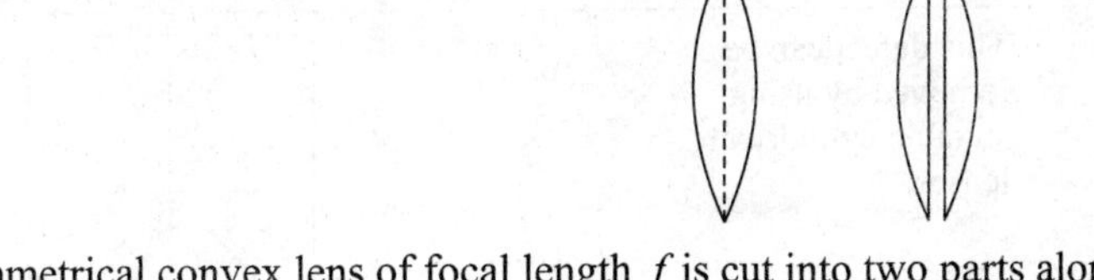

(ii) If a symmetrical convex lens of focal length f is cut into two parts along the principal axis, then focal length of each part remain unchanged to f.

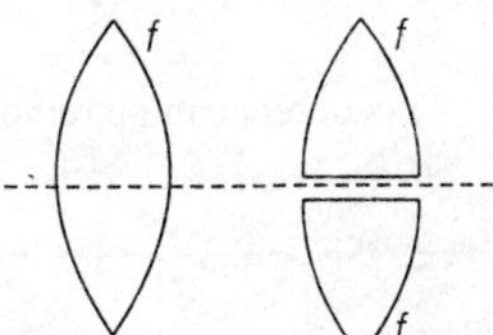

Scattering of Light

- If the molecules of a medium after absorption of incoming radiations (light) emit them in all directions, then the phenomenon takes place is called scattering of light.
- The intensity of scattered light depends on both, nature of molecules and wavelength of light.

  Intensity of scattered light $\propto \dfrac{1}{\lambda^4}$

Human Eye and Its Defects

- The eye is an organ which give us sense of sight. The eye behaves as a convex lens of refractive index 1.437, image formed by this lens is real and inverted and formed at retina.
- Eye lens is fixed between ciliary muscles, its radius of curvature can be changed by applying the pressure through ciliary muscles .
- Different defects of human eye along with their causes and remedies are given below

Defect of Vision	Causes	Remedy	Ray Diagram
Myopia or Short-Sightedness It is a defect of eye due to which a person can see near by objects clearly but cannot see far away objects clearly. In this defect, the far point of eye shifts from infinity to a nearer distance.	Increase in curvature of eye lens due to which its focal length decreases.	This defect can be removed by using a concave lens of appropriate power.	Myopic eye Corrected eye
Hypermetropia or Long-Sightedness In this defect, a person can see far away objects clearly but cannot see near by objects clearly. In this defect, the near point of eye shifts away from the eye.	Decrease in curvature of eye lens due to which its focal length increases.	This defect can be removed by using a convex lens of appropriate power.	Hypermetropic eye Corrected eye
Astigmatism In this defect, a person cannot focus on horizontal and vertical lines at the same distance at the same time.	Due to non-spherical shape of cornea.	This defect can be removed by using suitable cylindrical lenses.	
Presbyopia	Due to weakness of ciliary muscle with age.	This defect can be removed by using bi-focal lens.	

Optical Instruments

Magnifying power and resolving power of different optical instruments are shown in tabular form below

Optical Instruments	Image formed at Near Point of Eye (*D*)	Final Image at Infinity	Resolving Power
Simple microscope	$m = 1 + \frac{D}{f}$ where D = least distance of distinct vision for human eye and f = focal length of simple microscope.	$m = \frac{D}{f}$	$R = \frac{1}{\Delta d} = \frac{2\mu_m \sin\theta}{1.22\lambda}$ where μ_m = refractive index between object & lens and θ = angle subtended by radius of objective on one of the objects.
Compound microscope ($L = v_o + f_e$)	$m = -\frac{L}{f_o}\left(1 + \frac{D}{f_e}\right)$ where, f_o and f_e = focal length of objective and eye-piece.	$m = -\frac{L}{f_o} \cdot \frac{D}{f_e}$ (approx)	
Astronomical telescope (refractive telescope) ($L = f_o + f_e$)	$m = \frac{f_o}{f_e}\left(1 + \frac{f_e}{D}\right)$	$m = -\frac{f_o}{f_e}$	$R = \frac{1}{d\theta} = \frac{D}{1.22\lambda}$, where D = aperture or diameter of objective.
Reflecting telescope		$m = \frac{f_o}{f_e}$	

Topical Practice Questions

All the exam questions of this chapter have been divided into 6 topics as listed below

Topic 1

Reflection of Light at Plane and Spherical Mirrors

2018

1 An object is placed at a distance of 40 cm from a concave mirror of focal length 15 cm. If the object is displaced through a distance of 20 cm towards the mirror, the displacement of the image will be [NEET]

(a) 30 cm towards the mirror
(b) 36 cm away from the mirror
(c) 30 cm away from the mirror
(d) 36 cm towards the mirror

2014

2 To get three images of single object, one should have two plane mirrors at an angle of [UK PMT]

(a) 60° (b) 90° (c) 120° (d) 30°

3 An object is placed at 20 cm infront of a concave mirror produces three times magnified real image. What is the focal length of the concave mirror? [KCET]

(a) −15 cm (b) 6.6 cm (c) 10 cm (d) 7.5 cm

2013

4 A man of height 1.6 m wishes to see his full image in a plane mirror placed at a distance of 2 m. The minimum length of the mirror should be [UP CPMT, Manipal]

(a) 0.4 m (b) 0.8 m (c) 1.6 m (d) 2.4 m

5 A person standing infront of a mirror finds his image larger than himself. This implies that the mirror is [KCET]

(a) convex (b) parabolic
(c) plane (d) concave

2012

6 A rod of length 30 cm lies along the principal axis of a concave mirror of focal length 10 cm in such a way that its end closer to the pole is 20 cm away from the mirror. The length of the image is [CBSE AIPMT]

(a) 10 cm (b) 15 cm (c) 2.5 cm (d) 7.5 cm

2011

7 An object 5 cm tall is placed 1 m from a concave spherical mirror which has a radius of curvature of 20 cm. The size of the image is [UP CPMT]

(a) 0.11 cm (b) 0.5 cm
(c) 0.55 cm (d) 0.60 cm

8 Two mirrors are placed at right angle to each other. A man is standing between them combing his hair. How many images will he see? [Manipal]

(a) 2 (b) 3
(c) 1 (d) zero

2010

9 Object is placed 15 cm from a concave mirror of focal length 10 cm, then the nature of image formed will be [OJEE]

(a) magnified and inverted
(b) magnified and erect
(c) small in size and inverted
(d) small in size and erect

10 Two mirrors at an angle θ produces 5 images of a point. The number of images produced when θ is decreased to $\theta - 30°$ is [WB JEE]

(a) 9 (b) 10
(c) 11 (d) 12

11 A square of side 3 cm is located at a distance 25 cm from a concave mirror of focal length 10 cm. The centre of square is at the axis of the mirror and the plane is normal to axis of mirror. The area enclosed by the image of the square is [BCECE]

(a) 4 cm^2 (b) 6 cm^2
(c) 16 cm^2 (d) 36 cm^2

12 A plane mirror produces a magnification of [JIPMER]

(a) zero
(b) −1
(c) +1
(d) between 0 and +1

2009

13 **Assertion** The formula connecting u, v and f for a spherical mirror is valid only for mirrors sizes which are very small compared to their radii of curvature.

Reason Laws of reflection are strictly valid for plane surfaces, but not for large spherical surfaces. [AIIMS]

(a) Both Assertion and Reason are correct and Reason is the correct explanation of Assertion.
(b) Both Assertion and Reason are correct but Reason is not the correct explanation of Assertion.
(c) Assertion is correct but Reason is incorrect.
(d) Assertion is incorrect but Reason is correct.

14 A ray of light is incident on a plane mirror at an angle of 60°. The angle of deviation produced by the mirror is **[AFMC]**
(a) 120° (b) 30°
(c) 60° (d) 90°

15 Ray optics is valid, when characteristic dimensions are **[UP CMPT]**
(a) of the same order as the wavelength of light
(b) much smaller than the wavelength of light
(c) of the order of one millimetre
(d) much larger than the wavelength of light

16 Two plane mirrors inclined to each other at an angle 72°. What is the number of images formed? **[OJEE]**
(a) 3 (b) 5
(c) 9 (d) 7

2008

17 An object is placed at the focus of a concave mirror. If its focal length is 20 cm, the distance of object is **[BCECE]**
(a) 10 cm (b) 20 cm
(c) 40 cm (d) None of these

18 A plane mirror reflects pencil of light to form a real image then the pencil of light incident on the mirror is **[DUMET]**
(a) parallel (b) convergent
(c) divergent (d) None of these

19 A clock hung on a wall has marks instead of numerals on its dial. On the adjoining wall, there is a plane mirror and the image of the clock in the mirror indicates the time 7:10. Then, the time on the clock is **[Manipal]**
(a) 7 : 10 (b) 4 : 50
(c) 5 : 40 (d) 10 : 7

2007

20 If in the following figure, height of object is $O = +2.5$ cm, then height of image I formed is **[UP CPMT]**

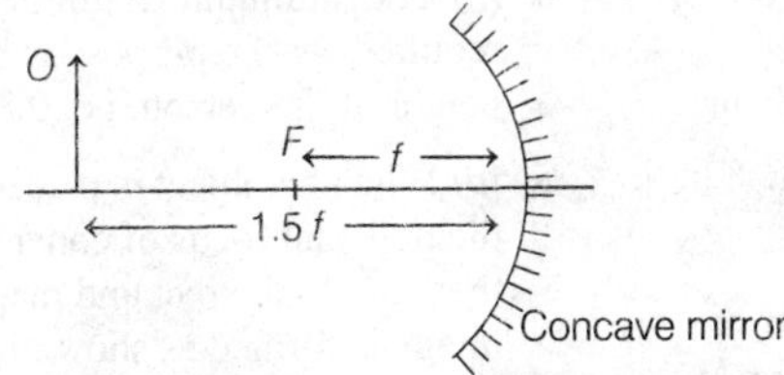

(a) – 5 cm (b) + 5 cm
(c) + 7.5 cm (d) – 7.5 cm

21 Two plane mirrors are perpendicular to each other. A ray after suffering reflection from the two mirrors will be **[MHT CET]**
(a) perpendicular to the original ray
(b) parallel to the original ray
(c) parallel to the first mirror
(d) at 45° to the original ray

22 A boy stands straight infront of a mirror at a distance of 30 cm from it. He sees his erect image whose height is $\frac{1}{5}$ of his real height. The mirror he is using, is **[AMU]**
(a) plane (b) convex
(c) concave (d) plano-concave

23 A bulb is placed between two plane mirrors inclined at an angle of 60°. The number of images formed is **[AMU]**
(a) 5 (b) 6 (c) 4 (d) 3

24 An object is placed at a distance of 40 cm infront of a concave mirror of focal length 20 cm. The image produced is **[Guj CET]**
(a) real, inverted and smaller in size
(b) real, inverted and of same size
(c) real and erect
(d) virtual and inverted

2006

25 A short linear object of length b lies along the axis of a concave mirror of focal length f at a distance u from the pole of the mirror, what is the size of image? **[Manipal]**
(a) $\left(\frac{f}{u-f}\right) b$ (b) $\left(\frac{f}{u-f}\right)^2 b$
(c) $\left(\frac{f}{u-f}\right) b^2$ (d) $\left(\frac{f}{u-f}\right)$

26 An object is placed at a distance equal to focal length of convex mirror. If the focal length of the mirror be f, then the distance of the image from the pole of the mirror is **[Manipal, Punjab PMET]**
(a) less than f (b) equal to f
(c) more than f (d) infinity

2005

27 Which of the following is not a property of light? **[AFMC]**
(a) It requires a material medium for propagation.
(b) It can travel through vacuum.
(c) It involves transportation of energy.
(d) It has finite speed.

28 A concave mirror of focal length 15 cm forms an image having twice the linear dimension of the object. The position of the object when the image is virtual will be **[RPMT]**
(a) 45 cm (b) 30 cm
(c) 7.5 cm (d) 22.5 cm

29 An object is placed at a distance $2f$ from the pole of a curved mirror (concave or convex) of focal length f. Then, **[Haryana PMT]**
(a) the linear magnification is 1 for both types of curved mirrors
(b) the linear magnification is 1 for a convex mirror
(c) the linear magnification is $\frac{1}{3}$ for a convex mirror
(d) None of the above

30 A man having height 6 m, observes image of 2 m height erect, then mirror used is **[Punjab PMT]**

(a) concave
(b) convex
(c) plane
(d) None of the above

31 A flat mirror revolves at a constant angular velocity making 4π rad s^{-1}. With what velocity will a light spot move along a spherical screen with a radius of 10 m, if the mirror is at a centre of curvature of the screen? **[DUMET]**

(a) 251.2 ms^{-1}
(b) 261.2 ms^{-1}
(c) 271.2 ms^{-1}
(d) 241.2 ms^{-1}

32 A vessel consists of two plane mirrors at right angle (as shown in figure). The vessel is filled with water. The total deviation in incident ray is **[DUMET]**

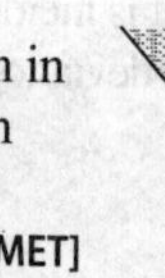

(a) 0° (b) 90°
(c) 180° (d) None of these

33 Which mirror is to be used to obtain a parallel beam of light from a small lamp? **[KCET]**

(a) Plane mirror
(b) Convex mirror
(c) Concave mirror
(d) Any one of the above

Answers

1	(b)	2	(b)	3	(a)	4	(b)	5	(d)	6	(d)	7	(c)	8	(b)	9	(a)	10	(c)
11	(a)	12	(c)	13	(c)	14	(c)	15	(d)	16	(b)	17	(b)	18	(b)	19	(b)	20	(a)
21	(b)	22	(b)	23	(a)	24	(b)	25	(b)	26	(a)	27	(a)	28	(c)	29	(c)	30	(b)
31	(a)	32	(c)	33	(c)														

Explanations

1 *(b)* ***Case* I** When the object distance,

$u_1 = -40$ cm

Focal length of mirror, $f = -15$ cm

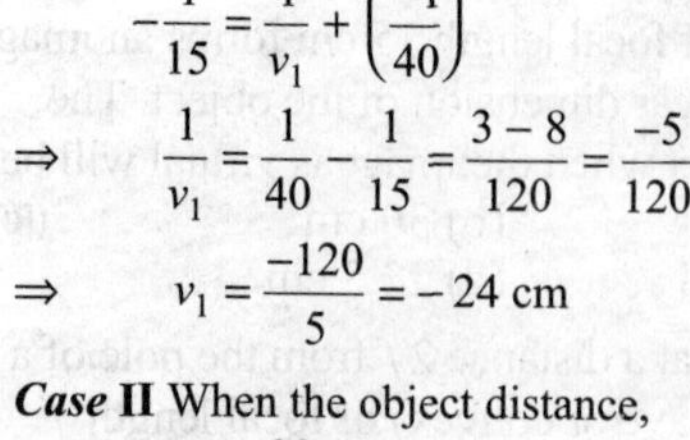

Using the mirror formula, we get

$$\frac{1}{f} = \frac{1}{v_1} + \frac{1}{u_1}$$

Substituting the given values, we get

$$-\frac{1}{15} = \frac{1}{v_1} + \left(\frac{-1}{40}\right)$$

$$\Rightarrow \frac{1}{v_1} = \frac{1}{40} - \frac{1}{15} = \frac{3-8}{120} = \frac{-5}{120}$$

$$\Rightarrow v_1 = \frac{-120}{5} = -24 \text{ cm}$$

***Case* II** When the object distance,

$u_2 = 20$ cm

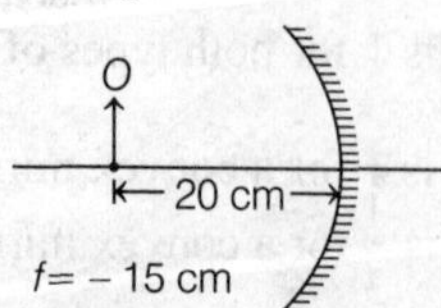

Using the mirror formula, we get

$$\frac{1}{f} = \frac{1}{v_2} + \frac{1}{u_2}$$

Substituting the given values, we get

$$-\frac{1}{15} = \frac{1}{v_2} + \left(-\frac{1}{20}\right)$$

$$\Rightarrow \frac{1}{v_2} = \frac{1}{20} - \frac{1}{15} = \frac{3-4}{60} = \frac{-1}{60}$$

$$\Rightarrow v_2 = -60 \text{ cm}$$

$\therefore$ The displacement of the image

$= v_2 - v_1$

$= -60 - (-24) = -60 + 24$

$= -36$ cm

or $= 36$ cm, away from the mirror

2 *(b)* Consider the diagram where two plane mirrors are inclined at angle θ.

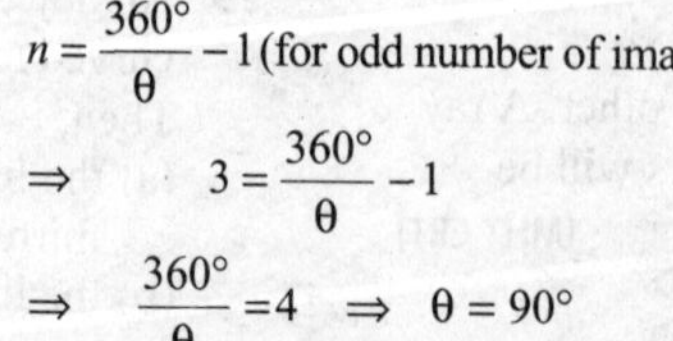

Number of images formed is given by

$$n = \frac{360°}{\theta} - 1 \text{(for odd number of images)}$$

$$\Rightarrow 3 = \frac{360°}{\theta} - 1$$

$$\Rightarrow \frac{360°}{\theta} = 4 \Rightarrow \theta = 90°$$

3 *(a)* We know that,

Linear magnification, $m = \dfrac{f}{f-u}$

Given, object distance, $u = -20$ cm

$m = -3$

($\because$ all real images are inverted)

So, $-3 = \dfrac{f}{f-(-20)}$

$$\Rightarrow -3 = \frac{f}{f+20} \Rightarrow -3f - 60 = f$$

$$4f = -60 \Rightarrow f = -\frac{60}{4} = -15 \text{ cm}$$

Since, mirror is concave, $f = -15$ cm

4 *(b)* The minimum length of the mirror required for the purpose is half the height of the person, i.e. 0.8 m.

5 *(d)* When an object is placed between the pole and focus of concave mirror, then a virtual, erect and magnified image is formed as shown below

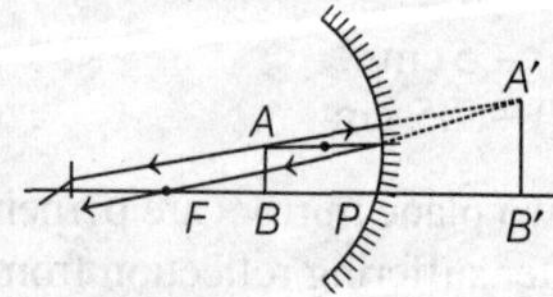

Thus, mirror is concave while convex mirror produce an image reduced in size.

For a plane mirror, the image is always at the same distance behind the mirror as the object is infront and of same size.

6 (*d*) By mirror formula, image distance of A

$$\frac{1}{v}+\frac{1}{u}=\frac{1}{f}$$

$$\Rightarrow \quad f=-10\text{ cm}$$

$$\frac{1}{v_A}+\frac{1}{u}=\frac{1}{f}$$

$$\Rightarrow \quad \frac{1}{v_A}=\frac{1}{-10}-\frac{1}{(-50)}$$

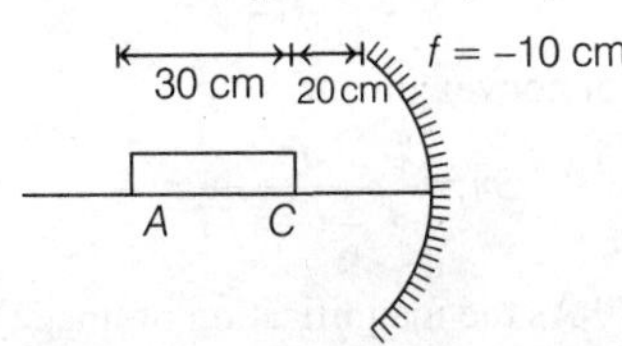

$$v_A=-12.5\text{ cm}$$

Also, image distance of C

$$\frac{1}{v_C}-\frac{1}{20}=\frac{-1}{10}$$

$$v_C=-20\text{ cm}$$

The length of image $=|v_A-v_C|$

$$=|-12.5-(-20)|=7.5\text{ cm}$$

7 (*c*) $\frac{I}{O}=\frac{f}{(f-u)}$

Since, radius of curvature $R=20$ cm,

then focal length, $f=\frac{R}{2}=\frac{20}{2}=10$ cm

$$u=1\text{ m}=100\text{ cm}$$

$$\Rightarrow \frac{I}{5}=\frac{-10}{-10-(-100)} \Rightarrow |I|=0.55\text{ cm}$$

8 (*b*) The number of images formed depends upon the angle between the mirrors. If two mirrors make an angle θ with each other, the number of images formed is

$$n=\frac{360°}{\theta}-1$$

When mirrors are kept mutually perpendicular to each other, then $\theta=90°$.

$$\Rightarrow n=\frac{360°}{\theta°}-1,\ n=\frac{360°}{90°}-1=3$$

9 (*a*) When object is placed between centre of curvature and focus, (i.e. $f<u$), then image will be between $2f$ and ∞, real, inverted and large in size or magnified ($m>-1$).

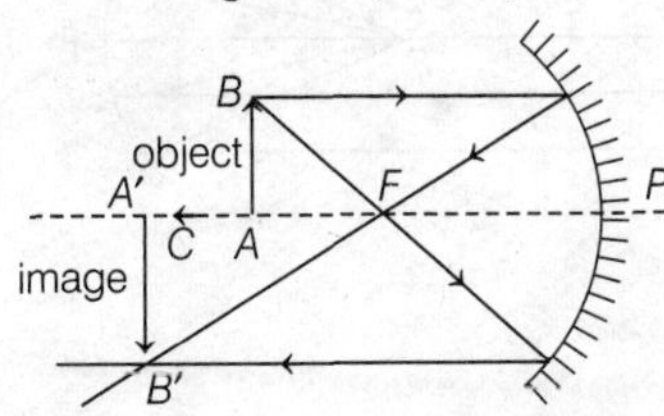

10 (*c*) The number of images produced by the two mirrors is

$$n=\frac{360°}{\theta}-1$$

$$\Rightarrow \quad 5=\frac{360°}{\theta}-1$$

$$\Rightarrow \quad \theta=60°$$

Now, $\theta-30°=60°-30°=30°$

$$\Rightarrow \quad n=\frac{360°}{(30)°}-1$$

$$=12-1=11$$

11 (*a*) Linear magnification,

$$m=\frac{I}{O}=\frac{f}{f-u}=\frac{10}{10-25}$$

$$\Rightarrow \quad m=\frac{-10}{15}=\frac{-2}{3}$$

Axial magnification $=m^2=\frac{4}{9}$

Area of image $=\frac{4}{9}\times$ Area of object

$$=\frac{4}{9}\times(3)^2=4\text{ cm}^2$$

12 (*c*) In a plane mirror, the image formed is erect and of same size as of object. Thus, magnification of plane mirror is 1.

13 (*c*) The mirror formula $\frac{1}{v}+\frac{1}{u}=\frac{1}{f}$ is valid only for mirror sizes which are very small compared to their radii of curvature to avoid spherical aberration. Also, the laws of reflection are valid for plane mirror as well as for curved surfaces.

Hence, Assertion is correct but Reason is incorrect.

14 (*c*) From geometry of figure, the angle of deviation produced by mirror

$$=30°+30°=60°$$

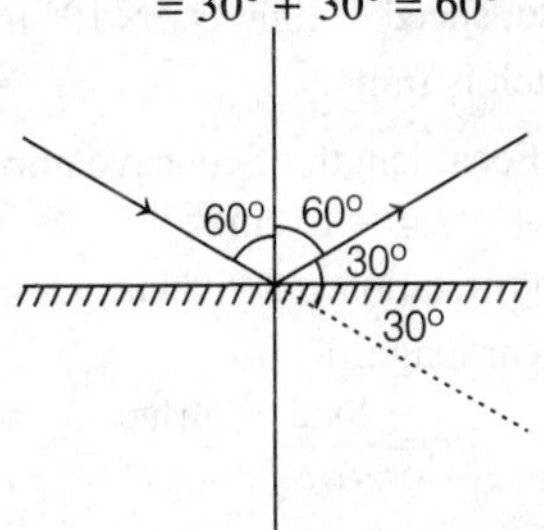

15 (*d*) Ray optics is valid when characteristics dimensions are much larger than the wavelength of light, otherwise diffraction will take place and laws of ray optics will fail.

16 (*b*)

$$n=\begin{cases}\frac{360°}{\theta°}-1, \text{ when } \frac{360°}{\theta°} \text{ is odd and the object lies symmetrically}\\ \frac{360°}{\theta°}, \text{ when } \frac{360°}{\theta°} \text{ is odd and the object lies unsymmetrically}\end{cases}$$

Here, $\frac{360°}{72}=5$, so number of images formed is either 5 or 4. Since, 4 is not available in option, so it is assumed that object lies unsymmetrically and number of image formed is 5.

17 (*b*) As the object is at focus and focal length of mirror is 20 cm. So, object is at a distance of 20 cm from mirror.

18 (*b*) When convergent beam incident on a plane mirror, then mirror forms real image, for a virtual object.

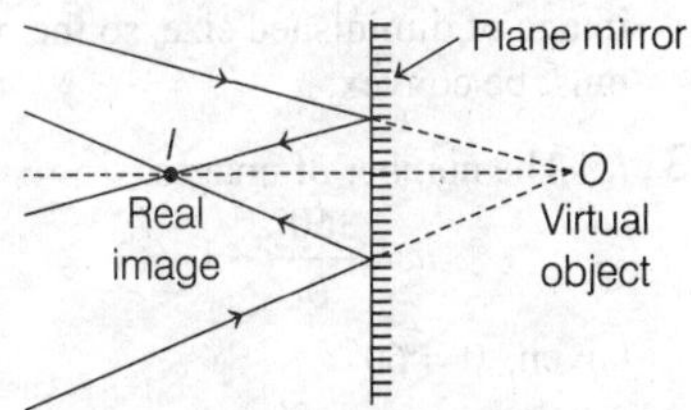

19 (*b*) In a plane mirror, the image undergoes depth inversion, hence the time on the image is as much ahead of 12 h and 0 min as the time on actual clock is behind 12 h and 0 min.

Time on the image clock = 7 h and 10 min

Time on the actual clock

= (12 h and 0 min) – (7 h and 10 min)

= 4 h and 50 min

20 (*a*) By concave mirror formula,

$$\frac{1}{f}=\frac{1}{v}+\frac{1}{u}$$

Here, $u=-1.5f$ and $f=-f$

We have, $\frac{1}{(-f)}=\frac{1}{v}+\frac{1}{(-1.5f)}$,

$$\frac{1}{v}=\frac{1}{-3f} \text{ or } v=-3f$$

Now, magnification in mirror is given by $m=\frac{I}{O}=\frac{v}{-u}$

where, I is size of image and O is size of object.

Here, $O=+2.5$ cm

$$\therefore \quad \frac{I}{2.5}=\frac{-3f}{-(-1.5f)}$$

or $I=-5$ cm

21 *(b)* Angular deviation, $\delta = 2\pi - 2\theta$ (θ is the angle between mirror)

$$= 2\pi - 2 \times \frac{\pi}{2} = \pi$$

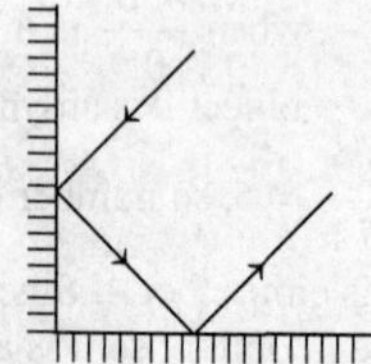

Hence, after suffering reflection from the two mirrors, the ray will travel in parallel direction to the original ray.

22 *(b)* Both concave and convex mirrors give virtual image but a concave mirror gives a magnified virtual image (when object is placed between F and P). Since, the boy sees his image of diminished size, so the mirror must be convex.

23 *(a)* The number of images,

$$n = \frac{360°}{\theta} - 1$$

Given, $\theta = 60°$

$$\Rightarrow \quad n = \frac{360°}{60°} - 1$$

$$\Rightarrow \quad n = 6 - 1 = 5$$

24 *(b)* Distance of object, $u = -40$ cm

Focal length of concave mirror, $f = -20$ cm

By mirror formula,

$$\frac{1}{f} = \frac{1}{v} + \frac{1}{u} \quad \text{or} \quad \frac{1}{v} = \frac{1}{f} - \frac{1}{u}$$

$$\therefore \quad \frac{1}{v} = \frac{1}{-20} - \frac{1}{(-40)} = \frac{1}{-20} + \frac{1}{40}$$

$$\therefore \quad v = -40 \text{ cm}$$

Negative sign implies that image is in front of concave mirror, hence image is real.

Magnification produced by concave mirror

$$m = -\frac{v}{u} = -\frac{(-40)}{(-40)} = -1$$

The image is of the same size and inverted.

25 *(b)* Using the relation for the focal length of concave mirror

$$\frac{1}{f} = \frac{1}{v} + \frac{1}{u} \quad \text{...(i)}$$

On differentiating Eq. (i), we get

$$0 = -\frac{1}{v^2}dv - \frac{1}{u^2}du$$

So, $dv = -\frac{v^2}{u^2} \times b$ (here, $du = b$) ...(ii)

From Eq. (i),

$$\frac{1}{v} = \frac{1}{f} - \frac{1}{u} = \frac{u - f}{fu}$$

or $$\frac{u}{v} = \frac{u - f}{f}$$

$$\frac{v}{u} = \frac{f}{u - f} \quad \text{...(iii)}$$

Now from Eqs. (ii) and (iii),

$$dv = -\left(\frac{f}{u - f}\right)^2 b$$

Therefore, size of image $= \left(\frac{f}{u - f}\right)^2 b.$

26 *(a)* Image formed by convex mirror is shown in figure.

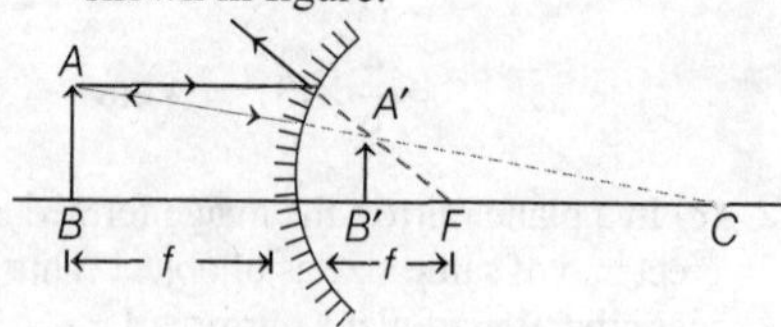

$$u = -f$$

By mirror formula,

$$\frac{1}{v} = \frac{1}{f} - \frac{1}{u} = \frac{1}{f} + \frac{1}{f} = \frac{2}{f} \Rightarrow v = \frac{f}{2}$$

i.e. the distance of the image formed is less than f.

27 *(a)* Light waves do not require a material medium for their propagation. Also, they travel through vacuum. A metallic plate kept in the path of light rays gets heated up, showing that light involves transportation of energy. Also, speed of light is 3×10^8 ms^{-1}, which is finite.

28 *(c)* Focal length of concave mirror,

$$f = -15 \text{ cm}$$

Magnification = 2 (for virtual image)

Linear magnification,

$$m = \frac{\text{Size of image}}{\text{Size of object}} = -\frac{v}{u}$$

$$2 = -\frac{v}{u} \quad \text{or} \quad v = -2u$$

Now, from the relation $\frac{1}{f} = \frac{1}{v} + \frac{1}{u}$

$$\Rightarrow \quad -\frac{1}{15} = \frac{1}{u} - \frac{1}{2u} = \frac{1}{2u}$$

$$2u = -15 \quad \text{or} \quad u = -7.5 \text{ cm}$$

29 *(c)* For a curved mirror, when object is placed at $2f$, the real image of the same size as that of object, is formed at 2C.

So, for a concave mirror,

$$m = \frac{-f}{-f - (-2f)} = -1$$

For convex mirror,

$$m = \frac{f}{f - (-2f)} = \frac{1}{3}$$

30 *(b)* As the magnification of image is less than 1 and positive, hence nature of image is erect, diminished but virtual, so this criteria of image formation is possible in convex mirror only.

31 *(a)* Angular velocity of mirror

$$= 4\pi \text{ rad s}^{-1}$$

Angular velocity of reflected ray

$$= 2 \times 4\pi = 8\pi \text{ rad s}^{-1}$$

$\therefore$ Velocity of spot,

$$v = 10 \times 8\pi = 80 \times 3.14$$
$$= 251.2 \text{ ms}^{-1}$$

32 *(c)* The deviation produced by combination of two plane mirrors is

$$\delta = 2\pi - 2\theta$$

$$= 2\pi - 2 \times \frac{\pi}{2} \quad (\theta = 90°)$$

90°

$$\Rightarrow \quad \delta = \pi = 180°$$

Hence, total deviation in incident ray is 180°.

33 *(c)* If lamp is placed at the focus of concave mirror, then we get parallel beam of light.

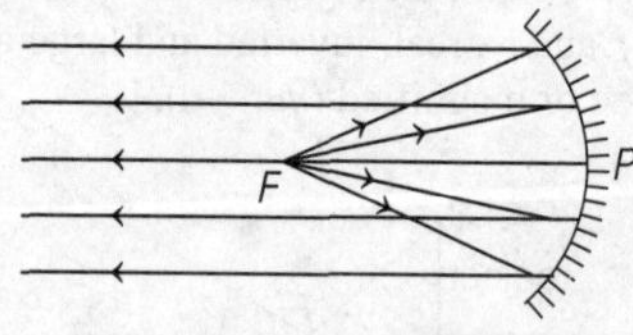

Topic 2

Refraction of Light at Plane Surface

2019

1 If velocity of light in air is c, what will be the velocity of light in a medium of refractive index 1.4? **[JIPMER]**

(a) 2.1×10^8 m/s (b) 1.4×10^8 m/s
(c) 2.8×10^8 m/s (d) None of these

2 If frequency (ν) of light is 5×10^{16} Hz and speed of light in air is 3×10^8 m/s. Find the ratio of wavelength of light in a medium of refractive index 2 to air. **[JIPMER]**

(a) $\frac{1}{2}$ (b) 3 (c) $\frac{3}{2}$ (d) 2

3 When a light ray enters from oil to glass on oil- glass interface, then velocity of light changes by a factor of [given, $\mu_{oil} = 2$ and $\mu_{glass} = 3/2$] **[JIPMER]**

(a) $\frac{4}{3}$ (b) $\frac{3}{4}$ (c) 3 (d) 1

2018

4 The refractive index of glass is 1.5. The speed of light in glass is **[AIIMS]**

(a) 3×10^3 m/s (b) 2×10^8 m/s
(c) 1×10^8 m/s (d) 4×10^8 m/s

2014

5 A glass slab consists of thin uniform layers of progressively decreasing refractive indices RI (see figure) such that the RI of any layer is $\mu - m\Delta\mu$. Here, μ and $\Delta\mu$ denote the RI of 0th layer and the difference in RI between any two consecutive layers, respectively. The integer $m = 0, 1, 2, 3, \cdots$ denotes the numbers of the successive layers. A ray of light from the 0th layer enters the 1st layer at an angle of incidence of 30°. After undergoing the mth refraction, the ray emerges parallel to the interface. If $\mu = 1.5$ and $\Delta\mu = 0.015$, then the value of m is **[WB JEE]**

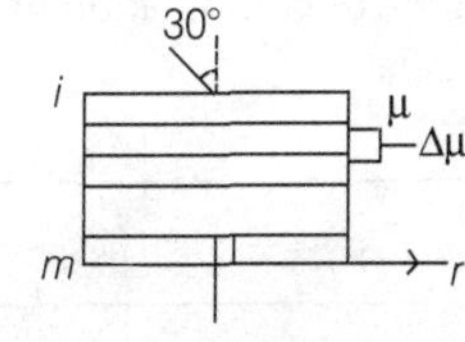

(a) 20 (b) 30 (c) 40 (d) 50

2011

6 Sun is visible a little before the actual sunrise and until a little after the actual sunset. This is due to **[J&K CET]**

(a) total internal reflection (b) reflection
(c) refraction (d) polarisation

7 The time required for the light to pass through a glass slab (refractive index = 1.5) of thickness 4 mm is ($c = 3\times10^8$ ms^{-1}, speed of light in free space) **[KCET]**

(a) 10^{-11} s (b) 2×10^{-11} s
(c) 2×10^{11} s (d) 2×10^{-5} s

2010

8 The optical path of a monochromatic light is same, if it goes through 4 cm of glass or 4.5 cm of water. If the refractive index of glass is 1.53, the refractive index of the water is **[AFMC]**

(a) 1.30 (b) 1.36
(c) 1.42 (d) 1.46

9 A beam of light composed of red and green rays is incident obliquely at a point on the face of a rectangular glass slab. When coming out on the opposite parallel face, the red and green rays emerge from **[AFMC]**

(a) two points propagating in two different non-parallel directions
(b) two points propagating in two different parallel directions
(c) one point propagating in two different directions
(d) one point propagating in the same direction

10 An objects is placed 21 cm infront of a concave mirror of radius of curvature 10 cm. A glass slab of thickness 3 cm and $\mu = 1.5$ is then placed close to the mirror in the space between the object and the mirror. The position of final image formed is **[BHU]**

(a) – 3.94 cm (b) – 4.3 cm
(c) – 4.93 cm (d) 3.94 cm

11 If angle of incidence is twice the angle of refraction in a medium of refractive index μ, then angle of incidence **[MHT CET]**

(a) $2\cos^{-1}\frac{\mu}{2}$ (b) $2\sin^{-1}\frac{\mu}{2}$
(c) $2\cos^{-1}\mu$ (d) $2\sin^{-1}\mu$

12 Wavelength of light in vacuum is 5890 Å, then its wavelength in glass ($\mu = 1.5$) will be **[OJEE]**

(a) 9372 Å (b) 7932 Å
(c) 7548 Å (d) 3927 Å

13 A transparent cube of 0.21 m edge contains a small air bubble. Its apparent distance when viewed through one face of the cube is 0.10 m and when viewed from the opposite face is 0.04 m. The actual distance of the bubble from the second face of the cube is **[JCECE]**

(a) 0.06 m (b) 0.17 m
(c) 0.05 m (d) 0.04 m

14 To a fish under water, viewing obliquely a fisherman standing on the bank of a lake, the man looks [JCECE]

(a) taller than what he actually is
(b) shorter that what he actually is
(c) the same height as he actually is
(d) depends on the obliquity

15 A ray of light is incident on surface of glass slab at an angle 45°. If the lateral shift produced per unit thickness is $\frac{1}{\sqrt{3}}$ m, the angle of refraction produced is [KCET]

(a) $\tan^{-1}\left(\frac{\sqrt{3}}{2}\right)$ (b) $\tan^{-1}\left(1-\sqrt{\frac{2}{3}}\right)$

(c) $\sin^{-1}\left(1-\sqrt{\frac{2}{3}}\right)$ (d) $\tan^{-1}\left(\sqrt{\frac{2}{\sqrt{3}-1}}\right)$

2009

16 The frequency of a light wave in a material is 2×10^{14} Hz and wavelength is 5000 Å. The refractive index of material will be [JIPMER]

(a) 1.4 (b) 1.5 (c) 3 (d) 1.33

2008

17 A fish in water (refractive index n) looks at a bird vertically above in the air. If y is the height of the bird and x is the depth of the fish from the surface, then the distance of the bird as estimated by the fish is [KCET]

(a) $x+y\left(1-\frac{1}{n}\right)$ (b) $x+ny$

(c) $x+y\left(1+\frac{1}{n}\right)$ (d) $y+x\left(1-\frac{1}{n}\right)$

2007

18 A ray of light is incident on the surface of a glass plate of thickness t. If the angle of incidence θ is small, the emerging ray would be displaced side ways by an amount (take, n = refractive index of glass) [AIIMS]

(a) $\frac{t\theta n}{(n+1)}$ (b) $\frac{t\theta(n-1)}{n}$ (c) $\frac{t\theta n}{(n-1)}$ (d) $\frac{t\theta(n+1)}{n}$

19 When light passes from one medium to other, then which will not change? [UP CPMT]

(a) Frequency (b) Wavelength
(c) Amplitude (d) Velocity

20 The refractive indices of glass and water with respect to air are $\frac{3}{2}$ and $\frac{4}{3}$, respectively. Then, the refractive index of glass with respect to water is [Kerala CEE]

(a) $\frac{8}{9}$ (b) $\frac{9}{8}$ (c) $\frac{7}{6}$ (d) 2
(e) 0.5

21 In refraction, light waves are bent on passing from one medium to the second medium, because in the second medium [RPMT]

(a) the frequency is different
(b) the coefficient of elasticity is different
(c) the speed is different
(d) the amplitude is smaller

22 A glass has refractive index $\frac{3}{2}$ and water has refractive index $\frac{4}{3}$. If the speed of light in glass is 2×10^8 ms^{-1}, then the speed of light in water in ms^{-1} is [AMU]

(a) 1.5×10^6 (b) 1.78×10^8
(c) 2.25×10^8 (d) 2.67×10^8

23 A vessel of height $2d$ is half-filled with a liquid of refractive index $\sqrt{2}$ and the other half with a liquid of refractive index n (the given liquids are immiscible). Then, the apparent depth of the inner surface of the bottom of the vessel (neglecting the thickness of the bottom of the vessel) will be [KCET]

(a) $\frac{n}{d(n+\sqrt{2})}$ (b) $\frac{d(n+\sqrt{2})}{n\sqrt{2}}$

(c) $\frac{\sqrt{2}n}{d(n+\sqrt{2})}$ (d) $\frac{nd}{d+\sqrt{2n}}$

2006

24 A transparent cube of 15 cm edge contains a small air bubble. Its apparent depth when viewed through one face is 6 cm and when viewed through the opposite face is 4 cm. Then, the refractive index of the material of the cube is [Manipal]

(a) 2.0 (b) 2.5
(c) 1.6 (d) 1.5

25 Maximum lateral displacement of a ray of light incident on a slab of thickness t is [J&K CET]

(a) $\frac{t}{2}$ (b) $\frac{t}{3}$ (c) $\frac{t}{4}$ (d) t

26 Considering normal incidence of ray, the equivalent refractive index of combination of two slabs shown in figure is [AMU]

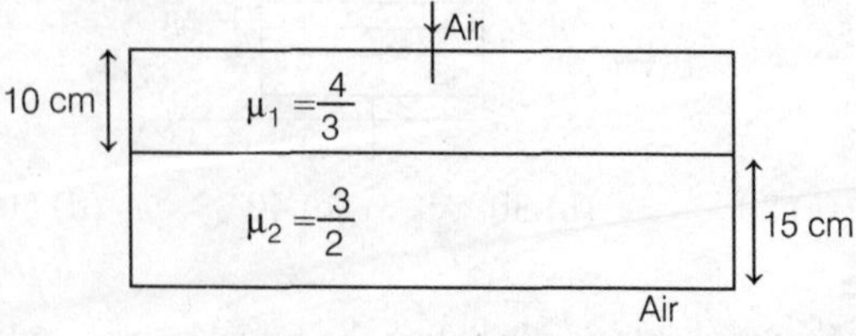

(a) 1.8 (b) 1.43
(c) 2 (d) None of these

27 A light ray in between two media as given below. The angle of incidence on the boundary in all the cases is 30°. Identify the correct sequence of increasing order of angles of refraction
(1) air to water
(2) water to glass
(3) glass to water
(Refractive indices of glass and water are respectively $\frac{3}{2}$ and $\frac{4}{3}$) **[EAMCET]**

(a) 1, 2, 3 (b) 2, 3, 1
(c) 3, 1, 2 (d) 1, 3, 2

2005

28 The apparent depth of water in cylindrical water tank of diameter $2R$ cm is reducing at the rate of x cm min^{-1} when water is being drained out at a constant rate. The amount of water drained in cc per minute is (n_1 = refractive index of air and n_2 = refractive index of water) **[AIIMS]**

(a) $\frac{x\pi R^2 n_1}{n_2}$ (b) $\frac{x\pi R^2 n_2}{n_1}$ (c) $\frac{2\pi R n_1}{n_2}$ (d) $\pi R^2 x$

29 A plane glass slab is kept over various colour letters, the letter which appears least raised is **[BHU]**

(a) red (b) violet (c) green (d) blue 3

Answers

1	(a)	2	(a)	3	(a)	4	(b)	5	(d)	6	(c)	7	(b)	8	(b)	9	(b)	10	(c)
11	(a)	12	(d)	13	(a)	14	(a)	15	(b)	16	(c)	17	(b)	18	(b)	19	(a)	20	(b)
21	(c)	22	(c)	23	(b)	24	(d)	25	(d)	26	(b)	27	(a)	28	(b)	29	(a)		

Explanations

1 (a) Refractive index of medium

$$= \frac{\text{Speed of light in vacuum}}{\text{Speed in medium}}$$

$\Rightarrow$ Speed of light in medium

$$= \frac{\text{Speed of light in vacuum}}{\text{Refractive index}}$$

$$\Rightarrow v = \frac{c}{n} = \frac{3\times 8^8}{1.4}$$

$$= 2.14\times 10^8 \text{ m/s}$$

2 (a) $v = \nu\lambda$, where ν is same for a source of light.

$$\Rightarrow \quad v \propto \lambda, \frac{v_1}{v_2} = \frac{\lambda_1}{\lambda_2}$$

But $v_1 = \frac{c}{n_1}$ and v_2 (in air) $= \frac{c}{n_2} = c$

$$\Rightarrow \frac{\lambda_1}{\lambda_2} = \frac{c/n_1}{c} = \frac{1}{n_1} = \frac{1}{2} \quad [\because n_1 = 2]$$

3 (a) Given, $\mu_{oil} = 2$ and $\mu_{glass} = 3/2$

Velocity of light in oil is given by

$$v_{oil} = \frac{\text{Velocity of light } (c)}{\mu_{oil}} = \frac{c}{\mu_{oil}}$$

Similarly, $v_{glass} = \frac{c}{\mu_{glass}}$

$$\therefore \quad \frac{v_{glass}}{v_{oil}} = \frac{c/\mu_{glass}}{c/\mu_{oil}} = \frac{\mu_{oil}}{\mu_{glass}}$$

$$= \frac{2}{3/2} = \frac{4}{3}$$

4 (b) From Snell's law of refraction,

$$\frac{\sin i}{\sin r} = \frac{\mu_2}{\mu_1} = \frac{v_1}{v_2}$$

Given, $v_1 = 3\times 10^8$ m/s

$$\frac{\mu_2}{\mu_1} = {}^1\mu_2 = 1.5$$

$$v_2 = \frac{v_1}{{}^1\mu_2} = \frac{3\times 10^8}{1.5} \text{ m/s} = \frac{3\times 10^8}{3/2}$$

$$= 2\times 10^8 \text{ m/s}$$

5 (d) By Snell's law,

$$\mu_1 \sin i = \mu_2 \sin r$$

$$\mu \sin i = (\mu - m\,\Delta\mu)\sin r$$

Given, $\mu = 1.5$, $i = 30°$, $r = 90°$

and $\Delta\mu = 0.015$

$$1.5 \sin 30° = (1.5 - m\times 0.015)\sin 90°$$

$$\frac{3}{2}\times\frac{1}{2} = (1.5 - m\times 0.015)\times 1$$

$$\frac{3}{4} - \frac{3}{2} = \frac{-15m}{1000}$$

$$\Rightarrow \quad 15m = \left(\frac{3}{2} - \frac{3}{4}\right)\times 1000$$

$$15m = \frac{6-3}{4}\times 1000$$

$$\Rightarrow \quad m = \frac{3}{4}\times\frac{1000}{15}$$

$$m = \frac{3000}{60}$$

$$\Rightarrow \quad m = 50$$

6 (c) Sun is visible a little before the actual sunrise and until a little after the actual sunset. This is due to refraction.

7 (b) We know that, $n_a c_a = n_g c_g$

$$\frac{n_g}{n_a} = 1.5 = \frac{3}{2}$$

$$\frac{n_g}{n_a} = \frac{c_a}{c_g} \Rightarrow \frac{3}{2} = \frac{3\times 10^8}{c_g}$$

$$\Rightarrow \quad c_g = 2\times 10^8$$

We have, Time $= \frac{\text{Distance}}{\text{Speed}}$

$$t = \frac{4\times 10^{-3}}{2\times 10^8} \quad \text{or} \quad t = 2\times 10^{-11}\text{s}$$

8 (b) As optical paths are equal, hence

$$n_g x_g = n_w x_w$$

$$\Rightarrow \quad n_w = n_g \frac{x_g}{x_w}$$

$$= 1.53\times\frac{4}{4.5} = 1.36$$

9 (b) In any medium other than air or vacuum, the velocities of different colours are different. Therefore, both red and green colours are refracted at different angles of refractions. Hence, after emerging from glass slab through opposite parallel face, they appear at two different points and move in two different parallel directions.

10 (c) Due to glass slab, increase in path

$= (\mu - 1)t = (1.5 - 1)\ 3\ \text{cm} = 1.5\ \text{cm}$

$\therefore \quad u' = -(21 + 1.5) = -22.5\ \text{cm}$

Now, $\dfrac{1}{-22.5} + \dfrac{1}{v} = \dfrac{1}{-5}$

$\Rightarrow \quad \dfrac{1}{v} = \dfrac{1}{22.5} - \dfrac{1}{5}$

$\Rightarrow \quad \dfrac{1}{v} = \dfrac{5 - 22.5}{22.5 \times 5}$

$\Rightarrow \quad v = \dfrac{22.5 \times 5}{-17.5} = -6.43\ \text{cm}$

Geometrical distance $= -(6.43 - 1.5)$

$= -4.93\ \text{cm}$

11 (a) According to Snell's law,

Refractive index,

$$\mu = \frac{\sin i}{\sin r}$$

Given, $\quad i = 2r$

$\Rightarrow \quad \mu = \dfrac{\sin 2r}{\sin r}$

$\Rightarrow \quad \mu = \dfrac{2 \sin r \cos r}{\sin r}$

$\Rightarrow \quad \cos^{-1} \dfrac{\mu}{2} = r$

$\Rightarrow \quad i = 2 \cos^{-1} \dfrac{\mu}{2}$

12 (d) Given, wavelength in vacuum

$= 5890\ \text{Å}$

In a medium of refractive index μ, the wavelength of light decreases to

$$\frac{\lambda}{\mu} = \frac{5890}{1.5} = 3927\ \text{Å}$$

13 (a) Refractive index $= \dfrac{\text{Real depth}}{\text{Apparent depth}}$

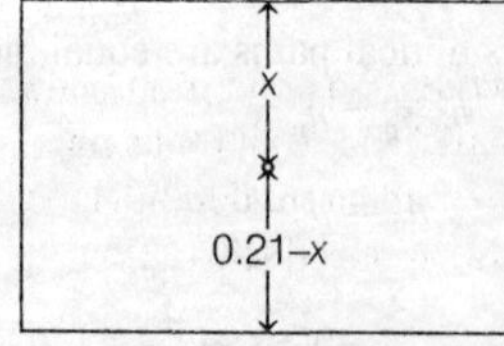

$\therefore \quad \dfrac{x}{0.04} = \dfrac{0.21 - x}{0.10}$

$\Rightarrow \quad 0.21 \times 0.04 - x \times 0.04 = 0.10\,x$

$\Rightarrow \quad x = \dfrac{0.21 \times 0.04}{0.14} = 0.06\ \text{m}$

14 (a) When a ray from man O in air (rarer medium) goes to water (denser medium), then it bends towards the normal. Extend MN backwards meet at point O'. Therefore, it appears to the fish as if the man is taller than what he actually is

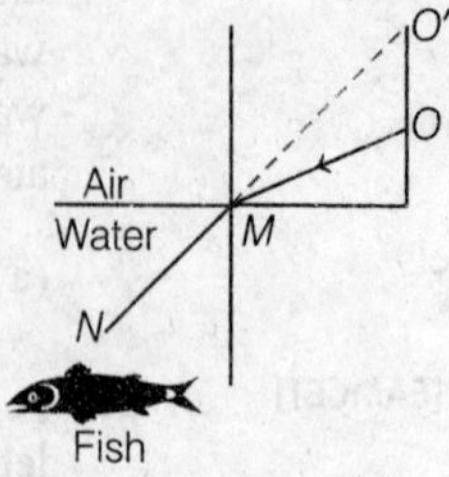

15 (b) Here, angle of incidence, $i = 45°$

$$\frac{\text{Lateral shift } (d)}{\text{Thickness of glass slab } (t)} = \frac{1}{\sqrt{3}}$$

Lateral shift, $\quad d = \dfrac{t \sin \delta}{\cos r} = \dfrac{t \sin(i - r)}{\cos r}$

$\Rightarrow \quad \dfrac{d}{t} = \dfrac{\sin(i - r)}{\cos r}$

$\Rightarrow \quad \dfrac{d}{t} = \dfrac{\sin i \cos r - \cos i \sin r}{\cos r}$

$\Rightarrow \quad \dfrac{d}{t} = \dfrac{\sin 45° \cos r - \cos 45° \sin r}{\cos r}$

$= \dfrac{\cos r - \sin r}{\sqrt{2} \cos r}$

$\Rightarrow \quad \dfrac{d}{t} = \dfrac{1}{\sqrt{2}}(1 - \tan r)$

$\Rightarrow \quad \dfrac{1}{\sqrt{3}} = \dfrac{1}{\sqrt{2}}(1 - \tan r)$

$\Rightarrow \quad \tan r = 1 - \dfrac{\sqrt{2}}{\sqrt{3}}$

$\therefore \quad r = \tan^{-1}\left(1 - \dfrac{\sqrt{2}}{\sqrt{3}}\right)$

16 (c) Velocity of light waves in material is

$$v = \nu\lambda \qquad \text{...(i)}$$

Refractive index of material is

$$\mu = \frac{c}{v} \qquad \text{...(ii)}$$

where, c is speed of light in vacuum or air, $\quad \mu = \dfrac{c}{\nu\lambda} \qquad$ ...(iii)

Given, $\quad \nu = 2 \times 10^{14}\ \text{Hz}$,

$\lambda = 5000\ \text{Å}$

$= 5000 \times 10^{-10}\ \text{m}$

and $\quad c = 3 \times 10^{8}\ \text{ms}^{-1}$

From Eq. (iii), we get

$$\mu = \frac{3 \times 10^{8}}{2 \times 10^{14} \times 5000 \times 10^{-10}} = 3$$

17 (b) When object is in rarer medium and observer is in denser medium, then normal shift,

$$d = (n - 1)h$$

where, h = real depth = y

Now, apparent depth or the apparent height of the bird from the surface of the water $= y + (n - 1)y = ny$.

The total distance of the bird as estimated by fish is $x + ny$.

18 (b) In ΔBCE,

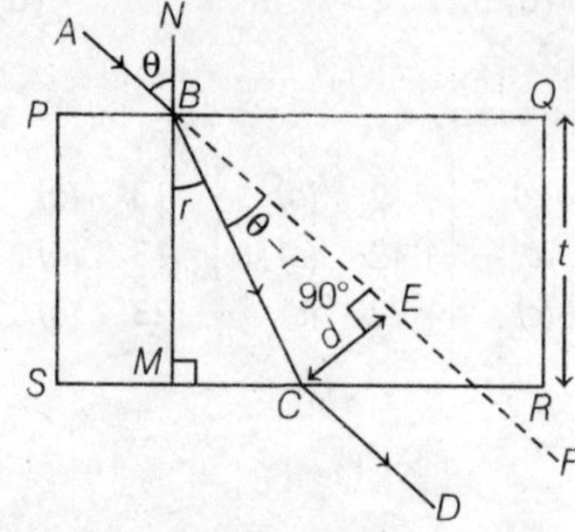

$\sin(\theta - r) = \dfrac{CE}{BC}$

$\Rightarrow \quad CE = BC \sin(\theta - r)$

$\Rightarrow \quad d = BC \sin(\theta - r) \qquad$ ...(i)

In ΔBMC, $\cos r = \dfrac{BM}{BC}$

$\Rightarrow \quad BC = \dfrac{BM}{\cos r} = \dfrac{t}{\cos r} \qquad$ ...(ii)

From Eqs. (i) and (ii), we get

$$d = \frac{t}{\cos r} \sin(\theta - r)$$

$\Rightarrow \quad d = \dfrac{t}{\cos r}(\sin\theta \cos r - \cos\theta \sin r)$

$\left\{\because \dfrac{\sin r}{\cos r} = \tan r\right\}$

$d = t(\sin\theta - \cos\theta \tan r)$

If n is the refractive index of material of slab (glass) w.r.t. air, then

$$n = \frac{\sin\theta}{\sin r}$$

For small angle, $n = \dfrac{\theta}{r}$

or $\quad r = \dfrac{\theta}{n}$ and $d = t(\theta - 1 \cdot r)$

($\because \sin\theta \approx \theta$ and $\cos\theta \approx 1$, if θ is small)

$$d = t\left(\theta - \frac{\theta}{n}\right) = t\theta\left(1 - \frac{1}{n}\right)$$

$\Rightarrow \quad d = \dfrac{t\theta(n - 1)}{n}$

19 *(a)* When light passes from one medium to another, its frequency does not change.

As intensity $\propto$ (amplitude)^2 and intensity changes in refraction so, amplitude also changes. The wavelength and velocity of light also changes with refractive index.

20 *(b)* Refractive index of glass with respect to air, ${}_a\mu_g = \frac{3}{2}$

Refractive index of water with respect to air, ${}_a\mu_w = \frac{4}{3}$

Refractive index of glass with respect to water,

$$ {}_w\mu_g = \frac{{}_a\mu_g}{{}_a\mu_w} = \frac{\left(\frac{3}{2}\right)}{\left(\frac{4}{3}\right)} = \frac{9}{8} $$

21 *(c)*

$$ {}_1\mu_2 = \frac{\text{Speed of light in first medium}}{\text{Speed of light in second medium}} $$

or

$$ {}_2\mu_1 = \frac{\text{Speed of light in second medium}}{\text{Speed of light in first medium}} $$

where, ${}_1\mu_2$ is refractive index of second medium relative to the first medium.

Hence, we see that on passing through another medium, speed of light changes due to which it bends, because wavelength changes.

22 *(c)* Since, μv = constant

$$ \therefore \quad \mu_g v_g = \mu_w v_w, \frac{3}{2}(2 \times 10^8) = \frac{4}{3} v_w $$

$$ \Rightarrow \quad v_w = 2.25 \times 10^8 \text{ ms}^{-1} $$

23 *(b)* Refractive index,

$$ \mu = \frac{\text{Real depth } (d)}{\text{Apparent depth } (x)} $$

For 1st liquid $\sqrt{2} = \frac{d}{x_1}$

$$ \Rightarrow \quad x_1 = \frac{d}{\sqrt{2}} $$

Similarly, for 2nd liquid,

$$ n = \frac{d}{x_2} $$

$$ \Rightarrow \quad x_2 = \frac{d}{n} $$

Total apparent depth $= x_1 + x_2$

$$ = \frac{d}{\sqrt{2}} + \frac{d}{n} $$

$$ = \frac{d(n + \sqrt{2})}{n\sqrt{2}} $$

24 *(d)* Let real depth of the bubble from one side is x and apparent depth is 6. Refractive index,

$$ \mu = \frac{\text{Real depth}}{\text{Apperent depth}} $$

Then, $\mu = \frac{x}{6} = \frac{15 - x}{4}$

$$ \Rightarrow \quad x = 9 \text{ cm} $$

Hence, $\mu = \frac{x}{6} = \frac{9}{6} = 1.5$

25 *(d)* As, lateral shift in rectangular glass slab, $d = t\frac{\sin(i - r)}{\cos r}$, maximum displacement will be $d = t$

Hence, maximum lateral displacement is t.

26 *(b)* The equivalent refractive index of combination of slabs for normal incidence is

$$ \mu = \frac{\Sigma t_i}{\Sigma \frac{t_i}{\mu_i}} $$

In this case, $\mu = \frac{t_1 + t_2}{\frac{t_1}{\mu_1} + \frac{t_2}{\mu_2}}$

$$ \Rightarrow \quad = \frac{10 + 15}{\frac{10}{4/3} + \frac{15}{3/2}} $$

$$ = \frac{25}{7.5 + 10} = \frac{25}{17.5} $$

$$ = 1.43 $$

27 *(a)* In case (i), ray travels from air (rarer) to water (denser) medium, so it bends towards the normal.

In case (ii), ray travels from water (less rarer than glass to glass (denser), so it bends (less than as in case (i)) towards the normal.

In case (iii), ray travels from glass (denser) to water (rarer), so it bends away from the normal. Hence, correct sequence will be (a).

28 *(b)* Let actual height of water in cylindrical tank be h.

$$ \frac{n_2}{n_1} = \frac{\text{Actual depth}}{\text{Apparent depth}} $$

or $\frac{n_2}{n_1} = \frac{h}{x}$

or $\frac{n_2}{n_1} = \frac{\frac{dh}{dt}}{\frac{dx}{dt}}$

$$ \therefore \quad \frac{dh}{dt} = \frac{n_2}{n_1} \times \frac{dx}{dt} $$

or Change in actual rate of flow

$= \frac{n_2}{n_1} \times$ Change in apparent rate of flow

or $\frac{dh}{dt} = \frac{n_2}{n_1} \times x \text{ cm min}^{-1}$ ...(i)

Thus, amount of water drained in cc per min

$$ = \frac{dh}{dt} \times \pi R^2 $$

$$ = \frac{n_2}{n_1} \times x \times \pi R^2 \quad \text{[from (i)]} $$

$$ \Rightarrow \quad = x \pi R^2 \frac{n_2}{n_1} $$

29 *(a)* We know that, $\mu = \frac{\text{Real depth}}{\text{Apparent depth}}$

Red colour has minimum value of refractive index and thus maximum value of apparent depth. Hence, it should be raised least.

Topic 3

Total Internal Reflection

2019

1 In total internal reflection, when the angle of incidence is equal to the critical angle for the pair of media in contact, what will be angle of refraction? **[NEET]**

(a) 0° (b) Equal to angle of incidence
(c) 90° (d) 180°

2 Find the value of θ in the given diagram. **[JIPMER]**

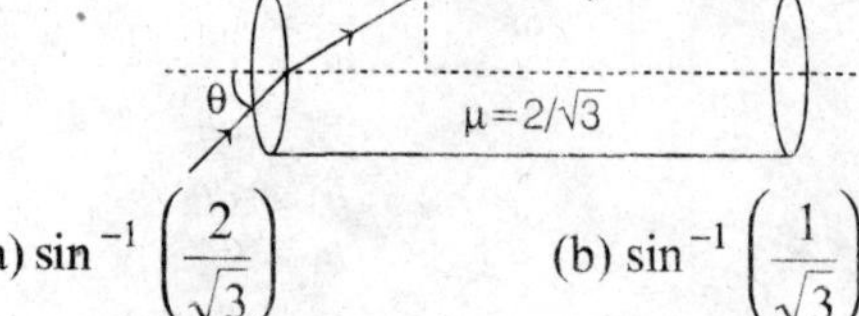

(a) $\sin^{-1}\left(\frac{2}{\sqrt{3}}\right)$ (b) $\sin^{-1}\left(\frac{1}{\sqrt{3}}\right)$
(c) $\sin^{-1}\left(\frac{1}{2}\right)$ (d) $\sin^{-1}\left(\frac{1}{\sqrt{2}}\right)$

2014

3 In vacuum, to travel distance d, light takes time t and in medium to travel $5d$, it takes time T. The critical angle of the medium is **[MHT CET]**

(a) $\sin^{-1}\left(\frac{5T}{t}\right)$ (b) $\sin^{-1}\left(\frac{5t}{3T}\right)$ (c) $\sin^{-1}\left(\frac{5t}{T}\right)$ (d) $\sin^{-1}\left(\frac{3t}{5T}\right)$

2013

4 If the critical angle for total internal reflection from medium to vacuum is 30°, the velocity of light in medium is **[Manipal]**

(a) 3×10^8 m/s (b) 1.5×10^8 m/s
(c) 6×10^8 m/s (d) $\sqrt{3}\times 10^8$ m/s

5 When a ray of light enters from one medium to another, then its velocity in second medium becomes double. The maximum value of angle of incidence, so that total internal reflection may not take place will be **[KCET]**

(a) 60° (b) 180° (c) 90° (d) 30°

2012

6 If the refractive index of water is 4/3 and that of given slab of glass immersed in it is 5/3, what is the critical angle for a ray of light tending to go from glass to water? **[UP CPMT]**

(a) $\sin^{-1}\left(\frac{3}{4}\right)$

(b) $\sin^{-1}\left(\frac{3}{5}\right)$

(c) $\sin^{-1}\left(\frac{4}{5}\right)$

(d) Data given are insufficient to make any calculation

2011

7 Light travels in two media A and B with speeds 1.8×10^8 ms^{-1} and 2.4×10^8 ms^{-1} respectively. Then, the critical angle between them is **[Kerala CEE]**

(a) $\sin^{-1}\left(\frac{2}{3}\right)$ (b) $\tan^{-1}\left(\frac{3}{4}\right)$
(c) $\tan^{-1}\left(\frac{2}{3}\right)$ (d) $\sin^{-1}\left(\frac{3}{4}\right)$
(e) $\sin^{-1}\left(\frac{1}{4}\right)$

8 A diver at a depth of 12 m in water $\left(\mu = \frac{4}{3}\right)$ sees, the sky in a cone of semi-vertical angle is **[WB JEE]**

(a) $\sin^{-1}\left(\frac{4}{3}\right)$ (b) $\tan^{-1}\left(\frac{4}{3}\right)$
(c) $\sin^{-1}\left(\frac{3}{4}\right)$ (d) 90°

2011

9 In optical fibres, the refractive index of the core is **[DUMET]**

(a) grater than that of the cladding
(b) equal to that of the cladding
(c) smaller than that of the cladding
(d) independent of that of the cladding

10 Wavelength of given light waves in air and in a medium are 6000 Å and 4000 Å respectively. The critical angle is **[KCET]**

(a) $\tan^{-1}\left(\frac{2}{3}\right)$ (b) $\tan^{-1}\left(\frac{3}{2}\right)$
(c) $\sin^{-1}\left(\frac{2}{3}\right)$ (d) $\sin^{-1}\left(\frac{3}{2}\right)$

2010

11 A ray of light travelling in transparent medium of refractive index μ falls on a surface separating the medium from air at an angle of incidence of 45°. For which of the following value of μ, the ray can undergo total internal reflection? **[CBSE AIPMT]**

(a) $\mu > 1.33$ (b) $\mu > 1.4$
(c) $\mu > 1.5$ (d) $\mu > 1.25$

12 Which one of the following is not associated with the total internal reflection? **[Manipal]**

(a) The mirage formation
(b) Optical fibre communication
(c) The glittering of diamond
(d) Dispersion of light

13 A ray of light strikes a plane water-air interface from within the water at an angle of incidence i. Which one of the following statements is correct? **[Manipal]**

(a) If i is $90°$, the angle of refraction will be the critical angle.

(b) If i is equal to the critical angle, the reflected and refracted rays will be at right angles to each other.

(c) If i is less than the critical angle, all the light is refracted and the angle of refraction is greater than i.

(d) If i is less than the critical angle, some light is refracted and the angle of reflection is less than the critical angle.

14 If refractive index of glass is 1.50 and of water is 1.33, then critical angle is **[Manipal]**

(a) $\sin^{-1}\left(\frac{8}{9}\right)$ (b) $\sin^{-1}\left(\frac{2}{3}\right)$

(c) $\cos^{-1}\left(\frac{8}{9}\right)$ (d) None of these

15 A light ray going from air is incident (as shown in figure) at one end of a glass fibre (refractive index, $\mu = 1.5$) making an incidence angle of $60°$ on the lateral surface, so that it undergoes a total internal reflection. How much time would it take to traverse the straight fibre of length 1 km? **[OJEE]**

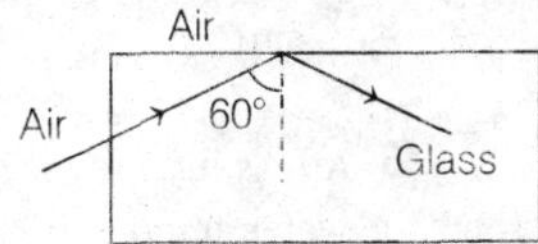

(a) 3.3 μs (b) 6.6 μs (c) 5.7 μs (d) 3.85 μs

16 A ray of light travels from an optically denser medium towards rarer medium. The critical angle for the two media is C. The maximum possible angle of deviation of the ray is **[EAMCET]**

(a) $\frac{\pi}{2} - C$ (b) $\pi - 2C$ (c) $2C$ (d) $\frac{\pi}{2} + C$

2009

17 **Assertion** Endoscopy involves use of optical fibres to study internal organs.

Reason Optical fibres are based on phenomenon of total internal reflection. **[AIIMS]**

(a) Both Assertion and Reason are correct and Reason is the correct explanation of Assertion.

(b) Both Assertion and Reason are correct but Reason is not the correct explanation of Assertion.

(c) Assertion is correct but Reason is not correct.

(d) Assertion is incorrect but Reason is correct.

18 The refractive index of water is 1.33. The direction in which a man under water should look to see the setting sun is **[Manipal]**

(a) $49°$ to the horizontal (b) $90°$ will be vertical

(c) $49°$ to the vertical (d) along the horizontal

19 The critical angle for total internal reflection in diamond is $24.5°$. The refractive index of the diamond is **[DUMET]**

(a) 2.45 (b) 1.41

(c) 2.59 (d) 1.59

2008

20 A fish looking up through the water sees the outside world, contained in a circular horizon. If the refractive index of water is $\frac{4}{3}$ and the fish is 12 cm below the water surface, the radius of this circle in cm is **[AIIMS]**

(a) $36\sqrt{7}$ (b) $\frac{36}{\sqrt{7}}$

(c) $36\sqrt{5}$ (d) $4\sqrt{5}$

21 Sparkling of diamond is because of **[DUMET]**

(a) total internal reflection (b) refraction

(c) diffraction (d) scattering

2007

22 A small coin is resting on the bottom of a beaker filled with a liquid. A ray of light from the coin travels upto the surface of the liquid and moves along its surface.

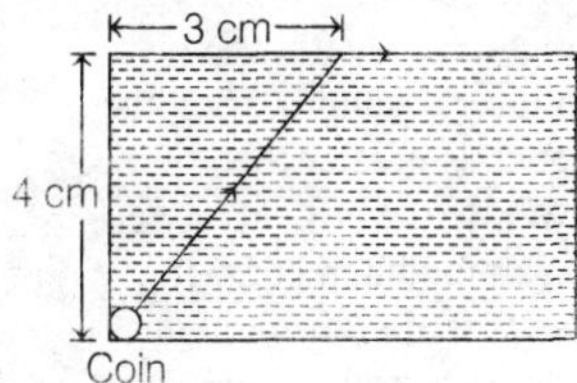

How fast is the light travelling in the liquid? **[CBSE AIPMT]**

(a) 1.8×10^8 ms^{-1} (b) 2.4×10^8 ms^{-1}

(c) 3.0×10^8 ms^{-1} (d) 1.2×10^8 ms^{-1}

23 Total internal reflection takes place **[AFMC]**

(a) when a ray moves from denser to rarer and incident angle is greater than critical angle

(b) when a ray moves from rarer to denser and incident angle is less than critical angle

(c) when a ray moves from rarer to denser and incident angle is equal to critical angle

(d) None of the above

24 A ray of light is travelling from glass to air (refractive index of glass = 1.5). The angle of incidence is $50°$. The deviation of the ray is **[KCET]**

(a) $0°$ (b) $80°$

(c) $50° - \sin^{-1}\left[\frac{\sin 50°}{1.5}\right]$ (d) $\sin^{-1}\left[\frac{\sin 50°}{1.5}\right] - 50°$

25 The instrument used by doctors for endoscopy works on the principle of **[BCECE]**

(a) total internal reflection

(b) reflection

(c) refraction

(d) None of the above

2006

26 Light enters at an angle of incidence in a transparent rod of refractive index of the material of the rod. The light once entered into it will not leave it through its lateral face so, whatever be the value of angle of incidence? **[AFMC]**

(a) $n > \sqrt{2}$ (b) $n = 1$

(c) $n = 1.1$ (d) $n = 1.3$

2005

27 **Assertion** Diamond glitters brilliantly.

Reason Diamond does not absorb sunlight. **[AIIMS]**

(a) Both Assertion and Reason are correct and Reason is the correct explanation of Assertion.

(b) Both Assertion and Reason are correct but Reason is not the correct explanation of Assertion.

(c) Assertion is correct but Reason is incorrect.

(d) Both Assertion and Reason are incorrect.

Answers

1 (c)	2 (b)	3 (c)	4 (b)	5 (d)	6 (c)	7 (d)	8 (c)	9 (a)	10 (c)
11 (b)	12 (d)	13 (c)	14 (a)	15 (d)	16 (a)	17 (a)	18 (c)	19 (a)	20 (b)
21 (a)	22 (a)	23 (a)	24 (b)	25 (a)	26 (a)	27 (b)			

Explanations

1 *(c)* The total internal reflection is the phenomenon of reflection back of light in the denser medium when it travels from denser to rarer medium, when the angle of incidence is greater than the critical angle. While the critical angle for a pair of given media in contact, the angle of incidence in denser medium for which the angle of refraction in rarer medium is 90°.

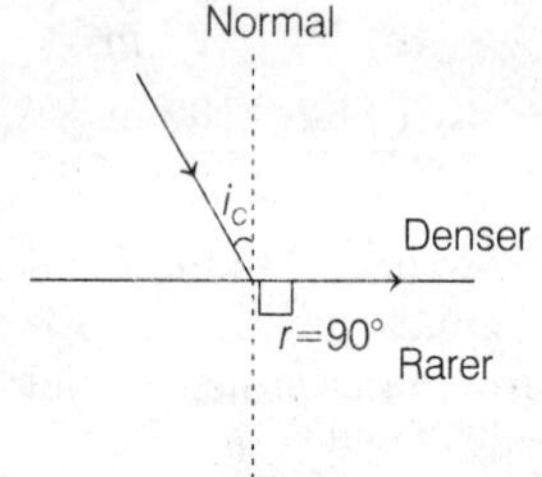

2 *(b)*

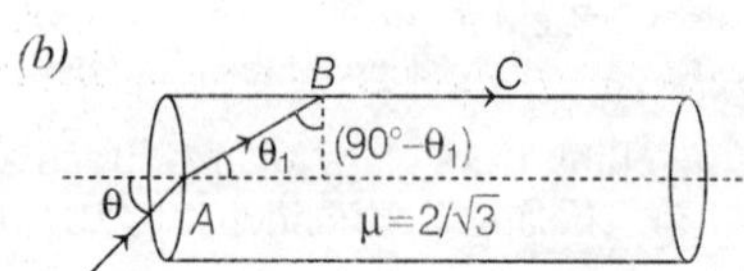

Since, BC grazes along surface

$\Rightarrow$ angle $(90 - \theta_1)$ = critical angle C

$\therefore \quad \sin C = \frac{1}{\mu}$

$\sin(90 - \theta_1) = \frac{\sqrt{3}}{2} \Rightarrow \cos\theta_1 = \frac{\sqrt{3}}{2}$

$\Rightarrow \quad \theta_1 = 30°$

Now, using Snells' law on 1st interface,

$n_1 \sin\theta = n_2 \sin\theta_1$

$\Rightarrow \quad (1) \sin\theta = \frac{2}{\sqrt{3}} \sin 30° = \frac{2}{\sqrt{3}} \cdot \frac{1}{2}$

$\Rightarrow \quad \sin\theta = \frac{1}{\sqrt{3}}$

$\Rightarrow \quad \theta = \sin^{-1}\left(\frac{1}{\sqrt{3}}\right)$

3 *(c)* In vacuum, $c = d/t$

In medium, $v = \frac{5d}{T}$

As refractive index,

$\mu = \frac{c}{v} = \frac{d/t}{5d/T} = \frac{T}{5t}$

Also, $\quad \sin C = \frac{1}{\mu}$

($\because$ C is critical angle)

$\therefore \quad C = \sin^{-1}\left[\frac{5t}{T}\right]$

4 *(b)* Refractive index of medium,

$\mu = \frac{1}{\sin C}$

where, C is critical angle.

Given, $\quad C = 30°$

$\therefore \quad \mu = \frac{1}{\sin 30°} = \frac{1}{1/2} = 2$

From Snell's law, $\mu = \frac{v_0}{v_m}$

where, v_0 is speed of light in vacuum and v_m the velocity in medium.

$\therefore \quad v_m = \frac{3 \times 10^8}{2} = 1.5 \times 10^8$ m/s

5 *(d)* $\mu = \frac{v_{rarer}}{v_{denser}} = \frac{2}{1}$

$\mu = \frac{1}{\sin C} = \frac{2}{1}$ ($\because$ C is critical angle)

$\sin C = \frac{1}{2} \Rightarrow C = 30°$

6 *(c)* As light ray is going from glass to water and if C is critical angle, then

$\sin C = \frac{1}{{}_g\mu_w} = \frac{\mu_w}{\mu_g}$

$C = \sin^{-1}\left(\frac{\mu_w}{\mu_g}\right) = \sin^{-1}\left(\frac{4/3}{5/3}\right)$

$= \sin^{-1}\left(\frac{4}{5}\right)$

7 *(d)* If C is critical angle, then speed of light, $v_1 = 1.8 \times 10^8$ m/s and $v_2 = 2.4 \times 10^8$ m/s

$C = \sin^{-1}\left(\frac{v_1}{v_2}\right)$

$= \sin^{-1}\left(\frac{1.8 \times 10^8}{2.4 \times 10^8}\right) = \sin^{-1}\left(\frac{3}{4}\right)$

8 *(c)* We can represent this diagrammatically as

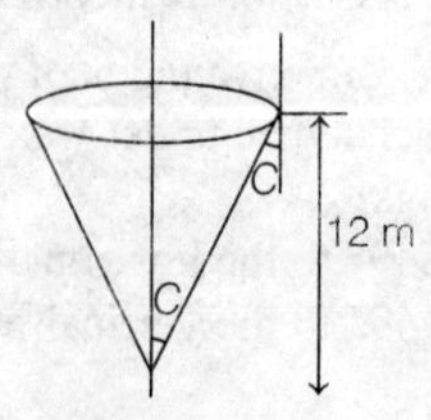

Thus, we see that

$$C = \sin^{-1}\left(\frac{1}{\mu}\right) = \sin^{-1}\left(\frac{3}{4}\right)$$

9 (a) In optical fibres, the refractive index of the core is greater than that of the cladding.
Thus, the core act as denser medium and cladding as rarer medium. For angle of incidence greater than critical angle, the ray forward through total internal reflection.

10 (c) $\frac{1}{\sin C} = \frac{\lambda_1}{\lambda_2}, \quad \frac{1}{\sin C} = \frac{6000}{4000}$

$\frac{1}{\sin C} = \frac{3}{2} \Rightarrow \sin C = \frac{2}{3}$

$\Rightarrow \quad C = \sin^{-1}\left(\frac{2}{3}\right)$

11 (b) For total internal reflection, $i > C$

$\Rightarrow \sin i > \sin C \Rightarrow \sin 45° > \frac{1}{\mu}$

$\Rightarrow \quad \mu > \sqrt{2} \Rightarrow \mu > 1.4$

12 (d) Dispersion of light is not associated with total internal reflection.

13 (c) If i is less than the critical angle, then all the light is refracted and the angle of refraction is greater than i.

14 (a) When a ray of light passes from a denser medium to a rarer medium, it bends away from the normal at the interface of the two media. The angle of incidence is measured with respect to the normal at the refractive boundary. It is given by

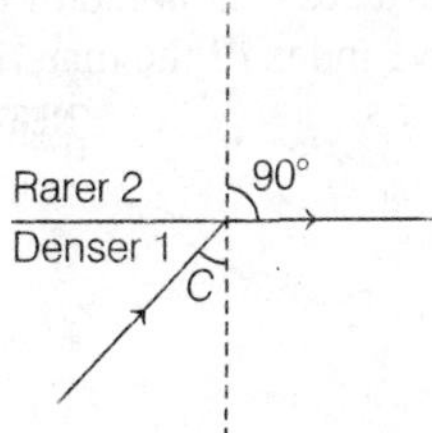

$$C = \sin^{-1}\left(\frac{n_2}{n_1}\right)$$

where, C is critical angle, n_2 is the refractive index of rarer medium and n_1 of the denser medium.

Given, $n_2 = 1.33$

and $n_1 = 1.50$

$$C = \sin^{-1}\left(\frac{1.33}{1.50}\right)$$

$$\Rightarrow \quad C = \sin^{-1}\left(\frac{8}{9}\right)$$

15 (d) When total internal reflection just takes place form lateral surface

$$i = C, \text{ i.e. } 60° = C$$

$\Rightarrow \quad \sin 60° = \sin C = \frac{1}{\mu}$

$\Rightarrow \quad \mu = \frac{2}{\sqrt{3}}$

and $\quad x = 1 \text{ km} = 1 \times 10^3 \text{ m}$

Time taken by light to traverse some distance in a medium,

$$t = \frac{\mu x}{c} = \frac{\frac{2}{\sqrt{3}} \times 10^3}{3 \times 10^8}$$

$$= 3.85 \ \mu\text{s}$$

16 (a) When the ray passes into the rarer medium, the deviation is $\delta = \phi - \theta$. This can have a maximum value of $\left(\frac{\pi}{2}\right) - C$,

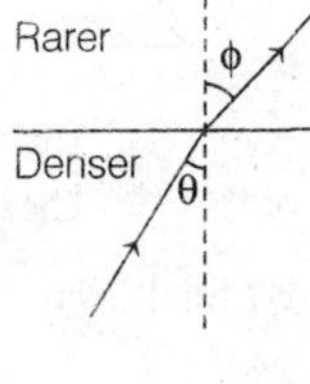

when $\theta = C$ and $\phi = \frac{\pi}{2}$.

17 (a) As optical fibre involves total internal reflection at each stage, hence a signal in the form of light is directed at one end of fibre at a suitable angle, undergoes repeated total internal reflection. Hence, this helps in visual examination of internal organs in endoscopy. Therefore, both Assertion and Reason are correct and Reason is the correct explanation of Assertion.

18 (c) $\sin \theta = \frac{1}{\mu_w} = \frac{1}{1.33}$

$\Rightarrow \theta = \sin^{-1}\left(\frac{1}{1.33}\right) = 49°$ to the vertical

19 (a) If μ is the refractive index and C is critical angle, then

$$\mu = \frac{1}{\sin C}$$

$\Rightarrow \quad \mu = \frac{1}{\sin 24.5}$

$\Rightarrow \quad \mu = 2.45$

20 (b) The situation is shown in figure

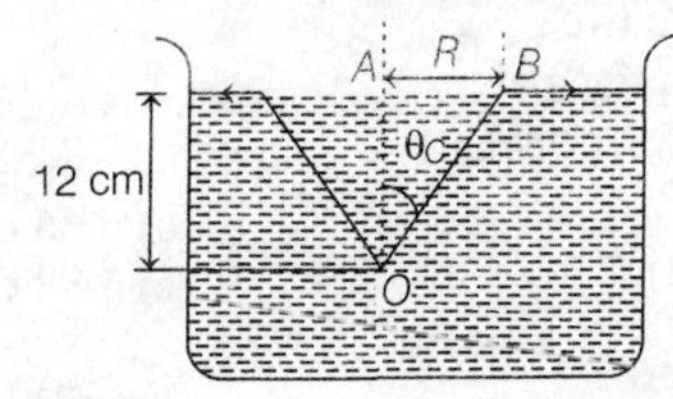

$$\sin \theta_C = \frac{1}{\mu} \Rightarrow \tan \theta_C = \frac{AB}{AO}$$

$\Rightarrow \quad AB = OA \tan \theta_C$

$$AB = \frac{OA}{\sqrt{\mu^2 - 1}} = \frac{12}{\sqrt{\left(\frac{4}{3}\right)^2 - 1}} = \frac{36}{\sqrt{7}}$$

$$\left[\because \tan \theta_C = \frac{1}{\sqrt{\mu^2 - 1}}\right]$$

21 (a) The brilliance of diamond is due to total internal reflection of light. μ for diamond is 2.42, so that critical angle for diamond-air interface as calculated is 24.4°.
The diamond is cut suitably so that light entering the diamond from any face falls at an angle greater than 24.4°; suffers multiple total internal reflection at the various faces and remains with in the diamond. Hence, the diamond sparkles.

22 (a) As shown in figure, a light ray from the coin will not emerge out of liquid, if $i > C$.
Therefore, minimum radius R corresponds to $i = C$.

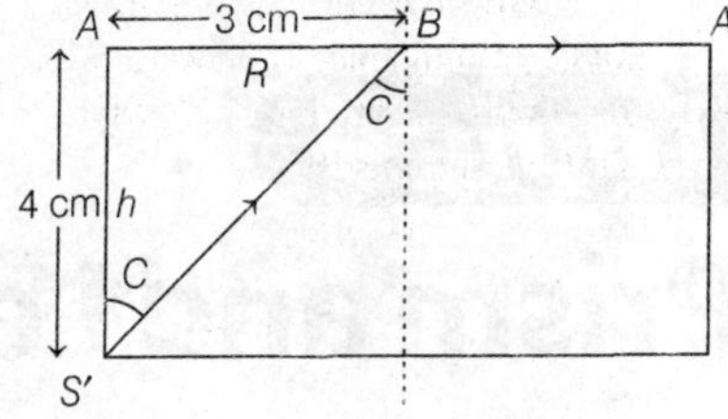

In ΔSAB, $\frac{R}{h} = \tan C$

$\Rightarrow \quad R = h \tan C$

$\Rightarrow \quad R = \frac{h}{\sqrt{\mu^2 - 1}}$

Given, $R = 3$ cm and $h = 4$ cm

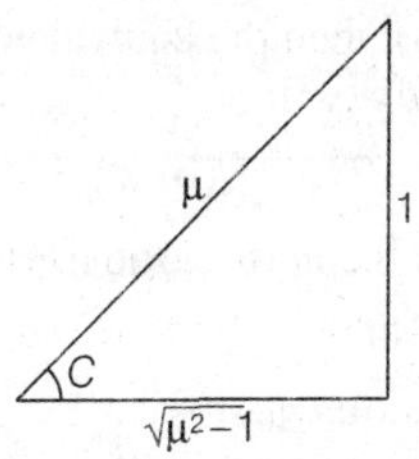

$$\therefore \frac{3}{4} = \frac{1}{\sqrt{\mu^2 - 1}} \Rightarrow \mu^2 = \frac{25}{9} \Rightarrow \mu = \frac{5}{3}$$

But $\mu = \frac{c}{v} \Rightarrow v = \frac{c}{\mu} = \frac{3 \times 10^8}{5/3}$

$$= 1.8 \times 10^8 \text{ ms}^{-1}$$

23 (a) Total internal reflection takes place when ray goes from denser to rarer medium and incident angle is greater than critical angle.

24 (b) Refractive index, $_a\mu_g = 1.5$

$$\frac{1}{\sin C} = 1.5$$

$$\Rightarrow \quad C = 42°$$

$\therefore$ Critical angle for glass = 42°

When the angle of incidence in the denser medium is greater than the critical angle, total internal reflection takes place inside the denser medium.

Hence, a ray of light, incident at 50° in glass medium undergoes total internal reflection.

Deviation, $\delta = (180° - (50° + 50°)$

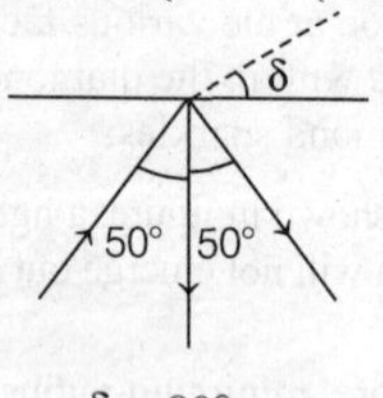

$$\therefore \quad \delta = 80°$$

25 (a) An endoscope is made by optical fibres and its interior surface is coated with a material which have the greater refractive index, than that of the outer cover (glass). Hence, it is based on total internal reflection.

26 (a) Let a light ray enters at A and refracted beam is AB. At the lateral face, the angle of incidence is θ. For no refraction at this face, $\theta > C$.

i.e. $\quad \sin\theta > \sin C$

but $\quad \theta + r = 90° \Rightarrow \theta = 90° - r$

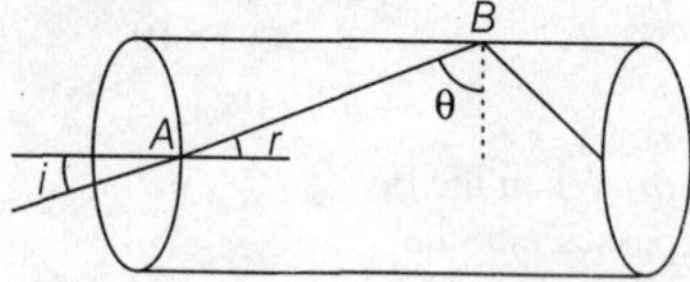

$$\therefore \quad \sin(90° - r) > \sin C$$

or $\quad \cos r > \sin C \quad$ ...(i)

By Snell's law, $\quad n = \dfrac{\sin i}{\sin r}$

$$\Rightarrow \quad \sin r = \frac{\sin i}{n}$$

$$\therefore \quad \cos r = \sqrt{1 - \sin^2 r} = \sqrt{\left(1 - \frac{\sin^2 i}{n^2}\right)}$$

From Eq. (i), $\sqrt{1 - \dfrac{\sin^2 i}{n^2}} > \sin C$

Also, $\quad \sin C = \dfrac{1}{n}$

$$\Rightarrow \quad 1 - \frac{\sin^2 i}{n^2} > \frac{1}{n^2}$$

or $\quad n^2 > \sin^2 i + 1$

The maximum value of $\sin i$ is 1.

$$\Rightarrow \quad n^2 > 2 \text{ or } n > \sqrt{2}$$

27 (b) The critical angle for diamond-air is nearly 24°. The faces of diamond are cut in such a way that the light ray entered inside the diamond falls on the diamond-air interface at an angle greater than the critical angle and so it suffers repeated total internal reflections and comes out of its faces only in some specific directions.

When diamond is seen in these directions, it appears bright and shining. It is understood that it absorbs no light falling on it.

Topic 4
Prism and Lens

2019

1 Two similar thin equi-convex lenses, of focal length f each, are kept co-axially in contact with each other such that the focal length of the combination is F_1. When the space between the two lenses is filled with glycerine (which has the same refractive index ($\mu = 1.5$) as that of glass), then the equivalent focal length is F_2. The ratio of $F_1 : F_2$ will be **[NEET]**

(a) 1 : 2 (b) 2 : 3 (c) 3 : 4 (d) 2 : 1

2 Which colour of the light has the longest wavelength? **[NEET]**

(a) Blue (b) Green
(c) Violet (d) Red

3 An equi-convex lens has power P. It is cut into two symmetrical halves by a plane containing the principal axis. The power of one part will be **[NEET(Odisha)]**

(a) 0 (b) $\dfrac{P}{2}$ (c) $\dfrac{P}{4}$ (d) P

4 A double convex lens has focal length 25 cm. The radius of curvature of one of the surfaces is doubled of the other. Find the radii, if the refractive index of the material of the lens is 1.5. **[NEET (Odisha)]**

(a) 100 cm and 50 cm
(b) 25 cm and 50 cm
(c) 18.75 cm and 37.5 cm
(d) 50 cm and 100 cm

5 Calculate the focal length of given lens, if the magnification is –0.5. **[AIIMS]**

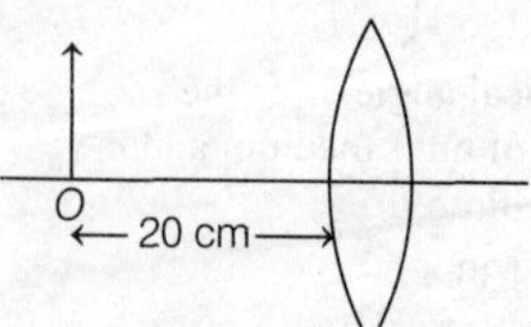

(a) 6.66 cm (b) 5.44 cm
(c) 3.88 cm (d) 1.38 cm

6 Find the position of final image from first lens. Given, focal length of each lens is 10 cm. **[JIPMER]**

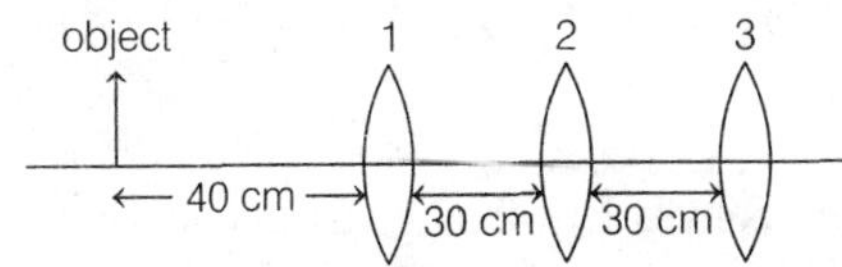

(a) 40 cm (b) 50 cm (c) 45 cm (d) 55 cm

2018

7 The refractive index of the material of a prism is $\sqrt{2}$ and the angle of the prism is 30°. One of the two refracting surfaces of the prism is made a mirror inwards by silver coating. A beam of monochromatic light entering the prism from the other face will retrace its path (after reflection from the silvered surface) if its angle of incidence on the prism is **[JIPMER]**

(a) 30° (b) 45°
(c) 60° (d) zero

8 **Assertion** Angle of deviation depends on the angle of prism.
Reasion For thin prism, $\delta = (\mu - 1) A$
where, δ = angle of deviation, μ = refractive index and A = angle of prism **[NEET]**

(a) Both Assertion and Reason are correct and Reason is the correct explanation of Assertion.
(b) Both Assertion and Reason are correct but Reason is not the correct explanation of Assertion.
(c) Assertion is correct but Reason is incorrect.
(d) Assertion is incorrect but Reason is correct.

9 A thin prism having refracting angle 10° is made of glass of refractive index 1.42. This prism is combined with another thin prism of glass of refractive index 1.7. This combination produces dispersion without deviation. The refracting angle of second prism should be **[NEET]**

(a) 4° (b) 6°
(c) 8° (d) 10°

10 A lens of refractive index μ is put in a liquid of refractive index μ'. If the focal length of lens in air f, then its focal length in liquid will be **[NEET]**

(a) $\dfrac{-f\mu'(\mu-1)}{(\mu'-\mu)}$ (b) $\dfrac{-f(\mu'-\mu)}{\mu'(\mu-1)}$

(c) $-\dfrac{\mu'(\mu-1)}{f(\mu'-\mu)}$ (d) $\dfrac{f\mu'\mu}{(\mu-\mu')}$

11 Two identical glass ($\mu_g = 3/2$) equi-convex lenses of focal length f each are kept in contact. The space between the two lenses in filled with water ($\mu_w = 4/3$). The focal length of the combination is **[NEET]**

(a) $f/3$ (b) f
(c) $\dfrac{4f}{3}$ (d) $\dfrac{3f}{4}$

12 If minimum deviation = 30°, then speed of light in shown prism will be **[JIPMER]**

(a) $\dfrac{3}{\sqrt{2}} \times 10^8$ m/s (b) $\dfrac{1}{\sqrt{2}} \times 10^8$ m/s

(c) $\dfrac{2}{\sqrt{3}} \times 10^8$ m/s (d) $\dfrac{2}{3} \times 10^8$ m/s

13 A prism of crown glass with refracting angle of 5° and mean refractive index = 1.51 is combined with a flint glass prism of refractive index = 1.65 to produce no deviation. Find the angle of flint glass. **[JIPMER]**

(a) 3.92° (b) 4.68° (c) 5.32° (d) 7.28°

2017

14 A thin prism P_1 of angle 4° and refractive index 1.54 is combined with another prism P_2 of refractive index 1.72 produce dispersion without deviation, the angle of P_2 is **[NEET]**

(a) 4° (b) 5.33 (c) 2.6° (d) 3°

15 A thin symmetrical double convex lens of refractive index $\mu_2 = 1.5$ is placed between a medium of refractive index $\mu_1 = 1.4$ to the left and another medium of refractive index $\mu_3 = 1 \cdot 6$ to the right. Then, the system behaves as

(a) a convex lens (b) a concave lens **[JIPMER]**
(c) a glass plate (d) a convexo concave lens

16 The plane face of a plano-convex lens is silvered. If μ be the refractive index and R be the radius of curvature of curved surface, then system will behave like a concave mirror of curvature **[JIPMER]**

(a) μR (b) R^2/μ
(c) $R/(\mu - 1)$ (d) $[(\mu + 1)/(\mu - 1)]R$

2016

17 The angle of incidence for a ray of light at a refracting surface of a prism is 45°. The angle of prism is 60°. If the ray suffers minimum deviation through the prism, the angle of minimum deviation and refractive index of the material of the prism respectively, are **[NEET]**

(a) 30° and $\sqrt{2}$ (b) 45° and $\sqrt{2}$

(c) 30° and $\dfrac{1}{\sqrt{2}}$ (d) 45° and $\dfrac{1}{2}$

18 The refracting angle of a prism is A and refractive index of the material of the prism is $\cot(A/2)$. The angle of minimum deviation is **[NEET]**

(a) 180°−3A (b) 180°−2A
(c) 90°−A (d) 180°+2A

2015

19 Two identical thin plano-convex glass lenses (refractive index 1.5) each having radius of curvature of 20 cm are placed with their convex surfaces in contact at the centre. The intervening space is filled with oil of refractive index 1.7. The focal length of the combination is **[NEET]**

(a) – 20 cm (b) – 25 cm (c) – 50 cm (d) 50 cm

2014

20 The angle of a prism is A. One of its refracting surfaces is silvered. Light rays falling at an angle of incidence $2A$ on the first surface returns back through the same path after suffering reflection at the silvered surface. The refractive index μ of the prism is **[CBSE AIPMT]**

(a) $2\sin A$ (b) $2\cos A$ (c) $\frac{1}{2}\cos A$ (d) $\tan A$

21 The equi-convex lens has focal length f. If it is cut perpendicular to the principal axis passing through optical centre, then focal length of each half is **[MHT CET]**

(a) $\frac{t}{2}$ (b) f (c) $\frac{3f}{2}$ (d) $2f$

22 Two lenses of power 15 D and −3 D are placed in contact. The focal length of the combination is **[Kerala CEE]**

(a) 10 cm (b) 15 cm (c) 12 cm (d) 18 cm
(e) 8.33 cm

23 A luminous object is separated from a screen by distance d. A convex lens is placed between the object and the screen such that it forms a distinct image on the screen. The maximum possible focal length of this convex lens is **[WB JEE]**

(a) $4d$ (b) $2d$ (c) $\frac{d}{2}$ (d) $\frac{d}{4}$

24 An object is placed 30 cm away from a convex lens of focal length 10 cm and a sharp image is formed on a screen. Now, a concave lens is placed in contact with the convex lens. The screen now has to be moved by 45 cm to get a sharp image again. The magnitude of focal length of the concave lens is (in cm) **[WB JEE]**

(a) 72 (b) 60
(c) 36 (d) 20

25 A thin glass (refractive index 1.5) lens has optical power of −5D in air. Its optical power in a liquid medium with refractive index 1.6 will be **[UK PMT]**

(a) 1 D (b) −1D (c) 25 D (d) −25 D

26 A concave lens of focal length f forms an image which is $\frac{1}{3}$ times the size of the object. Then, the distance of object from the lens is **[EAMCET]**

(a) $2f$ (b) f (c) $\frac{2}{3}f$ (d) $\frac{3}{2}f$

27 A focal length of a lens is 10 cm. What is power of a lens in dioptre? **[KCET]**

(a) 0.1 D (b) 10 D (c) 15 D (d) 1 D

2013

28 A plano-convex lens fits exactly into a plano-concave lens. Their plane surfaces are parallel to each other. If lenses are made of different materials of refractive indices μ_1 & μ_2 and R is the radius of curvature of the curved surface of the lenses, then the focal length of the combination is **[NEET]**

(a) $\frac{R}{2(\mu_1 + \mu_2)}$ (b) $\frac{R}{2(\mu_1 - \mu_2)}$

(c) $\frac{R}{(\mu_1 - \mu_2)}$ (d) $\frac{2R}{(\mu_1 - \mu_2)}$

29 A hollow prism is filled with water and placed in air. It will deviate the incident rays **[AIIMS]**

(a) towards the base
(b) away from base
(c) parallel to base
(d) towards or away from base depending on the location

30 The graph between the image distance (v) and object distance (u) from the convex lens is **[AIIMS]**

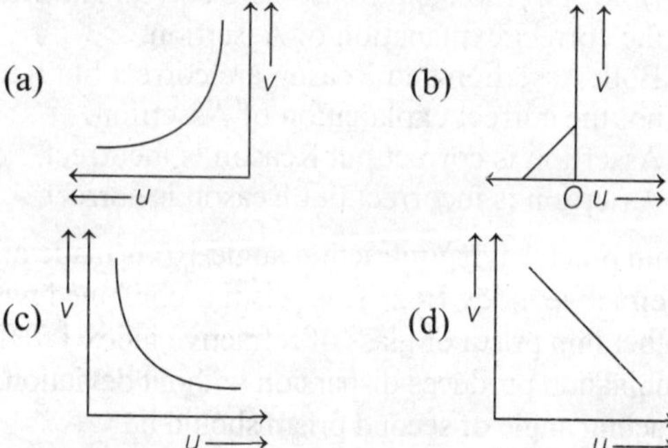

31 A concave mirror of focal length f in vacuum is placed in a medium of refractive index 2. Its focal length in the medium is **[WB JEE]**

(a) $\frac{f}{2}$ (b) f (c) $2f$ (d) $4f$

32 A balloon is filled with hydrogen. For sound waves, this balloon behaves like **[KCET]**

(a) a converging lens (b) a diverging lens
(c) a concave mirror (d) None of these

2012

33 When a biconvex lens of glass having refractive index 1.47 is dipped in a liquid, it acts as a plane sheet of glass. This implies that the liquid must have refractive index **[CBSE AIPMT]**

(a) equal to that of glass
(b) less than one
(c) greater than that of glass
(d) less than that of glass

34 For the angle of minimum deviation of a prism to be equal to its refracting angle, the prism must be made of material whose refractive index **[CBSE AIPMT]**

(a) lies between $\sqrt{2}$ and 1
(b) lies between 2 and $\sqrt{2}$
(c) is less than 1
(d) is grater than 2

35 A ray of light is incident at an angle of incidence on one face of a prism of angle A (assumed to be small) and emerges normally from the opposite face. If the refractive index of the prism is μ, the angle of incidence i, is nearly equal to **[CBSE AIPMT]**

(a) μA (b) $\frac{\mu A}{2}$
(c) $\frac{A}{\mu}$ (d) $\frac{A}{2\mu}$

36 A thin convex lens of refractive index 1.5 has 20 cm focal length in air. if the lens is completely immersed in a liquid of refractive index 1.6, its focal length will be **[AIIMS]**

(a) −160 cm (b) −100 cm (c) + 10 cm (d) + 100 cm

37 The focal length of an equi-convex lens is greater than the radius of curvature of any of the surfaces. Then, the refractive index of the material of the lens is **[AFMC]**

(a) greater than zero but less than 1.5
(b) greater than 1.5 but less than 2.0
(c) greater than 2.0 but less than 2.5
(d) greater than 2.5 but less than 2.0

38 A thin plano-convex lens acts like a concave mirror of focal length 0.2 m when silvered from its plane surface. The refractive index of the material of the lens is 1.5. The radius of curvature of the convex surface of the lens will be **[Manipal]**

(a) 0.1 m (b) 0.75 m
(c) 0.4 m (d) 0.2 m

2011

39 A convex lens has a radius of curvature of magnitude 20 cm. Which one of the following options describe best the image formed of an object of height 2 cm placed 30 cm from the lens? **[CBSE AIPMT]**

(a) Virtual, upright and height = 0.5 cm
(b) Real, inverted and height = 4 cm
(c) Real, inverted and height = 1
(d) Virtual, upright and height = 1

40 A ray of light is incident at an angle 60° on one face of a prism of angle 30° and the emergent ray makes 30° with the incident ray. The refractive index of the prism is **[Kerala CEE]**

(a) 1.732 (b) 1.414 (c) 1.5 (d) 1.33
(e) 1.6

41 Two thin lenses of focal lengths 20 cm and 25 cm are placed in contact. The effective power of the combination is **[WB JEE]**

(a) 9 D (b) 2 D (c) 3 D (d) 7 D

42 A convex lens of focal length 30 cm produces 5 times magnified real image of an object. What is the object distance? **[WB JEE]**

(a) 36 cm (b) 25 cm (c) 30 cm (d) 150 cm

43 A plano-concave lens is made of glass of refractive index 1.5 and the radius of curvature of its curved face is 100 cm. What is the power of the lens? **[WB JEE]**

(a) + 0.5 D (b) − 0.5 D (c) − 2D (d) + 2D

44 A transparent plastic bag filled with air forms a concave lens. Now, if this bag is completely immersed in water, then it behaves as **[J&K CET]**

(a) divergent lens (b) convergent lens
(c) equilateral prism (d) rectangular slab

45 Given figures show the arrangements of two lenses. The radii of curvature of all the curved surfaces are same. The ratio of the equivalent focal length of combinations P, Q and R is **[J&K CET]**

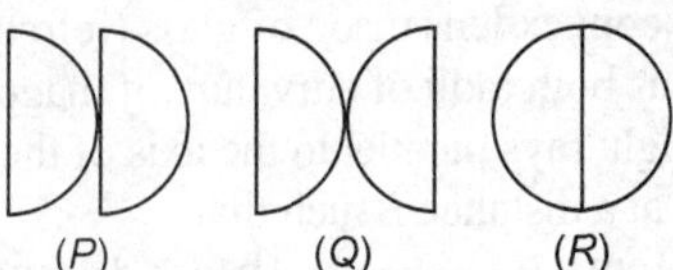

(a) 1 : 1 : 1 (b) 1 : 1 : −1
(c) 2 : 1 : 1 (d) 2 : 1 : 2

46 Two thin lenses have a combined power of +9 D. When they are separated by a distance of 20 cm, their equivalent power becomes $+\frac{27}{5}$ D. Their individual powers (in dioptre) are **[KCET]**

(a) 1, 8 (b) 2, 7 (c) 3,6 (d) 4, 5

47 A plano-convex lens has a maximum thickness of 6 cm. When placed on a horizontal table with the curved surface in contact with the table surface, the apparent depth of the bottom most point of the lens is found to be 4 cm. If the lens is inverted such that the plane face of the lens is in contact with the surface of the table, the apparent depth of the centre of the plane face is found to be $\frac{17}{4}$ cm. The radius of curvature of the lens is **[KCET]**

(a) 68 cm (b) 75 cm (c) 128 cm (d) 34 cm

48 A prism having refractive index 1.414 and refracting angle 30° has one of the refracting surfaces silvered. A beam of light incident on the other refracting surface will retrace its path, if the angle of incidence is **[KCET]**

(a) 0° (b) 30° (c) 60° (d) 45°

2010

49 A lens having focal length f and aperture of diameter d forms an image of intensity I. Aperture of diameter $\frac{d}{2}$ in central region of lens is covered by black paper. Focal length of lens and intensity of image now will be respectively **[CBSE AIPMT]**

(a) f and $\frac{I}{4}$ (b) $\frac{3f}{4}$ and $\frac{I}{2}$

(c) f and $\frac{3I}{4}$ (d) $\frac{f}{2}$ and $\frac{I}{2}$

50 **Assertion** There is no dispersion of light refracted through a rectangular glass slab.

Reason Dispersion of light is the phenomenon of splitting of a beam of white light into its constituent colours.

(a) Both Assertion and Reason are correct and Reason is the correct explanation of Assertion. **[AIIMS]**
(b) Both Assertion and Reason are correct but Reason is not the correct explanation of Assertion.
(c) Assertion is correct but Reason is not correct.
(d) Assertion is incorrect but Reason is correct.

51 A double convex lens made of glass (refractive index $n = 1.5$) has both radii of curvature of magnitude 20 cm incident light rays parallel to the axis of the lens will converge at a distance L such that **[AFMC]**

(a) $L = 20$ cm (b) $L = 10$ cm

(c) $L = 40$ cm (d) $L = \frac{20}{3}$ cm

52 A convex lens of focal length 1.0 m and a concave lens of focal length 0.25 m are 0.75 m apart. A parallel beam of light is incident in the convex lens. The beam emerging after refraction from both lenses is **[BHU]**

(a) parallel to principal axis
(b) convergent
(c) divergent
(d) None of the above

53 The radii of curvature of the two surfaces of a lens are 20 cm and 30 cm and the refractive index of the material of the lens is 1.5. If the lens is concavo-convex, then the focal length of the lens is **[BHU]**

(a) 24 cm (b) 10 cm
(c) 15 cm (d) 120 cm

54 A lens behaves as a converging lens in air and a diverging lens in water. The refractive index of the material is **[UP CPMT]**

(a) equal to unity
(b) equal to 1.33
(c) between unity and 1.33
(d) greater than 1.33

55 A convex lens has mean focal length of 20 cm. The dispersive power of the material of the lens is 0.02. The longitudinal chromatic aberration for an object at infinity is **[Manipal]**

(a) 10^3 (b) 0.80
(c) 0.40 (d) 0.20

56 A convex lens of focal length f is placed some where in between an object and a screen. The distance between object and screen is x. If numerical value of magnification produced by lens is m, focal length of lens is **[Manipal]**

(a) $\frac{mx}{(m+1)^2}$ (b) $\frac{mx}{(m-1)^2}$

(c) $\frac{(m+1)^2}{m}x$ (d) $\frac{(m-1)^2}{m}x$

57 How many images are formed by the lens shown, if an object is kept on its axis? **[Manipal]**

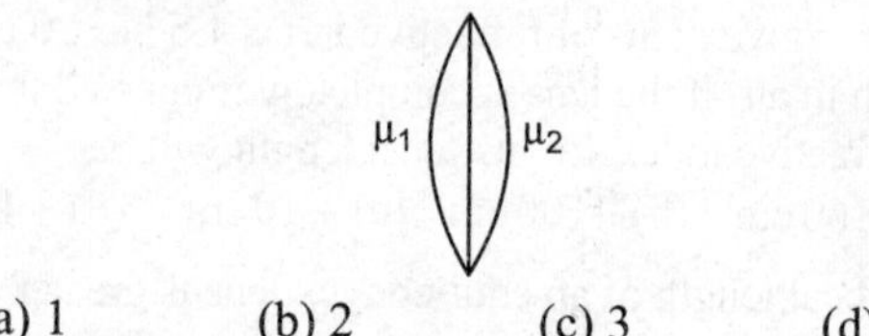

(a) 1 (b) 2 (c) 3 (d) 4

58 When white light passes through a glass prism, one gets spectrum on the other side of the prism. In the emergent beam, the ray which is deviating least is **[OJEE]**

(a) violet ray (b) green ray
(c) red ray (d) yellow ray

59 For an angle of incidence θ, on an equilateral prism of refractive index $\sqrt{3}$, the ray refracted is parallel to the base inside the prism. The value of θ is **[Kerala CEE]**

(a) 30° (b) 45° (c) 60° (d) 75°
(e) 15°

60 The power of a bi-convex lens is 10 D and the radius of curvature of each surface is 10 cm, then the refractive index of the material of the lens is **[Kerala CEE]**

(a) $\frac{3}{2}$ (b) $\frac{4}{3}$

(c) $\frac{9}{8}$ (d) $\frac{5}{3}$

(e) $\frac{3}{4}$

61 If x_1 be the size of the magnified image and x_2 be the size of the diminished image in lens displacement method, then the size of the object is **[WB JEE]**

(a) $\sqrt{x_1 x_2}$ (b) $x_1 x_2$

(c) $x_1^2 x_2$ (d) $x_1 x_2^2$

62 A plano-convex lens ($f = 20$ cm) is silvered at plane surface. Now, focal length will be **[WB JEE]**
(a) 20 cm (b) 40 cm (c) 30 cm (d) 10 cm

63 A thin convergent glass lens $\mu = 1.5$ has a power of + 5.0 D. When this lens is immersed in a liquid of refractive index μ_l it acts as diverging lens of focal length 100 cm. The value of μ_l should be **[Punjab PMET]**
(a) $\frac{3}{2}$ (b) $\frac{4}{3}$ (c) $\frac{5}{3}$ (d) 2

64 When a lens of refractive index n_1 is placed in a liquid of refractive index n_2, the lens looks to be disappeared only if **[DUMET]**
(a) $n_1 = n_2/2$
(b) $n_1 = 3n_2/2$
(c) $n_1 = n_2$
(d) $n_1 = 5n_2/2$

65 Two beams of red and violet colours made to pass separately through a prism of $A = 60°$. In the minimum deviation position, the angle of refraction inside the prism will be **[KCET]**
(a) greater for red colour
(b) equal but not 30° for both the colours
(c) greater for violet colour
(d) 30° for both the colours

66 A ray PQ incident on the refracting face BA is refracted in the prism BAC as shown in the figure and emerges from the other refracting face AC as RS, such that $AQ = AR$. If the angle of prism $A = 60°$ and the refractive index of the material of prism is $\sqrt{3}$, then the angle of deviation of the ray is **[JCECE]**

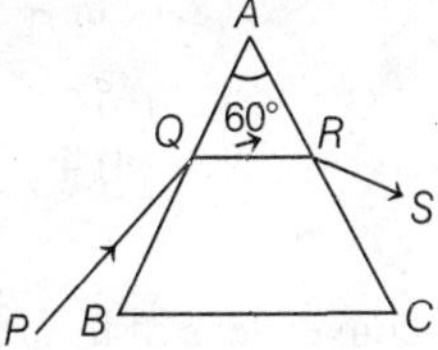

(a) 60° (b) 45°
(c) 30° (d) None of these

67 A thin lens made of glass of refractive index $\mu = 1.5$ has a focal length equal to 12 cm in air. It is now immersed in water $\left(\mu = \frac{4}{3}\right)$. Its new focal length is **[JCECE]**
(a) 48 cm (b) 36 cm
(c) 24 cm (d) 12 cm

68 When a thin convex lens is put in contact with a thin concave lens of the same focal length (f), the resultant combination has focal length equal to **[CG PMT]**
(a) $\frac{f}{2}$ (b) $2f$ (c) 0 (d) ∞

2009

69 A beam of light consisting of red, green and blue colours is incident on a right angled prism as shown in figure. The refractive indices of the material of prism for red, green and blue colours respectively are 1.33, 1.44, 1.47. The prism will **[AIIMS]**

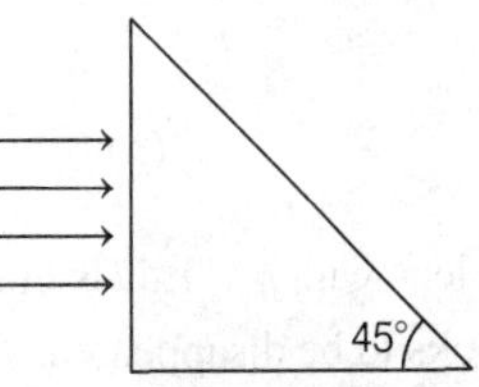

(a) separate part of blue colour from red and green colour
(b) separate all the three colours from one another
(c) separate part of the red colour from green and blue colours
(d) not separate even partially any colour from the other two colours

70 A symmetric double convex lens is cut in two equal parts by a plane perpendicular to the principal axis. If the power of the original lens is 4D, the power of a cut lens will be **[UP CPMT]**
(a) 2D (b) 3D (c) 4D (d) 5D

71 A convex lens of focal length 20 cm placed in contact with a plane mirror acts as a **[UP CPMT]**
(a) convex mirror of focal length 10 cm
(b) concave mirror of focal length 40 cm
(c) concave mirror of focal length 60 cm
(d) concave mirror of focal length 10 cm

72 If I_1 and I_2 be the size of the images respectively for the two positions of lens in the displacement method, then the size of the object is given by **[Manipal]**
(a) $\frac{I_1}{I_2}$ (b) $I \times I_2$
(c) $\sqrt{I_1 \times I_2}$ (d) $\sqrt{\frac{I_1}{I_2}}$

73 In the measurement of the angle of a prism using a spectrometer, the readings of first reflected image are Vernier I : 320° 40′, Vernier II : 140° 30′ and those of the second reflected image are Vernier I : 80° 38′, Vernier II : 260° 24′. Then, the angle of the prism is **[Kerala CEE]**
(a) 59° 58′ (b) 59° 56′ (c) 60° 2′
(d) 60° 4′ (e) 60° 0′

74 An equilateral prism has $\mu = \sqrt{2}$. Angle of incidence for minimum deviation is **[OJEE]**
(a) 45° (b) 30° (c) 60° (d) 90°

75 A glass slab of thickness 8 cm contains the same number of waves as 10 cm long path of water when both are traversed by the same monochromatic light. If the refractive index of water is $\frac{4}{3}$, then the refractive index of glass is **[EAMCET]**

(a) $\frac{5}{3}$ (b) $\frac{5}{4}$
(c) $\frac{16}{15}$ (d) $\frac{3}{2}$

76 When a glass lens with $n = 1.47$ is immersed in a trough of liquid, it looks to be disappeared. The liquid in the trough could be **[DUMET]**

(a) water (b) kerosene
(c) glycerine (d) alcohol

77 The distance between an object and a divergent lens is m times the focal length of the lens. The linear magnification produced by the lens is **[KCET]**

(a) m (b) $\frac{1}{m}$
(c) $m+1$ (d) $\frac{1}{m+1}$

78 The angle of minimum deviation for an incident light ray on an equilateral prism is equal to its refracting angle. The refractive index of its material is **[KCET]**

(a) $\frac{1}{\sqrt{2}}$ (b) $\sqrt{3}$ (c) $\frac{\sqrt{3}}{2}$ (d) $\frac{3}{2}$

2008

79 Two thin lenses of focal lengths f_1 and f_2 are in contact and co-axial. The power of the combination is **[CBSE AIPMT]**

(a) $\sqrt{\frac{f_1}{f_2}}$ (b) $\sqrt{\frac{f_2}{f_1}}$
(c) $\frac{f_1 - f_2}{f_1 f_2}$ (d) $\frac{f_1 + f_2}{f_1 f_2}$

80 A thin glass (refractive index 1.5) lens has optical power of -5 D in air. Its optical power in a liquid medium with refractive index 1.6 will be **[AIIMS]**

(a) 1 D (b) $-$ 1D (c) 25 D (d) $-$ 25 D

81 **Assertion** A concave mirror and convex lens both have the same focal length in air. When they are submerged in water, they will have same focal length.

Reason The refractive index of water is smaller than the refractive index of air. **[AIIMS]**

(a) Both Assertion and Reason are correct and Reason is the correct explanation of Assertion.
(b) Both Assertion and Reason are correct but Reason is not the correct explanation of Assertion.
(c) Assertion is correct but Reason is incorrect.
(d) Both Assertion and Reason are incorrect.

82 Given, ${}_a\mu_g = \frac{3}{2}$ and ${}_a\mu_w = \frac{4}{3}$. There is an equiconvex lens with radius of each surface equal to 20 cm. There is air in the object space and water in the image space. The focal length of lens is **[Manipal]**

(a) 80 cm (b) 40 cm (c) 20 cm (d) 10 cm

83 A diverging meniscus lens of 1.5 refractive index has concave surface of radii 3 and 4 cm. The position of the image, if an object is placed 12 cm infront of the lens is

(a) 7 cm (b) $-$ 8 cm **[Punja b PMT]**
(c) 9 cm (d) 10 cm

84 The angle of minimum deviation for a prism is 40° and the angle of the prism is 60°. The angle of incidence in this position will be **[DUMET]**

(a) 30° (b) 60° (c) 50° (d) 100°

85 A convex and a concave lens separated by distance d are then put in contact. The focal length of the combination

(a) decreases (b) increases **[KCET]**
(c) becomes zero (d) remains the same

86 A convex lens is made of 3 layers of glass of 3 different materials as in the figures. A point object is placed on its axis. The number of images of the object are **[KCET]**

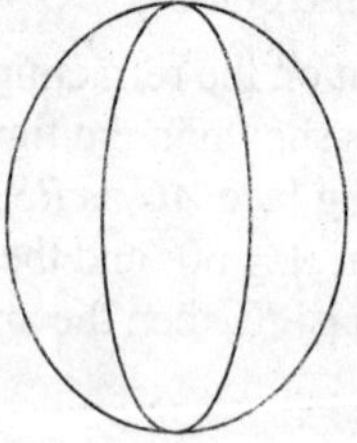

(a) 1 (b) 2
(c) 3 (d) 4

2007

87 **Assertion** A bi-convex lens of focal length 10 cm is split into two equals parts by a plane parallel to its principal axis. The focal length of the each part will be 20 cm.

Reason Focal length does not depend on the radii of curvature of two surfaces. **[AIIMS]**

(a) Both Assertion and Reason are correct and Reason is the correct explanation of Assertion.
(b) Both Assertion and Reason are correct but Reason is not the correct explanation of Assertion.
(c) Assertion is correct but Reason is incorrect.
(d) Both Assertion and Reason are incorrect.

88 A convex lens is dipped in a liquid whose refractive index is equal to the refractive index of the lens, then its focal length will **[AFMC]**

(a) become small, but non-zero
(b) remain unchanged
(c) become zero
(d) become infinite

89 An equi-convex lens is cut into two halves along (i) XOX' and (ii) YOY' as shown in the figure. Let f, f' and f'' be the focal lengths of the complete lens, of each half in case (i), and of each half in case (ii) respectively.

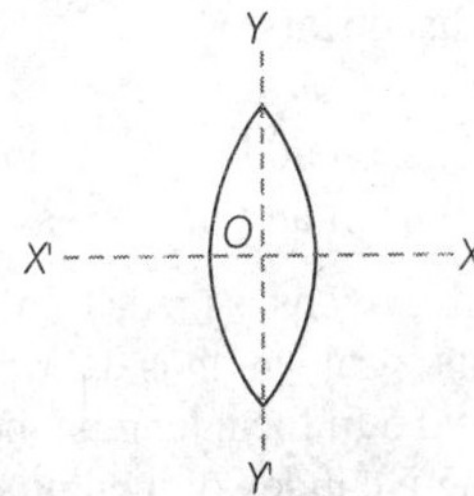

Choose the correct statement from the following **[BHU]**

(a) $f' = f, f'' = f$ (b) $f' = 2f, f'' = 2f$
(c) $f' = f, f'' = 2f$ (d) $f' = 2f, f'' = f$

90 An air bubble is contained inside water. It behave as a **[UP CPMT]**

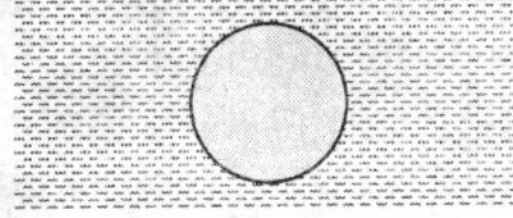

(a) concave lens
(b) convex lens
(c) Neither convex nor concave
(d) Cannot say

91 An object is placed at a distance of $\frac{f}{2}$ from a convex lens. The image will be **[Punjab PMET]**

(a) at one of the foci, virtual and double its size
(b) at $\frac{3f}{2}$, real and inverted
(c) at $2f$, virtual and erect
(d) None of the above

92 A ray of light is incident normally on one face of a right angled isosceles prism. It then grazes the hypotenuse. The refractive index of the material of the prism is **[KCET]**

(a) 1.33 (b) 1.414
(c) 1.5 (d) 1.732

93 Two thin equi-convex lenses each of focal length 0.2 m are placed co-axially with their optic centres 0.5 m apart. Then, the focal length of the combination is **[KCET]**

(a) – 0.4 m (b) 0.4 m
(c) – 0.1m (d) 0.1m

94 A prism of a certain angle deviates the red and blue rays by 8° and 12°, respectively. Another prism of the same angle deviates the red and blue rays by 10° and 14°, respectively. The prisms are small angled and made of different materials. The dispersive powers of the materials of the prisms are in the ratio **[KCET]**

(a) 5 : 6 (b) 9 : 11
(c) 6 : 5 (d) 11 : 9

2006

95 A wire mesh consisting of very small squares is viewed at a distance of 8 cm through a magnifying converging lens of focal length 10 cm, kept close to the eye. The magnification produced by the lens is **[AIIMS]**

(a) 5 (b) 8 (c) 10 (d) 20

96 A leaf which contains only green pigments, is illuminated by a laser light of wavelength 0.6328 μm. It would appear to be **[AFMC]**

(a) brown (b) black (c) red (d) green

97 Which of the following is true for rays coming from infinity? **[AFMC]**

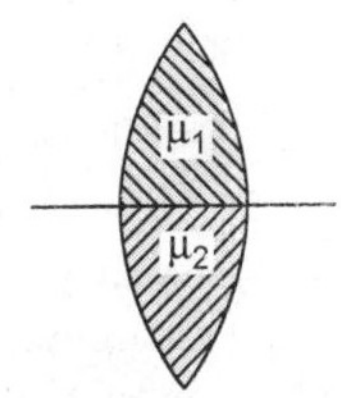

(a) Two images are formed
(b) Continuous image is formed between focal points of upper and lower lens
(c) One image is formed
(d) None of the above

98 If the focal length of the lens is 20 cm, what is the distance of the image from the lens in the following figure? **[BHU]**

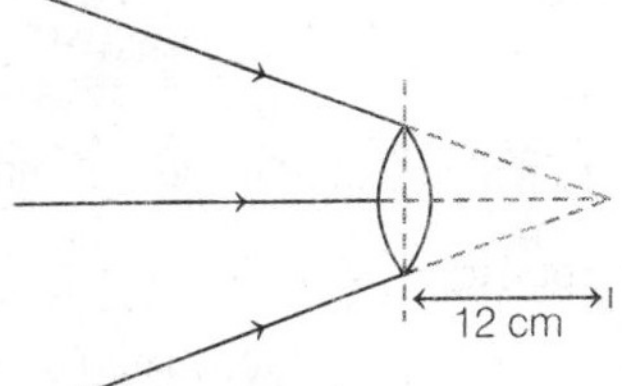

(a) 5.5 cm (b) 7.5 cm (c) 12 cm (d) 20 cm

99 The image of a small electric bulb fixed on the wall of a room is to be obtained on the opposite wall 4 m away by means of a large convex lens. The maximum possible focal length of the lens required for this purpose will be

(a) 0.5 m (b) 1 m (c) 1.5 m (d) 2 m **[BHU]**

100 The correct arrangement of colours in the descending order of their wavelength is **[Kerala CEE]**

(a) yellow, violet, green, orange
(b) orange, yellow, green, violet
(c) violet, green, yellow, orange
(d) yellow, green, orange, violet
(e) orange, green, violet, yellow

101 A concave lens of focal length 20 cm produces an image half the size of the real object. The distance of the real object is **[Kerala CEE]**

(a) 20 cm (b) 30 cm (c) 10 cm (d) 60 cm
(e) 40 cm

102 If a ray of light is incident on an equilateral glass prism PQR placed on a horizontal table, then for the minimum deviation which of the following is correct? **[RPMT]**

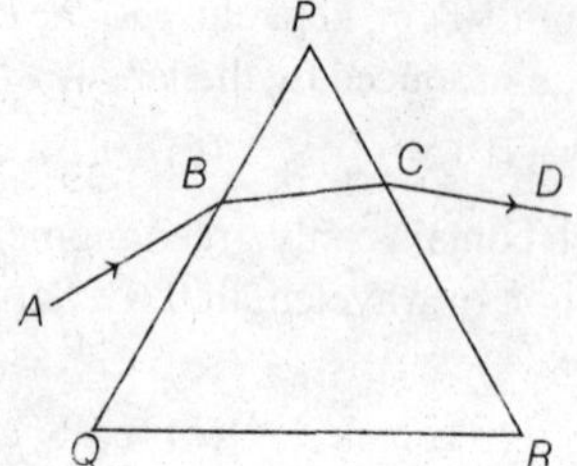

(a) AB is horizontal
(b) CD is horizontal
(c) Either AB or CD is horizontal
(d) BC is horizontal

103 The refractive index of the material of the prism and liquid are 1.56 and 1.32, respectively. What will be the value of θ for the following refraction? **[MP PMT]**

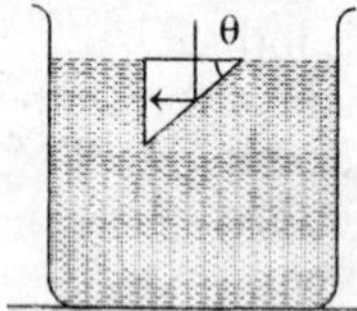

(a) $\sin\theta \geq \frac{13}{11}$ (b) $\sin\theta \geq \frac{11}{13}$
(c) $\sin\theta \geq \frac{\sqrt{3}}{2}$ (d) $\sin\theta \geq \frac{1}{\sqrt{2}}$

104 The effective focal length of the lens combination shown in the figure is – 60 cm. The radii of curvature of the curved surfaces of the plano-convex lenses are 12 cm each and refractive index of the material of the lens is 1.5. The refractive index of the liquid is **[EAMCET]**

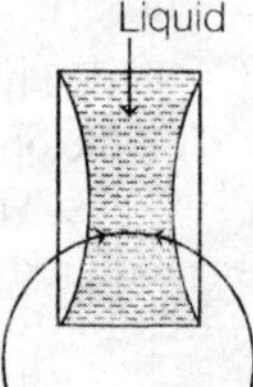

(a) 1.33 (b) 1.42 (c) 1.53 (d) 1.6

105 If the refractive index of a glass prism is $\cot\left(\frac{A}{2}\right)$ and A is angle of prism, then angle of minimum deviation is **[JCECE]**

(a) $\left(\frac{\pi}{2} - A\right)$ (b) $\left(2\pi - \frac{A}{2}\right)$
(c) $\left(\frac{\pi - A}{2}\right)$ (d) $(\pi - 2A)$

2005

106 A convex lens forms a full image of the object on a screen. If half of the lens is covered with an opaque object, then **[BHU]**

(a) the image disappears
(b) half of the image is seen
(c) full image is seen and of same intensity
(d) full image is seen and of decreased intensity

107 A thin equi-convex lens is made of glass of refractive index 1.5 and its focal length is 0.2 m. If it acts as a concave lens of 0.5 m focal length when dipped in a liquid, the refractive index of the liquid is **[EAMCET]**

(a) $\frac{17}{8}$ (b) $\frac{15}{8}$
(c) $\frac{13}{8}$ (d) $\frac{9}{8}$

108 If the focal length of a double convex lens for red light is f_R, its focal length for the violet light is **[EAMCET]**

(a) f_R
(b) greater than f_R
(c) less than f_R
(d) $2f_R$

109 A ray falls on a prism ABC ($AB = BC$) and travels as shown in figure. The least value of refractive index of material of the prism, should be **[DUMET]**

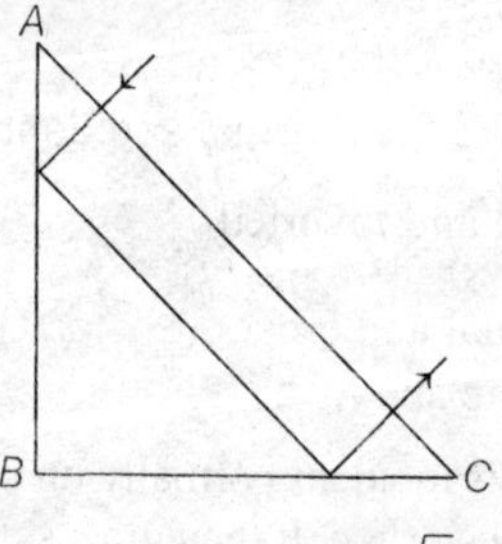

(a) 1.5 (b) $\sqrt{2}$
(c) 1.33 (d) $\sqrt{3}$

110 White light is incident on one of the refracting surfaces of a prism of angle 5°. If the refractive indices for red and blue colours are 1.641 and 1.659 respectively, the angular separation between these two colours when they emerge out of the prism is **[KCET]**

(a) 0.9° (b) 0.09°
(c) 1.8° (d) 1.2°

111 For a given lens, the magnification was found to be twice as large as when the object was 0.15 m distant from it as when the distance was 0.2 m. The focal length of the lens is **[KCET]**

(a) 1.5 m (b) 0.20 m
(c) 0.10 m (d) 0.05 m

Answers

1 (a)	2 (d)	3 (d)	4 (c)	5 (a)	6 (b)	7 (b)	8 (a)	9 (b)	10 (a)
11 (d)	12 (a)	13 (a)	14 (d)	15 (c)	16 (c)	17 (a)	18 (b)	19 (c)	20 (b)
21 (d)	22 (e)	23 (d)	24 (d)	25 (a)	26 (a)	27 (b)	28 (c)	29 (a)	30 (a)
31 (b)	32 (b)	33 (a)	34 (b)	35 (a)	36 (a)	37 (a)	38 (d)	39 (b)	40 (a)
41 (a)	42 (a)	43 (b)	44 (b)	45 (a)	46 (c)	47 (d)	48 (d)	49 (c)	50 (b)
51 (a)	52 (a)	53 (d)	54 (c)	55 (c)	56 (a)	57 (a)	58 (c)	59 (c)	60 (a)
61 (a)	62 (d)	63 (c)	64 (c)	65 (d)	66 (a)	67 (a)	68 (d)	69 (c)	70 (a)
71 (d)	72 (c)	73 (a)	74 (a)	75 (a)	76 (c)	77 (d)	78 (b)	79 (d)	80 (a)
81 (d)	82 (b)	83 (b)	84 (c)	85 (a)	86 (a)	87 (d)	88 (d)	89 (c)	90 (a)
91 (a)	92 (b)	93 (a)	94 (c)	95 (a)	96 (b)	97 (a)	98 (b)	99 (b)	100 (b)
101 (a)	102 (d)	103 (b)	104 (d)	105 (d)	106 (d)	107 (b)	108 (c)	109 (b)	110 (b)
111 (c)									

Explanations

1 (a) ***Case* I** When two equi-convex lens of focal length f_1 and f_2 respectively, are kept co-axially in contact, then the equivalent focal length of combination is

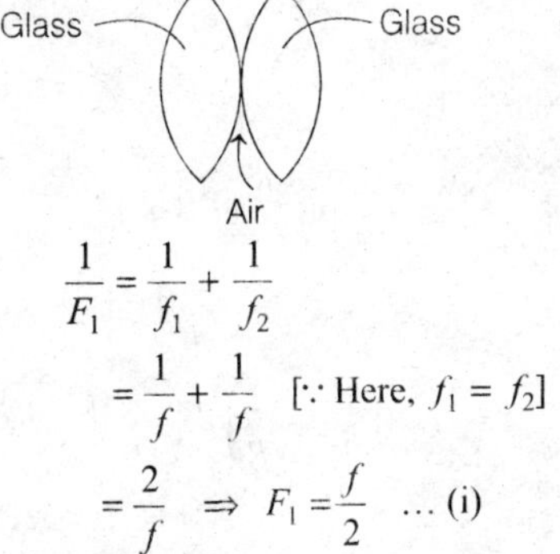

$$\frac{1}{F_1} = \frac{1}{f_1} + \frac{1}{f_2}$$

$$= \frac{1}{f} + \frac{1}{f} \quad [\because \text{Here, } f_1 = f_2]$$

$$= \frac{2}{f} \Rightarrow F_1 = \frac{f}{2} \quad \ldots \text{(i)}$$

***Case* II** When glycerine of same refractive index at that of the glass is filled in the space between two lens, then the combination will now comprises of three lenses; first bi-convex, second bi-concave and third is bi-convex. So, the focal length of the combination now is given as

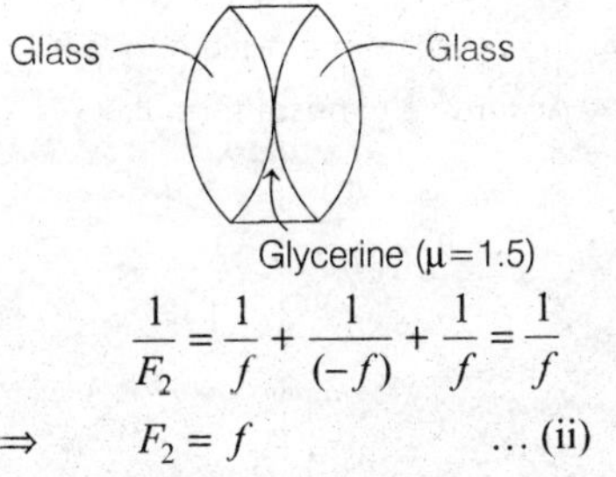

$$\frac{1}{F_2} = \frac{1}{f} + \frac{1}{(-f)} + \frac{1}{f} = \frac{1}{f}$$

$$\Rightarrow F_2 = f \quad \ldots \text{(ii)}$$

From Eqs. (i) and (ii), we get

$$F_1 : F_2 = 1 : 2$$

2 (d) Different colours of white light have different wavelengths. The descending order of the wavelength of the component of white light is

$$\lambda_{red} > \lambda_{green} > \lambda_{blue} > \lambda_{violet}$$

3 (d) When the lens is cut along its principal axis, the focal length of the two halves will remain same because the radius of curvature of both the surfaces are still same. So, the power also remains same as

$$P = \frac{1}{f}$$

4 (c) Using the lens Maker's formula

$$\frac{1}{f} = \left(\frac{\mu_2 - \mu_1}{\mu_1}\right)\left(\frac{1}{R_1} - \frac{1}{R_2}\right)$$

Given, $f = 25$ cm

$$\mu_2 = 1.5, \mu_1 = 1 \text{ (for air)}$$

let $R_1 = R$ and $R_2 = -2R$

$$\Rightarrow \frac{1}{25} = \left(\frac{1.5-1}{1}\right)\left[\frac{1}{R} - \left(-\frac{1}{2R}\right)\right]$$

$$\frac{1}{25 \times 0.5} = \frac{1}{R} + \frac{1}{2R}$$

$$\Rightarrow R = \frac{3}{2} \times 25 \times 0.5$$

$$= 18.75 \text{ cm}$$

$$\therefore R_1 = 18.75 \text{ cm}$$

$$R_2 = 2 \times 18.75$$

$$= 37.5 \text{ cm}$$

5 (a) From figure,

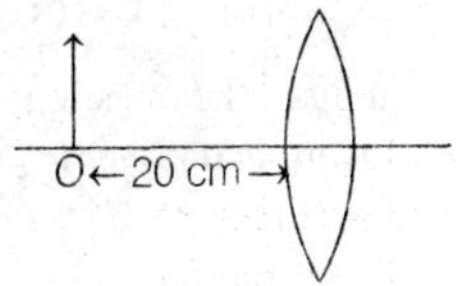

Distance of object, $u = -20$ cm

Magnification, $m = -0.5$

Magnification of lens in terms of u and f is given by

$$m = \frac{f}{u+f} \quad -0.5 = \frac{f}{-20+f}$$

$$\Rightarrow 10 - 0.5f = f$$

$$\Rightarrow 1.5f = 10$$

$$f = \frac{10}{1.5}$$

$$f = 6.66 \text{ cm}$$

6 (b)

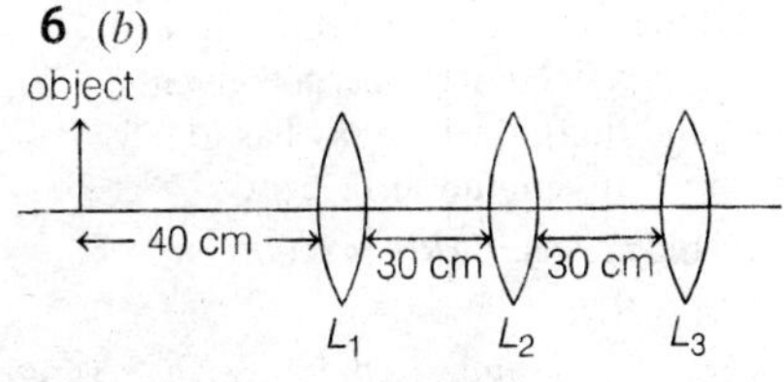

(i) For refraction from 1st lens,

$$\frac{1}{f} = \frac{1}{v} - \frac{1}{u}$$

$$\Rightarrow \frac{1}{v} = \frac{1}{f} + \frac{1}{u} = \frac{1}{10} - \frac{1}{40} = \frac{3}{40} \text{ cm}$$

$$\Rightarrow v = \frac{40}{3} \text{ cm}$$

This image acts as object for 2nd lens.

$\therefore$ Object distance for 2nd lens L_2

$$= 30 - \frac{40}{3} = \frac{50}{3} \text{ cm}$$

(ii) Now for refraction from L_2,

$$\frac{1}{v} - \frac{1}{u} = \frac{1}{f}$$

$$\Rightarrow \quad \frac{1}{v} = \frac{1}{u} + \frac{1}{f} = \frac{1}{10} - \frac{3}{50} = \frac{2}{50}$$

$$\Rightarrow \quad v = 25 \text{ cm}$$

This image is object for 3rd lens L_3

$(u = 30 - 25 = 5 \text{ cm})$

$$\Rightarrow \frac{1}{v} = \frac{1}{f} + \frac{1}{u} = \frac{1}{10} - \frac{1}{5}$$

or $\quad v = -10$ cm

(location of final image = 10 cm to left of L_3)

$\therefore$ Distance from L_1

$$= 30 + (30 - 10) = 50 \text{ cm.}$$

7 (b) According to the question, the figure of mentioned prism is given as

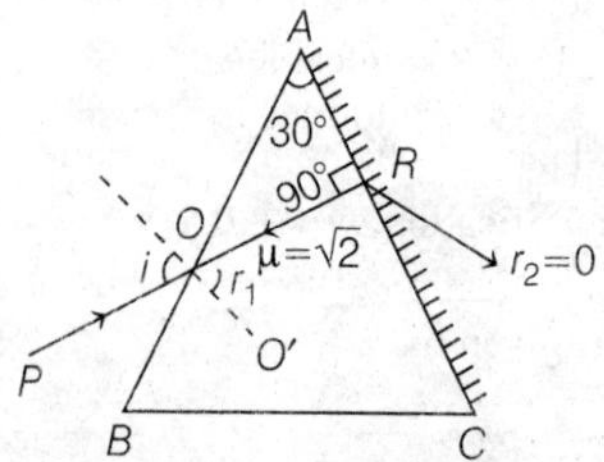

(since, there is no refraction at the face AC)

Given, refractive index of the material of prism, $\mu = \sqrt{2}$

and angle of prism, $A = 30°$.

If the ray OR has to retrace its path after reflection (as per the given condition), then the ray has to fall normally on the surface AC.

This means $\angle ARO = \angle ORC = 90°$

In ΔAOR,

$$\angle AOR + \angle ARO + \angle OAR = 180°$$

$$\Rightarrow \quad \angle AOR + 90° + 30° = 180°$$

$$\Rightarrow \quad \angle AOR = 180° - 120° = 60° \quad \ldots\text{(i)}$$

As we know, $\angle AOR + \angle r_1 = 90°$

$\Rightarrow \angle r_1 = 90° - 60° = 30°$ [from Eq. (i)]

Applying Snell's law at the face AB, we get $\quad \mu = \dfrac{\sin i}{\sin r}$

Substituting the given values, we get

$$\sqrt{2} = \frac{\sin i}{\sin 30°}$$

$$\Rightarrow \quad \sin i = \sin 30° \times \sqrt{2}$$

$$= \frac{1}{2} \times \sqrt{2} \quad \left(\because \sin 30° = \frac{1}{2}\right)$$

$$= \frac{1}{\sqrt{2}}$$

or $\quad i = \sin^{-1}\left(\dfrac{1}{\sqrt{2}}\right) = 45°$

$$\left(\because \sin 45° = \frac{1}{\sqrt{2}}\right)$$

Thus, the angle of incidence of the ray on the prism is 45°.

8 (a) The relation between angle of deviation δ for a thin prism of angle of prism A and refractive index (μ) of material of prism is given by $\delta = (\mu - 1)A$. Thus, angle of deviation depends on the angle of prism.

9 (b) For dispersion without deviation, net deviation produced by the combination of prisms must be zero.

Let prism angle of the first and second prisms are A_1 and A_2, respectively. Similarly, their refractive indices are μ_1 and μ_2.

Condition for dispersion without deviation is

$$\delta_1 - \delta_2 = 0$$

$$\Rightarrow (\mu_1 - 1) A_1 - (\mu_2 - 1) A_2 = 0$$

$$\Rightarrow \quad A_2 = \left(\frac{\mu_1 - 1}{\mu_2 - 1}\right) A_1 = \left(\frac{1.42 - 1}{1.7 - 1}\right)(10°)$$

$$\Rightarrow A_2 = 6°$$

10 (a) According to the question,

Here, μ = refractive index of lens

μ′ = refractive index of liquid and focal length of lens in air = f

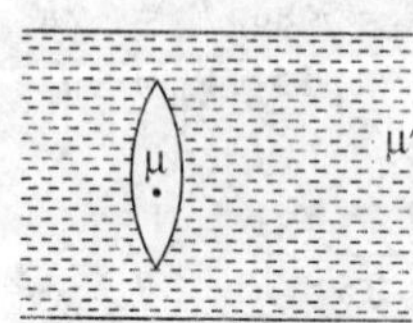

We have, by lens Maker's formula

$$\frac{1}{f} = (\mu - 1)\left(\frac{1}{R_1} - \frac{1}{R_2}\right)$$

When lens is dipped in water,

$$\frac{1}{f'} = \left(\frac{\mu_g}{\mu_l} - 1\right)\left(\frac{1}{R_1} - \frac{1}{R_2}\right)$$

or $$\left(\frac{\mu_g - \mu_l}{\mu_l}\right)\left(\frac{1}{R_1} - \frac{1}{R_2}\right)$$

$$\therefore \quad \frac{f'}{f} = \frac{(\mu - 1)\mu'}{(\mu - \mu')} = \frac{-(\mu - 1)\mu'}{(\mu' - \mu)}$$

$$(\because \mu_l = \mu')$$

or $$f' = \frac{-f\mu'(\mu - 1)}{(\mu' - \mu)}$$

11 (d) Consider the situation shown in figure.

Let radius of curvature of lens surfaces is R.

The combination is equivalent to three lenses in contact,

$$\therefore \quad \frac{1}{f_{eq}} = \frac{1}{f_1} + \frac{1}{f_2} + \frac{1}{f_3} = \frac{2}{f_1} + \frac{1}{f_2}$$

$$(\because f_1 = f_3)$$

μ = 3/2

f_1 $\quad f_2 \quad$ f_3

Now, $$\frac{1}{f_1} = \frac{1}{f_3} = (\mu - 1)\left(\frac{2}{R}\right) = \frac{1}{f} \quad \ldots\text{(i)}$$

$$\frac{1}{f_2} = (\mu_w - 1)\left(-\frac{2}{R}\right) = \left(\frac{4}{3} - 1\right)\left(\frac{-2}{R}\right)$$

$$= \left(\frac{1}{3}\right)\left(-\frac{2}{R}\right) = \left(\frac{-2}{3}\right)\left(\frac{1}{2f(\mu - 1)}\right)$$

[from Eq. (i)]

$$\Rightarrow \frac{1}{f_2} = \left(-\frac{1}{3}\right)\left(\frac{1}{\frac{3}{2} - 1}\right)\left(\frac{1}{f}\right) = -\frac{2}{3} \times \frac{1}{f}$$

$$\therefore \quad \frac{1}{f_{eq}} = \frac{2}{f} - \frac{2}{3} \times \frac{1}{f} = \frac{6 - 2}{3f} = \frac{4}{3f}$$

$$\Rightarrow f_{eq} = \frac{3f}{4}$$

12 (a) Given, $A = 60°$ and $\delta_m = 30°$

According to prism formula,

$$\mu = \frac{\sin\left(\frac{A + \delta_m}{2}\right)}{\sin\left(\frac{A}{2}\right)}$$

or $\mu = \dfrac{\sin\left(\dfrac{60°+30°}{2}\right)}{\sin\dfrac{60°}{2}} = \dfrac{\sin 45°}{\sin 30°}$

or $\mu = \sqrt{2}$

$\because \quad \mu = \dfrac{\text{Speed of light in air } (c)}{\text{Speed of light in prism } (v)}$

$$v = \frac{c}{\mu} = \frac{3\times10^8}{\sqrt{2}} = \frac{3}{\sqrt{2}}\times10^8 \text{ m/s}$$

13 *(a)* Let A' be the angle of flint glass prism.

Here, $A = 5°$ and $\mu = 1.51$ for crown glass prism.

Deviation produced by flint glass,

$\delta' = (\mu - 1)A = (1.51 - 1)\times 5 = 2.55°$

For no deviation, $\delta' = \delta$

or $0.65\, A' = 2.55$

$$A' = \frac{2.55}{0.65} = 3.92°$$

14 *(d)* Given, angle of prism, $A_1 = 4°$

$A_2 = ?,\ N_1 = 1.54,\ N_2 = 1.72$

Angle of deviation, $\delta = (n-1)A$

Dispersion produced by both the prism will be equal

i.e. $(n_1 - 1)\, A_1 = (n_2 - 1)\, A_2$

$\Rightarrow \quad A_2 = \dfrac{(n_1 - 1)A_1}{(n_2 - 1)}$

$$= \frac{(1\cdot 54 - 1)\times 4}{(1\cdot 72 - 1)} = 3°$$

Hence, the angle of prism P_2 is 3°.

15 *(c)* For first refracting surface,

For parallel beam of light,

$$-\frac{\mu_1}{u} + \frac{\mu_2}{v} = \frac{\mu_2 - 1}{R}$$

$\Rightarrow \quad -\dfrac{1\cdot 4}{(-\infty)} + \dfrac{1\cdot 5}{v} = \dfrac{1\cdot 5 - 1\cdot 4}{R}$

$$v = 15R$$

For second refracting surface,

$$\frac{\mu_2}{-15R} + \frac{\mu_3}{v'} = \frac{\mu_3 - \mu_2}{R}$$

$\Rightarrow \quad \dfrac{1\cdot 5}{15R} + \dfrac{1\cdot 6}{v'} = \dfrac{1\cdot 6 - 1\cdot 5}{R}$

$\Rightarrow \quad v' = \infty$

Hence, the combination behaves as glass plate.

16 *(c)* When an object is placed infront of such a lens,the rays first of all refracted from the convex surface, then reflect from the polished plane surface and again refracts from convex surface. If f_l and f_m be the focal lengths of lens (convex surface) and mirror (plane polished surface) respectively, then effective focal length F is given by

$$\frac{1}{F} = \frac{1}{f_l} + \frac{1}{f_m} + \frac{1}{f_l}$$

$$\frac{1}{F} = \frac{2}{f_l} + \frac{1}{f_m} = \frac{2}{f_l}\left(\because f_m = \frac{R}{2} = \infty\right)$$

As, $\dfrac{1}{f_l} = (\mu - 1)\left(\dfrac{1}{R}\right)$

$\therefore \quad \dfrac{1}{F} = \dfrac{2(\mu - 1)}{R}$ or $F = \dfrac{R}{2(\mu - 1)}$

or $\quad R = 2F = \dfrac{R}{(\mu - 1)}$

17 *(a)* Consider a ray of light PQ incident on the surface AB and moves along RS, after passing through the prism ABC.

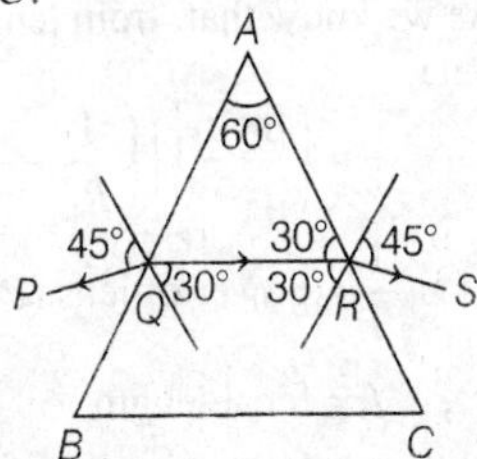

It is given that, the incident ray suffers minimum deviation. Therefore, the ray inside the prism must be parallel to the base BC of the prism from the geometry of the prism and the ray diagram, it is clear that

angle of incidence, $i = 45°$

angle of refraction, $r = r' = 30°$

angle of emergence, $e = 45°$

Therefore, minimum deviation angle suffered by the ray is

$$\delta_{\min} = i + e - (r + r')$$
$$= 90° - 60° = 30°$$

Also, we know that,

$$\mu = \frac{\sin\left(\dfrac{A + \delta_m}{2}\right)}{\sin\dfrac{A}{2}}$$

where, μ = refractive index of the material of the prism.

A = angle of prism = 60°

$$\therefore \quad \mu = \frac{\sin\left(\dfrac{60°+30°}{2}\right)}{\sin\dfrac{60°}{2}}$$

$$= \frac{\sin 45°}{\sin 30°} = \frac{1/\sqrt{2}}{1/2}$$

$$= \frac{2}{\sqrt{2}} = \sqrt{2}$$

18 *(b)* As, we know that,

$$\mu = \frac{\sin\left(\dfrac{A + D_m}{2}\right)}{\sin\dfrac{A}{2}}$$

$\Rightarrow \quad \cot\dfrac{A}{2} = \dfrac{\sin\left(\dfrac{A + D_m}{2}\right)}{\sin\dfrac{A}{2}}$

$\Rightarrow \quad \dfrac{\cos\dfrac{A}{2}}{\sin\dfrac{A}{2}} = \dfrac{\sin\left(\dfrac{A + D_m}{2}\right)}{\sin\dfrac{A}{2}}$

$$\sin\left(\frac{\pi}{2} - \frac{A}{2}\right) = \sin\left(\frac{A + D_m}{2}\right)$$

$\Rightarrow \quad \dfrac{\pi}{2} - \dfrac{A}{2} = \dfrac{A}{2} + \dfrac{D_m}{2}$

$\Rightarrow \quad D_m = \pi - 2A = 180° - 2A$

19 *(c)* Given, $\mu_g = 1.5$

$\mu_{\text{oil}} = 1.7$ and $R = 20$ cm

From lens Maker's formula for the plano-convex lens

$$\frac{1}{f} = (\mu - 1)\left[\frac{1}{R_1} - \frac{1}{R_2}\right]$$

Here, $R_1 = R$

and for plane surface, $R_2 = \infty$

$\therefore \quad \dfrac{1}{f_{\text{lens}}} = (1.5 - 1)\left(\dfrac{1}{R} - 0\right)$

$\Rightarrow \quad \dfrac{1}{f_{\text{lens}}}$ or $\dfrac{1}{f_l} = \dfrac{0.5}{R}$

When the intervening medium is filled with oil, then focal length of the concave lens formed by the oil

$$\frac{1}{f_{\text{concave}}} \text{ or } \frac{1}{f_c} = (1.7 - 1)\left(-\frac{1}{R} - \frac{1}{R}\right)$$

$$= -0.7 \times \frac{2}{R} = \frac{-1.4}{R}$$

Here, we have two concave surfaces,

so $\quad \dfrac{1}{f_{\text{eq}}} = 2\times\dfrac{1}{f_l} + \dfrac{1}{f_c}$

$$= 2\times\frac{0.5}{R} + \left(\frac{-1.4}{R}\right)$$

$$= \frac{1}{R} - \frac{1.4}{R}$$

$$= -\frac{0.4}{R}$$

$\therefore \quad f_{\text{eq}} = -\dfrac{R}{0.4}$

$$= -\frac{20}{0.4} = -50 \text{ cm}$$

20 (b) For the condition giving in question, ray diagram will be shown as

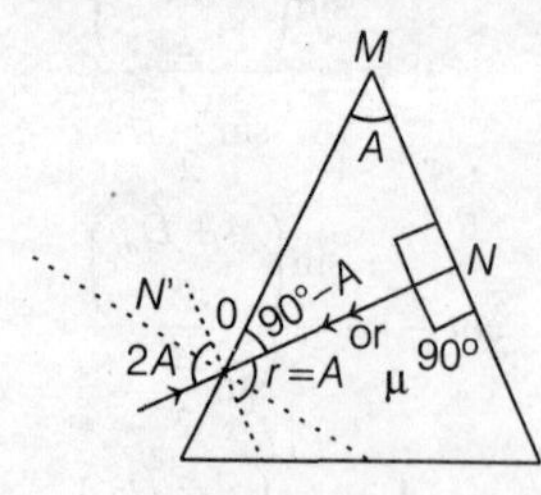

$\angle MON = 90° - A$

So, $\angle r = 90° - (90° - A)$

$\Rightarrow \angle r = A$

By Snell's law, $\dfrac{\sin i}{\sin r} = \mu$

$\Rightarrow \dfrac{\sin(2A)}{\sin(A)} = \mu$

$\dfrac{2\sin A\cos A}{\sin A} = \mu \Rightarrow \mu = 2\cos A$

21 (d) When an equi-convex lens is cut parallel to principal axis, focal length remains the same and when the lens is cut perpendicular to principal axis, its focal length becomes twice the original.

22 (e) Given, $P_1 = 15\text{D}$ and $P_2 = -3\text{D}$

$\because P = P_1 + P_2 = 15\,\text{D} - 3\text{D} = 12\text{D}$

$P = \dfrac{1}{f(\text{m})} \Rightarrow P = \dfrac{100}{f(\text{cm})}$

$\Rightarrow 12 = \dfrac{100}{f}$

$f = \dfrac{100}{12} = 8.33$ cm

23 (d) Focal length of a convex lens by displacement method.
Focal length of the convex lens,

$$f = \frac{a^2 - b^2}{4a}$$

where, a = distance between the image and object and b = distance between two positions of lens.
Here, $a = d$ and to form a distinct image $b = 0$, so the maximum possible focal length is $\dfrac{d}{4}$.

24 (d) For the first condition,
$f_1 = 10$ cm, $u = -30$ cm,

then $\dfrac{1}{f_1} = \dfrac{1}{v} - \dfrac{1}{u} \Rightarrow \dfrac{1}{10} = \dfrac{1}{v} + \dfrac{1}{30}$

$\dfrac{1}{v} = \dfrac{1}{10} - \dfrac{1}{30} \Rightarrow v = \dfrac{30}{2} = 15$

For the second condition when concave lens is placed,

$v' = (15 + 45) = 60$ cm

$\Rightarrow \dfrac{1}{F} = \dfrac{1}{v'} - \dfrac{1}{u}$

where, F = focal length of combination.

$\therefore \dfrac{1}{F} = \dfrac{1}{60} + \dfrac{1}{30}$

$\Rightarrow F = \dfrac{60}{3} = 20$ cm

The magnitude of focal length of concave lens,

$\dfrac{1}{F} = \dfrac{1}{f_1} + \dfrac{1}{f_2}$

$\Rightarrow \dfrac{1}{20} = \dfrac{1}{10} + \dfrac{1}{f_2}$

$\Rightarrow f_2 = -20$ cm

(negative sign for concave lens)

25 (a) As we know that, from lens Maker formula,

$$\frac{1}{f} = \left(\frac{\mu_2}{\mu_1} - 1\right)\left(\frac{1}{R_1} - \frac{1}{R_2}\right)$$

As, $\dfrac{1}{f}$ = power of lens (P)

where, f = focal length.
μ_2 & μ_1 = refractive index of 2nd & 1st medium.
and R_1 & R_2 = radius of curvature of 1st & 2nd curved surface of lens.
So, for 1st case

$$P_1 = \left(\frac{1.5}{1} - 1\right)\left(\frac{1}{R_1} - \frac{1}{R_2}\right) \quad \text{...(i)}$$

As, $\mu_2 = 1.5$
$\mu_1 = 1$ (air)
P_1 = power in initial condition.
Now, for 2nd case

$$P_2 = \left(\frac{1.5}{1.6} - 1\right)\left(\frac{1}{R_1} - \frac{1}{R_2}\right) \quad \text{...(ii)}$$

P_2 = power in 2nd condition.
On dividing Eq. (i) by Eq. (ii), we get

$$\frac{P_1}{P_2} = \frac{\dfrac{1.5 - 1}{1}}{\dfrac{1.5 - 1.6}{1.6}} = \frac{0.5 \times 1.6}{-0.1}$$

$\Rightarrow \dfrac{-5}{P_2} = \dfrac{-0.8}{0.1}$ (as $P_1 = -5\text{D}$)

$\Rightarrow P_2 = \dfrac{+5 \times 0.1}{0.8} = \dfrac{5}{8} = 0.625\text{D}$

So, option (a) is close to 0.625 as 0.625 D ≈ 1D.

26 (a) Given, $f = -f$ (for concave)

$v = \dfrac{1}{3}u$

According to the lens formula,

$\dfrac{1}{f} = \dfrac{1}{v} - \dfrac{1}{u} \Rightarrow \dfrac{1}{f} = \dfrac{1}{-\dfrac{1}{3}u} + \dfrac{1}{u}$

$\dfrac{1}{f} = \dfrac{-3 + 1}{u} \Rightarrow \dfrac{1}{f} = -\dfrac{2}{u}$

$\Rightarrow u = 2f$ $\quad [\because f = -f]$

27 (b) Given, $f = 10$ cm and power, $P = ?$

Power of lens, $P = \dfrac{1}{\text{Focal length (m)}}$

$P = \dfrac{1}{f(\text{m})} \Rightarrow P = \dfrac{100}{f(\text{cm})} = \dfrac{100}{10} = 10$ D

28 (c) Focal length of the combination,

$$\frac{1}{F} = \frac{1}{f_1} + \frac{1}{f_2} \quad \text{....(i)}$$

We have, $f_1 = \dfrac{R}{(\mu_1 - 1)}$

and $f_2 = \dfrac{-R}{(\mu_2 - 1)}$

or $\dfrac{1}{f_1} = \left(\dfrac{\mu_1 - 1}{R}\right)$

or $\dfrac{1}{f_2} = \dfrac{-(\mu_2 - 1)}{R}$

On putting these values in Eq. (i), we get

$$\frac{1}{F} = \frac{(\mu_1 - 1)}{R} - \frac{(\mu_2 - 1)}{R}$$

$$= \frac{[\mu_1 - 1 - \mu_2 + 1]}{R} = \frac{\mu_1 - \mu_2}{R}$$

$\Rightarrow F = \dfrac{R}{\mu_1 - \mu_2}$

29 (a) The propagation of light ray through a prism is shown below

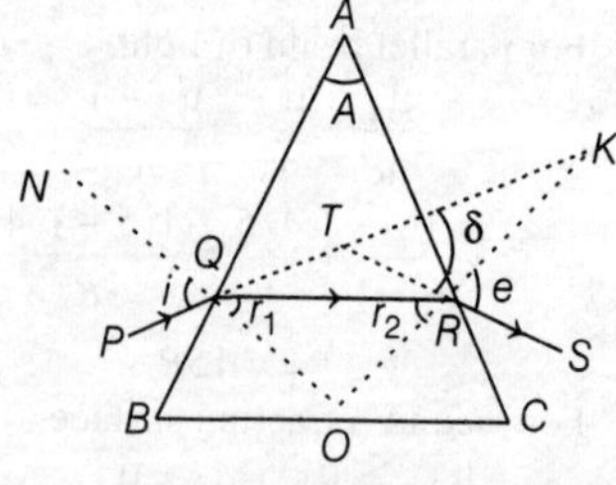

When a light ray travel from air (rarer) to prism filled with water (denser) of higher refractive index, then it bends towards the normal inside it. At other face, the light is travelling from denser to rarer medium, so it bends away from normal. Thus, the prism deviates the incident ray towards the base of prism as shown in figure above.

30 (a) For convex lens as object comes closer to lens image runs away from it and also object distance is always negative, so correct graphs in option (a).

31 (*b*) Focal length of mirror is independent of the refractive index of medium in which it is placed. So, focal length of mirror in any medium is same as the focal length of mirror in vacuum.

32 (*b*) The density of hydrogen is less than the density of air, so velocity of sound in hydrogen is greater than velocity of sound in air. Therefore, hydrogen acts as a rarer medium and the balloon behaves as a diverging lens.

33 (*a*) If bi-convex lens behave like plane sheet, ray will pass undeviated through it only when medium has same refractive index as that of biconvex lens. If f_l and f_a be the focal length in liquid and air respectively and $f_l = \infty$ (for plane sheet)

Thus, $f_l = \dfrac{({}_a\mu_g - 1)\,{}_a\mu_l\, f_a}{({}_a\mu_g - {}_a\mu_l)} \Rightarrow {}_a\mu_g = {}_a\mu_l$

34 (*b*) Refractive index,

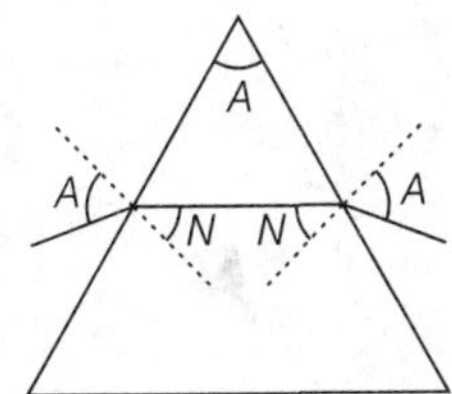

$$\mu = \frac{\sin\left(\dfrac{A + \delta m}{2}\right)}{\sin A/2} = \frac{\sin\left(\dfrac{A + A}{2}\right)}{\sin A/2}$$

$$= \frac{\sin A}{\sin A/2} = \frac{2\sin A/2 \cos A/2}{\sin A/2}$$

$$= 4\cos A/2$$

In given situation, value of A varies from 0 to 90°.

$$\mu_{\min} = 2\cos\frac{90°}{2} = \sqrt{2}$$

and $\mu_{\max} = 2\cos 0° = 2$

35 (*a*) Refractive index, $\mu = \dfrac{\sin i}{\sin r}$

or $\mu = \dfrac{\sin i}{\sin A}$

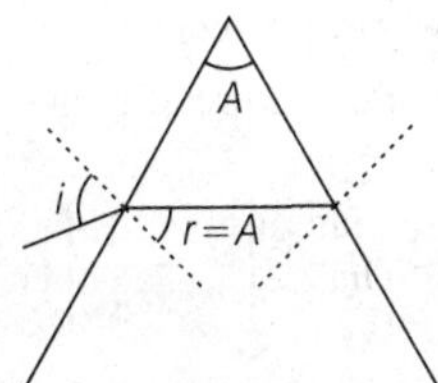

In case of small angle,

$\sin i \approx i$ and $\sin A \approx A \Rightarrow \mu = \dfrac{i}{A}$

Incident angle, $i = \mu A$

36 (*a*) From lens formula,

$$\frac{1}{f} = ({}_a\mu_g - 1)\left(\frac{1}{R_1} - \frac{1}{R_2}\right)$$

$$= (1.5 - 1)\left(\frac{1}{R_1} - \frac{1}{R_2}\right) \quad \text{...(i)}$$

Also, ${}_l\mu_g = \dfrac{\mu_g}{\mu_l} = \dfrac{1.5}{1.6} = \dfrac{15}{16}$

$$\therefore \quad \frac{1}{f'} = ({}_l\mu_g - 1)\left(\frac{1}{R_1} - \frac{1}{R_2}\right)$$

$$\frac{1}{f'} = \left(\frac{15}{16} - 1\right)\left(\frac{1}{R_1} - \frac{1}{R_2}\right) \quad \text{...(ii)}$$

On dividing Eq. (i) by Eq. (ii), we get

$$\frac{f}{f'} = \frac{\left(\frac{15}{16} - 1\right)}{(1.5 - 1)} = -\frac{1}{16 \times 0.5}$$

$$\Rightarrow \quad f' = -8 \times 20 = -160\text{ cm}$$

37 (*a*) Focal length of lens,

$$\frac{1}{f} = (\mu - 1)\left(\frac{1}{R_1} - \frac{1}{R_2}\right)$$

For equi-convex

$$R_1 = +R, R_2 = -R$$

$$\therefore \quad \frac{1}{f} = (\mu - 1)\left(\frac{1}{R} - \frac{1}{-R}\right) = (\mu - 1)\left(\frac{2}{R}\right)$$

$$f = \frac{R}{2(\mu - 1)} \Rightarrow f > R, \text{ so } 2(\mu - 1) < 1$$

i.e. $(\mu - 1) < \dfrac{1}{2} \Rightarrow (\mu - 1) < 0.5$

$\Rightarrow \quad \mu < 1.5$

Focal length of convex lens is positive, so u cannot be negative. Hence, μ should be greater than zero but less than 1.5.

38 (*d*) After silvering the plane surface, plano convex lens behaves as a concave mirror of focal length

$$\frac{1}{f'} = \frac{2}{f_{\text{lens}}}$$

But $\quad f' = 0.2\text{m}$

$\Rightarrow \quad f_{\text{lens}} = 2f' = 2 \times 0.2 = 0.4$ m

Now, from lens Maker's formula,

$$\frac{1}{f_{\text{lens}}} = (\mu - 1)\left(\frac{1}{R_1} - \frac{1}{R_2}\right)$$

$$\therefore \quad \frac{1}{0.4} = (1.5 - 1) \times \frac{1}{R_1} \quad (\because R_2 = \infty)$$

$$\Rightarrow \quad R_1 = 0.5 \times 0.4 = 0.2\text{ m}$$

39 (*b*) In general, we have assumed, $\mu = 1.5$

$$\frac{1}{f} = (1.5 - 1)\left(\frac{1}{20} + \frac{1}{20}\right)$$

So, $\quad f = 20\text{ cm} \Rightarrow \dfrac{1}{f} = \dfrac{1}{v} - \dfrac{1}{u}$

$$\frac{1}{20} = \frac{1}{v} - \frac{1}{(-30)}$$

$$\Rightarrow \quad \frac{1}{v} = \frac{1}{20} - \frac{1}{30} = \frac{10}{600}$$

$$v = 60\text{ cm} \Rightarrow \frac{h_i}{h_o} = \frac{60}{30} = 2$$

$$\Rightarrow \quad h_i = 2 \times |h_o| \Rightarrow h_i = 4\text{ cm}$$

Here, image is real, inverted, magnified and height of image is 4 cm.

40 (*a*) $A + \delta = i + e \quad$ ...(i)

Put the given values in Eq. (i)

$$30° + 30° = 60° + e$$

$$\Rightarrow \quad e = 60° - 60°$$

$$e = 0 \Rightarrow r_1 = A = 30°$$

$$\therefore \quad \mu = \frac{\sin i}{\sin r} = \frac{\sin 60°}{\sin 30°} = \sqrt{3} = 1.732$$

41 (*a*) We have, the effective power given by

$$P_{\text{eff}} = P_1 + P_2$$

Also, we know, $P = \dfrac{1}{f}$

Hence, $\quad P_{\text{eff}} = \dfrac{1}{f_1} + \dfrac{1}{f_2}$

$$\Rightarrow \quad = \frac{1}{0.20} + \frac{1}{0.25} = 5 + 4 = 9\text{D}$$

42 (*a*) We have a lens of focal length 30 cm that produces 5 times magnified real image.

We have, $\quad \dfrac{1}{5u} - \left(\dfrac{1}{-u}\right) = \dfrac{1}{30}$

$$\Rightarrow \quad \frac{1}{5u} + \frac{1}{u} = \frac{1}{30}$$

So, $\quad u = 36\text{ cm}$

43 (*b*) The refractive index is 1.5 and the radius of curvature of the curved face is 100 cm and of the plane side is ∞, hence

$$P = \frac{1}{f} = (\mu - 1)\left(\frac{1}{R_1} - \frac{1}{R_2}\right)$$

$$= (1.5 - 1)\left(\frac{1}{\infty} - \frac{1}{1}\right) = -0.5\text{ D}$$

44 (*b*) After completely immersed in water this bag will behave as convergent lens. Since, bag filled with air has lower refractive index than water, hence its nature reverses.

45 (*a*) In given images P, Q and R lenses are in contact.

$\therefore$ For P combination of lenses,

$$\frac{1}{F_P}=\frac{1}{f}+\frac{1}{f}=\frac{2}{f}$$

$$\left(\because \frac{1}{F}=\frac{1}{f_1}+\frac{1}{f_2} \text{ for combination of lenses}\right)$$

$$F_P=\frac{f}{2}$$

Similarly, for Q and R combinations,

$$F_Q=\frac{f}{2} \text{ and } F_R=\frac{f}{2}$$

Then, $F_P : F_Q : F_R :: 1:1:1$

46 *(c)* Given, $P_1+P_2=9$

$$P=P_1+P_2-dP_1P_2$$

$$\Rightarrow \frac{27}{5}=9-\frac{20}{100}\times P_1P_2$$

$$\Rightarrow P_1P_2=18$$

Hence, the above equation is correct for

$$P_1=3 \text{ and } P_2=6$$

47 *(d)* $n=\dfrac{\text{Real depth}}{\text{Apparent depth}}$

$$n_1=\frac{6}{4}=\frac{3}{2}=1.5$$

and $$n_2=\frac{6\times4}{17}=\frac{24}{17}$$

$$\Rightarrow \frac{n_1}{u}-\frac{n_2}{v}=\frac{n_1-n_2}{R}$$

$$\Rightarrow \frac{1.5}{6}-\frac{24}{17\times6}=\frac{1.5-1}{R}$$

$$\frac{15}{60}-\frac{24}{17\times6}=\frac{0.5}{R}$$

$$\Rightarrow \frac{1}{4}-\frac{4}{17}=\frac{1}{2R}\Rightarrow\frac{17-16}{68}=\frac{1}{2R}$$

$$\Rightarrow \frac{1}{34}=\frac{1}{R}$$

$$\Rightarrow R=34 \text{ cm}$$

48 *(d)* At second surface, there is no refraction.

So, $r_2=0 \Rightarrow r_1=A=30°$

From Snell's law,

$$n=\frac{\sin i_1}{\sin r_1} \Rightarrow n=\frac{\sin i_1}{\sin 30°}$$

$$\sin i_1=\sqrt{2}\times\frac{1}{2}=\frac{1}{\sqrt{2}}$$

$$\Rightarrow \sin i_1=\frac{1}{\sqrt{2}}\Rightarrow i_1=45°$$

49 *(c)* Intensity, $I \propto A^2$

$$\Rightarrow \frac{I_2}{I_1}=\left[\frac{A_2}{A_1}\right]^2=\frac{\pi r^2-\dfrac{\pi r^2}{4}}{\pi r^2}=\frac{3}{4}$$

$$(\because I_1=I)$$

$I_2=\dfrac{3}{4}I$ and focal length remains unchanged.

50 *(b)* Dispersion is caused due to the difference in the angle of deviation for different colours. In the case of glass slab, the opposite sides are parallel and therefore different colours emerge parallel to each other and are seen simultaneously.

Therefore, dispersion does not occur in glass slab, hence both Assertion and Reason are correct but Reason is not the correct explanation of Assertion.

51 *(a)* Here, $n=1.5$, as per sign convention followed

$$R_1=+20 \text{ cm} \text{ and } R_2=-20 \text{ cm}$$

$$\frac{1}{f}=(n-1)\left(\frac{1}{R_1}-\frac{1}{R_2}\right)$$

$$=(1.5-1)\left[\frac{1}{(+20)}-\frac{1}{(-20)}\right]$$

$$=0.5\times\frac{2}{20}=\frac{1}{20} \Rightarrow f=+20 \text{ cm}$$

Incident rays travelling parallel to the axis of lens will converge at its second principal focus.

$$\therefore L=+20 \text{ cm}$$

52 *(a)* Power of system $=\dfrac{1}{f_1}+\dfrac{1}{f_2}-\dfrac{d}{f_1f_2}$

$$=\frac{1}{1}+\left(\frac{1}{-0.25}\right)-\frac{0.75}{(1)(-0.25)}$$

$$=1-4+3=-3+3=0$$

Since, power of the system is zero, so its focal length is infinity. Hence, it acts like a plane glass sheet. Therefore, the incident parallel beam of light will remain parallel after emerging from the system.

53 *(d)* The focal length of the lens,

$$\frac{1}{f}=(\mu-1)\left(\frac{1}{R_1}-\frac{1}{R_2}\right)$$

$$\Rightarrow \frac{1}{f}=(1.5-1)\left(\frac{1}{20}-\frac{1}{30}\right)$$

$$\Rightarrow \frac{1}{f}=0.5\left(\frac{30-20}{600}\right)$$

$$\Rightarrow \frac{1}{f}=\frac{1}{2}\times\frac{10}{600}=\frac{1}{120}$$

or $f=120$ cm

54 *(c)* If $\mu_g<\mu_l$, then f_l and f_a have opposite signs and the nature of lens changes, i.e. a convex lens diverges the light rays and concave lens converges the light rays

$$\mu_{\text{air}}<\mu_{\text{lens}}<\mu_{\text{water}}$$

i.e. $1<\mu_{\text{lens}}<1.33$

55 *(c)* The refractive index of the material of a lens varies slightly with the wavelength and hence, the focal length is also different for different wavelengths. The separation between the images formed by extreme wavelengths of visible range is called the longitudinal chromatic given by

$$f_1-f_2=\omega\times f$$

where, ω is dispersive power.

Given, $\omega=0.02$

and $f=20$

$$f_1-f_2=0.02\times20=0.40$$

56 *(a)* Here, $x=u+v$ ...(i)

$$m=\frac{f}{f-u}=\frac{f-v}{f} \quad \text{...(ii)}$$

Image is real, magnification is negative

$$-m=\frac{f}{f-u} \Rightarrow u=\frac{(m+1)}{m}f$$

From Eq. (ii), we get $-m=\dfrac{f-v}{f}$

$$\Rightarrow v=(m+1)f$$

Put in Eq. (i), we get

$$x=\frac{(m+1)}{m}f+(m+1)f$$

$$\Rightarrow f=\frac{mx}{(m+1)^2}$$

57 *(a)* Only one converging point is found by this lens. Therefore, only one image is formed.

58 *(c)* $\delta \propto (\mu-1)$

μ_R is least, so δ_R is also least. So, red ray is deviating least.

59 *(c)* Given, $\mu=\sqrt{3}$ and $A=60°$

For minimum deviation, $r=\dfrac{A}{2}=30°$

From Snell's law, $\mu=\dfrac{\sin i}{\sin r}$

$$\Rightarrow \sqrt{3}=\frac{\sin i}{\sin 30°}\Rightarrow i=\sin^{-1}\left(\frac{\sqrt{3}}{2}\right)=60°$$

We have, $i=\theta \Rightarrow \theta=60°$

60 *(a)* Power of a bi-convex lens is 10 D.

Radius of curvature of each surface = 10 cm

$$\Rightarrow \frac{1}{f}=(\mu-1)\left[\frac{1}{R_1}-\frac{1}{R_2}\right]$$

$$\Rightarrow 10=(\mu-1)\left[\frac{100}{10}-\left(-\frac{100}{10}\right)\right]$$

$$\Rightarrow 10=(\mu-1)[20] \Rightarrow (\mu-1)=\frac{1}{2}$$

$$\Rightarrow \mu=\frac{3}{2}$$

61 (a) The size of the object in accordance with the Fresnel's displacement law is given by $\sqrt{x_1 x_2}$.

62 (d) The focal length of the plano-convex lens is 20 cm with the plane surface being silvered.
So, the net power of the lens is given by $P = \frac{1}{f} \times 2 = \frac{2}{f}$
Thus, the net focal length is

$$\frac{f}{2} = \frac{20}{2} = 10 \text{ cm}$$

63 (c) When the lens is in air, we have

$$P_a = \frac{1}{f_a} = \frac{\mu_g - \mu_a}{\mu_a}\left[\frac{1}{R_1} - \frac{1}{R_2}\right]$$

When the lens is in liquid, we have

$$P_l = \frac{1}{f_l} = \frac{\mu_g - \mu_l}{\mu_l}\left[\frac{1}{R_1} - \frac{1}{R_2}\right]$$

Given, $P_a = 5, P_l = -1$
and $\mu_a = 1, \mu_g = 1.5$
On solving, we get $\mu_l = \frac{5}{3}$.

64 (c) If refractive index of lens n_1 is equal to refractive index of liquid n_2, then lens behaves as a plane glass plate and becomes invisible in the medium.

65 (d) Here, angle of prism, $A = 60°$
For minimum deviation, $A = 2r$
or $r = \frac{A}{2} = \frac{60°}{2} = 30°$ for both colours.

66 (a) For a given prism, the angle of deviation depends upon the angle of incidence of the light rays falling on the prism. Taking triangle FQR, we have, $d = \angle FQR + \angle FRQ$

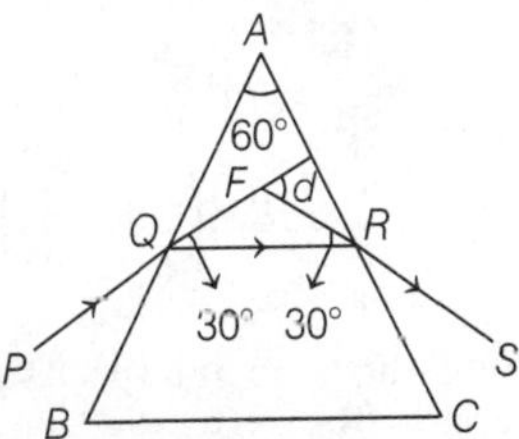

Since, ΔAQR is an equilateral triangle, therefore

$$\angle FQR = \frac{60°}{2} = 30° = \angle FRQ$$

$\Rightarrow \quad d = 30° + 30° = 60°$

Hence, angle of deviation of the ray is 60°.

67 (a) Focal length in air is given by

$$\frac{1}{f_a} = ({}_a\mu_g - 1)\left(\frac{1}{R_1} - \frac{1}{R_2}\right)$$

The focal length of lens immersed in water is given by

$$\frac{1}{f_l} = ({}_l\mu_g - 1)\left(\frac{1}{R_1} - \frac{1}{R_2}\right)$$

where, R_1 & R_2 are radii of curvatures of the two surfaces of lens and ${}_l\mu_g$ is refractive index of glass with respect to liquid.

Also, ${}_l\mu_g = \frac{{}_a\mu_g}{{}_a\mu_l}$

Given,
${}_a\mu_g = 1.5$, $f_a = 12$ cm and ${}_a\mu_l = \frac{4}{3}$

$$\therefore \quad \frac{f_l}{f_a} = \frac{({}_a\mu_g - 1)}{({}_l\mu_g - 1)}$$

$$\Rightarrow \quad \frac{f_l}{12} = \frac{(1.5-1)}{\left(\frac{1.5}{4/3} - 1\right)} = \frac{0.5 \times 4}{0.5}$$

$$\Rightarrow \quad f_l = 4 \times 12 = 48 \text{ cm}$$

68 (d) $F_{comb} = \frac{f_1 f_2}{f_1 + f_2} = \frac{f(-f)}{f + (-f)} = \infty$

69 (c) For $i > i_C$, as all rays incident at 45° on face AC.
So, $\sin 45° > \sin i_C$

$$\Rightarrow \sin 45° > \frac{1}{\mu} \Rightarrow \frac{1}{\sqrt{2}} > \frac{1}{\mu} \Rightarrow \mu > \sqrt{2}$$

or $\quad \mu > 1.41$

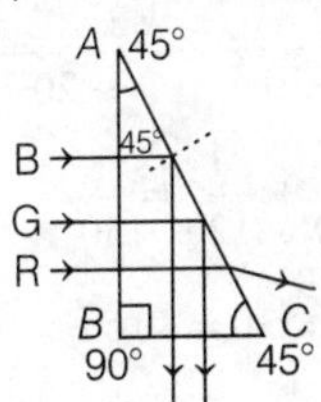

The deviation for red in comparison to other colour is less, whereas deviation for green and blue are nearly same so, prism will separate part of red colour from green and blue colours.

70 (a) Bi-convex lens is cut perpendicularly to the principal axis, it will become a plano-convex lens.
Focal length of bi-convex lens,

$$\frac{1}{f} = (n-1)\left(\frac{1}{R_1} - \frac{1}{R_2}\right)$$

$$\Rightarrow \quad \frac{1}{f} = (n-1)\frac{2}{R}$$

$(\because R_1 = R \text{ and } R_2 = -R)$

$$\Rightarrow \quad f = \frac{R}{2(n-1)} \quad \text{...(i)}$$

For plano-convex lens,

$$\frac{1}{f_1} = (n-1)\left(\frac{1}{R} - \frac{1}{\infty}\right)$$

$$f_1 = \frac{R}{(n-1)} \quad \text{...(ii)}$$

On comparing Eqs. (i) and (ii),we see the focal length become doubled.

As power of lens, $P \propto \frac{1}{\text{Focal length}}$.

Hence, power will become half.

New power $= \frac{4}{2} = 2$ D

71 (d) The equivalent combination will act as a mirror

Now, $\frac{1}{v} + \frac{1}{u} = \frac{1}{f_{equivalent}}$

$$\Rightarrow \quad \frac{1}{f_{equivalent}} = \left(\frac{1}{-f}\right) + \left(\frac{1}{-f}\right)$$

$$\Rightarrow \quad f_{equivalent} = -\frac{f}{2} = -\frac{20}{2} = -10 \text{ cm}$$

So, combination will act as concave mirror of focal length 10 cm.

72 (c) In reactants displacement experiment size of object is given by $h_0 = \sqrt{I_1 \times I_2}$.

73 (a) Angle of the prism, $A = \frac{\phi}{2}$

Now, $\phi = \frac{\phi_1 + \phi_2}{2}$

where, $\phi_1 = x_2 - x_1$
$= (360° + 80°38') - (320° 40')$
$= 119° 58'$
and $\phi_2 = y_2 - y_1$
$= 260° 24' - 140° 30' = 119° 54'$

$$\phi = \frac{119° 58' + 119° 54'}{2} = \frac{239° 52'}{2}$$

$$A = \frac{\phi}{2} = \frac{239° 52'}{4} = 59° 58'$$

74 (a) $\because \quad \mu = \frac{\sin\left(\frac{A + \delta_m}{2}\right)}{\sin\left(\frac{A}{2}\right)}$

Here, $\quad \mu = \sqrt{2}, A = 60°$

$$\text{So,} \quad \sqrt{2} = \frac{\sin\left(\frac{60° + \delta_m}{2}\right)}{\sin\left(\frac{60°}{2}\right)}$$

$$\Rightarrow \sqrt{2} \times \frac{1}{2} = \sin\left(\frac{60° + \delta_m}{2}\right)$$

$$\Rightarrow \quad \frac{1}{\sqrt{2}} = \sin\left(\frac{60° + \delta_m}{2}\right)$$

$$\Rightarrow \sin 45° = \sin\left(\frac{60° + \delta_m}{2}\right)$$

$$\Rightarrow 45° = 30° + \frac{\delta_m}{2} \Rightarrow \delta_m = 30°$$

$$i = \frac{A+\delta_m}{2} = \frac{60+30}{2} = 45°$$

75 *(a)* $_an_w = \frac{4}{3}$ and $_wn_g = \left(\frac{10}{8}\right)$

$$\therefore {}_an_g = {}_an_w \times {}_wn_g = \frac{4}{3} \times \frac{10}{8} = \left(\frac{5}{3}\right)$$

76 *(c)* The refractive index of liquid must be equal to that of glass, so glycerine is appropriate choice from given option.

77 *(d)* Given, $u = mf$

$$\therefore \frac{1}{v} - \frac{1}{(-mf)} = -\frac{1}{f}$$

$$\Rightarrow \frac{1}{v} = -\frac{1}{f}\left(1+\frac{1}{m}\right)$$

$$\Rightarrow -v = \frac{mf}{m+1} \Rightarrow -\frac{v}{u} = \frac{1}{1+m}$$

Thus, linear magnification

$$= \frac{v}{u} = \frac{-1}{m+1}$$

78 *(b)* $\because$ Refractive index,

$$\mu = \frac{\sin\left(\frac{A+\delta_m}{2}\right)}{\sin A/2}$$

Here, $A = \delta_m = 60^o$

So, $$\mu = \frac{\sin\left(\frac{A+A}{2}\right)}{\left(\sin\frac{A}{2}\right)} = \frac{\sin 60°}{\sin 30°}$$

$$\Rightarrow \mu = \sqrt{3}$$

79 *(d)* If two thin lenses of focal lengths f_1, f_2 are placed in contact co-axially, then equivalent focal length of combination (here, $d = 0$)

$$\frac{1}{F} = \frac{1}{f_1} + \frac{1}{f_2} - \frac{0}{f_1 f_2} = \frac{1}{f_1} + \frac{1}{f_2}$$

Power for the combination,

$$P = \frac{1}{F} = \frac{1}{f_1} + \frac{1}{f_2} = \frac{f_1 + f_2}{f_1 f_2}$$

80 *(a)* $$\frac{1}{f_a} = (\mu - 1)\left(\frac{1}{R_1} - \frac{1}{R_2}\right)$$

$$= (1.5 - 1)\left(\frac{1}{R_1} - \frac{1}{R_2}\right) \quad \ldots\text{(i)}$$

and $$\frac{1}{f_m} = \left(\frac{\mu_g - \mu_m}{\mu_m}\right)\left(\frac{1}{R_1} - \frac{1}{R_2}\right)$$

$$\frac{1}{f_m} = \left(\frac{1.5}{1.6} - 1\right)\left(\frac{1}{R_1} - \frac{1}{R_2}\right) \quad \ldots\text{(ii)}$$

Thus, $$\frac{f_m}{f_a} = \frac{(1.5 - 1)}{\left(\frac{1.5}{1.6} - 1\right)} = -8$$

$$\Rightarrow f_m = -8 \times f_a$$

$$= -8 \times \frac{-1}{5}\left[\because f_a = \frac{1}{P} = -\frac{1}{5}\text{ m}\right]$$

$$= 1.6\text{ m}$$

$$\therefore P_m = \frac{\mu}{f_m} = \frac{1.6}{1.6} = 1\text{ D}$$

81 *(d)* If a mirror is placed in a medium other than air, its focal length does not change as $f = \frac{R}{2}$. But for the lens

$$\frac{1}{f_a} = ({}_an_g - 1)\left(\frac{1}{R_1} - \frac{1}{R_2}\right)$$

and $$\frac{1}{f_w} = ({}_wn_g - 1)\left(\frac{1}{R_1} - \frac{1}{R_2}\right)$$

As $_wn_g < {}_an_g$, hence focal length of lens in water increase.

The refractive index of water is $\frac{4}{3}$ and that of air is 1.

Hence, $\mu_w > \mu_a$.

82 *(b)* $$\frac{_a\mu_w}{f} = \frac{({}_a\mu_g - 1)}{R_1} - \frac{({}_a\mu_g - {}_a\mu_w)}{R_2}$$

$$= \frac{\left(\frac{3}{2} - 1\right)}{20} - \frac{\left(\frac{3}{2} - \frac{4}{3}\right)}{-20}$$

$$= \frac{1}{40} + \frac{1}{120} = \frac{1}{30}$$

$$\therefore f = \frac{4}{3} \times 30 = 40\text{ cm}$$

83 *(b)* $$\frac{1}{f} = (\mu - 1)\left(\frac{1}{R_1} - \frac{1}{R_2}\right)$$

For given concave lens,

$R_1 = -3$ cm, $R_2 = -4$ cm

and $u = -12$ cm

$$\therefore \frac{1}{v} - \frac{1}{u} = (\mu - 1)\left(\frac{1}{-3} + \frac{1}{4}\right)$$

or $$\frac{1}{v} - \frac{1}{(-12)} = (1.5 - 1)\left(\frac{-4+3}{12}\right)$$

or $$\frac{1}{v} + \frac{1}{12} = 0.5 \times \frac{-1}{12} = \frac{-1}{24}$$

or $$\frac{1}{v} = -\frac{1}{24} - \frac{1}{12} = \frac{-1-2}{24} = -\frac{1}{8}$$

or $v = -8$ cm

84 *(c)* Angle of incidence,

$$i = \frac{A + \delta_m}{2} = \frac{40° + 60°}{2} = 50°$$

85 *(a)* $$\frac{1}{F} = \frac{1}{f_1} + \frac{1}{f_2} - \frac{d}{f_1 f_2}$$

When the lenses are put together, then $d = 0$, i.e. the focal length of the combination will decrease.

86 *(a)* A lens made of three different materials as shown have only one focal length. Thus, for a given object there is only one image.

87 *(d)* Since, lens is cut into two equal parts by a plane parallel to its principal axis, so both the part still to be biconvex.

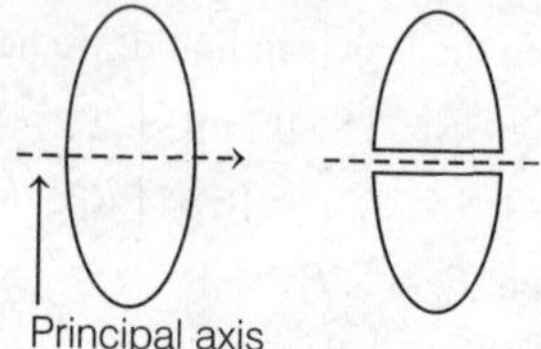

Hence, focal length of each part will remain as before, i.e. 10 cm.
Focal length of bi-convex lens,

$$\frac{1}{f} = (\mu - 1)\left(\frac{1}{R_1} - \frac{1}{R_2}\right)$$

where R_1 and R_2 be the radii of curvature of two surfaces.
Hence, focal length depends on radii of curvature of lens.

88 *(d)* By lens maker's formula,

$$\frac{1}{f} = (\mu_g - 1)\left(\frac{1}{R_1} - \frac{1}{R_2}\right) \quad \ldots\text{(i)}$$

When convex lens is dipped in a liquid of refractive index (μ_l), then its focal length,

$$\frac{1}{f_l} = \left(\frac{u_g}{\mu_l} - 1\right)\left(\frac{1}{R_1} - \frac{1}{R_2}\right)$$

or $$\frac{1}{f_l} = \frac{(\mu_g - \mu_l)}{\mu_l}\left(\frac{1}{R_1} - \frac{1}{R_2}\right) \quad \ldots\text{(ii)}$$

Dividing Eq. (i) by Eq. (ii), we get

$$\frac{f_l}{f} = \frac{(\mu_g - 1)\,\mu_l}{(\mu_g - \mu_l)} \quad \ldots\text{(iii)}$$

But it is given that refractive index of lens is equal to refractive index of liquid, i.e. $\mu_g = \mu_l$.

Hence, Eq. (iii) gives,

$$\frac{f_l}{f} = \frac{(\mu_g - 1)\,\mu_l}{0} = \infty \text{ (infinity).}$$

89 (c) The focal length of equi-convex lens,

$$\frac{1}{f}=(\mu-1)\left(\frac{1}{R_1}-\frac{1}{R_2}\right) \quad \ldots(i)$$

$$\frac{1}{f}=(\mu-1)\left(\frac{1}{R}-\frac{1}{-R}\right)=\frac{2(\mu-1)}{R}$$

***Case* I** When lens is cut along XOX', then each half is again equi-convex with

$$R_1=+R,\ R_2=-R$$

$$\therefore \quad \frac{1}{f}=(\mu-1)\left[\frac{1}{R}-\frac{1}{(-R)}\right]$$

$$\Rightarrow \quad =(\mu-1)\left[\frac{1}{R}+\frac{1}{R}\right]$$

$$=(\mu-1)\frac{2}{R}=\frac{1}{f'} \Rightarrow f'=f$$

***Case* II** When lens is cut along YOY', then each half becomes plano-convex with

$$R_1=+R,\ R_2=\infty$$

$$\therefore \quad \frac{1}{f''}=(\mu-1)\left(\frac{1}{R_1}-\frac{1}{R_2}\right)$$

$$=(\mu-1)\left(\frac{1}{R}-\frac{1}{\infty}\right)$$

$$\Rightarrow \quad =\frac{(\mu-1)}{R}=\frac{1}{2f}$$

Hence, $f''=2f$.

90 (a) Air bubble contains air whose refractive index is less than its surrounding medium, (i.e. water), so it will behave as concave lens.

91 (a) By lens formula,

$$\frac{1}{f}=\frac{1}{v}-\frac{1}{u} \quad \left(\text{given, } u=-\frac{f}{2}\right)$$

$$\Rightarrow \quad \frac{1}{f}=\frac{1}{v}+\left(\frac{1}{f/2}\right) \Rightarrow \frac{1}{v}=\frac{1}{f}-\frac{2}{f}$$

$$\Rightarrow \quad \frac{1}{v}=-\frac{1}{f} \text{ and } m=\frac{v}{u}=\frac{f}{f/2}=2$$

So, the image will be virtual at the focus and of double size.

92 (b) Refractive index, $\mu=\dfrac{1}{\sin C}$

where, C is the critical angle.

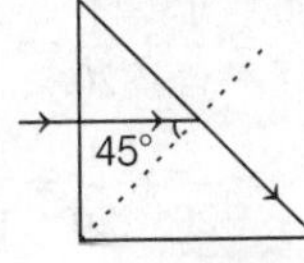

Here, $C=45°$ (as shown)

$$\therefore \quad \mu=\frac{1}{\sin 45°}$$

or $\quad \mu=\sqrt{2}$ or $\mu=1.414$

93 (a) $$\frac{1}{F}=\frac{1}{f_1}+\frac{1}{f_2}-\frac{d}{f_1f_2}$$

$$=\frac{1}{0.2}+\frac{1}{0.2}-\frac{0.5}{(0.2)(0.2)}=-2.5$$

$$F=-\frac{1}{2.5}=-0.4 \text{ m}$$

94 (c) Dispersive power, $\omega=\dfrac{\delta_B-\delta_R}{\delta}$

For 1st prism

$$\omega_1=\frac{\delta_B-\delta_R}{\delta}=\frac{12°-8°}{10°}=\frac{2}{5}$$

where, $\quad \delta=\dfrac{\delta_B+\delta_R}{2}$

Similarly, for 2nd prism

$$\omega_2=\frac{14°-10°}{12°}=\frac{1}{3}$$

$$\Rightarrow \quad \frac{\omega_1}{\omega_2}=\frac{2}{5}\times\frac{3}{1}=\frac{6}{5}$$

95 (a) Lens formula is given by

$$\frac{1}{f}=\frac{1}{v}-\frac{1}{u} \quad \ldots(i)$$

Given, $f=10$ cm (as lens is converging)
$u=-8$ cm (as object is placed on left side of the lens)

Substituting these values in Eq. (i), we get

$$\frac{1}{10}=\frac{1}{v}-\frac{1}{-8} \Rightarrow \frac{1}{v}=\frac{1}{10}-\frac{1}{8}$$

$$\Rightarrow \quad \frac{1}{v}=\frac{8-10}{80} \Rightarrow v=\frac{80}{-2}=-40 \text{ cm}$$

Hence, magnification produced by the lens,

$$m=\frac{v}{u}=\frac{-40}{-8}=5$$

96 (b) If an object reflects the colour of light incident on it, it will appear with that colour but if object absorbs the colour of light, it will appear to be black.

Since, the given wavelength does not belong to green, so it will be absorbed by the leaf and hence, it would appear to be black.

97 (a) Since, lens is made of two layers of different refractive indices, for a given wavelength of light it will have two focal lengths or will form two images at two different points.

98 (b) According to figure, the point on the right side of the lens of which rays converge will behave as virtual object at the lens.

$$\therefore \quad u=+12 \text{ cm},\ f=20 \text{ cm}$$

By lens formula, $\dfrac{1}{f}=\dfrac{1}{v}-\dfrac{1}{u}$

$$\therefore \quad \frac{1}{20}=\frac{1}{v}-\frac{1}{12}$$

or $$\frac{1}{v}=\frac{1}{20}+\frac{1}{12}=\frac{3+5}{60}=\frac{8}{60}$$

or $$v=\frac{60}{8}=7.5 \text{ cm}$$

So, image will be formed on same side of the virtual object at a distance of 7.5 cm from the lens.

99 (b) Let a large convex lens is placed between two walls at a distance x from wall on which an electric bulb is fixed.

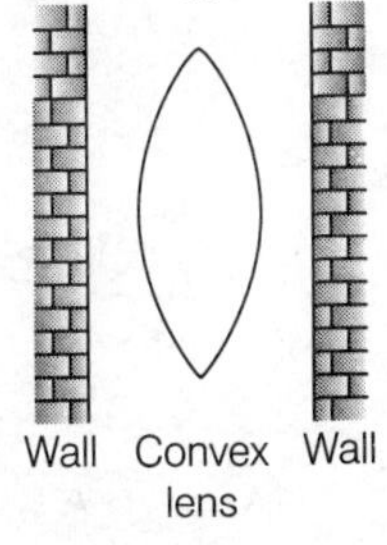

Using lens formula,

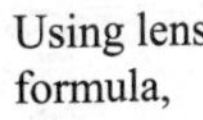

$$\frac{1}{f}=\frac{1}{v}-\frac{1}{u}$$

Putting $u=x$ and $v=4-x$

$$\therefore \quad \frac{1}{f}=\frac{1}{4-x}-\frac{1}{-x}$$

or $$\frac{1}{f}=\frac{x+4-x}{(4-x)(x)} \text{ or } \frac{1}{f}=\frac{4}{(4-x)(x)}$$

or $$f=\frac{(4-x)x}{4} \quad \ldots(i)$$

Now, magnification,

$$m=\frac{v}{u}=\frac{4-x}{x} \text{ or } 1=\frac{4-x}{x}$$

or $x=4-x$ or $2x=4$ or $x=2$m

From Eq. (i), we get

$$f=\frac{(4-2)(2)}{4}=\frac{2\times 2}{4}=1\text{m}$$

100 (b) Correct order of wavelength is orange > yellow > green > violet

101 (a) From lens formula, $\dfrac{1}{f}=\dfrac{1}{v}-\dfrac{1}{u}$

Given, $v=\dfrac{u}{2}$ and $f=20$ cm

$$\Rightarrow \quad \frac{1}{20}=\frac{1}{u/2}-\frac{1}{u}=\frac{1}{u}$$

$$\Rightarrow \quad u=20 \text{ cm}$$

102 (d) For minimum deviation position the refracted ray passes parallel to the base of the prism. Hence, BC is horizontal.

103 (b) Using the formula,

$$_{\text{prism}}\mu_{\text{liquid}} = \frac{\mu_{\text{liquid}}}{\mu_{\text{prism}}} = \frac{1.32}{1.56} = \frac{11}{13} \quad \ldots(i)$$

Now, the condition for the total internal reflection occurs when

$$\sin\theta \geq \mu, \text{ so } \sin\theta \geq \frac{11}{13}.$$

104 (d) The system is equivalent to combination of three lenses in contact, i.e.

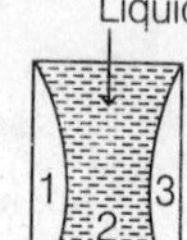

$$\frac{1}{F} = \frac{1}{f_1} + \frac{1}{f_2} + \frac{1}{f_3}$$

By lens Maker's formula

$$\frac{1}{f_1} = (1.5-1)\left(\frac{1}{-\infty} - \frac{1}{-12}\right)$$

$$= 0.5 \times \frac{1}{12} = \frac{1}{24}$$

$$\frac{1}{f_2} = (\mu - 1)\left(\frac{1}{-12} - \frac{1}{12}\right) = -\frac{(\mu-1)}{6}$$

$$\frac{1}{f_3} = (1.5-1)\left(\frac{1}{12} - \frac{1}{\infty}\right) = \frac{1}{24}$$

Also, $F = -60$ cm

$$\therefore \quad \frac{1}{-60} = \frac{1}{24} - \frac{(\mu-1)}{6} + \frac{1}{24}$$

$$= -\frac{(\mu-1)}{6} + \frac{1}{12}$$

or $\quad \dfrac{(\mu-1)}{6} = \dfrac{1}{12} + \dfrac{1}{60}$

or $\quad \dfrac{(\mu-1)}{6} = \dfrac{5+1}{60} = \dfrac{6}{60}$

or $\quad (\mu - 1) = \dfrac{36}{60} = 0.6$

or $\quad \mu = 0.6 + 1 = 1.6$

105 (d) The refractive index (μ) of a prism of angle A and minimum deviation δ_m is given by

$$\mu = \frac{\sin\left(\frac{A+\delta_m}{2}\right)}{\sin A/2}$$

Given, $\mu = \cot\dfrac{A}{2}$

$$\therefore \quad \cot\frac{A}{2} = \frac{\sin\frac{(A+\delta_m)}{2}}{\sin(A/2)}$$

$$\Rightarrow \quad \frac{\cos A/2}{\sin A/2} = \frac{\sin\frac{(A+\delta_m)}{2}}{\sin(A/2)}$$

$$\Rightarrow \quad \cos\frac{A}{2} = \sin\left(\frac{A+\delta_m}{2}\right)$$

$$\therefore \quad \sin\left(90° - \frac{A}{2}\right) = \sin\left(\frac{A+\delta_m}{2}\right)$$

$$\Rightarrow \quad 90° - \frac{A}{2} = \frac{A+\delta_m}{2}$$

$$\Rightarrow \quad 180° - A = A + \delta_m$$

$$\Rightarrow \quad \delta_m = 180° - 2A = \pi - 2A$$

106 (d) The various rays from the object, after refraction through different parts of the lens, will still converge at the same point, only their number will be less, when half of the lens is covered with an opaque object. Hence, still the full image of the object is obtained but its intensity will be less.

107 (b) The focal length of a convex lens of refractive index μ_g in air,

$$\frac{1}{f_{\text{air}}} = (\mu_g - 1)\left(\frac{1}{R_1} - \frac{1}{R_2}\right) \quad \ldots(i)$$

where R_1 and R_2 are the radius of curvatures of its first and second surface. When lens immersed in a liquid of refractive index μ_l, then refractive index of material of lens (glass) with respect to liquid is

$$_l\mu_g = \frac{\mu_g}{\mu_l} \quad \ldots(ii)$$

$\therefore$ Focal length of lens in liquid

$$\frac{1}{f'} = ({_l\mu_g} - 1)\left(\frac{1}{R_1} - \frac{1}{R_2}\right) \quad \ldots(iii)$$

Dividing Eq. (i) by Eq. (iii), we get

$$\frac{f'}{f_{\text{air}}} = \frac{\mu_g - 1}{({_l\mu_g} - 1)} = \frac{\mu_g - 1}{\left(\frac{\mu_g}{\mu_l} - 1\right)}$$

$$\frac{f'}{f_{\text{air}}} = \frac{-0.5}{0.2} = \frac{1.5-1}{\left(\frac{1.5}{\mu_l} - 1\right)} = \frac{0.5}{\left(\frac{1.5}{\mu_l} - 1\right)}$$

$$\frac{1.5}{\mu_l} - 1 = -0.2$$

$$\Rightarrow \quad \frac{1.5}{\mu_l} = 1 - 0.2 = 0.8 \quad \text{or} \quad \mu_l = \frac{15}{8}$$

$\therefore$ Refractive index of liquid $= \dfrac{15}{8}$

108 (c) In a double convex lens, the speed of violet light is minimum while that of red light is maximum. So, the refractive index (n) of glass is maximum for violet light and minimum for red light ($n_V > n_R$).

Hence, according to the formula, $\dfrac{1}{f} = (n-1)\left(\dfrac{1}{R_1} - \dfrac{1}{R_2}\right)$ the focal length f_V of the lens for violet light is least and the focal length f_R for the red light is largest i.e. $f_R > f_V$.

109 (b) The given prism is a right angled prism and angle $\angle LMN = 45°$. Since, the ray is suffering total internal reflection and the critical angle is the angle of incidence in the denser medium for which the angle of refraction in the rarer medium is 90°, i.e. $C = 45°$ and

$$\mu = \frac{1}{\sin C} = \frac{1}{\sin 45°} = \sqrt{2}.$$

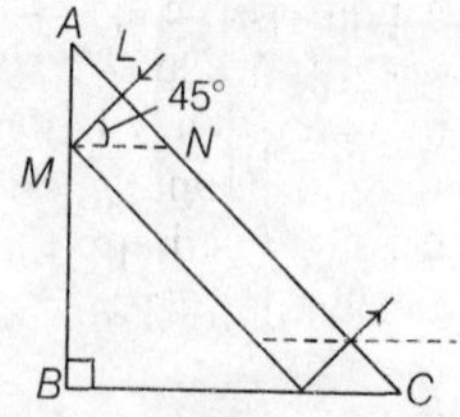

110 (b) Angular dispersion,

$$\delta_b - \delta_r = (\mu_b - \mu_r)A$$

$$\Rightarrow \quad = (1.659 - 1.641)5° = 0.09°$$

111 (c) Let as shown 1 and 2 are positions of objects and images in two different situations.

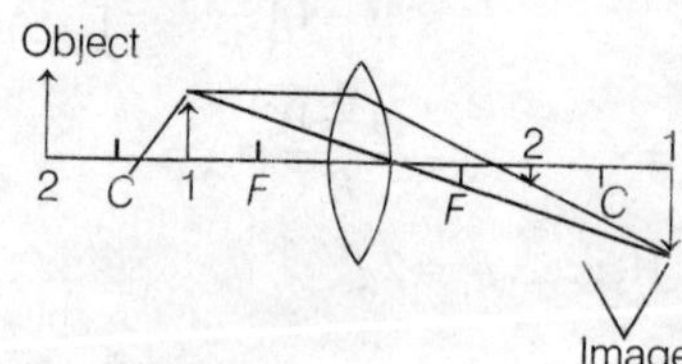

It is given, $\left|\dfrac{v_1}{u_1}\right| = 2\left|\dfrac{v_2}{u_2}\right|$

Here, $u_1 = -15$ cm

and $u_2 = -20$ cm

$$\therefore \quad v_1 = 2v_2 \times \frac{u_1}{u_2}$$

$$= 2v_2 \times \frac{15}{20} = \frac{3}{2}v_2$$

Now, $\dfrac{1}{f} = \dfrac{1}{v} - \dfrac{1}{u}$

$$\Rightarrow \quad \frac{1}{f} = \frac{1}{v_1} - \frac{1}{u_1}$$

and $\quad \dfrac{1}{f} = \dfrac{1}{v_2} - \dfrac{1}{u_2}$

So, $\quad \dfrac{1}{v_1} - \dfrac{1}{u_1} = \dfrac{1}{v_2} - \dfrac{1}{u_2}$

$$\Rightarrow \quad \frac{2}{3v_2} + \frac{1}{15} = \frac{1}{v_2} + \frac{1}{20} \Rightarrow v_2 = 20 \text{ cm}$$

$$\frac{1}{f} = \frac{1}{v_2} - \frac{1}{u_2} = \frac{1}{20} + \frac{1}{20} = \frac{1}{10}$$

$$\Rightarrow \quad f = 10 \text{ cm} = 0.10 \text{ m}$$

Topic 5

Scattering of Light

2019

1 Pick the incorrect statement in the context with rainbow.

(a) The order of colours is reversed in the secondary rainbow. [NEET]

(b) An observer can see a rainbow when his front is towards the sun.

(c) Rainbow is a combined effect of dispersion refraction and reflection of sunlight.

(d) When the light rays undergo two internal reflections in a water drop, a secondary rainbow is formed.

2010

2 When sunlight is scattered by minute particles of atmosphere, the intensity of light scattered away is proportional to [CG PMT]

(a) $(\text{wavelength of light})^4$ (b) $(\text{frequency of light})^4$

(c) $(\text{wavelength of light})^2$ (d) $(\text{frequency of light})^2$

2009

3 When sunlight is scattered by atmospheric atoms and molecules, the amount of scattering of light of wavelength 440 nm is A. The amount of scattering for the light of wavelength 660 nm is approximately [Kerala CEE]

(a) $\frac{4}{9}A$ (b) $2.25A$ (c) $1.5A$ (d) $0.66A$

(e) $\frac{A}{6}$

4 What will be the colour of the sky as seen from the earth, if there were no atmosphere? [BCECE]

(a) Black (b) Blue (c) Orange (d) Red

2008

5 The coming rays are forming rainbows [BHU]

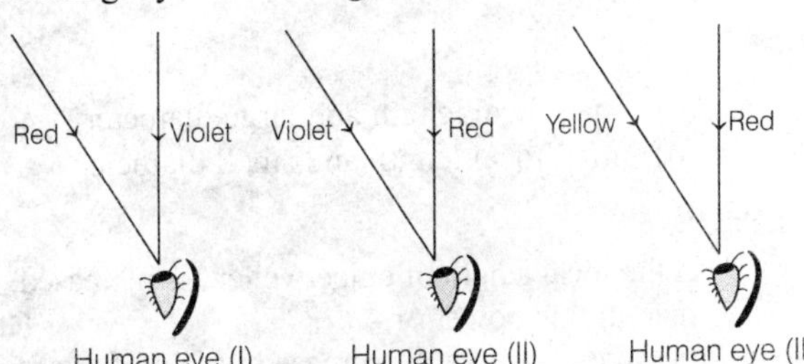

(a) Fig. (I) forms primary rainbow

(b) Fig. (I) and (III) form primary rainbow

(c) Fig. (II) forms secondary rainbow

(d) Fig. (I) forms secondary rainbow

6 Blue colour of sea water is due to [KCET]

(a) interference of sunlight reflected from the water surface

(b) scattering of sunlight by the water molecules

(c) image of sky in water

(d) refraction of sun light

2007

7 Red colour is used for danger signals, because [J&K CET]

(a) it causes fear

(b) it undergoes least scattering

(c) it undergoes maximum scattering

(d) it is in accordance with international convention

2006

8 Pick the correct statement from the following. [J&K CET]

(a) Primary rainbow is a virtual image and secondary rainbow is a real image .

(b) Primary rainbow is a real image and secondary rainbow is a virtual image .

(c) Both primary and secondary rainbows are virtual images.

(d) Both primary and secondary rainbows are real images.

2005

9 **Assertion** By roughening the surface of a glass sheet, its transparency can be reduced.

Reason Glass sheet with rough surface absorbs more light. [AIIMS]

(a) Both Assertion and Reason are correct and Reason is the correct explanation of Assertion.

(b) Both Assertion and Reason are correct but Reason is not the correct explanation of Assertion.

(c) Assertion is correct but Reason is incorrect.

(d) Both Assertion and Reason are incorrect.

10 **Assertion** The clouds in sky generally appear to be whitish.

Reason Diffraction due to clouds is efficient in equal measure at all wavelengths. [AIIMS]

(a) Both Assertion and Reason are correct and Reason is the correct explanation of Assertion.

(b) Both Assertion and Reason are correct but Reason is not the correct explanation of Assertion.

(c) Assertion is correct but Reason is incorrect.

(d) Both Assertion and Reason are incorrect.

Answers

1 (b)	2 (b)	3 (e)	4 (a)	5 (d)	6 (b)	7 (b)	8 (c)	9 (c)	10 (c)

Explanations

1 *(b)* The necessary conditions for the rainbow to take place are as follows

(*i*) Sun should be shining in part of the sky while it is raining in opposite part of the sky.

(*ii*) The observer must stand with his back towards the sun.

$\therefore$ Statement in option (b) is incorrect. However, rest statements regarding the rainbow are correct.

2 *(b)* Molecules of a medium after absorbing incoming light radiations, emit them in all directions. This phenomenon is called scattering. According to scientist Rayleigh, the intensity of scattered light $\propto \frac{1}{\lambda^4} \propto \nu^4$.

3 *(e)* By Rayleigh's law of scattering,

$$I \propto \frac{1}{\lambda^4} \quad \text{or} \quad \frac{I_2}{I_1} = \left(\frac{\lambda_1}{\lambda_2}\right)^4$$

or $$\frac{I_2}{A} = \left(\frac{440}{660}\right)^4$$

or $$I_2 \simeq \frac{A}{6}$$

4 *(a)* As there is no atmosphere, so no scattering of colours of white light occurs, hence the sky will appear black.

5 *(d)* In primary rainbow, red is on the top and violet is below, while in secondary rainbow violet is on top and red is below. So, Fig (I) forms secondary rainbow and Fig. (II) forms primary rainbow.

6 *(b)* Blue colour of sea water is due to scattering of sunlight by water molecules.

7 *(b)* Red light is used in danger signals, so that the danger signals can be seen distinctly upto large distances. The light used in the danger signals should not get scattered much, while passing through the atmosphere. Since, the red colour is scattered through a small amount due to its longer wavelength, the danger signals make use of red light.

8 *(c)* The rainbow is seen as a virtual image in the form of a coloured arc centered on the anti-solar point that is the point below the horizon, directly opposite the sun in the sky.

When conditions are favourable two rainbows are seen, the brighter one is the primary and a fainter one with reversed colours. Hence, both primary and secondary rainbows are virtual images.

9 *(c)* When glass surface is made rough, then light incident on it is scattered in different directions. Due to which, its transparency decreases.

There is no effect of roughness on absorption of light.

10 *(c)* The clouds consist of dust particles and water droplets. The scattering of sunlight by the big dust particles and water drops is not in accordance with the Rayleigh law. But they scatter the light of all the colours by the same amount, i.e. they are not efficient in diffraction by equal measures at all wavelength. Hence, the clouds are seen generally white. Hence, option (c) is correct.

Topic 6

Human Eye and Optical Instruments

2019

1 If focal length of objective and eye lenses are 10 cm and 10 mm respectively and tube length is 11 cm, then angular magnification of telescope is **[AIIMS]**

(a) 10 (b) 5 (c) 100 (d) 50

2018

2 An astronomical refracting telescope will have large angular magnification and high angular resolution when it has an objective lens of **[NEET]**

(a) large focal length and large diameter
(b) large focal length and small diameter
(c) small focal length and large diameter
(d) small focal length and small diameter

2014

3 If the focal length of objective lens is increased, then magnifying power of **[CBSE AIPMT]**

(a) microscope will increase but that of telescope decrease
(b) microscope and telescope both will increase
(c) microscope and telescope both will decrease
(d) microscope will decrease but that of telescope will increase

4 Astigmatism is corrected using [Kerela CEE]
(a) cylindrical lens (b) plano-convex lens
(c) plano-concave lens (d) convex lens
(e) concave lens

5 The intermediate image formed by the objective of a compound microscope is [WB JEE]
(a) real, inverted and magnified
(b) real, erect and magnified
(c) virtual, erect and magnified
(d) virtual, inverted and magnified

6 An astronomical telescope arranged for normal adjustment has a magnification of 6. If the length of the telescope is 35 cm, then the focal lengths of objective and eye-piece, respectively are [EAMCET]
(a) 30 cm, 5 cm (b) 5 cm, 30 cm
(c) 40 cm, 5 cm (d) 30 cm, 6 cm

7 A microscope is having objective of focal length 1 cm eye-piece of focal length 6 cm. If tube length is 30 cm and image is formed at the least distance of distinct vision, what is the magnification produced by the microscope? (Take, $D = 25$ cm) [KCET]
(a) 6 (b) 150 (c) 25 (d) 125

8 Diameter of the objective of a telescope is 200 cm. What is the resolving power of a telescope? (Take, wavelength of light = 5000Å) [KCET]
(a) 6.56×10^6 (b) 3.28×10^5
(c) 1×10^6 (d) 3.28×10^6

2013

9 For a normal eye, the cornea of eye provides a converging power of 40 D and the least converging power of the eye lens behind the cornea is 20 D. Using this information, the distance between the retina and cornea-eye lens can be estimated to be [NEET]
(a) 5 cm (b) 2.5 cm (c) 1.67 cm (d) 1.5 cm

10 A least distance of distinct vision is 25 cm. The focal length of a convex lens is 5 cm. It can act as a simple microscope of magnifying power. [UP CPMT]
(a) 4 (b) 5
(c) 6 (d) None of these

11 For a telescope, larger the diameter of the objective lens [KCET, Manipal]
(a) greater is the resolving power
(b) smaller is the resolving power
(c) greater is the magnifying power
(d) smaller is the magnifying power

2012

12 The magnifying power of a telescope is 9. When it is adjusted for parallel rays, the distance between the objective and eyepiece is 20 cm. The focal length of lenses are [CBSE AIPMT]
(a) 10 cm, 10 cm (b) 15 cm, 5 cm
(c) 18 cm, 2 cm (d) 11 cm, 9 cm

2011

13 If the focal length of the eyepiece of a telescope is doubled, its magnifying power (m) will be [WB JEE]
(a) $2m$ (b) $3m$
(c) $\frac{m}{2}$ (d) $4m$

14 A microscope is focussed on an ink mark on the top of a table. If we place a glass slab of 3 cm thick on it, how should the microscope be moved to focus the ink spot again? The refractive index of glass is 1.5. [J&K CET]
(a) 2 cm upwards (b) 2 cm downwards
(c) 1 cm upwards (d) 1 cm downwards

2010

15 If f_o and f_e are the focal lengths of the objective and eyepiece, respectively of a telescope, then its magnifying power will be [UP CPMT]
(a) $f_o + f_e$ (b) $f_o \times f_e$
(c) f_o / f_e (d) $\frac{1}{2}(f_o + f_e)$

16 If the aperture of a telescope is decreases, then resolving power will be [MHT CET]
(a) increases (b) decreases
(c) remain same (d) zero

17 Angular resolving power of human eye is [MP PMT]
(a) 3.4×10^3 (b) 3.6×10^2
(c) 3.6×10^4 (d) 3.6×10^6

18 A telescope using light having wavelength 5000 Å and using lenses of focal lengths 2.5 cm and 30 cm. If the diameter of the aperture of the objective is 10 cm, then the resolving limit of telescope is [Haryana PMT]
(a) 6.1×10^{-6} rad (b) 5.0×10^{-6} rad
(c) 8.3×10^{-4} rad (d) 7.3×10^{-3} rad

19 Mark the correct one. [Punjab PMET]
(a) Our eyes can distinguish between real and virtual image.
(b) Virtual image can also be taken on screen.
(c) If the incident rays are converging at a point, then the object is real.
(d) None of the above.

20 If the red light is replaced by blue light illuminating the object in a microscope, the resolving power of the microscope [Punjab PMET]
(a) decreases (b) increases
(c) gets halved (d) remains unchanged

21 The magnification produced by an astronomical telescope for normal adjustment is 10 and the length of the telescope is 1.1 m. The magnification, when the image is formed at least distance of distinct vision is [EAMCET]
(a) 6 (b) 14
(c) 16 (d) 18

22 An astronomical telescope in normal adjustment receives light from a distance source S. The tube length is now decreased slightly, then [BCECE]

(a) no image will be formed
(b) a virtual image of S will be formed at a finite distance
(c) a large, real image of S will be formed behind the eyepiece, far away from it
(d) a small, real image of S will be formed behind the eyepiece closes to it

23 An astronomical telescope has an angular magnification of magnitude 5 for distant objects. The separation between the objective and the eye-piece is 36 cm and the final image is formed at infinity. The focal length f_o of the objective and the focal length f_e of eye-piece are [JCECE]

(a) $f_o = 45$ cm and $f_e = -9$ cm
(b) $f_o = -7.2$ cm and $f_e = 5$ cm
(c) $f_o = 50$ cm and $f_e = 10$ cm
(d) $f_o = 30$ cm and $f_e = 6$ cm

24 The nearer point of hypermetropia eye is 40 cm. The lens to be used for its correction should have the power [CG PMT]

(a) + 1.5 D (b) – 1.5 D
(c) + 2.5 D (d) + 0.5 D

2009

25 An eye specialist prescribes spectacles having a combination of a convex lens of focal length 40 cm in contact with a concave lens of focal length 25 cm. The power of this lens combination will be [AFMC]

(a) + 1.5 D (b) – 1.5 D
(c) + 6.67 D (d) – 6.67 D

26 The magnifying power of telescope is high, if [AFMC]

(a) both objective and eyepiece have short focal length
(b) both objective and eyepiece have large focal length
(c) the objective has a large focal length and the eyepiece has a short focal length
(d) the objective has a short focal length and the eyepiece has a large focal length.

27 A telescope has an objective of focal length 50 cm and an eyepiece of focal length 5 cm. The least distance of distinct vision is 25. The telescope is focussed for distinct vision on a scale 200 cm away. The separation between the objective and the eyepiece is [Manipal]

(a) 75 cm (b) 60 cm
(c) 71 cm (d) 74 cm

28 An electron microscope is superior to an optical microscope in [Haryana PMT, CG PMT]

(a) having high resolving power
(b) being easy to handle
(c) low cost
(d) quickness of observation

29 If the telescope is reversed, i.e. seen from the objective lens, then [AFMC]

(a) object will appear very small
(b) object will appear very large
(c) there will be no effect on image
(d) image will be slightly greater than the earlier one

30 In a laboratory four convex lenses L_1, L_2, L_3 and L_4 of focal lengths 2, 4, 6 and 8 cm, respectively are available. Two of these lenses form a telescope of length 10 cm and magnifying power is 4. The objective and eye lenses are respectively [JIPMER]

(a) L_2, L_3 (b) L_1, L_4 (c) L_1, L_2 (d) L_4, L_1

2008

31 An observer looks at a tree of height 15 m with a telescope of magnifying power 10. To him the tree appears [Manipal]

(a) 10 times taller (b) 15 times taller
(c) 10 times nearer (d) 15 times nearer

32 The resolution limit of the eye is 1 min. At a distance x km from the eye, two persons stand with a lateral separation of 3 m. For the two persons to be just resolved by the naked eye, x should be [Manipal]

(a) 10 km (b) 15 km (c) 20 km (d) 30 km

33 In Ramsden eyepiece, the focal length of each lens is F. The distance of the image formed by the objective lens from the eye lens is [Punjab PMET]

(a) $\frac{14F}{15}$ (b) $\frac{13F}{14}$ (c) $\frac{12F}{13}$ (d) $\frac{11F}{12}$

34 In Ramsden eyepiece, the two plano-convex lenses each of focal length f are separated by a distance 12 cm. The equivalent focal length (in cm) of the eyepiece is [Punjab PMET]

(a) 10.5 (b) 12.0
(c) 13.5 (d) 15.5

35 In Huygens' eyepiece, [Punjab PMET]

(a) the cross wires are outside the eyepiece
(b) condition for achromatism is satisfied
(c) condition for minimum spherical aberration is not satisfied
(d) the image formed by the objective is a virtual image

2007

36 Identify the wrong description of the below figures. [AIIMS]

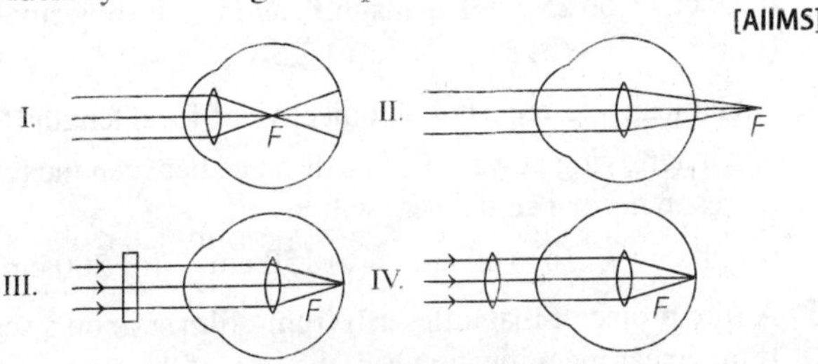

(a) I represents far-sightedness
(b) II correction for short-sightedness
(c) III represents far-sightedness
(d) IV correction for far-sightedness

37 Diameter of human eye lens is 2 mm. What will be the minimum distance between two points to resolve them, which are situated at a distance of 50 m from eye ? The wavelength of light is 5000Å. [AFMC]
(a) 2.32 m (b) 4.28 mm
(c) 1.25 cm (d) 12.48 cm

38 A telescope has an objective lens of 10 cm diameter and is situated at a distance of one kilometre from two objects. The minimum distance between these two objects, which can be resolved by the telescope, when the mean wavelength of light is 5000 Å, of the order of [Manipal]
(a) 0.5 m (b) 5 m
(c) 5 mm (d) 5 cm

39 How should people wearing spectacles work with a microscope? [MP PMT]
(a) They should keep on wearing their spectacles
(b) They should take off their spectacles
(c) They may keep on wearing or take off their spectacles, it makes no difference
(d) They cannot use a microscope at all

40 A simple telescope consisting of an objective of focal length 60 cm and a single eye lens of focal length 5 cm is focussed on a distant object in such a way that parallel rays comes out from the eye lens. If the object subtends an angle 2° at the objective, the angular width of the image [Punjab PMET]
(a) 10° (b) 24° (c) 50° (d) $\frac{1}{6}^\circ$

41 The head lights of a jeep are 1.2 m apart. If the pupil of the eye of an observer has a diameter of 2 mm and light of wavelength 5896 Å is used, what should be the maximum distance of the jeep from the observer if the two head lights are just separated ? [KCET]
(a) 33.9 km (b) 33.9 m (c) 3.34 km (d) 3.39 m

42 The limit of resolution of an optical instrument arises on account of [Guj CET]
(a) reflection (b) diffraction
(c) polarisation (d) interference

2006

43 A telescope has focal length of objective and eyepiece as 200 cm and 5 cm, respectively. What is magnification of telescope? [AFMC]
(a) 40 (b) 80 (c) 50 (d) 0.01

44 A person who can see things most clearly at a distance of 10 cm, requires spectacles to enable to see clearly things at a distance of 30 cm. What should be the focal length of the spectacles? [Manipal]
(a) 15 cm (concave) (b) 15 cm (convex)
(c) 10 cm (d) zero

45 The magnifying power of objective of a compound microscope is 5. If the magnifying power of microscope is 30, then magnifying power of eyepiece will be [Kerala CEE]
(a) 0.17 (b) 6 (c) 3 (d) 25
(e) 35

46 Ability of the eye to see objects at all distance is called [Punjab PMET]
(a) binocular vision (b) myopia
(c) hypermetropia (d) accommodation

47 A person sees clearly at a distance of 100 cm, then power of lens used to see object at 40 cm is [JCECE]
(a) 3 D (b) −3 D (c) − 1.5 D (d) + 1.5 D

48 The power of a lens, a short sighted person uses is − 2 D. Find the maximum distance of an object which he can see without spectacles. [JCECE]
(a) 25 cm (b) 50 cm
(c) 100 cm (d) 10 cm

2005

49 The angular resolution of a 10 cm diameter telescope at a wavelength of 5000 Å is of the order of [CBSE AIPMT]
(a) 10^6 rad (b) 10^{-2} rad
(c) 10^{-4} rad (d) 10^{-6} rad

50 A telescope has an objective lens of focal length 200 cm and an eyepiece with focal length 2 cm. If this telescope is used to see a 50 m tall building at a distance of 2 km, what is the height of the image of the building formed by the objective lens? [AIIMS]
(a) 5 cm (b) 10 cm (c) 1 cm (d) 2 cm

51 **Assertion** The resolving power of a telescope is more, if the diameter of the objective lens is more.

Reason Objective lens of large diameter collects more light. [AIIMS]
(a) Both Assertion and Reason are correct and Reason is the correct explanation of Assertion.
(b) Both Assertion and Reason are correct but Reason is not the correct explanation of Assertion.
(c) Assertion is correct but Reason is incorrect.
(d) Both Assertion and Reason are incorrect.

52 Large aperture telescopes are used for **[Haryana PMT]**
(a) greater resolution
(b) greater magnification
(c) reducing lens aberration
(d) ease of manufacturer

53 In a reflecting astronomical telescope, if the objective (a spherical mirror) is replaced by a parabolic mirror of the same focal length and aperture, then **[Punjab PMET]**
(a) the telescope will gather more light
(b) spherical aberration will be absent
(c) the larger image will be obtained
(d) the final image will be erect

54 Magnification of a compound microscope is 30. Focal length of eyepiece is 5 cm and the image is formed at a distance of distinct vision 25 cm. The magnification of the objective lens is
(a) 6 (b) 5 (c) 7.5 (d) 10 **[DUMET]**

55 A Galilean telescope has an objective of focal length 100 cm and magnifying power 50. The distance between the two lenses in normal adjustment will be **[BCECE]**
(a) 98 cm (b) 100 cm (c) 150 cm (d) 200 cm

56 A film projector magnifies a 100 cm^2 film strip on a screen. If the linear magnification is 4, the area of the magnified film on the screen is **[BCECE]**
(a) 1600 cm^2 (b) 400 cm^2 (c) 800 cm^2 (d) 200 cm^2

Answers

1 (a)	2 (a)	3 (d)	4 (a)	5 (a)	6 (a)	7 (b)	8 (d)	9 (c)	10 (c)
11 (a)	12 (c)	13 (c)	14 (c)	15 (c)	16 (b)	17 (a)	18 (a)	19 (a)	20 (b)
21 (b)	22 (b)	23 (d)	24 (c)	25 (b)	26 (c)	27 (c)	28 (a)	29 (a)	30 (d)
31 (c)	32 (a)	33 (d)	34 (c)	35 (b)	36 (a)	37 (c)	38 (c)	39 (b)	40 (b)
41 (c)	42 (b)	43 (a)	44 (a)	45 (b)	46 (d)	47 (d)	48 (b)	49 (d)	50 (a)
51 (a)	52 (a)	53 (b)	54 (b)	55 (a)	56 (a)				

Explanations

1 (a) Given, focal length of objective lens,

$$f_o = 10 \text{ cm}$$

Focal length of eye lens,

$$f_e = 10 \text{ mm} = 1 \text{ cm}$$

Total length $= f_o + f_e = 10 + 1$ cm $= 11$

This is the case when the final image is formed at infinity, therefore

Angular magnification,

$$|m| = \left|\frac{f_o}{f_e}\right| = \frac{10}{1} = 10$$

2 (a) Angular magnification of an astronomical refracting telescope is given as

$$M = \frac{f_o}{f_e}$$

where, f_o and f_e are the focal length of objective and eyepiece, respectively.

From the given relation, it is clear that for large magnification either f_o has to be large or f_e has to be small.

Angular resolution of an astronomical refracting telescope is given as

$$R = \frac{a}{1.22\lambda}$$

where, a is the diameter of the objective.

Thus, to have large resolution, the diameter of the objective should be large.

Hence, from the above, objective lens should have large focal length (f_o) and large diameter (a).

3 (d) For microscope,

$$m = \frac{L}{f_o}\frac{D}{f_e}$$

$$\Rightarrow \quad m \propto \frac{1}{f_o}$$

For telescope, $m = \dfrac{f_o}{f_e}$, $m \propto f_o$

The magnifying power of microscope will decrease but the magnifying power of telescope will increase.

4 (a) In this defect, eye cannot see horizontal and vertical lines clearly, simultaneously. It is due to imperfect spherical nature of eye lens.

This defect can be removed by using cylindrical lenses (Torric lenses).

5 (a) The intermediate image formed by the objective of a compound microscope is real, inverted and magnified.

6 (a) In normal adjustment, the object and the final image are both at infinity and the separation between the objective and the eyepiece is $f_o + f_e$.

Thus,

$$f_o + f_e = 35 \text{ cm} \quad \text{...(i)}$$

Also, the magnifying power of the telescope in normal adjustment is

$$m = -\frac{f_o}{f_e} = -6 \text{ (given)}$$

$$f_o = 6f_e \quad \text{...(ii)}$$

Solving Eqs. (i) and (ii), we get

$$f_o = 30 \text{ cm and } f_e = 5 \text{ cm}$$

7 (b) By compound microscope,

$$m = \frac{L}{f_o}\left(1 + \frac{D}{f_e}\right)$$

(where length of tube $L = 30$ cm, focal length of objective lens $f_o = 1$ cm, focal length of eye-piece $f_e = 6$ cm and $D = 25$ cm)

$$m = \frac{30}{1}\left(1 + \frac{25}{6}\right)$$

$$= 30 \times \frac{(6 + 25)}{6}$$

$$= 5 \times 31 = 155 \cong 150$$

8 (*d*) Given, wavelength of light,
$\lambda = 5000\,Å = 5000 \times 10^{-10} = 5\times10^{-7}$ m
Diameter of telescope, $D = 200$ cm $= 2$ m
Resolving power of a telescope

$$= \frac{1}{d\theta} = \frac{D}{1.22\lambda}$$

where, $d\theta$ = limit of resolution
λ = wavelength of light used
and D = diameter of aperture of objective.

$$\text{So, } \left(\frac{1}{d\theta}\right) \text{RP} = \frac{2}{1.22 \times 5 \times 10^{-7}}$$
$$= \frac{2\times10^7}{6.1} = \frac{20\times10^6}{6.1}$$
$$= 3.278\times10^6 = 3.28\times10^6$$

9 (*c*) Given, $P_1 = 40$ D and $P_2 = 20$ D
We have, $P_{\text{eff}} = 40\text{ D} + 20\text{ D} = 60\text{ D}$

$$\Rightarrow \quad f = \frac{100}{P_{\text{eff}}} = \frac{100}{60} = 1.67 \text{ cm}$$

10 (*c*) Magnifying power, $m = 1 + \frac{D}{f}$
Given, $D = 25$ cm, $f = 5$ cm

$$\therefore \quad m = 1 + \frac{25}{5} \Rightarrow m = 1 + 5 = 6$$

11 (*a*) The resolving power of a telescope is its ability to show two distant closely lying objects as just separate. The reciprocal of resolving power is the limit of resolution of the telescope.

Limit of resolution $= 1.22 \frac{\lambda}{d}$ rad,

where λ is wavelength and d the aperture (diameter). Hence, to reduce the limit of resolution of a telescope, we must use objective lens of large aperture (d).

Larger the aperture of the objective lens, smaller the limit of resolution or greater the resolving power of the telescope.

12 (*c*) Given, $M = \frac{f_o}{f_e} = 9$ and

$$f_o + f_e = 20$$
$$f_o = 9f_e$$
$$\text{So,} \quad 9f_e + f_e = 20$$
$$\Rightarrow \quad f_e = 2 \text{ cm}$$
$$\therefore \quad f_o = 9 \times 2 = 18 \text{ cm}$$

13 (*c*) We know that, the magnifying power (m) is given by $m = -\frac{f_o}{f_e}$.

Now, if the focal length of the eyepiece (f_e) is doubled, then the new magnification would be equal to

$$m' = -\frac{f_o}{2f_e} = \frac{m}{2}.$$

14 (*c*) Given, $n = 1.5$, $h_o = 3$ cm

Refractive index, $n = \frac{h_o}{h_i}$

$$\Rightarrow \quad 1.5 = \frac{3}{h_i}$$
$$\Rightarrow \quad h_i = \frac{3}{1.5} = 2 \text{ cm}$$

Hence, microscope is moved
$3 - 2 = 1$ cm upwards

15 (*c*) Magnification of a telescope is given by $m = \frac{f_o}{f_e}$, where f_o is the focal length of the objective lens and f_e is the focal length of eyepiece.

16 (*b*) The resolving power $= \frac{a}{1.22\,\lambda}$

where, a = aperture of telescope.
$\therefore$ Resolving power $\propto$ Aperture of telescope

If aperture is decreased, then resolving power will decrease.

17 (*a*) The minimum angular separation between two objects, so they are just resolved is called resolving limit. For eye it is $1 = \left[\frac{1}{60}\right]^\circ$. Reciprocal of resolving limit is called Resolving Power (RP)

$$= \frac{1}{\left(\frac{1}{60}\right)^\circ} = \frac{1}{\frac{1}{60} \times \frac{\pi}{180}}$$
$$= \frac{10800}{\pi} = 3.436\times10^3 \text{ rad}$$

18 (*a*) Given, $\lambda = 5000Å = 5000\times10^{10}$ m and $a = 10$ cm $= 0.1$ m.
Resolving limit

$$= \frac{1.22\lambda}{a} = \frac{1.22\times(5000\times10^{-10})}{0.1}$$
$$= 6.1\times10^{-6} \text{ rad}$$

19 (*a*) Only real image can be taken on screen. Object is real only when incident rays are diverging from it. Our eyes can distinguish between real and virtual image.

20 (*b*) Resolving power $= \frac{2\mu \sin\theta}{1.22\lambda}$

Since, $\lambda_R > \lambda_B$, hence resolving power increases.

21 (*b*) Magnification, $\frac{f_o}{f_e} = 10$

or $\quad f_o = 10\,f_e$
Given, $\quad f_e + f_o = 1.1$ m
$\Rightarrow \quad f_e + 10\,f_e = 1.1\times100$ cm
$\quad 11f_e = 110 \Rightarrow f_e = 10$ cm

Magnification at least distance of distinct vision,

$$m_b = \frac{f_o}{f_e}\left(1 + \frac{f_e}{D}\right)$$
$$= 10\left(1 + \frac{10}{25}\right) = 10\left(\frac{35}{25}\right) = 14$$

22 (*b*) In an astronomical telescope,

$$L = f_o + f_e$$

When tube length is decreased, the image formed by the objective lens will lie between principal focus and optical centre of eye-lens instead of lying at the focus of eye-lens. Therefore, a virtual image will be formed at a finite distance from the eye-lens.

23 (*d*) In this case $|m| = \frac{f_o}{f_e} = 5$ ...(i)

and length of telescope $= f_o + f_e = 36$ ...(ii)

Solving Eqs. (i) and (ii), we get
$f_e = 6$ cm, $f_o = 30$ cm

24 (*c*) Hypermetropia can be removed by using a convex lens.
Focal length of used lens,
$f = +d = +40$ cm
(defected near point)

$$\therefore \text{ Power of lens} = \frac{100}{f\text{ (cm)}} = \frac{100}{40}$$
$$= 2.5 \text{ D}$$

25 (*b*) Power $= \frac{1}{\text{Focal length}}$

Focal length of combination of convex and concave lenses is given by

$$\frac{1}{F} = \frac{1}{f_1} + \frac{1}{f_2}$$

where, f_1 and f_2 be the focal lengths of convex and concave lenses, respectively.

Now, $\frac{1}{F} = \frac{1}{0.4} + \frac{1}{(-0.25)}$

$\Rightarrow \frac{1}{F} = -1.5$

Power, $P = -1.5$ D

26 (c) In telescope for high magnifying power, size of objective lens, i.e.(f_o) should be large whereas size of eyepiece, i.e. (f_e) should be small.

[$\because$ Magnifying power, $|M| = \frac{f_o}{f_e}$ is normal adjustement]

27 (c) Given, $f_o = 50$ cm, $f_e = 5$ cm, $d = 25$ cm, $u_o = 200$ cm, $L = ?$

As, $\frac{1}{v_o} - \frac{1}{u_o} = \frac{1}{f_o}$

$\therefore \frac{1}{v_o} = \frac{1}{f_o} + \frac{1}{u_o}$

$= \frac{1}{50} - \frac{1}{200} = \frac{4-1}{200} = \frac{3}{200}$

$v_o = \frac{200}{3}$ cm

Linear magnification produced by objective lens,

$m_o = \frac{v_o}{u_o} = -\frac{200/3}{200} = -\frac{1}{3}$

Now, $v_e = d = -25$ cm

From $\frac{1}{v_e} - \frac{1}{u_e} = \frac{1}{f_e}$

$\Rightarrow \frac{-1}{u_e} = \frac{1}{f_e} - \frac{1}{v_e}$

$= \frac{1}{5} + \frac{1}{25} = \frac{5+1}{25}$

$u_e = -\frac{25}{6}$ cm

Distance between objective and eye piece

$L = |v_o| + |u_e| = \frac{200}{3} + \frac{25}{6}$

$= \frac{400+25}{6} = \frac{425}{6}$

$= 70.8 \text{ cm} \approx 71 \text{ cm}$

28 (a) Electron microscope has very high resolving power.

29 (a) If the telescope is reversed, i.e. seen from the objective side, then object will appear very small because in this case magnification becomes reciprocal of initial value.

30 (d) Here, length of telescope of $f_o + f_e = 10$ cm and magnitude of magnifying power $= \frac{f_o}{f_e} = 4$.

Both conditions are satisfied, if $f_o = L_4 = 8$ cm and $f_e = L_1 = 2$ cm.

31 (c) The angle subtended at the eye becomes 10 times larger. This happens only when the tree appears 10 times nearer.

32 (a) $\theta = \frac{l}{r}$, $\theta = 1$ min.

So, $\theta = \frac{1}{60°} = \frac{\pi}{180} \times \frac{1}{60}$ rad

and $l = 3$ m

$\therefore x = r = \frac{l}{\theta}$

$\Rightarrow x = \frac{3}{\frac{\pi}{180} \times \frac{1}{60}} = 10$ km

33 (d) The distance of image formed by the objective lens from the eye-lens

$= \frac{2F}{3} + \frac{F}{4} = \frac{8F + 3F}{12} = \frac{11F}{12}$

34 (c) $d = \frac{2f}{3}$

or $f = \frac{3d}{2} = \frac{3 \times 12}{2} = 18$ cm

Equivalent focal length.

$f' = \frac{f_1 f_2}{f_1 + f_2} + \frac{f}{4} = \frac{18 \times 18}{18 + 18} + \frac{18}{4}$

$= 9 + 4.5 = 13.5$ cm

35 (b) In Huygens' eyepiece, a telescope eyepiece consisting of two plano-convex lenses separated by a distance equal to half the sum of their focal lengths. Its chromatic and spherical aberration is also eliminated.

36 (a) Fig. I shows near sightedness, so option (a) is wrong.

37 (c) Angular limit of resolution of eye

$= \frac{\text{Wavelength of light}}{\text{Diameter of eye lens}}$

i.e. $\theta = \frac{\lambda}{d}$ ...(i)

If y is the minimum resolution between two objects at distance D from eye, then

$\theta = \frac{y}{D}$ ...(ii)

From Eqs. (i) and (ii), we have

$\frac{y}{D} = \frac{\lambda}{d}$ or $y = \frac{\lambda D}{d}$ ...(iii)

Given, $\lambda = 5000$ Å $= 5 \times 10^{-7}$ m,

$D = 50$ m

and $d = 2$ mm $= 2 \times 10^{-3}$ m

Substituting in Eq. (iii), we get

$y = \frac{5 \times 10^{-7} \times 50}{2 \times 10^{-3}} = 12.5 \times 10^{-3}$ m

$= 1.25$ cm

38 (c) Resolving limit of telescope,

$\theta \propto \frac{x}{D} = \frac{\lambda}{d}$

$\Rightarrow x = \frac{\lambda D}{d}$

Given, $\lambda = 5000$Å $= 5000 \times 10^{-10}$m,

$D = 1$ km $= 1000$ m and

$d = 10$ cm $= 0.1$ m

$\therefore x = \frac{5000 \times 10^{-10} \times 1000}{0.1}$

$= 5 \times 10^{-3}$ m $= 5$ mm

39 (b) Microscope is an optical instrument used to increase the visual angle of near objects which are too small to be seen by naked eye. So, spectacles should be removed while working with a microscope as image is magnified.

40 (b) Magnification, $m = \frac{f_o}{f_e}$

Also $m = \frac{\text{Angle subtanded by the image}}{\text{Angle subtended by the object}}$

$\therefore \frac{f_o}{f_e} = \frac{\alpha}{\beta}$

$\Rightarrow \alpha = \frac{f_o \times \beta}{f_e} = \frac{60 \times 2}{5}$

$= 24°$

41 (c) Distance of jeep, $x = \frac{D \times d}{1.22 \times \lambda}$

where, D = diameter of lens, = 2 mm

$= 2 \times 10^{-3}$ m

d = separation between sources = 1.2 m

$\lambda = 5896$ Å $= 5896 \times 10^{-10}$ m

$\Rightarrow x = \frac{(2 \times 10^{-3}) \times 1.2}{1.22 \times 5896 \times 10^{-10}}$

$\Rightarrow x = 3.34$ km

42 (b) According to ray optics, the image of a point object formed by an ideal lens is a point only. However, because of the diffraction effects, the image of a single point in the object formed by a circular lens will actually be a bright central circular region surrounded by concentric dark and light rings. The minimum distance between these two rings which can just be seen as separate by the optical instrument is called the limit of resolution.

43 (a) $|M| = \frac{f_o}{f_e}$

where, f_o = focal length of objective = 200 cm

and f_e = focal length of eyepiece = 5 cm.

$\therefore \quad |M| = \frac{200}{5} = 40$

44 (a) Since, the person is not able to see distant objects beyond 10 cm so, he should use concave lens in his spectacles. Concave lens will form the image of object distant 30 cm, at 10 cm it means $u = -30$ cm, $v = -10$ cm

$$\frac{1}{f} = \frac{1}{v} - \frac{1}{u} = \frac{1}{-10} - \frac{1}{-30} = -\frac{2}{30}$$

or $\frac{1}{f} = -\frac{1}{15}$

So, $f = -15$ cm

Minus sign signifies that lens used in concave.

45 (b) Total magnification, $M = M_o \times M_e$

Given, $M = 30$ and $M_o = 5$

$\Rightarrow \quad M_e = \frac{M}{M_o} = \frac{30}{5} = 6$

46 (d) Accommodation is ability of eye to see object at all distance.

47 (d) By lens formula, $\frac{1}{f} = \frac{1}{v} - \frac{1}{u}$

Given, $v = -100$ cm and $u = -40$ cm

$$\therefore \quad \frac{1}{f} = -\frac{1}{100} - \frac{1}{-40}$$

$$\Rightarrow \quad \frac{1}{f} = -\frac{1}{100} + \frac{1}{40}$$

$$\Rightarrow \quad \frac{1}{f} = \frac{-1 + 2.5}{100} = \frac{1.5}{100}$$

Hence, power of lens is

$$P = \frac{100}{f\text{ (cm)}} = 100 \times \frac{1.5}{100} = 1.5 \text{ D}$$

48 (b) Power $(P) = \frac{1}{\text{Focal length (m)}}$

Given, $P = -2$D

$\therefore$ Focal length $= -\frac{1}{2} = -0.5$ m

$\Rightarrow \quad F = -50$ cm

Hence, maximum distance of an object, which he can see without spectacles is 50 cm.

49 (d) Angular resolution $= \frac{1.22\lambda}{d}$

$$= \frac{1.22 \times 5000 \times 10^{-10}}{10 \times 10^{-2}}$$

$$= 6.1 \times 10^{-6} \approx 10^{-6} \text{ rad}$$

50 (a) For objective (convex) lens,

$$\frac{1}{f_o} = \frac{1}{v_o} - \frac{1}{u_o}$$

or $\frac{1}{v_o} = \frac{1}{f_o} + \frac{1}{u_o}$

Here, $f_o = 200$ cm,

$u_o = -2$ km $= -2 \times 10^5$ cm

and $O = 50$ m $= 5 \times 10^3$ cm

$$\therefore \quad \frac{1}{v_o} = \frac{1}{200} + \frac{1}{-200 \times 10^3}$$

$$\Rightarrow \quad = \frac{10^3 - 1}{200 \times 10^3} = \frac{999}{200 \times 10^3}$$

or $v_o = \frac{200 \times 10^3}{999}$ cm

Magnification, $m = \left|\frac{v_o}{u_o}\right| = \frac{I}{O}$

$$\therefore \quad \frac{200 \times 10^3}{999 \times 200 \times 10^3} = \frac{I}{5 \times 10^3}$$

or $I = \frac{5 \times 10^3}{999} \approx 5$ cm

51 (a) Resolving power of telescope $= \frac{a}{1.22\lambda}$

where, a is the diameter of objective lens and λ is the wavelength of light used. It is obvious that on increasing a, more light is collected by objective lens and so the image formed is more bright. Thus, resolving power of telescope increases.

52 (a) A telescope will have small value of angular limit of resolution and hence high resolving power, if objective of large diameter is used.

53 (b) When a spherical objective mirror is replaced by a parabolic mirror, it eliminates the spherical aberration.

54 (b) The image formed in a microscope at least distance of distinct vision ($D = 25$ cm) has magnification, $M = M_o \times M_e$ where M_o is magnification of objective lens and M_e that of eyepiece.

Given, $f_e = 5$ cm, $D = 25$ cm and $M = 30$

Also, $M = M_o\left(1 + \frac{D}{f_e}\right)$

$$\Rightarrow \quad 30 = M_o \times \left(1 + \frac{25}{5}\right)$$

$$\Rightarrow \quad M_o = \frac{30}{6} = 5$$

55 (a) In Galilean telescope, a convergent lens is used as the objective and a divergent lens as the eyepiece. Magnifying power and length of telescope are written as

$$M = \frac{f_o}{u_e}$$

and $L = f_o - u_e$

In normal adjustment, i.e. in relaxed eye state

$$u_e = f_e$$

So, $M_\infty = \frac{f_o}{f_e} = 50$

or $f_e = \frac{f_o}{50} = \frac{100}{50} = 2$ cm

and $L_\infty = f_o - f_e$

$\Rightarrow \quad L_\infty = 100 - 2 = 98$ cm

56 (a) Linear magnification = 4

Areal magnification

= (Linear magnification)^2

$= (4)^2 = 16$

Therefore, area of magnified film on the screen

= areal magnification × area

$= 16 \times 100 = 1600 \text{ cm}^2$

24

Wave Optics

Quick Review

According to wave theory of light, light is a form of energy which travels in the form of transverse waves. Wave theory introduced the concept of wavefront.

Wavefront

- It is the locus of all those points (wavelets or particles) which are vibrating in the same **phase condition**. The shape of the wavefront depends on a nature and dimension of source of light.
- Types of wavefront are classified according to the table given below

	Source of Light	Shape of Wavefronts	Figure	Amplitude (A)	Intensity (I)
(*i*)	Point source (rays are radial emerging from centre).	Spherical and ecentric with point source at their centre.	1 2 3 4 r Direction of propagation	$A \propto \frac{1}{r}$	$I \propto \frac{1}{r^2}$
(*ii*)	Linear and all points are equidistant from the source.	Cylindrical and co-axial with the source as their common axis.	1 2 3 r	$A \propto \frac{1}{\sqrt{r}}$	$I \propto \frac{1}{r}$
(*iii*)	Very far off source (emitting parallel rays).	Plane	Light rays Plane wavefronts	$A \propto r^0$	$I \propto r^0$

Huygens' Principle

According to Huygens' principle,

(i) Each point on the given wavefront (called primary wavefront) is the source of a secondary disturbance (called secondary wavelets) and the wavelets emanating from these points spread out in all directions with the speed of the wave.

(ii) A surface touching these secondary wavelets, tangentially in the forward direction at any instant gives the shape of a new wavefront at that instant. This is called secondary wavefront.

On the basis of the above principle, many optical phenomena like interference, diffraction as well as refraction can be explained.

This principle could not explain electromagnetic nature of light.

Coherent and Incoherent Sources of light

(i) The sources of light which is continuously emitting light waves of same frequency with a zero or constant phase difference are called **coherent sources**.

(ii) The sources of light which do not maintain constant phase difference are called **incoherent sources**.

Principle of Superposition of Waves

According to superposition principle, at a particular point in the medium, the resultant displacement y produced by a number of waves is the vector sum of the displacements produced by each of the waves ($y_1, y_2, \ldots$).

i.e. $$y = y_1 + y_2 + y_3 + y_4 + \ldots$$

Interference of Light

- Superimposition of two light waves of same frequency (or same wavelength) emitted by two coherent sources, travelling in a given direction is called interference.
- The intensity of resultant wave does not remain uniform, at some points, intensity is maximum, while at some points, intensity is minimum.
- Amplitude and intensity of interference of two waves are expressed as

$$A_R = \sqrt{a_1^2 + a_2^2 + 2a_1 a_2 \cos\phi} \text{ and}$$

$$I_R = I_1 + I_2 + 2\sqrt{I_1 I_2} \cos\phi$$

where a_1, a_2 = amplitude of two light waves, ϕ = phase difference between them and I_1, I_2 = intensities of two light waves.

The resultant intensity is just the sum of intensities, i.e.

$$I = I_1 + I_2 + I_3 + \ldots$$

- According to phase difference in superimposing waves, interference is divided into two categories in the given table

Types of Interference	Phase Difference	Intensities
(i) Constructive (when two waves meet in same phase)	$\phi = 2n\pi$, for $\cos\phi$ = maximum $\phi = 0, 2\pi, 4\pi \ldots$	$I_{max} = (\sqrt{I_1} + \sqrt{I_2})^2$
(ii) Destructive (when two waves meet in opposite phase)	$\phi = (2n-1)\pi$, for $\cos\phi$ = minimum $= -1$ $\phi = \pi, 3\pi, 5\pi, \ldots$	$I_{min} = (\sqrt{I_1} - \sqrt{I_2})^2$

- Comparison of intensities of maxima and minima

$$\frac{I_{max}}{I_{min}} = \frac{I_1 + I_2 + 2\sqrt{I_1 I_2}}{I_1 + I_2 - 2\sqrt{I_1 I_2}} = \left(\frac{\sqrt{I_1} + \sqrt{I_2}}{\sqrt{I_1} - \sqrt{I_2}}\right)^2 = \left(\frac{a_1 + a_2}{a_1 - a_2}\right)^2$$

$$\therefore \quad \frac{I_{max}}{I_{min}} = \left(\frac{r+1}{r-1}\right)^2$$

where, $r = \frac{a_1}{a_2}$ = amplitude ratio.

- For two interfering waves, if ϕ_0 is the originating phase difference and Δ be the path difference between them, then total phase difference between them is given by,

$$\phi = (\phi_0 + 2\pi/\lambda)\Delta$$

Young's Double Slit Experiment

The experimental arrangement is shown in figure below. In this experiment, the monochromatic light is used. The following terms are expressed below

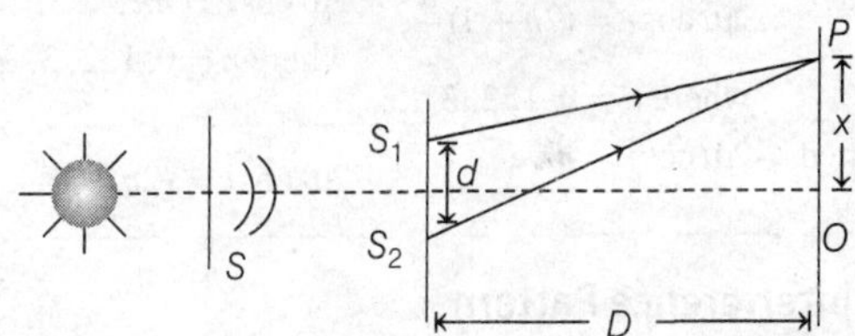

- For light waves reaching at a point P, situated at a distance x from central point O, the path difference (Δ) is given by

$$\Delta = S_2P - S_1P = \frac{xd}{D}$$

- If $\frac{xd}{D} = n\lambda$, then we get nth **bright fringe**, where $n = 1, 2, 3, 4 \ldots$
- If $\frac{xd}{D} = (2n-1)\frac{\lambda}{2}$, then we get nth **dark fringe**, where $n = 1, 2, 3, 4 \ldots$
- **Fringe Width** (β) The separation between any two consecutive bright or dark fringes is called fringe width (β) and it is given by

$$\beta = \frac{D\lambda}{d}$$

- **Angular Fringe Width** (θ) Its width is expressed as
$$\theta = \frac{\beta}{D} = \frac{\lambda}{d}$$
- The maximum and minimum intensity of the fringes are expressed as follows
$$I = I_{max} \cos^2 \frac{\phi}{2} \text{ and } I_{min} = 0$$
- The fringe width in a medium of refractive index (μ), when whole apparatus of Young's double slit experiment is immersed, will be expressed as $\beta_m = \frac{D\lambda}{\mu d}$.
- Distribution of intensity in Young's double slit experiment is shown graphically below

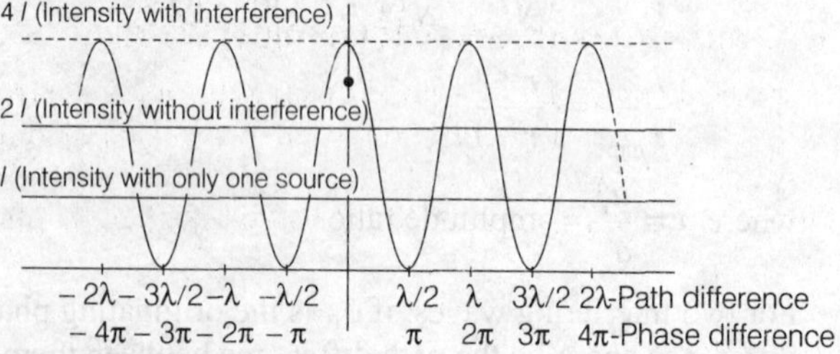

Interference in Thin Films

A thin film (soap or oil film) spread over water produce bright or dark fringes due to interference between from upper and lower surface which are shown in table given below

Interference	Bright Fringe	Dark Fringe
Reflected light	$2\mu t \cos r = (2n+1)\frac{\lambda}{2}$, where $n = 0, 1, 2, 3, \ldots$	$2\mu t \cos r = n\lambda$, where $n = 0, 1, 2, 3, \ldots$
Transmitted light	$2\mu t \cos r = n\lambda$	$2\mu t \cos r = (2n+1)\frac{\lambda}{2}$

Shift in Interference Pattern

When a thin transparent sheet of thickness t and refractive index μ is inserted in one of the interfering beams, then following terms can be calculated

(*i*) Additional path difference due to sheet = $(\mu - 1)t$

(*ii*) Fringe shift = $\frac{D}{d}(\mu - 1)t = \frac{\beta}{\lambda}(\mu - 1)t$

(*iii*) If due to presence of thin film, the fringe pattern shifts by n fringes, then
$$n = \frac{(\mu - 1)t}{\lambda} \Rightarrow t = \frac{n\lambda}{(\mu - 1)}$$

P
S_1 t y
S_2 O
D

Doppler's Effect of Light

- The apparent change in frequency or wavelength of light due to relative motion between the source of light and observer is called doppler's effect.
- Depending on the relative motion between source of light and stationary observer, the following terms obtained can be shown in tabular form below

Relative Position	Apparent Frequency	Apparent Wavelength	Fractional Change in Frequencies/ Wavelength	Doppler's Shift
Source moving towards observer	$\nu' = \nu\left(1 + \frac{v}{c}\right)$	$\lambda' = \lambda\left(1 - \frac{v}{c}\right)$	$\frac{\Delta\lambda}{\lambda} = \frac{\Delta\nu}{\nu} = \frac{v}{c}$	Violet shift (Apparent wavelength < Actual wavelength)
Source moving away from the observer	$\nu' = \nu\left(1 - \frac{v}{c}\right)$	$\lambda' = \lambda\left(1 + \frac{v}{c}\right)$	$-\frac{\Delta\lambda}{\lambda} = \frac{\Delta\nu}{\nu} = \frac{v}{c}$	Red shift (Apparent wavelength < Actual wavelength)

where, ν = actual frequency, ν' = apparent frequency, v = speed of source w.r.t. stationary observer and c = speed of light.

Diffraction of Light

- The phenomena of bending of light around the corners of an obstacle/aperture of the size of the wavelength is called diffraction of light.
- In the figure given alongside, diffraction pattern due to single slit is shown.

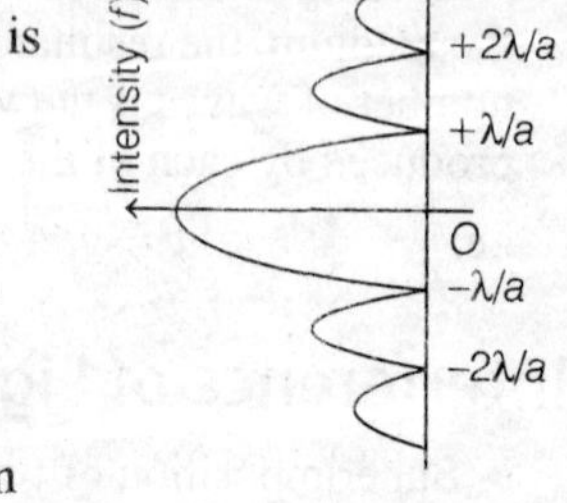

For a central bright fringe (central maxima) surrounded by dark and bright lines (secondary minima and maxima).

In the given figure of diffraction fringe pattern, intensity is maximum at point O.

- Width of the central maxima, $2y = \frac{2D\lambda}{a}$
- Angular width, $2\theta = \frac{2\lambda}{a}$.
- Angular position and distance of nth secondary minima and maxima from central maxima are shown in tabular form below

Pattern of Fringe	Path Difference	Angular Position	Distance from Central Maxima
Secondary maxima	$a \sin\theta = \frac{(2n+1)\lambda}{2}$	$\sin\theta \approx \theta \approx \frac{(2n+1)\lambda}{2a}$	$y_n = \frac{(2n+1)\lambda f}{2a}$
Secondary minima	$a \sin\theta = \pm n\lambda$, where $n = 1, 2, 3, \ldots$	$\sin\theta \approx \theta \approx \frac{n\lambda}{a}$	$y_n = D \cdot \theta = \frac{n\lambda f}{a}$

- The angular width of central maxima is double as compared to the angular width of secondary diffraction maxima.

Fresnel's Distance (z_F)

The distance travelled by a beam of width (x) before spreading out due to diffraction is known as Fresnel's distance. It is expressed as $z_F = \frac{d^2}{\lambda}$

where, d = size of slit or hole.

- Spreading due to diffraction is prominent for distances much greater than z_F.
- Image formation can be explained in ray optics for distances much lesser than z_F, i.e. $d >>> \lambda$.

Diffraction Grating

- It consists of large number of equally spaced parallel slits, used for measuring wavelengths accurately.
- Resolving power of the diffraction grating is expressed as

$$R = \frac{\lambda}{\lambda_2 - \lambda_1} = \frac{\lambda}{\Delta\lambda}$$

where, λ_1, λ_2 = two nearly equal wavelength ($\Delta\lambda = \lambda_2 - \lambda_1$).

Resolving Power of Optical Instruments

- It is the ability of optical instruments to observe the separate images of two close objects.
- **Resolving Power of Microscope** $R = \frac{1}{\Delta d} = \frac{2\mu \sin\theta}{\lambda}$,

  where μ = refractive index of medium between object and objective

  and θ = angle subtended by a radius of objective lens on one of the objects.
- **Resolving Power of Telescope**

$$R = \frac{1}{\Delta\theta} = \frac{D}{1.22\lambda},$$

where D = aperture diameter of objective.

Polarisation of Light

- The phenomena of limiting the vibration of electric vector in one direction in a plane perpendicular to the direction of propagation of light wave is called polarisation of light.
- The plane perpendicular to the plane of oscillation is called **plane of polarisation**.
- Thin film of ultramicroscopic crystals used to produce the plane polarised light is known as **polaroids**.
- The crystal or polaroid on which unpolarised light is incident is called **polariser**.
- Crystal or polaroid on which polarised light in incident is called **analyser**.

Malus's Law

According to Malus's law, the intensity of emergent light out of analyser varies as $I \propto \cos^2\theta$ or $I = I_0 \cos^2\theta$, where θ is the angle between the planes of transmission of polariser and analyser.

Figure given below explains Malus law

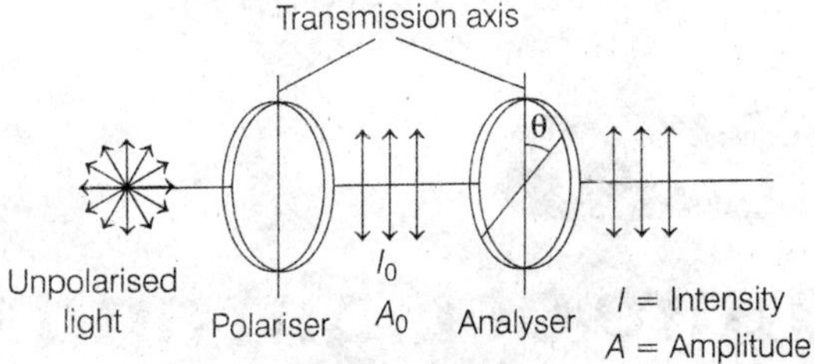

Polarisation of Transverse Mechanical Waves

If a transverse mechanical wave is passed through a narrow slit, so that the plane of vibration of the wave is parallel to the slit, then the wave passes through the slit with its vibrations being unaffected and the wave is said to be **plane polarised.**

Polarisation by Reflection

When a beam of unpolarised light is reflected from the surface (unpolished) of a transparent medium of refractive index n at the polarising angle i_p, the reflected light is completely plane polarised, shown in the following figure

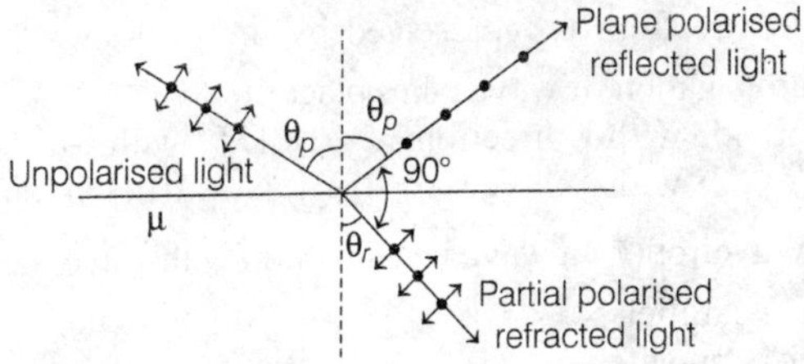

Brewster's Law

According to Brewster's law, a reflected light is completely plane polarised at certain angle of incidence (i_p) when a beam of unpolarised light is reflected from a transparent medium (refractive index = μ). It can be expressed as $\tan i_p = \mu$

- Accordingly, the reflected and transmitted rays are mutually perpendicular,
- Thus, angle of refraction, $r = 90° - i_p$.

Polarisation of Light by Scattering

It is the phenomena of bluish appearance of reflected light in the direction perpendicular to the incident beam.

Topical Practice Questions

All the exam questions of this chapter have been divided into 4 topics as listed below

Topic 1

Nature of Light and Huygens' Principle

2019

1 Huygens' principle does not use [JIPMER]
(a) reflection (b) refraction
(c) diffraction (d) point of spectra origin

2014

2 Wavefront is the locus of all points, where the particles of the medium vibrate with the same [KCET]
(a) phase (b) amplitude
(c) frequency (d) period

2009

3 A wavefront is represented by the plane $y = 3 - x$. The propagation of wave takes place at [MGIMS]
(a) 45° with x-direction (b) 135° with x-direction
(c) 60° with x-direction (d) No sufficient data

4 Wavefront of a wave has direction with wave motion [MGIMS]
(a) parallel (b) perpendicular
(c) opposite (d) at an angle of θ

5 Huygens' principle of secondary wavelets may be used to [Manipal]
(a) find the velocity of light in vacuum
(b) explain the particle's behaviour of light
(c) find the new position of a wavefront
(d) explain photoelectric effect

6 Which one of the following property of light does not support wave theory of light? [DCE]
(a) Light obeys laws of reflection and refraction.
(b) Light waves get polarised.
(c) Light shows photoelectric effect.
(d) Light shows interference.

7 According to Newton's corpuscular theory, the speed of light is [KCET]
(a) same in all the media
(b) lesser in rarer medium
(c) lesser in denser medium
(d) independent of the medium

2008

8 Wave theory cannot explain the phenomena of
I. Polarisation II. Diffraction
III. Compton effect IV. Photoelectric effect
Which of the following is correct? [EAMCET]
(a) I and II (b) II and III
(c) III and IV (d) IV and I

2007

9 Which of the following phenomenon exhibits particle's nature of light? [MHT CET]
(a) Interference
(b) Diffraction
(c) Polarisation
(d) Photoelectric effect

2006

10 Which of the following generates a plane wavefront? [MHT CET]
(a) α-rays (b) β-rays
(c) γ-rays (d) None of these

11 Light waves travel in vacuum along the Y-axis. Which of the following may represent the wavefront? [RPMT]
(a) $y =$ constant
(b) $x =$ constant
(c) $z =$ constant
(d) $x + y + z =$ constant

12 The wavefront due to a source situated at infinity is [Haryana PMT]
(a) spherical (b) cylindrical
(c) planar (d) None of these

2005

13 When a ray of light is incident normally on a surface, then [J&K CET]
(a) the total internal reflection takes place
(b) it passes undeviated
(c) it undergoes dispersion
(d) it gets absorbed by the surface

Answers

1 (d)	2 (a)	3 (b)	4 (b)	5 (c)	6 (c)	7 (b)	8 (c)	9 (d)	10 (d)
11 (a)	12 (c)	13 (b)							

Explanations

1 *(d)* Huygens' principle use the phenomenon of light as reflection, refraction and diffraction but does not use point of spectra origin.

2 *(a)* On the wavefront, all the points are in the same phases.

3 *(b)* Equation of plane is given as

$$y = -x + 3 \quad \text{...(i)}$$

On comparing Eq. (i) with the equation of straight line,

$$y = mx + c \quad \text{...(ii)}$$

Here, $m = -1$

$\Rightarrow \tan\theta = -1$

$\theta = 135^\circ$ with x-direction

4 *(b)* Wavefront of a wave is perpendicular to the direction of motion of wave.

5 *(c)* Every point on a given wavefront act as a secondary source of light and emits secondary wavelets which travels in all directions with the speed of light in the medium. A surface touching are these secondary wavelets tangentially in the forward direction, gives the shape of a new wavefront at that instant of time.

Hence, secondary wavelets may be used to find the new position of the wavefront.

6 *(c)* Photoelectric effect does not support the wave theory of light.

7 *(b)* According to Newton's corpuscular theory, the speed of light is lesser in rarer medium and more in denser medium. This was the main reason of failure of this theory.

8 *(c)* The wave theory cannot explain the phenomena of Compton effect and photoelectric effect.

9 *(d)* Photoelectric effect states that the light travels in the form of bundles or packets of energy called photons.

This effect is explained on the basis of quantum nature of light. So, it clearly explains the particle's nature of light.

10 *(d)*

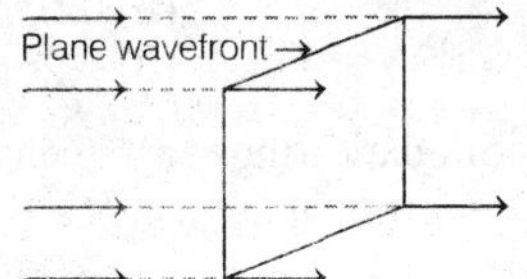

When the point source or linear source of light is at very large distance, a small portion of spherical or cylindrical wavefront appears to be plane, such a wavefront is called a plane wavefront. From the given options none of the sources generates plane wavefront, but it can be artificially produced by reflection from a mirror or by refraction through a lens.

11 *(a)* As, velocity of light is perpendicular to the wavefront and light wave is travelling in vacuum along the Y-axis, therefore, the wavefront is represented by $y =$ constant.

12 *(c)* As the parallel rays, will come from the source situated at infinity, hence the wavefront is planar and it is perpendicular to the rays.

13 *(b)* From Huygens' principle, if the incident wavefront is parallel to the interface of the two media ($i = 0$), then the refracted wavefront will also be parallel to the interface ($r = 0$). In other words, if light rays fall normally on the surface, then on passing to the second medium, they will not deviate from their original path.

Topic 2

Interference of Light

2019

1 In a double slit experiment, when light of wavelength 400 nm was used, the angular width of the first minima formed on a screen placed 1 m away, was found to be 0.2°. What will be the angular width of the first minima, if the entire experimental apparatus is immersed in water? ($\mu_{water} = 4/3$) **[NEET]**

(a) 0.15° (b) 0.051°
(c) 0.1° (d) 0.266°

2 Distance of 5th dark fringe from centre is 4 mm. If $D = 2\,\text{m}$, $\lambda = 600\,\text{nm}$, then distance between slits is **[AIIMS]**

(a) 1.35 mm (b) 2.00 mm
(c) 3.25 mm (d) 10.35 mm

3 A light of wavelength 500 nm is incident on a Young's double slit. The distance between slit and screen is $D = 1.8\,\text{m}$ and distance between slits is $d = 0.4$ mm. If screen moves with a speed of 4 ms^{-1}, then with what speed first maxima will move? **[AIIMS]**

(a) 5 mms^{-1} (b) 4 mms^{-1}
(c) 3 mms^{-1} (d) 2 mms^{-1}

4 **Assertion** Distance between position of bright and dark fringe remain same in Young's double slit experiment.

Reason Fringe width, $\beta = \frac{\lambda D}{d}$ **[AIIMS]**

(a) Both Assertion and Reason are correct and Reason is the correct explanation of Assertion.
(b) Both Assertion and Reason are correct but Reason is not the correct explanation of Assertion.
(c) Assertion is correct but Reason is incorrect.
(d) Both Assertion and Reason are incorrect.

5 In a Young's double slit experiment, if there is no initial phase difference between the light from the two slits, a point on the screen corresponding to the 5th minimum has path difference. **[NEET (Odisha)]**

(a) $5\frac{\lambda}{2}$ (b) $10\frac{\lambda}{2}$ (c) $9\frac{\lambda}{2}$ (d) $11\frac{\lambda}{2}$

2018

6 In Young's double slit experiment, the separation d between the slits is 2 mm, the wavelength λ of the light used is 5896 Å and distance D between the screen and slits is 100 cm. It is found that, the angular width of the fringes is 0.20°. To increase the fringe angular width to 0.21° (with same λ and D), the separation between the slits needs to be changed to **[NEET]**

(a) 2.1 mm (b) 1.9 mm (c) 1.8 mm (d) 1.7 mm

2017

7 Young's double slit experiment is first performed in air and then in a medium other than air. It is found that 8th bright fringe in the medium lies, where 5th dark fringe lies in air. The refractive index of the medium is nearly **[NEET]**

(a) 1.25 (b) 1.59 (c) 1.69 (d) 1.78

8 White light is used to illuminate two slits in Young's double slit experiment. The separation between the slits is b and the screen is at a distance $d(>> b)$ from the slits. At a point on the screen directly in front of one of the slits, which wavelengths are missing? **[JIPMER]**

(a) $\frac{b}{d}, \frac{b}{3d}, \frac{b}{5d}$ (b) $\frac{b^2}{2d}, \frac{b^2}{4d}, \frac{b^2}{6d}$
(c) $\frac{b^2}{d}, \frac{b^2}{3d}, \frac{b^2}{5d}$ (d) $\frac{b}{2d}, \frac{b}{4d}, \frac{b}{6d}$

9 An interference pattern is observed by Young's double slit experiment. If now the separation between coherent source is halved and the distance of screen from coherent sources is doubled, then new fringe width **[AIIMS]**

(a) becomes double (b) becomes one-fourth
(c) remains same (d) becomes four times

10 The Young's double slit experiment is performed with blue and green light of wavelengths 4360 Å and 5460 Å respectively. If x is the distance of 4th maxima from the central one, then **[AIIMS]**

(a) $x_{blue} = x_{green}$ (b) $x_{blue} > x_{green}$
(c) $x_{blue} < x_{green}$ (d) x_{blue} / x_{green}

11 The maximum numbers of possible interference maxima for slit separation equal to twice the wavelength in Young's double slit experiment is **[JIPMER]**

(a) infinite (b) five
(c) three (d) zero

2016

12 The intensity at the maximum in a Young's double slit experiment is I_0. Distance between two slits is $d = 5\lambda$, where λ is the wavelength of light used in the experiment. What will be the intensity infront of one of the slits on the screen placed at a distance $D = 10\,d$? **[NEET]**

(a) $\frac{I_0}{4}$ (b) $\frac{3}{4}I_0$
(c) $\frac{I_0}{2}$ (d) I_0

13 The interference pattern is obtained with two coherent light sources of intensity ratio n. In the interference pattern, the ratio $\frac{I_{max} - I_{min}}{I_{max} + I_{min}}$ will be **[NEET]**

(a) $\frac{\sqrt{n}}{n+1}$ (b) $\frac{2\sqrt{n}}{n+1}$ (c) $\frac{\sqrt{n}}{(n+1)^2}$ (d) $\frac{2\sqrt{n}}{(n+1)^2}$

2014

14 In the Young's double slit experiment, the intensity of light at a point on the screen (where the path difference is λ) is K, (λ being the wavelength of light used). The intensity at a point where the path difference is $\lambda/4$, will be **[J&K CET]**

(a) K (b) $K/4$ (c) $K/2$ (d) zero

15 A fringe width of a certain interference pattern is $\beta = 0.002$ cm. What is the distance of 5th dark fringe from centre? **[KCET]**

(a) 9×10^{-3} cm (b) 11×10^{-2} cm
(c) 1.1×10^{-2} cm (d) 3.28×10^{6} cm

16 Two coherent monochromatic beams of intensities I and $4I$ respectively are superposed. Then, the maximum and minimum intensities in the resulting pattern are **[WB JEE]**

(a) $5I$ and $3I$ (b) $9I$ and $3I$ (c) $4I$ and I (d) $9I$ and I

17 Colours appear on a thin soap film and soap bubbles due to the phenomenon of **[UK PMT]**

(a) interference (b) scattering
(c) diffraction (d) dispersion

18 In Young's double slit experiment, the ratio of maximum and minimum intensities in the fringe system is 9 : 1. The ratio of amplitudes of coherent sources is **[UK PMT]**

(a) 9 : 1 (b) 3 : 1 (c) 2 : 1 (d) 1 : 1

19 In Young's double slit interference experiment, using two coherent waves of different amplitudes, the intensities ratio between bright and dark fringes is 3. Then, the value of the ratio of the amplitudes of the wave that arrive there is **[EAMCET]**

(a) $\left(\frac{\sqrt{3}+1}{\sqrt{3}-1}\right)$ (b) $\left(\frac{\sqrt{3}-1}{\sqrt{3}+1}\right)$ (c) $\sqrt{3}:1$ (d) $1:\sqrt{3}$

20 A fringe width of a certain interference pattern is $\beta = 0.002$ cm. What is the distance of 5th dark fringe centre? **[CET]**

(a) 1×10^{-2} cm (b) 11×10^{-2} cm
(c) 1.1×10^{-2} cm (d) 3.28×10^{6} cm

2013

21 The Young's double slit experimental arrangement is shown in figure below. If λ is the wavelength of light used and $\angle S_1CS_2 = \theta$, then the fringe width will be **[AIIMS]**

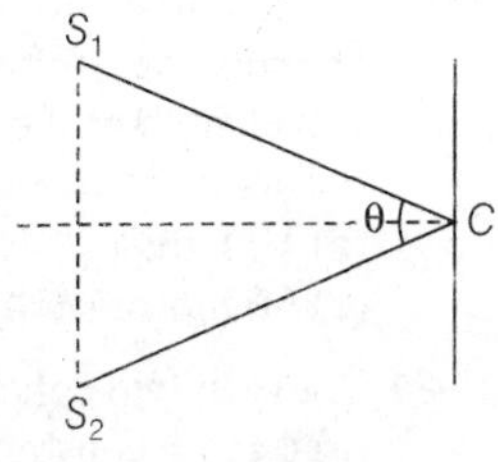

(a) $\frac{\lambda}{\theta}$ (b) $\frac{\lambda}{2\theta}$ (c) $\lambda\theta$ (d) $\frac{2\lambda}{\theta}$

22 In Young's double slit experiment, the slits are 2 mm apart and are illuminated by photons of two wavelengths $\lambda_1 = 12000$ Å and $\lambda_2 = 10000$ Å. At what minimum distance from the common central bright fringe on the screen 2 m from the slit will a bright fringe from one interference pattern coincide with a bright fringe from the other? **[NEET]**

(a) 8 mm (b) 6 mm
(c) 4 mm (d) 3 mm

23 The ratio of intensity at the centre of a bright fringe to the intensity at a point distance one-fourth of the distance between two successive bright fringes will be **[WB JEE]**

(a) 4 (b) 3 (c) 2 (d) 1

24 Two beams of light of intensities I_1 and I_2, interfere to give an interference pattern, if the ratio of the maximum intensity to the minimum intensity is $\frac{25}{9}$, then $\frac{I_1}{I_2}$ is **[KCET]**

(a) $\frac{5}{3}$ (b) 4 (c) $\frac{81}{625}$ (d) 16

2012

25 **Assertion** The pattern and the position of fringes always remain same even after the introduction of transparent medium in a path of one of the slit.

Reason The central fringe is bright or dark depends upon the initial phase difference between the two coherent sources. **[AIIMS]**

(a) Both Assertion and Reason are correct and Reason is the correct explanation of Assertion.
(b) Both Assertion and Reason are correct but Reason is not the correct explanation of Assertion.
(c) Assertion is correct but Reason is incorrect.
(d) Assertion is incorrect but Reason is correct.

26 In Young's double slit experiment, the fringe width is β. If the entire arrangement is placed in a liquid of refractive index n, the fringe width becomes **[AFMC]**

(a) $n\beta$ (b) $\frac{\beta}{n+1}$ (c) $\frac{\beta}{n-1}$ (d) $\frac{\beta}{n}$

27 In a Young's double slit experiment, the separation between the two slits is 0.9 mm and the fringe are observed 1 m away. If it produces the second dark fringe at a distance of 1 mm from the central fringe, the wavelength of the monochromatic source of light used is **[Manipal]**

(a) 450 nm (b) 400 nm (c) 500 nm (d) 600 nm

28 In Young's double slit experiment, the two slits are d distance apart, interference pattern is observed on a screen at a distance D from the slits. A dark fringe is observed on the screen directly opposite to one of the slits, the wavelength of light is **[WB JEE]**

(a) $\frac{D^2}{2d}$ (b) $\frac{d^2}{2D}$ (c) $\frac{D^2}{d}$ (d) $\frac{d^2}{D}$

2011

29 In a double slit interference experiment, the fringe width obtained with a light of wavelength 5900 Å was 1.2 mm for parallel narrow slits placed 2 mm apart. In this arrangement, if the slit separation is increased by one-and-half times the previous value, then the fringe width is **[EAMCET]**

(a) 0.9 mm (b) 0.8 mm
(c) 1.8 mm (d) 1.6 mm

30 In Young's double slit experiment, the angular width of the fringes is 0.20° for the sodium light ($\lambda = 5890$ Å). In order to increase the angular width of the fringes by 10%, the necessary change in wavelength is **[Manipal]**

(a) zero (b) increased by 6479 Å
(c) decreased by 589 Å (d) increased by 589 Å

31 In Young's double slit experiment, the intensity of light coming from one of the slits is doubled the intensity from the other slit. The ratio of the maximum intensity to the minimum intensity in the interference fringe pattern observed is **[Punjab PMET, Manipal]**

(a) 34 (b) 40
(c) 25 (d) 38

32 In Young's double slit experiment, if d, D and λ represents, the distance between the slits, the distance of the screen from the slits and wavelength of light used respectively, then the bandwidth is inversely proportional to **[Kerala CEE]**

(a) λ (b) d (c) D (d) λ^2
(e) D^2

33 A Young's double slit set up for interference is shifted from air to within water, then the fringe width **[J&K CET]**

(a) becomes infinite (b) decreases
(c) increases (d) remain unchanged

34 In Young's double slit experiment, the two slits are separated by 1 mm and the screen is placed 1m away. The fringe separation for blue and green light of wavelength 500 nm is **[J&K CET]**

(a) 10 mm (b) 0.5 mm
(c) 20 mm (d) 15 mm

35 In the case of light waves from two coherent sources S_1 and S_2, there will be constructive interference at an arbitrary point P, if the path difference, $S_1P - S_2P$ is **[J&K CET]**

(a) $\left(n+\frac{1}{2}\right)\lambda$ (b) $n\lambda$ (c) $\left(n-\frac{1}{2}\right)\lambda$ (d) $\frac{\lambda}{2}$

36 In Young's double slit experiment, fringes of width β are produced on a screen kept at a distance of 1 m from the slit. When the screen is moved away by 5×10^{-2} m, fringe width changes by 3×10^{-5} m. The separation between the slits is 1×10^{-3} m. The wavelength of the light used is ... nm. **[KCET]**

(a) 400 (b) 500
(c) 600 (d) 700

37 Consider the following statements in case of Young's double slit experiment. **[EAMCET]**

I. A slit S is necessary, if we use an ordinary extended source of light.
II. A slit S is not needed, if we use an ordinary but well collimated beam of light.
III. A slit S is not needed, if we use a spatially coherent source of light.

(a) I, II and III (b) I and II
(c) II and III (d) I and III

38 Two monochromatic light waves of amplitudes $3A$ and $2A$ interfering at a point have a phase difference of 60°. The intensity at that point will be proportional to **[KCET]**

(a) $5A^2$ (b) $13A^2$
(c) $7A^2$ (d) $19A^2$

2010

39 If the 8th bright band due to light of wavelength λ_1 coincides with 9th bright band from light of wavelength λ_2 in Young's double slit experiment, then the possible wavelengths of visible light are **[Manipal]**

(a) 400 nm and 450 nm (b) 425 nm and 400 nm
(c) 400 nm and 425 nm (d) 450 nm and 400 nm

40 The Young's double slit experiment is performed with light of wavelength 6000 Å, where in 16 fringes occupy a certain region on the screen. If 24 fringes occupy the same region with another light of wavelength λ, then λ is **[Kerala CEE]**

(a) 6000 Å (b) 4500 Å
(c) 5000 Å (d) 4000 Å
(e) 5500 Å

41 If the ratio of maximum and minimum intensities of an interference pattern is 36 : 1, then the ratio of amplitudes of the two interfering waves will be **[EAMCET]**

(a) 3 : 7 (b) 7 : 4
(c) 4 : 7 (d) 7 : 5

42 The wavelength of the light used in Young's double slit experiment is λ. The intensity at a point on the screen is I, where the path difference is $\frac{\lambda}{6}$. If I_0 denotes the maximum intensity, then the ratio of I and I_0 is **[KCET]**

(a) 0.866 (b) 0.5 (c) 0.707 (d) 0.75

43 What is the minimum thickness of a thin film required for constructive interference in the reflected light from it? Given, the refractive index of the film = 1.5 and wavelength of the light incident on the film = 600 nm. **[KCET]**

(a) 100 nm (b) 300 nm
(c) 50 nm (d) 200 nm

44 Between two coherent sources, the phase difference is **[JIPMER]**

(a) $\phi(x) =$ constant
(b) $\phi(t) =$ constant
(c) $\phi(x) = \phi(t) =$ constant
(d) $\phi(x) \neq \phi(t)$

45 If Young's double slit experiment is performed in water instead of air, then **[JIPMER]**
(a) no fringes would be seen
(b) fringe width would decrease
(c) fringe width would increase
(d) fringe width would remain unchanged

2008

46 Two periodic waves of intensities I_1 and I_2 pass through a region at the same time in the same direction. The sum of the maximum and minimum intensities is **[CBSE AIPMT]**
(a) $(I_1 + I_2)$ (b) $(\sqrt{I_1} + \sqrt{I_2})^2$
(c) $(\sqrt{I_1} - \sqrt{I_2})^2$ (d) $2(I_1 + I_2)$

47 **Assertion** In Young's double slit experiment, the two slits are at distance d apart. Interference pattern is observed on a screen at a distance D from the slits. At a point on the screen when it is directly opposite to one of the slits, a dark fringe is observed. Then, the wavelength of wave is proportional to the square of distance of two slits.
Reason For a dark fringe intensity is zero. **[AIIMS]**
(a) Both Assertion and Reason are correct and Reason is the correct explanation of Assertion.
(b) Both Assertion and Reason are correct but Reason is not the correct explanation of Assertion.
(c) A is correct but Reason is incorrect.
(d) Both Assertion and Reason are incorrect.

48 A beam of light of wavelength 600 nm from a distant source falls on a single slit 1 mm wide and the resulting diffraction pattern is observed on a screen 2 m away. The distance between the first dark fringes on either side of the central bright fringe is **[AFMC]**
(a) 1.2 cm (b) 1.2 mm (c) 2.4 cm (d) 2.4 mm

49 If white light is used in the Newton's rings experiment, the colour observed in the reflected light is complementary to that observed in the transmitted light through the same point. This is due to **[AFMC]**
(a) 90° change of phase in one of the reflected waves
(b) 180° change of phase in one of the reflected waves
(c) 145° change of phase in one of the reflected waves
(d) 45° change of phase in one of the reflected waves

50 White light may be considered to be mixture of wave with wavelength ranging between 3000 Å and 7800 Å. An oil film of thickness 10000 Å is examined normally by the reflected light. If $\mu = 1.4$, then the film appears bright for **[BHU]**
(a) 3733 Å, 4308 Å, 5091 Å, 6222 Å
(b) 4000 Å, 5091 Å, 5600 Å
(c) 4667 Å, 6222 Å, 7000 Å
(d) 4000 Å, 4667 Å, 5600 Å, 7000 Å

51 In an interference experiment, the spacing between successive maxima or minima is **[MHT CET]**
(a) $\frac{\lambda d}{D}$ (b) $\frac{\lambda D}{d}$ (c) $\frac{dD}{\lambda}$ (d) $\frac{\lambda d}{4D}$

52 The necessary condition for an interference by two sources of light is that **[Manipal]**
(a) two light sources must have the same wavelength
(b) two point sources should have the same amplitude and same wavelength
(c) two sources should have the same wavelength, nearly the same amplitude and have a constant phase difference
(d) two point sources should have a randomly varying phase difference

53 Colours in thin films are due to **[J&K CET]**
(a) diffraction phenomenon
(b) scattering phenomenon
(c) interference phenomenon
(d) polarisation phenomenon

54 In Young's double slit experiment, the distance between two slits is halved and the distance between the screen and slit is made three times. Then, the width of the fringe **[Guj CET]**
(a) becomes half (b) remains the same
(c) becomes 6 times (d) becomes 4 times

55 In Young's double slit experiment, two coherent sources are placed 0.90 mm apart and the fringes are observed 1m away. If it produces the second dark fringe at a distance of 1 mm from the central fringe, the wavelength of monochromatic light used would be **[BCECE]**
(a) 60×10^{-4} cm (b) 10×10^{-4} cm
(c) 10×10^{-5} cm (d) 6×10^{-5} cm

2007

56 In Young's double slit experiment, the distance between two slits is 0.6 mm and these are illuminated with a light of wavelength 4800 Å. The angular width of first dark fringe on the screen distant 120 cm from slits will be **[BHU]**
(a) 8×10^{-4} rad (b) 6×10^{-4} rad
(c) 4×10^{-4} rad (d) 16×10^{-4} rad

57 What causes change in the colours of the soap or oil films for the given beam of light? **[BHU]**
(a) Angle of incidence (b) Angle of reflection
(c) Thickness of film (d) None of these

58 In a double slit experiment, the distance between slits is increased 10 times, whereas their distance from screen is halved, then what is the fringe width? **[MHT CET]**
(a) It remains same (b) Becomes $\frac{1}{10}$
(c) Becomes $\frac{1}{20}$ (d) Becomes $\frac{1}{90}$

59 In a Fresnel's biprism experiment, the two positions of lens give separation between the slits as 16 cm and 9 cm, respectively. What is the actual distance of separation? **[MHT CET]**
(a) 12.5 cm (b) 12 cm
(c) 13 cm (d) 14 cm

60 In a certain double slit experiment arrangement, interference fringes of width 1.0 mm each are observed when light of wavelength 5000 Å is used. Keeping the set up unaltered, if the source is replaced by another source of wavelength 6000 Å, the fringe width will be **[Kerala CEE]**
(a) 0.5 mm (b) 1.0 mm
(c) 1.2 mm (d) 1.5 mm
(e) 1.8 mm

61 Separation between slits is halved and between screen and slits is doubled, then find the value of final fringe width if original is w. **[RPMT]**
(a) w (b) $9w$
(c) $4w$ (d) $2w$

62 If white light is used in Young's double slit experiment **[J&K CET]**
(a) no interference pattern is formed
(b) white fringes are formed
(c) central bright fringe is white
(d) central bright fringe is coloured

63 What happens to the fringe pattern when the Young's double slit experiment is performed in water instead of air? **[Punjab PMET]**
(a) Shrinks (b) Disappear
(c) Unchanged (d) Enlarged

64 If L is the coherence length and c is the velocity of light, the coherent time is **[Punjab PMET]**
(a) cL (b) $\frac{L}{c}$ (c) $\frac{c}{L}$ (d) $\frac{1}{Lc}$

65 The maximum intensity of fringes in Young's experiment is I. If one of the slits is closed, then the intensity at that place becomes I_0. Which of the following relations is true? **[Punjab PMET]**
(a) $I = I_0$
(b) $I = 2I_0$
(c) $I = 4I_0$
(d) There is no relation between I and I_0

66 Light from two coherent sources of the same amplitude A and wavelength λ illuminates the screen. The intensity of the central maxima is I_0. If the sources were incoherent, the intensity at the same point will be **[KCET]**
(a) $4I_0$ (b) $2I_0$
(c) I_0 (d) $I_0/2$

67 In Young's double slit experiment with sodium vapour lamp of wavelength 589 nm and the slits 0.589 mm apart, the half angular width of the central maxima is **[KCET]**
(a) $\sin^{-1}(0.01)$ (b) $\sin^{-1}(0.0001)$
(c) $\sin^{-1}(0.001)$ (d) $\sin^{-1}(0.1)$

68 $100\,\pi$ phase difference = ... path difference. **[Guj CET]**
(a) 10λ (b) 25λ
(c) 50λ (d) 100λ

2006

69 The path difference produced by two waves is 3.75 μm and the wavelength is 5000 Å. The point is **[MHT CET]**
(a) uncertain (b) dark
(c) partially bright (d) bright

70 Two light rays having the same wavelength λ in vacuum are in phase initially. Then, the first ray travels a path L_1 through a medium of refractive index n_1 while the second ray travels a path of length L_2 through a medium of refractive index n_2. The two waves are then combined to produce interference. The phase difference between the two waves is **[MHT CET]**
(a) $\frac{2\pi}{\lambda}(L_2 - L_1)$ (b) $\frac{2\pi}{\lambda}(n_1L_1 - n_2L_2)$
(c) $\frac{2\pi}{\lambda}(n_2L_1 - n_1L_2)$ (d) $\frac{2\pi}{\lambda}\left(\frac{L_1}{n_1} - \frac{L_2}{n_2}\right)$

71 In Young's double slit experiment when sodium light of wavelength 5893 Å is used, then 62 fringes are seen in the field of view. Instead, if violet light of wavelength 4358 Å is used, then the number of fringes that will be seen in the field of view will be **[MP PMT]**
(a) 54 (b) 64 (c) 74 (d) 84

72 Two coherent sources of intensity ratio β interfere, then the value of $(I_{max} - I_{min})/(I_{max} + I_{min})$ is **[Haryana PMT]**
(a) $\frac{1+\beta}{\sqrt{\beta}}$ (b) $\sqrt{\left(\frac{1+\beta}{\beta}\right)}$
(c) $\frac{1+\beta}{2\sqrt{\beta}}$ (d) $\frac{2\sqrt{\beta}}{1+\beta}$

73 In Young's double slit experiment with monochromatic light, the central fringe will be **[J&K CET]**
(a) coloured (b) white (c) bright (d) black

74 In the phenomenon of interference, energy is **[J&K CET]**
(a) destroyed at bright fringes
(b) created at dark fringes
(c) conserved, but it is redistributed
(d) same at all points

75 In a Young's double slit experiment, one of the slit is covered with a transparent sheet of thickness 3.6×10^{-3} cm due to which position of central fringe shifts to a position originally occupied by 30th bright fringe. The refractive index of the sheet, if $\lambda = 6000$ Å is **[AMU]**
(a) 1.5 (b) 1.2 (c) 1.3 (d) 1.7

76 Two coherent monochromatic light sources are located at two vertices of an equilateral triangle. If the intensity due to each of the sources independently is 1 Wm^{-2} at the third vertex, the resultant intensity due to both the sources at that point (i.e. at the third vertex) is (in Wm^{-2}) **[EAMCET]**
(a) zero (b) $\sqrt{2}$ (c) 2 (d) 4

77 The relationship between phase difference $\Delta\phi$ and the path difference Δx between two interfering waves is given by (λ = wavelength) **[J&K CET]**

(a) $\Delta x = \left(\frac{\lambda}{2\pi}\right)\Delta\phi$
(b) $\Delta x = \left(\frac{2\pi}{\lambda}\right)\Delta\phi$
(c) $\Delta\phi = \left(\frac{\lambda}{2\pi}\right)\Delta x$
(d) $\Delta\phi = 2(2\pi)\Delta x$

2005

78 If two waves represented by $y_1 = 4\sin\omega t$ and $y_2 = 3\sin\left[\omega t + \frac{\pi}{3}\right]$ interfere at a point, the amplitude of resulting wave will be about **[KCET]**

(a) 7 (b) 6 (c) 5 (d) 3.5

79 In Young's double slit experiment, the aperture screen distance is 2 m. The slit width is 1 mm and light of 600 nm is used. If a thin plate of glass ($\mu = 1.5$) of thickness 0.06 mm is placed over one of the slits, then there will be a lateral displacement of the fringes by **[BCECE]**

(a) zero (b) 6 cm
(c) 10 cm (d) 15 cm

80 In Young's double slit experiment, the slit width and the distance of slits from the screen both are doubled. The fringe width **[BCECE]**

(a) increases
(b) decreases
(c) remains unchanged
(d) None of these

Answers

1 (a)	2 (a)	3 (a)	4 (a)	5 (c)	6 (b)	7 (d)	8 (c)	9 (d)	10 (c)
11 (b)	12 (c)	13 (b)	14 (c)	15 (a)	16 (d)	17 (a)	18 (c)	19 (a)	20 (c)
21 (a)	22 (b)	23 (c)	24 (d)	25 (c)	26 (d)	27 (d)	28 (d)	29 (b)	30 (d)
31 (a)	32 (b)	33 (b)	34 (b)	35 (b)	36 (c)	37 (d)	38 (d)	39 (d)	40 (d)
41 (d)	42 (d)	43 (a)	44 (a)	45 (b)	46 (d)	47 (a)	48 (b)	49 (b)	50 (a)
51 (b)	52 (c)	53 (c)	54 (c)	55 (d)	56 (a)	57 (c)	58 (c)	59 (b)	60 (c)
61 (c)	62 (c)	63 (a)	64 (b)	65 (c)	66 (d)	67 (c)	68 (c)	69 (b)	70 (b)
71 (d)	72 (d)	73 (c)	74 (c)	75 (a)	76 (d)	77 (a)	78 (a)	79 (b)	80 (c)

Explanations

1 *(a)* The angular width in YDSE is given by

$$\theta = \frac{\beta}{D}$$

where, β is the separation between two fringes. D is the distance between the slits and screen. If YDSE apparatus is immersed in a liquid of refractive index μ, then the wavelength of light and hence the angular width decreases μ times.

i.e.

and $\theta' = \frac{\beta}{\mu D} = \frac{\theta}{\mu}$

Here, μ (for water) = 4 / 3 and

$$\theta = 0.2°$$

$$\Rightarrow \quad \theta' = \frac{0.2}{4/3} = 0.15°$$

2 *(a)* Given, distance between source and observer,

$$D = 2\,\text{m}$$

Distance of 5th dark fringe from centre

$$= 4 \times 10^{-3}\,\text{m}$$

Wavelength, $\lambda = 600\,\text{nm} = 6 \times 10^{-7}\,\text{m}$

Distance of 5th dark fringe from centre

$$= \beta + \beta + \beta + \beta + \frac{\beta}{2} = \frac{9\beta}{2}$$

where, β = fringe width.

According to question, $\frac{9\beta}{2} = 4 \times 10^{-3}$

$$\frac{9}{2} \times \frac{D\lambda}{d} = 4 \times 10^{-3}$$

$$\frac{9}{2} \times \frac{2 \times 6 \times 10^{-7}}{d} = 4 \times 10^{-3}$$

$$\Rightarrow \quad d = 1.35 \times 10^{-3}\,\text{m} = 1.35\,\text{mm}$$

3 *(a)* Given, wavelength of light,

$$\lambda = 500\,\text{nm} = 5 \times 10^{-7}\,\text{m}$$

Distance between slit and screen,

$$D = 1.8\,\text{m}$$

Distance between two slits,

$$d = 0.4\,\text{mm} = 4 \times 10^{-4}\,\text{m}$$

Velocity of screen $= \frac{dD}{dt} = 4\,\text{ms}^{-1}$

Speed of first maxima $= \frac{d\beta}{dt} = ?$

In Young's double slit experiment,

fringe width, $\beta = \frac{D\lambda}{d}$

Differentiating with respect to t, we get

$$\frac{d\beta}{dt} = \frac{\lambda}{d} \cdot \frac{dD}{dt} = \frac{5 \times 10^{-7}}{4 \times 10^{-4}} \times 4$$

$$= 5 \times 10^{-3}\,\text{ms}^{-1} = 5\,\text{mms}^{-1}$$

4 *(a)* Distance between position of bright and dark fringe is called fringe width in Young's double slit experiment, which is given by $\beta = \frac{D\lambda}{d}$

where, β = fringe width,
D = distance between source and screen,
d = distance between two slits
and λ = wavelength of monochromatic light wave.

Therefore, in Young's double slit experiment, fringes are of equal width, i.e., width of bright and dark fringes are same.

Hence, both Assertion and Reason are correct and Reason is the correct explanation of Assertion.

5 *(c)* In a Young's double slit experiment, the path difference for nth minima is given by, $\Delta y = (2n-1)\frac{\lambda}{2}$

For 5th minima, $n = 5$

$$\therefore \quad \Delta y = [2(5)-1]\frac{\lambda}{2} = \frac{9\lambda}{2}$$

6 *(b)* In a Young's double slit experiment, angular width of a fringe is given as

$$\theta = \frac{\lambda}{d}$$

where, λ is the wavelength of the light source and d is the distance between the two slits.

$$\Rightarrow \quad \theta \propto \frac{1}{d} \text{ or } \frac{\theta_1}{\theta_2} = \frac{d_2}{d_1} \quad \ldots(i)$$

Given, $\theta_1 = 0.20^\circ$, $\theta_2 = 0.21^\circ$, $d_1 = 2$ mm

Substituting the given values in Eq. (i), we get

$$\frac{0.20^\circ}{0.21^\circ} = \frac{d_2}{2 \text{ mm}}$$

$$\Rightarrow \quad d_2 = 2 \times \frac{0.20}{0.21} = \frac{0.40}{0.21}$$

$$\therefore \quad = 1.9 \text{ mm}$$

7 *(d)* According to question,

5th dark fringe in air = 8th bright fringe in the medium

$$(2n-1)\frac{D\lambda}{2d} = \frac{nD\lambda}{\mu d}$$

$$(2\times 5-1)\frac{\lambda D}{2d} = 8\frac{\lambda D}{\mu d}$$

$$9\frac{\lambda D}{2d} = 8\frac{\lambda D}{\mu d}$$

$$\Rightarrow \quad \frac{9}{2} = \frac{8}{\mu} \Rightarrow \mu = \frac{8\times 2}{9}$$

$\therefore$ Refractive index of the medium,

$$\mu = \frac{16}{9} = 1.7777 \approx 1.78$$

8 *(c)* The situation is shown in the figure

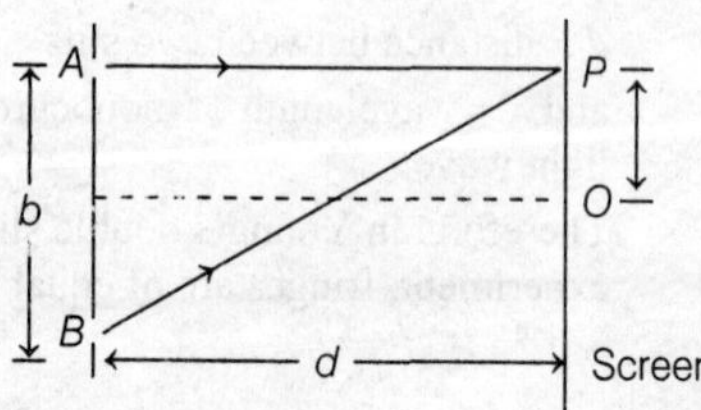

The path difference between the waves reaching the point P is

$$\Delta p = BP - AP$$

$$= (d^2 + b^2)^{1/2} - d$$

$$= d\left(1 + \frac{b^2}{d^2}\right)^{1/2} - d$$

$$\approx d\left[1 + \frac{1}{2}\cdot\frac{b^2}{d^2}\right] - d = \frac{b^2}{2d}$$

For a dark band,

$$\Delta p = \frac{b^2}{2d} = (2n-1)\frac{\lambda}{2}$$

where, $n = 1, 2, 3$ or $\lambda = \frac{1}{(2n-1)}\cdot\frac{b^2}{d}$

Hence, the missing wavelengths are

$$\frac{b^2}{d}, \frac{b^2}{3d}, \frac{b^2}{5d}, \ldots$$

9 *(d)* Fringe width $(w) = \frac{D\lambda}{d}$

Now, distance between the coherent sources is halved, i.e. $d' = d/2$ and distance of coherent source and screen is doubled, i.e. $D' = 2D$.

$$\therefore \quad w' = \frac{D'\lambda}{d'} = \frac{2D\lambda}{(d/2)} = \frac{4D\lambda}{d}$$

$$\Rightarrow \quad \frac{w'}{w} = 4$$

$$\Rightarrow \quad w' = 4w$$

(becomes four times)

10 *(c)* In Young's double slit experiment position of bright fringes on the screen are given by

$$x = \frac{nD\lambda}{d}$$

Hence, distance of nth maxima will be

$$x = n\lambda\frac{D}{d} \propto \lambda$$

$$\lambda_{\text{blue}} = 4360 \text{ Å}, \ \lambda_{\text{green}} = 5480 \text{ Å}$$

where, x = distance of 4th maxima from the central one

As, $\lambda_{\text{blue}} < \lambda_{\text{green}} \ \therefore \ x_{\text{blue}} < x_{\text{green}}$

11 *(b)* The condition of interference maxima is

$$d\sin\theta = n\lambda, \quad \sin\theta = \frac{n\lambda}{d}$$

Given, $d = 2\lambda$ and $\sin\theta = \frac{n\lambda}{2\lambda} = \frac{n}{2}$

The magnitude of $\sin\theta$ lies between 0 and 1.

When $n = 0$, $\sin\theta = 0 \Rightarrow \theta = 0^\circ$

When $n = 1$, $\sin\theta = 1/2 \Rightarrow \theta = 30^\circ$

When $n = 2$, $\sin\theta = 1 \Rightarrow \theta = 90^\circ$

Thus, there is central maximum ($\theta = 0^\circ$), on either side of it maxima lie at $\theta = 30^\circ$ and $\theta = 90^\circ$, so maximum number of possible interference maxima is 5.

12 *(c)*

Screen
S_1
S_2
5λ
2.5λ
O
50λ

In the above figure, S_1 and S_2 are the two different slits.

Given, distance between slits S_1 and S_2, $d = 5\lambda$. Distance between screen and slits, $D = 10d = 50\lambda$, where λ is the wavelength of light used in the experiment. According to question, the intensity at maximum in this Young's double slit experiment is I_0.

$$\Rightarrow I_{\max} = I_0$$

$\because$ Path difference

$$= \frac{dY_n}{D} = \frac{d\times\frac{d}{2}}{10d} = \frac{d}{20} = \frac{\lambda}{4} \quad \{\because d = 5\lambda\}$$

A path difference of λ corresponds to phase difference 2π, so for path difference $\lambda/4$.

Phase difference,

$$\phi = \frac{2\pi}{\lambda}\times\frac{\lambda}{4} = \pi/2 = 90^\circ$$

As we know,

$$I = I_0\cos^2\phi/2$$

$$\Rightarrow \quad I = I_0\cos^2\frac{90^\circ}{2}$$

$$\Rightarrow \quad I = I_0\times\left(\frac{1}{\sqrt{2}}\right)^2$$

$$\Rightarrow \quad I = \frac{I_0}{2}$$

13 *(b)* It is given that, $\frac{I_2}{I_1} = n \Rightarrow I_2 = nI_1$

$\therefore$ Ratio of intensities is given by

$$\frac{I_{\max} - I_{\min}}{I_{\max} + I_{\min}}$$

$$= \frac{(\sqrt{I_2}+\sqrt{I_1})^2 - (\sqrt{I_2}-\sqrt{I_1})^2}{(\sqrt{I_1}+\sqrt{I_2})^2 + (\sqrt{I_2}-\sqrt{I_1})^2}$$

$$= \frac{\left(\sqrt{\frac{I_2}{I_1}}+1\right)^2 - \left(\sqrt{\frac{I_2}{I_1}}-1\right)^2}{\left(\sqrt{\frac{I_2}{I_1}}+1\right)^2 + \left(\sqrt{\frac{I_2}{I_1}}-1\right)^2}$$

$$= \frac{(\sqrt{n}+1)^2 - (\sqrt{n}-1)^2}{(\sqrt{n}+1)^2 + (\sqrt{n}-1)^2} = \frac{2\sqrt{n}}{n+1}$$

14 *(c)* For net intensity, $I' = 4I_0 \cos^2 \frac{\phi}{2}$

Case I $K = 4I_0 \cos^2\left(\frac{2\pi}{2}\right)$

$$\left(\because \phi = \frac{2\pi}{\lambda} \times \lambda\right)$$

$$K = 4I_0 \cos^2(\pi)$$

$$\Rightarrow \quad K = 4I_0 \quad \ldots(i)$$

Case II $K' = 4I_0 \cos^2\left(\frac{\pi/2}{2}\right)$

$$\left(\because \phi = \frac{2\pi}{\lambda} \times \frac{\lambda}{4}\right)$$

$$K' = 4I_0 \cos^2(\pi/4)$$

$$\Rightarrow \quad K' = 2I_0 \quad \ldots(ii)$$

Comparing Eqs. (i) and (ii), we get

$$K' = K/2$$

15 *(a)* The distance of 5th dark fringe from centre is given by

$$x_n = (2n+1)\frac{\lambda l}{2d}$$

As, $n = 4$ for 5th dark fringe.

So, $x_5 = \frac{9}{2}\frac{\lambda D}{d}$

As, $\frac{\lambda D}{d} = \beta$

So, $x_5 = 9/2\,\beta = 9/2 \times 0.002$
$= 9 \times 10^{-3}$ cm

16 *(d)* We know that,

The maximum intensity,

$$I_{max} = (\sqrt{I_1} + \sqrt{I_2})^2 \quad \ldots(i)$$

The minimum intensity,

$$I_{min} = (\sqrt{I_1} - \sqrt{I_2})^2 \quad \ldots(ii)$$

So, the ratio of the maximum and minimum intensities is

$$\frac{I_{max}}{I_{min}} = \frac{(\sqrt{I_1} + \sqrt{I_2})^2}{(\sqrt{I_1} - \sqrt{I_2})^2} = \frac{(\sqrt{4I} + \sqrt{I})^2}{(\sqrt{4I} - \sqrt{I})^2} \quad \text{(given)}$$

$$\frac{I_{max}}{I_{min}} = \left(\frac{3\sqrt{I}}{\sqrt{I}}\right)^2 = \frac{9}{1} = 9:1$$

Hence, the maximum and minimum intensities in the resulting pattern are $9I$ and I.

17 *(a)* The diagram below shows a thin soap film.

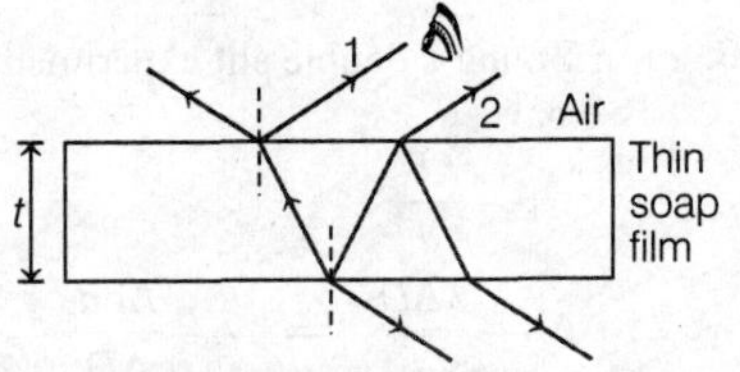

Consider the case, when the thin soap film is viewed by the light reflected by it (1 and 2).

Due to the reflection, from a denser medium (film) ray 1 suffers additional phase change of π, apart from the phase change due to the path difference between 1 and 2.

So, the rays 1 and 2 produce the phenomenon of interference when they meet.

When white light is to used, the path difference (phase difference) will satisfy the condition of maxima for certain wavelengths and condition of minima for other wavelengths. This gives coloured appearance of the film.

Similarly, in the case with soap bubble, the film between the inner and outer surfaces acts as a thin film and phenomenon can be explained as previous case.

18 *(c)* Let in Young's double slit experiment, amplitudes corresponding to the sources S_1 and S_2 be a_1 and a_2 and intensities be I_1 and I_2 respectively.

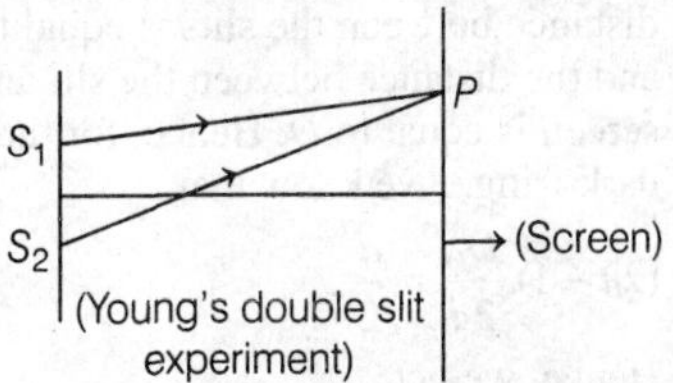

We know that, the intensity for a source (I) having an amplitude a are related as, $I \propto a^2$

From maximum intensity,

$$a_{max} = a_1 + a_2$$

i.e. sources are in phase.

For minimum intensity, $a_{min} = a_1 - a_2$

i.e. sources are out of phase.

So, $I_{max} \propto a_{max}^2$ and $I_{min} \propto a_{min}^2$

$$\Rightarrow \frac{I_{max}}{I_{min}} = \left(\frac{a_{max}}{a_{min}}\right)^2 = \left(\frac{a_1 + a_2}{a_1 - a_2}\right)^2$$

According to given question,

$$\frac{I_{max}}{I_{min}} = \frac{9}{1}$$

$$\Rightarrow \quad 9 = \left(\frac{a_1/a_2 + 1}{a_1/a_2 - 1}\right)^2$$

$$\Rightarrow \quad (3)^2 = \left(\frac{a_1/a_2 + 1}{a_1/a_2 - 1}\right)^2 \quad \text{(given)}$$

$$\Rightarrow \quad 3 = \frac{a_1/a_2 + 1}{a_1/a_2 - 1}$$

$$3 = \frac{\frac{a_1 + a_2}{a_2}}{\frac{a_1 - a_2}{a_2}}$$

$$\Rightarrow \quad 3 = \frac{a_1 + a_2}{a_1 - a_2}$$

$$\Rightarrow \quad 3(a_1 - a_2) = a_1 + a_2$$

$$\Rightarrow \quad 3a_1 - 3a_2 = a_1 + a_2$$

$$\Rightarrow \quad 2a_1 = 4a_2$$

$$\Rightarrow \quad \frac{a_1}{a_2} = \frac{4}{2}$$

$$\Rightarrow \quad a_1 : a_2 = 2:1$$

19 *(a)* $\frac{I_{bright}}{I_{dark}} = \frac{I_{max}}{I_{min}} = 3$ (given)

$$\Rightarrow \frac{(a_1 + a_2)^2}{(a_1 - a_2)^2} = \frac{3}{1}$$

$$\Rightarrow \frac{a_1 + a_2}{a_1 - a_2} = \sqrt{3}$$

$$\Rightarrow a_1 + a_2 = \sqrt{3}(a_1 - a_2)$$

$$\Rightarrow \frac{a_1}{a_2} = \frac{\sqrt{3} + 1}{\sqrt{3} - 1}$$

20 *(c)* The distance of 5th dark fringe from centre is given by

$$x_n = (2n+1)\frac{\lambda D}{2d}$$

As, $n = 5$ for 5th dark fringe

So, $x_5 = \frac{11}{2}\frac{\lambda D}{d} = \frac{11}{2}\beta \quad \left(\because \frac{\lambda D}{d} = \beta\right)$

Given, $\beta = 0.002$ cm

So, $= 11/2 \times 0.002 = 0.011$ cm
$= 1.1 \times 10^{-2}$ cm

21 *(a)* Fringe width, $\beta = \frac{D\lambda}{d}$

But, here $\theta = \frac{d}{D} \Rightarrow d = D\theta$

$$\therefore \quad \beta = \frac{D\lambda}{D\theta} = \frac{\lambda}{\theta}$$

22 *(b)* Given, $\lambda_1 = 12000$ Å,
$\lambda_2 = 10000$ Å, $D = 2$ m
and $d = 2$ mm $= 2 \times 10^{-3}$ m

We have, $\frac{\lambda_2}{\lambda_1} = \frac{n_1}{n_2} = \frac{10000}{12000} = \frac{5}{6}$

$$\left(\because x_n = \frac{n\lambda D}{d}\right)$$

As, $x = \frac{n_1\lambda_1 D}{d} = \frac{5 \times 12000 \times 10^{-10} \times 2}{2 \times 10^{-3}}$
$= 5 \times 1.2 \times 10^4 \times 10^{-10} \times 10^3$ m
$= 6 \times 10^{-3}$ m $= 6$ mm

23 (c) Intensity at the centre be bright fringe,

$$I_0 = I + I + 2\sqrt{I \cdot I}\cos 0^\circ$$

$$I_0 = 2I + 2I \Rightarrow I_0 = 4I \quad ...(i)$$

Intensity at a point distance $\frac{\beta}{4}$ with a phase difference $= \frac{2\pi}{4} = \frac{\pi}{2}$ is

$$I' = I + I + 2\sqrt{I \cdot I}\cos\frac{\pi}{2}$$

$$= 2I + 2\sqrt{I \cdot I} \times 0$$

$$\Rightarrow I' = 2I \quad ...(ii)$$

On dividing Eq. (i) by Eq. (ii), we get

$$\therefore \frac{I_0}{I'} = \frac{4I}{2I} = 2$$

24 (d) $\frac{I_{max}}{I_{min}} = \frac{25}{9}$ or $\left(\frac{a_1 + a_2}{a_1 - a_2}\right)^2 = \frac{25}{9}$

where, a is amplitude.

or $\frac{a_1 + a_2}{a_1 - a_2} = \frac{5}{3}$

$$\Rightarrow 3a_1 + 3a_2 = 5a_1 - 5a_2$$

$$\Rightarrow 5a_1 - 3a_1 = 3a_2 + 5a_2$$

$$\Rightarrow 2a_1 = 8a_2 \Rightarrow a_1 = 4a_2$$

$$\frac{a_1}{a_2} = 4$$

As, $(\text{amplitude})^2 \propto (\text{intensity})$

Hence, $\frac{I_1}{I_2} = \left(\frac{a_1}{a_2}\right)^2 = 16$

25 (c) If a transparent medium of thickness t and refractive index μ is introduced in the path of one of the slit, then effective path in air is increased by an amount $(\mu - 1)t$ due to introduction of plate. Therefore, the zeroth fringe shifts to a new position where the two optical paths are equal. In such cases, fringe width remains unchanged.

26 (d) Fringe width,

$$\beta = D\lambda/d \quad ...(i) \text{ (for air)}$$

When entire arrangement is placed in a liquid of refractive index n, then it becomes

$$\beta' = \frac{D\lambda}{nd} \quad ...(ii)$$

$$\frac{\beta'}{\beta} = \frac{D\lambda}{nd} \times \frac{d}{D\lambda} \Rightarrow \beta' = \frac{\beta}{n}$$

27 (d) The distance between two consecutive dark fringes or bright fringes are recognised as β (fringe width) and that between central fringe and first dark fringe on either side is $\beta/2$.

Given, $d = 0.9$ mm $= 0.9 \times 10^{-3}$ m and $D = 1$ m

Spacing between second dark fringe and central fringe

$$= \beta + \frac{\beta}{2} = \frac{3\beta}{2} = 1 \text{ mm}$$

$$\Rightarrow \beta = \frac{2}{3} \times 1 \text{ mm}$$

$$\Rightarrow \frac{\lambda D}{d} = \frac{2}{3} \text{ mm}$$

$$\therefore \lambda = \frac{2}{3} \times 10^{-3} \times \frac{0.9 \times 10^{-3}}{1}$$

$$= 600 \times 10^{-9} = 600 \text{ nm}$$

28 (d) According to given question, Young's double slit experiment is given by the diagram alongside.

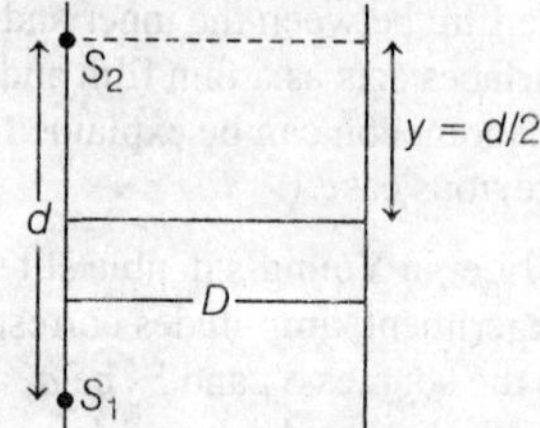

From the given figure, we see that the distance between the slits is equal to d and the distance between the slit and screen is equal to D. Hence, for the nth dark fringe, we know that

$$(2n - 1)\frac{D\lambda}{2d} = \frac{d}{2}$$

Hence, we get

$$\lambda = \frac{d^2}{(2n-1)D} = \frac{d^2}{D} \text{ for } n = 1$$

29 (b) By Young's double slit interference experiment, $\beta = \frac{\lambda D}{d}$

Given, $\beta_1 = 1.2$ mm

$$\frac{d_2}{d_1} = 1\frac{1}{2} = 1.5$$

So, $\beta \propto \frac{1}{d} \Rightarrow \frac{\beta_1}{\beta_2} = \frac{1/d_1}{1/d_2}$

$$\Rightarrow \frac{\beta_1}{\beta_2} = \frac{d_2}{d_1} = 1.5 \Rightarrow \frac{1.2}{\beta_2} = 1.5$$

$$\Rightarrow \beta_2 = \frac{1.2}{1.5} = \frac{4}{5} = 0.8 \text{ mm}$$

30 (d) Let λ be the wavelength of monochromatic light incident on slit S, then the angular distance between two consecutive fringes, i.e. the angular fringe width is

$$\theta = \lambda/d \quad ...(i)$$

where, d is distance between coherent sources.

Given, $\frac{\Delta\theta}{\theta} = \frac{10}{100}$

So, from Eq. (i)

$$\frac{\Delta\lambda}{\lambda} = \frac{\Delta\theta}{\theta} = \frac{10}{100} = 0.1$$

$$\Rightarrow \Delta\lambda = 0.1\lambda = 0.1 \times 5890 \text{ Å}$$

$$= 589 \text{ Å (increases)}$$

31 (a) $\frac{I_{max}}{I_{min}} = \frac{(\sqrt{2I} + \sqrt{I})^2}{(\sqrt{2I} - \sqrt{I})^2} = \left(\frac{\sqrt{2}+1}{\sqrt{2}-1}\right)^2$ (given)

Now, rationalising the denominator by multiplying the denominator with numerator and with denominator itself.

$$= \left[\frac{(\sqrt{2}+1)(\sqrt{2}+1)}{(\sqrt{2}-1)(\sqrt{2}+1)}\right]^2$$

$$= \left(\frac{2 + 1 + 2\sqrt{2}}{2 - 1}\right)^2 = \frac{9 + 8 + 12\sqrt{2}}{1}$$

$$= 34$$

32 (b) The bandwidth is inversely proportional to the distance between the slits d as $\beta = \frac{\lambda D}{d} \Rightarrow \beta \propto \frac{1}{d}$

33 (b) When a Young's double slit set up for interference is shifted from air to within water, then the fringe width decreases.

34 (b) Given,

$$d = 1 \times 10^{-3} \text{ m}, \lambda = 500 \times 10^{-9} \text{ m}$$

and $D = 1$ m

Fringe separation,

$$\beta = \frac{\lambda D}{d} = \frac{500 \times 10^{-9} \times 1}{1 \times 10^{-3}} = 500 \times 10^{-6}$$

$$= 0.5 \times 10^{-3} \text{ m} = 0.5 \text{ mm}$$

35 (b) The path difference $S_1P - S_2P$ is a whole number of wavelength, for the interference at an arbitrary point P. So,

$S_1P - S_2P = n\lambda$ (for maximum intensity)

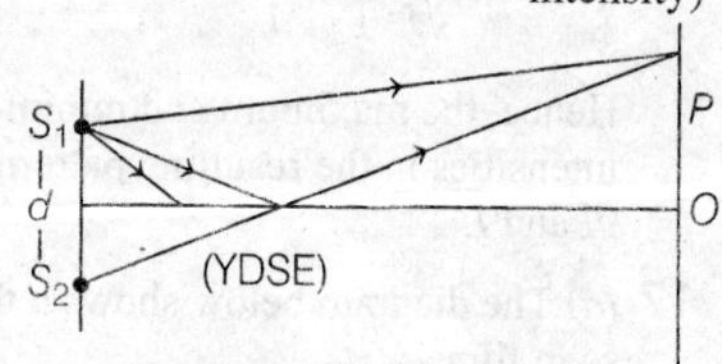

36 (c) In Young's double slit experiment, we have

$$\beta = \frac{\lambda D}{d}$$

$$\Delta\beta = \frac{\lambda \Delta D}{d} \Rightarrow \lambda = \frac{\Delta\beta d}{\Delta D}$$

$$\lambda = \frac{3\times10^{-5}\times1\times10^{-3}}{5\times10^{-2}} = 6\times10^{-7}\text{ m}$$

or $\lambda = 600$ nm

37 *(d)* In the case of Young's double slit experiment, a slit S is necessary, if we use an ordinary extended source of light and slit S is not needed, if we use a spatially coherent source of light.

38 *(d)* Given, $A_1 = 3A = A_2 = 2A$

and $\theta = 60^\circ$

We know that,

$$A = \sqrt{A_1^2 + A_2^2 + 2A_1A_2\cos\theta}$$

$$A^2 = A_1^2 + A_2^2 + 2A_1A_2\cos 60^\circ$$

$$I = 9A^2 + 4A^2 + 2\times 3A\times 2A\times\frac{1}{2}$$

$$I = 19A^2$$

39 *(d)* Position of nth bright fringe from central maxima is $\frac{n\lambda D}{d}$.

$$\therefore \frac{8\lambda_1 D}{d} = \frac{9\lambda_2 D}{d} \Rightarrow \frac{\lambda_1}{\lambda_2} = \frac{9}{8} \quad \text{(given)}$$

Hence, the possible wavelengths of visible light is of the ratio of $9:8$. Therefore, only option (d) is correct because ratio of $\frac{450\text{ nm}}{400\text{ nm}} = \frac{9}{8}$

40 *(d)* Given, $\lambda_1 = 6000\text{Å}$, $n_1 = 16$ fringes and $n_2 = 24$ fringes

[Position of n th fringe $= \frac{nD\lambda}{d}$

$\Rightarrow n_1\lambda_1 = n_2\lambda_2$]

$$\Rightarrow \frac{\lambda_1}{\lambda_2} = \frac{n_2}{n_1} \Rightarrow \frac{6000}{\lambda_2} = \frac{24}{16}$$

$$\Rightarrow \lambda_2 = \frac{6000\times16}{24} = \frac{96000}{24} = 4000\text{ Å}$$

41 *(d)* $\frac{I_{max}}{I_{min}} = \left(\frac{a_1+a_2}{a_1-a_2}\right)^2$

$$\Rightarrow \frac{a_1+a_2}{a_1-a_2} = \sqrt{\frac{36}{1}} \quad \text{(given)}$$

$$\Rightarrow \frac{a_1+a_2}{a_1-a_2} = 6$$

$$a_1 + a_2 = 6a_1 - 6a_2$$

$$\Rightarrow 7a_2 = 5a_1$$

$$\frac{a_1}{a_2} = \frac{7}{5} \Rightarrow a_1 : a_2 = 7:5$$

42 *(d)* Phase difference,

$$\phi = \frac{2\pi}{\lambda}\times\text{Path difference}$$

$$= \frac{2\pi}{\lambda}\times\frac{\lambda}{6} = \frac{\pi}{3} = 60^\circ$$

Intensity, $I = I_0\cos^2\left(\frac{\phi}{2}\right)$

$$\Rightarrow \frac{I}{I_0} = \cos^2(30^\circ) = \left(\frac{\sqrt{3}}{2}\right)^2 = 0.75$$

43 *(a)* Given, $\lambda = 600\text{ nm} = 600\times10^{-9}$ m and $u = 1.5$

Condition for constructive interference,

$$2\mu t = (2n+1)\frac{\lambda}{2}$$

where, $n = 0, 1, 2, 3$

For minimum thickness, $n = 0$

$$2\mu t = \frac{\lambda}{2}$$

$$\Rightarrow t = \frac{\lambda}{4\mu} = \frac{600\times10^{-9}}{4\times1.5} = 100\text{ nm}$$

44 *(a)* Two sources are said to be coherent, if they emit light waves of same frequency or wavelength and of a stable phase difference. i.e. $\phi(x) =$ constant.

45 *(b)* Fringe width, $\beta = \frac{D\lambda}{d}$ or $\beta \propto \lambda$

If the Young's double slit experiment is performed in water, wavelength λ decreases, so fringe width also decreases.

46 *(d)* Resultant intensity of two periodic waves is given by

$$I = I_1 + I_2 + 2\sqrt{I_1I_2}\cos\delta$$

where, δ is the phase difference between the waves.

For maximum intensity, $\delta = 2n\pi$, $n = 0, 1, 2,\ldots$ etc.

Therefore, for zero order maxima, $\cos\delta = 1$

$$I_{max} = I_1 + I_2 + 2\sqrt{I_1I_2} = (\sqrt{I_1}+\sqrt{I_2})^2$$

For minimum intensity, $\delta = (2n-1)\pi$, where, $n = 1, 2, \ldots$ etc.

Therefore, for 1st order minima, $\cos\delta = -1$

$$I_{min} = I_1 + I_2 - 2\sqrt{I_1I_2} = (\sqrt{I_1}-\sqrt{I_2})^2$$

Therefore, $I_{max} + I_{min}$

$$= (\sqrt{I_1}+\sqrt{I_2})^2 + (\sqrt{I_1}-\sqrt{I_2})^2$$

$$= 2(I_1 + I_2)$$

47 *(a)* When a dark fringe is obtained at the point on the screen opposite to one of the slits, then $S_1P = D$ and $S_2P = \sqrt{D^2+d^2}$

$$= D\left(1+\frac{d^2}{D^2}\right)^{1/2} = D\left(1+\frac{d^2}{2D^2}\right)$$

Path difference $= S_2P - S_1P$

$$= D\left(1+\frac{d^2}{2D^2}\right) - D = \frac{d^2}{2D} = \frac{\lambda}{2}$$

or $\lambda = \frac{d^2}{D} \Rightarrow \lambda \propto d^2$

Also, intensity of a dark fringe is zero.

48 *(b)* Given, $\lambda = 600\text{ nm} = 600\times10^{-9}$ m

$D = 2$ m and $d = 1$ m

Fringe width,

$$\beta = \frac{\lambda D}{d} = \frac{600\times10^{-9}\times2}{1\times10^{-3}}$$

$$= 12\times10^{-4}\text{ m}$$

So, the distance between the first dark fringes on either side of the central bright fringe is

$$x = \beta = 12\times10^{-4}\text{ m} = 1.2\text{ mm}$$

49 *(b)* Newton's ring is a phenomena in which an interference pattern is created by reflection of light between spherical surface and an adjacent touching flat surface. There is a phase reversal of π at two places as reflected and transmitted part and total phase difference is 0.

The ray reflected at the upper surface of the air film suffers no phase change, while the ray reflected internally at the lower surface suffers a phase change of π.

50 *(a)* The film appears bright, if the path difference is

$$2\mu t\cos r = (2n-1)\frac{\lambda}{2},$$

where, $n = 1, 2, 3, \ldots$

$$\therefore \lambda = \frac{4\mu t\cos r}{(2n-1)}$$

$$\lambda = \frac{4\times1.4\times10000\times10^{-10}\cos 0^\circ}{(2n-1)}$$

$$= \frac{56000}{(2n-1)}\text{ Å}$$

$\therefore \lambda = 56000$ Å, 18666 Å, 11200 Å, 8000 Å, 6222 Å, 5091 Å, 4308 Å, 3733 Å

The wavelengths which are not within specified ranges are to be rejected, hence option (a) is the correct answer

51 *(b)* In an interference experiment, the spacing between successive maxima and minima is called the fringe width and it is given by $\beta = \frac{D\lambda}{d}$

52 (c) Two sources should have the same wavelength, nearly the same amplitude and have a constant phase difference. If the phase difference between two interfering waves does not remain constant, interference pattern will not be sustained.

53 (c) When the light rays fall on thin film of oil, then rays are reflected from upper and lower layer of the thin films. These reflected rays produce interference pattern due to which the surface of thin film appears as coloured.

54 (c) Given that, the distance between two slits $d' = \frac{d}{2}$

and the distance between screen and slit $D' = 3D$

We know that, the fringe width is

$$\beta = \frac{D\lambda}{d} \quad \ldots(i)$$

According to question

$$\Rightarrow \quad \beta' = \frac{D'\lambda}{d'} \Rightarrow \beta' = \frac{3D \cdot \lambda}{d/2}$$

$$\Rightarrow \quad \beta' = \frac{6D\lambda}{d} \quad \ldots(ii)$$

On dividing Eq. (ii) by Eq. (i), we get

$$\frac{\beta'}{\beta} = \frac{\frac{6D\lambda}{d}}{\frac{D\lambda}{d}} \Rightarrow \frac{\beta'}{\beta} = 6 \Rightarrow \beta' = 6\beta$$

Hence, the width of the fringe becomes 6 times.

55 (d) Given, $d = 0.9\text{ mm} = 0.9 \times 10^{-3}$ m,

$x_2 = 1\text{ mm} = 1 \times 10^{-3}$ m and $D = 1$ m.

Distance of nth dark fringe from central fringe

$$x_n = \frac{(2n-1)\lambda D}{2d}$$

$$\therefore \quad x_2 = \frac{(2 \times 2 - 1)\lambda D}{2d} = \frac{3\lambda D}{2d}$$

$$\Rightarrow 1 \times 10^{-3} = \frac{3\lambda \times 1}{2 \times 0.9 \times 10^{-3}}$$

$$= 6 \times 10^{-5}\text{ cm}$$

56 (a) Angular fringe width of first minima

$$\frac{2x}{D} = 2(2n-1)\frac{\lambda}{2d} = (2n-1)\frac{\lambda}{d}$$

Given, $d = 0.6\text{ mm} = 0.6 \times 10^{-3}$ m

$\lambda = 4800\text{ Å} = 4.8 \times 10^{-7}$ m, $n = 1$

$$\therefore \quad \frac{2x}{D} = \frac{(2 \times 1 - 1) \times 4.8 \times 10^{-7}}{0.6 \times 10^{-3}}$$

$$= 8 \times 10^{-4}\text{ rad}$$

57 (c) When a thin film of oil spreads over the surface of water and observed in broad day light, then brilliant colours are observed. These colours arise due to the interference of sunlight reflected from lower surface and upper surface of the film.

If thickness of film at a point is such that optical path difference $\delta = 0, \lambda, 2\lambda, 3\lambda, \ldots$ then, the film appears dark and if $\delta = \frac{\lambda}{2}, \frac{3\lambda}{2}, \frac{5\lambda}{2}, \ldots$ film will appear bright.

Hence, colours of soap film change because of thickness of film.

58 (c) Let λ be the wavelength of monochromatic light, d be the distance between coherent sources and D be the distance between the screen and source, then fringe width is

$$\beta = \frac{D\lambda}{d} \Rightarrow \beta' = \frac{D'\lambda}{d'}$$

$$\left(\text{given, } d' = 10d, D' = \frac{D}{2}\right)$$

$$\therefore \quad \beta' = \frac{\frac{D}{2}\lambda}{10d} = \frac{D\lambda}{20d}$$

$$\Rightarrow \quad \beta' = \frac{\beta}{20} \quad \left(\because \beta = \frac{D\lambda}{d}\right)$$

59 (b) Fresnel used a biprism to obtain the two coherent sources for producing interference fringes in the laboratory. In biprism, the virtual images act as two coherent sources are superimposed and interference fringes are formed in overlapping region PQ on a screen placed at O.

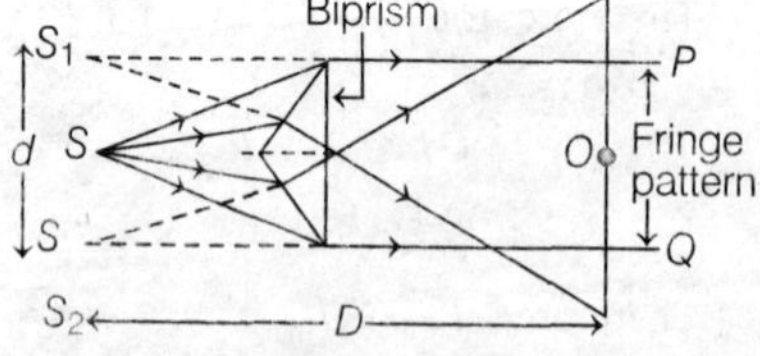

In order to measure the distance d between the virtual sources S_1 and S_2, Glazebrook gave a method, known as magnification method due to Glazebrook. If d_1 and d_2 are the distance between real images of S_1 and S_2, then $d = \sqrt{d_1 d_2}$

Given, $\quad d_1 = 16\text{ cm}, d_2 = 9\text{ cm}$

$$\therefore \quad d = \sqrt{16 \times 9} = 12\text{ cm}$$

60 (c) The fringe width obtained in a two slit experiment is given by

$$\beta = \frac{D\lambda}{d} \text{ or } \beta \propto \lambda$$

Given, $\beta_1 = 1.0$ mm, $\lambda_1 = 5000$ Å and $\lambda_2 = 6000$ Å

$$\therefore \quad \frac{\beta_1}{\beta_2} = \frac{\lambda_1}{\lambda_2} \text{ or } \frac{1.0}{\beta_2} = \frac{5000}{6000}$$

$$\Rightarrow \quad \beta_2 = \frac{6000}{5000} = 1.2\text{ mm}$$

61 (c) In interference pattern,

$$\text{Fringe width} = \frac{\lambda D}{d} = w$$

According to the given condition,

$$w' = \frac{\lambda \times 2D}{d/2} \quad \text{(given)}$$

$$= 4 \times \frac{\lambda D}{d} = 4w$$

62 (c) When a white light is used in Young's double slit experiment, then different component colours of white light produce their own interference pattern. The path difference for all colours is zero at the centre of screen, so bright fringes of different colours overlap at the centre. Consequently, the central fringe is white.

63 (a) In Young's double slit experiment, let a screen be placed at a distance D, d be the distance between coherent sources.

The fringe width is given by $\beta = D\lambda/d$, where λ is the wavelength of light used.

When the entire setup is dipped in water, wavelength, $\lambda_w = \frac{\lambda_a}{\mu}$ is decreases.

Therefore, fringe width decreases and hence fringe pattern shrinks.

64 (b) Coherent time $= \frac{\text{Coherence length}}{\text{Velocity of light}}$

$$= \frac{L}{c}$$

65 (c) Suppose slit width's are equal, so they produce waves of equal intensity say I'. Resultant intensity at any point, $I_R = 4I'\cos^2\phi$, where ϕ is the phase difference between the waves at the point of observation.

For maximum intensity, $\phi = 0°$

$$\Rightarrow \quad I_{max} = 4I' = I \quad \ldots(i)$$

If one of slits is closed, resultant intensity at the same point will be I' only, i.e.

$$I' = I_0 \quad \text{...(ii)}$$

Comparing Eqs. (i) and (ii), we get

$$I = 4I_0$$

66 *(d)* The rays of light from two coherent sources superimpose each other on the screen forming alternate maxima (with maximum intensity I_0) and minima (with intensity zero). If two non-coherent sources superimpose, there will be no maxima and minima, instead the intensity will be $\frac{I_0}{2}$ throughout.

67 *(c)* Given, $\lambda = 589 \text{ nm} = 589 \times 10^{-9} \text{m}$

and $d = 0.589 \text{ mm} = 0.589 \times 10^{-3} \text{ m}$

In Young's double slit experiment, half angular width is given by,

$$\sin\theta = \frac{\lambda}{d}$$

$$\Rightarrow \quad \sin\theta = \frac{589 \times 10^{-9}}{0.589 \times 10^{-3}} = 10^{-3}$$

$$\Rightarrow \quad \theta = \sin^{-1}(0.001)$$

68 *(c)* Given, phase difference $= 100\pi$

$$\text{Path difference} = \frac{\lambda}{2\pi} \times \text{Phase difference}$$

$$= \frac{\lambda}{2\pi} \times 100\,\pi = 50\lambda$$

69 *(b)* Given, path difference, $\Delta x = 3.75\ \mu\text{m} = 3.75 \times 10^{-6}$ m and wavelength, $\lambda = 5000\ \text{Å} = 5 \times 10^{-7}$ m

$$\frac{\Delta x}{\lambda} = \frac{3.75 \times 10^{-6}}{5 \times 10^{-7}} = \frac{37.5}{5} = 7.5$$

$$\Rightarrow \quad \Delta x = 7.5\,\lambda$$

Here, Δx is odd multiple of λ, so point is dark.

70 *(b)* The optical path between any two points is proportional to the time of travel. The distance traversed by light in a medium of refractive index μ in time t is given by

$$d = vt \quad \text{...(i)}$$

where, v is velocity of light in the medium. The distance traversed by light in a vacuum in this time, $d' = ct$

$$d' = c \cdot \frac{d}{v} \quad \text{[from Eq. (i)]}$$

$$d' = d\frac{c}{v} = \mu d \quad \text{...(ii)}$$

$$\left(\text{Since } \mu = \frac{c}{v}\right)$$

This distance is the equivalent distance in vacuum and is called optical path.

Here, optical path for first ray $= n_1L_1$, optical path for second ray $= n_2L_2$

Path difference $= n_1L_1 - n_2L_2$

Now, phase difference

$= 2\pi/\lambda \times$ path difference

$$= \frac{2\pi}{\lambda} \times (n_1L_1 - n_2L_2)$$

71 *(d)* Given, $\lambda_1 = 5893$ Å, $n_1 = 62$, $\lambda_2 = 4358$ Å

As field of view in case of both the wavelengths is same, hence

$$n_1\beta_1 = n_2\beta_2$$

$$\text{As, } n_1\left(\frac{D\lambda_1}{d}\right) = n_2\left(\frac{D\lambda_2}{d}\right)$$

$$\Rightarrow \quad n_2 = n_1\left(\frac{\lambda_1}{\lambda_2}\right) = 62 \times \frac{5893}{4358} \approx 84$$

72 *(d)* We know that,

$$I \propto a^2 \quad \text{or} \quad a \propto \sqrt{I} \quad \text{or} \quad \frac{a_1}{a_2} = \sqrt{\left(\frac{I_1}{I_2}\right)}$$

$$\text{So,} \quad \frac{I_{max}}{I_{min}} = \frac{(a_1 + a_2)^2}{(a_1 - a_2)^2} = \frac{(1+\sqrt{\beta})^2}{(1-\sqrt{\beta})^2}$$

Applying componendo and dividendo, we get

$$\frac{I_{max} + I_{min}}{I_{max} - I_{min}} = \frac{(1+\sqrt{\beta})^2 + (1-\sqrt{\beta})^2}{(1+\sqrt{\beta})^2 - (1-\sqrt{\beta})^2} = \frac{2+2\beta}{4\sqrt{\beta}}$$

$$\text{or} \quad \frac{I_{max} - I_{min}}{I_{max} + I_{min}} = \frac{2\sqrt{\beta}}{1+\beta}$$

73 *(c)* In Young's double slit experiment, for maximum intensity (bright fringe)

$$x = m\frac{D\lambda}{d} \quad \text{... (i)}$$

where, m is the path difference, D is the distance between screen and coherent sources, d is the distance between coherent sources and λ is the wavelength.

Putting $m = 0$ in Eq. (i) we get the position of the central bright fringe (which is called zero order fringe).

Hence, at point O the path difference between two wavelets is zero, then at O there is always a bright fringe. This is called the central fringe.

74 *(c)* As, average of I_{max} and I_{min} is given as

$$\frac{I_{max} + I_{min}}{2} = \frac{(a_1 + a_2)^2 + (a_1 - a_2)^2}{2}$$

$$= \frac{2(a_1^2 + a_2^2)}{2} = a_1^2 + a_2^2$$

$$\Rightarrow \quad = I_1 + I_2$$

Hence, during phenomenon of interference, energy is conserved, but it is redistributed.

75 *(a)* The position of 30th bright fringe

$$y_{30} = \frac{30\lambda D}{d}$$

Now, position shift to central fringe is

$$y_0 = \frac{30\lambda D}{d}$$

But we know that,

$$y_0 = \frac{D}{d}(\mu - 1)t$$

$$\frac{30\lambda D}{d} = \frac{D}{d}(\mu - 1)t$$

$$\Rightarrow \quad (\mu - 1) = \frac{30\lambda}{t}$$

Given, $\lambda = 6000\,\text{Å} = 6000 \times 10^{-10}$ m,

$$t = 3.6 \times 10^{-3} \text{ cm} = 3.6 \times 10^{-5} \text{ m}$$

$$(\mu - 1) = \frac{30 \times 6000 \times 10^{-10}}{3.6 \times 10^{-5}} = 0.5$$

$$\Rightarrow \quad \mu = 1.5$$

76 *(d)* $I_1 = I_2 = 1 \text{ Wm}^{-2}$

So, resultant intensity at third vertex

$$I = (\sqrt{I_1} + \sqrt{I_2})^2$$

$$= (\sqrt{1} + \sqrt{1})^2 \quad \text{(given)}$$

$$= (1+1)^2 = 4 \text{ Wm}^{-2}$$

77 *(a)* As, $\Delta\phi$ = phase difference and Δx = path difference.

$$\therefore \quad \Delta\phi = \frac{2\pi}{\lambda}[\Delta x]$$

$$\Rightarrow \quad \Delta x = \left(\frac{\lambda}{2\pi}\right)\Delta\phi$$

78 *(a)* Given,

$$\phi = \frac{\pi}{3}, a_1 = 4 \text{ and } a_2 = 3$$

Amplitude,

$$A = \sqrt{a_1^2 + a_2^2 + 2a_1a_2\cos\phi}$$

$$= \sqrt{4^2 + 3^2 + 2\times4\times3\times\cos\left(\frac{\pi}{3}\right)}$$

$$= 6.7 \simeq 7$$

79 *(b)* When a thin glass plate of thickness t is placed over one of the slits, then lateral displacement is given by

$$x = \frac{(\mu - 1)tD}{d}$$

Given, $\mu = 1.5$, $t = 0.06$ mm

$$= 6 \times 10^{-5}\text{m}$$

and $D = 2$ m, $d = 1$ mm

$$= 1 \times 10^{-3}\text{ m}$$

Putting the values in the above relation, we get

$$x = \frac{(1.5 - 1) \times 6 \times 10^{-5} \times 2}{1 \times 10^{-3}}$$

$$= 0.5 \times 12 \times 10^{-2} = 6 \text{ cm}$$

80 *(c)* Distance between two adjacent bright (or dark) fringes is called the fringe width. It is denoted by β, thus,

$$\beta = \frac{D\lambda}{d}$$

where, D is the distance between the slit source and screen and d is the separation of slits.

Since D and d are increased to same extent, so fringe width (β) will remain unchanged.

Topic 3

Diffraction of Light

2019

1 Angular width of the central maxima in the Fraunhoffer diffraction for $\lambda = 6000$ Å is θ_0. When the same slit is illuminated by another monochromatic light, the angular width decreases by 30%. The wavelength of this light is **[NEET (Odisha)]**

(a) 1800 Å (b) 4200 Å (c) 6000 Å (d) 420 Å

2016

2 In a diffraction pattern due to a single slit of width a, the first minimum is observed at an angle 30°, when light of wavelength 5000 Å is incident on the slit. The first secondary maximum is observed at an angle of **[NEET]**

(a) $\sin^{-1}\left(\frac{2}{3}\right)$ (b) $\sin^{-1}\left(\frac{1}{2}\right)$ (c) $\sin^{-1}\left(\frac{3}{4}\right)$ (d) $\sin^{-1}\left(\frac{1}{4}\right)$

3 A linear aperture whose width is 0.02 cm is placed immediately infront of a lens of focal length 60 cm. The aperture is illuminated normally by a parallel beam of wavelength 5×10^{-5} cm. The distance of the first dark band of the diffraction pattern from the centre of the screen is **[NEET]**

(a) 0.10 cm (b) 0.25 cm (c) 0.20 cm (d) 0.15 cm

2015

4 For a parallel beam of monochromatic light of wavelength λ diffraction is produced by a single slit whose width a is of the order of the wavelength of the light. If D is the distance of the screen from the slit, then the width of the central maxima will be **[NEET]**

(a) $\frac{2D\lambda}{a}$ (b) $\frac{D\lambda}{a}$ (c) $\frac{Da}{\lambda}$ (d) $\frac{2Da}{\lambda}$

5 In a double slit experiment, the two slits are 1 mm apart and the screen is placed 1 m away. A monochromatic light of wavelength 500 nm is used. What will be the width of each slit for obtaining ten maxima of double slit within the central maxima of single slit pattern? **[NEET]**

(a) 0.2 mm (b) 0.1 mm (c) 0.5 mm (d) 0.02 mm

2013

6 In single slit diffraction pattern, **[UP CPMT]**

(a) central fringe has negligible width than others

(b) all fringes are of same width

(c) central fringes do not exist

(d) None of the above

2012

7 A parallel beam of monochromatic light is incident normally on a narrow slit. A diffraction pattern is formed on a screen placed perpendicular to the direction of the incident beam. At the first minimum of the diffraction pattern, the phase difference between the rays coming from the two edges of the slit is **[AMU]**

(a) zero (b) $\pi/2$ (c) π (d) 2π

8 For a wavelength of light λ and scattering object of size a, all wavelengths are scattered nearly equally, if **[DUMET]**

(a) $a = \lambda$ (b) $a >> \lambda$ (c) $a << \lambda$ (d) $a \geq \lambda$

9 If two sources have a randomly varying phase difference $\phi(t)$, the resultant intensity will be given by **[DUMET]**

(a) $1/2I_0$ (b) $I_0/2$ (c) $2I_0$ (d) $I_0/\sqrt{2}$

10 For an aperture of size a illuminated by a parallel beam of light having wavelength λ, the Fresnel distance is **[DUMET]**

(a) $\approx a/\lambda$ (b) $\approx a^2/\lambda$

(c) $\approx a^2\lambda$ (d) $\approx a/\lambda^2$

2011

11 Assertion The clouds in sky generally appear to be whitish.

Reason Diffraction due to clouds is efficient in equal measure at all wavelengths. [AIIMS]

(a) Both Assertion and Reason are correct and Reason is the correct explanation of Assertion.
(b) Both Assertion and Reason are correct but Reason is not the correct explanation of Assertion.
(c) Assertion is correct but Reason is incorrect.
(d) Both Assertion and Reason are correct.

12 In a single slit diffraction of light of wavelengths by a slit of width e, the size of the central maxima on a screen at a distance b is [MP PMT]

(a) $2b\lambda + e$ (b) $\frac{2b\lambda}{e}$ (c) $\frac{2b\lambda}{e} + e$ (d) $\frac{2b\lambda}{e} - e$

13 A parallel beam of monochromatic light of wavelength 5000 Å is incident normally on a single narrow slit of width 0.001 mm. The light is focussed by a convex lens on a screen placed on the focal plane. The first minima will be formed for the angle of diffraction equal to [Manipal]

(a) 0° (b) 15° (c) 30° (d) 60°

14 A grating which would be most suitable for constructing a spectrometer for the visible and ultraviolet region, should have [Haryana PMT, CG PMT]

(a) 100 lines cm^{-1} (b) 1000 lines cm^{-1}
(c) 10000 lines cm^{-1} (d) 1000000 lines cm^{-1}

15 In a single slit diffraction experiment, the width of the slit is made double its original width. Then, the central maxima on the diffraction pattern will become [BCECE, J&K CET]

(a) narrower and fainter (b) narrower and brighter
(c) broader and fainter (d) broader and brighter

16 The slit width, when a light of wavelength 6500 Å is incident on a slit, if first minima for red light is at 30°, is

(a) 1×10^{-6} m (b) 5.2×10^{-6} m [DUMET]
(c) 1.3×10^{-6} m (d) 2.6×10^{-6} m

2010

17 Red light of wavelength 625 nm is incident normally on an optical diffraction grating with 2×10^5 lines m^{-1}. Including central principal maxima, how many maximas may be observed on a screen which is far from the grating?

(a) 15 (b) 17 (c) 8 (d) 16 [KCET]

18 A parallel monochromatic beam of light is incident normally on a narrow slit. A diffraction pattern is formed on a screen placed perpendicular to the direction of incident beam. At the first maxima of the diffraction pattern, the phase difference between the rays coming from the edges of the slit is [JCECE]

(a) 0 (b) $\frac{\pi}{2}$ (c) π (d) 2π

19 The angular width of the central maxima of the diffraction pattern in a single slit (off width a) experiment, with λ as the wavelength of light, is [JCECE]

(a) $\frac{3\lambda}{2a}$ (b) $\frac{\lambda}{2a}$ (c) $\frac{2\lambda}{a}$ (d) $\frac{\lambda}{a}$

20 In a single slit diffraction pattern, the distance between the first minima on the left and the first minima on the right is 5 mm. The screen on which the diffraction pattern is displayed is at a distance of 80 cm from the slit. The wavelength is 6000 Å. The slit width (in mm) is about [MGIMS]

(a) 0.576 (b) 0.348 (c) 0.192 (d) 0.096

2008

21 The width of the diffraction band varies [AFMC]

(a) inversely as the wavelength
(b) directly as the width of the slit
(c) directly as the distance between the slit and the screen
(d) inversely as the size of the source from which the slit is illuminated

22 The source is at some distance from an obstacle. Distance between obstacle and the point of observation is b and wavelength of light is λ. Then, the average distance of nth Fresnel zone will be at a distance (from the point of observation) [Punjab PMET]

(a) $\frac{bn\lambda}{2}$ (b) $b - \frac{n\lambda}{2}$ (c) $b + \frac{n\lambda}{2}$ (d) $b - n\lambda$

2007

23 A single slit Fraunhofer diffraction pattern is formed with white light. For what wavelength of light, the third secondary maxima in the diffraction pattern coincides with the second secondary maxima in the pattern for red light of wavelength 6500 Å? [KCET]

(a) 4400 Å (b) 4100 Å (c) 4642.8 Å (d) 9100 Å

2006

24 In a Fraunhofer diffraction at a single slit of width d with incident light of wavelength 5500 Å, the first minima is observed, at an angle 30°. The first secondary maxima is observed at an angle θ equals [Kerala CEE]

(a) $\sin^{-1}\left(\frac{1}{\sqrt{2}}\right)$ (b) $\sin^{-1}\left(\frac{1}{4}\right)$
(c) $\sin^{-1}\left(\frac{3}{4}\right)$ (d) $\sin^{-1}\frac{\sqrt{3}}{2}$ (e) $\sin^{-1}\left(\frac{3}{8}\right)$

2005

25 A single slit of width d is illuminated by violet light of wavelength 400 nm and the width of the diffraction pattern is measured as y. When half of the slit width is covered and illuminated by yellow light of wavelength 600 nm, the width of the diffraction pattern is [KCET]

(a) the pattern vanishes and the width is zero
(b) $\frac{y}{3}$ (c) $3y$ (d) None of these

Answers

1 (b)	2 (c)	3 (d)	4 (a)	5 (a)	6 (d)	7 (c)	8 (b)	9 (d)	10 (b)
11 (a)	12 (c)	13 (c)	14 (d)	15 (a)	16 (c)	17 (b)	18 (d)	19 (c)	20 (c)
21 (c)	22 (c)	23 (c)	24 (c)	25 (c)					

Explanations

1 *(b)* The angular width of central maxima is given by

$$2\theta = \frac{2\lambda}{a} \quad \ldots(i)$$

where, λ = wavelength of light used

and a = width of the slit.

Angular width, $2\theta = \theta_0$ (given)

So, $$\theta_0 = \frac{2\lambda_1}{a} \quad \ldots(ii)$$

[from Eq. (i)]

For another light of wavelength λ_2 (says), the angular width decreases by 30%, so

$$2\theta = \left(\frac{100-30}{100}\right)\theta_0$$

$$2\theta = \frac{70}{100}\theta_0 = 0.7\theta_0$$

$\therefore$ Angular width, $0.7\theta_0 = \frac{2\lambda_2}{a}$ ...(iii)

As slit width is constant, so on dividing Eq. (ii) by Eq. (iii), we get

$$\frac{\theta_0}{0.7\theta_0} = \frac{\lambda_1}{\lambda_2}$$

$$\Rightarrow \lambda_2 = \lambda_1 \times 0.7$$

$$= 6000 \times 0.7 = 4200 \text{ Å}$$

2 *(c)* As, the first minimum is observed at an angle of 30° in a diffraction pattern due to a single slit of width a.

i.e. $n = 1$ and $\theta = 30°$.

$\because$ According to Bragg's law of diffraction,

$$a\sin\theta = n\lambda$$

$$\Rightarrow a\sin 30° = (1)\lambda \quad (n = 1)$$

$$\Rightarrow a = 2\lambda \quad \ldots(i) \quad \left\{\because \sin 30° = \frac{1}{2}\right\}$$

For first secondary maxima,

$$\Rightarrow a\sin\theta_1 = \frac{3\lambda}{2}$$

$$\Rightarrow \sin\theta_1 = \frac{3\lambda}{2a} \quad \ldots(ii)$$

Substitute value of a from Eq. (i) to Eq. (ii), we get

$$\sin\theta_1 = \frac{3\lambda}{4\lambda}$$

$$\Rightarrow \sin\theta_1 = \frac{3}{4}$$

$$\Rightarrow \theta_1 = \sin^{-1}\left(\frac{3}{4}\right)$$

3 *(d)* For the distance of the first dark band of the diffraction pattern from the centre of the screen is given by the position of first minima.

i.e. $Y = \lambda D / a$

where, λ = wavelength of parallel beams,

D = focal length

and a = width of linear aperture.

Given, $\lambda = 5 \times 10^{-5}$ cm,

$D = 60 \text{ cm} = 0.6 \text{ m}$

and $a = 0.02 \text{ cm} = 0.02 \times 10^{-2}$ m

$$\Rightarrow Y = \frac{(5 \times 10^{-5})(0.6)}{0.02 \times 10^{-2}}$$

$$\Rightarrow Y = 0.15 \text{ cm}$$

4 *(a)* For the condition of maxima,

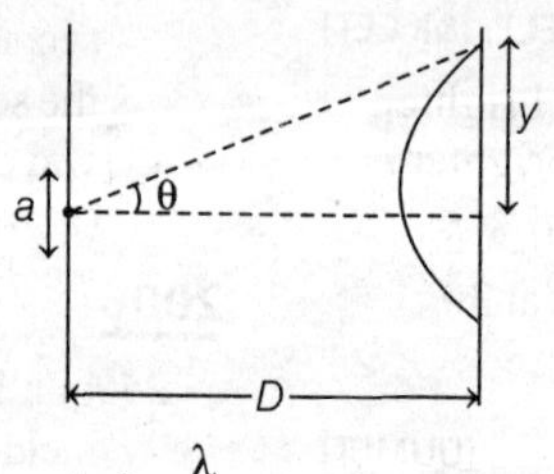

$$\sin\theta = \frac{\lambda}{a}$$

From the geometry,

$$\sin\theta = \theta = \frac{Y}{D} \quad \text{(for small angle)}$$

So $$\frac{Y}{D} = \frac{\lambda}{a}$$

$$\Rightarrow Y = \frac{\lambda D}{a}$$

Hence, width of central maxima

$$= 2Y = \frac{2\lambda D}{a}$$

5 *(a)* Given, $d = 1 \text{ mm} = 1 \times 10^{-3}$ m,

$D = 1$ m

and $\lambda = 500 \text{ nm} = 5 \times 10^{-7}$ m

As, width of central maxima = width of 10 maxima

$$\therefore \frac{2D\lambda}{a} = 10\left(\frac{\lambda D}{d}\right)$$

$$\Rightarrow a = \frac{d}{5} = \frac{10^{-3}}{5}$$

$$= 0.2 \times 10^{-3} \text{ m}$$

$$a = 0.2 \text{ mm}$$

6 *(d)* The following diagram shows a single slit diffraction pattern

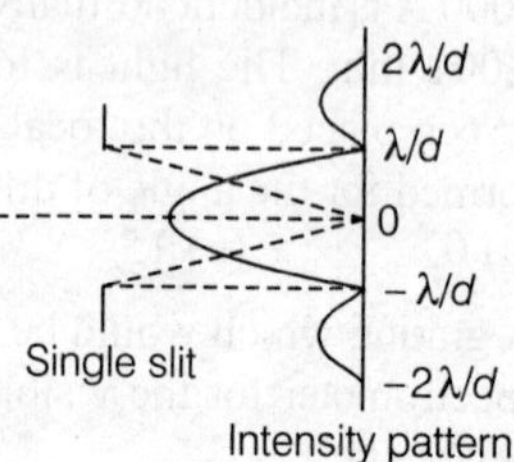

As, it is clear from above diagram, in single slit diffraction, the central fringe has maximum intensity and has width double than other fringes.

7 *(c)* The phase difference (ϕ) between the wavelength from the top edge and bottom edge of the slit is

$$\phi = \frac{2\pi}{\lambda}(d\sin\theta)$$

where, d is the width from minima of the diffractions pattern.

At $\lambda = \lambda/2$, $\sin\theta = \frac{\lambda}{2d}$

$$\Rightarrow \phi = \frac{2\pi}{\lambda}\left(d \times \frac{\lambda}{2d}\right) = \pi$$

8 *(b)* All the wavelengths are scattered nearly equally, if $a >> \lambda$.

9 *(d)* If two sources have a randomly varying phase difference $\phi(t)$, then the resultant intensity will be $\frac{I_0}{\sqrt{2}}$.

10 *(b)* In this case, the Fresnel distance is equivalent to a^2/λ.

11 *(a)* As, the water droplets in cloud is responsible for diffraction of light and is efficient in equal measure at all wavelength and hence cloud look whitish.

12 (c) The direction in which the first minima occurs is θ (say). The $e \sin \theta = \lambda$

or $\quad e\theta = \lambda$ or $\theta = \dfrac{\lambda}{e}$

($\because \theta = \sin \theta$, when θ is small)

Width of the central maxima

$$= 2b\theta + e = \frac{2b\lambda}{e} + e$$

13 (c) For the first minima, $d \sin \theta = \lambda$

$$\Rightarrow \quad \sin \theta = \frac{\lambda}{d}$$

Given, $\lambda = 5000 \text{Å} = 5000 \times 10^{-10}$ m

and $d = 0.001 \text{ mm} = 0.001 \times 10^{3}$ m.

$$\Rightarrow \theta = \sin^{-1}\left[\frac{5000 \times 10^{-10}}{0.001 \times 10^{-3}}\right]$$

$$= \sin^{-1}(0.5) = 30^\circ$$

14 (d) Grating with 10^6 lines/cm is suitable for constructing spectrometer for visible and ultraviolet region because this corresponds to the wavelength equivalent to the wavelengths of visible and ultraviolet region.

15 (a) Width of central maxima,

$$\beta = \frac{2D\lambda}{d}$$

As, we increase d to $2d$, β becomes $\dfrac{\beta}{2}$.

So, it becomes narrower and fainter.

16 (c) When rays of monochromatic light of wavelength λ are incident on a diffraction grating in which slit separation is d, then for angle of diffraction θ, the following relation holds true.

$$d \sin \theta = n\lambda$$

where, n is called the spectrum order.

Given, $n = 1$, $\lambda = 6500$ Å

$$= 6500 \times 10^{-10} \text{ m}$$

and $\quad \sin 30^\circ = \dfrac{1}{2}$

$$\Rightarrow \quad d = \frac{n\lambda}{\sin 30^\circ} = \frac{6500 \times 10^{-10}}{(1/2)}$$

$$\Rightarrow \quad d = 1.3 \times 10^{-6} \text{ m}$$

17 (b) For principal maxima in grating spectra,

$$\frac{\sin \theta}{N} = n\lambda$$

where, $n = (1, 2, 3...)$ is the order of principal maximum and θ is the angle of diffraction.

Given, $\lambda = 625 \text{ nm} = 6.25 \times 10^{-7}$ m,

$N = 2 \times 10^5$ line/m and $\theta = 90^\circ$

$$\Rightarrow n = \frac{1}{\lambda N} = \frac{1}{6.25 \times 10^{-7} \times 2 \times 10^5} = 8$$

$\therefore$ Number of maxima

$$= 2n + 1 = 2 \times 8 + 1 = 17$$

18 (d) The phase difference (ϕ) between the wavelets from the top edges and the bottom edges of the slit is

$$\phi = \frac{2\pi}{\lambda}(d \sin \theta)$$

where, d is the slit width.

The first minima of the diffraction pattern occurs at $\sin \theta = \dfrac{\lambda}{d}$

So, $\quad \phi = \dfrac{2\pi}{\lambda}\left(d \times \dfrac{\lambda}{d}\right) = 2\pi$

19 (c) The central maxima lies between the first minima on both sides. The angular width of central maxima

$$= 2\theta = \frac{2\lambda}{a}$$

20 (c) Slit width, $d = \dfrac{2D\lambda}{\beta}$

Given, $\quad D = 80 \text{ cm} = 80 \times 10^{-2}$ m,

$$\lambda = 6000 \text{ Å} = 6000 \times 10^{-10} \text{m}$$

and $\quad \beta = 5 \text{ mm} = 5 \times 10^{-3}$ m

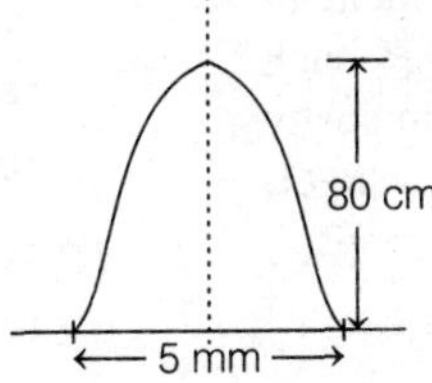

$$\therefore d = \frac{80 \times 10^{-2} \times 6000 \times 10^{-10} \times 2}{5 \times 10^{-3}}$$

$$= 0.192 \text{ mm}$$

21 (c) Width of the diffraction band is given by

$$\beta = \frac{\lambda D}{d}$$

where, D = distance between slit and the screen, λ = wavelength of light used and d = width of slit.

Hence, width of the diffraction band varies directly as the distance between the slit and the screen.

22 (c) The average distance of nth Fresnel zone from observation point will be at a distance is $b + \dfrac{n\lambda}{2}$.

23 (c) We know that, position of nth maximum where, $n = 1, 2, ...$ corresponds to central maxima.

For red light, $x = \dfrac{(4+1)D}{2a} \times 6500$

[$\because$ for 2nd maxima, $n = 2$]

For unknown wavelength of light,

$$x = \frac{(6+1)D}{2a} \times \lambda$$

[$\because$ for 3rd maxima, $n = 3$]

Accordingly, equating the equations

$\therefore 5 \times 6500 = 7 \times \lambda$

$$\Rightarrow \quad \lambda = \frac{5}{7} \times 6500 = 4642.8 \text{ Å}$$

24 (c) Condition for nth secondary minima is that path difference

$$= a \sin \theta_n = n\lambda$$

For n th secondary maxima is path difference $= a \sin \theta_n = (2n+1)\dfrac{\lambda}{2}$

For 1st minima,

$$\lambda = 5500 \text{ Å}, \theta_n = 30^\circ$$

$$a \sin 30^\circ = \lambda \quad \text{...(i)}$$

For 2nd maxima, path difference

$$= a \sin \theta_n = (2+1)\frac{\lambda}{2} \quad \text{...(ii)}$$

Dividing Eq. (i) by Eq. (ii), we get

$$\frac{\frac{1}{2}}{\sin \theta_n} = \frac{2}{3} \Rightarrow \sin \theta_n = \frac{3}{4}$$

$$\Rightarrow \quad \theta_n = \sin^{-1}\left(\frac{3}{4}\right)$$

25 (c) In single slit diffraction experiment, width of central maxima,

$$y = \frac{2\lambda D}{d}$$

where d = slit of width.

Given, $\lambda_1 = 4000$ Å

and $\lambda_2 = 6000$Å, when $d = \dfrac{d}{2}$.

Case I $\quad y = \dfrac{2 \times 4000}{d} = \dfrac{8000D}{d} \quad \text{...(i)}$

Case II

$$y' = \frac{2 \times 6000 \times D}{\frac{d}{2}} = \frac{24000D}{d} \quad \text{...(ii)}$$

From Eqs. (i) and (ii), we get

$$y' = 3y$$

Topic 4

Polarisation of Light

2019

1 **Assertion** Incoming light reflected by earth is partially polarised.

Reason Atmospheric particle polarise the light. **[AIIMS]**

(a) Both Assertion and Reason are correct and Reason is the correct explanation of Assertion.
(b) Both Assertion and Reason are correct but Reason is not the correct explanation of Assertion.
(c) Assertion is correct but Reason is incorrect.
(d) Both Assertion and Reason are incorrect.

2018

2 Unpolarised light is incident from air on a plane surface of a material of refractive index μ. At a particular angle of incidence i, it is found that the reflected and refracted rays are perpendicular to each other. Which of the following options is correct for this situation? **[NEET]**

(a) $i = \sin^{-1}\left(\frac{1}{\mu}\right)$
(b) Reflected light is polarised with its electric vector perpendicular to the plane of incidence
(c) Reflected light is polarised with its electric vector parallel to the plane of incidence
(d) $i = \tan^{-1}\left(\frac{1}{\mu}\right)$

2017

3 Two polaroids P_1 and P_2 are placed with their axis perpendicular to each other. Unpolarised light I_0 is incident on P_1. A third polaroid P_3 is kept in between P_1 and P_2 such that its axis makes an angle 45° with that of P_1. The intensity of transmitted light through P_2 is **[NEET]**

(a) $\frac{I_0}{2}$ (b) $\frac{I_0}{4}$
(c) $\frac{I_0}{8}$ (d) $\frac{I_0}{16}$

2014

4 The angle of incidence at which reflected light is totally polarised for refraction from air to glass (refractive index μ) is **[UK PMT]**

(a) $\sin^{-1}\mu$ (b) $\sin^{-1}(1/\mu)$
(c) $\tan^{-1}(1/\mu)$ (d) $\tan^{-1}(\mu)$

5 A polarised light of intensity I_0 is passed through another polariser whose pass axis makes an angle of 60° with the pass axis of the former. What is the intensity of emergent polarised light from second polariser? **[KCET]**

(a) $I = I_0$ (b) $I = I_0/6$
(c) $I = I_0/5$ (d) $I_0/4$

2013

6 An unpolarised beam of intensity I_0 is incident on a pair of nicols making an angle of 60° with each other. The intensity of light emerging from the pair is **[AFMC]**

(a) I_0 (b) $I_0/4$ (c) $I_0/2$ (d) $I_0/8$

7 The Brewster angle for the glass-air interface is 54.74°. If a ray of light going from air to glass strikes at an angle of incidence 45°, then the angle of refraction is (given, $\tan 54.74° = \sqrt{2}$) **[Manipal]**

(a) 60° (b) 30° (c) 25° (d) 54.74°

2011

8 The critical angle of a certain medium is $\sin^{-1}\left(\frac{3}{5}\right)$. The polarising angle of the medium is **[KCET]**

(a) $\sin^{-1}\left(\frac{4}{5}\right)$ (b) $\tan^{-1}\left(\frac{5}{3}\right)$
(c) $\tan^{-1}\left(\frac{3}{4}\right)$ (d) $\tan^{-1}\left(\frac{4}{3}\right)$

2010

9 Critical angle for certain medium is $\sin^{-1}(0.6)$. The polarising angle of that medium is **[KCET]**

(a) $\tan^{-1}(1.5)$ (b) $\sin^{-1}(0.8)$
(c) $\tan^{-1}(1.6667)$ (d) $\tan^{-1}(0.6667)$

10 When the angle of incidence on a material is 60°, the reflected light is completely polarised. The velocity of the refracted ray inside the material is (in ms^{-1}) **[JCECE]**

(a) 3×10^8 (b) $\left[\frac{3}{\sqrt{2}}\right] \times 10^8$
(c) $\sqrt{3} \times 10^8$ (d) 0.5×10^8

11 Which of the following phenomena is not common to sound and light waves? **[CG PMT]**

(a) Interference (b) Diffraction
(c) Polarisation (d) Reflection

2009

12 Specific rotation of sugar solution is 0.01 SI units. $200\,kg\,m^{-3}$ of impure sugar solution is taken in a polarimeter tube of length 0.25 m and an optical rotation of 0.4 rad is observed. The percentage of purity of sugar in the sample is **[AIIMS]**

(a) 11% (b) 20% (c) 80% (d) 89%

13 The graph showing the dependence of intensity of transmitted light on the angle between polariser and analyser, is **[AIIMS]**

(a) 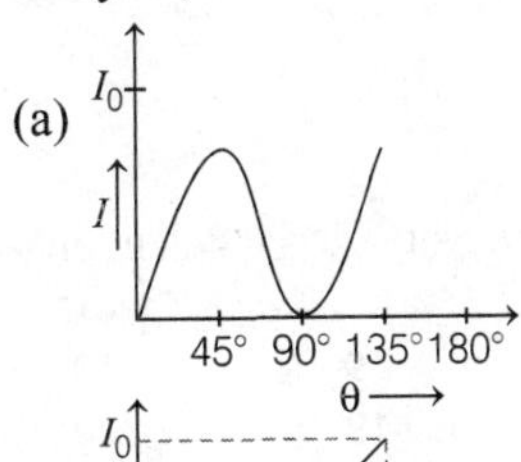

(b) 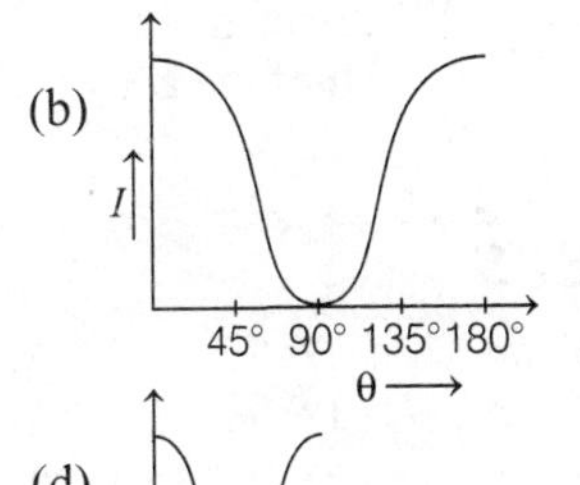

(c) 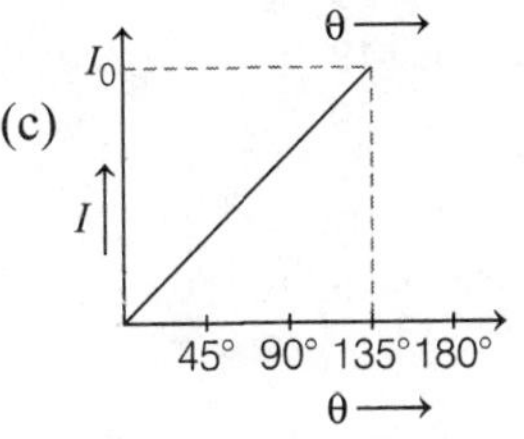

(d) 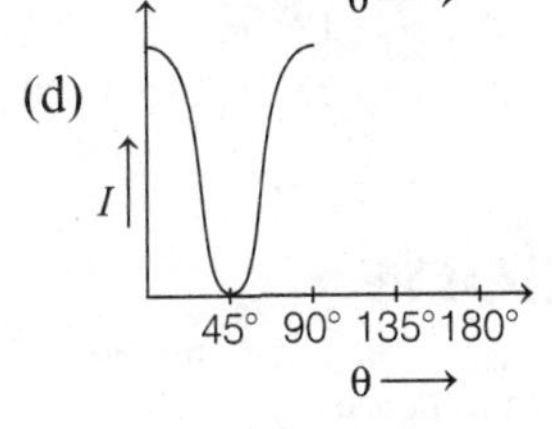

14 Two nicols are oriented with, then principal planes making an angle of 60°. The percentage of incident unpolarised light which passes through the system is **[Manipal]**

(a) 50% (b) 100% (c) 12.5% (d) 37.5%

15 In case of linearly polarised light, the magnitude of the electric field vector **[Manipal]**

(a) does not change with time
(b) varies periodically with time
(c) increases and decreases linearly with time
(d) is parallel to the direction of propagation

16 Transverse nature of the light was confirmed by the phenomenon of **[J&K CET]**

(a) refraction of light (b) diffraction of light
(c) dispersion of light (d) polarisation of light

2008

17 When an unpolarised light of intensity I_0 is incident on a polarising sheet, the intensity of the light which does not get transmitted is **[MHT CET]**

(a) $\frac{1}{2}I_0$ (b) $\frac{1}{4}I_0$ (c) zero (d) I_0

18 Light is incident on a glass surface at polarising angle of 57.5°. Then, the angle between the incident ray and the refracted ray is **[Kerala CEE]**

(a) 57.5° (b) 115° (c) 65° (d) 145°
(e) None of these

19 The angle of incidence of light is equal to Brewster's angle, then **[J&K CET]**

I. reflected ray is perpendicular to refracted ray
II. refracted ray is parallel to reflected ray
III. reflected light is polarised having its electric vector in plane of incidence
IV. refracted light is polarised

(a) I and IV are correct (b) I and II are correct
(c) I and III are correct (d) II and III are correct

20 An unpolarised beam of intensity I_0 falls on a polaroid. The intensity of the emergent light is **[KCET]**

(a) $\frac{I_0}{2}$ (b) I_0
(c) $\frac{I_0}{4}$ (d) zero

21 Which of the following is a dichroic crystal? **[KCET]**

(a) Quartz (b) Tourmaline
(c) Mica (d) Selenite

2007

22 Brewster's angle in terms of refractive index (μ) of the medium **[AFMC]**

(a) $\tan^{-1}\sqrt{\mu}$ (b) $\sin^{-1}\mu$
(c) $\sin^{-1}\sqrt{\mu}$ (d) $\tan^{-1}\mu$

23 Sound wave in air cannot be polarised because **[J&K CET]**

(a) their speed is small
(b) they require medium
(c) these are longitudinal
(d) their speed is temperature dependent

2006

24 Which one of the following statements is true? **[CBSE AIPMT]**

(a) Both light and sound waves in air are transverse.
(b) The sound waves in air are longitudinal while the light waves are transverse.
(c) Both light and sound waves in air are longitudinal.
(d) Both light and sound waves can travel in vacuum.

25 Which of the following diagrams represent the variation of electric field vector with time for a circularly polarised light? **[AIIMS]**

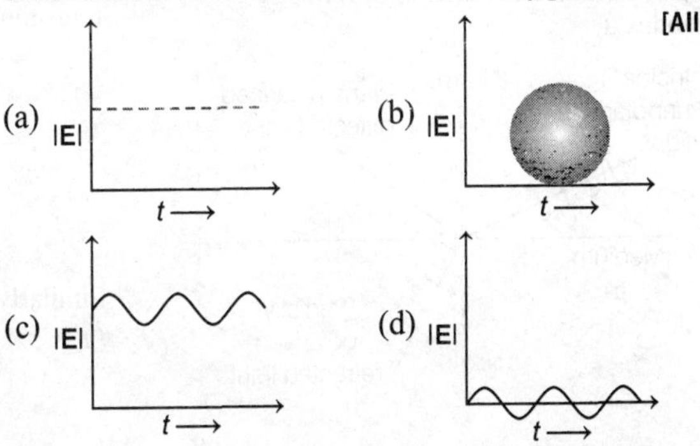

26 In the propagation of light waves, the angle between the direction of vibration and plane of polarisation is **[UP CPMT]**

(a) 0° (b) 90°
(c) 45° (d) 80°

27 Two polaroids are oriented with their planes perpendicular to incident light and transmission axis making an angle of 30° with each other. What fraction of incident unpolarised light is transmitted? **[KCET]**

(a) $\frac{1}{2}$ (b) $\frac{3}{4}$
(c) $\frac{7}{8}$ (d) $\frac{3}{8}$

2005

28 For the study of the helical structure of nucleic acids, the property of electromagnetic radiation, generally used is **[EAMCET]**

(a) reflection (b) interference
(c) diffraction (d) polarisation

29 When unpolarised light beam is incident from air onto glass ($n = 1.5$) at the polarising angle **[KCET]**

(a) reflected beam is polarised 100%
(b) reflected and refracted beams are partially polarised
(c) the reason for option (a) is that almost all the light is reflected
(d) All of the above

Answers

1 (b)	2 (b)	3 (c)	4 (d)	5 (d)	6 (d)	7 (b)	8 (b)	9 (c)	10 (c)
11 (c)	12 (c)	13 (b)	14 (c)	15 (b)	16 (d)	17 (a)	18 (e)	19 (c)	20 (a)
21 (b)	22 (d)	23 (c)	24 (b)	25 (a)	26 (a)	27 (d)	28 (d)	29 (a)	

Explanations

1 *(b)* When unpolarised light coming from sun, enters into atmosphere of earth, then it scatters due to presence of atmospheric particles. The scattered light seen in a direction perpendicular to the direction of incidence is found to be plane polarised.

When the light from the sun incident on reflecting surface of earth at an angle of polarisation, then reflecting light is polarised. Little amount of light is incident on polarising direction, hence reflected light is partially polarised.

Hence, Assertion and Reason both are correct but Reason is not the correct explanation of Assertion.

2 *(b)* The figure shown below represents the course of path an unpolarised light follows, when it is incident from air on plane surface of material of refractive index μ.

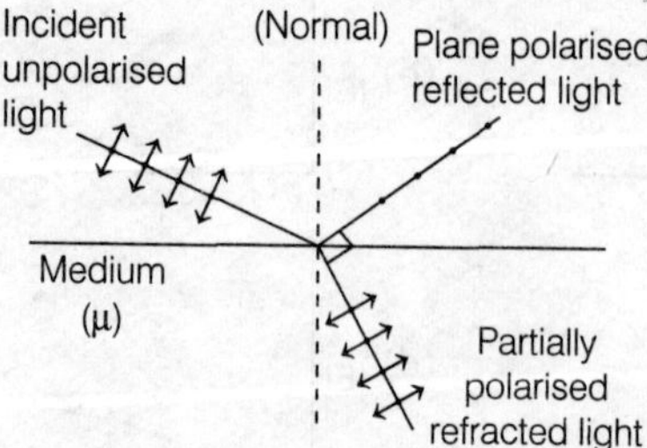

If reflected and refracted light are perpendicular to each other, then the reflected light is completely plane polarised at a certain angle of incidence. This means, the reflected light has electric vector perpendicular to incidence plane.

3 *(c)* According to the question,

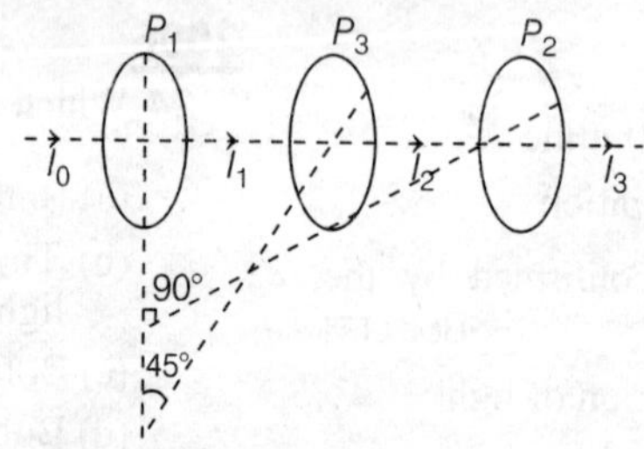

Given, θ = 45°

From the above diagram, intensity transmitted through P_3,

$$I_2 = \frac{I_0}{2}\cos^2 45°$$

$$\Rightarrow \quad I_2 = \frac{I_0}{2} \times \left(\frac{1}{\sqrt{2}}\right)^2$$

$$\Rightarrow \quad I_2 = \frac{I_0}{4}$$

Similarly, intensity transmitted through P_2,

$$I_3 = \frac{I_0}{4}\cos^2 45°$$

$$\Rightarrow \quad I_3 = \frac{I_0}{4} \times \left(\frac{1}{\sqrt{2}}\right)^2$$

$$\Rightarrow \quad I_3 = \frac{I_0}{4} \times \frac{1}{2}$$

$$\Rightarrow \quad I_3 = \frac{I_0}{8}$$

4 *(d)* Suppose, i_p is the Brewster's angle, when unpolarised light is incident at polarising angle, the reflected component along OB and refracted component along OC can be shown in the given figure as follows

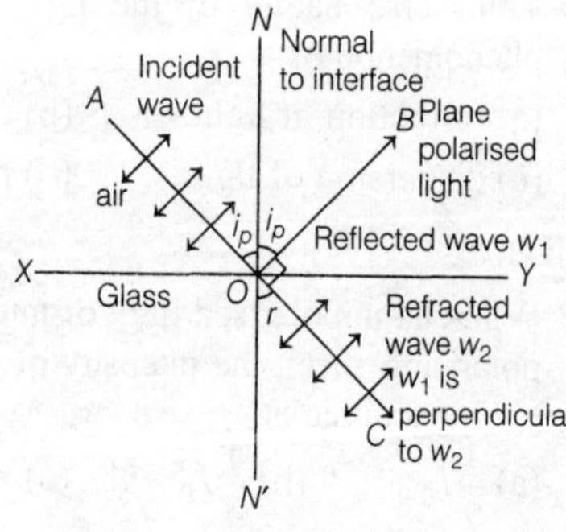

Now, $\angle BOY + \angle YOC = 90°$

$(90° - i_p) + (90° - r) = 90°$

Here, r is the angle of refraction.

i.e. $90° - i_p = r$

According to Snell's law,

$$\mu = \frac{\sin i}{\sin r}$$

When, $i = i_p, r = 90° - i_p$

Then, $\mu = \frac{\sin i_p}{\sin (90° - i_p)} = \frac{\sin i_p}{\cos i_p}$

$= \tan i_p$

$\therefore \quad i_p = \tan^{-1} (\mu)$

where, i_p is polarised angle.

5 *(d)* By law of Malus, $I = I_0 \cos^2 \theta$

where, I = intensity of emergent polarised light and I_0 = intensity passed through polariser.

Given, $\theta = 60°, I = ?$

$$I = I_0 \times \cos^2 60°$$

$$= I_0 \times \left(\frac{1}{2}\right)^2 = \frac{I_0}{4}$$

6 *(d)* Since the incident light beam is unpolarised, the intensity of light, on being transmitted through first nicol polaroid, will become

$$I = \frac{I_0}{2} \quad \text{...(i)}$$

Then, the intensity of light on passing through the second nicol is given by,

$$I' = I \cos^2 60 \quad \left(\because \cos 60° = \frac{1}{2}\right)$$

$$= \frac{I_0}{2}\left(\frac{1}{2}\right)^2 = \frac{I_0}{8}$$

7 *(b)* Refractive index, $\mu = \tan \theta = \sqrt{2}$

and $i = 45°$

Now according to Snell's law,

$$\sqrt{2} = \frac{\sin 45°}{\sin r} \quad \left[\because \mu = \frac{\sin i}{\sin r}\right]$$

$$\sin r = \frac{\frac{1}{\sqrt{2}}}{\sqrt{2}}$$

$\Rightarrow \quad \sin r = 0.5$

$r = 30°$

8 *(b)* Polarising angle, $\mu = \tan i$

and $\quad \mu = \frac{1}{\sin C}$

$$\tan i = \frac{1}{\sin C}$$

where, C = critical angle.

$\therefore \quad \cot i = \sin\left(\sin^{-1}\left(\frac{3}{5}\right)\right)$

$\Rightarrow \quad \cot i = \frac{3}{5}$ or $\tan i = \frac{5}{3}$

or $\quad i = \tan^{-1}\left(\frac{5}{3}\right)$

9 *(c)* Critical angle,

$$C = \sin^{-1} (0.6)$$

$$\sin C = 0.6$$

$$\mu = \frac{1}{\sin C} = \frac{1}{0.6}$$

Polarising angle,

$$i_p = \tan^{-1} (\mu)$$

$$= \tan^{-1}\left(\frac{1}{0.6}\right)$$

$$= \tan^{-1} (1.6667)$$

10 *(c)* From Brewster's law, $\mu = \tan i_p$

$\Rightarrow \quad \frac{c}{v} = \tan 60° = \sqrt{3}$

$\Rightarrow \quad v = \frac{c}{\sqrt{3}} = \frac{3 \times 10^8}{\sqrt{3}}$

$= \sqrt{3} \times 10^8 \text{ ms}^{-1}$

11 *(c)* Polarisation is not shown by sound waves because sound waves are longitudinal waves.

12 *(c)* Given, $\theta = 0.4$ rad, $l = 0.25$ m

and $\alpha = 0.01$.

Specific rotation of sugar solution,

$$\alpha = \frac{\text{Angle of rotation}}{\text{Length of tube} \times \text{Concentration}}$$

$$= \frac{\theta}{l \times C}$$

$\therefore \quad C = \frac{\theta}{l\alpha} = \frac{0.4}{0.25 \times 0.01}$

$= 160 \text{ kg m}^{-3}$

Thus, purity of sugar solution

$$= \frac{160}{200} \times 100 = 80\%$$

13 *(b)* According to law of Malus, when a beam of completely plane polarised light is incident on an analyser, the resultant intensity of light (I) transmitted from the analyser varies directly as the square of the cosine of the angle (θ) between planes of transmission of analyser and polariser.

$$I \propto \cos^2 \theta$$

and $\quad I = I_0 \cos^2 \theta \quad \text{...(i)}$

where, I_0 = intensity of the light from polariser.

From Eq. (i), we note that if the transmission axes of polariser and analyser are parallel (i.e. $\theta = 0°$ or $180°$), then $I = I_0$. It means that intensity of transmitted light is maximum.

When the transmission axis of polariser and analyser are perpendicular (i.e. $\theta = 90°$), then

$$I = I_0 \cos^2 90° = 0.$$

It means the intensity of transmitted light is minimum.

On plotting a graph between I and θ as given by relation (i), we get the curve as shown in figure

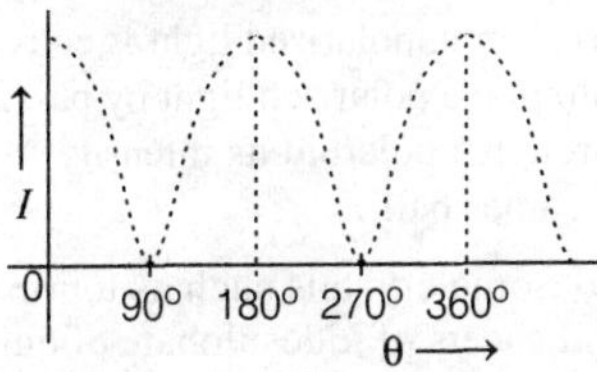

14 *(c)* Intensity of polarised light from first polariser $= \frac{100}{2} = 50$

$$I = I_0 \cos^2 \theta = 50 \cos^2 60°$$

$$= \frac{50}{4} = 12.5\%$$

15 *(b)* The magnitude of electric field vector varies periodically with time, because it is a form of electromagnetic wave.

16 *(d)* Transverse nature of light was confirmed by the polarisation of light.

17 *(a)* According to law of Malus,

$$I = I_0 \cos^2 \theta$$

Intensity of polarised light $= \frac{I_0}{2}$

$\left[\because \text{average value of } \cos\theta = \frac{1}{2}\right]$

$\therefore$ Intensity of untransmitted light

$$= I_0 - \frac{I_0}{2} = \frac{I_0}{2}$$

18 *(e)* When light ray incident at polarising angle, then angle of incidence (i) and angle of reflection (r) are equal. Also, angle between reflected and refracted ray is 90°.

Thus, angle between incident ray and refracted ray

$$= 57.5° + 57.5° + 90° = 205°$$

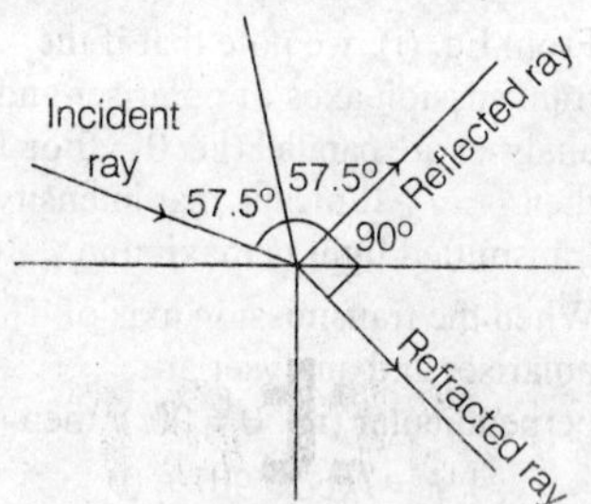

19 *(c)* By Brewster's law, reflected ray is perpendicular to refracted ray.

The reflected ray so obtained is plane polarised having its electric vector in the plane of incidence.

20 *(a)* If an unpolarised light is converted into plane polarised light by passing through a polaroid its intensity becomes half.

21 *(b)* Some crystals such as tourmaline and sheets of iodosulphate of quinine have the property of strongly absorbing the light with vibrations perpendicular to a specific direction (called transmission axis) transmitting the light with vibration parallel to it. This selective absorption of light is called dichroism.

22 *(d)* Refractive index of a medium,

$$\mu = \tan i_p$$

where, i_p = Brewster's angle.

$$\Rightarrow \quad i_p = \tan^{-1}\mu$$

23 *(c)* Sound waves are longitudinal and cannot be polarised.

24 *(b)* Sound waves are longitudinal in nature. Light waves are transverse in nature.
Sound waves need medium to travel. So, they cannot move in space.

25 *(a)* When two plane polarised waves are superimposed, then under certain conditions, the resultant light vector rotates with a constant magnitude in a plane perpendicular to the direction of propagation. The tip of the vector traces a circle and the light is said to be circularly polarised.

To form circularly polarised light,

$$E_x = E_0 \sin \omega t$$

$$\Rightarrow \quad E_y = E_0 \cos \omega t = E_0 \sin\left(\omega t + \frac{\pi}{2}\right)$$

where, E_0 is amplitude.

Resultant amplitude,

$$\mathbf{E} = \mathbf{E}_x + \mathbf{E}_y$$

$$|\mathbf{E}|^2 = E_0 + E_0 + 2E_0 \cdot E_0 \cos\frac{\pi}{2}$$

$$|\mathbf{E}|^2 = E_0\sqrt{2} = \text{constant}$$

26 *(a)* Plane containing the direction of vibration and wave motion is called plane of polarisation. Plane of vibration is perpendicular to the direction of propagation and also perpendicular to the plane of polarisation.

Therefore, angle between plane of polarisation and direction of propagation is 0°.

27 *(d)* Suppose, intensity of unpolarised light = I_0

$\therefore$ Intensity of polarised light = $\frac{I_0}{2}$

Intensity of emergent light,

$$I = \frac{I_0}{2}\cos^2 30°$$

$$= \frac{I_0}{2}\cdot\left(\frac{\sqrt{3}}{2}\right)^2$$

$$I = \frac{3I_0}{8}$$

$$\frac{I}{I_0} = \frac{3}{8}$$

$\therefore$ Fraction of incident unpolarised light of transmitted

$$= \frac{I}{I_0} = \frac{3}{8}$$

28 *(d)* For the study of the helical structure of nucleic acids, polarisation property of electromagnetic radiation is generally used.

29 *(a)* If unpolarised light is incident at polarising angle, then reflected light is completely, i.e. 100% polarised.

25

Dual Nature of Matter and Radiation

Quick Review

Electron Emission

- It is the phenomenon of emission of electrons from the surface of the metal.
- The minimum energy required for the electron emission from the metal's surface can be supplied to the free electrons by the following processes given in tabular form below

Physical Processes	Definitions
(*i*) Thermionic emission	Emission of electrons (thermions) due to heating the metals.
(*ii*) Field emission	Emission of electrons from a metal surface by applying strong electric field ($\approx 10^8$ V/m).
(*iii*) Secondary emission	Emission of electrons from a metal surface by bombardment of high speed electrons or other particles.
(*iv*) Photoelectric emission	Emission of electrons from metal surface when light radiations of suitable frequency fall on it.

Photoelectric Effect

- It is the phenomenon of emission of photoelectrons from the surface of metal when radiation of suitable frequency fall on it.
- This suitable or minimum frequency of radiation which can emit photoelectrons from the material is called **threshold frequency** (ν_0).
- Also, the minimum energy required for this emission of electron is known as **work function**. It is mathematically expressed as $\phi_0 = h\nu_0$, where h is Planck's constant.

  Work function depends on the properties of the metal and nature of its surface. It decreases with the increase in temperature.
- The maximum wavelength of light which can eject photoelectrons from a metal surface is called **threshold wavelength** (λ_{max}) of that metal.
- For a particular frequency of incident radiation, the minimum negative (retarding) potential V_0 for which photoelectric current becomes zero is known as **cut-off potential** or **stopping potential**.
- Relation between work function, threshold frequency and threshold wavelength is

$$\phi = h\nu_0 = \frac{hc}{\lambda_{max}}$$

Laws of Photoelectric Effect

(*i*) For a given material and a given frequency of incident radiation, the photoelectric current or number of photoelectrons ejected per second is directly proportional to the intensity of the incident light.

(*ii*) For a given material and frequency of incident radiation, saturation current is found to be proportional to the intensity of incident radiation, whereas the stopping potential is independent of its intensity.

(*iii*) For a given material, there exists a certain minimum frequency of the incident radiation below which no emission of photoelectrons takes place. This frequency is called threshold frequency.

Above the threshold frequency, the maximum kinetic energy of the emitted photoelectrons or equivalent stopping potential is independent of the intensity of the incident light but depends upon only the frequency (or wavelength) of the incident light.

(*iv*) The photoelectric emission is an instantaneous process. The time lag between the incidence of radiations and emission of photoelectrons is very small, less than even 10^{-9} s.

Einstein's Photoelectric Equation

- Einstein's photoelectric equation is given as

$$\frac{1}{2}mv^2_{max} = K_{max} = h(\nu - \nu_0) = h\nu - \phi_0$$

where, ν is the frequency and K_{max} is the maximum kinetic energy of the incident photon, respectively.

- In terms of threshold wavelength (λ_0) above equation can be written as

$$eV_0 = hc\left(\frac{1}{\lambda} - \frac{1}{\lambda_0}\right)$$

where, λ is the wavelength of incident photon.

Graphs Related to Photoelectric Effect

Given below are few graphs related to this effect

Name of the graph	Nature of Graph
(*i*) Photoelectric current (*i*) *versus* intensity (*I*)	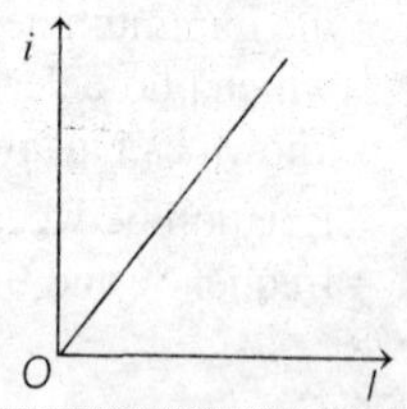
(*ii*) Photoelectric current (*i*) *versus* retarding potential (*V*) for different intensities but constant frequency.	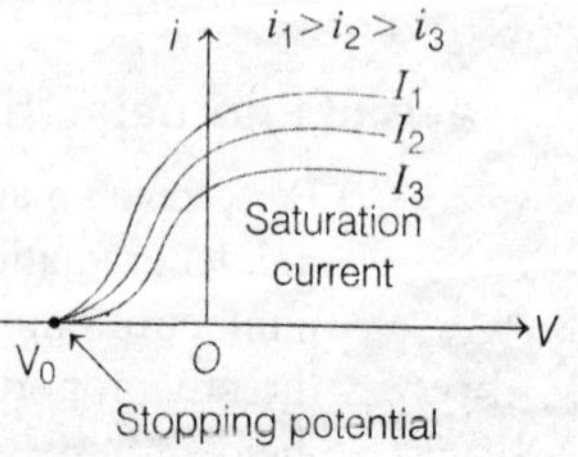
(*iii*) Photoelectric current (*i*) *versus* retarding potential (*V*) for different frequencies but constant intensity.	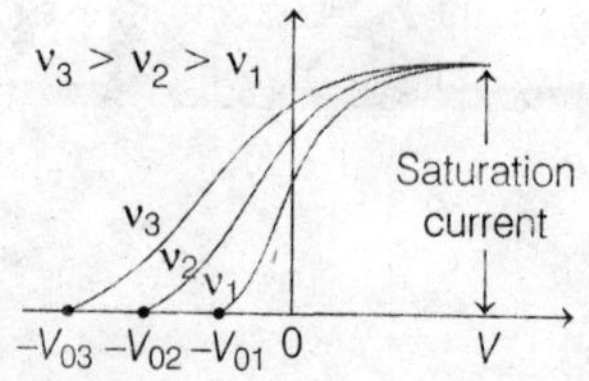
(*iv*) Stopping potential (V_0) *versus* frequency (ν) of incident radiation.	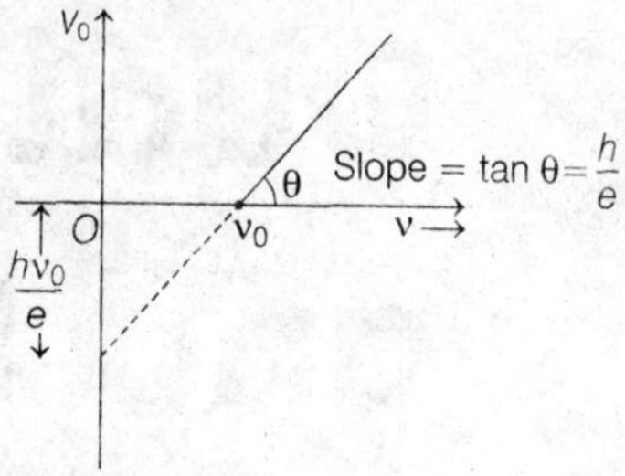

Planck's Quantum Theory

(Particle Nature of Light : Photon)

- Photoelectric effect had given evidence that light consists of packet of energy.
- Thus, in interaction of radiation with matter, radiation behaves as it made up of particles (or packets of energy) known as **photons.**

Following are the different characteristics properties of the photons

(*i*) It travels with the speed of light (c), i.e. 3×10^8 m/s.

(*ii*) It cannot exist at rest, i.e. its mass is zero.

(*iii*) Irrespective of the intensity of radiation, all the photons of particular frequency (ν), wavelength (λ) have same energy $E\left(= h\nu = \frac{hc}{\lambda}\right)$ and momentum $p\left(= \frac{h\nu}{c} = \frac{h}{\lambda}\right)$.

(*iv*) It is not deflected by electric and magnetic fields, thus it is electrically neutral.

(*v*) Intensity associated with a photon, $I = \frac{nh\nu}{A}$, where A is the area of normal incident light and n is the number of photons.

(*vi*) Pressure exerted by N photons on a perfectly reflecting surface is $\frac{2I}{c}$. However, pressure exerted by these photons on a perfectly absorbing surface is $\frac{I}{c}$.

Note Photocell is a device which converts light energy into electrical energy. It is used in burglar alarms, fire alarms, etc.

Dual Nature of Radiation

With the experimental verification, it was proved that light has dual nature, in some phenomena, it behaves like wave and in some phenomena, it behaves like particle depending upon the dimensions of object with which the particle interacts.

In 1924, French physicist Lewis de-Broglie suggested like radiation, matter too should have dual nature, i.e. the particles like electrons, protons, neutrons, etc., can have particle as well as wave nature.

Matter Waves : de-Broglie Waves

- These are the waves associated with moving particle. Its wavelength is expressed as

$$\lambda = \frac{h}{mv} = \frac{h}{p} \qquad [\because p = mv]$$

- For charged particles accelerated through a potential,

$$\lambda = \frac{h}{\sqrt{2meV}}$$

Following table represents the de-Broglie wavelength associated with various particles

	Name of the Particle	de-Broglie Wavelength
	Charged Particle	
(*i*)	For electrons	$\lambda = \frac{12.27}{\sqrt{V}}$ Å
(*ii*)	For protons	$\lambda = \frac{0.286}{\sqrt{V}}$ Å
(*iii*)	For deuterons	$\lambda = \frac{0.202}{\sqrt{V}}$ Å
(*iv*)	For α-particles	$\lambda = \frac{0.101}{\sqrt{V}}$ Å
	Uncharged Particle	
(*i*)	For photons	$\lambda = \frac{h}{mc}$ Å
(*ii*)	For neutrons	$\lambda = \frac{0.286}{\sqrt{E(\text{in eV})}}$ Å
(*iii*)	For thermal neutrons	$\lambda = \frac{25.17}{\sqrt{7}}$ Å

Heisenberg's Uncertainty Principle

- According to this principle, it is impossible to measure position and momentum of the microscopic particle simultaneously.
- According to this principle, $\Delta x \cdot \Delta p > \frac{\hbar}{2}$, where $\hbar = \frac{h}{2\pi}$

  i.e. if $\Delta x = 0$, then $\Delta p = \infty$ and if $\Delta p = 0$, then $\Delta x = \infty$.
- This principle is also applicable to energy and time, angular momentum and angular displacement by the relation $\Delta E \cdot \Delta t \geq \frac{h}{2\pi} = \hbar$ and $\Delta L \cdot \Delta\theta \geq \frac{h}{2\pi}$.
- Probability of finding the electron inside the nucleus is $\Delta x = 2r$

  (r = radius of nucleus) and uncertainty in momentum, $\Delta p = \frac{h}{4\pi}$.

Davisson and Germer Experiment

- This experiment predicted the wave nature of material particle as predicted by de-Broglie by studying the scattering of electrons from a solid.
- de-Broglie wavelength of moving electron at V = 54V is 1.67Å which is in close agreement with 1.67Å from Bragg's equation of diffraction.
- Davisson-Germer electron diffraction arrangement alongwith intensity *versus* voltage graph is shown below

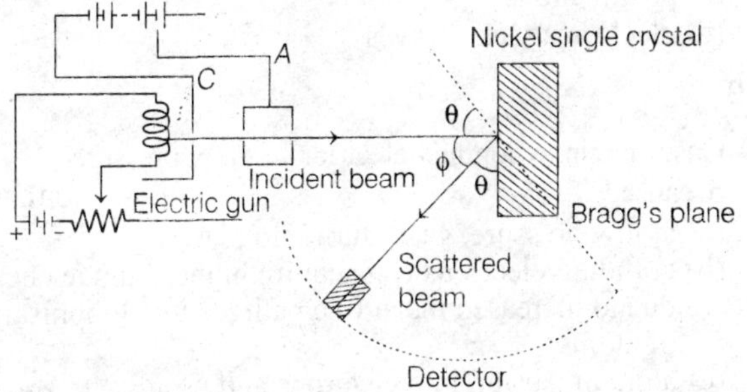

- Intensity of scattered beam of electrons was found to be maximum when angle of scattering is 50° and accelerating potential is 54 V.

Topical Practice Questions

All the exam questions of this chapter have been divided into 3 topics as listed below

Topic 1

Cathode Rays and Positive Rays

2010

1 A beam of cathode rays is subjected to crossed electric field (E) and magnetic field (B). The fields are adjusted such that the beam is not deflected. The specific charge of the cathode rays is given by [CBSE AIPMT]

(a) $\frac{B^2}{2VE^2}$ (b) $\frac{2VB^2}{E^2}$ (c) $\frac{2VE^2}{B^2}$ (d) $\frac{E^2}{2VB^2}$

2 Assertion The specific charge for positive rays is a characteristic constant.

Reason The specific charge depends on charge and mass of positive ions present in positive rays. [AIIMS]

(a) Both Assertion and Reason are correct and Reason is the correct explanation of Assertion.
(b) Both Assertion and Reason are correct but Reason is not the correct explanation of Assertion.
(c) Assertion is correct but Reason is incorrect.
(d) Assertion and Reason are incorrect.

3 Canal rays consist of [UP CPMT]
(a) electrons
(b) neutrons
(c) positive ions
(d) electromagnetic waves

2009

4 Gases begin to conduct electricity at low pressure because [UP CPMT]
(a) at low pressure, gases turn into plasma
(b) colliding electrons can acquire higher kinetic energy due to increased mean free path leading to ionisation of atoms
(c) atom breaks up into electrons and protons
(d) the electrons in atoms can move freely at low pressure

5 Positive rays are very identical to [MP PMT]
(a) α-rays (b) β-rays
(c) γ-rays (d) None of these

6 In Millikan's oil drop experiment, a charged oil drop of mass 3.2×10^{-14} kg is held stationary between two parallel plates 6 mm apart, by applying a potential difference of 1200 V between them.

How many electrons does the oil drop carry? (Take, $g = 10\ \text{ms}^{-2}$) [EAMCET]

(a) 7 (b) 8 (c) 9 (d) 10

7 In Millikan's oil drop experiment, an oil drop is observed to move vertically upwards. The upward motion of the drop is due to [BCECE]
(a) gravity (b) viscosity
(c) buoyancy (d) electric field

8 JJ Thomson's cathode ray tube experiment demonstrated that [JIPMER]
(a) cathode rays are streams of negatively charged ions
(b) all the mass of an atom is essentially in the nucleus
(c) the e/m of electrons is much greater than the e/m of protons
(d) the e/m ratio of the cathode ray particles changes when a different gas is placed in the discharged tube

2008

9 In the phenomenon of electric discharge through gases at low pressure, the coloured glow in the tube appears as a result of [CBSE AIPMT]
(a) excitation of electrons in the atoms
(b) collision between the atoms of the gas
(c) collisions between the charged particles emitted from the cathode and the atoms of the gas
(d) collision between different electrons of the atoms of the gas

10 The specific charge of a proton is $9.6 \times 10^7\ \text{C kg}^{-1}$. The specific charge of an alpha particle will be [AFMC]
(a) $9.6 \times 10^7\ \text{C kg}^{-1}$ (b) $19.2 \times 10^7\ \text{C kg}^{-1}$
(c) $4.8 \times 10^7\ \text{C kg}^{-1}$ (d) $2.4 \times 10^7\ \text{C kg}^{-1}$

11 The material used for making thermionic cathode in discharge-tube experiment must have [MHT CET]
(a) low work function and low melting point
(b) low work function and high melting point
(c) high work function and high melting point
(d) high work function and low melting point

12 In a discharge tube, ionisation of enclosed gas is produced due to collisions between [Haryana PMT]
(a) positive ions and neutral atoms/molecules
(b) negative electrons and neutral atoms/molecules
(c) photons and neutral atoms/molecules
(d) neutral gas atoms/molecules

13 The resistance of a discharge tube is [J&K CET]
(a) zero (b) ohmic
(c) non-ohmic (d) infinity

14 What is e/m ratio of electron? **[DUMET]**

(a) 2.76×10^{10}

(b) 2.76×10^{11}

(c) 1.76×10^{10}

(d) 1.76×10^{11}

2007

15 Three particles having charges in the ratio of 2 : 3 : 5, produce the effect at the same point on the photographic film in Thomson experiment. Their masses are in the ratio of **[Manipal]**

(a) 2 : 3 : 5 (b) 5 : 3 : 2

(c) 15 : 10 : 6 (d) 3 : 5 : 2

16 In a Thomson set up, $E = 30\,\text{Vcm}^{-1}$ and $B = 6$ G. Then, speed of the electron that goes undeflected in the common region of the two fields will be **[CET (J&K) 2002]**

(a) 1×10^6 m/s (b) 5×10^6 m/s

(c) 1.5×10^6 m/s (d) 25×10^6 m/s

17 Cathode rays of velocity $10^6\ \text{ms}^{-1}$ describe an approximate circular path of radius 1 m in an electric field 300 Vcm^{-1}. If the velocity of the cathode rays are doubled, the value of electric field, so that the rays describe the same circular path, will be **[BCECE]**

(a) 2400 V cm^{-1} (b) 600 V cm^{-1}

(c) 1200 V cm^{-1} (d) 12000 V cm^{-1}

Answers

1 (d)	2 (a)	3 (c)	4 (d)	5 (a)	6 (d)	7 (d)	8 (c)	9 (c)	10 (c)
11 (b)	12 (b)	13 (c)	14 (d)	15 (a)	16 (b)	17 (c)			

Explanations

1 *(d)* As the electron beam is not deflected, then

$$F_m = F_e$$

or $$Bev = Ee$$

or $$v = E/B \quad \ldots\text{(i)}$$

Since, as the electron moves from cathode to anode, its potential energy at the cathode appears as its kinetic energy at the anode. If V is the potential difference between the anode and cathode, then potential energy of the electron at cathode = eV.

Also, kinetic energy of the electron at anode = $\frac{1}{2}mv^2$.

According to law of conservation of energy,

$$\frac{1}{2}mv^2 = eV \quad \text{or} \quad v = \sqrt{\frac{2eV}{m}} \quad \ldots\text{(ii)}$$

From Eqs. (i) and (ii), we have

$$\sqrt{\frac{2eV}{m}} = \frac{E}{B} \quad \text{or} \quad \frac{e}{m} = \frac{E^2}{2\,VB^2}$$

2 *(a)* A positive ray consists of positive ions, whose specific charge depends on charge and mass of ion and is given by

$$\text{Specific charge} = \frac{e}{m}$$

For a specific positive ray, the charge and mass are constant and thus specific charge is a constant characteristic of positive rays.

3 *(c)* Canal rays/Anode rays/Positive ray are beam of positive ions that is created by a certain type of gas-discharge tubes.

4 *(d)* When a subatomic particle like an electron moves through the gas, it undergoes lots of collisions with the gas molecules in it and thereby losing energy and sometimes even failing to reach the other end of the tube. If the gas is at low pressure, molecules are quite apart and when an electron travels, the number of collisions are reduced and more number of electrons are able to reach the other end and that is why we say gases at low pressure conduct electricity better.

5 *(a)* Charges of positive rays and α-ray, i.e. helium atom are same. Moreover the mass of helium atom = 2 × mass of proton + 2 × mass of neutron. Therefore, it can be concluded that positive rays are very identical to α-rays.

6 *(d)* According to figure, it is clear that electrical force is balanced by weight of body, i.e.

E

mg

$$qE = mg \quad \text{or} \quad ne\frac{V}{l} = mg$$

$$\therefore\ n \times 1.6 \times 10^{-19} \times \frac{1200}{6 \times 10^{-3}} = 3.2 \times 10^{-14} \times 10$$

$$\Rightarrow \quad n = \frac{3.2 \times 10^{-13} \times 6 \times 10^{-3}}{1.6 \times 10^{-19} \times 1200} = 10$$

7 *(d)* In Millikan's oil drop experiment, the electric field is applied between the plates, where the negatively charged oil drop carrying a charge (q) will experience electrostatic force of attraction. If the magnitude of electrostatic force is greater than that of gravitational force, the oil drop will start moving in upward direction.

8 *(c)* JJ Thomson's cathode ray tube experiment demonstrated the relation for e/m of charged particles. The relation is

$$\frac{e}{m} = \frac{E^2}{2B^2V}$$

Thus, knowing E, B and V, the value of $\frac{e}{m}$ for electrons and for protons can be calculated. It was then found that the $\frac{e}{m}$ of electrons is much greater than the $\frac{e}{m}$ of protons.

9 *(c)* In discharge tube, collisions between the charged particles emitted from the cathode and the atoms of the gas results to the coloured glow in the tube. This coloured glow appears as the result of excitations of electrons in the atoms.

10 *(c)* Specific charge of proton

$$= \left(\frac{e}{m}\right)_p = 9.6 \times 10^7\ \text{C kg}^{-1}$$

Specific charge of α-particle

$$= \left(\frac{q}{m}\right)_\alpha = \frac{2e}{4m} = \frac{1}{2}\left(\frac{e}{m}\right)_p$$

$$= \frac{1}{2} \times 9.6 \times 10^7 = 4.8 \times 10^7 \text{ C kg}^{-1}$$

11 *(b)* A cathode should have following properties:

(i) **Low Work Function** The substance selected as cathode should have low work function, so that electron emission takes place by applying small amount of heat energy, i.e. at low temperature.

(ii) **High Melting Point** As electron emission takes place at very high temperatures (> 1500° C), therefore the substance used as a cathode should have high melting point.

12 *(b)* In a discharge tube, the electron in the gas tube after being accelerated through a high potential difference, strike the atom with huge kinetic energy. This collision liberates electrons from the atom. These free electrons can further liberate electrons from gas molecules through collisions. This results in the formation of positive ions.

These positive ions are then attracted towards the cathode and negatively electrons move towards anode.

Thus, ionisation of gas results due to collision between neutral atom or molecules and negative electrons.

13 *(c)* In discharge tube, the current is due to flow of positions ions and electrons. Moreover, secondary emission of electrons is also possible. So, V-I curve is non-linear, hence its resistance is non-ohmic.

14 *(d)* The accurate value of $\frac{e}{m}$ for electron is found to be 1.7589×10^{11} C kg^{-1}

or $\approx 1.76 \times 10^{11}$ C kg^{-1}

15 *(a)* As we know, particles having same $\frac{e}{m}$ ratio are deflected to the same extent in the Thomson experiment.

So, $\frac{e}{m}$ = constant $\Rightarrow e \propto m$

So, their masses are in the ratio of 2 : 3 : 5.

16 *(b)* $v = \frac{E}{B}$

Given, $E = 30$ V/cm $= 30 \times 10^2$ V/m

$B = 6\text{ G} = 6 \times 10^{-4}$ Wb/m^2

$$\therefore \quad v = \frac{30 \times 10^2}{6 \times 10^{-4}} = 5 \times 10^6 \text{ m/s.}$$

17. *(c)* Cathode rays are composed of electrons, when they move in electric field, a force,

$$F = eE \quad \text{...(i)}$$

acts on them, this provides the necessary centripetal force to the particles.

$$\therefore \quad F = mv^2/r \quad \text{...(ii)}$$

From Eqs. (i) and (ii), we get

$$eE = \frac{mv^2}{r}$$

$$\Rightarrow \quad r = \frac{mv^2}{eE} = \frac{m(10^6)^2}{e(300)} \quad \text{...(iii)}$$

When velocity is doubled same circular path is followed, hence radius is same

$$r = \frac{m(2 \times 10^6)^2}{eE} \quad \text{...(iv)}$$

Equating Eqs. (iii) and (iv), we get

$$\frac{m \times (10^6)^2}{300e} = \frac{m \times (2 \times 10^6)^2}{eE}$$

$$\Rightarrow \quad E = 300 \times 4 = 1200 \text{ V cm}^{-1}$$

Topic 2

Photoelectric Effect

2019

1 The work function of a photosensitive material is 4.0 eV. This longest wavelength of light that can cause photon emission from the substance is (approximately) **[NEET (Odisha)]**

(a) 3100 nm (b) 966 nm (c) 31 nm (d) 310 nm

2 If frequency of a photon is 6×10^{14} Hz, then find its wavelength. [Take, speed of light, $c = 3 \times 10^8$ m/s] **[JIPMER]**

(a) 500 Å (b) 500 nm (c) 200 Å (d) 200 nm

2018

3 When the light of frequency $2\nu_0$ (where, ν_0 is threshold frequency), is incident on a metal plate, the maximum velocity of electrons emitted is v_1. When the frequency of the incident radiation is increased to $5\nu_0$, the maximum velocity of electrons emitted from the same plate is v_2. The ratio of $v_1 : v_2$ is **[NEET]**

(a) 4 : 1 (b) 1 : 4 (c) 1 : 2 (d) 2 : 1

2017

4 The photoelectric threshold wavelength of silver is 3250×10^{-10} m. The velocity of the electron ejected from a silver surface by ultraviolet light of wavelength 2536×10^{-10} m is (Take, $h = 4.14 \times 10^{-15}$ eV-s and $c = 3 \times 10^8$ ms^{-1}) **[NEET]**

(a) $\approx 6 \times 10^5$ ms^{-1} (b) $\approx 0.6 \times 10^6$ ms^{-1}

(c) $\approx 61 \times 10^3$ ms^{-1} (d) $\approx 0.3 \times 10^6$ ms^{-1}

5 **Assertion** Photoelectric effect can take place only with an electron bound in the atom. **[AIIMS]**

Reason Electron is a fermion, whereas proton is a boson.

(a) Both Assertion and Reason are true and Reason is the correct explanation of Assertion

(b) Both Assertion and Reason are true but Reason is not the correct explanation of Assertion

(c) Assertion is true but Reason is false.

(d) Both Assertion and Reason are false.

2016

6 When a metallic surface is illuminated with radiation of wavelength λ, the stopping potential is V. If the same surface is illuminated with radiation of wavelength 2λ, the stopping potential is $\frac{V}{4}$. The threshold wavelength for the metallic surface is **[NEET]**

(a) 5λ (b) $\frac{5}{2}\lambda$ (c) 3λ (d) 4λ

2015

7 A certain metallic surface is illuminated with monochromatic light of wavelength λ. The stopping potential for photoelectric current for this light is $3V_0$. If the same surface is illuminated with light of wavelength 2λ, the stopping potential is V_0. The threshold wavelength for this surface for photoelectric effect is **[CBSE AIPMT]**

(a) 6λ (b) 4λ
(c) $\frac{\lambda}{4}$ (d) $\frac{\lambda}{6}$

2014

8 When the energy of the incident radiation is increased by 20%, the kinetic energy of the photoelectrons emitted from a metal surface increased from 0.5 eV to 0.8 eV. The work function of the metal is **[UP CPMT]**

(a) 0.65 eV (b) 1 eV
(c) 1.3 eV (d) 1.5 eV

9 Light of wavelengths λ_A and λ_B fall on two identical metal plates A and B, respectively. The maximum kinetic energy of photoelectrons is K_A and K_B respectively, then which one of the following relations is true? $(\lambda_A = 2\lambda_B)$ **[MHT CET]**

(a) $K_A < \frac{K_B}{2}$ (b) $2K_A = K_B$
(c) $K_A = 2K_B$ (d) $K_A > 2K_B$

10 If the wavelength of incident light falling on a photosensitive material decreases, then **[Kerala CEE]**

(a) photoelectric current increases
(b) stopping potential decreases
(c) stopping potential remains constant
(d) stopping potential increases
(e) photoelectric current remains constant

11 Find the correct statement(s) about photoelectric effect. **[WB JEE]**

(a) There is no significant time delay between the absorption of a suitable radiation and the emission of electrons
(b) Einstein analysis gives a threshold frequency above which no electron can be emitted
(c) The maximum kinetic energy of the emitted photoelectrons is proportional to the frequency of incident radiation
(d) The maximum kinetic energy of electrons does not depend on the intensity of radiation

12 When monochromatic light falls on a photosensitive material, the number of photoelectron emitted per second is n and their maximum kinetic energy is K_{max}. If the intensity of incident light is doubled, then **[EAMCET]**

(a) n is doubled but K_{max} remains same
(b) K_{max} is double but n remains same
(c) Both n and K_{max} are doubled
(d) Both n and K_{max} are halved

13 The maximum kinetic energy of the photoelectrons depends only on **[KCET]**

(a) charge (b) frequency
(c) incident angle (d) pressure

14 For photoelectric emission from certain metal, the cut-off frequency is ν. If radiation of frequency 2ν impinges on the metal plate, the maximum possible velocity of the emitted electron will be (m is the electron mass) **[NEET]**

(a) $\sqrt{\frac{h\nu}{(2m)}}$ (b) $\sqrt{\frac{h\nu}{m}}$ (c) $\sqrt{\frac{2h\nu}{m}}$ (d) $2\sqrt{\frac{h\nu}{m}}$

15 A light of wavelength 5000 Å falls on a sensitive plate with photoelectric work function 1.90 eV. Kinetic energy of the emitted photoelectrons will be (Take, $h = 6.62 \times 10^{-34}$ J-s) **[UP CPMT]**

(a) 0.1 eV (b) 2 eV (c) 0.58 eV (d) 1.581 eV

2013

16 The number of photons of wavelength 660 nm emitted per second by an electric bulb of 60 W is (Take, $h = 6.6 \times 10^{-34}$ J-s) **[Guj CET]**

(a) 3×10^{20} (b) 1.5×10^{20} (c) 2×10^{-20} (d) 2×10^{20}

2012

17 Light from a hydrogen discharge tube is made incident on the cathode of a photoelectric cell. The work function of the cathode surface is 3.1 eV. In order to reduce the photoelectric current to zero value, the minimum potential applied to anode with respect to cathode should be **[DCE]**

(a) – 3.1 V (b) – 10.5 V (c) + 10.5 V (d) – 16.7 V

18 A 200 W sodium street lamp emits yellow light of wavelength 0.6 μm. Assuming it to be 25% efficient in converting electrical energy to light, the number of photon of yellow light, it emits per second is **[CBSE AIPMT]**

(a) 1.5×10^{20} (b) 6×10^{18} (c) 6.2×20^{20} (d) 3×10^{19}

19 Photoelectric emission is observed from a metallic surface for frequencies ν_1 and ν_2 of the incident light $(\nu_1 > \nu_2)$. If the maximum values of kinetic energy of the photoelectrons emitted in the two cases are in the ratio $1 : n$, then the threshold frequency of the metallic surface is **[AFMC]**

(a) $\frac{(\nu_1 - \nu_2)}{(n-1)}$ (b) $\frac{(n\nu_1 - \nu_2)}{(n-1)}$
(c) $\frac{(n\nu_2 - \nu_1)}{(n-1)}$ (d) $\frac{(\nu_1 - \nu_2)}{n}$

20 When a certain metal surface is illuminated with light of frequency ν, the stopping potential for photoelectric current is V_0. When the same surface is illuminated by light of frequency $\frac{\nu}{2}$, the stopping potential is $\frac{V_0}{4}$. The threshold frequency for photoelectric emission is **[WB JEE]**
(a) $\frac{\nu}{6}$ (b) $\frac{\nu}{3}$ (c) $\frac{2\nu}{3}$ (d) $\frac{4\nu}{3}$

21 The threshold frequency for a certain photosensitive metal is ν_0. When it is illuminated by light of frequency $\nu = 2\nu_0$, the maximum velocity of photoelectrons is v_0. What will be the maximum velocity of the photoelectrons when the same metal is illuminated by light of frequency $\nu = 5\nu_0$? **[AMU]**
(a) $\sqrt{2}\, v_0$ (b) $2\, v_0$ (c) $2\sqrt{2}\, v_0$ (d) $4\, v_0$

2011

22 Photoelectric emission occurs only, when the incident light has more than a certain minimum **[CBSE AIPMT]**
(a) wavelength (b) intensity
(c) frequency (d) power

23 The work functions for metals A, B and C are respectively, 1.92 eV, 2 eV and 5 eV. According to Einstein's equation, the metal(s) which will emit photoelectrons for a radiation of wavelength 4100 Å is/are **[AIIMS]**
(a) Only A (b) A and B
(c) All of these (d) None of these

24 Work function of nickel is 5.01 eV. When ultraviolet radiation of wavelength 2000 Å is incident on it, electrons are emitted. What will be the maximum velocity of emitted electrons? **[AIIMS]**
(a) 3×10^{8} ms^{-1} (b) 6.46×10^{5} ms^{-1}
(c) 10.36×10^{5} ms^{-1} (d) 8.54×10^{6} ms^{-1}

25 If 5% of the energy supplied to a bulb is irradiated as visible light, how many quanta are emitted per second by a 100 W lamp? (Assume, wavelength of visible light as 5.6×10^{-5} cm) **[AIIMS]**
(a) 1.4×10^{19} (b) 3×10^{3} (c) 1.4×10^{-19} (d) 3×10^{4}

26 The threshold frequency for a metallic surface corresponds to an energy of 6.2 eV and the stopping potential for a radiation incident on this surface is 5 V. The incident radiation lies in **[AFMC]**
(a) ultraviolet region (b) infrared region
(c) visible region (d) X-ray region

27 When 1 cm thick surface is illuminated with light of wavelength λ, the stopping potential is V. When the same surface is illuminated by light of wavelength 2λ, the stopping potential is $V/3$. Threshold wavelength for metallic surface is **[BHU]**
(a) $4\lambda/3$ (b) 4λ (c) 6λ (d) $8\lambda/3$

28 The momentum of a photon in an X-ray beam of 10^{-10} m wavelength is **[UP CPMT]**
(a) 1.5×10^{-23} kg-ms^{-1} (b) 6.6×10^{-24} kg-ms^{-1}
(c) 6.6×10^{-44} kg-ms^{-1} (d) 2.2×10^{-52} kg-ms^{-1}

29 The frequency of a photon having energy 100 eV is (Take, $h = 6.62\times10^{-34}$ J-s, 1 eV $= 1.6\times10^{-19}$ J) **[J&K CET]**
(a) 2.417×10^{-16} Hz (b) 2.417×10^{16} Hz
(c) 2.417×10^{17} Hz (d) 10.54×10^{17} Hz

30 A photosensitive metallic surface has work function φ. If photon of energy 3 φ fall on this surface, the electron comes out with a maximum velocity of 6×10^{6} ms^{-1}. When the photon energy is increased to 9 φ, then maximum velocity of photoelectron will be **[J&K CET]**
(a) 12×10^{6} ms^{-1} (b) 6×10^{6} ms^{-1}
(c) 3×10^{6} ms^{-1} (d) 24×10^{6} ms^{-1}

31 Monochromatic light of wavelength 667 nm is produced by a helium neon laser. The power emitted is 9 mW. The number of photons arriving per second on the average at a target irradiated by this beam is **[CBSE AIPMT]**
(a) 9×10^{17} (b) 3×10^{16}
(c) 9×10^{15} (d) 3×10^{19}

32 The figure shows a plot of photocurrent *versus* anode potential for a photosensitive surface for three different radiations. Which one of the following is a correct statement?

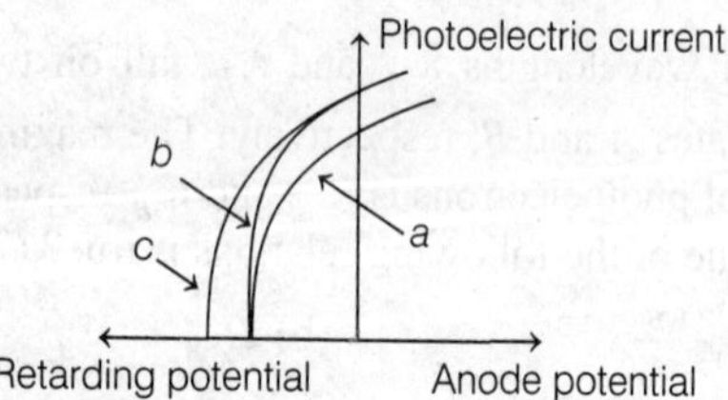

[CBSE AIPMT]
(a) Curves a and b represent incident radiations of different frequencies and different intensities
(b) Curves a and b represent incident radiations of same frequency but of different intensities
(c) Curves b and c represent incident radiations of different frequencies and different intensities
(d) Curves b and c represent incident radiations of same frequency having same intensity

33 Light of two different frequencies whose photons have energies 1 eV and 2.5 eV respectively, illuminate a metallic surface whose work function is 0.5 eV, successively. Ratio of maximum speeds of emitted electrons will be **[CBSE AIPMT]**
(a) 1 : 2 (b) 1 : 1 (c) 1 : 5 (d) 1 : 4

34 In photoelectric emission process from a metal of work function 1.8 eV, the kinetic energy of most energetic electrons is 0.5 eV. The corresponding stopping potential is **[CBSE AIPMT]**
(a) 1.3 V (b) 0.5 V
(c) 2.3 V (d) 1.8 V

2010

35 When ultraviolet light of wavelength 100 nm is incident upon silver plate, a potential of 7.7 V is required to stop the photoelectrons from reaching the collector plate. How much potential will be required to stop the photoelectrons when light of wavelength 200 nm is incident upon silver? **[Manipal]**
(a) 1.5 V (b) 3.85 V
(c) 2.35 V (d) 15.4 V

36 Radiations of two photon of energies twice and five times the work function of metal are incident successively on the metal surface. The ratio of the maximum velocity of the photoelectrons emitted in the two cases will be **[Manipal]**
(a) 1 : 1 (b) 1 : 2 (c) 1 : 3 (d) 1 : 4

37 Photoelectric effect experiments are performed using three different metal plates p, q and r having work functions $\phi_p = 2.0\,\text{eV}$, $\phi_q = 2.5\,\text{eV}$ and $\phi_r = 3.0\,\text{eV}$, respectively. A light beam containing wavelengths of 550 nm, 450 nm and 350 nm with equal intensities illuminates each of the plates. The correct I-V graph for the experiment is **[Main (IIT) JEE]**

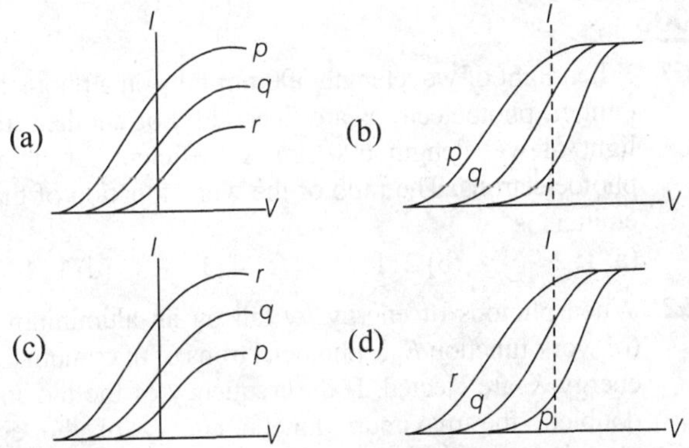

38 Calcium plate has maximum possible radiation of wavelength λ of 400 nm to eject electrons. Its work function is **[Manipal]**
(a) 2.3 eV (b) 3.1 eV
(c) 4.5 eV (d) None of these

39 Momentum of photon is **[MP PMT]**
(a) $\frac{h\nu}{c^2}$ (b) $\frac{h\nu}{c^3}$ (c) $\frac{h\nu}{c}$ (d) $\frac{h}{c}$

40 If the work function of the photoelectric surface is 3.3 eV, then the value of threshold frequency is **[MP PMT]**
(a) 8×10^{14} Hz (b) 5×10^{16} Hz
(c) 4×10^{11} Hz (d) 8×10^{10} Hz

41 Minimum light intensity that can be perceived by normal human eye is about 10^{-10} Wb m^{-2}. What is the minimum number of photons of wavelength 660 nm that must enter the pupil in 1 s for one to see the object? Area of cross-section of the pupil is 10^{-4} m^2. **[Punjab PMET]**
(a) 3.3×10^2 (b) 3.3×10^3
(c) 3.3×10^4 (d) 3.3×10^5

42 The threshold frequency of the metal of the cathode in a photoelectric cell is 1×10^{15} Hz. When a certain beam of light is incident on the cathode, it is found that a stopping potential 4.144 V is required to reduce the current to zero. The frequency of the incident radiation is **[EAMCET]**
(a) 2.5×10^{15} Hz (b) 2×10^{15} Hz
(c) 4.144×10^{15} Hz (d) 3×10^{16} Hz

43 According to Einstein's photoelectric equation, the graph of kinectic energy of the photoelectron emitted from the metal *versus* the frequency of the incident radiation gives a straight line graph, whose slope **[KCET]**
(a) depends on the intensity of the incident radiation
(b) depends on the nature of the metal and also on the intensity of incident radiation
(c) is same for all metals and independent of the intensity of the incident radiation
(d) depends on the nature of the metal

44 Light of wavelength λ, strikes a photoelectric surface and electrons are ejected with an energy E. If E is to be increased to exactly twice its original value, the wavelength changes to λ', where **[BCECE]**
(a) λ' is less than $\lambda/2$
(b) λ' is greater than $\lambda/2$
(c) λ' is greater than $\lambda/2$ but less than λ
(d) λ' is exactly equal to $\lambda/2$

45 The work function for aluminium surface is 4.2 eV. The cut-off wavelength for the photoelectric effect is **[CG PMT]**
(a) 2955 Å (b) 4200 Å
(c) 2000 Å (d) 1000 Å

46 The energy of a photon corresponding to the visible light of maximum wavelength is approximately **[MGIMS]**
(a) 1 eV (b) 1.6 eV
(c) 3.2 eV (d) 7 eV

47 A radio transmitter radiates 1 kW power at a wavelength 198.6 m. How many photons does it emit per second? **[VMMC]**
(a) 10^{10} (b) 10^{20} (c) 10^{30} (d) 10^{40}

48 If the distance of 100 W lamp is increased from a photocell, the saturation current i in the photocell varies with the distance d as **[VMMC]**
(a) $i \propto d^2$ (b) $i \propto d$
(c) $i \propto \frac{1}{d}$ (d) $i \propto \frac{1}{d^2}$

2009

49 Let K_1 be the maximum kinetic energy of photoelectrons emitted by light of wavelength λ_1 and K_2 corresponding to wavelength λ_2. If $\lambda_1 = 2\lambda_2$, then **[AIIMS]**
(a) $2K_1 = K_2$ (b) $K_1 = 2K_2$
(c) $K_1 < K_2/2$ (d) $K_1 > 2K_2$

50 The curve drawn between velocity and frequency of photon in vacuum will be a **[AIIMS]**
(a) straight line parallel to frequency axis
(b) straight line parallel to velocity axis
(c) straight line passing through origin and making an angle of 45° with frequency axis
(d) hyperbola

51 The work function of a substance is 4 eV. The longest wavelength of light that can cause photoelectron emission from this substance is approximately **[AFMC]**
(a) 540 nm (b) 400 nm (c) 310 nm (d) 220 nm

52 Sodium and copper have work functions 2.3 eV and 4.5 eV, respectively. Then, the ratio of their threshold wavelengths is nearest to **[UP CPMT]**
(a) 1 : 2 (b) 2 : 1 (c) 1 : 4 (d) 4 : 1

53 The energy of photon of light is 3 eV. Then, the wavelength of photon must be **[UP CPMT]**
(a) 4125 nm (b) 412.5 nm
(c) 41.250 nm (d) 4 nm

54 Choose the correct statement. **[BVP]**
(a) Photoelectric effect can take place from bound electrons.
(b) Photoelectric effect can take place from free electrons.
(c) Photoelectric effect can take place from bounded or free electrons.
(d) None of the above

55 Monochromatic light of frequency f is incident on emitter having threshold frequency f_0. The kinetic energy of ejected electron will be **[OJEE]**
(a) hf (b) $h(f - f_0)$
(c) hf_0 (d) $h(f + f_0)$

56 The photons in a radio wave of wavelength 3×10^4 cm have energy **[Haryana PMT]**
(a) 6.62×10^{-10} J (b) 19.86×10^{-24} J
(c) 6.62×10^{-28} J (d) 2.2×10^{-35} J

57 In a photoelectric experiment, the relation between applied potential difference between cathode and anode V and the photoelectric current I was found to be shown in graph below. If Planck's constant $h = 6.6 \times 10^{-34}$ Js^{-1} and work function is 4 eV, then the frequency of incident radiation would be nearly (in second^{-1}) **[Haryana PMT, CG PMT]**

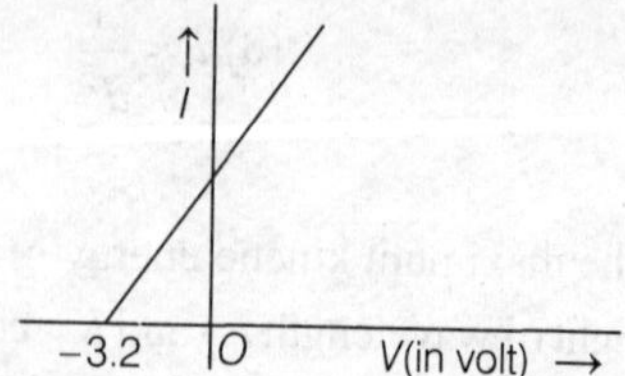

(a) 0.436×10^{18} (b) 1.436×10^{17}
(c) 1.939×10^{14} (d) 0.775×10^{16}

58 If the photoelectric work function for a metallic surface is 4.125 eV, the cut-off wavelength for photoelectric phenomenon for the surface is **[J&K CET]**
(a) 4500 Å (b) 1700 Å
(c) 2800 Å (d) 3000 Å

59 In photoelectric effect, if the intensity of light is doubled, then maximum kinetic energy of photoelectrons will become **[MHT CET]**
(a) double (b) half
(c) four times (d) no change

60 Light of wavelength 330 nm falling on a piece of metal ejects electrons with sufficient energy which requires voltage V_0 to prevent them from reaching a collector. In the same set up, light of wavelength 220 nm, ejects electrons which require twice the voltage V_0 to stop them in reaching a collector. The numerical value of voltage V_0 is **[AIIMS]**
(a) $\frac{16}{15}$ V (b) $\frac{15}{16}$ V (c) $\frac{15}{8}$ V (d) $\frac{8}{15}$ V

2008

61 When light of wavelength 300 nm falls on a photoelectric emitter, photoelectrons are liberated. For another emitter, light of wavelength 600 nm is sufficient for liberating photoelectrons. The ratio of the work function of the two emitters is **[AFMC]**
(a) 1 : 2 (b) 2 : 1 (c) 4 : 1 (d) 1 : 4

62 When photons of energy $h\nu$ fall on an aluminium plate (of work function E_0), photoelectrons of maximum kinetic energy K are ejected. If the frequency of the radiation is doubled, the maximum kinetic energy of the ejected photoelectrons will be **[Haryana PMT]**
(a) $K + E_0$ (b) $2K$ (c) K (d) $K + h\nu$

63 The velocity of the most energetic electrons emitted from a metallic surface is doubled when the frequency ν of the incident radiation is doubled. The work function of this metal is **[Punjab PMET]**
(a) $\frac{h\nu}{4}$ (b) $\frac{h\nu}{3}$ (c) $\frac{h\nu}{2}$ (d) $\frac{2h\nu}{3}$

64 The threshold frequency for a certain metal is ν_0. When a certain radiation of frequency $2\nu_0$ is incident on this metal surface, the maximum velocity of the photoelectrons emitted is 2×10^6 ms^{-1}. If a radiation of frequency $3\nu_0$ is incident on the same metal surface, the maximum velocity of the photoelectrons emitted (in ms^{-1}) is **[EAMCET]**
(a) 2×10^6 (b) $2\sqrt{2} \times 10^6$
(c) $4\sqrt{2} \times 10^6$ (d) $4\sqrt{3} \times 10^6$

65 Calculate the linear momentum of a 3 MeV photon. **[AMU]**
(a) 0.01 eV-s/m (b) 0.02 eV-s/m
(c) 0.03 eV-s/m (d) 0.04 eV-s/m

66 A photon of energy 8 eV is incident on a metal surface of threshold frequency 1.6×10^{15} Hz. The maximum kinetic energy of photoelectrons emitted is
(take, $h = 6.6\times10^{-34}$ J-s, $1\text{eV} = 1.6\times10^{-19}$ J) **[Guj CET]**
(a) 1.4 eV (b) 0.8 eV (c) 4.2 eV (d) 2.8 eV

67 Ultraviolet light of wavelength 200 nm is incident on polished surface of Fe (iron). Work function of the surface is 4.71 eV. What will be its stopping potential?
(Take, $h = 6.626\times10^{-34}$ J-s, 1 eV= 1.6×10^{-19} J and $c = 3\times10^{8}$ ms^{-1}) **[Guj CET]**
(a) 0.5 V (b) 2.5 V
(c) 1.5 V (d) None of these

2007

68 A 5 W source emits monochromatic light of wavelength 5000 Å. When placed 0.5 m away, it liberates photoelectrons from a photosensitive metallic surface. When the source is moved to a distance of 1 m, the number of photoelectrons liberated will be reduced by a factor of **[CBSE AIPMT]**
(a) 4 (b) 8
(c) 16 (d) 2

69 Energy from the sun is received on earth at the rate of 2 cal cm^{-2} min^{-1}. If average wavelength of solar light be taken as 5500 Å, then how many photons are received on the earth (cm^{-2} min^{-1})?
(Take, $h = 6.6\times10^{-34}$ J-s, 1 cal = 4.2 J) **[AIIMS]**
(a) 1.5×10^{13} (b) 2.9×10^{13}
(c) 2.3×10^{19} (d) 1.75×10^{19}

70 An X-ray pulse of wavelength 4.9 Å is sent through a section of Wilson cloud chamber containing a super saturated gas and tracks of photoelectron ejected from the gaseous atoms are observed. Two groups of tracks of lengths 1.40 cm and 2.02 cm are noted. If the range-energy relation for cloud chamber is given by $R = \alpha E$ with $\alpha = 1\text{cm keV}^{-1}$, obtain the binding energies of the two levels from which electrons are emitted.
(Take, $h = 6.63\times10^{-34}$ J-s, $1\text{eV} = 1.6\times10^{-19}$ J) **[AIIMS]**
(a) 0.52 keV (b) 0.75 eV (c) 0.52 eV (d) 0.75 keV

71 In a p-n junction photocell, the value of the photo-electromotive force produced by monochromatic light is proportional to **[AFMC]**
(a) the barrier voltage at the p-n junction
(b) this intensity of the light falling on the cell
(c) the frequency of the light falling on the cell
(d) the voltage applied at the p-n junction

72 A light of wavelength 5000 Å falls on a sensitive plate with photoelectric work function 1.90 eV. Kinetic energy of the emitted photoelectrons will be
(Take, $h = 6.62\times10^{-34}$ J-s) **[RPMT]**
(a) 0.1 eV (b) 2 eV (c) 0.58 eV (d) 1.581 eV

73 Which one of the following graph represents the variation of maximum kinetic energy (E_K) of the emitted electrons with frequency (ν) in photoelectric effect correctly? **[KCET]**

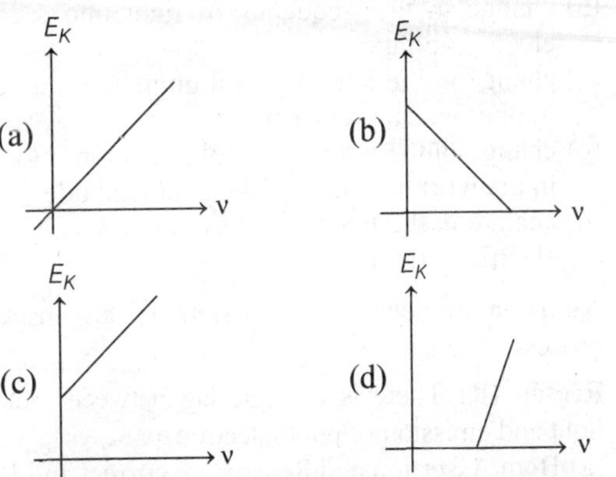

74 A and B are two metals with threshold frequencies 1.8×10^{14} Hz and 2.2×10^{14} Hz. Two identical photons of energy 0.825 eV each are incident on them. Then, photoelectrons are emitted by (Take, $h = 6.6\times10^{-34}$ J-s) **[KCET]**
(a) Only B (b) Only A
(c) Neither A nor B (d) Both A and B

75 The electromagnetic theory of light failed to explain **[KCET]**
(a) photoelectric effect (b) polarisation
(c) diffraction (d) interference

76 Light of wavelength 0.6 μm from a sodium lamp falls on a photocell and causes the emission of photoelectrons for which the stopping potential is 0.5 V. With light of wavelength 0.4 μm from a sodium lamp, the stopping potential is 1.5 V, with this data, the value of h/e is **[Punjab PMET]**
(a) 4×10^{-19} V-s (b) 0.25×10^{-15} V-s
(c) 4×10^{-15} V-s (d) 4×10^{-8} V-s

77 A metal surface is illuminated by light of two different wavelengths 248 nm and 310 nm. The maximum speeds of the photoelectrons corresponding to these wavelengths are u_1 and u_2, respectively. If the ratio $u_1 : u_2 = 2:1$ and $hc = 1240$ eV nm, then the work function of the metal is nearly **[EAM CET]**
(a) 3.7 eV (b) 3.2 eV (c) 2.8 eV (d) 2.5 eV

78 A photosensitive surface is receiving light of wavelength 5000 Å at the rate of 10^{-7} J-s. The number of photons ejected per second is **[AMU]**
(a) 2.5×10^{12} (b) 2.5×10^{11}
(c) 2.5×10^{10} (d) 2.5×10^{9}

79 The threshold wavelength for a metal having work function W_0 is λ_0. What is the threshold wavelength for a metal whose work function is $W_0/2$? **[Guj CET]**
(a) $4\lambda_0$ (b) $2\lambda_0$ (c) $\frac{\lambda_0}{2}$ (d) $\frac{\lambda_0}{4}$

2006

80 A photocell employs photoelectric effect to convert **[CBSE AIPMT]**

(a) change in the frequency of light into a change in electric voltage
(b) change in the intensity of illumination into a change in photoelectric current
(c) change in the intensity of illumination into a change in the work function of the photocathode
(d) change in the frequency of light into a change in the electric current

81 **Assertion** Photoelectric emission is an instantaneous process.

Reason (R) There is no time lag between incidence of light and emission of photoelectron. **[AIIMS]**

(a) Both Assertion and Reason are correct and Reason is the correct explanation of Assertion
(b) Both Assertion and Reason are correct but Reason is not the correct explanation of Assertion
(c) Assertion is correct but Reason is incorrect
(d) Both Assertion and Reason are incorrect

82 The threshold frequency for certain metal is 3.3×10^{14} Hz. If light of frequency 8.2×10^{14} Hz is incident on the metal, then the cut-off voltage of the photoelectric current will be **[BHU]**

(a) 4.9 V (b) 3 V
(c) 2 V (d) 1 V

83 For photoelectric emission, tungsten requires light of wavelength 2300 Å. If light of 1800 Å wavelength is incident, then emission **[Punjab PMET]**

(a) takes place
(b) does not take place
(c) may or may not take place
(d) depends on frequency

84 Light of frequency ν falls on material of threshold frequency ν_0. Maximum kinetic energy of emitted electron is proportional to **[DUMET]**

(a) $\nu - \nu_0$ (b) ν
(c) $\sqrt{\nu - \nu_0}$ (d) ν_0

85 Maximum velocity of the photoelectrons emitted by a metal surface is 1.2×10^6 ms^{-1}. Assuming the specific charge of an electron to be 1.8×10^{11} C kg^{-1}, the value of the stopping potential (in volt) will be **[KCET]**

(a) 2 (b) 3
(c) 4 (d) 6

86 Monochromatic light frequency f_1 incident on a photocell and the stopping potential is found to be V_1. What is the new stopping potential of the cell, if it is radiated by monochromatic light of frequency f_2? **[Guj CET]**

(a) $V_1 - \frac{h}{e}(f_2 - f_1)$ (b) $V_1 + \frac{h}{e}(f_1 + f_2)$
(c) $V_1 - \frac{h}{e}(f_1 + f_2)$ (d) $V_1 + \frac{h}{e}(f_2 - f_1)$

2005

87 A photosensitive metallic surface has work function $h\nu_0$. If photons of energy $2h\nu_0$ fall on this surface, the electrons come out with a maximum velocity of 4×10^6 ms^{-1}. When the photon energy is increased to $5h\nu_0$, then maximum velocity of photoelectrons will be **[CBSE AIPMT]**

(a) 2×10^6 ms^{-1} (b) 2×10^7 ms^{-1}
(c) 8×10^5 ms^{-1} (d) 8×10^6 ms^{-1}

88 The graph between KE $\left(\frac{1}{2}mv^2_{max}\right)$ of ejected photoelectrons and the frequency (ν) of incident radiation for a material exhibiting photoelectric effect is shown in the figure. The work function of the material is

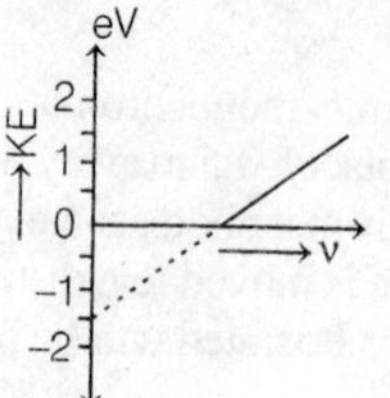

[AFMC]

(a) 1.5 eV (b) 1 eV (c) 3 eV (d) 2 eV

89 The light rays having photons of energy 1.8 eV are falling on a metal surface having a work function 1.2 eV. What is the stopping potential to be applied to stop the emitting electrons? **[BHU]**

(a) 3 eV (b) 1.2 eV (c) 0.6 V (d) 1.4 V

90 The correct curve between the stopping potential (V_s) and intensity (I) of incident light is **[Haryana PMT]**

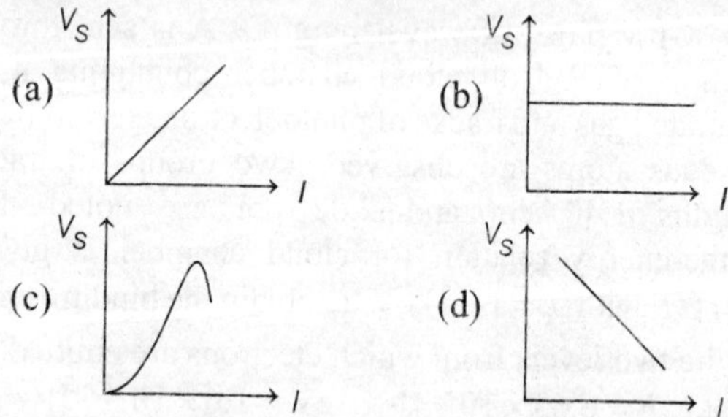

91 From the figure describing photoelectric effect, we may infer correctly that **[KCET]**

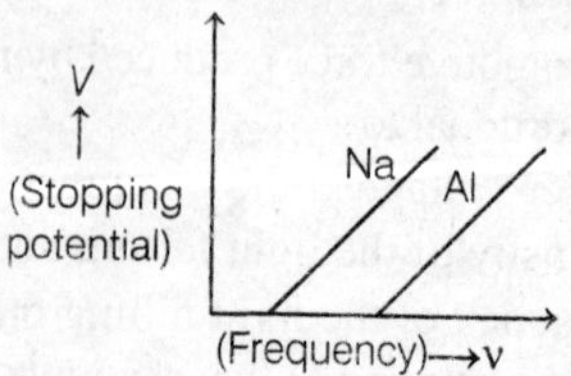

(a) Na and Al both have the same threshold frequency
(b) maximum kinetic energy for both the metals depend linearly on the frequency
(c) the stopping potentials are different for Na and Al for the same change in frequency
(d) Al is a better photosensitive material than Na

Answers

1 (d)	2 (b)	3 (c)	4 (a)	5 (c)	6 (c)	7 (b)	8 (b)	9 (a)	10 (d)
11 (a,c,d)	12 (a)	13 (b)	14 (c)	15 (c)	16 (d)	17 (a)	18 (a)	19 (b)	20 (b)
21 (b)	22 (c)	23 (b)	24 (b)	25 (a)	26 (a)	27 (b)	28 (b)	29 (b)	30 (a)
31 (b)	32 (b)	33 (a)	34 (b)	35 (a)	36 (b)	37 (a)	38 (b)	39 (c)	40 (a)
41 (c)	42 (b)	43 (c)	44 (c)	45 (a)	46 (b)	47 (c)	48 (d)	49 (c)	50 (a)
51 (c)	52 (b)	53 (b)	54 (b)	55 (b)	56 (c)	57 (c)	58 (d)	59 (d)	60 (c)
61 (b)	62 (d)	63 (d)	64 (b)	65 (a)	66 (a)	67 (c)	68 (a)	69 (c)	70 (a)
71 (b)	72 (c)	73 (d)	74 (b)	75 (a)	76 (c)	77 (a)	78 (b)	79 (b)	80 (b)
81 (a)	82 (c)	83 (a)	84 (a)	85 (c)	86 (d)	87 (d)	88 (a)	89 (c)	90 (b)
91 (b)									

Explanations

1 *(d)* The work function of material is given by

$$\phi = h\nu$$

$$\phi = \frac{hc}{\lambda} \quad \ldots(i) \left[\because \nu = \frac{c}{\lambda}\right]$$

where,

h = Planck's constant = 6.63×10^{-34} J-s,

c = speed of light = 3×10^8 ms^{-1} and

λ = wavelength of light.

Here, $\phi = 4 \text{ eV} = 4 \times 1.6 \times 10^{-19}$ J

Substituting the given values in Eq. (i), we get

$$4 \times 1.6 \times 10^{-19} = \frac{6.63 \times 10^{-34} \times 3 \times 10^8}{\lambda}$$

$$\Rightarrow \lambda = \frac{6.63 \times 10^{-34} \times 3 \times 10^8}{4 \times 1.6 \times 10^{-19}}$$

$$= 3.108 \times 10^{-7} \text{ m} \simeq 310 \text{ nm}$$

2 *(b)* Given, frequency of photon, $\nu = 6 \times 10^{14}$ Hz

Speed of light, $c = 3 \times 10^8$ m/s

$\therefore$ Wavelength of photon,

$$\lambda = \frac{c}{\nu}$$

$$= \frac{3 \times 10^8}{6 \times 10^{14}} = 0.5 \times 10^{-6}$$

$$= 500 \times 10^{-9} = 500 \text{ nm}$$

3 *(c)* According to the Einstein's photoelectric equation,

$$K_{\max} = \frac{1}{2}mv_{\max}^2 = h\nu - \phi_0$$

$$= h\nu - h\nu_0 \quad \ldots(i)$$

where, $K_{\max}$ is the maximum kinetic energy of photoelectrons having maximum velocity $v_{\max}$.

When incident frequency of light,

$$\nu = 2\nu_0$$

Substituting the value of ν in Eq. (i), we get

$$\frac{1}{2}mv_1^2 = h(2\nu_0) - h\nu_0$$

$$= 2h\nu_0 - h\nu_0 = h\nu_0 \quad \ldots(ii)$$

If incident frequency of radiation,

$$\nu = 5\nu_0$$

Substituting the value of ν in Eq. (i), we get

$$\frac{1}{2}mv_2^2 = h(5\nu_0) - h\nu_0$$

$$= 5h\nu_0 - h\nu_0$$

$$= 4h\nu_0 \quad \ldots(iii)$$

On dividing Eq. (ii) by Eq (iii), we get

$$\frac{\frac{1}{2}mv_1^2}{\frac{1}{2}mv_2^2} = \frac{h\nu_0}{4h\nu_0}$$

$$\Rightarrow \frac{v_1^2}{v_2^2} = \frac{1}{4} \text{ or } \frac{v_1}{v_2} = \frac{1}{2}$$

$$\therefore \quad v_1 : v_2 = 1:2$$

4 *(a)* Given, threshold wavelength,

$$\lambda_0 = 3250 \times 10^{-10} \text{ m}$$

Wavelength of ultraviolet light,

$$\lambda = 2536 \times 10^{-10} \text{ m}$$

Let velocity of ejected electron be v.

Now, applying Einstein's photoelectric equation, we have

$$E = K + \phi_0$$

$$\Rightarrow h\nu = \frac{1}{2}m_e v^2 + h\nu_0$$

$$\Rightarrow \frac{1}{2}m_e v^2 = h\nu - h\nu_0 = hc\left(\frac{1}{\lambda} - \frac{1}{\lambda_0}\right)$$

$\Rightarrow$ Velocity of electron,

$$v = \sqrt{\frac{2hc}{m_e}\left(\frac{1}{\lambda} - \frac{1}{\lambda_0}\right)}$$

$$= \sqrt{\frac{2 \times 4.14 \times 10^{-15} \times 1.6 \times 10^{-19} \times 3 \times 10^8}{9.1 \times 10^{-31} \times 10^{-20}}\left(\frac{3250 - 2536}{3250 \times 2536}\right)}$$

$$\approx 0.6 \times 10^6 \text{ ms}^{-1} \approx 6 \times 10^5 \text{ ms}^{-1}$$

5 *(c)* The photoelectric effect is the emission of electrons (called photoelectrons) when light strikes a metal surface. Hence, photoelectric effect can take place only with an electron bound in the atom. However, electron is a lepton, whereas proton is fermion.

6 *(c)* ***Case* I** When a metallic surface is illuminated with radiation of wavelength λ, the stopping potential is V.

So, photoelectric equation can be written as

$$eV = \frac{hc}{\lambda} - \frac{hc}{\lambda_0} \quad \ldots(i)$$

***Case* II** When the same surface is illuminated with radiation of wavelength 2λ, the stopping potential is $\frac{V}{4}$. So, photoelectric equation can be written as

$$\frac{eV}{4} = \frac{hc}{2\lambda} - \frac{hc}{\lambda_0}$$

$$\Rightarrow eV = \frac{4hc}{2\lambda} - \frac{4hc}{\lambda_0} \quad \ldots(ii)$$

From Eqs. (i) and (ii), we get

$$\Rightarrow \frac{hc}{\lambda} - \frac{hc}{\lambda_0} = \frac{4hc}{2\lambda} - \frac{4hc}{\lambda_0}$$

$$\Rightarrow \frac{1}{\lambda} - \frac{1}{\lambda_0} = \frac{2}{\lambda} - \frac{4}{\lambda_0} \Rightarrow \lambda_0 = 3\lambda$$

7 *(b)* From photoelectric equation,

$$h\nu = W + eV_0$$

(where, W = work function)

So firstly, $\frac{hc}{\lambda} = W + 3eV_0$ ...(i)

Also, $\frac{hc}{2\lambda} = W + eV_0$

$\Rightarrow \frac{hc}{\lambda} = 2W + 2eV_0$ ...(ii)

Subtracting Eq. (i) from Eq. (ii), we get

$0 = W - eV_0 \Rightarrow W = eV_0$

From Eq. (i), we get

$\frac{hc}{\lambda} = eV_0 + 3eV_0 = 4eV_0$

Threshold wavelength is given by

$\lambda_{th} = \frac{hc}{W} = \frac{4eV_0\lambda}{eV_0} = 4\lambda$

8 *(b)* From Einstein's photoelectric equation,

$(KE)_{max} = h\nu - \phi_0$

For first condition,

$0.5 = E - \phi_0$ ...(i)

For second condition,

$0.8 = \left(E + \frac{E \times 20}{100}\right) - \phi_0$

$\Rightarrow 0.8 = 1.2E - \phi_0$ ...(ii)

From Eqs. (i) and (ii), we get

$0.3 = 0.2E \Rightarrow E = \frac{3}{2} = 1.5$ eV

From Eq. (i), we get

$\phi_0 = E - 0.5 = 1.5 - 0.5 = 1$ eV

9 *(a)* Accroding to Einstein photoelectric equation,

$K_A = \frac{hc}{\lambda_A} - \phi$

$\Rightarrow 2K_A = \frac{2hc}{\lambda_A} - 2\phi$

or $2K_A + \phi = \frac{2hc}{\lambda_A} - \phi$

Wavelength of metal *B* is half of metal *A*, therefore

$K_B = \frac{2hc}{\lambda_A} - \phi \Rightarrow 2K_A + \phi = K_B$

$\Rightarrow K_A < K_B/2$

10 *(d)* The stopping potential is given as

$V_0 = \frac{h}{e}(\nu - \nu_0)$

$\Rightarrow V_0 = \frac{h}{e}\left(\frac{c}{\lambda} - \frac{c}{\lambda_0}\right) \Rightarrow V_0 \propto \frac{1}{\lambda}$

Thus, if the wavelength of incident light falling on a photosensitive material decreases, then stopping potential increases.

11 *(a, c d)* There is no significant time delay between the absorption of a suitable radiation and the emission of electrons and the maximum kinetic energy of electrons does not depend on the intensity of radiation. Also, the maximum kinetic energy of emitted photoelectrons is proportional to frequency of incident radiation.

So, (a), (c) and (d) are the correct options.

However, Einstein analysis gives a threshold frequency below which no electron can be emitted.

12 *(a)* We know that, $K_{max} = eV_0$

where, *e* is the charge of the electron. Since, at the stopping potential, the photoelectric current cannot be obtained by increasing the intensity of the incident. So, light, it is clear that the stopping potential or the maximum kinetic energy of the photoelectrons, does not depend upon the intensity of the incident light. However, if the intensity of light be doubled, then the number of photoelectrons emitted per second is doubled.

So, *n* is doubled but K_{max} remains same.

13 *(b)* Above the threshold frequency, the maximum kinetic energy of the emitted photoelectrons depends on the frequency of the incident light, but is independent of the intensity of the incident light.

14 *(c)* As, $(KE)_{max} = h\nu - \phi_0 = h(\nu - \nu_0)$

Here, $\frac{1}{2}mv_{max}^2 = h[2\nu - \nu] = h\nu$ $[\because \nu_0 = \nu]$

$\Rightarrow v_{max}^2 = \frac{2h\nu}{m} \Rightarrow v_{max} = \sqrt{\frac{2h\nu}{m}}$

15 *(c)* From photoelectric equation,

$E_K = E - W$

where, E_K is kinetic energy of emitted photoelectrons, *W* is the work function and *E* is the energy supplied.

$E = h\nu = \frac{hc}{\lambda}$

where, *h* is Planck's constant, *c* is the speed of light in vacuum and λ is the wavelength.

$\therefore E = \frac{6.6 \times 10^{-34} \times 3 \times 10^8}{5000 \times 10^{-10}}$

$= 3.96 \times 10^{-19}$ J

Also, 1 eV $= 1.6 \times 10^{-19}$ J

$\therefore E = \frac{3.96 \times 10^{-19}}{1.6 \times 10^{-19}} = 2.48$ eV

Hence, $E_K = 2.48 - 1.90 = 0.58$ eV

16 *(d)* Given, wavelength of photons,

$\lambda = 660 \text{ nm} = 660 \times 10^{-9}$ m

Energy of photons,

$E = nh\nu$

But $E = P \times t$

$\therefore P \times t = nh\nu$

$\Rightarrow P \times t = \frac{nhc}{\lambda}$ $[\because \nu = c/\lambda]$

$\therefore 60 \times 1 = \frac{n \times 6.6 \times 10^{-34} \times 3 \times 10^8}{660 \times 10^{-9}}$

$\Rightarrow 60 = \frac{n \times 6.6 \times 3 \times 10^{-19}}{6.6}$

$\Rightarrow n = \frac{60}{3 \times 10^{-19}} = 2 \times 10^{20}$ photons

17 *(a)* As, $E_K = eV_s$

$\Rightarrow V_s = \frac{E_K}{e} = \frac{3.1 \times 1.6 \times 10^{-19}}{1.6 \times 10^{-19} \text{ C}}$

$V_s = 3.1$ V

The stopping potential should be negative, so that it can stop the electrons to reach the anode.

18 *(a)* Efficient power,

$P = \frac{N}{t} \times \frac{hc}{\lambda} = 200 \times 0.25 = 50$ $\left[\because P = \frac{E}{t}\right]$

$\frac{N}{t} = 50 \times \frac{\lambda}{hc}$

$\Rightarrow \frac{N}{t} = \frac{50 \times 0.6 \times 10^{-6}}{6.6 \times 10^{-34} \times 3 \times 10^8}$

$= 1.5 \times 10^{20}$

19 *(b)* By using equation,

$h\nu - h\nu_0 = K_{max}$, we have

$h(\nu_1 - \nu_0) = K_1$ and $h(\nu_2 - \nu_0) = K_2$

$\therefore \frac{\nu_1 - \nu_0}{\nu_2 - \nu_0} = \frac{K_1}{K_2} = \frac{1}{n}$

or $\nu_0 = \frac{(n\nu_1 - \nu_2)}{(n-1)}$

20 *(b)* We know that,

$eV_0 = h\nu - \phi_0$

where, V_0 = stopping potential

and ν = frequency of light.

***Case* I** $eV_0 = h\nu - \phi_0$ ...(i)

***Case* II** $\frac{eV_0}{4} = \frac{h\nu}{2} - \phi_0$

$\Rightarrow eV_0 = 2h\nu - 4\phi_0$ ...(ii)

From Eqs. (i) and (ii), we get

$h\nu - \phi_0 = 2h\nu - 4\phi_0$

$\Rightarrow h\nu = 3\phi_0$

$\Rightarrow h\nu = 3h\nu_0$ $(\because \phi_0 = h\nu_0)$

$\Rightarrow \nu_0 = \frac{h\nu}{3h} \Rightarrow \nu_0 = \frac{\nu}{3}$

21 (*b*) Maximum velocity of a photoelectron,

$$v_{max} = \sqrt{\frac{2h(\nu - \nu_0)}{m}}$$

$$\therefore \quad v_{max} = v_0 = \sqrt{\frac{2h(2\nu_0 - \nu_0)}{m}}$$

(given, $\nu = 2\nu_0$)

$$v_0 = \sqrt{\frac{2h\nu_0}{m}} \quad \text{...(i)}$$

Again, $\nu = 5\nu_0$

$$\therefore \quad v_{max} = \sqrt{\frac{2h(5\nu_0 - \nu_0)}{n}}$$

$$= \sqrt{\frac{2h^4\nu^0}{m}} = 2v_0 \quad \text{[by Eq. (i)]}$$

22 (*c*) For a given material, there exists a certain minimum frequency of the incident radiations below which no emission of photoelectrons takes place. This frequency is also known as threshold frequency.

23 (*b*) Energy incident by the radiation of wavelength 4100 Å is

$$E = \frac{hc}{\lambda} = \frac{6.67 \times 10^{-34} \times 3 \times 10^8}{4100 \times 10^{-10}}$$

$$= 4.8 \times 10^{-19} \text{ J}$$

$$= \frac{4.8 \times 10^{-19}}{1.6 \times 10^{-19}} \text{ eV} = 3 \text{ eV}$$

Now, we have $W_A = 1.92$ eV, $W_B = 2$ eV and $W_C = 5$ eV

Since, $W_A < E$ and $W_B < E$

Hence, A and B will emit photoelectrons.

24 (*b*) Energy corresponding to 2000 Å

$$E = \frac{12375}{\lambda(\text{in Å})} = \frac{12375}{2000} \text{ eV} = 6.2 \text{ eV}$$

Maximum kinetic energy

$$K = h\nu - h\nu_0$$

$$\Rightarrow \quad K = E - W$$

$$K_{max} = (6.2 - 5.01) \text{ eV} = 1.19 \text{ eV}$$

Now, $K_{max} = \frac{1}{2} m v_{max}^2$

$$1.19 \times 1.6 \times 10^{-19} = 1/2 \times 9.1 \times 10^{-31} \times v_{max}^2$$

or $$v_{max}^2 = \frac{1.19 \times 1.6 \times 10^{-19} \times 2}{9.1 \times 10^{-31}}$$

$$= 0.418 \times 10^{12} = 41.8 \times 10^{10}$$

or $$v_{max} = 6.46 \times 10^5 \text{ ms}^{-1}$$

25 (*a*) Energy radiated as visible light

$$= \frac{5}{100} \times 100 = 5 \text{ Js}^{-1}$$

Let n be the number of photons emitted per second. Then,

$$nh\nu = E = 5$$

$$\therefore \quad n = \frac{5\lambda}{hc} = \frac{5 \times 5.6 \times 10^{-7}}{(6.62 \times 10^{-34})(3 \times 10^8)} \quad \left[\because E = \frac{hc}{\lambda}\right]$$

$$= 1.4 \times 10^{19}$$

26 (*a*) From Einstein's photoelectric equation, $h\nu = h\nu_0 + eV_0$

$$= 6.2 + 5 = 11.2 \text{ eV}$$

$$\Rightarrow \quad \frac{hc}{\lambda} = 11.2 \text{ eV or } \lambda = \frac{hc}{11.2 \text{ eV}}$$

$$= \frac{6.6 \times 10^{-34} \times 3.0 \times 10^8}{11.2 \times 1.6 \times 10^{-19}}$$

$$= 1.1049 \times 10^{-7} = 1104.9 \text{ Å}$$

This incident radiation lies in ultraviolet region.

27 (*b*) According to the question,

$$eV = hc\left(\frac{1}{\lambda} - \frac{1}{\lambda_0}\right) \quad \text{...(i)}$$

and $$\frac{eV}{3} = hc\left(\frac{1}{2\lambda} - \frac{1}{\lambda_0}\right) \quad \text{...(ii)}$$

Dividing Eq. (i) by Eq. (ii), we get

$$3 = \frac{\left(\frac{1}{\lambda} - \frac{1}{\lambda_0}\right)}{\left(\frac{1}{2\lambda} - \frac{1}{\lambda_0}\right)}$$

or $$3\left(\frac{1}{2\lambda} - \frac{1}{\lambda_0}\right) = \left(\frac{1}{\lambda} - \frac{1}{\lambda_0}\right)$$

or $$\frac{3}{2\lambda} - \frac{1}{\lambda} = \frac{3}{\lambda_0} - \frac{1}{\lambda_0}$$

or $$\frac{1}{2\lambda} = \frac{2}{\lambda_0}$$

Threshold wavelength for metallic surface, $\lambda_0 = 4\lambda$.

28 (*b*) Momentum of photon,

$$p = \frac{h}{\lambda} = \frac{6.6 \times 10^{-34}}{10^{-10}}$$

$$= 6.6 \times 10^{-24} \text{ kg-ms}^{-1}$$

29 (*b*) Given, $E = 100$ eV

$$= 100 \times 1.6 \times 10^{-19} \text{J}$$

and $$h = 6.62 \times 10^{-34} \text{ J-s}$$

$$\Rightarrow \quad E = h\nu$$

or $$\nu = \frac{E}{h} = \frac{100 \times 1.6 \times 10^{-19}}{6.62 \times 10^{-34}}$$

$$= 0.2417 \times 10^{17}$$

$$= 2.417 \times 10^{16} \text{ Hz}$$

30 (*a*) Work function of metal = ϕ

From Einstein's photoelectric equation,

$E_i = \phi + (\text{KE})_{max}$, where E_i = energy of incident photon

***Case* I** $\quad 3\phi = \phi + K_1$

$$\Rightarrow \quad 2\phi = K_1 = \frac{1}{2} m_p (v_1)^2 \quad \text{...(i)}$$

***Case* II** $\quad 9\phi = \phi + K_2$

$$\Rightarrow \quad 8\phi = K_2 = \frac{1}{2} m_p (v_2)^2 \quad \text{...(ii)}$$

From Eqs. (i) and (ii), we get

$$\frac{1}{4} = \frac{K_1}{K_2} = \frac{(v_1)^2}{(v_2)^2}$$

$$\Rightarrow \quad v_2 = 2v_1 = 2 \times 6 \times 10^6 \text{ ms}^{-1}$$

Hence, maximum velocity

$$= 12 \times 10^6 \text{ ms}^{-1}$$

31 (*b*) Given, $\lambda = 667$ nm $= 667 \times 10^{-9}$m,

$P = 9$ mW $= 9$ mJs^{-1}

Now, $$E = \frac{hc}{\lambda} = \frac{6.6 \times 10^{-34} \times 3 \times 10^8}{667 \times 10^{-9}}$$

$$= \frac{19.8 \times 10^{-17}}{667} = 3 \times 10^{-19}$$

Now, number of photons

$$= \frac{9 \times 10^{-3}}{3 \times 10^{-19}} \quad \left[\because n = \frac{P}{E}\right]$$

$$= 3 \times 10^{16}$$

32 (*b*) Here, curves a and b represent incident radiations of same frequency because they are having same retarding potential, but of different intensities. However, curves b and c represent incident radiations of same intensity but of different frequencies.

33 (*a*) Kinetic energy, KE = $\phi - \phi_0$

Here, $\text{KE}_1 = 1 - 0.5 = 0.5$ eV

$\text{KE}_2 = 2.5 - 0.5 = 2$ eV

$$\therefore \quad \frac{\text{KE}_1}{\text{KE}_2} = \frac{0.5}{2} = \frac{1}{4} \text{ or } \frac{v_1^2}{v_2^2} = \frac{1}{4}$$

or $$\frac{v_1}{v_2} = \sqrt{\frac{1}{4}} = \frac{1}{2}$$

34 (*b*) We know that, $eV_0 = h\nu - \phi_0$

Also, $K_{max} = h\nu - \phi_0$

$$\Rightarrow \quad eV_0 = K_{max} = 0.5 \text{ eV (given)}$$

$$\Rightarrow \quad V_0 = \frac{0.5 \text{ eV}}{e} = 0.5 \text{ V}$$

35 (*a*) $$\lambda_1 = \frac{12375}{E_1 \text{ (eV)}} \text{ Å}$$

$$\Rightarrow \quad E_1 = \frac{12375}{\lambda_1(\text{Å})} = \frac{12375}{1000}$$

$\therefore \quad E_1 = 12.375 \text{ eV}$

Similarly, $E_2 = \dfrac{12375}{\lambda_2(\text{Å})} \text{ eV}$

$= \dfrac{12375}{2000} = 6.1875 \text{ eV}$

Now, $E_1 - W_0 = eV_{s_1}$

and $E_2 - W_0 = eV_{s_2}$

Hence, $12.375 - W_0 = 7.7\, e$

and $6.1875 - W_0 = eV_{s_2}$

Solving, we get $V_{s_2} = 1.5 \text{ V}$

36 *(b)* $E - W_0 = (1/2)\, mv^2$

***Case* I** $2W_0 - W_0 = (1/2)\, mv_1^2$ ...(i)

***Case* II** $5W_0 - W_0 = (1/2)\, mv_2^2$ ...(ii)

Therefore, from Eqs. (i) and (ii), we get

$$\frac{2W_0 - W_0}{5W_0 - W_0} = \frac{v_1^2}{v_2^2} \Rightarrow \frac{v_1}{v_2} = \frac{1}{2}$$

37 *(a)* $E_1 = \dfrac{1240}{550} = 2.25 \text{ eV}$,

$E_2 = \dfrac{1240}{450} = 2.75 \text{ eV}$

$E_3 = \dfrac{1240}{350} = 3.54 \text{ eV}$

E_1 cannot emit photoelectrons from q and r plates. E_2 cannot emit photoelectrons from r. Thus, the stopping potential and saturation current is minimum for plate r.

Further, work function of p is least and it can emit photoelectrons from all three wavelengths. Hence, magnitude of its stopping potential and saturation current both will be maximum.

This is correctly shown in graph (a).

38 *(b)* The minimum energy required for the emission of photoelectron from a metal is called the work function W of that metal. If ν_0 is threshold frequency, then

$$W = h\nu_0$$

But frequency $(\nu_0) = \dfrac{\text{velocity } (c)}{\text{wavelength } (\lambda)}$

$\therefore \quad W = \dfrac{hc}{\lambda}$

Given, $h = 6.6 \times 10^{-34}$ J-s,

$c = 3 \times 10^8$ m/s, $\lambda = 400$ nm

$= 400 \times 10^{-9}$ m

$\therefore \quad W = \dfrac{6.6 \times 10^{-34} \times 3 \times 10^8}{400 \times 10^{-9}}$

$= 4.95 \times 10^{-19}$ J

$\Rightarrow \quad W = \dfrac{4.95 \times 10^{-19}}{1.6 \times 10^{-19}} = 3.1 \text{ eV}$

39 *(c)* Momentum of photon,

$$p = m \times c = \frac{E}{c} = \frac{h\nu}{c}.$$

40 *(a)* $\because E = h\nu$

$\Rightarrow \quad 3.3 \times 1.6 \times 10^{-19} = 6.6 \times 10^{-34} \times \nu$

$\Rightarrow \quad \nu = \dfrac{3.3 \times 1.6 \times 10^{-19}}{6.6 \times 10^{-34}}$

$= 0.8 \times 10^{15} = 8 \times 10^{14}$ Hz

41 *(c)* Intensity, $I = 10^{-10} \text{ Wbm}^{-2}$

$= 10^{-10} \text{ Js}^{-1}\text{m}^{-2}$

Let the number of photons required be n.

Then, $\dfrac{nh\nu}{10^{-4}} = 10^{-10}$

Hence, $n = \dfrac{10^{-10} \times 10^{-4}}{h\nu} = \dfrac{10^{-14} \times \lambda}{hc}$

$= \dfrac{10^{-14} \times 660 \times 10^{-9}}{6.6 \times 10^{-34} \times 3 \times 10^8} = 3.3 \times 10^4$

42 *(b)* $V_0 = \dfrac{h}{e}(\nu - \nu_0)$

or $(\nu - \nu_0) = \dfrac{V_0 \times e}{h}$

$= \dfrac{4.144 \times 1.6 \times 10^{-19}}{6.63 \times 10^{-34}}$

$\Rightarrow \quad \nu - 1 \times 10^{15} = 10^{15}$

$\nu = 10^{15} + 1 \times 10^{15} = 2 \times 10^{15}$ Hz

43 *(c)* According to Einstein's photoelectric equation,

$KE_{max} = h\nu - \phi_0$

Comparing with the equation of straight line,

$$y = mx + c$$

We get, slope of graph $= h$

So, the slope is a constant and same for all metals and independent of the intensity of the incident radiation.

44 *(c)* Energy of photoelectrons,

$$E = \frac{hc}{\lambda} - W \Rightarrow \frac{hc}{\lambda} = E + W \quad ...(i)$$

where, W is the work function for the metal surface (constant).

$$2E = \frac{hc}{\lambda'} - W \Rightarrow \frac{hc}{\lambda'} = 2E + W \quad ...(ii)$$

Dividing Eq. (i) by Eq. (ii), we get

$$\frac{\lambda'}{\lambda} = \frac{E + W}{2E + W} \Rightarrow \frac{\lambda'}{\lambda} = \frac{(E + W)}{2\left(E + \frac{W}{2}\right)}$$

$$\therefore \frac{\lambda'}{\lambda} > \frac{1}{2} \text{ or } \lambda' > \frac{\lambda}{2} \Rightarrow \lambda > \lambda' > \frac{\lambda}{2}$$

45 *(a)* If λ_0 is threshold wavelength, then work function

$$\phi_0 = \frac{hc}{\lambda_0} \Rightarrow \lambda_0 = \frac{hc}{\phi_0}$$

$$= \frac{6.6 \times 10^{-34} \times 3 \times 10^8}{4.2 \times 1.6 \times 10^{-19}} \approx 2955 \text{ Å}$$

46 *(b)* Energy of photon, $E = \dfrac{12375}{\lambda \text{ (in Å)}}$ eV

For red light, the wavelength is maximum.

$\because \lambda_R = 7900$ Å

$\therefore \quad E = \dfrac{12375}{7900} \text{ eV} = 1.56 \text{ eV} \simeq 1.6 \text{ eV}$

47 *(c)* Number of photons,

$$n = \frac{P}{E} = \frac{P}{h\nu} = \frac{P\lambda}{hc}$$

$$= \frac{1000 \times 198.6}{6.6 \times 10^{-34} \times 3 \times 10^8} \approx 10^{30}$$

48 *(d)* Photoelectric current depends on the intensity of incident radiation,

i.e. $\quad i \propto I$

But, intensity of radiation, $I \propto 1/d^2$

$\therefore \quad i \propto 1/d^2$

49 *(c)* Here, $K_1 = \dfrac{hc}{\lambda_1} - W$ ...(i)

and $K_2 = \dfrac{hc}{\lambda_2} - W$ ...(ii)

Substituting $\lambda_1 = 2\lambda_2$ in Eq. (i), we get

$$K_1 = \frac{hc}{2\lambda_2} - W$$

$$\Rightarrow K_1 = \frac{1}{2}\left(\frac{hc}{\lambda_2}\right) - W = \frac{1}{2}(K_2 + W) - W$$

$$K_1 = \frac{K_2}{2} - \frac{W}{2} \Rightarrow K_1 < \frac{K_2}{2}$$

50 *(a)* The curve drawn between velocity and frequency of photon in vacuum will be a straight line parallel to frequency axis as velocity of photon in a vacuum is constant and it is independent of frequency.

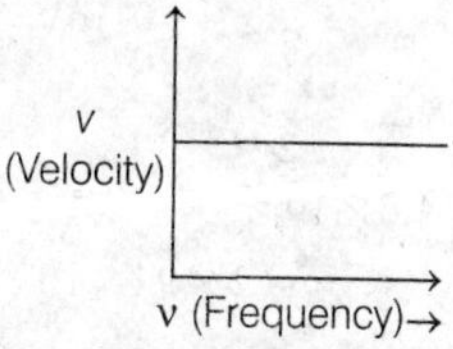

51 *(c)* Given, work function, $\phi = 4$ eV

Longest wavelength of light $= \lambda_m$

$\therefore \quad \dfrac{hc}{\lambda_m} = \phi$

$\therefore \quad \lambda_m = \dfrac{hc}{\phi} = \dfrac{(6.63 \times 10^{-34} \times 3 \times 10^8)}{4.0 \times 1.6 \times 10^{-19}}$

$= 310$ nm

52 (b) We know that, work function $= \dfrac{hc}{\lambda}$

$$\frac{W_{Na}}{W_{Cu}} = \frac{hc/\lambda_{Na}}{hc/\lambda_{Cu}} = \frac{hc}{\lambda_{Na}} \times \frac{\lambda_{Cu}}{hc}$$

$$\Rightarrow \quad \frac{\lambda_{Cu}}{\lambda_{Na}} = \frac{2.3}{4.5} \approx \frac{1}{2}$$

$$\therefore \quad \lambda_{Na} : \lambda_{Cu} = 2:1$$

53 (b) Given, $E = 3 \text{ eV} = 3 \times 1.6 \times 10^{-19}$ J

We know that, $E = hc/\lambda \Rightarrow \lambda = hc/E$

$$= \frac{6.6 \times 10^{-34} \times 3 \times 10^8}{3 \times 1.6 \times 10^{-19}} = \frac{19.8 \times 10^{-26}}{4.8 \times 10^{-19}}$$

$$= 4.125 \times 10^{-7} = 412.5 \times 10^{-9} \text{m}$$

$$= 412.5 \text{ nm}$$

54 (b) Photoelectric effect can take place from free electrons.

55 (b) Given, frequency, $\nu = f$

Threshold frequency, $\nu_0 = f_0$

We know that,

Maximum kinetic energy,

$$K_{max} = h\nu - \phi_0 = h\nu - h\nu_0$$
$$= hf - hf_0 = h(f - f_0)$$

56 (c) Given, wavelength, $\lambda = 3 \times 10^4$ cm

$$= 3 \times 10^4 \times 10^{-2} \text{ m} = 3 \times 10^2 \text{ m}$$

We know that, energy,

$$E = \frac{hc}{\lambda} = \frac{6.62 \times 10^{-34} \times 3 \times 10^8}{3 \times 10^2}$$

$$= 6.62 \times 10^{-28} \text{ J}$$

57 (c) Given, $V_0 = -3.2$V,

$$h = 6.6 \times 10^{-34} \text{ Js}^{-1}$$

and $\phi_0 = 4$ eV

We know that, $eV_0 = h\nu - \phi_0$

$\nu = eV_0 + \phi_0/h$

$$= -\frac{1.6 \times 10^{-19} \times 3.2 + 4 \times 1.6 \times 10^{-19}}{6.6 \times 10^{-34}}$$

$$= 1.939 \times 10^{14} \text{ s}^{-1}$$

58 (d) Given, work function, $\phi = 4.125$ eV

We know that, work function, $\phi = \dfrac{hc}{\lambda}$

$$\Rightarrow \lambda = \frac{hc}{\phi} = \frac{6.6 \times 10^{-34} \times 3 \times 10^8}{4.125 \times 1.6 \times 10^{-19}}$$

$$= \frac{19.8 \times 10^{-7}}{6.6} = 3 \times 10^{-7}$$

$$= 3000 \times 10^{-10} = 3000 \text{ Å}$$

59 (d) The maximum kinetic energy of emitted photoelectrons depends on the radiation source and nature of material of plate but is independent of the intensity. So, it will remain unchanged.

60 (c) Let W be the work function of metal, then

$$eV_0 = \frac{hc}{330 \times 10^{-9}} - W$$

and $$e(2V_0) = \frac{hc}{220 \times 10^{-9}} - W$$

Solving these two equations, we get

$$V_0 = \frac{10^9 \times h \times c}{110 \times e \times 6}$$

$$= \frac{10^9 \times 6.6 \times 10^{-34} \times 3 \times 10^8}{110 \times 1.6 \times 10^{-19} \times 6} = \frac{15}{8} \text{V}$$

61 (b) Given, $\lambda_1 = 300$ nm

and $\lambda_2 = 600$ nm

We know that, work function,

$$\phi = hc/\lambda$$

So, to find ratio between them,

$$\frac{\phi_1}{\phi_2} = \frac{hc}{\lambda_1} \times \frac{\lambda_2}{hc} = \frac{\lambda_2}{\lambda_1} = \frac{600}{300} = 2:1$$

62 (d) According to Einstein's photoelectric effect,

Energy of photon

= KE of photoelectron + work function of metal

or $\quad h\nu = K_{max} + E_0 \quad$ ...(i)

Now, we have given, $\nu' = 2\nu$

Therefore, $K'_{max} = 2h\nu - E_0 \quad$ ...(ii)

From Eqs. (i) and (ii), we have

$$K'_{max} = 2(K_{max} + E_0) - E_0$$
$$= 2K_{max} + E_0$$
$$= K_{max} + (K_{max} + E_0)$$
$$= K_{max} + h\nu$$

Putting $K_{max} = K$

$$\therefore \quad K'_{max} = K + h\nu$$

63 (d) We have,

$$\frac{\frac{1}{2}mv^2}{\frac{1}{2}m(2v)^2} = \frac{h\nu - \phi}{h(2\nu) - \phi}$$

$$\left[\because K_{max} = h\nu - \phi = \frac{1}{2}mv^2\right]$$

or $$\frac{1}{4} = \frac{h\nu - \phi}{2h\nu - \phi} \text{ or } \phi = \frac{2h\nu}{3}$$

64 (b) Kinetic energy (KE),

$$\frac{1}{2}mv_1^2 = 2h\nu_0 - h\nu_0 = h\nu_0$$

and $$\frac{1}{2}mv_2^2 = 3h\nu_0 - h\nu_0 = 2h\nu_0$$

$$\therefore \quad \frac{1}{2}mv_2^2 = 2\left[\frac{1}{2}mv_1^2\right]$$

$$\Rightarrow \quad v_2^2 = 2v_1^2$$

or $$v_2 = \sqrt{2}v_1 = \sqrt{2} \times 2 \times 10^6$$

$$\Rightarrow \quad v_2 = 2\sqrt{2} \times 10^6 \text{ ms}^{-1}$$

65 (a) Momentum, $p = \dfrac{E}{c} = \dfrac{3 \text{ MeV}}{3 \times 10^8 \text{ m/s}}$

$$= \frac{3 \times 10^6 \text{ eV}}{3 \times 10^8 \text{ m/s}} = 0.01 \text{ eV-s/m}$$

66 (a) Given, energy of photon,

$$E = h\nu = 8 \text{ eV}$$

Threshold frequency,

$$\nu_0 = 1.6 \times 10^{15} \text{ Hz}$$

From Einstein's photoelectric equation,

$$KE_{max} = h\nu - h\nu_0$$

$$\Rightarrow KE_{max} = 8 - \frac{6.6 \times 10^{-34} \times 1.6 \times 10^{15}}{1.6 \times 10^{-19}}$$

$$= 8 - 6.6 = 1.4 \text{ eV}$$

67 (c) Given, the wavelength of incident light, $\lambda = 200 \text{ nm} = 200 \times 10^{-9}$ m

Work function, $\phi = 4.71$ eV

From Einstein's photoelectric equation,

$$KE_{max} = h\nu - \phi \quad \text{...(i)}$$

But $KE_{max} = eV_0 \quad$ ...(ii)

So, $\quad eV_0 = h\nu - \phi$

where, V_0 = stopping potential.

or $$eV_0 = \frac{hc}{\lambda} - \phi$$

$$\therefore \quad 1.6 \times 10^{-19} V_0 = \frac{6.6 \times 10^{-34} \times 3 \times 10^8}{200 \times 10^{-9}} - 4.71 \times 1.6 \times 10^{-19}$$

$$\Rightarrow V_0 = \frac{6.6 \times 10^{-34} \times 3 \times 10^8}{2 \times 10^{-7} \times 1.6 \times 10^{-19}} - \frac{4.71 \times 1.6 \times 10^{-19}}{1.6 \times 10^{-19}}$$

$$\Rightarrow V_0 = (6.19 - 4.71) = 1.48 \approx 1.5 \text{ V}$$

68 (a) Intensity of light is inversely proportional to square of distance.

i.e. $$I \propto \frac{1}{r^2} \text{ or } \frac{I_2}{I_1} = \frac{(r_1)^2}{(r_2)^2}$$

Given, $r_1 = 0.5$ m, $r_2 = 1.0$ m

Therefore, $$\frac{I_2}{I_1} = \frac{(0.5)^2}{(1)^2} = \frac{1}{4}$$

Now, since number of photoelectrons emitted per second is directly proportional to intensity, so number of electrons emitted would decrease by factor of 4.

69 (c) Energy received from the sun

$$= 2 \text{ cal cm}^{-2} \text{ min}^{-1}$$
$$= 8.4 \text{ J-cm}^{-2} \text{ min}^{-1}$$

Energy of one photon received from sun,

$$E = \frac{hc}{\lambda} = \frac{6.6 \times 10^{-34} \times 3 \times 10^8}{5500 \times 10^{-10}} = 3.6 \times 10^{-19} \text{ J}$$

$\therefore$ Number of photons reaching the earth per cm^2 per minute will be

$$n = \frac{\text{Energy received from sun}}{\text{Energy of one photon}}$$

$$n = \frac{8.4}{3.6 \times 10^{-19}} = 2.3 \times 10^{19}$$

70 *(a)* Binding energy, $W = \frac{hc}{\lambda} - E$

Here, $\lambda = 4.9 \times 10^{-10}$ m,

$R_1 = 1.40$ cm, $R_2 = 2.02$ cm,

$\alpha = 1$ cm keV^{-1}

For cloud chamber, the range-energy relation is

$R = \alpha E$ or $E = \frac{R}{\alpha}$

$$\therefore E_1 = \frac{R_1}{\alpha} = \frac{1.40}{1} = 1.40 \text{ keV} \quad \ldots\text{(i)}$$

$$\text{and } E_2 = \frac{R_2}{\alpha} = \frac{2.02}{1} = 2.02 \text{ keV} \quad \ldots\text{(ii)}$$

Energy of the incident photon,

$$h\nu = \frac{hc}{\lambda} = \frac{6.63 \times 10^{-34} \times 3 \times 10^8}{4.9 \times 10^{-10}} \text{ J}$$

$$= \frac{6.63 \times 3 \times 10^{-16}}{4.9 \times 1.6 \times 10^{-19}} \text{ eV}$$

$$= 2.54 \text{ keV} \quad \ldots\text{(iii)}$$

From Einstein's photoelectric equation, $h\nu = W + E$

$\therefore$ Binding energy, $W = h\nu - E$

From Eqs. (i), (ii) and (iii), we get

$W_1 = 2.54 - 1.40 = 1.14$ keV

and $W_2 = 2.54 - 2.02 = 0.52$ keV

71 *(b)* In a photoconductive cell, when monochromatic light is incident on the transparent metallic film, a force produced called the photo-electromotive, stimulates the emission of an electric current when photovoltaic action creates a potential difference between two points.

The magnitude of this current depends upon the intensity of incident light. Hence, photo-electromotive force produced by monochromatic light is proportional to the intensity of the light falling on the cell.

72 *(c)* From photoelectric equation,

$$E = h\nu = \frac{hc}{\lambda}$$

$$\therefore E = \frac{6.6 \times 10^{-34} \times 3 \times 10^8}{5000 \times 10^{-10}} = 3.96 \times 10^{-19} \text{ J}$$

$$\text{or} \quad E = \frac{3.96 \times 10^{-19}}{1.6 \times 10^{-19}} = 2.48 \text{ eV}$$

Hence, $E_K = 2.48 - 1.90 = 0.58$ eV

73 *(d)* According to photoelectric equation,

$$E_K = h\nu - h\nu_0 \quad \ldots\text{(i)}$$

If the energy of photon ($h\nu$) is less than the work function ($h\nu_0$) of metallic surface, then electrons will never be ejected from surface regardless of intensity of incident light.

Also, from Eq. (i), we get

When $\nu = \nu_0$, $E_k = 0$

and for $\nu > \nu_0$, $E_k \propto \nu$

$\therefore$ Graph (d) represents variation of E_K with ν.

74 *(b)* Threshold energy of A is

$$E_A = h\nu_A = 6.6 \times 10^{-34} \times 1.8 \times 10^{14} = 11.88 \times 10^{-20} \text{ J}$$

$$= \frac{11.88 \times 10^{-20}}{1.6 \times 10^{-19}} \text{ eV} = 0.74 \text{ eV}$$

Similarly, $E_B = h\nu_B / e = 0.91$ eV

Since, the incident photons have energy greater than E_A but less than E_B.

So, photoelectrons will be emitted from metal A only.

75 *(a)* The electromagnetic theory of light failed to explain photoelectric effect.

76 *(c)* According to photoelectric equation,

$$eV = \frac{hc}{\lambda} - W_0$$

$$\Rightarrow 0.5\, e = \frac{hc}{6 \times 10^{-7}} - W_0$$

$$\Rightarrow 0.5 = \frac{h}{e} \times \frac{c}{6 \times 10^{-7}} - \frac{W_0}{e} \quad \ldots\text{(i)}$$

Similarly,

$$1.5 = \frac{h}{e} \times \frac{c}{4 \times 10^{-7}} - \frac{W_0}{e} \quad \ldots\text{(ii)}$$

From Eqs. (i) and (ii), we get

$$1 = \frac{h}{e} \times \frac{c}{10^{-7}} \left(\frac{1}{4} - \frac{1}{6} \right)$$

$$\Rightarrow \frac{h}{e} = \frac{12 \times 10^{-7}}{3 \times 10^8} = 4 \times 10^{-15} \text{ V-s}$$

77 *(a)* Energy corresponding to 248 nm

$$\text{wavelength} = \frac{1240}{248} \text{ eV} = 5 \text{ eV}$$

Energy corresponding to 310 nm

$$\text{wavelength} = \frac{1240}{310} \text{ eV} = 4 \text{ eV}$$

$$\frac{(\text{KE})_1}{(\text{KE})_2} = \frac{u_1^2}{u_2^2} \Rightarrow \frac{4}{1} = \frac{5 \text{ eV} - W}{4 \text{ eV} - W}$$

$$\Rightarrow 16 - 4W = 5 - W \quad \Rightarrow 11 = 3W$$

$$\Rightarrow W = \frac{11}{3} = 3.67 \text{ eV} \cong 3.7 \text{ eV}$$

78 *(b)* According to Planck's quantisation law,

$$E = nh\nu = n\left(\frac{hc}{\lambda}\right)$$

$$\Rightarrow \frac{E}{t} = \left(\frac{n}{t}\right)\left(\frac{hc}{\lambda}\right)$$

$$\Rightarrow 10^{-7} = \left(\frac{n}{t}\right) \frac{6.626 \times 10^{-34} \times 3 \times 10^8}{5000 \times 10^{-10}}$$

$$\Rightarrow \frac{n}{t} = \frac{5000 \times 10^{-10} \times 10^{-7}}{6.626 \times 10^{-34} \times 3 \times 10^8} = 2.5 \times 10^{11} \text{ s}^{-1}$$

79 *(b)* Work function of a metal is given by

$$W = h\nu_0 = hc/\lambda_0$$

where, λ_0 is the threshold wavelength.

$$\text{or} \quad W_0 \propto \frac{1}{\lambda_0}$$

$$\therefore \frac{W_0}{W'_0} = \frac{\lambda'_0}{\lambda_0} \text{ or } \frac{W_0}{\left(\frac{W_0}{2}\right)} = \frac{\lambda'_0}{\lambda_0}$$

$$\Rightarrow \lambda'_0 = 2\lambda_0$$

80 *(b)* A photocell employs photoelectric effect to convert change in the intensity of illumination into a change in photoelectric current. In other words, it converts light energy into electrical energy.

81 *(a)* There is no time lag between the instant, the photon of light falls on the metal surface and the instant a photoelectron is emitted from the metal surface.

Hence, the photoelectric emission is an instantaneous process.

82 *(c)* In photoelectric effect, Einstein's equation is given by

Photon energy = KE of electron + work function

i.e. $h\nu = eV_s + h\nu_0$

where, V_s is stopping potential and ν_0 is the threshold frequency.

$$\therefore V_s = \frac{h}{e}(\nu - \nu_0) \quad \ldots\text{(i)}$$

Given, $\nu_0 = 3.3 \times 10^{14}$ Hz,

$\nu = 8.2 \times 10^{14}$ Hz, $h = 6.6 \times 10^{-34}$ J-s

and $e = 1.6 \times 10^{-19}$ C

Substituting the values in Eq. (i), we get

$$V_s = \frac{6.6 \times 10^{-34} \times (8.2 \times 10^{14} - 3.3 \times 10^{14})}{1.6 \times 10^{-19}} \approx 2 \text{ V}$$

83 *(a)* If kinetic energy of photoelectrons emitted from metal surface is E_K and W is the minimum energy required to eject photoelectrons from the metal, then from Einstein's photoelectric equation

$$E_K = h\nu - W$$

Also, $E = \frac{hc}{\lambda}$

where, h is Planck's constant and c is speed of light and λ is wavelength.

Since, wavelength is reduced from 2300 Å to 1800 Å, energy increases, hence emission takes place.

84 *(a)* When light falls on a metallic surface, then it results ejection of photoelectron. In this process, conservation of energy hold. Thus, from law of conservation of energy, energy imparted by the photon = maximum kinetic energy of the emitted electron + work function of the metal

or $h\nu = (\text{KE})_{max} + \phi$

But $\phi = h\nu_0$

where, ν_0 being threshold frequency.

or $(\text{KE})_{max} = h\nu - h\nu_0$

$\Rightarrow (\text{KE})_{max} \propto \nu - \nu_0$

85 *(c)* Specific charge of an electron,

$$\frac{e}{m} = 1.8 \times 10^{11}\ \text{C kg}^{-1}$$

Maximum kinetic energy of photoelectron, $\frac{1}{2} mv_{max}^2 = eV_s$

where, V_s is the stopping potential.

$$\Rightarrow V_s = \frac{mv_{max}^2}{2e} = \frac{v_{max}^2}{2(e/m)}$$

$$= \frac{(1.2 \times 10^6)^2}{2 \times 1.8 \times 10^{11}} = 0.4 \times 10 = 4\ \text{V}$$

86 *(d)* Einstein's photoelectric equation can be written as

$$hf = k + \phi$$

But, $k = eV_s$, V_s being stopping potential

$\therefore \quad hf = eV_s + \phi \quad \ldots(\text{i})$

So, $hf_1 = eV_1 + \phi \quad \ldots(\text{ii})$

and $hf_2 = eV_2 + \phi \quad \ldots(\text{iii})$

Subtracting Eq. (ii) from Eq. (iii), we get

$h(f_1 - f_2) = e(V_1 - V_2)$

or $eV_2 = eV_1 - h(f_1 - f_2)$

or $V_2 = V_1 + \frac{h}{e}(f_2 - f_1)$

87 *(d)* Einstein's photoelectric equation can be written as $\frac{1}{2}mv^2 = h\nu - \phi$

$\Rightarrow \frac{1}{2} m \times (4 \times 10^6)^2 = 2h\nu_0 - h\nu_0 \quad \ldots(\text{i})$

and $\frac{1}{2} m \times v^2 = 5h\nu_0 - h\nu_0 \ldots(\text{ii})$

Dividing Eq. (ii) by Eq. (i), we get

$$\frac{v^2}{(4 \times 10^6)^2} = \frac{4h\nu_0}{h\nu_0}$$

$\Rightarrow v^2 = 4 \times 16 \times 10^{12}$

$\Rightarrow v^2 = 64 \times 10^{12}$

$v = 8 \times 10^6\ \text{ms}^{-1}$

88 *(a)* As per Einstein's photoelectric equation,

$$h\nu = \phi_0 + 1/2\ mv^2$$

The intercept of KE-ν graph on KE axis gives the value of work function. Hence, work function, $W = 1.5$ eV

89 *(c)* From Einstein's photoelectric equation, we have $E_K = h\nu - W$

where, $h\nu$ is energy of photon absorbed by the electron in the metal, W is the work function of the metal.

Also, the potential at which the photoelectric current becomes zero, is called stopping potential or cut-off potential.

Given, $h\nu = 1.8$ eV, $W = 1.2$ eV

$\therefore E_K = 1.8 - 1.2 = 0.6$ eV

Thus, stopping potential,

$$V_0 = \frac{E_K}{e} = \frac{0.6 \times 1.6 \times 10^{-19}}{1.6 \times 10^{-19}} = 0.6\ \text{V}$$

90 *(b)* The magnitude of the stopping potential is independent of the intensity of the incident radiation, irrespective of the change in the frequency of the incident radiation. Hence, V *versus* I curve is constant and correctly shown by graph (b).

91 *(b)* The graph between stopping potential and frequency is a straight line, so stopping potential and hence maximum kinetic energy of photoelectrons depends linearly on the frequency.

Topic 3

Dual Nature of Matter : de-Broglie Waves

2019

1 An electron is accelerated through a potential difference of 10000 V. Its de-Broglie wavelength is (nearly) (Take, $m_e = 9 \times 10^{-31}$ kg) **[NEET (National)]**

(a) 12.2×10^{-12} m (b) 12.2×10^{-14} m

(c) 12.2 nm (d) 12.2×10^{-13} m

2 A proton and an α-particle are accelerated from rest to the same energy. The de-Broglie wavelengths λ_p and λ_α are in the ratio **[NEET (Odisha)]**

(a) 2 : 1 (b) 1 : 1 (c) $\sqrt{2} : 1$ (d) 4 : 1

2018

3 The graph between the energy log E of an electron and its de-Broglie wavelength log λ will be **[AIIMS]**

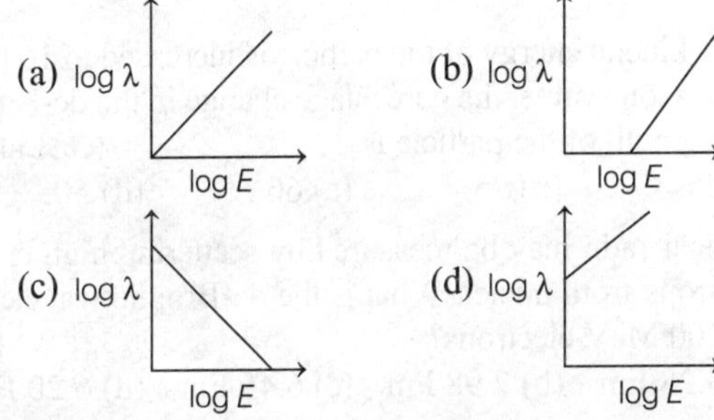

2017

4 The de-Broglie wavelength of a neutron in thermal equilibrium with heavy water at a temperature T (kelvin) and mass m is [NEET]

(a) $\frac{h}{\sqrt{mkT}}$ (b) $\frac{h}{\sqrt{3mkT}}$ (c) $\frac{2h}{\sqrt{3mkT}}$ (d) $\frac{2h}{\sqrt{mkT}}$

5 The wavelength λ of a photon and the de-Broglie wavelength of an electron have the same value. Find the ratio of energy of photon to the kinetic energy of electron in terms of mass m, speed of light c and Planck's constant (h). [JIPMER]

(a) $\lambda mc/h$ (b) hmc/λ (c) $2hmc/\lambda$ (d) $2\lambda mc/h$

2016

6 Electrons of mass m with de-Broglie wavelength λ fall on the target in an X-ray tube. The cut-off wavelength (λ_0) of the emitted X-ray is [NEET]

(a) $\lambda_0 = \frac{2mc\lambda^2}{h}$ (b) $\lambda_0 = \frac{2h}{mc}$

(c) $\lambda_0 = \frac{2m^2c^2\lambda^3}{h^2}$ (d) $\lambda_0 = \lambda$

7 An electron of mass m and a photon have same energy E. The ratio of de-Broglie wavelengths associated with them is [NEET]

(a) $\left(\frac{E}{2m}\right)^{1/2}$ (b) $c(2mE)^{1/2}$

(c) $\frac{1}{c}\left(\frac{2m}{E}\right)^{1/2}$ (d) $\frac{1}{c}\left(\frac{E}{2m}\right)^{1/2}$

2015

8 Which of the following figures represent the variation of particle momentum and the associated de-Broglie wavelength? [AIPMT]

(a) 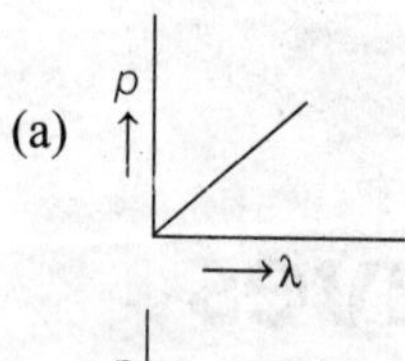

(b) $p \uparrow$, $\rightarrow \lambda$

(c) $p \uparrow$, $\rightarrow \lambda$

(d) 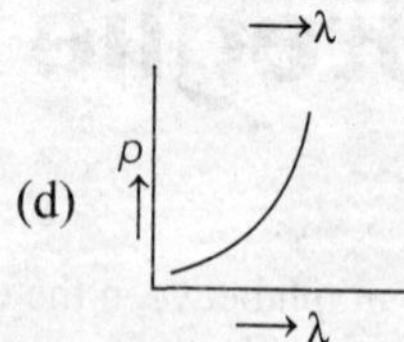

2014

9 If the kinetic energy of the particle is increased to 16 times its previous value, the percentage change in the de-Broglie wavelength of the particle is [CBSE AIPMT]

(a) 25 (b) 75 (c) 60 (d) 50

10 Nuclear radii may be measured by scattering high energy electrons from nuclei. What is the de-Broglie wavelength for 200 MeV electrons? [BVP]

(a) 8.28 Fm (b) 7.98 Fm (c) 6.45 Fm (d) 6.20 Fm

11 The de-Broglie wavelength of an electron is the same as that of a 50 keV X-ray photon. The ratio of the energy of the photon to the kinetic energy of the electron is (the energy equivalent of electron mass is 0.5 MeV) [WB JEE]

(a) 1 : 50 (b) 1 : 20

(c) 20 : 1 (d) 50 : 1

12 What is the de-Broglie wavelength of the electron accelerated through a potential difference of 100 V? [KCET]

(a) 12.27 Å (b) 1.227 Å

(c) 0.1227 Å (d) 0.001227 Å

2012

13 If the momentum of an electron is changed by p, then the de-Broglie wavelength associated with it changes by 0.5%. The initial momentum of electron will be [CBSE AIPMT]

(a) $200p$ (b) $400p$ (c) $p/200$ (d) $100p$

14 Photon and electron are given same energy (10^{-20} J). Wavelength associated with photon and electron are λ_p and λ_e, the correct statement will be [AIIMS]

(a) $\lambda_p > \lambda_e$ (b) $\lambda_p < \lambda_e$ (c) $\lambda_p = \lambda_e$ (d) $\frac{\lambda_e}{\lambda_p} = c$

15 The de-Broglie wavelength of an electron moving with a velocity 1.5×10^8 ms^{-1} is equal to that of a photon. The ratio of the kinetic energy of the electron to the energy of the photon is [J&K CET]

(a) $\frac{1}{4}$ (b) $\frac{1}{2}$ (c) 2 (d) 4

2011

16 Electrons used in an electron microscope are accelerated by a voltage of 25 kV. If the voltage is increased to 100 kV, then the de-Broglie wavelength associated with the electrons would [CBSE AIPMT]

(a) decrease by 2 times (b) decrease by 4 times

(c) increase by 4 times (d) increase by 2 times

17 If a proton and an electron have the same de-Broglie wavelength, then [Kerala CEE]

(a) kinetic energy of electron < kinetic energy of proton

(b) kinetic energy of electron = kinetic energy of proton

(c) momentum of electron > momentum of proton

(d) momentum of electron = momentum of proton

(e) momentum of electron < momentum of proton

18 If the particles listed below all have the same kinetic energy, which one would possess the shortest de-Broglie wavelength? [J&K CET]

(a) Deuteron (b) α-particle (c) Proton (d) Electron

19 The de-Broglie wavelength λ of an electron accelerated through a potential V (in volt) is [J&K CET]

(a) $\frac{1.227}{\sqrt{V}}$ nm (b) $\frac{0.1227}{\sqrt{V}}$ nm

(c) $\frac{0.01227}{\sqrt{V}}$ nm (d) $\frac{0.1227}{\sqrt{V}}$ Å

20 An electron and a proton are moving in the same direction with same kinetic energy. The ratio of the de-Broglie wavelength associated with these particles is **[J&K CET]**

(a) $\frac{m_e}{m_p}$ (b) $\frac{m_p}{m_e}$ (c) $\sqrt{m_p/m_e}$ (d) $m_p m_e$

21 An electron of mass m_e and a proton of mass m_p are moving with the same speed. The ratio of their de-Broglie wavelengths λ_e/λ_p is **[KCET]**

(a) 1 (b) 1836 (c) $\frac{1}{1836}$ (d) 918

22 In Davisson and Germer experiment, the velocity of electrons emitted from the electron gun can be increased by **[CBSE AIPMT]**

(a) increasing the filament current
(b) decreasing the filament current
(c) decreasing the potential difference between the anode and filament
(d) increasing the potential difference between the anode and filament

2010

23 If K be the kinetic energy and m be the mass of a moving particle, then the de-Broglie wavelength of the particle is **[Manipal]**

(a) $\lambda = \frac{h}{\sqrt{mK}}$ (b) $\lambda = \frac{2h}{\sqrt{mK}}$
(c) $\lambda = \frac{h}{2\sqrt{mK}}$ (d) $\lambda = \frac{h}{\sqrt{2mK}}$

24 The de-Broglie wavelength of neutrons in thermal equilibrium is **[Manipal]**

(a) $\frac{30.8}{\sqrt{T}}$ Å (b) $\frac{3.08}{\sqrt{T}}$ Å
(c) $\frac{0.308}{\sqrt{T}}$ Å (d) $\frac{0.0308}{\sqrt{T}}$ Å

25 An electron and a photon possess the same de-Broglie wavelength. If E_e and E_p are the energies of electron and photon respectively and v and c are their respective velocities, then $\frac{E_e}{E_p}$ is equal to **[Manipal]**

(a) $\frac{v}{c}$ (b) $\frac{v}{2c}$ (c) $\frac{v}{3c}$ (d) $\frac{v}{4c}$

26 The idea of matter waves was given by **[J & KCET]**

(a) Davisson and Germer (b) de-Broglie
(c) Einstein (d) Planck

27 An electron of mass m when accelerated through a potential difference V has de-Broglie wavelength λ. The de-Broglie wavelength associated with a proton of mass M accelerated through the same potential difference will be **[AIIMS]**

(a) $\lambda \frac{m}{M}$ (b) $\lambda \sqrt{\frac{m}{M}}$ (c) $\lambda \frac{M}{m}$ (d) $\lambda \sqrt{\frac{M}{m}}$

28 λ_e, λ_p and λ_α are the de-Broglie wavelength of electron, proton and α-particle. If all are accelerated by same potential, then **[Kerala CEE]**

(a) $\lambda_e < \lambda_p < \lambda_\alpha$ (b) $\lambda_e < \lambda_p > \lambda_\alpha$
(c) $\lambda_e > \lambda_p < \lambda_\alpha$ (d) $\lambda_e = \lambda_p > \lambda_\alpha$
(e) $\lambda_e > \lambda_p > \lambda_\alpha$

29 The de-Broglie wavelength of a ball of mass 120 g, moving at a speed of 20 m/s is **[Haryana PMT]**

(a) 3.5×10^{-34} m (b) 2.8×10^{-34} m
(c) 1.2×10^{-34} m (d) 2.1×10^{-34} m

30 The masses of two particles having same kinetic energies are in the ratio 1 : 2. Then, their de-Broglie wavelengths are in the ratio **[J&K CET]**

(a) 2 : 1 (b) 1 : 2 (c) $\sqrt{2}$: 1 (d) $\sqrt{3}$: 1

2009

31 Calculate the momentum and de-Broglie wavelength of electrons accelerated through a potential difference of 56 V. **[BVP]**

(a) λ = 0.164 nm (b) λ = 1 nm
(c) λ = 0.5 nm (d) λ = 5 mm

32 Which of these particles (having the same kinetic energy) has the largest de-Broglie wavelength? **[DUMET]**

(a) Electron (b) α-particle (c) Proton (d) Neutron

33 The de-Broglie wavelength of an electron having 80 eV of energy is nearly (1 eV = 1.6×10^{-19} J, mass of electron = 9.1×10^{-31} kg, Planck's constant = 6.6×10^{-34} J-s) **[MGIMS]**

(a) 150 Å (b) 0.15 Å
(c) 15 Å (d) 1.5 Å

34 The de-Broglie wavelength of a neutron at 927° C is λ. What will be its wavelength at 27° C? **[BCECE]**

(a) λ/a (b) λ (c) 2λ (d) 4λ

2008

35 A particle of mass 1 mg has the same wavelength as an electron moving with a velocity of 3×10^6 ms^{-1}. The velocity of the particle is **[CBSE AIPMT]**

(Take, mass of electron = 9.1×10^{31} kg)

(a) 2.7×10^{-18} ms^{-1} (b) 9×10^{-2} ms^{-1}
(c) 3×10^{-31} ms^{-1} (d) 2.7×10^{-21} ms^{-1}

36 A proton accelerated through a potential V has de-Broglie wavelength λ. Then, the de-Broglie wavelength of an α-particle, when accelerated through the same potential V is **[Kerala CEE]**

(a) $\frac{\lambda}{2}$ (b) $\frac{\lambda}{\sqrt{2}}$
(c) $\frac{\lambda}{2\sqrt{2}}$ (d) $\frac{\lambda}{8}$
(e) $\frac{\lambda}{4}$

37 The de-Broglie wavelength associated with a particle moving with momentum (p) and mass (m) is **[J&K CET]**

(a) $\frac{h}{p}$ (b) $\frac{h}{mp}$ (c) $\frac{h}{p^2}$ (d) $\frac{h^2}{p^2}$

38 What should be the velocity of an electron, so that its momentum becomes equal to that of a photon of wavelength 5200 Å? **[AMU]**

(a) 700 ms^{-1} (b) 1000 ms^{-1}
(c) 1400 ms^{-1} (d) 2800 ms^{-1}

39 If an electron and a proton have the same de-Broglie wavelength, then the kinetic energy of the electron is **[KCET]**

(a) zero
(b) less than that of a proton
(c) more than that of a proton
(d) equal to that of a proton

40 The wavelength λ_e of an electron and λ_p of a photon of same energy E are related by **[NEET]**

(a) $\lambda_e^2 \propto \lambda_p$ (b) $\lambda_e \propto \lambda_p$
(c) $\sqrt{\lambda_e} \propto \lambda_p$ (d) $1/\sqrt{\lambda_e} \propto \lambda_p$

41 An α-particle and a deuteron are moving with velocities v and $2v$, respectively. What will be the ratio of their de-Broglie wavelengths? **[Guj CET]**

(a) 1:1 (b) $\sqrt{2}:1$ (c) $1:\sqrt{2}$ (d) 2:1

2007

42 The uncertainty in the momentum of a particle is 10^{-30} kg - ms^{-1}. The minimum uncertainty in its position will be **[UP CPMT]**

(a) 10^{-8} m (b) 10^{-12} m
(c) 10^{-16} m (d) 10^{-4} m

43 We wish to see inside an atom. Assuming the atom to have a diameter of 100 pm, this means that one must be able to resolve a width of say 10 pm. If an electron microscope is used, the minimum electron energy required is about **[UP CPMT]**

(a) 1.5 keV (b) 15 keV
(c) 150 keV (d) 1.5 MeV

44 An electron and a proton are possessing same amount of kinetic energies. The de-Broglie wavelength is greater for **[RPMT]**

(a) electron (b) proton
(c) Both (a) and (b) (d) None of these

45 Davisson-Germer's electron diffraction arrangement is as shown **[AIIMS]**

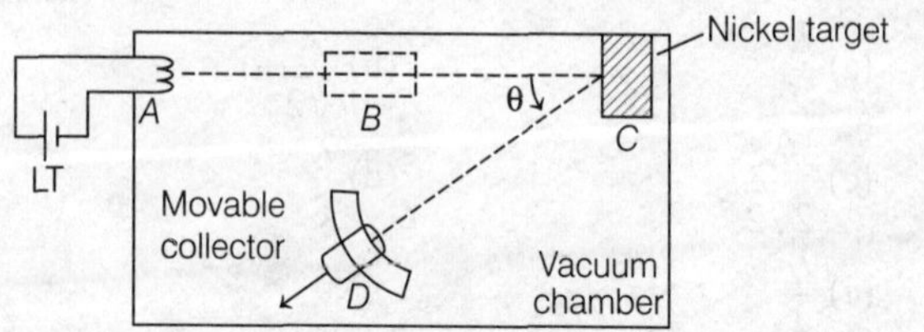

Correct labelling is

(a) A-electron source, B-metal crystal, C-reflector, D-detector
(b) A-electron source, B-hollow tube, C-wall, D-reflector
(c) A-electron gun, B-electron accelerator, C-detector, D- counter
(d) A-electron gun, B-collimating and accelerating tube, C-metal target, D -movable collector

46 An electron, accelerated by a potential difference V, has de-Broglie wavelength λ. If the electron is accelerated by a potential difference $4V$, its de-Broglie wavelength will be **[AMU]**

(a) 2λ (b) 4λ (c) $\frac{\lambda}{2}$ (d) $\frac{\lambda}{4}$

47 A material particle with a rest mass m_0 is moving with speed of light c. The de-Broglie wavelength associated is given by **[AMU]**

(a) h/m_0c (b) m_0c/h (c) zero (d) infinite

48 The de-Broglie wavelength of a proton (charge $= 1.6 \times 10^{-19}$ C, mass $= 1.6 \times 10^{-27}$ kg) accelerated through a potential difference of 1 kV is **[KCET]**

(a) 600 Å (b) 0.9×10^{-12} m
(c) 7 Å (d) 0.9 nm

49 Which of the following has the longest de-Broglie wavelength, if they are moving with same velocity? **[Guj CET]**

(a) Neutron (b) Proton
(c) α-particle (d) β-particle

2006

50 If alpha, beta and gamma rays carry same momentum, which has the longest wavelength? **[AFMC]**

(a) Alpha rays (b) Beta rays
(c) Gamma rays
(d) All have same wavelength

51 The de-Broglie wavelengths of an electron, α-particle and a proton all having the same kinetic energy is respectively given as $\lambda_e, \lambda_\alpha$ and λ_p. Then, which of the following is true? **[BHU]**

(a) $\lambda_e < \lambda_p$ (b) $\lambda_p < \lambda_\alpha$
(c) $\lambda_e > \lambda_\alpha$ (d) $\lambda_\alpha < \lambda_p > \lambda_e$

52 A particle of mass M at rest decays into two particles of masses m_1 and m_2 having non-zero velocities. The ratio of the de-Broglie wavelengths of the particles λ_1/λ_2 is **[AIIMS]**

(a) m_1/m_2 (b) m_2/m_1
(c) 1 (d) $\sqrt{m_2}/\sqrt{m_1}$

53 The de-Broglie wavelength of an electron and the wavelength of a photon are the same. The ratio between the energy of that photon and the momentum of that electron is (c = velocity of light, h = Planck's constant) **[EAMCET]**

(a) h (b) c (c) $1/h$ (d) $1/c$

2005

54 Assertion The energy (E) and momentum (p) of a photon are related by $p = E/c$.

Reason The photon behaves like a particle. [AIIMS]

(a) Both Assertion and Reason are correct and Reason is the correct explanation of Assertion.

(b) Both Assertion and Reason are correct but Reason is not the correct explanation of Assertion.

(c) Assertion is correct but Reason is incorrect.

(d) Both Assertion and Reason are incorrect.

55 In Davisson-Germer experiment, the wavelength associated with nickel crystal is [J&K CET]

(a) 1.66 Å (b) 2Å (c) 2.3 Å (d) 3.86 Å

56 The dual nature of light is exhibited by [Punjab PMET]

(a) diffraction (b) diffraction and reflection

(c) refraction and interference (d) photoelectric effect

57 The energy that should be added to an electron to reduce its de-Broglie wavelength from 1 nm to 0.5 nm is [KCET]

(a) four times the initial energy

(b) equal to the initial energy

(c) twice the initial energy

(d) thrice the initial energy

Answers

1 (a)	2 (a)	3 (c)	4 (b)	5 (d)	6 (a)	7 (d)	8 (b)	9 (b)	10 (d)
11 (c)	12 (b)	13 (a)	14 (a)	15 (a)	16 (a)	17 (d)	18 (b)	19 (a)	20 (c)
21 (b)	22 (d)	23 (d)	24 (a)	25 (b)	26 (b)	27 (b)	28 (e)	29 (b)	30 (c)
31 (a)	32 (a)	33 (a)	34 (c)	35 (a)	36 (c)	37 (a)	38 (c)	39 (c)	40 (a)
41 (a)	42 (d)	43 (b)	44 (a)	45 (d)	46 (c)	47 (c)	48 (b)	49 (d)	50 (d)
51 (c)	52 (c)	53 (b)	54 (a)	55 (a)	56 (d)	57 (d)			

Explanations

1 *(a)* Given, potential difference, $V = 10000$ V

If electron is accelerated through a potential of V volt, then the wavelength associated with it is given by

$$\lambda = \frac{h}{\sqrt{2eVm_e}} \quad \text{... (i)}$$

where, h = Planck's constant $= 6.63 \times 10^{-34}$ J-s,

e = electronic charge $= 1.6 \times 10^{-19}$C

and m_e = mass of electron $= 9 \times 10^{-31}$ kg

Substituting these values in Eq. (i), we get

$$\lambda = \frac{12.27}{\sqrt{V}} \text{Å} = \frac{12.27}{\sqrt{10000}} \times 10^{-10}$$

$$= \frac{12.27 \times 10^{-10}}{100} = 12.2 \times 10^{-12} \text{ m}$$

2 *(a)* The de-Broglie wavelength associated with a charged particle is given by

$$\lambda = \frac{h}{p}$$

where, h = planck's constant

and p = momentum $= \sqrt{2m\text{KE}}$ (here, KE is the kinetic energy of the charged particle).

$$\Rightarrow \quad \lambda = \frac{h}{\sqrt{2m\text{KE}}}$$

For proton and α-particle, the wavelengths are respectively given as

$$\lambda_p = \frac{h}{\sqrt{2m_p\text{KE}_p}} \text{ and } \lambda_\alpha = \frac{h}{\sqrt{2m_\alpha \text{KE}_\alpha}}$$

$$\therefore \frac{\lambda_p}{\lambda_\alpha} = \frac{\sqrt{2m_\alpha\text{KE}_\alpha}}{\sqrt{2m_p\text{KE}_p}} \quad \text{...(i)}$$

Here, $\text{KE}_\alpha = \text{KE}_p$ and $m_\alpha = 4m_p$

Substituting these above mentioned relations in Eq. (i), we get

$$\Rightarrow \frac{\lambda_p}{\lambda_\alpha} = \sqrt{\frac{4m_p}{m_p}} = \frac{2}{1} \text{ or } \lambda_p : \lambda_\alpha = 2:1$$

3 *(c)* As we know that, wavelength of a particle,

$$\lambda = \frac{h}{\sqrt{2mE}} = \frac{h}{\sqrt{2m}} \cdot \frac{1}{\sqrt{E}}$$

$$\Rightarrow \log\lambda = \log\left(\frac{h}{\sqrt{2m}} \cdot \frac{1}{\sqrt{E}}\right)$$

$$\Rightarrow \log\lambda = \log\frac{h}{\sqrt{2m}} + \log\frac{1}{E^{1/2}}$$

$$\Rightarrow \log\lambda = \log\left(\frac{h}{\sqrt{2m}}\right) - \frac{1}{2}\log E$$

$$\Rightarrow \log\lambda = -\frac{1}{2}\log E + \log\frac{h}{\sqrt{2m}}$$

Comparing the above equation with the equation of straight line, i.e. $y = mx + c$.

We can conclude that, logλ varies linearly with log$E$, with slope $-1/2$.

It is correctly shown in graph (c).

4 *(b)* de-Broglie wavelength associated with a moving particle can be given as

$$\lambda = \frac{h}{p}$$

At thermal equilibrium, temperature of neutron and heavy water will be same. This common temperature is given as, T. Also, we know that, kinetic energy of a particle,

$$\text{KE} = \frac{p^2}{2m}$$

where, p = momentum of the particle and m = mass of the particle.

Kinetic energy of the neutron at T is

$$\text{KE} = \frac{3}{2}kT$$

$\therefore$ de-Broglie wavelength of the neutron,

$$\lambda = \frac{h}{p} = \frac{h}{\sqrt{2m(\text{KE})}}$$

$$= \frac{h}{\sqrt{2m \times 3/2\, kT}} = \frac{h}{\sqrt{3mkT}}$$

5 *(d)* The de-Broglie wavelength of an electron,

$$\lambda = \frac{h}{mv} \Rightarrow v = \frac{h}{m\lambda} \quad \text{...(i)}$$

Energy of photon,

$$E_p = \frac{hc}{\lambda} \text{ (since, } \lambda \text{ is same)} \quad \dots \text{(ii)}$$

Kinetic energy of photon to kinetic energy of electron

$$= \frac{E_p}{E_e} = \frac{\frac{hc}{\lambda}}{\left(\frac{1}{2}\right)mv^2} = \frac{2hc}{\lambda mv^2}$$

Substituting the value of v from Eq. (i), we get

$$\frac{E_p}{E_e} = \frac{2hc}{\lambda m\left(\frac{h}{m\lambda}\right)^2} = \frac{2\lambda mc}{h}$$

6 (a) Cut-off wavelength occurs, when incoming electron losses its complete energy in collision. This energy appears in the form of X-rays.

Given, mass of electrons = m

de-Broglie wavelength = λ

So, kinetic energy of electron = $p^2/2m$

$$= \frac{(h/\lambda)^2}{2m} = \frac{h^2}{2m\lambda^2}$$

Now, maximum energy of photon can be given by

$$E = \frac{hc}{\lambda_0} = \frac{h^2}{2m\lambda^2}$$

$$\Rightarrow \lambda_0 = \frac{hc \times 2\lambda^2 \cdot m}{h^2} = \frac{2mc\lambda^2}{h}$$

7 (d) Since, it is given that electron has mass m.

de-Broglie's wavelength for an electron will be given as

$$\lambda_e = \frac{h}{p} \quad \dots \text{(i)}$$

where, h = Planck's constant and p = linear momentum of electron.

As kinetic energy of electron,

$$E = \frac{p^2}{2m} \Rightarrow p = \sqrt{2mE} \quad \dots \text{(ii)}$$

From Eqs. (i) and (ii), we get

$$\lambda_e = \frac{h}{\sqrt{2mE}} \quad \dots \text{(iii)}$$

Energy of a photon can be given as

$$E = h\nu \Rightarrow E = \frac{hc}{\lambda_p}$$

$$\Rightarrow \lambda_p = \frac{hc}{E} \quad \dots \text{(iv)}$$

Here, λ_p = de-Broglie's wavelength of photon.

Now, dividing Eq. (iii) by Eq. (iv), we get

$$\frac{\lambda_e}{\lambda_p} = \frac{h}{\sqrt{2mE}} \cdot \frac{E}{hc}$$

$$\Rightarrow \frac{\lambda_e}{\lambda_p} = \frac{1}{c} \cdot \sqrt{\frac{E}{2m}}$$

8 (b) The de-Broglie wavelength is given by

$$\lambda = \frac{h}{p} \Rightarrow p\lambda = h$$

This equation is in the form of $yx = c$, which is the equation of a rectangular hyperbola. Hence, the graph given in option (b) is the correct one.

9 (b) For de-Broglie wavelength,

$$\lambda_1 = \frac{h}{p} = \frac{h}{\sqrt{2mK}} \quad \dots \text{(i)}$$

$$\lambda_2 = \frac{h}{\sqrt{2m\,16K}} = \frac{h}{4\sqrt{2mk}} = \frac{\lambda_1}{4} \quad \dots \text{(ii)}$$

$\lambda_2 = 25\%$ of λ_1

There is 75% change in the wavelength.

10 (d) de-Broglie wavelength,

$$\lambda = \frac{hc}{E} = \frac{1240}{200 \times 10^6} = 6.20 \times 10^{-6} \text{ nm}$$

$= 6.20$ Fm

11 (c) de-Broglie wavelength, $\lambda = \frac{h}{\sqrt{2mK}}$

The kinetic energy of the electron,

$$K_{\text{electron}} = \frac{h^2}{2m \cdot \lambda^2} \quad \dots \text{(i)}$$

where, h = Planck's constant and λ = wavelength.

The photon energy, $E_{\text{photon}} = ch/\lambda$ ...(ii)

From Eqs. (i) and (ii), we get

$$\frac{E_{\text{photon}}}{K_{\text{electron}}} = \frac{ch/\lambda}{h^2/2m \cdot \lambda^2} = \frac{hc \cdot \lambda^2 2m}{h^2 \cdot \lambda} = \frac{2m\lambda c}{h}$$

where, $E = m = 0.5$ MeV $= 5 \times 10^5$ eV

$$\frac{h}{c\lambda} = 50 \times 10^3 \text{ eV}$$

$$\frac{E_p}{K_e} = \frac{2E}{h/\lambda c} = \frac{2 \times 5 \times 10^5}{50 \times 10^3} = 20$$

$= 20:1$

12 (b) de-Broglie wavelength of an electron is given by

$$\lambda = \frac{h}{mv} = \frac{h}{\sqrt{2meV}} = \frac{12.27}{\sqrt{V}} \text{ Å}$$

where, h = Planck's constant,
m = mass of electron,
e = electronic charge
and V = potential difference with which electron is accelerated.

$$\lambda = \frac{12.27}{\sqrt{100}} = \frac{12.27}{10} = 1.227 \text{ Å}$$

13 (a) We know that, $\lambda = \frac{h}{p}$

Here, $\left|\frac{\Delta\lambda}{\lambda}\right| = \left|\frac{\Delta p}{p}\right| \Rightarrow \frac{0.5}{100} = \frac{p}{p_i}$

$$p_i = \frac{100}{0.5}p \Rightarrow p_i = 200p$$

14 (a) We have, $\lambda_p = hc/E$; E = energy given to photon

$$\lambda_e = \frac{h}{\sqrt{2M_e E}};$$

E = energy given to electron

$$\Rightarrow \frac{\lambda_p}{\lambda_e} = c\sqrt{\frac{2M_e}{E}} > 1 \Rightarrow \lambda_p > \lambda_e$$

15 (a) We know that, $K_e = \frac{1}{2}mv^2$

Also, $\lambda = \frac{h}{mv} \Rightarrow m = \frac{h}{\lambda v}$

$$\therefore K_e = \frac{1}{2}\left(\frac{h}{\lambda v}\right) \cdot v^2 = \frac{vh}{2\lambda}$$

Similarly, $K_p = hc/\lambda$

$$\therefore \frac{K_e}{K_p} = \frac{v}{2c} = \frac{1.5 \times 10^8}{2 \times 3 \times 10^8} = \frac{1}{4}$$

16 (a) We have, $\lambda = \frac{12.27}{\sqrt{V}}$ Å

$$\therefore \frac{\lambda_1}{\lambda_2} = \sqrt{\frac{V_2}{V_1}}$$

$$\Rightarrow \lambda_2 = \lambda_1\sqrt{\frac{V_1}{V_2}}$$

$$\Rightarrow \lambda_2 = \lambda_1\sqrt{\frac{25}{100}}$$

$$\Rightarrow \lambda_2 = \lambda_1\sqrt{\frac{1}{4}} = \frac{\lambda_1}{2}$$

17 (d) If a proton and electron have the same de-Broglie wavelength, then momentum of electron equals to momentum of proton as, de-Broglie wavelength $\propto$ 1/momentum.

18 (b) KE $= \frac{1}{2}mv^2$ (same for all particles)

The de-Broglie wavelength,

$$\lambda = \frac{h}{p} = \frac{h}{\sqrt{2m(\text{KE})}}$$

$$\Rightarrow \lambda \propto 1/\sqrt{m}$$

Here, mass of α-particle is highest, hence it has lowest wavelength.

19 *(a)* The de-Broglie wavelength of an electron accelerated through potential V is

$$\lambda = \frac{h}{\sqrt{2m_eV_e}} = \frac{1.227}{\sqrt{V}}\text{ nm} = \frac{12.27}{\sqrt{V}}\text{ Å}$$

20 *(c)* de-Broglie wavelength,

$$\lambda_e = \frac{h}{\sqrt{2m_eE}} \text{ and } \lambda_p = \frac{h}{\sqrt{2m_pE}}$$

$$\Rightarrow \frac{\lambda_e}{\lambda_p} = \sqrt{\frac{m_p}{m_e}}$$

21 *(b)* de-Broglie wavelength, $\lambda = \frac{h}{mv}$

For electron, $\lambda_e = \frac{h}{m_ev}$

For photon, $\lambda_p = \frac{h}{m_pv}$

$$\Rightarrow \frac{\lambda_e}{\lambda_p} = \frac{h/m_ev}{h/m_pv} \Rightarrow \frac{\lambda_e}{\lambda_p} = \frac{m_p}{m_e}$$

$$\frac{\lambda_e}{\lambda_p} = \frac{1.67\times10^{-27}}{9.1\times10^{-31}} = 0.1836\times10^4 = 1836$$

22 *(d)* In the Davisson and Germer experiment, the velocity of electron emitted from the electron gun can be increased by increasing the potential difference between the anode and filament.

23 *(d)* Given, K = kinetic energy, m = mass

Then, $K = \frac{1}{2}mv^2$ ...(i)

But we know that, $\lambda = \frac{h}{mv}$ ...(ii)

Now, from Eq. (i), $v^2 = \frac{2K}{m}$

$\Rightarrow v = \sqrt{2K/m}$

Putting this in Eq. (ii), we get

$$= \frac{h}{\sqrt{2mK}}$$

24 *(a)* de-Broglie wavelength,

$$\lambda = \frac{h}{\sqrt{3mkT}}$$

where, T = temperature

and k = Boltzmann constant

$$= \frac{6.62\times10^{-34}}{\sqrt{3\times1.67\times10^{-27}\times1.38\times10^{-23}\,T}} = \frac{6.62\times10^{-34}}{2.15\times10^{-25}\sqrt{T}}$$

$$= \frac{3.08}{\sqrt{T}}\times10^{-9} = \frac{30.8}{\sqrt{T}}\text{ Å}$$

25 *(b)* de-Broglie wavelength,

$$\lambda = \frac{h}{\sqrt{2mE_e}} = \frac{hc}{E_p} \text{ or } 2mE_e = \frac{E_p^2}{c^2} \quad ...(i)$$

But $E_e = \frac{1}{2}mv^2$ or $m = \frac{2E_e}{v^2}$

From Eq. (i), we get

$$2\left[\frac{2E_e}{v^2}\right]E_e = \frac{E_p^2}{c^2} \text{ or } \frac{4E_e^2}{v^2} = \frac{E_p^2}{c^2}$$

or $\frac{E_e^2}{E_p^2} = \frac{v^2}{4c^2}$ or $\frac{E_e}{E_p} = \frac{v}{2c}$

26 *(b)* Idea of matter waves was given by de-Broglie.

27 *(b)* As, $\lambda = \frac{h}{\sqrt{2mE}}$

$$\Rightarrow \lambda \propto \frac{1}{\sqrt{m}} \Rightarrow \frac{\lambda_1}{\lambda_2} = \sqrt{\frac{m_2}{m_1}}$$

So, $\frac{\lambda}{\lambda_2} = \sqrt{\frac{M}{m}}$

$\therefore \lambda_2 = \lambda\sqrt{\left(\frac{m}{M}\right)}$

28 *(e)* de-Broglie wavelength for particle,

$$\lambda = \frac{h}{p} = \frac{h}{\sqrt{2mk}} = \frac{h}{\sqrt{2mqV_0}}$$

Here, $K = qV_0$, where q = charge of particle and V_0 = potential.

$\Rightarrow \lambda \propto \frac{1}{\sqrt{qm}}$

Since, $q_em_e < q_pm_p < q_\alpha m_\alpha$

So, $\lambda_e > \lambda_p > \lambda_\alpha$

29 *(b)* de-Broglie wavelength,

$$\lambda = \frac{h}{mv} = \frac{6.6\times10^{-34}}{120\times10^{-3}\times20} = 2.8\times10^{-34}\text{ m}$$

30 *(c)* Given, $(\text{KE})_1 = (\text{KE})_2 = \frac{1}{2}mv^2$ ...(i)

$\Rightarrow m_1v_1^2 = m_2v_2^2$

$\Rightarrow \frac{m_1}{m_2} = \left(\frac{v_2}{v_1}\right)^2$

$\Rightarrow \frac{v_1}{v_2} = \sqrt{\frac{m_2}{m_1}}, \frac{v_1}{v_2} = \sqrt{2}$

We know that, $\lambda = \frac{h}{mv} \Rightarrow mv = \frac{h}{\lambda}$

Putting this in Eq. (i), we get

$$\frac{1}{2}\frac{h}{\lambda_1}v_1 = \frac{1}{2}\frac{h}{\lambda_2}v_2$$

$\Rightarrow \frac{v_1}{\lambda_1} = \frac{v_2}{\lambda_2}$

$\Rightarrow \frac{\lambda_1}{\lambda_2} = \frac{v_1}{v_2} = \frac{\sqrt{2}}{1} = \sqrt{2}:1$

31 *(a)* Given, potential difference, $V = 56$ V

de-Broglie wavelength of electron,

$$\lambda = \frac{12.27}{\sqrt{V}}\text{ Å} = \frac{12.27}{\sqrt{56}} = 0.164\times10^{-9}\text{m} = 0.164\text{ nm}$$

32 *(a)* de-Broglie wavelength,

$$\lambda = \frac{h}{mv} = \frac{h}{\sqrt{2mE}}$$

E is same for all, so $\lambda \propto \frac{1}{\sqrt{m}}$

Hence, de-Broglie wavelength will be maximum for particle with lesser mass. Mass of the given particles in increasing order are given as

$$m_e < m_p < m_n < m_\alpha$$

Thus, de-Broglie wavelength will be maximum for electron.

33 *(a)* Given, $E = 80$ eV

$= 80\times1.6\times10^{-19}\text{ J} = hc/\lambda$

Now, de-Broglie wavelength

$$\lambda = \frac{h}{mv} = \frac{hc}{E} = \frac{6.6\times10^{-34}\times3\times10^8}{80\times1.6\times10^{-19}} = \frac{19.82\times10^{-7}}{128} \approx 0.15\times10^{-7}$$

$= 150\times10^{-10} = 150$ Å

34 *(c)* de-Broglie wavelength, $\lambda \propto \frac{1}{\sqrt{T}}$

$$\Rightarrow \frac{\lambda_1}{\lambda_2} = \sqrt{\frac{T_2}{T_1}} \Rightarrow \frac{\lambda_1}{\lambda_2} = \sqrt{\frac{273+27}{273+927}} = \sqrt{\frac{300}{1200}} = \frac{1}{2} \text{ or } \lambda_2 = 2\lambda$$

35 *(a)* Wavelength of an electron is given by

$\lambda_e = \frac{h}{p_e}$, where h is Planck's constant.

But $\lambda = \lambda_e$

So, $p = p_e$ or $mv = m_ev_e$

or $v = \frac{m_ev_e}{m}$

Putting the under given data,

$m_e = 9.1\times10^{-31}$ kg,

$v_e = 3\times10^6\text{ ms}^{-1}$,

$$m = 1 \text{ mg} = 1 \times 10^{-6} \text{ kg}$$

$$\therefore \quad v = \frac{9.1 \times 10^{-31} \times 3 \times 10^{6}}{1 \times 10^{-6}}$$

$$= 2.7 \times 10^{-18} \text{ ms}^{-1}$$

36 *(c)* de-Broglie wavelength of proton given by

$$\lambda_p = \frac{h}{\sqrt{2mqV}} = \lambda \text{ (given)}$$

So, for α-particle,

$$\lambda_\alpha = \frac{h}{\sqrt{2m_\alpha q_\alpha V}} = \frac{h}{\sqrt{2(4m)(2q)V}}$$

$$= \frac{h}{\sqrt{8(2mqV)}} = \frac{\lambda}{2\sqrt{2}}$$

37 *(a)* de-Broglie wavelength associated with a moving particle,

$$\lambda = \frac{h}{mv} \quad \text{or} \quad \lambda = \frac{h}{p}$$

where, p is momentum of the particle.

38 *(c)* Momentum, $p = mv = \frac{h}{\lambda}$

$$\Rightarrow \quad v = \frac{h}{m\lambda}$$

$$\therefore \quad v = \frac{6.62 \times 10^{-34}}{9.1 \times 10^{-31} \times 5.2 \times 10^{-7}}$$

$$\Rightarrow \quad v = \frac{6.62 \times 10^{4}}{9.1 \times 5.2}$$

$$\Rightarrow \quad v = 1.4 \times 10^{3} \text{ ms}^{-1}$$

$$\Rightarrow \quad v = 1400 \text{ ms}^{-1}$$

39 *(c)* Given, $\lambda = \frac{h}{mv} = \frac{h}{\sqrt{2mK}}$

$$\Rightarrow \quad K = \frac{h^2}{2m\lambda^2}$$

As, λ is same for both electron and proton.

So, $\quad K \propto \frac{1}{m}$

Hence, kinetic energy will be maximum for particle with lesser mass, i.e. electron.

40 *(a)* Wavelength of electron,

$$\lambda_e = \frac{h}{\sqrt{2mE}} \qquad \ldots\text{(i)}$$

and photon,

$$\lambda_p = \frac{hc}{E} \text{ or } E = \frac{hc}{\lambda_p} \qquad \ldots\text{(ii)}$$

[illegible] value of E in Eq. (i), we get

$$\Rightarrow \lambda_e^2 = \frac{h^2}{2mE} = \frac{h^2}{2m(hc/\lambda_p)} = \frac{h^2\lambda_p}{(2mhc)}$$

$$\Rightarrow \lambda_e^2 = \frac{h\lambda_p}{2mc} \Rightarrow \lambda_e^2 \propto \lambda_p$$

41 *(a)* Given, the velocity of α-particle [nucleus of $_2He^4$] = v

The velocity of the deuteron ($_1D^2$) = $2v$

We know that, the de-Broglie wavelength,

$$\lambda = h/mv \qquad \ldots\text{(i)}$$

So, the de-Broglie wavelength for α-particle

$$\lambda_\alpha = \frac{h}{4\, m_p \times v} \qquad \ldots\text{(ii)}$$

$$(\because m_\alpha = 4\, m_p)$$

where, m_p is the mass of proton and the de-Broglie wavelength for deuteron,

$$\lambda_D = \frac{h}{2m_p \times 2v} \qquad \ldots\text{(iii)}$$

$$(\because m_D = 2m_P)$$

On dividing Eq. (ii) by Eq. (iii), we get

$$\frac{\lambda_\alpha}{\lambda_D} = \frac{\frac{h}{4vm_p}}{\frac{h}{4vm_p}} = \frac{1}{1}$$

$$\Rightarrow \quad \lambda_\alpha : \lambda_D = 1:1$$

42 *(d)* The product of uncertainties in the simultaneous measurement of position and momentum, energy and time, angular momentum and angular displacement is of the order of $\hbar$ (or h).

where, $\quad \hbar = \frac{h}{2\pi}$

$$\therefore \quad \Delta p \cdot \Delta x \geq \hbar$$

where, Δp is uncertainty in the measurement of momentum of particle.

The minimum uncertainty in position of particle will be

$$\Delta x = \hbar / \Delta p$$

$$\because \quad \Delta p = 10^{-30} \text{ kg-ms}^{-1},$$

$$\hbar = 1.03 \times 10^{-34}$$

$$\therefore \quad \Delta x = \frac{1.034 \times 10^{-34}}{10^{-30}} \approx 10^{-4} \text{ m}$$

43 *(b)* From de-Broglie equation, we have

$$\lambda = \frac{h}{p} = \frac{h}{mv}$$

Given, $\lambda = 10 \text{ pm} = 10^{-11}$ m,

$$m = 9.1 \times 10^{-31} \text{ kg},$$

and $\quad h = 6.6 \times 10^{-34}$ J-s

$$\therefore \quad v = h/m\lambda = \frac{6.6 \times 10^{-34}}{9.1 \times 10^{-31} \times 10^{-11}}$$

$$= 7.25 \times 10^{7} \text{ ms}^{-1}$$

Energy of electron, $E = \frac{1}{2}mv^2$

$$= \frac{1}{2} \times \frac{9.1 \times 10^{-31} \times (7.25 \times 10^{7})^2}{1.6 \times 10^{-19}}$$

$$= 15 \text{ keV}$$

44 *(a)* According to de-Broglie hypothesis, wavelength, $\lambda = h/p$

where, h is Planck's constant.

Also, $\quad E = \frac{p^2}{2m} \Rightarrow \lambda = \frac{h}{\sqrt{2mE}}$

$$\Rightarrow \quad \lambda \propto 1/\sqrt{m}$$

Mass of electron is 9.1×10^{-31} kg and of proton is 1.6×10^{-27} kg, hence mass of electron is less than that of proton, so electron will have greater wavelength.

45 *(d)*

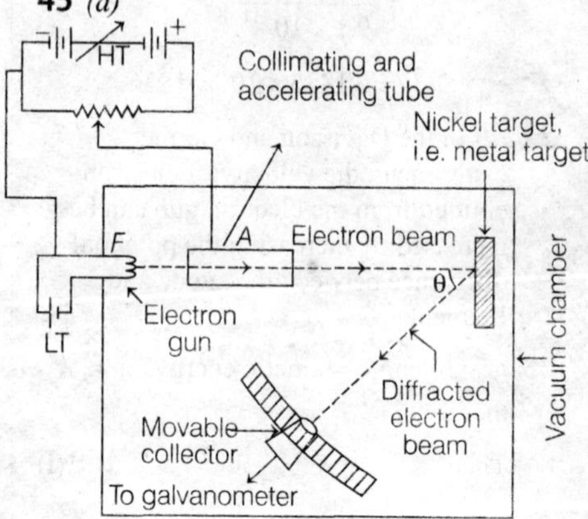

46 *(c)* From the relation,

$$\lambda = \frac{h}{\sqrt{2meV}} \qquad \ldots\text{(i)}$$

So, when V becomes $4V$, then

$$\lambda' = \frac{h}{\sqrt{2me(4V)}}$$

$$\Rightarrow \quad \lambda' = \frac{h}{2\sqrt{2meV}}$$

$$\Rightarrow \quad \lambda' = \frac{\lambda}{2}$$

47 *(c)* $\lambda = \frac{h}{mv}$

where, $m = \frac{m_0}{\sqrt{1 - v^2/c^2}}$,

As $\quad v = c$, then

$\Rightarrow \quad m = \dfrac{m_0}{\sqrt{1-\dfrac{c^2}{c^2}}} = \dfrac{m_0}{\sqrt{1-1}} = \dfrac{m_0}{0}$

$\Rightarrow \quad m = \infty,$

Hence, $\lambda = \dfrac{h}{\infty} = 0$

48 *(b)* According to de-Broglie hypothesis,

$$\lambda = \frac{h}{p} = \frac{h}{\sqrt{2mE}} = \frac{h}{\sqrt{2mqV}}$$

$$\therefore \quad \lambda = \frac{6.6\times10^{-34}}{\sqrt{2\times(1.6\times10^{-27})(1.6\times10^{-19})\times1000}}$$

$$= \frac{6.6\times10^{-34}}{7.16\times10^{-22}} = 0.9\times10^{-12}\text{ m}$$

49 *(d)* According to de-Broglie hypothesis, the wavelength of the wave associated with particle moving with velocity v is given by

$$\lambda = h/mv$$

Since, v remains the same, therefore

$$\lambda \propto \frac{1}{m}$$

As $m_\alpha > m_n > m_p > m_\beta$

$\therefore \quad \lambda_\alpha < \lambda_n < \lambda_p < \lambda_\beta$

Therefore, β-particle has longest wavelength. Since, it has minimum mass.

50 *(d)* We know that, $\lambda = h/p$

Given, $\quad p_\alpha = p_\beta = p_\gamma$

So, all have same wavelength.

51 *(c)* We know that,

$$\lambda = \frac{h}{mv} \quad \text{...(i)}$$

or $\quad \lambda \propto \dfrac{1}{m}$

Therefore, $\lambda_e \propto \dfrac{1}{m_e}$

$\lambda_\alpha \propto \dfrac{1}{m_\alpha}$

and $\quad \lambda_p \propto \dfrac{1}{m_p}$

As we know that, $m_e < m_p < m_\alpha$

$\therefore \quad \lambda_e > \lambda_p > \lambda_\alpha$

or $\quad \lambda_e > \lambda_\alpha$

or $\quad \lambda_p > \lambda_\alpha$

or $\quad \lambda_e > \lambda_p$

52 *(c)* From law of conservation of momentum,

$p_1 = p_2$ (in opposite directions)

Now, de-Broglie wavelength is given by

$\lambda = \dfrac{h}{p}$, where h = Planck's constant.

Since, magnitude of momentum (p) of both the particles is equal, therefore

$$\lambda_1 = \lambda_2$$

or $\quad \lambda_1/\lambda_2 = 1$

53 *(b)* $\lambda_e = \dfrac{h}{mv}$ and $\lambda_p = \dfrac{hc}{E_p}$

Given, $\lambda_e = \lambda_p$

$\Rightarrow \quad \dfrac{h}{mv} = \dfrac{hc}{E_p}$

$\Rightarrow \quad \dfrac{h}{p_e} = \dfrac{hc}{E_p} \quad [\because p_e = mv]$

or $\quad E_p/p_e = c$

54 *(a)* Momentum of photon, according to de-Broglie,

i.e. $\quad p = h/\lambda \quad$ ...(i)

But photon moves in the form of energy packet called quanta and behaves as a particle whose energy is given by

$$E = \frac{hc}{\lambda} \text{ or } \frac{h}{\lambda} = \frac{E}{c} \quad \text{...(ii)}$$

Thus, $p = E/c$ [from Eqs. (i) and (ii)]

55 *(a)* For the nickel crystal, the interatomic separation is

$d = 0.91$ Å

According to Bragg's law, for first order diffraction maxima ($n = 1$), we have

$2\,d \sin\theta = 1\times\lambda$

$\therefore \lambda = 2\times0.91\times\sin 65^\circ = 1.65$ Å

56 *(d)* The dual nature of light, i.e. both particle and wave nature is exhibited by photoelectric effect.

57 *(d)* de-Broglie wavelength,

$$\lambda = \frac{h}{\sqrt{2mE}}$$

$\therefore \quad \dfrac{\lambda_1}{\lambda_2} = \sqrt{\dfrac{E_2}{E_1}}$

$\Rightarrow \quad \dfrac{1\times10^{-9}}{0.5\times10^{-9}} = \sqrt{\dfrac{E_2}{E_1}}$

$\Rightarrow \quad 2 = \sqrt{\dfrac{E_2}{E_1}} \Rightarrow \dfrac{E_2}{E_1} = 4$

$\therefore \quad E_2 = 4E_1$

$\therefore$ Energy to be added $= E_2 - E_1$

$= 4E_1 - E_1 = 3E_1$

26

Atoms and Nuclei

Quick Review

Dalton's Atomic Theory

All elements are consists of very small invisible particles, called **atoms**. Atoms of same elements are exactly same and atoms of different elements are different.

Thomson's Atomic Model

Every atom is uniformly positive charged sphere of radius of the order of 10^{-10} m, in which entire mass is uniformly distributed and negative charged electrons are embedded randomly. The atom as a whole is neutral.

Rutherford α-particle Scattering Experiment

According to this experiment, following observations and conclusions were made

(*i*) Most α-particles passes straight without deflection, while a few deflected at small angles and a very few return back.

(*ii*) Number of α-particles scattered through an angle θ varies inversely as $\sin^4\left(\frac{\theta}{2}\right)$.

(*iii*) The positively charged nucleus concentrated at centre has size of order of 10^{-15} m and is about 10^{-12} of the total volume of atom.

(*iv*) The minimum distance from the nucleus upto which the α-particles approaches, i.e. **distance of closest approach** of α-particle is expressed as $r_0 = \frac{4kZe^2}{mv^2}$

where, m and v is the mass and velocity of α-particle and $k = \frac{1}{4\pi\varepsilon_0} = 9 \times 10^9 \text{ Nm}^2\text{C}^{-2}$, respectively.

(*v*) Perpendicular distance of the velocity vector of α-particle from the central line of the nucleus of atom, i.e. the **impact parameter** is given mathematically as

$$b = \frac{kZe^2 \cot\left(\frac{\theta}{2}\right)}{\text{KE}}$$

Note Smaller the impact parameter (b), greater the scattering angle (θ) and kinetic energy (KE) of α-particle.

(*vi*) Force between α-particle and nucleus is given by

$$F = \frac{1}{4\pi\varepsilon_0}\frac{2Ze^2}{r^2}$$

Limitations of Rutherford's Atomic Model

(*i*) **About the Stability of Atom** According to Maxwell's electromagnetic wave theory, electron should emit energy in the form of electromagnetic wave during its orbital motion. Therefore, orbit radius of electron will decrease gradually and ultimately it will fall in the nucleus.

(*ii*) **About the Line Spectrum** Rutherford atomic model cannot explain atomic line spectrum.

Bohr's Atomic Model

Bohr's model of atom was based on the following three postulates

(*i*) Electrons move around nucleus in certain circular stable orbits.

(*ii*) Electrons can revolve around in only those orbits in which their angular momentum (mvr) is an integral multiple of $\frac{h}{2\pi}$.

Thus, $$mvr = \frac{nh}{2\pi}$$

where, h = Planck's constant

and n = principal quantum number (1, 2, 3, ...).

(*iii*) When atom receives some energy from outside, then one or more of its outer electron leaves its orbit and move to higher orbit, i.e. it is in excited state.

Note When electron returns back to its initial state from higher orbit, it radiates energy in form of electromagnetic wave of frequency is given by

$$\nu = \frac{E_2 - E_1}{h}$$

- There are some characteristics associated with Bohr's atomic model as given in the table below

Characteristics	Formula	For Hydrogen Like Atom
Orbital radius	$r_n = \frac{n^2h^2\varepsilon_0}{\pi m Z e^2}$	$r_n = 0.53 \frac{n^2}{Z}$ Å
Orbital speed	$v_n = \frac{Ze^2}{2n\varepsilon_0} \cdot \frac{1}{n}$	$v_n = 2.2 \times 10^6 \frac{Z}{n}$ ms^{-1}
Time period	$T_n = \frac{4\varepsilon_0^3 n^3 h^3}{mZ^2e^4}$	$T_n = 1.52 \times 10^{-6} \frac{n^3}{Z^2}$ s
Kinetic energy	$(KE)_n = \frac{RhcZ^2}{n^2}$	$(KE)_n = \frac{13.6Z^2}{n^2}$ eV
Potential energy	$(PE)_n = \frac{-2RhcZ^2}{n^2}$	$(PE)_n = \frac{-13.6Z^2}{n^2}$ eV
Total energy	$E_n = \frac{-RhcZ^2}{n^2}$	$E_n = \frac{-13.6Z^2}{n^2}$ eV
Ionisation energy	$E_{ion} = E_\infty - E_n = \frac{RhcZ^2}{n^2}$	$E_{ion} = \frac{13.6Z^2}{n^2}$ eV
Ionisation potential	$V_{ion} = \frac{RhcZ^2}{en^2}$	$V_{ion} = \frac{13.6Z^2}{n^2}$ V

Note Rhc = 1Rydberg = 13.6 eV.

Hydrogen Spectrum

- When an electron of an atom jumps from some ground state (n_i) to its excited state (n_f), then the energy of photon emitted is given by

$$\Delta E = \frac{hc}{\lambda} = \frac{Z^2me^4}{8\varepsilon_0^2h^2}\left[\frac{1}{n_f^2} - \frac{1}{n_i^2}\right]$$

- The wave number, i.e. reciprocal of wavelength is expressed as

$$\bar{\nu} = \frac{1}{\lambda} = RZ^2\left[\frac{1}{n_f^2} - \frac{1}{n_i^2}\right]$$

- In case of hydrogen, the emission spectrum obtained for different energy level contains five series as shown below

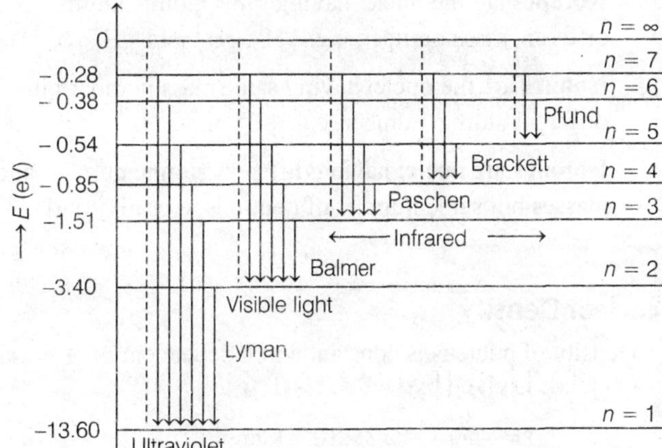

- The wavelength or wave number of lines of these series is obtained as

(*i*) For Lyman series, $n_f = 1$ and $n_i = 2,3,4......$.

(*ii*) For Balmer series, $n_f = 2$ and $n_i = 3,4,5......$.

(*iii*) For Paschen series, $n_f = 3$ and $n_i = 4,5,6......$.

(*iv*) For Brackett series, $n_f = 4$ and $n_i = 5,6,7......$.

(*v*) For Pfund series, $n_f = 5$ and $n_i = 6,7,8......$.

Note To calculate the series limit of a series, we use $n_i = \infty$.

The lines of Balmer series are found in the visible part of the spectrum and other series in invisible parts. Lyman series is found in ultraviolet region and Paschen, Brackett and Pfund series in infrared region.

Limitations of Bohr's Model

The limitations of Bohr's model are as follows

(*i*) This model is applicable only to a simple atom like hydrogen having $Z = 1$.

This theory fails, if $Z > 1$.

(*ii*) It does not explain the fine structure of spectral lines in H-atom.

(*iii*) This model does not explain why orbits of electrons are taken as circular whereas elliptical orbits are also possible.

Nucleus

The entire positive charge and nearly the entire mass of atom is concentrate in a very small space called nucleus of an atom.

- Nucleus is composed of two type of particles; positively charged particle **protons** and neutral particle **neutrons**.
- Radius of a nucleus is expressed as
  $R = R_0 A^{1/3}$, where A is mass number
  and $R_0 = 1.2 \times 10^{-15}$ m (range of nuclear size).
- **Atomic number** is equal to the number of protons present inside while the atomic mass is equal to the total number of neutrons and protons.
- **Isotopes** are the nuclei having same atomic number but different mass number, e.g. ${}_1H^1$, ${}_1H^2$ and ${}_1H^3$.
- **Isobars** are the nuclei having same mass number but different atomic number, e.g. ${}_1H^3$ and ${}_2He^3$.
- **Isotones** are nuclei having different atomic number and masses but same number of neutrons, e.g. ${}_1H^3$ and ${}_2He^4$.

Nuclear Density

Density of nucleus is constant and independent of A for all nuclei. It is given by

$$\rho = \frac{3m}{4\pi R_0^3} \simeq 2.3 \times 10^{17} \text{ kgm}^{-3}$$

Mass Defect

Difference between the sum of the masses of the nucleons constituting a nucleus and the rest mass of nucleus is called mass defect (Δm). It is expressed as

$$\Delta m = Zm_{\text{proton}} + (A - Z)m_{\text{neutrons}} - m_{\text{nucleus}}$$

1 atomic mass unit (amu) = 931.5 MeV

- Packing fraction is given as $\frac{m - A}{A}$, where m is actual isotopic mass.

Einstein's Mass-Energy Relation

According to Einstein's mass-energy relation, the equation is expressed as

$$E = \Delta mc^2$$

where, c = speed of light.

Binding Energy

The binding energy of a nucleus may be defined as the energy equivalent to the mass defect of the nucleus.

If Δm is mass defect, then according to Einstein's mass-energy relation

Binding energy $= \Delta mc^2 = [\{Zm_p + (A - Z)m_n\} - m_N] \cdot c^2$

This binding energy is expressed in joule, if Δm is measured in kg.

If Δm is measured in amu, then binding energy

$$E_b = \Delta m \text{ amu} = [\{Zm_p + (A - Z)m_n\} - m_N] \text{ amu}$$

$$E_b = \Delta m \times 931 \text{ MeV}$$

Binding Energy Curve

It is the graph between binding energy per nucleon and total number of nucleons (i.e. mass number A).

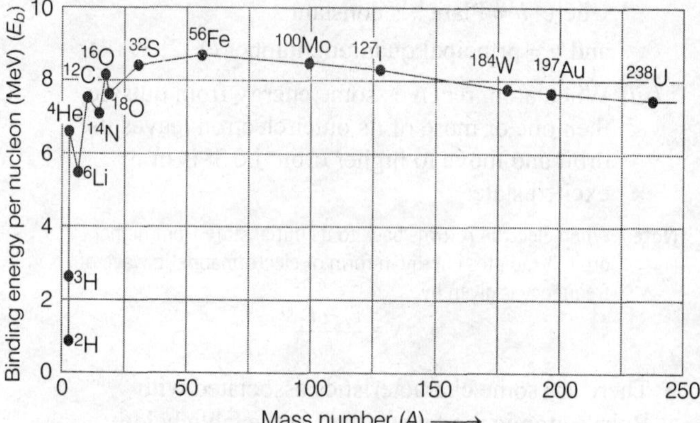

Some features of this curve are given below

(i) The curve has almost a flat maximum roughly from $A = 50$ to $A = 80$ corresponding to an average BE/nucleon of about 8.5 MeV. So, the nuclei having mass number between 50 to 80 are most stable. Iron (Fe^{56}, i.e. $A = 56$), having a BE/nucleon of about 8.8 MeV has maximum stability.

(ii) For nuclei having mass number more than 80, the average binding energy per nucleon decreases slowly and drop to about 7.6 MeV for Uranium ($A = 238$). The lower value of binding energy per nucleon fails to overcome the repulsion among protons in nuclei having large number of protons, i.e. the nuclei of heavier atoms beyond ${}_{83}Bi^{209}$ are radioactive.

(iii) For nuclei having mass number below 20, it decreases sharply, e.g. for heavy hydrogen (${}_1H^2$), it is only about 1.1 MeV. This shows that the nuclei having mass number below 20 are comparatively less stable.

(iv) Below $A = 50$, the curve does not fall continuously, but has subsidiary peaks at ${}_8O^{16}$, ${}_6C^{12}$ and ${}_2He^4$. This shows that these (even-even) nuclei are more stable than their immediate neighbours.

Nuclear Force and Nuclear Stability

Nuclear Force

The forces that holds the nucleons together inside the nucleus of an atom are called nuclear forces.

Some important properties of nuclear forces are given below

(*i*) Nuclear forces are charge independent.

(*ii*) Nuclear forces are short range forces. These do not exist at large distances greater than 10^{-15} m.

(*iii*) These are attractive force and cause stability of the nucleus.

(*iv*) Nuclear forces are non-central force.

(*v*) Nuclear forces are the strongest forces in nature.

(*vi*) Nuclear forces depends on the direction of the spins of the nucleons. The force is stronger, if the spin of nucleons is parallel and is weak, if it is anti-parallel.

(*vii*) Electrical and gravitational forces follows inverse square law (i.e. $F \propto 1/r^2$), but nuclear forces are complicated in nature and does not follow it.

Nuclear Stability

The stability of a nucleus is determined by the value of its binding energy per nucleon. Higher the binding energy of nucleon, nucleus is more stable. The stability of nucleus is also determined by its neutron to proton ratio. A plot of number of neutrons and number of protons is shown in the figure below.

In the figure, the solid line shows the nuclei with equal number of protons and neutrons ($N = Z$). Only light nuclei are on this line, i.e. they are stable if they contain approximately same number of protons and neutrons.

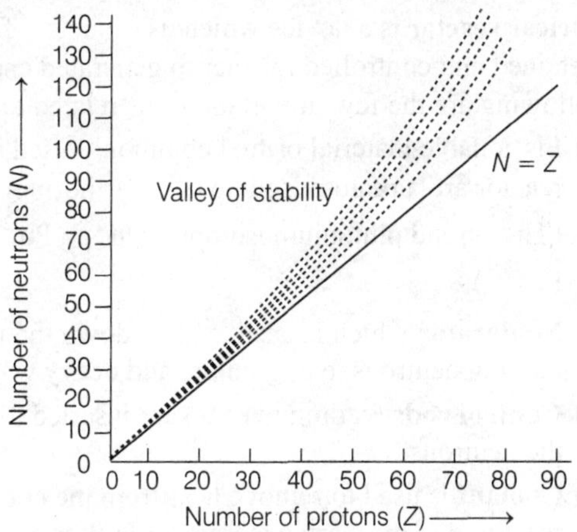

Heavy nuclei are stable only when they have more neutrons than protons.

The long narrow region shown in the figure, which contains the cluster of short lines representing stable nuclei is referred to as the valley of stability.

Radioactivity

- It is the phenomenon of spontaneous emission of radiations by nucleus of some elements. Generally, three types of emission are emitted namely α, β and γ-radiations.

Few properties of these radiations are listed below in the tabular form below

S.No.	Property	α-particle	β-particle	γ-rays
(*i*)	Nature	Helium nucleus	Fast moving electrons	Electromagnetic waves
(*ii*)	Charge	$+2e$	$-e$	zero
(*iii*)	Rest mass	6.67×10^{-27} kg	9.1×10^{-31} kg	zero
(*iv*)	Speed	1.4×10^7 to 2.2×10^7 ms^{-1}	1 to 99% of c	$c = 3 \times 10^8 \text{ms}^{-1}$
(*v*)	Ionising power	10^4	10^2	1
(*vi*)	Penetrating power	1	10^2	10^4

- Radioactive nucleus decays into another nucleus by emission of these particles known as **radioactive decay**. The reaction of the three types of decays are as follows

  (*i*) **α-decay** A nucleus emitting an alpha particle loses two protons and two neutrons. Therefore, the atomic number Z decreases by 2, the mass number A decreases by 4 and the neutron number N decreases by 2. The decay can be written as

$$_ZX^A = {}_{Z-2}Y^{A-4} + {}_2\text{He}^4$$

  (*ii*) **β-decay** Beta decay involves the emission of electrons or positron. A positron is a form of anti-matter, which has a charge equal to $+e$ and a mass equal to that of electron. The electrons and positrons emitted in β-decay do not exist inside the nucleus. They are created at the time of emission.

  It is further of three types which are as follows

  - **β^--decay** A parent nucleus with atomic number Z and mass number A decays by β^- emission into a daughter nuclei with atomic number $Z+1$ and the same mass number A.

$$_ZX^A \xrightarrow{\beta^-} {}_{Z+1}Y^A + e^- + \bar{\nu}$$

- **β^+-decay** Positron (e^+) emission from a nucleus decreases the atomic number Z by 1 while keeping the same mass number A.

$$_ZX^A \xrightarrow{\beta^+} {}_{Z-1}Y^A + e^+ + \overline{\nu}$$

- **Electron Capture** This occurs when a parent nucleus captures one of its own orbital electrons and emits a neutrino.

$$_ZX^A + e^{-1} \longrightarrow {}_{Z-1}Y^A + \nu$$

where, ν = neutrino and $\overline{\nu}$ = anti-neutrino.

(*iii*) **γ-decay** These rays are emitted when a nucleus in excited state by radioactive transformation decays to ground state.

Law of Radioactive Decay

- According to the law of radioactive decay, the number of nuclei present after time t is given by $N = N_0 e^{-\lambda t}$, where N_0 = number of nuclei present at $t = 0$ and λ = decay constant.
- Number of decayed nuclei after time t,

$$N_0 - N = N_0(1 - e^{-\lambda t})$$

Activity of Radioactive Substance

Rate of decay of radioactive substance is called activity of the substance. It is given as

$$R = -dN/dt = R_0 e^{-\lambda t}$$

Unit of activity, 1 Bq = 1 decay/s, 1 Ci = 3.7×10^{10} Bq and 1 Rd = 10^6 Bq.

Half-Life and Mean Life

- **Half-life** The time interval in which the mass of a radioactive substance or the number of its atom, is reduced to half its initial value is called half-life of that substance.

$$T_{1/2} = \frac{0.6931}{\lambda}$$

- After n half-life, the number of nuclei left undecayed is given as $t = nT_{1/2}$,

$$N = N_0\left(\frac{1}{2}\right)^n \text{ and } R = R_0\left(\frac{1}{2}\right)^n.$$

- **Mean life** The average of the lives of all the nuclei in a radioactive substance is called the **mean life** or **average life** of that substance. It is denoted by τ.

$$\tau = \frac{T_{1/2}}{0.6931} = 1.443\,T_{1/2}$$

Nuclear Reaction

The process by which the identity of a nucleus is changed when it is bombarded by an energetic particle is called nuclear reaction. Its general expression is

$$\underset{\text{(parent nucleus)}}{X} + \underset{\text{(incident particle)}}{a} \longrightarrow \underset{\text{(compound nucleus)}}{c} \longrightarrow \underset{\text{(product nucleus)}}{Y} + \underset{\text{(daughter nucleus)}}{b} + \underset{\text{(energy)}}{Q}$$

All nuclear reactions obeys basic conservation laws that includes conservation of mass number, electric charge, linear & angular momentum and total energy.

***Q*-value** means the difference between the rest mass energy of the initial constituents and that of the final constituents of a nuclear reaction.

Nuclear Energy

Nuclear energy is the energy released during a nuclear reaction and can be obtained through nuclear fission and fusion.

Nuclear Fission

- It is the process of splitting of heavy nucleus into lighter nucleus of comparable masses with liberation of energy. It can lead to chain reactions under favourable conditions.
- Reproduction factor (R) of chain reaction is given as

$$R = \frac{\text{Rate of production of neutrons}}{\text{Rate of loss of neutrons}}$$

If $R = 1$, the reaction is steady, $R > 1$, the reaction grows faster and $R < 1$, the reaction comes to halt.

- **Nuclear reactor** is a device which uses nuclear fission in sustained and controlled manner to generated energy. Following are the few important terms related to it
  - (*i*) Fissionable material or fuel commonly used in a reactor are uranium isotope (U^{235}), thorium isotope (Th^{232}) and plutonium isotopes (Pu^{239}, Pu^{240} and Pu^{241}).
  - (*ii*) **Moderator** which is used to slow down the fast moving neutrons, e.g. graphite and heavy water.
  - (*iii*) **Control rods** (cadmium rods) are inserted to absorb the neutrons.
  - (*iv*) **Coolant** is used to remove heat from the core of the reactor, e.g. ordinary water under high pressure.
- **Atom bomb** has an increasing uncontrolled chain reaction occuring for a short time.

Nuclear Fusion

- It is the process of combining of two light nuclei to form a heavy nuclei.
- In this process, mass of single nucleus so formed is less than the sum of the masses of parent nuclei and this difference in mass, result in release of tremendous amount of energy.
- It is also known as **thermonuclear reaction** as it is only carried at high pressure and temperature of order 10^7 K to 10^8 K.
- **Hydrogen bomb** is based on the fusion process.

X-rays

- These are the electromagnetic waves of high penetration power with wavelength range of 0.1 Å to 100 Å.
- X-rays are classified as : continuous and characteristics, while the former depends on the accelerating voltage only and the latter depends on the target used.
- The minimum wavelength of emitted X-ray, when an electron incident through a potential V on the target is given by

$$\lambda_{\min} = \frac{hc}{eV} = \frac{1240}{V} \text{ nm or } \frac{12375}{V} \text{ Å}.$$

Note X-rays of high frequency are known as **hard X-rays** while X-rays of low frequency are known as **soft X-rays.**

- Intensity of X-rays beam emerging from a material after some absorption of these rays into it, is given as $I = I_0 e^{-\mu t}$, where I_0 is the intensity of incident X-rays, t is the thickness of material and μ is absorption coefficient of material.

Moseley's Law

According to Moseley's law, the frequency of characteristic X-ray emitted is given by

$$\sqrt{\nu} = a(Z - b)$$

where, a = proportionality constant

and b = screening constant.

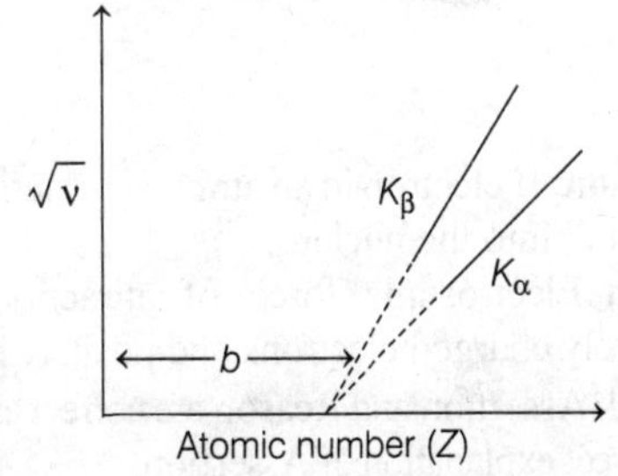

Bragg's Law

According to Bragg's law of X-ray diffraction, the path difference between the diffracted rays from a crystal is given as $2d \sin\theta = n\lambda$, where d is the interatomic distance.

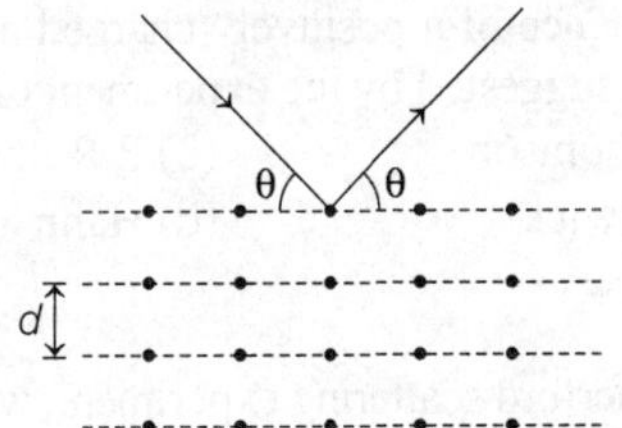

Topical Practice Questions

All the exam questions of this chapter have been divided into 5 topics as listed below

Topic 1

Rutherford α-Particle Scattering Experiment and Atomic Model

2018

1 **Assertion** If electron in an atom were stationary, then they would fall into the nucleus.

Reason Electrostatic force of attraction acts between negatively charged electrons and positive nucleus. **[AIIMS]**

(a) Both Assertion and Reason are correct and Reason is the correct explanation of Assertion.
(b) Both Assertion and Reason are correct but Reason is not the correct explanation of Assertion.
(c) Assertion is correct but Reason is incorrect.
(d) Assertion is incorrect but Reason is correct.

2013

2 The existence of a positively charged nucleus in an atom was first suggested by the experiment of **[WB JEE]**

(a) J J Thomson (b) E Rutherford
(c) Chadwick (d) Hahn and Strassman

2011

3 In a Rutherford scattering experiment, when a projectile of charge Z_1 and mass M_1 approaches a target nucleus of charge Z_2 and mass M_2, the distance of closest approach is r_0. The energy of the projectile is **[CBSE PMT]**

(a) directly proportional to $M_1 \times M_2$
(b) directly proportional to $Z_1 Z_2$
(c) inversely proportional to Z_1
(d) directly proportional to mass M_1

4 A beam of fast moving alpha particles were directed towards a thin film of gold. The parts A', B' and C' of the transmitted and reflected beams corresponding to the incident parts A, B and C of the beam are shown in the adjoining diagram. The number of alpha particles in **[RPET]**

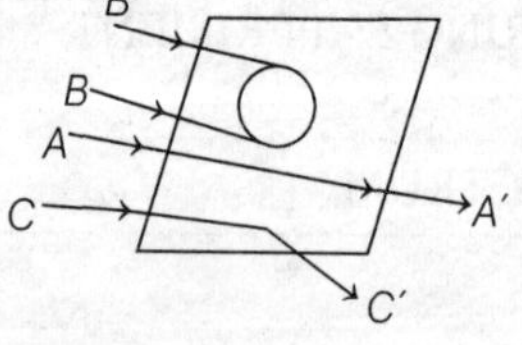

(a) B' will be minimum and in C' maximum
(b) A' will be maximum and in B' minimum
(c) A' will be minimum and in B' maximum
(d) C' will be minimum and in B' maximum

5 Rutherford's atomic model could account for **[KCET]**

(a) stability of atoms
(b) origin of spectra
(c) the positive charged central core of an atom
(d) concept of stationary orbits

2010

6 In Rutherford scattering experiment, what will be the correct angle for α scattering for an impact parameter $b = 0$? **[JCECE]**

(a) 90° (b) 270° (c) 0° (d) 180°

2009

7 If an α-particle of mass m, charge q and velocity v is incident on a nucleus charge Q and mass m, then the distance of closest approach is **[BVP]**

(a) $\frac{Qq}{4\pi\varepsilon_0 m^2}$ (b) $\frac{Qq}{2\pi\varepsilon_0 mv^2}$ (c) $\frac{Qq\,mv^2}{2}$ (d) $\frac{Qq}{mv^2}$

8 In Rutherford's α-particle experiment with thin gold foil, 8100 scintillations per minute are observed at an angle of 60°. The number of scintillations per minute at an angle of 120° will be **[BCECE]**

(a) 900 (b) 2025 (c) 32400 (d) 4050

9 An alpha nucleus of energy $\frac{1}{2}mv^2$ bombards a heavy nuclear target of charge Ze. Then, the distance of closest approach for the alpha nucleus will be proportional to **[JIPMER]**

(a) v^2 (b) $\frac{1}{m}$
(c) $\frac{1}{v^4}$ (d) $\frac{1}{Ze}$

10 According to classical theory of Rutherford's model, the path of electron will be **[AFMC]**

(a) parabolic (b) hyperbolic
(c) circular (d) elliptical

11 An α-particle of energy 5 MeV is scattered through 180° by a fixed uranium nucleus. The distance of the closest approach is of the order of **[MP PMT]**

(a) 1 Å (b) 10^{-10} cm (c) 10^{-12} cm (d) 10^{-15} cm

Answers

1 (a)	2 (b)	3 (b)	4 (b)	5 (c)	6 (d)	7 (b)	8 (a)	9 (b)	10 (d)
11 (c)									

Explanations

1 (a) In an atom, electron revolves around nucleus, for this required centripetal forces is provided by electrostatic force of attraction between electron and nucleus. If electrons were stationary, then due to this force they would fall into the nucleus.

2 (b) A positively charged nucleus in an atom was first suggested by E Rutherford through its gold foil experiment.

3 (b) The energy of the projectile will be equivalent to potential energy of the charge system,

$$E = \frac{1}{4\pi\varepsilon_0}\frac{(Z_1 e)(Z_2 e)}{r_0}$$

$$\Rightarrow \quad E \propto Z_1 Z_2$$

4 (b) A' will be maximum and minimum in B' because atom is hollow and whole mass of atom is concentrated in a small centre called nucleus.

5 (c) Rutherford's atomic model could account for the positive charged central core of an atom.

6 (d) We know that, impact parameter,

$$b \propto \cot\frac{\theta}{2} \Rightarrow b = K\cot\frac{\theta}{2}$$

where, K is a constant.

Given, $b = 0$, hence $\theta = 180°$.

7 (b) According to the question, for the distance of closest approach kinetic energy will totally be converted to potential energy.

Hence, $$\frac{1}{2}mv^2 = \frac{1}{4\pi\varepsilon_0}\frac{Qq}{r_0}$$

$$\Rightarrow \quad r_0 = \frac{Qq}{2\pi\varepsilon_0 mv^2}$$

8 (a) Number of α-particles scattered through at an angle θ, $N \propto \frac{1}{\sin^4\left(\frac{\theta}{2}\right)}$

$$\Rightarrow \quad \frac{N_1}{N_2} = \frac{\left(\sin^4\frac{\theta_2}{2}\right)}{\left(\sin^4\frac{\theta_1}{2}\right)}$$

Given, $N_1 = 8100$, $\theta_1 = 60°$

and $\theta_2 = 120°$

$$\Rightarrow \quad \frac{8100}{N_2} = \frac{\left(\sin^4\frac{120°}{2}\right)}{\left(\sin^4\frac{60°}{2}\right)}$$

$$\Rightarrow \quad \frac{8100}{N_2} = \frac{\sin^4 60°}{\sin^4 30°}$$

$$\Rightarrow \quad N_2 = \frac{8100\times\frac{1}{16}}{\frac{9}{16}} = 900$$

9 (b) For the distance of closest approach, we can write,

$$\frac{1}{2}mv^2 = \frac{K\times(Ze)\,2e}{r_0}$$

$$\Rightarrow \quad r_0 \propto \frac{1}{m}$$

10 (d) According to classical theory of Rutherford model, the path of electron will be elliptical.

11 (c) According to law of conservation of energy, kinetic energy of α-particle = potential energy of α-particle at distance of closest approach

i.e. $$\frac{1}{2}mv^2 = \frac{1}{4\pi\varepsilon_0}\frac{q_1 q_2}{r}$$

$$\therefore \quad 5\text{ MeV} = \frac{9\times10^9\times(2e)\times(92e)}{r}$$

$$\left(\because \frac{1}{2}mv^2 = 5\text{ MeV}\right)$$

$$\Rightarrow \quad r = \frac{9\times10^9\times2\times92\times(1.6\times10^{-19})^2}{5\times10^6\times1.6\times10^{-19}}$$

$$\therefore \quad r = 5.3\times10^{-14}\text{ m}$$

$$= 5.3\times10^{-12}\text{ cm}$$

Topic 2

Bohr Model and Hydrogen Spectrum

2019

1 The total energy of an electron in an atom in an orbit is −3.4 eV. Its kinetic and potential energies are, respectively **[NEET]**

(a) −3.4 eV, −6.8 eV (b) 3.4 eV, −6.8 eV
(c) 3.4 eV, 3.4 eV (d) −3.4 eV, −3.4 eV

2 The radius of the first permitted Bohr orbit for the electron, in a hydrogen atom equals 0.51 Å and its ground state energy equals − 13.6 eV. If the electron in the hydrogen atom is replaced by muon (μ^{-1}) [Charge same as electron and mass 207 m_e], the first Bohr radius and ground state energy will be **[NEET (Odisha)]**

(a) 0.53×10^{-13} m, − 3.6 eV (b) 25.6×10^{-13} m, − 2.8 eV
(c) 2.56×10^{-13} m, − 2.8 keV (d) 2.56×10^{-13} m, − 13.6 eV

3 15 eV is given to electron in 4th orbit, then find its final energy when it comes out of H-atom. **[AIIMS]**

(a) 14.15 eV (b) 13.6 eV
(c) 12.08 eV (d) 15.85 eV

2018

4 The ratio of kinetic energy to the total energy of an electron in a Bohr orbit of the hydrogen atom is **[NEET]**

(a) 2, −1 (b) 1, −1 (c) 1, 1 (d) 1, −2

2017

5 The ratio of wavelength of the last line of Balmer series and the last line of Lyman series is **[NEET]**

(a) 2 (b) 1 (c) 4 (d) 0.5

2016

6 If an electron in a hydrogen atom jumps from the 3rd orbit to the 2nd orbit, then it emits a photon of wavelength λ. When it jumps from the 4th orbit to the 3rd orbit, then the corresponding wavelength will be [NEET]

(a) $\frac{16}{25}\lambda$ (b) $\frac{9}{16}\lambda$
(c) $\frac{20}{7}\lambda$ (d) $\frac{20}{13}\lambda$

2015

7 Consider 3rd orbit of helium using non-relativistic approach the speed of electron in this order will be (take, $k = 9\times10^9$ constant, $Z = 2$ and h = Planck's constant $= 6.64\times10^{-34}$ J-s) [CBSE]

(a) $2.92\times10^6\ \text{ms}^{-1}$ (b) $1.46\times10^6\ \text{ms}^{-1}$
(c) $0.73\times10^6\ \text{ms}^{-1}$ (d) $3\times10^6\ \text{ms}^{-1}$

2014

8 Hydrogen atom in ground state is excited by a monochromatic radiation of $\lambda = 975$ Å. Number of spectral lines in the resulting spectrum emitted will be [CBSE AIPMT]

(a) 3 (b) 2
(c) 6 (d) 10

9 If an electron in hydrogen atom jumps from an orbit of level $n = 3$ to an orbit of level $n = 2$, emitted radiation has a frequency (R = Rydberg's constant, c = velocity of light) [MHT CET]

(a) $\frac{3Rc}{27}$ (b) $\frac{Rc}{25}$
(c) $\frac{8Rc}{9}$ (d) $\frac{5Rc}{36}$

10 The ionisation energy of hydrogen is 13.6 eV. The energy of the photon released when an electron jumps from the first excited state ($n = 2$) to the ground state of hydrogen atom is [WB JEE]

(a) 3.4 eV (b) 4.53 eV
(c) 10.2 eV (d) 13.6 eV

2013

11 The energy E of a hydrogen atom with principal quantum number n is given by

$$E = \frac{13.6}{n^2}\ \text{eV}$$

The energy of a photon ejected when the electron jumps from $n = 3$ state to $n = 2$ state of hydrogen is approximately [AIIMS]

(a) 1.5 eV (b) 0.85 eV (c) 3.3 eV (d) 1.9 eV

12 Outside a nucleus, [AIIMS]

(a) neutron is stable
(b) neutron is unstable
(c) proton and neutron both are stable
(d) proton and neutron both are unstable

13 **Assertion** Balmer series lies in the visible region of electromagnetic spectrum.

Reason $\frac{1}{\lambda} = R\left(\frac{1}{2^2} - \frac{1}{n^2}\right)$, where, $n = 3, 4, 5 \ldots \infty$

(a) Both Assertion and Reason are correct and Reason is the correct explanation of Assertion. [AIIMS]
(b) Both Assertion and Reason are correct but Reason is not the correct explanation of Assertion.
(c) Assertion is correct but Reason is incorrect.
(d) Both Assertion and Reason are incorrect.

14 According to Bohr's theory (assuming infinite mass of the nucleus), the frequency of the second line of the Balmer series is [UP CPMT]

(a) 6.16×10^{14} Hz (b) 6.16×10^{13} Hz
(c) 6.16×10^{10} Hz (d) 6.16×10^{16} Hz

15 In the lowest energy level of hydrogen atom, the electron has the angular momentum [WB JEE]

(a) $\frac{\pi}{h}$ (b) $\frac{h}{\pi}$ (c) $\frac{h}{2\pi}$ (d) $\frac{2\pi}{h}$

16 Band spectrum is also called [KCET]

(a) molecular spectrum (b) atomic spectrum
(c) flash spectrum (d) line absorption spectrum

2012

17 The transition from the state $n = 3$ to $n = 1$ in a hydrogen like atom results in ultraviolet radiation. Infrared radiation will be obtained in the transition from [CBSE AIPMT]

(a) $2 \to 1$ (b) $3 \to 2$ (c) $4 \to 2$ (d) $4 \to 3$

18 An electron of a stationary hydrogen atom passes from the 5th energy level to the ground level. The velocity that the atom acquired a result of photon emission will be [CBSE AIPMT]

(a) $\frac{24hR}{25m}$ (b) $\frac{25hR}{24m}$
(c) $\frac{25m}{24hR}$ (d) $\frac{24m}{25hR}$

19 Electron in hydrogen atom first jumps from third excited state to second excited state and then from second excited to the first excited state. The ratio of the wavelengths $\lambda_1 : \lambda_2$ emitted in the two cases is [CBSE AIPMT]

(a) 7 : 5 (b) 27 : 20
(c) 27 : 5 (d) 20 : 7

20 Which state of triply ionised Beryllium (Be^{3+}) has the same orbital radius as that of the ground state of hydrogen? [CBSE AIPMT]

(a) $n = 3$ (b) $n = 4$ (c) $n = 1$ (d) $n = 2$

21 For a hydrogen atom, in which of the following transitions will the wavelength of emitted photon be minimum? [MP PET]

(a) $n = 5$ to $n = 4$ (b) $n = 4$ to $n = 3$
(c) $n = 3$ to $n = 2$ (d) $n = 2$ to $n = 1$

22 The radius of the smallest electron orbit in hydrogen like ion is $(0.51 \times 10^{-10} / 4)$ m, then it is **[Manipal]**

(a) hydrogen atom (b) He^{+}
(c) Li^{2+} (d) Be^{3+}

23 The electron of a hydrogen atom revolves around the proton in a circular nth orbit of radius $r_n = \varepsilon_0 n^2 h^2 / \pi m e^2$ with speed $v_n = \dfrac{e^2}{2\varepsilon_0 nh}$.

The current due to the circulating charge is proportional to

(a) n^2 (b) n^3 (c) n^{-3} (d) n^{-2} **[AMU]**

2011

24 The wavelength of the first line of Lyman series for H- atom is equal to that of the second line of Balmer series for a H-like ion. The atomic number Z of H-like ion is **[CBSE AIPMT]**

(a) 4 (b) 1 (c) 2 (d) 3

25 The energy of a hydrogen atom in the ground state is -13.6eV. The energy of a He^{+} ion in the first excited state will be **[CBSE AIPMT]**

(a) -13.6eV (b) -27.2eV
(c) -54.4eV (d) -6.8eV

26 The first emission of hydrogen atomic spectrum in Lyman series appears at a wavelength of **[Odisha JEE]**

(a) $\dfrac{3R}{4}$ cm^{-1} (b) $\dfrac{4}{3R}$ cm (c) $\dfrac{7R}{144}$ cm^{-1} (d) $\dfrac{400}{9R}$ cm

27 When an electron in hydrogen atom is excited from its 4th to 5th stationary orbit, the change in angular momentum of electron is (Planck's constant, $h = 6.6 \times 10^{-34}$ J-s) **[CBSE AIPMT]**

(a) 4.16×10^{-34} J-s (b) 3.32×10^{-34} J-s
(c) 1.05×10^{-34} J-s (d) None of these

28 When an electron jumps from the orbit $n = 2$ to $n = 4$, then wavelength of the radiations absorbed will be (where, R is Rydberg's constant) **[KCET, CBSE AIPMT]**

(a) $\dfrac{16}{3R}$ (b) $\dfrac{16}{5R}$ (c) $\dfrac{5R}{16}$ (d) $\dfrac{3R}{16}$

29 In an inelastic collision, an electron excites a hydrogen atom from its ground state to a M-shell state. A second electron collides instantaneously with the excited hydrogen atom in the M-shell state and ionizes it. At last how much energy the second electron transfers to the atom in the M-shell state? **[WB JEE]**

(a) $+3.4$ eV (b) $+1.51$ eV
(c) -3.4 eV (d) -1.51 eV

30 According to the Bohr's atomic model, the relation between principal quantum number (n) and radius of orbit (r) is **[J&K CET]**

(a) $r \propto n^2$ (b) $r \propto \dfrac{1}{n^2}$ (c) $r \propto \dfrac{1}{n}$ (d) $r \propto n$

31 Which of the following postulates of the Bohr model led to the quantisation of energy of the hydrogen atom? **[J & K CET]**

(a) The electron goes around the nucleus in circular orbits.
(b) The angular momentum of the electron can only be an integral multiple of $h / 2\pi$.
(c) The magnitude of the linear momentum of the electron is quantised.
(d) Quantisation of energy is itself a postulate of the Bohr model.

2010

32 The ionisation energy of the electron in the hydrogen atom in its ground state is 13.6 eV. The atoms are excited to higher energy levels to emits radiations of 6 wavelengths. Maximum wavelength of emitted radiation corresponds to the transition between **[CBSE AIPMT]**

(a) $n = 3$ and $n = 2$ states
(b) $n = 3$ and $n = 1$ state
(c) $n = 2$ and $n = 1$ state
(d) $n = 4$ and $n = 3$ states

33 An electron jumps from 4th orbit to 2nd orbit of the hydrogen atom. Given, Rydberg's constant $R = 10^5$ cm^{-1}, the frequency in hertz of emitted radiation will be **[AFMC]**

(a) $\dfrac{3}{16} \times 10^5$ (b) $\dfrac{3}{16} \times 10^{15}$ (c) $\dfrac{9}{16} \times 10^{15}$ (d) $\dfrac{3}{4} \times 10^{15}$

34 In figure the energy levels of the hydrogen atom have been shown along with some transitions marking A, B, C. The transitions A, B and C respectively represents **[AFMC]**

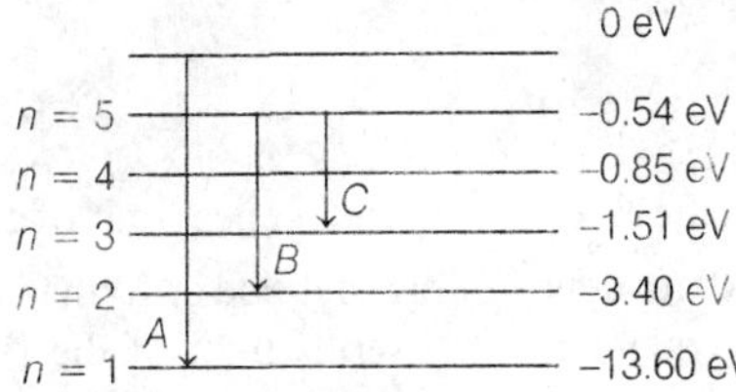

(a) the first member of the Lyman series, third member of Balmer series and second member of Paschen series
(b) the ionisation potential of H, second member of Balmer series and third member of Paschen series
(c) the series limit of Lyman series, second member of Balmer series and second member of Paschen series
(d) the series limit of Lyman series, third member of Balmer series and second member of Paschen series

35 A hydrogen-like atom emits radiations of frequency 2.7×10^{15} Hz, when it makes a transition from $n = 2$ to $n = 1$. The frequency emitted in a transition from $n = 3$ to $n = 1$ will be **[BHU]**

(a) 1.8×10^{15}Hz (b) 3.2×10^{15} Hz
(c) 4.7×10^{5}Hz (d) 6.9×10^{15} Hz

36 The minimum energy to ionise an atom is the energy required to [BHU]
(a) add one electron to the gaseous state of atom
(b) excite the atom from its ground state to its first excited state
(c) remove one outermost electron from the gaseous state of atom
(d) remove one innermost electron from the gaseous state of atom

37 In the following atoms, the molecules for the transition from $n=2$ to $n=1$, the spectral line of minimum wavelength will be produced by [UP CPMT]
(a) hydrogen atom (b) deuterium atom
(c) uni-ionised helium (d) di-ionised lithium

38 The orbital frequency of an electron in the hydrogen atom is proportional to [MHT CET]
(a) n^3 (b) n^{-3} (c) n (d) n^0

39 A hydrogen atom emits a photon corresponding to an electron transition from $n=5$ to $n=1$. The recoil speed of hydrogen atom is almost (mass of proton $\approx 1.6\times10^{-27}$ kg) [Haryana PMT]
(a) 10 ms^{-1} (b) 2×10^{-2} ms^{-1}
(c) 4 ms^{-1} (d) 8×10^2 ms^{-1}

40 The following diagram indicates the energy levels of a certain atom when the system moves from $4E$ level to E. A photon of wavelength λ_1 is emitted. The wavelength of photon produced during its transition from $(7/3)E$ level to E is λ_2. The ratio λ_1/λ_2 will be [Punjab PMET]

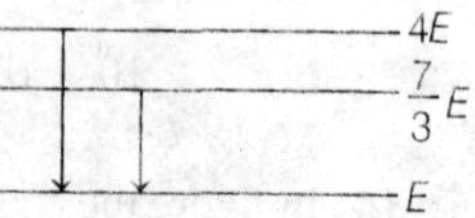

(a) $\frac{9}{4}$ (b) $\frac{4}{9}$ (c) $\frac{3}{2}$ (d) $\frac{7}{3}$

41 If ν_1 is the frequency of the series limit of Lyman series, ν_2 is the frequency of the first line of Lyman series and ν_3 is the frequency of the series limit of the Balmer series. Then, [KCET]
(a) $\nu_1 - \nu_2 = \nu_3$ (b) $\nu_1 = \nu_2 - \nu_3$
(c) $\frac{1}{\nu_2} = \frac{1}{\nu_1} + \frac{1}{\nu_3}$ (d) $\frac{1}{\nu_1} = \frac{1}{\nu_2} + \frac{1}{\nu_3}$

42 An electron is moving in an orbit of a hydrogen atom from which there can be a maximum of six transitions. An electron is moving in an orbit of another hydrogen atom from which there can be a maximum of three transitions. The ratio of the velocities of the electron in these two orbits is [KCET]
(a) $\frac{1}{2}$ (b) $\frac{2}{1}$ (c) $\frac{5}{4}$ (d) $\frac{3}{4}$

43 The spectrum of an oil flame is an example for [KCET]
(a) line emission spectrum
(b) continuous emission spectrum
(c) line absorption spectrum
(d) band emission spectrum

44 An electron jumps from the first excited state to the ground state of hydrogen atom. What will be the percentage change in the speed of electron? [BCECE]
(a) 25 (b) 50 (c) 100 (d) 200

45 If the potential energy of the electron in the hydrogen atom is $\frac{-Ke^2}{r}$, its kinetic energy is [CG PMT]
(a) $\frac{-Ke^2}{2r}$ (b) $\frac{-Ke^2}{r}$ (c) $\frac{Ke^2}{2r}$ (d) $\frac{Ke^2}{r}$

46 The ground state energy of hydrogen atom is -13.6 eV. The kinetic energy of the electron in this state is [MGIMS]
(a) 27.2 eV (b) 13.6 eV
(c) 6.8 eV (d) 3.4 eV

47 If the radius of the 1st Bohr orbit of the hydrogen atom is 5.29×10^{-11} m, the radius of the 2nd orbit will be [MGIMS]
(a) 21.16×10^{-11} m (b) 15.87×10^{-11} m
(c) 10.58×10^{-11} m (d) 2.64×10^{-11} m

2009

48 In the Bohr's model of a hydrogen atom, the centripetal force is furnished by the Coulomb attraction between the proton and the electron. If a_0 is the radius of the ground state orbit, m is the mass, e is the charge on electron and ε_0 is the permittivity of free space, the speed of the electron is [AIIMS]
(a) $\frac{e}{\sqrt{\varepsilon_0 a_0 m}}$ (b) zero
(c) $\frac{e}{\sqrt{4\pi\varepsilon_0 a_0 m}}$ (d) $\frac{\sqrt{4\varepsilon_0 a_0 m}}{e}$

49 A hydrogen atom is in excited state of principal quantum number n. It emits a photon of wavelength λ, when returns to ground state. The value of n is [AIIMS]
(a) $\sqrt{\lambda R(\lambda R-1)}$ (b) $\sqrt{\frac{\lambda R-1}{\lambda R}}$
(c) $\sqrt{\frac{\lambda R}{\lambda R-1}}$ (d) $\sqrt{\lambda(R-1)}$

50 The energy of hydrogen atom in ground state is 13.6 eV. The ionisation energy of singly ionised helium He^{2+} will be [AIIMS]
(a) 13.6 eV (b) 3.4 eV (c) 27.2 eV (d) 54.4 eV

51 **Assertion** It is essential that all the lines available in the emission spectrum will also be available in the absorption spectrum.
Reason The spectrum of hydrogen atom is only absorption spectrum. [AIIMS]
(a) Both Assertion and Reason are correct and Reason is the correct explanation of Assertion.
(b) Both Assertion and Reason are correct but Reason is not the correct explanation of Assertion.
(c) Assertion is correct but Reason is incorrect.
(d) Both Assertion and Reason are incorrect.

52 If elements with principal quantum number $n > 4$ were not allowed in nature, then the number of possible elements would be **[AFMC]**
(a) 32 (b) 60 (c) 18 (d) 4

53 The shortest wavelength of the Brackett series of hydrogen like atom (atomic number = Z) is the same as the shortest wavelength of the Balmer series of hydrogen atom. The value of Z is **[UP CPMT]**
(a) 3 (b) 4 (c) 5 (d) 2

54 If an electron is revolving around the hydrogen nucleus at a distance of 0.1 nm, what should be its speed? **[MHT CET]**
(a) 2.188×10^6 ms^{-1} (b) 1.094×10^6 ms^{-1}
(c) 4.376×10^6 ms^{-1} (d) 1.60×10^6 ms^{-1}

55 The spectral series of the hydrogen atom that lies in the visible region of the electromagnetic spectrum **[MHT CET]**
(a) Paschen (b) Balmer
(c) Lyman (d) Brackett

56 In a hydrogen like atom, electron make transition from at energy level with quantum number n to another with quantum number $(n-1)$. If $n >> 1$, the frequency of radiation emitted is proportional to **[JEE (Main)]**
(a) $\frac{1}{n}$ (b) $\frac{1}{n^2}$ (c) $\frac{1}{n^3/2}$ (d) $\frac{1}{n^3}$

57 The radius of hydrogen atom in its ground state is 5.3×10^{-11} m. After collision with an electron, it is found to have a radius of 21.2×10^{-11} m. What is the principal quantum number n of the final state of atom? **[MHT CET]**
(a) $n = 4$ (b) $n = 2$ (c) $n = 16$ (d) $n = 3$

58 The energy of an electron in excited hydrogen atom is -3.4 eV. Then, according to Bohr's theory, the angular momentum of the electron is **[Manipal]**
(a) 2.1×10^{-34} J-s (b) 3×10^{-34} J-s
(c) 2×10^{-34} J-s (d) 0.5×10^{-34} J-s

59 The shortest wavelength which can be obtained in hydrogen spectrum is ($R = 10^7$ m^{-1}) **[Haryana PMT, CG PMT]**
(a) 1000 Å (b) 800 Å (c) 1300 Å (d) 2100 Å

60 According to Bohr's theory of hydrogen atom, for the electron in the nth allowed orbit the
I. linear momentum is proportional to $1/n$.
II. radius is proportional to n.
III. kinetic energy is proportional to $1/n^2$.
IV. angular momentum is proportional to n.
Choose the correct option from the codes given below **[Haryana PMT, CG PMT]**
(a) I, III and IV (b) only I
(c) I and II (d) only III

61 The radius of an electron orbit in a hydrogen atom is of the order of **[DUMET]**
(a) 10^{-8} m (b) 10^{-9} m (c) 10^{-11} m (d) 10^{-10} m

62 Maximum energy is evolved during which of the following transitions? **[MGIMS]**
(a) $n = 1$ to $n = 2$ (b) $n = 2$ to $n = 6$
(c) $n = 2$ to $n = 1$ (d) $n = 6$ to $n = 2$

2008

63 The ground state energy of hydrogen atom is -13.6 eV. When its electron is in the first excited state, its excitation energy is **[CBSE AIPMT]**
(a) 3.4 eV (b) 6.8 eV (c) 10.2 eV (d) zero

64 White light is passed through a dilute solution of potassium permanganate. The spectrum produced by the emergent light is **[AFMC]**
(a) band emission spectrum
(b) line emission spectrum
(c) band absorption spectrum
(d) line absorption spectrum

65 If λ_1 and λ_2 are the wavelengths of the first members of the Lyman and Paschen series respectively, then $\lambda_1 : \lambda_2$ is **[AFMC]**
(a) 1 : 3 (b) 1 : 30
(c) 7 : 50 (d) 7 : 108

66 If the series limit wavelength of the Lyman series for hydrogen atom is 912 Å, then the series limit wavelength for the Balmer series for the hydrogen atom is **[BHU]**
(a) 912 Å (b) 912×2 Å (c) 912×4 Å (d) $\frac{912}{2}$ Å

67 Ionisation potential of hydrogen atom is 13.6eV. Hydrogen atoms in the ground state are excited by monochromatic radiation of photon energy is 12.1 eV. According to Bohr's theory, the spectral lines emitted by hydrogen will be **[Haryana PMT]**
(a) two (b) three
(c) four (d) one

68 The angular momentum (L) of an electron moving in a stable orbit around nucleus is **[J&K CET]**
(a) half integral multiple of $\frac{h}{2\pi}$
(b) integral multiple of h
(c) integral multiple of $\frac{h}{2\pi}$
(d) half integral multiple of h

69 Solar spectrum is an example for **[KCET]**
(a) line emission spectrum
(b) continuous emission spectrum
(c) band absorption spectrum
(d) line absorption spectrum

70 The ratio of minimum wavelengths of Lyman and Balmer series will be **[KCET]**
(a) 1.25 (b) 0.25 (c) 5 (d) 10

71 The wavelength of the first spectral line in the Balmer series of hydrogen atom is 6561Å. The wavelength of the second spectral line in the Balmer series of single ionised helium atom is **[IIT-JEE]**
(a) 1215Å (b) 1640Å (c) 2430Å (d) 4687Å

72 What will be the angular momentum in 4th orbit, if L is the angular momentum of the electron in the 2nd orbit of hydrogen atom? [Guj CET]

(a) $2L$ (b) $\frac{3}{2}L$ (c) $\frac{2}{3}L$ (d) $\frac{L}{2}$

73 The diagram shows the energy levels for an electron in a certain atom. Which transition shown represents the emission of a photon with the most energy? [JCECE]

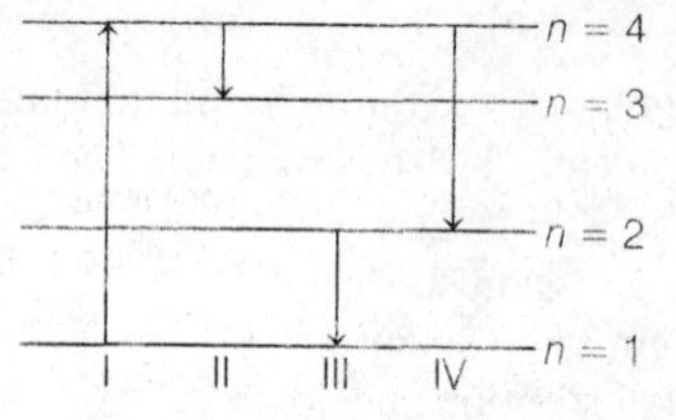

(a) III (b) IV (c) I (d) II

2007

74 The total energy of electron in the ground state of hydrogen atom is − 13.6 eV. The kinetic energy of an electron in the first excited state is [CBSE AIPMT]

(a) 3.4 eV (b) 6.8 eV
(c) 13.6 eV (d) 1.7 eV

75 The shortest wavelength in hydrogen spectrum of Lyman series, when $R_H = 109678 \text{cm}^{-1}$ is [Kerala PET]

(a) 1002.7 Å (b) 1215.67 Å
(c) 1127.30 Å (d) 911.7 Å
(e) 1234.7 Å

76 If the energy of hydrogen atom in nth orbit is E_n, then energy in the nth orbit of a singly ionised helium atom will be [AFMC]

(a) $4E_n$ (b) $E_n / 4$ (c) $2E_n$ (d) $E_n / 2$

77 In which of the following systems will the radius of the first orbit ($n = 1$) be minimum? [AFMC]

(a) Deuterium atom
(b) Hydrogen atom
(c) Doubly ionised lithium
(d) Singly ionised helium

78 The wavelength of K_α-line in copper is 1.54 Å. The ionisation energy of K-electron in copper in joule is [UP CPMT]

(a) 11.2×10^{-17} (b) 12.9×10^{-16}
(c) 1.7×10^{-15} (d) 10×10^{-16}

79 The Bohr model of atoms [Manipal]

(a) assumes that the angular momentum of electrons is quantised
(b) uses Einstein's photoelectric equation
(c) predicts continuous emission spectra for atoms
(d) predicts the same emission spectra for all types of atoms

80 The ionisation energy of Li^{2+} is equal to [KCET]

(a) $9hcR$ (b) $6hcR$ (c) $2hcR$ (d) hcR

81 The state of the triply ionised beryllium (Be^{3+}) has the same orbital radius as that of the ground state of hydrogen is [WB JEE]

(a) 4 (b) 1 (c) 2 (d) 3

82 The ratio of areas between the electron orbits for the first excited state to the ground state for the hydrogen atom is [AMU]

(a) 2 : 1 (b) 4 : 1
(c) 8 : 1 (d) 16 : 1

83 The ionisation energy of 10 times ionised sodium atom is [RPMT]

(a) $\frac{13.6}{11}$ eV (b) $\frac{13.6}{(11)^2}$ eV
(c) $13.6 \times (11)^2$ eV (d) 13.6 eV

84 An electron with kinetic energy 5 eV is incident on an H-atom in its ground state. The collision [RPMT]

(a) must be elastic
(b) may be partially elastic
(c) may be completely elastic
(d) may be completely inelastic

85 The wavelength of the first spectral line of sodium 5896 Å. The first excitation potential of sodium atom will be (Planck's constant, $h = 6.63 \times 10^{-34}$ J-s) [BCECE]

(a) 4.2 V (b) 3.5 V
(c) 2.1 V (d) None of these

86 At the time of total solar eclipse, the spectrum of solar radiation will have [MP PMT]

(a) a large number of dark Fraunhoffer lines
(b) a smaller number of dark Fraunhoffer lines
(c) no lines at all
(d) all Fraunhoffer lines changed into bright coloured lines

87 Mercury vapour lamp gives [J&K CET]

(a) continuous spectrum (b) line spectrum
(c) band spectrum (d) absorption spectrum

88 The first member of the Balmer's series of the hydrogen has a wavelength λ, the wavelength of the second member of its series is [J&K CET]

(a) $\frac{27}{20}\lambda$ (b) $\frac{20}{27}\lambda$
(c) $\frac{27}{10}\lambda$ (d) None of these

89 The shortest wavelength in Lyman series is 91.2 nm. The longest wavelength of the series is [J&K CET]

(a) 121.6 nm (b) 182.4 nm
(c) 243.4 nm (d) 364.8 nm

90 The values $+\frac{1}{2}$ and $-\frac{1}{2}$ of spin quantum number show [RPMT]

(a) rotation of electron clockwise and anti-clockwise directions, respectively
(b) rotation of electron anti-clockwise and clockwise directions, respectively
(c) rotation in any direction according to convention
(d) None of the above

91 As the quantum number increases, the difference of energy between consecutive energy levels **[Guj CET]**
(a) decreases
(b) increases
(c) first decreases and then increases
(d) remains the same

92 Emission of light stops as the incident light is cut-off in **[Guj CET]**
(a) phosphorescence (b) fluorescence
(c) luminescence (d) efflorescence

2006

93 In terms of Rydberg constant R, the waves number of the first Balmer line is **[AMU]**
(a) R (b) $3R$ (c) $\frac{5R}{36}$ (d) $\frac{8R}{9}$

2005

94 Energy levels A, B and C of a certain atom correspond to increasing values of energy, i.e. $E_A < E_B < E_C$. If λ_1, λ_2 and λ_3 are wavelengths of radiations corresponding to transitions C to B, B to A and C to A respectively, which of the following relations is correct? **[CBSE AIPMT]**
(a) $\lambda_3 = \lambda_1 + \lambda_2$ (b) $\lambda_3 = \frac{\lambda_1 \lambda_2}{\lambda_1 + \lambda_2}$
(c) $\lambda_1 + \lambda_2 + \lambda_3 = 0$ (d) $\lambda_3^2 = \lambda_1^2 + \lambda_2^2$

95 The ground state energy of hydrogen atom is – 13.6 eV. What is the potential energy of the electron in this state? **[AIIMS]**
(a) 0 eV (b) – 27.2 eV
(c) 1 eV (d) 2 eV

96 Calculate the highest frequency of the emitted photon in the Paschen series of spectral lines of the hydrogen atom. **[AMU (Engg.)]**
(a) 3.7×10^{14} Hz
(b) 9.1×10^{15} Hz
(c) 10.23×10^{14} Hz
(d) 29.7×10^{15} Hz

97 The electron in a hydrogen atom makes a transition from $n = n_1$ to $n = n_2$ state. The time period of the electron in the initial state (n_1) is eight times that in the final state (n_2). The possible values of n_1 and n_2 are **[KCET]**
(a) $n_1 = 8, n_2 = 1$
(b) $n_1 = 4, n_2 = 2$
(c) $n_1 = 2, n_2 = 4$
(d) $n_1 = 1, n_2 = 8$

98 Bohr's atom model assumes **[KCET]**
(a) the nucleus is of infinite mass and is at rest
(b) electrons in a quantised orbit will not radiate energy
(c) mass of electron remains constant
(d) All the above conditions

Answers

1 (b)	2 (c)	3 (a)	4 (b)	5 (c)	6 (c)	7 (b)	8 (a)	9 (d)	10 (c)
11 (d)	12 (b)	13 (a)	14 (a)	15 (c)	16 (a)	17 (d)	18 (a)	19 (d)	20 (d)
21 (d)	22 (d)	23 (c)	24 (c)	25 (a)	26 (b)	27 (c)	28 (a)	29 (d)	30 (d)
31 (b)	32 (d)	33 (c)	34 (d)	35 (b)	36 (b)	37 (d)	38 (b)	39 (c)	40 (b)
41 (a)	42 (d)	43 (b)	44 (b)	45 (c)	46 (b)	47 (a)	48 (c)	49 (c)	50 (d)
51 (d)	52 (b)	53 (d)	54 (d)	55 (b)	56 (d)	57 (b)	58 (a)	59 (a)	60 (a)
61 (c)	62 (c)	63 (c)	64 (c)	65 (d)	66 (c)	67 (b)	68 (c)	69 (d)	70 (b)
71 (a)	72 (a)	73 (a)	74 (a)	75 (d)	76 (a)	77 (c)	78 (c)	79 (a)	80 (a)
81 (c)	82 (d)	83 (c)	84 (a)	85 (c)	86 (d)	87 (b)	88 (b)	89 (a)	90 (a)
91 (a)	92 (b)	93 (c)	94 (b)	95 (b)	96 (a)	97 (b)	98 (b)		

Explanations

1 *(b)* According to Bohr's model, the kinetic energy of electron in term of Rydberg constant R is given by

$$\text{KE} = \frac{Rhc}{n^2} \quad \ldots \text{(i)}$$

where, h = Planck's constant, c = speed of light and n = principal quantum number.

Similarly, potential energy is given by

$$\text{PE} = -\frac{2Rhc}{n^2} \quad \ldots \text{(ii)}$$

$\therefore$ Total energy, E = PE + KE

$$= -\frac{Rhc}{n^2}$$

[from Eqs. (i) and (ii)]

$\Rightarrow$ KE = – E and PE = 2E

Given, E = – 3.4 eV

$\therefore$ KE = – (–3.4) = 3.4 eV

and PE = 2 (– 3.4) = – 6.8 eV

2 *(c)* Given, radius of first orbit for electron, $r_1 = 0.51$ Å,

Ground state energy of electron, $E_1 = -13.6$ eV,

Mass of electron = m_e

Mass of muon, $m_\mu = 207 m_e$

and Mass of nucleus, $M = 1836 m_e$

When electron in hydrogen atom is replaced by muon, the reduced mass of muon is

$$m_\mu' = \frac{m_\mu M}{m_\mu + M} \quad \ldots \text{(i)}$$

Substituting the given values in Eq. (i), we get

$$m_\mu' = \frac{207 m_e \times 1836 m_e}{207 m_e + 1836 m_e} \approx 186\, m_e \quad \ldots \text{(ii)}$$

The radius of first orbit in hydrogen atom for electron is given by

$$r_1 = \frac{h^2\varepsilon_0}{\pi m_e e^2} \quad \text{...(iii)}$$

The radius of first orbit for muon is given by

$$r_1' = \frac{h^2\varepsilon_0}{\pi m_\mu' e^2}$$

[$\because$ charge of μ = charge of e^-]

$$= \frac{h^2\varepsilon_0}{\pi \times 186 m_e e^2} \quad \text{[from Eq. (ii)]}$$

$$= \left(\frac{h^2\varepsilon_0}{\pi m_e e^2}\right)\frac{1}{186} = \frac{r_1}{186}$$

[from Eq. (iii)]

$$= \frac{0.51}{186}\text{Å} \quad [\because r_1 = 0.51\text{Å}]$$

$$= 2.74 \times 10^{-13}\text{ m}$$

[$\because$ 1 Å $= 10^{-10}$ m]

The total energy of electron is given by

$$E_n = \frac{-mZ^2e^4}{8\varepsilon_0^2h^2}\left(\frac{1}{n^2}\right)$$

$$\Rightarrow \quad E_n \propto m$$

For electron in first orbit of hydrogen atom,

$$E_1 = km_e \quad \text{...(iv)}$$

where, $k = \frac{e^4}{8\varepsilon_0^2h^2}$ = constant.

For muon in first orbit

$$E_1' = km_\mu'$$
$$= k \times 186m_e \quad \text{[from Eq. (i)]}$$
$$= 186km_e$$
$$= 186E_1 \quad \text{[from Eq. (iv)]}$$
$$= 186(-13.6)\text{ eV(given)}$$
$$= -2529.6\text{ eV} = -2.5\text{ keV}$$

$\therefore$ The values are closest to that of option (c).

3 (a) Given, total energy given to e^- in 4th orbit, $E = 15$ eV

Energy of nth orbit of H-atom,

$$E' = -\frac{13.6}{n^2}$$

So, energy of 4th orbit of H-atom,

$$E' = \frac{-13.6}{4^2} = -0.85\text{ eV}$$

$\therefore$ Ionisation energy of 4th orbit $= -E'$

$$= (-0.85\text{ eV})$$
$$= 0.85\text{ eV}$$

$\therefore$ Final energy of electron, when it comes out of H-atom,

E = Total energy given to electron–Ionsiation energy of 4th orbit.

$$= 15 - 0.85 = 14.15\text{ eV}$$

4 (b) kinetic energy of an electron in a Bohr orbit of a hydrogen atom is given as

$$(\text{KE})_n = \frac{Rhc}{n^2} \quad \text{...(i)}$$

Total energy of an electron in a Bohr orbit of a hydrogen atom is given as

$$(\text{TE})_n = \frac{-Rhc}{n^2} \quad \text{...(ii)}$$

Dividing Eq. (i) by Eq. (ii), we get

$$\frac{(\text{KE})_n}{(\text{TE})_n} = \frac{(Rhc/n^2)}{(-Rhc/n^2)}$$

So, $\quad (\text{KE})_n : (\text{TE})_n = 1 : -1$

5 (c) Wavelength of spectral lines are given by

$$\frac{1}{\lambda} = Z^2R\left(\frac{1}{n_1^2} - \frac{1}{n_2^2}\right)$$

For last line of Balmer series, $n_1 = 2$ and $n_2 = \infty$

$$\Rightarrow \quad \frac{1}{\lambda_B} = Z^2R\left(\frac{1}{2^2} - \frac{1}{\infty^2}\right) = \frac{R}{4}$$

Similarly, for last line of Lyman series, $n_1 = 1$ and $n_2 = \infty$

$$\Rightarrow \quad \frac{1}{\lambda_L} = Z^2R\left(\frac{1}{1^2} - \frac{1}{\infty^2}\right) = R$$

$$\Rightarrow \quad \frac{\lambda_L}{\lambda_B} = \frac{1}{4} \Rightarrow \frac{\lambda_B}{\lambda_L} = 4$$

6 (c) Excess energy of electron appears as photon.

Given, $n_1 = 2$ and $n_2 = 3$

From Rydberg's formula,

$$\frac{1}{\lambda} = R\left(\frac{1}{n_2^2} - \frac{1}{n_1^2}\right) = R\left(\frac{1}{2^2} - \frac{1}{3^2}\right) = \frac{5R}{36}$$

and $n_1 = 3$ and $n_2 = 4$

$$\Rightarrow \quad \frac{1}{\lambda'} = R\left(\frac{1}{3^2} - \frac{1}{4^2}\right) = \frac{7R}{144}$$

$$\Rightarrow \quad \frac{1}{\lambda}\Big/\frac{1}{\lambda'} = \frac{5R}{36}\Big/\frac{7R}{144}$$

$$\Rightarrow \quad \frac{\lambda'}{\lambda} = \frac{20}{7}$$

$$\Rightarrow \quad \lambda' = \frac{20}{7}\lambda$$

7 (b) Energy of electron in the 3rd orbit of He,

$$E_3 = -13.6 \times \frac{Z^2}{n^2}\text{ eV}$$

$$= -13.6 \times \frac{4}{9} \times 1.6 \times 10^{-19}\text{ J (given)}$$

From Bohr's model,

$$E_3 = -\text{KE}_3 = -\frac{1}{2}m_e v^2$$

$$= \frac{1}{2} \times 9.1 \times 10^{-31} \times v^2$$

$$= -13.6 \times \frac{4}{9} \times 16 \times 10^{-19}$$

($\because m_e = 9.1 \times 10^{-31}$ kg)

$$\Rightarrow \quad v^2 = \frac{13.6 \times 16 \times 4 \times 2 \times 10^{-11}}{9 \times 91}$$

$$v = 1.46 \times 10^6\text{ ms}^{-1}$$

8 (a) Given, $\lambda = 975\text{Å} = 975 \times 10^{-10}$ m

Energy provided to the ground state electron

$$= \frac{hc}{\lambda} = \frac{6.6 \times 10^{-34} \times 3 \times 10^8}{975 \times 10^{-10}}$$

($\because c = 3 \times 10^8$ ms^{-1} and $h = 6.6 \times 10^{-34}$ Js-)

$$= \frac{6.6 \times 3}{975} \times 10^{-16}$$

$$= 0.020 \times 10^{-16} = 2 \times 10^{-18}\text{ J}$$

$$= \frac{20 \times 10^{-19}}{1.6 \times 10^{-19}}\text{ eV} = \frac{20}{1.6} = 12.5\text{ eV}$$

It means the electron jumps to $n = 3$ from $n = 1$.

The number of possible spectral lines from $n = 3$ to $n = 1$ is 3.

i.e. $\quad (n = 3) \longrightarrow (n = 1)$

$\quad (n = 3) \longrightarrow (n = 2)$

and $\quad (n = 2) \longrightarrow (n = 1)$

9 (d) When an electron jumps from orbit n_i to orbit n_f ($n_i > n_f$), the frequency of emitted photon is given by

$$\nu = cR\left(\frac{1}{n_f^2} - \frac{1}{n_i^2}\right) \Rightarrow \nu = cR\left(\frac{1}{2^2} - \frac{1}{3^2}\right)$$

(given)

$$\nu = cR\left(\frac{5}{36}\right) \quad \Rightarrow \quad \nu = \frac{5Rc}{36}$$

10 (c) The energy of the photon

$$= Rhc\left(\frac{1}{1^2} - \frac{1}{n^2}\right)$$

$$= 13.6\left(\frac{1}{1} - \frac{1}{4}\right) \quad (\because n = 2)$$

$$= 13.6\left(\frac{4-1}{4}\right)$$

$$= 13.6 \times \frac{3}{4} = \frac{40.8}{4} = 10.2\text{ eV}$$

11 (d) The energy of ejected photon,

$$E = Rhc\left(\frac{1}{n_1^2} - \frac{1}{n_2^2}\right)$$

where, transition takes place from n_1 to n_2.

$$= 13.6\left(\frac{1}{2^2} - \frac{1}{3^2}\right)$$

$$= 13.6 \times \frac{5}{36} = 1.9\text{ eV}$$

12 (b) Outside a nucleus, neutron is unstable.

13 (a) The wavelength in Balmer series is given by

$$\frac{1}{\lambda}=R\left(\frac{1}{2^2}-\frac{1}{n^2}\right)$$

where, $n = 3, 4, 5 \ldots \infty$

$$\Rightarrow \frac{1}{\lambda_{max}}=R\left(\frac{1}{2^2}-\frac{1}{3^2}\right)$$

$$\lambda_{max}=\frac{36}{5R}=\frac{36}{5\times1.097\times10^7}=6563\,\text{Å}$$

and $\frac{1}{\lambda_{min}}=R\left(\frac{1}{2^2}-\frac{1}{\infty^2}\right)$

$$\lambda_{min}=\frac{4}{R}=\frac{4}{1.097\times10^7}=3646\,\text{Å}$$

The wavelength 6563 Å and 3646 Å lies in visible region.
Therefore, Balmer series lies in visible region.

14 (a) Wavelength of the Balmer series is given by

$$\frac{1}{\lambda}=R\left(\frac{1}{n_1^2}-\frac{1}{n_2^2}\right)$$

$$\Rightarrow \frac{v}{c}=R\left(\frac{1}{n_1^2}-\frac{1}{n_2^2}\right) \quad (\because c=v\lambda)$$

$$\Rightarrow v=cR\left(\frac{1}{n_1^2}-\frac{1}{n_2^2}\right)$$

For second line of Balmer series, $n_1 = 2, n_2 = 4$

$$\therefore v=3\times10^8\times10967800\left(\frac{1}{2^2}-\frac{1}{4^2}\right)$$

$$=6.16\times10^{14}\text{ Hz}$$

15 (c) Angular momentum of electron in nth orbit is given by $mvr_n=\frac{nh}{2\pi}$.

In the lowest energy level, $n = 1$, then

$$mvr_1=1\left(\frac{h}{2\pi}\right)=\frac{h}{2\pi}$$

16 (a) Band spectrum is also called as molecular spectrum. They are produced by molecules radiating their rotational or vibrational energies or both simultaneously.

17 (d) Infrared radiation found in Paschen, Brackett and Pfund series and it is obtained when electron transition high energy level to minimum third level.

18 (a) Given, $E_5-E_1=\frac{hc}{\lambda}$ and

$$\frac{Rhc}{25}-Rhc=\frac{hc}{\lambda}$$

$$\frac{24}{25}R=\frac{1}{\lambda}$$

But, $p=\frac{h}{\lambda}\Rightarrow v=\frac{h}{m\lambda}=\frac{24\,hR}{25\,m}$

19 (d) Here, for wavelength λ_1, $n_1 = 4$ and $n_2 = 3$ and for wavelength λ_2, $n_1 = 3$ and $n_2 = 2$

We know that, $\frac{hc}{\lambda}=-13.6\left(\frac{1}{n_2^2}-\frac{1}{n_1^2}\right)$

So, for wavelength λ_1

$$\Rightarrow \frac{hc}{\lambda_1}=-13.6\left[\frac{1}{(4)^2}-\frac{1}{(3)^2}\right]$$

$$\Rightarrow \frac{hc}{\lambda_1}=13.6\left(\frac{7}{144}\right) \quad \ldots(i)$$

Similarly, for wavelength λ_2

$$\Rightarrow \frac{hc}{\lambda_2}=-13.6\left[\frac{1}{(3)^2}-\frac{1}{(2)^2}\right]$$

$$\Rightarrow \frac{hc}{\lambda_2}=13.6\left(\frac{5}{36}\right) \quad \ldots(ii)$$

Hence, from Eqs. (i) and (ii), we get

$$\frac{\lambda_1}{\lambda_2}=\frac{20}{7}\Rightarrow \lambda_1:\lambda_2=20:7$$

20 (d) Radius of orbit of electron in nth excited state of hydrogen,

$$r=\frac{\varepsilon_0h^2n^2}{\pi mZe^2}\Rightarrow r\propto\frac{n^2}{Z} \quad \ldots(i)$$

$$\therefore \frac{r_1}{r_2}=\frac{n_1^2}{n_2^2}\times\frac{Z_2}{Z_1}$$

So, $n_2^2=n_1^2\times\frac{Z_2}{Z_1} \quad (\because r_1=r_2)$

Here, $n_1 = 1$ (ground state of hydrogen)
$Z_1 = 1$ (atomic number of hydrogen)
$Z_2 = 4$ (atomic number of beryllium)

$$\therefore n_2^2=(1)^2\times\frac{4}{1}\text{ or } n_2^2=4\text{ or } n_2=2$$

So, the atom is triply ionised beryllium (Be^{3+}).

21 (d) According to Bohr's theory, the wavelength of the radiation emitted from hydrogen atom is given by

$$\frac{1}{\lambda}=R\left[\frac{1}{n_1^2}-\frac{1}{n_2^2}\right]$$

Then, λ is minimum for minimum value of n_1 and n_2, hence $n = 2$ to $n = 1$.

22 (d) For hydrogen like atom the radius of nth orbit, $r_n^2=\frac{n^2}{Z}a_0$

Given, $a_0=0.51\times10^{-10}$ m,

$$r_n^2=\frac{0.51\times10^{-10}}{4}\text{ m}$$

In the ground state, $n = 1$

$$\therefore \frac{0.51\times10^{-10}}{4}=\frac{1^2}{Z}\times0.51\times10^{-10}$$

$$\therefore Z=4$$

23 (c) Time period of electron,

$$T=\frac{2\pi r}{v}=\frac{\frac{2\pi\times\varepsilon_0n^2h^2}{\pi me^2}}{\frac{e^2}{2\varepsilon_0nh}}=\frac{4\varepsilon_0^2n^3h^3}{me^4}$$

$$\left(\because r=\frac{\varepsilon_0n^2h^2}{\pi me^2}\text{ and } v=\frac{e^2}{2\varepsilon_0nh}\right)$$

Now current,

$$i=\frac{e}{T}=\frac{e}{\frac{4\varepsilon_0^2n^3h^3}{me^4}}=\frac{me^5}{4\varepsilon_0^2n^3h^3}$$

$$\left(\frac{m}{4\varepsilon_0^2n^3h^3}=\text{constant for a particular atom}\right)$$

Thus, $i\propto n^{-3}$

24 (c) Lyman series of H-atom, we can write

$$\frac{hc}{\lambda}=Rhc\left(\frac{1}{1^2}-\frac{1}{2^2}\right)$$

where, symbols have their usual meaning and for second line of Balmer series of H-like ion

$$\frac{hc}{\lambda}=Z^2Rhc\left(\frac{1}{2^2}-\frac{1}{4^2}\right).$$

Therefore $\left(\frac{1}{1^2}-\frac{1}{2^2}\right)=Z^2\left(\frac{1}{4}-\frac{1}{16}\right)$

$$\left(1-\frac{1}{4}\right)=Z^2\left(\frac{1}{4}-\frac{1}{16}\right)$$

$$\Rightarrow Z=2.19\simeq2$$

25 (a) Energy E of an atom with principal quantum number n is given by

$$E=\frac{-13.6}{n^2}Z^2$$

For first excited state $n = 2$ and for He^+, $Z = 2$

$$\Rightarrow E=\frac{-13.6\times(2)^2}{(2)^2}=-13.6\text{ eV}$$

26 (b) We know that, $\frac{1}{\lambda}=R\left(\frac{1}{n_1^2}-\frac{1}{n_2^2}\right)$

$$\Rightarrow \frac{1}{\lambda}=R\left(\frac{1}{1_1^2}-\frac{1}{2^2}\right)=\frac{3R}{4}$$

$$\Rightarrow \lambda=\frac{4}{3R}\text{ cm}$$

27 (c) Change in the angular momentum,

$$\Delta L=L_2-L_1=\frac{n_2h}{2\pi}-\frac{n_1h}{2\pi}$$

$$\Delta L=\frac{h}{2\pi}(n_2-n_1)=\frac{6.6\times10^{-34}}{2\times3.14}(5-4)$$

$$=1.05\times10^{-34}\text{ J-s}$$

28 (a) Wavelength is given by

$$\frac{1}{\lambda}=R\left(\frac{1}{n_1^2}-\frac{1}{n_2^2}\right)$$

$$\Rightarrow \quad \frac{1}{\lambda}=R\left[\frac{1}{(2)^2}-\frac{1}{(4)^2}\right]$$

$$\Rightarrow \quad \frac{1}{\lambda}=R\left(\frac{1}{4}-\frac{1}{16}\right)$$

$$\Rightarrow \quad \frac{1}{\lambda}=R\left(\frac{4-1}{16}\right)$$

$$\Rightarrow \quad \frac{1}{\lambda}=\frac{3R}{16} \Rightarrow \lambda=\frac{16}{3R}$$

29 (d) The ground state of hydrogen ($n=1$) is represented by K, the first excited state ($n=2$) is represented by L, the second excited state ($n=3$) is represent by M. So, the energy transferred by the second electron can be given by

$$E=-13.6\left(\frac{1}{n_1^2}-\frac{1}{n_2^2}\right)$$

$$=-13.6\left(\frac{1}{3^2}-\frac{1}{\infty^2}\right)$$

$$\simeq -1.51 \text{ eV}$$

30 (d) Electron angular momentum (mvr) about the nucleus is an integer multiple of $\frac{h}{2\pi}$, where h is Planck's constant.

Thus, angular momentum,

$$I\omega = mvr = \frac{nh}{2\pi}$$

Hence, $\quad r \propto n$

31 (b) Bohr's quantisation condition of angular momentum,

i.e. $L=n\frac{h}{2\pi}$ led to the quantisation of energy.

32 (d) We know that, the wavelength of emitted radiation is given by

$$\frac{1}{\lambda}=R\left(\frac{1}{n_1^2}-\frac{1}{n_2^2}\right)=R\times K$$

where, $K=\frac{1}{n_1^2}-\frac{1}{n_2^2}$

For λ_{max}, K should be minimum which corresponds to $n_1=3$, $n_2=4$. So, transition takes place between $n=4$ and $n=3$ states.

33 (c) We know that, frequency,

$$\nu=\frac{c}{\lambda}=c\cdot R\left(\frac{1}{n_1^2}-\frac{1}{n_2^2}\right)$$

$$=3\times10^8\times10^7\left(\frac{1}{2^2}-\frac{1}{4^2}\right)$$

$$=\frac{9}{16}\times10^{15}\text{ Hz}$$

34 (d) The transition mark, A represents series limit of Lyman series, B represents third member of Balmer series and C represents second member of Paschen series.

35 (b) According to Bohr's theory, the wavelength of the radiation

$$\frac{1}{\lambda}=Z^2R\left(\frac{1}{n_1^2}-\frac{1}{n_2^2}\right)$$

$$\Rightarrow \quad \frac{\nu}{c}=Z^2R\left(\frac{1}{n_1^2}-\frac{1}{n_2^2}\right)$$

$$\nu=cZ^2R\left(\frac{1}{n_1^2}-\frac{1}{n_2^2}\right)$$

Case I

$$\Rightarrow \quad 2.7\times10^{15}=cZ^2R\left(\frac{1}{1^2}-\frac{1}{2^2}\right)$$

$$\Rightarrow cZ^2R=\frac{4}{3}\times2.7\times10^{15}$$

Case II $\nu=cZ^2R\left(\frac{1}{1^2}-\frac{1}{3^2}\right)$

$$\Rightarrow \quad \nu=\frac{32}{27}\times2.7\times10^{15}$$

$$=3.2\times10^{15}\text{ Hz}$$

36 (b) The minimum energy to ionise an atom is the energy required to excite an electron in the atom from its ground state corresponding to $n=1$, to its ionisation level corresponding to $n=\infty$. If the atom is given an amount of energy equal to the ionisation energy, the electron is just able to become a free electron and the atom is about to be ionised.

When this occurs, one outermost electron from the atom is just to be removed from the atom. Much higher energy is necessary to free an innermost electron from the atom because this will occur only after the outermost electrons are all removed.

37 (d) As, $\frac{1}{\lambda}=RZ^2\left(\frac{1}{1^2}-\frac{1}{2^2}\right)$

$$\frac{1}{\lambda}\propto Z^2$$

$$\Rightarrow \quad \lambda\propto\frac{1}{Z^2}$$

For di-ionised lithium, the value of Z is maximum.

Hence, λ is minimum.

38 (b) Time period for orbital motion of electron,

$$T=\frac{4\varepsilon_0^2n^3h^3}{mZ^2e^4}$$

$$\Rightarrow \quad T\propto n^3$$

$$\Rightarrow \quad \frac{1}{\text{Frequency }(f)}\propto n^3$$

$$\Rightarrow \quad f\propto n^{-3}$$

39 (c) The hydrogen atom before the transition was at rest. Therefore, from conservation of momentum

So, $\quad p_{\text{H-atom}}=p_{\text{photon}}=\frac{E_{\text{radiated}}}{c}$

$$=\frac{13.6\left(\frac{1}{n_1^2}-\frac{1}{n_2^2}\right)\text{eV}}{c}$$

$$\Rightarrow 1.6\times10^{-27}\times\nu$$

$$=\frac{13.6\left(\frac{1}{1^2}-\frac{1}{5^2}\right)\times1.6\times10^{-19}}{3\times10^8}$$

$$\therefore \quad \nu=4.352\text{ ms}^{-1}\simeq4\text{ ms}^{-1}$$

40 (b) For transition from $4E$ to E,

$$(4E-E)=\frac{hc}{\lambda_1}$$

$$\Rightarrow \quad \lambda_1=\frac{hc}{3E} \quad \ldots(\text{i})$$

For transition from $\frac{7}{3}E$ to E,

$$\left(\frac{7}{3}E-E\right)=\frac{hc}{\lambda_2}$$

$$\Rightarrow \quad \lambda_2=\frac{3hc}{4E} \quad \ldots(\text{ii})$$

From Eqs. (i) and (ii), we get

$$\frac{\lambda_1}{\lambda_2}=\frac{4}{9}$$

41 (a) We know that, frequency,

$$\nu=Rc\left(\frac{1}{n_1^2}-\frac{1}{n_2^2}\right) \quad \ldots(\text{i})$$

ν_1 is frequency of the series limit of Lyman series, hence put $n_1=1$ and $n_2=\infty$ in Eq. (i), this gives

$$\nu_1=Rc\left(1-\frac{1}{\infty}\right)=Rc$$

Similarly, for first line of Lyman series, put $n_1=1$ and $n_2=2$ in Eq. (i), this gives

$$\nu_2=Rc\left(1-\frac{1}{4}\right)=\frac{3}{4}Rc$$

Similarly, for v_3, put $n_1 = 2$ and $n_2 = \infty$ in Eq. (i), this gives

$$v_3 = Rc\left(\frac{1}{4} - \frac{1}{\infty}\right) = \frac{Rc}{4}$$

$\Rightarrow v_1 - v_2 = v_3$

42 *(d)* Number of spectral lines obtained due to transition of electrons from nth orbit to lower orbit is given by

$$N = \frac{n(n-1)}{2}$$

Case I $6 = \dfrac{n_1(n_1-1)}{2}$

$\Rightarrow n_1^2 - n_1 - 12 = 0$

$\Rightarrow (n_1 - 4)(n_1 + 3) = 0 \Rightarrow n_1 = 4$

Because n_1 cannot be negative, i.e. -3.

Case II $3 = \dfrac{n_2(n_2-1)}{2}$

$\Rightarrow n_2^2 - n_2 - 6 = 0$

$\Rightarrow (n_2 + 2)(n_2 - 3) = 0$

$n_2 = 3$

Because n_2 cannot be negative, i.e. -2.

Velocity of electron in hydrogen atom in nth orbit,

$$v_n \propto \frac{1}{n} \Rightarrow \frac{v_n}{v_n'} = \frac{n_2}{n_1} \Rightarrow \frac{v_6}{v_3} = \frac{3}{4}$$

43 *(b)* Since, spectrum of an oil flame consists of continuously varying wavelength in a definite wavelength range, it is an example for continuous emission spectrum.

44 *(b)* Velocity of electron in nth shell can be related as

$$v_n \propto \frac{1}{n}$$

So, $\dfrac{v_2}{v_1} = \dfrac{1}{2} \Rightarrow v_2 = \dfrac{v_1}{2}$

$$\Rightarrow \Delta v = v_1 - v_2 = \frac{v_1}{2}$$

Hence, percentage change in the speed of electron = 50

45 *(c)* The kinetic energy is equal to half of magnitude of potential energy.

So, $\text{KE} = \dfrac{1}{2}\left|\dfrac{Ke^2}{r}\right| = \dfrac{Ke^2}{2r}$

46 *(b)* Since, we know $\text{KE} = -E_0$

$= -(-13.6\text{ eV}) = 13.6\text{eV}$

The kinetic energy of the electron in this state is 13.6 eV.

47 *(a)* Radius of Bohr's orbit, $r \propto n^2$

$$\Rightarrow \frac{r_1}{r_2} = \left(\frac{n_1}{n_2}\right)^2$$

$$\Rightarrow \frac{5.29\times 10^{-11}}{r_2} = \left(\frac{1}{2}\right)^2$$

$\Rightarrow r_2 = 5.29\times 10^{-11} \times 4$

$= 21.16\times 10^{-11}$ m

48 *(c)* We can write the expression for the circular motion of electron around the nucleus

$$F_{\text{electrostatic}} = F_{\text{centripetal}}$$

$$\Rightarrow \frac{1}{4\pi\varepsilon_0}\frac{e^2}{a_0^2} = \frac{mv^2}{a_0}$$

$$\Rightarrow v^2 = \frac{1}{4\pi\varepsilon_0}\frac{e^2}{ma_0}$$

$$\Rightarrow v = \frac{e}{\sqrt{4\pi\varepsilon_0 a_0 m}}$$

49 *(c)* Energy of photon can be given by

$$E = Rhc\left(1 - \frac{1}{n^2}\right)$$

$$\Rightarrow \frac{hc}{\lambda} = Rch\left(1 - \frac{1}{n^2}\right)$$

$$\Rightarrow \frac{1}{\lambda} = R\left(1 - \frac{1}{n^2}\right)$$

$$\Rightarrow \frac{1}{\lambda R} = 1 - \frac{1}{n^2} \Rightarrow \frac{1}{n^2} = 1 - \frac{1}{\lambda R}$$

$$\Rightarrow \frac{1}{n^2} = \frac{(\lambda R - 1)}{\lambda R} \Rightarrow n = \sqrt{\frac{\lambda R}{(\lambda R - 1)}}$$

50 *(d)* Energy of the ionised He^{2+},

$E = (E_0)Z^2 = (13.6)(4) = 54.4$ eV

51 *(d)* **Assertion** It is not essential that all the lines available in the emission spectrum will also be available in the absorption spectrum.

Reason The spectrum of hydrogen atom may not be absorption spectrum.

52 *(b)* If all the elements having $n > 4$ are removed the number of elements that will be present in the periodic table are calculated as

(i) $n = 1$, represents K shell and the number of elements having K shell $= 2$ [in accordance with $2n^2$]

(ii) $n = 2$, represents L shell and the number of elements having L shell $= 8$

(iii) $n = 3$, represents M shell and the number of elements having M shell $= 18$

(iv) $n = 4$, represents N shell and the number of elements having N shell $= 32$

So, the total number of elements having $n < 5$ are

$2 + 8 + 18 + 32 = 60$

53 *(d)* According to the question,

$(\lambda_{\text{shortest}})$ Brackett $= (\lambda_{\text{shortest}})$ Balmer

$$\Rightarrow \frac{1}{(\lambda_{\text{shortest}})} = \frac{1}{(\lambda_{\text{shortest}})}$$

$$\Rightarrow Z^2R\left(\frac{1}{4^2}\right) = R\left(\frac{1}{4}\right)$$

$$\Rightarrow Z^2 = 4 \Rightarrow Z = 2$$

54 *(d)* Given, radius, $r = 0.1$ nm

We know that, $r_n = \dfrac{n^2}{Z}r_0$

$\therefore \quad n = \sqrt{\dfrac{r}{r_0}} \qquad (\because Z = 1)$

We know,

By putting the values,

$$v_n = \frac{c_0}{137}\cdot\frac{Z}{n} = \frac{3\times 10^8}{137}\sqrt{\frac{r_0}{r}}$$

$$= \frac{3\times 10^8}{137}\sqrt{\frac{53\times 10^{-12}}{0.1\times 10^{-9}}} = 1.60\times 10^6 \text{ m/s}$$

55 *(b)* The electromagnetic spectrum in this case lies in Balmer series.

56 *(d)* $\Delta E = hv$

$$v = \frac{\Delta E}{h} = k\left[\frac{1}{(n-1)^2} - \frac{1}{n^2}\right]$$

$$= k\frac{(2n-1)}{n^2(n-1)^2} = \frac{k\cdot 2n}{n^2\cdot n^2} \quad (\because n >> 1)$$

$$\approx \frac{2k}{n^3}$$

$$\Rightarrow v \propto \frac{1}{n^3}$$

57 *(b)* We know that, $r_n = \dfrac{n^2}{Z}r_0$

According to the question,

$r_n = 21.2\times 10^{-11}$

$$\Rightarrow 21.2\times 10^{-11} = \frac{n^2}{1}\times 5.3\times 10^{-11}$$

$$\Rightarrow n^2 = \frac{21.2}{5.3} \Rightarrow n = 2$$

58 *(a)* According to the question, energy, $E = -3.4$ eV

This corresponds to $n = 2$.

So, the angular momentum of the electron, $mvr = \dfrac{nh}{2\pi} = \dfrac{2\times 6.626\times 10^{-34}}{2\times 3.14}$

$$= \frac{6.626\times 10^{-34}}{3.14}$$

$= 2.1\times 10^{-34}$ J-s

59 *(a)* The wavelength can be given as

$$\frac{1}{\lambda} = Z^2R\left(\frac{1}{n_1^2} - \frac{1}{n_2^2}\right) \quad \ldots\text{(i)}$$

For λ to be shortest, if $\left(\frac{1}{n_1^2}-\frac{1}{n_2^2}\right)$ should be maximum

So, $n_2=\infty$ and $n_1=1$

Now, from Eq. (i)

$$\frac{1}{\lambda}=R\left(\frac{1}{1}\right)$$

$$\Rightarrow \quad \lambda=\frac{1}{R}=\frac{1}{10^7}\text{ m}\simeq 1000\text{ Å}$$

60 *(a)* According to Bohr's theory of hydrogen atom, we know that,

Angular momentum, $mvr=\frac{nh}{2\pi}$

$$\Rightarrow \quad mv=\frac{nh}{2\pi r}$$

Linear momentum, $p=mv=\frac{nh}{2\pi r}$

$$\Rightarrow \quad p\propto\frac{n}{r}$$

As, $r\propto n^2$

Hence, $p\propto\frac{1}{n}$

We know that, kinetic energy

$$\text{KE}\propto\frac{1}{r}\quad\text{and}\quad r\propto n^2$$

Hence, $\text{KE}\propto\frac{1}{n^2}$

61 *(c)* Radius of nth orbit, $r_n=0.53\frac{n^2}{Z}$ Å

Here, $n=1$ and for hydrogen atom, $Z=1$

$$\therefore \quad r_1=0.53\frac{(1)^2}{1}\text{ Å}=0.53\times10^{-10}\text{ m}$$
$$=5.3\times10^{-11}\text{ m}$$

62 *(c)* When transition is from upper state to lower state, the energy is evolved. Therefore, options (c) and (d) are practicable. In option (c),

$$E=-Rch\left(\frac{1}{1^2}-\frac{1}{2^2}\right)=-\frac{3}{4}Rch$$

In option (d), $E=-Rch\left(\frac{1}{2^2}-\frac{1}{6^2}\right)$

$$=-\frac{2}{9}Rch$$

Thus, maximum energy is evolved in option (c), when transition takes place between $n=2$ to $n=1$.

63 *(c)* Given, ground state energy of hydrogen atom,

$$E_1=-13.6\text{ eV}$$

Energy of electron in first excited state, i.e. $n=2$

$$E_2=-\frac{13.6}{(2)^2}\text{ eV}$$

Therefore, excitation energy,

$$\Delta E=E_2-E_1=-\frac{13.6}{4}-(-13.6)$$
$$=-3.4+13.6=10.2\text{ eV}$$

64 *(c)* The spectrum produced by emergent light is band absorption spectrum.

65 *(d)* For first line of Lyman series,

$n_1=1$ and $n_2=2$

$$\therefore \quad \frac{1}{\lambda_1}=R\left(\frac{1}{1^2}-\frac{1}{2^2}\right)$$
$$=R\left(1-\frac{1}{4}\right)=\frac{3R}{4}$$

For first line of Paschen series, $n_1=3$ and $n_2=4$

$$\therefore \quad \frac{1}{\lambda_2}=R\left(\frac{1}{3^2}-\frac{1}{4^2}\right)$$
$$=R\left(\frac{1}{9}-\frac{1}{16}\right)=\frac{7R}{144}$$
$$\therefore \quad \frac{\lambda_1}{\lambda_2}=\frac{7R}{144}\times\frac{4}{3R}=\frac{7}{108}$$
$$\lambda_1:\lambda_2=7:108$$

66 *(c)* Since, we know, limiting wavelength of the Lyman series,

$$\lambda=\frac{1}{R}=912\text{Å}$$

For series limit of Balmer series, we can write, $n_2=2$, $n_1=\infty$

$$\Rightarrow \quad \frac{1}{\lambda}=R\left(\frac{1}{n_2^2}-\frac{1}{n_1^2}\right)$$
$$=R\left[\frac{1}{(2)^2}-\frac{1}{(\infty)^2}\right]=\frac{R}{4}$$
$$\therefore \quad \lambda=\frac{4}{R}=4\times912\times10^{-10}\text{m}$$
$$=912\times4\text{Å}$$

67 *(b)* Ionisation energy corresponding to ionisation potential $=-13.6$ eV

Photon energy incident $=12.1$ eV

So, the energy of electron in excited state

$$=-13.6+12.1=-1.5\text{ eV}$$

i.e. $E_n=-\frac{13.6}{n^2}$ eV

$$-1.5=\frac{-13.6}{n^2}$$
$$\Rightarrow \quad n^2=\frac{-13.6}{-1.5}=9$$
$$\Rightarrow \quad n=3$$

i.e. the energy of electron in excited state corresponds to third orbit.

The possible spectral lines are when electron jumps from orbit 3rd to 2nd, 3rd to 1st and 2nd to 1st. Thus, three spectral lines are emitted.

68 *(c)* For an electron to remain orbiting around the nucleus, the angular momentum (L) should be an integral multiple of $\frac{h}{2\pi}$.

i.e. $mvr=\frac{nh}{2\pi}$

where, $n=$ principal quantum number for electron (1, 2 ...)

and $h=$ Planck's constant.

69 *(d)* Solar spectrum is an example for line absorption spectrum.

70 *(b)* The series end of Lyman series corresponds to transition from $n_i=\infty$ to $n_f=1$, corresponding to the wavelength,

$$\frac{1}{(\lambda_{\min})_L}=R\left(\frac{1}{1}-\frac{1}{\infty}\right)=R$$
$$\Rightarrow \quad (\lambda_{\min})_L=\frac{1}{R}=912\text{ Å} \qquad \text{...(i)}$$

For last line of Balmer series,

$$\frac{1}{(\lambda_{\min})_B}=R\left[\frac{1}{(2)^2}-\frac{1}{(\infty)^2}\right]=\frac{R}{4}$$
$$\Rightarrow \quad (\lambda_{\min})_B=\frac{4}{R}=3636\text{ Å} \qquad \text{...(ii)}$$

Dividing Eq. (i) by Eq. (ii), we get

$$\frac{(\lambda_{\min})_L}{(\lambda_{\min})_B}=0.25$$

71 *(a)* $\frac{1}{\lambda_{H_2}}=RZ_H^2\left[\frac{1}{4}-\frac{1}{9}\right]=R(1)^2\left[\frac{5}{36}\right]$

$$\frac{1}{\lambda_{He}}=RZ_{He}^2\left[\frac{1}{4}-\frac{1}{16}\right]=R(4)\left[\frac{3}{16}\right]$$
$$\frac{\lambda_{He}}{\lambda_{H_2}}=\frac{1}{4}\left[\frac{16}{3}\times\frac{5}{36}\right]=\frac{5}{27}$$
$$\Rightarrow \quad \lambda_{He}=\frac{5}{27}\times6561=1215\text{Å}$$

72 *(a)* We know that, the angular momentum of the electron of hydrogen atom,

$$L_n=\frac{nh}{2\pi} \qquad \text{...(i)}$$

But according to question, the angular momentum in 2nd orbit is L.

So, $L=\frac{2h}{2\pi}=\frac{h}{\pi}$ ...(ii)

Hence, the angular momentum in 4th orbit is

$$L_4'=\frac{4h}{2\pi}=\frac{2h}{\pi}=2L$$

73 (a) Energy of emitted radiation,

$$E = Rhc\left(\frac{1}{n_1^2} - \frac{1}{n_2^2}\right)$$

$$\Rightarrow R_{(4\to 3)} = Rhc\left(\frac{1}{3^2} - \frac{1}{4^2}\right)$$

$$= Rhc\left(\frac{7}{9\times 16}\right) = 0.05\ Rhc$$

$$E_{(4\to 2)} = Rhc\left(\frac{1}{2^2} - \frac{1}{4^2}\right)$$

$$= Rhc\left(\frac{3}{16}\right) = 0.2Rhc$$

$$E_{(2\to 1)} = Rhc\left[\frac{1}{(1)^2} - \frac{1}{(2)^2}\right]$$

$$= Rhc\left(\frac{3}{4}\right) = 0.75Rhc$$

and $E_{(1\to 4)} = Rhc\left[\frac{1}{(4)^2} - \frac{1}{(1)^2}\right]$

$$= -\frac{8}{9}Rhc = -0.9Rhc$$

Thus, transition III gives largest amount of energy.

74 (a) The energy of hydrogen atom when the electron revolves in nth orbit is

$$E = \frac{-13.6}{n^2}\ \text{eV}$$

In the ground state, $n = 1$

$$\therefore \quad E = \frac{-13.6}{1^2} = -13.6\ \text{eV}$$

For $n = 2$, $E = \frac{-13.6}{2^2} = -3.4$ eV

So, kinetic energy of electron in the first excited state, i.e. for $n = 2$ is

$$K = -E = -(-3.4) = 3.4\ \text{eV}$$

75 (d) The wavelength of different spectral lines of Lyman series is given by

$\frac{1}{\lambda} = R_H\left[\frac{1}{1^2} - \frac{1}{n^2}\right]$, where $n = 2, 3, 4, \ldots\ldots$

For shortest wavelength, $n = \infty$

$$\therefore \quad \frac{1}{\lambda} = \frac{R_H}{1}$$

or $\lambda = \frac{1}{R_H} = \frac{1}{109678\ \text{cm}^{-1}}$

$$= 9.117\times 10^{-6}\ \text{cm}$$

$$= 9.117\times 10^{-8}\ \text{m}$$

$$= 911.7\times 10^{-10}\ \text{m} = 911.7\ \text{Å}$$

76 (a) Since, we know, the energy of an electron in H-like atom in nth orbit,

$$E_n = \frac{-13.6}{n^2}Z^2$$

For hydrogen atom,

$$E_{n_1} = \frac{-13.6}{n^2} \quad (Z = 1)\ldots\text{(i)}$$

For He$^+$ ion,

$$E_{n_2} = \frac{-13.6(2)^2}{n^2} \quad \ldots\text{(ii)}$$

From Eqs. (i) and (ii), we get

$$\frac{E_{n_2}}{E_{n_1}} = (2)^2$$

$$\Rightarrow \quad E_{n_2} = 4E_{n_1}$$

77 (c) Radius of nth Bohr's orbit of hydrogen like atom,

$$r_n \propto \frac{n^2}{Z}$$

where, Z is the atomic number.

For first orbit.

$$n = 1$$

$$\therefore \quad r_n \propto \frac{1}{Z}$$

Now, for radius of 1st orbit to be minimum, its atomic number must be greater. Here, in the problem, atomic number Z is greater for double ionised lithium, i.e. $Z = 3$. Hence, for the radius of 1st orbit will be minimum.

78 (c) For K_α-line, we can write,

$$\frac{1}{\lambda_\alpha} = R(Z-1)^2\left(\frac{1}{1^2} - \frac{1}{2^2}\right)$$

$$\frac{1}{\lambda_\alpha} = R(Z-1)^2 \times \frac{3}{4}$$

$$\Rightarrow \quad R(Z-1)^2 = \frac{4}{3\lambda_\alpha}$$

Ionisation energy is given by

$$E = Rhc(Z-1)^2\left(\frac{1}{1^2} - \frac{1}{\infty}\right)$$

$$= hc\frac{4}{3\lambda_\alpha}$$

$$= \frac{6.6\times 10^{-34}\times 3\times 10^8\times 4}{3\times 1.54\times 10^{-10}}$$

$$= 1.7\times 10^{-15}\ \text{J}$$

79 (a) According to Bohr's hypothesis, electron can revolve only in those orbits in which its angular momentum is an integral multiple of $\frac{h}{2\pi}$, where h being the Planck's constant.

In these orbits, angular momentum of electron can have magnitude as $\frac{h}{2\pi}, \frac{2h}{2\pi}, \frac{3h}{2\pi}, \ldots$, etc, but can never have magnitude as $\frac{1.5h}{2\pi}, \frac{2.5h}{2\pi}, \frac{3.5h}{2\pi}, \ldots$, etc.

This is called the quantisation of angular momentum.

80 (a) As, ionisation energy $= hcRZ^2$

For Li^{2+}, $Z = 3$

$\therefore$ Ionisation energy $= (3)^2 hcR = 9hcR$

81 (c) Since, radius of nth orbit is given by $r_n \propto \frac{n^2}{Z}$

$$\left(\frac{n^2}{Z}\right)_{\text{for Be}^{3+}} = \left(\frac{n^2}{Z}\right)_{\text{for H}}$$

$$\frac{n^2}{4} = \frac{1^2}{1} \Rightarrow n = 2$$

82 (d) We know that, radius of nth orbit,

$$r_n \propto n^2$$

Hence, area, $A_n \propto n^4$

Hence, $\quad \frac{A_2}{A_1} = \frac{n_2^4}{n_1^4} = \frac{(2)^4}{(1)^4}$

$$\Rightarrow \quad \frac{A_2}{A_1} = \frac{16}{1}$$

$$A_2 : A_1 = 16 : 1$$

83 (c) The Bohr model of hydrogen atom can be extended to hydrogen like atoms.

Energy of such an atom is given by

$$E_n = -13.6\frac{Z^2}{n^2}$$

Here, $Z = 11$ for Na-atom, 10 electrons are removed already, so it is 10 times ionised. For the last electron to be removed,

$$\therefore \quad E_n = -\frac{13.6(11)^2}{(1)^2}\ \text{eV}$$

$$\Rightarrow \quad E_n = -13.6\times (11)^2\ \text{eV}$$

Hence, ionisation energy is $13.6\times (11)^2$ eV.

84 (a) In H-atom, $E_2 - E_1 = 10.2$ eV.

Since, energy difference is 10.2 eV which is greater than kinetic energy 5 eV, thus the electron excites the hydrogen atom. Hence, collision must be elastic.

85 (c) The energy of first excitation of sodium is

$$E = h\nu = \frac{hc}{\lambda}$$

$\therefore \quad E = \dfrac{6.63 \times 10^{-34} \times 3 \times 10^8}{5896 \times 10^{-10}}$ J

$E = 3.37 \times 10^{-19}$ J

Also, since 1.6×10^{-19} J = 1 eV

$\therefore \quad E = \dfrac{3.37 \times 10^{-19}}{1.6 \times 10^{-19}}$

$\Rightarrow \quad E = 2.1$ eV

Hence, corresponding first excitation potential is 2.1 V.

86 *(d)* At the time of solar eclipse, all Fraunhoffer lines changed into bright coloured lines.

87 *(b)* When an electric discharge is passed through mercury vapour lamp, eight to ten lines from red to violet are seen in its spectrum. In some line spectrum there are only a few lines, while in many of them there are hundereds of them. Hence, mercury vapour lamp gives line spectrum.

88 *(b)* The wavelength of Balmer's series for n is given by

$$\frac{1}{\lambda} = R\left(\frac{1}{2^2} - \frac{1}{n^2}\right)$$

where, R is Rydberg's constant.

For Balmer series, $n = 3$ gives the first member of series and $n = 4$ gives the second member of series.

Hence,

$$\frac{1}{\lambda_1} = R\left(\frac{1}{2^2} - \frac{1}{3^2}\right) = R\left(\frac{5}{36}\right) \quad \text{...(i)}$$

$$\Rightarrow \frac{1}{\lambda_2} = R\left(\frac{1}{2^2} - \frac{1}{4^2}\right)$$

$$= R\left(\frac{12}{16 \times 4}\right) = \frac{3R}{16} \quad \text{...(ii)}$$

$$\Rightarrow \frac{\lambda_2}{\lambda_1} = \frac{16}{3} \times \frac{5}{36} = \frac{20}{27}$$

Given, $\lambda_1 = \lambda$

$$\Rightarrow \lambda_2 = \frac{20}{27}\lambda$$

89 *(a)* The wavelength (λ) of lines is given by

$$\frac{1}{\lambda} = R\left(\frac{1}{1^2} - \frac{1}{n^2}\right)$$

For Lyman series, the shortest wavelength is for $n = \infty$ and longest is for $n = 2$.

$$\therefore \frac{1}{\lambda_S} = R\left(\frac{1}{1^2}\right) \quad \text{...(i)}$$

$$\frac{1}{\lambda_L} = R\left(\frac{1}{1^2} - \frac{1}{2^2}\right) = \frac{3}{4}R \quad \text{...(ii)}$$

On dividing Eq. (ii) by Eq. (i), we get

$$\frac{\lambda_L}{\lambda_S} = \frac{4}{3}$$

Given, $\lambda_S = 91.2$ nm

$$\Rightarrow \lambda_L = 91.2 \times \frac{4}{3}$$

$$= 121.6 \text{ nm}$$

90 *(a)* The clockwise rotation is assigned by $+\frac{1}{2}$ while the anti-clockwise rotation is assigned by $-\frac{1}{2}$.

91 *(a)* Total energy in nth Bohr's orbit,

$$E_n = -\frac{13.6}{n^2} \text{ eV}$$

where, n is the principal quantum number.

$$E_2 - E_1 = -13.6\left(\frac{1}{(2)^2} - \frac{1}{(1)^2}\right)$$

$$= -13.6\left(\frac{1}{4} - \frac{1}{1}\right) = \frac{13.6 \times 3}{4}$$

$$= 0.75 \times 13.6 \text{ eV}$$

$$E_3 - E_2 = -13.6\left(\frac{1}{3^2} - \frac{1}{2^2}\right)$$

$$= -13.6\left(\frac{1}{9} - \frac{1}{4}\right)$$

$$= 13.6 \times \frac{5}{36}$$

$$= 0.14 \times 13.6 \text{ eV}$$

Therefore, the energy difference between consecutive energy levels decreases with increase in quantum number.

92 *(b)* In fluorescence, emission of light stops as soon as incidence of light stops.

93 *(c)* Wave number is given by

$$\nu = \frac{1}{\lambda} = R\left(\frac{1}{n_1^2} - \frac{1}{n_2^2}\right)$$

Given $n_1 = 2$, $n_2 = 3$

$$\Rightarrow \nu = R\left(\frac{1}{2^2} - \frac{1}{3^2}\right)$$

$$\therefore \nu = \frac{5R}{36}$$

94 *(b)* From the energy level diagram as shown below

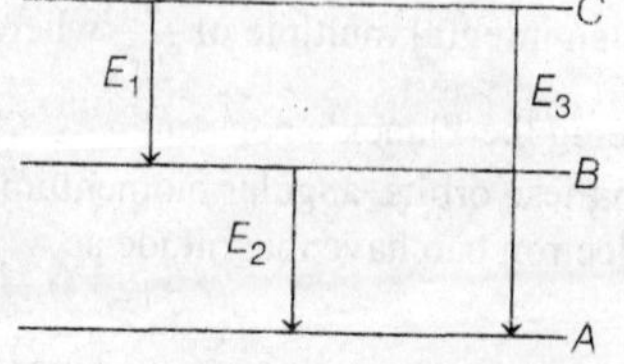

According to question,

$$\frac{1}{\lambda_1} = Z^2R\left(\frac{1}{n_C^2} - \frac{1}{n_B^2}\right) \quad \text{...(i)}$$

$$\frac{1}{\lambda_2} = Z^2R\left(\frac{1}{n_B^2} - \frac{1}{n_A^2}\right) \quad \text{...(ii)}$$

$$\frac{1}{\lambda_3} = Z^2R\left(\frac{1}{n_C^2} - \frac{1}{n_A^2}\right) \quad \text{...(iii)}$$

Adding Eqs. (i) and (ii), we have,

$$\frac{1}{\lambda_1} + \frac{1}{\lambda_2} = Z^2R\left(\frac{1}{n_C^2} - \frac{1}{n_B^2}\right) + Z^2R\left(\frac{1}{n_B^2} - \frac{1}{n_A^2}\right)$$

$$\Rightarrow \frac{\lambda_2 + \lambda_1}{\lambda_1\lambda_2} = Z^2R\left[\frac{1}{n_C^2} - \frac{1}{n_B^2} + \frac{1}{n_B^2} - \frac{1}{n_A^2}\right]$$

$$\Rightarrow \frac{\lambda_1 + \lambda_2}{\lambda_1\lambda_2} = Z^2R\left[\frac{1}{n_C^2} - \frac{1}{n_A^2}\right]$$

$$\frac{\lambda_1 + \lambda_2}{\lambda_1\lambda_2} = \frac{1}{\lambda_3} \quad \text{[from Eq. (iii)]}$$

$$\Rightarrow \lambda_3 = \frac{\lambda_1\lambda_2}{\lambda_1 + \lambda_2}$$

95 *(b)* Potential energy of electron in ground state = 2 × total energy in this state = 2 × (− 13.6 eV) = − 27.2 eV

96 *(a)* The frequencies of the emitted photon in the Paschen series are given by,

$$\nu = Rc\left(\frac{1}{3^2} - \frac{1}{n^2}\right), \text{ where } n = 4, 5, 6, \ldots$$

The highest frequency corresponds to $n = \infty$.

$$\therefore \nu_{\text{highest}} = \frac{Rc}{9} = \frac{1.097 \times 10^7 \times 3 \times 10^8}{9}$$

$$= 0.37 \times 10^{15} \text{ s}^{-1}$$

$$= 3.7 \times 10^{14} \text{ s}^{-1}$$

$$= 3.7 \times 10^{14} \text{ Hz}$$

97 *(b)* In a hydrogen atom, the time period is given by $T \propto n^3$

$$\frac{T_1}{T_2} = \left(\frac{n_1}{n_2}\right)^3$$

$$\Rightarrow \frac{8}{1} = \left(\frac{n_1}{n_2}\right)^3$$

$$\Rightarrow \frac{n_1}{n_2} = \frac{2}{1}$$

The values in the given option (b) gives this ratio for n_1 and n_2, hence it is correct.

98 *(b)* Bohr's atom model assumes that electron is in a quantised orbit will not radiate energy.

Topic 3

Nucleus and Radioactivity

2019

1 α-particle consists of [NEET]
(a) 2 electrons, 2 protons and 2 neutrons
(b) 2 electrons and 4 protons only
(c) 2 protons only
(d) 2 protons and 2 neutrons only

2 The rate of radioactive disintegration at an instant for a radioactive sample of half-life 2.2×10^9 s is $10^{10}\ s^{-1}$. The number of radioactive atoms in that sample at that instant is [NEET (Odisha)]
(a) 3.17×10^{20} (b) 3.17×10^{17}
(c) 3.17×10^{18} (d) 3.17×10^{19}

3 Ba-122 has half-life of 2 min. Experiment has to be done using Ba-122 and it takes 10 min to set up the experiment. If initially 80 g of Ba-122 was taken, how much Ba was left when experiment was started? [JIPMER]
(a) 2.5 g (b) 5 g
(c) 10 g (d) 20 g

4 In which radiation atomic number and mass number are not affected? [JIPMER]
(a) α-radiation (b) γ-radiation
(c) β- radiation (d) None of these

5 If half-life of an element is 69.3 h, then how much of its per cent will decay in 10th to 11th h? (Initial activity = 50 μCi) [AIIMS]
(a) 1% (b) 2% (c) 3% (d) 4%

6 **Assertion** In both radioactivity and photoelectric effect, electrons may be ejected.
Reason In photoelectric effect and radioactivity emission occurs only of unstable elements. [JIPMER]
(a) Both Assertion and Reason are correct and Reason is the correct explanation of Assertion.
(b) Both Assertion and Reason are correct but Reason is not the correct explanation of Assertion.
(c) Assertion is correct but Reason is incorrect.
(d) Both Assertion and Reason are incorrect.

7 **Assertion** For an element generally $N \geq Z$
(N = number of neutrons, Z = atomic number).
Reason Neutrons always experience attractive nuclear force. [JIPMER]
(a) Both Assertion and Reason are correct and Reason is the correct explanation of Assertion.
(b) Both Assertion and Reason are correct, but Reason is not the correct explanation of Assertion.
(c) Assertion is true but Reason is incorrect.
(d) Both Assertion and Reason are incorrect.

2018

8 For a radioactive material, half-life is 10 minutes. If initially there are 600 number of nuclei, the time taken for disintegration of 450 nuclei is [NEET]
(a) 30 (b) 10 (c) 20 (d) 15

9 The half-life a radioactive substance is 20 min. The approximate time interval $(t_2 - t_1)$ between the time t_2, when $\frac{2}{3}$ of it has decayed and time t_1, when $\frac{1}{3}$ of it had decayed is [AIIMS]
(a) 14 min (b) 20 min (c) 28 min (d) 7 min

10 **Assertion** Radioactive nuclei emits β-particles.
Reason Electron exist inside the nucleus. [AIIMS]
(a) Both Assertion and Reason are correct and Reason is correct explanation of Assertion.
(b) Both Assertion and Reason are correct but Reason is not the correct explanation of Assertion.
(c) Assertion is correct but Reason is incorrect.
(d) Assertion is incorrect but Reason is correct.

2017

11 Radioactive material (A) has decay constant 8λ and material (B) has decay constant λ. Initially, they have same number of nuclei. After what time, the ratio of number of nuclei of material B to that A will be I/e? [NEET]
(a) $\frac{1}{\lambda}$ (b) $\frac{1}{7\lambda}$ (c) $\frac{1}{8\lambda}$ (d) $\frac{1}{9\lambda}$

12 **Assertion** In α-decay, atomic number of daughter nucleus reduces by a unit from the parents nucleus.
Reason An α-particle carriers four units of mass. [AIIMS]
(a) Both Assertion and Reason are correct and Reason is correct explanation of Assertion.
(b) Both Assertion and Reason are correct but Reason is not the correct explanation of Assertion.
(c) Assertion is correct but Reason is incorrect.
(d) Assertion is incorrect but Reason is correct.

13 When the radioactive isotope $_{85}Ra^{225}$ decays in a series by emission of three alpha (α) and a beta (β) particle, the isotope X which remains undecay is [JIPMER]
(a) $_{80}X^{213}$ (b) $_{84}X^{218}$ (c) $_{84}X^{225}$ (d) $_{83}X^{223}$

14 Radioactive decay will occur as follows

$_{86}Rn^{220} \longrightarrow {}_{84}Po^{216} + {}_2He^4$, half-life = 55 s

$_{84}Po^{216} \longrightarrow {}_{82}Pb^{212} + {}_2He^4$, half-life = 0.66 s

$_{82}Pb^{212} \longrightarrow {}_{82}B^{212} + {}_{-1}^{0}e$, half-life = 10.6 h

If a certain mass of radon (Rn = 220) is allowed to decay, then after 5 min the element with greater mass will be [JIPMER]

(a) radon (b) lead
(c) polonium (d) bismuth

15 The half-life period of a radioactive element X is same as the mean life of another radioactive element Y. Initially, both of them have same number of atoms, then [JIPMER]

(a) X and Y have same decay rate initially
(b) X and Y have same decay rate always
(c) Y will decay faster
(d) X will decay faster

2016

16 The half-life a radioactive substance is 30 min, the time taken between 40% decay and 85% decay is [NEET]

(a) 15 (b) 30 (c) 45 (d) 60

2015

17 If radius of the $_{13}Al^{27}$ nucleus is taken to be R_{Al}, then the radius of $_{53}Te^{125}$ is nearly [CBSE]

(a) $\left(\frac{53}{13}\right)^{1/3} R_{Al}$ (b) $\frac{5}{3} R_{Al}$ (c) $\frac{3}{5} R_{Al}$ (d) $\left(\frac{13}{53}\right) R_{Al}$

2014

18 A radio isotope X with a half-life 1.4×10^9 yr decays of Y which is stable. A sample of the rock from a cave was found to contain X and Y in the ratio 1 : 7. The age of the rock is [CBSE AIPMT]

(a) 1.96×10^9 yr (b) 3.92×10^9 yr
(c) 4.20×10^9 yr (d) 8.40×10^9 yr

19 After 300 days, the activity of a radioactive sample is 5000 dps (disintegration per second). The activity becomes 2500 dps after another 150 days. The initial activity of the sample (in dps) is [Kerala CEE]

(a) 20000 (b) 10000
(c) 7000 (d) 25000
(e) 15000

20 For the radioactive nuclei that undergo either α or β decay, which one of the following cannot occur? [WB JEE]

(a) Isobar of original nucleus is produced
(b) Isotope of the original nucleus is produced
(c) Nuclei with higher atomic number than that of the original nucleus is produced
(d) Nuclei with lower atomic number than that of the original nucleus is produced

21 In a given reaction,

$$_ZX^A \rightarrow {}_{Z+1}Y^A \rightarrow {}_{Z-1}K^{A-4} \rightarrow {}_{Z-1}K^{A-4}$$

The radioactive radiations are emitted in the sequence of [UK PMT]

(a) α, β, γ (b) γ, α, β
(c) β, α, γ (d) γ, β, α

2013

22 The mother and daughter elements, with emission of γ-rays are [AIIMS]

(a) isotopes (b) isobars
(c) isomers (d) isodiapheres

23 The half-life of a radioactive isotope X is 20 yr. It decays to another element Y which is stable. The two elements X and Y were found to be in the ratio 1 : 7 in a sample of a given rock. The age of the rock is estimated to be [NEET]

(a) 40 yr (b) 60 yr
(c) 80 yr (d) 100 yr

24 The half-value period of a radioactive nuclide is 3 h. In 9 h, its activity will be reduced by a factor of [UP CPMT]

(a) $\frac{1}{9}$ (b) $\frac{1}{27}$ (c) $\frac{1}{6}$ (d) $\frac{1}{8}$

25 A radioactive element has half-life period of 600 yr, what amount will remain in 3000 yr? [UP CPMT, KCET]

(a) $\frac{1}{2}$ (b) $\frac{1}{16}$
(c) $\frac{1}{8}$ (d) $\frac{1}{32}$

26 In a sample of radioactive material, what percentage of the initial number of active nuclei will decay during one mean life? [KCET]

(a) 37% (b) 50%
(c) 63% (d) 69.3%

2012

27 A mixture consists of two radioactive materials A_1 and A_2 with half lives of 20 s and 10 s respectively. Initially, the mixture has 40 g of A_1 and 160 g of A_2. The amount of the two in the mixture will become equal after [CBSE AIPMT]

(a) 60 s (b) 80 s (c) 20 s (d) 40 s

28 Two radioactive samples A and B have decay constant 6λ and 2λ, respectively. If initially they have the same number of nuclei, then the ratio of the number nuclei A to that of B will be $\frac{1}{e}$ after a time [MP PMT]

(a) $\frac{1}{\lambda}$ (b) $\frac{1}{4\lambda}$ (c) $\frac{1}{2\lambda}$ (d) $\frac{1}{3\lambda}$

29 A count rate metre shows a count of 240/min from a given radioactive source. One hour later, the metre shows a count rate of 30/min. The half-life of the source is [Manipal]

(a) 80 min (b) 120 min
(c) 20 min (d) 30 min

30 Two radioactive substances A and B have decay constants 5λ and λ respectively. At $t = 0$, they have the same number of nuclei. The ratio of number of nuclei of A to that of B will be $(1/e)^2$ after a time interval of [WB JEE]

(a) $\frac{1}{\lambda}$ (b) $\frac{1}{2\lambda}$ (c) $\frac{1}{3\lambda}$ (d) $\frac{1}{4\lambda}$

2011

31 In the nuclear reaction ${}_{7}^{14}N + X \longrightarrow {}_{6}^{14}C + {}_{1}^{1}C + {}_{1}^{1}H$, the X will be **[WB JEE]**
(a) ${}_{-1}^{0}e$ (b) ${}_{1}^{1}H$ (c) ${}_{1}^{2}H$ (d) ${}_{0}^{1}n$

32 Which of the following quantities for a nucleus is independent of its mass number? **[J&K CET]**
(a) Density (b) Volume (c) Mass (d) Radius

33 A radioactive nucleus of mass M emits a photon of frequency ν and the nucleus recoils. The recoil energy will be **[CBSE AIPMT]**
(a) $h^2\nu^2/2Mc^2$ (b) zero
(c) $h\nu$ (d) $Mc^2 - h\nu$

34 The radioactivity of a sample is I_1 at a time t_1 and I_2 at a time t_2. If the half-life of the sample is $T_{1/2}$, then the number of nuclei that have disintegrated in the time $t_2 - t_1$ is proportional to **[J&K CET]**
(a) $I_1t_2 - I_2t_1$ (b) $I_1 - I_2$
(c) $\frac{I_1 - I_2}{T_{1/2}}$ (d) $(I_1 - I_2)T_{1/2}$

35 A radioactive nucleus of mass number A, initially at rest, emits an α-particle with a speed v. The recoil speed of the daughter nucleus will be **[J&K CET]**
(a) $\frac{2v}{A-4}$ (b) $\frac{2v}{A+4}$ (c) $\frac{4v}{A-4}$ (d) $\frac{4v}{A+4}$

36 The fraction of the initial number of radioactive nuclei which remain undecayed after half of a half-life of the radioactive sample is **[KCET]**
(a) $\frac{1}{4}$ (b) $\frac{1}{2\sqrt{2}}$ (c) $\frac{1}{2}$ (d) $\frac{1}{\sqrt{2}}$

37 1 curie represents **[KCET]**
(a) 3.7×10^7 dps (b) 3.7×10^{10} dps
(c) 10^6 dps (d) 1 dps

38 A nucleus ${}_{n}^{m}X$ emits one α-particle and two β^--particles. The resulting nucleus is **[CBSE AIPMT]**
(a) ${}_{n}Z^{m-6}$ (b) ${}_{n}X^{m-4}$ (c) ${}_{n-2}Y^{m-4}$ (d) ${}_{n-4}Z^{m-6}$

39 In beta minus decay, a neutron transforms with the nucleus according to **[J&K CET]**
(a) $p \rightarrow n + e^+ + \nu$ (b) $n \rightarrow p + e^- + \overline{\nu}$
(c) $n \rightarrow p + e^+ + \overline{\nu}$ (d) $n \rightarrow p + e^- + \overline{\nu}$

40 Following process is known as $h\nu \longrightarrow e^+ + e^-$ **[BVP]**
(a) pair production (b) photoelectric effect
(c) Compton effect (d) Zeeman effect

41 Particles that are exchanged in weak interaction are **[Manipal]**
(a) mesons (b) photons
(c) bosons (d) gravitons

42 If the radius of a nucleus of mass number 3 is R, then the radius of a nucleus of mass number 81 is **[Manipal]**
(a) $3R$ (b) $9R$ (c) $(27)^{1/2}R$ (d) $27R$

43 A luminous body radiates energy at a rate 3.6×10^{28} J / s, then loss of the mass of the body per second is **[OJEE]**
(a) 2×10^3 kg/s (b) 3×10^4 kg/s
(c) 4×10^{11} kg / s (d) 5×10^5 kg/s

44 The nucleus which has radius one-third of the radius of Os^{189} is **[Kerala CEE]**
(a) Be^9 (b) Li^7 (c) F^{19} (d) C^{12}
(e) O^{16}

45 The density of a nucleus of mass number A is proportional to **[DUMET]**
(a) A^3 (b) $A^{1/3}$ (c) A (d) A^0

46 The radius of a copper nucleus is of the order of **[DUMET]**
(a) 10^{-16} m (b) 10^{-14} m
(c) 10^{-12} m (d) 10^{-9} m

47 Radius of ${}_{2}He^4$ nucleus is 3 Fm. The radius of ${}_{82}Pb^{206}$ nucleus will be **[JCECE]**
(a) 5 Fm (b) 6 Fm
(c) 11.16 Fm (d) 8 Fm

48 The element ${}_{92}U^{238}$ on absorbing a neutron goes over to ${}_{92}U^{239}$. The nucleus emits an electron to go over to neptunium which on further emitting an electron goes over to plutonium. The resulting plutonium can be expressed as **[MGIMS]**
(a) ${}_{94}Pb^{239}$ (b) ${}_{92}Pb^{219}$
(c) ${}_{93}Pb^{240}$ (d) ${}_{92}Pb^{240}$

49 The disintegration rate of a certain radioactive sample at any instant is 5400 disintegrations per minute. 5 min later, the rate becomes 600 disintegrations per minute. Half-life of sample is **[EAMCET]**
(a) $\frac{\ln 3}{\ln 2}$ (b) $\frac{\ln 3}{\ln 5}$ (c) $\frac{\ln 32}{\ln 9}$ (d) $\frac{\ln 9}{\ln 32}$

2010

50 The activity of a radioactive sample is measured as N_0 counts per minute at $t = 0$ and N/e counts per minute at $t = 5$ min. The time (in minute) at which the activity reduces to half its value is **[CBSE AIPMT]**
(a) $\log_e 2/5$ (b) $\frac{5}{\log_e 2}$ (c) $5\log_{10} 2$ (d) $5\log_e 2$

51 **Assertion** The mass of β-particles when they are emitted is higher than the mass of electrons obtained by other means.
Reason β-particle and electron, both are similar particles. **}[AIIMS]**
(a) Both Assertion and Reason are correct and Reason is the correct explanation of Assertion.
(b) Both Assertion and Reason are correct but Reason is not the correct explanation of Assertion.
(c) Assertion is correct but Reason is incorrect.
(d) Both Assertion and Reason are incorrect.

52 The half-life of radioactive radon is 3.8 days. The time at the end of which (1/20) th of the radon sample will remain undecayed is (given, $\log_{10} e = -0.4343$). [AFMC]
(a) 13.8 days (b) 16.5 days (c) 33 days (d) 76 days

53 A uranium nucleus $_{92}U^{238}$ emits an α-particle and a β- particle in succession. The atomic number and mass number of the final nucleus will be [Kerala CEE]
(a) 90, 233 (b) 90, 238
(c) 91, 234 (d) 93, 238

54 In a reaction $_{92}Be^{234} \longrightarrow {}_{88}Y^{218}$, the number of α and β-particles emitted respectively, are [Manipal]
(a) 4, 4 (b) 1, 6 (c) 4, 8 (d) 4, 2

55 The fraction of a sample of radioactive nuclei that remains undecayed after one mean-life is [Manipal]
(a) $\frac{1}{e}$ (b) $1-\frac{1}{e}$ (c) $\frac{1}{e^2}$ (d) $1-\frac{1}{e^2}$

56 If 20% of a radioactive substance decay in 10 days. The amount of the original material left after 30 days is [Manipal]
(a) 51.2% (b) 62.6% (c) 15% (d) 21.2%

57 1 mg gold undergoes decay with 2.7 days half-life period, amount left after 8.1 days is [Manipal]
(a) 0.125 mg (b) 0.5 mg (c) 0.25 mg (d) 0.91 mg

58 Pick out the incorrect statement from the following. [Kerala CEE]
(a) β^- emission from the nucleus is always accompanied with a neutrino.
(b) The energy of the α-particle emitted from a given nucleus is always constant.
(c) γ-rays emission makes the nucleus more stable
(d) Nuclear force is charge independent.
(e) Fusion is the main process by which energy is released from a star.

59 Half-life of a radioactive substance is 20 min. The time between 20% and 80% decay will be [WB JEE]
(a) 20 min (b) 30 min (c) 40 min (d) 25 min

60 When a neutron is disintegrated to give a β-particle, [KCET]
(a) a anti-neutrino alone is emitted
(b) a proton and neutrino are emitted
(c) a proton alone is emitted
(d) a proton and an anti-neutrino are emitted

61 A radioactive sample, S_1 having the activity A_1 has twice the number of nuclei as another sample S_2 of activity A_2. If, $A_2 = 2A_1$, then the ratio of half-life of S_1 to the half-life of S_2 is [KCET]
(a) 4 (b) 2 (c) 0.25 (d) 0.75

62 The activity of a radioactive sample is measured as 9750 count/min at $t = 0$ and 975 count/min at $t = 5$ min. The decay constant is nearly [BCECE]
(a) 0.922 min^{-1} (b) 0.691 min^{-1}
(c) 0.461 min^{-1} (d) 0.230 min^{-1}

63 The ratio of molecular masses of two radioactive substances is 3/2 and the ratio of their decay constants is 4/3. Then, the ratio of their initial activities per mole will be [BCECE]
(a) 2 (b) 4/3
(c) 8/9 (d) 9/8

64 A radioactive isotope has a half-life of T yr. How long will it take the activity to reduce to 1% of its original value? [DUMET]
(a) 3.2 T yr (b) 4.6 T yr
(c) 6.6 T yr (d) 9.2 T yr

65 A radioactive material decays by simultaneous emission of two particles with half-lives 1620 yr and 810 yr respectively. The time in year after which one-fourth of the material remains is [JCECE]
(a) 4860 yr (b) 3240 yr
(c) 2340 yr (d) 1080 yr

66 The half-life of the isotope $_{11}Na^{24}$, is 15 h. How much time does it take for $(7/8)$th of a sample of this isotope to decay? [CG PMT]
(a) 75 h (b) 65 h
(c) 55 h (d) 45 h

67 If $_{92}U^{238}$ emits 8 α-particles and 6 β-particles, then the resulting nucleus is [JIPMER]
(a) $_{82}X^{206}$ (b) $_{82}Pb^{206}$
(c) $_{82}X^{210}$ (d) $_{82}Z^{214}$

68 Number of nuclei of a radioactive substance at time $t = 0$ are 2000 and 1800 at time $t = 2$ s. Number of nuclei left after $t = 6$ s is [MGIMS]
(a) 1442 (b) 1554
(c) 1652 (d) 1458

2009

69 A sample of radioactive elements contains 3×10^9 nuclei. If half-life time of element is 20 days, then the number of decayed nuclei after 60 days is [KCET]
(a) 2.6×10^9 (b) 2×10^9
(c) 7.5×10^8 (d) 3.6×10^8

70 A nucleus at rest breaks into two nuclear parts which have their velocities ratio equal to 2 : 1. What will be the ratio of their radii of the nuclei? [AIIMS]
(a) $2^{1/3}:1$ (b) $1:2^{1/3}$
(c) $2^{3/2}:1$ (d) $1:2^{3/2}$

71 **Assertion** Electron capture occurs more than positron emission in a heavy nucleus.
Reason In a heavy nucleus, electrons are relatively close to nucleus. [AIIMS]
(a) Both Assertion and Reason are correct and Reason is the correct explanation of Assertion.
(b) Both Assertion and Reason are correct but Reason is not the correct explanation of Assertion.
(c) Assertion is correct but Reason is incorrect.
(d) Both Assertion and Reason are incorrect.

72 The mass defect in a particular nuclear reaction is 0.3 g. The amount of energy liberated (in kWh) is (velocity of light = 3×10^8 m/s) **[Manipal]**
(a) 1.5×10^6 (b) 2.5×10^6
(c) 3×10^6 (d) 7.5×10^6

73 Number of neutrons in C^{12} and C^{14} are **[OJEE]**
(a) 8 and 6 (b) 6 and 8
(c) 6 and 6 (d) 8 and 8

74 The amount of energy released when one microgram of matter is annihilated is **[KCET]**
(a) 25 J (b) 9×10^{10} J
(c) 3×10^{10} J (d) 0.5×10^5 J

75 The nuclear force **[J&K CET]**
(a) is purely an electrostatic force
(b) obeys inverse square law of distance
(c) is equal in strength to gravitational force
(d) is short range force

76 The number of beta particles emitted by a radioactive substance is twice the number of alpha particles emitted by it. The resulting daughter is an **[CBSE AIPMT]**
(a) isobar of parent (b) isomer of parent
(c) isotone of parent (d) isotope of parent

77 The electron emitted in beta radiation originates from **[AFMC]**
(a) inner orbits of atoms
(b) free electron existing in nuclei
(c) decay of neutron in the nucleus
(d) photon escaping from the nucleus

78 A radioactive element x converts into another stable element y. Half-life of x is 2 h, initially only x is present. After time t, the ratio of atoms of x and y is found to be 1 : 4, then t (in hour) is **[UP CPMT]**
(a) 2 (b) 4
(c) between 4 and 6 (d) 6

79 A radioactive isotope A with a half-life of 1.25×10^{10} yr decays into B which is stable. A sample of rock from a planet is found to contain both A and B present in the ratio 1 : 15. The age of the rock (in years) **[J&K CET]**
(a) 9.6×10^{10} (b) 4.2×10^{10}
(c) 5×10^{10} (d) 1.95×10^{10}

80 A free neutron decays spontaneously into **[JCECE]**
(a) a proton, an electron and anti-neutrino
(b) a proton, an electron and a neutrino
(c) a proton and electron
(d) a proton, an electron, a neutrino and an anti-neutrino

81 One Becquerel is defined as **[Haryana PMT, CG PMT]**
(a) 1 dps (b) 10^6 dps
(c) 3.7×10^{10} dps (d) 10^3 dps

82 In radioactive decay process, the negatively charged emitted β-particles are **[JIPMER]**
(a) the electrons present inside the nucleus
(b) the electrons produced as a result of the decay of neutrons inside the nucleus
(c) the electrons produced as a result of collisions between atoms
(d) the electrons orbiting around the nucleus

83 In gamma ray emission from a nucleus **[JIPMER]**
(a) both the neutron number and the proton number change
(b) there is no change in the proton number and the neutron number
(c) only the neutron number changes
(d) only the proton number changes

2008

84 Two nuclei have their mass numbers in the ratio of 1 : 3. The ratio of their nuclear densities would be
(a) 1 : 3 (b) 3 : 1 **[CBSE AIPMT]**
(c) $(3)^{1/3}:1$ (d) 1 : 1

85 What is the size of gold nuclei? **[DUMET]**
(a) $3R_0$ (b) $4R_0$ (c) $5R_0$ (d) $5.8R_0$

86 Which one of the following is a possible nuclear reaction?
(a) ${}^{10}_{5}B+{}^{4}_{2}He\longrightarrow{}^{13}_{7}N+{}^{1}_{1}H$ **[BCECE]**
(b) ${}^{23}_{11}Na+{}^{1}_{1}H\longrightarrow{}^{20}_{10}Ne+{}^{4}_{2}He$
(c) ${}^{239}_{93}Np\longrightarrow{}^{239}_{94}Pu+b^-+\overline{\nu}$
(d) ${}^{11}_{7}N+{}^{1}_{1}H\longrightarrow{}^{12}_{6}C+b^-+\nu$

87 Activity of a radioactive sample decreases to (1/3)rd of its original value in 3 days, then in 9 days its activity will become
(a) (1/27) of the original value **[AFMC]**
(b) (1/9) of the original value
(c) (1/18) of the original value
(d) (1/3) of the original value

88 A radioactive sample with a half-life of 1 month has the label activity = 2μCi on 1-8-1991. What was its activity two months earlier? **[Manipal]**
(a) 1 μCi (b) 0.5 μCi
(c) 4 μCi (d) 8 μCi

89 The masses of two radioactive substances are same and their half-lives are 1 yr and 2 yr, respectively. The ratio of their activities after 4 yr will be **[KCET]**
(a) 1 : 4 (b) 1 : 2 (c) 1 : 3 (d) 1 : 6

90 If λ is decay constant and N is the number of radioactive nuclei of an element, then the decay rate R of that element is **[J&K CET]**
(a) λN^2 (b) λN (c) $\dfrac{\lambda}{N}$ (d) $\lambda^2 N$

91 The ratio of half-life times of two elements A and B is $\frac{T_A}{T_B}$. The ratio of respective decay constants $\frac{\lambda_A}{\lambda_B}$ is **[J&K CET]**

(a) $\frac{T_B}{T_A}$ (b) $\frac{T_A}{T_B}$ (c) $\frac{T_A + T_B}{T_A}$ (d) $\frac{T_A - T_B}{T_A}$

92 For a nucleus to be in critical condition, the value of neutron multiplication factor (k) must be **[J&K CET]**

(a) $k > 1$ (b) $k < 1$ (c) $k = 1$ (d) $k = 0$

93 Which of the following cannot be emitted by radioactive substances during their decay? **[RPMT]**

(a) Protons (b) Neutrons
(c) Helium nuclei (d) Electrons

94 A nucleus with $Z = 92$ emits the following in a sequence : $\alpha, \alpha, \beta^-, \beta^-, \alpha, \alpha, \alpha, \alpha; \beta^-, \beta^-, \alpha, \beta^+, \beta^+, \alpha$. The Z of the resulting nucleus is **[RPMT]**

(a) 76 (b) 78
(c) 82 (d) 74

95 A radioactive sample at any instant has its disintegration rate 5000 disintegrations per min. After 5 min, the rate is 1250 disintegrations per min. Then, the decay constant (per minute) is **[RPMT]**

(a) 0.4 ln 2 (b) 0.2 ln 2 (c) 0.1 ln 2 (d) 0.8 ln 2

2007

96 The number of electrons, neutrons and protons in a species are equal to 10, 8 and 8 respectively. The proper symbol of the species is **[Kerala PET]**

(a) ${}^{16}O_8$ (b) ${}^{18}O_8$ (c) ${}^{18}Ne_{10}$ (d) ${}^{16}O_8^-$
(e) ${}^{16}O_8^{2-}$

97 If the nucleus ${}^{27}_{13}Al$ has a nuclear radius of about 3.6 Fm, then ${}^{125}_{52}Te$ would have its radius approximately as **[CBSE AIPMT]**

(a) 6 Fm (b) 9.6 Fm
(c) 12 Fm (d) 4.8 Fm

98 When a sample of solid lithium is placed in a flask of hydrogen gas, then following reaction happened

$${}^1_1H + {}_3Li^7 \longrightarrow {}_2He^4 + {}_2He^4$$

This statement is **[AFMC]**

(a) true
(b) false
(c) May be true at a particular pressure
(d) None of the above

99 The volume occupied by an atom is greater than the volume of the nucleus by factor of about **[BHU]**

(a) 10^{10} (b) 10^{15} (c) 10^1 (d) 10^5

100 A nucleus represented by the symbol ${}^A_Z X$ has **[Manipal]**

(a) Z neutrons and $A - Z$ protons
(b) Z protons and $A - Z$ neutrons
(c) Z protons and A neutrons
(d) A protons and $Z - A$ neutrons

101 The volume of a nucleus is directly proportional to (where, A = mass number of the nucleus) **[KCET]**

(a) A (b) A^3
(c) $\sqrt{A}$ (d) $A^{1/3}$

102 The nucleus ${}_6C^{12}$ absorbs an energetic neutron and emits a beta particle (β). The resulting nucleus is **[Kerala CEE]**

(a) ${}_7N^{14}$ (b) ${}_7N^{13}$ (c) ${}_5B^{13}$ (d) ${}_6C^{13}$
(e) ${}_5B^{12}$

103 Select the true statement from the following. Nuclear force is **[Kerala CEE]**

(a) strong, short range and charge independent force.
(b) charge independent, attractive and long range force.
(c) strong, charge dependent and short range attractive force.
(d) long range, charge dependent and attractive force.
(e) charge independent, short range and strong repulsive force.

104 The masses of proton and neutron are m_p and m_n, respectively. An element M of Z protons and N neutrons, then **[MHT CET]**

(a) $M > (Zm_p + Nm_n)$
(b) $M = (Zm_p + Nm_n)$
(c) $M < (Zm_p + Nm_n)$
(d) M may be greater than less than or equal to $Zm_p + Nm_n$, depending on nature of element

105 The radius of germanium (Ge) nuclide is measured to be twice the radius of ${}^9_4Be$. The number of nucleons in Ge are **[MP PMT]**

(a) 73 (b) 74
(c) 75 (d) 72

106 All nucleus in an atom are held by **[J&K CET]**

(a) nuclear forces (b) van der Waals' forces
(c) tensor forces (d) Coulomb's forces

107 The nucleus, ${}_7N^{14}$ is bombarded with ${}_2He^4$. The resulting nucleus is ${}_8O^{17}$ with the emission of **[BCECE]**

(a) neutrino (b) anti-neutrino
(c) proton (d) neutron

108 The energy spectrum of β-particles [number $N(E)$ as a function of β-energy E] emitted from a radioactive source is **[AIIMS]**

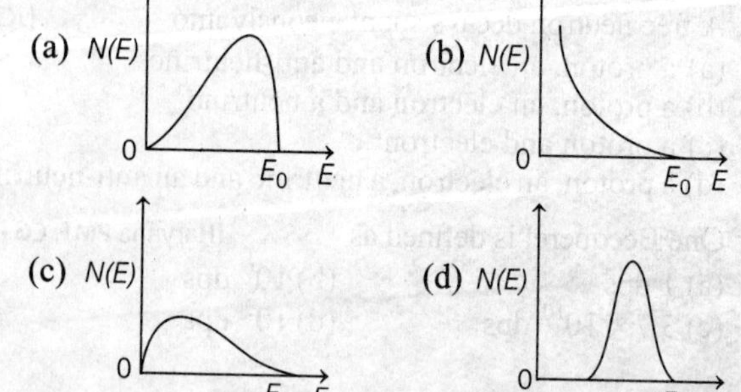

109 We have seen that a gamma-ray dose of 3 Gy is lethal to half the people exposed to it. If the equivalent energy were absorbed as heat, what rise in body temperature would result? [AIIMS]
(a) 300 μK (b) 700 μK (c) 455 μK (d) 390 μK

110 Mass spectrometric analysis of potassium and argon atoms in a moon rock sample shows that the ratio of the number of (stable) ^{40}Ar atoms present to the number of (radioactive) ^{40}K atoms is 10.3. Assume that all the argon atoms were produced by the decay of potassium atoms, with a half-life of 1.25×10^9 yr. How old is the rock?
(a) 2.95×10^{11} yr (b) 2.95×10^9 yr [AIIMS]
(c) 4.37×10^9 yr (d) 4.37×10^{11} yr

111 A sample of radioactive element has a mass of 10 g at an instant $t = 0$. The approximate mass of this element in the sample after two mean lives is [BHU]
(a) 3.70 g (b) 6.30 g (c) 1.35 g (d) 2.50 g

112 In a radioactive material, the activity at time t_1 is R_1 and at a later time t_2, it is R_2. If the decay constant of the material is λ, then [MHT CET]
(a) $R_1 = R_2 e^{-\lambda(t_1 - t_2)}$ (b) $R_1 = R_2 e^{\lambda(t_1 - t_2)}$
(c) $R_1 = R_2 (t_2 / t_1)$ (d) $R_1 = R_2$

113 A radioactive element forms its own isotope after 3 consecutive disintegrations. The particles emitted are [KCET]
(a) 3 β-particles
(b) 2 β-particles and 1 α-particle
(c) 2 β-particles and 1 γ-particle
(d) 2 α-particles and 1 β-particle

114 A radioactive substance has half-life of 60 min. During 3 h, the fraction of the substance that has to be decayed, will be [BCECE]
(a) 87.5% (b) 52.5%
(c) 25.5% (d) 8.5%

115 Half-lives of two radioactive substances *A* and *B* are respectively 20 min and 40 min. Initially, the samples of *A* and *B* have equal number of nuclei. After 80 min, the ratio of remaining number of *A* and *B* nuclei is [JCECE]
(a) 1 : 16 (b) 4 : 1 (c) 1 : 4 (d) 1 : 1

116 If the half-life of any sample of radioactive substance is 4 days, then the fraction of sample will remain undecayed after 2 days, will be [RPMT]
(a) $\sqrt{2}$ (b) $\frac{1}{\sqrt{2}}$ (c) $\frac{\sqrt{2}-1}{\sqrt{2}}$ (d) $\frac{1}{2}$

2006

117 Electrons in the atom are held to the nucleus by [J&K CET]
(a) Coulomb's forces (b) nuclear forces
(c) van der Waals' forces (d) gravitational forces

118 Mass of the nucleons together in a heavy nucleus is
(a) greater than mass of nucleus [J&K CET]
(b) equal to mass of nucleus
(c) less than mass of nucleus
(d) None of the above

119 In nuclear reaction,
$${}_2\text{He}^4 + {}_Z X^A \longrightarrow {}_{Z+2}Y^{A+3} + {}_Z M^A$$
M denotes [AMU]
(a) electron (b) positron (c) proton (d) neutron

120 The γ-rays are originated from [DUMET]
(a) nucleus
(b) outermost shell of atom
(c) innermost shell of atom
(d) None of the above

121 The mass number of nucleus is [MHT CET]
(a) sometimes equal to its atomic number
(b) sometimes less than and sometimes more than its atomic number
(c) always less than its atomic number
(d) always more than its atomic number

122 M_p and M_n are masses of proton and neutron, respectively at rest. If they combine to form deuterium nucleus. The mass of the nucleus will be [RPMT]
(a) less than M_p
(b) less than $(M_p + M_n)$
(c) less than $(M_p + 2M_n)$
(d) greater than $(M_p + 2M_n)$

123 The nucleus ${}^{238}_{92}$U has 92 protons and 238 nucleons. It decays by emitting an α-particle and becomes [AIIMS]
(a) ${}^{234}_{92}$U (b) ${}^{234}_{90}$Th (c) ${}^{235}_{92}$U (d) ${}^{237}_{93}$Np

124 The fossil bone has a ^{14}C : ^{12}C ratio, which is $\left[\frac{1}{16}\right]$ of that in a living animal bone. If the half-life of ^{14}C is 5730 yr, then the age of the fossil bone is [AIIMS]
(a) 11460 yr (b) 17190 yr
(c) 22920 yr (d) 45840 yr

125 **Assertion** Cobalt-60 is useful in cancer therapy.
Reason Cobalt-60 is source of γ-radiations capable of killing cancerous cell. [AIIMS]
(a) Both Assertion and Reason are correct and Reason is the explanation of Assertion.
(b) Both Assertion and Reason are correct but Reason is not the correct explanation of Assertion.
(c) Assertion is correct but Reason is incorrect.
(d) Both Assertion and Reason are incorrect.

126 What is the disintegration constant of radon, if the number of its atoms diminishes by 18% in 24 h? [BHU]
(a) $2.1\times 10^{-3}\,\text{s}^{-1}$ (b) $2.1\times 10^{-4}\,\text{s}^{-1}$
(c) $2.1\times 10^{-5}\,\text{s}^{-1}$ (d) $2.1\times 10^{-6}\,\text{s}^{-1}$

127 n α-particles per second are being emitted by N atoms of a radioactive element. The half-life of element will be
(a) (n/N) s (b) (N/n) s [UP CPMT]
(c) $\frac{0.693N}{n}$ s (d) $\frac{0.693\,n}{N}$ s

128 The half-life of thorium X is 3.64 days. After how many days will 0.1 of the mass of a sample of the substance remain undecayed? [Kerala CEE]
(a) 12.1 days (b) 24 days (c) 60 days (d) 4 days
(e) 14 days

129 The radioactivity of a sample is x at time t_1 and is y at time t_2. If the mean-life of the specimen is τ, the number of atoms that have disintegrated in the time interval $(t_2 - t_1)$ is [Guj CET]
(a) $x - y$ (b) $(x - y)/\tau$ (c) $(x - y)\tau$ (d) $xt_1 - yt_2$

2005

130 The nuclei of which one of the following pairs of nuclei are isotones? [CBSE AIPMT]
(a) ${}_{34}Se^{74}, {}_{31}Ga^{71}$ (b) ${}_{42}Mo^{92}, {}_{40}Zr^{92}$
(c) ${}_{38}Sr^{84}, {}_{38}Sr^{86}$ (d) ${}_{20}Ca^{40}, {}_{16}S^{32}$

131 Which of the following is most unstable? [AFMC]
(a) Electron (b) Proton
(c) Neutron (d) α-particle

132 The particle A is converted into C *via* following reaction,
$$A \longrightarrow B + {}_2He^4,\ B \longrightarrow C + 2e^-$$
Then, [J&K CET]
(a) A and C are isobars (b) A and C are isotopes
(c) A and B are isobars (d) A and B are isotopes

133 In a nuclear reaction $C_6^{11} \longrightarrow B_5^{11} + \beta^+ + X$,
what does X stand for? [Haryana PMT]
(a) An electron (b) A proton
(c) A neutron (d) A neutrino

134 The phenomenon of radioactivity is [BHU]
(a) exothermic change which increases or decreases with temperature
(b) increases on applied pressure
(c) nuclear process does not depend on external factors
(d) None of the above

135 Mean life of a radioactive sample is 100 s, then its half-life (in min) is [KCET]
(a) 0.693 (b) 1 (c) 10^{-4} (d) 1.155

136 Consider two nuclei of the same radioactive nucleid. One of the nuclei was created in a supernova explosion 5 billion years ago. The other was created in a nuclear reactor 5 min ago. The probability of decay during the next time is
(a) different for each nuclei [KCET]
(b) nuclei created in explosion decays first
(c) nuclei created in the reactor decays first
(d) independent of the time of creation

137 Two radioactive materials A and B have decay constants 10λ and λ respectively. If initially they have the same number of nuclei, then the ratio of the number of nuclei of A to that of B will be $1/e$ after a time [Haryana PMT]
(a) $\frac{1}{10\lambda}$ (b) $\frac{1}{11\lambda}$ (c) $\frac{11}{10\lambda}$ (d) $\frac{1}{9\lambda}$

138 At a specific instant, emission of a radioactive compound is not deflected in a magnetic field. The compound can emit [Haryana PMT]
(a) electrons (b) protons (c) neutrons (d) deuterons

139 In the nuclear reaction,
$${}_{72}X^{180} \xrightarrow{-\alpha} Y \xrightarrow{-\beta} Z \xrightarrow{-\alpha} A \xrightarrow{-\gamma} P$$
the atomic mass and atomic number of P are respectively
(a) 170, 69 (b) 172, 69 [DUMET]
(c) 172, 70 (d) 170, 70
(e) 91, 234

140 A nuclide X with mass number A and charge number Z, disintegrates into one α-particle and one β-particle. The resulting nuclide R has atomic mass and atomic number, equal to [RPMT]
(a) $(A - Z)$ and $(Z - 1)$ (b) $(A - Z)$ and $(Z - 2)$
(c) $(A - 4)$ and $(A - 2)$ (d) $(A - 4)$ and $(Z - 1)$

Answers

1 (d)	2 (d)	3 (a)	4 (b)	5 (a)	6 (c)	7 (d)	8 (c)	9 (b)	10 (c)
11 (b)	12 (d)	13 (a)	14 (b)	15 (c)	16 (d)	17 (b)	18 (c)	19 (a)	20 (b)
21 (c)	22 (c)	23 (b)	24 (d)	25 (d)	26 (c)	27 (d)	28 (b)	29 (c)	30 (b)
31 (c)	32 (a)	33 (a)	34 (d)	35 (c)	36 (d)	37 (b)	38 (b)	39 (d)	40 (a)
41 (c)	42 (a)	43 (c)	44 (b)	45 (d)	46 (b)	47 (c)	48 (a)	49 (c)	50 (d)
51 (b)	52 (b)	53 (c)	54 (a)	55 (b)	56 (a)	57 (a)	58 (a)	59 (c)	60 (a)
61 (a)	62 (c)	63 (b)	64 (c)	65 (d)	66 (d)	67 (b)	68 (d)	69 (a)	70 (b)
71 (d)	72 (d)	73 (b)	74 (b)	75 (d)	76 (d)	77 (c)	78 (b)	79 (c)	80 (a)
81 (a)	82 (b)	83 (b)	84 (d)	85 (d)	86 (c)	87 (a)	88 (d)	89 (a)	90 (b)
91 (a)	92 (c)	93 (a)	94 (b)	95 (a)	96 (e)	97 (a)	98 (a)	99 (b)	100 (b)
101 (a)	102 (b)	103 (a)	104 (c)	105 (d)	106 (a)	107 (c)	108 (c)	109 (b)	110 (c)
111 (c)	112 (a)	113 (b)	114 (a)	115 (c)	116 (b)	117 (a)	118 (a)	119 (d)	120 (a)
121 (a)	122 (b)	123 (b)	124 (c)	125 (a)	126 (d)	127 (c)	128 (a)	129 (c)	130 (a)
131 (c)	132 (b)	133 (d)	134 (c)	135 (d)	136 (d)	137 (d)	138 (c)	139 (b)	140 (d)

Explanations

1 *(d)* α-particles are doubly ionised helium nucleus (He^{2+}) which are emitted in any radioactive process. So, they have 2 protons, 2 neutrons in its nucleus and no electron.

2 *(d)* Given, half-life, $T_{1/2} = 2.2 \times 10^9$ s

Rate of disintegration, $R = 10^{10}\ s^{-1}$

If N be the number of nuclei present, then the rate of disintegration is

$$\frac{dN}{dt} = \lambda N \quad (\lambda = \text{decay constant})$$

$$\Rightarrow \quad R = \lambda N \text{ or } N = \frac{R}{\lambda} \quad \ldots\text{(i)}$$

Also, the half-life is given by

$$T_{1/2} = \frac{0.693}{\lambda}$$

$$\Rightarrow \quad \lambda = \frac{0.693}{T_{1/2}} \quad \ldots\text{(ii)}$$

From Eqs (i) and (ii), we get

$$N = \frac{R}{0.693} \times T_{1/2} = \frac{10^{10} \times 2.2 \times 10^9}{0.693} = 3.17 \times 10^{19}$$

3 *(a)* As, $T_{1/2} = 2\text{ min} \Rightarrow 10\text{ min} = 5$ half-lives

We know, $\frac{N}{N_0} = \left(\frac{1}{2}\right)^n$

where, N = remaining of nuclei,

N_0 = initial number of nuclei

and n = number of half-lives.

$$\Rightarrow N = \frac{N_0}{2^n} = \frac{80}{2^5} = \frac{80}{32} = 2.5\text{ g}$$

4 *(b)* In γ-radiation, no change occurs in mass number and atomic number because its rest mass is zero and it is neutral for electric and magnetic fields.

In α-radiation, atomic number is decreased by 2 units and atomic mass is decreased by 4 units.

In β-radiation, no change occurs in atomic mass but atomic number increases by 1 unit.

5 *(a)* Given, half-life of an element, $T_{1/2} = 69.3$ h

Let initial amount (at $t = 0$) of radioactive element is N_0

Active nuclei at $t = 10$ h,

$$N_1 = N_0 e^{-10\lambda}$$

Active nuclei at $t = 11$ h, $N_2 = N_0 e^{-11\lambda}$

% decay in 10th to 11th hours

$$= \frac{N_1 - N_2}{N_1} \times 100$$

$$= \frac{N_0 e^{-10\lambda} - N_0 e^{-11\lambda}}{N_0 e^{-10\lambda}} \times 100$$

$$= (1 - e^{-\lambda}) \times 100$$

$$= \left[1 - e^{\frac{-0.693}{69.3}}\right] \times 100$$

$$\left[\because \text{ where, } \lambda = \frac{0.693}{T_{1/2}}\right]$$

$$= [1 - e^{-0.01}] \times 100$$

$$= [1 - 0.99] \times 100$$

$$= 0.01 \times 100 = 1\%$$

6 *(c)* In radioactivity, electrons are emitted in the form of $\beta\,({}_{-1}e^0)$ particles. It is also called negative β-decay, where an unstable nucleus emits an energetic electron and an anti-neutrino and a neutron in the nucleus becomes a proton that remains in the product nucleus.

In photoelectric effect, when light rays of frequency greater than or equal to threshold frequency incident on metal surface, then electrons are emitted from metal surface. This phenomenon is called photoelectric effect. For photoelectric emission it is not necessary that element is unstable but for radioactivity, it is necessary that elements are unstable.

7 *(d)* For an element, it is not always true that number of neutrons (N) are greater than or equal to atomic number (Z). For example, in hydrogen atom, there is no neutron but it has one proton. Therefore, atomic number of hydrogen atom is greater than number of neutrons.

i.e., $Z > N$ for hydrogen atom.

The force between neutrons in the nucleus is attractive only upto the range of 1 fm. But this attractive force become highly repulsive when neutrons came nearer to about 0.6 to 0.7 fm. Therefore, neutrons do not always experience attractive nuclear force.

Hence, both Assertion and Reason are incorrect.

8 *(c)* After n half-life, the number of nuclei left undecayed is given as

$$N = N_0 (1/2)^n$$

where, $n = \frac{t}{T_{1/2}}$

Here, intially number of nuclei, $N_0 = 600$. Disintegrated number of nuclei in time $t = N' = 450$

∵ Number of nuclei left undecayed,

$$N = N_0 - N'$$

$$N = 600 - 450 = 150$$

As, we know,

$$\frac{N}{N_0} = \left(\frac{1}{2}\right)^{t/T_{1/2}}$$

Substituting the given values, we get

$$\frac{150}{600} = \left(\frac{1}{2}\right)^{t/T_{1/2}} \text{ or } \frac{1}{4} = \left(\frac{1}{2}\right)^{t/T_{1/2}}$$

$$\text{or} \quad \left(\frac{1}{2}\right)^2 = \left(\frac{1}{2}\right)^{t/10} \Rightarrow 2 = \frac{t}{10}$$

$$\Rightarrow \quad t = 20 \text{ min}$$

9 *(b)* $N_1 = N_0 - \frac{1}{3}N_0 = \frac{2}{3}N_0$

and $N_2 = N_0 - \frac{2}{3}N_0 = \frac{1}{3}N_0$

$$\because \frac{N_2}{N_1} = \frac{1}{2} = \left(\frac{1}{2}\right)^{t/T_{1/2}} \Rightarrow t/T_{1/2} = 1$$

$$\Rightarrow \quad t = 20$$

where $t = t_2 - t_1$

Therefore, the time interval $(t_2 - t_1)$ = 20 min

10 *(c)* For a β-decay, ${}_0^1n \longrightarrow {}_1^1p + {}_{-1}^{0}e$

where, ${}_{-1}e^0$ is a positron having mass equal to an electron. But electron does not exist inside the nucleus.

11 *(b)* Let initial number of nuclei in A and B is N_0. Number of nuclei of A after time t is

$$N_A = N_0 e^{-8\lambda t} \quad \ldots\text{(i)}$$

Similarly, number of nuclei of B after time t is

$$N_B = N_0 e^{-\lambda t} \quad \ldots\text{(ii)}$$

It is given that $\frac{N_A}{N_B} = \frac{1}{e} \quad (\because N_B > N_A)$

Now, from Eqs. (i) and (ii), $\frac{e^{-8\lambda t}}{e^{-\lambda t}} = \frac{1}{e}$

Rearranging, we get

$$e^{-1} = e^{-7\lambda t} \Rightarrow 7\lambda t = 1$$

Time, $t = \frac{1}{7\lambda}$.

12 (d) We know that, α-particle carries two units of positive charge and four units of mass. In α-decays, charge or atomic number of parent nucleus decreased by two units. Also, mass number reduces by four units.

13 (a) Due to emission of 3α-particles, the mass number is reduced by 12, while atomic number is decreased by 6. Due to emission of β-particle, the atomic number is increased by one while there is no change in mass number.

Now, resulting mass will be decreased by 12 and atomic number is decreased by 5, so isotopes X is ${}_{80}X^{213}$.

14 (b) Let M_0 be initial mass of Rn - 220.

Number of half-lives of Rn in 5 min,

$$= \frac{5 \text{ min}}{55 \text{ s}} = \frac{5 \times 60}{55} = 5.5$$

∵ Mass of Rn – 220 (left)

$$= \left(\frac{1}{2}\right)^{5.5} M_0 = \frac{M_0}{45}$$

∵ The mass converted is Po = 216 is $(44/45)M_0$. The number of half-lives of Po-216 in 5 min

$$= \frac{5 \text{ min}}{0.66} = \frac{300}{0.66} = 455$$

∵ Mass of Po = 216 (left)

$$= \left(\frac{1}{2}\right)^{455} \times \frac{44}{55} M_0 \to 0$$

This means that Po-216 formed will soon decay to lead. Hence, lead will have maximum mass nearly $\left(\frac{44}{45}\right)M_0$.

15 (c) Half-life of X = Mean life of Y.

Let λ_X and λ_Y be decay constants of X and Y, then condition (1) implies

$$\frac{0.693}{\lambda_X} = \frac{1}{\lambda_Y} \Rightarrow \lambda_Y = \frac{\lambda_X}{0.693}$$

$$\Rightarrow \lambda_Y > \lambda_X$$

Hence, Y will decay faster.

16 (d) The number of nuclei left undecayed is given as

$$N = N_0\left(\frac{1}{2}\right)^{t/T_{1/2}} \quad \text{...(i)}$$

Given, $N_1 = 0.6 N_0$ (∵ 40% decay)

and $N_2 = 0.15 N_0$ (∵ 85% decay)

From Eq. (i), $$\frac{N_2}{N_1} = \frac{N_0\left(\frac{1}{2}\right)^{\frac{t_2}{T_{1/2}}}}{N_0\left(\frac{1}{2}\right)^{\frac{t_1}{T_{1/2}}}} = \left(\frac{1}{2}\right)^{\frac{t_2 - t_1}{T_{1/2}}}$$

or $$2^{\frac{t_2 - t_1}{T_{1/2}}} = \frac{N_1}{N_2}$$

Taking log on both sides, we get

$$\Rightarrow \frac{(t_2 - t_1)}{T_{1/2}} \log_{10} 2 = \log_{10} \frac{N_1}{N_2}$$

$$\Rightarrow t_2 - t_1 = T_{1/2} \log_2 \frac{N_1}{N_2}$$

$$\Rightarrow t_2 - t_1 = 30 \times \log_2 \frac{N_1}{N_2}$$

$$= 30 \log_2 \left(\frac{0.6}{0.15} \cdot \frac{N_0}{N_0}\right)$$

$$= 30 \log_2 2^2$$

$$= 30 \times 2 = 60 \text{ min}$$

17 (b) Radius of the nucleus is given by

$$R = R_0 A^{+1/3} \Rightarrow R \propto A^{1/3}$$

$$\Rightarrow \frac{R_{\text{Al}}}{R_{\text{Te}}} = \frac{(A_{\text{Al}})^{1/3}}{(A_{\text{Te}})^{1/3}} = \left(\frac{27}{125}\right)^{1/3} = \frac{3}{5}$$

$$R_{\text{Te}} = \frac{5}{3} R_{\text{Al}}$$

18 (c) According to the question, ratio of $X : Y$ is $1 : 7$

$$\Rightarrow \frac{m_x}{m_y} = \frac{1}{7} \Rightarrow 7m_x = m_y$$

Let the initial total mass is m.

$$\Rightarrow m_x + m_y = m$$

$$\Rightarrow \frac{m_y}{7} + m_y = m$$

$$\Rightarrow \frac{8m_y}{7} = m$$

$$\Rightarrow m_y = \frac{7}{8} m$$

Only $\left(\frac{1}{8}\right)$th part remains left undisintegrated.

Number of half-lives involve are three as

$$1 \xrightarrow{T_{1/2}} \frac{1}{2} \xrightarrow{T_{1/2}} \frac{1}{4} \xrightarrow{T_{1/2}} \frac{1}{8}$$

So, time taken to become $\frac{1}{8}$ unstable part

$$= 3 \times T_{1/2} = 3 \times 1.4 \times 10^9$$

$$= 4.2 \times 10^9 \text{ yr}$$

19 (a) As, activity droped from 5000 dps to 2500 dps in 150 day means

$T_{1/2} = 150$ day

$\Rightarrow$ 300 day $= 2T_{1/2}$

So, initial activity $= 5000 \times (2)^2$

$= 20000$ dps

20 (b) In radioactive, α or β-decay, the mass number and atomic number changes and one nucleus decays into another nucleus. But isotopes are the nuclei of same atom having same atomic number and different mass number. Hence, it will not be produced in radioactive decay.

21 (c) Suppose a given nucleus is ${}_ZX^A$.

In α-decay, the mass number of the product nucleus is four less than that of decaying nucleus while the atomic number decreases by two.

$${}_ZX^A \xrightarrow{\alpha\text{-decay}} {}_{Z-2}X^{A-4} + {}_2\text{He}^4 (\alpha)$$

In β-decay, the mass number of product nucleus remains same but atomic number increases or decreases by one.

$${}_Z^AX \xrightarrow{\beta^-\text{-decay}} {}_{Z+1}^{A}Y + {}_{-1}^{0}e + \nu$$

or $${}_Z^AX \xrightarrow{\beta^+\text{-decay}} {}_{Z-1}^{A}Y + {}_{+1}^{0}e + \nu$$

Gamma decay is the phenomenon of emission of gamma rays or photon from a radioactive nucleus.

$${}_ZX^A \longrightarrow {}_ZX^A + \gamma$$

Hence, the given reaction will have sequence as follows

$${}_ZX^A \xrightarrow{\beta^-\text{-emission}} {}_{Z+1}Y \xrightarrow{\alpha\text{-emission}}$$

$${}_{Z-1}K^{A-4} \xrightarrow{\gamma\text{-emission}} {}_{Z-1}K^{A-4}$$

22 (c) The mother and daughter elements after the emission γ-rays are called isomers having same atomic number and mass number. Isotopes have same atomic number but different atomic mass and isobars have same mass number but different atomic number,

23 (b) Ratio of X and $Y = 1 : 7$, let the initial total mass $= m$

$$\frac{m_X}{m_Y} = \frac{1}{7}$$

$$m_Y = 7m_X$$

$$\Rightarrow m_X + m_Y = m$$

$$\frac{m_Y}{7} + m_Y = m$$

$$\frac{8m_Y}{7} = m \Rightarrow m_Y = \frac{7}{8} m$$

Only $\left(\frac{1}{8}\right)$th part remains undisintegrated, number of half lives involved are

$$1 \xrightarrow{T_{1/2}} \frac{1}{2} \xrightarrow{T_{1/2}} \frac{1}{4} \xrightarrow{T_{1/2}} \frac{1}{8}$$

So, total time taken to become $\frac{1}{8}$ unstable part will be

$3 \times T_{1/2} = 3 \times 20 = 60\text{yr}$

24 *(d)* As, $\frac{N}{N_0} = \left(\frac{1}{2}\right)^{t/T_{1/2}}$

Given, $T_{1/2} = 3$ h and $t = 9$ h

$$\therefore \frac{N}{N_0} = \left(\frac{1}{2}\right)^{9/3} = \left(\frac{1}{2}\right)^3$$

$$\Rightarrow \frac{N}{N_0} = \frac{1}{8}$$

$$\text{Activity} = \left|\frac{-dN}{dt}\right| = N\lambda$$

$$\Rightarrow \frac{A}{A_0} = \frac{N\lambda}{N_0\lambda} = \frac{N}{N_0} = \frac{1}{8}$$

25 *(d)* We know that, $n = \frac{t}{T}$

Given, $t = 3000$ yr and $T = 600$ yr

$$\Rightarrow n = \frac{3000}{600} = 5$$

Then, $\frac{N}{N_0} = \left(\frac{1}{2}\right)^n = \left(\frac{1}{2}\right)^5 = \frac{1}{32}$

26 *(c)* From Rutherford-Soddy law,

$$N = N_0 e^{-\lambda\tau}$$

where, N_0 is the initial number of atoms present, λ is the decay constant and τ is the mean life-time.

Using $\tau = \frac{1}{\lambda}$, we have

$$N = N_0 e^{-\lambda\tau} = N_0 e^{-1} = \frac{N_0}{e}$$

Percentage of active nuclei decayed

$$= \frac{N_0 - N}{N_0} \times 100$$

$$= \frac{(N_0 - N_0/e)}{N_0} \times 100$$

$= 63\%$

27 *(d)* For 40 g amount,

$$40 \text{ g} \xrightarrow[\text{half-life}]{20 \text{ s}} 20 \text{ g} \xrightarrow{20 \text{ s}} 10 \text{ g}$$

For 160 g amount,

$$160 \text{ g} \xrightarrow{10 \text{ s}} 80\text{g} \xrightarrow{10 \text{ s}} 40\text{g} \xrightarrow{10 \text{ s}} 20 \text{ g} \xrightarrow{10 \text{ s}} 10 \text{ g}$$

So after 40 s, A_1 and A_2 become equal.

28 *(b)* If N be the number of radioactive nuclei at time t, then

$$N = N_0 e^{-\lambda t}$$

[where, N_0 = initial amount]

$$\therefore \frac{N_1}{N_2} = \frac{e^{-\lambda_1 t}}{e^{-\lambda_2 t}}$$

Given, $\frac{N_1}{N_2} = \frac{1}{e}$

$$\therefore \frac{1}{e} = \frac{e^{-\lambda_1 t}}{e^{-\lambda_2 t}}$$

$$e^{-1} = e^{-(\lambda_1 - \lambda_2)t}$$

$$1 = (\lambda_1 - \lambda_2)t$$

$$\Rightarrow t = \frac{1}{\lambda_1 - \lambda_2} = \frac{1}{6\lambda - 2\lambda} = \frac{1}{4\lambda}$$

29 *(c)* The number of counts left after time t,

$$N = N_0 \left(\frac{1}{2}\right)^{t/T_{1/2}}$$

$$\therefore 30 = 240 \left(\frac{1}{2}\right)^{60/T_{1/2}}$$

$(\because t = 1 \text{ h} = 60 \text{ min})$

$$\Rightarrow \frac{30}{240} = \left(\frac{1}{2}\right)^{60/T_{1/2}} \Rightarrow \left(\frac{1}{2}\right)^3 = \left(\frac{1}{3}\right)^{60/T_{1/2}}$$

On comparing the powers, we get

$$\frac{60}{T_{1/2}} = 3 \Rightarrow T_{1/2} = \frac{60}{3} = 20 \text{ min}$$

30 *(b)* We know that, $N = N_0 e^{-\lambda t}$

For A, $N_A = N_0 e^{-5\lambda t}$

For B, $N_B = N_0 e^{-\lambda t}$

Given, $\frac{N_A}{N_B} = \frac{1}{e^2}$ ...(i)

and $\frac{N_A}{N_B} = \frac{1}{e^{4\lambda t}}$ ...(ii)

From Eqs. (i) and (ii), we get

$$t = \frac{1}{2\lambda}$$

31 *(c)* Given reaction is

$${}^{14}_{7}\text{N} + X \rightarrow {}^{14}_{6}\text{C} + {}^{1}_{1}\text{H} + {}^{1}_{1}\text{C}$$

Clearly, X is ${}^{2}_{1}\text{H}$.

32 *(a)* Nuclear density is given by

$$\rho = \frac{m}{\frac{4}{3}\pi R_0^3}$$

which is independent of mass number A.

33 *(a)* Momentum of a photon, $p = \frac{h\nu}{c}$

Hence, recoil energy,

$$E = \frac{p^2}{2M} = \frac{\left(\frac{h\nu}{c}\right)^2}{2M} = \frac{h^2\nu^2}{2Mc^2}$$

34 *(d)* Half-life, $T_{1/2} = \frac{0.693}{\lambda}$

Activity, $I_1 = N_1\lambda$ and $I_2 = N_2\lambda$

where, λ is disintegration constant.

$$\therefore (I_1 - I_2) = (N_1 - N_2)\frac{0.693}{T_{1/2}}$$

or $(N_1 - N_2) \propto (I_1 - I_2) T_{1/2}$

35 *(c)* The initial momentum of the nucleus would be equal to $4u_H v$, where, u_H is the unit mass of hydrogen. Since, the mass of hydrogen is 1, so the initial momentum can be given by $4v$. The final momentum of the nucleus would be equal to $(A-4)V$, where V is the final velocity. Thus, we get from the conservation of momentum

$$(A-4)V = 4v, \text{ so } V = \frac{4v}{(A-4)}.$$

36 *(d)* As, we know

$$N = N_0 \left(\frac{1}{2}\right)^{t/T_{1/2}}$$

Given, $t = T_{1/2}/2$

$$\therefore N = N_0 \left(\frac{1}{2}\right)^{\frac{T_{1/2}/2}{T_{1/2}}} = N_0 \left(\frac{1}{2}\right)^{1/2} = \frac{N_0}{\sqrt{2}}$$

37 *(b)* 1 Curie $= 3.7 \times 10^{10}$ disintegration s^{-1}

i.e. 1 Curie $= 3.7 \times 10^{10}$ dps

38 *(b)* The nuclear reaction can be given as

$${}^{m}_{n}X \xrightarrow{\alpha} {}_{n-2}X^{m-4} \xrightarrow{2\beta} {}_{n}X^{m-4}$$

39 *(d)* A beta minus particle (β^-) is like an electron. Emission of β^- involves transformation of a neutron into a proton, an electron and third particle called an anti-neutrino.

$$n = p + {}_{-1}\beta^0 + \bar{\nu}$$

or $n \rightarrow p + e^- + \bar{\nu}$

40 *(a)* Pair production refers to the creation of an elementary particle and its anti-particle usually from a photon (or another neutral boson). This is allowed, provided there is enough energy available to create the pair.

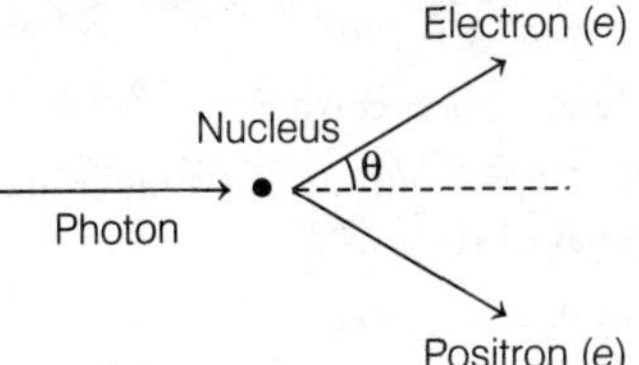

41 *(c)* The particles those are involved in the weak interaction are bosons.

42 *(a)* Nuclear radius is proportional to $A^{1/3}$, where A is the mass number of nucleus.

i.e. $R \propto A^{1/3}$

$$\Rightarrow \frac{R_1}{R_2} = \left(\frac{A_1}{A_2}\right)^{1/3}$$

$$\Rightarrow \quad \frac{R_1}{R_2} = \left(\frac{3}{81}\right)^{1/3}$$

$$\Rightarrow \quad R_1/R_2 = 1/3$$

$$\therefore \quad R_2 = 3R_1 = 3R \quad (\because R_1 = R)$$

43 (c) Energy and mass are related by the relation, $E = mc^2$

Differentiating, we get

$$\frac{dE}{dt} = m \times [0] + c^2 \frac{dm}{dt}$$

$$\Rightarrow \quad 3.6 \times 10^{28} = 9 \times 10^{16} \frac{dm}{dt}$$

$$\Rightarrow \quad \frac{dm}{dt} = 4 \times 10^{11} \text{ kg/s}$$

44 (b) The radius of a nucleus is given by the relation,

$$r = r_0 (A)^{1/3} \text{ (key concept)}$$

where, r_0 = constant.

For Os^{189}, $A_1 = 189$ and $r_1 = r$ (say)

Thus, using $r_2 = \frac{r}{3}$, we know that,

$$\frac{r_1}{r_2} = \left(\frac{A_1}{A_2}\right)^{1/3}$$

$$\Rightarrow \quad 3 = \left(\frac{189}{A_2}\right)^{1/3}$$

$$\Rightarrow \quad 27 = \frac{189}{A_2} \Rightarrow A_2 = 7$$

Thus, the answer is Li^7.

45 (d) Radius of nucleus is given by $R = R_0 A^{1/3}$

So, the volume of the nucleus is given by

$$V \propto R^3, \quad V \propto R_0^3 A$$

Hence, the density is given by

$$\rho = \frac{A}{kR_0^3 A} \propto \frac{1}{R_0^3}$$

$$\Rightarrow \quad \rho \propto A^0 \quad \left(\because A \propto \frac{1}{R_0^3}\right)$$

Here, k = constant

46 (b) Copper nucleus has a radius of the order of 10^{-14} m.

47 (c) We have, $r \propto A^{1/3}$

$$\Rightarrow \quad \frac{r_2}{r_1} = \left(\frac{A_2}{A_1}\right)^{1/3} = \left(\frac{206}{4}\right)^{1/3}$$

$$\therefore \quad r_2 = 3\left(\frac{206}{4}\right)^{1/3} = 11.16 \text{ Fm}$$

48 (a) The reaction can be shown as

$$_{92}U^{238} + {}_0n^1 \longrightarrow {}_{92}U^{239}$$

$$\longrightarrow {}_{93}Ne^{239} + {}_{-1}e^0$$

$$\longrightarrow {}_{94}Pb^{239} + {}_{-1}e^0$$

49 (c) From the relation,

$$R = R_0 e^{-\lambda t}$$

[where, R = activity of sample]

Given, $R_0 = 5400$ dis/min

$R = 600$ dis/min

and $t = 5$ min

$$\therefore \quad 600 = 5400\, e^{-5\lambda}$$

$$\frac{1}{9} = e^{-5\lambda} \Rightarrow \lambda = \frac{\ln 9}{5}$$

$\therefore$ Half-life of the sample

$$T_{1/2} = \frac{\ln 2}{\frac{\ln 9}{5}} = \frac{5 \ln 2}{\ln 9} = \frac{\ln 2^5}{\ln 9} = \frac{\ln 32}{\ln 9}$$

50 (d) Fraction remains after n half-lives,

$$\frac{N}{N_0} = \left(\frac{1}{2}\right)^n = \left(\frac{1}{2}\right)^{t/T}$$

Given, $N = \frac{N_0}{e}$

$$\Rightarrow \quad \frac{N_0}{eN_0} = \left(\frac{1}{2}\right)^{5/T} \text{ or } \frac{1}{e} = \left(\frac{1}{2}\right)^{5/T}$$

Taking log on both sides, we get

$$\log 1 - \log e = \frac{5}{T} \log \frac{1}{2}$$

$$-1 = \frac{5}{T}(-\log 2)$$

$$\Rightarrow \quad T = 5 \log_e 2$$

Now, let t' be the time after which activity reduces to half

$$\left(\frac{1}{2}\right) = \left(\frac{1}{2}\right)^{t'/5 \log_e 2} \Rightarrow t' = 5 \log_e 2$$

51 (b) As, β-particles are emitted with very high velocity (upto 0.99 c, where c is the speed of the light in air). So, according to Einstein's theory of relativity, the mass of a β-particle is much higher compared to its rest mass (m_0). The velocity of electrons obtained by other means is very small compared to c (velocity of the light). So, its mass remains nearly m_0. Also, β-particle and electrons are similar particles.

52 (b) By formula, $N = N_0 \left(\frac{1}{2}\right)^{t/T_{1/2}}$

$$\left(\frac{1}{2}\right)^n = \frac{N}{N_0} = \frac{1}{20}, \text{ which give } n = 4.3$$

$$t = nT_{1/2} = 4.3 \times 3.8 \simeq 16.5 \text{ days}$$

53 (c) Simply, we can analyse from the equation

$$_{92}U^{238} \xrightarrow{-\alpha} {}_{90}U^{234} \xrightarrow{-\beta} {}_{91}Y^{234}$$

54 (a) When α-particles are emitted, the mass number decreases by 4 units and atomic number decreases by 2 units and for β-particle, atomic number is increased by 1 and mass number remains the same.

Given reaction is

$$_{92}Be^{234} \longrightarrow {}_{88}Y^{218}$$

Number of α-particles

$$= \frac{234 - 218}{4} = \frac{16}{4} = 4$$

Decreases in atomic number = 4 × 2 = 8

From atomic number 88, number of β-particles emitted

$$= \frac{88 - 84}{1} = 4$$

Hence, 4α and 4β-particles are emitted.

55 (b) By using, $N = N_0 e^{-\lambda t}$ and average life-time, $t = \frac{1}{\lambda}$

So, $N = N_0 e^{-\lambda \times 1/\lambda} = N_0 e^{-1}$

$$\Rightarrow \quad \frac{N}{N_0} = e^{-1} = \frac{1}{e}$$

Now, disintegrated fraction

$$= 1 - \frac{N}{N_0} = 1 - \frac{1}{e}$$

56 (a) Fraction left, $f = 1 - \frac{20}{100} = \frac{8}{10}$

Hence, $N = \frac{8}{10} N_0$, $t = 10$ days

Now, $N = N_0^{-\lambda t}$

$$\frac{8}{10} N_0 = N_0 e^{-\lambda t}$$

$$\Rightarrow \quad e^{\lambda t} = \frac{10}{8}$$

$$\therefore \quad \lambda = \frac{\log_e (10/8)}{10} = \frac{2.303 \log (10/8)}{10}$$

$$\lambda = 0.022$$

If $T_{1/2}$ is half-life period,

$$T_{1/2} = \frac{0.693}{\lambda} = \frac{0.693}{0.022}$$

$$T_{1/2} = 31.5 \text{ days}$$

Again, $N = N_0 \left(\frac{1}{2}\right)^n = N_0 \left(\frac{1}{2}\right)^{31.5/30}$

$$\simeq 51.2\%$$

57 (a) 8.1 days are equivalent to three half days.

Hence, amount left after three half days

$$= \left(\frac{1}{2}\right)^3 (1 \text{ mg}) = \left(\frac{1}{8}\right)(1 \text{ mg})$$

$$= 0.125 \text{ mg}$$

58 (a) In a radioactive emission, the emission of a β-particle is accompanied with the emission of an anti-neutrino. It is represented as

$$n \longrightarrow p + \underset{\text{electron}}{\overset{\uparrow}{e^-}} + \underset{\text{anti-neutrino}}{\overset{\uparrow}{\bar{\nu}}}$$

59 (c) Given that the half-life of a radioactive substance is 20 min.

So, $T_{1/2} = 20$ min.

For 20% decay, we have 80% of the substance left, hence

$$\frac{80N_0}{100} = N_0 e^{-\lambda t_{20}} \quad \ldots\text{(i)}$$

where, N_0 = initial undecayed substance and t_{20} is the time taken for 20% decay.

For 80% decay, we have 20% of the substance left, hence

$$\frac{20N_0}{100} = N_0 e^{-\lambda t_{80}} \quad \ldots\text{(ii)}$$

On dividing Eq. (i) and Eq. (ii), we get

$$4 = e^{\lambda(t_{80} - t_{20})}$$

Taking log on both sides, we get

$$\Rightarrow \quad \ln 4 = \lambda (t_{80} - t_{20})$$

$$\Rightarrow \quad 2 \ln 2 = \frac{0.693}{T_{1/2}} (t_{80} - t_{20})$$

$$\Rightarrow \quad t_{80} - t_{20} = 2 \times T_{1/2} = 40 \text{ min}$$

60 (a) When a neutron is disintegrated to give β-particle following reaction involves

$$\underset{\text{neutron}}{n} \longrightarrow \underset{\text{proton}}{p} + \underset{\text{electron or } \beta^-}{e^-} + \underset{\text{anti-neutrino}}{\bar{\nu}}$$

In this decay, a neutron is converted into a proton with the emission of an anti-neutrino only.

61 (a) Activity, $A = \lambda N = \frac{0.693}{t_{1/2}} N$, where $T_{1/2}$ is the half-life of a radioactive sample.

$$\therefore \quad \frac{A_1}{A_2} = \frac{N_1}{t_1} \times \frac{t_2}{N_2}$$

$$\Rightarrow \quad \frac{t_1}{t_2} = \frac{A_2}{A_1} \times \frac{N_1}{N_2} = \frac{2A_1}{A_1} \times \frac{2N_2}{N_2} = \frac{4}{1}$$

62 (c) As we know that,

$$A = \lambda N$$

$$\Rightarrow \quad A \propto N$$

$$\Rightarrow \quad \frac{A_1}{A_2} = \frac{N_1}{N_2}$$

Now, for a radioactive disintegration

$$t = \frac{2.303}{\lambda} \log \frac{N_o}{N_t}$$

$$\Rightarrow \quad 5 = \frac{2.303}{\lambda} \log \frac{9750}{975} = \frac{2.303}{\lambda} \log 10$$

$$\therefore \lambda = \frac{2.303}{5} \simeq 0.461 \text{min}^{-1} \quad (\because \log 10 = 1)$$

63 (b) Activity, $A = \frac{-dN}{dt} = \lambda N$

As, the number of nuclei (N) per mole are equal for both the substances, irrespective of their molecular mass, therefore

$$A \propto \lambda$$

$$\frac{A_1}{A_2} = \frac{\lambda_1}{\lambda_2} = \frac{4}{3}$$

64 (c) From the question,

$$N = \frac{N_0}{100}$$

and $\quad T_{1/2} = T$ yr

So, $\quad \lambda = \frac{0.693}{T}$

$$\therefore \quad t = \frac{2.303}{\lambda} \log \left[\frac{N_0}{N}\right]$$

$$= \frac{2.303\text{T}}{0.693} \log 100$$

$$= 6.65\, T$$

65 (d) From Rutherford-Soddy law, the number of atoms left after n half-lives is given by

$$N = N_0 \left(\frac{1}{2}\right)^n$$

where, N_0 is the original number of atoms.

The number of half-life,

$$n = \frac{\text{Time of decay}}{\text{Effective half-life}}$$

Relation between effective disintegration constant (λ) and half-life (T) is

$$\lambda = \frac{\ln 2}{T}$$

$$\therefore \lambda_1 + \lambda_2 = \frac{\ln 2}{T_1} + \frac{\ln 2}{T_2}$$

Effective half-life,

$$\frac{1}{T} = \frac{1}{T_1} + \frac{1}{T_2} = \frac{1}{1620} + \frac{1}{810}$$

$$\Rightarrow \quad \frac{1}{T} = \frac{1+2}{1620}$$

$$\Rightarrow \quad T = 540 \text{ yr}$$

$$\therefore \quad n = \frac{t}{540}$$

$$\therefore \quad N = N_0 \left(\frac{1}{2}\right)^{t/540}$$

$$\Rightarrow \quad \frac{N}{N_0} = \left(\frac{1}{2}\right)^2 = \left(\frac{1}{2}\right)^{t/540}$$

$$\Rightarrow \quad \frac{t}{540} = 2$$

$$\Rightarrow \quad t = 2 \times 540 = 1080 \text{ yr}$$

66 (d) Undecayed isotope $= 1 - \frac{7}{8} = \frac{1}{8}$

$$\therefore \quad \frac{N}{N_0} = \left(\frac{1}{2}\right)^{t/T}$$

$$\Rightarrow \quad \frac{1}{8} = \left(\frac{1}{2}\right)^{t/15}$$

$$\Rightarrow \quad \frac{t}{15} = 3$$

$$\Rightarrow \quad t = 45\text{h}$$

67 (b) After one α-emission, the daughter nucleus reduces in mass number by 4 unit and in atomic number by 2 units. In β-emission the atomic number of daughter nucleus increases by 1 unit. The reaction can be written as

$${}_{92}\text{U}^{238} \xrightarrow{-8\alpha} {}_{76}X^{206} \xrightarrow{-6\beta} {}_{82}Y^{206}$$

Thus, the resulting nucleus is ${}_{82}Y^{206}$, i.e. ${}_{82}\text{Pb}^{206}$.

68 (d) From, $N = N_0 e^{-\lambda t}$

$$1800 = 2000\, e^{-\lambda \times 2}$$

$$\Rightarrow \quad \frac{9}{10} = e^{-2\lambda} \quad \Rightarrow \quad e^{-\lambda} = \left(\frac{9}{10}\right)^{1/2}$$

Number of nuclei left after 6 s,

$$N = N_0 e^{-\lambda t'} = 2000\, e^{-\lambda \times 6}$$

$$= 2000 (e^{-\lambda})^6 = 2000 \left[\left(\frac{9}{10}\right)^{1/2}\right]^6$$

$$= 2000 \times \left(\frac{9}{10}\right)^3 = 2000 \times \frac{729}{1000} = 1458$$

69 (a) Number of half-lives,

$$n = \frac{t}{T_{1/2}} = \frac{60}{20} = 3$$

Initial amount, $N_0 = 3 \times 10^9$

Number of undecayed nuclei is N, then

$$N = N_0 \left(\frac{1}{2}\right)^n = 3 \times 10^9 \left(\frac{1}{2}\right)^3$$

$$N = \frac{3}{8} \times 10^9$$

Thus, number of nuclei decayed after 60 days

$$= N_0 - N = 3 \times 10^9 - \frac{3}{8} \times 10^9$$

$$= 3 \times 10^9 \left(1 - \frac{1}{8}\right) = \frac{21}{8} \times 10^9$$

$$= 2.625 \times 10^9 \simeq 2.6 \times 10^9$$

70 *(b)* According to the law of conservation linear momentum,

$$m_1 v_1 = m_2 v_2$$

$$\therefore \quad \frac{m_1}{m_2} = \frac{v_2}{v_1} = \frac{1}{2} \quad \left(\text{given}, \frac{v_1}{v_2} = 2\right)$$

Since, we know

$$R = R \cdot (A)^{1/3}$$

$$A \approx m$$

$$\text{Thus,} \quad \frac{R_1}{R_2} = \left(\frac{m_1}{m_2}\right)^{1/3} = \left(\frac{1}{2}\right)^{1/3}$$

$$\therefore \quad R_1 : R_2 = 1 : 2^{1/3}$$

71 *(d)* Electron capture generally occurs for small atoms and positron emission occur for heavy nucleus.
This is because as in heavy nucleus, the electrons are loosely bound to nucleus and at a distance from it.

72 *(d)* According to mass energy equivalence, $E = \Delta mc^2$

$$= \frac{0.3}{1000} \times (3 \times 10^8)^2 = 2.7 \times 10^{13} \text{ J}$$

$$= \frac{2.7 \times 10^{13}}{3.6 \times 10^6} = 7.5 \times 10^6 \text{ kWh}$$

73 *(b)* These are isotopes having same atomic number, i.e., 6.
Number of neutrons = Atomic mass − Atomic number

For C^{12}, $= 12 - 6 = 6$
For C^{14}, $= 14 - 6 = 8$

74 *(b)* The amount of energy released,

$$E = \Delta mc^2 = (1 \times 10^{-6})(3 \times 10^8)^2 = 9 \times 10^{10} \text{ J}$$

75 *(d)* Nuclear forces are short range forces having range upto 10^{-15} m. These are charge independent, hence they are not electrostatic in nature. These are the strongest forces in nature. They are complicated in nature and so does not follow inverse square law $\left(\text{i.e.} F \propto \frac{1}{r^2}\right)$.

76 *(d)* In emission of α-particle, following process involves

$$_Z X^A \xrightarrow{\alpha} {}_{Z-2}Y^{A-4}$$

In emission of β-particle,

$$_{Z-2}Y^{A-4} \xrightarrow{2\beta} {}_Z Z^{A-4}$$

(given, $\alpha = 2\beta$)

Thus, the resulting daughter nuclei by two process is the isotopes (having same atomic number but different mass) of parent nuclei.

77 *(c)* The electron emitted by beta radiation originates from decay of neutron in the nucleus.

78 *(b)* Consider the radioactive conversion is $x \to y$

$$y_{1/2} = 2h \quad \text{(half-life)}$$

$$\text{Given,} \quad \left(\frac{N_x}{N_y}\right) = \frac{1}{4} = \left(\frac{1}{2}\right)^2$$

Hence, number of half-lives are 2.

$$\therefore \quad t = 2 \times t_{1/2} = 2 \times 2 = 4 \text{ h}$$

79 *(c)* According to Rutherford and Soddy law for radioactive decay,
Number of atoms remained undecayed after time *t* are

$$N = N_0 e^{-\lambda t}$$

$$\text{or} \quad \lambda = \frac{2.303}{t} \log \frac{N_0}{N} \quad \text{...(i)}$$

$$\text{and} \quad \lambda = \frac{0.693}{T_{1/2}} = \frac{0.693}{1.25 \times 10^{10}} \quad \text{...(ii)}$$

From Eqs. (i) and (ii), we get

$$t = \frac{2.303 \times 1.25 \times 10^{10}}{0.693} \log \frac{16}{1}$$

$$= 5 \times 10^{10} \text{ yr}$$

80 *(a)* A free neutron decays into a proton, an electron and anti-neutrino.

81 *(a)* The becquerel is taken as SI unit of radioactive disintegration which means 1 dps.

82 *(b)* Beta decay can involve the emission of either electrons or positrons. The electrons or positrons emitted in a β-decay do not exist inside the nucleus. They are only created at the time of emission, just as photons are created when an atom makes a transition from higher to a lower energy state. In negative β-decay a neutron in the nucleus is transformed into a proton, an electron and an anti-neutrino.
Hence, in radioactive decay process, the negatively charged emitted β-particles are the electrons produced as a result of the decay of neutrons present inside the nucleus.

83 *(b)* A excited nucleus attains ground state by emitting γ-rays. γ-rays does not change nucleus atomic number or its mass number.

84 *(d)* Nuclear density is independent of mass number and have the ratio

$$\rho_1 : \rho_2 = 1 : 1$$

85 *(d)* Nuclear radius of gold ($_{79}Au^{198}$),

$$R_{Au} = R_0(A^{1/3}) = R_0 (198)^{1/3} = 5.8 R_0$$

where, $R_0 = 1.2 \times 10^{-15}$ m = 1.2 Fm

86 *(c)* In any nuclear reaction, mass number and atomic number should remain conserved. Reaction (c) satisfies this condition. Also, for $^{239}_{93}Np$, neutron to proton ratio is greater than 1.52, which makes it unstable.

87 *(a)* Activity, $R = R_0 e^{-\lambda t}$

$$\Rightarrow \quad \left(\frac{1}{3}\right) = e^{-\lambda \times 3} = e^{-3\lambda} \quad \text{...(i)}$$

$$\text{Again,} \quad \frac{R'}{R_0} = e^{-\lambda \times 9} = e^{-9\lambda} = (e^{-3\lambda})^3$$

[from Eq. (i)]

$$= \left(\frac{1}{3}\right)^3 = \frac{1}{27} \Rightarrow R' = \frac{R_0}{27}$$

Hence, in 9 days activity will become $\left(\frac{1}{27}\right)$ of the original value.

88 *(d)* Two months mean 2 half-life periods.
Two months earlier, the activity

$$= 2 \times 2^2 = 8 \mu\text{Ci}$$

89 *(a)* Let initial activity of both substances are same.

$$\therefore \quad R = R_0 \left(\frac{1}{2}\right)^n = R_0 \left(\frac{1}{2}\right)^{t/T_{1/2}}$$

$$\Rightarrow \quad \frac{R_1}{R_2} = \frac{\left(\frac{1}{2}\right)^{4/1}}{\left(\frac{1}{2}\right)^{4/2}} = \frac{\left(\frac{1}{2}\right)^4}{\left(\frac{1}{2}\right)^2} = \left(\frac{1}{2}\right)^2 = \frac{1}{4}$$

90 *(b)* At any instant the rate of decay of radioactive atoms is proportional to the number of atoms present at that instant, i.e.

$$-\frac{dN}{dt} \propto N \quad \text{or} \quad -\frac{dN}{dt} = R = \lambda N$$

where, λ is decay constant.

91 *(a)* Half-life of a radioactive element,

$$T = \frac{0.693}{\lambda} \quad \text{or} \quad T \propto \frac{1}{\lambda}$$

$$\therefore \quad \frac{\lambda_A}{\lambda_B} = \frac{T_B}{T_A}$$

92 *(c)* In critical condition, $k = 1$. The chain reaction will be steady. The size of the fissionable material used is said to be the critical size and its mass the critical mass.

93 *(a)* Protons cannot be emitted by radioactive substances during their decay.

94 (b) Since, 8α-particles $4\beta^-$-particles and $2\beta^+$-particles are emitted, so, new atomic number

$$Z' = Z - 8 \times 2 + 4 \times 1 - 2 \times 1$$
$$= 92 - 16 + 4 - 2$$
$$= 92 - 14 = 78$$

95 (a) Given, $N_0\lambda = 5000$, $N\lambda = 1250$

$$N = N_0 e^{-\lambda t} = N_0 e^{-5\lambda}$$

where, λ is decay constant per minute.

$$N\lambda = N_0 \lambda e^{-5\lambda}$$
$$\Rightarrow \quad 1250 = 5000 e^{-5\lambda}$$
$$\therefore \quad e^{5\lambda} = \frac{5000}{1250} = 4 \Rightarrow e^{5\lambda} = 4$$
$$\Rightarrow \quad 5\lambda = 2\log_e 2$$
$$\therefore \quad \lambda = 0.4 \ln 2$$

96 (e) Number of electrons = 8 + 2 = 10
Number of protons = 8
Number of neutrons, N = 8
Atomic number, Z = number of protons = 8
Mass number, $A = Z + N = 8 + 8 = 16$
The proper symbol of the species is $^{16}O_8^{2-}$.

97 (a) If R is the radius of the nucleus, the corresponding volume $\frac{4}{3}\pi R^3$ has been found to the proportional to A.
This relationship is expressed in inverse form as

$$R = R_0 A^{1/3}$$

The value of R_0 is 1.2×10^{-15} m, i.e. 1.2 Fm.

$$\text{Therefore, } \frac{R_{Al}}{R_{Te}} = \frac{R_0 (A_{Al})^{1/3}}{R_0 (A_{Te})^{1/3}}$$
$$\frac{R_{Al}}{R_{Te}} = \frac{(A_{Al})^{1/3}}{(A_{Te})^{1/3}} = \frac{(27)^{1/3}}{(125)^{1/3}} = \frac{3}{5}$$
$$\Rightarrow R_{Te} = \frac{5}{3} \times R_{Al} = \frac{5}{3} \times 3.6 = 6 \text{ Fm}$$

(given, $R_{Al} = 3.6$ Fm)

98 (a) The given reaction is a nuclear reaction, which can take place only if a proton (a hydrogen nucleus) comes into contact with a lithium nucleus. If the hydrogen is in the atomic form, the interaction between its electron cloud and the electron cloud of a lithium atom keeps the two nuclei close to each other. Even, if isolated protons are used, they must be fired at the Li-atom with enough kinetic energy to overcome the electric repulsion between the proton and Li-atom. Hence, given statement is true.

99 (b) Radius of atom $\simeq 10^{-10}$ m and radius of nucleus $\simeq 10^{-15}$ m

$$\therefore \text{ Required ratio} = \frac{\text{Volume of atom}}{\text{Volume of nucleus}}$$
$$= \frac{\frac{4}{3}\pi r_1^3}{\frac{4}{3}\pi r_2^3} = \left(\frac{10^{-10}}{10^{-15}}\right)^3 = 10^{15}$$

100 (b) The nucleus, $_ZX^A$ has number of protons = Z and number of neutrons = $A - Z$, where A is the total number of protons and neutrons, i.e. $A = Z + N$.

101 (a) Radius of nucleus, $R = R_0 A^{1/3}$

where, $R_0 = 1.2 \times 10^{-15}$ m

Volume of nucleus, (V)

$$= \frac{4}{3}\pi R^3 = \frac{4}{3}\pi [R_0 A^{1/3}]^3$$
$$= \frac{4}{3}\pi R_0^3 A$$
$$\therefore \quad V \propto A$$

102 (b) The nuclear reaction can be given by

$$_6C^{12} + \underset{\text{(Neutron)}}{_0n^1} \longrightarrow {_7N^{13}} + \underset{\text{(Beta particle)}}{_{-1}e^0} + \underset{\text{(Anti-neutrino)}}{\bar{\nu}}$$

On equating atomic numbers and atomic masses, for resulting nucleus is 7 and 13, which is for nitrogen nucleus.

103 (a) Nuclear force has the following properties

(i) Nuclear force is a short range force whose range is of the order of 2 to 3 femtometre.

(ii) Nuclear force is the strongest force in nature.

(iii) Nuclear force is an attractive force acting between nucleons, which is charge independent.

Therefore, nuclear force is strong, short range and charge independent force.

104 (c) When a nucleus is formed, then the mass of nucleus is slightly less than the sum of the mass of Z protons and N neutrons.

i.e. $\quad M < (Zm_p + Nm_n)$

105 (d) Let radius of $^9_4$Be nucleus be r.

Then, radius of germanium (Ge) nucleus will be $2r$.

Radius of a nucleus is given by $R = R_0 A^{1/3}$

$$\therefore \quad \frac{R_1}{R_2} = \left(\frac{A_1}{A_2}\right)^{1/3}$$
$$\Rightarrow \quad \frac{r}{2r} = \left(\frac{9}{A_2}\right)^{1/3} \quad (\because A_1 = 9)$$
$$\Rightarrow \quad \left(\frac{1}{2}\right)^3 = \frac{9}{A_2}$$
$$\text{Hence,} \quad A_2 = 9 \times (2)^3$$
$$= 9 \times 8 = 72$$

Thus, in germanium (Ge) nucleus number of nucleons is 72.

106 (a) Nuclear forces are the strong attractive forces between nucleons in the atomic nucleus that hold the nucleons together.

107 (c) The nuclear reaction is as follows

$$_7N^{14} + {_2He^4} \longrightarrow {_8O^{17}} + {_qX^p}$$

Conservation of mass number gives, $p = 14 + 4 - 17 = 1$

Conservation of atomic number give, $Z = 7 + 2 - 8 = 1$

Hence, particle is a proton, i.e. $_1H^1$.

108 (c) Energy spectrum of emitted β-particles from a radioactive source is drawn as

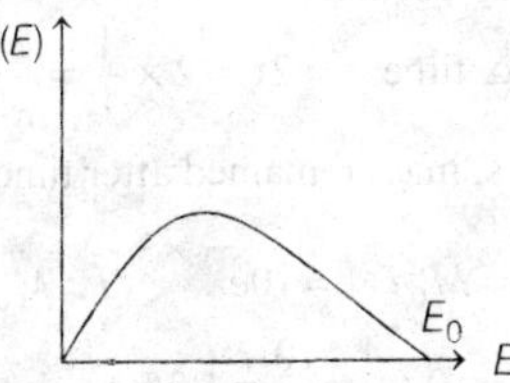

109 (b) We can relate an absorbed energy Q and the resulting temperature increase ΔT with relation $Q = cm\,\Delta T$. In this equation, m is the mass of the material absorbing the energy and c is the specific heat of that material. An absorbed dose of 3 Gy corresponds to an absorbed energy per unit mass of 3 J kg^{-1}. Let us assume that c is the specific heat of human body, is the same as that of water, 4180 J kg^{-1} K^{-1}. Then, we find that

$$\Delta T = \frac{Q/m}{c} = \frac{3}{4180}$$
$$= 7.2 \times 10^{-4} \text{K} \simeq 700\,\mu\text{K}$$

Obviously, the damage done by ionising radiation has nothing to do with thermal heating. The harmful effects arises, because the radiation damages DNA and thus interferes with the normal functioning of tissues in which it is absorbed.

110 (c) If N_0 potassium atoms were present at the time of the rock was formed by solidification from a molten form, the number of potassium atoms remaining at the time of analysis is

$$N_K = N_0 e^{-\lambda t} \quad \text{...(i)}$$

in which t is the age of the rock.

For every potassium atom that decays, an argon atom is produced. Thus, the number of argon atoms present at the time of the analysis is

$$N_{Ar} = N_0 - N_K \quad \text{...(ii)}$$

We cannot measure N_0, so let's eliminate it from Eqs. (i) and (ii), we get

$$\lambda t = \ln\left(1 + \frac{N_{Ar}}{N_K}\right),$$

in which N_{Ar}/N_K can be measured. Solving for t, we get

$$t = \frac{T_{1/2} \ln(1 + N_{Ar}/N_K)}{\ln 2}$$

$$= \frac{(1.25 \times 10^9)[\ln(1 + 10.3)]}{\ln 2}$$

$$= 4.37 \times 10^9 \text{ yr}$$

111 (c) As, mean life, $\tau = \frac{1}{\lambda}$ where λ being decay constant.

Also, time, $t = 2\tau = 2 \times \frac{1}{\lambda} = \frac{2}{\lambda}$

Thus, mass remained after time t,

$$M = M_0 e^{-\lambda t} = 10 e^{-\lambda \times \frac{2}{\lambda}} \quad (\because M_0 = 10 \text{g})$$

$$= 10e^{-2} = \frac{10}{e^2} = 1.35 \text{ g}$$

112 (a) The decay rate R of a radioactive material is the number of decays per second.

From radioactive decay law,

$$-\frac{dN}{dt} \propto N \text{ or } -\frac{dN}{dt} = \lambda N$$

Thus, $R = -\frac{dN}{dt} \Rightarrow R = \lambda N$

$$\Rightarrow \quad R = \lambda N_0 e^{-\lambda t} \quad \text{...(i)}$$

where, $R_0 = \lambda N_0$ is the activity of the radioactive material at time $t = 0$.

At time t_1, $R_1 = R_0 e^{-\lambda t_1}$ ...(ii)

At time t_2, $R_2 = R_0 e^{-\lambda t_2}$ ...(iii)

On dividing Eq. (ii) by Eq. (iii), we have

$$\frac{R_1}{R_2} = \frac{e^{-\lambda t_1}}{e^{-\lambda t_2}} = e^{-\lambda(t_1 - t_2)}$$

or $R_1 = R_2 e^{-\lambda(t_1 - t_2)}$

113 (b) To form its own isotope, atomic number (Z) should remain same. So, the emission of one α-particle and two β-particles will maintain the Z same.

where, α-particle $= {}_2He^4$ and

β-particle $= {}_{-1}\beta^0$

114 (a) From Rutherford and Soddy law, the rate of decay of a radioactive substance is proportional to number of atoms left at that instant, using this we can arrive at

$$N = N_0\left(\frac{1}{2}\right)^n$$

where, N_0 is original number of atoms and n is the number of half-lives.

$$n = \frac{t}{T_{1/2}} = \frac{180}{60} = 3$$

$$\therefore \quad \frac{N}{N_0} = \left(\frac{1}{2}\right)^n = \left(\frac{1}{2}\right)^3 = \frac{1}{8}$$

$$\Rightarrow \quad N = \frac{N_0}{8} = 0.125 N_0$$

$$= 12.5\%$$

$\therefore$ Amount decayed

$$= 100 - 12.5 = 87.5\%$$

115 (c) Given, total time = 80 min

Number of half-lives of A,

$$n_A = \frac{80}{20} = 4$$

Number of half-lives of B, $n_B = \frac{80}{40} = 2$

Number of nuclei remains undecayed,

$$N = N_0\left(\frac{1}{2}\right)^n$$

where, N_0 is initial number of nuclei.

$$\therefore \quad \frac{N_A}{N_B} = \frac{\left(\frac{1}{2}\right)^{n_A}}{\left(\frac{1}{2}\right)^{n_B}} = \frac{\left(\frac{1}{2}\right)^4}{\left(\frac{1}{2}\right)^2} = \frac{\left(\frac{1}{16}\right)}{\left(\frac{1}{4}\right)} = \frac{1}{4}$$

116 (b) From Rutherford-Soddy law, the fraction left after n half-lives is

$$N = N_0\left(\frac{1}{2}\right)^n$$

where, n is number of half-lives.

$$n = \frac{\text{time } (t)}{\text{half-life } (T_{1/2})} = \frac{2}{4} = \frac{1}{2}$$

$$\Rightarrow \quad \frac{N}{N_0} = \left(\frac{1}{2}\right)^{1/2} = \frac{1}{\sqrt{2}}$$

117 (a) Atom with positively charged nucleus has electrons revolving around it in stationary orbits. The Coulomb's forces provides the necessary centripetal force of attraction to keep the electrons in orbits.

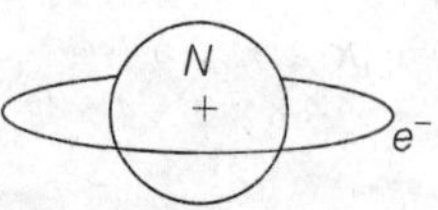

118 (a) When nuclear masses are measured, the mass is always found to be less than the sum of the masses of the individual nucleons bound in the nucleus. This difference between the nuclear mass and the sum of individual masses is known as mass defect.

Mass of nucleons = Isotopic mass + Mass defect

Hence, mass of nucleons together in a heavy nucleus is greater than the mass of nucleus.

119 (d) Applying charge and mass conservation,

$$4 + A = A + 3 + A' \Rightarrow A' = 1$$

$$2 + Z = Z + 2 + Z' \Rightarrow Z' = 0$$

Hence, M is neutron.

120 (a) When an alpha or a beta decay takes place, the daughter nucleus is generally formed in one of its excited states eventually comes to its ground state by emitting a photon or electromagnetic radiation. The process of a nucleus coming down to a lower energy level by emitting a photon is called gamma decay. Hence, γ-rays are originated from excited nucleus.

121 (a) Mass number of an element is the total number of protons and neutrons present inside the atomic nucleus of the element. It is represented by A with A is different for different elements. Mass number of a nucleus is sometimes equal to its atomic number, e.g. in case of hydrogen, number of neutrons = 0.

So, mass number = atomic number.

122 (b) On combination, some energy is released, which is obtained from mass energy conversion of particles, so the mass of nucleus is less than the sum of mass of protons and neutrons.

123 (b) Let the daughter nucleus be , so reaction can be shown as

$${}^{238}_{92}U \longrightarrow {}^{A}_{Z}X + {}^{4}_{2}He$$

From conservation of atomic mass

$$238 = A + 4 \Rightarrow A = 234$$

From conservation of atomic number

$$92 = Z + 2 \Rightarrow Z = 90$$

So, the resultant nucleus is ${}^{234}_{90}X$,

i.e. ${}^{234}_{90}Th$.

124 (c) After n half-lives (i.e. at $t = nT$), the number of nuclides left undecayed,

$$N = N_0(1/2)^n$$

Given, $\frac{N}{N_0} = \frac{1}{16}$

$\Rightarrow \frac{1}{16} = \left(\frac{1}{2}\right)^n$ or $\left(\frac{1}{2}\right)^4 = \left(\frac{1}{2}\right)^n$

Equating the powers, we obtain, $n = 4$

i.e. $\frac{t}{T} = 4$

$\Rightarrow t = 4T$

$\therefore t = 4 \times 5730 = 22920$ yr $(\because T = 5730 \text{ yr})$

125 (a) Radiotherapy is exposing tumours/ cancer cells to radiations, from radioactive elements like, Cobalt-60, Radon-120 and I-131.

Cobalt-60 is a source of γ-radiations. These radiations kill cancer cells much rapidly. However, healthy cells in vicinity of cancer cells are also damaged.

126 (d) The percentage of radioactive substance left behind after time t,

$$\frac{N}{N_0} = (100 - 18)\% = 82\%$$

Also, $\frac{N}{N_0} = e^{-\lambda t}$

$\Rightarrow \frac{82}{100} = e^{-(\lambda \times 24 \times 60 \times 60)}$

$\Rightarrow (24 \times 60 \times 60 \times \lambda) = \log\left(\frac{82}{100}\right)$

$\Rightarrow \lambda = 2.1 \times 10^{-6}\ s^{-1}$

127 (c) The decay rate R of a radioactive element is the number of decays per second.

$$n = R = \lambda N$$

where, λ = decay constant.

$$= \frac{0.693}{\text{half-life}} = \frac{0.693}{T}$$

$\therefore n = \frac{0.693}{T} N$

or $T = \frac{0.693\,N}{n}$ s

128 (a) Decay constant,

$$\lambda = \frac{0.693}{T} = \frac{0.693}{3.64} = 0.1904 \text{ per day}$$

Also, $N = N_0 e^{-\lambda t}$

Given, $\frac{N}{N_0} = 0.1 = 10^{-1}$

$\Rightarrow 10^{-1} = e^{-\lambda t}$

$\Rightarrow e^{\lambda t} = 10$

$\Rightarrow \lambda t = \log_e 10$

$= 2.3026 \times \log_{10} 10$

$= 2.3026 \times 1$

$\therefore t = \frac{2.3026 \times 1}{\lambda}$

$= \frac{2.3026 \times 1}{0.1904}$

$= 12.1$ days

129 (c) The activity, $\frac{dN}{dt} = -\lambda N$

As per question,

$$x = -\lambda N_{t_1},\ y = -\lambda N_{t_2}$$

$\Rightarrow N_{t_1} = -\frac{x}{\lambda},\ N_{t_2} = -\frac{y}{\lambda}$

The number of atoms disintegrated in time interval,

$$N_{t_2} - N_{t_1} = -\frac{y}{\lambda} - \left(-\frac{x}{\lambda}\right)$$

$$= \frac{x - y}{\lambda} = (x - y)\tau$$

where, τ = mean life of the sample.

130 (a) The nuclei which have same number of neutrons but different atomic number and mass number are known as isotones. In choice (a) nuclei of $_{34}Se^{74}$ and $_{31}Ga^{71}$ are isotones as

$$A - Z = 74 - 34 = 71 - 31 = 40$$

131 (c) (i) Electron revolves around the nucleus of an atom. It is a stable particle.

(ii) Proton has positive charge and its mass is 1836 times the electronic mass. In free state, the proton is a stable particle.

(iii) Neutron carries no charge. Its mass is 1839 times the electronic mass (1.675×10^{-27} kg). In free state, the neutron is unstable (its mean life is about 17 min), but it constitutes a stable nucleus along with proton.

(iv) α-particle stable is helium nucleus whose atomic number is 2 and mass number is 4.

Hence, out of the given four options neutron is most unstable.

132 (b) Let x be the mass number of A and y the atomic number. Then, since atomic number and mass number remain conserved, we have

$$_yA^x \longrightarrow {}_{y-2}B^{x-4} + {}_2He^4$$

$$_{y-2}B^{x-4} \longrightarrow {}_yC^{x-4} + 2\,{}_{-1}e^0$$

Hence, we observed that A and C are isotopes as their atomic numbers are same but mass numbers are different.

133 (d) X is neutrino because mass number and atomic number of neutrino is zero.

134 (c) The radioactivity does not depend on external factors.

135 (d) Mean life, $\tau = 1.44\,T_{1/2}$

$\therefore T_{1/2} = \frac{100}{1.44}$

$= 69.44\text{ s} = \frac{69.44}{60} \simeq 1.155$ min

136 (d) Radioactive decay does not depend upon the time of creation.

137 (d) Number of nuclei remain undecayed,

$$N_A = N_0 e^{-10\lambda t}$$

and $N_B = N_0 e^{-\lambda t}$

$\Rightarrow \frac{N_A}{N_B} = \frac{1}{e} = e^{(-10\lambda + \lambda)t}$

or $9\lambda t = 1$

$\Rightarrow t = \frac{1}{9\lambda}$

138 (c) The compound can emit neutrons. This is because neutrons are neutral particles, i.e. they do not have any charge on them, so do not deflected in a magnetic field.

139 (b) When an atom emits an α-particle its mass number decreases by 4 and atomic number by 2. When it emits a β-particle its atomic number increases by 1, while there is no change in mass number and atomic number in γ-rays emission.

$$_{72}X^{180} \xrightarrow{-\alpha} {}_{70}Y^{176} \xrightarrow{-\beta}$$

$$_{71}Z^{176} \xrightarrow{-\alpha} {}_{69}A^{172} \xrightarrow{-\gamma} {}_{69}P^{172}$$

140 (d) When an α-particle is emitted, mass number of nuclide X is reduced by 4, and its charge number reduced by 2. But when a β-particle is emitted, mass number of nuclide remains the same and its charge number is increased by 1. Hence, the resulting nuclide has atomic mass $A - 4$ and atomic number $Z - 1$.

Topic 4

Nuclear Fission & Fusion and Binding Energy

2019

1 **Assertion** Heavy water is used to slow neutron in nuclear reactor.

Reason It does not react with slow neutron and mass of deuterium is comparable to the neutron. [JIPMER]

(a) Both Assertion and Reason are correct and Reason is the correct explanation of Assertion.
(b) Both Assertion and Reason are correct but Reason is not the correct explanation of Assertion.
(c) Assertion is correct but Reason is incorrect.
(d) Both Assertion and Reason are incorrect.

2018

2 An atomic power nuclear reactor can deliver 300 MW. The energy released due to fission of each nucleus of uranium atoms fissioned per hour will be [JIPMER]

(a) 30×10^{25} (b) 10×10^{25} (c) 4×10^{22} (d) 5×10^{15}

3 In the fusion reaction, the masses of deuteron, helium and neutron expressed in amu are 2.015, 3.017 and 1.009, respectively . If 1 kg of deuterium undergoes complete fusion, then find the amount of total energy released. (1 amu = 931.5 MeV) [JIPMER]

(a) 9×10^{13} J (b) 20×10^{5} J (c) 4×10^{22} (d) 5×10^{15}

2017

4 A nucleus $_ZX^A$ has mass represented by $m(A,Z)$. If m_p and m_n denote the mass of proton and neutron respectively and BE the binding energy (in MeV), then [JIPMER]

(a) $BE = [m(A,Z) - Zm_p - (A-Z)m_p]c^2$
(b) $BE = [Zm_p + (A-Z)m_n - m(A,Z)]c^2$
(c) $BE = [Zm_p + Am_p - m(A,Z)]c^2$
(d) $BE = m(A,Z) - Zm_p - (A-Z)m_n$

5 A nuclear explosive is designed to deliver 1MW power in the form of heat energy. If the explosion is designed with nuclear fuel consisting of U^{235} to run a reactor at this power level for one year, then the amount of fuel needed is (take, energy per fission is 200 MeV) [AIIMS]

(a) 1 kg (b) 0.01 kg (c) 3.84 kg (d) 0.384 kg

2014

6 The binding energy per nucleon of $^7_3$Li and $^4_2$He nuclei are 5.60 MeV and 7.06 MeV respectively. In the nuclear reaction $^7_3\text{Li} + ^1_1\text{H} \rightarrow ^4_2\text{He} + ^4_2\text{He} + Q$, the value of energy Q released is [CBSE AIPMT]

(a) 19.6 MeV (b) – 2.4 MeV
(c) 8.4 MeV (d) 17.3 MeV

7 For the stability of any nucleus, [KCET]

(a) binding energy per nucleon will be more
(b) binding energy per nucleon will be less
(c) number of electrons will be more
(d) None of the above

8 The total binding energy of $_1H^2$, $_2He^4$, $_{28}Fe^{56}$ and $_{92}U^{235}$ nuclei are 2.22, 28.3, 492 and 786 MeV respectively. Identify the most stable nucleus of the following. [UP CPMT]

(a) $_{28}Fe^{56}$ (b) $_1H^2$
(c) $_{92}U^{238}$ (d) $_2He^4$

9 The control rods used in a nuclear reactor can be made up of [Kerala CEE]

(a) graphite (b) cadmium
(c) uranium (d) barium
(e) lead

10 The fusion reaction in the sun is a multi-step process in which the [Kerala CEE]

(a) helium is burned into deuterons
(b) helium is burned into hydrogen
(c) deuteron is burned into hydrogen
(d) hydrogen is burned into helium
(e) helium is burned into neutrons

11 The nuclear fusion reaction between deuterium and tritium takes place [EAMCET]

(a) at low temperature and low pressure
(b) at very high temperature and very high pressure
(c) when the temperature is near absolute zero
(d) at ordinary temperature and pressure

2011

12 The element with maximum value of binding energy per nucleon is [J&K CET]

(a) iron (b) aluminium (c) uranium (d) hydrogen

13 When two nuclei (with $A = 8$) join to form a heavier nucleus, the Binding Energy (BE) per nucleon of the heavier nuclei is [DUMET]

(a) more than the BE per nucleon of the lighter nuclei
(b) same as the BE per nucleon of the lighter nuclei
(c) less than the BE per nucleon of the lighter nuclei
(d) double the BE per nucleon of the lighter nuclei

14 Fusion reaction takes place at high temperature, because [CBSE AIPMT]

(a) atoms get ionised at high temperature
(b) kinetic energy is high enough to overcome the coulomb repulsion between nuclei
(c) molecules break up at high temperature
(d) nuclei break up at high temperature

15 Which one of the following cannot be used as a moderator in a nuclear reactor? **[Manipal]**
(a) Water (b) Heavy water
(c) Molten sodium (d) Graphite

16 Pick out the correct statement from the following. **[KCET]**
(a) Energy released per unit mass of the reactant is less in case of fusion reaction.
(b) Packing fraction may be positive or may be negative.
(c) Pu^{239} is not suitable for a fission reaction.
(d) For stable nucleus, the specific binding energy is high.

2010

17 The mass of a ${}_3^7Li$ nucleus is 0.042u less than the sum of the masses of all its nucleons. The binding energy per nucleon of ${}_3^7Li$ nucleus is nearly **[CBSE AIPMT]**
(a) 46 MeV (b) 5.6 MeV
(c) 3.9 MeV (d) 23 MeV

18 Binding energy of nucleus is defined as **[Punjab PMET]**
(a) the energy released, when the nucleus has been separated into its constituent particle
(b) the energy required, to separate the nucleus from the constituent particles
(c) the energy required to form the nucleus from its constituent particle
(d) None of the above

19 The energy released by the fission of one uranium atom is 200 MeV. The number of fission per second required to produce 3.2 W of power is (take, 1 eV = 1.6×10^{-19} J) **[WB JEE]**
(a) 10^7 (b) 10^{10}
(c) 10^{15} (d) 10^{11}

20 If 200 MeV of energy is released in the fission of 1 nucleus of ${}_{92}U^{235}$, then the number of nuclei that undergo fission to produce energy of 10 kWh in 1 s, is **[EAMCET]**
(a) 11.25×10^{18} (b) 22.5×10^{17}
(c) 11.25×10^{17} (d) 22.5×10^{18}

2009

21 Atomic mass of ${}_6^{13}C$ is 13.00335 amu and its mass number is 13. If, 1 amu = 931MeV, binding energy of the neutrons presents in the nucleus is **[EAMCET]**
(a) 0.24 MeV (b) 1.44 MeV
(c) 1.68 MeV (d) 3.12 MeV

22 Fusion reaction is initiated with the help of **[Manipal]**
(a) low temperature (b) high temperature
(c) neutrons (d) any particle

23 If the speed of light was 2/3 of its present value, then the energy released in a given atomic explosion would **[KCET]**
(a) decrease by a factor 2/3
(b) decrease by a factor 4/9
(c) decrease by a factor 5/9
(d) decrease by a factor $\sqrt{5/9}$

24 Pick out the unmatched pair. **[Kerala CEE]**
(a) Moderator-heavy water
(b) Nuclear fuel - ${}_{92}U^{235}$
(c) Pressurised water reactor-Water as the heat exchange system
(d) Safety rods-Carbon
(e) Reactor is critical-Multiplication factor is unity

25 Enriched uranium is used in nuclear reactors, because it contains greater proportion of **[J&K CET]**
(a) U^{238} (b) U^{235} (c) U^{239} (d) U^{233}

2008

26 If $M(A,Z)$, M_p and M_n denote the masses of the nucleus ${}_Z^AX$, proton and neutron respectively in units of u (1 u= 931.5 MeV/c^2) and BE represents its binding energy in MeV, then **[CBSE AIPMT]**
(a) $M(A,Z)=ZM_p+(A-Z)M_n-\text{BE}/c^2$
(b) $M(A,Z)=ZM_p+(A-Z)M_n+\text{BE}$
(c) $M(A,Z)=ZM_p+(A-Z)M_n-\text{BE}$
(d) $M(A,Z)=ZM_p+(A-Z)M_n+\text{BE}/c^2$

27 The binding energies of the atoms of elements A and B are E_a and E_b, respectively. Three atoms of the element B fuse to give one atom of element A. This fusion process is accompanied by release of energy e. Then, E_a, E_b and e are related to each other as **[Manipal]**
(a) $E_a+e=3E_b$ (b) $E_a=3E_b$
(c) $E_a-e=3E_b$ (d) $E_a+3E_b+e=0$

28 If M_o is the mass of an oxygen isotope ${}_8O^{17}$, M_p and M_n are the masses of a proton and a neutron respectively, the nuclear binding energy of the isotope is **[UP CPMT]**
(a) $(M_o-8M_p)c^2$ (b) $(M_o-8M_p-9M_n)c^2$
(c) M_oc^2 (d) $(M_o-17M_n)c^2$

29 The binding energy of deuteron is 2.2 MeV and that of ${}_2^4He$ is 28 MeV. If two deuterons are fused to form one ${}_2^4He$, then the energy released is **[Haryana PMT]**
(a) 25.8 MeV (b) 23.6 MeV
(c) 19.2 MeV (d) 30.2 MeV

30 Assuming that about 20 MeV of energy is released per fusion reaction

$${}_1H^2+{}_1H^3\rightarrow{}_0n^1+{}_2He^4,$$

then the mass of ${}_1H^2$ consumed per day in a fusion reactor of power 1 MW will approximately be **[BHU]**
(a) 0.001 g (b) 0.1 g
(c) 10.0 g (d) 1000 g

31 On bombarding U^{235} by slow neutron, 200 MeV energy is released. If the power output of atomic reactor is 1.6 MW, then the rate of fission will be **[KCET]**
(a) $5\times 10^{22}\ s^{-1}$ (b) $5\times 10^{16}\ s^{-1}$
(c) $8\times 10^{16}\ s^{-1}$ (d) $20\times 10^{16}\ s^{-1}$

32 If 200 MeV energy is released in the fission of a single nucleus of $_{92}U^{235}$, then how many fissions must occur per second to produce a power of 1 kW? [BCECE]
(a) 3.12×10^{13} (b) 3.12×10^{3}
(c) 3.1×10^{17} (d) 3.12×10^{19}

2007

33 The mass of proton is 1.0073 u and that of neutron is 1.0087 *u* (*u* = atomic mass unit). The binding energy of $_2He^4$ is [BHU]
(a) 28.4 MeV (b) 0.061 u
(c) 0.0305 J (d) 0.0305 erg

34 What is the *Q*-value of the reaction

$$p + {}^7Li \longrightarrow {}^4He + {}^4He$$

The atomic masses of ^1H, ^4He and ^7Li are 1.007825 u, 4.002603 u and 7.016004 u respectively [UP CPMT]
(a) 17.35 MeV (b) 18.06 MeV
(c) 177.35 MeV (d) 170.35 MeV

35 Binding energy per nucleon relation with mass number (given, mass of helium nucleus $\simeq$ 4.0015 u) [UP CPMT]
(a) first decreases then increases
(b) first increases then decreases
(c) increases
(d) decreases

36 The fission of ^{235}U can be triggered by the absorption of a slow neutron by a nucleus. Similarly a slow proton can also be used. This statement is [AFMC]
(a) correct
(b) incorrect
(c) information is insufficient
(d) None of the above

37 Solar energy is mainly caused due to [BHU]
(a) fusion of protons during synthesis of heavier elements
(b) gravitational contraction
(c) burning of hydrogen in the oxygen
(d) fission of uranium present in the sun

38 If in a nuclear fusion process, the masses of the fusing nuclei be m_1 and m_2 and the mass of the resultant nucleus be m_3, then [Manipal]
(a) $m_3 = m_1 + m_2$ (b) $m_3 = |m_1 - m_2|$
(c) $m_3 < (m_1 + m_2)$ (d) $m_3 > (m_1 + m_2)$

39 Nuclear fission can be explained based on [J&K CET]
(a) Millikan's oil drop method
(b) Liquid drop model
(c) Shell model
(d) Bohr's model

2006

40 **Assertion** The binding energy per nucleon, for nuclei with atomic mass number $A > 100$, decreases with A.
Reason The nuclear forces are weak for heavier nuclei. [AIIMS]
(a) Both Assertion and Reason are correct and Reason is the correct explanation of Assertion.
(b) Both Assertion and Reason are correct but Reason is not the correct explanation of Assertion.
(c) Assertion is correct but Reason is incorrect.
(d) Both Assertion and Reason are incorrect.

41 Hydrogen bomb is based upon [AFMC]
(a) fission (b) fusion
(c) chemical reaction (d) transmutation

42 Nuclear fusion is common to the pair [Manipal]
(a) thermonuclear reactor, uranium based nuclear reactor
(b) energy production in the sun, uranium based nuclear reactor
(c) energy production in the sun, hydrogen bomb
(d) disintegration of heavy nuclei, hydrogen bomb

43 Which is nuclear fusion reaction? [JCECE]
(a) Hydrogen to helium
(b) Uranium to krypton
(c) Hydrogen to water
(d) Neutron to proton

44 Two nucleons are at a separation of 1 Fm. The net force between them is F_1, if both are neutrons, F_2, if both are protons and F_3, if one is a proton and the other is a neutron, then [MHT CET]
(a) $F_1 > F_2 > F_3$ (b) $F_2 > F_1 > F_3$
(c) $F_1 = F_3 = F_2$ (d) $F_1 = F_2 > F_3$

45 **Assertion** Nuclear forces arise from strong interactions between protons and neutrons.
Reason Nuclear forces are independent of the charge of the nucleons. [EAMCET]
(a) Both Assertion and Reason are correct and Reason is the correct explanation of Assertion.
(b) Both Assertion and Reason are correct but Reason is not the correct explanation of Assertion.
(c) Assertion is correct but Reason is incorrect.
(d) Both Assertion and Reason are incorrect.

2005

46 In the reaction ${}^2_1H + {}^3_1H \rightarrow {}^4_2He + {}^1_0n$, if the binding energies of ${}^2_1H$, ${}^3_1H$ and ${}^4_2He$ are respectively a, b and c (in MeV), then the energy (in MeV) released in this reaction is [CBSE AIPMT]
(a) $c + a - b$ (b) $c - a - b$
(c) $a + b + c$ (d) $a + b - c$

47 If the binding energies of a deuteron and an α-particle are 1.125 MeV and 7.2 MeV, respectively, then the more stable of the two is **[J&K CET]**
(a) deuteron
(b) α-particle
(c) Both (a) and (b)
(d) sometimes deuteron and sometimes alpha-particle

48 The curve of binding energy per nucleon as a function of atomic mass number has a sharp peak for helium nucleus. This implies that helium **[UP CPMT]**
(a) can easily be broken up
(b) is very stable
(c) can be used as fissionable material
(d) is radioactive

49 Fission of nuclei is possible, because the binding energy per nucleon in them **[CBSE AIPMT]**
(a) increases with mass number at high mass numbers
(b) decreases with mass number at high mass numbers
(c) increases with mass number at low mass numbers
(d) decreases with mass number at low mass numbers

50 In any fission process, the ratio $\dfrac{\text{mass of fission products}}{\text{mass of parent nucleus}}$ is **[CBSE AIPMT]**
(a) less than 1
(b) greater than 1
(c) equal to 1
(d) depend on the mass of parent nucleus

51 The fusion process is possible at high temperatures, because at higher temperatures **[J&K CET]**
(a) the nucleus disintegrates
(b) the molecules disintegrates
(c) atoms become ionised
(d) the nucleus get sufficient energy to overcome the strong forces of repulsion

52 For maintaining sustained chain reaction, the following is required **[J&K CET]**
(a) protons (b) electrons
(c) neutrons (d) positrons

53 Atomic reactor is based on **[J&K CET]**
(a) controlled chain reaction
(b) uncontrolled chain reaction
(c) nuclear fission
(d) nuclear fusion

54 A chain reaction in fission of uranium is possible, because **[RPMT]**
(a) two intermediate sized nuclear fragments are formed
(b) three neutrons are given out in each fission
(c) fragments in fission are radioactive
(d) large amount of energy is released

55 The functions of moderators in nuclear reactor is to **[RPMT]**
(a) decrease the speed of neutrons
(b) increase the speed of neutrons
(c) decrease the speed of electrons
(d) increase the speed of electrons

56 The nuclear energy produced in nuclear reactor is used to run **[Punjab PMET]**
(a) AC motor
(b) induction generator
(c) electric generator
(d) DC motor

57 When helium nuclei bombard Beryllium nuclei, then **[DUMET, CBSE AIPMT]**
(a) electrons are emitted
(b) protons are emitted
(c) neutrons are emitted
(d) protons and neutrons are emitted

58 The thermonuclear reaction of hydrogen inside the stars is taking place by a cycle of operations. The particular element which acts as a catalyst is **[KCET]**
(a) nitrogen (b) oxygen
(c) helium (d) carbon

59 A neutron breaks into a proton, an electron (β-particle) and anti-neutrino $({}_0n^1 \longrightarrow {}_1\text{H}^1 + {}_1\beta^0 + \bar{\nu})$. The energy released in the process in MeV is **[AIIMS]**
(a) 731 MeV (b) 7.31 MeV
(c) 0.731 MeV (d) 1.17 MeV

Answers

1 (a)	2 (c)	3 (a)	4 (b)	5 (d)	6 (d)	7 (a)	8 (a)	9 (b)	10 (d)
11 (b)	12 (a)	13 (a)	14 (b)	15 (a)	16 (d)	17 (b)	18 (d)	19 (d)	20 (c)
21 (d)	22 (b)	23 (c)	24 (d)	25 (b)	26 (a)	27 (a)	28 (b)	29 (b)	30 (b)
31 (b)	32 (a)	33 (a)	34 (a)	35 (b)	36 (b)	37 (a)	38 (c)	39 (d)	40 (c)
41 (b)	42 (c)	43 (a)	44 (c)	45 (b)	46 (b)	47 (b)	48 (b)	49 (b)	50 (a)
51 (d)	52 (c)	53 (a)	54 (b)	55 (a)	56 (c)	57 (c)	58 (d)	59 (c)	

Explanations

1 (a) Heavy water (D_2O) is used to slow down fast moving neutrons in nuclear reactor, hence it is called moderator. It does remove neutrons from the system by absorbing them. When fast moving neutrons are passed through heavy water (D_2O), then they make elastic collisions with protons or deuterium having mass comparable to neutrons, which have comparatively much smaller than velocities. In few interactions, the velocities of neutrons get interchanged with those of protons. Heavy water does not react with slow moving neutrons, i.e. it slow down-fast moving neutrons.

Hence, Assertion and Reason both are correct and Reason is the correct explanation of Assertion.

2 (c) Power $= \dfrac{\text{Energy}}{\text{Time}}$

$= 300 \times 10^6$ W

$= 3 \times 10^8$ J/s

Energy released due to fission

$= 170$ MeV

$= 170 \times 10^6 \times 1.6 \times 10^{-19}$

$= 27.2 \times 10^{-12}$ J

Number of atoms fissioned per second,

$$\frac{3 \times 10^8}{27.2 \times 10^{-12}} = \frac{3 \times 10^{20}}{27.2}$$

Number of atoms fissioned per hour

$$= \frac{3 \times 10^{20} \times 3600}{27.2}$$

$= 4 \times 10^{22}$ m

3 (a) $\Delta m = 2(2.015) - (3.017 + 1.009)$

$= 0.004$ amu

$\because$ Energy released

$= (0.004 \times 931.5)$ MeV

$= 3.726$ MeV

Energy released per deuterium,

$$= \frac{3.726}{2} = 1.863 \text{ MeV}$$

Number of deuterons in 1 kg

$$= \frac{6.02 \times 10^{26}}{2}$$

$= 3.01 \times 10^{26}$.

$\because$ Energy released per kg of deuterium fusion

$= (3.01 \times 10^{26} \times 1.863)$

$= 5.6 \times 10^2$ MeV

$= 9 \times 10^{13}$ J

4 (b) According to mass defect, if the quantity of mass disappearing is Δm, then the binding energy is

$$BE = \Delta mc^2$$

From the above discussion, the Δm is given by

$$\Delta m = Zm_p - Nm_n - m(A, Z)$$

where, $m(A, Z)$ is the mass of the atom of mass number A and atomic number Z.

Hence, the BE of nucleus is

$$BE = (Zm_p + Nm_n - m(A, Z))c^2$$

$$BE = [Zm_p + (A - Z)m_n - m(A, Z)]c^2$$

5 (d) Energy released per fission,

$E = 200$ Mev $= 200 \times 1.6 \times 10^{-13}$.

$= 3.2 \times 10^{-11}$ J

Total energy required to run a 1 MW reaction for one year

$= 10^6$ J s^{-1} $\times (365 \times 24 \times 60 \times 60)$

$= 3.15 \times 10^{13}$ J

Since, 1 fission (atom of U^{235}) produces 3.2×10^{-11} J of energy.

So, total number of U^{235} atoms required is $\dfrac{3.15 \times 10^{13}}{3.2 \times 10^{-11}} = 9.84 \times 10^{23}$.

$\because$ Mass of U^{235} containing 9.84×10^{23} atom,

$$M = \frac{235}{6.02 \times 10^{23}} = 9.84 \times 10^{23}$$

$= 384$ g $= 0.384$ kg

6 (d) The binding energy for $_1H^1$ is around zero and also not given in the question, so we can ignore it

$Q = 2(4 \times 7.06) - 7 \times (5.60)$

$= (8 \times 7.06) - (7 \times 5.60)$

$= 56.48 - 39.2$

$= 17.28$ MeV

$\simeq 17.3$ MeV

7 (a) The binding energy of a nucleus is the energy required to take its nucleons away from one another. It is generally expressed as binding energy per nucleon. It is a measure of the stability of the nucleus. Higher the binding energy per nucleon, more stable is the nucleus.

8 (a) Binding energy per nucleon

For $_1H^2$, $\quad E_1 = \dfrac{2.22}{2} = 1.11$ MeV

For $_1He^4$, $\quad E_2 = \dfrac{28.3}{4} = 7.08$ MeV

For $_{28}Fe^{56}$, $E_3 = \dfrac{492}{56} = 8.80$ MeV

For $_{92}U^{235}$, $E_4 = \dfrac{786}{235} = 3.35$ MeV

Hence, it is obvious that $_{28}Fe^{56}$ is most stable as its binding energy per nucleon is highest.

9 (b) The control rods used in a nuclear reactor can be made up of cadmium, because control rods have to absorb fast moving neutrons.

10 (d) The fusion reaction in the sun is a multi-step process in which the hydrogen is burned into helium. Because in fusion, lighter nuclei combine to form heavier nucleus.

11 (b) In practical, the nuclear fusion is a very difficult process. Since, the nuclei to be fused are positively charged, they would repel one another strongly. Hence, they must be brought very close together not only by high pressure, but also with high kinetic energy ($\simeq 0.1$ MeV).

For this, a temperature of the other of 10^8 K is required.

So, the nuclear fusion reaction between deuterium and tritium takes place at very high temperature and very high pressure.

12 (a) We have to consider binding energy per nucleon curve, where we can find that iron (Fe) is having maximum binding energy per nucleon.

13 (a) When two nuclei join to form a heavier nucleus the binding energy (BE) per nucleon of the heavier nuclei is more than the BE per nucleon of the lighter nuclei.

14 (b) Fusion reaction takes place at high temperature because kinetic energy is high enough to overcome the Coulomb repulsion between nuclei.

15 (a) Moderator is used to slow down the fast moving neutrons. Most commonly used moderator are graphite and heavy water (D_2O). Water cannot be used as moderator in a nuclear reactor.

16 (d) For stable nucleus, specific binding energy is high.

17 (b) If $m = 1$ u, $c = 3 \times 10^8$ ms^{-1}, then
$E = 931$ MeV i.e. 1u = 931 MeV
Binding energy
$= 0.042 \times 931 = 39.10$ MeV
$\therefore$ Binding energy per nucleon
$= \frac{39.10}{7} = 5.58$
$\simeq 5.6$ MeV

18 (d) The binding energy of nucleus is the energy released in formation of nucleus by combining its constituent particles, i.e. nucleons. In other words, it is that external energy which is required to isolate the nucleons of the nucleus from each other.

19 (d) We have, the energy released by fission of one uranium atom is 200 MeV, so
$E = 200 \times 10^6 \times 1.6 \times 10^{-19}$
$= 3.2 \times 10^{-11}$ J

The power required = 3.2 W
Thus, the number of fission required is equal to $\frac{3.2}{3.2 \times 10^{-11}} = 10^{11}$ fissions.

20 (c) As, $P = n\left(\frac{E}{t}\right)$
$\Rightarrow 10 \text{ kWh} = n\left[\frac{200 \text{ MeV}}{t}\right]$
$\Rightarrow 10 \times 10^3 \times 60 \times 60 = n \times 200 \times 10^6 \times 1.6 \times 10^{-19}$ ($\because t = 1$)
$\therefore \quad n = \frac{10 \times 10^3 \times 60 \times 60}{200 \times 10^6 \times 1.6 \times 10^{-19}}$
$= \frac{36 \times 10^{19}}{200 \times 1.6} = \frac{360 \times 10^{18}}{200 \times 1.6}$
$= 1.125 \times 10^{18}$
$= 11.25 \times 10^{17}$

21 (d) Binding energy of neutron,
$E = \Delta m \times 931$ MeV
$= (13.00335 - 13) \times 931$ MeV
$= 3.12$ MeV

22 (b) Fusion reaction is initiated with the help of high temperature.

23 (c) Energy released
$\Delta E = mc^2 - mc^2 \times \left(\frac{2}{3}\right)^2$
$= \left(1 - \frac{4}{9}\right) mc^2 = \frac{5}{9} mc^2$

Hence, energy relased decrease by a factor of $\frac{5}{9}$.

24 (d) Carbon rods are not used as safety rods.
For this, cadmium rods are used because they can absorb the neutrons.

25 (b) Enriched uranium is used in nuclear reactors, because it contains greater proportion of U^{235}.

26 (a) Binding energy of a nucleus containing N neutrons and Z protons is
$BE = [NM_n + ZM_p - M(A, Z)]c^2$
$\Rightarrow \frac{BE}{c^2} = NM_n + ZM_p - M(A, Z)$
$\Rightarrow \frac{BE}{c^2} = (A - Z)M_n + ZM_p - M(A, Z)$
(As, $N = A - Z$)
$\Rightarrow M(A,Z) = ZM_p + (A-Z)M_n - BE/c^2$

27 (a) As, $Q = \Sigma B_r - \Sigma B_p$
Here, $\Sigma B_r = 3E_b, \Sigma B_p = E_a, Q = e$
$\therefore \quad e = 3E_b - E_a \Rightarrow E_a + e = 3E_b$

28 (b) Binding energy,
$BE = (M_{\text{nucleus}} - M_{\text{nucleons}})c^2$
$= (M_o - 8M_p - 9M_n)c^2$

29 (b) The reaction can be written as
${}_1H^2 + {}_1H^2 \longrightarrow {}_2He^4 + \text{Energy}$
The energy released in the reaction is difference of binding energies of daughter and parent nuclei.
Hence, energy released = binding energy of ${}_2He^4$ $- 2\times$ Binding energy of ${}_1H^2$
$= 28 - 2 \times 2.2 = 23.6$ MeV

30 (b) Energy produced, $U = Pt$
$= 10^6 \times 24 \times 36 \times 10^2$
$= 24 \times 36 \times 10^8$ J
Energy released per fusion reaction
$= 20 \text{ MeV} = 20 \times 10^6 \times 1.6 \times 10^{-19}$
$= 32 \times 10^{-13}$ J
Energy released per atom of ${}_1H^2$
$= 32 \times 10^{-13}$ J
Number of ${}_1H^2$ atoms used
$= \frac{24 \times 36 \times 10^8}{32 \times 10^{-13}} = 27 \times 10^{21}$
Mass of 6×10^{23} atoms = 2 g
$\therefore$ Mass of 27×10^{21} atoms
$= \frac{2}{6 \times 10^{23}} \times 27 \times 10^{21} = 0.1$ g

31 (b) Energy released on bombarding U^{235} by neutron = 200 MeV
Power output of atomic reactor = 1.6 MW
$\therefore$ Rate of fission
$= \frac{1.6 \times 10^6}{200 \times 10^6 \times 1.6 \times 10^{-19}}$
$= 5 \times 10^{16}$ s^{-1}

32 (a) Total energy/s = 1000 J
Energy released/fission
$= 200$ MeV
$= 200 \times 1.6 \times 10^{-13}$
$= 3.2 \times 10^{-11}$ J
$\therefore$ Number of fission/s
$= \frac{1000}{3.2 \times 10^{-11}} = 3.12 \times 10^{13}$

33 (a) The nucleus of ${}_2He^4$ contains 2 neutrons and 2 protons.
Mass of 2 protons $= 2 \times 1.0073$ $= 2.0146$ u
Mass of 2 neutrons
$= 2 \times 1.0087 = 2.0174$ u
Total mass of 2 protons and 2 neutrons
$= (2.0146 + 2.0174) = 4.032$ u
Mass of helium nucleus = 4.0015 u
Thus, mass defect is lacking of mass in forming the helium nucleus from 2 protons and 2 neutrons.
$\therefore \Delta m =$ Mass defect
$= (4.032 - 4.0015)$ u $= 0.0305$ u
$= 0.0305$ amu
but 1 amu = 931 MeV
Hence, binding energy,
$\Delta E = (\Delta m) \times 931$
$= 0.0305 \times 931 = 28.4$ MeV

34 (a) The total mass of the initial particles,
$m_i = 1.007825 + 7.016004$
$= 8.023829$ u
and the total mass of the final particles,
$m_f = 2 \times 4.002603$
$= 8.005206$ u
Difference between initial and final mass of particles,
$\Delta m = m_i - m_f$
$= 8.023829 - 8.005206$
$= 0.018623$ u
The Q-value is given by
$Q = (\Delta m)u^2$
$= 0.018623 \times 931.5$
$= 17.35$ MeV

35 *(b)* The variation of average binding energy per nucleon with mass number A is shown in figure. Average binding energy per nucleon for light nuclei like ${}_1H^1, {}_1H^2, {}_1H^3$ is small. For mass numbers, ranging from 2 to 20, there are sharply defined peaks corresponding to ${}_2He^4, {}_6C^{12}, {}_8O^{16}$ etc. The binding energy curve has a broad maximum in the range $A = 30$ to $A = 120$ corresponding to average binding energy per nucleon = 8.5 MeV. The peak value of the curve is 8.8 MeV/ nucleon for ${}_{26}Fe^{56}$. As the mass number increases, the binding energy per nucleon decreases gradually falling to about 7.6 MeV/ nucleon for ${}_{92}U^{238}$.

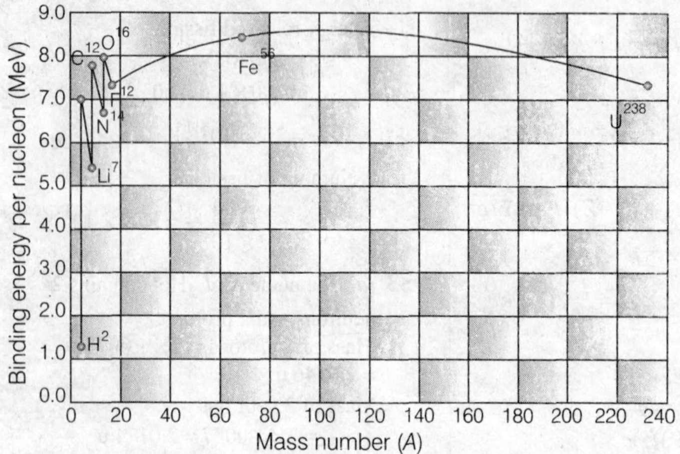

36 *(b)* Because the neutron has no electric charge, it experiences no electric repulsion from a U^{235} nucleus. Hence, a slow moving neutron can approach and enter a U^{235} nucleus, thereby providing the excitation needed to trigger fission. In contrast, a slow moving proton feels a strong repulsion from a U^{235} nucleus. It never gets close to the nucleus, so it cannot trigger nuclear fission. Hence, given statement is incorrect.

37 *(a)* In solar energy huge amount is produced due to fusion of 4 protons (hydrogen nuclei) into a heavier element (helium nucleus) according to the reaction

$${}_1H^1 + {}_1H^1 + {}_1H^1 + {}_1H^1 \rightarrow {}_2He^4 + 2\ {}_{+1}\beta^0 + \gamma\ (\text{energy}) + 2\nu$$

38 *(c)* In a nuclear fusion, when two light nuclei of different masses are combined to form a stable nucleus, then some mass is lost and appears in the form of energy, called the mass defect. So, the mass of resultant nucleus is always less than the sum of masses of initial nuclei, i.e.

$$m_3 < (m_1 + m_2)$$

39 *(d)* The nuclear fission can be explained on the basis of Bohr's model of atom.

40 *(c)* A better measure of the force between the constituents of the nucleus is the binding energy per nucleon, which is the ratio of the binding energy of a nucleus to the number of the nucleons in that nucleus. For heavy nuclei ($A > 100$), Coulomb repulsion between the protons inside the nucleus increases. This results in decrease in binding energy per nucleon. Now, nuclear force is the familiar Coulomb force that determines the motion of atomic electrons. Nuclear force is nearly same for all nuclei.

41 *(b)* Hydrogen bomb is based on nuclear fusion.

42 *(c)* The energy released in the sun and hydrogen bomb are due to nuclear fusion.

43 *(a)* Hydrogen bomb is also known as nuclear fusion bomb based upon nuclear fusion of hydrogen nuclei to helium. Since, fusion takes place under the extreme conditions of high pressure and high temperature, a fission bomb must be used as ignitor of a fusion bomb.

44 *(c)* Nuclear forces are the strong forces of attraction which hold together the nucleons (neutrons and protons) in the tiny nucleus of an atom, inspite of strong electrostatics forces of repulsion between protons. Nuclear forces act between a pair of neutrons, a pair of protons and also between a neutron, proton pair with the same strength. This shows that the nuclear forces are independent of charge.

Hence, $$F_1 = F_3 = F_2$$

45 *(b)* The nuclear force is responsible to bind the nucleons (protons and neutrons) within the nucleus. This force does not depend on the charge.

46 *(b)* Binding energy of $({}_1^2H + {}_1^3H) = a + b$

Binding energy of ${}_2^4He = c$

In a nuclear reaction, the resultant nucleus is more stable than the

reactants. Hence, binding energy of ${}_2^4He$ will be more than that of $({}_1^2H + {}_1^3H)$.

Thus, energy released per nucleon

= resultant binding energy

$= c - (a + b) = c - a - b$

47 *(b)* In order to compare the stability of the nuclei of different atoms, binding energy per nucleon is determined. Higher the binding energy per nucleon more stable is the nucleus.

$\therefore$ BE per nucleon of deuteron $= \frac{1.125}{2} = 0.5625$ MeV

BE per nucleon of alpha particle $= \frac{7.2}{4} = 1.8$ MeV

Since, binding energy per nucleon of α-particle is more, hence it is more stable.

48 *(b)* The elements higher on the binding energy *versus* mass number plot are very tightly bound and hence are stable of the element those are lower on this plot are lightly bond and hence are unstable. Hence, helium having sharp peak is very stable.

49 *(b)* The binding energy per nucleon for the middle nuclides (from $A = 20$ to $A = 56$) is maximum. Hence, these are more stable.

As the mass number increases, the binding energy per nucleon gradually decreases and ultimately binding energy per nucleon of heavy nuclides (such as uranium etc.) is comparatively low. Hence, these nuclides are relatively unstable. So, they can be fissioned easily.

50 *(a)* In fission process, when a parent nucleus breaks into daughter products, then some mass is lost in the form of energy. Thus, mass of fission products < mass of parent nucleus

$$\Rightarrow \frac{\text{Mass of fission products}}{\text{Mass of parent nucleus}} < 1$$

51 *(d)* At high temperatures, the nucleus get sufficient energy to overcome the strong forces of repulsion between them and hence fuses to give a heavier nuclei.

52 *(c)* When uranium is bombarded by neutrons, each uranium nucleus is broken into two nearly equal fragments and along with it huge energy and two or three fresh neutrons are liberated. Under favourable conditions, these neutrons produce fission with other uranium nuclei in the same way. Thus, a chain of nuclear fission is established which continues till the whole of uranium is consumed.

53 *(a)* An atomic reactor or a nuclear pile is a device in which a self-sustaining controlled chain reaction is produced in a fissionable material.

It is thus a source of controlled energy which is utilised for many useful purposes.

54 *(b)* In fission of uranium, there are three neutrons produced in each fission which further initiates fission process. Hence, this reaction becomes a chain reaction.

55 *(a)* In nuclear reactors, the moderators are used to slow down the speed of neutrons. Heavy water, graphite are used for this purpose because they are the best moderators.

56 *(c)* The nuclear energy produced in nuclear reactor is used to run electric generator.

57 *(c)* When helium nuclei bombard beryllium nuclei, then neutrons are emitted.

58 *(d)* In the cycle of operation carbon is a reactant and as well as an end product. Hence, it acts as a catalyst.

59 *(c)* According to the question,

$$_0n^1 \longrightarrow {}_1H^1 + {}_1\beta^0 + \bar{\nu}$$

The energy released can be calculated by using,

$\Delta E = \Delta mc^2 = m\,({}_1H^1 + {}_1\beta^0) - m\,({}_0n^1)$

By putting values, we get ,

$$\Delta E \simeq 0.731 \text{ MeV}$$

Topic 5
X-Rays

2013

1 **Assertion** X-rays are used for studying the structure of crystals.

Reason The difference between the atoms of crystal is of the order of wavelength of X-rays. **[AIIMS]**

(a) Both Assertion and Reason are correct and Reason is the correct explanation of Assertion.
(b) Both Assertion and Reason are correct but Reason is not the correct explanation of Assertion.
(c) Assertion is incorrect but Reason is incorrect.
(d) Both Assertion and Reason are incorrect.
(e) Assertion is incorrect but Reason is correct.

2 The difference between soft and hard X-rays is of **[RPMT]**

(a) velocity (b) intensity
(c) frequency (d) polarisation

3 The wavelength of the K_α line for an element of atomic number 43 is λ. Then, the wavelength of the K_α line for an element of atomic number 29, is **[UP CPMT, AIPMT]**

(a) $\left(\frac{43}{29}\right)\lambda$ (b) $\left(\frac{42}{28}\right)\lambda$ (c) $\left(\frac{9}{4}\right)\lambda$ (d) $\left(\frac{4}{9}\right)\lambda$

4 The intensity of X-rays from a coolidge tube is plotted against wavelength as shown in the figure. The minimum wavelength found is λ_c and the wavelength of the K_α line is λ_k. As the accelerating voltage is increased **[UP CPMT]**

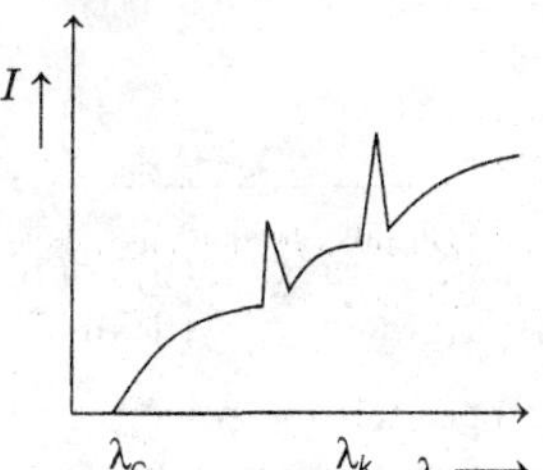

(a) $(\lambda_k - \lambda_c)$ increases (b) $(\lambda_k - \lambda_c)$ decreases
(c) λ_k increases (d) λ_k decreases

2010

5 The crystal structure can be studied using **[Manipal]**

(a) UV rays (b) X-rays
(c) IR radiation (d) Microwave

6 The potential difference between the cathode and the target electrode in a coolidge tube is 24.75 kV. The minimum wavelength of the emitted X-rays is **[Manipal]**
(a) 0.1 Å (b) 0.5 Å
(c) 1 Å (d) 5 Å

7 If maximum velocity with which an electron can be emitted from photocell is 4×10^8 cm/s, the stopping potential is (mass of electron = 9×10^{-31} kg) **[Haryana PMT]**
(a) 30 V (b) 45 V (c) 59 V
(d) Information is insufficient

8 For characteristic X-ray **[Haryana PMT]**
(a) $E(K_\gamma) < E(K_\beta) < E(K_\alpha)$
(b) $E(K_\alpha) < E(L_\alpha) < E(M_\alpha)$
(c) $\lambda(K_\gamma) < \lambda(K_\beta) < \lambda(K_\alpha)$
(d) $\lambda(M_\alpha) < \lambda(L_\alpha) < \lambda(K_\alpha)$

9 X-rays are being produced in a tube operating at 10^5 V. The velocity of X-rays produced is **[CG PMT]**
(a) 3×10^8 m/s (b) 2.8×10^8 m/s
(c) 3.1×10^8 m/s (d) 3×10^{10} m/s

2009

10 Absorption of X-rays is maximum in which of the following material sheets of same thickness? **[AFMC]**
(a) Cu (b) Au (c) Be (d) Pb

11 The wavelengths of K_a X-rays for lead isotopes Pb^{208}, Pb^{206} and Pb^{204} are λ_1, λ_2 and λ_3 respectively. Then
(a) $\lambda_1 = \lambda_2 = \lambda_3$ (b) $\lambda_1 > \lambda_2 > \lambda_3$ **[UP CPMT]**
(c) $\lambda_1 < \lambda_2 < \lambda_3$ (d) $\lambda_1 = \lambda_2 > \lambda_3$

12 Sharp peak point A represents

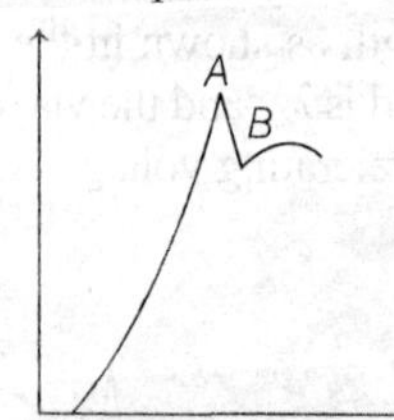

(a) characteristic X-rays (b) continuous X-rays
(c) Band spectrum (d) discontinuous spectrum

13 The spacing between the principal planes of a crystal is 4 Å. It is found that first order Bragg reflection of a beam of monochromatic X-rays occurs at an angle of 30°. The wavelength of X-rays is **[Haryana PMT, CG PMT]**
(a) 4 Å (b) 2 Å (c) 1 Å (d) 1.5 Å

14 The shortest wavelength of X-rays coming from an X-ray tube depends on the **[J&K CET]**
(a) voltage applied to the tube
(b) current in the tube
(c) atomic number of target element
(d) nature of gas in the tube

15 The energy in monochromatic X-rays of wavelength 1 Å is roughly equal to **[BCECE]**
(a) 2×10^{-15} J (b) 2×10^{-16} J
(c) 2×10^{-17} J (d) 2×10^{-18} J

2008

16 According to Moseley's law of X-ray, the frequency (ν) of a particular characteristic X-ray and the atomic number (Z) of the element depend on each other as **[J&K CET]**
(a) $\sqrt{\nu} = kZ^2$ (b) $\sqrt{\nu} = \dfrac{h}{Z^2}$
(c) $\nu = kZ$ (d) $\sqrt{\nu} = kZ$

17 Hydrogen atom does not emit X-rays, because **[KCET]**
(a) it contains only a single electron
(b) energy levels in it are far apart
(c) its size is very small
(d) energy levels in it are very close to each other

2007

18 A beam of 35.0 keV electrons strikes a molybdenum target and generate the X-rays. What is the cutoff wavelength?
(a) 35.5 Å (b) 40.0 Å **[AIIMS]**
(c) 15.95 Å (d) 18.2 Å

19 The distance between two successive atomic planes of a calcite crystal is 0.3 nm. The minimum angle for Bragg scattering of 0.3 Å X-rays will be **[RPMT]**
(a) 1.43° (b) 1.56° (c) 2.86° (d) 30°

20 An X-ray machine is opearated at 40 kV. The short wavelength limit of continuous X-rays will be (take, $h = 6.63 \times 10^{-34}$ J-s, $c = 3 \times 10^8$ ms^{-1} and $e = 1.6 \times 10^{-19}$ C) **[BCECE]**
(a) 0.31Å (b) 0.62 Å (c) 0.155 Å (d) 0.62 Å

21 Hard X-rays for the study of fractures in bones should have a minimum wavelength of 10^{-11} m. The accelerating voltage for electrons in X-ray machine should be **[JCECE]**
(a) < 124 kV
(b) > 124 kV
(c) between 60 kV and 70 kV
(d) 100 kV

2006

22 **Assertion** Standard optical diffraction cannot be used for discriminating between different X-ray wavelengths.
Reason The grating spacing is not of the order of X-ray wavelengths. **[AIIMS]**
(a) Both Assertion and Reason are correct and Reason is the correct explanation of Assertion.
(b) Both Assertion and Reason are correct but Reason is not the correct explanation of Assertion.
(c) Assertion is correct but Reason is incorrect.
(d) Both Assertion and Reason are incorrect.

23 X-rays are used in determining the molecular structure of crystalline because **[UP CPMT]**
(a) its energy is high
(b) it can penetrate the material
(c) its wavelength is comparable to interatomic distance
(d) its frequency is low

24 The minimum wavelength of X-rays emitted by X-ray tube is 0.4125 Å. The accelerating voltage is **[Manipal]**
(a) 30 kV (b) 50 kV (c) 80 kV (d) 60 kV

25 In X-ray spectrum, transition of an electron from an outer shell to an inner shell gives a characteristics X-ray spectral line. If we consider the spectral line K_β, L_β and M_α, then **[EAMCET]**
(a) K_β and L_β have a common inner shell
(b) K_β and L_β have a common outer shell
(c) L_β and M_α have a common outer shell
(d) L_β and M_α have a common inner shell

2005

26 The X-ray beam coming from an X-ray tube will be **[BHU]**
(a) monochromatic
(b) having all wavelengths lying between a minimum and a maximum wavelength
(c) having all wavelengths larger than a certain minimum wavelength
(d) having all wavelengths smaller than a certain maximum wavelength

27 Who discovered X-rays? **[BHU]**
(a) Roentgen (b) Madam Curie
(c) Rutherford (d) All of these

28 The X-ray cannot be diffracted by means of an ordinary grating due to **[Punjab PMET]**
(a) large wavelength (b) high speed
(c) short wavelength (d) All of these

Answers

1 (a)	2 (c)	3 (c)	4 (a)	5 (b)	6 (b)	7 (b)	8 (c)	9 (a)	10 (d)
11 (a)	12 (a)	13 (a)	14 (a)	15 (a)	16 (d)	17 (d)	18 (a)	19 (c)	20 (a)
21 (a)	22 (a)	23 (c)	24 (a)	25 (b)	26 (c)	27 (a)	28 (c)		

Explanations

1 *(a)* In crystal, the difference between the atoms of crystal is of the order of wavelength of X-rays. When X-rays fall on a crystal, they are diffracted. The diffraction pattern is helpful in the study of crystal structure.

2 *(c)* The penetrating power of X-rays depends upon their wavelength, which depends upon frequency. The frequency of X-rays having longer wavelength is lower and so their energy is smaller. Hence, their penetrating power is weaker and they are called soft X-rays.

While the penetrating power of X-rays, having shorter wavelength or higher frequency is stronger and they are called hard or highly penetrating X-rays.

3 *(c)* Moseley's law is given by

$$\sqrt{v} = a(Z-b)$$

For K_α line, $b = 1$

$$\therefore \quad \sqrt{v} = a(Z-1)$$

Squaring both sides, we get

$$v = a^2(Z-1)^2$$

or $$\frac{c}{\lambda} = a^2(Z-1)^2$$

or $$\lambda = \frac{c}{a^2(Z-1)^2}$$

For $Z = 43$,

$$\therefore \text{ Wavelength, } \lambda = \frac{c}{a^2(43-1)^2}$$

or $$\lambda = \frac{c}{a^2(42)^2} \quad \text{...(i)}$$

For $Z = 29$,

$$\therefore \text{ Wavelength, } \lambda' = \frac{c}{a^2(29-1)^2}$$

or $$\lambda' = \frac{c}{a^2(28)^2} \quad \text{...(ii)}$$

Dividing Eq. (ii) by Eq. (i), we get

$$\frac{\lambda'}{\lambda} = \left(\frac{42}{28}\right)^2 = \left(\frac{3}{2}\right)^2 \Rightarrow \lambda' = \left(\frac{9}{4}\right)\lambda$$

4 *(a)* Wavelength λ_k is independent of the accelerating voltage (V), while the minimum wavelength λ_c is inversely proportional to V. Therefore, as V increases λ_k remains unchanged whereas λ_c decreases as $\lambda_k - \lambda_c$ will increase.

5 *(b)* The crystal structure can be studied using X-rays.

6 *(b)* Given, $V = 24.75$ kV
$= 24.75 \times 10^3$ V

We know that,

$$\text{Minimum wavelength, } \lambda_{min} = \frac{hc}{eV}$$

$$= \frac{6.64 \times 10^{-34} \times 3 \times 10^8}{1.6 \times 10^{-19} \times 24.75 \times 10^3}$$

$$= \frac{6.64 \times 3}{1.6 \times 24.75} \times 10^{-10}$$

$$= 0.50 \times 10^{-10} = 0.5 \text{ Å}$$

7 *(b)* Given, $v_{max} = 4 \times 10^8$ cm/s
$= 4 \times 10^6$ m/s

$$\therefore \quad K_{max} = \frac{1}{2} m v_{max}^2$$

$$= \frac{1}{2} \times 9 \times 10^{-31} \times (4 \times 10^6)^2$$

$$= 7.2 \times 10^{-18} \text{ J} = 45 \text{ eV}$$

We know that,

$$K_{max} = |V_0| e$$

Hence, stopping potential

$$|V_0| = \frac{K_{max}}{e} = \frac{45 \text{ eV}}{e}$$

$$= 45 \text{ V}$$

8 *(c)* As, $E(K_\gamma) > E(K_\beta) > E(K_\alpha)$

$$\Rightarrow \lambda(K_\gamma) < \lambda(K_\beta) < \lambda(K_\alpha) \left(\because \lambda \propto \frac{1}{E}\right)$$

9 (a) X-rays travel in straight line with speed of light, i.e. 3×10^8 m/s. Because this is a part of electromagnetic radiation.

10 (d) Absorption of X-rays is maximum in the material sheets of Pb of same thickness.

11 (a) The wavelength of K_a X-rays for lead isotopes Pb^{208}, Pb^{206} and Pb^{204} will be same for all i.e. $\lambda_1 = \lambda_2 = \lambda_3$, because it does not change on changing mass number it depends only on Z, i.e. atomic number.

12 (a) Sharp peak point A represents characteristic X-rays.

13 (a) We know that, $n\lambda = 2d \sin\theta$

Given, $\theta = 30°$, $d = 4$ Å

$$\therefore \lambda = \frac{2d \sin\theta}{n} = \frac{2 \times 4 \times 10^{-10} \sin 30°}{1}$$
$$= 2 \times 4 \times 10^{-10} \times \frac{1}{2}$$
$$= 4 \times 10^{-10} \text{ m} = 4 \text{ Å}$$

14 (a) When the electron loses whole of its energy in a single collision with the atoms, an X-ray photon of maximum energy $h\nu_{max}$ is emitted i.e.

$$\frac{1}{2}mv^2 = eV = h\nu_{max} = hc/\lambda_{min}$$

Minimum wavelength = cut-off wavelength of X-ray

$$\lambda_{min} = \frac{hc}{eV} = \frac{12375}{V(\text{in volt})} \text{ Å}$$

Thus, shortest wavelenth of X-rays coming from an X-rays tube depends on the voltage applied to the tube.

15 (a) We know that, $E = \frac{hc}{\lambda}$

Given, $\lambda = 1 \text{ Å} = 1 \times 10^{-10}$ m

$$\Rightarrow \quad E = \frac{6.64 \times 10^{-34} \times 3 \times 10^8}{1 \times 10^{-10}}$$
$$= 6.64 \times 3 \times 10^{-16}$$
$$= 19.92 \times 10^{-16} = 2 \times 10^{-15} \text{ J}$$

16 (d) According to Moseley's law of X-rays, $\sqrt{\nu} = k(Z - b)$

where, k = proportionality constant

and b = shielding constant.

Here, $b = 0$

$\therefore \quad \sqrt{\nu} = kZ$

17 (d) In order for an atom to emit X-rays, an electron must jump from a high to low energy level. The difference in that energy needs to be large, enough to produce an X-ray photon, which means a jump of about 100 eV or more. In an hydrogen atom, the largest energy drop is about 10.2 eV. So, hydrogen atom does not emit X-rays due to the fact that energy levels in it are very close to each other.

18 (a) The cut-off wavelength λ_{min} corresponds to an electron transferring (approximately) all of its energy to an X-ray photon, thus producing a photon with the greatest possible frequency and least possible wavelength.

From relation

$$\lambda_{min} = \frac{hc}{K_0} = \frac{(4.14 \times 10^{-15})(3 \times 10^8)}{35.0 \times 10^3}$$
$$= 3.55 \times 10^{-11} \text{m} = 35.5 \text{ Å}$$

19 (c) For constructive interference, we have

$$2d \sin\theta = n\lambda$$

Given, $\lambda = 0.3 \text{ Å} = 0.3 \times 10^{-10}$ m

$d = 0.3 \text{ nm} = 0.3 \times 10^{-9}$ m

$$\sin\theta = \frac{n\lambda}{2d} = \frac{1 \times 0.3 \times 10^{-10}}{2 \times 0.3 \times 10^{-9}}$$
$$= 0.05 \text{ rad}$$
$$= \frac{0.05 \times 180}{\pi} = 2.86°$$

20 (a) For the most favourable collision in which the electron loses the whole of its energy in a single collision with the target atom, an X-ray photon of maximum energy $h\nu_{max}$ emitted. Thus, for an accelerating voltage V, the maximum X-ray photon energy is given by $h\nu_{max} = eV$

Also, $\lambda_{min} = \frac{hc}{eV}$

$$= \frac{6.63 \times 10^{-34} \times 3 \times 10^8}{1.6 \times 10^{-19} \times 40 \times 10^3}$$
$$= 0.31 \times 10^{-10} \text{ m} \approx 0.31 \text{ Å}$$

21 (a) From conservation of energy, the kinetic energy of electron equals the maximum photon energy (we neglect the work function ϕ because it is normally so small compared to eV_0).

$$\therefore \quad eV_0 = \frac{hc}{\lambda_{min}}$$
$$\therefore \quad V_0 = \frac{hc}{e\lambda_{min}}$$
$$\text{or} \quad V_0 = \frac{12400 \times 10^{-10}}{10^{-11}} = 124 \text{ kV}$$

Hence, accelerating voltage for electrons in X-ray machine should be less than 124 kV.

22 (a) X-rays are electromagnetic radiations whose wavelengths are of the order of 1 Å (= 10^{-10} m). A standard optical diffraction grating cannot be used to discriminate between different wavelengths in the X-ray wavelength range. For $\lambda = 1$ Å (= 0.1 nm) and $d = 3000$ nm, for example, the first order maximum occurs at

$$\theta = \sin^{-1}\left(\frac{m\lambda}{d}\right) = \sin^{-1}\frac{(1)(0.1)}{3000}$$
$$= 0.0019°$$

This is too close to the central maximum to be practical. A grating with $d \approx \lambda$ is desirable, but, since X-ray wavelengths are about equal to atomic diameter, such gratings cannot be constructed directly.

23 (c) Crystal structure is explored through the diffraction of waves having a wavelength comparable with the interatomic spacing (10^{-10} m) in crystals. Radiation of longer wavelength cannot resolve the details of structure, while radiation of much shorter wavelength is diffracted through inconveniently small angles. Usually diffraction of X-ray is employed in the study of crystal structure as X-rays have wavelength comparable to interatomic spacing.

24 (a) From the formula,

$$eV = \frac{hc}{\lambda} \Rightarrow V = \frac{hc}{e\lambda}$$
$$= \frac{6.6 \times 10^{-34} \times 3 \times 10^8}{1.6 \times 10^{-19} \times 0.4125 \times 10^{-10}}$$
$$= 30 \times 10^3 \text{ V} = 30 \text{ kV}$$

25 (b) If K_β and L_β have a common outer shell, then in X-rays spectrum, transition of an electron from an outer shell to inner shell gives a characteristics X-rays spectral line.

26 (c) The X-ray spectrum is continuous i.e. we have all wavelengths larger than a certain minimum wavelength

$$\lambda_{min} = \frac{hc}{eV},$$

where, V = accelerating potential.

27 (a) Roentgen discovered X-rays.

28 (c) For diffraction, the edges of the obstacle should be comparable to the wavelength of radiation. Wavelength of X-rays is very low, so they cannot be diffracted through ordinary grating.

27

Semiconductor Electronics

Quick Review

Among the various states of matter, electrical conductivity in solids is due to both electrons and holes and this can be understood by the help of energy band theory.

Energy Band Theory

- According to Bohr's theory, each and every shell and subshell of atoms contains a discrete amount of energy. When atoms are brought together, electrons of outermost shell interact each other. This interaction change the energy level, which give rise to energy band theory.

- Some important terms used in energy band theory are shown in tabular form below

Terms	Definitions
Energy band	A group of large number of closely spaced energy levels.
Valence band	The highest energy band occupies by the valence electrons.
Conduction band	The lowest unoccupied or empty band next to the valence band.
Forbidden band	The amount of energy needed to release an electron from valence band to conduction band.

- Classification of solids on the basis of energy band theory are given in flow chart

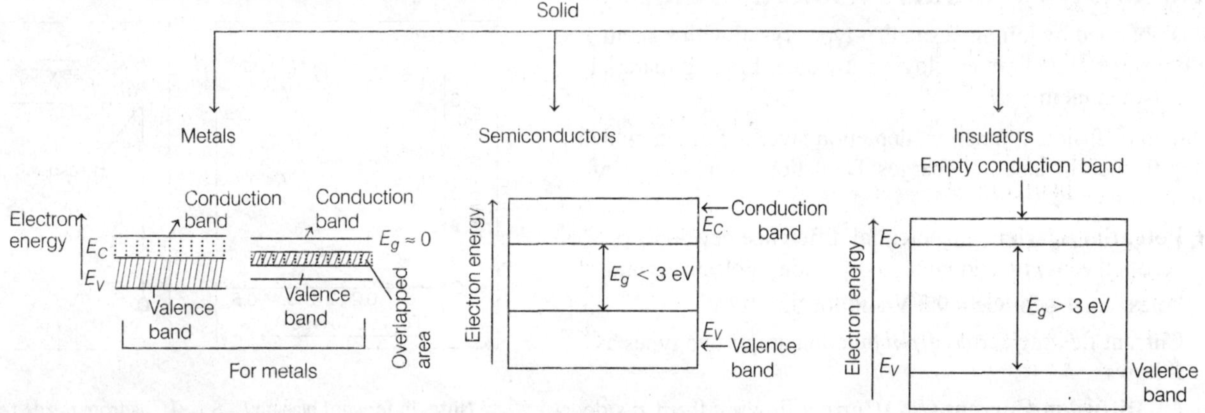

Semiconductors

These are the substances like silicon, germanium, etc. that offer resistance that lies in between that, offered by conductors and insulators.

Some important properties of semiconductors are given below

(*i*) They have negative temperature coefficient of resistance.

(*ii*) At 0K, these behave as a 100% insulator.

(*iii*) Its conductivity σ is $(10^{-5} - 10^{-6}\ \text{Sm}^{-1})$ and resistivity ρ is $(10^{-5} - 10^{6}\ \Omega\text{-m})$

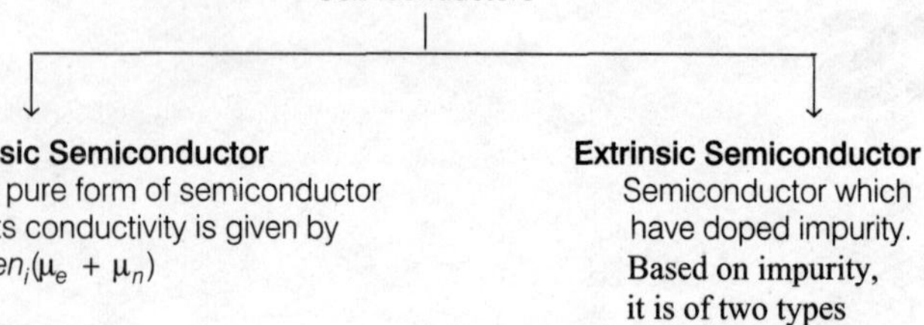

n-type Semiconductor	*p*-type Semiconductor
• In it pentavalent impurity, e.g. P, As, Sb is used as a dopant with Si or Ge.	• In it trivalent impurity, e.g. B, Al, In, Ga etc., is used as a dopant with Si or Ge.
• Pentavalent impurity is called **donor impurity** because each dopant atom provides one free **electron**.	• Trivalent impurity is called **acceptor impurity** because each dopant atom provides a **hole**.
• In it electrons are majority charge carriers and the holes are minority charges carries such that, $n_e \cdot n_h = n_i^2$.	• In it holes are majority charge carries and electrons are minority charge carriers such that $n_h \cdot n_e = n_i^2$.
• It is electrically neutral and is not negatively charged.	• It is electrically neutral and is not positively charged.

Semiconductor diode/p-n Junction diode

It is obtained by joining a small *p*-type crystal with a small *n*-type crystal without employing any other binding material in between them.

Due to diffusion at junction, depletion layer is formed, which stop further diffusion of charges. Depletion layer is made of immobile ions.

- **Potential Barrier** The potential difference developed across the *p*-*n* junction due to diffusion of electrons and holes. e.g. V_b for Ge = 0.3 V and for Si = 0.7 V.
- Current flowing across a *p*-*n* junction are of two types as follows

(*i*) **Diffusion Current** (I_{df}) Current flowing from *p*-side to *n*-side due to diffusion of electrons and holes because of concentration difference.

(*ii*) **Drift Current** (I_{dr}) Current flowing from *n*-side to *p*-side due to electron-hole pairs (because of thermal collision) created in depletion region.

- It is represented by the symbol given below

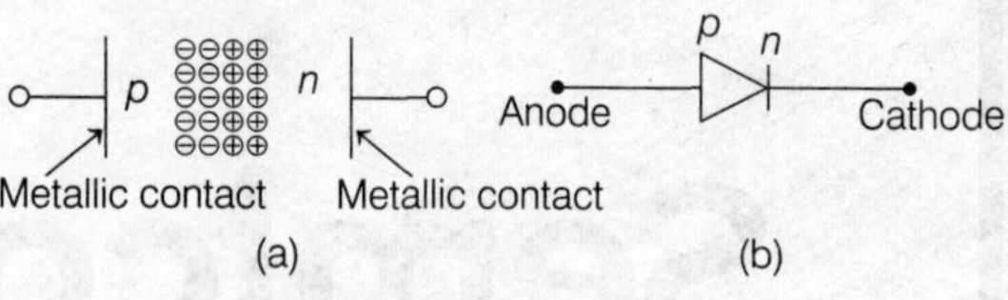

- **Dynamic resistance** (r_d) offered by junction diode will depend on applied voltage and is expressed as

$$r_d = \frac{\Delta V}{\Delta I}$$

Biasing of Junction Diode

- Biasing of junction diode is the method of connecting external battery or emf source to *p*-*n* junction.
- Biasing are of two types as given in following flow chart

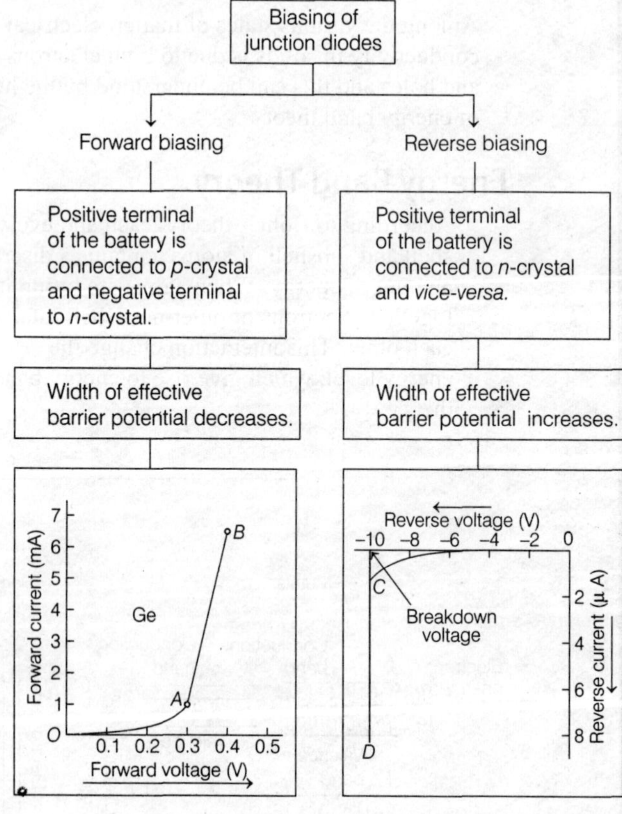

Note In forward biasing $I_{df} > I_{dr}$, I_{net} is from *p*-side to *n*-side but in reverse bias $I_{dr} > I_{df}$ or I_{net} is from *n*-side to *p*-side.

V-I Characteristic of Junction Diode

Complete *V-I* characteristic of a junction diode is shown below which does not obey Ohm's law.

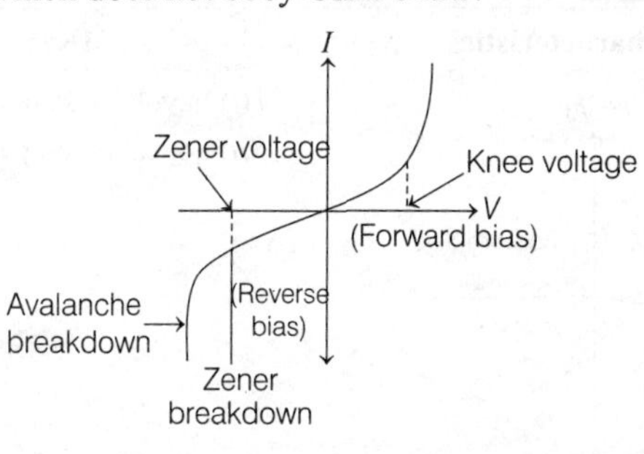

- A large current produced due to high electric field breaking the covalent bonds and producing large number of carriers in **reverse bias** is known as **zener breakdown.**
- At high **reverse voltage,** due to high electric field generating more carriers give rise to high current. This mechanism is knwon as **Avalanche breakdown.**

Diode as a Rectifier

The use of diode to rectify AC voltage and the circuit used for this purpose is known as rectifier. There are two types of it, which are given below in tabular form

	Half-Wave Rectifiers	**Full Wave Rectifiers**
Types	It uses one diode which converts the positive half cycle of the input signal into pulsating DC output as in figure.	It uses two diodes which convert the both half cycles of the input signal into a pulsating DC output, as in figure.
Circuit diagram	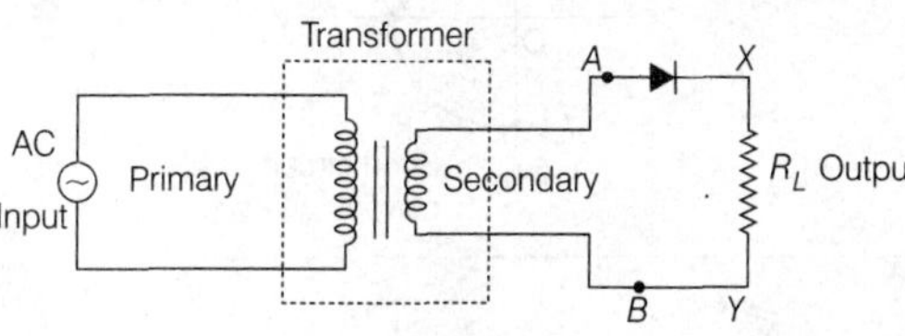	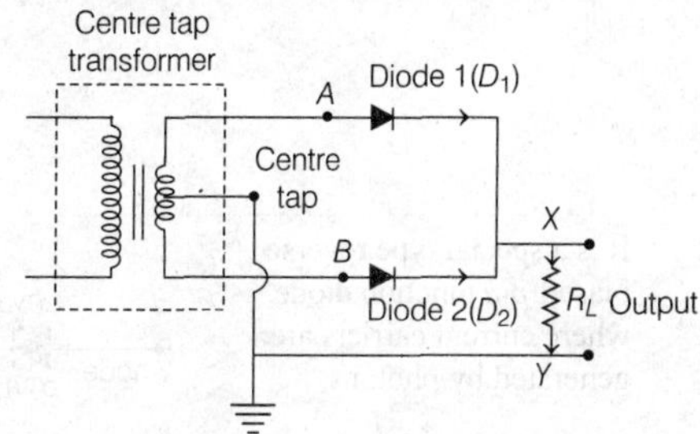
Input-Output waveforms	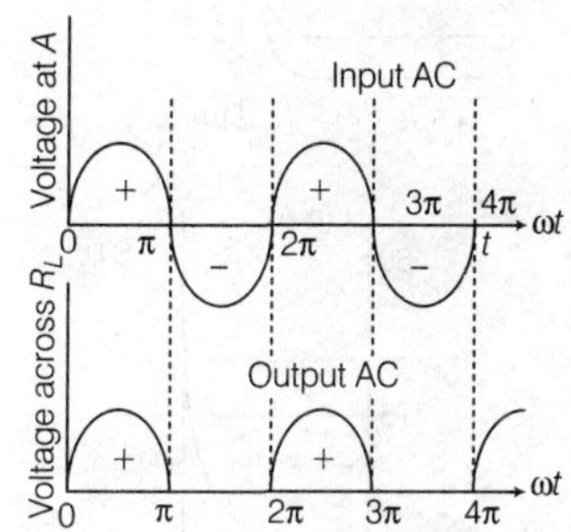	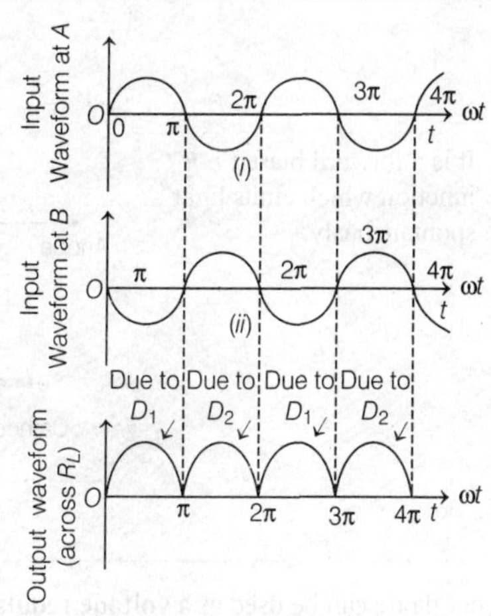
Important Terms	• The **ripple factor** $= \dfrac{\text{Effective AC component of voltage}}{\text{Effective DC component of voltage}}$ • The **average output** in one cycle is $V_{DC} = \dfrac{V_0}{\pi}$ and $I_{DC} = \dfrac{I_0}{\pi}$	• **Ripple factor** in full wave rectifier, $\dfrac{V_{AC}}{V_{DC}} = 0.48 = 48\%$ • The **average output** in one cycle is $V_{DC} = \dfrac{2}{\pi} V_0$ and $I_{DC} = \dfrac{2}{\pi} I_0$

Special Purpose *p-n* Junction Diodes

There are many types of *p-n* junction diode based on their purpose, some of them are discussed here

Devices	Description	Symbols	*V-I* Characteristics	Uses
Zener diode	It is a heavily doped *p-n* junction diode and operated in reverse bias.		I (mA) Reverse bias V_Z Forward bias O → V I (μA)	(*i*) In voltage stabilisers. (*ii*) For calibrating voltmeters.
Solar cell	It is a *p-n* junction diode that converts solar energy into electrical energy.	$h\nu$ + –	I Open circuit voltage (V_{oc}) O V I_{sc} Short circuit current	In space vehicles.
Photodiode	It is a special type reverse biased *p-n* junction diode where current carriers are generated by photons.	$h\nu$ Anode *p* *n* Cathode	mA Reverse bias volt I_1 I_2 I_3 I_4 Reverse current $I_4 > I_3 > I_2 > I_1$ μA	(*i*) In light-operated switches (*ii*) Light-detection systems. (*iii*) Computer punch cards.
Light Emitting Diode (LED)	It is a forward biased *p-n* junction which emits light spontaneously.	$h\nu$ Anode *p* *n* Cathode Cathode Anode	I (mA) 30 Silicon 20 15 10 –10V 0 0.5 0.8 V (volt) 1 μA	(*i*) As bulb. (*ii*) In optical communication.

Note Zener diode can be used as a **voltage regulator**, in which the constant output voltage is taken across a load resistance connected in parallel with it.

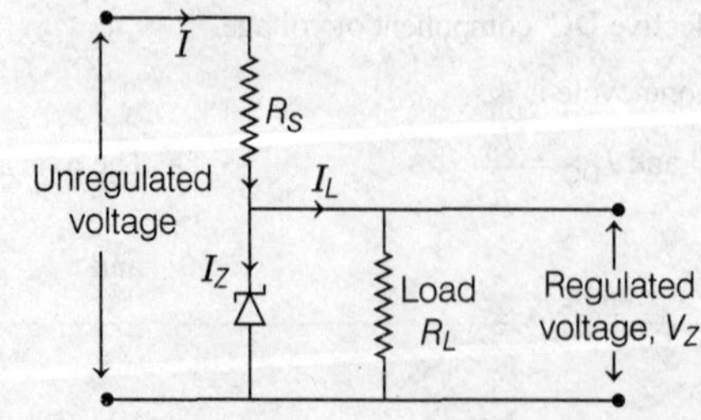

Junction Transistors

- A three terminal device formed by sandwiching a thin wafer of one type of semiconductors between two layers of another type.
- Its three terminals and their functions are as follows
  (*i*) **Emitter** (E) Heavily doped, moderate in size and emits the majority charge carriers into the base due to which current flows.
  (*ii*) **Base** (B) Lightly doped, thin and passes charge carriers from emitter to collector.
  (*iii*) **Collector** (C) Moderately doped, lies between the doping levels of emitter and base. Its size is larger as it collects the charge carriers from base.
- Circuit diagrams of *n-p-n* and *p-n-p* transistors along with other features are shown below

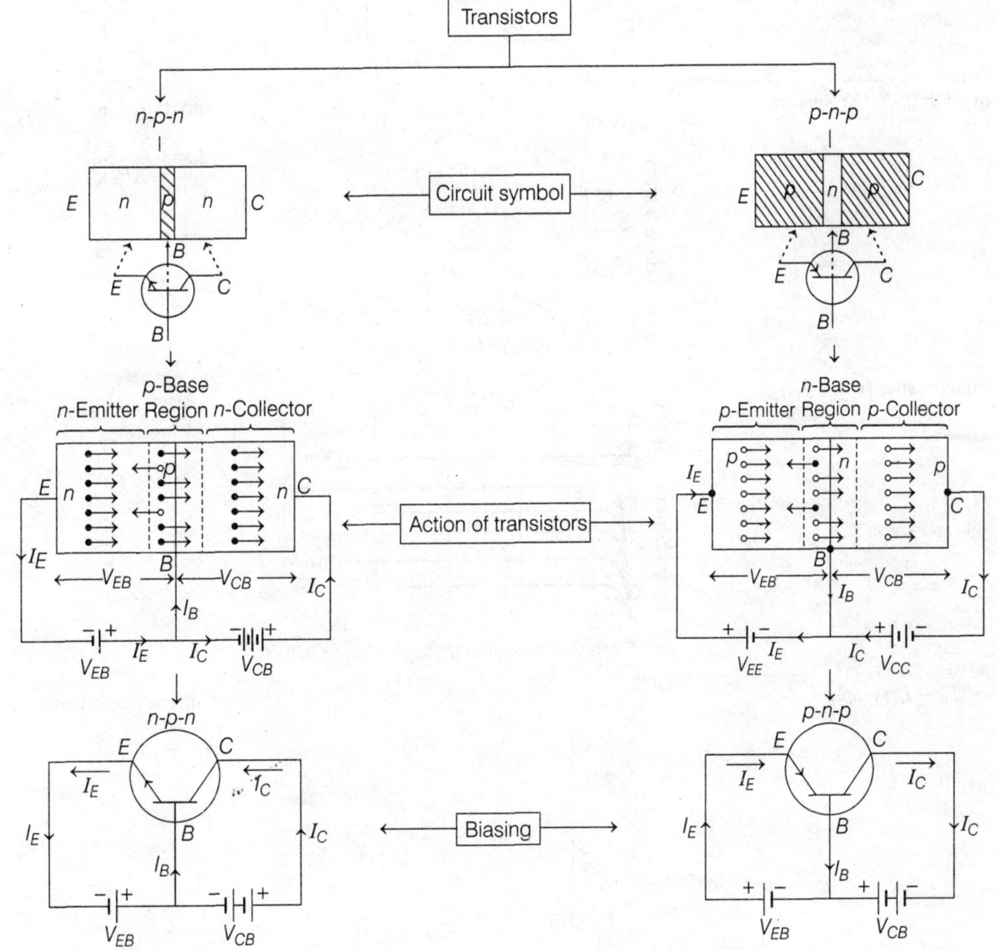

Note In *n-p-n* transistor $I_C >> I_B$ but in *p-n-p* transistor $I_C << I_B$ as emitter current $I_E = I_C + I_B$.

- Transistor configuration are of three types shown in following flow chart

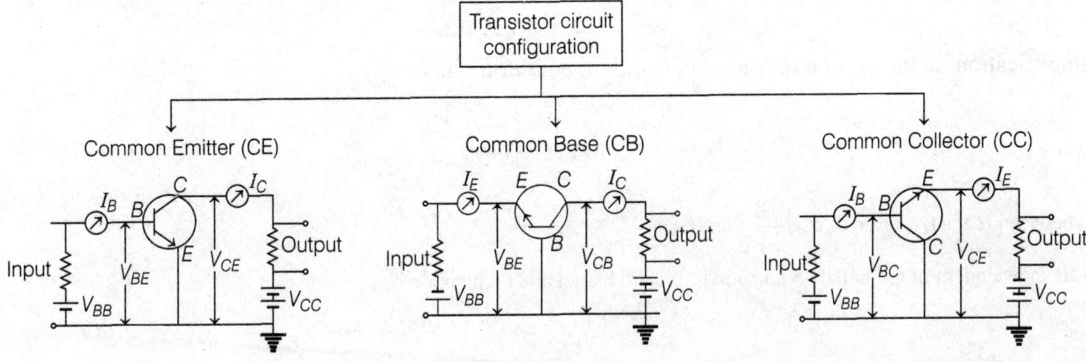

Various Characteristics of Transistor

The graphical relations are shown in tabular form below, for common emitter (CE) characteristics of a *n-p-n* transistor.

Characteristics	Diagram	Parameters
Circuit diagram of *n-p-n* transistor in CE mode	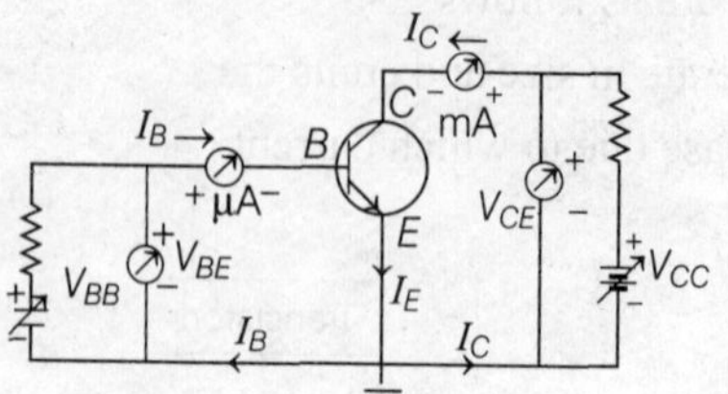	
Input characteristics of a CE (*n-p-n*) transistor ($V_{BE} \sim I_B$) graph	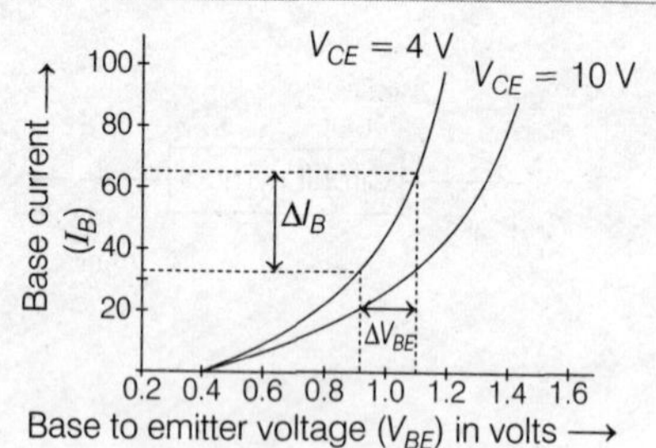	Input resistance, $R_i = \left(\frac{\Delta V_{BE}}{\Delta I_B}\right)_{V_{CE} = \text{constant}}$
Output or collector characteristics ($V_{CE} \sim I_C$) graph	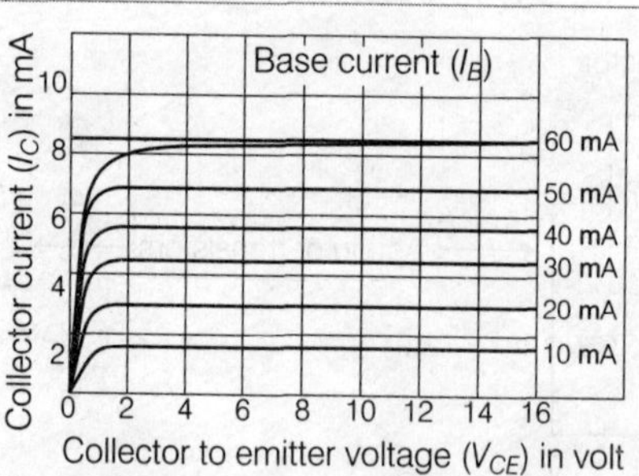	Output resistance, $r_o \left(\frac{\Delta V_{CE}}{\Delta I_C}\right)_{I_B = \text{constant}}$ = Reciprocal of slope of $I_C \sim V_{CE}$ curve
Transfer characteristics ($I_B \sim I_C$) graph	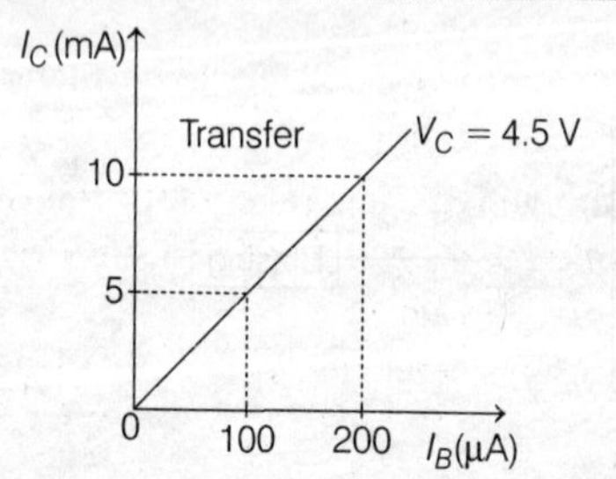	Current amplification factor (β), $\beta_{AC} = \left(\frac{\Delta I_C}{\Delta I_B}\right)_{V_{CE} = \text{constant}}$ ($\beta_{AC} >> 1$)

- Current amplification factor (α) of a transistor in common base mode is

$$\alpha = \left[\frac{\Delta I_C}{\Delta I_E}\right]_{V_{CB} = \text{constant}}$$

- Current amplification factor (β) of a transistor in common emitter mode is

$$\beta = \left[\frac{\Delta I_C}{\Delta I_B}\right]_{V_{CE} = \text{constant}}$$

Note

- Relation between α and β is given as $\alpha = \frac{\beta}{1+\beta}$ and $\beta = \frac{\alpha}{1-\alpha}$.
- α and β are independent of current, if *EB* junction is forward biased and *CB* junction is reverse biased.

Transistor as an Amplifier

- Transistor can be used as an amplifier for increasing the amplitude of input signal.
- Circuit diagrams of *n-p-n* transistor (in CE mode) along with power gains are shown in following table

Features	Circuits and gains
Circuit diagram (*n-p-n*) in CE mode	I_B B C I_C *n-p-n* R_L E V_{BE} V_{CE} I_C I_E V_{CC} Input AC Signal I_B V_{BB} I_C Amplified Output AC Signal
DC current gain	$\beta_{DC} = \left(\frac{I_C}{I_B}\right)_{V_{CE}=\text{constant}}$
AC current gain	$\beta_{AC} = \left(\frac{\Delta I_C}{\Delta I_B}\right)_{V_{CE}=\text{constant}}$
AC voltage gain	$A_V = \frac{\Delta I_C}{\Delta I_B} \times \frac{R_{out}}{R_{in}}$ = current gain × resistance gain
AC power gain	AC power gain = $\beta_{AC} A_V$ $= \beta_{AC}^2 \times$ resistance gain

Transistor as a Switch

- Transistor can be used as a **switch** because its I_C is directly controlled by I_B.
- CE(*n-p-n*) transistor along with its characteristic and other parameters are shown in following table

Features	Parameters
Circuit diagram of *n-p-n* in (CE) mode as a switch	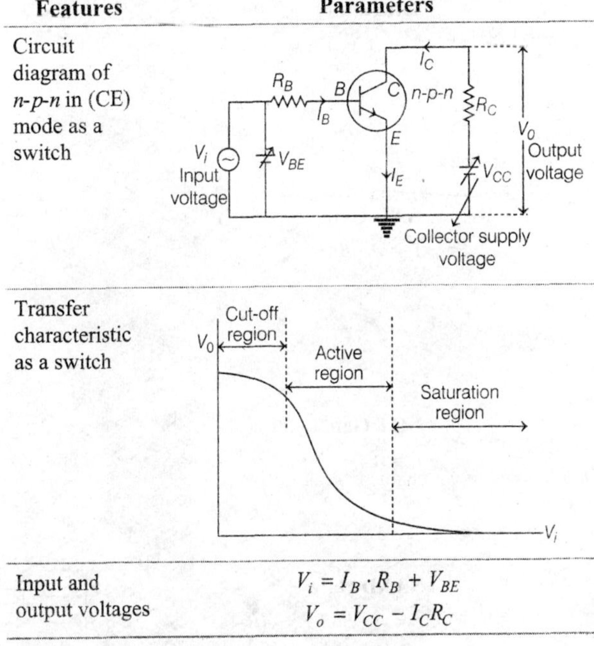
Transfer characteristic as a switch	
Input and output voltages	$V_i = I_B \cdot R_B + V_{BE}$ $V_o = V_{CC} - I_C R_C$

Note In case of silicon transistor, if $V_i < 0.6$ V, $I_B = 0$, $I_C = 0$ and transistor will operate in cut off state and $V_0 = V_{CC}$.

Transistor as an Oscillator

- Transistor can be used as an oscillator which produces electrical oscillation of constant frequency and amplitude without any external input signal.
- Block diagram of transistor oscillator along with its several components are shown in following flow chart

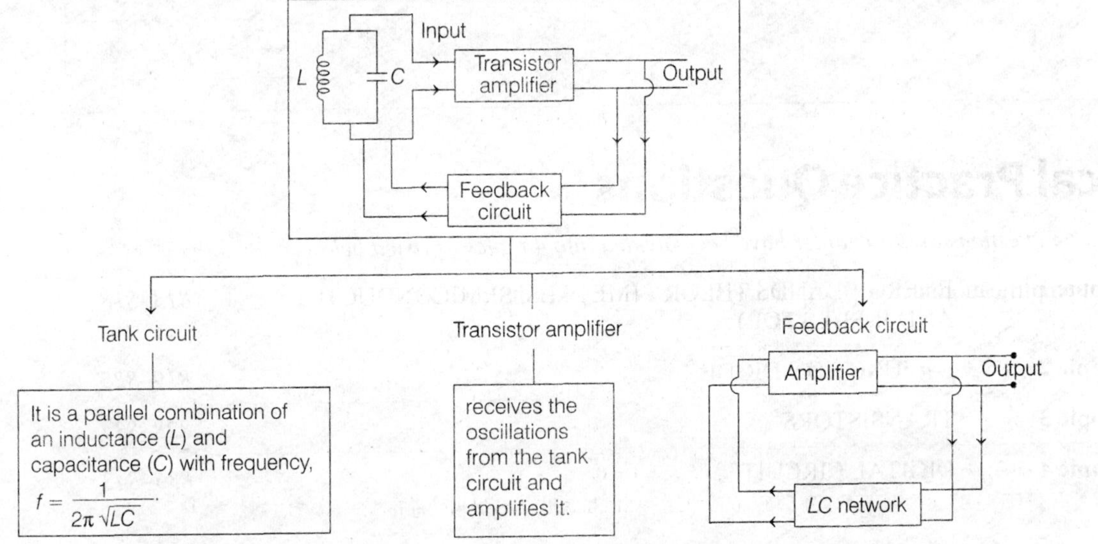

Note An oscillator may be regarded as an amplifier which provides its own input signal.

Logic Gates

These are the building blocks of digital circuits using diodes and transistors to perform switching function. A logic gate (a digital circuit) has one output but one or more inputs. Three basic gates along with two combination gates with their truth tables and logic symbols are shown in following table

Boolean Expressions | **Logic Symbols** | **Truth Tables**

OR Gate

$Y = A + B$

A, B → $Y = A + B$

Input		Output
A	B	$Y = A + B$
0	0	0
0	1	1
1	0	1
1	1	1

AND Gate

$Y = A \cdot B$

A, B → $Y = A \cdot B$

Input		Output
A	B	$Y = A \cdot B$
0	0	0
0	1	0
1	0	0
1	1	1

NOT Gate

$Y = \overline{A}$

A → $Y = \overline{A}$

Input	Output
A	$Y = \overline{A}$
0	1
1	0

Combination of Gates

NAND Gate

$Y = \overline{A \cdot B}$ or $Y = \overline{AB}$

A, B → AND → NOT → $Y = \overline{AB}$

$Y' = A \cdot B$

A, B → $Y = \overline{AB}$

Input			Output
A	B	$Y' = A \cdot B$	$Y = \overline{AB}$
0	0	0	1
0	1	0	1
1	0	0	1
1	1	1	0

NOR Gate

$Y = \overline{A + B}$

A, B → $Y' = A + B$ → $Y = \overline{A + B}$

A, B → $Y = \overline{A + B}$

Input			Output
A	B	$Y' = A + B$	$Y = \overline{A + B}$
0	0	0	1
0	1	1	0
1	0	1	0
1	1	1	0

Topical Practice Questions

All the exam questions of this chapter have been divided into 4 topics as listed below

Topic 1

Energy Bands Theory

(Metals, Semiconductors and Insulator)

2019

1 For a p-type semiconductor, which of the following statements is true ? **[NEET]**

(a) Holes are the majority carriers and trivalent atoms are the dopants.
(b) Holes are the majority carriers and pentavalent atoms are the dopants.
(c) Electrons are the majority carriers and pentavalent atoms are the dopants.
(d) Electrons are the majority carriers and trivalent atoms are the dopants.

2017

2 A specimen of silicon is to be made p-type semiconductor, for this one atom of indium, on an average, is doped in 5×10^7 silicon atoms. If the number density of silicon is 5×10^{28} atom/m^3, then the number of acceptor atoms per cm^3 will be **[AIIMS]**

(a) 2.5×10^{30} (b) 1.0×10^{13}
(c) 1.0×10^{15} (d) 2.5×10^{36}

2014

3 A piece of semiconductor is connected in series in an electric circuit. On increasing the temperature, the current in the circuit will **[EAMCET]**

(a) decrease
(b) remain unchanged
(c) increase
(d) stop flowing

4 In insulators (CB is Conduction Band and VB is Valence Band) **[MHT CET]**

(a) VB is partially filled with electrons
(b) CB is partially filled with electrons
(c) CB is empty and VB is filled with electrons
(d) CB is filled with electrons and VB is empty

5 Identify the wrong statement. **[Kerala CEE]**

(a) In conductors, the valence and conduction bands overlap.
(b) Substances with energy gap of the order of 10 eV are insulators.
(c) The resistivity of semiconductors is lower than metals.
(d) The conductivity of metals is high.
(e) The resistivity of a semiconductor is lower than that of an insulator.

6 In the band gap between valence band and conduction band in a material is 5.0 eV, then the material is **[WB JEE]**

(a) semiconductor (b) good conductor
(c) superconductor (d) insulator

7 In n-type semiconductor, electrons are majority charge carriers but it does not show any negative charge. The reason is **[KCET]**

(a) electrons are stationary
(b) electrons neutralise with holes
(c) mobility of electrons is extremely small
(d) atom is electrically neutral

2013

8 In a n-type semiconductor, which of the following statement is true? **[NEET]**

(a) Electrons are majority carriers and trivalent atoms are dopants
(b) Electrons are minority carriers and pentavalent atoms are dopants
(c) Holes are minority carriers and pentavalent atoms are dopants
(d) Holes are majority carriers and trivalent atom are dopants

9 The electrical conductivity of semiconductor increases when electromagnetic radiation of wavelength shorter than 2480 nm is incident on it. The band gap (in eV) for the semiconductor is

(a) 0.9 (b) 0.7 (c) 0.5 (d) 1.1 **[AIIMS]**

2012

10 The elements C and Si both have same lattice structure, having 4 bonding electrons in each. However, C is insulator, whereas Si is intrinsic semiconductor. This is because **[CBSE AIPMT]**

(a) in case of C, the valence band is not completely filled at absolute zero temperature
(b) in case of C, the conduction band is partly filled even at absolute zero temperature
(c) the four bonding electrons in the case of C lie in the second orbit, whereas in the case of Si, they lie in the third orbit
(d) the four bonding electrons in the case of C lie in the third orbit, whereas for Si, they lie in the fourth orbit

2011

11 If a small amount of antimony is added to germanium crystal **[CBSE AIPMT]**

(a) the antimony becomes an acceptor atom
(b) there will be more free electrons than holes in the semiconductor
(c) its resistance is increased
(d) it becomes a p-type semiconductor

2010

12 Which one of the following statement is false? [CBSE AIPMT]
(a) Pure Si doped with trivalent impurities gives a *p*-type semiconductor.
(b) Majority carriers in a *n*-type semiconductor are holes.
(c) Minority carriers in a *p*-type semiconductor are electrons.
(d) The resistance of intrinsic semiconductor decreases with increase of temperature.

13 The typical ionisation energy of a donor in silicon is [AFMC]
(a) 10.0 eV (b) 1.0 eV
(c) 0.1 eV (d) 0.001 eV

14 Based on the energy band description, a solid can be classified as an insulator. The energy gap between the valence band and conduction band is [Manipal]
(a) $3\,\text{eV} < E_g < 6\,\text{eV}$ (b) $E_g > 6\,\text{eV}$
(c) $E_g < 3\,\text{eV}$ (d) $E_g = 0$

15 A *p*-type semiconductor can be obtained by adding [OJEE]
(a) arsenic to pure silicon
(b) aluminium to pure silicon
(c) antimony to pure germanium
(d) phosphorous to pure germanium

16 The forbidden energy gap in Ge is 0.72 eV. Given, $hc = 12400$ eV-Å. The maximum wavelength of radiation that will generate electron hole pair is [KCET]
(a) 172220 Å (b) 172.2 Å
(c) 17222 Å (d) 1722 Å

17 The energy gap between the valence band and the conduction band for a material is 6 eV. The material is [MGIMS]
(a) an insulator
(b) a metal
(c) an intrinsic semiconductor
(d) a superconductor

18 Band gap of silicon is E_g (Si) of germanium is E_g (Ge) and of carbon is E_g (C). The correct order of band gap is [DUMET]
(a) E_g (Si) < E_g (Ge) < E_g (C)
(b) E_g (Si) > E_g (Ge) < E_g (C)
(c) E_g (Si) < E_g (Ge) > E_g (C)
(d) E_g (Si) > E_g (Ge) > E_g (C)

19 **Assertion** The resistivity of a semiconductor decreases with temperature.
Reason The atoms of a semiconductor vibrate with larger amplitudes at higher temperature there by increasing its resistivity. [NMMC]
(a) Both Assertion and Reason are correct and Reason is the correct explanation of Assertion.
(b) Both Assertion and Reason are correct but Reason is not the correct explanation of Assertion.
(c) Assertion is correct but Reason is incorrect.
(d) Assertion is incorrect but Reason is correct.

20 An *n*-type semiconductor is formed [CG PMT]
(a) when germanium crystal is doped with an impurity containing 3 valence electrons
(b) when germanium crystal is doped with an impurity containing 5 valence electrons
(c) from pure germanium
(d) from pure silicon

21 The contribution in the total current flowing through a semiconductor due to electrons and holes are 3/4 and 1/4, respectively. If the drift velocity of electrons is 5/2 times that of holes at this temperature, then the ratio of concentration of electrons and holes is [JCECE]
(a) 6 : 5 (b) 5 : 6
(c) 3 : 2 (d) 2 : 3

2009

22 Suitable impurities are added to a semiconductor depending on its use. This is done to [AFMC]
(a) increase its life
(b) enable it to withstand high voltage
(c) increase its electrical conductivity
(d) increase its electrical resistivity

23 The energy band gap (distance between the conduction band and valence band) in conductor is [MHT CET]
(a) zero (b) 4 Å
(c) 10 Å (d) 100 Å

24 A semiconductor has an electron concentration of $8 \times 10^{13}\,/\text{m}^3$ and hole concentration of $5.5 \times 10^{12}\,/\text{m}^3$. The semiconductor is [Manipal]
(a) *n*-type (b) *p*-type
(c) intrinsic semiconductor (d) *p-n* junction

25 In semiconducting material, 1/5th of the total current is carried by the holes and the remaining is carried by the electrons. The drift speed of electrons is twice that of holes at this temperature. The ratio between the number densities of electrons and holes is [J&K CET]
(a) 21/6 (b) 5
(c) 3/8 (d) 2

26 The electrical conductivity of semiconductor increases, when electromagnetic radiation of wavelength shorter than 24800 Å is incident on it. The band gap for the semiconductor is [MGIMS]
(a) 0.9 eV (b) 0.7 eV
(c) 0.5 eV (d) 1.1 eV

2008

27 A pure semiconductor behaves slightly as a conductor at [BHU]
(a) room temperature (b) low temperature
(c) high temperature (d) Both (b) and (c)

28 The process of adding impurities to the pure semiconductor is called [BHU]
(a) biasing (b) cotting
(c) doping (d) None of these

29 The charge carriers in a p-type semiconductor are [MHT CET]
(a) electrons only
(b) holes only
(c) holes in larger numbers and electrons in smaller numbers
(d) holes and electrons in equal numbers

30 The difference in variation of resistance with temperature in a metal and a semiconductor arises essentially due to the difference in the [RPMT]
(a) crystal structure
(b) variation of the number of charge carriers with temperature
(c) type of bonding
(d) variation of scattering mechanism with temperature

31 An intrinsic semiconductor at 0 K temperature behaves like [J&K CET]
(a) conductor
(b) p-type semiconductor
(c) n-type semiconductor
(d) insulator

32 If n_e and n_h represent the number of free electrons and holes respectively in a semiconducting material, then for n-type semiconducting material [J&K CET]
(a) $n_e << n_h$ (b) $n_e >> n_h$
(c) $n_e = n_h$ (d) $n_e = n_h = 0$

33 If an intrinsic semiconductor is heated, the ratio of free electrons to holes is [EAMCET]
(a) greater than one
(b) less than one
(c) equal to one
(d) decreases and becomes zero

34 A pure Ge specimen is doped with Al. The number density of acceptor atoms is approximately 10^{21} m^{-3}. If density of electron hole pair in an intrinsic semiconductor is approximately 10^{19} m^{-3}, the number density of electrons in the specimen is [Guj CET]
(a) 10^4 m^{-3} (b) 10^2 m^{-3}
(c) 10^{17} m^{-3} (d) 10^{15} m^{-3}

35 Pure silicon at 300 K has equal electron (n_e) and hole (n_h) concentration of 1.5×10^{16} m^{-3}. Doping by indium increases n_h to 4.5×10^{22} m^{-3}. The n_e in doped silicon is (in m^{-3}) [AMU]
(a) 9×10^5 (b) 5×10^9
(c) 2.25×10^{11} (d) 3×10^{19}

36 In intrinsic semiconductor at room temperature, number of electrons and holes are [AMU]
(a) equal (b) zero
(c) unequal (d) infinite

2007

37 In the energy band diagram of a material shown below, the open circles and filled circles denote holes and electrons, respectively. The material is a/an [CBSE AIPMT]

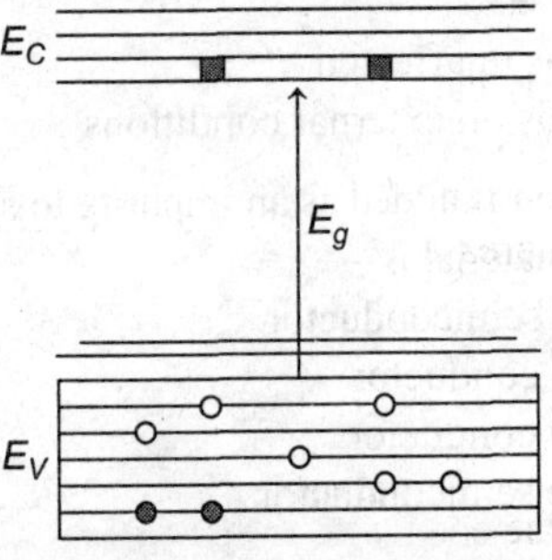

(a) p-type semiconductor (b) insulator
(c) metal (d) n-type semiconductor

38 **Assertion** The energy gap between the valence band and conduction band is greater in silicon than in germanium.
Reason Thermal energy produces fewer minority carriers in silicon than in germanium. [AIIMS]
(a) Both Assertion and Reason are correct and Reason is the correct explanation of Assertion.
(b) Both Assertion and Reason are correct but Reason is not the correct explanation of Assertion.
(c) Assertion is correct but Reason is incorrect.
(d) Both Assertion and Reason are incorrect.

39 Would there be any advantage to add n-type or p-type impurities to copper? [AFMC]
(a) Yes
(b) No
(c) May be
(d) Information is insufficient

40 In semiconductor, the concentrations of electrons and holes are 8×10^{18} m^{-3} and 5×10^{18} m^{-3} respectively. If the mobilities of electrons and holes are 2.3 m^2 V^{-1}s^{-1} and 0.01 m^2 V^{-1}s^{-1} respectively, then semiconductor is [AFMC]
(a) n-type and its resistivity is 2.95 Ω-m
(b) p-type and its resistivity is 0.034 Ω-m
(c) n-type and its resistivity is 0.34 Ω-m
(d) p-type and its resistivity is 3.4 Ω-m

41 Choose the only false statement from the following. [Manipal]
(a) Substances with energy gap of the order of 10 eV are insulators.
(b) The conductivity of a semiconductor increases with increase in temperature.
(c) In conductors, the valence and conduction bands may overlap.
(d) The resistivity of a semiconductor increases with increase in temperature.

42 The temperature of germanium is decreased from room temperature to 100 K. The resistance of germanium [J&K CET]
(a) decreases
(b) increases
(c) remains unaffected
(d) depends on external conditions

43 When boron is added as an impurity to silicon, the resulting material is [J&K CET]
(a) *n*-type semiconductor
(b) *n*-type conductor
(c) *p*-type conductor
(d) *p*-type semiconductor

44 In a semiconductor, electron concentration is 7×10^{13} cm^{-3} and hole concentration is 5×10^{12} cm^{-3}. Then the semiconductor is [DUMET]
(a) *n*-type (b) *p*-type
(c) intrinsic (d) *p*-*n* type

45 *n*-type semiconductor is obtained on doping intrinsic germanium by [Guj CET]
(a) gold (b) boron
(c) aluminium (d) phosphorus

2006

46 In a semiconducting material, the mobilities of electrons and holes are μ_e and μ_h respectively. Which of the following is true? [AIIMS]
(a) $\mu_e > \mu_h$ (b) $\mu_e < \mu_h$
(c) $\mu_e = \mu_h$ (d) $\mu_e < 0, \mu_h > 0$

47 **Assertion** The number of electrons in a *p*-type silicon semiconductor is less than the number of electrons in a pure silicon semiconductor at room temperature.
Reason It is due to the law the of mass - action. [AIIMS]
(a) Both Assertion and Reason are correct and Reason is the correct explanation of Assertion.
(b) Both Assertion and Reason are correct but Reason is not the correct explanation of Assertion.
(c) Assertion is correct but Reason is incorrect.
(d) Both Assertion and Reason are incorrect.

48 Which of the following statement is true for an *n*-type semiconductor? [BHU]
(a) The donor level lies closely below the bottom of the conduction band.
(b) The donor level lies closely above the top of the valence band.
(c) The donor level lies at the halfway mark of the forbidden energy gap.
(d) None of the above

Answers

1 (a)	2 (c)	3 (c)	4 (c)	5 (c)	6 (d)	7 (d)	8 (c)	9 (c)	10 (c)
11 (b)	12 (b)	13 (c)	14 (b)	15 (b)	16 (c)	17 (a)	18 (b)	19 (c)	20 (b)
21 (a)	22 (c)	23 (a)	24 (a)	25 (d)	26 (c)	27 (a)	28 (c)	29 (c)	30 (b)
31 (d)	32 (b)	33 (c)	34 (c)	35 (b)	36 (a)	37 (a)	38 (b)	39 (b)	40 (c)
41 (d)	42 (b)	43 (d)	44 (a)	45 (d)	46 (a)	47 (a)	48 (a)		

Explanations

1 (a) *p*-type semiconductors are obtained when a trivalent impurity (e.g. boron, aluminium, gallium or indium) is added to a intrinsic semiconductor (e.g. germanium or silicon).
In other words, the dopants in *p*-type semiconductor is trivalent atom.
Thus, this addition creates deficiencies of valence electron which are most commonly known as holes. These are the majority charge carriers in this type of semiconductor.
However, in *n*-type semiconductors, the dopants are pentavalent impurities. Also, the majority charge carriers are electrons.

2 (c) Given, one indium atom to be doped in 5×10^7 silicon atoms.
Number density of silicon
$= 5 \times 10^{28}$ atom m^{-3}
$\approx 5 \times 10^{22}$ atom cm^{-3}
Number of acceptor atom cm^{-3}
$$= \frac{5 \times 10^{22}}{5 \times 10^7} = 1 \times 10^{15} \text{cm}^{-3}$$
Hence, number of acceptor atom/cm^3 is 1×10^{15} cm^{-3}.

3 (c) On increasing the temperature, the current in the circuit will increase because with rise in temperature, resistance of semiconductor decreases.
Hence, overall resistance of the circuit decreases, which in turn increases the current in the circuit.

4 (c) In insulators, conduction band is empty and valence band is filled with electrons.

5 (c) At room temperature in semiconductor, some electrons in the valence band acquire thermal energy greater than energy band gap and jump over to conduction band.
Here they are free to move under the influence of even a small electric field thus acquires small conductivity. But their resistivity is not lower than metals.

Because in metals conduction band is partially filled and valence band is partially empty or conduction and valence band overlap, thus large number of electrons are available for conduction.

6 (d) The minimum energy required for shifting electrons from valence to conduction band is band gap. For semiconductor it is less than 3eV, for conductors it is 0 eV. The band gap of 5 eV corresponds to that of an insulator.

7 (d) The n-type semiconductor region has (negative) electrons as majority charge carriers and an equal number of fixed positively charged donor ions. Again, the material as a whole is neutral. That is the reason that atom is electrically neutral.

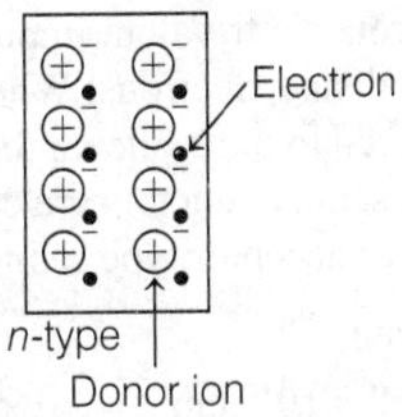

8 (c) The n-type semiconductor can be produced by doping an impurity atom of valency 5, i.e. pentavalent atoms such as phosphorus. In this, electrons are majority charge carriers and holes are minority charge carriers.

9 (c) Band gap, $E = \frac{hc}{\lambda}$

$$= \frac{6.6 \times 10^{-34} \times 3 \times 10^8}{2480 \times 10^{-9}}$$

$$= \frac{19.8 \times 10^{-17}}{2480}$$

$$= 8 \times 10^{-20} \text{ J} = \frac{8 \times 10^{-20}}{1.6 \times 10^{-19}} \text{ eV}$$

$$= 5 \times 10^{-1} = 0.5 \text{ eV}$$

10 (c) The four bonding electrons in the case of C lie in the second orbit, whereas in case of Si they lie in the third orbit. So Si has loosely bounded valence electron as compared to C.

11 (b) When a small amount of antimony is added to germanium crystal, the crystal becomes n-type semiconductor, because antimony is a pentavalent substrate and act as donor atom. So, there will be more free electrons than hole in the semiconductor.

12 (b) A p-type semiconductor is obtained by adding a small amount of trivalent impurity to a pure sample of semiconductor (Ge).

In this, majority charge carriers are holes and minority charge carriers are electrons.

An n-type semiconductor is obtained by adding a small amount of pentavalent impurity to a pure sample of semiconductor (Ge).

In this, majority charge carriers are electrons and minority charge carriers are holes. The resistance of intrinsic semiconductors decreases with increase of temperature.

13 (c) The typical ionisation energy of donor in silicon is of the order of 0.1 eV.

14 (b) In insulators, the forbidden energy gap is quite large, e.g. the forbidden energy gap for diamond is 6 eV, which means that minimum of 6 eV energy is required to make the electron jump from the completely filled valence band to the conduction band.

15 (b) Trivalent atoms have 3 valence electrons such as aluminium (Al). Such atom on being added to a pure semiconductor (silicon), instead of producing free electrons, accept electrons from the semiconductor and creates holes. For this reason, trivalent impurity atoms are called acceptor impurity atoms. The semiconductor so produced is called p-type semiconductor.

16 (c) Energy gap, $E_g = hc/\lambda$

$$\Rightarrow \quad \lambda = \frac{hc}{E_g} = \frac{12400}{0.72}$$

$$= 17222 \text{ Å}$$

17 (a) Insulators have large energy gap between valence and conduction bands (about 6 eV), while semiconductors have a smaller one and conductors have the smallest energy gap.

18 (b) Energy band gap at 0 K in eV for silicon and germanium is 1.17 eV and 0.74 eV, respectively. Band gap for carbon is much higher (5.2 eV).

Thus, correct sequence is

$$E_g(\text{Si}) > E_g(\text{Ge}) < E_g(\text{C})$$

19 (c) Resistivity of a semiconductor decreases with rise in the temperature. The atoms of a semiconductor vibrate with larger amplitudes at higher temperature thereby increasing its conductivity not resistivity.

20 (b) Pentavalent impurity atom, i.e. atoms having 5 valence electrons such as antimony (Sb) or arsenic (As), when added to a pure semiconductor (Ge), produce excess of free electrons, i.e. donate electrons to the semiconductor. For this reason, pentavalent impurity atoms are called donor impurity atom. The semiconductor so produced is called n-type extrinsic semiconductor.

21 (a) As we know, current density, $J = nqv$

$$\Rightarrow \quad J_e = n_e q v_e$$

and $\quad J_h = n_h q v_h$

$$\Rightarrow \quad \frac{J_e}{J_h} = \frac{n_e}{n_h} \times \frac{v_e}{v_h}$$

$$\Rightarrow \quad \frac{3/4}{1/4} = \frac{n_e}{n_h} \times \frac{5/2 v_h}{v_h} \quad \left(\because v_e = \frac{5}{2} v_h\right)$$

$$\Rightarrow \quad \frac{3}{1} = \frac{n_e}{n_h} \times \frac{5}{2}$$

$$\Rightarrow \quad \frac{n_e}{n_h} = \frac{6}{5}$$

22 (c) Impurities added to semiconductors increase their electrical conductivity by increasing the number of charge carriers, i.e. holes and electrons.

23 (a) Energy band gap in case of conductor is zero. In conductor, the valence and conduction band overlap with each other.

24 (a) As, $\quad n_e = 80 \times 10^{12}/\text{m}^3$ and

$$n_h = 5.5 \times 10^{12}/\text{m}^3$$

$$\Rightarrow \quad n_e > n_h$$

Hence, it is a n-type semiconductor.

25 (d) As, we know,

$$I = An\, ev_d$$

As, $\quad I = I_h + I_e$

Now, $I_h = An_h ev_h = \frac{1}{5} I \quad \text{...(i)}$

$$I_e = An_e ev_e = \frac{4}{5} I \quad \text{...(ii)}$$

Given, $\quad v_e = 2v_h$

Dividing Eq. (i) by Eq. (ii),we get

$$\Rightarrow \quad \frac{n_e}{n_h} = 2$$

26 (c) As, $E_g = hc/\lambda$

$$\Rightarrow E_g = \frac{6.6\times10^{-34}\times3\times10^8}{24800\ \text{Å}}$$

$$= \frac{19.8\times10^{-20}}{2.48}\ \text{J}$$

$$= \frac{7.98\times10^{-20}}{1.6\times10^{-19}}$$

$$= 5\times10^{-1}\ \text{eV}$$

$$\Rightarrow E_g = 0.5\ \text{eV}$$

27 (a) At room temperature, a few electrons in valence band acquire energy greater than the forbidden energy gap and move to conduction band.

Hence, at room temperature, a pure semiconductor behaves slightly as a conductor.

28 (c) Dopant elements are called impurities, therefore the process of adding impurities to the pure semiconductor is known as doping.

29 (c) In a p-type semiconductor, holes are the majority charge carriers and electrons are minority charge carriers.

So, holes are in larger numbers and electrons in smaller numbers.

30 (b) The difference in the variation of resistance with temperature in metal and semiconductor is caused due to the difference in the variation of the number of charge carriers with temperature.

31 (d) At 0 K, there is no free electrons for conduction. Therefore, at 0 K an intrinsic semiconductor behaves as an insulator.

32 (b) In an n-type semiconductor, majority charge carriers are electrons and minority charge carriers are holes.

Therefore, $n_e >> n_h$.

33 (c) A semiconductor in which electrons and holes are created by thermal excitation across the energy gap is called an intrinsic semiconductor.

The electrons reaching conduction band due to thermal excitation leave equal number of vacancies or holes in valence band, i.e. in intrinsic semiconductor concentration of holes and electrons must always be the same. Hence, ratio of free electrons to holes is one.

34 (c) Given, the density of electron-hole pair in an intrinsic semiconductor,

$$n_i = \frac{10^{19}}{\text{m}^3}$$

Density of holes (number of acceptor atom), $n_h = 10^{21}/\text{m}^3$

We know that,

$$n_h \cdot n_e = n_i^2$$

$$\therefore\ 10^{21}\times n_e = (10^{19})^2$$

$$\Rightarrow n_e = \frac{10^{19}\times10^{19}}{10^{21}} = 10^{17}\ \text{m}^{-3}$$

35 (b) In an extrinsic semiconductor,

$$n_e n_h = n_i^2$$

$$\Rightarrow n_e\times4.5\times10^{22} = (1.5\times10^{16})^2$$

$$n_e = \frac{2.25\times10^{32}}{4.5\times10^{22}}$$

$$\Rightarrow n_e = 5\times10^9\ \text{m}^{-3}$$

36 (a) At room temperature, due to thermal vibrations, the few bonds of intrinsic semiconductor are broken, producing equal number of electrons and holes in the semiconductor.

37 (a) The given figure in question represents a p-type semiconductor as there are majority of holes present in valence band.

38 (b) The energy gap between valence band and conduction band in germanium is 0.76 eV and the energy gap between valence band and conduction band in silicon is 1.1 eV. Also, it is true that thermal energy produces fewer minority carriers in silicon than in germanium.

39 (b) Pure Cu is already an excellent conductor, since it has a partially filled conduction band.

Further more, Cu forms a metallic crystal as compared to the covalent crystals of silicon or germanium, so the scheme of using an impurity to donate or accept an electron does not work for copper.

In fact adding impurities to copper decreases the conductivity, because an impurity tends to scatter electrons, impeding the flow of current.

So, there is no advantage of adding n-type or p-type impurities to copper.

40 (c) As, $n_e > h_h$, so semiconductor is n-type.

Also, conductivity $(\sigma) = \dfrac{1}{\text{resistivity }(\rho)}$

$$\sigma = e(n_e\mu_e + n_h\mu_h)$$

$$= 1.6\times10^{-19}\times[8\times10^{18}\times2.3 + 5\times10^{18}\times0.01]$$

$$= 2.95\ \Omega\text{-m}$$

So, $\rho = \dfrac{1}{\sigma} = \dfrac{1}{2.95} = 0.34\ \Omega\text{-m}$

41 (d) In semiconductor, resistivity decreases with increase in temperature.

42 (b) Germanium is a semiconductor and possesses negative temperature coefficient. Therefore, when temperature of germanium is decreased its resistance increases.

43 (d) Boron is a trivalent impurity having three valence electrons. When it is introduced to pure silicon, then such type of semiconductors are called p-type or acceptor type semiconductors.

44 (a) Given,

$$n_e = 7\times10^{13}\ \text{cm}^{-3} = 70\times10^{12}\ \text{cm}^{-3}$$

$$n_h = 5\times10^{12}\ \text{cm}^{-3}$$

$$n_e > n_h$$

So, the semiconductor must be n-type.

45 (d) When a small amount of pentavalent impurity is added to intrinsic germanium, it is known as n-type semiconductor. Typical examples of pentavalent impurities are arsenic, antimony, phosphorus etc.

46 (a) Hole is massive than electron, thus mobility of holes is less than that of electrons, i.e. $\mu_h < \mu_e$.

47 (a) According to law of mass-action, $n_i^2 = n_e n_h$.

For p-type semiconductor, number of electrons is less than the number of electrons in a pure silicon semiconductor as for p-type semiconductor, $n_e < n_h$.

48 (a) The donor level is found only in n-type semiconductors. The donor level lies closely below the bottom of the conduction band.

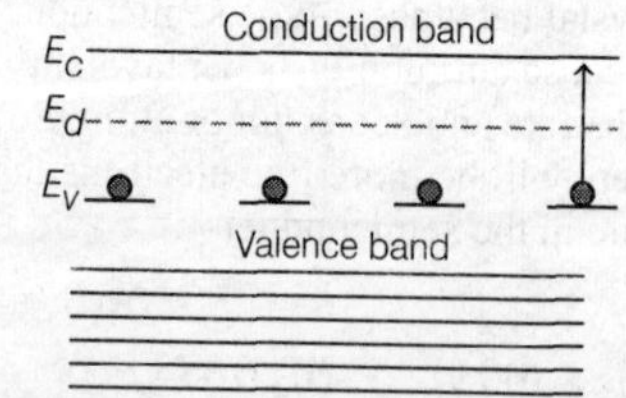

Topic 2

p-n Junction Diode

2019

1 An LED is constructed from a *p-n* junction diode using GaAsP. The energy gap is 1.9 eV. The wavelength of the light emitted will be equal to **[NEET (Odisha)]**

(a) 10.4×10^{-26} m (b) 654 nm

(c) 654 Å (d) 654×10^{-11} m

2 If voltage across a zener diode is 6V, then find out the value of maximum resistance in this condition. **[AIIMS]**

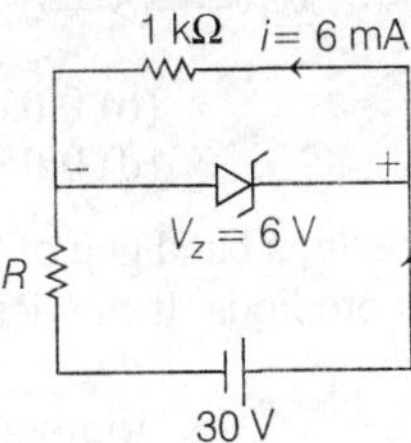

(a) 2 kΩ (b) 2 kΩ (c) 5 kΩ (d) 4 kΩ

3 **Assertion** Photodiode and solar cell works on same mechanism.

Reason Area is large for solar cell. **[AIIMS]**

(a) Both Assertion and Reason are correct and Reason is the correct explanation of Assertion.

(b) Both Assertion and Reason are correct but Reason is not the correct explanation of Assertion.

(c) Assertion is correct but Reason is incorrect.

(d) Both Assertion and Reason are incorrect.

2018

4 In a *p-n* junction diode, change in temperature due to heating **[NEET]**

(a) does not affect resistance of *p-n* junction

(b) affects only forward resistance

(c) affects only reverse resistance

(d) affects the overall *V-I* characteristics of *p-n* junction

5 The diode used at a constant potential drop of 0.5 V at all currents and maximum power rating of 100 mW. What resistance must be connected in series to diode to so that current in circuit is maximum? **[AIIMS]**

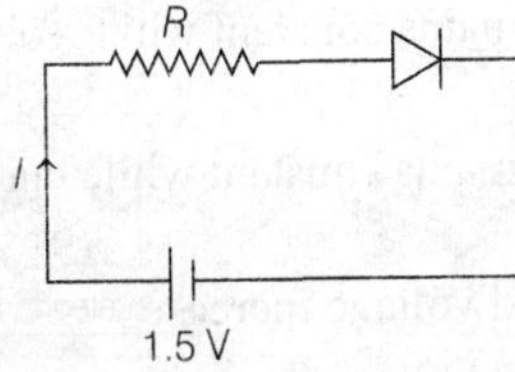

(a) 200 Ω (b) 6.67 Ω (c) 5 Ω (d) 15 Ω

2017

6 Which one of the following represents forward bias diode? **[NEET]**

(a) 0V —▷|— R —2 V

(b) −4V —▷— R −3 V

(c) −2V —▷|— R +2 V

(d) 3V —▷|— R 5 V

2016

7 The given circuit has two ideal diodes connected as shown in the figure below. The current flowing through the resistance R_1 will be **[NEET]**

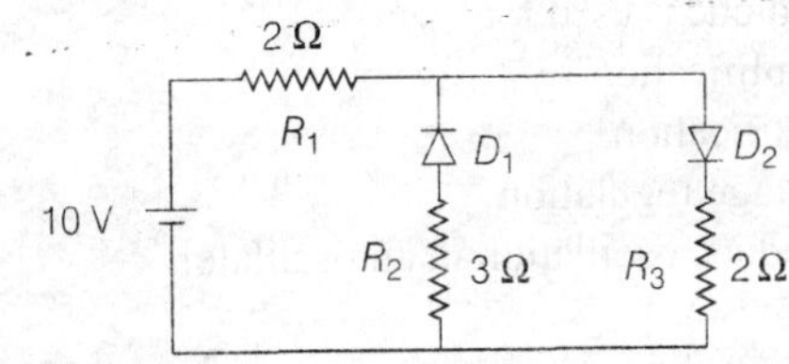

(a) 2.5 A (b) 10.0 A

(c) 1.43 A (d) 3.13 A

2014

8 The barrier potential of a *p-n* junction depends on

I. type of semiconductor material

II. amount of doping III. temperature

Which one of the following is correct? **[CBSE AIPMT]**

(a) I and II (b) Only II

(c) II and III (d) All of these

9 Identify the incorrect statement with reference to solar cell. **[Kerala CEE]**

(a) It is a *p-n* junction diode with no external bias.

(b) It uses materials of high optical absorption.

(c) It uses materials with band gap of 5 eV.

(d) It converts light energy into electrical energy.

(e) It uses materials such as GaAs, Si.

10 In the circuit shown below, assume the diode to be ideal. When V_i increases from 2 V to 6 V, the change in the current is (in mA) **[WB JEE]**

V_i o— 150 Ω —▷|— o +3 V

(a) zero (b) 20

(c) 80/3 (d) 40

11 The given graph represents V-I characteristic for a semiconductor device. Which of the following statements is correct? **[CBSE AIPMT]**

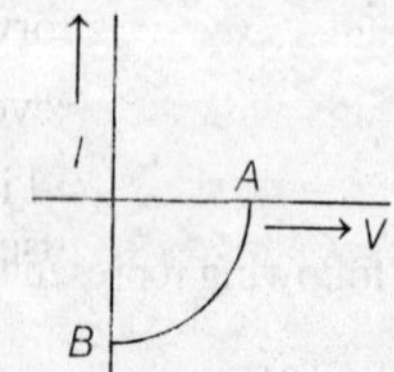

(a) It is V-I characteristic for solar cell, where point A represents open circuit voltage and point B short circuit current.
(b) It is for a solar cell and points A and B represent open circuit voltage and current, respectively.
(c) It is for a photodiode and points A and B represent open circuit voltage and current, respectively.
(d) It is for a LED and points A and B represents open circuit voltage and short circuit current respectively.

12 Zener diode is used for **[UK PMT]**
(a) amplification
(b) rectification
(c) voltage regulation
(d) produce oscillation in an oscillator

2013

13 When two semiconductors of p-type and n-type are brought into contact, they form a p - n junction which acts like a **[AIIMS]**
(a) conductor (b) oscillator
(c) amplifier (d) rectifier

14 For the given circuit shown below, to act as full wave rectifier, the AC input should be connected across ... & ... and the DC output would appear across ... & ... . **[Manipal]**

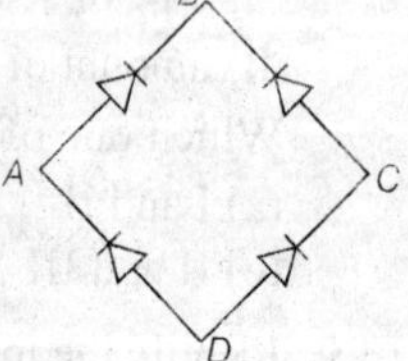

(a) B & D, A & C
(b) B & C, A & D
(c) A & C, B & D
(d) A & D, B & C

15 On increasing the reverse bias to a large value in a p-n junction diode, current **[WB JEE]**
(a) increases slowly
(b) remains fixed
(c) suddenly increases
(d) decreases slowly

16 On applying reverse bias to a junction diode, it **[KCET]**
(a) lowers the potential barrier
(b) raises the potential barrier
(c) increases the majority carrier current
(d) increases the minority carrier current

2012

17 Find the current in the circuit. **[CBSE AIPMT]**

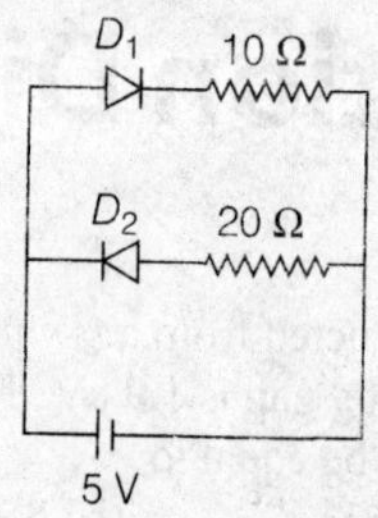

(a) 0.75 A (b) Zero (c) 0.25 A (d) 0.5 A

18 As shown in figure, the current in the part of circuit is **[OJEE]**

(a) 0.03 A (b) 0.02 A
(c) 0.04 A (d) 0.05 A

19 A semiconductor with a band gap of 2.5 eV is used to fabricate a p-n photodiode. It can detect a signal of wavelength **[Kerala CEE]**
(a) 4000 nm (b) 6000 Å
(c) 6000 nm (d) 4950 Å
(e) 5500 Å

20 In which of the following figures, the p-n diode is forward biased? **[J&K CET]**

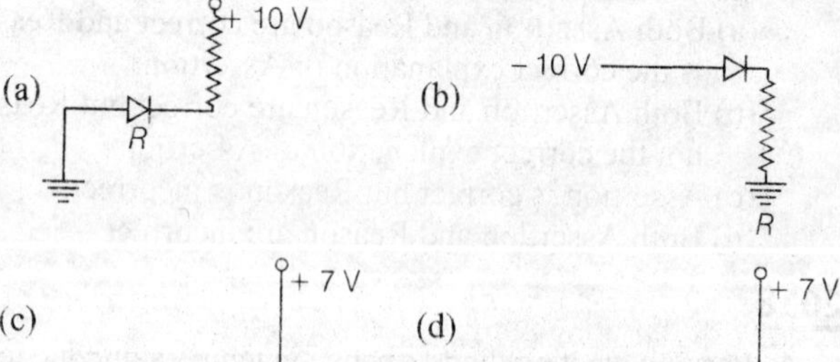

21 The p-n junction which generates an emf when solar radiation falls on it, with no external bias applied, is a **[J&K CET]**
(a) light emitting diode
(b) photodiode
(c) solar cell
(d) zener diode

22 In a reverse biased p-n junction, when the applied bias voltage is equal to the breakdown voltage, then **[DUMET]**
(a) current remains constant while voltage increases sharply
(b) voltage remains constant while current increases sharply
(c) current and voltage increase
(d) current and voltage decrease

23 In forward biasing of the p-n junction, **[CBSE AIPMT]**
(a) the positive terminal of the battery is connected to n-side and the depletion region becomes thin
(b) the positive terminal of the battery is connected to n-side and the depletion region becomes thick
(c) the positive terminal of the battery is connected to p-side and the depletion region becomes thin
(d) the positive terminal of the battery is connected to p-side and the depletion region becomes thick

2011

24 In the case of forward biasing of a p-n junction diode, which one of the following figures correctly depicts the direction of conventional current (indicated by an arrow mark)? **[KCET]**

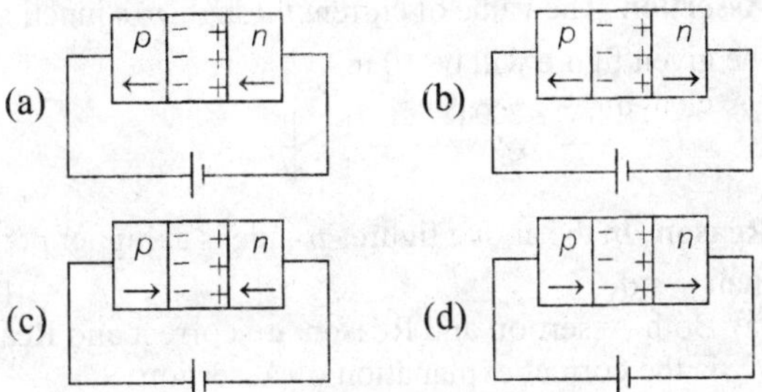

2010

25 The output form of a full wave rectifier is **[AFMC]**
(a) an AC voltage
(b) a DC voltage
(c) zero
(d) a pulsating unidirectional voltage

26 Which circuit will not show current in ammeter ? **[BVP]**

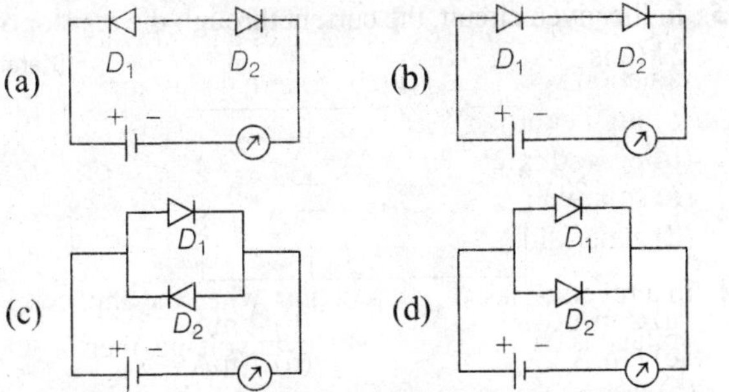

27 LED is a p-n junction diode which is **[MHT CET]**
(a) forward biased
(b) Either forward biased or reverse biased
(c) reverse biased
(d) Neither forward biased nor reverse biased

28 Which one of the following statement is correct in the case of light emitting diodes? **[Manipal]**
(a) It is a heavily doped p-n junction.
(b) It emits light only when it is forward biased.
(c) It emits light only when it is reverse biased.
(d) The energy of the light emitted is less than the energy of the semiconductor used.

29 In the figure given below, the input is across the terminals A & C and the output is across B & D. Then, the output is **[OJEE]**

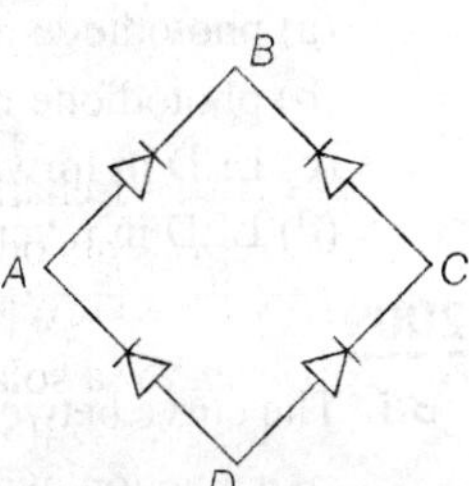

(a) zero
(b) same as the input
(c) full wave rectified
(d) half-wave rectified

30 When the voltage drop across a p-n junction diode is increased from 0.65 V to 0.70 V, the change in the diode current is 5 mA. The dynamic resistance of the diode is **[Kerala CEE]**
(a) 20 Ω (b) 50 Ω (c) 10 Ω (d) 80 Ω
(e) 100 Ω

31 GaAs (with a band gap = 1.5 eV) as an LED can emit **[Kerala CEE]**
(a) blue light (b) ultraviolet rays
(c) X-rays (d) infrared rays
(e) None of these

32 What controls the conduction of p-n junction? **[MP PMT]**
(a) Majority carriers (b) Minorty carriers
(c) Holes (d) Both (a) and (b)

33 The value of DC voltage in half-wave rectifier in converting AC voltage $V = 100 \sin(314\,t)$ into DC is **[MP PMT]**
(a) 100 V (b) 50 V (c) 30.3 V (d) zero

34 If the voltage between the terminals A and B is 17 V and zener breakdown voltage is 9 V, then the potential across R is **[EAMCET]**

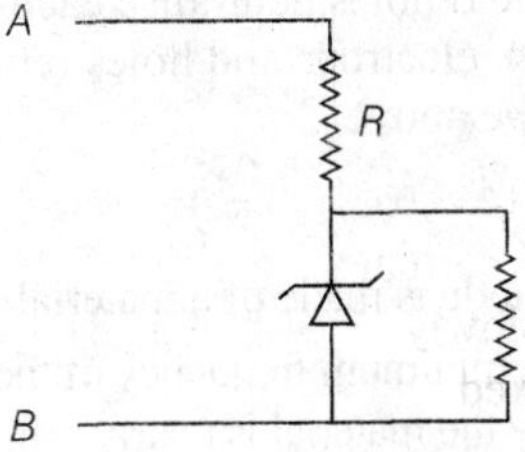

(a) 6 V (b) 8 V (c) 9 V (d) 17 V

35 An AC signal of 50 Hz frequency is input of a full wave rectifier using two diodes. The output frequency after full wave rectification is **[MGIMS]**
(a) 25 Hz (b) 50 Hz
(c) 100 Hz (d) 200 Hz

36 Avalanche breakdown in a *p-n* junction diode is due to [MGIMS]
(a) shift of fermi level
(b) widening of forbidden gap
(c) high impurity concentration
(d) cummulative effect of conduction band electrons collision

37 For detecting intensity of light, we use [VMMC]
(a) photodiode in forward bias
(b) photodiode in reverse bias
(c) LED in forward bias
(d) LED in reverse bias

2009

38 The curve between charge density (ρ) and distances near *p-n* junction, will be [AIIMS]

(a) 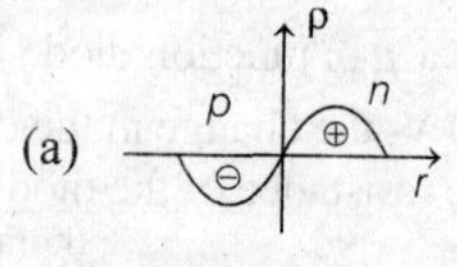
(b) 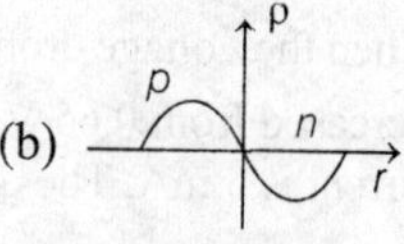
(c) 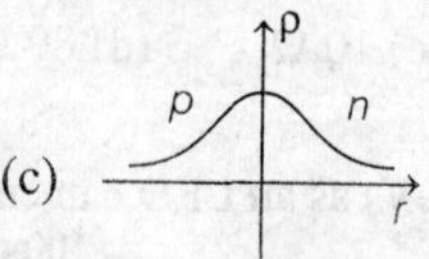
(d) 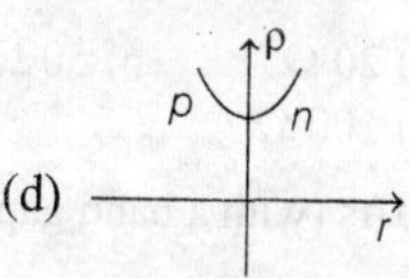

39 What is the current through an ideal *p-n* junction diode shown in figure below ? [AFMC]

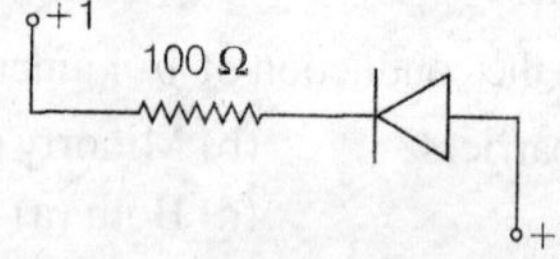

(a) Zero (b) 10 mA
(c) 20 mA (d) 50 mA

40 When LED is forward biased, then [MGIMS]
(a) electrons from the *n*-type material cross the *p-n* junction and recombine with holes in the *p*-type material
(b) electrons and holes neutralise each other
(c) at junction, electrons and holes remains at rest
(d) None of the above

2008

41 A *p-n* photodiode is made of a material with a band gap of 2.0 eV. The minimum frequency of the radiation that can be absorbed by the material is nearly [CBSE AIPMT]
(a) 10×10^{14} Hz
(b) 5×10^{14} Hz
(c) 1×10^{14} Hz
(d) 20×10^{14} Hz

42. If in a *p-n* junction diode, a square input signal of 10 V is applied as shown below.

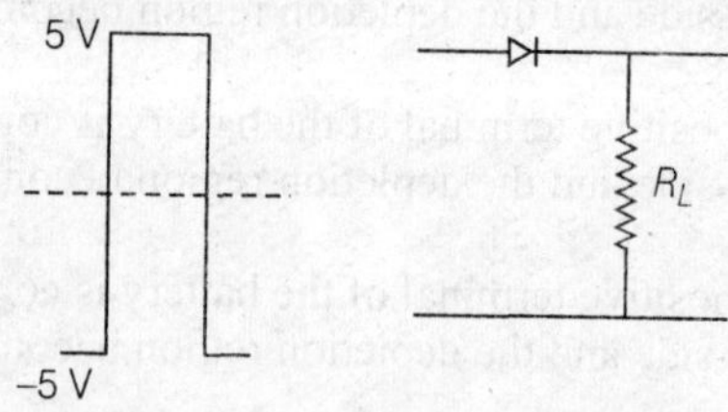

Then, the output signal across R_L will be [AIIMS]

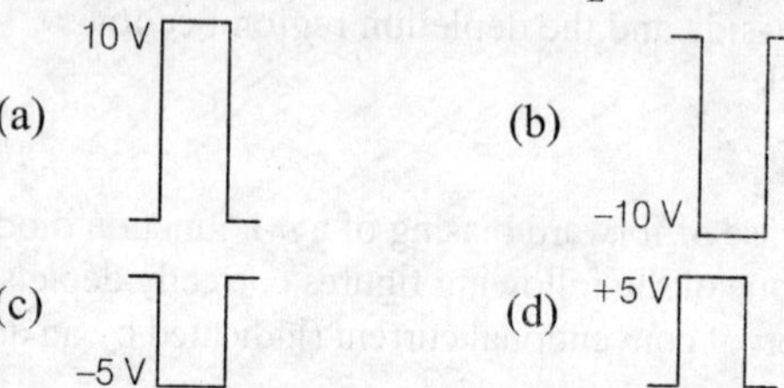

43. **Assertion** The value of current through *p-n* junction in the given figure will be 10 mA.

+ 5 V 300 Ω + 2 V

Reason In the above figure, *p*-side is at higher potential than *n*-side. [AIIMS]
(a) Both Assertion and Reason are correct and Reason is the correct explanation of Assertion.
(b) Both Assertion and Reason are correct but Reason is not the correct explanation of Assertion.
(c) Assertion is correct but Reason is incorrect.
(d) Assertion is incorrect but Reason is correct.

44 In an unbiased *p-n* junction, [KCET]
(a) potential at *p* is more than that at *n*
(b) potential at *p* is less than that at *n*
(c) potential at *p* is equal to that at *n*
(d) potential at *p* is positive and that at *n* is negative

45 In the given circuit, the current through the resistor of 2 kΩ is [Kerala CEE]

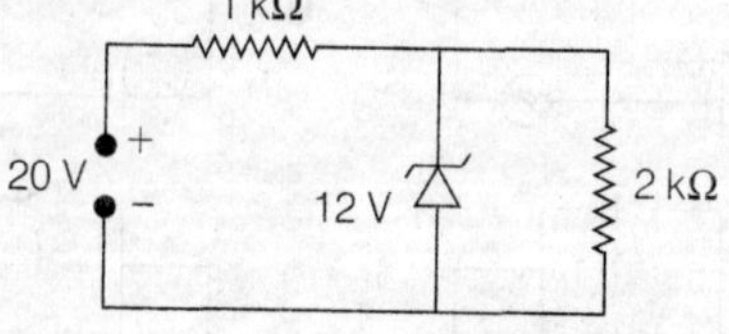

(a) 2 mA (b) 4 mA
(c) 6 mA (d) 1 mA
(e) 10 mA

46 In the middle of the depletion layer of reverse biased *p-n* junction, the [RPMT]
(a) electric field is zero (b) potential is maximum
(c) electric field is maximum (d) potential is zero

47 When a p-n junction diode is connected in forward bias, its barrier potential **[J&K CET]**
(a) decreases and less current flows in the circuit
(b) decreases and more current flows in the circuit
(c) increases and more current flows in the circuit
(d) decreases and no current flows in the circuit

48 The main cause of zener breakdown is **[J&K CET]**
(a) the base semiconductor being germanium
(b) production of electron-hole pairs due to thermal excitation
(c) low doping
(d) high doping

49 The depletion layer in a silicon diode is 1 μm wide and its knee voltage is 0.6 V, then the electric field in the depletion layer will be **[J&K CET]**
(a) $0.6\ \text{Vm}^{-1}$ (b) $6\times 10^4\ \text{Vm}^{-1}$
(c) $6\times 10^5\ \text{Vm}^{-1}$ (d) zero

50 Zener diode acts as **[DUMET]**
(a) voltage regulator in reverse biasing
(b) voltage regulator in forward biasing
(c) current regulator in reverse biasing
(d) current regulator in forward biasing

51 **Assertion** Light Emitting Diode (LED) emits spontaneous radiation.
Reason LED are forward biased p-n junctions. **[AIIMS]**
(a) Both Assertion and Reason are correct and Reason is the correct explanation of Assertion.
(b) Both Assertion and Reason are correct but Reason is not the correct explanation of Assertion.
(c) Assertion is correct but Reason is incorrect.
(d) Assertion is incorrect but Reason is correct.

52 Barrier potential of a p-n junction diode does not depend on **[BHU]**
(a) forward bias (b) doping density
(c) diode design (d) temperature

53 If a full wave rectifier circuit is operating from 50 Hz mains, the fundamental frequency in the ripple will be **[MHT CET]**
(a) 70.7 Hz (b) 100 Hz
(c) 25 Hz (d) 59 Hz

54 In a diode, when there is a saturation current, the plate resistance will be **[MHT CET]**
(a) data insufficient (b) zero
(c) finite quantity (d) infinite quantity

55 The peak voltage in the output of a half-wave diode rectifier fed with a sinusoidal signal without filter is 10 V. The DC component of the output voltage is **[Manipal]**
(a) $\frac{10}{\sqrt{2}}$ V (b) $\frac{10}{\pi}$ V
(c) 10 V (d) $\frac{20}{\pi}$ V

56 Of the diodes shown in the following diagrams, which one is reverse biased? **[Manipal]**

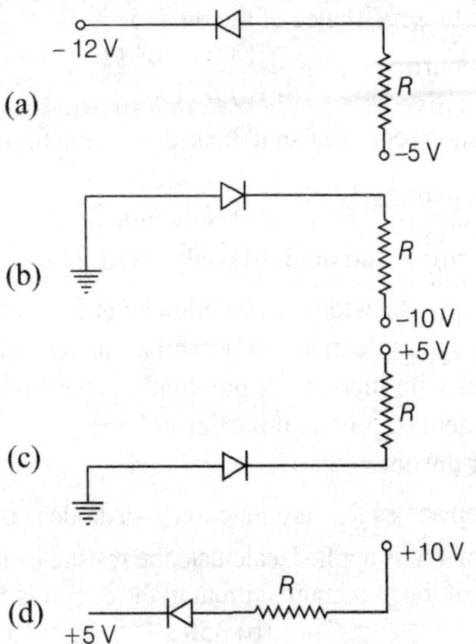

57 A Light Emitting Diode (LED) has a voltage drop of 2 V across it and passes a current of 10 mA. When it operates with a 6 V battery through a limiting resistor R, the value of R is **[RPMT]**
(a) 40 kΩ (b) 4 kΩ
(c) 200 Ω (d) 400 Ω

58 When a p-n junction diode is reverse biased, then **[RPMT]**
(a) no current flows
(b) the depletion region is increased
(c) the depletion region is reduced
(d) the height of the potential barrier is reduced

59 The potential in depletion layer is due to **[J&K CET]**
(a) electrons (b) holes
(c) ions (d) forbidden band

60 In breakdown region, a zener diode behaves as a **[J&K CET]**
(a) constant current source
(b) constant voltage source
(c) constant resistance source
(d) constant power source

61 Two identical capacitors A and B are charged to the same potential V and are connected in two circuits at $t = 0$, as shown in figure. The charge on the capacitors at time $t = CR$ are respectively **[Punjab PMET]**

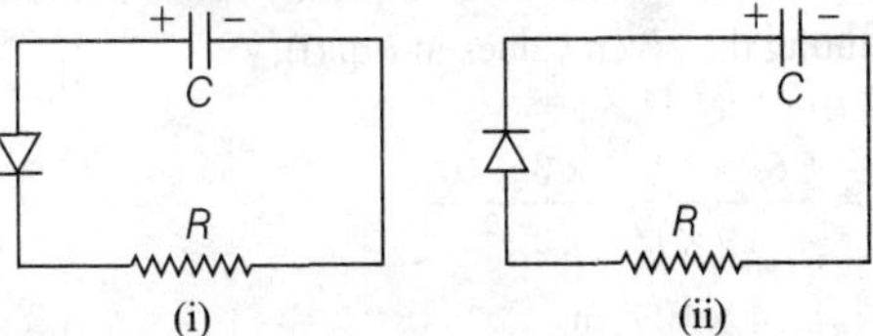

(a) VC, VC (b) $\frac{VC}{e}, VC$ (c) $VC, \frac{VC}{e}$ (d) $\frac{VC}{e}, \frac{VC}{e}$

62 In a reverse biased diode when the applied voltage changes by 1 V, the current is found to change by 0.5 μA. The reverse bias resistance of the diode is **[KCET]**

(a) $2 \times 10^5\ \Omega$ (b) $2 \times 10^6\ \Omega$
(c) $200\ \Omega$ (d) $2\ \Omega$

63 In the depletion region of an unbiased *p-n* junction diode, there are **[AMU]**

(a) only electrons (b) only holes
(c) both electrons and holes (d) only fixed ions

64 In forward bias, the width of depletion layer is **[DUMET]**

(a) decreases with decrease in potential barrier voltage
(b) increases with increase in potential barrier voltage
(c) independent of potential barrier voltage
(d) None of the above

65 Potential drop across forward junction *p-n* diode is 0.7 V. If a battery of 4 V is applied, calculate the resistance to be put in series, if the maximum current in the circuit is 5 mA. **[DUMET]**

(a) $660\ \Omega$ (b) $350\ \Omega$
(c) $475\ \Omega$ (d) $500\ \Omega$

2006

66 Assertion A *p-n* junction with reverse bias can be used as a photodiode to measure light intensity.

Reason In a reverse bias condition, the current is small but it is more sensitive to change in incident light intensity. **[AIIMS]**

(a) Both Assertion and Reason are correct and Reason is the correct explanation of Assertion.
(b) Both Assertion and Reason are correct but Reason is not the correct explanation of Assertion.
(c) Assertion is correct but Reason is incorrect.
(d) Assertion is incorrect but Reason is correct.

2005

67 Zener diode is used for **[CBSE AIPMT]**

(a) producing oscillations in an oscillator
(b) amplification
(c) stabilisation
(d) rectification

Answers

1 (b)	2 (d)	3 (b)	4 (d)	5 (c)	6 (a)	7 (a)	8 (d)	9 (c)	10 (b)
11 (a)	12 (c)	13 (d)	14 (c)	15 (c)	16 (b)	17 (d)	18 (b)	19 (d)	20 (c)
21 (c)	22 (b)	23 (c)	24 (d)	25 (d)	26 (a)	27 (a)	28 (b)	29 (c)	30 (c)
31 (d)	32 (d)	33 (c)	34 (b)	35 (c)	36 (d)	37 (b)	38 (a)	39 (c)	40 (a)
41 (b)	42 (d)	43 (a)	44 (b)	45 (c)	46 (a)	47 (b)	48 (b)	49 (c)	50 (a)
51 (a)	52 (c)	53 (b)	54 (d)	55 (b)	56 (c)	57 (d)	58 (b)	59 (c)	60 (b)
61 (b)	62 (b)	63 (d)	64 (a)	65 (a)	66 (a)	67 (c)			

Explanations

1 *(b)* The energy of light of wavelength λ is given by

$$E = h\nu = \frac{hc}{\lambda}$$

$$\Rightarrow \quad \lambda = \frac{hc}{E} \quad \ldots\text{(i)}$$

Here, h = Planck's constant $= 6.63 \times 10^{-34}$ J-s

c = speed of light $= 3 \times 10^8$ m/s

E = energy gap = 1.9 eV $= 1.9 \times 1.6 \times 10^{-19}$ J

Substituting the given values in Eq. (i), we get

$$\Rightarrow \lambda = \frac{6.63 \times 10^{-34} \times 3 \times 10^8}{1.9 \times 1.6 \times 10^{-19}}$$

$$= 6.54 \times 10^{-7}\ \text{m}$$

$$\approx 654\ \text{nm}$$

Thus, the wavelength of light emitted from LED will be 654 nm.

2 *(d)* Given, voltage across zener diode, $V_Z = 6$ V

Since, zener diode provide stabilised supply of 6 V.

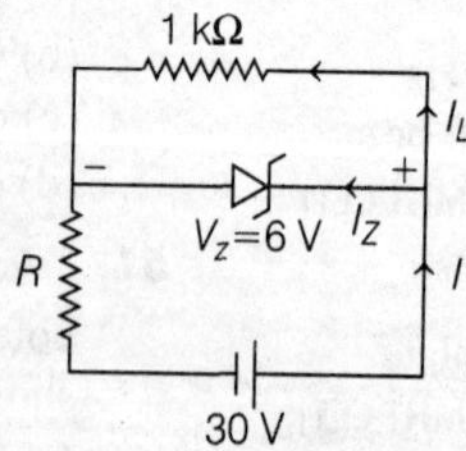

In this case, the value of R should be chosen such that negligible current flows through the zener diode.

$$\therefore \quad I = I_Z + I_L = 0 + I_L$$

$$I = \frac{30}{R + 10^3}$$

But $\quad I = 6\text{mA} = 6 \times 10^{-3}$ A

$$\therefore \quad 6 \times 10^{-3} = \frac{30}{R + 10^3}$$

$$\Rightarrow \quad R = 4 \times 10^3\ \Omega = 4\ \text{k}\Omega$$

3 *(b)* A *p-n* junction photodiode can be operated under photovoltaic conditions similar to that of a solar cell. The current-voltage characteristics of a photodiode and solar cell under illumination are also similar.

When light energy falls on the solar cell, then it converts solar energy into electrical energy.

The area of solar cell is larger, so that it could absorbed more amount of sunlight and hence more amount of electrical energy is obtained.

Hence, Assertion and Reason both are true but Reason is not the correct explanation of Assertion.

4 *(d)* Due to increase in temperature because of heating, thermal collision between the electron and holes increases. Thus, net electron-hole pairs increase. This leads to increase in the current in diode and overall resistance of the diode changes. This in turn changes both the forward biasing and the reverse biasing. Thus, the overall I-V characteristics of p-n junction diode gets affected.

5 (c) Current passing in the circuit,

$$I = \frac{P}{V} = \frac{100 \times 10^{-3}}{0.5} = 0.2 \text{ A}$$

Value of connected series resistance,

$$R = \frac{1.5 - 0.5}{0.2} \Rightarrow R = \frac{1}{0.2}$$

$$\therefore \ R = 5\,\Omega$$

6 (a) In the forward biasing of p-n junction, p-side of junction diode is connected to higher potential and n-side of junction diode is connected to lower potential. As $0 \text{ V} > -2 \text{ V}$, hence option (a) is the correct answer.

7 (a) We know that, a diode only conducts in forward biased condition. In the given circuit, the diode D_1 is in reverse bias, so it will block the current and diode D_2 is in forward bias, so it will pass the current,

$$i = \frac{V}{R_1 + R_3} = \frac{10}{2+2} = 2.5 \text{A}$$

8 (d) Barrier potential depend on all the three given points, i.e. barrier potential depends on the material used to make p-n junction diode (whether it is Si or Ge). It also depends on amount of doping due to which the number of majority carriers will change. It also depends on temperature due to which number of charge carriers will change.

9 (c) The incorrect statement with reference to a solar cell is that, it uses materials with band gap of 5 eV. Because for solar cell, band gap < 3 eV.

10 (b) The initial current, $I_{in} = 0$, for $V_i = 2$ V [$\because D$ = reverse biased]

V_i — 150 Ω — D — +3 V

and the final current,

$$I_f = \frac{3}{150} = 0.02 \text{ A}$$

So, change in current,

$$\Delta I = I_f - I_{in} = 0.02 \text{ A} = 20 \text{ mA}$$

11 (a) V-I characteristics of solar cell is drawn in fourth quadrant of coordinate axes, because a solar cell does not draw current but supplies the same to the load. Hence, options (c) and (d) are incorrect.

Point A represents the open circuit voltage as current is zero and point B represents short circuit current as voltage is zero at this point.

12 (c) When the applied reverse voltage (V) reaches the breakdown voltage (V_Z) of the zener diode, there is a large change in the current, for almost insignificant change in the reverse bias voltage.

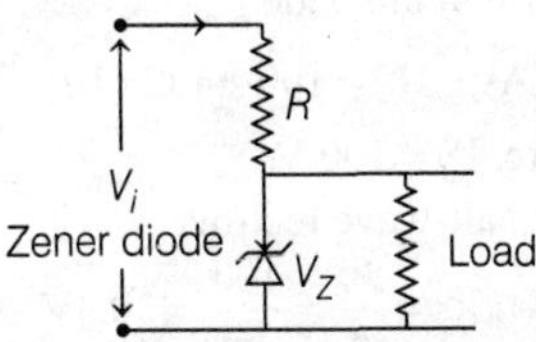

As zener voltage remains constant even though the current through the zener diode varies over a wide range, hence it is used to obtain regulated output voltage as shown in the above diagram.

13 (d) A p-n junction acts as a rectifier.

14 (c) The full wave diode bridge rectifier is shown below

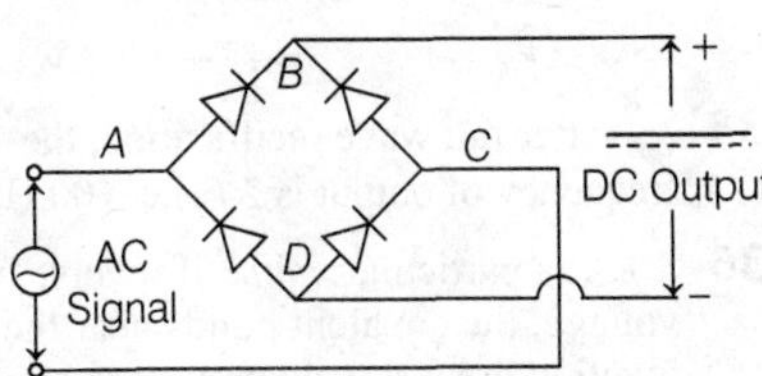

So, AC input is connected across A & C and DC output would appears across B & D.

15 (c) On increasing the reverse bias (voltage) to a large value in a p-n junction diode, the junction breaks down.

Now, a large reverse current is set up due to minority charge carriers.

16 (b) When positive terminal of battery is connected to n-side and negative to p-side of the junction, it is said to be reverse biased. In this case, both electrons and holes move away from each other.

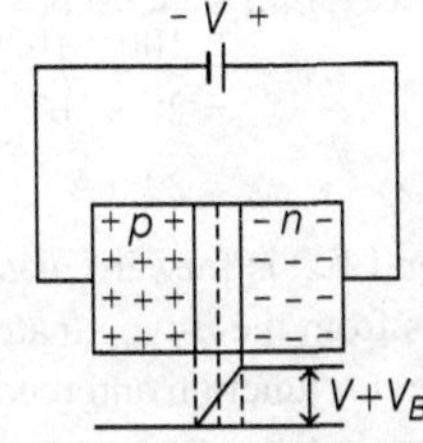

Since there is no electron-hole combination, no current flows and junction offers high resistance. Hence, width of the depletion layer is increased because of increased barrier width or potential barrier.

17 (d) In the given circuit, diode D_1 is forward bias and diode D_2 is reverse bias. So, current will flow only in diode D_1.

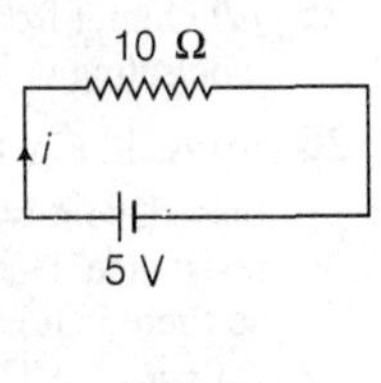

The current supplied by the battery,

$$i = \frac{5}{10} = 0.5 \text{ A}$$

18 (b) From Kirchhoff's law, algebraic sum of changes in potential around any closed loop involving resistors and the cells in the loop is zero. i.e. algebraic sum of emf's is equal to algebraic sum of products of current and resistances.

Hence, $6 - i \times 150 - 3 = 0$

$$\Rightarrow \quad i = \frac{3}{150} = \frac{1}{50} = 0.02 \text{ A}$$

19 (d) Given, $E = 2.5$ eV

$$= 2.5 \times 1.6 \times 10^{-19} \text{ V}$$

Now, $E = \dfrac{hc}{\lambda}$

$$\Rightarrow \quad \lambda = \frac{hc}{E}$$

$$= \frac{6.6 \times 10^{-34} \times 3 \times 10^8}{2.5 \times 1.6 \times 10^{-19}}$$

$$= 4950 \text{ Å}$$

20 (c) As in Fig. (c), p-side is connected to $+7$ V which is more than the n-side which is connected to $+5$V, hence potential at p-side is more than the n-side. Hence, it follows the criteria of forward biasing.

21 (c) The p-n junction which generates an emf when solar radiation falls on it, with no external bias applied is a solar cell.

In LED, photodiode and zener diode external bias is applied.

22 (b) In a reverse biased p-n junction, when the applied bias voltage is equal to the breakdown voltage, then voltage remains constant while current increases sharply.

23 (c) In forward biasing of p-n junction, the positive terminal of the battery is connected to p-side and negative terminal to the n-side, thus decreasing the barrier potential. So, the depletion region becomes thin.

24 (d) In p-region, direction of conventional current is same as the flow of holes and in n-region direction of conventional current is opposite to the direction of electron's flow. Hence, option (d) is correct.

25 (d) Output from of a full-wave rectifier is a pulsating unidirectional voltage.

26 (a) As in Fig. (a), diode D_1 is reversed biased, so it will offer infinite resistance. Hence, current will be zero, so there is no deflection in ammeter.

27 (a) When a junction diode is forward biased, energy is released at the junction due to recombination of electrons and holes. In the junction diode made of gallium arsenide or indium phosphide, the energy is released in visible region. Such a junction diode is called a Light Emitting Diode (LED).

28 (b) Light emitting diodes are specially designed diodes which give out light radiations when forward biased. LED's are made of GaAsP, GaP, etc.

29 (c) The figure shown below has AC input connected to A & C and output is taken across B & D.

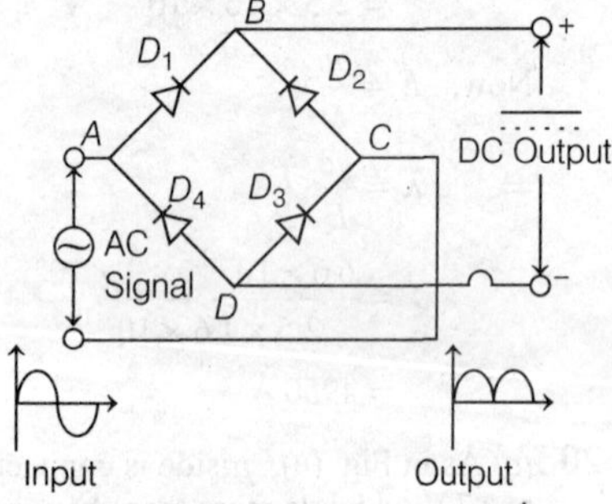

For positive half-cycles D_1 and D_3 are forward biased and hence give output across BD.

For negative half-cycles D_2 and D_4 are forward biased and hence give output across BD.

Therefore, output is obtained for both cycles and we get full-wave rectified output.

30 (c) The dynamic resistance of a diode is defined as

$$r_d = \frac{\Delta V}{\Delta i}$$

$$= \frac{0.70 - 0.65}{5 \times 10^{-3}} = 10\ \Omega$$

31 (d) The band gap = 1.5 eV

$$= 1.5 \times 1.6 \times 10^{-19}$$

$$E = 2.40 \times 10^{-19}\ \text{J}$$

Wavelength of radiation emitted,

$$\lambda = \frac{hc}{E} = \frac{6.6 \times 10^{-34} \times 3 \times 10^8}{2.4 \times 10^{-19}}$$

$$= 8.25 \times 10^{-7}\ \text{m} = 8250\ \text{Å}$$

This wavelength belongs to infrared rays.

32 (d) Conduction is controlled by both the carriers like electron (majority carriers) in n-side and holes (minority carriers) in p-side.

33 (c) As, $V = 100 \sin (314\, t)$

Here, $V_0 = 100$ V

For half-wave rectifier,

$$V_{DC} = \frac{V_0}{\pi} = \frac{100}{\pi} = 30.3\text{V}$$

34 (b) Here, $V = V_R + V_Z$

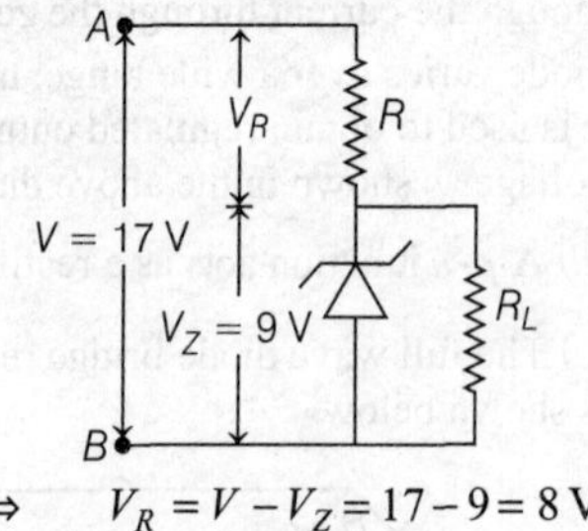

$$\Rightarrow \quad V_R = V - V_Z = 17 - 9 = 8\ \text{V}$$

35 (c) After full wave rectification, the frequency of output is $2f$, i.e. 100 Hz.

36 (d) At a particular value of reverse bias voltage, the covalent bonds near the junction break, so electron-hole pairs get liberated, this process rapidly multiplies and an avalanche of electron-hole pairs is produced. Clearly, avalanche breakdown in p-n diode is cummulative effect of conduction band electrons collision.

37 (b) To detect the intensity of light photodiode is used in reverse bias.

38 (a) The n-side of p-n junction has stationary positive ions and p-side has stationary negative ions. So, the correct graph between charge density and distance near p-n junction is shown in option (a).

39 (c) Applying KVL, $1 + 100\, i - 3 = 0$

$$i = \frac{2}{100} \times \frac{1000}{1000}$$

$$= 20 \times 10^{-3}\text{A}$$

$$= 20\ \text{mA}$$

40 (a) When LED is forward biased, then electrons from the n-type material cross the p-n junction and recombine with holes in the p-type material.

41 (b) An p-n photodiode is a semiconductor diode that produces a significant current when illuminated. It is reverse biased and it is operated below the breakdown voltage.

Energy of radiation = Band gap energy

i.e. $h\nu = 2.0\,\text{eV}$

$$\text{or } \nu = \frac{2.0 \times 1.6 \times 10^{-19}}{6.6 \times 10^{-34}} \approx 5 \times 10^{14}\ \text{Hz}$$

42 (d) For $V_i < 0$, ($V_i = -5$ V), the diode is reverse biased and hence offer infinite resistance and does not conduct.

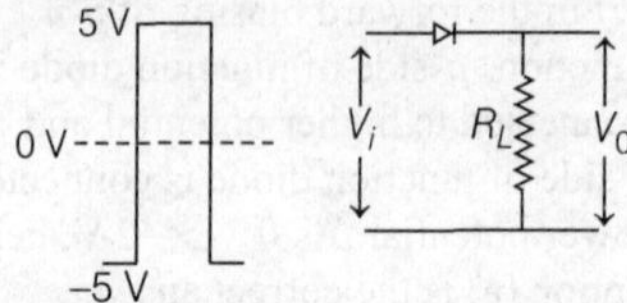

For $V_i > 0$ ($V_i = +5$ V), the junction diode is forward biased and hence conducts. The amplitude of the input signal is 5 V, hence output obtained is 5 V.

43 (a) In the given figure, p-side of p-n junction is at higher potential than n-side, so p-n junction is forward biased. Taking its resistance to be zero and applying Ohm's law,we get

$$I = \frac{V}{R} = \frac{5-2}{300} = 10^{-2}\ \text{A}$$

$$= 10^{-2} \times 10^3\ \text{mA} = 10\ \text{mA}$$

44 (b) Graph between potential and distance in a p-n junction diode is given by

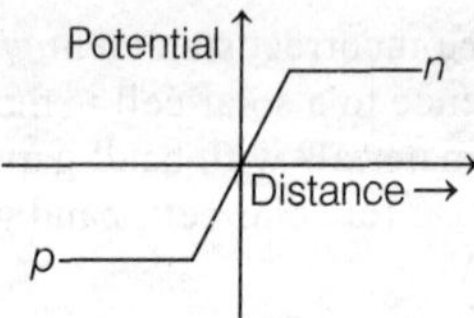

∴ Potential at p-side is less than that at n-side.

45 (c) The voltage across 2 kΩ resistor = 12 V (since applied voltage is more than breakdown voltage for zener diode).

Therefore, current passing through 2 kΩ resistor

$$= \frac{12}{2 \times 10^3} = 6 \times 10^{-3}$$

$$\text{A} = 6\,\text{mA}$$

46 (a) Due to reverse biasing, the width of depletion region increases and current flowing through the diode is almost zero. In this case, electric field is almost zero at the middle of the depletion region.

47 *(b)* When *p-n* junction diode is forward biased, more number of charge carriers (electrons in *n*-side and holes in *p*-side) moves through the junction. Therefore, in forward biasing barrier potential decreases. Thus, more current flows in the circuit.

48 *(b)* The main cause of zener breakdown is production of electron-hole pairs due to thermal excitation.

49 *(c)* Electric field, $E = -\frac{dV}{dr} = \frac{0.6}{10^{-6}}$

$= 6 \times 10^5 \text{ Vm}^{-1}$.

50 *(a)* Zener diode works as a voltage regulator under reverse biasing condition. It is based on the fact that in the breakdown region, for quite large changes in the zener current, the voltage across the diode remains almost constant.

51 *(a)* When a junction diode is forward biased as shown in figure, energy is released at the junction due to recombination of electrons and holes. In the junction diode made of gallium arsenide or indium phosphide, the energy is released in visible region. Such a junction diode is called light emitting diode or LED. It is a heavily doped *p-n* junction diode. So, the radiations emitted are spontaneous in forward biasing.

52 *(c)* Barrier potential does not depend on diode design while it depends on temperature, doping density and forward biasing.

53 *(b)* For full wave rectifier,

Ripple frequency = 2× Input frequency

= 2 × 50 = 100 Hz

54 *(d)* In a diode, in case of saturation current established, the plate resistance will be infinite, i.e. its conductivity is zero.

55 *(b)* The output DC component

$= \frac{\text{Peak voltage}}{\pi} = \frac{10}{\pi} \text{ V}$

56 *(c)* In reverse biasing condition, the potential at *p*-side is lower than that at *n*-side. In option (c), the *p*-side is grounded or at zero potential and *n*-side is at +5 V which is higher. So, it is reverse biased.

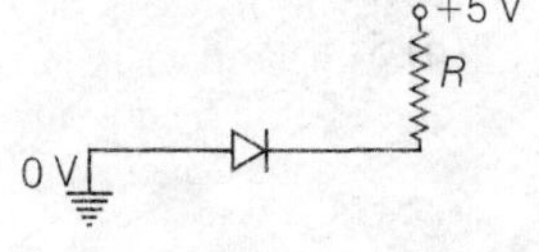

57 *(d)* Given, current in the circuit

$= 10 \text{ mA} = 10 \times 10^{-3} \text{ A}$

Voltage in the circuit = 6 − 2 = 4 V

From Ohm's law, $V = IR$

$\Rightarrow R = \frac{V}{I} = \frac{4}{10 \times 10^{-3}} = 400 \ \Omega$

58 *(b)* In reverse biasing, the applied voltage V on the *n*-side is positive and on the *p*-side is negative. The applied bias voltage V and the barrier potential V_B are in the same direction making the effective junction potential $V + V_B$. As a result, the junction width or depletion region will increase. The higher junction potential restricts the flow of majority carriers to a much greater extent and current flows due to minority carriers.

59 *(c)* The potential in depletion layer is due to ions. It appears as if some fictitious battery is connected across the junction with its negative pole connected to *p*-region and positive pole connected to *n*-region. The potential difference developed across the junction due to migration of majority charge carriers is potential barrier.

60 *(b)* When the reverse voltage across a zener diode exceeds the breakdown voltage V_Z, the current increases very sharply. In this region, the curve is almost vertical. It means voltage across zener diode is constant at V_Z even though the current through it changes. Therefore, a zener diode behaves as a constant voltage source.

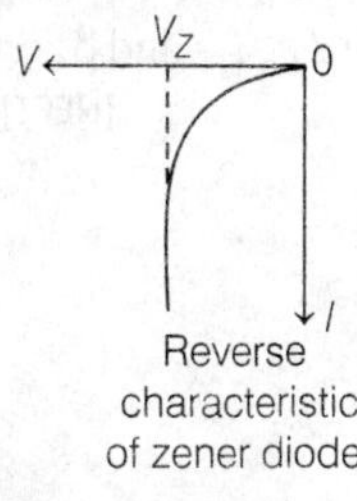

Reverse characteristic of zener diode

61 *(b)* The time, $t = CR$ is known as time constant. It is time in which charge on the capacitor decreases to $\frac{1}{e}$ times of its initial charge (steady state charge).

In Fig. (i), *p-n* junction diode is in forward bias, so current will flow in the circuit, i.e. charge on the capacitor decrease and in time t_0 it becomes,

$$Q = \frac{1}{e}(Q_0)$$

where, $Q_0 = CV$ and $Q = \frac{CV}{e}$

In Fig. (ii), the diode is reverse biased. Hence, the capacitor doesn't discharged as no current flows in the circuit. So, $Q = CV$.

62 *(b)* Reverse bias resistance

$= \frac{\Delta V}{\Delta I} = \frac{1}{0.5 \times 10^{-6}} = 2 \times 10^6 \ \Omega$

63 *(d)* Depletion layer contains only fixed positive and negative ions. Positive ions are on *n*-side and negative ions are on *p*-side.

64 *(a)* In forward biasing, the forward bias voltage opposes the potential barrier V_B. Due to it, the potential barrier is considerably reduced and the depletion region becomes thin. The potential barrier at some forward voltage (0.1 to 0.3 V), is eliminated altogether.

65 *(a)* The circuit can be drawn as

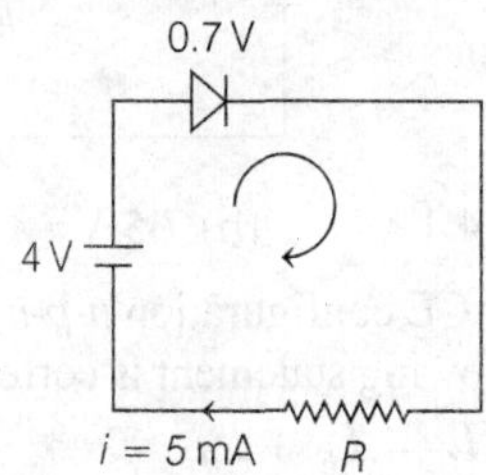

Applying KVL,

$-0.7 + 4 - 5 \times 10^{-3} R = 0$

$\Rightarrow \qquad R = 660 \ \Omega$

66 *(a)* At the *p-n* junction with reverse bias, there exists a junction field which at equilibrium does not permit the flow of charge carriers across the junction. When such a *p-n* diode is illuminated with light photons having energy, $h\nu > E_g$ and intensities I_1, I_2, I_3, etc, the electron and hole pairs generated in the depletion layer (or near the junction) and made to flow across the junction.

This produces current in the circuit depending on light intensity. Thus, a reverse biased *p-n* junction is used as a photodiode to measure light intensity.

67 *(c)* Zener diode is a silicon crystal diode having an unusual reverse current characteristic which is particularly suitable for voltage regulating purposes. Due to this characteristic, it is used as voltage stabiliser in many appliances in electronics.

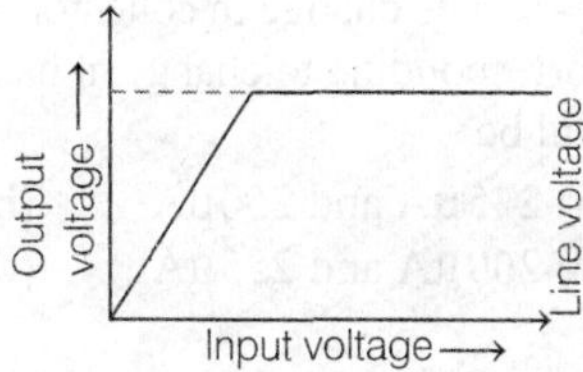

Topic 3

Transistors

2019

1 The given transistor operates in saturation region, then what should be the value of V_{BB}? ($R_{\text{out}} = 200\,\Omega$, $R_{\text{in}} = 100\,\text{k}\Omega$, $V_{CC} = 3$ V, $V_{BE} = 0.7$ V, $V_{CE} = 0$ V and $\beta = 200$)

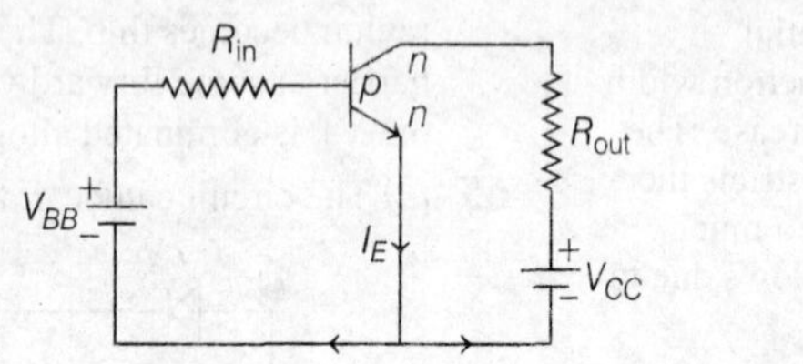

[AIIMS]

(a) 4.1 V (b) 7.5 V (c) 8.2 V (d) 6.8 V

2 For CE configuration *n-p-n* transistor. Which of the following statement is correct? [JIPMER]

(a) $I_C = I_E + I_B$ (b) $I_B = I_E + I_C$
(c) $I_E = I_C + I_B$ (d) All of these

2018

3 In the circuit shown in the figure, the input voltage V_i is 20 V, $V_{BE} = 0$ and $V_{CE} = 0$. The values of I_B, I_C and β are given by [NEET]

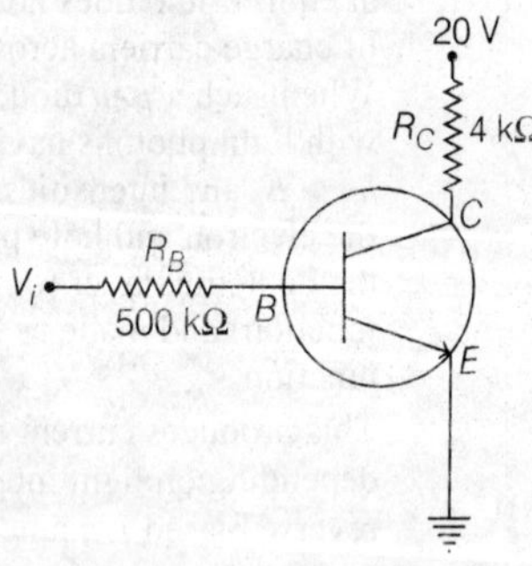

(a) $I_B = 20\,\mu\text{A}$, $I_C = 5$ mA and $\beta = 250$
(b) $I_B = 25\,\mu\text{A}$, $I_C = 5$ mA and $\beta = 200$
(c) $I_B = 40\,\mu\text{A}$, $I_C = 10$ mA and $\beta = 250$
(d) $I_B = 40\,\mu\text{A}$, $I_C = 5$ mA and $\beta = 125$

2017

4 The current gain of a transistor in common emitter mode is 49. The change in collector current and emitter current corresponding to change in base current by $5.0\,\mu\text{A}$, will be [AIIMS]

(a) $245\,\mu\text{A}$ and $250\,\mu\text{A}$ (b) $240\,\mu\text{A}$ and $235\,\mu\text{A}$
(c) $260\,\mu\text{A}$ and $255\,\mu\text{A}$ (d) None of these

5 In a common emitter transistor amplifier, the audio signal voltage across the collector is 3 V. The resistance of collector is 3 kΩ. If current gain is 100 and the base resistance is 2 kΩ, the voltage and power gain of the amplifier is [NEET]

(a) 200 and 1000 (b) 15 and 200
(c) 150 and 15000 (d) 20 and 2000

2016

6 A *n-p-n* transistor is connected in common emitter configuration in a given amplifier. A load resistance of 800 Ω is connected in the collector circuit and the voltage drop across it is 0.8V. If the current amplification factor is 0.96 and the input resistance of the circuits is 192 Ω, the voltage gain and the power gain of the amplifier will respectively be [NEET]

(a) 3.69, 3.84 (b) 4, 4
(c) 4, 3.69 (d) 4, 3.84

7 For CE transistor amplifier, the audio signal voltage across the collector resistance of 2 kΩ is 4 V. If the current amplification factor of the transistor is 100 and the base resistance is 1 kΩ, then the input signal voltage is [NEET]

(a) 10 mV (b) 20 mV
(c) 30 mV (d) 15 mV

2014

8 In common base circuit of a transistor, current amplification factor is 0.95. Calculate the emitter current, if base current is 0.2 mA. [MHT CET]

(a) 2 mA (b) 4 mA
(c) 6 mA (d) 8 mA

9 In a transistor output characteristics commonly used in common emitter configuration, the base current I_B, the collector current I_C and the collector-emitter voltage V_{CE} have values of the following orders of magnitude in the active region [WB JEE]

(a) I_B and I_C both are in μA and V_{CE} in V
(b) I_B is in μA, I_C is in mA and V_{CE} in V
(c) I_B is in mA, I_C is in μA and V_{CE} in mV
(d) I_B is in mA, I_C is in mA and V_{CE} in mV

10 If α (current gain) of transistor is 0.98. What is the value of β (current gain) of the transistor? [KCET]

(a) 0.49 (b) 49
(c) 4.9 (d) 5

11 For the action of a common base (CB) transistor, (E = emitter, B = base and C = collector) the required CB, EB junction bias conditions are **[EAMCET]**
(a) Both EB and CB junction-forward bias
(b) Both EB and CB junction-reverse bias
(c) EB junction forward bias, CB junction reverse bias
(d) EB junction reverse bias, CB junction forward bias

2013

12 In a common emitter (CE) amplifier having a voltage gain G, the transistor used has transconductance 0.03 mho and current gain 25. If the above transistor is replaced with another one with transconductance 0.02 mho and current gain 20, the voltage gain will be **[NEET]**
(a) $\frac{2}{3}G$ (b) $1.5G$
(c) $\frac{1}{3}G$ (d) $\frac{5}{4}G$

13 In the case of constants α and β of a transistor **[AIIMS]**
(a) $\alpha\beta = 1$ (b) $\beta > 1, \alpha < 1$
(c) $\alpha = \beta$ (d) $\beta < 1, \alpha > 1$

2012

14 The input resistance of a silicon transistor is 100 Ω. Its base current is changed by 40 μA, which results in a change in collector current by 2 mA. This transistor is used as a common emitter amplifier with a load resistance of 4 kΩ. The voltage gain of the amplifier is **[CBSE AIPMT]**
(a) 2000 (b) 3000
(c) 4000 (d) 1000

15 In a CE transistor amplifier, the audio signal voltage across the collector resistance of 2 kΩ is 2V. If the base resistance is 1 kΩ and the current amplification of the transistor is 100, the input signal voltage is **[CBSE AIPMT]**
(a) 0.1 V (b) 1.0 V
(c) 1 mV (d) 10 mV

2011

16 A transistor is operated in common emitter configuration at $V_C = 2$ V such that a change in the base current from 100μA to 300 μA produces a change in the collector current from 10 mA to 20 mA. The current gain is **[CBSE AIPMT]**
(a) 75 (b) 100
(c) 25 (d) 50

17 The current gain of a common base transistor circuit is 0.96. On changing the emitter current by 10.0 mA, the change in the collector current will be **[J&K CET]**
(a) 9.6 mA (b) 0.4 mA
(c) 19.6 mA (d) 24 mA

18 The transfer characteristics of a base biased transistor has the operations, namely, cut-off, active region and saturation region. For using the transistor as an amplifier, it has to operate in the **[J&K CET]**
(a) active region (b) cut-off region
(c) saturation region (d) cut-off and saturation

19 An n-p-n transistor can be consider to be equivalent to two diodes connected. Which of the following figures is the correct one? **[KCET]**

(a) 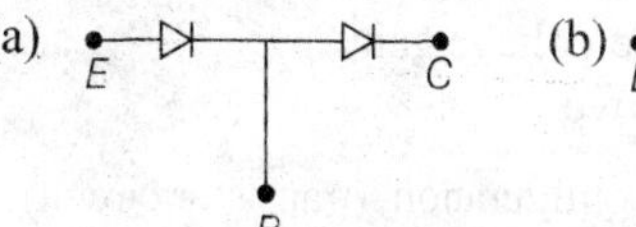

(b) 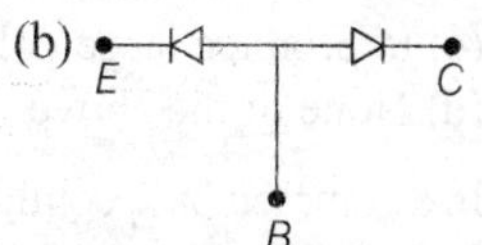

(c) 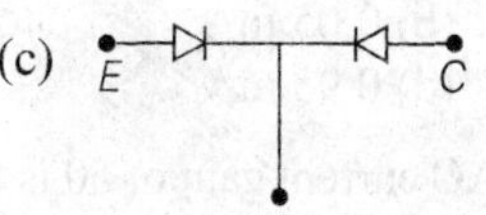

(d) 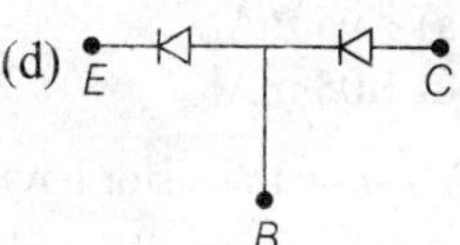

20 The device that can act as a complete electronic circuit is **[CBSE AIPMT]**
(a) junction diode (b) integrated circuit
(c) junction transistor (d) zener diode

21 The current gain α of a transistor in common-base mode is 0.995. Its current gain β in the common emitter mode is **[Manipal]**
(a) 200 (b) 90.5
(c) 100 (d) 1.005

22 The current gain in the common-emitter mode of a transistor is 10. The input impedance is 20 kΩ and load of resistance is 100 kΩ. The power gain is **[Manipal]**
(a) 300 (b) 500 (c) 200 (d) 100

23 If β, R_L and r are the AC current gain, load resistance and the input resistance of a transistor, respectively in CE configuration, the voltage and the power gains respectively are **[Manipal]**
(a) $\beta\frac{R_L}{r}$ and $\beta^2\frac{R_L}{r}$
(b) $\beta\frac{r}{R_L}$ and $\beta^2\frac{r}{R_L}$
(c) $\beta\frac{R_L}{r}$ and $\beta\left(\frac{R_L}{r}\right)^2$
(d) $\beta\frac{r}{R_L}$ and $\beta\left(\frac{r}{R_L}\right)^2$

2010

24 If parameter $\alpha = 0.9$, then the value of the parameter β is **[OJEE]**
(a) 0.1 (b) 1
(c) 0.9 (d) 9

25 In a common emitter configuration, a transistor has $\beta = 50$ and input resistance is $1\,k\Omega$. If the peak value of AC input is 0.01 V, then the peak value of collector current is [WB JEE]
(a) $0.01\,\mu A$ (b) $0.25\,\mu A$
(c) $100\,\mu A$ (d) $500\,\mu A$

26 In transistor, forward bias is always smaller than the reverse bias. The correct reason is [Haryana PMT]
(a) to avoid excessive heating of transistor
(b) to maintain a constant base current
(c) to produce large voltage gain
(d) None of the above

27 In a common base configuration, (transistor circuit) $I_E = 1\,mA$ and $I_C = 0.95\,mA$. The value of base current is [CG PMT]
(a) 1.95 mA (b) 0.05 mA
(c) 1.05 mA (d) 0.95 mA

28 A *p-n-p* transistor having AC current gain of 50 is used to make an amplifier of a voltage gain of 5. What will be the power gain of the amplifier? [DUMET]
(a) 125 (b) 178
(c) 250 (d) 354

2009

29 A transistor is operated in common emitter configuration at $V_c = 2\,V$ such that a change in the base current from $100\,\mu A$ to $200\,\mu A$ produces a change in the collector current from 5 mA to 10 mA. The current gain [CBSE AIPMT]
(a) 75 (b) 100
(c) 150 (d) 50

30 In a transistor, the collector current is always less than the emitter current, because [AFMC]
(a) collector side is reverse biased and the emitter side is forward biased
(b) a few electrons are lost in the base and only remaining ones reach the collector
(c) collector being reverse biased, attracts less electrons
(d) collector side is forward biased and emitter side is reverse biased

2008

31 The voltage gain of an amplifier with 9% negative feedback is 10. The voltage gain without feedback will be [CBSE AIPMT]
(a) 90 (b) 10
(c) 1.25 (d) 100

32 The input resistance of a common emitter transistor amplifier, if the output resistance is $500\,k\Omega$, the current gain is $\alpha = 0.98$ and power gain is 6.0625×10^6 is [AIIMS]
(a) $198\,\Omega$ (b) $300\,\Omega$
(c) $100\,\Omega$ (d) $400\,\Omega$

33 A change of 8.0 mA in the emitter current brings a change of 7.9 mA in the collector current. The values of α and β are [MHT CET]
(a) 0.99, 90 (b) 0.96, 79
(c) 0.97, 99 (d) 0.99, 79

34 In a common emitter configuration of a transistor, the voltage drop across a $500\,\Omega$ resistor in the collector circuit is 0.5 V when the collector supply voltage is 5 V. If the current gain in the common base mode is 0.96, the base current is [Kerala CEE]
(a) $\frac{1}{20}\,\mu A$ (b) $\frac{1}{5}\,\mu A$ (c) $\frac{1}{20}\,mA$ (d) $\frac{1}{10}\,mA$
(e) $\frac{1}{24}\,mA$

35 In a transistor circuit, the base current changes from $30\,\mu A$ to $90\,\mu A$. If the current gain of the transistor is 30, the change in the collector current is [Punjab PMET]
(a) 4 mA (b) 2 mA
(c) 3.6 mA (d) 1.8 mA

36 A common emitter amplifier has a voltage gain of 50, an input impedance of $100\,\Omega$ and an output impedance of $200\,\Omega$. The power gain of the amplifier is [JCECE]
(a) 500 (b) 1000 (c) 1250 (d) 100

2007

37 In the following common emitter circuit, if $\beta = 100, V_{CE} = 7\,V, V_{BE}$ = negligible, $R_C = 2\,k\,\Omega$, then $I_B = ?$ [Punjab PMET]

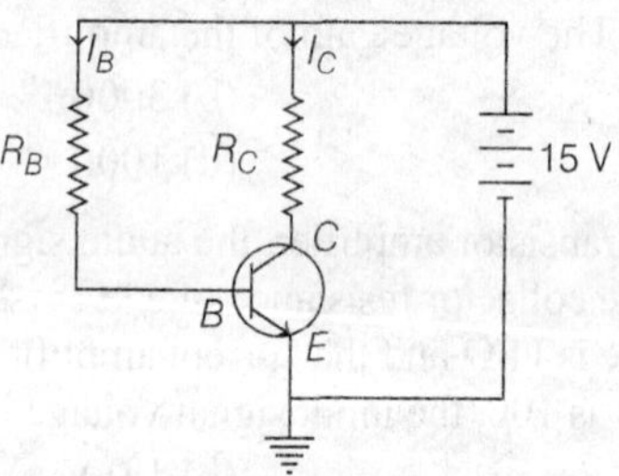

(a) 0.01 mA (b) 0.04 mA (c) 0.02 mA (d) 0.03 mA

38 Graph of input characteristics of common emitter amplifier is [DUMET]

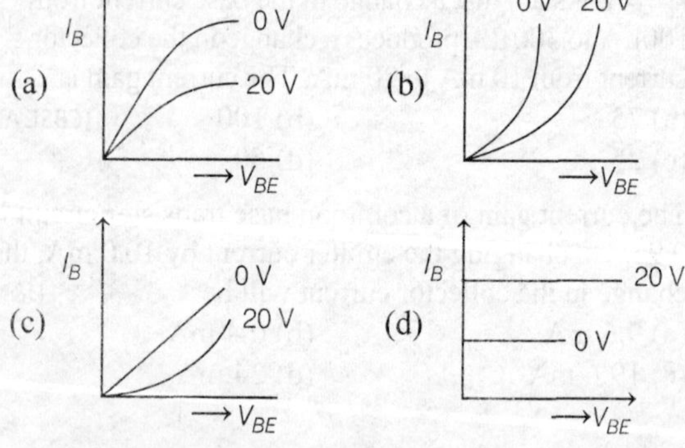

39 The minimum potential difference between the base and emitter required to switch a silicon transistor ON is approximately **[AIIMS]**
(a) 1 V (b) 3 V
(c) 5 V (d) 4.2 V

40 **Assertion** In common base configuration, the current gain of the transistor is less than unity. **[AIIMS]**
Reason The collector terminal is reverse biased for amplification.
(a) Both Assertion and Reason are correct and Reason is the correct explanation of Assertion.
(b) Both Assertion and Reason are correct but Reason is not the correct explanation of Assertion.
(c) Assertion is correct but Reason is incorrect.
(d) Assertion is incorrect but Reason is correct.

2006

41 An amplifier has a voltage gain $A_V = 1000$. The voltage gain in dB is **[AFMC]**
(a) 30 dB (b) 60 dB (c) 3 dB (d) 20 dB

42 In a transistor amplifier, the two AC current gains α and β are defined as $\alpha = \frac{\partial I_C}{\partial I_E}$ and $\beta = \frac{\partial I_C}{\partial I_B}$. The relation between α and β is **[Guj CET]**
(a) $\beta = \frac{1-\alpha}{\alpha}$ (b) $\beta = \frac{\alpha}{1-\alpha}$ (c) $\beta = \frac{\alpha}{1+\alpha}$ (d) $\beta = \frac{1+\alpha}{\alpha}$

43 A *p-n-p* transistor is said to be in active region of operation, when **[EAMCET]**
(a) both emitter junction and collector junction are forward biased
(b) both emitter junction and collector junction are reverse biased
(c) emitter junction is forward biased and collector junction is reverse biased
(d) emitter junction is reverse biased and collector junction is forward biased

2005

44 The voltage gain of the following amplifier is **[AIIMS]**

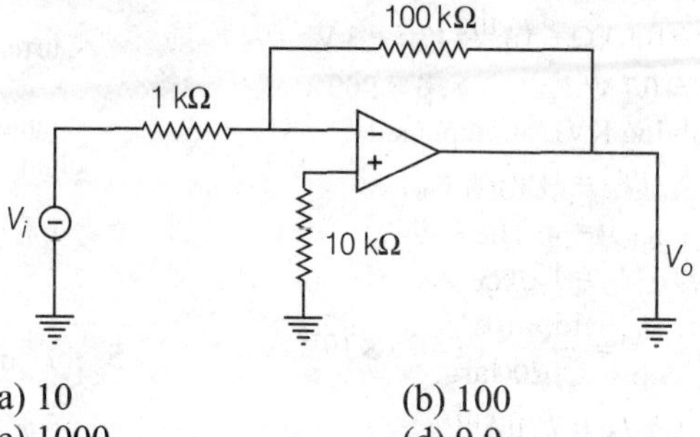

(a) 10 (b) 100
(c) 1000 (d) 9.9

45 Consider an *n-p-n* transistor amplifier in common emitter configuration. The current gain of the transistor is 100. If the collector current changes by 1 mA, what will be the change in emitter current? **[AIIMS]**
(a) 1.1 mA (b) 1.01 mA
(c) 0.01 mA (d) 10 mA

46 In *n-p-n* transistor, the collector current is 10 mA. If 90% of the electrons emitted reach the collector, then **[Kerala CEE]**
(a) emitter current will be 9 mA
(b) emitter current will be 11.1 mA
(c) base current will be 0.1 mA
(d) base current will be 0.01 mA
(e) emitter current will be 11.3 mA

47 **Assertion** In a common emitter transistor amplifier, the input current is much less than the output current.
Reason The common emitter transistor amplifier has very high input impedance. **[Manipal]**
(a) Both Assertion and Reason are correct and Reason is the correct explanation of Assertion.
(b) Both Assertion and Reason are correct but Reason is not the correct explanation of Assertion.
(c) Assertion is correct but Reason is incorrect.
(d) Assertion is incorrect but Reason is correct.

Answers

1 (c)	2 (c)	3 (d)	4 (a)	5 (c)	6 (d)	7 (b)	8 (b)	9 (b)	10 (b)
11 (c)	12 (a)	13 (b)	14 (a)	15 (d)	16 (d)	17 (a)	18 (a)	19 (b)	20 (b)
21 (a)	22 (b)	23 (a)	24 (d)	25 (d)	26 (a)	27 (b)	28 (c)	29 (d)	30 (b)
31 (d)	32 (a)	33 (d)	34 (e)	35 (d)	36 (c)	37 (b)	38 (b)	39 (a)	40 (b)
41 (a)	42 (b)	43 (c)	44 (b)	45 (b)	46 (b)	47 (c)			

Explanations

1 (c) Given, $R_{out} = 200\Omega$,

$R_{in} = 100\,k\Omega = 10^5\,\Omega\; V_{CC} = 3\,V$,

$V_{BE} = 0.7\,V, V_{CE} = 0V, \beta = 200$

Applying KVL at output side,

$$V_{CE} = V_{CC} - I_C R_{out}$$
$$0 = 3 - I_c \times 200$$
$$\Rightarrow \quad I_C = 15\,mA$$
$$\therefore I_B = \frac{I_C}{\beta} = \frac{15\times10^{-3}}{200} = 75\times10^{-6}\,A$$
$$\therefore \quad I_B = 75\,\mu A$$

Again, Applying KVL at input side,

$$V_{BE} = V_{BB} - I_B R_{in}$$
$$\Rightarrow V_{BB} = V_{BE} + I_B R_{in}$$
$$= 0.7 + 75\times10^{-6}\times10^5$$
$$= 0.7 + 7.5 = 8.2\,V$$

2 (c) In CE configuration *n-p-n* transistor, emitter current (I_E) is equal to sum of collector current (I_C) and base current (I_B), i.e $I_E = I_C + I_B$

3 (d) Given, $V_{BE} = 0$ V, $V_{CE} = 0$ V and $V_i = 20$ V

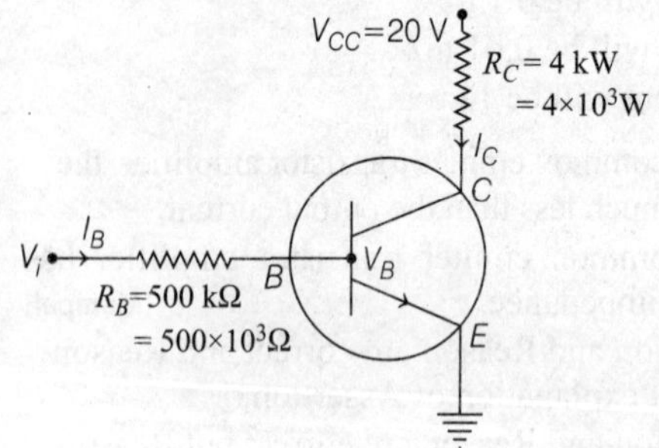

Applying Kirchhoff's law to the base emitter loop, we get

$$V_i = I_B R_B + V_{BE}$$

Substituting the values, we get

$$20 = I_B \times (500\times10^3) + 0$$
$$\Rightarrow I_B = \frac{20}{500\times10^3} = 0.04\times10^{-3}$$
$$= 40\times10^{-6} = 40\,\mu A \quad \ldots(i)$$

Similarly, $V_{CC} = I_C R_C + V_{CE}$

Substituting the given values, we get

$$20 = I_C\times(4\times10^3) + 0$$
$$\Rightarrow I_C = \frac{20}{4\times10^3} = 5\times10^{-3} = 5\,mA \ldots(ii)$$

Current gain is given as $\beta = \dfrac{I_C}{I_B}$

Substituting the value of I_B and I_C from Eqs. (i) and (ii), we get

$$\Rightarrow \beta = \frac{5\times10^{-3}}{40\times10^{-6}} = 0.125\times10^3 = 125$$

4 (a) Given, $\beta = 49$ and $\Delta I_B = 5\mu A$

Current gain, $\beta = \dfrac{\Delta I_C}{\Delta I_B}$, where ΔI_C is change in collector current and ΔI_B is change in base current.

$$\Delta I_C = \beta\Delta I_B = 49\times5 = 245\mu A$$
$$\Delta I_E = \Delta I_B + \Delta I_C = (245+5)\,\mu A$$
$$= 250\,\mu A$$

5 (c) Collector current,

$$i_C = \frac{V}{R} = \frac{3}{3\times10^3} = 10^{-3}\,A$$

Now, base current,

$$i_B = \frac{i_C}{\beta} = \frac{10^{-3}}{100} = 10^{-5}\,A$$

As, voltage, $V_{in} = i_B R_B$

$$\therefore \quad V_{in} = 10^{-5}\times2\times10^3$$
$$= 2\times10^{-2}\,V$$

So, voltage gain,

$$A_V = \frac{V_{out}}{V_{in}} = \frac{3}{2\times10^{-2}} = 150$$

Power gain $= A_V \times \beta$

$$= 150\times100 = 15000$$

6 (d) Given, resistance across load, $R_L = 800\,\Omega$

Voltage drop across load, $V_L = 0.8$ V

Input resistance of circuit, $R_i = 192\,\Omega$.

Collector current is given by

$$I_C = \frac{V_L}{R_L} = \frac{0.8}{800} = \frac{8}{8000} = 1\,mA$$

$\because$ Current amplification

$$= \frac{\text{Output current}}{\text{Input current}} = \frac{I_C}{I_B} = 0.96$$
$$\Rightarrow I_B = \frac{1\,mA}{0.96}$$

$\because$ Voltage gain, $A_V = \dfrac{V_L}{V_{in}} = \dfrac{V_L}{I_B R_i}$

$$= \frac{0.8\times0.96}{10^{-3}\times192} = 4 \Rightarrow A_V = 4$$

and power gain,

$$A_P = \frac{I_C^2 R_L}{I_B^2 R_i} = \left(\frac{I_C}{I_B}\right)^2 \cdot \frac{R_L}{R_i}$$
$$= (0.96)^2 \times 800/192$$
$$A_P = 3.84$$

7 (b) Voltage amplification,

$$A_V = \beta\frac{R_{out}}{R_{in}} = \frac{(V_{out})_{AC}}{(V_{in})_{AC}}$$

Given, collector resistance $= R_{out} = 2\,k\Omega$

Current amplification factor, $\beta = 100$

Base resistance, $R_{in} = 1\,k\Omega$

Output signal voltage = 4 V

Putting all the values in given equation, we get

$$A_V = \beta\frac{R_{out}}{R_{in}} = 100\times\frac{2\,k\Omega}{1\,k\Omega}$$
$$\Rightarrow A_V = 200$$

Now, $A_V = \dfrac{(V_{out})_{AC}}{(V_{in})_{AC}} = 200$

$$\Rightarrow (V_{in})_{AC} = 4/200 = 20\,mV$$

8 (b) Given, $\alpha = 0.95$ and $I_b = 0.2$ mA

As, $\quad \alpha = \dfrac{I_c}{I_e} = \dfrac{I_e - I_b}{I_e} = 1 - \dfrac{I_b}{I_e}$

$$\Rightarrow \quad \frac{I_b}{I_e} = 1-\alpha = 1-0.95 = 0.05$$
$$\Rightarrow \quad I_e = \frac{I_b}{0.05} = \frac{0.2}{0.05} \Rightarrow I_e = 4\,mA$$

9 (b) In active region values are as I_B is in μA, I_C is in mA and V_{CE} in V.

10 (b) α and β are the AC current gains of a transistor in the common base configuration and in the common emitter configuration, respectively and are related as

$$\beta = \frac{\alpha}{1-\alpha} = \frac{0.98}{1-0.98} \quad [\because \alpha = 0.98]$$
$$\Rightarrow \quad = \frac{0.98}{0.02} = \frac{98}{2} = 49$$

11 (c) A common base circuit of a *p-n-p* transistor is shown in figure. The emitter base (*p-n*) junction on the left is given a small forward bias (fraction of a volt) by an emitter base battery V_{EB}, while the base collector (*n-p*) junction is given a large reverse bias (a few volt) by another battery V_{CB}.

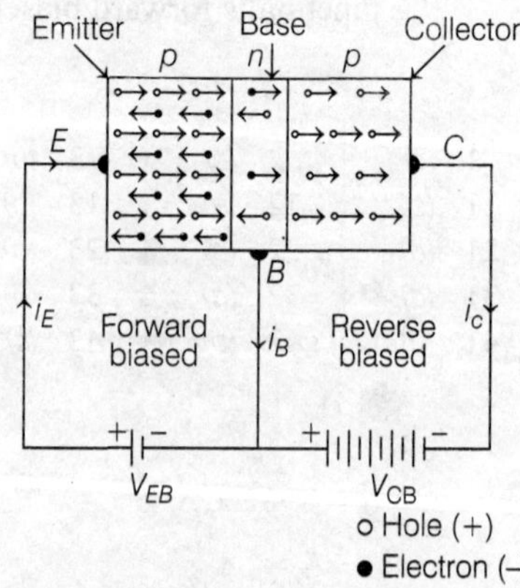

So, the required solution is emitter-base (EB) junction is forward bias and collector-base (CB) junction is reverse bias.

12 (a) As voltage gain,

$$G = \left(\frac{\beta}{R_i}\right) R_L \quad \left[\because g_m = \frac{\beta}{R_i}\right]$$

$$\Rightarrow \quad G = g_m R_L \Rightarrow G \propto g_m$$

$$\therefore \quad \frac{G_2}{G_1} = \frac{g_{m_2}}{g_{m_1}} \Rightarrow G_2 = \frac{0.02}{0.03} \times G$$

$\therefore$ Voltage gain, $G_2 = \frac{2}{3} G$

13 (b) In case of transistor, constant α is current gain in common base configuration and constant β is current gain in common emitter configuration. Also, α is always less than 1, while β is always greater than 1.

14 (a) We know that, voltage gain,

$$A_V = \beta \frac{R_L}{R_i}$$

On putting given values, we get

$$A_V = \frac{2 \times 10^{-3}}{40 \times 10^{-6}} \times \frac{4 \times 10^3}{100} \left[\because \beta = \frac{\Delta I_C}{\Delta I_B}\right]$$

$$A_V = 2000$$

15 (d) Current amplification factor,

$$\beta = \frac{\Delta I_C}{\Delta I_B} \quad \ldots\text{(i)}$$

Collector current,

$$\Delta I_C = \frac{V_C}{R_C} = \frac{2\text{V}}{2 \times 10^3\ \Omega} = 1 \times 10^{-3}\ \text{A}$$

Base current,

$$\Delta I_B = \frac{V_B}{R_B} = \frac{V_B}{1 \times 10^3} = V_B \times 10^{-3}\ \text{A}$$

Given, $\beta = 100$

$$\therefore \quad 100 = \frac{1 \times 10^{-3}}{V_B \times 10^{-3}} \Rightarrow V_B = \frac{1}{100}$$

$$\Rightarrow V_B = \frac{10}{1000} = 10 \times 10^{-3}\ \text{V} = 10\ \text{mV}$$

16 (d) Current gain,

$$\beta = \frac{\Delta I_C}{\Delta I_B} = \frac{(20 - 10)\ \text{mA}}{(300 - 100)\ \mu\text{A}}$$

$$= \frac{10 \times 10^{-3}}{200 \times 10^{-6}} = 50$$

17 (a) Current gain for common base transistor, $\alpha = \left(\frac{\Delta I_C}{\Delta I_E}\right)_{V_C}$

Given, $\alpha = 0.96$ and $\Delta I_E = 10.0$ mA

$$0.96 = \frac{\Delta I_C}{10.0}$$

$$\Delta I_C = 0.96 \times 10.0 = 9.6\ \text{mA}$$

18 (a) For using the transistor as an amplifier, it has to operate in the active region, because in this region, it shows linear characteristics between input and output voltage.

19 (b) Fig. (b) shows the correct diagram of the circuit.

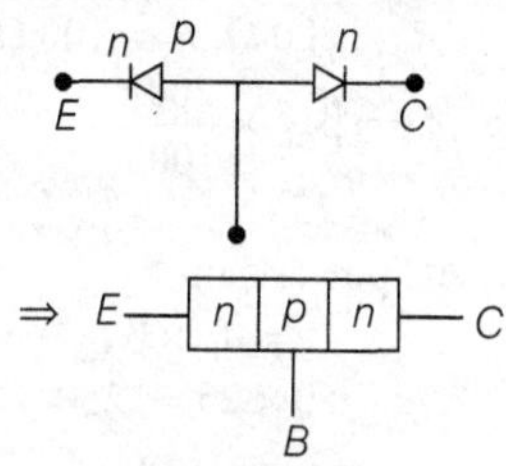

20 (b) Integrated circuits are miniature electronic circuit produced within a single crystal of a semiconductors such as silicon. They contain a million or so transistors and resistors or capacitors. They are widely used in memory circuits, micro computers, pocket calculators and electronic watches, on account of their low cost and reliability into specific regions of the semiconductor crystals.

21 (a) Given, current gain α of a transistor is in common base mode, $\alpha = 0.995$

We have to find, current gain in common emitter mode β.

We know that,

$$\beta = \frac{\alpha}{1 - \alpha} = \frac{0.995}{1 - 0.995} \approx 200$$

22 (b) The power gain is defined as the ratio of change in output power to the change in input power.

Since, $P = Vi$

Therefore, power gain = current gain $\times$ voltage gain

$$= \beta \times \beta \left(\frac{R_{\text{out}}}{R_{\text{in}}}\right)$$

$$= \beta^2 \left(\frac{R_{\text{out}}}{R_{\text{in}}}\right)$$

Given, $\beta = 10$, $R_{\text{in}} = 20\ \text{k}\Omega$

and $R_{\text{out}} = 100\ \text{k}\Omega$

$$\therefore \text{Power gain} = (10)^2 \left(\frac{100}{20}\right)$$

$$= 100 \times 5 = 500$$

23 (a) Transistor as a common emitter amplifier,

Voltage gain, $A_V = \frac{\Delta V_o}{\Delta V_i}$

$$= \beta_{\text{AC}} \times \text{Resistance gain} = \beta \times \frac{R_L}{r}$$

Power gain $= \frac{\Delta P_o}{\Delta P_i}$

$$= \beta_{\text{AC}}^2 \times \text{Resistance gain} = \beta^2 \times \frac{R_L}{r}$$

24 (d) Relation between α and β is given by

$$\alpha = \frac{\beta}{1 + \beta} \Rightarrow 0.9 = \frac{\beta}{1 + \beta} \Rightarrow \beta = 9$$

25 (d) Given, the current gain of the transistor is $\beta = 50$,

input resistance = 1 kΩ

and input voltage = 0.01 V

Hence, $\beta = \frac{\Delta i_C}{\Delta i_B} = 50 \Rightarrow \Delta i_C = 50\ \Delta i_B$

Also, the change in base current is

$$\Delta i_B = \frac{\text{Input voltage}}{\text{Input resistance}} = \frac{0.01}{1 \times 10^3}$$

$$= 10^{-5}\ \text{A}$$

So, $\Delta i_C = 50 \times 10^{-5} = 500\ \mu\text{A}$

26 (a) If forward bias is made large, the majority charge carriers would move from the emitter to the collector through the base with high velocity. This would give rise to excessive heat causing damage to transistor.

27 (b) For a common base transistor,

$$I_E = I_B + I_C$$

$$\Rightarrow 1\ \text{mA} = I_B + 0.95\ \text{mA}$$

$$I_B = 0.05\ \text{mA}$$

28 (c) For the amplifier,

Power gain = Current gain $\times$ Voltage gain = $50 \times 5 = 250$

29 (d) Current gain is given as

$$\beta = \left|\frac{\Delta I_C}{\Delta I_B}\right|_{V_{CE} = \text{constant}}$$

$$\Rightarrow \frac{(10 - 5) \times 10^{-3}}{(200 - 100) \times 10^{-6}} = \frac{5 \times 10^3}{100} = 50$$

30 (b) Due to forward bias at the emitter-base junction (in *n-p-n*), the majority charge carrier (electrons) of emitter get repelled from the negative terminal and move towards base. Some of these electrons combine with the majority charge carrier (holes) present in the base and most of the electrons reach the collector, crossing the collector-base junction. This implies that collector current is always less than the emitter current as a few electrons are lost in the base and only remaining ones reach the collector.

31 (d) The process of injecting a fraction of output energy of some device back to the input is known as feedback. When the feedback energy (voltage or current) is out of phase with the input signal and thus opposes it, is called negative feedback.

Voltage gain with feedback is

$$A_{Vf} = \frac{A_V}{1 + \beta A_V}$$

where, A_V is the voltage gain without feedback and β is the negative feedback.

Given, $A_{Vf} = 10, \beta = 9\% = \frac{9}{100}$

$\therefore \quad 10 = \dfrac{A_V}{1 + \frac{9}{100} A_V}$

or $10 + \frac{9}{10} A_V = A_V$

or $\quad 0.1\, A_V = 10$ or $A_V = 100$

32 (a) Voltage gain, $A_V = \beta \frac{R_2}{R_1}$

where, R_1 = input resistance

and $\quad R_2$ = output resistance

Also, current gain,

$$\beta = \frac{\alpha}{1-\alpha} = \frac{0.98}{1-0.98} = 49$$

$\therefore \quad A_V = (49)\left[\dfrac{500 \times 10^3}{R_1}\right]$

$\Rightarrow$ Power gain $= \beta\, A_V \Rightarrow 6.0625 \times 10^6$

$$= 49 \times \left[\frac{500 \times 10^3}{R_1}\right] \times 49$$

$\Rightarrow \quad R_1 = 198\, \Omega$

33 (d) Given, change in emitter current,

$$\Delta I_E = 8 \text{ mA}$$

and change in collector current,

$$\Delta I_C = 7.9 \text{ mA}$$

We know that, $\alpha = \dfrac{\Delta I_C}{\Delta I_E} = \dfrac{7.9}{8} \simeq 0.99$

Also we know that,

$$\beta = \frac{\alpha}{1-\alpha} = \frac{\frac{7.9}{8}}{1-\frac{7.9}{8}} = \frac{7.9}{8-7.9}$$

$$= \frac{7.9}{0.1} = 79$$

Hence, the required answer is $\alpha = 0.99$ and $\beta = 79$.

34 (e) In common emitter configuration,

$$I_C = \frac{\Delta V_C}{R_L} = \frac{0.5}{500} = 1 \text{ mA}$$

Given, $\quad \alpha = 0.96$

$\Rightarrow \quad \beta = \dfrac{\alpha}{1-\alpha} = \dfrac{0.96}{0.04} = 24$

$\because \quad \beta = \dfrac{I_C}{I_B} \Rightarrow I_B = \dfrac{I_C}{\beta} = \dfrac{1}{24}$ mA

35 (d) The current gain, $\beta = \dfrac{\Delta I_C}{\Delta I_B}$

$\therefore \quad 30 = \dfrac{\Delta I_C}{90-30}$

$$\Delta I_C = 30 \times 60 = 1800\, \mu\text{A} = 1.8 \text{ mA}$$

36 (c) As, A_V is voltage gain and β_{AC} is AC current gain.

$A_V = \beta_{AC} \times$ Resistance gain $\left(= \dfrac{R_0}{R_i}\right)$

Given, $A_V = 50$,

$$R_0 = 200\, \Omega, R_i = 100\, \Omega$$

Hence, $50 = \beta_{AC} \times \dfrac{200}{100}$

$\therefore \quad \beta_{AC} = 25$

Now, AC power gain

$$= A_V \times \beta_{AC}$$
$$= 50 \times 25 = 1250$$

37 (b) Here, $\quad V = V_{CE} + I_C R_C$

$\Rightarrow \quad 15 = 7 + I_C \times 2 \times 10^3$

$$I_C = 4 \text{ mA}$$

$\Rightarrow \quad I_B = \dfrac{4}{100} = 0.04 \text{ mA} \quad \left(\because \beta = \dfrac{I_C}{I_B}\right)$

38 (b) The input characteristics of common emitter amplifier is the curve between base current, I_B and base emitter voltage, V_{BE} at constant collector emitter voltage, V_{CE}.

The input characteristics can be determined by the circuit as shown in figure. Keeping V_{CE} constant (say at 0 V), note the base current I_B for various values of V_{BE}.

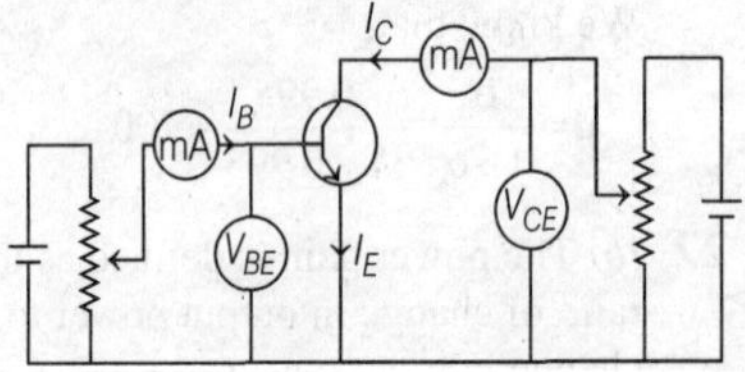

Then, plot the readings obtained on the graph, taking I_B along Y-axis and V_{BE} along X-axis.

Its slope is given by reverse of graph, i.e.

$$\left(\frac{\Delta V_{BE}}{\Delta I_B}\right)_{V_{CE} = \text{constent}} = R_i \text{ (input resistance)}$$

With increasing value of V_{CE}, the slope of graph increases, so correct graph is shown in (b).

39 (a) To switch on the transistor, the emitter-base junction of a transistor is forward biased, while collector-base junction is reverse biased. The cut-off voltage for silicon is 1V. So to switch on a silicon transistor a potential difference of 1V approximately is required between the base and emitter.

40 (b) The input current flowing into emitter is quite large as it is the sum of both the base current and the collector current respectively, therefore the collector current output is less than emitter current and hence $\alpha < 1$.

Because, $\alpha = \dfrac{\Delta I_C}{\Delta I_E}$.

For amplification, the collector terminal of the transistor is reverse biased.

41 (a) Voltage gain, $A_V = 1000$

In dB, voltage gain,

$$A = 10 \log_{10} 1000 \text{ dB}$$
$$= (10 \times 3) \log_{10} 10 \text{ dB} = 30 \text{ dB}$$
$$(\because \log_{10} 10 = 1)$$

42 (b) Given, $\alpha = \dfrac{\partial I_C}{\partial I_E}$ and $\beta = \dfrac{\partial I_C}{\partial I_B}$,

We know that, in a transistor amplifier,

$$I_E = I_C + I_B$$

$\Rightarrow \quad \partial I_E = \partial I_C + \partial I_B$

Now, $\beta = \dfrac{\partial I_C}{\partial I_B} = \dfrac{\partial I_C}{\partial I_E - \partial I_C} = \dfrac{\partial I_C / \partial I_E}{1 - \partial I_C / \partial I_E}$

$\therefore \quad \beta = \dfrac{\alpha}{1-\alpha}$

43 (c) For amplification of a *p-n-p* transistor, emitter junction is forward biased and collector junction is reverse biased. In this state, *p-n-p* transistor is said to be in active region of operation.

44 (b) The given circuit is an operational amplifier (Op-amp). The voltage gain of this amplifier

$$A_V = \frac{V_o}{V_i} = \frac{R_f}{R_i} = \frac{100 \text{ k}\Omega}{1 \text{k}\Omega} = 100$$

45 (b) Current gain in common emitter mode, $\quad \beta = \Delta I_C / \Delta I_B$

But $\quad \Delta I_B = \Delta I_E - \Delta I_C$

$\therefore \quad \beta = \dfrac{\Delta I_C}{\Delta I_E - \Delta I_C}$

Here, $\beta = 100$ and $\Delta I_C = 1$ mA

$\therefore \quad 100 = \dfrac{1}{\Delta I_E - 1}$ or $(\Delta I_E - 1) = \dfrac{1}{100}$

$\Rightarrow \Delta I_E - 1 = 0.01$

or $\quad \Delta I_E = 1 + 0.01 = 1.01$ mA

46 (b) Collector current, $I_C = 10$ mA

Given, $\quad I_C = (90/100) I_E$

$\therefore I_E = \dfrac{100}{90} \times 10 = \dfrac{100}{9}$ mA $= 11.1$ mA

Also, $I_B = I_E - I_C = 11.1 - 10 = 1.1$ mA

47 (c) The common emitter transistor amplifier has input resistance equal to 1 k Ω (approx.) and output resistance equal to 10 k Ω (approx.). Also, the output current in common emitter amplifier is much larger than the input current because current gain $\beta > 1$.

Topic 4
Digital Circuit

2019

1

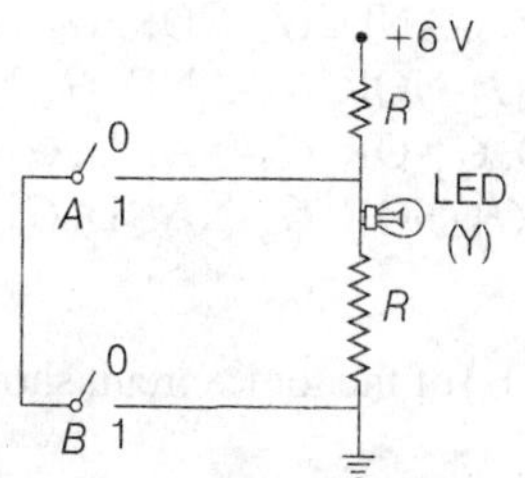

The correct boolean operation represented by the circuit diagram drawn is **[NEET]**

(a) OR (b) NAND
(c) NOR (d) AND

2 The circuit diagram shown here corresponds to the logic gate **[NEET (Odisha)]**

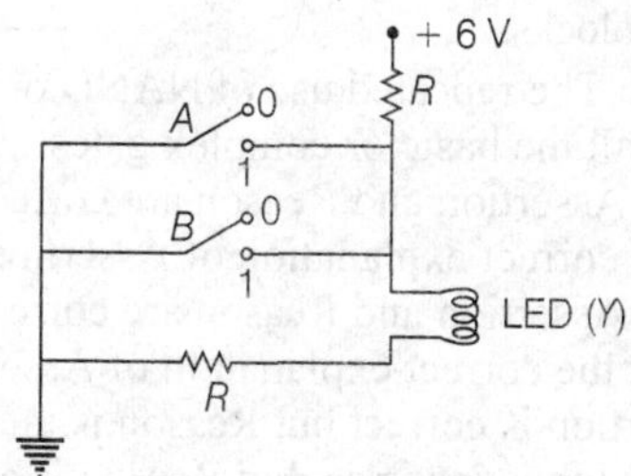

(a) NOR (b) AND
(c) OR (d) NAND

3 Following circuit will act as **[JIPMER]**

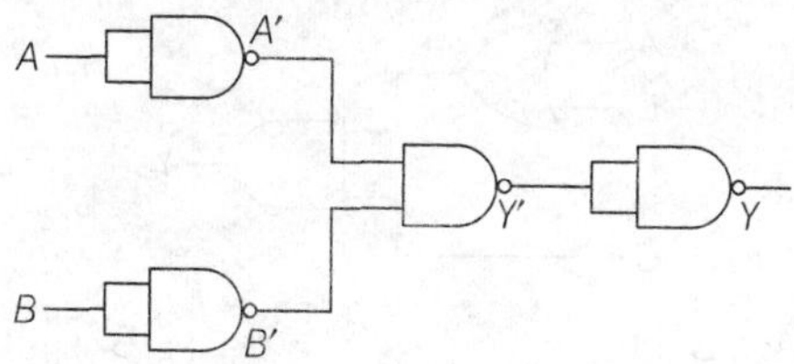

(a) NOR gate
(b) NAND gate
(c) AND gate
(d) OR gate

4 The given combination will work as **[JIPMER]**

(a) NAND gate (b) OR gate
(c) AND gate (d) NOR gate

2018

5 In the combination of the following gates, the output Y can be written in terms of inputs A and B as

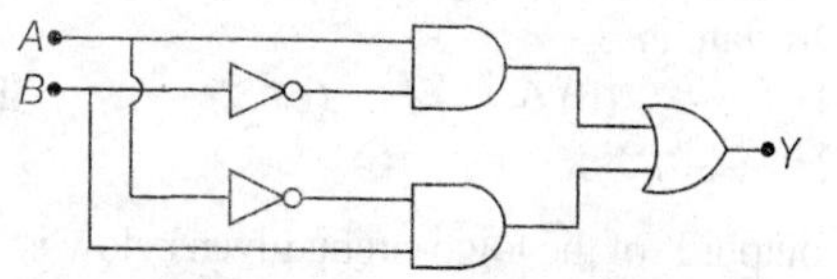

[NEET]

(a) $\overline{A \cdot B} + A \cdot B$ (b) $A \cdot \overline{B} + \overline{A} \cdot B$
(c) $\overline{A \cdot B}$ (d) $\overline{A + B}$

2017

6 The following circuit represents

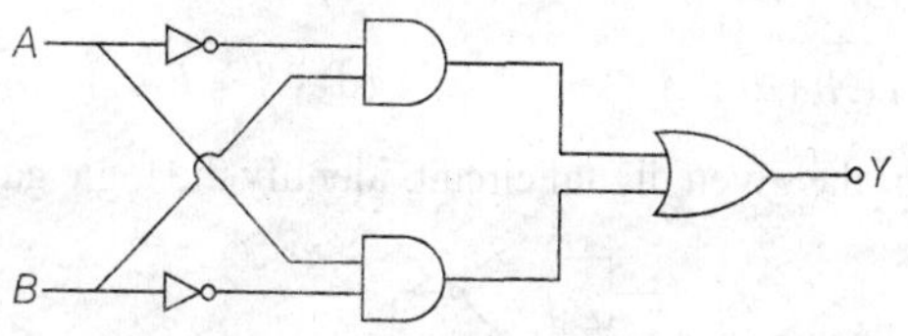

[JIPMER]

(a) OR gate (b) XOR gate
(c) AND gate (d) NAND gate

7 A proper combination of 3 NOT and 1 NAND gates is shown in figure. If $A = 0$, $B = 1$, $C = 1$, then the output of this combination is **[AIIMS]**

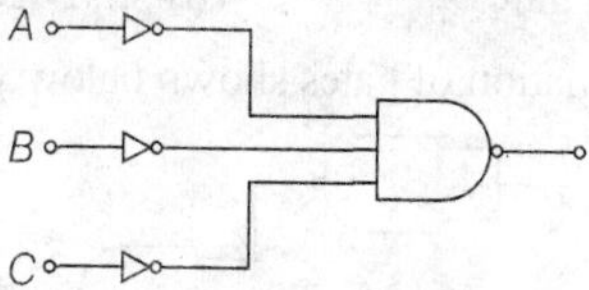

(a) 1 (b) 0
(c) not predictable (d) None of these

8 The given electrical network is equivalent to **[NEET]**

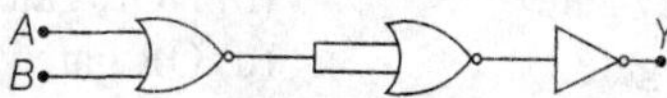

(a) AND gate (b) OR gate (c) NOR gate (d) NOT gate

2016

9 To get output 1 for the following circuit, the correct choice for the input is **[NEET]**

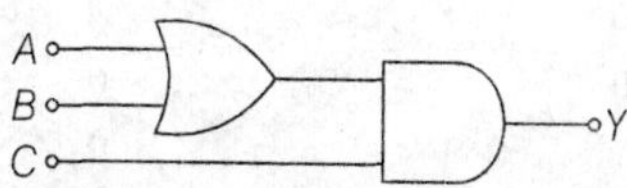

(a) $A = 1$, $B = 0$ and $C = 0$ (b) $A = 1$, $B = 1$ and $C = 0$
(c) $A = 1$, $B = 0$ and $C = 1$ (d) $A = 0$, $B = 1$ and $C = 0$

10 What is the output Y in the following circuit, when all the three inputs A, B, C are first 0 and then 1? **[NEET]**

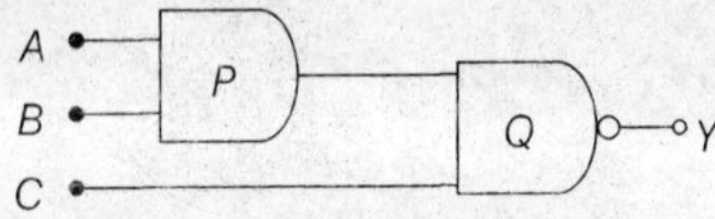

(a) 0, 1 (b) 0, 0 (c) 1, 0 (d) 1, 1

2014

11 The minimum number of NAND gates used to construct an OR gate is **[Kerala CEE]**

(a) 4 (b) 6 (c) 5 (d) 3
(e) 2

12 The output Y of the logic circuit given below is **[J&K CET]**

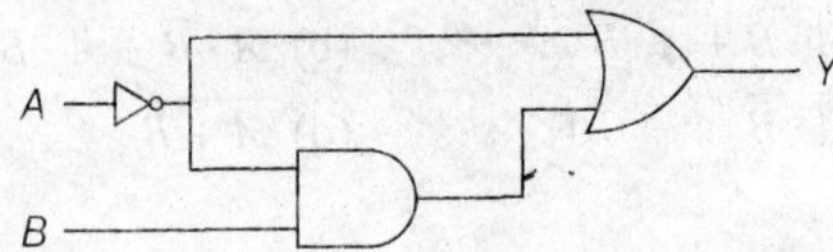

(a) $\overline{A} + B$ (b) $\overline{A}$

(c) $\overline{(\overline{A} + B)} \cdot \overline{A}$ (d) $\overline{(\overline{A} + B) \cdot A}$

13 For the given digital circuit, identify the logic gate

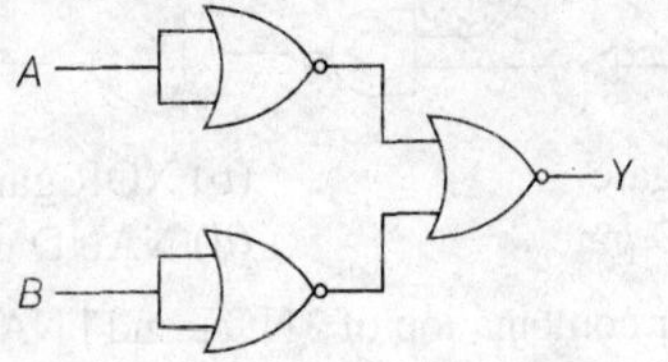

[KCET]

(a) OR gate (b) NOR gate
(c) NAND gate (d) AND gate

14 The combination of gates shown below yields **[UK PMT]**

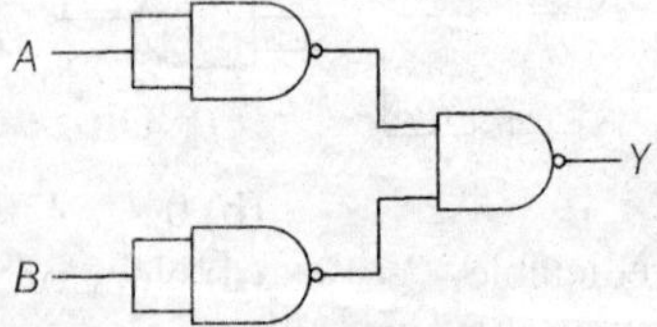

(a) NAND gate (b) NOR gate
(c) XOR gate (d) OR gate

15 The truth tables of logic gates G_1, G_2, G_3 and G_4 are given here. Identify them correctly. **[EAMCET]**

G_1

Inputs		Output
A	*B*	*Y*
0	0	0
0	1	1
1	0	1
1	1	1

G_2

Inputs		Output
A	*B*	*Y*
0	0	0
0	1	0
1	0	0
1	1	1

G_3

Inputs		Output
A	*B*	*Y*
0	0	1
0	1	0
1	0	0
1	1	0

G_4

Inputs		Output
A	*B*	*Y*
0	0	1
0	1	1
1	0	1
1	1	0

(a) G_1-OR, G_2-AND, G_3-NOR, G_4-NAND
(b) G_1-OR, G_2-NOR, G_3-AND, G_4-NAND
(c) G_1-AND, G_2-OR, G_3-NAND, G_4-NOR
(d) G_1-OR, G_2-NOR, G_3-NAND, G_4-AND

2013

16 The output (Y) of the logic circuit shown in figure will be

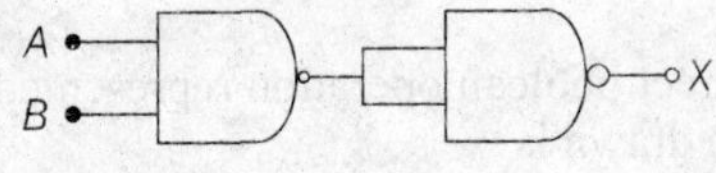

[NEET]

(a) $Y = \overline{\overline{A}} \cdot \overline{\overline{B}}$ (b) $Y = \overline{A \cdot B}$
(c) $Y = A \cdot B$ (d) $Y = \overline{A + B}$

17 **Assertion** NAND or NOR gates are called digital building blocks.

Reason The repeated use of NAND or NOR gates can produce all the basic or complex gates. **[AIIMS]**

(a) Both Assertion and Reason are correct and Reason is the correct explanation of Assertion.
(b) Both Assertion and Reason are correct but Reason is not the correct explanation of Assertion.
(c) Assertion is correct but Reason is incorrect.
(d) Assertion is incorrect but Reason is correct.

2012

18 To get an output, $Y = 1$ in given circuit, which of the following input will be correct? **[CBSE AIPMT]**

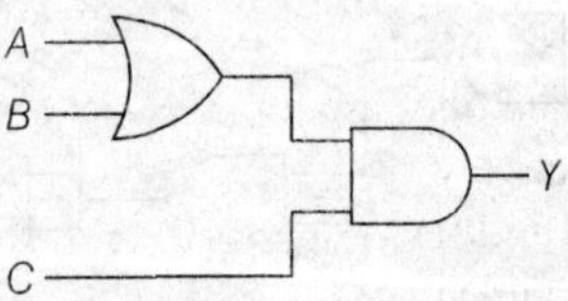

	A	B	C		A	B	C
(a)	1	0	0	(b)	1	0	1
(c)	1	1	0	(d)	0	1	0

19 The figure shows a logic circuit with two inputs A and B and the output C. The voltage waveforms across A, B and C are as given. The logic circuit gate is **[CBSE AIPMT]**

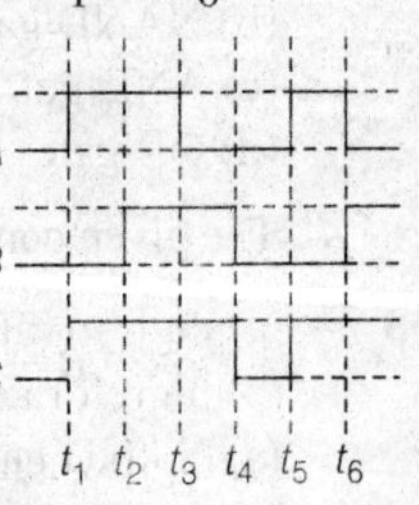

(a) OR gate (b) NOR gate
(c) AND gate (d) NAND gate

20 The truth table given below is for (A & B are the inputs and Y is the output) **[AFMC]**

A	B	Y
0	0	1
0	1	1
1	0	1
1	1	0

(a) NOR (b) AND (c) XOR (d) NAND

21 When the inputs of a two input logic gate are 0 and 0, the output is 1. When the inputs are 1 and 0, the output is 0. The logic gate is of the type **[Manipal]**

(a) AND (b) NAND (c) NOR (d) OR

22 The given below truth table shows

A	B	Y
0	0	0
1	0	1
0	1	1
1	1	0

(a) XOR gate (b) NAND gate
(c) OR gate (d) AND gate

23 The decimal number equivalent to a binary number 1011001 is **[WB JEE]**

(a) 13 (b) 17 (c) 89 (d) 178

2011

24 Symbolic representation of four logic gates are shown as **[CBSE AIPMT]**

(i) 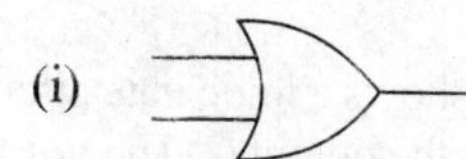 (ii) 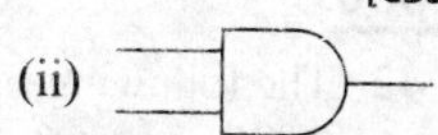

(iii) 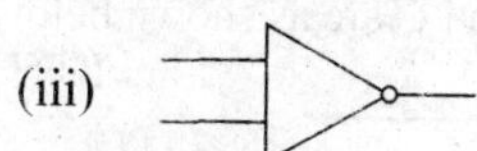 (iv) 

Pick out which ones are for AND, NAND and NOT gates, respectively.

(a) (iii), (ii) and (i) (b) (iii), (ii) and (iv)
(c) (ii), (iv) and (iii) (d) (ii), (iii) and (iv)

25 In the circuit given A, B & C are inputs and Y is the output. The output of Y is **[Kerala CEE]**

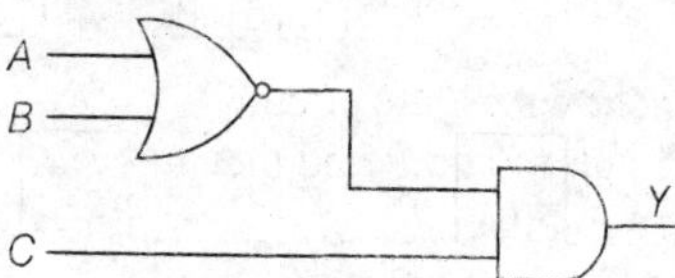

(a) high for all the high inputs
(b) high for all the low inputs
(c) high when $A = 0$, $B = 0$ and $C = 1$
(d) low when $A = 0$, $B = 0$ and $C = 1$
(e) None of the above

26 The output Y of the circuit shown is **[J&K CET]**

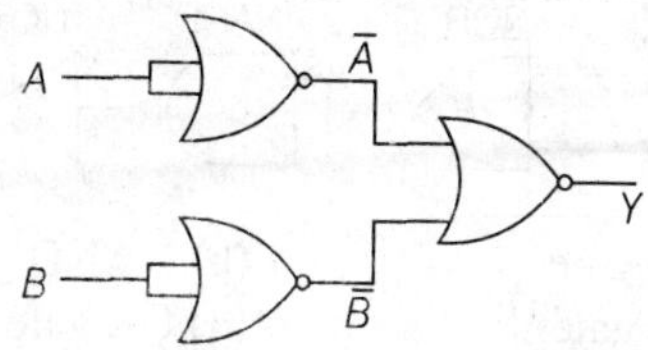

(a) $Y = A \cdot B$ (b) $Y = \overline{A} \cdot \overline{B}$
(c) $Y = \overline{A + B}$ (d) $Y = A + B$

27 The output Y of given logic circuit is  **[KCET]**

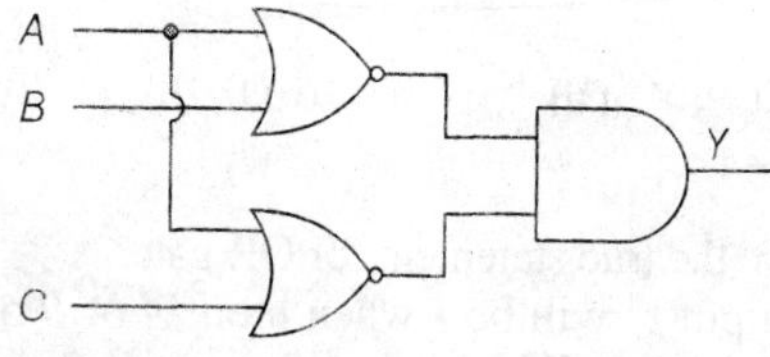

(a) $A \cdot \overline{(B + C)}$ (b) $A \cdot (B \cdot C)$
(c) $\overline{(A + B)} \cdot \overline{(A + C)}$ (d) $A + B + C$

28 Given below are four logic gate symbols. Those for OR, NOR and NAND are respectively. **[Manipal]**

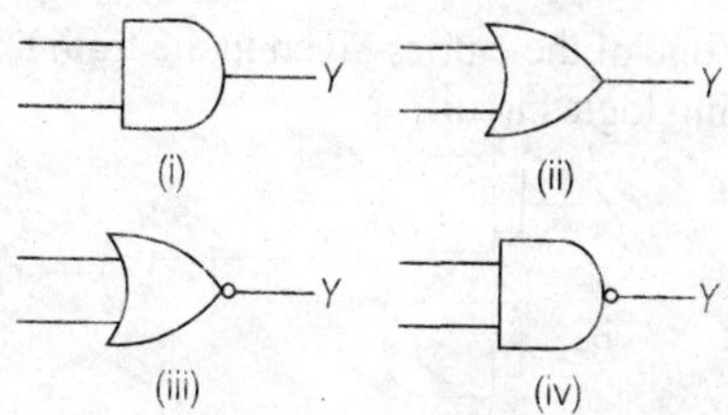

(a) (i), (iv) and (iii) (b) (iv), (i) and (ii)
(c) (i), (iii) and (iv) (d) (ii), (iii) and (iv)

29 If the two inputs of a NAND gate are shorted, the gate is equivalent to **[Kerala CEE]**

(a) XOR (b) OR (c) NOR (d) NOT
(e) AND

30 Which logic gate is represented by the following combination of logic gates? **[Punjab PMET]**

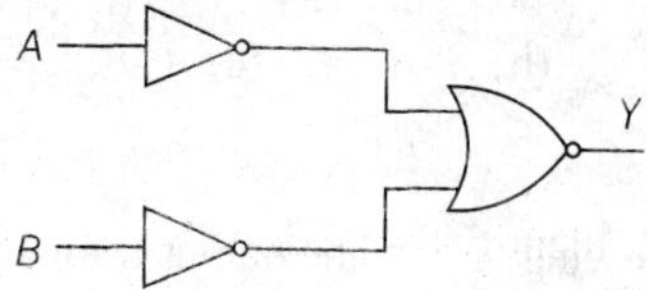

(a) OR (b) NAND (c) AND (d) NOR

2010

31 Identify the logic operation performed by the circuit given here. **[KCET]**

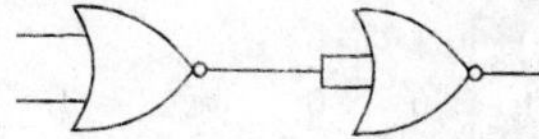

(a) OR (b) NOR (c) NOT (d) NAND

32 The circuit is equivalent to [CBSE AIPMT]

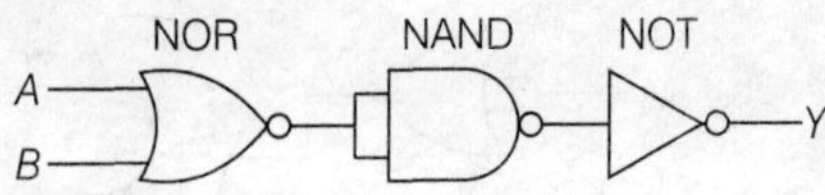

(a) AND gate (b) NAND gate
(c) NOR gate (d) OR gate

33 The output Y, when all the three inputs are first high and then low, will respectively be [Kerala CEE]

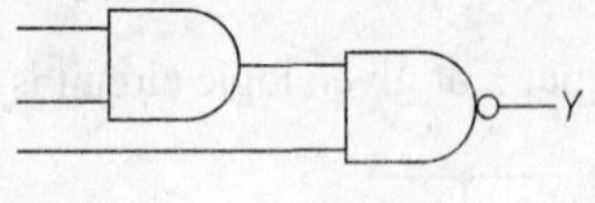

(a) 1, 0 (b) 1, 1 (c) 0, 0 (d) 0, 1
(e) 1, – 1

34 Identify the true statement for OR gate. [J&K CET]
(a) Output Y will be 1 when input A or B or both are 1.
(b) Output Y will be 0 when the either of the inputs A or B is 1.
(c) Output Y will be 1 only when both the inputs A and B are 1.
(d) Output Y will be 1 only when either of the inputs A and B are 1.

35 Which one of the entries given in the truth table is true for the following logic circuit? [Guj CET]

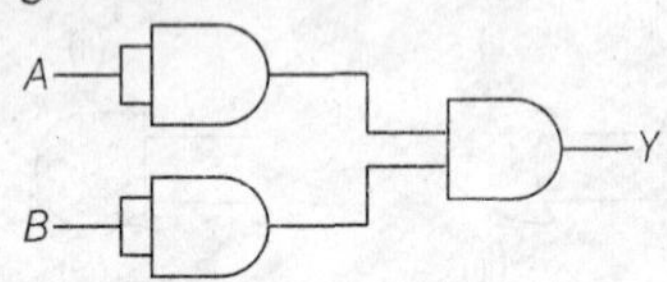

Entry No.	Input A	Input B	Output Y
1.	0	0	1
2.	0	1	0
3.	1	0	1
4.	1	1	0

(a) 3 (b) 4 (c) 1 (d) 2

36 An AND gate is followed by a NOT gate in series. With two inputs A and B, the Boolean expression for the output Y will be [Guj CET]

(a) $\overline{A+B}$ (b) $\overline{A \cdot B}$ (c) $A \cdot B$ (d) $A+B$

2007

37 In the following circuit, the output Y for all possible inputs A and B is expressed by the truth table [CBSE AIPMT]

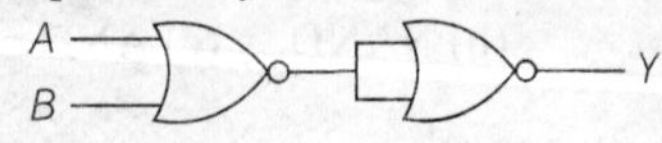

(a)

A	B	Y
0	0	0
0	1	0
1	0	0
1	1	1

(b)

A	B	Y
0	0	1
0	1	1
1	0	1
1	1	0

(c)

A	B	Y
0	0	1
0	1	0
1	0	0
1	1	0

(d)

A	B	Y
0	0	0
0	1	1
1	0	1
1	1	1

38 The following configuration of gate is equivalent to [Punjab PMET]

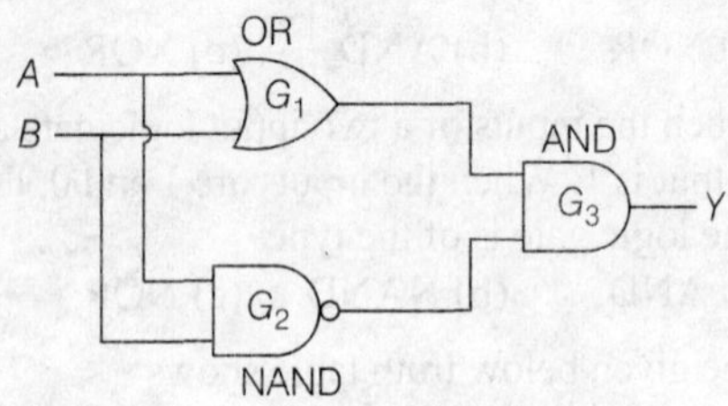

(a) NAND (b) XOR
(c) OR (d) None of these

39 The output is low when either of the input is high, then this represents which of the following gates? [DUMET]
(a) OR (b) NOR
(c) AND (d) NAND

40 8 bits form [DUMET]
(a) 1 byte (b) 1 diction
(c) 1 nibble (d) 1 binary

41 Boolean expression for OR gate is [Guj CET]
(a) $Y = A \cdot B$ (b) $Y = \overline{A} + \overline{B}$
(c) $Y = A + B$ (d) $Y = \overline{A}$

2006

42 The following figure shows a logic gate circuit with two inputs A & B and the output C. The voltage waveforms of A, B and C are as shown below. [CBSE AIPMT]

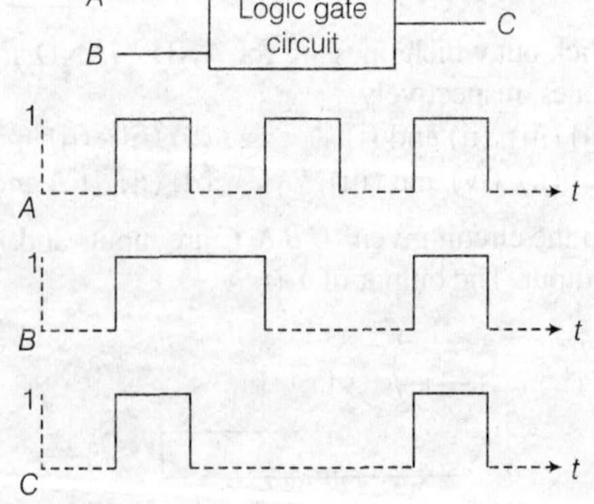

(a) AND gate
(b) NAND gate
(c) NOR gate
(d) OR gate

2005

43 **Assertion** The logic gate NOT can be built using diode.
Reason The output voltage and the input voltage of the diode have 180° phase difference. **[AIIMS]**

(a) Both Assertion and Reason are correct and Reason is the correct explanation of Assertion.
(b) Both Assertion and Reason are correct but Reason is not the correct explanation of Assertion.
(c) Assertion is correct but Reason is incorrect.
(d) Both Assertion and Reason are incorrect.

44 In the following circuit the output Y becomes one for the inputs **[Kerala CEE]**

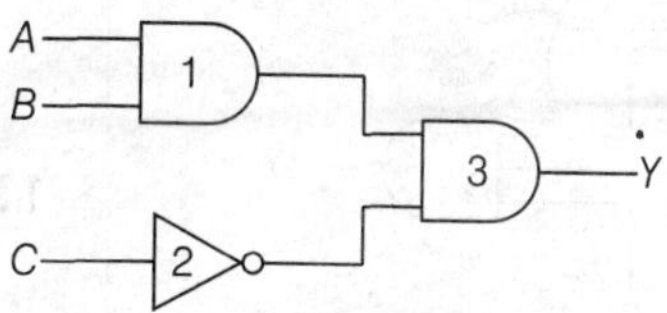

(a) $A = 1, B = 0$ and $C = 0$ (b) $A = 0, B = 1$ and $C = 1$
(c) $A = 0, B = 0$ and $C = 0$ (d) $A = 1, B = 1$ and $C = 0$
(e) $A = 1, B = 1$ and $C = 1$

Answers

1 (b)	2 (a)	3 (a)	4 (c)	5 (b)	6 (b)	7 (a)	8 (c)	9 (c)	10 (c)
11 (d)	12 (b)	13 (d)	14 (d)	15 (a)	16 (c)	17 (a)	18 (b)	19 (a)	20 (d)
21 (c)	22 (a)	23 (c)	24 (c)	25 (c)	26 (a)	27 (c)	28 (d)	29 (d)	30 (c)
31 (a)	32 (c)	33 (d)	34 (a)	35 (d)	36 (b)	37 (d)	38 (b)	39 (b)	40 (a)
41 (c)	42 (a)	43 (d)	44 (d)						

Explanations

1 *(b)* The LED will glow when the current flows through it, i.e. when the voltage across it is high.

The truth table can be formed from this

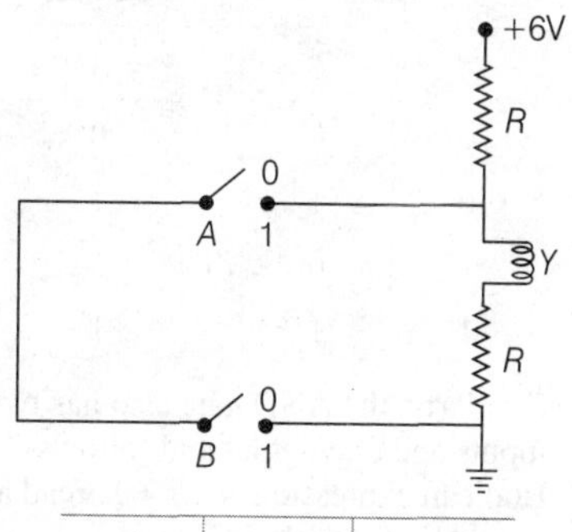

A	B	Y
0	0	1
0	1	1
1	0	1
1	1	0

The output Y is same as that come from NAND gate.

2 *(a)* From the circuit diagram given below, it can be seen that the current will flow to ground if any of the switch is closed. Also, the LED will only glow when current flows through it, i.e. both the switches should be open.

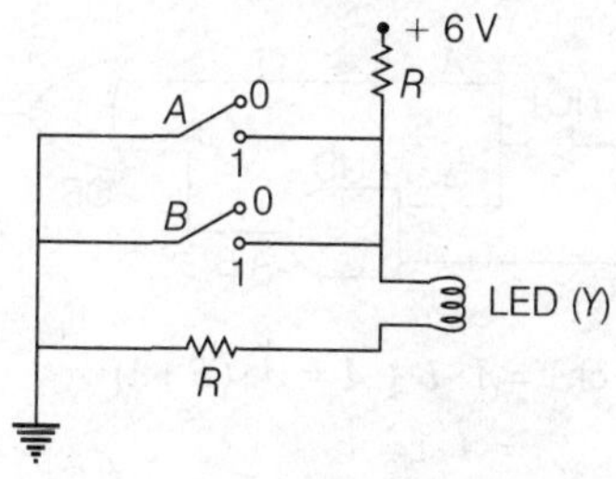

Thus, the truth table for the circuit diagram can be formed as

A	B	Y
0	0	1
0	1	0
1	0	0
1	1	0

The output (Y) is equivalent to that of NOR gate.

3 *(a)* The truth table for the circuit is as

A	B	A'	B'	Y'	Y
1	1	0	0	1	0
1	0	0	1	1	0
0	1	1	0	1	0
0	0	1	1	0	1

The Y-output is of NOR gate.

4 *(c)* The given combination is written as

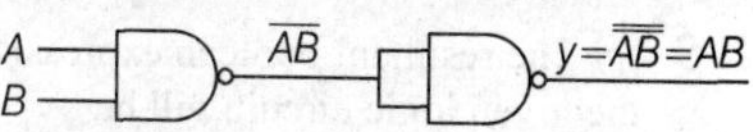

i.e. Output of the combination of gates

$Y = \overline{\overline{AB}} = AB$

= output of AND gate.

5 *(b)* According to the question, the figure of combination of gates in terms of inputs and outputs can be given as

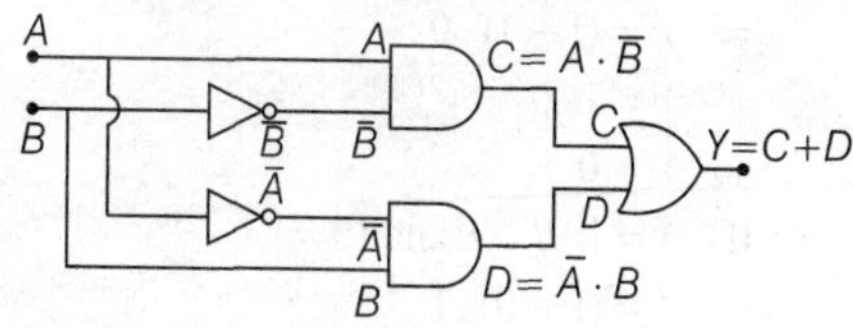

Thus, $Y = A \cdot \overline{B} + \overline{A} \cdot B$

6 *(b)* Output of upper AND gate $= \overline{A}B$

Output of lower AND gate $= A\overline{B}$

Thus, output of OR gate $= \overline{A}B + A\overline{B}$

This is the boolean expression for XOR gate.

7 *(a)* The simplified circuit is shown in figure below

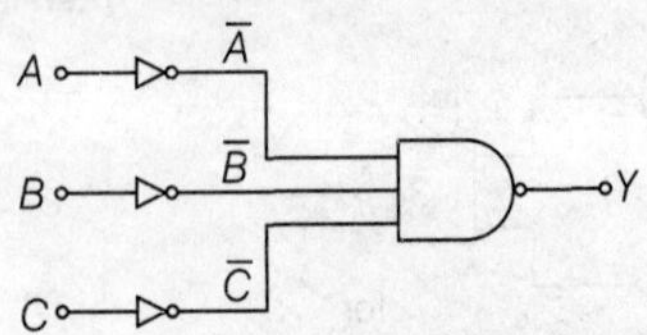

So, output $y=\overline{\overline{A}\cdot\overline{B}\cdot\overline{C}}$

If $A=0$, $B=1$, $C=1$

$\therefore \quad y=\overline{\overline{0}\cdot\overline{1}\cdot\overline{1}}=\overline{1\cdot 0\cdot 0}=\overline{0}=1$

8 *(c)* Truth table for given network is

A	B	Y_1	Y_2	Y
0	0	1	0	1
1	0	0	1	0
0	1	0	1	0
1	1	0	1	0

Output Y of network matches with that of NOR gate.

9 *(c)* The resultant boolean expression of the given logic circuit will be

$Y=(A+B)\cdot C$

Now, let us try with inputs *A*, *B* and *C* given in the options and lets see, which one of them will give output 1 at *Y*.

If $A=1$, $B=0$ and $C=0$

$\Rightarrow Y=(1+0)\cdot 0$

$\Rightarrow Y=0$

If $A=1$, $B=1$ and $C=0$

$\Rightarrow Y=(1+1)\cdot 0$

$\Rightarrow Y=1\cdot 0$

$\Rightarrow Y=0$

If $A=1$, $B=0$ and $C=1$

$\Rightarrow Y=(1+0)\cdot 1$

$\Rightarrow Y=1\cdot 1$

$\Rightarrow Y=1$

If $A=0$, $B=1$ and $C=0$

$\Rightarrow Y=(0+1)\cdot 0$

$\Rightarrow Y=1\cdot 0$

$\Rightarrow Y=0$

So, we have seen that among the given options, only option (c) is the correct choice, i.e., output $Y=1$ only when inputs $A=1$, $B=0$ and $C=1$.

10 *(c)* Output of the given circuit is given by

$y=\overline{(AB)\,(C)}$

When $A=B=C=0$,

$Y_1=\overline{(0)\,(0)\,(0)}=\overline{0}=1$

When $A=B=C=1$,

$Y_2=\overline{(1)\,(1)\,(1)}=0$

11 *(d)* If the two inputs of a NAND gate are joined together, it works as a NOT gate. Now, if the inputs *A* and *B* are inverted by using two NOT gates (obtained from two NAND gates) and the resulting output $\overline{A}$ and $\overline{B}$ are fed to a third NAND gates, then output is

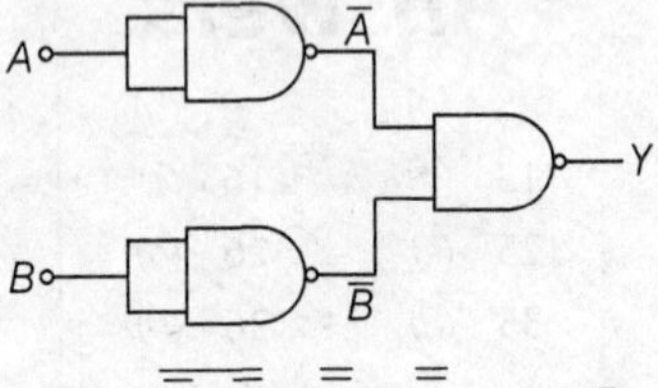

$Y=\overline{\overline{A}\cdot\overline{B}}=\overline{\overline{A}}+\overline{\overline{B}}=A+B$

So, three NAND gates are required to make an OR gate.

12 *(b)* By absorption law, output,

$Y=\overline{A}+\overline{A}\cdot B$

or $Y=\overline{A}\cdot B+\overline{A}=\overline{A}\cdot(B+1)$

$=\overline{A}\cdot 1=\overline{A}$

13 *(d)* According to the logical relationship,

$\overline{\overline{A}+\overline{B}}=\overline{\overline{A}}\cdot\overline{\overline{B}}=A\cdot B$

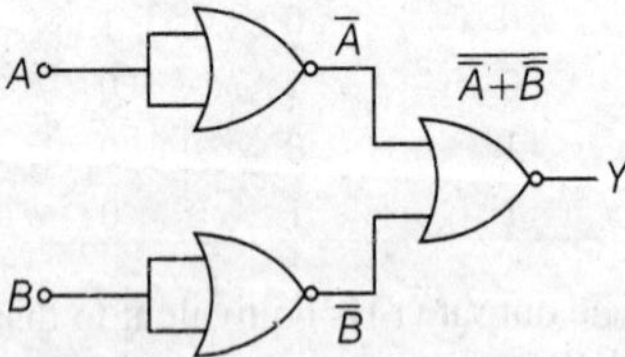

So, it is AND gate.

14 *(d)* The combination of three NAND gates are shown in the diagram.

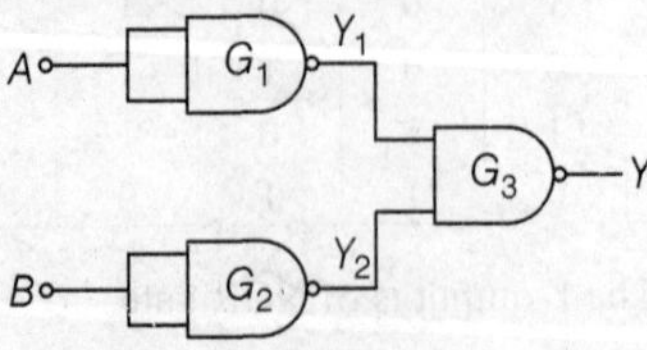

$Y_1=$ Output due to NAND gate 1

$=\overline{A\cdot A}=\overline{A}$

$Y_2=$ Output due to the NAND gate 2

$=\overline{B.B}=\overline{B}$

Output due to NAND gate 3

$Y=\overline{Y_1\cdot Y_2}=\overline{Y_1}+\overline{Y_2}$

$=\overline{\overline{A}}+\overline{\overline{B}}$

$=A+B$

This is OR gate.

Alternate Method The combination is equivalent to an OR gate. Truth table for given gate combination is

Inputs		Output		
A	B	Y_1	Y_2	Y
1	1	0	0	1
1	0	0	1	1
0	1	1	0	1
0	0	1	1	0

15 *(a)* The OR gate is a device that has two (or more) input variables *A* and *B* and one output variable *Y* and follows the Boolean expression, $A+B=Y$, read as '*A* OR *B* equals *Y*'.

Truth table for given gate combination is

Inputs		Output
A	B	$Y=A+B$
0	0	0
0	1	1
1	0	1
1	1	1

Similarly, the AND gate also has two inputs and one output and follows Boolean expression $A\cdot B=Y$, read as "*A* AND *B* equals *Y*".

Truth table for given gate combination is

Inputs		Outputs
A	B	$Y=A\cdot B$
0	0	0
0	1	0
1	0	0
1	1	1

The NOR gate is a combination of OR and NOT gates.

The boolean expression for the NOR gate is $\overline{A+B}=Y$.

Truth table for given gate combination is

Inputs		Output
A	B	$Y=\overline{A+B}$
0	0	1
0	1	0
1	0	0
1	1	0

The NAND gate is a combination of AND and NOT gates.

The boolean expression for the NAND gate is

$$\overline{A \cdot B} = Y$$

Truth table for given gate combination is

Inputs		Output
A	B	$Y=\overline{A \cdot B}$
0	0	1
0	1	1
1	0	1
1	1	0

So, the required solution is

$G_1 \rightarrow$ OR gate,

$G_2 \rightarrow$ AND gate,

$G_3 \rightarrow$ NOR gate

and $G_4 \rightarrow$ NAND gate.

16 *(c)* As, $Y = \overline{\overline{A \cdot B}} = A \cdot B$

i.e. AND gate

17 *(a)* The NAND or NOR gates are called universal (digital) building blocks, because using these two types of gates we can produce all the basic gates namely OR , AND, NOT or complex gates.

18 *(b)* The boolean expression for output of the given combination is

$$Y = (A + B) \cdot C$$

The truth table for the given combination is

A	B	C	$Y = (A+B) \cdot C$
0	0	0	0
1	0	0	0
0	1	0	0
0	0	1	0
1	1	0	0
0	1	1	1
1	0	1	1
1	1	1	1

Hence, $A = 1$, $B = 0$ and $C = 1$, gives output $Y = 1$.

19 *(a)* From the given waveforms, the following truth table can be made

Time	Inputs		Output
	A	B	C
t_1	1	0	1
t_2	1	1	1
t_3	1	1	1
t_4	0	1	1
t_5	1	0	1
t_6	1	1	1

This truth table is equivalent to OR gate. So, logic circuit is OR gate.

Note The logic of the OR gate is, if any of the input is one, then output is one.

20 *(d)* The output $Y = \overline{(A \cdot B)}$ is a combination of AND and NOT gates. Hence, the truth table is for NAND gate.

21 *(c)* The NOR gate is obtained when the output of OR gate is made as the input of NOT gate. Boolean expression for NOR gate is $Y = \overline{A + B}$. The logic symbol of NOR gate as shown below

Truth table for given gate combination is

Inputs		Output
A	B	$Y=\overline{A+B}$
0	0	1
1	0	0
0	1	0
1	1	0

Hence, the logic gate is of NOR type.

22 *(a)* In XOR gate, if both the inputs are high or low, then the output is low, so the truth table shows the XOR gate.

23 *(c)* Given, binary number = 1011001

Its equivalent decimal number

$$= 1\times2^0 + 0\times2^1 + 0\times2^2 + 1\times2^3 + 1\times2^4 + 0\times2^5 + 1\times2^6$$

$$= 2^0 + 0 + 0 + 2^3 + 2^4 + 0 + 2^6$$

$$= 1 + 8 + 16 + 64 = 89$$

24 *(c)* Symbols given in the problem are

(i) OR gate *(ii)* AND gate

(iii) NOT gate *(iv)* NAND gate

25 *(c)* The output of the circuit is

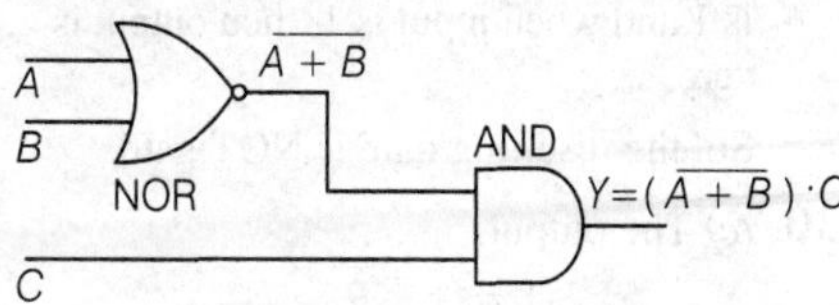

$$Y = (\overline{A + B}) \cdot C$$

Now checking for each option,

When $A = B = C = 1$, then

$$Y = (\overline{1 + 1}) \cdot 1 = 0 \cdot 1 = 0$$

When $A = B = C = 0$, then

$$Y = (\overline{0 + 0}) \cdot 0 = 1 \cdot 0 = 0$$

When $A = 0$, $B = 0, C = 1$, then

$$Y = (\overline{0 + 0}) \cdot 1 = 1 \cdot 1 = 1$$

Hence, output is high, when $A = 0$, $B = 0$ and $C = 1$, then option (c) is correct.

26 *(a)* The gate circuit is as shown below

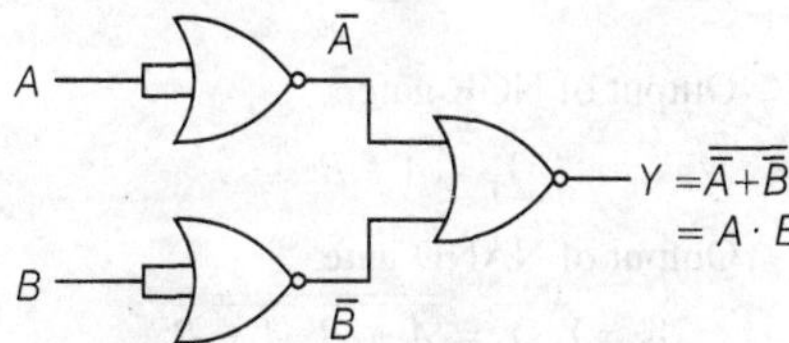

The output of the circuit, $Y = A \cdot B$

27 *(c)* The gate circuit is shown as

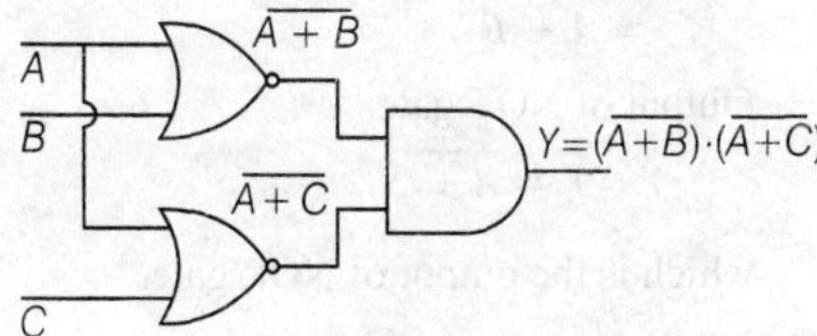

For this circuit, output,

$$Y = (\overline{A + B}) \cdot (\overline{A + C})$$

28 *(d)* Gate (i) $\rightarrow$ AND, Gate (ii) $\rightarrow$ OR,

Gate (iii) $\rightarrow$ NOR and

Gate (iv) $\rightarrow$ NAND

29 *(d)* The circuit diagram of a NAND gate when its two inputs are shorted is given as

NAND = AND + NOT

The gate circuit is given as

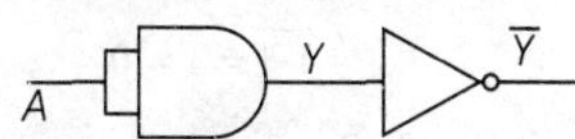

Truth table for given gate combination is

A	Y	$\bar{Y}$
0	0	1
1	1	0

Hence, if the inputs is zero, then output is 1 and when input is 1, then output is zero.

So, the resulting gate is NOT gate.

30 *(c)* The output,

$$Y = \overline{\overline{A} + \overline{B}}$$

$$= \overline{\overline{A}} \cdot \overline{\overline{B}} = A \cdot B$$

This is the boolean expression for AND gate.

31 *(a)* The given gate circuit is a combination of NOR and NOT gates.

$\therefore \quad Y = \overline{\overline{A+B}} = A + B$

This is the boolean expression for OR gate.

32 *(c)* The gate circuit can be shown by given two inputs A and B.

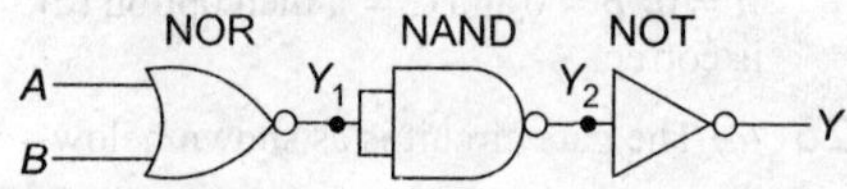

Output of NOR gate,

$$Y_1 = \overline{A + B}$$

Output of NAND gate,

$$Y_2 = \overline{Y_1 \cdot Y_1} = \overline{\overline{A+B} \cdot \overline{A+B}}$$

$$= \overline{\overline{A+B}} + \overline{\overline{A+B}}$$

$$= (A + B) + (A + B)$$

$$= A + B$$

Output of NOT gate,

$$Y = \overline{Y_2} = \overline{A + B}$$

which is the output of NOR gate.

33 *(d)* Let inputs A, B and C are given to the circuit.

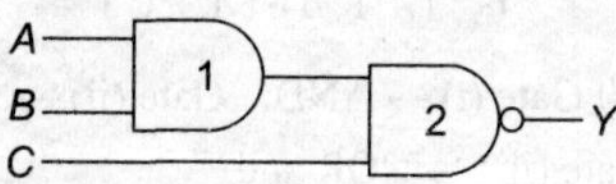

Gate-1 is AND gate and Gate-2 is NAND gate.

Output, $\quad Y = (\overline{A \cdot B \cdot C})$

When, $A = 1$, $B = 1$ and $C = 1$, then

$$Y = \overline{(1 \cdot 1) \cdot 1}$$

$$= \overline{1 \cdot 1} = \overline{1} = 0$$

when, $A = 0$, $B = 0$ and $C = 0$, then

$$Y = \overline{(0 \cdot 0) \cdot 0}$$

$$= \overline{0 \cdot 0} = \overline{0} = 1$$

34 *(a)* In an OR gate, output Y is 1, only when either or both the inputs A and B are 1.

The truth table is shown below

A	*B*	*Y*
0	0	0
0	1	1
1	0	1
1	1	1

35 *(d)* When the inputs of a AND gate are shorted, then there are two conditions arise

(*i*) When the input is 0, then the output is 0.

(*ii*) When the input is 1, then the output is 1.

Hence, by using these two conditions, the ouptut is 0 for the given logic circuit.

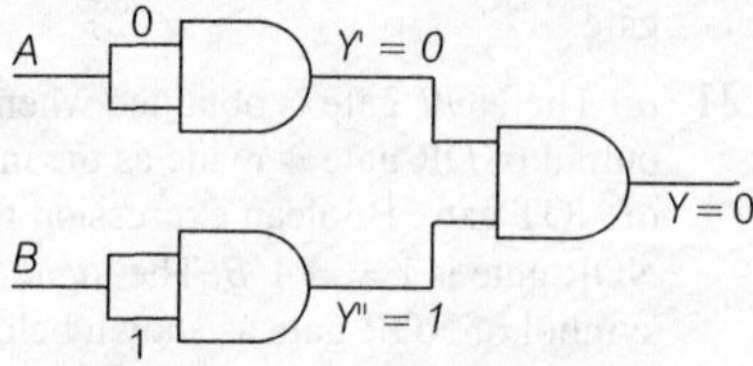

Boolean expression for AND gate is $Y = A \cdot B$

Then, the truth table for the above logic circuit is given below

A	*B*	*Y'* = 0	*Y''* = *B*	*Y* = *A*· *B*
0	0	0	0	0
1	0	1	0	0
0	1	0	1	0
1	1	1	1	1

Therefore, the required entry for the given logic circuit is 2.

36 *(b)* The inputs for AND gate is given by

$$Y' = A \cdot B$$

Y' is the input for NOT gate

$$\therefore \quad Y = \overline{Y'}$$

$$\Rightarrow \quad Y = \overline{A \cdot B}$$

37 *(d)* We can simplify the gate circuit as

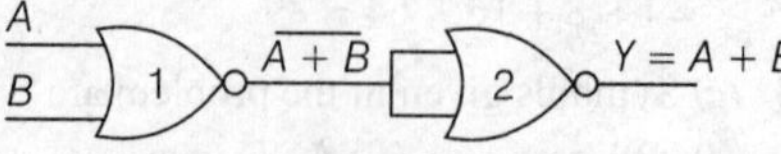

Here, gate-1 and gate-2 are NOR gates. The output $\overline{(A + B)}$ of gate-1 will be appeared as input of gate-2.

The final output is

$$Y = \overline{\overline{A + B}} = A + B$$

This is the boolean expression for OR gate whose truth table is given below.

A	*B*	*Y*
0	0	0
0	1	1
1	0	1
1	1	1

38 *(b)* The output, $Y = (A + B) \cdot \overline{AB}$

The given output equation can also be written as

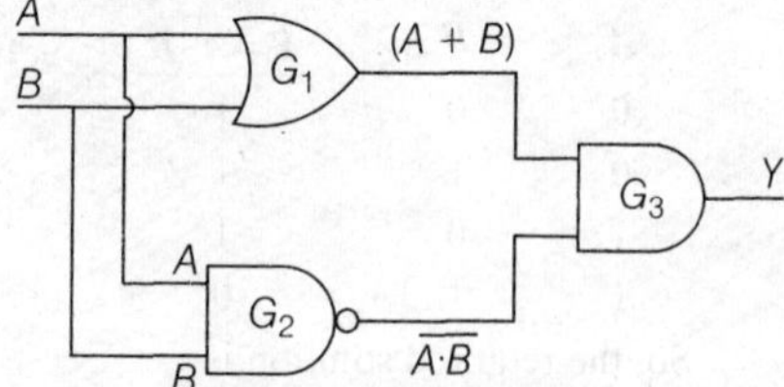

Boolean expression for XOR gate is

$$Y = (A + B) \cdot \overline{AB}$$

(De-Morgan's theorem)

$$= A\,\overline{AB} + \overline{AB}\,B$$

$$= A(\overline{A} + \overline{B}) + (\overline{A} + \overline{B})B$$

$$= A\overline{A} + A\overline{B} + \overline{A}B + B\overline{B}$$

$$= 0 + A\overline{B} + \overline{A}B + 0$$

$$= \overline{A}B + A\overline{B}$$

$$= A \oplus B$$

which is the output of XOR gate.

39 *(b)* Figure shows that an N input $(N \geq 2)$ OR gate followed by a NOT gate. The operation of this circuit can be described in the following way

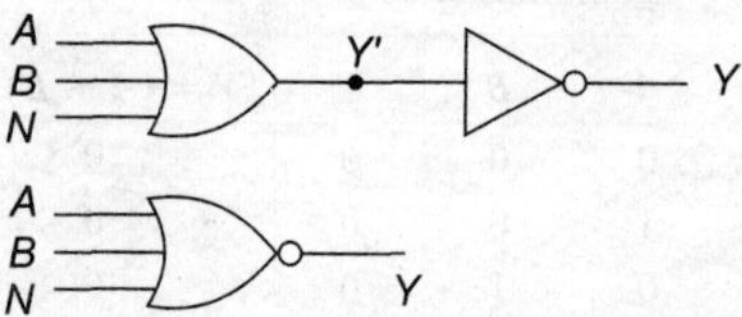

This output of the OR gate Y' can be written as

$$Y' = A + B + \ldots + N \qquad \ldots\text{(i)}$$

The output of the NOT gate (Y) can be written using

$$Y = \overline{Y'} = \overline{A + B + \dots + N} \quad \dots\text{(ii)}$$

The logic operation represented by Eq. (ii) is known as the NOR operation.

Logic operation gives the truth table of a 2-input NOR gate.

Inputs		Output
A	B	Y
0	0	1
0	1	0
1	0	0
1	1	0

It indicates that when either of input is high, the output is low.

40 *(a)* 8 bits form 1 byte.

41 *(c)* In boolean algebra, addition symbol (+) is referred to as OR function.
The boolean expression for OR gate is given by
$A + B = Y$, indicates Y equals to A or B.

42 *(a)* The boolean expression which satisfies the output of this logic gate is $C = A \cdot B$, which indicates for AND gate. We can see, output C is zero when either of A or B (inputs) is zero.

43 *(d)* An NOT gate inverts the signal applied to it. But in diode, the input and output are in same phase. Thus, NOT gate cannot be built by a diode.

44 *(d)* The output of gate-1, $Y_1 = A \cdot B$

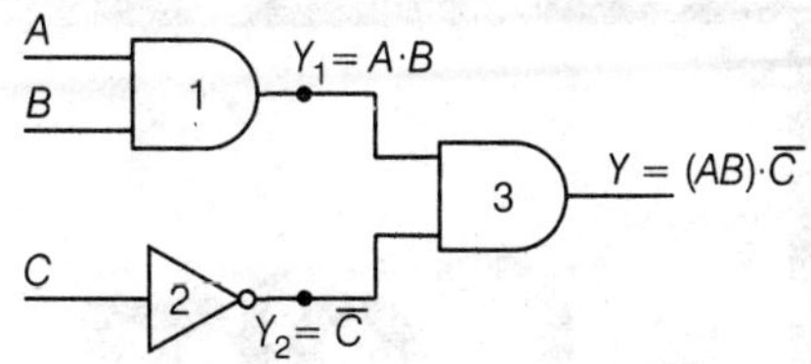

Output of gate-2, $Y_2 = \overline{C}$

Output of gate-3, $Y = Y_1 \cdot Y_2$
$= (A \cdot B) \cdot \overline{C}$

Thus, output will be one, if

$A = 1, B = 1$ and $C = 0$

28

Communication System

Quick Review

The word communication refers the act of transmission of information in an intelligible form, whereas communication system is the collection of all individual system elements required for the process of transmission.

Elements of Communication System

- Every communication system has three essential elements
  (*i*) Transmitter (*ii*) Medium/Channel
  (*iii*) Receiver
- The **block diagram** of generalised communication system is given below

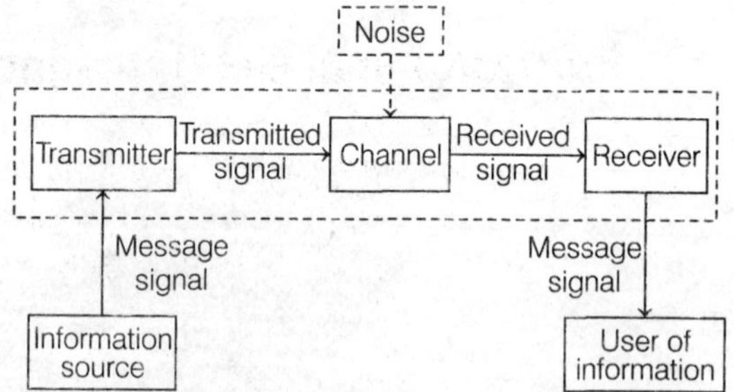

- Sources or devices used in communication system are shown in following table

Sources of Information	Speech, pictures, commands, data.
Transmitter	Oscillators, amplifiers, filters, antenna.
Channel	Wire, links, wireless, optical fibres.
Receiver	Radio, TV, computer.

- Few basic modes of communication system are given in tabular form below

Systems	Specifications	Examples
Point to point	Link between single transmitter and a receiver.	Telephony
Broadcast	A large number of receivers corresponding to a single transmitter.	TV, Radio

Basic Terminology Used In Electronic Communication System

Basic terms used in electronic communication system are listed below

(*i*) **Transducer** A device that converts one form of energy into another form.

(*ii*) **Signal** It is the information converted in electric form which is suitable for transmission.

(*iii*) **Noise** It refers to the unwanted signals that tend to disturb the transmission and processing of information.

(*iv*) **Transmitter** It processes the incoming message signals so as to make it suitable for transmission through a channel.

(*v*) **Receiver** It extracts the desired message signals from the received signal at the channel output.

(*vi*) **Attenuation** Loss of strength of signal while propagating through a medium.

(*vii*) **Amplification** Process of increasing the strength of a signal using an amplifier.

(*viii*) **Range** The largest distance between a source and a destination upto which the signal is received with sufficient strength.

(*ix*) **Bandwidth** The frequency range over which an equipment operates or the portion of the spectrum occupied by the signal.

i.e. $$\Delta f = f_2 - f_1$$

(*x*) **Repeater** It picks up the signal from the transmitter, amplifies and retransmits it to the receiver sometimes with a change in carrier frequency.

(*xi*) **Message Signals** A time varying electrical signal generated by a transducer out of original signal.

Note Message signals can be voice, picture or computer data.

Bandwidth of Signals

The bandwidth for different types of signals are shown in following table

Types of Signal	Frequency Range	Bandwidth
Speech signal	300-3100 Hz	2800 Hz
Music	20-20000 Hz	20 kHz
Video	—	4.2 MHz
TV	—	6 MHz

- Bandwidth = Highest frequency – Lowest frequency
- A digital signal in the form of a rectangular wave which can be obtained by the superposition of sine waves (ν_0) and their higher harmonics ($2\nu_0, 3\nu_0 \ldots, m\nu_0$). This implies a infinite bandwidth as shown in the following graph

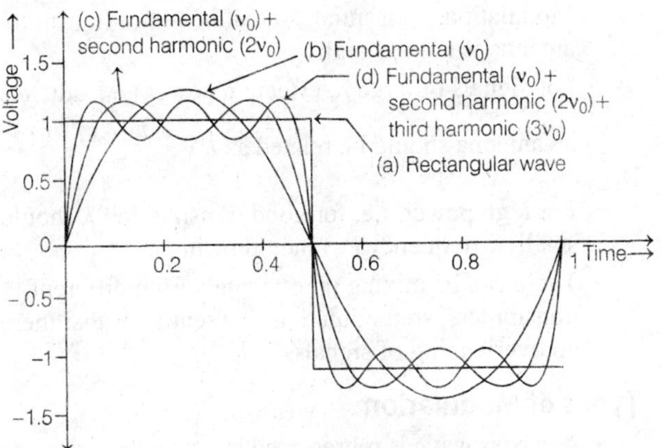

- However, bandwidth is limited, so the received waves are a distorted version of the transmitted one.

Bandwidth of Transmission Medium

- Some important bandwidths of transmission medium along with their allocated services are shown in following table

Services	Frequency Bands	Remarks
Standard AM broadcast	540-1600 kHz	Radio broadcast
FM broadcast	88-108 MHz	Music channel
Television	54-72 MHz	VHF (Very High Frequencies)
	76-88 MHz	TV
	174-216 MHz	UHF (Ultra High Frequencies)
	420-890 MHz	TV
Cellular mobile radio	896-901 MHz	Mobile to base station
	840-935 MHz	Base station to mobile
Satellite	5.925-6.425 GHz	Uplink
Communication	3.7-4.2 GHz	Downlink

- **Antenna** is an important device which acts as an emitter of electromagnetic waves and first receiver of energy.
- Types of antenna are shown in following table relating its length with wavelength

Types of Antenna	Relation of Length (l) with Wavelength (λ)
Hertz antenna	$l = \lambda / 2$
Marconi antenna	$l = \lambda / 4$

- Two commonly used antenna are dipole and dish type antenna.

Propagation of Electromagnetic Waves

- Three modes of propagation of electromagnetic waves are shown pictorially below, which are described as

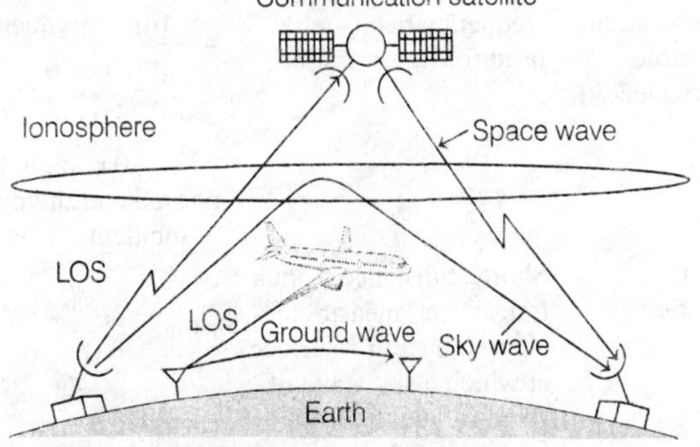

1. Ground Wave Propagation

- Radio waves guided along the earth's surface, following curvature of earth.
- These waves are limited to frequency of 1.5 MHz (1500 kHz) or wavelength of 200 m.
- Used for low or medium frequency band for radio navigation.

2. Sky Wave Propagation

- Propagation of AM radio waves signals from one point to another *via* reflection from **ionosphere.** Their frequency range is from 3 to 30 MHz.
- The different layers of atmosphere and their interaction with the propagating electromagnetic waves are shown below

Name of the Stratum (layers) (Parts of Ionosphere)	Approximate Height over the Earth's Surface	Exists During	Frequencies most Affected
Troposphere	10 km	Day and night	VHF (upto several GHz)
D (Part of stratosphere)	65-75 km	Day only	Reflects LF, absorbs MF and HF to some degree
E (Part of stratosphere)	100-125 km	Day only	Helps surface waves, reflects HF
F_1 (Part of mesosphere)	170-190 km	Day time, merges with F_2 at night	Partially absorbs HF waves yet allowing them to reach F_2
F_2 (Part of thermosphere)	300 km at night, 250-400 km during day time	Day and night	Efficiently reflects HF waves, particularly at night

- Terms related to sky wave propagation along with their definitions are shown below

Terms	Definitions	Expressions
(*i*) Critical Frequency	Maximum frequency of radio waves reflected from ionosphere	$\nu_C \approx 9(N_{max})^{1/2}$ where, N_{max} = maximum electron density of ionosphere.
(*ii*) MUF (Maximum Usable Frequency)	The highest radio frequency that can be used for transmission.	MUF $= \dfrac{\text{Critical frequency}}{\cos\theta}$ $= \nu_C \sec\theta$ where, θ = angle between normal and the direction of incident wave.
(*iii*) Skip distance	Shortest distance from a transmitter, measured along the earth's surface at which a sky wave of fixed frequency will be first received after reflection from ionosphere.	$D_{skip} = 2h\sqrt{\left(\dfrac{\nu_{max}}{\nu_c}\right)^2 - 1}$

3. Space Wave Propagation

- The mode of propagation in which the radio waves emitted from the **transmitter antenna** reach the **receiving antenna** through space waves.
- Range of frequency of space waves 54 MHz - 4.2 GHz.
- Range of a transmitting antenna, called radio horizon,

$$d_T = \sqrt{2Rh_T}$$

where, R = radius of earth

and h_T = height of transmitting antenna.

- Maximum line of sight distance between two antenna (transmitting and receiving) as per diagram,

$$d_{max} = d_T + d_R = \sqrt{2Rh_T} + \sqrt{2Rh_R}$$

where, d_T = radio horizon of transmitting antenna, d_R = radio horizon of recieving antenna and d_{max} = maximum line of sight distance between two antennas.

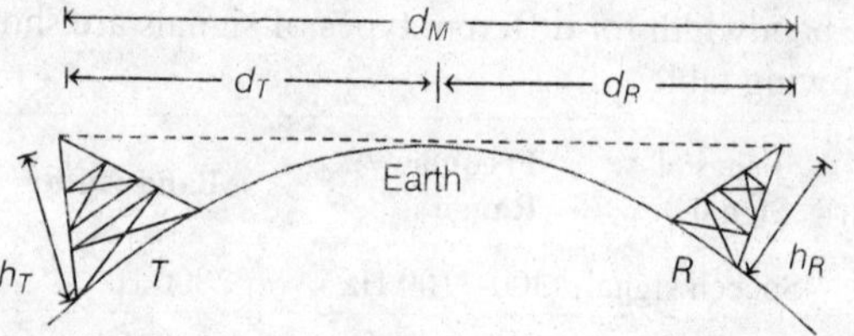

Modulation

The process of superposing a low frequency message signal on a high frequency wave (carrier wave) is called modulation.

Need for Modulation

- Size of the antenna should be comparable to the wavelength of signal (at least $\lambda/4$ in size) in order to sends the signal properly.
- Modulation is essential, so that height of transmitting antenna is not too high.
- For signals of large λ, effective power (P) radiated by an antenna should be related as $P \propto \left(\dfrac{l}{\lambda}\right)^2$.

  For high power, i.e. for good transmission λ should be small or frequency (ν) should be high.
- There can be mixing up of signals from different transmitters, so modulation is essential so that there is no overlapping of signals.

Types of Modulation

- A carrier wave is represented by

$$c(t) = A_c \sin(\omega_c t + \phi)$$

where, $c(t)$ = signal strength of carrier wave,

A_c = amplitude, ω_c = angular frequency

and ϕ = initial phase of carrier wave.

- Three types of modulation along with diagrams are shown below

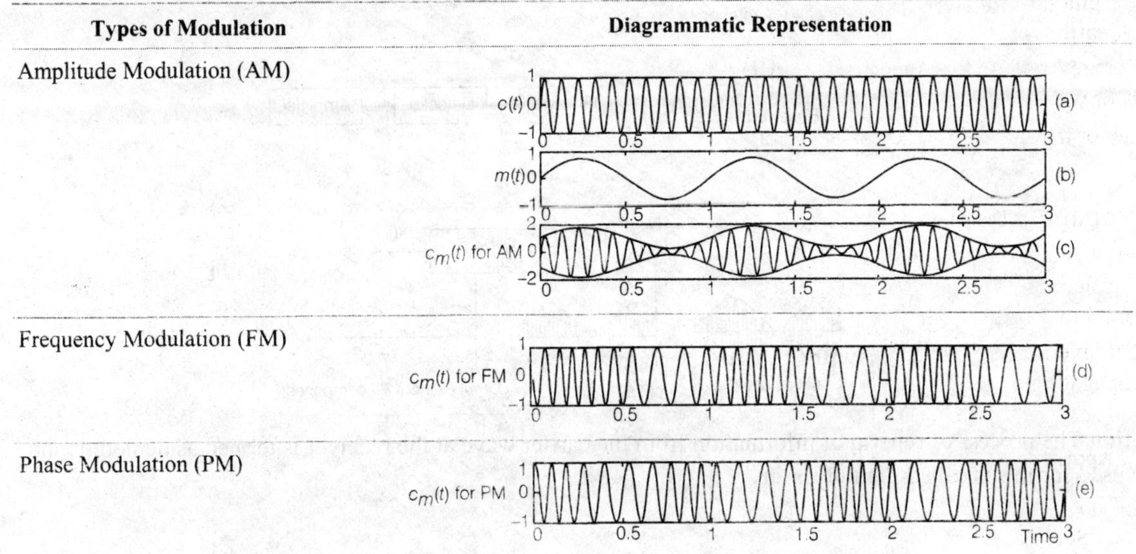

Types of Modulation	Diagrammatic Representation
Amplitude Modulation (AM)	(a), (b), (c)
Frequency Modulation (FM)	(d)
Phase Modulation (PM)	(e)

Amplitude Modulation (AM)

- It is the process of changing the amplitude (A_c) of a carrier wave linearly in accordance with the amplitude of message signal (A_m).
- The modulated signal can be written as

$$c_m(t) = (A_c + A_m \sin \omega_m t) \sin \omega_c t$$

$$= A_c \left(1 + \frac{A_m}{A_c} \sin \omega_m t\right) \sin \omega_c t$$

$$= A_c \sin \omega_c t + \frac{\mu A_c}{2} \cos(\omega_c - \omega_m) t - \frac{\mu A_c}{2} \cos(\omega_c + \omega_m) t$$

- The ratio $\mu = \frac{A_m}{A_c}$ is called the **modulation index** and in practice we maintain $\mu \leq 1$, so as to avoid distortion.
- **Modulation Index** In terms of amplitude,

$$\mu = \frac{A_m}{A_c} = \frac{A_{max} - A_{min}}{A_{max} + A_{min}}$$

- In AM modulated wave signal, we have carrier wave of frequency ω_c and two side bands of frequencies $(\omega_c - \omega_m)$ and $(\omega_c + \omega_m)$, respectively. Thus, total bandwidth of AM signals is $2\omega_m$.
- AM technique is simpler and cost effective, however it suffers from noisy reception, low efficiency, small operating range and poor audio quality.
- In AM technique, power dissipated depends on modulation index (μ).
- A plot of amplitude *versus* ω for an amplitude modulated signal is represented as

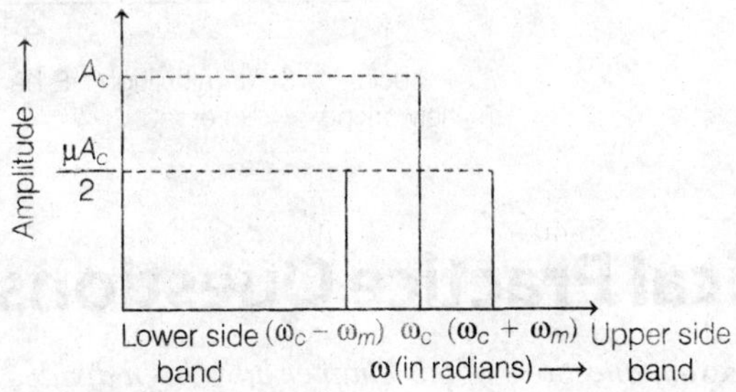

- Block diagrams of the devices (systems) used for obtaining AM signals are given below

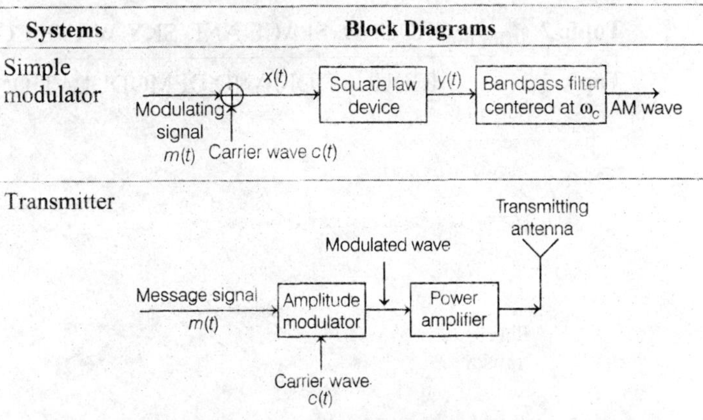

Systems	Block Diagrams
Simple modulator	Modulating signal m(t) → x(t) → Square law device → y(t) → Bandpass filter centered at ω_c → AM wave; Carrier wave c(t)
Transmitter	Message signal m(t) → Amplitude modulator → Modulated wave → Power amplifier → Transmitting antenna; Carrier wave c(t)

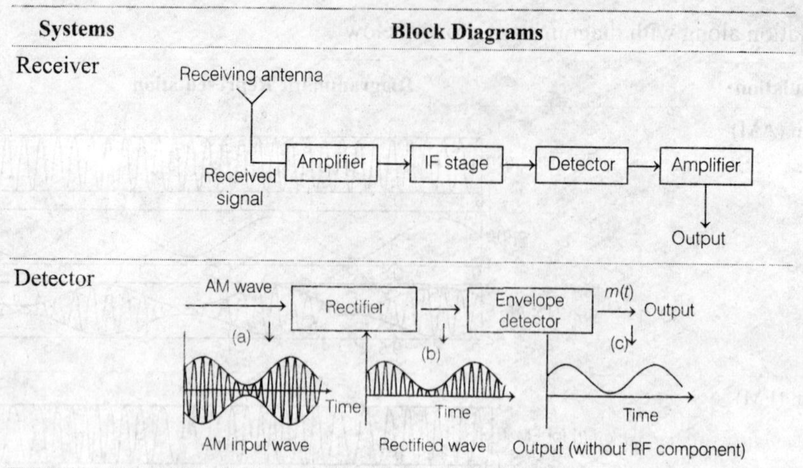

- **Demodulation** The process of retrival of information from the carrier wave at the receiver is termed as demodulation. The device used for this is called **demodulator.**

Internet

- It is a global networking of computers which are interconnected networks world wide.
- Local area network is known as LAN where networking of computers at small scale is possible, e.g. school and office.
- A Wide Area Network (WAN) is the connection between various LANs.

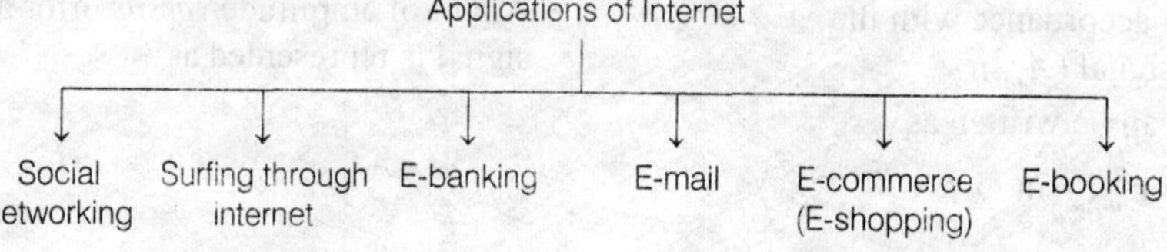

Topical Practice Questions

All the exam questions of this chapter have been divided into 3 topics as listed below

Topic 1

Basics of Communication System and Optical Fibre Communication

2014

1 Which of the following is not a transducer? **[UK PMT]**

(a) Loudspeaker (b) Amplifier
(c) Microphone (d) All of these

2 A transducer, in communication system is a device that **[Kerala CEE]**

(a) is a part of the antenna
(b) is a combination of a receiver and a transmitter
(c) converts audio signals into video signals
(d) converts physical variable into corresponding variations in the electrical signal

2013

3 **Assertion** Endoscopy involves use of optical fibres to study internal organs.

Reason Optical fibres are based on phenomenon of total internal reflection. **[WB JEE]**

(a) Both Assertion and Reason are correct and Reason is the correct explanation of Assertion.
(b) Both Assertion and Reason are correct but Reason is not the correct explanation of Assertion.
(c) Assertion is correct but Reason is incorrect.
(d) Both Assertion and Reason are incorrect.
(e) Assertion is incorrect but Reason is correct.

2011

4 The mobile telephones operate typically in the range of **[Kerala CEE]**

(a) 1-100 MHz (b) 100-200 MHz
(c) 1000-2000 MHz (d) 800-950 MHz
(e) 10-1000 kHz

2010

5 1% of 10^{12} Hz of a satellite link was used for telephony. Find the number of channels (or subscribers) if each channel is 8 kHz. **[BVP]**

(a) 2.5×10^7 (b) 1.25×10^7 (c) 2.5×10^8 (d) 1.25×10^6

6 A radio transmitter radiated 1 kW power at a wavelength 198.6 m. How many photons does it emit per second? **[Manipal]**

(a) 10^{10} (b) 10^{20} (c) 10^{30} (d) 10^{40}

7 An optical fibre communication system works on a wavelength of 1.3 μm. The number of subscribers it can feed, if a channel requires 20 kHz are **[Haryana PMT]**

(a) 2.3×10^{10} (b) 1.15×10^{10}
(c) 1×10^5 (d) None of these

8 In a point to point communication mode, communication takes place over a link between **[Manipal]**

(a) transmitter and channel (b) channel and transmitter
(c) transmitter and receiver (d) channel and receiver

9 Pick up the correct statements about optical fibres from the following. **[Guj CET]**

S1 : Optical fibres are used for the transmission of optical signals only.

S2 : Optical fibres are used for transmitting and receiving electrical signals.

S3 : The intensity of light signals sent through optical fibres suffer very small loss.

S4 : Optical fibres effectively employ the principle of multiple total internal reflections.

S5 : Optical fibres are glass fibres coated with a thin layer of a material with lower refractive index.

(a) S1 and S2 (b) S2 and S3
(c) S3 and S4 (d) S1, S3, S4 and S5

10 Which one of the following is a full duplex transmission system? **[Guj CET]**

(a) TV (b) Radio
(c) Telephone
(d) Walky-talky (wireless used in the Army)

2009

11 The frequency of audio analog signals lies in the range of **[Guj CET]**

(a) 20 kHz to 20 MHz (b) 12 Hz to 20 MHz
(c) 20 Hz to 20 MHz (d) 20 Hz to 20 kHz

2008

12 Consider telecommunication through optical fibres. Which of the following statements is not true? **[RPMT]**

(a) Optical fibres can be of graded refractive index.
(b) Optical fibres are subjected to electromagnetic interference from outside.
(c) Optical fibres have extremely low transmission loss.
(d) Optical fibres may have homogeneous core with a suitable cladding.

13 What happen, if the bandwidth is large enough to accommodate a few harmonics? **[RPMT]**

(a) The information is not lost
(b) The rectangular signal is more or less recovered
(c) Both (a) and (b)
(d) None of the above

14 Advantages of optical fibre communications over two wire transmission line or coaxial cable transmission are [Guj CET]
(a) low bandwidth, low transmission loss
(b) high bandwidth, high transmission loss
(c) high bandwidth, low transmission loss
(d) low bandwidth, high transmission loss

2007

15 Identify the parts X and Y in the block diagram of a generalised communication system. [J & K CET]

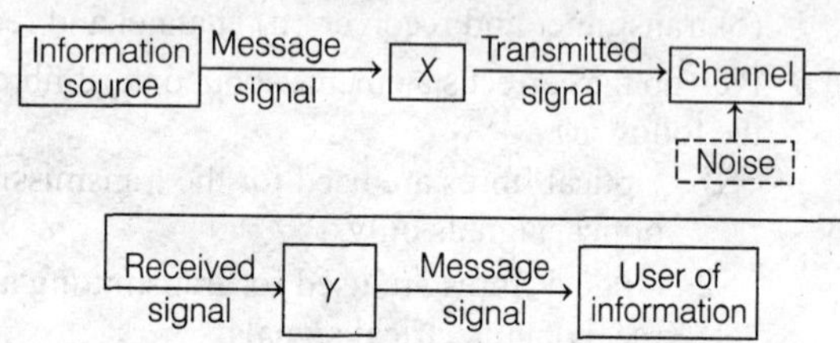

(a) channel, transmitter (b) transmitter, receiver
(c) receiver, channel (d) receiver, transmitter

16 **Assertion** Optical fibre communication has immunity to cross-talk.
Reason Optical interference between fibres is zero. [AIIMS]
(a) Both Assertion and Reason are correct and Reason is the correct explanation of Assertion.
(b) Both Assertion and Reason are correct but Reason is not the correct explanation of Assertion.
(c) Assertion is correct but Reason is incorrect.
(d) Both Assertion and Reason are incorrect.

17 The cladding material of optical fibre has refractive index [J&K CET]
(a) greater than that of core (b) infinity
(c) equal to that of core (d) less than that of core

18 The glass of optical fibre has refractive index 1.55 and is clad with another glass of refractive index 1.51. When the surrounding is air, the numerical aperture will be [Guj CET]
(a) 0.625 (b) 0.350 (c) 0.528 (d) 0.704

2006

19 **Assertion** In optical fibre, the diameter of the core is kept small.
Reason This smaller diameter of the core ensures that the fibre should have incident angle more than the critical angle required for total internal reflection. [AIIMS]
(a) Both Assertion and Reason are true and Reason is the correct explanation of Assertion.
(b) Both Assertion and Reason are correct but Reason is not the correct explanation of Assertion.
(c) Assertion is correct but Reason is incorrect.
(d) Both Assertion and Reason are incorrect.

2005

20 What should be the maximum acceptance angle at the air-core interface of an optical fibre, if n_1 and n_2 are the refractive indices of the core and the cladding respectively? [AIIMS]
(a) $\sin^{-1}(n_2/n_1)$ (b) $\sin^{-1}\sqrt{n_1^2 - n_2^2}$
(c) $\left[\tan^{-1}\frac{n_2}{n_1}\right]$ (d) $\left[\tan^{-1}\frac{n_1}{n_2}\right]$

Answers

1 (b)	2 (d)	3 (a)	4 (d)	5 (d)	6 (c)	7 (b)	8 (c)	9 (d)	10 (c)
11 (d)	12 (b)	13 (c)	14 (c)	15 (b)	16 (a)	17 (d)	18 (b)	19 (a)	20 (b)

Explanations

1 *(b)* Transducers are devices which are used to convert one form of energy (disturbance) to other form of energy, e.g. loudspeaker converts electrical energy to sound energy (mechanical vibrations). In a microphone, a series of energy conversions occurs in reverse order.

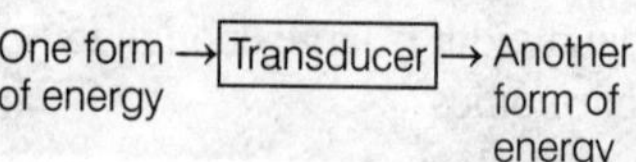

Amplifier is a device which increases (amplifies) the amplitude of a signal.

In this, the nature of the signal in output and input remains same.

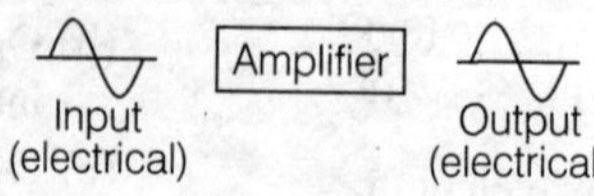

2 *(d)* Transducer is a device that converts variations in a physical quantity such as pressure or brightness into an electrical signal or *vice-versa*.

3 *(a)* Endoscopy is process for viewing internal organs of human body. This device uses optical fibres, which works on the principle of total internal reflection.

4 *(d)* The mobile telephones operate typically in the range of 800-950 MHz.

5 *(d)* Given, 1% of 10^{12} Hz $= 10^{10}$Hz

Now, number of channels

$$= \frac{\text{Total bandwidth}}{\text{Bandwidth per channel}}$$

⇒ Number of channels

$$= \frac{10^{10}}{8 \times 10^3} \quad \text{(given)}$$

$$= 1.25 \times 10^6$$

6 (*c*) Given, $P = 1$ kW $= 1000$ W and $\lambda = 198.6$ m

Number of photons emitted per second

$$n = \frac{P}{E} = \frac{P}{h\nu} = \frac{P\lambda}{hc}$$

$$= \frac{1000 \times 198.6}{6.6 \times 10^{-34} \times 3 \times 10^8} = 10^{30}$$

7 (*b*) Given, $\lambda = 1.3\ \mu\text{m} = 1.3 \times 10^{-6}$ m

Optical source frequency,

$$f = \frac{c}{\lambda} = \frac{3 \times 10^8}{1.3 \times 10^{-6}}$$

$$= 2.3 \times 10^{14} \text{ Hz}$$

$\therefore$ Number of channels,

$$n = \frac{2.3 \times 10^{14}}{20 \times 10^3}$$

$$= 1.15 \times 10^{10}$$

8 (*c*) In a point-to-point communication mode, communication takes place over a link between a transmitter and a receiver. It is also known as peer-to-peer communication.

9 (*d*)

(*i*) The optical fibres are used to transmit optical signal from one place to another without any practical loss in the intensity of light signal.

(*ii*) Optical fibre is made of a thin glass core surrounded by a layer of material of lower refractive index.

(*iii*) It works on the principle of multiple internal reflection.

Hence, statements S1, S3, S4 and S5 are correct.

10 (*c*) The telephone is a full duplex transmission system, because in it data signal can be transmitted between two stations synchronised in both directions at the same instant of time.

11 (*d*) We know that, the frequency range of audio analog signals is 20 Hz to 20 kHz.

12 (*b*) Some of the characteristics of an optical fibre are as follows

(*i*) It work on the principle of total internal reflection.

(*ii*) It consists of core made up of glass/silica/plastic with refractive index n_1, which is surrounded by a glass or plastic cladding with refractive index $n_2 (n_1 > n_2)$. The refractive index of cladding can be either changing abruptly or gradually changing (graded index fibre).

(*iii*) There is a very little transmission loss through optical fibres.

(*iv*) There is no interference from electric and magnetic fields to the signals through optical fibres.

Hence, option (b) is not true.

13 (*c*) The information is not lost and the rectangular signal is more of less recovered. This is so because the higher the harmonic less is its contribution to the waveform.

14 (*c*) In optical communication, light is transmitted in the form of light pulses along an optical fibre as transmission medium. Since, wavelength of the light is very small, it provides a very large bandwidth and can carry a huge amount of information.

The main merits of optical fibre over two wire transmission line or co-axial cable transmission are that they are quite cheap, very easy to install and less energy loss during transmission. So, the required answer is high bandwidth and low transmission loss.

15 (*b*) The message signal has to be converted into electrical signal before being sent to the channel. This is done by a transmitter. A transmitter consists of an amplitude modulation, power amplifier and transmitting antenna. Received signal is sent to the receiver which amplifies the signal, detects it and then sends is to the user. So, correct option is (b).

16 (*a*) Optical communication is a system by which we transfer the informations over any distance from one location to other through optical range of frequency using optical fibre. The optical interference between fibres is zero. Hence, optical fibre communication has immunity to cross talk.

17 (*d*) In optical fibre, the core (refractive index μ_1) is surrounded by cladding (refractive index μ_2) made up of transparent glass or plastic such that $\mu_2 < \mu_1$.

18 (*b*) For air, $\mu_0 = 1$.

Given, $\mu_1 = 1.55$ and $\mu_2 = 1.51$

Numerical aperture

$$= \frac{\sqrt{\mu_1^2 - \mu_2^2}}{\mu_0}$$

$$= \frac{\sqrt{(1.55)^2 - (1.51)^2}}{1}$$

$$= 0.350$$

19 (*a*) The core diameter of optical fibres is so small ($\sim 10\mu\text{m}$) that the light entering will almost essentially be having incident angle more than the critical angle and will suffer total internal reflection at the core-cladding boundary. The successive total reflections at opposite boundaries will confine the light to the core as shown in figure

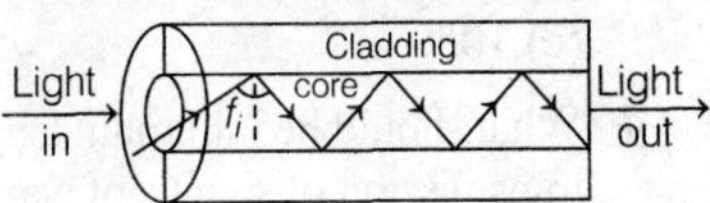

20 (*b*) The maximum angle of incidence (*i*) in air for which all the incident light is totally reflected at the interface of a pair of media having refractive indices n_1 and n_2 is given by

$$i = \sin^{-1}(\sqrt{n_1^2 - n_2^2})$$

This value of the maximum angle of incidence is known as acceptance angle.

Topic 2

Ground, Space and Sky Wave Communication

2019

1 **Assertion** In ionospheric reflection, phase change does not occur with the radio wave.

Reason The ionosphere reflection is similar to the total internal reflection in mirage. **[AIIMS]**

(a) Both Assertion and Reason are correct and Reason is the correct explanation of Assertion.
(b) Both Assertion and Reason are correct but Reason is not the correct explanation of Assertion.
(c) Assertion is correct but Reason is incorrect.
(d) Both Assertion and Reason are incorrect.

2014

2 The maximum distance upto which TV transmission from a TV tower of height h can be received is proportional to **[UP CPMT]**

(a) $h^{1/2}$ (b) h
(c) $h^{3/2}$ (d) h^2

2011

3 If the TV telecast is to cover a radius of 120 km, then the height of the transmitting antenna is (take, the radius of the earth = 6400 km), **[Kerala CEE]**

(a) 1280 m (b) 1125 m (c) 1560 m (d) 79 m
(e) 1050 m

4 What should be minimum length of antenna for efficient transmission of signals of wavelength λ? **[J&K CET]**

(a) $\frac{\lambda}{2}$ (b) $\frac{\lambda}{3}$ (c) $\frac{\lambda}{4}$ (d) $\frac{\lambda}{5}$

5 What fraction of the surface area of the earth can be covered to establish communication by a geo-stationary satellite? **[J&K CET]**

(a) $\frac{1}{2}$ (b) $\frac{1}{3}$ (c) $\frac{1}{4}$ (d) $\frac{1}{8}$

6 A TV tower has a height 150 m. What is the total population covered by the TV tower, if the population density around the TV tower is $10^3\ \text{km}^{-2}$? (Take radius of the earth as 6.4×10^6 m) **[J&K CET]**

(a) 60.288 lakh (b) 40.192 lakh
(c) 100 lakh (d) 20.22 lakh

7 A radio wave that travels in a straight line from the transmitting antenna to the receiving antenna is known as **[J&K CET]**

(a) sky wave (b) ground wave
(c) space wave (d) ionospheric wave

8 For a radio signal to travel 150 km from the transmitter to a receiving antenna, it takes **[DUMET]**

(a) 5×10^{-4} s (b) 4.5×10^{-3} s
(c) 5×10^{-8} s (d) 4.5×10^{-6} s

2010

9 The relation between the maximum electron density N_{max} and the critical frequency f_c for the ionosphere can be given as **[Guj CET]**

(a) $f_c = \sqrt{9N_{max}}$ (b) $f_c = \sqrt{9N}_{max}$
(c) $f_c = 9\sqrt{N_{max}}$ (d) None of these

2008

10 If electron density of the layer of ionosphere is 10×10^{11} and k is a constant, then critical frequency for reflection of radio waves is **[Kerala CEE]**

(a) $k\times 10^{18}$ Hz (b) $k\times 10^{12}$ Hz
(c) $k\times 10^{7}$ Hz (d) $k\times 10^{6}$ Hz

11 A transmitting antenna of height h and the receiving antenna of height 45 m are separated by a distance of 40 km for satisfactory communication in line-of-sight mode. Then, the value of h is (take, radius of the earth is 6400 km) **[Kerala CEE]**

(a) 15 m (b) 20 m (c) 30 m (d) 25 m
(e) 40 m

12 If the critical frequency for sky wave propagation is 12 MHz, then the maximum electron density in the ionosphere is **[Kerala CEE]**

(a) $1.78\times 10^{12}\ \text{m}^{-3}$ (b) $0.178\times 10^{10}\ \text{m}^{-3}$
(c) $1.12\times 10^{12}\ \text{m}^{-3}$ (d) $0.56\times 10^{12}\ \text{m}^{-3}$
(e) $0.148\times 10^{12}\ \text{m}^{-3}$

13 Beyond which frequency, the ionosphere bends any incident electromagnetic radiation but does not reflect it back towards the earth? **[AMU]**

(a) 50 MHz (b) 40 MHz (c) 30 MHz (d) 20 MHz

14 Sky waves are reflected by **[DUMET]**

(a) stratosphere (b) mesosphere
(c) ionosphere (d) None of these

15 A TV tower has a height of 75 m. What is the maximum distance upto which this TV transmission can be received? (Take radius of the earth = 6.4×10^6 m) **[Guj CET]**

(a) 30.98 km (b) 38.98 km
(c) 40.98 km (d) 50.98 km

16 The sky wave propagation is suitable for radio waves of frequency **[Kerala CEE]**
(a) upto 2 MHz
(b) from 2 MHz to 20 MHz
(c) from 2 MHz to 30 MHz
(d) from 2 MHz to 50 MHz
(e) from 2 MHz to 80 MHz

17 For sky wave propagation of 10 MHz signal, what should be the maximum electron density in ionosphere? **[JCECE]**
(a) $\sim 1.2 \times 10^{12}\ m^{-3}$ (b) $\sim 10^{6}\ m^{-3}$
(c) $\sim 10^{14}\ m^{-3}$ (d) $\sim 10^{22}\ m^{-3}$

18 What minimum frequency can be reflected from ionosphere? **[JCECE]**
(a) 2 MHz (b) 6 GHz (c) 5 kHz (d) 500 MHz

2006

19 **Assertion** Electromagnetic waves with frequencies more than the critical frequency of ionosphere cannot be used for communication using sky wave propagation.
Reason The refractive index of the ionosphere becomes very high for frequencies higher than the critical frequency. **[AIIMS]**
(a) Both Assertion and Reason are correct and Reason is the correct explanation of Assertion.
(b) Both Assertion and Reason are correct but Reason is not the correct explanation of Assertion.
(c) Assertion is correct but Reason is incorrect.
(d) Both Assertion and Reason are incorrect.

20 The radio waves which are received after reflection in ionosphere are known as **[BHU]**
(a) surface waves (b) sky waves
(c) ground waves (d) space waves

21 The area of the region covered by the TV broadcast by a TV tower of 100 m height is (take, radius of the earth $= 6.4 \times 10^6$ m) **[Kerala CEE]**
(a) $12.8\pi \times 10^8\ km^2$ (b) $1.28\pi \times 10^3\ km^2$
(c) $0.644\pi \times 10^3\ km^2$ (d) $1.28 \times 10^3\ km^2$
(e) $2.56\pi \times 10^3\ km^3$

22 Refractive index of ionosphere is **[Guj CET]**
(a) zero (b) more than one
(c) less than one (d) one

2005

23 Audio signal cannot be transmitted, because **[Kerala CEE]**
(a) the signal has more noise
(b) the signal cannot be amplified for distance communication
(c) the transmitting antenna length is very small to design
(d) the transmitting antenna length is very large and impracticable
(e) the signal is not a radio signal

24 The region of the atmosphere above troposphere is known as **[Punjab PMET]**
(a) lithosphere
(b) upper sphere
(c) ionosphere
(d) stratosphere

25 If the area to be covered for TV telecast is doubled, then height of transmitting antenna (TV tower) will have to be **[J&K CET]**
(a) doubled
(b) halved
(c) quadrupled
(d) kept unchanged

Answers

1 (a)	2 (a)	3 (b)	4 (c)	5 (b)	6 (a)	7 (c)	8 (a)	9 (c)	10 (d)
11 (b)	12 (a)	13 (b)	14 (c)	15 (a)	16 (c)	17 (a)	18 (a)	19 (a)	20 (b)
21 (b)	22 (c)	23 (d)	24 (d)	25 (a)					

Explanations

1 *(a)* The ionosphere reflection is similar to the total internal reflection and also similar to the total internal reflection in mirage. In total internal reflection, there is no phase change after reflection. So, in ionospheric reflection also frequency and phase do not change of the reflected radio wave. Hence, both Assertion and Reason are correct and Reason is the correct explanation of Assertion.

2 *(a)* Consider the diagram, let the receiving antenna is at ground level.

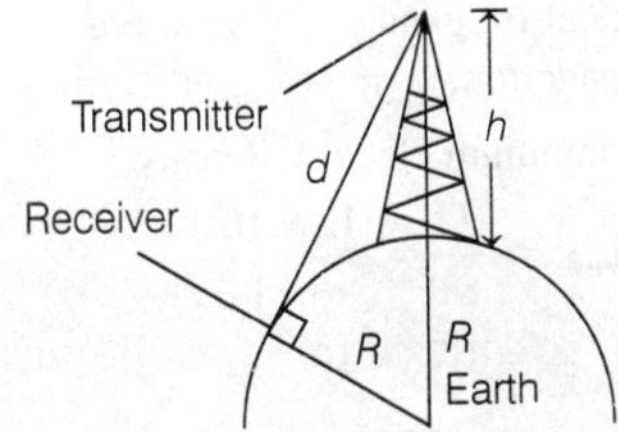

The range of an antenna is given by
$\Rightarrow d = \sqrt{2R}\,(\sqrt{h_t} + \sqrt{h_r})$ ...(i)

where, d = maximum distance upto which signals can be received,
h_t = height of the transmitter,
h_r = height of the receiver.
and R = radius of the earth $\simeq$ 6400 km.
Let $h_r \simeq 0$ (for ground level)
From Eq. (i), we get

$$d \approx \sqrt{2R}\,(\sqrt{h})$$
$$= \sqrt{2R}\,(h)^{1/2} \quad [\because h_t = h]$$
$$\Rightarrow d \propto h^{1/2} \quad (\because \sqrt{2R} = \text{constant})$$

Alternate Method

$$d^2 + R^2 = (R + h)^2$$

(using pythagoras theorem)

$$\Rightarrow \quad d^2 + R^2 = R^2 + 2hR + h^2$$

$$\Rightarrow \quad d = \sqrt{h^2 + 2hR}$$

$$d = h\sqrt{1 + \frac{2R}{h}}$$

$$\simeq h\sqrt{\frac{2R}{h}} = \sqrt{2hR}$$

$$\Rightarrow \quad d \propto h^{1/2}$$

3 (*b*) Given, $d = 120\text{ km} = 120 \times 10^3\text{ m}$ and $R = 6400\text{ km} = 6400 \times 10^3\text{ m}$

Distance covered by transmitting signal, i.e.

$$d = \sqrt{2hR}$$

Height of an antenna, i.e.

$$h = \frac{d^2}{2R} = \frac{(120 \times 1000)^2}{2 \times 6400 \times 1000} = 1125\text{ m}$$

4 (*c*) For efficient radiation and reception, the height of transmitting and receiving antenna should be comparable to a quarter of wavelength of the signal used. So, for efficient transmission of signals of wavelength λ, the minimum length of antenna should be $\lambda/4$.

5 (*b*) We use three geo-stationary satellites placed at the vertices of an equilateral triangle, then the entire surface area of the earth can be covered by the communication network, each satellite covers 1/3 on the globe.

6 (*a*) Given, height of a tower, i.e.

$$h = 150\text{ m}, R = 6.4 \times 10^6\text{ m}$$

and average population density

$$= 10^3\text{ km}^{-2} = (10^3)(10^{-6})\text{ m}^{-2} = 10^{-3}\text{ m}^{-2}$$

Distance upto which the transmission could be viewed,

$$d = \sqrt{2hR}$$

Total area over which transmission could be viewed

$$= \pi d^2 = 2\pi hR$$

Population covered $= 10^{-3} \times 2\pi hR$

$$= 10^{-3} \times 2 \times 3.14 \times 150 \times 6.4 \times 10^6 = 60.288\text{ lakh}$$

7 (*c*) Space waves are used for very long distance radio communication at high frequencies.

A radio wave that travels in a straight line from the transmitting antenna to the receiving antenna is known as space wave.

8 (*a*) Velocity of radio wave,

$$v = 3 \times 10^8\text{ ms}^{-1}$$

$$\therefore \text{ Time, } t = \frac{\text{Distance }(s)}{\text{Velocity }(v)} = \frac{150 \times 1000}{3 \times 10^8} = 5 \times 10^{-4}\text{ s}$$

9 (*c*) If maximum electron density of the ionosphere is N_{max} per m^3, then

$$f_c = 9\,(N_{max})^{1/2}.$$

Above f_c a wave will penetrate the ionosphere and is not reflected by it.

10 (*d*) Given, $N = 10 \times 10^{11} = 10^{12}$

By the relation, $f_c = kN^{1/2}$

We have critical frequency, i.e.

$$f_c = k\,(10^{12})^{1/2} = k \times 10^6\text{ Hz}$$

11 (*b*) The situation can be shown as

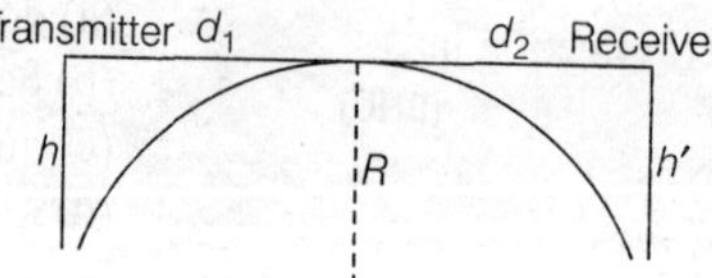

Here, total distance travelled by a signal, i.e.

$$d = d_1 + d_2 = \sqrt{2hR} + \sqrt{2h'R}$$

Given, $d = 40\text{ km} = 40 \times 10^3\text{ m}$

$$\therefore 40 \times 10^3 = \sqrt{2 \times 6400 \times 10^3} \cdot (\sqrt{h} + \sqrt{45})$$

On solving, we get

$$h = 20\text{ m}$$

12 (*a*) Given, $f_c = 12\text{ MHz} = 12 \times 10^6\text{ Hz}$

Critical frequency for sky wave propagation, $f_c = 9(N_{max})^{1/2}$

$\therefore$ Maximum electron density,

$$N_{max} = \frac{f_c^2}{81} = \frac{(12 \times 10^6)^2}{81} = 1.78 \times 10^{12}\text{ m}^{-3}$$

13 (*b*) The ionosphere can reflect electromagnetic waves of frequency less than 40 MHz but waves does not reflect electromagnetic of frequency more than 40 MHz.

14 (*c*) Sky waves are the radio waves which are directed towards the sky and reflected back by the ionosphere towards the desired location on the earth.

15 (*a*) Given, height of a TV tower,

$$h = 75\text{ m}$$

and radius of the earth, $R = 6.4 \times 10^6\text{m}$

The distance upto which TV transmission can be received,

$$d = \sqrt{2hR} = \sqrt{2 \times 75 \times 6.4 \times 10^6} = \sqrt{15} \times 8 \times 10^3\text{m} = 30.98\text{ km}$$

16 (*c*) The sky waves are the radio waves of frequency between 2 MHz to 30 MHz. These waves cannot propagate through the atmosphere but are reflected back by the ionosphere of the earth's atmosphere.

These waves can propagate from transmitter to receiver through sky, therefore their propagation is called sky wave propagation.

17 (*a*) The critical frequency of sky wave undergoing reflection from a layer of atmosphere is

$$f_c = 9\,(N_{max})^{1/2}$$

where, N_{max} is electron density (per m^3).

$$\Rightarrow N_{max} = \frac{f_c^2}{81} = \frac{(10 \times 10^6)^2}{81} = 1.2 \times 10^{12}\text{ m}^{-3}$$

18 (*a*) By the ionosphere, the range of frequency lying between 2 MHz to 20MHz can be reflected back . The given frequency range waves are the sky waves. So, a minimum of about 2 MHz frequency can be reflected by ionosphere.

19 (*a*) The sky waves are the radio waves of frequency range between 2 MHz to 20 MHz. The ionosphere reflects these radio waves back to the earth during their propagation through atmosphere.

The refractive index of ionosphere is less than its free space value, i.e. it behaves as a rarer medium. As we go deep into the ionosphere (electron density N is large), the refractive index keeps on decreasing.

If the frequency is too high, then after a certain value, the electron density N may never be so high as to produce enough bending for attainment of critical angle or condition of reflection. This is called critical frequency.

For frequencies higher than critical one, the refractive index of the ionosphere becomes very high, so the wave crosses the ionosphere and does not return back to the earth.

20 (b) The radio waves which are received after reflection in ionosphere are called sky waves. Sky waves are used for very long distance radio communication at medium and high frequency (i.e. at medium waves and short waves).

21 (b) Area of broadcast is

$$A = \pi d^2 = \pi(2hR)$$

Given, $h = 100$ m and $R = 6.4 \times 10^6$ m

$$\Rightarrow \quad A = \pi(2 \times 100 \times 6.4 \times 10^6)$$
$$= 1.28\pi \times 10^3 \text{ km}^2$$

22 (c) Refractive index of ionosphere,

$$\mu = \mu_0 \sqrt{1 - \frac{80.6N}{\nu^2}}$$

where, N is free electron density typically equal to 10^{11} m^{-3} and ν is frequency of waves in kHz.

So, we have $\mu < 1$.

Hence, refractive index of ionosphere is less than one.

23 (d) Height of antenna is proportional to $\lambda/4$, where λ is the wavelength of signal. Audio signal have very large wavelength (2-2kHz). So, the height of antenna required would also be very large which is not practicable.

24 (d) The stratosphere is the second major layer of the earth's atmosphere, just above the troposphere and below the mesosphere.

It is stratified in temperature, with warmer layers higher up and cooler layers farther down.

25 (a) Area A covered by TV signal is given by

$$A = \pi d^2$$

where, d is range given by $d = \sqrt{2Rh}$

where, R is radius of the earth and h is the height of antenna.

$$\therefore \quad A = \pi(2Rh)$$

Given, $A_1 = A, A_2 = 2A$

$$\therefore \quad \frac{A_1}{A_2} = \frac{h_1}{h_2} \Rightarrow \frac{h_1}{h_2} = \frac{1}{2}$$

$$\Rightarrow \quad h_2 = 2h_1$$

Hence, height of transmitting antenna will have to be doubled.

Topic 3

Modulation and Demodulation

2019

1 If modulation index $\mu = \frac{1}{2}$ and $V_m = 2$, then V_C is **[AIIMS]**

(a) 4 (b) 2
(c) 6 (d) 8

2 **Assertion** Amplitude modulation shows more interference than frequency modulation with noise. **[AIIMS]**

Reason Interference is function of ratio of amplitude of modulation wave with carrier wave.

(a) Both Assertion and Reason are correct and Reason is the correct explanation of Assertion.
(b) Both Assertion and Reason are correct but Reason is not the correct explanation of Assertion.
(c) Assertion is correct, but Reason is incorrect.
(d) Both Assertion and Reason are incorrect.

2014

3 If in an amplitude modulated wave, the maximum amplitude is 10 V and the modulation index is (2/3), then the minimum amplitude is (in volt) **[EAMCET]**

(a) 7 (b) 9 (c) 6 (d) 2

2011

4 Identify the incorrect statement from the following. **[Kerala CEE]**

(a) AM detection is carried out using a rectifier and an envelope detector.
(b) Pulse position denotes the time of rise or fall of the pulse amplitude.
(c) Modulation index μ is kept ≥ 1, to avoid distortion.
(d) Facsimile (FAX) scans the contents of the document to create electronic signals.
(e) Detection is the process of recovering the modulating signal from the modulated carrier wave.

2009

5 The modulation in which pulse duration varies in accordance with the modulation signal is called **[Kerala CEE]**

(a) PAM (b) PPM
(c) PWM (d) PCM
(e) PFM

2008

6 A 1000 kHz carrier wave is modulated by an audio signal of frequency range 100-5000 Hz. Then, the width of the channel in kHz is **[Kerala CEE]**

(a) 10 (b) 20 (c) 30 (d) 40
(e) 50

2007

7 In a detector, output circuit consists of $R = 10\ \text{k}\Omega$ and $C = 100\,\text{pF}$. The frequency of carrier signal it can detect is **[AIIMS]**

(a) >> 1 MHz (b) 0.1 kHz
(c) >> 1 GHz (d) 10^3 Hz

8 **Assertion** A portable AM radio set must be kept horizontal to receive the signals properly.
Reason Radio waves are polarised electromagnetic waves. **[AIIMS]**

(a) Both Assertion and Reason are correct and Reason is the correct explanation of Assertion.
(b) Both Assertion and Reason are correct but Reason is not the correct explanation of Assertion.
(c) Assertion is correct but Reason is incorrect.
(d) Both Assertion and Reason are incorrect.

9 Modulation is the process of superimposing **[Kerala CEE]**

(a) low frequency audio signal on high frequency waves
(b) low frequency radio signal on low frequency audio waves
(c) high frequency radio signal on low frequency audio signal
(d) high frequency audio signal on low frequency radio waves
(e) low frequency radio signal on high frequency audio waves

2006

10 Given below is a circuit diagram of an AM demodulator.

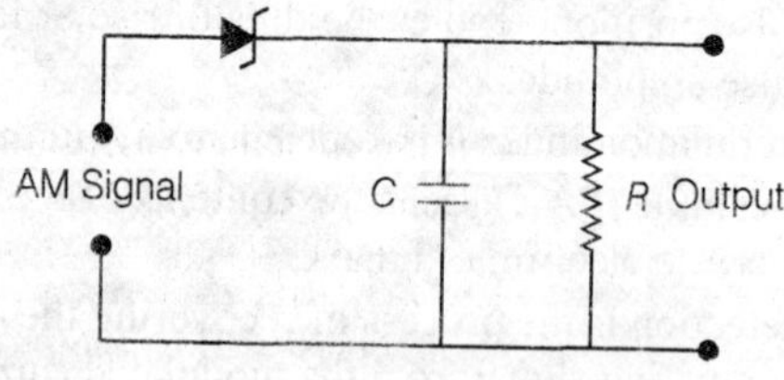

For good demodulation of AM signal of carrier frequency f, the value of RC should be **[AIIMS]**

(a) $RC = \frac{1}{f}$ (b) $RC < \frac{1}{f}$
(c) $RC \geq \frac{1}{f}$ (d) $RC >> \frac{1}{f}$

11 Of the following which is preferred modulation scheme for digital communication? **[Kerala CEE]**

(a) Pulse Code Modulation (PCM)
(b) Pulse Amplitude Modulation (PAM)
(c) Pulse Position Modulation (PPM)
(d) Pulse Width Modulation (PWM)
(e) Pulse Time Modulation (PTM)

2005

12 In frequency modulation, **[Kerala CEE]**

(a) the amplitude of modulated wave varies as frequency of carrier wave
(b) the frequency of modulated wave varies as amplitude of modulating wave
(c) the amplitude of modulated wave varies as amplitude of carrier wave
(d) the frequency of modulated wave varies as frequency of modulating wave
(e) the frequency of modulated wave varies as frequency of carrier wave

13 **Assertion** Transducer in communication system converts electrical signal into a physical quantity.
Reason For information signal to be transmitted directly to long distances, modulation is not a necessary process. **[AIIMS]**

(a) Both Assertion and Reason are correct and reason is the correct explanation of Assertion.
(b) Both Assertion and Reason are correct but Reason is not the correct explanation of Assertion.
(c) Assertion is true but Reason is incorrect.
(d) Both Assertion and Reason are incorrect.

Answers

1 (a)	2 (a)	3 (d)	4 (c)	5 (c)	6 (a)	7 (a)	8 (a)	9 (a)	10 (d)
11 (a)	12 (b)	13 (c)							

Explanations

1 (a) Given, modulation index, $\mu = \frac{1}{2}$

Amplitude of modulation voltage,

$$V_m = 2$$

$$\therefore \quad \mu = \frac{V_m}{V_c}$$

$$\therefore \quad V_c = \frac{V_m}{\mu} = \frac{2}{1/2} = 4$$

2 (a) Amplitude modulation has less noise immunity than frequency modulation, hence amplitude modulation shows more interference with noise than frequency modulation. Interference (noise) depends mostly upon ratio of amplitudes of modulation wave and carrier wave and not their frequency ratio.

In amplitude modulation, the change in amplitude can actually modulate the signal and be picked up in the AM system. As a result, AM systems are very sensitive to random noise.

In FM system, mostly frequency of carrier wave is changed according to the modulating signal, hence noise does not interfere FM signal directly. Therefore, FM systems are far better at rejecting noise than AM systems.

Hence, both Assertion and Reason are correct and Reason is the correct explanation of Assertion.

3 (d) Given, modulation index, $\mu = 2/3$

and $E_{max} = 10$ V

We know that,

$$\mu = \frac{E_{max} - E_{min}}{E_{max} + E_{min}}$$

$$\Rightarrow \quad \frac{2}{3} = \frac{10 - E_{min}}{10 + E_{min}}$$

$$\Rightarrow \quad 20 + 2E_{min} = 30 - 3E_{min}$$

$$\Rightarrow \quad 5\,E_{min} = 10$$

or $\quad E_{min} = 10/5 = 2$ V

4 (c) Modulation index, μ cannot be greater than one, i.e. $\mu \geq 1$ to avoid distortion in a signal is wrong.

5 (c) In Pulse Width Modulation (PWM), the samples of the message signal are used to vary the width or duration of the individual pulse in accordance with the modulating signal.

6 (a) Given, maximum frequency range,

$f_{m(max)} = 5000$ Hz

As we know, width of the channel

$= 2f_{m\,(max)} = 2 \times 5000 = 10000$ Hz

$= 10$ kHz

7 (a) Given, $R = 10\ k\Omega = 10^4\ \Omega$

and $C = 100$ pF $= 10^{-10}$ F

The time constant of the RC circuit,

$$\tau = RC$$

$$= 10^4 \times 10^{-10}$$

$$= 10^{-6}\ s$$

For demodulation, $1/f_C << RC$

or $\quad f_C >> \frac{1}{RC}$

or $\quad f_C >> \frac{1}{10^{-6}} = 10^6$ Hz

$= 1$MHz

Therefore, frequency of carrier signal must be much greater than 1 MHz.

8 (a) It is true that the radio waves are polarised electromagnetic waves. The antenna of portable AM radio is sensitive to only magnetic components of electromagnetic waves. On account of this, the set should be put horizontal so that the signals are received properly from radio station.

9 (a) Low frequency audio signal cannot be transmitted as such over long distances. Therefore, to overcome this difficulty, the low frequency audio signal is superposed on a high frequency carrier wave. This process is called modulation.

10 (d) From the modulated signal, we can demodulate or detect the modulating or message signal by using a diode and a suitable capacitor filter. The AM signal given to the input of the circuit appears at the output of the diode as a rectified wave as shown

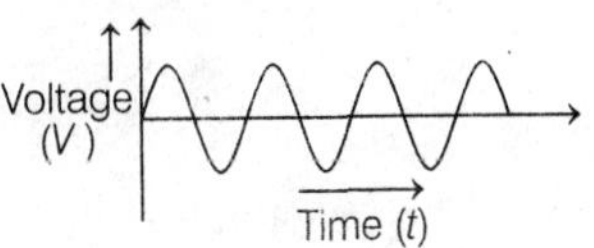

For good demodulation of AM signal, the value of RC (which is a time-constant) is chosen such that

$$\frac{1}{f} << RC \text{ or } RC >> \frac{1}{f}$$

where, f is the frequency of the carrier signal or wave

11 (a) Pulse Code Modulation (PCM) is a digital representation of an analog signal where the magnitude of the signal is sampled regularly at uniform intervals, then quantised to a series of symbols in a digital code.

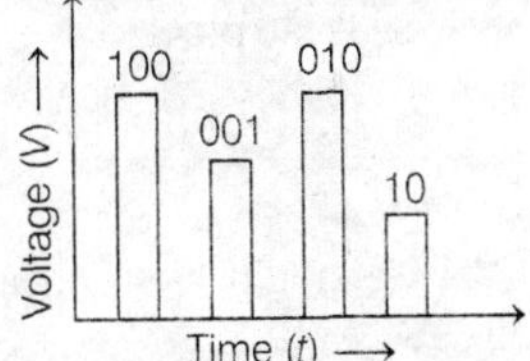

12 (b) The phenomenon of superposition of information signal over a high frequency carrier wave such that the frequency of the modulated wave is modified according to amplitude of modulating wave, keeping the amplitude constant is called frequency modulation.

13 (c) In any communication system, information (a physical quantity) is converted into an electrical signal by a device called transducer or *vice-versa*. Most of the speech or information signal cannot be directly transmitted to long distances.

For this, an intermediate step of modulation is necessary in which the information signal is loaded or superimposed on a high frequency wave which acts as a carrier wave.

NEET

SOLVED PAPER 2020

1. The phase difference between displacement and acceleration of a particle in a simple harmonic motion is

(a) $\frac{3\pi}{2}$ rad (b) $\frac{\pi}{2}$ rad

(c) zero (d) π rad

2. A long solenoid of 50 cm length having 100 turns carries a current of 2.5 A. The magnetic field at the centre of solenoid is (Take, $\mu_0 = 4\pi \times 10^{-7}$ T m A^{-1})

(a) 3.14×10^{-4} T

(b) 6.28×10^{-5} T

(c) 3.14×10^{-5} T

(d) 6.28×10^{-4} T

3. Two bodies of mass 4 kg and 6 kg are tied to the ends of a massless string. The string passes over a pulley which is frictionless (see figure). The acceleration of the system in terms of acceleration due to gravity g is

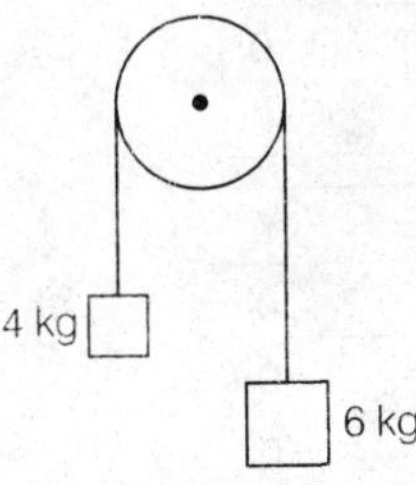

(a) $g/2$ (b) $g/5$

(c) $g/10$ (d) g

4. The ratio of contributions made by the electric field and magnetic field components, to the intensity of an electromagnetic wave is

(where, c = speed of electromagnetic waves)

(a) 1 : 1 (b) 1 : c

(c) 1 : c^2 (d) c : 1

5. In a certain region of space with volume 0.2 m^3, the electric potential is found to be 5 V throughout. The magnitude of electric field in this region is

(a) 0.5 N/C (b) 1 N/C

(c) 5 N/C (d) zero

6. The average thermal energy for a monoatomic gas is (where, k_B is Boltzmann constant and T is absolute temperature.)

(a) $\frac{3}{2}k_BT$ (b) $\frac{5}{2}k_BT$

(c) $\frac{7}{2}k_BT$ (d) $\frac{1}{2}k_BT$

7. Find the torque about the origin when a force of $3\hat{\mathbf{j}}$ N acts on the particle whose position vector is $2\hat{\mathbf{k}}$ m.

(a) $6\hat{\mathbf{j}}$ N-m (b) $-6\hat{\mathbf{i}}$ N-m

(c) $6\hat{\mathbf{k}}$ N-m (d) $6\hat{\mathbf{i}}$ N-m

8. The mean free path λ for a gas, with molecular diameter d and number density n can be expressed as

(a) $\frac{1}{\sqrt{2}\, n\pi d^2}$ (b) $\frac{1}{\sqrt{2}\, n^2\pi d^2}$

(c) $\frac{1}{\sqrt{2}\, n^2\pi^2 d^2}$ (d) $\frac{1}{\sqrt{2}\, n\pi d}$

9. The energy equivalent of 0.5 g of a substance is

(a) 4.5×10^{13} J (b) 1.5×10^{13} J

(c) 0.5×10^{13} J (d) 4.5×10^{16} J

10. A screw gauge has least count of 0.01 mm and there are 50 divisions in its circular scale.

The pitch of the screw gauge is

(a) 0.25 mm (b) 0.5 mm

(c) 1.0 mm (d) 0.01 mm

11. Two cylinders A and B of equal capacity are connected to each other *via* a stop cock. A contains an ideal gas at standard temperature and pressure. B is completely evacuated. The entire system is thermally insulated. The stop cock is suddenly opened. The process is

(a) adiabatic (b) isochoric

(c) isobaric (d) isothermal

12. A cylinder contains hydrogen gas at pressure of 249 kPa and temperature 27°C.

Its density is ($R = 8.3$ J mol^{-1} K^{-1})

(a) 0.2 kg/m^3 (b) 0.1 kg/m^3

(c) 0.02 kg/m^3 (d) 0.5 kg/m^3

13. When a uranium isotope $^{235}_{92}U$ is bombarded with a neutron, it generates $^{89}_{36}Kr$, three neutrons and

(a) $^{91}_{40}Zr$ (b) $^{101}_{36}Kr$
(c) $^{103}_{36}Kr$ (d) $^{144}_{56}Ba$

14. A charged particle having drift velocity of 7.5×10^{-4} ms^{-1} in an electric field of 3×10^{-10} Vm^{-1}, has a mobility (in m^{2}V^{-1}s^{-1}) of

(a) 2.5×10^{6} (b) 2.5×10^{-6}
(c) 2.25×10^{-15} (d) 2.25×10^{15}

15. Taking into account of the significant figures, what is the value of 9.99 m − 0.0099 m?

(a) 9.98 m (b) 9.980 m
(c) 9.9 m (d) 9.9801 m

16. An iron rod of susceptibility 599 is subjected to a magnetising field of 1200 A m^{-1}. The permeability of the material of the rod is
(Take, $\mu_0 = 4\pi \times 10^{-7}$ T m A^{-1})

(a) 8.0×10^{-5} T m A^{-1}
(b) $2.4\pi \times 10^{-5}$ T m A^{-1}
(c) $2.4\pi \times 10^{-7}$ T m A^{-1}
(d) $2.4\pi \times 10^{-4}$ T m A^{-1}

17. A spherical conductor of radius 10 cm has a charge of 3.2×10^{-7} C distributed uniformly. What is the magnitude of electric field at a point 15 cm from the centre of the sphere?
$\left(\frac{1}{4\pi\varepsilon_0} = 9 \times 10^9 \text{ Nm}^2/\text{C}^2\right)$

(a) 1.28×10^{5} N/C
(b) 1.28×10^{6} N/C
(c) 1.28×10^{7} N/C
(d) 1.28×10^{4} N/C

18. A series *L-C-R* circuit is connected to an AC voltage source. When *L* is removed from the circuit, the phase difference between current and voltage is $\frac{\pi}{3}$. If instead *C* is removed from the circuit, the phase difference is again $\frac{\pi}{3}$ between current and voltage. The power factor of the circuit is

(a) 0.5 (b) 1.0
(c) −1.0 (d) zero

19. A capillary tube of radius *r* is immersed in water and water rises in it to a height *h*. The mass of the water in the capillary tube is 5 g. Another capillary tube of radius 2*r* is immersed in water. The mass of water that will rise in this tube is

(a) 5.0 g (b) 10.0 g
(c) 20.0 g (d) 2.5 g

20. In Young's double slit experiment, if the separation between coherent sources is halved and the distance of the screen from the coherent sources is doubled, then the fringe width becomes

(a) half (b) four times
(c) one-fourth (d) double

21. For the logic circuit shown, the truth table is

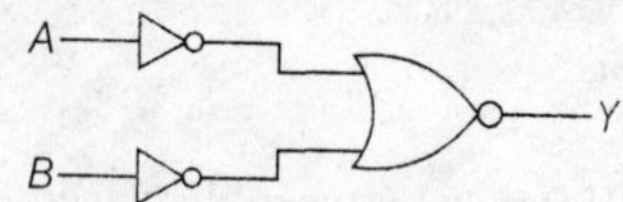

(a)

A	B	Y
0	0	0
0	1	1
1	0	1
1	1	1

(b)

A	B	Y
0	0	1
0	1	1
1	0	1
1	1	0

(c)

A	B	Y
0	0	1
0	1	0
1	0	0
1	1	0

(d)

A	B	Y
0	0	0
0	1	0
1	0	0
1	1	1

22. The color code of a resistance is given below

The values of resistance and tolerance respectively, are

(a) 47 kΩ, 10% (b) 4.7 kΩ, 5%
(c) 470 Ω, 5% (d) 470 kΩ, 5%

23. The capacitance of a parallel plate capacitor with air as medium is 6 μF. With the introduction of a dielectric medium, the capacitance becomes 30 μF. The permittivity of the medium is
($\varepsilon_0 = 8.85 \times 10^{-12}$ C^{2}N^{-1}m^{-2})

(a) 1.77×10^{-12} C^{2}N^{-1}m^{-2} (b) 0.44×10^{-10} C^{2}N^{-1}m^{-2}
(c) 5.00 C^{2}N^{-1}m^{-2} (d) 0.44×10^{-13} C^{2}N^{-1}m^{-2}

24. A ball is thrown vertically downward with a velocity of 20 m/s from the top of a tower. It hits the ground after some time with a velocity of 80 m/s. The height of the tower is $(g = 10 \text{ m/s}^2)$

(a) 340 m (b) 320 m
(c) 300 m (d) 360 m

25. A body weighs 72 N on the surface of the earth. What is the gravitational force on it, at a height equal to half of radius of the earth?

(a) 32 N (b) 30 N
(c) 24 N (d) 48 N

26. Two particles of mass 5 kg and 10 kg respectively are attached to the two ends of a rigid rod of length 1 m with negligible mass.
The centre of mass of the system from the 5 kg particle is nearly at a distance of

(a) 50 cm (b) 67 cm
(c) 80 cm (d) 33 cm

27. The increase in the width of the depletion region in a *p-n* junction diode is due to

(a) reverse bias only
(b) both forward bias and reverse bias
(c) increase in forward current
(d) forward bias only

28. Light of frequency 1.5 times the threshold frequency is incident on a photosensitive material. What will be the photoelectric current if the frequency is halved and intensity is doubled?

(a) Four times (b) One-fourth
(c) Zero (d) Doubled

29. Assume that, light of wavelength 600 nm is coming from a star. The limit of resolution of telescope whose objective has a diameter of 2 m is

(a) 1.83×10^{-7} rad (b) 7.32×10^{-7} rad
(c) 6.00×10^{-7} rad (d) 3.66×10^{-7} rad

30. A resistance wire connected in the left gap of a metre bridge balances a 10 Ω resistance in the right gap at a point which divides the bridge wire in the ratio 3 : 2. If the length of the resistance wire is 1.5 m, then the length of 1 Ω of the resistance wire is

(a) 1.0×10^{-1} m (b) 1.5×10^{-1} m
(c) 1.5×10^{-2} m (d) 1.0×10^{-2} m

31. Light with an average flux of 20 W/cm^2 falls on a non-reflecting surface at normal incidence having surface area 20 cm^2. The energy received by the surface during time span of 1 min is

(a) 12×10^3 J (b) 24×10^3 J
(c) 48×10^3 J (d) 10×10^3 J

32. A ray is incident at an angle of incidence i on one surface of a small angle prism (with angle of prism A) and emerges normally from the opposite surface. If the refractive index of the material of the prism is μ, then the angle of incidence is nearly equal to

(a) $\frac{2A}{\mu}$ (b) μA
(c) $\frac{\mu A}{2}$ (d) $\frac{A}{2\mu}$

33. A 40 μF capacitor is connected to a 200 V, 50 Hz AC supply. The rms value of the current in the circuit is, nearly

(a) 2.05 A (b) 2.5 A
(c) 25.1 A (d) 1.7 A

34. Dimensions of stress are

(a) $[ML^2T^{-2}]$ (b) $[ML^0T^{-2}]$
(c) $[ML^{-1}T^{-2}]$ (d) $[MLT^{-2}]$

35. The Brewster's angle i_b for an interface should be

(a) $30° < i_b < 45°$
(b) $45° < i_b < 90°$
(c) $i_b = 90°$
(d) $0° < i_b < 30°$

36. A wire of length L, area of cross-section A is hanging from a fixed support. The length of the wire changes to L_1 when mass M is suspended from its free end. The expression for Young's modulus is

(a) $\frac{Mg(L_1 - L)}{AL}$ (b) $\frac{MgL}{AL_1}$
(c) $\frac{MgL}{A(L_1 - L)}$ (d) $\frac{MgL_1}{AL}$

37. A short electric dipole has a dipole moment of 16×10^{-9} C-m. The electric potential due to the dipole at a point at a distance of 0.6 m from the centre of the dipole, situated on a line making an angle of 60° with the dipole axis is $\left(\frac{1}{4\pi\varepsilon_0} = 9 \times 10^9 \text{ Nm}^2/\text{C}^2\right)$

(a) 200 V (b) 400 V
(c) zero (d) 50 V

38. In a guitar, two strings A and B made of same material are slightly out of tune and produce beats of frequency 6 Hz. When tension in B is slightly decreased, the beat frequency increases to 7 Hz. If the frequency of A is 530 Hz, the original frequency of B will be

(a) 524 Hz
(b) 536 Hz
(c) 537 Hz
(d) 523 Hz

39. An electron is accelerated from rest through a potential difference of V volt. If the de-Broglie wavelength of the electron is 1.227×10^{-2} nm, the potential difference is

(a) 10^2 V
(b) 10^3 V
(c) 10^4 V
(d) 10 V

40. The solids which have the negative temperature coefficient of resistance are

(a) insulator only
(b) semiconductors only
(c) insulators and semiconductors
(d) metals

41. The energy required to break one bond in DNA is 10^{-20} J. This value (in eV) is nearly

(a) 0.6 (b) 0.06
(c) 0.006 (d) 6

42. The quantities of heat required to raise the temperature of two solid copper spheres of radii r_1 and r_2 ($r_1 = 1.5\, r_2$) through 1 K are in the ratio

(a) $\frac{9}{4}$ (b) $\frac{3}{2}$
(c) $\frac{5}{3}$ (d) $\frac{27}{8}$

43. Which of the following graph represents the variation of resistivity (ρ) with temperature (T) for copper?

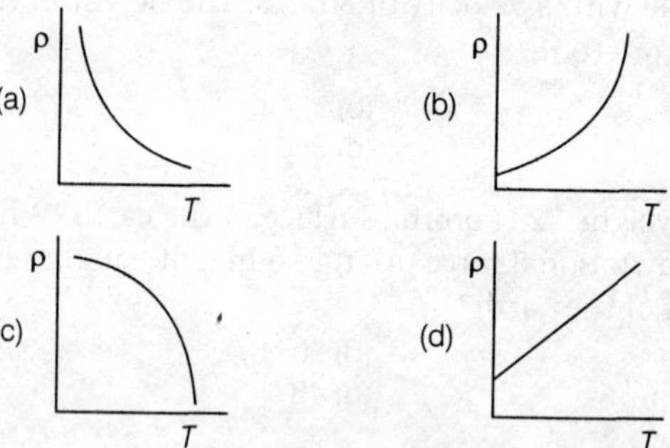

44. For transistor action, which of the following statements is correct?

(a) Base, emitter and collector regions should have same size.
(b) Both emitter junction as well as the collector junction are forward biased.
(c) The base region must be very thin and lightly doped.
(d) Base, emitter and collector regions should have same dopping concentrations.

45. For which one of the following, Bohr model is not valid?

(a) Singly ionised helium atom (He^+)
(b) Deuteron atom
(c) Singly ionised neon atom (Ne^+)
(d) Hydrogen atom

Answers

1.	(d)	2.	(d)	3.	(b)	4.	(d)	5.	(d)	6.	(a)	7.	(b)	8.	(a)	9.	(a)	10.	(b)
11.	(a)	12.	(a)	13.	(d)	14.	(a)	15.	(a)	16.	(d)	17.	(a)	18.	(b)	19.	(d)	20.	(b)
21.	(d)	22.	(c)	23.	(b)	24.	(c)	25.	(a)	26.	(b)	27.	(a)	28.	(c)	29.	(d)	30.	(a)
31.	(b)	32.	(b)	33.	(b)	34.	(c)	35.	(b)	36.	(c)	37.	(a)	38.	(a)	39.	(c)	40.	(c)
41.	(b)	42.	(d)	43.	(b)	44.	(c)	45.	(c)										

Answer *with* Explanations

1. *(d)* In SHM, equation of displacement of a particle is $y = a \sin \omega t$

and equation of acceleration of a particle is

$$A = a\omega^2 \sin \omega t = a\omega^2 \sin(\omega t + \pi)$$

$\therefore$ Phase difference between displacement and acceleration of a particle is

$$= (\omega t + \pi) - \omega t = \pi \text{ rad}$$

Hence, correct option is (d).

2. *(d)* Given, $l = 50$ cm $= 0.5$ m, $N = 100$ turns and $I = 2.5$A

$\therefore$ Magnetic field at the centre of solenoid is

$$= \mu_0 nI = \mu_0 \left(\frac{N}{l}\right) \cdot I$$

$$= 4\pi \times 10^{-7} \times \frac{100}{0.5} \times 2.5$$

$$= 6.28 \times 10^{-4} \text{T}$$

Hence, correct option is (d).

3. *(b)* Given, $m_1 = 4$ kg, $m_2 = 6$ kg and $a = ?$

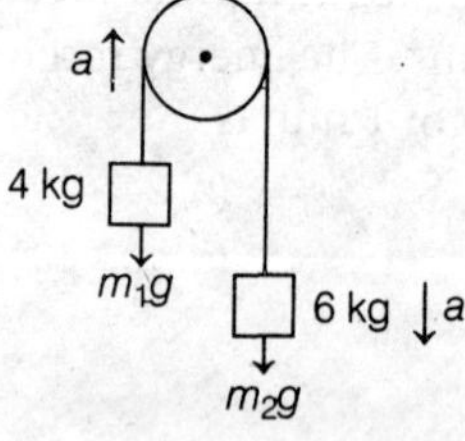

From the above free body diagram, the relation for acceleration of the given system can be given as

$$a = \left(\frac{m_2 - m_1}{m_1 + m_2}\right) \cdot g = \left(\frac{6-4}{4+6}\right) \times g = \frac{g}{5}$$

Hence, correct option is (b).

4. *(d)* We know that,

$$\frac{E_0}{B_0} = c$$

where, E_0 and B_0 are the peak values of electric field and magnetic field, respectively.

$\therefore \quad E_0 : B_0 = c : 1$

Hence, correct option is (d).

5. *(d)* Given, volume, $V = 0.2\,\text{m}^3$

Electric potential = 5 V = constant

Electric field = ?

We know that, for constant electric potential the value of electric field is zero.

i.e., $\quad E = \frac{-dV}{dr} = \frac{-d(5)}{dr} = 0$

Hence, correct option is (d).

6. *(a)* The average thermal energy of a system with degree of freedom f is equals to its average energy, which is given as

$$= \frac{f}{2} k_B \cdot T$$

For monoatomic gas, $f = 3$

$\therefore$ Average thermal energy $= \frac{3}{2} k_B \cdot T$

Hence, correct option is (a).

7. *(b)* Given, position vector, $\mathbf{r} = 2\hat{\mathbf{k}}$ m

Force, $\mathbf{F} = 3\hat{\mathbf{j}}$ N

As, torque, $\tau = \mathbf{r} \times \mathbf{F} = 2\hat{\mathbf{k}} \times 3\hat{\mathbf{j}}$

$= 6(-\hat{\mathbf{i}}) = -6\hat{\mathbf{i}}$ N-m

Hence, correct option is (b).

8. *(a)* The mean free path λ for a gas, with molecular diameter d and number density n is given by the relation

$$\lambda = \frac{1}{\sqrt{2} n \pi d^2}$$

Hence, correct option is (a).

9. *(a)* Given, $m = 0.5\,\text{g} = 0.5 \times 10^{-3}$ kg

Relation for energy equivalent of mass is

$$E = mc^2$$

where, c is speed of light.

$$= 0.5 \times 10^{-3} \times (3 \times 10^8)^2$$

$$= 4.5 \times 10^{13}\,\text{J}$$

Hence, correct option is (a).

10. *(b)* Given, least count = 0.01 mm

Number of divisions on circular scale = 50

Pitch of the screw gauge = least count × number of division on circular scale

$= 0.01 \times 50 = 0.5\,\text{mm}$

Hence, correct option is (b).

11. *(a)* Since, the entire system is thermally insulated. Thus, their will be no transfer of heat between the system and the surrounding. Hence, when the stop cock is suddenly opened, a sudden process of expansion will takes place with no heat transfer. Thus, the given process will be adiabatic, as it is a process that occurs without transferring heat or mass between a thermodynamic system and its surroundings.

Hence, correct option is (a).

12. *(a)* Given, pressure $p = 249\,\text{kPa} = 249 \times 10^3$ Pa

Temperature, $T = 27°\text{C} = 273 + 27\,\text{K} = 300$ K

Density, $\rho = ?$

As, from ideal gas equation,

$$pV = nRT$$

$\Rightarrow \quad pV = \frac{m}{M} RT \quad \left[\text{as } n = \frac{m}{M}\right]$

$\Rightarrow \quad pVM = mRT$

$\Rightarrow \quad pM = \frac{m}{V} RT = \rho RT \quad \left[\text{as } \frac{m}{V} = \rho\right]$

$\Rightarrow \quad \rho = \frac{pM}{RT} = \frac{249 \times 10^3 \times 2 \times 10^{-3}}{8.3 \times 300}$

[$\because$ for hydrogen gas, $M = 2\,\text{g} = 2 \times 10^{-3}$ kg]

$\Rightarrow \quad \rho = 0.2\,\text{kg/m}^3$

Hence, correct option is (a).

13. *(d)* Here,

$${}^{235}_{92}\text{U} + {}^{1}_{0}n \longrightarrow {}^{89}_{36}\text{Kr} + {}^{A}_{Z}X + 3({}^{1}_{0}n)$$

According to the law of conservation,

$(\text{Atomic number})_{\text{Reactant}} = (\text{Atomic number})_{\text{Product}}$

$92 + 0 = 36 + Z \quad \Rightarrow \quad Z = 92 - 36 = 56$

Similarly,

$(\text{Atomic masses})_{\text{Reactant}} = (\text{Atomic masses})_{\text{Product}}$

$235 + 1 = 89 + A + 3 \times 1 \quad \Rightarrow \quad A = 144$

$\therefore$ Other element is ${}^{144}_{56}\text{Ba}$.

Hence, correct option is (d).

14. *(a)* Given, drift velocity, $v_d = 7.5 \times 10^{-4}$ m/s

Electric field, $E = 3 \times 10^{-10}$ V-m

Mobility, $\mu = ?$

As, $\quad \mu = \frac{v_d}{E} = \frac{7.5 \times 10^{-4}}{3 \times 10^{-10}}$

$= 2.5 \times 10^6\,\text{m}^2\text{V}^{-1}\text{s}^{-1}$

Hence, correct option is (a).

15. *(a)* The difference between 9.99 m and 0.0099 m is

$= 9.99 - 0.0099 = 9.9801\,\text{m}$

Taking significant figures into account, as both the values has two significant figures after decimal.

So, their difference will also have two significant figures after decimal, i.e. 9.98 m.

Hence, correct option is (a).

16. (d) Given, susceptibility, $\chi = 599$

Magnetic field, $B = 1200\ \text{Am}^{-1}$

Permeability of the material of the rod = ?

As, $\mu_m = \mu_0(1 + \chi)$

$= 4\pi \times 10^{-7}(1 + 599)$

$= 2.4\pi \times 10^{-4}\ \text{TmA}^{-1}$

Hence, correct option is (d).

17. (a) Given, radius, $r = 10\ \text{cm} = 10 \times 10^{-2}\ \text{m}$

Charge, $q = 3.2 \times 10^{-7}\ \text{C}$

Electric field, $E = ?$

Electric field at a point ($x = 15\text{cm}$) from the centre of the sphere is

$$E = \frac{1}{4\pi\varepsilon_0} \cdot \frac{q}{x^2} = 9 \times 10^9 \times \frac{3.2 \times 10^{-7}}{(15 \times 10^{-2})^2}$$

$$= 1.28 \times 10^5\ \text{N/C}$$

Hence, correct option is (a).

18. (b) For *L-C-R* circuit, phase difference,

$$\phi = \tan^{-1}\left(\frac{X_L - X_C}{R}\right)$$

When *L* is removed, then $X_L = 0$

$$\therefore \quad \phi = \tan^{-1}\left(\frac{-X_C}{R}\right)$$

$$\Rightarrow \quad \tan\phi = \left|\frac{X_C}{R}\right| \quad \ldots\text{(i)}$$

When *C* is removed, then $X_C = 0$

$$\therefore \quad \phi = \tan^{-1}\left(\frac{X_L}{R}\right)$$

$$\Rightarrow \quad \tan\phi = \frac{X_L}{R} \quad \ldots\text{(ii)}$$

From Eqs. (i) and (ii), we get

$$X_L = X_C$$

$\therefore$ Impedance, $Z = \sqrt{R^2 + (X_L - X_C)^2} = R$

Power factor, $\cos\phi = \frac{R}{Z} = \frac{R}{R} = 1$

Hence, correct option is (b).

19. (d) Relation for height of water in capillary tube is

$$h = \frac{2S\cos\theta}{\rho g r}$$

$$\Rightarrow \quad h \propto \frac{1}{r}$$

$$\Rightarrow \quad \frac{h_1}{h_2} = \frac{r_2}{r_1} = \frac{2r}{r} = 2$$

As $\quad m = A \cdot h \cdot \rho$

$$\therefore \quad \frac{m_2}{m_1} = \frac{Ah_2\rho}{Ah_1\rho}$$

$$= \frac{h_2}{h_1} = \frac{1}{2}$$

$$\Rightarrow \quad m_2 = \frac{m_1}{2} = \frac{5}{2} = 2.5\text{g}$$

Hence, correct option is (d).

20. (b) Fringe width, $\beta = \frac{\lambda D}{d}$

$$\therefore \quad \frac{\beta_2}{\beta_1} = \frac{\frac{\lambda_2 D_2}{d_2}}{\frac{\lambda_1 D_1}{d_1}}$$

[As $\lambda_1 = \lambda_2$, $D_2 = 2D_1$ and $d_2 = \frac{d_1}{2}$]

$$\therefore \quad \frac{\beta_2}{\beta_1} = \frac{2D_1}{\left(\frac{d_1}{2}\right)} \times \frac{d_1}{D_1} = 4$$

$$\Rightarrow \quad \beta_2 = 4\beta_1$$

i.e., fringe width becomes four times.

Hence, correct option is (b).

21. (d) Given logic circuit is

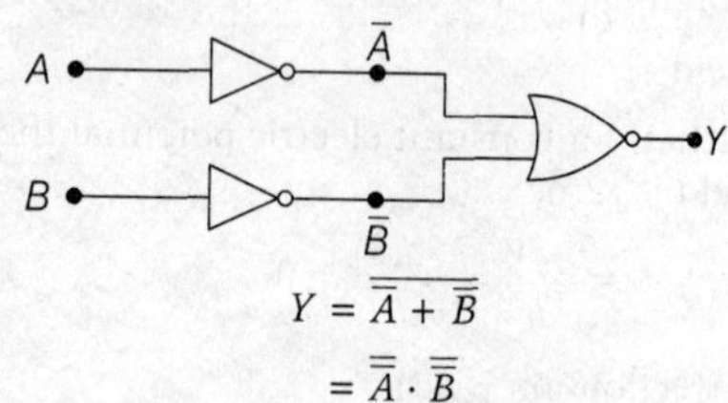

$$Y = \overline{\bar{A} + \bar{B}}$$

$$= \bar{\bar{A}} \cdot \bar{\bar{B}}$$

[using de-Morgan's theorem, $\overline{x + y} = \bar{x} \cdot \bar{y}$]

$$= A \cdot B \quad [\because \bar{\bar{x}} = x]$$

Truth table for above given logic circuit is

A	B	$\bar{A}$	$\bar{B}$	$Y = A \cdot B$
0	0	1	1	0
0	1	1	0	0
1	0	0	1	0
1	1	0	0	1

$\Rightarrow$

A	B	Y
0	0	0
0	1	0
1	0	0
1	1	1

Hence, correct option is (d).

22. (c) According to the carbon color code for resistors,

Code of yellow = 4

Code of violet = 7

Code of brown, i.e. multiplier = 10^1

Code of gold, i.e. tolerance = $\pm$ 5%

Hence, resistance of resistor = $47 \times 10^1\ \Omega$, 5%

$= 470\ \Omega$, 5%

Hence, correct option is (c).

23. (b) Given, $C_0 = 6\mu\text{F}$

$$C_m = 30\mu\text{F}$$

$\therefore$ As, dielectric constant

$$K = \varepsilon_r = \frac{C_m}{C_0} = \frac{30}{6} = 5$$

Permittivity of the medium,

$$\varepsilon_m = K \times \varepsilon_0 = 5 \times \varepsilon_0$$
$$= 5 \times 8.85 \times 10^{-12}$$
$$= 0.44 \times 10^{-10} C^2 N^{-1} m^{-2}$$

Hence, correct option is (b).

24. **(c)** Given, $u = 20$ m/s, $v = 80$ m/s and $h = ?$

From kinematic equation of motion,

$$v^2 = u^2 + 2gh$$

$$\Rightarrow \quad h = \frac{v^2 - u^2}{2g} = \frac{(80)^2 - (20)^2}{2 \times 10} \quad (\because \text{ given, } g = 10 \text{ m/s}^2)$$

$$= 300 \text{m}$$

Hence, correct option is (c).

25. **(a)** Given, $w = mg = 72$ N (on the surface of earth).

At height equal to half of radius of the earth, $\left(\text{i.e. } h = \frac{R}{2}\right)$

Acceleration due to gravity,

$$g' = g\left(\frac{R}{R+h}\right)^2$$

$$= g\left(\frac{R}{R + R/2}\right)^2 = g\left(\frac{4R^2}{9R^2}\right)$$

$$\Rightarrow \quad g' = \frac{4}{9} g$$

$$\Rightarrow \quad mg' = \frac{4}{9} mg = \frac{4}{9} \times 72 = 32 \text{N}$$

$$w' = 32 \text{N}$$

Hence, correct option is (a).

26. **(b)** Given, $m_1 = 5$ kg, $m_2 = 10$ kg and $r = 1$ m $= 100$ cm

Let the centre of mass lies at origin O.

$$\therefore \quad \frac{m_1 r_1 - m_2 r_2}{m_1 + m_2} = 0$$

$$\Rightarrow \quad 5r_1 - 10r_2 = 0$$

$$\Rightarrow \quad r_2 = \frac{r_1}{2}$$

Also,
$$r_1 + r_2 = 100$$

$$\Rightarrow \quad r_1 + \frac{r_1}{2} = 100$$

$$\Rightarrow \quad 3r_1 = 200$$

$$\Rightarrow \quad r_1 = \frac{200}{3} \simeq 67 \text{cm}$$

Hence, correct option is (b).

27. **(a)** Under reverse bias condition, the holes of p-side are attracted towards the negaive terminal of the battery and electrons of the n-side are attracted towards the positive terminal of the battery. This increases the width of the depletion layer.
However, in the case of forward biasing, the width of the depletion layer decreases.
Hence, correct option is (a).

28. **(c)** Initially, frequency of light, $\nu = 1.5\nu_0$

But when the frequency of incident light is halved, then $\nu' = \frac{\nu}{2} = 0.75\nu_0$. Thus, it becomes less than the threshold frequency. In that case, no photoelectric effect takes place.
Hence, photoelectric current becomes zero.
Hence, correct option is (c).

29. **(d)** Given, light of wavelength, $\lambda = 600 \text{ nm} = 600 \times 10^{-9}$ m

Diameter, $\quad d = 2$ m

As, limit of resolution of telescope, $d\theta = \frac{1.22\lambda}{d}$

$$= \frac{1.22 \times 600 \times 10^{-9}}{2}$$

$$= 3.66 \times 10^{-7} \text{ rad}$$

Hence, correct option is (d).

30. **(a)** According to the question, the metre bridge is shown below,

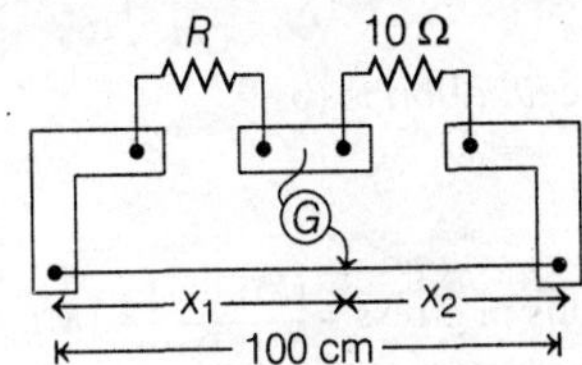

Given, $\frac{x_1}{x_2} = \frac{3}{2}$

At balance condition in metre bridge,

$$\frac{R}{10} = \frac{x_1}{x_2}$$

$$\Rightarrow \quad R = \frac{x_1}{x_2} \times 10 = \frac{3}{2} \times 10 = 15 \Omega$$

Now, length of given wire whose resistance 15Ω is 1.5 m.
Therefore, length of 1Ω resistance wire is

$$= \frac{1.5}{15} = \frac{1}{10} = 0.1 = 1 \times 10^{-1} \text{ m}$$

Hence, correct option is (a).

31. **(b)** Given, average flux $= 20 \text{ W/cm}^2$

Surface area $= 20 \text{cm}^2$

Time $= 1 \text{min} = 60$ s

For non-reflecting surface,
energy received = average flux × surface area × time

$$= 20 \times 20 \times 60 = 24 \times 10^3 \text{ J}$$

32. **(b)** According to the question, the ray diagram can be shown as

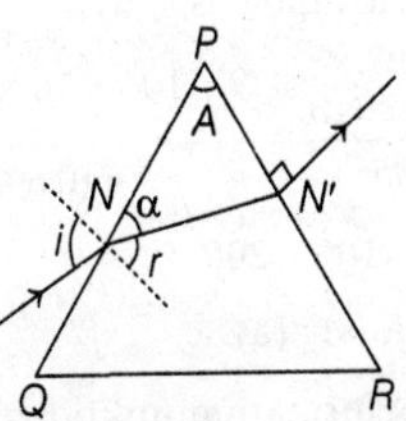

From figure in $\Delta PNN'$,

$$A + \alpha + 90° = 180°$$

$$\Rightarrow \quad \alpha = 90° - A \quad \text{...(i)}$$

Also, $r + \alpha = 90^\circ$

$\Rightarrow \quad r = 90^\circ - \alpha$

$= 90^\circ - (90^\circ - A) = A \quad$ [$\because$ from Eq. (i)]

$\Rightarrow \quad r = A$

From Snell's law,

$$\mu_1 \sin i = \mu_2 \sin r$$

$\Rightarrow \quad \sin i = \mu \sin A \quad$ (here, $\mu_1 = 1$ and $\mu_2 = \mu$)

For small angle, $\sin\theta \simeq \theta \Rightarrow i = \mu A$

Hence, correct option is (b).

33. *(b)* Given, $C = 40\,\mu F = 40 \times 10^{-6}$ F

$V_{rms} = 200$V

$\nu = 50$Hz

As, $$X_C = \frac{1}{2\pi\nu C} = \frac{1}{2\pi \times 50 \times 40 \times 10^{-6}}$$

$$= \frac{10^6}{100\pi \times 40} = \frac{250}{\pi}\Omega$$

$\therefore$ $$I_{rms} = \frac{V_{rms}}{X_C} = \frac{200}{\left(\frac{250}{\pi}\right)} = 2.5\text{A}$$

Hence, correct option is (b).

34. *(c)* $\because$ Stress $= \frac{\text{Force}}{\text{Area}}$

$\therefore$ Dimensions of stress $= \frac{[MLT^{-2}]}{[L^2]} = [ML^{-1}T^{-2}]$

Hence, correct option is (c).

35. *(b)* The Brewster's angle i_b for an interface should lies between 45° to 90°, i.e. $45^\circ < i_b < 90^\circ$.

Hence, correct option is (b).

36. *(c)* Here, change in length, $\Delta L = (L_1 - L)$

Area $= A$

Force, $F = Mg$

Young's modulus, $Y = \frac{\text{Normal stress}}{\text{Longitudinal strain}}$

$\Rightarrow$ $$Y = \frac{(F/A)}{\left(\frac{\Delta L}{L}\right)} = \frac{\frac{Mg}{A}}{\left(\frac{L_1 - L}{L}\right)} = \frac{MgL}{A(L_1 - L)}$$

Hence, correct option is (c).

37. *(a)* Given, electric dipole moment, $p = 16 \times 10^{-9}$ C-m

Distance, $r = 0.6$ m

Angle, $\theta = 60^\circ \Rightarrow \cos 60^\circ = \frac{1}{2}$

Electric potential at a point which is at a distance r at some angle θ from electric dipole is

$$V = \frac{p\cos\theta}{4\pi\varepsilon_0 r^2} = \frac{9 \times 10^9 \times 16 \times 10^{-9} \times \frac{1}{2}}{(0.6)^2}$$

$= 2 \times 10^2 = 200$ V

Hence, correct option is (a).

38. *(a)* In case of beats formation unknown frequency $(\nu_B) = \nu_A \pm$ beats

where, $\nu_A = 530$ Hz and beats $= 6$ Hz.

$\Rightarrow \nu_B = 530 \pm 6 = 536$ or 524 Hz

When tension in B is slightly decreased, then beats frequency increases to 7 Hz. This is possible if we take original frequency of B as 524 Hz.

Hence, correct option is (a).

39. *(c)* Given, $\lambda = 1.227 \times 10^{-2}$ nm $= 1.227 \times 10^{-11}$ m

Potential difference, $V = ?$

Relation for de-Broglie wavelength for moving electron is

$$\lambda = \frac{12.27}{\sqrt{V}}\text{Å}$$

$\Rightarrow$ $$\sqrt{V} = \frac{12.27}{\lambda} \times 10^{-10} = \frac{12.27 \times 10^{-10}}{1.227 \times 10^{-11}} = 10^2$$

$\Rightarrow \quad V = 10^4$ V

Hence, correct option is (c).

40. *(c)* Insulators and semiconductors are those solids, which have negative temperature coefficient of resistance. As, when temperature increases number of free electrons increases in both insulator and semiconductor.

Hence, correct option is (c).

41. *(b)* Given, $E = 10^{-20}$ J

In terms of eV, we get

$$E = \frac{10^{-20}}{1.6 \times 10^{-19}}\text{eV} = 0.06\text{eV}$$

Hence, correct option is (b).

42. *(d)* Since, heat required, $Q = mc\Delta T$

$$= \left(\frac{4}{3}\pi r^3 \cdot \rho\right)c\Delta T \quad [\because m = V_{sphere}\,\rho]$$

Since, π, ρ, c and T are constant.

$\Rightarrow \quad Q \propto r^3$

or $$\frac{Q_1}{Q_2} = \frac{r_1^3}{r_2^3} = \left(\frac{r_1}{r_2}\right)^3 = \left(\frac{1.5r_2}{r_2}\right)^3 = \frac{27}{8}$$

Hence, correct option is (d).

43. *(b)* Resistivity of copper (a metal) as a function of temperature increases with the increase in temperature as shown below,

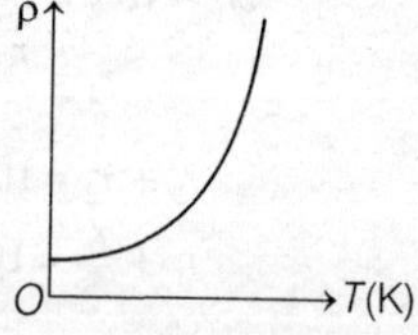

For copper at 0K, value of resistivity is $1.7 \times 10^{-8}\,\Omega$-m.

Hence, correct option is (b).

44. *(c)* In case of transistor action, base region is thin and lightly dopped. While, emitter region is heavily dopped and collector region is moderately dopped. Also, the size of collector is slightly more than the size of emitter.

Hence, option (c) is correct.

45. *(c)* Since, Bohr's model is valid for hydrogen and hydrogen like atoms He^+, deuteron, etc. So, it is not valid for singly ionised neon atom (Ne^+).

Hence, correct option is (c).

NEET

SOLVED PAPER 2021

NEET SOLVED PAPER 2021

Instruction

- This question paper contains of 50 Multiple Choice Questions of Physics, divided into two Sections; section A and section B.
- Section A contains 35 questions and all questions are compulsory.
- Section B contains 15 questions out of which only 10 questions are to be attempted.
- Each question carries 4 marks.

Section-A

1. An inductor of inductance L, a capacitor of capacitance C and a resistor of resistance R are connected in series to an AC source of potential difference V volts as shown in figure.

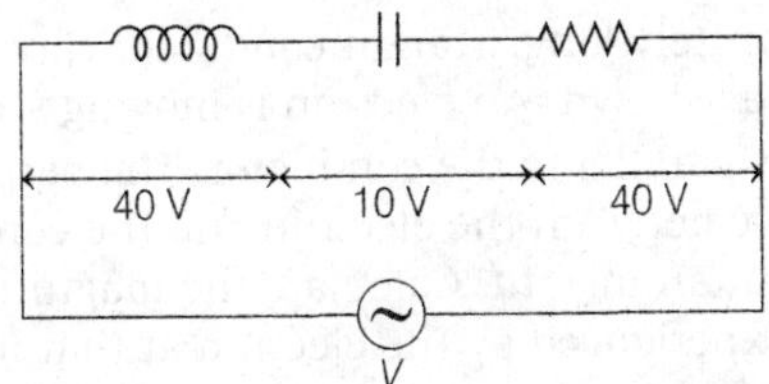

Potential difference across L, C and R is 40 V, 10 V and 40 V, respectively. The amplitude of current flowing through L-C-R series circuit is $10\sqrt{2}$ A. The impedance of the circuit is

(a) $4\sqrt{2}\ \Omega$ (b) $5\sqrt{2}\ \Omega$
(c) $4\ \Omega$ (d) $5\ \Omega$

2. Find the value of the angle of emergence from the prism. Refractive index of the glass is $\sqrt{3}$.

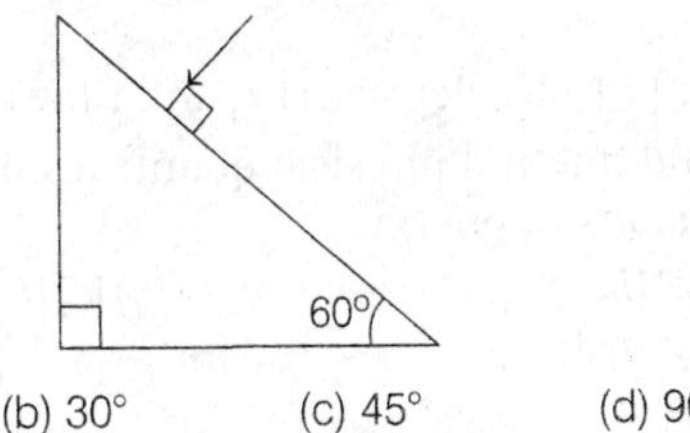

(a) 60° (b) 30° (c) 45° (d) 90°

3. A dipole is placed in an electric field as shown. In which direction will it move?

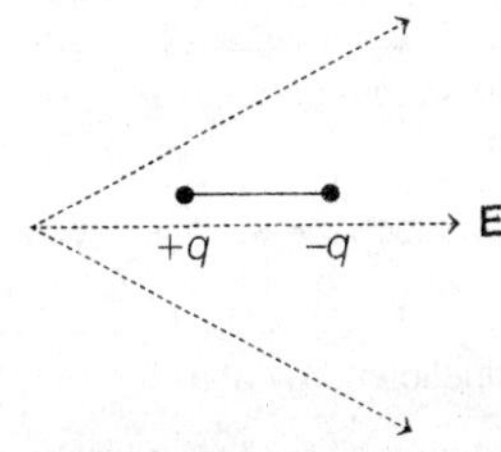

(a) Towards the left as its potential energy will increase
(b) Towards the right as its potential energy will decrease
(c) Towards the left as its potential energy will decrease
(d) Towards the right as its potential energy will increase

4. A capacitor of capacitance C, is connected across an AC source of voltage V, given by $V = V_0 \sin \omega t$

The displacement current between the plates of the capacitor, would then be given by

(a) $I_d = V_0 \omega C \cos \omega t$ (b) $I_d = \dfrac{V_0}{\omega C} \cos \omega t$
(c) $I_d = \dfrac{V_0}{\omega C} \sin \omega t$ (d) $I_d = V_0 \omega C \sin \omega t$

5. A thick current carrying cable of radius R carries current I uniformly distributed across its cross-section. The variation of magnetic field B due to the cable with the distance r from the axis of the cable is represented by

(a)
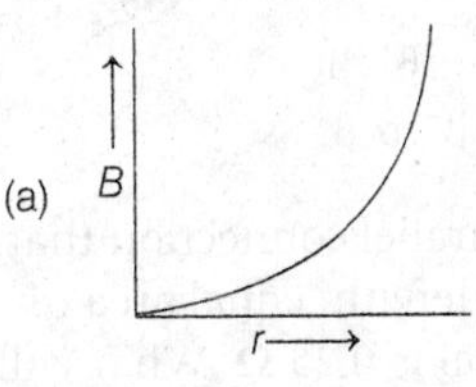

(b)
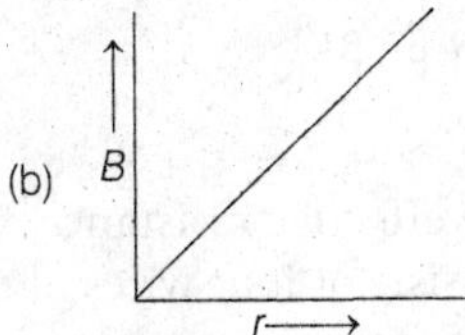

(c)
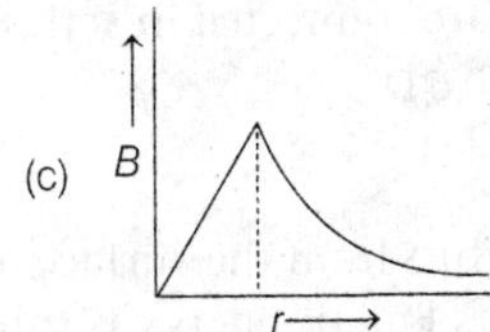

(d)
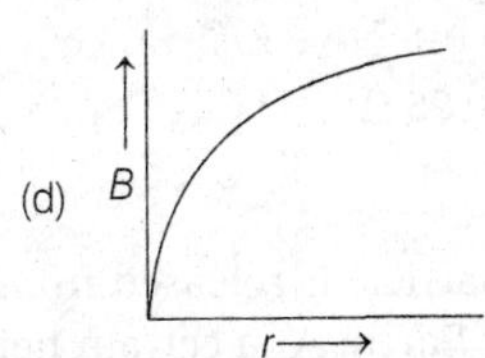

6. A convex lens A of focal length 20 cm and a concave lens B of focal length 5 cm are kept along the same axis with a distance d between them. If a parallel beam of light falling on A leaves B as a parallel beam, then the distance d (in cm) will be

(a) 25 (b) 15
(c) 50 (d) 30

7. An electromagnetic wave of wavelength λ is incident on a photosensitive surface of negligible work function. If m mass is of photoelectron emitted from the surface has de-Broglie wavelength λ_d, then

(a) $\lambda = \left(\dfrac{2m}{hc}\right)\lambda_d^2$ (b) $\lambda_d = \left(\dfrac{2mc}{h}\right)\lambda^2$
(c) $\lambda = \left(\dfrac{2mc}{h}\right)\lambda_d^2$ (d) $\lambda = \left(\dfrac{2h}{mc}\right)\lambda_d^2$

8. **Column I** Gives certain physical terms associated with flow of current through a metallic conductor.
Column II Gives some mathematical relations involving electrical quantities. Match Column I and Column II with appropriate relations.

Column I	Column II
A. Drift velocity	1. $\frac{m}{ne^2\rho}$
B. Electrical resistivity	2. nev_d
C. Relaxation period	3. $\frac{eE}{m}\tau$
D. Current density	4. $\frac{E}{J}$

Codes

	A	B	C	D
(a)	3	4	1	2
(b)	3	4	2	1
(c)	3	1	4	2
(d)	3	2	4	1

9. A radioactive nucleus ${}^A_Z X$ undergoes spontaneous decay in the sequence
${}^A_Z X \longrightarrow {}_{Z-1}B \longrightarrow {}_{Z-3}C \longrightarrow {}_{Z-2}D$, where Z is the atomic number of element X. The possible decay particles in the sequence are
(a) α, β^-, β^+
(b) α, β^+, β^-
(c) β^+, α, β^-
(d) β^-, α, β^+

10. The effective resistance of a parallel connection that consists of four wires of equal length, equal area of cross-section and same material is 0.25 Ω. What will be the effective resistance if they are connected in series?
(a) 0.25 Ω
(b) 0.5 Ω
(c) 1 Ω
(d) 4 Ω

11. A particle is released from height S from the surface of the Earth. At a certain height its kinetic energy is three times its potential energy. The height from the surface of earth and the speed of the particle at that instant are respectively
(a) $\frac{S}{4}, \frac{3gS}{2}$
(b) $\frac{S}{4}, \frac{\sqrt{3gS}}{2}$
(c) $\frac{S}{2}, \frac{\sqrt{3gS}}{2}$
(d) $\frac{S}{4}, \sqrt{\frac{3gS}{2}}$

12. The half-life of a radioactive nuclide is 100 h. The fraction of original activity that will remain after 150 h would be
(a) $\frac{1}{2}$
(b) $\frac{1}{2\sqrt{2}}$
(c) $\frac{2}{3}$
(d) $\frac{2}{3\sqrt{2}}$

13. A cup of coffee cools from 90°C to 80°C in t minutes, when the room temperature is 20°C. The time taken by a similar cup of coffee to cool from 80°C to 60°C at a room temperature same at 20°C, is
(a) $\frac{13}{10}t$
(b) $\frac{13}{5}t$
(c) $\frac{10}{13}t$
(d) $\frac{5}{13}t$

14. The number of photons per second on an average emitted by the source of monochromatic light of wavelength 600 nm, when it delivers the power of 3.3×10^{-3} W will be ($h = 6.6 \times 10^{-34}$ J-s)
(a) 10^{18}
(b) 10^{17}
(c) 10^{16}
(d) 10^{15}

15. A body is executing simple harmonic motion with frequency n, the frequency of its potential energy is
(a) n
(b) $2n$
(c) $3n$
(d) $4n$

16. An infinitely long straight conductor carries a current of 5 A as shown. An electron is moving with a speed of 10^5 m/s parallel to the conductor. The perpendicular distance between the electron and the conductor is 20 cm at an instant. Calculate the magnitude of the force experienced by the electron at that instant.

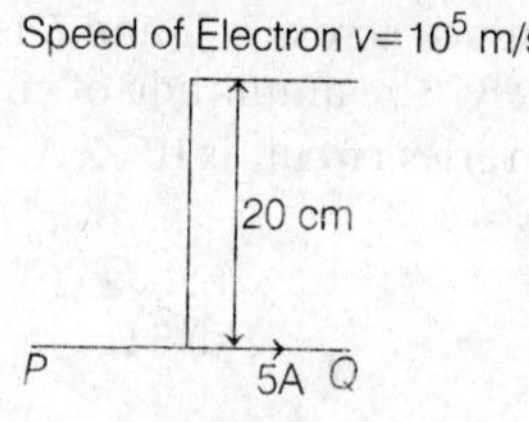

(a) 4×10^{-20} N
(b) $8\pi \times 10^{-20}$ N
(c) $4\pi \times 10^{-20}$ N
(d) 8×10^{-20} N

17. If force $[F]$, acceleration $[a]$ and time $[T]$ are chosen as the fundamental physical quantities. Find the dimensions of energy.
(a) $[F][a][T]$
(b) $[F][a][T^2]$
(c) $[F][a][T^{-1}]$
(d) $[F][a^{-1}][T]$

18. Match Column I with Column II and choose the correct match from the given choices.

Column I	Column II
A. Root mean square of gas molecules	1. $\frac{1}{3}nm\bar{v}^2$
B. Pressure exerted by ideal gas	2. $\sqrt{\frac{3RT}{M}}$
C. Average kinetic energy of a molecule	3. $\frac{5}{2}RT$
D. Total internal energy of 1 mole of a diatomic gas	4. $\frac{3}{2}k_BT$

Codes

	A	B	C	D
(a)	3	1	4	2
(b)	2	3	4	1
(c)	2	1	4	3
(d)	3	2	1	4

19. A small block slides down on a smooth inclined plane, starting from rest at time $t = 0$. Let s_n be the distance travelled by the block in the interval $t = n - 1$ to $t = n$.

Then, the ratio $\frac{s_n}{s_{n+1}}$ is

(a) $\frac{2n-1}{2n}$ (b) $\frac{2n-1}{2n+1}$

(c) $\frac{2n+1}{2n-1}$ (d) $\frac{2n}{2n-1}$

20. A nucleus with mass number 240 breaks into two fragments each of mass number 120, the binding energy per nucleon of unfragmented nuclei is 7.6 MeV while that of fragments is 8.5 MeV. The total gain in the binding energy in the process is

(a) 0.9 MeV (b) 9.4 MeV

(c) 804 MeV (d) 216 MeV

21. A screw gauge gives the following readings when used to measure the diameter of a wire

Main scale reading : 0 mm

Circular scale reading : 52 divisions

Given that, 1 mm on main scale corresponds to 100 divisions on the circular scale. The diameter of the wire from the above data is

(a) 0.52 cm (b) 0.026 cm

(c) 0.26 cm (d) 0.052 cm

22. The equivalent capacitance of the combination shown in the figure is

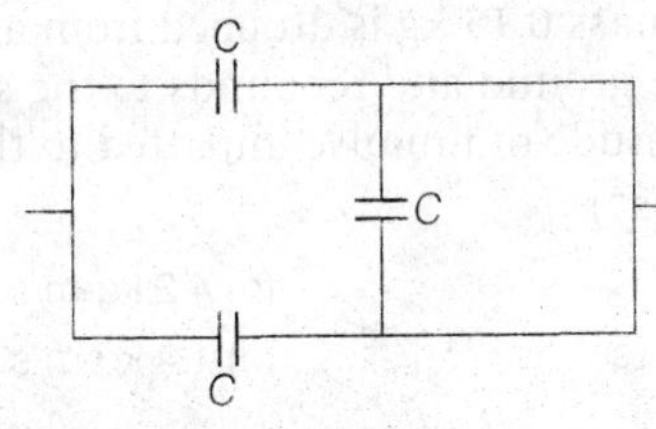

(a) 3C (b) 2C

(c) $\frac{C}{2}$ (d) $\frac{3C}{2}$

23. A lens of large focal length and large aperture is best suited as an objective of an astronomical telescope, since

(a) a large aperture contributes to the quality and visibility of the images

(b) a large area of the objective ensures better light gathering power

(c) a large aperture provides a better resolution

(d) All of the above

24. Two charged spherical conductors of radii R_1 and R_2 are connected by a wire. Then, the ratio of surface charge densities of the spheres (σ_1/σ_2) is

(a) $\frac{R_1}{R_2}$ (b) $\frac{R_2}{R_1}$

(c) $\sqrt{\left(\frac{R_1}{R_2}\right)}$ (d) $\frac{R_1^2}{R_2^2}$

25. A spring is stretched by 5 cm by a force 10 N. The time period of the oscillations when a mass of 2 kg is suspended by it is

(a) 0.0628 s (b) 6.28 s

(c) 3.14 s (d) 0.628 s

26. For a plane electromagnetic wave propagating in x-direction, which one of the following combination gives the correct possible directions for electric field (E) and magnetic field (B) respectively?

(a) $\hat{j}+\hat{k}, \hat{j}+\hat{k}$ (b) $-\hat{j}+\hat{k}, -\hat{j}-\hat{k}$

(c) $\hat{j}+\hat{k}, -\hat{j}-\hat{k}$ (d) $-\hat{j}+\hat{k}, -\hat{j}+\hat{k}$

27. The escape velocity from the Earth's surface is v. The escape velocity from the surface of another planet having a radius, four times that of Earth and same mass density is

(a) v (b) $2v$

(c) $3v$ (d) $4v$

28. In a potentiometer circuit, a cell of emf 1.5 V gives balance point at 36 cm length of wire. If another cell of emf 2.5 V replaces the first cell, then at what length of the wire, the balance point occurs?

(a) 60 cm (b) 21.6 cm

(c) 64 cm (d) 62 cm

29. The velocity of a small ball of mass M and density d when dropped in a container filled with glycerine becomes constant after some time. If the density of glycerine is $d/2$, then the viscous force acting on the ball will be

(a) $\frac{Mg}{2}$ (b) Mg

(c) $\frac{3}{2}Mg$ (d) $2Mg$

30. A parallel plate capacitor has a uniform electric field **E** in the space between the plates. If the distance between the plates is d and the area of each plate is A, the energy stored in the capacitor is (ε_0 = permittivity of free space).

(a) $\frac{1}{2}\varepsilon_0 E^2$ (b) $\varepsilon_0 EAd$

(c) $\frac{1}{2}\varepsilon_0 E^2 Ad$ (d) $\frac{E^2 Ad}{\varepsilon_0}$

31. The electron concentration in an n-type semiconductor is the same as hole concentration in a p-type semiconductor. An external field (electric) is applied across each of them. Compare the currents in them.

(a) Current in n-type = Current in p-type
(b) Current in p-type > Current in n-type
(c) Current in n-type> Current in p-type
(d) No current will flow in p-type. current will only flow in n-type

32. Consider the following statements (A) and (B) and identify the correct answer.

(A) A Zener diode is connected in reverse bias, when used as a voltage regulator.

(B) The potential barrier of p-n junction lies between 0.1 V to 0.3 V.

(a) (A) and (B) both are correct.
(b) (A) and (B) both are incorrect.
(c) (A) is correct and (B) is incorrect.
(d) (A) is incorrect but (B) is correct.

33. Polar molecules are the molecules

(a) having zero dipole moment
(b) acquire a dipole moment only in the presence of electric field due to displacement of charges.
(c) acquire a dipole moment only when magnetic field is absent
(d) having a permanent electric dipole moment

34. If E and G respectively denote energy and gravitational constant. then $\frac{E}{G}$ has the dimensions of

(a) $[M^2]\ [L^{-1}]\ [T^0]$
(b) $[M]\ [L^{-1}]\ [T^{-1}]$
(c) $[M]\ [L^0]\ [T^0]$
(d) $[M^2]\ [L^{-2}]\ [T^{-1}]$

35. Water falls from a height of 60 m at the rate of 15 kg/s to operate a turbine. The losses due to frictional force are 10% of the input energy. How much power is generated by the turbine? ($g = 10\ m/s^2$)

(a) 10.2 kW
(b) 8.1 kW
(c) 12.3 kW
(d) 7.0 kW

Section-B

36. A car starts from rest and accelerates at $5\ m/s^2$. At $t = 4s$, a ball is dropped out of a window by a person sitting in the car. What is the velocity and acceleration of the ball at $t = 6$ s? (Take, $g = 10\ m/s^2$)

(a) 20 m/s, 5 m/s^2
(b) 20 m/s, 0
(c) $20\sqrt{2}$ m/s, 0
(d) $20\sqrt{2}$ m/s, 10 m/s^2

37. For the given circuit, the input digital signals are applied at the terminals A, B and C. What would be the output at the terminal?

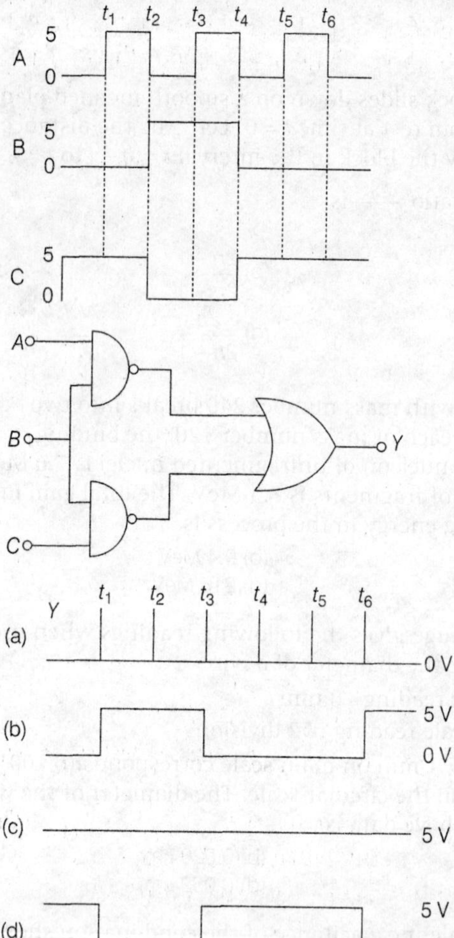

38. A ball of mass 0.15 kg is dropped from a height 10 m, strikes the ground and rebounds to the same height. The magnitude of impulse imparted to the ball is nearly ($g = 10\ m/s^2$)

(a) 0
(b) 4.2 kg-m/s
(c) 2.1 kg-m/s
(d) 1.4 kg-m/s

39. A uniform rod of length 200 cm and mass 500 g is balanced on a wedge placed at 40 cm mark. A mass of 2 kg is suspended from the rod at 20 cm and another unknown mass m is suspended from the rod at 160 cm mark as shown in the figure. Find the value of m such that the rod is in equilibrium. ($g = 10\ m/s^2$)

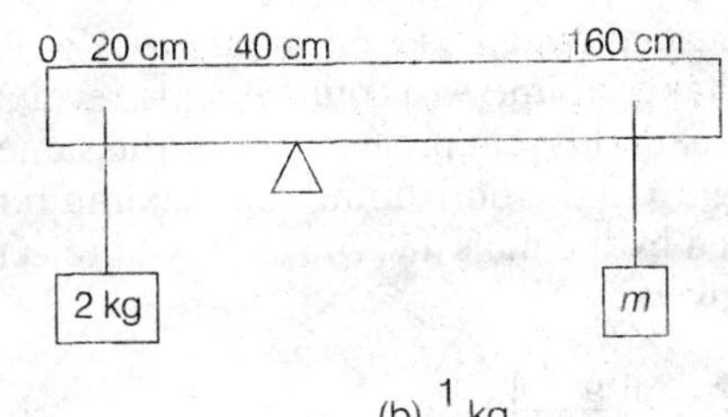

(a) $\frac{1}{2}$ kg
(b) $\frac{1}{3}$ kg
(c) $\frac{1}{6}$ kg
(d) $\frac{1}{12}$ kg

40. A point object is placed at a distance of 60 cm from a convex lens of focal length 30 cm. If a plane mirror were put perpendicular to the principal axis of the lens and at a distance of 40 cm from it, the final image would be formed at a distance of

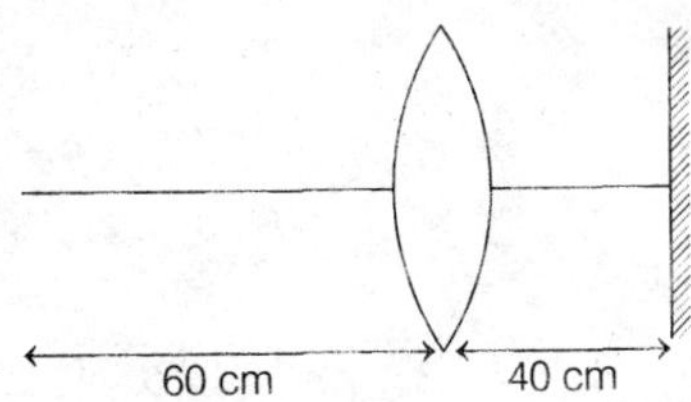

(a) 20 cm from the lens, it would be a real image
(b) 30 cm from the lens, it would be a real image
(c) 30 cm from the plane mirror, it would be a virtual image
(d) 20 cm from the plane mirror, it would be a virtual image

41. A step down transformer connected to an AC mains supply of 220 V is made to operate at 11 V, 44 W lamp. Ignoring power losses in the transformer, what is the current in the primary circuit ?

(a) 0.2 A
(b) 0.4 A
(c) 2 A
(d) 4 A

42. Three resistors having resistances r_1, r_2 and r_3 are connected as shown in the given circuit. The ratio i_3/i_1 of currents in terms of resistances used in the circuit is

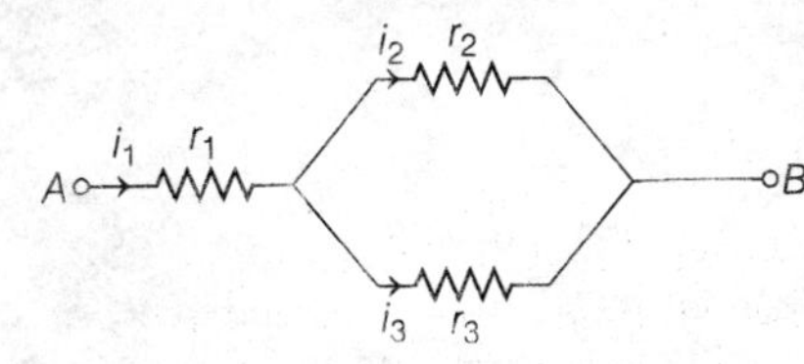

(a) $\frac{r_1}{r_2 + r_3}$
(b) $\frac{r_2}{r_2 + r_3}$
(c) $\frac{r_1}{r_1 + r_2}$
(d) $\frac{r_2}{r_1 + r_3}$

43. In the product

$$\mathbf{F} = q(\mathbf{v} \times \mathbf{B}) = q\mathbf{v} \times (B\hat{\mathbf{i}} + B\hat{\mathbf{j}} + B_0\hat{\mathbf{k}})$$

For $q = 1$ and $\mathbf{v} = 2\hat{\mathbf{i}} + 4\hat{\mathbf{j}} + 6\hat{\mathbf{k}}$ and $\mathbf{F} = 4\hat{\mathbf{i}} - 20\hat{\mathbf{j}} + 12\hat{\mathbf{k}}$

What will be the complete expression for **B**?

(a) $-8\hat{\mathbf{i}} - 8\hat{\mathbf{j}} - 6\hat{\mathbf{k}}$
(b) $-6\hat{\mathbf{i}} - 6\hat{\mathbf{j}} - 8\hat{\mathbf{k}}$
(c) $8\hat{\mathbf{i}} + 8\hat{\mathbf{j}} - 6\hat{\mathbf{k}}$
(d) $6\hat{\mathbf{i}} + 6\hat{\mathbf{j}} - 8\hat{\mathbf{k}}$

44. A particle of mass m is projected with a velocity $v = kv_e (k < 1)$ from the surface of the Earth.
(Here, v_e = escape velocity)
The maximum height above the surface reached by the particle is

(a) $R\left(\frac{k}{1-k}\right)^2$
(b) $R\left(\frac{k}{1+k}\right)^2$
(c) $\frac{R^2 k}{1+k}$
(d) $\frac{Rk^2}{1-k^2}$

45. Twenty seven drops of same size are charged at 220 V each. They combine to form a bigger drop. Calculate the potential of the bigger drop.

(a) 660 V
(b) 1320 V
(c) 1520 V
(d) 1980 V

46. A series L-C-R circuit containing 5.0 H inductor, 80 μF capacitor and 40 Ω resistor is connected to 230 V variable frequency AC source. The angular frequencies of the source at which power transferred to the circuit is half the power at the resonant angular frequency are likely to be

(a) 25 rad/s and 75 rad/s
(b) 50 rad/s and 25 rad/s
(c) 46 rad/s and 54 rad/s
(d) 42 rad/s and 58 rad/s

47. A uniform conducting wire of length $12a$ and resistance R is wound up as a current (I) carrying coil in the shape of

1. an equilateral triangle of side a.
2. a square of side a.

The magnetic dipole moments of the coil in each case respectively are

(a) $\sqrt{3}\, Ia^2$ and $3\, Ia^2$
(b) $3\, Ia^2$ and Ia^2
(c) $3\, Ia^2$ and $4\, Ia^2$
(d) $4\, Ia^2$ and $3\, Ia^2$

48. From a circular ring of mass M and radius R, an arc corresponding to a 90° sector is removed. The moment of inertia of the remaining part of the ring about an axis passing through the centre of the ring and perpendicular to the plane of the ring is K times MR^2. Then, the value of K is

(a) $\frac{3}{4}$ (b) $\frac{7}{8}$

(c) $\frac{1}{4}$ (d) $\frac{1}{8}$

49. Two conducting circular loops of radii R_1 and R_2 are placed in the same plane with their centres coinciding. If $R_1 >> R_2$, the mutual inductance M between them will be directly proportional to

(a) $\frac{R_1}{R_2}$ (b) $\frac{R_2}{R_1}$

(c) $\frac{R_1^2}{R_2}$ (d) $\frac{R_2^2}{R_1}$

50. A particle moving in a circle of radius R with a uniform speed takes a time T to complete one revolution.
If this particle were projected with the same speed at an angle θ to the horizontal, the maximum height attained by it equals $4R$. The angle of projection θ is then given by

(a) $\theta = \cos^{-1}\left(\frac{gT^2}{\pi^2 R}\right)^{1/2}$

(b) $\theta = \cos^{-1}\left(\frac{\pi^2 R}{gT^2}\right)^{1/2}$

(c) $\theta = \sin^{-1}\left(\frac{\pi^2 R}{gT^2}\right)^{1/2}$

(d) $\theta = \sin^{-1}\left(\frac{2gT^2}{\pi^2 R}\right)^{1/2}$

Answers

1.	(d)	2.	(a)	3.	(b)	4.	(a)	5.	(c)	6.	(b)	7.	(c)	8.	(a)	9.	(c)	10.	(d)
11.	(d)	12.	(b)	13.	(b)	14.	(c)	15.	(b)	16.	(d)	17.	(b)	18.	(c)	19.	(b)	20.	(d)
21.	(d)	22.	(b)	23.	(d)	24.	(b)	25.	(d)	26.	(b)	27.	(d)	28.	(a)	29.	(a)	30.	(c)
31.	(c)	32.	(c)	33.	(d)	34.	(a)	35.	(b)	36.	(d)	37.	(c)	38.	(b)	39.	(d)	40.	(d)
41.	(a)	42.	(b)	43.	(b)	44.	(d)	45.	(d)	46.	(c)	47.	(a)	48.	(a)	49.	(d)	50.	(d)

Answer *with* Explanations

1. *(d)* The given circuit diagram as shown below

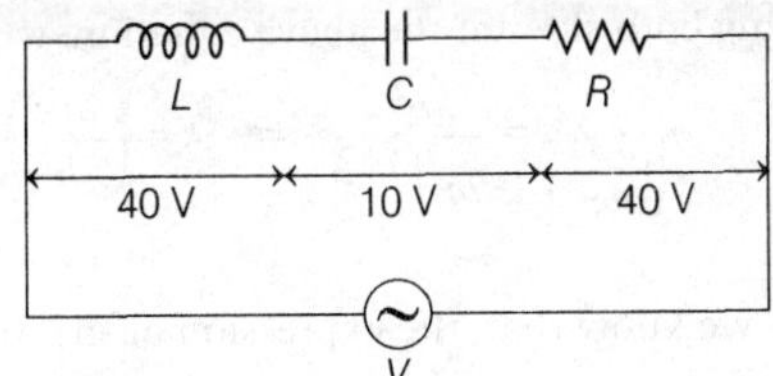

Given,

$$V_L = 40\text{ V},\ V_C = 10\text{ V}$$

and $$V_R = 40\text{ V}$$

The amplitude of the current flowing in the *L-C-R* series circuit,

$$I_0 = 10\sqrt{2}\text{ A} \quad \ldots(\text{i})$$

We know that, rms current in the *L-C-R* series circuit,

$$I_{\text{rms}} = \frac{I_0}{\sqrt{2}}$$

$$\Rightarrow \quad I_{\text{rms}} = \frac{10\sqrt{2}}{\sqrt{2}} \quad [\text{from Eq. (i)}]$$

$$\Rightarrow \quad I_{\text{rms}} = 10\text{ A}$$

$$\therefore \quad V_{\text{rms}} = \sqrt{V_R^2 + (V_L - V_C)^2}$$

$$\Rightarrow \quad V_{\text{rms}} = \sqrt{(40)^2 + (40-10)^2}$$

$$\Rightarrow \quad V_{\text{rms}} = 50\text{ V}$$

The impedance of the *L-C-R* series circuit,

$$Z = \frac{V_{\text{rms}}}{I_{\text{rms}}} \Rightarrow Z = \frac{50\text{ V}}{10\text{ A}} \quad \text{or} \quad Z = 5\Omega$$

2. *(a)* Given, the refractive index of the glass, $n_2 = \sqrt{3}$

The refractive index of the air, $n_1 = 1$

The path of ray incident on the prism is as shown below

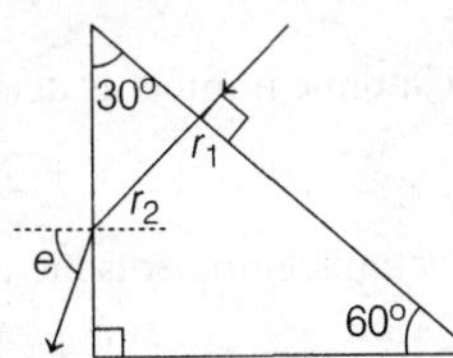

From the given figure, $r_1 = 0°$

As, $$A = r_1 + r_2$$

where, *A* is the angle of prism .

$$30° = 0° + r_2 \Rightarrow r_2 = 30°$$

Using the Snell's law, in glass and air interference,

$$n_2 \sin\theta_2 = n_1 \sin\theta_1$$

$$\Rightarrow \quad n_2 \sin r_2 = n_1 \sin e$$

$$\Rightarrow \quad \sqrt{3}\sin 30° = 1 \times \sin e \Rightarrow \sin e = \frac{\sqrt{3}}{2}$$

$$\Rightarrow \quad \sin e = \sin 60° \Rightarrow e = 60°$$

3. *(b)* We know that, the direction of electric dipole moment is from negative charge to positive charge.

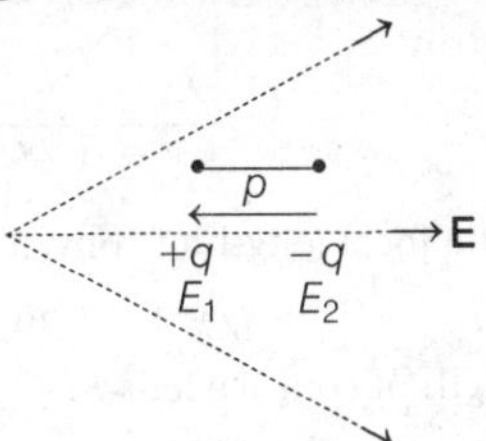

The strength of the electric field at $+q$ is greater than that of $-q$ charge, i.e. $|E_1| > |E_2|$.

So, the net force on the dipole act towards the right side.

We know that, a system always moves to decrease in its potential energy.

So, the given dipole move towards right side as its potential energy will decreases.

4. *(a)* Given, AC source voltage,

$$V = V_0 \sin\omega t \quad \ldots(\text{i})$$

We know that,

$$Q = CV \quad \ldots(\text{ii})$$

Here, *Q* is the charge on the capacitor,

C is the capacitance of the capacitor,

V is the AC source voltage.

On differentiate Eq. (ii) w.r.t. time, we get

$$\frac{dQ}{dt} = \frac{d(CV)}{dt}$$

$$\Rightarrow \quad \frac{dQ}{dt} = \frac{Cd(V_0 \sin\omega t)}{dt} \quad [\text{from Eq. (i)}]$$

$$\Rightarrow \quad \frac{dQ}{dt} = C\omega V_0 \cos\omega t$$

As we know, the displacement current,

$$I_d = \frac{dQ}{dt} \Rightarrow I_d = V_0\,\omega\,C\cos\omega t$$

5. *(c)* Magnetic field inside the conducting cylindrical cable,

$$B = \frac{\mu_0 I}{2\pi R^2} r$$

Here, *R* is the radius of the cylindrical cable,

r is the distance from the axis of the cylinder,

I is the current carrying in the cylindrical cable.

$$\Rightarrow \quad B \propto r$$

$\therefore$ The graph of magnetic field *B* with *r* is a straight line passing through origin.

For a point outside the cylinder,

$$B = \frac{\mu_0 I}{2\pi R} \Rightarrow B \propto \frac{1}{R}$$

The graph of magnetic field (*B*) with *r* is a rectangular hyperbola passing through the outer surface of the cylinder.

$\therefore$ The variation of the magnetic field B due to the cable with the distance r from the axis of the cylindrical cable is as shown in the figure.

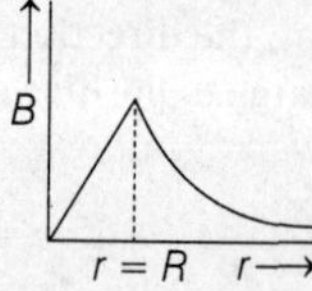

6. *(b)* Given, the focal length of convex lens A,

$$f_1 = +20 \text{ cm}$$

The focal length of concave lens B,

$$f_2 = -5 \text{ cm}$$

The convex lens is the converging lens and the concave lens is the diverging lens.

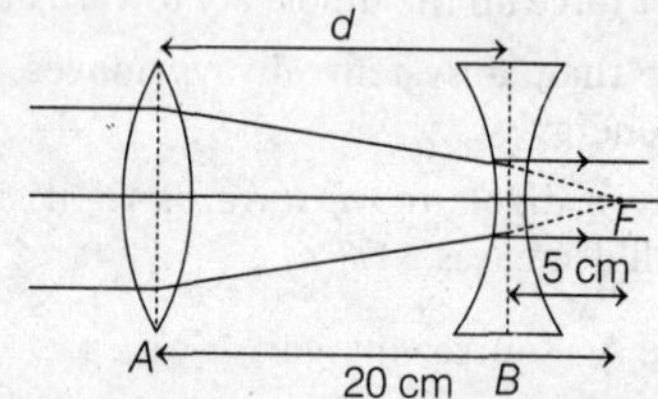

When the parallel beam of light passes through the convex lens, it converges at the focal point F and the distance between lens A to F point is 20 cm.

Now, after emerging from the lens B, the beam is still parallel in nature. So, the net focal length of the lens A and B will be infinite.

As we know,

$$\frac{1}{f} = \frac{1}{f_1} + \frac{1}{f} - \frac{d}{f_1 f_2}$$

$$\Rightarrow \quad \frac{1}{\infty} = \frac{1}{20} - \frac{1}{5} + \frac{d}{20 \times 5}$$

$$\Rightarrow \quad \frac{3}{20} = \frac{d}{20 \times 5}$$

or $\quad d = 3 \times 5 = 15 \text{ cm}$

7. *(c)* We know that, de-Broglie wavelength,

$$\lambda_d = \frac{h}{mv}$$

Kinetic energy of the photoelectrons,

$$\text{KE} = \frac{1}{2} mv^2 \Rightarrow v = \sqrt{\frac{2 \times \text{KE}}{m}}$$

Here, m is the mass of photoelectrons.

Substituting the value of v in de-Broglie wavelength equation, we get

$$\lambda_d = \frac{h}{\sqrt{2m\text{KE}}} \quad \text{.... (i)}$$

Since, work-function of photosensitive surface is negligible, hence the kinetic energy of photoelectron is equal to the energy of the photon of electromagnetic wave,

$$\text{KE} = \frac{1}{2} mv^2 = \frac{hc}{\lambda}$$

Substituting in the Eq. (i), we get

$$\lambda_d = \frac{h}{\sqrt{2m\left(\frac{hc}{\lambda}\right)}}$$

Squaring both sides of the above equation, we get

$$\lambda_d^2 = \frac{h^2}{2m\left(\frac{hc}{\lambda}\right)} \Rightarrow \lambda = \left(\frac{2mc}{h}\right) \times \lambda_d^2$$

8. *(a)* As we know that, the expression of the drift velocity,

$$v_d = \frac{eE}{m} \tau$$

Here, e is the electric charge,

E is the electric field,

m is the mass of an electron,

τ is the relaxation time.

Consider the conductor having length l, area of the cross-section A and the charge density n.

Electrical resistivity, $\rho = \dfrac{m}{ne^2\tau}$

Rearranging the above expression,

Relaxation period, $\quad \tau = \dfrac{m}{ne^2\rho}$

As we know that, the expression of current density,

$$J = \frac{I}{A} = \frac{neAv_d}{A} = nev_d$$

Again, $\dfrac{E}{J} = \dfrac{E}{\sigma E} = \dfrac{1}{\sigma} = \rho$

$\therefore$ Electrical resistivity, $\rho = \dfrac{E}{J}$

The correct match is A$\rightarrow$3, B$\rightarrow$4, C$\rightarrow$1, D$\rightarrow$2.

9. *(c)* As we know that,

In α-decay, the atomic number is decreased by 2 units.

$$X_Z^A \longrightarrow {}_{Z-2}^{A-4}Y + {}_2^4\text{He}$$

In β^+-decay, the atomic number is decreased by 1 unit.

$$X_Z^A \longrightarrow {}_{Z-1}^{A}Y + {}_{+1}^{0}e + \bar{\nu}$$

In β^--decay, the atomic number is increased by 1 unit.

$$X_Z^A \longrightarrow {}_{Z+1}^{A}Y + {}_{-1}^{0}e + \bar{\nu}$$

From the above relations, the spontaneous decay given in question can be written as

$$X_Z^A \xrightarrow{\beta^+} {}_{Z-1}B \xrightarrow{\alpha} {}_{Z-3}C \xrightarrow{\beta^-} {}_{Z-2}D$$

The possible decay particles in the sequence are β^+, α, β^-.

10. *(d)* The four resistances have equal length, equal cross-sectional area and same material.

So, $\quad R_1 = R_2 = R_3 = R_4 = R \quad$ (say)

Given, the effective resistance,

$$R_{\text{eq}} = 0.25\,\Omega$$

For parallel arrangement,

$$\frac{1}{R_{eq}} = \frac{1}{R_1} + \frac{1}{R_2} + \frac{1}{R_3} + \frac{1}{R_4}$$

$$\Rightarrow \frac{1}{R_{eq}} = \frac{1}{R} + \frac{1}{R} + \frac{1}{R} + \frac{1}{R}$$

$$\Rightarrow \frac{1}{0.25\Omega} = \frac{4}{R} \Rightarrow R = 1\,\Omega$$

For series combination,

$$R_{eq} = R_1 + R_2 + R_3 + R_4$$

$$\Rightarrow R_{eq} = R + R + R + R$$

$$\Rightarrow R_{eq} = 4R \Rightarrow R_{eq} = 4(1) = 4\Omega$$

11. **(d)** Let the particle at height S from the surface of the Earth is as shown.

Given, at height x, kinetic energy

= 3 (potential energy)

$$\Rightarrow \text{KE} = 3mgx$$

At height S, total energy, TE = PE + KE

$$\text{TE} = mgS + 0 = mgS$$

At height x, total energy,

$$\text{TE} = \text{PE} + \text{KE}$$

$$\text{TE} = mgx + 3mgx$$

$$mgS = 4mgx$$

$$\Rightarrow x = \frac{S}{4} \quad \text{...(i)}$$

Now, we shall determine the speed of the particle at this height.

As, $\text{KE} = 3 \times mgx$

$$\text{KE} = 3 \times mg\frac{S}{4} \quad \text{[from Eq. (i)]}$$

$$\frac{1}{2}mv^2 = \frac{3}{4}mgS$$

$$\Rightarrow v = \sqrt{\frac{3}{2}gS}$$

12. **(b)** Given, the half-life of a radioactive nuclide, $t_{1/2} = 100$ h

As we know,

$$A = \frac{A_0}{2^{t/t_{1/2}}}$$

Here, A_0 is the original activity of the nuclide,

A is the activity of the nuclide after time t.

$$\Rightarrow \frac{A}{A_0} = 2^{-t/t_{1/2}} = 2^{-\frac{150}{100}} = 2^{-3/2} = \frac{1}{2\sqrt{2}}$$

So, the fraction of original activity that will remain after 150 h will be $\frac{1}{2\sqrt{2}}$.

13. **(b)** In first conditions;

Given, the initial temperature of the cup of coffee, $T_i = 90°C$

The final temperature of the cup of coffee, $T_f = 80°C$

The time taken to drop the temperature 90°C to 80°C is t.

The temperature of the surrounding, $T_0 = 20°C$

Using the Newton's law of cooling,

$$\text{rate of cooling} = \frac{dT}{dt} = K\left[\frac{T_i + T_f}{2} - T_0\right]$$

Substituting the values in the above equation, we get

$$\frac{90-80}{t} = K\left[\frac{90+80}{2} - 20\right]$$

$$\Rightarrow \frac{10}{t} = K[65] \Rightarrow K = \frac{2}{13t}$$

In second conditions;

The initial temperature of the cup of coffee, $T_i' = 80°C$

The final temperature of the cup of coffee, $T_f' = 60°C$.

Using the Newton's law of cooling,

$$\text{rate of cooling} = \frac{dT}{dt} = K\left[\frac{T'_i + T'_f}{2} - T_0\right]$$

Substituting the values in the above equation, we get

$$\frac{80-60}{t_1} = \frac{2}{13t}\left[\frac{60+80}{2} - 20\right]$$

$$\frac{20}{t_1} = \frac{2}{13t}[50] \Rightarrow t_1 = \frac{13}{5}t$$

14. **(c)** Given, the monochromatic light of the wavelength, $\lambda = 600$ nm

The power of the source,

$$P = 3.3 \times 10^{-3}\text{ W}$$

We know that, $P = \frac{nhc}{\lambda}$

Here, P is the power of the source,

n is the number of photons per second,

h is the Planck's constant,

c is the speed of the light in vacuum,

λ is the wavelength of the monochromatic light.

Substituting the values in the above equation, we get

$$3.3 \times 10^{-3} = \frac{n \times 6.6 \times 10^{-34} \times 3 \times 10^8}{600 \times 10^{-9}}$$

$$\Rightarrow n = 10^{16}$$

15. **(b)** In simple harmonic motion, both kinetic energy and potential energy attains their maximum value two times in one complete oscillation. Hence, frequency of kinetic energy and potential energy is 2 for one complete oscillation. So, the frequency of the potential energy of a body executing SHM with frequency n is $2n$.

16. **(d)** Given, the current carrying in infinitely long straight conductor, $I = 5$A

The electron is moving with speed, $v = 10^5$ m/s

The perpendicular distance between the electron and the conductor, r = 20 cm = 0.20 m

Now, the magnetic field experience by electron due to infinitely long straight conductor,

$$B = \frac{\mu_0 I}{2\pi r} \Rightarrow B = \frac{4\pi \times 10^{-7} \times 5}{2\pi (0.20)}$$

$$\Rightarrow \quad B = 5 \times 10^{-6}\ T$$

The magnetic force experience by an electron,

$$F = evB$$

Here, e is the charge of an electron,
v is the velocity of an electron,
B is the magnetic field experience by an electron.
Substituting the values in the above equation, we get

$$F = 1.6 \times 10^{-19} \times 10^5 \times 5 \times 10^{-6}$$

$$F = 8 \times 10^{-20}\ N$$

17. *(b)* Given, fundamental physical quantities are force $[F]$, acceleration $[a]$ and time $[T]$.

Now, we shall determine the dimensions of the energy.

Energy depends on force, acceleration and time as,

$$[E] = [F]^a [a]^b [T]^c$$

$$\Rightarrow \quad [ML^2T^{-2}] = [MLT^{-2}]^a [LT^{-2}]^b [T]^c$$

$$\Rightarrow \quad [ML^2T^{-2}] = [M]^a [L]^{a+b} [T]^{-2a-2b+c}$$

Comparing the powers of M, L and T on both sides, we get

$$a = 1, a + b = 2 \text{ and } -2a - 2b + c = -2$$

$$\Rightarrow \quad 1 + b = 2$$

$$\Rightarrow \quad b = 1,$$

$$\Rightarrow \quad -2(1) - 2(1) + c = -2 \Rightarrow c = 2$$

The dimensions of the energy are $[F^1][a]^1[T]^2$.

18. *(c)* We know that, the rms speed of the gas molecules,

$$v_{rms} = \sqrt{3RT/M}$$

Here, T is the temperature of the gas,

R is the universal gas constant,

M is the molar mass of the gas.

Pressure exerted by an ideal gas,

$$p = \frac{1}{3} nm\bar{v}^2$$

Here, n is the number of moles,

m is the mass of the gas,

$\bar{v}$ is the average speed of the gas molecules.

The average kinetic energy of a molecule,

$$KE_{av} = \frac{3}{2} k_B T$$

Here, k_B is the Boltzmann constant,

T is the temperature of the gas.

For diatomic gas, degree of freedom, $f = 5$

As, total internal energy of 1 mole of diatomic gas,

$$\Delta U = \frac{nfRT}{2}$$

$$\Rightarrow \quad \Delta U = \frac{1(5)RT}{2} \Rightarrow \Delta U = \frac{5RT}{2}$$

The correct match is A $\rightarrow$ 2, B $\rightarrow$ 1, C $\rightarrow$ 4 and D $\rightarrow$ 3.

19. *(b)* Distance covered nth seconds is s_n.

Distance covers in $(n+1)$ th seconds is s_{n+1}.

Initial velocity of small block, $u = 0$

Distance cover in nth seconds,

$$s_n = u + \frac{a}{2}(2n-1)$$

$$\Rightarrow \quad s_n = 0 + \frac{a}{2}(2n-1)$$

$$\Rightarrow \quad s_n = \frac{a}{2}(2n-1) \quad \text{...(i)}$$

Distance cover in $(n+1)$th seconds,

$$s_{n+1} = u + \frac{a}{2}[2(n+1) - 1]$$

$$\Rightarrow \quad s_{n+1} = 0 + \frac{a}{2}(2n + 2 - 1)$$

$$\Rightarrow \quad s_{n+1} = \frac{a}{2}(2n+1) \quad \text{...(ii)}$$

On dividing Eq. (i) by Eq. (ii), we get

$$\frac{s_n}{s_{n+1}} = \frac{\frac{a}{2}(2n-1)}{\frac{a}{2}(2n+1)}$$

$$\Rightarrow \quad \frac{s_n}{s_{n+1}} = \frac{(2n-1)}{(2n+1)}$$

20. *(d)* A nucleus with mass number 240 breaks into two fragment each of mass number 120.

$$X^{240} \longrightarrow Y^{120} + Z^{120}$$

Given, the binding energy per nucleon of unfragmented nuclei, $X = 7.6$ MeV

The binding energy per nucleon of fragmented nuclei, $Y = Z = 8.5$ MeV

Now, we shall determine the total gain in binding energy.

Gain in binding energy = Binding energy of products – Binding energy of reactants

Gain in binding energy $= 2 \times 120 \times 8.5 - 240 \times 7.6 = 216$ MeV

21. *(d)* Given, the main scale reading, MSR = 0

The circular scale reading, CSR = 52 divisions

Now, we shall determine the least count of the screw gauge,

$$LC = \frac{p}{n}$$

Here, p is the pitch of the screw,

n is the number of circular divisions in one complete revolution.

$$LC = \frac{1}{100}\ \text{mm}$$

$$\Rightarrow \quad LC = 0.01\ \text{mm} \Rightarrow LC = 0.001\ \text{cm}$$

Thus, the least count of the screw gauge is 0.001 cm.

Therefore, diameter of the wire of screw gauge,

$$D = MSR + (CSR \times LC)$$

$$\Rightarrow \quad D = 0 + (52 \times 0.001)$$

$$\Rightarrow \quad D = 0.052\ \text{cm}$$

22. *(b)* Consider the nodes be *A, B, E* and *F* as shown in the figure

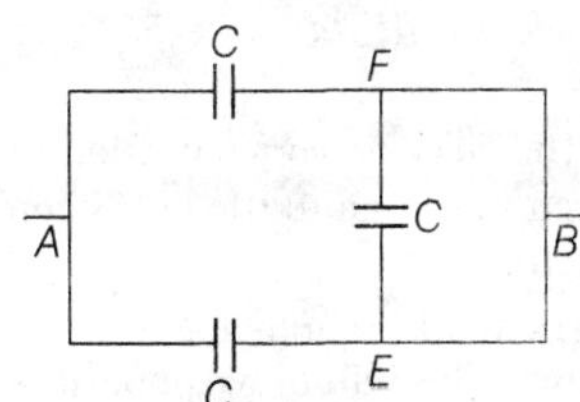

The potential at node *A* is equal to the potential at node *B*.

Similarly, the potential at *F* is equal to the potential at node *E*.

So, there is no potential difference between the *EF* arms, thus, no current (hence, charge) will flow in the circuit.

So, *EF* behave as open circuit.

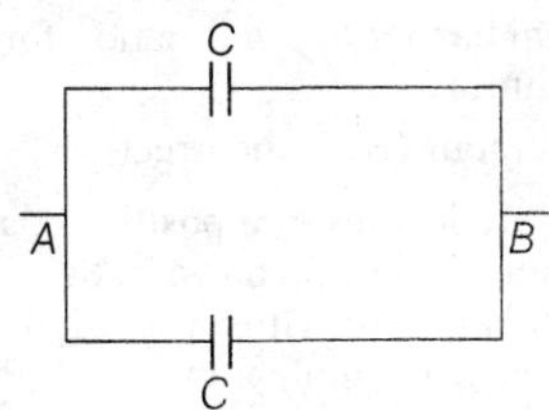

Now, the two capacitors are arranged in parallel.

The net equivalent capacitors,

$$C_{eq} = C_1 + C_2$$

$$\Rightarrow \quad C_{eq} = C + C$$

$$\Rightarrow \quad C_{eq} = 2C$$

23. *(d)* The objective of an astronomical telescope has large focal length and large aperture. Because the lens used is convex lens and the magnification of an astronomical telescope is directly proportional to the focal length of the objective lens.

This large aperture also contributes to the better quality and visibility of the images. Thus, it provides better resolution.

Due to large focal length of the objective, it covers large area which ensures better light gathering power.

Thus, all options (a), (b) and (c) are correct.

24. *(b)* When two charged spherical conductors are connected by a conducting wire, then the potential becomes same in both the spherical conductor, i.e.

$V_1 = V_2$

$$\Rightarrow \quad \frac{Kq_1}{R_1} = \frac{Kq_2}{R_2} \Rightarrow \frac{q_1}{q_2} = \frac{R_1}{R_2} \quad \ldots\text{(i)}$$

As we know that, the surface charge density of the charged spherical conductor,

$$\sigma = \frac{q}{4\pi R^2}$$

where, q is the charge on the spherical conductor,

r is the radius of the spherical conductor.

$$\therefore \quad \frac{\sigma_1}{\sigma_2} = \frac{\frac{q_1}{4\pi R_1^2}}{\frac{q_2}{4\pi R_2^2}}$$

$$\Rightarrow \quad \frac{\sigma_1}{\sigma_2} = \frac{q_1}{q_2}\frac{R_2^2}{R_1^2}$$

$$\Rightarrow \quad \frac{\sigma_1}{\sigma_2} = \frac{R_1}{R_2}\frac{R_2^2}{R_1^2} \quad \text{[from Eq. (i)]}$$

$$\Rightarrow \quad \frac{\sigma_1}{\sigma_2} = \frac{R_2}{R_1}$$

25. *(d)* Given, the mass of suspended, $m = 2\,\text{kg}$

The spring is stretched, $x = 5\text{ cm} = 0.05\text{ m}$

The constant force applied on the spring, $F = 10\text{ N}$

As we know that, spring force,

$$F = kx \Rightarrow 10\text{ N} = k\,(0.05\text{ m})$$

$$\Rightarrow \quad k = 200\text{ N/m}$$

Now, time period of the oscillation,

$$T = 2\pi\sqrt{\frac{m}{k}} \Rightarrow T = 2\pi\sqrt{\frac{2}{200}}$$

Time period, $T = 0.628\text{ s}$

26. *(b)* We know that, in electromagnetic wave, the electric field (E) and magnetic field (B) are perpendicular to each other,

$$\mathbf{E}\cdot\mathbf{B} = 0$$

Consider the option (a);

$$(\hat{\mathbf{j}} + \hat{\mathbf{k}})\cdot(\hat{\mathbf{j}} + \hat{\mathbf{k}}) = 1 + 1 = 2 \neq 0$$

So, it is incorrect option.

Consider the option (b);

$$(-\hat{\mathbf{j}} + \hat{\mathbf{k}})\cdot(-\hat{\mathbf{j}} - \hat{\mathbf{k}}) = 1 - 1 = 0$$

Hence, it satisfies the condition $\mathbf{E}\cdot\mathbf{B} = 0$

Similarly, options (c) and (d) are incorrect.

So, the correct option is (b).

27. *(d)* We know that,

escape velocity from Earth's surface, $v_e = \sqrt{\frac{2GM_e}{R_e}}$

where, G is the gravitational constant,

R_e is the radius of the Earth,

M_e is the mass of the Earth.

Also, $\quad \text{density} = \frac{\text{mass}}{\text{volume}}$

$$\Rightarrow \quad \text{Mass} = \text{Density} \times \text{Volume}$$

$$\text{or} \quad M_e = \rho \times V$$

$$\text{or} \quad M_e = \rho \times \frac{4}{3}\pi R_e^3 \quad \left(\because V = \frac{4}{3}\pi R_e^3\right)$$

Substituting the values in the escape velocity expression, we get

$$v_e = \sqrt{\frac{2G\rho \times \frac{4}{3}\pi R_e^3}{R_e}}$$

$$v_e = \sqrt{2G\rho \times \frac{4}{3}\pi R_e^2} \quad \ldots\text{(i)}$$

Now, we shall determine the escape velocity for another planet. Given, radius of another planet is 4 times the radius of the Earth,

$$\Rightarrow \quad v_p = \sqrt{2G\rho \times \frac{4}{3}\pi R_p^2}$$

$$v_p = \sqrt{2G\rho \times \frac{4}{3}\pi(4R_e)^2} \quad (\because R_p = 4R_e)$$

$$v_p = 4\sqrt{2G\rho \times \frac{4}{3}\pi(R_e)^2} \quad \text{...(ii)}$$

On dividing Eq. (ii) by Eq. (i), we get

$$\frac{v_p}{v_e} = \frac{4\sqrt{2G\rho \times \frac{4}{3}\pi(R_e)^2}}{\sqrt{2G\rho \times \frac{4}{3}\pi R_e^2}}$$

$$\Rightarrow \quad v_p = 4v_e = 4v$$

28. *(a)* Given, length of balancing point, $L_1 = 36$ cm

$$E_1 = 1.5\text{V}$$
$$E_2 = 2.5\text{V}$$

We know that,

Potential gradient $= \frac{E}{L}$

$$\because \quad \frac{E_1}{L_1} = \frac{E_2}{L_2}$$

where, L_2 is the length of the balancing point for cell of emf E_2.

Substituting the values in the above equation, we get

$$\frac{1.5}{36} = \frac{2.5}{L_2} \Rightarrow L_2 = 60 \text{ cm}$$

29. *(a)* Given, the density of the small ball is d

The mass of the small ball is M

The density of the glycerine is $d/2$.

As we know that,

viscous force = weight – buoyant force

Viscous force $= Vd_1g - Vd_2g$

Here, V is the volume of submerged bodies,

g is the acceleration due to gravity,

d_1 is the density of the small ball,

d_2 is the density of the glycerine,

$$d_1 = d \text{ and } d_2 = d/2$$

Substituting the given values in the viscous force expression, we get

Viscous force $= Vdg - V\frac{d}{2}g$

Viscous force $= \frac{Vdg}{2} = \frac{Mg}{2} \quad (\because M = d \times V)$

30. *(c)* We know that, capacitance of a parallel plate capacitor,

$$C = \frac{A\varepsilon_0}{d} \quad \text{...(i)}$$

The relation between the potential difference (V) and electric field (E),

$$V = Ed \quad \text{...(ii)}$$

The energy stored in the capacitor,

$$U = \frac{1}{2}CV^2$$

$$U = \frac{1}{2}\left(\frac{\varepsilon_0 A}{d}\right)(Ed)^2 \quad [\because \text{from Eqs. (i) and (ii)}]$$

$$U = \frac{1}{2}(\varepsilon_0 A)(E)^2 d = \frac{1}{2}\varepsilon_0 E^2 Ad$$

31. *(c)* Given, the electron concentration in n- type semiconductor is equal to the hole's concentration in p-type semiconductor.

When electric field is applied across the semiconductor, the electrons and holes will move opposite to each other. The mobility of n-type semiconductor is greater than mobility of p-type semiconductor.

So, the current in the n-type semiconductor is greater than current in the p-type semiconductor.

32. *(c)* Zener diode is a type of special p-n junction diode that operates in reverse bias. Thus, it is used as a voltage regulator. So, the statement (A) is correct.

The potential barrier of p-n junction for silicon is 0.6-0.7 V and for germanium is 0.2-0.35 V.

So, the statement (B) is incorrect.

33. *(d)* In polar molecules, the positive charge and negative charge do not overlap each other. So, the total charge on the polar molecule is zero. Thus, these types of molecules have permanent electric dipole moment. e.g. Water is polar molecule.

34. *(a)* The dimensions of energy $[E] = [F] \cdot [d]$

$$\Rightarrow \quad [E] = [\text{MLT}^{-2}][\text{L}] \Rightarrow [E] = [\text{ML}^2\text{T}^{-2}]$$

As we know that, the expression of gravitational force,

$$F = \frac{GM_1M_2}{r^2} \Rightarrow G = \frac{Fr^2}{M_1M_2}$$

$$\therefore \quad [G] = \frac{[F][r^2]}{[M_1][M_2]} \Rightarrow [G] = \frac{[\text{MLT}^{-2}][\text{L}]^2}{[\text{M}][\text{M}]}$$

$$\Rightarrow \quad [G] = [\text{M}^{-1}\text{L}^3\text{T}^{-2}]$$

The dimensions of

$$\frac{E}{G} = \frac{[\text{ML}^2\text{T}^{-2}]}{[\text{M}^{-1}\text{L}^3\text{T}^{-2}]} \Rightarrow \left[\frac{E}{G}\right] = [\text{M}^2\text{L}^{-1}\text{T}^0]$$

35. *(b)* Given, the flow rate of the water, $\frac{m}{t} = 15$ kg/s

The height of the water fall, $h = 60$ m

Loss due to frictional force = 10%

The power used in the turbine

= (100 – 10) % = 90%

The acceleration due to gravity, $g = 10 \text{ m/s}^2$

We know that, power generated by the turbine

$$= \text{change in potential energy} = 0.90 \frac{mgh}{t}$$

$$= 0.90 \times 15 \times 10 \times 60 = 8100 \text{ W} = 8.1 \text{ kW}$$

36. *(d)* Given, the initial velocity of a car, $u = 0$

The acceleration of a car, $a = 5 \text{ m/s}^2$

At $\quad t = 4$ s, $v = u + at$

$$\Rightarrow \quad v = 0 + (5)4 \Rightarrow v = 20 \text{ m/s}$$

Thus, the final velocity of car at $t = 4$ s is 20 m/s.

At $t = 4$ s, the ball is dropped out of a window by a person sitting in the car.

The velocity of the ball in the x-direction,

$v_x = 20$ m/s (due to the car)

Therefore, in the y-direction, the acceleration is equal to the acceleration due to gravity,

$$a_y = g = 10 \text{ m/s}^2$$

The velocity of the ball in the y-direction,

$$v_y = u + a_y t \quad \Rightarrow \quad v_y = 0 + 10 \times 2$$

$$\Rightarrow \quad v_y = 20 \text{ m/s}$$

Thus, the velocity of the ball in y-direction is 20 m/s.

The net velocity at $t = 6$s,

$$v = \sqrt{v_x^2 + v_y^2} \quad \Rightarrow \quad v = \sqrt{(20)^2 + (20)^2}$$

$$\Rightarrow \quad v = 20\sqrt{2} \text{ m/s}$$

Thus, the velocity of the ball at $t = 6$ s is $20\sqrt{2}$ m/s.

and there is no acceleration in the x-direction, $a_x = 0 \text{ ms}^{-2}$

In y-direction, $a_y = 10 \text{ ms}^{-2}$

Now, we shall determine the net acceleration at $t = 6$ s,

$$a = \sqrt{a_x^2 + a_y^2} \Rightarrow a = \sqrt{(0) + (10)^2} \quad \Rightarrow a = 10 \text{ ms}^{-2}$$

37. **(c)** Output of the given logic circuit is given as

$$Y = \overline{AB} + \overline{BC}$$

Truth table for the given input waveforms A, B and C.

Time interval	A	B	C	AB	BC	$\overline{AB}$	$\overline{BC}$	$Y = \overline{AB} + \overline{BC}$
$0\text{-}t_1$	0	0	1	0	0	1	1	1
$t_1\text{-}t_2$	1	0	1	0	0	1	1	1
$t_2\text{-}t_3$	0	1	0	0	0	1	1	1
$t_3\text{-}t_4$	1	1	0	1	0	0	1	1
$t_4\text{-}t_5$	0	0	1	0	0	1	1	1
$t_5\text{-}t_6$	1	0	1	0	0	1	1	1

Hence, output waveform will be 5V.

Thus, option (c) is correct.

38. **(b)** Given, the mass of the ball dropped from the height, $m = 0.15$ kg

The height from the ball dropped, $h = 10$ m

We know that,

$$|\text{Impulse}| = m\,|\Delta\bar{v}|$$

where, $\Delta\bar{v} = v_2 - v_1$

Here, v_2 is velocity reaches to the same height,

v_1 is velocity just before striking to the ground.

For case (1), ball dropped from the 10m height and strikes to the ground.

Now, the velocity of the ball just before striking to the ground is

$$v_1 = -\sqrt{2gh}$$

$$\Rightarrow \quad v_1 = -\sqrt{2(10)(10)}$$

$$\Rightarrow \quad v_1 = -10\sqrt{2} \text{ m/s}$$

For case (2), ball rebounds to the same height.

The velocity with which the ball just reaches to the same height,

$$v_2 = \sqrt{2gh}$$

$$\Rightarrow \quad v_2 = \sqrt{2(10)(10)}$$

$$\Rightarrow \quad v_2 = 10\sqrt{2} \text{ m/s}$$

Now, magnitude of the impulse imparted to the ball,

$$|\text{Impulse}| = m\,|\Delta\bar{v}|$$

$$= 0.15\,|10\sqrt{2} - (-10\sqrt{2})|$$

$$= 0.15|2 \times 10\sqrt{2}|$$

$$= 4.2 \text{ kg - m/s}$$

39. **(d)** Given, the length of a uniform rod, $L = 200$ cm

The wedge is placed at the mark = 40 cm

The balanced mass placed at 100 cm mark on wedge = 500 g = 0.5 kg

The mass suspended from the rod at 20 cm distance from the end, $M = 2$ kg

Another unknown mass suspended from the rod at 160 cm distance from the end = m

Let's draw the diagram of the uniform rod suspended with mass.

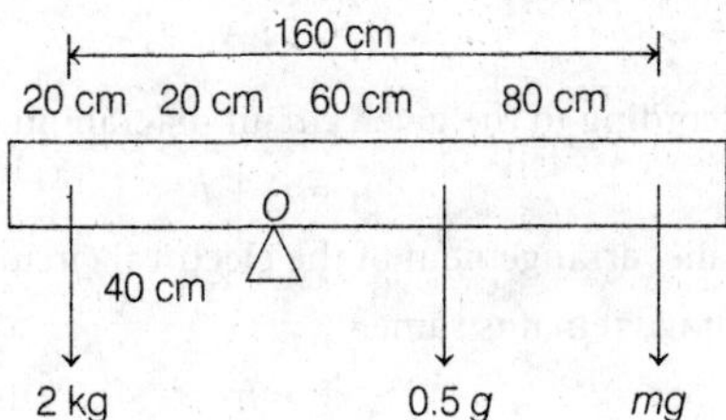

As we know in equilibrium net moment of force is equals to zero.

$$\Rightarrow \quad 0.5\,g\,(0.60) + mg\,(1.20) - 2g\,(0.20) = 0$$

$$\Rightarrow \quad 0.3 + 1.20\,m - 0.4 = 0$$

$$\Rightarrow \quad 1.20m = 0.1 \quad \Rightarrow \quad m = \frac{1}{12} \text{ kg}$$

40. **(d)** Given, the focal length of the convex lens, $f = +30$ cm

The object distance from the lens, $u = -60$ cm

The image formed by the lens be at distance v, then by using lens formula,

$$\frac{1}{f} = \frac{1}{v} - \frac{1}{u}$$

$$\frac{1}{+30} = \frac{1}{v} - \frac{1}{(-60)}$$

$$\Rightarrow \quad \frac{1}{+30} = \frac{60 + v}{60v}$$

$$\Rightarrow \quad 2v = 60 + v \quad \Rightarrow \quad v = 60 \text{ cm}$$

Let's draw the ray diagram of the convex lens and mirror.

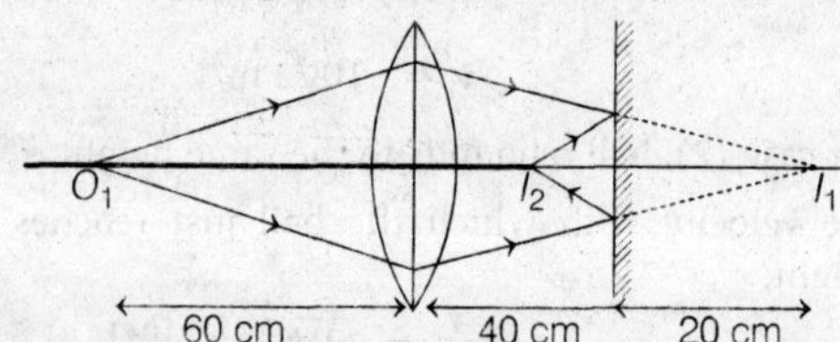

This real image will now act as a virtual object for the mirror. Thus, a real image from the mirror is formed 20 cm in front of the mirror. Hence, at 20 cm distance from the lens. Also, this real image acts as an object for lens for final image.

Again by using lens formula,

$$\frac{1}{v} + \frac{1}{20} = \frac{1}{30}$$

or $\quad v = -60$ cm from the lens

i.e., 20 cm from the plane mirror and virtual in nature.

41. *(a)* Given, the main supply line voltage in transformer,

$$V = 220 \text{ V}$$

The rating of the lamp = 11 V, 44 W

We know that,

$$P = VI_P \qquad \ldots(i)$$

Here, P is the power that operates the lamp,

V is the supply line voltage,

I_P is the primary current in the transformer.

From Eq. (i), we get

$$\Rightarrow \quad 44 = I_P \times 220$$

$$\Rightarrow \quad I_P = 0.2 \text{ A}$$

42. *(b)* According to the given circuit diagram in question,

$$i_1 = i_2 + i_3 \qquad \ldots(i)$$

In parallel arrangement of the electrical circuit, the voltage remains same.

$$\therefore \quad V = ir \qquad \text{(using Ohm's law)}$$

$$\Rightarrow \quad i_2 r_2 = i_3 r_3$$

$$\Rightarrow \quad i_2 = \frac{i_3 r_3}{r_2}$$

Substituting the values in the Eq. (i), we get

$$i_1 = \frac{i_3 r_3}{r_2} + i_3 \Rightarrow \frac{i_1}{i_3} = \frac{r_3}{r_2} + 1$$

$$\Rightarrow \quad \frac{i_1}{i_3} = \frac{r_3 + r_2}{r_2} \Rightarrow \frac{i_3}{i_1} = \frac{r_2}{r_3 + r_2}$$

43. *(b)* Given, velocity, $\mathbf{v} = 2\hat{\mathbf{i}} + 4\hat{\mathbf{j}} + 6\hat{\mathbf{k}}$

Force, $\mathbf{F} = 4\hat{\mathbf{i}} - 20\hat{\mathbf{j}} + 12\hat{\mathbf{k}}$

As we know,

$$\mathbf{F} = q\,(\mathbf{v} \times \mathbf{B})$$

Here, $q = 1$ (given)

Substituting the values in the above equation, we get

$$4\hat{\mathbf{i}} - 20\hat{\mathbf{j}} + 12\hat{\mathbf{k}} = (1)\,[(2\hat{\mathbf{i}} + 4\hat{\mathbf{j}} + 6\hat{\mathbf{k}}) \times (B\hat{\mathbf{i}} + B\hat{\mathbf{j}} + B_0\hat{\mathbf{k}})]$$

$$4\hat{\mathbf{i}} - 20\hat{\mathbf{j}} + 12\hat{\mathbf{k}} = \begin{pmatrix} \hat{\mathbf{i}} & \hat{\mathbf{j}} & \hat{\mathbf{k}} \\ 2 & 4 & 6 \\ B & B & B_0 \end{pmatrix}$$

$$\Rightarrow 4\hat{\mathbf{i}} - 20\hat{\mathbf{j}} + 12\hat{\mathbf{k}} = \hat{\mathbf{i}}(4B_0 - 6B) - \hat{\mathbf{j}}(2B_0 - 6B) + \hat{\mathbf{k}}\,(2B - 4B)$$

Comparing the LHS and RHS of the above equation, we get

$\hat{\mathbf{i}}$ terms:

$$4B_0 - 6B = 4 \qquad \ldots(i)$$

$\hat{\mathbf{j}}$ terms:

$$2B_0 - 6B = 20 \qquad \ldots(ii)$$

$\hat{\mathbf{k}}$ terms:

$$2B - 4B = 12$$

$$\Rightarrow \quad B = -6$$

Substituting the value of B in the Eq. (ii), we get

$$2B_0 - 6(-6) = 20 \Rightarrow B_0 = -8$$

Thus, the magnetic field vector, $B = -6\hat{\mathbf{i}} - 6\hat{\mathbf{j}} - 8\hat{\mathbf{k}}$

44. *(d)* Given, the mass of the particle $= m$

The velocity of the projected particle, $v = kv_e$

Initial energy at the time of projection

$$= \frac{1}{2}mv^2 - \frac{GMm}{R}$$

Final energy at the maximum height h from surface of the Earth $= \frac{1}{2}mv^2 - \frac{GMm}{R+h}$

$$= \frac{1}{2}m(0)^2 - \frac{GMm}{R+h}$$

($\because$ final velocity is zero at height h from the surface of the Earth)

$$= -\frac{GMm}{R+h}$$

Using the law of conservation of energy,

initial energy at the time of projection = final energy at the maximum height h from the surface of the Earth

$$\frac{1}{2}mv^2 - \frac{GMm}{R} = -\frac{GMm}{R+h}$$

Substituting the values in the above equation, we get

$$\frac{1}{2}m(kv_e)^2 - \frac{GMm}{R} = -\frac{GMm}{R+h}$$

$$\Rightarrow \quad \frac{1}{2}mk^2\left(2\frac{GM}{R}\right) - \frac{GMm}{R} = -\frac{GMm}{R+h} \qquad \left(\because v_e = \sqrt{\frac{2GM}{R}}\right)$$

$$\Rightarrow \quad \frac{k^2}{R} - \frac{1}{R} = -\frac{1}{R+h}$$

$$\Rightarrow \quad \frac{1}{R+h} = \frac{1}{R} - \frac{k^2}{R}$$

$$\Rightarrow \quad \frac{R}{1-k^2} = R + h$$

$$\Rightarrow \quad h = \frac{R}{1-k^2} - R$$

$$\Rightarrow \quad h = R\left(\frac{1}{1-k^2} - 1\right)$$

$$\Rightarrow \quad h = R\left(\frac{1-1+k^2}{1-k^2}\right)$$

$$\Rightarrow \quad h = R\left(\frac{k^2}{1-k^2}\right)$$

45. *(d)* Given, the number of small drops, $n = 27$

Potential on each charged drop, $V = 220$ V

Consider r be the radius of the small drops and R be the radius of the bigger drop.

According to the question, 27 small drops of same size combine to form a bigger drop. So, the volume remains same, i.e.

$$V_{\text{bigger}} = 27 \times V_{\text{small}}$$

$$\Rightarrow \quad \frac{4}{3}\pi R^3 = 27 \times \frac{4}{3}\pi r^3$$

$$\Rightarrow \quad R^3 = 27 \times r^3 \Rightarrow R = 3r$$

Now, the potential of the small drop,

$$V = \frac{Kq}{r} \quad \ldots\text{(i)}$$

Here, q is the charge on the small drop.

The potential of the bigger drop,

$$V' = \frac{KQ}{R}$$

Here, Q is the charge on the bigger drop.

The charge on the bigger drop is 27 times the charge on the smaller drop, i.e. $Q = 27q$

So, the potential of the bigger drop,

$$V' = \frac{K \times 27q}{3r}$$

$$\Rightarrow \quad V' = 9\frac{Kq}{r}$$

$$V' = 9V \quad \text{[from Eq. (i)]}$$

$$= 9 \times 220 = 1980 \text{ V}$$

46. *(c)* Given, in the L-C-R series circuit, $L = 5$ H,

$C = 80\ \mu$F, $R = 40\ \Omega$

Supply voltage, $V = 230$ V

We know that, resonance frequency, $\omega_r = \frac{1}{\sqrt{LC}}$

Substituting the values in the above equation, we get

$$\omega_r = \frac{1}{\sqrt{5 \times 80 \times 10^{-6}}} = 50 \text{ rad/s}$$

Therefore, the angular frequencies of the source at which power transferred to the circuit is half the power at the resonant angular frequency are

$$\omega = \omega_r \pm \Delta\omega \quad \ldots\text{(i)}$$

We know that,

$$\Delta\omega = \frac{R}{2L} \Rightarrow \Delta\omega = \frac{40}{2(5)} \Rightarrow \Delta\omega = 4$$

Using the Eq. (i), we get

$$\omega = \omega_r \pm \Delta\omega$$

$$\omega = (50 \pm 4) \text{ rad/s}$$

So, the angular frequency is likely to be 46 rad/s and 54 rad/s.

47. *(a)* Given, the length of a uniform conducting wire, $L = 12a$

The resistance of a uniform conducting wire $= R$

We know that, magnetic dipole moment, $M = nIA$

Here, I is the current in the loop,

A is the area of the coil,

n is the number of loops.

For case (1):

An equilateral triangle of side a.

Total wire length $= n \times$ Perimeter of the triangle

$$12a = n \times 3a \Rightarrow n = 4$$

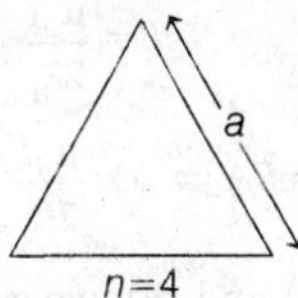

Area of the triangle, $A = \frac{\sqrt{3}}{4}a^2$

Magnetic dipole moment, $M = nIA$

$$\Rightarrow \quad M = 4I \times \frac{\sqrt{3}}{4}a^2$$

$$\Rightarrow \quad M = \sqrt{3}Ia^2$$

For case (2) :

A square of side a.

Total wire length $= n \times$ Perimeter of the square

$$12a = n \times 4a \Rightarrow n = 3$$

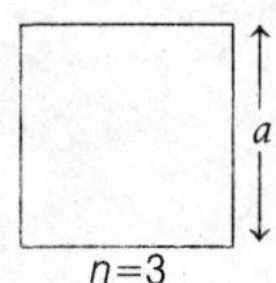

Area of the square loop, $A = a^2$

Magnetic dipole moment, $M = nIA \Rightarrow M = 3Ia^2$

48. *(a)* Given, the mass of the circular ring $= M$

The radius of the circular ring $= R$

We know that, the moment of inertia of the circular ring, $I = MR^2$

An arc corresponding to a 90° sector in the circular ring is removed, means one-fourth part of circular ring is removed. Then, the remaining mass of the circular ring,

$$M' = \frac{M}{4}$$

The new moment of inertia, $I' = M'R^2 = \frac{MR^2}{4}$

Now, the moment of inertia of the remaining part,

$$I'' = I - I' = MR^2 - \frac{MR^2}{4}$$

$$\Rightarrow \quad I'' = \frac{3MR^2}{4}$$

Comparing with $I'' = KMR^2$

The value of $K = 3/4$.

49. ***(d)*** Since, both conducting circular loops are in same plane and their centres are coinciding.

Hence, magnetic flux, $\phi = Mi$ ...(i)

Here, M is the mutual inductance.

Also, the magnetic flux, $\phi = BA$

Here, B is the magnetic field and

$A (= \pi R_2^2)$ is the area of the inner circular loop.

If the current passing through the outer loop is i, then the magnetic field,

$$B = \frac{\mu_0 i}{2R_1}$$

Magnetic flux, $\phi = BA \Rightarrow \phi = \frac{\mu_0 i}{2R_1} \pi R_2^2$ ...(ii)

Comparing Eqs. (i) and (ii), we get

$$M = \frac{\mu_0}{2R_1} \pi R_2^2$$

Thus, the mutual inductance is directly proportional to the $\frac{R_2^2}{R_1}$.

50. ***(d)*** Given, the radius of the circular path $= R$

The time taken by the particle to complete one revolution $= T$

When the particle is projected with the same speed (by which it is moving in circular orbit) at angle θ to the horizontal, the maximum height attained it is given as

$$H_{max} = \frac{u^2 \sin^2 \theta}{2g} \quad \text{...(i)}$$

$$H_{max} = 4R \quad \text{(given)}$$

Also, we know that,

speed of the particle in circular path, $u = \frac{2\pi R}{T}$

Substituting the values in the Eq. (i), we get

$$4R = \frac{\left(\frac{2\pi R}{T}\right)^2 \sin^2 \theta}{2g}$$

$$\Rightarrow \quad \sin \theta = \left(\frac{2gT^2}{\pi^2 R}\right)^{1/2}$$

$$\Rightarrow \quad \theta = \sin^{-1}\left(\frac{2gT^2}{\pi^2 R}\right)^{1/2}$$

NEET

SOLVED PAPER 2022

NEET SOLVED PAPER 2022

nstruction

This question paper contains 50 Multiple Choice Questions of Physics, divided into two Sections; section A and section B.

Section A contains 35 questions and all questions are compulsory.

Section B contains 15 questions out of which 10 questions are to be attempted.

Each question carries 4 marks.

ection-A

1. If a soap bubble expands, the pressure inside the bubble

(a) increases

(b) remains the same

(c) is equal to the atmospheric pressure

(d) decreases.

2. The graph which shows the variation of the de-Broglie wavelength (λ) of a particle and its associated momentum (p) is

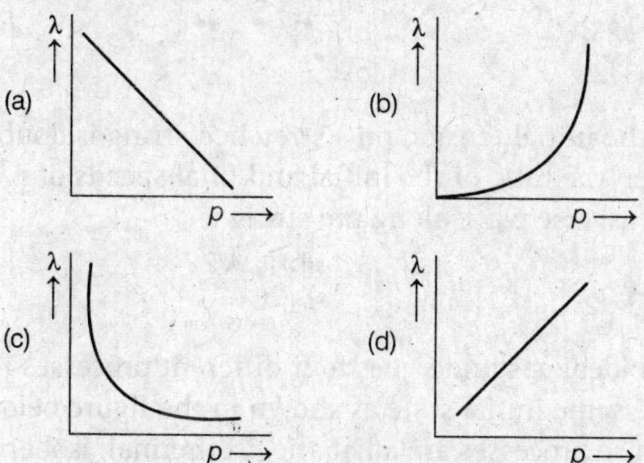

3. A body of mass 60 g experiences a gravitational force of 3.0 N, when placed at a particular point. The magnitude of the gravitational field intensity at that point is

(a) 50 N/kg (b) 20 N/kg

(c) 180 N/kg (d) 0.05 N/kg

4. Given below are two statements

Statement I Biot-Savart's law gives us the expression for the magnetic field strength of an infinitesimal current element (Idl) of a current carrying conductor only.

Statement II Biot-Savart's law is analogous to Coulomb's inverse square law of charge q, with the former being related to the field produced by a scalar source, Idl while the latter being produced by a vector source, q. In light of above statements choose the most appropriate answer from the options given below

(a) Both Statement I and Statement II are incorrect.

(b) Statement I is correct and Statement II is incorrect.

(c) Statement I is incorrect and Statement II is correct.

(d) Both Statement I and Statement II are correct.

5. The ratio of the distances travelled by a freely falling body in the 1st, 2nd, 3rd and 4th second

(a) 1 : 4 : 9 : 16 (b) 1 : 3 : 5 : 7

(c) 1 : 1 : 1 : 1 (d) 1 : 2 : 3 : 4

6. In half wave rectification, if the input frequency is 60 Hz, then the output frequency would be

(a) 30 Hz (b) 60 Hz

(c) 120 Hz (d) zero

7. A spherical ball is dropped in a long column of a highly viscous liquid. The curve in the graph shown, which represents the speed of the ball (v) as a function of time (t) is

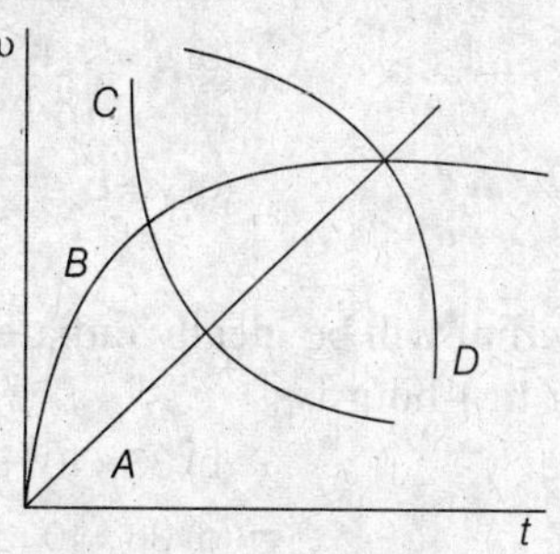

(a) B (b) C

(c) D (d) A

8. The angle between the electric lines of force and the equipotential surface is

(a) 45° (b) 90°
(c) 180° (d) 0°

9. As the temperature increases, the electrical resistance

(a) decreases for both conductors and semiconductors.
(b) increases for conductors but decreases for semiconductors.
(c) decreases for conductors but increases for semiconductors.
(d) increases for both conductors and semiconductors.

10. In the given nuclear reaction, the element X is

$$^{22}_{11}\text{Na} \longrightarrow X + e^{+} + \nu$$

(a) $^{23}_{10}\text{Ne}$ (b) $^{22}_{10}\text{Ne}$
(c) $^{22}_{12}\text{Mg}$ (d) $^{23}_{11}\text{Na}$

11. Let T_1 and T_2 be the energy of an electron in the first and second excited states of hydrogen atom, respectively. According to the Bohr's model of an atom, the ratio of $T_1 : T_2$ is:

(a) 4 : 1 (b) 4 : 9
(c) 9 : 4 (d) 1 : 4

12. The ratio of the radius of gyration of a thin uniform disc about an axis passing through its centre and normal to its plane to the radius of gyration of the disc about its diameter is

(a) $\sqrt{2} : 1$ (b) 4 : 1
(c) $1 : \sqrt{2}$ (d) 2 : 1

13. When light propagates through a material medium of relative permittivity $\in_r$ and relative permeability μ_r, the velocity of light, v is given by (c-velocity of light in vacuum)

(a) $v = \sqrt{\frac{\mu_r}{\in_r}}$ (b) $v = \sqrt{\frac{\in_r}{\mu_r}}$
(c) $v = \frac{c}{\sqrt{\in_r \mu_r}}$ (d) $v = c$

14. The energy that will be ideally radiated by a 100 kW transmitter in 1 hour is :

(a) 36×10^4 J (b) 36×10^5 J
(c) 1×10^5 J (d) 36×10^7 J

15. An electric lift with a maximum load of 2000 kg (lift + passengers) is moving up with a constant speed of 1.5 ms^{-1}. The frictional force opposing the motion is 3000 N. The minimum power delivered by the motor to the lift in watts is ($g = 10$ ms^{-2})

(a) 20000 (b) 34500
(c) 23500 (d) 23000

16. Two resistors of resistance, 100 Ω and 200 Ω are connected in parallel in an electrical circuit, The ratio of the thermal energy developed in 100 Ω to that in 200 Ω in a given time is

(a) 2 : 1
(b) 1 : 4
(c) 4 : 1
(d) 1 : 2

17. The peak voltage of the AC source is equal to

(a) the rms value of the AC source
(b) $\sqrt{2}$ times the rms value of the AC source
(c) $1/\sqrt{2}$ times the rms value of the AC source.
(d) the value of voltage supplied to the circuit.

18. A shell of mass m is at rest initially. It explodes into three fragments having mass in the ratio 2 : 2 : 1. If the fragments having equal mass fly off along mutually perpendicular directions with speed v, the speed of the third (lighter) fragment is

(a) $\sqrt{2}\,v$ (b) $2\sqrt{2}\,v$
(c) $3\sqrt{2}\,v$ (d) v

19. If the initial tension on a stretched string is doubled then the ratio of the initial and final speeds of a transverse wave along the string is

(a) $\sqrt{2} : 1$ (b) $1 : \sqrt{2}$
(c) 1 : 2 (d) 1 : 1

20. An ideal gas undergoes four different processes from the same initial state as shown in the figure below. Those processes are adiabatic, isothermal, isobaric and isochoric. The curve which represents the adiabatic process among 1, 2, 3 and 4 is

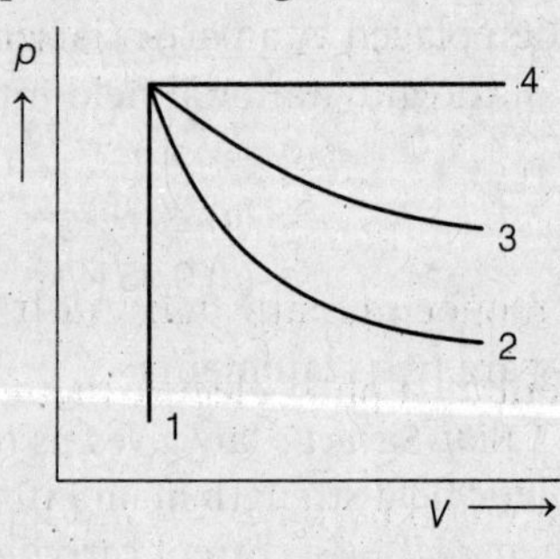

(a) 2 (b) 3
(c) 4 (d) 1

21. The angular speed of a fly wheel moving with uniform angular acceleration changes from 1200 rpm to 3120 rpm in 16 seconds. The angular acceleration in rad/s^2 is

(a) 4π (b) 12π

(c) 104π (d) 2π

22. Plane angle and solid angle have

(a) Dimensions but no units

(b) No units and no dimensions

(c) Both units and dimensions

(d) Units but no dimensions

23.

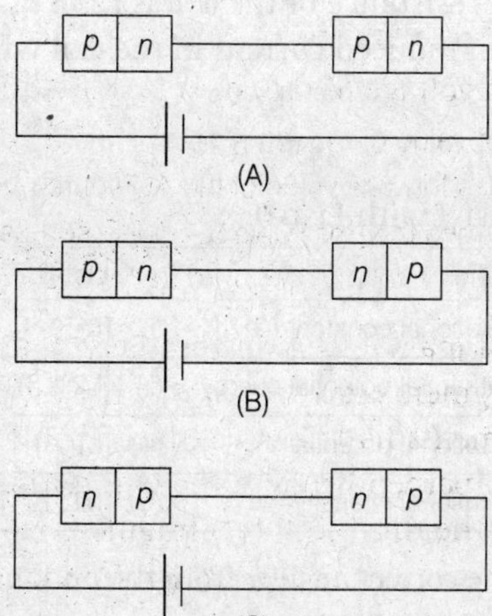

In the given circuits (A), (B) and (C) the potential drop across the two *p-n* junctions are equal in

(a) Circuit (B) only

(b) Circuit (C) only

(c) Both circuits (A) and (C)

(d) Circuit (A) only

24. In a Young's double slit experiment, a student observes 8 fringes in a certain segment of screen when a monochromatic light of 600 nm wavelength is used. If the wavelength of light is changed to 400 nm, then the number of fringes he would observe in the same region of the screen is

(a) 8 (b) 9

(c) 12 (d) 6

25. When two monochromatic lights of frequency, ν and $\frac{\nu}{2}$ are incident on a photoelectric metal, their stopping potential becomes $\frac{V_s}{2}$ and V_s respectively. The threshold frequency for this metal is :

(a) 3ν (b) $\frac{2}{3}\nu$

(c) $\frac{3}{2}\nu$ (d) 2ν

26. A square loop of side 1 m and resistance $1\,\Omega$ placed in a magnetic field of 0.5 T. If the plane of loop is perpendicular to the direction of magnetic field, the magnetic flux through the loop is

(a) 0.5 Wb (b) 1 Wb

(c) zero Wb (d) 2 Wb

27. Two hollow conducting spheres of radii R_1 and $R_2 (R_1 > R_2)$ have equal charges. The potential would be

(a) more on smaller sphere

(b) equal on both the spheres

(c) dependent on the material property of the sphere

(d) more on bigger sphere

28. A Copper wire of length 10m and radius $(10^{-2}/\sqrt{\pi})$ m has electrical resistance of $10\,\Omega$. The current density in the wire for an electric field strength of 10 (V / m) is

(a) 10^6 A / m^2 (b) 10^{-5} A / m^2

(c) 10^5 A / m^2 (d) 10^4 A / m^2

29. A long solenoid of radius 1 mm has 100 turns per mm. If 1A current flows in the solenoid, the magnetic field strength at the centre of the solenoid is

(a) 12.56×10^{-2} T (b) 12.56×10^{-4} T

(c) 6.28×10^{-4} T (d) 6.28×10^{-2} T

30. Two objects of mass 10 kg and 20 kg, respectively are connected to the two ends of a rigid rod of length 10 m with negligible mass. The distance of the center of mass of the system from the 10 kg mass is

(a) $\frac{20}{3}$ m (b) 10 m

(c) 5 m (d) $\frac{10}{3}$ m

31. A light ray falls on a glass surface of refractive index $\sqrt{3}$ at an angle 60°. The angle between the refracted and reflected rays would be

(a) 60° (b) 90°

(c) 120° (d) 30°

32. The dimensions $[MLT^{-2}A^{-2}]$ belong to the

(a) self inductance
(b) magnetic permeability
(c) electric permittivity
(d) magnetic flux

33. The displacement-time graph of two moving particles make angles of 30° and 45° with the X-axis as shown in the figure. The ratio of their respective velocity is

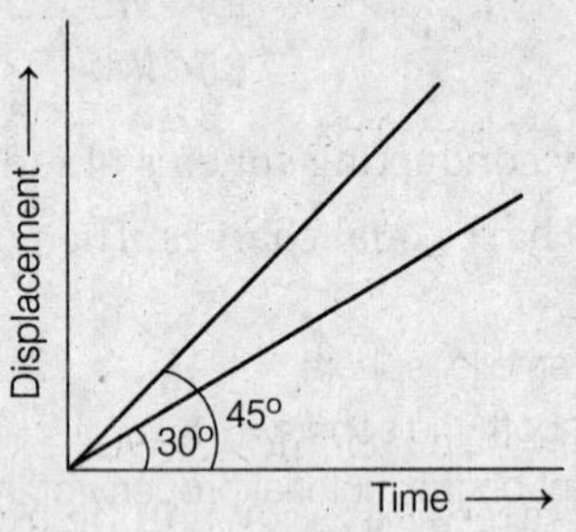

(a) 1 : 1 (b) 1 : 2
(c) $1 : \sqrt{3}$ (d) $\sqrt{3} : 1$

34. A biconvex lens has radii of curvature, 20cm each. If the refractive index of the material of the lens is 1.5, the power of the lens is

(a) + 20 D (b) + 5 D
(c) infinity (d) + 2 D

35. Match List - I with List - II

	List-I (Electromagnetic waves)		List-II (Wavelength)
(A)	AM radio waves	(i)	10^{-10}m
(B)	Microwaves	(ii)	10^{2}m
(C)	Infrared radiations	(iii)	10^{-2}m
(D)	X-rays	(iv)	10^{-4}m

Choose the correct answer from the options given below

(a) (A) - (iii), (B) - (ii), (C) - (i), (D) - (iv)
(b) (A) - (iii), (B) - (iv), (C) - (ii), (D) - (i)
(c) (A) - (ii), (B) - (iii), (C) - (iv), (D) - (i)
(d) (A) - (iv), (B) - (iii), (C) - (ii), (D) - (i)

Section-B

36. A nucleus of mass number 189 splits into two nuclei having mass number 125 and 64. The ratio of radius of two daughter nuclei, respectively is:

(a) 4 : 5 (b) 5 : 4
(c) 25 : 16 (d) 1 : 1

37. Two transparent media A and B are separated by a plane boundary. The speed of light in those media are 1.5×10^8 m/s and 2.0×10^8 m/s, respectively. The critical angle for a ray of light for these two media is

(a) $\sin^{-1}(0.750)$ (b) $\tan^{-1}(0.500)$
(c) $\tan^{-1}(0.750)$ (d) $\sin^{-1}(0.500)$

38. A big circular coil of 1000 turns and average radius 10m is rotating about its horizontal diameter at 2 rad s^{-1}. If the vertical component of earth's magnetic field at that place is 2×10^{-5}T and electrical resistance of the coil is 12.56 Ω, then the maximum induced current in the coil will be

(a) 1.5 A (b) 1 A
(c) 2 A (d) 0.25 A

39. Match List-I with List-II.

	List-I		List-II
(A)	Gravitational constant (G)	(i)	$[L^2T^{-2}]$
(B)	Gravitational potential energy	(ii)	$[M^{-1}L^3T^{-2}]$
(C)	Gravitational potential	(iii)	$[LT^{-2}]$
(D)	Gravitational intensity	(iv)	$[ML^2T^{-2}]$

Choose the correct answer from the options given below

(a) (A) - (ii), (B) - (iv), (C) - (i), (D) - (iii)
(b) (A) - (ii), (B) - (iv), (C) - (iii), (D) - (i)
(c) (A) - (iv), (B) - (ii), (C) - (i), (D) - (iii)
(d) (A) - (ii), (B) - (i), (C) - (iv), (D) - (iii)

40. Given below are two statements: One is labelled as Assertion (A) and the other is labelled as Reason (R)

Assertion (A) The stretching of a spring is determined by the shear modulus of the material of the spring.

Reason (R) A coil spring of copper has more tensile strength than a steel spring of same dimensions.

In the light of the above statements, choose the most appropriate answer from the options given below

(a) Both A and R are true and R is not the correct explanation of A.
(b) A is true but R is false.
(c) A is false but R is true.
(d) Both A and R are true and R is the correct explanation of A.

41. The area of a rectangular field (in m^2) of length 55.3m and breadth 25m after rounding off the value for correct significant digits is

(a) 1382 (b) 1382.5 (c) 14×10^2 (d) 138×10^1

42. 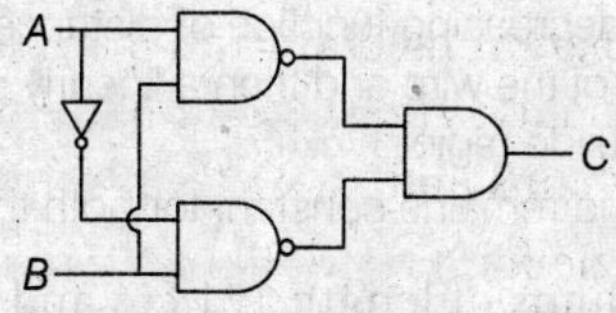

The truth table for the given logic circuit is

(a)

A	B	C
0	0	1
0	1	0
1	0	0
1	1	1

(b)

A	B	C
0	0	1
0	1	0
1	0	1
1	1	0

(c)

A	B	C
0	0	0
0	1	1
1	0	0
1	1	1

(d)

A	B	C
0	0	0
0	1	1
1	0	1
1	1	0

43. The volume occupied by the molecules contained in 4.5 kg water at STP, if the intermolecular forces vanish away is

(a) $5.6 \times 10^3 \text{ m}^3$ (b) $5.6 \times 10^{-3} \text{ m}^3$
(c) 5.6 m^3 (d) $5.6 \times 10^6 \text{ m}^3$

44. A wheatstone bridge is used to determine the value of unknown resistance X by adjusting the variable resistance Y as shown in the figure. For the most precise measurement of X, the resistances P and Q

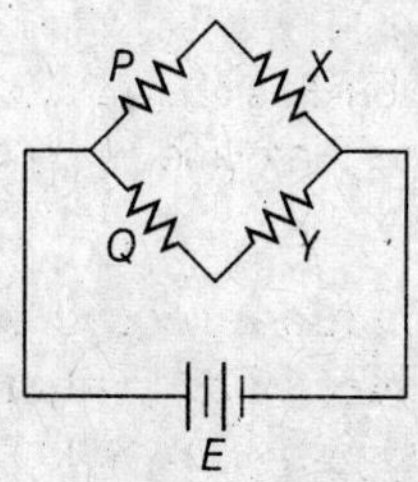

(a) should be approximately equal and are small
(b) should be very large and unequal
(c) do not play any significant role
(d) should be approximately equal to $2X$

45. A series L-C-R circuit with inductance 10 H, capacitance 10 μF, resistance 50Ω is connected to an AC source of voltage, $V = 200 \sin(100\, t)$ volt. If the resonant frequency of the LCR circuit is ν_0 and the frequency of the AC source is ν, then

(a) $\nu_0 = \nu = \dfrac{50}{\pi}$ Hz

(b) $\nu_0 = \dfrac{50}{\pi}$ Hz, $\nu = 50$ Hz

(c) $\nu = 100$ Hz; $\nu_0 = \dfrac{100}{\pi}$ Hz

(d) $\nu_0 = \nu = 50$ Hz

46. A capacitor of capacitance $C = 900$ pF is charged fully by 100 V battery B as shown in figure (a). Then, it is disconnected from the battery and connected to another uncharged capacitor of capacitance $C = 900$ pF as shown in figure (b). The electrostatic energy stored by the system (b) is

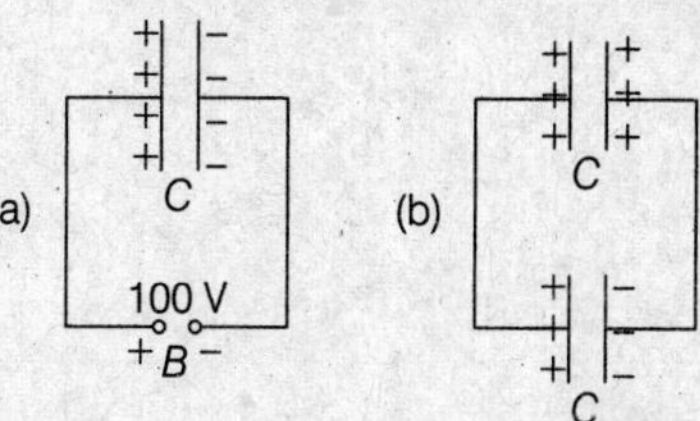

(a) 3.25×10^{-6} J (b) 2.25×10^{-6} J
(c) 1.5×10^{-6} J (d) 4.5×10^{-6} J

47. Two point charges $-q$ and $+q$ are placed at a distance of L, as shown in the figure.

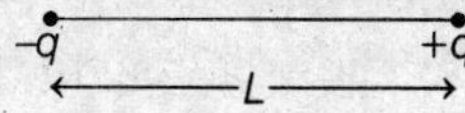

The magnitude of electric field intensity at a distance $R (R >> L)$ varies as

(a) $\dfrac{1}{R^3}$ (b) $\dfrac{1}{R^4}$
(c) $\dfrac{1}{R^6}$ (d) $\dfrac{1}{R^2}$

48. A ball is projected with a velocity, 10 ms^{-1}, at an angle of 60° with the vertical direction. Its speed at the highest point of its trajectory will be

(a) $5\sqrt{3}\ \text{ms}^{-1}$ (b) $5\ \text{ms}^{-1}$
(c) $10\ \text{ms}^{-1}$ (d) Zero

49. From Ampere's circuital law for a long straight wire of circular cross-section carrying a steady current, the variation of magnetic field in the inside and outside region of the wire is :

(a) a linearly increasing function of distance upto the boundary of the wire and then linearly decreasing for the outside region.

(b) a linearly increasing function of distance r upto the boundary of the wire and then decreasing one with $1/r$ dependence for the outside region.

(c) a linearly decreasing function of distance upto the boundary of the wire and then a linearly increasing one for the outside region.

(d) uniform and remains constant for both the regions.

50. Two pendulums of length 121 cm and 100 cm start vibrating in phase. At some instant, the two are at their mean position in the same phase. The minimum number of vibrations of the shorter pendulum after which the two are again in phase at the mean position is

(a) 9 (b) 10 (c) 8 (d) 11

Answers

1.	(d)	2.	(c)	3.	(a)	4.	(b)	5.	(b)	6.	(b)	7.	(a)	8.	(b)	9.	(b)	10.	(b)
11.	(c)	12.	(a)	13.	(c)	14.	(d)	15.	(b)	16.	(a)	17.	(b)	18.	(b)	19.	(b)	20.	(a)
21.	(a)	22.	(d)	23.	(c)	24.	(c)	25.	(*)	26.	(a)	27.	(a)	28.	(c)	29.	(a)	30.	(a)
31.	(b)	32.	(b)	33.	(c)	34.	(b)	35.	(c)	36.	(b)	37.	(a)	38.	(b)	39.	(a)	40.	(b)
41.	(c)	42.	(*)	43.	(c)	44.	(a)	45.	(a)	46.	(b)	47.	(a)	48.	(b)	49.	(b)	50.	(d)

Note (*) None of the option is correct.

Answer *with* Explanations

1. *(d)* We know that pressure inside the soap bubble of radius r is given as,

$$p = \frac{4T}{r}$$

where, T is surface tension.

$$\Rightarrow \quad p \propto \frac{1}{r} \quad \text{... (i)}$$

Therefore, when soap bubble expands, then its radius increases, hence from Eq. (i), pressure inside it will decrease.

2. *(c)* de-Broglie wavelength (λ) of a moving particle is given as

$$\lambda = \frac{h}{p}$$

$$\therefore \quad \lambda \propto \frac{1}{p}$$

Hence, the graph showing the variation of de-Broglie wavelength (λ) of a moving particle with its momentum (p) is shown below.

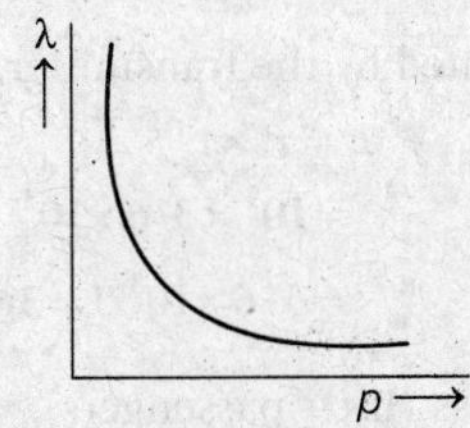

3. *(a)* Given, mass of body, $m = 60$ g

$$= 6 \times 10^{-2} \text{ kg}$$

Gravitational force, $F = 3 \cdot 0$ N

Magnitude of gravitational field intensity

$$I = \frac{F}{m} = \frac{3}{6 \times 10^{-2}}$$

$$= 50 \text{ N / kg}$$

4. *(b)* According to Biot-Savart's law, magnetic field due to small current element $Id\mathbf{l}$, at a distance r from it is given as

$$dB = \frac{\mu_0 (Id\mathbf{l} \times \mathbf{r})}{4\pi r^3}$$

Thus, current element $Id\mathbf{l}$ is a vector quantity. Hence, statement-I is correct and statement-II is incorrect.

5. *(b)* Initial speed of freely falling body,

$$u = 0$$

We know that, distance travelled by freely falling body in nth second

$$s_n = u + \frac{1}{2} g(2n - 1)$$

$$= 0 + \frac{1}{2} g(2n - 1)$$

$$s_n = \frac{1}{2} g(2n - 1)$$

Distance travelled by body in first second ($n = 1$ s)

$$s_1 = \frac{1}{2} g(2 \times 1 - 1) = \frac{g}{2}$$

Distance travelled by body in 2nd second ($n = 2$ s)

$$s_2 = \frac{1}{2} g(2 \times 2 - 1) = \frac{3g}{2}$$

Distance travelled by body in 3rd second ($n = 3$ s)

$$s_3 = \frac{1}{2} g(2 \times 3 - 1) = \frac{5g}{2}$$

Distance travelled by body in 4th second ($n = 4$ s)

$$s_4 = \frac{1}{2} g(2 \times 4 - 1) = \frac{7g}{2}$$

$$\therefore \quad s_1 : s_2 : s_3 : s_4 = \frac{g}{2} : \frac{3g}{2} : \frac{5g}{2} : \frac{7g}{2}$$

$$= 1 : 3 : 5 : 7$$

6. *(b)* In half wave rectification, input frequency,

$$f_{in} = 60 \text{Hz}$$

Since, frequency of output voltage obtained from the half wave rectifier is same as frequency of input AC voltage.

Hence, $f_{out} = 60$Hz

7. *(a)* When a spherical ball is dropped in a long column of a highly viscous liquid, then its velocity first increases and after sometime, it moves with constant velocity, known as terminal velocity (v).

Hence, correct variation of speed of ball in liquid column with time is given as

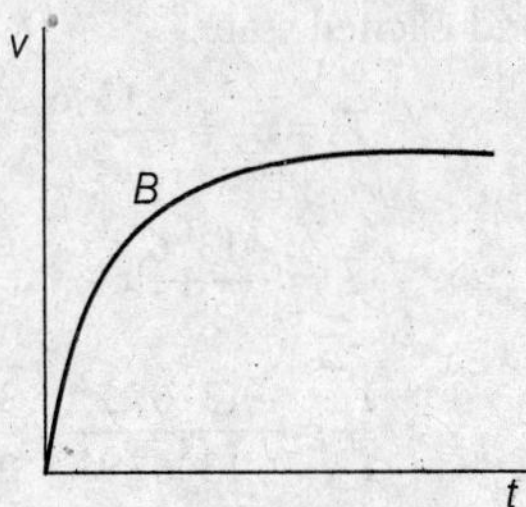

8. *(b)* Work done to move a charge (q) particle between any two points on equipotential surface is zero.

i.e. $\quad W = q(V_2 - V_1)$

$\Rightarrow \quad \mathbf{F} \cdot d\mathbf{s} = q(V - V) \quad [\because V_1 = V_2 = V]$

$\Rightarrow \quad q(\mathbf{E} \cdot d\mathbf{s}) = 0 \quad [\because \mathbf{F} = \mathbf{E} \cdot d\mathbf{s}]$

$\Rightarrow \quad \mathbf{E} \cdot d\mathbf{s} = 0$

Therefore, $\mathbf{E} \perp d\mathbf{s}$

i.e., electric field is perpendicular to displacement vector ($d\mathbf{s}$).

Since, ds lies in the plane of equipotential surface. Thus, angle between the electric lines of force and the equipotential surface is 90°.

9. *(b)* Coefficient of thermal resistance α is positive for conductor and negative for semiconductor. Thus, on increasing temperature, resistance of conductor increases and resistance of semiconductor decreases.

10. *(b)* The given nuclear reaction is represented as

$$^{22}_{11}\text{Na} \longrightarrow {}^{M}_{Z}X + e^{+} + \nu$$

Since, atomic number and mass number are same for both side of reaction.

Hence, for atomic number,

$$11 = Z + 1$$

$$\Rightarrow \quad Z = 10$$

For mass number,

$$22 = M$$

$$\Rightarrow \quad M = 22$$

$$\therefore \quad {}^{M}_{Z}X = {}^{22}_{10}\text{Ne}$$

11. *(c)* For the first excited state of hydrogen atom,

$$n_1 = 2$$

For the second excited state of hydrogen atom,

$$n_2 = 3$$

According to Bohr's model of H-atom, energy of an electron revolving in nth orbit.

$$E = \frac{-13 \cdot 6}{n^2} \text{ eV}$$

Here, for the first excited state.

$$T_1 = E_1 = \frac{-13 \cdot 6}{n_1^2}$$

$$= \frac{-13 \cdot 6}{2^2} \quad [\because n_1 = 2]$$

For the second excited state,

$$T_2 = E_2 = \frac{-13 \cdot 6}{n_2^2}$$

$$= \frac{-13 \cdot 6}{3^2} \text{ eV} \quad [\because n_2 = 3]$$

$$\therefore \quad \frac{T_1}{T_2} = \frac{-13 \cdot 6/2^2}{-13 \cdot 6/3^2} = \frac{3^2}{2^2} = \frac{9}{4}$$

$$\Rightarrow \quad T_1 : T_2 = 9 : 4$$

12. *(a)* Radius of gyration of a body is given as

$$K = \sqrt{\frac{I}{m}}$$

Where, I is moment of inertia and m is mass of body.

$$\therefore \quad \frac{K_1}{K_2} = \sqrt{\frac{I_1}{I_2}} \quad \ldots \text{(i)}$$

I_1 = Moment of inertia of thin uniform disc about an axis passing through its centre and normal to plane.

$$= \frac{MR^2}{2} \quad \begin{pmatrix}\text{where, } R = \text{radius of disc} \\ \text{and } M = \text{mass of disc}\end{pmatrix}$$

I_2 = Moment of inertia of disc about its diameter.

$$= \frac{MR^2}{4}$$

$\therefore$ From Eq. (i),

$$\frac{K_1}{K_2} = \sqrt{\frac{MR^2/2}{MR^2/4}} = \sqrt{2}$$

$$\therefore \quad K_1 : K_2 = \sqrt{2} : 1$$

13. *(c)* When light (EM wave) propagates through a material medium of relative permittivity ε_r and relative permeability μ_r, then velocity of light (EM wave) is given by

$$v = \frac{c}{\sqrt{\mu_r \varepsilon_r}}$$

where, c is speed of light in vacuum.

14. *(d)* Given, power radiated by transmitter, $P = 100 \text{ kW} = 10^5 \text{ W}$

$\therefore$ Time, $\quad t = 1 \text{ h} = 60 \times 60 \text{ s} = 3 \cdot 6 \times 10^3 \text{ s}$

$\therefore$ Energy radiated by the transmitter,

$$E = P \times t$$

$$= 10^5 \times 3 \cdot 6 \times 10^3$$

$$= 3 \cdot 6 \times 10^8 \text{ J} = 36 \times 10^7 \text{ J}$$

15. *(b)* Given, mass (lift + passengers), $m = 2000$ kg

$\therefore$ Weight (lift + passengers),

$$w = mg = 2000 \text{ g N}$$

$$v = 1 \cdot 5 \text{ m/s}$$

Frictional force, $f = 3000$ N

Since, lift is moving with constant velocity, hence net applied force on the lift = friction force + weight.

$$F = 3000 + 2000 \text{ g}$$

$$= 3000 + 2000 \times 10$$

$$= 23000 \text{ N}$$

$\therefore$ Minimum power delivered, $P = F \times v$

$$= 23000 \times 1.5$$

$$= 34500 \text{ W.}$$

16. *(a)* The given situation is shown in the following circuit diagram.

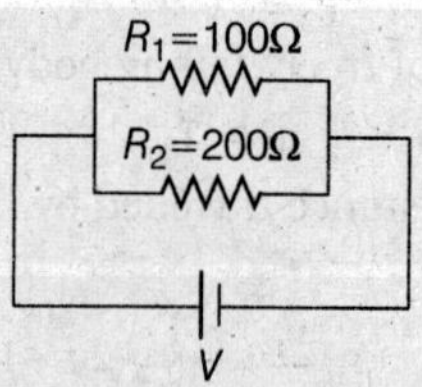

Let, these two resistors are connected with a battery of voltage V volts. We know that, in parallel combination, potential difference across each resistor is same.

Hence, potential difference across R_1, and R are given as,

$$V_1 = V_2 = V \text{ volts}$$

If H_1 and H_2 are thermal energy produced through resistances R_1 and R_2 in time t, then

$$H_1 = \frac{V_1^2}{R_1} t = \frac{V^2 t}{100}$$

and $$H_2 = \frac{V_2^2 t}{R_2} = \frac{V^2 t}{200}$$

Hence, $$\frac{H_1}{H_2} = \frac{V^2 t/100}{V^2 t/200}$$

$$= \frac{200}{100} = \frac{2}{1}$$

$\Rightarrow$ $$H_1 : H_2 = 2:1$$

17. **(b)** We know that, peak voltage (V_0) and rms voltage (V_{rms}) are related as,

$$V_0 = \sqrt{2}\, V_{rms}$$

Thus, peak voltage of the AC source is equal to $\sqrt{2}$ times the rms value of the AC source.

18. **(b)** Let total mass of the shell be m.

$\therefore$ The ratio of the masses of the fragment is 2 : 2 : 1

$$m_1 + m_2 + m_3 = m$$

$$2k + 2k + k = m$$

$\Rightarrow$ $$k = 0.2 \text{ m}$$

$\therefore$ Mass of lighter fragment, $m_3 = k = 0.2$ m

$$m_1 = m_2 = 2 \times 0.2 \text{ m} = 0.4 \text{ m}$$

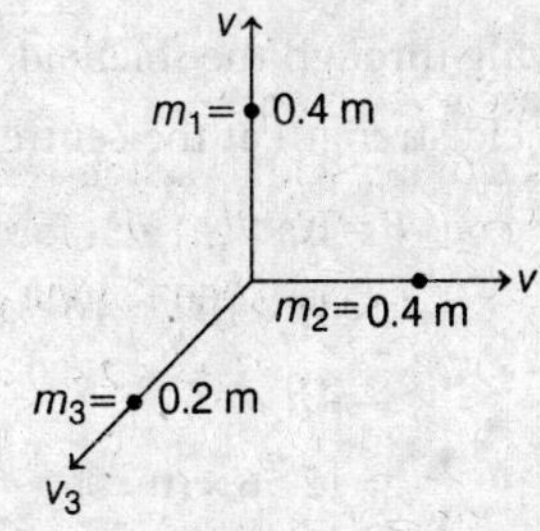

$\therefore$ Let the velocity of lighter fragment is v_3,

Since, $$p_3 = \sqrt{p_1^2 + p_2^2}$$

$\Rightarrow$ $$0.2mv_3 = \sqrt{(0.4mv)^2 + (0.4mv)^2}$$

$\Rightarrow$ $$v_3 = 2\sqrt{2}\, v$$

19. **(b)** We know that, velocity of transverse wave in the string, $v \propto \sqrt{T}$

Where, T is tension in the string.

$\therefore$ $$\frac{v_1}{v_2} = \sqrt{\frac{T_1}{T_2}} = \sqrt{\frac{T_1}{2T_1}} \quad [\because T_2 = 2T_1]$$

$$= \frac{1}{\sqrt{2}}$$

$$v_1 : v_2 = 1 : \sqrt{2}$$

20. **(a)** When a thermodynamic system undergoes a change in such a way that no exchange of heat takes place between it and the surrounding, the process is known as adiabatic process.

Curve 4 is isobaric process because pressure is constant.

Curve 1 is isochoric process because volume is constant.

In curve 2 and 3, curve 3 has smaller slope than curve 2. Hence, curve 3 represents isothermal process and curve 2 represents adiabatic process.

21. **(a)** Given, initial angular velocity of fly wheel,

$$\omega_0 = 2\pi\text{rad} \times 1200\text{rpm}$$

$$= 2\pi \text{ rad} \times \frac{1200}{60} \text{ rps}$$

$$= 40\,\pi \text{ rad/s}$$

Similarly, final angular velocity of fly wheel,

$$\omega = 2\pi\text{rad} \times 3120\text{rpm}$$

$$= 2\pi\text{rad} \times \frac{3120}{60} \text{rps}$$

$$= 104\,\pi\,\text{rad/s}$$

Time, $t = 16$ s

If α be the angular acceleration, then using the equation of rotational motion,

$$\omega = \omega_0 + \alpha t$$

$\Rightarrow$ $$104\pi = 40\pi + \alpha \times 16$$

$\Rightarrow$ $$\alpha = \frac{104\,\pi - 40\,\pi}{16}$$

$$= \frac{64\,\pi}{16} = 4\pi \text{ rad/s}^2$$

22. **(d)** Plane angle is measured in radian whereas solid angle is measured in steradian.

Therefore, plane angle and solid angle have units but no dimensions.

23. **(c)** In the circuit diagram (A) and (C), both the p-n junction diodes are in same biasing conditions.

So, both diodes offers equal resistances.

Since, both diodes are in series, therefore equal potential will drop across the junction.

24. **(c)** In Young's double slit experiment, wavelength of light used is inversely proportional to the number of fringes observed.

i.e. $$\lambda_1 n_1 = \lambda_2 n_2$$

$$n_2 = \frac{n_1 \lambda_1}{\lambda_2}$$

Here, $\lambda_1 = 600 \text{ nm} = 6 \times 10^{-7}$ m

$$\lambda_2 = 400 \text{ nm} = 4 \times 10^{-7} \text{m}$$

$$n_1 = 8$$

$$\therefore \quad n_2 = \frac{8 \times 6 \times 10^{-7}}{4 \times 10^{-7}} = 12$$

25. **(*)** Using Einstein's photoelectric equation,

$$eV' = h\nu' - h\nu_0$$

when $\nu' = \nu$ and $V' = V_s$, then

$$\therefore \quad eV_s = h\nu - h\nu_0 \quad \text{... (i)}$$

Again when $\nu' = \frac{\nu}{2}$ and $V' = \frac{V_s}{2}$

$$\therefore \quad \frac{eV_s}{2} = \frac{h\nu}{2} - h\nu_0 \quad \text{... (ii)}$$

Dividing Eq. (i) by Eq. (ii), we have

$$\frac{eV_s}{eV_s / 2} = \frac{h\nu - h\nu_0}{\frac{h\nu}{2} - h\nu_0}$$

$$2 = \frac{h(\nu - \nu_0)}{h\left(\frac{\nu}{2} - \nu_0\right)}$$

$$\Rightarrow \quad 2\left(\frac{\nu}{2} - \nu_0\right) = \nu - \nu_0$$

$$\nu - 2\nu_0 = \nu - \nu_0$$

$$\Rightarrow \quad \nu_0 = 0$$

Hence, question is wrong.

26. **(a)** Side of square loop, $a = 1$ m

$\therefore$ Area of square loop, $A = a^2 = 1^2 = 1 \text{ m}^2$

Resistance of square loop, $R = 1\,\Omega$

Magnetic field, $B = 0.5$ T

Since, plane of loop is perpendicular to the direction of magnetic field, hence angle made by the normal to the loop with the direction of magnetic field will be 0°.

i.e., $\theta = 0$

$\therefore$ Magnetic flux passing through the loop,

$$\phi = BA\cos\theta = 0.5 \times 1 \times \cos 0^\circ$$
$$= 0.5 \text{Wb}$$

27. **(a)** Potential on the hollow conducting sphere of radius R due to charge Q is

$$V = \frac{1}{4\pi\varepsilon_0} \cdot \frac{Q}{R}$$

$$\Rightarrow \quad V \propto \frac{1}{R} \quad \text{[For same charge } Q\text{]}$$

$$\Rightarrow \quad \frac{V_1}{V_2} = \frac{R_2}{R_1}$$

Since, $R_1 > R_2$

$$\therefore \quad \frac{R_1}{R_2} > 1$$

$$\Rightarrow \quad \frac{R_2}{R_1} < 1$$

$$\therefore \quad \frac{V_1}{V_2} < 1$$

$$\therefore \quad V_1 < V_2$$

Hence, potential will more on smaller sphere.

28. **(c)** Given, radius, $r = \frac{10^{-2}}{\sqrt{\pi}}$ m

$$\therefore \quad R = 10\,\Omega$$
$$E = 10 \text{ V/m}$$
$$l = 10 \text{ m}$$

$\therefore$ Area of cross-section of copper wire,

$$A = \pi r^2$$
$$= \pi \times \left(\frac{10^{-2}}{\sqrt{\pi}}\right)^2$$
$$= 10^{-4} \text{ m}^2$$

$\therefore$ Current density,

$$J = \frac{i}{A} = \frac{V/R}{A} \quad \left[\because i = \frac{V}{R}\right]$$

$$= \frac{V}{RA} = \frac{El}{RA} \quad [\because V = El]$$

$$= \frac{10 \times 10}{10 \times 10^{-4}} = 10^5 \text{ A/m}^2$$

29. **(a)** Given, Radius of solenoid, $r = 1$ mm

Number of turns per mm $= \frac{100}{1 \text{ mm}}$

$\therefore$ Number of turns per metre $= \frac{100}{1 \times 10^{-3} \text{m}}$

i.e., $n = 10^5$ turns/m

Current flowing through the solenoid, $I = 1$ A

$\therefore$ Magnetic field strength at the centre of the solenoid

$$B = \mu_0 nI$$
$$= 4\pi \times 10^{-7} \times 10^5 \times 1$$
$$= 4\pi \times 10^{-2} \text{ T}$$
$$= 12.56 \times 10^{-2} \text{ T}$$

30. **(a)** The given situation is shown below.

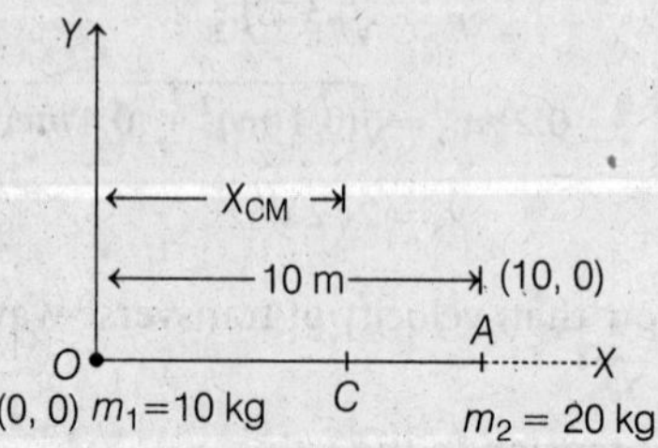

Let X_{CM} be the position of centre of mass from 10 kg mass.

$$\therefore \quad X_{CM} = \frac{m_1 x_1 + m_2 x_2}{m_1 + m_2}$$

$$= \frac{10 \times 0 + 20 \times 10}{10 + 20} = \frac{200}{30} = \frac{20}{3} \text{ m}$$

31. *(b)* Given, refractive index of glass surface

$$\mu = \sqrt{3}$$

Angle of incidence, $i = 60^\circ$

Since, above situation follows Brewster's law because,

$$\mu = \tan i = \tan 60^\circ = \sqrt{3}$$

Hence, angle i is equal to polarising angle i_p.

i.e., $i_p = i = 60^\circ$

By snell's law

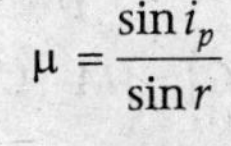

$$\mu = \frac{\sin i_p}{\sin r}$$

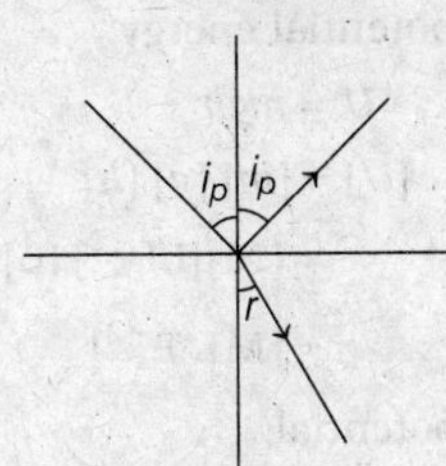

$$\Rightarrow \quad \tan i_p = \frac{\sin i_p}{\sin r} \qquad [\text{Since, } \mu = \tan i_p]$$

$$\Rightarrow \quad \frac{\sin i_p}{\cos i_p} = \frac{\sin i_p}{\sin r}$$

$$\Rightarrow \quad \cos i_p = \sin r$$

$$\Rightarrow \quad \cos i_p = \cos(90^\circ - r)$$

$$\Rightarrow \quad i_p = 90^\circ - r$$

$$\Rightarrow \quad r + i_p = 90^\circ$$

Hence, angle between the refracted and reflected rays

$$= 180^\circ - (r + i_p) = 180^\circ - (90^\circ) = 90^\circ$$

It is also called Brewster's law.

32. *(b)* We know that, magnetic field due to current carrying solenoid,

$$B = \mu_0 n I$$

$$\Rightarrow \quad \mu_0 = \frac{B}{nI}$$

$$\Rightarrow \quad [\mu_0] = \frac{[B]}{[n]\,[I]}$$

$$= \frac{\left[\frac{F}{IL}\right]}{[n]\,[I]} \qquad \left[\because F = IBL \Rightarrow B = \frac{F}{IL}\right]$$

$$= \frac{[F]}{[n]\,[L]\,[I^2]} = \frac{[\text{MLT}^{-2}]}{[\text{L}^{-1}]\,[\text{L}]\,[\text{A}^2]}$$

$$= [\text{MLT}^{-2}\text{A}^{-2}]$$

Hence, option (b) is correct.

Dimensional formula of self inductance,

$$[L] = [\text{M}^1\text{L}^2\text{T}^{-2}\text{A}^{-2}]$$

Dimensional formula of electric permittivity,

$$[\varepsilon_0] = [\text{M}^{-1}\text{L}^{-3}\text{T}^4\text{A}^2]$$

Dimensional formula of magnetic flux,

$$[\phi] = [\text{ML}^2\text{T}^{-2}\text{A}^{-1}]$$

33. *(c)* We know that, slope of displacement-time graph for a moving object gives velocity of moving object.

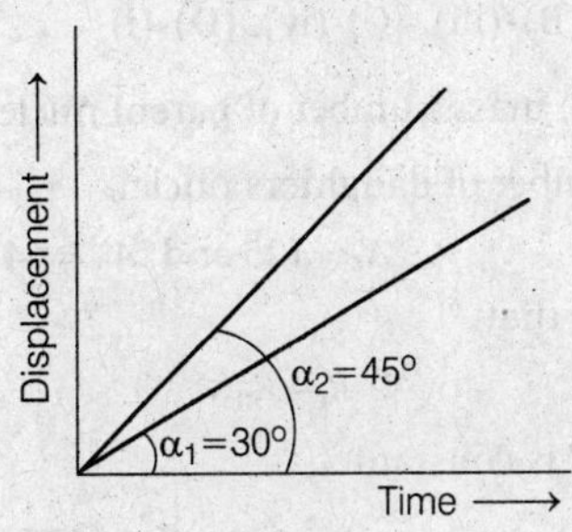

$\therefore$ Velocity of first moving particle,

$$v_1 = \tan \alpha_1$$

$$= \tan 30^\circ = \frac{1}{\sqrt{3}}$$

Velocity of second moving particle,

$$v_2 = \tan \alpha_2 = \tan 45^\circ = 1$$

$$\therefore \quad \frac{v_1}{v_2} = \frac{1/\sqrt{3}}{1}$$

$$= \frac{1}{\sqrt{3}}$$

$$\therefore \quad v_1 : v_2 = 1 : \sqrt{3}$$

34. *(b)* For a biconvex lens,

$R_1 = +\,20$ cm, $R_2 = -\,20$ cm and $\mu = 1.5$

By using lens maker's formula, we have,

$$\frac{1}{f} = (\mu - 1)\left(\frac{1}{R_1} - \frac{1}{R_2}\right)$$

$$= (1.5 - 1)\left(\frac{1}{20} - \frac{1}{-20}\right)$$

$$= 0.5\left(\frac{2}{20}\right)$$

$$\Rightarrow \quad \frac{1}{f} = 0.5 \times \frac{1}{10}$$

$$\Rightarrow \quad f = \frac{10}{0.5}$$

$$\Rightarrow \quad f = 20 \text{ cm} = 0.2 \text{ m}$$

$\therefore$ Power of the lens, $P = \dfrac{1}{f}$ (in metre)

$$= \frac{1}{0.2} = +\,5 \text{ D}$$

35. (c)

A. Wavelength range of AM radio waves lies between 10^2 m to 10^3 m.

B. Wavelength range of microwaves lies between 10^{-3} m to 10^{-1} m.

C. Wavelength range of infrared radiations lies between 10^{-5} m to 10^{-3} m.

D. Wavelength range of X-rays lies between 10^{-12} m to 10^{-8} m.

Therefore, correct matching pairs are (A)-(ii), (B)-(iii), (C)-(iv), (D)-(i)

36. (b) Given, mass number of parent nucleus, $A = 189$

Mass number of daughters nuclei,

$$A_1 = 125 \text{ and } A_2 = 64$$

We know that,

$$R = R_0(A^{1/3})$$

where, R_0 is constant.

$$\therefore \quad \frac{R_1}{R_2} = \left(\frac{A_1}{A_2}\right)^{1/3} = \left(\frac{125}{64}\right)^{1/3}$$

$$= \left[\left(\frac{5}{4}\right)^3\right]^{1/3} = \frac{5}{4}$$

$$\therefore \quad R_1 : R_2 = 5 : 4$$

37. (a) Given, speed of light in transparent medium A,

$$v_A = 1.5 \times 10^8 \text{ m/s}$$

Speed of light in transparent medium B,

$$v_B = 2 \times 10^8 \text{ m/s}$$

Refractive index (μ) and critical angle (i_c) are related as

$$\mu = \frac{1}{\sin i_c}$$

$$\Rightarrow \quad \sin i_c = \frac{1}{\mu} = \frac{1}{(v_B / v_A)} \quad \left[\because \mu = \frac{v_B}{v_A}\right]$$

$$= \frac{v_A}{v_B} = \frac{1.5 \times 10^8}{2 \times 10^8}$$

$$= 0.750$$

$$\Rightarrow \quad i_c = \sin^{-1}(0.750)$$

38. (b) Given, number of turns in big circular coil, $N = 1000$

Average radius, $r = 10$ m

Vertical component of Earth's magnetic field,

$$B_V = 2 \times 10^{-5} \text{ T}$$

Resistance of coil, $R = 12.56\,\Omega$

Angular velocity, $\omega = 2$ rad/s

Maximum induced emf in the coil

$$e_{max} = NBA\omega = NB_vA\omega$$

$$= 1000 \times 2 \times 10^{-5} \times \pi(10)^2 \times 2 \quad [\because A = \pi r^2]$$

$$e_{max} = 4\pi \text{V}$$

$\therefore$ Maximum induced current in the coil

$$I_{max} = \frac{e_{max}}{R} = \frac{4\pi}{12.56} = 1 \text{ A}$$

39. (a) A. According to Newton's law of gravitation,

$$F = G\frac{m_1 m_2}{r^2}$$

$$\Rightarrow \quad G = \frac{Fr^2}{m_1 m_2}$$

$$\Rightarrow \quad [G] = \frac{[F][r^2]}{[m_1][m_2]}$$

$$= \frac{[MLT^{-2}][L^2]}{[M][M]}$$

$$\Rightarrow \quad [G] = [M^{-1}L^3T^{-2}]$$

B. Gravitational potential energy,

$$U = mgh$$

$$[U] = [m][g][h]$$

$$= [M][LT^{-2}][L]$$

$$= [ML^2T^{-2}]$$

C. Gravitational potential,

$$V = -\frac{Gm}{r}$$

$$\therefore \quad [V] = \frac{[G][m]}{[r]}$$

$$= \frac{[M^{-1}L^3T^{-2}][M]}{[L]} = [L^2T^{-2}]$$

D. Gravitational intensity,

$$I = \frac{GM}{r^2}$$

$$\therefore \quad [I] = \frac{[G][M]}{[r^2]}$$

$$= \frac{[M^{-1}L^3T^{-2}][M]}{[L^2]} = [LT^{-2}]$$

Hence, correct matching pair is (A)-(ii), (B)-(iv), (C)-(i), (D)-(iii)

40. (b) When a coil spring is stretched, neither its length nor its volume changes, but there is only the change in its shape. Therefore, stretching of coil spring is determined by shear modulus.

Young's modulus of steel spring is more than Young's modulus of copper spring, therefore tensile strength of steel spring is more than tensile strength of copper spring. Hence, Assertion is true but Reason is false.

41. (c) Area = Length $\times$ Breadth

$$= 55.3 \times 25$$

$$= 1382.5$$

$$= 13.825 \times 10^2$$
$$= 13.83 \times 10^2$$
$$= 13.8 \times 10^2$$
$$= 14 \times 10^2$$

42. *(*)* The given logic circuit is represented as

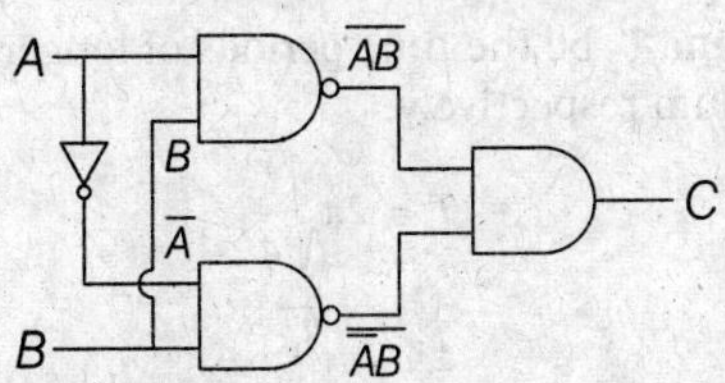

Output of logic circuit,

$$C = \overline{AB} + \overline{\overline{A}B} = (\overline{A} + \overline{B}) + \overline{\overline{A}} + \overline{B}$$

[Using De-morgan's law $\overline{xy} = \overline{x} + \overline{y}$]

$$= \overline{A} + \overline{B} + A + \overline{B}$$
$$C = \overline{A} + A + \overline{B} = 1 + \overline{B} \; [\because \overline{A} + A = 1]$$

Truth table is given as

A	B	$\overline{B}$	$C = 1 + \overline{B}$
0	0	1	1
0	1	0	1
1	0	1	1
1	1	0	1

Hence, no option is correct.

43. *(c)* Molecular weight of water $= 18\text{ g} = 1.8 \times 10^{-2}$ kg

$\therefore$ Mass of water, $M = 4.5$ kg

$\therefore$ number of moles of water,

$$n = \frac{\text{Mass of water}}{\text{Molecular weight of water}}$$
$$= \frac{4.5}{1.8 \times 10^{-2}} = 250$$

At STP, $T = 273$ K, $p = 10^5 \text{ N/m}^2$

Using equation, $pV = nRT$

$$\Rightarrow \quad V = \frac{nRT}{p}$$
$$= \frac{250 \times 8.3 \times 273}{10^5}$$
$$= 5.6 \text{ m}^3$$

44. *(a)* For the most precise measurement of unknown resistance X, the resistances P and Q should be approximately equal and should be small so that it could decrease error in experiment.

45. *(a)* Given, In series L-C-R circuit,

$$L = 10\text{ H}, C = 10\,\mu\text{F} = 10^{-5}\text{ F}$$
$$R = 50\,\Omega$$

Source voltage, $V = 200\sin(100\,t)$ volt.

$$\omega = 100 \text{ rad/s}$$
$$\therefore \quad 2\pi\nu = 100$$
$$\Rightarrow \quad \nu = \frac{100}{2\pi} = \frac{50}{\pi}\text{ Hz}$$

Resonance frequency,

$$\nu_0 = \frac{1}{2\pi\sqrt{LC}} = \frac{1}{2\pi\sqrt{10 \times 10^{-5}}}$$
$$= \frac{1}{2\,\pi \times 10^{-2}} = \frac{50}{\pi}\text{ Hz}$$

Hence, $\nu = \nu_0 = \dfrac{50}{\pi}$ Hz

46. *(b)* The given situation is shown below.

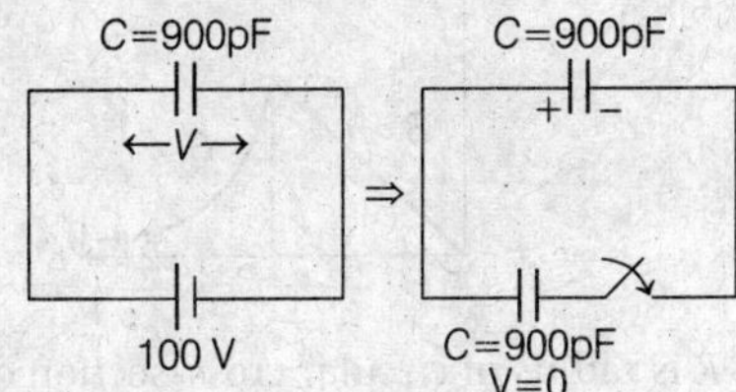

After combination,

Common potential,

$$V = \frac{C_1V_1 + C_2V_2}{C_1 + C_2}$$
$$= \frac{C \times 100 + C \times 0}{C + C} = 50\text{V}$$

$\therefore$ Electrostatic stored potential energy,

$$U = 2 \times \frac{1}{2}CV^2 = CV^2$$
$$= 9 \times 10^{-10} \times 50^2$$
$$= 2.25 \times 10^{-6}\text{ J}$$

47. *(a)* The arrangement of charges shown in the figure is an electric dipole. Hence, electric field at point P at a distance $R(R >> L)$ from the dipole is equal to electric field due to electric dipole on axial position.

−q   +q   P
←R→
←L→

i.e., $$E = \frac{1}{4\pi\varepsilon_0} \cdot \frac{2p}{R^3}$$

where, $p = qL$ (Electric dipole moment)

$$\therefore \quad E \propto \frac{1}{R^3}$$

48. *(b)* Initial speed of ball, $u = 10\text{ ms}^{-1}$

Angle of projection, $\theta = 60°$

At highest point of the trajectory of ball, its vertical component of velocity becomes zero and only horizontal component of velocity exists, which is equal to horizontal component of velocity at the time of projection.

i.e., speed of ball at highest point

$$= u\cos\theta = 10\cos 60^{\circ}$$

$$= 10 \times \frac{1}{2} = 5 \text{ ms}^{-1}$$

49. *(b)* According to Ampere's circuital law, magnetic field inside the current carrying long straight wire of circular cross-section is a linearly increasing function of distance $r(r < R)$ upto the boundary of the wire and magnetic field outside the wire at distance $r(r > R)$ from its axis is decreasing one with $\frac{1}{r}$ dependence as shown in figure.

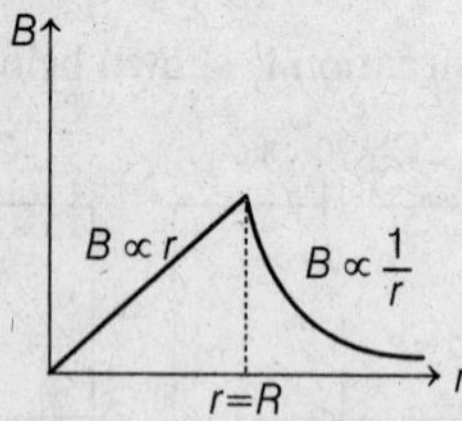

where, R is radius of circular cross-section of wire.

50. *(d)* Given, length of first pendulum,

$$l_1 = 121 \text{ cm} = 1\cdot 21 \text{ m}$$

length of second pendulum,

$$l_2 = 100 \text{ cm} = 1 \text{ m}$$

According to given situation, both pendulums are again in phase if vibrations made by the shorter pendulum will be known.

Let T_1 and T_2 be the time periods of longer and shorter pendulum respectively.

Since, $$T = 2\pi\sqrt{\frac{l}{g}}$$

$$\Rightarrow \quad \frac{T_1}{T_2} = \sqrt{\frac{l_1}{l_2}}$$

$$= \sqrt{\frac{1\cdot 21}{1}} = 1\cdot 1 = \frac{11}{10}$$

$$\Rightarrow \quad 10T_1 = 11T_2$$

$\therefore$ 10 vibrations of longer pendulum

= 11 vibrations of shorter pendulum

$\therefore$ Minimum number of vibrations of shorter pendulum = 11

NEET

SOLVED PAPER 2023

NEET SOLVED PAPER 2023

Instruction

This question paper contains 50 Multiple Choice Questions of Physics, divided into two Sections; section A and section B.

Section A contains 35 questions and all questions are compulsory.

Section B contains 15 questions out of which 10 questions are to be attempted.

Each question carries 4 marks.

PHYSICS

Section-A

1. If the galvanometer (G) does not show any deflection in the circuit shown, the value of R is given by

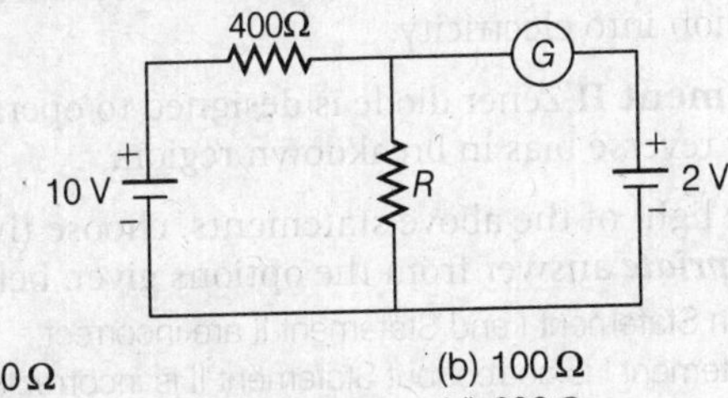

(a) $50\,\Omega$ (b) $100\,\Omega$
(c) $400\,\Omega$ (d) $200\,\Omega$

2. A full wave rectifier circuit consists of two p-n junction diodes, a centre-tapped transformer, capacitor and a load resistance. Which of these components remove the AC ripple from the rectified output?

(a) p-n junction diodes
(b) Capacitor
(c) Load resistance
(d) A centre-tapped transformer

3. A Carnot engine has an efficiency of 50% when its source is at a temperature 327°C. The temperature of the sink is

(a) 15°C (b) 100°C
(c) 200°C (d) 27°C

4. Light travels a distance x in time t_1 in air and $10x$ in time t_2 in another denser medium. What is the critical angle for this medium?

(a) $\sin^{-1}\left(\frac{10t_2}{t_1}\right)$

(b) $\sin^{-1}\left(\frac{t_1}{10t_2}\right)$

(c) $\sin^{-1}\left(\frac{10t_1}{t_2}\right)$

(d) $\sin^{-1}\left(\frac{t_2}{t_1}\right)$

5. The angular acceleration of a body, moving along the circumference of a circle, is

(a) along the radius towards the centre
(b) along the tangent to its position
(c) along the axis of rotation
(d) along the radius, away from centre

6. The venturimeter works on

(a) Bernoulli's principle
(b) the principle of parallel axes
(c) the principle of perpendicular axes
(d) Huygen's principle

7. The half-life of a radioactive substance is 20 minutes. In how much time, the activity of substance drops to (1/16)th of its initial value?

(a) 40 minutes (b) 60 minutes
(c) 80 minutes (d) 20 minutes

8. The errors in the measurement which arise due to unpredictable fluctuations in temperature and voltage supply are

(a) personal errors
(b) least count errors
(c) random error
(d) instrumental errors

9. An electric dipole is placed at an angle of 30° with an electric field of intensity $2\times10^5\,\text{NC}^{-1}$. It experiences a torque equal to 4 N m. Calculate the magnitude of charge on the dipole, if the dipole length is 2 cm.

(a) 6 mC (b) 4 mC
(c) 2 mC (d) 8 mC

10. A football player is moving southward and suddenly turns eastward with the same speed to avoid an opponent. The force that acts on the player while turning is

(a) along northward
(b) along north-east
(c) along south-west
(d) along eastward

11. In hydrogen spectrum, the shortest wavelength in the Balmer series is λ. The shortest wavelength in the Bracket series is

(a) 4λ
(b) 9λ
(c) 16λ
(d) 2λ

12. The magnitude and direction of the current in the following circuit is

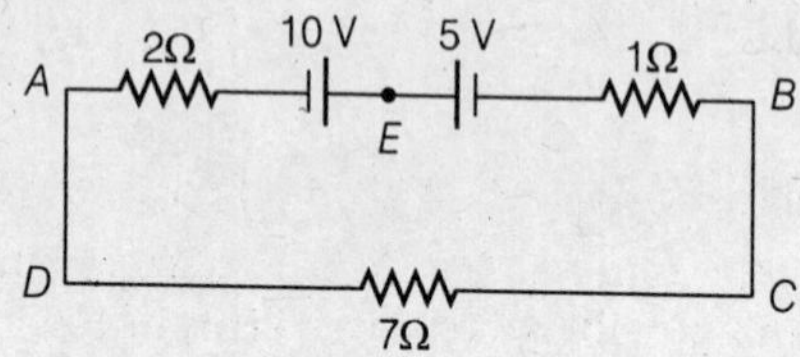

(a) 0.5 A from *A* to *B* through *E*
(b) 5/9 A from *A* to *B* through *E*
(c) 1.5 A from *B* to *A* through *E*
(d) 0.2 A from *B* to *A* through *E*

13. A 12 V, 60 W lamp is connected to the secondary of a step down transformer, whose primary is connected to AC mains of 220 V. Assuming the transformer to be ideal, what is the current in the primary winding?

(a) 2.7 A
(b) 3.7 A
(c) 0.37 A
(d) 0.27 A

14. The work functions of caesium (Cs), Potassium (K) and sodium (Na) are 2.14 eV, 2.30 eV and 2.75 eV respectively. If incident electromagnetic radiation has an incident energy of 2.20 eV. Which of these photosensitive surfaces may emit photoelectrons?

(a) Both Na and K
(b) K only
(c) Na only
(d) Cs only

15. The potential energy of a long spring when stretched by 2 cm is *U*. If the spring is stretched by 8 cm, potential energy stored in it will be

(a) 4 *U*
(b) 8 *U*
(c) 16 *U*
(d) 2 *U*

16. The net magnetic flux through any closed surface is

(a) positive
(b) infinity
(c) negative
(d) zero

17. The amount of energy required to form a soap bubble of radius 2 cm from a soap solution is nearly (surface tension of soap solution $= 0.03 \text{ N m}^{-1}$)

(a) 5.06×10^{-4} J
(b) 3.01×10^{-4} J
(c) 50.1×10^{-4} J
(d) 30.16×10^{-4} J

18. Let a wire be suspended from the ceiling (rigid support) and stretched by a weight *w* attached at its free end. The longitudinal stress at any point of cross-sectional area *A* of the wire is

(a) w/A
(b) $w/2A$
(c) zero
(d) $2w/A$

19. Two bodies of mass *m* and 9*m* are placed at a distance *R*. The gravitational potential on the line joining the bodies where the gravitational field equals zero, will b (*G* = gravitational constant)

(a) $-\dfrac{12\,Gm}{R}$
(b) $-\dfrac{16\,Gm}{R}$
(c) $-\dfrac{20\,Gm}{R}$
(d) $-\dfrac{8\,Gm}{R}$

20. The temperature of a gas is –50°C. To what temperature the gas should be heated so that the rms speed is increased by 3 times?

(a) 3295°C
(b) 3097 K
(c) 223 K
(d) 669°C

21. Given below are two statements.

Statement I Photovoltaic devices can convert optical radiation into electricity.

Statement II Zener diode is designed to operate under reverse bias in breakdown region.

In the light of the above statements, choose the ***most appropriate*** answer from the options given below

(a) Both Statement I and Statement II are incorrect.
(b) Statement I is correct but Statement II is incorrect.
(c) Statement I is incorrect but Statement II is correct.
(d) Both Statement I and Statement II are correct.

22. If $\oint \mathbf{E} \cdot d\mathbf{S} = 0$ over a surface, then:

(a) the magnitude of electric field on the surface is constant.
(b) all the charges must necessarily be inside the surface.
(c) the electric field inside the surface is necessarily uniform.
(d) the number of flux lines entering the surface must be equal to the number of flux lines leaving it.

23. In a series *L-C-R* circuit, the inductance *L* is 10 mH, capacitance *C* is 1 μF and resistance *R* is 100 Ω. The frequency at which resonance occurs is

(a) 15.9 kHz
(b) 1.59 rad/s
(c) 1.59 kHz
(d) 15.9 rad/s

24. An AC source is connected to a capacitor *C*. Due to decrease in its operating frequency

(a) displacement current increases.
(b) displacement current decreases.
(c) capacitive reactance remains constant.
(d) capacitive reactance decreases.

25. A bullet is fired from a gun at the speed of 280 m s^{-1} in the direction 30° above the horizontal. The maximum height attained by the bullet is ($g = 9.8 \text{ m s}^{-2}$, $\sin 30° = 0.5$)

(a) 2000 m
(b) 1000 m
(c) 3000 m
(d) 2800 m

26. A vehicle travels half the distance with speed v and the remaining distance with speed $2v$. Its average speed is

(a) $\frac{2v}{3}$ (b) $\frac{4v}{3}$
(c) $\frac{3v}{4}$ (d) $\frac{v}{3}$

27. Resistance of a carbon resistor determined from colour codes is $(22000 \pm 5\%)\ \Omega$. The colour of third band must be

(a) green (b) orange
(c) yellow (d) red

28. The equivalent capacitance of the system shown in the following circuit is

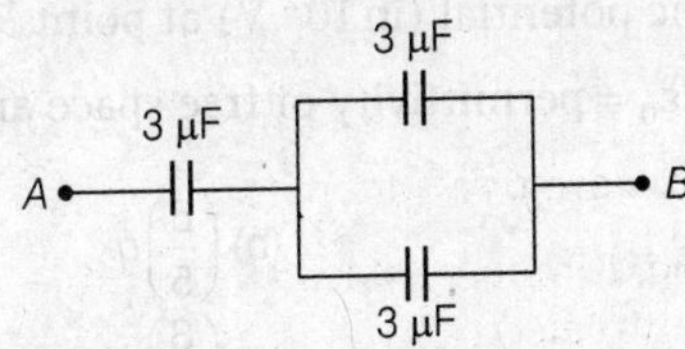

(a) 3 μF (b) 6 μF
(c) 9 μF (d) 2 μF

29. The minimum wavelength of X-rays produced by an electron accelerated through a potential difference of V volts is proportional to

(a) $1/V$ (b) $1/\sqrt{V}$
(c) V^2 (d) $\sqrt{V}$

30. The magnetic energy stored in an inductor of inductance 4 μH carrying a current of 2 A is

(a) 4 mJ (b) 8 mJ
(c) 8 μJ (d) 4 μJ

31. For Young's double slit experiment, two statements are given below:

Statement I If screen is moved away from the plane of slits, angular separation of the fringes remains constant.

Statement II If the monochromatic source is replaced by another monochromatic source of larger wavelength, the angular separation of fringes decreases.

In the light of the above statements, choose the correct answer from the options given below

(a) Both Statement I and Statement II are false.
(b) Statement I is true but Statement II is false.
(c) Statement I is false but Statement II is true.
(d) Both Statement I and Statement II are true.

32. The ratio of radius of gyration of a solid sphere of mass M and radius R about its own axis to the radius of gyration of the thin hollow sphere of same mass and radius about its axis is

(a) 5 : 3 (b) 2 : 5
(c) 5 : 2 (d) 3 : 5

33. In a plane electromagnetic wave travelling in free space, the electric field component oscillates sinusoidally at a frequency of 2.0×10^{10} Hz and amplitude 48 V m^{-1}. Then the amplitude of oscillating magnetic field is (Speed of light in free space $= 3 \times 10^8$ m s^{-1})

(a) 1.6×10^{-8} T
(b) 1.6×10^{-7} T
(c) 1.6×10^{-6} T
(d) 1.6×10^{-9} T

34. A metal wire has mass (0.4 ± 0.002) g, radius (0.3 ± 0.001) mm and length (5 ± 0.02) cm. The maximum possible percentage error in the measurement of density will nearly be

(a) 1.3% (b) 1.6%
(c) 1.4% (d) 1.2%

35. The ratio of frequencies of fundamental harmonic produced by an open pipe to that of closed pipe having the same length is

(a) 2 : 1 (b) 1 : 3
(c) 3 : 1 (d) 1 : 2

Section-B

36. Two thin lenses are of same focal lengths (f), but one is convex and the other one is concave. When they are placed in contact with each other, the equivalent focal length of the combination will be

(a) $\frac{f}{4}$ (b) $\frac{f}{2}$
(c) infinite (d) Zero

37. A satellite is orbiting just above the surface of the earth with period T. If d is the density of the earth and G is the universal constant of gravitation, the quantity $3\pi/Gd$ represents

(a) T^2 (b) T^3
(c) $\sqrt{T}$ (d) T

38. In the figure shown here, what is the equivalent focal length of the combination of lenses (Assume that, all layers are thin)?

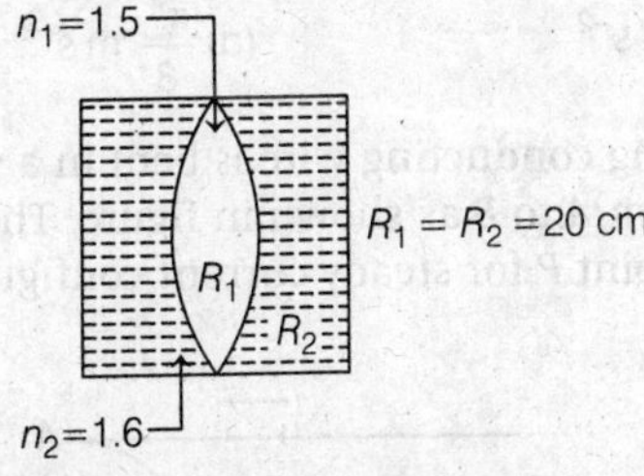

(a) – 40 cm
(b) – 100 cm
(c) – 50 cm
(d) 40 cm

39. A bullet from a gun is fired on a rectangular wooden block with velocity u. When bullet travels 24 cm through the block along its length horizontally, velocity of bullet becomes $\frac{u}{3}$. Then it further penetrates into the block in the same direction before coming to rest exactly at the other end of the block. The total length of the block is

(a) 24 cm (b) 28 cm
(c) 30 cm (d) 27 cm

40. 10 resistors, each of resistance R are connected in series to a battery of emf E and negligible internal resistance. Then those are connected in parallel to the same battery, the current is increased n times. The value of n is

(a) 100 (b) 1
(c) 1000 (d) 10

41. The net impedance of circuit (as shown in figure) will be

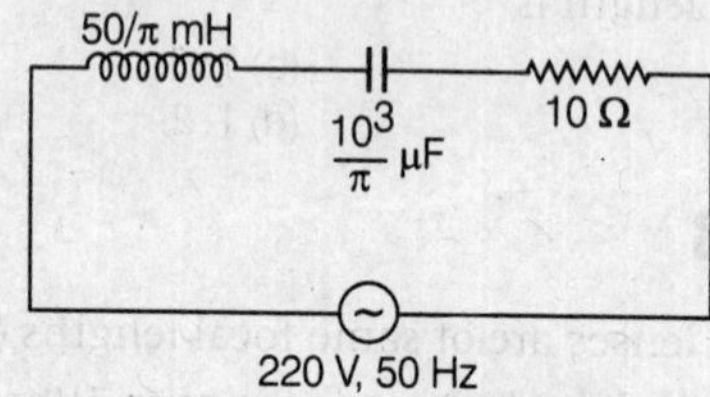

(a) 15 Ω (b) $5\sqrt{5}$ Ω
(c) 25 Ω (d) $10\sqrt{2}$ Ω

42. The x-t graph of a particle performing simple harmonic motion is shown in the figure. The acceleration of the particle at $t = 2$ s is

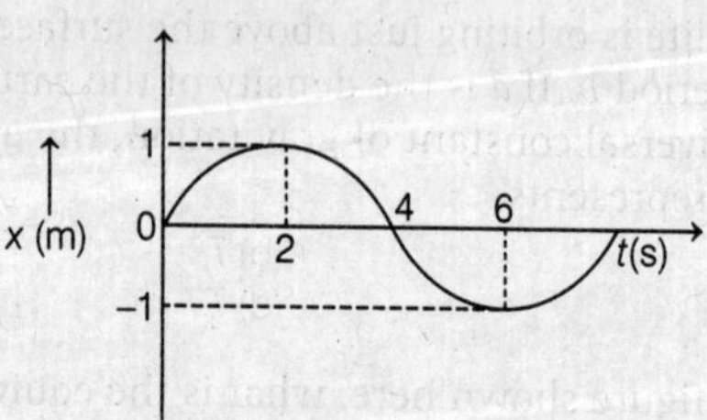

(a) $-\frac{\pi^2}{8}$ m s^{-2} (b) $\frac{\pi^2}{16}$ m s^{-2}
(c) $-\frac{\pi^2}{16}$ m s^{-2} (d) $\frac{\pi^2}{8}$ m s^{-2}

43. A very long conducting wire is bent in a semi-circular shape from A to B as shown in figure. The magnetic field at point P for steady current configuration is given by

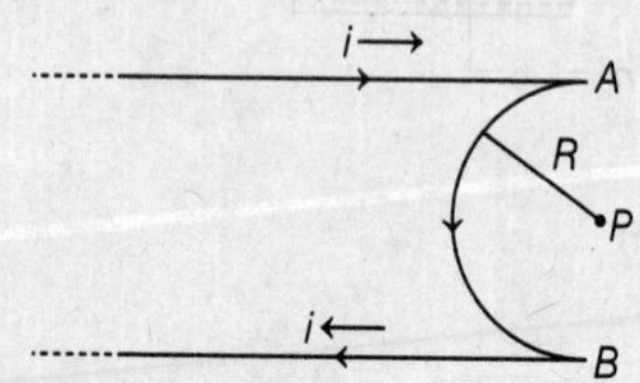

(a) $\frac{\mu_0 i}{4R}$ pointed away from the page
(b) $\frac{\mu_0 i}{4R}\left[1-\frac{2}{\pi}\right]$ pointed away from page
(c) $\frac{\mu_0 i}{4R}\left[1-\frac{2}{\pi}\right]$ pointed into the page
(d) $\frac{\mu_0 i}{4R}$ pointed into the page

44. An electric dipole is placed as shown in the figure.

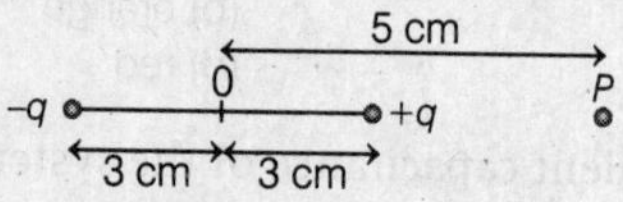

The electric potential (in 10^2 V) at point P due to the dipole is (ε_0 = permittivity of free space and $\frac{1}{4\pi\varepsilon_0} = K$)

(a) $\left(\frac{5}{8}\right)qk$ (b) $\left(\frac{8}{5}\right)qk$
(c) $\left(\frac{8}{3}\right)qk$ (d) $\left(\frac{3}{8}\right)qk$

45. The resistance of platinum wire at 0°C is 2 Ω and 6.8 Ω at 80°C. The temperature coefficient of resistance of th wire is

(a) 3×10^{-3} °C^{-1} (b) 3×10^{-2} °C^{-1}
(c) 3×10^{-1} °C^{-1} (d) 3×10^{-4} °C^{-1}

46. A wire carrying a current I along the positive X-axis h length L. It is kept in a magnetic field $\mathbf{B} = (2\hat{\mathbf{i}} + 3\hat{\mathbf{j}} - 4\hat{\mathbf{k}}$ T. The magnitude of the magnetic force acting on the wire is

(a) $\sqrt{5}\,IL$ (b) 5 IL
(c) $\sqrt{3}\,IL$ (d) 3 IL

47. Calculate the maximum acceleration of a moving car s that a body lying on the floor of the car remains stationary. The coefficient of static friction between th body and the floor is 0.15 ($g = 10$ m s^{-2}).

(a) 150 m s^{-2} (b) 1.5 m s^{-2}
(c) 50 m s^{-2} (d) 1.2 m s^{-2}

48. The radius of inner most orbit of hydrogen atom is 5.3×10^{-11} m. What is the radius of third allowed orbit of hydrogen atom?

(a) 1.06 Å (b) 1.59 Å
(c) 4.77 Å (d) 0.53 Å

49. For the following logic circuit, the truth table is

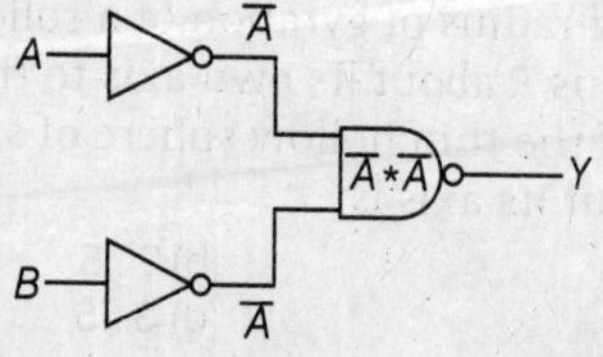

(a)

A	B	Y
0	0	0
0	1	1
1	0	1
1	1	1

(b)

A	B	Y
0	0	1
0	1	0
1	0	1
1	1	0

(c)

A	B	Y
0	0	0
0	1	0
1	0	0
1	1	1

(d)

A	B	Y
0	0	1
0	1	1
1	0	1
1	1	0

50. A horizontal bridge is built across a river. A student standing on the bridge throws a small ball vertically upwards with a velocity 4 m s^{-1}. The ball strikes the water surface after 4 s. The height of bridge above water surface is (Take, $g = 10 \text{ m s}^{-2}$)

(a) 60 m
(b) 64 m
(c) 68 m
(d) 56 m

Answers

1.	*(b)*	**2.**	*(b)*	**3.**	*(d)*	**4.**	*(c)*	**5.**	*(c)*	**6.**	*(a)*	**7.**	*(c)*	**8.**	*(c)*	**9.**	*(c)*	**10.**	*(b)*
11.	*(a)*	**12.**	*(a)*	**13.**	*(d)*	**14.**	*(d)*	**15.**	*(c)*	**16.**	*(d)*	**17.**	*(b)*	**18.**	*(a)*	**19.**	*(b)*	**20.**	(*)
21.	*(d)*	**22.**	*(d)*	**23.**	*(c)*	**24.**	*(b)*	**25.**	*(b)*	**26.**	*(b)*	**27.**	*(b)*	**28.**	*(d)*	**29.**	*(a)*	**30.**	*(c)*
31.	*(b)*	**32.**	(*)	**33.**	*(b)*	**34.**	*(b)*	**35.**	*(a)*	**36.**	*(c)*	**37.**	*(a)*	**38.**	(*)	**39.**	*(d)*	**40.**	*(a)*
41.	*(b)*	**42.**	*(c)*	**43.**	*(b)*	**44.**	(*)	**45.**	*(b)*	**46.**	*(b)*	**47.**	*(b)*	**48.**	*(c)*	**49.**	*(a)*	**50.**	*(b)*

Note (*) None of the option is correct.

Answer *with* Explanations

1. *(b)* The given situation is shown below.

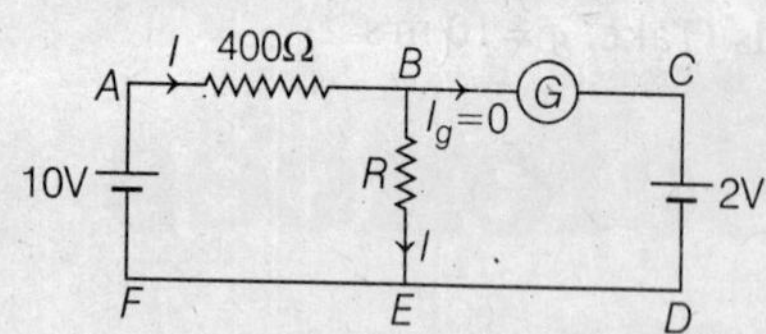

Applying Kirchhoff's voltage law in the loop *ABCDEFA*, we get

$$400I + 2 - 10 = 0$$

$$\Rightarrow \quad I = \frac{8}{400} = \frac{1}{50}\text{ A}$$

Applying Kirchhoff's voltage law in loop *ABEFA*, we get

$$400I + RI - 10 = 0$$

$$\Rightarrow \quad (400 + R)I = 10$$

$$\Rightarrow \quad (400 + R) \times \frac{1}{50} = 100$$

$$\Rightarrow \quad 400 + R = 500$$

$$\Rightarrow \quad R = 100\,\Omega$$

2. *(b)* When AC is converted into DC using a rectifier circuit, then converted DC is an unstable current that includes ripples. A capacitor is used to remove these ripples and maintain a constant voltage across load.

3. *(d)* Efficiency of carnot engine,

$$\eta = 50\% = 0.5$$

Temperature of source,

$$T_1 = 327°\text{C}$$
$$= (327 + 273)\text{ K}$$
$$= 600\text{ K}$$

If T_2 be the temperature of sink, then

$$\eta = 1 - \frac{T_2}{T_1}$$

$$\Rightarrow \quad 0.5 = 1 - \frac{T_2}{600}$$

$$\Rightarrow \quad \frac{T_2}{600} = 0.5$$

$$\Rightarrow \quad T_2 = 300\text{ K}$$
$$= (300 - 273)°\text{C}$$
$$= 27°\text{C}$$

4. *(c)* According to given situation,

$$c = \frac{x}{t_1} \text{ and } v = \frac{10x}{t_2}$$

Since, $\sin i_c = \frac{1}{\mu} = \frac{1}{\left(\frac{c}{v}\right)}$

$$= \frac{v}{c} = \frac{\frac{10x}{t_2}}{\frac{x}{t_1}}$$

$$= \frac{10t_1}{t_2}$$

$$\Rightarrow \quad i_c = \sin^{-1}\left(\frac{10t_1}{t_2}\right)$$

5. *(c)* The direction of angular acceleration of a body moving along the circumference of the circular path is perpendicular to the plane in which rotation takes place i.e. along the axis of rotation.

6. *(a)* Venturimeter is a device used to measure the flow speed (flow rate) of incompressible fluid. It works on the Bernoulli's principle.

7. *(c)* Given, $T_{1/2} = 20$ minutes

According to given condition,

$$R = \frac{R_0}{16}$$

But, $\quad R = R_0\left(\frac{1}{2}\right)^n$

$$\Rightarrow \quad \frac{R_0}{16} = R_0\left(\frac{1}{2}\right)^n$$

$$\Rightarrow \quad \left(\frac{1}{2}\right)^4 = \left(\frac{1}{2}\right)^n$$

$$\Rightarrow \quad n = 4$$

$$\Rightarrow \quad \frac{t}{T/2} = 4$$

$$\Rightarrow \quad t = 4T_{1/2}$$
$$= 4 \times 20 = 80\text{ minutes}$$

8. *(c)* Random errors can arise due to random and unpredictable fluctuations in temperature and voltage supply.

9. *(c)* Given,

$$\theta = 30°$$
$$E = 2 \times 10^5\text{ NC}^{-1}$$

Dipole length,

$$2l = 2\text{ cm}$$
$$= 2 \times 10^{-2}\text{ m}$$

Torque, $\tau = 4$ N-m

We know that,

$$\Rightarrow \quad \tau = pE\sin\theta$$

$$\Rightarrow \quad p = \frac{\tau}{E\sin\theta}$$

$$= \frac{4}{2 \times 10^5 \times \sin 30°}$$

$$\Rightarrow \quad p = 4 \times 10^{-5}\text{ C-m}$$

$$\Rightarrow \quad 2l \cdot q = 4 \times 10^{-5}$$

$$\Rightarrow \quad q = \frac{4 \times 10^{-5}}{2l}$$

$$= \frac{4 \times 10^{-5}}{2 \times 10^{-2}}$$
$$= 2 \times 10^{-3}\ C$$
$$= 2\ mC$$

0. *(b)* Friction force always works against the motion of the football player. Here, football player is moving in the southward, so friction will act in northword. From the Newton's law of motion, force is in the direction of change in momentum. Since, the football player is just trying to move in the east direction in which no initial momentum was present, so force will be in north-east direction.

1. *(a)* In hydrogen spectrum,

$$\frac{1}{\lambda} = R\left(\frac{1}{n_1^2} - \frac{1}{n_2^2}\right)$$

For shortest wavelength in the Balmer series,

$$n_1 = 2 \text{ and } n_2 = \infty$$
$$\therefore \quad \frac{1}{\lambda} = R\left(\frac{1}{2^2} - \frac{1}{\infty^2}\right)$$
$$\Rightarrow \quad \frac{1}{\lambda} = \frac{R}{4}$$
$$\Rightarrow \quad R = \frac{4}{\lambda} \quad \ldots(i)$$

For the shortest wavelength of Bracket series,

$$n_1 = 4 \text{ and } n_2 = \infty$$
$$\therefore \quad \frac{1}{\lambda_B} = R\left(\frac{1}{4^2} - \frac{1}{\infty^2}\right)$$
$$= \frac{R}{16} = \frac{\frac{4}{\lambda}}{16}$$
$$\Rightarrow \quad \frac{1}{\lambda_B} = \frac{1}{4\lambda}$$
$$\Rightarrow \quad \lambda_B = 4\lambda$$

12. *(a)* The circuit diagram is shown as

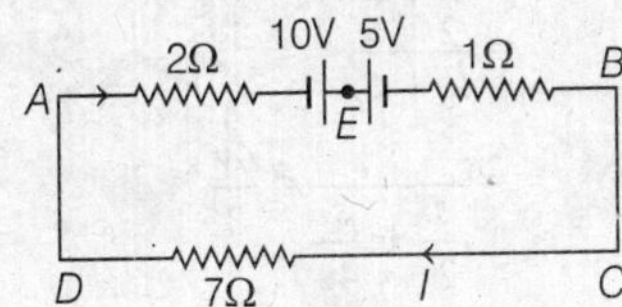

Applying KVL in the closed loop $AEBCDA$,

$$2I - 10 + 5 + I \cdot 1 + 7I = 0$$
$$\Rightarrow \quad 10I = 5$$
$$\Rightarrow \quad I = 0.5\ A$$

Since, current is positive, hence direction of current is from A to B through E.

13. *(d)* According to given situation,

$$V_S = 12\ V,$$
$$\therefore \quad I_S = \frac{P}{V_S} = \frac{60}{12} = 5\ A$$

$\therefore$ Given, $V_P = 220$ V

For ideal transformer.

$$I_P V_P = I_S V_S$$
$$\Rightarrow \quad I_P = \frac{I_S V_S}{V_P}$$
$$= \frac{5 \times 12}{220} = 0.27\ A$$

14. *(d)* For photoelectric emission, energy of incident electromagnetic radiation must be greater than or equal to work function of photosensitive surface. Thus, only Cs can emit photoelectrons.

15. *(c)* Given, when $x_1 = 2$ cm

Then, $\quad U_1 = U$

$$\Rightarrow \quad \frac{1}{2}kx_1^2 = U$$
$$\Rightarrow \quad K = \frac{2U}{x_1^2} \quad \ldots(i)$$

When $x_2 = 8$ cm, then $U = \frac{1}{2}kx_2^2$

$$= \frac{1}{2} \times \frac{2U}{x_1^2} \times x_2^2 \quad \text{[From Eq. (i)]}$$
$$= U \cdot \left(\frac{x_2}{x_1}\right)^2 = U\left(\frac{8}{2}\right)^2 = 16\,U$$

16. *(d)* Net magnetic flux through a closed surface is zero because the number of field lines leaving the surface are equal to the number of field lines entering the surface.

17. *(b)* Given, surface tension,

$$T = 0.03\ Nm^{-1}$$

Radius of soop bubble,

$$r = 2\text{cm} = 2 \times 10^{-2}\text{m}$$

$\therefore$ Amount of energy required,

$$E = 2TA = 2 \times 0.03 \times 4\pi\,(2 \times 10^{-2})^2$$
$$= 3.01 \times 10^{-4}\ J$$

18. *(a)* Longitudinal stress $= \frac{\text{Weight}}{\text{Area}} = \frac{w}{A}$

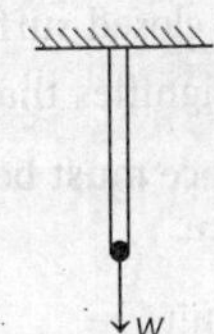

19. *(b)* The given situation is shown below.

Since, gravitational field at point O is zero, hence

$$\frac{Gm}{x^2} = \frac{G(9m)}{(R-x)^2}$$
$$\Rightarrow \quad \left(\frac{1}{x}\right)^2 = \left(\frac{3}{R-x}\right)^2$$
$$\Rightarrow \quad \frac{1}{x} = \frac{3}{R-x}$$
$$\Rightarrow \quad 3x = R - x$$

$\Rightarrow \quad x = \frac{R}{4}$

∴ Gravitational potential at point O,

$$V = \frac{-Gm}{x} + \left[\frac{-G(9m)}{R-x}\right]$$

$$= \frac{-Gm}{\frac{R}{4}} - \frac{9Gm}{R-\frac{R}{4}}$$

$$= -\frac{4Gm}{R} - \frac{12Gm}{R}$$

$$= -\frac{16Gm}{R}$$

20. (*) Initial temperature of the gas,

$T_1 = -50°C = (-50 + 273)K = 223K$

Final temperature of the gas,

$T_2 = ?;\ (v_{rms})_1 = v;\ (v_{rms})_2 = 3v$

We know that, $v_{rms} = \sqrt{\frac{3RT}{m}}$

$\Rightarrow \quad V_{rms} \propto \sqrt{T}$

$\Rightarrow \quad \frac{(v_{rms})_2}{(v_{rms})_1} = \sqrt{\frac{T_2}{T_1}}$

$\Rightarrow \quad \frac{3v}{v} = \sqrt{\frac{T_2}{223}}$

$\Rightarrow \quad 9 = \frac{T_2}{223}$

$\Rightarrow \quad T_2 = 2007K$

21. **(d)** Photovoltaic devices can convert optical radiation into electricity. The basic example of such device is solar photovoltaic system which converts solar energy directly into electrical energy.
Zener diode is heavily doped *p-n* junction diode operating in reverse biased condition in breakdown region.

22. **(d)** According to Gauss's law, $\oint \mathbf{E} \cdot dS$ represents total electric flux passing through a closed surface.
If $\oint \mathbf{E} \cdot dS = 0$, then it signifies that the number of electric flux lines entering the surface must be equal to the number of flux lines leaving the surface.

23. **(c)** In series *L-C-R* circuit,

$L = 10 \text{ mH} = 10^{-2} \text{ H}$

$\Rightarrow \quad C = 1 \text{ F} = 10^{-6} \text{ F}$

$R = 100\,\Omega$

∴ Resonance frequency,

$$f = \frac{1}{2\pi\sqrt{LC}}$$

$$= \frac{1}{2\pi\sqrt{10^{-2} \times 10^{-6}}}$$

$$= \frac{1}{2\pi \times 10^{-4}} = \frac{10^4}{2\pi}$$

$$= 1.59 \times 10^3 \text{ Hz}$$

$$= 1.59 \text{ kHz}$$

24. **(b)** We know that, capacitive reactance,

$$X_C = \frac{1}{\omega C} = \frac{1}{2\pi f C}$$

i.e., due to decrease in operating frequency (f), X_C increases. X_C increases, the conduction current decreases. Since, in case capacitor, conduction current is equal to displacement curre[nt]. Thus, with the decrease of operating frequency, displaceme[nt] current decreases.

25. **(b)** Given, $u = 280 \text{ ms}^{-1}, \theta = 30°$

∴ Maximum height attaiend by the bullet.

$$H_{max} = \frac{u^2 \sin^2\theta}{2g}$$

$$= \frac{(280)^2 \sin^2 30°}{2 \times 9.8}$$

$$= \frac{(280)^2 \times (0.5)^2}{2 \times 9.8} = 1000 \text{ m}$$

26. **(b)** A —— v —— C —— 2v —— B; $\frac{s}{2}$ (A to C), $\frac{s}{2}$ (C to B)

Time taken by vehicle to cover first half,

$$t_1 = \frac{\frac{s}{2}}{v} = \frac{s}{2v}$$

Time taken by vehicle to cover second half,

$$t_2 = \frac{\frac{s}{2}}{2v} = \frac{s}{4v}$$

∴ Average speed,

$$v_{avg} = \frac{\text{Total distance covered}}{\text{Total time taken}}$$

$$= \frac{\frac{s}{2} + \frac{s}{2}}{t_1 + t_2}$$

$$= \frac{s}{\frac{s}{2v} + \frac{s}{4v}} = \frac{4v}{3}$$

27. **(b)** Given, $R = (22000 \pm 5\%)\,\Omega$

$= (22 \times 10^3 \pm 5\%)\,\Omega$

Here, colours of four bands are

Red	Red	Orange	Gold
↓	↓	↓	↓
2	2	3	± 5%

Thus, colour of third band is orange.

28. **(d)** Equivalent capacitance of the system,

$$C_{AB} = \frac{3 \times (3+3)}{3 + (3+3)} = \frac{18}{9} = 2\mu\text{F}$$

29. *(a)* The minimum wavelength of X-rays produced by an electron accelerated through a potential difference V is given as

$$\lambda_{min} = \frac{hc}{eV}$$

$$\Rightarrow \quad \lambda_{min} \propto \frac{1}{V}$$

30. *(c)* Stored magnetic energy,

$$U = \frac{1}{2}LI^2$$

Here, $L = 4\mu H = 4 \times 10^{-6}$ H

$I = 2$ A

$$\therefore \quad U = \frac{1}{2} \times 4 \times 10^{-6} \times 2^2$$

$$= 8 \times 10^{-6} \text{ J}$$

$$= 8 \, \mu\text{J}$$

31. *(b)* Angular separation of fringes,

$$\theta = \frac{\lambda}{d}$$

i.e., Angular separation does not depend on the distance between screen and plane of slits. Thus, statement I is correct.

Since, $\theta \propto \lambda$

Thus, if the monochromatic source is replaced by another monochromatic source of larger wavelength, then angular seperation of fringes increases. Hence, statement II is incorrect.

32. (*) Radius of gyration of solid sphere and hollow sphere are K_1 and K_2 respectively, then

$$MK_1^2 = \frac{2}{5}MR^2$$

$$\Rightarrow \quad K_1 = \sqrt{\frac{2}{5}}R$$

and $$MK_2^2 = \frac{2}{3}MR^2$$

$$\Rightarrow \quad K_2 = \sqrt{\frac{2}{3}}R$$

$$\therefore \quad \frac{K_1}{K_2} = \frac{\sqrt{2/5R}}{\sqrt{2/3R}} = \sqrt{\frac{3}{5}}$$

33. *(b)* Given, $E_0 = 48 \text{ Vm}^{-1}$

$c = 3 \times 10^8$ m/s

$\therefore$ Amplitude of oscillating magnetic field,

$$B_0 = \frac{E_0}{c} = \frac{48}{3 \times 10^8}$$

$$= 1.6 \times 10^{-7} \text{ T}$$

34. *(b)* Given, $M = (0.4 \pm 0.002)$ g

$R = (0.3 \pm 0.001)$ mm

$L = (5 \pm 0.02)$ cm

$\therefore$ Density of wire,

$$\rho = \frac{M}{\pi r^2 L}$$

$\therefore$ Maximum percentage error in the measurement of density of wire.

$$\frac{\Delta\rho}{\rho} \times 100 = \frac{\Delta M}{M} \times 100 + 2 \times \frac{\Delta r}{r} \times 100 + \frac{\Delta L}{L} \times 100$$

$$= \frac{0.002}{0.4} \times 100 + 2 \times \frac{0.001}{0.3} \times 100 + \frac{0.02}{5} \times 100$$

$$= 0.5 + 0.67 + 0.4$$

$$= 1.57\% \approx 1.6\%$$

35. *(a)* Fundamental frequency of an open pipe,

$$f_0 = \frac{v}{2l}$$

and fundamental frequency of an closed pipe,

$$f_c = \frac{v}{4l}$$

$$\therefore \quad \frac{f_0}{f_c} = \frac{\frac{v}{2l}}{\frac{v}{4l}} = \frac{2}{1}$$

$$\therefore \quad f_0 : f_c = 2:1$$

36. *(c)* Focal length of convex lens,

$$f_1 = + f$$

Focal length of concave lens,

$$f_2 = - f$$

When both lenses are kept in contact, then equivalent focal length (F) is given by

$$\frac{1}{F} = \frac{1}{f_1} + \frac{1}{f_2} = \frac{1}{f} + \frac{1}{-f} = 0$$

$$\Rightarrow \quad F = \infty$$

37. *(a)* Time period of satellite,

$$T = \frac{2\pi r}{v_0}$$

$$\Rightarrow \quad T = \frac{2\pi(R_e + h)}{v_0} \quad \text{...(i)}$$

Orbital velocity, $v_0 = \sqrt{\frac{GM_e}{r}}$

$$\Rightarrow \quad v_0 = \sqrt{\frac{GM_e}{(R_e + h)}} \quad \text{...(ii)}$$

From Eqs. (i) and (ii), we get

$$T = \frac{2\pi(R_e + h)}{\sqrt{\frac{GM_e}{R_e + h}}}$$

$$T = 2\pi\sqrt{\frac{(R_e + h)^3}{GM_e}} \quad \text{...(iii)}$$

Since, $M_e = \frac{4}{3}\pi R_e^3 d$

$\therefore$ Putting the value of M_e in Eq. (iii), we get

$$T = 2\pi\sqrt{\frac{(R_e + h)^3}{G \cdot \frac{4}{3}\pi R_e^3 d}}$$

$$= \sqrt{\frac{3\pi(R_e + h)^3}{GdR_e^3}}$$

Since, satellite is orbiting just above the surface of the earth, hence $h = 0$

$$\therefore \quad T = \sqrt{\frac{3\pi R_e^3}{GdR_e^3}} = \sqrt{\frac{3\pi}{Gd}}$$

38. (*) The given situation is shown below.

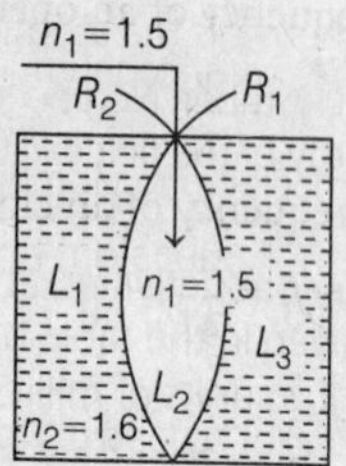

$$\therefore \quad R_1 = 20\,\text{cm}$$

$$\Rightarrow \quad R_2 = -20\,\text{cm}$$

Lens L_1 and L_3 are plano concave lens.

Focal length of lens L_1 is given as

$$\frac{1}{f_1} = (n_2 - 1)\left(\frac{1}{\infty} - \frac{1}{R_1}\right)$$

$$= (1.6 - 1)\left(-\frac{1}{20}\right) = -\frac{1}{25}$$

$$\Rightarrow \quad f_1 = -25\text{ cm}$$

Similarly, focal length of lens L_3,

$$f_3 = -25\text{ cm}$$

Now, focal length of convex lens L_2 is given as

$$\frac{1}{f_2} = (n_1 - 1)\left(\frac{1}{R_1} - \frac{1}{R_2}\right)$$

$$= (1.5 - 1)\left(\frac{1}{20} - \frac{1}{-20}\right) = \frac{1}{20}$$

$$\Rightarrow \quad f_2 = 20\text{ cm}$$

If F be the focal length of combination, then

$$\frac{1}{F} = \frac{1}{f_1} + \frac{1}{f_2} + \frac{1}{f_3}$$

$$= \frac{1}{-25} + \frac{1}{20} + \frac{1}{-25} = -\frac{3}{100}$$

$$\Rightarrow \quad F = \frac{-100}{3}\text{ cm}$$

39. *(d)* The given situation is shown below.

block
u
$v_1 = u/3$
$v_2 = 0$
24 cm
s_2

$$s_1 = 24\text{ cm}$$

Using, $v^2 = u^2 - 2as$

$$\Rightarrow \quad v_1^2 = u^2 - 2as$$

$$\Rightarrow \quad \left(\frac{u}{3}\right)^2 = u^2 - 2a \times 0.24$$

$$\Rightarrow \quad 0.48a = \frac{8}{9}u^2$$

$$\Rightarrow \quad a = \frac{8u^2}{9 \times 0.48} = \frac{u^2}{0.54}$$

According to second condition,

$$0 = v_1^2 - 2as_2$$

$$\Rightarrow \quad 0 = \left(\frac{u}{3}\right)^2 - 2 \times \frac{u^2}{0.54} \times s_2$$

$$\Rightarrow \quad \frac{u^2}{9} = \frac{2u^2}{0.54}s_2$$

$$\Rightarrow \quad s_2 = \frac{0.54}{9 \times 2} = 0.03\text{ m}$$

$$= 3\text{ cm}$$

$\therefore$ Total length of the block $= s_1 + s_2$

$$= 24 + 3 = 27\text{ cm}$$

40. *(a)* When 10 resistors, each of resistance R is connected in series, then equivalent resistance.

$$R_s = R + R + R + \ldots 10\text{ times}$$

$$\Rightarrow \quad R_s = 10R$$

$\therefore$ Current drawn from the battery,

$$I_s = \frac{E}{R_S} = \frac{E}{10R}$$

$$\Rightarrow \quad I_s = \frac{E}{10R} \quad \ldots\text{(i)}$$

In second case, when resistors are connected in parallel, then equivalent resistance,

$$\frac{1}{R_p} = \frac{1}{R} + \frac{1}{R} + \frac{1}{R} + \ldots 10\text{ times} = \frac{10}{R}$$

$$\Rightarrow \quad R_p = \frac{R}{10}$$

$\therefore$ Current drawn from the battery,

$$I_p = \frac{E}{R_p} = \frac{E}{R/10}$$

$$= 10 \times \frac{E}{R}$$

$$= 100 \times \frac{E}{10R}$$

$$\Rightarrow \quad I_p = 100I$$

$$\therefore \quad n = 100$$

41. *(b)* Given, $L = \frac{50}{\pi}\text{ mH} = \frac{5}{\pi} \times 10^{-2}\text{ H}$

$$C = \frac{10^3}{\pi}\,\mu\text{F} = \frac{1}{\pi} \times 10^{-3}\text{ F}$$

$$R = 10\,\Omega,$$

$$f = 50\text{ Hz},$$

$$V = 220\text{ V}$$

$$\therefore \quad X_L = 2\pi fL$$
$$= 2\pi \times 50 \times \frac{5}{\pi} \times 10^{-2} = 5\,\Omega$$
$$X_C = \frac{1}{\omega C} = \frac{1}{2\pi fC}$$
$$= \frac{1}{2\pi \times 50 \times \frac{1}{\pi} \times 10^{-3}}$$
$$= \frac{1}{10^{-1}} = 10\,\Omega$$

$\therefore$ Net impedance the circuit,

$$Z = \sqrt{R^2 + (X_C - X_L)^2}$$
$$= \sqrt{10^2 + (10-5)^2}$$
$$= \sqrt{125} = 5\sqrt{5}\,\Omega$$

42. *(c)* The motion of the particle performing S.H.M. is represented by

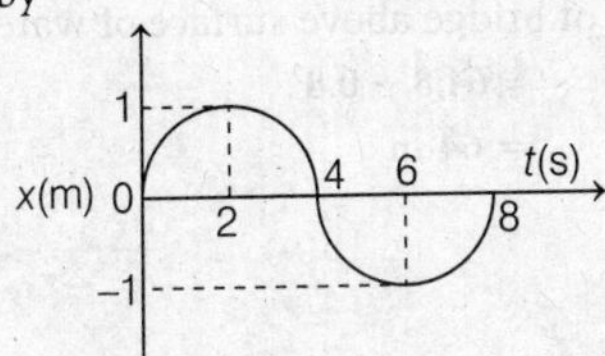

$$x = A\sin\omega t = 1\sin\frac{2\pi}{T}t$$
$$= 1\sin\frac{2\pi}{8}t$$
$$\Rightarrow \quad x = \sin\left(\frac{\pi}{4}t\right)$$

$$\therefore \text{ velocity, } v = \frac{dx}{dt} = \frac{d}{dt}\sin\left(\frac{\pi}{4}\right)t$$
$$= \frac{\pi}{4}\cos\left(\frac{\pi}{4}\right)t$$

$\therefore$ Acceleration of the particle,

$$a = \frac{dv}{dt} = \frac{d}{dt}\left[\frac{\pi}{4}\cos\left(\frac{\pi}{4}\right)t\right]$$
$$= -\frac{\pi}{4}\cdot\frac{\pi}{4}\cdot\sin\left(\frac{\pi}{4}t\right)$$
$$\Rightarrow \quad a = -\frac{\pi^2}{16}\sin\left(\frac{\pi}{4}\cdot t\right)$$

At $\quad t = 2\,\text{s}$

$$a = -\frac{\pi^2}{16}\cdot\sin\left(\frac{\pi}{4}\cdot 2\right) = -\frac{\pi^2}{16}\ \text{ms}^{-2}$$

43. *(b)*

Net magnetic field at point P,

$$B = B_{\text{semicircle}} - B_{XA} - B_{YB}$$
$$= \frac{\mu_0 i}{4R} - \frac{\mu_0 i}{4\pi R} - \frac{\mu_0 i}{4\pi R}$$
$$= \frac{\mu_0 i}{4R}\left[1 - \frac{2}{\pi}\right] \text{ pointed away from the page.}$$

44. (*) Electric potential at point P due to electric dipole.

$$V = \frac{1}{4\pi\varepsilon_0}\cdot\frac{p}{r^2}$$
$$= K\cdot\frac{p}{r^2} = K\cdot\frac{(q\cdot 2a)}{r^2}$$

Here, $r = 5\,\text{cm} = 5\times10^{-3}$ m

$$2a = (3+3)\,\text{cm} = 6\,\text{cm}$$
$$= 6\times10^{-2}\ \text{m}$$
$$\therefore \quad V = K\cdot q\cdot\frac{6\times10^{-2}}{(5\times10^{-2})^2}$$
$$= Kq\cdot\frac{6}{25}\times10^2$$
$$= Kq\left(\frac{6}{25}\right)\times(10^2\ \text{V})$$
$$= \left(\frac{6}{25}\right)Kq\times(10^2\ \text{V})$$

45. *(b)* Given, $R_0 = 2\,\Omega$

At $t = 80°\text{C}$, $R_t = 6.8\,\Omega$

We know that,

$$R_f = R_0(1 + \alpha t)$$
$$\Rightarrow \quad R_t = R_0 + R_0\alpha t$$
$$\therefore \quad \alpha = \frac{R_t - R_0}{R_0 t} = \frac{6.8-2}{2\times 80}$$
$$= \frac{4.8}{2\times 80} = 0.03$$
$$= 3\times10^{-2}\,°\text{C}^{-1}$$

46. *(b)* Given, $\mathbf{L} = L\hat{\mathbf{i}}$

$$\mathbf{B} = 2\hat{\mathbf{i}} + 3\hat{\mathbf{j}} - 4\hat{\mathbf{k}}$$
$$\therefore \quad \mathbf{F} = \mathbf{I}(\mathbf{L}\times\mathbf{B}) = I\,[L\hat{\mathbf{i}}\times(2\hat{\mathbf{i}} + 3\hat{\mathbf{j}} - 4\hat{\mathbf{k}})]$$
$$= I\,[L(\hat{\mathbf{i}}\times\hat{\mathbf{i}}) + 3L(\hat{\mathbf{i}}\times\hat{\mathbf{j}}) - 4L(\hat{\mathbf{i}}\times\hat{\mathbf{k}})]$$
$$= I\,[0 + 3L\hat{\mathbf{k}} + 4L\hat{\mathbf{j}}]$$
$$= I\,[4L\hat{\mathbf{i}} + 3L\hat{\mathbf{k}}]$$
$$\therefore \quad F = |\mathbf{F}| = \sqrt{(4LI)^2 + (3LI)^2}$$
$$= 5LI$$

47. *(b)* Given, $\mu = 0.15$

For the given situation,

$$F = ma = \mu mg$$
$$\Rightarrow \quad a = \mu g = 0.15\times10$$
$$= 1.5\ \text{ms}^{-2}$$

48. *(c)* Radius of innermost orbit of H-atom

$$r_0 = 5.3\times10^{-11}\ \text{m}$$

$\therefore$ Radius of third allowed orbit of H-atom,

$$r_3 = r_0 n^2 = r_0(3)^2 = 9r_0$$
$$= 9\times5.3\times10^{-11}$$
$$= 47.7\times10^{-11}$$

$= 4.77 \times 10^{-10}$ m

$= 4.77$ Å

49. ***(a)*** Output of the logic circuit is

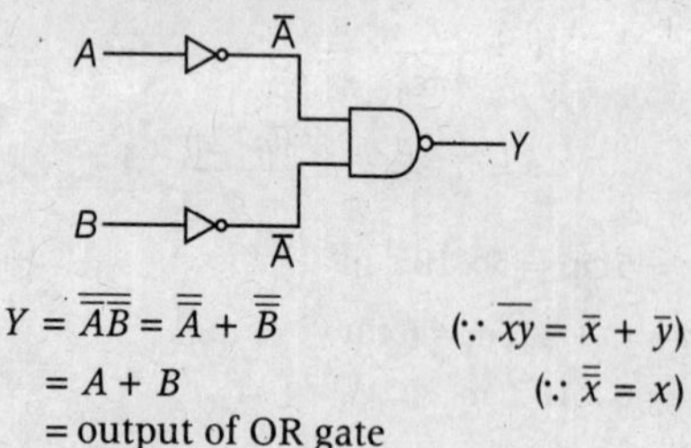

$Y = \overline{\overline{A}\,\overline{B}} = \overline{\overline{A}} + \overline{\overline{B}}$ $\quad (\because \overline{xy} = \overline{x} + \overline{y})$

$= A + B$ $\quad (\because \overline{\overline{x}} = x)$

= output of OR gate

Truth table is

A	B	$Y = A + B$
0	0	0
0	1	1
1	0	1
1	1	1

50. ***(b)*** Maximum height attaine by the ball,

$$h' = v^2/2g$$

$$= \frac{4^2}{2 \times 10} = 0.8 \text{ m}$$

Time of flight from bridge to bridge

$$t_1 = \frac{2v}{g} = \frac{2 \times 4}{10} = 0.8 \text{ s}$$

Total time of flight is given as 4 s.

Time taken by the ball to reach at the surface of water from highest point, $t_2 = 4 - \frac{t_1}{2} = 4 - \frac{0.8}{2} = 3.6 \text{ s}$

$$\therefore \quad h = 0 \times t_2 + \frac{1}{2} g t_2^2$$

$$= 0 + \frac{1}{2} \times 10 \times (3.6)^2$$

$$= 64.8 \text{ m}$$

$\therefore$ The height of bridge above surface of water $= h - h'$

$$= 64.8 - 0.8$$

$$= 64 \text{ m}$$